THE GUINNESS ENCYCLOPEDIA *of* POPULAR MUSIC

Edited by
COLIN LARKIN

VOLUME 4

Lincoln, Abe –
Primettes

GUINNESS PUBLISHING

First edition published in 1992
Second impression 1994
Second edition published in 1995 by
GUINNESS PUBLISHING LTD
33 London Road, Enfield, Middlesex EN2 6DJ, England

Published in the United States by
STOCKTON PRESS
an imprint of Grove's Dictionaries Inc.
345 Park Avenue South, New York, NY 10010, USA

British Library Cataloguing-in-Publication data
A catalogue record for this book is available from the British Library

ISBN 0-85112-662-6 (UK)

Library of Congress Cataloging-in-Publication Data
A catalog record for this book is available from the Library of Congress

ISBN 1-56159-176-9 (USA)

Conceived and edited by Colin Larkin for
SQUARE ONE BOOKS LTD
to whom all editorial correspondence should be sent
Iron Bridge House, 3 Bridge Approach, Chalk Farm, London NW1 8BD
Production Editor: Susan Pipe
Desk Editor: Miles Hutchinson
Senior contributors: Alex Ogg, John Martland and Brian Hogg
Special thanks to John Reiss and to David Roberts of Guinness Publishing
This book has been designed on Apple Macintosh computers
using 4th Dimension, Quark XPress and Microsoft Word

Printed and bound in Great Britain by the Bath Press

Contents

Lincoln, Abe

b. Abraham Lincoln, 29 March 1907, Lancaster, Pennsylvania, USA. Lincoln started playing the trombone as a small child and by his late teens was proficient enough to follow **Tommy Dorsey** into the **California Ramblers**. He played in various other bands and in the 20s was with those led by **Roger Wolfe Kahn** and **Paul Whiteman**. During the late 30s he played with **Ozzie Nelson**'s popular dance band and also became a studio musician in Los Angeles where he recorded alongside such luminaries as Bing Crosby in 1937 and again in 1941, Hoagy Carmichael in 1938 and Judy Garland in 1939. During the 40s he returned to jazz during the dixieland revival and recorded with Wingy Manone in 1944. He was also active in film studio work and continued to make occasional record dates with singers and a handful of jazz musicians. In the 50s he made rather more jazz dates, including well-known sessions of traditional jazz with the Rampart Street Paraders in 1953, **Pete Fountain** 1956, **Matty Matlock** in 1957 and again in 1958 and **Bob Scobey**. In the 60s, he played club and festival dates with several bands including brief stints with **Wild Bill Davison** in 1967 and Fountain. He appeared at a dixieland jazz festival in Sacramento, California in 1976. Although Lincoln was capable of playing in the legato style achieved by such notable contemporaries as Dorsey and **Jack Teagarden**, it is probably as a bristling dixieland master of the trombone that he is at his most exciting and for which he will be longest remembered.

Album: with the Rampant Street Preachers, *Jam Session Coast To Coast* (1953).

Lincoln, Charley

b. Charley Hicks, 11 March 1900, Lithonia, Georgia, USA, d. 28 September 1963, Cairo, Georgia, USA. Like his younger brother Robert '**Barbecue Bob**' Hicks, Lincoln learned guitar from **Curley Weaver**'s mother, but was less accomplished than Bob. He recorded from 1927-30, probably thanks to his brother's hit-making status, and his blues are a mix of the sad and the mildly risqué, backed by simple 12-string guitar. Despite being billed as 'Laughing Charley' on a duet with Bob, Lincoln was a man whose mood changed under the influence of drink from introverted to choleric, a trait exacerbated by the alcoholism that followed various family tragedies, notably the premature death of his brother in 1929. On Christmas Day, 1955, he senselessly murdered a man, and spent the rest of his life in prison, repentant and performing only religious songs.

Compilations: *Charley Lincoln* (1983), *Complete Recordings 1927-1930* (1984).

Lind, Bob

b. 25 November 1944, Baltimore, Maryland, USA. Lind is now best known for writing and recording the folk-rock song 'Elusive Butterfly' which reached number 5 in the US in 1966. He moved around often with his family, and while settled in Denver, Colorado, he began singing folk music in clubs. He moved to the west coast and was signed to World Pacific Records, a division of the larger **Liberty Records**. Produced by **Jack Nitzsche**, Lind played guitar on his recordings for the label, while piano was handled by **Leon Russell**. His first single, 'Cheryl's Goin' Home', failed to catch on but was later covered by **Cher** and the **Blues Project**. 'Elusive Butterfly' was its b-side and became an international Top 10 hit. Lind was widely touted as 'the new **Bob Dylan**' and the latest spokesperson for youth during 1966. Despite his pop star looks and sensitive lyrics, however, his subsequent singles, 'Remember The Rain' and 'Truly Julie's Blues (I'll Be There)' reached only number 64 and 65 respectively. The album *Don't Be Concerned* contained a number of sentimental, but largely attractive songs. His compositions continued to find numerous interpreters, among them the **Turtles**, **Noel Harrison**, **Nancy Sinatra** and **Bobby Sherman**. Bob Lind continued to record into the early 70s, having switched to **Capitol Records**, but there was no revival of his commercial fortunes. However, he did in fact continue performing live at folk and country music venues well into the 80s.

Albums: *Don't Be Concerned* (1966), *The Elusive Bob Lind* (1966), *Photographs Of Feeling* (1966), *Since There Were Circles* (1971).

Lindenberg, Udo

b. 17 May 1946, Gronau, Germany. Udo Lindenberg is hugely popular in his native country: From the time of *Lindenberg*, released in 1971, to the late 80s when his recorded output was directed towards the English-speaking market, Lindenberg has accumulated sales of over 15 million albums in Germany alone. His early career included a spell as the drummer in a local jazz group who played mainstream standards such as 'The Shadow Of Your Smile' that would later find a place in his singing repertoire. He would perform the standard 'Lover Man (Where Can You Be)' with no alterations to the lyrics to reflect what he called his 'flexible' sexuality. Alongside this, other aspects of **David Bowie**'s artistic presentation were featured in Lindenberg's multi-media concerts which would sometimes include wrestlers, trampolinists and similar non-musical support acts. Another influence was a less famous friend, Jean-Jacques Kravetz, whom Udo assisted willingly on three albums recorded in the 70s. His interest in national left-wing politics manifested itself in active membership of the Green party and its

peace movement - with compositions such as 'Father You Should Have Killed Hitler' and 'They Don't Need Another Fuehrer' expressing his concern about the German renaissance of Nazism. This was balanced with the pride apparent in 1984's 'Germans' which lauded Goethe, Kafka, Mozart, Schumann and other cultural icons. Though this single - buttressed by a promotional visit - made ripples in Britain, a duet with Leata Galloway ('Gesang'), 'Berlin', the lighter 'Special Train To Pankow' (portraying a prominent East German leader 'as a closet rock 'n' roller') and other worthy singles together made less worldwide impact than his characteristically controversial appearance, backed by the Panik Orchestra, as his country's representative on **Live Aid**. Nevertheless, if not neglecting a still huge home following, releases such as 1987's *All Clear!* (which embraced a revival of **Steppenwolf**'s 'Born To Be Wild') demonstrate a continued wooing of a wider audience.
Albums: *Galaxo Gang* (1976), *Lindenberg* (1971), *Daumen Im Wind* (1972), *Alles Klar Auf Der Andrea Doria* (1973), *Ball Pompos* (1974), *Votan Wahnwitz* (1975), *Das Sind Die Herrn Vom Andern Stern* (1976), *Sister King Kong* (1977), *No Panic* (1977), *Lindenbergs Rock Revue* (1978), *Droehnland Symponie* (1978), *Odyssee* (1979), *Livehaftig* (1979), *Der Detektiv* (1979), *Panische Zeiten* (1980), *Udopia* (1981), *Intensivstationen* (1982), *Keule* (1982), *Lindstarke 10* (1983), *Gottewrhammerung* (1984), *Udo Lindenberg Und Das Panik Orchestra* (1985), *Feuerlamnd* (1987), *All Clear!* aka *Alles Klar!* (1987), *Lieder Statt Briefe* (1988), *CasaNova* (1988), *Hermine* (1988), *Bunte Republik Deutschland* (1989), *Niemandsland* (1990), *Ich Will Dich Haben* (1991), *Gustav* (1991), *Panik-Panther* (1992).

Lindisfarne

Based in Newcastle, UK, this quintet consisted primarily of **Alan Hull** (b. 20 February 1945, Newcastle-Upon-Tyne, Tyne And Wear, England; vocals/guitar/piano), Simon Cowe (b. 1 April 1948, Jesmond Dene, Tyne And Wear, England; guitar), Ray Jackson (b. 12 December 1948, Wallsend, Tyne And Wear, England; harmonica/mandolin), Rod Clements (b. 17 November 1947, North Shields, Tyne And Wear, England; bass/violin) and Ray Laidlaw (b. 28 May 1948, North Shields, Tyne And Wear, England; drums). The band was originally known as the Downtown Faction, but changed their name to Lindisfarne in 1968. Their debut *Nicely Out Of Tune*, was issued the following year and this brash mixture of folk-rock and optimistic harmonies is arguably the group's most satisfying set. The album contained the wistful and lyrically complex 'Lady Eleanor'. Their popularity flourished with the release of *Fog On The Tyne* the humorous title track celebrating life in Newcastle and containing lyrics such as: 'Sitting in a sleazy snack-bar sucking sickly sausage rolls'. The album reached number one and the attendant single, 'Meet Me On The Corner' reached the UK Top 5 in 1972 where it was followed by a re-released 'Lady Eleanor'. The debut album, *Nicely Out Of Tune,* was reissued in 1972 and this time reached number 8 in the UK. *Fog On The Tyne* was produced by Bob Johnston, and although they pursued this relationship on a third selection, *Dingly Dell*, the group was unhappy with his work and remixed the set prior to release. The final results were still disappointing, although the album still managed to reach number 5 in the UK, and tensions within the line-up were exposed during an ill-fated tour of the USA. In 1973, Laidlaw, Cowe and Clements left for a new venture, **Jack The Lad**. Kenny Craddock (keyboards), Charlie Harcourt (guitar), Tommy Duffy (bass) and Paul Nichols (drums) were brought in as replacements but this reconstituted line-up lacked the charm of its predecessor and was overshadowed by Alan Hull's concurrent solo career. A 1974 release, *Happy Daze*, offered some promise, but did not sell at all well and as a result Lindisfarne was disbanded the following year. The break, however, proved to be merely temporary and the original quintet later resumed working together. They secured a recording deal with **Mercury Records** and in 1978 enjoyed a UK Top 10 single with the hugely catchy 'Run For Home'. Despite further releases, Lindisfarne was unable to repeat this success and subsequently reached an artistic nadir with *C'mon Everybody*, a medley of rock 'n' roll party favourites with six of the group's own best-known songs saved for the finale. In November 1990, Lindisfarne were back in the UK charts, joined together by the England international footballer, and fellow Geordie, Paul Gascoigne. Their re-worked, and much inferior, reworking of their classic of 'Fog On The Tyne' reached number 2, although this probably reflected post-World Cup euphoria for the skills of Gascoigne rather than any musical merit in the song. Although they are now restricted to only the occasional chart success, the group's following remains strong, particularly in the north-east of England, and is manifested in their annual Christmas concerts. Hull maintains an independent solo career although he still performs Lindisfarne classics, as heard on his *Back To Basics* in 1994.
Albums: *Nicely Out Of Tune* (1970), *Fog On The Tyne* (1971), *Dingly Dell* (1972), *Lindisfarne Live* (1973), *Roll On Ruby* (1973), *Happy Daze* (1974), *Back And Fourth* (1978), *Magic In The Air* (1978), *The News* (1979), *Sleepless Nights* (1982), *Lindisfarne Tastic Live* (1984), *Lindisfarne Tastic Volume 2* (1984), *Dance Your Life Away* (1984), *C'mon Everybody* (1987), *Amigos* (1989), *Elvis Lives On The Moon* (1993). Compilations: *Take Off Your Head* (1974), *Finest Hour* (1975), *Singles Album* (1981), *Buried Treasures Vol. 1* (1993), *Buried Treasures Vol. 2* (1993), *On Tap* (1994).

Lindley, David

Guitarist Lindley first attracted attention for his work in

a multitude of traditional USA groups, including the Smog City Trestle Hangers, the Mad Mountain Ramblers and the Dry City Scat Band. Having embraced rock music in the short-lived Rodents, he became a founder member of **Kaleidoscope** (USA), one of the 60s most enduring, and enigmatic, acts. Lindley's skills as a guitarist, violinist and banjo player were crucial to the eclectic approach of the group, which he led until its demise in 1970. During the 70s his talents were much in demand and David appeared as an accompanist for such diverse acts as **Terry Reid**, **David Blue**, **Linda Ronstadt**, **James Taylor** and **Crosby And Nash**. However, Lindley is best-recalled for his association with **Jackson Browne** which spanned seminal releases such as *Late For The Sky*, *The Pretender* and *Running On Empty*. His wailing falsetto on Browne's version of 'Stay' (1978) brought an unlikely UK/US Top 20 hit. In 1981, the guitarist released his first solo album, *El Rayo-X*. The set featured a mixture of New Orleans, Latin and reggae styles and included versions of 'Mercury Blues', 'Twist And Shout' and 'Petit Fleur', the last of which he also recorded with Kaleidoscope. Although several writers criticized its unadventurous content, there was no denying the infectious enthusiasm which Lindley clearly delighted in. Having formed a group around Bernie Larsen (guitar), Jorge Calderon (bass), Ian Wallace (drums) and Ras 'Baboo' Pierre (percussion), David began extensive touring. The excitement they generated was captured on *El Rayo-X Live* while further studio selections continued the eclectic mix of his debut. Lindley remains a consummate and skilled musician, never more apparent than in the 90s when he undertook live dates with **Ry Cooder**.

Albums: *El Rayo-X* (1981), *Win This Record* (1982), *El Rayo-X Live* (1983), *Mr. Dave* (1985), *Very Greasy* (1988), with Hani Naser *Official Bootleg* (Pleemhead 1994).

Lindsay, Erica

b. 5 June 1955, San Francisco, California, USA. Lindsay spent her childhood in Europe, her parents being teachers in American schools there. She took up clarinet at high school, then alto and tenor saxophones. At this time she was studying with **Mal Waldron**. In 1973, she went to the **Berklee College Of Music** in Boston for a year, then returned to Europe to tour with her own quartet and to freelance as soloist, composer and arranger. She came back to New York in 1980, composing for television, video and ballet, and playing with **Melba Liston**, **Clifford Jordan**, **Ted Curson** and **McCoy Tyner**. As a composer of well-crafted and atmospheric tunes, her influences include Waldron, **Gene Ammons**, **Johnny Griffin**, **Dexter Gordon**, **Wayne Shorter**, **John Coltrane** and **Miles Davis**.

Album: *Dreamer* (1989).

Lindsay, Jimmy

b. 1950, Kingston, Jamaica, West Indies. At the age of nine Lindsay and his family relocated to the UK. His first venture into music began in 1965 with a soul group named the Healers, followed by a short term with the Nighthawks. Other ventures included a spell with the rock band Pure Medicine, back to soul with the Garments, and notably as part of the more successful group Cymande. In the early 70s his first recordings surfaced, 'Tribute To Jimi Hendrix' and on the Cymande album, *Promised Heights*. By 1976 he began concentrating on reggae and the **sound system** hit, 'What You Gonna Do' with Lindsay on lead vocals. This encouraged **Lloyd Coxsone** to produce him as a soloist. The first release, 'Motion', surfaced through Cactus, followed by 'Easy', a cover of the **Commodores** hit, on Lloyd's own Tribesman label. The latter was picked up for release by **Island Records** appearing on the revived Black Swan logo. The single's success led Lindsay to put his energies into his own Music Hive label and sharing lead vocals with Larry Walker under the collective name of Dambala they enjoyed a big hit with 'Zimbabwe'. The lyrics, 'Crucify Smith and take back Zimbabwe, crucify Smith and take back Namibia, crucify Vorster and take back Anzania' was released shortly before **Bob Marley**'s plea for the country then known as Rhodesia. The group consisted of a multi racial line-up including members from Nigeria, Guyana, St. Lucia, Barbados and the UK. The group were commissioned by the BBC to record a theme to a six-part current affairs programme, *Babylon*. Lindsay began to concentrate on his solo career when he signed a contract with the Gem label and in the autumn of 1979 he released, *Where Is Your Love* produced by Lloyd Coxsone. To promote the album he toured with his new band Rasuji including members from Dambala in the line-up. In 1980 he released *Children Of Rastafari* empathizing a more spiritual message, notably on the track 'It's Hard (For A Dread To Live In Babylon)'. It was lifted for single release and promoted on a tour of the UK when supporting **Steel Pulse**.

Albums: *Where Is Your Love* (Gem 1979), *Children Of Rastafari* (Gem 1980).

Lindsay, Mark

b. 9 March 1942, Eugene, Oregon, USA. Lindsay first achieved recognition as the lead vocalist of the US rock group **Paul Revere And The Raiders**. While with that group he launched a solo career. He first sang publicly in 1956 at a high school talent contest. Receiving a favourable response, he started a rock band. In 1958, he moved to Caldwell, Idaho, he sat in with an early band of Revere's, and was soon asked to replace singer Red Hughes. Lindsay also became the band's saxophonist. In the early 60s the group became one of the most popular in its region and ultimately one of the most popular in the USA. Lindsay made three singles in 1966 with Keith Allison and **Steve Alaimo**, as the Unknowns, but these were recorded as side projects; he was still very much at the helm of the Raiders. Lindsay announced his decision to begin an official solo career in April 1969 and for some time worked both as a soloist and the Raiders' singer. Lindsay's first solo single for **Columbia Records** was a **Jimmy Webb** composition, 'First Hymn From Grand Terrace' (1969), but it failed to make any impression upon the charts. His next, 'Arizona', signalled the true start of his solo success by reaching number 10 in the USA, remaining his most successful solo single. At that point, Columbia opted to shorten the group's name simply to the Raiders, to denigrate Revere's involvement (Revere was primarily the keyboardist and bandleader, while Lindsay sang all of their material.) Despite that action, Lindsay's *Arizona* outperformed the Raiders' own *Collage* in early 1970, the former reaching number 36 on the US charts while the latter stalled at number 154.

This pattern continued, with Lindsay's single 'Silver Bird' reaching number 25 that year and the album of the same title hitting number 82. Oddly, in 1971, the Raiders' career received a great boost with the success of the single 'Indian Reservation (The Lament Of The Cherokee Reservation Indian)', a cover of a song which English singer **Don Fardon** had taken to number 20 in 1968. It became the Raiders' only number 1 single and sparked a Top 20 album of the same title. But that was to be a last gasp for both the Raiders and Lindsay. Although Lindsay returned to working with the group, neither party scored another major hit record. Lindsay failed to make either the singles or albums charts after 1971, and the Raiders' own run ended in 1973. Lindsay finally left the group in early 1975, making two unsuccessful singles for **Warner Brothers Records** in 1977. He quit performing and recording altogether when that contract expired, and did not make another appearance until the late 80s. In 1990, he began work on what would be his first solo album in 18 years.

Albums: *Arizona* (1970), *Silverbird* (1970), *You've Got A Friend* (1971).

Lindsay, Reg

b. 7 July 1930, Parkes, New South Wales, Australia. The family's ancestors had arrived from the UK to seek gold but found only hard work which led ultimately to the boy growing up in an inland farming area known as the Golden West. He learned to play fiddle and mandolin from his father and is reputed to have played 'The Wheel Of The Wagon Is Broken' on the harmonica at the age of four. He developed a great interest in country music from the recordings of such singers as **Wilf Carter** and **Tex Morton**. The family relocated to Adelaide but whenever possible, Lindsay spent his free time out of town, working on farms and learning the life of a cowboy. During this time, he mastered the banjo and guitar and worked hard on his singing and yodelling. After leaving school, he worked in the shearing sheds and as a fencing contractor before being hurt in a rodeo accident. In 1951, while confined to bed recuperating, he heard of a major talent show being held in Sydney that was organised by top country singer **Tim McNamara**. He made the long trip to Sydney and singing 'Streamlined Yodel Song', won the contest, pushing **Shorty Ranger** into second place. The prize was a recording contract with Rodeo Records but the win also led to a demand for personal appearances and considerable radio work. Throughout the 50s and 60s, he had popular radio shows on major Australian stations including 2CH, 2SM and 2KY. In the mid-60s, he also added television work to his busy schedules, which included touring with his own show. In 1954, he married Heather McKean (**Slim Dusty**'s sister-in-law) and worked some tours with his brother-in-law. (The marriage produced three daughters but the couple later divorced). The same year, Lindsay was booked to accompany his idol, Wilf Carter, on his Australasian tour and when (after a week) Carter was forced through throat problems to quit, Lindsay continued the tour with his own show. He proved so popular that the 'tour' went on for over five years. In 1968, he made his first visit to the USA, where he appeared on the ***Grand Ole Opry***. A later appearance saw him become the first Australian country artist to play the networked Saturday Night *Opry* segment. He has since made many trips to the USA and has made several recordings in Nashville and even worked on record production there.

Over the years, he has turned out a steady stream of records. He left Rodeo in the late 50s and recorded with **EMI** until the late 60s, when he moved to the Festival label. After another spell with EMI, he began recording for the Seven label, which lead to his recordings being released in America on Con Brio. He is probably the first Australian artist to use an electric lead guitar and he even used a didgeridoo on records (on 'Walkabout Rock 'n' Roll'). His many recordings have included rockabilly, bluegrass, boogie and on occasions, he has used orchestral backings. Though rated by many to be one of the best exponents around, he dropped the yodel during the late 50s because he reckoned there were too many singers yodelling but in more recent times, he has used it again to great effect. In a career now lasting over four decades, he has become one of Australia's most popular and versatile entertainers. He has won many awards, including being made an honorary citizen of Tennessee for his promotion of country music world wide. He also starred on the first ever country music show at the Sydney Opera House. In 1984, he became the ninth artist to be elected to the Country Music Roll Of

Renown (Australia's equivalent to Nashville's Country Music Hall Of Fame). Surprisingly, although he is a major star in his own hemisphere and well known in the USA, he is still relatively unknown in the UK except to the devout band of followers of Australian country music. There seems little doubt that his all round entertaining abilities would soon change that should he ever tour the British country club scene.

Albums: *Country Music Comes To Town* (EMI 1961), *Reg Lindsay Favourites* (EMI 1962), *Country And Western Singalong* (EMI 1963), *Songs For Country Folk* (EMI 1964), *Another Country And Western Singalong* (EMI 1964), *Reg Lindsay Encores* (EMI 1964), *20 Golden Country Greats* (Festival 60s), *Reg Lindsay's National Country & Western Hour* (Festival 1965), *Country & Western Million Sellers* (Festival 1966), *Glory Land Way* (Festival 1967), with Heather McKean *Country Duets From Reg And Heather* (Festival 1968), *TV Requests* (Festival 60s), *Roadside Mail Box* (Festival 60s), *Reg Lindsay On Tour* (Festival 60s), *Australia's Country Music Man* (Festival 60s), *Hot Shot Country* (Festival 60s), *She Taught Me To Yodel* (Festival 1970), *Armstrong* (Festival 1970), *Out On The Lone Prairie* (CBS 70s), *Country & Western Greats* (WRC 1972), *Country Music Jamboree* (Summit 1973), *Australia's King Of The Road* (Summit 1973), *21st Anniversary Album* (Festival 1973), *Country Favourites* (Summit 1974), *Country Classics* (Summit 1974), *Reg Lindsay* (Festival 1974), *Country And Western Greats* (Calendar 1974), *Reg Lindsay In Nashville* (Festival 1975), *The Travellin' Man* (Festival 1976), *Silence On The Line* (EMI 1977), *Play Me A Simple Song* (EMI 1978), *The World Of Rodeo* (EMI 1978), *Some Of The Best* (EMI 1978), *Standing Tall* (Brook 1979), *Ten Ten Two And A Quarter* (Brook 1980), *Classics* (EMI 1981), *If You Could See Me Now* (Telmak 1981), *Will The Real Reg Lindsay* (Powderworks 1982), *I've Always Wanted To Do That* (RCA 1985), *Lifetime Of Country Music* (Hammard 1987).

Lindsey, LaWanda

b. 12 January 1953, Tampa, Florida, USA. LaWanda's family moved to Savannah, Georgia soon after her birth. Lindsey's father was the manager of a local country music radio station and he played on air with his group, the Dixie Showboys. From the age of five, Lindsey was featured with the band. **Conway Twitty** was impressed by her talent and, through his help, she signed with Chart Records in 1967. Her first singles included 'Beggars Can't Be Choosers', 'Wave Bye Bye To The Man' and two duets with Kenny Vernon, 'Eye To Eye' and 'Pickin' Wild Mountain Berries', which was her biggest-selling record. In 1970, she had a solo hit on the US country charts with 'Partly Bill'. Although she continued to record and has had several minor successes, she has not manage to establish herself as an adult country artist.

Albums: *Swingin' And Singin' My Songs* (1969), *We'll Sing In The Sunshine* (1970), with Kenny Vernon *Pickin' Wild Mountain Berries* (1970), *This Is LaWanda Lindsey* (1974).

Line Records

Germany's leading independent label, Line Records was founded in Hamburg in 1979 by Uwe Tessnow, a former A&R representative of **Decca Records**' German branch. Initially the label was launched as an outlet for long-deleted gems licensed by Anglo-American companies, featuring artists including **Link Wray**, **Terry & The Pirates**, **Jon Lord**, **Michael Bloomfield**, **Randy California**, Jon Mark and others. Tessnow specialised in re-activating yesterday's heroes, relaunching the careers of **Family** singer Roger Chapman, **Mickey Jupp**, Chris Youlden (ex-**Savoy Brown**) and **Mitch Ryder**, the latter still contracted to the label into the 90s. One of Line's outstanding landmarks was the highly recommended 50 CD series, *Rock File*, comprising 800 rare classics from the American Top 40 of the 50s and early 60s. In the second half of the 80s Line concentrated on acquiring rights to new material, having signed Iain Matthews, Plainsong and Richard Barone since.

Linkchain, Hip

b. Willie Richard, 10 November 1936, near Jackson, Mississippi, USA, d. 13 February 1989, Chicago, Illinois, USA. As a baby, Linkchain was known as Long Linkchain. Hip heard the blues at home and learned to play acoustic guitar, switching to electric after settling in Chicago in the early 50s. He formed his first band in 1959 and recorded singles in the 60s for the Lola and Sann labels, under the name 'Hip Lanchan'. In the 70s he had a single issued by Blues King, and on the JSP label, an album featuring further titles from this session plus earlier tracks. Albums also appeared on MCM, Rumble (with **Jimmy Dawkins**), Teardrop (including a collaboration with Jimmy Rogers) and a highly-acclaimed set for Black Magic. Hip died of cancer in 1989. Linkchain's guitar style was unique in the west-side Chicago tradition, and he was a talented songwriter and singer.

Album: *Airbuster* (1987).

Linn County

Formed in Chicago, Illinois, USA, this powerful, blues-based quintet - Stephen Miller (organ/vocals), Fred Walk (guitar/sitar), Larry Easter (saxophones/flute), Dino Long (bass) and Jerome 'Snake' McAndrew (drums) - subsequently moved to San Francisco. Their impressive debut *Proud Flesh Soothsayer*, included the lengthy 'Protect And Serve/Bad Things' which showcased the exhilarating interplay between the unit's instrumental protagonists. A more orthodox collection, *Fever Shot*, nonetheless featured several hard-edged, disciplined performances, while a final release, *Till The Break Of Dawn*, offered a vibrant reading of **John Lee Hooker**'s 'Boogie Chillun' as its highlight. By this

point McAndrew had been replaced by Clark Pierson, but the group was unable to capitalize upon their cult status and broke up soon afterwards. Miller completed a solo album, which featured the entire Linn County line-up, before joining the **Elvin Bishop** group. Pierson subsequently drummed in **Janis Joplin**'s Full Tilt Boogie Band.
Albums: *Proud Flesh Soothsayer* (1968), *Fever Shot* (1969), *Till The Break Of Dawn* (1970).

Linx

One of the leading lights in the brief but high-profile Brit-funk movement of the early 80s (with Light Of The World, its spin-offs Beggar And Co, **Imagination** and **Freeez**), Linx were based around the duo of **David Grant** (b. 8 August, 1956, Kingston, Jamaica, West Indies; vocals) and Sketch Martin (b. 1954, Antigua, West Indies; bass), and completed by Bob Carter (keyboards) and Andy Duncan (drums). Grant came to the UK in the late 50s and grew up in north London. Sketch came over when he was four, and was based in West Ham, east London. They met while working in a hi-fi shop. Grant later opened a record shop with his cousin, and became a junior reporter on a local paper, before working at **Island**'s press office. Martin worked for the civil service, a film company, and the Performing Rights Society. They had their debut single, 'You're Lying' released as a private pressing (1,000 copies) and sold through a specialist funk shop before **Chrysalis** picked up on it and enabled it to be a hit. They were the first of the Brit Funk bands to make an impression in the USA, when 'You're Lying' made the R&B charts. Further singles included 'Intuition', and 'So This Is Romance'. The video for 'Intuition' featured the late Bertice Reading, while their stage performances harked back to the best traditions of the **Glitter Band** and **Adam And The Ants** by employing twin drummers. Grant moved on to a solo career with Chrysalis and had hit duets with Jaki Graham. He moved to **Polydor** in 1987 then Fourth and Broadway in 1990.
Albums: *Intuition* (1981), *Go Ahead* (1981).

Lion

After the demise of the largely overlooked UK hard rock band **Tytan**, vocalist Kal Swan left England for Los Angeles to put together his own band. Formed in 1983, Lion consisted of Swan (vocals), Doug Aldrich (guitar), Jerry Best (bass) and ex-**Steeler** drummer Mark Edwards. The band quickly produced a self-financed EP, *Powerlove* (only available as a Japanese release), which gained them a strong following in the Far East. Due to the interest being shown towards them, primarily through their contributions to the soundtracks of two films, *The Wraith* and *Transformers*, they attracted the attention of the Scotti Brothers label. This resulted in the band's debut, *Dangerous Attraction*, released in 1987. This proved to be a strong, melodic hard rock effort, on which Swans' soaring vocals came to the fore. However, Scotti Brothers failed to promote the record fully and album sales suffered. The band signed a new recording agreement with Grand Slamm Records after disentangling themselves from their former employers, resulting in *Trouble At Angel City* being released in 1989. Unfortunately soon after release the band folded due to drummer Mark Edwards experiencing a debilitating accident and guitarist Doug Aldrich leaving to join **Hurricane**.
Albums: *Power Love* (Lion 1985, Japan only), *Dangerous Attraction* (Scotti Bros 1987), *Trouble At Angel City* (Grand Slam 1989).

Lion King, The

'Prepare to be awed', was *Time* magazine's warning when the latest **Walt Disney** blockbuster was preparing to dominate the world's cinema screens in 1994. Unlike the Studio's previous feature length animated triumphs, *The Lion King* is not based on an established fairy tale or children's book. Instead, the witty screenplay, by Irene Mecchi, Jonathan Roberts and Linda Woolverton, weaves a timeless tale of 'monarchical principal, family unity and male supremacy', and has 'lions dancing with zebras, monkeys aping around with warthogs and ostriches, and giraffes performing as in the *Folies Bergère*'. With a soundtrack full of perfectly selected, familiar voices, the Hamlet-style hero, Simba the lion cub (Jonathan Taylor Thomas), is cheated out of his inheritance by his wicked Uncle Scar (Jeremy Irons), after he has seen his regal father, Mufasa (James Earl Jones), killed while trying to rescue him from a stampeding herd of hyenas and wildebeests. It takes a long period in the wilderness, where he meets up with Pumbaa, the weird and wonderful warthog (Ernie Sabella) and Timon, the marvellous meercat (Nathan Lane), before the grown Simba (now voiced by Matthew Broderick), urged by the ghost of his dead father, returns to dispose of his murdering uncle and take his rightful place in the scheme of things. Also contributing their vocal talents to a heartwarming range of characters, are Rowan Atkinson (as Zazu the hornbill) and Whoopi Goldberg, Cheech Marin and Jim Cummings as a trio of a leering hyenas. The critics were unanimous in their praise of the film's 'technical wizardry and rich imagery, the late 20th century sophistication', and 'the lurid colours, that are so right for the African subject matter', although some of them had reservations about the degree of violence involved in some scenes, and the lack of political correctness. The general feeling seemed to be that the film's music was not in the same class as that which graced two of Disney's other recent animated successes, ***The Little Mermaid*** and ***Beauty And The Beast***. Even so, **Hans Zimmer**'s score, and one of **Elton John** and **Tim Rice**'s songs, 'Can You Feel

The Love Tonight', won Oscars, and the soundtrack was awarded two Grammys. With forecasts in the order of 'this will be the most successful film of the century', *The Lion King*, which was directed by Roger Allers and Rob Minkoff, grossed £21 million over the first weekend of its release.

Lioness

Founded by lead singer/songwriter Teri Owens, and largely inspired by her staunch Rastafarian beliefs and morals, Lioness' sound is rendered unique by the employment of instrumentation drawn from outside of reggae's normal canon, notably Janet Irvine's flute. Their 'cultural' lyrics are equally refreshing, a return to the roots flavour which has been overshadowed by modern **dancehall** tastes.

Albums: *Jah Works* (1989), *Jah Victory* (Dawter 1991).

Lionheart

Formed in 1980 by Dennis Stratton (guitar) on his exit from **Iron Maiden**, he was joined in this crusade by vocalist Jess Cox (**Tygers Of Pan Tang**), Frank Noon (Next Band/**Def Leppard**) on drums, Steve Mann (Liar) on guitar and Rocky Newton (**Wildfire**) on bass. They made their highly impressive debut one Saturday night at the Marquee, London, but suffered from bad press thanks to their opinions on Cox. This led to the cancellation of the next two appearances and saw Cox replaced by Reuben Archer (Lautrec). Noon quit in 1981 to join **Paul Di'Anno**'s band before setting off for **Waysted**. The nucleus of Stratton/Mann and Newton continued with various line-ups that included drummers Les Binks (**Judas Priest**) and Clive Edwards (**Grand Prix**). In 1982 they signed to Heavy Metal Records but only managed to release one track, on the *Heavy Metal Heroes Vol 2* compilation. That track, 'Lionheart', remains the only representative recording of their early sound, as later they would significantly adapt their style. With the addition of Chad Brown on vocals and session drummer Robert Jenkins, they went on to record an album with producer Kevin Beamish (**REO Speedwagon**). This was a slick, Americanized effort which failed to capture the old fans' interest or that of their target audience in the US. In 1985 they continued with drummer Andy Bierne and Phil Lanzon (keyboards) who had been playing with reformed glam rockers **Sweet**. After a while Lanzon also left and was replaced by Steve Mann from Stratus and new vocalist Keith Murrell. They split up finally in 1986, with Bierne going into management, Murrell to **Mama's Boys** and Newton and Mann joining **MSG**. Stratton later found fame in Japan as part of the British All Stars/**Praying Mantis** line-up which featured a number of ex-**N.W.O.B.H.M.** musicians.

Album: *Die For Love* (Epic 1984).

Lionsheart

Following his departure from UK heavy metal thrashers **Onslaught,** ex-**Grim Reaper** vocalist Steve Grimmett set about forming a more melodic band to better suit his vocal abilities and musical inclinations, enlisting twin brothers Mark (guitar) and Steve Owers (bass), Graham Collet (keyboards) and Anthony Christmas (drums). Lionsheart signed to **Music For Nations**, but the Owers brothers departed before the release of their self-titled debut, with illness leaving Mark Owers unable to tour, and they were replaced by Nick Burr (guitar; ex-**Killers/**Idol Rich) and Zak Bajjon (bass). Lionsheart ignored grunge trends in favour of guitar-driven melodic hard rock with quality songwriting, and despite minimal reaction at home and in the USA, the band achieved deserved success in Europe and major status in Japan. *Pride In Tact* saw Lionsheart extending their approach from almost AOR balladry to harder blues-rock, with Burr proving equal to the task of following Mark Owers' performance on the debut.

Albums: *Lionsheart* (Music For Nation 1993), *Pride In Tact* (Music For Nations 1994).

Lipscomb, Mance

b. 9 April 1895, Navasota, Texas, USA, d. 30 January 1976, Navasota, Texas, USA. The son of a former slave and professional fiddle player, Lipscomb initially learned that instrument and later the guitar. For many years he played on a solely local basis, while working as a farmer, and only made his first recordings at the age of 65, in 1960. Over the following 15 years, he made a series of highly regarded albums, mainly for Chris Strachwitz's **Arhoolie** label. On the strength of these and his frequent live performances, he built up a very strong reputation for his skills as a singer of a wide range of material. His remarkably extensive repertoire encompassed gospel, rags, ballads and other traditional songs, as well as Texas-style blues. He also appeared in several films, including one biopic, *A Well Spent Life*.

Albums: *You'll Never Find Another Man Like Mance* (1964), *Texas Songster, Volumes 1 - 6* (60s/70s), *Texas Blues* (60s/70s). Compilations: *Texas Songster* (1990, CD compilation of the *Texas Songster* series), *You Got To Reap What You Sow* (Arhoolie 1993).

Lipton, Sydney

b. 4 January 1906, London, England. A popular and stylish dance band leader, Lipton learned to play the violin as a child, and was a member of cinema ensembles accompanying silent films in his early teens. His interest in dance band music led him to work in the 20s with Murray Hedges and **Billy Cotton**, before forming his own band in the early 30s. His first recordings to be released were made in 1932, and from then, until 1941, Sydney Lipton And His Orchestra were resident at the Grosvenor House in London, from where they broadcasted regularly. In the early days Lipton's signature tune was 'I'll See You In My Dreams', but in later years he used two others, 'Just Dance And Leave The Music To Me' and 'Sweet Harmony'. After service in the Royal Artillery and the Royal Signals during World War II, Lipton returned to the Grosvenor House, and continued to purvey his particular brand of sophisticated dance music until 1967. He then formed his own successful entertainment agency, as well as serving as musical director for various prestige venues and cruise ships. Top sidemen who played in his bands over the years included **Ted Heath**, Harry Hayes, **Bill McGuffie**, Freddy Gardner, George Evans, Max Goldberg, Billy Munn and many more, along with vocalists such Anona Wynn, Primrose Hayes, Les Allen, Chips Chippindall, and Lipton's daughter, Celia. An accomplished dancer and singer, Celia appeared in London shows such as *Get A Load Of This* and ***The Quaker Girl,*** and was a notable Peter Pan at the Scala Theatre, before moving to America while in her 20s. After appearing in cabaret, on television and starring in straight roles on Broadway, she retired from show business and settled in California, living the life of a society hostess, raising millions of dollars for charity. After her husband died in 1985 (leaving her a reported $200 million), Celia recorded two albums for her Independent label, *The London I Love* and *The Best Of Times*, and appeared in her own television special. In the late 80s she was joined in America by Sydney Lipton.

Selected albums: *Sweet Harmony* (Decca 1959), *Dancing At The Grosvenor House Volumes 1, 2* and *3* (Decca 1960-61), *Sydney Lipton And His Orchestra 1932-3* (Retrospect 1977), *Just Dance* (Decca 1982), *Beautiful Melodies From Around The World* (Horatio Nelson 1985).

Liquid

Group who originally comprised Eamon Downes and Shane Honegan, until the latter party left. They had become one of the first progressive house acts in the Top 20, with 1992's 'Sweet Harmony', recorded while they were still a duo, as a reaction to the 'louder faster' rules of hardcore techno. It cost only £200 to record yet saw them grace UK television's *Top Of The Pops* stage. Downes re-emerged in 1993 on the **XL** roster, after a period in the shadows with the *Time To Get Up* EP. He maintains that he calls himself Liquid because he 'likes the odd drink'. Early influences were dub maestros such as **Barrington Levy** and **Scientist**.

Liquid Jesus

This experimental, Los Angeles-based quintet were formed in 1990 by bassist Johnny Lonely and guitarist Scott Tracey. Adding Todd Rigione (guitar), Buck Murphy (vocals) and John Molo (drums), they gigged incessantly on the LA bar and club circuit. Fusing psychedelic, blues, jazz and metal influences to bizarre extremes, they debuted with an independently released live album. Tipped by some as the next **Jane's Addiction**, they were signed by **Geffen Records** in 1991 and delivered *Pour In The Sky*. This pooled their influences of **Jimi Hendrix**, **Led Zeppelin**, the **Red Hot Chili Peppers** and **Queen**, but accusations of plagiarism were sidestepped by virtue of their totally deranged and unpredictable delivery.

Albums: *Liquid Jesus Live* (Liquid Jesus 1990), *Pour In The Sky* (Geffen 1991).

Lisa Lisa And Cult Jam

Formed in Brooklyn, New York, USA, consisting of Lisa Velez (b. 1967, New York City, USA), the youngest of 10 children in her family, plus Mike Hughes (b. 1963) and Alex 'Spanador' Mosely (b. 1962). The two men in the group were members of the New York funk/soul group Full Force. Lisa Lisa And Cult Jam were signed to **Columbia Records** in 1985 and recorded their debut single, 'I Wonder If I Take You Home', only a week after forming. The single, which rose to the Top 10 of the black charts in the USA and the national UK Top 20, was produced, written and recorded with the complete Full Force aggregation - only in concert did Lisa Lisa work strictly in the reduced trio format. Lisa Lisa And Cult Jam continued to achieve US Top 10 singles in the national and dance charts throughout the late 80s, including two US number 1 hits in 1987, 'Head To Toe' and 'Lost In Emotion' as well as, 'All Cried Out', 'Someone To Love Me For Me' and 'Everything Will B-Fine'. Their 1985, self-titled debut album was only moderately successful but 1987's *Spanish Fly* reached the US Top 10. In 1989, their third album, *Straight To The Sky*, stalled at number 77 and produced no hit singles.

Albums: *Lisa Lisa And Cult Jam With Full Force* (1985), *Spanish Fly* (1987), *Straight To The Sky* (1989). Solo: Lisa Lisa *LL-77* (Pendulum 1994).

Lisberg, Harvey

b. 1940, Manchester, England. A chartered accountant turned pop manager, Lisberg entered the music business in 1964 after signing the Heartbeats (better known as **Herman's Hermits**). He took them to producer **Mickie Most** and by the end of the year they were number 1 in the UK with 'I'm Into Something Good'. Lisberg later teamed-up with the renowned agent **Danny Betesh** and became involved in his Kennedy Street Enterprises. During one week in early 1965, agent and manager found themselves on the top of the world when three of their acts, **Freddie And The Dreamers**, **Wayne Fontana And The Mindbenders** and Herman's Hermits held the first three places in the US chart. As manager of Herman's Hermits, Lisberg took full advantage of singer **Peter Noone**'s stardom in America, and supervised his entry into films by negotiating with the renowned producer, Sam Katzman. Lisberg was also responsible for directly selecting three of Herman's Hermits biggest world hits: 'Mrs Brown You've Got A Lovely Daughter', 'I'm Henry VIII, I Am' and 'Listen People'. While enjoying amazing success with Noone, Lisberg was less lucky with another Manchester group, the **Mockingbirds**, who failed to chart despite the presence of top songwriter **Graham Gouldman**. After briefly managing the **Herd**, Lisberg signed songwriters **Andrew Lloyd Webber** and **Tim Rice**, but abandoned them just before they completed the astonishingly successful musical, ***Jesus Christ Superstar***. A brief association with vocalist **Tony Christie** was followed by another spectacular run of hits with **10cc**. Lisberg managed them from their early days as **Hotlegs** right through to the emergence of **Godley And Creme**. Along the way, he entered the 'progressive' market with acts such as **Julie Driscoll** and **Barclay James Harvest**, before finding another major hit act with **Sad Cafe**. For a time, Lisberg abandoned pop management in favour of looking after the careers of various snooker players, but sought new pop acts in the late 80s.

Lisbon Story, The (Film Musical)

Released by British National in 1946, this war-time story of intrigue set in Lisbon and Paris in 1940, was adapted by Jack Whittingham from Harold Purcell's long-running musical which opened in London in 1943. The delightful Patricia Burke recreated her stage role as Gabrielle Gerard, a French actress and singer, who risks accusations of collaborating with the invading Germans to assist a member of British Intelligence, David Warren (David Farrar), in his successful efforts to smuggle atom scientist Pierre Sargon (John Ruddock) back to England. David returns to Gabrielle after Paris has been liberated by the Allies, and they are married. The celebrated tenor, Richard Tauber, played Andre Joubert, Gabrielle's singing partner, and Walter Rilla was suitably evil as Karl von Schriner, Director of German Propaganda in Paris. Other roles went to Lawrence O'Madden, Austin Trevor, Harry Welchman, Paul Bonifas, Esme Percy, Noele Gordon, John Ruddock, and Joan Seton. Violin virtuoso **Stéphane Grappelli** was in it too, and so were two of the original show's hit songs, 'Pedro the Fisherman', 'Never Say Goodbye' (music Harry Parr-Davies, lyrics Harold Purcell). The former song was enormously popular during and after the war, especially in a recording by **Gracie Fields**. The picture itself, which was directed by Paul Stein, was pretty popular as well.

Lisbon Story, The (Stage Musical)

One of the most popular West End musicals during World War II, *The Lisbon Story* opened at the London Hippodrome on 17 June 1943. Fifty years on, it is still recalled fondly because of the inclusion of the jaunty 'Pedro The Fisherman', which almost immediately became an enormous hit. The song was part of a score written by composer Harry Parr-Davies and lyricist Harry Purcell, who also provided a book in which wartime drama was mixed with sentimental music and lavish dance sequences in a spectacular and entertaining fashion. The story concerns a Parisian prima ballerina, Gabrielle Gerard (Patricia Burke), who colludes with the Nazis in an effort to secure the release of an important French scientist. When her deceit is discovered, she is executed. Albert Lieven played her German go-between, Carl von Shriner, and the cast also included Arséne Kiriloff, Zulia, Noele Gordon, Jack Livesey, Margaret McGrath, Reginald Long, and Joseph Dollinger. There were two major dance scenes and a lovely operetta sequence. The score contained several attractive numbers, including the waltz, 'Someday We Shall Meet Again', 'Never Say Goodbye', 'For The First Time (I've Fallen In Love)', 'Follow The Drum', 'Happy Days', and 'A Serenade For Sale', but it was 'Pedro The Fisherman', which was sung in the show by Vincent Tildsley's Master Singers, in sailor rig, that audiences were whistling when they left the theatre. Patricia Burke made a successful recording of the song, as did the distinguished tenor, Richard Tauber, who appeared with her in the 1946 film of *The Lisbon Story*. Probably the version that endured the most, and which received consistent exposure on BBC Radio's *Family Favourites* programme, was that by **Gracie Fields**.

Liston, Melba

b. 13 January 1926, Kansas City, Missouri, USA. Although she was born and spent her childhood in Kansas City during its hottest jazz years, Liston's entry into music began in Los Angeles where her family moved when she was 11 years old. At the age of 16, she joined the pit band, playing trombone, at the Lincoln Theatre and the following year, 1943, joined **Gerald Wilson**'s orchestra. With Wilson's guidance and encouragement, she began arranging but remained an active performer, appearing on record with an old school friend, **Dexter Gordon**. When the Wilson band folded while on a tour of the east coast, Liston was hired by **Dizzy Gillespie**. This was in 1948 and the following year she toured briefly with Wilson who was leading a band accompanying **Billie Holiday**. The tour was a disaster and the experience led to Liston quitting music for a while. She worked as an educational administrator in California, played occasionally in clubs, and also worked as an extra in films. In 1956, and again in 1957, she returned to Gillespie for his State Department tours of the Middle East, Asia and South America. She then began a musical association with **Quincy Jones**, writing scores for his band and working on the show *Free And Easy*

with which they toured Europe. In the 60s, she wrote extensively for **Randy Weston** and occasionally for **Duke Ellington**, **Solomon Burke** and **Tony Bennett**. Her arrangements were used on **Johnny Griffin**'s *White Gardenia.* In the 70s she was involved in a number of jazz educational projects, especially in Jamaica where, for almost six years, she ran the pop and jazz division of the country's School of Music. She continued to write charts for the bands of Ellington and **Count Basie** and singers such as **Abbey Lincoln** and **Diana Ross**. At the end of the 70s she was persuaded to return to the USA as the headline attraction at the first Kansas City Women's Jazz Festival. There, she led her own band, with an all-woman line-up, and made a great impact. Her successful return to playing led to a revitalisation of her performing career and although her band later developed into a 'mixed' group, she has continued to play an important role in furthering the role of women in jazz. A sound section player whose ballad solos are particularly effective, Liston is one of the best latter-day arrangers in jazz. Unfortunately, the male domination of so many aspects of the jazz life has resulted in this enormously talented artist remaining little-known, even within the jazz community itself.
Albums: with Dexter Gordon *The Chase* (1947), *Dizzy Gillespie At Newport* (1957), *Melba Liston And Her Orchestra* (1958), with Randy Weston *Uhuru Afrika* (1960), with Weston *Volcano Blues* (1993).

Lisztomania

In his early carreer the maverick British film director Ken Russell made several controversial biographies of revered classic composers. These early films were noteable for introducing previously unknown aspects of the composers' private lives. This reached a peak with the Tchaikovsky feature, *The Music Lovers.* Russell's later work was often criticised as excessive, particularly in the wake of his film of the **Who** rock-opera, ***Tommy*** (1975). The group's lead singer, **Roger Daltrey** starred in *Lisztomania,* which was released that same year. However, the director's attempt to portray the composer as a hedonistic rock star was artistically unsatisfying, and did much to undermine Russell's reputation. **Ringo Starr** and **Paul Nicholas** were part of an uninspired cast while ex-**Yes** keyboard player **Rick Wakeman** provided a score comprising of heavy-handed treatments of Liszt and Wagner compositions. *Lisztomania* played upon the artistic flaws of all the participants.

Litter

Based in Minneapolis, Minnesota, USA, Denny Waite (vocals/organ), Tom Kaplan (lead guitar), Dan Rinaldi (rhythm guitar/vocals), Jim Kane (bass) and Tom Murray (drums) won cult acclaim for the impressive *Distortions.* Inspired by British favourites the **Who**, **Spencer Davis Group** and **Yardbirds**, the Litter drew material from such mentors, infusing it with garage band simplicity and a penchant for feedback. The same style prevailed on *$100 Fine,* on which the quintet's own songwriting flourished, although the set lacked the naive charm of its predecessor. This artistic demise was confirmed with *Emerge,* the group's first recording for a major label. With a new lead vocalist in Mark Gallagher, the brand of progressive hard rock on offer here was indistinguishable from a myriad of contemporaries and Litter ceased recording with its release.
Albums: *Distortions* (1968), *$100 Fine* (1969), *Emerge* (1969).

Little Angels

This UK heavy rock quintet were formed in Scarborough, Yorkshire, during 1985, originally under the title Mr Thrud. Comprising Toby Jepson (vocals), Bruce John Dickinson (guitar), Mark Plunkett (bass), Jimmy Dickinson (keyboards) and Dave Hopper (drums) they were a youthful outfit, whose energy and enthusiasm in the live setting won them a loyal fan base in their native north east. Following a series of independent releases, notably the seven-track *Too Posh To Mosh,* they attracted the attention of **Polydor Records**. *Don't Prey For Me,* which featured new drummer Michael Lee, included a dozen gems of melodic, but rough-shod rock 'n' roll, characterized by Jepson's raucous and charismatic vocals. The big budget follow-up, mixed by the Steve Thompson/Michael Barbiero partnership, was a disappointment. Abandoning their roots, this set saw them made a concerted attempt to break into the American FM radio market. Internal disputes began to manifest themselves in 1991. Drummer Michael Lee secretly auditioned for the **Cult**, and was ejected from the band as a result. His replacement would be Mark Richardson. *Jam* regained much of the lost ground in 1993, entering the UK charts at number 1 and winning them the support slot on **Van Halen**'s European tour. However, having found their niche, effectively refining it while still enlarging their fan-base, they nevertheless elected to go their separate ways in 1994. Several farewell gigs were played, with a final album release housed on Castle.
Albums: *Too Posh To Mosh* (Powerstation 1987), *Don't Prey For Me* (Polydor 1989), *Young Gods* (Polydor 1991), *Jam* (Polydor 1993), *Little Of The Past* (Polydor 1994).
Compilation: *Too Posh To Nosh* (Castle 1994).
Video: *Big Bad Video* (1991).

Little Anthony And The Imperials

Formed in Brooklyn, New York, USA in 1957 and originally called the Chesters, the group comprised 'Little' Anthony Gourdine (b. 8 January 1940, Brooklyn, New York, USA), Ernest Wright Jnr. (b. 24 August 1941, Brooklyn, New York, USA), Clarence

Collins (b. 17 March 1941, Brooklyn, New York, USA), Tracy Lord and Glouster Rogers (b. 1940). A vital link between doo-wop and sweet soul, the Imperials were the prototype for the **Delfonics** and **Stylistics**. Gourdine first recorded in 1956 as a member of the Duponts. From there he helped form the Chesters, who became the Imperials on signing to the End label. The 'Little Anthony' prefix was subsequently added at the suggestion of the influential disc jockey **Alan Freed**. The group's first hit, the haunting 'Tears On My Pillow' (1958), encapsulated the essence of street-corner harmony. Further success came with 'So Much' (1959) and 'Shimmy Shimmy Ko-Ko-Bop' (1960), before Gourdine was persuaded to embark on an ill-fated solo career. In 1964, he formed a 'new' Imperials around Wright, Collins and Sammy Strain (b. 9 December 1940). Their first hit, 'I'm On The Outside (Looking In)' showcased Anthony's dazzling falsetto, a style continued on 'Goin' Out Of My Head' and 'Hurt So Bad' (both of which reached the US pop Top 10). Complementing these graceful releases were such uptempo offerings as 'Better Use Your Head' and 'Gonna Fix You Good' (both 1966). The line-up later drifted apart and in 1974 Sammy Strain replaced William Powell in the **O'Jays**. Three years later, Collins formed his own 'Imperials', touring Britain on the strength of two hit singles, a reissued 'Better Use Your Head', and a new recording, 'Who's Gonna Love Me'. In the 80s Gourdine released *Daylight* on the religious outlet, Songbird.

Albums: *We Are Little Anthony And The Imperials* (1959), *Shades Of The 40's* (1961), *I'm On The Outside Looking In* (1964), *Goin' Out Of My Head* (1965), *Paying Our Dues* (1967), *Reflections* (1967), *Movie Grabbers* (1968), *Out Of Sight, Out Of Mind* (1969), *On A New Street* (1974). Compilations: *Outside Looking In* (1984), *The Best Of Little Anthony And The Imperials* (1989). Solo: Anthony Gourdine *Daylight* (1980).

Little Beaver

b. William Hale, 15 August 1945, Forest City, Arkansas, USA. Little Beaver, a singer and guitarist, made his mark on the tail end of the soul era in the early 70s with a typical southern-style body of work that included both blues and soul traditions. Little Beaver grew up in Arkansas but when a teenager moved to Florida. He recorded some local hits for various labels, with a **Bobby Bland**-type gospel-blues voice. He then joined Henry Stone's TK complex of labels in 1971, and penned some hits for **Betty Wright** as well as playing on innumerable sessions. By the time Little Beaver first recorded on his own for TK's Cat subsidiary in 1972 he had found his own voice and style and scored nationally with 'Joey' (number 48 R&B). His biggest hit was 'Party Down' (number 2 R&B) from 1974. His deep southern sound was not all that compatible with the emerging disco and funk trends and Beaver had his last chart record in 1976.

Albums: *Joey* (Cat 1972). *Black Rhapsody* (Cat 1973), *Little Beaver* (Cat 1974), *Party Down* (Cat 1975), *Party Down* (Collectables 1994).

Little Big Band

A pseudonym for the talented folk/blues musician, Rob Gray, from Manchester, England. Between high level gigs, he busks in city centre shopping arcades.

Album: *Little Big Band* (1989).

Little Caesar

A highly underrated R&B-influenced rock band from Los Angeles, Little Caesar made their recorded debut with one track, 'Down To The Wire', on *Street Survivors*, a compilation showcasing the best unsigned local bands. With a line-up of Ron Young (vocals), Apache (guitar/steel guitar), Louren Molinaire (guitar), Fidel Paniagua (bass) and Tom Morris (drums), an EP, *Name Your Poison*, was recorded, helping the band sign a major deal with **Geffen**. The self-titled debut, produced by Bob Rock, deservedly received excellent reviews. Packed with good material, from the basic rock 'n' roll of 'Down-N-Dirty' to the more soulful R&B of 'In Your Arms', plus two **Motown** covers in 'Chain Of Fools' and 'I Wish It Would Rain', the album displayed the band's strong songwriting talents and sense of melody, coupled with an emotive performance from the smoky-voiced Young. However, despite praise in the press for both live and recorded work, the album failed to take off. As it was released, **Guns N'Roses** were attaining enormous mass popularity, and the band's tattooed biker image, unpremeditated though it may have been, probably worked against them, allowing many to dismiss them as yet another Guns N'Roses clone band without hearing the evidence. Little was heard from the group for some time, although Young made a cameo appearance in *Terminator 2: Judgement Day*, and 'Down To The Wire' featured on the *Point Break* soundtrack, until they reappeared with ex-**David Bowie**/**Dirty White Boy** guitarist Earl Slick replacing the departed Apache for some live shows prior to recording *Influence*. Boasting a harder sound than the debut, the album was another high-quality outing, but despite further good press, sales were again disappointing. When Geffen failed to take up a third album option, the band split up, with Young going on to front the similarly ill-fated Manic Eden.

Albums: *Little Caesar* (Geffen 1990), *Influence* (Geffen 1992).

Little Caesar And The Romans

The roots of doo-wop group Little Caesar And The Romans are found in a 50s vocal group from Los Angeles called the Cubans, featuring David Caesar

Johnson (b. 16 June 1934, Chicago, Illinois, USA), Leroy Sanders (bass), Johnny O'Simmons and Early Harris (both tenors). The group first recorded in 1959. When Cuba underwent a political revolution that year the group became the Upfronts. Two years later they met songwriter Paul Politi, who had penned a song called 'Those Oldies But Goodies (Remind Me Of You)'. After personnel changes they became Little Caesar And The Romans with a faintly ludicrous gimmick of dressing up in togas and sandals and recorded Politi's ballad for Del-Fi Records. It reached the US Top 10 and they followed with one other minor hit single, 'Hully Gully Again', before disbanding in 1962. In 1975, Johnson put together a new Little Caesar And The Romans and recorded a single called 'Disco Hully Gully'. For a while they toured as **Marvin Gaye**'s opening act and in the late 70s, one of the backing singers for the group was **Rickie Lee Jones**. Little Caesar And The Romans were still active in the early 90s.

Album: *Memories Of Those Oldies But Goodies, Volume 1* (1961).

Little Charlie And The Nightcats

Rick Estrin (b. 5 October 1950, San Francisco, California, USA; vocal/harmonica), Charlie Baty (b. 10 July 1953, Birmingham, Alabama, USA; guitar), Brad Lee Sexton (b. 11 November 1948, South Carolina, USA; bass), Dobie Strange (b. 15 November 1948, Red Bluff, California, USA; drums). One of the most popular bands performing in the west coast 'Chicago blues' style, the Nightcats grew out of a 1973 meeting between Estrin and Baty, at that time a harmonica player himself. Estrin had been professional since 1968, when a jam with **Lowell Fulson** turned into a three-week booking. By 1975, he had turned down the opportunity to join **Muddy Waters**' band, while Baty was in Sacramento, where he had started a band. When Estrin tired of San Francisco a year later, he contacted Baty with the idea of getting a group together. In 1982, the band pressed up a single which they sold at gigs and began to put together a tape which in 1986 they submitted to Bruce Iglauer at Alligator. A year later, *All The Way Crazy* was released. With their succeeding albums, the band established a reputation for hard driving music with a humorous edge to their lyrics. Estrin is their principal composer; **Robert Cray** recorded his 'I'm Just Lucky That Way', while 'My Next Ex-Wife' won the 1993 **W.C. Handy** award for Best Blues Song Of The Year.

Albums: *All The Way Crazy* (Alligator 1987), *Disturbing The Peace* (Alligator 1988), *The Big Break* (Alligator 1989), *Captured Live* (Alligator 1991), *Night Vision* (Alligator 1993), *Straight Up!* (Alligator 1995).

Little Dippers

One of several groups of singers formed by successful backup vocalist/group leader/producer **Anita Kerr**, the Little Dippers had one US Top 10 single, 'Forever', in 1960, before disappearing forever themselves. The quartet consisted of Delores Dinning, Emily Gilmore, Darrell McCall and Hurshel Wigintin. Written by popular Nashville writer/producer Buddy Killen, 'Forever' was released on University Records. Although it reached number 9 in 1960, no other record by that particular aggregation ever charted.

Little Egypt

Claiming their initial notoriety from the fact that lead guitarist/vocalist Nick Rossi is the son of Francis Rossi of **Status Quo**, Little Egypt formed in the early 90s as a similarly inclined metal/boogie affair. The nepotism extended further: the group supported Quo on their 1993 tour, while father, who wrote several of their early songs, also co-produced their debut album. Bob Young, famed for his harmonica contributions to the denim warriors, is their manager. The other members of Little Egypt include Duncan Turmain (guitar/vocals), Dan Eames (drums) and 'Flying' Dave Conti (bass).

Album: *Little Egypt* (1994).

Little Eva

b. Eva Narcissus Boyd, 29 June 1943, Bellhaven, North Carolina, USA. Discovered by songwriters **Carole King** and **Gerry Goffin**, Little Eva burst to fame in 1962 with the international hit, 'The Loco-Motion', a driving, dance-based song. Its ebullient, adolescent approach was muted on a follow-up single, 'Keep Your Hands Off My Baby', but although further releases from the following year, 'Let's Turkey Trot' and 'Old Smokey Locomotion', revived its novelty appeal, they lacked its basic excitement. Eva continued to record until 1965, but her only other substantial hit came with 'Swinging On A Star', a duet with **Big Dee Irwin** on which she was, unfortunately, uncredited. She made a UK chart comeback in 1972 with 'The Loco-Motion' re-issue peaking at number 11 and the song's lasting appeal was reaffirmed in 1988 when **Kylie Minogue** emulated Eva's original UK chart position.

Album: *Loco-Motion* (1962). Compilations: *Lil' Loco'Motion* (1982), *The Best Of Little Eva* (1988), *Back On Track* (1989).

Little Feat

The compact rock 'n' roll funk displayed by Little Feat put them out of step with other Californian rock bands of the early 70s. By combining elements of country, folk, blues, soul and boogie they unwittingly created a sound that became their own, and has to date never been replicated or bettered. The band comprised **Lowell George** (b. 13 April 1945, Hollywood, California, USA, d. 29 June 1979) who had already found experience with the earthy garage band the **Standells** and with the **Mothers Of Invention**, plus, Roy Estrada (b. Santa Ana, California, USA; bass), Bill Payne (b. 12 March 1949, Waco, Texas, USA; keyboards) and Richie Haywood (drums). Although they signed to the mighty **Warner Brothers** label in 1970, no promotional push was given to the band until their second album in 1972. The public later latched on to the debut, *Little Feat.* It remains a mystery why the band were given such a low profile. George had already been noticed as potentially a major songwriter; two of his songs were taken by the **Byrds**, 'Truck Stop Girl' and 'Willin''.

The debut sold poorly, and quite inexplicably, so did their second and third albums. The band were understandably depressed and began to fragment. Lowell began writing songs with **John Sebastian** amid rumours of a planned supergroup adding Phil Everly. Fortunately, their record company made a further advance to finance *Feats Don't Fail Me Now*; the revised band was now Paul Barrere (b. 3 July 1948, Burbank, California, USA; guitar), Kenny Gradney (b. New Orleans, Louisiana, USA; bass) and Sam Clayton (b. New Orleans, Louisiana, USA; percussion). Deservedly, they made the album charts in the USA, although the excellent material was no better than their three previous albums. *Feats Don't Fail Me Now* marked the growth of other members as credible songwriters and George's role began to diminish. The European critics were unanimous in praising the band in 1975 on the 'Warner Brothers Music Show'. This impressive package tour contained **Graham Central Station**, Bonaroo, **Tower Of Power**, **Montrose**, Little Feat and the headliners, the **Doobie Brothers**, who were then enjoying unprecedented acclaim and success. Without exaggeration, Little Feat blew everyone off the stage with a series of outstanding concerts, and from that moment on they could do no wrong. *The Last Record Album* in 1975 contained Lowell's finest (albeit short), winsome love song, 'Long Distance Love'; the sparseness of the guitar playing and the superb change of tempo with drum and bass, created a song that courted melancholy and tenderness. The opening question and answer line 'Ah Hello, give me missing persons, tell me what is it that you need, I said oh, I need her so, you've got to stop your teasing', is full of emotional pleading.

George meanwhile was overindulging with drugs and his contribution to *Time Loves A Hero* was minimal. Once again they delivered a great album, featuring the by now familiar and distinctive cover artwork by Neon Park. Following the double live *Waiting For Columbus*, the band disintegrated and George started work on his solo album, *Thanks, I'll Eat It Here*, (which sounded like a Little Feat album); two notable tracks were 'Missing You', and '20 Million Things To Do'. During a solo concert tour George had a heart attack and died; years of abuse had taken their toll. The remaining band reformed for a benefit concert for his widow and at the end of a turbulent year the barrel was scraped to release *Down On The Farm*. The record became a considerable success, as did the compilation *Hoy-Hoy*.

In 1988, almost a decade after they broke up, the band re-formed and *Let It Roll* became their biggest album by far. The band had ex-**Pure Prairie League** Craig Fuller taking Lowell's place, and the musical direction was guided by the faultless keyboard playing of Bill Payne. A second set from the re-formed band came in 1990, and although it disappointed many, it added fuel to the theory that this time they intended to stay together. *Shake Me Up* finally buried the ghost of George, as the critics accepted that the band are a credible force once again and can claim rightful ownership of both its name and history, without forgetting Lowell George's gigantic contribution. Fuller was not present on *Ain't Had Enough Fun*, instead the band recruited a female lead singer, Shaun Murphy

Albums: *Little Feat* (Warner 1971), *Sailin' Shoes* (Warner 1972), *Dixie Chicken* (Warner 1973), *Feats Don't Fail Me Now* (Warner 1974), *The Last Record Album* (Warner 1975), *Time Loves A Hero* (Warner 1977), *Waiting For Columbus* (Warner 1978), *Down On The Farm* (Warner 1979), *Let It Roll* (Warner 1988), *Representing The Mambo* (Warner 1990), *Shake Me Up* (1991), *Ain't Had Enough Fun* (Zoo 1995). Compilation: *Hoy Hoy* (Warner 1981), *As Time Goes By - The Best Of Little Feat* (Warner 1986). Solo: Lowell George *Thanks I'll Eat It Here* (Warner 1979).

Little Joe And The Thrillers

This R&B vocal group came from Philadelphia, Pennsylvania, USA. The group was formed in 1956 by Joe Cook (b. 29 December 1922, Philadelphia, Pennsylvania, USA), who had made his first record in 1949 as lead of a gospel group, the Joe Cook Quartet. While recording as a member of a later gospel group, the Evening Star Quartet, Cook formed the Thrillers, which besides Cook consisted of Farris Hill (tenor), Richard Frazier (tenor), Donald Burnett (baritone) and Harry Pascle (bass). Their only real claim to fame was 'Peanuts', which entered the US Top 30 in 1957 on the **OKeh** label. Cook's piercing falsetto lead became the standard for many R&B doo-wop groups from the late 50s through the 70s. The first release of the group was a dance number, called 'The Slop' that achieved some local east coast recognition in 1956. The Thrillers never hit the charts after 'Peanuts' and they broke up, Little Joe continued recording up to 1966 on various small Philadelphia labels. In 1964, Cook organized an all-girl group, the **Sherrys**, two of whom were his daughters, and enjoyed a Top 40 national hit with 'Pop Pop Pop-Pie'.

Album: *Little Joe Cook-In* (1981).

Little Joey And The Flips

This US vocal group from Philadelphia, Pennsylvania,

comprised Joey Hall (b. 1943; lead), Fred Garace (b. 1947; first tenor), James Meagher (b. 1946; second tenor), John Smith (b. 1946; baritone) and Jeff Leonard (b. 1946; bass). Hall, the lone black member, was from west Philadelphia, while the remainder of the group was from the Philadelphia suburb of Upper Darby. The group's only chart record was 'Bongo Stomp', which went to number 33 in 1962, a classic in the teen-lead genre made famous by **Frankie Lymon And The Teenagers**. Amazingly, Hall who sounded as though he was a 13-year-old, was actually a diminutive 19-year-old when he made the record. The group came together in 1959 as the Elads, but after the group was signed by their manager he replaced their original lead, Jimmy Dilks, with Joey Hall and renamed the group Little Joey And The Flips. Two more releases followed - 'Bongo Gully' (1962) and 'Fool, Fool, Fool' (1964) - but the group could not repeat the magic and broke up in 1967. Joey Hall died in 1974.

Little John

b. John McMorris, c.1970, Kingston, Jamaica, West Indies. McMorris first recorded with **Captain Sinbad** for the Youth In Progress label at the tender age of nine, where his piping interjections contrasted neatly with Sinbad's gruff style, and throughout the 80s he was seldom out of the reggae charts. Claimed by many to be the first **dancehall** singer, his ability to fit lyrics over any rhythm or backing track became something of a legend in a business that has scant regard for second takes and 'dropping in'. Little John did it every time - and he rode on the crest of the 80s dancehall music explosion, becoming a superstar by the age of 17.

He began his career on Romantic Hi Fi, moving up through Killermanjaro, Gemini and Volcano Hi Power (the importance of **sound systems** such as these to the rise in popularity of Little John and dancehall music cannot be overstated) where he honed and perfected his craft with a constant string of live appearances. Simultaneously he was recording for just about every producer in Jamaica, notably **Henry 'Junjo' Lawes**, **Joe Joe Hookim**, George Phang, Jah Thomas and **Jammys**, and he has released countless records on a bewildering string of labels. He no longer records as extensively as he once did, and limits his live appearances these days too - a stance that is only fitting for a veteran of his status. He's certainly not living on past glories either, as recent hits for **Exterminator** proved, and his talent, warm personality and skill as a raconteur are bound to ensure his place at the top for a long time to come.

Albums: *True Confession* (Power House 1984), *Unite* (Vista Sounds 1984), *Clark's Booty* (Live & Love/Jammys 1985), *River To The Bank* (Power House 1985), *Warriors & Trouble* (World Enterprise 1986), *Youth Of Today* (Skengdon 1987), *Reggae Dance* (Midnight Rock 1989). Compilations: *Best Of Little John* (R&M 1985), *Junjo Presents A Live Session With Aces International* (Volcano/Greensleeves; includes Little John).

Little Johnny Jones

George M. Cohan's first Broadway hit, and the beginning of his long association with producer Sam H. Harris. The show opened at the Liberty Theatre in New York on 7 November 1904, and, as was to become the norm throughout his career, Cohan provided the book, music and lyrics, as well directing and appearing in the piece. He is said to have got the idea for the plot from a newspaper account about an American jockey, Tod Sloane, who rode in the English Derby race in 1903. In Cohan's version, Johnny Jones refuses to be bribed to throw the race, but he loses anyway. When he arrives at Southampton docks to board a ship for his return to America, he is besieged by an angry crowd. Eventually they disperse and he is left alone waiting for a signal from his friend on the ship, now some way out at sea, to indicate that his innocence has been proved. The moment when the rocket soars into the sky and Jones goes into an exhuberant rendering of 'Give My Regards To Broadway', is one of the most memorable sequences in musical comedy history. It was recreated superbly by **James Cagney** when he starred in the George M. Cohan biopic, ***Yankee Doodle Dandy***, in 1942. The latter film got it's title from 'The Yankee Doodle Boy', which Cohan introduced in *Little Johnny Jones*, along with other numbers such as 'Life's A Funny Proposition After All', 'If Mr. Boston Lawson Got His Way', and 'I'm Might Glad I'm Living And That's All'. Cohan's wife, Ethel Levy, had a leading role, and so did his mother and father, Helen and Jerry Cohan. Also in the cast was Donald Brian, the actor, singer, and dancer who was to appear in Cohan's next Broadway musical, ***Forty-Five Minutes From Broadway***, before going on to star in other important shows such as ***The Merry Widow*** and ***The Girl From Utah***, in which he introduced **Jerome Kern** and Herbert Reynolds' lovely song, 'They Didn't Believe Me'. Although Cohan is often criticized for his sentimental, flag-waving approach, *Little Johnny Jones*, with its strong score and solid, believable book is considered to a be significant landmark in development of the indigenous American musical. It ran for only 52 performances in its first outing on Broadway, but Cohan brought it back twice during 1905, and toured it extensively. The 1930 film version starred Alice Day and Eddie Buzzell. A 1981 revival of the show which began its life at the Goodspeed Opera House, Connecticut, amended the original plot and introduced some other Cohan songs. After using several actors in the lead role during its pre-Broadway tour, **Donny Osmond**, a former member of the **Osmond Brothers**, was chosen to play the part at the Alvin Theatre in New York - but for the one-night run only.

Little Louie Vega

A New York-based DJ, Vega's career began at high school at the age of 18, after watching his friends spin records. He played high school parties before eventually establishing his own label. He went on to DJ at the Devil's Nest (regarded as the birthplace of the New York 'freestyle' approach, alongside TKA and Sa-Fire), then Hearthrob and 1018. By the time he had reached the 4,000 capacity Studio 54 **Todd Terry** would pass Vega his new mixes to try out on the crowd. His first remix job was 'Running' by Information Society, then Noel's 'Silent Morning'. He even worked **Debbie Gibson**'s first record. He began his own-name productions with the instrumental 'Don't Tell Me' for SBK in 1989 and 'Keep On Pumpin' It Up' (as Freestyle Orchestra), before signing to **CBS** subsidiary WTG Records with singer Mark Anthony. He had previously been commissioned to write songs for the movie *East Side Story*, where he first met the singer. Together they hooked up for a Latin R&B flavoured album and single, 'Ride On The Rhythm'. He also worked with his girlfriend, 'India', and Todd Terry for the latter's 'Todd's Message'. Together with **Barbara Tucker**, Vega runs the Underground Network Club in New York, and he has also produced 'Beautiful People' for that artist. Despite this background as an established house star, he is probably best known now for his work alongside **Kenny 'Dope' Gonzalez** as half of the **Masters At Work** remix team. He is not to be confused with Chicago house veteran **Lil' Louis**, or, for that matter, with the Louie Vega who remixed for **Lakim Shabazz**, despite the fact that both shared the same management. Vega's most recent remix clients include **Juliet Roberts** and **Urban Species**.

Little Mary Sunshine

On first sight a show with a title like that, and characters with names such as Mme. Ernestine Von Liebedich and General Oscar Fairfax, plus songs with titles like 'Do You Ever Dream Of Vienna?', the casual observer could be forgiven for thinking that this is an operetta. It is the date that gives the game away: *Little Mary Sunshine* opened Off Broadway (another clue) at the Orpheum Theatre on 19 November 1959. With rock 'n' roll already into its stride, there was not much of an audience in those days for genuinely new operetta, and, sure enough, this show turned out to be an elaborate spoof of the real thing. Sub titled A New Musical About An Old Operetta, *Little Mary Sunshine* unmercifully sends up prime examples of the genre such as ***Rose Marie*** and ***Naughty Marietta***. Set in the upper reaches of the Colorado Rockies, Rick Besoyan's book tells the hot-blooded story of Mary Potts (Eileen Brennan), the hostess of the local hostelry, who makes it quite clear to the Rangers' Captain Big Jim Warrington (William Graham), that there is always plenty of room at her inn, for him. However, Big Jim is more interested in capturing the despicable Indian, Yellow Feather (Ray James), who has indicated on more than one occasion that he would like to get Mary into his wigwam. Fortunately for our heroine, she and Big Jim give out with the 'Colorado Love Call', which proves to have more of a deterrent effect on amorous, ambitious Indians than a whole company of cavalry. The sub-plot involves another young loving couple Nancy Twinkle (Elmarie Wendel) and Corporal Billy Jester (John McMartin), who promise to be true to each other 'Once In A Blue Moon'. The remainder of Rick Besoyan's score was in that same mocking vein, and included 'Look For Sky Of Blue', 'Playing Croquet', 'Tell A Handsome Stranger', 'Every Little Nothing', 'Naughty Naughty, Nancy', and 'Such A Merry Party', and 'In Izzenschnooken On The Lovely Ezzenzook Zee', which is 'authentically' rendered by a visiting opera star of yesterday (or the day before), Mme. Ernestine Von Liebedich (Elizabeth Parrish). It all must have touched the right nerve, because *Little Mary Sunshine* became one of the longest-running Off Broadway musicals ever, during its run of 1,143 performances. Londoners did not seem to see the joke, and, despite the presence in the cast of comedy stalwarts such as Patricia Routledge and Bernard Cribbins, the show folded there after five weeks.

Little Me

Conceived as a vehicle for one of US television's favourite performers, Sid Caesar, the versatile comedian needed all his skills and ingenuity to cope with a scenario that called upon him to play seven different characters. The leading female role, on the other hand, is shared by two different actresses. *Little Me* opened at the Lunt-Fontanne Theatre in New York on 17 November 1962. Neil Simon's book, which was based on the play by Patrick Dennis, opens with the older Belle Poitrine (Nancy Andrews), 'queen of the silver screen', dictating her memoirs ('The Truth'). The young, ambitious Belle Schlumpfort (Virginia Martin) then relives the scenes as they actually occurred, and in each one she is accompanied by a male admirer played by Caesar. These range from her first love, the snobby 16-years-old Noble Eggleston, from whom she gets a taste for the high-life ('Rich Kids Rag') and yearns to be 'On The Other Side Of The Tracks', to the geriatric banker Amos Pinchley, who is surely a good person 'Deep Down Inside', the 'great French entertainer', Val du Val, ('Boom-Boom'), her temporary husband, Fred Poitrine a World War I sad soldier who yearns for a 'Real Live Girl', a dominating film director, ('Poor Little Hollywood Star'), and Prince Cherney 'the expiring regent of Rosenzweig' ('Goodbye'). George Musgrove, a childhood admire of Belle's, and now a big-time gambler, comes back into her life at one point and tries to seduce her with the sensuous 'I've Got

Your Number'. This was the only major male role not played by Sid Caesar. At the end, the two Belles get together to try and make sense of it all and unite in 'Little Me'. The older Belle is then left alone, seated in her Beverly Hill mansion, realising that she has achieved her aims of 'wealth, culture and social position' - but not, unfortunately, Noble Eggleston. **Cy Coleman** and **Carolyn Leigh**'s score was, in turn, witty and tender, especially in numbers such as 'Real Live Girl' ('Speaking of miracles, this must be it/Just when I started to learn how to knit/I'm all in stitches from finding what riches a waltz, can reveal/With a real, live girl'), and 'The Other Side Of The Tracks', which became popular through a recording by **Tony Bennett**. **Bob Fosse** won a **Tony Award** for his ingenious choreography, and the Broadway run of only 257 performances was followed by a much better reception in London, where the show stayed at the Cambridge Theatre for 10 months. It proved to be a personal triumph for Bruce Forsyth, the young comedian and television comperé. In 1982, a Broadway revival, starring James Coco and Victor Garber, lasted for only a month, but, two years later, London audiences approved of the show again, with Russ Abbott, Lynda Baron, and Sheila White. In 1993, another, more 'intimate' musical entitled *Little Me*, with a score by Brad Ross, Ellen Greenfield, Hal Hackady, *et al*, played at Steve McGraw's in New York.

Little Mermaid, The

Based on the Hans Christian Andersen fairytale, this 1989 **Walt Disney** release was the Studio's 28th animated feature, and a reminder of that golden era during which cinema audiences of all ages all over the world were enchanted with the immortal stories of ***Snow White And The Seven Dwarfs***, ***Peter Pan***, ***Cinderella***, and ***Sleeping Beauty***. This particular tale concerns the 16-year-old mermaid Ariel, who, after a series of exciting watery adventures, takes on a human form and marries the handsome and heroic Prince Eric. The action is enhanced by the 'contemporary songs and score ranging from English folk to French cabaret, from lively Caribbean to showstopping Broadway'. The composer **Alan Menken** won an Academy Award for his original score, and he and lyricist **Howard Ashman** gained another Oscar for the song, 'Under The Sea'. 'Kiss The Girl' was also nominated, and there were other attractive numbers such as 'Poor Unfortunate Souls' and 'Part Of Your World'. All these contributed to a soundtrack album which won a Grammy for the 'Best Recording For Children'. The film's spectacular animation, particularly in the underwater sequences, was widely applauded, and as usual the Disney organization selected appropriate voices for characters such as Ariel (Jodi Benson), her father King Triton (Kenneth Mars), Ursula (Pat Caroll), Prince Eric (Christopher Daniel Barnes), and Flotsam/Jetsam (Paddi Edwards). No one could mistake the distinctive tones of Ariel's friend Scuttle the seagull, which were provided by comedian Buddy Hackett. He has also made several impressive on-screen performances in movies such as ***The Music Man*** and *It's A Mad Mad Mad Mad World. The Little Mermaid*, which was directed by John Musker and Ron Clements who also wrote the screenplay, enjoyed substantial success in the US and abroad, and set up audiences nicely for Disney's sensational early 90s trio of ***Beauty And The Beast***, ***Aladdin*** and *The Lion King.*

Little Milton

b. James Milton Campbell Jnr., 7 September 1934, Inverness, Mississippi, USA. Having played guitar from the age of 12, Little Milton (he legally dropped the James when he discovered that he had a brother of the same name on his father's side) made his first public appearances as a teenager in the blues bars and cafes on Greenville's celebrated Nelson Street. He first appeared on record accompanying pianist **Willie Love** in the early 50s, then under his own name appearing on three singles issued on **Sam Phillips**'s **Sun** label under the guidance of **Ike Turner**. Although their working relationship continued throughout the decade, it was on signing to Chicago's **Chess**/Checker outlet that Milton's career flourished. An R&B-styled vocalist in the mould of **Bobby 'Blue' Bland** and **'T-Bone' Walker**, his work incorporated sufficient soul themes to maintain a success denied less flexible contemporaries. Propelled by an imaginative production, Milton scored a substantial hit in 1965 with the optimistic 'We're Gonna Make It', and followed with other expressive performances, including 'Who's Cheating Who?' (1965) plus the wry 'Grits Ain't Groceries' (1968). Campbell remained with Chess until 1971, whereupon he switched to **Stax**. 'That's What Love Will Do' returned the singer to the R&B chart after a two-year absence, but despite his appearance in the pivotal *Wattstax* film, Little Milton was unable to maintain a consistent recording career. A series of ill-fitting funk releases from the late 70s reinforced the perception that the artist is at his peak with blues-edged material, something proved by his excellent contemporary work for the **Malaco** label.

Albums: *We're Gonna Make It* (1965), *Little Milton Sings Big Blues* (1966), *Grits Ain't Groceries* (1969), *If Walls Could Talk* (1970), *Blues 'N' Soul* (1974), *Waiting For Little Milton* (1973), *Montreux Festival* (1974), *Friend Of Mine* (1976), *Me For You, You For Me* (1976), *In Perspective* (1981), *I Need Your Love So Bad* (1982), *Age Ain't Nothing But A Number* (1983), *Playin' For Keeps* (1984), *Annie Mae's Cafe* (1987), *Movin' To The Country* (1987), *I Will Survive* (1988), *Too Much Pain* (1990), *Reality* (1992). Compilations: *Little Milton's Greatest Hits* (1972), *Little Milton* (1976), *Sam's Blues* (1976), *Walkin' The Back Streets* (1981), *Raise A Little*

Sand (1982), *His Greatest Hits* (1987), *Chicago Golden Years* (1988), *Hittin' The Boogie* (1988, Sun recordings), *The Sun Masters* (1990).

Little Miss Marker

That old show-biz maxim about not working with animals or children must have crossed Adolphe Menjou's mind more than once during the filming of this Paramount musical which was released in 1934. He was top-billed, but, although she was only six years old, **Shirley Temple** dominated this Damon Runyon story in which she is adopted by bookmaker Sorrowful Jones (Menjou), after being used as security for a losing bet. Shirley then proceeds to look after Jones while having a far more beneficial effect on the New York gambling fraternity than any government commission could hope for. Shell-shocked as he must have been, Menjou gave a creditable performance under heavy fire. Also suffering from the tremendous impact of this little blonde bombshell were Charles Bickford, Dorothy Dell, Lynne Overman, Willie Best, and Frank McGlynn Snr. **Leo Robin** and **Ralph Rainger** wrote the songs which included 'Low Down Lullaby', 'I'm A Black Sheep Who Is Blue', and 'Laugh, You Son-Of-A-Gun'. William R. Lipman, Sam Hellman and Gladys Lehman were responsible for the neat screenplay, and the director was Alexander Hall. The 'marker' of the title being an indigenous American term for IOU, the name of the film was changed to *The Girl In Pawn* for UK distribution. *Little Miss Marker* was remade in 1949 as *Sorrowful Jones*, in 1963 as *40 Pounds Of Trouble*, and again in 1980 under its original title, but none of them made anything like the impact of the 1934 version.

Little Richard

b. Richard Wayne Penniman, 5 December 1935, Macon, Georgia, USA. The wildest and arguably the greatest and most influential of the 50s rock 'n' roll singers and songwriters. He first recorded in late 1951 in Atlanta for **RCA**, cutting eight urban blues tracks with his mentor **Billy Wright**'s Orchestra; 'Taxi Blues' being the first of four unsuccessful single releases on the label. He moved to Houston, Texas in 1953 and with the Tempo Toppers (vocals) and the Duces of Rhythm (backing) recorded four R&B tracks including 'Ain't That Good News'. Eight months later he recorded another four with **Johnny Otis**' Orchestra but none of these were released at the time. In February 1955, at the suggestion of **Lloyd Price**, he sent a demo to **Specialty Records** who realized his potential and in September, under the guidance of producer **Robert 'Bumps' Blackwell**, recorded a dozen tracks in New Orleans. The classic 'Tutti Frutti', which was amongst them gave him his first R&B and pop hit in the USA. The follow-up 'Long Tall Sally' topped the R&B chart and was the first of his three US Top 10 hits, despite being covered by **Pat Boone** whose previous record, a cover of 'Tutti Frutti', was still charting. Richard's string of Top 20 hits continued with the double-sider 'Rip It Up'/'Ready Teddy', the former being his first UK release and chart entry in late 1956. Richard's frantic, no-holds barred performance of his first two hits 'Long Tall Sally' and 'Tutti Frutti' in the film *Don't Knock The Rock* undoubtedly helped push his next UK single, which coupled the tracks, into the Top 3.

His next film and single was *The Girl Can't Help It* which missed the US Top 40 but together with its b-side 'She's Got It' (a re-working of his earlier track 'I Got It') gave him two more UK Top 20 hits. The remainder of 1957 saw him notch up three more huge transatlantic hits with the rock 'n' roll classics 'Lucille', 'Keep A Knockin'' (he featured both in the movie *Mr. Rock & Roll*) and 'Jenny Jenny' and a Top 20 album with *Here's Little Richard.* At the very height of his career, the man with the highest pompadour in the business, shocked the rock world by announcing, during an Australian tour, that he was quitting music to go into a theological college. In 1958, previously recorded material like the transatlantic Top 10 hit 'Good Golly Miss Molly' kept his name on the chart and a year later he had his biggest UK hit with a 1956 recording of the oldie 'Baby Face' which reached number 2. Between 1958 and 1962 Richard recorded only gospel music for Gone, **Mercury** (with producer **Quincy Jones**) and **Atlantic**. In late 1962, Richard toured the UK for the first time and the now short-haired wild-man who pounded pianos and pierced eardrums with his manic falsetto was a huge success. In 1963, he worked in Europe with the **Beatles** and the **Rolling Stones**, who were both great admirers of his music. His first rock recordings in the 60s were made back at Speciality and resulted in the UK Top 20 hit 'Bama Lama Bama Loo'. In 1964, he signed with **VeeJay** where he re-recorded all his hits, revived a few oldies and cut some new rockers - but the sales were unimpressive. In the mid-60s, soul music was taking hold worldwide and Richard's soulful VeeJay tracks, 'I Don't Know What You've Got But It's Got Me' (which included **Jimi Hendrix** on guitar) and 'Without Love', although not pop hits, were among the best recordings of the genre. For the rest of the 60s he continued to pack in the crowds singing his old hits and in the studios mixed 50s rock and 60s soul for Modern in 1965, **OKeh** a year later and **Brunswick** in 1967. The best of these were his OKeh tracks which included 'Poor Dog', 'Hurry Sundown' and the UK recorded 'Get Down With It' (which gave **Slade** their first hit in the 70s).

Reprise Records, whom he joined in 1970, tried very hard to get him back at the top and under the expertise of producer **Richard Perry** he managed minor US hits 'Freedom Blues' and 'Greenwood, Mississippi' but his three albums sold poorly. The rest of the 70s was spent jumping from label to label, recording in supergroup-type projects and playing oldies shows. When he desired, he could still 'out rock' anyone, but often there was too much Las Vegas glitter, excessive posturing and an element of self-parody. In 1976, he re-joined the church and for the next decade preached throughout America. In 1986, Richard was among the first artists inducted into the Rock 'n' Roll Hall of Fame and he successfully acted in the film *Down And Out In Beverly Hills* which included the rocking 'Great Gosh A'Mighty', which just missed the US Top 40. Renewed interest, spurred **WEA** to sign him and release, *Lifetime Friend*, which included the chart record 'Operator'. Since the mid-80s he has become a frequent visitor on chat shows, an in-demand guest on other artist's records and an often seen face on videos (of acts ranging from **Hank Williams Jnr.** to **Living Colour** to **Cinderella**), He even has his own star on the Hollywood Walk of Fame and a boulevard named after him in his hometown. Nowadays a regular presenter of music awards, he has also been the star of **Jive Bunny** hits. The leader of rebellious 50s rock 'n' roll, the man who shook up the music business and the parents of the period, is now a much-loved personality accepted by all age groups.

Selected albums: *Here's Little Richard* (1957), *Little Richard Volume 2* (1958), *The Fabulous Little Richard* (1959), *Little Richard Is Back* (1965), *The Explosive Little Richard* (1967), *The Little Richard Story* (1970), *Good Golly Miss Molly* (1969), *Rock Hard Rock Heavy* (1970), *Mr Big* (1971), *The Original Little Richard* (1972), *Rip It Up* (1973), *Slippin' And Slidin'* (1973), *Keep A Knockin'* (1975), *Dollars Dollars* (1975), *The Great Ones* (1976), *Little Richard And Jimi Hendrix Together* (1977), *Whole Lotta Shakin' Goin' On* (1977), *Greatest Hits Recorded Live* (1977), *The Georgia Peach* (1980), *Little Richard And His Band* (1980), *Get Down With It* (1982), *Ooh! My Soul* (1982), *The Real Thing* (1983), *He's Got It* (1984). Compilations: *20 Classic Cuts* (1986), *The Collection* (1989), *The Specialty Sessions* (1989, CD box set), *The Formative Years, 1951-53* (1989), *The EP Collection* (1993).

Films: *The Girl Can't Help It* (1956), *Don't Knock The Rock* (1956), *Catalina Caper* (1967).

Little River Band

Prior to the success of **AC/DC**, **Air Supply**, **Men At Work** and **INXS**, the Little River Band were probably Australia's most successful international rock band. Evolving out of the group Mississippi, who had previously spent much time working in London, former members Graham Goble (b. 15 May 1947, Adelaide, South Australia, Australia; guitar), Beeb Birtles (b. Gerard Birtlekamp, 28 November 1948, Amsterdam, Netherlands; guitar) and Derek Pellicci (drums) met up with Glen Shorrock (b. 30 June 1944, Rochester, Kent, England; vocals) in Melbourne in 1975. With a name change to the Little River Band and the addition of Rick Formosa (guitar) and Roger McLachlan (bass) the band boasted years of experience and chose the US west coast harmony and guitar sound as their major influence. They had immediate success in Australia with their first single and album. Under the guidance of Glen Wheatley (ex-**Masters Apprentices**), the band was soon aiming for the overseas market, the USA in particular, and by the end of 1976 they had enjoyed their first appearance in the US charts. With Formosa and McLachlan being replaced respectively by David Briggs (b. 26 January 1951, Melbourne, Victoria, Australia) and George McArdle (b. 30 November 1954, Melbourne, Victoria, Australia), the second album *Diamantina Cocktail* went gold in the USA in 1977, the first time an Australian act had managed this. The band followed this with another hugely successful album in 1978, *Sleeper Catcher*, and they found themselves also selling well in Latin-America and Europe, especially France. The band's popularity waned a little in Australia but continued unabated in the USA. In 1983, lead vocalist Glen Shorrock left to pursue a solo career and was replaced by **John Farnham**, one of Australia's most popular singers. By 1986 Farnham had left to pursue his solo career and the band continued with a low profile, playing live occasionally at up-market venues but still releasing records. In 1988, with the return of Shorrock, the group signed to MCA Records, releasing *Get Lucky* two years later.

Albums: *Little River Band* (1975), *After Hours* (1976), *Diamantina Cocktail* (1977), *Sleeper Catcher* (1978), *First Under The Wire* (1979), *Backstage Pass* (1980), *Time Exposure* (1981), *The Net* (1983), *Playing To Win* (1984), *No Reins* (1986), *Monsoon* (1988), *Too Late To Load* (1989), *Get Lucky* (1990). Compilation: *Greatest Hits* (1982).

Little Roy

b. Earl Lowe, c.1950, Jamaica, West Indies. Little Roy is perhaps the archetypal roots reggae artist, with a career that stretches back to the early 70s, and hardly a non-'cultural' lyric on any of his records. He first recorded for producer **Lloyd 'Matador' Daley** in 1969, both as a solo act and alongside Joy Lindsay as Roy And Joy. From the outset he wrote about Rasta themes - slavery, the wearing of dreadlocks, exile - his best record of the period was 'Righteous Man'. By 1972 he had formed the Tafari label with the help of **Lloyd Barnes** and Munchie Jackson, and his records soon received simultaneous release in New York through Barnes' Aries label. Often part of a trio alongside two mysterious characters, Ian and Rock, he recorded some alluring and atmospheric tracks: 'Tribal War', 'Blackbird' and 'Prophecy'. Barnes put them together to form an album, *Tribal War*, a record of a decidedly limited pressing. In 1978 he recorded *Columbus Ship*, a far less artistically successful set, and then dropped below reggae's horizon altogether, though there were occasional sightings of him confined to New York. His business associate Munchie Jackson was shot by his own son in a bizarre Brooklyn domestic killing in 1977. However, in one of those twists unique to reggae, ragga rulers **Steely And Clevie** decided to remake the 'Prophecy' rhythm in 1990, and it was an instant hit for **Freddie McGregor**. Not slow to spot an opportunity, Little Roy emerged from nowhere with a 10-track compilation of his now in-demand old material, *Prophecy*, and then cut the extremely good *Live On* the following year. He is rumoured to be assembling yet another comeback set.

Albums: *Tribal War* (Tafari 1975), *Free For All Dub* (1975), *Columbus Ship* (Copasetic 1978), *Prophecy* (1990), *Live On* (1991).

Little Shop Of Horrors (Film Musical)

As a film to put audiences off gardening for life, *Little Shop Of Horrors*, released in December 1986, is top of the heap. It tells the story of Seymour (Rick Moranis), a rather sweet but accident-prone character - a sort of **Norman Wisdom** of the 80s - whose working life at Mushnik's Skid Row flower shop just is not going to plan. On to the scene comes Audrey II, named after the girl Seymour adores, who changes from a tiny shrub to a sinister blood sucking flytrap. When Seymour has bled his fingers dry in an attempt to feed it, the plant forces him to find some human meat to satisfy its hunger. In return Seymour is to have as much success in love and life as he can handle. Eventually, realising that the man-eating plant really wants to take over the world, Seymour faces up to its menace and, with the help of a few volts of electricity, blows Audrey II into oblivion. ***Little Shop Of Horrors*** was first seen Off Broadway in 1982, and that production itself was based on Roger Corman's 60s low budget horror movie. Directed by Frank Oz, and produced by **David Geffen** for the Geffen Company, the show's author and lyricist, **Howard Ashman**, also wrote the movie's screenplay. It is interesting to note that the film's ending is distinctly different in tone from its stage predecessor, when Seymour and Audrey are both eaten and Audrey II succeeds. It appears the preview audiences preferred a happy ending and so it was changed. Ashman was joined by **Alan Menken** to write the quirky, clever and often extremely funny score. Highlights included 'Skid Row', the film's only real production number of any sorts, involving most of the cast, and 'Suddenly Seymour', by no means an average love song. A host of guest stars joined in the fun, among them Steve Martin, James Belushi, John Candy, and Bill Murray. Ellen Greene recreated her stage role as Audrey. Martin plays Audrey's sadistic dentist boyfriend (in 'Somewhere's That Green', she sings 'I know Seymour's the greatest, but I'm dating a semi-sadist'). Consequently it is not surprising that Martin becomes Audrey II's first human victim. The plant's big number is 'Mean Green Mother From Outer Space' (the voice is that of the **Four Tops**' Levi Stubbs). The song was written especially for the film, and is quite a treat, especially its flower bud chorus. The rest of the score included 'Little Shop Of Horrors', 'Grow For Me', 'Dentist', 'Feed Me', and 'Suppertime'. Pat Garrett was the choreographer, and the film was photographed in Technicolor and Panavision by Robert Paynter.

Little Shop Of Horrors (Stage Musical)

After making its debut at the tiny WPA Theatre in New York, *Little Shop Of Horrors* moved to the Orpheum Theatre on the Lower East Side on 27 July 1982. The book, by **Howard Ashman**, was based on Charles Griffith's screenplay for the 1960 spoof of the horror movie genre, which had become a cult classic. Hardly the usual Broadway - or Off-Broadway - fare, the grisly tale tells of Seymour Krelbourn (Lee Wilkof), an assistant at Mushnik's florist shop on Skid Row, who decides to boost sales by producing a strange houseplant. He names it Audrey II, because of his love for sales assistant Audrey (Ellen Greene), and finds that it grow faster if it is fed with a few drops of blood - and subsequently, human flesh. Things rapidly get out of hand as the monster - and the business - thrives, eventually devouring just about everything and everyone in sight. The amusing and imaginative score by Ashman and composer **Alan Menken** had some 'good rock in the **Phil Spector** Wall of Sound idiom', and included 'Grow For Me', 'Suddenly Seymour', 'Skid Row', 'Somewhere That's Green', and 'Little Shop Of Horrors'. The show's bizarre humour caught on in a big way, as Audrey II and Little Shop Of Horrors became a sort of phenomenon. It continued to amaze and delight Off Broadway audiences for 2,209 performances, and was awarded the New York Drama Critics Circle Award for best musical. The 1984 London production, which ran for over a year, also received the Evening Standard prize for outstanding musical. Ellen Greene reprised her role in London, and for the 1986 film version which also starred Rick Moranis, Vincent Gardenia and Steve Martin. In 1994, a 'gorgeously funny' revival toured the UK starring Sue Pollard, better know for her role as Peggy, the zany chalet maid, in the popular television comedy series Hi-Di-Hi.

Little Show, The

Composer **Arthur Schwartz** and lyricist **Howard Dietz**, one of the top Broadway songwriting teams of the 30s, got together for the first time to write several songs for this smart, classy revue which opened at the Music Box Theatre on 30 April 1929. Dietz also wrote most of the sketches, along with **George S. Kaufman** and others. He and Schwartz contributed 'I've Made A Habit Of You', 'Hammacher-Schlemmer, I Love You', and 'I Guess I'll Have To Change My Plan', ('I should have realized there'd be another man/Why did I buy those blue pajamas/Before the big affair began?'), which, for obvious reasons became known as 'The Blue Pajama Song', and, while never becoming a big hit, was one of the songwriters' hardy standards. It was very effectively sung by a couple of song-and-dance-men, **Fred Astaire** and **Jack Buchanan** in the film of ***The Band Wagon*** in 1953. It was introduced in *The Little Show* by Clifton Webb, who finally became recognized as a star in this revue, as did the resident funny man, 'dead-pan' Fred Allen. The third leading player, Libby Holman, had 'Can't We Be Friends?' (written by **Kay Swift** and Paul James - a pseudonym for her husband, James Warburg), which was quite a jolly little song for many years until **Frank Sinatra** turned it into a lonely ballad on his *In The Wee Small Hours*. Holman also sang the show's big hit, 'Moanin' Low', which had music and lyric by **Ralph Rainger** and Dietz. One of the other songs, 'A Little Hut In Hoboken', was one of a the relatively few numbers written by **Herman Hupfield** in his career; two years later he produced another, 'As Time Goes By', which was later immortalised in the film, *Casablanca*. *The Little Show* ran for 321 performances. Without Holman, Webb, and Allen neither of the sequels did well. *The Second Little Show* (1929), again had some songs by Schwartz and Dietz ('You're The Sunshine', 'What A Case I've Got On You', and 'Lucky Seven') and one by Hupfield ('Sing Something Simple'), but only ran for 63 performances; and *The Third Little Show* (1930), starred Beatrice Lillie who introduced **Noël Coward**'s 'Mad Dogs And Englishmen' to the American public. The show also contained another rare Hupfield number, 'When Yuba Plays The Rhumba On His Tuba', and stayed at Music Box Theatre for four months.

Little Son Joe

b. Ernest Lawlars, 18 May 1900, Hughes, Arkansas, USA, d. 14 November 1961, Memphis, Tennessee, USA. Lawlars is best known for his musical partnership with his wife, **Memphis Minnie**, but he had been playing guitar and singing blues for some years around Memphis before they got together, including a period with **Rev. Robert Wilkins**, whom he accompanied on record in 1935. He took up with Minnie in the late 30s, replacing her previous husband and partner, **Joe McCoy**. Like McCoy, Lawlars also made records under his own name, including the well known 'Black Rat Swing', but he mainly appeared in the supporting role, on a large number of sides covering most of the 40s and the early years of the following decade. As their popularity in Chicago waned, they settled back in Memphis and retired from music in the 50s.

Albums: *Memphis Minnie* (1964), *Chicago Blues* (1982), *World Of Trouble* (1982).

Little Sonny

b. Aaron Willis, 6 October 1932, Greensboro, Alabama, USA. Despite the claims of his first album, its evidence shows that Little Sonny Willis is an adequate harmonica player and reluctant singer whose music career has been at best intermittent. With little experience in music apart from singing in church choirs, Willis moved to Detroit in 1954. Working as a photographer in the bars of the Hastings Street area, he also picked up the rudiments of the harmonica. His first gig was in the Good Time Bar with **Washboard Willie's** band. Willis gained some harmonica tuition from **Sonny Boy (Rice Miller) Williamson**, from whom he adopted his nickname. In March 1956, he formed his own band with pianist Chuck Smith, guitarist Louis (Big Bo) Collins and drummer Jim Due Crawford. Two years later Smith, Crawford and **Eddie Burns** backed Willis on his debut record, 'I Gotta Find My Baby', for Duke Records. Another record, 'Love Shock', recorded by **Joe Von Battle**, was leased to Excello. An unissued 1961 session for **Chess Records** resaged a five-year record silence, followed by singles for Speedway, Revilot (including the instrumental 'The Creeper') and Wheel City at the end of the decade. In 1969 he recorded his first album for the **Stax** subsidiary, Enterprise. *New King Of The Blues Harmonica*, an album of mostly uninventive instrumentals, evoked the Hans Christian Andersen fairy tale. A second album released in 1973, *Hard Goin' Up*, was a more honest, balanced exercise. **Albert King** recorded Willis' 'Love Shock' and 'Love Mechanic' for Tomato in 1978. The album, *King Albert*, was recorded in Detroit and used Willis' songs, Aaron Jnr., Anthony and Eddie in the backup band. Perhaps their father had read *King Lear*.

Selected album: *New King Of The Blues Harmonica/Hard Goin' Up* (1991).

Little Steven And The Disciples Of Soul

(see **Van Zandt, Steven**)

Little Texas

Since their 1992 debut album, *First Time For Everything*, Little Texas have emerged as one of America's biggest 'new country' phenomena. The band comprise Tim Rushlow (vocals), Del Gray (drums), Peter Howell (guitar/bass), Dwayne Propes (bass/backing vocals) and Brady Seals (keyboards/guitar/backing vocals), and they were rewarded soon after their debut with the American Country Music award for Top Vocal Group. With sales of the album reaching gold status, Little Texas toured the US with artists including **Travis Tritt** and **Trisha Yearwood**. *First Time For Everything* produced a run of successful singles, as did its follow-up, *Big Time*, whose sales figures would reach platinum status. They started recording a third set, *Kick A Little*,

straightaway and this, their first collection to be released outside of the USA, contained more strong material, including 'Your Days Are Numbered', 'A Night I'll Never Remember' and 'Southern Grace'.
Albums: *First Time For Everything* (Warners 1992), *Big Time* (Warners 1993), *Kick A Little* (Warners 1994).
Video: *Kick A Little* (Warner Reprise 1994).

Little Tony

b. Antonio Ciacci, 1940, San Marino, Italy. Little Tony and his two brothers formed a vocal group and were 'discovered' by **Jack Good** in 1959. Despite profound language difficulties, the trio - as Little Tony And His Brothers - won female hearts with their Latinate charm on UK television; toured with **Cliff Richard**, and recorded 'Foxy Little Mama', **Chan Romero**'s 'Hippy Hippy Shake' and other singles under Good's supervision in London. However, it was without his siblings that Ciacci grazed the UK Top 20 with 1960's 'So Good'. With the withdrawal of Good's support, he returned to Italy where he was runner-up in 1961's San Remo Song Festival with a song translated as '42,000 Kisses' when covered by Liverpudlian vocalist Paul Rogers. Little Tony became a regular performer at this event - even after 1967 brought a million-seller in 'Cuore Matto' (composed by Ambrosino and Tito Savio). Nevertheless, this was covered in the English-speaking market, where the song appeared as **Tony Hatch** and **Jackie Trent**'s 'Long Is The Lonely Night'.

Little Village

(see **Cooder, Ry**)

Little Walter

b. Marion Walter Jacobs, 1 May 1930, Marksville, Louisiana, USA, d. 15 February 1968. A major figure of post-war blues, Little Walter is credited for bringing the harmonica, or 'French harp', out from its rural setting and into an urban context. His career began at the age of 12 when he left home for New Orleans, but by 1946 Jacobs was working in Chicago's famed Maxwell Street. Early recordings for the Ora Nelle label were the prelude to his joining the **Muddy Waters** band where he helped forge what became the definitive electric Chicago blues group. The harmonica player emerged as a performer in his own right in 1952 when 'Juke', an instrumental recorded at the end of a Waters' session, topped the R&B chart where it remained for eight consecutive weeks. Little Walter And The Night Caps - David Myers (guitar), Louis Myers (guitar) and Fred Below (drums) - enjoyed further success when 'Sad Hours' and 'Mean Old World' reached the Top 10 in the same chart. The group then became known as Little Walter And The Jukes and although obliged to fulfil recording agreements with Waters, Jacobs actively pursued his own career. He enjoyed further R&B hits with 'Blues With A Feeling' (1953), 'Last Night' (1954) and the infectious 'My Babe' (1955). The last song, patterned on a spiritual tune, 'This Train', was a second number 1 single and became much-covered during later years. Other notable releases included 'Mellow Down Easy' and 'Boom Boom (Out Go The Lights)' which were later recorded, respectively, by **Paul Butterfield** and the **Blues Band**. A haunting version of 'Key To The Highway' (1958), previously recorded by **Big Bill Broonzy**, gave Walter his final Top 10 entry. He nonetheless remained a pivotal figure, undertaking several tours including one of Britain in 1964. His career, however, was undermined by personal problems. A pugnacious man with a quick temper and a reputation for heavy drinking, he died on 15 February 1968 as a result of injuries sustained in a street brawl. This ignominious end should not detract from Little Walter's status as an innovative figure. The first musician to amplify the harmonica, his heavy, swooping style became the lynchpin for all who followed him, including Norton Buffalo, Butterfield and **Charlie Musselwhite**.
Compilations: *The Best Of Little Walter* (1964), *Hate To See You Go* (1969), *On The Road Again* (1979), *Quarter To Twelve* (1982), *Chess Masters* (1983), *Boss Blues Harmonica* (1986), *Confessin' The Blues* (1986), *Windy City Blues* (1986), *Collection: Little Walter 20 Blues Greats* (1987), *The Blues World Of Little Walter* (1988), *Boss Blues Harmonica* (1988), *The Best Of Little Walter Volume 2* (1989), *The Chess Years 1952 - '63* (1993, 4-CD box set).

Little, Booker

b. 2 April 1938, Memphis, Tennessee, USA, d. 5 October, 1961. One of the most promising of all trumpeters in the second bebop wave of the 50s, Booker Little was equipped with a superb technique, crystal clarity of intonation and rhythmic originality. His imagination extended beyond the strict harmonic disciplines of bop however, and hinted at the vision of **Ornette Coleman** or **Miles Davis**, but an early death from uraemia consigned such promise to the realm of speculation. Little was born into a musical family, and played clarinet before taking up the trumpet at the age of 12. He was involved in Memphis jam sessions with local pianist **Phineas Newborn Jnr.** in his teens, but moved to Chicago in 1957 to enrol at the city's Conservatory. During this period Little worked with **Johnny Griffin**'s band, but his most significant engagement of the period was with **Max Roach**, replacing another gifted trumpeter, **Clifford Brown**. His recordings with Roach include *Deeds Not Words*, *We Insist!*, *Freedom Now Suite* and *Percussion Bitter Sweet*. Little's originality quickly marked him out, as did his flexibility about non-bop settings, and he collaborated with **Eric Dolphy** on *Far Cry* and *Live At The Five Spot* (reissued as *The Great Concert Of Eric*

Dolphy) and **John Coltrane** on the *Africa/Brass* recording. Little's own recordings featured some outstanding players, including Roach, Dolphy (*Out Front*), **Booker Ervin** and the 'legendary quartet' of **Scott La Faro**, **Roy Haynes** and both **Wynton Kelly** and **Tommy Flanagan** taking turns on piano. He worked too with **Donald Byrd** (*The Third World*), **Abbey Lincoln** (*Straight Ahead*) and **Frank Strozier**. By the time of his death Little was balancing tonality and dissonance with an insight that suggested his influence on jazz directions in general might have been even more substantial.

Albums: *Booker Little 4 And Max Roach* (Blue Note 1959), *Booker Little* (Time 1960), *In New York* (Jazz View 1960), *The Legendary Quartet Album* (1960), *Out Front* (Candid 1961), with Booker Ervin *Sounds Of The Inner City* (1961), *Victory And Sorrow* (Affinity 1961).

Littlefield, 'Little' Willie

b. 16 September 1931, El Campo, Texas, USA. By the age of 16, Littlefield was emulating his hero **Amos Milburn**, shouting the blues and hammering the pianos of nearby Houston's Dowling Street clubs. He made his recording debut the following year for the local Eddie's Records and for the Freedom label. In August 1949, Littlefield was discovered by the Bihari brothers, who had flown to Houston to find their own version of Aladdin's Amos Milburn, and signed him to their Los Angeles-based Modern label. Littlefield's first Modern session, recorded in Houston, resulted in the huge hit 'It's Midnight' which featured his school friend, Don Wilkerson, on tenor saxophone. From October 1949, Littlefield was recording in Los Angeles, but subsequent releases did not match the promise of the debut single, in spite of bands which included **Jimmy 'Maxwell Street' Davis**, Chuck Norris and **Johnny Moore**. In 1952, Littlefield signed with Federal Records and continued to make fine records in his own right and in duets with Lil Greenwood and **Little Esther Phillips**. His first Federal session resulted in his best-known recording, 'K.C. Lovin'' which was later altered slightly by **Leiber And Stoller** and recorded by **Wilbert Harrison** as 'Kansas City'. By 1957, Littlefield had moved to northern California, where he recorded for the Rhythm label. He stayed in San José throughout the 60s and 70s, making the occasional club appearance, but in the early 80s he moved with his family to the Netherlands and has since experienced a minor comeback with new material on various European labels and frequent appearances at jazz and blues festivals.

Albums: *K.C. Loving* (1977), *It's Midnight* (1979), *Little Willie Littlefield - Volume One* (1980), *Little Willie Littlefield - Volume Two* (1981), *I'm In The Mood* (1984), *Jump With Little Willie Littlefield* (1984), *Happy Pay Day* (1986), *House Party* (1988), ... *Plays Boogie Woogie* (1988).

Littlejohn, Johnny

b. John Wesley Funchess, 16 April 1931, Learned, Mississippi, USA, d. 1 February 1994, Chicago, Illinois, USA. Littlejohn taught himself to play guitar, and was inspired by Henry Martin, a blues guitarist friend of his father. In 1946, he left home and was an itinerant worker before settling in Gary, Indiana, in 1951 and taking up the guitar seriously. He quickly became a popular attraction and later relocated to Chicago. A chronically underrated slide guitarist/singer, Littlejohn has recorded for numerous labels, including Ace, Margaret, Bluesway, and Wolf, but his best work is to be found on **Arhoolie** and Rooster. Although often categorized as an **Elmore James** influenced player, he can also recall the smooth approach of **B.B. King** with his picking and singing.

Albums: *John Littlejohn's Chicago Blues Stars* (1968), *So-Called Friends* (1985).

Live

US rock band from York, Pennsylvania, Live comprise Ed Kowalcyzk (vocals), with Patrick Dahlheimer, Chad Taylor and Chad Gracey. The group was formed out of blue-collar friends attending high school because 'we share the same ignorance'. The group's dynamic is one of fraught pop which occasionally expands into full blown rock mode - with lyrics striking an idealistic tone. This was particularly true of the group's 1991 debut, the largely ignored *Mental Jewelery*, where spiritual overtones were also present. No less intense was the subsequent *Throwing Copper*, which would go on to sell over 2 million copies in the USA by 1995. However, by now Kowalcyzk's lyrics had developed a less literal level: 'I'm more into letting my subconscious write, I want to let go completely, without becoming addicted to anything - which is a danger'. Another danger was a track like 'Shit Towne', which addressed the populace of hometown York, and did little to ingratiate the band to their old community.

Albums: *Mental Jewelry* (Radioactive 1991), *Throwing Copper* (Radioactive 1994).

Live Aid

Millions saw the 1984 BBC television news report narrated by Michael Buerk, showing the appalling famine in Ethiopia. **Bob Geldof** was so moved that he organized, promoted and produced a fund-raising enterprise that the world had never seen before. Geldof's likeable bullying and eloquently cheeky publicity endeared him to millions. The song 'Do They Know It's Christmas?' co-written with **Midge Ure**, assembled a cavalcade of rock and pop stars under the name **Band Aid**. It included members from: **Status Quo**, **Culture Club**, **Bananarama**, **Style Council**, **Duran Duran**, **Spandau Ballet**, **Heaven 17** and **U2**. Solo stars included **Phil Collins**, **Sting**, **George**

Michael, and **Paul Young**. Geldof brilliantly bludgeoned artists, record companies, pressing plants, distributors and record shops to forego their profit. The record scaled the UK charts and stayed on top for 5 weeks, eventually selling millions of copies. Geldof topped this masterstroke in July 1985 by organizing Live Aid. This spectacular rock and pop concert was televised world-wide, live from London and Philadelphia. Among the stellar cast were: **Sade**, **Queen**, **Bob Dylan**, **Neil Young**, the **Cars**, **Beach Boys**, **Pat Metheny**, **Santana**, **Madonna**, **Kenny Loggins**, **Bryan Adams**, **Crosby, Stills And Nash**, **Eric Clapton**, Phil Collins (who via Concorde appeared at both venues), **Judas Priest**, **REO Speedwagon**, **Jimmy Page**, **Robert Plant**, Status Quo, **Elvis Costello**, **Bryan Ferry**, Sting, Paul Young, **Adam Ant**, **Simple Minds**, **U2**, the **Who**, **Paul McCartney**, **Mick Jagger**, **Tina Turner**, **Elton John**, Spandau Ballet and **David Bowie**. The event had the largest television viewing figure of all time and raised over £50 million through pledged donations. Geldof carried through his sincere wish to help starving children with integrity, passion and a sense of humour. The Live Aid concert remains one of the greatest musical events of all-time.
Further reading: *Live Aid: The Greatest Show On Earth*, Peter Hillmore.

Liverpool Express

Liverpool Express centred on singer/guitarist Billy Kinsley (b. 28 November 1946, Liverpool, England), veteran of 60s groups the **Merseybeats**, the **Merseys** and the **Swinging Blue Jeans**. He later formed Rockin' Horse with songwriter **Jimmy Campbell**, before embarking on a solo career in 1973 with 'Annabella'. Liverpool Express evolved out of the club group Kinsley had been working with and this new venture made its debut in 1975 with 'Smile (My Smiler's Smile)'. The quartet scored four chart hits between 1976-77, two of which, 'You Are My Love' and 'Every Man Must Have A Dream', reached the UK Top 20. The resulting touring schedule brought success in South America and on the European continent. A brief hiatus was followed by a modest UK chart position for 'So What?' in 1983. Liverpool Express have continued to perform and record into the 90s.
Albums: *Tracks* (1977), *Dreamin'* (1977, issued only in South America), *ELX* (1978, issued only in Europe).

Liverpool Scene

The name 'Liverpool Scene' was derived from a poetry anthology which featured Roger McGough, Adrian Henri and Brian Patten. The writers subsequently appeared on UK television's *Look Of The Week*, where their readings were accompanied by guitarist **Andy Roberts**. McGough and Henri then recorded *The Incredible New Liverpool Scene*, which included definitive performances of their best-known work, including 'Let Me Die A Young Man's Death' (McGough) and 'Tonight At Noon' (Henri). While McGough pursued a career within **Scaffold**, Henri and Roberts added Mike Hart (guitar/vocals), Mike Evans (saxophone/vocals) Percy Jones (bass) and Brian Dodson (drums) to create an explicitly rock-based ensemble. UK disc jockey **John Peel** was an early patron and the group quickly found itself an integral part of music's underground circuit, culminating in their impressive appearance at the 1969 Isle Of Wight Festival. *The Amazing Adventures Of...* captured the sextet at their most potent, but successive albums, although worthwhile, failed to match the crucial balance between musical and lyrical content and the group broke up in 1970. Hart embarked on a solo career, but while Roberts initially found fame in Plainsong, he was later reunited with both Henri and McGough in **Grimms**.
Albums: *The Incredible New Liverpool Scene* (1967), *The Amazing Adventures Of...* (1968), *Bread On The Night* (1969), *Saint Adrian Co. Broadway And 3rd* (1970), *Heirloom* (1970). Compilation: *Recollections* (1972).

Livgren, Kenny

The former **Kansas** guitarist (b. 18 September 1949, Kansas, USA) departed the fold in the early 80s to put on record his new-found religious beliefs as a born-again Christian. His debut solo effort saw him keeping a nucleus of Kansas personnel in support, adding the vocals of **Ronnie James Dio** on a competent set. Afterwards Livgren indulged in some tepid AOR albums, often allied to grandiose orchestral concepts, both solo and with his spin-off project, **AD**.
Album: *Seeds Of Change* (Kirshner 1980).

Living Colour

This US rock band was originally formed by Vernon Reid (b. England; guitar), Muzz Skillings (bass) and William Calhoun (drums). Reid had studied performing arts at Manhattan Community College, having moved to New York at the age of two. His first forays were in experimental electric jazz with Defunk, before he formed Living Colour as a trio in 1984. Both Skillings and Calhoun were experienced academic musicians, having studied and received acclaim at City College and **Berklee College Of Music** respectively. The line-up was completed by the induction of vocalist Corey Glover, who had just finished his part in Oliver Stone's *Platoon* movie, and whom Reid had originally encountered at a friend's birthday party. Their first major engagement came when **Mick Jagger** caught them performing at **CBGB's** and invited them to the studio for his forthcoming solo album. Jagger's patronage continued as he produced two demos for the band, which would secure them a deal with **Epic**

Records. Their debut, *Vivid*, earned them early critical favour and rose to number 6 in the US charts. Fusing disparate black musical formats like jazz, blues and soul, alongside commercial hard rock, its diversity was reflected in the support slots the band acquired to promote it; **Cheap Trick**, **Robert Palmer** and **Billy Bragg** among them. Musically, the band is aligned primarily to the first named of that trio of acts, although their political edge more closely mirrors the concerns of Bragg. In 1985 Reid formed the *Black Rock Coalition* pressure movement alongside journalist Greg Tate, and Living Colour grew to be perceived as their nation's most articulate black rock band. Two subsequent singles, 'Cult Of Personality' (which included samples of John F. Kennedy and won a Grammy award) and 'Open Letter (To A Landlord)' were both provocative but intelligent expressions of urban concerns. The ties with the **Rolling Stones** remained strong, with Reid collaborating on **Keith Richards**' solo album. They also joined the Stones on their *Steel Wheels* tour. After sweeping the boards in several Best New Band awards in such magazines as ***Rolling Stone***, *Time's Up* was released in 1990, and afforded another Grammy Award. Notable contributions, apart from the omnipresent Jagger, included **Little Richard** on the controversial 'Elvis Is Dead'. 1991 saw worldwide touring establish them as a highly potent force in the mainstream of rock. Bassist Doug Wimbish from **Tackhead** joined them for *Stain* which added a sprinkling of studio gimmickry on a number of tracks. The band announced its dissolution early in 1995. Vernon Reid issued a statement thus: '...Living Colour's sense of unity and purpose was growing weaker and fuzzier, I was finding more and more creative satisfaction in my solo projects. Finally it became obvious that I had to give up the band and move on'.

Albums: *Vivid* (Epic 1988), *Time's Up* (Epic 1990), *Stain* (Epic 1993).

Living In A Box

This Sheffield, UK-based pop group comprised Richard Darbyshire (b. 8 March 1960, Stockport, Cheshire, England; vocal/guitar), Marcus Vere (b. 29 January 1962; keyboard) and Anthony Critchlow (drums). Their first single, the self-referential, 'Living In A Box' was a UK Top 10 hit in the spring of 1987 and further successes followed over the next two years, most notably, 'Blow The House Down' and 'Room In Your Heart'. Meanwhile, vocalist Richard Darbyshire guested on John 'Jellybean' Benitez's *Jellybean Rocks The House.* Having enjoyed a hit album with their self-titled debut, the group consolidated their success with *Gatecrashing.*

Albums: *Living In A Box* (1987), *Gatecrashing* (1989).

Living It Up

One of the best films that **Dean Martin** and Jerry Lewis made together in the early-middle 50s, this 1954 Paramount release was twice blessed - with an amusing story and a set of good songs. Jack Rose and Melville Shavelson's screenplay was based on James Street's story *Letter To The Editor* and the 1937 movie *Nothing Sacred* which starred Fredric March and Carole Lombard. Proving that nothing really is sacred in Hollywood, Lombard's role was played this time by Jerry Lewis who gave a typically zany performance as a man who thinks he has a hefty dose of radiation poisoning. Encouraged by his doctor (Martin), who knows very well it is only a sinus condition, and a newspaper reporter (Janet Leigh), who believes he is going to die and knows a good story when she sees one, Lewis takes a press-sponsored trip to New York for one final all-out binge. It was all very entertaining, but much of the original film's bite and satire seemed to get lost on the journey. Two of **Jule Styne** and **Bob Hilliard**'s songs, 'How Do You Speak To An Angel?' and 'Money Burns A Hole In My Pocket' became popular record hits, and Martin's relaxed and easy manner was ideal for the engaging 'That's What I Like' and a duet with Lewis, 'Ev'ry Street's A Boulevard (In Old New York)'. The other songs were 'Champagne And Wedding Cake' and 'You're Gonna Dance With Me, Baby'. Also featured were Edward Arnold, Fred Clark, Sheree North, Sig Ruman, and Sammy White. Norman Taurog was the director and the film was shot in Technicolor. Jule Styne and Bob Hilliard also wrote the score for a 1953 Broadway musical based on this story. It was called *Hazel Flagg*, and ran for just 190 performances.

Livingston, Jay

b. 28 March 1915, Pittsburgh, Pennsylvania, USA. After studying music at school, Livingston attended the University of Pennsylvania where he met and formed a lasting friendship with Ray Evans (b. 4 February 1915, Salamanca, New York, USA) with whom he worked in shipboard bands on transatlantic and cruise liners. Their joint careers as songwriters were barely under way when they were interrupted by World War II. In the post-war years Livingston and Evans worked in Hollywood, writing songs for films. Their major success during this period was the title song from *To Each His Own* (1946). Other films they contributed to included *The Cat And The Canary*, *On Stage Everybody*, *The Stork Club*, *My Favourite Brunette*, *Dream Girl*, *Whispering Smith*, *Samson And Delilah*, *Bitter Victory*, *The Great Lover*, *Sorrowful Jones*, *My Friend Irma*, *Fancy Pants*, *The Lemon Drop Kid*, *Here Comes The Groom*, *Aaron Slick From Punkin Crick*, *Thunder In The East*, *Here Come The Girls*, and *Red Garters*. While continuing their partnership, in which Livingston usually wrote the music and Evans the words, both men occasionally worked with other composers. Their joint successes included the Oscar-winning songs 'Buttons And Bows' (*The Paleface* 1948) and 'Mona Lisa' (*Capt. Carey, USA* 1950). Among their other movie songs were 'Golden Earrings' (music by **Victor Young**), 'My Love Loves Me', 'Silver Bells', 'I'll Always Love You', 'Home Cookin'', 'A Place In The Sun' (music by **Franz Waxman**), 'Never Let Me Go', and another Oscar winner and **Doris Day** hit, 'Whatever Will Be, Will Be (Que Sera, Sera)'. Throughout the 50s Livingston and Evans continued to turn out film songs such as 'Tammy' and 'Almost In Your Arms'. In 1958 they wrote the score for a Broadway show *Oh, Captain!*, which included 'Femininity'. In the 60s came 'The Arms Of Love' and 'Wait Until Dark', and the duo also wrote the themes for the television series *Bonanza* and *Mr. Ed.* In the 70s Livingston and Evans continued to write occasional material for films and television, and contributed to the Broadway musical ***Sugar Babies*** (1979).

Livingstone, Dandy

b. 1944, Kingston, Jamaica, West Indies. Livingstone was at one time a member of the 60s duo, Sugar And Dandy with Sugar Simone and he was a very popular performer in the UK as a solo artist after he relocated there at the age of 15. His records appeared on a variety of different labels under different names and he was responsible for many of the UK's **rocksteady** and reggae hits throughout the 60s, 'Reggae In Your Jeggae' proving particularly popular in 1969. His first UK chart entry was 'Suzanne Beware of the Devil' in 1972, when reggae was briefly enjoying great popularity in the charts due to the skinhead connection. The follow up, 'Big City', was a smaller hit the following year. His name was revered by many **ska/2-Tone** fans who recalled his 60s heyday, and the **Specials** recorded a cover of his 'A Message To You Rudy'.

Selected albums: *Your Musical Doctor* (Downtown 1965), *Dandy Livingstone* (Trojan 1972), *South African Experience* (Night Owl 1978).

Lizzy Borden

This theatrical heavy rock band formed in Los Angeles in 1983, and took their name from the infamous axe murderess. Utilizing strong sexual and horror imagery, their visual deportment owed much to **Alice Cooper**. The group featured Lizzy Borden (vocals), his brother Joey Scott Harges (drums), Mike Kenny (bass) and Tony Matuzak (guitar). Their contribution to the *Metal Massacre IV* compilation impressed **Metal Blade** boss Brian Slagel enough to offer them a contract. The mini-album, *Give 'Em The Ax,* emerged in the summer of 1984, followed a year later by *Love You To Pieces*, their official full-length debut. Both were highly derivative of **Rainbow/Iron Maiden**, with Lizzy's vocals sounding similar to Geoff Tate's of **Queensrÿche**. Alex Nelson replaced Tony Matuzak on guitar at a juncture before the recording of *The Murderess Metal Roadshow*. This was a double live collection whose low-tech origins did little to flatter the band. Two more studio albums followed, including the abbreviated *Terror Rising*, which saw Betsy from **Bitch** duetting on a cover of the **Tubes**' kitsch classic, 'Don't Touch Me There'. Gene Allen was added as a second guitarist and Jesse Holmes and Mychal Davis replaced Nelson and Kenny respectively, before the recording of what is arguably the band's most enduring set, *Visual Lies*. Loosely based around a central theme of illusions, the album was varied and hard-hitting, characterized by infectious hooks, anthemic choruses and smouldering guitar breaks. They played the Reading Festival in 1987 to an indifferent reaction and Lizzy disbanded the group shortly afterwards (Holmes and Allen having already departed, with guitarist Ron Cerito replacing Mike Davis). Concentrating on a solo career he released the ambitious concept album, *Master Of Disguise*.

Albums: *Give 'Em The Axe* (Metal Blade 1984, mini-album), *Love You To Pieces* (Metal Blade 1985), *The Muderess Metal Roadshow* (Roadrunner 1986), *Menace To Society* (Roadrunner 1986), *Terror Rising* (Metal Blade 1987, mini-album), *Visual Lies* (Roadrunner 1987). Compilation: *Best Of* (Metal Blade 1994). Solo: Lizzy Borden *Master Of Disguise* (Roadrunner 1989).

Video: *Murdress Metal Roadshow* (1986).

LL Cool J

b. James Todd Smith, 16 August 1969, St. Albans, Queens, New York, USA. Long-running star of the rap scene, LL Cool J found fame at the age of 16, his pseudonym standing for 'Ladies Love Cool James'. As might be inferred by this, LL is a self-professed ladykiller in the vein of **Luther Vandross** or **Barry White**, yet he retains a superior rapping agility. Smith started rapping at the age of nine, after his grandfather bought him his first DJ equipment. From the age of 13 he was processing his first demos. The first to respond to his mail-outs was Rick Rubin of **Def Jam**, then a senior at New York University, who signed him to his fledgling label. The first sighting of LL Cool J came in 1984 on a 12-inch, 'I Need A Beat', which was the label's first such release. However, it was 'I Just Can't Live Without My Radio', which established his gold-chained, bare-chested B-boy persona. The song was featured in the *Krush Groove* film, on which the rapper also performed. In its wake he embarked on a 50 city US tour alongside the **Fat Boys**, **Whodini**, **Grandmaster Flash** and **Run DMC**. The latter were crucial to LL Cool J's development: his *modus operandi* was to combine their beatbox cruise control with streetwise B-boy raps, instantly making him a hero to a new generation of black youth. As well as continuing to tour with the trio, he would also contribute a song, 'Can You Rock It Like This', to Run DMC's *King Of Rock.* His debut album too, would see Rubin dose the grooves with heavy metal guitar breaks first introduced by Run DMC. LL Cool J's other early singles included 'I'm Bad', 'Go Cut Creator Go', 'Jack The Ripper' and 'I Need Love' (the first ballad rap, recorded with the **Los Angeles Posse**), which brought him a UK Top 10 score. Subsequent releases offered a fine array of machismo funk-rap, textured with personable charm and humour. Like many of his bretherin, LL Cool J's career has not been without incident. Live appearances in particular have been beset by many problems. Three people were shot at a date in Baltimore in December 1985, followed by an accusation of 'public lewdness' after a 1987 show in Columbus, Ohio. While playing rap's first concert in Cote d'Ivoire, Africa, fights broke out and the stage was stormed. Most serious, however, was an incident in 1989 when singer David Parker, bodyguard Christopher Tsipouras and technician Gary Saunders were accused of raping a 15-year old girl who attended a backstage party after winning a radio competition in Minneapolis. Though LL Cool J's personal involvement in all these cases was incidental, they undoubtedly have tarnished his reputation. He has done much to make amends, including appearances at benefits including Farm Aid, recording with the Peace Choir, and launching his *Cool School Video Program*, in an attempt to encourage children to stay at school. Even Nancy Reagan invited him to headline a 'Just Say No' concert at Radio City Music Hall. Musically, Cool is probably best sampled on his 1990 set, *Mama Said Knock You Out*, produced by the omnipresent **Marley Marl**, which as well as the familiar sexual braggadocio included LL's thoughts on the state of rap past, present and future. The album went triple platinum, though the follow-up, *14 Shots To The Dome*, was a less effective attempt to recycle the formula. Some tracks stood out: 'A Little Something', anchored by a sample of **King Floyd**'s soul standard 'Groove Me', being a good example. Like many of rap's senior players, he has also sustained an acting career, with film appearances in *The Hard Way* and *Toys*, playing a cop in the former and a military man in the latter.

Albums: *Radio* (Columbia 1985), *Bigger And Deffer* (Def Jam 1987), *Walking With A Panther* (Def Jam 1989), *Mama Said Knock You Out* (Def Jam 1990), *14 Shots To The Dome* (Def Jam 1993).

Lloyd Webber, Andrew

b. 22 March 1948, London, England. The 'Sir Arthur Sullivan' of the rock age was born the son of a Royal College of Music professor and a piano teacher. His inbred musical strength manifested itself in a command of piano, violin and French horn by the time he had spent a year at Magdalen College, Oxford, where he penned *The Likes Of Us* with lyricist (and law student) **Tim Rice**. As well as his liking for such modern composers as Hindemith, Ligeti and Penderecki, this first musical also revealed a captivation with pop music that surfaced even more when he and Rice collaborated in 1967 on ***Joseph And The Amazing Technicolor Dreamcoat***, a liberal adaptation of the scriptures. Mixing elements of psychedelia, country and French *chanson*, it was first performed at a London school in 1968 before reaching a more adult audience, via fringe events, the West End theatre (starring **Paul Jones**, **Jess Conrad** and Maynard Williams), an album, and, in 1972, national television.

In the early 70s, Lloyd Webber strayed from the stage, writing the music scores for two British films, *Gumshoe* and *The Odessa File*. His next major project with Rice was the audacious ***Jesus Christ Superstar*** which provoked much protest from religious groups. Among the studio cast were guest vocalists **Michael d'Abo**, **Yvonne Elliman**, **Ian Gillan** and Paul Raven (later **Gary Glitter**), accompanied by a symphony orchestra under the baton of **André Previn** - as well as members of **Quatermass** and the **Grease Band**. Issued well before its New York opening in 1971, the tunes were already familiar to an audience that took to their seats night after night as the show ran for 711 performances. A less than successful film version was released in 1976.

After the failure of ***Jeeves*** in 1974 (with Alan Ayckbourn replacing Rice) Lloyd Webber returned to form with ***Evita***, an approximate musical biography of Eva Peron, self-styled 'political leader' of Argentina. It was preceded by high chart placings for its album's much-covered singles, most notably **Julie Covington**'s 'Don't Cry For Me Argentina' and 'Oh! What A Circus' from **David Essex**. *Evita* was still on Broadway in 1981 when ***Cats***, based on T.S. Eliot's *Old Possum's Book Of Practical Cats*, emerged as Lloyd Webber's most commercially satisfying work so far. It was also the composer's second musical without Rice, and included what is arguably his best-known song, 'Memory', with words by Eliot and the show's director, **Trevor Nunn**. **Elaine Paige**, previously the star of *Evita*, and substituting for the injured Judi Dench in the feline role of Grizabella, took the song into the UK Top 10. Subsequently, it became popular for **Barbra Streisand**, amongst others. With ***Song And Dance*** (1982), which consisted of an earlier piece, *Tell Me On Sunday* (lyrics by **Don Black**), and *Variations* composed on a theme by Paganini for his cellist brother, Julian, Lloyd Webber became the only theatrical composer to have three works performed simultaneously in both the West End and Broadway. Two items from *Song And Dance*, 'Take That Look Off Your Face' and 'Tell Me On Sunday' became hit singles for one of its stars, **Marti Webb**. Produced by **Cameron Mackintosh** and Lloyd Webber's Really Useful Company, it was joined two years later by ***Starlight Express*** (lyrics by **Richard Stilgoe**), a train epic with music which was nicknamed 'Squeals On Wheels' because the cast dashed around on roller skates pretending to be locomotives. Diversifying further into production, Lloyd Webber presented the 1983 comedy *Daisy Pulls It Off*, followed by ***The Hired Man***, *Lend Me A Tenor* and **Richard Rodgers** and **Lorenz Hart**'s ***On Your Toes*** at London's Palace Theatre - of which he had become the new owner.

Like Sullivan before him, Lloyd Webber indulged more personal if lucrative artistic whims in such as *Requiem*, written for his father, which, along with *Variations*, became a best-selling album. A later set, *Premiere Collection*, went triple platinum. A spin-off from *Requiem*, 'Pie Jesu' (1985), was a hit single for Paul Miles-Kington and **Sarah Brightman**, the composer's second wife. She made the UK Top 10 again in the following year, with two numbers from Lloyd Webber's ***The Phantom Of The Opera*** (adapted from the Gaston Leroux novel), duetting with **Steve Harley** on the title theme, and later with **Cliff Richard** on 'All I Ask Of You'. The original 'Phantom', **Michael Crawford**, had great success with his recording of another song hit from the show, 'The Music Of The Night'. Controversy followed, with Lloyd Webber's battle to ensure that Brightman re-created her role in the Broadway production in 1988. His US investors capitulated, reasoning that future Lloyd Webber creations were guaranteed box office smashes before their very conception. Ironically, ***Aspects Of Love*** (lyrics by Charles Hart and Don Black), which also starred Brightman (by now Lloyd Webber's ex-wife), was rated as one of the failures (it did not recoup its investment) of the 1990/1 Broadway season, although it eventually ran for over 300 performances. In London, the show, which closed in 1992 after a three year run, launched the career of **Michael Ball**, who had a UK number 2 with its big number, 'Love Changes Everything'. In April 1992, Lloyd Webber intervened in the Tate Gallery's attempt to purchase a Canaletto painting. Anxious, that it should remain in Britain, he bought the picture for £10 million. He was reported to have commented: 'I'll have to write another musical before I do this again'. That turned out to be ***Sunset Boulevard***, a stage adaptation of Billy Wilder's 1950 Hollywood classic, with Lloyd Webber's music, and book and lyrics by Don Black and Christopher Hampton. It opened in London on 12 July 1993 with **Patti LuPone** in the leading role of Norma Desmond, and had its American premiere in Los Angeles five months later, where Desmond was played by Glenn Close. Legal wrangles ensued when Lloyd Webber chose Close to star in the 1994 Broadway production instead of LuPone (the latter is said to have received 'somewhere in the region of $1 million compensation'), and there was further controversy when he closed down the Los Angeles production after having reservations about the vocal talents of its prospective new star, Faye Dunaway. She too, is said to have received a 'substantial settlement'. Meanwhile, *Sunset Boulevard* opened at the Minskoff Theatre in New York on November 17 with a record box office advance of $37.5 million. Like *Cats* and *The Phantom Of The Opera* before it, the show won seven **Tony Awards**, including best musical, score and book. Lloyd Webber was living up to his rating as the most powerful person in the American theatre in a list compiled by *TheaterWeek* magazine. His knighthood was awarded for services to the theatre, not only in the US and UK, but throughout the world - at any one time there are dozens of his productions touring, and resident in main cities. Among his other honours have been Drama Desk and **Ivor Novello** Awards. *Cats*, complete with its billing of 'Now And Forever', celebrated 14 years in the West End in 1995, and together with *Starlight Express* and *Jesus Christ Superstar*, gave Lloyd Webber the three longest-running musicals in British theatre history for a time, before the latter show was overtaken by ***Les Misérables*** in January of that year. *Jesus Christ Superstar* celebrated its 20th anniversary in 1992 with a UK concert tour. Other Lloyd Webber highlights of just that one year included a series of concerts entitled *The Music Of Andrew Lloyd Webber* (special guest star Michael Crawford), a smash hit revival of *Joseph And The Amazing Technicolor Dreamcoat* at the London Palladium, and the recording, by Sarah Brightman and José Carreras, of Lloyd Webber's Barcelona Olympic Games anthem 'Friends For Life' ('Amigos Para Siempre'). In the mid-90s Lloyd Webber is said to be planning to build theatres around the world in which to house his musicals, and extending his empire into feature films.

Further reading: *Andrew Lloyd Webber*, G. McKnight. *Fanfare: The Unauthorized Biography Of Andrew Lloyd Webber*, J. Mantle. *Andrew Lloyd Webber: His Life And Works*, M. Walsh.

Video: *The Premier Collection Encore* (1994).

Lloyd, A.L.

b. February 1908, London, England. Bert Lloyd was one of the prime movers of the 50s folk song revival in Britain. He returned to England in 1935 with a collection of some 500 songs and a determination to study and research into folk music. In 1937, he sailed to Antarctica with a whaling fleet, adding further songs to his repertoire. On his return he joined BBC radio as a scriptwriter. During the 40s he wrote *The Singing Englishman*, the first general book on folk song since **Cecil Sharp**'s in 1909. He also compiled the *Penguin Book Of English Folk Song* with the composer Ralph Vaughan Williams. By the 50s, Lloyd was a full-time folklorist, making several field trips to record material in Bulgaria and Albania as well as publishing a selection of coalfield ballads which provided repertoire for young singers in the growing number of folk song clubs. At this time he met **Ewan MacColl**, with whom he made his own first recordings, as part of the *Radio Ballads* series. During the 60s he made a series of solo albums for **Topic Records**, with accompanists including singers **Anne Briggs** and **Frankie Armstrong**, Alf Edwards (accordion), **Martin Carthy** (guitar/mandolin), **Dave Swarbrick** (fiddle) and actor/singer Harry H. Corbett. They covered drinking songs, industrial songs and selections from his sheep-shearing and whaling exploits. Lloyd also arranged compilation albums of sea shanties, industrial songs (*The Iron Muse*) and recordings from the Balkan field trips.

Albums: *Selections From The Penguin Book Of English Folk Songs* (1960), *The Iron Muse* (1963), *All For Me Grog* (1964), *The Bird In The Bush* (1965), *First Person* (1966), *Leviathan* (1968), *The Great Australian Legend* (1969), with Ewan MacColl *English And Scottish Popular Ballads* (1974), *Sea Songs And Shanties* (1981).

Lloyd, Charles

b. 15 March 1939, Memphis, Tennessee. Lloyd was self-taught on tenor saxophone, which he played in his high school band. He gained a Masters Degree at the University of Southern California and became a music teacher at Dorsey High in Los Angeles. In October 1960, he joined the **Chico Hamilton** Quintet, where he played flute, alto and clarinet as well as tenor, and soon became the band's musical director. In January 1964, he joined the **Cannonball Adderley** Sextet, where he stayed until forming his own quartet with guitarist **Gabor Szabo**, bassist **Ron Carter** and drummer **Tony Williams** in July 1965. Soon Szabo was replaced by pianist **Keith Jarrett** and Carter and Williams returned to the **Miles Davis** group. At the start of 1966 **Cecil McBee** came in on bass (he was replaced by **Ron McClure** in 1967), **Jack DeJohnette** took the drum chair and the stage was set for a jazz phenomenon. Manager George Avakian decided to market the band in the same way he would a rock group, and the tactic paid off. In modern jazz terms the Quartet was hugely successful, playing to massive rock audiences at the Fillmore Stadium in San Francisco and becoming the first American band to appear in a Soviet festival. While the public and musicians such as Miles Davis and **Ian Carr** admired the band, the critics were predictably cynical, criticizing the musicians' clothes, hair styles and hippy attitudes but ignoring the basic virtues of the music itself, which included rhythmic vitality, a sound foundation in bop and the blues, and Lloyd's surging and emotionally affecting tenor sound. In due course his public looked elsewhere and, eventually, Lloyd left music to pursue his interest in philosophy and meditation, although during this period he did work and record with the **Beach Boys** (*Surf's Up*) as a result of his friendship with Mike Love. In the early 80s he edged back onto the jazz scene, notably with a **Montreux Festival** performance featuring **Michel Petrucciani**, and he began to tour again with a quartet containing Palle Danielson and **Jon Christensen**. During his semi-retirement his flute playing had become stronger whilst his tenor took on some of the ethereal quality his flute formerly had.

Albums: with Chico Hamilton *Passing Thru'* (1963), *Discovery!* (1964), *Of Course Of Course* (1965), *Dream Weaver* (Atlantic 1966), *Live At Antibes* (1966), *Forest Flower* (1966), *Charles Lloyd In Europe* (1966), *Love-In* (1967), *Live In The Soviet Union* (1967), *Journey Within* (1969), *The Flowering Of The Original Charles Lloyd Quartet* (1971), *Moonman* (1971), *Warm Waters* (1971), *Geeta* (1972), *Waves* (1972), *Weavings* (1978), *Big Sur Tapestry* (1979), *Montreux '82* (1982), *A Night In Copenhagen* (Blue Note 1989), *Fish Out Of Water* (ECM 1990), *Notes From Big Sur* (ECM 1992), *The Call* (EMC 1994).

Lloyd, Jon

b. 20 October 1958, Stratford-upon-Avon, Warwickshire, England. Lloyd dabbled with piano at the age of 12, and then taught himself tenor saxophone at 23. His first public appearances were with a pop/soul band in the mid-80s and with an **ECM**-inspired duo, Confluence. His first professional job was with a duo playing standards on the restaurant/wine-bar/pub circuit. Despite his relatively late start on saxophone he has developed an individual style of music that is exhibited to especially good advantage on his first, privately-produced recording. His influences include **Jan Garbarek**, **John Surman**, **Trevor Charles Watts** and, 'more for affirmation than emulation', **Eric Dolphy**, **Evan Parker**, **Jimmy Lyons**, **Anthony Braxton** and **Arthur Blythe**. He has also been inspired by composers Olivier Messiaen (who has influenced several non-classical figures, notably Mike Ratledge of the **Soft Machine** and **Mike Gibbs**) and Benjamin Britten. He has organized several worthy attempts at regular venues for improvised music, including the 'Sun Sessions' in Clapham, south London. Apart from his own trio and quartet he has worked with Dave Fowler and in duos with **Evan Shaw Parker** and **Phil Wachsmann**, and organizes Anacrusis, a nine-piece improvising group containing several major names.

Albums: *Pentimento* (1988), *Syzygy* (Leo 1990), with Dave Fowler *As It Was* (1990), *Head* (Leo 1993).

Lloyd, Richard

Having established himself as a rhythm guitarist of standing in **Television**, Lloyd embarked on a solo career in 1979, releasing an album whose quality rivalled the efforts of his more illustrious ex-partners, **Tom Verlaine** and **Richard Hell**. *Alchemy* should

have projected Lloyd towards a bigger audience but its reviews were not matched by its sales and Richard failed to exploit the work due to an alarming slump into drug addiction. It was five years before a chemical-free Lloyd returned with a new album, *Field Of Fire*, but since the mid-80s his output remained decidedly low. By 1991, he had joined Verlaine, Ficca and Smith in a reformed Television, spending much of the first part of 1992 rehearsing and recording.
Albums: *Alchemy* (Elektra 1979), *Field Of Fire* (Mistlur/Moving Target 1985), *Real Time* (Celluloid 1987, live album).

Lloyd, Robert

Inspired by **T. Rex** and the fact that girls tended to pin posters of pop stars on their walls and not the professional footballers that Robert Lloyd (b. 1959, Cannock, Staffordshire, England) aspired to emulate, the teenager switched his allegiance from the football field to concert hall. Between 1974 and 1976 he played in several bands that never escaped the rehearsal room. He left school at the age of 16 and in 1976 attended a concert by the **Sex Pistols**. He started to follow the Pistols around on the Anarchy Tour and at one of the gigs, he persuaded a promoter to offer him some gigs. The result was the hurriedly assembled Prefects in February 1977, consisting of Lloyd, Alan and Paul Appelby, and Joe Crow. After one performance at a private party and one at the famous Barbarella's club in Birmingham, the Prefects were offered the chance of standing in for the **Slits** at a **Clash** concert. When the **Buzzcocks** dropped out of the subsequent tour, the Prefects were offered a permanent place. Although the band recorded two **John Peel** BBC radio sessions, no records were released until after the band's split in 1979. Lloyd's next move was to form the **Nightingales** and his own Vindaloo label. When the Nightingales fell apart in the mid-80s he concentrated on the label and songwriting, the results of which surfaced in further Peel sessions (he holds the record for the most sessions for Peel in his various forms) under the name Robert Lloyd And The New Four Seasons. This led to a single with the In-Tape label and in 1989 he signed to **Virgin Records**. After a few false starts, the album emerged in 1990 and featured Steve Nieve and Pete Thomas (the **Attractions**), Andy Scott (the **Sweet**) and Craig Gannon (formerly of the **Bluebells**, **Aztec Camera**, the **Colourfield** and the **Smiths**) amongst others. However, when it came to promoting the album, Lloyd had to assemble a new band centred around former Nightingale guitarist, The Tank.
Album: *Me And My Mouth* (Virgin 1990).

Loaded Records

Record label which is also the home of the Brighton-based remix team of JC Reid and Tim Jeffreys (also a *Record Mirror* journalist), who operate under the name Play Boys. Their first production work together was for the London Community Gospel Choir in 1992 with 'I'll Take You There' and 'Ball Of Confusion', before they set up the Loaded imprint. Titles like 'Ransom' and 'Suggestive', co-produced with Pizzaman, aka **Norman Cook**, emerged. Their next work was on a hot re-activated version of 'Love So Strong' by **Secret Life** which proved more than merely a remix, with re-recorded Paul Bryant vocals. Other remix projects included Brother Love Dub's 'Ming's Incredible Disco Machine', **PM Dawn**'s 'When Midnight Says' and Talizman. As the Play Boys they also released in their own right, included 'Mindgames' from 1992. They also returned the compliment to Norman Cook by remixing his **Freak Power** track, 'Turn On, Tune In, Cop Out'. The Loaded release schedule continued apace too, with records like those from Key Largo (Eddie Richards) and the garage house of Wildchild Experience (the *Wildtrax* EP, which ran to several volumes, created by Southampton-born DJ Roger McKenzie). Other artists included Jason Nevins ('The Upper Room').

Loading Zone

The Loading Zone - Linda Tillery (vocals), Paul Fauerso (keyboards), Steve Dowler (guitar), Patrick O'Hara (trombone), Todd Anderson (wind instruments), Bob Kridle (bass) and George Newcom (drums) - were one of several R&B-based US groups popular in San Francisco's ballrooms during the late 60s. Although signed to **RCA Records** in 1968, their jazz/blues debut album failed to capture an onstage verve. Tillery's powerful voice provided much of the unit's identity, but their potential was undermined by several changes in personnel and the band collapsed following the release of a second album on the Umbrella label. The singer has remained a popular figure on the Bay Area circuit.
Albums: *The Loading Zone* (1968), *One For All* (1968).

Lobo

b. Roland Kent Lavoie, 31 July 1943, Tallahassee, Florida, USA. Lobo was the pseudonym of Roland Lavoie a singer-songwriter who was successful in the early 70s. He was raised in the town of Winter Haven, Florida, where he began his musical career as a member of the Rumors. He apprenticed in several other groups during the 60s as well, notably, the Legends from Tampa, Florida, which included **Gram Parsons** and **Jim Stafford**; who would also enjoy success in the early 70s with two US Top 10 hits, produced by Lavoie. (Other members of the Legends included Gerald Chambers and Jon Corneal, the latter remaining an associate of Parsons for many years.) Lavoie also performed with bands called the Sugar Beats and Me And The Other Guys, neither of which had any success outside of their region. In 1971, former

Sugar Beats member Phil Gernhard signed Lavoie, calling himself Lobo (Spanish for wolf) to Big Tree Records, where he was an executive, and released their first single, 'Me And You And A Dog Named Boo'. It reached number 5 in the US and launched a successful series of singles. The song became his only hit in the UK, where it reached number 4. Back to back Top 10 hits in 1972, 'I'd Love You To Want Me' and 'Don't Expect Me To Be Your Friend', were the last major hits for Lobo. However, he continued to chart with Big Tree until 1975 (six albums also charted, but only the second, *Of A Simple Man,* in 1972, made the Top 40). In 1979, Lobo resurfaced on MCA Records, 'Where Were You When I Was Falling In Love', reached number 23. After the end of that decade his recording career ended.

Albums: *Introducing Lobo* (1971), *Of A Simple Man* (1972), *Calumet* (1973), *Just A Singer* (1974), *A Cowboy Afraid Of Horses* (1975), *Lobo* (1979). Compilation: *The Best Of Lobo* (1975).

Lock Up Your Daughters

This show was the first to be presented at the new Mermaid Theatre in the City of London on 28 May 1959, and was, appropriately enough, the brainchild of the Mermaid's founder, Bernard (later, Sir Bernard) Miles. His adaptation of Henry Fielding's *Rape Upon Rape*, was an extremely bawdy tale in which a gentle maiden, Hilaret (Stephanie Voss), and her would-be rapist, Ramble (Frederick Jaeger), appear before the lecherous Justice Squeezum (Richard Wordsworth). Squeezum's efforts to inflict his own individual brand of custodial sentence on Hilaret lead to highly complicated manoeuvres which involve the far-from-innocent Mrs Squeezum (Hy Hazell), and result in the Justice himself going to prison. The object of his affections is then reunited with her true love, Captain Constant (Terence Cooper). The score, by two young newcomers, composer **Laurie Johnson** and lyricist **Lionel Bart** (Bart's ***Fings Ain't Wot They Used T'Be*** was just starting out at the Theatre Royal Stratford) complemented perfectly the lusty outrages of the story, in songs such as 'Lock Up Your Daughters' ('Here comes a rake!'), 'When Does The Ravishing Begin?', 'Red Wine And A Wench', and 'I'll Be There'. Hilaret *almost* seduces Squeezum 'On A Sunny Sunday Morning', and the other delights included 'Lovely Lover', 'Kind Fate', 'A Proper Man', 'It Must Be True', ''Tis Plain To See', and 'Mr. Jones'. The show ran for 330 performances, and subsequently had its US premiere in New Haven in April 1960. *Lock Up Your Daughters* returned to the Mermaid two years later before transferring to the Her Majesty's theatre in the West End for a stay of some 16 months, and called in at the Mermaid again in 1969 for just a brief stay. Another American production, with 50s film star, Carleton Carpenter as Squeezum, was presented at the Goodspeed Opera House in 1982.

Locke, Josef

b. Joseph McLaughlin, 23 March 1917, Londonderry, Northern Ireland. A extremely popular ballad singer in the UK from the 40s through to the 60s, with an impressive tenor voice and substantial stage presence, Locke sang in local churches as a child, and, when he was 16, added two years to his age in order to enlist in the Irish Guards. Later, he served abroad with the Palestine Police before returning to Ireland in the late 30s to join the Royal Ulster Constabulary. Nicknamed the 'Singing Bobby', he became a local celebrity in the early 40s, and then toured the UK variety circuit. In the following year, he played the first of 19 seasons at the popular northern seaside resort of Blackpool. He made his first radio broadcast in 1949 on the famous *Happydrome*, which starred the trio of 'Ramsbottom, Enoch and Me', and subsequently appeared on television programmes such as *Rooftop Rendezvous*, *Top Of The Town*, *All-Star Bill* and the *Frankie Howerd Show*. In 1947, Locke released 'Hear My Song, Violetta', which became forever associated with him. His other records were mostly a mixture of Irish ballads such as 'I'll Take You Home Again Kathleen', 'Dear Old Donegal' and 'Galway Bay'; excerpts from operettas, including 'The Drinking Song', 'My Heart And I' and 'Goodbye'; along with familiar Italian favourites such as 'Come Back To Sorrento' and 'Cara Mia'. He also made several films, including the comedy, *Holidays With Pay*. In 1958, after appearing in five Royal Command Performances, and while still at the peak of his career, the Inland Revenue began to make substantial demands that Locke declined to meet. Eventually he 'fled from public view to avoid tax-evasion charges'. Meanwhile, on the television talent show, *Opportunity Knocks*, the host, Hughie Green introduced 'Mr. X', a Locke look-alike, as a 'is-he-or-isn't-he' gimmick. He was in reality, Eric Lieson, who carved a long and lucrative career out of the impersonation. When Locke's differences with the tax authorities were settled, he retired to County Kildare, emerging for the occasional charity concert. He attracted some attention in 1984 when he was the subject of a two-hour birthday tribute on Gay Bryne's talk show, *The Late, Late Show*, on Irish television, but faded into the background once more until 1992, when the Peter Chelsom film *Hear My Song*, was released in the UK. It was an 'unabashed romantic fantasy based on the exuberant notion of Locke returning to Britain to complete an old love affair and save a Liverpool-based Irish night-club from collapse'. Locke was flown to London for the royal premiere, which was attended by Princess Diana, and became the 'victim' of television's *This Is Your Life*. In the movie, the songs are dubbed by the operatic tenor Vernon Midgely. Although determined not to become a celebrity all over again, during the spring of 1992,

Locke found himself in the UK Top 10 album chart with *Hear My Song*.
Selected albums: *My Many Requests* (1964), *I'll Sing It My Way* (1974), *Josef Locke Sings Favourite Irish Songs* (1978), *Let There Be Peace* (1980), *In Concert* (1989). Compilations: *The World Of Josef Locke Today* (1969), *Hear My Song* (1983), *34 Great Singalong Songs* (1988), *Hear My Song: The Best Of* (1992), *Take A Pair Of Sparkling Eyes* (1992), *A Tear, A Kiss, A Smile* (1993).

Locklin, Hank

b. Lawrence Hankins Locklin, 15 February 1918, McLellan, Florida, USA. A farm boy, Locklin worked in the cottonfields as a child and on the roads during the Depression of the 30s. He learned to play the guitar at the age of 10 and soon after performed on local radio and at dances. His professional career started in 1938 and after an interruption for military service, he worked various local radio stations, including WALA Mobile and KLEE Houston. In 1949, he joined the *Louisiana Hayride* on KWKH Shreveport and achieved his first country chart entry with his Four Star recording of his self-penned 'The Same Sweet One'. In 1953, 'Let Me Be The One' became his first country number 1. After moving to **RCA** in the mid-50s, he had Top 10 US country hits with 'Geisha Girl', his own 'Send Me The Pillow You Dream On', both also making the US pop charts, and 'It's A Little More Like Heaven'. His biggest chart success came in 1960, when his million-selling recording of 'Please Help Me I'm Falling' topped the US country charts for 14 successive weeks and also reached number 8 in the pop charts. It also became one of the first modern country songs to make the British pop charts, peaking at number 9 in a 19-week chart stay. (An answer version by **Skeeter Davis** called '(I Can't Help You) I'm Falling Too' also became a US country and pop hit the same year.) Locklin became a member of the *Grand Ole Opry* in 1960 and during the next decade, his fine tenor voice and ability to handle country material saw him become one of the most popular country artists. He registered over 20 US chart entries including 'We're Gonna Go Fishing' and a number 8 hit with the now country standard 'The Country Hall Of Fame' in 1967. He hosted his own television series in Houston and Dallas in the 1970s and during his career has toured extensively in the States, Canada and in Europe. He is particularly popular in Ireland, where he has toured many times and, in 1964, recorded an album of Irish songs. Although a popular artist in Nashville, he always resisted settling there. In the early 60s, he returned to his native Florida and built his home, the Singing L, on the actual cottonfield where he had once worked as a boy. After becoming interested in local affairs, his popularity saw him elected mayor of his home town of McLellan. Although Locklin's last chart success was a minor hit in 1971, he remains a firm favourite with the fans and still regularly appears on the *Opry*.
Albums: *Foreign Love* (1958), *Please Help Me I'm Falling* (1960), *Encores* (1961), *Hank Locklin* (1962), *Happy Journey* (1962), *10 Songs* (1962), *This Song Is Just For You* (1962), *A Tribute To Roy Acuff* (1962), *The Ways Of Life* (1963), *Irish Songs, Country Style* (1964), *Sings Hank Williams* (1964), *Born To Ramble* (1965), *My Kind Of Country Music* (1965), *Down Texas Way* (1965), *Sings Eddy Arnold* (1965), *The Girls Get Prettier* (1966), *The Gloryland Way* (1966), *Bummin' Around* (1967), *Send Me The Pillow You Dream On* (1967), *Sings Hank Locklin* (1967), *Nashville Women* (1967), *Wabash Cannonball* (1968), *Country Hall Of Fame* (1968), *Queen Of Hearts* (1968), *My Love Song For You* (1968), *Softly - Hank Locklin* (1969), *Best Of Today's Country Hits* (1969), *Lookin' Back* (1969), *That's How Much I Love You* (1969), *Candy Kisses* (1970), *Bless Her Heart - I Love Her* (1970), *Hank Locklin & Danny Davis & The Nashville Brass* (1970), *The First Fifteen Years (1971), The Mayor Of McLellan, Florida* (1972), *Hank Locklin* (1975), *The Golden Hits* (1977), *There Never Was A Time* (1977), with various artists *Carol Channing & Her Country Friends* (1977), *All Kinds Of Everything* (1979), *Please Help Me I'm Falling* (1986). Compilation: *20 Of The Best* (1982).

Lockran, Gerry

b. Gerald Loughran, 19 July 1942, Yeotmal, Central Province, India, d. 17 November 1987. Born to an Irish father and an Indian mother, Lockran and his family moved to England in 1953. Two years later, aged just 13, Lockran was playing guitar in a skiffle band called the Hornets. However, it was not until he heard **Elvis Presley**'s guitarist **Scotty Moore** that Lockran really took interest in the instrument. What clinched it for Lockran was hearing **Big Bill Broonzy** and **Brownie McGhee**. They, he claimed, were his greatest influences. He regularly played in clubs in Europe through the early 60s, and the latter half of the period saw him consolidate his popularity in the UK and on the continent. In 1974 Lockran toured the US with **Joe Cocker**, and at one stage was offered the chance of replacing the headlining artist, who had fallen ill, but declined saying that he 'didn't want to be Joe Cocker' as he had his own loyal following. Lockran also supported artists such as **Stevie Wonder**, the **Eagles**, **Rod Stewart**, and at one time the American press likened Lockran to another great blues man, **Taj Mahal**. Lockran gradually moved away from the British folk scene, finding himself able to make a better living playing in the US. This decision was also prompted by the fact that the British folk scene had largely scorned blues through the early 70s, preferring to retain its traditional image. It was while returning from a German tour in October 1981 that Lockran suffered a heart attack, and not long after this, a stroke left him partially paralyzed down the left side. In 1982 another heart attack left him unable to perform, cruelly ensuring that his legacy of country-blues and rag-time were confined to his recorded works. Lockran's albums featured a veritable who's who of the music business, notably **Cliff Aungier**, **Henry McCullough**, **Pete Wingfield**, and **Neil Hubbard**. A collection of Lockran's poems were published in 1983 under the title *Smiles And Tears*. Lockran died in November 1987 following another heart attack. Such was the respect that he was held in that a benefit night held for his family on 24 January 1988 at the Half Moon, Putney, London, saw artists such as Cliff Aungier, **Gordon Giltrap**, **Wizz Jones**, **Bert Jansch**, **Dave Kelly**, **Alexis Korner** and Henry McCullough turn out to play.

Albums: *Hold On I'm Coming* (Philips 1963), *The Essential Gerry Lockran* (Pye 1966), *Blues Vendetta* (EMI 1967), *Wun* (Polydor 1968), *Rags To Glad Rags* (Decca 1970), *Blues Blast Off* (Autogram 1972), *Live/Rally Round The Flag* (Autogram 1973), *No More Cane On The Brazos* (Munich 1976), *The Shattered Eye* (Autogram 1977), *Total* (Autogram 1978), *Across The Tracks* (BML 1981), with Hans TheesinkL *Cushioned For A Soft Ride* (Autogram 1981).

Further reading: *Smiles And Tears*, Gerry Lockran.

Locks, Fred

b. Stafford Elliot, c.1955, Kingston, Jamaica, West Indies. Locks began his sporadic career as a member of the Lyrics, who recorded tracks like 'A Get It', 'Girls Like Dirt', and 'Hear What The Old Man Say' for **Coxsone Dodd** in the late 60s, 'Give Praises' for Randy's, and the self-financed 'Sing A Long', both in 1971. The Lyrics disbanded shortly afterwards, and Locks, discouraged by the lack of financial reward endemic to the Jamaican music business, immersed himself in the Rasta faith then gaining significant ground amongst Jamaica's ghetto youth, and retired to live a spartan existence out on the beach at Harbour View. Whilst enduring this bucolic lifestyle, Locks allowed his dreads to grow to formidable proportions - hence his nickname - and continued to write songs, one of which, a prophetic Garveyite vision of repatriation entitled 'Black Star Liners', he was persuaded to record by producer Hugh Boothe.

Released in 1975 on the Jahmikmusic label in Jamaica, and on Grounation in the UK, 'Black Star Liners' struck a resounding chord amongst the new generation of Rastafarian youth on both islands, propelling Locks to cult figure status in the process. Two years later Grounation off-shoot Vulcan finally officially released the long awaited *Black Star Liners/True Rastaman*, a classic example of 70s roots Rasta reggae, packed with fine songs including former singles 'Last Days' (retitled 'Time To Change') and 'Wolf Wolf', and raw, guileless vocals. Throughout this time Locks had also been a member of the vocal trio Creation Steppers with Eric Griffiths and Willy Stepper, who had been releasing singles on their Star Of The East imprint in Jamaica, achieving considerable local success with 'Stormy Night' - later covered at **Channel One** by the Rolands. A various artists album entitled *Love & Harmony* featured the title track (also a 12-inch in Jamaica) credited to Fred Locks, and 'Kill Nebuchadnezzar' by the Creation Steppers also emerged, in 1979. In 1980 Locks and the Creation Steppers went to the UK for several shows and linked up with the legendary **sound system** operator and record producer, **Lloydie Coxsone**, who released a number of discs by both the group and Locks including the classic 'steppers' 'Homeward Bound', 'Love And Only Love' and 'Voice Of The Poor'. These and other tracks were eventually released on *Love And Only Love*. Locks moved to the USA in 1982, effectively halting his and the Steppers career. Settling in Philadelphia, he immersed himself in the local Twelve Tribes organisation, after which he recorded only sporadically.

Albums: *Black Star Liners/True Rastaman* (Vulcan 1977), *Love And Only Love* (Tribesman 1981).

Lockwood, Didier

b. 11 February 1956, Calais, France. Lockwood studied classical violin at the Conservatoire de Musique de Paris, but exposure to the blues of **Johnny Winter** and **John Mayall** persuaded him to cut short formal study in 1972 and form a jazz-rock group with his brother, Francis. A three-year stint with **Magma** followed, but Lockwood was more excited by the improvising of **Jean-Luc Ponty**, whom he heard on **Frank Zappa**'s 'King Kong'. He listened to other jazz violinists, particularly the Pole, **Zbigniew Seifert** and the veteran **Stéphane Grappelli**. The latter quickly realised the talent in Lockwood and played with him whenever possible. During the late 70s Lockwood played and recorded with many major European and American artists including **Tony Williams**, **Gordon Beck**, **John Etheridge**, **Daniel Humair** and **Michal Urbaniak**. In 1981, Lockwood recorded *Fusion*, which typified the approach he has followed throughout the 80s: a solid rock-based rhythm with plenty of soloing room for Lockwood's lightning improvisations on the 160-year-old violin he continues to use, emphasizing the long tradition of French jazz violinists of which he is a part and which his love of the music of **John Coltrane**, and his rock influences have helped to update.

Albums: with Magma *New World* (MPS 1979), *Fusion* (1981), *New World* (1984), *1,2,3,4* (JMS 1987), *Pheonix 90* (1990), *DLG* (JMS 1993), *Martial Solal* (JMS 1993).

Lockwood, Robert

b. 27 March 1915, Marvell, Arkansas, USA. In his youth, Lockwood learned some guitar from **Robert Johnson** who was evidently a major influence. Lockwood's earliest recordings emphasize that debt. He worked the Mississippi Delta area throughout the 30s,

playing with musicians such as **Sonny Boy 'Rice Miller' Williamson** and **Howlin' Wolf**. In 1941, he was in Chicago, Illinois making his first records as a solo artist, as well as some accompaniments to **Peter J. 'Doctor' Clayton**. Lockwood spent some time as one of the resident musicians on the famous *King Biscuit Time* radio programme, from Helena, Arkansas. In the early 50s he settled in Chicago where he recorded with **Sunnyland Slim**. Johnson's influence was detectable, but the style was becoming distinctly urban in orientation. Throughout that decade he played the blues clubs, and often accompanied **Little Walter** on record. As his status as one of Chicago's master guitarists grew, he also contributed to material from **Muddy Waters**, **Eddie Boyd** and others. In 1960, he made some classic recordings with **Otis Spann**, his delicate runs and big, chunky chords betraying a more sophisticated, jazzy direction. Indeed, these sessions are considered by many to be among the greatest piano/guitar duo recordings of all time. He has continued to be very active in music through the ensuing years, working with **Willie Mabon** among others. In the late 70s he formed a touring and recording partnership with **John Ed 'Johnny' Shines**, and into the 90s he was still producing high-calibre work, notably on an album with **Ronnie Earl**.
Selected albums: *Windy City Blues* (1976), *Does 12* (1977), *Johnny Shines & Robert Lockwood - Dust My Broom* (Flyright 1980, rec.50s), *Johnny Shines & Robert Lockwood: Mr Blues Is Back To Stay* (Rounder 1981), *Robert & Robert* (Black & Blue, rec.1982), *What's The Score* (1990), *Steady Rolling Man* (Delmark 1992, rec.1970), *Plays Robert Johnson & Robert Lockwood Jr.* (1992).

Lockyer, Malcolm

b. Malcolm Neville Lockyer, 5 October 1923, Greenwich, London, England, d. 28 June 1976, England. Trained as an architect, Lockyer's interest in dance music dated from the age of 12, and he played semi-professionally until called up for war service as a musician in the Royal Air Force at the age of 19. He played with Sid Phillips And His Quintet, and in 1944 he joined the Buddy Featherstonehaugh Sextet and recorded with them for Radion and HMV. After leaving the RAF, Lockyer worked as pianist with **Ambrose**, **Cyril Stapleton** and **Robert Farnon**. He started with BBC radio in 1945, and during his career he worked on almost 6,000 broadcasts. He formed his own orchestra in 1951. A prolific composer (often under the pseudonym Howard Shaw), his biggest successes were 'Friends And Neighbours' (for the 1954 BBC television series), 'Fiddler's Boogie' and 'The Big Guitar' (for the BBC television series *Stranger Than Fiction* - 1955). Lockyer scored over 30 feature films and also the television series *The Pursuers* and *The Pathfinders*. Together with **Reg Owen** he made a collection of albums for Top Rank with the Knightsbridge Strings and the Cambridge Strings. He succeeded **Harry Rabinowitz** as conductor of the BBC Revue Orchestra in 1960, and was associated with many radio shows, among them *Mid-day Music Hall*, *Take It From Here* and *Beyond Our Ken*. When the Revue and Variety orchestras were amalgamated in 1966 to form the new Radio Orchestra, Lockyer became associate conductor. His connection with **Glenn Miller** began in 1944, when he was stationed in Bedford at the same time as the famous American band leader. He was able to study at first-hand how that unmistakeable sound was achieved. Shortly before his death in 1976 he conducted the Million Airs Orchestra in 26 highly-successful Glenn Miller Tribute Concerts.

Locomotive

Formed in Birmingham, England, Locomotive initially achieved fame as a **ska**/bluebeat band and by the fact that one of their early members, Chris Wood had departed in 1967 to join the fledgling **Traffic**. Having made their debut with 'Broken Heart' on the dance-oriented Direction label, they switched to **Parlophone** for 'Rudi's In Love'. This enchanting rock-steady ballad reached the UK Top 30 in 1968, but by the following year the group had completely changed its musical direction. Norman Haines (guitar/vocals) took control of the band on 'Mr. Armageddon', a haunting progressive rock piece drawing an air of mystery from its pulsating, yet distant, horn section. Mick Taylor (trumpet), Bill Madge (saxophone), Mick Hincks (bass) and Bob Lamb (drums) completed the line-up featured on *We Are Everything You See* which, despite contemporary commercial indifference, has become one of the era's most fêted releases. Locomotive split up soon after its release and while its erstwhile leader founded the Norman Haines Band. Lamb, Hincks and associate member Keith Millar formed the Dog That Bit People. The drummer then went on to join the **Steve Gibbons** Band.
Album: *We Are Everything You See* (1969).

Locust

In the accelerating flurry of ambient dance releases following the **Orb**'s breakthrough, at least the work of Mark Van Hoen contains a snatch of humour. The track 'Xenophobia', for example: 'I started with this Japanese vocal sample, and began thinking I'd have to surround it with five-note Japanese pentatonik scales. Then I gave up and called myself xenophobic'. Elsewhere the musical territory on his debut album was mapped out in traditional genre style, eerie mood pieces with more than a passing nod to composers like **Steve Reich**. Diverting enough, but hardly a substantial listening experience. He originally came to prominence through the heavily-imported *Skyline* EP, before a deal with **R&S** subsidiary Apollo for six albums. Unlike many similar artists, however, Van

Hoen has no ambitions to remix other people's music, preferring instead to concentrate on his own music (though he does plan to produce other artists, from outside the house/techno sphere).
Album: *Weathered Well* (R&S 1994).

Lodge, J.C.

b. June Carol, hence the JC initials. JC's entrance into the reggae world came courtesy of an audition for **Joe Gibbs**, who was won over by her voice. Their first recording together was a version of **Charley Pride**'s 'Someone Loves You, Honey', which went straight to the top of the Jamaican charts. Ironically, the result for Gibbs was bankruptcy, after he failed to pay royalties to the songwriter. In 1988 she recorded 'Telephone Love' for **Gussie Clarke**, which subsequently became a big hit in Jamaica and America, where, after being housed on the Pow Wow imprint, it achieved crossover status. Its success brought her to the attention of the predominantly hip hop-focused Warners owned Tommy Boy subsidiary. In the process she became the first female reggae star to pick up a major label deal. Her debut for Tommy Boy played safe by revisiting 'Telephone Love', and branching out musically to encompass soul and rock. Also a talented painter, Lodge has exhibited in Kingston art galleries, and appeared as an actor in several theatrical productions.
Selected albums: *I Believe In You* (Greensleeves 1987), *Revealed* (RAS 1988), *Tropic Of Love* (Tommy Boy 1992).

Loesser, Frank

b. Henry Frank Loesser, 29 June 1910, New York City, New York, USA, 28 July 1969. A leading songwriter for the stage, films and Tin Pan Alley from the 30s through to the 60s. Initially he only wrote lyrics, but later in his career he provided both words and music, and sometimes co-produced through his Frank Productions. Born into a musical family, (his father was a music teacher, and his brother a music critic and pianist), Loesser declined a formal musical education, and trained himself. During the Depression years of the early 30s, following a brief spell at City College, New York, Loesser worked in a variety of jobs including city editor for a local newspaper, a jewellery salesman, and a waiter. His first published song, written with William Schuman in 1931, was 'In Love With A Memory Of You'. Loesser also wrote for vaudeville performers and played piano in nightclubs around New York's 52nd Street. In 1936, he contributed some lyrics to *The Illustrators Show*, with music by Irving Actman, including 'Bang-The Bell Rang!' and 'If You Didn't Love Me'; but the show closed after only five Broadway performances.
In 1937, Loesser went to Hollywood and spent the next few years writing lyrics for movies such as *Cocoanut Grove* ('Says My Heart'), *College Swing* ('Moments Like This' and 'How'dja Like To Make Love To Me?'), ***Sing You Sinners*** (**Bing Crosby** singing 'Small Fry'), *Thanks For The Memory* (**Bob Hope** and Shirley Ross singing 'Two Sleepy People'), *The Hurricane* (**Dorothy Lamour** singing 'Moon Of Manakoora'), *Man About Town* ('Fidgety Joe' and 'Strange Enchantment'), *Some Like It Hot* (1939 film starring Bob Hope and Shirley Ross singing 'The Lady's In Love With You'), *Destry Rides Again* (**Marlene Dietrich** with a memorable version of 'See What The Boys In The Backroom Will Have'), *Dancing On A Dime* ('I Hear Music'), *Las Vegas Nights* ('Dolores'), ***Kiss The Boys Goodbye*** ('I'll Never Let A Day Pass By', 'Sand In My Shoes' and the title song), *Sweater Girl* ('I Don't Want To Walk Without You' and 'I Said No'), *Forest Rangers* ('Jingle Jangle Jingle'), *Happy-Go-Lucky* ('Let's Get Lost' and "Murder' She Says'), *Seven Days Leave* ('Can't Get Out Of This Mood') and *Thank Your Lucky Stars* ('They're Either Too Young Or Too Old', sung by Bette Davis, and including one of Loesser's most amusing lyrics, which contained the couplet: 'I either get a fossil, or an adolescent pup/I either have to hold him off, or have to hold him up!'). These songs were written in collaboration with composers **Burton Lane**, **Hoagy Carmichael**, **Alfred Newman**, Matty Malneck, Frederick Hollander, Louis Alter, **Victor Schertzinger**, **Jule Styne**, Joseph Lilley, **Jimmy McHugh** and **Arthur Schwartz**.
The first song for which Loesser wrote both music and lyrics is said to be 'Praise The Lord And Pass The Ammunition', and when he left Hollywood for military service during World War II he added some more service songs to his catalogue, including 'First Class Private Mary Brown', 'The Ballad Of Roger Young', 'What Do You Do In The Infantry?' and 'Salute To The Army Service Forces'. He also continued to write for films such as *Christmas Holiday* (1944, 'Spring Will Be A Little Late This Year') and *The Perils Of Pauline* (1947), the bio-pic of silent movie-queen Pearl White, with Loesser's songs, 'Poppa Don't Preach To Me' and 'I Wish I Didn't Love You So', which was nominated for an Academy Award. Loesser finally received his Oscar in 1949 for 'Baby It's Cold Outside', from the **Esther Williams**/Red Skelton movie, ***Neptune's Daughter***. In 1948, Loesser wrote 'On A Slow Boat To China', which became a hit for several US artists including **Kay Kyser**, **Freddy Martin**, **Eddy Howard** and **Benny Goodman**. In the same year he again turned his attention to the Broadway stage, writing the score for a musical adaptation of Brandon Thomas's classic English farce, *Charley's Aunt*. ***Where's Charley?***, starring **Ray Bolger**, included the songs, 'My Darling, My Darling', 'Once In Love With Amy', 'The New Ashmoleon Marching Society And Student Conservatory Band' and 'Make A Miracle'. The show ran for a creditable 792 performances.
Far more successful, two years later, was ***Guys And Dolls***, a musical setting of a Damon Runyon fable,

starring Robert Alda, **Vivian Blaine**, Sam Levene, Isabel Bigley and **Stubby Kaye**. It ran for 1,200 performances, and is generally considered to be Loesser's masterpiece. As with *Where's Charley?*, he was now writing both music and lyrics, and the show is such a legend that it is worth listing all the principal songs; they were 'Fugue For Tinhorns', 'The Oldest Established', 'I'll Know', 'A Bushel And A Peck', 'Adelaide's Lament', 'Guys And Dolls', 'If I Were A Bell', 'My Time Of Day', 'I've Never Been In Love Before', 'Take Back Your Mink', 'More I Cannot Wish You', 'Luck Be A Lady', 'Sue Me', 'Sit Down, You're Rockin' The Boat' and 'Marry The Man Today'. The original cast album is still available in the 90s, and among the other associated issues was an all-black cast album, released on the **Motown** label, and *Guys And Dolls: The Kirby Stone Four.* A film adaptation of *Guys And Dolls* was released in 1955, starring **Frank Sinatra**, Marlon Brando, Jean Simmons, and **Vivian Blaine**. The movie version left out some of the original songs, and Loesser replaced them with 'A Woman In Love' and 'Adelaide'. In 1952, *Where's Charley?* was released on film, and the same year saw a movie of the ***Hans Christian Andersen*** fairy tale, starring **Danny Kaye** in the title role, and a Loesser score which included 'Wonderful Copenhagen', 'No Two People', 'Anywhere I Wander', 'Inchworm' and 'Thumbelina'. Loesser's next Broadway project was ***The Most Happy Fella***, for which he also wrote the libretto. The show was adapted from the original story, *They Knew What They Wanted*, by Sidney Howard, which told the tale of an elderly Italian winegrower living in California, who falls in love at first sight with a waitress. Loesser created what has been called 'one of the most ambitiously operatic works ever written for the Broadway musical theatre'. Arias such as 'Rosabella' and 'My Heart Is So Full Of You' are contrasted with more familiar Broadway fare such as 'Standing On the Corner', 'Big D' and 'Happy To Make Your Acquaintance'. The show ran for 676 performances, far more than Loesser's 1960 production of the folksy ***Greenwillow***, which closed after less than three months. It starred Anthony Perkins in his first musical, and contained a religious hymn, the baptism of a cow, and wistful ballads such as 'Faraway Boy' and 'Walking Away Whistling', along with 'Never Will I Marry' and 'Summertime Love', both sung by Perkins. A 3-album set, was issued, containing the complete score. In terms of the number of performances, (1,417), Loesser's last Broadway show, which opened in 1961, was his most successful. ***How To Succeed In Business Without Really Trying*** was a satire on big business which starred Robert Morse as the aspiring executive, J. Pierpont Finch, and **Rudy Vallee** as his stuffy boss, J. B. Biggley. The songs which, most critics agreed, fitted the plot completely, included 'The Company Way', 'A Secretary Is Not A Toy', 'Grand Old Ivy', 'Been A Long Day', 'I Believe In You' and 'Brotherhood Of Man'. The show became one of the select band of American musicals to be awarded a Pulitzer Prize; a film version was released in 1967. Loesser died of lung cancer on 28 July 1969, with cigarettes by his side. A life-long smoker, with a contentious, volatile temperament, he is regarded as one of the most original, innovative men of the musical theatre. In the early 90s the *The Most Happy Fella, Guys And Dolls*, and *How To Succeed In Businese Without Even Trying*, were all revived on Broadway, and Loesser's second wife, Jo Sullivan, and one of his daughters, Emily Loesser, appeared in a provincial production of *Where's Charley?* In 1993, the two ladies also featured on the album *An Evening With Frank Loesser*, singing medleys of songs from his shows. Of even more interest, in the same year a fascinating album consisting of demo recordings by Loesser himself was released.

Selected album: *Loesser By Loesser* (DRG 1993).

Further reading: *A Most Remarkable Fella*, Susan Loesser.

Loewe, Frederick

b. 10 June 1901, Vienna, Austria, d. 14 February 1988. A distinguished composer for the musical theatre, Loewe was born into a musical family, (his father was a professional singer). He studied piano as a child, appearing with the Berlin Symphony Orchestra in 1917. In 1924, he visited the USA, but was unable to find work in a classical enviroment. Instead, he eked out a living playing piano in restaurants and bars, then roamed throughout the USA, tackling a variety of jobs, including prospecting and cowpunching. As a young teenager he had written songs and he resumed this activity in New York in the early 30s. Later in the decade he contributed to various musical shows, and in 1942 began to collaborate with lyricist **Alan Jay Lerner**. Their first Broadway score was for *What's Up?* in 1943, which was followed two year later with *The Day Before Spring*. From then, on they wrote the music and lyrics (Lerner also contributed the librettos) for some of the most memorable productions in the history of the American musical theatre. They had their first hit in 1947 with ***Brigadoon***, from which came 'The Heather On The Hill', 'From This Day On' and 'Almost Like Being In Love', and the association was renewed in 1951 with ***Paint Your Wagon***, containing such lovely songs as 'They Call The Wind Maria', 'I Talk To The Trees' and 'Wand'rin' Star'. In 1956, the team had a major triumph with the legendary ***My Fair Lady***, which ran on Broadway for 2,717 performances. The score included such lasting favourites as 'On The Street Where You Live', 'Get Me To The Church On Time', 'With A Little Bit Of Luck', 'Wouldn't It Be Loverly?', 'The Rain In Spain', 'Why Can't The English?', 'I'm An Ordinary Man' and 'I Could Have Danced All Night'. After the huge success of *My Fair Lady*, Lerner and Loewe were invited to write the script, music and lyrics for a musical film, and while Lerner was keen on the idea, Loewe was somewhat reluctant. Eventually he agreed, and together they created the incomparable ***Gigi*** (1958), one of the final flourishes of the old-style Hollywood musical. The magnificent score included 'Thank Heaven For Little Girls', 'I'm Glad I'm Not Young Anymore', 'I Remember It Well', 'The Night They Invented Champagne', and the charming title song. After being hospitalized with serious heart trouble, Loewe collaborated with Lerner on ***Camelot***, which opened in 1960, and ran for over two years. Although the show's preproduction was marred with problems, the result was another success, with such outstanding songs as 'If Ever I Would Leave You' and 'How To Handle A Woman'. After that Loewe decided to retire, emerging briefly in the early 70s to work with Lerner on two unsucessful projects: a stage adaptation of *Gigi* (1973) and the film *The Little Prince* (1974).

Lofgren, Nils

b. 21 June 1951, Chicago, Illinois, USA. In the late 60s, Lofgren first recorded as Paul Dowell And The Dolphin before forming Grin. The latter made several excellent albums during the early 70s and although a critics' favourite they never quite managed to receive the recognition they deserved. Lofgren, meanwhile, was already branching out into other ventures after making a guest appearance on **Neil Young**'s *After The Goldrush.* He briefly teamed-up with Young's backing group **Crazy Horse** for their critically-acclaimed debut album. Lofgren's association with Young continued in 1973 when he was invited to join the *Tonight's The Night* tour. By now, Lofgren was a highly-respected guitarist and it was widely speculated that he might be joining the **Rolling Stones** as **Mick Taylor**'s replacement. Instead, he signed to **A&M Records** as a solo artist and recorded a self-titled album, which included the tribute 'Keith Don't Go (Ode To The Glimmer Twin)'. The album was applauded on its release, as were Lofgren's solo tours during which he would astound audiences with his acrobatic skills, often propelling himself in the air from a trampoline. An 'official bootleg' from the tour *Back It Up* captured some of the excitement. Lofgren's *Cry Tough*, displayed his power as a writer, arranger and musician. It was a best seller on both sides of the Atlantic and momentarily placed Lofgren on a level with the other acclaimed new guitar-playing artists such as **Bruce Springsteen**. With *I Came To Dance* and *Nils*, the singer/guitarist consolidated his position without breaking any new ground. The latter included some lyrics from **Lou Reed** which added some bite to the proceedings. By the end of the 70s, Lofgren left A&M and found himself recording for the **MCA** subsidiary, Backstreet. By the early 80s, his reputation as a solo artist had declined and it was generally accepted that his real genius lay as a 'right-hand man' to other artists. In early 1983 he embarked on Neil Young's *Trans* tour and the following year joined Bruce Springsteen's E Street Band. By this point, his solo standing was such that he was recording for an independent label, Towerbell. During the late 80s, he continued to work with Springsteen, but also undertook occasional low-key solo tours. In 1991, he ended a six-year hiatus from recording with *Silver Lining*, which included guest appearances from Springsteen and various members of **Ringo Starr**'s All Starr Band.
Albums: *Nils Lofgren* (1975), *Back It Up (Official Bootleg)* (1976), *Cry Tough* (1976), *I Came To Dance* (1977), *Night After Night* (1977), *Nils* (1979), *Night Fades Away* (1981), *Wonderland* (1983), *Flip* (1985), *Code Of The Road* (1986), *Silver Lining* (1991), *Crooked Line* (1992), *Everybreath* (Permanent 1994).

Loft

The Loft were formed in 1980 when Bill Prince (b. 19 July 1962, Devon, England) and Andy Strickland (b. 16 July 1959, Isle Of Wight, England; guitar/vocals) met with **Peter Astor** (b. 1959, Colchester, Essex, England), then singing in the group News Of Birds. Later joined by drummer Dave Morgan (drums), the band's first gig was under the name the Living Room which, by sheer coincidence, was also the banner of a small but significant London venue set up by Scottish entrepreneur, Alan McGee. Fortunately, the freshly-named Loft linked up with McGee's nascent **Creation Records** label to release the single, 'Why Does The Rain?', which encapsulated their stylishly downbeat driving guitar sound. A year later, the follow-up, 'Up The Hill And Down The Slope', furthered the Loft's cause and strengthened their cult-status, bolstered by championing from BBC disc jockey, Janice Long. As their reputation grew, so did tensions within the band, causing them to split just as their career appeared to be in full flow. As Astor recalled: 'We split for the same reason all bands do - people's feet smell.' Both Strickland and Prince pursued journalistic vocations and started up the **Caretaker Race** and the Wishing Stones respectively. Peter Astor and Dave Morgan formed the marginally successful **Weather Prophets** until they disbanded at the end of the 80s, allowing Astor to embark upon a solo career whilst Morgan went on to join the country-flavoured **Rockingbirds**. He would leave that band in 1994 to concentrate on a B.Sc in psychology, managing Bingo Salad, and playing sessions with several artists. After the demise of the Wishing Stones Prince would record a 1992 solo album for **Heavenly Records**. He became production editor for *Q* magazine in 1993.
Compilation: *Once Around The Fair* (Creation 1989).

Lofton, Cripple Clarence

b. 28 March 1887, Kingsport, Tennessee, USA, d. 9 January 1957. Living and playing in Chicago from the age of 20, pianist and vocalist Lofton became a popular

accompanist to visiting blues singers, in many instances appearing in this role on record. He worked steadily through the 30s, proving very popular in the Windy City, and enjoyed the fleeting benefits of the boogie-woogie craze. Influenced by **Charles 'Cow Cow' Davenport** and **Jimmy Yancey**, he in turn influenced a number of other pianists, notably **Meade 'Lux' Lewis**.
Compilation: *Clarence's Blues (1930s)* (1988).

Logan, Josh

b. Richmond, Kentucky, USA. He is one of New Country's hat brigade with a difference - his hat is of the Humphrey Bogart variety. Logan's favourite country performer was **Mel Street** and his own vocals are very close to Street's. He had the misfortune of having 1981 single, 'I Made You A Woman For Somebody Else', covered by **Conway Twitty** and thereby lost any possible success. He eventually made the US charts with 'Everytime I Get To Dreamin''. His debut album included Street's 'Easy Lovin' Kind' and the good-natured 'Somebody Paints The Wall': 'Everytime I make my mark, somebody paints the wall.' There has been an excellent cover by **George Jones** under the title, 'Somebody Always Paints The Wall'.
Album: *Somebody Paints The Wall* (Curb 1989).

Loggins And Messina

This duo featured **Kenny Loggins** and Jim Messina (b. 5 December 1947, Maywood, California, USA). Following his premature departure from **Poco**, Messina intended to resume his career as a record producer, a role he had previously carried out by producing the final **Buffalo Springfield** album, *Last Time Around.* Songwriter Loggins, who had recently experienced success when the **Nitty Gritty Dirt Band** took his whimsical song 'House At Pooh Corner' into the US charts, was signed by **CBS** and was introduced to Messina who was now a staff producer. This started a partnership which lasted six years and produced numerous gold albums. By combining country rock with hints of Latin, Mexican and R&B, the duo hit upon a strong formula. All nine albums reached high US chart positions and spawned a number of hit singles including 'Your Mama Don't Dance' and 'My Music'. As seasoned performers, their regular tours of North America made them a major attraction during the first half of the 70s. Following an amicable split, Loggins embarked on a solo career. Messina, following three moderately successful albums, instigated the reformation of the much-loved Poco in 1989 to considerable acclaim and a successful album.
Albums: *Kenny Loggins With Jim Messina Sittin' In* (1972), *Loggins And Messina* (1972), *Full Sail* (1973), *On Stage* (1974), *Mother Lode* (1974), *So Fine* (1975), *Native Sons* (1976), *Finale* (1977). Compilation: *The Best Of Friends* (1977). Solo: Jim Messina *Oasis* (Columbia 1979), *Messina* (Warner 1981), *One More Mile* (Warner 1983), with the Jesters *Jim Messina And The Jesters* (The Dragsters (Audio Fidelity 1966).

Loggins, Kenny

b. 7 January 1948, Everett, Washington, USA. Loggins came to prominence as a member of **Loggins And Messina** from 1972-77. After separating from Messina, he set out on a solo recording career, specialising in rock ballads such as 'Whenever I Call You Friend', a 1978 Top 10 hit in the US which was co-written by **Melissa Manchester** and had harmony vocals by **Stevie Nicks**. There was subsequent success with 'This Is It' and Loggins co-wrote with **Michael McDonald** 'What A Fool Believes', a million-seller and a US number 1 for the **Doobie Brothers**. Don't Fight It' (1982) was a collaboration with **Journey** singer Steve Ferry. During the 80s, Loggins came to prominence as a writer and performer of theme songs for the new breed of Hollywood action movies. Beginning with 'I'm Alright' (from *Caddyshack*, 1980) and the chart-topping title song from *Footloose* (1984), he reached his peak with the soundtrack of *Top Gun* (1986). As well as co-writing several of the songs used in the film, Loggins recorded the best-selling 'Danger Zone'. This was followed by music for *Caddyshack II*, including another hit single, 'Nobody's Fool'. He had a minor hit with 'Convictions Of The Heart' in 1991.
Albums: *Celebrate Me Home* (1977), *Nightwatch* (1978), *Keep The Fire* (1979), *Alive* (1980), *High Adventure* (1982), *Footloose* (1984), *Vox Humana* (1985), *Top Gun* (1986, soundtrack), *Back To Avalon* (1988), *Leap Of Faith* (1991), *Outside From The Redwoods - An Acoustic Afternoon* (1993).
Film: *Footloose* (1984).

Logic Records

Run in Frankfurt, Germany, by Luca Anzilotti and Michael Munzig, Logic was the original home to their mega-successful Euro-techno creations like **Snap!**'s 'Exterminate'. The label also released **Blake Baxter**'s 'One More Time', Noys' 'Ave Maria' and Rapination featuring **Kym Mazelle**'s 'Love Me The Right Way' in 1992. Others included **Pressure Drop**'s 'Release Me', 2 Funk 2 ('Brothers And Sisters') and Durga McBroom (ex-**Blue Pearl**)'s solo debut. Mark Spoon of **Jam & Spoon** fame held the A&R post for a number of years. However, Logic is just as well known for its impressive compilations like *Logic Trance 1 & 2.* There is also a successful subsidiary imprint, Save The Vinyl, which produces work on vinyl only.

Lolita

b. Ditta Zuza Einzinger, 17 January 1931, St. Poelten, Austria. Lolita Ditta was not expected to enter showbusiness by her civil servant father. She worked as a children's nurse and then a secretary. Yet her soloing in a local church choir earned her a regular spot on Radio Linz, which prompted Lolita to take her chances as a full-time cabaret singer. Subsequent recordings for **Polydor** made her a star in German-speaking Europe. However, a grander destiny awaited her in 1960 when 'Seeman' (composed by Werner Scharfenberger and Fini Busch) managed the hitherto impossible as the first German-made single by a female artist to reach the US Hot 100 - climbing to number 5. This triumph was dampened slightly when simultaneous covers (translated as 'Sailor (Your Home Is The Sea)' by lyricist Norman Newell) by **Anne Shelton** and **Petula Clark** stole her thunder in the UK chart. Indeed, Lolita was to enjoy no more big hits in English-speaking regions while remaining a top domestic attraction - epitomized when her detailing of a 'Gateau a la Lolita' recipe on Danish television was headlined in a national newspaper.

Lomax, Alan And John A.

A well-known and well-read folklorist, Alan Lomax (b. 15 January 1915, Austin, Texas, USA), travelled with his father, John A. Lomax (b. John Avery Lomax, 23 September 1875, Goodman, Mississippi, USA, d. 26 January 1948, Greenville, Mississippi, USA), on field recording trips during the 30s, collecting folk songs and tunes from various States in the USA. They collected songs for the Library of Congress Archive for which **Woody Guthrie** was later recorded. Until that time, John Lomax had been an administrator at college, who had collected cowboy songs, including 'Home On The Range', as a hobby. As a result of the Depression and crash of the 30s, John Lomax, now jobless, started collecting folk songs and material on a full-time basis. By the time Alan was 23 years old he was assistant director of the Archive of Folk Song at the Library of Congress. The Lomaxes met a number of singers, who were later to become almost household names, including Huddie '**Leadbelly**' Ledbetter, and **Muddy Waters**. Leadbelly was discovered in a Louisiana prison, but John Lomax managed to obtain his release, employing him as a chauffeur. Lomax later took him to New York where he performed to college audiences. In 1934, John Lomax became honorary consultant and head of the Library of Congress archive of folk song. Alan Lomax travelled to Britain during the 50s and collaborated with **Ewan MacColl** on the radio series *Ballads And Blues*. Lomax later returned to the USA to conduct field recordings in the southern States. The results were subsequently released on **Atlantic Records** as part of a series called 'Southern Folk Heritage'. John and Alan Lomax were also responsible for collecting a number of the songs of the Ritchie Family of Kentucky. In addition to his many other activities, Alan Lomax was still a fine performer in his own right, as can be heard on *Texas Folk Songs*, which contains the standards 'Ain't No More Cane On The Brazo's' and 'Billy Barlow'. *Alan Lomax Sings Great American Ballads*, on **HMV**, included **Guy Carawan** (banjo), and Nick Wheatstraw (guitar). It featured such classics as 'Frankie', 'Darlin' Corey' and 'Git Along Little Doggies'. The latter song had been recorded by John Lomax in 1908, and originates from an Irish ballad, converted and adapted by cowboys. After World War II, Alan was the Director of Folk Music for **Decca**, and then he worked for the Office of War Information from 1943-44 and then for the Army's Special Services Section until 1945. As a singer, Alan had performed both in the USA and Britain. Twelve years of research culminated in *Cantometrics*, a set of seven cassettes with a book.

Albums: John A. Lomax *The Ballad Hunter, Lectures On American Folk Music* (date unavailable, 10 record set). Alan Lomax *Alan Sings Great American Ballads* (1958), *Texas Folk Songs* (1958), *Folk Song Saturday Night* (60s), *Murderer Is Home* (1976).

Further reading: Alan Lomax: *Amercian Folk Song And Folk Lore*, with Sidney Robertson Cowell. *Mister Jelly Roll - The Fortunes Of Jelly Roll Morton, New Orleans, Creole And Inventor Of Jazz, The Folksongs Of North America.* Editor of: *Folk Songs Of North America In The English Language, Folk Song Style And Culture, Cantometrics - An Approach To The Anthropology Of Music.* John A. Lomax: *Cowboy Songs, Adventures Of A Ballad Hunter, Cowboy Songs And Other Frontier Ballads, Songs Of The Cattle Trail And Cow Camp,* John and Alan Lomax: *American Ballads And Folk Songs, Cowboy Songs And Other Frontier Ballads, Negro Folk Songs As Sung By Leadbelly, Folksong USA, Our Singing Country, The Penguin Book Of American Folk Songs*

Lomax, Jackie

b. 10 May 1944, Wallasey, Merseyside, England. A former vocalist with the 60s beat group the **Undertakers**, Lomax began a new career in America when this respected Liverpool unit disbanded. Spells with two short-lived bands, the Mersey Lads and the Lost Souls, preceded a return to England where the singer worked with his own group, the Lomax Alliance, and as a solo act. Two strong, but unsuccessful, singles followed before he was signed to the fledgling Apple label but his opening release, 'Sour Milk Sea', written for him by **George Harrison**, was unfortunately overshadowed by hits for stablemates the **Beatles** and **Mary Hopkin**. Jackie's debut *Is This What You Want*, featured contributions from a host of star names including Harrison, **Paul McCartney**, **Ringo Starr** and **Eric Clapton**. The artist's stylish compositions and superb voice were equal to such esteemed company. Sadly, Apple's internal problems doomed his undoubted potential and following an interlude as part of the elusive **Heavy Jelly**, Lomax returned to America where he completed two more excellent albums, *Home Is In My Head* and *Three*. In 1973, the

singer joined the British-based Badger, a group formed by ex-**Yes** organist, Tony Kaye. Lomax helped transform them from a progressive rock band into a more soulful aggregation, exemplified on *White Lady*, which was produced by **Allen Toussaint** and consisted solely of Jackie's songs. Badger then split into two factions, with Lomax and bassist Kim Gardner instigating an offshoot unit named after the album. Jackie subsequently resumed his solo career, but the releases which followed were disappointing and the ill-luck which had often dogged this worthwhile performer further undermined his career. Lomax did resurface in 1990 as one of several acts contributing to the 'tribute' album *True Voices* wherein he sang a version of **Tim Buckley**'s 'Devil Eyes'.
Albums: *Is This What You Want* (1969), *Home Is In My Head* (1971), *Three* (1972), with Badger *White Lady* (1974), *Livin' For Lovin'* (1976), *Did You Ever* (1977).

Lombardo, Guy

b. 19 June 1902, London, Ontario, Canada, d. 5 November 1977, Houston, Texas, USA. A celebrated bandleader and impresario, early in the 20s, Lombardo formed a dance band in collaboration with his brothers Carmen and Lebert (a fourth brother, Victor, joined later). After some limited success in their own country they travelled across the border and secured a regular radio engagement in Cleveland, Ohio, where they adopted the name 'Guy Lombardo And His Royal Canadians'. The band played in Chicago before moving to New York where they remained, mostly enjoying very long residencies, until 1963. Frequent broadcasts and their immaculately played dance music, which was billed as 'the sweetest music this side of heaven', appealed to a huge audience. He is probably best remembered for his theme tune, 'Auld Lang Syne', and 'Boo-Hoo' which was written by Carmen Lombardo, Edward Heyman and John Jacob Loeb. However, from 1927-54, he had an enormous number of hits, including 'Charmaine', 'Sweethearts On Parade', 'You're Driving Me Crazy', 'By the River St. Marie', '(There Ought To Be) A Moonlight Saving Time', 'Too Many Tears', 'Paradise', 'We Just Couldn't Say Goodbye', 'The Last Roundup', 'Stars Fell On Alabama', 'What's The Reason (I'm Not Pleasin' You')', 'Red Sails In The Sunset', 'Lost', 'When Did You Leave Heaven?', 'September In The Rain', 'It Looks Like Rain In Cherry Blossom Lane', 'So Rare', 'Penny Serenade', 'The Band Played On', 'It's Love-Love-Love', 'Managua, Nicaragua', and 'The Third Man Theme'. The band's worldwide record sales were extraordinary - published estimates vary between 100 and 300 million copies. Lombardo also appeared in several films such as *Many Happy Returns* (1934), *Stage Door Canteen* (1943), and *No Leave, No Love* (1946). From 1954 Lombardo took over the operation of the Marine Theatre at New York's Jones Beach, and continued to produce all manner of spectacular musical extravaganzas adaptations for successive seasons until shortly before his death. He also had extensive business interests, and was a long-time speedboat racing enthusiast, a pastime which brought him many awards, including that of National Champion in the late 40s.
Selected albums: *Your Guy Lombardo Medley* (1957), *Berlin By Lombardo* (1958), *The Sounds Of The Swing Years* (1960), *Every Night Is New Year's Eve* (1973), *Guy Lombardo And The Royal Canadians, 1950* (1988). Compilations: *Guy Lombardo In Hi-Fi* (c.1955), *The Uncollected* (1986), *All Time Favourites* (1988).
Further reading: *Auld Acquaintance: An Autobiography*, Guy Lombardo and J. Altschue.

London

As punk sent an electric shock through a complacent late 70s UK music scene, major labels were to be found signing acts, regardless of ability. London, like many other second division new wavers, were scooped up only to disappear after all the fuss had died down. Two releases in 1977, 'Everyone's A Winner' and 'No Time', were both of their time; punchy and urgent but ultimately lacking in substance. *Animal Games*, London's one and only album (and accompanying single) in 1978 followed suit, its power-pop feel lacking the true bite of punk's pioneers. Lead singer Riff Regan later had a stab at a solo career, while drummer Jon Moss joined the **Edge** before making his name in the early 80s with **Culture Club**.
Album: *Animal Games* (1978).

London Calling!

The name '**Noël Coward**' went up in West End lights for the first time when this André Charlot revue opened at the Duke of York's Theatre on 4 September 1923. Coward also co-wrote the book, with Ronald Jeans, and the music and lyrics with Philip Braham. Also in the cast was Coward's favourite leading lady, **Gertrude Lawrence**, along with Maisie Gay, Eileen Molyneux, and comedian Tubby Edlin. **Fred Astaire**, who was appearing with his sister Adele in ***Stop Flirting*** at the Shaftesbury Theatre, arranged some of the dances. The songs included 'What Love Means To Girls Like Me', 'Carrie', 'Life In The Old Girl Yet', 'Sentiment', and 'Other Girls'. Gertrude Lawrence introduced one of Coward's most enduring numbers, 'Parisian Pierrot', and together they sang 'You Were Meant For Me', another future standard, written by **Arthur Freed** and **Nacio Herb Brown**. The show was a great success until Charlot decided to transfer Gertrude Lawrence and several other members of the company to the Broadway production of *André Charlot's London Revue Of 1924* which opened in January. After Joyce Barbour replaced Lawrence, *London Calling!* soon ran out of steam.

London Jazz Composers Orchestra

(see **Guy, Barry**)

London Posse

One of Britain's first credible rap acts, utilising rhymes built over expertly executed ragamuffin breaks, with cockney accents thrown in for good measure. Unfortunately, London Posse were not free of the misogyny made more explicit by the gangsta rappers (tracks like 'Sexy Gal' and 'Living' imply that the entire female gender is out *en masse* to rob them of their money). London Posse at least possess wit and a nose for rhythm to dilute their urban warnings. Stylistically it could be dated by its **Eric B And Rakim**-styled delivery. The band comprise Rodney and Bionic (who is titled thus due to the artificial limb he wields).
Album: *Gangster Chronicles* (Mango/Island 1990).

London Records

Founded in 1947, this renowned label was established in the USA by British **Decca** to provide an outlet for its domestic releases. The UK counterpart was introduced in 1949 when the parent company began recording American acts, including **Teresa Brewer** and **Josh White**. London began licensing material from other US outlets in October 1951 and within two years had acquired the rights to Essex and **Imperial**, with which it laid the foundations of its impressive rock 'n' roll catalogue. **Bill Haley And His Comets** and **Fats Domino** were an important part of its early roster, but the label enjoyed commercial success with releases by **Slim Whitman** and the bright pop of **Pat Boone**. The addition of **Atlantic Records** (1955), **Chess**, **Specialty** (both 1956) and **Sun** (1957) ensured a virtually peerless position. **Little Richard**, **Chuck Berry**, **Bo Diddley**, **Jerry Lee Lewis**, the **Everly Brothers**, **Rick Nelson** and the **Coasters** were among the many artists introduced to British audiences by this cogent outlet whose reputation flourished as the 50s progressed.
London's eminent position continued into the 60s. Success with **Duane Eddy**, **Del Shannon** and **Roy Orbison** was derived by distributing the Jamie, Big Top and Monument labels and the girl-group genre was satisfied through releases drawn from **Phil Spector**'s Philles label. However, several other licencees felt the wide roster jeopardized their individuality. **Berry Gordy** removed his fledgling Tamla/**Motown** empire after a mere handful of releases, **EMI** acquired the rights to **Liberty**, United Artists, Imperial and Minit, while the defection of Chess to Pye International was particularly ill-timed, given that the emergent British R&B movement brought renewed interest to a catalogue London had failed to exploit fully. Another crucial loss was that of Atlantic and although London had secured a measure of success with **Otis Redding**, the US company took its catalogue to **Polydor** in 1966, just as the soul style it contained began a commercial ascendancy. **Elektra** made a similar move, thus depriving London of a prime outlet for folk-rock and the emergent US underground scene, and by 1967 releases on this once-prolific outlet had lessened dramatically. Minor labels - White Whale, Bang and Laurie - provided occasional hits, but London's sole remaining jewel was the Memphis-based **Hi Records**, home of **Al Green**, **Ann Peebles** and **Willie Mitchell**. Releases by these artists provided commercial and artistic success, but the company's decline during the 70s mirrored that of Decca itself. This once-mighty concern had failed to adapt to the changing face of pop and was sold to Phonogram in 1980 upon the death of its patriarch, Sir Edward Lewis. Although initially reserved - two singles were released bearing the London imprint between 1980 and 1981 - the new owners resurrected the name fully in 1982 for a new generation of British-based acts. Hits for the **Bluebells**, **New Edition**, **Blancmange**, **Bronksi Beat**, **Communards** and Glenn Medeiros ensued, but **Bananarama** enjoyed the most comprehensive success with a run of 17 Top 40 hits for the label between 1982-1988.
Albums: *London American Legend, Part One* (1975), *London American Legend, Part Two* (1976).

London SS

Historically London SS were one of the most important British bands of the punk era despite never playing in front of a paying audience, nor releasing any recordings. Musically they were either 'raw rock 'n' roll' or 'pretty crap' depending on which of their many members you care to ask. An *ad hoc* combo of London youth (or migrants drifting in from elsewhere), they were started around March 1975 by Tony James and Mick Jones. They spent the entire 10 months or so of the group's life auditioning musicians and rehearsing 60s beat and R&B classics. The only other semi-permanent member they found was guitarist Bryan James but amongst the others who traded licks and rimshots were: Terry Chimes (drums), who was rejected; Paul Simenon (vocals) rejected as well; Nicky Headon (drums) turned the gig down; Tony James tried out for bass; Rat Scabies (b. Chris Miller) had a bash at the drum stool despite being in his own proto-punk group - Rot; Matt Dangerfield and Casino Steel of the **Hollywood Brats** popped in for two rehearsals on their way to forming the **Boys**; Roland Hot warmed the drum seat briefly as did Andy (whose surname has been lost to the mists of time; and another long-forgotten soul called George had a spell on the guitar). The only recording they ever made was a demo featuring the James/Jones/James/Hot line-up which was the penultimate assembly. In January 1976 they kicked Hot out, Bryan James went off with Rat Scabies to join the Subterraneans and then form the **Damned**. That left the two originators on their own again so James eventually went off and got a job before running into **Billy Idol** and joining **Chelsea** with him. They soon split Chelsea to form **Generation X.** Messrs Jones, Simenon and Chimes teamed up with **101ers** vocalist Joe Strummer to form the **Clash**, and when Chimes left to form Jem, another London SSer, Nicky 'Topper' Headon, replaced him.

London Town

This 1946 release, the first picture be made at 'Sound City Studios', Shepperton, England, after World War II, was an attempt to mount a lavish Technicolor British musical to rival the legendary Hollywood productions. It failed dismally, even though the American producer-director Wesley Ruggles was joined by several of his fellow countrymen including highly experienced songwriters **Johnny Burke** and **Jimmy Van Heusen**, and musical director-arranger **Salvador 'Tutti' Camarata**. The dreary and overly sentimental screenplay by Elliot Paul and Siegfried Herzig concerns ambitious comedian Jerry Ruggles (Sid Field), who is merely the understudy for star Charlie DeHaven (Sonnie Hale) in the West End production of *London Town*, until his fawning daughter, Peggy (14-years-old **Petula Clark**), gets to work. She persuades Charlie's dresser, Belgrave (Claude Hulbert), to feed him a potion which makes his face go green. Naturally, he cannot go on stage like that, so, step forward Jerry, the world of show business is at your feet. The delectable Kay Kendall rose above it all, and also trying their best were Greta Gynt, **Tessie O'Shea**, **Sonnie Hale**, and Mary Clare. Jerry Desmonde, Sid Field's regular straight man, was also on hand to assist him in several of the celebrated comedian's classic routines, including his famous golfing sketch. 'My Heart Goes Crazy' was the big number, and it was reprised several times. Burke and Van Heusen's other songs consisted of an appealing ballad, 'So Would I' (introduced by Beryl Davis) 'You Can't Keep A Good Dreamer Down', and 'Any Way The Wind Blows'. Drummer-singer **Jack Parnell** turned up in 'The 'Amstead Way' production number which topped and tailed a knees-up medley of Cockney favourites such as 'Don't Dilly Dally On The Way' (Fred W. Leigh-Charles Collins), 'Any Old Iron' (Collins-Fred Terry-E.A. Sheppard), and 'Wot Cher' ('Knock 'Em In The Old Kent Road') (Albert Chevalier-Charles Ingle). The finalé, which featured an enormous grand piano with 10 men seated at the keyboard, reminded many of previous films in which the instrument was featured in a visually effective fashion, such as ***King Of Jazz*** and ***Gold Diggers Of 1935***. Unfortunately, *London Town* was just not in the same class as either of those pictures. In America it was re-titled *My Heart Goes Crazy*.

London, Julie

b. June Webb, 26 September 1926, Santa Rosa, California, USA. Actress-singer London is inextricably linked to the sultry Andy Hamilton song, 'Cry Me A River' which gave the artist her sole million-seller in 1955. Her memorable performance of the song in the film *The Girl Can't Help It*, defined a lachrymose delivery best exemplified on *Julie Is Her Name*, which also featured the talent of jazz guitarist **Barney Kessel**. London continued to record prodigiously throughout the late 50s to the mid-60s, but this aspect of her career vied with roles in films, notably: *The Great Man* and *A Question Of Adultery*. She later appeared in several television series, often alongside her second husband and longtime producer and songwriter **Bobby Troup**. Her popularity underwent a revival in the UK in the early 80s after **Mari Wilson** scored a hit with London's classic lament.

Albums: *Julie Is Her Name* (1955), *Lonely Girl* (1956), *Calendar Girl* (1956), *About The Blues* (1957), *Make Love To Me* (1957), *Julie* (1957), *Julie Is Her Name, Volume 2* (1958), *London By Night* (1958), *Sing Me An Old Song* (1959), *Your Number Please* (1959), *Julie London At Home* (1959), *Around Midnight* (1960), *Send For Me* (1960), *Whatever Julie Wants* (1961), *Sophisticated Lady* (1962), *Love Letters* (1962), *Latin In A Satin Mood* (1963), *The End Of The World* (1963), *The Wonderful World Of Julie London* (1963), *Julie London* (1964), *In Person At The Americana* (1964), *Our Fair Lady* (1965), *All Through The Night* (1965), *For The Night People* (1966). Compilations: *Julie's Golden Greats* (1963), *Great Performances* (1968), *The Best Of Julie London* (1984)

Film: *The Girl Can't Help It* (1956).

London, Laurie

b. 19 January 1944, London, England. At the age of 13, this pop singer who had the confidence and showmanship of a veteran, appeared in a closed circuit transmission of *6.5 Special* at the BBC stand at the 1958 Radio Show. He so impressed producer John Warrinton that he was invited back every day and therefore came to the attention of **EMI**, who put him in the studio with producer Norman Newell. The result was a **Geoff Love** arranged revival of the spiritual 'He's Got The Whole World In His Hands'. The record climbed to number 12 in the UK and went on to become the most successful record by a British male in the 50s in the USA, topping the ***Billboard*** chart. Fame forced London to leave school and his father Will gave up his sales management job to manage him but refused the chance of a US tour in 1958 for the 14-year-old. London recorded a handful of other pop/gospel singles including 'Joshua', 'The Gospel Train' and 'I Gotta Robe' but the adolescent, who for an all too brief time had the whole world in his hands, never charted again. He released one album for

Capitol Records. He was later reported successfully working in the clothing industry in London.
Album: *Laurie London* (1958).

Londonbeat

This group featured a white English guitarist and three black American singers. Their line-up comprises Jimmy Chambers (b. 20 January 1946), **Jimmy Helms** (b. Florida, USA) and George Chandler (b. Atlanta, Georgia, USA), plus Willy M, (b. William Henshall, London, England). Helms was best known for his UK Top 10 hit in 1973 with 'Gonna Make You An Offer You Can't Refuse'. He released several other singles at the time, including 'Jack Horner's Holiday'. Chandler was in 60s soul group the Four Kents who were American but based in northern Italy as servicemen. He too had released solo singles in the 70s. They came together and settled in London where they signed to **David A. Stewart**'s Anxious label. Much of their material was close to **a cappella** though they used session musicians when necessary. Their debut '9am (The Comfort Zone)' was a strong piece, and it reached the UK number 21 spot in 1988. It was 1990's 'I've Been Thinking About You' that gave the band their biggest hit, rising to number 2. They also appeared with BBC Radio 1 disc jockeys, Liz Kershaw and Bruno Brooks on the Christmas 1989 charity record 'It Takes Two Baby' which was a minor hit in the UK.
Albums: *Speak* (1987), *In The Blood* (1990), *Harmony* (1992).

Lone Justice

This group of US country-rockers were fronted by **Maria McKee** (b. 17 August 1964, Los Angeles, California, USA) who is the half-sister of **Love**'s Bryan MacLean. When she was just three-years-old her brother would take her to the various clubs along Los Angeles' Sunset Strip and she was befriended by the likes of **Frank Zappa** and the **Doors**. When she grew up, she and MacLean formed a duo initially called the Maria McKee Band, but later changed to the Bryan MacLean Band to cash in on *his* slightly higher profile. Heavily immersed in country music, McKee formed the first incarnation of Lone Justice with Ryan Hedgecock (guitar), Don Heffington (drums), Marvin Etzioni (bass) and Benmont Tench (keyboards, ex-**Tom Petty And The Heartbreakers**). The group were signed to the **Geffen** label at the recommendation of **Linda Ronstadt**. McKee's talents were also admired by artists such as **Bob Dylan**, **U2**'s Bono, who offered them a support slot on tour, and Tom Petty, who donated songs to the first album. One of these, 'Ways To Be Wicked', while not achieving any notable chart status, was responsible for bringing the group to the attention of the UK audience via an imaginative black-and-white, cut-up-and-scratched video. The band's more established line-up transmuted to that of ex-patriot Brit Shayne Fontayne (guitar), Bruce Brody (keyboards, ex-**Patti Smith** and **John Cale**), Greg Sutton (bass) and Rudy Richardson (drums). They were managed by the respected producer, Jimmy Iovine. In 1985, former **Undertones** singer **Feargal Sharkey** scored a UK number 1 hit with McKee's 'A Good Heart'. Lone Justice split suddenly in 1987 with McKee going on to a solo career, taking only Brody with her from the remnants of Lone Justice.
Albums: *Lone Justice* (1985), *Shelter* (1987).

Lone Ranger

b. Anthony Waldron, the Lone Ranger was one of the most lyrically inventive late 70s DJs, with a considerable influence on the British school of MCing. Waldron spent a large proportion of his formative years in the UK, which perhaps accounted for his radically different stance, and, like so many others, he began his own recording career at **Studio One**. Welton Irie partnered him at first, but he soon graduated to working solo, setting himself loose on several classic Studio One rhythms, after which he became virtually unstoppable. His version of **Slim Smith**'s seminal 'Rougher Yet', re-titled 'Love Bump', was a major success. So too his reading of **Slim Smith**'s 'Never Let Go', a version known as 'The Answer', which has become more famous than the original. As top DJ for Kingston's Virgo Sound, he kept up appearances in the dance halls and Virgo Hi Fi were voted the top sound of 1980.
His recordings for Alvin 'GG' Ranglin assured his legendary status. 'Barnabas Collins' (about a vampire show on television) contained the immortal line: 'chew ya neck like a Wrigley's', and was a UK reggae chart number 1 in 1980. His additional work for **Winston Riley** and **Channel One**, which included the memorable 'M16', proved almost as popular. His tour of the UK that year reiterated that he could do it on stage as well as on record and for the **sound systems**. Any performer who could deliver priceless lyrics such as 'Lightning clap and thunder roll . . . Noah at the ark control', would always be guaranteed a receptive audience. His repertoire of strange voices, 'oinks' and 'ribbits', were widely imitated. Ranger recorded sparingly, sometimes branching out in keeping with other DJs into self-production, and his catalogue has always been assembled with style, class and a dash of great humour.
Selected albums: *Barnabas Collins* (GG's 1980), *On The Other Side Of Dub* (Studio One 1981), *M16* (Channel One 1982), *Hi-Yo Silver Away!* (Greensleeves 1982), *Badda Dan Dem* (Studio One 1982), *Dee Jay Daddy* (Techniques 1984), *Learn To Drive* (Bebo's Music 1985).

Lone Star

This traditional UK hard rock quintet was formed in

1975 by Kenny Driscoll (lead vocals), Tony Smith (guitar), Paul 'Tonka' Chapman (guitar), Pete Hurley (bass) and Dixie Lee (drums). Specializing in dynamic heavy rock, they attracted considerable attention with their Roy Thomas Baker-produced debut, offering an approach and sound not dissimilar to early **Queen**'s pomp/hard rock formula. Driscoll was replaced by John Sloman in 1977 before the release of *Firing On All Six*. This album pushed the dual guitars of Chapman and Smith to the forefront and concentrated on heavier material by dropping the delicate touches that appeared on their debut. Shortly after its release the band disintegrated, with Sloman joining **Uriah Heep**, Chapman replacing **Michael Schenker** in UFO and Dixie Lee teaming up with **Wild Horses**.
Albums: *Lone Star* (CBS 1976), *Firing On All Six* (CBS 1977), *BBC Radio 1 Live* (Windsong 1994).

Lonesome Strangers

Lonesome Strangers is a Los Angeles-based country band and their lead vocalist, Jeff Rhymes, writes most of their material. Other members include Randy Weeks, Lorne Rail and Mike McLean. They have had minor US country hits with 'Goodbye Lonesome, Hello Baby Doll' and 'Just Can't Cry No More'.
Albums: *Lonesome Pine* (Special Delivery 1988), *The Lonesome Strangers* (Special Delivery 1989).

Lonesome Sundown

b. Cornelious Green, 12 December 1928, Donaldsonville, Louisiana, USA. Green taught himself piano while growing up, then took guitar lessons in his early 20s. He joined **Clifton Chenier**'s band in 1955, and can be heard on several of that artist's recordings on the **Specialty** label. The following year he recorded for the first time in his own right and 16 singles were issued over the next nine years under the name given to him by producer **Jay Miller** - Lonesome Sundown. Many of these, such as 'My Home Is A Prison' and 'Lonesome Lonely Blues', were classic examples of that uniquely Louisiana sound, swamp blues - a resonant production, featuring a strong, booming rhythm section, rippling piano and support from **Lazy Lester** or John Gradnigo on harmonica and Lionel Prevost on tenor saxophone. Green's vocals and biting lead guitar invariably provide just the right gritty edge. A religious conversion towards the end of this period led to his withdrawal from the music scene, but he returned, if only briefly, to record an excellent album for the Joliet label in the late 70s.
Albums: *Been Gone Too Long* (1977), *Lonesome Whistler* (1983), *If Anybody Asks You* (1988).

Loney, Roy (And The Phantom Movers)

b. San Francisco, California, USA. Forsaking an early experience as an actor, Loney turned to music during the folk boom of the early 60s. Impressed by the **Beatles** and the **Rolling Stones**, he later formed the Chosen Few, a high school band which evolved into the **Flamin' Groovies**. Loney's voice and compositions provided the focal point for this cult-favourite act during its early history, but internal tension led to his departure in 1971. Roy then retired from professional music until 1977 when various ex-colleagues backed him on *Artistic As Hell*, an EP invoking the artist's love of classic rockabilly. The following year he formed the Phantom Movers with James Ferrall (guitar) and Danny Mihm (drums), plus two further ex-Groovies' alumni, Larry Lea (guitar) and Maurice Tani (bass). *Out After Dark* fully captured the spirit and style of the singer's former group and was the subject of critical acclaim. Despite innumerable changes in personnel, Loney continued to pursue his unique blend of 50s rock 'n' roll and tongue-in-cheek humour through successive, often excellent albums and a powerful stage show. The singer disbanded his backing group in 1981 following the artistic failure of *Contents Under Pressure*, a flawed 'power-pop' experiment. A second period of retirement ended with the release of *Scientific Bombs Away*, which also marked the reinstatement of the 'Phantom Movers' name. Although denied widespread popularity, Loney has nonetheless retained a small, but highly loyal, following.
Albums: *Out After Dark* (1979), *Phantom Tracks* (1980), *Contents Under Pressure* (1981), *Rock 'N' Roll Dance Party With Roy Loney*, (1982), *Fast And Loose* (1983), *Scientific Bombs Away* (1988).

Long And The Short

The Long And The Short enjoyed a brief spell in the UK pop spotlight when 'The Letter' reached number 30 in September 1964. The song was originally recorded by R&B act **Don And Dewey**, but was revived by its composer, **Sonny Bono**, as the debut release by Caesar And Cleo, the duo he had formed with his wife, **Cher**. The Long And The Short, meanwhile, broached the UK Top 50 in December with a follow-up single, 'Choc Ice', but their perky, 'beat' intonations were quickly overtaken by newer, more exciting styles of music
Film: *Gonks Go Beat* (1965).

Long Ryders

Formed in November 1981, the Long Riders (as they were then known), initially included three ex-members of the Unclaimed - Sid Griffin (guitar/vocals), Barry Shank (bass/vocals) and Matt Roberts (drums). **Steve Wynn** completed this early line-up, but the guitarist was replaced by Stephen McCarthy on leaving to form the **Dream Syndicate**. Griffin and McCarthy remained at the helm throughout the group's turbulent history. As part of Los Angeles' 'paisley underground' movement, the Long Ryders' history is linked with, not only that of the Dream Syndicate, but also that of other

guitar-oriented bands such as **Rain Parade**, (early) **Bangles**, **Green On Red** and **Blood On The Saddle**. A mini-album, *The Long Ryders*, was completed with Des Brewer (bass) and Greg Sowders (drums), although by the time the quartet secured a permanent deal, Tom Stevens had joined in place of Brewer. *Native Sons*, an excellent set influenced by **Buffalo Springfield** and **Gram Parsons**, suggested a promising future, but the Long Ryders were unable to repeat its balance of melody and purpose. They withered on record company indecision and, unable to secure a release from their contract, the group broke up in 1987.
Albums: *The Long Ryders* (1983), *Native Sons* (1984), *State Of Our Union* (1985), *Two-Fisted Tales* (1987), *10-5-60* (1987), *Metallic B.O.* (1989, early recordings).

Long, Shorty

b. Frederick Earl Long, 20 May 1940, Birmingham, Alabama, USA, d. 29 June 1969, Detroit, Michigan, USA. Multi-instrumentalist Long received tutelage from **W.C. Handy** and **Alvin Robinson** before joining **Harvey Fuqua**'s Tri-Phi label in 1961. This Detroit-based company was later acquired by Tamla/**Motown** and Long acted as master of ceremonies on his new outlet's touring revues before recording 'Devil With The Blue Dress On' in 1964 for the Motown subsidiary, Soul. The singer's slow, blues-based interpretation was not a hit, but the song became successful in the hands of **Mitch Ryder** and **Bruce Springsteen**. Long enjoyed minor chart entries with 'Function At The Junction' (1966) and 'Night Fo' Last' (1968) before reaching the US Top 5 in 1968 with a version of 'Here Comes The Judge'. His premature death as a result of a boating accident on the Detroit River robbed Motown of an ebullient, but sadly unfulfilled, talent.
Albums: *Here Comes The Judge* (1968), *The Prime Of Shorty Long* (1969).

Longbranch Pennywhistle

This Los Angeles-based duo is better recalled for the member's subsequent escapades. **Glenn Frey** (b. 6 November 1948, Detroit, Michigan, USA; guitar/vocals) arrived in California in 1968 where he met **J.D. Souther** (b. John David Souther, c.1946, Texas, USA; guitar/vocals), an aspiring singer-songwriter. The pair then began performing together as Longbranch Pennywhistle. They secured a record deal with the Amos label, but although pleasant, the resultant album lacked identity and distinctiveness. A contract dispute then ensued, preventing the duo from further recording and they broke up in 1971. Frey subsequently joined **Linda Ronstadt**'s backing group, from which the **Eagles** evolved, while Souther forged a successful solo career as both singer/songwriter and with the Souther-Hillman-Furay Band.
Album: *Longbranch Pennywhistle* (1969).

Longdancer

A short-lived English folk-rock band, Longdancer were best remembered as the first professional band to feature **David A. Stewart** (b. 9 September 1952, Sunderland, England). The group grew out of a folk duo comprising Stewart and Brian Harrison, formerly with the London-based band Ball Of Yarn. The pair played clubs and support gigs in the north east of England and in 1971 recorded an EP for the local Multichord label. Soon afterwards they added further singer/guitarists Steve Sproxton and Kai Olsson and became Longdancer. In 1973, they became the first artists to sign to **Elton John**'s Rocket label, touring with Elton before Olsson left to be replaced by Matt Irving (keyboards) and Charlie Smith (drums). The new line-up made a second album and released an unsuccessful single, 'Puppet Man' in 1974. Shortly afterwards, Longdancer split up. Kai Olsson made a 1979 solo album for **Chrysalis** (*Crazy Love*) while Harrison and Smith later played with folk singers Robin and Barry Dransfield before Smith joined **Blue**. Irving recorded with Phil Rambow before joining the **Lords Of The New Church** in the 80s. In 1977, Stewart would form the **Tourists** and in 1981, with Annie Lennox, the **Eurythmics**.
Albums: *If It Was So Simple* (1973), *Trailer For A Good Life* (1974).

Longo, Pat

b. 11 September 1929, Passaic, New Jersey, USA. Adept on several reed instruments, Longo concentrated on alto saxophone and clarinet. During military service he played in the band of the 2nd Marine Airwing and following his discharge studied music full-time. Although intent on a career in music, throughout the 60s and into the early 70s Longo found it necessary to support himself by working in a bank. However, in 1974 and resident in Los Angeles, he decided the time was right to give up banking and just play music. He joined the **Harry James** band but had ambitions to lead his own big band. In 1979, he achieved his goal and formed a big band which quickly gained regular bookings in and around LA. In the late 70s and early 80s Longo's Super Big Band successfully blended the more traditional aspects of big band music with currently popular jazz-rock funkiness. His line-ups usually featured many of the best west coast session men and a useful handful of talented jazzmen, including **Gordon Brisker**, **Lanny Morgan**, **Bob Efford**, **Buddy Childers**, Frank Szabo and **Nick Ceroli**. Intent on developing other areas of exposure for the band, Longo has recently been involved in the planning of a television series.
Albums: *Crocodile Tears* (1980), *Billy May For President* (1982), *Chain Reaction* (1983).

Lonzo and Oscar

A vocal and instrumental comedy duo that for many years consisted of John Sullivan (b. 7 July 1917, d. 5 June 1967, Nashville, Tennessee, USA; bass fiddle/guitar) and his brother Rollin Sullivan (b. 19 January 1919, mandolin/guitar), both at Edmonton, Kentucky, USA. The brothers toured the south as a duo in the late 30s and appeared on WTJS Jackson, Tennessee, where they worked with **Eddy Arnold**. In 1942, Rollin played on the ***Grand Ole Opry*** as a member of **Paul Howard**'s band but the following year, he joined that of Eddy Arnold. A fellow band member was Ken Marvin (b. Lloyd George, 27 June 1924, Haleyville, Alabama, USA, bass fiddle/guitar) and the two men immediately resumed a comedy act that they had started at WTJS. Initially known as Cicero (Marvin) And Oscar (Sullivan), they were soon renamed Lonzo And Oscar by Arnold. Dressed in ill-fitting costumes and singing novelty songs in country harmony, interspersed by inane banter (John Sullivan wrote material for them), they were a well established act when war service intervened. After their discharge, they resumed as part of Arnold's touring show and played with him at WAVE Louisville but in 1946, Marvin retired. John Sullivan assumed the role of Lonzo and they remained as part of Arnold's group until they became regular *Opry* members in their own right in 1947. In January 1948, an **RCA**-Victor recording of 'I'm My Own Grandpa' charted to give them a major Top 5 hit on both jukebox and country charts. (The song, attributed to Dwight Latham and Moe Jaffe was based on a humorous Mark Twain anecdote). The original single was made by Ken Marvin and Rollin but the brothers later made their own version. Their partnership lasted two decades until John's death, following a heart attack in 1967. During this period they maintained their *Opry* status, proved a very popular touring act and appeared frequently on network television. They recorded for several other labels including Starday, **Decca** and their own Nugget label but only achieved one further chart hit 'Country Music Time'. Their songs varied from the sublime 'Ole Buttermilk Sky' to the ridiculous 'You Blacked My Blue Eyes Once Too Often' and 'There's A Hole In The Bottom Of The Sea'. Late in 1967, the act was reformed when David Hooten (b. St. Claire, Missouri, USA) took over the role of Lonzo. They resumed the touring and the *Opry* shows and recording for **Columbia**, they found some success with 'Did You Have To Bring That Up While I Was Eating?'. The comedy continued but surprisingly, on a 1974 GRC album, the hillbilly harmony is completely missing. Some of the material may almost be classed as gospel and their fine harmony work saw them chart with the title track 'Traces Of Life'. Further recordings appeared in the early 80s on the Brylen label. The original 'I'm My Own Grandpa' appears on RCA's mid-60s compilation *Stars Of The Grand Ole Opry*.

Albums: *America's Greatest Country Comedians* (Starday 1960), *Lonzo & Oscar* i (Starday 1961), *Country Comedy Time* (Decca 1963), *Country Music Time* (Starday 1963), *Hole In The Bottom Of The Sea* (Nugget 60s), *Lonzo & Oscar* ii (Hilltop 1965), *Mountain Dew* (Columbia 1968), *Traces Of Life* (GRC 1974), *Old & New Songs* (Brylen 1982).

Looking Glass

This New Jersey, USA-based quartet was led by vocalist/guitarist Elliot Lurie (b. 19 August 1948, Brooklyn, New York, USA) with backing from Larry Gonsky (keyboards), Pieter Swerval (bass) and Jeffrey Grob (drums). Initially as a mid-heavy rock band, they played the east coast bar circuit for many months before refining their act for record company consumption. An audition for **CBS Records**' president **Clive Davis** proved successful and in 1972 the group recorded Lurie's melodic 'Brandy (You're A Fine Girl)' for the CBS subsidiary, Epic. Within a few weeks it had topped the US charts, but the group was unprepared for what was to follow. Bracketed as a soft rock act, their live act was confusingly guitar heavy and drew only lukewarm support. They continued to adopt a lighter approach on record, but their follow-up 'Jimmy Loves Mary-Anne' proved only a minor hit. Bereft of ideas, the group split and Lurie went on to pursue an unsuccessful solo career.

Album: *Looking Glass* (1972).

Looking Through A Glass Onion

Subtitled '**John Lennon** In Word And Music', this one-man show consisted of 'a series of wry monologues spliced with the singer's songs, which attempted to unearth the man beneath the mythology'. It was written by the Australian-based, British-born actor John Waters, and toured successfully for two years in Australia before opening at the 600-seater newly-refurbished subterranean Criterion Theatre in London on 18 October 1993. Waters himself starred in the piece, backed by a band which included Stewart D'Arrietta on keyboards and Hamish Stewart on drums. The title image, from the song 'Glass Onion', 'seems to promise a peeling away of the layers of a crystal ball', but what actually transpires is as non-chronological narrative framework around the songs, beginning at the end with Lennon at the door of his New York apartment block watching an autograph hound coming towards him. Waters' 'exaggerated Liverpudlian twang' in the spoken passages, supplemented by a 'good bluesy voice' for the classic **Beatles** and later, subtler songs, brought him some critical appreciation, but the concept as a whole was generally considered to be 'charmless and depressing - a fraction of the real thing'. Reportedly capitalised at

£160,000 and expected to make a profit after three months, closure on 1 January 1994 presumably resulted in a small loss.

Loop

Along with **Spacemen 3**, Loop, from Croydon, London, England, proved to be the UK's answer to the onslaught of harsh, guitar-wielding acts that dominated the late 80s independent scene. Like the Spacemen, Loop refined fuzz-laden, pulsing guitar riffs, monotonous vocals and distinctive drum patterns to build bruised and intimidating soundscapes. An uncompromising blend of late 60s Detroit rock (**Stooges** and **MC5**) and Germany's early 70s *avant garde* (**Can** and **Faust**), the result was a dense, brooding mantra-like noise, not unlike early **Hawkwind**. Loop have always revolved around singer and guitarist Robert Wills (b. Robert Hampson), who formed the band with his wife, drummer Bex, and bassist Glen Ray in 1986. After the garage-like feedback on '16 Dreams' began their recording legacy in 1987, Bex was replaced by John Wills, who introduced a harder, rhythmic sound. This was further strengthened when James Endicott joined as second guitarist, after the reverberating psychedelia of 'Spinning' set the scene for Loop's impressive debut, *Heavens End*, in November. Alongside a cover of **Suicide**'s 'Rocket USA' came a barrage of layered guitar noise awash with distortion and wah-wah. With a new bassist, John McKay, Loop moved to Midlands label Chapter 22 for April 1988's dynamic 'Collision', backed by a cover of the **Pop Group**'s 'Thief Of Fire'. After the departure of James Endicott, and the Head label's compilation of their singles on *The World In Your Eyes* in August, Loop were ready to skirt the national charts with *Fade Out* in November. Its sparser, more discordant sound pushed the Can influence to the fore. Indeed, a cover of Can's hypnotic magnum opus, 'Mother Sky', turned up on the b-side of 'Black Sun' the following month. After a quiet year, Loop ended 1989 with the powerful 'Arc-Lite', their first single for Situation Two and with new guitarist Scott. Chapter 22 signalled their departure with another collection of two 12-inch singles, but this time, Loop publicly denounced the set. *A Gilded Eternity*, in 1990, again fared well commercially, and moved further towards ethereal soundscapes and away from the aggression of *Fade Out*. Since then, Loop have coveted a decidedly low profile with rumours of a split, with only 1991's *Wolf Flow*, a double set of sessions for BBC disc jockey **John Peel**, to indicate otherwise.

Albums: *Heavens End* (Head 1987), *Fade Out* (Chapter 22 1988), *A Gilded Eternity* (Beggars Banquet 1990). Compilations: *The World In Your Eyes* (Head 1988), *Eternal* (Chapter 22 1989), *Wolf Flow* (Reactor 1991, rec. 1987-90).

Loop Guru

The listening tastes of spokesman Jal Muud (South American pipe music, Morrocan indigenous sounds) has informed the career of Nation Records' Loop Guru. Together with Salman Gita he forms the core of the band, aided by up to ten guest musicians for various events (who include former **Pigbag** drummer Chip Carpenter and percussionist Mad Jym). The duo have been involved in music since 1980 when they were early members of the Megadog enclave, meeting through mutual friend Alex Kasiek (**Trans-Global Underground**). It was at this time that Jamuud: '...stopped listening to Western music altogether. I foudn that the wealth of sound and mood in Asian and African music was vastly more alive than its Western counterparts.' Offering their listeners 'total enlightenment through music', Loop Guru have perfected a package of chants, laments, tablas, Eastern religion and ethnic samples, which was first brought to the public's attention via their *Sus-San-Tics* EP, which featured the guest vocals of Sussan Deheim (b. Iran). A debut album was recorded, its title, *Duniya*, translating from Urdu as 'The World'. Part of the methodology evolved from **Brian Eno**'s 'Choice Cards' ethos, wherein different instructions on musical structure are carried out via the turn of a set of cards. It placed them at the forefront of the 'world dance' movement. Arguably their most effective and popular single to date has proved to be 'Paradigm Shuffle', which included at its core Martin Luther King's 'I Have A Dream' speech.

Album: *Duniya* (Nation 1994).

Loose Tubes

Appearing on the London scene in 1984 this big (20-piece plus) band appealed to (and reflected) the new, smart young audience jazz was attracting at the time, and seemed likely to prove a considerable 'crossover' success. It was run as a collective, although trombonist Ashley Slater acted as 'frontman' and **Django Bates** emerged as a main writer for the band. Characterized by clever arrangements, technically slick soloing and an urbane stage-presence, Loose Tubes was acclaimed by many critics and created interest in jazz among sections of the public which had not previously paid the genre any attention. It spawned several other successful units, which indulged in various styles (funk, African, soca, bebop and so on), including Human Chain, Pig Head Son, Lift, the **Iain Ballamy** Quartet, the Steve Berry Trio, the **Tim Whitehead** Band, Parker Bates Stubbs and the **Julian Argüelles** Quartet. By the early 90s the parent group had disbanded - although reunions should never be ruled out.

Albums: *Loose Tubes* (Loose Tubes 1986), *Delightful Precipice* (Loose Tubes 1986), *Open Letter* (Editions EG 1988).

López, Israel 'Cachao'

b. 14 September 1918, Havana, Cuba. The name of revered bassist Cachao (who also arranges, composes and plays piano, tres, bongo, trumpet and trombone) is linked with the origins of mambo and is virtually synonymous with descarga, which was defined by pianist/bandleader **Charlie Palmieri** as having '. . . no music written. It's a soloists freedom of expression, ad-libs, an improvisation of the melody . . . whatever he (she) feels at the moment . . .' (quoted by Latin music historian Max Salazar). Leading Cuban bandleader of the 50s, Bebo Valdés said in 1991: '. . . if Cachao and **Arsenio Rodríguez** had not been born, the Cuban music of the 50s and perhaps the last 30 years, would have sounded like the music of the 30s'.

López was born to a musical family and started learning guitar when he was six years of age. When he was about eight he played guitar and bongo with Conjunto Miguel De Seste. This was followed by a stint with Ignacio Villa (who later became popular as Bola de Nieve; also see **Ernesto Lecuona**), whose band provided the music for silent films at a movie house in Guanabacoa, Havana. In 1931, he joined the Havana Symphonic Orchestra and remained a member for over 30 years. Meanwhile, López performed with the dance band of violinist Marcelino González, turning out exciting bass solos that earned him the nickname 'Cachao' (derived from 'cachandeo', meaning 'lively with joy'). Between 1934 and 1936 he worked with Ernesto Muñoz, Antonio Maria Cruz and Orquesta Antillana. In 1937, he joined La Maravilla del Siglo, a flute, strings and rhythm section band led by singer Fernando Collazo. The following year, the musicians mutinied after a row with Collazo and formed themselves into a co-operative directed by Antonio Arcaño Betancourt, which became known as Arcaño y sus Maravillas. Besides Cachao and Arcaño, membership of the band included Orestes López (Cachao's brother; b. 29 August 1908, Havana, Cuba; cello/bass/piano/composer/arranger); Enrique Jorrín (b. 1926, Cuba, d. 1988, Cuba; violin; he later joined Orquesta América, developed the cha cha chá rhythm and became a bandleader in his own right); Félix Reina (violin; he went on to work with Orquesta América, **José Fajardo** and lead Estrellas Cubanas); Elizardo Aroche (violin); Jesús López (piano); Ulpiano Díaz (timbales) and Oscar Pelegrin (güiro). The band, along with other flute and strings outfits of the era, specialized in performing the Cuban ballroom dance form called the danzón, which was descended from the 17th and 18th century French contradanza.

Amid the ongoing controversy about the creation of the mambo, Orestes López's 1938 danzón composition called 'Mambo', which had its debut performance on the radio station Mil Diez, has been cited as one of the earliest examples of the rhythm. In a 1979 interview with Erena Hernández, Orestes said: '. . . I must give Arcaño credit in the development of my mambo. When I played it for him, he blew flute montunos (improvisations) I had never heard before. His floreos (ad-libs) are what enhanced my mambo'. In addition to Orestes and Arcaño, two leading contenders for the title of likely inventor of the mambo are regarded to be **Pérez Prado** and Arsenio Rodríguez. Cachao stated his position in the debate to Max Salazar: 'Prado's mambo is different to my brother's mambo . . . he's deserved all the fame and wealth with his new sound . . . we Cubans are proud of him . . . Arcaño y su Maravillas were the first to play the mambo . . . we played it before Arsenio's diablo (his initial name for the rhythm) and we did it over the radio.' The new danzón-mambo sound took a while to gain acceptance. Inspired by Arsenio, who was the first bandleader to incorporate the conga into a trumpet-led conjunto (group/band), Arcaño added the conga of Eliseo El Colorao to his line-up in 1939. By 1943, Arcaño's band rivalled Arsenio as the top orchestra in Cuba. However, working with a popular dance band eventually took its toll on Cachao. 'In 1943, I couldn't take the pressure of arranging music, playing every day, and being on the move all day long. I was on the verge of a nervous breakdown' (quote from 'El Gran Cachao', 1991). After a break in Miami, he returned to the arduous routine. In 1948, Cachao suffered a further stress-related bout of depression and despite another respite, which included a period in New York and a stint with an American ice follies orchestra back in Cuba, he eventually quit Arcaño's band on amicable terms in 1949. Stints with Mariano Mercerón and José Fajardo followed; with the latter he played at New York's famed Palladium Ballroom in 1954.

The earliest pieces that could be described as Latin jam or descarga (which literally means 'discharge') were recorded in New York in the 40s. It is currently believed that the first descarga to be recorded in Cuba was probably 'Con Coco Poco' in 1952 by Bebo Valdés and members of the Tropicana nightclub orchestra, performing under the name of the Andres All Stars. The number was later included on the 10-inch album *Cubano* released on the Panart label. In 1956, Panart used the bait of a well-advertised 'party' to attract some of Cuba's leading musicians to a jam session for which they received a nominal payment. The participants were told that the recording being made was for private use but shortly afterwards Panart released *Cuban Jam Session Vol. 1*. The album was a huge success and was closely followed by volume two. Popular musician Julio Gutiérrez was credited as the director on both volumes. However, the extent of his involvement later became the subject of speculation.

Panart continued with *Cuban Jam Session Vol. 3* directed by Niño Rivera. In 1957, Cachao organized a group to record *Cuban Jam Session In Miniature 'Descargas'* for

Panart. The album, which sold well over a million copies, achieved the status of a classic and acted as the launch-pad for Cachao's widespread acclaim. Cachao followed up with further descarga releases: *Jam Sessions With Feeling* on the Maype label and *Cuban Music In Jam Session* on the Bonita label. The final volume in the Panart *Cuban Jam Session* series was provided by José Fajardo and his All-Stars. In the late 50s, Cachao reassembled the disbanded members of Arcaño y sus Maravillas for two albums of danzones on the Kubaney label. Cachao performed with **Chico O'Farill**'s Cuban All Stars on 'Descarga Numero Uno' and 'Descarga Numero Dos' for the Gema label, which were included on the various artists collection *Los Mejores Musicas de Cuba* (c.1960, reissued by Palladium Records in 1988). He played bass on *Cuban Jazz* (c.1961, aka *Sabor Cubano*) on Gema (reissued by Palladium in 1988) by percussionist Walfredo de los Reyes, who appeared on the first two Panart *Cuban Jam Session* volumes. The album also featured pianist Paquito Echavarría. Meanwhile in New York, the *Cuban Jam Session* releases inspired the first in a series of Latin jam albums by the Alegre All-Stars in 1961. Descarga recordings by other New York-based artists and bands followed, including albums by **Kako**, **Johnny Pacheco**, percussionist Osvaldo 'Chi Hua Hua' Martínez, Tico All-Stars, Cesta All-Stars, Salsa All-Stars, Fania All Stars and SAR All Stars.

In 1963, Cachao took up residence in New York and was initially desperate for work. Charlie Palmieri persuaded his regular bassist to stand down for a while (he had gigs with other bands available) so that Cachao could step-in to earn some money. Stints with various bandleaders followed, including Johnny Pacheco, **Tito Rodríguez**, **Candido**, **Eddie Palmieri**, Julio Gutiérrez, Lou Pérez, George Hernández and Pupi Campo (he worked with the latter two in Las Vegas), before he relocated to Miami. Rodríguez paid tribute to him with the track 'Descarga Cachao' on his 1964 release *Tito Tito Tito*. Cachao received the opportunity to record with the Alegre All-Stars in 1965. **Al Santiago** explained: '. . . we decided to do a tribute to **Noro Morales** and we called it the Kako After Hours Orchestra; picking up the musicians at five in the morning after everyone was done with their regular gigs. We had Cachao there, and Bobby Rodríguez, one played one side of the record and one played the other! . . .' (quote from 1990 interview with Nancy Rodríguez). He appeared on recordings by the Tico All-Stars in 1966, at New York's Village Gate, and in 1974 at Carnegie Hall. Cachao again shared bass playing chores with Bobby Rodríguez on 1968's *Salsa All-Stars* produced by Al Santiago.

Cachao appeared at the memorable March 1977 *Lo Dice Todo* (*This Says It All*) concert at the Avery Fisher Hall, New York. Shortly afterwards, some of the musicians who participated in the concert, such as Charlie Palmieri; Don Gonzalo Fernández (flute); **Pupi Legarreta**, **Alfredo de la Fé** and Eddie Drennon (violins); and Chi Hua Hua and Rolando Valdés (percussionists), were amongst the personnel on Cachao's *Cachao y su Descarga '77 Vol. 1* and *Dos, Vol. 2* on Salsoul Records. In 1981, Cachao collaborated with Walfredo de los Reyes, Paquito Echavarría and Cuban percussionist Tany Gil on the Latin jam oriented *Walpataca* on the Miami-based Tania Records label. In 1986, he led a descarga group on *Maestro de Maestros/Israel López 'Cachao' y su Descarga '86* also on the Tania label, which included José Fajardo, de los Reyes and Echavarría. In November 1987, Cachao journeyed to New York to perform at a tribute to him at Hunter College Auditorium, which featured **Tito Puente**, Charlie Palmieri, Pupi, José Fajardo, **Alfredo 'Chocolate' Armenteros**, saxophonist/violinist José 'Chombo' Silva, trombonist Barry Rogers and others. During his years in New York and Miami, Cachao sessioned on albums by a string of artists and bands, including Carlos 'Patato' Valdez and Eugenio Arango 'Totico', Candido, **Hubert Laws**, Eddie Palmieri, **Mongo Santamaría**, Lou Pérez, Pedro Rafael Chaparro, Héctor Rivera, Charlie Palmieri, Chano Montes, Pepe Mora, Hernán Gutiérrez, Ñico Rojas, La India de Oriente, **Roberto Torres**, Hansel And Raúl and **Grupo Niche**. He also performed with the Miami Symphony Orchestra.

Selected albums: with Arcaño y sus Maravillas *Danzón Mambo* (1974), *Arcaño y sus Maravillas 1944-47/La Radiofonica* (1976); *Cuban Jam Sessions In Miniature 'Descargas'* (1957), *Jam Session With Feeling* (c.1958), *Con El Ritmo De Cachao* (1959, aka *Cachao y su Típica*), *El Gran Cachao* (1959, aka *Cachao y su Típica Vol. 2*), *Cuban Music In Jam Session* (c.1961), *Cachao y su Descarga '77 Vol. 1* (1977), *Dos, Vol. 2* (1977), *Walpataca* (1981), *Maestro de Maestros/Israel López 'Cachao' y su Descarga '86* (1986).

Lopez, Trini

b. Trinidad Lopez III, 15 May 1937, Dallas, Texas, USA. Trini Lopez took folk songs and rocked them up into Latin rhythms, recording 14 chart albums and 13 chart singles between 1963 and 1968. Propelled by a strong R&B-influenced backbeat (usually provided by bassist Dave Shriver and drummer Gene Riggio) and his own incessantly rhythmic guitar, Lopez was at his best when playing live. A number of his nightclub performances were recorded and released as albums. Lopez listened to R&B music while growing up, and formed his first band in Wichita Falls, Texas at the age of 15. At the recommendation of **Buddy Holly**, Lopez went to the producer **Norman Petty** in Clovis, New Mexico, but Lopez did not record with him as Petty wanted to record only instrumental music. In 1958, however, Petty did secure Lopez and his group the Big Beats a deal with **Columbia Records**, which released the single 'Clark's Expedition'/'Big Boy', ironically an instrumental. Lopez made his first solo recording, his own composition 'The Right To Rock', for the Dallas-based Volk Records, and then signed with King Records in 1959, recording more than a dozen singles for that label, none of which charted. In late 1962, after the King deal expired, Lopez followed up on an offer by producer **Snuff Garrett** to join the post-Holly **Crickets** as vocalist. After a couple of weeks of auditions in Los Angeles that idea did not bear fruit and Lopez formed his own group.

He landed a steady engagement at the nightclub PJ's, where his audience soon grew. He was heard there by **Frank Sinatra**, who had started his own label, **Reprise Records**, and signed Lopez. He was placed with arranger/producer **Don Costa**, who wisely chose to record Lopez in concert at the club. His first album, *Trini Lopez At PJ's*, rose to number 2 in the summer of 1963 and stayed in the US charts for nearly two years. The first single from the album, an uptempo party-like version of **Pete Seeger**'s 'If I Had A Hammer', reached number 3, (number 4 in the UK) out-performing **Peter, Paul And Mary**'s more sedate rendering a year earlier. Lopez's subsequent recordings for Reprise displayed a musical eclecticism - he recorded a folk album, an R&B album, two Latin albums, country, in foreign languages (Spanish and German) and even Broadway show tunes, all in his infectiously simple sing-along style. Only one other Top 20 single resulted, 'Lemon Tree' in 1965, and he appeared in a number of films, including *The Dirty Dozen* and *Marriage On The Rocks*, but by the end of the 60s Lopez had largely disappeared from public view. He recorded sporadically in the 70s, including *Viva* and a number of singles for **Capitol Records** in 1971-72, and *Transformed By Time* for Roulette Records in 1978, and although he continued to sing in Las Vegas during the 80s little has been heard from Lopez since his heyday. There are numerous budget-label album releases of his music available, and several anthologies on European labels.

Selected albums: *Trini Lopez At PJ's* (1963), *More Trini Lopez At PJ's* (1963), *On The Move* (1964), *The Latin Album* (1964), *Live At Basin St. East* (1964), *The Folk Album* (1965), *The Love Album* (1965), *The Rhythm & Blues Album* (1965), *The Sing-Along World Of Trini Lopez* (1965), *Trini* (1966), *The Second Latin Album* (1966), *Trini Lopez In London* (1967), *Now!* (1967), *It's A Great Life* (1968), *Trini Country* (1968), *Viva* (1972), *Transformed By Time* (1978). Compilations: *Greatest Hits!* (1966), *La Bamba - 28 Greatest Hits* (1988).

Lopez, Vincent

b. 30 December 1898, New York City, New York, USA, d. 20 September 1975, North Miami, Florida, USA. The celebrated pianist and leader of a highly popular 'sweet style' danceband, Lopez originally intended to go into the church, and also tried his hand as a businessman. However, his father was a bandsman in the US Navy, and urged his son into a musical career, apparently forcing him to practice incessantly. He had his first professional job when he was 17-years-old and by 1916 was leading his own band at the prestigious Pekin Restaurant. By 1921, he was bandleading at the Statler Hotel where his was among the first dance bands to receive national fame through remote radio link-ups (outside broadcasts). Lopez became a national name, his opening remark, 'Hello everybody, Lopez speaking,' appealing to the public. During the 20s the band appeared in the Broadway musicals *Love Birds*, ***Greenwich Village Follies*** *Of 1924*, and ***Earl Carroll's Vanities*** *Of 1928*, and the early movie musical ***The Big Broadcast*** *Of 1932*. Among his many record hits, from 1922 to 1939, were 'Nola' (his theme tune), 'Teasin'', 'I'm Just Wild About Harry', 'I Want To Be Happy', 'Show Me The Way To Go Home', 'Always', 'Hello, Bluebird', 'My Angel (Angela Mia)', and 'There's Honey On The Moon Tonight'. He and his band appeared at the Hippodrome in London but it was as a stalwart of radio and the plush hotel circuit in America that he was best noted. In 1941, he took the band into New York's Hotel Taft where he remained for 25 years. From 1949, he appeared regularly on television. Among the well known musicians and vocalists who played and sang with the Lopez band at various stages of their careers were **Glenn Miller**, **Artie Shaw** and **Xaviar Cugat**, and **Betty** and **Marion Hutton**. Defying the radical changes that took place in popular music over the years, Lopez led his band into the 70s

Further reading: *Lopez Speaking*, V. Lopez.

Lora Logic

London art student Susan Whitby originally adopted the pseudonym Lora Logic during her stint as saxophonist in **X-Ray Spex**. After leaving that group following their debut single, she soon re-emerged in 1978 with her own outfit, **Essential Logic**, who quickly recorded a couple of hard-edged EPs, *Aerosol Burns* and *Wake Up*. One album was recorded, *Beat Rhythm News* (1979), before Lora commenced on a series of solo recordings in 1981. Her quirky, occasionally arresting, vocals were in evidence on her sole album, *Pedigree Charm*, and she can also be heard on a number of recordings by other artists including the **Raincoats**, **Stranglers**, **Swell Maps** and **Red Crayola**.

Album: *Pedigree Charm* (Rough Trade 1982).

Lorber, Jeff

b. 4 November 1952, Philadelphia, USA. Lorber started playing the piano when he was four and played in local R&B bands while he was still at school. While studying at the **Berklee College Of Music** in Boston he came under the influence of **Herbie Hancock** and his contemporaries. When he left Berklee he studied privately with **Ran Blake**. In 1979, he moved to Portland, Oregon and taught improvisation at Lewis and Clark College. In 1977, he had recorded *Jeff Lorber Fusion* and in 1979 he was able to form a band of the same name. Lorber's compositions are characterized by syncopated, chromatic melody and modal writing which facilitated a funk style. In the early 80s he started singing on record and playing the guitar and his music incorporated increasing pop elements.

Albums: *Jeff Lorber Fusion* (1977), *Soft Space* (1978), *Water Sign* (1978), *Jeff Lorber Fusion* (1979), *Wizard Island* (1979), *Galaxian* (1980), *Its A Fact* (1981), *In The Heat Of The Night* (1983), *Step By Step* (1984), *Worth Waiting For* (1993).

Lord Creator

b. Kentrick Patrick, c.1940, Trinidad, West Indies. As his imperious name makes clear, Lord Creator began his career as a calypso singer. Some time in the mid-to-late 50s he arrived in Jamaica where the music scene was just starting its own recording business. Lord Creator's smooth, honeyed tones were not ideal for the raucous jump to R&B soon to emerge from **ska**, but as a big band crooner in Jamaica, he had no equal. 'Evening News' (1959) was his first massive hit, and it was a song he returned to at several points in his career. The storyline of a barefoot kid feeding his siblings by selling newspapers he could not even read, had greater resonance at a time when Jamaica was struggling for its independence. In 1962 his 'Independent Jamaica' was the first single on the **Island** label in the UK, although legend has it that **Owen Gray**'s 'Twist Baby', scheduled as Island 002, made it to the shops first. 'Don't Stay Out Late' (1963) was a major Jamaican hit, and Lord Creator was generally regarded as the island's biggest star of the time. 'Little Princess' (1964) helped maintain his status. He also released a calypso album for the **Studio One** label. He was overtaken by other smooth voices such as **Ken Boothe** and **Bob Andy**, both of which offered more contemporary songs. In 1969, he teamed up with producer **Clancy Eccles** and recorded the single 'Kingston Town', perhaps the finest sentimental reggae record ever released. However, by this time Creator was hardly well-off and a week after recording the record, he borrowed $30 from Eccles. A couple of months later Eccles spotted Creator in a Kingston street and the singer ran off. Eventually Eccles caught him, and Creator immediately began to make excuses for not paying back the money he owed. Eccles explained that he owed Creator $1,000 in royalties for 'Kingston Town'. The record had sold thousands of copies in Britain without ever making the charts. During the 70s, Lord Creator's croon became rare in a reggae music obsessed with roots, Rasta and heavy dub. He did record one powerful single in 1977, 'Life', a new version of a 1967 single, 'Such Is Life'. During the 80s rumour had it that Lord Creator had succumbed to the life of the homeless rum drinker on the streets of Kingston, and eventually Clancy Eccles helped organise enough money for Creator to be returned to his family in Trinidad. That seemed to be the end of the story, but in 1989 **UB40** covered 'Kingston Town', and Clancy Eccles and Creator were recruited to give their seal of approval in the accompanying video. While it seems sadly ironic that he never got the hit he deserved with his own version, at least UB40's success meant that a royalty cheque would go to the song's creator.

Albums: *Songs My Mother Never Taught Me* (Port O Jam 1964), *Big Bamboo* (Dynamic 1974).

Lord Rockingham's XI

Scottish bandleader Harry Robinson and his band took the pseudonym of Lord Rockingham's XI (after a genuine historical character) to appear on the **Jack Good** UK television pop programme, *Oh Boy*, playing 'novelty' rock instrumentals. Other key members were Chery Wainer (organ), and Red Price (saxophone) as well as renowned British rock 'n' roll drummer Rory Blackwell, the former two of which would feature in their own spots on *Oh Boy*. The first release was 'Fried Onions' in May 1958 but in September **Decca** released the Robinson penned 'Hoots Mon' complete with Scottish accented cries of 'Hoots mon, there's a moose in the hoose!'. It was a UK number 1 hit but the follow-up, 'Wee Tom', only made number 16. They featured on an *Oh Boy* EP but after a further attempt to have a hit with 'Ra Ra Rockingham' failed, Robinson reverted to more straight forward orchestra names like Harry Robinson's XV and the Robinson Crew. He later revived the Lord Rockingham monicker in an attempt to cash in on the 1962 Twist phenomenon with 'Newcastle Twist'/'Rockingham Twist'. **Benny Green** played tenor sax with Rockingham before he realized he could make more money writing and talking about jazz than performing. He is now a respected author and broadcaster, but still plays saxophone semi-professionally. Robinson was later involved with another UK number 1 when he provided the musical accompaniment to **Millie**'s 'My Boy Lollipop'.

Lordan, Jerry

b. 1933, London, England. After leaving the Royal Air Force in 1955, Lordan sought work as a comedian before forming a short-lived duo, Lee And Jerry Elvin. One of their demos, the Lordan composition 'A Home, A Car And A Wedding Ring', with **Emile Ford** guesting on piano, became a minor US hit for **Mike Preston**. When **Anthony Newley** took Lordan's 'I've Waited So Long' to number 3 in the UK, the composer was signed as a soloist by **Parlophone**. Five low-ranking Top 50 hits in the first six months of 1960

confirmed Lordan's promise but it was as a songwriter that he shone. The shimmering 'Apache' gave the **Shadows** a momentous UK number 1, while Jorgen Ingmann almost achieved the same position in the USA. Thereafter, Lordan was lauded as the great composer of instrumentals, enjoying chart toppers with the Shadows' 'Wonderful Land', and **Jet Harris And Tony Meehan**'s 'Diamonds'. He still wrote lyrics for artists including **Cleo Laine**, **Petula Clark**, **Matt Monro** and **Shane Fenton**. At the end of the 60s, two more Lordan hits were high in the charts, courtesy of **Cilla Black** ('Conversations') and **Cliff Richard** ('Good Times'). After an all too brief recording comeback in 1970 with *Old Man And The Sea,* Lordan's disc career tailed-off and he ceased writing altogether.
Albums: *Old Man Of The Sea* (1970), *All My Own Work* (1981).

Lords

Formed in 1959 as the Skiffle Lords, this German act dropped the prefix four-years-later, upon adopting a style more in keeping with British beat. In September 1964 they won a 'Battle Of The Bands' contest at Hamburg's famed *Star Club*, the prize for which was a recording contract. Although their debut single, 'Hey Baby, Lass Den Ander'n', was sung in German, subsequent releases featured their highly-stylized version of English. However, despite a lack of subtlety, 'Shakin' All Over', 'Poor Boy' and 'Boom Boom' were highly accomplished. The Lords - Ulrich Gunther (vocals), Rainer Petry (guitar), Klaus Peter Leitz (guitar), Knud Kuntz (bass) and Peter Donath (drums) - were later viewed as Germany's leading group and successful tours of other European countries ensued. In 1965, Kuntz was replaced by Bernd Zamulo, but the promise of their early work was undermined by increasingly substandard fair, including 'Have A Drink On Me' (1966), 'John Brown's Body' and 'Gloryland' (both 1967). The Lords nonetheless embraced psychedelia with *Ulleogmamaxbe*, but having failed to revive their reputation, were supplanted by newer, progressive rock acts. The group has been revived on several occasions to exploit the nostalgia market.
Albums: *In Black And White, In Beat In Sweet* aka *Deutschland's Beatband Nr. 1* (1965), *2 - Shakin' All Over* (1966), *Some Folks By The Lords* (1967), *Good Side Of June* (1967), *Ulleogmamaxbe* (1968), *Shakin' All Over '70* (1970).

Lords Of The New Church

This UK rock band was made up of several well-known personalities, and often described as a punk 'supergroup'. The personnel was; Brian James (b. 18 February 1961; guitar, ex-**Damned**), **Stiv Bators** (b. 22 October 1956, Cleveland, Ohio, USA; vocals, ex-**Dead Boys**, Wanderers), Dave Treganna (b. 1954, Derby, England; bass, ex-**Sham 69**, Wanderers) and drummer Nicky Turner (b. 4 May 1959, ex-**Barracudas**). When **Jimmy Pursey** left Sham 69, the rest of the band had continued in the Wanderers, drafting in Stiv Bators. It was at this point that James contacted Bators with the view to setting up a group. Miles Copeland took on their management, their name coming from his original suggestion, Lords Of Discipline. They made their live debut in Paris in 1981. Their debut vinyl, 'New Church', helped to increase criticisms about the band's apparent blasphemy, hardly dispelled when the album appeared with lines like: 'Greed and murder is forgiven when in the name of the Church'. The self-titled debut premiered an authentic rock band with dark shades, flirting with apocalyptic and religious imagery. The single, 'Dance With Me', from *Is Nothing Sacred*, gained several **MTV** plays with a video directed by Derek Jarman. Unfortunately its success was scuppered after mistaken allegations about paedophilia saw it taken off air. Their final studio album, *Method To Our Madness*, revealed a band treading water with stifled heavy rock routines. They did not split officially until 1989, but before that Treganna had departed for **Cherry Bombz**, while Alistair Ward contributed some second guitar.
Albums: *Lords Of The New Church* (IRS 1982) *Is Nothing Sacred* (IRS 1983) *Method To Our Madness* (IRS 1984), *Live At The Spit* (Illegal 1988, rec. 1982). Compilation: *Killer Lords* (IRS 1985).

Lords Of The Underground

Based in Newark, New Jersey, USA, Lords Of The Underground came to prominence via tours with **Cypress Hill** and **Funkdoobiest**, with whom their music shares more than a passing acquaintance. The group first met at college where all the band were majoring in radio communication. The frontmen are Doitall and Mr Funke (aka Mr Funky). The former also has acting interests, taking his first role in the film *The School Game*. They are backed by their DJ, Lord Jazz. Doitall and Mr Funke were originally solo artists, collaborating for the first time on a cut called 'Psycho'. 'Flow On' was eventually issued as a single, remixed by **Pete Rock**, while the debut collection was produced by **Marley Marl**. They have also been responsible for fostering the career of Rated R.
Album: *Here Come The Lords* (Pendulum/Elektra 1993).

Lords, Traci

US actor Traci Lords made her recording debut as guest vocalist on the **Manic Street Preachers**' 'Little Baby Nothing'. For her solo career she signed to the Los Angeles, California based Radioactive Records label, enlisting several high profile musical personnel to back her on her debut album, *1000 Fires*. The participants included Mike Edwards (**Jesus Jones**), Tom Bailey and Alannah Currie (**Thompson Twins**) and Ben Watkins (**Juno Reactor**). The latter penned 'Control', which reached number 2 in the ***Billboard***

Dance Charts before the album's release. Lords' peculiar story began in the late 80s with an under-age porn career which ended in a well publicised drug overdose. She emerged from the wreckage with the help of therapy and began to attend acting and vocal classes. Appearances in a variety of film and television shows, including *Roseanne* and *Melrose Place*, saw her re-establish herself, though journalists were reluctant to let her escape the shadow of her past totally. Rather than pursue the mainstream direction which her standing now warranted, Lords and her A&R director, Brendan Bourke, opted for a techno-dance slant for *1000 Fires*. This decision followed the artist's own conversion to dance music when she came to London in 1992 on a modelling assignment.

Album: *1000 Fires* (Radioactive 1995).

Lore And The Legends

Lore Cayote Orion (b. Ramona, California, USA) developed an esoteric form of country music by including his Spanish influences and his love of rock music. He wrote 'That's What Made Me Love You', a US country hit for **Bill Anderson** and Mary Lou Turner. He worked as part of Bandera in the early 80s and then built up a UK following as Lore And The Legends. One UK single was released as a picture disc. Lore currently manages a dude ranch.

Albums: *One Step Ahead Of The Law* (Colt 1987), *Lore Cayote Orion* (PT 1988).

Lori And The Chameleons

Formed in 1979 in Liverpool, England, the group was a vehicle for the evocative teenage singer Lori Larty. With backing, production and songwriting provided by former **Big In Japan** alumni David Balfe and **Bill Drummond**, Lori emerged with an appealing, almost spoken-word tribute to Japan (the country), entitled 'Touch'. A sparkling arrangement, the disc entered the bottom of the UK charts and appeared to signal the emergence of a new talent. The concept of the group appeared to revolve vaguely around exotic, travelogue pop with each song title set in a specific geographical location: Japan, Peru, Russia and the Ganges River in India. The second single, 'The Lonely Spy', boasted another impressive, atmospheric vocal from Lori and an astonishing backing which emulated the bombastic scores associated with *James Bond* films. After four superb tracks, which represented some of the best UK pop of the period, the group ceased operating. The journeyman Troy Tate reappeared in the **Teardrop Explodes**, while Drummond turned to management and was later the brains behind a series of pseudonymous groups including the **Justified Ancients Of Mu Mu** (JAMS) and the **Timelords** who later emerged as the very successful **KLF**. Lori, meanwhile, spurned imminent pop success by returning to art college and effectively retiring from the music business. Her fleeting career provided as much mystery and instant appeal as the extraordinary discs on which she appeared.

Los Bravos

Originally known as Los Sonor, Mike Kogel (b. 25 April 1945, Beuliu, Germany; vocals), Antonio Martinez (b. 3 October 1945, Madrid, Spain; guitar), Manolo 'Manuel' Fernandez (b. 29 September 1943, Seville, Spain; organ), Miguel Vicens Danus (b. 21 June 1944, Palma de Mallona, Spain; bass) and Pablo 'Gomez' Samllehi (b. 5 November 1943, Barcelona, Spain; drums) were voted Spain's top beat group following two Top 10 hits in their own country. They achieved international recognition in 1966 when 'Black Is Black', a song composed by two Englishmen, Tony Hayes and Steve Wadey, rose to number 2 in the UK charts in the wake of heavy promotion on **pirate radio**. The song's compulsive hookline proved equally popular in the USA where it reached number 4, but the quintet was sadly unable to repeat this success. Despite a series of superior pop performances, including an effervescent reading of an **Easybeats**' composition, 'Bring A Little Lovin''; 'I Don't Care' (1966) was the group's last UK Top 20 entry.

Albums: *Black Is Black* (1966), *Los Bravos* aka *Bring A Little Lovin'* (US) (1968).

Los Indios Tabajaras

Musiperi and Herundy (b. Ceara, Brazil) were sons of a Tabajaras Indian chieftain of an isolated jungle tribe. The story circulated by their publicist was that they found guitars mislaid by European explorers, and taught themselves to play. Next, they travelled the 1,000-odd miles to Rio de Janiero to perform South American folk ditties in the city's clubland where they were noticed by a showbusiness agent who polished both their act and cultural education. As 'Natalicio and Antenor Lima', they toured other South American regions including Mexico before a trip to Europe where they proved particularly popular in Italy and Spain. It was, therefore, hardly surprising that, as Los Indios Tabajaras, they began recording principally for the Latin market in 1943. After 20 years, however, their instrumental revival of **Jimmy Dorsey**'s 'Maria Elena' - dedicated to the wife of a Mexican president - was issued in the USA on **RCA Records** where, with no obvious precedent, it was a huge hit. In Britain and Australasia too, it reached the Top 10, but its ear-catching extraneousness was regarded as a one-off novelty and the duo made no further impact on charts in English-speaking territories.

Albums: *Maria Elena* (1963), *Always In My Heart* (1964).

Los Lobos

This group were leaders of the Tex-Mex brand of rock 'n' roll, which is Latin-based Chicano music built around accordion and guitar. They were formed in 1974 in Los Angeles by Cesar Rosas (b. 1954, Los Angeles, California, USA; vocals/guitar/mandolin), David Hidalgo (b. c.1954, Los Angeles, California, USA; vocals/guitar/accordion), Luis (Louie) Perez (b. c. 1953, Los Angeles, California, USA; drums/guitar/quinto), Conrad Lozano (b. c.1952, Los Angeles, California, USA; vocals/bass/guitarron) and Steve Berlin (b. c.1957, Philadelphia, Pennsylvania, USA). Their mixture of **Clifton Chenier** zydeco and **Richie Valens** rock was a totally refreshing new sound. Their debut album came in 1978 with the self-financed *Just Another Band From East LA*, although not a hit it was a critical success. The reviewers welcomed their second *How Will The Wolf Survive?* with open arms, but still it only made moderate sales. The superb title track vocal has an uncanny resemblance to **Steve Winwood**. The band continued to receive excellent reviews of their stage act, but it was not until 1987 that they found commercial success. Following their major contribution to the film soundtrack *La Bamba* the title single was released. It became an international number 1 and the first song in Spanish to top the pop charts. *La Pistola Y El Corazon* was a deliberate attempt to go back to their roots following their recent overwhelming profile. *Kiko* in 1992 was an excellent record, moving them back to a varied rock approach with delightful hints of cajun, straight rock and even soul music.

Albums: *Just Another Band From East LA* (1978), *How Will The Wolf Survive?* (1984), *By The Light Of The Moon* (1987), *La Bamba* (1987), *La Pistola Y El Corazon* (1988), *The Neighbourhood* (1990), *Kiko* (1992).

Loss, Joe

b. Joshua Alexander Loss, 22 June 1909, Spitalfields, London, England, d. 6 June 1990, London, England. One of the most popular bandleaders in the UK over a period of many years, Loss was taught to play the violin with a view to a classical career, He won a scholarship to the Trinity College of Music, and later studied at the London School of Music before forming his own band at the age of 16, playing local halls and for silent movies. In 1930 he moved into London's Astoria Ballroom, and played at the Kit-Kat Club a year later. His band made its broadcasting debut in 1933, and, early in 1934, topped the variety bill at the Holborn Empire. Later that year, he returned to the Astoria for a long residency, and while there adopted 'Let's Dance At The Make Believe Ballroom' as his first proper signature tune. Also in 1934 he started recording for the Regal-Zonophone label, later part of **EMI**, and stayed with the company for over 50 years. A large part of the Loss band's popularity during the 30s was due to the many featured vocalists including Paula Greene, Betty Dale, **Adelaide Hall**, Shirley Lenner, Elizabeth Batey, Marjorie Kingsley, Monte Rey (with his big hit 'The Donkey Serenade') and especially Chick Henderson, later killed while in the Royal Navy, who recorded the very popular 'Begin The Beguine'. Some of the band's other successes were 'Woodchopper's Ball' and 'Honky Tonk Train Blues'. Loss also gave **Vera Lynn** her first broadcast in 1935, when she sang 'Red Sails In The Sunset'. In 1940, Loss left the Astoria and went to France to play for the British Expeditionary Forces before returning to the UK, and spending the rest of World War II successfully touring the UK's ballrooms. After the war he was resident at the Hammersmith Palais, and later, during the 50s, lived through the onslaught of rock 'n' roll, and survived. By now he also had a successful band agency. In the early 60s he had chart hits with 'Wheels Cha Cha', 'Sucu Sucu', 'The Maigret Theme', 'Must Be Madison', 'The March Of The Mods', and many best-selling albums. During the war Loss had adopted the **Glenn Miller** favourite 'In The Mood' as his theme tune, and it was his recording which topped and tailed the Jive Bunny And The Mastermixers novelty single in 1989. His series of *World Championship Ballroom Dances* albums reflected his many appearances on BBC television's *Come Dancing*, and the 14 Carl Alan Awards presented by the industry. During one of his annual working holidays on the QE2 in 1978, he became the first dance bandleader to play in communist China. His post-war singers included Howard Jones (the vocalist on the 1948 Loss US hit 'A Tree In A Meadow'), Larry Gretton, **Rose Brennan** (who stayed with the band for over 15 years), and Ross McManus, (father of **Elvis Costello**). McManus and Costello sang together for the first time on stage in a charity tribute to Joe Loss which was presented at the Barbican Theatre in London in 1994. Loss played at many Royal functions, including The Queen's 50th birthday celebrations and the Queen Mother's 80th birthday. The most energetic and mobile of bandleaders officially retired in 1989 after 60 years at the top. Among his many awards were an OBE in 1978, Her Majesty's Silver Medal in 1977 and a Lieutenancy in the Royal Victorian Order in 1984.

Selected albums: *Dancing Time For Dancers, Number 11* (1957), *Dancing Time For Dancers, Number 12* (1957), *Dancing Time For Dancers, Number 13* (1958), *Dancing Time For Dancers, Number 14* (1958), *36 All-Time Hits* (1960), *Come Dancing* (1960), *Party Dance Time - Another 36 All-Time Hits* (1961), *Dancing Party* (1962), *Must Be Madison - Must Be Twist* (1963), *Go Latin With Loss* (1964), *Joe Loss Plays Glenn Miller* (1969), *Latin A La Loss* (1969), *Latin Like Loss* (1970), *Play It Latin* (1971), *All-Time Party Hits* (1971), *The Loss Concertium* (1972), *Dances For The World Ballroom Championship* (1972), *Non-Stop Latin Lovelies* (1973), *Joe Loss Hits The Road To Songland* (1974), *Dance At Your Party* (1975), *Top Pop Party Time* (1975), *Jitterbug And Jive With Joe Loss* (1976), *Swing Is The Thing* (1976), *World Ballroom Championship Dances* (1977), *Championship Dances For The World Ballroom* (1978), *New World*

Championship Ballroom Dances (1979). Compilations: *The Very Best Of Joe Loss And His Big Band* (1976), *Let's Dance At The Make-Believe Ballroom 19434-40* (1977), *50 Fabulous Years* (1980), *The Golden Age Of Joe Loss* (1985), *Isn't It Heavenly* (1986), *In A Romantic Mood* (1987).

Lost And Found

This US group was formed in Houston, Texas in 1965 and originally known as the Misfits. The quartet - Jimmy Frost (lead guitar), Peter Black (guitar/vocals), James Harrell (bass) and Steve Webb (drums) - enjoyed a residency at the city's Living Eye Club and became friendly with the **Thirteenth Floor Elevators** following frequent trips to Austin. The latter's guitarist, **Roky Erickson**, introduced Lost And Found to the International Artists label, a debt they repaid by including the Elevators' 'Don't Fall Down' on *Everybody's Here.* Although pleasant, the album lacked incisiveness, but a later single, 'When Will You Come Through?'/'Professor Black', showed a greater sense of purpose. Lost And Found split up in 1968, although Black and Harrell resurfaced in stablemates Endle (later Potter) St. Cloud.
Album: *Everybody's Here* (1968). Compilation: *Forever Lasting Plastic Words* (1988).

Lost Generation

An R&B vocal group from Chicago, Illinois, USA. The Lost Generation bucked the early 70s major trend in sweet falsetto-led vocal groups to provide a fresh sound of the dry hard lead. Members were Lowrell Simon (lead), his brother Fred Simon, Larry Brownlee (ex-**CODs**), and Jesse Dean. Lowrell and Dean had earlier been in the group, the Vondells, who had a local Chicago hit in 1964 with 'Lenore'. The Lost Generation established themselves with the 'The Sly, Slick, And The Wicked' (number 14 R&B, number 30 pop) in 1970, and although they were never able to penetrate the national pop charts again managed to sustain themselves on R&B hits for the next several years, notably with 'Wait A Minute' (number 25 R&B) in 1970, and 'Talking The Teenage Language' (number 35 R&B) in 1971. The group broke up after their last chart record in 1974. Lowrell Simon under the name of 'Lowrell' went on to establish a solo career, having a solid hit with 'Mellow Mellow Right On' (number 32 R&B) in 1979, and AVI released *Lowrell* the same year.
Albums: *The Sly, Slick And The Wicked* (Brunswick 1970), *Young, Tough And Terrible* (Brunswick 1971).

Lost In The Stars

Following their collaboration on ***Knickerbocker Holiday*** in 1938, composer **Kurt Weill** and librettist and lyricist Maxwell Anderson renewed their association more than a decade later for this show which opened at the Music Box Theatre in New York on 30 October 1949. It was a musical adaptation of Alan Paton's novel, *Cry, The Beloved Country*, which was set in apartheid South Africa, and told the powerful story of a black Anglican minister, Stephen Kumalo (Todd Duncan), whose son, Absalom (Julian Mayfield), is sentenced to hang after accidentally killing a young white man - a liberal - during an attempted robbery in Johannesburg. A few minutes before Absalom is due to die, the victim's father, James Jarvis (Leslie Banks), who is a supporter of apartheid, calls at Stephen Kumalo's house, and the two men unite in their grief. The music score reflected the show's brooding, tragic mood, and included ''Thousands Of Miles', 'Cry, The Beloved Country', 'The Hills Of Ixipo', 'Train To Johannesburg', 'Stay Well', 'The Little Gray House', 'Trouble Man', 'Big Mole', 'A Bird Of Passage', 'The Wild Justice, 'Who Will Buy', and the haunting ballad, 'Lost In The Stars', which was sung in the piece by Todd Duncan, and has been recorded many times over the years by artists such as **Tony Bennett**, **Vic Damone**, **Dick Haymes**, **Frank Sinatra**, Lotte Lenya, and Singers Unlimited. It was to be Kurt Weill's last Broadway show - he died during the run of 273 performances, on 3 April 1950. Eight years later, *Lost In The Stars* entered the repertory of the New York City Opera, and, in 1972, it returned to Broadway for a month, starring Brock Peters as Stephen Kumalo. He also appeared in the 1974 film version, along with **Melba Moore**, Raymond St. Jacques, Clifton Davis, and Paula Kelly. The Long Wharf Theatre, New Haven, Connecticut, presented a 'chamber version' of the show in 1986, and the work received its UK professional premiere in a production by the New Sussex Opera at the Gardner Centre, Brighton, in 1991. Three years later, a new musical adaptation of Alan Paton's novel, by Frank Galati, was presented by the Goodman Theatre in Chicago. It used the book's title, *Cry, The Beloved Country*, and re-arranged the original score to such an extent that the Kurt Weill Foundation demanded that an apology be included in the showbill. Also in 1993, a 'fine new recording' of the score was issued, with a cast which included Arthur Woodley, Gregory Hopkins, Cynthia Clarey, Reginald Pindell, and Carol Woods, who had impressed in recent years in ***Blues In The Night*** and ***The Goodbye Girl***.

Lost Jockey

(see **Man Jumping**)

Lost Tribe

This New York City, New York, USA group escape easy categorisation, their armoury spanning funk, soul, hardcore punk and hip hop. 'Our music is a reflection of who we are, where we live, and what we've been through. That has an effect on the kind of music we play. It's a very intense environment'. Comprising

David Benney (alto saxophone), Fima Ephron (bass), David Gilmore (guitar), Ben Perowsky (drums) and Adam Rogers (guitar), each contributes to the group's songwriting platform, bringing diverse personal influences to bear. Lost Tribe began by jamming in local New York clubs and Central Park, with members involved in sundry side projects. It was not until 1988 that the core of the group was cemented when Ephron, Perowsky and Rogers decided to put previous collaborations on a more permanent footing. By 1989 Binney and Gilmore had cemented the line-up. By this time members had amassed considerable and varying experience playing with **John Cale**, **George Russell**, **Me'shell NdegéOcello**, **Roy Ayers**, **Steve Coleman**, **Rickie Lee Jones** and **Walter Becker**, among others. The latter produced their self-titled debut album at his Maui studio. This mesh of contrasting influences was quickly followed by *Souflish* a year later. This time working with Joseph Marciano at Brooklyn's Systems Two enclave, guests included Benny Nitze and Joe Mendelson of Rise Robots Rise, with whom Ephron, Rogers and Gilmore had formerly participated. *Soulfish* duly included several memorable songs, not least Perowsky's 'Daze Of Ol'' and Rogers' 'Steel Orchards'.
Albums: *Lost Tribe* (High Street 1994), *Soulfish* (High Street 1995).

Lothar And The Hand People

Although this splendidly-named quintet became fixtures of New York's underground circuit, they were formed in Denver, Colorado, USA in 1965. College drop-out John Arthur Emelin (vocals/theremin) was initially joined by Richard Lewis (rhythm guitar), Russell 'Rusty' Ford (bass) and Tom Lyle (drums), before William C. Wright (lead guitar) completed the line-up. Lewis and Wright were later replaced by Kim King (guitar) and Paul Conly (keyboards). Much attention to the group was given due to Emelin's use of the Theremin, an instrument capable of eerie electronic 'cries' similar to those used in horror movies and previously heard on the **Beach Boys**' 'Good Vibrations'. Lothar headed east at the behest of the **Lovin' Spoonful** whom they supported on a provincial tour. The new arrivals quickly secured a recording deal, but the apathy which greeted their first three singles delayed a debut album. *Presenting Lothar And The Hand People* was not issued until late 1968, although its simple, folksy atmosphere recalled a more innocent era. The album was produced by Robert Margouleff who went on to form the experimental **Tonto's Expanding Headband**. A second collection, *Space Hymn,* followed within a matter of months and showed a group embracing synthesized technology. The set maintained a love of melody, but despite positive reviews, the album was not a commercial success and Lothar And The Hand People broke up in 1971.
Albums: *Presenting Lothar And The Hand People* (1968), *Space Hymn* (1969). Compilation: *This Is It...Machines* (1986).

Lotis, Dennis

b. 8 March 1925, Johannesburg, South Africa. An extremely popular singer in the UK, particularly in the 50s, with a sophisticated style which was particularly attractive to the young female population. Lotis trained for four years as a boy soprano, and won several cups and medals. He made his first stage appearance at the age of seven, and his first broadcast when he was nine. After leaving school, he worked as a bus conductor and electrician, and sang in cinemas and nightclubs in Johannesburg. When he moved to the UK in the early 50s, he carried with him a letter of introduction to **Ted Heath** from the former London saxophonist and bandleader, Don Barrigo. Following a couple of broadcasts with **Henry Hall**, Lotis joined the Heath band, and, together with the other resident vocalists **Lita Roza** and **Dickie Valentine**, became one of the most popular singers on the circuit. Lotis's vocal talents were evident on such records as 'Sam's Song', 'Goodnight Irene', 'Nevertheless', and 'She's A Lady' (with Roza and Valentine). After scoring a hit with 'Cuddle Me', he went solo, and during the late 50s toured the UK variety circuit, appeared in his first Royal Command Performances, and rejoined the Heath band for a tour of the USA, including an appearance at Carnegie Hall. He was also voted Top Male Singer in the 1957 *Melody Maker* poll. In 1956 he appeared in a touring production of the stage musical *Harmony Close* and, two years later, starred in John Osborne's *The World Of Paul Slickey*, a 'musical comedy of manners' that was poorly-received in Britain. Lotis also made several films, a mixture of drama, comedy, musicals and horror, including *The Extra Day*, *It's A Wonderful World*, *City Of The Dead* and *She'll Have To Go.* Among his other stage roles was an appearance as Lucio in John Neville's Playhouse Production of Shakespeare's *Measure For Measure.* Adversely affected by the changing face of popular music, he played the working men's clubs, and ran his own antiques and restaurant businesses for a time. Eventually, in the 80s and 90s, he returned to the theatres, singing in nostalgic shows with contemporaries such as **Joan Regan** and **Russ Conway**. He also frequently joined Lita Roza and some of Britain's top musicians in concerts commemorating the great Ted Heath band.
Selected albums: *How About You?* (1958), *Bidin' My Time* (1959), *Night And Day* (1983), *Get Happy* (1994).

Lottin, Eboa

b. 1942, Douala, Cameroon. A gifted guitarist and harmonica player, Lottin was a popular, albeit second division, makossa bandleader of the 70s and early 80s.

Albums: *Bessombe I* (1975), *Tete Youngo* (1979), *Les Trois Visages* (1983), *Disque D'Or* (1986).

Lotus Eaters

UK band who rose from the ashes of the **Wild Swans**, Liverpool's Lotus Eaters enjoyed instant commercial success with a fragrant pop song, 'The First Picture Of You', their debut single from June 1983. Revolving around Peter Coyle (vocals) and Jeremy Kelly (guitar), plus Alan Wills (drums), Gerard Quinn (keyboards) and Phil (bass), the rhythm section was later replaced by Michael Dempsey (bass) and Steve Creese (drums). However, the band never managed to repeat their Top 20 status, despite four catchy follow-ups; 'You Don't Need Someone New' later in 1983, 'Set Me Apart' and 'Out On Your Own' (both 1984) and a final stab, 'It Hurts' (1985). Those who appreciate well-crafted, quality melodic pop should look no further than their only album, *No Sense Of Sin*, from 1984. Coyle and Kelly later reactivated the Wild Swans but were again unable to sustain significant interest.

Album: *No Sense Of Sin* (Sylvan 1984).

Loudermilk, John D.

b. 31 March 1934, Durham, North Carolina, USA. Loudermilk's first musical experience was banging a drum for the Salvation Army and he played various instruments as a child and appeared regularly on the radio from the age of 11. In 1956, **George Hamilton IV** recorded his song, 'A Rose And A Baby Ruth', which went from the local to the national charts, reaching number 6. A few months later **Eddie Cochran** made his debut in the US Top 20 with 'Sittin' In The Balcony', another Loudermilk song which he had recorded himself under the pseudonym, Johnny D.

When Loudermilk moved to Nashville, a stream of hits followed, the UK chart successes being 'Waterloo' (**Stonewall Jackson**, 1959); 'Angela Jones' (**Michael Cox**, 1960); 'Tobacco Road' (**Nashville Teens**, 1964); 'Google Eye' (which was a catfish, Nashville Teens, 1964); 'This Little Bird' (**Marianne Faithfull**, 1965, and subsequently parodied by the **Barron Knights**); 'Then You Can Tell Me Goodbye' (**Casinos**, 1967, and a US country number l for **Eddy Arnold**); 'It's My Time' (the **Everly Brothers**, 1968); 'Indian Reservation (The Lament Of The Cherokee Reservation Indian)' (**Don Fardon**, 1970 and a US number l for the **Raiders**, 1971) and 'Sunglasses' (a revival of a **Skeeter Davis** record by **Tracey Ullman**, 1984). His controversial 'death' song, 'Ebony Eyes', was the b-side of the **Everly Brothers**' 1961 number l, 'Walk Right Back'. Other successful b-sides include 'Weep No More My Baby' (**Brenda Lee**'s 'Sweet Nuthins'); 'Stayin' In' (**Bobby Vee**'s 'More Than I Can Say'); 'Heaven Fell Last Night' (the **Browns**' 'The Three Bells') and 'In A Matter Of Moments' (**Louise Cordet**'s 'I'm Just A Baby'). Near misses include 'All Of This For Sally' (**Mark Dinning**), 'The Guitar Player (Him And Her)' for **Jimmy Justice** and 'To Hell With Love' for **Adam Faith**. He arranged an old song, 'Abilene', for George Hamilton IV, and it made the US charts in 1963 and became a country standard. His other country music successes include 'Talk Back Trembling Lips' (**Ernest Ashworth** and **Johnny Tillotson**); 'Bad News' (**Johnny Cash** and **Boxcar Willie**); 'Break My Mind' (George Hamilton IV, **Gram Parsons** and the **Hillsiders**); 'You're Ruinin' My Life' (**Hank Williams Jnr.**) and 'Half-Breed' (**Marvin Rainwater**). He wrote clever novelty songs for **Bob Luman** ('The Great Snowman' and 'The File') and for **Sue Thompson** ('Sad Movies (Make Me Cry)', 'Norman', 'James (Hold The Ladder Steady)' and 'Paper Tiger', all US Top 30 hits).

Loudermilk had his own hit with 'The Language Of Love', which made number 13 in the UK in 1962. He made several albums of his own material and they have been collected onto two Bear Family compilations, *Blue Train* and *It's My Time*, which contain two previously unreleased tracks in 'The Little Wind Up Doll' and 'Giving You All My Love'. He has often worked in the UK and performs his songs in a similar manner to Burl Ives. He produced Pete Sayers' best album, *Bogalusa Gumbo*, in 1979 but an album which he recorded at the same sessions has not been released.

Albums: *The Language Of Love* (1962), *Twelve Sides Of Loudermilk* (1962), *John D. Loudermilk Sings A Bizarre Collection Of Unusual Songs* (1965), *Suburban Attitudes In Country Verse* (1967), *Country Love Songs* (1968), *The Open Mind Of John D. Loudermilk* (1969), *Elloree* (70s), *Just Passing Through* (1977). Compilations: *Blue Train* (1989), *It's My Time* (1989).

Louis, Joe Hill

b. Lester Hill, 23 September 1921, Whitehaven Tennessee, USA, d. 5 August 1957. He learned blues harmonica from **Will Shade** as a teenager and was given the name Joe Hill Louis after victory in a boxing match. He performed in Memphis in the late 40s, where he became known as 'The Be-Bop Boy' and developed a one-man band act, with guitar, foot-drum and harmonica. Louis's first recordings were made for **Columbia** in 1949 before he took over **B.B. King**'s radio spot as the Pepticon Boy on WDIA in Memphis. This led to 'Boogie in the Park', a single produced by **Sam Phillips** for his short-lived Phillips label in 1950. Next, Phillips signed Louis to the **Bihari Brothers**' Modern label, for which 'I Feel Like A Million' was a local hit. By 1952, Phillips was recording him with a backing group on tracks like 'We All Gotta Go Sometime' and using Louis to accompany such artists as the **Prisonaires** and **Rufus Thomas** for whose 'Tiger Man' (1953), he supplied a scintillating guitar

solo. There were other tracks for Checker, Meteor and Ace. His final records were made for House Of Sound shortly before his death from tetanus in Memphis in August 1957.
Albums: *Blues In The Morning* (1972, reissue), *The One Man Band 1949-56* (1979, resissue).

Louisiana Hayride, The

This popular radio show was first broadcast on station KWKH Shreveport on 3 April 1948, the brainchild of the manager Henry Clay, the programme director Horace Logan and the commercial manager Dean Upson (a former member of the ***Grand Ole Opry*** singing trio, the **Vagabonds**). The programme, a three-hour Saturday night show, broadcast live from Shreveport's Municipal Auditorium, quickly attracted the public's attention. It was soon rated by many to be second only to Nashville's *Opry*, as the important venue for would-be country stars to reach. The *Opry* had already been established for over 20 years but the *Hayride* did not have the budget to compete with the mighty WSM to keep its stars. Consequently, it became the expected norm that artists first established themselves on the *Hayride* and then moved up to the *Opry*. In its way, therefore, if only as a final grooming place for stardom, the show became a very important part of country music and soon acquired the nickname of 'the cradle of the stars'. The first *Hayride* show actually featured some established acts, including the **Bailes Brothers** and **Johnny And Jack** (plus Johnny's then unknown wife, **Kitty Wells**) but within four months, under the careful management of its director and compere Horace Logan, the show had its own first star in **Hank Williams**. (Hank would later return to play the *Hayride* in November 1952, after he was dropped by the *Opry*). From that point, the country music side of KWKH's programming saw a steady progression of future stars including **Red Sovine**, **Webb Pierce**, **George Jones**, **Faron Young**, **Johnny Horton**, **Jimmy C. Newman**, **Floyd Cramer**, **Hank Locklin**, **Slim Whitman** and **Elvis Presley**. (Whitman actually recorded two of his biggest hits 'Indian Love Call' and 'Love Song Of The Waterfall' for **Imperial Records** in the studio of KWKH). **Jim Reeves** launched his career with KWKH, first as an announcer and DJ before being given the chance to sing one night on the *Hayride* in 1952, when Hank Williams failed to show. **Johnny Cash** also started on the road to stardom as a member of the *Hayride* in 1955. In its heyday, the Hayride show was broadcast over CBS national network and also carried internationally on the Armed Forces Network. Recordings of performances on the show by some artists, including one by Elvis have been issued on CD. When the show finally ended, after undergoing various formats, in the early 90s, it marked the end of a piece of country music history.

Louisiana Purchase

This show, which made its debut at the Imperial Theatre in New York on 28 May 1940, was **Irving Berlin**'s first Broadway score since his successful revue ***As Thousands Cheer*** brightened up America's gradual emergence from the Depression in 1933. In the intervening years, the prolific songwriter had scored several Hollywood films, including the classic **Fred Astaire-Ginger Rogers** musicals, ***Top Hat***, ***Follow The Fleet***, and ***Carefree***. Morrie Riskin's humorous and satirical book was based on a story by **B.G. 'Buddy' De Sylva**, and was said to have been influenced by a recent political scandal involving Huey Long, a well-known Louisiana politician. The upstanding and incorruptible Senator Oliver P. Loganberry (Victor Moore), travels to New Orleans in an effort to disentangle the somewhat unconventional business methods practised by the Louisiana Purchase Company. The firm's lawyer, Jim Taylor (William Gaxton), tries to deflect the heat by putting the Senator in a series of compromising situations with the titillating trio of Marina Van Linden (Vera Zorina), Mme. Boredelaise (Irene Bordoni), and Beatrice (Carol Bruce). Happily, Loganberry emerges with his honour intact. As usual, Berlin's score complemented the story perfectly. Two of the numbers, 'It's A Lovely Day Tomorrow', sung by Bordini, and 'You're Lonely And I'm Lonely', which served as a duet for Moore and Zorina, became quite popular - the latter for **Tommy Dorsey**'s Orchestra, with a vocal by the young **Frank Sinatra**. Carol Bruce made a memorable musical comedy debut, and sang the chirpy title song. The rest of the score included 'Outside Of That I Love You', 'Latins Know How', 'The Lord Done Fixed Up My Soul', 'Fools Fall In Love', 'What Chance Have I?', and 'You Can't Brush Me Off'. Chorus members, Hugh Martin and Ralph Blane, later went on to write the scores for ***Best Foot Forward*** on Broadway, and ***Meet Me In St. Louis*** in Hollywood. The presence of the familiar team of Gaxton and Moore ensured that *Louisiana Purchase* had a lot of laughs, and a successful run of 444 performances.

Louisiana Red

b. Iverson Minter, 23 March 1936, Vicksburg, Mississippi, USA. Although beginning as a sincere imitator of his various heroes, including **Muddy Waters**, **Lightnin' Hopkins** and **John Lee Hooker**, **Louisiana Red** has gained stature of his own as an instinctual and creative blues singer and guitarist. Red spent his earliest years in a variety of orphanages, his mother having died a week after his birth, his estranged father a victim of Ku Klux Klan violence. Raised in Pittsburg by an aunt, Corrine Driver, he got his first guitar at the age of 11 and instruction from the veteran Crit Walters. At 16, he joined the army and served in Korea. On his return, though claiming to have recorded with Waters and **Little Walter,** his first known record, 'Gonna Play My Guitar', was released as by Playboy Fuller on his own Fuller label. Another session for Checker as Rocky Fuller yielded a single, 'Soon One Morning'; further titles were reissued during the 80s. Working alongside Hooker and **Eddie Kirkland,** he gained a reputation as 'a guitar fiend'. Much of the 50s were spent travelling throughout the south. In 1960 he moved to New Jersey and made his first record as Louisiana Red for Atlas; 'I Done Woke Up' was backed by James Wayne & The Nighthawks. After recording an unissued session for **Bobby Robinson**'s Fury label, Red was signed to Roulette in 1962 by veteran producer Henry Glover. His album, *The Lowdown Backporch Blues* brought him much critical praise. During 1965 he was comprehensively recorded for Festival Records by **Herb Abramson**, from which the **Atco** album, *Louisiana Red Sings The Blues*, was assembled. Further titles appeared on the Red Lightnin' *Hot Sauce* album. Other sessions took place in 1967, 1971 and 1973. He recorded a number of sessions in 1975 for Blue Labor, from which two volumes of *The Blues Purity Of Louisiana Red* were issued; he also participated on albums by **Peg Leg Sam**, **Johnny Shines**, **Roosevelt Sykes** and **Brownie McGhee**. In 1976 he moved to Germany, where he has remained, touring Europe extensively and recording for several labels, including Black Panther, JSP, L+R, Orchid, MMG and Blues Beacon. He is a dependable if mercurial performer, his spontaneity sometimes a brick wall but often a springboard.

Selected albums: *Midnight Rambler* (1989), *Live At 55* (1991), *The Lowdown Backporch Blues* (1992).

Lounge Lizards

(see **Lurie, Evan**)

Loussier, Jacques

b. 26 October 1934, Angers, France. A classically taught pianist, he found a career in commercial popular music more lucrative. Then, in 1959, he hit upon the idea of performing the classical piano works of Johann Sebastian Bach in a quasi-jazz style. Together with **Pierre Michelot** and Christian Garros, the trio had enormous international success with the wider public. Their records were popular and they toured extensively. The concept, the low-key detached style, and possibly the huge commercial success, failed to endear the group to the hardcore jazz audience. The trio played on into the mid-70s.

Albums: *Play Bach* i (Decca 1960), *Play Bach* ii (Decca 1961), *Play Bach* iii (Decca 1962), *Play Bach* iv (London 1963), *The World Of Jacques Loussier - Live* (Decca 70s), *Bach To The Future* (State Of The Art 70s), *The Jacques Loussier Trio In Concert At The Royal Festival Hall* (Philips 70s).

Louvin Brothers

Brothers Lonnie Ira Loudermilk (b. 21 April 1924) and Charlie Elzer Loudermilk (b. 7 July 1927, both Rainesville, Alabama, USA). They were raised on a forty-acre farm in Henegar, Alabama, but only half of it could be cultivated. Despite their poverty, their parents sang gospel songs and encouraged their sons' musical talents. Ira took up the mandolin and Charlie the guitar and they created perfect harmonies for country and gospel music, inspired, in particular, by the **Blue Sky Boys**. In 1943, after winning a talent contest in Chattanooga, they began broadcasting regularly, leading to three shows a day for WMPS in Memphis. They recorded for **Decca**, **MGM** and **Capitol** but they found it hard to make ends meet and worked night shifts in the Post Office. Some radio broadcasts to promote a songbook, *Songs That Tell A Story*, have been released and show the Louvin Brothers at their best, with no additional instruments. Their career was also interrupted by Charlie's military service in Korea. (Their 'Weapon Of Prayer' is an emotional plea for peace.) They performed as the Louvin Brothers because the family name was considered too long for stage work, although their cousin, **John D. Loudermilk**, was to have no such qualms. Capitol Records re-signed the brothers as gospel artists but a tobacco company sponsoring a portion of the *Grand Ole Opry* told them to sing secular songs as 'you can't sell tobacco with gospel music'. They crossed over to the country market with their own composition 'When I Stop Dreaming', which is now a standard. Their secular US country hits included 'I Don't Believe You've Met My Baby' (their only number 1), 'Hoping That You're Hoping', 'You're Running Wild' and 'My Baby's Gone', but Charlie says, 'I don't think we ever did a show without some gospel music. Our mother would have thrashed us if we hadn't done that!'

By the late 50s, their sound was old-fashioned and their songs too melodramatic for the rock 'n' roll era. The **Everly Brothers**, who acknowledged their debt to the Louvins, may also have contributed unwittingly to their downfall. Charlie says, 'Ken Nelson told Ira, in 1958, that the mandolin was hindering the sales of our music, so my brother lost total interest in the mandolin and never picked another note on it on a record. He had put 25 years of his life into mastering that instrument, and it messed his head to hear a good friend whose opinion he respected say, 'You're the problem, you've got to throw that thing away.' Ira's drink problem worsened, their own relationship deteriorated and their last success together was, ironically, 'Must You Throw Dirt In My Face?'. Charlie broke up the partnership on 18 August 1963. '*He* had said a lot of times he was going to quit, but it was the first time *I* had ever said it.' Charlie went on to have solo hits with 'I Don't Love You Anymore' and 'See The Big Man Cry, Mama'. Ira started his solo career with 'Yodel Sweet Molly' but he was shot and badly injured by his wife, Faye, whom he then divorced. He then married Florence, who sang on his shows as Anne Young, but soon afterwards they both perished in a car crash in Jefferson City, Missouri, USA on 20 June 1965. Ira and **Bill Monroe** had pledged that whoever lived the longest would sing at the other's funeral, and Monroe sang 'Where No One Stands Alone'.

Gram Parsons introduced their songs to a new audience, recording 'The Christian Life' with the **Byrds**, and 'Cash On The Barrelhead' and 'The Angels Rejoiced In Heaven Last Night' with **Emmylou Harris**. After Parsons' death, Harris continued recording their songs: 'If I Could Only Win Your Love', 'When I Stop Dreaming', 'You're Learning' and, with Don Everly, 'Everytime You Leave'. Charlie Louvin had a country hit with 'You're My Wife, She's My Woman' and made two successful albums with **Melba Montgomery**. A single, 'Love Don't Care' with Emmylou Harris, made the US country charts.

Albums: by the Louvin Brothers *Tragic Songs Of Life* (1956), *Nearer My God To Thee* (1957), *The Louvin Brothers* (1957, MGM recordings), *Ira And Charlie* (1958), *The Family Who Prays* (1958), *Country Love Ballads* (1959), *Satan Is Real* (1960), *Those Louvin Brothers Sing The Songs Of The Delmores* (1960), *My Baby's Gone* (1960), *Encore* (1961), *Country Christmas With The Louvin Brothers* (1961), *Weapon Of Prayer* (1962), *Keep Your Eyes On Jesus* (1963), *The Louvin Brothers Sing And Play Their Current Hits* (1964), *Thank God For My Christian Home* (1965), *Two Different Worlds* (1966), *The Louvin Brothers Sing The Great Roy Acuff Songs* (1967), *Country Heart And Soul* (1968), *The Great Gospel Singing Of The Louvin Brothers* (1973), *Songs That Tell A Story* (1981), *Radio Favourites* (1987), *Live At The New River Ranch* (1989), *Running Wild* (1992), *Close Harmony* (1992), *Capitol Country Music Classics* (1993); by Charlie Louvin *Charlie Louvin* (1965), *Less And Less/I Don't Love You Anymore* (1965), *The Many Moods Of Charlie Louvin* (1966), *Lonesome Is Me* (1966), *I'll Remember Always* (1967, a tribute to Ira Louvin), *I Forgot To Cry* (1967), *Will You Visit Me On Sundays?* (1968), *Here's A Toast To Mama* (1969), *Hey Daddy* (1969), *The Kind Of Man I Am* (1969), *Ten Times Charlie* (1970), with Melba Montgomery *Something To Brag About* (1971), with Montgomery *Baby, You've Got What It Takes* (1971), *It Almost Felt Like Love* (1974), *Country Souvenirs* (1981), *Charlie Louvin* (1982), *Jim And Jesse And Charlie Louvin* (1982), *Charlie Louvin* (1989), *Then, Now And Forever* (1990), *50 Years Of Making Music* (1991); by Ira Louvin *The Unforgettable Ira Louvin* (1965).

Lovano, Joe

b. 29 December 1952, Cleveland, Ohio, USA. Lovano grew up to the sounds of jazz, thanks to a father who played tenor saxophone professionally and also owned a large record collection. In 1971, he went to the **Berklee College Of Music**, where he studied with **Gary Burton** and first met with future collaborators **Bill Frisell** and **John Scofield**. Returning to Ohio in the mid-70s, he played tenor saxophone with **Lonnie Liston Smith**, making his recording debut with him on 1974's *Aphrodisiac For A Groove Merchant*, and later toured with another organist, **Brother Jack McDuff**. Lovano moved to New York in 1976 and, after work with Albert Dailey and **Chet Baker**, played with the **Woody Herman** band until 1979. The following year he joined the **Mel Lewis** big band (with which he still works on occasion) and a little later met up with **Paul Motian**, in whose groups he has played and recorded for the last decade, renewing his acquaintance with Frisell in the process. (Motian and Frisell also play on Lovano's own *Worlds*.) In 1987, he toured Europe with **Elvin Jones** and in the late 80s worked with **Charlie Haden**'s Liberation Music Orchestra (*Dream Keeper*) and recorded a duo album with drummer **Aldo Romano**. Reuniting with Scofield, he played on the guitarist's highly-acclaimed **Blue Note Records** debut *Time On My Hands* together with the follow-up *What We Do*, and was signed by the label himself, his *Landmarks* appearing in 1991. Lovano's third album on Blue Note, *Universal Language*, comprised a line-up of **Jack DeJohnette**, Charlie Haden, **Steve Swallow**, **Tim Hagans**, Scott Lee, Kenny Werner and Judi Silverman.

An admirer of **Hank Mobley**, **Sonny Stitt**, **John Coltrane** and **Sonny Rollins**, Lovano's own saxophone playing is distinguished by a lovely tone, fluent line and lucid sense of time - still showcased to best advantage, perhaps, in the company of Motian and Frisell on recordings such as *One Time Out*, *On Broadway* and *Bill Evans* (all under the drummer's name). Lovano's output with Blue Note during the early 90s is particularly inspiring especially *From The Soul* and *Rush Hour* (Orchestrated by **Gunther Schuller**). He now stands in the very top league of tenor players, side by side amongst the finest artists of the century.

Albums: *Tones, Shapes And Colours* (Soul Note 1986), *One Time Out* (Soul Note 1988), *Village Rhythm* (Soul Note 1989), with Aldo Romano *Ten Tales* (Owl 1989), *Worlds* (1990), *Landmarks* (Blue Note 1991), *Sounds Of Joy* (Enja 1991), with Paul Motian, Bill Frisell *Motian In Tokyo* (1992), *From The Soul* (Blue Note 1992), *Universal Language* (Blue Note 1993), *Tenor Legacy* (Blue Note 1994), *Rush Hour* (Blue Note 1995).

Love

For many, the doyens of Los Angeles progressive rock in the 60s, brilliantly erratic and producers of one of the finest rock albums ever made: *Forever Changes*. Love were formed in 1965 as the Grass Roots by Bryan Maclean (b. 1947 Los Angeles, California, USA; guitar/vocals), **Arthur Lee** (b. 1945, Memphis,

Tennessee, USA; guitar/vocals), John Echols (b. 1945, Memphis, Tennessee, USA; lead guitar). Don Conka (drums) and Johnny Fleckenstein were soon replaced by Alban 'Snoopy' Pfisterer (b. 1947, Switzerland) and Ken Forssi (b. 1943, Cleveland, Ohio, USA). They become the first rock band to be signed by the expanding **Elektra Records**, just beating the **Doors** by a whisker. Their debut single was **Burt Bacharach** and **Hal David**'s 'My Little Red Book', in a different form from the way the writers imagined it. Love were an instant sensation on the LA club scene, outrageous, loud, innovative and stoned. The furiously energetic '7 And 7 Is' was released in the summer of 1966 and became their second hit. Although 'The Castle' on *Da Capo* pointed to a new direction it was *Forever Changes* that put them in the history books. That album, 25 years later, is still found on most critics' recommended list and no comprehensive record collection should be without it. It is a superlative record, unassumingly brilliant, gentle, biting and full of surprises. It proved to be Arthur Lee's finest work and marked the end of the partnership with Bryan Maclean. A new Love featuring Lee, Frank Fayad (bass), Jay Donnellan (guitar) and the drumming pyrotechnics of George Suranovitch, proved to be the most stable line-up and lasted for two albums. Both records contained rare glimpses of *Forever Changes*, but ultimately they were bitter disappointments. *False Start* featured few memorable moments, one being a guitar solo from **Jimi Hendrix**. *Reel To Real* is a truly wretched affair. The long-held opinion that Arthur Lee had become a casualty of too many chemicals was strengthened throughout the 70s, 80s and 90s with various stories chronicling his erratic and eccentric behaviour. Many attempts to resurrect his career have faltered, although there are hopeful signs that his comeback started in 1992 will be more lasting.
Albums: *Love* (1966), *Da Capo* (1967), *Forever Changes* (1967), *Four Sail* (1969), *Out Here* (1969), *False Start* (1970), *Reel To Real* (1974), *Love Live* (1982), *Love* (1982), as Arthur Lee And Love *Arthur Lee And Love* (1992). Compilations: *Love Revisited* (1970), *Love Masters* (1973), *Out There* (1988, a compilation culled from *Out Here* and *False Start*), *Comes In Colours* (1993).

Love Affair

Originally formed in 1966, this London-based quintet comprised Steve Ellis (vocals), **Morgan Fisher** (keyboards), Rex Brayley (guitar), Mick Jackson (bass) and Maurice Bacon (drums). Although Ellis was barely 16 years old, the group performed frequently in clubs on a semi-professional basis. Fisher was briefly replaced by Lynton Guest and the following year Ellis, backed by session musicians, recorded a sparkling cover of **Robert Knight**'s 'Everlasting Love' for **CBS Records**. By January 1968, the single unexpectedly hit number 1 in the UK and Love Affair became instant pop stars with Ellis' cherubic looks gracing teen magazines throughout the nation. With Mo Bacon's father Sid overseeing the management, the group resisted the solicitations of more powerful entrepreneurs, yet failed to exploit their potential. Four more hits followed, 'Rainbow Valley', 'A Day Without Love', 'One Road' and 'Bringing On Back The Good Times', but by the end of the 60s, the lead singer quit to form his own group, Ellis. Fisher reappeared in **Mott The Hoople**, Bacon became a music publisher and the group name was successively plundered for cabaret/revivalist bookings.
Compilations: *Greatest Hits* (1985), *Everlasting Hits* (1993).

Love And Money

After the break-up of the Glasgow band, **Friends Again** in the mid-80s, guitarist James Grant formed the pop/funk influenced Love And Money, taking with him erstwhile 'Friends', Paul McGeechan (keyboards) and Stuart Kerr (drums), plus Bobby Patterson (bass). The group were named after Grant's personal pledge as to what he wanted to achieve in the coming year. Since then, the group have achieved a string of minor hit singles in the UK starting with 'Candybar Express' (1986) released on the **Mercury** label, followed by the Fontana issued 'Love And Money' (1987), 'Hallelujah Man' (1988), 'Strange Kind Of Love', 'Jocelyn Square' (both 1989) and 'Winter' (1991). Stuart Kerr left the group in 1987 and subsequently joined the Glasgow-based, **Texas**. Love And Money recorded their second album as a trio. By the time of *Dogs In The Traffic* the line-up was bolstered by the addition of Douglas McIntyre (guitar/vocals) and Gordon Wilson (drums). Seemingly, forever on the fringes of success, Love And Money have yet to achieve that major breakthrough
Albums: *All You Need Is Love And Money* (1986), *A Strange Kind Of Love* (1988), *Dogs In The Traffic* (1991), *Little Death* (Iona 1994).

Love And Rockets

This *avant garde* UK rock band formed in Christmas 1985 from the ashes of **Bauhaus**. When David Jay (aka David J) had finished working with the **Jazz Butcher** on the *Sex And Travel* and *A Scandal In Bohemia* albums, he linked up once more with old colleague **Daniel Ash**, who had been working with **Tones On Tail**. Kevin Haskins also came with Ash, forming the band's nucleus of David Jay (vocals, bass, keyboards), Daniel Ash (vocals, guitar, keyboards) and Haskins (drums, keyboards). Early singles included 'Kundiluni Express', concerning Tuntric meditation, and a cover of the **Temptations** 'Ball Of Confusion'. The band's debut *Seventh Dream Of Teenage Heaven*, was a celebration of the rituals of youth, based loosely on their own experiences of going to rock concerts to see bands like **Roxy Music**. Like all of the post-Bauhaus projects, the band have failed to cultivate a UK audience to rival their previous standing. However, they scored a big hit

single in the US with 'So Alive', where their work still sells moderately well.
Albums: *Seventh Dream Of Teenage Heaven* (1986), *Express* (1986), *Earth Sun Moon* (1987), *Love And Rockets* (1989), *Hot Trip To Heaven* (Beggars Banquet 1994).

Love City Groove

The UK's entrants in the 1995 **Eurovision Song Contest**, dance/rap collective Love City Groove originally entered the competition 'for a bit of a laugh'. Certainly their stylised but effusive distillation of the **Stereo MC's** formula proved an unexpected hit in the qualifying stages, competing against the more standard array of MOR ballads and a hilarious token 'grunge' song. Led by Beanz (b. Stephen Rudden), with fellow rappers Jay Williams, Paul Hardy and 'Reason', the song, a half rapped/half sung affair also titled 'Love City Groove', found favour in the UK charts. It also served to give the competition some unexpected credibility and became a staple of the UK's summer 1995 pop radio schedules. There was some controversy over the single in the press, however, when runners up Dear Jon argued that the single had already been released to club DJ's in January 1995 (though this did not infract standing rules). Speculating on its Eurovision chances, **Jonathon King** commented that the song would 'either win or come last'. It did neither, managing a respectable Top 5 placing. Prior to the group's Eurovision success the members had all been struggling fruitlessly as musicians, but now found the opportunity to record their debut album at London's Nomis Studios, with all of the group members contributing to the writing process.

Love In Las Vegas

(see ***Viva Las Vegas***)

Love Life

A most unusual show, with music by **Kurt Weill**, and a book and lyrics by **Alan Jay Lerner**, *Love Life* opened at the 46th Street Theatre in New York on 7 October 1948 - just 18 months after ***Brigadoon***, the author's first big Broadway success with Frederick Loewe. Contrasting sharply with ***Kiss Me, Kate***, and ***South Pacific***, which both made their debut in the same season, this unconventional show deals with a fantasy situation in which a married couple, Sam and Susan Cooper (Nanette Fabray and Ray Middleton) with their two children, reflect on their lives from the year 1791 until the present day - initially a happy, satisfying relationship, which declines into a pointless cynical arrangement - but without the protagonists aging at all. The individual scenes are linked by vaudeville acts, and no attempt is made to integrate the songs into the plot, such as it is - rather, they provide a commentary on the action that is taking place on the stage. Fabray had 'Green-Up Time' and 'Here I'll Stay' (which became a hit for **Jo Stafford**), and she won the 1949 Tony Award for best actress in a musical. The rest of the score included 'Progress', 'Economics', 'Mr. Right', and 'I Remember It Well', a title that Lerner remembered well enough to use it again in the Oscar-winning film, ***Gigi***, in 1958. Considering the style and tone of the piece, a run of 252 performances seems to have been a reasonable outcome.

Love Me Or Leave Me

This realistic bio-pic of the popular 20 and 30s torch singer **Ruth Etting** was produced by Joe Pasternak for MGM in 1955. Daniel Fuchs won an Oscar for his original story which he and Isobel Lennart adapted for the absorbing screenplay. **Doris Day** shrugged off her 'goody-goody' image and gave a fine performance as the singer whose dramatic rise from dancehall hostess to nightclub and Ziegfeld star was masterminded by her gangster husband Martin 'Moe the Gimp' Snyder. **James Cagney** was outstanding as the domineering Snyder whose response to his wife's relationship with her pianist (Cameron Mitchell) was to shoot him. Although cinematic convention (and box office returns) required a happy ending, there was enough reality left to make this an unusual film. Most of the songs were authentic Etting favourites, too, and included 'Ten Cents A Dance' (**Richard Rodgers-Lorenz Hart**), 'Shaking The Blues Away' (**Irving Berlin**), 'It All Depends On You' (**De Sylva, Brown And Henderson**), 'You Made Me Love You' (**Jimmy Monaco-Joseph McCarthy**), 'Everybody Loves My Baby' (Jack Palmer-Spencer Williams), 'Mean To Me' (**Roy Turk-Fred Ahlert**), 'Sam The Old Accordion Man' (**Walter Donaldson**), 'My Blue Heaven' (Donaldson-George Whiting), 'At Sundown' (Donaldson), and the singer's theme song 'Love Me Or Leave Me' (Donaldson-**Gus Kahn**). One of the new songs, 'I'll Never Stop Loving You', which was written by **Nicholas Brodszky** and **Sammy Cahn**, became a US Top 20 record hit for Doris Day. The strong supporting cast featured Robert Keith, Tom Tully, Harry Bellaver, Claude Stroud, Richard Gaines, Peter Leeds, and Audrey Young. Alex Romero was the choreographer and Charles Vidor directed this popular, and sometimes intriguing film which grossed over $4 million in the US alone.

Love Me Tender

Elvis Presley's first feature, released in 1956, cast the singer as one of three brothers who rob a bank. Strife over a share of the spoils is compounded by conflicting love interests culminating with the Elvis character's slaying, although he appears as a wraith in the final reel. Although cast as a miscreant, the singer had opted for a more conservatively-styled film, a western, rather than embrace contemporary teen sub-cultures in the manner of *Rebel Without A Cause*. Indeed he did not enjoy top billing - Richard Egan was the star - but interest naturally focused on Presley's performance. Critics were generally impressed, citing great potential, something tossed to the wind by much of the singer's subsequent output. Although not a musical, the film's mournful title track gave the singer his third US chart-topper and *Love Me Tender* also featured the well-known 'weepie' 'Old Shep'. Again, by avoiding 'controversial' musical content, the Presley industry showed that, even at this early stage, a wider audience was being sought.

Love Me Tonight

This stylishly adventurous musical which was released by Paramount in 1932, bore many of the hallmarks of **Ernst Lubitsch**. However, it was, in fact, superbly directed by **Rouben Mamoulian** whose innovative work on dramatic films such as *Applause*, *City Streets* and *Dr. Jekyll And Mr. Hyde*, had already marked him out as a master of the medium. The sometimes risqué and satirical screenplay, by Samuel Hoffenstein, Waldemar Young, and George Marion Jnr., was set in France where a simple tailor (**Maurice Chevalier**) is passed off as a baron by the Vicomte de Vareze (Charlie Ruggles) who owes him a great deal of money. Chevalier is eventually paid in full and also wins the hand of Princess Jeanette (**Jeanette MacDonald**). The film is brimful of memorable scenes, such as in the early moments when the city of Paris rouses itself from sleep, and especially the sequence in which one song, 'Isn't It Romantic?', is used to transport the action from place to place - a technique which was, at the time, entirely original. The lyric for that song was inextricably linked to the film's story, referring as it did to Chevalier's occupation as a 'tailor', and its composers, **Richard Rodgers** and **Lorenz Hart**, wrote a new set of words for the number's wider publication. Their score also contained another enduring standard, 'Lover', which was introduced by Jeanette MacDonald, and she had 'The Son Of A Gun Is Nothing But A Tailor', as well as duetting with Chevalier and others on 'A Woman Needs Something Like That', 'Love Me Tonight', and 'Song Of Paree'. Chevalier was his charming self on 'The Poor Apache', and, especially, 'Mimi'. Also among the cast were Charles Butterworth, Myrna Loy, C. Aubrey Smith, Elizabeth Patterson, and George 'Gabby' Hayes, who would eventually become a respected character actor in Western movies. *Love Me Tonight*, which is regarded by film buffs all over the world as one of the most perfect and important films in the history of the cinema, was photographed by Victor Milner and produced, as well as directed, by Rouben Mamoulian.

Love Parade, The

Sometimes called 'the first truly cinematic screen musical in America', *The Love Parade* was released by Paramount in 1929. **Jeanette MacDonald**, who was making her screen debut, co-starred with **Maurice Chevalier** in Ernest Vajda and **Guy Bolton**'s adaptation of the French play, *Le Prince Consort*. The somewhat bawdy story concerned the Queen of Sylvania (Macdonald), who, having heard on the royal grapevine that her emissary-at-large, Count Alfred (Chevalier), is engaging in the wrong kind of foreign affairs, recalls him so that he can devote more of his energies to her. After he has measured up to her exacting standards, they marry, although her domination extends to the marriage certificate which reads 'wife and man'. Among the rest of the cast were British comedian **Lupino Lane**, Lillian Roth, Edgar Norton, Lionel Belmore, Virginia Bruce, and Jean Harlow. The score was written by **Victor Schertzinger** (music) and Clifford Grey (lyrics), and included 'Paris, Stay The Same', 'Dream Lover', 'Nobody's Using It Now', 'The Queen Is Always Right', 'March Of The Grenadiers', and 'Let's Be Common'. Chevalier and MacDonald excelled on 'Anything To Please The Queen' and 'My Love Parade', and the combination of the jaunty boulevardier and the unsophisticated, shrill soprano helped *The Love Parade* to become an enormous box-office winner. Much of the film's success was due to the innovative direction of **Ernst Lubitsch**, whose lavish settings, and consummate skill in the seamless blending of music, dialogue and action is constantly admired.

Love Sculpture

Having recorded as the Human Beans, **Dave Edmunds** (b. 15 April 1944, Cardiff, South Glamorgan, Wales; guitar) and John Williams (bass) formed Love Sculpture in 1967 with Bob 'Congos' Jones (drums). This Cardiff-based trio enjoyed modest airplay with their debut single, 'River To Another Day', before a rousing interpretation of Aram Khachaturian's 'Sabre Dance', initially aired as a radio session by BBC disc jockey **John Peel**, became a surprising hit single. Its success bestowed a novelty tag on a group already hampered by a lack of musical direction and although their debut album offered worthy blues interpretations, the psychedelic tinges on a second set were somewhat anachronistic. This impasse led to a split in the original line-up and Mickey Gee (bass) and Terry Williams (drums, later of **Man** and **Dire Straits**) joined the guitarist for a final flourish. Edmunds then disbanded the group and embarked on a solo career.

Albums: *Blues Helping* (1968), *Forms And Feelings* (1969). Compilations: *The Classic Tracks 1968/72* (1974), *The Dave Edmunds And Love Sculpture Singles As And Bs* (1990).

Love To Infinity

UK garage production duo comprising the brothers Andrew and Peter Lee, who have been working together since the late 80s. Both were trained in classical music, while their modern work recalls the heyday of disco, with strings, diva vocals and uptempo rhythms. Peter is responsible for programming, while Andrew acts as engineer. In addition to remixing for the **Other Two**, **Melanie Williams, D:Ream** and **Grace Jones**, they have also worked as a band in their own right, notably with Bruce Forest in 1990. They co-wrote with **Boy George**, and released their own album in Japan. They also released a solitary 12-inch for **Big Life**, before eeking out a living with engineering work for **Sub Sub** and the **Mock Turtles**. They returned to their own recording work in the early-90s, alongside vocalist Louise Bailey, on singles like 'Somethin' Outta Nothin'' for **Pigeon Pie**.

Love Unlimited

Formed in 1969 in San Pedro, California, USA, under the aegis of singer/producer **Barry White**, the group consisted of Diane Taylor, Linda James and her sister Glodean James who married White on 4 July 1974. The trio scored an early hit with 'Walkin' In The Rain With The One I Love' (1972), an imaginatively arranged performance which married contemporary soul to the aura of the now-passed girl-group genre, reminiscent of the **Shangri-Las**. Love Unlimited's later releases included 'It May Be Winter Outside, (But In My Heart It's Spring)' (1973) and 'Under The Influence Of Love' (1974), both of which White had previously recorded with **Felice Taylor**. The care the producer lavished on such releases equalled that of his own, but despite further R&B hits, 'I Belong To You' (1974) was the trio's final US pop chart entry.
Albums: *Love Unlimited* (1972), *Under The Influence Of...* (1973), *In Heat* (1974), *He's All I Got* (1977), *Love Is Back* (1980).

Love Unlimited Orchestra

This 40-piece orchestra was pieced together by singer **Barry White** to back his girl trio proteges, **Love Unlimited**. The unit also supplied the silky backing to several of White's singles and enjoyed an international hit in 1974 in their own right with 'Love Theme'. Later releases, including 'Rhapsody In White' and 'Satin Soul', were less successful, although they did provide the theme song to the Dino DeLaurentis remake of *King Kong* (1977). One member, saxophonist **Kenny G**, later embarked on a solo career.
Albums: *Rhapsody In White* (1974), *Together Brothers* (1974), *White Gold* (1974), *Music Maestro Please* (1975), *My Sweet Summer Suite* (1976), *My Musical Bouquet* (1978), *Super Movie Themes* (1979), *Let 'Em Dance* (1981), *Welcome Aboard* (1981), *Rise* (1983).

Love, Clayton

b. 15 November 1927, Mattson, Mississippi, USA. While studying as a medical student at Alcorn, Love formed the Shufflers with some of his fellow students, including Jesse Flowers and Henry Reed, to play clubs and colleges around Vicksburg. His cousin, Earl Reed, had a big band which had recorded for Trumpet Records in Jackson. With his encouragement, Love contacted Lillian McMurray and a session was arranged. 'Shufflin' With Love', released in 1951, was a ragged imitation of bands led by Louis Jordan and Roy Milton that toured the South. Other records, for **Aladdin**, Modern and Groove, followed over the next years. By then, he had met **Ike Turner**, a childhood friend from his Clarksdale days. Turner's band, the Kings Of Rhythm, was based in St. Louis and in 1957, with Love as their lead vocalist, the band recorded three singles for Federal, including the regional hit 'The Big Question'. He then joined pianist Roosevelt Marks' group and sang on two singles for Bobbin. Love became a full-time teacher in the 60s and only resumed a music career on his retirement. In 1990, along with fellow pianists **Johnnie Johnson** and Jimmy Vaughn, he cut four titles for *Rockin' Eighty-Eights*, including a remake of 'The Big Question' and **Fats Domino**'s 'Goin' Home'.
Albums: *Strange Kind Of Feelin'* (Acoustic Archives/Alligator 1990/1993), with Johnnie Johnson, Jimmy Vaughn *Rockin' Eighty-Eights* (Modern Blues Recordings 1991), with Ike Turner *Trailblazer* (Charly 1991), with Little Milton *The Bobbin Blues Masters Parts 1 & 2* (Collectables 1995).

Love, Darlene

b. Darlene Wright, 26 July 1938, Los Angeles, California, USA. A prolific vocalist, Love began her career in 1957 as a founder member of the **Blossoms**. This influential girl-group not only enjoyed an extensive recording career in its own right, but also appeared on scores of sessions and as the resident singers on US television's *Shindig*. Darlene also enjoyed a fruitful association with producer **Phil Spector**, and sang lead vocals on the **Crystals**' 'He's A Rebel' and 'Zip-A-Dee-Doo-Dah' by **Bob B. Soxx And The Bluejeans**. Love completed six singles in her own right for Spector's Philles label, including 'Christmas (Baby Come Home)', '(Today I Met) The Boy I'm Gonna Marry' and 'Wait Til' My Bobby Gets Home', the latter reaching the US Top 30 in 1963. Darlene subsequently pursued her solo career on a variety of outlets before being reunited with Spector in 1977 for 'Lord, If You're A Woman'. She continued her demanding session-singer schedule and in the 80s branched into acting with film roles in *Lethal Weapon* and *Lethal Weapon 2* as well as the Royal Shakespeare Company's co-production of Stephen King's horror-novel, *Carrie*. In 1990, Love completed the long-awaited *Paint Another Picture*, before touring the USA as a back-up vocalist for **Cher**.
Albums: *Darlene Love* (1981), *Paint Another Picture* (1990). Compilations: *Masters* (1981), *The Best Of* (1992).

Love, Geoff

b. 4 September 1917, Todmorden, Yorkshire, England, d. 8 July 1991, London, England. Love was a musical director, arranger, composer and one of the UK's most popular easy-listening music personalities. His father, Kid Love, was World Champion sand dancer, and came to the UK from the USA. Geoff Love learned to play the trombone in his local brass band and made his first broadcast in 1937 on Radio Normandy. He moved to the south of England, and played with violinist Jan Ralfini's Dance Orchestra in London and with the Alan Green Band in Hastings. After six years in the army during World War II, he joined **Harry Gold**'s Pieces Of Eight in 1946, and stayed with them until 1949, providing the vocal on their successful record, 'Blue Ribbon Gal'. In 1955, Love formed his own band for the television show *On The Town*, and soon afterwards started recording for **EMI**/Columbia with his Orchestra and Concert Orchestra. He had his first hit in 1958, with a cover-version of **Perez Prado**'s cha-cha-cha 'Patricia', and made several albums including *Enchanted Evenings*, *Our Very Own* and *Thanks For The Memory (Academy Award Winning Songs)*. In 1959, Love started to release some recordings under the pseudonym, **Manuel And His Music Of The Mountains**, which proved be immensly successful. Besides his own orchestral records, Love provided the accompaniment and arrangements on record, and in concert, for many popular artists such as **Connie Francis**, **Russ Conway**, **Paul Robeson**, **Judy Garland**, **Frankie Vaughan**, **Johnny Mathis**, **Des O'Connor**, **Ken Dodd**, **Marlene Dietrich** and **Gracie Fields**. In the 70s, he formed yet another group, Billy's Banjo Band, later known as Geoff Love's Banjo Band, while still having hits under his own name with *Big War Themes*, *Big Western Movie Themes* and *Big Love Movie Themes*. He also capitalized on the late 70s dance fad with several volumes of *Geoff Love's Big Disco Sound*, while retaining his more conservative image with *Waltzes With Love* and *Tangos With Love*. He was consistently popular on radio, and on television, where, besides conducting the orchestra, he was especially effective as a comic foil to **Max Bygraves** on his *Singalongamax*, and similar series. Love's compositions range from the Latin-styled 'La Rosa Negra' to the theme for the hit television situation comedy, *Bless This House*. His prolific album output included mostly film or television themes.

Selected albums: recorded variously under names of the Geoff Love Orchestra, Singers, Sound, Ragtime Band, Big Disco Sound, Big Band Dixieland, Banjos, and Mandolins; *Banjo Party Time* (1968), *Big Western Movie Themes* (1969), *Great TV Western Themes* (1970), *Big War Movie Themes* (1971), *Big Western Movie Themes, Number Two* (1971), *Big Love Movie Themes* (1971), *Banjo Movie Parade* (1971), *In Romantic Mood - Love With Love* (1972), *Big Concerto Movie Themes* (1972), *Your Top TV Themes* (1972), *Big Suspense Movie Themes* (1972), *Christmas With Love* (1972), *Sing-Along Banjo Party* (1973), *Melodies That Live Forever* (1973), *Somewhere My Love* (1973), *Showbusiness* (1973), *The Music Of Ennio Morricone* (1973), *The Music Of Michael Legrand* (1973), *Latin With Love* (1973), *Your Favourite TV Themes* (1973), *Big Musical Movie Themes* (1973), *Mandolin Magic* (1974), *Concert Waltzes* (1974), *Bridge Over Troubled Water* (1974), *All-Time Orchestral Hits* (1974), *Ragtime With Love* (1974), *Sing-Along Minstrel Party* (1974), *Sing-Along Western Party* (1974), *Sing-Along Banjo Party, Number Two* (1975), *More Mandolin Magic* (1975), *The Golden World Of Puccini* (1975), *The Golden World Of Opera* (1975), *Big Bond Movie Themes* (1975), *Close To You* (1975), *Waltzes With Love* (1975), *Big Hollywood Movie Themes* (1975), *Dreaming With Love* (1976), *Big Terror Movie Themes* (1976), *The Big, Big Movie Themes* (1976), *Magic Mandolins* (1976), *A Jolson Sing-Along* (1976), *Big Band Dixieland* (1976), *Geoff Love Plays Elton John* (1976), *Dance, Dance, Dance* (1976), *Take Me Home Country Roads* (1976), *Very Special Love Songs* (1977), *You Should Be Dancing* (1977), *Geoff Love Plays The Beatles* (1977), *Star Wars And Other Space Themes* (1978), *Tangos With Love* (1978), *Close Encounters Of The Third Kind And Other Disco Galactic Themes* (1978), *South Of The Border* (1978), *Big Disco Movie Hits* (1978), *The Biggest Pub Party In The World* (1979), *Music From Mandingo (Tiger In The Night)* (1979), *20 Explosive TV Themes* (1979), *Gold And Silver* (1979), *We're Having A Party* (1979), *More Waltzes With Love* (1979), *Themes For Super Heroes* (1979), *Your 100 Instrumental Favourites, Volume One* (1980), *Your 100 Favourite Love Songs, Volume One* (1980), *Your 100 Favourite Love Songs, Volume Two* (1980), *Your 100 Instrumental Favourites, Volume Two* (1981), *Your 100 Instrumental Favourites, Volume Three* (1981), *Your 100 Favourite Love Songs, Volume Three* (1981), *Your 100 Instrumental Favourites, Volume Four* (1982), *Your 100 Favourite Love Songs, Volume Four* (1982), *Your 100 Instrumental Favourites, Volume Five* (1982), *Your 100 Favourite Love Songs, Volume Five* (1982), *A String Of Pearls* (1983), *Sing-Along Banjo Party, Volume Three* (1983), *Your 100 Instrumental Favourites, Volume Six* (1983), *Your 100 Favourite Love Songs, Volume Six* (1983), *Your 100 Instrumental Favourites, Volume Seven* (1983), *Your 100 Favourite Love Songs, Volume Seven* (1983), *50 Dancing Favourites* (1984), *The Best Of British* (1985), *An Hour Of Geoff Love's Piano Party* (1987), with Shirley Bassey, Howard Keel, Alma Cogan, *et al Geoff Love With Friends* (MFP 1993 2-CD set).

Film: *It's All Happening* (1963).

Love, M'Pongo

b. 5 June 1956, Kinshasa, Zaire. Crippled by polio as a young child, but, determined to become a professional vocalist, Love overcame her disability and began working at the nightclubs in the Zairean capital of Kinshasa in her mid-teens. By the mid-70s she was known throughout the country as La Voix Du Zaire,

and in 1977 was invited to represent her country at the pan-African arts and culture festival FESTAC in Lagos, Nigeria - where she appeared alongside **OK Jazz**. She released her first album, *L'Afrique Dance*, the same year. On the 1980 set *La Voix Du Zaire* she was accompanied by a galaxy of stars including Jules Kamga, Vicky Edimo and Eko Roosevelt - some of whom were also featured on the follow-up *Femme Commercante.* In 1984, she drafted in **Les Quatres Etoiles**' Bopol and Wuta May for the superb *Basongeur.* Later that year, she toured widely in Europe, supporting fund-raising activities for the International Year Of The Child.
Albums: *L'Afrique Dance* (1977), *La Voix Du Zaire* (1980), *Femme Commercante* (1982), *Basongeur* (1984), *Une Seule Femme* (1985), *Mokili Complique* (1986), *Remercients* (1989).

Love, Monie

b. Simone Johnson, 2 July 1970, Battersea, London, England. Monie Love is a female rapper who has lived in New York since 1989. Her first recordings were with childhood friend **MC Mell 'O'**, Sparki and **DJ Pogo**, under the banner Jus Bad Productions, who formed in 1987. They released a solitary single 'Freestyle'. Love started recording solo with DJ Pogo in 1988, releasing 12-inch singles on obscure underground labels which were eventually spotted by DJ Tim Westwood, who asked them to do a single for his Justice label. There were several delays in releasing it, so instead they approached **Cooltempo** with 'I Can Do This', which became a hit in early 1989. Love has since worked with many other rap groups including the **Jungle Brothers**, who she met at a London gig in September 1988. They subsequently introduced her to the **Native Tongues Posse**, while Afrika Baby Bambaataa would produce her debut album. There have also been collaborations with Andy Cox and David Steele of the **Fine Young Cannibals** on the summer 1990 single 'Monie In The Middle', and with the band True Image, who are best known for performing the theme to the *Cosby Show.* They featured on Monie's Christmas 1990 single, 'Down To Earth'. Previous hits included 'I Can Do This', 'Grandpa's Party' (a tribute to the original **Afrika Bambaataa**), and her biggest hit, the **Spinners**' cover - 'It's A Shame (My Sister)'. In 1991 she teamed up with **Adeva**, as well as working with **Queen Latifah** and Almond Joy on the Bold Soul Sisters feminist project. Tracks on her debut album like 'RU Single' were intelligent attacks on the expectations and stereotypes of black women. Despite maturity beyond her years, she recognised that this phase of her career was still an apprenticeship; 'To me, rap is a school. The heads are split between **Public Enemy** and **KRS-1**'s **Boogie Down Productions**. The students are me, Jungle Brothers, **De La Soul**... but the best thing about it is that the classroom is open to all'. She would go on to appear in Forest Whittaker's Harlem film, *Strapped.*
Albums: *Down To Earth* (Warners 1990), *In A Word Or 2* (Cooltempo 1993).

Love, Preston

b. 26 April 1921, Omaha, Nabraska, USA. He inherited an alto saxophone from his older brother 'Dude' and obtained his first professional job in 1940, after which he took lessons from **Illinois Jacquet**'s brother Julius. Inspired further by **Count Basie**'s **Earle Warren**, Love played with Lloyd Hunter, Nat Towles and Snub Mosely before replacing Warren in Basie's band briefly in 1943. He worked with **Lucky Millinder** in 1944 and rejoined Basie for a longer spell from 1945-47, after which he played on-and-off in the band of his friend, **Johnny Otis**. Love also led his own orchestra (recording for his own Spin label and Federal Records) until 1962. Moving to California in 1962, he became a top session-player until he joined **Ray Charles**' band in 1966, going on to become the west coast house bandleader at **Motown**. Today, he lectures in African-American music at colleges and writes for local newspapers while maintaining a healthy touring schedule, including frequent trips to Europe.
Albums: *Omaha Barbeque* (60s), *Strictly Cash* (1982).

Love, Willie

b. 4 November 1906, Duncan, Mississippi, USA, d. 19 August 1953, Jackson, Mississippi, USA. A musician from an early age, Love's career was spent almost entirely in and around the Mississippi Delta country. In the 40s and 50s, he was a regular performer on the famous radio show, *King Biscuit Time*, but his music is known to us now only because of a handful of records issued on the Trumpet label in the mid-50s. These are tough, downhome blues, on which he demonstrated considerable proficiency on the piano, as well as an effective singing voice. 'Nelson Street Blues', in which he describes the street of that name in Greenville, Mississippi, is particularly notable for its strong and fascinating evocation of the time and place. Among his accompanists were **Elmore James**, **Little Milton** and Joe Willie Wilkins.
Compilations: *Clownin' With The World* (1990), *Delta Blues 1951* (1990).

Love/Hate

This Los Angeles, California-based quartet, formerly known as Data Clan, originally comprised Jizzy Pearl (lead vocals), Jon E. Love (guitar), Skid Rose (bass) and Joey Gold (drums). Proudly sub-titling themselves the 'stoopidest band in the world', the new name was first invoked in 1986. With a streetwise attitude and a highly talented frontman, their debut album, produced by Tom Werman, was released to widespread critical acclaim. A hybrid of **Guns N'Roses** and **Mötley Crüe**, their songs dealt with the well-worn themes of sex, drugs, drink and rock 'n' roll. It was in a live setting

that the band truly excelled, however, playing with genuine commitment and generating real intensity with their brand of funk-infused, jitterbug rock. The visual spectacle of a cross constructed from empty Budwiser cans also appealed. *Wasted In America* confirmed their fan's faith in them and recruited many new converts, but nevertheless saw them dropped by **Columbia**. They regrouped for *Let's Rumble*, with Love replaced by Darren Housholder, but by this point some of the earlier momentum, if not their native talent, had dispersed.
Albums: *Blackout In The Red Room* (Columbia 1990), *Wasted In America* (Columbia 1992), *Let's Rumble* (1993).

Lovebug Starski

b. Kevin Smith, 13 July 1961, New York, USA. One of the pioneering forefathers of hip hop culture, Starski has seen commerce move rap away from what he originally envisioned. Still remembering the days in the Black Spades when 'we used to push refrigerator-size speakers through the blocks', his role in the developmental parties was pivotal. At the age of 13 he began spinning records on the playground of the Forrest Housing Project (at which time he also adopted his stage name, from the popular television show *Starsky & Hutch*). The *modus operandi* would be to set up two turntables in the South Bronx parks, or mix live at parties. He was among the first to begin 'rapping' over the records he played. Although technically too young, Starski would sneak into a West Bronx club, 371, where his friends **DJ Hollywood** and **Peter 'DJ' Jones** worked, initially under the guise of roadie. From there his reputation brought him prestige placements at upmarket venues like Dancetaria and Stardust Ballroom, before eventually being offered a residency at Disco Fever - rap's first proper home. In 1981, he released his first single, 'Positive Life', quickly followed by 'Funky Pledge', a typical Lovebug message rap preaching the virtues of education, responsibility and self-respect. By 1983, with hip-hop showing signs of moving overground, Starksi cut his first proper record deal with Fever Records, owned by Sal Abatiello, the manager of Disco Fever. 'You Gotta Believe', on which he collaborated with producer **Larry Smith** (**Whodini** etc) would go on to sell nearly a million copies. It also became the theme for WABC-television's *Big Break Dance Contest*. It was followed by the masterful 'Do The Right Thing' (produced by **Kurtis Blow**) and the title theme for the movie, *Rappin'*. In 1986 he enjoyed crossover hits with 'House Rocker' and 'Amityville'. For a period in the mid-80s it looked as though Starski would truly break through. He was to be seen in the same company as **Luther Vandross**, **Sade** and **Michael Jackson**, and found a one-off album deal with **Epic**. Unfortunately, the resulting record sunk without trace, and Starski became another hip hop pioneer to fall by the wayside. His slide into cocaine dependency was complete, and he returned to the streets until he was busted for possession in 1987. He was finally released in December 1991. He returned, fittingly, to his old haunt, Disco Fever.
Albums: *House Rocker* (Epic 1986), *Lovebug* (Epic 1987).

Loved Ones

Formed in Melbourne, Australia in 1965. The raucous Gerry Humphries was the vocal and focal point of this group, and with a good-time band behind him the Loved Ones had success in the Australian charts with their first two singles 'The Loved One' and 'Everlovin' Man'. The five-piece band, which also comprised Rob Lovett (guitar), Ian Clyne (piano), Kim Lynch (bass) and Gavin Anderson (drums), was formed by musicians from traditional jazz bands including the successful Red Onion Jazz Band. It was probably this jazz background which gave the group a more distinctive sound than that of many in the post-**Beatles** beat groups explosion. An EP and two more singles were successful and then in 1967 an album was released. This album has proven to be something of an evergreen, being released several times and still being available today. The band petered out by the year's end and Humphries moved into management. Humphries re-formed the band in 1972, as the Joy Band and managed briefly to recapture the atmosphere of the original band. Despite Humphries' inconsistency, on a good night he could enthrall a rowdy public hotel audience in a fashion that few of his contemporaries could match. Many critics regard the Loved Ones as Australia's finest 60s band surpassed only by the **Easybeats**.
Album: *Magic Box* (1967).

Loveless, Patty

b. Patricia Ramey, 4 January 1957, Pikeville, Kentucky, USA. The youngest of eight children, she began to write songs and sing in local venues with her brother Roger, after the family relocated to Louisville. When she was 14 years old they visited Nashville, where her singing and songwriting so impressed the **Wilburn Brothers** (although they felt she was not mature enough to record), that they offered her the opportunity to work on their shows. She combined singing and schooling but in 1973, after marrying Terry Lovelace, who played drums with the Wilburns, she relocated to North Carolina and for a time finding the current country music did not suit her more traditional preferences, she left the music scene. During this time her marriage ended and a second marriage to a rock musician also floundered in the mid-80s, seemingly because he told her to give up country. Eventually, she resumed her singing career (even singing some rock 'n' roll in local clubs) and using the name Loveless to avoid being confused with porn actress Linda Lovelace, she moved to Nashville in

1985. She became a staff writer at **Acuff-Rose** and her brother Roger (acting as her manager) persuaded his friend Emory Gordy Jnr., a producer and musician at MCA, to record her. She made her chart debut in 1985 with 'Lonely Days, Lonely Nights' and her career was firmly established by her debut album *Patty Loveless* in 1987. In 1988, she scored her first Top 10 successes with 'If My Heart Had Windows', which **George Jones** had first charted 21 years earlier and her version of **Steve Earle**'s 'A Little Bit Of Love'. Patty established herself with UK audiences by her fine performances at the 1987 and 1988 Wembley Festivals. She became a member of the ***Grand Ole Opry*** in 1988 and in 1989, she married Emory Gordy Jnr. She continued to record chart making songs scoring number 1s with 'Timber, I'm Falling In Love' and 'Chains'. In 1992, she recorded a successful duet 'Send A Message To My Heart' with **Dwight Yoakam** Also late in 1992, she underwent surgery for a leaking blood vessel on her vocal chords and in spite of some initial concern, she soon recovered. She believed it was time to make some changes and after reluctantly dispensing with her brother's management she moved to the Epic label. She is quoted as saying 'The goal was to find a real good style and just have a lot of fun with it'. She quickly scored a number 1 country hit 'Blame It On Your Heart', which also nudged the pop charts. There seems little doubt that her vocal stylings will see her continued successes, in fact, her early 1995 hit 'Here I Am' seems to sum things up admirably. Sticking to her belief in hard country music she says, 'You're gonna hear that old bluegrass style, those blues licks when I sing. It's who I am - and I can't leave that behind. What we sang growing up was more old mountain style music, white man's blues, and that'll always be in there'. Although she never mentioned it when she was struggling to make her name, she actually is a cousin of **Loretta Lynn, Crystal Gayle, Peggy Sue** and **Jay Lee Webb**. Cousin Loretta finally broke the news one day on live television.

Albums: *Patty Loveless* (MCA 1987), *If My Heart Had Windows* (MCA 1988), *Honky Tonk Angels* (MCA 1988), *On Down The Line* (MCA 1990), *Up Against My Heart* (MCA 1991), *Only What I Feel* (Epic 1993), *When Fallen Angels Fly* (Epic 1994).

Video: *You Don't Even Know My Name* (Sony 1995).

Lovelites

An R&B female group from Chicago, Illinois, USA. The Lovelites epitomized a Chicago approach to soul music that married teenage voices to bright sounding horn arrangements and mid-tempos. The architect of the group was Patti Hamilton, who was the principal songwriter and whose emotive lead voice helped immeasurably ensure the success of the Lovelites. She formed the original group in 1967, with herself, her sister Rozena Petty, and Barbara Peterman. Ardell McDaniel replaced Peterman in 1968, who in turn was replaced by Rhonda Grayson in 1971. Petty was replaced by Joni Berlmon in 1970. The trio had two magnificent hits, 'How Can I Tell My Mom And Dad' (number 15 R&B) from 1969, and 'My Conscience' (number 36 R&B) from 1971. Their one album, *With Love From The Lovelites*, only yielded one national hit yet is loaded with fine songs that were frequently played in many locales. The group broke up in 1973.

Album: *With Love From The Lovelites* (Uni 1970).

Lovens, Paul

b. 6 June 1949, Aachen, Germany. Self-taught Lovens grew up listening to his sister's **Elvis Presley** records and BFR hit parades. While at school he played drums in dixieland and dance groups. His earliest jazz influences included **Chris Barber**, **Art Blakey** and **Thelonious Monk**. In 1969, he met German improvisers **Manfred Schoof** and **Alexander von Schlippenbach**. Thereafter, he established himself as one of the leading percussionists in improvised music. Lovens has toured worldwide, making numerous collaborations and recordings; most notably with Schlippenbach's trio, quartet and **Globe Unity Orchestra**, and duos with Paul Lytton, Toshinori Kondo, Urs Voerkel and the influential pianist, **Cecil Taylor**. In 1976, he founded the Po Torch label with Lytton. His playing is likely to veer, without a moment's notice, from unrestrained tumult to the most delicate use of a horsehair bow drawn across tiny cymbals.

Albums: with the Globe Unity Orchestra *Live In Wuppertal* (1973), with Paul Lytton *The Fetch* (1980), with Toshinori Kondo *The Last Supper* (1980), with the Alexander von Schlippenbach Trio *Detta Fra Di Noi* (1981), with Cecil Taylor *Regalia* (1988), with Urs Voerkel *Goldberg* (1989).

Lover Speaks

This acoustic duo featuring David Freeman (vocals/lyrics) and Joseph Hughes (various instruments) rose to prominence by supporting the **Eurythmics** in 1986 at a series of large arenas, after they had been 'discovered' by **Dave Stewart** on an early demo. He played this demo tape to producer **Jimmy Iovine**, who was in London recording material with the **Pretenders**. The result was a debut album and the single 'No More I Love You's', although other singles 'Terrible Dancing', 'Every Lover's Sign' and 1987's 'I Close My Eyes And Count To Ten' failed to match that song's impact. The future for the band seemed bright with dates lined up to work with **Alison Moyet** on album tracks and production work with **Maria Vidal** and others. However, the partnership dissolved soon after. While Hughes gave up the music business in favour of carpentry, Freeman continued to write songs at Dave Stewart's studio, recording some ten album's

worth of material. However, with one or two exceptions these compositions remained unreleased. In 1991 he did release *Balance*, a 1,000-copy pressing credited to Free-Man-Creese. A cassette credited to The Lover Speaks, but actually solely the work of Freeman, titled *Under A Tall Tree*, was also given a limited (500 copy) release. However, with **Annie Lennox** reaching number 2 in 1995 with a cover version of 'No More I Love You's', the group was once again the subject of some interest. Freeman used the resultant publicity to search for a major recording contract and pieced together a 'greatest hits' selection from his unissued archive recordings.
Album: *The Lover Speaks* (A&M 1986).

Loverboy

Loverboy were formed in Toronto, Canada, in 1980, by Mike Reno (vocals), Paul Dean (guitar), Doug Johnston (keyboards), Scott Smith (bass) and Matthew Frenette (drums). Reno was formerly with Moxy, and Dean and Frenette had been members of Sweetheart, a melodic AOR/heavy rock band. With this pedigree Loverboy were signed by **CBS Records** as soon as they were formed. Producer Bruce Fairbairn helped them record a self-titled album that was to set Loverboy's standard for years to come. It was an American-styled melodic hard rock collection that also dipped into reggae and jazz moods. With the hit singles 'Turn Me Loose' and 'The Kid Is Hot Tonite', *Loverboy* went platinum. After touring the group re-entered the studio in 1981, with Fairbairn again producing, to record the follow-up, *Get Lucky*. The album lived up to its name by selling over two million copies, helped by the singles chart progress of 'Working For The Weekend'. The only territory where the band had failed to take off was Europe. After further touring Fairbairn produced the multi-platinum *Keep It Up* in 1983, from which 'Hot Girls In Love' charted. Loverboy's inviting blend of melodic AOR had now been honed to a fine art, the album's success keeping the band on the road for nearly two years. On *Lovin' Every Minute Of It* they were joined by Tom Allom, the best known for his work with **Judas Priest**. The result was a musically tougher album which proved to be the band's least successful, though it still sold well over a million copies. The title-track, released as a single, was written by **Def Leppard** producer, Robert John 'Mutt' Lange. Fairbairn had by now made his name as the producer of **Bon Jovi**, but returned to the helm for Loverboy's *Wildside*, released in 1987, and their most complete album to date. **Bryan Adams**, **Richie Sambora** and **Jon Bon Jovi** all co-wrote various tracks. 'Notorious' also proved the band's most successful single, achieving platinum status three times over. This was followed by a marathon two-year tour, their longest yet. They did, however, take a break for two months to record tracks with producer Bob Rock before they came over to support Def Leppard on their European tour in the spring of 1988. After this, Loverboy returned home to Canada and an uncertain future. Dean and Reno announced plans to record solo and this left the rest of the band in limbo. In 1989 a compilation album was released by CBS, *Big Ones*, which also contained three new tracks that had been recorded with Bob Rock. Later that year Dean released a solo effort assisted by Loverboy drummer Frenette and Jon Bon Jovi on harmonica. The parent band, meanwhile, have remained inactive.
Albums: *Loverboy* (CBS 1980), *Get Lucky* (CBS 1981), *Keep It Up* (CBS 1983), *Lovin' Every Minute Of It* (CBS 1985), *Wildside* (CBS 1987). Compilation: *Big Ones* (CBS 1989). Solo: Paul Dean *Hard Core* (CBS 1989).

Lovers Rock

Although love songs have been staple fare in reggae, and other musics, since time began, lovers rock as a genre emerged in the mid-70s, chiefly in London. Mixing Philly soul with sweet skanking rhythms, it was the antithesis of the roots reggae movement and provided non-Rasta reggae fans with something to identify with, and party to, in an era otherwise dominated by **dub**. Early exponents such as 15-16-17, Brown Sugar (who featured **Caron Wheeler**, later of **Soul II Soul**) and Carroll Thompson, all sold incredibly well. The critics reviled them for their sickly, barely-trained harmonies and schoolgirl voices, but meanwhile, this truly working class music was to be found in teenagers' bedrooms in every British city centre. There were few lovers chart hits, one exception being **Janet Kay**'s 'Silly Games' (number 2 in 1979), but the music thrived away from the mainstream music business, and some records, such as Louisa Mark's 'Caught You In A Lie' and 'Six Sixth Street' were real artistic successes, albeit largely unheralded ones. Throughout the 80s and early 90s lovers has remained a largely underground music, while artists like Winsome, The Investigators, The Instigators, **Deborahe Glasgow** and Sandra Cross have built huge followings. One international success has been **Maxi Priest**, who combined lovers with **ragga**, roots and soul to produce that long-awaited breakthrough fusion.
Selected albums: Various: *Pure Lovers Volume 2* (Charm 1992), *Lovers For Lovers Volume 6* (Business 1992), *Fashion Revives Classic Lovers* (Fashion 1989). Deborahe Glasgow: *Deborahe Glasgow* (Greensleeves 1989). Sandra Cross: *Country Life* (Ariwa 1985).

Lovett, Lyle

b. 1 November 1957, Houston, Texas, USA. Singer/songwriter Lovett grew up 25 miles north of Houston in the rural Klein community (an area largely populated by farmers of German extraction) which was named after his grandfather, Adam Klein. During his teenage years, as Houston's borders expanded, Lovett was exposed to more urban influences, and attended Texas A&M University where he studied journalism and then German. During this period (late 70s), he began writing songs, his early heroes included **Guy Clark** (who later wrote a dedication on the sleeve of Lovett's first album), **Jerry Jeff Walker** and **Townes Van Zandt**. Having visited Europe (to improve his German) in the late 70s, he met a local country musician named Buffalo Wayne (who apparently took his name from his favourite western heroes), and remained in touch after returning to Texas - when Wayne was organizing an event in Luxembourg in 1983, he booked Lovett, and also on the bill was an American band from Phoenix whose members included Matt Rollings (keyboards) and Ray Herndon (guitar) who were later involved with Lovett's albums.

Lovett worked the same Texas music circuit as **Nanci Griffith**, singing on two of her early albums, *Once In A Very Blue Moon* (1984, which included one of his songs, 'If I Were The Woman You Wanted') and *Last Of The True Believers* (1985), on which he is pictured on the front of the sleeve. When Guy Clark heard a demo tape by Lovett in 1984, he passed it onto Tony Brown of MCA Records, and by 1986, Lovett had signed to MCA/Curb. His self-titled debut album was idiosyncratic, to say the least, including both the song covered by Griffith and 'Closing Time', which was covered by **Lacy J. Dalton**, as well as a fine song he co-wrote with fellow singer/songwriter **Robert Earl Keen Jnr.**, 'This Old Porch'. However, his acceptance was slow in US country music circles, and Lovett first received substantial critical acclaim when the album was eventually released in Europe. 1987 brought a follow-up, *Pontiac*, after Lovett had successfully toured Europe backed only by 'cellist John Hagen. The album made it clear that Lovett was rather more than a folk or country artist, with such songs as the surreal 'If I Had A Boat' and 'She's Hot To Go', while guests on the album included **Emmylou Harris**. By this time, Lovett was talking about both recording and touring with what he called His Large Band, with several saxophone players and a female backing singer, Francine Reed, as well as a regular rhythm section, and his third album, released in 1989, was indeed titled *Lyle And His Large Band.* Including an insidiously straight cover of the **Tammy Wynette** standard 'Stand By Your Man', and a version of the R&B oldie, 'The Glory Of Love', this again delighted critics by its very humour and eclecticism, but further confused record buyers, especially in the USA, who were unsure whether this was a country record or jazz or something quite different.

At this point Lovett moved away from Nashville, where he was regarded as too weird, and as a result, his fourth album, produced by Los Angeles heavyweight George Massenburg, was not released until early 1992. Its title *Joshua Judges Ruth* (three consecutive books in the Old Testament, but meaning something very difference if read as a phrase) was symptomatic of Lovett's intelligence, but perhaps equally so of his idiosyncratic approach. As usual, critics loved it, although it included hardly any traces of country music, and seemed to portray him as a **Tom Waits**-like figure - ultra sophisticated, but somewhat off the wall. In 1992, Lovett was chosen as the opening act for many of the dates on the first world tour during the 90s by **Dire Straits**. This exposed him to a huge international audience, but seems to have done little to extend his cult following. In the same year, Lovett met the Hollywood actress, Julia Roberts, on the set of *The Player*, a high-grossing film, in which Lovett played the role of a detective. They married in June 1993, the following year their marriage was floundering, by 1995 it appeared to be over. Presumably Lovett will now resume his career as one of the sharpest and wittiest songwriters to come out of America in recent times.

Albums: *Lyle Lovett* (1986), *Pontiac* (1987), *Lyle Lovett And His Large Band* (1989), *Joshua Judges Ruth* (1992), *I Love Everybody* (MCA 1994).

Lovich, Lene

Vocalist Lovich was one of several acts launched by the **Stiff** label in 1978. The former horror-film soundtrack screamer joined new signings **Mickey Jupp**, **Rachel Sweet** and **Jona Lewie** on the *Be Stiff* national tour, of which this charismatic performer emerged as the undoubted star. Her arresting, gypsy-like appearance, and warbled intonation was matched by a sense of pop's dynamics, as evinced by her UK Top 3 hit, 'Lucky Number'. Shaven-head guitarist Les Chappell provided a visual and compositional foil to a singer who enjoyed further, albeit minor, hits with 'Say When', 'Bird Song' (both 1979) and 'New Toy' (1981). Lovich also entered the album charts with *Stateless*, which derived its title from the air of mystery the artist cultivated about her origins. Subsequent releases fared less well and her 1982 single, 'It's You Only You (Mein Schmerz)', provided Lovich with her final chart entry. Problems within Stiff undermined the progress of a singer who sadly failed to maintain early promise.

Albums: *Stateless* (1978), *Flex* (1979), *No Man's Land* (1982).

Lovin' Spoonful

Few American pop groups have gathered as much universal affection over the years as the brilliant and underrated Lovin' Spoonful. Their back catalogue of hits is constantly repackaged and reissued, as their stature increases. They were formed in 1965 by **John Sebastian** (b. 17 March 1944, New York, USA; vocal/guitar/harmonica/autoharp) and **Zalman Yanovsky** (b. 19 December 1944, Toronto, Canada; guitar/vocals) following their time together in the

Mugwumps (as eulogized in the **Mamas And The Papas** hit 'Creeque Alley'). The band were completed by Steve Boone (b. 23 September 1943, Camp Lejeune, North Carolina, USA; bass) and Joe Butler (b. 19 January 1943, Long Island, New York, USA; drums/vocals). Their unique blend of jug-band, folk, blues and rock 'n' roll synthesized into what was termed as 'electric good-time music' kept them apart from every other American pop group at that time. In two years they notched up 10 US Top 20 hits, all composed by John Sebastian. From the opening strum of Sebastian's autoharp on 'Do You Believe In Magic?' the party began; from the evocative 'You Didn't Have To Be So Nice', to the languid singalong 'Daydream'. From the punchy and lyrically outstanding 'Summer In The City'; 'Hot town summer in the city, back of my neck getting dirt and gritty', to the gentle romanticism of 'Rain On The Roof'; 'You and me and the rain on the roof, caught up in a summer shower, drying while it soaks the flowers, maybe we'll be caught for hours'. Their four regular albums were crammed full of other gems in addition to the hits. Additionally Sebastian wrote the music for two films; Woody Allen's *What's Up Tiger Lily* and Francis Ford Coppola's *You're A Big Boy Now*, the latter featuring the beautiful 'Darling Be Home Soon'. Sadly the non-stop party came to an end in 1968 following the departure of Yanovsky and the arrival, albeit briefly, of Jerry Yester. The quality of Sebastian's lyrics and melodies makes him one of the finest American songwriters. In 1991, Steve Boone, Joe Butler and the Yester brothers announced the reformation of the band for a tour - however, without Yanovsky and Sebastian, the 'magic' cannot be present.
Albums: *Do You Believe In Magic* (1965), *Daydream* (1966), *What's Shakin'* (1966), *What's Up Tiger Lily* (1966, film soundtrack), *Hums Of The Lovin' Spoonful* (1966), *You're A Big Boy Now* (1967, film soundtrack), *Everything Playing* (1968), *Revelation: Revolution* (1968). Selected compilations: *The EP Collection* (1988), *Collection: Lovin' Spoonful, 20 Hits* (1988), *The Very Best Of The Lovin' Spoonful* (1988), *Go To The Movies* (1991).

Low

Based in Duluth, Minneapolis, USA, Low consist of Alan Sparhawk (vocals/guitar), his wife Mimi Parker (drums/vocals) and Zak Scalley (bass), who joined in time for the group's second album. Formed in 1993, Low were initially influenced by **Brian Eno** and **Joy Division** and 'the boredom of living in Duluth'. A demo tape was subsequently passed to underground producer/artist **Kramer**, who invited the band to his New York studio to record their debut album. This revealed a band who specialise in a uniquely uncommercial songwriting process, 'We just wanted to annoy people by building up all this tension and not giving them any release.' However, over the course of a full album, they mellowed, with their minimal instrumentation similar to the slow-burning power of **Morphine**. Similarly, Low conducted themselves without recourse to conventional formats - Parker's drum kit consisting merely of one snare and a cymbal. By the second album they had dispensed to some degree with the reverb-dominated sound, although this was still not music for the faint-hearted, with the band opting for a moribund but hypnotic groove. The band spent part of 1995 touring with **Spectrum**.
Albums: *I Could Live In Hope* (Vernon Yard/Virgin 1993), *Long Division* (Vernon Yard/Virgin 1995).

Lowe, Frank

b. 24 June 1943, Memphis, Tennessee, USA. Although originally categorized as a 'new thing' (the US 60s free-jazz movement) player, Lowe has grown into one of the most distinctive and thoughtful of contemporary tenor saxophonists. Growing up in Memphis, one of his first jobs was at the Satellite record shop and its offshoot label, **Stax**. A liking for the records of **Gene Ammons** developed into a fascination with the newer musics of **John Coltrane**, **Ornette Coleman** and the **AACM**. He attended the University of Kansas, then moved to San Francisco and studied with Rafael Garrett, **Sonny Simmons** and Bert Wilson. Moving to New York in the mid-60s, he worked with **Sun Ra** then, after a spell at the San Francisco Conservatory, he settled in New York, playing with numerous musicians from the jazz *avant garde*, including **Rashied Ali** (*Duo Exchanges*), **Alice Coltrane** (*World Galaxy*) and **Don Cherry** (*Relativity Suite*, *Brown Rice*), while his own debut as leader - *Black Beings* - had **Joseph Jarman** guesting. In the mid-70s he formed a group with **Joe Bowie** and **Charles 'Bobo' Shaw**, recording *Fresh* (which also featured **Lester Bowie**) and *The Flam* (with **Leo Smith**). While in San Francisco, he had met **Lawrence 'Butch' Morris**, who has become one of his most frequent collaborators (*Current Trends In Racism In Modern America*), as has **Billy Bang**, with whom he plays in the collective quartet Jazz Doctors (*Intensive Case*) and in the violinist's own group (*Valve No 10*). Always open to new ideas, Lowe has played with leftfield rock musicians such as **Eugene Chadbourne** and seems as comfortable with New York's 80s *avant garde* downtown scene as he does with 60s jazzers such as Cherry and **Charles Moffett**: indeed, his own recordings feature a diverse array of artists, from **John Zorn** (*Lowe And Behold*) to **Geri Allen** and **Grachan Moncur III** (*Decision In Paradise*). As he told *Cadence* magazine, 'I've always tried to go in *and* out', though adding that even when playing in, he likes to 'experiment with time and colours'.
Albums: *Black Beings* (ESP 1973), *Fresh* (Freedom 1975), *The Flam* (Black Saint 1976), *Lowe And Behold* (1977), *The Other Side* (1977), *Tricks Of The Trade* (1977), *Doctor Too-Much* (1977), *Don't Punk Out* (1977), *Skizoke* (1981), *Exotic Heartbreak* (Soul Note 1982), with the Jazz Doctors

Intensive Care (1984), *Decision In Paradise* (Soul Note 1985), *Inappropriate Choices* (ITM Pacific 1991).

Lowe, Jez

b. 14 July 1955, County Durham, England. Having played on the folk circuit, with various groups from 1973, Lowe also worked for a time with Ged Foley, who was later to join the **House Band**. In 1979, Jez, performing mainly traditional songs, turned professional. His first release, in 1980, was on Fellside Records, and included three Lowe originals. He was supported on *Jez Lowe* by Jim Barnes (cittern, guitar) and Sylvia Barnes (whistle, vocals). Both had previously been members of the **Battlefield Band**. From 1981, Lowe pursued a largely solo career, but performed at festivals and concerts, both at home and in the USA and Europe, with Jake Walton (hurdy gurdy). However, Jez continued to record with Fellside, releasing *Old Durham Road* and the highly acclaimed *Galloways*, which contains the much covered Lowe composition 'Old Bones'. Subsequent releases contained more Lowe originals, and, following the release of *Bad Penny*, Jez formed Jez Lowe And The Bad Pennies, taking on Bev Sanders (vocals, percussion, whistle) and Rob Kay (vocals, keyboards, melodeon, recorder, percussion) who was in turn replaced in 1991 by Bob Surgeoner (bass, accordian, banjo, keyboards). They recorded *Briefly On The Street*, which contained the excellent 'The Famous Working Man' and 'Davis And Golightly'. Lowe has had songs recorded by artists such as **Gordon Bok** and **Mary Black** among others, and he continues to be a popular figure on the folk circuit. Billy Surgeoner (fiddle, whistle, keyboards, bass) joined in 1991.

Albums: *Jez Lowe* (1980), *The Old Durham Road* (1983), *Galloways* (1985), with Martin Carthy, Roy Harris *The Penguin Book Of English Folk Songs* (1985), with Jake Walton *Two A Roue* (1986), *Bad Penny* (1988), with the Bad Pennies *Briefly On The Street* (1990), with the Bad Pennies *Bede Weeps* (1993). Compilation: *Back Shift* (1992).

Lowe, Mundell

b. 21 April 1922, Laurel, Mississippi, USA. Guitarist Lowe began playing at the age of six and seven years later, left home and headed for New Orleans, Louisiana. He listened and learned at many of the city's clubs before he was found by his Baptist minister father and taken back home. He soon made another try for an early career in music, this time visiting Nashville where he played in the **Pee Wee King** band. Taken home again he graduated from school in 1940 and promptly joined the **Jan Savitt** band. Drafted for military service, Lowe was posted to a camp near New Orleans. At a nearby camp the entertainments officer was **John Hammond Jnr.** and their meeting helped Lowe establish his career after the war. Hammond introduced him to **Ray McKinley** who was leading the postwar **Glenn Miller** band and thereafter the guitarist worked with **Benny Goodman**, **Wardell Gray**, **Fats Navarro** and **Red Norvo** among many leading jazz musicians. During the late 40s and early 50s, Lowe worked mostly in New York, playing club dates and recording sessions with a remarkable array of top-flight artists, including **Lester Young**, **Buck Clayton**, **Charlie Parker** and **Billie Holiday**. During the 50s Lowe played in the NBC studio orchestra, was musical director on the *Today* show on television, acted on and off Broadway and continued to play and record with such well-known jazz musicians as **Georgie Auld**, **Ruby Braff**, **Ben Webster**, **Carmen McRae** and **Harold Ashby**.

Since 1965, Lowe has been based in Los Angeles, again working in television and radio and also establishing himself as a writer of scores for films and television. He also became active as an educator but despite his busy schedule found time to continue his recording career, accompanying such musically diverse artists as **Sammy Davis Jnr.**, **Tony Bennett**, **Bill Berry**, **Richie Kamuca** and many others. In the early 80s he formed a small band he named TransitWest, in which he was joined by Sam Most, **Monty Budwig** and **Nick Ceroli**, which made its first major appearance at the 1983 **Monterey Jazz Festival**. A quietly elegant player with a cool but surging swing, Lowe's playing style, with its deceptively sparse exploration of the often-overlooked subtleties of many standards from the jazz and popular song repertoires, is in the great tradition of jazz guitar. Nevertheless, his experimentations with 12-tone compositions have also put him in the forefront of jazz-guitar thinking.

Albums: *The Mundell Lowe Quartet* (Original Jazz Classics 1955), *Guitar Moods* (Riverside 1956), *The Mundell Lowe Trio* (1956), *New Music Of Alec Wilder* (1956), *A Grand Night For Swinging* (1957), *Porgy And Bess* (RCA 1958), with Donald Byrd and others *TV Themes* (1959), *The Mundell Lowe All Stars* (1960), *Mundell Lowe And His Orchestra* i (1961), *Mundell Lowe And His Orchestra* ii (1962), *California Guitar* (1974), *Guitar Player* (1976), with Richie Kamuca *Richie* (1977), with Bill Berry *Shortcake* (1978), *TransitWest* (1983), *Souvenirs A Tribute To Nick Carroll* (Jazz Alliance 1992).

Lowe, Nick

b. 25 March 1949, Woodbridge, Suffolk, England. Lowe has for many years been held in high esteem by a loyal band of admirers aware of his dexterity as producer, musician, vocalist and songwriter. His early apprenticeship as bass player/vocalist with **Kippington Lodge**, which evolved into **Brinsley Schwarz**, made him a seasoned professional by the mid-70s. He then started a career as record producer, making his debut with the **Kursaal Flyers**' *Chocs Away*, followed by **Dr. Feelgood**'s *Malpractice*. He also owns up to being responsible for an appalling novelty record, 'We Love You', a parody of the **Bay City Rollers**, recorded under the name the Tartan Horde. He formed **Stiff Records** with Jake Riviera and Dave Robinson in 1976 and was an early pioneer of punk music. His own singles were unsuccessful, but he was critically applauded for the catchy 'So It Goes', backed with the prototype punk song, 'Heart Of The City'. He was an important catalyst in the career of **Elvis Costello**, producing his first five albums and composing a modern classic with 'What's So Funny 'Bout (Peace Love And Understanding)'. Lowe became a significant figure in the UK, producing albums for the **Damned**, **Clover** and **Dave Edmunds**. In 1977, Lowe co-founded **Rockpile** and also managed to join the legendary 'Live Stiffs' tour. His own debut, *Jesus Of Cool* (US title: *Pure Pop For Now People*) was a critics' favourite and remains a strong collection of unpretentious rock 'n' pop. The hit single, 'I Love The Sound Of Breaking Glass', is still a disc-jockey favourite, although the equally impressive 'Little Hitler' failed miserably. In 1979 he produced another important single, 'Stop Your Sobbing', by the **Pretenders**, and released another excellent collection, *Labour Of Lust,* which contained the sparkling 'Cruel To Be Kind' and 'Cracking Up'. Lowe was indeed cracking up, from a surfeit of alcohol, as his brother-in-arms Dave Edmunds intimated in the UK television documentary, *Born Fighters*. Towards the end of a hectic year he married **Carlene Carter**. In the early 80s, as well as continuing his work with Costello, he additionally produced albums with **John Hiatt**, **Paul Carrack**, Carlene Carter and the **Fabulous Thuderbirds**. His own recordings suffered and were rushed efforts. In 1986 he reunited with Costello for *Blood And Chocolate*, although his own albums were virtually ignored by the public. He returned in 1988 with *Pinker And Prouder Than Previous*, with contributions from Edmunds, but once again it was dismissed, making his catalogue of flop albums embarrassingly large, a fact that Lowe observes with his customary good grace and humour. In 1992 Lowe formed a loose band with **Ry Cooder**, Jim Keltner and **John Hiatt**, known as Little Village, whose debut album received a lukewarm response. Light years better was *The Impossible Bird* with some of his best lyrics in years notably 'Lover Don't Go' and 'Love Travels On A Gravel Road'.

Albums: *Jesus Of Cool* aka *Pure Pop For Now People* (Radar 1978), *Labour Of Lust* (Radar 1978), *Nick The Knife* (F-Beat 1982), *The Abominable Showman* (F-Beat 1983), *Nick Lowe And His Cowboy Outfit* (RCA 1984), *Rose Of England* (RCA 1985), *Pinker And Prouder Than Previous* (Demon 1988), *Party Of One* (Reprise 1990), *The Impossible Bird* (Demon 1995). Compilations: *16 All Time Lowes* (Demon 1984), *Nick's Knacks* (Demon 1986), *Basher: The Best Of Nick Lowe* (Demon 1989), *The Wilderness Years* (Demon 1991).

Film: *Americation* (1979).

Lowrell

(see **Lost Generation**)

Lowther, Henry

b. 11 July 1941, Leicester, England. As a child Lowther learned trumpet from his father and took private violin lessons before going on to study with Manoug Parakian at London's Royal Academy of Music. From the mid-60s on he worked with **Mike Westbrook**, the **New Jazz Orchestra**, **Keef Hartley**, **John Mayall**, **Manfred Mann**, **Michael Garrick**, **Norma Winstone** (in *Edge Of Time*), **John Dankworth**, **Art Themen**, **Alan Jackso**n (in the superb *Kinkade*), **Barbara Thompson** (*Jubiaba*), **John Stevens**, **Kenny Wheeler**, **Mike Gibbs**, **Tony Coe**, **John Surman**, **Gordon Beck**, **Gil Evans**, **John Taylor**, the BBC Symphony Orchestra and the London Brass Virtuosi as well as his own groups, Quarternity and Group Sounds Five. That list is in itself a testimony to his versatility and craftsmanship. As well as playing trumpet, flügelhorn, cornet and violin he has composed for jazz and orchestral groups. Influenced by sources as varied as Indian music, Karlheinz Stockhausen, **Joe 'King' Oliver**, **Weather Report** and the **Average White Band**, Lowther is still playing with as much freshness and directness as ever, touring in the early 90s with Kenny Wheeler and **Barry Guy**'s **London Jazz Composers Orchestra**.

Selected albums: with Keef Hartley *The Battle Of North West Six* (Deram 1969), *Child Song* (1970).

Lubinsky, Herman

b. 30 August 1896, USA, d. 16 March 1974. Lubinsky formed Savoy Records in 1942 in Market Street, Newark, New Jersey after running a record shop on the site for many years. He had previously been responsible for operating New Jersey's first radio station in 1924. Savoy scored a number 1 hit from its first recording session and, bolstered by this success, went on to build a peerless jazz, gospel and R&B roster in the late 40s with top-selling records by such artists as, on the jazz roster: **Charlie Parker**, **Lester Young**, **Dexter Gordon**, **Erroll Garner**, **J.J. Johnson**, **Fats Navarro**, **Miles Davis**, **Leo Parker**, **Eddie 'Lockjaw' Davis**; gospel: the Kings Of Harmony and the Deep Tones (on the King Solomon subsidiary); and R&B: Dusty Fletcher, **Paul Williams**, **Wild Bill Moore**, **Hal Singer** and **Brownie McGhee**. In 1948, Savoy opened a successful west coast office under **Ralph Bass** who continued in Savoy's excellent tradition of recording the finest R&B and bebop, having big hits with **Johnny Otis**/Little **Esther Phillips** and **Big Jay McNeely**. In the 50s, Savoy largely eschewed rock 'n' roll, concentrating on its jazz and ever-expanding gospel catalogue - the latter of which now included **Clara Ward**, the Drinkard Singers, the Davis Sisters, the Selah Jubilee Singers and, later, Alex Bradford and **Jimmy Cleveland**. This catalogue would prove to be the company's 'bread and butter' through the 60s and 70s. However, they continued to enjoy R&B success with **Nappy Brown**, Big Maybelle and **Varetta Dillard**, as well as making several brilliant territorial forays into the Atlanta and New Orleans musical communities and purchasing important smaller independents labels such as National. Lubinsky remained a strong character, fronting Savoy until just a few months before his death from cancer in March 1974. Savoy Records was purchased by **Arista** in 1975, and a large-scale reissue programme was commenced.

Lubitsch, Ernst

b. 28 January 1892, Berlin, Germany, d. 30 November 1947, Bel Air, Los Angeles, California, USA. A celebrated film director who took Hollywood by storm after moving to America in 1923. His reputation was based mainly on a series of sophisticated comedies, first with silents, and then with talkies such as *Trouble In Paradise* (1932). However, in the early 30s, he did grace several immensely successful Paramount musicals - all of which starred **Maurice Chevalier** - with his highly individual, innovative and delightfully risqué 'Lusbitsch touch'. These were ***The Love Parade***, *Paramount On Parade* (co-directed), ***Monte Carlo***, ***The Smiling Lieutenant***, ***One Hour With You***, and *The Merry Widow* (1934). For a time during the 30s Lubitsch was the director of production at Paramount, and he continued work as a director on a variety of films into the 40s. The sole musical among them was 20th Century-Fox's *That Lady In Ermine*, starring **Betty Grable**, Douglas Fairbanks Jnr., and Cesar Romero. Sadly, it had to be completed by Otto Preminger after Lubitsch's death from a heart attack in 1947. A year earlier he had received a special Academy Award for 'his distinguished contributions to the art of the motion picture'.

Lucas

b. c.1970, Copenhagen, Denmark. His mother an artist and his father a writer, Lucas moved around the world from an early age, finding his most permanent port of call in New York. There he immersed himself in the prevailing hip hop culture on the Lower East Side, rubbing shoulders with old school crews like Kid Crush as he became first a breakdancer, secondly a DJ, and finally a rapper. By 1990 he was signed to **Uptown** Records as part of **Key West**, billed as the label's 'first white artist'. When that band fell from favour Lucas worked briefly with **Chubb Rock** and **Kool Keith** (**Ultramagnetic MCs**), DJing for The Lifers Project, before leaving New York for England. His debut single for **WEA**, 'Wau Wau Wau'/'Work In Progress', revealed the experience he had gained. While the a-side was an easily likeable jazz-tinged affair, distinguished by a sample left on his answaphone by a drunken kid, the b-side cut, featuring the vocals of Fay Simpson (**Nu Colours**) and Junior Dangerous, spanned rap, soul and ragga. Lucas also became prominent in UK hip hop circles for his production skills (**Nu Colours**, **Shara Nelson**).

Albums: *Living In A Sillicone Dream* (WEA 1994), *Lucacentric* (WEA 1994).

Lucas, Carrie

b. Carmel, California, USA. This sensuous soul and disco stylist started as a backing singer with the **Whispers** and did backing vocals on record for D.J. Rogers. She also wrote songs recorded by R&B acts, the Whispers, the Soul Train Gang and South Shore Commission before joining the Soul Train label in 1976. Her first chart record and biggest hit was the disco smash 'I Gotta Keep Dancin'', released simply under the name Carrie in 1977. Two years later 'Dance With You' on **Solar**, (formerly Soul Train) also made the lower reaches of the Top 100 and gave her a UK Top 40 entry. Over the next six years she registered four US Top 200 album entries and a further five R&B chart singles. The biggest of these being her revival (with the Whispers) of **Barbara Lewis**'s 'Hello Stranger', which reached the Top 20 in 1985 on Constellation Records. Lucas, who is married to Solar Records head Dick Griffey, has now put her singing career on ice.

Albums: *Simply Carrie* (1977), *In Danceland* (1979), *Portrait Of Carrie* (1980), *Still In Love* (1982).

Lucas, Dick

Rarely gaining the recognition as an innovative, intelligent singer/songwriter with a strong social conscience that his work deserves, Lucas started his career as a teenager in anarcho-punks the **Subhumans** in the early 80s. During this initial period, it became clear that his lyrics and musical ambitions stretched beyond the usual punk rut. The 1983 mini-album, *Time Flies But Aeroplanes Crash*, included the melancholy 'Susan', a moving tale of a young girl resorting to suicide in order to escape from the restrictions of conventional life. It was something most of the Subhumans' contemporaries would never have dreamed of attempting. With his own record label - Bluurg - now established within the alternative scene, Lucas moved onto the upbeat tempo of ska, mixed with reggae references and punk politics. The vehicle for this was Culture Shock, arguably the most interesting and entertaining underground group of the late 80s, providing welcome relief from the usual uniformity and drabness of so-called 'political punk'. With Culture Shock, Lucas produced three fine albums, the best of which was undoubtedly *Onwards And Upwards*. On this excellent collection listeners were treated to lyrics on personal, emotional and socio-political subjects without ever devolving into empty rhetoric or personal deification. The stand-out tracks, 'You Are Not Alone' and 'Don't Worry About It', showed an extraordinary gift for tapping into the minds of isolated young listeners, marking Lucas as a **Morrissey** for the 'crusty' generation. Lucas decided to start the 90s with a new project, named Citizen Fish, embracing his philosophy that anarchists and libertarians are free-flowing souls trapped by the rules of civilisation. *Free Souls In A Trapped Environment* confirmed this stance, as Lucas struggled with the dilemma of expressing strong political views in an exciting way without losing the fun by being too rhetorical or burying the meaning with flippancy. A heavy dose of thrashing guitars/drums, offset by rootsy ska/dance tones proved to be the perfect solution. The lyrics, of course, were as astute as ever: 'Just to know that every up and down must balance out somehow/And there's a smile to end a conversation that was full of frowns/And here's a major chord to lift the minors up and dance around/And if the song seems far too long then tune in to another sound.' 1992's *Wider Than A Postcard* continued the social theory and skanky music, while the music press, whenever they deigned to actually write about them, compared Citizen Fish with the much-vaunted **Manic Street Preachers** - 'these are the REAL Generation Terrorists!'

Albums: Subhumans: *The Day The Country Died* (Spiderleg 1981), *Time Flies But Aeroplanes Crash* (Bluurg 1983), *From The Cradle To The Grave* (Bluurg 1984), *Worlds Apart* (Bluurg 1985), *EP-LP* (Bluurg 1986), *29:29 Split Vision* (Bluurg 1987). Culture Shock: *Go Wild!* (Bluurg 1987), *Onwards And Upwards* (Bluurg 1988), *All The Time* (Bluurg 1989). Citizen Fish: *Free Souls In A Trapped Environment* (Bluurg 1990), *Wider Than A Postcard* (Bluurg 1992).

Lucas, Nick

b. 22 August 1897, Newark, New Jersey, USA, d. 28 July 1982. Lucas was a vocalist/guitarist/banjoist whose easy-going style made him a massive record seller in the late 20s and early 30s. Initially in vaudeville, he played clubs before becoming banjoist with the Dan Russo-**Ted Fio Rito** Oriole Orchestra in the early 20s and was known as the 'Singing Troubador'. Lucas signed to **Brunswick** and had his first hit with 'My Best Girl' in 1925. This was followed by a string of best-sellers through to 1931, including 'Brown Eyes Why Are You Blue', 'I'm Looking Over A Four Leaf Clover', 'Tiptoe Through The Tulips' and 'Painting The Clouds With Sunshine'. He appeared in the Broadway musical *Showgirl* in 1929 along with **Ruby Keeler**, **Jimmy Durante** and the **Duke Ellington** Orchestra. That same year he featured in two early 'talkies' ***Gold Diggers Of Broadway*** and *Show Of Shows*. During the 30s he settled in Hollywood making movie shorts and playing clubs. In 1934, he headed a dance band for a while and by 1937 was resident on the Al Pearce radio show. He became inactive in the 50s and 60s apart from the occasional one-off show, but **Tiny Tim**'s late 60s version of 'Tiptoe Through The Tulips' rekindled interest in Lucas and in 1974 he sang on the soundtrack of the film *The Great Gatsby*.

Album: *Painting The Clouds With Sunshine* (1957). Compilation: *The Singing Troubador* (1983).

Lucas, Robert

b. 1962, Long Beach, California, USA. A 13-year-old Lucas watched **Jimi Hendrix** play 'Hear My Train A-Comin'' in the documentary about his life and asked his local record store for more acoustic blues. He was sold **Robert Johnson**'s *King Of The Delta Blues Singers* and a compilation of **Leroy Carr/Scrapper Blackwell** recordings. His hands were too small to properly learn the guitar, so he took up the harmonica instead. But by the age of 20, he was playing harmonica and guitar with the Bernie Pearl Blues Band behind such bluesmen as **Big Joe Turner**, **George Smith**, **Lowell Fulson**, **Pee Wee Crayton** and **Percy Mayfield**. In 1983 he joined the Confessors, an R&B band with whom he stayed for three years. He then formed his own band, Luke And The Locomotives, but also performed solo gigs at which he demonstrated a comprehensive slide guitar technique. His first solo release in 1989 was a self-produced cassette on Delta Man Music, *Across The River*, which was followed a year later by the first of a series of albums on Audioquest which combined solo and small group recordings. *Luke And The Locomotives* dispensed with acoustic playing and featured amplified blues. Having dispensed with the band, Lucas has returned to playing solo. On *Layaway* he further expanded his musical horizons by featuring keyboards and a horn section.

Albums: *Usin' Man Blues* (Audioquest 1990), *Luke And The Locomotives* (Audioquest 1991), *Built For Comfort* (Audioquest 1992), *Across The River* (Delta Man Music 1993), *Dodgin' The Dirt* (Roadrunner 1993), *Layaway* (Audioquest 1994).

Lucas, Trevor

b. 25 December 1943, Bungaree, Victoria, Australia, d. 4 February 1989. Lucas began as a singer-songwriter, performing contemporary folk songs, in the cafes and clubs of Melbourne, Australia. He recorded one obscure album before moving to the UK in 1964, where he established himself on the folk circuit, as a duo with fellow Australian Kerilee Male. They formed one of the first electric folk groups, **Eclection**, in 1967 and later formed **Fotheringay** with **Sandy Denny**,

who he married. Lucas then became a producer at **Island Records** for 18 months until he joined **Fairport Convention** in 1972. He left the band in early 1976 to take up production work again. He returned to Australia in 1978, after Sandy Denny's death. His time fully engaged in the production of such bands as **Paul Kelly**, **Bushwackers**, **Goanna**, and **Redgum**, plus film documentaries and children's dramas. He died in Sydney, Australia of a suspected heart attack.
Albums: *See That My Grave Is Kept Clean* (mid-60s), *Overlander* (1966).

Lucas, William 'Lazy Bill'

b. 29 May 1918, Wynne, Arkansas, USA. Bill Lucas's first instrument was a guitar, financed by selling a pig, but he really wanted a piano. Living on a farm with five siblings it seemed like a dream when his father actually bought him one in 1932. However, when the family moved to Cape Girardeau, Missouri, the piano was left behind. Lazy Bill had no real contact with the blues until he met **Big Joe Williams** in St. Louis in 1940. Converted, he moved to Chicago in 1941 and turned back to the piano after playing guitar in support of many of the famous artists of the day. He was one of Little Hudson's Red Devils and recorded with his own Blue Rhythms for the Chance label in 1954. Experiencing difficulties, due, in part to the nervous condition that had rendered him almost blind since childhood, he moved to Minneapolis, Minnesota, in 1964 where he continued to play, appearing at festivals and recording for his own Lazy label in 1970 and later for the Philo label.
Albums: *The News About The Blues* (Wild 1970), *Lazy Bill And His Friends* (Lazy 1971), *Lazy Bill Lucas* (Philo 1974).

Lucca, Papo (and Sonora Ponceña)

b. Enrique Arsenio Lucca Jnr., 1946, Ponce, Puerto Rico. A remarkable pianist (he also plays percussion, vibes, tres, synthesizer and flugelhorn), gifted soloist and innovative arranger, Lucca is musical director, arranger and producer of Puerto Rico's oldest active band, Sonora Ponceña. In 1944, his father, Enrique 'Quique' Lucca, founded the two trumpet, rhythm section and voices band, Orquesta Internacional, which was entirely composed of musicians from Ponce. They specialized in the typical Cuban song-and-dance form called son, and Quique played guitar with the band. Out of deference to the internationally famous Cuban band, Sonora Matancera, they were renamed Sonora Ponceña (Son Orchestra of Ponce) for their 1954 recording debut. A third trumpet was added to their line-up during the 50s, and in the 60s they had a four-trumpet front-line. Papo was a child musical prodigy. He started playing congas at the age of four. When he was six years old he began formal musical education at the Free School of Music in Ponce, run by the famous Puerto Rican music teacher Don Julio Alvarado. Lucca commenced intensive piano, clarinet, saxophone and theoretical tuition, and within his first month, he performed a classical piece on the local radio station. Attending the school at the same time were singer **Héctor Lavoe** and trumpeter/arranger José Febles.
Lucca first performed with Sonora Ponceña at the age of eight. In the mid-50s, he played solo piano on the television show of Ruth Fernández (b. Ponce, Puerto Rico). Ruth was blessed with a rich golden voice and recorded with Obdulio Morales, Orquesta Panamericana and **Machito**. Lucca made his recording debut at the age of 11 when the band accompanied bolero singers, Felipe Rodríguez and Davilita (Pedro Ortiz Dávila) on *Al Compás de Las Sonoras*, released on the Marvela label. His first arrangement for the band was transcribed from the record of **Tito Puente**'s hit 'Caramelos' (contained on *Pachanga Con Puente*). Papo graduated from the University of Puerto Rico and studied at Puerto Rico's Conservatory of Music. Sonora Ponceña recorded for the Marvela and Inca labels. They remained with the latter into the 90s. The band's career really took off after Inca was sold to Jerry Masucci, co-founder (with **Johnny Pacheco**) of the Fania Records label. Masucci did a great deal to promote them, and Latin music in general. They became especially popular with the Latino audience in New York. Success boosted their confidence and inspired others, demonstrating that it was possible to make a living from the music.
In the late 60s, Sonora Ponceña had big hits with interpretations of a couple of **Arsenio Rodríguez** classics: 'Hachero Pa' Un Palo' and 'Fuego En El 23'. The original recordings are still available on the 1975 compilation *Lo Mejor De Sonora Ponceña*. Bandleader/pianist **Larry Harlow** produced the band's albums between 1972 and 1975. Ponceña had returned to a three-trumpet section, comprised of José A. (Joe) Rodríguez, Ramón A. (Tony) Rodríguez and Delfin 'El del Café' Pérez , for *Desde Puerto Rico a Nueva York* (*From Puerto Rico To New York*) in 1972. Lead vocals were provided by the raw and earthy voice of Luis Guillermo 'Luigui' Texidor (b. 1940, Puerto Rico; joined Ponceña in the mid-60s), and Humberto Luis 'Tito' Gómez (b. 1948, Juana Díaz, Puerto Rico; joined Ponceña in 1968), the latter whose voice has a haunting, melancholic timbre. Both singers were ex-members of Conjunto Antoanetti.
Trumpeter Joe Rodríguez left to lead La Terrifica, taking Tito Gómez and percussionist Miguel 'Mikey' Ortiz with him. They debuted on the Larry Harlow produced *Terrifica* in 1974. Gómez split from La Terrifica, did a brief stint with **Ray Barretto** and recorded as a solo artist, ie. *Para Gozar Borinquen* (1977), produced by Harlow. Miguel A. Ortiz 'Miguelito', who possesses a high-pitched voice, filled Gómez's vacancy on Ponceña's 1974 release *Sabor Sureño*. Conga player

Vicente Rivero 'Little Johnny' joined the band on 1975's *Tiene Pimienta.* In 1976, Lucca made his debut as producer, in association with **Louie Ramírez**, on *Musical Conquest/Conquista Musical.* The album contained the smash hit 'El Pio Pio', composed by the Mexican duo Lobo y Melón (Angel Luis Silva). That year, Lucca and Texidor participated in the first Puerto Rico All Stars album. In 1977, Papo assisted Ramírez with the production of *El Gigante Del Sur.* The hit track 'Boranda', was about Puerto Rico's then frequent droughts, and commented on the migration of the country people (jibaros) and abandonment of the land. Yolanda Rivera joined Ponceña as a third lead vocalist on this album; formerly a member of La Terrifica, she had appeared on their *Sabor A Pueblo* in 1976. Texidor left to join **Bobby Valentín** on his *Musical Seduction* (1978), on which he sang the hit 'Naci Moreno' (Born Brown), an affirmation of the racial mixture that is Puerto Rico's identity. Texidor later recorded as a solo artist and with Tito Puente and El Combo Del Ayer. He has now retired from the business.

Although intimated on earlier albums, Ponceña's present bright, mellow, laid-back, yet relentlessly swinging style noticeably started to coalesce on *Explorando* in 1978. A further trumpet was added, and with his arranger's pen, Lucca began developing a unique, well-blended four-trumpet sound of elaborate, interweaving lines. Lucca told UK salsa broadcaster Tomek, in May 1991, that he had got the idea for four trumpets from Conjunto Casino, a popular Cuban band of the 40s and 50s. 'I'm honest', he said.

Lucca was the sole producer on *Explorando* and all Ponceña's subsequent recordings. Tito Gómez returned to fill Texidor's vacated slot and sang lead on the hit track 'Moreno Soy' (I Am Brown), which was Lucca's arrangement of 'Naci Moreno'. Gómez sang in the chorus on *La Orquesta De Mi Tierra* in 1978, before leaving to work with Tito Valentín, La Amistad (see **Nati**) and Grupo Niche. In 1979, Sonora Ponceña teamed up with **Celia Cruz** for *La Ceiba.* That year, Jeremy Marre's television film *Salsa,* featured a tantalizing glimpse of the band backing Celia, with Yolanda Rivera in the chorus. Also in 1979, Texidor and Lucca reunited in the context of the Fania All Stars to perform a 'live' version of 'Naci Moreno' on *Habana Jam*, recorded in Cuba. In 1980, Alberto Antonio Ledeé 'Toñito' (b. Salinas, Puerto Rico) joined Yolanda and Miguelito as a third lead singer on Ponceña's *New Heights.* Their second release in 1980, *Unchained Force,* was dedicated to longstanding members Tony 'El Cordobes' Rodríguez, Delfin Pérez and bassist Antonio Santaella (Tato).

Lucca is a great admirer of his Cuban contemporary, composer/bandleader/pianist **Adalberto Alvarez**. Lucca and Sonora Ponceña recorded interpretations of Alvarez's compositions on six out of seven of their albums between 1981 and 1990.

Yolanda departed after 1982's *Determination* and relocated to Miami, USA, where she sang coro (chorus) with **Gabino Pampini** and Fuerza Noble. She sang lead vocals with bandleader/trombonist Rubby Haddock, on *Otra Vez!* (1988) and *Salsa Tropical* (1990), and also performed as a solo artist in 1990 with the Hermanos Rivera Orchestra. Her vacancy was filled by another ex-La Terrifica member, Héctor 'Pichy' Pérez, on *Future* in 1984. Yet another former La Terrifica member, Manuel Martínez Roldan 'Mannix', replaced Miguelito Ortiz on Ponceña's 30th anniversary release *Jubilee*, which contained an updated version of their 60s hit 'Fuego En El 23'. 1988's *On The Right Track* contained a tribute poem and song to Toñito Ledeé, a devoted family man, who was tragically killed in a car crash on 28 May 1986. After a 15-year tenure, conguero Johnny Rivero walked out on Ponceña following a row with Quique, while the band were at the airport waiting for a flight to Tenerife in 1990 - something he apparently later regretted. Lucca and the band made a foray into salsa romántica territory on *Into The 90's.* He has described the popular style as 'salsa monga' - a term coined by **Willie Rosario** - which politely translates as 'flaccid salsa'. The album was partly recorded in their own Pianissimo Studios in Ponce. In 1990, Pichy Pérez left to join **Tommy Olivencia**'s band. He was replaced by Luisito Carrión, who worked previously with Julio 'Gunda' Merced's Salsa Fever, La Terrifica, Bobby Valentín and Don Perignon. In 1976, Lucca replaced Larry Harlow as the pianist with the Fania All Stars and made his UK debut with them the same year. He continued to gig and record with them into the 90s. Lucca and Sonora Ponceña made their UK debut in May 1991 with an outstanding concert at London's Empire Ballroom.

Selected albums by Sonora Ponceña, unless otherwise stated: *Hachero Pa' Un Palo* (c.1968), *Fuego En El 23* (c.1969), *Algo De Locura* (c.1970), *Navidad Criolla* (c. 1971, reissued 1978), *Desde Puerto Rico a Nueva York* (1972), *Sonora Ponceña* (1972), *Sabor Sureño* (1974), *Tiene Pimienta* (1975), *Musical Conquest/Conquista Musical* (1976), with Celia Cruz, Johnny Pacheco, Justo Betancourt and Papo *Recordando El Ayer* (1976), *El Gigante Del Sur* (1977), *Explorando* (1978), *La Orquesta De Mi Tierra* (1978), Ponceña with Celia Cruz *La Ceiba* (1979), *New Heights* (1980), *Unchained Force* (1980), *Night Raider* (1981), *Determination* (1982), with Ismael Quintana and Papo *Mucho Talento* (1983), *Future* (1984), *Jubilee* (1985), *Back To Work* (1987), *On The Right Track* (1988), *Into The 90's* (1990). Compilations: *Lo Mejor De Sonora Ponceña* (1975), *Energized* (1979).

Luciano

b. Jepther McClymont, Davey Town, Jamaica, West Indies. Luciano was one of the most promising new singer/songwriters to emerge in 1993. He began

singing in his local parish church before assuming the name of Stepper John and migrating to Kingston in April 1992. There he voiced his debut tune for **Herman Chin-Loy** at Aquarius, then half an album with Pressley for Mau Mau producer Sky High. Homer Harris of Blue Mountain had by now changed McClymont's name to Luciano. His first Jamaican hit, 'Give My Love A Try', was for Castro Brown and a clutch of ballads and self-penned reality songs soon followed, initially for Brown's New Name label. **Phillip 'Fatis' Burrell** produced his first two UK hits, 'Chant Out' and 'Poor And Simple', in the summer of 1993 on **Exterminator**, and was later to release his debut solo album *Moving Up*. Singles for Exterminator, Blacka Dread ('Time Is The Master') and **Sly And Robbie**'s Taxi label helped establish Luciano's fast-growing reputation before he joined **Freddie McGregor**'s Big Ship organisation, 'Shake It Up Tonight' becoming his first UK reggae number 1 and leading to a well-received album of the same name.
Selected albums: *Moving Up* (RAS/Exterminator 1993), *Shake It Up Tonight* (Big Ship 1993), with Pressley *Meets Pressley* (Sky High 1993), *Moving Up* (Xterminator 1994).

Lucky People Center

Swedish dance exponents whose samples on their debut album built on the best traditions of **Test Department** by using speeches from world leaders, in this case marrying George Bush and Saddam Hussein to a backbeat on 'It's Still Cloudy In Saudi Arabia'. The group were formed in 1992 by Johan Söderburg (percussion), Lars Åkerlund (samples) and Sebastian Öberg (electric cello). The relentless barrage of samples (Rodney King, Bishop Desmond Tutu, the lawyer of massacre-priest Jim Jones) were adopted in a vein more prevalent within hip-hop than the dance scene, though Lucky People Center are firmly placed in the latter tradition by their cutting rhythms.
Album: *Welcome To Lucky People* (MNW 1993).

Ludus

Founded in 1978, this Manchester, England-based quartet was consistently fronted by the enigmatic lyricist/vocalist Linder (b. Linda Mulvey, 1954, Liverpool, England). The backing was provided by Arthur Cadmon (b. Peter Sadler, Stockport, England), formerly of Manicured Noise and originally the musical genius behind the group. The line-up was completed by bassist Willie Trotter (b. 1959, Manchester, England) and drummer Phil 'Toby' Tolman (ex-Ed Banger And The Nosebleeds). With their jazz-influenced forays and Linder's strong, sloganeering, elliptical feminist lyrics, the group were one of the most interesting of the Manchester new wave of the late 70s. The departure of Cadmon and later Trotter, replaced by Ian Devine (Ian Pincombe), saw the group change direction, though the jazz influence remained. Linder, a former girlfriend of the **Buzzcocks**' **Howard Devoto**, later became a well-publicized confidante of **Morrissey**. In spite of some inspired moments with Ludus, the group almost wilfully avoided the mainstream. As manager Richard Boon concluded: 'Ludus were totally improvisational and their set list would read: bass, drums, voice, next number. There was something self-limiting about Linder. Any time she seemed on the brink of a breakthrough, even if that meant selling 50 extra records, she would retreat, just like the poet Stevie Smith'. Ian Devine teamed-up in 1989 with ex-**Weekend** singer, Alison Statton, to form **Devine And Statton**.
Albums: *Pickpocket* (New Hormones 1981).

Lukather, Steve

b. USA. Perhaps best known for his accomplished guitar work with AOR supremos, **Toto**, Lukather started out as a session player. Indeed, the first Toto album was originally intended to be a one-off project and brought together the talents of some of the most notable Californian session musicians. Such was the success of the project that the arrangement soon became permanent and Toto went on to record many albums. Later albums saw varying musical styles and fluctuating commercial success. In 1989, Lukather released his first solo album. The album saw him joined by a whole host of guest players including fellow guitar maestros **Eddie Van Halen** and Steve Stevens, **Richard Marx** on vocals and **Jan Hammer** on keyboards. Lukather's recent live work with Toto has seen them once again adopt a heavier musical stance.
Albums: *Lukather* (1989), *Candyman* (Columbia 1994).

Luke, Robin

b. 20 March 1942, Los Angeles, California, USA. Luke was a rockabilly-style singer who scored with one Top 5 hit, 'Susie Darlin'', in 1958. His family moved often, and in 1953 settled in Hawaii, where he learned to play guitar and ukulele. He was discovered by entertainer Kimo McVay, who introduced him to Bob Bertram, who recorded Luke in his own Bertram International studio. The simplistic 'Susie Darlin'', named after Luke's younger sister, was recorded using a great deal of echo, with Bertram singing behind him and percussion created by simply banging two pens on a box. (Bertram later reported that some 75 takes of the song were recorded.) The single was issued on the Bertram International label and became a local favourite. It was then picked up by the larger **Dot Records** and began its 1958 ascent to number 5. (A few other singles were issued on Bertram while the Dot contract was already in effect.) In 1959, Luke moved to California and continued to record, now backed by top session musicians such as **Glen Campbell** and **Barney Kessel**. Luke remained with Dot until 1962, but never had another hit, possibly because the more

elaborate productions lacked the charm of the minimal Bertram record. In the early 60s, Luke moved to Missouri to complete his education and he then became a teacher in that State's university system. His only recording after leaving Dot was a remake of 'Susie Darlin" for **K-Tel Records** in the 70s.
Album: *Susie Darlin'* (1958). Compilation: *Susie Darlin'* (1991).

Lulu

b. Marie MacDonald McLaughlin Lawrie, 3 November 1948, Lennox Castle, Glasgow, Scotland. Lulu was originally a beat group vocalist with her own backing group the Luvvers, who comprised, Ross Nelson (guitar), Jim Dewar (rhythm guitar), Alec Bell (keyboards), Jimmy Smith (saxophone), Tony Tierney (bass) and David Miller (drums). The 15-year-old singer first came to prominence with a rasping version of the **Isley Brother**s' 'Shout' in 1964. Under the tutelage of manager Marian Massey she survived a stormy couple of years during which only two of her eight singles charted. Abandoning the Luvvers along the way, she switched record labels from **Decca** to **EMI**/Columbia Records and found a new hitmaker in the form of **Mickie Most**. A cover of **Neil Diamond**'s 'The Boat That I Row' saw an upsurge in her career during 1967, which was punctuated by an acting part in the movie *To Sir With Love.* The theme tune from the film gave her a million-selling US number 1, and in the UK it reached number 6, despite being relegated to b-side of the inferior 'Let's Pretend'. Further UK hits followed, notably 'Me, The Peaceful Heart', 'Boy' and 'I'm A Tiger'. Having established herself as an entertainer of wide appeal, Lulu was granted her own television series and later represented Britain in the Eurovision Song Contest. The painfully trite 'Boom-Bang-A-Bang' tied for first place and provided her highest UK chart placing at number 2. Her brief marriage to Maurice Gibb of the **Bee Gees** was followed by another switch of labels and musical styles when she worked with famed producer **Jerry Wexler** on two albums. A lean period of flop singles ended when **David Bowie** intervened to produce and arrange her hit version of 'The Man Who Sold The World'. During the 70s, she concentrated increasingly on stage work and developed her career as an all-round entertainer, a spin-off which was becoming the long-standing model/endorser for the Freeman's mail-order catalogue. Appearances in *Guys And Dolls, Song And Dance* and the television programme, *The Secret Diary Of Adrian Mole* distracted her from the studio but a disco re-recording of 'Shout', in 1986, repeated the Top 10 success of 22 years before. In 1993, Lulu released *Independence*, an album of 'modern disco-pop with a flavour of classic soul and R&B'. Co-produced by **Bobby Womack** and Londonbeat, the title track registered strongly in the UK and US charts, and was followed by another single, 'I'm Back For More', on which Lulu duetted with Womack. She was, by then, creating some of her own material, and one of her songs, 'I Don't Wanna Fight Any More', written with her brother, Billy Laurie, was recorded by Tina Turner.
Albums: *Something To Shout About* (Decca 1965), *Love Loves To Love Lulu* (Columbia 1967), *Lulu's Album* (Columbia 1969), *New Routes* (Atco 1970), *Melody Fair* (Atco 1971), *Don't Take Love For Granted* (Rocket 1979), *Lulu* (Alfa 1981), *Take Me To Your Heart Again* (Alfa 1982), *Shape Up And Dance With Lulu* (Life Style 1984), *The Man Who Sold The World* (Start 1989), *Independence* (Dome 1993). Compilations: *The World Of Lulu* (Decca 1969), *The World Of Lulu Vol 2* (Decca 1970), *The Most Of Lulu* (MFP 1971), *The Most Of Lulu Vol 2* (MFP 1972), *The Very Best Of Lulu* (Warwick 1980), *Shout* (MFP 1983), *I'm A Tiger* (MFP 1989)
Film: *Gonks Go Beat* (1965).

Lulu Belle And Scotty

Lulu Belle (b. Myrtle Eleanor Cooper, 24 December 1913, Boone, North Carolina, USA) and Scott Wiseman (b. 8 November 1909, Spruce Pine, near Ingalls, North Carolina, USA, d. 31 January 1981). Lulu Belle learned to play the guitar and sing mountain songs as a child but after the family relocated to Evanston, Illinois in 1929, she first worked as a clerk. In 1932, she successfully auditioned at WLS television company Chicago and was given a spot on the *National Barn Dance* programme, where as Lulu Belle, she initially worked with **Red Foley**. Wiseman grew up on the family farm and developed his first musical skills by learning to play a home-made banjo. He became interested in a musical career after seeing **Bradley Kincaid** perform and by working in his school holidays, he bought himself a guitar. In 1927, he made his radio debut, singing and playing in a manner that showed a distinct Kincaid influence, on WRVA Richmond. Initially doubtful that he could make his living by music, he decided to study for a teaching career. From 1929-32, he attended the Teachers College at Fairmont, West Virginia and obtained a degree. During these years, he wrote songs and, appearing as Skyland Scotty, was regularly featured on WMMN Fairmont. In 1933, he joined the *National Barn Dance*, where he began to work with Lulu Belle. He made his first recordings (solo) in December 1933, when playing his guitar for one of the few times on record, he cut four songs for **RCA**-Victor. One of the songs was 'Home Coming Time In Happy Valley', which soon became a popular song for the duo. They were married on 13 December 1934, by which time they had become a very popular act. On stage, Scotty wore plain, casual attire and played banjo, while Lulu Belle dressed in old gingham styled dresses, pantalettes and usually wore pigtails. Their simple harmony singing, interspersed with comedy and novelty songs, endeared them to the network audience and gained them the nickname of the Sweethearts of Country Music.

In 1936, Lulu Belle was voted the most popular woman on American radio and between 1938 and 1944, their national popularity saw them appear in seven films including *Shine On Harvest Moon.* They remained stars of the WLS *National Barn Dance* from 1933-58 but also had a spell on the *Boone County Jamboree* (later the *Midwestern Hayride*) on WLW Cincinnati as well as playing on the *Grand Ole Opry* and the *Ozark Jubilee.* They were also regulars on WNNBQ-TV Chicago from 1949-57. Over the years, they recorded for various labels including Conqueror, Vocalion, and Bluebird. They popularized many songs including 'Mountain Dew' (written by Scotty with Bascombe Lunsford), 'Remember Me', 'My Heart Cries For You', 'Tying The Leaves' and 'Does Your Spearmint Lose Its Flavour On The Bed Post Overnight?'. (A UK pop hit for **Lonnie Donegan** with 'Chewing Gum' substituted for 'Spearmint' in 1959.) Perhaps their best-known song is one that originated at a time when Scotty was hospitalized with appendix trouble. During a visit Lulu Belle said 'Have I told you lately that I love you' and it inspired him to write a song. **Gene Autry** recorded it in November 1945 and in 1946, it was a Top 5 US country hit for Autry, **Tex Ritter**, **Red Foley** and Foy Willing. It went on to become a country standard and has been recorded over the years by many artists, including **Bing Crosby** with the **Andrews Sisters**, **Jim Reeves**, **Van Morrison** and **Elvis Presley**. In 1958, after Scotty had obtained an MA Teaching degree at Northwestern University at Evanston, they semi-retired from the entertainment business. They moved back to Spruce Pine, where Scotty taught people with speech problems at the college. They also bought a cattle farm but still made a few concert appearances and recorded for the Starday label in the 60s. At one time, they presented their *Breakfast In The Blue Ridge* radio show, supposedly live from their home but, in reality, taped in Chicago. They appeared at the 1975 *Fan Fair* in Nashville and on the *Opry* but generally, during the 70s, Scotty continued to teach and they restricted themselves to local appearances. In 1971, his many songs saw him elected to the Nashville Songwriters International Hall of Fame. Lulu Belle became interested in politics and in 1974, she was elected to the North Carolina House of Representatives. Scotty died following a heart attack, when driving home from Gainsville, Florida. Lulu Belle remarried in 1983 (Ernest Stamey, an old family friend) and in 1986, she recorded a solo album for the Old Homestead label.

Albums: *Lulu Belle & Scotty* (1963), *The Sweethearts Of Country Music* (1963), *Down Memory Lane* (1964), *Lulu Belle & Scotty (Sweethearts Still)* (1965), *Just A Closer Walk With Thee* (60s), *Have I Told You Lately That I Love You* (1974), *Early And Great Volume 1* (1985), *Country & Western Memories, Volume 3 Lulu Belle & Scotty* (c.1986), *Tender Memories Recalled Volumes 1 & 2* (1989), *Tender Memories Recalled Volumes 2 & 3* (1991). Solo: Lulu Belle *Snickers & Tender Memories* (1986).

Luman, Bob

b. Robert Glynn Luman, 15 April 1937, Blackjack, near Nacogdoches, Texas, USA, d. 27 December 1978. Luman's father, Joe, a school caretaker, bus driver and gifted musician, taught his son country music, but Luman's first love was baseball, which he played on a semi-professional basis until 1959. He was influenced by seeing **Elvis Presley** in concert, later saying, 'That was the last time I tried to sing like **Webb Pierce** or **Lefty Frizzell**'. His band then won a talent contest sponsored by the Texas Future Farmers of America and judged by **Johnny Horton**. In 1955, Luman recorded the original version of 'Red Cadillac And A Black Moustache' and also a scorching 'Red Hot' for **Imperial Records**. He joined *Louisiana Hayride* as replacement for **Johnny Cash** and came into contact with guitarist **James Burton** and bass player James Kirkland, whom he recruited for his band. Unfortunately for Luman, **Ricky Nelson** was so impressed by Luman's musicians that he made them a better offer. After a brief, unsuccessful period with **Capitol Records**, Luman moved to **Warner Brothers**, who released 'Class Of '59' and 'Dreamy Doll', both featuring **Roy Buchanan**. He had a transatlantic hit with **Boudleaux Bryant**'s satire on 'death discs' like 'El Paso' and 'One Of Us (Will Weep Tonight)' in 'Let's Think About Living'. 'If we keep losing our singers like this,' he concluded, 'I'll be the only one you can buy.' He failed to repeat his success, despite such clever novelties as 'The Great Snowman' and 'Private Eye'. After spending part of the early 60s in the army due to the draft laws, he became a member of the *Grand Ole Opry* in 1964 and made many country records for the Hickory label, including **John D. Loudermilk**'s witty 'The File'. He became a big-selling US country artist via his Epic recordings, 'When You Say Love', 'Lonely Women Make Good Lovers' and 'Neither One Of Us Wants To Be The First To Say Goodbye', subsequently a pop hit for **Gladys Knight And The Pips**. In 1976, he underwent major surgery and then, prompted and produced by Johnny Cash, he recorded *Alive And Well.* Despite the title, he collapsed and died shortly after an appearance at the *Grand Ole Opry*. In recent years, Luman's work has been reassessed with retrospectives and, like **Johnny Burnette**, it is his early, rockabilly work that most interests collectors. To quote one of his country hits, 'Good Things Stem From Rock 'n' Roll.'

Albums: *Let's Think About Living* (1960), *Livin' Lovin' Sounds* (1965), *Ain't Got Time* (1968), *Come On Home And*

Sing The Blues To Daddy (1969), *Getting Back To Norman* (1970), *Is It Any Wonder That I Love You?* (1971), *A Chain Don't Talk To Me* (1971), *When You Say Love* (1972), *Lonely Women Make Good Lovers* (1972), *Neither One Of Us* (1973), *Red Cadillac And A Black Moustache* (1974), *Still Loving You* (1974), *A Satisfied Mind* (1976), *Alive And Well* (1977), *Bob Luman* (1978), *The Pay Phone* (1978), *Try Me* (1988). Compilations: *The Rocker* (1984), *More Of That Rocker* (1984), *Still Rockin'* (1984), *Carnival Rock* (1988), *Wild-Eyed Woman* (1988).
Film: *Carnival Rock* (1957).

Lunachicks

Legend has it that New York's Lunachicks were rescued from a life of streetgangs, drinking, idolatry and terrorism against humanity by being discovered by **Sonic Youth**, who recommended the all-female band to Blast First Records so vociferously that the Lunachicks' debut, *Babysitters On Acid*, was barely recorded before it was let loose upon an unsuspecting public. The 'not-at-all-nice-girls' turned their rebellious behaviour into a stage act. Becky (drums), Squid Sid (bass), Gina (lead guitar) and Sindi (guitar) were the musicians with a taste for excessive volume. Theo was the singer with a prediliction for blood-splattered wedding gowns. The Lunachicks can only be described as 'different'.
Albums: *Babysitters On Acid* (Blast First 1990), *Binge Purge* (Blast First 1993), *Jerk Of All Trades* (Go Kart 1995).

Lunceford, Jimmie

b. 6 June 1902, Fulton, Mississippi, USA, d. 12 July 1947. At school in Denver, Colorado, Lunceford studied under Wilberforce Whiteman, father of **Paul Whiteman**. He later read for a degree in music at Fisk University, where his studies included composition, orchestration and musical theory and he also developed his precocious ability as a performer on many instruments although he preferred alto saxophone. After leaving Fisk, he worked briefly in New York in bands led by **Elmer Snowden** and others before taking up a teaching post at Manassas High School in Memphis, Tennessee. He formed a band at the school which included Moses Allen (bass) and **Jimmy Crawford** (drums). Later, **Willie Smith** and pianist Eddie Wilcox were added before Lunceford took the band on tour. They became very popular and after several such tours Lunceford decided in 1929 to make the band his full-time activity. For the next few years, with the same nucleus of musicians, he toured and broadcast throughout the mid-west. In 1933, the band reached New York and quickly established a reputation. More broadcasts, national tours and, eventually, some successful records made Lunceford's one of the most popular black bands of the swing era. The band's arrangers were originally Wilcox and Smith but later additions were **Eddie Durham** and **Sy Oliver**. It was the arrival of Oliver that set the seal on Lunceford's greatest period. Thanks to excellent charts, brilliantly performed by a meticulously rehearsed reed section (credit due largely to Smith), biting brass and a powerful rhythm section sparked by Crawford, the band became one of the best of the period. In addition to the band's sound they also looked good on stage. The Lunceford band was chiefly responsible for the showmanship which crept into many subsequent big band performances, but although many copied, none ever equalled the *élan* of Lunceford's band, especially the members of the trumpet section who would toss their horns high into the air, catching them on the beat. Apart from Smith, the band had good soloists in tenor saxophonist **Joe Thomas** and trombonist **Trummy Young** who gave the band a hit recording with his own composition, 'Tain't What You Do (It's The Way That You Do It'. Oliver's departure in mid-summer 1939 to join **Tommy Dorsey** was a blow but the band continued to use his arrangements. How long this state of affairs could have continued is debatable because the band's days were numbered. Lunceford's personal behaviour was distressing many of his long-serving sidemen. Their dismay at the manner in which he spent money (on buying airplanes for example), while refusing to meet what they saw as reasonable pay demands led, in 1942, to a mass walk-out. The band continued with replacements but the flair and excitement had gone. Although recordings over the next few years show a new promise any further improvement was forestalled when Lunceford died suddenly in July 1947. Although often overlooked in surveys of swing era big bands, during its glory days Lunceford's was one of the best in its precision playing of superbly professional arrangements, it had no betters and very few equals.
Selected compilations: *Jimmie Lunceford And Louis Prima 1945* (1979), *The Golden Swing Years* (1981), *Jimmie Lunceford (1935-41)* (1982), *Strictly Lunceford* (Jasmine 1983), *The Complete Jimmie Lunceford (1935-41)* (Jasmine 1986), *Oh Boy* (Happy Days 1987), *Runnin' A Temperature* (Affinity 1986), *Oh Boy!* (1987), *Stomp It Off Vol 1 1934-1935* (Decca 1992), *Jimmie Lunceford And His Orchestra Vol. 1 1934 - 1939* (Black And Blue 1993), *For Dancers Only* (Charly 1993).

Lunch, Lydia

b. Lydia Koch, 1959, Rochester, New York, USA. The provocative Lydia Lunch was a pivotal figure in New York's 'no wave' scene of the late 70s and has worked with an array of talent since then. After spells with **Teenage Jesus And The Jerks** and Beirut Slump (the latter were restricted to one US single, 'Try Me'), Lydia Lunch opted for the freedom of solo work with 1980's acclaimed *Queen Of Siam* on the Ze label. Her next project, Eight-Eyed Spy, toyed with funk and R&B while retaining her uncompromising vocal style and violent, experimental musical approach. Then came *13:13* on the Ruby label, which benefited from a harder, more co-ordinated feel. In 1982 she shared a 12-inch EP with the **Birthday Party** on **4AD Records**, *The Agony Is The Ecstacy*, revealing her increasing fascination with the baser instincts of human nature. Members of the Birthday Party also backed Lydia on 'Some Velvet Morning', while **Einsturzende Neubauten** joined her for 'Thirsty'. This marriage of the New York and Berlin undergrounds was further demonstrated on 'Der Karibische Western', on Zensor with Die Haut. Lunch continued this collaborative stance in 1983, working with Danish band Sort Sol. 1984's *In Limbo*, a mini-album for **Cabaret Voltaire**'s Doublevision label, re-introduced her to solo work, and she soon founded Widowspeak Productions in 1985 as an outlet to document her work, starting appropriately with the *Uncensored Lydia Lunch* cassette. After a project with Michael Gira, entitled *Hard Rock* (a cassette on Ecstatic Peace), Lydia homed in on New York pranksters **Sonic Youth** for 'Death Valley '69', a menacing start for Blast First Records in the UK. A sinister solo offering, *The Drowning Of Lady Hamilton*, was followed by a 10-inch EP recorded with No Trend, entitled *Heart Of Darkness* (1985). The next release for Widowspeak was a limited edition box, *The Intimate Diaries Of The Sexually Insane*, containing a cassette of chronic case histories, a booklet and a book, *Adulterers Anonymous*, co-written by Lydia. 1987's remixed and remastered double album retrospective, *Hysterie*, summarized her work from 1976-86, before she paired with the man behind **Foetus** and Clint Ruin, Jim Thirlwell, for the awesome Stinkfist project in 1989. That year also witnessed Harry Crews, an all-female wall of guitar sound for which Lunch was joined by Sonic Youth bassist, Kim Gordon. 1993 was spent working on a film script, *Psychomenstruum*. Lunch, in conjunction with her soul-mate Thirlwell, has also become known as an avid opponent of censorship. Her own work is uncompromisingly confrontational and lurid, including videos featuring highly explicit sexual activity. The politics of outrage remain her gospel.

Albums: *Queen Of Siam* (Ze 1980), *13:13* (Ruby 1982), *In Limbo* (Doublevision 1984), *Uncensored Lydia Lunch* (Widowspeak 1985), *The Drowning Of Lady Hamilton* (Widowspeak 1985), *Honeymoon In Red* (Widowspeak 1988), *Oral Fixation* (Widowspeak 1989), with Rowland S. Howard *Shotgun Wedding* (UFO 1991). Compilations: *Hysterie (1976-1986)* (Widowspeak 1989), *Crimes Against Nature* (Triple X, 3-CD set).

Further reading: *Incriminating Evidence (Last Gasp)*, Lydia Lunch.

Video: *Lydia Lunch: The Gun Is Loaded* (1993).

Lundberg, Victor

b. 1923, Grand Rapids, Michigan, USA. Victor Lundberg provided the inevitable response to the protest recordings of the mid-60s, 'An Open Letter To My Teenage Son'. Lundberg was a former news reporter and radio announcer who owned a company which created radio and television commercials when, in 1967, he sought to address the current 'generation gap' with his patriotic spoken-word 'letter' addressing the youth of America on how to 'straighten up and fly right'. Whether his words of advice were observed by the kids or their parents, enough copies of the single, on **Liberty Records**, sold to push it into the US Top 10. Lundberg attempted other similar recordings but was unable to repeat his initial success.

Album: *Open Letter To My Teenage Son* (1967).

Lunn, Robert

b. Robert Rainey Lunn, 28 November 1912, Franklin, Tennessee, USA, d. 1966. Little is known of his early life probably owing to the fact that Lunn seemingly expected writers to pay for interviews. He may well have worked in vaudeville before he arrived on the ***Grand Ole Opry*** in 1930, with an act that included comedy and ventriloquism but mainly, the gimmick that led to him acquiring the pseudonym of the Talking Blues Man. A left-handed guitarist, he used a heavy guitar vamp as a backing, while he talked his way through recitations that sometimes contained countless verses. (The practice had previously been used in the 20s, by a vaudeville artist called Chris Bouchillon, who Lunn may have seen). It is unlikely that comedy numbers such as 'Tooth Picking Time In False Teeth Valley' would ensure stardom today but, by the mid-30s, with his band the Talking Blue Boys, he was a very popular *Opry* act and remained so for many years. (He also worked on occasions with **Roy Acuff** and his talking blues style was used later by folksinger **Woody Guthrie**). A noted practical joker, Lunn would sometimes stand at the stage door and audition any would-be *Opry* members, who wrongly assumed him to be the stage manager, in the street. Apart from a break during military service in World War II, he remained on the *Opry* until 1958 and toured with Acuff to Australia and Hawaii in 1959. He very rarely sang and his recording career consisted of a single Starday album. Lunn died following a heart attack in 1966.

Album: *The Original Talking Blues Man* (Starday 1962).

Lupino, Stanley

(see **Lane, Lupino**)

LuPone, Patti

b. 21 April 1949, Northport, New York, USA. An actress and singer who left several well-known Hollywood and Broadway stars feeling bitterly disappointed and distraught when she won the role of Norma Desmond in **Andrew Lloyd Webber**'s 1993 London production of ***Sunset Boulevard***. LuPone

made her stage debut, tap dancing, at the age of four, and later took dancing classes with Martha Graham. She trained for the stage at the Juilliard School where she met the actor Kevin Kline. A six-year personal relationship was supplemented by a joint association with John Housman's Actor's Company, which gave them both invaluable experience in the straight theatre, and resulted in their appearance together - as the bride and bridegroom - in a short-lived Broadway musical, *The Robber Bridegroom* (1975). After several other flops, including ***The Baker's Wife*** (1976) and *Working* (78), LuPone won Tony and Drama Desk Awards for her performance in the leading role of ***Evita*** (1979) on Broadway, and stayed with the show 'until the strain of being obnoxious and dying from cancer every night got too much'. She returned to serious theatre in the provinces and had an occasionally effective part in films such as *1941* and *Witness*. In 1985 LuPone moved to London and appeared firstly in ***The Cradle Will Rock***. In the same year, she became the first American actress and singer to gain a principal role with the Royal Shakespeare Company, in the the hit musical ***Les Misérable.*** The names of both shows appeared on her 1985 Olivier Award. In complete contrast to those two roles, in 1986 she played Lady Bird Johnson in a US mini-series based on the ex-President's life, and, a year later, was back on Broadway in an acclaimed revival of ***Anything Goes***. In the late 80s and early 90s LuPone had a major role in the popular US situation comedy *Life Goes On*, and experienced some difficulty breaking free from her contract when the call came from Lloyd Webber. She first played Norma Desmond at the composer's Sydmonton Festival in the summer of 1992. Declining the use of the book on stage, she learnt the part and gave what was regarded as a 'sensational' performance. Soon afterwards it became obvious that she had stolen the role-of-a-lifetime from 'under the noses' of bigger names such as Meryl Streep, **Angela Lansbury**, **Liza Minnelli**, and **Julie Andrews**. *Sunset Boulevard* opened in the West End in July 1993, and although LuPone enjoyed a personal triumph, her contract to take the show to Broadway was cancelled, resulting in a payoff 'in the region of $1 million'.
Selected albums: *Patti LuPone Live* 2-CD set (RCA Victor 1993), *Heatwave: Sings Irving Berlin* (Philips 1995), and Original Cast recordings.

Lurie, Evan

Lurie was a part of a group of young New York musicians, including his brother, John Lurie (saxophone) plus **Arto Lindsay** and **Henry Kaiser** (guitars), and Anton Fier (drums). They were unwilling to recognize the boundaries between different forms of popular and not-so-popular music and so happily mixed *avant garde* techniques with pop music and jazz. Lurie became the keyboard player with the Lounge Lizards, a band led by his brother John, which was one of the first New York bands to play jazz with a pop sensibility and present it in that adaptation of 50s style which became fashionable in the 80s. The black-and-white cover on the band's first album showed them in a picture reminiscent of the 50s and this was typical of the approach. Lurie is a technically able pianist who is able to adapt his playing to the very varied repertoire encompassed by the band, everything from 'Harlem Nocturne' to **Thelonious Monk** pieces like 'Epistrophy'. Lurie also wrote music for the band.
Albums: with the Lounge Lizards *The Lounge Lizards* (1981), *Live From The Drunken Boat* (1983), *Live In Berlin 1991 Vol. II* (1993); solo *Pieces Of Bandoneon* (1989), *Selling Water By The Side Of The River* (1990).

Lurkers

This first-generation UK punk quartet formed during 1977 in Uxbridge, London. Comprising Arturo Bassick (b. Arthur Billingsley; bass), Howard Wall (lead vocals), Pete Stride (guitar) and Manic Esso (b. Pete Haynes; drums), they were heralded as the British answer to the **Ramones**. They scored four minor UK hit singles between 1978-79, with 'Ain't Got A Clue' and 'I Don't Need To Tell Her' proving the most successful. Bassick had departed quickly, and was replaced first by Kim Bradshaw (ex-**Saints**) then, more permanently, Nigel Moore. The Lurkers specialized in two-minute blasts of punky rock 'n' roll, delivered with almost naive charm. Their simple, yet effective style was instantly accessible and exuded warmth as well as energy. They never received the recognition their talents deserved, however, because of a lack of image and media support. Pete Stride teamed-up with John Plain (the **Boys**) in 1980 to record *New Guitar In Town*. The material on this album was very much in a Lurkers vein, but again it met with limited success. The Lurkers were inactive for a short time at this juncture, with Stride and Moore then bringing in new singer Mark Fincham. The group reformed in 1988 (with the Stride/Bassick/Esso/Moore line-up) appearing on punk nostalgia bills and touring widely in Europe as well as recording new material.
Albums: *Fulham Fallout* (Beggars Banquet 1978), *God's Lonely Men* (Beggars Banquet 1979), *This Dirty Town* (Clay 1982), *King Of The Mountain* (Link 1989), *Wild Times Again* (Wesserlabel 1989, live album), *Powerjive* (Released Emotions 1990). Compilations: *Greatest Hit, Last Will And Testament* (Beggars Banquet 1980), *Totally Lurkered* (Dojo 1992).

Luscious Jackson

The New York-based band Luscious Jackson enjoyed almost universal press acclaim in the 90s with their spacious, bass-driven hip hop/rock crossover. Their sound sampled New York life first-hand, with breakbeats married to traffic noise and overheard conversation, coupled with a slouching bass and guitar that managed to effect a Brooklyn drawl of its own. The band were actually most heavily influenced by UK groups such as **Delta 5**, the **Slits** and **Gang Of Four**. Thus inspired, Jill Cunniff (vocals/bass), Gabrielle Glaister (vocals/guitar) and Kate Schellenbach (drums) used to forge ID to get into Manhatten's Lower East Side's punk clubs, as a result of which Schellenbach was recruited as drummer by the **Beastie Boys**, in their original hardcore guise. Having worked on their first two releases, *Pollywog Stew* and *Cookie Puss*, she later drummed with Hippies With Guns before rejoining her old friends. However, the trio then went off to separate art schools. (Cunniff and Glaister also formed a punk band, Jaws, in San Francisco, and Cunniff edited the fanzines *Decline of Art* and *The Golfing Experience*.) They returned to New York in 1991, and Cunniff and Glaister began to write short sketches, songs and rhymes together, recruiting Cunniff's art school friend, the classically trained musician Vivian Trimble, to add keyboards for their first shows. With a guitar and beatbox as their musical foundation, they added primal but amusing sampling on their first demo tape. Old friend Mike D heard it and was impressed enough to release it, virtually unchanged, as the group's 1992 debut mini-album on the Beastie Boys' Grand Royal imprint. Many were impressed by their erudite wit displayed in both the songs themselves and in the choice of samples. *Natural Ingredients* was more reserved musically, but was just as barbed lyrically, concentrating on nostalgia, romance and relationships. 'A lot of the lyrics on this record are about coming to terms with womanhood and the search for the identity and confusion that women tend to experience in adolescence or in long-term relationships.' Not that the band made it sound as prosaic as that, with their clever use of irresistible harmonies and low-slung bass on the fine track 'Energy Sucker' and promotional single, 'Deep Shag'.

Albums: *In Search Of Manny* (Grand Royal 1992, mini-album), *Natural Ingredients* (Grand Royal 1994).

Lush

Though they made their live debut at the Camden Falcon public house in London on 6 March 1988, little was heard of the UK-based Lush's serene pop qualities and full-bodied guitar sound until their mini-album, *Scar*, was issued in October 1989 on **4AD Records**. It was a critically acclaimed debut, and red-haired Miki Berenyi (b. 18 March 1967, St Stephen's, London, England; vocals/guitar), Emma Anderson (b. 10 June 1964, Raynes Park, London, England; guitar/backing vocals), Steve Rippon (bass guitar) and Christopher Acland (b. 7 September 1966, Lancaster, Lancashire, England; drums) found themselves topping the independent charts. Previously Anderson, a former DHSS clerical assistant, had been bass player for the Rover Girls, Berenyi had played with I-Goat, Fuhrer Five and the Lillies, while Acland had been a member of Infection, Panik, A Touch Of Hysteria, Poison In The Machine and others. Tours with the **Darling Buds** and **Loop** followed Lush's initial breakthrough, plus an appearance on BBC2's *Snub TV* and a **John Peel** radio session. The EP, *Mad Love*, issued in February 1990, was less raw but soared to new heights with the help of producer Robin Guthrie from the **Cocteau Twins**. Lush's consistent coverage in the music press, not least for their perpetual appearances at pre/post-gig parties, made them one of the leading UK independent groups of the year; one that was taken up with tours in the UK and Europe and an appearance at the Glastonbury Festival. Another EP, *Sweetness And Light*, offered a further move towards a commercial pop sound and only narrowly missed the national charts. The three EPs were compiled, originally for the US market, on *Gala*. Much of 1991 was spent recording the long-awaited full debut album, during which time they also issued an EP, *Black Spring* (which included a cover of **Dennis Wilson**'s 'Fallin' In Love'). When *Spooky* was finally released, many were disappointed, some insisting that Guthrie's production had swamped the group sound. Nevertheless, the album reached the national Top 20 and number 1 in the UK independent chart. During the winter of 1991/2 the group line-up changed when bassist Steve Rippon left amicably, to be replaced by ***New Musical Express*** picture researcher, Phil King (b. 29 April 1960, Chiswick, London, England). His musical apprenticeship had already included stints in the **Servants**, **Felt**, **Biff Bang Pow!** and **See See Rider**. The critical reception which awaited 1994's second album, *Split*, was fervent, with its cool guitar textures winning over many who had doubted their staying power. Berenyi and Anderson, dismissed in some quarters as 'two pissheads from London', had dispelled not only that notion, but also that of them being a 'typically glacial post-punk 4AD band' with a stunningly evocative collection of pop songs.

Albums: *Scar* (4AD 1989, mini-album), *Spooky* (4AD 1992), *Split* (4AD 1994). Compilation: *Gala* (4AD 1990).

Lusher, Don

b. 6 November 1923, Peterborough, Cambridgeshire, England. Lusher grew up in a musical family, his grandfather, father and mother playing and singing in Salvation Army bands. Lusher learned to play trombone and pursued his musical interests at school. At the age of 18, he went into the army but contrived to keep up his playing by joining Salvation Army bands in any town he happened to be near. A visit to a camp he was at by **Geraldo** And His Orchestra, in whose trombone section was **Ted Heath**, convinced Lusher that once the war was over that was how he would make his career. In 1947, he left the army, bought a

secondhand trombone, and joined a band led by an army friend in Tenby, Wales. He then joined **Joe Daniels** And His Hot Shots, but only a few weeks later the band folded. Lusher's next professional engagement was with Lou Preager at London's leading dancehall, the Hammersmith Palais. He then worked in a band led by Maurice Winnick at Ciro's Club, following this with important and career-moulding engagements with the **Squadronaires** and the Ted Heath band, with which he visited the USA. By the 60s Lusher was one of the UK's best-known trombonists, touring extensively with prominent artists, such as **Frank Sinatra**. Subsequently, Lusher led big bands for special television and radio appearances and for limited concert work, activities which continued into the early 90s. He also established a reputation as an educator, working in this capacity in the USA, Japan and Australia as well as in the UK. Despite his international fame, Lusher has never lost contact with his musical origins and regularly performs and records with brass bands. An outstanding technician, Lusher's flowing, precisely articulated playing style remains an object lesson to fellow trombonists in all areas of music.
Selected albums: *Lusher & Lusher & Lusher* (1972), *Collection* (1976), *Don Lusher Big Band* (1981), *Don Lusher Pays Tribute To The Great Bands* (c.1986) *Don Lusher Pays Tribute To The Great Bands, Volume 2* (1988), with Maurice Murphy *Just Good Friends* (1993).
Further reading: *The Don Lusher Book*, Don Lusher.

Lusk, Professor Eddie

b. 21 September 1948, Chicago, Illinois, USA, d. 26 August 1992, Chicago, Illinois, USA. Lusk's parents were both ministers in the Pentecostal Church and ran The Lusk Bible Way Center on Chicago's South Side. When he was old enough, his mother delegated the piano-playing duties to her son. Lusk was also tempted by the blues sounds emanating from Pepper's Lounge nearby and spent his teenage years struggling against their influence. He was ordained in the Pentecostal faith in 1968 but found the temptation of the blues too strong. He became music director at the Shiloh Academy, thus inspiring the nickname given to him by **Professor Longhair**. He worked with **Luther Allison** for three years and throughout the 80s recorded with artists such as **Fenton Robinson**, **Syl Johnson**, **Koko Taylor**, **Buddy Guy** and **Michael Coleman**, and toured with **Jimmy Dawkins**, **Phil Guy** and **Otis Rush**. He formed his own band, the Professor's Blues Review with vocalist Gloria Hardiman, and recorded 'Meet Me With Your Black Drawers On' for the 1987 anthology, *The New Bluebloods*. On his only solo album, *Professor Strut*, Hardiman was replaced by Karen Carroll. He continued to be in demand for sessions, some of which remain unissued. He and his band appeared in the 1991 film, *V. I. Warshawski*, and later in the year toured Europe with Coleman and **Kenny Neal**. In the summer of 1992, Lusk was diagnosed with colon cancer, brought on by AIDS. In desperation, he took his own life by jumping into the Chicago River.
Albums: *The New Bluebloods* (Alligator/Sonet 1987), *Professor Strut* (Delmark 1988).

Lutcher, Joe

Brother of **Nellie Lutcher**, Joe moved from Lake Charles, Louisiana to California where he played his alto saxophone with the **Nat 'King' Cole** Trio, the **Will Mastin** Trio and the **Mills Brothers**. He then signed for **Capitol Records** in the summer of 1947 (at the same time as Nellie) and had strong sellers with his 'Strato Cruiser', 'No Name Boogie' and the US Top 10 hit 'Shuffle Boogie'. Leaving Capitol in 1948, Lutcher's Jump Band went on to record for **Specialty Records**, Modern (resulting in a moderate hit with 'Mardi Gras' in 1949, which uncovered his Louisiana connections), London, Peacock and several small obscure independent labels. Meanwhile, Joe undertook some session work, before giving up the 'devil's music' and becoming an evangelist in the mid-50s; he is said to be responsible for converting **Little Richard** from secular to spiritual music in the late 50s.
Album: *Joe Joe Jump* (1982).

Lutcher, Nellie

b. 15 October 1915, Lake Charles, Louisiana, USA. A singer/pianist notable for her percussive piano playing and distinctive scat-vocal approach. Initially, Lutcher played in a big band with her bass-playing father before moving on to join the Southern Rhythm Boys band. She played clubs on the west coast during the late 30s/early 40s and signed to **Capitol Records** in 1947 following an appearance on a *March Of Dimes* charity show. Her first release, the R&B styled 'Hurry On Down', became a US Top 20 hit that same year and was followed by 'He's A Real Gone Guy', 'The Song Is Ended' and 'Fine Brown Frame'. The latter was a cover of an earlier hit by bandleader **Buddy Johnson**. She later moved on to **Liberty Records** recording a highly-rated album, *Our New Nellie*. But her popularity had faded, and during the late 60s and early 70s she took a staff job with the Hollywood Local Branch of the Musician's Union, still occasionally playing clubs such as the New York Cookery.
Albums: *Real Gone* (mid-50s), *Our New Nellie* (mid-50s). Compilations: *Real Gone Gal* (1985), *My Papa's Got To Have Everything* (1985), *Ditto From Me To You* (1987).

Luther, Frank

b. Frank Luther Crow, 5 August 1900, near Hutchinson, Kansas, USA, d. 16 November 1980. A competent musician, Luther was one of the early pioneers, who popularised western songs to city dwellers, by his personal appearances and radio performances. Sometimes working with his brother Phil, he toured and by the mid-20s, he had built himself a considerable reputation. He had noted the success of **Carson Robison** and **Vernon Dalhart** with their country ballads and cowboy songs and performed similar material. In 1928, Robison and Dalhart split and Luther and Robison began to work together. They recorded under various names including the Highhatters, the Homespun Trio and Men About Town. They even used the same pseudonyms as Dalhart used and Luther was very adept at imitating the nasal tones of Dalhart. They are perhaps best remembered though for their fine recordings as Bud and Joe Billings. Their recordings proved good sellers and were released in various countries; the 1929 Regal Zonophone recording, 'Will The Angels Play Their Harps For Me', being very popular in the UK. Another combination in 1931 saw 'In The Cumberland Mountains' listed as Bud And Joe Billings and Carson Robison (brother Phil Crow being the extra vocalist). They sometimes performed as the Carson Robison Trio with Luther's wife, Zora Layman, as the third member. (Zora Layman, a Kansas born singer and fiddler, also recorded in her own right, being especially remembered for her recording of 'Seven Years With The Wrong Man'. She and Luther divorced in 1940, but continued to worked together for several years. A pioneer of early country music, she later worked as a singing teacher and died in October 1981). In 1934, he made recordings with singing cowboy **Ray Whitley**. The use of pseudonyms and the fact that, in those days, artist recorded for different labels saw Luther appear on a vast number of recordings. It has been suggested that, in one year, he made over 500 recordings and it has been estimated that he probably appeared on 3,000 in all. In the mid-30s, he became interested in recording cowboy and other songs especially for children. He finally worked on the production of children's material for **Decca**. He co-wrote 'Barnacle Bill The Sailor' with Robison and some of their recordings may be found on *Just A Melody* (Old Homestead).

Luvdup Twins

Twins Mark and Adrian Luvdup, who won numerous UK music press Single Of The Week plaudits with their debut 12-inch, 'Good Times'. This was released on Manchester's UFG label (set up by **E-Lustrious**), and featured mixes from Jon Dasilva and John McCready. The duo play out at the Jolly Roger night in their native Manchester's Paradise Factory venue, review for *Mixmag Update* (having formerly run the well-regarded Luvdup fanzine), and have remixed for Awesome 3 among others.

Lyman, Arthur, Group

b. 1936, Kauai, Hawaii, USA. Lyman popularized a jazzy style of Hawaiian music during the 50s, and gathered a following as a purveyor of so-called exotic music. As a child, Lyman moved to the large Hawaiian city of Honolulu, where he became interested in the music of **Benny Goodman** and **Lionel Hampton**. He learned to play along with their records on a toy marimba. At the age of 14, he joined a jazz group and by his early 20s was performing with 'mood music' king Martin Denny. Lyman was signed to the Hi-Fi record label in 1957 and released his debut *Taboo,* the following year. It ultimately reached number 6 in the USA and remained on the chart for over a year. Lyman led a quartet: himself on four-mallet vibes, guitar and percussion, John Kramer (bass, ukulele, guitar, flute, clarinet, percussion), Alan Soares (piano, celeste, guitar, glockenspiel, chimes, clavinet, percussion) and Harold Chang (percussion). Because of its superior production - all of their music was recorded at the Henry J. Kaiser Aluminum Dome in Hawaii - and the unusual orchestral sounds created by the group, the record was particularly popular among consumers purchasing the then-new stereo equipment. In 1961, Lyman's single 'Yellow Bird' reached number 4 in the USA, one of the most uncharacteristic hits of the era. The album of the same name reached number 10. Lyman's last charting album in 1963 was *I Wish You Love* but Lyman continued to record into the 60s.
Selected albums: *Taboo* (1958), *Leis Of Jazz* (1959), *Yellow Bird* (1961), *Many Moods Of* (1962), *I Wish You Love* (1963), *Blowin' In The Wind* (1964), *Cast Your Fate* (1988, reissue), *Pearly Shells* (1988, reissue), *Puka Shells* (1988, reissue). Compilation: *The Exotic Sound Of The Arthur Lyman Group* (1991).

Lymon, Frankie, And The Teenagers

b. 30 September 1942, Washington Heights, New York, USA, d. 28 February 1968, New York City, New York, USA. Often billed as the 'boy wonder', Lymon first entered the music business after teaming-up with a local all-vocal quartet the Premiers. The latter comprised Jimmy Merchant (b. 10 February 1940, New York, USA), Sherman Garnes (b. 8 June 1940, New York, USA, d. 1978), Herman Santiago (b. 18 February 1941, New York, USA) and Joe Negroni (b. 9 September 1940, New York, USA, d. 1977). Lymon joined them in 1954 and soon after they were signed to the Gee label as the Teenagers. Their debut, the startling 'Why Do Fools Fall In Love?' was issued on 1 January 1956 and soon climbed into the US Top 10, alongside the early recordings of **Elvis Presley** and **Carl Perkins**. The song went on to reach number 1 in the UK and sold two million copies. Lymon soon left school and the group toured extensively. For their second single, 'I Want You To Be My Girl', the 13-year-old boy wonder was given superior billing to the group. With their use of high tenor, deep bass and soprano and teenage-orientated lyrics, the Teenagers

boasted one of the most distinctive sounds in 50s pop. After registering chart entries in the USA with 'I Promise To Remember' and 'The ABCs Of Love', they found greater acclaim in England. The soaring 'I'm Not A Juvenile Delinquent' (from the film *Rock Rock Rock*) hit the UK Top 12 and Lymon was afforded the honour of appearing at the London Palladium. So strong was his appeal at this point that the single's b-side 'Baby Baby' received separate promotion and outshone the a-side by climbing to number 4. During his celebrated UK tour, Lymon recorded as a soloist with producer **Norrie Paramor** and the resulting 'Goody Goody' reached the Top 30 on both sides of the Atlantic. By the summer of 1957, he had split from the Teenagers, and thereafter his career prospects plummeted. He enjoyed the excesses of stardom, smoking cigars, drinking heavily and enjoying under-age sex with women old enough to be his mother. Despite recording a strong album, his novelty appeal waned when his voice broke. By 1961, the teenager was a heroin addict and entered Manhattan General Hospital on a drug rehabilitation programme. Although he tried to reconstruct his career with the help of **Dizzy Gillespie** and even took dancing lessons and studied as a jazz drummer, his drug habit remained. In 1964, he was convicted of possessing narcotics and his finances were in a mess. His private life was equally chaotic and punctuated by three marriages. In February 1968, he was discovered dead on the bathroom floor of his grandmother's New York apartment with a syringe by his side. The Teenager who never grew up was dead at the tragically early age of 25. His former group continued to record sporadically and in the 80s, surviving members Santiago and Merchant formed a new Teenagers and Pearl McKinnon took Lymon's part.
Album: *The Teenagers Featuring Frankie Lymon* (1956), *The Teenagers At The London Palladium* (1958), *Rock 'N' Roll With Frankie Lymon* (1960). Compilations: *Frankie Lymon And The Teenagers* (1987, 61-track set), *The Best Of* (1990).

Lymon, Louis, And The Teen-Chords

An R&B vocal group from New York, New York, USA. Members were Louis Lymon (lead), Ralph Vaughan (first tenor), Rossilio Rocca (second tenor), Lyndon Harold (baritone), and David Little (bass). Lymon, the youngest brother of the great **Frankie Lymon**, built a remarkably top-notch group modelled on the pre-teen girlish sound of his brother and his group the Teenagers, even though he lacked the range and commanding stage presence of Frankie. The Teen-Chords never got a national hit, but were extremely popular on the east coast, where doo-wop groups had their biggest following. They got together in 1956 and were signed by Bobby Robinson and he formed the Fury label to launch the group. They achieved two New York hits for Robinson, with 'I'm So Happy' (1956) and 'Honey Honey' (1957), and then the group were signed to George Goldner's End label. They promoted their first End release, 'Your Last Chance', by making an imposing appearance in a quirky rock 'n' roll film, *Jamboree*. But that was the peak of their success. After scoring with 'Dance Girl' in 1958, the group disillusioned by lack of national success broke up.
Compilation: *I'm So Happy* (Relic 1992).
Film: *Jamboree* aka *Disc Jockey Jamboree* (1957).

Lynch Mob

Following **Dokken**'s acrimonious split, guitarist George Lynch and drummer Mick Brown recruited bassist Anthony Esposito and tempted vocalist Oni Logan away from the embryonic **Cold Sweat** to complete Lynch Mob. *Wicked Sensation* was a decent hard rock debut, carried by Lynch's considerable ability, but youthful vocalist Logan's inexperience began to show through on the road. The band felt particularly uncomfortable when comparing Logan with Geoff Tate during a European tour with **Queensrÿche**, where the highlight of the set tended to be a rendition of 'Mr Scary', Lynch's Dokken-era instrumental guitar workout, and Logan was replaced by another relative unknown, Robert Mason, when touring was complete. *Lynch Mob* incorporated more R&B influences, moving further from the Dokken sound, and this suited Mason's bluesy tones, while the band paid tribute to their influences with a cover of **Queen**'s 'Tie Your Mother Down'. However, neither album really took off, and Lynch split the band, opting to go solo while Brown rejoined Don Dokken.
Albums: *Wicked Sensation* (Elektra 1990), *Lynch Mob* (Elektra 1992).

Lynch, Kenny

b. 18 March 1939, Stepney, London, England. Britain's best-known black all-round entertainer has been a television personality for three decades. The youngest of 13 children, he first appeared on stage at the age of 12 with his sister, singer **Maxine Daniels**. At 16 he joined Ed Nichol's Band and before going into the services in 1957 worked in a string of bands including **Bob Miller**'s. He joined **HMV Records** and hit the UK Top 40 in 1960 with his debut single, a cover of 'Mountain Of Love'. He appeared in several films and hit his recording peak in 1963 with two successive Top 10 entries - a cover of 'Up On The Roof' and 'You Can Never Stop Me Loving You' (which made the US Top 20 when covered by **Johnny Tillotson**). Over the next 20 years he was one of the UK's busiest and most popular entertainers and was also awarded an OBE. He co-wrote the **Small Faces** number 1, 'Sha La La La Lee' and has recorded spasmodically since then on **Columbia**, **Atlantic Records**, **Polydor**, Laser, Towerbell and Spartan. In 1983, he had a surprise chart return with a Brit-funk

track 'Half The Day's Gone And We Haven't Earned A Penny' on Satril.
Selected albums: *We Love Kenny* (1966), *Half The Day's Gone And We Haven't Earned A Penny* (1983). Compilation: *The Very Best Of Kenny Lynch* (1987).

Lynch, Ray

b. Texas, USA. One of the most prominent and influential of the new age musicians of the 80s, Lynch's initial training was on piano, before he switched to classical guitar at age 12 after hearing Adrés Segovia's work. Later he moved to Barcelona, Spain, studying guitar technique for three years under Eduardo Sainz de la Maza. His studies continued back in America with a three year course at the University of Texas, learning composition of symphonic and chamber music. Some of these scores were later performed by the Dallas Symphony Orchestra. He also joined a group of madrigal singers as an auxiliary lutenist. This led to an invitation to join the Renaissance Quartet in New York. He consequently relocated to the east coast and spent seven years performing with the Quartet and other sympathetic 'early music' groups, with interest in medieval and baroque music undergoing something of a revival. Purchasing a 125-acre farm in Maine, Lynch concurrently toured the country giving virtuoso solo performances, until he found something lacking in his life and dropped everything to move to California. His recording career was well under way at this point, having started in 1983 with *The Sky Of The Mind*, a reflective piece of mood music, with Tibetan bells merging with classically formed song structures. *Deep Breakfast* became a certified Platinum album in the aftermath, mainly on the strength of the accompanying hit single, 'Celestial Soda Pop'. The five year delay before *No Blue Thing* engendered a much expanded sound, with evocative melodies fashioning a full, adroit range of moods and atmospherics. It quickly became a runaway success in US new age circles, staying on ***Billboard***'s genre chart for 122 weeks. Lynch also won *Billboard*'s award for New Age Album of The Year, an honour which the same record was awarded again the following year. 1993's *Nothing Above My Shoulders But The Evening* reflected on the trials of the human spirit, with Lynch commenting: 'The mind filters out so much of our humanity. Great art, if we participate fully in it, gives us permission to feel, and creates a space in which we can feel at a depth not ordinarily allowed.'
Albums: *The Sky Of Mind* (Ray Lynch Productions 1983), *Deep Breakfast* (Ray Lynch Productions 1984), *No Blue Thing* (Windham Hill 1989), *Nothing Above My Shoulders But The Evening* (Windham Hill 1993).

Lynn, Barbara

b. Barbara Lynn Ozen, 16 January 1942, Beaumont, Texas, USA. Barbara was signed up by producer **Huey P. Meaux** after hearing a demo tape and watching her perform in a Texas club. Her early records were recorded at Cosimo's New Orleans' studio and leased to the Jamie label. Composed by Lynn, 'You'll Lose A Good Thing' (1962) was an R&B chart topper and pop Top 10 in the USA, and was followed by 'You're Gonna Need Me' and 'Oh! Baby (We Got A Good Thing Goin')'. The last of these was revived by the **Rolling Stones** on *Out Of Our Heads*. Barbara issued several singles on Meaux's own label, Tribe, amongst which was her version of 'You Left The Water Running' (1966). Subsequent releases for **Atlantic Records** included 'This Is The Thanks I Get' (1968), '(Until Then) I'll Suffer' (1972), both of which reached the R&B chart for this accomplished singer, songwriter and guitarist, who continued to tour, including visits to Japan, and also cut albums for Ichiban and Rounder/Bullseye.
Albums: *You'll Lose A Good Thing* (Jamie 1962), *Here Is Barbara Lynn* (Atlantic 1968), *You Don't Have To Go* (Ichiban 1988), *So Good* (1994). Compilations: *The Barbara Lynn Story* (1965), *Elegant Soul* (1982, six tracks plus 6 by Bettye Swann), *We Got A Good Thing Goin'* (1984, double album), *Barbara Lynn* (Good Thing 1989), *You'll Lose A Good Thing* (Sound Of The Fifties 1992), *Barbara Lynn Live In Japan* (c.1993, rec. 1984), *The Atlantic Years* (Ichiban/Soul Classics 1994).

Lynn, Cheryl

b. Cheryl Lynn Smith, 11 March 1957, Los Angeles, California, USA. The full-throated Lynn became a hitmaker at the height of disco's popularity singing dance tunes that retained the gospel vocal approach of classic soul. Lynn grew up in the church where her mother was a minister of music. Her break in the business came in 1976 after she won as a contestant on the US television amateur contest show *The Gong Show*. Before signing with **Columbia**, however, she spent half a year with a touring company of ***The Wiz***, a black musical based on the *Wizard Of Oz* story. Lynn achieved a million-seller with her very first record, 'Got To Be Real', hitting number 1 R&B and number 12 pop in 1978. Other chart entries followed, notably 'Shake It Up Tonight' (US R&B number 5), 'Encore' (US R&B number 1), and 'If You Were Mine' (US R&B number 11). She also scored in 1982 with an excellent remake of the **Marvin Gaye** and **Tammi Terrell** hit, 'If This World Was Mine' (US R&B number 4), on which she duetted with **Luther Vandross**. Her success in the UK was minimal, with only 'Encore' briefly entering the charts in 1984.
Albums: *Cheryl Lynn* (1978), *In Love* (1980), *In The Night* (1981), *Instant Love* (1982), *Preppie* (1984), *It's Gonna Be Alright* (1985), *Start Over* (1987), *Whatever It Takes* (1989).

Lynn, Judy

b. Judy Voiten, 12 April 1936, Boise, Idaho, USA. The daughter of bandleader Joe Voiten (he once worked with **Bing Crosby**) she grew up to be a teenage rodeo rider. She also became a yodelling champion and in 1955, she represented her State in the Miss America contest. Later the same year, when the touring *Grand Ole Opry* show played Boise, she deputised for indisposed **Jean Shepard**, which resulted in her joining the show. In 1957, she co-hosted with **Ernest Tubb** the first national television showing of the *Opry*. This led to appearances on many major television shows and after leaving the touring *Opry* show, in 1960, she formed her own band and started her own television series. 'Footsteps Of A Fool' became her first and only US country Top 10 hit, when it charted in 1962. Noted for her beauty and elegance, her colourful western-style Nudie costumes and with a repertoire that ran from big ballads to yodels, she became very popular. She was one of the first country singers to appear in Las Vegas and was actually a featured artist around the Nevada casino circuit for over twenty years, being a frequent performer at such major venues as the Golden Nugget Club and Caesar's Palace. She recorded for several labels including ABC, United Artists, Musicor and **Columbia Records** and her last country chart hit was 'Padre' in 1975. She retired from the music industry in 1980 to become a church minister. (She is not related to country star **Loretta Lynn**.)

Albums: with the Sunshine Boys *Sings At The Golden Nugget* (1962), *Here Is Our Girl Judy Lynn* (1963), *The Judy Lynn Show* (1964), *The Judy Lynn Show Act 2* (1965), *The Judy Lynn Show Plays Again* (1966), *Number One Most Promising New Country And Western Girl Singer* (1964), *Honey Stuff* (1966), *Judy Lynn In Las Vegas* (1967), *Golden Nuggets* (1967), *Sings At Caesar's Palace* (1969), *Parts Of Love* (1971), *Naturally* (1973).

Lynn, Loretta

b. Loretta Webb, 14 April 1935, Butcher Hollow, Kentucky, USA. Lynn is a coal miner's daughter, being the second of the eight children of Ted and Clara Webb. She is one-quarter Cherokee and her name came from her mother's fondness for film star, Loretta Young. She was raised in a small shack during the Depression and was attracted to country music as an 11-year-old, when the family acquired a radio and she heard the singing of Molly O'Day. Her autobiography tells of her makeshift wardrobe and how, at the age of 13, she married a serviceman, Oliver Vanetta Lynn, known to his friends as Doolittle or Mooney, which was short for Moonshine. He took her to Custer, Washington, and she had four children and several miscarriages by the time she was 18. They had six children and Lynn was a grandmother at the age of 29. 'Mooney', recognizing her talent, encouraged her to sing in local clubs and her band, the Trailblazers, included her brother, Jay Lee Webb, on guitar. Her talent was recognized by Don Grashey of Zero Records, who took her to Los Angeles in February 1960 where she recorded four of her own songs. Zero had no money for promotion so she and Mooney promoted 'I'm A Honky Tonk Girl' themselves, the song taking its style from **Kitty Wells**'s 'It Wasn't God Who Made Honky Tonk Angels'. Mooney said that 'they drove 80,000 miles to sell 50,000 copies' but it reached number 14 in the US country charts and enabled her to appear regularly on *Grand Ole Opry*. Many female singers were jealous of her success, but **Patsy Cline** sprang to her defence and they became close friends. (Lynn released a tribute album to her in 1977.)

When they moved to Nashville, she became a regular on a weekly television show with the **Wilburn Brothers**, who also managed her. Kitty Wells and Patsy Cline were two of her major influences and she was pleased to be assigned to their producer, **Owen Bradley**, by USA **Decca Records**. 'Success', her second country hit, peaked at number 6 in 1962, and she had further hits with 'Before I'm Over You' and 'Blue Kentucky Girl'. She then developed a hard-hitting persona as the wife who stood no nonsense from her rivals ('You Ain't Woman Enough', 'Fist City') or her husband (her first country number 1 'Don't Come Home A-Drinkin' (With Lovin' On Your Mind)' from 1966, 'Your Squaw Is On The Warpath'). Her best-known record, the autobiographical 'Coal Miner's Daughter', was a US country number 1 in 1970. **Shel Silverstein**, ironically a *Playboy* cartoonist, wrote 'One's On The Way' in which she was harassed by her children and an insensitive husband. She answered **Tammy Wynette**'s 'Stand By Your Man' in 1975 with the double standards of 'The Pill', which was banned by several USA radio stations. By way of contrast, she subsequently had a country hit with a song called 'Pregnant Again'.

Although her first duets were with **Ernest Tubb**, she formed a regular team with **Conway Twitty** and the combination of the two distinctive voices worked well, especially in 'After The Fire Is Gone', 'As Soon As I Hang Up The Phone', 'The Letter' and the amusingly-titled 'You're The Reason Our Kids Are Ugly'. When she fell out with the Wilburn Brothers, she formed United Talent Inc. with Twitty. As the brothers still owned her publishing, she was reluctant to record her own material, although subsequently she was elected to the Nashville Songwriters International Hall of Fame. In 1972, Lynn was the first woman to become the Country Music Association's Entertainer of the Year and she also shared the Vocal Duo of the Year award with Twitty. In 1973, she made the cover of *Newsweek* and was the first woman in country music to become a millionaire. However, she met with little UK success and some of her UK releases sold less than 200 copies. Her best-selling autobiography, *Coal Miner's Daughter*, showed how the human spirit could combat poverty and sickness, but also illustrated that the problems of endless touring could be as traumatic. Lynn's musicians call her 'Mom' and share their problems with her. Sissy Spacek won an Oscar for her portrayal of Lynn, which included reproducing her singing, in the 1980 film *Coal Miner's Daughter*, and the film also featured Tommy Lee Jones as her husband and Levon Helm of the **Band** as her father. Her country music success includes 16 number 1 singles, 60 other hits, 15 number 1 albums and numerous awards, but she has never sought pop success. She owns a huge ranch, 70 miles outside of Nashville, which has the whole town of Hurricane Mills in its grounds. Another part of the property, the Loretta Lynn Dude Ranch, is a tourist attraction with camping facilities. Despite her prolific output in the 60s and 70s, she has not recorded much recently but she is considering an album of traditional country music with her sisters, **Crystal Gayle** and Peggy Sue Wright. To quote **Roy Acuff**, 'A song delivered from Loretta is from the deepest part of her heart.'

Albums: *Loretta Lynn Sings* (1963), *Before I'm Over You* (1964), *Songs From My Heart* (1965), *Blue Kentucky Girl* (1965), *Hymns* (1965), with Ernest Tubb *Mr. And Mrs. Used To Be* (1965), *I Like 'Em Country* (1966), *Country Christmas* (1966), *You Ain't Woman Enough* (1966), with Tubb *Singin' Again* (1967), *Don't Come Home A-Drinkin'* (1967), *Singin' With Feelin'* (1967), *Who Says God Is Dead* (1968), *Fist City* (1968), *Your Squaw Is On The Warpath* (1969), *Woman Of The World/To Make A Man* (1969), *Here's Loretta Singing 'Wings Upon Your Horns'* (1969), with Tubb *If We Put Our Heads Together* (1969), *Loretta Writes 'Em And Sings 'Em* (1970), *Coal Miner's Daughter* (1971), *I Want To Be Free* (1971), *You're Lookin' At Country* (1971), *One's On The Way* (1971), with Conway Twitty *We Only Make Believe* (1971), with Twitty *Lead Me On* (1971), *God Bless America Again* (1972), *Alone With You* (1972), *Here I Am Again* (1972), *Entertainer Of The Year* (1973), with Twitty *Louisiana Woman, Mississippi Man* (1973), *Love Is The Foundation* (1973), *They Don't Make 'Em Like My Daddy* (1974), with Twitty *Country Partners* (1974), with Twitty *Feelins'* (1975), *Back To The Country* (1975), *Home* (1975), *When The Tingle Becomes A Chill* (1976), *Somebody Somewhere* (1976), *On The Road With Loretta And The Coal Miners* (1976), with Twitty *United Talent* (1976), *I Remember Patsy* (1977), with Twitty *Dynamic Duo* (1977), *Out Of My Head And Back In My Bed* (1978), with Twitty *Honky Tonk Heroes* (1978), with Twitty *Diamond Duets* (1979), *We've Come A Long Way Baby* (1979), *Loretta* (1980), *Lookin' Good* (1980), with Twitty *Two's A Party* (1981), *Making Love From Memory* (1982), *I Lie* (1982), *Lyin', Cheatin', Woman Chasin', Honky Tonkin', Whiskey Drinkin' You* (1983), *Just A Woman* (1985), with Twitty *Making Believe* (1988), with Tammy Wynette, Dolly Parton *Honky Tonk Angels* (1993). Compilations: *Great Country Hits* (1985), *Golden Greats* (1986), *The Very Best Of Loretta Lynn* (1988), *20 Greatest Hits* (1989), *Coal Miner's Daughter: The Best Of...* (Music Collection 1993).

Further reading: *Coal Miner's Daughter*, Loretta Lynn with George Vecsey. *The Story Of Loretta Lynn*, Robert K. Krishef. *Loretta Lynn's World Of Music: Including An Annotated Discog*, Laurence J. Zwisohn.

Videos: *Loretta Lynn Live* (1988), *Coal Miners Daughter* (1991), *Loretta Lynn* (1992).

Lynn, Tami

Tami Lynn was one of several New Orleans, Louisiana, USA-based artists who worked for **Harold Battiste**'s AFO (All For One) label during the early 60s. She sang on *A Compendium*, an album which featured the co-operative's crack houseband, but this phase in her career was forestalled when the company folded. Tami's best-known single, 'I'm Gonna Run Away From You', was originally released in 1967. This powerful **Bert Berns** composition failed to register in America, but became a belated UK hit in 1971, when it reached number 4. Its popularity was confirmed four years later when it again entered the Top 40. Lynn had meanwhile continued to record, but this excellent performance remains her most lasting legacy.

Albums: *A Compendium* (1963), *Love Is Here And Now You're Gone* (1972).

Lynn, Vera

b. Vera Welch, 20 March 1917, London, England. A much-loved singer with a clear, strong, plaintive voice, who is held in great esteem by British audiences because of her work in entertaining service personnel during World War II. At the age of seven she was singing regularly in working men's clubs, and later joined a dancing troupe until she was 15. She made her first broadcast in 1935, singing with the **Joe Loss** Orchestra, and later worked with **Charlie Kunz** and **Ambrose**. While she was with Ambrose she met saxophonist Harry Lewis, who later became her husband and manager. She went solo in 1940, and with the help of producer Howard Thomas, launched her own BBC radio series entitled *Sincerely Yours*. Introducing each programme with the signature tune 'Wishing', she attempted to become the musical link between the girls 'back home' and their men overseas, by reading out personal messages and singing sentimental favourites such as 'Yours', 'We'll Meet Again' and 'White Cliffs Of Dover'. In 1941, she appeared in the revue *Applesauce* at the London Palladium, with Florence Desmond and the 'Cheekie Chappie', comedian Max Miller. By now, she was the most popular female vocalist in Britain and with UK Forces overseas, to whom she was known as 'The Forces Sweetheart'. One comedian was heard to remark: 'The war was started by Vera Lynn's agent!'. She also made three films, *We'll Meet Again* (1942), which featured **Geraldo**'s Orchestra, *Rhythm Serenade* (1943) with comedy duo Jewell and Warriss, and *One Exciting Night* (1944) with top wartime comedian

Richard Murdoch. Lynn toured Burma with ENSA, entertaining the troops, and shortly after the war ended she retired, temporarily. She returned to the UK variety circuit in 1947, and soon had her own BBC radio series again, this time with Canadian **Robert Farnon** as musical director. Partly because a musicians' strike was causing disruption in the USA, UK **Decca Records** decided to issue some of her material on their US **London** label. From 1948-54, she had several US Top 30 hits there, including 'You Can't Be True, Dear', 'Again', 'Auf Wiederseh'n Sweetheart' (the first record by a UK artist to top the US charts), 'Yours', 'We'll Meet Again', 'If You Love Me, Really Love Me' and 'My Son, My Son'. She promoted the records by making regular guest appearances on Tallulah Bankhead's US radio programme *The Big Show*.

In the UK during the 50s, besides 'Auf Wiederseh'n' and 'My Son, My Son' (a UK number 1), Vera Lynn had Top 30 entries such as 'Homing Waltz', 'Forget Me Not', 'Windsor Waltz', 'Who Are We', 'A House With Love In It', 'The Faithful Hussar (Don't Cry My Love)' and 'Travellin' Home'. From 1952-54 she appeared at London's Adelphi Theatre in the revue *London Laughs*, which also featured young English comedians Jimmy Edwards and Tony Hancock. In the late 50s, with the UK variety theatres in decline, Lynn appeared mainly on radio and television. In 1960, after 20 years with Decca, she joined **EMI**, a move that prompted the album *Hits Of The Sixties*, which contained contemporary ballads such as 'By the Time I Get To Phoenix', 'Everybody's Talking' and 'Fool On The Hill'. In 1962, her recorded voice was used to evoke memories of the war years each night in **Lionel Bart**'s West End musical ***Blitz!*** In 1969 she launched her first television series for seven years, and in the following year was unable to sing for four months after developing the lung condition emphysema. In the same year she was awarded the OBE. Since then she has worked less and less, preferring to save her performances for nostalgic occasions organized by bodies such as the Burma Star Association at London's Royal Albert Hall, and shows to mark the 50th anniversaries of the outbreak of World War II, the D-Day landings, and VE Day. She was created a Dame of the British Empire in 1975, and is still fondly regarded as a legend by a large proportion of the British public. The **Pink Floyd** wrote 'Vera' for *The Wall*, which accurately satirised her importance during World War II.

Selected albums: *Hits Of The Blitz* (1962), *The Wonderful Vera* (1963), *Favourite Sacred Songs* (1972), *Unforgettable Songs* (1972), *Remembers The World At War* (1974), *Sing With Vera* (1974), with Kenneth McKellar *World Nursery Rhymes* (1976), *I'll Be Seeing You* (1976), *Christmas With Vera Lynn* (1976), *Vera Lynn In Nashville* (1977), *Thank You For The Music* (1979), *Singing To The World* (1981), *In Concert: Guard's Depot, Caterham* (1984). Compilations: *The World Of Vera Lynn* (1969), *The World Of Vera Lynn, Volume Two* (1970), *The World Of Vera Lynn, Volume Three* (1971), *The World Of Vera Lynn, Volume Four* (1972), *The World Of Vera Lynn, Volume Five* (1974), *The Great Years* (1975), *Focus On Vera Lynn* (1977), *We'll Meet Again* (1980), *This Is Vera Lynn* (1980), 20 *Family Favourites* (1981), *The Vera Lynn Songbook* (1981, five-album box set), *We'll Meet Again* (1989), *Vera Lynn Remembers - The Songs That Won World War II* (1994), *We'll Meet Again - The Early Years* (1994).

Further reading: *Vocal Refrain*, Vera Lynn. *We'll Meet Again*, R. Cross.

Lynne, Gillian

b. 1926, Bromley, Kent, England. An internationally acclaimed director and choreographer with over 40 London and Broadway shows to her credit. Gillian Lynne was originally a dancer and made her stage debut with the Sadlers Wells Ballet in 1944, remaining with the company for seven years, during which time she played several leading roles. During the 50s she danced many times at the London Palladium, and played Claudine in ***Can-Can*** at the Coliseum. In 1960 she appeared in John Cranko's *New Cranks* at the Lyric, Hammersmith, and choreographed her first ballet, *Owl And The Pussycat*, for the Western Theatre Ballet. Since that time Lynne has worked as a choreographer and/or director on musical productions such as ***The Roar Of The Greasepaint - The Smell Of The Crowd***, *The Match Girls*, ***Pickwick***, *How Now Dow Jones*, ***Tonight At Eight***, *Songbook*, *Tomfoolery*, *Once Upon A Time*, ***My Fair Lady***, ***Cabaret***, ***Cats***, and ***The Phantom Of The Opera***. Her work on *Cats* earned her an **Laurence Olivier Award** - one of four she owns - and the Austrian Government's Order of Merit for a production of the show which was presented in Vienna and subsequently played in East Berlin and Moscow. Her Paris production won the prestigious Moliére Award. She has also worked extensively for the Royal Shakespeare Company, the Royal Opera House, Covent Garden, and on more than 10 films including ***Half A Sixpence***, ***Man Of La Mancha***, and ***Yentl***. Her television credits include *The Muppet Show* series, her own creation, *The Fool On The Hill*, which was based on the **Beatles'** music, and her BAFTA award-winning ballet *A Simple Man*. In the early 90s, as well as supervising and working on many other productions world-wide, she re-staged and choreographed a UK revival of *Pickwick*, starring **Harry Secombe**, and devised her first full-length ballet, *The Brontës*, which had its world premiere in Leeds early in 1995.

Lynne, Jeff

b. 30 December 1947, Birmingham, England. Lynne's long and varied musical career began in 1966 when he joined the Nightriders, a popular beat group still

reeling from the loss of their leader, Mike Sheridan, and guitarist, **Roy Wood**. Having completed all contractual obligations, the band took the name, **Idle Race** and, under Lynne's guidance, became a leading exponent of classic late 60s pop. Frustrated at a lack of commercial success, the artist opted to join the **Move** in 1970, where he was teamed with the aforementioned Wood. Lynne's contributions to the unit's late-period catalogue included the riff-laden 'Do Ya', but this era is also marked by the duo's desire to form a more experimental outlet for their talents. This resulted in the launch of the **Electric Light Orchestra**, or ELO, of which Lynne took full control upon Wood's early and sudden departure. The group gradually developed from cult favourites into one of the 70s' leading recording acts, scoring international success with several platinum-selling albums, including *A New World Record* and *Out Of The Blue*. Lynne's dual talents as a composer and producer ensured the group's status but, sensing an artistic sterility, he abandoned his creation in 1986. The artist then assumed an increasingly backroom role, but won praise for his production work with **George Harrison** (*Cloud Nine*), **Randy Newman** (*Land Of Dreams*) and **Roy Orbison** (*Mystery Girl*) and he has also contributed his distinctive production qualities to much of **Tom Petty**'s recent output. Lynne's work with Orbison coincided with his position as 'Otis Wilbury' in the **Traveling Wilburys**, an informal 'supergroup' completed by Orbison, Harrison, Tom Petty and **Bob Dylan**. This particularly prolific period was also marked by Jeff's work with **Brian Wilson** on the ex-**Beach Boys**' first long-awaited solo album. In 1990, Lynne also unveiled his own solo debut, *Armchair Theatre*, on which his gifts for pop melody remained as sure as ever.
Album: *Armchair Theatre* (1990). Compilation: *Message From The Country (The Jeff Lynne Years 1968-1973)* (1989, spans Lynne's career with Idle Race, the Move and early ELO).

Lynne, Shelby

b. Shelby Lynn Moore, 22 October 1968, Quantico, Virginia, USA. The exceptionally talented Lynne was raised in Jackson, Alabama and her life reads like a soap opera: there were long arguments with her father who had her jailed on a trumped-up charge. She saw her father shoot her mother dead and then commit suicide. When she appeared on the *Nashville Now* talent show at the age of 18, it was evident that she was a very good singer with a rather unusual, deep voice. **Billy Sherrill** offered to produce her records and her first album included the standards, 'I Love You So Much It Hurts Me' and 'I'm Confessin''. Her first single, 'If I Could Bottle This Up', was with another of Sherrill's artists, **George Jones**. She is a very determined country performer who does not cowtow to the media by turning on smiles for the photographers. Her reputation made it difficult to obtain a record contract after parting with Epic. *Temptation* is a radical album, employing a full horn section and closer to **Harry Connick Jnr.** than country music. Her video for 'Feelin' Kind Of Lonely Tonight' indicates her wish to tour with an orchestra.
Albums: *Sunrise* (Epic 1989), *Tough All Over* (Epic 1990), *Soft Talk* (Epic 1991), *Temptation* (Morgan-Creek 1993).
Video: *Tell Me I'm Crazy* (1993).

Lynott, Phil

b. 20 August 1951, Dublin, Eire, d. 4 January 1986. Having enjoyed considerable success in **Thin Lizzy**, Lynott first recorded solo in 1980, the same year that he married Caroline Crowther, daughter of the television celebrity, Leslie Crowther. Lynott's first single, 'Dear Miss Lonely Hearts', reached number 32 in the UK charts and was followed by an album, *Solo In Soho*. A tribute to **Elvis Presley**, 'King's Call' also reached number 35. Lynott had to wait until 1982 for his next hit, 'Yellow Pearl', which reached the UK Top 20 after being used as the theme tune to television show *Top Of The Pops*. In the summer of 1983 Thin Lizzy broke up and it was widely anticipated that Lynott would go on to solo fame. A new group, Grand Slam, failed to develop and Lynott's subsequent solo single, 'Nineteen', did not sell. The last notable instalment in his career arrived in May 1985 when he partnered **Gary Moore** on the number 5 hit, 'Out In The Fields'. He played his last gig with Grand Slam at the Marquee in London on 3 December 1985. At the turn of the following year he suffered a drug overdose and, following a week in a coma, died of heart failure, exacerbated by pneumonia.
Albums: *Solo In Soho* (Vertigo 1981), *The Phillip Lynott Solo Album* (Vertigo 1992).
Further reading: *Phillip Lynott: The Rocker*, Mark Putterford. *Songs For While I'm Away*, Phillip Lynott.

Lynyrd Skynyrd

Formed in Jacksonville, Florida, in 1964, this US boogie/hard rock band took their (slightly corrupted) name from their Physical Education teacher, Leonard Skinner. The group initially comprised Ronnie Van Zant (b. 15 January 1948, Jacksonville, Florida, USA, d. 20 October 1977; vocals), Gary Rossington (b. 4 December 1951, Jacksonville, Florida, USA; guitar), Allen Collins (b. 19 July 1952, Jacksonville, Florida, USA, d. 23 January 1990; guitar; ex-Mods), Larry Jungstrom (bass) and Bob Burns (drums; ex-Me, You & Him), the quintet meeting through minor league baseball connections. Together they played under various names, including Noble Five, Wildcats, Sons Of Satan and My Backyard, releasing one single, 'Need All My Friends', in 1968, before changing their name to Lynyrd Skynyrd. After playing the southern states during the late 60s they released a second single, 'I've

Been Your Fool', in 1971, after recording demos in Sheffield, Alabama. The group were discovered in Atlanta by **Al Kooper** in 1972 while he was scouting for new talent for his Sounds Of The South label. Signed for $9,000, the group's ranks were swollen by the addition of Leon Wilkeson (b. 2 April 1952; bass), who replaced Jungstrom (who went on to work with Van Zant's brother, Donnie, in **.38 Special**). Kooper produced the group's debut album, *Pronounced Leh-Nerd Skin-Nerd*, which also featured former **Strawberry Alarm Clock** guitarist Ed King (originally standing in on bass for Wilkeson, who dropped out of the band for six months) and Billy Powell (b. 3 June 1952; keyboards). Their three-guitar line-up attracted a great deal of attention, much of it generated through support slots with the **Who**, and the combination of blues, honky tonk and boogie proved invigorating. Their momentous anthem, 'Free Bird' (a tribute to **Duane Allman**), included a superb guitar finale, while its gravity and durability were indicated by frequent reappearances in the chart years after. In 1974 the group enjoyed their biggest US hit with 'Sweet Home Alabama', an amusing and heartfelt response to **Neil Young** who had criticized the south in his compositions 'Southern Man' and 'Alabama'. After the release of parent album *Second Helping* drummer Bob Burns was replaced by Artimus Pyle (b. 15 July 1948, Spartanburg, South Carolina, USA). The group were by now renowned as much for their hard-living as their music, and Ed King became the first victim of excess when retiring from the band in May 1975 (Van Zant's name was also regularly to be found in the newspapers through reports of bar brawls and confrontations with the law). *Gimme Back My Bullets* arrived in March of the following year, with production expertise from Tom Dowd. In September 1976 Rossington was injured in a car crash, while Steve Gaines (b. 14 September 1949, Seneca, Missouri, d. 20 October 1977; guitar) became King's replacement. With their tally of gold discs increasing each year and a series of sell-out tours, the band suffered an irrevocable setback in late 1977. On 20 October, Van Zant, Gaines, his sister Cassie (one of three backing singers) and personal manager Dean Kilpatrick were killed in a plane crash *en route* from Greenville, South Carolina, to Baton Rouge, Louisiana. Rossington, Collins, Powell and Wilkeson were all seriously injured, but each would recover. That same month the group's new album, *Street Survivors*, was withdrawn as the sleeve featured an unintentionally macabre design of the band surrounded by flames. With their line-up devastated, the group dispersed and the remaining members went on to join the **Rossington-Collins Band** (with the exception of Pyle). In 1987 the name Lynyrd Skynyrd was revived for a 'reunion' tour featuring Rossington, Powell, Pyle, Wilkeson and King, with Ronnie's brother Johnny Van Zant (vocals) and Randell Hall (guitar). One of their performances was later issued as the live double set, *For The Glory Of The South*. Collins had earlier been paralysed, and his girlfriend killed, during an automobile accident in 1986. When he died in 1990 from pneumonia, this only helped to confirm Lynyrd Skynyrd's status as a 'tragic' band. However, members were still performing, and recording, in the early 90s, after disentangling themselves from legal complications over the use of the name caused by objections from Van Zant's widow. The most spectacular aspect of which was a 20th Anniversary performance live on cable television in February 1993, with Rossington, Powell, Wilkeson, King and Johnny Van Zant joined by guests including **Peter Frampton**, Brett Michaels (**Poison**), **Charlie Daniels** and Tom Kiefer (**Cinderella**), the latter having also written new songs with Rossington. Pyle was conspicuous by his absence, having been charged with a sexual assault on a four year old girl the previous year.

Albums: *Pronounced Leh-Nerd Skin-Nerd* (Sounds Of The South/MCA 1973), *Second Helping* (Sounds Of The South/MCA 1974), *Nuthin' Fancy* (MCA 1975), *Gimme Back My Bullets* (MCA 1976), *One More From The Road* (MCA 1976), *Street Survivors* (MCA 1977), *First And Last* (MCA 1978, rec. 1970-72), *For The Glory Of The South* (MCA 1987, double album), *The Last Rebel* (MCA 1993). Compilations: *Gold And Platinum* (MCA 1980, double album), *Best Of The Rest* (MCA 1982), *Legend* (MCA 1987), *Anthology* (Raw Power 1987), *Lynyrd Skynyrd 1991* (MCA 1991, 3-CD set), *Definitive* (MCA 1992).

Lyons, James L.

b. 18 November 1916, USA, d. 10 April 1994. One of the greatest of jazz's promotors and impressarios, Lyons was first employed in 1941 as a publicity agent for a dance hall venue offering **Stan Kenton**'s 'Artistry In Rhythm Orchestra'. Already a jazz enthusiast, and impressed by Kenton's craft, he took a DJ job in California, where he persuaded the management to give Kenton a live spot. This helped bring the bandleader to the public's attention, and Lyons too was well served by his success, graduating to NBC where he worked as a presenter and producer, notably on New York's *The Jubilee Show* for Armed Forces Radio. Post-war, Lyons returned to his native California, hosting the NBC show *Discapades*, where he proved a major influence on the jazz scene's transition from dixieland to bebop (the **Gerry Mulligan/Chet Baker** group famously paying tribute in 'Line For Lyons'). Lyons also played a crucial role in bringing to light the talents of **Dave Brubeck** and his octet, when everybody else was turning a deaf ear. However, Lyons greatest triumph still lay ahead of him. In 1958 he programmed the first line-up of the **Monterey Festival**, boasting the discovery of vibraharpist and drummer **Cal Tjader** in addition to new work from

Duke Ellington. Other artists included **Billie Holiday** and **Dizzy Gillespie**. Lyons remained the captain of the Monterey event up until the early 90s, when he was forced to retire after being criticised for his conservative and intransient booking policies. Whilst this was perhaps true, the sniping should not rob him of his status as a vital component in the emergence of the west coast jazz scene.

Lyons, Jimmy

b. 1 December 1933, Jersey City, New Jersey, USA, d. 19 May 1986. A self-taught alto saxophone player, Lyons was encouraged while still in his early teens by such leading jazzmen as **Buster Bailey**, **Bud Powell** and **Thelonious Monk**. He first worked with **Cecil Taylor** in 1960 and through this association became known as a leading exponent of free-jazz. In the early 70s he was actively engaged in musical education while simultaneously pursuing his own studies. This period saw him broadening his musical base but he retained his links with Taylor, touring with him in various parts of the world. In the early 80s Lyons formed a quartet with **Andrew Cyrille**, **Joseph Jarman** and **Don Moye**. Soon thereafter his health began to fail and he died of cancer in 1986.

Albums: with Cecil Taylor *Nefertiti, The Beautiful One Has Come* (1962), with Taylor *Conquistador* (1966), *Other Afternoons* (Affinity 1969), *Push Pull* (1978), *Jump Up/What To Do About* (1980), with Taylor *Calling It The 8th* (1981), *Jump It Up* (Hat Art 1981), *Something In Return* (Black Saint 1981), *Wee Sneezawee* (1983), *Give It Up* (Black Saint 1985), with Andrew Cyrille *Burnt Offering* (Black Saint 1991).

Lyons, Willie James

b. 5 December 1938, Alabama, USA, d. 26 December 1980, Chicago, Illinois, USA. A west side Chicago blues guitarist from the 50s, Lyons worked as a accompanist with many artists, including **Luther Allison**, **Jimmy Dawkins** and Bobby Rush. Unaccountably ignored by Chicago record companies, he was taken up by French blues enthusiasts in the 70s. He recorded as an accompanist, made a disappointing half album, and in 1979 visited Europe, where he recorded his only full album. This proved to be the work of a fine singer and guitarist, influenced by **B.B. King** and **Freddie King**, **'T-Bone' Walker** and **Lowell Fulson**.

Albums: *Ghetto* (1976), *Chicago Woman* (1980).

Lyttelton, Humphrey

b. 23 May 1921, Eton, Buckinghamshire, England. Raised in an academic atmosphere, his father was a Housemaster at Eton College, he taught himself to play a variety of instruments including the banjolele. His prodigious talent was spotted early and he was given formal lessons on piano and, a little later, in military band drumming. Eventually, his education took him back to Eton College this time as a pupil. He joined the school orchestra as a timpanist but after a while drifted away from the orchestra and the instrument. At the age of 15 he discovered jazz, thanks to records by trumpeters **Nat Gonella** and, decisively, **Louis Armstrong**. By this time Lyttelton had switched to playing the mouth-organ but realizing the instrument's limitations, he acquired a trumpet which he taught himself to play. Forming his own small jazz band at the college, he developed his playing ability and his consuming interest in jazz. With the outbreak of World War II he joined the Grenadier Guards, continuing to play whenever possible. After the war he resumed playing, this time professionally and in 1947 became a member of **George Webb**'s Dixielanders. The following year he formed his own band and quickly became an important figure in the British revivalist movement. In the late 40s and through to the mid-50s Lyttelton's stature in British jazz increased. Significantly, his deep interest in most aspects of jazz meant that he was constantly listening to other musicians, many of whom played different forms of the music. Although he was never to lose his admiration for Armstrong he refused to remain rooted in the revivalist tradition. His acceptance and absorption of music from the jazz mainstream ensured that when the trad boom fizzled out, Lyttelton continued to find an audience. In the mid-50s he added alto saxophonist **Bruce Turner** to his band, outraging some reactionary elements in British jazz circles, and a few years later added **Tony Coe**, **Joe Temperley** and other outstanding and forward-thinking musicians.

In the early 60s Lyttelton's reputation spread far beyond the UK and he also developed another important and long-term admiration for a trumpet player, this time **Buck Clayton**. By this time, however, Lyttelton's personal style had matured and he was very much his own man. He was also heavily involved in many areas outside the performance of music. In 1954, he had published his first autobiographical volume and in the 60s he began to spread his writing wings as essayist, journalist and critic. He also broadcast on radio and television, sometimes as a performer but also as a speaker and presenter. These multiple activities continued throughout the next two decades, his UK BBC Radio 2 series, *The Best Of Jazz*, running for many years. His writings included further autobiographical work and his ready wit found outlets in such seemingly unlikely settings such as the quizmaster on the long-running radio comedy-panel series, *I'm Sorry I Haven't A Clue*. During this time he continued to lead a band, employing first-rate musicians with whom he toured and made numerous records. Amongst the sidemen of the 70s and 80s were **Dave Green**, **Mick Pyne**, **John Surman**, **John Barnes**, **Roy Williams** and Adrian Macintosh. He also toured and recorded with singers **Helen Shapiro**, **Carol Kidd** and **Lillian Boutté**.

Back in the late 40s Lyttelton had recorded with **Sidney Bechet** and in the 70s and 80s he made occasional albums with other American jazz stars including **Buddy Tate**, on *Kansas City Woman*, and **Kenny Davern**, *Scatterbrains* and *This Old Gang Of Ours.* In the early 80s Lyttelton formed his own recording company, Calligraph, and by the end of the decade numerous new albums were available. In addition to these came others, mostly on the Dormouse label, which reissued his earlier recordings and were eagerly snapped up by fans of all ages. Although he has chosen to spend most of his career in the UK, Lyttelton's reputation elsewhere is extremely high and thoroughly deserved. As a trumpet player and bandleader, and occasional clarinettist, he has ranged from echoing early jazz to near-domination of the British mainstream. For more than 40 years he has succeeded in maintaining the highest musical standards, all the while conducting himself with dignity, charm and good humour. In the early 90s touring with **Kathy Stobart**, he showed no signs of letting up and barely acknowledged the fact that he had sailed passed his 70th birthday.

Selected albums: *Humph At The Conway* (Calligraph 1954), *I Play As I Please* (1957), *Triple Exposure* (1959), *Back To The 60s* (Philips 1960-63 recordings), *Humphrey Lyttelton And His Band 1960-63* (Philips), *21 Years On* (1969), *South Bank Swing Session* (1973), *Kansas City Woman* (1974), *Spreadin' Joy* (1978), *One Day I Met An African* (Black Lion 1980), *It Seems Like Yesterday* (1983), *Movin' And Groovin'* (1983), *Scatterbrains* (1984), *Humph At The Bull's Head* (Calligraph 1985), *...This Old Gang Of Ours...* (1985) with Helen Shapiro *Echoes Of The Duke* (Calligraph 1985), *Gonna Call My Children Home: The World Of Buddy Bolden* (1986), *Movin' And Groovin'* (Black Lion 1986), *Gigs* (1987), *Doggin Around* (Wam 1987), *The Dazzling Lillian Boutté* (1988), *In Canada* (Sackville 1980), *The Beano Boogie* (Calligraph 1989), with Helen Shapiro *I Can't Get Started* (Calligraph 1990), *Rock Me Gently* (Calligraph 1991), *Hook Line And Sinker* (Angel 1991), *At Sundown* (Calligraph 1992), *Rent Party* (Stomp Off 1992), *Movin' And Groovin'* (1993), *Hear Me Talkin' To Ya* (Calligraph 1994). Compilations: *Delving Back And Forth With Humph* (1948-86 recordings), *Bad Penny Blues: The Best Of Humph* (1949-56 recordings), *Tribute To Humph Vols 1-8* (1949-56 recordings), *The Parlophone Years* (Dormouse 1989, 1949-56 recordings), *Jazz At The Royal Festival Hall & Jazz At The Conway Hall* (1951-54 recordings), *Dixie Gold* (1960-63 recordings).

Further reading: *I Play As I Please*, Humphrey Lyttelton. *Second Chorus*, Humphrey Lyttelton. *Take It From The Top*, Humphrey Lyttelton. *Humph*, Julian Purser.

M

M

M was the brainchild of former art school student and folk singer Robin Scott. He started out as manager of the R&B band **Roogalator** and formed the Do It label to release an album by them. Do It later found critical success with the band **Adam And The Ants**. Scott moved to Paris in 1978, where he produced the **Slits** and several French bands. It was here that he got the idea for the band M, whose name was taken from the signs for the Paris Metro. Their debut single 'Moderne Man' was not successful and was released at the same time as a single by Comic Romance in which Scott also featured. However M's quirky and hook-laden second single 'Pop Musik' was a massive hit both in the UK and the USA as well as across Europe. As a gimmick, some copies of the single featured both a and b-sides on the one playing surface with the listener taking pot luck as to which groove the needle dropped on to. An album was released to capitalize on the hit and, as well as the singles, also featured a re-recording of the track 'Cowboys And Indians' - previously the b-side of the 'Comic Romance' single. The album was recorded using session musicians Wally Badarov (keyboards), Gary Barnacles (saxophone/flute), Philip Gould (drums), Julian Scott of **Roogalator** (bass), and Betty Vinchon (vocals). Among the musicians on the second album were **Level 42**'s Mark King. After a couple of minor hit follow-ups, M's career slipped into rapid decline with subsequent singles (including a release on **Stiff Records**) failing to chart. Only a 1989 remix of 'Pop Musik' returned the name of M to the charts. Meanwhile, Scott worked with **Ryûichi Sakamoto** on two albums and put out his own solo album - *The Kiss Of Life* - in 1985.
Albums: *New York - London - Paris - Munich* (1979), *The Official Secrets Act* (1980).

M People

The key component of M People is Mike Pickering (b. March 1958, Manchester, England; keyboards, programming), a man of many talents and former DJ at the **Factory** owned Hacienda club in Manchester. *The Face* magazine went as far as to describe Pickering as 'England's most revered DJ'. After school Pickering worked in a fish factory and engineering warehouse, and became a Northern Soul fan. He played saxophone for mid-80s indie dance forerunners **Quando Quango** and had various connections with **New Order**, including sharing a flat with their manager, Rob Gretton. Among several weighty notches on his bedpost was the distinction of having booked the **Smiths** for their first Manchester gigs. He had also signed **James** and **Happy Mondays** in his role as Factory's A&R man. After Factory he became a junior director at the **DeConstruction** label, where he brought **Black Box** and **Guru Josh**, the label's two most important early successes. He provided DeConstruction with *North - The Sound Of The Dance Underground*, arguably the first UK house compilation, though it was Pickering and his band T-Coy behind seven of the eight cuts. He is also the founder member, and songwriter for M People - the M standing for his Christian name - who also record for DeConstruction. The band includes ex-Hot House vocalist Heather Small (b. Heather Margeurita Small, 20 January 1965, London, England) and Paul Heard (b. 5 October 1960, Hammersmith, London, England; keyboards, programming), formerly of **Orange Juice** and **Working Week**. They debuted in May 1991 with 'Colour My Life', scoring with the club hit 'How Can I Love You More' at the end of the year. These singles promoted a first album which took its name from Pickering's early musical leanings, *Northern Soul*. 1993 was M People's breakthrough year. On the back of colossal UK hits like 'Movin' On Up', they were afforded a BRIT Award for Best UK Dance Act. The album which housed the hits, *Elegant Slumming* (whose title was taken from a Tom Woolfe book), included a cover of Dennis Edwards' 'Don't Look Any Further', and vocal support from **Nu Colours**.
Albums: *Northern Soul* (DeConstruction 1992), *Northern Soul Extended* (DeConstruction 1992), *Elegant Slumming* (DeConstruction 1993), *Bizarre Fruit* (DeConstruction (1994).
Video: *Elegant TV* (1994).

M&O Band

This UK studio act was assembled by studio owner and producer Muff Murfin and his engineer and assistant Colin Owen. Murfin, who ran a recording studio at the back of a department store in Worcester, England, recorded many acts under various names before becoming involved with the burgeoning northern soul scene in the mid-70s. A specialist at duplicating sounds, he recorded tracks for Disco Demand under names like the Jezebelles and the Sounds Of Lancashire and also worked with Wigan's Ovations. He then built the Old Smithy studio in his large garden and produced television personality John Asher's 1975 Top 20 revival of 'Let's Twist Again'. In 1976 he covered **Eddie Drennon**'s 'Let's Do The Latin Hustle' as the M&O Band and made it a bigger hit. He was accused of sampling part of Drennon's track on his record which he took as a compliment on his close duplication of Drennon's rhythm track. The publicity, however, harmed the act and future records failed to chart. Today Murfin continues to run a successful studio and publishing operation.

M.A.R.S.

This short-lived UK heavy rock supergroup project was assembled in 1987. Featuring **Tony Macalpine** (guitar), Tommy Aldridge (drums), Robert Rock (vocals) and Rudi Sarzo (bass), their collective pedigrees promised more than they delivered. Produced by Mike Varney, their sole album would have been indistinguishable from **Vinnie Moore**'s, Tony Macalpine's, **Marty Friedman**'s, **Jason Becker**'s or Greg Howe's instrumental sets, were it not for the additional vocals of Rock. *Project Driver* seriously lacked identity, with the all-too transparent influences of **Yngwie Malmsteen** and **Rainbow** unbalancing the collection. The band dissolved soon after the release, with Sarzo and Aldridge joining **Whitesnake**, Rock taking over vocals in **Joshua** and Macalpine picking up his solo career once more.

Album: *Project Driver* (Roadrunner 1987).

M.O.P.

Their name standing for Mash Out Posse, Lil' Fame and Billy Danzenie were the faces behind one of Select Records' freshest hardcore arrivals of 1994. They came to prominence when 'How About Some Hardcore', included on the *House Party 3* soundtrack, took off. Fame had already made his debut with three cuts on 4th & Broadway's *The Hill That's Real*. After a projected solo deal with the label fell through, he hooked up with old friend Danzenie, then fresh out from a prison stretch. When 'Hardcore' succeeded they elected to make the partnership a permanent one. Both had grown up in Brownsville, Brooklyn, New York, and brought a sense of justice to their summaries of urban life. M.O.P. was the title of the gang they ran with, who in turn descended from the Tomahawks. M.O.P. thus started life as an 11-piece, but, according to legend, four of that number were cut down in gang fights, and five more are in jail. The sole remainder numbered Fame and Danzenie, alongside producer/manager Lazy Laz. Their debut album, produced by Darryl D, included the predictable put-downs of 'F.A.G.''s (fake-ass gangstas), while 'Blue Steel' confirmed that 'Nowadays shit is for real - so I'm packin' blue steel'.

Album: *To The Death* (Select 1994).

Maal, Baaba

b. 12 November 1960, Fouata, Senegal. After winning a scholarship to the Ecole Des Beaux Arts in Dakar, the capital of Senegal, vocalist and guitarist Maal travelled widely throughout Senegal and neighbouring Mali and Mauritania, studying the traditional musics of the area. He spent a further two years of academic study at the Paris Conservatoire, learning European theory and composition, before returning to Dakar in the early 80s. In 1982 he released the first of six cassette-only albums that would, by mid-decade, establish him as a potential rival to **Youssou N'Dour**, the reigning king of Senegalese youth music. In 1985, he formed the band Dande Lenol ('voice of the race') and signed to the Paris-based label Syllart, releasing three superb albums: *Wango*, *Nouvelle Generation* and *Taara*. In 1991 he signed to London-based Mango Records.The impressive *Lam Toro* was a more modern Senegalese sound, with synthesizers and programmed percussion, than his previous accoustic albums. *Firin' In Fouta* was also well received by the critics and introduced freeform jazz and reggae beats into Maal's sound. A hugely impresive mix of the new and the old, it was his most complete statement to date.

Albums: *Demgala* (1983), *Djam Leelii* (1984), *Wango* (1986), *Nouvelle Generation* (1988), *Taara* (1990), *Lam Toro* (1992), *Lam Toro - The Remix Album* (1993), *Firin' In Fouta* (Mango 1995).

Mabley, Moms 'Jackie'

b. Loretta Mary Aiken, 19 March 1894, Brevard, North Carolina, USA, d. 23 May 1975. Mabley was raised in Washington, DC. Her 1969 mauldin recitation of the **Dion** hit, 'Abraham, Martin And John' somewhat obscured her history as the most successful comedienne on the black theatre circuit. The song made her a one-hit-wonder, when it hit number 18 R&B and number 35 pop, yet she had been performing for almost 40 years and had already charted with 13 comedy albums on the pop album charts. She was masterful at blue humour but less effective with suitable family fare. Mabley entered the Chitlin' Circuit in 1921 when she toured with **Butterbeans And Susie**. She also appeared in bit parts in films - *Emperor Jones* (1933), *Killer Diller* (1947), *Boarding House Blues* (1948). *Amazing Grace* (1974) was her only starring appearance.

Mabon, Willie

b. 24 October 1925, Hollywood, Tennessee, USA, d. 19 April 1986, Paris, France. Accompanying himself on piano and secondly on harmonica, Mabon sang an urbane blues style similar to **Charles Brown**. He moved from Memphis, Tennessee, to Chicago in 1942 and first got on record in 1949 as a member of the Blues Rockers group. After military service he became a popular entertainer in Chicago's Black Belt, and by the early 50s, was well-established as an R&B singer with a number of successful records to his credit. Signed as a solo artist to **Chess Records** in 1951, Mabon immediately hit with a novelty blues, 'I Don't Know' (R&B number 1, 1952), a remake of a **Cripple Clarence Lofton** record from 1938. Mabon had other hits with 'I'm Mad' (R&B number 1, 1953), 'Poison Ivy' (R&B Top 10, 1954), and 'Seventh Son' (1955). After leaving Chess in 1956, he continued to record on various small labels, getting his best success on Formal in 1962 with 'Got To Have Some'. During the 70s and 80s, Mabon would flit back and forth between Chicago and Europe, making an occasional album for German and French labels, most of which were poorly received. He found a wider audience in Europe, playing the Montreux Jazz Festival and festivals in Berlin and Holland. A polished performer, with a measure of glossy sophistication to his singing, Mabon retained a strong affinity with the earthier aspects of the blues and was an influence upon **Mose Allison**.

Albums: *Funky* (1972), *Cold Chilly Woman* (1973), *Come Back* (1973), *The Comeback* (1973), *Live And Well* (1974), *Shake That Thing* (1975), *Sings 'I Don't Know' And Other Chicago Blues Hits* (70s), *Chicago Blues Session* (1980). Compilations: *Chicago 1963* (1974), *I'm The Fixer: Original USA Recordings 1963-64* (1981), *The Seventh Son* (1982), *Blues Roots Volume 16* (1982).

Mabsant

This Welsh trio took their name from the Patron Saint of festivals in Wales. The current line-up includes Siwsann George (b. Suzanne George, 2 April 1956, East Glamorgan Hospital, Church Village, Wales; guitar, harp, concertina, spoons, vocals), Stuart Brown (b. 7 May 1956, Springburn, Glasgow, Scotland; recorder, bouzouki, whistle, keyboards); and Steve Whitehead (b. 10 March 1960, Coventry, Warwickshire, England; clarinet/saxophone). The group was formed in mid-1978, playing Welsh and Irish songs and tunes in Cardiff pubs. The line-up at the time was Siwsann George, together with Pete Meazey (mandolin, banjo, mouth organ, dulcimer, vocals), Alun Roberts (mandolin) and Chris Jones. Following the departure of Jones, and Roberts falling ill, Stuart Brown joined the group, this was to be the first of a number of personnel changes. After a three-week tour of Brittany in 1980, Meazey stayed behind, making way for Duncan Brown (Stuart's older brother) to join on double bass. Later the same year, Gareth Westacott (mandolin) and Non Harris (vocals) were added. Their debut album was followed by television work and touring. The following year, Siwsann won the Pan-Celtic traditional singing competition (solo category) with a song called 'Aberfan'. Mabsant were the first Welsh group to appear at the Inverness Folk Festival in Scotland in 1982. The group turned fully professional in 1984 and toured extensively. In November 1986, Robin Huw Bowen (b. 7 June 1957, Liverpool, England; harp), joined the group, and in 1987 Mabsant toured the Far East for the British Council. In 1988, they appeared at London's Royal Albert Hall and toured Hungary, Ireland, Denmark and Brittany. Bowen left in 1989 to pursue a solo career and continue his research work of Welsh folk tunes. Peter Stacey (pipes/saxophone/flute) joined temporarily, but family commitments forced him to play less and less and Steve Whitehead was recruited. In December 1989, Mabsant toured Germany for the first time, and by 1990 they were recording music for television. Despite the changes in personnel, Mabsant's sound has continued to develop with each change, without losing sight of the original feel for the music. *Cofeb* was almost folk/jazz, but still had the unmistakable Mabsant touch. Owing to Mabsant's success, the folk world at large now acknowledges that (good) folk music exists outside Scotland and Ireland; the group has paved the way for a number of other highly talented Welsh artists.

Albums: *Cwlwm Pedwar* (Sain 1982), *Trip I Forgannwg* (Folktracks 1983), *Gwyl Mabsant* (Gwerin 1984), *Chware Chwyldro* (Gwerin 1986), *Valley Lights* (Sain 1986), *Trwy'r Weiar* (Sain 1987), *Chwedlau Cymru I Ddysgwyr* (1989), *Cofeb* (1989), *Ton Gron* (Cwmni Fflach 1990). Siwsann George: *Traditional Songs Of Wales* (Saydisc 1994).

Mabuse, Sipho

b. 6 February 1950, Cape Town, South Africa. Vocalist, guitarist, keyboard player, drummer. One of the giants of South African township pop, Mabuse began his career in the late 60s, as drummer with the Beaters, a band heavily influenced by the **Beatles**, **Rolling Stones** and, to a lesser extent, South African groups like the **Manhattan Brothers** and the Skylarks. By the early 70s, township music was increasingly rejecting imported music in favour of indigenous, traditionally-rooted styles, and the Beaters were no exception. A three-month tour of Zimbabwe in 1973 did much to influence this development, with the band becoming deeply influenced by the Afro-rumba style of Harare bands like OK Success. In 1974, their single 'Harari', became a huge hit throughout Southern Africa and provided a new African sound and name for the band, as the tide of black consciousness rose around them. Harari enjoyed widespread success, despite a number of personal problems, not least the deaths of two leading members. By the late 70s their style had moved away from Afro-rumba towards a more overtly mbaqanga sound.

In 1984 - the same year **Hugh Masekela** recorded three Mabuse compositions on his *Techno Bush* album - Harari disbanded and Mabuse decided to pursue a solo career as a vocalist and instrumentalist. His first release,

'Rise', became a major hit later the same year. In 1985, his album *Burn Out* followed suit, selling an unprecedented 230,000 copies in South Africa alone and subsequently being picked up for American release by **CBS**. The album charted a new path for South African pop, with Mabuse focussing his arrangements on keyboards rather than guitars, in addition to saxophones, previously the great staple of township music. In 1986, he enjoyed substantial success on the British independent charts with the single 'Jive Soweto'; the following year he was signed to **Virgin**, who released the single 'Shikisha' and the album *Sipho Mabuse*. In 1986, Mabuse became a leading figure in the South African Musicians Against Apartheid organisation, which campaigned for greater freedom of movement and opportunity for black musicians.

Albums: *Burn Out* (1985), *Afrodizzia* (1986), *Sipho Mabuse* (1987).

McAfee, Johnny

b. 24 July 1913, Dallas, Texas, USA. McAfee, this highly respected ballad singer, also played alto saxophone with several bands during the 30s and 40s. He studied music at Baylor University, Waco, Texas, before working for the bands of Paul Pendarvis, Johnny Hamp, Leighton Noble and **Eddy Duchin**. In the early 40s he led Tony Pastor's saxophone section for a while, and sang on their hit, 'That Ain't The Way I Dreamed It'. After replacing **Dick Haymes** when Haymes left **Tommy Dorsey** at the end of 1941, McAfee supplied the vocals on 'Daybreak', and 'Moonlight Becomes You', which was on the other side of the **Harry James** million-seller, 'I've Heard That Song Before'. After military service during World War II, McAfee played with **Buddy Morrow** and **Horace Heidt** and, in the 50s McAfee appeared frequently on television, often on **Sammy Kaye**'s popular shows.

McAlmont

David McAlmont's first exposure to the music industry came as half of the highly-praised but under-achieving London duo **Thieves**, who split up in 1994. McAlmont has said about the Thieves split, 'It was just a case of who jumped first. I was very cowardly because I did it on the phone.' He subsequently teamed up with ex-**Suede** guitarist Bernard Butler. The relationship was never intended to be permanent, as both parties were unhappy about the dissolution of their former band. The two singles, 'Yes' and 'You Do', they co-wrote featured on McAlmont's typically lush solo debut.

Album: *McAlmont* (Hut 1995).

Macalpine, Tony

Initially trained as a pianist, Tony Macalpine graduated to the electric guitar with an ambition to fuse rock and classical influences into a musical form that would have widespread appeal. Teaming up with ex-**Journey** drummer Steve Smith and ex-**Dave Lee Roth** bassist Billy Sheehan, he recorded *Edge Of Insanity*, which featured a set of classical-jazz-rock fusion instrumental numbers. The album was characterized by Macalpine's ability to improvise and imbue feeling and emotion into songs, even at break-neck speed. He experimented with the idea of forming a straightforward rock band as a consequence, and signed up Tommy Aldridge (drums), Rudi Sarzo (bass) and Robert Rock (vocals) to record *Project Driver* under the **M.A.R.S.** alias; a disappointing **Rainbow**-style collection of hard rock numbers. The band split soon after the release and Macalpine returned to solo status, forming his own Squawk label. He released another all-instrumental album but it was readily apparent, not least to the artist, that he had taken this particular format as far as it could go. On *Eyes Of The World* he added Alan Schorn on lead vocals, Mark Robertson (keyboards), Billy Carmassi (drums) and Mike Jacques (drums) to form Macalpine, the band, specializing in highly polished melodic rock, punctuated by fluid but economical guitar breaks.

Albums: *Edge Of Insanity* (Roadrunner 1986), *Maximum Security* (Vertigo 1987). As Macalpine: *Eyes Of The World* (Vertigo 1990).

McAnally, Mac

b. Lyman McAnally Jnr., 1 July 1959, Belmont, Mississippi, USA. You can find out about McAnally's early life by listening to his US country hit song, 'Back Where I Came From'. Inspired by his mother's gospel piano playing, he started working in clubs from a young age. He had a US pop hit in 1977 with 'It's A Crazy World'. His first album for **Geffen Records** featured the quaintly-titled 'E=MC Squared'. *Simple Life* included harmonies from **Tammy Wynette** and **Ricky Skaggs** but he is better known for his songwriting, which, unusually for Nashville, he generally does on his own. He has written 'It's My Job', 'Back Where I Come From' (both **Jimmy Buffett**), 'Two Dozen Roses' and 'She's All I Got Going' (both **Shenandoah**) and the classic story-song, 'Crime Of Passion' for **Ricky Van Shelton**. He wrote 'Company Time' for **Linda Davis** and the amusing video showed an MCP receiving a public humiliation for his behaviour. He also co-produced Ricky Skaggs' album, *My Father's Son*.

Album: *It's A Crazy World* (Ariola 1977), *Finish Lines* (Geffen), *Simple Life* (Warner 1990), *Live And Learn* (MCA 1992), *Knots* (MCA 1994).

MacArthur, Neil

(see **Blunstone, Colin**)

Macauley, Tony

b. Anthony Instone, 21 April 1944, Fulham, London,

England. Originally a song-plugger for Essex Music, Macauley became one of the UK's leading pop composers of the late 60s and early 70s. He burst onto the scene in 1967 with two number 1 hits, 'Baby Now That I've Found You' for the **Foundations** and 'Let The Heartaches Begin' for **Long John Baldry**. With uncomplicated lyrics by John MacLeod, the songs were bouncy and melodic, setting the pattern for much of Macauley's subsequent output. The run of hits continued in 1968-69 with songs for **Herman's Hermits** ('I Can Take Or Leave Your Loving'), the **Hollies** ('Sorry Suzanne' with lyrics by Geoff Stephens) and the Foundations again ('Back On My Feet Again' and 'Build Me Up Buttercup'). Another good-time pop band, **Johnny Johnson And The Bandwagon**, became a vehicle for Macauley's compositions in 1970 when they recorded 'Sweet Inspiration' and 'Blame It On The Pony Express'. But his biggest songs of the year were **Pickettywitch**'s 'That Same Old Feeling' and 'Love Grows (Where My Rosemary Goes)' by **Edison Lighthouse**, while the most accomplished was the reflective 'Home Lovin' Man', recorded by **Andy Williams**. During the early 70s, Macauley's progress was interrupted by a lengthy legal dispute with his publishers, which the songwriter won on appeal in 1974. The case had staggering implications for the music industry, presaging similar actions from **Gilbert O'Sullivan** and **Elton John**. Macauley's later successes were almost all in association with American artists. For the **Drifters** he wrote 'Kissin In The Back Row Of The Movies' and 'You're More Than A Number In My Little Red Book' and he helped to revive **Duane Eddy**'s career by providing him with 'Play Me Like You Play Your Guitar'. Geoff Stephens rejoined Macauley for the biggest hits of this phase of his career and the pair provided a series of soft ballads for actor **David Soul** (star of television's *Starsky & Hutch*), the most successful of which were 'Goin' In With My Eyes Open' and the 1976 transatlantic number 1, 'Don't Give Up On Us'. With the arrival of disco, Macauley turned away from the pop scene, to write stage musicals and film music but none of these projects achieved the popularity of his earlier hits.

McAuliffe, Leon

b. William Leon McAuliffe, 1 March 1917, Houston, Texas, USA, d. 20 August 1988, Tulsa, Oklahoma, USA. McAuliffe learned both guitar and steel guitar while at school, and when aged 16 joined the Light Crust Doughboys. In March 1935, he joined **Bob Wills**' Texas Playboys as steel guitarist, remaining with him until December 1942, when military service intervened. Wills' entreaties of 'Take It Away Leon' became an expected shout, both on live and recorded performances. He formed his own band, the Western Swing Band, in 1946, but after becoming the owner of the Cimarron Ballroom, Tulsa, in the early 50s, changed the band's name to the Cimarron Boys. He recorded for Majestic, **Columbia**, **Dot** and Starday finding success with such numbers as 'Steel Guitar Rag' and 'Panhandle Rag', and played regularly on KVOO and KRMG, Tulsa. In the late 50s and for most of the 60s, McAuliffe and his band toured extensively in the USA, appeared on many television shows and even visited Europe. He formed Cimarron Records in 1961, and the next year had US country chart success with his version of 'Faded Love', before moving to **Capitol** in 1964. He retired in the late 60s, but in 1973, he played on the famous last recordings made by Wills and soon afterwards was persuaded to front a line-up of ex-Texas Playboys. This band played successfully during the 70s and early 80s, and recorded for **Capitol** and Delta. He died in August 1988, and is remembered as one of the all-time great steel guitarists.

Albums: *Take Off* (1958), *The Swinging Western Strings Of Leon McAuliffe* (1960), *Cozy Inn* (1961), *Mister Western Swing* (1962), *The Swinging West With Leon McAuliffe & His Cimarron Boys* (1964), *The Dancin'est Band Around* (1964), *Everybody Dance, Everybody Swing* (1964), *The Swinging Western Strings Of Leon McAuliffe* (1960), *Golden Country Hits* (1966), *Take It Away, Leon* (1973), *For The Last Time* (1975), *Steel Guitar Rag* (1982), *Leon McAuliffe & His Western Swing Band* (1984).

McBee, Cecil

b. 19 May 1935, Tulsa, Oklahoma, USA. A full-toned bassist who creates rich, singing phrases in a wide range of contemporary jazz contexts, McBee studied clarinet at school, but switched to bass at the age of 17, playing in local nightclubs. He gained a degree in music from Ohio Central State University, then spent two years in the army, conducting the band at Fort Knox. Moving to Detroit in 1962, he worked with **Paul Winter** (1963-64), then went to New York and played with **Jackie McLean** (1964), **Wayne Shorter** (1965-66), **Charles Lloyd** (1966), **Yusef Lateef** (1967-69) and **Alice Coltrane** (1969-72). He established his own group in 1975, but, as one of the most in-demand sidemen in jazz, has continued to work with others, including **Chico Freeman**, **Freddie Hubbard**, **Grachan Moncur III**, **Miles Davis**, **Bobby Hutcherson**, Charles Tolliver, **Pharoah Sanders**, **Lonnie Liston Smith**, **Sonny Rollins**, **Michael White**, **JoAnne Brackeen**, **Horace Tapscott**, **Anthony Braxton**, **Abdullah Ibrahim**, **Buddy Tate** and **Harry 'Sweets' Edison**.

Albums: *Mutima* (Strata East 1975), *Music From The Source* (Enja 1977), *Compassion* (Enja 1977), *Alternate Spaces* (India Navigation 1979), *Flying Out* (India Navigation 1982).

Macbeth, David

b. 1935, Newcastle-upon-Tyne, England. Macbeth was on Newcastle United Football Club's books before being conscripted into the army. He was discovered as a pop singer when he appeared on the *Carroll Levis Talent Show* which led to him making several appearances on local Tyne-Tees Television (some under the pseudonym David North). In 1959, while still working as a commercial traveller, he made his debut single for Pye Records, 'Mr. Blue', a cover of the **Fleetwood**'s US number 1, which proved to be his only Top 20 success. In 1962 he represented Britain at the European Knokke Festival in Belgium and later that year his cover of **Bobby Vinton**'s US chart-topper 'Roses Are Red' entered the Top 40. He worked the cabaret circuit and recorded on **Decca** and Piccadilly in the early 60s before going into the agency side of the music business in 1965. He returned briefly to recording in 1969, under the guidance of producer **Tony Hatch**, but further chart success was not forthcoming.

McBride And The Ride

Terry McBride (b. 16 September 1958, Austin, Texas, USA; lead vocals/bass), Ray Herndon (b. 14 July 1960, Scottsdale, Arkansas, USA; guitar/vocals), Billy Thomas (b. 24 October 1953, Fort Myers, Florida, USA; drums/vocals). MCA producer Tony Brown noticed that **Alabama** were losing their appeal and so he formed a new country group to take over the market. He experimented with McBride, Herndon and Thomas, liked what he heard and gave them a contract and within two months, they were making their first album. The title track of *Sacred Ground* is a neat twist on adultery, written by Kix Brooks of **Brooks And Dunn** and Vernon Rust. Herndon and Thomas left in 1993 and were replaced by Kenny Vaughn (guitar), Randy Frazier (bass) and Keith Edwards (drums). They are featured performing 'No More Cryin'' in the rodeo film, *8 Seconds*. Terry McBride's father, incidentally, was Dale McBride, an original member of the Downbeats who scored several minor country successes in the 70s.
Albums: *Burnin' Up The Road* (MCA 1990), *Sacred Ground* (MCA 1992), *Hurry Sundown* (MCA 1993), *Terry McBride And The Ride* (MCA 1994).

McBride, Frankie

b. 1944, Omagh, Northern Ireland. Originally a member of the Polka Dots Showband, McBride found solo fame in 1967 after working with producer **Tommy Scott** on the ballad 'Five Little Fingers'. Signed by Dick Katz of the Harold Davison Agency, McBride seemed a likely bet to cross over into mainstream cabaret success in the UK, but a follow-up hit proved elusive. His fortunes in Ireland, where he enjoyed a hit with 'Burning Bridge', continued for a period, and his 1968 album, *Frankie McBride Sings,* was a moderate seller.
Album: *Frankie McBride Sings* (1968).

McBride, Laura Lee

b. Laura Frances Owens, 16 May 1920, Bridport, Oklahoma, USA. McBride first sang with her sister as Joy And Jane on her father **Tex Owens**' radio programme on KMBC Kansas City, Missouri in the mid-30s. When, in 1943, she was hired by **Bob Wills**, she became not only the first female vocalist with Wills but, in fact, the first featured woman singer of western swing music. She devoted her life to the genre and became affectionately known as the Queen of Western Swing. She recorded with Wills on Armed Forces Radio Transcriptions in 1943/4 and some **MGM** recordings in 1950. In the late 40s, she married guitarist/bandleader Dickie McBride who, as a member of **Cliff Bruner**'s Texas Wanderers, provided the vocal for the first recording of the country standard 'It Makes No Difference Now' in September 1938. (Between 1938 and 1941, Dickie McBride fronted his own band the Village Boys and recorded for **Decca**). In the late 70s, Laura Lee McBride made some appearances with surviving members of Bob Wills' Texas Playboys at various functions.

McCafferty, Dan

This gritty vocalist gained early experience as a member of the Shadettes, a mid-60s' beat group based in Dunfermline, Scotland. By 1968, the act had evolved into **Nazareth,** which grew from provincial origins into a leading international attraction. McCafferty's throaty rasp was an integral part of the unit's best-known hits, notably 'Broken Down Angel' and 'This Flight Tonight' (both 1973), but he undertook a concurrent solo project in 1975. *Dan McCafferty* comprised several of the artist's favourite songs, including 'Out Of Time', which broached the UK Top 50 as a single. The singer then resumed his commitment to the parent group, but re-embarked on an independent career in 1987 with *Into The Ring.*
Albums: *Dan McCafferty* (1975), *Into The Ring* (1987).

McCain, Jerry

b. 19 June 1930, Gadsden, Alabama, USA. From a musical family, McCain learned harmonica as a child, and played with local group the Upstarts in the early 50s. He first recorded in Jackson, Mississippi for Lillian McMurry's Trumpet label in 1954 ('Wine-O-Wine', 'Stay Out Of Automobiles', 'East Of The Sun'). A competent singer and fiery harmonica player, McCain next signed to Excello where he recorded a number of songs from 1956-59. After other tracks for **Cosimo Mattasa**'s Rex label and for **OKeh**, McCain left music in the early 60s. He returned to the studio in 1965, cutting '728 Texas' for Stan Lewis's Jewel label. In the 70s and 80s he worked as a private investigator while continuing to make occasional records and perform at blues festivals. The **Atlanta Rhythm**

Section provided the backing for McCain's cover versions of **Slim Harpo**'s hits, while *Love Desperado* contained some of his best work including an anti-drug piece, 'Burn The Crackhouse Down'.
Albums: *Sings Slim Harpo* (1973), *Blues 'N' Stuff* (Ichiban 1989), *Love Desperado* (Ichiban 1992).

McCall, C.W.

b. William Fries, 15 November 1928, Audubon, Iowa, USA. Fries loved country music as a child, but had a successful career in advertising in Omaha, culminating in a 1973 campaign for the Metz bread company which involved a truckdriver called C.W. McCall. 'It was just a name that came out of thin air,' says Fries. He had done the voice-over himself and developed the character on record. McCall had a US country hit with 'The Old Home Filler-Up And Keep On A-Truckin' Cafe', and then made the pop chart with a tale of brake failure on 'Wolf Creek Pass'. President Nixon had imposed a 55-mph speed limit during an oil shortage; CB radio, which had been confined to farmers and radio hams, was in demand so that motorists could warn each other of radar traps. McCall told the story of 'Convoy' in CB jargon and the accompanying press release enabled DJs to explain the song to their listeners. 'Convoy' took the hammer down and soared to number 1 on both the US pop and country charts, also making number 2 in the UK. A parody 'Convoy G.B.' by Laurie Lingo And The Dipsticks (in actuality, BBC Radio 1 disc jockeys Dave Lee Travis and Paul Burnett) made number 4. McCall's record was the inspiration for a film of the same name, directed by Sam Peckinpah and starring **Kris Kristofferson**. The soundtrack featured 'Convoy' and previously released material by other artists. McCall went to number 2 on the US country charts with the narration, 'Roses For Mama', and scored a minor US pop hit with 'There Won't Be No Country Music (There Won't Be No Rock'n'Roll)', but he soon returned to advertising. In 1982, he moved to Ouray, Colorado and was elected mayor in 1986.
Albums: *Wolf Creek Pass* (1975), *Black Bear Road* (1975), *Wilderness* (1976), *Rubber Duck* (1976), *Roses For Mama* (1977), *C.W. McCall And Co.* (1978).

McCall, Cash

b. Maurice Dollison, 28 January 1941, New Madrid, Missouri, USA. McCall was a songwriter, session musician and vocalist in the R&B and gospel fields. Best known for his 1966 R&B hit 'When You Wake Up', McCall began singing with the gospel Belmont Singers at the age of 12. Moving to Chicago in the 60s, he played guitar for the Five Blind Boys of Mississippi, Pilgrim Jubilee Singers and Gospel Songbirds. His secular recording career began in 1963 for One-derful Records. He next signed to the small Thomas label, for which he recorded his only R&B chart hit. Subsequent releases for labels such as Checker, Ronn, Paula, and **Columbia Records** did not fare as well. In 1967, McCall wrote 'That's How Love Is', a hit for **Otis Clay**, and also penned songs for artists including **Etta James** and **Tyrone Davis**.
Albums: *Omega Man* (1973), *No More Doggin'* (1983).

McCall, Mary Ann

b. 4 May 1919, Philadelphia, Pennsylvania, USA, d. 14 December 1994, Los Angeles, California, USA. McCall's early career was spent singing with the bands of **Buddy Morrow**, **Tommy Dorsey**, **Woody Herman** and **Charlie Barnet**. During this period, which ended in 1940, she was regarded as an average big band singer. Her return to the spotlight, when she rejoined Herman in 1946, saw her maturing and by the time she left the band in 1950, she was an able, original and forthright jazz singer. She recorded with several leading beboppers in the late 40s and early 50s, including **Howard McGhee**, **Dexter Gordon**, **Charlie Ventura** and her then husband, **Al Cohn**. During the next three decades, McCall worked extensively as a soloist, making occasional records with jazz musicians such as **Jake Hanna** and **Nat Pierce** and singing in jazz clubs and at festivals.
Albums: *An Evening With Charlie Ventura And Mary Ann McCall* (1954), *Easy Living* (1956), *Detour To The Moon* (1958), with Jake Hanna *Kansas City Express* (1976), with Nat Pierce *5400 North* (1978).

McCall, Steve

b. 30 September 1933, Chicago, Illinois, USA, d. 25 May 1989. McCall studied music at conservatory and university, though his first professional gig was with blues singer Lucky Carmichael. In 1964, he recorded with soul/jazz pianist **Ramsey Lewis**. McCall was not only a founder member of the **AACM**, but also a member of its predecessor, the legendary Experimental Band. He brought to both years of experience with blues, dance and show bands, having worked with **Gene Ammons**, **Dexter Gordon** and **Arthur Prysock**. His incisive, precise drumming always had the ability to boil up when necessary. In Chicago, he played with **Muhal Richard Abrams** and **Joseph Jarman**. Between 1967 and 1970 he lived in Paris, where he played and recorded with **Anthony Braxton** on his recordings for the BYG label. When the Chicago musicians played in New York in 1971 under the name of Creative Construction Company, McCall again played drums, relating to the established New York bassist **Richard Davis** with no problems at all. McCall's most visible gig after that was with **Henry Threadgill** in the trio **Air**, a group that rapidly became festival favourites. McCall supplied magically sensitive percussion to the group, so important to their collective sound that when he left in 1982 - to be replaced by Pheeroan akLaff - they changed their name

to New Air. He worked, too, with **Marion Brown**, **Chico Freeman**, **Arthur Blythe** and **David Murray**'s Octet: McCall's creative drumming, with its irreverent enthusiasm for past styles, was the ideal accompaniment for Murray's great 'jazz consolidation' band of the 80s. He returned to Chicago later in the 80s, giving solo concerts and leading his own sextet.
Albums: with Anthony Braxton *B-X/N-O-1-47A* (1969), with Marion Brown *Geechee Recollections* (1973), with Brown *Sweet Flying Earth* (1974), with Creative Construction Company *CCC* (1975, rec 1970), with CCC *CCC Vol II* (1976, rec 1970), with Muhal Richard Abrams *I-OQA+19* (1979), with David Murray Octet *Ming* (1980), with Murray Octet *Home* (1981), with Murray *Murray's Steps* (1982).

McCall, Toussaint

b. 1934, Monroe, Louisiana, USA. McCall's haunting hypnotic 'Nothing Takes The Place Of You' (number 5 R&B) was one of the highlights of a golden year in soul, 1967. Six other singles followed and one album but McCall could not recapture the magic of that one hit. He attempted to revive his career in 1976 with an album on McGowan, but it met with little acceptance. In 1988 he made a surprise appearance in the John Waters film, *Hairspray*, where his lip-sync cameo to 'Nothing Can Take The Place Of You', was a most memorable moment even if it was outside the time frame of the movie.
Albums: *Nothing Takes The Place Of You* (Ronn 1967), *Make Love To Me* (McCowan 1976).

McCalmans

Formed on 6 October 1964, the original line-up of this Scottish trio was Hamish Bayne (b. Nairobi, Kenya), Ian McCalman (b. 1 September 1946, Edinburgh, Scotland; vocals, guitar, bodhran), and Derek Moffat (b. near Dundee, Fife, Scotland; vocals, guitar, mandolin, bodhran). All three met, in 1964, at the Edinburgh School of Architecture, where they called themselves the Ian McCalman Folk Group. Within the year the trio was regularly playing clubs and concerts, and signed a recording deal with **EMI** in 1967. The group secured its first television series in 1970, on BBC Scotland, and worked in Europe. In 1982, Bayne left the group, to be replaced by Nick Keir (b. Edinburgh, Scotland; vocals/guitar/mandolin/tenor banjo/whistles/recorder). Throughout their career, the group have continued to base their style around three-part vocal harmony, both with and without instruments, performing traditional and contemporary material. *Flames On The Water*, featuring contemporary Scottish songs, was highly regarded, and in 1991 the group were given their own series on BBC Radio 2.
Albums: *All In One Mind* (1967), *McCalmans Folk* (1968), *Singers Three* (1969), *Turn Again* (1970), *No Strings Attached* (1971), *An Audience With The McCalmans* (1973), *Side By Side By Side* (1977), *Burn The Witch* (1978), *Smuggler* (1975), *House Full* (1976), *McCalmans Live* (1980), *The Ettrick Shepherd* (1980), *Bonnie Bands Again* (1982), *Ancestral Manoeuvres* (1984), *Peace And Plenty* (1986), *Scottish Songs* (1986), *Listen To The Heat* (1988), *Flames On The Water* (1990), *Honest Poverty* (1993). Compilation: *The Best Of The McCalmans* (1979).

McCandless, Paul

b. 24 March 1947, Indiana, Pennsylvania, USA. The distinctive, curling sound of Paul McCandless on English horn, oboe, saxophones, flute, clarinet, musette (a French bagpipe from the last century) and wind-driven synthesizers has done much to define the fusion music of **Oregon**. The nucleus of the group, **Ralph Towner**, **Collin Walcott**, and McCandless, came together as members of the influential **Paul Winter** Consort. Just as the part-time nature of Oregon has enabled its members to undertake other projects, so, too, has McCandless taken that opportunity to work with Art Lande and **David Samuels**; he also re-united with ex-Consort cellist, **David Darling** in the Gallery project.
Selected albums: with Cyrus *Cyrus* (1971), with Oregon *Music of Another Present Era* (1973), *Distant Hills* (1974), *Winter Light* (1974), *In Concert* (1975), *Friends* (1975), *Together* (1977), *Violin* (1978), *Out Of The Woods* (1978), *Roots In The Sky* (1979), *In Performance* (1980), *Oregon* (1983), *Crossing* (1984), *Ecotopia* (1987), *45th Parallel* (1989), *Always, Never, And Forever* (1991), *Premonition* (1993).

McCann, Eamon

b. 6 November 1955, Creggan, Omagh, Co. Tyrone, Northern Ireland. His interest in music came from his father, who played in a ceilidh band. After learning to play guitar as a boy, he gained his first experiences of country music playing local venues with his two brothers. He recorded a demo cassette *Eamon McCann Sings Country* in 1990 on No Sweat, which led to him being signed to the Harmac label the following year. In 1992, he formed his own band, Pure Country, and soon became a popular touring band around the Irish country scene. He joined Ritz Records in 1994 and has collected several awards for his modern approach to country music. He sings in a style that strongly suggests the influence of **Randy Travis** and **Merle Haggard**. *Everything That I Am*, includes seven of his own songs. It has also led Irish devotees of line dancing, to create a new dance routine, The Eamon McCann Shuffle, which they perform to his recording of 'Its All Over Now'. McCann now regularly tours in the UK and his growing popularity and the airplay his records are receiving should ensure future success.
Albums: *Gold In The Mountains* (Harmac 1991), *Everything That I Am* (Ritz 1994).

McCann, Les

b. Leslie Coleman McCann, 23 September 1935, Lexington, Kentucky, USA. 'There is no end to the possibilities (and fun) in music. So, why don't we get on in there and get it?' McCann's comment highlights two distinctive elements of his music: an interest in innovation, particularly in new technology, and a preference for the dance-based rhythms of gospel and funk. Self-taught as a pianist, he played and sang in school bands and in the navy where a talent contest won him a spot on the ***Ed Sullivan*** *Show*. Moving to California in the late 50s, he formed a successful trio with which he first recorded in 1960. A series of popular albums followed and, in the late 60s, McCann had two hit singles with the protest song 'Compared To What' and the ballad 'With These Hands'. The early 70s saw the pianist exploring electronic keyboards and synthesizers and, while still recording, performing in films such as *Soul To Soul* and shows like the all-star *Black Music Show* from 1972-74. McCann also practiced as a photographer, exhibiting on a number of occasions, and worked as a volunteer teacher with his wife in Mexico. His recording diminished in the late 70s, following an unsuccessful foray into soul and R&B.
Albums: *Les McCann Plays the Truth* (1960), *In New York* (1961), *Swiss Movement* (1971).

McCann, Peter

b. Connecticut, USA. Peter McCann was best known for his 1977 Top 5 single 'Do You Wanna Make Love', and as the author of 'Right Time Of The Night', a Top 10 hit for **Jennifer Warnes** that same year. McCann joined a folk-rock group called the Repairs in 1971, while attending college, and in 1973, when the group split, he joined the staff of ABC Music Publishers. He wrote and recorded 'Do You Wanna Make Love' while employed by that firm (it was issued on 20th Century Fox Records), and simultaneously Warnes scored a hit with his other composition. After his glory year of 1977, however, McCann never wrote or sang another hit.
Album: *Peter McCann* (1977).

McCarters

Jennifer and twins Lisa and Teresa were born in the late 60s, in **Dolly Parton**'s home town of Sevierville, Sevier County, Tennessee, USA. Their father, a factory foreman, played banjo in local bands, and their mother was a gospel singer. When Jennifer was 11 years old and her siblings were nine, they were performing clog dancing routines they had learned from watching the groups on the *Grand Ole Opry*. Three years later, realizing that they would not make a living by that occupation, Jennifer learned to play the guitar and sing, and soon the twins were adding harmony vocals. Around 1984, they made their debut on a Knoxville television station and gained further experience working with *Opry* stars Stu Philips and **Archie Campbell**, as well as busking on the streets of their home town. In 1986, after some persistent and persuasive telephoning by Jennifer, the girls managed to get an audition with Kyle Lehning, **Randy Travis**' record producer, which led to them signing for **Warner Brothers**. They made their US country chart debut in January 1988, with Top 10 hits named 'Timeless And True Love' and 'The Gift', the title track of their first album. Soon after, they became part of the Randy Travis show and toured extensively in the USA and Europe. They have also appeared on many top US network television shows. Their close-harmony singing is similar to the 'Trio' recordings of Dolly Parton, **Linda Ronstadt** and **Emmylou Harris**. Jennifer also showed a talent for songwriting and with Carl Jackson co-wrote their beautifully descriptive ballad 'Letter From Home'. By the time their second album appeared in 1990, they had become known as Jennifer McCarter And The McCarters.
Albums: *The Gift* (1988), *Better Be Home Soon* (1990).

McCarthy

Barking Abbey Comprehensive school, in Essex, England, acted as a meeting point for McCarthy in the early part of the 80s. Eventually, in 1984, Malcolm Eden (b. 1 September 1963, Ilford, Essex, England; vocals), Tim Gane (b. 12 July 1964, Barking, Essex, England; guitar), John Williamson (b. 28 December 1963, Ilford, Essex, England; bass) and Gary Baker (b. 8 September 1963, Barking, Essex, England; drums) formed McCarthy and released a self-financed single, limited to 485 copies. The quartet's profile was further raised with the inclusion of 'Celestial City' on the ***New Musical Express***' influential *C86* cassette, but while McCarthy certainly shared many contemporary bands' tastes for rough-edged guitars, they forced themselves away from the crowd by anointing their music with an extreme left wing political stance. Perhaps it was pure coincidence that the similarly-minded songwriter **Billy Bragg** attended the very same school, yet the 'Red Sleeping Beauty' single - a poetically-veiled commentary on the Thatcher government of the time - was just one of a series of sharply-toned releases where the message never suffocated McCarthy's melodic instinct. After a series of label changes and a highly successful last gasp evolution towards the more fashionable, upbeat sounds of 1990, McCarthy finally tired of battling against their apathetic surroundings and dissolved, playing their final gig at the London School of Economics at the start of the new decade. Baker turned to radiography, Eden concentrated on literary writing, while Gane remained in music and started receiving numerous critical recommendations for his new band, **Stereolab**. He would also use his Duophonic imprint to release Malcolm Eden's first post-McCarthy venture, Herzfield.

Albums: *I'm A Wallet* (Pink 1987), *The Enraged Will Inherit The Earth* (September Records 1989), *Banking, Violence And The Inner Life Today* (Midnight 1990). Compilations: *That's All Very Well But* (Midnight 1989), *We'll Get You Soon You Creeps* (Midnight 1991).

McCarthy, Joseph

b. 27 September 1885, Somerville, Massachusetts, USA, d. 18 December 1943, New York, USA. An important lyricist in the 20s and 30s, McCarthy sang in cafes and worked for music publishers before writing songs such as 'That Dreamy Italian Waltz', 'That's How I Need You' and 'I Miss You Most Of All'. In 1913, with **Jimmy Monaco**, he produced one of popular music's all-time standards, 'You Made Me Love You', memorably sung and recorded by hundreds of artists, including **Al Jolson**, **Harry James**, **Judy Garland** and Grace La Rue. Three years later, again with Monaco, and Howard Johnson, McCarthy wrote 'What Do You Want To Make Those Eyes At Me For?' for **Betty Hutton** to sing in the 1945 movie *Incendiary Blonde*, the bio-pic of nightclub queen Texas Guinan. The song resurfaced in the UK in 1959, as a number 1 for **Emile Ford** And The Checkmates, and again in 1987, when it was a hit for rock 'n' roll revivalist, **Shakin' Stevens**.

In 1919, McCarthy and **Harry Tierney** contributed songs to the ***Ziegfeld Follies*** of that year, and wrote the score for the hugely successful ***Irene***, which was filmed in 1940, starring **Anna Neagle** and Ray Milland, and successfully revived at the Minskoff Theatre in 1973, with **Debbie Reynolds** as Irene. In 1920, Tierney and McCarthy had several numbers, including 'Why Don't You?', interpolated in the European score of Charles Cuvillier's *Afgar* when it was staged on Broadway, starring the toast of London and Paris, Alice Delysia. They also contributed to the revues *The Broadway Whirl*, *Up She Goes* and *Glory*, before writing the score for **Florenz Ziegfeld**'s 1923 hit, *Kid Boots*. After a brief break, McCarthy resumed his association with Tierney in 1927 for the operetta ***Rio Rita***, the season's biggest musical success. McCarthy and Tierney's songs included 'The Rangers' Song', 'If You're In Love, You'll Waltz', 'You're Always In My Arms', 'Following The Sun Around', 'The Kinkajou' and the main duet, 'Rio Rita', which was sung by Ethelind Terry and J. Harold Murray. It ran for nearly 500 performances and was filmed in 1929, and again in 1942. Tierney and McCarthy's last Broadway show together was *Cross My Heart* in 1928, which closed after only eight weeks.

In the 30s, McCarthy collaborated with James Hanley on the songs for the film *High Society Blues* ('I'm In The Market for You', 'Eleanor', 'Just Like A Story Book', 'I Don't Know You Well Enough For That') and *Listen, Darling*, starring **Judy Garland** ('Ten Pins In the Sky'), and in 1940 had 'You Think Of Ev'rything and 'When The Spirit Moves Me' in *Billy Rose's Aquacade* water carnival. McCarthy's other songs included the poignant ballad 'I'm Always Chasing Rainbows' (with Harry Carroll), 'They Go Wild, Simply Wild, Over Me' (a hit for Marion Harris), 'Through', 'Ireland Must Be Heaven For My Mother Came From There', Night Time In Italy', 'I'm In The Market For You', and 'Underneath The Arches'. Among his other collaborators were **Fred Fisher** and Al Piantadosi.

McCartney, Paul

b. 18 June 1942, Liverpool, England. Although commitments to the **Beatles** not unnaturally took precedence, bassist/vocalist McCartney nonetheless pursued several outside projects during this tenure. Many reflected friendships or personal preferences, ranging from production work for **Cliff Bennett**, **Paddy, Klaus And Gibson** and the **Bonzo Dog Doo-Dah Band** to appearances on sessions by **Donovan**, **Paul Jones** and **Steve Miller**. He also wrote 'Woman' for **Peter And Gordon** under the pseudonym Bernard Webb, but such contributions flourished more freely with the founding of Apple Records, where Paul guided the early careers of **Mary Hopkin** and **Badfinger** and enjoyed cameos on releases by **Jackie Lomax** and **James Taylor**. However, despite this well-documented independence, the artist ensured a critical backlash by timing the release of *McCartney* to coincide with that of the Beatles' *Let It Be* and his announced departure from the group. His low-key debut was labelled self-indulgent, yet its intimacy was a welcome respite from prevailing heavy rock, and in 'Maybe I'm Amazed', offered one of Paul's finest songs. *Ram*, credited to McCartney and his wife Linda (b. Linda Eastman, 24 September 1942, Scarsdale, New York, USA), was also maligned as commentators opined that the singer lacked an acidic riposte to his often sentimental approach. The album nonetheless spawned a US number 1 in 'Uncle Albert/Admiral Halsey', while an attendant single, 'Another Day', reached number 2 in the UK. Drummer Denny Seiwell, who had assisted on these sessions, was invited to join a projected group, later enhanced by former **Moody Blues**' member **Denny Laine**. The quartet, dubbed **Wings**, then completed *Wildlife*, another informal set marked by an indifference to dexterity and the absorption of reggae and classic rock 'n' roll rhythms. Having expanded the line-up to include **Henry McCullough** (ex-**Grease Band**; guitar), McCartney took the group on an impromptu tour of UK colleges, before releasing three wildly contrasting singles, 'Give Ireland Back To The Irish' (banned by the BBC), 'Mary Had A Little Lamb' and 'Hi Hi Hi'/'C Moon' (all 1972). The following year, Wings completed 'My Love', a sculpted ballad in the accepted McCartney tradition, and *Red Rose Speedway*, to that date his most formal set. Plans for the unit's fourth album were undermined by the defection of McCullough and Seiwell, but the remaining trio emerged triumphant from a series of productive sessions undertaken in a Lagos studio.

Band On The Run was undeniably a major achievement, and did much to restore McCartney's faltering reputation. Buoyed by adversity, the artist offered a passion and commitment missing from earlier albums and, in turn, reaped due commercial plaudits when the title song and 'Jet' reached both US and UK Top 10 positions. The lightweight, 'Junior's Farm' provided another hit single before a reconstituted Wings, which now included guitarist Jimmy McCulloch (d. 28 September 1979)(ex-**Thunderclap Newman** and **Stone The Crows**) and Joe English (drums), completed *Venus And Mars*, *Wings At The Speed Of Sound* and the expansive on-tour collection, *Wings Over America*. Although failing to scale the artistic heights of *Band On The Run*, such sets re-established McCartney as a major figure and included best-selling singles such as 'Listen To What The Man Said' (1975), 'Silly Love Songs' and 'Let 'Em In' (both 1976). Although progress was momentarily undermined by the departures of McCulloch and English, Wings enjoyed its most spectacular success with 'Mull Of Kintyre' (1977), a saccharine paean to Paul and Linda's Scottish retreat which topped the UK charts for nine consecutive weeks and sold over 2.5 million copies in Britain alone. Although regarded as disappointing, *London Town* nevertheless included 'With A Little Luck', a US number 1, but although Wings' newcomers Laurence Juber (guitar) and Steve Holly (drums) added weight to *Back To The Egg*, it, too, was regarded as inferior. Whereas the group was not officially disbanded until April 1981, McCartney's solo recordings, 'Wonderful Christmastime' (1979), 'Coming Up' (1980) and *McCartney II*, already heralded a new phase in the artist's career. However, if international success was maintained through duets with **Stevie Wonder** ('Ebony And Ivory'), **Michael Jackson** ('The Girl Is Mine') as well as 'Say Say Say' and 'Pipes Of Peace', attendant albums were marred by inconsistency. McCartney's feature film, *Give My Regards To Broadstreet*, was maligned by critics, a fate befalling its soundtrack album, although the optimistic ballad, 'No More Lonely Nights', reached number 2 in the UK. The artist's once-prolific output then noticeably waned, but although his partnership with **10cc** guitarist Eric Stewart gave *Press To Play* a sense of direction, it failed to halt a significant commercial decline. *Choba B CCCP*, a collection of favoured 'oldies' solely intended for release in the USSR, provided an artistic respite and publicity, before a much-heralded collaboration with **Elvis Costello** produced material for the latter's *Spike* and McCartney's own *Flowers In The Dirt*, arguably his strongest set since *Venus And Mars*. Paradoxically, singles culled from the album failed to chart significantly, but a world tour, on which Paul and Linda were joined by Robbie McIntosh (ex-**Pretenders**; guitar), Wix (keyboards), Hamish Stuart (ex-**Average White Band**; bass/vocals) and Chris Whitten (drums), showed that McCartney's power to entertain was stil intact. By drawing on material from the Beatles, Wings and solo recordings, this enduring artist demonstrated a prowess which spans over a quarter of a century. The extent of his diversity was emphasized by his collaboration with Carl Davis on the classical 'Liverpool Oratorio', which featured opera singer Dame Kiri Tekanewa. *Off The Ground* received lukewarm reviews and soon dropped of the charts after a brief run. The accompanying tour however, was a different story. The ambitious stage show and effects undertook a world tour in 1993 and was one of the highest grossing tours in the USA during tht year. Various rumours circulated in 1994 about a reunion with surviving members of his most famous group. Both he and **Yoko Ono** appeared to have settled their longstanding differences, as had **George Harrison** and Paul. The success in 1994/95 of the *Beatles At The BBC* would indicate a ripe time for some kind of musical reunion.

Albums: *McCartney* (1970), *McCartney II* (1980), *Tug Of War* (1982), *Pipes Of Peace* (1983), *Give My Regards To Broad Street* (1984), *Press To Play* (1986), *Choba B CCCP* (1989), *Flowers In The Dirt* (1989), *Tripping The Live Fantastic* (1990), *Unplugged - The Official Bootleg* (1991), *Off The Ground* (1992), *Paul Is Live* (1993). As Wings *Ram* (1971), *Wildlife* (1971), *Red Rose Speedway* (1973), *Band On The Run* (1973), *Venus And Mars* (1975), *Wings At The Speed Of Sound* (1976), *Wings Over America* (1976), *London Town* (1978), *Back To The Egg* (1979). Compilations: *Wings Greatest* (1978), *All The Best* (1987).

Video: *Paul Is Live In Concert On The New World Tour (PMI)* (1994).

Films: *A Hard Day's Night* (1964), *Help!* (1965), *Give My Regards To Broad Street* (1985).

Further reading: *Body Count*, Francie Schwartz. *The Paul McCartney Story*, George Tremlett. *The Facts About A Pop Group: Featuring Wings*, David Gelly. *Paul McCartney In His Own Words*, Paul Gambaccini. *Paul McCartney: A Biography In Words & Pictures*, John Mendelsohn. *Paul McCartney & Wings*, Tony Jasper. *Hands Across The Water: Wings Tour USA* (no author listed). *Paul McCartney: Beatle With Wings*, Martin A. Grove. *Paul McCartney: Composer/Artist*, Paul McCartney. *The Ocean View: Paintings And Drawings Of Wings American Tour April To June 1976*, Humphrey Ocean. *Paul McCartney: The Definitive Biography*, Chris Welch. *McCartney*, Chris Salewicz. *McCartney: The Biography*, Chet Flippo. *Blackbird: The Unauthorized Biography of Paul McCartney*, Geoffrey Giuliano. *Paul McCartney: Behind The Myth*, Ross Benson.

McCarty, Jim

b. 25 July 1943, Liverpool, England. This ex-**Yardbird**'s musical career resumed after his departure from **Renaissance** when, in an unfamiliar role on lead vocals and keyboards, he recorded 1973's *On The Frontier* with Shoot before concentrating on writing for other artists such as **Dave Clark** and **Dave Berry**. Plans to reform the original Renaissance line-up were quashed by **Keith Relf**'s death in 1976, but the survivors continued as Illusion. Lingering enthusiasm for this outfit culminated in 1990's posthumous *Enchanted Caress,* which contained demos mostly composed and sung by McCarty, whose *curriculum vitae* by then included leadership of Ruthless Blues and later combos who, if popular club attractions, leaned heavily on the repertoires of the Yardbirds and their R&B contemporaries. This tendency also pervaded the British Invasion All-Stars which, financed by an American 60s fan, was a studio amalgam of McCarty and certain middle-aged peers. Earlier delvings into the past included 1981's *Afternoon Tea*, a spoken-word album of reminiscences with Chris Dreja (with whom McCarty also co-authored the Yardbirds' biography), and a *Guide To Yardbirds Drumming* video. Moreover, he was one of the Yardbirds who performed two UK concerts in 1983 and made an album under the guise of A Box Of Frogs. By the later 80s, the multi-talented McCarty emerged on yet another artistic front - as a colossus of new age music - when, as a mainstay of Stairway, his output was as strong in its way as anything in the Yardbirds/Renaissance canon.
Albums: *Out Of The Dark* (Higher Octave 1994).

McClain, Charly

b. Charlotte Denise McClain, 26 March 1956, Jackson, Tennessee, USA. McClain began her musical career when only nine years old with her brother in a band called Charlotte And The Volunteers. For six years they worked locally and also had television appearances. She then started modelling swimsuits, changed her name to Charly and was signed to Epic in 1976. She had US country hits with 'Lay Down', 'Make The World Go Away', 'Surround Me With Love' and a duet with **Johnny Rodriguez**, 'I Hate The Way I Love It'. McClain had her first US country number 1 with the soap opera saga of 'Who's Cheatin' Who'. This was followed by 'Sleepin' With The Radio On' and two duets with **Mickey Gilley**, 'Paradise Tonight' (a number 1) and 'Candy Man'. In 1983, she married Wayne Massey, a star of the television soap *One Life To Live*, and they scored with the duets 'With Just One Look In Your Eyes' and 'You Are My Music, You Are My Song'. Massey encouraged her to record 'Radio Heart', also a US country number 1, and he became her record producer when she switched from Epic to **Mercury Records**. McClain has appeared in the television series, *Hart To Hart* and *Fantasy Island*, and has been featured in numerous commercials.
Albums: *Here's Charly McClain* (1977), *Let Me Be Your Baby* (1978), *Alone Too Long* (1979), *Women Get Lonely* (1980), *Who's Cheatin' Who* (1981), *Encore* (1981), *Surround Me With Love* (1981), *Too Good To Hurry* (1982), *Paradise* (1983), *The Woman In Me* (1983), with Mickey Gilley *It Takes Believers* (1984), *Charly* (1984), *Radio Heart* (1985), *Still I Stay* (1987), *Charly McClain* (1988).

McClean, Bitty

b. c.1972, Birmingham, England. Bitty was so named by his grandmother because he was underweight as a baby. As a teenager he went on to study Sound Recording and Media at Sandwell College in Birmingham. He impressed in his studies, and lecturer Alan Cave, previously engineer to **UB40** on *Labour Of Love*, recommended him to his former employers as a tape operator. He went down to the band's Abattoir Studio and remained there for three years. Although nominally recording local bands, Bitty would more often find himself sneaking back into the studio late at night to record demos. By chance the band's Ali Campbell got to hear some of his material and was impressed enough to invite Bitty to provide backing vocals and harmonies on UB40's UK number 1, 'Can't Help Falling In Love'. He also co-produced and engineered their subsequent album, *Promises And Lies.* Having given notice of his talents, he was signed by the newly invoked Brilliant Record Company in June 1993. His debut single, 'It Keeps Rainin', surged to number 2 in the UK charts in September of that year, and was a good example of the fare on offer for his debut long playing set. As Bitty himself described it: 'Fresh, infectious, accessible reggae'. The immediate follow-ups were versions of **Bunny Wailer**'s 'Pass It On' and **Justin Hinds**' 'Here I Stand', both of which followed a similar pattern.
Album: *Just To Let You Know* (Brilliant 1994).

McClennan, Tommy

b. 8 April 1908, Yazoo City, Mississippi, USA, d. c.1960 Chicago, Illinois, USA. McClennan's biography is fairly typical of many blues singers of his time and place. He was raised on the J. F. Sligh farm in rural Mississippi and learned to play the guitar at an early age. Working for tips on the streets and at private parties, he became acquainted with other performers such as **Honeyboy Edwards** and Robert Petway. Petway and McClennan shared a style so close that, later on record, it became difficult to tell them apart, a confusion they sometimes compounded by recording together. McClennan had a limited but effective percussive guitar style, often played by working on a single string. His voice was rough but full of humour, and also capable of expressing poignancy and subtle emotions. Around 1939, he moved to Chicago (as did

Petway) and made a name for himself playing at clubs where expatriate southerners gathered to hear the 'down home' sounds of their younger days. McClennan was an uncompromising character, who, according to a famous story told by **Big Bill Broonzy,** got into trouble by refusing to adapt his songs to conform with northern sensibilities. His refusal to be impressed by the big city found expression in his often used, self-addressed, facetious aside, 'Play it right, you're in Chicago'. Although his 40-track career on record ended in 1942, he continued to play in the clubs into the post-war boom typified by **Muddy Waters** and **Howlin' Wolf**. One of his two known photographs shows him in the company of **Sonny Boy Williamson** (Rice Miller), **Little Walter** and **Elmore James**. His death is unconfirmed, but word of mouth suggests he died, in poverty, around 1960.
Albums: *Travelin' Highway Man* (1990), *I'm A Guitar King* 1990).

McClintock, Harry

b. 8 October 1882, Knoxville, Tennessee, USA, d. 24 April 1957, San Francisco, California, USA. He learned guitar and sang as a child but left home in 1896 to travel. He worked briefly with a travelling show, before he hoboed his way to New Orleans. During his career, he was referred to as Haywire Mac, Radio Mac and sometimes just plain Mac. By 1897, he was busking on the streets where, for the first time, he sang his self-penned 'Big Rock Candy Mountain'. (The song later became internationally popular and has been recorded by many artists.) In 1898, he worked as a mule driver, in the Philippines, delivering supplies to American troops involved in the war with Spain. In 1899, he assisted journalists reporting on the Boxer Rebellion in China, before visiting Australia. He moved to Africa and worked for the railroad delivering supplies to the British during the Boer War. In 1902, after visiting London to watch the coronation of Edward VII, he worked in Argentina, Barbados and St. Croix before returning to the USA to work on the west coast and in Alaska. He became involved with the Industrial Workers of the World and wrote several songs and poems for their publications, including his famous 'Hallelujah, I'm A Bum'. In 1925, whilst working as a brakeman, he gained a daily programme on KFRC San Francisco where both he and the aforementioned song soon proved very popular. In 13 sessions, between 1928 and 1932, he recorded 41 sides for **Victor,** including 'Hallelujah, I'm A Bum', 'The Bum Song' and 'The Bum Song #2'. The material also included hobo songs ('My Last Dollar'), cowboy ballads ('The Texas Rangers') and novelty numbers ('Ain't We Crazy'). Some were recorded with what was described as his Haywire Orchestra. In 1938, he re-recorded his three 'Bum' songs and 'Big Rock Candy Mountain' for **Decca**. He relocated to Hollywood in 1938 and made some film appearances, including several with **Gene Autry**. He also did regular radio work and wrote articles, plays and stories for several publications, sometimes under pseudonyms. His popular column, 'The Railroad Boomer', for *Railroad Magazine,* ran for 10 years and in 1953, he returned to San Francisco to appear on the radio and television show *The Breakfast Hour,* until he officially retired in 1955. He continued however, by request, to make appearances whenever he felt inclined.
Album: *Hallelujah, I'm A Bum* (Rounder 1975, covers 1928-29).

McClinton, Delbert

b. 4 November 1940, Lubbock, Texas, USA. This white R&B artist honed his craft working in a bar band, the Straitjackets, backing visiting blues giants such as **Sonny Boy Williamson**, **Howlin' Wolf**, **Lightnin' Hopkins** and **Jimmy Reed**. McClinton made his first recordings as a member of the Ron-Dels, and was noted for his distinctive harmonica work on **Bruce Channel**'s 'Hey Baby', a Top 3 single in the UK and number 1 in the US in 1962. Legend has it that on a tour of the UK with Channel, McClinton met a young **John Lennon** and advised him on his harmonica technique, resulting in the sound heard on 'Love Me Do'. Relocating to Los Angeles in the early 70s, McClinton emerged in a partnership with fellow Texan Glen Clark, performing country/soul. They achieved a degree of artistic success, releasing two albums before splitting, with Delbert embarking on a solo career. His subsequent output reflects several roadhouse influences. Three gritty releases, *Victim Of Life's Circumstances*, *Genuine Cowhide* and *Love Rustler,* offered country, R&B and southern-style funk, while a 1980 release, *Keeper Of The Flame*, contained material written by **Chuck Berry** and **Don Covay**, as well as several original songs, including loving re-makes of two compositions from the Delbert and Glen period. **Emmylou Harris** scored a C&W number 1 with McClinton's 'Two More Bottles Of Wine' in 1978 and 'B Movic Boxcar Blues' was used in the John Belushi-Dan Aykroyd film, ***The Blues Brothers***. His 1980 album, *The Jealous Kind*, contained his solitary hit single, a Jerry Williams song, 'Givin' It Up For Your Love' which reached the US Top 10. After a lay-off for much of the 80s, this rootsy and largely underrated figure made a welcome return in 1989 with the fiery, *Live From Austin.*
Albums: as Delbert And Glen *Delbert And Glen* (1972), *Subject To Change* (1973). Solo *Victim Of Life's Circumstances* (1975), *Genuine Cowhide* (1976), *Love Rustler* (1977), *Second Wind* (1978), *Keeper Of The Flame* (1979), *The Jealous Kind* (1980), *Plain' From The Heart* (1981), *Live From Austin* (1989), *I'm With You* (1990). Archive collection: *Very Early Delbert McClinton With The Ron-Dels* (1978).

McClinton, O.B.

b. Obie Burnett McClinton, 25 April 1940, Senatobia, Mississippi, USA, d. 23 September 1987. The son of a Baptist preacher, McClinton was dissuaded from listening to R&B, but took solace in country music. Having worked for a time as a disc jockey at radio-station WDIA in Memphis, he forged a career as a songwriter, penning country-soul ballads for **Otis Redding** ('Keep Your Arms Around Me'), before finding the ideal foil in **James Carr**. Two of McClinton's compositions, 'You've Got My Mind Messed Up' (1966) and 'A Man Needs A Woman' (1968), stand among this singer's finest work. McClinton then became a staff writer at the **Stax** label and, in January 1971, began recording as a C&W artist on the company's Enterprise subsidiary. His four albums there offered varied material, including versions of **Wilson Pickett**'s 'Don't Let The Green Grass Fool You' (1972) - his most successful country chart single - and **Merle Haggard**'s 'Okie From Muskogee'. McClinton briefly moved to **Mercury** in 1976, where he had a hit with 'Black Speck', before moving to Epic, where he scored a half-dozen minor C&W hits. One of the few successful black country singers, McClinton died of abdominal cancer in September 1987.
Albums: *O.B. Clinton Country* (1972), *Obie From Senatobie* (1973), *O.B. McClinton Live At Randy's Rodeo* (1973), *Chocolate Cowboy* (1981).

McClure, Bobby

b. 21 April 1942, Chicago, Illinois, USA, d. 13 November 1992, Los Angeles, California, USA. McClure's family moved to East St. Louis when he was two years old, and he was singing in church by the time he was nine. A year later, he provided the unbroken high-tenor lead in the otherwise all-female Spirit Of Illinois gospel group, which went on to tour the 'programs' with better-known gospel quartets like the Swan Silvertones, the Pilgrim Travellers and the **Soul Stirrers**, for whom McClure's then-idol **Sam Cooke** was singing lead. By the late-50s, McClure was involved in R&B, and formed the doo-wop group, Bobby And The Vocals. Subsequently, he sang with East St. Louis drummer Big Daddy Jenkins' band, before replacing vocalist Bernard Mosley with Oliver Sain's famous revue. Sain launched two other major blues/soul names, **Little Milton** and **Fontella Bass**. Bass and McClure duetted on his first recording, 'Don't Mess Up A Good Thing', which was released in January 1965 on Checker, and made the US Top 30. In the mid-60s, McClure moved to Chicago to gig with the likes of **Otis Clay** and Little Milton, but by the early 70s he was back in East St. Louis singing for Sain, sometimes duetting with **Shirley Brown**, and recording for Sain's Vanessa label as well as February 15 Records. He also cut for Sedgwick, Klondike, and **Willie Mitchell**'s by now predominantly soul-orientated Memphis-based Hi label, for whom he recorded four good, but unsuccessful sides. By the 80s McClure was working as a correction officer in an Illinois penitentiary, but still cut two singles for B-Mac, before quitting his job and moving to Los Angeles where he recorded for Jerry '**Swamp Dogg**' Williams and for ex-**Stax** man, Al Bell's Edge Records. Sadly, Bobby McClure was only 50 when he died from a stroke following a brain aneurysm.
Album: *The Cherry LP* (1988). Compilations: *The Rough Edge* (1989, 2 tracks), *Bobby McClure & Willie Clayton* (1992, 8 tracks).

McClure, Ron

b. 22. November 1941, New Haven, Connecticut, USA. McClure started playing the accordion when he was five years old, and played the piano at high school. He studied the bass at the Julius Hartt Conservatory in Hartford, and when he left in 1963 went on to study composition with Hall Overton and Don Sebesky. By the time he joined **Charles Lloyd** in 1967, he had played with **Buddy Rich**, **Herbie Mann** and **Wynton Kelly** backing **Wes Montgomery**. Lloyd's enormously successful group took McClure on worldwide tours before he returned to San Francisco, where he was a founder member of the fusion group Fourth Way. Later on, he played with the group **Blood, Sweat And Tears** before settling to studio work in New York. McClure played with musicians as diverse as vocalists **Tony Bennett**, **Dionne Warwick** and the **Pointer Sisters**, and instrumentalists **Thelonious Monk**, **Gary Burton** and **Joe Henderson**. In 1985, he joined the group of **Al DiMeola** and then worked with **Michel Petrucciani** and **George Russell**. His firm bass lines are characterized by rhythmic fills on open strings against the fretboard. He has taught at the **Berklee College Of Music** (1971) and Long Island University (1983-85).
Albums: with Charles Lloyd *Love In* (1967), *Charles Lloyd In The Soviet Union* (1967), with Fourth Way *Sun And Moon* (1969), with Joe Henderson *In Pursuit Of Blackness* (1971), *Descendants* (Ken Music 1992), *Yesterday's Tomorrow* (EMP 1992).

MacColl, Ewan

b. Jimmie Miller, 25 January 1915, Salford, Manchester, England, d. 22 October 1989. Having parents who sang enabled MacColl to learn many of their songs while he was still young. He subsequently wrote many classic and regularly covered songs of his own, including 'Dirty Old Town' which was inspired by his own home town of Salford. The song was later made popular by the **Dubliners**, among others. Having left school at the age of 14, MacColl joined the Salford Clarion Players, and by the age of 16 he was already actively involved in street theatre. His lifelong allegiance to the Communist Party was influenced by what he experienced first-hand during the Depression years, and by seeing what it had done to his own father and others around him. As a result of his early involvement in political theatre, MacColl, as playwright, actor, director and singer, co-founded the Theatre Workshop at Stratford, London, with Joan Littlewood, who became his first wife. A meeting with folklorist and collector **Alan Lomax** in the 50s persuaded MacColl to become involved in the revival of British folk songs, which at the time took a back seat to the wealth of American folk material that had arrived via the skiffle boom. The Critics Group was formed by MacColl in 1964, in an effort to analyze folk song and folk singing technique. This had its critics, who felt that MacColl and the group were setting themselves up as an elitist authority on folk music. It was in the Critics Group that he met Jean Newlove, who was to be his second wife. They had two children, Hamish and **Kirsty MacColl**. In 1965, a series of programmes called *The Song Carriers* was broadcast on Midlands Radio. Later, the innovative *Radio Ballads* was formulated, combining the voice of the ordinary working man with songs and music relevant to their work. The first series, *The Ballad Of John Axon*, was broadcast in 1958. This brought together **Peggy Seeger** and radio producer Charles Parker. Despite the success of these programmes, no more were commissioned by the BBC on the grounds of expense. It is more likely, however, that the views and opinions of the working man did not conform to the Establishment's idea of what was suitable for broadcast. Unlike many, MacColl believed that it was not sufficient to only perform old songs, but that new material should be aired and 'The Travelling People' emerged from these ideas. Both Seeger and MacColl continued to perform professionally throughout the 70s and 80s, having wed following the break-up of his second marriage. Together they set up Blackthorne Records. They were particularly noticeable during the UK miners' strike of 1984, recording and appearing at benefits.

Outside folk music circles, MacColl is probably best remembered for the beautiful 'The First Time Ever I Saw Your Face' which he wrote in 1957 for Peggy Seeger. **Roberta Flack** reached the top of the US charts with the song in 1972, as well as the UK Top 20. MacColl received an **Ivor Novello** Award for the song in 1973. He died in October 1989, having only recently completed an autobiography. *Black And White* is a compilation of live and studio recordings from 1972-86 and was compiled by his sons, Calum and Neill. In addition to the three children born to him and Peggy, songs such as 'My Old Man' and 'The Joy Of Living', and a pride in British traditional song are just part of the considerable legacy he left behind.

Selected albums: with Dominic Behan *Streets Of Song* (1959), with Peggy Seeger *Chorus From The Gallows* (1960), *Haul On The Bowlin'* (1962), with Peggy Seeger *Jacobite Songs* (1962), *Off To Sea Once More* (1963), *Fourpence A Day-British Industrial Folk Songs* (1963), with A.L. Lloyd *English And Scottish Folk Ballads* (1964), *The Ballad Of John Axon* (1965), *The Long Harvest 1* (1966), with Seeger *The Amorous Muse* (1966), *A Sailor's Garland* (1966), with Seeger *The Manchester Angel* (1966), *The Long Harvest 2* (1967), *Blow Boys Blow* (1967), *Singing The Fishing* (1967), *The Big Hewer* (1967), *The Fight Game* (1967), *The Long Harvest 3* (1968), *The Wanton Muse* (1968), with Seeger *The Angry Muse* (1968), *Paper Stage 1* (1969), *Paper Stage 2* (1969), *The Long Harvest 4* (1969), *The Travelling People* (1969), *The Long Harvest 5* (1970), *On The Edge* (1970), *The World Of Ewan MacColl And Peggy Seeger 1* (1970), *The Long Harvest 6* (1971), *The Long Harvest 7* (1972), *The World Of Ewan MacColl And Peggy Seeger 2* (1972), *Solo Flight* (1972), *The Long Harvest 8* (1973), *The Long Harvest 9* (1974), *The Long Harvest 10* (1975), with Seeger *Saturday Night At The Bull And Mouth* (1977), *Cold Snap* (1977), *Hot Blast* (1978), *Blood And Roses* (1979), with Seeger *Kilroy Was Here* (1980), *Blood And Roses Vol.2* (1981), *Blood And Roses Vol.3* (1982), *Blood And Roses Vol.4* (1982), *Blood And Roses Vol.5* (1983), *Daddy, What Did You Do In The Strike?* (1985), *Items Of News* (1986), with Seeger *Naming Of Names* (1990). Compilations: *Black And White - The Definitive Collection* (Cooking Vinyl 1990), *The Real MacColl* (1993).

Further reading: *Journeyman*, Ewan MacColl. *Traveller's Songs From England And Scotland*, Ewan MacColl and Peggy Seeger

MacColl, Kirsty

b. 10 October 1959, England. The daughter of the celebrated folk singer **Ewan MacColl**, Kirsty has enjoyed success in her own right as an accomplished songwriter and pop vocalist. Originally signed to **Stiff Records** as a 16-year-old, she was most unfortunate not to secure a massive hit with the earnest 'They Don't Know'. Many years later, the television comedienne **Tracey Ullman** took an inferior rendition of the song to number 2 in the UK charts. MacColl had to wait until 1981 for her first chart hit. A change of label to Polydor brought her deserved UK Top 20 success with the witty 'There's A Guy Works Down The Chip Shop Swears He's Elvis'. Her interest in country and pop influences was discernible on her strong debut *Desperate Characters*. In 1984, MacColl married producer Steve Lillywhite, and during the same year she returned to the charts with a stirring version of **Billy Bragg**'s 'A New England'. During the next couple of years, she gave birth to two children but still found herself in-demand as a backing singer. She guested on recordings by a number of prominent artists, including **Simple Minds**, the **Smiths**, the **Rolling Stones**, **Talking Heads**, **Robert Plant**, **Van Morrison** and

Morrissey. In December 1987, she enjoyed her highest ever chart placing at number 2 when duetting with Shane MacGowan on the **Pogues**' evocative vignette of Irish emigration, 'Fairytale Of New York'. In 1989, she returned to recording solo with the highly-accomplished *Kite*. The album included the powerful 'Free World' and an exceptionally alluring version of the **Kinks**' 'Days', which brought her back to the UK Top 20. Smiths guitarist Johnny Marr guested on several of the album's tracks and appeared on the excellent follow-up released in 1991. *Electric Landlady*, an amusing pun on the **Jimi Hendrix** Experience's *Electric Ladyland*, was another strong album which demonstrated MacColl's diversity and songwriting talent. The haunting, dance-influenced 'Walking Down Madison' gave her another Top 40 UK hit. Her career to date was sympathetically compiled on *Galore*, which demonstrated a highly accomplished artist even though four albums in fifteen years is hardly prolific.

Albums: *Desperate Characters* (1981), *Kite* (1989), *Electric Landlady* (1991), *Titanic Days* (ZTT 1994). Compilation: *Galore* (Virgin 1995).

McConnell, Rob

b. 14 February 1935, London, Ontario, Canada. After playing valve trombone in various bands in his homeland during the mid- and late 50s, McConnell joined fellow-Canadian **Maynard Ferguson**'s New York Band in 1964. Despite the attention he attracted there, he returned to Canada to work with the Phil Nimmons band; he also played in studio orchestras and wrote many arrangements. Towards the end of the 60s he formed a band, the Boss Brass, playing his own charts of currently popular music for a 15-piece brass and rhythm group. In the early 70s McConnell added a reed section and, with the band's musical policy slanted strongly towards jazz, he made a series of outstanding albums. Among the musicians in the band were **Sam Noto**, Guido Basso, Don Thompson and **Ed Bickert**. Apart from its own albums, the band also made records with Singers Unlimited, the **Hi-Lo's**, **Phil Woods** and **Mel Tormé**. He also made *Old Friends/New Music*, using a sextet drawn from the big band. Despite the popularity of the Boss Brass and the success of its albums, by the late 80s McConnell decided it was time to make changes. He accepted a teaching post at the Dick Grove Music School in Los Angeles, where he relocated at the end of 1988. In the early 90s, he was active in the southern California jazz scene, playing with various rehearsal bands and seriously considering the reformation of his own big band. An excellent arranger with a real affection for hard-swinging, contemporary, big band jazz, McConnell has made an outstanding contribution to the development of this area of music. His decision to enter teaching (while stopping, at least temporarily) the flow of outstanding big band albums, should ensure that a future generation of musicians will develop some of the theories he has already put into practice.

Albums: *The Rob McConnell-Guido Basso Quintet* (1963), *Rob McConnell And His Orchestra* (1965), *The Boss Brass* i (1968), *The Boss Brass* ii (1972), *The Best Damn Band In The Land* (1974), *Satin Sheets* (1975), *The Jazz Album* (1976), *Big Band Jazz* (1977), *Nobody Does It Better* (1977-78), *The Boss Brass Again* (1978), *Are Ya Dancin' Disco* (1979), *Present Perfect* (MPS 1979), *The Brass Connection* (1980), *Live In Digital* (Sea Breeze 1980), *Tribute* (1980), *All In Good Time* (1982), *Atras Da Porta* (1983), *Old Friends, New Music* (Unisson 1984), *All In Good Time* (Innovation 1984), *Boss Brass And Woods* (1985), *Again* (Pausa 1985), *Big Band Jazz* (Pausa 1985), *Mel Tormé/Rob McConnell* (1986), *Boss Of The Boss Brass* (1988), *The Rob McConnell Jive Five* (Concord 1990), *The Brass Is Back* (Concord 1991), *Live At The 1990 Concord Jazz Festival* (Concord 1991), *Brassy And Sassy* (Concord 1992), *Our 25th Year* (Bellaphon 1993).

McConville, Tom

b. 6 November 1950, Newcastle-Upon-Tyne, England, to a Scottish mother, and an Irish father. During the 70s, this fiddle player toured with comedian **Mike Elliott**, then teamed up with Bob Fox (guitar/vocals) to form a duo. McConville then worked briefly with **Magna Carta** in 1977. During 1979, he got together with songwriter **Kieran Halpin** to play clubs and festivals. Apart from the domestic circuit, they often performed on the Continent, particularly in Germany. They released two albums before reverting to solo work. In 1983, McConville formed Dab Hand with **Jez Lowe** and Tom Napper (b. England; tenor banjo). With only the one album to this line-up's credit, and insufficient work as a three-piece, McConville left in 1987, again returning to solo performances. In 1988, he released *Straight From The Shoulder*. The excellent follow-up *Cross The River* saw the fiddler establishing himself on the club and festival circuit. The album was produced, arranged and recorded by **Chris Newman**.

Albums: with Kieran Halpin *Port Of Call* (1981), with Halpin *Streets Of Everywhere* (1983), *Straight From The Shoulder* (1988), *Cross The River* (Old Bridge Music 1990, with Chris Newman *Fiddler's Fancy - The Music Of James Hill* (Old Bridge Music 1993). With Dab Hand *High Rock And Low Glen* (1987).

McCoo, Marilyn

b. 30 September 1943, Jersey City, New Jersey, USA. McCoo first reached stardom as a founding member of the **Fifth Dimension**. That group was formed in 1965 as the Versatiles in Los Angeles and scored a number of Top 10 hits between 1967 and 1972, including 'Up-Up And Away', 'Stoned Soul Picnic', 'Aquarius/Let The Sunshine In' and 'Wedding Bell Blues'. McCoo married Fifth Dimension member Billy

Davis Jnr in 1969, and together they left the group in 1975 to form an act as a duo. Signed to **ABC Records**, their first single, 'I Hope We Get To Love On Time', was a minor chart entry in 1976, but the album of the same title yielded 'You Don't Have To Be A Star (To Be In My Show)', a number 1 hit. The couple then hosted their own television show for six weeks in 1977. They released two further albums together in 1977 and 1978, and both recorded solo albums in the 80s. In 1981, McCoo hosted the popular television musical programme *Solid Gold*, with which she remained until 1984, then returned to in 1987-88. She released a gospel-orientated album in 1991.

Albums: *Solid Gold* (1981), *The Me Nobody Knows* (1991). With Billy Davis Jnr. *I Hope We Get To Love On Time* (1976), *The Two Of Us* (1977), *Marilyn & Billy* (1978).

McCook, Tommy

b. c.1932, Jamaica, West Indies. From the age of 10, McCook attended the Alpha Catholic School For Boys, where he learnt tenor saxophone, flute and music theory. He left Alpha at 14, and played with the dance bands of Eric Deans and Ray Coburn, subsequently developing into a fine jazz player. During the late 40s and early 50s he was a frequent visitor to **Count Ossie**'s camp, where he would jam with Ossie's Rastafarian hand-drummers, developing a deep love for their music in the process. In 1954 McCook joined a dance band in the Bahamas, and further developed his jazz technique. On his return to Jamaica in 1962, he became involved in the development of **ska**, emerging as a founder member of the **Skatalites** in 1963. His understanding of jazz, R&B and Jamaican musical forms enabled him to make a huge contribution to the group, which changed the course of Jamaican music. The group backed all of the major ska vocalists, and recorded a huge body of instrumental music. Some of the best examples of his work with the Skatalites are compiled on *Ska Authentic*. After the Skatalites split up in 1965, McCook formed the Supersonics, who became **Duke Reid**'s houseband at Treasure Isle studios. Their sublime, cool style made Treasure Isle the most popular studio of the **rocksteady** era with hits from the **Techniques**, **Alton Ellis** And The Flames, **Justin Hinds** And The Dominoes and many more. A compilation of Supersonics instrumentals from this period, simply entitled *Tommy McCook*, was later released in the UK. Since this time, he has played on many recordings for **Coxsone Dodd**, **Bunny Lee**, **Channel One**, **Joe Gibbs**, Randys and other producers. Solo albums released by Bunny Lee include *Cookin'*, *Brass Rockers* and *Hot Lava*. **Glen Brown** also issued an excellent blank-labelled album, usually called *Horny Dub* (1976), and with trumpeter Bobby Ellis he made an album for **Yabby You**, *Blazing Horns* (1978). He is also a featured soloist on most **Aggrovators**, Revolutionaries and Professionals instrumentals from this period. He continues to tour and work as a session player.

Albums: *Tommy McCook* (Attack 1974, rec. 1965-6), *Cookin'* (c.1974), *Brass Rockers* (1975), *Horny Dub* (Grounation white label 1976), *Hot Lava* (Third World 1977) *Instrumental* (Justice 1978). With Bobby Ellis: *Blazing Horns* (1978).

McCorkle, Susannah

b. 1 January 1949, Berkeley, California, USA. In the late 60s, McCorkle lived for a while in Paris. It was during this sojourn that she heard **Billie Holiday** on records and decided to take up singing. Multi-lingual, she lived for a while in Italy, working as a translator and taking any singing jobs she could find. In 1972, she moved to the UK, singing in clubs and pubs and learning about what she had determined would be her future career. She also made two albums which, although well received, enjoyed only limited circulation. In the late 70s, McCorkle returned to the USA and settled in New York, where a five-month engagement at the Cookery in Greenwich Village brought her to wider public attention and elicited rave reviews from critics. She continued to record during the 80s, and her maturing style and the darkening timbre of her voice greatly enhanced her performances. By the early 90s, with the release by Concord Records of *No More Blues* and *Sabia*, two enormously successful albums, McCorkle was poised to make her name known to the wider world. Indeed, her linguistic abilities, skills which enabled her to translate lyrics, notably the Brazilian songs on *Sabia*, make her a likely candidate for international success. In the meantime, she is consolidating her status in jazz with awards, including the 1989 New York Music Award, and is being recorded by the Smithsonian Institute, the youngest singer ever to be included in their popular music series. A graduate of the University of California at Berkeley, McCorkle has also had several short stories published and, in 1991, was working on her first novel.

Albums: *The Music Of Harry Warren* (1976), *There Will Never Be Another You* (Retrospect 1976), *The Quality Of Mercer* (Black Lion 1977), *Over The Rainbow - Songs Of E.Y. Harburg* (1980), *The People That You Never Get To Love* (1982), *How Do You Keep The Music Playing?* (c.1982), *Thanks For The Memory - Songs Of Leo Robin* (1986), *As Time Goes By* (1987), *Dream* (1987), *No More Blues* (Cocord 1989), *Sabia* (Concord 1990), *I'll Take Romance* (Concord 1992), *From Bessie To Brasil* (Cocord 1993).

McCormack, Count John

b. 14 June 1884, Athlone, Eire, d. 16 September 1945. McCormack was one of the most renowned tenors of the first part of the 20th century, as well as an early recording star. After winning a singing competition in Dublin, he made his first records in London in 1904. He studied opera singing in Milan, and regularly appeared at Covent Garden in London after 1909. From 1907 he had a dual recording career, releasing both operatic arias and popular songs. Among those most associated with McCormack were 'The Minstrel Boy', 'The Irish Immigrant' and 'The Sunshine Of Your Smile'. He made hundreds of records, covering virtually the whole repertoire of Victorian parlour ballads and Irish folk songs and ballads. During World War I, he enjoyed tremendous success with his version of 'It's A Long, Long Way To Tipperary' and **Ivor Novello**'s 'Keep The Home Fires Burning'. He also gave numerous fundraising concerts in the USA. In 1928, McCormack became a Papal Count and the following year made his film debut in *Song O'My Heart.* During the 30s he gave numerous radio broadcasts and continued to record and give recitals. During his lifetime, over 200 million copies of McCormack's recordings were sold and his continuing popularity is proven by the 15 reissued albums of his work released during the 80s.

Compilations: *John McCormack In Irish Song* (1974), *John McCormack Sings Ballads* (1974), *Golden Voice Of John McCormack* (1978), *John McCormack Sings Of Old Scotland* (1980), *20 Golden Pieces* (1982), *Popular Songs & Irish Ballads* (1984), *Art Of John McCormack* (1984), *Golden Age Of John McCormack* (1985), *Golden Songs* (1988), *John McCormack in Opera* (1988), *Rarities* (1988), *Turn Ye To Me* (1988).

McCoy, Charlie

b. 28 March 1941, Oak Hill, West Virginia, USA. When McCoy was eight years old, he ordered a harmonica for 50 cents and a box-top, but he was more interested in the guitar. He played in rock 'n' roll bands in Miami, where **Mel Tillis** heard him and suggested that he came to Nashville to work as a singer. This did not work out, but he played drums for US hitmakers **Johnny Ferguson** and **Stonewall Jackson**. In 1961, McCoy recorded as a singer for US Cadence Records and entered the charts with 'Cherry Berry Wine'. He then formed a rock 'n' roll band, Charlie McCoy And The Escorts, which played in Nashville clubs for several years. McCoy played harmonica on **Ann-Margret**'s 'I Just Don't Understand' and **Roy Orbison**'s 'Candy Man', and the success of the two records led to offers of session work. McCoy became the top harmonica player in Nashville playing up to 400 sessions a year. He worked with **Bob Dylan**, playing harmonica on 'Obviously Five Believers', trumpet on 'Rainy Day Women, Nos. 12 And 35', and bass on several other tracks. The success of Dylan and other rock musicians in Nashville prompted McCoy and other sessionmen to form **Area Code 615**. McCoy had a US chart hit in 1972 with a revival of 'Today I Started Loving You Again', but, considering his love of blues harmonica player **Little Walter**, his records are unadventurous and middle-of-the-road. Nevertheless, he often made the US country charts with instrumental interpretations of over-worked country songs. McCoy joined **Barefoot Jerry** and was featured on the group's 1974 US country hit, 'Boogie Woogie'. He now limits his session appearances, largely because he is musical director of the television series, *Hee-Haw.* McCoy frequently visits the UK and has played the Wembley Country Festival with other Nashville musicians.

Albums: *The Real McCoy* (1969), *Charlie McCoy* (1972), *Goodtime Charlie* (1973), *Fastest Harp In The South* (1973), *The Nashville Hit Man* (1974), *Christmas Album* (1974), *Harpin' The Blues* (1975), *Charlie My Boy* (1975), *Play It Again, Charlie* (1976), *Country Cookin'* (1977), *Appalachian Fever* (1979), *One For The Road* (1986), *Charlie McCoy's 13th* (1988), *Beam Me Up, Charlie* (1989).

McCoy, Clyde

b. 29 December 1903, Ashland, Kentucky, USA, d. 1 June 1990, Memphis, Tennessee, USA. McCoy grew up in Portsmouth, Ohio, bought his first trumpet at the age of nine and taught himself to play. While in his teens he formed his own small group, and by the late 20s, led a full orchestra, playing clubs and ballrooms. Using a mute, he developed a distinctive hiccuping, growling, 'wah-wah' trumpet sound, exemplified by his first big hit in 1931, 'Sugar Blues'. This first McCoy recording of the number on **Columbia Records**, (he re-recorded it several times), reputedly sold several million copies and became his theme tune. His other hits during the 30s included **Glen Gray**'s signature tune 'Smoke Rings', 'In The Cool Of The Night', 'Wah Wah Lament', 'The Goona Goo' and 'Sugar Blues', this time on **Decca**. In 1937, McCoy added a female vocal group, the Bennett Sisters, and later married the lead singer. During World War II McCoy took his band and vocalists into the Navy's Special Services as a complete unit. He re-formed after the war and during the 50s had an especially successful band, working major clubs, ballrooms and concert halls throughout the USA and Canada. In later years he often led a small Dixieland outfit, and was still performing up to the mid-80s.

Album: *Sammy Kaye And His Orchestra With Clyde McCoy And His Orchestra* (1987).

McCoy, Joe

b. 11 May 1905, Raymond, Mississippi, USA, d. 28 January 1950, Chicago, Illinois, USA. An early start learning guitar prepared McCoy for a diverse recording career. At first, he partnered his wife, **Memphis Minnie**, and they made many blues records together in the late 20s and early 30s. McCoy (under the pseudonym Kansas Joe) played beautifully tight, two-guitar arrangements, sometimes one on lead vocals, sometimes the other and occasionally a duet. When the couple split up, McCoy was well-established

in Chicago and continued to record as accompanist to other artists, under his own name or a variety of pseudonyms (including religious records as Hallelujah Joe). He adopted a more urbane blues style as time went on and, in 1936, he began a long and successful series of recordings with the jazz-orientated group, the **Harlem Hamfats**.
Albums: *Memphis Minnie And Kansas Joe, Complete Recordings* (1991, four vols), *Harlem Hamfats* (1984).

McCoy, Neal

b. Hubert Neal McGauhey Jnr. (surname pronounced McGoy), Jacksonville, Texas, USA. Neal grew up with a love of country as well as pop and big band music. He started performing as Neal McGoy and his break came when **Janie Fricke** was a judge in a talent contest that he won. She mention Neal to **Charley Pride**, who signed him to a booking and management contract and asked him to be his opening act. His debut single was 'That's How Much I Love You' on 16th Avenue Records, but, in 1991, he moved to **Atlantic** and adjusted his name to Neal McCoy. After several minor hits, he had his first US country number 1 with 'No Doubt About It'.
Albums: *At This Moment* (Atlantic 1991), *Where Forever Begins* (Atlantic 1992), *No Doubt About It* (Atlantic 1994).
Video: *You Gotta Love That! (Warner)* (1994).

McCoy, Robert

b. 31 March 1912, Aliceville, Alabama, USA, d. 1978, Birmingham, Alabama, USA. Jabbo Williams was a family friend, and **Cow Cow Davenport** and **Pinetop Smith** were visitors to the McCoy home. McCoy claimed to have played piano on record behind **Jaybird Coleman** in 1930 and, in 1937, he accompanied a number of Birmingham artists at a session organised by **Lucille Bogan,** of whose band he was a member. After war service, McCoy largely retired (though he claimed to have recorded with **Jerry McCain**). In the early 60s he was extensively recorded by a local enthusiast; attempts to commercialize his sound with R&B musicians and songs failed, but his exploration of the older repertoire resulted in some valuable performances. Heavily indebted to Race Records for material, and stylistically influenced by **Leroy Carr**, McCoy nevertheless preserved the rough, percussive piano styles of Birmingham. He had become a church deacon by 1975.
Albums: *Blues And Boogie Woogie Classics* (c.1975), *Birmingham Sessions* (1988).

McCoy, Van

b. 6 January 1944, Washington, DC, USA, d. 6 July 1979. This successful artist had been a member of several groups prior to announcing his solo career with 'Hey Mr DJ'. Released in 1959, the single was distributed by Sceptre Records, with which McCoy subsequently served in an A&R capacity. He also branched out into writing and production work, making contributions to hits by the **Drifters**, **Gladys Knight And The Pips** and **Barbara Lewis**. Following that, McCoy embarked on a fruitful relationship with **Peaches And Herb**. In 1968, he established VMP (Van McCoy Productions) and enjoyed further success with **Jackie Wilson** ('I Get The Sweetest Feeling') and **Brenda And The Tabulations** ('Right On The Tip Of My Tongue'). He later became the musical arranger for the **Stylistics**, on the departure of **Thom Bell**, and emphasized the sweet, sentimental facets of their sound. McCoy was also encouraged to record under his own name and, fronting the Soul Symphony, secured an international smash in 1975 with the multi-million-selling, disco-dance track, 'The Hustle'. This perky performance set the pattern for further releases but the style grew quickly anonymous. McCoy continued his successful production career with, among others, Faith, Hope And Charity, until his premature death from a heart attack in 1979.
Albums: *Soul Improvisations* (1972), *From Disco To Love* (1972), *Disco Baby* (1975), *Disco Kid* (1975), *The Real McCoy* (1976), *The Hustle* (1976), *Rhythms Of The World* (1976), *Lonely Dancer* (1979), *My Favourite Fantasy* (1978), *Van McCoy And His Magnificent Movie Machine* (1978), *Sweet Rhythm* (1979). Compilation: *The Hustle And Best Of Van McCoy* (1976).

McCoys

Formed in Union City, Indiana, USA, in 1962, this beat group initially comprised Rick Zehringer (b. 5 August 1947, Fort Recovery, Ohio, USA; guitar), his brother Randy (b. 1951, Union City, Indiana, USA; drums) and bassist Dennis Kelly. Known variously as Rick And The Raiders or the Rick Z Combo, the group later added Ronnie Brandon (organ), becoming the McCoys soon after Randy Hobbs replaced the college-bound Kelly. The quartet became a popular attraction throughout America's midwest, and were brought to **Bert Berns**' Bang label by producers **Feldman/Gottherer/Goldstein**. The group's debu 'Hang On Sloopy' (1965), topped the US chart and reached the UK Top 5, but if successive releases in a similar gutsy style fared less well, an early b-side, 'Sorrow', was later adopted by the **Merseys**, which in turn was covered by **David Bowie** on his 1973 *Pin-Ups*. The unit threw off its bubblegum image with the progressive *Infinite McCoys*, and, as the houseband at New York's popular Scene club. Owner/entrepreneur Steve Paul later paired the group with blues protege **Johnny Winter**, whose *Johnny Winter And* featured the Zehringer siblings and Randy Hobbs, with Rick, now **Rick Derringer**, handling production. When this group was disbanded Derringer joined **Edgar Winter** before embarking on a solo career.

Albums: *Hang On Sloopy* (1965), *You Make Me Feel So Good* (1966), *Infinite McCoys* (1968), *Human Ball* (1969).

McCracken, Bob

b. 23 November 1904, Dallas, Texas, USA, d. 4 July 1972, Los Angeles, California, USA. McCracken's early clarinet playing included work in Doc Ross's band with **Jack Teagarden**. He worked in Chicago and New York with Willard Robison's Band in the late 20s before returning to Texas. It was only in 1939 that he settled in Chicago and worked with various artists including trumpeters **Jimmy McPartland** and **Wingy Manone**. His elegant playing fitted well with the **Louis Armstrong** All Stars with whom he played in the early 50s, touring Europe in 1952-53. He played with **Kid Ory**'s Band before settling in California, where he continued playing with Ben Pollack (drums), Pete Dailey (cornet), Jack Teagarden and **Wild Bill Davison**.

Album: *Henry 'Red' Allen And The Kid* (1959).

McCracklin, Jimmy

b. James David Walker, 13 August 1921, St. Louis, Missouri, USA. A former professional boxer, McCracklin began his singing career in 1945. Four years later he formed his own band, the Blues Blasters, in San Francisco, but almost a decade would pass before the artist secured minor fame for his single, 'The Walk'. This gritty slice of R&B crossed over into the pop charts via **Dick Clark**'s *American Bandstand* show where it was favoured by the resident dancers. In the wake of this success, McCracklin continued to enjoy intermittent chart success. 'Just Got To Know' (1961) and 'Think' (1965) reached the US R&B Top 10, but later blues/soul-styled releases fared less well and confined this underrated performer's appeal to a more specialist audience.

Albums: *Jimmy McCracklin Sings* (1961), *I Just Gotta Know* (1961), *Every Night, Every Day* (1965), *Think* (1965), *My Answer* (1966), *New Soul Of Jimmy McCracklin* (1966), *A Piece Of Jimmy McCracklin* (c.1967), *Let's Get Together* (1968), *Stinger Man* (1969), *High On The Blues* (1971), *Yesterday Is Gone* (1972), *Same Lovin'* (1989). Compilations: *Jimmy McCracklin And His Blues Blasters* (1981), *Blues And Soul* (1986), *I'm Gonna Have My Fun* (1986), *You Deceived Me* (1986), *Blast 'Em Dead* (1987).

McCrae, George

b. 19 October 1944, West Palm Beach, Florida, USA. A member of a vocal group, the Stepbrothers, while at elementary school, McCrae later joined the Jivin' Jets. This unit broke up on his induction into the US Navy, but was reformed by the singer on completing his service in 1967. McCrae's wife, **Gwen McCrae**, joined the line-up, but after six months the couple began work as a duo. Together they recorded two singles, the second of which, 'Lead Me On', won Gwen a contract as a solo artist with **Columbia Records**. She received sole credit on the song's ensuing re-release which reached the R&B Top 40. McCrae then began managing his wife's career, but following an R&B Top 20 hit with 'For Your Love' (1973), the pair resumed their singing partnership. McCrae was responsible for one of soul's memorable releases when Gwen failed to meet a particular studio session. He was obliged to sing lead on 'Rock Your Baby', a melodic composition written and produced by Harry Wayne (KC) Casey and Rick Finch, the two protagonists of **KC And The Sunshine Band**. This soaring, buoyant song topped both the US and UK charts, while two further releases, 'I Can't Leave You Alone' (1974) and 'It's Been So Long' (1975) also reached the UK Top 10. McCrae's work was less well-received at home but he continued to manage and record with his wife, appearing on her US number 1 R&B hit 'Rockin' Chair' (1975). In 1984, George McCrae enjoyed a final minor UK chart entry with 'One Step Closer (To Love)', but is still recording and touring in the mid-90s.

Albums: *Rock Your Baby* (1974), *George McCrae* i (1975), *Diamond Touch* (1977), *George McCrae* ii (1978), *We Did It* (1979). With Gwen McCrae *Together* (1975), *One Step Closer To Love* (1984). Compilation: *The Best Of George McCrae* (1984), *The Best Of George And Gwen McCrae* (1993).

McCrae, Gwen

b. 21 December 1943, Pensacola, Florida, USA. Then wife of **George McCrae,** Gwen made her mark in the mid-70s with a delightful series of southern-style soul numbers produced by **Steve Alaimo** and **Clarence Reid** for Henry Stone's Miami-based TK operation. She first hit with a remarkable remake of the old **Bobby 'Blue' Bland** gospel-blues, 'Lead Me On' (R&B number 32, 1970). The record was recorded for TK Records, but leased to **Columbia**. The following year, now on TK's subsidiary label Cat, she followed with an equally remarkable remake of the **Ed Townsend** oldie, 'For Your Love' (R&B number 17). McCrae had her only pop hit with 'Rockin' Chair' in 1975, when the number 1 R&B hit crossed-over reaching the US Top 10. 'Love Insurance' (R&B number 16) was a respectable follow-up in 1975. TK collapsed in 1980, and McCrae moved to New Jersey, and while there signed with **Atlantic**, after which they entered the charts with 'Funky Sensation' (number 22 R&B) in 1981. McCrae's last US chart record was in 1984, but in the UK she scored with 'All This Love That I'm Giving' (number 63), in 1988. Ironically it was her only UK chart record.

Albums: *Gwen McCrae* (1974), *Rockin' Chair* (1975), with George McCrae *Together* (1975), *Something So Right* (1976), *Let's Straighten It Out* (1978), *Melody Life* (1979), *Gwen McCrae* (1981), *On My Way* (1982). Compilation: *The Best Of George And Gwen McCrae* (1993).

McCray, Larry

b. 5 April 1960, Magnolia, Arkansas, USA. McCray was given his first guitar by his sister Clara when he was 12 years old. Soon after the pair moved to Saginaw, Michigan, to be followed over several months by the rest of the family. He played saxophone in high school, but at home he persevered with the guitar, with his brothers Carl and Steve on bass and drums. Like most of his generation, he listened to funk music as well as blues and liked **Eric Clapton** and **Jeff Beck** as much as **Albert King**, **B.B. King** and **Albert Collins**. While working a day job, he gigged with **Lazy Lester** and jammed with his brothers. A basement tape from those sessions brought about his contract with PointBlank. *Ambition* was the label's initial release and to promote it, McCray toured Europe with **Gary Moore**. While that album was heavily rock orientated, *Delta Hurricane*, recorded in Memphis with production assistance by **Mike Vernon**, reverted to a more traditional blues stance, with McCray paying homage to the guitarists that influenced him.

Albums: *Ambition* (PointBlank 1990), *Delta Hurricane* (PointBlank 1993).

McCulloch, Ian

(see **Echo And The Bunnymen**)

McCullough, Henry

b. 1943, England. In 1975, former **Joe Cocker** guitarist McCullough completed a solo album for **George Harrison**'s Dark Horse label. The set featured contributions from many of his ex-colleagues in the **Grease Band**, as well as vocalist **Frankie Miller**.

Album: *Mind Your Own Business* (1975).

McCurdy, Ed

b. 11 January 1919, Willow Hill, Pennsylvania, USA. McCurdy started out as a gospel singer on radio station WKY in Oklahoma City, and went on to work as a night-club and theatre performer, and radio announcer. Married in 1945, it was in 1946 that McCurdy began singing folk-songs on Canadian radio, and later recorded his first album for the Whitehall label. In 1952, he started writing and performing, for children's programmes, both on radio and on television, and, in 1954, moved to New York City. For *A Ballad Singer's Choice*, he was accompanied by **Erik Darling** on guitar and banjo. The album included folk standards such as 'Barbara Allen' and 'Pretty Saro'. McCurdy performed at the 1959 Newport Folk Festival, and appeared on four tracks on *Folk Festival At Newport Vol.3*. The album was recorded on 11-12 July 1959, and released the following year. McCurdy also played the festival in 1960 and 1963. He wrote the song 'Last Night I Had The Strangest Dream' in 1950. The song has been covered by many singers, including **Simon And Garfunkel**, and was especially popular with the peace movements of the 60s. Despite health problems during the 60s, McCurdy was able to undertake a European tour in 1976.

Albums: *Sings Songs Of The Canadian Maritimes* (c.50s), *The Ballad Record* (1955), *Bar Room Ballads* (c.50s), *A Ballad Singer's Choice* (1956), *The Folk Singer* (c.50s), *Frankie And Johnnie* (c.50s), *Sin Songs* (c.50s), *Children's Songs* (1958), *When Dalliance Was In Flower* (c.50s), *When Dalliance Was In Flower Vol. 2* (1958), *Son Of Dalliance* (1959), with Michael Kane *The Legend Of Robin Hood* (c.50s), with other artists *Folk Festival At Newport Vol.3* (1960), *Last Night I Had The Strangest Dream* (1967). Compilations: *Best Of Ed McCurdy* (1967).

Further reading: *Ed McCurdy's Song Book Of Wit And Mirth*, Ed McCurdy.

McCutcheon, John

b. 14 August 1952, Wisconsin, USA. McCutcheon, whose family background encompasses farmers and shoemakers, started playing guitar in the early 60s. He picked up a great number of traditional American songs and tunes from the Appalachians, and learned a wealth of instruments, including fiddle, banjo, autoharp, dulcimer. He is especially regarded for his songwriting and hammer-dulcimer playing, as can be heard on *Step By Step*. His dulcimer playing encompasses folk, classical, jazz and many other elements. *Fine Times At Our House* received a Grammy nomination on release, while *Step By Step* received the NAIRD Award, in 1987, for string music album of the year. In 1986, *Frets* magazine readers poll named McCutcheon the String Instrumentalist of the Year. 'Christmas In The Trenches', from *Winter Solstice*, tells the story from a soldier's point of view of the day when opposing troops got together in no-man's land during World War I, to celebrate Christmas. *Mail Myself To You*, and *Howjadoo*, in contrast, consisted of children's songs, both traditional and contemporary. In 1984, McCutcheon co-produced, co-wrote and arranged *Watch Out* by **Holly Near**. Occasionally, he tours the UK. He has also recorded with songwriter **Si Kahn**, including *Signs Of The Times*. John also collected and recorded a good deal of Nicaraguan music, which was released on Rounder as a double album *Nicaragua Presente!* in 1989. Since 1989, he has been co-editor for 'Folk Blues And Bayond', a regular piece in *International Musician* magazine.

Albums: *How Can I Keep From Singing* (1974), *The Wind That Shakes The Barley* (1977), *Barefoot Boy With Boots On* (1980), *Fine Times At Our House* (1982), *Winter Solstice* (1984), *Howjadoo!* (1985), *Signs Of The Times* (1986), *Step By Step* (1986), *Gonna Rise Again* (1987), *Grandma's Patchwork Quilt* (1987), *Mail Myself To You* (1988), *Water From Another Time* (1989), *What It's Like* (1990), *Live At Wolf Trap* (1991), *Family Garden* (1993).

Further reading: *Water From Another Time*, John McCutcheon.

McDaniel, Mel

b. 6 September 1942, Checotah, Oklahoma, USA. McDaniel began working in bands around Tulsa - first on trumpet, then on guitar - and **J.J. Cale** wrote and produced his first single, 'Lazy Me'. He moved to Nashville in 1969, and, after two years of banging on doors, his brother found him steady work at a club in Anchorage, Alaska. In the mid-70s, he began recording demos for a Nashville publisher and his singing talents were then recognised. In 1976 he entered the US country charts with 'Have A Dream On Me' and he had a considerable success with 'Gentle To Your Senses'. A record about a synthetic lover, 'Plastic Girl', was banned by radio stations. He recorded many songs by Bob McDill including 'Louisiana Saturday Night', 'Right In The Palm Of Your Hand', 'I Call It Love' and his US country number 1, 'Baby's Got Her Blue Jeans On'. He wrote **Conway Twitty**'s tribute to the *Grand Ole Opry*, 'The Grandest Lady Of Them All', while his hippie anthem 'Roll Your Own', has been recorded by **Hoyt Axton**, **Arlo Guthrie** and **Commander Cody**.

Albums: *Gentle To Your Senses* (1977), *Mello* (1978), *The Farm* (1978), *Countrified* (1981), *Take Me To The Country* (1982), *Naturally Country* (1983), *Mel McDaniel & Oklahoma Wind* (1984), *Let It Roll* (1985), *Stand Up* (1985), *Just Can't Sit Down Music* (1986), *Now You're Talkin'* (1988), *Rockabilly Boy* (1989), *Country Pride* (1991).

McDaniels, Gene

b. Eugene B. McDaniels, 12 February 1935, Kansas City, Kansas, USA. A former gospel singer and bandleader, McDaniels completed studies at Omaha's Conservatory of Music before embarking on a recording career. Signed to **Liberty** in the late 50s, he enjoyed several local hits, including 'In Times Like These' and 'The Green Door', prior to securing two US Top 5 entries in 1961 with 'A Hundred Pounds Of Clay' and 'Tower Of Strength'. Both singles fared less well in Britain, where cover versions by **Craig Douglas** and **Frankie Vaughan** took the plaudits, but Gene's influence on British music was acknowledged by his appearance in the film *It's Trad, Dad*. McDaniels' last US chart entry came the following year with 'Point Of No Return', a smooth, jazz-based performance and arguably the singer's finest release. He sadly fell from favour when tastes changed following the rise of the **Beatles** and his subsequent efforts at soul, tinged with social consciousness, paled beside these early recordings.

Albums: *In Times Like These* (1960), *Sometimes I'm Happy (Sometimes I'm Blue)* (1960), *100 lbs Of Clay* (1961), *Gene McDaniels Sings Movie Memories* (1962), *Tower Of Strength* (1962), *Spanish Lace* (1963), *The Wonderful World Of Gene McDaniels* (1963), *Facts Of Life* (1968), *Outlaw* (1970), *Natural Juices* (1975). Compilations: *Hit After Hit* (1962), *Another Tear Falls* (1986).

Film: *It's Trad, Dad a.k.a. Ring-A-Ding Rhythm* (1962).

MacDermot, Galt

b. 18 December 1928, Montreal, Canada. Nostalgia reared its grey and grizzly head at the Palace Theatre in New York when ***George M!***, a celebration of the life and works of **George M. Cohan**, opened on 10 April 1968. Just under three weeks later, audiences at the nearby Biltmore Theatre came face to face (and other parts of the anatomy) with what many theatregoers felt was the 'grim reality' of the present and future, in the full-frontal shape of ***Hair***, the 'American Tribal Rock Musical'. Galt MacDermot wrote the music for what was not so much a show as a social phenomenon, and the book and lyrics were by Gerome Ragni (b. 1943, Pittsburg, USA, d. 10 July 1991, New York, USA) and James Rado. The trio won Grammy Awards for the cast album which spent over a year in the US chart and spawned several hit singles, the most succesful of which was probably the **Fifth Dimension**'s 'Aquarius/Let The Sunshine In'. During the 1970s, MacDermot's compositions featured in a variety of productions, including *Isabel's A Jezebel* (1970, London), ***Two Gentlemen Of Verona*** (**Tony Award**), *Dude*, *Via Galactica*, *Take This Bread*, an oritorio, *Vieux Carré*, *I Took Panama*, and *The Sun Always Shines On The Cool* (1979). In 1984, his musical *The Human Comedy*, lasted for less than two weeks on Broadway, and was revived by the West Coast Ensemble in Hollwood as part of their 1993 season. For some considerable time during the late 80s MacDermot collaborated with the West Indian poet and playwright Derek Walcott on the score for *Steel*, which eventually had its world premiere at Cambridge, Massachusetts, in May 1991. His music for the show was a cosmopolitan mixture of calypso, blues, gospel, and ballads. A reminder, perhaps, of his early days - even before *Hair* - when his instrumental composition, 'African Waltz', won two Grammys and an **Ivor Novello** Award, and became a UK hit in 1961 for British jazzman **Johnny Dankworth**.

Selected abums: *Disin-Hair-ited* (c.70s), *Haircuts* (c.70s).

McDermott's Two Hours

A thumping, jig along Celtic folk/rock pub band, that began on the Levellers' label. They featured a high percentage of political protest songs in their repertoire, but have since disappeared from the music scene.

Album: *The Enemy Within* (1989).

McDevitt, Chas

b. 1935, Glasgow, Scotland. McDevitt was the banjo player with the Crane River Jazz Band in 1955 before forming a skiffle group which won a talent contest organised by **Radio Luxembourg**. Another

contestant, vocalist **Nancy Whiskey** (b. 1936, Glasgow, Scotland) joined the McDevitt group which included guitarists Tony Kohn and Bill Branwell (from the **Cotton Pickers** skiffle group), Marc Sharratt (d. May 1991; washboard) and Lennie Hanson (bass). The group appeared in the film *The Tommy Steele Story* in 1957, performing 'Freight Train', a song introduced to Britain by **Peggy Seeger** who had learned it from its composer, black American folk singer **Elizabeth Cotten**. Issued by Oriole, the McDevitt/Whiskey version was a Top 10 hit in the UK and reached the US charts, although McDevitt did receive a lawsuit from America over the ownership of the copyright. After the release of a version of 'Greenback Dollar' and an EP as follow-ups, Whiskey left the group. With a studio group, the Skifflers, she made a series of singles for Oriole from 1957-59, including 'He's Solid Gone' and the folk song 'I Know Where I'm Going' and also released *The Intoxicating Miss Whiskey*. Having opened a Freight Train coffee bar in London, McDevitt continued to perform and record with new vocalist Shirley Douglas, (b. 1936, Belfast, Northern Ireland) whom he later married. He briefly followed the rock 'n' roll trend with conspicuous lack of success and later performed duets with Douglas after the manner of **Nina And Frederik**. Among his later efforts were 'It Takes A Worried Man' (Oriole 1957), 'Teenage Letter' (1959) and 'One Love' (**HMV** 1961). Both McDevitt and Douglas recorded for Joy Records in the 70s enlisting session support from **Joe Brown** and **Wizz Jones**.
Albums: *The Intoxicating Miss Whiskey* (1957), *The Six-Five Special* (50s), *Sing Something Old, New, Borrowed & Blue* (1972), *Takes Ya Back Don't It* (1976).

McDonald And Giles

Ian McDonald (b. 25 June 1946, London, England; keyboards/woodwind) and Mike Giles (b. 1942, Bournemouth, Dorset, England; drums) were founder members of **King Crimson**, but they left the group in December 1969, following an ill-tempered tour of the USA. Their lone album, *McDonald And Giles*, displayed similarities to their former incarnation, while adding a freer, jazz-like atmosphere. The duo was assisted by Mike's brother, Peter, and **Steve Winwood**, but despite their potential, the partners embarked on separate careers. McDonald later became a founder member of **Foreigner**.
Album: *McDonald And Giles* (1970).

McDonald, Brian, Group

This melodic USA pop-rock outfit was put together in 1987 by keyboard wizard Brian McDonald. Enlisting the services of Will Hodges (guitar), Andrew G. Wilkes (bass), and D.W. Adams (drums), they signed to **Capitol Records** and released *Desperate Business* the same year. Influenced by **Nightranger**, **Bryan Adams** and **Jeff Paris**, the album was a solid musical statement, marred only by McDonald's vocals, which lacked both power and range. However, the set did feature singer/actress **Fiona** on backing vocals, which helped the cause.
Album: *Desperate Business* (Capitol 1987).

McDonald, Country Joe

b. 1 January 1942, El Monte, California, USA. Named Joe in honour of Joseph Stalin by his politically active parents, McDonald became immersed in Berkeley's folk and protest movement during the early 60s. In 1964, he made a low-key album with fellow performer Blair Hardman, and later founded the radical pamphlet, *Rag Baby*. An early copy included a four-track record which featured the original version of the singer's celebrated anti-Vietnam War song, 'I Feel Like I'm Fixin' To Die Rag'. In 1965, he formed the Instant Action Jug band, which later evolved into **Country Joe And The Fish**. This influential acid-rock band was one of the era's finest, but by 1969, McDonald had resumed his solo career. Two tribute albums, *Thinking Of Woody Guthrie* and *Tonight I'm Singing Just For You* (a selection of C&W favourites) presaged his first original set, *Hold On, It's Coming*, which was recorded in London with several British musicians. This was followed by *Quiet Days In Clichy*, the soundtrack to a film of Henry Miller's novel, and *War, War, War*, an evocative adaptation of the work of poet Robert Service. The acclaimed *Paris Sessions* was a critical success, but subsequent releases lacked the artist's early purpose. He has remained a popular live attraction and his commitment to political and environmental causes is undiminished, as exemplified on a 1989 release, *Vietnam Experience*.
Albums: *Country Joe And Blair Hardman* (1964), *Thinking Of Woody Guthrie* (1969), *Tonight I'm Singing Just For You* (1969), *Hold On It's Coming* (1971), *Quiet Days In Clichy* (1971), *War, War, War* (1971), *Incredible Live* (1972), *The Paris Sessions* (1973), *Country Joe* (1975), *Paradise With An Ocean View* (1976), *Love Is A Fire* (1976), *Goodbye Blues* (1977), *Rock 'N' Roll From Planet Earth* (1978), *Leisure Suite* (1979), *On My Own* (1980), *Into The Fray* (1982), *Child's Play* (1983), *Animal Tracks* (1983), *Peace On Earth* (1989), *Vietnam Experience* (1989). Compilations: *The Best Of Country Joe McDonald* (1973), *The Essential Country Joe McDonald* (1976), *Collectors' Items* (1981), *Classics* (1992).

MacDonald, Jeanette

(see **Eddy, Nelson, And Jeanette MacDonald**)

MacDonald, Laurel

b. Halifax, Nova Scotia, Canada. The singer-songwriter and multi-instrumentalist Laurel MacDonald is the cousin of the east coast folk singer **Mary Jane Lamond**. She learned piano and ukulele as a child, and in the 60s played guitar in folk clubs. It

was not until the late 80s, though, that she decided to pursue a career in music. MacDonald and her producer Philip Strong (whom she met in 1992 while he was mixing her score for Mehra Meh's film *Siblings*) recorded her debut in 1994, with MacDonald herself distributing it to local shops until Cargo Records signed her. The album was firmly in the Celtic folk tradition, albeit with an *avant garde* edge, and its mix of musical styles, including Turkish, Balkan, Indian and Celtic, soon won her many admirers. MacDonald played bodhran, bouzouki and harmonium, Catherine Keenana played the hurdy-gurdy, Loretto Reid the Irish tin whistle and Rob Piltch the electric guitar. MacDonald has said of her writing, 'Primarily the album is me telling a story about my life and about my reality.'
Album: *Kiss Closed My Eyes* (Improbable/Cargo 1994).

McDonald, Michael

b. 1952, St. Louis, Missouri, USA. Following his departure from the **Doobie Brothers** in 1982, McDonald, the former **Steely Dan** keyboard player, embarked on a popular solo career. He had already won a Grammy for his song, co-written with **Kenny Loggins**, 'What A Fool Believes', but during the 80s he had his compositions recorded by a plethora of artists, including **Aretha Franklin**, **Millie Jackson** and **Carly Simon**. He almost made the top of the US charts in 1982 with his soulful 'I Keep Forgettin' (Every Time You're Near)'. It is not often that a white singer is able to write and sing black soul music with conviction and integrity. His 'Yah Mo B There', recorded with **James Ingram** in 1984, is a modern soul classic. The 1985 *No Lookin' Back* was a dance favourite, shortly to be followed by his epic number 1 hit with **Patti LaBelle**, 'On My Own'. During that year, he scored an international hit with the theme from *Running Scared*, the graceful 'Sweet Freedom'. McDonald has one of the best voices in modern soul/rock; it is effortless and powerful. Additionally he has honed his ability in order to become a major songwriter, but can be accused of selling himself short.
Albums: *If That's What It Takes* (1982), *No Looking Back* (1985), *Lonely Talk* (1989), *Take It To Heart* (1990), *Blink Of An Eye* (1993). Compilation: *Sweet Freedom: Best Of Michael McDonald* (1986).

MacDonald, Ralph

b. 15 March 1944, New York City, New York, USA. MacDonald learnt the conga while listening to his father's band playing in Harlem. His own playing reflects interests in both African and West Indian music. When he was 17, he joined **Harry Belafonte**'s band and stayed with him for 10 years (1961-71). After that he played with **Roberta Flack** before leading his own band right through to the 80s. His main work was as a producer in his own studio (Rosebud Recording Studio), with a team of writers that included William Salter and William Eaton. **Donny Hathaway** had a huge hit with their 'Where Is the Love' which sold 10 million copies. MacDonald went on to write songs on eight million-selling records and produced seven gold records, including **Grover Washington**'s *Mr. Magic* and Rod Stewart's *Trade Winds*. He has also worked with saxophonists **Roland Kirk**, **Paul Desmond**, **David Sanborn** and **Randy** and **Michael Brecker**.
Album: *The Brecker Brothers* (1975).
Film: *Body Rock* (1984).

McDonald, Shelagh

One of the leading females from the UK during the brief early 70s folksinger/songwriter boom, McDonald signed to B&C Records where she cut a couple of coyly appealing, self-penned and traditional albums. She sang a particularly fine version of the traditional ballad 'Dowie Dens Of Yarrow', but has been absent from the music scene for some time.
Selected album: *Stargazer* (1971).

McDonough, Dick

b. 1904, USA, d. 25 May 1938. Guitarist McDonough began on banjo and by the mid-20s was in great demand on record sessions by jazz groups, popular singers and dancebands of the day. Among the artists with whom he recorded were **Red Nichols**, **Red McKenzie**, **Connee Boswell**, **Benny Goodman**, **Mildred Bailey** and **Glenn Miller**. His career continued into the 30s, which saw a particularly fruitful musical partnership with fellow-guitarist **Carl Kress**. McDonough's high-pressure musical life was matched by equally high living, and his health finally gave out. He died in May 1938. Although often overlooked, McDonough was an important figure in the development of jazz guitar and his recorded work, especially that with Kress, is worthy of study.
Compilation: *The Guitar Genius Of Dick McDonough And Carl Kress In The Thirties* (1934-37).

McDowell, Mississippi Fred

b. 12 January 1904, Rossville, Tennessee, USA, d. 3 July 1972, Memphis, Tennessee, USA. A self-taught guitarist, McDowell garnered his early reputation in the Memphis area by appearances at private parties, picnics and dances. He later moved to Como, Mississippi, and was employed as a farmer until discovered by field researcher **Alan Lomax** in 1959. Sessions for **Atlantic** and Prestige confirmed the artist as one of the last great exponents of the traditional bottleneck style and McDowell became a leading light of the 60s blues renaissance. He undertook several recordings with his wife, Annie Mae and, in 1964, appeared at the *Newport Folk Festival* alongside other major 'rediscoveries' **Mississippi John Hurt** and **Sleepy John Estes**; a portion of his performance was captured on the attendant film. The following year he completed the first of several releases for the California-based **Arhoolie** label. These recordings introduced a consistency to his work which deftly combined blues and spiritual material. McDowell also became a frequent visitor to Europe, touring with the American Folk Blues Festival and later appearing in concert in London, where he was supported by **Jo Ann Kelly**. He appeared on several Dutch television programmes and in two documentary films, *The Blues Maker* (1968) and *Fred McDowell* (1969). The artist was then signed to the **Capitol** label, for which he recorded *I Don't Play No Rock 'N' Roll.* Arguably one of the finest releases of its genre, its intimate charm belied the intensity the performer still brought to his work. Despite ailing health McDowell continued to follow a punishing schedule with with performances at festivals throughout the USA, but by the end of 1971, such work had lessened dramatically. He died of cancer in July 1972. Although his compositions were not widely covered, the **Rolling Stones** recorded a haunting version of 'You've Got To Move' on *Sticky Fingers* (1971). McDowell's influence is also apparent in the approach of several artists, notably that of **Bonnie Raitt**.

Albums: *Mississippi Delta Blues* (1964), *My Home Is In The Delta* (1964), *Amazing Grace* (1964), *Mississippi Delta Blues Volume 2* (1966), *I Don't Play No Rock 'N' Roll* (1969), *Mississippi Fred McDowell And His Blues Boys* (1969), *Mississippi Fred McDowell In London 1* (1970), *Mississippi Fred McDowell In London 2* (1970), *Going Down South* (1970), *Mississippi Fred McDowell* (1971), *Mississippi Fred McDowell 1904-1972* (1974), *Mississippi Fred McDowell And Johnny Woods* (1977), *Miss Delta Blues* (1981), *Miss Delta Blues, Volume Two* (1981), *Keep Your Lamps Trimmed* (1981), *A Double Dose Of Dynamite* (1986), *Fred McDowell 1959* (1988), *When I Lay My Burden Down* (1988), *1962* (1988), with Jo Ann Kelly *Standing At The Burying Ground* (1989), *The Train I Ride* (1993).

McDowell, Ronnie

b. Fountain Head, Tennessee, USA. McDowell initially built his career on his ability to imitate the voice of **Elvis Presley**, a talent he was called upon often to utilize in films and television programmes. He also recorded his own music, however, and, by the 80s, was a major star in his own right in the country field. McDowell began trying out his Presley imitation while in the US Navy in 1968. Upon his discharge, he worked as a sign painter in Nashville while trying to sell his songs. Among the country artists who recorded his compositions were **Roy Drusky** and **Billy Walker**. He recorded for minor record labels such as Chart and Scorpion during the mid-70s, with no success, and released a cover version of **Roy Orbison**'s 'Only The Lonely' in 1976, which also did not chart. McDowell's first single to chart was 'The King Is Gone', his tribute to his departed hero, which he wrote (with **Lee Morgan**) and recorded on Scorpion two months after Presley's death. It reached number 13 on both the country and pop charts. His real breakthrough came later that year, with 'I Love You, I Love You, I Love You', which reached number 5 on the country chart (it was also his last single to cross over to pop, although it placed near the bottom of that chart). McDowell continued to place singles on the country charts through 1980, having switched to Epic Records in 1979. That same year he supplied the voice of Presley for the soundtrack of the film *Elvis.*

At the start of 1981, he began a long string of country Top 10 singles with 'Wandering Eyes', which was followed by the number 1 'Older Women' and 10 other Top 10 country hits. By the middle of the 80s, he was able to release music with little remaining of the Elvis sound, and could finally claim to have succeeded on the merits of his own voice. Later, he returned to his early vocation as the voice of Elvis in the short-lived 1989 television series titled *Elvis.* McDowell switched labels to **MCA Records**' Curb division in 1986. One of his biggest hits of the late 80s was a remake of the old **Conway Twitty** hit 'It's Only Make Believe', with the originator supplying a guest vocal.

Albums: *The King Is Gone* (1977), *Live At The Fox* (1978), *Tribute To The King* (1979), *I Love You, I Love You, I Love You* (1978), *Elvis* (1979, film soundtrack), *Rockin' You Easy, Lovin' You Slow* (1979), *Love So Many Ways* (1980), *Going, Going...Gone* (1980), *Good Time Lovin' Man* (1981), *Greatest Hits* (1982), *Love To Burn* (1982), *Personally* (1985), *Country Boy's Heart* (1983), *Willing* (1984), *In A New York Minute* (1985), *All Tied Up In Love* (1986), *Older Women And Other Greatest Hits* (1987), *Best Of Ronnie McDowell* (1990), *Unchained Melody* (1991), *Country Dances* (1993).

Film: *Elvis - The Movie* (1979).

McDuff, Brother Jack

b. Eugene McDuff, 17 September 1926, Champaign, Illinois, USA. McDuff adopted a professional name which reflects the racial consciousness of the 60s. Self-taught on piano, he became adept on the Hammond organ, an instrument associated with the church and hence with black music at its most heated. He took time out from touring to study music at the New York Technical College in Cincinnati, Ohio. He toured with various R&B bands from 1948, then formed his own jazz group in 1954, playing in the midwest. In 1957, he broke up the group and left music, but returned in 1958 as a bass player. This was the ideal introduction to taking up the Hammond, where the organist supplies bass with foot pedals. In 1961, he recorded an album with **Roland Kirk**, *Kirk's Works.* In that year he also worked with guitarist **Grant Green** and, from 1962 to 1965, with superstar-to-be **George Benson**. 1964's *The Dynamic Jack McDuff* was a highly successful encounter of organ and big band, featuring arrangements by **Benny Golson**. In the 80s McDuff started playing electric piano and working with vocalists.

Selected albums: *Brother Jack* (Prestige 1960), *Tough Duff* (Prestige 1960), *The Honeydripper* (Prestige 1961), *Goodnight, It's Time To Go* (Prestige 1961), *Mellow Gravy-Brother Jack Meets The Boss* (Prestige 1962), *Screanin'* (Prestige 1963), *Somethin' Slick!* (Prestige 1963), *Brother Jack McDuff Live!* (Prestige 1960), *Live! At The Jazz Workshop* (Prestige 1963), *The Dynamic Jack McDuff* (Prestige 1964), *Prelude* (Prestige 1964), *The Concert McDuff Recorded Live* (Prestige 1965), *Silk And Soul* (Prestige 1965), *Hot Barbeque* (Prestige 1966), *A Change Is Gonna Come* (Atlantic 1966), *Walk On By* (Prestige 1967), *Brother Jack McDuff's Greatest Hits* (Prestige 1967), *Hallelujah Time* (Prestige 1967), *Tobacco Road* (Atlantic 1967), The *Midnight Sun* (Prestige 1967), *Getting Our Thing Together* (1968), *Soul Circle* (Prestige 1968), *Jack McDuff Plays For Beautiful People* (Prestige 1969), *I Got A Woman* (Prestige 1969), *Steppin' Out* (Prestige 1969), *Live, The Best Of Brother Jack McDuff* (Prestige 1969), *Down Home Style* (Blue Note 1969), *Moon Rappin'* (Blue Note 1969), *The Fourth Dimension* (1974), *Heatin' System* (1975), *Another Real Good'un* (1992).

McEachern, Murray

b. 16 August 1915, Toronto, Canada, d. 28 April 1982. After learning to play a wide range of musical instruments, McEachern began playing in dancebands during the early 30s. In 1936, he joined the **Benny Goodman** Orchestra, where he played trombone. After Goodman he was with the **Casa Loma Orchestra**, playing trombone and alto saxophone; following this there was a short spell with **Paul Whiteman**. By 1942 McEachern was settled on the west coast and for much of the next three decades he was active in film and television studio work. In 1972, he took the lead alto chair when **Bill Berry** reformed his big band on moving to Los Angeles, but soon afterwards, McEachern went on the road as leader of the reformed **Tommy Dorsey** band - this time, naturally enough, playing trombone. A remarkably polished player on trombone with a contrastingly strong and gutsy saxophone style, McEachern was one of the outstanding sidemen in the history of big band music.

Compilations: *The Indispensable Benny Goodman Vols. 1/2* (1935-36), *The Indispensable Benny Goodman Vols. 3/4* (1936-37).

McEnery, David (Red River Dave)

b. David McEnery, 15 December 1914, San Antonio, Texas, USA, close to the Alamo. Being a Texan, McEnery naturally became interested in things appertaining to the western life and as a boy at school, took to playing the guitar and singing cowboy songs. His fondness for 'Red River Valley' led to his nickname when he started his professional career. He played on local radio in the early 30s, but during the decade he also played many stations in various places, including New York State where the northern audiences were taken with the singing cowboy and his strange saga songs. He developed a penchant for writing songs of historic events such as 'The Battle Of The Alamo' and 'Pony Express' and his first real break came in 1937, with his saga song 'Amelia Earhart's Last Flight'. Following this, he moved to Chicago for a time and in 1939, was invited to New York to sing his song of the lost aviator and others on the first commercial television broadcast at the World's Fair. In the early 40s, he returned to San Antonio, Texas and began regular appearances on Border Radio station XERF where, billing himself as 'your favourite Texas Farmboy', he sang his songs and sold his sets of six songbooks, which he classed as 'a complete library of cowboy, hillbilly and sacred songs'. He also appeared on local US stations and during the 40s and 50s, recorded for several labels. He wrote many songs including 'I'm A Convict With Old Glory In My Heart' (about the man who wanted to fight but was in jail) and as the war ended, he tugged at his listeners heartstrings' with such maudlin numbers as 'The Blind Boy's Dog' (later recorded with success by **Hank Snow**). He has never been short on gimmicks. In 1936, he claimed to be the first (and probably the last) singing cowboy to broadcast from an airship when high above Miami, he sang 'Way Out There', over the airwaves of CBS, from the Goodyear blimp. In 1946, he was handcuffed to a piano for 12 hours and wrote songs from titles that people selected from magazines. By the end, he claimed a total of 52 completed songs.

In the 40s, he appeared in several films, including *Swing In The Saddle, Hidden Valley* and *Echo Ranch* but had made some appearances in earlier films in the 30s. Although he was a singer of cowboy songs for many years and is an expert on them, he is probably now best remembered for his saga songs. After the success of the Amelia Earhart song, he continued over the years to turn out such numbers of news interest including 'Ballad Of Emmett Till', 'The Flight Of Gary Powers', 'The Flight Of Apollo Eleven' and 'The Ballad Of Patty Hearst'. He has appeared on countless radio and television programmes and built the reputation of being something of a character, as well as becoming an ordained Pentecostal minister. Many of the major stars have recorded his songs and amongst his many tribute songs, he once recorded a dedication to his friend, **Bob Wills,** called 'Somewhere I Hear Angels Singing The San Antone Rose'. He moved to Nashville in the mid 70s, where he became noted for his flamboyant western dress with gold boots, his long white hair and goatee beard, all of which made him look a most distinctive resident somewhat like a modern Buffalo Bill Cody. He later returned to his native Texas, where he dispensed with the white locks and beard and reverted to more

normal attire but still maintained his regular public appearances at folk festivals and similar events in many parts of the USA.
Albums: with the Texas Tophands *Songs Of The Rodeo* (1961), *Red River Dave Sings* (1962), *Red River Dave Volumes 1* and *2* (mid-60s), *Days Of The Yodeling Cowboys* (80s), *More Days Of Yodeling Cowboys Volume 2* (80s), *Yodelin' Cowboy Memories* (80s).

McEntire, Pake

b. Dale Stanley McEntire, 1952, Chockie, Oklahoma, USA. Brother of **Reba McEntire**, Pake sang at rodeos with her and their other sister Susie as the Singing McEntires in the early 70s. He has competed professionally in roping events for many years. McEntire had his first US country success with 'Every Night' in 1986; 'Savin' My Love For You' went to number 3. Reba sang harmony on his 1987 entry, 'Heart Vs. Heart'.
Albums: *Too Old To Grow Up Now* (1986), *My Whole World* (1988).

McEntire, Reba

b. Reba Nell McEntire, 28 March 1955, Chockie, Oklahoma, USA. One of four children, McEntire recorded 'The Ballad Of John McEntire', which was about her grandfather. The family owned a 7,000 acre ranch and participated in rodeos; hence McEntire's song 'Daddy'. She sang with her sister Susie and brother **Pake McEntire** as the Singing McEntires and, in 1972, they recorded for the small Boss label. In 1974, she was asked to sing 'The Star-Spangled Banner' at the National Rodeo Finals in Oklahoma City. Honky-tonk singer **Red Steagall** heard her, which led to a recording contract with **Mercury**. Her first single, 'I Don't Want To Be A One Night Stand', made the US country charts in 1976, the year in which she married rodeo rider Charlie Battles. It was followed by several minor successes, including a revival of 'Sweet Dreams' and two duets with Jacky Ward ('Three Sheets To The Wind', 'That Makes Two Of Us'). She made the US country Top 10 with '(You Lift Me) Up To Heaven', the Top 5 with 'Today All Over Again' and, in 1982, number 1 with 'Can't Even Get The Blues'. She often recorded country waltzes and had another chart-topper in 1983 with 'You're The First Time I've Thought About Leaving'. She then left Mercury for **MCA**, although the label was to release an album of outtakes, *Reba Nell McEntire*, in 1986. She continued her country hits with 'Just A Little Love', 'He Broke Your Memory Last Night', 'Have I Got A New Deal For You', and the number 1 hits, 'How Blue' and 'Somebody Should Leave'. Her best-known single and title track of a best-selling album was 'Whoever's In New England'. McEntire's own battles with Battles ended in their divorce in 1987, and she married her bandleader, Narvel Blackstock in 1989. Several of her successes, although they were not written for her ('I Know How He Feels' and 'New Fool At An Old Game'), have overtones from her own life. She has won numerous country music awards, but her 1988 album, *Reba*, although very successful, irritated traditionalists who questioned her revival of a pop hit, 'Sunday Kind Of Love', and her version of **Otis Redding**'s 'Respect'. McEntire was adamant: 'I can sing any kind of song, but whatever I sing, it'll come out country.' She appeared, killing graboids with an elephant gun, in the well-reviewed horror film *Tremors*. In March 1991, tragedy struck when seven of the nine members of McEntire's band died in a plane crash shortly after taking off from San Diego.
The following year, McEntire herself was involved in a forced landing at Nashville airport, evoking memories of the earlier tragedy. She dedicated her next album, *For My Broken Heart*, to her friends and collegues. It proved to be one of her most successful projects, and the title track was a major hit single.
Albums: *Reba McEntire* (1977), *Out Of A Dream* (1979), *Feel The Fire* (1980), *Heart To Heart* (1981), *Unlimited* (1982), *Behind The Scenes* (1983), *Just A Little Love* (1984), *Have I Got A Deal For You* (1985), *My Kind Of Country* (1986), *Whoever's In New England* (1986), *Reba Nell McEntire* (1986), *What Am I Gonna Do About You* (1986), *The Last One To Know* (1987), *So So So Long* (1988), *Merry Christmas To You* (1988), *Reba* (1988), *Sweet Sixteen* (1989), *Live* (1989), *Rumour Has It* (1990), *For My Broken Heart* (1991), *It's Your Call* (1992), *Greatest Hits Vol. 2* (1993), *Read My Mind* (MCA 1994).
Videos: *Reba In Concert* (1992), *For My Broken Heart* (1993), *Greatest Hits* (1994), *Why Haven't I Heard From You* (1994), *And Still (MCA)* (1995).
Further reading: *Reba: Country Music's Queen*, Don Cusic. *Reba - My Story*, Reba McEntire with Tom Carter.

McEvoy, Johnny

b. Banagher, Co. Offaly, Eire. After serving an apprenticeship around the Irish folk clubs, McEvoy established himself on the country music scene in the mid-60s. Since then he has become one of the most important and respected Irish country singer/songwriters. He made his first recordings in 1965 and topped the Irish charts the following year with 'Mursheen Durkin'. In the mid-70s, he furthered his reputation by his popular country show on British television and had his own series *My Ireland* on RTE. He has toured extensively in the UK and the USA and Canada. He has written and recorded many fine songs often based on true life incidents. They range from 'The Ballad Of John Williams' (the story of a couple who sailed on the Titanic), 'Lincoln's Army' (a song of an Irish emigrant to the USA), 'Michael' (the story of Irish patriot, Michael Collins), 'I'll Write Whenever I Can' (written after he saw homeless living on London's streets), to the beautifully descriptive 'Rich Man's

Garden', about childhood memories and 'Leaves In The Wind', a moving story of old Rosie Atkinson who had been widowed by the war. McEvoy has become something of a living legend in Ireland and many artists including Foster And Allen have recorded his songs.
Albums: *Johnny McEvoy* (Hawk 1973), *Sings Country* (Hawk 1974), *Sounds Like McEvoy* (Hawk 1974), *All Our Wars Were Merry, All Our Songs Were Sad* (Hawk 1974), *Sings Hank Williams* (Hawk 1975), *Where My Eileen Is Waiting* (Hawk 1975), *Long Before Your Time* (Hawk c.1976), *Christmas Dreams* (Hawk c.1976), *Leaves In The Wind* (Hawk c.1977), *I'll Spend A Time With You* (Hawk 1978),with Gloria *Golden Duets* (Pickwick/Harp 1980), *Johnny McEvoy Goes Country* (Pickwick/Harp 1980), *My Favourite Irish Songs* (Pickwick/Harp c.1981), *20 Greatest Hits* (Dolphin 80s), *20 More Hits* (Dolphin 80s), *Since Maggie Went Away* (MCA 1985), *Songs Of Ireland* (MCA 1986), *Golden Hour Of Johnny McEvoy* (Polydor 80s, covers 70s), *Sings For You* (Play c.1988), *The Original* (Play 1991).

McFadden And Whitehead

Gene McFadden and John Whitehead (both b. 1948, Philadelphia, Pennsylvania, USA), were former members of the Epsilons, a group managed by **Otis Redding**, prior to joining the Philadelphia International label. Here they forged a career as producers, playing a major role in the development of the label's 'sound' and as songwriters, penning hits for **Harold Melvin And The Blue Notes** ('Bad Luck', 'Wake Up Everybody') and the **O'Jays** ('Back Stabbers'), ultimately being responsible for over 20 gold discs. As performers, MacFadden and Whitehead enjoyed an international smash with 'Ain't No Stoppin Us Now' (1979), a defiant, post-disco anthem, highlighted by the latter's magnificent, exhorting delivery. The duo's later releases, however, were less successful, and, after serving time in prison for tax evasion, Whitehead embarked on a solo career in 1988.
Albums: *McFadden And Whitehead* (1979), *I Heard It In A Love Song* (1980), *Ain't No Stoppin' Us Now* (1993).

McFarland, Gary

b. 23 October 1933, Los Angeles, California, USA, d. 3 November 1971, New York City, New York, USA. McFarland was a vibraphonist, arranger and orchestra leader. He moved to Grants Pass in Oregon when he was 15 years old, and became interested in jazz while studying at the University of Oregon. He began to play the vibes during a stint in the US Army at Fort Sill, Oklahoma, in 1954, and, three years later, joined a group led by Santiago Gonzalez. Encouraged by musicians such as **John Lewis**, Buddy Montgomery and fellow vibes player **Cal Tjader**, McFarland won scholarships to the School of Jazz in Lennox and the **Berklee College Of Music** in Boston (1959). In the early 60s he blossomed into a fine young jazz writer, contributing arrangements and compositions to albums including those of the **Modern Jazz Quintet**, **Gerry Mulligan**, and John Lewis. He also wrote all the charts, and conducted the orchestra for **Anita O'Day**'s *All The Sad Young Men* - although, according to O'Day, she sang to pre-recorded tapes, and did not meet McFarland until four or five years after the record had been released! Presumably he did get personally involved when working on albums with **Stan Getz**, **Bill Evans** and other leading musicians. In 1961, he recorded his own jazz version of the **Frank Loesser**-Abe Burrows Broadway Musical, *How To Succeed In Business Without Really Trying*, and subsequent releases included *Soft Samba*, *Point Of Departure*, *Profiles*, *Simpatico*, *Tijuana Jazz* and *America the Beautiful* and *Does The Sun Real, Shine On The Moon?* for the Skye Label, of which he was the co-founder. During the mid-60s, McFarland toured with his own quintet, and, in 1966, wrote the score for the Deborah Kerr-David Niven thriller movie, *Eye Of The Devil*. His latest film music was for another 'whodunnit', *Who Killed Mary What's'ername?* in 1971. He died in November of that year. The cause of death was given as a heart attack, although it is rumoured that methadone, a synthetic drug similar to morphine, was put in his drink by a 'joker'.

McFerrin, Bobby

b. 11 March 1950, New York City, New York, USA. To call Bobby McFerrin a jazz vocalist is hardly to do him justice, for when McFerrin performs - he usually appears solo in lengthy concerts-he uses his entire body as a sound-box, beating noises out of his slender frame while emitting a constant accompaniment of guttural noises, clicks and popping sounds. To all this he adds a vocal technique that owes a slight debt to the bop vocalist **Betty Carter** and her daring swoops and scat vocals. McFerrin was brought up in a musical family-both his parents are opera singers, his father performing on the film sound-track of ***Porgy And Bess*** in 1959 - but his main jazz influence came from the jazz-rock of **Miles Davis**' *Bitches Brew* album. Training as a pianist at the Juilliard School and later at Sacramento State College, he worked first as an accompanist, then as a pianist and singer during the 70s. He came to public notice in 1979, when he performed in New York with the singer **Jon Hendricks**, from whom he learnt much, but it was his accompanied appearance at the 1981 Kool Jazz Festival which brought him widespread acclaim. By 1983, he had perfected his solo style of wordless, vocal improvisations. His debut album contained a dramatic reworking of **Van Morrison**'s 'Moondance', while *The Voice* mixed his fondness for pop classics - this time, the **Beatles**' 'Blackbird' - with more adventurous pieces, notably the self-descriptive 'I'm My Own Walkman'. The 1988 album *Simple Pleasures* shows off his wide range with its mixture of pop classics and self-composed material. The highlight of the album was his idiosyncratic version of **Cream**'s 'Sunshine Of Your Love', complete with a vocal electric guitar. Since he experienced a surprise major hit record with 'Don't Worry Be Happy' in 1988 (US number 1, UK number 2) McFerrin has seemingly dried up.

Albums: *Bobby McFerrin* (Elektra 1982), *The Voice* (Elektra 1984), *Spontaneous Inventions* (Blue Note 1986), *Simple Pleasures* (EMI Manhattan 1988), *Medicine Man* (EMI Manhattan 1990), with Chick Corea *Play* (Blue Note 1992).

McGann, Bernie

b. 22 June 1937, Sydney, New South Wales, Australia. Arguably Australia's premier saxophonist, McGann began on drums, taking lessons from his father, who was a professional musician. He switched to alto saxophone in 1955, initially inspired by **Paul Desmond**, though later influences were **Sonny Rollins** and *avant garde* players such as **Ornette Coleman** and **Albert Ayler**. In the late 50s, McGann began a long association with drummer John Pochée, and in 1964, joined him in a group called the Heads which also featured pianist Dave MacRae. McGann played regularly at Sydney's El Roco club, but when it closed in 1969, he found jazz gigs extremely scarce and for a while worked as a postman. From 1975, he played in Pochée's group, the Last Straw, and also led his own trio into the 80s, recording with **Sonny Stitt** on the latter's 1981 Australian tour. He has worked with other visiting Americans, notably **Dewey Redman** and **Red Rodney**, continues to perform both with the Last Straw and Pochée's big band, Ten Part Invention, and still leads his own small groups, which usually feature Pochée and bassist Lloyd Swanton. Although active since the 50s and a striking soloist, whose lines have the gnarled beauty of a truly original talent, McGann has rarely recorded. *At Long Last,* on the Emanem label, was his first album as leader after 30 years on the scene and remains his best to date - a twisting, eloquent bebop spiced with modernity.

Albums: *With The Ted Vining Trio* (1986, rec 1983), *At Long Last* (1987, rec 1983), *Kindred Spirits* (1987), *The Last Straw* (1991, rec 1987), *Ten Part Invention* (1991, rec 1987), *Ugly Beauty* (1992).

McGarity, Lou

b. 22 July 1917, Athens, Georgia, USA, d. 28 August 1971. After playing in dancebands in and around Atlanta, Georgia, trombonist McGarity moved north. In 1938, he joined **Ben Bernie**'s popular recording unit and, two years later, became a member of the **Benny Goodman** band. After military service in World War II, McGarity again played with Goodman, then divided his time between west coast studio work and playing in small jazz groups, often those under the nominal leadership of **Eddie Condon**, **Yank Lawson** and **Bob Haggart**. In the 60s, he played with **Bob Crosby** And The Bobcats and was with Lawson and Haggart in the **World's Greatest Jazz Band**. His warm sound and sometimes aggressive style made McGarity a welcome member of any dixieland-orientated jazz band. He worked until the day of his death in August 1971.

Albums: with Lawson-Haggart *Jelly Roll's Jazz* (1951), with Eddie Condon *Jammin' At Condon's* (1954), *Blue Lou* (1959), *Jazz Master* (1970), *In Celebration* (IAJRC 1989).

McGarrigle, Kate And Anna

Kate (b. 1944, St Sauveur, Montreal, Canada; keyboards, guitar, vocals), and her sister Anna (b. 1946, St. Sauveur, Montreal, Canada; keyboards, banjo, vocals), were brought up in the French quarter of Quebec. As a result they learned to sing and perform in both French and English. It was their father who first encouraged them in their musical pursuits, rewarding them with nickels when they learnt harmonies from him. While still in Montreal, after mastering the guitar in their teens, the sisters became members of the Mountain City Four, before they went their separate ways, Anna to art college and Kate to McGill University to study engineering. As a duo, Kate and Anna came to public notice after other artists, including **Linda Ronstadt** and **Maria Muldaur**, recorded and performed their songs. Kate McGarrigle met Muldaur after moving to New York, and Muldaur recorded 'Work Song' as the final track on her debut album. When Ronstadt scored a hit with Anna's 'Heart Like A Wheel', record companies began to express an interest in the duo's talents. As a result, Muldaur's label, **Warner Brothers**, asked the McGarrigle sisters to record an album. *Kate And Anna McGarrigle*, their first release, was produced by **Joe Boyd**, and contained their own take of 'Heart Like A Wheel'. The album's disparate musical styles spanned everything save rock, yet that did not prevent *Melody Maker* magazine naming it the 1976 Rock Record Of The Year. Apart from *Dancer With Bruised Knees*, which made the Top 40 in the UK, none of their subsequent releases has had any significant impact in the charts in either the USA or Britain. The long break between *Love Over And Over* was put down to the strong-minded duo fighting the promotional machine that was building around them: 'We just weren't prepared to be in that mould, of "Hey, now you're being professional". It took a lot of the fun out of it.' However, they have retained a strong following and their concerts, albeit on a smaller scale, consistently sell out. They first came to the UK to perform in 1976, with Kate then married to **Loudon Wainwright III**, and they toured consistently until they arrived to support the release of *Love Over And Over*. In the meantime they had raised four children between them, penned movie soundtracks and written songs. The McGarrigle sisters have an instantly recognizable sound, with a distinctive harmonic blend, and incisive lyrics which defy expectations. Their early promise has never been realized, but they still command respect, and a loyal following.

Albums: *Kate And Anna McGarrigle* (1975), *Dancer With Bruised Knees* (1977), *Pronto Monto* (1978), *French Record* (1980), *Love Over And Over* (1982), *Heartbeats Accelerating* (1990).

McGear, Mike

b. Peter Michael McCartney, 7 January 1944, Liverpool, England. The younger brother of the **Beatles**' **Paul McCartney**, McGear adopted his tongue-in-cheek appellation in order to avoid unwarranted associations. In 1962, he joined John Gorman and Roger McGough in the **Scaffold**, a satirical revue which later enjoyed success as a pop group with 'Thank U Very Much' (1967) and the chart-topping 'Lily The Pink' (1968). With Gorman in absentia and Paul as producer, the remaining pair recorded McGough And McGear (1968), a mixture of songs and poetry which featured support from **Jimi Hendrix**, **Dave Mason**, **John Mayall** and **Graham Nash**. McGear later joined the multi-faceted troupe **Grimms**, many of whom appeared on the artist's solo debut *Woman*. A subsequent single, 'Sweet Baby', led to the recording of **McGear*. Paul not only produced this set, but wrote or co-wrote all but one of its songs, adding bass, guitar and backing vocals, before inviting Wings to provide further support. A critical success, the album failed commercially and McGear, who reverted to his McCartney surname, has since pursued an informal career, including work as a photographer.

Albums: *Woman* (1972), **McGear* (1974). With Roger McGough *McGough & McGear* (1968).

Further reading: *Thank U Very Much: Mike McCartney's Family Album*, Mike McCartney.

McGee, Alan

b. 29 September 1960, Glasgow, Scotland. After leaving school at the age of 17, McGee became an electrician, then relocated to London where he worked as a clerk for British Rail. In his spare time, he promoted gigs for his nomadic club, the Living Room, booking acts such as the **Nightingales** and the **Television Personalities**. To his surprise, he found that he was making a profit, so elected to release records and formed the label **Creation**. During the early phase of the label's history, McGee issued singles by artists such as the **Loft**, the **Pastels**, **Primal Scream**, the Jasmine Minks and his own venture, **Biff Bang Pow**. After signing the **Jesus And Mary Chain** in 1984, McGee's credibility as a manager and label owner escalated dramatically. He stayed with the group for two, often stormy, years and along the way issued some fascinating product by Felt, the **Bodines** and the Weather Prophets. The ill-fated tie-up with **Warner Brothers**, Elevation Records, encouraged McGee to pursue the independent route with more vigour. During the latter half of the 80s, the Creation roster extended to include **Nikki Sudden**, **Momus**, Clive Langer and, most crucially, the **House Of Love**. After one album and two excellent singles, the latter signed to Phonogram. After 1988, McGee turned increasingly to the dance floor for inspiration. Initial releases by Love Corporation, Hynotone, JBC and DJ Danny Rampling were not commercial successes, but the new direction was sound. Ironically, it was former psychedelic outfit Primal Scream who embraced the dance culture most effectively, providing the label with hits such as 'Loaded'. Further success followed with the critically acclaimed and best-selling **My Bloody Valentine**, **Ride**, **Oasis**, **Teenage Fanclub**, and the **Boo Radley's** as Creation entered its most productive phase yet during the mid-90s. McGee's genuine love of music and thrust for innovation has made him one of the most influential music business entrepreneurs to emerge in the UK over the past decade.

McGee, Sam And Kirk

Samuel Fleming McGee (b. 1 May 1894, d. 21 August 1975) and David Kirkland McGee (b. 4 November 1899, d. 24 October 1983) were both born and raised on the family farm near Franklin, Williamson County, Tennessee, USA. Their father was a noted fiddle player, and the brothers learned to play the banjo as children but changed their style in their teens. Sam worked as a blacksmith, but around 1910, he became interested in the guitar and learned to play from black street musicians. During his career he became so proficient that he has been a major influence to many musicians and was most likely the first white musician to use the guitar as a solo instrument, instead of a mere accompaniment for vocals or fiddle music. Kirk concentrated on the banjo, although he later played guitar, mandolin and fiddle, and also developed into a fine vocalist. In 1925, Sam first met and played with **Uncle Dave Macon** and, the following year, made his first appearance with Macon on the *Grand Ole Opry*. Soon after, they were joined by Kirk and both played with Macon, as well as performing as a duo. In 1927, together with fiddler Mazy Todd, they went to New York with Macon and recorded as Uncle Dave Macon And His Fruit Jar Drinkers. They recorded with Macon until the mid-30s, as well as recording as a duo, including their noted 1934 recording of 'Brown's Ferry Blues'. They were among the first members of the *Opry* ever to record, which later led to Sam stating, 'They recorded us because we were outstanding in the field and that's where they found us - outstanding in the field'. In 1930, they also teamed up with Fiddlin' **Arthur Smith** and both toured and played the *Opry* with him as the Dixieliners. They worked with Smith until 1938, when he left for Hollywood. Strangely, though recognized as one of the *Opry*'s most influential bands, they never actually recorded with Smith until years later in the 60s, when they were reunited by **Mike Seeger**.

During the 40s, they toured with **Bill Monroe**, appeared occasionally with Macon and still played the *Opry*. It seems likely that Sam was the first member to play an electric guitar on the *Opry*. It was only the use of an amplified Spanish guitar and an early electric lap steel, but the action soon incurred the wrath of **George D. Hay**, who quickly told Sam to 'Keep it down to earth'. In the 50s and 60s, the folk revival found them touring and still on the *Opry*. In later years, Kirk went into the property business and Sam continued to work the farm until he died in a tractor accident in 1975, at the age of 82. After Sam's death, Kirk played the *Opry* as a member of the *Opry*'s own Fruit Jar Drinkers String Band, frequently playing fiddle rather than banjo. He died after a heart attack at his home in Franklin in 1983, having appeared on the *Opry* only a few days previously. It is interesting to note that, in 1924, Sam had learned to play the guitar-banjo, and his recordings using it, made with Macon in 1926 and 1927, are probably the only known examples ever made by a white musician with this difficult instrument. The brothers contribution to the history of country music, with their gospel, blues, instrumentals and old folk ballads, is considerable and, although they made many recordings during their long careers, few are now available.

Albums: one side each act *Opry Old Timers Sam & Kirk McGee And The Crook Brothers* (1962), *Fiddlin' Arthur Smith & His Dixieliners* (1962), *Rare Old Fiddle Tunes (Fiddlin' Arthur Smith & His Dixieliners)* (1962), *Old Timers Of The Grand Ole Opry* (1964), with Arthur Smith *Milk 'Em In The Evening Blues* (1965), *Opry Old Time Songs And Guitar Tunes, Volume One* (1985). Sam McGee: *The Grandad Of The Country Guitar Pickers* (1963). Kirk McGee: *Mister Kirk* (1980). They also appear on several album releases of Uncle Dave Macon and sundry individual tracks appear on various artists albums of old time music.

McGhee, Granville 'Sticks'

b. 23 March 1918, Knoxville, Tennessee, USA, d. 15 August 1961, New York City, New York, USA. Like his more famous brother, **Brownie McGhee**, Granville learned guitar from his father. After seeing action in the World War II, he moved to New York in 1946. The following year, he made his first record, 'Drinkin' Wine Spo-Dee-O-Dee', under his own name. However, it was a later cut of the same song, made for **Atlantic** in 1949, with a group that included **Big Chief Ellis** as well as Brownie, that gave him his biggest success. Over the next few years, he made several more records, and appeared as accompanist on others, most notably to **Sonny Terry**. However, he did not manage to make the move to the new, young, white audience that his brother tapped into so successfully in the late 50s and onwards.

Album: *Drinkin' Wine Spo-Dee-O-Dee* (1982).

McGhee, Howard

b. 6 March 1918, Tulsa, Oklahoma, USA, d. 17 July 1987. During the late 30s, McGhee played trumpet in several **territory bands** in the Midwest before moving to Detroit, where he became well known in that city's lively jazz scene. He first enjoyed major success with **Lionel Hampton** in 1941; however, he quickly moved on, joining **Andy Kirk**, for whom he wrote arrangements and was featured soloist. Although he was to work in other big bands of the early 40s, including **Charlie Barnet**'s and **Georgie Auld**'s, McGhee soon became most closely associated with bebop. From the mid-40s he could be heard playing in clubs and on records with **Charlie Parker**, **Fats Navarro** and others. He was present on the notorious Parker recording date for Dial which produced 'Lover Man' and was, in fact, largely responsible for salvaging the session from potential disaster when Parker broke down. During the 50s, McGhee's career was damaged by drug addiction and his private life was blighted by some of the worst excesses of racism: his marriage to a white woman resulted in his wife being beaten up and he himself was framed on drugs-related charges. However, he survived and, in the early 60s, was making records with **Teddy Edwards**, **George Coleman** and others and later returned to regular playing. A big band he formed at this time and a 1969 appearance at the **Newport Jazz Festival** with **Buddy Tate** helped to prove that he still had talent to spare. One of the most melodic of bebop trumpeters, McGhee was an important influence on two major figures, Navarro and **Clifford Brown**, both of whom, ironically, were to die many years before him.

Albums: *The Howard McGhee Sextet With Milt Jackson* (Savoy 1948), *The Howard McGhee All Stars* (1949), *Maggie* (Savoy 1950), *The Howard McGhee Korean All Stars* (1951), *The Howard McGhee Sextet With Gigi Gryce* (1953), *That Bop Thing* (1955), *Howard McGhee And His Orchestra* (1960), *The Howard McGhee Quintet* (1960), *Dusty Blue* (Affinity 1960), with Teddy Edwards *Together Again!* (1961), *The Bop Master* (Affinity 1961), *Maggie's Back In Town* (Original Jazz Classics 1961), *Shades Of Blue/Sharp Edge* (Black Lion 1961), *House Warmin'* (1962), *Cookin' Time* (Hep Jazz 1966), *Here Comes Freddy* (Sonet 1976), with Charlie Rouse *Jazzbrothers* (1977), *Just Be There* (Steeplechase 1977), *Home Run* (1978), *Live At Emerson's* (Zim 1978), with Edwards *Young At Heart* (1979), *Trumpet At Tempo* (Spotlite 1983). Compilations: with Andy Kirk *Walkin' And Swingin'* (1942), with Charlie Parker *The Legendary Dial Masters Vol. 1* (1946-47), *Howard McGhee And His Band* (1945), *Trumpet At Tempo* (1946).

McGhee, Walter Brown 'Brownie'

b. 30 November 1915, Knoxville, Tennessee, USA. McGhee learned guitar from his father, and started early on a musical career, playing in church before he was 10 years old, and on the road with medicine shows, carnivals and minstrel troupes in his early teens. His travels took him into the Carolinas, and his time there proved very influential in moulding his musical style. He met **Sonny Terry** in 1939, and their partnership was to become one of the most enduring in blues. The following year, he made his first records, reminiscent of those of **Blind Boy Fuller**; indeed some of them bore the credit 'Blind Boy Fuller No.2'. Also around this time, he settled in New York, where his career took a rather different turn, as he took up with a group of black musicians - including Terry, **Leadbelly** and **Josh White** - favoured by the then small white audience for the blues. For a number of years, he catered very successfully both for this audience, playing acoustic blues in an older style, and for an entirely separate one. Through the late 40s and early 50s, he recorded electric blues and R&B aimed at black record buyers. In retrospect, it is this second type that stands up best, and indeed, some of his records from this period rank among the finest blues to come out of New York in the post-war years. He was also very prolific as an accompanist, playing superb lead guitar on records by other artists such as **Champion Jack Dupree**, **Big Chief Ellis** and Alonzo Scales, as well as his brother **Stick**. His partnership with Terry became more firmly established during this period, and, as the original market for blues and R&B faded, they carved a very strong niche for themselves, playing concerts, festivals and clubs, and making albums aimed at the growing audience for folk music. For many years, they travelled the world and made record after record, establishing their names among the best-known of all blues artists. However, critical opinion seems agreed that their music suffered to a large degree during this period, as it was diluted for such a wide, international audience and as successive recordings trod similar ground. McGhee seems to have been inactive since Terry's death in 1986, although in fact their partnership broke up shortly before this.

Selected albums: *1944-1955* (1990), *Home Town Blues* (1990), *The 1958 London Sessions* (1990), *Carolina Blues* (1992).

McGhee, Wes

b. 26 October, 1948, Lutterworth, Leicestershire, England. One of the very few British performers whose Texas-inspired country music is regarded as creditable in the USA. McGhee has suffered more than most from the British refusal to accept homegrown country music as genuine. He has worked with noted Texan artists including Ponty Bone and Freddie Kre (for both of whom he produced albums in the 80s), Butch Hancock, **Jimmie Dale Gilmore** and Kimmie Rhodes. As a promising teenage guitarist, McGhee was involved with the celebrated **Reg Calvert**, (who worked as patron for a number of emergent musicians in the 60s from a large country house where several groups, none of which became famous, lived communally). During the late 60s, McGhee worked in Hamburg as one of many musicians following the Merseybeat trail - his first wife was German. During the early 70s, he fronted an early pub/rock combo known as McGhee, but management problems, among other things, conspired to sabotage the recording contract which he was promised. By the mid-70s, McGhee had become friendly with Arthur Anderson, a musician he had met on the gig circuit, and they joined forces to record an album of McGhee's original material, with Anderson engineering and producing. The result, *Long Nights And Banjo Music*, was released on their own label, Terrapin Records, in 1978, with McGhee as lead vocalist and lead guitarist, plus assistance from, among others, Bob Loveday (violin, later with the Penguin Cafe Orchestra and the post **Boomtown Rats Bob Geldof** band) and Rick Lloyd (later a member of the chart-topping **Flying Pickets**). The achievement of completing the album was of far greater significance than much of the self-conscious country/rock it contained, and McGhee and Anderson scraped together enough finance - by renting out their homemade studio and by McGhee writing and recording radio commercials - to release a second album in 1980, *Airmail*, which gave notice that he was a considerable songwriting talent.

Before *Landing Lights* was released in 1983, Anderson had left the partnership, although he worked on part of the album, some of which was recorded in Texas with local musicians like Kre (ex-**Jerry Jeff Walker**), Bone and Lloyd Maines (ex-**Joe Ely**), Gilmore and Rhodes. Probably McGhee's best original studio album to date in terms of original songs, it was released on his own TRP label, as was 1985's *Thanks For The Chicken*, a live double album made in Texas with a mixed British/Texan band including Kre, Bone, Rhodes and Texan fiddler Alvin Crow, plus McGhee's long-time backing vocalist, Ian Bartholomew (primarily an actor), Patti Vetta, and Irish multi-instrumentalist Dermot O'Conner. As well as numerous fine McGhee originals, the album included covers of **Richard Thompson**'s 'Tear Stained Letter', Joe 'King' Carrasco's 'Mexcal Road' and the sublime 'Contrabandistas', written by record producer and Rhodes's husband, Joe Gracey, and his partner, Bobby Earl Smith. The album even included a song sung in Mexican - McGhee had developed a cult following in Mexico owing to his semi-successful attempts to cater for the Hispanic audience.

Although he remained virtually unknown in Britain, his talent was recognized by pioneering American music publisher Bug Music, which signed him during the second half of the 80s, as his fifth album *Zacatecas*, was released in 1986. A much more measured collection, it was his first studio album made without cost-cutting, and included a remarkable epic titled 'Monterey', plus a cover of the 60s hit by **Troy Shondell**, 'This Time'. As usual, there was little commercial interest in Britain, although McGhee began working frequently in Texas, both on his own account and as lead guitarist with Kimmie Rhodes, who had duetted with him on a track from *Thanks For The Chicken*, and with whom he played on several of her albums. Finally, in 1991, a UK label, Minidoka, was interested enough in McGhee to release a compilation of remixed tracks from his previous studio albums titled *Neon And Dust*, although at the time of writing, this again has not achieved the success its quality so richly deserves. His acoustic album in 1995 featured Kimmie Rhodes, Freddie Kre and Ponty Bone.

Albums: *Long Nights And Banjo Music* (1978), *Airmail* (1980), *Landing Lights* (1983), *Thanks For The Chicken* (1985) *Zacatecas* (1986), *Neon And Dust* (1991), *Border Guitars* (Road Goes On Forever 1994).

McGovern, Maureen

b. Maureen Therese McGovern, 27 July 1949, Youngstown, Ohio, USA. The possessor of 'one of the most technically proficient singing voices in all of pop', with a four-octave, coloratura range, as a young girl Maureen McGovern was influenced by **Barbra Streisand**. After graduating from high school in 1967, she she worked as a typist, and perfomed folk songs in the evenings. She then embarked on a six-year tour of hotels and holiday camps in the midwest of America, performing contemporary material with a rock band. She came to the attention of 20th Century-Fox Records, who signed her to a contract. Her first recording, in 1972, was Al Kasha and Joel Hirschhorn's 'The Morning After', which was used as the love theme for the 'disaster' film *The Poseidon Adventure*. It won an Academy Award for best song, and McGovern's version topped the US chart. In 1974, the media began calling her the 'disaster queen' after she sang the Oscar-winning 'We May Never Love Like This Again' (Kasha -Hirschhorn) on the soundtrack of *The Towering Inferno* (McGovern also played a cameo role in the picture), and 'Wherever Love Takes Me' (**Leslie Bricusse-Don Black**), the theme from *Gold*, a British film starring Roger Moore and Susannah York, in which a South African gold mine is destroyed. Given her recent career history, it was hardly surprising that McGovern was cast as the singing nun, Sister Angelina, in the 'disaster-spoof' movie *Airplane!* in 1980. By that time, she had begun to be known in Britain through her version of 'The Continental', and reached the US Top 10 with 'Different Worlds', the theme from the television series *Angie*. She had also recorded 'Can You Read My Mind' (Bricusse-**John Williams**), the love theme from *Superman*. In the early 80s, as well as appearing in regional productions of ***The Sound Of Music*** and ***South Pacific***, McGovern attracted much acclaim for her performance as the ingénue, Mabel, in Joe Papp's revival of *The Pirates Of Penzanze* on Broadway. She replaced Karen Akers in the **Tony Award**-winning musical, ***Nine***, toured with ***Guys And Dolls***, and appeared in a revival of the two-hander musical, ***I Do! I Do!*** Around this time McGovern was beginning to establish herself as classy nightclub performer, singing mainly a blend of jazz and beloved Broadway standards. In particular, she has come to be regarded by many as 'the quintessential interpreter of **Gershwin**', although her programmes also include songs by writers such as **Sergio Mendes**, **John Lennon** and **Paul McCartney**, and **Shelby Flint**. In 1989 McGovern made her solo debut at Carnegie Hall, and as Polly Peachum, with **Sting** as Macheath, in *3 Penny Opera* (a new production of ***The Threepenny Opera***) on Broadway. In the early 90s, she made her London concert debut at the Barbican theatre, and also played in cabaret at the Pizza On The Park and the Café Royal. Her honours include a Canadian Gold Leaf Award (1973), an Australian Gold Award (1975), and the Grand Prize in the 1975 Tokyo Music Festival for her performance of **Paul Williams**' 'Even Better Than I Know Myself'.

Selected albums: *The Morning After* (1973), *Nice To Be Around* (1974), *Academy Award Performance* (1975), *Maureen McGovern* (1979), *Christmas With Maureen McGovern* (c.80s), with Sarah Vaughan, Placido Domingo, Mandy Patinkin *Love Songs* (c.80s), *Another Woman In Love* (1987), *State Of The Heart* (1988), *Naughty Baby-Sings Gershwin* (1988), *Greatest Hits* (Curb 1990), *Baby I'm Yours* (BMG 1992).

MacGowan, Shane, And The Popes

There are doubtless those in the music industry, particularly some vulture-like members of the press, who never expected Shane MacGowan to survive, never mind record again, after the **Pogues** splintered in the early 90s. Following a promotional single, 'That Woman's Got Me Drinking' ('she must have been employed by the brewing industry', as one wag in the press noted), MacGowan unveiled his new group, the Popes, and debut solo album, *The Snake*, in October 1994. The Popes included Paul McGuinness (guitar), Bernie France (bass), Tom McManamon (banjo) and Danny Pope (drums). Unsurprisingly given MacGowan's collaborative track record, there was also an array of guest musicians in attendance, including Barney McKenna and John Sheahan (**Dubliners**), Jem Finer and Spider Stacy (Pogues) and the actor Johnny Depp, who directed and starred in the video for 'That Woman's Got Me Drinking', also contributing some elementary guitar on the track. *The Snake*

additionally featured eleven other original compositions, and was co-produced with Dave Jordan in London and Ireland. The range of musical styles on offer was typically impressive, running from the raucous cow punk of 'Mexican Funeral In Paris', which could have graced any Pogues album, as could more reflective and traditional songs such as 'Donegal Express'.
Album: *The Snake* (ZTT/WEA 1994).

McGraw, Tim

b. 1 May 1967, Delhi, Louisiana, USA. He was raised in Start, Louisiana and is the son of Frank Edwin 'Tug' McGraw, a noted left-handed relief pitcher for the New York Mets and Philadelphia Phillies, who retired in 1984, after a 19 year major league baseball career. Tim began his musical career singing in local clubs and also worked as a demo singer. He was signed to **Curb Records** in 1990 but did not achieve his first chart entry until 1992, with 'Welcome To The Club'. In 1993, he had two further minor hits with 'Memory Lane' and 'Two Steppin' Mind', all three of these songs coming from his debut album. He appeared on the Honky Tonk Attitude tour with **Joe Diffie**. His career really took off because of the release, early in 1994, of a single 'Indian Outlaw'. The song, written by **John D. Loudermilk**, caused considerable controversy in the USA, where some claimed that it degraded the accepted image of the American Indian. Controversy always helps sales and the recording, with its war dance rhythmic drum beat, quickly gave McGraw his first country number 1 record. The song naturally appeared on his second album, from which he also gained further chart success with the recording of 'Down On The Farm' and the title track. The album, *Not A Moment Too Soon*, actually went straight in at number 1. The album sales have topped four million and after 63 weeks of chart life, it was still occupying the number five position in the album chart.
Albums: *Tim McGraw* (Curb 1993), *Not A Moment Too Soon* (Curb 1994).
Videos: *Indian Outlaw* (1994), *Refried Dreams* (1995), *An Hour With Tim* (1995).

McGregor, Chris

b. 24 December 1936, Somerset West, South Africa, d. 27 May 1990. In his early years in the Transkei, McGregor studied classical piano music, but was more significantly affected by the hymns in his father's Church of Scotland mission and the music of the Xhosa people. At the 1962 Johannesburg Jazz Festival, he selected five of the best players (**Mongezi Feza**, **Dudu Pukwana**, Nick Moyake, **Johnny Dyani** and **Louis Moholo**) and invited them to join him in a new band. Thus, the legendary Blue Notes were created. Apartheid made it impossible for them, as a mixed-race band, to work legally in South Africa, and so, while touring Europe in 1964, they decided not to return home. After a year in Switzerland, they settled in London, where, evolving into the Chris McGregor Group (with Ronnie Beer replacing Moyake on tenor), they made a huge impact with their exhilarating mixture of free jazz and kwela, the South African Township dance music. During that period McGregor established a big band for gigs at **Ronnie Scott**'s Old Place and, in 1970, he formed a regular big band, the Brotherhood Of Breath. He moved to Aquitaine, France, in 1974, often playing solo gigs, although from time to time he revived the Brotherhood. McGregor was an exciting piano player whose style encompassed the power of **Cecil Taylor** and the gentleness of African folk melodies, but it was as leader of a series of joyful, powerful bands that he made his main reputation. He once told Valerie Wilmer, 'Real musical freedom is the ability to look inside your own personal experience and select from it at will.' He died of lung cancer in May 1990.
Albums: *The African Sound* (1963), *Very Urgent* (1968), *Brotherhood Of Breath* (1971), *Brotherhood* (1972), *Live At Willisau* (1975), *Blue Notes For Mongezi* (1976), *Piano Song Volumes 1 & 2* (1977), *Procession* (Ogun 1977), *Blue Notes In Concert* (1978), *In His Good Time* (Ogun 1979), *Yes, Please* (1982), *Blue Notes For Johnny* (Ogun 1987), *Country Cooking* (Venture 1990), *Grandmother's Teaching* (ITM 1991).

McGregor, Freddie

b. c.1955, Clarendon, Jamaica, West Indies. McGregor entered the Jamaican music business at the precocious age of seven, singing backing vocals with **ska** duo the **Clarendonians** at **Coxsone Dodd**'s **Studio One**. He stayed with Dodd throughout the rest of the decade and into the early 70s, acting as a session drummer and backing singer as well as cutting sides such as 'Why Did You Do It', and 'Do Good' (c.1965) with Clarendonian Ernest 'Fitzroy' Wilson as Freddie And Fitzy, versions of **Johnny Ace**'s 'Pledging My Love' and **Junior Byles**' 'Beat Down Babylon' (c.1972), and his own compositions, 'Go Away Pretty Woman', 'What Difference Does It Make' and 'Why Is Tomorrow Like Today'. In 1975, after adopting the Rasta faith through the Twelve Tribes organisation, he recorded two of his finest singles, 'I Man A Rasta' and 'Rastaman Camp', both heavyweight slices of roots Rasta reggae. In the early 70s he worked stage shows as lead singer with the Generation Gap and **Soul Syndicate** bands and maintained strong links with both sets of musicians throughout his career. The late 70s saw his star rise with excellent singles such as 'Jogging' for Tuff Gong, the herbsman anthem 'Natural Collie', based around the melody and arrangement of Norman Collins' soul opus, 'You Are My Starship', and 'Mark Of The Beast', 'Leave Yah', and a cover of **George Benson**'s 'Love Ballad', all for Earl 'Chinna' Smith. **Winston**

'Niney' Holness produced his debut set *Mr McGregor* and there were further recordings for Studio One including 'Homeward Bound', 'Come Now Sister', 'Africa Here I Come', and the classic *Boby Babylon.* In 1979 McGregor was also involved in the production of **Judy Mowatt**'s excellent *Black Woman.*
McGregor's reputation as one of the most vocally gifted singers in reggae, able to turn his hand to lovers or roots material with equal potency, had been increasing steadily when he recorded *Big Ship* for Linval Thompson. Released in the UK on **Greensleeves**, the album was a great success. He followed this up with *Love At First Sight* (1982) for **Joe Gibbs**. Coxsone capitalized on McGregor's popularity, which by now was rivalling that of **Dennis Brown** and **Gregory Isaacs**', with *I Am Ready* (1982), like its predecessor comprised mainly of singles and previously unreleased tracks from the singers sojourn at Studio One in the early 70s. In 1984 McGregor inaugurated his own Big Ship label with *Across The Border*, and completed a licensing deal with RAS Records in the US for the release of *Come On Over.* In 1985 he recorded the duet 'Raggamuffin' with Dennis Brown for **Gussie Clarke**, and the **dancehall** hit 'Don't Hurt My Feelings' for George Phang's Powerhouse label. Throughout the 80s McGregor enjoyed a position as one of reggae's most popular performers touring the world with the Studio One Band, and scoring a huge hit in Colombia with a version of the **Sandpipers**' 'Guantanamera', sung in Spanish, for RAS. He signed a contact with **Polydor** which resulted in the UK chart-nudging 'Push Come To Shove' (1987) and 'That Girl', finally scoring a UK hit with a cover of **Main Ingredient**'s 'Just Don't Wanna Be Lonely', which reached number 9 in August 1987. Now established as a senior reggae statesman McGregor completed a pair of albums, *Sings Jamaican Classics* (1991) and *Jamaican Classic Vol. 2* (1992), on which he offers his interpretations of reggae standards such as **Little Roy**'s 'Prophecy' and **Derrick Harriott's** 'The Loser', re-titled 'The Winner'. McGregor again narrowly missed the UK charts with his interpretation of**Justin Hinds** And The Dominoes' 'Carry Go Bring Come' (1993), but has since had huge success in the reggae charts with his production of **Luciano**'s 'Shake It Up Tonight', sung over the rhythm used for his own 'Seek And You Will Find', which also provides the vehicle for **Big Youth**'s excellent 'Jah Judgement'. Already a veteran in the business at the age of 37, McGregor's future as a reggae superstar looks assured.
Selected albums: *Mr Macgregor* (Observer 1979), *Boby Babylon* (Studio One 1980), *Lovers Rock Showcase JA Style* (Third World 1981), *Love At First Sight* (Intense/Vista Sounds 1982), *Big Ship* (Greensleeves 1982), *I Am Ready* (Studio One 1982), *Come On Over* (RAS 1983), *Freddie* (Vista Sounds 1983), *Across The Border* (RAS 1984), *All In The Same Boat* (RAS 1986), *Freddie MacGregor* (Dynamic/Polydor 1987), *Rhythm So Nice* (Dynamic 1988), *Don't Want To Be Lonely* (Studio One 1988), *Now* (Steelie & Clevie/VP 1991), *Sings Jamaican Classics* (Jetstar/VP 1991), *Hard To Get* (Greensleeves 1992), *Jamaican Classics Vol. 2* (Jetstar/VP 1992), *Push On* (Big Ship 1994). Compilation: *Reggae Rockers* (Rohit 1989). Video: *So I Wait* (1989).

McGriff, Jimmy

b. James Herrell, 3 April 1936, Philadelphia, Pennsylvania, USA. Encouraged by a musical home environment (both his parents were pianists), by the time he left school, McGriff played not only piano but bass, vibes, drums and saxophone. He played with **Archie Shepp**, **Reggie Workman**, Charles Earland and Donald Bailey in his youth, but after two years as an MP in the Korean War he decided to take up law enforcement rather than music as a career. This did not satisfy him in the event, and he began moonlighting as a bassist, backing blues stars like **Big Maybelle**. He left the police force and studied organ at Combe College, Philadelphia, and New York's Juilliard. He also took private lessons with **Jimmy Smith**, **Richard 'Groove' Holmes** and **Milt Buckner**, as well as from classical organist Sonny Gatewood. His career first took off with the single 'I Got A Woman' in 1962, and he had a string of hits released through the legendary Sue label. During this decade Jimmy was arguably the crown prince of the soul jazz organ movement (the King being Jimmy Smith). His stabbing style and shrill tone was much copied, particularly in the UK with the rise of the beat R&B scene. **Georgie Fame** and **Brian Auger** were greatly influenced by McGriff. His memorable 'All About My Girl' remains one of his finest compositions, and has become a minor classic. In the late 80s he experienced a revival in his commercial success, collaborating with **Hank Crawford** on record and in concert. He tours for most of the year, still concentrating on Hammond organ, but also using synthesizers. A fine, bluesy player, he helped popularize a jazz-flavoured style of R&B which is still gathering adherents and is influential in London clubland's so-called 'acid jazz' circles.
Selected albums: *I've Got A Woman* (1962), *Gospel Time* (c.1963), *Topkapi* (1964), *One Of Mine* (c.60s), *At The Apollo* (c.60s), *At The Organ* (c.60s), *Blues For Mister Jimmy* (Stateside 1965), *The Worm* (1968), *The Last Minute* (1983), *The Countdown* (Milestone 1983), *Skywalk* (1985), *State Of The Art* (Milestone 1986), with Hank Crawford *Soul Survivors* (Milestone 1986), Fly Dude (1987), *The Starting Five* (1987), *Jimmy McGriff Featuring Hank Crawford* (LRC 1990), *Georgia On My Mind* (LRC 1990), *Tribute To Basie* (LRC 1991), *Funkiest Little Band In The Land* (LRC 1992), *Electric Funk* (Blue Note 1993). Compilation: *A Toast To Jimmy McGriffs Golden Classics* (Collectable 1989).

McGuffie, Bill

b. 11 December 1927, Carmyle, near Glasgow, Scotland, d. 22 March 1987, Chertsey, Surrey, England. A highly accomplished pianist, composer and arranger in the UK from the 40s through to the 80s. Although the third finger of his right hand was amputated following a playtime accident as a child, McGuffie persevered with his music studies, and at the age of 11 was awarded the Victoria Medal for his piano proficiency by the Victoria College, Glasgow. A year later he made his first broadcast on *Childrens' Hour*, and at the age of 14 was playing regularly with the BBC Scottish Variety Orchestra. For a while he studied to be a naval architect, before moving to Ayr to join the Miff Hobson Orchestra. Early in 1944, he moved to London and played with Teddy Foster at the Lyceum, and then spent four years with **Joe Loss,** before joining Maurice Winnick and **Sidney Lipton**. He also led his own ensemble at the Mayfair Club, but really came to prominence during a three-year spell as a featured soloist with **Cyril Stapleton**'s BBC Showband in the early 50s. When the band was taken off the air, McGuffie joined **Kenny Baker**'s Dozen, and then, in the early 60s, played with the orchestra of **Robert Farnon**, who, together with composer Phil Green, was one of McGuffie's main influences, particularly in the area of film music. Widening his field into composing and arranging, he is said to have worked on over 50 movies, including *The Boys* (1961), *The Leatherboys* (1963), *The Asphyx* (1972) and *The Small Miracle* (1973). He also assisted Farnon on many projects, such as ***Gentlemen Marry Brunettes*** (1955) and the final 'Road' film, *Road To Hong Kong*, in which **Frank Sinatra** joined the regular team of **Bing Crosby**, **Bob Hope** and **Dorothy Lamour**. In the early 70s he played with **Benny Goodman**'s British Band and American Sextet on their European tours, but a stroke in 1974 laid him low for a while. When he recovered, McGuiffie continued to work regularly until 1983, and the onset of cancer, from which he died four years later. During his wide- ranging career, he played jazz, both sweet and swinging, show music and concertos for films. He recorded as a solo pianist, and fronted a variety of ensembles including the Bill McGuffie Big Band, Trio, and Quintet. He broadcast regularly with his own show, and contributed to programmes such as *Breakfast (And Bedtime) With Braden*, *Round The Horne*, *King Of The Keyboard*, *Piano Playtime* and *Week Ending*. His compositions included 'Dear Dave', 'Up On the Hill', 'Gentle Gataa', 'It Zoot Sims' and 'Sweet September', for which he won an **Ivor Novello** Award in 1963. In 1980, the British Academy of Composers Songwriters and Authors awarded him its Gold Badge of Merit. He was also a founder member of the Niner Club, so called because of his missing finger. The organization raises substantial sums of money for autistic children.

Albums: *West End Mood* (1954), *Bill McGuffie Solo* i (1959), *Bill McGuffie Solo* ii (1960), *McGuffie At The Mayfair* (c.50s/60s), *Continental Tour* (c.50s/60s), *Isn't It Romantic* (c.50s/60s), *Film Themes* (c.50s/60s), *Playing for Pleasure* (c.50s/60s), *Bill McGuffie And Big Band* (c.50s/60s), *McGuffie And Big Band* (1975), *Playing Piano Greats* (1978).

McGuinn, Clark And Hillman

This aggregation of ex-**Byrds** came together at the end of 1977 and signed a major deal with **Capitol Records**. Their debut, *McGuinn, Clark & Hillman* had a distinctly late 70s production courtesy of Ron and Howard Albert, which contrasted markedly with their previous work in such outfits as the **Flying Burrito Brothers, Manassas** and **Dillard And Clark.** A catchy single, 'Don't You Write Her Off', written by **Roger McGuinn,** gave the trio its first ***Billboard*** hit since the Byrds days. After touring extensively, **Gene Clark** left his colleagues during the recording of their second album, *City*. McGuinn and Hillman soldiered on for one last album which did little to enhance their reputation. The experiment had clearly run its course and when **Chris Hillman** lashed out against a Capitol Records promotions person, the weary McGuinn announced that their latest partnership was at an end. Thereafter, they returned to various small-time solo ventures. It would be another decade before the two came together again for a brief series of shows with **David Crosby**.

Albums: *McGuinn, Clark & Hillman* (1979), *City* (1980), *McGuinn/Hillman* (1981), *Return 2 Flight* (1993).

McGuinn, Roger

b. James Joseph McGuinn, 13 July 1942, Chicago, Illinois, USA. After a period playing at various folk clubs in Chicago, lead guitarist Jim McGuinn briefly joined the **Limeliters** before accepting a job as an accompanist in the **Chad Mitchell Trio** in 1960. He played on two of their albums, *Mighty Day On Campus* and *Live At The Bitter End*, but after a couple of years became frustrated with his limited role in the ensemble. **Bobby Darin,** having switched from pop to folk, also recruited McGuinn for a spell, and the guitarist continued to learn his craft by appearing on sessions for artists such as **Hoyt Axton, Judy Collins** and Tom And Jerry (alias **Simon And Garfunkel**). By 1964, McGuinn was playing regularly as a soloist at the Troubadour in Hollywood, and it was there that he formed the Jet Set with **Gene Clark** and **David Crosby**. Following the recruitment of bassist **Chris Hillman** and drummer Michael Clarke, the quintet emerged as the chart-topping **Byrds**. McGuinn was a focal point in the group from the outset, thanks largely to his distinctive 12-string **Rickenbacker** guitar playing, Dylanesque vocal style and rectangular glasses. The only Byrd actually to play an instrument on 'Mr

Tambourine Man', McGuinn was often nominated 'leader' at recording sessions - though his authority was largely illusory during the early stages of the group's career. Never a prolific songwriter, McGuinn's importance to the Byrds lay largely in his playing and arranging skills. Always professing an interest in religion, he became involved in the sect Subud and changed his name to Roger before recording the celebrated *The Notorious Byrd Brothers*.
By 1968, he was the sole-surviving, original Byrd and kept the group going until as late as 1973. That same year, he launched his solo career with a self-titled album which ably displayed his musical versatility - combining folk, surf and even space rock. The Rickenbacker twang was even more evident on his second album, *Peace On You* (1974), but he lost critical ground with a hastily produced third album. A starring spot in **Bob Dylan**'s Rolling Thunder Revue, in 1975, revitalized his career at a crucial time, laying the foundations for the excellent *Cardiff Rose* (1976), his most complete work as a soloist. The patchy *Thunderbyrd* (1977), which included McGuinn's version of **Tom Petty**'s 'American Girl', coincided with a UK tour which brought together three ex-Byrds in different groups on the same bill. Within a year, the trio united as **McGuinn, Clark & Hillman**, re-enacting the Byrds' stormy career in microcosm when Gene Clark again left after the second album, *City*. Meanwhile, McGuinn had undergone another religious conversion, this time emerging as a born-again Christian. For virtually the whole of the 80s he performed solo without a recording contract, and avoided any ill-advised Byrds reunions. A legal dispute with his former colleague Michael Clarke briefly saw McGuinn re-establish the Byrds with Chris Hillman and David Crosby. After losing the Byrds' name at the injunction stage, a proposed world tour and live album failed to materialize. Instead, McGuinn won a major deal with **Arista Records** and set about recording his first album in over a decade. McGuinn's 'legendary' reputation as an innovative guitarist has grown to the extent that, during the late 80s, Rickenbacker manufactured a 'Roger McGuinn' production model. This guitar is pre-set to give a replica of his trademark 12-string sound. In 1990, McGuinn returned to the recording scene with the release of his first album in over a decade, *Back From Rio*. Critically acclaimed, the album charted on both sides of the Atlantic.
Albums: *Roger McGuinn* (1973), *Peace On You* (1974), *Roger McGuinn And Band* (1975), *Cardiff Rose* (1976), *Thunderbyrd* (1977), *Back From Rio* (1990). Compilation: *Born To Rock 'n' Roll* (1992).
Further reading: *Timeless Flight: The Definitive Biography of the Byrds*, Johnny Rogan.

McGuinness Flint

Formed in 1969 by Tom McGuinness (b. 2 December 1941, London, England; bass, ex-**Manfred Mann**) and Hughie Flint (b. 15 March 1942; drums, ex-**John Mayall**). Dennis Coulson (keyboards), Benny Gallagher (b. Largs, Scotland; guitar/vocals), Graham Lyle (b. Largs, Scotland; guitar/vocals) and Paul Rutherford (saxophone) completed the original line-up, although the latter dropped out the following year. The group enjoyed immediate success with 'When I'm Dead And Gone' and 'Malt And Barley Blues', both of which reached the UK Top 5 and established their brand of light, folksy pop. Two excellent albums confirmed their undoubted promise, although a succession of disastrous live performances undermined progress. Further problems occurred in 1971, when principle songwriters **Gallagher And Lyle** left to pursue a career as a duo, but although Dixie Dean (bass/harmonica), John Bailey (guitar) and **Neil Innes** (piano, ex-**Bonzo Dog Doo-Dah Band**) replaced them, the group broke up at the end of the year. A resurrection of sorts occurred in 1972, when Coulson, Dean, McGuinness and Flint recorded *Lo And Behold*, a selection of **Bob Dylan** songs unavailable commercially. Coulson was then replaced by Lou Stonebridge, and with the addition of guitarist Jim Evans, a revamped McGuinness Flint re-emerged the following year. Two more albums were completed, but the unit was unable to recapture that first flush of success and broke up in 1975. Flint, Stonebridge and McGuinness later enjoyed fruitful periods with the **Blues Band**, albeit at different times.
Albums: *McGuinness Flint* (1971), *Happy Birthday Ruthie Baby* (1971), *Lo And Behold* (1972), *Rainbow* (1973), *C'est La Vie* (1974).

McGuire Sisters

b. Middletown, Ohio, USA. This close-harmony vocal group, popular in the 50s and early 60s, consisted of three sisters, Chris (Christine) (b. 30 July 1929), Dorothy (Dotty) (b. 13 February 1930) and Phyllis (b. 14 February 1931). While in their teens the sisters sang with church choirs, and won an amateur talent contest at their local cinema for three consecutive weeks. After singing on their local radio station, the McGuires had their first big break, entertaining at army camps and hospitals during a nine-month tour in 1950-51. Then they played club and radio dates in Cincinnati before moving to New York in 1952, and successfully auditioning for the *Arthur Godfrey Talent Scouts* contest. They subsequently became regulars on the show, and also appeared for eight weeks on singer **Kate Smith**'s top-rated radio programme. Signed to the Coral label, they had their first minor hit in 1954 with 'Pine Tree, Pine Over Me', in collaboration with **Johnny Desmond** and Eileen Barton. During the rest of that year they had further successes with their version of the **Spaniels**' R&B hit, 'Goodnight Sweetheart, Goodnight', followed by 'Muskrat Ramble', 'Lonesome

Polecat' and 'Christmas Alphabet'. In 1955 the sisters had their first million-seller with another cover, 'Sincerely', originally recorded by the **Moonglows**. The McGuires' version stayed at number 1 in the US for 10 weeks, and accelerated their breakthrough into the big time in clubs, theatres and on television. They sang on the *Red Skelton Show* and the *Phil Silvers Show* and appeared at the Waldorf Astoria, the Desert Inn, Las Vegas and the Coconut Grove in Los Angeles. They made their first visit to London in 1961, and played a season at the Talk Of The Town. Their other hits, up until 1961, included 'No More', 'It May Sound Silly', 'Something's Gotta Give', 'He', 'Moonglow And The Theme From *Picnic*', 'Delilah Jones'; 'Weary Blues' (with **Lawrence Welk**), 'Ev'ry Day Of My Life', 'Goodnight My Love, Pleasant Dreams', 'Sugartime', 'Ding Dong', 'May You Always' and 'Just For Old Times Sake'. When the McGuires' sweet style was overtaken by the harder sounds of the **Crystals**, **Shirelles** and **Supremes** during the 60s, they turned to cabaret, and eventually disbanded. Phyllis continued as a single, appearing regularly in Las Vegas and other cities. In 1985 the McGuire Sisters re-formed and, in the following year, undertook a national tour, stopping off at Bally's Reno to headline in Donn Arden's lavish revue *Hello, Hollywood, Hello*. Their well- received act continued into the 90s, leaning heavily on their old catalogue, along with more contemporary material from ***Cats*** and ***Les Miserables***, and an **a cappella** version of 'Danny Boy'. In January 1986, Murray Kane, their personal manager and arranger since 1952, died in Las Vegas. He was responsible for writing the arrangements that won the sisters a spot on the *Arthur Godfrey Show*, their first break in New York. Prior to that, Kane had worked with **Fred Waring**, and had been a member of the Crew Chiefs, **Glenn Miller**'s vocal group during World War II.

Selected albums: *By Request* (1955), *Children's Holiday* (c.50s), *Do You Remember When?* (c.50s), *He* (c.50s), *Sincerely* (c.50s), *Teenage Party* (c.50s), *When The Lights Are Low* (1958) *Musical Magic* (c.50s), *Sugartime* (1958), *Greetings From The McGuire Sisters* (late 50s), *Our Golden Favourites* (late 50s), *May You Always* (1959), *In Harmony With Him* (1960) *His And Her's* (early 60s), *Just For Old Times Sake* (1961), *Subways Are For Sleeping* (1962), *Songs Everybody Knows* (1962), *Showcase* (early 60s), *The McGuire Sisters Today* (1966). Compilation: *The Best Of The McGuire Sisters* (1982), *Greatest* (1989).

McGuire, Barry

b. 15 October 1935, Oklahoma City, Oklahoma, USA. McGuire first came to prominence as a minor actor in *Route 66* before teaming up with singer Barry Kane as Barry And Barry. In 1962, he joined the **New Christy Minstrels** and appeared as lead singer on several of their hits, most notably, 'Green Green' and 'Saturday Night'. He also sang the lead on their comic but catchy 'Three Wheels On My Wagon'. While still a Minstrel, he composed the hit 'Greenback Dollar' for the **Kingston Trio**. After leaving the New Christy Minstrels, McGuire signed to **Lou Adler**'s Dunhill Records and was assigned to staff writers **P.F. Sloan** and **Steve Barri**. At the peak of the folk-rock boom, they wrote the rabble-rousing protest 'Eve Of Destruction', which McGuire took to number 1 in the USA, surviving a blanket radio ban in the process.The anti-establishment nature of the lyric even provoked an answer record, 'Dawn Of Correction', written by John Madara and Dave White under the pseudonym the Spokesmen. Ironically, 'Eve Of Destruction' had originally been conceived as a flip-side and at one stage was offered to the **Byrds**, who turned it down. Coincidentally, both Barry McGuire and Byrds leader Jim (later **Roger**) **McGuinn** received a flattering namecheck on the **Mamas And The Papas**' hit 'Creeque Alley' ('McGuinn and McGuire were just a-getting higher in LA, you know where that's at'). McGuire, in fact, played a significant part in bringing the million-selling vocal quartet to Adler and they later offered their services as his backing singers.

McGuire attempted unsuccessfully to follow-up his worldwide hit with other Sloan material, including the excellent 'Upon A Painted Ocean'. He continued to pursue the protest route on the albums *Eve Of Destruction* and *This Precious Time*, but by 1967 he was branching out into acting. A part in *The President's Analyst* led to a Broadway appearance in the musical ***Hair***. After the meagre sales of *The World's Last Private Citizen*, McGuire ceased recording until 1971, when he returned with former Mamas And The Papas sideman Eric Hord on *Barry McGuire And The Doctor*. The work featured backing from the cream of the 1965 school of folk-rock, including the Byrds' **Chris Hillman** and Michael Clarke. Soon afterwards, McGuire became a Christian evangelist and thereafter specialized in gospel albums.

Albums: *Eve Of Destruction* (1965), *This Precious Time* (1966), *The World's Last Private Citizen* (1967), *Barry McGuire And The Doctor* (1971), *Seeds* (1973), *Finer Than Gold* (1981), *Inside Out* (1982), *To The Bride* (1982), *Best Of Barry* (1982).

McHugh, Jimmy

b. James Francis McHugh, 10 July 1894, Boston, Massachusetts, USA, d. 23 May 1969, Beverly Hills, California, USA. A prolific composer for films and the Broadway stage, McHugh was educated at St. John's Preparatory School and Holy Cross College, where he graduated with an honours degree in music. After receiving professional tuition, he worked as a rehearsal pianist at the Boston Opera House, and later as a song-plugger for the Boston office of **Irving Berlin** Music. Moving to New York, he wrote for Harlem's Cotton Club revues, and had some success with 'When My Sugar Walks Down The Street' (lyric by **Irving Mills** and Gene Austin) and 'I Can't Believe That You're In Love With Me' (lyric by Clarence Gaskill). His first Broadway success came with the score for the all-black revue, ***Blackbirds Of 1928***, in collaboration with **Dorothy Fields**, who became his first main lyricist. The songs included 'I Can't Give You Anything But Love', 'Diga Diga Doo', 'I Must Have That Man', 'Doin' The New Low-Down' and 'Porgy'. The original stars, **Adelaide Hall** and **Bill 'Bojangles' Robinson** were joined by the **Mills Brothers**, **Ethel Waters**, and the orchestras of **Cab Calloway**, **Duke Ellington**, and **Don Redman** on a rare reissue album. The McHugh/Fields team wrote the scores for two more Broadway shows, *Hello Daddy* (1929, 'In A Great Big Way' and 'Let's Sit And Talk About You'), and *International Revue* (1930), which starred **Gertrude Lawrence** and **Harry Richman**, and featured two important McHugh numbers, 'On The Sunny Side Of The Street' and 'Exactly Like You'. McHugh and Fields also contributed songs to the Chicago revue *Clowns In Clover* (1933), in which Jeanette Leff introduced the lovely ballad 'Don't Blame Me'. During the 30s and 40s McHugh is said to have written songs for over 50 films, initially with Fields. These included *The Cuban Love Song* and *Dinner At Eight* (title songs), *Singin' The Blues* (title song, 'Its The Darndest Thing'), *Have A Heart*, ('Lost In A Fog'), *Every Night At Eight*, starring **Alice Faye** ('I'm In The Mood For Love', 'I Feel A Song Coming On'), ***Dancing Lady*** (title song), and ***Roberta*** ('Lovely To Look At', 'I Won't Dance', with **Jerome Kern**). McHugh's other chief collaborator was **Harold Adamson**. Together they wrote numerous songs for films such as *Banjo On My Knee* ('There's Something In The Air'), *You're A Sweetheart*, starring **Alice Faye** and George Murphy (title song, 'My Fine Feathered Friend'). *That Certain Age* ('My Own'), ***Mad About Music***, starring **Deanna Durbin** ('A Serenade To The Stars', 'I Love To Whistle'), *Four Jills In A Jeep*, starring **Dick Haymes**, Alice Faye, and **Betty Grable** ('How Blue The Night'), ***Higher And Higher***, an early **Frank Sinatra** film ('The Music Stopped', 'I Couldn't Sleep A Wink Last Night', 'A Lovely Way To Spend An Evening', 'I Saw You First'), *Calendar Girl* ('Have I Told You Lately That I Love You', 'A Lovely Night To Go Dreaming'), *Smash Up* ('Red Hot And Beautiful', 'Hushabye Island'), *Something For The Boys* ('In The Middle Of Nowhere', 'Wouldn't It Be Nice?'). Two other well-known McHugh/Adamson songs were 'Comin' In On A Wing And A Prayer', and 'Love Me As Though There Were No Tomorrow'. In 1939, McHugh collaborated with **Al Dubin** on 'South American Way', which was introduced by **Carmen Miranda**, Ramon Vinay, Della Lind, and the Hylton Sisters in the Broadway revue *Streets Of Paris*. Miranda gave it the full treatment again in the 1940 movie ***Down Argentine Way***. In the same year, McHugh and Dubin worked with **Howard Dietz** on the score for the stage musical *Keep Off the Grass*, which included 'Clear Out Of This World' and 'A Latin Tune, A Manhattan Moon, And You'. Other popular McHugh songs include 'I'm Shooting High', 'Let's Get Lost', I'd Know You Anywhere', 'You've Got Me This Way', 'Sing A Tropical Song, ''Murder' She Says', 'Say A Prayer For The Boys Over There', 'Can't Get Out Of This Mood', 'In A Moment Of Madness', 'Blue Again', 'Goodbye Blues', 'I've Just Found Out About Love And I Like It', 'Warm and Willing', 'The Star You Wished Upon Last Night', 'Where The Hot Wind Blows' and 'Massachusetts'. McHugh's collaborators during his long career included **Ted Koehler**, **Frank Loesser**, **Johnny Mercer**, **Herb Magidson**, Ralph Freed, **Ned Washington** and Arnold Johnson.

During World War II, McHugh wrote several US Government-commissioned 'War Savings Bond' songs such as 'Buy, Buy, Buy A Bond' and 'We've Got Another Bond To Buy'. For his work during the war he was awarded the Presidential Certificate Of Merit. He continued writing well into the 50s, and in 1955 had a hit with 'Too Young To Go Steady' (with Adamson), which was recorded by **Patti Page** and **Nat 'King' Cole**.

Macintosh, Adrian

b. 7 March 1942, Tadcaster, Yorkshire, England. Macintosh began playing drums as a child and worked with various bands locally before moving to London in the mid-60s. He played with several small, mainstream bands but attracted most attention during a stint with **Alan Elsdon**'s more traditionally oriented group. He gained further experience backing visiting American jazz musicians at various London clubs, and in 1982 joined **Humphrey Lyttelton**. His work with Lyttelton drew widespread attention to his fine musicianship and subtle swing. His playing on the band's many concert and recording sessions of the late 80s helped to consolidate critical and audience opinion that Macintosh was the best of all the drummers to accompany Lyttelton over the years.

Albums: all with Lyttelton *It Seems Like Yesterday* (1983), *Gigs* (1987), *Rock Me Gently* (1991).

McIntyre, Hal

b. 29 November 1914, Cromwell, Connecticut, USA, d. 5 May 1959, Los Angeles, California, USA. After playing alto saxophone and clarinet in several groups, McIntyre formed his own big band in 1935. Although fairly popular on the one-night-stand dancehall circuit, the band folded, and in 1937, McIntyre joined **Glenn Miller**. He remained with Miller until 1941, when he reformed his own band. This time he enjoyed considerably more success, making records and playing on the radio. Although still orientated towards dance music, McIntyre's was always a very sophisticated outfit

and the employment of leading jazz players such as **Eddie Safranski** and **Allen Eager** ensured that the band swung. Arrangements were largely the responsibility of tenor saxophonist Dave Matthews, whose love of **Duke Ellington**'s music was apparent in much of his work. In the mid-40s McIntyre took his band on overseas trips to entertain US servicemen. He managed to keep the group together into the 50s, but he died in a fire at his home in May 1959.
Compilations: *One Night Stand With Hal McIntyre* (1943), *Broadcasts 1943-1946* (1943-46), *Hal McIntyre And His Orchestra* I (1943-47), *Hal McIntyre And His Orchestra* II (1944-45), *Hal McIntyre And His Orchestra* iii (1945), *Hal McIntyre At The Hotel Commodore* (1946), *Hal McIntyre At Frank Dailey's Meadowbrook* (1946).

McIntyre, 'Kalaparush' Maurice

b. 24 March 1936, Clarksville, Arkansas, USA. McIntyre's family moved to Chicago when he was six weeks old, and he grew up on the city's south side. He began to play drums at the age of seven, and clarinet two years later, but he did not really study music seriously until his mid-teens, when he concentrated on tenor saxophone. After a drugs problems in the early 60s, he worked on the Chicago blues scene - performing with **Little Milton**, recording with **J.B. Hutto** - and also joined **Muhal Richard Abrams**'s Experimental Band, becoming one of the first members of the **AACM** in 1965. He played with **Roscoe Mitchell**'s sextet (*Sound*) and with Abrams (*Levels And Degrees Of Light*) before forming his own group, the Light, and recording his first session as leader in 1969 (*Humility In The Light Of The Creator*). That same year he underwent a form of spiritual conversion and changed his name to Kalaparush (or Kalaparusha) Ahrah Difda (or Defda), though subsequent recordings have usually been credited to Kalaparush(a) Maurice McIntyre. He later spent time in New York, recording there for the *Wildflower* series of compilations (volume 1); but he was mostly based in Chicago throughout the 70s and 80s, during which time he played with a variety of artists, including Abrams again, **Julius Hemphill**, Jerome Cooper, Warren Smith, Roland Alexander, Sonelius Smith and Wilbur Morris. In 1982, he replaced 'Light' Henry Huff in the **Ethnic Heritage Ensemble**, recording with them on *Welcome* (but did not play on the later *Ancestral Song*). A robust, inventive tenor saxophonist, McIntyre cites his chief influences as **Sonny Rollins**, **Charlie Parker**, **John Coltrane** and **Sam Rivers**, but he has evolved a personal, rhythmically assured style, bristling with authority on his own *Ram's Run*, waxing more tenderly on *Welcome*. Regrettably, he is one of several AACM stalwarts who has not been recorded as frequently as their talent deserves.
Albums: *Humility In The Light Of The Creator* (1969), *Forces And Feelings* (1972), *Peace And Blessings* (1979), *Ram's Run* (1982), with the Ethnic Heritage Ensemble *Welcome* (1983).

McIntyre, Ken

b. 7 September 1931, Boston, Massachusetts, USA. McIntyre was born into a musical family (his father played mandolin) and took lessons in classical piano between 1940 and 1945. At the age of 19 he began alto saxophone lessons with Andrew McGhee, **Gigi Gryce** and **Charlie Mariano**. In 1954, he attended the Boston Conservatory, and after graduating with an MA in composition, he studied at Brandeis University for two years. He formed his own group in Boston and recorded his debut, *Stone Blues*, for the Prestige label in 1959. In 1960, he moved to New York and met **Eric Dolphy**, who played on his *Looking Ahead* in June of that year. Discouraged by the poor financial returns of the jazz life, McIntyre decided to make teaching his full-time profession. However, he continued to record, releasing *The Years Of The Iron Sheep* and *Way, Way Out* (the latter featuring his own flute, oboe, bass-clarinet and alto sax plus his arrangements for strings). In 1964, McIntyre recorded with the **Bill Dixon** Septet, and in 1965, he played with the Jazz Composers Guild Orchestra. He was also in the **Cecil Taylor** group that recorded *Unit Structures* in 1966, a monumental work of intricate jazz modernism. Having taught in schools in New York, he obtained a post at Wilberforce University in Ohio between 1967 and 1969, and taught at the Wesleyan University for two years after that. Since 1971, he has been director of the African-American Music and Dance Department at Old Westbury. The Danish label Steeplechase documented his playing and compositions on a series of five albums in the 70s, since when he has played with **Charlie Haden**'s Liberation Music Orchestra, but made only one more recording under his own name (taken from a 1990 tribute concert to Dolphy, with French reeds player Thierry Bruneau). Although a less innovative talent than Eric Dolphy or **Ornette Coleman**, McIntyre's work represents an equally valid extension of the music of **Charlie Parker** and often includes elements of African-Caribbean musics in recognition of the West Indian cultural heritage.
Albums: *Stone Blues* (Original Jazz Classics 1959), *Looking Ahead* (Original Jazz Classics 1960), *The Years Of The Iron Sheep* (1962), *Way, Way Out* (1963), *Hindsight* (1974), *Home* (1975), *Open Horizon* (1976), *Introducing The Vibrations* (Steeplechase 1977), *Chasing The Sun* (1979), with Thierry Bruneau *Tribute* (Serene 1991).

McKagan, Duff

b. Michael McKagan, 5 February 1964, Seattle, Washington, USA. **Guns N'Roses**' bass player who has served time in more *ad hoc* bands than anybody can care to remember. It was once said of McKagan that there were few punk/hard rock outfits in Seattle whose

line-up he had not passed through at some point, including the Fartz, Ten Minute Warning, Thankless Dogs, Silly Killers and Wandering Bandeleros. However, in 1993 McKagan decided to take the big step up to a solo career. Writing and playing most of the instruments, his debut included guest appearances by a fine array of rock's glitterati, **Jeff Beck**, **Lenny Kravitz**, Sebastian Bach (**Skid Row**) among them. There were also appearances from his Guns N'Roses workmates Matt Sorum, Gilby Clarke and Slash, just to prove there were no bad feelings about his off-season foray. Despite the strength of the largely power-pop musical backing, McKagan's lyrics revealed only feint flashes of insight, notably on 'Man In The Meadow', dedicated to his former best friend, Todd Crew, who died of an overdose in 1987. It also disappointed those expecting him to return to his punk roots (he sang half of the tracks on Guns N'Roses punk tribute album, *The Sphaghetti Incident*).
Album: *Believe In Me* (Geffen 1993).

Mackay, Andy

b. 23 July 1946, London, England. Originally a classical musician, Mackay switched to rock, and while at Reading University, played saxophone in R&B group, the Nova Express. After answering an advertisement placed by **Bryan Ferry**, Mackay was offered a place in **Roxy Music**. Within a year and a half, the group were acclaimed as one of the most exciting new prospects on the UK rock scene. Much of their power came from the breathtaking saxophone work of Mackay. Such was his credibility that, in 1974, he was given leave to release a solo album, *In Search Of Eddie Riff*. With a wealth of backing musicians, including **Brian Eno**, **Phil Manzanera**, Eddie Jobson, Paul Thompson and John Porter, Mackay recorded an instrumental album on which he demonstrated his musical talent. It was an idiosyncratic work containing a selection of rock numbers and updated classics such as **Jimmy Ruffin**'s 'What Becomes Of The Broken Hearted?' and the **Beatles**' 'The Long And Winding Road'. The classical pieces featured an arrangement of Schubert's 'An Die Musik' and a startling adaptation of Wagner's 'Ride Of The Valkyries'. The musical concoction was completed by some self-penned compositions, most notably, 'Pyramid Of The Night (Past, Present And Future)'. When Roxy Music temporarily retired during 1976-78, Mackay composed the music for the television series *Rock Follies*. He also worked with **Mott The Hoople**, **John Cale** and **Pavlov's Dog** and produced and played on **Eddie And The Hot Rods**' reworking of 'Wooly Bully'. In 1978, a second album of saxophone instrumentals emerged with *Resolving Contradictions*. In the wake of Roxy's final split, Mackay formed the Explorers with Phil Manzanera and released an album of the same title, which sold moderately.
Albums: *In Search Of Eddie Riff* (1974), *Resolving Contradictions* (1982), *The Explorers* (1985).
Further reading: *Electronic Music*, Andy Mackay.

McKay, Freddie

b. 1947, St Catherine, Jamaica, West Indies. McKay recorded for producer **Prince Buster** in 1967 and scored his first hit, 'Love Is A Treasure', for **Duke Reid** in that same year. Later he moved from Treasure Isle to **Coxsone Dodd**'s **Studio One** to record a number of popular titles in the early reggae idiom, including 'High School Dance', 'Sweet You Sour You', 'Drunken Sailor' and 'Picture On The Wall', which was also the title of a debut album which remains McKay's most consistent set. Never in the major league of Jamaican singers, Freddie nevertheless commanded a faithful following and continued to make excellent records right up to his untimely death in the mid-80s.
Albums: *Picture On The Wall* (Studio One 1971), *Lonely Man* (Dragon 1974), *The Best Of Freddie McKay* (GG's 1977), *Creation* (Plant 1979), *Tribal In A Yard* (Move/Charly 1983).

McKee, Maria

Before her solo career McKee was the singer with **Lone Justice**, a band formed by her brother, Brian McLean, the former **Love** guitarist and vocalist. After the break up of the band McKee took time to compose herself, and her debut solo album gave a good platform for her powerful voice and distinctive register with more pop-orientated hooks. Predominantly concerned with romance and heartbreak, it included an unrepresentative UK number 1 single, 'Show Me Heaven', taken from the soundtrack to the Tom Cruise motor racing film, *Days Of Thunder*. Touring extensively in support of the album, McKee eventually decided to move to Ireland. This period also saw McKee collaborate with a variety of Irish musicians, including **Gavin Friday** at a series of gigs for the Dublin A.I.D.S. Alliance. She also recorded the UK club hit, 'Sweetest Child', with the help of noted producer Youth (**Killing Joke**, **Brilliant**). She eventually returned to Los Angeles in 1992 to begin work on a follow-up set. This time she recruited producer George Drakoulias, veteran of successful albums by **Black Crowes** and the **Jayhawks** both of whom sounded similar to Lone Justice. *You Gotta Sin To Get Saved* reunited three-quarters of the original line-up of that band: Marvin Etzioni (bass), Don Heffington (drums) and Bruce Brody (keyboards), alongside Gary Louris and Mark Olsen (guitar/vocals) of the Jayhawks. As McKee noted, 'We had everything in common musically so it just happened.' Bob Fisher provided guitar on live dates, with McKee seemingly much more comfortable with the return to rootsy material.
Albums: *Maria McKee* (Geffen 1989), *You Gotta Sin To Get Saved* (Geffen 1993).

McKellar, Kenneth

b. 1927, Paisley, Renfrewshire, Scotland. An accomplished tenor, McKellar first achieved fame as an interpreter of Scottish songs, notably those by poet Robert Burns. Although later work encompassed light opera, sacred songs and popular material, he remained associated with the heritage of his homeland and was an endemic part of the country's entertainment industry. Despite a plethora of contemporaneous pop acts, McKellar was surprisingly nominated as Britain's representative in the 1966 Eurovision Song Contest. His entry, 'A Man Without Love', fared poorly and at a time such records invariably sold well domestically, the ensuing single struggled to reach the Top 30. This aberration apart, the singer has continued to enjoy a successful international career, particularly in countries boasting expatriate Scots.

Albums: *A Tribute To Robert Burns* (1959), *Kenneth McKellar, Roamin' In The Gloamin'* (1959), *The Songs Of Robert Burns*, *The Songs Of Ireland* (1960), *The Tartan* (1960), *Famous Handel Songs And Arias* (1961), *Songs Of The Hebrides* (1961), *The Songs Of John McCormack* (1962), *Scottish Saturday Night* (1962), *Favourite Ballads And Songs* (1963), *Scotland's Heritage* (1964), *Concert Classics* (1965), *Songs Of The British Isles* (1965), *Great Love Songs* (1965), *Kenneth McKellar's Scotland* (1967), *Sacred Songs*, *Lollipops And Roses*, *Kenneth McKellar's People* (1969), *'Eco Di Napoli* (1970), with Patricia Cahill *Great Duets* (1971), *A Dream O Hame* (1971), *Famous Sacred Songs* (1972), *Great Serenades* (1973), *Willie McCulloch: A Tribute* (1973), *On Wings Of Song* (1975), with Patsy Gilland *Among Your Souvenirs* (1977), *I Belong To Scotland* (1978), *Hosanna* (1979), *McKellar In Scotland* (1984), *Highland Journey* (1985), *The Road To The Isles* (1985), *Sacred Songs Of Scotland* (1985), *Scotland The Brave* (1986), *To Robert Burns: A Tribute* (1987), *Kenneth McKellar Today* (1988). Compilations: *The World Of Kenneth McKellar* (1969), *The World Of Kenneth McKellar Volume 2* (1970), *The Evergreen World Of Kenneth McKellar* (1971), with Vera Lynn *The World Of Nursery Rhymes* (1976) *Focus On Kenneth McKellar* (1976), *Kenneth McKellar Sings Robert Burns* (1978), *The Operatic World Of Kenneth McKellar* (1980).

McKenna, Dave

b. 30 May 1930, Woonsocket, Rhode Island, USA. By his late teens, McKenna was active in and around Boston, playing piano with Boots Mussulli's band. In 1949, he joined **Charlie Ventura**, then worked with **Woody Herman** until drafted during the Korean War. From 1953 until well into the 60s he was mostly engaged in small group work, playing with Ventura again and with several major artists, including **Gene Krupa**, **Stan Getz** and **Zoot Sims**. From the late 60s until the end of the 70s, he played long residencies at bars and restaurants in the Boston and Cape Cod areas of Massachusetts. His return to the national and international scene happened on several fronts, with record dates, tours and festival appearances with **Bob Wilber**, **Scott Hamilton**, **Warren Vaché** and many other musicians associated with Concord Records. An exceptionally accomplished pianist whether playing solo, as accompanist or in an ensemble role, McKenna's range is wide - although he is clearly happiest playing ballads to which he brings a delightfully melodic touch.

Albums: *Dave McKenna* i (1955), *The Dave McKenna Trio* (1958), with Hal Overton *Dual Piano Jazz* (1960), *Dave McKenna* ii (1963), *Cookin' At Michael's Pub* (1973), *Solo Piano* (1973), *Both Sides Of Dave McKenna* (c.1973), *The Dave McKenna Quartet Featuring Zoot Sims* (1974), *By Myself* (1976), *Dave 'Fingers' McKenna* (1977), *No Holds Barred* (1977), *McKenna* (1977), with Joe Venuti *Alone At The Palace* (1977), *This Is New* (1977), *One Bass Hit* (Concord 1979), *Giant Strides* (1979), *Oil And Viegar* (Honeydew 1979), *Left Handed Compliment* (Concord 1979), *Piano Mover* (1980), *Dave McKenna Plays The Music Of Harry Warren* (1981), *A Celebration Of Hoagy Carmichael* (Concord 1983), *The Keyman* (1984), *The Key Man* (Concord 1985), *Dancing In The Dark And Other Music Of Arthur Schwarz* (Concord 1985), *My Friend The Piano* (Concord 1986), *No More Ouzo For Puzo* (Concord 1988), *Live At Maybeck Recital Hall Vol 2* (Concord 1989), *Shadows 'N' Dreams* (Concord 1990), *Hanging Out* (Concord 1992), with Gary Sargeant *Concord Duo Series Vol. 2* (1993).

McKenna, Mae

A contemporary Scottish vocalist who contributed an impressive performance on Contraband's sole album in 1973. Shortly after they disbanded, Transatlantic launched McKenna as a singer-songwriter. She recorded a series of competent, but undistinguished albums before spending most of the 80s as a session singer with pop artists such **Rick Astley**, and **Ultravox**. In 1988 she surprisingly reappeared on **Virgin**'s Venture offshoot with the Celtic, new age *Nightfallers*. The ensuing album, *Mirage & Reality*, displayed her **Enya**-like qualities and while not as strong as its predecessor, included a stunning interpretation of the Gaelic 'St. Columbia's Hymn'.

Albums: *Mae McKenna* (1975), *Everything That Touches Me* (1976), *Walk On Water* (1977), *Nightfallers* (1988), *Mirage & Reality* (1991).

McKenzie, Bob And Doug

Bob and Doug McKenzie were actually pseudonyms for comedians Dave Thomas and Rick Moranis, two Canadians who gained fame on the popular *SCTV* television programme in the USA. They left their mark in the music world with the 1982 single 'Take Off', which reached the Top 20 in the US, and *Great White North*, which made the Top 10. Thomas, a former scriptwriter for the Canadian Broadcasting Company,

and Moranis, a comedy writer, actor, stand-up comic, included a routine on the television show in which they parodied Canadians. In 1982, they recorded the *Great White North* based on their characters, and it became a hit. The single featured Geddy Lee of **Rush** on vocals; the pair never charted again after their initial success. However, Moranis went on to greater success, as an actor who starred in films including *Ghostbusters*, *Parenthood*, and *Honey I Shrunk The Kids*.
Album: *Great White North* (1982).

McKenzie, Julia

b. 17 February 1941, Enfield, Middlesex, England. An actress, singer, and director, Julia McKenzie is one of the most accomplished leading ladies in the British (and occasionally Broadway) musical theatre. She started to perform at an early age, and attended the Sylvia Spriggs Dancing School. She was about to begin training to become a French teacher when she was offered a scholarship to study opera. After spending four years at the Guildhall School Of Music, she performed in provincial theatres and toured in operettas and musical comedies for a good number of years before coming to prominence in 1969 in the London production of ***Mame***, which starred **Ginger Rogers**. In the early 70s she had her first introduction to **Stephen Sondheim**'s work - with which she has since become indelibly associated - when she took over one of the leading roles in ***Company***. She also replaced Patricia Routledge in *Cowardy Custard*, and, in 1974, appeared in *Cole*, another of the Mermaid Theatre's excellent anthology productions. McKenzie's biggest break came two years later when she co-starred with Millicent Martin, David Kernan, and Ned Sherrin in yet another celebratory revue - *Side By Side By Sondheim* . A surprise hit in London, the show was also well-received in New York where it ran for 384 performances. During the 80s, McKenzie gave a 'dazzling performance' as Lily Garland in ***On The Twentieth Century***, won Variety Club and **Laurence Olivier Awards** for her portrayal of Miss Adelaide in ***Guys And Dolls*** at the National Theatre, and resumed her association with Sondheim in ***Follies*** and ***Into The Woods***. The 90s could well be another Sondheim decade for McKenzie. In 1993 she played Mrs. Lovett in the Royal National Theatre's highly acclaimed production of ***Sweeney Todd***, a performance which won her another Olivier Award. And in the same year she directed the New York premiere of *Putting It Together*, a revue based on the composer's songs, which tempted **Julie Andrews** back to the New York musical stage for the first time since ***Camelot*** (1960). Julia McKenzie has also worked extensively in the straight theatre, and on television where she was voted 'Favourite Comedy Performer' three times in the 80s for her appearances in sitcoms such as *Maggie And Her*, *Fresh Fields*, and *French Fields*. In 1994, she devised (with Kit Hesketh-Harvey) and directed the well-received *Mercury Workshop Musical Revue* at London's Jermyn Street Theatre.
Selected album: *Show Stoppers* (Telstar 1993), and Original Cast recordings.

McKenzie, Red

b. William McKenzie, 14 October 1899, St. Louis, Missouri, USA, d. 7 February 1948. Very much a Jazz Age figure, McKenzie was an ordinary singer and something of a hustler. His principal contribution to jazz lay in his associations with several leading jazzmen of his day for whom he worked tirelessly, promoting record dates and gigs often against reluctance and indifference. In the early 20s, he formed the **Mound City Blue Blowers**, a group which became enormously popular with the fringe audience. McKenzie's singing and playing of an improvised comb-and-paper instrument, together with other instrumentation such as the kazoo, sometimes militated against a true jazz feel, but among the musicians he hired to augment the band for record dates were some of the best available. The results included two tracks featuring **Coleman Hawkins**, 'Hello Lola' and 'If I Could Be With You One Hour Tonight', which became classics. A later band, the Rhythm Kings, featured **Bunny Berigan**. A close associate of McKenzie's was **Eddie Condon**, for whom he arranged a record date, Condon's first, which helped show the outside world what was happening in the white jazz scene in Chicago. By the early 30s, McKenzie's star had waned, but he returned to limited prominence in the mid-40s, playing at Condon's club and making a handful of records.
Compilations: with the Rhythm Kings *Bunny And Red* (1935-36), with Eddie Condon *Chicagoans* (Jazzology 1988).

McKenzie, Scott

b. Philip Blondheim, 1 October 1944, Arlington, Virginia, USA. McKenzie began his professional career in the **Journeymen**, a clean-cut folk group. He later recorded some undistinguished solo material before fellow ex-member **John Phillips**, currently enjoying success with the **Mamas And The Papas**, invited the singer to join him in Los Angeles. Although the folk/rock-inspired 'No No No No No' failed to sell, the pairing flourished spectacularly on 'San Francisco (Be Sure To Wear Some Flowers In Your Hair)'. This altruistic hippie anthem, penned by Phillips, encapsulated the innocent wonderment felt by many onlookers of the era and the single, buoyed by an irresistible melody, reached number 4 in the US chart, but climbed to the dizzy heights of number 1 in the UK and throughout Europe. Meritorious follow-ups, 'Like An Old Time Movie' and 'Holy Man', failed to emulate such success, and although McKenzie briefly

re-emerged with the low-key, country-influenced *Stained Glass Morning*, he remained out of the public eye until the 80s, when he joined Phillips in a rejuvenated Mamas And Papas.
Albums: *The Voice Of Scott McKenzie* (1967), *Stained Glass Morning* (1970).

Mackenzie Theory

Formed in Melbourne, Australia in 1971, Mackenzie Theory remain one of the few totally instrumental bands in Australia to achieve recognition in the mainstream rock and pop music industry since the demise of non-vocal rock 'n' roll and surf bands of the early 60s. In 1973, they recorded a fully instrumental album in Australia, which charted. Rob Mackenzie led the band with his inspired, ethereal guitar playing, but the band also owed much of its distinctive sound to the viola playing of Cleis Pearce. The band, which included Andy Majewski (drums) and Mike Leadabrand (bass), folded in mid-1974 when Mackenzie was awarded an Arts Council grant to study guitar in Europe and America. He currently resides in Los Angeles, USA, performing and doing recording sessions with emerging bands, providing guitar solo embellishments on their demo tapes, or recording eastern and other exotic ethnic styles. Pearce turned her talent to folk music and other eclectic work and she has recorded regularly.
Albums: *Out Of The Blue* (1973), *Bon Voyage* (1974).

Mackenzies

One of the more refreshing aspects of the ***New Musical Express***/ICA Rock Week and accompanying *C86* cassette compilation was the Ron Johnson camp. This Manchester label threw up a handful of manic guitar acts whose shared sources appeared to be the **Fall** and **Captain Beefheart**. The Mackenzies were no exception. 'Big Jim (There's No Pubs In Heaven)' on *C86* started as a quirky thrash similar to the **Fire Engines**, then switched to militant jazz funk groove and back again. Similar ingredients were also found on 'New Breed' in April 1986 and the excellent 'Mealy Mouths' the following February. But the Mackenzies failed to capitalize on these, and nothing was heard from them, apart from a remix of 'Mealy Mouths' exactly a year later, in February 1988.

McKibbon, Al

b. Alfred Benjamin McKibbon, 1 January 1919, Chicago, Illinois, USA. After playing bass in various mid-west bands in the late 30s and early 40s, McKibbon moved to Nw York where he established a solid reputation with leaders of large and small bands, such as **Lucky Millinder** and **Coleman Hawkins**. His musical interests were, however, moving away from such late swing era stylists and from the late 40s he became a prominent member of important bop groups including **Dizzy Gillespie**'s big band and the studio band assembled for the **Miles Davis-Gil Evans** *Birth Of The Cool* sessions. He also worked with **Thelonious Monk** but maintained his connection with the mainstream and in 1951 joined **George Shearing**'s quintet for a seven-year stint. Throughout the 60s and succeeding decades, McKibbon played and recorded with leading jazzmen, including Monk, **Benny Carter** and Gillespie. A meticulous sense of time, allied to a robust style has made McKibbon a much sought-after session musician, able to adapt readily to mainstream and bop demands.
Albums: with Dizzy Gillespie *Salle Pleyel Concert* (1948), with Miles Davis *Classics In Jazz* (1949-50), with George Shearing *Latin Escapade* (1956), with Cal Tjader *In A Latin Bag* (1961), with Thelonious Monk *Something In Blue* (1971), *Carter, Gillespie, Inc.* (1976).

McKinlay, Bob

b. 13 May 1942, Ashton-in-Makerfield, near Wigan, Lancashire, England. Like many others, McKinlay learned guitar from **Bert Weedon**'s *Play In A Day*. He was a member of the northwest beat group, The Long And The Short, which made the UK Top 30 in 1964 with 'The Letter', featuring session musician **Jimmy Page** on lead guitar. They appeared in the film, *Gonks Go Beat*, and then McKinlay was offered a place in the **Mojos**. He soon, however, returned to Wigan and a job in a printing works. He became a mature student and gained a degree in sociology and a teaching diploma. He visited Nashville in 1977 and, on his return, formed a country group. He decided to become a full-time professional and toured the UK country clubs with American singer-songwriter, **Steve Young**. McKinley is enormously popular around country clubs and he manages to support a band. His songs include his personal credo, 'English Born - Dixie Fried', and this Wigan peer has made several cassettes to sell at his shows. He has emulated Bert Weedon by issuing his own guitar tutor.
Albums: *English Born - Dixie Fried* (1979), *Country Good And Rollin'* (1982), *My Songbird* (1984), *Country Tapestry* (1985), *Roots And Offshoots* (1987), *Once More* (1989), *Singer-Songwriter* (1990).

McKinley, L.C.

b. between 1914 and 1920, Winona, Mississippi, USA, d. 19 January 1970. McKinley is one of the mystery figures of the post-war Chicago blues. He had a much smoother style than most of his contemporaries and was obviously influenced by **T-Bone Walker**. McKinley was playing in Chicago in the 40s, and recorded as an accompanist to **Tampa Red** in 1953 and then, under his own name, for States the following year and for **VeeJay Records** in 1955, and finally for Bea And Baby in 1959, before he dropped out of the music scene. **Willie Dixon** reputedly attempted to revive his musical career in the 60s, but to little avail. Compilations: *Chicago Bluesmasters Volume Four* (1985), two Bea And Baby tracks *Meat And Gravy From Cadillac Baby Volume Three: Trying To Make A Living* (1978).

McKinley, Ray

b. 18 June 1910, Fort Worth, Texas, USA, d. 7 May 1995, Largo, Florida, USA. After drumming in the danceband led by fellow Texan, singer **Smith Ballew**, McKinley joined the Dorsey Brothers orchestra in 1934. When the band became **Jimmy Dorsey**'s, after his brother **Tommy** walked out, McKinley remained in the drum chair until 1939. In the autumn of that year he formed a band which he co-led with **Will Bradley**. A string of successful novelty songs, and the use of orchestral arrangements which capitalized on the current boogie-woogie craze, helped the band to become very popular. In 1942, he briefly led a band on his own but was then drafted into the US Army Air Force. He became a key member of **Glenn Miller**'s USAAF band and, following Miller's death, took over leadership of the danceband unit. After the war, McKinley led his own outfit for a number of years, then formed a Miller-style unit which he led until 1966. Thereafter he continued to lead bands, large and small, often geared to Miller's music, until the late 70s. He was still active, playing at Miller reunion sessions, into the mid-80s. A fine, swinging drummer, equally at home in big bands and small groups, playing four-beat or two-beat with consummate ease, and an engaging singer, McKinley made a substantial contribution to American dance music.

Albums: *One Night Stand With Ray McKinley* (1948-49), *The Swingin' 30s* (1955), *Ray McKinley's Greatest Hits* (c.1956), *Glenn Miller Time* (1965). Compilations: The *Will Bradley-Ray McKinley Orchestra* (1940-41), *Glenn Miller And His Army Air Force Orchestra* (1944), *Howdy Friends* (1946), *Ray McKinley And His Musicians 1946-1949* (1946-49), *Blue Skies* (1948), *Ray McKinley And His Orchestra Play The Arrangements And Compositions Of Eddie Sauter* (1949), *Ray McKinley And His Orchestra* (1949), *A Legend* (1949).

McKinney's Cotton Pickers

Originally formed shortly after the end of World War I by drummer Bill McKinney (b. 17 September 1895, d. 14 October 1969), the band adopted their name in 1926. By this time McKinney was manager, having hired **Cuba Austin** to replace himself on the drums. Although geared towards harmless hokum, novelty songs and other aspects of currently popular entertainment, the arrival in 1927 of arranger **Don Redman** turned the band onto a jazz course. Among the many fine musicians who played in the band in its earlier years were **Joe Smith**, **Doc Cheatham**, **Claude Jones** and **Fats Waller**. Resident for several years at Detroit's Graystone Ballroom, promoter **Jean Goldkette**'s flagship venue, the unit made a huge impression upon other bands and their arrangers. In 1931, Redman left, forming his own outfit from a nucleus of McKinney musicians. This was a blow from which the band never fully recovered. Even though several important jazzmen played in later editions, among them **Benny Carter**, who became its musical director, the glory days were over. Indeed, the band made no more records even though it stayed in existence for a few more years. McKinney managed to continue leading a band into the early 40s, but by then it was a shadow of what had gone before. During the four years of its supremacy, the Cotton Pickers established new standards towards which all later big bands would strive. Although history would later credit the period Don Redman spent with the **Fletcher Henderson** Orchestra as being the start of big band music as it is known today, the arranger's work with this earlier band should not be overlooked. In particular, the lively, skilful manner in which they played Redman's arrangements suggest a band well ahead of its time and place in the story of big band jazz. McKinney himself remained only sporadically active in music for the rest of his life. A year or two after his death in 1969, a number of musicians from Detroit formed the New McKinney's Cotton Pickers, using Redman's and Carter's old scores for successful engagements at jazz festivals in America and Europe.

Compilations: *The Complete McKinney's Cotton Pickers Vols 1/2, 3/4, 5* (RCA 1983, 1928-31 recordings), *The Band Don Redman Built* (Bluebird 1990, 1928-30 recordings), *1928-29* (Original Jazz Classics 1992).

Further reading: *McKinney's Music: A Bio-discography Of McKinney's Cotton Pickers*, John Chilton.

McKinney, Bill

(see **McKinney's Cotton Pickers**)

Mackintosh, C.J.

One of the UK's most widely revered DJs and remixers, to whom major record companies regularly indulge their A&R budgets. Chris 'C.J' Mackintosh's standard approach, that of radio-friendly, lush garage arrangements, is too MOR for many of the nation's more underground clubbers, but his technique has become the epitome of taste in the mainstream. Clients have included **Whitney Houston**, **Lisa Stansfield** and **Janet Jackson**. Mackintosh actually started out as a hip hop DJ, going on to win the 1987 finals of the DMC mixing championships. After this initial success he provided hip hop megamixes for labels such as **Champion**. His first venture into remixing proved even more rewarding. Together with Dave Dorrell, he mixed **MARRS**' 'Pump Up The Volume', one of dance music's seminal moments. Mackintosh happily continues his day time job, that of club DJ, and on this basis is one of the first of the UK's 'names' to play in the States. However, it is as a remixer he has won fame and fortune, although he also sees the dangers inherent in a DJ-led music scene: 'With remixing, everyone's doing it and it's wrong, but I think it'll go on because there's nothing to stop it...All sorts of bands are depending on it, they all want a dance mix... remixing's easy because you're using someone else's ideas. Production, and writing, is a totally different thing.' A list of his credits could fill a small book, but some of the most important include **Inner City** ('Good Life'), **Dina Carroll** ('Ain't No Man'), **PM Dawn** ('Reality'), **A Tribe Called Quest** ('Bonita Applebum'), **De La Soul** ('Ring, Ring, Ring'), **Digital Underground** ('Packet Man'), **Simple Minds** ('Sign Of The Times), **Gang Starr** ('Take A Rest'), Whitney Houston ('Queen Of The Night') and **Luther Vandross** and Janet Jackson ('The Best Things In Life Are Free').

Mackintosh, Cameron

b. 17 October 1946, Enfield, England. 'The Czar of theatrical producers' - that is what the American magazine *TheatreWeek* called him in 1993 when they rated him number 3 in their list of the 100 Most Powerful People in American Theatre. The son of a Maltese-born mother and a Scottish father, Mackintosh attended a small public school in Bath and became obsessed by the musical theatre at the age of eight after being taken to see a production of **Julian Slade**'s ***Salad Days*** at Bristol Old Vic in 1954. After leaving school, where he was known as Darryl F. Mackintosh, he attended the Central School for Speech and Drama for a year before becoming an assistant stage manager at the Theatre Royal, Drury Lane when ***Camelot*** was running. His first forays into producing came with some budget-priced touring shows before he moved into the West End in 1969 with a revival of ***Anything Goes***. It proved to be a disaster and was withdrawn after 27 performances. *Trelawny* (1972) and ***The Card*** (1973) fared better, and, after a number of provincial productions of varying degrees of profitability, Mackintosh's breakthrough finally came in 1976 with *Side By Side By Sondheim*. During the next few years he mounted successful revivals of ***Oliver!***, ***My Fair Lady,*** and ***Oklahoma!***, before his meeting with **Andrew Lloyd Webber** resulted in ***Cats*** in 1981. The show transformed the lives of both men, and became the prototype for future productions which overthrew the old style of musical and provided a simple and vivid theatrical experience that did not rely on big name stars, and was easily exportable. In the 80s Mackintosh went from strength to strength with ***Song And Dance***, ***Les Misérables***, ***The Phantom Of The Opera***, and ***Miss Saigon*** (1989). In 1990 the latter show provided an example of just how powerful Mackintosh had become when American Equity initially objected to the casting of Jonathan Pryce in the Broadway production 'because it would be an affront to the Asian community'. After the producer threatened to withdraw the show altogether - and one or two others as well - capitulation was more or less immediate. The incident did nothing to improve the producer's ruthless (he prefers 'relentless') reputation with the New York theatre community, many of whom object to his dictatorial attitude and 'flashy' marketing methods. For some reason he deliberately did not use those ploys when his London hit, ***Five Guys Named Moe***, transferred to Broadway, and that may well be one of the reasons for its relatively poor showing. In 1992 Mackintosh was involved with a rare flop which some say marked the beginning of his decline. ***Moby Dick*** ('a damp squib . . . garbage') is reported to have cost him £1 million and a great deal of pride during its 15-week run, and he hinted at the time that he may be past his peak. However, the highly impressive monetary facts continued to emerge: a personal salary of over £8 million in 1991, the 39th richest man in Britain, and the acquisition of a substantial stake in two West End theatres, the Prince of Wales and the Prince Edward. His love of musicals - that is all he seems to be interested in producing - has caused Mackintosh to divert some of his reported £300 million wealth to a number of extremely worthy causes. As well as numerous donations to small theatrical projects, he provided £2 million to endow Oxford University's first professorship in drama and musical theatre, and his £1 million gift to the Royal National Theatre has enabled it to mount highly acclaimed revivals of ***Carousel*** and ***Sweeney Todd***, the first two in a series of five classic musicals. It is not all philanthropy: Mackintosh is reported to retain the rights to the productions when they are eventually produced in the commercial sector. A knighthood is inevitable, but until then his kudos have included the 1991 *Observer* Award for Outstanding Achievement, and the prestigious **Richard Rodgers** Award for Excellence in Musical Theatre (1992). Previous recipients have been **Harold Prince**, **Julie Andrews** and **Mary Martin**. In 1994, Mackintosh's major revival of *Oliver!* opened at the London Palladium, starring Jonathan Pryce, and in 1995 his production company, Cameron Mackintosh Limited, earned a Queen's Award for Export Achievement. Two years earlier, for the benefit of an awe-struck journalist, he had attempted to remember all the musicals he had running in various parts of the world. They included six ***Cats***, 20 *Phantom Of The Opera*, 12 *Les Misérables*, seven *Miss Saigon*, four *Five Guys Named Moe*, two ***Follies*** . . . et cetera, et cetera, as **Yul Brynner** used to say.

Mackintosh, Ken

b. 4 September 1919, Liversedge, West Yorkshire, England. Mackintosh began playing alto saxophone as a child and worked with various bands in Yorkshire in his teens. In 1939, he joined the army and towards the

end of the war was playing in military bands. He formed his own unit in 1948 and enjoyed a measure of local popularity in dancehalls and on regional radio. In 1950, his band was booked to open the Wimbledon Palais in London and met with immediate success. The band broadcast regularly and won a recording contract with **HMV**. The Wimbledon engagement lasted three years. During the last year, Mackintosh had a record hit with 'The Creep', his own composition, and this led to a bill-topping tour of the UK. Throughout the 50s the band toured, recorded, broadcast extensively on radio and television, where it headlined its own show, *Flying Standards*, and was featured in the film *An Alligator Named Daisy* (1955). Mackintosh was able to give an early career boost to **Frankie Vaughan** and **Alma Cogan**, making records with both artists. Among the band's record successes of the 50s were 'Harlem Nocturne' and 'Raunchy', which reached number 8 in 1958. In 1963, Mackintosh was hired to open the new Empire Ballroom in London's Leicester Square, at the time billed as the world's greatest and most expensive ballroom. This engagement lasted for seven years, after which the band moved to the Hammersmith Palais for a further seven-year stint. Late in the 70s, Mackintosh took his band on the road where he frequently backed touring singers, including **Matt Monro**, **Pat Boone**, **Tom Jones** and **Shirley Bassey**. Throughout the 80s and into the 90s, Mackintosh continued on the road with his band, playing dances at which he acknowledged contemporary sounds while nostalgically recreating the best popular dance music of earlier years. His son is Andy Mackintosh.
Albums: *Skyliner* (1980s), *The Very Thought Of You* (1985), *Blue Skies* (1990).

Mackness, Vanessa

b. Christchurch, Hampshire, England. Mackness grew up in Ipswich, Suffolk, and studied painting in the late 70s at the celebrated Camberwell School of Art, London. She later shared a studio with **Maggie Nicols** and met Phil Minton (then singing with **Mike Westbrook**, but also exploring freely improvised vocals), who gave Mackness the idea of using her voice. She asked Minton for lessons, some of which were conducted under bridges to gain greater resonance. She later studied with the Hungarian mezzo-soprano Julianna Bethlen and the French composer/singer Gilles Petit, another influence was Indian classical music, through Imrat Khan and the teachings of Pandit Ravi Shankar. The London free improvisation scene embraced her wide-ranging vocal palette and sensitivity. In 1990 and 1991, she sang at Company Week and also broadcast a 'Music In Our Time' programme organized by **Derek Bailey** for the BBC's Radio 3. Duos with bassist and composer **Barry Guy** (formed in 1989), violinist **Phil Wachsmann**, pianist **Keith Tippett** and saxophonist John Butcher have produced astonishingly varied and powerful music. Mackness remains open to a wide variety of vocal styles and musics - she declares she has an 'endless preoccupation with sound in all contexts, including everyday sounds' - and her cornucopia of vocalism has attracted much attention. In 1991, she initiated a duet with Alexander Balanescu, leader of one of the pre-eminent contemporary classical quartets.

McKuen, Rod

b. Rodney Marvin McKuen, 29 April 1933, Oakland, California, USA. One of the revered poets of the late 60s love generation, Rod McKuen took a slow route to the top. He performed various manual jobs as a young man and embarked on both a pop career ('Happy Is A Boy Named Me' was released in the UK in 1957) and an attempted acting career, combining both by appearing as a musician in the rock 'n' roll exploitation movie *Rock Pretty Baby* in 1957. He also spent a spell as a disc jockey before heading to Paris in the 60s. It was here, in the company of **Jacques Brel** and **Charles Aznavour**, that he began writing poetry in a free verse form very typical of the times. Described by *Newsweek* as 'the king of kitsch', McKuen became one of the few poets able to sell his work in large volumes, and he became a wealthy man. His 60s books included *Lonesome Cities*, *Stanyan Street And Other Sorrows* and *Listen To The Warm*. His musical career continued when he wrote the score for the movie *The Prime Of Miss Jean Brodie* including the title song 'Jean' and contributed six songs to the soundtrack of *A Boy Named Charlie Brown*. The most interesting of his albums is *McKuen Country*, on which he enlists the aid of **Glenn Campbell**, **Big Jim Sullivan** and **Barry McGuire** in a perfectly acceptable stab at country rock. Among his best remembered compositions are 'Seasons In The Sun' (music by Brel and a hit for **Terry Jacks**), 'If You Go Away', 'Love's Been Good To Me' (recorded by **Frank Sinatra** on an album of McKuen songs, *A Man Alone*), 'I Think Of You (music by Francis Lai and a hit for **Perry Como**), 'Soldiers Who Want To Be Heros', 'Doesn't Anybody Know My Name', and 'The Importance Of The Rose'.
Selected albums: *Rod McKuen Live In London!* (Warner Brothers 1970), *At Carnegie Hall* (Warner Brothers 1974), *McKuen Country* (1976), *Rod McKuen 77* (1977), *McKuen* (1982). Compilation: *Greatest Hits* (1973).
Further reading: all by Rod McKuen *Listen To The Warm*, *Stanyan Street And Other Sorrows*, *In Someone's Shadow*, *Lonesome Cities*, *Fields Of Wonder*, *Twelve Years Of Christmas*, *Caught In The Quiet*, *Moment To Moment*, *Come To Me In Silence*, *Seasons In The Sun*, *Alone*, *The Sea Around Me: The Hills Above*, *Coming Close To Earth*, *Finding My Father: One Man's Search For Identity*, *We Touch The Sky*, *Beyond The Boardwalk*.

McLachlan, Sarah

b. 28 January 1968, Bedford, Halifax, Nova Scotia, Canada. Singer-songwriter Sarah McLachlan has featured on the Canadian folk scene since she was a 20-year-old, and through a series of well-received albums and tours has blossomed into a well-rounded folk-rock artist and a confident live performer. 1994's *Fumbling Towards Ecstasy* was produced by **Daniel Lanois**' protégé Pierre Marchand and was inspired partly by a disturbing trip the singer undertook with the World Vision charity to Cambodia and Thailand. The album blends her pastoral and reflective mood with a high-tech production that gives her sound a sophisticated edginess. As on all her releases her earthy voice is the perfect vehicle for her songs about the deeper, darker aspects of the human condition.

Albums: *Touch* (Arista 1988), *Solace* (Arista 1992), *Fumbling Towards Ecstasy* (Arista 1994), *The Freedom Sessions* (Nettwork 1995).

McLagan, Ian

b. 12 May 1945, London, England. The organist in the Muleskinners and Boz And The Boz People, McLagan was an established musician prior to joining the **Small Faces** in 1965. His distinctive style, redolent of **Jimmy Smith**, quickly became an integral part of the group's overall sound, and he remained an influential figure on their mutation into the **Faces**. When the latter group split in 1975, McLagan was tempted into the ill-fated Small Faces reunion before embarking on a solo album. *Troublemaker* featured assistance from several star names, including **Keith Richards**, **Ron Wood** and **Stanley Clarke**, but was a largely disappointing collection. The organist's distinguished work as part of the **Rolling Stones**' touring ensemble enabled him to relocate to the USA in the late 70s, where he carved out a successful career as a session musician playing alongside countless names such as **Jackson Browne**, **Bonnie Raitt**, the **Everly Brothers**, **Bob Dylan** and more recently, **Georgia Satellites**, **Dogs D'Amour**, **Stray Cats** and **Bruce Springsteen**.

Albums: *Troublemaker* (1979), *Bump In The Night* (1980).

McLain, Tommy

b. 15 March 1940, Jonesville, Louisiana, USA. McLain was a practitioner of a musical style briefly popular in that state during the 50s and 60s called 'swamp pop'. He is best known for his 1966 hit 'Sweet Dreams', written by country singer **Don Gibson** and previously a hit for **Patsy Cline**. It peaked at number 15 in the US charts. McLain first came to notice as bassist for Clint West And The Boogie Kings, a popular Louisiana 'blue-eyed soul' band. He recorded 'Sweet Dreams' on his own, and news of its modest sales was brought to the attention of producer Floyd Soileau, who re-recorded the song for his Jin label. The subsequent national success of the disc forced the distribution onto the newly formed MSL Records, and eventually sold a million copies. McLain released six further singles on Soileau's Jin Records label and Soileau later released two albums of his material but none charted. He was still performing in Louisiana in the early 90s.

Albums: *Tommy McLain* (1973) Compilation: *The Best of Tommy McLain* (1977).

McLaren, Malcolm

b. 22 January 1946, London, England. After a tempestuous childhood, during which he was reared by his eccentric grandmother, McLaren spent the mid-late 60s at various art colleges. In 1969 he became romantically involved with fashion designer Vivienne Westwood and they subsequently had a son together, Joseph. Malcolm was fascinated by the work of the Internationale Situationist, a Marxist/Dadaist group which espoused its doctrines through sharp political slogans such as 'be reasonable - demand the impossible'. Their use of staged 'situations', designed to gain the attention of and ultimately enlighten the proletariat, impressed McLaren, and would significantly influence his entrepreneurial career. In 1971 he opened the shop Let It Rock in Chelsea's Kings Road, which catered for Teddy Boy fashions. Among the shop's many visitors were several members of the **New York Dolls**, whose management McLaren took over in late 1974. It was to prove an ill-fated venture, but McLaren did spend some time with them in New York and organized their 'Better Dead Than Red' tour. After returning to the UK, he decided to find a new, young group whose power, presence and rebelliousness equalled that of the Dolls. The result was the **Sex Pistols**, whose brief spell of public notoriety ushered in the era of punk. McLaren was at the peak of his powers during this period, riding the wave of self-inflicted chaos that the Pistols spewed forth. The highlights included McLaren taking sizeable cheques from both **EMI** and **A&M Records**, who signed then fired the group in quick succession. The creation of the tragic caricature **Sid Vicious**, the conflict with Johnny Rotten, the involvement with Great Train Robber Ronnie Biggs and, finally, a self-glorifying film *The Great Rock 'n' Roll Swindle*, were all part of the saga. Following the Sex Pistols' demise, McLaren launched **Bow Wow Wow**, heavily promoting the 14-year-old singer Annabella Lu Win. Although their recordings were highly original for the period, the dividends proved unimpressive and the group split. In the meantime, McLaren had served as 'advisor' to and let slip through his hands 80s stars such as **Adam Ant** and **Boy George** (**Culture Club**). Eventually, he decided to transform himself into a recording star, despite the fact that he could not sing (ample evidence of which had appeared on his *Great Rock 'n' Roll Swindle* out-take, 'You Need Hands'). His singular ability to predict trends saw him assimilating various styles of music, from the Zulu tribes in Africa to the ethnic sounds of the Appalachian Mountains. The arduous sessions finally came to fruition with *Duck Rock*, which featured two UK Top 10 singles, 'Buffalo Girls' and 'Double Dutch'. The work pre-empted rock's interest in world music, as exemplified on *Graceland* by **Paul Simon**. McLaren next persisted with the music of urban New York and was particularly interested in the 'scratching' sounds of street hip hop disc jockeys. *Would Ya Like More Scratchin'* again anticipated the strong dance culture that would envelop the UK pop scene in the late 80s. Ever restless, McLaren moved on to a strange fusion of pop and opera with *Fans*, which featured a startling version of 'Madam Butterfly' that became a UK Top 20 hit. Following his experimental forays in the music business, McLaren relocated to Hollywood for a relatively unsuccessful period in the film industry. Nothing substantial emerged from that sojourn, but McLaren remains as unpredictable and innovative as ever. Another unlikely coupling was in 1995 when he duetted with **Francoise Hardy** on 'Revenge Of The Flowers'.

Albums: *Duck Rock* (Island 1983), *Would Ya Like More Scratchin'* (Island 1984), *Fans* (Island 1984), *Waltz Darling* (Epic 1989), *Paris* (Disques Vogue 1994). Malcolm McLaren Presents The World Famous Supreme Team Show: *Round The Outside! Round The Outside!* (Virgin 1990).

Further reading: *Starmakers & Svengalis: The History Of British Pop Management*, Johnny Rogan. *The Wicked Ways Of Malcolm McLaren*, Craig Bromberg.

McLaughlin, John

b. 4 January 1942, Yorkshire, England. Born into a musical family - his mother played violin - McLaughlin studied piano from the age of nine. He then took up the guitar because, like so many of his generation, he was inspired by the blues. By the time he was 14 years old, he had developed an interest in flamenco - the technical guitarist's most testing genre - and later started listening to jazz. He moved to London and his first professional gigs were as part of the early 60s blues boom, playing with **Alexis Korner**, **Georgie Fame** and **Graham Bond**. As the 60s progressed, McLaughlin became interested in more abstract forms, working and recording with **John Surman** and **Dave Holland**. He also spent some time in Germany playing free jazz with **Gunter Hampel**. His *Extrapolation*, recorded in 1969, with Surman and drummer **Tony Oxley**, was a landmark in British music. McLaughlin's clean, razor-sharp delivery wowed a public for whom guitars had become an obsession. The rock music of the **Beatles** and the **Rolling Stones** seemed to be adding something to R&B that the Americans had not thought of, so when **Tony Williams** - the drummer who had played on **Eric Dolphy**'s *Out To Lunch* - formed his own band, Lifetime, it seemed natural to invite the young English guitarist aboard. McLaughlin flew to New York in 1969, but left the band the following year. His own *My Goal's Beyond* (1970) flanked his guitar with the bass of **Charlie Haden** and the percussion of **Airto Moreira**. Meanwhile, ever conscious of new directions, **Miles Davis** had used McLaughlin on *In A Silent Way*, music to a rock beat that loosened rhythmic integration (a nod towards what Dolphy and **Ornette Coleman** were doing). However, it was McLaughlin's playing on the seminal *Bitches Brew* (1970) that set the jazz world alight: it seemed to be the ideal mixture of jazz chops and rock excitement. Nearly everyone involved went off to form fusion outfits, and McLaughlin was no exception. His **Mahavishnu Orchestra** broke new boundaries in jazz in terms of volume, brash virtuosity and multi-faceted complexity. The colossal drums of **Billy Cobham** steered McLaughlin, violinist Jerry Goodman and keyboard player **Jan Hammer** into an explosive creativity bordering on chaos. The creation of rock superstars had found its equivalent for jazz instrumentalists. McLaughlin sported a custom-built electric guitar with two fretboards. By this time, too, his early interest in Theosophy had developed into a serious fascination with Eastern mysticism: McLaughlin announced his allegiance to guru Snr i Chinmoy and started wearing white clothes. When Cobham and Hammer left to form their own bands, a second Mahavishnu Orchestra formed, with ex-**Frank Zappa** violinist **Jean-Luc Ponty** and drummer Michael Walden. This group never quite recaptured the over-the-top glory of the first Orchestra, and compositional coherence proved a problem. In the mid-70s, McLaughlin renounced electricity and formed Shakti with Indian violinist **L. Shankar** and tabla-player **Zakir Hussain**. This time McLaughlin's customized guitar had raised frets, allowing him to approximate sitar-like drone sounds. In 1978, McLaughlin made another foray into the world of electricity with the One Truth Band, but punk had made the excesses of jazz-rock seem old-fashioned and the band did not last long. In 1978, he teamed up with **Larry Coryell** and Paco De Lucia as a virtuosic guitar trio. Guitar experts were astonished, but critics noted a rather dry precision in his acoustic playing: McLaughlin seemed to need electricity and volume to really spark him. After two solo albums (*Belo Horizonte*, *Music Spoken Here*), he played on Miles Davis's *You're Under Arrest* in 1984. In November 1985, he performed a guitar concerto written for him and the LA Philharmonic by **Mike Gibbs**. The same year he joined forces with Cobham again to create a violin-less Mahavishnu that featured saxophonist **Bill Evans** as an alternate solo voice. In 1986, they were joined by keyboardist Jim Beard. Two years later, McLaughlin toured with **Trilok Gurtu**, a percussionist trained in Indian classical music, and was again playing acoustic guitar; a 1989 trio concert (with Gurtu) at London's Royal Festival Hall was later released on record. McLaughlin was back in the UK in 1990, premiering his *Mediterranean Concerto* with the Scottish National Orchestra at the Glasgow Jazz Festival.

Albums: *When Fortune Smiles* (1967), *Extrapolation* (Polydor 1969), *Devotion* (CBS 1969), *My Goal's Beyond* (CBS 1970), *Birds Of Fire* (CBS 1973), *Shakti With John McLaughlin* (Columbia 1975), *A Handful Of Beauty* (CBS 1976), with Shakti *Natural Elements* (CBS 1977), *Johnny McLaughlin, Electric Guitarist* (Columbia 1978), with Al Di Meola, Paco De Lucia *Friday Night In San Francisco* (1978), *Electric Dreams* (CBS 1979), *Belo Horizonte*, (WEA 1982) *Music Spoken Here*, (WEA 1982), with Al DiMeola and Paco De Lucia *Passion Grace And Fire* (Mercury 1983), *Mahavishnu* (1984), *Inner Worlds* (CBS 1987), *Adventures In Radioland* (Polygram 1987), *Live At The Royal Festival Hall* (JMT 1990), *Que Alegria* (Verve 1992), *Time Remembered: John McLaughlin Plays Bill Evans* (1993), *Tokyo Live* (Verve 1994), *After The Rain* (Verve 1995). Compilations: *The Best Of* (CBS 1981), *Compact Jazz* (Verve 1989), *The Collection* (Castle 1991), *Greatest Hits* (CBS 1991), *Where Fortune Smiles* (Beat Goes On 1993).

Further reading: *John McLaughlin And The Mahavishnu Orchestra*, John McLaughlin.

McLaughlin, Ollie

b. 24 March 1925, Carthage, Mississippi, USA, d. 19 February 1984. McLaughlin was a record producer whose list of credits included artists such as **Del Shannon,** the **Capitols, Deon Jackson** and jazz great **Chet Baker**. McLaughlin moved to Michigan in his youth and, upon graduating high school and spending time in the army, he moved to Chicago, where he became a disc jockey. With his brother Maxie, he began promoting concerts. A move to Ann Arbor, Michigan, found him promoting some of the area's hottest jazz and R&B concerts. He produced an album by the Chet Baker Quartet, *Jazz At Ann Arbor*, for the Pacific Jazz label. **Dave Brubeck**'s *Jazz Goes To College* was recorded at a McLaughlin-produced concert. By 1958, he had given up promotion, but in 1960 he heard a country band led by Charles Westover, better known as Del Shannon, and convinced the artist to allow McLaughlin to produce him. 'Runaway' was McLaughlin's first major production and drew him into the business full-time. He produced other hits for Shannon, as well as 'Hello Stranger' by **Barbara Lewis**, Deon Jackson's 'Love Makes The World Go Round', the Capitols' 'Cool Jerk' and others. He remained active until his death in 1984, but had no other major hits after the 60s.

McLean, Don

b. 2 October 1945, New Rochelle, New York, USA. McLean began his recording career performing in New York clubs during the early 60s. A peripatetic singer for much of his career, he was singing at elementary schools in Massachusetts when he wrote a musical tribute to Van Gogh in 1970. After receiving rejection slips from countless labels, his debut *Tapestry* was issued by Mediarts that same year, but failed to sell. United Artists next picked up his contract and issued an eight-minutes plus version of 'American Pie'. A paean to **Buddy Holly**, full of symbolic references to other performers such as **Elvis Presley** and **Bob Dylan**, the song topped the US chart and reached number 2 in the UK. The album of the same name was also an enormous success. In the UK, 'Vincent' fared even better than in his home country, reaching number 1. By 1971, McLean was acclaimed as one of the most talented and commercial of the burgeoning singer-songwriter school emerging from the USA. According to music business legend, the song 'Killing Me Softly With His Song' was written as a tribute to McLean, and was subsequently recorded by Lori Lieberman and **Roberta Flack**. McLean's affection for Buddy Holly was reiterated in 1973, with a successful cover of 'Everyday'. Meanwhile, his song catalogue was attracting attention, and **Perry Como** registered a surprise international hit with a cover of McLean's 'And I Love You So'. Despite his promising start, McLean's career foundered during the mid-70s, but his penchant as a strong cover artist held him in good stead. In 1980, he returned to the charts with a revival of **Roy Orbison**'s 'Crying' (UK number 1/US number 2). Thereafter, his old hits were repackaged and he toured extensively. As the 80s progressed, he moved into the country market, but remained popular in the pop mainstream. In 1991, his 20-year-old version of 'American Pie' unexpectedly returned to the UK Top 20, once again reviving interest in his back catalogue.

Albums: *Tapestry* (1970), *American Pie* (1971), *Don McLean* (1973), *Playin' Favorites* (1974), *Homeless Brother* (1974), *Solo* (1976), *Prime Time* (1977), *Chain Lightning* (1980), *Believers* (1982), *Love Tracks* (1987). Compilations: *The Very Best Of Don McLean* (1980), *Don McLean's Greatest Hits - Then And Now* (1987), *The Best Of Don McLean* (1991).

MacLean, Dougie

b. 27 September 1954, Dunblane, Scotland. Before he was two years old, MacLean moved to Butterstone, near Dunkeld, Perthshire, and now lives in the old schoolhouse there. He was formerly a member of both the **Tannahill Weavers** and **Silly Wizard**, and an early Euro-band, Mosaic, in the mid-80s. The latter band included **Andy Irvine**, Donal Lunny and Márta

Sebestyén. MacLean went solo in 1979 and released the excellent *Caledonia.* He formed Dunkeld Records in 1983, with the aim of promoting other Scottish performers. MacLean had one of his own compositions recorded by **Kathy Mattea** in 1990, for release on her album. Mattea also appears on backing vocals on *Whitewash,* in what is perhaps a classic parting song, 'Until We Meet Again'. *The Search* came out of a commision to write and record music for the official Loch Ness Monster Exhibition. In some ways a departure for MacLean, the album is highly atmospheric. MacLean has also completed music for a BBC television series, *MacGregor Across Scotland,* and his album *Real Estate* won a silver disc in 1988. Whether playing guitar, fiddle, bouzouki or didgeridoo, Dougie MacLean's songs combine a love of tradition with the contemporary.

Albums: with Alex Campbell, Alan Roberts *CRM* (1979), *Caledonia* (1979), *Snaigow* (Plant Life 1980), *On A Wing And A Prayer* (Plant Life 1981), *Craigie Dhu* (Dunkeld 1982), *Butterstone* (1983), *Fiddle* (Dunkeld 1984), *Singing Land* (Dunkeld 1985), *Real Estate* (Dunkeld 1988), *Whitewash* (Dunkeld 1990), *The Search* (Dunkeld 1990), *Indigenous* (1991).

McLean, Jackie

b. 17 May 1932, New York City, New York, USA. Coming as he did from a musical background (McLean's father played guitar with the **Tiny Bradshaw** band), Jackie was encouraged by family friends who included **Bud Powell**. It was through Powell that alto saxophonist McLean came to the attention of **Miles Davis**, with whom he played in 1951, having previously gigged with **Sonny Rollins**. Throughout the 50s McLean performed and recorded with numerous leading jazzmen, among them **Charles Mingus** and **Art Blakey**. He also led his own groups, touring internationally, and from the early 70s became active in musical education. In the late 70s, he had a surprising entry in the UK pop charts with his 'Dr Jackyll And Mr Funk', a disco favourite, which reached number 53. Strongly influenced by **Charlie Parker** and **Ornette Coleman**, McLean's forceful and highly personal playing style reflects his interest in several schools of modern jazz. McLean's son, Rene, is a jazz saxophonist.

Selected albums: *The Jackie McLean Quintet* (1955), *Lights Out* (Original Jazz Classics 1956), *Jackie McLean 4, 5 & 6* (Original Jazz Classics 1956), *Jackie's Pal* (Original Jazz Classics 1956), *McLean's Scene* (Original Jazz Classics 1956), *Jackie McLean & Co* (Original Jazz Classics 1957), *Alto Madness* (Original Jazz Classics 1957), *Makin' The Changes* (Original Jazz Classics 1957), *A Long Drink Of The Blues* (Original Jazz Classics 1957), *Strange Blues* (Original Jazz Classics 1957), *New Soil* (Blue Note 1959), *Swing, Swang, Swingin'* (Boplicity 1959), *Jackie's Bag* (1959), *Capuchin Swing* (1960), *Bluesnik* (Blue Note 1961), *A Fickle Sonance* (Blue Note 1961), *Let Freedom Ring* (Blue Note 1962), *Tippin' The Scales* (Blue Note 1962), *Hipnosis* (1962-67), *Vertigo* (1963), *One Step Beyond* (1963), *Destination Out* (1963), *It's Time* (1964), *Action* (1964), *Right Now!* (New Note 1965), *Consequence* (Liberty 1965), *Jacknife* (1965-66), *Dr Jackle* (Steeplechase 1966), with others *Charlie Parker Memorial* (1967), *New And Old Gospel* (1967), *'Bout Soul* (1967), *Demon's Dance* (Blue Note 1967), *Live At Montmartre* (Steeplechase 1972), *Ode To Super* (Steeplechase 1973), *A Ghetto Lullaby* (1973), with Dexter Gordon *The Meeting* (Steeplechase 1974) with Gordon *The Source* (Steeplechase 1974), *New York Calling* (Steeplechase 1975), *Antiquity* (1975), *New Wine, Old Bottles* (1978), *Monuments* (1979), *Contour* (Prestige 1980), with others *One Night With Blue Note* (1985), with Mal Waldron *Left Alone '86* (1986), *Fat Jazz* (Fresh Sounds 1988), *Rites Of Passage* (Triloka 1992, rec 1991), *Dynasty* (Triloka 1992, rec live 1988), *Rhythm Of The Earth* (Birdology 1992), *The Jackie Mac Attack* (Birdology 1993).

McMahon, Andrew 'Blueblood'

b. 12 April 1926, Delhi, Louisiana, USA, d. 17 February 1984, Monroe, Louisiana, USA. McMahon played blues and hillbilly music in Mississippi and worked with **Bukka White** in Memphis, Tennessee, before moving to Chicago in 1949. During the 50s he worked with **J.B. Hutto** and **Jimmy Dawkins**, and played bass guitar for **Howlin' Wolf** and recorded during 1960-73. McMahon recorded under his own name for the Bea And Baby label in 1971, and as 'Blueblood' for Dharma Records in 1973. After leaving Wolf, he led a band around the Chicago clubs and recorded a live album for MCM in 1976, following which he returned to his home state and left music. Although he was a limited singer, McMahon always seemed to attract all-star line-ups for his recording sessions.

Albums: *Blueblood* (1973), *Go Get My Baby* (1976).

McMorland, Alison

b. 12 November 1940, Clarkston, Renfrewshire, Scotland. When McMorland was aged four, her family moved to Strathaven, where she spent most of her school days. Later, when living in Helston, Cornwall, during the 60s, she became involved in the folk revival. In 1967, McMorland produced a teaching manual for the Smithsonian Institute in Washington DC, USA, to accompany a video made a year earlier, *British Traditional Singing Games.* It was not until 1970, however, that she first performed at a Scottish festival in Irvine. The following year, she won the women's traditional singing trophy at the Kinross folk festival. During the early 70s, McMorland worked on a project for the York Museum, producing a sound tape of songs and memories of old York called *These Times Be Good Times.* She also spent a great deal of time researching Scottish folk song tradition, as well as collecting songs on children's games and stories. In 1974, McMorland made a film on this particular subject, *Pass It On*, and was later invited by the Smithsonian Institute to appear in the Festival of American Folk Life. She also initiated workshops for children at festivals, specializing in songs and games. With **Frankie Armstrong**, she ran voice workshops, very innovative in the 70s, but now regarded as normal. For seven years, until the series ended, she presented *Listen With Mother* for BBC radio. For the series, she chose all the music, and always made a point of including folk material in the programme. Alison sang with the **Albion Band** at the National Theatre debut of *Lark Rise To Candleford*, and later went on a European tour with *The Passion And Creation*, produced by Bill Bryden. *Belt Wi' Colours Three*, an album of Scottish traditional songs, included **Aly Bain** on fiddle, and Rab Wallace on pipes. *My Song Is My Own* featured songs from a women's perspective, ranging from the traditional 'John Anderson, My Jo' to the 1977 composition 'Lady Bus Driver'. Both Alison and **Peta Webb** were the subject of one of a series of a films, made in 1980, by Phillip Donnelly, called *Pioneers Of The Folk Revival*. Others featured in the series were **Martin Carthy**, **Peggy Seeger**, **Leon Rosselson** and **Roy Bailey**, Frankie Armstrong and **Ewan MacColl**. McMorland also contributed to *That'd Be Telling-Tales Of Britain*, in 1985, a multi-cultural collection compiled by Mike Rosen and John Griffiths for the Cambridge University Press.

One of McMorland's more recent projects, resulted in the book *Memories*, a reminiscence project on Humberside of old people's musical memories, which were also recorded. In 1986, sheheaded another project called *Threads*, featuring Grand Union, a group of exiled musicians from different ethnic communities, who fused Scottish and Asian musical styles. The project told the story of the cotton trade and slavery in music. In 1990, Alison took up the post of Traditional Folk Arts Lecturer for the Strathclyde Region.

Albums: with various artists *Scots Songs And Music-Live From Kinross* (1975), *Songs And Rhymes From Listen With Mother* (1977), *Belt Wi' Clours Three* (1977), *Alison McMorland Presents The Funny Family* (songs, rhymes and games for children 1977), with various artists *Freedom Come All Ye-Poems And Songs Of Hamish Henderson* (1977), with various artists *The Good Old Way-The Best Of British Folk* (1980), *Alison McMorland And Peta Webb* (1980), with Frankie Armstrong, Kathy Henderson, Sandra Kerr *My Song Is My Own-Songs From Women* (1980), with various artists *Nuclear Power No Thanks!* (1981), with various artists *Glasgow Horizons* (1990).

Further reading: *British Traditional Singing Games* (1967), *The Funny Family* (1978), *Brown Bread And Butter* (1982), *Memories* (1987), *The Herd Laddie O' The Glen-Songs And Stories Of Willie Scott, A Border Shepherd* (1988).

McMullen, Fred

A shadowy figure, McMullen recorded for ARC in New York in January 1933, playing immaculate bottleneck blues guitar, whether behind his own vocals or with one or other of the Atlanta guitarists, **Curley Weaver** and **Buddy Moss**. They also recorded as a trio, with Moss on harmonica. McMullen was listed only once in the 1932 Atlanta City Directory, and Moss maintained that he had returned to his hometown, Macon, Georgia, after the session. The intensity of 'De Kalb Chain Gang' ('They whipped me and they slashed me, 45 all in my side') suggests that it was autobiographical, and that he may have been on his way home after release from prison when he encountered the Atlanta musicians.

Albums: *Georgia Blues Guitars* (1988), *Buddy Moss* (1990).

McNabb, Ian

b. 3 November 1962, Liverpool, Merseyside, England. Former **Icicle Works** guitarist, singer and songwriter Ian McNabb never earned the commercial rewards he deserved first time round with his highly individual, under-rated band. The Liverpool group's back-catalogue reputedly continues to sell better since their demise than it ever did while active, but more pertinent compensation for McNabb has arrived in a highly visible solo career. Though he has steered closer to the mainstream since the Icicle Works dissolved, he remains essentially the same prolific and acute songwriting commentator that many critics adored in the previous decade. His debut album, *Truth And Beauty*, was recorded on a small budget (allegedly with a loan secured by the artist's own mortgage) in Oldham, Lancashire. Andrew Lauder of This Way Up Records was the only one to express any interest, and the record was eventually released early in 1993. It housed one notable single, 'If Love Was Like Guitars'. His breakthrough album, *Head Like A Rock*, was afforded a much grander platform. It was recorded over three weeks in Los Angeles, California, USA, with expert help from **Meters**' drummer Joseph Modeliste, pedal steel guitar player Greg Leisz (of **kd Lang** fame), plus Hutch Hutchings (rhythm guitar), Ralph Molina (drums) and Billy Talbot (bass) of **Neil Young**'s **Crazy Horse** band. Amazingly, nobody had ever asked Crazy Horse to play on anybody else's record before, but they were happy to oblige, despite the near 20 year age gap. The album, with sonic similarities to Neil Young which proved inescapable, earned rave critical reviews, ensuring a Mercury Prize nomination for a man whose career looked unlikely to be sustainable just a few months previously.

Albums: *Truth And Beauty* (This Way Up 1993), *Head Like A Rock* (This Way Up 1994).

McNamara, Robin

McNamara was an original member of the cast of the Broadway musical ***Hair*** in the 60s, before placing two singles on the charts in 1970. The same year, he signed with the New York-based Steed Records, owned by songwriter **Jeff Barry**, and recorded 'Lay A Little Lovin' On Me', written by the two of them plus Jim Cretecos. It reached number 11 in the US that summer, and was followed by 'Got To Believe In Love', which featured other singers from ***Hair*** on back-up vocals. The second single did not reach number 80, however, and McNamara's recording career ended.

Album: *Lay A Little Lovin' On Me* (1970).

McNamara, Tim

b. Timothy Edmund McNamara, 10 October 1922, Lucknow, near Orange, New South Wales, Australia, d. 16 April 1983, Sydney, Australia. A pioneer of Australian country music, not only by his own performances but by the help he gave fellow performers. The youngest of 11 children, he worked as a boundary rider on a sheep station when he was 12. The following year, when the family relocated to Sydney, he refused to accompany them. Instead, having quit school, he spent the next four or five years working on dairy farms. He learned to play guitar, sing and yodel the hillbilly songs that he heard on the radio by such singers as **Tex Morton**. In 1940, he married Daphne Ford, a top horse rider and she encouraged him to pursue a singing career. He saw service with the Air Force during World War II, some of it overseas but sang whenever the opportunity arose. Returning to civilian life in 1945, writing much of his own material, he resumed the life of an entertainer, sometimes working as a duo with his brother Tommy Mack. By 1948, he was a well established artist and appeared in the film *Into The Straight*. He sang two of his own songs, 'Riding Along' and 'We're Going To The Rodeo Today', both of which he later recorded, with four other songs, at his first recording session in August that year. In 1949, he joined 2SM Sydney, as the presenter of their country show. Here he played records, sang a few songs and interviewed any available guests. Both **Slim Dusty** and **Gordon Parsons** gained initial career boosts by their appearances on the programme. In August 1950, McNamara persuaded 2SM and Rodeo Records to sponsor a national talent show, with a recording contract as the prize to be won at the grand final in Sydney's Town Hall. The first show attracted massive interest, eventually being won by **Reg Lindsay** with **Shorty Ranger** in second place. The process was repeated in other years and many artists achieved a breakthrough following appearances on McNamara's show. In 1950, McNamara had joined Rodeo Records and during the 50s, he recorded around 52 sides for the label, with many being self-penned numbers. In 1952, he became more active in production and with his wife, promoted shows in many areas that featured most of the top Australian artists. He recorded six sides for Festival in 1956 but made no further recordings until the 70s, when he recorded albums for **EMI** and Picture before returning to EMI. He maintained regular appearances around the Australian country circuit and even played the ***Grand Ole Opry*** in 1959 during an American visit. In 1981, his dedicated commitment to the Australian country music scene saw him become only the sixth person elected to the Country Music Roll Of Renown (Australia's equivalent to Nashville's **Country Music Hall Of Fame**). McNamara remained active promoting shows and helping fellow artists, until he finally lost his battle against cancer and with his wife, son Tim and old friend **Smoky Dawson** at his bedside, died in a Sydney hospital on 16 April 1983.

Albums: *Relaxin'* (EMI 1971), *Campfire Of Dreams* (Picture 1974).

McNeely, Big Jay

b. Cecil James McNeely, 29 April 1927, Los Angeles, California, USA. As a tenor saxophonist McNeely was one of the pioneers of the wild, honking style that emerged in the dance halls during the late 40s. The definitive tune of this style was 'Deacon's Hop', which reached number 1 R&B in 1949. His 'Wild Wig', which went to number 12 R&B the same year, was McNeely's only other chart record in this style. He returned to the charts in 1959 with the classic 'There Is Something On Your Mind' (number 5 R&B/number 44 pop), but vocalist Sonny Warner was the focus rather than McNeely. During the 80s McNeely revived his career with a series of reissue albums. His new recordings were mainly released in Europe only.

Albums: *Big Jay McNeely* (1954), *A Rhythm And Blues Concert* (1955), *Big Jay McNeely In 3-D* (1956), *Big Jay McNeely* (1963). Compilations: *From Harlem To Camden* (1984), *Road House Boogie* (1985), *Golden Classics* (1989), *Live At Birdland 1957* (1989), *Welcome To California* (1990), *Live And Rare* (1991), *Blow The Wall Down* (1991).

McNeil, Rita

b. Big Pond, Cape Breton Island, Nova Scotia, Canada. McNeil appeared on the music scene in Britain almost overnight, and has had a degree of success in the field of country and folk music. In 1985, she went to Tokyo to perform at the Canada Expo pavilion, and in 1987, *Flying On Your Own* was released. The title track was also recorded by fellow Canadian **Anne Murray**. That same year, McNeil sang at the Edinburgh Folk Festival, and won a Canadian Juno award as Most Promising Female Vocalist. She first appeared in London, England, in September 1990, and **Polydor** released three of her albums, *Flying On Your*

Own, *Reason To Believe* and *Rita*. In the same year, McNeil's *Reason To Believe* toppled **Madonna** from the top of the Australian album charts. Mixing country, folk and elements of Gaelic drawn from the fact that her family originally came from Scotland, McNeil has had less success in Britain than on her home ground, but still charted with 'Working Man', which reached the UK Top 20. Her albums have achieved platinum sales in Canada and she was the subject of a 1991 documentary, *Home I'll Be*.
Albums: *Flying On Your Own* (1987), *Reason To Believe* (1990), *Home I'll Be* (1991).

McNulty, Chris

b. 23 December 1953, Melbourne, Victoria, Australia. Starting to sing professionally when she was aged 15, McNulty quickly developed a reputation in and around Melbourne. In the early 70s, while still singing in clubs and hotels, she studied musical theory. Tours of Australia and South-east Asia extended her experience and popularity and in 1975 she helped form a jazz group which performed in the jazz-funk idiom. Simultaneously, McNulty was also in growing demand as a studio singer, working on radio and television. In 1980 she moved to Sydney where she formed a new jazz group which was highly successful during the next few years. In 1985 she visited New York where she sang at the Bluenote club. By the late 80s McNulty was back in New York, this time picking up a contract to record for Trend/Discovery. She has continued to sing in the New York area, working with such leading musicians as Peter Leitch, Cecil McBee, **George Mraz** and Kenny Washington. McNulty's repertoire ranges over the great standards and modern jazz classics. She has also written lyrics for various songs including **Miles Davis**'s 'A Kind Of Blue'. Singing in a rich contralto with a pleasing hint of toughness, McNulty ably interprets the lyrics she sings while giving full rein to her ability to phrase imaginatively in the jazz idiom.
Album: *Waltz For Debby* (1990).

McPartland, Jimmy

b. 15 March 1907, Chicago, Illinois, USA, d. 13 March 1991. McPartland began playing cornet while still at Austin High School in Chicago, and became a founding member of both the Austin High School Gang (not all of whom were pupils there) and the Blue Friars. At the age of 17, he replaced **Bix Beiderbecke** in the **Wolverines**, and two years later was with Art Kassell's Castles In The Air band. In 1927, he joined **Ben Pollack** for a two-year stint, then freelanced with numerous bands, small and large, playing on many record dates, until World War II. While still on active service, he married British pianist Marian Turner (see **Marian McPartland**). After the war he returned to playing in small dixieland-orientated bands, toured many countries, and was still entertaining audiences in the mid-80s with appearances at prestigious events such as the Nice Jazz Festival. A fiery, exuberant player, McPartland was also capable of playing with a wistful elegance that recalled his earliest and greatest influence, Bix Beiderbecke.
Selected albums: *Shades Of Bix* (1953), *Jimmy McPartland's Dixieland* (1957), *Meet Me In Chicago* (1959), with Marian McPartland *The McPartlands Live At The Monticello* (1972). Selected compilations: *The Wolverines Orchestra* (1924-25), *One Night Stand* (Jazzology 1987), *On Stage* (Jazzology 1990).

McPartland, Marian

b. Marian Margaret Turner, 20 March 1920, Windsor, Berkshire, England. Prior to World War II, McPartland played British music halls as a member of a four-piano group led by Billy Mayer. While touring with ENSA (the British equivalent of America's USO), she met and married **Jimmy McPartland**. At the end of the war she went to the USA with her husband, quickly establishing a reputation in her own right. During the late 40s and throughout the following decade, she worked steadily, usually leading a trio, holding down several long residencies, notably an eight-year spell at the Hickory House. During the 60s and 70s she developed a long-lasting interest in education, established her own recording company, Halcyon Records, performed extensively in clubs and at festivals and also began parallel careers as a writer and broadcaster on jazz. A very gifted pianist, rhythmically near-perfect and with a seemingly endless capacity for intelligent improvising, her long-running radio show, *Piano Jazz*, has helped establish her as one of the best-known jazz artists in America. Although divorced from her husband Jimmy, she has latterly made occasional concert appearances with him. She is also a familiar figure at many important jazz festivals around the world. McPartland has also worked successfully in duos with **Joe Venuti**, and with fellow pianists **Teddy Wilson** and **George Shearing**. In addition to her other many activities, she has also made a successful crossover into classical music, performing such works as the Grieg Piano Concerto, **George Gershwin**'s 'Rhapsody in Blue', and a series of popular songs arranged for piano and orchestra by **Robert Farnon**. Although relatively little known in the country of her birth, McPartland continues to prove herself to be one of the outstanding pianists in jazz. A collection of her articles on jazz, *All In Good Time*, was published in 1987.
Selected albums: *Jazz At Storyville* (1951), *Moods Vol. 2* (1952), *The Magnificent Marian McPartland At The Piano* (1952), *Great Britons* (1952, one side only), *Lullaby Of Birdland* (1953), *Jazz At The Hickory House* i (Savoy 1953), *Jazz At The Hickory House* ii (Savoy 1954), *The Marian McPartland Trio* i (1955), *The Marian McPartland Trio* ii (1956), *With You In My Mind* (1957), *At The London House*

(1958), *The Music Of Leonard Bernstein* (1960), *The Marian McPartland Quintet* (1963), *Marian McPartland And Her Orchestra/Marian McPartland January 6th & 8th 1964* (1964), *The Marian McPartland Trio* iii (1968), *Interplay* (c.1969), *Ambiance* (1970), *A Delicate Balance* (c.1971-72), with Teddy Wilson *Elegant Piano* (1972), with Jimmy McPartland *The McPartlands Live At The Monticello* (1972), *Marian McPartland Plays The Music Of Alec Wilder* (Jazz Alliance 1973), *Marian Remembers Teddi* (1973), *Swingin'* (1973), *Solo Concert At Haverford* (1974), *Concert In Argentina* (1974, one side only), *Joe Venuti & Marian McPartland* (1974), *Send In The Clowns* (1976), *Wanted!* (1977), *Make Magnificent Music* (1977), *Now's The Time* (1977), *From This Moment On* (Concord 1978), *Portrait Of Marian McPartland* (Concord 1979), *At The Festival* (1979), *Live At The Carlyle* (1979), *Alone Together* (1981), *Personal Choice* (Concord 1982), *Willow Creek And Other Ballads* (Concord 1985), *Marian McPartland Plays The Music Of Billy Strayhorn* (Concord 1987), *Marian McPartland Plays The Benny Carter Songbook* (Concord 1990), *Live At Maybeck Recital Hall* (Concord 1991), *Piano Jazz With Guest Dave Brubeck* (Bellaphon 1993), *With Rosemary Clooney* (Jazz Alliance 1993), *In My Life* (Concord 1993).
Further reading: *All In Good Time*, Marian McPartland.

McPhatter, Clyde

b. Clyde Lensley McPhatter, 15 November 1932, Durham, North Carolina, USA, d. 13 June 1972. For three years, McPhatter was the lead singer in the R&B vocal group, **Billy Ward And His Dominoes**. He left in 1953 to form the **Drifters**, whose early releases were enhanced the singer's emotional, gospel-drenched delivery. In 1954 McPhatter was drafted into the US Army, where he entertained fellow servicemen. Such work prompted a solo career, and the vibrant 'Seven Days' (1956), was followed by several other superb performances, many of which, including 'Treasure Of Love', 'Without Love (There Is Nothing)' and 'A Lover's Question', became R&B standards. A hugely influential figure, McPhatter inspired a generation of singers. His work was covered by **Elvis Presley**, **Ry Cooder** and **Otis Redding**, but his departure from the **Atlantic** label for **MGM** in 1959 precipitated an artistic decline. Although he scored several minor hits during the early 60s, arguably his finest work was the US Top 10 hit 'Lover Please' in 1962. Its follow-up 'Little Bitty Pretty One' became standard fodder for many UK beat groups in the early 60s (recorded by the **Paramounts**). The singer became increasingly overshadowed by new performers and his career started to wane in the mid-60s. Beset by personal problems, he came to Britain in 1968, but left two years later without an appreciable change in fortune. A 1970 album, on **Decca**, *Welcome Home*, was his last recording. McPhatter, one of R&B's finest voices, died from a heart attack as a result of alcohol abuse in 1972.

Albums: *Clyde McPhatter And The Drifters* (1958), *Love Ballads* (1958), *Clyde* (1959), *Let's Start Over Again* (1959), *May I Sing For You* (1960), *Ta Ta* (1960), *Golden Blues Hits* (1962), *Lover Please* (1962), *Rhythm And Soul* (1963), *Songs Of The Big City* (1964), *Live At The Apollo* (1965), *Welcome Home* (1970). Compilations: *Greatest Hits* (1963), *The Best Of Clyde McPhatter* (1964), *Greatest Recordings* (1972), *A Tribute To Clyde McPhatter* (1973), *Rock And Cry* (1984), *Rhythm And Soul* (1987, eight album set of MGM/Mercury recordings), *Deep Sea Ball - The Best Of* (1993).

McPhee, Joe

b. 3 January 1939, Miami, Florida, USA. McPhee played the trumpet in his school band and studied music theory and harmony in his Division Band while he was with the army in Germany (1964-65). His first recording was with fellow trumpeter **Clifford Thornton** in 1967. While he was playing with the Matt Jordan Orchestra in the late 60s, he took up the saxophone as he became interested in free jazz. He gave a lecture course entitled 'The Revolution In Sound' when he taught at Vassar College (1969-71). McPhee has sought to extend the tonal range of the saxophone, introducing grainy effects into his playing and extending his phrasing by using circular breathing. The freedom he seeks is often clearly tied to melody. Though his first recording on saxophone was with Shakey Jake (vocal/harmonica) in 1972, he soon moved to New York to work with trumpeter **Don Cherry**, Thornton and the **Jazz Composers Orchestra**. In the mid-70s he worked in Europe with **Steve Lacy**, among others.
Selected albums: *Black Magic Man* (1970), *Graphics 3/4* (1977), *Topology* (1981), *Oleo & A Future Retrospective* (1993), with André Jaume, Raymond Boni *Impressions Of Jimmy Giuffre* (1993).

McPherson, Charles

b. 24 July 1939, Joplin, Missouri, USA. Often dismissed as a **Charlie Parker** copyist, McPherson is in fact more than a simple revivalist. While the style in which he plays, bebop, is now outmoded, it is one with which he grew up, and he plays it with fire and conviction. His family moved to Detroit when he was aged nine, and it was at high school, a few years later, that he started playing trumpet and flügelhorn. McPherson took up alto saxophone in his early teens (although he had wanted to play tenor), but his vocation for alto was confirmed, however, when he heard Parker. While in Detroit he spent some time studying with Barry Harris, and then, after moving to New York, he worked in Greenwich Village with Lonnie Hillyer in the early 60s. Fellow Detroit saxophonist **Yusef Lateef** suggested to **Charles Mingus** that he should hear McPherson when he was looking for a replacement for **Eric Dolphy**, and thus McPherson began the first of his stints with Mingus's band, garnering some critical plaudits for his work with one of the more adventurous bop-based leaders. Almost a forgotten man until the late 80s, he deservedly came back into the limelight as a result of a couple of successful European tours. He also played on part of the soundtrack for Clint Eastwood's bio-pic of Parker, ***Bird***.

Albums: *Be-Bop Revisited* (Original Jazz Classics 1964), *Con Alma* (1965), *The Quintet Live!* (Original Jazz Classics 1966), *Live At The Five Spot* (Prestige 1966), *From This Moment On* (1968), *Horizons* (1968), *McPherson's Mood* (1969), *Beautiful* (Xanadu 1975), *Live In Tokyo* (Xanadu 1976), *Siku Ya Bibi* (Mainstream 1976).*New Horizons* (Xanadu 1977), *Free Bop!* (1978), *The Prophet* (Discovery 1983).

McQuater, Tommy

b. Thomas Mossie, 4 September 1914, Maybole, Ayrshire, Scotland. A self-taught trumpeter, he gained wide professional experience in the mid-30s playing in many leading British dancebands. These included **Jack Payne**, **Lew Stone** and **Ambrose**. During World War II he was in the Royal Force's noted danceband, the **Squadronaires**. In the late 40s and on for the next four decades, he worked extensively in theatre, radio and television bands. A highly accomplished lead trumpeter, McQuater's solo work in a jazz context was fiery and exhilarating and he played and recorded with many notable leaders including **George Chisholm**, **John Dankworth** and visiting Americans such as **Benny Carter** in the 30s and **Benny Goodman** in the 60s. In 1995 he was still enjoying life and helping fellow octogenarian Chisholm celebrate his birthday. McQuater's enthusiasm and skills as a teacher brought him the respect of many younger musicians and his pupils include distinguished trumpeters such as **Ian Carr** and **Digby Fairweather**.

Compilations: *Swing' Britain: The Thirties* (Deccas 1935-38).

McRae, Carmen

b. 8 April 1922, New York City, New York, USA, d. 10 November 1994, Beverly Hills, California, USA. One of the best American jazz singers, McRae was also an accomplished pianist and songwriter. Early in her career she sang with bands led by **Benny Carter**, **Mercer Ellington**, **Charlie Barnet** and **Count Basie** (sometimes under the name of Carmen Clarke, from her brief marriage to **Kenny Clarke**). Although a familiar figure on the New York jazz club scene, including a spell in the early 50s as intermission pianist at Minton's Playhouse, her reputation did not spread far outside the jazz community. In the 60s and 70s she toured internationally and continued to record - usually accompanied by a small group - but joined on one occasion by the **Clarke-Boland Big Band**. By the 80s, she was one of only a tiny handful of major jazz singers whose work had not been diluted by commercial pressures. One of her early songs, 'Dream Of Life', written when she was just 16 years old, was recorded in 1939 by **Billie Holiday**. Although very much her own woman, McRae occasionally demonstrated the influence of Holiday through her ability to project a lyric with bittersweet intimacy. She also sang with remarkable rhythmic ease and her deft turns-of-phrase helped conceal a relatively limited range, while her ballad singing revealed enormous emotional depths. Her repertoire included many popular items from the Great American Songbook, but her jazz background ensured that she rarely strayed outside the idiom. Relaxed and unpretentious in performance and dedicated to her craft, McRae secured a place in the history of jazz singing.

Albums: *Carmen McRae* i (1954), *By Special Request* (1955), *Torchy* (1955), *Blue Moon* (1956), *After Glow* (1957), *Carmen For Cool Ones* (1957), *Mad About The Man* (1957), with Sammy Davis Jnr. *Boy Meets Girl* (1957), *Book Of Ballads* (1958), *Birds Of A Feather* (1958), *Carmen McRae* ii (1958), *When You're Away* (1958), *Something To Swing About* (1959), *Carmen McRae Sings Lover Man And Other Billie Holiday Classics* (1961), *Carmen McRae Live At The Flamingo Club, London* (1961), *Carmen McRae* iii (1962), *In Person* (1963), *Carmen McRae Live At Sugar Hill* (c.1963), *Carmen McRae* iv (1964), *Carmen McRae* v (1964), *Carmen McRae* vi (1964), *Carmen McRae* vii (1964), *Woman Talk: Carmen McRae Live At The Village Gate* (1965), *Carmen McRae* viii (1965), *Live And Doin' It* (c.1965-66), *Carmen McRae* ix (1967), *Portrait Of Carmen* (1967), *Carmen McRae* x (1968), with Kenny Clarke, Francy Boland *November Girl* (1970), *Just A Little Lovin'* (1970), *The Great American Songbook* (1971), *As Time Goes By* (1973), *It Takes A Whole Lot Of Human Feeling* (1973), *Carmen McRae And Zoot Sims* (1973), *I Am Music* (1975), *Can't Hide Love* (1976), *Carmen McRae At The Great American Music Hall* (1976), *Live At The Roxy* (1976), *Ronnie Scott Presents Carmen McRae 'Live'* (1977), *For Carmen McRae* (1977), *I'm Coming Home Again* (1978), *Two For The Road* (1980), *Recorded Live At Bubba's* (1981), *Heat Wave* (1982), *You're Lookin' At Me (A Collection Of Nat 'King' Cole Songs)* (1983), *Any Old Time* (1986), *Fine And Mellow: Live At Birdland West* (1987), *Velvet Soul* (Denon 1988, 1973 recording), *Carmen Sings Monk* (Novus 1989), *Sarah Dedicated To You* (Novus 1991), *Woman Talk* (Mainstream 1991), *Sings Great American Songwriters* (GRP 1994, 1955-59 recordings).

MacRae, Dave

b. 2 April 1940, Aukland, New Zealand. Following an appearance in 1971 on an album by Mike Maran, MacRae embarked upon a busy period of session activity throughout that decade. His keyboards (usually electric piano) can be heard on recordings by **Back Door**, the **Walker Brothers**, and **Max Merritt And The Meteors**. Additionally, MacRae also found time to join **Ian Carr**'s **Nucleus**, **Robert Wyatt**'s

post-**Soft Machine** band, Matching Mole, and the equally short-lived **Pacific Eardrum**. Most recently David MacRae has written music for UK television series, notably the ***Goodies*** and *Bread.*
Albums: with Mike Maran *Fair Warning* (1971), with Schunge *Ballad Of A Simple Love* (1972), with Matching Mole *Matching Mole* (1972), *Little Red Record* (1973), with Nucleus *Belladonna* (1972), *Labyrinth* (1973), *Roots* (1973), *Direct Hits* (1976), with Back Door *Another Fine Mess* (1975), with the Walker Brothers *No Regrets* (1975), *Lines* (1976), *Nite Flights* (1978), with Max Merritt And The Meteors *A Little Easier* (1975), with Joe Breen *More Than Meets the Eye* (1976), with the Goodies *Nothing to Do With Us* (1976), with Pacific Eardrum *Pacific Eardrum* (1977), *Beyond Panic* (1978).

MacRae, Gordon

b. 12 March 1921, East Orange, New Jersey, USA, d. 24 January 1986, Lincoln, Nebraska, USA. A popular singer on records, radio and in films during the 50s, MacRae was the son of local radio celebrity, Wee Willie MacRae, and often worked on radio as a child actor before joining the Millpond Playhouse, New York. There he met actress Sheila Stephens who became his first wife in 1941. After winning an amateur singing contest at the 1939/40 New York World's Fair, he sang for two weeks with the **Harry James** and **Les Brown** bands. While working as a pageboy at NBC Radio, he was heard by bandleader **Horace Heidt** who signed him for two years, during which time he appeared with Heidt, James Stewart and Paulette Goddard in a movie about Heidt's radio giveaway show, *Pot O' Gold.* After serving in the US Army Air Force Corps in World War II, MacRae returned to New York to take a singing role in the 1946 Broadway revue *Three To Make Ready*, starring **Ray Bolger**. In 1947, he signed to **Capitol Records** and had a string of hits up until 1954, including 'I Still Get Jealous', 'At The Candlelight Cafe', 'It's Magic', 'Hair Of Gold, Eyes Of Blue', 'So In Love', 'Mule Train'/'Dear Hearts And Gentle People' and 'Rambling Rose'. After a four-year gap, he entered the US charts again in 1958 with 'The Secret'. MacRae also made a series of successful singles with ex-**Tommy Dorsey** singer, **Jo Stafford**. These included 'Say Something Sweet To Your Sweetheart', 'Bluebird Of Happiness', 'My Darling, My Darling' (a US number 1), 'A-You're Adorable', 'Need You', 'Whispering Hope', 'Bibbidi-Bobbidi-Boo' and 'Dearie'. MacRae's film career, mostly for Warner Brothers, started in 1948 with a non-singing role in *The Big Punch.* This was followed by a series of musicals which included *Look For The Silver Lining* (1949) and *The Daughter Of Rosie O'Grady* (1950), both co-starring **June Haver**, and four films in which he was partnered by **Doris Day**: *Tea For Two* (1950), *West Point Story* (1950), *On Moonlight Bay* (1951) and *By The Light Of The Silvery Moon* (1953). Among his other screen appearances were roles in *The Desert Song*, (1953) co-starring **Kathryn Grayson**, and *Three Sailors And A Girl* (1953), with **Jane Powell**. In 1955 and 1956 he had the two most satisfying film parts of his career, when he played opposite **Shirley Jones** in highly successful adaptations of the Broadway shows ***Oklahoma!*** and ***Carousel***. Also in 1956, MacRae appeared in his last film musical as **Buddy De Sylva**, in ***The Best Things In Life Are Free***, a bio-pic of the 20s/30s songwriting team of **De Sylva, Brown And Henderson**. In 1979, he made one final film appearance, in a dramatic role, in *The Pilot.* In the mid-50s, MacRae was also popular on US television as the singing host of *The Railroad Hour*, *The Colgate Comedy Hour*, and his own *Gordon MacRae Show*. After he divorced his first wife, he was remarried in 1967 to Elizabeth Lambert Schrafft. In the same year he made his first Broadway musical appearance since 1946, replacing **Robert Preston** in ***I Do! I Do!*** In the 70s he struggled with alcoholism and, in the early 80s, claimed that he had won the battle. He died from cancer of the mouth and jaw in January 1986.
Albums: with Lucille Norman *New Moon/Vagabond King* (1950), with Jo Stafford *Sunday Evening Songs* (1953), with various artists *The Desert Song* (1953), with Stafford *Memory Songs* (mid-50s), *Romantic Ballads* (1956), *Oklahoma!* (1956, film soundtrack), *Carousel* (1956, film soundtrack), *Operetta Favourites* (1956), *The Best Things In Life Are Free* (1956), *Motion Picture Soundstage* (1957), *Gordon MacRae In Concert* (1958), *Cowboy's Lament* (1958), *Seasons Of Love* (1959), *This Is Gordon MacRae* (1960), with Stafford *Whispering Hope* (1962), with Stafford *Peace In The Valley* (1963), with Stafford *Old Rugged Cross* (1978), *Best Of The Capitol Years* (1990).
Further reading: *Hollywood Mother Of The Year: Sheila MacRae's Own Story*, Sheila MacRae with Paul Jeffers.

McShann, Jay 'Hootie'

b. 12 January 1909, Muskogee, Oklahoma, USA. After playing in many **territory bands** in the southwest and midwest, pianist McShann settled in Kansas City in the mid-30s, playing in **Buster Smith**'s band, which also included **Charlie Parker**, in 1937. The following year, McShann formed his own unit which included **Gene Ramey** and **Gus Johnson** as well as Parker. By 1941, with the departure from Kansas City of **Harlan Leonard**, McShann's became the city's top band, **Count Basie** having moved on to greater things a few years earlier. The most popular member of the band was singer **Walter Brown**, who was featured on a handful of hit records, although McShann was himself an above-average blues shouter. In retrospect, the 1941 band is regarded as the most interesting of those McShann led because the saxophone section included the fast-developing and revolutionary talent of Parker. In fact, all McShann's bands had the virtues common to most Kansas City bands, those of lithely swinging, blues-based, exciting jazz. In 1944, McShann folded the band to enter the armed forces, reforming in 1945 on the west coast. Once again he showed himself to have a good ear for singers by hiring **Jimmy Witherspoon**. During the 50s and 60s, McShann was active, sometimes leading small groups, sometimes working as a solo act, but the jazz world was largely indifferent. By the 70s, however, he had become a popular figure on the international festival circuit, playing piano and singing the blues with flair and vigour. His recording career was also revitalized, and the 70s and 80s saw a steady stream of fine recordings, many of which were in the authentic tradition of the blues.

Selected albums: *McShann's Piano* (1966), *Confessin' The Blues* (1969), *Live In France* (1969), *Roll 'Em* (1969-77), *With Kansas City In Mind* (Swaggie 1969-72 recordings), *Jumpin' The Blues* (1970), *The Man From Muskogee* (1972), *Going To Kansas City* (1972), *Kansas City Memories* (Black And Blue 1973), *Vine Street Boogie* (1974), *Kansas City Joys* (1976), *Crazy Legs And Friday Strut* (1976), *Live At Istres* (1977), *Kansas City On My Mind* (1977), *After Hours* (1977), *The Last Of The Blue Devils* (1977), *Blues And Boogie* (1978), *Kansas City Hustle* (1978), *A Tribute To Fats Waller* (1978), *The Big Apple Bash* (1978), *Tuxedo Junction* (1980), with Al Casey *Best Of Friends* (JSP 1982), *Swingmatism* (Sackville 1982), *Just A Lucky So And So* (1983), *At The Cafe Des Copains* (Sackville 1983-89), *Magical Jazz* (1984), *Airmail Special* (Sackville 1985), *A Tribute To Charlie Parker* (S&R 1991), *Some Blues* (Chiaroscuro 1993), *The Missouri Connection* (Reervoir 1993). Selected compilations: *Hootie's KC Blues* (1941-42), *Blues From Kansas City* (MCA 1941-1943 recordings), *The Band That Jumps The Blues* (1947-49).

McTell, 'Blind' Willie

b. 5 May 1901, McDuffie County, Georgia, USA, d. 19 August 1959, Almon, Georgia, USA. Blind from birth, McTell began to learn guitar in his early years, under the influence of relatives and neighbours in Statesboro, Georgia, where he grew up. In his late teens, he attended a school for the blind. By 1927, when he made his first records, he was already a very accomplished guitarist, with a warm and beautiful vocal style, and his early sessions produced classics such as 'Statesboro Blues', 'Mama Tain't Long Fo Day' and 'Georgia Rag'. During the 20s and 30s, he travelled extensively from a base in Atlanta, making his living from music and recording, on a regular basis, for three different record companies, sometimes using pseudonyms which included Blind Sammie and Georgia Bill. Most of his records feature a 12-string guitar, popular among Atlanta musicians, but particularly useful to McTell for the extra volume it provided for singing on the streets. Few, if any, blues guitarists could equal his mastery of the 12-string. He exploited its resonance and percussive qualities on his dance tunes, yet managed a remarkable delicacy of touch on his slow blues. In 1934, he married, and the following year recorded some duets with his wife, Kate, covering sacred as well as secular material. In 1940, **John Lomax** recorded McTell for the Folk Song Archive of the Library of Congress, and the sessions, which have since been issued in full, feature him discussing his life and his music, as well as playing a variety of material. These offer an invaluable insight into the art of one of the true blues greats. In the 40s, he moved more in the direction of religious music, and when he recorded again in 1949 and 1950, a significant proportion of his songs were spiritual. Only a few tracks from these sessions were issued at the time, but most have appeared in later years. They reveal McTell as commanding as ever. Indeed, some of these recordings rank amongst his best work. In 1956, he recorded for the last time at a session arranged by a record shop manager, unissued until the 60s. Soon after this, he turned away from the blues to perform exclusively religious material. His importance was eloquently summed up in **Bob Dylan**'s strikingly moving elegy, 'Blind Willie McTell'.

Selected albums: *Last Session* (1960), *Complete Library Of Congress Recordings* (1969), *Complete Recorded Works 1927-1935* (1990, 3-CD), *Pig 'N Whistle Red* (1993).

McTell, Ralph

b. 3 December 1944, Farnborough, Kent, England. Having followed the requisite bohemian path, busking in Europe and living in Cornwall, McTell emerged in the late 60s as one of Britain's leading folksingers with his first two albums, *Eight Frames A Second* and *Spiral Staircase*. The latter collection was notable for the inclusion of 'Streets Of London', the artist's best-known composition. He re-recorded this simple, but evocative, song in 1974, and was rewarded with a surprise number 2 UK hit. Its popularity obscured McTell's artistic development from acoustic troubadour to thoughtful singer/songwriter, exemplified on *You Well-Meaning Brought Me Here*, in which the singer tackled militarism and its attendant political geography in an erudite, compulsive manner. During live performances McTell demonstrated considerable dexterity on acoustic guitar. He was particularly proficient when playing ragtime blues. Subsequent releases included the excellent *Not Until Tomorrow*, which featured the infamous 'Zimmerman Blues', and *Easy*, but McTell was unable to escape the cosy image bestowed by his most successful song. During the 80s he pursued a career in children's television, and his later releases have featured songs from such work, as well as interpretations of other artist's compositions. Touring occasionally, McTell is still able to comfortably fill concert halls.

Albums: *Eight Frames A Second* (1968), *Spiral Staircase* (1969), *My Side Of Your Window* (1970), *You Well-Meaning*

Brought Me Here (1971), *Not Till Tomorrow* (1972), *Easy* (1973), *Streets* (1975), *Right Side Up* (1976), *Ralph, Albert And Sydney* (1977), *Slide Away The Screen* (1979), *Love Grows* (1982), *Water Of Dreams* (1982), *Weather The Storm* (1982), *Songs From Alphabet Zoo* (1983), *The Best Of Alphabet Zoo* (1984), *At The End Of A Perfect Day* (1985), *Tickle On The Tum* (1986), *Bridge Of Sighs* (1987), *The Ferryman* (1987), *Blue Skies, Black Herdes* (1988), *Stealin' Back.* (1990), *The Boy With The Note* (1992), *Alphabet Zoo* (The Road Goes On Forever 1994). Compilations: *Ralph McTell Revisited* (1970), *The Ralph McTell Collection* (1978), *Streets Of London* (1981), *71/72* (1982), *At His Best* (1985).

McVea, Jack

b. 5 November 1914, Los Angeles, California, USA. Starting out on banjo, McVea played in his father's band before he reached his teenage years. In the late 20s, he began playing reed instruments, eventually concentrating on tenor saxophone. In the early 30s, after graduating from high school, he turned professional and worked with a number of bands, including that led by Charlie Echols. In 1936, he was with **Eddie Barefield** and, after a brief spell leading his own unit, joined **Lionel Hampton** in 1940. With Hampton he mostly played baritone saxophone. After a short stint with **Snub Mosley**, he became interested in new developments in jazz and worked with **Dizzy Gillespie** and **Charlie Parker**. McVea was also featured at an early **Jazz At The Philharmonic** concert. Despite his interest in bop, McVea appreciated current popular tastes, and his R&B single, 'Open The Door, Richard', a massive hit in 1946, brought him international attention. This celebrity allowed him to maintain a small R&B band for the next several years, playing clubs, hotels, casinos and concerts in various parts of the USA. In the late 50s he also played in bands led by **Benny Carter** among others. In the mid-60s McVea led a trio at Disneyland, a gig he retained into the 80s.

Album: *Nothin' But Jazz* (Harlequin 1962). Compilations: *Open The Door, Richard* (Jukebox Lil 1985, 1940s), *Come Blow Your Horn* (Ace 1985), *Two Timin' Baby* (Jukebox Lil 1986), *New Deal* (Jukebox Lil 1989).

McVie, Christine

b. Christine Perfect, 12 July 1944, Birmingham, England. Having begun her musical career playing bass in the Birmingham-based Shades Of Blue, Perfect joined two other ex-members, Andy Sylvester and Stan Webb, in **Chicken Shack**, a blues group signed to **Mike Vernon**'s nascent **Blue Horizon** label. Between April 1967 and August 1969, she was featured on piano and vocals, and her impassioned reading of the **Etta James** classic, 'I'd Rather Go Blind', became the band's best-known and most successful release. Perfect left Chicken Shack on completion of *O.K. Ken.* Now married to **John McVie**, bassist in **Fleetwood Mac**, she had tired of the couple's alternating lives on the road. A 1969 poll in ***Melody Maker*** voted her 'Female Vocalist Of The Year', and in deference to the publicity surrounding this award, the singer instigated the Christine Perfect Band, which included former **Yardbirds**' guitarist 'Top' Topham. She made her solo recording debut with *Christine Perfect*, a low-key but absorbing collection, before joining Fleetwood Mac in August 1970 in place of guitarist **Peter Green**. Christine's skills as a pianist, vocalist and composer were steadying influences during the group's turbulent years. Although the arrival of **Stevie Nicks** and **Lindsey Buckingham** introduced a musical consistency, personal problems now wracked the band. Her marriage to John McVie ended, a break-up detailed on the singer's stellar contributions to the phenomenally successful *Rumours*. Although several members of Fleetwood Mac began pursuing their own directions in the early 80s, it was not until 1984, following the release of the group's *Mirage* album, that Christine unveiled her second solo selection. The album confirmed her varied prowess and McVie's in-concert appearances proved highly popular. However, her contributions to the film soundtrack of *A Fine Mess* aside, the singer has since concentrated on Fleetwood Mac's career. Indeed, the departure of Buckingham in the wake of *Tango In The Night*, coupled with Nick's divided loyalties between her own recordings and those of the band allowed Christine's talent to flourish on the 1990 release, *Behind The Mask*.

Albums: *Christine Perfect* (1970), *Christine McVie* (1984).

McVie, John

b. 26 November 1945, London, England. Having served his musical apprenticeship in an amateur group inspired by the **Shadows**, bassist McVie joined **John Mayall**'s Bluesbreakers in 1963. Barring interludes during which he was suspended for over-indulging in alcohol - Mayall was a notorious teetotaller - this excellent musician provided the backbone to one of the era's most influential acts. He appeared on releases such as *John Mayall's Bluebreakers With Eric Clapton* (1966), *A Hard Road* (1967) and *Crusade* (1968), and despite repeated overtures, initially preferred to remain in the group rather than join ex-members **Peter Green** and Mick Fleetwood in **Fleetwood Mac**. However, the temptation became too strong to resist and, in September 1967, he joined the new venture. Despite the interminable changes which have afflicted this band, the bassist is still an integral part of its line-up. This position has been maintained despite considerable personal difficulties, in particular his battle against alcoholism and his divorce from **Christine McVie**, who was added to the line-up in 1970. The latter chronicled their marital problems on *Rumours* (1976). John McVie has yet to record as a solo act and has deferred a compositional role within the group. However, his interest in penguins inspired the title of their 1973 release and a recurrent motif which has appeared on each subsequent album.

McWilliams, David

b. 4 July 1945, Cregagh, Belfast, Northern Ireland. The subject of an overpowering publicity campaign engineered by his manager **Phil Solomon**, McWilliams was featured on the front, inside and back covers of several consecutive issues of the ***New Musical Express***, which extolled the virtues of a new talent. He was incessantly plugged on the **pirate Radio** Caroline. Much was made of his rebellious youth and affinity with Irish music, yet the singer's debut release, 'Days Of Pearly Spencer'/'Harlem Lady', revealed a grasp of pop's dynamics rather than those of folk. The former song was both impressive and memorable, as was the pulsating follow-up, '3 O'Clock Flamingo Street', but McWilliams was unable to shake the 'hype' tag which accompanied his launch. His manager believed that Williams was a more promising protege than his other star artist, **Van Morrison** of **Them**, but his faith was unrewarded. Williams disliked live performance and failed to show his true talent in front of an audience. Neither single charted and a period of reassessment followed before the artist re-emerged the following decade with a series of charming, folk-influenced collections. In April 1992 **Marc Almond** took 'Days Of Pearly Spencer' back into the UK charts.

Albums: *David McWilliams Sings* (1967), *David McWilliams Volume 2* (1967), *Days Of Pearly Spencer* (1971), *Lord Offaly* (1972), *The Beggar And The Priest* (1973), *Living Is Just A State Of Mind* (1974), *David McWilliams* (1977), *Don't Do It For Love* (1978), *Wounded* (1982). Compilation: *Days Of Pearly Spencer* (1971).

Macabre

Chicago-based specialists in the field of sick rock, Macabre's chief obsession is with serial killers. The positive response to their mass murderer-fixated demos on the fanzine network, demonstrated the degree to which Macabre had tapped into a fascination of the heavy metal underground. During the late 80s serial killers were becoming the ultimate villains - icons of anti-sociability - and serial killer T-shirts, magazines and books were doing a brisk trade on the darker fringes of youth culture. In 1987 Macabre released their official debut, the self-financed EP, *Grim Reality*, which featured ditties about such deviants as German cannibal Fritz Haarmann, and Harvey Glatman 'the Want Ad killer'. Macabre's material often sounds like punk nursery rhymes: serial killer tributes which drip with black humour and kitsch crudity, delivered with frantic speed, minimal polish and a total disregard for any standards of good taste. As their career has progressed, their style has veered away from their more punkish roots to include a few death metal flourishes, but is still decidedly rough. With the stable line-up of Dennis the Menace (drums), Corporate Death (vocals, lead guitar) and Nefarious (bass guitar), Macabre remain a morbid gag of extravagant proportions.

Albums: *Gloom* (Vinyl Solution 1989), *Sinister Slaughter* (Nuclear Blast 1992).

Macc Lads

This trio from Macclesfield, Cheshire, England, comprised pseudonymous chancers The Beater (guitar/vocals), Muttley McLad (bass/vocals) and Chorley The Hord (drums). With a musical brief that incorporated elements of three-chord boogie, metallic riffs and punk, they insulted and entertained their audiences with a barrage of foul-mouthed one-liners and rock 'n' roll rugby songs. Lyrically, they extolled and exaggerated the virtues of the northern, macho, male-dominated pub scene: drinking real ale, 'pulling' women, Chinese takeaways and homophobia. Sample song titles include: 'Now He's A Poof', 'Eh Up Let's Sup', 'Dan's Big Log' and 'No Sheep Till Buxton'. Releasing a series of albums full of schoolboy humour, they gradually ran out of ideas. Shunned by nearly every record company and live venue in the land, the Macc Lads' grim philosophy, if such a polysyllabic word is appropriate, endures.

Albums: *Beer & Sex & Chips 'N' Gravy* (FM Revolver 1985), *Bitter, Fit, Crack* (FM Revolver 1987), *Live At Leeds - The Who?* (FM Revolver 1988), *From Beer To Eternity* (Hectic House 1989), *The Beer Necessities* (Hectic House 1990), *Turtle's Heads* (Hectic House 1991), *Alehouse Rock* (Up Not Down 1994). Compilation: *20 Golden Crates* (1991).

Videos: *Come To Brum* (1989), *Quality Of Mersey* (1990), *Three Bears* (1990), *Sex, Pies And Videotape* (1992).

Maceo And The King's Men

This group was formed in 1970 by Maceo Parker (b. 14 February 1943, Kinston, North Carolina, USA; tenor saxophone) and Melvin Parker (b. Kinston, North Carolina, USA; drums). Former members of various high school bands, the brothers joined the **James Brown** revue in 1964, and were featured on several of the artist's seminal recordings before embarking on an independent career in March 1970. The new group, Maceo And The King's Men, was completed by other defecting members of Brown's troupe. Richard 'Kush' Griffiths (trumpet), Joseph 'Joe' Davis (trumpet), L.D. 'Eldee' Williams (tenor saxophone), Jimmy 'Chank' Nolen (guitar), Alphonso 'Country' Kellum (guitar) and Bernard Odum (bass) were all serving members of the James Brown Orchestra, and similarities between both groups' music were thus inevitable. Despite this, however, neither King's Men album sold well, and several musicians drifted back to their former employer. Both Maceo and Melvin also rejoined Brown, but in deference to their obvious frustration, he wrote, arranged and produced several tracks for a spin-off project, Maceo And The Macks. Two singles, 'Party - Part 1' and 'Soul Power 74 - Part 1', reached the R&B Top 30, before an album entitled *Us*, credited solely to Maceo, was released in 1974. The brothers left the fold again in 1976, whereupon the saxophonist joined **George Clinton**'s **Funkadelic** empire. Maceo did, however, rejoin Brown briefly in the 80s. 'Cross The Track (We Better Go Back)', a track by Maceo And The Macs, was reissued in 1987 and reached number 54 in the UK chart. In the early 90s Maceo Parker joined with fellow Brown alumni, tenor saxophonist Pee Wee Ellis and trombonist **Fred Wesley**, to make the well-received *Roots Revisited* and *Mo' Roots*.

Albums: as Maceo And The King's Men *Doing Their Own Thing* (1970), *Funky Music Machine* (1975). As Maceo *Us* (1974). As Maceo Parker *For All The King's Men* (1999), *Roots Revisited* (1990), *Mo' Roots* (1991), *Life On Planet Groove* (1992), *Southern Exposure* (1993).

Macero, Teo

b. Attilio Joseph Macero, 30 October 1925, Glens Fall, New York, USA. A member of the first **Charles Mingus** Jazz Composers' Workshop in 1953, saxophonist Macero's keen interest in composition led to an involvement in the Third Stream Music and Guggenheim Awards for composition in 1957 and 1958. It was arguably after he joined **CBS** as a producer in 1957 that Macero had his greatest influence. Working on many of **Miles Davis**' finest albums, he played a particularly important role in *In A Silent Way* and *Bitches Brew*, where his editing gave the albums their form.

Albums: *Explorations* (1953), *Teo Macero With The Prestige Jazz Quartet* (1957), *Impressions Of Charles Mingus* (1983).

Machine Head

Formed in Oakland, California, USA, in June 1992, Machine Head comprise Robb Flynn (vocals/guitar; ex-**Violence**), Logan Mader (guitar), Adam Duce (bass) and Chris Kontos (drums). Specializing in angry, violent scenarios, their debut album relied heavily on Flynn's 'reflections about the self and some of my personal experiences'. These were accompanied by overdriven guitars in the tradition of a fresh-faced **Anthrax**, with a level of guile that few had anticipated. European touring with **Slayer** brought the band rave reviews the following year, before Roadrunner released 'Old', backed by cover versions of hardcore material by **Poison Idea** and the **Cro-Mags**. Meanwhile *Burn My Eyes* picked up third place in *Kerrang!* Magazine's critics lists for 1994, describing the band as 'the HM discovery of the year'.

Album: *Burn My Eyes* (Roadrunner 1994).

Machito

b. Frank Raul Grillo, 16 February 1912, Tampa, Florida, USA, d. 15 April 1984. Raised in Cuba, Machito became a singer and maracas player, working with many of the best-known bands on the island. After arriving in New York in the late 30s, he became similarly well-known as an accomplished player in various Latin-American dancebands. In 1941 he formed his own unit, the Afro-Cubans, and the following year his brother-in-law, **Mario Bauza**, until then lead trumpeter with **Chick Webb**, joined him. Under Bauza's watchful eye, the Afro-Cubans became one of the leading exponents of their particular form of Latin-American music. In the late 40s, and throughout the 50s, Machito's band regularly teamed up with leading jazz musicians, especially beboppers, for recording sessions, some of the earliest of which were produced by **Norman Granz**. These artists included **Charlie Parker**, **Dizzy Gillespie**, **Joe 'Flip' Phillips**, **Buddy Rich** and **Howard McGhee**. His music appealed greatly to **Stan Kenton**, helping prompt Kenton's long-lasting love affair with Latin rhythms. Machito played percussion instruments on some of Kenton's recordings, including the original version of 'Peanut Vendor'. Machito had a number of successful records during the mambo craze of the 60s, but it was the increasing popularity of salsa which helped keep him in the front rank of popular entertainment until his death in April 1984, which occurred during an engagement in London.

Selected albums: *Afro-Cubop* (1949), *Macho Mambo* (1949), *Machito* i (1952), *Kenya/Latin Soul Plus Jazz* (1957), *With Flute To Boot* (1958), *Machito At The Crescendo* (late 50s), *The World's Greatest Latin Band* (early 60s), *Machito* ii (1967), *Machito* iii (1971), *Fireworks* (early 70s), *Afro-Cuban Jazz Moods* (1975), *Machito And His Salsa Big Band 1982* i (1982), *Live At North Sea '82* (1982) *Machito And His Salsa Big Band* ii (1983), *Cubop City* (1992), *The Original Mambo Kings* (1993), *Tremendo Cumban 1949-52* (1993).

Mack And Mabel

High up on the list of fondly remembered flops - mainly through the medium of its superb Original Cast recording - this show ran on Broadway for only two months. It opened at the Majestic Theatre in New York on 6 October 1974, with what must have seemed a stellar cast. It had David Merrick, the premiere producer of musicals throughout the 60s, director and choreographer **Gower Champion**, a book by Michael Stewart, a score by **Jerry Herman** (***Mame*** and ***Hello, Dolly!***), and, best of all, two outstanding performers, **Robert Preston** and **Bernadette Peters**, supported by Lisa Kirk and James Mitchell - and it still failed. The story is told in flashback: one of the great comedy silent movie innovators, Mack

Sennett (Preston), remembers the early days and his first studio in Brooklyn ('Movies Were Movies'). He takes a sandwich delivery girl, Mabel Normand (Bernadette Peters), and puts her into pictures, but neither their private or professional relationship is satisfactory ('I Won't Send Roses'), and when Mabel gets the offer of a serious part, she walks out on him. The story ends in 1938, with Sennett leaving the movie business for ever. As well as Preston's 'Movies Are Movies' and 'I Won't Send Roses', (which is reprised as 'Who Needs Roses?' by Peters), the delightful and lively score included 'Look What Happened To Mabel', 'Big Time', 'I Wanna Make The World Laugh', 'Wherever He Ain't', 'Hundreds Of Girls', 'When Mabel Comes Into The Room', 'My Heart Leaps Up', 'Time Heals Everthing', 'Tap Your Troubles Away', and 'I Promise You A Happy Ending'. In spite of receiving several Tony nominations (none of which were for Herman), it just did not catch on and closed after 65 performances, losing an estimated $800,000. Two years later a new production, with a revised book, toured with David Cryer, Lucie Arnez, and **Tommy Tune**, and, since that time, there have been several US provincial presentations, including one at the Paper Mill Playhouse in 1988, with Lee Horsley as Sennett and Janet Metz as Mabel. In the UK, interest was aroused in the show when its overture was used by Torvill and Dean, in their successful bid for a gold medal in the Olympic Ice Dancing Championship in 1984. A BBC Radio 2 disc jockey, David Jacobs, began playing tracks from the album, and 'I Won't Send Roses', in particular, became one of the station's easy-listening favourites. After both amateur and one-night concert versions attracted a good deal of attention in Britain over the years, persistent calls for the show to be mounted professionally seemed to have been answered when a Leicester Haymarket production was announced for autumn 1995.

Mack, Lonnie

b. 1941, Harrison, Indiana, USA. Lonnie Mack began playing guitar while still a child, drawing early influence from a local blues musician, Ralph Trotts, as well as established figures **Merle Travis** and **Les Paul**. He later led a C&W act, Lonnie And The Twilighters, and by 1961 was working regularly with the **Troy Seals** Band. The following year, Mack recorded his exhilarating instrumental version of **Chuck Berry**'s 'Memphis'. By playing his Gibson 'Flying V' guitar through a Leslie cabinet, the revolving device which gives the Hammond organ its distinctive sound, Mack created a striking, exciting style. 'Memphis' eventually reached the US Top 5, while an equally urgent original, 'Wham', subsequently broached the Top 30. *The Wham Of That Memphis Man* confirmed the artist's vibrant skill, which drew on blues, gospel and country traditions. Several tracks, notably 'I'll Keep You Happy', 'Where There's A Will' and 'Why', also showed Mack's prowess as a soulful vocalist, and later recordings included a rousing rendition of **Wilson Pickett**'s 'I Found A Love'. The guitarist also contributed to several sessions by **Freddy King** and appeared on **James Brown**'s 'Kansas City' (1967). Mack was signed to **Elektra** in 1968 following a lengthy appraisal by **Al Kooper** in ***Rolling Stone*** magazine. *Glad I'm In The Band* and *Whatever's Right* updated the style of early recordings and included several notable remakes, although the highlight of the latter set was the extended 'Mt. Healthy Blues'. Mack also added bass to the **Doors**' *Morrison Hotel* (1970) and undertook a national tour prior to recording *The Hills Of Indiana*. This low-key, primarily country album was the prelude to a six-year period of seclusion which ended in 1977 with *Home At Last*. Mack then guested on **Michael Nesmith**'s *From A Radio Engine To The Photon Wing*, before completing *Lonnie Mack And Pismo*, but this regeneration was followed by another sabbatical. He re-emerged in 1985 under the aegis of Texan guitarist **Stevie Ray Vaughan**, who co-produced the exciting *Strike Like Lightning*. Released on the Alligator label, a specialist in modern blues, the album rekindled this talented artist's career a rebirth that was maintained on the fiery *Second Sight*.

Albums: *The Wham Of That Memphis Man* (1963), *Glad I'm In The Band* (1969), *Whatever's Right* (1969), *The Hills Of Indiana* (1971), *Home At Last* (1977), *Lonnie Mack And Pismo* (1977), *Strike Like Lightning* (1985), *Second Sight* (1987). Compilations: *For Collectors Only* (1970), *The Memphis Sound Of Lonnie Mack* (1974), *Sixteen Rock Guitar Greats* (c.70s).

Mack, Warner

b. Warner McPherson, 2 April 1938, Nashville, Tennessee, USA. Warner Mack is one of the few country musicians to be born in Nashville, although at the age of seven he moved to Jackson, Tennessee, and at nine, to Vicksburg, Mississippi. Mack, whose father was a minister, tells his story in the song 'Tennessee Born, Mississippi Raised'. He played at various school functions and started performing on the radio show *Louisiana Hayride*. In 1957, he wrote and recorded 'Is It Wrong (For Loving You)?', which was later a number 1 country hit for **Sonny James**. In 1964 Mack had success with a **Jim Glaser** song, 'Sitting In An All Night Cafe', but while it was climbing the country charts, he suffered serious injuries in a car accident. Mack, whose stage name came about through a mistake on a record label, had a US country number 1 with his own composition, 'The Bridge Washed Out', and had further success with 'Talking To The Walls' and 'How Long Will It Take?'. He was the first country artist to record a national commercial for Coca-Cola. His last US country chart entry was 'These Crazy Thoughts' in 1977. Mack has completed successful

tours of UK country clubs, always closing with an emotional version of 'He Touched Me'.
Albums: *Warner Mack's Golden Country Hits, Vol. 1* (1961), *Warner Mack's Golden Country Hits, Vol. 2* (1962), *Great Country And Western Hits* (1964), *The Bridge Washed Out* (1965), *The Country Touch* (1966), *Everybody's Country Favourites* (1966), *Drifting Apart* (1967), *The Many Moods Of Warner Mack* (1968), *The Country Beat Of Warner Mack* (1969), with his sister Dean *Songs We Sang In Church And Home* (1969), *I'll Still Be Missing You* (1969), *Love Hungry* (1970), *You Make Me Feel Like A Man* (1971), *Great Country* (1973), *The Best Of The Best Of Warner Mack* (1978), *The Prince Of Country Blues* (1983), *At Your Service* (1984), *Warner Mack - The England Tour* (1984).

Macka B

Macka B is the most productive, distinctive and certainly among the most talented of MCs to emerge in Britain in the 1980s. Born Christopher MacFarlane, Wolverhampton, England, he first rose to local fame chatting for Birmingham-based Wassifa hi-fi, with a melodic but gruff voice which perhaps most closely resembled that of **Prince Far-I**, although Macka B was of the new breed and capable of a pace of delivery that made his predecessors look lazy by comparison. His large physique, stunning, topical lyrics and dreadlocked features made him an imposing presence on the mic, and after one local release his fame quickly spread to London, occasioning the release of a well-received 45, 'Bible Reader', for **Fashion** Records (1985). Perhaps recognising that Macka B's future did not lay in the **dancehall** MC trade the label were currently having hits with, Fashion suggested that Macka B try his luck at **Ariwa Records**, their South London rivals.
With the help of fellow Wolverhamptonite Macka Dub, **Ariwa** producer Mad Professor unleashed a monster with Macka B's debut LP, *Sign Of The Times*, which remains a classic to this day. Mixing comic material with roots anthems like 'Invasion', drenched in tight horns and heavy dub mixing, the album was a huge hit in the reggae community. Macka B appeared on ITV's *Club Mix* and was something of a celebrity, but he shunned the limelight, preferring instead to work in the roots market, issuing a series of strong albums over the next five years, among them *We've Had Enough*, *Natural Suntan* and *Peace Cup*. He retains his credibility and goodwill, and has even made the occasional trip to Jamaica to record with producer Black Scorpio on a couple of sides, as well as cutting 'DJ Unity' at **Penthouse** Studio, Kingston, with Jamaican counterpart **Tony Rebel**.
Albums: *Sign Of the Times* (Ariwa 1986), *We've Had Enough* (Ariwa 1987), *Looks Are Deceiving* (Ariwa 1988), *Buppie Culture* (Ariwa 1989), *Natural Suntan* (Ariwa 1990), *Peace Cup* (Ariwa 1991), *Jamaica No Problem* (Ariwa 1992), *Here Comes Trouble* (Ariwa 1993).

Macon, John Wesley 'Shortstuff'

b. 1933, Crawford, Mississippi, USA, d. 28 December 1973, Macon, Mississippi, USA. In the mid-60s, Macon was brought briefly to public attention by his cousin **Big Joe Williams**. Although 30 years younger than Williams, he performed a remarkably archaic style of blues, featuring simple, insistently rhythmic guitar, often without chord changes, and mode packed vocals which often recalled the field holler. After the trip north with Joe that resulted in his too few recordings, Macon returned home to undeserved obscurity until his death.
Albums: *Mr. Shortstuff & Big Joe Williams* (c.1965), *Hell Bound & Heaven Sent* (1967).

Macon, Uncle Dave

b. David Harrison Macon, 7 October 1870, Smart Station, Warren County, Tennessee, USA, d. 22 March 1952. Macon's family moved to Nashville when his father, a Confederate captain in the Civil War, bought the city's Broadway Hotel. Macon learned to play the banjo and acquired songs from the vaudeville artists who stayed at the hotel. He married in 1889 and started the Macon Midway Mule And Wagon Transportation Company, which was later described in the song 'From Here To Heaven'. His mule-drawn wagons carried goods between Murfreesboro and Woodbury. Macon performed at venues along the way. However, the business collapsed following the advent of a motorized competitor in 1920. Although he had worked as a jovial entertainer for many years, he never thought of turning professional until a pompous farmer asked him to play at a wedding. Macon demanded $15 in the sure knowledge he would be turned down: it was accepted and became his first professional booking. At the age of 52, when Uncle Dave Macon launched his professional career, his songs and humour proved so popular that he was soon known all over the south. He became the first star of the *Grand Ole Opry* when it was launched in 1925 with material covering folk tunes, vaudeville, blues, country and gospel music. In 1927, Macon formed the Fruit Jar Drinkers with Sam And Kirk McGee and Mazy Todd - their tracks among the finest produced by old-time string bands. In 1931 he was the main attraction of the *Opry*'s first touring show, working with his son, Dorris, and the **Delmore Brothers**. Between 1924 and 1938, he recorded over 170 songs, which makes him among the most recorded of the early-day country stars. Despite the age of the recordings, his whooping and hollering brings them to life, and notable successes included 'Arkansas Traveller' and 'Soldier's Joy'. 'Hill Billie Blues' is possibly the first recorded song ever to use hillbilly in its title. His 1927 recording of 'Sail Away Ladies' was converted into the 50s skiffle hit, 'Don't You Rock Me, Daddy-O'. Macon appeared with **Roy Acuff** in the 1939 film, *Grand Ole Opry*, which showed that, even at an advanced age, he

was a fine showman. Macon stopped touring in 1950 and he made his last appearance at the *Opry* on 1 March 1952. After his death at Murfreesboro in 1952, a monument was erected near Woodbury by his fellow *Opry* associates and he was elected to the Country Music Hall Of Fame in 1966.
Albums: *Uncle Dave Macon - First Featured Star Of The Grand Ole Opry* (1966), *Uncle Dave Macon - Early Recordings, 1925-1935* (1971), *Go Long Mule* (1972), *The Gayest Old Dude In Town* (1974), *Dixie Dewdrop* (1975), *Uncle Dave Macon At Home - His Last Recordings* (1976), *Keep My Skillet Good And Greasy* (1979), *Laugh Your Blues Away* (1979).

Mad About Music

Deanna Durbin was only 17 years old when she made this film in 1938, but her 'significant contribution in bringing to the screen the spirit and personification of youth', gained her a special Academy Award in the same year. In *Mad About Music* she once again plays a character bursting with imagination and energy, who, after being deposited in a swanky Swiss finishing school by her narcissistic actress mother (Gail Patrick), comes up with a father who is simply the product of that same fertile imagination. Invited to produce him for inspection, the youngster offers a rather puzzled visitor (Herbert Marshall) as her partner in the collusion. It was all good fun, and also taking part were Jackie Moran, Arthur Treacher, William Frawley, Helen Parrish, Marcia Mae Jones. The musical highlight was Miss Durbin's spirited rendering of 'I Love To Whistle' with Cappy Barra's Harmonica Band. **Harold Adamson** and **Jimmy McHugh** wrote that tune, along with 'Serenade To The Stars', 'Chapel Bells', and 'There Isn't A Day Goes By'. Durbin also joined the Vienna Boys' Choir in a beautiful version of 'Ave Maria' (Charles Gounod). Norman Taurog directed this highly popular feature which attracted several Oscar nominations, two of which went to Marcella Burke and Frederick Kohner, the writers of the story on which Bruce Manning and Felix Jackson's screenplay was based. It received another airing in 1956 when *Mad About Music* was remade as *Toy Tiger* starring Jeff Chandler and Laraine Day, with Tim Hovey in the Deanna Durbin part.

Mad Lads

Hailing from Memphis, Tennessee, USA, the Mad Lads comprised John Gary Williams, Julius Green, William Brown and Robert Phillips. Although not one of the premier **Stax**/Volt acts, this quartet scored seven R&B hits between 1965 and 1969. After changing their name from the Emeralds, their first single, 'The Sidewalk Surf', flopped, but the group placed three singles in the R&B Top 20 in 1965-66, the best known being 'I Want Someone'. Their first hit, 'Don't Want To Shop Around', was curiously anachronistic, owing more to doo-wop than southern soul. Later releases, including the perky 'Sugar Sugar', were more typical, but the group was increasingly obscured by its more successful counterparts. In 1966, Williams and Brown were drafted and replaced by Sam Nelson and Quincy Clifton Billops Jnr. A version of the **Jimmy Webb** standard 'By The Time I Get To Phoenix' proved the Mad Lads' last chart entry in 1969; after that they broke up. A new line-up was put together in 1972, but disbanded after completing one album. Former member Billops joined another Stax group, Ollie And The Nightingales, and from there moved into a reformed version of the **Ovations**. A new Mad Lads built around Williams and Gary formed in 1984, with a new Volt album, *Madder Than Ever*, released in 1990.
Albums: *In Action* (1966), *The Mad, Mad, Mad, Mad, Mad Lads* (1969), *A New Beginning* (1972), *A New Beginning* (1973), *Madder Than Ever* (1990).

Mad Professor

(See **Ariwa Sounds**)

Mad River

Laurence Hammond (vocals/harmonica), David Robinson (lead guitar), Greg Druian (rhythm guitar), Tom Manning (bass) and Greg Dewey (drums) formed the Mad River Blues Band in 1965. Initially based in Yellow Springs, Ohio, USA, the group subsequently moved to California, by which time Druian had been replaced by Rick Bockner. The quintet, now dubbed simply Mad River, initially struggled to assert themselves, but a privately pressed EP helped secure a series of gigs at prestigious San Franciscan venues. Mad River's debut album was released in 1968. Although mastered too fast owing to a technical error, it remains an enthralling slice of vintage acid rock, where traces of **Country Joe And The Fish** and **Quicksilver Messenger Service** blend with Hammond's reedy, quivering voice. A second album, *Paradise Bar And Grill*, was an altogether different affair. A handful of the tracks echoed the style of that first selection, while others were indebted to C&W, a genre the singer was increasingly drawn towards. Two haunting acoustic instrumentals and a cameo appearance by the late writer Richard Brautigan completed one of the late 60s most engaging collections. Mad River broke up soon after its release. Dewey later joined Country Joe And The Fish, and has subsequently played with numerous Bay Area groups. Hammond pursued his love of country music with his Whiplash Band and recorded an engaging album, *Coyote's Dream*, in 1976. The remainder of the group retired from active performance.
Albums: *Mad River* (1968), *Paradise Bar And Grill* (1969).

Mad Season

Mad Season were formed as an offshoot of **Pearl Jam** when their lead guitarist, Mike McCready, was on holiday in Minneapolis. There he met John Baker Saunder, the bass player with Lamont Cranston. The rest of Mad Season consist of Seattle luminaries Barrett Martin (drums; also **Screaming Trees**) and Layne Staley (vocals; **Alice In Chains**). They played their first gig with just three days notice as the Gacy Bunch (a halfway house name between television serial *The Brady Bunch* and serial killer John Wayne Gacy) at Seattle's Crocodile Cafe. There had still been no proper rehearsals when they played their second gig, two weeks later. By the recording of the album they were called Mad Season, which McCready first heard in Surrey when Pearl Jam were mixing their first album. 'It's the time when the psychedelic mushrooms grow. And it's a Hunter S. Thompson thing, and it certainly describes my years of alcohol, so it had stuck in my mind for a long time.' The group's debut featured Screaming Trees' vocalist Mark Lanegan duetting with Staley. The understated performances from the star personnel helped to create an impressive and relaxed album.

Album: *Above* (Columbia 1995).

Madam X

One of Madam X's more distinctive songs, 'Come One, Come All', contained the line 'We're bad, we're good, that's all we ever wanted'. Sadly for them, most people thought they belonged chiefly to the first category. The group were formed in New York in 1983 by sisters Maxine and Roxy Petrucci on guitar and drums respectively, along with vocalist Bret Kaiser and bassist Christopher 'Godzilla' Doliber. They subsequently moved to Los Angeles where their brand of glam metal was better accepted. In February 1985 they released an anthemic single, 'High In High School', backed with a suitably grandiose video. The single was produced by **Rick Derringer** who also performed the same task on the album. Both, however, were very average affairs and live shows fell short of the expected excitement. In 1986 Roxy departed to form **Vixen** and Kaiser quit the scene with ego suitably deflated. Mark McConnell took over the drums whilst vocal duties were handled by Sebastian Bach. Within the year the band disintegrated with Doliber forming a wild and heavy band called **Godzilla** (which failed). Maxine remained in the shadow of her sister, but Bach found stardom with **Skid Row**.

Album: *We Reserve The Right* (Jet 1984).

Madame Sherry

With music by Hugo Felix and a book by Maurice Ordonneau, this 'Musical Vaudeville' or 'French Vaudeville', was presented in Paris and Berlin in 1902, and in London a year later. By the time it opened at the New Amersterdam Theatre in New York on 30 August 1910, it had been radically reworked, and had music by Karl Hoschna and a book and lyrics by **Otto Harbach**. The complicated story involves Edward Sherry (Jack Gardner), whose wealthy uncle Theophilus (Ralph Herz), sets him up in his own Sherry School of Aesthetic Dancing. Edward succeeds in convincing his uncle that his houskeeper, Catherine (Elizabeth Murray), is his wife and two of the dancing pupils are his children. At the time, Edward loves Lulu (Frances Demarest), one of his terpsichorean teachers, but, by the end of the piece he has transferred his affections to Yvonne (Lina Abarbanell), who, fresh from the convent school, accedes to the title of Madame Sherry. Hoschna and Harbach's score contained 'Every Little Movement' ('Has a meaning of its own'), which became an enormous hit and a firm favourite in vaudeville and music halls through the years. The **Dorsey** Brothers Orchestra had some success with it, and the number was also featured in several 40s film musicals such as *Presenting Lily Mars* (Judy Garland), *Shine On Harvest Moon*, and ***The Jolson Story***. The rest of the composers' score included 'The Smile She Means For You, 'I Want To Play House With You', and 'The Birth Of Passion'. Another song, 'Put You Arms Around Me Honey', which was written by **Albert Von Tilzer** and Junie McCree, and interpolated into the show, became extremely popular. It also turned up in several movie musicals including two Betty Grable vehicles, ***Coney Island*** and ***Mother Wore Tights***. Lina Abarbanell was the main star of the piece, but comedienne Elizabeth Murray also made a strong impression, and helped the show enjoy a run of 231 performances. She went on to further success in *High Jinks*, ***Watch Your Step***, and *Sidewalks Of New York*.

Madball

Singer Freddy Cricien (b. Florida, USA), brother of **Agnostic Front**'s Roger Miret, was unsurprisingly influenced by his imposing sibling. So much so that when he put his own band together after following the New York legends across the country, Madball would operate in a similar, all-out hardcore vein. In fact Cricien had made his debut at an Agnostic Front show at the age of seven, when visiting his New York-based brethren, getting up on stage to offer a rendition of the **Animals**' It's My Life'. Eventually he would move to the US capital, spending many of his evenings at the city's home for hardcore, **CBGB's**. In fact, it would be Vinnie Stigma of Agnostic Front who would give him his nickname, 'Madball', after harassing the young Cricien to the point at which his face resembled such an object, in the back of the tour van. When Madball was put together, it included Vinnie on guitar, with brother Roger on bass and Will Shepler on drums.

Their first release, 'Ball Of Destruction', was unveiled in 1989 on In-Effect Records, and is now a genuine rarity. However, there was a three-year gap before a second 7-inch, 'Droppin' Many Suckers', this time for Wreck-age Records. It prefaced a switch to **Roadrunner** and a long-playing set which, predictably, accented machismo and power over subtlety, but was an energizing collection for all that. It saw the debut of the current line-up; Cricien (vocals), Shepler (drums), Stigma (guitar), Matt Henderson (guitar), Hoya (bass).
Album: *Set It Off* (Roadrunner 1993).

Madder Rose

Spuriously lauded on their arrival in 1993 as the 'new **Velvet Underground**', Manhattan-based New Yorkers Madder Rose comprised Billy Coté (b. New Jersey, USA; guitar), Mary Lorson (vocals), Matt Verta-Ray (bass) and Johnny Kick (b. Chicago, ex-Speedball; drums). The initial ripples were caused by singles such as 'Swim', a yearning, slow burning torch song reminiscent of **Lou Reed**'s craft. However, they could hardly be described as anyone's 'new young thing', with all of the members aged over 30 at this early stage in their career. Each boasted an interesting, non-musical background. Lorson was an ex-busker and film student, while both Matt and Johnny worked at the **Andy Warhol** silk-screen factory and met the great man several times (a fact which helped to encourage the Velvet Underground comparisons). Coté had additionally spent much of the 80s working in No/New Wave bands Hammerdoll and Coté Coté, whilst struggling to overcome his heroin addiction. Covers of **PiL**'s 'Rise' and the **Cars**' 'My Best Friends Girl' on stage further revealed Madder Rose's diversity, while their debut album was trumpeted by ***Melody Maker*** magazine as '*the* debut album of 1993'. Released on **Atlantic Records**' independently distributed subsidiary Seed, production was overseen by Kevin Salem of **Dumptruck**. Matt Verta-Ray left in February 1994, the departure agreed before the band recorded their second album, to concentrate on his own project, Speedball Baby. He was replaced for *Panic On* by Chris Giammalvo (ex-Eve's Plum), on a set co-produced with **Clash/Breeders/Th' Faith Healers** veteran, Mark Freegard. This saw Lorson emerge as a songwriting force to rival Coté on some of the album's best numbers, including the appealing 'Foolish Ways'.
Albums: *Bring It Down* (Seed 1993), *Panic On* (Atlantic 1994).

Maddox, Rose

b. Roselea Arbana Maddox, 15 December 1926, near Boaz, Alabama, USA. In the Depression days of 1933, Charlie and Lula Madox took their five young children (Cal, Henry, Fred, Don and Rose), whose ages ranged from 7 to 16, illegally boarded freight trains and headed for California, eventually settling near Bakersfield. They followed the various harvests, working as 'fruit tramps', and were soon joined by eldest son, Cliff. All were musical, and to help their income, they began to play for local dances with the 12-year-old Rose providing the vocals, even in noisy honky tonks. They first appeared on radio on KTRB Modesto in 1937, but by 1941, when they disbanded owing to Cal, Fred, and Don being drafted, they had become a popular act, due initially to appearances on the powerful KFBK Sacramento station. In 1946, they reformed as the Maddox Brothers And Rose and became popular over a wide area. Their bright and garish stage costumes earned them the title: 'the most colourful hillbilly band in America'. Cliff died in 1948,and his place was taken by Henry. By the early 50s, with an act that included comedy as well as songs, they were regulars on the *Louisiana Hayride*, played concerts and also appeared on the *Grand Ole Opry*. In 1947, they recorded for Four Star before moving to Columbia in 1951. Their successes included Rose's stirring recordings of 'The Philadelphia Lawyer' and 'The Tramp On The Street'. Rose also recorded with her sister-in-law, Loretta, as Rosie And Rita. By the mid-50s, Rose was beginning to look to a solo career. In 1957, she signed for **Capitol** and about that time the Maddox Brothers nominally disbanded. Rose soon established herself as a solo singer and, during the 60s, had several chart hits including 'Gambler's Love', 'Conscience I'm Guilty' and her biggest hit 'Sing A Little Song Of Heartache'. She also had four very successful duet recordings with **Buck Owens**, namely 'Mental Cruelty', 'Loose Talk', 'We're The Talk Of The Town' and 'Sweethearts In Heaven'. In the late 60s, she suffered the first of several heart attacks which have affected her career, but by 1969 she had recovered and made the first of her visits to Britain. She continued to work when health permitted throughout the 70s, but had no chart success. After leaving Capitol in 1967, she recorded for several labels including Starday, **Decca** and King. In the 80s, she recorded two albums for **Arhoolie Records** and her famous Varrick album *Queen Of The West*, on which she was helped by **Merle Haggard** and the Strangers and **Emmylou Harris**. Her son, Donnie, died in 1982 and she sang gospel songs with the Vern Williams band at his funeral. She frequently appeared with Williams, a popular west coast bluegrass musician who also provided the backing on some of her 80s recordings. In 1987, Maddox suffered a further major heart attack which left her in a critical condition for some time. Her situation was aggravated by the fact that she had no health insurance but benefit concerts were held to raise the funds. Rose Maddox possessed a powerful, emotive voice and was gifted with the ability to sing music of all types. Her recordings range from early hillbilly songs and gospel tunes through to rockabilly numbers that have endeared her to followers of that genre. Later she worked with long-time friend and rockabilly artist Glen Glenn, recording the album *Rockabilly Reunion* with him at the Camden Workers Club, London in March 1987. Many experts rate the album *Rose Maddox Sings Bluegrass* as her finest recorded work. On it she is backed by such outstanding bluegrass musicians as Don Reno, Red Smiley and **Bill Monroe**.

Albums: *Precious Memories* (1958), *Glorybound Train* (1960), *The One Rose* (1960), *A Big Bouquet Of Roses* (1961), with Bill Monroe *Sings Bluegrass* (1962), *Rosie* (1970), *Alone With You* (1963), *Reckless Love & Bold Adventure* (1977), *This Is Rose Maddox* (1980), *A Beautiful Bouquet* (1983), with Merle Haggard & The Strangers, Emmylou Harris *Queen Of The West* (1983), with Glen Glenn *Live In London - Rockabilly Reunion* (1988), *Rose Of The West Coast Country* (1991) with Fred Maddox *50 Years Of Country Music* (1993), *The One Rose - The Capitol Years* (Bear Family 1994, 4 CD set), *$35 And A Dream* (Arhoolie 1995), As The Maddox Brothers & Rose: *A Collection Of Standard Sacred Country Songs* (1956), *I'll Write Your Name In The Sand* (1961), *The Maddox Brothers & Rose* (1961), *The Maddox Brothers & Rose* (1962), *The Maddox Brothers & Rose 1946-1951 Vols. 1 & 2* (1964), *The Maddox Brothers & Rose Go Honky Tonkin'* (1965), *Family Folks* (1982), *Rockin' Rollin'* (1982), *The Maddox Brothers & Rose On The Air Vol. 1* (1985), *The Maddox Brothers & Rose On The Air Vol. 2* (1982), *The Maddox Brothers & Rose* (1986).

Made

A cheerless 1972 film, *Made* starred Carol White (*Cathy Come Home*, ***Poor Cow***) as a struggling single parent mistreated by those around her. The role of her musician lover was initially offered to **Marc Bolan**, but it was desolate folk singer **Roy Harper** who secured the part. Both he and White were excellent in their roles, although the depressing situation of the latter ensures that watching *Made*, although thought-provoking, is not a pleasurable experience. Harper contributed several songs, marked by *de rigueur* personal ruminations, but the power of the film is derived from its script and John Mackenzie's sympathetic direction. A minor classic, *Made* continues the atmosphere of early 60s' 'kitchen sink' drama.

Madness

This highly-regarded UK pop group evolved from the London-based Invaders in the summer of 1979. Their line-up comprised Suggs McPherson (b. Graham McPherson, 13 January 1961, Hastings, Sussex, England; vocals), Mark Bedford (b. 24 August 1961, London, England; bass), Mike Barson (b. 21 April 1958, London, England; keyboards), Chris Foreman (b. 8 August 1958, London, England; guitar), Lee Thompson (b. 5 October 1957, London, England; saxophone), Chas Smash (b. Cathal Smythe, 14 January 1959; vocals/trumpet) and Dan Woodgate (b. 19 October 1960, London, England; drums). After signing a one-off deal with **2-Tone** they issued 'The Prince', a tribute to blue beat maestro **Prince Buster** (whose song, 'Madness', had inspired the group's name). The single reached the UK Top 20 and the follow-up, 'One Step Beyond' (a Buster composition) did even better, peaking at number 7, the first result of their new deal with **Stiff Records**. An album of the same title revealed Madness' charm with its engaging mix of ska and exuberant pop, a fusion they humorously dubbed 'the nutty sound'. Over the next two years the group enjoyed an uninterrupted run of Top 10 UK hits, comprising 'My Girl', *Work Rest And Play* (EP) (which included 'Night Boat To Cairo'), 'Baggy Trousers', 'Embarrassment', 'The Return Of The Los Palmas Seven', 'Grey Day', 'Shut Up' and 'It Must Be Love' (originally a hit for its composer, **Labi Siffre**). Although Madness appealed mainly to a younger audience and were known as a zany, fun-loving group, their work occasionally took on a more serious note. Both 'Grey Day' and 'Our House' (number 5, 1992) showed their ability to write about working-class family life in a fashion that was piercingly accurate, yet never patronizing. At their best, Madness were the most able commentators on London life since the **Kinks** in the late 60s. An ability to tease out a sense of melancholy beneath the fun permeated their more mature work, particularly on the 1982 album, *The Rise And Fall.* That same year Suggs married singer **Bette Bright** and the group finally topped the charts with their 12th chart entry, 'House Of Fun' (which concerned the purchase of prophylactics and teenage sexuality). More UK hits followed, including 'Wings Of A Dove' and 'The Sun And The Rain', but in late 1983 the group suffered a serious setback when founding member Barson quit. The group continued to release some exceptional work in 1984 including 'Michael Caine' and 'One Better Day'. At the end of that year, they formed their own label, Zarjazz. It's first release was **Feargal Sharkey**'s 'Listen To Your Father' (written by the group), which reached the UK Top 30. Madness continued to enjoy relatively minor hits by previous standards with the contemplative 'Yesterday's Men', the exuberant 'Uncle Sam' and a cover of the former **Scritti Politti** success, 'The Sweetest Girl'. In the autumn of 1986, the group announced that they were splitting. Seventeen months later, they reunited as a four-piece under the name The Madness, but failed to emulate previous successes. One of Mark Bedford's projects was a collaboration with ex-**Higson** member Terry Edwards in **Butterfield 8**. Lee Thompson and Chris Foreman later worked under the appellation the Nutty Boys, releasing one album, *Crunch* (1990), and played to capacity crowds in London clubs and pubs. In June 1992 the original Madness reformed for two open air gigs in Finsbury Park, London, which resulted in *Madstock*, a 'live' document of the event. The group's renewed public image was rewarded with four chart entries during the year; three re-issues, 'It Must Be Love', 'House Of Fun', and 'My Girl'; along with 'The Harder They Come'. In 1993, a 'musical about homelessness', *One Step Beyond*, by Alan Gilbey, incorporated 15 Madness songs when it opened on the London Fringe. Further evidence, as if any was needed, of the enduring brilliance of Madness' irresistable songcraft.

Albums: *One Step Beyond* (Stiff 1979), *Absolutely* (Stiff 1980), *Madness 7* (Stiff 1981), *The Rise And Fall* (Stiff 1982), *Keep Moving* (Stiff 1984), *Mad Not Mad* (Zarjazz 1985), *Madstock* (Go! Discs 1992), *The Madness* (Virgin 1988). Compilations: *Complete Madness* (Stiff 1982), *Utter Madness* (Zarjazz 1986), *Divine Madness* (Virgin 1992), *The Business - The Definitive Singles Collection* (Virgin 1993). Videos: *Complete Madness* (1984), *Utter Madness* (1988), *Complete And Utter Madness* (1988), *Divine Madness* (1992). Further reading: *A Brief Case Of Madness*, Mark Williams, *Total Madness*, George Marshall.

Madonna

b. Madonna Louise Vernon Ciccione, 16 August 1958, Rochester Michigan, USA. Madonna excelled at dance and drama at high school and during brief periods at colleges in Michigan and North Carolina. In 1977 she went to New York, studying with noted choreographer Alvin Ailey and taking modelling jobs. Two years later, Madonna moved to France to join a show featuring disco singer Patrick Hernandez. There she met Dan Gilroy and, back in New York, the pair formed club band the Breakfast Club. Madonna played drums and sang with the band before setting up Emmy in 1980 with Detroit-born drummer Steve Bray. Together, Madonna and Bray created dance tracks which led to a recording deal with **Sire Records**. With leading New York disc jockey Mark Kamins producing, she recorded 'Everybody', a US club hit in 1982. Madonna broke out from the dance scene into mainstream pop with 'Holiday' written and produced by John 'Jellybean' Benitez. It reached the US Top 20 and was a Top 10 hit across Europe in 1984. By now, her tough, raunchy persona was coming across to international audiences and the attitude was underlined by the choice of Tom Kelly and Billy Steinberg's catchy 'Like A Virgin' as a 1984 single. It was the first of five US number 1 hits for Madonna. Among these was 'Material Girl', the video for which introduced one of her most characteristic visual styles, the mimicking of Marilyn Monroe's 'blonde bombshell' image. By the time of the ***Live Aid*** concert, at which she appeared, and her high-profile wedding to actor Sean Penn, Madonna had become an internationally recognized superstar, known to millions of tabloid newspaper readers without any interest in her music. Among the fans of her work were a growing number of 'wannabees', teenage girls who aped her independent and don't-care stance.

From 1985-87, she turned out a stream of irresistibly catchy hit singles. 'Crazy For You' was co-written by ex-**Carpenters**' collaborator John Bettis, while she and Steve Bray wrote 'Into The Groove'. These were followed by 'Dress You Up' and 'Papa Don't Preach', with its message of generational rebellion. 'True Blue', 'Open Your Heart' and 'La Isla Bonita' were later successes. Like an increasing number of her songs, 'Who's That Girl' (1987) were tied-in to a film - in this instance, a poorly received comedy in which she starred with Sir John Mills. Madonna's film career had begun in 1980 with a bit part in the b-movie *A Certain Sacrifice* before she starred in *Desperately Seeking Susan* (1985). In *Shanghai Surprise* (1986), Madonna appeared with Penn, from whom she separated in 1988. In that year, she also appeared on Broadway in the play *Speed The Plow* by David Mamet. Madonna continued to attract controversy when in 1989 the video for 'Like A Prayer', with its links between religion and eroticism, was condemned by the Vatican and caused Pepsi-Cola to cancel a sponsorship deal with the star. The resulting publicity helped the album of the same title - co-produced with new collaborator Patrick Leonard - to become a global best-seller. 1990 saw her career reach a new peak of publicity and commercial success. She starred with Warren Beatty in the blockbuster film *Dick Tracy* while the extravagant costumes and choreography of the Blond Ambition world tour were the apotheosis of Madonna's uninhibited melange of sexuality, song, dance and religiosity. The tour was commemorated by a documentary film, *Truth Or Dare On The Band Behind The Scenes, And In Bed With Madonna*, released in 1991. Among the hits of the early 90s were 'Vogue', devoted to a short-lived dance craze, 'Justify My Love' (co-written with **Lenny Kravitz**) and 'Rescue Me', produced by Madonna and Shep Pettibone. Madonna's reputation as a strong businesswoman, in control of each aspect of her career, was confirmed in 1992 when she signed a multi-million dollar deal with the Time-Warner conglomerate, parent company of Sire. This guaranteed the release of albums, films and books created by her own Maverick production company. The publication of her graphic and erotic book *Sex* put her back on top of the charts, though this time it was in the bestselling book lists. The book was an unprecidented success, selling out within hours and needing an immediate reprint. *Bedtime Stories* saw her team up with **Soul II Soul** producer Nellie Hooper, who wrote the title-track in conjunction with **Björk**. It was prefaced by the Top 10 performance of 'Secret', and boasted 11 tracks which combined, by her own description, pop, R&B, hip hop and Madonna.

Albums: *Madonna* (1983), *Like A Virgin* (1984), *True Blue* (1986), *You Can Dance* (1987), *Who's That Girl* (1987, film

soundtrack), *Like A Prayer* (1989), *I'm Breathless* (1990), *Erotica* (1992), *Bedtime Stories* (WEA 1994). Compilations: *The Immaculate Collection* (1991), *Best Of The Rest Vol. 2* (1993).
Videos: *The Virgin Tour* (1986), *Ciao Italia* (1988), *Immaculate Collection* (1990), *The Real Story* (1991), *Madonna Video EP* (1991), *In Bed With Madonna* (1991), *Madonna Exposed* (1993), *Madonna: The Unauthorised Biography (MIA Video)* (1994), *Madonna: The Girlie Show* (1994).
Further reading: *Madonna: Her Story*, Michael McKenzie. *Madonna: The New Illustrated Biography*, Debbi Voller. *Madonna: In Her Own Words*, Mick St Michael. *Madonna: The Biography*, Robert Matthew-Walker. *Madonna*, Marie Cahill. *Madonna: The Style Book*, Debbi Voller. *Like A Virgin: Madonna Revealed*, Douglas Thompson. *Sex*, Madonna. *Madonna Unathorized*, Christopher Anderson. *I Dream Of Madonna: Women's Dreams Of The Goddess Of Pop*, Kay Turner. *Madonna: The Girlie Show*, Glenn O'Brien. *Deconstructing Madonna*, Fran Lloyd.

Madriguera, Enric

b. 17 February 1904, Barcelona, Spain, d. 7 September 1975. A child prodigy on violin, Madriguera played concerts in Spain and France before studying music with Leopold Auer at Barcelona Conservatory. After emigrating to the USA, he played as soloist with the Boston and Chicago Symphony Orchestras and, while still in his 20s, became conductor of the Cuban Philharmonic, later joining NBC in New York as concertmaster. While visiting Colombia he worked as musical director for the Columbia Records' subsidiary there; as a result Madriguera became interested in dance music, forming his first band for the Havana Casino. Back in New York, he recorded with the group for the parent Columbia company. Madriguera's occupation for the eight years of his popular career was as leading violinist of a society band, which debuted in 1932 at the Commodore, Biltmore and Weylin hotels in New York. **Helen Ward** was his vocalist in her pre-**Benny Goodman** days; her place was later taken by Patricia Gilmore, who subsequently married Madriguera. In 1940, his musical policy became almost exclusively Latin-American for recording contracts with **RCA** and **Brunswick** as well as for the usual Columbia releases, so much so that he was known as 'Musical Ambassador Of The Americas'. Madriguera compositions include a stage musical *The Moor And The Gipsy*, a ballet *Follies Of Spain*, and many popular songs including 'Adios' and 'The Minute Samba'. When the band business had no more to offer, Mr. and Mrs. Madriguera retired to an old inn and country house in Connecticut where they continued to entertain visitors until his death in 1975.

Maestro Fresh Wes

Until the release of his self-proclaiming 1994 album, Fresh Wes had been one of the Canadian hip hop fraternity's most closely guarded secrets. With production aid from DJ Showbiz (of **Showbiz and AG** fame), the MC's rhymes were delivered in old school New York style, emphasising a punning ability and freestyle approach, which was competent though hardly innovative. The introduction of jazzy overtones too, was not exactly revolutionary by this stage, though the single 'Fine Tune Da Mic' was well-received.
Album: *Nah! Dis Kid Can't Be From Canada* (LMR 1994).

Maestro, Johnny

b. John Mastrangelo, 7 May 1939, Brooklyn, New York, USA. Maestro led two singing groups to the Top 10: the **Crests** in the 50s and **Brooklyn Bridge** in the 60s and 70s. With the Crests, whom he joined in 1956, Maestro's voice was heard on the number 2 doo-wop classic '16 Candles' in 1958, as well as lesser hits 'The Angels Listened In', 'Step By Step' and 'Trouble In Paradise'. (NB: Maestro spelled his stage name Mastro during his tenure with the Crests). Maestro signed as a solo artist to the Coed label, the same for which the Crests recorded, in 1960, while still with the Crests (the group backed him vocally). That year he placed three singles on the charts: the Top 20 'Model Girl', the Top 40 'What A Surprise' and the lesser entry 'My Happiness'. He left the group and the label in 1962 and continued to record singles for Apt Records, **Cameo-Parkway Records**, Sceptre Records and United Artists Records, some with new line-ups of Crests, but none were successful. He was absent from the national scene until 1968, when he combined two groups from Long Island, New York: the Del Satins (who had backed **Dion** on some recordings) and the Rhythm Method, into the Brooklyn Bridge. The 11-piece group immediately logged its biggest hit, 'The Worst That Could Happen', followed by six lesser chart entries, including 'Blessed Is The Rain', 'Welcome My Love' and 'Your Husband-My Wife'. The group's chart run stopped in 1970 but Maestro continued to appear with revamped Brooklyn Bridge line-ups into the 90s.
Album: *The Johnny Maestro Story* (1971).

Maffay, Peter

b. Peter Makkay, 30 August 1949, Kronstadt, Romania. This popular German-based singer arrived in his adopted country in 1963, beginning his apprenticeship by playing folk clubs in Bavaria. It was while undertaking these endeavours that he was spotted by lyricist/composer Michael Kunze in 1969, who became a powerful advocate. Maffay's debut single, 'Du', charted at number 1 in Germany and went gold almost instantaneously. It was accompanied by a debut

solo album, *Feur Das Maedchen, Das Ich Liebe* (For The Girl That I Love), in 1970. The next few years were surprisingly quiet, however, until he teamed up with rock band Sahara in 1974. Three years later he collaborated with Johnny Tame, using English lyrics for the first time in an attempt to broaden his appeal beyond the domestic market. The same year he also formed the Peter Maffay Band with local accomplices. The group's faithful translation of American MOR rock proved immensely popular, with their career receiving a huge upswing when *Steppenwolf* became a major seller. The band continued to sustain this success throughout the 80s, and by 1987 Maffay had also launched an acting career, appearing in the critically acclaimed *The Joker*. By the time he came to renegotiate his contract with BMG Ariola it was to the tune of a guaranteed 11 million Deutschmarks (approximately £4 million) over five years. By the advent of the 90s the artist had a prolific track record of European sales which amounted to over 30 million units, nearly 20 platinum records and a clutch of major industry awards.
Albums: *Feur Das Maedchen, Das Ich Liebe* (1970), *Samstag Abend In Unserer Strasse* (1974), *Meine Freiheit* (1975), *Tame & Maffay* (1977), *Steppenwolf* (1979), *Ich Will Leben* (1982), *Tabaluga* (1983), *Sonn In Der Nacht* (1985), *Lange Schatten* (1988), *Kein Weg Zu Weit* (1989), *38317 - Liebe* (1991), *Freunde & Propheten* (1992).

Mafia And Fluxy

Initially inspired by **Sly And Robbie**, brothers Mafia (b. Leroy Heywood, 1962, London, England; bass) and Fluxy (b. David Heywood, 1963, London, England; drums) are the UK's foremost rhythm section, and are becoming increasingly well-known for their own productions. Early encouragement came via Uncle Wizard's **sound system** and then Fatman, who released their debut, 'Let's Make Love', after they had formed Tottenham, London, band the Instigators in 1977. By 1985 they had earned several hits and gained valuable experience backing touring Jamaican acts, quickly coming to terms with the new digital technology. In 1987 they visited Jamaica, building rhythm tracks for **Bunny Lee**, Blacker Dread, **King Jammys** and **Exterminator**. That year they started their own self-titled label, producing Cinderella, Billy Melody, **Sugar Minott** and later Private Collection ('Dreamer'). Their debut album *Dancehall Connection Vol. 1* featured such diverse talents as General Trees, **King Kong** and **General Levy** when released in 1990. That year Mafia And Fluxy returned to Jamaica, providing many notable hits for Penthouse, Black Scorpio, King Jammys, **Gussie Clarke**, Mikey Bennett, Mr Doo and Roy Francis. In the UK they backed **Maxi Priest** and Lloyd Brown while being voted Producers Of The Year, the Instigators winning the Best Reggae Band Award. On their own label tracks by **Tiger** ('Winery'), **Gregory Isaacs**, **Johnny Osbourne**, Sugar Black, **Cornell Campbell**, **Sanchez** ('Whip Appeal') and Sugar Minott were released at regular intervals. In 1992 Mafia issued his debut album, *Finders Keepers*, while hits by **Cobra** ('Off Guard'), **Dirtsman**, Poison Chang ('Do Me A Favour'), Sweetie Irie, **Red Dragon**, **Cutty Ranks** ('Armed And Dangerous'), Tenor Fly and **Chaka Demus And Pliers** ('Wining Machine') witnessed no shortage of success throughout 1992/3. Back in Jamaica Mafia And Fluxy laid further tracks for **Bobby Digital**, **Penthouse** and Stone Love, with whom they won a Jamaican award for 'Best Juggling (mixing) Record'. By 1994 they were remixing the likes of **Boy George**, **Barrington Levy** and the Rhythm Kings, Mega Banton's 'First Position' was a number 1 hit and they had become one of the most in-demand rhythm sections in reggae music, even occasionally pairing with Sly (Mafia) and Steely (Fluxy).
Selected albums: Various: *Danchall Collection Vol. 1* (Mafia & Fluxy 1990). Mafia solo: *Finders Keepers* (Mafia & Fluxy 1992). Mafia And Fluxy: *Revival Hits Vol. 1* (Mafia & Fluxy 1992).

Magazine

The **Buzzcocks** vocalist **Howard Devoto** left that group in January 1977, although he continued to be involved on the fringe of their activities for some time. In April he met guitarist John McGeogh and together they started writing songs. They formed Magazine with Devoto on vocals, McGeogh on guitar, **Barry Adamson** on bass, Bob Dickinson on keyboards and Martin Jackson on drums. The group played their debut live gig at the closing night of the Electric Circus, Manchester, in the autumn of 1977 as a last-minute addition to the bill. Their moody, cold keyboards and harsh rhythms were in sharp contrast to the mood of the day: 'Everybody was playing everything ultra fast, as fast as they could. I thought we could begin to play slow music again.' They were signed to **Virgin Records** but Dickinson left in November and, as a result, their debut, 'Shot By Both Sides', was recorded by the four remaining members. Dave Formula was recruited in time to play on *Real Life*. Next to leave was Jackson who departed after their first tour. Paul Spencer came in temporarily before John Doyle was recruited in October 1978. This line-up remained for the next couple of years, although McGeogh was also playing with **Siouxsie And The Banshees**, and, along with Adamson and Formula, in Steve Strange's **Visage**. Their albums received universal acclaim but only their first single and 1980's 'Sweetheart Contract' dented the charts. As the latter was released McGeogh left to join Siouxsie full-time and Robin Simon (ex-Neo and **Ultravox**) was brought in on guitar. A tour of the USA and Australia - where a live album was recorded - led to Simon's departure and Ben Mandelson (ex-

Amazorblades) came in for the band's last few months. The departure of Devoto in May 1981 signalled the unit's death knell. The body of work they left behind, however, is surprisingly enduring given its angular and experimental slant. Devoto went on to a solo career before forming **Luxuria**.

Albums: *Real Life* (Virgin 1978), *Secondhand Daylight* (Virgin 1979), *The Correct Use Of Soap* (Virgin 1980), *Play* (Virgin 1980), *Magic, Murder And The Weather* (Virgin 1981). Compilations: *After The Fact* (Virgin 1982), *Rays & Hail 1978-81* (Virgin 1987), *Scree: Rarities 1978-1981* (Virgin 1990), *BBC Radio 1 Live In Concert* (Windsong 1993).

Magellan

Formed in Vacaville, California, USA, in the mid-80s, Magellan was originally a project put together by brothers Wayne (electric and acoustic guitar) and Trent (lead vocals/keyboards) Gardner. Together with Hal Stringfellow Imbrie (bass/vocals) they set out to reinstate the progressive rock tradition of the 70s which married riffs to jazz and classical flourishes. This combination was finely executed on their 1991 debut, *Hour Of Restoration*, which added modern, computer-generated possibilities to the equation. August 1993 saw the release of its follow-up, *Impending Ascension*, which earned comparisons to **Dream Theater**'s crafted electro-rock. Opponents of grandiose musical statements were rewarded with much to scoff at, including quotes drawn from Shakespeare, Poe and Magellan, the historical explorer from whom the group took their name. The subject matter, however, was far from trite mysticism, and included topics like virtual reality and social alienation.

Albums: *Hour Of Restoration* (Magna Carta/Roadrunner 1991), *Impending Ascension* (Magna Carta/Roadrunner 1993).

Maggie May

Lionel Bart, who liked to have a hand in most aspects of his shows, concentrated on writing just the music and lyrics for this one which opened at the Adelphi Theatre in London on 22 September 1964. His librettist was the Liverpudlian playwright Alun Owen, an appropriate choice considering that the story was set in and around the Liverpool Docks. Bart's project was inspired by the traditional ballad about a local prostitute, which was sung by the sailors and dockworkers in the area. In Owen's dramatic book dealing with trades union ethics and disputes, the streetwalker, Margaret Mary Duffy (Rachel Roberts), loses her childhood sweetheart, Patrick Casey (Kenneth Haigh), after he dies trying to prevent a shipload of arms going to South America. As in previous shows such as ***Fings Ain't Wot They Used T'Be***, ***Blitz!***, and ***Oliver!***, Bart's score caught the mood and the style of the piece perfectly. The songs ranged from attractive ballads such as 'It's Yourself', 'The Land Of Promises', 'Lullaby', 'I Love A Man', and 'The Ballad Of The Liver Bird', to the more lively 'I Told You So', 'Dey Don't Do Dat T'day', 'Leave Her, Johnny, Leave Her', 'Shine, You Swine', 'We Don't All Wear D'Same Size Boots', 'Maggie, Maggie May', and 'It's Yourself'. The critics were divided, but the public took to the show, partly perhaps because anything to do with Liverpool was of interest while the **Beatles**, and several other local groups, were constantly storming the pop charts. *Maggie May* had a highly respectable run of 501 performances, and also introduced a future star to the West End in the shape of **Julia McKenzie** who took over from Rachel Roberts occasionally. Part of Bart's score reached a wider audience when **Judy Garland** recorded four of the songs from the show, 'Maggie May', 'There's Only One Union', 'Land Of Promise', and 'It's Yourself', on an EP record. In 1992, nearly 30 years later, the National Youth Theatre of Great Britain mounted an acclaimed production of *Maggie May* at London's Royalty Theatre. It was a welcome feature of Lionel Bart's UK renaissance.

Magic Christian, The

During his period in the **Beatles**, **Ringo Starr** had emerged as the quartet's most natural actor. In his first sideline project, he appeared as a gardener in *Candy* (1968), which was written by Terry Southern. *The Magic Christian* was based on a novel by the same US author, who penned the ensuing screenplay with Peter Sellers, star of the film. The latter plays an eccentric millionaire, determined to spend his fortune by compromising the greed of others. Starr relishes his role as the adopted, savant son who helps oversee a variety of loosely satirical 'happenings'. These reach a climax when an assembly wades through a mixture of blood and ordure in order to gain their fortune. A galaxy of co-stars, including Richard Attenborough, Lawrence Harvey, Yul Brinner and Roman Polanski, were cast alongside a host of British actors, notably Spike Milligan, John Cleese, Graham Chapman, John Le Mesurier and Dennis Price. The result is an entertaining period-piece, released in 1970, but fired by the charm and excess of the decade which had passed. The Beatles' connection was furthered by a soundtrack which featured **Apple** label protégés, **Badfinger**. 'Come And Get It', written for the quartet by **Paul McCartney**, reached number 4 in the UK singles chart, and the album also includes 'Something In The Air' a chart-topper in 1969 for **Thunderclap Newman**.

Magic Lanterns

Formed in the UK and based in the Manchester area, this soft rock band were formed from the Sabres who were in existence around 1962. At one point the Sabres also included Kevin Godley and Lol Creme, later of

10cc and **Godley And Creme**. After the temporary title of the Hammers, they became the Magic Lanterns. Their founding members were Jimmy Bilsbury (vocals), Peter Shoesmith (guitar), Ian Moncur (bass) and Allan Wilson (drums). While working in a local nightclub they were approached by compere Roy Hastings who liked Bilsbury's songs and introduced them to his publisher, Mike Collier. Collier got them to record a new version of **Artie Wayne**'s US release 'Excuse Me Baby' on the strength of which **CBS** signed them and released 'Excuse Me Baby' as a single in June 1966. It was a minor hit and was followed by such misses as 'Knight In Rusty Armour', 'Rumplestiltskin', and 'Auntie Griselda', by which time they were sounding increasingly psychedelic. In 1969, Collier switched their management to American Ronnie Oppenheimer who got Steve Rowland (**Family Dogg**) and **Albert Hammond** involved. They co-wrote 'Shame Shame' which became the band's first US hit. Moncur left in 1969 and sometime later Shoesmith and Wilson followed suit. The band struggled on for a few more months, but split while in Hamburg. The final line-up was Bilsbury, Alistair Beveridge (guitar), Paul Garner (guitar), Mike Osbourne (bass) and Paul Ward (drums). Bilsbury joined the Les Humphries Singers who were popular on the continent and had several singles released in the UK in the 70s. **Boney M**'s Liz Mitchell was a founding member, along with Humphreys.
Album: *Lit Up With The Magic Lanterns* (1968).

Magic Muscle

Formed in the west country of England in 1969, Magic Muscle mixed classical nuances with **Blue Cheer** noise levels, thus creating a musical paradox enhanced by the band's peculiar abilities. With so many musicians passing through over the years, Magic Muscle were more of a community than a band, but at the centre of all activities was guitarist and vocalist Rod Goodway (ex-**Artwoods**, White Rabbit, J.P. Sunshine, **Rustic Hinge**), Adrian Shaw (later **Hawkwind**) on bass and drummer Kenny Wheeler. Working with Drachen Theaker (**Crazy World Of Arthur Brown**) and members of **High Tide** they began to gig and record, coming to the attention of disc jockey **John Peel**, who nearly signed them to his **Dandelion** label. By 1972 they had built a strong cult following and earned themselves the nickname 'Bastard Sons Of Hawkwind' when they joined the latter on their *Space Ritual* tour (tracks from which are present on *Laughs & Thrills*). They also started a partnership with **Keith Christmas**. This brought them to the attention of **Island Records** - though proprietor **Chris Blackwell** eventually chose to promote Jamaican music at this stage instead, signing **Bob Marley**. In 1973 Magic Muscle gigged with the **Pink Fairies** and for a while were joined by John Perry (**Only Ones**) and violinist Simon House (High Tide/**Third Ear Band**/Hawkwind/**David Bowie**). By the end of the year Goodway was ill in hospital and ended the band. It was 1987 before the name returned, thanks to the surge in interest in the recording activities of many ex-members connected with Hawkwind. After the relative success of *Laughs & Thrills* Goodway undertook the compilation of an album released in 1988 which featured 1970-1973 recordings. A year later he reformed the band with Gower/Shaw/House and drummer **Twink** (Pink Fairies/**Pretty Things/Tomorrow**). Their debut concert was held in Bath on 1 August and was recorded and released as *One Hundred Miles Below*. Dave Brock of Hawkwind played keyboards at the gig but his contribution did not appear on the finished album. Riding high on their new found fame Goodway released a second compilation set, *Living Weeds From Ancient Seeds*, some of the tracks therein featuring members of Elias Hulk and **Dr. John**'s band. In 1991 he returned with a new line-up which featured Steve Broughton on drums (**Edgar Broughton Band**) and guitarist Nick Saloman (aka **Bevis Frond**). By 1994 Goodway had returned to other pursuits while the rest of the band effectively became the new line-up for the Bevis Frond.
Albums: *Laughs And Thrills* (Acid 1987), *One Hundred Miles Below* (1 Big Guitar 1989), *Gulp!* (Woronzow 1990). Compilations: *The Pipe, The Roar, The Grid* (5 Hours Back 1988), *Living Weeds From Ancient Seeds* (Pilgrim 1990).

Magic Sam

b. Samuel Maghett, 14 February 1937, Grenada, Mississippi, USA, d. 1 December 1969. Although Sam's immediate family were not musical, he received encouragement from his uncle, 'Shakey Jake' Harris, a popular blues singer on Chicago's west side. Maghett arrived in the city in 1950 and by the age of 20 had secured a recording deal with Cobra Records, an emergent independent label. His debut single, 'All Your Love', a compulsive, assured performance which highlighted Sam's crisp guitar figures, set the pattern for several subsequent releases, but progress faltered upon his induction into the army in 1959. Not a natural soldier, Sam deserted after a couple of weeks' service and was subsequently caught and sentenced to six months' imprisonment. He was given a dishonourable discharge on release, but the experience had undermined Sam's confidence and his immediate recordings lacked the purpose of their predecessors. However, his debut album, *West Side Soul*, encapsulated an era when Maghett not only re-established his reputation in Chicago clubs, but had become an attraction on the rock circuit with appearances at the Fillmore and Winterland venues in San Francisco. This vibrant record included 'Sweet Home Chicago', later revived by the **Blues Brothers**. A second collection, *Black Magic*, confirmed his new-found status but its

release was overshadowed by Sam's premature death from a heart attack in December 1969. Only days before, Maghett had agreed to sign with the renowned **Stax** label. His passing robbed the blues genre of a potentially influential figure.
Albums: *West Side Soul* (1968), *Black Magic* (1969). Compilations: *Sweet Home Chicago* (1968), *Magic Sam (1937-1969)* (1969), *Magic Sam Live* (1981, live recordings from 1964), with Earl Hooker *Calling All Blues* (1986), *The Magic Sam Legacy* (1989), *Give Me Time* (1992), *West Side Soul* (1992).

Magic Show, The

Proof of the unpredictablity of musical theatre audiences, this show, which was merely a series of spectacular set-piece magical illusions linked by a flimsy plot, opened at the Cort Theatre in New York on 28 May 1974, and closed over four-and-a-half years later after an incredible 1,920 performances. **Stephen Schwartz**, who can usually be relied upon to conjure up something out of the ordinary himself, wrote the music and lyrics, and the book was the work of Bob Randall. The latter dealt with the sad tale of a New Jersey nightspot, The Passaic Top Hat, which is saved from debt and the road to the depths of degradation, by the arrival of a magic act. Doug Henning was the wizard who made everything well, and he really was the star of the show, with a supporting cast made up of Dale Soules, David Ogden Stiers, and Anita Morris. The songs included 'Up To His Old Tricks', 'Lion Tamer', 'Style', 'West End Avenue', and 'The Goldfarb Variations'. 'Goldfarb' is a familiar name in musical comedy history. **George** and **Ira Gershwin** immortalised the taxi driver-turned sheriff in ***Girl Crazy*** (1930), with their song, 'Goldfarb! That's I'm!'

Magic Slim

b. Morris Holt, 7 August 1937, Torrence, Mississippi, USA. Blues guitarist/vocalist Magic Slim became interested in music during childhood. He moved first to nearby Grenada, Mississippi, and then to Chicago in 1955, where he worked as bassist for **Magic Sam**, who gave Holt his name. He obtained a false identity card so that he was able to play bass with Sam in the bars and clubs. After completing that stay, he switched back to guitar and performed with a Chicago band called Mr. Pitiful And The Teardrops. When that band split up, he moved back to Mississippi, before returning to Chicago once again in 1965, where he reformed the Teardrops with his two brothers (Nick, the bassist, became a permanent member). The band recorded its first single for the local Wes label in 1966, and another for the equally small Mean Mistreater label in 1970. It was not until 1978 that Magic Slim And The Teardrops began recording in earnest, contributing four tracks to an Alligator Records anthology. That was followed by a live album for the small Candy Apple label as well as recordings made in France, which were released in the USA on Alligator as *Raw Magic* in 1982. That same year he recorded the highly-praised *Grand Slam* for Rooster Blues Records. A live album recorded in Austria, *Chicago Blues Session*, followed in 1987. *Gravel Road*, released on the small Blind Pig label in the USA, was issued in 1990. His sound is perhaps the tightest of any Chicago blues band working at the present time. This consistently satisfying blues musician recorded singles for numerous labels and, since 1976, he recorded an album for the collector market.
Albums: *Live 'N Blue* (1980), *Raw Magic* (1982), *Grand Slam* (1982), *Chicago Blues Session Volume Three* (1986), *Highway Is My Home* (1978 recordings), *Son Of A Gun* (1988), *Gravel Road* (1990).

Magicians

Formed in New York in 1964, the Magicians comprised Allan Jacobs (lead guitar), Gary Bonner (rhythm guitar), John Townley (bass) and Alan Gordon (drums). They were briefly the houseband at the famed Night Owl Cafe, but despite becoming the subject of a WCBS-television documentary, *Four To Go!* (1966), the quartet was unable to achieve a commercial breakthrough. They completed four folk-rock/pop singles, including 'An Invitation To Cry' (1965) and 'I'd Like To Know' (1966). The latter was penned by **David Blue**. The group disbanded following the release of 'Double Good Feeling'. **Bonner And Gordon** subsequently forged a successful songwriting team whose several hits included 'Happy Together' and 'She'd Rather Be With Me' for the **Turtles**.

Magidson, Herb

b. 7 January 1906, Braddock, Pennsylvania, USA, d. 5 January 1986, Beverly Hills, California, USA. A leading composer and lyricist in the 30s and 40s, particularly remembered for 'The Continental', which he wrote Con Conrad for the **Fred Astaire-Ginger Rogers** picture ***The Gay Divorcée***. It became the first winner of the 'Best Song' Academy Award in 1934. The team also wrote another good song for Astaire to sing in the film - 'Needle In A Haystack'. Magidson studied journalism at the University of Pittsburg before moving to New York and writing special material for **Sophie Tucker**. In the late 20s and early 30s he contributed a few numbers to Broadway shows such as ***Earl Carroll's Vanities*** *Of 1928* and ***George White****'s Musical Hall Varieties*, but the majority of his output was for movies. Through to 1939 he wrote single songs or complete scores for *The Time, The Place And The Girl* (1929), *Show Of Shows*, ***Little Johnny Jones***, ***No, No, Nanette***, *I Like It That Way*, *The Gift Of Gab*, *George White's 1935 Scandals*, *Here's To Romance*, ***The Great Ziegfeld***, *Hats Off*, *Music For Madame*, *Life Of The Party*, *Radio City Revels*, and *George White's Scandals Of 1939*. From these films came songs such as 'The

Racoon', 'Somebody To Love', 'Dance Of The Wooden Shoes', 'Singin' In The Bathtub', 'Talkin' To Myself', 'Oh, I Didn't Know', 'According To The Moonlight', 'Here's To Romance', 'Midnight In Paris', 'Twinkle, Twinkle, Little Star' (not the nursery rhyme), 'Where Have You Been All My Life?', 'Let's Have Another Cigarette', 'Roses In December', 'Goodnight Angel', 'When The Cat's Away', and 'Something I Dreamed Last Night'. In the 40s, two of Magidson's wartime songs, 'Say A Prayer For The Boys Over There' (written with **Jimmy McHugh** for *Hers To Hold*) and 'I'll Buy That Dream' (with **Allie Wrubel** for *Sing Your Way Home*) were nominated for Oscars, and he also had numbers in *Sleepy Time Gal*, *Music In Manhatten*, *Do You Love Me?*, and *Make Mine Laughs*, amongst others. Throughout his career Magidson did not neglect Tin Pan Alley, and several of his best songs, unassociated with either films or shows, have been sung and played by the finest vocalists and bands. Among them are 'Gone With The Wind', 'Music, Maestro Please', '(I'm Afraid) The Masquerade Is Over', 'How Long Has This Been Going On?', 'I Can't Love You Anymore', 'A Pink Cocktail For A Blue Lady', 'I'm Stepping Out With A Memory Tonight', 'I'll Dance At Your Wedding', 'Enjoy Yourself (It's Later Than You Think)', and one of his earliest successes, 'Black-Eyed Susan Brown'. Besides the ones already mention, his many collaborators included Carl Sigman, Michael Cleary, **Sammy Fain**, Ben Oakland, **Sam Stept**, and **Jule Styne**. Like so many of the Old Guard, he seems to have been a casualty of rock 'n' roll, and there is no apparent record of him composing songs after the early 50s.

Magma

This challenging Parisian combo was assembled in the late 60s by classically-trained drummer Christian Vander to perform a lengthy oratorio expressing laudable anxiety about the future of our abused planet. Much of its libretto was in the language of Kobaia, Earth's imaginary rival world. The first fifth of the work filled Magma's first two albums, but by 1973's overblown *Mekanik Destrucktiw Kommandoh* (for which a choir was hired) the idea was wearing thin. The group's line-up included Vander's singing wife Stella and Klaus Blasquiz, whose *bel canto* baritone became Magma's most identifiable idiosyncrasy. Apart from Vander, the most representative instrumental line-up during the band's 10-year history was Gabriel Federow (guitar), **Didier Lockwood** (violin), Jean-Paul Asseline (keyboards), Benoit Widemann (keyboards) and Bernard Paganotti (bass). After transferring from **A&M Records** to Utopia in the summer of 1975, **Giorgio Gomelsky**, the new label's supremo, was often heard smiting percussion on subsequent discs, such as an in-concert offering from the French capital's Taverne de l'Olympia.

Rather than individual pieces, it was the sound of Magma's records that mattered. Among the most apparent of stylistic reference points were the **John Coltrane/Ornette Coleman** end of jazz and the stubbornly chromatic tonalities of Stravinsky, Bartok and Stockhausen - hardly the stuff of hit singles. Musical and lyrical themes and leitmotivs connected each album *à la* **Mothers Of Invention** - even if Magma's humour was radically different from that of the US act. Continued repackaging of the band's output has enhanced their reputation.

Albums: *Magma* (1970), *1001 Centigrade* (1971), *Mekanik Destructiw Kommandoh* (1973), *Kohntarkosz* (1974), *Live* (1975), *Udu Wudu* (1976), *Edits* (1977). Compilations include *Retrospective* (1979).

Magna Carta

Magna Carta were renowned for their gentle ballad style and, often, mythical subject matter. Although they were never purely a folk group, they successfully bridged the gap between folk and folk-rock. They originally formed as a duo, in London, in 1969, with Chris Simpson (b. 13 July 1942, Harrogate, North Yorkshire, England; guitar/vocals), and Lyell Tranter (guitar/vocals). They obtained a deal with **Fontana**, and then Glen Stuart (vocals) joined them. In August 1970, *Seasons* made 55 in the UK album charts. *Times Of Change* was released on Fontana, and the highly regarded *Seasons* appeared on the Vertigo label. Tranter then returned to Australia. The group played the Royal Albert Hall in 1971, with the Royal Philharmonic Orchestra, but the tapes of the recording were lost by Phonogram. Texts from *Seasons* and *Lord Of The Ages*, have been used as part of the English syllabus in several European countries. Davy Johnstone (guitar/vocals) then joined the line-up, recording, *In Concert* and *Songs From Wasties Orchard*, with them before leaving to work with **Elton John** and **Kiki Dee**. The latter album was regarded by many as the group's finest work. Simpson and Stuart were then joined by Stan Gordon (guitar), recording and releasing the much-lauded *Lord Of The Ages*. Graham Smith (bass), who had been on the sessions for this album, then joined the group. Shortly afterwards both he and Stan Gordon left, so by 1974, it was back to square one as a duo. There followed a period of much change and upheaval, as, in following more of a rock path, they added Mohammed Amin (bass), and a drummer, but Glen Stuart did not feel comfortable with the new direction. This short-lived set-up soon gave way to Simpson and Stuart being joined by Tom Hoy (b. 5 February 1950, Glasgow, Scotland; guitar/vocals). Stuart then left to run a pet shop in Richmond, Surrey.

In 1977, former Natural Acoustic Band member Robin Thyne (b. 1 November 1950, Newcastle Upon Tyne, England; guitar/vocals), joined the group, along with Lee Abbott (b. 21 January 1950, Gravesend, Kent,

England; fretless bass/vocals). Soon afterwards, Pick Withers (drums) was added. Withers stayed only briefly, leaving to join **Dire Straits**. There followed upheavals in 1979, when Thyne and Hoy left to form Nova Carta. There had been much acrimony leading to the split. **Tom McConville** appeared on the *Live In Bergen* release, before the line-up changed again to include Al Fenn (b. Alastair Fenn, 9 March 1947, Chingford, Essex, England; guitar/vocals), and George Norris (b. 30 December 1945, Cowes, Isle Of Wight, England; guitar/vocals). Between 1980 and 1982, Doug Morter (electric and acoustic guitar) was added, together with a variety of drummers, one of whom was Paul Burgess (b. 28 September 1950, Stockport, Cheshire, England), who had formerly been with **10cc**. The 1981 release, *Midnight Blue*, contained 'Highway To Spain', a track consistently on radio station playlists around the world. Subsequently, despite much touring and recording, Simpson pursued a solo career, while Norris and Burgess both left.

Eventually, Morter left to join the **Albion Band**. Simpson's solo release, *Listen To The Man* came out with Magna Carta now including, in addition to Simpson and Abbott, Linda Taylor (b. 28 June 1953, Halifax, West Yorkshire, England; guitar/vocals), and Willie Jackson (b. 18 February 1954, York, England; guitars). Between 1984 and 1986, Chris and Linda went to the Middle East, running a music club, eventually deciding to return home and re-form Magna Carta. In 1986, the extremely fluid line-up now included, in addition to Simpson, Taylor and Abbott, Glyn Jones (keyboards), John Carey (fiddle), Paul Burgess, again, (drums), and Simon Carlton (lead guitar). In 1987, *One To One* was finished, for the Tembo record label. The same year, Jones left the group, and the band played the Cambridge Festival, and the album was released in 1988. In 1990, Simpson and Taylor married, and with the semi-retirement of Lee Abbott, they continued as a duo touring worldwide. Phonogram then released the compilation *Old Masters/New Horizons*, in Europe only. *Heartlands* followed soon after, released in Holland in 1992, followed by a sell-out tour of Holland, with Will Jackson (keyboards/guitars) and Paul Burgess (drums) returning, together with Jonathan Barrett (b. 16 August 1962, Leeds, West Yorkshire, England; bass). Will's brother Eddie Jackson (b. 23 April 1957, York, England; bass), played on the *Heartlands* album, and on their January 1992 tour. In January 1994, Mike Bedford took over on drums from Burgess. Chris and Linda still work as a duo, as well as with the larger line-up for extensive touring. Over the years, the group has toured over 151 countries.

Albums: *Magna Carta* (Mercury 1969), *Times Of Change* (Fontana 1969), *Seasons* (Vertigo 1970), *Songs From Wasties Orchard* (Vertigo 1971), *Magna Carta In Concert* (Vertigo 1972), *Lord Of The Ages* (Vertigo 1974), *Martin's Cafe* (Vertigo 1974), *Putting It Back Together* (Polydor 1975), *Prisoner's On The Line* (Phillips 1978), *Live In Bergen* (Fontana 1978), *Midnight Blue* (1981), *Sweet Deceiver* (1981), *No Truth In The Rumour* (Ariola 1979), *One To One* (1988), *Heartlands* (Sound Products Holland 1992), *State Of The Art - Magna Carta Live* (D&K 1993). Compilations: *Greatest Hits 1* (1975), *Greatest Hits 2* (1977), *Spotlight On Magna Carta* (Phillips 1977), *Old Masters/New Horizons* (1992). Solo: Chris Simpson *Listen To The Man* (1983).

Magnapop

Based in Watkinsville, Athens, Georgia, USA, Magnapop's personnel is composed of Ruthie Morris (b. Florida, USA; guitar), Shannon Mulvaney (bass), David McNair (drums) and Linda Hopper (vocals). Linda had originally met Michael Stipe (**R.E.M.**) at art college in the early 80s, where he persuaded her to form a band with his sister (also called Linda), who were titled Oh OK. They lasted three years and briefly included McNair on drums. Mutual friends introduced her to Morris in Atlanta, and they started to write songs together in 1988, with their first demos produced by Stipe. Their debut single, 'Merry', was followed by the *Kiss My Mouth* EP, which found instant success in Holland and Belgium, their popularity demanding the release of a premature mini-album, essentially of demo tracks, in that area. This celebrity was based in part on an appearance at a Rotterdam festival, where **Bob Mould**, **Nirvana** and **Frank Black** were all playing. Magnapop created such a buzz that the promotor shifted them from a smaller platform to the main stage the following night, and Mould took an interest in the group, agreeing to produce their debut album proper. Mould proved not to be Magnapop's only star fan. **Juliana Hatfield** spoke highly of them whenever the opportunity arose, and even wrote a song, 'Ruthless', about their guitarist Ruthie Morris ('We're all suckers for a girl who really plays guitar/We're all pining for Ruthie/We all wish we were Ruthie/We're all dying for Ruthie').

Album: *Hot Boxing* (Play It Again Sam 1994).

Magnetic North

ThisUK techno record label run by Dave Clarke is and distinguished by releases by Woody MC Bride ('Rattlesnake'), who also works under the title DJ ESP. The label's first two releases were from the acid-fixated Directional Force and Graphite ('Pure'), in 1993. By 1994 the roster included material by **DJ Hell** and Christian Vogel.

Magnificents

An R&B vocal group formed in 1953 from Chicago, Illinois, USA. The Magnificents in their uptempo songs brought rock 'n' roll to their doo-wop and in their ballads stayed true to their R&B roots. Members were Johnny Keyes, Thurman 'Ray' Ramsey, Fred

Rakestraw, and Willie Myles. Singing as the Tams, they were discovered by disc jockey Magnificent Montague, who gave them their name and became their manager. Their one hit, 'Up On The Mountain' (number 9 R&B) in 1956 has come to be remembered as a goldie oldie, but also outstanding was their great ballad b-side, 'Why Did She Go', lead by Ramsey. But then Ramsey left to be replaced by L.C. Cooke (brother of **Sam Cooke**), and Barbara Arrington was added to the group as lead, the successful sound of the group was lost on the next record, 'Caddy Bo'. The third single 'Off The Mountain', deserved to restore the group to prominence, but that was not to be. Keyes and rest of the group broke from Montague, who then formed a new Magnificents, whose individuals identity remains unknown. Their 'Don't Leave Me' is one of the most beloved of the doo-wop oldies that never was a hit.
Compilation: *Magnificents & Rhythm Aces: 15 Cool Jewels* (Solid Smoke 1984).

Magnum

The Birmingham, England-based pomp rockers were formed in 1972 by Tony Clarkin (guitar), Bob Catley (vocals), Kex Gorin (drums) and Dave Morgan (bass). They remained unsigned, undertaking various engagements including acting as **Del Shannon**'s backing band, until 1978, when they were picked up by **Jet** Records. By this time Morgan had departed, to be replaced by Colin 'Wally' Lowe, and Richard Baily had joined as keyboard player. Between 1978 and 1980, Magnum released three albums to a moderate degree of success, and toured relentlessly with **Judas Priest**, **Blue Öyster Cult**, and **Def Leppard**. *Chase The Dragon* was released in 1982, with new keyboard player Mark Stanway, and gave them their first Top 20 album; it featured the grandiose pomp of 'Sacred Hour' and 'The Spirit', both of which still appear in their current live set. Following the release of *Eleventh Hour* problems beset the band: Clarkin became ill, and a dispute with Jet Records ensued. These combined to cause the band to fragment. The troubles were soon resolved, and a number of low-key club dates persuaded them to continue. FM Revolver Records signed the band in 1985 for *On A StoryTeller's Night.* Its Top 40 success, along with a highly successful tour of the UK, prompted **Polydor** Records to offer a long-term contract. *Vigilante*, which featured new drummer Mickey Barker, was the first release under a new deal, and was produced by **Queen**'s **Roger Taylor**. The backing of a major label paid immediate dividends with a Top 30 album and a sold-out UK tour. This success was taken one step further with *Wings Of Heaven* (1988), their first gold album and UK Top 10 hit. Top 40 single success came with 'Days Of No Trust', 'Start Talkin' Love', and 'It Must Have Been Love'. Numerous compilation albums, including *Mirador* and *Anthology*, were released, along with re-issues of their now extensive back-catalogue from Jet Records. A two-year gap between official releases resulted in the Keith Olsen-produced *Goodnight L.A.* and again Top 40 success was achieved with a single, 'Rocking Chair', the album also enjoying Top 10 status. Extensive touring promoted *Goodnight L.A.* and several shows were recorded for a double live set, *The Spirit.* After years of struggle and setbacks, Magnum's popularity has been achieved the hard way, by dint of constant touring and a series of quality albums.
Albums: *Kingdom Of Madness* (Jet 1978), *Magnum II* (Jet 1979), *Marauder* (Jet 1980), *Chase The Dragon* (Jet 1982), *The Eleventh Hour* (Jet 1983), *On A StoryTeller's Night* (Polydor 1985), *Vigilante* (Polydor 1986), *Wings Of Heaven* (Polydor 1988), *Goodnight L.A.* (Polydor 1990), *Invasion - Magnum Live* (Receiver 1990), *The Spirit* (Polydor 1991, double album), *Sleepwalking* (Polydor 1992), *Rock Art* (EMI 1994). Compilations: *Anthology* (Raw Power 1986), *Collection* (Castle 1990), *Box Set* (Castle 1992), *Chapter And Verse - Best Of* (Polydor 1993), *Uncorked* (Jet 1994).
Videos: *The Sacred Hour Live* (1986), *On The Wings Of Heaven* (1988), *From Midnight To LA* (1990).

Maguire, Alex

b. 6 January 1959, Croydon, Surrey, England. Maguire remembers improvising at the piano before he received any lessons, which began at the age of eight. He studied music at the University of London and gained a BA degree; he also took lessons from Wanda Jeziorska, Andrew Ball and **Howard Riley**. He names as his inspiration a number of respected figures in the free improvising scene, such as **Tony Oxley** and **Evan Parker,** as well as jazz players **Cecil Taylor** and **Eric Dolphy**. McGuire says he is interested in 'pre-literate music, anything original rather than imitative (irrespective of idiom)'. He has studied with classical composers John Cage and Michael Finnissy and his arsenal of techniques and figures, which stretch from *avant garde* classical piano to jazz, from kwela to R&B, has made him much in demand. His sympathy as an accompanist is only matched by his imagination, perverse and frequently humorous. He formed a partnership with drummer **Steve Noble** and played with him at Company Week 1989. He is also a member of Tony Oxley's Celebration Orchestra and plays with Sean Bergin's MOB groups. In 1989, he toured with his own nine-piece, the Cat O' Nine Tails, which featured drummer **Louis Moholo** and saxophonist **Alan Wilkinson**.
Albums: with Steve Noble *Live At Oscars* (1987), with Cat O'Nine Tails *Hoki Poki* (1990), with Luc Houtcomp, Willie Kellers *HKM* (1990).

Mahavishnu Orchestra

Led by guitarist **John McLaughlin**, (b. 4 January 1942, Yorkshire, England), between 1972 and 1976 the Mahavishnu Orchestra played a leading part in the creation of jazz/rock fusion music. Mahavishnu was the name given to McLaughlin by his Hindu guru Snr i Chimnoy, and the group's early work showed the influence of Indian ragas. The first line-up included several musicians who had played on McLaughlin's previous solo album, *Inner Mounting Flame.* The high-energy electric music created by keyboardist **Jan Hammer**, ex-**Flock** violinist Jerry Goodman, bassist Rick Laird and drummer **Billy Cobham** made *Birds Of Fire* a Top 20 hit in the USA. After releasing the live *Between Nothingness And Eternity*, whose lengthy 'Dreams' sequence featured spectacular duetting between the guitarist and Cobham, McLaughlin split the group. A year later he re-formed Mahavishnu with an entirely new personnel. **Jean-Luc Ponty** replaced Goodman, Narada Michael Walden took over on drums, with Gayle Moran on keyboards/vocals, and there was also a four-piece string section. This group made *Apocalypse* with producer **George Martin**. In 1975, Ponty left and keyboardist Stu Goldberg played on the final albums. McLaughlin next decided to pursue classical Indian music more rigorously in the acoustic quartet Shakti, but Cobham and Hammer in particular carried on the Mahavishnu approach to jazz/rock in their later work. Moran played with **Chick Corea**'s **Return To Forever** while Walden became a noted soul music producer in the 80s.

Albums: *The Inner Mounting Flame* (1972), *Birds Of Fire* (1973), *Between Nothingness And Eternity* (1973), *Apocalypse* (1974), *Visions Of The Emerald Beyond* (1975), *Inner Worlds* (1976).

Mahlathini, Simon Nkabinde

b. 1950, Natal, South Africa. The most distinguished of the basso-profundo 'groaners' of black South African vocal music - and the acknowledged originator of an mbaqanga sub-style known mgqashiyo ('indestructible beat'), Mahlathini began performing in the late 60s, touring townships in package shows which often featured the **Mahotella Queens**, with whom he occasionally recorded, and using the legendary **Makgona Tshole Band** for back-up. A dynamic dancer, Mahlathini would create a frenzy of joyous mayhem in beer halls, the venues for many township concerts in the 60s and 70s, and was on several occasions arrested for 'inciting unrest' (despite the apolitical nature of most of his material). He toured Europe in 1987, in the wake of the international profile achieved by **Paul Simon**'s *Graceland* guest artists **Ladysmith Black Mambazo**, but has yet to match their overseas breakthrough.

Albums: *Guga Mzimba* (1976), with the Mahotella Queens *Mahlamini And The Queens* (1976), *Kudala Besibiza* (1977), with the Mahotella Queens and Makgona Tshole Band *Uhambo Lwami* (1983), *Ejerusalem Siyakhona* (1986), with the Mahotella Queens *The Best Of* (1992).

Mahogany

Released in 1975, *Mahogany* reunited **Diana Ross** and Billy Dee Williams, co-stars of the **Billie Holiday** biopic, ***Lady Sings The Blues***. Tamla/**Motown** founder **Berry Gordy** produced this rather insubstantial vehicle and assumed the role of director when a disaffected Tony Richardson walked out of the project. The wafer-thin plot - Ross rises from department store secretary to top-line model while falling in and out of love - recalled those of the 'classic' Hollywood era, but the film lacked wit and charm while the actors seemed uninspired. However the theme from the film, 'Do You Know Where You're Going To', written by **Gerry Goffin** and Michael Masser, secured an Academy Award as Best Song. It provided Ross with a US chart-topper and an ensuing number 5 hit in the UK, giving commercial boost to a part of her career in temporary abeyance.

Mahogany Rush

Recovering in hospital from a bad drugs experience, **Frank Marino** (b. 22 August 1954, Canada) claimed he was visited by an apparition of **Jimi Hendrix**. After leaving hospital he picked up a guitar for the first time and was able to play Hendrix riffs, or so the legend runs. The group was formed in Montreal during 1970 when Marino recruited bassist Paul Harwood and drummer Jim Ayoub to fulfil his desire to work in a power trio format. Their first three albums were derivative in the extreme; every component of Hendrix's unique style had been dismantled, adapted, then re-built under new song titles. Nevertheless, they were not condemned as copyists, but revered instead for paying tribute to the great man in such an honest and sincere fashion. By 1976 Marino had started to develop his own style, based on an extension of the Hendrix tricks he had already acquired. This is clearly evident on *Mahogany Rush IV* and *World Anthem*, released in 1976 and 1977 respectively. Eventually he outgrew the comparisons as his own style began to dominate the band's material. The name was amended to Frank Marino and Mahogany Rush, then to Frank Marino, following the release of *What's Next* and the departure of Ayoub.

Albums: *Maxoom* (Kotai 1971), *Child Of The Novelty* (20th Century 1974), *Strange Universe* (20th Century 1975), *Mahogany Rush IV* (CBS 1976), *World Anthem* (CBS 1977), *Live* (CBS 1978), *Tales Of The Unexpected* (CBS 1979), *What's Next* (CBS 1980).

Mahotella Queens

South Africa's leading mbaqanga harmony group in the late 60s and throughout the 70s, the Queens' featured groaners (basso profundos) and have at various times included the great **Mahlathini**, Potatoes Mazambane, Mbazo Mkhize and Joseph Mthimkhulu.

On most of the their 70s records, the Queens were backed by Marks Mankwane and his **Makgona Tshole Band**, one of mbaqanga's hardest instrumental outfits. Like Mahlathini, the Queens called their style 'the indestructible beat', a reference to its solid, four-on-the-floor rhythm and the spirit of the oppressed township people who are its prime audience.
Selected albums: *Marks Umthamkithi* (1972), *Phezulu Eqhudeni* (1975), *Best Of The Mahotella Queens* (1978), *Peggy & The Mahotella Queens* (1984), *Putting On The Light* (1993), *Women Of The World* (1993).

Maid Of The Mountains, The

A favourite with amateur operatic societies throughout the world, this show was first presented in London at Daly's Theatre on 10 February 1917. The score was mainly by Harold Fraser-Simpson and James Tate (music) and Harry Graham (lyrics), with additional songs by F. Clifford Harris, James W. Tate, and (Arthur) 'Valentine'. Frederick Lonsdale's book was set in the high mountains of 'brigand land', and concerned the lovely Teresa (José Collins) who is arrested by General Malona (Mark Lester), the Governor of Santo, and is promised her freedom if her lover, the outlaw Baldasarre (Arthur Wontner), is captured. Complications arise when Teresa learns that Baldasarre has eyes for another, and in a fit of pique, she exposes him. Whereupon he is captured, and incarcerated on Devil's Island. All ends well when Teresa engineers his release, and they board a small boat and sail to the mainland - and into the sunset. The enchanting score included memorable songs such as Fraser-Simpson and Graham's 'Love Will Find A Way'and 'Live For Today', along with the engaging 'A Bachelor Gay', 'My Life Is Love', and 'A Paradise For Two' by Tate, Harris, and Valentine. the show was an enormous success and ran for a record 1,352 performances - even longer than the other big London hit of World War I, ***Chu Chin Chow***. It made a star of the fiery José Collins, who had already enjoyed a prosperous Broadway career before she appeared in *The Maid Of The Mountains*, but is always remembered for introducing 'Love Will Find A Way'. Perhaps if she had recreated her role in New York, the 1918 production of *The Maid Of The Mountains* would have stayed at the Casino Theatre more than 37 performances. In the event Collins did appear in the 1921 London revival, the first of several that were produced through until 1942. Thirty years after that, a revised version, with additional songs by Harry Parr-Davies, Harold Purcell, **Rudolph Friml**, and Brian Hooker, and starring Lynne Kennington, Gordon Clyde, Neville Jason, Jimmy Thompson, and Janet Mahoney, was presented at London's Palace Theatre. Compared to contemporary musicals such as ***Jesus Christ Superstar*** it was considered to be out of place and somewhat old-fashioned. The original concept was nicely captured in the 1932 film with Nancy Brown and Harry Welchman.

Maiden, Sidney

b. 1923, Mansfield, Louisiana, USA. A shadowy figure about whom little has been written, Maiden was evidently influenced by **John Lee (Sonny Boy) Williamson** when learning the harmonica. Sometimes in the Forties, he made the journey west to work in the shipyards around Richmond, California. There he met **K.C. Douglas** and the pair began to work clubs in the area. In 1948 he and Douglas recorded for **Bob Geddins**' Down Town, with his 'Eclipse Of The Sun' becoming a notable performance amongst collectors. He next recorded in April 1952 for Imperial, an eight-track session with The Blues Blowers, perhaps including Douglas and Otis Cherry on drums, from which just one single was released. Moving to Los Angeles the following year, he joined up with drummer B. Brown and guitarist Haskell Sadler to inaugurate the Flash label, each man recording one single. 'Hurry Hurry Baby' was an unsteady boogie piece distantly akin to **Jimmy Reed**'s 'You Don't Have To Go'. In 1957, he recorded 'Hand Me Down Baby' for Dig, with guitarist Slim Green. Four years later, he was recruited by **Arhoolie** boss Chris Strachwitz to participate in sessions with Douglas and **Mercy Dee**, during which he also recorded an album leased to Bluesville. During the 60s, he formed his own group and worked the Fresno area, since when his whereabouts and fate are unknown.
Album: *Jericho Alley Blues Flash* (1988).

Main

This UK 90s ambient dance band were formed by Robert Hampson of **Loop**. Taking the repetitive motifs from that band, Main refined the formula to accentuate the aesthetics of post-rave dance 'chill'. They draw heavily on environmental sounds (ie a road at night) on which they dub synths and electronically generated effects as well as guitars. Their first EP, *Hydra*, was dedicated to the German composer Karlheinz Stockhausen. Follow-up EPs included *Dry Stone Feed* and *Firmament*.

Main Ingredient

This New York-based trio, Donald McPherson (b. 9 July 1941, d. 4 July 1971), Luther Simmons Jnr. (b. 9 September 1942) and Tony Sylvester (b. 7 October 1941, Panama) made their recording debut in 1965. One of several groups using the name 'the Poets', they decided to become the Main Ingredient and signed with producer Bert DeCoteaux, whose lush arrangements provided the requisite foil for their excellent harmonies. This skill was particularly apparent on such early releases as 'I'm So Proud' (1970), 'Spinning Around (I Must Be Falling In Love)'

and 'Black Seeds Keep On Growing' (both 1971). McPherson died from leukaemia in 1971 and, ironically, it was his replacement, **Cuba Gooding**, who sang on the group's million-seller 'Everybody Plays The Fool'. Although the Ingredient went on to enjoy further commercial success, their work grew increasingly bland and lacked the purpose of those early releases. Gooding embarked on a solo career with **Motown** in 1977, but reunited with Sylvester and Simmons in 1979, continuing to record under the Main Ingredient name into the 80s.
Albums: *The Main Ingredient LTD* (1970), *Black Seeds* (1971), *Tasteful Soul* (1971), *Bitter Sweet* (1972), *Afrodisiac* (1973), *Euphrates River* (1974), *Rolling Down A Mountainside* (1975), *Shame On The World* (1975), *Music Maxiums* (1977), *Ready For Love* (1980), *I Only Have Eyes For You* (1981), *I Just Wanna Love You* (1989).

Main Source

There has been much swapping and shifting in the constantly evolving line-ups of the rap band Main Source, formed in Toronto, Canada, but based in New York. The original MCs were K-Cut and Sir Scratch, though **Large Professor** (b. Paul Mitchell) excused himself after their first album, which included choice cuts like 'Just A Friendly Game Of Baseball'. Professor would go on to work with **A Tribe Called Quest**, **Nas**, who had first arrived on the debut album's 'Live At The BBQ' cut, and others. He was replaced by Mikey D, who was installed in time to become chief rapper on their second set, the invitingly titled *Fuck What You Think*, on which they were also joined by Shaheem, a female MC recruited straight from high school (on the title-track and 'Set It Off'). Their fresh, jazzy platform was well served by the indignant, often complex lyrical matter they pursued. In the light of delays over the release of their *Fuck What You Think* set they parted company with label **Wild Pitch**, and Mikey D also broke ranks - claiming he did not get along with K-Cut and Scratch, looking for a solo deal instead.
Albums: *Breaking Atoms* (Wild Pitch 1990), *Fuck What You Think* (Wild Pitch 1994).

Mainer, J.E.

b. Joseph Emmett Mainer, 20 July 1898, in a one room log house in Buncombe County, North Carolina, USA, d. 12 June 1971. Mainer played banjo at the age of nine but later became an accomplished fiddle player. He worked in textile mills from the age of 12 but began playing locally with other musicians in the 20s. He eventually formed Mainer's Mountaineers which consisted of his banjo playing brother **Wade Mainer** and guitarists Daddy John Love and Claude 'Zeke' Morris. In 1932, Mainer played regularly on radio in Gastonia but in 1934, sponsored by Crazy Water Crystals, and performing as the Crazy Mountaineers, they became regulars on WBT Charlotte. They later moved to WPTF Raleigh but also played in New Orleans and on the Mexican border stations. Over the years there were various changes of personnel including Steve Ledford, Snuffy Jenkins and Morris's brothers Wiley and George. They first recorded as J.E. Mainer's Mountaineers for Bluebird in 1935 and are still remembered for their recordings of 'Johnsons's Old Grey Mule', 'Take Me In The Lifeboat' and 'Maple On The Hill'. By the end of the 40s, Mainer's RCA recordings exceeded 200 but he later recorded for King and during the 60s, made recordings for the folk music archives of the Library of Congress and a whole series of albums for Rural Rhythm. Mainer's Mountaineers were one of the most important of all the early day string bands and greatly influenced later bands and musicians. Mainer remained active and regularly appeared at bluegrass and folk festivals until his death from a heart attack.
Albums: *Good Ole Mountain Music* (1960), *Variety Album* (1961), *Legendary Family From The Blue Ridge Mountains* (1963), *J.E. Mainer's Crazy Mountaineers. Volumes 1 & 2* (1963), *The Legendary J.E. Mainer Volumes 1-20* (1966-71), *70th Happy Birthday* (1968), *J.E. Mainer* (1968), *At Home With Family And Friends Volumes 1 & 2* (c.1981).

Mainer, Wade

b. 21 April 1907, near Weaverville, North Carolina, USA. The younger brother of **J.E. Mainer** and a fine singer and talented banjoist who developed a clever two-fingered style that made his playing readily identifiable. In 1937, after initially playing with his brother's Mountaineers, he formed his own Sons of The Mountaineers, which at times included Wade Morris, Jay Hugh Hall, Steve Ledford and **Clyde Moody**. He recorded for Bluebird until 1941, being especially remembered for his 1939 recording of 'Sparkling Blue Eyes'. He later made some recordings for King before moving in the 50s to work for Chevrolet in Flint, Michigan. After retirement from that in the 70s, he returned to recording with the Old Homestead label.
Albums: *Soulful Sacred Songs* (1961), *Early Radio* (c.1971), *Wade Mainer & The Mainer Mountaineers* (1971), *Sacred Songs Of Mother And Home* (1972), *Rock Of My Soul* (1972), *Mountain Sacred Songs* (1972), *From The Maple On The Hill* (c.1973), *Wade Mainer & The Sons Of The Mountaineers* (1979), *Old Time Songs* (1982), *Early And Great Volumes 1 & 2* (1983), *Wade & Julia Mainer* (1985).

Mainieri, Mike

b. 24 July 1938, the Bronx, New York, USA. Mainieri was playing the vibraphone by the time he was 10 years old and performing publicly at 14. He studied at the Juilliard School and then joined the **Paul Whiteman** Band before touring with the **Buddy Rich** Orchestra (1956-62). He left Rich to become a session musician in

New York. During the 70s he wrote music for television and films. He played with Jeremy Steig's band Jeremy And The Satyrs at the Cafe A Go Go, formed a 16-piece rock band and led his own quartet with **Steve Gadd** on drums. He invented the synthi-vibe, which not only allowed him to treat the sound of the vibes electronically but also to be heard in high-volume situations. In 1979, he brought together a group of session musicians to tour Japan. The unit included Gadd (later replaced by **Peter Erskine**), **Michael Brecker**, Don Grolnick (piano), and **Eddie Gomez**. They were named Steps, later to be **Steps Ahead**, and were described as 'a contemporary bebop band'.
Albums: *Free Smiles* (1978), *Wanderlust* (NYC 1981), *Steps Ahead* (1983), *Modern Times* (1984), *Magnetic Love* (1986), *Come Together* (NYC 1993).
Video: *Mike Mainieri Quintet* (Kay Jazz 1988).

Maisonettes

Based in Birmingham, England, this 60s-influenced pop group reached number 7 in the UK chart in 1983 with 'Heartache Avenue'. The group consisted of Lol Mason (vocals), Elaine Williams (vocals), Denise Ward (vocals), Mark Tibbenham (keyboards), and Nick Parry (drums). Mason, the driving force behind the band, was no stranger to chart success, having previously been the singer with **City Boy**. Two follow-up singles, 'Where I Stand' and 'Say It Again', and an album, all for the Birmingham independent label Ready Steady Go!, flopped, and the band broke up.
Albums: *For Sale* (1983), *Heartache Avenue* (1993).

Major Surgery

A four-piece outfit based in Croydon, Surrey, England, during the latter part of the 70s, Major Surgery comprised **Don Weller**, Tony Marsh (drums), Bruce Collcutt (bass guitar) and Jimmy Roche (guitar). Roche had a blues background, having been a brief member of an early **Colosseum** line-up; he subsequently joined **East Of Eden**, where he played with Weller. This pair also played together in Boris prior to forming Major Surgery. Thus Major Surgery drew on the blues, rock, and *avant garde* music, reconstituting them as a muscular blend of intellectual electric jazz.
Album: *First Cut* (1977).

Majors

Formed in Philadelphia, Pennsylvania, USA, in 1959, the Majors were an R&B quintet which crossed over to the US pop charts three times in 1962, most notably with their debut, 'A Wonderful Dream'. The group consisted of lead singer Rick Cordo, Ron Gathers, Gene Glass, Idella Morris and Frank Troutt, and was produced by the influential **Jerry Ragavoy** - 'A Wonderful Dream' was his first Top 40 success. The Majors had their roots in a harmony group called the Premiers. Upon recording their first single, 'Lundee Dundee', for Rocal Records in 1960, they changed their name to the Versatiles. The next time the group entered the studio was in 1962 for the Ragavoy-produced tracks for **Imperial Records**. During 1963, they recorded eight singles for the label, as well as one album. The group resurfaced with a single on **ABC**-Paramount in 1966, under the name the Performers. They toured throughout the 60s but split by the end of that decade.
Album: *Meet The Majors* (Imperial 1962, reissued as *A Golden Classics Edition* on Collectables in 1991).

Make Me An Offer

One of that band of typically English musicals that were around in the late 50s, which included ***Fings Ain't Wot They Used T'Be*** and ***Expresso Bongo***. The creative team behind the latter came together again for this show which began its life at the innovative Theatre Royal, Stratford East, before opening in the West End at the New Theatre on 16 December 1959. The book was adapted by Wolf Mankowitz from his own slim 1952 novel and the 1959 film starring Peter Finch and Adrienne Corri, and was set in the world of small-time antique dealers based around London's Portobello Road market. Charlie (Daniel Massey), an expert in Wedgwood china, longs to own a beautiful piece for himself. His chance comes when he is involved with an auction (a particularly effective scene) for a complete (fake) Wedgwood room - and he ends up with a valuable (genuine) vase. Charlie's main rival dealer in the saga is the stunning Redhead (Dilys Laye), and his wife, Sally, was played by Diana Coupland. Some 20 songs, by **David Heneker** and Monty Norman, were skilfully incorporated into the plot, pointing up the various characters and situations as they occurred. They consisted of a blend of amusing and sentimental items, such as 'Make Me An Offer', Redhead's proposal that Charlie gallantly turns down; 'The Pram Song', 'I Want A Lock-Up', 'Portobello Road', 'Business Is Business', 'Whatever You Believe', 'It's Sort Of Romantic', 'If I Was A Man', 'Dog Eat Dog', 'All Big Fleas', and 'Love Him'. *Make Me An Offer* had decent run of 267 performances, and won the 1959 *Evening Standard* Award for best musical.

Make Mine Manhattan

Sid Caesar, a comedian who specialized in subjects satirical, was on the brink of television super-stardom when he appeared with a clutch of fellow clowns, including Joshua Shelley and David Burns, in this show which opened at the Broadhurst Theatre in New York on 15 January 1948. It was Caesar's debut on Broadway, and in a format - the revue - that was on its last legs. The music was by Richard Lewine, with lyrics and sketches by Arnold B. Horwitt, and it went for all the usual New York targets in a pleasant and amusing way. The songs included 'Saturday Night In Central Park', 'Subway Song', 'Phil The Fiddler', 'Gentleman Friend', 'My Brudder And Me', and 'I Fell In Love With You'. It is ironic that a fairly simple, lightweight production such as this should run for 429 performances, when Caesar's triumphant return to Broadway 14 years later in ***Little Me*** could only manage 257.

Makeba, Miriam

b. 4 March 1932, Johannesburg, South Africa. The vocalist who first put African music on the international map in the 60s, Makeba began her professional career in 1950, when she joined Johannesburg group the Cuban Brothers. She came to national prominence during the mid-50s as a member of leading touring group the **Manhattan Brothers**, an 11-piece close harmony group modelled on African-American line-ups such as the **Mills Brothers**. She performed widely with the outfit in South Africa, Rhodesia and the Congo until 1957, when she was recruited as a star attraction in the touring package show African Jazz And Variety. She remained with the troupe for two years, again touring South Africa and neighbouring countries, before leaving to join the cast of the 'township musical' *King Kong,* which also featured such future international stars as **Hugh Masekela** and **Jonas Gwangwa**.

By now one of South Africa's most successful performers, Makeba was nonetheless receiving just a a few dollars for each recording session, with no additional provision for royalties, and was increasingly keen to settle in the USA. The opportunity came following her starring role in American film-maker Lionel Rogosin's semi-documentary *Come Back Africa,* shot - in defiance of the Pretorian government - in South Africa. When the Italian government invited Makeba to attend the film's premiere at the Venice Film Festival in spring 1959, she privately decided not to return home. Shortly afterwards, furious at the international furore created by the film's powerful exposé of apartheid, her South African passport was withdrawn. In London after the Venice Festival, Makeba met **Harry Belafonte**, who offered to help her gain an entry visa and work permit to the USA. Arriving in New York in autumn 1959, Belafonte further assisted Makeba by securing her a guest spot on the popular *Steve Allen Show* and an engagement at the prestigious Manhattan jazz club the Village Vanguard. As a consequence of these exposures, Makeba became a nationally-feted performer within a few months of arriving in the USA, combining her musical activities - such as major chart hits like 'Patha Patha', 'The Click Song' and 'Malaika' - with outspoken denunciations of apartheid. In 1963, after an impassioned testimony before the United Nations Committee Against Apartheid, all her records were banned in South Africa. Married for a few years to fellow South African emigre Masekela, in 1968 Makeba divorced him in order to marry the Black Panther activist Stokeley Carmichael - a liaison which severely damaged her following amongst older white American record buyers. Promoters were no longer interested, and tours and record contracts were cancelled. Consequently, she and Carmichael, from whom she is now divorced, moved to Guinea in West Africa. Fortunately, Makeba continued to find work outside the USA, and during the 70s and 80s spent most of her time on the international club circuit, primarily in Europe, South America and black Africa. She has also been a regular attraction at world jazz events such as the Montreux Jazz Festival, the Berlin Jazz Festival and the Northsea Jazz Festival. In 1977, she was the unofficial South African representative at the pan-African festival of arts and culture, Festac, in Lagos, Nigeria. In 1982, she was reunited with Masekela at an historic concert in Botswana. As previously in the USA, Makeba combined her professional commitments with political activity, and served as a Guinean delegate to the United Nations. In 1986, she was awarded the Dag Hammarskjold Peace Prize in recognition of this work. In 1987, Makeba was invited to appear as a guest artist on **Paul Simon**'s Graceland tour, which included emotional returns to the USA and Zimbabwe (she had been banned from the then Rhodesia in 1960). While some anti-apartheid activists, mostly white Westerners, criticized her for allegedly breaking the African National Congress' cultural boycott by working with Simon (whose *Graceland* album had been part-recorded in South Africa), Makeba convincingly maintained that the Graceland package was substantially helping the anti-apartheid movement by drawing attention to the culture and plight of black South Africans.

Selected albums: *The World Of Miriam Makeba* (1962), *Makeba* (1963), *The Click Song* (1965), *Pata Pata* (1972), *Live At Conakry* (1975), *Festac 77* (1978), *Greatest Hits From Africa* (1985), *Sangoma* (1989), *Sing Me A Song* (Sonodisc 1993). Compilation: *The Best Of Miriam Makeba And The Sklarks* (1993).

Further reading: *Makeba, My Story* Miriam Makeba with James Hall.

Makowicz, Adam

b. 18 August 1940, Czechoslovakia. Makowicz's piano teacher mother taught him to play. He studied classical music at the Fryderyck Chopin School in Kracow, but left when he became interested in jazz. His first work was with **Tomasz Stanko** (trumpet) in one of the first European groups to be influenced by the free style of **Ornette Coleman**. In 1965, he moved to Warsaw, where he had his own trio and played with **Zbigniew Namyslowski** (alto) with whom he toured worldwide. Makowicz's interest in composition grew during this period and he became involved with electric keyboards.

In 1970, he joined **Michal Urbaniak** in his new group Constellation and recorded an album with Urbaniak's wife, **Urszula Dudziak**. Between 1973 and 1976 he played in a group called Unit with **Tomasz Stanko** and played the piano with the **Duke Ellington** Orchestra at a concert in Prague (1976). In 1977 he went to the USA as a solo performer, playing in a way which reflected his interest in **Art Tatum**, **Keith Jarrett** and romantic piano music. He settled in New York in 1977 and became an American citizen in 1986.

Albums: with Urszula Dudziak *Newborn Light* (1972), with Michel Urbaniak *Michal Urbaniak Fusion* (1975), *Live Embers* (1975), *Winter Flowers* (1978), *From My Window* (1980), *Naughty Baby* (1987), *The Solo Album: Adam In Stockholm* (Verve 1987), with George Mraz *Classic Jazz Duets* (Stash 1987), *Name Is Makowitz* (Sheffield Lab 1988), *Solo* (Sonet 1988), *Live At The Maybank Recital Hall Series, Vol 24* (Concord 1993), *Music Of Jerome Kern* (Concord 1993).

Mákvirág

Formed in 1973, this trio from Hungary and Romania, have reached a wider audience due to the increasing interest shown in European and world music during the late 80s. The group won first prize in 1974 in a folk-jazz competition in Gyor, Hungary. They were subsequently afforded the accolade Young Master Of Folk Art in 1976. Then, in 1978, they won the Lászl Lajtha Award at Szombathely, Hungary. They appeared in Britain in 1988, while undertaking their first major UK and Irish tour. All multi-instrumentalists, Csaba Szijjártó (b. Budapest, Hungary), Zoltán Kátai, and Károly Horváth (b. Romania) have recorded a number of albums, each combining music from their own backgrounds as well as from other Eastern European countries. Instrumentation is supplemented by recorders, ocarina and pan pipes. All three members have spent time in various orchestras and choirs and music conservatories. Mákvirág have since played the UK again on a number of occasions, largely at festivals.

Albums: *Trifa* (Hungaroton 1978), *Palóc Lakodalmas* (Hungaroton 1978), *Mákvirág 1* (Hungaroton 1979), *Mákvárig 2* (1981), *Mákávirag In Brazil* (Espe Music-Stockfisch 1988), *Mákvirágék* (Sugas Prod. 1988), *Népszokások-Jeles Napok* (Radioton 1988), *Békesség-Peacefulness* (Trax 1991).

Malaco Records

An independent soul, blues and gospel label based in Jackson, Mississippi, USA, Malaco Records was founded in 1962 by Tommy Couch from Tucombia, Alabama, and by Gerald "Wolf" Stephenson from Columbia, Mississippi, as a booking agency for local and touring acts visiting Mississippi. It started recording relatively obscure talent and leasing recordings to more established labels, as well as allowing other labels and artists to use their recording studios. Its first release was 'Misty Blue' by **Dorothy Moore** in 1975. Dave Clark joined the label in 1980, after which Malaco built a formidable roster of soul and blues artists, including Denise Latimore, Johnnie La Salle, Dorothy Taylor, Shirley Moore, Bobby Brown 'Blue Band', Little Milton, **Artie 'Blues Boy' White** and Poonanny. It has become one of the major labels catering for the audience interested in this form of music. Malaco's biggest hit came with **Z.Z. Hill**'s 'Down Home Blues' in 1982 which sold more than 500,000 copies. Malaco bought the **Muscle Shoals** Studio in 1985 and so became associated with the Muscle Shoals Sound that musicians such as **Jimmy Johnson**, David Hood, Roger Hawkins, Harrison Calloway. It has recently established a subsidiary, Waldoxy. The gospel division of Malaco started in 1976 and within a few years it had become the third largest gospel label in the USA. Its subsidiaries also include Savoy and Blackberry records. The Malaco gospel label has 165 artists and 500 releases in its catalogue headed by Jerry Mannery. Its artists include **Mississippi Mass Choir**, **Rev. James Cleveland**, **Rev. James Moore**, **Williams Brothers**, Dorothy Norwood, Albertina Walker, Florida Mass Choir, Rev. Clay Evans, Sensational Nightingales, Jackson Southernairs, Philadelphia Mass Choir.

Malcom, Carl

b. July 1952, Black River, St. Elizabeth, Jamaica, West Indies. Malcom learnt to play the keyboard by ear at the local Methodist church and his musical talents were recognised by those around him from an early age. After leaving the St. Elizabeth Technical High School he spent two years working for a shoe company in Kingston and was a reserve for the Jamaica Defence Force. Music was his passion and in 1965 he became involved in a band called the Volcanoes alongside **Al Brown**. The two artists shared vocal duties and stayed with the group until they disbanded four years later. Malcom retired from music and went back to studying. It was in his second year that he became involved in an automobile accident where he sustained a broken leg and cracked ribs. Returning to music at this time he joined a band called Big Relations led by **Jo Jo Bennett**. Malcom recorded with **Coxsone Dodd** on his first tune, 'Father Free Us' before leaving the island for the USA. While in America he performed at various clubs and house parties. He then returned to Jamaica where he found employment with **Rupie Edwards** as the branch manager of Success Records located at Half Way Tree. Whilst working for Rupie he was allowed studio time to record 'Make It When You Try' but, like his earlier effort, it was overlooked by Jamaican music lovers. Accompanied by Skin Flesh And Bones in 1973 he recorded 'No Jestering', and two years later when released in the UK it held the number 1 position in the reggae charts. Malcom's career took off in a big way with the follow-up, 'Miss Wire Waist', which demonstrated his smooth vocals when he sang, 'Miss wire waist, you lickle but you chalawah'. In an effort to appease his fans he also acknowledged his love of bigger women in the song 'Fattie Bum Bum' which became a UK Top 10 hit in September 1975. The lyrics, 'Hey fatty bum bum, you sweet sugar dumpling, hey fatty bum bum let me tell you something, no not because your so big and fat, don't believe I'm afraid of that, never let the big size fool you', appealed to many but in the eyes of the British record buying public he was a one-hit-wonder. The song was covered by a UK-based group, the Diversions, who diverted enough sales from Malcom to enjoy a chart hit alongside the original version. He returned to the reggae charts in the late 70s with the release of 'Repatriation' with **Ranking Trevor** and 'Take A Tip From Me', with the intention of further releases but since that time Carl has remained incognito. In 1992 **Scotty** re-activated his career when he covered, 'Miss Wire Waist'. Even though Malcom had a UK Top 10 hit no album was released to coincide with his success. *DJ Specials* (VP 1981) featured both 'No Jestering' and 'Miss Wire Waist' providing the foundation to the DJ tracks.

Malevolent Creation

Formed in Buffalo, New York, in 1987, it took Malevolent Creation four years to secure a deal and release their official debut. This gore-fixated recording, *The Ten Commandments*, was mixed at Morrisound Studios in Florida by Scott Burns. Burns' distinctive production more or less defined the death metal sound, and he was in great demand among death metal bands. But his work, like the genre, has become increasingly formulaic. Despite this, Malevolent Creation were an above average example of the genre, and attracted a degree of critical acclaim. They arrived on the death metal scene too late, however, to establish themselves among the front-runners and as its popularity waned, the band found themselves without a deal in 1994 and have since broken up.

Albums: *The Ten Commandments* (Roadrunner 1991), *Retribution* (Roadrunner 1992), *Stillborn* (Roadrunner 1993).

Malice

This Los Angeles band emerged from the local club scene of the early 80s with a sound influenced by European metal, particularly **Judas Priest**. Indeed Malice were widely described as Priest clones, not only for their twin guitar-based sound and James Neal's vocal similarities to Rob Halford, but also for their leather-clad image and guitarist Jay Reynolds' distinct resemblance to KK Downing. Malice, completed by Mick Zane (guitar), Mark Behn (bass) and Peter Laufman (drums), recorded a five-track demo with producer Michael Wagener of stunning quality, which had independent labels clamouring to release it in its own right, but the band instead signed to **Atlantic Records**. The demo formed half of *In The Beginning*, with the remaining five tracks produced by Ashley Howe, an excellent debut built on a solid base of power metal guitars, although the Priest comparison remained obvious. However, cracks were beginning to show by *License To Kill*, as internal conflicts began to divide the band, and the split came in late 1987, as Malice divided into two warring camps. Reynolds later joined **Megadeth** for a brief period.

Albums: *In The Beginning* (Atlantic 1985), *License To Kill* (Atlantic 1987).

Malicorne

The brainchild of French music genius Gabriel Yacoub, Malicorne was formed after he and his then wife, Marie, spent some time in **Alan Stivell**'s pioneering Breton unit. The original, innovative line-up, used antique instruments to play peasant songs, haunting harmonies and integrated rock rhythms. *Pierre De Grenoble* (1973), although recorded before Malicorne came into being, set the style and manner of the band. Initially a four piece, the Yacoubs were joined by Laurent Vercambe (violin) and Hugh De Courson (bass/woodwinds). Their finest set in this form was *Almanach*, a song cycle based on the turning year, and based on rustic folklore. A commercially successful tour of France was followed, in 1978, by the recuitment of a fifth member, Oliver Zdrzalik (bass). Subsequently, an excellent live recording, *En Public A Montreal*, preceded further fundamental personnel changes, and the birth of a new seven-piece unit, which included ex-**Gryphon** bassoonist Brian Gulland. Following *Le Bestiare*, which proved to be an 'animalistic album, a story of French country folk', the band cut one final set before splitting up, but came together again in 1986 when an intended Gabriel Yacoub solo session was reorganized as a Malicorne piece. The Yacoubs, with Oliver Kowalski (bass), Jean Pierre Arnoux (drums) and Michel Le Cam (fiddle), recorded the industrial sounding *Les Cathedrales De L'industrie*. This line-up became Gabriel Yacoub's own band, and, with the addition of Nikki Matheson (keyboards), played both Malicorne and Yacoub material. Yacoub's own albums are all distinct; ranging from traditional folk and chamber music, to bizarre electronic pieces. Yacoub married Matheson in the late 80s, and they toured as an acoustic duo.

Selected albums: *Almanach* (1976), *Le Extraordinaire Tour De France D' Adeland Rousseau* (1978), *En Public A Montreal* (1979), *Le Bestiare* (1980), *Les Cathedrales De L'industrie* (1986). Compilation: *Légende* (1989). Gabriel & Marie Yacoub: *Pierre De Grenoble* (1973). Gabriel Yacoub: *Elementary Level Of Faith* (1987), *Bel* (1990).

Mallard

This short-lived group was the result of an acrimonious split between **Captain Beefheart** and the most renowned of his backing groups, the Magic Band. Their split had occurred in 1974, following the release of *Unconditionally Guaranteed*. Bill Harkleroad (aka Zoot Horn Rollo; guitar), Mark Boston (aka Rockette Morton; bass) and Ed Marimba (aka Art Tripp III; drums) formed Mallard with vocalist Sam Galpin, but although their debut album offered a glimpse of the inspired interplay shown on their previous incarnation, its overall lack of passion justified Beefheart's assertion that he taught the two guitarists by rote. Tripp was replaced by George Draggota for a second Mallard album, *In A Different Climate*. This set was an even greater disappointment and the group broke up soon after its release.

Albums: *Mallard* (1975), *In A Different Climate* (1977).

Malmsteen, Yngwie

b. 30 June 1963. This Swedish-born guitar virtuoso was the originator of the high-speed, technically precise, neo-classical style that developed during the 80s. Influenced by **Jimi Hendrix, Ritchie Blackmore** and **Eddie Van Halen**, Malmsteen first picked up a guitar at the age of five and had formed his first band, Powerhouse, by the time he entered his teens. At age 14 he formed Rising, named after **Rainbow**'s second album, and recorded a series of demo tapes. One of these was picked up by producer and guitar specialist Mike Varney. Malmsteen was persuaded by Varney to relocate to Los Angeles and join Ron Keel's **Steeler** as lead guitarist, and went straight into the studio to record the band's debut album. Following this he was approached by **Kiss**, **UFO** and **Ozzy Osbourne**, but declined their offers in favour of teaming up with **Graham Bonnet** in a new group called **Alcatrazz**. This association lasted for one studio album and a live set, recorded in Japan. After the dissolution of that band Malmsteen was immediately offered a solo deal by **Polydor** Records, just as his reputation and stature were beginning to escalate. He released the self-produced *Rising Force*, utilizing ex-**Jethro Tull** drummer Barriemore Barlow, vocalist Jeff Scott Soto and keyboardist Jens Johansson. This comprised a mixture of new songs and re-worked demo material that had been available for several years. Deciding to work within a band framework once more, but this time exercising tight control, Malmsteen formed Rising Force with Soto and Johansson, plus bassist Marcel Jacob and drummer Anders Johansson. This basic formation recorded two albums, the second of which, *Trilogy*, saw Soto replaced by ex-**Ted Nugent** vocalist Mark Boals, which showcased Malmsteen's amazing virtuosity and ability to combine speed with melody. Following an 18-month break after a serious road accident involving Malmsteen, Rising Force was resurrected again with ex-Rainbow vocalist **Joe Lynn Turner**. Produced by Jeff Glixman and mixed by the Thompson/Barbiero team, *Odyssey* was released in 1988 to widespread acclaim. At last Malmsteen's guitar pyrotechnics had been anchored within commercial hard rock structures. The guitar solos, for once, were economical, and did not detract from the songs. The album reached number 40 on the USA *Billboard* album chart and brought many new fans to the guitarist. Eager to capitalize on this success, Malmsteen then issued a disappointing and self-indulgent live album recorded in Leningrad. The momentum was lost and Joe Lynn Turner was dismissed, to be replaced with a Swedish vocalist, Goran Edman. *Eclipse* emerged in 1990 with weak vocals and an unusually restrained Malsteen on guitar, and it appeared that he was suppressing his real desires and ability in the search for commercial success. *Fire And Ice* debuted at number 1 in the Japanese charts, and introduced new vocalist Mike Vescera. He switched back to his old flamboyant style on *No Mercy*, however, which featured classical material and a string orchestra.

Albums: *Yngwie Malmsteen's Rising Force* (Polydor 1984), *Marching Out* (Polydor 1985), *Trilogy* (Polydor 1986), *Odyssey* (Polydor 1988), *Live In Leningrad* (Polydor 1989), *Eclipse* (Polydor 1990), *Fire & Ice* (Elektra 1992), *Seventh Sign* (Elektra 1994), *No Mercy* (CMC International 1994).

Videos: *Rising Force Live 85* (1989), *Trial By Fire* (1989), *Collection* (1992).

Malombo Jazz

Formed in Pretoria, South Africa, in 1962, the original - and definitive - Malombo Jazz was a three-piece comprising guitarist Philip Tabane, flautist Abe Cindi and traditional drummer and percussionist Julian Bahula. The group's repertoire drew heavily on the ancient folk music of South Africa's Venda and Pedi peoples, but also used as an immensely appropriate backdrop for Tabane's exquisite jazz-based improvisations, which were capable of moving through every emotional area from the loud and lascivious to the pastoral and delicate. In a country long racked by tribal rivalries, jazz had served since the 30s to unite various ethnic groups, and Malombo achieved much the same success in the 60s. In 1964, the band won first prize at the prestigious Castle Lager Jazz Festival (their set was included on the live album of the event, which can still be found in the second-hand racks of specialist record stores). Bahula and Cindi left Malombo in the late 60s to base themselves in London, where they formed the short-lived Malombo Jazzmen prior to Bahula setting up his own band, Jabula. Malombo's line-up underwent numerous personnel changes in subsequent years, as Tabane strove to recapture the magic of the original trio. His first replacement for

Bahula was Gabriel Thobejani, who later left to join fusion outfit Sakhile. In 1981, Cindi briefly rejoined the band. In 1986, Thobejani returned. In the late 80s, Tabane began leading an occasional big band, the Homeland Symphony Orchestra, re-interpreting Venda and Pedi folk music in jazz-influenced orchestral style. Sadly, the project remains unrecorded.
Albums: *Castle Lager Jazz Festival 1964* (1964), *The Indigenous Afro-Jazz Sounds Of Philip Tabane And His Malombo Jazzmen* (1968), *Sangoma* (1972), *Pele Pele* (1974), *Malombo* (1984), *Man Phily* (1986).

Malone, J.J.

b. 20 August 1935, Pete's Corner, Alabama, USA. Malone was playing guitar and harmonica before his 13th birthday, and he began performing at dances and parties when he was 17. In the mid-50s he spent a year in the Air Force and formed his first band the Rockers, later called Tops In Blues. Once out of the Service in 1957, he formed the Rhythm Rockers in Spokane, Washington, and they worked all over the west coast. In 1966, he settled in Oakland, California, and recorded for the Galaxy label, enjoying a hit with 'Its A Shame' in 1972, and he subsequently had records issued by the Red Lightnin', Cherrie, Paris Album, and Eli Mile High labels. Malone is a soulful vocalist, adept on both piano and guitar and playing straight blues, rocking R&B, or funk-influenced material.
Albums: *Bottom Line Blues* (1991), with Troyce Key *I've Gotta New Car* (1980).

Malopoets

Formed in Johannesburg in 1978 by vocalist Patrick Sefolosha and guitarist Kenny Mathaba, the Malopoets were, until their demise in 1986, one of the most significant and rewarding groups at the rootsier end of the township pop movement, playing a lighter, more relaxed form of mbaqanga. Sefolosha and Mathaba had paid their dues in the rock and soul-orientated band Purple Haze before, alongside their audience, becoming increasingly frustrated in the mid-70s with imported styles and making a decision to strive for greater authenticity in their music.
By 1983, however, the band were close to breaking up, finding it practically impossible to make a living under apartheid, where black bands were denied freedom to tour the country or promote their records on state radio. Sefolosha accordingly left South Africa and teamed up with producer Martin Meissonnier in Paris. A few months later the rest of the group joined him, signed to **EMI** and, in 1984, released the album *Malopoets*. The set failed to make any impact on the burgeoning African music scene in Europe, however, being adjudged too pop-orientated by white audiences craving for 'roots', and early in 1986 the Malopoets broke up.
Album: *Malopoets* (1984).

Maltby, Richard

b. 26 June 1914, Chicago, Illinois, USA, d. 19 August 1991, Santa Monica, California, USA. Maltby started playing cornet in his school band, going onto Northwest University Music School, before his first professional experience with 'Little' Jack Little and his band. He was musical director for **CBS** radio in Chicago (1940-45), and during this period he wrote 'Six Flats Unfurnished' for the **Benny Goodman** band, and then he spent 10 years working as musical associate for **Paul Whiteman** at ABC radio in New York. During 1950-65, Maltby was also musical director for SESAC Jazz Classics, recording radio transcriptions with a big band which he took on the road from 1955, encouraged by the success of his 'St Louis Blues Mambo' which had charted the previous year, followed in 1956 by 'The Man With The Golden Arm'. The band recorded prolifically for various **RCA** labels and **Columbia** during the 50s, and Maltby was active on many different labels, directing backings for artists **Peggy Lee**, Gisele Mackenzie, **Sarah Vaughan**, **Gordon MacRae**, **Johnnie Ray**, **Vic Damone** and **Ethel Merman**. *Downbeat* voted his unit 'Best New Swing Band', but, the swing era having long since passed, he found more financial reward, if less musical satisfaction, as **Lawrence Welk**'s arranger and conductor on records and television. Maltby's original compositions (mostly for the SESAC transcriptions) for his own orchestra and big band must number in the hundreds, although few measured-up to the commercial success of his first Goodman hit and its successor, 'Five Flats Unfurnished', for **Sy Oliver**. Maltby's only venture into 'serious music' was his threnody 'Requiem For John Fitzgerald Kennedy'. He suffered from ill-health in the 80s, enduring five bouts of open-heart surgery until his death in 1991. His son, Richard Maltby Jnr., is a Broadway director and lyricist.
Selected albums: *Manhattan Bandstand* (Viking c.50s), *Hello, Young Lovers* (Columbia 1959), *A Bow To The Big Name Bands* (Camden 1959), *Swings For Dancers* (Roulette c.50s), *Mr Lucky* (Camden 1960), *Swingin' Down The Lane* (Columbia 1961), *Swings Folk Songs* (Roulette 1961), *Most Requested* (1962), *Music From Mr. Lucky* (Camden c.60s).

Maltby, Richard, Jnr.

(see **Shire, David**)

Mama's Boys

The three McManus brothers began their musical careers as folk musicians, playing the local dance hall and club circuit in their native Northern Ireland. After experiencing the Irish electric folk-rock outfit **Horslips** in concert in 1978, they decided to abandon their acoustic guitars and tambourines and become a hard rock power trio. John took on vocals and bass, Pat picked up lead guitar and Tommy occupied the drumstool. Merging traditional Irish influences with blues and heavy rock, they quickly developed a unique style that echoed **Thin Lizzy**. Their first two albums contained high-energy boogie and driving blues, but from *Turn It Up* onwards, they began to show a greater awareness of melody and veered towards AOR. Realizing the limitations of John as a vocalist, they expanded to a quartet in 1987, adding ex-**Airrace** singer Keith Murrell. *Growing Up The Hard Way* followed and was undoubtedly the band's most accomplished album to date, with a sophisticated approach reminiscent of **Foreigner**. After four years of recording inactivity, *Live Tonite* emerged. Recorded on their 1990 European tour, it featured latest vocalist Mike Wilson, plus four brand new songs. On 16 November 1994 drummer Tommy McManus died of a lung infection following a bone marrow transplant, having for several years been plagued by leukaemia.

Albums: *Official Bootleg* (Pussy 1980), *Plug It In* (Albion 1982), *Turn It Up* (Spartan 1983), *Mama's Boys* (Jive 1984), *Power And The Passion* (Jive 1985), *Growing Up The Hard Way* (Jive 1987), *Live Tonite* (Music For Nations 1991), *Relativity* (CTM 1992).

Mama, I Want To Sing

Conceived, so it said, on a beach in Jamaica in 1980, and subsequently showcased at various provincial theatres in the USA, this 'multi-cultural gospel musical' finally opened in New York, Off-Broadway, at the Heckscher Theatre, the former home of Joe Papp's New York Shakespeare Festival, on 23 March 1983. Set in Harlem in the late 40s and 50s, Vy Higginsen and Ken Wydro's book is based the life of **Doris Troy**, Higginsen's sister, who emerged from her gospel church choir to become an accomplished R&B songwriter and session singer with one or two substantial hits of her own, including 'Just One Look' in 1963. Early in 1984, Doris Troy herself joined the cast in the role of her mother, and stayed with the company over the years. She is credited, along with Rudolph V. Hawkins, Pat Holley and Stephen Taylor, with composing the music to Higginsen and Wydro's lyrics for the 'rhythmical foot-stomping, hand-clapping score', which is supplemented by some familar gospel tunes. The musical numbers included 'You Are My Child', 'Faith Can Move A Mountain', 'My Faith Looks Up To Thee', 'I Don't Worry About Tomorrow', 'God Will Be', 'Gifted Is', 'What Do You Win When You Win?', 'Precious Lord', 'Know When To Leave The Party', 'The One Who Will Love Me', and the title song. With audiences flocking to see 'this morally uplifting entertainment', by the end of 1984 *Time Magazine* had selected *Mama, I Want To Sing* as one of the Top 10 theatrical productions of the year, and 1985 saw the show playing 10 performances a week with two different casts. A year later, while the New York cast was still in residence at the Heckscher Theatre, the first US national tour opened. This was followed over the next few years by productions in Tokyo, Osaka, Athens, Zurich, Munich, Venice, Berlin, Frankfurt, Palermo, Sicily, Istanbul and many other cities around the world. When the New York production closed in 1991 (after playing in repertory for a while with *Mama, I Want To Sing Part II*) the show had played more than 2,400 performances over eight consecutive years, and become 'the longest-running, best-loved black Off-Broadway musical in the history of the American theatre'. Four years later, when it arrived in London, it was estimated that *Mama, I Want To Sing* had played to more than 3,000,000 people and grossed £38 million. Doris Troy was still present when the West End production opened at the Cambridge Theatre on 1 February 1995, with Stacy Francis as the young Doris, and soul star **Chaka Khan**, in the principal role of Sister Carrie, singing 'a couple of real stompers'.

Mamas And The Papas

Formed in Los Angeles in 1965, this enthralling harmony group embodied the city's astute blend of folk and pop. **John Phillips** (b. 30 August 1935, Parris Island, South Carolina, USA) had been a founder member of the popular **Journeymen**, before establishing this new attraction with his wife **Michelle Phillips** (b. Holly Michelle Gilliam, 6 April 1944, Long Beach, California, USA), and former **Mugwumps**' members Denny Doherty (b. 29 November 1941, Halifax, Nova Scotia, Canada) and **Cass Elliot** (b. Ellen Naimoi Cohen, 19 September 1943, Alexandria, Virginia, USA, d. 29 July 1974, London, England). Although drawing inspiration from the flourishing milieu of New York's Greenwich Village, the quartet quickly moved to California, where they met producer **Lou Adler** through the interjection of mutual acquaintance **Barry McGuire**. The then unnamed Mamas And Papas contributed backing vocals to the latter's second album, which in turn inspired the group's own career. Their debut single, 'California Dreamin'', was originally recorded by McGuire, whose voice was simply erased and replaced by that of Doherty. Penned by Phillips and Gilliam, the song provided a vivid contrast between the cold New York winter and the warmth and security of life on the west coast and effectively established the group as arguably the finest vocal ensemble form their era working in the pop field. The group's bohemian image was reinforced by their compositional skill and distinctive individual personalities. Visually, they seemed eccentrically contrasting: John, a towering 6 foot 4 inches, thin as a rake, and cast in the role of group intellectual; Denny the 'good-looking Canadian' and master of the sarcastic one-liner; Cass, overweight,

uproarious and charming; and Michelle, quiet, beautiful and 'angelic when she wants to be'. With 'California Dreamin'' they infiltrated the US Top 5 and the song became a standard, covered by many artists, most notably **Jose Feliciano**. The richly-harmonic follow-up, 'Monday Monday' reached number 1 in the US and also established the group in the UK. Further timeless hit singles followed, including the soaring 'I Saw Her Again' and a brilliant revival of the **Shirelles** 'Dedicated To The One I Love'. Michelle's sensual, semi-spoken introduction, backed by a solitary acoustic guitar remains one of the most classic and memorable openings to any pop recording. The group's albums achieved gold status and while the first was sprinkled with cover versions, the second documented Phillips' development as a songwriter. He was involved in no less than 10 compositions, two of which ('No Salt On Her Tail' and 'Strange Young Girls') were particularly outstanding. Marital problems between John and Michelle eroded the stability of the group and she was fired in 1966 and briefly replaced by lookalike Jill Gibson. The group reconvened for *Deliver*, another strong album, which was followed by the autobiographical 'Creeque Alley', which humorously documented their rise to fame. During the summer of 1967 Phillips organized the **Monterey Pop Festival** and helped launch the career of former Journeymen **Scott McKenzie** by writing the chart-topping hippie anthem 'San Francisco'. In the winter of 1967, the group arrived in the UK for concerts at London's Royal Albert Hall. After docking at Southampton, Cass was arrested by police, charged with stealing blankets and keys from the Royal Garden Hotel in Kensington on an earlier visit. The charges were dropped but the concerts were subsequently cancelled, amid beak-up rumours. The unit managed to complete one last album, *The Papas And Mamas*, a superb work that highlighted Phillips' brilliance as a songwriter. 'Safe In My Garden', 'For The Love Of Ivy' and the sublime 'Twelve Thirty' were all minor classics, while 'Rooms' and 'Mansions' incisively documented the spiritual isolation that accompanied their rise to international stardom: 'Limousines and laughter, parties ever after/If you play the game you pay the price/purchasing our piece of paradise'. It was a fitting valediction.
After splitting up in 1968, the quartet embarked on solo careers, with varying success. Three years later, the group briefly reformed for *People Like Us*, but their individual contributions were taped separately and the results were disappointing. Cass enjoyed the greatest success as a solo artist but her career was tragically cut short by sudden death in July 1974. Michelle continued to pursue an acting career, while John plummeted into serious drug addiction, near- death and arrest. He subsequently recovered and in 1982 he and Denny reformed the Mamas And Papas. The new line-up featured Phillips' actress daughter Laura McKenzie (McKenzie Phillips) and Elaine 'Spanky' McFarlane of **Spanky And Our Gang**. Doherty left when the band began touring full-time, and was replaced by the aforementioned McKenzi.
Albums: *If You Can Believe Your Eyes And Ears* (1966), *The Mamas And The Papas* aka *Cass, John, Michelle, Denny* (1966), *The Mamas And The Papas Deliver* (1967), *The Papas And The Mamas* (1968), *Monterey International Pop Festival* (1971), *People Like Us* (1971). Compilations: *Farewell To The First Golden Era* (1967), *Golden Era Volume 2* (1968), *16 Of Their Greatest Hits* (1969), *A Gathering Of Flowers* (1971), *20 Golden Hits* (1973), *The ABC Collection: Greatest Hits* (1976), *Creeque Alley: The History Of The Mamas And Papas* (1991).
Further reading: *Papa John*, John Phillips with Jim Jerome. *California Dreamin' - The True Story Of The Mamas And Papas*, Michelle Phillips.

Mambo Kings, The

Adapted by Cynthia Cidre from Oscar Hijuelos' Pulitzer Prize-winning novel *The Mambo Kings Play Songs Of Love*, this 1992 Warner Brothers production tells of two Cuban brothers, trumpet player Nestor and mambo singer and percussionist Cesar Castillo (Antonio Banderas and Armand Assante). In 1952 they leave Cuba for New York where Cesar demonstrates his skills at the swish Palladium club with the renowned **Tito Puente** Orchestra. After forming their own group The Mambo Kings, fellow Cuban **Desi Arnaz** - who is played by his real-life son Desi Arnaz Jnr. - hears them singing Nestor's composition 'Beautiful Maria Of My Soul' (Robert Kraft-Arne Glimcher) and invites them to appear on the top-rated *I Love Lucy* television show. Their subsequent rise to fame and fortune is shattered when Nestor dies in a car crash. Cesar buys a bar of his own, the Club Havana, and on the opening night, at the request of his late brother's girl, Delores Fuentes (Maruschka Detmers), he sings Nestor's lovely bolero 'Beautiful Maria Of My Soul'. The song had been dedicated to Maria Rivera (Talisa Soto) Nestor's former lover in Cuba. Other roles in the large cast went to Cathy Moriarty, Pablo Calogero, Scott Cohen, Mario Grillo, Ralph Irizzary, Pete MacNamara, and Jimmy Medina. The mostly South American songs included 'Mambo Caliente' (Arturo Sandoval), 'Tanga, Rumba-Afro-Cubana' (**Mario Bauza**), 'Guantanamera' (Fernandez Diaz', 'Perfidia' (Alberto Dominguez), 'Quiereme Mucho' (Gonzalo Roig-Augustin Rodriguez), and 'Cuban Pete' (José Norman). The exotic background score was written by Robert Kraft and Carlos Franzetti. Michael Peters was the choreographer, and the film was photographed in Technicolor by Michael Ballhouse. The director was Arne Glimcher. 'Beautiful Maria Of My Soul' was nominated for the best song Oscar, but, unlike the original book, no other prizes came the way of this brash and colourful film.

Mame

Opening at the Winter Garden Theatre in New York on 24 May 1966 to excellent reviews, the stage show *Mame* was another hit for composer and lyricist **Jerry Herman**. Robert E. Lee and Jerome Lawrence's book was based on the play *Auntie Mame*, which was in turn adapted from Patrick Dennis's novel. Mame (**Angela Lansbury**) is an eccentric lady of indeterminate years but with a decidedly youthful approach to life, and her efforts to impart the elements of her lifestyle and philosophy to her young nephew, Patrick Dennis (Frank Michaels) and her Texan husband, Beauregard Burnside (Charles Braswell), made for a delightful show. There were some memorable songs in a score which included 'Open A New Window', 'The Man In The Moon', 'It's Today', 'We Need A Little Christmas', 'That's How Young I Feel', 'My Best Girl', and the poignant 'If He Walked Into My Life', which later received sympathetic readings from **Matt Monro** and **Scott Walker**. The enormously likeable title number was a US hit for **Herb Alpert**, and Herman won a Grammy for the Original Cast album. Another outstanding number in the show was the amusingly bitchy 'Bosom Buddies', sung by Mame and her lifelong 'chum', Vera Charles (Beatrice Arthur), in which they swopped compliments such as 'If I say that your tongue is vicious, if I call you uncouth/It's simply that who else but a bosom buddy will sit down and tell you the truth?'. *Mame* ran for 1,508 performances on Broadway and won **Tony Awards** for best actress (Lansbury), and featured actor and actress (Michaels and Arthur). Hollywood superstar **Ginger Rogers** played the lead in the 1969 London production, various touring versions of the show have proved convenient vehicles for several other 'maturing' ladies of the stage and screen, including Janis Paige, **Jane Morgan**, **Ann Miller**, Rosalind Russell (who had starred in the long-running *Auntie Mame* and its film version), **Dolores Gray**, Greer Garson, Eve Arden and Sylvia Sidney. Angela Lansbury reprised her role for the short-lived 1983 Broadway revival. A 1974 film version starred Lucille Ball and **Robert Preston**.

Mammoth

The prerequisite for joining this appropriately titled UK band was, as legend has it, to weigh in excess of 20 stone. Consequently potential members were few and far between, but compensated for in girth what they lacked in number. Vocalist Nicky Moore (ex-**Samson**) and bassist John McCoy (ex-**Gillan**) eventually found guitarist Big Mac Baker and drummer 'Tubby' Vinnie Reid large enough for their requirements. The idea behind Mammoth was to present an alternative to 'pouting' rock bands such as **Poison** and **Bon Jovi**, with the music, rather than the image, topping the agenda. Unfortunately, due to contractual problems with their record company **Jive**, their debut album was delayed for 10 months and the interest they generated had evaporated by the time it was released. It comprised a poorly produced but workmanlike selection of hard rock and R&B numbers, with guitarists **Bernie Torme** and **Kenny Cox** guesting on a couple of tracks. The single, 'Can't Take The Hurt Anymore', was included on the soundtrack to *Nightmare On Elm Street 5, The Dream Child*. The band collapsed shortly after the album's release.
Album: *Mammoth* (Jive 1988).

Mamoulian, Rouben

b. 8 October 1898, Tbilisi, Georgia, Russia, d. 4 December 1987, Los Angeles, California, USA. A distinguished stage and film director whose name is particularly associated with two masterpieces of the American musical theatre - ***Porgy And Bess*** and ***Oklahoma!***- and a legendary Hollywood movie, ***Love Me Tonight***. Mamoulian spent part of his childhood in Paris before studying at Moscow University, and running his own drama school in Tbilisi. In 1920 he toured Britain with a Russian theatre group and subsequently studied drama at London University. He moved to the USA in 1923 and operettas at the George Eastman Theatre in Rochester, New Jersey, before going to New York where he became a leading light with the prestigious Theatre Guild. His reputation as a theatre director led him to Hollywood at the beginning of the talkie era, and he immediately impressed with his innovative and audacious approach to the medium. His first film, *Applause* (1929) starring **Helen Morgan**, was followed by a series of highly acclaimed pictures - sophisticated comedies, dramas, gangster movies - featuring the biggest stars of the day, including Fredric March, **Marlene Dietrich**, Tyrone Power, and Greta Garbo. Among them were several musicals, such as the charming *Love Me Tonight* (1932) with **Jeanette MacDonald** and **Maurice Chevalier** (which Mamoulian also produced), *The Gay Desperado* (1936), ***High, Wide And Handsome*** (1937), ***Summer Holiday*** (1947), and the elegant ***Silk Stockings*** (1957) starring **Fred Astaire** and **Cyd Charisse**. His relatively small cinema output is said to be due to persistent disagreements and confrontations with producers. He was hired and quickly fired from movies such as *Laura*, ***Porgy And Bess***, and the Elizabeth Taylor-Richard Burton epic *Cleopatra* (1963). In parallel with his Hollywood career, Mamoulian directed major works on Broadway, including *Porgy And Bess* (1935), *Oklahoma!* (1943), *Sadie Thompson* (1944), ***Carousel*** (1945), ***St. Louis Woman*** (1946), ***Lost In The Stars*** (1949), and *Arms And The Girl* (1950). On the latter show, and on *Sadie Thompson*, he also served as co-librettist, and in later years wrote and adapted several plays and children's stories.

Man

Man evolved from the **Bystanders**, a Swansea, Wales-based group specializing in close harmony pop. They latterly grew tired of this direction and, by 1969, were performing a live set at odds with their clean-cut recordings. Producer John Schroeder was inclined to drop the unit from his roster, but on hearing this contrary material, renewed their contract on the understanding they pursue a more progressive line. Micky Jones (b. 7 June 1946, Merthyr Tydfil, Mid-Glamorgan, Wales; lead guitar/vocals), **Deke Leonard** (b. Roger Leonard, Wales; guitar), Clive John (guitar/keyboards), Ray Williams (bass) and Jeff Jones (drums) completed Man's debut, *Revelation*, a concept album based on evolution. One of the tracks, 'Erotica', became a substantial European hit, but the single, which featured a simulated orgasm, was denied a British release. Man abandoned much of *Revelation*'s gimmicky frills for *2ozs Of Plastic With A Hole In The Middle*, which captured something of the group's live fire. Having suppressed the British feel prevalent on that first outing, the quintet was establishing its improvisatory preferences, akin to those associated with America's 'west coast' bands, exemplified by the **Quicksilver Messenger Service**. The first in a flurry of line-up changes began when Martin Ace (bass) and Terry Williams (drums) joined the group. *Man* and *Do You Like It Here, Are Your Settling In?* contained several established stage favourites, including 'Daughter Of The Fireplace' and 'Many Are Called But Few Get Up', but the band only prospered as a commercial force with the release of *Live At the Padgett Rooms, Penarth.* This limited-issue set created considerable interest but coincided with considerable internal unrest. With the departure of Deke Leonard in pursuit of a solo career, the 1972 line-up of Micky Jones, Clive John, Will Youatt (b. Michael Youatt, 16 February, 1950, Swansea, West Glamorgan, Wales; bass/vocals), Phil Ryan (b. 21 October 1946, Port Talbot, West Galmorgan, Wales; keyboards) and Terry Williams (b. 11 January 1948, Swansea, West Glamorgan, Wales) released what is generally considered to be Man's most popular album, the live set, *Be Good To Yourself...At Least Once A Day*, which contained lengthy guitar/keyboard work-outs typified by the classic track 'Bananas'. The next album, *Back To The Future* gave Man their highest UK album chart position, which was almost emulated the following year with *Rhinos, Winos And Lunatics*. The latter saw the return of Leonard and found Man at the height of their success. During this period the nomadic habits of various members were unabated due to the comings and goings between variously related groups such as **Help Yourself**, the **Neutrons**, **Alkatraz** and the **Flying Aces**. Throughout the band's history, Mickey Jones was Man's unifying factor as they lurched from one change to the next. Following the group's success in the USA promoting their well-received album, *Slow Motion*, an ill-fated project with Quicksilver's **John Cippolina** resulted in the unsatisfactory *Maximum Darkness*. The group's demise came in 1976 when, after the release of the *Welsh Connection*, having lost their momentum, the group ground to a halt. During the late 80s, Jones, Leonard, Ace and drummer John 'Pugwash' Weathers (ex-**Gentle Giant**), resuscitated the Man name, regularly appearing on the UK pub/club circuit and on the Continent. Terry Williams had in the meantime found security in **Rockpile** and **Dire Straits**. In 1993 the unit released their first studio album in 16 years, *The Twang Dynasty Road Goes On Forever*. Much-loved, the band's activities are still chronicled in Michael Heatley's fanzine, *The Welsh Connection.*

Albums: *Revelation* (1969), *2ozs Of Plastic With A Hole In The Middle* (1969), *Man* aka *Man 1970* (1970), *Do You Like It Here Are You Settling In?* (1971), *Live At The Padgett Rooms, Penarth* (1972), *Be Good To Yourself...At Least Once A Day* (1972), *Back To The Future* (1974), *Rhinos, Winos And Lunatics* (1975), *Slow Motion* (1975), *Maximum Darkness* (1976), *The Welsh Connection* (1976), *All's Well That Ends Well* (1977), *Live At Reading 1983* (1993), *The Twang Dynasty Road Goes On Forever* (1993). Compilations: *Golden Hour* (1973), *Green Fly* (1986), *Perfect Timing (The UA Years: 1970-75)* (1991).

Further reading: *Mannerisms*, Martin Mycock.

Man Jumping

Once described by **Brian Eno** as the most interesting band in the world, Man Jumping evolved out of the cooperative band, Lost Jockey. Lost Jockey had been set up in 1980 to perform the music of American Minimalist/Systems composers (**Steve Reich**, **Philip Glass**, **Terry Riley**), together with works by members of the ensemble, such as Andrew Poppy and Orlando Gough. Growing to over 30 musicians, it became unmanageable and collapsed in 1983 after producing two excellent albums: *Hoovering The Beach* (1981) and the 10-inch *Lost Jockey* (1982). Saxophonist Andy Blake, bassist and keyboardist John Lunn and Gough, Schaun Tozer, Charlie Seaward and Glyn Perrin (all keyboards) decided to pull a more viable unit out of the ashes, planning a more varied repertoire with emphasis on original pieces. Martin Ditcham came in on drums (replaced in 1986 by Simon Limbrick, from the Lumiere Theatre Company). They had problems getting their recordings promulgated (A&R people liked their mix of Systems, funk, jazz, Afro and the 'classical' *avant garde*, but did not know how to label or, consequently, how to market it) and the band started doing live gigs in late 1985. The following summer they opened the Covent Garden Music Festival with a free open-air concert, and took part in the Summerscope season at London's South Bank Centre. The band and individual members have also done much fine work

with dance companies such as Second Stride (eg Weighing The Heart) and the London Contemporary Dance Theatre (eg *Unfolding Field*).
Albums: *Jump Cut* (1984), *World Service* (1987).

Man Of La Mancha

Staged at the ANTA Washington Square Theater, and hence just a little off-Broadway, *Man Of La Mancha* opened on 22 November 1965. Dale Wasserman's book combined elements of Miguel de Cervantes's classic novel, *Don Quixote*, with the troubled life of the author. Wasserman had earlier written a straight dramatic play which was televised in 1959, and was persuaded by producer-director Albert Marre to adapt it into a musical version. With music by **Mitch Leigh** and lyrics by Joe Darion, the show opened to good reviews and quickly built a following at the comparatively small ANTA Theater. Starring Richard Kiley as Cervantes/Quixote and Joan Diener as Aldonza, the story interweaved episodes in the life of Cervantes, who endured slavery and imprisonment, often for debt, before achieving success with the publication of his masterpiece. It proved to be an unexpected hit and won Tony Awards for best musical, actor (Kiley), score, director (Marre), and scenic design (Howard Bay). The careful integration of songs and lyrics into the development of the plot made it difficult for most of them to gain life outside the show, but there were several admirable numbers, including 'I'm Only Thinking Of Him', 'The Dubbing', 'Little Bird, Little Bird', 'What Do You Want From Me?', and 'I Really Like Him'. Another of the songs, 'The Impossible Dream', did achieve some measure of popularity especially in a recording by **Jack Jones**. It endured, and became a UK hit in 1992 for the local eccentric band **Carter USM**. *Man Of La Mancha* stayed at the ANTA theatre until March 1968 when it transferred to the larger Martin Beck Theatre where it continued its run for a total of 2,328 performances. The London production opened in March 1968 with Joan Diener and Keith Michell; Richard Kiley took over the lead in 1969. A 1992 Broadway revival, which starred Raul Julia and pop singer **Sheena Easton**, folded after 108 performances. Peter O'Toole appeared in the 'plodding, abysmal' film version in 1972.

Man Who Fell To Earth, The

Nicolas Roeg, already responsible for ***Performance***, *Walkabout* and *Don't Look Now*, directed this elliptical 1976 feature. His decision to cast **David Bowie** as Thomas Jerome Newton, an angel/alien on an ill-defined mission, was inspired. The singer's gaunt features and flaxen hair combined well with his chameleon musical persona. Bowie's chillingly austere *Station To Station* appeared the same year as *The Man Who Fell To Earth*, and an atmosphere of disengagement permeates both projects. Roeg's camerawork and direction are suitably enigmatic, resulting in one of the era's most perplexing, but absorbing, films. **John Phillips**, formerly of the **Mamas And The Papas**, helped assemble the soundtrack selections, which included four of his own performances; 'Hello Mary Lou', 'Boys From The South', Rhumba Boogie' and 'Bluegrass Breakdown', as well as material by Japanese percussionist **Stomu Yamash'ta**, 50s' college-folk act the **Kingston Trio** and **Roy Orbison**. This beguiling collection was completed by MOR songs, excerpts from Holtz's *Planet Suite* and recordings of the humpback whale. The music proved as eclectic as the film itself.

Manassas

The multi-talented **Stephen Stills** founded this highly-regarded unit in October 1971, during sessions for a projected album. **Chris Hillman** (guitar/vocals), Al Perkins (pedal steel guitar), both formerly of the **Flying Burrito Brothers**, and percussionist Jo Lala joined the singer's regular touring band of Paul Harris (b. New York City, New York, USA; keyboards), Calvin 'Fuzzy' Samuels (bass) and Dallas Taylor (drums), although Samuels was latterly replaced by Kenny Passarelli. The group's disparate talents were best displayed in their remarkably accomplished live shows and on *Manassas*, a diverse double-album selection brilliantly encompassing country, rock, R&B and latin styles. The septet displayed a remarkable unity of purpose despite the contrasting material, a cohesion which endowed the set with its lasting quality. *Down The Road* could not quite match the standards set by the debut and Manassas was brought to an end in September 1973, with the sudden departure of Hillman, Perkins and Harris for the ill-fated Souther Hillman Furay Band. Many mourn the fact that Stills seemed at his most creative when fronting this band and those who were lucky enough to have seen them during their brief career can testify that they were indeed a spectacular rock/country/blues band.
Albums: *Manassas* (1972), *Down The Road* (1973).

Mance, Junior

b. Julian Clifford Mance, Jnr., 10 October 1928, Chicago, Illinois, USA. Taught piano by his father, a professional jazz musician, Mance was playing professionally long before he entered his teenage. In the late 40s, still in his teens, he joined a band led by **Gene Ammons** and in 1950 worked with **Lester Young**. After military service he became a resident at a Chicago jazz club before becoming **Dinah Washington**'s accompanist. In the mid-60s he played with **Cannonball** and **Nat Adderley**, whom he had first met in an army band, then joined **Dizzy Gillespie**. By the early 60s, Mance had decided on a career as leader and from then onwards worked clubs throughout the USA. Although primarily known for his

work in bop and post-bop groups, Mance's playing reveals echoes of his father's early instruction which drew heavily upon the blues piano tradition. A gifted player with a fluent technique and subtle touch, Mance's reputation worldwide is somewhat less than his talent deserves.
Albums: *The Soulful Piano Of Junior Mance* (1960), with Eddie 'Lockjaw' Davis, Johnny Griffin *Tough Tenors* (1960), *Junior Mance Trio At The Village Vanguard* (Carrere 1961), *Holy Mama* (1976), *Smokey Blues* (JSP 1980), *Deep* (JSP 1982), with Martin Rivera *For Dancers Only* (1983), with Rivera *The Tender Touch Of* (Niva 1984), *Junior Mance Special* (Sackville 1989), *Play The Music Of Dizzy Gillespie* (Sackville 1993).

Mancha, Steve

b. Clyde Wilson, 25 December 1945, Walhall, South Carolina, USA. As lead vocalist of the group **100 Proof Aged In Soul** on their big 1970 hit 'Somebody's Been Sleeping', Mancha probably achieved his most significant commercial success; but soul fans, and especially Detroit soul fans, remember him from his days as writer and performer Clyde Wilson in Detroit, where his family had moved to in 1954. Signing first with **Harvey Fuqua**, together with friend Wilbert Jackson, Clyde and Wilbert performed as the Two Friends for Fuqua's HPC label. Soon, this and other Fuqua labels were incorporated by **Berry Gordy** into his fledgling **Motown** empire, and, in 1965, Wilson moved to the Wheelsville label, owned by Don Davis, where he recorded 'Did My Baby Call' coupled with 'Whirlpool'. In 1966 he had a hit as a member of the Holidays (other memebers were **J.J. Barnes** and **Edwin Starr**) with 'I'll Love You Forever' (number 7 R&B). That year Clyde Wilson became Steve Mancha, and joined Don Davis's Groovesville Records as a solo artist in 1966, together with J.J. Barnes and Melvin Davis. Mancha cut five singles for the label, with 'I Don't Wanna Lose You' and 'Don't Make Me A Storyteller' making the national R&B charts. Then Davis formed Groove City for which Mancha cut just one single, 'Hate Yourself In The Morning'/'A Love Like Yours'. Six of these Groovesville and Groove City sides appeared on the **Stax**/Volt album, *Rare Stamps*, after Don Davis began leasing his product to the Memphis-based label. (The other tracks on the album were Davis-produced items by J.J. Barnes). Subsequently, Mancha signed for **Holland/Dozier/Holland**'s Hot Wax, which the famous trio had formed on splitting with Motown. Here, Mancha became lead vocalist on all but three of 100 Proof Aged In Soul's recordings, as well as co-writing seven of their sides. When Holland/Dozier/Holland moved to California, Mancha stayed in Detroit and became involved in gospel music, returning to the secular scene in 1986 when UK soul entrepreneur, Ian Levine, recorded him on 'It's All Over The Grapevine' for EMI.
Compilations: *Rare Stamps* (1969, 6 tracks), *Don Davis Presents The Sound Of Detroit* (1993, 6 tracks).

Manchester, Melissa

b. 15 February 1951, the Bronx, New York, USA. A former staff writer at Chappel Music and back-up singer for **Bette Midler**, Manchester launched her own career in 1973 with *Home To Myself*. Her intimate style showed a debt to contemporary New York singer/songwriters, but later releases, including her self-titled third album, were more direct. This collection, produced by **Richard Perry** and **Vini Poncia**, yielded the artist's first major hit, 'Midnight Blue' (US Top 10), and set the pattern for her subsequent direction which, if carefully performed, lacked the warmth of those early recordings. Success as a performer and songwriter continued into the 70s and 80s. 'Whenever I Call You Friend', co-written with **Kenny Loggins**, was a best-selling single for him in 1978, while in 1979 Melissa's second US Top 10 was achieved with 'Don't Cry Out Loud' (composed by **Carole Bayer Sager** and **Peter Allen**). Three years later she scored another hit with 'You Should Hear How She Talks About You'. Although she has since diversified into scriptwriting and acting, Manchester remains a popular recording artist.
Albums: *Home To Myself* (1973), *Bright Eyes* (1974), *Melissa* (1975), *Better Days And Happy Endings* (1976), *Help Is On The Way* (1976), *Singin'* (1977), *Don't Cry Out Loud* (1978), *Melissa Manchester* (1979), *For The Working Girl* (1980), *Hey Ricky* (1982), *Emergency* (1983), *Mathematics* (1985). Compilation: *Greatest Hits* (1983).

Mancini, Henry

b. Enrico Mancini, 16 April 1924, Cleveland, Ohio, USA, d. 14 June 1994, Los Angeles, California, USA. Prompted by his father, a steelworker who loved music, Mancini learned to play several musical instruments while still a small child. As a teenager he developed an interest in jazz and especially music of the big bands. He wrote some arrangements and sent them to **Benny Goodman**, from whom he received some encouragement. In 1942, he became a student at the Juilliard School of Music, but his career was interrupted by military service during World War II. Immediately following the war he was hired as pianist and arranger by **Tex Beneke**, who was then leading the **Glenn Miller** orchestra. Later in the 40s Mancini began writing arrangements for studios, prompted initially by a contract to score for a recording date secured by his wife, singer Ginny O'Connor (of the **Mel-Tones**). He was also hired to work on films (the first of which was the Abbott and Costello comedy *Lost In Alaska*), and it was here that his interest in big band music paid off. He wrote the scores for two major Hollywood bio-pics, ***The Glenn Miller Story*** (1954)

and ***The Benny Goodman Story*** (1956), as well as Orson Welles' *Touch Of Evil* classic (1958). Mancini also contributed jazz-influenced scores for television, including those for the innovative *Peter Gunn* series and *Mr Lucky*. His film work continued with scores and songs for such films as ***Breakfast At Tiffany's*** (1961), from which came 'Moon River', (the Oscar winner that year), and the title songs for *Days Of Wine And Roses* (1962), which again won an Oscar, and *Charade* (1963). His other film compositions included 'Baby Elephant Walk' from *Hatari!* (1962), the theme from *The Pink Panther* (1964), 'Sweetheart Tree' from *The Great Race* (1965), and scores for *Man's Favourite Sport?*, *Dear Heart*, *Wait Until Dark*, *Darling Lili*, *Mommie Dearest*, ***Victor/Victoria*** (1982), for which he won an Oscar for 'Original Song Score' with **Leslie Bricusse**, *That's Dancing*, *Without A Clue*, *Physical Evidence*, *Blind Date*, *That's Life*, *The Glass Menagerie*, *Sunset*, *Fear*, *Switch*, and *Tom And Jerry: The Movie*, on which he again teamed with Leslie Bricusse. One of the most respected film and television composers - and the winner of 20 Grammy Awards - Mancini acknowledged his greatest legacy to be '...my use of jazz - incorporating various popular idioms into the mainstream of film scoring. If that's a contribution, then that's mine'. In addition he also regularly conducted orchestras in the USA and UK in concerts of his music, most of which stood comfortably on its own merits outside the context for which it was originally conceived. In the months prior to his death, Mancini was working with Leslie Bricusse on the score for the stage adaption of *Victor/Victoria*.
Selected albums: *The Music From Peter Gunn* (1959), *The Blues And The Beat* (1960), *The Mancini Touch* (1960), *Mr Lucky Goes Latin* (1961), *Breakfast At Tiffany's* (1961), *Hatari* (1962), *Combo!* (1962), *Uniquely Mancini* (1963), *Our Man In Hollywood* (1963), *The Second Time Around* (1963), *Marches* (1963), *The Concert Sound Of Henry Mancini* (1964), with his orchestra and chorus *Dear Heart-And Other Songs About Love* (1965), *The Latin Sound Of Henry Mancini* (1965), *Sounds And Voices* (1966), *Two For The Road* (1967), *Encore!* (1967), *A Warm Shade Of Ivory* (1969), *Mancini Country* (1970), *Themes From Love Story* (1971), *This Is Henry Mancini* (1971, 2 LP set), *The Mancini Generation* (1972), with Doc Severinsen *Brass, Ivory & Strings* (1973), *The Academy Award Winning Songs* (1975), *Mancini's Angels* (1977), *Just You And Me Together Love* (1979), *Pure Gold* (1980), *Victor/Victoria* (1982), *Best Of* (1984), *A Man And His Music* (1985, 2 LP set), with James Galway *In The Pink* (1985), *Merry Mancini Christmas* (1985), *At The Movies* (1986), with Johnny Mathis *The Hollywood Musicals* (1986), *Henry Mancini And The Royal Philharmonic Pops Orchestra* (1988), *Diamond Series* (1988), with The Royal Philharmonic Pops Orchestra *Premier Pops* (1988) and *Mancini Rocks The Pops* (1989), *Theme Scene* (1989), *Mancini In Surround Sound* (1990), and various other film and television soundtracks.

Further reading: *Henry Mancini*, Gene Lees. *Did They Mention The Music?*, Henry Mancini and Gene Lees.

Mandel, Harvey

b. 11 March 1945, Detroit, Michigan, USA. This fluent, mellifluous guitarist was one of several young aspirants learning their skills in Chicago blues clubs. A contemporary of **Paul Butterfield** and **Michael Bloomfield**, Mandel was a member of both the **Charlie Musselwhite** and **Barry Goldberg** blues bands, before moving to the west coast in 1967. His debut album, *Christo Redentor*, was released the following year. This wholly instrumental set, which included contributions from Musselwhite, **Graham Bond**, and the Nashville musicians later known as **Area Code 615**, is arguably the guitarist's definitive release, but *Righteous* and *Baby Batter* are equally inventive. Between 1969 and 1971, Mandel was a member of **Canned Heat** wherein he struck an empathy with bassist Larry Taylor. Both subsequently joined **John Mayall** for *USA Union* and *Back To The Roots* before the guitarist formed the short-lived Pure Food And Drug Act. He also remained a popular session musician, contributing to albums by **Love**, the **Ventures** and **Don 'Sugarcane' Harris** during this highly prolific period. Mandel continued to record his stylish solo albums throughout the early 70s, and was one of several candidates mooted to replace **Mick Taylor** in the **Rolling Stones**. The results of his audition are compiled on the group's 1976 album, *Black And Blue*. This dalliance with corporate rock was Harvey's last high-profile appearance. In 1985 he signed a recording deal with the newly-founded Nuance label, but no new release has been forthcoming.
Albums: *Christo Redentor* (Philips 1968), *Righteous* (Philips 1969), *Games Guitars Play* (Philips 1970), *Baby Batter* aka *Electric Progress* (Janus 1971), *The Snake* (Janus 1972), *Shangrenade* (Janus 1973), *Feel The Sound Of...* (Janus 1974), *Live Boot: Harvey Mandel Live In California* (Fresh Squeezed 1990), *Twist City* (Western Front 1993). Compilation: *Best Of...* (Janus 1975).

Mandel, Johnny

b. 23 November 1935, New York City, New York, USA. After playing trumpet and trombone while still in his pre-teenage years (a period in which he began to write music), Mandel played with various bands in and around New York, including those led by **Boyd Raeburn** and **Jimmy Dorsey**. In the mid- to late 40s Mandel played in the bands of **Buddy Rich, Alvino Rey** and others, and in the early 50s, he worked with **Elliott Lawrence** and **Count Basie**. He began to establish himself both as an arranger, contributing charts to the Basie and **Artie Shaw** bands, and also as a songwriter. By the mid-50s he was writing music for films and was working less in the jazz field, although his film music often contained echoes of his background.

Much respected by singers and jazz instrumentalists, Mandel has a particular facility for ballads. He also orchestrated scores for Broadway and for television specials. His film work, from the 50s through to the 80s, includes music for *I Want To Live*, *The Third Voice*, *The Americanization Of Emily*, *The Sandpiper*, *The Russians Are Coming*, *Point Blank*, *MASH*, *The Last Detail*, *Escape To Witch Mountain*, *Freaky Friday*, *Agatha*, *Being There*, *The Baltimore Bullet*, *Caddyshack*, *Deathtrap*, *The Verdict*, *Staying Alive*, and *Brenda Starr* (1987). He also scored for television movies such as *The Trackers*, *The Turning Point Of Jim Molloy*, *A Letter To Three Wives*, *Christmas Eve*, *LBJ - The Early Years*, *Assault And Matrimony*, *Foxfire*, *Agatha*, *The Great Escape II - The Untold Story*, and *Single Men - Married Women* (1989). Among his songs are 'Emily', 'A Time For Love' and, perhaps his best-known, 'The Shadow Of Your Smile' (lyrics by **Paul Francis Webster**), written for *The Sandpiper* (1965). The latter won a Grammy for song of the year, and and the Oscar for best song.

Mandingo Griot Society

Formed in Chicago, USA in 1977 by the Gambian kora player **Foday Musa Suso**, the Mandingo Griot Society were a flexible line-up of like-minded African, Caribbean and American musicians who played a fusion of rock, funk, reggae and traditional Gambian styles, and who did much to foster the spirit of stylistic eclecticism and multi-cultural collision then emerging amongst *avant garde* Western musicians and audiences. Their music was both lyrical and irresistibly danceable and, unlike so many subsequent fusion attempts, retained the rough edges of its many constituent styles rather than attempting to make them blandly acceptable to mainstream listeners. In addition to the Western instruments of bass, guitar and kit drums, the group employed a wide range of ethnic instruments, including the West African dusungoni (seven-stringed hunter's harp), bala (xylophone), djembe (hand drum), bolon (three-stringed warrior's harp), dundungo (bass drum), tamo (talking drum) and, of course, Suso's kora (21-stringed harp). North Indian tabla drums and Afro-Cuban timbales, bongos and congas were also employed from time to time.

Aside from Suso, key members of the group included percussionist Adam Rudolph, who had previously played with numerous jazz, latin and new music ensembles including Chevere, Streetdancer, Eternal Wind and Detroit's Contemporary Jazz Quintet. He had also performed in Europe and the USA with trumpeter **Don Cherry.** Drummer Hamid Drake had been an important part of numerous Chicago jazz and R&B groups, working with **Muhal Richard Adams, Douglas Ewart** and **George Lewis.** He had also toured Europe and West Africa with Don Cherry. Bassist Joseph Thomas and guitarist John Markiss had previously worked together in bands led by **Sun Ra, Lonnie Liston Smith** and **Peter Tosh,** and in **Tower Of Power** and **Earth Wind And Fire**. Mandingo Griot Society recorded two outstanding albums before disbanding in 1983. Suso then moved to New York to work with **Bill Laswell** and **Herbie Hancock,** while the other members subsequently pursued solo and guest artist careers on the Chicago jazz and R&B scenes.

Albums: *Mandingo Griot Society* (1978), *Mighty Rhythm* (1981).

Mandrake Memorial

Formed in 1967 in Philadelphia, USA, Mandrake Memorial was a progressive-rock quartet which helped pioneer the use of electronics in rock music. The group consisted of guitarist Craig Anderton, keyboardist/vocalist Michael Katz, bassist Randy Monaco and drummer Kevin Lally. Using such psychedelic music techniques as feedback, sitars, orchestras and backwards tape loops, the group added the sound of synthesizers, one of the first bands to do so on a regular basis. Signed to Poppy Records, they released their self-titled first album in 1968, after which Katz departed and the group continued as a trio. Two more albums were issued in 1969 and 1970 before the group disbanded. Anderton became a producer, designer of musical electronics and journalist specializing in electronic music and technology.

Albums: *Mandrake Memorial* (1968), *Medium* (1969), *Puzzle* (1970).

Mandrell, Barbara

b. 25 December 1948, Houston, Texas, USA, but raised in Oceanside, near Los Angeles, California. Mandrell comes from a musical family: her father, Irby, sang and played guitar and her mother, Mary, played piano and taught music. At the age of 12, Mandrell demonstrated the steel guitar at a national convention and then worked in Las Vegas with **Joe Maphis** and **Tex Ritter**. By her teens, she also played saxophone, guitar, banjo and bass. Her parents formed the Mandrells with herself and two boys, one of whom, drummer Ken Dudney, became her husband in 1967. Their extensive touring schedule included forces bases in Vietnam. Mandrell first recorded in 1966 for the small Mosrite label, and her sobbing 'Queen For A Day', with **Glen Campbell** on guitar, was reissued with a revised accompaniment in 1984. Mandrell signed with **Columbia** in 1969, and, for a time, she concentrated on country versions of soul hits - 'I've Been Lovin' You Too Long', 'Treat Him Right', 'Show Me' and 'Do Right Woman - Do Right Man'. Despite her glossy Las Vegas look, she joined the *Grand Ole Opry* in 1972, switched to **ABC-Dot** in 1975 and had her first Top 5 country single with 'Standing Room Only'. In 1977 she had her first US country number 1 with 'Sleepin' Single In A Double Bed', which was written by Kye Fleming and Dennis Morgan, who also wrote further number 1 hits, including 'Years' and 'I Was Country When Country Wasn't Cool', which was released during *Urban Cowboy*'s popularity and featured **George Jones**. Her version of the soul hit, '(If Loving You Is Wrong) I Don't Want To Be Right', was another country number 1 and also a US pop hit, leading her to name her band, the Do-Rites. Mandrell also covered **Poacher**'s 'Darlin'' for the US country market. Her television series, *Barbara Mandrell And The Mandrell Sisters*, ran from 1980-82 and was screened in the UK. There was good-humoured interplay between Mandrell and her sisters, Irlene (b. Ellen Irlene Mandrell, 29 January 1956, California, USA) and **Louise Mandrell**, and the diminutive Barbara had the same vivacious appeal as **Dolly Parton**. She had further US country number 1 singles, 'Til You're Gone' and 'One Of A Kind Pair Of Fools', and also fared well with 'To Me', a duet with **Lee Greenwood**. In 1984 she and her two children were badly injured when her car was hit head-on. She was unable to work for a year, although she had another child, and she lost much credibility when she sued, on her insurer's advice, the late driver's family for $10 million. Her records for **Capitol** have not seen much chart success, but she maintains that the accident has strengthened her faith.

Albums: *Treat Him Right* (1971), with David Houston *A Perfect Match* (1972), *The Midnight Oil* (1973), *This Time I Almost Made It* (1974), *This Is Barbara Mandrell* (1976), *Midnight Angel* (1976), *Lovers, Friends And Strangers* (1977), *Love's Ups And Downs* (1978), *Moods* (1978), *Just For The Record* (1979), *Love Is Fair* (1980), *Looking Back* (1981), *Live* (1981), *In Black And White* (1982), *He Set My Life To Music* (1982), *Spun Gold* (1983), with Houston *Back To Back* (1983), *Clean Cut* (1984), with Lee Greenwood *Meant For Each Other* (1984), *Christmas At Our House* (1984), *Get To The Heart* (1985), *Moments* (1986), *Sure Feels Good* (1987), *I'll Be Your Jukebox Tonight* (1988), *Morning Sun* (1990), *No Nonsense* (1991), *Key's In The Mailbox* (1991).

Further reading: *Get To The Heart: My Story*, Barbara Mandrell with George Vecsey. *The Barbara Mandrell Story*, Charles Paul Conn.

Mandrell, Louise

b. Thelma Louise Mandrell, 13 July 1954, Corpus Christi, Texas, USA. Mandrell began playing guitar, banjo and fiddle as a child and joined her sister, **Barbara Mandrell**, in the latter's band on bass in 1969. She had a short-lived marriage with Ronny Shaw, who opened for Barbara Mandrell, and her second marriage also failed. She was a featured singer with **Merle Haggard**'s roadshow in the mid-70s. She signed to Epic and had US country hits with 'Put It On Me', 'Everlasting Love' and 'Reunited' (which was a duet with her third husband, **R.C. Bannon**). She had further success with **RCA** and was the butt of her sister's jokes on the television series, *Barbara Mandrell And The Mandrell Sisters*. In 1983, she had solo country hits with 'Save Me' and 'Too Hot To Sleep', which led to her own television series. Her 1988 single with **Eric Carmen**, 'As Long As We Got Each Other', made the US country charts despite only promotional copies being issued.

Albums: with R.C. Bannon *Inseparable* (1979), with Bannon *Love Won't Let Us Go* (1980), *Louise Mandrell* (1981), with Bannon *Me And My R.C.* (1982), with Bannon *(You're My) Superwoman, (You're My) Incredible Man* (1982), *Close Up* (1983), *Too Hot To Sleep* (1983), *I'm Not Through Loving You Yet* (1984), *Maybe My Baby* (1985).

Manfred Mann

During the UK beat boom of the early 60s, spearheaded by the **Beatles**, a number of R&B groups joined the tide with varying degrees of achievement. Of these, Manfred Mann had the most commercial success. The band was formed as the Mann-Hugg Blues Brothers by Manfred Mann (b. Manfred Lubowitz, 21 October 1940, Johannesburg, South Africa; keyboards) and Mike Hugg (b. 11 August 1942, Andover, Hampshire, England; drums/vibraphone). They became Manfred Mann shortly after adding **Paul Jones** (b. Paul Pond, 24 February 1942, Portsmouth, Hampshire, England; harmonica/vocals). The line-up was completed by Mike Vickers (b. 18 April 1941, Southampton, Hampshire, England; flute/guitar/saxophone) and Tom McGuinness (b. 2 December 1941, London, England; bass), following the departure of Dave Richmond. After being signed by a talent hungry **HMV Records** and following one unsuccessful instrumental, they made an impression with the catchy 'Cock-A-Hoop'. The prominent use of Jones' harmonica gave them a distinct sound and they soon became one of Britain's leading groups. No less than two of their singles were used as the theme music to the pioneering British television music programme, *Ready Steady Go*. '5-4-3-2-1' provided the breakthrough Top 10 hit in early 1964. By the summer, the group registered their first UK number 1 with the catchy 'Do Wah Diddy Diddy'. Over the next two years, they charted regularly with memorable hits such as 'Sha La La', 'Come Tomorrow', 'Oh No! Not My Baby' and **Bob Dylan**'s 'If You Got To Go, Go Now'. In May 1966, they returned to number 1 with the sublime 'Pretty Flamingo'. It was to prove the last major hit on which Jones appeared. His departure for a solo career was a potential body blow to the group at a time when personnel changes were regarded as anathema by the pop media and fans. He was replaced by **Michael D'Abo** recruited from A Band Of Angels in preference to **Rod Stewart**, who failed the audition. Mike Vickers had previously departed for a lucrative career as a television composer. He was replaced by **Jack Bruce** on bass, allowing Tom McGuinness to move to lead guitar, a role he was happier with. Additionally,

Henry Lowther (trumpet) and **Lyn Dobson**, (saxophone) enlarged the line-up for a time and **Klaus Voorman** replaced Bruce on bass. D'Abo's debut with the group was another hit rendering of a Dylan song, 'Just Like A Woman' their first for the Fontana label. He fitted in surprisingly well with the group, which surprised many critics by maintaining their hit formulae despite the departure of the charismatic Jones. Both 'Semi-Detached Suburban Mr. Jones' and 'Ha! Ha! Said The Clown' were formidable Top 5 hits in the classic Mann tradition. Along with America's **Byrds**, the group were generally regarded as the best interpreters of Dylan material, a view endorsed by the songwriter himself. This point was punctuated in 1968 when the group registered their third number 1 with the striking reading of his 'Mighty Quinn'. They ended the 60s with a final flurry of Top 10 hits, 'My Name Is Jack', 'Fox On The Run' and 'Raggamuffin Man' before abdicating their pop crown in favour of a heavier approach. Their albums had always been meatier and showed off their considerable dexterity as musicians working with jazz and blues-based numbers. Mann went on to form the jazz/rock unit **Chapter Three** and the highly successful **Manfred Mann's Earth Band**. Still highly respected, Manfred Mann remain one of the finest beat groups of the 60s.

Albums: *Five Faces Of Manfred Mann* (1964), *Mann Made* (1965), *Mann Made Hits* (1966), *As Is* (1966), *Soul Of Mann* (1967), *Up The Junction* (1967), *The Mighty Garvey* (1968), *The R&B Years* (1986). Compilations: *This Is Manfred Mann* (1971), *Semi-Detached Suburban* (1979), *The Singles Plus* (1987), *The EP Collection* (1989), *The Collection* (1990), *Ages Of Mann* (1992), *Best Of The EMI Years* (1993).

Manfred Mann Chapter Three

Following the demise of **Manfred Mann**, Hugg (b. 11 August 1942, Andover, Hampshire, England; drums/vibraphone) and Mann (b. Manfred Lubowitz, 21 October 1940, Johannesburg, South Africa; keyboards) pursued their jazz/rock path by forming Chapter Three as a sideline to their lucrative career writing successful television jingles. This brave project was originally called Enamel and included Bernie Living (alto saxophone/flute), Steve York (bass), Craig Collinge (drums) and featured sessions from some of the finest contemporary jazz musicians including Harold Beckett, Derek Wadsworth, **Chris Pyne** and Dave Quincey. They immediately established themselves on the progressive rock circuit, but could not break out of the small club environment. Their two albums were excellent and imaginative but came as a considerable shock to those old fans who expected anything akin to Manfred Mann. The band weas blighted with problems; due to Mann and Hugg having to support the venture financially, and because of trying to establish themselves as something other than a pop group. Those that supported the endeavour were not disappointed, although Manfred soon returned to a more commercial path with **Manfred Mann's Earth Band**.

Albums: *Manfred Mann Chapter Three* (1969), *Manfred Mann Chapter Three Volume Two* (1970).

Manfred Mann's Earth Band

The fourth incarnation of Manfred Mann (the second being only a change of singer) has been the longest, surviving for almost 20 years. The original Earth Band was formed after Mann's bold attempt at jazz/rock with **Manfred Mann Chapter Three** had proved financially disastrous. The new band was comprised of Manfred (b. Manfred Lubowitz, 21 October 1940, Johannesburg, South Africa; keyboards), Mick Rogers (vocals/guitar), Colin Pattenden (bass) and Chris Slade (drums). Their debut was with the **Bob Dylan** song 'Please Mrs Henry' and following its poor showing they quickly released a version of **Randy Newman**'s 'Living Without You', again to apathy. Whilst the band gradually won back some of the fans who had deserted the Chapter Three project, it was not until their third offering, *Messin'*, that both success and acclaim arrived. The title track was a long, rambling but exciting piece, reminiscent of Chapter Three, but the band hit the mark with a superb interpretation of Holst's Jupiter, entitled 'Joybringer'. It became a substantial UK hit in 1973. From then on the band forged ahead with gradual rather than spectacular progress and built a loyal following in Europe and America. Their blend of rock still contained strong jazz influences, but the sound was wholeheartedly accessible and rock based. *Solar Fire* featured yet another Dylan song, 'Father Of Day', complete with heavenly choir. Rogers departed in 1976. Just as **Bruce Springsteen** fever started, the band had a transatlantic hit with a highly original reading of his 'Blinded By The Light' with vocals from Chris Thompson. The record, with its lengthy, spacey instrumental introduction, reached the top spot in the US chart and worldwide sales exceeded two million.

The Roaring Silence became the band's biggest album, and featured the most assured line-up to date. Other hits followed, including the **Robbie Robertson/John Simon** composition 'Davey's On The Road Again' in 1978 and Dylan's 'You Angel You' and 'Don't Kill It Carol' in 1979. Further personnel changes came with Pat King (bass), ex-**Wings** and **East Of Eden** drummer Geoff Britton and Steve Waller (ex-**Gonzalez**). After a lengthy absence, they made the US chart in 1984 with 'Runner', featuring the vocals of the returning Mick Rogers. Mann's homage to his former homeland *Somewhere In Afrika* was well received that year, although *Criminal Tango*, a collection of non-originals, *Budapest* and *Masque* were commercial failures. The band remain highly popular in Germany and retain the respect of the critics, having never produced

a poor album during their long career.
Albums: *Manfred Mann's Earth Band* (1972), *Glorified Magnified* (1972), *Messin'* (1973), *Get Your Rocks Off* (1973), *Solar Fire* (1973), *The Good Earth* (1974), *Nightingales And Bombers* (1975), *The Roaring Silence* (1976), *Watch* (1978), *Angel Station* (1979), *Chance* (1980), *Somewhere In Afrika* (1983), *Budapest* (1984), *Criminal Tango* (1986), *Masque* (1987). Compilations: *The New Bronze Age* (1977), *Manfred Mann's Earth Band* (1992, 13-CD box set).

Manga, Bebe

b. 1948, Mante, Cameroon. Vocalist Manga was already well known in Cameroon and Gabon before she moved to Paris in 1980 and recorded her classic debut album. A tough mix of makossa, funk and soukous musics. The title track sold over one million copies on single release and spawned over 50 cover versions, including the 1985 club hit by **Nyanka Bell**. A late 80s move to New York, from where she intented to further her international breakthrough, came to nothing and Manga has faded into semi-obscurity.
Album: *Amie* (1983).

Mangelsdorff, Albert

b. 5 September 1928, Frankfurt-Am-Main, Germany. From a musical family, Mangelsdorff and his brother, saxophonist Emil, learned about jazz from secret meetings of the Frankfurt Hot Club, since jazz was banned by the Nazis. He has subsequently become one of the most important and distinctive European jazz players. After playing violin and danceband guitar, he took up the trombone at the age of 20 and extended its range with the use of multiphonics (playing more than one note at a time) through his technique of humming and growling while playing, so that the brass-generated note is augmented by the vocal sound. He won awards in Germany in 1954, and in 1958 gained attention in the USA as a member of the Newport International Band. In 1962 he recorded with **John Lewis**. In 1964 he toured Asia with his own band and at that time began to move towards free jazz. He also recorded an album with **Ravi Shankar**. In the late 60s he joined the **Globe Unity** Orchestra. In 1975, he joined the United Jazz And Rock Ensemble. From 1976-82 Mangelsdorff worked with **Michel Portal**, and in 1981 he co-founded the French/German Jazz Ensemble with J.F. Jenny-Clark. In the mid-70s he augmented **John Surman**'s The Trio (with **Barre Phillips** and Stu Martin) to create MUMPS. In 1986 he and Surman joined with **Elvin Jones** and **Dave Holland** for a tour of Europe.
Selected albums: with John Lewis *Animal Dance* (Atlantic 1962), *Tension* (1963), *New Jazz Ramwong* (L+R 1964), with Lee Konitz, Attila Zoller *ZO-KO-MA* (1967), *And His Friends* (1967), *Wild Goose* (1969), *Never Let It End* (1970), *Live In Tokyo* (Enja 1971), *Spontaneous* (Enja 1971), *Birds Of Underground* (1972), *Trombirds* (1973), *The Wide Point* (MPS 1975), *Solo Now* (1976), *Tromboneliness* (1976), with Alphonse Mouzon, Jaco Pastorious *Trilogue-Live* (1976), with MUMPS *A Matter Of Taste* (1977), *A Jazz Tune I Hope* (1978), *Albert Live In Montreux* (1980), *Eternal Rhythm* (MPS 1981), *Three Originals* (MPS 1981), *Triple Entente* (1983), with Wolfgang Dauner *Two Is Company* (1983), with Peter Brötzmann, Günter Sommer Pica *Pica* (1983), *Hot Hut* (1985), with Konitz *The Art Of The Duo* (1988, rec 1983), *Internationales Jazzfestival Munster* (Tutu 1989), with John Surman *Room 1220* (Konnek 1993, 1970 recording).

Mangione, Chuck

b. Charles Frank Mangione, 29 November 1940, Rochester, New York, USA. Mangione began playing trumpet as a child, studying formally at the Eastman School of Music. He gained experience accompanying visiting jazzmen, then in 1960 went to New York where he formed a band with his brother, pianist Gap Mangione. The band, the Jazz Brothers, remained in existence for five years, playing hard bop. In 1965, Mangione played in the trumpet sections of the **Woody Herman** and **Maynard Ferguson** bands and later that year he joined **Art Blakey**, with whom he remained until 1967. After leaving Blakey, Mangione taught at his old school and again formed his own small band. He began making albums with which he achieved considerable popular success. He had started to dabble on flügelhorn and eventually abandoned the trumpet altogether in favour of the more mellow-sounding instrument. Throughout the 70s and into the 80s Mangione continued to capitalize upon his successful recordings, appearing widely in concert and making more records which again appealed to a wide audience. To a great extent, Mangione achieved his popular success by offering melodic and uncluttered music, sometimes with interesting hints of Latin influence. Although much of his popular material failed to excite the hardcore jazz audience, there can be little doubt that he helped to introduce the music to many who might otherwise have passed it by. His compositions have appealed to a wide range of musicians, being played by artists as different as **Percy Faith** and **Cannonball Adderley**. Perhaps the best known of his compositions is 'Land Of Make Believe', which has frequently been recorded. Additionally, Mangione has written for films, notably *The Children Of Sanchez* (1978).
Selected albums: *The Jazz Brothers* (Milestone 1960), *Hey Baby!* (Original Jazz Classics 1961), *Spring Fever* (Original Jazz Classics 1961), *Recuerdo* (Original Jazz Classics 1963), with Art Blakey *Buttercorn Lady* (1966), *Land Of Make Believe* (1972), *Bellavia* (1975), *Feels So Good* (1977), *Feels So Good* (A&M 1978), *The Children Of Sanchez* (1978), *An Evening Of Magic* (A&M 1979), *Tarentella* (A&M 1981), *Love Notes* (Columbia 1982), *Journey To A Rainbow*

(CBS 1983), *Disguise* (1984), *Save Tonight For Me* (CBS 1987), *Eyes Of The Veiled Temptress* (CBS 1988). Compilations: *The Best Of Chuck Mangione* (Mercury 1983), *Compact Jazz* (Mercury 1984).

Mangwana, Sam

b. 18 July 1945, Kinshasa, Zaire. A protege of **Rochereau** and **Franco**, vocalist and composer Mangwana is one of Zaire's least conventional stars. He is known as Le Pigeon Voyageur, the travelling pigeon, a musician who constantly travels, side-stepping the usual stereotypes. Big stars have regular bands - Mangwana has none. They buy hotels, houses, clubs - Mangwana places no value on them. In Zaire, he stays with friends. His career has provoked controversy, rumour and violence - plus a new Zairean style which mixes the rumba with beguine and gives a distinctive Afro-Antillean mixture.

He started his career with a five-year stint with Rochereau, before leaving for L'Orchestre Maquisards. In 1969, after several hits, including 'Zelangaina Sala', the band folded. Mangwana formed Vox Afrique, with **Dalienst**, then went solo, working as musical director and arranger for Rochereau, standing in for him during his absences abroad and recording the harmony parts for him in the studio. In 1972, he changed camps and moved to Franco's TPOK Jazz. Such a change caused unheard-of controversy. Rochereau and Franco were considered to be poles apart: they had their own individual styles, and their own fans in opposing camps. The change was simply unthinkable. Mangwana even received threatening letters; he was forced to hide in a hotel guarded by gendarmes. Finally the dispute grew too much for him and, in 1976, he embarked on a tour of Africa which took him from Zaire to Ghana, Nigeria, Cameroon, Togo, Lome and finally Cote D'lvoire. In the latter country, he formed a band called Amida, with the intention of modernizing Zairean music. When that group fell apart, he formed the African All Stars, with guitarist Syran Mbenza and a large fluctuating membership that included, at various times, Nyboma, Lokassa Ya Mbongo, Syran Mbenza and Bopol (some of whom would later form **Les Quatre Etoiles**). The new band created a hugely influential new style of soukous. Rather than stick to the old Zairean rumba, African All Stars blended it with highlife, Afrobeat and, above all, biguine, to create a solid Afro-Antilles crossover. The African All Stars, however, ran into problems. When the band performed at a reception for the Zairean Ambassador to Cote D'Ivoire, they were accused of neglecting their own national music and asked to play **Zaiko Langa Langa** songs. Back in Zaire, the accusation was at first equally pronounced, until the massive hit 'Georgette Eckins' swept such petty-minded nationalism aside and established Mangwana and his band as major stars and stylists.

Out of the post-Cote D'Ivoire music came a string of hits, each mixing Zairean guitars with a solid beat and a singing style - from the sweetest of tenors to the most swaggering of middle registers - that has become Mangwana's hallmark. Throughout the late 70s, Mangwana remained a vital force on the African scene, influencing such musicians as Quatre Etoiles' Bopol and Nyboma and **Souzy Kasseya**. In 1979, Mangwana arrived in Paris with a slimmer line-up of Syran, Bopol and Pablo. He re-recorded 'Georgette Eckins' and cut the album *Maria Tebbo*, which mixed the tenderness of the title track with the political exultation of 'Chimurenga Zimbabwe' - a celebration of that country's new-found independence. In 1982, Mangwana travelled to southern Africa to throw himself further into the great political struggles of the region. In 1982, he released *Co-Operation* with Franco, and joined him onstage at a concert in Kinshasa. Politically, Mangwana has shown himself as a strong champion of African liberation, through albums like 1983's *Canta Mocambique*, which he recorded as a tribute and an encouragement to the revolution that had ousted the Portuguese in favour of a new, independent Mozambique. He continues his peripatetic career across Africa and Europe, constantly re-energizing his bands with infusions of young, radical musicians.

Albums: *Sam Mangwana With Festival Maquisards* (1977), *Maria Tebbo* (1979), *IMatinda* (1979), *Affaire Video* (1982), with Franco *Co-Operation* (1982), *Canta Mocambique* (1983), *In Nairobi* (1985), *Les Champions Pt. 3* (1988), *Cantabile* (1990).

Manhattan Brothers

Formed in Johannesburg in 1946 by Joseph Mogotsi, Nathan Mdedle, Ronnie Majola and Rufus Khoza, the Manhattan Brothers were the greatest South African vocal group of the 50s and 60s, whose jazz-influenced style nonetheless blazed a trail for later, more traditionally-orientated vocal outfits such as **Ladysmith Black Mambazo**. They were also the first South African group, vocal or instrumental, to achieve any significant international profile. Signed by leading South African label Gallo in 1948, the Manhattan Brothers were marketed as the home-grown answer to American vocal outfits such as the **Mills Brothers** and the **Ink Spots**, and through sheer musical talent quickly outsold their role models. As well as record releases and radio broadcasts, the group put together elaborate variety shows, and created their own backing band, the Jazz Dazzlers, which was led by Mackay Davashe and went on to feature at various times **Hugh Masekela**, Dollar Brand (now **Abdullah Ibrahim**) and **Jonas Gwangwa**. They also recruited **Miriam Makeba** as a young singer, launching her career and, in the process, encouraging her to become one of the first women to perform the traditionally male gumboot dance, a staple of Zulu street music.

The group's material included covers of popular Ink Spots and Mills Brothers songs usually rewritten in Zulu, Sotho or Xhosa - and traditional African folk songs. Their first records were accompanied by a single, acoustic guitar, but by the early 50s a rhythm section and one or two horns had been added. In 1959, the group, with Makeba, took part in the township musical *King Kong*, based on the true story of a township boxing champion who, denied by apartheid the opportunity to face his white peers, fell into crime and was eventually executed for murder. The Brothers came to Britain with the show, while Makeba went to America. In 1964, the group recorded a live album at London's **Cecil Sharp** House (home of the English Folk Song & Dance Society). In 1965, **EMI** released a compilation set featuring some of their greatest hits (notably 'Kilimanjaro', 'Mdube' and 'Thimlela'). By the early 70s, the Manhattan Brothers had pretty much disappeared from the South African and international scenes, though they came together for occasional reunion concerts. Their legacy, however, and the doors they opened for younger South African groups and solo artists, should not be forgotten.
Albums: *Kilimanjaro* (1962), *Manhattan Brothers Live In London* (1964), *Kilimanjaro And Other Hits* (1965).

Manhattan Transfer

The original band was formed in 1969, performing good-time, jugband music. By 1972, the only surviving member was Tim Hauser (b. 1940, Troy, New York, USA; vocals), accompanied by Laurel Masse (b. 1954, USA; vocals) Alan Paul (b. 1949, Newark, New Jersey, USA; vocals) and Janis Siegel (b. 1953, Brooklyn, New York, USA; vocals). Although they covered a variety of styles, their trademark was their use of exquisite vocal harmony. Like their **Atlantic** stablemate, **Bette Midler**, they were selling nostalgia, and they were popular on the New York cabaret circuit. An unlikely pop act, they nonetheless charted on both sides of the Atlantic. It was symptomatic of their lack of crossover appeal that the hits were different in the UK and the USA. Their versatility splintered their audience. Fans of the emotive ballad, 'Chanson D'Amour', were unlikely to go for the brash gospel song 'Operator', or a jazz tune like 'Tuxedo Junction'. In 1979, Cheryl Bentyne replaced Masse without noticeably affecting the vocal sound. Their stunning version of **Weather Report**'s 'Birdland' remains a modern classic. The power of the band is in their sometimes breathtaking vocal abilities, strong musicianship and slick live shows.
Albums: *Jukin'* (1971/75), *Manhattan Transfer* (1975), *Coming Out* (1976), *Pastiche* (1978), *Live* (1978), *Extensions* (1979), *Mecca for Moderns* (1981), *Bodies And Souls* (1983), *Bop Doo-wop* (1985), *Vocalese* (1985), *Live In Tokyo* (1987), *Brazil* (1988). Compilations: *Best Of Manhattan Transfer* (1983), *The Christmas Album* (1992). Solo album: Janis Siegel *Experiment In White* (1982).

Manhattans

Formed in 1962 in Jersey City, New Jersey, USA, about 10 miles south of New York City's borough of Manhattan, the Manhattans were a soul group whose greatest success came during the 70s. The original members were lead vocalist George Smith, bass singer Winfred 'Blue' Lovett (b. 16 November 1943), tenor Edward Bivins (b. 15 January 1942), tenor Kenneth Kelley (b. 9 January 1943) and baritone Richard Taylor (d. 7 December 1987). Specializing in smooth ballads, the group recorded first for the Newark, New Jersey-based Carnival label, on which they placed eight singles on the US R&B charts, beginning with 1965's 'I Wanna Be (Your Everything)'. In 1969, they changed to Deluxe Records, on which they recorded their first Top 10 R&B hit, 'One Life To Live', in 1972. In 1971, Smith died, and was replaced by Gerald Alston (b. 8 November 1942). The group left Deluxe for Columbia in 1973, where their now-sweetened soul style resulted in a string of Top 10 R&B hits, including the 1976 number 1 'Kiss And Say Goodbye', which also made number 1 on the pop charts, and 1980's 'Shining Star' (number 4 R&B/number 5 pop). After 1983's number 4 'Crazy', the group's chart popularity waned, although they continued to release recordings for Columbia. Taylor left the group in 1976 and was not replaced; he died in 1987.
Albums: *Dedicated To You* (Carnival 1964), *For You And Yours* (Carnival 1965), *With These Hands* (1970), *A Million To One* (1972), *There's No Me Without You* (Columbia 1973), *Summertime In The City* (1974), *That's How Much I Love You* (Columbia 1975), *The Manhattans* (Columbia 1976), *It Feels So Good* (Columbia 1977), *There's No Good In Goodbye* (Columbia 1978), *Love Talk* (Columbia 1979), *After Midnight* (Columbia 1980), *Black Tie* (Columbia 1981), *Follow Your Heart* (Columbia 1981), *Forever By Your Side* (Columbia 1983), *Too Hot To Stop It* (Columbia 1985), *Back To Basics* (1986), *Sweet Talk* (1989), *Now* (c.1994). Compilations: *Greatest Hits* (1980), *Best Of* (Columbia 1981), *Dedicated To You/For You And Yous* (1993), *Black Tie* (c.1994).

Manic Street Preachers

These UK punk revivalists enjoyed a love-hate relationship with the music press which opened with a bizarre encounter in 1991. The catalyst was Richey Edwards, who cut the words '4 Real' into his forearm to the amazement of ***New Musical Express*** critic Steve Lamacq, when he dared to call into question the band's authenticity. The group hails from Blackwood, Gwent, Wales, and is comprised of James Dean Bradfield (b. 21 February 1969; vocals/guitar), Richey Edwards (b. 27 December 1969; rhythm guitar), Nicky Wire (b. Nick Jones; bass) and Sean Moore (b. 30 July 1970; drums). Their calculated insults at a wide variety of targets, particularly their peers, had already won them infamy following the release of their debut *New Art Riot* EP, and the **Public Enemy**-sampling 'Motown Junk' (a previous single, 'Suicide Alley', had been a limited pressing distributed to journalists only). Their personal manifesto was equally explicit: rock bands should cut down the previous generation, release one explosive album then disappear. Although the music press pointed out the obvious contradictions and naivete of this credo, the band polarized opinion to a degree which far outweighed their early musical proficiency. The singles, 'Stay Beautiful' and 'Love's Sweet Exile' (backed by the superior 'Repeat' - 'Repeat after me, fuck Queen and Country') were inconclusive, but the reissued version of 'You Love Us', with its taut, vicious refrain, revealed a band beginning to approach in power what they had always had in vision. Their debut album, too, was an injection of bile which proved perversely refreshing in a year of industry contraction and self-congratulation. Unfortunately, it never quite achieved its intention to outsell **Guns N'Roses**' *Appetite For Destruction*, nor did the band split immediately afterwards as stated. The polished, less caustic approach of *Gold Against The Soul* saw the Manics hitting a brick wall in expectation and execution, though as always there were moments of sublime lyricism (notably the singles 'Roses In The Hospital' and 'Life Becoming A Landslide'). *The Holy Bible* returned the group to the bleak worldview of yesteryear, notably on the haunting '4st 7lb', written by a near-anorexic Richey James before a nervous breakdown which saw him temporarily admitted to a mental facility. Other subject matter was drawn from prostitution, the holocaust and the penal system. Never easy listening at the best of times (despite the ability to write genuinely affecting songs like 'Motorcycle Emptiness'), the Manics have already produced enough inspired moments to justify their protracted early claims. However, all that seemed somehow irrelevant following Edwards' disappearance on 1 February 1995, with several parties expressing concern as to his well-being.

Albums: *Generation Terrorists* (Columbia 1992, double album), *Gold Against The Soul* (Columbia 1993), *The Holy Bible* (Columbia 1994).

Manifold, Keith

b. Keith Cyril Manifold, 2 April 1947, Biggin By Hartington, near Buxton, Derbyshire, England. Manifold learned to play guitar and after completing his education, he sought a singing career. He was influenced by such artists as **Jimmie Rodgers** and **Hank Williams**. He was also greatly inspired by the recordings and particularly the yodels of **Wilf Carter** (Montana Slim) and quickly became one of the few British artists to become completely proficient in the art of yodelling. He made his professional debut at a local club in Derbyshire in June 1965. In 1974, he became the first UK country artist to benefit from appearances on television's *Opportunity Knocks*, eventually finishing second to the series' overall winner **Lena Zavaroni**. He made his first recordings for the Westwood label in 1974. In 1975, he performed the winning song, 'Who's Gonna Bring Me Laughter', in the 1975 *Opportunity Knocks* Songwriters Competition, which led him to record for a major label, and he was also voted the *Billboard* Best British Solo Artist at London's Wembley Festival. In 1977, he recorded for DJM and in September 1978, he was sponsored and taken to the USA to record an album in Nashville, using Nashville musicians. In 1986, he varied his style to record a gospel album, whereon he was backed by the Pilling Brass Ensemble. Manifold has maintained his popularity over the years, still tours extensively in the British Isles and has also regularly played in several European venues. Occasionally he is joined on stage by his two daughters. He also owns an entertainments agency and is involved with promotional work and a recording studio.

Albums: *Casting My Lasso* (1974), *Let's Sit Down* (1974), *Yodelling Just For You* (1975), *Danny Boy* (1975), *Inheritance* (1977), *In Nashville* (1978), *Remembering* (1979), *Old Folks Home* (1983), *Time* (1985), *Keith Manifold & White Line Fever* (1986), *Old Rugged Cross* (1986), *She's Mine* (1989), *I Dreamed About Mama Last Night* (1989), *Love Hurts* (1991).

Manilow, Barry

b. Barry Alan Pinkus, 17 June 1946, Brooklyn, New York, USA. An immensely popular singer, pianist, and composer from the mid-70s onwards, Manilow studied music at the Juilliard School and worked as an arranger for CBS-TV. During the 60s, he also became a skilled composer of advertising jingles. In 1972 he served as accompanist to **Bette Midler**, then a cult performer in New York's gay bath-houses. Manilow subsequently arranged Midler's first two albums and gained his own recording contract with Bell. After an unsuccessful debut album, he took the powerful ballad 'Mandy' to number 1 in America. The song had previously been a UK hit for its co-writer Scott English, as 'Brandy'. This was the prelude to 10 years of remarkable hit parade success. With his strong, pleasant tenor, well-constructed love songs and ingratiating manner in live shows, Manilow was sneered at by critics but adored by his fans, who were predominantly female. Among the biggest hits were 'Could It Be Magic' (1975), 'I Write The Songs' (composed by the **Beach Boys**' **Bruce Johnston** (1976), 'Tryin' to Get The Feeling Again' (1976), 'Looks Like We Made It' (1977), 'Can't Smile Without You' (1978), the upbeat 'Copacabana (At The Copa' (1978), 'Somewhere In The Night' (1979), 'Ships' (1979), and 'I Made It Through The Rain' (1980). Two albums, *2am Paradise Cafe* and *Swing Street*, marked a change of direction as Manilow underlined his jazz credentials in collaborations with **Gerry**

Mulligan and **Sarah Vaughan**. He also appeared on Broadway in two one-man shows, the second of which, *Showstoppers* (1991), was a schmaltzy tribute to great songwriters of the past. During the 80s, Manilow was invited by the widow of one of those writers, **Johnny Mercer**, to set to music lyrics unpublished during Mercer's lifetime. A selection of these were recorded by **Nancy Wilson** on her 1991 album *With My Lover Beside Me*. In June 1994, the stage musical *Copacabana*, for which Manilow composed the music and co-wrote the book, opened in London starring Gary Wilmot and Nicola Dawn. In the same year he was the supervising composer, and collaborated on several of the songs, for the animated feature *Thumbelina*.

Albums: *Barry Manilow* (1973), *Barry Manilow II* (1974), *Tryin' To Get The Feeling* (1975), *This One's For You* (1976), *Live* (1977), *Even Now* (1978), *One Voice* (1979), *Barry* (1980), *If I Should Love Again* (1981), *Barry Live In Britain* (1982), *2am Paradise Cafe* (1984), *Swing Street* (1988), *Songs To Make The Whole World Sing* (1989), *Live On Broadway* (1990), *Showstoppers* (1991), *Hidden Treasures* (1993), *Singin' With The Big Bands* (Arista 1994). Compilation: *The Complete Collection And Then Some* (1992, 4-CD set).

Videos: *The Greatest Hits...And Then Some* (1994).

Further reading: *Barry Manilow*, Ann Morse. *Barry Manilow: An Autobiography*, Barry Manilow with Mark Bego. *Barry Manilow*, Howard Elson. *The Magic Of Barry Manilow*, Alan Clarke. *Barry Manilow For The Record*, Simon Weir. *The Barry Manilow Scrapbook: His Magical World In Works And Pictures*, Richard Peters. *Barry Manilow*, Tony Jasper.

Mann, Aimee

Having begun performing with the punk-inspired Young Snakes, Aimee Mann achieved recognition as the lead vocalist of the critically-acclaimed 'Til Tuesday. Frustrated with the an industry trying to push a more mainstream approach - and suggestion that writers outside the group should contribute material - Mann left for a solo career in 1990. *Whatever* was a remarkable set, drawing rave reviews and the generous plaudits of **Elvis Costello**. A literate and skilled composer, Mann attacked the corporate music business on 'I've Had It' and detailed estrangement and heartbreak on 'I Should've Known' and 'I Know There's A Word' (allegedly concerning her former relationship with **Jules Shear**). Former **Byrds**' guitarist **Roger McGuinn** was persuaded to contribute distinctive 12-string backing on a set reviving pop's traditions of melody and chorus, while placing them in an unquestionably contemporary context.

Album: *Whatever* (Imago 1993).

Mann, Barry

b. 9 February 1939, Brooklyn, New York, USA. One of the leading pop songwriters of his generation. Although trained as an architect, Mann began his career in music following a summer singing engagement in the Catskills resort. He initially composed material for **Elvis Presley**'s publishers Hill & Range, before briefly collaborating with Howie Greenfield. In 1961, he enjoyed a Top 10 hit in his own right with 'Who Put The Bomp?', but thereafter it was as a composer that he dominated the Hot 100. During the same year as his solo hit, Mann had found a new songwriting partner in **Cynthia Weil**, whom he soon married. Their first success together was **Tony Orlando**'s 'Bless You' (1961), a simple but effective love song, which endeared them to their new employer, bubblegum genius **Don Kirschner**, who housed a wealth of songwriting talent in the cubicles of his **Brill Building** offices. With intense competition from those other husband-and-wife teams **Jeff Berry** and **Ellie Greenwich**, and **Gerry Goffin** and **Carole King**, Mann and Weil responded with a wealth of classic songs which still sound fresh and impressive to this day. Like all great songwriters, they adapted well to different styles and themes, and this ensured that their compositions were recorded by a broad range of artists. There was the evocative urban romanticism of the **Crystals**' 'Uptown' (1962) and the **Drifters**' 'On Broadway' (1963), novelty teen fodder such as **Eydie Gorme**'s 'Blame It On The Bossa Nova' (1963) and **Paul Petersen**'s 'My Dad' (1963), the desolate neuroticism of **Gene Pitney**'s 'I'm Gonna Be Strong' (1964) and the **Righteous Brothers**' 'You've Lost That Lovin' Feelin''(1964), and classic mid-60s protest songs courtesy of the **Animals**' 'We Gotta Get Out Of This Place', **Jody Miller**'s 'Home Of The Brave', 'Only In America' (**Jay And The Americans**) and 'Kicks' (**Paul Revere And The Raiders**)

By the late 60s, Mann and Weil left Kirschner and moved to Hollywood. Throughout this period, they continued to enjoy hit success with **Bobby Vinton**'s 'I Love How You Love Me'(written with Larry Kolber in 1968), **Jay And The Americans**' 'Walking In The Rain' (1969) and **B.J. Thomas**' 'I Just Can't Help Believing' (1970). Changes in the pop marketplace subsequently reduced their hit output, but there were some notable successes such as **Dan Hill**'s 'Sometimes When We Touch' (1977). Mann himself still craved recognition as a performer and won a recording contract, but his album work, most notably 1977's aptly titled *Survivor* failed to match the sales of his and his wife's much covered golden hits. *Survivor* was produced by **Bruce Johnson** and **Terry Melcher**, and was regarded as a leading example of the 70s' singer/songwriter oeuvre.

Albums: *Who Put The Bomp* (1961), *Lay It All Out* (1971), *Survivor* (1975).

Mann, C.K.

b. 1957, Accra, Ghana. Singer/saxophonist Mann was

a member of the **Sweet Talks** before setting out on a solo career singing that she describes as 'refined highlife'. One album that soulfully captured the highlife before it was overwhelmed by refinement in a fruitless search for international mainstream success was *Wamaya*.
Album: *Wamaya* (1981).

Mann, Carl

b. 24 August 1942, Huntingdon, Tennessee, USA. Mann was a rockabilly artist who recorded his only two chart singles for the Phillips International label, owned by **Sam Phillips**, proprietor of the legendary **Sun Records**. Mann was a singer and pianist whose group, the Kool Kats, was based in Jackson, Tennessee, when they recorded their first tracks for the small Jaxon label, owned by Jim Stewart (who later founded **Stax Records**). Those songs were published by Knox Music, owned by Phillips, who had started Sun and launched the careers of artists including **Elvis Presley, Jerry Lee Lewis,** and **Johnny Cash**. Phillips signed Mann and had him record the standard 'Mona Lisa', which had been a hit for **Nat 'King' Cole** in the early 50s. It reached number 25 in the US in 1959 and became Mann's biggest record. Mann recorded a total of seven singles and an album for Phillips International before leaving in 1962, but only one other single, 'Pretend', another Cole song, charted, also in 1959. He toured with fellow rockabilly artist **Carl Perkins** from 1962-64 and left music between 1967-74, after which he returned on the **ABC/Dot Records** label, placing a remake of the **Platters**' 'Twilight Time' at number 100 on the US country charts.
Albums: *Like Mann* (1960), *Gonna Rock 'N' Roll Tonight* (1985). Archival albums: *The Sun Story, Vol. 6* (1977), *14 Unissued Sides* (1985).

Mann, Herbie

b. 16 April 1930, New York City, New York, USA. After learning to play the clarinet while still a small child, Mann took up the flute. He developed his musical experience during military service. After leaving the US army, he was active in film and television studios as both performer and composer. He played in several small jazz groups during the late 50s, including his own Afro-Jazz Sextet with which he toured internationally. Early in the 60s, his interest in Brazilian music led to a series of profitable recordings, notably 'Coming Home Baby'. Although rooted in bop and recording with leading jazzmen such as **Bill Evans**, by the late 60s, Mann's writing and playing had broadened to include musical influences from many lands - especially those of the Middle East. He was also open-minded about rock and by the early 70s was a leading figure in jazz-rock fusion. Indeed, his wide acceptance of areas of popular music outside jazz created some difficulties of categorization, especially when he embraced, however briefly, reggae and disco-pop. He has become one of the widest known flautists in jazz, gaining a considerable measure of credibility for an instrument which has always had an uncertain status in jazz circles. In addition to his performing and writing, Mann has also been active as a record producer, running his own label, Embryo, under the **Atlantic** aegis for a decade. Subsequently, he formed his own independent label, Herbie Mann Music.
Selected albums: *Mann In The Morning* (1956), *Salute To The Flute* (1956), *Mann Alone* (1957), *Yardbird Suite* (Savoy 1957), *Flute Souffle* (Original Jazz Classics 1958), *Just Wailin'* (1958), with Bill Evans *Nirvana* (Atlantic 1961-62), *Herbie Mann At The Village Gate* (Atlantic 1962), *Herbie Mann Today* (1965), *Memphis Underground* (Atlantic 1968), *Push* (WEA 1971), *Mississippi Gambler* (Atlantic 1972), *London Underground* (Atlantic 1973), *Reggae* (1973), *Gagaku And Beyond* (1974), *Discotheque* (1974-75), *Surprises* (c.1976), *Brazil - Once Again* (1978), *Astral Island* (1983), *Opalescence* (Kokopelli 1989), *Caminho De Casa* (Chesky 1990), *The Jazz We Heard Last Summer* (Savoy 1993), with Bobby Jaspar *Deep Pocket* (Kokopelli 1994). Compilation: *Best Of Herbie Mann* (WEA 1993).

Mann, Johnny, Singers

This US male/female vocal group, popular in the 60s, specialized in lively, swinging arrangements, in complete contrast to the prevailing beat music scene. The group released several popular albums, including *Roar Along With The Singing 'Twenties* and *Swing Along With The Swingin' 'Thirties*, and also had a US Top 10 chart single in 1967 with **Jimmy Webb**'s 'Up, Up And Away'. Nearly 20 years later, their album *The Johnny Mann Singers* (1984), featured their interpretations of 60s classics, such as 'Portrait Of My Love', 'A Taste Of Honey', 'Dedicated To The One I Love', 'Yesterday' and 'A World Without Love'.
Albums: *Golden Folk Songs, Volume Two* (1963), *Invisible Tears* (1964), *We Can Fly! Up-Up And Away* (1967), *The Church's One Foundation* (1975), with Si Zenter And His Orchestra *Great Band With Great Voices Swing* (1985).

Mann, Manfred

(see **Manfred Mann**)

Mann, Peggy

b. Margaret Germano. An excellent band singer, especially on ballads, during the 'Big Band Era'. Mann worked for the outfits of Henry Halstead, **Ben Pollack** and Enoch Light in the late 30s, and sang with **Larry Clinton**, **Teddy Powell** and **Gene Krupa** in the early 40s before she left to work as a soloist. She sang with the Pollack band just after its prime, but was on recordings such as 'I'm In My Glory', 'If It's The Last Thing I Do' and 'You Made Me Love You'. With Clinton she appeared on several recordings, including

'Because Of You', 'You'll Never Know' and 'Isn't It Time To Fall In Love'. For Teddy Powell's sweet band she duetted with Dick Judge on the hit, 'Goodbye, Mama (I'm Off To Yokohama)' and also sang on 'Somebody's Thinking Of You Tonight' and 'Be Careful, It's My Heart'. Peggy Mann also recorded with **Russ Case** ('Crying For Joy'), **Tommy Dorsey** ('Bill'), the **Benny Goodman** Quintet ('Ev'ry Time We Say Goodbye') and under her own name ('Changeable' and 'When Somebody Thinks You're Wonderful'). She retired from the music business in the early 50s, but made a comeback for a while three years later, despite swimming against the prevailing musical tide.

Manne, Shelly

b. Sheldon Manne, 11 June 1920, New York City, New York, USA, d. 26 September 1984. After switching to drums from saxophone, Manne worked with a number of dance and swing bands of the late 30s and early 40s, including **Joe Marsala**'s big band. He was also active in small groups in New York, accompanying **Coleman Hawkins** as well as some of the upcoming bebop artists. He first attracted widespread attention in 1946, the year he joined **Stan Kenton**. On and off, he was with Kenton until 1952, finding time in between stints to work in bands led by **George Shearing**, **Woody Herman** and others. From the early 50s, he was resident in Los Angeles, working in the studios by day and gradually becoming one of the most important musicians in the rising west coast school of jazz. In 1951, he had recorded with **Shorty Rogers** and become a member of the house band at Howard Rumsey's Lighthouse Cafe at Hermosa Beach. During the next few years he took part in many fine record sessions, notably for Contemporary, with **Teddy Edwards**, **Jimmy Giuffre**, **Art Pepper**, **Lennie Niehaus**, **Bud Shank**, **Bob Cooper**, **Maynard Ferguson**, **Hampton Hawes** and most of the other west coast stars. Among the most successful of these recordings were those made with Rogers in 1951 and 1955/6, a set he recorded with **Russ Freeman** and **Chet Baker**, and an album of tunes from the Broadway Show, ***My Fair Lady***, which he recorded with **Leroy Vinnegar** and **André Previn**. This set, the first ever complete album of jazz versions of tunes from a single show, was particularly successful. Almost as popular was another album made by the same trio with visiting guest, **Sonny Rollins**. Although recording with many different musicians, Manne kept a fairly constant personnel together for his regular working band, and towards the end of 1959 was booked into the Blackhawk in San Francisco. The band comprised trumpeter Joe Gordon, **Richie Kamuca**, **Monty Budwig**, who had recently taken over from Vinnegar, and Freeman's replacement, **Vic Feldman**. It was immediately apparent to Manne that the band he had assembled for this two-week engagement was something special, and he persuaded Les Koenig of Contemporary to travel to San Francisco to record them. The resulting four albums became some of the most successful in Contemporary's catalogue and an outstanding example of the west coast's so-called 'cool' sounds at their smokiest. In 1960, Manne opened his own nightclub, Shelly's Manne-Hole, which remained in existence until the middle of the following decade. In the 60s he recorded with **Bill Evans** and in 1974 was a founder member of the LA Four, with Shank, **Ray Brown** and **Laurindo Almeida**. By the late 70s Manne was a familiar figure on the international jazz festival circuit, appearing at the 1980 Aurex festival in Japan with **Benny Carter**'s Gentlemen of Swing. Although deeply rooted in the swinging tradition of drumming, Manne's sensitive, explorative playing made him an ideal accompanist in almost any setting and one of the finest drummers of the post-war period.

Selected albums: with Shorty Rogers *Modern Sounds* (1951), with Rogers *Cool And Crazy* (1953), *The Three And The Two* (1954), with Lennie Niehaus *The Quintet* (1954), *The Shelly Manne-Russ Freeman Duo* (1954), with Rogers *The Swinging Mr Rogers* (1955), *Concerto For Clarinet And Combo* (1955), *The West Coast Sound* (Original Jazz Classics 1955), with Rogers *Martians Come Back!* (1955), with Rogers *Big Band Express/Blues Express* (1956), *Swinging Sounds* (1956), *Quartet: Russ Freeman And Chet Baker* (1956), *Shelly Manne And His Friends* (Original Jazz Classics 1956), *More Swinging Sounds* (Contemporary 1956), *My Fair Lady* (Original Jazz Classics 1957), *The Gambit* (1957), with Sonny Rollins *Way Out West* (1957), *The Bells Are Ringing* (1958), *Shelly Manne And His Men Play Peter Gunn* (1959), *Son Of Gun* (1959), *Shelly Manne And His Men At The Blackhawk Vols 1-4* (Original Jazz Classics 1959), *The Proper Time* (1960), *West Coast Jazz In England* (1960), *Shelly Manne And His Men Live At The Manne-Hole* Vols 1 and 2 (Original Jazz Classics 1961), *Checkmate* (1961), *Sounds Unheard Of* (1962), with Bill Evans *Empathy* (1962), *My Son, The Jazz Drummer* (1962), *Shelly Manne And His Orchestra* i (1964), *Shelly Manne And His Orchestra* ii (1965), *Manne - That's Gershwin!* (1965), *Perk Up* (1967), *Shelly Manne And His Orchestra* iii (1967), *Jazz Gun* (Atlantic 1968), *Outside* (1969), *Alive In London* (Original Jazz Classics 1970), *A Night On The Coast* (Moon 1969-1970 recordings), *Mannekind* (Original Master Recordings 1972), *Hot Coles* (1975), *The LA Four Scores!* (1975), *Rex - Shelly Manne Plays Richard Rodgers* (1976), *Essence* (Galaxy 1977), *French Concert* (1977), *Jazz Crystallizations* (1978), *The Manne We Love* (1978), *Interpretations Of Bach And Mozart* (Trend 1980), *In Concert At Carmelo's/Double Piano Jazz Quartet Vol. 1* (Trend 1980), *Double Piano Jazz Quartet Vol. 2* (Trend 1980), with Benny Carter *The Gentlemen Of Swing* (1980), *Hollywood Jam* (1981), *Fingering* (1981), *Remember* (1984), *In Concert At Carmelo's Vols 1 and 2* (Trend 1986).

Manners, Zeke

b. Leo Mannes, San Francisco, California, USA. An accordion and piano playing vocalist, songwriter and co-founder, with Glen Rice, of the Beverly Hill Billies, who made their debut on KMPC Los Angeles in April 1930. Manners had originally gone to Hollywood in the hope of making a career in films and initially had no interest in country music. With the Hill Billies, he became known as Leo 'Zeke Craddock' Manners, which eventually led to the permanent change of surname. It was Manners who discovered **Elton Britt** and brought him to the Hill Billies. When the original group split in late 1932, Rice moved to San Francisco forming a new Beverly Hill Billies, whilst Manners remained on KMPC with a new group, Zeke And His City Fellers, which included Elton Britt. They also recorded transcriptions as the Langworth Hill Billies. Eventually, around 1933, Manners and Britt moved to New York where, under various aliases, they performed and recorded for ARC. They eventually went their own way with Britt going on to solo stardom. Zeke Manners later recorded for several labels, including **RCA** but they were reunited in 1959, when Britt recorded an album with Manner's band.

Albums: with Elton Britt *The Wandering Cowboy* (ABC-Paramount 1959), *Those Fabulous Beverly Hill Billies* (Rar Arts 1961, gold vinyl).

Manning, Bob

b. Manny Levin, 1 February 1926, Philadelphia, Pennsylvania, USA. A highly accomplished, but underrated ballad singer, whose career has probably suffered because his voice bore an uncanny similarity to that of the more popular **Dick Haymes**. Influenced by the singers and bands of the 'Swing Era', Manning sang in Philadephia hotels and had his own show on a local radio station before joining the newly formed **Ziggy Elman** outfit in 1947. He then worked for short periods with **Art Mooney** and **Tommy Dorsey**, and made an impressive appearance on the *Arthur Godfrey Talent Scouts* programme. Unable to obtain a deal with a major record company, Manning persuaded a friend to finance a recording session, out of which came 'The Nearness Of You', a classic performance, and reportedly composer **Hoagy Carmichael**'s favourite version of his song. It was picked up by **Capitol Records**, and entered the US Top 20 in 1953. The singer had further success with 'All I Desire' and 'Venus De Milo', and also released a tasteful collection of standards entitled *Lonely Spell*. Like so many other classy singers, Manning was overtaken by the advent of rock 'n' roll in the late 50s, and faded into the background.

Selected albums: *Lonely Spell* (Capitol c.50s), *Our Wedding Songs* (Everest c.50s), *Great Gentlemen Of Song-Spotlight On Bob Manning*, (Capitol 1994).

Manning, Dick

b. Samuel Medoff, 12 June 1912, Gomel, Russia, d. 11 April 1991, Marietta, Georgia, USA. A popular songwriter during the late 40s and 50s, who sometimes wrote both music and lyrics, and was probably best-known for his novelty songs. Born into a theatrical family, Manning was taken to the USA when he was six years old, and studied at the Philadelphia Conservatory and Juilliard. A gifted pianist at an early age, he gave concerts and later served as an accompanist, arranger and music coach for singers, while working in theatre and television as an arranger and conductor. One of his first compositions, with F.D. Marchetti and Maurice De Feraudy, was 'Fascination' (1932). He hosted *Sam Medoff And His Yiddish Swing Orchestra* on radio station WHN, before changing his name in 1948. In the same year his composition, 'The Treasure Of Sierra Madre', written with Buddy Kaye, was a hit for Buddy Cole and **Freddy** Martin, and became the title song for John Huston's film starring Humphrey Bogart. Manning's other 40s songs included 'While The Angelus Was Ringing', 'A Carnival In Venice' (a hit for the **Mills Brothers**), 'Donna Bella' and the jaunty 'One More Dream (And She's Mine)'. It was during the 50s, though, that Manning made his greatest impact, mostly in collaboration with lyricist **Al Hoffman**. Their novelty songs included 'Takes Two To Tango', which became a hit in the US for **Pearl Bailey** and **Louis Armstrong,** and somewhat surprisingly, was recorded in the UK by Hermione Gingold and the grumpy television personality, Gilbert Harding; and 'Papa Loves Mambo' and 'Hot Diggity', both of which were successful for **Perry Como**. The latter song was also a hit in the UK for **Michael Holliday** and the **Stargazers**. Other ballads written by Manning included 'Allegheny Moon' (which **Patti Page** took almost to the top of the US chart in 1956), 'Hawaiian Wedding Song' (successful for **Andy Williams** in 1959) and 'The Morning Side Of The Mountain' (a US hit for **Tommy Edwards** in 1959, and revived by **Donny** and **Marie Osmond** in 1975). In the 60s, Manning (with Fred Wise) contributed '(There's) No Room To Rhumba In A Sports Car' to the **Elvis Presley** movie *Fun In Acapulco* (1963). Manning' songs, which are said to have been published in 27 languages, also included 'Like I Do' (UK Top 5 for **Maureen Evans**), 'Festival Of Roses', 'I Still Feel The Same About You', 'I Can't Get You Out Of My Heart', 'Redwood Smoke', 'When You Kiss Me', 'Oh, Oh, I'm Falling In Love Again', 'Torero' (a hit for Renato Carosone and Julius La Rosa), 'Jilted' (popular for **Teresa Brewer**), 'Underneath The Linden Tree', 'Don't Stay Away Too Long', 'Mama, Teach Me To Dance' and 'Nickelodeon Song'. He also wrote the score for the television production *The Boys From Boise*, and a symphonic piece for piano and orchestra entitled

'Nightbird'. Among his other collaborators were Kay Twomey and Al Stillman.

Manning, Phil, Band

Australian Maning emerged as an inventive guitarist in several pop and club bands before playing with the heavy rock/blues band **Chain**. After leaving Chain in 1974, Manning fronted several different line-ups of his own band which showcased his excellent playing. However, the songs on the albums were not very strong and the band did not achieve commercial acclaim. Manning lives near Brisbane, occasionally performing solo.

Albums: *I Wish There Was A Way* (1974), *Manning* (1978), *Live* (1979), with the Manning Taylor Band *Oz Blues* (1981), *It's Blues* (1989).

Manone, Joseph 'Wingy'

b. 13 February 1900, New Orleans, Louisiana, USA, d. 9 July 1982. Manone lost his right arm in a road accident while still a child, but took up trumpet playing, turning professional in his mid-teens. The 20s were hectic times for Manone. He worked with many riverboat and **territory bands**, visited St. Louis where he made his first records in 1924, moved on to New York in 1929 to record with **Benny Goodman**, and settled in Chicago. He led his own band at nightclubs, then took it to New York for a string of successful engagements which were enhanced by the popularity of his recording of 'The Isle Of Capri'. By the early 40s he was in California, appearing in films and becoming a regular on **Bing Crosby**'s radio show, visiting New York and other centres for concerts and record dates with, for example, **Sidney Bechet**. In the mid-50s Manone moved to Las Vegas, playing there for several years but making occasional trips to New York and visiting Europe for festivals and tours of clubs. Manone's vocal style, although popular with audiences, was filled with rather forced humour. Contrastingly, he played trumpet with a forthright, honest style which compounded his love for the playing of **Louis Armstrong** with the New Orleans tradition he heard in his childhood. His early recordings are solidly entertaining.

Albums: *Wingy Manone And His Band* i (1954), *Wingy Manone And His Band* ii (1957), *Wingy Manone And His Band* iii (1957), *Wingy Manone And His Band* iv (1959-60), *Wingy Manone And His Band* v (1960), with Papa Bue Jensen *A Tribute To Wingy Manone* (1966), *Jazz From Italy* (1975). Compilations: *Wingy Manone Vol. 1* (1928-34), *Wingy Manone Vol. 2* (1934-35), *Wingy Manone/Sidney Bechet - Together at Town Hall, 1947* (1947), *Collection Vols 1-3* (Collectors Classics 1989).

Manowar

This traditionalist heavy metal quartet from the USA (whose motto is 'Death To False Metal') was formed in 1981 by bassist Joey Demaio (a former **Black Sabbath** roadie) and ex-**Shakin' Street** and **Dictators**' guitarist Ross The Boss (b. Ross Friedman). Recruiting vocalist Eric Adams and drummer Donnie Hamzik, they decided on an approach that was to be the total antithesis of melodic AOR. Dressed in animal skins, they delivered a brutal series of riffs that were characterized by Adam's barbaric vocals and the dense bass-work of Demaio. They debuted in 1982 with *Battle Hymns*, a milestone in the metal genre. With subject material firmly centred on fighting, bloodshed, death and carnage, they came over as a turbo-charged hybrid of **Ted Nugent** and Black Sabbath. The album was notable for an amazing version of the 'William Tell Overture', played as an electric bass solo, while the voice of actor Orson Welles appeared on 'Dark Avenger'. *Battle Hymns* failed to sell, however, and with the press treating the band as an absurd joke, they were dropped by **Liberty Records** in 1982. They subsequently signed to Megaforce (**Music For Nations** in the UK) using their own blood on the contract, their veins opened via a ceremonial dagger. Scott Columbus took over the drumstool on *Into Glory Ride*, another intensely heavy, chest-beating collection of metal epics. They built up a small yet loyal cult following, but were generally panned by the rock mainstream. *Sign Of The Hammer,* released in 1985, featured some excellent guitar work from Ross The Boss and contained the band's most accessible compositions to date, including the archetypal metal boast, 'All Men Play On 10'. Once again it flopped, and after a serious re-think they returned two years later with *Fighting The World* (in the meantime they had entered the *Guinness Book Of Records* for playing live at 160 decibels). On this album they incorporated elements borrowed from **Kiss** and **Judas Priest** into their songwriting, but although it was aimed at the rock mainstream, it failed to win many new fans. *Kings Of Metal* was released the following year and met with a similar fate. Disillusioned, Ross The Boss quit in 1988, with Scott Columbus following suit two years later (Ross was replaced by Death Dealer, aka Dave Shankel, Columbus by Rhino). The future of the group is still uncertain. Manowar are colourful, flamboyant and rather kitsch, but nevertheless an essential component in the music industry; the perfect antidote to the sometimes conservative rock fraternity.

Albums: *Battle Hymns* (Liberty 1982), *Into Glory Ride* (Megaforce 1983), *Hail To England* (Megaforce 1984), *Sign Of The Hammer* (Virgin 1985), *Fighting The World* (Atco 1987), *Kings Of Metal* (Atlantic 1988), *Triumph Of Steel* (Atlantic 1992).

Mantas

This short-lived hard rock quartet from the north of England was formed by Mantas after quitting the demonic thrash metallers **Venom**. Enlisting the help of

vocalist Pete Harrison, second guitarist Al Barnes and Keith Nichol on keyboards, their debut and only release comprised nine new originals penned by Mantas. Moving away from the one-dimensional approach of Venom, they straddled the ground between AOR and the more commercial slant of **Rainbow**, **Saxon** and **Dio**. *Winds Of Change* featured computerized drums and extensive use of keyboards, but Harrison's vocals lacked distinction and the material was ultimately dull. The album was ignored by mainstream record purchasers aside from diehard Venom fans. After a careful re-think, Mantas disbanded the group and re-joined Venom in 1989.
Album: *Winds Of Change* (Neat 1988).

Mantler, Michael

b. 10 August 1943, Vienna, Austria. Mantler took up trumpet at the age of 12, and from 14 worked in dance bands, playing stock arrangements with little opportunity for creative jazz. He found more musical freedom after moving to the USA in 1962. After what he regarded as educationally barren years at the **Berklee College Of Music** in Boston, he moved to New York in 1964 and immediately became involved with musicians such as **Paul Bley**, **Carla Bley** (whom he would later marry) and **Cecil Taylor**. In 1965-66 he toured Europe with Carla Bley and **Steve Lacy** in the Jazz Realities quintet. In more recent times, he has toured with Carla Bley's Sextet and **Charlie Haden**'s Liberation Music Orchestra, and has recorded several albums of his own pieces. Although a striking trumpet player, he concentrates most of his energy on organizing, producing and composing (often setting the words of Samuel Beckett, Harold Pinter and Edward Gorey to music). He was a co-founder of the Jazz Composers' Guild and the **Jazz Composers' Orchestra Association**. He also set up two record labels with Carla Bley: Watt, for their own recordings, and JCOA Records, to promote the work of others.
Albums: *Jazz Composers' Orchestra* (1968), *No Answer* (1974), with Carla Bley *13 & 3/4* (1975), *The Hapless Child* (Watt 1976), *Silence* (1977), *Movies* (1978), *More Movies* (1980), *Something There* (ECM 1982), *Alien* (Watt 1985), *Live* (Watt 1987), *Many Have No Speech* (Watt 1988), *Folly Seeing All This* (ECM 1993).

Mantovani

b. Annunzio Paolo Mantovani, 15 November 1905, Venice, Italy, d. 30 March 1980, Tunbridge Wells, Kent, England. A violinist, pianist, musical director, conductor, composer and arranger, Mantovani was one of the most successful orchestra leaders and album sellers in the history of popular music. His father was principal violinist at La Scala, Milan, under Arturo Toscanini, and also served under Mascagni, Richter and Saint-Saens and, subsequently, led the Covent Garden Orchestra. It is said that Mantovani received encouragement to become a professional musician from his mother, rather than his father. He began his musical training on the piano, and later learned to play the violin. After the family moved to England in 1912, he made his professional debut at the age of 16, playing the Bruch Violin Concerto Number 1. Four years later he had installed his own orchestra at London's Hotel Metropole, and began his broadcasting career. In the early 30s he formed the Tipica Orchestra and began a series of lunch-time broadcasts from the famous Monseigneur Restaurant, in Piccadilly, London, and started recording for Regal Zonophone. He had two US hits in 1935-36, with 'Red Sails In The Sunset' and 'Serenade In The Night'. Samples of his work around this time are on *The Young Mantovani 1935-39*. In the 40s, Mantovani served as musical director for several London West End shows, including *Lady Behave*, *Twenty To One*, *Meet Me Victoria*, *And So To Bed*, *Bob's Your Uncle* and *La-Di-Da-Di-Da*. He was also involved in **Noël Coward**'s *Pacific 1860* and ***Ace Of Clubs***; conducting from the theatre pit for artists such a **Lupino Lane**, **Pat Kirkwood**, **Mary Martin**, Sally Gray, **Leslie Henson** and many others. His records, for UK **Decca**, included 'The Green Cockatoo', 'Hear My Song, Violetta' and 'Tell Me, Marianne' (vocal by Val Merrall). Experimenting with various arrangements with which to target the lucrative USA market, he came up with what has been called variously, the 'cascading strings', 'cascading violins', or 'tumbling strings' effect, said to be an original idea of arranger Ronnie Binge. It became the Orchestra's trademark and was first used to great effect in 1951, on Mantovani's recording of 'Charmaine', a song originally written to promote the 1926 silent film classic *What Price Glory?*. The Mantovani recording was the first of several million-selling singles for his orchestra, which included 'Wyoming', (another 20s number), 'Greensleeves', 'Song From Moulin Rouge' (a UK number 1), 'Swedish Rhapsody' and 'Lonely Ballerina'. Mantovani's own compositions included 'Serenata d'Amore', 'A Poem To The Moon', 'Royal Blue Waltz', 'Dance Of The Eighth Veil', 'Toy Shop Ballet' (**Ivor Novello** Award 1956), 'Red Petticoats', 'Brass Buttons', 'Tango In the Night' and 'Cara Mia', written with UK record producer/manager, Bunny Lewis. **David Whitfield**'s 1954 recording of 'Cara Mia', with Mantovani's orchestra accompaniment, sold over a million copies, and stayed at number 1 in the UK charts for a record (at the time) 10 weeks. It also made Whitfield one of the earliest UK artists to break into the US Top 10. Mantovani issued an instrumental version of the number, featuring himself on piano. This was most unusual in that the instrument was rarely a part of his 40-piece orchestral set-up. Singles apart, it was as an album artist that Mantovani excelled around the world, and especially in the USA. He is said to have been the first to sell over a million stereo units, aided in no small measure by the superb quality of sound obtained by **Decca**. Between 1955 and 1966 he had 28 albums in the US Top 30. Although he toured many countries of the world, including Russia, his popularity in the USA, where his kind of orchestral offerings are often referred to as 'the beautiful music', was unique. An indication of that audience's devotion can be gained from a story by George Elrick, Mantovani's manager of 21 years. Elrick claims that, at the beginning of one tour of the USA, the maestro was taken ill and a few concerts had to be cancelled. The prospective capacity audience at one of them, the University of Minnesota and Minneapolis, refused to claim refunds, preferring to retain their tickets for the following year. Mantovani continued to perform throughout the ever-changing musical climate of the 60s and 70s. He was awarded a special Ivor Novello Award in 1956 for services to popular music.

Albums: *Mantovani Plays Tangos* (1953), *Strauss Waltzes* (1953), *Christmas Carols* (1953), *The Music Of Rudolph Friml* (1955), *Waltz Time* (1955), *Song Hits From Theatreland* (1955), *Ballet Memories* (1956), *Waltzes Of Irving Berlin* (1956), *Film Encores* (1957), *Gems Forever* (1958), *Continental Encores* (1959), *Film Encores, Volume 2* (1959), *The American Scene* (1960), *Songs To Remember* (1960), *Mantovani Plays Music From Exodus And Other Great Themes* (1960), *Concert Spectacular* (1961), *Operetta Memories* (1961), *Italia Mia* (1961), *Themes From Broadway* (1961), *Songs Of Praise* (1961), *American Waltzes* (1962), *Moon River And Other Great Film Themes* (1962), *Stop The World - I Want To Get Off/Oliver!* (1962), *Latin Rendezvous* (1963), *Classical Encores* (1963), *Mantovani/Manhattan* (1963), *Christmas Greetings From Mantovani* (1963), *Kismet* (1964), *Folk Songs Around The World* (1964), *The Incomparable Mantovani* (1964), *The Mantovani Sound - Big Hits From Broadway And Hollywood* (1965), *Mantovani Olé* (1965), *Mantovani Magic* (1966), *Mr. Music...Mantovani* (1966), *Mantovani Hollywood* (1967), *Old And New Fangled Tangos* (1967), *The Mantovani Touch* (1968), *Mantovani/Tango* (1968), *Mantovani Memories* (1968), *The Mantovani Scene* (1969), *The World Of Mantovani* (1969), *Mantovani Today* (1970), *Mantovani Presents His Concert Successes* (1971), *To Lovers Everywhere USA* (1971), *To Lovers Everywhere* (1972), *Annunzio Paolo Mantovani* (1972), *Cascade Of Praise* (1985). Compilations: *Mantovani Stereo Showcase* (1959), *All-American Showcase* (1959), *Mantovani's Greatest Hits* (1967), *The World Of Mantovani* (1969), *The World Of Mantovani, Volume 2* (1969), *From Monty, With Love* (1971), *Focus On Mantovani* (1975), *Twenty Golden Greats* (1979), *Young Mantovani 1935-1939* (1980), *Mantovani Magic* (1985), *The Unforgettable Sounds Of Mantovani* (1984), *Collection: Mantovani* (1987).

Mantra, Michael

A California-based musician/experimentalist who has sought to advance on the ambient ethic of **Brian Eno** and more recent 'chill-out' arists such as the **Orb**. Mantra describes his methods as 'Brain Hemisphere Harmonic Healing', which spells out his intention to create sound structures that 'induce a meditative state that synchronises brain wave frequencies'. After synchronising the mind and the body, Mantra's work claims to release endorphines (part of the human body's natural pharmacy which work at the level of opiates). To achieve this electronics are combined with field recordings of the Pacific sea, seagulls, and natural instruments such as the didgeridoo. Such experiments in the neural affects of sound could well represent a previously unchartered future for music.

Album: *Sonic Alter* (Silent Records 1994).

Mantronix

DJ Curtis Mantronik (b. Kurtis Kahleel, 4 September 1965, Jamaica, West Indies, moving to Canada at age seven, then New York as a teenager) is the creative force behind these New York-based hip hop innovators, a multi-instrumental talent whose knowledge of electronics is instrumental to the band's sound. That sound, electro rap in its purest form, as suggested by the band's name, was highly popular in the mid-80s. Kahleel's use of samplers and drum machines proved.pivotal to the genre's development, not least on tracks like 'Music Madness', which used a snatch of 'Stone Fox Chase' by **Area Code 615** (better known in the UK as the theme to *The Old Grey Whistle Test*). Indeed, the raps of MC Tee (b. Tooure Embden) often seemed incidental to the formula. The duo met at Manhattan's Downtown Record Store in 1985, where Mantronik was mixing records behind the turntables and introducing customers to new releases. A few weeks later, they made a demo tape and started looking for a label. Soon afterwards, William Socolov, the astute founder of independent label **Sleeping Bag**, was in the store and was sufficiently impressed with the demo tape Mantronik played him to offer a deal. The group's first single, 1985's 'Fresh Is The Word', was a huge street and dancefloor hit, as was their production of Tricky Tee's 'Johnny The Fox'. In late 1985 they released their first album, the adventurous *Mantronix*, which included the hit singles 'Bassline' and 'Ladies', and took the marriage of street rhyme and electronic studio wizardry to new heights. Mantronix further built their reputation with their production of **Joyce Sims**' 'All And All' and 12.41's 'Success Is The Word', before going on to record their second album, the competent but relatively disappointing *Music Madness*. The duo were one of the most popular acts at the historic UK Fresh hip hop festival at London's Wembley Arena in the summer of 1986, but were dropped by Sleeping Bag a year later. Mantronix appeared to have run out of fresh ideas and had been overtaken by a new generation of rappers/studio maestros. In the late 80s Tee signed up to the USAF, to be replaced by two stand-in rappers, Bryce Luvah (b. c.1970; cousin of **LL**

Cool J) and DJ Dee (b. c.1969, Mantronik's cousin). They did hit the UK charts with *This Should Move Ya*'s promotional single, 'Got To Have Your Love'. The latter featured the vocal sheen of Wondress, while the attendant album featured a cover of **Ian Dury And The Blockheads**' 'Sex And Drugs And Rock 'n' Roll'. The distinctive Mantronix bass lines were still in place, though by now Kahleel was branching out into soul and R&B horizons. Possibly their best material in this format is 1991's *The Incredible Sound Machine*, which saw the introduction of singer Jade Trini. Kahleel continues to produce for others, notably English vocalist **Mica Paris**. In the modern age he composes all his music on an Apple Macintosh computer, a trait he shares with many of techno's leading lights.

Albums: *Mantronix* (Sleeping Bag 1985), *Music Madness* (Sleeping Bag 1986), *In Full Effect* (Capitol 1988), *This Should Move Ya* (Capitol 1990), *The Incredible Sound Machine* (Capitol 1991). Compilation: *The Best Of (1986-1988)* (1990).

Manuel And His Music Of The Mountains

Orchestra leader **Geoff Love** (b. 1916, d. July 1991) initially used the above name pseudonymously. The British-born son of a black American dancer, he took to music at an early age and by the late 50s/early 60s joined **Joe Loss** and **Ted Heath** as one of the country's leading bandleaders. Love's Manuel appellation allowed him an artistic freedom to draw influence from South American music and, although early releases did not reveal its creator's identity (Love was 'unmasked' during a cameo appearance on BBC television's *Juke Box Jury*), such recordings later became the natural outlet for his talents. A prodigious output, notably for **EMI**'s prestigious *Studio Two* stereo series, ensured that the attraction remained one of Britain's most popular light orchestral attractions throughout the 60s and 70s.

Albums: *Manuel And His Music Of The Mountains* (c.60s), *Mountain Carnival* (c.60s), *Ecstasy* (c.60s), *Mountain Fiesta* (c.60s), *Blue Waters* (1966), *Reflections* (1969), *This Is Manuel* (1971), *Carnival* (1971), *Mardi Gras* (1972), *Shangri-La* (1973), *Sun, Sea And Sky* (1973), *Y Viva Espana* (1974), *You, The Night And Music* (1975), *El Bimbo* (1975), *Manuel And The Voices Of Mountains* (1975), *Masquerade* (1976), *Mountain Fire* (1977), *Blue Tangos* (1977), *Bossa Nova* (1978), *Cha Cha* (1978), *Music Of Manuel* (1978), *Supernatural* (1979), *Viva Manuel* (1979), *Manuel Movie Hits* (1979), *Fiesta* (1980), *Digital Spectacular* (1981), *Bolero* (1984), *Latin Hits* (1988). Compilation: *The Very Best Of Manuel* (1976).

Manzanera, Phil

b. Philip Targett-Adams, 31 January 1951, London, England. A guitarist at the age of 12, Manzanera gradually progressed to vocals, bass and drums. After forming the *avant garde* group Quiet Sun, he was recruited to **Roxy Music** as a guitarist in February 1972. By the mid-70s, he had established himself as one of Britain's most respected rock musicians. Manzanera's guitar virtuosity quickly established him as a sought-after session player. In 1974 alone, he appeared as either guitarist, co-composer or producer on Roxy Music's *Country Life*, **Brian Eno**'s *Here Come The Warm Jets* and *Taking Tiger Mountain (By Strategy)*, **Bryan Ferry**'s *Another Time Another Place* and **Nico**'s *The End*. Further sessions included **John Cale**'s *Slow Dazzle* before he was drafted back into Roxy Music for *Siren*. He then produced the bizarre New Zealand pop group **Split Enz**, whom he had discovered in 1974. During the Roxy Music hiatus of 1975, he recorded his first solo work, *Diamond Head*, as well as working on a reunion album with Quiet Sun, *Mainstream*. Both works were well-received. More work followed, including a major role in the presentation of **Stomu Yamash'ta**'s *Go* at London's Royal Albert Hall, in conjunction with **Steve Winwood**. Following the 'devolution' of Roxy Music in 1976, Manzanera formed the eclectic **801** with Bill MacCormick, Simon Phillips, Lloyd Watson, Francis Monkman and Eno. The band was originally for a complete tour but their live performances were wittled down to three shows: a warm-up gig in Norfolk, a guest appearance at the 1976 Reading Festival and a sell-out concert at the Queen Elizabeth hall, London. The latter was recorded for *801 Live*. The group then folded with Manzanera re-uniting with Ferry. One year later, the guitarist issued a new 801 recording *Listen Now!!* Its theme was life in a totalitarian society. The work was notable for the use of **Godley And Creme**'s famous Gizmo gadget, which produced the sound of strings from a guitar. After taking 801 back on the road, Phil issued the less adventurous *K Scope*. In the wake of Roxy's final split, he teamed up with **Andy Mackay** in the **Explorers** before returning to solo work.

Albums: *Diamond Head* (1975), *K Scope* (1978), *Primitive Guitars* (1987), *Guitarissimo* (1987), *Southern Cross* (1990). As 801: *801 Live* (1976), *Listen Now!!* (1977). As the Explorers: *The Explorers* (1985).

Further reading: *Roxy Music: Style With Substance - Roxy's First Ten Years*, Johnny Rogan.

Mapfumo, Thomas

b. October 1945, Marondera, Zimbabwe. Mapfumo, known domestically as The Lion Of Zimbabwe, is to the music of the Shona people what **Fela Kuti** is to Nigeria or **Franco** to Zaire: simultaneously a modernizer and preserver of tradition, and the single most important figure on the local music scene for decades (in Mapfumo's case, since the early 70s). Brought up for the first few years of his life in the small town of Marondera, his family moved to the capital, Salisbury (now Harare), in 1950, where he remained until he left school in 1964. He spent 1965 in neighbouring Zambia, before returning to Harare and starting to sing with local bands such as the Cosmic Dots and the Springfields. As their names suggest, both bands were heavily influenced by imported music, and Mapfumo acquired his early reputation for convincing cover versions of **Elvis Presley, Otis Redding** and **Sam Cooke** tracks. His first tentative step towards the musical revolution that he would instigate in the early 70s occurred when he began to translate the lyrics of songs like 'A Change Is Gonna Come' into the Shona language, immediately giving USA-located protest material an added relevance for black Africans languishing under Ian Smith's neo-apartheid Rhodesian regime.

In 1973, Mapfumo left the Springfields, no longer prepared to devote his career to even Africanized interpretations of overseas material. Forming the rootsier Hallelujah Chicken Run Band, he started to seriously research traditional Zimbabwean, and in particular Shonan, folk styles. The key instrument in practically all this music is the mbira or 'thumb piano', a gourd soundbox with a set of tuned metal keys which produces a part melodic, part rhythmic effect. Mapfumo, together with the Chicken Run's lead guitarist Jonah Sithole, translated the mbira's complex patterns on to electric guitars, dampening the strings to produce a near-precise copy of the mbira's tonal quality. At the same time, he reappraised the band's kit drum style, changing it to fall in with traditional percussion rhythms and the structured stamping of dancers' feet. At first, these innovations failed to make much impact on local club-goers and record buyers: brainwashed and demoralized by decades of white colonialist supremacy, most indigenous Africans felt their own music to be inferior to imported white styles and found the Chicken Run's championing of it, even through a filter of electric guitars and kit drums, embarrassing. Gradually, however, attitudes changed. As the political situation worsened, Mapfumo's lyrics - thinly disguised criticisms of white supremacy, incomprehensible to white ears through their use of the Shona language - converged with newly emergent nationalist sentiments. By 1975, via singles like 'Morento' (a warning that war was on the way) and 'Ngoma Yarira' (an exhortation to fight for civil rights), Chicken Run were no longer disdained but seen as stylish and innovative. In 1977, after putting together the short-lived Pied Pipers Band, Mapfumo formed the Acid Band and released his first album, *Hokoyo!* (Watch Out!). The album established him as the most celebrated performer on the national scene. By this time, the white Rhodesian power structure had been alerted to the subversive nature of Mapfumo's material and, failing to persuade his record label, Teal, to stop their release, achieved the next best thing, which was to deny them airplay on state-controlled radio. At the end of 1977, Mapfumo was jailed for three months on charges of subversion. He was not to be intimidated, however, and once free, began releasing a string of chimurenga ('struggle') singles which offered support to ZANU freedom fighters and their supporters throughout Zimbabwe. Airtime continued to be denied, but the records became huge hits nonetheless - championed by club disc jockeys and widely heard on programmes broadcast by the Voice Of Mozambique radio station. In 1978, as the war of liberation reached its climax, Mapfumo renamed the Acid Band as Blacks Unlimited.

After 1980, and the birth of independent Zimbabwe, Mapfumo maintained the political orientation of his music, while resisting attempts to have it hijacked by supporters of the rival ZANU and ZAPU parties. The lyrics on albums like *Mabasa* and *Ndangariro* were non-sectarian exhortations to the people to rebuild their country and its culture. In 1983, the British label Earthworks released a compilation album, *The Chimurenga Singles*, and in 1984 and 1985, Mapfumo made his first British and European tours. African music was at the time enjoying a major growth of interest in the West and this, coupled with Mapfumo's dreadlocked appearance and the reggae-ish shangara beat used in many of his songs, gave him an immediate impact amongst black and white music audiences. In 1986, he made what arguably remains his most outstanding work, *Chimurenga For Justice*, where his updating of traditional Shona music reached full and glorious maturity, with keyboards as well as guitars reinterpreting the ancient lines of the mbira. The political orientation of Mapfumo's lyrics shifted once more in the late 80s, this time to embrace overt criticism of Zimbabwean President Robert Mugabe's regime. On the 1989 album *Corruption,* he pointedly contrasted the Mercedes-and-swimming-pool lifestyles of Harare bureaucrats and politicians with the still pitiful condition of the urban and rural working classes, suggesting that a one-party state might make such polarization a permanent feature of Zimbabwean life.

Albums: *Hokoyo!* (1977), *Gwindingwe* (1980), *Mabasa* (1983), *Congress* (1983), *The Chimurenga Singles* (1983), *Ndangariro* (1984), *Mr Music* (1985), *Chimurenga For Justice* (1986), *Corruphon* (1989), *Chamunorwa* (1990).

Maphis, Joe, And Rose Lee

b. Otis W. ('Joe') Maphis, 12 May 1921, near Suffolk, Virginia, USA, d. 27 June 1986, Nashville, Tennessee, USA. His father taught him to play the fiddle as a child and he was performing at local dances by the age of 10. At 16, Maphis was a featured musician on WBRA Richmond, by which time he also played guitar, mandolin and bass. During the 40s, he starred on several top country shows, including *Boone County Jamboree* (later the *Midwestern Hayride*) (WLW Cincinnati), *National Barn Dance* (WLS Chicago) and *Old Dominion Barn Dance* (WRVA Richmond), where he first met his future wife Rose Lee (b. 29 December 1922, Baltimore, Maryland, USA). She was singing and playing the guitar before she reached her teens and at the age of 15, as Rose Of The Mountains, she had her own show on radio in Hagerstown, Maryland. In 1948, she met Joe and they were soon married. They moved to Los Angeles in 1951, where they became regulars on **Cliffie Stone**'s *Hometown Jamboree* and later stars of the televised *Town Hall Party* from KFI Compton. Joe also worked with **Merle Travis** on occasion and they recorded two duet albums together. In the 50s, apart from their own recordings they worked as session musicians. Joe, with his super-fast picking on his unusual double-necked guitar, was much in demand by both country and pop artists and he recorded with rockabilly singers such as **Wanda Jackson** and **Ricky Nelson**, with whom he also toured. Maphis appeared with many of the major country stars, including **Jimmy Dean** and **Jerry Lee Lewis** on network television shows. From the 50s, for almost 30 years, he and Rose Lee toured with their own show, joined later by their three children Jody, Dale and Lorrie. During this time they not only played in every state but also in Europe and the Far East. They made their home in Nashville in the 60s, where Joe's multi-instrumental skills were much in demand for session work. He played the background music on several films and television series, including *Thunder Road*, *Have Gun Will Travel*, *The Virginian* and *The FBI Story*. Their abilities won them the nickname of Mr & Mrs Country Music. Over the years, they recorded in their own right for several labels, including **Capitol**, Starday and CMH. In 1960, Joe gave 11-year-old **Barbara Mandrell** her first big break in country music when he included her on his show at the Showboat Hotel and Casino, Las Vegas. (Contrary to many reference books, although Barbara referred to him as Uncle Joe, he was not her real uncle) Joe Maphis, who was **Bert Weedon**'s favourite picker, became known as the King Of The Strings and ranks with Merle Travis and **Chet Atkins** as one of the finest guitarists of all time. He died in June 1986.

Albums: by Joe Maphis *Fire On The Strings* (1957), *Hi-Fi Holiday For Banjo* (1959), with Merle Travis *Two Guitar Greats* (1964), *Hootenanny Star* (1964), *Golden Gospel Guitar* (1965), *The Amazing Joe Maphis* (1965), *Country Guitar Goes To The Jimmy Dean Show* (1966), *New Sound Of Joe Maphis* (1967), *Gospel Guitar* (1970), *Gospel Guitar Vol.2* (1971), with Jody Maphis *Guitaration Gap* (1971), *Grass 'N' Jazz* (1977), with Merle Travis *Country Guitar Giants* (1979, double album), *Flat Picking Spectacular* (1982, double album); by Joe and Rose Lee Maphis: *Rose Lee Maphis* (1961), *Rose Lee & Joe Maphis with the Blue Ridge Mountain Boys* (1962), *Mr & Mrs Country Music* (1964), with Dale Maphis *Dim Lights, Thick Smoke* (1978), *Boogie Woogie Flat Top Guitar Pickin' Man* (1979), *Honky Tonk Cowboy* (1980).

Maple Oak

This obscure Canadian group gained short-lived minor fame when former **Kinks**' bassist, Pete Quaife, joined their ranks in 1969. He contributed to Maple Oak's lone British single, 'Son Of A Gun', but although the ensemble completed an album, Quaife abandoned them for a more conventional life as a commercial artist. Although he initially settled in Denmark, Pete later moved to Montreal, where he made an impromptu live appearance with the Kinks when a 80s tour reached the city. Maple Oak dissolved several years beforehand.

Mar-Keys

Formed in Memphis, Tennessee, USA, and originally known as the Royal Spades, their line-up comprised: **Steve Cropper** (b. 21 October 1941, Willow Spring, Missouri, USA; guitar), Donald 'Duck' Dunn (b. 24 November 1941, Memphis, Tennessee, USA; bass), Charles 'Packy' Axton (tenor saxophone), Don Nix (b. 27 September 1941, Memphis, Tennessee, USA; baritone saxophone), Wayne Jackson (trumpet), Charlie Freeman (b. Memphis, Tennessee, USA; guitar), Jerry Lee 'Smoochy' Smith (organ) and Terry Johnson (drums). Although their rhythmic instrumental style was not unique in Memphis, (**Willie Mitchell** followed a parallel path at Hi Records), the **Mar-Keys** were undoubted masters. Their debut hit, 'Last Night', reached number 3 in the US ***Billboard*** pop chart during the summer of 1961, establishing Satellite, its outlet, in the process. Within months, Satellite had altered its name to **Stax** and the Mar-Keys became the label's houseband. Initially all-white, two black musicians, Booker T. Jones (organ) and Al Jackson (drums), had replaced Smith and Johnson by 1962. The newcomers, along with Cropper and Dunn, also worked as **Booker T. And The MGs**. A turbulent group, the Mar-Keys underwent several changes. Freeman left prior to the recording of 'Last Night' (but would later return for live work), Nix and Axton also quit, while Joe Arnold and Bob Snyder joined on tenor and baritone saxophone. They in turn were replaced by Andrew Love and Floyd Newman, respectively. Although commercial success under their own name was limited, the group provided the backbone to sessions by **Otis Redding**, **Sam And Dave**, **Wilson Pickett**, **Carla Thomas** and many others, and were the pulsebeat to countless classic records. Axton, the son of Stax co-founder Estelle, later fronted the Packers, who hit with 'Hole In The Wall' (1965). The single, released on Pure Soul, featured a not-inconspicuous MGs. Line-ups bearing the Mar-Keys' name continued to record despite the desertion of most of the original members. Nix later became part of the **Delaney And Bonnie/Leon Russell** axis while Charlie Freeman was later part of the **Dixie Flyers**,

one of the last traditional housebands. Both he and Axton died in the early 70s, victims, respectively, of heroin and alcohol. Jackson, Love and Newman, meanwhile, continued the Mar-Keys legacy with releases on Stax and elsewhere, while simultaneously forging a parallel career as the **Memphis Horns**.
Albums: *Last Night* (1961), *Do The Popeye With The Mar-Keys* (1962), *The Great Memphis Sound* (1966), with Booker T. And The MGs *Back To Back* (1967), *Damifiknow* (1969), *Memphis Experience* (1971).

Mara

This Australian group was formerly known as Tensey's Fancy. **Danny Thompson** (double bass), had earlier been a member of the group. His place was taken by Steve Elphick. The group recorded one album as Tansey's Fancy before changing their name. This new line-up comprised James Llewelyn Kiek (bouzouki, guitar, bass), Jim Denly (flute, alto-saxophone, darrabukka, denleyphone), Mike Haughton (recorder, tenor, soprano saxophone, vocals) and Mara Kiek (vocals, tapan, darrabukka, tambourine). Mara have adopted a highly original style encompassing a whole range of musical influences, including material from France, Persia, Greece and Macedonia. Whether performing the 15th-century ballad 'Riturnella' or a more contemporary song, the group displays a clever marriage of European music and jazz influences.
Albums: *Tansey's Fancy* (1983), *Images* (1984), *On The Edge* (1987), *Don't Even Think* (1990).

Marathons

The brief history of the Marathons is shrouded in mystery and confusion. Long thought to be a pseudonym for the **Olympics**, the US R&B group which had recorded 'Western Movies' in 1958, the Marathons was actually a pseudonym for the **Vibrations**, a Los Angeles vocal group which had a 1961 dance hit with 'The Watusi', and in a previous incarnation, as the Jayhawks who hit the US singles charts in 1956 with 'Stranded In The Jungle'. The convoluted story of the Marathons' only hit, 1961's 'Peanut Butter', is that the Olympics' record company, Arvee, needed a new release from the group while they were on the road. In the Olympics' place, Arvee hired the Vibrations to record 'Peanut Butter', a virtual soundalike of the Olympics' own '(Baby) Hully Gully'. 'Peanut Butter' reached number 20 on Arvee, but when the Vibrations' own label found out that its group had been moonlighting, it took over distribution of the record, issuing it on both the **Chess** and Argo labels. With that decision, the career of the non-existent Marathons came to an end. However, an attempt by Arvee to cash-in on the success of the group resulted in a bogus version of the Marathons along with an album and a series of single releases, including 'C. Percy Mercy Of Scotland Yard' and 'Tight Sweater'.

Marauders

Formed in Stoke-on-Trent, England, this superior beat group enjoyed a minor hit in 1963 with 'That's What I Want'. Penned by the prolific **Carter And Lewis** team, the song boasted an effective hookline, while the quartet's understated, acoustic-based interpretation invoked that of contemporaries, the **Merseybeats**. When a promising follow-up, 'Always On My Mind', failed to chart, the Marauders tried to redress the balance with two established stage favourites. Their version of **Little Richard**'s 'Lucille' boasted an impressive guitar solo, while its coupling, 'Little Egypt', is arguably the finest British reading of a much-covered classic. The single, sadly, failed to become a hit and the Marauders broke up without realizing their full potential.

Marbles

Trevor Gordan (b. 5 May 1948) and Graham Bonnet (b. 12 December 1947) were cousins from the UK seaside town of Skegness, Yorkshire. The former had moved to Australia, where he worked as a compere and recorded with the **Bee Gees**. It was this connection which brought Gordan to the attention of manager **Robert Stigwood**, who agreed to sign the duo when they formed in England in 1968. By further coincidence, Bonnet was a distant cousin of the Gibb brothers. With a name provided by **Barry Gibb** and a song written by the Bee Gees, the group had an excellent chance of success, and so it proved. The powerful 'Only One Woman' was a Top 10 UK hit in the autumn of 1968, but the group could only scrape the charts once more with the prophetically titled, 'The Walls Fell Down'. In 1979, Bonnet joined **Ritchie Blackmore's Rainbow** as lead vocalist.

Marc And The Mambas

Formed by **Marc Almond** (b. Peter Marc Almond, 9 July 1956, Southport, Lancashire, England), Marc And The Mambas was a pseudonym that the singer employed for his more arcane and adventurous work. Weary of the restrictions that came with his pop star role in **Soft Cell**, the Mambas project enabled him to attempt more daring and original ideas without compromise. With the assistance of Annie Hogan, Almond completed *Untitled* in which he unveiled spirited revivals of material by artists such as **Lou Reed** and **Jacques Brel**. By 1983, Almond was plunging far deeper into the Marc And The Mambas project, despite the continued success of Soft Cell. This phase culminated in the release of a double album, *Torment And Toreros*. This was unquestionably Almond's most extreme and personal recording, full of melodrama with a burningly revealing glimpse into the singer's darker side. When the album received a poor review in one music paper, Almond was so despondent

and incensed that he announced his retirement. What that comment actually meant was the imminent dissolution of Marc And The Mambas and a final return to Soft Cell. When they, too, collapsed at the end of 1983, Almond embarked on a solo career, although his first post-Soft Cell recording, *Vermin In Ermine* was credited to Marc And The Willing Sinners and featured several musicians who had joined in the Mambas experiment.
Albums: *Untitled* (1982), *Torment And Toreros* (1983).

Marcels

The Marcels were one of several doo-wop influenced American vocal groups to score success in the early 60s, despite the passing of the genre's golden age. Cornelius 'Nini' Harp (lead singer), Ronald 'Bingo' Mundy (tenor), Fred Johnson (bass), Gene Bricker (tenor) and Richard Knauss (baritone), all native to Pittsburg, Pennsylvania, USA, achieved fame for their distinctive version of **Richard Rodgers/ Lorenz Hart**'s classic 'Blue Moon', previously a UK Top 10 hit for **Elvis Presley** in 1956, which topped both the US and UK charts in 1961. Johnson's distinctive bass introduction to the song has remained as one of most enduring vocal phrases of the time. The quartet scored a further US Top 10 hit that year with 'Heartaches', but its personnel was unstable, with Allen Johnson replacing Knauss and Walt Maddox replacing Bricker. Mundy walked out on the group during this same period, and this did nothing to prepare them for the ever-changing trends prevalent during the early 60s, and, eventually undermined the Marcels' long-term aspirations.
Album: *Blue Moon* (Colpix 1961). Compilations: *Heartaches* (1987), *The Best Of The Marcels* (1990), *The Complete Colpix Sessions* (Sequel 1994).

March Of The Falsettos

The second in a series of musicals with music and lyrics by William Finn, all of which began Off Broadway at the experimental and innovative centre, Playwrights Horizons. The first of what is sometimes called 'The Marvin Trilogy', *In Trousers*, played for 16 performances from 26 March 1985 at the Promenade Theatre in New York, and has rarely been presented since. The third, and last, in the trilogy is entitled *Falsettoland*, and that piece is sometimes combined with *March Of The Falsettos* under the title of *Falsettos*.
March Of The Falsettos, a piece which William Finn himself has called 'a passionate work about being scared to death of love', gave a total of 298 performances at Playwrights Horizons and the West Side Arts Centre from April 1981. It was set in 1979, and told of a Jewish father, Marvin (Michael Rupert), who discovers that he is homosexual, and leaves his wife, Trina (Alison Fraser) and young son, Jason (James Kushner), to go and live with his male lover, Whizzer Brown (Stephen Bogardus). In a neat twist, Marvin's wife marries his psychiatrist, Mendel (Chip Zien), and he is left alone. What has been called 'the most powerful and emotional score of the 80s, (there is no spoken dialogue) included 'Four Jews In A Room Bitching', 'This Had Better Stop', 'The Games I Play', 'The Chess Game, 'I Never Wanted To Love You', 'Trina's Song', 'This Had Better Come To A Stop', 'Love Is Blind', 'My Father's A Homo', and 'The Thrill Of First Love'.
Falsettoland, which opened in 1990, begins two years after *March Of The Falsettos*. Rupert, Bogardus and Zien recreated their original roles, and added to the cast was a doctor, Charlotte (Heather MacRae), and her lesbian lover, Cordelia (Janet Metz). After the excruciatingly difficult adjustments that all the characters had been forced to make in the previous show, the early mood in *Falsettoland* is one of 'whimsical goofiness', but that changes swiftly when Whizzer is diagnosed as having a deadly disease soon to be identified as AIDS. The family gather round his bedside, and the show culminates in young Jason's bar mitzvah in Whizzer's hospital room. The songs included 'Falsettoland', 'Year Of The Child', 'The Baseball Game', 'Everyone Hates His Parents', 'What More Can I Say?', 'Something Bad Is Happening', 'Days Like This', 'Unlikely Lovers,' 'You Gotta Die Sometime', and 'What Would I Do?'. Opinions as to the two shows' merit and value varied widely. To many, *March Of The Falsettos* was 'not just a musical about gay life in modern times, but a masterly feat of comic storytelling and a visionary musical theatre work', while others dismissed both *March Of The Falsettos* and *Falsettoland* as 'overrated Off Broadway cult items'. *Falsettoland* won **Tony Awards** for best book (Finn and James Lapine, who also directed) and score, and ran for a total of 245 performances. After over a decade on the Fringe, Finn and Lapine's audacious and original concept finally graduated to Broadway in April 1992, when *March Of The Falsettos* and *Falsettoland* were presented under the title of *Falsettos* at the John Golden Theatre for nearly 500 performances, and was rewarded with Tony Awards for book and score. A London production of *March Of The Falsettos*, with Simon Green, Paddy Navin, Barry James, Martin Smith, and Damien Walker, played 29 performances at the Albery Theatre in 1987.

March Violets

This rock band with definite 'gothic' leanings was formed in England during 1982. Hugh (bass) met Simon (vocals) in Leeds, and the latter recruited an old friend, Tom (guitar). Together with a hastily recruited female singer they entered the studios to record an EP which brought them subsequent exposure on BBC disc jockey **John Peel**'s show. After further releases on the fashionable Merciful Release label, they acquired the services of Travis when he replaced the original drum machine in late 1984. Simon left owing to a 'mutual

decision', while vocalist Cleo joined for their 'Snakedance' single in 1983. By this time the band behind her only retained Tom from the original line-up, with Loz the latest recruit on bass. In 1986, they signed to **London Records**, releasing 'Turn To The Sky', which just failed to scrape the charts. By this time they were trying to shake off the taint of the 'goth' tag, emphasizing that their influences were bands like **Z.Z. Top**, **Led Zeppelin** and the **Pretenders**. Critics used Cleo's blonde hair as justification for comparisons to **Blondie**, while musically they were somewhere between the two.
Album: *Natural History* (1984).

March, Little Peggy

b. Margaret Battavio, 7 March 1948, Lansdale, Pennsylvania, USA. A child prodigy, at the age of five, March was a regular cast member of Rex Trailer's television show. She subsequently won a talent contest, before securing a recording deal with **RCA Records**. The singer secured her sole million-selling disc in 1963 when 'I Will Follow Him' topped the US charts. This memorable song had been adapted from 'Chariot', a gold-disc in France for British vocalist **Petula Clark** the previous year. March enjoyed other minor chart entries, most notably with 'Hello Heartache, Goodbye Love', her sole UK hit, but she is forever linked to her major success. Moving to Germany in the late 60s, she sang frequently on television shows; as a songwriter, she is credited to two European number 1 hits: 'When The Rain Begins To Fall (**Jermaine Jackson** and **Pia Zadora**) and 'Manuel Goodbye' (Audrey Landers). She returned to the USA in the 80s. She performed 'I Will Follow Him' in the 1987 John Waters' film, *Hairspray*, a tongue-in-cheek homage to pre-**Beatles** 60s America.
Albums: *Little Peggy March* (1962), *I Will Follow Him* (RCA Victor 1963), with Bennie Thomas *In Our Fashion* (RCA Victor 1965), *No Foolin'* (RCA Victor 1968).

Marchan, Bobby

b. 30 April 1930, Youngstown, Ohio, USA. Marchan was a New Orleans entertainer who had moderate success both as a rock 'n' roller and a soul singer. His long-time career as a female impersonator reflected a time-honored tradition in black entertainment going back to medicine shows. He began performing in Ohio as a drag comic singer, and in 1954 made his way to New Orleans as a member of a drag-queen troupe called the Powder Box Revue. Also during that year, he made his first records for California-based Aladdin Records. In 1957, he joined **Huey 'Piano' Smith** and the Clowns as lead vocalist and, with his distinctive vocals and pianist Smith's boogie-woogie stylings, recorded a succession of infectious rock 'n' roll hits, notably 'Rocking Pneumonia And The Boogie Woogie Flu' and 'Don't You Just Know It'. Marchan left the Clowns in 1960 after leaping on the charts with a melodramatic version of 'There Is Something On Your Mind' (number 1 R&B and number 31 pop), a cover of **Big Jay McNeely**'s hit of the previous year. Marchan's version made an impact because of an impassioned recitation involving sexual jealousy and murder that was lifted from an earlier New Orleans hit, **Larry Darnell**'s 'I'll Get Along Somehow' from 1949. He had a moderate hit in 1966 with 'Shake Your Tambourine' (number 14 R&B). He continued to record into the mid-70s, but with no further success. In between singing engagements, Marchan worked as a female impersonator on New Orleans' Bourbon Street, and was a master of ceremonies at many clubs.
Albums: *There's Something On Your Mind* (1964), *Golden Classics* (1988).

Marcus, Steve

b. 18 September 1939, New York, USA. Marcus studied at the **Berklee College Of Music** in Boston (1959-61) before joining **Stan Kenton**'s Orchestra in 1963. From 1967-70 he played with the **Herbie Mann** Group as well as for bands as diverse as those of **Woody Herman** and the **Jazz Composers Orchestra**. In the early 70s, he played with **Larry Coryell** (1971-73) before forming his own Count's Rock Band (1973-75). He joined **Buddy Rich** in 1975, and played with him regularly over the next 10 years. His tenor playing blends R&B stylings with the influence of **John Coltrane** in much the way **Sal Nistico**, another Rich tenor, does: it is a style which can punch its way through the ebullient backings of the big band in full swing.
Albums: *Count's Rock Band* (1974), *Buddy Rich Plays And Plays And Plays* (1975), *Lionel Hampton Presents Buddy Rich* (1977), *201* (Red Baron 1992).

Mardi Gras

Pop crooner **Pat Boone** forged his career by recording antiseptic cover versions of R&B hits. He became the clean-cut face of rock 'n' roll, acceptable to a moral majority fearful of black musicians and the ebullient talent of, for example, **Elvis Presley** and **Jerry Lee Lewis**. Boone was thus quickly embraced by Hollywood, but his ventures into pop films proved equally insubstantial. *Mardi Gras*, released in 1958, co-starred aspiring singers Gary Crosby (the son of **Bing Crosby** and **Tommy Sands**, the first husband of **Nancy Sinatra**. Boone portrays a cadet who wins a date with a movie star; the film's title is inspired by footage of the New Orleans festival which provides momentarily relief from this anodyne plot. The soundtrack includes the risible 'A Fiddle, A Rifle, An Axe And A Bible', the last of which Boone grasped in real-life when he opted to record religious material.

Maresca, Ernie

b. 21 April 1939, Bronx, New York, USA. Maresca's one hit was the rousing rock 'n' roll tune, 'Shout! Shout! (Knock Yourself Out),' from 1962, which went to number 6 on the US chart. With great support from the vocal group, Del Satins, Maresca created a piece that epitomized the spirit of early rock 'n' roll with its sense of fun and enthusiasm for dance. But he was mainly a behind-the-scenes talent, writing and producing acts for the Laurie label in New York City. The songs he composed included 'No One Knows' for **Dion And The Belmonts**; 'Runaround Sue' and 'The Wanderer' for **Dion**, and 'Runaround' for the **Regents**. Most of the acts he worked with were hard-hitting, Italian-American, doo-wop groups who came from the Bronx, notably the Belmonts, Regents, Camelots, Del Satins, Nino And The Ebbtides, and the Five Discs. In the UK, 'Shout! Shout' (Knock Yourself Out)' was remade in 1982 by **Rocky Sharpe And The Replays**, who took it to number 19.
Album: *Shout! Shout! Knock Yourself Out* (Seville 1962).

Margo

b. Margaret O'Donnell, 6 February 1951, Kincasslagh, County Donegal, Eire. Influenced by **Patsy Cline** and whilst still at school, she began her own musical career in 1964, as a member of a local showband, the Keynotes. Her first success came with her recordings of 'Bonny Irish Boy' and 'Road By The River' in 1968, which led to appearances on major television shows. In the early 70s, she formed her own band, Country Folk, topped the Irish charts with an old Irish ballad 'I'll Forgive And I'll Try To Forget' and registered a very successful appearance at the 1972 Wembley Festival. Margo was the victim of a road accident in the mid-70s, which saw her hospitalized for months and inactive for over a year. In 1976, she fronted the Country Blue Boys, toured extensively and scored a major duet hit, 'Hello Mr Peters', with Larry Cunningham. Since that time, she has continued to entertain audiences, not only in the UK but also in the USA and Australia. Her major achievements include appearances at Carnegie Hall, New York and London's Royal Albert Hall, plus a very successful series on RTE television. In 1983, her younger brother, **Daniel O'Donnell**, joined her band and gained some experience before launching his own solo career. In 1988, after joining the Ritz label, Margo recorded 'Two's Company' with Daniel. In 1989, she was honoured, in Kincasslagh, at an event that included a surprise appearance from her brother, in recognition of her 25 years in show business. In 1991, she formed a new band, Sweet Dreams, which featured John Glenn as her co-vocalist but she later reverted to using her original band name of Country Folk. In 1994, Ritz released *New Beginnings*, which included her hit single, 'The Eyes Of My Child', as well as a new version of her old hit 'I'll Forgive And Try To Forget' but in 1995, she joined the Hazel label. Once asked for a comment on her successful longevity in the business, she is quoted as saying 'Keep your head very level and stay away from the drink at all costs.' A very accomplished entertainer, she has never strayed far from her early influences, in either her concert appearances or her recorded output of almost 30 albums, which has led many people to affectionately call Margo, The Queen of Country and Irish.
Albums: *Margo And The Country Folk* (Ruby 1971), *From Margo With Love* (ARA 1972), *Country Lovin'* (ARA 1973, issued in UK, One Up 1973), *At Home In Ireland* (ARA 1974), *Margo - The Girl From Donegal* (IRL 1975), with Larry Cunningham *Yes Mr Peters* (Release 1977), *A Toast To Claddagh* (ARA 1978), *Galway Bay* (ARA 1978), *Irish Requests* (ARA 1979), *Country Style* (ARA 1979), *All Time Hits* (ARA 1979), *Country Girl* (Homespun 1980), *Margo's Favourites* (Harp 1980), *Trip To Ireland* (Homespun 1982), *Three Leaf Shamrock* (Homespun early-80s), *Just Margo* (Homespun early-80s), *I'll Settle For Old Ireland* (Homespun early-80s), *Destination Donegal* (ARA 1982), *18 Irish Songs* (ARA 1982), *Toast From An Irish Colleen* (Stoic 1984), *Girl From Donegal* (IMHC 1987), *Margo Now* (Unicorn 1987, reissued with different sleeve Ritz 1988), *I Long To See Old Ireland Free Once More* (Outlet 1988), *Ireland Must Be Heaven* (EMI-Ireland 1988), *A Trip Through Ireland* (I&B 1989), *Ireland On My Mind* (Ritz 1992), *New Beginnings* (Ritz 1994).

Margolin, Bob

b. 9 May 1949, Brookline, Massachusetts, USA. Margolin's right of passage to the blues came through **Chuck Berry**, who sparked his interest in the guitar and introduced him to the music of the classic **Muddy Waters** band. After working in local blues outfits, Margolin worked alongside **Luther 'Georgia Boy' Johnson**, who had been in Muddy's band during the 60s. In 1973, he received the call to join Muddy Waters and played with the band until the early 80s, appearing on seven albums for **Chess** and Blue Sky and backing Muddy on his appearance in ***The Last Waltz***, the **Band**'s farewell concert film. He had begun to front his own band by then and when Muddy died in 1983 took up a full-time solo career. Now calling himself Steady Rollin' Bob Margolin, his first two albums pay more than ample tribute to his former boss and to post-war Chicago blues, and feature men such as **Jimmy Rogers**, **Pinetop Perkins** and **Willie Smith**. *Down In The Alley*, with guest vocalists **Nappy Brown** and **John Brim**, broadened its perspective, but live Margolin remains a sincere recreator of his primary influences.
Albums: *The Old School* (Powerhouse 1989), *Chicago Blues* (Powerhouse 1991), *Down In The Alley* (Alligator 1994).

Mariano, Charlie

b. 12 November 1923, Boston, Massachusetts, USA. One of many fine students to emerge from Boston's **Berklee College Of Music**, Mariano gained most of his early experience in and around his home town. Among the musicians with whom he played in the formative years of the late 40s and early 50s were **Herb Pomeroy**, **Nat Pierce**, **Gigi Gryce**, **Quincy Jones** and **Jackie Byard**. In 1953, he joined **Stan Kenton** for a two-year spell and then worked in Los Angeles with **Shelly Manne**. By 1958 he was back in Boston, this time teaching at **Berklee College Of Music**. The following year he was briefly with Kenton again, then met, married and formed a band with **Toshiko Akiyoshi**. This association lasted into the mid-60s, with part of that time spent in Japan. During the 60s Mariano also played with **Charles Mingus**, spent more time teaching at Berklee, travelled extensively in the far-east, and led his own jazz-rock group. In the 70s and 80s Mariano lived mostly in Europe, leading bands with **Philip Catherine** and others, continuing to explore eastern music and playing many kinds of fusion music with, among other groups, the **United Jazz And Rock Ensemble** and **Eberhard Weber**'s Colours. Throughout his career, Mariano has displayed a striking ability to encompass many diverse musical forms and incorporate them into jazz without losing the emotional intensity of his early bebop-orientated playing style. Through his continued exploration of ethnic musical forms, particularly those of eastern origin, Mariano has established a secure and significant place as a truly international jazz artist.

Selected albums: *Charlie Mariano With His Jazz Group* (1950-51), *The Modern Saxophone Stylings Of Charlie Mariano* (1950-51), *Charlie Mariano* i (1951), *Charlie Mariano Boston All Stars* (Original Jazz Classics 1953), *Charlie Mariano* ii (1953), *Swinging With Mariano* (Affinity 1954), *Charlie Mariano* Plays (Fresh Sound 1954), *Alto Sax For Young Moderns/Johnny One-note* (Affinity 1954), with Stan Kenton *Contemporary Concepts* (1955), *Charlie Mariano* iv (1957), *Toshiko-Mariano Quartet* i (1960), with Charles Mingus *The Black Saint And The Sinner Lady* (1963), *Toshiko-Mariano Quartet* (1963), *A Jazz Portrait Of Charlie Mariano* (1963), *Folk Soul* (1967), with Sadao Watanabe *Iberian Waltz* (1967-68), *Charlie Mariano And His Orchestra* (c.1970), *Cascade* (1974), *Reflektions* (1974), *Jazz Confronto 15/JaC's Group Featuring Charlie Mariano* (1975), *The Door Is Open/Pork Pie* (1975), *Helen 12 Trees* (1976), *October* (1977), with United Jazz And Rock Ensemble *Teamwork* (1978), *Crystal Bells* (1979), *Tea For Four* (1980), *Some Kind Of Changes* (c.1982), *Jyothi* (ECM 1983), *The Charlie Mariano Group* (1985), *Mariano* (Intuition 1987), *Charlie Mariano And The Karnataka College Of Percussion: Live* (1989), *Live* (Verabra 1990), *It's Standard Time* (Fresh Sound 1990), *Innuendo* (Lipstick 1992).

Mariano, Torcuato

b. 1963, Buenos Aires, Argentina. A powerful and talented advocate of Brazilian instrumental jazz, Mariano moved to that country from his native Argentina at the age of 14. By this time already a fluent, self-taught performer, under the tutelage of guitarist Claudio Gabis he studied music theory and harmony. By 1980 he was a regular at various night clubs, performing alongside bossa nova legends including **Johnny Alt**. However, his other influences were drawn from a wide musical vocabulary, and he delighted in mixing his South American heritage with the rock, blues, jazz and funk traditions of the US. Numbering **Santana**, **Pat Metheny**, **Jeff Beck**, Ivan Luis and **Djavan** among his primary influences, he was pleased to oblige when the opportunity arose to accompany the last named pair in the studio. They were impressed enough by his emerging technique to invite Mariano to join their respective touring bands. Further sessions in Brazil's music capital, Rio de Janeiro, confirmed his new-found status, and brought him into harness with names such as **Sergio Mendez**, Xuxa, **Cal Costa** and Leo Gandelman. The first to use his own compositions was saxophonist Gandelman, before he teamed up with lyricist Claudio Rabello to produce a powerful songwriting partnership, benefiting the careers of Xuxa, Angelica, Rosana and others. These successes awoke the interest of VISOM Records, and they duly released a debut solo album, *Paradise Station*. Written, arranged and co-produced by Mariano, it became a welcome addition to the artist's growing legacy and furthered Brazil's discourse with other musical forms and countries. His growing professionalism in producing and composing material with Brazil's major record companies was reflected on *Last Look*. The most poignant track, 'Everything I Couldn't Say With Words', saw him combine his guitar with the flute of Marcelo Martins. Just as affecting was the hip-hop based 'In The Rhythm Of My Heart'.

Albums: *Paradise Station* (VISOM 1993), *Last Look* (Windham Hill 1995).

Marie, Kelly

b. Jacqueline McKinnon, 23 October 1957, Paisley, Scotland. The disco/Hi-NRG singer Kelly Marie won the *Opportunity Knocks* talent competition on British television at the age of 15, but it was in France that she first enjoyed any success on vinyl when 'Who's The Lady With My Man?' was awarded a gold disc. However, 'Feels Like I'm In Love' topped the UK singles chart in 1980. The song, written by former **Mungo Jerry** leader Ray Dorset, had originally been intended for **Elvis Presley** who died before he could record it. Minor hits followed with 'Loving Just For Fun', 'Hot Love' and 'Love Trial', before Kelly's chart career came to an end. She made a part-time return to

the club circuit in the 90s generally to appreciative gay Hi-NRG audiences, such as those at the G.A.Y. venue. Her last record was a cover of **Billy Fury**'s 'Halfway To Paradise' in 1989.
Albums: *Who's That Lady With My Man* (Pye 1977), *Feels Like I'm In Love* (Calibre 1980).

Marie, Teena

b. Mary Christine Brocker, 1957, Santa Monica, California, USA. A singer, songwriter, multi-instrumentalist, arranger and producer, Teena Marie is one of the few white artists to sustain a consistent career in the US soul market. Spotted by **Motown Records**' Berry Gordy in the 70s, he put her in touch with funk star and label-mate **Rick James**, and her early career strongly reflected their joint influence. The highly commercial *Wild And Peaceful* saw her backed by James and the Stone City Band on a set which included their hit duet, 'I'm A Sucker For Your Love'. She returned the favour by partnering James on 'Fire And Desire' on his *Street Songs* album in 1981. Afterwards Marie took increasing control of her career and songwriting, singing both ballads and funk. Both 'I Need Your Lovin'' and 'Square Biz' reached the Top 20 of the US ***Billboard*** charts in 1980 and 1981 respectively. In the UK 'Behind The Groove', a surprise disco smash at number 6 in the singles chart, led to confusion in public minds over her and the similarly titled **Kelly Marie** (it also, accidentally, picked up on the prevalent UK disco trend for songs with 'Groove' in the title). However, her greatest success followed her move to **Epic Records**, which some saw as an assertion of her independence, and the number 4-peaking US hit, 'Lovergirl'. Afterwards her chart career declined. *Emerald City* was a funky outing, notable particularly for **Stevie Ray Vaughan** guitar solo on 'You So Heavy'. Demonstrating her talent to modernise her technique with the advent of each new instalment in R&B's development, *Ivory* was produced by **Soul II Soul**'s Jazzie B.
Albums: *Wild And Peaceful* (Gordy 1979), *Lady T* (Gordy 1980), *Irons In The Fire* (Gordy 1980), *It Must Be Magic* (Gordy 1981), *Robbery* (Epic 1983), *Starchild* (Epic 1984), *Emerald City* (Epic 1986), *Naked To The World* (Epic 1988), *Ivory* (Epic 1990). Compilations: *Greatest Hits* (Motown 1985), *Greatest Hits* (Epic 1991; different track-listing to Motown issue).

Marillion

Frontrunners of the short-lived UK progressive rock revival of the early 80s, Marillion survived unfavourable comparisons with **Genesis** to become a popular melodic rock group, notching up several successful singles plucked from their grandiose concept albums. The group formed in Aylesbury, Buckinghamshire, originally as Silmarillion, a name taken from the novel by J.R.R. Tolkien. The group featured Doug Irvine (bass), Mick Pointer (b. 22 July 1956; drums), Steve Rothery (b. 25 November 1959, Brampton, South Yorkshire, England; guitar) and Brian Jelliman (keyboards). After recording the instrumental demo, 'The Web', the band recruited **Fish** (b. Derek William Dick, 25 April 1958, Dalkeith, Edinburgh, Scotland; vocals) and Diz Minnett (bass) and began building a strong following through almost continuous gigging. Before recording their debut, 'Market Square Heroes', Jelliman and Minnitt were replaced by Mark Kelly (b. 9 April 1961; keyboards) and Pete Trewavas (b. 15 January 1959, Middlesbrough, Cleveland, England; bass). Fish wrote all the lyrics for *Script For A Jester's Tear* and became the focal point of the group, often appearing on stage in garish make-up, echoing the style, both visually and vocally, of Genesis' singer **Peter Gabriel**. In 1983 Pointer was sacked and replaced for brief stints by Andy Ward of **Camel**, then John Marter and Jonathan Mover before the arrival of Ian Mosley (b. 16 June 1953, London, England), a veteran of many progressive rock bands, including **Curved Air** and the **Gordon Giltrap** band. Marillion's second album embraced a more straightforward hard rock sound and yielded two hits, 'Assassin' and 'Punch And Judy'. 1985's *Misplaced Childhood* was Marillion's biggest-selling album - surprisingly so, as it featured an elaborate concept, being virtually one continuous piece of music based largely on Fish's childhood experiences. 'Kayleigh', a romantic ballad extracted from this mammoth work, reached number 2 in the UK charts. By 1988 Fish was becoming increasingly dissatisfied with the group's musical development and left to pursue a solo career. The live double album, *Thieving Magpie*, was his last recorded contribution, and provided a fitting overview of the group's past successes. Marillion acquired Steve Hogarth (b. Doncaster, England), formerly of the **Europeans**, who made his debut on *Seasons End*, proving himself equal to the daunting task of fronting a well-established band. The 90s have found Marillion as popular as ever, with the ghost of Fish receding into the distance. With Hogarth fronting the band consistent success has continued to acrue, including chart status for 'Sympathy', 'The Hollow Man' and 'Alone Again In The Lap Of Luxury'. Unusually for a band rooted in the progressive rock subculture, a genre dominated by the album, Marillion continue to be distinguished as much for their single output.
Albums: *Script For A Jester's Tear* (EMI 1983), *Fugazi* (EMI 1984), *Real To Real* (EMI 1984), *Misplaced Childhood* (EMI 1985), *Brief Encounter* (EMI 1986), *Clutching At Straws* (EMI 1987), *B Sides Themselves* (EMI 1988), *The Thieving Magpie* (EMI 1988), *Seasons End* (EMI 1989), *Holidays In Eden* (EMI 1991), *Brave* (EMI 1994, *Afraid Of Sunlight* (EMI 1995). Compilation: *A Singles Collection* (EMI 1992).

Videos: *1982-1986 The Videos* (1986), *Live From Loreley* (1987), *From Stoke Row To Ipanema* (1990).
Further reading: *Market Square Heroes*, Mick Wall. *Marillion*, Carol Clerk. *The Authorized Story Of Marillion*, Mick Wall. *Marillion: The Script*, Clive Gifford.

Marilyn Manson

Controversial by design rather than accident, Florida group Marilyn Manson were formed in 1990 with the express intention of 'exploring the limits of censorship'. In keeping with this image, they were the first band to be signed to Trent Reznor (**Nine Inch Nails**) and John A. Malm Jr's Nothing label. Support slots with the likes of **Suicidal Tendencies**, **Meat Beat Manifesto**, **Murphy's Law** and the **Genitorturers** brought them considerable local recognition, in the form of the 1993 'Slammy' awards (taking the song of the year nomination for 'Dope Hat') and sundry other baubles (not least short-heading **Gloria Estefan** for the Best Local Musician category in *South Flordia* Magazine). Reznor also acted as guest musician and executive producer on the group's 1994 debut album, with half of the tracks mixed at the Sharon Tate house where NIN have also recorded. The group comprises Mr Manson (vocals, tape loops), Daisy Berkowitz (guitar), Twiggy Ramirez (bass), Madonna Wayne Gacy (Hammond organ, samples) and Sara Lee Lucas (drums).
Album: *Portrait Of An American Family* (Nothing/East West 1994).

Marine Girls

This UK quartet was formed by four Hertfordshire school friends: Jane Fox (b. c.1963; bass/vocals), her sister Alice (b. c.1966; vocals/percussion), **Tracey Thorn** (b. 26 September 1962; guitar/vocals) and the soon-to-depart, Gina (percussion/vocals). The Marine Girls recorded their homemade *Beach Party* in a garden shed. Musically competent, within limitations, their lyrics showed remarkable strength and eloquence in dealing with the age-old problems of difficult boyfriends, new love and loneliness, often using the symbolic context of the sea and all its mysteries. With initial encouragement from the **Television Personalities**, the album was released by the Whaam! label and was later picked up Cherry Red Records, who signed the group for a second album. By this time, Tracey had left school to go to Hull University, where she struck up a romantic and artistic relationship with Cherry Red stable-mate **Ben Watt**. They recorded the **Cole Porter** song, 'Night And Day' under the name of **Everything But The Girl**. Thorn had also released a solo album in 1982, *A Distant Shore*, which was well-received by the critics and public. Pursuing a parallel career as a Marine Girl and as a duettist with Watt at first proved comfortable, but with the increasing popularity and media attention of Everything But The Girl, an amicable split with the Fox sisters came in late 1983, after the release of the successful *Lazy Ways*. Continuing their seaside/oceanic fixation, the sisters formed Grab Grab The Haddock, which produced two fine EPs on Cherry Red before folding in 1986. The line-up of Grab Grab The Haddock was notable for the inclusion of Lester Noel, who later joined former **Housemartin** Norman Cook in **Beats International**.
Albums: *Beach Party* (1981), *Lazy Ways* (1983).

Marino, Frank

b. 22 August 1954, Canada. This formidible guitarist initially based his style obsessively on **Jimi Hendrix**. Forming **Mahogany Rush** in 1970 (later known as Frank Marino And Mahogany Rush), he decided to work solely under his own name from 1980 onwards. Playing the Heavy Metal Holocaust Festival in Port Vale during 1981, he was the surprise success of the day, upstaging headliners **Triumph** with a truly dazzling display of guitar pyrotechnics and showmanship. *The Power Of Rock 'N' Roll* was the first release under Marino's own name and featured a more aggressive style, coupled with lyrical references to sensitive social and political issues of the time. *Juggernaut* built on this success, but increased the tempo and introduced a greater degree of melody in the material. A four year break from recording ensued, owing to business and management setbacks, before *Full Circle* appeared in 1986. A stunning double live album was issued two years later, but nothing further appeared until a single track contribution to the *Guitar Speak Vol.2* album was released in 1990.
Albums: *The Power Of Rock 'N' Roll* (CBS 1981), *Juggernaut* (CBS 1982), *Full Circle* (Maze 1986), *Double Live* (Maze 1988).

Marion

Macclesfield, England quintet comprising Jamie Harding (b. c.1975; vocals), Anthony Grantham (guitar), Phil Cunningham (guitar), Julian Phillips (bass) and Murad Mousa (drums), who created an immediate stir in 1994 with the release of two independent singles ('Violent Men' and 'The Only Way'). This brace of fierce, anthemic songs, together with the fact that they were represented by ex-**Smiths** manager Joe Moss, helped ensure a frenzied A&R chase in the summer of that year, which was eventually concluded at the In The City seminar in September when they were signed by **London Records**. However, there was a degree of longevity to Marion's pursuits which might not have been suggested by their average age of 20 - Harding, Cunningham and Grantham had been in youthful bands together for nine years before this current incarnation. Their new label sent them to work with **Stephen Street**, provoking further Smiths' comparisons, which were hardly deflated by the news that **Morrissey** had attended two of their early gigs (he subsequently invited them to support him on UK dates). The first result of the new deal was the single, 'Toys For Boys'.

Marionette

Formed in the early 80s in Islington, London, Marionette were a four-piece group in the tradition of the **New York Dolls** and **Faces**. The main strength of the band, fronted by vocalist Ray Zell along with Dave Veal on guitar, KK on bass and Pig on drums, was in their live performances - which at times recalled the punk gigs of the mid to late 70s. Their first release was *Provocatively Trashy*, a live cassette, soon after which they ventured into the recording studio for 'My Baby Sucks', which was a proposed single at the time, but did not materialise. By 1985 Zell was making a name for himself as a journalist in the music press, eventually working for *Kerrang!* magazine where he created the cartoon character, Pandora Peroxide, which is still a weekly feature today. Heavy Metal Records did release one album by them, but UK glam had long since given way to American imports. Zell has revived the band on occasions, but now seems content with writing.
Album: *Blonde Secrets And Dark Bombshells* (Heavy Metal 1985).

Marionettes

Based in London, England, this Gothic rock band were formed by singer Sean Cronin in February 1986, and were originally titled the Screaming Marionettes. The full line-up consisted of Paul Newton (drums), Barry Downes (bass; ex-**Weapon**) and Vile Gold (guitar). After embarking on a tough gigging schedule, the band signed to the record label Lambs To The Slaughter. 'Obsession' was released in April 1988, along with a video made by cult film director David McGillivery. Despite the media paying no attention whatsoever, the Marionettes had no troubling building a live following. 'Goth' audiences had, after all, been largely deserted by old favourites such as the **Mission** and **Cult**, whose style the Marionettes revisited, and the band were easily able to attract 1,500 fans to a gig at Hammersmith Palais, London, in August 1988. A second single, 'Like Christabel', made the UK independent charts in July of the following year. Rainer Hensal invited them to record their debut album for his Maze Music label (through **Virgin Records**). Germany proved to have a great affection for the group, and after playing three festivals under the auspices of the *Zillo* magazine, the group signed to the inter-connected Mephisto's Mob label. *Book Of Shadows*, produced by John McGowan (**Metallica** and **Ozzy Osbourne**) was released in late 1992, after which they hit the European festival trail, playing shows with **Pearl Jam** and the **Sisters Of Mercy** to audiences of over 50,000.
Albums: Ave Dementia (Maze/Virgin 1990), Book Of Shadows (Mephisto's Mob/Jungle 1992).

Mark IV

This rock 'n' roll group from Berkhampsted, Hertfordshire, England was formed in 1961, around a nucleus of William Rawlinson and Beverly Brown. However, during 1963 - the exact circumstances are unclear and lost even to the memory of some of the protagonists - members of the group Jimmy Virgo And The Bluejacks seemed to take over Mark IV squeezing the old members out. The line-up evolved into Kenny Pickett (b. 3 September 1947, Ware, Hertfordshire, England; vocals), Eddie Phillips (b. 15 August 1945, Leytonstone, London, England; guitar), Mick Thompson (rhythm guitar), John 'Nobby' Dalton (bass), and Jack Jones (b. Northampton, England; drums). Initially managed by **Robert Stigwood**, they released two singles on **Mercury** and then further releases on **Decca** and Fontana. It was during the Mark IV days that guitarist Phillips first conceived the idea of playing his guitar with a violin bow after previous attempts with a fret saw had damaged the instrument. Mark IV later came under the managerial auspices of **Tony Stratton-Smith** and on 6 June 1966 played their last gig under that name. Dalton left to join the **Kinks**, Thompson left the music business completely and the remaining members went on to form **Creation**.

Mark, Louisa

b. 1960, Shepherds Bush, London, England. Mark first ventured into show business through the regular talent competitions held at the Four Aces Club in London where she accomplished victory for 10 consecutive weeks. Competitors would sing over acetates provided by **Lloyd Coxsone** who, impressed with her popularity, took her into Gooseberry Studios for a recording session. The result was a cover version of the soul hit by **Robert Parker**, 'Caught You In A Lie'. With backing provided by **Matumbi** it was an instant hit almost breaking through into the pop charts. The second release with Coxsone was 'All My Loving' but it lacked the original winning formula. As Mark was only 15 years old and attending Hammersmith County School at the time, she became quite a celebrity among the pupils. After leaving school further releases surfaced including the Clement Bushay-produced, 'Keep It Like It Is', which was later used by **Trinity** for his hit 'Step It Brother Clem'. Her preference for lyrics relating to infidelity continued unabashed when she released 'Six Sixth Street' continuing with the theme of her debut hit. 'I know your having an affair - And I know who and I know where - It's that easy going chick just down there - She lives at number six sixth street - Oh why, oh why just down the road from me - So I could see'. The song, comparable to her debut outing, was beautifully crafted and resulted in another successful hit. In 1980

Bushay released *Markswoman*, which ensued with the artist not recording the following year as she felt the album was rush released and not properly mixed. By 1982 their differences were resolved and she recorded a version of the **Jones Girls**' 'Mum And Dad' arranged by **Sly And Robbie**. As one of the forerunners of Lovers Rock, before the phrase was inaugurated by Dennis Harris, Mark is still held in high esteem as demonstrated by the popularity of her debut single which is still played in dancehalls 20 years after the initial release.
Albums: *Markswoman* (Bushranger 1980), *Breakout* (Bushays 1982).

Marketts

This Hollywood, California-based instrumental group rose to prominence during the surfing craze of the early 60s. Ben Benay (guitar), Mike Henderson (saxophone), Ray Pohlman (bass), Gene Pello (drums) and Richard Hobriaco, then Tom Hensey (keyboards), enjoyed two minor US hits with 'Surfer's Stomp' and Balboa Blue' (both 1962), before scoring a million-seller the following year with the pulsating 'Out Of Limits'. They secured another US Top 20 entry in 1966 with the then-popular 'Batman Theme', but were usurped by newer styles of Californian music. A unit dubbed the New Marketts surfaced during the 70s, by which point Benay was established in Los Angeles session circles. Pohlman pursued a similar career, working with, among others, **Emmylou Harris**, while Hensey became **Neil Diamond**'s keyboard player.
Albums: *Surfer's Stomp* (1962), *The Surfing Scene* (1963), *Take To Wheels* (1963), *Out Of Limits!* (1964), *The Batman Theme* (1966), *Sun Power* (1967), *AM/FM* (1973), *The New Marketts* (mid-70s).

Markham, Pigmeat

b. Dewey Markham, 1904, Durham, North Carolina, USA, d. 13 December 1981. Best known as a comedian, Markham began his long career in 1917, dancing in travelling shows. He travelled the southern 'race' circuit with blues singer **Bessie Smith** and later appeared on burlesque bills with Milton Berle, Red Buttons and **Eddie Cantor**. By the 50s, Markham was one of Black America's most popular entertainers through his shows at the Regal in Chicago, the Howard in Washington and, in particular, New York's famed **Apollo**. Despite being black, he applied burnt cork make-up to his face, a device which caused many of his fans to believe he was actually white. He later made several successful appearances on the influential ***Ed Sullivan*** television show and was signed by **Chess** during the 60s. The Chicago-based label issued several in-concert albums and his 1968 novelty hit, 'Here Comes The Judge'. This tongue-in-cheek recording was inspired by the artist's catch-phrase which was used extensively on the American television comedy series, *Rowan And Martin's Laugh-In*. Although hampered by a competitive version by **Shorty Long**, Markham enjoyed a Top 20 hit in the US and UK. Although this was a one-off achievement, Pigmeat Markham remained a well-known figure until his death in December 1981.

Marlene, Das Musical

Originally titled *Sag Mir Wo Die Blumen Sind* (Where Have All The Flowers Gone?), this musical is based on British author Laurence Roman's biography of the legendary entertainer **Marlene Dietrich**. It opened at the small (785-seater) Theatre am Kurfürstendamm, Berlin, Germany, on 7 April 1993, almost a year after her death. Somewhat optimistically, in the light of subsequent events, the show's producer, Friedrich Kurz, booked the theatre, where Dietrich herself had performed in 1928, until the year 2000. Reportedly capitalized at between £1.5-2 million and directed by Terry Hands, formerly Artistic Director of the Royal Shakespeare Company, the production 'fast-frames 40 years of Dietrich's life, interspersed with a contemporary sub-plot about a troupe of drama students planning a tribute to her'. Along with the 'clumsy political allegories', there is a scene in which Dietrich romps in bed with her husband and his mistress, and, towards the end, **Edith Piaf**, played by a man wearing a white wedding dress, is brought on in a wheel chair. The 'charming, slightly plump' Jutta Habicht plays Dietrich in a cast of six which is accompanied by seven musicians. Most of the 20 songs are by Frederick Hollander, and include his bitter-sweet 'Falling In Love Again' from the memorable Dietrich film, *The Blue Angel*. Two months after the show opened it was retitled *Marlene, Das Musical* and drastically revised so that it became a more straight forward chronological life story, while still retaining plenty of sex and innuendo. More songs were added, but the enormous helium-filled Dietrich model which almost seemed to fill the stage was now missing. In any event, the changes were to no avail, and the show, which it was hoped would go some way towards re-estabishing Marlene Dietrich's reputation in a city that once reviled her, closed on 30 June 1993.

Marley Marl

b. Marlon Williams, 30 September 1962, Queens, New York, USA. Widely revered for his considerable production skills, notably for his cousin **MC Shan**, **Big Daddy Kane**, **Master Ace**, **Roxanne Shanté** and **Biz Markie**, Marl's work is inhabited by a spirit of accessible, old school gusto. He has been widely congratulated for his innovative sampling techniques, using the SP1200 on hip hop landmarks like *Eric B For President*. He also acts as host on the weekly *Rap Attack* radio programme on the WBLS-FM station in New York. The selected albums listed below sample some of

this work, including contributions from Shanté and Kane, plus **Kool G. Rap**, Chuck D, **LL Cool J**, **King Tee** and **Chubb Rock**.
Selected albums: *In Control Volume 1* (Cold Chillin' 1988), *In Control Volume II* (Cold Chillin' 1991).

Marley, Bob, And The Wailers

This legendary vocal group originally comprised six members: Robert Nesta Marley (b. 6 February 1945, St. Anns, Jamaica, West Indies, d. 11 May 1981, Miami, Florida, USA), **Bunny Wailer** (b. Neville O'Riley Livingston, 10 April 1947, Kingston, Jamaica), **Peter Tosh** (b. Winston Hubert McIntosh, 19 October 1944, Westmoreland, Jamaica, d. 11 September 1987, Kingston, Jamaica), Junior Braithwaite, Beverley Kelso, and Cherry Smith. Bob Marley And The Wailers are the sole Jamaican group to have achieved global superstar status together with genuine penetration of world markets. The original vocal group was formed during 1963. After extensive tuition with the great vocalist **Joe Higgs**, they began their recording career later that year for **Coxsone Dodd**, although Marley had made two singles for producer **Leslie Kong** in 1962 - 'Judge Not' and 'One Cup Of Coffee'. Their first record, 'Simmer Down', released just before Christmas 1963 under the group name Bob Marley And The Wailers, went to number 1 on the JBC Radio chart in January 1964, holding that position for the ensuing two months and reputedly selling over 80,000 copies. This big local hit was followed by 'It Hurts To Be Alone', featuring Junior Braithwaite on lead vocal, and 'Lonesome Feeling', with lead vocal by Bunny Wailer. During the period 1963-66, the Wailers made over 70 tracks for Dodd, over 20 of which were local hits, covering a wide stylistic base; from covers of US soul and doo-wop with **ska** backing to the newer, less frantic 'rude-boy' sounds which presaged the development of **rocksteady**, and including many songs which Marley would re-record in the 70s. In late 1965, Braithwaite left to go to America, and Kelso and Smith also departed that year.
On 10 February 1966, Marley married Rita Anderson, at the time a member of the Soulettes, later to become one of the **I-Threes** and a solo vocalist in her own right. The next day he left to join his mother in Wilmington, Delaware, returning to Jamaica in October 1966; the Wailers were now a vocal trio. They cut the local hit 'Bend Down Low' at Studio One late in 1967 (though it was actually self-produced and released on their own label, Wail 'N' Soul 'M'). This and other self-produced output of the time is amongst the rarest, least re-issued Wailers music, and catches the group on the brink of a new maturity; for the first time there were overtly Rasta songs. By the end of that year, following Bunny Wailer's release from prison, they were making demos for Danny Sims, the manager of soft-soul singer **Johnny Nash**, who would hit the UK charts in April of 1972 with the 1968 Marley composition, 'Stir It Up'. This association proved incapable of supporting them, and they began recording for producer Leslie Kong, who had already enjoyed international success with **Desmond Dekker**, the **Pioneers**, and **Jimmy Cliff**. Kong released several singles and an album called *The Best Of The Wailers* in 1970. By the end of 1969, wider commercial success still eluded them. Marley, who had spent the summer of 1969 working at the Chrysler car factory in Wilmington, Delaware, returned to Jamaica, and the trio began a collaboration with **Lee Perry** that was to prove crucially important to their future development. Not only would Perry help focus the trio's rebel stance more effectively, but they would work with the bass and drum team of the Barrett brothers, Aston 'Family Man' (b. 22 November 1946, Kingston, Jamaica) and Carlton (b. 17 December 1950, Kingston, Jamaica, d. 1987, Kingston, Jamaica), who would become an integral part of the Wailers' sound.
The music Bob Marley And The Wailers made with Perry during 1969-71 represents possibly the height of their respective collective powers. Combining brilliant new songs like 'Duppy Conqueror', 'Small Axe' and 'Sun Is Shining' with definitive reworkings of old material, backed by the innovative rhythms of the **Upsetters** and the equally innovative influence of Perry, this body of work stands as a zenith in Jamaican music. It was also the blueprint for Bob Marley's international success. The group continued to record for their own Tuff Gong label after the Perry sessions and came to the attention of **Chris Blackwell**, then owner of **Island Records**. Island had released much of the Wailers' early music from the Studio One period, although the label had concentrated on the rock market since the late 60s. Their first album for the company, *Catch A Fire* (1973), was packaged like a rock album, and targeted at the album market in which Island had been very successful. The band arrived in the UK in April 1973 to tour and appear on television. In July 1973 they supported **Bruce Springsteen** at Max's Kansas City club in New York. Backed by an astute promotional campaign, *Catch A Fire* sold well enough to warrant issue of *Burnin'*, adding Earl 'Wire' Lindo to the group, which signalled a return to a militant, rootsy approach unencumbered by any rock production values whatsoever.
The rock/blues guitarist **Eric Clapton** covered 'I Shot The Sheriff' from this album, taking the tune to the number 9 position in the UK chart during the autumn of 1974, and reinforcing the impact of the Wailers in the process. Just as the band was poised on the brink of wider success internal differences caused Tosh and Livingston to depart, both embarking on substantial solo careers, and Lindo left to join **Taj Mahal**. The new Wailers band, formed mid-1974, included Marley, the Barrett brothers and Bernard

'Touter' Harvey on keyboards, with vocal harmonies by the **I-Threes**, comprising **Marcia Griffiths**, **Rita Marley** and **Judy Mowatt**. This line-up, with later additions, would come to define the so-called 'international' reggae sound that Bob Marley and the Wailers played until Marley's death in 1981. In establishing that form, not only on the series of albums recorded for Island but also by extensive touring, the band moved from the mainstream of Jamaican music into the global market. As the influence of Bob Marley spread, not only as a musician but also as a symbol of success from the so-called 'Third World', the music made locally pursued its own distinct course. 1975 was the year in which the group consolidated their position, with the release of the massively successful *Natty Dread* and rapturously-received concerts at London Lyceum. These concerts attracted both black and white patrons; the crossover had begun. At the end of the year Marley scored his first UK chart hit, the autobiographical 'No Woman No Cry'. His first live album, comprising material from the Lyceum concerts, was also released this year. He continued to release an album a year until his death, at which time a spokesman for Island Records estimated worldwide sales of $190 million. Marley survived an assassination attempt on 3rd December 1976, leaving Jamaica for 18 months early in 1977. In July he had an operation in Miami to remove cancer cells from his right toe.

His albums *Exodus* and *Kaya* enjoyed massive international sales. In April 1978, he played the One Love Peace Concert in Kingston, bringing the two leaders of the violently-warring Jamaican political parties together in a largely symbolic peacemaking gesture. The band then undertook a huge worldwide tour that took in the USA, Canada, Japan, Australia and New Zealand. His own label, Tuff Gong, was expanding its interests, developing new talent. The album *Survival* was released to the usual acclaim, being particularly successful in Africa. The song 'Zimbabwe' was subsequently covered many times by African artists. In 1980, Marley and the Wailers played a momentous concert in the newly-liberated Zimbabwe to an audience of 40,000. In the summer of 1980, his cancer began to spread; he collapsed at Madison Square Garden during a concert. Late in 1980 he began treatment with the controversial cancer specialist, Dr Josef Issels. By the 3rd of May, the doctor had given up. Marley flew to Miami, Florida, where he died on the 11th. Marley was rightly celebrated in 1992 with the release of an outstanding CD box set chronicling his entire career, athough his discography remains cluttered due to the legal ramifications of his estate. His global success had been an inspiration to all Jamaican atists; his name became synonymous with Jamaican music, of which he had been the first authentic superstar. His contribution is thus immense: his career did much to focus attention on Jamaican music and establish credibility for it. In addition, he was a charismatic performer, a great singer and superb songwriter; a hard act to follow for other Jamaican artists.

Albums: *Wailing Wailers* (Studio One c.1965), *The Best Of The Wailers* (Beverley's 1970), *Soul Rebels* (Trojan/Upsetter 1970), *Catch A Fire* (Island 1973), *Burnin'* (Island 1973), *African Herbsman* (Trojan 1974), *Rasta Revolution* (Trojan 1974), *Natty Dread* (Island 1975), *Live* (Island 1975, later re-titled *Live At The Lyceum*), *Rastaman Vibration* (Island 1976), *Exodus* (Island 1977), *Kaya* (Island 1978), *Babylon By Bus* (Island 1978, live double album), *Survival* (Tuff Gong/Island 1979), *Uprising* (Tuff Gong/Island 1980), *Marley, Tosh Livingston & Associates* (Studio One 1980). Compilations: *In The Beginning* (Psycho/Trojan 1979), *Chances Are* (WEA 1981), *Bob Marley - The Boxed Set* (Island 1982, 9-album box set), *Confrontation* (Tuff Gong/Island 1983), *Legend* (Island 1984), *Mellow Mood* (Topline 1984), *Reggae Greats* (Island 1985), *Soul Revolution I & II* (Trojan 1988, the first UK release of the 70s Jamaican double album), *Interviews* (Tuff Gong 1988), *Talkin' Blues* (Tuff Gong 1991), *All The Hits* (Rohit 1991), *Upsetter Record Shop Parts 1&2* (Esoldun 1992), *Songs Of Freedom* (Island 1992, 4-CD box set), *Never Ending Wailers* (RAS 1993), *Natural Mystic: The Legend Continues* (Island 1995).

Videos: *One Love Peace Concert* (1988), *Live At The Rainbow* (1988), *Caribbean Nights* (1988), *Legend* (1991), *Time Will Tell* (1992), *The Bob Marley Story (Island Video)* (1994).

Further reading: *Bob Marley: The Roots Of Reggae*, Cathy McKnight & John Tobler. *Soul Rebel - Natural Mystic*, Adrian Boot & Vivien Goldman. *Bob Marley: The Biography*, Stephen Davis. *Catch A Fire, The Life Of Bob Marley*, Timothy White. *Bob Marley: Reggae King Of The World*, Malika Lee Whitney. *Bob Marley: In His Own Words*, Ian McCann. *The Music Of Bob Marley*, Ian McCann. *Bob Marley: Music, Myth & The Rastas*, Henderson Dalrymple. *Bob Marley: Conquering Lion Of Reggae*, Stephen Davis. *The Illustrated Legend 1945-1981*, Barry Lazell. *Sprit Dancer*, Bruce W. Talamon.

Marley, Cedella Booker

The mother of **Bob Marley**, Cedella invoked her own musical career after her son's death by recording a gospel/reggae set in tribute to her late son. Backed by the **Wailers**, her big, sweeping vocals revealed how great Bob Marley's debt was to his maternal forebear.

Album: *Awake Zion* (Rykodisc 1990).

Marley, Rita

Wife of **Bob Marley**, Rita (b. Rita Anderson, Jamaica, West Indies) has enjoyed a successful solo career in her own right, both before and after her husband's death. She had originally worked with the Soulettes, a **Studio One** trio, where she first met Bob. She subsequently enjoyed several solo hits in Jamaica, among them 'Pied Piper'. Prophetically, she would back the Wailers on

several early recordings before hooking up with **Marcia Griffiths** and **Judy Mowatt** to form the **I-Threes**. Perhaps her most poignant statement is the album, *Who Feels It Knows It*, recorded while Bob was dying of cancer. Rita's biggest hit came with 'One Draw', a pro-marijuana lyric recorded in 1981, shortly after Bob's death. However, she continued to score single successes with 'Many Are Called' and 'Play Play'. By the mid-80s she was largely retired, concentrating on untangling Bob's legal estate, and fostering the career of her children, **Ziggy Marley And The Melody Makers**.
Albums: *Who Feels It Knows It* (Shanachie 1980), *Harambe* (Teldec 1984).

Marley, Ziggy, And The Melody Makers

b. 1968, Kingston, Jamaica, West Indies. Stephen Marley, one of **Bob Marley**'s four children with his wife **Rita Marley**, started his career as one of the Melody Makers with siblings Sharon, Cedella and Stevie, whose appearance at their father's funeral in 1981 was their first introduction to the rest of the world. The following year 'What A Plot', released on Rita's label, was a big hit, and Ziggy's lead vocals sounded so uncannily like his late father's as to be almost frightening. The Melody Makers were allowed the time and space to mature and practise before committing themselves needlessly to vinyl - unlike so many of their Jamaican counterparts where recording activities were an economic necessity - and by the late 80s they were a headline act - especially in the USA. Their *Play The Game Right* debut, the only album to be credited simply to the Melody Makers, included one notable excerpt from their father's songbook, 'Children Playing In The Street', which he had originally written for them. Despite their tender years, the record stands up to repeated listening and suggests that Marley's maturity and wisdom may well be hereditary. The album to confirm this was *Conscious Party*. Produced by Chris Frantz and Tina Weymouth from **Talking Heads**, and featuring an inspired selection of backing musicians, the set boasted high-calibre material like 'Tomorrow People' and 'We Propose', which would not have disgraced any **Wailers** album. *One Bright Day* is a similarly delightful collection, comprising slick dance reggae with articulate rebuttals of the South African apartheid system.
The Melody Makers have resisted the obvious temptation to re-record too many of their father's songs, and instead forged a career in their own right. Stephen Davis recounts in his excellent book - *Bob Marley - Conquering Lion Of Reggae* - just how popular they are in America by detailing a short exchange between two youngsters after seeing Bob Marley on video. One's question: 'Who's that?', being met by the cursory response: 'Ziggy Marley's father'. In his own lifetime Bob and the Wailers never really cracked the American market in the way that the Melody Makers have done. It must be pointed out that they are also very popular in Jamaica too - and not just because of Ziggy's lineage, though his ability to sing over his father's songs as 'specials' for some of Kingston's top **sound systems**, adapting the lyrics to espouse the prowess of a particular system, has made him widely popular. Irie FM have been known to play their favourite Ziggy songs such as 'Garden' three times in a row when the vibes are right. Ziggy & The Melody Makers have transcended the 'famous parent' tag to become stars in their own right, following on from their fathers' tradition without ever leaning too heavily on it. As Bob once remarked: 'All a my family are music'.
Albums: *Play The Game Right* (EMI 1985), *Hey World* (EMI 1986), *Conscious Party* (Virgin 1988), *One Bright Day* (Virgin 1989), *Jahmekya* (Virgin 1991), *Joy & Blues - Ghetto Youths United* (Virgin 1993). Compilation: *Time Has Come: The Best Of Ziggy Marley And The Melody Makers* (EMI/Manhattan 1988).

Marmalade

Originally known as Dean Ford And The Gaylords, this Glasgow-based quintet enjoyed considerable success on the Scottish club circuit between 1961 and 1967. Eventually, they were signed by agent/manager **Peter Walsh** and, after moving to London, changed their name to Marmalade. The line-up then comprised: Dean Ford (b. Thomas McAleese, 5 September 1946, Coatbridge, Glasgow; lead singer), Graham Knight (b. 8 December 1946, Glasgow, Scotland; vocals/bass), Pat Fairley (b. 14 April 1946, Glasgow, Scotland; rhythm guitar), Willie **Junior Campbell** (b. 31 May 1947, Glasgow, Scotland; lead vocals) and Alan Whitehead (b. 24 July 1946, Oswestry, Shropshire, England; drums). Unpretentious and irresistibly commercial, the group reached the UK charts in May 1968 with 'Lovin' Things' and enjoyed a number 1 with an opportunist cover of **John Lennon/Paul McCartney's** 'Ob-La-Di, Ob-La-Da'. After several successes with **CBS**, Walsh negotiated a deal with **Decca** via **Dick Rowe** and Marmalade became the first ***New Musical Express*** UK chart toppers of the 70s by displacing **Rolf Harris**'s 'Two Little Boys' with the moving 'Reflections Of My Life', a more serious work which ably displayed their underused compositional skills. In 1971, the group suffered a severe setback when Campbell, their producer and main songwriter, quit to attend the Royal College of Music. With replacement Hugh Nicolson (formerly of the **Poets**), they enjoyed several more hits, including 'Cousin Norman', 'Radancer' and 'Falling Apart At The Seams'. The latter proved a prophetic title, for the group were dogged by line-up changes during the 70s. Changes in the pop marketplace lessened their appeal, and a saucy 'sex on tour' story in the salacious Sunday papers caused them considerable embarrassment. With Knight

and Whitehead surviving from the original line-up, Marmalade was resuscitated for cabaret purposes later in the decade.
Albums: *There's A Lot Of It* (1969), *Reflections Of My Life* (1970), *Songs* (1971), *Our House Is Rockin'* (1974), *Only Light On My Horizon* (1977), *Doing It All For You* (1979).

Marmarosa, Dodo

b. Michael Marmarosa, 12 December 1925, Pittsburgh, Pennsylvania, USA. After formal studies and gigging with local bands, Marmarosa played piano with a succession of name big bands of the early and mid-40s, including those of **Gene Krupa**, **Tommy Dorsey** and **Artie Shaw**. In 1946, he settled in Los Angeles, playing and recording with several leading jazz musicians, including **Barney Kessel**, **Lester Young** and **Charlie Parker**. His affinity with bebop made him, briefly, one of the outstanding exponents of the form, but ill-health drove him from the scene around 1948. Marmarosa returned to music in 1961, recording alone and with **Gene Ammons**. Within a couple of years he was again forced into retirement.
Selected albums: *Dodo's Back!/The Return Of Dodo Marmarosa* (1961), with Gene Ammons *Jug & Dodo* (1962), *The Chicago Sessions* (Affinity 1989, 1961-62). Compilations: with Barney Kessel, others *Central Avenue Breakdown Vols 1 & 2* (1945-46), *The Dial Masters* (1946), *Piano Man* (Phoenix 1981, 1946 recording), with Charlie Parker *The Legendary Dial Masters* (1946-47), *A 'Live Dodo'* (Swing House 1979, 1947 recording), *Experiment In Bop* (Raretone 1989).

Marr, Johnny

(see **Smiths**; **Electronic**; **The The**)

Marriott, Steve

b. 30 January 1947, London, England, d. 20 April 1991, Essex, England. As a child actor, Marriott appeared in *The Famous Five* television series in the late 50s and made a West End theatre debut as the Artful Dodger in **Lionel Bart**'s ***Oliver!*** in 1962. That same year, **Decca** engaged him as an **Adam Faith** soundalike for two unsuccessful singles. Next, as singing guitarist in the Moments, he had another miss with a sly cover of the **Kinks**' 'You Really Got Me' for the USA market. Then followed Steve Marriott and the Frantic Ones (amended to just the Frantics). This venture was, however, less lucrative than his daytime job in an East Ham music equipment shop where, in 1964, he met fellow mod **Ronnie Lane** (bass) with whom he formed the **Small Faces** after recruiting Kenny Jones (drums) and ex-Moment Jimmy Winston (keyboards). Knock-kneed and diminutive, Steve emerged as the outfit's public face, attacking the early smashes with a strangled passion revealing an absorption of R&B, and an exciting (if sometimes slipshod) fretboard style that belied the saccharine quality of such songs as 'Sha-La-La-La-Lee' and 'My Mind's Eye'. With Lane, he composed the unit's later output as well as minor hits for **Chris Farlowe** and **P.P. Arnold**.
On leaving the Small Faces in 1969, Marriott, as mainstay of **Humble Pie**, acquired both a solitary UK Top 20 entry and a reputation for boorish behaviour on BBC's *Top Of The Pops* before building on his previous group's small beginnings. In North America, by 1975, he earned a hard-rock stardom accrued over 22 USA tours when Humble Pie disbanded. He put himself forward as a possible replacement when **Mick Taylor** left the **Rolling Stones**, played concerts with his All-Stars (which included **Alexis Korner**) and recorded a patchy solo album before regrouping the Small Faces, but poor sales of two 'comeback' albums blighted their progress. A link-up with Leslie West was mooted and a new Humble Pie released two albums but, from the early 80s, Marriott was heard mostly on the European club circuit, fronting various short-lived bands, including Packet Of Three, with a repertoire that hinged on past glories. Shortly before he perished in a fire in his Essex home in April 1991, Marriot had been attempting to reconstitute Humble Pie with **Peter Frampton**. Frampton was among the many famous friends attending the funeral where the Small Faces' 'All Or Nothing' was spun as Steve Marriott's requiem. Since his death his standing has steadily increased, cruel irony for a man who found it hard to get a recording contract for much of the past decade.
Albums: *Marriott* (1975), *30 Seconds To Midnite* (1993).
Film: *Be My Guest* (1965).

MARRS

A collaboration between two **4AD** bands, **Colourbox** and **AR Kane** which, though a one off, was enough to set both the Uk independent, dance and national charts alight during Autumn 1987. 'Pump Up The Volume' was augmented on the a-side by UK champion scratch mixer **Chris 'C.J' Mackintosh** and London disc jockey/journalist Dave Dorrell. Primarily aimed at the dance market, the record was originally mailed to the 500 most influential regional club and dance DJs on an anonymous white label, in order that it received exposure six weeks prior to its stock version. On official release it entered the charts at number 35, a figure attained on 12-inch sales only. Daytime radio play ensured the single was the next weeks' highest climber, rising 24 places to number 11. The following two weeks it stayed at number 2 before reaching the number 1 spot on 28th September 1987. Originally the idea of 4AD supremo Ivo, the single featured samples of **James Brown**, a practice already common in hip hop which would soon come into vogue for an avalanche of dance tracks: 'We've used a lot of rhythms and time signatures from old records, classic soul records, but mixed that with modern electronic instruments and AR

Kane's guitar sound', was how the single was described. The single was never followed-up, apparently due to acrimony between the involved personnel over finance, which was a great shame. As such the MARRS discography is a brief but blemishless one. Dorrell would go on to manage **Bush** while Mackintosh returned to the club circuit.

Mars

Led by Sumner Crane and completed by China Burg, Nancy Arlen and Mark Cunningham, Mars made its debut on *No New York*, the pivotal compilation of New York's leading 'no-wave' acts, produced by **Brian Eno**. Even more dissonant than contemporaries **Teenage Jesus And The Jerks**, Mars rampaged a way through their four contributions with no regard for melody or formal musical training. Briefly signed to the Ze label, the quartet completed a single, '3E'/'11,000 Volts', before imploding. A 1978 appearance at CBGB's, recorded by **Arto Lindsay**, was issued as the *Live EP*, but this was superseded by *78*. Jim **Foetus** Thirwell took both sides of the Ze 45, remixed the contributions to *No New York* and added all but one track from the previous EP to create the definitive Mars collection. In 1981 Crane recorded a version of Don Giovanni, *John Gavanti*, with the aid of sundry like-minded musicians. It has been dubbed the most unlistenable record ever made.
Compilation: *78* (Widowspeak 1986).

Mars, Chris

b. USA. Formerly drummer with the **Replacements**, by the time Mars quit that groundbreaking band he had also left behind his drinking and drug-taking excesses. 'I got a little constipated with the Replacements, and it's been a release to get out a lot of ideas I've had,' he commented at the time. He left his former employers in 1990 with no idea of what to do, until his wife sent some of his home-recorded demo tapes to **Island Records** subsidiary, Smash. The result was *Horseshoes And Hand Grenades*, the first of his albums to boast his distinctive caricature drawings in its artwork. The title of his second album, *75% Less Fat*, meanwhile, was taken by some analysts as an indication of his diminished circumstances. The intention was to tour with the album whilst also displaying his paintings in local galleries. 1995's *Tenterhooks* was his first collection for Hoboken, New Jersey independent, Bar/None Records. Written, performed, produced and engineered by Mars himself, this was the first collection to see Mars put distance between himself and the Replacements, focusing instead on the strong pop hooks which propelled songs such as 'Forkless Tree'. His contract with the label came with the invitation to build his own 24 track studio in lieu of an advance, which suited Mars who was keen not to tour again following over ten years on the road with the Replacements. In a novel marketing coup, Bar/None sent out another of its roster, the Wallmen, to tour performing covers of the Mars songs, with a cardboard cut-out of the artist erected centre-stage.
Albums: *Horseshoes And Hand Grenades* (Smash 1992), *75% Less Fat* (Smash 1993), *Tenterhooks* (Bar/None 1995).

Mars, Johnny

b. 7 December 1942, Laurens, South Carolina, USA. During his youth, his family moved around the southeast, and Mars began playing harmonica before he was in his teens, influenced by older, local players and his sister's collection of blues records. He moved to New Paltz, New York, in 1958 and joined a high school band. In 1961, he was in the Train Riders and a few years later in Burning Bush (as bass guitarist and occasional harmonica player). In 1967, Mars settled in San Francisco, where he led his own band, then moved to England in 1972, working as a singer/harmonica player. He has subsequently recorded for the Big Bear, JSP, Ace, Sundance, President, and Lamborghine labels, sometimes with guitarist Ray Fenwick. Mars is a fine vocalist and a modern, adventurous, blues harmonica player.
Albums: *Oakland Boogie* (1976), *King Of The Blues Harp* (1980), *Life On Mars* (1984).

Marsala, Joe

b. 4 January 1907, Chicago, Illinois, USA, d. 4 March 1978. After playing locally, Marsala's first name-band job was with **Wingy Manone** in 1929. In the early 30s he gigged in Chicago and elsewhere, returning several times to Manone, with whom he appeared at a number of leading New York nightspots. In 1935, he played and recorded with **Adrian Rollini**'s Tap Room Gang before yet another spell with Manone, this time at the Hickory House. Taking over the band on Manone's departure in 1936, Marsala became one of the first bandleaders on 52nd Street to regularly front a racially-mixed band which included **Red Allen**. The Hickory House engagement was another long-running affair, extending into the mid-40s, but interspersed with leading bands on cruise ships he also briefly led a big band which played charts commissioned from **Don Redman**. In some of these bands, Marsala was joined by his brother, trumpeter Marty Marsala (b. 2 April 1909, d. 27 April 1975). In 1938, Marsala married harpist **Adele Girard** with whom he recorded and later collaborated on the composition of a number of songs, including such popular hits as 'Little Sir Echo' and 'Don't Cry, Joe'. During the early 40s, the bands Marsala led at the Hickory House included not only swing era veterans but also several younger musicians in transition to bebop and the mainstream, among them **Buddy Rich**, **Charlie Byrd** and **Shelly Manne**. He was also instrumental in giving an early

career boost to **Frankie Laine**. The Hickory House job finally ended in 1947; thereafter, Marsala redirected his career to songwriting and administrative work in music publishing and related businesses. During the 60s, he sometimes played on recording sessions, on one occasion teaming up with **Bobby Hackett** to accompany **Tony Bennett**. Although he deliberately ended his full-time playing career while still at his peak, Marsala left some very good recordings featuring his **Jimmie Noone**-inspired clarinet playing.
Compilations: *Joe Marsala And His Orchestra Featuring Adele Girard* (Aircheck 1979, 1942 recording), *Joe Marsala And His Band* (Jazzology 1986, 1944), *Hickory House Jazz* (Affinity 1991).

Marsalis, Branford

b. 26 August 1960, Breaux Bridge, Louisiana, USA. With their father, Ellis Marsalis, a bop pianist, composer and teacher, it is not surprising that his sons Branford, Delfeayo and **Wynton Marsalis** all took up music in childhood. Branford Marsalis's first instrument was the alto saxophone, which he played during his formative years and while studying at **Berklee College Of Music**. In 1981, he played in **Art Blakey**'s **Jazz Messengers** and the following year began a spell with a small band led by Wynton. During this period Marsalis switched instruments, taking up both soprano and tenor saxophones. He also played on record dates with leading jazzmen such as **Miles Davis** and **Dizzy Gillespie**. After three years in his brother's band, he began a period of musical searching. Like many young musicians of his era, Marsalis often played in jazz-rock bands, including that led by **Sting**. He also formed his own small group with which he toured and recorded. By the late 80s he had established a reputation as a leading post-bop jazz saxophonist, but also enjoyed status in fusion and even classical circles (*Romances For Saxophone*). Like most jazzmen, Marsalis drew early inspiration from the work of other musicians, amongst them **John Coltrane**, **Ben Webster**, **Wayne Shorter**, **Ornette Coleman** and especially **Sonny Rollins**. In some of his recordings these influences have surfaced, leading to criticisms that he has failed to build a personal style. Closer attention reveals that these stylistic acknowledgements are merely that and not an integral part of his musical make-up. His 1993 outing with *I Heard You Twice The First Time* showed a strong leaning towards the blues, both **John Lee Hooker** and **B. B. King** are featured in addition to his brother. Perhaps of more significance to Marsalis's development as a musician is the fact that his career appears fated to be constantly compared to and contrasted with that of his virtuoso brother Wynton. If this should result in his long-term overshadowing it will be, at least, unfortunate, because by the early 90s Branford Marsalis had proved himself to be an inventive soloist with considerable warmth. His best work contains many moments of powerful emotional commitment.
Albums: *Wynton Marsalis* (1981), *Scenes In The City* (Columbia 1983), with Dizzy Gillespie *New Faces* (1984), with Wynton Marsalis *Black Codes (From The Underground)* (1985), with Sting *Bring On The Night* (c.1986), *Royal Garden Blues* (Columbia 1986), *Random Abstract* (Columbia 1987), *Renaissance* (Columbia 1987), *Trio Jeepy* (Columbia 1988), *Crazy People Music* (Columbia 1990), *The Beautyful Ones Are Not Yet Born* (Columbia 1992), *I Heard You Twice The First Time* (Columbia 1993), *Bloomington* (Columbia 1993), *Spike Lee's Mo Better Blues* (1993).
Videos: *Steep* (1989), *The Music Tells You* (1993).

Marsalis, Ellis

b. 14 November, 1934, New Orleans, Louisiana, USA. Although he has never really been a revolutionary band-leader or pianist, Ellis Marsalis' influence on the American mainstream jazz scene cannot be over-estimated. As an inspirational figure to a new generation of artists, and an educator and spokesman, this New Orleans-born pianist is unrivalled. Marsalis' professional music career began on tenor saxophone while still in high school, but he changed to piano a few years later, performing with such New Orleans-based modern jazz luminaries as clarinettist **Alvin Batiste** and drummer **Ed Blackwell**. He spent a brief spell on the west coast (he accompanied Blackwell out there, who was going out to meet up with **Ornette Coleman**), before signing up for military service with the marines in the mid-50s. His musical career was hardly interrupted by the services, and he soon found himself accompanying singers on CBS television, on the Marine-sponsored *Dress Blues* show. Back in New Orleans during the early 60s, Marsalis' reputation as a sensitive and versatile accompanist led to a job fronting the house trio at the Playboy Club, where he accompanied stars vocalists such as **Ernestine Anderson** and **Jimmy Rushing**. He joined trumpeter **Al Hirt**'s showboating trad band during the late 60s, and appeared with the group on many popular American television shows, before leaving to join Bob French's Storyville Jazz Band in 1970, continuing the all-round jazz education and understanding that has made him such a unique figure on the current scene. He went on to lead his own highly successful modern jazz band with drummer James Black, enjoying a residency at one of New Orleans' premier jazz clubs for a year and a half. In the mid-70s, Marsalis began to turn his attention toward furthering his involvement in education. He had been teaching since the mid-50s, but now he began working in earnest on a jazz curriculum, and was taken on by the New Orleans Centre for the Creative Arts (NOCCA) in 1975. As a teacher, Marsalis' students have included many of the new generation of New Orleans-based modern jazz stars,

including saxophonist Victor Goines, bassist Reginald Veal, flautist Kent Jordan, trumpeter **Terence Blanchard**, pianist/vocalist **Harry Connick Jnr.** and, of course, his stellar progeny **Wynton Marsalis** (trumpet), **Branford Marsalis** (saxophones), Delfayo Marsalis (trombone) and Jason Marsalis (drums), who have affected the US jazz scene permanently, with their emphasis on craftsmanship and learning. Ellis Marsalis is head of jazz studies at the University of New Orleans and a panellist, grant evaluator and board member for the National Endowment for the Arts and the Southern Arts Federation.
Albums: *Piano In E* (Rounder 1984), *Ellis Marsalis Trio* (Blue Note 1990), *Heart Of Gold* (Columbia 1991), *The Classic Marsalis* (Boplicity 1993), with Wynton Marsalis *Joe Cool's Blues* (Columbia 1995).

Marsalis, Wynton

b. 18 October 1961, New Orleans, Louisiana, USA. Marsalis took up the trumpet at the age of six, encouraged by his father, Ellis Marsalis, a pianist, composer and teacher. His brothers, Delfeayo and **Branford Marsalis** are also musicians. Before entering his teenage years he was already studying formally, but had simultaneously developed an interest in jazz. The range of his playing included performing with a New Orleans marching band led by **Danny Barker**, and playing trumpet concertos with the New Orleans Philharmonic Orchestra. Marsalis later extended his studies at two of the USA's most prestigious musical education establishments, Berkshire Music Center at Tanglewood and the Juilliard School of Music in New York City. By the age of 19, he was already a virtuoso trumpeter, a voracious student of jazz music, history and culture, and clearly destined for great things. It was then that he joined **Art Blakey**'s **Jazz Messengers**, perhaps the best of all finishing schools for post-bop jazzmen. During the next two years he matured considerably as a player, touring and recording with Blakey and also with other leading jazzmen, including **Herbie Hancock** and **Ron Carter**. He also made records under his own name and, encouraged by his success, decided to form his own permanent group. In this he was joined by his brother Branford. During 1983, he again worked with Hancock. The following year he recorded in London with Raymond Leppard and the National Philharmonic Orchestra, playing concertos by Hayden, Hummell and Leopold Mozart - a side-step which led to his becoming the unprecedented recipient of Grammy Awards for both jazz and classical albums. He next toured Japan and Europe, appearing at many festivals, on television and making many recording sessions. By 1991, and still only just turned 30, he had become one of the best- known figures on the international musical stage. Insofar as his classical work is concerned, Marsalis has been spoken of in most glowing terms. In his jazz work his sublime technical ability places him on a plateau he shares with very few others. Nevertheless, despite such extraordinary virtuosity, the emotional content of Marsalis's work often hints only lightly at the possibilities inherent in jazz. Sometimes, the undeniable skill and craftsmanship are displayed at the expense of vitality. If compared to, say, **Jon Faddis**, eight years his senior, or **Clifford Brown**, who died at the age of only 26, then there is clearly some distance to go in his development as a player of emotional profundity.
Selected albums: with Art Blakey *Recorded Live At Bubba's* (1980), with Blakey *Straight Ahead* (1981), *Wynton Marsalis* (Columbia 1981), *Think Of One* (Columbia 1982), with Branford and Ellis Marsalis *Fathers And Sons* (Columbia 1982), *The Herbie Hancock Quintet* (1982), with Blakey *Keystone 3* (1982), *Hot House Flowers* (Columbia 1984), *Black Codes (From The Underground)* (Columbia 1985), *J Mood* (Columbia 1986), *Marsalis Standard Time; Volumes 1-3* (Columbia 1986), *Live At Blues Alley* (Columbia 1987), *The Majesty Of The Blues* (Columbia 1988), *Crescent City Christmas Card* (1989), *Thick In The South* (Columbia 1991), *Uptown Ruler* (Columbia 1991), *Levee Low Moan* (Columbia 1991), *Tune In Tomorrow* (Columbia 1991), *Blue Interlude* (Columbia 1992), *Citi Movement* (Columbia 1993, 2-CD), *Resolution To Swing* (Columbia 1993), *In This House, On This Morning* (Columbia 1994, 2-CD).
Video: *The London Concert (Sony Classical)* (1994).

Marsden, Bernie

This masterly UK guitarist rose to prominence during his stints with **Babe Ruth**, **UFO** and **Whitesnake**. At the turn of the 70s Marsden took time out between Whitesnake projects to record solo material. He was assisted by several noteworthy musicians who included Ian Paice, **Cozy Powell**, Simon Phillips, **Don Airey**, Neil Murray and **Jack Bruce**. The albums featured melodic hard rock, with Marsden successfully handling the vocals as well as some extended guitar workouts. He subsequently formed Bernie Marsden's **S.O.S.** which later became known as **Alaska**. Marsden remains an accomplished musician able to offer enormous variety and depth to heavy rock, though the solo trail was never his most rewarding enterprise.
Albums: *And About Time Too* (Sunburst 1979), *Look At Me Now* (Sunburst 1981).

Marsden, Beryl

b. Beryl Hogg, 1947, Liverpool, England. One of a handful of female singers to emerge during the Mersey boom, Marsden made her debut in January 1963 with the powerful 'I Know'. A vivacious performance earned her the title 'Britain's **Brenda Lee**', but subsequent releases showed an empathy with soul material and included versions of 'Whenever The Lovelight Starts Shining Through His Eyes' (originally recorded by the **Supremes**), and 'Break-A-Way', an

Irma Thomas song later revived by **Tracey Ullman**. In 1966, Marsden joined the **Shotgun Express**, a revue-styled act which initially featured **Rod Stewart** and **Peter Bardens**. Beryl appeared on both of the group's singles before joining the She Trinity. She then retired from music for several years but resumed performing in the 70s as a member of Sinbad, a Liverpool group which also featured Paddy Chambers (of **Paddy Klaus And Gibson**). She later recorded two Peter Bardens' songs, 'I Video'/'Hungry For You', appeared regularly as a Vandella with **Martha Reeves** and joined fellow-Buddhist **Sandie Shaw** at several charity concerts.

Marsden, Gerry

(see **Gerry And The Pacemakers**)

Marseille

This band was formed in London, England, in 1976, ostensibly to record the soundtrack to the Jane Birkin film, *The French Way*. The original line-up consisted of Paul Dale (vocals), Neil Buchanan (guitar), Andy Charters (guitar), Steve Dinwoodie (bass) and Keith Knowles (drums). Signing to the now-defunct Mountain Records label, the band released their debut album in 1978. *Red, White And Slightly Blue* was a subtle blend of melodic rock and pop. A couple of tours followed, supporting **UFO** among others, who the band were later to model themselves on. This was most noticeable on *Marseille* where a more traditional hard rock sound was embraced. The group then ran into difficulties as Mountain Records went bankrupt. This left Marseille in limbo but they resurfaced in 1983 with new personnel and a record deal. The new line-up consisted of ex-Savage Lucy vocalist Sav Pearse, Mark Hays (guitar), Neil Buchanan (guitar), Steve Dinwoodie (bass) and Keith Knowles (drums). They went on to record the band's third and final album, *Touch The Night*, which appeared on the Ultra Noise Records label in 1984. Still failing to make any real impact with either press or public, the band folded soon after.

Albums: *Red, White And Slightly Blue* (Mountain 1978), *Marseille* (Mountain 1979), *Touch The Night* (Ultra Noise 1984).

Marsh, Warne

b. 26 October 1927, Los Angeles, California, USA, d. 18 December 1987, Los Angeles, California, USA. Tenor saxophonist Marsh first played professionally in the early 40s with the Hollywood Canteen Kids, later working with **Hoagy Carmichael**'s Teenagers. By the end of the decade, he had spent time in **Buddy Rich**'s band and had also begun an important association as student and sideman of **Lennie Tristano**. In the late 40s and early 50s, he made a number of milestone recordings with temporary musical partners such as **Lee Konitz**, among them 'Wow', 'Crosscurrent' and 'Marshmallow'. The 50s and 60s saw Marsh active mainly in teaching and there were only occasional forays into playing and recording with, among a few others, **Art Pepper** and **Joe Albany**. In the 70s he became rather more prominent, working with **Supersax**, **Lew Tabackin** and Konitz. He also toured overseas, attracting considerable attention from the more discerning members of his audiences as well as from among his fellow musicians who held him in highest regard. Also in the 70s, he recorded rather more extensively, including material from an especially successful engagement in London with Konitz. A meticulously accurate yet free-flowing improviser, Marsh was comfortable in most bebop-orientated settings. His ballad playing was especially attractive, replete with clean and highly individual phrasing which constantly and consistently demonstrated his total command of instrument and genre. He died on-stage at Donte's, a Los Angeles jazz club, in December 1987.

Selected albums: *Live In Hollywood* (Xanadu 1952), *Lee Konitz With Warne Marsh* (1955), *Jazz Of Two Cities* (1956), with Art Pepper *The Way It Was!* (1956-57), *Warne Marsh Quartet* i (1957), *Warne Marsh Quartet* ii (1958), *The Art Of Improvising Vols 1 & 2* (Revelation 1959), *New York* (1959-60), *Jazz From The East Village* (Wave 1960), *Live At The Montmartre Club* (Storyville 1965), *Ne Plus Ultra* (Hat Art 1969), *Warne Marsh Quintet* (Storyville 1975), *All Music* (Nessa 1976), with Lee Konitz *London Concert* (1976), with Lew Tabackin *Tenor Gladness* (1977), *Warne Out* (1977), *How Deep/How High* (1977-79), *Star Highs* (Criss Cross 1982), *A Ballad Album* (Criss Cross 1983), *In Norway/Sax Of A Kind* (1983), *Posthumous* (Interplay 1985), *Back Home* (Criss Cross 1986), *Two Days In The Life Of...* (Storyville 1987), *Music For Prancing* (Criss Cross 1988), *Noteworth* (Discovery 1988), *For The Time Being* (1987), *Newly Warne* (Storyville 1990).

Marshall Hain

This UK pop duo consisted of Julian Marshall and Kit Hain, b. 15 December 1956, Cobham, Surrey, England, who enjoyed a hit in 1979 with the memorable 'Dancing In The City'. The equally smooth and emotional follow-up 'Coming Home' was also a minor hit. Their only album enlisted the credible support of **Frank Ricotti** (percussion), Dave Olney (guitar), Harold Fisher (drums) and Glen Nightingale (guitar). However, as their grip on the pop charts slackened the duo's record company cancelled their second album. Marshall left to play piano for the **Flying Lizards** and following the breakup of their personal relationship his partner embarked on a solo career. Hain's first release was 'The Joke's On You', for **Harvest**, before she signed to **Decca** and subsequently **Mercury** for several singles and albums. Kit Hain moved to the USA in 1985 and has forged a

successful career as a songwriter. Her portfolio includes 'Fires Of Eden' for **Cher**, 'Back To Avalon' for **Heart**, 'Rip In Heaven' and 'Crash And Burn' for **Til Tuesday**, 'Further From Fantasy' for Annie Haslam, 'Remind My Heart' and 'Every Time We Fall' for Lea Salonga (Miss Saigon). Her songs have also been recorded by **Roger Daltrey**, **Kiki Dee**, **Barbara Dickson**, Nicki Gregoroff, Cheryl Beattie and Kim Criswell.
Albums: *Free Ride* (1978). Kit Hain: *Spirits Walking Out* (1981), *Looking For You* (1981), *School For Spies* (1983).

Marshall Law

This Birmingham, England-based heavy metal quintet comprised Andy Pike (vocals), Dave Martin (guitar), Andy Southwell (guitar), Rog Davis (bass) and Mick Donovan (drums). Following in the tradition of UK rockers such as **Judas Priest**, **Saxon** and **Iron Maiden**, they transposed melody onto infectious, circular power-riffs, cleverly avoiding any monotony by the injection of twin lead guitar solos between rousing choruses. Signing to the Heavy Metal Records label, they released their self-titled debut in 1989 to considerable critical acclaim. Touted as the spearhead of a new revival in traditional British heavy rock, it all went a little quiet shortly thereafter.
Album: *Marshall Law* (Heavy Metal 1989).

Marshall Tucker Band

Formed in 1971 in South Carolina, USA, the Marshall Tucker Band was a 'southern-rock' style outfit which maintained modest popularity from the early to late 70s. The band consisted of Toy Caldwell (b. 1948, Spartanburg, South Carolina, USA, d. 25 February 1993, Moore, South Carolina, USA; lead guitarist), his brother, Tommy Caldwell, (b. 1950, Spartanburg, South Carolina, USA; bass), vocalist/keyboardist Doug Gray, rhythm guitarist George McCorkle, saxophonist/flautist Jerry Eubanks and drummer Paul Riddle. There was no member named Marshall Tucker; the group was named after the owner of the room in which they practiced their music. Like the **Allman Brothers Band**, **Wet Willie** and several others, the band signed with Capricorn Records and established the southern-rock style that emphasized lengthy improvisations built around soul-influenced rock and boogie songs. Prior to the formation of the Marshall Tucker Band, from 1962-65, Toy Caldwell had played with a local group called the Rants. He was in the Marines from 1965-69, and then the Toy Factory, which also included Gray and Eubanks. McCorkle (another ex-Rant), Riddle and Tommy Caldwell were then added in 1972, and the new name was adopted. The group's first Capricorn album was self-titled and reached number 29 in the US in 1973. The following year *A New Life* and *Where We All Belong* were released, a two-album set featuring one studio and one live disc. Their highest-charting album, *Searchin' For A Rainbow*, came in 1975. Their first single to chart was 'This Ol' Cowboy', also in 1975.
Most of the group's albums were gold or platinum sellers through 1978, and the 1977 single 'Heard It In A Love Song' was their best-selling, reaching number 14 (although they were primarily considered an 'album' band). Following their 1978 *Greatest Hits* album, the band switched to **Warner Brothers Records** and released three final chart albums through 1981. The group continued to perform after the death of Tommy Caldwell in an auto crash on 28 April 1980, but never recaptured their 70s success. (Caldwell was replaced by Franklin Wilkie, ex-Toy Factory) By the early 80s they had largely disappeared from the national music scene. They released new albums, first on **Mercury Records** in 1988, and then on Sisapa Records in 1990, with no notable success. All of the group's Capricorn albums were reissued on the AJK Music label in the USA in the late 80s.
Albums: *The Marshall Tucker Band* (1973), *A New Life* (1974), *Where We All Belong* (1974), *Searchin' For A Rainbow* (1974), *Long Hard Ride* (1976), *Carolina Dreams* (1977), *Together Forever* (1978), *Greatest Hits* (1978), *Running Like The Wind* (1979), *Tenth* (1980), *Dedicated* (1981), *Tuckerized* (1981), *Just Us* (1983), *Greetings From South Carolina* (1983), *Still Holdin' On* (1988), *Southern Spirit* (1990), *Still Smokin'* (1993).
Videos: *This Country's Rockin'* (1993), *Then And Now, Cabin Fever* (1993).

Marshall, Jim

b. 29 July 1923, Kensington, London, England. The legendary amplifier manufacturer began his career as a vocalist and became a successful drummer in the 50s. Additionally, he founded his own drum school, teaching up to 65 pupils a week. In 1960, capitalizing on the rock 'n' roll craze, he opened his first retail music shop, and it was through this that he started making speaker cabinets in his garage to fulfil requests from his customers. Marshall paid great attention to the sound that guitarists wanted, and tailor-made the units. The first Marshall amplifier went into production in 1962 and, following his design of a 4x12 speaker cabinet, he was swamped with orders. By 1964, he had opened his first factory since Marshall had already become a considerable name with the beat boom of the early 60s. The **Who** were early converts; it was **Pete Townshend** who wanted more power from his amplifier to increase the feedback sound. Jim Marshall responded to his request and produced a 100-watt version. Similarly, when Townshend asked for a cabinet containing eight speakers, this impractical request led to the birth of the famous Marshall stack: two 4x12 speakers on top of each other. The astonishing success over the next decade resulted in the Marshall amplifier becoming the rock world's most famous piece of equipment, endorsed by **Cream** and **Jimi Hendrix**. The original facia shape and design has barely changed in almost 30 years - the dated facia is still part of the charm. In 1984 and 1992, Marshall received the Queen's Award for Export, with thousands of his units being sold worldwide. The benchmark of most heavy metal groups is a Marshall, which gives a loud, dirty sound from within the famous black and gold box.

Marshall, John

b. 28 August 1941, London, England. Marshall is one of the most impressive drummers Britain has produced, equally powerful, flexible and reliable in rock, jazz or fusion. He played at school, but became more heavily involved with music while reading psychology at university. He studied drums privately with **Allan Ganley** and **Philly Joe Jones**, and worked with **Alexis Korner**'s Blues Incorporated (1964), **Graham Collier** (1965-70), **Nucleus** (of which he was a founder member with **Ian Carr** in 1969, and which he returned to in 1982), **Mike Gibbs**, **Jack Bruce** (1971-72), and, in February 1972, he began his long-term membership of **Soft Machine**. On leaving the band he joined **Eberhard Weber**'s Colours (1977-81). He has been a regular associate of **John Surman** over many years, and has also worked with **Michael Garrick**, **Keith Tippett**, **Chris McGregor**, **John McLaughlin**, **John Taylor**, **Graham Bond**, **Mike Westbrook**, **Tubby Hayes**, **Jaspar Van't Hof**, **Kenny Wheeler**, **Gil Evans**, **Alan Skidmore**, **Ronnie Scott** and many others, including those in the contemporary classical field and in session work.

Marshall, Kaiser

b. Joseph Marshall, 11 June 1899, Savannah, Georgia, USA, d. 3 January 1948. While he was still a child Marshall's family moved to Boston, Massachusetts, where he began playing drums, tutored by George L. Stone. In 1923, by now in New York, he joined **Fletcher Henderson**'s band during its rise to fame and prominence but left in 1930 just as Henderson entered his headiest period. In the late 20s, Marshall made some landmark recordings with **Louis Armstrong**'s small studio groups. A solid reliable drummer, in the late 30s and early 40s he found regular work, playing and recording with many leading figures of the jazz world including **Duke Ellington**, **Cab Calloway**, **Wild Bill Davison**, **Art Hodes**, **Sidney Bechet** and **Bunk Johnson**. Marshall's work was thought of sufficiently highly for him to be called upon to deputize for **Chick Webb** when the more famous drummer was too sick to play all night with his own band.

Compilations: with Fletcher Henderson *A Study In Frustration* (1923-38), *The Louis Armstrong Legend Vols 1-4* (1925-29).

Marshall, Keith

Marshall was originally the guitarist for UK glam rock band **Hello**. When the band finally collapsed, he turned to singing and walked straight into a successful solo career in Germany with his first single 'Remember Me'. It was followed by another three chart contenders including the 1981 worldwide hit, 'Only Crying'. While Germany continued to hold him dear, Marshall was not content to spend the rest of his career rewriting his greatest hit and has continued to move on musically, releasing records mainly in Europe, leaving the UK with only the occasional single.

Albums: *Keith Marshall* (1981), *Tonight We Dance* (1988).

Marshall, Larry

b. c.1945, St. Anns, Jamaica, West Indies. In 1963, Marshall had minor hits with 'Too Young To Love' for E Henry, and 'Please Stay' for **Coxsone Dodd**'s **Studio One** label. Subsequently he enjoyed a big hit with 'Snake In The Grass', a Top Deck production, and, in 1967, recorded 'I've Got Another Girl' and 'Suspicion' for **Prince Buster**. However, he had his greatest successes at Studio One where, in addition to singing in a duo with Alvin Leslie, he also worked as an engineer. Larry And Alvin had a massive hit with 'Nanny Goat' (1968), and followed with 'Hush Up' (1968), 'Your Love' (1969) and 'Mean Girl' (1969). Another of their songs, 'Throw Me Corn', became hugely popular at dances through 1969-70 when played on acetate, and was eventually released in 1971. Marshall then recorded solo, and had a further hit with 'Thelma'. A compilation of his Studio One recordings, *Presenting Larry Marshall*, was issued around 1973. By this time, he was also doing production work at Studio One. He left around 1974, and had success with his self-produced 'I Admire You' (1975), with a strong album of the same name following. Since then, he has issued a steady stream of singles, and had moderate hits with remakes of 'Throw Me Corn' (1984) and 'I Admire You' (1985), both **Gussie Clarke** productions.

Albums: *Presenting Larry Marshall* (Studio One 1973, covers 1968-1971), *I Admire You* (Java 1975), *Dance With Me Across The Floor* (1988), *Come Let Us Reason* (1992).

Marshall, Wendell

b. 24 October 1920, St. Louis, Missouri, USA. He took up the bass thanks to the example of his cousin, **Jimmy Blanton**, who was also his first tutor. Although Wendell played regularly in his younger years, including brief stints with **Lionel Hampton**, **Stuff Smith** and others, he did not fully enter the bigtime until the late 40s when he moved to New York. Briefly with **Mercer Ellington**, he joined **Duke Ellington** in 1948 where he remained until 1955. During the rest of the 50s he worked with many

important jazz artists including **Carmen McRae**, **Hank Jones** and **Art Blakey**. By the end of the decade, however, he was turning more and more to work in New York theatre pit bands where he remained until his retirement from regular playing in the late 60s. A gifted soloist with a full tone, Marshall's solid rhythmic playing and adaptable style made him a valuable member of any band in which he played.
Albums: with Duke Ellington *Seattle Concert* (1952), *Duke Ellington Plays Duke Ellington* (1953), *Wendell Marshall With The Billy Byers Orchestra* (1955), with Mary Lou Williams *A Keyboard History* (1955), with Carmen McRae *By Special Request* (1955).

Martell, Lena

A much-loved British cabaret singer, her polished interpretations of contemporary, easy-listening items popularized by others - with a bias towards country-tinged material - filled 13 Pye albums that rose successively higher in the national list throughout the 70s to culminate with 1979's prosaically-titled *Lena's Music Album*. The latter included **Kris Kristofferson**'s 'One Day At A Time'. Produced, like all her output, by her bandleader, George Elrick, it was issued as a single and, blessed by many spins on BBC Radio 2, spent three weeks at number 1 - her sole entry in the UK singles chart. An ill-advised attempt at 'Don't Cry For Me Argentina' and the title track of 1980's *Beautiful Sunday* - a revival of a Daniel Boone hit - were among subsequent misses, but her albums still reached the Top 50 until her retirement in the late 80s.
Selected albums: *That Wonderful Sound Of Lena Martell* (1974), *The Best Of Lena Martell* (1977), *The Lena Martell Collection* (1978), *Lena's Music Album* (1979), *By Request* (1980), *Beautiful Sunday* (1980).

Martell, Linda

b. Leesville, South Carolina, USA. Initially a R&B singer who included some country material in her repertoire. In 1969, while working the clubs and military bases in her home State, she attracted the attention of **Shelby Singleton**, who signed her to his Plantation label. In 1969 and 1970, she registered three ***Billboard*** country hits namely 'Color Him Father', her version of the **Freddy Fender** hit, 'Before The Next Teardrops Falls' and 'Bad Case Of the Blues'. Further chart success eluded her but she is credited with being the first black female country singer to appear on the *Grand Ole Opry* after her appearance there in August 1969.
Album: *Color Me Country* (1970).

Marterie, Ralph

b. Ralph Martin, 24 December 1914, Accerra, near Naples, Italy, d. 10 October 1978, Dayton, Ohio, USA. While Marterie was still a child his parents emigrated to the USA, where his father joined the orchestra of the Chicago Civic Opera. Ralph was still a teenager when he started playing trumpet with Dan Russo's Otriole Orchestra. He went on to play in local theatres and with other bands in Chicago, which was at that time the country's largest musical centre outside New York. Consequently Marterie never had to leave the city to find work, joining the NBC staff orchestra where he played under conductors such as **Percy Faith** and **André Kostelanetz**. During World War II Marterie led a US Navy band, then postwar he returned to Chicago as a leader with ABC radio. In 1949 he started recording for **Mercury** with his own band, fwhich featured his brassy open trumpet. He did not achieve instant success but in 1952 the band spent 10 weeks in the US charts with 'Caravan', earning a second Gold Disc the following year with 'Pretend'. His album and singles output varied between swing standards, novelties and pop instrumentals that highlighted his trademark of trumpet and guitar voiced together (compare his temporary partnership with guitarist/musical director **Al Caiola** on a cover version of 'Acapulco 22'). There were moderate hits with 'Guaglione', 'Skokiaan' and 'Tequila', which were successful enough to maintain his reputation and keep him working through changing fashions in pop music. Marterie was still touring with a band until his death in Dayton, where he had just played a one-nighter in October 1978.

Martha And The Muffins

The roots of this Canadian new wave band stem back to the mid-70s, when Martha Johnson was the organist with Oh Those Pants, a 10-piece 60s covers/send-up band which also included future members of the Cads. This was followed by a spell in another Toronto band the Doncasters, who specialized in revamping 60s garage band material. In 1977, Johnson joined up with Mark Gane (guitar), Carl Finkle (bass), Andy Haas (saxophone), and Tim Gane (drums) to form Martha and the Muffins. They were later joined by Martha Ladly, who initially played guitar but later moved to keyboards and trombone. They sent a tape to New York journalist Glenn O'Brien, who referred them to the fledgling DinDisc label. This led to the release of their debut single 'Insect Love'. Success came in 1980 with 'Echo Beach' which was a big hit in the UK. Follow-ups, including 'Saigon' (with its double groove b-side - playable backwards and forwards) fared less well. In 1981, Ladly left to work with the **Associates** and formed the Scenery Club who released a single on DinDisc. The Muffins signed to **RCA** and session player Clara Hurst played keyboards temporarily but joined the **Belle Stars** in 1982, when Martha And The Muffins split up. Johnson and Mark Gane formed M+M, who had a hit with 'Black Stations White Stations'.
Albums: *Metro Music* (1980), *Trance And Dance* (1980),

This Is The Ice Age (1981), *Danseparc* (1983). Compilation: *Far Away In Time* (1993).

Martha And The Vandellas

Martha Reeves, Annette Sterling Beard, Gloria Williams and Rosalind Ashford formed the Del-Phis in 1960, one of the scores of female vocal groups then operating in Detroit, Michigan, USA. After Reeves began working as a secretary at **Motown Records**, they were offered a one-off single release on the label's Melody subsidiary, for which they were credited as the Vels. Gloria Williams left the group when the single flopped, but the remaining trio were allowed a second opportunity, recording 'I'll Have To Let Him Go' in late 1962, when the artist for whom it had been intended, **Mary Wells**, failed to turn up for the session. Renamed Martha And The Vandellas, the group divided their time between backing other Motown artists and recording in their own right. They were featured on **Marvin Gaye**'s 1962 hit, 'Stubborn Kind Of Fellow', before the US Top 30 success of their own release, 'Come And Get These Memories', brought their career as second-string vocalists to an end. Their next single, the dynamic 'Heat Wave', was masterminded by the **Holland/Dozier/Holland** production team, and epitomized the confidence and verve of the Vandellas' finest work. 'Quick Sand' repeated the hit formula with a US Top 10 chart placing, while it was 'Dancing In The Street' which represented the pinnacle of their sound. The song, co-written by Marvin Gaye and **William Stevenson**, was an anthemic invitation to party, given added bite by the tense, political situation in the black ghettos. Holland/Dozier/Holland's production exploited all the potential of the music, using clunking chains to heighten the rhythmic feel, and a majestic horn riff to pull people to their feet. 'Dancing In The Street' was the most exciting record Motown had yet made, and it was a deserved number 2 hit in America.

Nothing the Vandellas recorded thereafter reached quite the same peak of excitement, though not for want of trying. 'Nowhere To Run' in 1965 was an irresistible dance hit, which again was given political connotations in some quarters. It introduced a new group member, former **Velvelette** Betty Kelly, who replaced Annette Sterling Beard. This line-up scored further Top 10 hits with 'I'm Ready For Love' and the infectious 'Jimmy Mack', and celebrated Motown's decision to give Martha Reeves individual credit in front of the group's name with another notable success, 'Honey Chile'. Reeves was taken seriously ill in 1968, and her absence forced the group to disband. By 1970, she was able to resume her career, recruiting her sister Lois and another former Velvelette, Sandra Tilley, to form a new Vandellas' line-up. No major US hits were forthcoming, but in Britain they were able to capitalize on the belated 1969 success of 'Dancing In The Street', and racked up several Top 30 entries in the early 70s. When Motown moved their headquarters from Detroit to Hollywood in 1972, Reeves elected to stay behind. Disbanding the group once again, she fought a lengthy legal battle to have her recording contract annulled, and was eventually free to begin an abortive solo career. Her sister Lois joined Quiet Elegance, while Sandra Tilley retired from the record business, and died in 1982. Motown retained the rights to the Vandellas' name, but chose not to sully the memory of their early 60's hits by concocting a new version of the group without Martha Reeves.

Albums: *Come And Get These Memories* (1963), *Heat Wave* (1963), *Dance Party* (1965), *Watchout!* (1966), *Live!* (1967), *Ridin' High* (1968), *Sugar'n'Spice* (1969), *Natural Resources* (1970), *Black Magic* (1972). Compilations: *Greatest Hits* (1966), *Anthology* (1974), *Come & Get These Memories* (c.90s), *Heatwave* (c.90s), *Compact Commmand Performances* (1992), *24 Greatest Hits* (1992), *Live Wire, 1962-1972* (c.1993, double CD).

Martika

b. Marta Marrero, 18 May 1969, California, USA. This pop singer grew up in California, her parents having fled Cuba shortly after the revolution. Her first experiences in show business came early, with an appearance as a dancer in the film *Annie*. Moving on to music, her debut single was the self-penned 'Toy Soldiers'. Although she has done little to please critics ('Love . . . Thy Will Be Done' was cited by one journalist as being 'sub-**Tiffany**'), her singles have become a fixture of the charts in the early 90s. Her profile has also been bolstered by consistent rumours of romances with pop stars (Nuno of **Extreme**, **Prince**). With the latter she co-wrote the hit single 'Martika's Kitchen', and he also helped out with several tracks on the album of the same name. She appeared in the US television show *Wiseguy* as a jazz singer.

Album: *Martika's Kitchen* (1991), *The 12 Mixes* (1993).

Martin, Benny

b. 8 May 1928, Sparta, Tennessee, USA. Martin grew up in a musical family (his father and two sisters played as the Martin Family) and he was taught to play the guitar, mandolin and fiddle as a child - receiving tuition on the latter from **Lester Flatt**'s father. After making his radio debut on WHUB Cookeville around 1939, he became a member of Big Jeff And The Radio Playboys on the *Mid-Day Merry-Go-Round* at WNOX Knoxville, and in 1942, moved with them to WLAC Nashville. They relocated to Chattanooga, playing WDOD and WAPO, and toured with Bisby's Comedians tent show, where they worked with **Rod Brasfield**. In 1946, they returned to WLAC and Martin left the band and joined WSM. He worked briefly as a member of the Musical Millers on the *Martha White Show* before his musical talents as a fiddle player and vocalist found him in demand. During the late 40s and 50s, he played with many famous acts, including **Bill Monroe, Roy Acuff,** Lester Flatt and **Earl Scruggs** (he also played on their **Columbia** recordings made between November 1952 and August 1953) and **Johnny And Jack**. He toured extensively, particularly during his time with Roy Acuff with whom he visited Germany in 1949. He made some solo vocal recordings for **Mercury Records** in the early 50s, and from 1953-60, he was a member of the *Grand Ole Opry*. He had minor US country hits in the 60s, with 'Rosebuds And You' and a duet with bluegrass musician Don Reno on the patriotic offering 'Soldier's Prayer in Viet Nam'. Martin, always a popular entertainer, continued to play with various acts throughout the 70s and 80s and has recorded albums with several other top instrumentalists, as well as appearing as a guest on other artists' albums. The *Tennessee Jubilee* album, made with **John Hartford** and Lester Flatt, includes his tribute to the early days of bluegrass, 'Lester, Bill And Me'. It is interesting to remember that, during the 50s, he worked on perfecting an unusual eight-string fiddle, which he often used on the *Opry*. He originally got the idea after playfully using his fiddle bow on Bill Monroe's mandolin.

Albums: *Country Music's Sensational Entertainer* (1961), *Old Time Fiddlin' & Singin'* (1964), *Benny Martin with Bobby Sykes* (1965), with Don Reno *Bluegrass Gospel Favorites* (1967), with John Hartford, Lester Flatt *Tennessee Jubilee* (1975), *The Fiddle Collection* (1976, double album), *Turkey In The Grass* (1977), *Big Daddy Of The Fiddle And Bow* (1979, double album), *Southern Bluegrass Fiddle* (1980), with Buddy Spicer *Great American Fiddle Collection* (1980), with Reno *Gospel Songs From Cabin Creek* (1990).

Martin, Bill

b. William Wylie, 9 November 1938, Glasgow, Scotland. A prolific and highly successful songwriter, record producer, and music publisher. Although he came from a musical family, and studied at the Royal Academy of Music, Martin first made his mark as a professional footballer for Partick Thistle. He subsequently played abroad in South Africa for three years, before returning to England intent on making a career as a songwriter. After being introduced to the Irish musician and arranger **Phil Coulter** by American lyricist Buddy Kaye, Martin and Coulter formed a publishing company in 1965. They had their first success with 'Hi Hi Hazel', which the **Troggs** and **Geno Washington** took into the UK chart. From then on, during the next 10 years, they wrote and/or produced a string of hit records for artists ranging from the **Bay City Rollers** to **Elvis Presley**. In 1967, **Sandie Shaw** won the Eurovision Song Contest with their infectious 'Puppet On A String' (UK number 1), which earned an **Ivor Novello** Award for 'Most Performed Work'. There was another 'Ivor' in the following year for 'Congratulations', with which **Cliff Richard** just failed to make it two Eurovision wins in a row for the songwriters, although it was another chart-topper. After providing **Cilla Black** with 'Surround Yourself With Sorrow' (UK number 3), Martin and Coulter came up with the immensely popular 'Back Home' for the 1970 England World Cup Squad. It too topped the chart (as did the associated album), and more or less took over as the UK 'National Anthem' for a few weeks, until the football team lost to Germany. A year later, Martin and Coulter wrote the English words to 'My Boy' (music by Jean Bourtayre and Claude Francois), which was popularized by **Richard Harris**, and revived in 1975 by Elvis Presley who took it into the US Top 20. Martin and Coulter had another US hit (a number 1) in the following year with the Bay City Rollers' 'Saturday Night'. By that stage, they had already given the Rollers several UK Top 20 entries, including 'All Of Me Loves All Of You', 'Remember (Sha-La-La)', 'Shang-A-Lang', and 'Summer Love Sensation'. Two of the other acts to enjoy success with Martin/Coulter songs in the 70s were, by a strange coincidence, both called Kenny. The Irish singer of that name went to number 11 with 'Heart Of Stone', while **Kenny**, the male vocal/instrumental group, had four Top 20 hits in a row with Martin and Coulter's 'The Bump', Fancy Pants', 'Baby I Love You OK', and 'Julie Ann'. Another UK group, Slik, also topped the UK chart in 1976 with the songwriters' 'Forever And Ever'. As a songwriter, music publisher, and record publisher Martin's worldwide sales have been estimated at over 35 million, and he is said to have had a number 1 record in every country in the Western world. Artists whom Martin has recorded, published or produced include **Elton John**, **Elkie Brooks**, **Rod Stewart**, the **New Seekers**, **Van Morrison**, **Buddy Greco**, **Billy Connelly**, the **Dubliners**, **B.A. Robertson**, **Isaac Hayes**, **Dana** and many more. He has also written for films and television. After selling his music business to EMI, he is now involved in television productions, character licensed merchandise and music publishing. A member of the Variety Club of Great Britain, a Freeman of the City of Glasgow and of London, and a director of the PRS, in 1975 Martin was the co-recipient - with Phil Coulter - of the Ivor Novello Award for 'Songwriter of the Year'.

Martin, C.F.

b. Christian Frederick Martin, 31 January 1796, Saxony, Germany. Martin established his guitar factory in 1833 at 196 Hudson Street, New York. By the time the company relocated to Nazareth, Pennsylvania, six years later, the organization was already on its way to becoming as synonymous to handmade acoustic guitars as Stradivarius was to violins. Its continued success was due to a refusal to change, cheapen or speed up the method in which the instrument was produced. During

the folk boom of the early 60s, demand was such that the factory was taking 36 months to fulfil orders. The most famous of Martin's many styles of guitar is the Dreadnought. First manufactured in 1931, this guitar set the standard which is copied by most other manufacturers. Today, it remains a popular instrument for bluegrass, folk, blues and rock artists. The Dreadnought is renowned for its booming bass sound, and for some, an uncomfortably high string action. However, such action provides a beautiful tone and arguably the finest in pure acoustic guitars. In addition to regular guitars, Martin has also been a leading maker of ukuleles and mandolins, applying similar painstaking standards to each instrument. During the acoustic rock boom of the 70s, the guitar to be seen with was a D45, with its beautiful pearl inlay. On the first D45, made in 1933, one of the Martin craftsmen inlaid **Gene Autry**'s name onto the fingerboard. This luxury is now particularly popular with US country singers. In recent years the company has adapted to changing demands by integrating an electro-acoustic device to amplify sound, competing with companies like Ovation, which pioneered this method. People will always pay more for the finest piece of craftsmanship, and Martin continues to lead the field.
Further reading: *Martin Guitars A History*, Mike Longworth.

Martin, Carl

b. 15 April 1906, Big Stone Gap, Virginia, USA, d. 1978. Like his father, the multi-instrumentalist Martin played in a string band, although he is also known for his work in the blues field. In his teens he met Howard Armstrong and, in 1930, the two musicians, along with Martin's brother Roland, recorded under the name of the Tennessee Chocolate Drops. It gives some indication of their sound that the record was also issued in the company's country music series (under a different credit). A couple of years later, Martin moved to Chicago and joined the blues circuit, recording under his own name as well as accompanying diverse artists such as **Tampa Red** and Freddie Spruell. In the 60s, Martin and Armstrong, with guitarist Ted Bogan, brought the old string band sound to a new audience.
Selected albums: *Martin, Bogan And Armstrong* (1973), *Carolina Blues* (1992).

Martin, Claire

b. 6 September 1967, Wimbledon, London, England. In 1982, after spending 10 years at stage school, Martin became resident singer at the Savoy Hotel in Bournemouth. In 1987 she sang on cruise liners for Cunard, including the *QE II.* In 1990 she visited the USA where she studied with Marilyn J. Johnson in New York. In 1991 she returned to the UK to form her own band, playing many prestigious London jazz venues including **Ronnie Scott**'s, the 100 Club and the Pizza On The Park, and also toured extensively. In 1992 she played a return engagement at Ronnie Scott's and also appeared at the Glasgow and Sheffield Jazz Festivals. In addition to leading her own band, Martin also works regularly with Mick Hutton's group, Straight Face, which includes **Steve Argüelles** and **Iain Ballamy**, with Ray Gelato's Giants Of Jive, and with a free-music band led by **John Stevens**. She has also recorded with **Bobby Wellins**. A remarkably versatile singer, Martin's repertoire ranges happily from R&B to free music, incorporating along the way the great standards of which she is an accomplished interpreter. Despite her youth, Martin's work displays exceptional maturity which, allied to her warm, sensual sound, makes her performances a constant delight. Her choice of musical associates (her own group comprises pianist **Jonathan Gee**, bassist Arnie Somogyi and **Clark Tracey**) reveals her commitment to jazz. Although still at the beginning of her career, Martin has already made it clear that she is one of the most important new singers to emerge on the jazz scene in recent years.
Albums: *The Waiting Game* (Linn 1991), with Bobby Wellins *Remember Me* (1992), *Devil May Care* (Linn 1993), *Old Boyfriends* (Linn 1994).

Martin, Dean

b. Dino Paul Crocetti, 7 June 1917, Steubenville, Ohio, USA. An extremely popular ballad singer and light comedian with a relaxed and easy style, who developed into an accomplished dramatic actor. After leaving school in the 10th grade, he worked as a shoe-shine boy and a gas station attendant before becoming an 'amateur' welterweight boxer, 'Kid Crochet', earning 10 dollars a fight. When he retired from the boxing arena, he became a croupier at a local casino. His first singing job is said to have been with the Sammy Watkins band in 1941, in which he was initially billed as Dino Martini, but the name was soon changed to Dean Martin. His earliest recordings were for the Diamond label, and they included 'Which Way Did My Heart Go'/'All Of Me' and 'I Got the Sun In The Morning'/'Sweetheart Of Sigma Chi'. He also recorded some tracks for the Apollo label, well known for its impressive roster of black talent. The Martin recordings included, 'Walkin' My Baby Back Home', 'Oh Marie', 'Santa Lucia', 'Hold Me', 'Memory Lane' and 'Louise'. In 1946, Martin first worked with comedian Jerry Lewis at the 500 Club in Atlantic City. Together they developed an ad-libbing, song and comedy act which became very popular on US television and radio in the late 40s. In 1949, they appeared in supporting roles in the film *My Friend Irma*, and in the sequel, *My Friend Irma Goes West*, the following year. The team then starred in another 14 popular comedies, with Martin providing the songs and

romantic interest, and Lewis contributing the zany fun. These films included *At War With The Army* (1950), *Jumping Jacks* (1952), *Sailor, Beware!*, *The Stooge*, *Scared Stiff* (1953), *The Caddy* (1953), ***Living It Up*** (1954), *Pardners* (1956) and *Hollywood Or Bust* (1956). Their parting was somewhat acrimonious, and it was widely felt that Martin would be the one to suffer most from the split. In fact, they both did well. Martin, after a shaky start in the comedy movie, *Ten Thousand Bedrooms* (1957), blossomed as a dramatic actor in *The Young Lions* (1958), *Some Came Running* (1958), *Rio Bravo* (1959), *Ada* (1961), *Toys In The Attic* (1963), *The Sons Of Katie Elder* (1965) and *Airport* (1970). He still retained his comedy touch in *Who Was That Lady?* (1960) and *What A Way To Go* (1964) but made surprisingly few musicals. The most notable were ***Bells Are Ringing*** (1960), with Judy Holliday, and *Robin And The Seven Hoods* (1964). Meanwhile, Martin had signed to **Capitol Records** in 1948, and for the next 10 years had a series of US Top 30 chart entries, including 'That Certain Party' (duet with Jerry Lewis), 'Powder Your Face With Sunshine', 'I'll Always Love You', 'If', 'You Belong To Me', 'Love Me, Love Me', 'That's Amore', 'I'd Cry Like A Baby', 'Sway', 'Money Burns A Hole In My Pocket, 'Memories Are Made Of This' (number 1), 'Innamorata', 'Standing On The Corner', 'Return To Me', 'Angel Baby' and 'Volare' ('Nel Blu Dipinto Di Blu'). Martin's version of 'That's Amore' surfaced again when it was featured in the 1987 hit movie, *Moonstruck*.
Although Martin was still a big attraction on film and in nightclubs, his records found difficulty in making the singles charts during the early part of the 60s. In 1961, **Frank Sinatra**, who had also been with Capitol Records, started his own **Reprise Records**. Martin, who was a member of Sinatra's 'Clan', or 'Ratpack', was one of the first recruits to the new label. In 1964, Martin was back in the US singles charts with a bang. His recording of 'Everybody Loves Somebody', produced by Jimmy Bowen, had a commercial country 'feel' about it, and knocked the **Beatles**' 'A Hard Day's Night' off the top of the chart. Martin's subsequent Top 30 entries were all in the same vein - records such as 'The Door Is Still Open To My Heart', 'You're Nobody Till Somebody Loves You', 'Send Me The Pillow You Dream On', 'Houston', 'In The Chapel In The Moonlight' and 'Little Ole Wine Drinker, Me'. The latter number was a fitting selection for an artist whose stage persona was that of a man more than slightly inebriated. 'Everybody Loves Somebody' became the theme song for *The Dean Martin Show* on NBC TV which started in 1964, ran for nine seasons and was syndicated world-wide. As well being a showcase for Martin's singing talents, the show gave him the opportunity to display his improvisation skills in comedy. He continued to be a big draw in clubs, especially in Las Vegas, and played the London Palladium in the summer of 1987, to favourable reviews. Later that year, he joined ex-Rat Pack colleagues, Sinatra and **Sammy Davis Jnr.**, in the 'Together Again' tour, involving 40 performances in 29 cities, but had to withdraw at an early stage because of a kidney ailment. In the autumn of 1993 it was reported that Martin had lung cancer.
Albums: *The Stooge* (1956, film soundtrack), *Swingin' Down Yonder* (mid-50s), *Pretty Baby* (mid-50s), *This Is Martin* (late 50s), *Sleep Warm* (1959), *Winter Romance* (1959), *The Bells Are Ringing* (1960, film soundtrack), *This Time I'm Swingin'* (1961), *Dean Martin* (1961), *Dino - Italian Love Songs* (1962), *French Style* (1962), *Dino Latino* (1963), *Country Style* (1963), *Dean 'Tex' Martin Rides Again* (1963), *Everybody Loves Somebody* (1964), *Hey Brother, Pour The Wine* (1964), *Dream With Dean* (1964), *The Door Is Still Open To My Heart* (1964), *Dean Martin Hits Again* (1965), *Dean Martin Sings, Sinatra Conducts* (1965), *Southern Style* (1965), *Holiday Cheer* (1965), *Lush Years* (1965), *(Remember Me) I'm The One Who Loves You* (1965), *Houston* (1965), *Somewhere There's A Someone* (1966), *Relaxin'* (1966), *Happy In Love* (1966), *The Silencers* (1966, film soundtrack), *The Hit Sound Of Dean Martin* (1966), *The Dean Martin TV Show* (1966), *The Dean Martin Christmas Album* (1966), *At Ease With Dean* (1967), *Happiness Is Dean Martin* (1967), *Welcome To My World* (1967), *Gentle On My Mind* (1968), *I Take A Lot Of Pride In What I Am* (1969), *My Woman, My Woman, My Wife* (1970), *For The Good Times* (1971), *Dino* (1972). Compilations: *The Best Of Dean Martin* (1966), *Dean Martin's Greatest Hits! Volume 1* (1968), *Dean Martin's Greatest Hits! Volume 2* (1968), *The Best Of Dean Martin, Volume 2* (1969), *20 Original Dean Martin Hits* (1976), *The Collection* (1989), *The Best Of The Capitol Years* (1989), *Singles* (1994).
Further reading: *Everybody Loves Somebody*, Arthur Marx. *Dino: Living High In The Dirty Business Of Dreams*, Nick Tosches.

Martin, Fiddlin' Joe

b. 8 January 1900, Edwards, Mississippi, USA, d. 21 November 1975, Walls, Mississippi, USA. Martin learned guitar and trombone as a boy, later adding mandolin and bass fiddle (hence his nickname). He switched to washboard and drums in the 40s after damaging his hands in a fire. He worked with many Delta blues singers, including **Charley Patton**, Willie Newbern, **Johnnie Temple**, **Memphis Minnie**, **Willie Brown** and **Son House**, recording with the last two for the Library of Congress in 1940. Martin played drums for **Howlin' Wolf** until Wolf went north, but his most enduring association was with **Woodrow Adams**; he appeared on all Adams' recordings, and they worked Mississippi juke joints together until Martin's death.
Album: *Walking Blues* (1979).

Martin, Freddy

b. 9 December 1906, Cleveland, Ohio, USA, d. 30

September 1983. After starting out on drums and C-melody saxophone, Martin switched to playing tenor saxophone. He led his own band while still at high school, then became a sideman in various local bands. After a few years, he began attracting attention for his smooth and competent musicianship. **Guy Lombardo** and his brothers heard and encouraged him and, in 1931, Martin formed his own band. He took the unit into a succession of engagements at prestigious hotels, including the Roosevelt Grill in New York's Manhattan Hotel, and was heard on the radio. He made his breakthrough into popular success with an arrangement the theme from the first movement of Tchaikovsky's B-flat piano concerto. This was followed by other arrangements of popular classics, usually featuring the band's current pianist - a role taken by, amongst others, Jack Fina and Barclay Allen. The Tchaikovsky piece was later re-recorded, this time with lyrics by Bobby Worth and retitled 'Tonight We Love', and became a hit all over again. Martin and his band appeared in a handful of films, including ***Stage Door Canteen*** (1943). Martin had a good ear for singers and at one time or another employed **Helen Ward**, Merv Griffin, **Buddy Clark** and Terry Shand. In the 50s and 60s Martin continued to perform on the radio and also appeared on television shows. Untroubled by changing musical tastes, he continued to work at major venues and was musical director for **Elvis Presley**'s first appearance in Las Vegas. Still in demand for hotel work, he entered the 70s with an engagement at the Ambassador in Los Angeles. Martin continued leading his band until shortly before his death in 1983.
Albums: incl. on *Ford Star Time Presents* (1960). Compilation: *The Uncollected Freddy Martin Vols.1-4* (1940-52).

Martin, George

b. 3 January 1926, London, England. Martin became the world's most famous record producer through his work with the **Beatles**. Classically-trained at London's Guildhall School of Music, he joined **EMI** in 1950 as a junior A&R man. Five years later, Martin was given charge of the **Parlophone** label where he produced a wide variety of artists. Among them were the ballad singers (**Shirley Bassey** and **Matt Monro**), skiffle groups (the **Vipers**), jazz bands (**Temperance 7**, **Johnny Dankworth**, **Humphrey Lyttelton**) and numerous comedy artists. Chief among these were Peter Sellers and Bernard Cribbins, whose 'Right Said Fred' and 'Hole In The Ground' were hits in 1962. By this time, Martin had signed the Beatles to Parlophone and begun a relationship which lasted until their demise in 1970. Apart from insisting that drummer **Pete Best** be replaced, Martin's main contribution to the group's music lay in his ability to translate their more adventurous ideas into practical terms. Thus, he added classical music touches to 'Yesterday' and 'For No One' and devised the tape loops and studio manipulations which created the stranger sounds on *Revolver* and *Sgt Pepper's Lonely Hearts Club Band*. Martin also made two orchestral albums of Beatles' tunes. As **Brian Epstein** signed **Cilla Black**, **Gerry And the Pacemakers** and **Billy J. Kramer And the Dakotas** to Parlophone, Martin supervised their recordings.
In 1965, he left EMI and set up his own studios, AIR London with fellow producers **Ron Richards** (**Hollies**) and John Burgess (**Manfred Mann**). He continued to work with several new EMI artists, notably the **Action**. In the 70s he produced a series of hit albums by **America**. During this period he worked with **Neil Sedaka**, **Ringo Starr**, **Jimmy Webb**, **Jeff Beck** and **Stackridge**,while producing the soundtrack to the 1978 film of *Sgt Pepper's Lonely Hearts Club Band*. He also maintained the Beatles connection and prepared the 1977 release of the live recording *At The Hollywood Bowl* and produced two of **Paul McCartney**'s solo efforts, *Tug Of War* (1981) and *Pipes Of Peace* (1983). He also produced the soundtrack to McCartney's film musical *Give My Regards To Broad Street*. In the late 70s, AIR was purchased by **Chrysalis** and Martin became a director of the company. He opened a second studio on the Caribbean island of Montserrat, which became a favoured recording centre for artists, including McCartney, **Dire Straits** and the **Rolling Stones**, before the island was devastated by a huricane in 1989. Those artists were among the musicians donating tracks for *After The Hurricane*, a benefit album organized by Martin. During the late 80s, he was less prolific as a producer, but created a version of Dylan Thomas's *Under Milk Wood* in 1988 and worked with ex-**Dexy's Midnight Runners** member Andy Leek on his debut solo album. In 1990, Martin announced plans to replace AIR Studios with a 'state of the art' audio-video complex in north London. Martin's quiet and intelligent persona has masked an extraordinary talent. His punctilious attention in remastering the entire Beatles' work for compact disc is demonstrated in the quite remarkable results he obtained. In 1992, he was instrumental in producing a television documentary to mark the 25th anniversary of the Beatles' Sgt. Pepper album.
Albums: *Off The Beatle Track* (1964), *A Hard Day's Night* (1964), *George Martin Scores Instrumental Versions Of The Hits* (1965), *Help!* (1965), *The Beatle Girls* (1966), *The Family Way* (1967), with the Beatles *Yellow Submarine* (1969), *By George!* (1970), *Live And Let Die* (1973), *Beatles To Bond And Bach* (1987).
Film: *Give My Regards To Broad Street* (1985).
Further reading: *All You Need Is Ears*, George Martin with Jeremy Hornsby. *All You Need Is Ears*, George Martin. *Summer Of Love: The Making Of Sgt Pepper*, George Martin.

Martin, Grady

b. Thomas Grady Martin, 17 January 1929, Chapel Hill, Marshall County, Tennessee, USA. As a boy, Martin was obsessed by both the fiddle and guitar, and he attended all the shows he could to watch and learn. When aged only 15, he was taken to Nashville to play with the **Bailes Brothers** on the *Grand Ole Opry*. He and his friend, Jabbo Arrington, travelled to Chicago to play on 1946 recordings by fiddler Curly Fox and his wife, Texas Ruby. He became a resident musician on the *Grand Ole Opry* but, in 1949, he and Arrington joined a band formed by **Little Jimmy Dickens**. Their twin guitars can be heard on Dickens' country hits, 'A-Sleepin' At The Foot Of The Bed' and 'Hillbilly Fever'. Martin formed a group of session musicians, the Slewfoot Five, who recorded in their own right and were credited on hit records by **Bing Crosby** ('Till The End Of The World') and **Burl Ives** ('The Wild Side Of Life'). Martin played on sessions for **Red Foley, Bobby Helms, Webb Pierce** and **Marty Robbins** ('El Paso'). He also played on **Buddy Holly**'s Nashville sessions, including 'Love Me' and 'Modern Don Juan', and the distinctive introduction to **Johnny Horton**'s 'Battle Of New Orleans'. A failure in electrical equipment led to him 'inventing' feedback on Marty Robbins' US hit, 'Don't Worry'. Martin and **Chet Atkins** are the only musicians to have accompanied both **Hank Williams** and **Elvis Presley**. Martin played on Presley's recording sessions from 1962-65, and he became a mainstay of the so-called Nashville sound. He also worked with **Joan Baez, J.J. Cale, Kris Kristofferson** ('Why Me Lord'), **Roy Orbison** ('Oh Pretty Woman') and **Leon Russell**. Martin has also toured with **Jerry Reed** and latterly with **Willie Nelson**, and can be seen in his film, *Honeysuckle Rose*. Nelson says, 'Grady Martin has been my hero forever. There's nobody to have in the studio than Grady Martin, because not only does he play great guitar, he knows what everybody else is supposed to be doing too.'

Albums: *Dance-O-Rama* (1955), *Powerhouse Dance Party* (1955), *Jukebox Jamboree* (1956), *The Roaring Twenties* (1957), *Hot Time Tonight* (1959), *Big City Lights* (1960), *Swinging Down The River* (1962), *Songs Everybody Knows* (1964), *Instrumentally Yours* (1965), *A Touch Of Country* (1967), *Cowboy Classics* (1967).

Martin, Hugh

b. 11 August 1914, Birmingham, Alabama, USA. A composer, lyricist, librettist, vocal arranger and singer, who has worked for stage and films, in the 30s Martin teamed up with Ralph Blane (b. Ralph Uria Hunsecker, 26 July 1914, Broken Arrow, Oklahoma, USA). They appeared together in ***Hooray For What!*** (1937) and ***Louisiana Purchase*** (1940), after which they formed a vocal quartet called the Martins. Blane also sang in Leonard Sillman's *New Faces Of 1936* and *The Lady Comes Across* (1942), while Martin wrote the fine vocal arrangements for a number of shows, including ***Too Many Girls***, ***Du Barry Was A Lady***, ***Pal Joey***, ***Cabin In The Sky***, *Very Warm For May*, and *Stars In Your Eyes*. In 1941 the team wrote the score for the Broadway musical ***Best Foot Forward*** ('Buckle Down, Winsocki', 'Ev'ry Time', 'That's How I Love The Blues'), which enjoyed a run of 326 performances and was filmed in 1943. One of the film's additional songs was the delightful 'Wish I Might'. Staying in Hollywood, Martin and Blane contributed songs to several other movies, including ***Thousands Cheer*** ('The Joint Is Really Jumpin' In Carnegie Hall'), ***Meet Me In St. Louis*** (three memorable songs for **Judy Garland**, 'Have Yourself A Merry Little Christmas', 'The Boy Next Door' and 'The Trolley Song'), ***Ziegfeld Follies*** ('Love'), and ***Good News*** ('Pass That Peace Pipe') (1947), Blane also worked with other composers, including **Harry Warren**, Kay Thompson, **Harold Arlen**, and Robert Wells, on numbers for movies such as ***Summer Holiday***, *One Sunday Afternoon*, *My Dream Is Yours*, *My Blue Heaven*, *Skirts Ahoy!*, and *The French Line* (1953). Martin returned to stage musicals with complete scores for *Look, Ma, I'm Dancin!'* ('The Little Boy Blues', 'Shauny O'Shay', 'Tiny Room') (1948) and *Make A Wish!* (1951), and collaborated with singer Timothy Gray on *Love From Judy* (London, 1952), which starred Jeannie Carson, Bill O'Connor and Adelaide Hall, and ran for 594 performances, and ***High Spirits*** (1964). Martin and Blane reunited in the mid-50s to write songs for the movies *Athena*, *The Girl Rush* ('An Occasional Man'), and *The Girl Most Likely*. In 1960 they wrote eight new songs for a stage adaptation of *Meet Me In St. Louis* when it was presented by the Municipal Opera in St. Louis, Missouri. Further changes were incorporated in the 1989 Broadway production, and two years later the show was again seen in St. Louis.

Album: *Martin & Blane Sing Martin & Blane* (DRG 1994, rec. 1956).

Martin, Jimmy

b. James Henry Martin, 10 August 1927, on a farm near Sneedville, Tennessee, USA. He learned to play the guitar as a boy and first appeared on radio in Morristown in 1948. He joined **Bill Monroe** in 1949 and remained with him (except for a short break) until 1954. Many rate Martin to be the finest lead singer and guitarist ever to work with Monroe. He played on some of Monroe's best recordings and sang notable duets with him including 'Memories Of Mother And Dad'. In the mid-50s, he worked with the **Osborne Brothers**, with whom he recorded '20-20 Vision', before eventually forming his own Sunny Mountain Boys. Martin went on to become a legend of bluegrass music, he played the WJR Detroit *Barn Dance*, *Louisiana Hayride* and all major venues. Over the years his band has contained some of the greatest bluegrass musicians including J.D. Crowe, Doyle Lawson and Alan Munde. He recorded for **Decca** and had some chart successes including 'Rock Hearts' (1958) and 'Widow Maker' (1964). He also achieved acclaim for his work on the **Nitty Gritty Dirt Band**'s legendary 1972 album, *Will The Circle Be Unbroken*. Many experts believe that Martin has never been afforded full credit for his contributions over the years. It may be that his frankness and the perfection that he expects from his musicians has at times gone against him.

Albums: *Good 'N' Country* (1960), *Country Music Time* (1962), *This World Is Not My Home* (1963), *Widow Maker* (1964), *Sunny Side Of The Mountain* (1965), *Mr. Good 'N' Country Music* (1966), *Big And Country Instrumentals* (1967), *Tennessee* (1968), *Free Born Man* (1969), *All Day Singing* (1970), *I'd Like To Be Sixteen Again* (1972), *Moonshine Hollow* (1973), *Jimmy Martin & The Sunny Mountain Boys* (1973), *Fly Me To Frisco* (1974), *Me 'N' Old Pete* (1978), *Greatest Bluegrass Hits* (1978), *To Mother At Christmas* (1980), with Ralph Stanley *First Time Together* (1980), Will *The Circle Be Unbroken* (1980), *One Woman Man* (1983), *With The Osborne Brothers* (1983), *Big Jam Session* (1984), *Stormy Waters* (1985), *Hit Parade Of Love* (1987).

Martin, Mac, And The Dixie Travelers

b. William D. Colleran, 26 April 1925, Pittsburg, Pennsylvania, USA. Colleran began his career as a teenager singing with Ed Brozi in a touring medicine show, and was influenced by acts such as the **Monroe Brothers** and the **Blue Sky Boys**. After World War II, he became interested in bluegrass music. In 1949, he and his band played regularly on WHJB Greensburg, Pennsylvania, and since there were three members of the band called Bill, he decided he would become Mac Martin. In the early 50s, he was noted for his banjo playing and fine vocal work, and in 1953, was playing with a band on WHOD Homestead, Pennsylvania, which was likened to that of **Lester Flatt** and **Earl Scruggs**. In 1957, he and his band took a residency at Walsh's Lounge in Pittsburg where they played weekly for the next 15 years. In 1963, the Travelers recorded two albums for Gateway records, although only one was released. A few years later, they recorded four albums for Rural Rhythm. Noted mandolin specialist Bob Artis (b. 26 July 1946, Santa Monica, California, USA) joined the band and when Mac Martin left for a time in 1972, Artis took over. In 1974, when the band recorded for County, Martin had returned. Apart from his playing Artis wrote many articles for publications such as *Bluegrass Unlimited* and *Muleskinner News* and his book *Bluegrass* was published in 1975.

Albums: *Folk And Bluegrass Favorites* (1966), *Traveling Blues* (1968), *Goin' Down The Country* (1968), *Just Like Old Times* (1970), *Back Trackin'* (1971), *Dixie Bound* (1974), *Travelin' On* (1978), *Basic Bluegrass* (1987), *Traveler's Portrait* (1989). Further reading: *Bluegrass*, Bob Artis.

Martin, Mary

b. Mary Virginia Martin, 1 December 1913, Weatherford, Texas, USA, d. 3 November 1990, Rancho Mirage, California, USA. A legendary star of the Broadway musical theatre during the 40s and 50s, and one of its most charming, vivacious and best-loved performers. Her father was a lawyer, and her mother a violin teacher. She took dancing and singing lessons from an early age, married at 16, and eventually ran a dancing school herself before moving to Hollywood where she auditioned constantly at the film studios, and worked in nightclubs and on radio. After being spotted by the producer Lawrence Schwab, her first big break came on Broadway in 1938 when she won a secondary role, as Dolly Winslow, in the **Cole Porter** musical ***Leave It To Me***. Almost every night she stopped the show with her 'sensational' rendering of 'My Heart Belongs To Daddy' while performing a mock striptease perched on top of a large cabin trunk at a 'Siberian' railway station. On the strength of her performance in that show she was signed to Paramount, and made 10 films over a period of four years, beginning with *The Great Victor Herbert* in 1939. Although her delightfuly warm personality and theatrical star quality, were not so effective on film, she did have her moments, particularly in *Rhythm On The River* (with **Bing Crosby** and **Oscar Levant**) and ***Birth Of The Blues***, in which she joined Crosby and **Jack Teagarden** for 'The Waiter, And The Porter And The Upstairs Maid'. She also sang the title song in ***Kiss The Boys Goodbye***, which became a big hit for **Tommy Dorsey**, and duetted with **Dick Powell** on 'Hit The Road To Dreamland' in ***Star Spangled Rhythm***. Other film appearances included *Love Thy Neighbour*, *New York Town*, *Happy-Go-Lucky*, *True To Life*, and *Main Street To Boradway* (1953). While on the west coast, she married for the second time, to a Paramount executive Richard Halliday, who became her manager. In 1943 she returned to the stage, and, after failing to reach Broadway with *Dancing In The Streets*, scored a great success with ***One Touch Of Venus*** which ran for 567 performances. The role of a glamorous statue that comes to life and falls in love with a human had originally been intended for **Marlene Dietrich**, but it fell to Martin to sing the haunting 'Speak Low,' and the show established her as a true star. She followed it with *Lute Song*, the show which introduced **Yul Brynner** to Broadway, before returning to Hollywood to reprise 'My Heart Belongs To Daddy' for the Cole Porter biopic ***Night And Day***. A trip to London in 1947 for an appearance in **Noël Coward**'s *Pacific 1860*, proved an unsatisfactory experience, and Martin returned to the USA to play the lead in a touring version of ***Annie Get Your Gun***. **Richard Rodgers** and **Oscar**

Hammerstein's smash hit ***South Pacific*** was next, and Martin's memorable performance, funny and poignant in turns, won her a **Tony Award**. Starred with opera singer Ezio Pinza, she introduced several of the composers' most endearing numbers, including 'I'm Gonna Wash That Man Right Out Of My Hair' (sung while she shampooed her hair on stage), 'A Wonderful Guy', 'A Cockeyed Optimist', and the hilarious 'Honeybun'. *South Pacific* ran for 1,925 performances in New York, and Martin recreated her role for the 1951 London production at Drury Lane where she was equally well received. During the rest of the 50s Mary Martin appeared in several straight plays, two highly regarded television spectaculars - one with **Ethel Merman** (which included a 35-song medley), and the other with Noël Coward - as well as starring on Broadway with Cyril Ritchard in a musical version of ***Peter Pan*** (1954) which was taped and shown repeatedly on US television. In November 1959 Martin opened at the Lunt-Fontanne Theatre in New York in what was to prove yet another blockbuster hit. Rodgers and Hammerstein's musical about the Trapp family of Austrian folk singers, ***The Sound Of Music***, immediately produced reactions ranging for raves to revulsion, but it gave Martin another Tony Award and the chance to display her homespun charm with songs such as 'My Favourite Things' and 'Do-Re-Mi'. From the 'hills that were alive with music', Mary Martin plummeted to the depths in *Jennie* (1963), her first real flop. Thereafter, she and her husband spent more time at their home in Brazil, but in 1965 she was persuaded to embark on a world tour in ***Hello, Dolly!*** which included a visit to Vietnam, and a five-month stay in London. Her final appearance in a Broadway musical was in 1966 with **Robert Preston** in the two-hander ***I Do! I Do!*** which ran for 560 performances. In the 70s she did more straight theatre and won a Peabody Award for the television film *Valentine*. After her husband's death in 1973, Martin moved to Palm Springs to be near her friend Janet Gaynor, but returned to New York in 1977 to star with Ethel Merman in a benefit performance of *Together Again*. In the early 80s, Martin and Janet Gaynor were severely injured in an horrific taxicab crash in San Francisco which took the life of her longtime aide Ben Washer. Martin recovered to receive the applause of her peers in *Our Heart Belongs To Mary*, and to make her final US stage appearance in 1986 with **Carol Channing** in a national tour of James Kirkwood's comedy *Legends*. For much of the time she had to wear a shortwave radio device to prompt her when she forgot her lines. Mary Martin made her final appearance on the London stage in the 1980 Royal Variety Performance when she performed a delightful version of 'Honeybun', and then had to suffer the embarrasment of watching her son from her first marriage, Larry Hagman (the notorious J. R Ewing from the television soap opera, *Dallas*), forget his lines in front of the celebrity audience.

Selected albums: *Adventures For Readers* (Harcourt 1958), *Mary Martin Sings-Richard Rodgers Plays* (RCA 1958), *Sings For You* (Columbia c.50s), *A Spoonful Of Sugar* (Kapp 1964), with Danny Kaye, Ethel Merman and others *Cole Porter Sings And Plays Jubilee* (Columbia 1972), with Noël Coward *Together With Music* (AMR 1976), *On Broadway* (Silva Screen 1989), *16 Most Requested Songs* (Columbia 1993), and stage cast recordings.

Further reading: *Mary Martin On Stage*, S. P. Newman, *My Heart Belongs*, Mary Martin.

Martin, Ray

b. Raymond Stuart Martin, 11 October 1918, Vienna, Austria, d. February 1988, South Africa. A composer, arranger, musical director and author. After studying violin, composition and orchestration at the State Academy for Music and Fine Arts in Vienna, Martin moved to Britain in 1937. He joined the *Carroll Levis Discoveries* show as a solo violin act, touring the UK Variety circuit, and was then chosen as the 'New Voice' in the popular BBC radio series *Bandwaggon*, which starred Arthur Askey and Richard Murdoch. After appearing in several editions of *Sidney Torch's Half Hour*, he enlisted in the British Army in 1940 and worked in the Intelligence Corps, aided by his fluency in German, French and English. Later, he became musical director of the Variety Department for the British Forces Network in Hamburg, Germany. He started broadcasting his *Melody From The Sky* programme from there, with a German string orchestra culled from the Hamburg Philharmonic Orchestra, and transferred the show to the BBC in December 1946, where it ran for over 500 broadcasts. Martin was also instrumental in founding the BBC Northern Variety Orchestra, and, from 1949-51, conducted at least six shows a week. He started recording for **Columbia Records** in 1949 with his own Concert Orchestra accompanying other artists including **Julie Andrews**, **Steve Conway** and **Jimmy Young**. Eventually he became the company's recording manager. His 50s instrumental hits included **Leroy Anderson**'s 'Blue Tango', 'Swedish Rhapsody' and 'Carousel Waltz'. Some of his many compositions and film scores are difficult to locate because, besides his own name, he wrote under several pseudonyms, such as Tony Simmonds, Buddy Cadbury, Lester Powell and Marshall Ross. In 1956 he wrote the background score, and served as musical director, for a British musical film called ***It's Great To Be Young***, starring John Mills. In addition to the title track, written under his own name, the film contained Martin's (Marshall Ross's) 1952 composition 'Marching Strings'; and his (Lester Powell's) romantic ballad 'You Are My First Love' (in collaboration with Paddy Roberts). Martin's other compositions included 'Melody From The Sky', 'Once Upon A Winter Time', 'Muriella', 'Begorra',

'Parlour Game', 'Blue Violins' (a US hit for Hugo Winterhalter's Orchestra), 'Any Old Time', 'Waltzing Bugle Boy', 'Airborne', 'Ballet Of The Bells', 'Tango Of The Bells', 'Big Ben Blues', 'Never Too Young' and 'Sounds Out Of Sight'. He composed the incidental music for over 20 BBC Sound cartoons, and wrote the scores for several films, including *Yield To The Night*, a prison melodrama in which ex-'glamour girl' Diana Dors gave a highly acclaimed dramatic performance; and the 1956 version of *My Wife's Father*. In 1957 Martin moved to America to work in New York and Hollywood. His US film scores included *The Young Graduates* and *The Hoax*. In 1972 he returned to work in the UK and, in 1980, appeared as himself in *The Baltimore Bullit*. During the 80s he settled in South Africa, and died there in 1988.

Selected albums: *Lehar, Strauss And Novello Melodies* (1956), *High Barbaree-12 Famous Sea Shanties* (1957), *Olives, Almonds And Raisins* (1958), *Million Dollar Melodies* (1959), *Melodies D'Amour* (1961), *Boots And Saddles* (1961), *I Could Have Danced All Night* (1961), *Dynamica* (1962), *We* (1962), *Spotlight On Strings* (1962), *Sounds Out Of Sight* (1963), *London Under The Stars* (1966), *Favourite TV Themes* (1973), *Favourite TV Themes, Volume 2* (1975), *Viva Mariachi* (1975), *Welcome Home* (1975).

Martin, Sara

b. 18 June 1884, Louisville, Kentucky, USA, d. 24 May 1955, Louisville, Kentucky, USA. A melodious but rather inflexible singer, Martin appears nevertheless to have been a popular success, recording over 120 tracks for **OKeh** between 1923 and 1928. These include the first recorded blues with guitar accompaniment (by **Sylvester Weaver**), and the first with a jug band (that of Clifford Hayes, billed as 'Sara Martin's Jug Band'). Although Chicago-based, Martin maintained close connections with Louisville, from where Hayes and Weaver also originated. She worked in vaudeville from 1915-31, thereafter devoting herself to the church and to running a nursing home in Louisville from the 40s until her death.

Albums: *Clifford Hayes Vol. 2* (c.1987), with Sylvester Weaver *The Accompanist* (1988), *Sara Martin* (c.1990).

Martin, Tony

An extremely popular singer from the 30s until the late 50s, with a powerful voice and an easy, romantic style. As a teenager, Martin became proficient on the saxophone and formed his own band, the Clarion Four. For some years he worked in the San Francisco area at the Palace Hotel, playing saxophone and singing with bands such as Anson Weeks, Tom Coakley, and Tom Guran, whose outfit included **Woody Herman**. Morris drove across country with Herman and other members of the band to the 1933 Chicago World Fair, and afterwards played the city's Chez Paree Club. In 1934 he changed his name to Tony Martin, and tried to break into films, without success. Two years later he landed a 'bit' part in the **Fred Astaire-Ginger Rogers** hit movie ***Follow The Fleet***, along with two other young hopefuls, Lucille Ball and **Betty Grable**. Later, in 1936, he signed for 20th Century-Fox, and sang 'When I'm With You' in ***Poor Little Rich Girl***, and 'When Did You Leave Heaven?' in *Sing, Baby, Sing*. The following year he married one of the film's stars, **Alice Faye**.

During the late 30s he achieved star status, thanks to film musicals such as *Pigskin Parade*, with **Judy Garland** and Betty Grable; *Banjo On My Knee*, with Barbara Stanwyck and Joel McCrea; *The Holy Terror* and *Sing And Be Happy*, with Leah Ray; *You Can't Have Everything* and *Sally, Irene And Mary* with Alice Faye; *Ali Baba Goes To Town*, starring **Eddie Cantor**; *Kentucky Moonshine* and *Thanks For Everything*. When Martin left Fox he appeared with **Rita Hayworth** in *Music In My Heart*, and introduced **Robert Wright** and **George Forrest**'s 'It's A Blue World' which was nominated for an Academy Award in 1940. In 1941, Martin appeared with the Marx Brothers in *the Big Store*, and sang what was to become one of his 'identity songs', 'The Tenement Symphony', described in some quarters, somewhat unkindly, as the comedy highlight of the film. Martin's other movie that year was ***Ziegfeld Girl***, with some spectacular **Busby Berkeley** production numbers, and starring, amongst others, Judy Garland, Hedy Lamarr and Lana Turner. After the attack on Pearl Harbour in December 1941, Martin enlisted in the US Armed Forces, serving first in the Navy, and then with the Army in the Far East. He also sang for a time with the Army Air Forces Training Command Orchestra directed by **Glenn Miller**. While in the Services, Martin received several awards, including the Bronze Star and other citations. At the end of World War II he returned to showbusiness, and starred in the **Jerome Kern** bio-pic, ***Till The Clouds Roll By*** (1946), which was followed by *Casbah* (1948), thought by many to have been his best role. The songs were by **Harold Arlen** and **Leo Robin**, and included another Martin all-time favourite, 'For Every Man There's A Woman'. In the same year Martin, having divorced Alice Faye, married dancer-actress **Cyd Charisse**, and later starred with her in *Easy To Love* (1953). Martin's other films during the 50s included *Two Tickets To Broadway* (with Janet Leigh), *Here Come The Girls* (with **Bob Hope** and **Rosemary Clooney**), the all-star **Sigmund Romberg** bio-pic ***Deep In My Heart***, the 1955 MGM re-make of ***Hit The Deck***, and a guest appearance in *Meet Me In Las Vegas* (which starred Cyd Charisse and **Dan Dailey**). In 1957 Martin starred with **Vera-Ellen** in *Let's Be Happy*, an unsuccessful British attempt to recreate the Hollywood musical. In addition to his film work, Martin has had a very successful recording career. His first hits, 'Now It Can Be Told' and 'South Of The

Border', came in the late 30s, and continued through to the mid-50s with songs such as 'It's A Blue World', 'Tonight We Love', 'To Each His Own', 'Rumours Are Flying', 'It's Magic', 'There's No Tomorrow', 'Circus', 'Marta (Rambling Rose Of The Wildwood)', 'I Said My Pyjamas (And Put On My Prayers)' and 'Take A Letter, Miss Smith' (both duets with Fran Warren), 'La Vie En Rose', 'Would I Love You (Love You Love You)', 'I Get Ideas' (adapted from the Argentine tango 'Adios Muchachos' and thought to be quite racy at the time), 'Over A Bottle Of Wine', 'Domino', 'Kiss Of Fire', 'Stranger In Paradise', 'Here', 'Do I Love You (Because You're Beautiful)' and 'Walk Hand In Hand'. He was also very active on radio in the 30s, 40s, and into the 50s on shows such as Walter Winchell's *Lucky Strike Hour*, and others featuring Burns And Allen, **André Kostelanetz** and **David Rose**, along with his own programmes. In the 50s and 60s Martin appeared frequently on television, and in 1964 formed a night club act with his wife. For many years they continued to tour the cabaret circuit in the USA and abroad. In 1986 Martin accompanied Charisse to London when she re-created the role first played by **Anna Neagle** over 20 years earlier in the **David Heneker**-John Taylor stage musical ***Charlie Girl*** at the Victoria Palace. The couple had first been in London in 1948 on their honeymoon when he was playing the first of several London Palladium seasons. Martin has come a long way since then, and is still regarded as one of the most accomplished and stylish vocalists of his era. He returned to London yet again in 1994 for a spell in cabaret at the Café Royal.
Selected albums: *A Night At The Copacabana* (1956), *Our Love Affair* (1957), *In The Spotlight* (1958), *Dream Music* (1959), *Mr. Song Man* (1960), *At The Desert Inn* (1960), *Tonight* (1960), *Fly Me To The Moon* (1962), *At Carnegie Hall* (1967). Selected compilations: *Greatest Hits* (1961), *Golden Hits* (1962), *Best Of* (1984), *Tenement Symphony* (1984), *Something In The Air* (1989), *This May Be The Night* (ASV 1993).
Further reading: *The Two Of Us*, Tony Martin and Cyd Charisse (with Dick Kleiner).

Martin, Vince

A folk singer who first surfaced in the mid-50s on the east coast club circuit, little is known about Vince Martin's background. His major claim to fame was as the singer on the 1956 Top 10 hit 'Cindy, Oh Cindy', on Glory Records. The folk song, written by Bob Baron and Burt Long, featured Martin backed by the **Tarriers**, which included Alan Arkin (who went on to become a successful actor), Erik Darling (who became a member of the folk group the **Rooftop Singers**), and Bob Carey. Martin made other recordings into the 70s, including singles for **ABC** Paramount and **Elektra Records**.
Album: *Vince Martin* (Capitol 1973).

Martindale, Wink

b. Winston Martindale, 1933, Jackson, Tennessee, USA. A 1959 revival of **T. Texas Tyler**'s 'Deck Of Cards' monologue is synonymous with this ex-Memphis radio presenter as the pyramids are to Egypt. While studying speech and drama at the state university, he had moonlighted at a city station, working his way up from music librarian. A meeting with **Dot Records** executive Randy Wood led to the release of 'Deck Of Cards' - a soldier answering a charge of playing cards in church by explaining each one's religious significance - an opus that appealed to Martindale, a former chorister and regular church-goer. Its worldwide success brought far-flung television appearances on Australia's *Bandstand* and UK's *Sunday Night At The London Palladium*, and also caused the artist to migrate to Hollywood, where he hosted the *Teenage Dance Party* television series in the early 60s. 'A Deck Of Cards' has been extraordinarily successful in the UK, re-entering the charts on several occasions in the 60s and in 1973. It peaked behind a more recently recorded rival recitation from **Max Bygraves**.

Martino, Al

b. Alfred Cini, 7 October 1927, Philadelphia, Pennsylvania, USA. The son of Italian immigrants, a fact that was always obvious in his style and manner, Martino worked as bricklayer in his father's construction business before being encouraged to become a singer by his friend, **Mario Lanza**. After singing in local clubs, and winning Arthur Godfrey's *Talent Scouts*, he recorded 'Here In My Heart' for the small BBS record label. It shot to number 1 in the US chart, and reputedly sold over a million copies. This disc was also the first ever record to top the ***New Musical Express*** UK listings, inaugurated in 1952. Martino's success led to a contract with **Capitol Records**, and more hits in 1953 with 'Take My Heart', 'Rachel' and 'When You're Mine'. For several years after that, the US record buyers apparently tired of Martino's soulful ballads, although he remained popular in Europe for a time - particularly in the UK, where he made the Top 20 with 'Now', 'Wanted', 'The Story Of Tina' and 'The Man From Laramie'. After some telling performances on US television, he made his recording comeback in 1963 with country singer Leon Payne's 'I Love You Because', followed by 'Painted, Tainted Rose', 'Living A Lie', 'I Love You More And More Every Day', 'Tears And Roses', 'Always Together', 'Think I'll Go And Cry Myself To Sleep' and 'Mary In The Morning'. His second million-seller, 'Spanish Eyes' (1965), was originally an instrumental piece, 'Moon Over Naples', written by the popular German orchestra leader, **Bert Kaempfert**. With lyrics by Charles Singleton and Eddy Snyder, Martino's version became, particularly in Europe, a dreamy dance favourite to rival **Charles Aznavour**'s, 'Dance In The Old Fashioned Way'. In 1964, Martino sang the title song for the Bette Davis/Olivia De Havilland film, *Hush...Hush Sweet Charlotte*, and this led to his playing singer Johnny Fontane in the smash hit movie *The Godfather* (1972). In the film, Martino sang the Italian number 'O Marenariello' ('I Have But One Heart'). He also recorded the film's love theme, 'Speak Softly Love', and had chart success with another couple of Italian songs, 'To The Door Of The Sun' ('Alle Porte Del Sole') and the old **Dean Martin** hit, Domenico Modugno's 'Volare'. In vogue once more, Martino played top night clubs and theatres, and continued to record with Capitol who have reissued many of his early albums on CD. In 1992 he played some UK dates, mixing selections from ***Cats*** and ***The Phantom Of The Opera*** with much requested favourites such as 'Granada'.

Selected albums: *The Exciting Voice Of Al Martino* (1962), *The Italian Voice Of Al Martino* (1963), *I Love You Because* (1963), *Painted, Tainted Rose* (1963), *Living A Lie* (1964), *I Love You More And More Every Day/Tears And Roses* (1964), *We Could* (1965), *Somebody Else Is Taking My Place* (1965), *My Cherie* (1965), *Spanish Eyes* (1966), *Think I'll Go Somewhere And Cry Myself To Sleep* (1966), *This Is Love* (1966), *This Love For You* (1967), *Daddy's Little Girl* (1967), *Mary In The Morning* (1967), *This Is Al Martino* (1968), *Love Is Blue* (1968), *Sausalito* (1969), *Jean* (1969), *Can't Help Falling In Love* (1970), *My Heart Sings* (1970), *Love Theme From 'The Godfather'* (1972), *Country Style* (1974), *To The Door Of The Sun* (1975), *Sing My Love Songs* (1977), *The Next Hundred Years* (1978). Compilations: *The Best Of Al Martino* (1968), *The Very Best Of Al Martino* (1974), *The Hits Of Al Martino* (1985), *Al Martino* (1992).

Martino, Pat

b. 25 April 1944, Philadelphia, Pennsylvania, USA. Martino's singer father encouraged him to play guitar and he received some instruction from his cousin. He was a professional guitarist at the age of 15, playing with saxophonists **Gator Jackson** and **Red Holloway**. He played in all the leading organ combos of the 60s: with **Don Patterson**, **Jimmy Smith**, **Brother Jack McDuff**, **Richard 'Groove' Holmes** and **Jimmy McGriff**. In 1966, after four months with **Sonny Stitt**'s band, he worked with **John Handy**'s rather more *avant garde* quintet. In the late 60s, Martino had his own bands with **Cedar Walton**, Richard Davis (bass) and **Billy Hart**. Main influences on Martino were **Wes Montgomery** and eastern music, but during the 70s he became interested in the music of composers such as Stockhausen and Elliott Carter. He taught and published a book called *Linear Expressions* with T. Baruso (1983). Martino had suffered a seizure in 1980 which led to a temporary loss of memory. He recovered and returned to playing in 1984. Martino's playing is characterized by fleet fingerwork and virtuoso flourishes, while his improvisations involve passages in octaves like Wes Montgomery, and are often influenced by his choice of the 12-string guitar. The trick of his dark and chunky sound is that he tunes the treble strings down and the bass strings up.

Selected albums: *El Hombre* (1966), *Strings!* (c.60s), *East* (c.60s), *Baiyana* (60s), *Live* (c60s), *Consciousness* (c.60s), *Exit* (c.70s), *The Visit* (c.70s), *Starbright* (c.70s), *Joyous Lake* (c.70s), *We'll Be Together Again* (1981), *Footprints* (1981), *Strings* (1986), with Stanley Clarke *Children Of Forever* (c.1982), *The Return* (1991), *Desperado* (1993).

Martyn, Barry

b. Barry Martin Godfrey, 23 February 1941, London, England. Martyn began playing drums in his early teens and was soon leading his own band and making records. Playing in the New Orleans tradition, Martyn's musical interest led him to visit New Orleans in the early 60s where he studied with **Josiah 'Cié' Frazier**. Martyn recorded in New Orleans with many leading local jazzmen and also organized and led international tours by major figures such as **George Lewis** and **Albert Nicholas**. Resident in the USA since the early 70s, Martyn has continued to play and record New Orleans jazz to a very high standard with the likes of **Barney Bigard** and the Eagle Brass Band. In addition to bands under his own name Martyn was also leader of the Legends Of Jazz, a group of elderly but still musically active New Orleans jazzmen. Deeply committed to preserving the great tradition of New Orleans jazz, over the years Martyn has done much more than play and record. He formed his own recording company, writes extensively, and, perhaps most importantly, has recorded for archive purposes numerous interviews with New Orleans jazz survivors.

Albums: *Barney Bigard And The Pelican Trio* (1976), with the Eagle Brass Band *Last Of The Line* (1983).

Martyn, Beverly

b. Beverly Kutner, Coventry, England. This underrated artist first attracted attention in 1966 when her anonymous demo tape solicited an inquiry by **Decca** employee Tony Hall in his *Record Mirror* column. She was subsequently signed to the label and, as Beverly, launched its **Deram Records** subsidiary with 'Happy New Year', a **Randy Newman** composition. The singer appeared at the **Monterey Pop Festival**, and enjoyed an uncredited cameo part on **Simon And Garfunkel**'s 'Fakin' It', prior to forming a duo with her husband, **John Martyn**. The couple recorded two albums, *Stormbringer* and *The Road To Ruin*, the latter of which featured Beverly's evocative song, 'Primrose Hill'. Their professional relationship was severed in 1971, and the couple were divorced later in the decade. Sadly, Beverly has subsequently failed to fulfil the promise shown in her early work.

Albums: with John Martyn *Stormbringer* (1970), *The Road To Ruin* (1970).

Martyn, John

b. Iain McGeachy, 11 September 1948, New Malden, Surrey, England, to musically-minded parents. At the age of 17, he started his professional career under the guidance of folk artist **Hamish Imlach**. The long, often bumpy journey through Martyn's career began when he arrived in London, where he was signed instantly by the astute **Chris Blackwell**, whose fledgling **Island Records** was just finding major success. Martyn became the first white solo artist on the label. His first album, the jazz/blues tinged *London Conversation* (1968), was released amidst a growing folk scene which was beginning to shake off its traditionalist image. The jazz influence was confirmed when, only nine months later, *The Tumbler* was released. A bold yet understated album, it broke many conventions of folk music, featuring the flute and saxophone of jazz artist Harold MacNair. The critics began the predictable **Bob Dylan** comparisons, especially as the young Martyn was not yet 20. Soon afterwards, Martyn married singer Beverly Kutner, and as John and **Beverly Martyn** they produced two well-received albums, *Stormbringer* and *Road To Ruin*. The former was recorded in Woodstock, USA, with a talented group of American musicians, including Levon Helm of the **Band** and keyboard player Paul Harris. Both albums were relaxed in approach and echoed the simple peace and love attitudes of the day, with their gently naive sentiments. Martyn the romantic also became Martyn the drunkard, and so began his conflict. The meeting with jazz bassist **Danny Thompson**, who became a regular drinking companion, led to some serious boozing and Martyn becoming a 'Jack the Lad'. Hard work in the clubs, however, was building his reputation, but it was the release of *Bless The Weather* and *Solid Air* that established him as a concert hall attraction. Martyn delivered a unique combination of beautifully slurred vocals and a breathtaking technique using his battered acoustic guitar played through an echoplex unit, together with sensitive and mature jazz arrangements. The track 'Solid Air' was written as a eulogy to his friend singer/songwriter **Nick Drake** who had committed suicide in 1974. Martyn was able to pour out his feelings in the opening two lines of the song: 'You've been taking your time and you've been living on solid air. You've been walking the line, you've been living on solid air'. Martyn continued to mature with subsequent albums, each time taking a step further away from folk music. *Inside Out* and the mellow *Sunday's Child* both confirmed his important musical standing, although commercial success still eluded him. Frustrated by the music business in general, he made and produced *Live At Leeds* himself. The album could be purchased only by writing to John and Beverly at their home in Hastings; they personally signed every copy of the plain record sleeve upon despatch. Martyn's dark side was beginning to get the better of him, and his alcohol and drug intake put a strain on his marriage. *One World*, in 1977, has subtle references to these problems in the lyrics, and, with **Steve Winwood** guesting on most tracks, the album was warmly received. Martyn, however, was going through serious problems and would not produce a new work until three years later when, following the break up of his marriage, he delivered the stunning *Grace And Danger* produced by **Phil Collins**. This was the album in which Martyn bared all to his listeners, a painfully emotional work, which put the artist in a class of his own. Following this collection Martyn ended his association with Chris Blackwell. Martyn changed labels to WEA and delivered *Glorious Fool* and *Well Kept Secret*, also touring regularly with a full-time band including the experienced Max Middleton on keyboards and the talented fretless bassist, Alan Thompson. These two albums had now moved him firmly into the rock category and, in live performance, his much- revered acoustic guitar playing was relegated to only a few numbers, such as his now-classic song 'May You Never', subsequently recorded by **Eric Clapton**. Martyn's gift as a lyricist, however, had never been sharper, and he injected a fierce yet honest seam into his songs.

On the title track to *Glorious Fool* he wrote a powerful criticism of the former American president, Ronald Reagan (in just one carefully repeated line Martyn states, 'Half the lies he tells you are not true'). Following another home-made live album *Philentropy*, Martyn returned to Island Records and went on to deliver more quality albums. *Sapphire*, with his evocative version of 'Somewhere Over The Rainbow', reflected a happier man, now re-married. The world's first commercially released CD single was Martyn's 'Angeline', a superbly crafted love song to his wife, which preceded the album *Piece By Piece* in 1986. With commercial success still eluding him, Martyn slid into another alcoholic trough until 1988, when he was given a doctor's ultimatum. He chose to dry out and live, returning in 1990 with *The Apprentice*. *Cooltide* was a fine album, expertly produced but contained songs that tended to last too long, this was also the case with *Couldn't Love You More* in 1992. The latter was a bonus for loyal fans as it was an album of re-recorded versions from Martyn's exquisite back catalogue. Perplexingly *No Little Boy* a year later was a re-recoding of many of the songs on the former album. Martyn was unhappy with some of the tracks on *Couldn't Love You More* and his tolerent record company allowed him this luxury. Interestingly many of the versions were better especially a moody and lengthy return to 'Solid Air'. Martyn has retained his loyal cult following for over 25 years, and remains a critics' favourite. It is difficult to react indifferently to his challenging and emotional work. He now possesses a voice that is a good octave lower than the young curly haired freshman of 60s folk clubs. Martyn is a major artist; although he has yet to receive major commercial success.

Albums: *London Conversation* (Island 1968), *The Tumbler* (Island 1968), *Stormbringer* (Island 1970), *The Road To Ruin* (Island 1970), *Bless The Weather* (Island 1971), *Solid Air* (Island 1973), *Inside Out* (Island 1973), *Sunday's Child* (Island 1975), *Live At Leeds* (Island 1975), *One World* (Island 1977), *Grace And Danger* (Island 1980), *Glorious Fool* (WEA 1981), *Well Kept Secret* WEA (1982), *Philentrophy* (1983), *Sapphire* (Island 19Island 84), *Piece By Piece* (Island 1986), *Foundations* (Island 1987), *The Apprentice* (Island 1990), *Cooltide* (1991), *BBC Radio 1 Live In Concert* (Windsong 1992), *Couldn't Love You More* (Permanent 1992), *No Little Boy* (Permanent 1993). Compilations: *So Far So Good* (Island 1977), *The Electric John Martyn* (Island 1982).

Marvelettes

The Marvelettes' career epitomized the haphazard progress endured by many of the leading girl groups of the early 60s. Despite scoring several major USA hits, they were unable to sustain a consistent line-up, and their constant shift in personnel made it difficult to overcome their rather anonymous public image. The group was formed in the late 50s by five students at Inkster High School in Michigan, USA: Gladys Horton, Georgeanna Marie Tillman, Wanda Young, Katherine Anderson and Juanita Grant. They were spotted at a school talent show by Robert Bateman of the **Satintones**, who introduced them to **Berry Gordy**, head of the fledgling **Motown** organization. Bateman co-produced their early releases with **Brian Holland**, and the partnership found immediate success with 'Please Mr Postman' - a US number 1 in 1961, and Motown's biggest-selling record up to that point. This effervescent slice of pop-R&B captivated teenage audiences in the USA, and the song was introduced to an even wider public when the **Beatles** recorded a faithful cover version on their second album.

After a blatant attempt to repeat the winning formula with 'Twistin' Postman', the Marvelettes made the Top 20 again in 1962 with 'Playboy' and the chirpy 'Beechwood 4-5789'. The cycle of line-up changes was already underway, with Juanita Grant's departure reducing the group to a four-piece. The comparative failure of the next few singles also took its toll, and by 1965, Tillman had also left. The remaining trio, occasionally augmented by **Florence Ballard** of the **Supremes**, were paired with producer/writer **Smokey Robinson**. He tailored a series of ambitious hit singles for the group, the most successful of which was 'Don't Mess With Bill' in 1966 - though 'The Hunter Gets Captured By The Game' was arguably a more significant achievement. Gladys Horton, the Marvelettes' usual lead singer, left the group in 1967, to be replaced by Anne Bogan. They continued to notch up minor soul hits for the remainder of the decade, most notably 'When You're Young And In Love', before disintegrating in 1970. Wanda Young completed the group's recording commitments with an album, *The Return Of The Marvelettes*, which saw her supported by session vocalists. In 1989 original members Wanda Rogers and Gladys Horton, plus Echo Johnson and Jean McLain, recorded for Ian Levine's Motor City label issuing the disco-sounding 'Holding On With Both Hands' and *Now*. Johnson and McLain were replaced by Jackie and Regina Holleman for subsequent releases.

Albums: *Please Mr Postman* (1961), *The Marvelettes Sing* (1962), *Playboy* (1962), *The Marvellous Marvelettes* (1963), *Recorded Live: On Stage* (1963), *The Marvelettes* (1967), *Sophisticated Soul* (1968), *In Full Bloom* (1969), *The Return Of The Marvelettes* (1970), *Now* (1990). Compilations: *Compact Command Perfomances - 23 Greatest Hits* (1992), *The Marvellous Marvelettes* (c.1993), *Deliver The Singles 1961-1971* (c.1993, double CD).

Marvellos

An R&B vocal group from Los Angeles, California, USA. Members were Jesse Harris, Milton Hayes, Harold Harris, Willie Holley, and Lance Porter. The group was formed in 1963 and first found success locally with 'She Told Me Lies' for Exodus. It raised enough interest for **Warner Brothers** to pick it up and release it on its **Reprise** label. The formation of Warner Brother's R&B subsidiary, Loma, had the Marvellos joining that label in 1965. The group immediately succeeded with 'We Go Together', styled after the **Temptations**' 'It's Growing'. Nothing much happened after 'We Go Together' had run its course and members of the Marvellos spent many years as background session singers. Then in 1975, Jesse Harris and Milton Hayes found new success in a highly respected vocal group, Street Corner Symphony, which had evolved out of the session group they were in. The outfit released *Harmony Grits* (1975) and *Little Funk Machine* (1976), reprising old songs and singing new material in a neo-doo-wop style.

Marvelows

Formed in Chicago Heights, Illinois, USA, in 1959, Melvin Mason, Willie 'Sonny' Stevenson, Frank Paden and Johnny Paden were originally known as the Mystics. They became the Marvelows in 1964, following the addition of Jesse Smith. The group was then signed to **ABC Records**, and scored a hit the following year with the euphoric 'I Do', which combined equal traces of doo-wop and Windy City soul. (This excellent song was later revived in 1977 by the **J. Geils Band**.) The Marvelows replaced Jesse

Smith with Andrew Thomas in 1967, and, the following year hit with a soft ballad, 'In The Morning'. The Marvelows broke-up in 1969.

Album: *The Mighty Marvelows* (1968). Compilation: shared with the Esquires *Chi-Town Showdown* (1982).

Marvin And Johnny

A R&B duo from Los Angeles, California, USA. Marvin Phillips (b. 23 October 31, Guthrie, Oklahoma, USA) and Emory 'Johnny' Perry (b. 1 March 1928, Sherman, Texas, USA) made a brief impact on the rock 'n' roll scene when Los Angeles was a major centre of the R&B recording scene during the late 40s and early 50s. Phillips and Perry had known each other since 1949, when they both played saxophones in the Richard Lewis Band. When Phillips formed the Marvin Phillips And His Men From Mars combo, Perry joined him. Meanwhile, Phillips obtained his first success in the recording business when teamed with **Jesse Belvin** in a duo called Marvin And Jesse, reaching the charts with the dreamy ballad 'Dream Girl' (number 2 R&B) in 1952 for **Specialty Records**. After Belvin was drafted into the army in 1953, Phillips at the behest of Specialty recruited a new partner, his old friend Perry, to form Marvin And Johnny. The duo immediately had a hit with 'Baby Doll' (number 9 R&B) in 1953. They moved to Modern in 1954 and released 'Tick Tock' (number 9 R&B). However, they are best remembered for 'Cherry Pie', the b-side to 'Tick Tock', which although did not make any national charts possibly achieved more radio airplay. The song was revived by **Skip And Flip** in 1960, putting it high on the pop charts.

Albums: *Marvin And Johnny* (Crown 1963). Compilation: *Flipped Out* (Specialty 1992).

Marvin, Hank B.

b. Brian Rankin, 28 October 1941, Newcastle-upon-Tyne, England. Marvin's metallic, echoed picking on a red Fender Stratocaster (with generous employment of tremelo arm) was the inspirational source of the fretboard pyrotechnics of **Jeff Beck**, **Ritchie Blackmore** and many other lead guitarists who began in groups imitating the **Shadows**, of whom Marvin, in his black, horn-rimmed glasses, was the principal public face. After teaching himself guitar, banjo and boogie-woogie piano at school, Marvin's father presented him with a Hofner Congress on his 16th birthday. When his Crescent City Skiffle Group won a South Shields Jazz Club talent contest, he was asked to join **Bruce Welch**'s Railroaders. On moving to London, Marvin and Welch operated briefly as the Geordie Boys before enlisting in an outfit called the Drifters, which evolved into the Shadows. While backing and, later, composing songs for **Cliff Richard**, the quartet recorded independently and became generally acknowledged as Britain's top instrumental act.

After their first disbandment in 1968, Marvin's subsequent solo career commenced with 'Goodnight Dick', but poor sales of this and two further singles were only surface manifestations of the deeper groundswell of support that hoisted 1969's *Hank Marvin* to number 14 in the UK album chart. Yet despite contrasting moods and styles, the album was not far removed from the Shadows with its **Norrie Paramor** arrangements and composing contributions by Brian Bennett, the group's drummer. Marvin's affinity with Richard continued via their hit duets with 'Throw Down A Line' and 'Joy Of Living', as well as Hank's residency as instrumentalist and comedian on Cliff's BBC television series. In the early 70s, seeking a fresh artistic direction, Marvin amalgamated with Welch and John Farrar for two albums (*Marvin, Welch And Farrar* and *Second Opinion*) dominated by vocals and another (*Marvin And Farrar*) with Farrar alone ('a bit like Frankenstein meets the **Beach Boys**', concluded Marvin) before this project was abandoned partly through Marvin's personal commitments - notably his indoctrination as a Jehovah's Witness in 1973, and the gradual reformation of the Shadows. After moving to Australia, Marvin turned out for the group's annual tour and studio album, while also recording albums such as *The Hank Marvin Guitar Syndicate*, on which he led nine noted session guitarists. In 1982, he charted with 'Don't Talk' - intended initially for Richard - from Words And Music, which contained only one instrumental ('Captain Zlogg'). Hank B. Marvin has long been assured a place in pop history and is unquestionably one of the major influences on rock guitarists over the past 30 years.

Albums: *Hank Marvin* (1969), *The Hank Marvin Guitar Syndicate* (1977), *Words And Music* (1982), *All Alone With Friends* (1983), *Into The Light* (1992), *Heartbeat* (1993). Compilation: *Would You Believe It . . . Plus!* (1988).

Film: *Expresso Bongo* (1959).

Marvin, Johnny And Frankie

Johnny (b. John Senator Marvin, 11 July 1897, Butler, Oklahoma, USA, d. 20 December 1945, Hollywood, California, USA) and brother Frankie (b. Frank James Marvin, 27 January 1904, Butler, Oklahoma, USA). Around 1913, Johnny (who played guitar and banjo and had previously left home at twelve to join a circus) joined a travelling show called the Royal Hawaiians, where he learned the steel guitar and ukulele. After naval service in World War I, he moved into vaudeville and as Honey Duke And His Uke, he worked his way to New York where, for five years, he had a daily radio show on network NBC. He made records and even appeared on Broadway in the musical *Honeymoon Lane*. In 1928, he was joined by Frankie (also a good steel guitarist) and using several differing names, he was soon recording for several labels. The Marvins befriended and arranged auditions for the young **Gene Autry**, when he first visited New York seeking a recording contract. Autry never forgot their help and from that time he began to provide work for them. In the late 20s, Frankie also worked with the Duke of Paducah (Benjamin Francis 'Whitey' Ford, b. 12 May 1901, DeSoto, Missouri, USA, d. 20 June 1986, Nashville, Tennessee, USA) in a comedy duo known as Ralph And Elmer. (Ford also later worked as MC on Autry's radio show before becoming a long time regular on the ***Grand Ole Opry***). The Marvins moved to Hollywood with Autry in 1934, and for about 20 years, Frankie's distinctive steel guitar was an important part of the Autry sound on recordings and radio shows. He also worked on Autry's films, both in acting roles and as a stuntman - a job that he reckoned paid better than acting. Although Johnny recorded for **Decca** in the mid-30s, the Depression had basically ended his solo career. He worked with Autry as a writer and producer on the *Melody Ranch Show* and wrote around 80 songs for Autry's films including 'Dust'. During World War II, Johnny made several tours to the South Pacific to entertain army personnel and in 1943, in the Papuan jungles, he contacted dengue fever, which ultimately led to his death from a heart attack in 1945. In the mid-50s, when the *Melody Ranch Show* was taken off air, Frankie become something of a recluse. However, when the television version of *Melody Ranch* appeared on Autry's own KTLA station, Frankie worked on it both on and off camera. In the early 70s, he retired to Frazier Park, California and underwent open heart surgery. He was not a prolific songwriter like his brother but he co-wrote the well-known song 'Cowboy's Heaven' with Autry in 1934. He was an avid angler all his life and when once asked why he never tried to resume his own recording career he replied 'Heck, I ain't got time. I'd rather go fishing'.

Marx, Richard

This Chicago, Illinois, USA bred singer/songwriter began his career at the age of five, singing on US advertising jingles. This became his professional vocation until he moved on to become a backing singer for **Lionel Richie**. Afterwards, Marx embarked on a solo career in his own right. A string of hits began with 'Don't Mean Nothing' before he put together a run of three successive US number 1 hits with 'Hold On To The Nights', 'Satisfied' and 'Right Here Waiting'. He also wrote the **Kenny Rogers** hit 'What About Me'. Seemingly unable to fail with his big ballad formula, Marx looks assured of continued success in the US market. He married Cynthia Rhodes of Animotion in August 1989.

Albums: *Richard Marx* (1987), *Repeat Offender* (1989), *Rush Street* (1991), *Paid Vacation* (Parlophone 1994).

Marxman

Irish/marxist rap crew whose political stance, in the final analysis, won them more fans than their music did. Yet for a period in late 1992/early 1993, they mounted an effective bid as supercharged champions of ultra left hip hop. Fronted by rappers MC Hollis and Phrase, plus musician Oisin, if Marxman's political motives weren't already guaranteed to stoke controversy, then the subject of their debut single, 'Sad Affair', was. Discussing Northern Ireland, with the explicit statement that English troops should be withdrawn, it was naturally banned by the BBC (one DJ attempted to play it but had it edited from his show - objections were made to the fact that the lyrics contained the IRA slogan 'tiocfaidh ar la' - 'Our Time Will Come'). Both sides of the debut used traditional Irish instruments (three quarters of the band are Irish-born), and the follow-up, 'Ship Ahoy', featured **Sinead O'Connor**. Other guest contributions have included the tin whistle of traditional Irish musician **Davy Spillane**. Contrastingly, both 45s emerged on Gilles Peterson's laid-back **Talkin' Loud** empire. A third, 'All About Eve', actually made the UK Top 30, before 'Ship Ahoy' was re-released. The sleeve of their debut LP confirmed their allegiances: 'Marx, Engels, Lenin, Rosa Luxemburg, Bobby Sands . . . and all those who have devoted themselves to the overthrow of the bourgeoisie'. Though they were allied to a major (**Polygram**), Marxman still set their sights on the death of capitalism. In the final analysis, however, there was simply too much analysis.

Album: *33 Revolutions Per Minute* (Talkin' Loud 1992).

Mary Poppins

There have been many occasions when performers who have triumphed in Broadway shows have been overlooked when the movie adaptations came along. While **Julie Andrews** would have no doubt dazzled as Eliza Doolittle in the film version of ***My Fair Lady***, it was not to be. Instead, Andrews made up for the disappointment in a big way by making her first screen appearance in this 1964 **Walt Disney** classic. With supreme irony, Andrews won the best actress Oscar for her debut performance, while Audrey Hepburn, who 'took her place' in the film of **Alan Jay Lerner** and **Frederick Loewe**'s masterpiece, was not even nominated. With a screenplay by Bill Walsh and Donald Da Gradi, adapted from the children's story by Pamela Travers, the action of *Mary Poppins* evolves around the Banks family, residents of 17 Cherry Tree Lane, London. Mr George Banks (David Tomlinson) is a banker by name, nature and occupation. He rules his house with a rod of iron, while Winifred, his wife (Glynis Johns), spends most of the time fighting for the Suffragettes' cause (the year is 1910). Both spend little time with their children Michael (Matthew Garber) and Jane (Karen Dotrice). Many nannies have come and gone (six in four months), and as the film begins, the time has come to employ another one. The children draw up their own advertisement, outlining what they want most in the new employee. In disgust Mr Banks throws the piece of paper into the fireplace, and unbeknown to him, it travels up the chimney, and, before you can say 'Mary Poppins', she floats down to earth, carrying her trusty umbrella, and appoints herself as the new nanny, giving the family a week's trial! Before long Mary has won the hearts of the children, tidying up by magic, and taking them on many an adventure. During one such trip she bumps into an old friend, Bert (Dick Van Dyke) who plays a number of different roles in the film), entertaining with his one-man band and drawing pictures on the pavement. As if by magic, Mary, Bert and the children escape from reality and step into the street painting. Here the movie really comes into its own as humans mix with all kinds of animated characters and animals. It is great fun to watch, as we see the group being waited on by penguins, and wooden horses galloping with freedom. Only when the pavement picture is washed away by rain, do the happy foursome have to return home. However, fun is frivolous to Mr Banks, and he decides to take the children along to his workplace to see what the real world is all about. Here Michael and Jane meet the bank president, Mr Dawes, (Dick Van Dyke again), but the trip turns into a disaster, and as a result their father is sacked. By the time he eventually gets his job back, the family have become much happier and tolerant of each other. Mary Poppins sees that her job has been accomplished and flies back to her cloud. Also among the cast were Hermione Baddeley, Ed Wynn, Arthur Treacher, Elsa Lanchester, Reginald Owen, and Reta Shaw. Directed by Robert Stevenson, this is an enchanting fairy tale, never losing its musical and comic pace for a moment. **Richard M.** and **Robert B Sherman**'s outstanding score included 'A Spoonful Of Sugar', 'Feed the Birds', the infamous 'Supercalifragilisticexpialidocious', 'The Perfect Nanny', 'Sister Suffragette', 'The Life I Lead', 'Fidelity Feduciary Bank', 'Lets' Go Fly A Kite', and 'Chim Chim Cheree' which won the Oscar for best song. One of the film's highlights comes when the energetic Dick Van Dyke (complete with an amusingly artificial Cockney accent) leads a band of chimney sweeps in a dance to 'Step In Time' over the rooftops of London. The scene is a joy, and a credit to choreographers Marc Breaux and DeeDee Wood. *Mary Poppins* won Academy Awards for its music score and (predictably) for special effects and film editing. Photographed in Technicolor by Edward Colman, it went on to become the third-highest grossing musical of the 60s.

Maschwitz, Eric

b. 10 June 1901, Birmingham, England, d. 27 October 1969, Ascot, Berkshire, England. A librettist, lyricist, author and producer. After studying at Cambridge University, Maschwitz joined the BBC in the late 20s, and was editor of *Radio Times* from 1927-33. For the next four years he served as BBC Radio's first Director of Variety. While with the Corporation he often used the pseudonym, Holt Marvell, for his songwriting activities. In 1932, his radio play *Goodnight Vienna*, written with composer George Posford, was turned into a musical film, and gave its star, **Jack Buchanan**, one of his biggest record hits. In the following year, again with Posford, Maschwitz wrote *The Gay Hussar*, which was staged in the West End. Revised, and with a new title, ***Balalaika***, and an additional composer, Bernard Grun, it ran for 570 performances from 1936-38. It became the first British Musical to be filmed in Hollywood, and starred **Nelson Eddy** singing the hit song, 'At The Balalaika'. In 1936, together with Jack Streachey and Harry Link, Maschwitz wrote the all-time standard, 'These Foolish Things', which was interpolated into the show *Spread It Abroad*. In the same year he received the OBE, and three years later was nominated for an Academy Award for co-writing the screenplay for the **MGM** classic *Goodbye, Mr Chips*. During World War II, Maschwitz served in the Intelligence Corps, but still found the time to write songs, including some of the era's most potent numbers, such as 'A Pair Of Silver Wings' (with **Michael Carr**), 'Room Five Hundred And Four' (Posford), and 'A Nightingale Sang In Berkeley Square' (with Jack Strachey and Manning Sherwin). The latter song turned up in the revue, *Strange Faces* (1940). Maschwitz's other stage shows included *Paprika*, *Magyar Melody* (*Paprika* revised), *Waltz Without End*, *Flying Colours*, *Evangeline*, *Starlight Roof*, *Carissima* and *Belinda Fair* (1949). In the 50s Maschwitz wrote the songs, with Posford, for **George Formby**'s first, and last, West End Musical, *Zip Goes A Million* (1951-53), and contributed librettos to *Love From Judy* (1952-54), and *Romance In Candlelight* (1955). His last London production, in 1956, was *Summer Song*, with music by Bernard Grun and Dvorak. In 1958 Maschwitz returned to the BBC as Head of Light Entertainment in television, and was partly responsible for the long-running *Black And White Minstrel Show*.

Further reading: *No Chip On My Shoulder*, Eric Maschwitz.

Masekela, Hugh

b. Hugh Rampolo Masekela, 4 April 1939, Witbank, Johannesburg, South Africa. South Africa's leading *émigré* trumpeter and bandleader was born into a musical family which boasted one of the largest jazz record collections in the city. One of Masekela's earliest memories is of winding up the household gramophone for his parents; by the age of 10, he was familiar with most of the 78s issued by **Duke Ellington**, **Count Basie**, **Cab Calloway** and **Glenn Miller**. Other early influences were the traditional musics of the

Swazis, Zulus, Sutus and Shangaan, all of which he heard at weekend musical gatherings in the township and neighbouring countryside. A difficult and rebellious schoolboy, Masekela was frequently given to playing truant. On one such occasion, he saw Kirk Douglas in the **Bix Beiderbecke** bio-pic *Young Man With A Horn* - and decided there and then that he wanted to become a trumpeter and bandleader when he grew up. His teacher, the anti-apartheid activist and Anglican priest Trevor Huddlestone, welcomed this enthusiasm and gave Masekela his first trumpet, a battered old instrument owned by a local bandleader. A year later, in 1955, Huddlestone was expelled from South Africa. In New York, he met **Louis Armstrong**, and enthused to him about Masekela's talents and persuaded Armstrong to send a trumpet over to Johannesburg for the boy. With trombonist **Jonas Gwangwa**, Masekela dropped out of school in 1955 to form his first group, the Merry Makers. His main influences at this time were the African-American bop trumpeters **Dizzy Gillespie** and **Clifford Brown** and by 1956, the Merry Makers were playing nothing but bop.

By 1958, apartheid had tightened up to the extent that it was very difficult for black bands to make a living - they were banned from the government-controlled radio and were not allowed to travel freely from one town to another. Masekela was obliged to leave the Merry Makers and join the African Jazz and Variety package tour (which also included his future wife, **Miriam Makeba**). Operated by a white man, Alfred Herbert, the troupe was able to circumvent some of the travel restrictions imposed on blacks and continued to tour the country. In 1959, with Makeba, Masekela left Herbert to join the cast of the 'township musical', *King Kong*. The same year, he formed the pioneering band, the Jazz Epistles, with Gwangwa and pianist Dollar Brand (now **Abdullah Ibrahim**). They became the first black band in South Africa to record an album, all previous releases having been 78s.

In 1960, the year of the Sharpeville massacre, the government extended the Group Areas Act to ban black musicians from working in inner city (that is, white) clubs. The move effectively ended the Jazz Epistles' ability to make a living, and Masekela decided the time had come to emigrate to the USA. With the help of Trevor Huddlestone and **Harry Belafonte** in New York, he obtained a passport and, after a brief period in London at the Guildhall School of Music, won a scholarship to New York's Manhattan School of Music.

Initially aspiring to become a sideman with **Art Blakey**, Masekela was instead persuaded by the drummer to form his own band, and put together a quartet which debuted at the Village Gate club in 1961. A year later, he recorded his first album, *Trumpet Africa*, a considerable critical success. In 1964, Masekela married Miriam Makeba, another of Belafonte's protegees (who was to divorce him a few years later to marry Black Panther activist Stokeley Carmichael). Continuing to lead his own band, Masekela also wrote arrangements for Makeba and toured with her backing group. Husband and wife became prominent critics of the South African regime, and donated part of their touring income to fund scholarships which enabled black musicians to leave South Africa. In 1964, Masekela also released his second solo album, *The Americanization Of Ooga Booga*, and appeared at the first Watts, Los Angeles, California Jazz Festival. In 1966, he linked up with old Manhattan School of Music classmate Stewart Levine to form the production company Chisa. The original idea was for Levine to be the artist and Masekela the producer, but the success of Chisa's debut release, an album called *The Emancipation Of Hugh Masekela*, lead to a role-reversal. (The Levine-Masekela partnership would continue through the 60s, 70s and 80s.)

In 1967, Masekela appeared at the legendary **Monterey Jazz Festival** and released two more albums, *Promise Of A Future* and *Coincidence*. Unable to find top-quality South African musicians to work with in the USA, Masekela became drawn into the lucrative area of lightweight jazz/pop. His first chart success in the genre was an instrumental version of 'Up Up And Away' in 1967, which reached number 71 in the US charts. In 1968, he had a number 1 hit with 'Grazin' In The Grass', selling four million copies. The follow-up, 'Puffin' On Down The Track', disappointingly only reached number 71. Not surprisingly, given the mood of the times, the latter two singles were widely perceived to carry pro-marijuana statements in their titles and, in autumn 1968, Masekela was arrested at his home in Malibu and charged with possession of the drug.

Despite the urging of the record business, Masekela refused to capitalize on the success of 'Grazin' In The Grass' with a lightweight album in the same vein, and instead recorded the protest album *Masekela*, which included track titles like 'Fuzz' and 'Riot'.

In 1970, Masekela signed with **Motown Records**, who released the album *Reconstruction*. Also that year, he formed the Union of South Africa band with fellow *émigrés* Gwangwa and Caiphus Semenya. The band was short-lived, however, following the lengthy hospitalization of Gwangwa from injuries sustained in a car crash. Frustrated in his attempt to launch an American-based, South African line-up, Masekela visited London to record the album *Home Is Where The Music Is* with exiled South African saxophonist **Dudu Pukwana**. Deciding to re-immerse himself in his African roots, Masekela set off in late 1972 on a 'pilgrimage' to Senegal, Liberia, Zaire and other countries. He worked for a year in Guinea (where his ex-wife Makeba was now living) as a music teacher, and spent some months in Lagos, Nigeria, playing in **Fela Anikulapo Kuti**'s band. He finally ended up in Ghana, where he joined the young highlife-meets-funk band **Hedzolleh Soundz**. Between 1974 and 1976, Masekela released five albums with the group - *Your Mama Told You Not To Worry*, *I Am Not Afraid*, *The Boys Doin' It*, *The African Connection* and *Colonial Man*. By 1975, however, leader and band had fallen out, with Hedzolleh accusing Masekela of financial mistreatment. In fact, the cost of supporting Hedzolleh in the USA during loss-making tours had drained Masekela's resources, and in 1976, he and Levine were obliged to wind up Chisa. Short of money, Masekela signed to **A&M Records**, where he recorded two lightweight albums with label boss **Herb Alpert** - *The Main Event* and *Herb Alpert/Hugh Masekela.*

In 1980, with Makeba, Masekela headlined a massive Goin' Home outdoor concert in Lesotho. In 1982, in a similar venture, they appeared in neighbouring Botswana. Both concerts were attended by large numbers of black and white South Africans, who gave the duo heroes' welcomes. Masekela decided to settle in Botswana, 20 miles from the South African border, and signed to the UK label Jive, who flew over to him in a state-of-the-art mobile studio. The sessions resulted in the albums *Technobush* and *Waiting For The Rain.* In 1983, he made his first live appearance in London for over 20 years, at the African Sounds for Mandela concert at Alexandra Palace. In 1986, Masekela severed his links with Jive and returned to the USA, where he signed with **Warner Brothers**, releasing the album *Tomorrow*, and joining label-mate **Paul Simon**'s Graceland world tour. In 1989, he co-wrote the music for the Broadway show *Sarafina*, set in a Soweto school during a state of emergency, and released the album *Up Township.*

Albums: *Jazz Epistles* (1959), *Trumpet Afnca* (1962), *The Americanization Of Ooga Booga* (1964), *The Emancipation Of Hugh Masekela* (1966), *Promise Of A Future* (1967), *Coincidence* (1967), *Masekela* (1968), *Reconstruction* (1970), with Dudu Pukwana *Home Is Where The Music Is* (1972), Your *Mama Told You Not To Worry* (1974), *I Am Not Afraid* (1974), *The Boys Doin' It* (1975), *The African Connection* (1975), *Colonial Man* (1976), with Herb Alpert *The Main Event* (1978), *Herb Alpert/Hugh Masekela* (1979), *Home* (1982), *Dollar Bill* (1983), *Technobush* (1984), *Waiting For The Rain* (1985), *Tomorrow* (1987), *Up Township* (1989), *Hope* (Triloka 1994).

Maskman And The Agents

An R&B vocal group from Washington, D.C., USA. Maskman And The Agents achieved success based on the nexus of two popular culture phenomenons, soul music and the spy craze. Members were Harmon Bethea, Tyrone Gay, Paul Williams, and Johnny Hood. Bethea was a veteran of the R&B business for some 25 years in the group the **Cap-Tans**, when in 1967 he formed from the remnants of the old group Maskman And The Agents. The outfit sang novelty soul songs and Harmon appeared masked, which fitted into the period when *I Spy* and *Get Smart* were popular US television spy shows, and James Bond films were highly successful. In the same period **Edwin Starr** had a hit with 'Agent Double-O Soul' and Jamo Thomas with 'I Spy (For The F.B.I.)'. Mask Man And The Agents succeeded with two moderate sized hits, 'One Eye Open' (number 20 R&B) in 1968 and 'My Wife, My Dog, My Cat' (number 22 R&B) in 1969. They never charted nationally again.

Albums: *One Eye Open* (Dynamo 1968), *Got To Find A Sweet Name* (Musicor 1970).

Maslak, Keshavan

b. 26 February 1947, Detroit, Michigan, USA, into a Ukrainian family. As a child, Keshavan 'spoke Ukrainian around the house, and Russian and Polish to the neighbours' and was regularly beaten up by his all-American contemporaries at elementary school for being different. He started playing saxophone at the age of eight. An early enthusiasm for polkas and mazurkas was soon replaced by an obsession with **John Coltrane**'s music, and some of Coltrane's yearning, burning passions infuse Maslak's best work (eg *Big Time*). The saxophonist has been a stylistic jack-of-all-trades, having performed with **Philip Glass**, the **Temptations**, and **Sam Rivers**, and rechristening himself Kenny Millions in a futile attempt to crack the punk/rock market. He has toured and performed extensively in Eastern Europe and Russia: 'I'm like **Mick Jagger** over there, I'm telling you.'

Albums: *Buddha's Hand* (1979), *Maslak One Thousand* (1979), *Mayhem In Our Streets* (1980), *Humanplexity* (1980), *Loved By Millions* (1981), *Blaster Master* (1981), *Big Time* (1981), *Better And Better* (1987), *Mother Russia* (1991), with Paul Bley *Not To Be A Star* (1993), with Bley *Romance In The City* (Leo 1993).

Mason Dixon

Jerry Dengler (b. 29 May 1955, Colorado Springs, Colorado, USA), Frank Gilligan (b. 2 November 1955, Queens, New York, USA), Rick Henderson (b. 29 May 1953, Beaumont, Texas, USA). Mason Dixon is the brainchild of three graduates of Lamar University in Beaumont, Texas. They recorded their mixture of folk and country for several small labels in the 80s and then signed with **Capitol Records** in 1988. Their most successful singles are '3935 West End Avenue', 'When Karen Comes Around' and 'Exception To The Rule'.

Album: *Exception To The Rule* (Capitol 1988).

Mason Proffit

Led by brothers Terry and John Talbot, country-rockers Mason Proffit formed in Chicago, Illinois, USA, in 1969 from the ashes of groups called the

Quinn Chords and Sounds Unlimited. The other members were Tim Ayers (bass), Ron Schetter (guitar/vocals) and Art Nash (drums). Originally called Mason Proffit Reunion, the group recorded its first album, *Wanted*, in 1969 for Happy Tiger Records. Mixing country, folk, bluegrass and rock touches, the group eventually placed three albums in the charts - on Happy Tiger, Ampex and **Warner Brothers** - before the Talbot Brothers left to pursue successful careers (both together and individually) performing religious songs.
Albums: *Wanted* (1969), *Movin' Toward Happiness* (1971), *Last Night I Had The Strangest Dream* (1971), *Rockfish Crossing* (1972), *Bareback Rider* (1973), *Come And Gone* (1974).

Mason, Barbara

b. 9 August 1947, Philadelphia, Pennsylvania, USA. Mason first recorded for Crusader Records in 1964, but did not achieve success until she began recording for the Philadelphia-based Artic label the following year. With her voice sounding young and innocent in its thinness and flatness, Mason reached the US charts with the marvellous 'Yes, I'm Ready' (R&B number 2, 1965) and excellent follow-ups, 'Sad, Sad Girl' (R&B number 12/pop Top 30, 1965), 'I Need Love' (R&B number 25, 1966), and 'Oh, How It Hurts' (R&B number 11, 1968). A brief stay at the National Records label yielded one moderate hit, 'Raindrops Keep Fallin' On My Head' (R&B number 38, 1970), a cover of the **B.J. Thomas** hit. In 1972, Mason signed with **Buddah Records** and obviously had fully blossomed with more mature material, such as 'Give Me Your Love' (R&B number 9/pop Top 40, 1972), a **Curtis Mayfield** song from the movie *Superfly*, 'From His Woman To You' (R&B number 3/pop Top 30, 1974), and 'Shackin Up' (R&B number 9, 1975), but she was much less interesting as a singer. She still had her thin-sounding voice, but what was fetching in an 18-year-old, sounded undeveloped for a woman in her late 20s. Also, her habit of including recitations ('raps') in the songs on man-woman relationships strongly dated the later material, most typically on 'She's Got The Papers (But I Got The Man)' (R&B number 29, 1981). Mason's last chart record was 'Another Man' (R&B number 68, 1984), which was the singer's only UK chart entry, reaching number 45 the same year.
Albums: *Yes, I'm Ready* (1965), *If You Knew Him Like I Do* (1970), *Give Me Your Love* (1973), *Love's The Thing* (1975), *Locked In This Position* (1977), *I Am Your Woman, She Is Your Wife* (1978), *A Piece Of My Life* (1980). Compilations: *Philadelphia's Lady Love* (1990), *Yes I'm Ready* (1994).

Mason, Dave

b. 10 May 1946, Worcester, England. Mason, the former guitarist of local band the Hellions, met **Steve Winwood** when he was employed as a road manager for the **Spencer Davis Group**. This legendary 60s R&B band was weakened in 1967 when Winwood, together with Mason, formed **Traffic**. They found instant success as one of the leaders of progressive pop in the late 60s, and went on to develop into a highly regarded unit in the 70s. Mason joined and left the band on numerous occasions. He subsequently settled in America and enjoyed considerable success as a solo artist. His excellent debut album, *Alone Together*, proved to be his most critically acclaimed work, and featured strong musical support from **Leon Russell**, **Rita Coolidge** and former Traffic colleague **Jim Capaldi**. Mason's melodic flair and fine guitar playing came to the fore on all eight tracks. The original record package was a triple fold, cut-out, hole-punched cover which attempted to encourage the listener to hang it on the wall. His second venture without Traffic was a collaboration with **'Mama' Cass Elliot**. The record suffered from poor marketing and indifferent reviews. By 1973, Mason had permanently settled in America, and he signed a long-term contract with **CBS**. The first record, *It's Like You Never Left*, put him back in favour. The recruitment of a number of name LA musicians gave the album a full and varied sound. **Graham Nash**, Greg Reeves, Jim Keltner, Carl Radle, Lonnie Turner and **Stevie Wonder** were just some of the artists who participated. Mason found greater success in his adopted country, and produced a series of successful records throughout the 70s. The albums formed a steady pattern that contained mostly Mason originals, regularly sprinkled with versions of oldies. 'All Along The Watchtower', 'Bring It On Home To Me', 'Crying, Waiting, Hoping' were just three of the songs he sympathetically interpreted. Mason kept a relatively low-profile during the 80s, making one album in 1987 on the small Voyager label. He was last heard on American television singing on a beer commercial.
Albums: *Alone Together* (1970), *Dave Mason And Cass Elliot* (1971), *Headkeeper* (1972), *Dave Mason Is Alive!* (1973), *It's Like You Never Left* (1973), *Dave Mason* (1974), *Split Coconut* (1975), *Certified Live* (1976), *Let It Flow* (1977), *Mariposa De Oro* (1978), *Old Crest On A New Wave* (1980). Compilations: *The Best Of Dave Mason* (1974), *Dave Mason At His Best* (1975), *The Very Best Of Dave Mason* (1978).
Further reading: *Keep On Running: The Steve Winwood Story*, Chris Welch. *Back In The High Life: A Biography Of Steve Winwood*, Alan Clayson.

Mason, Harvey

b. 22 February 1947, Atlantic City, New Jersey, USA. Mason began playing the drums when he was four years old. He studied at the **Berklee College Of Music** in Boston and later gained a degree in education at New England Conservatory. He worked with pianists **Errol Garner**, **George Shearing** and

Jan Hammer before moving to Los Angeles in 1971, where he worked as a studio musician covering music such as jazz, pop/rock and orchestral. He played with a wide range of bandleaders and musicians, including **Duke Ellington**, **Quincy Jones**, **Gunther Schuller**, **Donald Byrd**, **Gerry Mulligan**, **Grover Washington**, **George Benson** and **Lee Ritenour**. His clear, strong rhythm playing was perfect for **Herbie Hancock**'s *Headhunters* in 1973, which also highlighted several of Mason's expert arrangements.
Albums: with Herbie Hancock *Headhunters* (1973), with Grover Washington *Mister Magic* (1974), with George Benson *Breezin* (1976), *World Class* (1981).

Mason, Nick

b. Nicholas Berkeley Mason, 27 January 1945, Birmingham, England. It was while studying architecture at a London polytechnic in 1965 that Mason joined what was to become **Pink Floyd** as drummer. Sixteen years later, he was the last member of the group to issue a solo album, *Nick Mason's Fictitious Sports*, a collection that bore the indelible jazz-pop mark of its pianist and composer, **Carla Bley**. Other contributors included **Robert Wyatt**, **Chris Spedding** and Bley's husband, **Michael Mantler**. Records, however, were of less importance to Mason than Formula 1 racing and vintage cars. These interests infiltrated 1985's *Profiles* with Rick Fenn (ex-**10cc**), which included a revival of the **Crew-Cuts**' 'Sh-boom' (sung by 10cc's Eric Stewart) and other items that had already featured in *Life Could Be A Dream*, a half-hour film documentary (directed by Mike Shackleton) about Mason's pastimes. The founders of Bamboo Music, Fenn and Mason also scored Donald Cammill's *White Of The Eye* as well as advertising jingles for Barclays Bank and the HMV record shop chain. As a producer, Mason has ministered to albums by **Gong**, **Steve Hillage** and the **Damned**. In 1985, **David Gilmour** appeared on Mason's 'Lie For A Lie' (from *Profile*). The following year, Pink Floyd reformed.
Albums: *Nick Mason's Fictitious Sports* (1981), *Profiles* (1985).

Mason, Rod

b. 28 September 1940, Plymouth, Devon, England. Mason worked first in 1959 with **Cy Laurie** before spending four years (1962-66) with the band of **Monty Sunshine**. When he contracted Bell's palsy, he had to adjust his embouchure which, luckily for him, improved his range. In 1970, he joined **Acker Bilk**'s band, but in the late 70s, was leading his own ensemble and playing all over Europe. He spent some time with the **Dutch Swing College Band** in the early 80s, but resumed leading his own outfit in 1985. His wide range and exceptional stamina make him a natural lead trumpeter who seems effortlessly to recreate the sound of **Louis Armstrong** in the 30s.
Albums: *Rod Mason/Ian Wheeler Band* (1974), *Great Having You Around* (1978), *Six For Two* (1979).

Mason, Wood, Capaldi And Frog

This short-lived group, aka Wooden Frog, was formed in January 1969 from the remnants of **Traffic**. Ex-members **Dave Mason** (guitar/vocals), **Jim Capaldi** (drums/vocals) and Chris Wood (saxophone) were joined by organist **Mick Weaver**, who had previously enjoyed a solo career under the pseudonym **Wynder K. Frog**. The new quartet lasted a mere three months, completing a handful of live dates and a radio session before disintegrating. Despite their potential, the group was overshadowed by Traffic's powerful legacy, and lacked the focus its former leader, **Steve Winwood**, provided. Mason and Weaver then resumed their independent solo pursuits while Capaldi and Wood reverted to session work before re-convening Traffic.

Mass Order

A Baltimore-based duo of Mark Valentine and Eugene Hayes, who grew up listening to the **O'Jays** and soul standards. Mass Order scored a huge Autumn 1991 'hit' with their gospel house cracker, 'Take Me Away', a popular but elusive disc. It was actually a bootleg which had been pirated from a DAT tape at New York's New Music Seminar. It was eventually given a proper release (under its full title, 'Lift Every Voice (Take Me Away)') with remixes from the **Basement Boys** and **Tony Humphries**. As a footnote the bootlegging incident went to court, but the miscreants, David Cooper and William Lynch, still escaped justice. They were acquitted because they 'did not know they were breaking the law'.
Album: *Maybe One Day* (Columbia 1992).

Massacre

Formed in the US in the mid-80s, Massacre were one of the earliest extreme thrash metal bands, acting as pioneers of a style which was a popular underground phenomenon long before gaining public attention and widespread success. Founder members Kam Lee (vocals) and Rick Rozz (guitar) had been two thirds of the first **Death** line-up with Chuck Schuldiner. When Schuldiner relocated to California, the duo put together Massacre with Terry Butler (bass) and Bill Andrews (drums). Like other early thrash/death metal bands from Florida, they spread their name by recording demo tapes which were sent around the world and traded with various contacts. In the late 80s death metal and extreme thrash were becoming increasingly popular, and bands were much more widespread than when Massacre began. After a period of non-activity (with Rozz, Butler and Andrews again joining *Leprosy*-era Death), this new attention provided an opportunity for Massacre to begin work again, and they succeeded in gaining a record deal with UK label

Earache, whose specialism in extreme music was now well established. Their debut album saw Lee and Rozz reunited with Butler and Andrews to record *From Beyond*, a set primarily based on original demo material which had never been given official release. Successful touring of the US preceded the April 1992 launch of a 12-inch, 'Inhuman Condition', which included a cover of the **Venom** standard, 'Warhead', with guest vocals from that band's Cronos. The recording of a second album introduced a new rhythm section in Pete Sison (bass) and Syrus Peters (drums).
Albums: *From Beyond* (Earache 1991), *Promise* (Earache 1995).

Massey, Cal

b. 11 January 1928, Philadelphia, USA, d. 25 October 1972, New York City, New York, USA. Despite having played trumpet in the big bands of **Jay McShann** and **Jimmy Heath**, Massey's interests were firmly in the field of composition by the mid-50s. Between 1956 and 1958, he led a group of distinguished musicians, including **McCoy Tyner**, **Jimmy Garrison**, and **Al Heath**, playing solely his own compositions. His tunes have since been recorded by countless musicians from **Philly Joe Jones** to **Archie Shepp**. When he died, Massey had just completed a musical play about Billie Holiday.
Albums: compositions featured on John Coltrane *Coltrane* (1957), Freddie Hubbard *Here To Stay* (1962).

Massey, Louise, And The Westerners

b. Victoria Louise Massey, 10 August 1902, Hart County, Texas, USA, d. 22 June 1983. The family relocated first to Midland and then to the K Bar Ranch, near Roswell, Lincoln County, New Mexico, to an area still full of the memories of Billy the Kid. The Masseys became a very popular vocal and instrumental family band of the 30s and 40s and one of the first to adopt overdressed cowboy outfits as their stage attire. The band originally comprised Henry 'Dad' Massey and three of his eight children, namely Louise (d. 22 June 1983, San Angelo, Texas) and brothers Curt (b. 3 May 1910) and Allen. 'Dad' taught his children to play various instruments, although Curt usually played fiddle but in later years, he also played trumpet and piano. When Louise was 15, she married Milton Mabie who then became the fifth member of the group. The Massey Five's career began in the 20s, when they played and sang at local shows and church socials. This led to a two year tour of the USA and Canada, as well as a radio show on KMBC Kansas City. In 1930, 'Dad' retired to his ranch and Californian, Larry Wellington, replaced him. In 1933, they became regulars on the ***National Barn Dance*** on WLS Chicago, before moving to New York in 1935, where they featured on the NBC networked *Show Boat* and the following year, they gained their own networked *Log Cabin Dude Ranch* on NBC-WJZ. They had, by this time, first become the Westerners but when Louise, with her flamboyant Spanish style costumes, became more and more the focal point of the act, she received lead billing. They made popular personal appearances over a wide area and even returned to WLS to star on *Plantation Party* and other shows. In 1938, they made a film appearance in **Tex Ritter**'s Monogram B-western *Where The Buffalo Roam*. They recorded for several labels including **Vocalion**, **OKeh** and Conqueror and are best remembered for their fine version of 'My Adobe Hacienda'. Louise wrote the song, based on a house that she and Milt were building in 1941. She needed the music properly transcribed for publication before it could be used on NBC and this was done by a family friend, Lee Penny. He had no professional connection with the band or with the writing of the song but Louise credited him as co-writer for his work. After the group disbanded, Curt became the musical director and theme songwriter for the television shows *Beverly Hillbillies* and *Petticoat Junction* (which he actually sang).

Massive Attack

This loose Bristol collective have grown to become one of the premier UK dance/rap outfits. The group features the talents of rapper '3D' Del Najo (b. c.1966), and Daddy G (b. c.1959) and Mushroom (b. c.1968, Knowle West, Bristol, England). They started in 1988 having spent several years working on various mobile sound systems, as well as releasing records under The Wild Bunch moniker ('Fucking Me Up', 'Tearing Down The Avenue'). Nellee Hooper, a former member of the Wild Bunch, left to work with **Soul II Soul**, while another original member, Milo Johnson, began work in Japan. 3D is also a well respected graffiti artist, having his work featured in art galleries and a television survey on Channel 4. Liaisons with **Neneh Cherry** eventually led to a meeting with Cameron McVey, who produced Massive Attack's debut album. The resultant *Blue Lines* boasted three hit singles; 'Daydreaming', 'Unfinished Sympathy' (which also featured an orchestral score) and 'Safe From Harm'. The blend of rap, deep reggae and soul was provocative and rich in texture, and featured singing from Cherry and **Shara Nelson**. An outstanding achievement, it had taken eight months to create 'with breaks for Christmas and the World Cup'. 'Unfinished Symphony' was particularly well received. ***Melody Maker*** magazine ranked it as the best single of 1991, and it remains a perennial club favourite. One minor hiccup arrived when they were forced, somewhat hysterically, to change their name during the Gulf War in order to maintain airplay. It was duly shortened to Massive. Their philosophy singled them out as dance music's new sophisticates, 'We don't ever make direct dance music. You've got to be able to listen and then dance.' That status was confirmed when **U2** asked them to remix their single 'Mysterious Ways'. Despite *Blue Lines* being widely acclaimed, the band disappeared shortly afterwards. Shara Nelson had a solo career, with Massive Attack put on hold until the mid-90s. Another early contributor, **Tricky**, launched himself to considerable fanfare, with Massive Attack widely credited as an influence on fellow-Bristolians **Portishead**. A second Massive Attack album finally arrived in 1994, with former collaborator Nellee Hooper returning as producer. The featured singers this time included Tricky, Nigerian-born Nicolette, **Everything But The Girl**'s Tracy Thorn and **Horace Andy** (who had also contributed to the debut) on a selection of tracks which sadly failed to capture the magic of *Blue Lines*. Many critics suggested that others had now run so far with the baton handed them by the collective that the instigators themselves were yet to catch up.

Album: *Blue Lines* (Wild Bunch/EMI 1991), *No Protection* (EMI 1994).

Masso, George

b. 17 November 1926, Cranston, Rhode Island, USA. Coming from a musical background, Masso began on trumpet, then became a competent multi-instrumentalist, playing piano and vibraphone. However, it was hearing a **Lou McGarity** trombone solo on **Benny Goodman**'s recording of 'Yours' which determined his final choice of instrument. Despite his background, and a two-year stint with **Jimmy Dorsey** in the late 40s, Masso opted for a career as a teacher of music. In 1973, with his family grown up, he decided to return to playing after persistent needling from **Bobby Hackett**. He spent a year and a half with Goodman's Sextet, played with the **World's Greatest Jazz Band** and on some of **Buck Clayton**'s later Jam Sessions. Since then, Masso has toured extensively, usually as a single, sometimes in harness with **Scott Hamilton**, **Warren Vaché**, **Spike Robinson**, **Bobby Rosengarden** and other mainstream artists, playing clubs and festivals around the world.

Albums: *Buck Clayton Jam Session* (1975), *Choice NYC 'Bone* (1978), *Dialogue At Condon's* (1979), *A Swinging Case Of Masso-ism* (1980), *Pieces Of Eight* (1982), *No Frills, Just Music* (1983).

Master Ace

Raised in Brooklyn, Master Ace (aka Masta Ace) became a hip hop DJ in the 70s before adjusting to MC status by 1983. He won a rapping competition two years later which earned him studio time with producer **Marley Marl**, before a collegiate interlude followed. He contributed to the *In Control Volume 1* set by Marl, and the latter's label, **Cold Chillin'**, offered him a deal. His debut album, *Take A Look Around*, was fuelled by Marley Marl's funk throb and included a duet with **Biz Markie**. Songs like 'Brooklyn Battles' attempted to look through the blood and rage circus of urban decadent rap. He had earlier contributed to the **Brand New Heavies**' *Heavy Rhyme Experience*. His second album was better yet, the title-track, 'Slaughtahouse', a clever parody on the absurd machismo of gangsta rap: '99 rappers wanna kill to sound ill, You couldn't find their brains with a drill'. However, the graphic presentation of the video failed to impress **MTV** who banned it. He enjoyed more success with the Crooklyn Dodgers project (alongside **Special Ed** and Buckshot of **Black Moon**), scoring with the Spike Lee soundtrack single, 'Crooklyn'. He describes himself as a hip-hop purist, and certainly his wordy, considered narratives owe a debt to **Gil Scott-Heron**.

Albums: *Take A Look Around* (Warners 1990), *Slaughtahouse* (Delicious Vinyl 1993).

Master Apprentices

Formed in Adelaide, Australia, in 1965, the Master Apprentices have often been regarded by many observers of the Australian music scene as one of that country's most outstanding bands. Because Australian music was influenced by both the American and the British music scene, there were occasions when local Australian trends swung between the two. This was particularly true in the late 60s, when pop/soft rock was the main radio fodder, and yet there was the heavy blues influence from the UK, as well as the US west coast psychedelic phenomenon bubbling underground. The Master Apprentices took notice of the latter two and created a unique sound which encompassed both styles. Thus their material is disjointed but individual, and their albums have stood up well since then, in addition to becoming collectors items. They evolved from the instrumental-surf band the Mustangs who, comprising Mick Bower (guitar), Gavin Webb (bass), Rick Morrison (guitar) and Brian Vaughton (drums), took on a lead vocalist, Jim Keays, adopted their new name and started playing raucous, energetic R&B-based songs written by Bower. The band moved to Melbourne in early 1967 to capitalize on the success of the first single, 'Undecided'. By mid-1967, the second single, 'Dead And Buried', and their debut album had been released, but the music scene had moved on and psychedelia now being in vogue. Like many others, the band followed suit and released the 'Living In A Child's Dream' single, their most successful yet. Several line-up changes had taken place, but the departure of songwriter Bower was a setback. More changes followed, and it was not until early 1968, with the arrival of guitarist Doug Ford, that the band got back into gear, with the Keays/Ford team providing songs for the rest of the band's existence. A couple of catchy singles followed, and the group was joined by former Bay City Union member Glen Wheatley (b. 23 January 1949, Australia) on bass. The band continued its success through 1969-70, with further Australian hit singles featuring their distinctive guitar riffing. The band journeyed to the UK in 1970, but fame eluded them. They returned to Australia and released *Choice Cuts*, which was released in the UK as the *Masters Apprentices*, to favourable critical reviews. The band returned to England, but by the time of its arrival, interest had waned. Nevertheless, the members stayed on, releasing *Toast To Panama Red*, to limited success. Keays and Wheatley departed in early 1972; Ford kept the name going with a trio for another year before the band faded out, an ignominious end to what had been one of Australia's best and most adventurous bands. Jim Keays continued with a lengthy and patchy solo career, while Wheatley became the most successful rock entrepreneur in Australia. The band later reformed in 1989.

Albums: *Master Apprentices* (1967), *Masterpiece* (1969), *Choice Cuts/Masters Apprentices* (1970), *Nickelodeon* (1971), *Toast To Panama Red* (1972), *Now That It's Over* (1979), *Hands Of Time* (1980), *Jam It Up* (1987), *Do What You Wanna Do* (1989). Compilation: *The Very Best Of The Master Apprentices* (1988).

Mastercuts Series

A Beechwood subsidiary UK record label masterminded by Ian Dewhirst, Mastercuts was launched in 1991 to document some of dance music's most essential moments, in all its myriad forms. Initial releases such as *Jazz Funk 1* sold 25,000 copies, while *New Jack Swing* climbed as high as number 8 in the *Music Week* compilation chart, showing well against much better-funded, television-advertised albums. The first record in the series had been Classic Mix, but other formats were explored in the following order: Jazz-Funk, Mellow, New Jack Swing, Funk, Salsoul, Rare Groove, P-Funk, 80s Groove, Electro and House. Each came complete with insightful sleevenotes and anecdotes, in a manner which suggested that at last dance music might be taking its history as seriously as other forms of music. In 1994 the label also reluanched the legendary **Streetsounds** label.

Masters At Work

aka **Lil' Louie Vega** and **Kenny 'Dope' Gonzalez**, who marked the inception of their partnership by releasing 'Ride On The Rhythm' in 1991. On the back of that and their well established personal reputations (appearances as extras in Spaghetti Westerns notwithstanding), they subsequently undertook a vast array of remix projects. These began with **St Ettienne** ('Only Love Can Break Your Heart'), plus **Chic**, **Debbie Gibson**, **Melissa Morgan**, **BG The Prince Of Rap** ('Take Control Of The Party'), **Lisa Stansfield**, **Deee-Lite** ('Bittersweet Loving') plus legendary Latin jazz player **Tito Puente**'s 'Ran Kan Kan'. In turn Puente contributed three times to Louie's 1992 album with singer Marc Anthony. They also recorded, in their own right, material like 'Can't Stop The Rhythm (with **Jocelyn Brown**) for US label **Cutting**. Widely regarded as the cream of the profession, not everybody was clamouring for their wares - **Jamiroquai**'s 'Emergency On Planet Earth' remix was rumoured to be hated by the artist concerned. His was a rare dissenting voice, however.

Masters Of Ceremony

Nowadays chiefly remembered for the exploits of lead rapper **Grand Puba** (b. Maxwell Dixon), who would go on to front **Brand Nubian** before selecting a solo career. Masters Of Ceremony's singular album release was a pedestrian affair, divorced of the religious dogma, or indeed the musical precision, which characterised the work of Brand Nubian. Without which their attempts to fascimile a **Public Enemy** sneer wore fatally thin. However, it did include a major hit in 'Sexy'.

Album: *Dynamite* (4th & Broadway 1988).

Masters Of Reality

This New York, USA-based quartet featured Chris Goss (vocals/guitar), Tim Harrington (guitar), Googe (bass) and Vinnie Ludovico (drums). Deriving their name from the title of **Black Sabbath**'s third album, they fused a diverse array of rock styles into a form that clearly invoked names such as the **Doors**, **Vanilla Fudge**, **Love** and **Deep Purple**. The group originally formed as early as 1980, after which they embarked on a long-haul club touring policy which finally brought them serious attention. With the aid of producer Rick Rubin, who signed them originally to his **Def Jam** enterprise before it became **Def American**, they distilled their influences into a potent and powerful sound which had its roots in the 70s but was delivered with the technology of the present. Their self-titled debut was released to widespread critical acclaim in 1989, but fans had to wait another four years for a follow-up, *Sunrise On The Sufferbus*. This featured the legendary **Ginger Baker** joining only surviving original member, Goss. The first line-up had imploded following disastrous touring engagements in support of their debut, and the intervening period had seen Masters Of Reality put on ice. Harrington and Ludovico formed the Bogeymen.

Album: *Masters Of Reality* (Def American 1989), *Sunrise On The Sufferbus* (Def American 1993).

Masters, Valerie

b. 24 April 1940, London, England. This red-headed pop singer from London's East End sang during her childhood in the local underground station during air raids and later became the private secretary to the Mayor of Stepney. She received her big musical break when she replaced **Marion Ryan** in the popular **Ray**

Ellington Quartet. Masters made her first recording, 'Ding Dong', for Fontana in 1958 and was first seen on television on the *Hughie Green Show*. She was given her own series on Radio Luxembourg in 1959, which ran for over two years. Her only chart success came in 1960 with her sixth single on Fontana, a version of the European song 'Banjo Boy'. This was the same song that gave much-loved singer/comedian **George Formby** his last chart hit. Masters represented Britain in the European (not Eurovision) Song Contest in Belgium in 1960, and this led to her working in Scandinavia, Germany, and the Netherlands. She recorded for **HMV** in 1963, Columbia in 1964, **Polydor** in 1966 and once more on Columbia in 1969 but not graced the chart since.

Matador

This show, which was 'inspired' by the life of the Spanish bullfighter El Cordobes, first surfaced in the form of a concept album recorded by **Tom Jones** in 1987. One of the tracks, 'A Boy From Nowhere', climbed to number 2 in the UK singles chart, and Jones was originally set to take the leading role in the stage production. Things did not work out that way, and when *Matador* opened at the Queens theatre in London on 16 April 1991, the central character of Domingo Hernandez was played by the young unknown John Barrowman, with Nicky Henson as his crafty manager. In an attempt to give the production some glamour, the actress Stephanie Powers, well-known in England for her appearances with Robert Wagner in the television series *Hart To Hart*, was brought in to play the part of an American film star Laura-Jane Wilding. The character was thought to be based on Ava Gardner with whom El Cordobes is said to have had an affair. The score was by Michael Leander and Edward Seago, who had written hits for **Gary Glitter**, **Engelbert Humperdinck** and **Cliff Richard**, and the book, by Peter Dukes, was based on Leander and Seago's original storyline. Domingo's rise from the obscure village of Andalucia to the top of the bullfighting world despite a background of illiteracy, was thrillingly staged against a background of spectacular sets, but it was the dancing - particularly the flamenco dancing choreographed by Rafael Aguilar - which proved to be the outstanding feature of the whole production. The score, which contained nothing else as memorable as 'A Boy From Nowhere', also included 'Panama Hat', 'No Way Out Of This Town', 'I Was Born To Be Me', 'I'll Take You Out To Dinner', 'Paseo And Corrida', 'To Be a Matador', 'Children Of The Sun', 'I'll Dress You In Mourning', and 'I'm You, You Are Me'. Critical reaction was mixed ('Risibly awful . . . a load of bull', was the worst), but the show never captured an audience and closed after three months with losses 'approaching £1 million'.

Matassa, Cosimo

Of Italian ancestry, Matassa ran a New Orleans juke-box company and a record store, J&M Amusement Services in the early 40s. In 1945 he opened a small recording studio behind the shop. For the next 20 years, Cosimo's studios were the focus of recording activity in the city. Among the first to produce at Cosimo's was **Dave Bartholomew** who recorded **Roy Brown** for De Luxe and **Tommy Ridgley** for Imperial. In 1949, Bartholomew began recording **Fats Domino** at the studio, and in 1952, he recorded **Lloyd Price**. There were other hits from J&M by **Shirley & Lee**. By the mid-50s, a studio band had emerged to accompany the growing number of singers working there. Led by saxophonists Red Tyler and **Lee Allen**, its members included Earl Palmer (drums) and Frank Fields (bass). In 1956, the studio moved to larger premises and was renamed Cosimo's. Soon afterwards, **Little Richard** made some of his most famous recordings there. During this time, Matassa had been engineer and studio owner but in 1957 he moved into management with white pop singer **Jimmy Clanton**. Two years later he started his own, shortlived, label Rex. Among its roster of artists was **Mickey Gilley**, **Earl King**, **Jerry McCain** and Mac Rebennack (**Dr. John**). Matassa returned to his recording work on hits like **Barbara Lynn**'s 'You'll Lose A Good Thing' (1962) until 1966 when he set up Dover Records, an ambitious distribution company for local New Orleans labels. There were big successes with **Robert Parker** ('Barefootin'') and **Aaron Neville** ('Tell It Like It Is') but by 1968 Dover too had become bankrupt. Afterwards, Matassa remained a part-owner of the Jazz City Studios in New Orleans, as well as working at Sea-Saint studios and forming the Jefferson Jazz company with Marshall Sehorn.

Matchbox

Named after a **Carl Perkins**' classic, Matchbox were one of several 70s rock 'n' roll revivalist bands from the UK to make the jump from club favourites to chart stars. The band was formed in 1971 by two former members of Contraband - bassist Fred Poke and his brother-in-law Jimmy Redhead. They were joined by an old school friend of Poke's called Steve Bloomfield. Capable of playing almost any stringed instrument, Bloomfield had made a living as a session player for Pye and was on several **Mungo Jerry** hits. Matchbox's debut single came out on Dawn in 1973, after which Redhead's departure left a line-up of Wiffle Smith (vocals), Rusty Lipton (piano), Bob Burgos (drums), Bloomfield (guitars), and Poke (bass). They subsequently recorded *Riders In The Sky* for Charly. (They had previously recorded a Dutch only album on Rockhouse.) Smith and Lipton then departed, and former Cruisers vocalist Gordon Waters joined. The band were signed to a minor label and completed *Setting The Woods On Fire* in just over two days in October 1977, but as the record company were virtually bankrupt Chiswick took over its distribution. By this time however, Matchbox had signed up with Raw Records - which issued a single - and this led to complications. Chiswick did not promote the band because Matchbox were not signed to the label, and Raw declined to promote them because they did not own the album. In desperation the group bought themselves out of their contract and signed a new deal with Magnet. At this point they had been joined by vocalist Graham Fenton, previously with the Wild Bunch, the Houseshakers and the Hellraisers, and now Redhead returned, along with another guitarist Gordon Scott. The first Magnet single, 'Black Slacks', missed out, but the second - a Steve Bloomfield original called 'Rockabilly Rebel' - made the charts. A string of hit singles followed. One further line-up change came about when Bloomfield decided he did not want to tour anymore, and Dick Callan was brought in as a replacement for live appearances. Apart from Matchbox recordings, the group also put out a version of **Freddie Cannon**'s 'Palisades Park' under the pseudonym Cyclone. Steve Bloomfield released a solo album entitled *Rockabilly Originals*. The group is known as Major Matchbox outside the UK.

Albums: *Riders In The Sky* (1978), *Setting The Woods On Fire* (1979), *Matchbox* (1980), *Midnite Dynamos* (1980), *Flying Colours* (1981), *Crossed Line* (1983), *Going Down Town* (1985), *Rockabilly Rebel* (1993).

Material

One of **Bill Laswell**'s projects, Material was mixing jazz, funk and punk with hip-hop and scratch before the terms were invented; the result was stunning and powerful music. Basically comprising Michael Beinhorn, Fred Maher and Laswell, Material has also included **Fred Frith**, Sonny Sharrock, **Shankar**, **George Lewis**, **Henry Threadgill** and Olu Daru. After a long hiatus in its career, Material reappeared in 1989 with *Seven Souls*, when it seemed to be evolving into a 'new age' band. However, on *Third Power*, Laswell has assembled a new, back-on-the-block version that includes Shabba Ranks, the Jungle Brothers, **Herbie Hancock**, **Sly And Robbie** and **Fred Wesley**.

Albums: *Temporary Music 1 & 2* (1979, reissued as *Secret Life*), *Memory Serves* (1981), *One Down* (1983), *Seven Souls* (1989), *Third Power* (1991), *Hallucination Engine* (Axiom 1994).

Material Issue

Belonging to the pop rock tradition of **Tom Petty** and **Big Star**, Material Issue arrived in the mid-80s from Chicago, Illinois, USA, to great critical fanfare. The band consist of songwriter Jim Ellison (vocals/guitar; previously a member of fellow Chicago band, Green), Fred Ansani (bass/vocals) and Michael Zeleneko (drums). *Material Issue* was a six-track mini-album, co-produced by Jeff Murphy of the **Shoes**. The promise was confirmed with the arrival of their first full-length album which illustrated Ellison's flair for power pop composition, with songs recalling a golden age of US pop with a focus on guys and girls which was both heartfelt and innocent.

Albums: *Material Issue* (Big Block/Landmind 1987, mini-album), *International Pop Overthrow* (Mercury 1991), *Freak City Soundtrack* (Mercury 1994).

Mathieu, Mireille

b. 24 July 1946, Avignon, France. It was convenient, if inaccurate, for the media to brand her a second **Edith Piaf**, but Mathieu shared a similar poor upbringing. One of 13 children of a stone mason, she used some of her factory wages for singing lessons, until she was noticed by one of **Johnny Hallyday**'s former managers, Johnny Stark. He groomed her for stardom via an 'urchin' hair style by Elrhodes and, from celebrated *couturier* Louis Feraud, trademark red-and-black stage costumes. A showcase at the Paris Olympia led to a deal with Barclay Records and a run of hits that began with 'Mon Credo' in 1965. After this and later singles such as 'C'Est Ton Nom', 'Qu'Elle Est Belle' and 'Funambule' sold over a million collectively within Europe alone, the organization directed its gaze overseas. While a domestic television spectacular (directed by François Reichenbach) served as a grassroots holding operation, the artist's appearances on networked US shows (hosted, respectively, by **Ed Sullivan** and **Andy Williams**) established vital links with that lucrative market. During the same lengthy world tour, Mathieu was even heard in concert in Moscow where she sang 'Quand Fera-T-Il Jour Comrade', Gaston Bonheur's tempestuous anthem commemorating the October Revolution. Her impact on Britain was less tangible, though healthy sales of her 1968 album indicated a deeper groundswell of support than was evidenced by a solitary entry in the singles Top 30 the previous Christmas with a French interpretation of **Engelbert Humperdinck**'s 'The Last Waltz'. Later, Humperdinck stole UK chart honours with his cover of Mathieu's 'Les Bicyclettes De Belsize'. Both vocalists were featured on 1972's *Top Star Festival*, a charity compilation of international entertainers on which Mirielle performed 'Where Do I Begin' (from *Love Story*) - a rare genuflexion towards English-speaking listeners from one who had achieved global fame with a recorded repertoire which was invulnerably French, no matter what language the actual lyrics she sang.

Selected albums: *Mireille Mathieu* (1968), with Paul Anka *You And I* (1979), *Les Contes De Cri-Cri* (1985), *Recontres De Femme* (1988), *Greatest Hits Vol. 1* (1989).

Mathis, Country Johnny

b. 28 September 1933, Maud, Texas, USA. Not to be confused with his more successful namesake, this Johnny Mathis is a country singer/songwriter. He appeared on the *Big D Jamboree*, Dallas but moved to Shreveport and made his debut on the *Louisiana Hayride* in 1953. In 1954, he and Jimmy Lee Fautheree recorded as Jimmy And Johnny and gained a number 3 US country chart hit with his song 'If You Don't Somebody Else Will'. During his days at Shreveport, Mathis worked with **Johnny Horton** and co-wrote some songs with him including 'I'll Do It Everytime'. Horton also recorded some of Mathis' songs. Although Mathis appeared on the *Grand Ole Opry*, He had no solo chart hits after 'Please Talk To My Heart' in 1963. The following year that song became a Top 10 hit for **Ray Price** and, 16 years later, charted again for **Freddy Fender**. His songs have been recorded by many stars, including **George Jones**, **Faron Young**, **Charley Pride** and **Engelbert Humperdinck**. Mathis recorded both country and gospel material for Little Darlin' and Hilltop Gospel during the 60s and 70s, but despite being around the country music scene for three decades, he remains basically an unknown.

Albums: *Great Country Hits* (1964), *Country Johnny Mathis* (1965), *He Keeps Me Singing* (1967), *Come Home To My Heart* (1970), *The Best Of My Country* (1973), *Heartfelt* (1981).

Mathis, Johnny

b. John Royce Mathis, 30 September 1935, San Francisco, California, USA. In 1956, the 19-year-old Mathis was signed to **Columbia Records** where he began his career with a jazz-tinged album. A US Top 20 hit with 'Wonderful! Wonderful!' saw him move adroitly towards the balladeer market, and before long he was a major concert attraction, with regular appearances on highly-rated American television shows. In 1957, together with his first hit, Mathis was barely absent from the US best-sellers, and that year had a further five hits, including the number 1 'Chances Are', 'The Twelfth Of Never' and 'It's Not For Me To Say'. Mathis had become a phenomenon; his popularity at that time ranked with that of **Frank Sinatra**. By May 1958, he was scraping the UK charts with 'Teacher, Teacher', and soon established himself with major hits such as 'A Certain Smile', 'Winter Wonderland', 'Someone', 'Misty' and 'My Love For You'. His appeal to the adult market ensured spectacular album success, and *Johnny's Greatest Hits* stayed a record 490 weeks in the US chart. With the beat boom and 60's pop explosion making it more difficult for visiting American balladeers to infiltrate the singles chart, Mathis concentrated increasingly on releasing albums. Indeed, he seemed willing to tackle a variety of concepts presented by his various producers and arrangers. *Away From Home*, produced by **Norman Newell,** saw the singer concentrating on the songs of European composers; *Olé*, the Latin-American outing, was sung in Portuguese and Spanish; *Wonderful World Of Make Believe* consisted entirely of songs based on fairy tales; and there were tribute albums to such composers as **Burt Bacharach** and **Bert Kaempfert**. Meanwhile, Mathis suffered serious drug addiction, but fortunately managed to kick the habit.

By the late 60's, Mathis seemed equally adept at tackling MOR standards and **John Lennon/Paul McCartney** songs, as well as hoping to update his image. He returned to the UK singles chart in 1974 for the first time in a decade with 'I'm Stone In Love With You' and, two years later, secured the Christmas number 1 with 'When A Child Is Born'. Back in the USA, he was still searching for new ideas and in 1978, collaborated with **Deniece Williams** on 'Too Much, Too Late'. This, his first duet, brought a surprise number 1, his first US chart-topper since 1957. Since then, Mathis has duetted incessantly with a list that includes **Gladys Knight**, Paulette McWilliams, Stephanie Lawrence, Jane Oliver, **Dionne Warwick**, Angela Bofill, **Natalie Cole**, **Barbara Dickson** and **Nana Mouskouri**. What has been overlooked is Mathis's incredible commercial success: he is said to be the third most successful recording artist of all time, behind Sinatra and **Elvis Presley** and ahead of the **Beatles** and the **Rolling Stones**. His remarkable durability and unfailing professionalism demand admiration.

Selected albums: *Johnny Mathis* (1957), *Wonderful! Wonderful!* (1957), *Warm* (1957), *Heavenly* (1958), *Merry Christmas* (1958), *Swing Softly* (1958), *Good Night, Dear Lord* (1958), *Open Fire, Two Guitars* (1959), *Ride On A Rainbow* (1960), *Faithfully* (1960), *The Rhythms And Ballads Of Broadway* (1960), *Johnny's Mood* (1960), *I'll Buy You A Star* (1961), *Portrait Of Johnny* (1961), *Live It Up* (1962), *Rapture* (1962), *Johnny* (1963), *Romantically* (1963), *I'll Search My Heart* (1964), *Sounds Of Christmas* (1964), *Tender Is The Night* (1964), *The Wonderful World Of Make Believe* (1964), *Olé* (1965), *This Is Love* (1964), *Away From Home* (1965), *Love Is Everything* (1965), *The Sweetheart Tree* (1965), *The Shadow Of Your Smile* (1966), *So Nice* (1966), *Up, Up And Away* (1967), *Johnny Mathis Sings* (1967), *Love Is Blue* (1968), *Those Were The Days* (1968), *Johnny Mathis Sings The Music Of Bert Kaempfert* (1969), *The Impossible Dream* (1969), *Love Theme From 'Romeo And Juliet'* (1969), *People* (1969), *Raindrops Keep Fallin' On My Head* (1970), *The Long And Winding Road* (1970), *Johnny Mathis Sings The Music Of Bacharach And Kaempfert* (1970), *Close To You* (1970), *Love Story* (1971), *Christmas With Johnny Mathis* (1972), *You've Got A Friend* (1971), *Johnny Mathis In Person* (1972), *The First Time Ever I Saw Your Face* (1972), *Make It Easy On Yourself* (1972), *Me And Mrs Jones* (1973), *Killing Me Softly With Her Song* (1973), *I'm Coming Home* (1973), *Johnny Mathis Sings The Great Songs* (1974), *Song Sung Blue*

(1974), *The Heart Of A Woman* (1974), *When Will I See You Again* (1975), *Feelings* (1975), *I Only Have Eyes For You* (1976), *Sweet Surrender* (1977), *Mathis Is . . .* (1977), *You Light Up My Life* (1978), *When A Child Is Born* (1978), *The Best Days Of My Life* (1979), *Mathis Magic* (1979), *Tears And Laughters* (1980), *All For You* (1980), *Different Kinda Different* (1980), *Friends In Love* (1982), *A Special Part Of Me* (1984), *Johnny Mathis Live* (1985), *Right From The Heart* (1985), *The Hollywood Musicals* (1986), *How Do You Keep The Music Playing?* (Columbia 1993)
Further reading: *Johnny: The Authorized Biography Of Johnny Mathis*, Jasper, Tony (1984).

Matsuda, Seiko

b. Noriko Kamachi, 1962, Fukuoka, Japan. As extremely popular as her precedent, Momoe Yamaguchi, Matsuda had her first single, 'Hadashi No Kisetsu' ('The Season For Bare Feet') was released in 1980. As the theme song for a television commercial it became a substantial hit. The second single, 'Aoi Sangoshô ('A Blue Coral Reef'), rose in the chart of *Original Confidence*, a smaller Japanese equivalent to ***Billboard*** magazine, to number 2. Her third single, released that same year 'Kaze Wa Akiiro' ('The Colour Of The Wind Is Autumn'), easily topped the chart and began her unprecedented run of 24 consecutive chart-toppers, the last one of which was 'Tabidachi Wa Freesia' ('Starting On A Journey Feels Like A Freesia') in 1988. The cuteness of her appearance and voice has often been criticized as feigned innocence and prudishness, especially by her female critics. Her national popularity, however, has never substantially waned, and her public and private affairs are routinely headlined in the entertainment journals, including her marriage to a popular actor, Masateru Kanda, the birth of her baby, and her residential and professional life in New York - a life-style regarded by many Japanese observers as feministic.
Albums: *Squall* (1980), *North Wind* (1980), *Silhouette* (1981), *Kaze Tachinu* (*A Wind Blows*) (1981), *Matsuda Seiko* (1981), *Pineapple* (1982), *Index* (1982), *Candy* (1982), *Kin'irono Ribbon* (*A Golden Ribbon*) (1982), *Utopia* (1983), *Plaza* (1983), *Canary* (1983), *Touch Me* (1984), *Tinker Bell* (1984), *Seiko Town* (1984), *Windy Shadow* (1984), *Seiko Train* (1985), *The 9th Wave* (1985), *Sound Of My Heart* (1985), *Supreme* (1986), *Strawberry Time* (1987), *Show Garden* (1987), *Citron* (1988), *Precious Moment* (1989), *Seiko* (1990), *Eternal* (1991).
Further reading: *Seiko*, Noriko Kanda. *Matsuda Seiko Ron (On Seiko Matsuda)*, Chikako Ogura.

Matt Bianco

This UK jazz/pop group was formed in 1984 by ex-**Blue Rondo A La Turk** members Mark Reilly (b. 20 February 1960, High Wycombe, Buckinghamshire, England; lead vocals) and Daniel White (b. 26 August 1959, High Wycombe, Hertfordshire, England; keyboards), with **Basia** (b. Basha Trzetrzelewska, 30 September 1954, Jaworzno, Poland; vocals). They emerged in the latter part of the UK jazz/pop scene in the early 80s, inhabitated by other acts such as **Sade** and **Animal Nightlife**. Signed to the WEA distributed YZ label, they achieved a run of hits with the breezy, samba-laced 'Get Out Of Your Lazy Bed' (1984), 'Sneaking Out The Back Door'/'Matt's Moods' (1984), 'Half A Minute (1984) and a cover of **Georgie Fame**'s 'Yeh Yeh' (1985). The initial employment of various session musicians was abandoned in favour of a full-time group, taking on Mark Fisher (who had connections to the group in the capacity of songwriter), as keyboard player, plus Kito Poncioni (b. Rio, Brazil; bass). Basia left in 1986 to forge her own solo career and was replaced by Jenni Evans. Daniel White also left around this time. Basia and White recorded *Time And Tide* together and, because of White's contractual problems the album, and various singles from it, came out as Basia solo releases. By now Matt Bianco was, in pop terms, unfashionable; yet Reilly's fascination, and adeptness with fusing Latin rhythms to pop, gave the group another UK hit in 1988 with the number 11 single, 'Don't Blame It On That Girl'. Increasingly driven to cater for a select audience, the group has continued to produce specialized, quality pop music.
Albums: *Whose Side Are You On?* (1984), *Matt Bianco* (1986), *Indigo* (1988), *Samba In Your Casa* (1991). Compilation: *The Best Of Matt Bianco* (1990), *Yeah Yeah* (1993).

Mattea, Kathy

b. 21 June 1959, Cross Lane, West Virginia, USA. During her teens, Mattea began playing with her guitar at church functions and, when she attended university, she joined a bluegrass group, Pennsboro. She decided to go with the bandleader to Nashville and, amongst several jobs, she worked as a tour guide at the Country Music Hall Of Fame. Despite the competition, her vocal talents were appreciated and she was soon recording demos, jingles and commercials. In 1982, she became part of **Bobby Goldsboro**'s road show. She signed with **Mercury** and worked with **Don Williams**' producer, **Allen Reynolds**. Her first single, 'Street Talk', made the US country charts, and then, after some minor successes, her version of **Nanci Griffith**'s 'Love At The Five And Dime' reached number 3. She topped the US country charts with 'Goin' Gone', written by the delightfully eccentric Fred Koller, and had further chart-toppers with '18 Wheels And A Dozen Roses', 'Life As We Knew It', 'Come From The Heart' and 'Burnin' Old Memories'. Mattea is married to Jon Vezner, who won awards for the best country song of the year with Mattea's 'Where've You Been', written about his grandparents' love. Her 1991 album, *Time Passes By*, includes her version of 'From A Distance' which she recorded in Scotland with her friend, folksinger **Dougie MacLean**. Her song, 'Leaving West Virginia', is used by the West Virginia Department of Tourism. Mattea overcame persistent throat problems to record *Lonesome Standard Time* in 1992. Since then she has become part of the new wave of contemporary country females currently leading the way.

Albums: *Kathy Mattea* (1984), *From My Heart* (1985), *Walk The Way The Wind Blows* (1986), *Untasted Honey* (1987), *Willow In The Wind* (1989), *Time Passes By* (1991), *Lonesome Standard Time* (1992), *Untold Stories* (1993), *Good News* (1993), *Walking Away A Winner* (Mercury 1994). Compilation: *A Collection Of Hits* (1990), *Ready For The Storm Favourite Cuts* (Mercury 1995).

Videos *The Videos* (1994).

Matthews Southern Comfort

Formed in 1969 by former **Fairport Convention** singer/guitarist **Iain Matthews**, the group comprised Mark Griffiths (guitar), Carl Barnwell (guitar), Gordon Huntley (pedal steel guitar), Andy Leigh (bass) and Ray Duffy (drums). After signing to **EMI Records**, they recorded their self-titled debut album in late 1969. Country-tinged rather than folk, it nevertheless displayed Matthews' songwriting talents. In the summer of 1970, their next album, *Second Spring* reached the UK Top 40 and was followed by a winter chart-topper, 'Woodstock'. The single had been written by **Joni Mitchell** as a tribute to the famous festival that she had been unable to attend. Already issued as a single in a harde -rocking vein by **Crosby, Stills, Nash & Young**, it was a surprise UK number 1 for Matthews Southern Comfort. Unfortunately, success was followed by friction within the group and, two months later, Matthews announced his intention to pursue a solo career. One more album by the group followed, after which they truncated their name to Southern Comfort. After two further albums, they disbanded in the summer of 1972.

Albums: *Matthews Southern Comfort* (1969), *Second Spring* (1970), *Later That Same Year* (1970). As Southern Comfort: *Southern Comfort* (1971), *Frog City* (1971), *Stir Don't Shake* (1972).

Matthews, Al

b. Brooklyn, New York, USA. An all-round entertainer, Matthews began singing in New York street groups before progressing to the folk scene. He was a member of bands who supported artists including **Bob Dylan, Tom Paxton** and **Peter, Paul And Mary**, before moving to France where as a leading member of Petit Conservatoire de Chanson, he became a familiar voice on radio and television. Between 1965 and 1971, he served in Vietnam becoming the first black to be promoted to sergeant while still in the field. He returned to Europe and became successful on the English folk scene, and he later was signed by **CBS Records**. A UK Top 20 hit followed with 'Fool'. It also reached the Top 10 in 15 European countries. Although he continued to record, Matthews never matched his initial chart entry. In 1979, he became the first black disc jockey on BBC Radio 1. Throughout the 80s he turned his career entirely towards acting, starring in movies including *Aliens*, *Superman 3* and *Yanks*.

Albums: *Al Matthews* (1975), *It's Only Love* (1977).

Matthews, Dave, Band

Dave Matthews (b. c.1967, South Africa) moved to New York from his native country when he was just two years old. When his father died he moved back to Johannesburg with his mother, where he finished high school. He finally settled back in Charlottesville, and assembled his self-titled multi-racial band in the late 80s. The line-up comprises; Boyd Tinsley (violin), Carter Beauford (drums), Stefan Lessard (bass) and Leroi Moore (saxophone/flute). These exceptional musicians forged a vibrant, individual sound from elements moved away from the traditional rock format. This eclectic mix significantly complemented Matthews own expanded world view. Together they built a formidable reputation on the back of a punishing touring schedule, which helped their self-produced and financed debut, *Remember Two Things*, sell over 100,000 copies. In its wake the group were afforded the luxury of picking from the major record labels. Eventually choosing **RCA Records** (who offered the most malleable contract), their major label debut, *Under The Table And Dreaming*, produced by **Steve Lillywhite**, entered the ***Billboard*** charts at number 34 (eventually reaching number 11). The band are impossible to pigeonhole as they embrace rock, jazz folk, blues and R&B with incredible confidence and yet end up sounding totally refreshing and original. By mid-1995 their reputation in the USA was considerable, following a punishing performance schedule in support of the album which was still hovering around the US Top 20. The Dave Matthews Band is one of the most exciting and fresh units currently working in the USA. It is hoped that their eclectic mix will be appreciated by the rest of the world.

Albums: *Remember Two Things* (Bama Rags 1993), *Under The Table And Dreaming* (RCA 1994).

Matthews, Iain

b. Ian Matthews McDonald, 16 June 1946, Scunthorpe, Lincolnshire, England. Matthews sang with small-time Lincolnshire bands, the Classics, the Rebels and the Imps, before moving to London in 1966, as one of the vocalists in a British surfing band Pyramid, who recorded a few tracks for **Deram Records**. To supplement his income, Iain worked in a shoe shop in London's famous Carnaby Street. He learnt of a vacancy for a vocalist in **Fairport**

Convention, which he joined in 1967 before they had recorded (and before **Sandy Denny** joined them). He appeared on the group's first single 'If I Had A Ribbon Bow', released on Track and produced by Joe Boyd, and on their debut album on **Polydor**. Fairport then moved to **Island Records** in 1968, and Matthews appeared on their early breakthrough album, *What We Did On Our Holidays*, but left the group during the recording of mid-1969's *Unhalfbricking*, because it had become obvious to him that the group's new-found traditional folk/rock direction would involve him less than its previous contemporary 'underground' work.

Matthews (who had changed his surname to avoid confusion with saxophonist Ian McDonald of **King Crimson**) then signed with starmakers **Howard And Blaikley**, who had been involved in the success story of **Dave Dee**, **Dozy**, **Beaky**, **Mick And Tich**. After making a solo album *Matthews Southern Comfort*, for MCA in 1970, a group, also called **Matthews Southern Comfort**, was formed around him, and released two more country/rock albums, *Second Spring* and *Later That Same Year*. The group also topped the UK singles chart with their version of **Joni Mitchell**'s 'Woodstock'. By 1971, Matthews had left the band, which continued with little success as Southern Comfort. Matthews, meanwhile, signed a solo deal with **Vertigo**, releasing two excellent but underrated solo albums, *If You Saw Through My Eyes* and *Tigers Will Survive*, both featuring many of his ex-colleagues from Fairport, before forming Plainsong, an ambitious quartet which included Andy Roberts (ex-**Liverpool Scene**), Dave Richards and Bob Ronga. Matthews was still obligated to make another album for Vertigo, but was unwilling to commit Plainsong to the label. As a result, he was given a small budget to make a contractual commitment album, *Journeys From Gospel Oak*, which Vertigo did not release but instead sold to Mooncrest, a label with which the album's producer Sandy Robertson was connected. Originally released in 1974, it became one of the earliest compact disc releases to feature Matthews' post-Fairport work. Plainsong then signed with **Elektra**, and released the magnificent *In Search Of Amelia Earhart* in 1972, before Bob Ronga left the band. During the recording of a second album (still unreleased, but supposedly titled *Plainsong III*, referring to the membership of the band rather than a third album), Matthews and Richards apparently fell out. To continue would have been difficult, and Matthews accepted an invitation to work with ex-**Monkee Michael Nesmith** in Los Angeles. An excellent solo album (organized and encouraged by Nesmith), *Valley Hi*, was followed by *Some Days You Eat The Bear*, which included the **Tom Waits** song, 'Ol' 55', which Matthews recorded a month earlier than label-mates the **Eagles**. He then signed with **CBS** for *Go For Broke* and *Hit And Run*, which were neither commercially successful nor artistically satisfactory. By 1978, Matthews was again 'available for hire', at which point Rockburgh (which was owned by Sandy Robertson) offered to re-sign him. The first fruit of this reunion was *Stealing Home*, on which the backing musicians included Bryn Haworth and Phil Palmer on guitar, and **Pete Wingfield** on piano. Robertson licensed the album for North America to a small Canadian label, Mushroom, which had been financed by the discovery of the group **Heart**. 'Shake It' was excerpted as a US single and reached the Top 10, but the founder and owner of Mushroom died suddenly, and the company virtually collapsed. A follow-up by Matthews, *Siamese Friends*, was already contracted to Mushroom, but swiftly vanished with little trace in the UK.

In 1980 came a third album for Rockfield, *A Spot Of Interference*, which was an ill-judged attempt to climb aboard the new wave. This also disappeared, and later that same year came *Discreet Repeat*, a reasonably selected double album 'Best Of' featuring post-Southern Comfort material, but this marked the parting of the waves between Matthews and Robertson. The former formed an unlikely band called Hi-Fi in Seattle, where he lived with ex-**Pavlov's Dog** vocalist David Surkamp. Two more contrasting vocal styles than those of Surkamp and Matthews could hardly be imagined, but the group made a live mini-album, *Demonstration Records*, in 1982, and followed it with a full- length studio album, *Moods For The Mallards* - both were released in the UK on the small independent label, Butt Records.

In 1983, Matthews signed with Polydor in Germany for a new album, *Shook*, which surprisingly remains unreleased in Britain, and more importantly from the artistic point of view, the USA. Matthews threw in the towel and took a job as an A&R man for Island Music in Los Angeles, but was made redundant in 1985. An appearance at the 1986 Fairport Convention Cropredy Festival in Oxfordshire convinced Matthews that he should return to singing, even though he had just ended a period of unemployment by starting to work for the noted new age label, Windham Hill. After a frustrating year during which it became clear that Matthews and the label were creatively at odds, Matthews left, but only after recording a vocal album for the predominantly instrumental label, *Walking A Changing Line* released in 1988, on which he interpreted a number of songs written by **Jules Shear** (ex-Funky Kings and Jules And The Polar Bears). While this was his best album to date according to Matthews, it sold little better than anything since *Stealing Home*.

In 1989, Matthews relocated to Austin, Texas, where he linked up with Mark Hallman, a guitarist and producer who had worked on 'Changing Line'. A cassette-only album by the duo, *Iain Matthews Live*, was made for sale at gigs, and Matthews signed in 1990 with US independent label Goldcastle, to which several comparative veterans, including **Joan Baez** and Karla Bonoff, were also contracted. *Pure And Crooked* was released in 1990, and later that same year, Matthews reunited with his Plainsong-era colleague, Andy Roberts, for a very popular appearance at Cambridge Folk Festival. By 1992, Goldcastle had gone out of business, leaving Matthews, an exceptional vocalist with excellent taste in both self-composed material and especially in cover versions, once again without a recording contract. In 1993 Matthews and Roberts released *Dark Side Of The Room* under the Plainsong monicker, which was funded by a German record-maker and supporter.

Albums: *If You Saw Through My Eyes* (1970), *Tigers Will Survive* (1971), *Journeys From Gospel Oak* (1972), *Valley Hi* (1973), *Somedays You Eat The Bear* (1974), *Go For Broke* (1975), *Hit And Run* (1976), *Stealing Home* (1978), *Siamese Friends* (1979), *A Spot Of Interference* (1980), *Shook* (1983), *Walking A Changing Line* (1988), *Pure And Crooked* (1990), *Nights In Manhattan - Live* (1991), *Orphans And Outcasts Vol. 1* (1991, *The Dark Ride* (Watermelon 1994). Compilation: *Discreet Repeat* (1980). With Plainsong *In Search Of Amelia Earhart* (1972), *Dark Side Of The Room* (1993).

Matthews, Jessie

b. 11 March 1907, London, England, d. 19 August 1981, Pinner, Middlesex, England. A member of a large and poor family, Matthews became a professional dancer at the age of 10. After a few years in the chorus of several shows in London's West End, she achieved recognition with a series of ingenue roles and some bit parts in films. After appearing in stage production such as *André Charlot's Revue Of 1926*, ***Earl Carroll****'s Vanities Of 1926*, *Jordan*, *This Year Of Grace*, *Wake Up And Dream* (London and New York), *Hold My Hand*, and *Sally Who?*, by the early 30s she had become one of London's most popular stars. At the height of her career, in such shows as the 1930 London production of ***Ever Green***, with a score by **Richard Rodgers** and **Lorenz Hart**, Matthews was the epitome of the English musical comedy star: her delicate build and translucent beauty fully matched songs such as that show's ethereal 'Dancing On The Ceiling'. Her film work also grew, and she made several British movies in which she shone effortlessly. Despite an appearance in the 1934 film version of her stage hit, slightly retitled as ***Evergreen*** - in which she introduced 'Over My Shoulder', one of 'identity songs - few of Matthews' film musicals were worthy of her talent. They included *Out Of The Blue*, *Waltzes From Vienna*, ***First A Girl***, *It's Love Again*, *Head Over Heels*, *Gangway*, and *Sailing Along* (1938). An outstanding dancer, the variable quality of her films militated against her continuing for long and by the 40s, her career was all but over. Her last appearance on a London stage in this part of her career was in the 1942 production of *Wild Rose*. After many years away from the public eye, spent mostly in Australia, she returned to the screen in 1958 as the mother in *Tom Thumb*, and in 1963 took over the title role in the daily BBC radio serial *Mrs Dale's Diary*. In the 70s she was seen on the London stage in *The Water Babies* and *Lady Windemere's Fan*, and also appeared on television in the series *Edward And Mrs. Simpson*. Her one-woman show *Miss Jessie Matthews In Concert*, which was produced in Los Angeles in 1979, won the US Drama Critics Award. In 1993/94, when the Adelphi Theatre in London was being lavishly restored under the supervision of its co-owner, the celebrated composer and producer **Andrew Lloyd Webber** - a great admirer of Jessie Matthews, one of the bars in the theatre was named in her honour.

Further reading: *Over My Shoulder: An Autobiography*, Jessie Matthews. *Jessie Matthews - A Biography*, Michael Thornton.

Matthewson, Ron

b. Rognuald Andrew Matthewson, 19 February 1944, Lerwick, Shetland Isles, Scotland. Matthewson began playing piano at the age of three, but switched to bass at 16. The first band he played with was a local quartet in which he was teamed with a violinist, pianist and an accordionist playing reels and old-time dances. His first jazz enthusiasm was for trad stars **Acker Bilk** and **Chris Barber**, and his first engagements with a well-known band were with the Clyde Valley Stompers, with whom he moved to London in 1962. After a spell back in the Shetlands working for the Herring Industry Board, he returned to London to work with **Alex Welsh** in 1964. He began to work in a modern jazz context with **John Stevens**, then returned to Welsh's band for a while before spending time with John Cox, **Tubby Hayes**, the **Kenny Clarke/Francy Boland** Big Band, **Philly Joe Jones**, **Phil Woods**' European Rhythm Machine, **Gordon Beck**'s Gyroscope, Stan Sulzmann, **Kenny Wheeler** and a long spell with **Ronnie Scott**'s Quintet. There was also a duo with bassist Ron Rubin.

Album: *All In The Morning* (1972).

Mattôya, Yumi

b. Yumi Arai, 29 January 1954, Tokyo, Japan. As the daughter of a rich draper who could afford to give her private lessons in music, Yumi developed into a female singer-songwriter, debuting in 1972 with 'Henji Wa Iranai' ('I Don't Want Any Reply'). Her fifth single, 'Anohi Ni Kaeritai' ('I Want To Go Back To That Day'), topped the Japan singles chart in 1975, after she married, taking the name Mattôya. The sense of airy urbanity that has characterized her lyrics and music, as well as the way they were performed, contributed towards turning what had usually been called 'folk' - a derivation of the kind of music earlier developed by **Bob Dylan** - into 'new music', a field that would later

overwhelm kayôkyoku, formerly the most common style of popular song in Japan. The eclectic music of Mattôya, who is fondly called Yûmin, has been especially popular among female listeners.
Albums: *Hikôkigumo* (*A Vapor Trail*) (1973), *Misslim* (1974), *Cobalt Hour* (1975), *Yuming Brand* (1976), *Jûyobanmeno Tsuki* (*The Fourteenth Moon*) (1976), *Album* (1977), *Kujaku* (*Peacock*) (1978), *Ryûsenkei* (*Streamline*) (1978), *Olive* (1979), *Kanashiihodono Otenki* (*Touchingly Fine Weather*) (1979), *Tokinonai Hotel* (*A Timeless Hotel*) (1980), *Surf And Snow* (1980), *Mizunonakano Asiae* (*Into Asia In Water*) (1981), *Sakuban Oaishimashô* (*See You Last Night*) (1981), *Pearl Pierce* (1982), *Reincarnation* (1983), *Voyager* (1983), *No-Side* (1984), *Da-Di-Da* (1985), *Alarm A La Mode* (1986), *Diamond Dustga Kienumani* (*Before The Diamond Dust Disperses*) (1987), *Delight Slight Light Kiss* (1988), *Love Wars* (1989), *Tenhokuno Door* (*Heaven's Door*) (1990).
Further reading: *Rouge-no Dengon* (*Message In Rouge*), Yumi Mattôya. *Yûminno Toiki* (*Sighs Of Yûmin*), Haruka Fukami.

Matumbi

Nowadays largely remembered for being home to **Dennis Bovell**'s first musical adventures, Matumbi should nevertheless be considered in their own right as a leading voice in the UK's 70s reggae scene. Formed in south London in 1971 by Tex Dixon (vocals), he pulled together a nucleus which comprised Uton Jones (drums), Errol Pottinger (guitar), Bevin Fagan, Glaister Fagan and Nicholas Bailey (vocals), alongside the aforementioned Bovell (guitar). They took their name from the African word for 'rebirth', and in the customary manner of early UK reggae bands, first found employment backing visiting Jamaican musicians. After signing to **Trojan** early singles included 'Brother Louie' and 'Wipe Them Out', but it was the subsequent singles, 'After Tonight' and 'Man In Me', which brought them major commercial recognition. The latter was the biggest selling UK reggae single of 1976. However, success almost immediately brought internal friction, exacerbated by Trojan's attitude. They were diquietened by the way individual members were partaking of several outside projects, rather than concentrating on establishing the band as a top name. An injunction was finally served, with the result that Bailey and Dixon quit, and Uton Jones was replaced on drums by Jah 'Bunny' Donaldson. Bailey would go on to solo 'pop' successes with **Nick Straker**. The remaining members moved on to a contract with **EMI** subsidiary Harvest, bolstering their profile by joining **Ian Dury And The Blockheads** on tour. *Seven Seals* was an effective long playing debut, but it was the follow-up, *Point Of View*, with garnered most plaudits. The title-track, a mix of reggae, soul and **Glen Miller**, reached the Top 40, and for a time it seemed Matumbi might occupy the commercial high ground which many UK reggae bands had aspired to. It was not to be, two albums followed but popular taste had bypassed Matumbi, and the members resumed their solo projects. Bunny joined the **Cimarons**, and Glaister Fagan and Blake came to be known as the Squad, seeing some chart success as such. Bovell pursued his own idiosyncratic vision working both inside and outside of the reggae medium.
Albums: *Seven Seals* (Harvest 1978), *Point Of View* (EMI 1979), *Dub Planet* (Extinguish 1980). Compilation: *Best Of* (Trojan 1978).

Maughan, Susan

b. 1 July 1942, Newcastle-upon-Tyne, Tyne And Wear, England. A popular and vivacious singing star in the UK during the 60s, Susan Maughan began her singing career in 1958 as a member of a popular midland band led by Ronnie Hancock. Their 1961 demonstration disc alerted the Philips label to her talent, and a year within the **Ray Ellington** Quartet ran concurrent with a nascent recording career which began with the timely 'Mama Do The Twist'. Maughan enjoyed chart success when the effervescent 'Bobby's Girl' reached the UK Top 3 in 1962, but although 'Hand A Handkerchief To Helen' and 'She's New To You' (both 1963) were minor hits, she was unable to repeat this early triumph. Maughan nonetheless continued to record, and albums featuring a full orchestra (*Swingin' Susan*) or a jazzband (*Hey Look Me Over*) showed her versatility. In 1965, along with a host of other pop stars such as **Billy J. Kramer**, the **Animals**, **Peter and Gordon**, **Matt Monro**, and **Herman's Hermits**, she appeared in the 'mock concert' film *Pop Gear*, which was hosted by Jimmy Savile. Nearly 30 years later, in 1992, Susan Maughan joined another survivor from those far off days, **Jess Conrad**, in the UK tour of *The Golden Sounds Of The Sixties*.
Albums: *Swingin' Susan* (1962), *Sentimental Susan* (1963), *Hey Look Me Over* (1966).

Maupin, Bennie

b. 29 August 1940, Detroit, Michigan, USA. Maupin played saxophone in high school before studying music at the Detroit Institute for Music Art. He came to New York, in 1963 making his living from commercial music while playing with saxophonists **Marion Brown** and **Pharoah Sanders**. In 1966, he played with **Roy Haynes** and in 1968 joined the **Horace Silver** Quintet. By 1969, drummer **Jack DeJohnette** had introduced him to **Miles Davis** who made his bass clarinet improvisations an integral part of *Bitches Brew*. He went on to play with pianists **Chick Corea** and **Andrew Hill** before joining **Herbie Hancock**'s sextet in 1970. He played with the band which recorded the influential *Headhunters*, and continued with Hancock when the sextet became the funk band. He settled in Los Angeles where he has worked ever since.

Albums: with Miles Davis *Bitches Brew* (1969), with Chick Corea *Sundance* (1969), with Andrew Hill *One For One* (1970), with Herbie Hancock *Mwandishi* (1971), *Crossings* (1972), *Sextant* (1973), *Headhunters* (1973), *The Jewel In The Lotus* (1974), *VSOP* (1976), *Slow Traffic To The Right* (1977).

Mauriat, Paul

b. 1925, France. A conductor, arranger and composer, descended from generations of classical musicians, Mauriat began to study music at the age of four, and continued his studies at the Conservatoire in Paris when his family moved there in 1935. His initial ambition to become classical pianist gave way to an interest in popular music and jazz. When he was 17, Mauriet formed his own orchestra and, for several years, toured concert halls and theatres in Europe. His big break came when he began arranging and conducting for recordings by **Charles Aznavour**, a relationship which endured, and led to him working with other French artists. In the 60s his distinctive, melodic, arrangements on his own instrumental albums with a contemporary beat, gained him a substantial following. In 1962, under the pseudonym Del Roma, Mauriat co-wrote 'Chariot', which, sung in French, became a big Continental hit for **Petula Clark**. In the following year, with an alternative lyric by Norman Gimbel and Arthur Altman, the song was re-titled 'I Will Follow Him', and was taken to the top of the US chart by **Little Peggy March**. Mauriat's own success in America was sparked off in 1968, when his enormous international hit version of 'L'Amour Est Bleu' ('Love Is Blue'), Luxembourg's entry in the 1963 Eurovision Song contest, spent five weeks in the number 1 spot. He repeated the feat with *Blooming Hits*, a collection of 60s favourites, including Eurovision winner 'Puppet On A String' and **John Lennon/Paul McCartney**'s 'Penny Lane', which is reputed to have sold well over two million copies. This all led to major television appearances and tours throughout the USA and Mexico, Latin America, Japan, and many other countries. Mauriat had two other minor US hit singles, 'Love In Every Room' and 'Chitty Chitty Bang Bang', but his albums continued to sell in large quantities.
Selected albums: *Memories of Russia* (early 60s), *Rhythm And Blues* (early 60s), *A Taste Of Paul Mauriat* (early 60s), *Blooming Hits* (1967), *More Mauriat* (1968), *Mauriat Magic* (1968), *Prevailing Airs* (1968), *Doing My Thing* (1969), *The Soul Of Paul Mauriat* (1969), *L.O.V.E.* (1969), *Gone Is Love* (1970), *El Condor Pasa* (1971), *Tout Pour La Musiique* (1982), *Magic* (1984), *I Love Breeze* (1984), *Penelope* (1984), *Magic Laser Hits* (1985), *The Seven Seas* (1985), *Windy* (1986).

Maurice And Mac

(Maurice McAlister and Green McLauren). One of the long lost soul duos of the 60s, Chicago-based Maurice And Mac's output for the Checker label between 1967 and 1970 contained both upbeat and slow-tempo examples of gospel-based soul as good as anything by better-known duos like **Sam And Dave** or **James And Bobby Purify**. Maurice And Mac were founder-members of the fine Chicago R&B/early soul group, the **Radiants**, who began recording for **Chess** in 1962. The group itself stemmed from the young people's choir of the local Greater Harvest Baptist Church. Both McAlister and McLauren sang with the choir, but Maurice McAlister first came to notice in gospel circles as early as 1956 when he formed the Golden Gospeltones quartet together with Leonard Caston. Caston, the son of famous bluesman, **Leonard 'Baby Doo' Caston**, and a long-time associate of **Willie Dixon**, later wrote and produced for ex-**Temptation Eddie Kendricks** at **Motown**, and formed Caston And Majors. In 1960, Caston and McAlister joined a doo-wop group, the Radiants, with McAlister on lead, plus Wallace Sampson, Jerome Brooks, Elzie Butler and Charles Washington, later replaced by Green 'Mac' McLauren. In 1962, they signed for Chess, and cut 'One Day I'll Show You', which combined doo-wop with soul, and 'Father Knows Best'. On the strength of their first secular recording, they appeared at Harlem's **Apollo**, but were still members of the Greater Harvest Baptist Church choir that recorded a gospel album and two singles for the Sharp label in the same year (1962), with McAlister taking lead on 'Steal Away' and McLauren on 'What A Difference In My Life'. By early 1963 they had left the Church, and a further nine Radiants Chess singles, chiefly featuring McAlister on lead, appeared up until 1966. Green McLauren enlisted in the US armed forces in late 1963, and was replaced for a time by Frank McCollum, before the Radiants continued to work as a trio. The group had some sucess in 1965 with 'Voice Your Choice' and 'It Ain't No Big Thing', both of which made the R&B and Hot 100 Charts. There were two further hits in 1967/8, but with a different Radiants lineup. Maurice McAlister left to go solo in mid-1966, and cut one recording for Chess later that year ('Baby Hang On'), but, after it flopped, he teamed up with the newly demobbed Green 'Mac' McLauren. As Maurice And Mac they were allotted to the Checker label and sent south to Rick Hall's 'Fame' studio in Muscle Shoals. The initial recordings contrasted the duo's churchy vocals with the sympathetic sound of Fame's premier soul-loving rhythm-section. They included the ultradeep 'Lean On Me' and 'You're The One', the slightly pacier but still deep cover of **Ben E. King**'s 'So Much Love', the lilting mid-tempo of 'Why Don't You Try Me', the driving soul of 'Try Me', and an excellent version of the much-covered 'You Left The Water Running', first recorded by Billy Young. They were followed by other great cuts such as the rhythmic 'Love Power', which was re-released on the

superb 1984 Japanese P-Vine album, containing all of Maurice And Mac's best material. Poor promotion by Chess/Checker affected those, and subsequent issues, such as their Chicago sides which included the deep *crie de coeur* 'What Am I Gonna Do', 'Lay It On Me', 'Oh What A Time', 'Baby You're The One' (arguably the duo's most beautiful deep ballad), 'Kick My Cat, I'll Beat Your Dog', and the very churchy, slow-building deepie, 'But You Know I Love You'. The latter single was released on Checker in 1970, and in the following year the Chess label reissued 'Lay It On Me' coupled with 'You Can't Say I Didn't Try'. McAlister's high pitched tenor and McLauren's deeper gospelly baritone, combined on one last single for Brown Sugar in 1972 ('Use That Good Thing'/'Ain't No Harm To Moan'), before the pair split up. McLauren disappeared completely from the music scene, and McAlister spent some time making television jingles, before working as an an appliance-repair man in Chicago. In the 80s, he was reported to be playing a few local clubs with a newly-formed band.
Compilation: *Lean On Me* (1984).

Maurizio

Berlin DJ and recording artist who runs the Basic Channel label. He is famed for placing only a large M on the centre of his records, then pressing them in America so they are presumed to have emerged from Detroit. Cuts like 'Domina' (1994) highlighted his experimental but accessible craft, while collaborations with genuine native Detroit man **Carl Craig** ('Mind') proffered further cult status.

Mauro, Turk

b. Mauro Turso, 11 June 1944, New York City, New York, USA. Mauro began playing clarinet while still in school and was largely self-taught. By the age of 15, he was sufficiently proficient both on this instrument and the alto saxophone to obtain his union card. In 1960, he joined **Red Allen**'s quartet, playing at clubs in Queens and Harlem. After graduation, Mauro decided to become a professional musician and around this time switched to tenor saxophone. Not surprisingly for a musician of his generation, he was attracted to jazz-rock, though between these gigs he would sit in at the Half Note club with jazzmen such as **Zoot Sims**, **Al Cohn**, **Nat Pierce** and **Dave Frishberg**. In the late 60s, he played at holiday resorts in upstate New York - originally as a sideman - but later leading a danceband playing Latin American music. Subsequently, he led a small group at the Half Note, then worked with **Richie Cole** before becoming resident at Sonny's Place, a club on Long Island where he remained for more than a dozen years. He found time, however, for appearances with the bands of **Dizzy Gillespie**, **Buddy Rich** and others. Of greater long-term significance were some appearances with **Billy Mitchell**, for whom he had to play baritone saxophone. Gradually, over the years, Mauro became steadily more proficient on the baritone until it eventually became his principal instrument. In the early 80s, he worked solo in New York and also toured Europe, both as a single performer and with Cole. He appeared in Paris and London and also at various festivals. Back in New York in the mid-80s, he had to take work outside of music to help make ends meet; but, in 1987, he decided to return to Europe and settle in Paris. Although of an age to have come under more modern influences, Mauro's chief musical mentors are great mainstreamers such as tenor saxophonists **Ben Webster**, **Coleman Hawkins**, **Lester Young**, **Stan Getz** and **Dexter Gordon** - though he also acknowledges debts to Sims, Cohn, Mitchell, **Gene Ammons** and others with whom he has worked. As such a list indicates Mauro still thinks of himself as a tenor player. Perhaps this is what has allowed him to develop an interesting and highly distinctive baritone style. His playing is forceful, fiery and committed, and his occasional vocal excursions show a tough, no-nonsense approach and considerable rhythmic vitality.
Selected albums: *The Underdog* (Storyville 1978), *The Heavyweight* (Phoenix 1980), *Live In Paris* (Bloomdido 1987), *Jazz Party* (Bloomdido 1993), *Plays Love Songs* (Bloomdido 1993).

Mavericks

This country-rock band were formed in Miami, Florida, a region better known for its dance and rock music than any fondness for country. Lead singer and songwriter Raul Malo (vocals/guitar) was born in Miami of Cuban descent. His parents' record collection was full of American roots music and rockabilly, and led to his discovery of **Johnny Cash**, **Elvis Presley** and **Bill Haley**. He also grew particularly fond of the dramatic intensity of the ballads sung by **Roy Orbison** and **Patsy Cline**. However, nobody at his school shared his taste, until he came across Robert Reynolds (bass). Reynolds was also a fan of older bands, and had previously been unable to find anyone to share his fascination with old country records. His best friend was Paul Deakin (drums), who had played with local progressive rock bands for several years. The played the Florida rock circuit having realised that the few country venues wanted covers bands only. They used the opportunity to set about building a set of strong original songs, steering away from too close an approximation of their heroes because, as Reynolds conceded, 'it's one thing to touch the nerve of older styles, it's another to let yourself be engulfed by them'. The band independently released a 13-song album in 1990. This eventually reached the ears of the Nashville record companies, and **MCA Records** flew them to the country music capital for a showcase. Legend has it that the company decided to make their offer before

the end of the band's sound check. Their debut for MCA, *From Hell To Paradise*, was a minor success, but it was with *What A Crying Shame* that they made their breakthrough when it sold over half a million copies. It was produced by Don Cook (who had also worked with **Mark Collie** and **Brooks & Dunn**) and it included covers such as **Bruce Springsteen**'s 'All That Heaven Will Allow' and **Jesse Winchester**'s 'O What A Thrill'. The group then added a second guitarist, Nick Kane. The Mavericks are not to be confused with the UK band of the same name formed in the 90s by the former **Sex Pistols**' bass player, Glenn Matlock.
Albums: *The Mavericks* (Y&T 1990), *From Hell To Paradise* (MCA 1992), *What A Crying Shame* (MCA 1994).

Max And The Broadway Metal Choir

'The Devil gave us Death Metal and God gave us Max' - that's how the publicity introduced us to Maximilan Gelt - a Jewish delicatessen owner from Miami, Florida, in his late 40s. It seems that Max was contacted by a friend to come to London to see a band, the Broadway Metal Choir, featuring Jan Cyrka (guitar), Kevin Riddles (ex-**Angelwitch/Tytan** bass), Kevin Fitzpatrick (keyboards) and Andy Beirne (drums). As they lacked a vocalist Max put himself up for the job and got it, but after six weeks of touring he broke his leg and returned to Miami. Later he returned to London armed with new songs, and together with **FM** and guitarist Steve Boltz, backing singers Suzie O'List and Gillian O'Donovan and recorded 10 tracks. The press loved the story but not the finished product and, dejected, Max returned home to face a different type of music. His wife, Shirly, had launched divorce proceedings, claiming his recent obsession with heavy metal music had driven him 'insane'. The rest of the band split and returned to session work.
Album: *And God Gave Us Max* (Powerstation 1986).

Max Frost And The Troopers

Max Frost And The Troopers were a fictional group created for the 1968 hippie-exploitation film, *Wild In The Streets*. Frost was actor Christopher Jones (more interestingly, the Troopers' drummer was a young Richard Pryor). Their role in the film was to gain voting rights for 14-year-olds. Frost is elected president of the USA at the film's climax, and he orders everyone over 30 into concentration camps, where they are forced to take LSD. His band's songs were equally absurd semi-political rants ('14 Or Fight') save for one bona fide folk-punk classic, 'Shape Of Things To Come'. Written by **Barry Mann** and **Cynthia Weil**, the song was actually recorded by a group called the 13th Power. However, it was released under the name Max Frost And The Troopers to capitalize on the film's success with the youth market, and eventually reached number 22 in the USA.
Album: *Wild In The Streets* (1968).

Max Webster

Toronto, Canada-based group put together by guitarist **Kim Mitchell**, who had worked with various bands over the years including **MC5** and **Alice Cooper**. Mitchell was very much the central figure due to his on-stage showmanship and guitar ability. He was backed by Dave Myles on bass, Terry Watkinson on keyboards and Gerry McCracken on drums. Their second album in particular is worthy of any record collection. The UK proved a hard nut to crack but they tried hard in 1979 with two albums and a single, 'Paradise Skies', that featured guest appearances from fellow Canadians, **Rush**. For some reason British audiences turned their back on the band and most of the tour was cancelled. 1980's *Universal Juveniles* did bring back some dignity but their career and songwriting was on the wane and by 1982 they had split up. Mitchell continued as a solo artist.
Albums: *Hangover* (Mercury 1976), *High Class In Borrowed Shoes* (Mercury 1977), *Mutiny Up My Sleeve* (Capitol 1978), *A Million Vacations* (Capitol 1979), *Live Magnetic Air* (Capitol 1979), *Universal Juveniles* (Mercury 1980).

Maximum Joy

Like other Y label acts **Shriekback** and **Pigbag**, Bristol-based Maximum Joy explored a refreshing brand of independent funk that was in vogue in the UK during the early 80s. Formed by ex-**Pop Group** members John Waddington (guitar/vocals) and Dan Katsis (bass), the band was swelled by Janine Rainforth (vocals/clarinet/violin), Tony Wrafter (saxophone/flute/trumpet) and Charles Llewellyn (drums/percussion). The group's first two singles 'Stretch' (1981), 'White And Green Place' (1982) featured in the UK Independent Top 20. Later in the year, 'In The Air' preceded what was to be Maximum Joy's sole album, by which time Katsis had been replaced by Kevin Evans. Produced by Adrian Sherwood, this encapsulated Maximum Joy's at times quirky blend of percussion and funky instrumental flair, characterized by distinctive horns. With the departure of Wrafter later in the year, Dan Katsis rejoined for saxophone duties. After a healthy rendition of **Timmy Thomas**' 70s soul classic, 'Why Can't We Live Together', Maximum Joy disbanded.
Album: *Station M.X.J.Y...* (1982).

Maxwell, Jimmy

b. 9 January 1917, Stockton, California, USA. After extensive studies in all aspects of brass playing, Maxwell established himself as a major-league trumpet player. Among his first professional engagements was one in the early 30s with **Gil Evans**, who was raised in Maxwell's home town. By the end of the decade he had played in the trumpet sections of several leading dance and swing bands, including those of **Jimmy Dorsey**

and **Benny Goodman**. His stint with Goodman lasted from 1939-43, when he joined **CBS**. During the 30 years this job lasted he found time to work with **Woody Herman**, **Count Basie**, **Gerry Mulligan**, **Duke Ellington**, **Quincy Jones** and others. Among his Ellington engagements was an informal appearance on stage at the famous Newport concert in 1956, when **Willie Cook** was late returning to the stand. In the 70s he played with the New York Jazz Repertory Company under **Dick Hyman**, with **Lionel Hampton**'s All-Star Big Band and with **Chuck Israels**'s National Jazz Ensemble. After Ellington's death, he also played in the band which continued for a while under **Mercer Ellington**. Since the late 70s, Maxwell has employed his early training and subsequent breadth of playing experience to good effect as a teacher. He has also published a trumpet manual.
Albums: with Benny Goodman *Benny And Sid 'Roll 'Em'* (1941), with Chuck Israels *National Jazz Ensemble* (1976), *Strong Trumpet* (1977), *Let's Fall In Love* (c.1980).

May Blitz

Formed in 1969, May Blitz comprised guitarist James Black and drummer Tony Newman, both veterans of **Sounds Incorporated** and the **Jeff Beck** Group. They were subsequently joined by Reid Hudson (bass). *May Blitz* showcased the trio's forceful sound and, in particular, Black's aggressive style, but it failed to emulate the success of stablemates **Uriah Heep** and **Black Sabbath**. *The Second Of May* was less satisfying and the group split up soon after its release. Newman subsequently joined Three Man Army and **Boxer**.
Albums: *May Blitz* (1970), *The Second Of May* (1971).

May, Billy

b. 10 November 1916, Pittsburgh, Pennsylvania, USA. May's first impact on the big band scene came in 1938, when he joined the trumpet section of the **Charlie Barnet** Band and, most notably, began contributing arrangements. Amongst his best-known charts was Barnet's hit record of the old **Ray Noble** song, 'Cherokee'. In 1939, he joined **Glenn Miller**, bringing a previously absent vitality to the trumpet section and more fine arrangements. In 1942, he also wrote arrangements for **Les Brown** and **Alvino Rey**. The early 40s found him in great demand in radio and film studios, but he continued to write for popular bands of the day. When **Capitol Records** was formed, with a policy which called for the highest standards of musicianship, May was employed to write and direct for many major singing stars, including **Frank Sinatra**, **Peggy Lee** and **Nat 'King' Cole**. During the 50s, May also began making big band albums, on which he gave full rein to his highly distinctive arranging style. Although adept at all kinds of big band music, he had a particular fondness for voicing the reed section in thirds, creating a so-called 'slurping' saxophone sound. Among his band's successes were arrangements of 'All Of Me', 'Lulu's Back In Town', 'Charmaine', 'When My Sugar Walks Down The Street', 'Lean Baby' and 'Fat Man Boogie' (the last two also his own compositions). His recording of the movie theme, 'The Man With The Golden Arm', made the UK Top 10 in 1956. For his studio band, May called upon such reliable sidemen as Murray McEachern, Ted Nash and Alvin Stoller. He also wrote for television, lending musical quality to series such as *Naked City* and to the occasional commercial. More recently, he was musical director on the recording dates on which swing era music was recreated for a series of albums issued by *Time-Life*.
Albums: *A Band Is Born* (1951-55), *Sorta May* (1954), *Sorta Dixie* (1955), *Billy May And His Orchestra* i (1956), *The Great Jimmie Lunceford* (1957), *Billy May And His Orchestra* ii (1958), *The Girls And Boys On Broadway* (1958), *Billy May And His Orchestra* iii (1963), *Billy May And His Orchestra* iv (1966), *I Believe In You* (c.70s), *You May Swing* (1980), *The Capitol Years* (1993).

May, Brian

b. 19 July 1947, Twickenham, Middlesex, England. Best known as the flamboyant and highly original guitarist in **Queen**, May has also recorded in his own right. In the summer of 1983 he teamed-up with **Eddie Van Halen** (guitar), **REO Speedwagon**'s Alan Gratzer (drums), Fred Mandel (keybords) and Phil Chen (bass) for a supergroup session, which was released under the title *Star Fleet Project*. He subsequently produced the spoof heavy metal group **Bad News** as well as the recording of 'Anyone Can Fall In Love' by his actress/lover Anita Dobson. He also worked with **Steve Hackett**, completed a solo album and, in 1991, wrote and recorded the score for a production of Shakespeare's *Macbeth*. Following a commission for an advertisement by the Ford Motor Company in 1991, May released a further single, 'Driven By You', which became a sizeable hit at the end of 1991. He was also one of the prime movers behind the **Freddy Mercury** Aid Benefit in 1992, and he has sustained himself admirably as a solo artist in the wake of the latter's death.
Albums: *Star Fleet Project* (EMI 1983), *Back To The Light* (EMI 1992), *Live At Brixton* (EMI 1994).
Video: *Live At The Brixton Academy* (1994).
Further reading: *Queen & I: The Brian May Story*, Laura Jackson.

May, Derrick

If one name crops up again and again in discussions of techno, it is that of Derrick 'Mayday' May (b. c.1964, USA). Alongside **Juan Atkins**, **Carl Craig** and **Kevin Saunderson**, with whom he ran the Music Institute club and attended high school, May is the king of the Detroit sound. His work in the late 80s/early

90s, especially as Rhythim Is Rhythim, has provided literally thousands with inspiration, cuts like 'The Dance', 'It Is What It Is' and 'Strings Of Life' (1989) defining a moment in time in dance music. In his youth he was inspired by **Yello** and **Kraftwerk**, and he began to make electronic music with Atkin and Saunderson while studying at Belleville High, Detroit. Recording as Mayday or Rhythim Is Rhythim, generally on his own **Transmat** label, he went on to carve out a new vein in dance music, which synthesised the advances of the electro movement with the more challenging end of the house movement. A music that was christened 'techno', though May conceded in 1992 that 'I don't even use the word techno anymore'. He has never proved prolific in his recordings, and aside from occasional European jaunts has proved an elusive spokesperson for 'techno' music. To such an extent that when Chris Peat of **Altern 8** stood for parliament, he made a manifesto commitment to use MI5 to track May down. A self-evident example of May's belief in Kraftwerk's 'less is more' mystique. After the success of 'Strings Of Life' he largely fled the dance scene, aside from a remix of Yello's 'The Race'. His chief notoriety rose from an argument at the 1990 New Music Seminar in New York when Factory personnel, Tony Wilson in particular, attempted to lecture the Americans on dance music (specifically that they did not know what they had created). Rhythim Is Rhythim did not follow up 'Strings Of Life' until 1990, when 'The Beginning' was released. May went on to cut three tracks on **System 7**'s debut album, before, in 1991, **Network** released *Innovator: Soundtrack For The Tenth Planet*, an EP which comprised some of May's definitive moments to date. It was followed in 1992 by *Transmat Relics*, a double album of the label's finest moments, heavily featuring Rhythim Is Rhythim. The Transmat logo had been reactivated via a deal with Belgium label Buzz. 'Strings Of Life' was also re-released in the same yearl after being heavily sampled on **Altern 8**'s 'Evapor 8' - this time in a new, drumless version. May, meanwhile, could not be found, having relocated to Amsterdam to play a leading role in that city's 'Hi-Tech Soul' movement in 1993.
Selected albums: *Relics: A Transmat Compilation* (Buzz 1992). As Rhythim Is Rhythim: *The Beginning* (Big Life 1990).

May, Wuta
(see **Les Quatre Etoiles**)

Mayall, John
b. 29 November 1933, Macclesfield, Cheshire, England. The career of England's premier white blues exponent and father of British blues has now spanned five decades and much of that time has been spent unintentionally acting as a musical catalyst. Mayall formed his first band in 1955 while at college, and as the Powerhouse Four the group worked mostly locally. Soon after Mayall enlisted for National Service. He then became a commercial artist and finally moved to London to form his Blues Syndicate, the forerunner to his legendary Bluesbreakers. Along with **Alexis Korner, Cyril Davies** and **Graham Bond**, Mayall pioneered British R&B. The astonishing number of musicians who have passed through his bands reads like a who's-who. Even more remarkable is the number of names who have gone on to eclipse Mayall with either their own bands or as members of highly successful groups. Pete Frame author of *Rock Family Trees* has produced a detailed Mayall specimen, which is recommended. His roster of musicians included, **John McVie**, Hughie Flint, Mick Fleetwood, **Roger Dean**, **Davey Graham**, **Eric Clapton**, **Jack Bruce**, **Aynsley Dunbar**, **Peter Green**, **Dick Heckstall-Smith**, **Keef Hartley**, **Mick Taylor**, **Henry Lowther**, Tony Reeves, Chris Mercer, **Jon Hiseman**, Steve Thompson, Colin Allen, **Jon Mark**, **Johnny Almond**, **Harvey Mandel**, Larry Taylor, and **Don 'Sugercane' Harris**.
His 1965 debut, *John Mayall Plays John Mayall*, was a live album which, although badly recorded, captured the tremendous atmosphere of an R&B club. His first single, 'Crawling Up A Hill', is contained on this set and it features Mayall's thin voice attempting to compete with an exciting, distorted harmonica and Hammond organ. *Bluesbreakers With Eric Clapton* is now a classic, and is highly recommended to all students of white blues. Clapton enabled his boss to reach a wider audience, as the crowds filled the clubs to get a glimpse of the guitar hero. *A Hard Road* featured some clean and sparing guitar from Peter Green, while *Crusade* offers a brassier, fuller sound. *The Blues Alone* showed a more relaxed style, and allowed Mayall to demonstrate his musical dexterity. *Diary Of A Band Vol. 1* and *Vol. 2* were released during 1968 and capture their live sound from the previous year; both feature excellent drumming from Keef Hartley, in addition to Mick Taylor on guitar. *Bare Wires*, arguably Mayall's finest work, shows a strong jazz leaning, with the addition of Jon Hiseman on drums and the experienced brass section of Lowther, Mercer and Heckstall-Smith. The album was an introspective journey and contained Mayall's most competent lyrics, notably the beautifully hymn-like 'I Know Now'. The similarly packaged *Blues From Laurel Canyon* (Mayall often produced his own artwork) was another strong album which was recorded in Los Angeles, where Mayall lived. This marked the end of the Bluesbreakers name and, following the departure of Mick Taylor to the **Rolling Stones**, Mayall pioneered a drumless acoustic band featuring Jon Mark on acoustic guitar, Johnny Almond on tenor saxophone and flute, and Stephen Thompson on string bass. The subsequent live album, *The Turning Point*, proved to be his biggest-selling album and almost reached the UK

Top 10. Notable tracks are the furious 'Room To Move', with Mayall's finest harmonica solo, and 'Thoughts About Roxanne' with some exquisite saxophone from Almond. The same line-up plus Larry Taylor produced *Empty Rooms,* which was more refined and less exciting.

The band that recorded *USA Union* consisted of Americans Harvey Mandel, 'Sugercane' Harris and Larry Taylor. It gave Mayall yet another success, although he struggled lyrically. Following the double reunion, *Back To The Roots,* Mayall's work lost its bite, and over the next few years his output was of poor quality. The halcyon days of name stars in his band had passed and Mayall had to suffer record company apathy. His last album to chart was *New Year, New Band, New Company* in 1975, featuring for the first time a female vocalist, Dee McKinnie, and future **Fleetwood Mac** guitarist Rick Vito. Following a run of albums which had little or no exposure, Mayall stopped recording, playing only infrequently close to his base in California. He toured Europe in 1988 to small but wildly enthusiastic audiences. That same year he signed to **Island Records** and released *Chicago Line.* Renewed activity and interest occurred in 1990 following the release of his finest album in many years, *A Sense Of Place.* Mayall was interviewed during a short visit to Britain in 1992 and sounded positive, happy and unaffected by years in the commercial doldrums. *Wake Up Call* changed everything once more. Released in 1993 the album is one of his finest ever, and became his biggest selling disc for over two decades. The 90s have so far been kind to Mayall, 1995 saw the birth of another child, and a solid new relases *Spinning Coin.* The replacement for the departing Coco Montoya is yet another highly talented guitarist, a knack with which Mayall is clearly blessed, Buddy Whittington is the latest, continuing a tradition which started with Clapton and Green. As the sole survivor from the four 60s UK R&B/Blues catalysts, Mayall has played the blues for so long without any deviation that it is hard to think of any other white artist to compare. He has outlived his contemporaries from the early days (Korner, Bond and Davis) and recent reappraisal has put the man clearly back on top of a genre that he can rightly claim to have furthered more than any other Englishman.

Albums: *John Mayall Plays John Mayall* (Decca 1965), *Bluesbreakers With Eric Clapton* (Decca 1966), *A Hard Road* (Decca 1967), *Crusade* (Decca 1967), *Blues Alone* (Ace Of Clubs 1967), *Diary Of A Band Vol.1* (Decca 1968), *Diary Of A Band Vol.2* (Decca 1968), *Bare Wires* (Decca 1968), *Blues From Laurel Canyon* (Decca 1968), *Turning Point* (Polydor 1969), *Empty Rooms* (Polydor 1970), *USA Union* (Polydor 1970), *Back To The Roots* (Polydor 1971), *Beyond The Turning Point* (Polydor 1971), *Thru The Years* (Decca 1971), *Memories* (Polydor 1971), *Jazz Blues Fusion* (Polydor 1972), *Moving On* (Polydor 1973), *Ten Years Are Gone* (Polydor 1973), *Down The Line* (London US 1973, double album), *The Latest Edition* (Polydor 1975), *New Year, New Band, New Company* (ABC 1975), *Time Expired, Notice To Appear* (ABC 1975), *John Mayall* (Polydor 1976), *A Banquet Of Blues* (ABC 1976), *Lots Of People* (ABC 1977), *A Hard Core Package* (ABC 1977), *Primal Solos* (London 1977), *Blues Roots* (Decca 1978), *Last Of The British Blues* (MCA 1978), *Bottom Line* (DJM 1979), *No More Interviews* (DJM 1979), *Roadshow Blues* (DJM 1980), *Last Edition* (Polydor 1983), *Behind the Iron Curtain* (PRT 1986), *Chicago Line* (Island 1988), *A Sense Of Place* (Island 1990), *Wake Up Call* (Silvertone 1993), *Spinning Coin* (Silvertone 1995). Selected compilations: *Looking Back* (Decca 1969), *World Of John Mayall* (Decca 1970), *World Of John Mayall Vol.2* (Decca 1971), *The John Mayall Story Vol.1* (Decca 1983), *The John Mayall Story Vol.2* (Decca 1983), *London Blues 1964-1969* (Polygram 1992, 2 CD box set), *Room To Move 1969-1974* (Polygram 1992, 2 CD box set).

Maye, Arthur Lee

b. 11 December 1934, Tuscaloosa, Alabama, USA. Maye had one of the most engaging lead voices on the west coast doo-wop scene and he put it to terrific use on many fine songs, usually recorded with his group the Crowns. His career was unique dual one, as a baseball player (as Lee Maye) and as a singer, and he was only able to record and tour during the off-seasons. In 1954, the same year he joined a Milwaukee Braves' minor league club he formed a trio in Los Angeles with bass Johnny Coleman and bass/baritone **Richard Berry**. They made some records for the Flair label that were released as by the Rams and as by the '5' Hearts (the company put the numeral in quotes for obvious reasons). Maye at the end of the 1954 baseball season organized the Crowns, which other than himself included Berry and Coleman, with new members Charles Colbert (tenor), Johnny Morris (tenor), and Joe Moore (baritone). Occasionally bass Randy Jones would substitute for Berry. The records they made for the RPM label were excellent, notably the classic 'Truly' and 'Love Me Always', but the Crowns only managed local success with them. At the end of the 1955 baseball season, Maye And The Crowns then joined the **Specialty** label, recording one of their finest songs, 'Gloria'. No hits resulted and at the end of the 1956 baseball season, Maye began an association with **Johnny Otis**, touring with him in a vocal ensemble called the Jayos. They recorded for Otis's Dig label without much success, but Maye also brought his group the Crowns on the label, recording several tracks, most notably 'This Is The Night For Love' (1956). Maye And The Crowns made further tracks in 1957 for Flip and in 1959 for Cash. In 1959 Maye was brought up from the minor leagues to play major league ball for the Milwaukee Braves. This served to end Maye's career with the Crowns, but as Maye played for various major league teams through 1971, each off season would find him recording some solo numbers for a record label. He made his last record for Dave Antrell's Antrell label in 1985.

Mayer, Nathaniel

b. 10 February 1944, Detroit, Michigan, USA. Mayer was a typical transitional artist, whose vocal intensity evoked both the doo-wop past and the emerging soul music. This style was magnificently realized in his lone hit, 'Village Of Love', which went to number 16 R&B and number 22 pop in 1962. It was recorded for a small Detroit company, Fortune, and proved to be the biggest hit the label ever had (after being leased to United Artists). Mayer started singing in high school, and recorded his first record, the wonderful 'My Last Dance With You', with a pick-up group, the Fabulous Twilights. It failed to attract buyers, but the follow-up, 'Village Of Love', also recorded with the group, gave him a national audience. Later releases, notably 'Leave Me Alone' (1962) and 'Going Back To The Village Of Love' (1964), could not return Mayer to the charts, probably because the primitive production of Fortune's records made them sound uncompetitive next to the increasingly sophisticated recording methods employed by rival firms. Mayer never recorded again after his stay at Fortune Records.
Album: *Going Back To The Village Of Love* (1964).

Mayerl, Billy

b. William Joseph Mayerl, 31 May 1902, London, England, d. March 1959, England. The most famous British pianist of the 20s and 30s, who was also a celebrated composer of piano pieces and light orchestral works. Mayerl gave the first British performance of **George Gershwin**'s 'Rhapsody In Blue' in 1925, and thereafter he was recognised as the leading exponent of syncopated piano playing in Britain. His influence on amateur pianists was so great that he was persuaded to form The Billy Mayerl School which supplied piano transcriptions by post, together with guidance on improving one's playing. Mayerl's best-known piece was 'Marigold' (1926) which he adopted as his signature tune. It was one of the earliest of a great string of piano successes, such as 'Autumn Crocus' (1932), 'Four Aces Suite' (1933), 'Bats In The Belfry' (1935), 'Aquarium Suite' (1937), 'From A Spanish Lattice' (1938), 'Parade Of The Sandwich Board Men' (1938) and 'Fireside Fusiliers' (1943). Mayerl's light orchestral works included 'Minuet By Candlelight' (1956), 'Waltz For A Lonely Heart' (1956), 'Busybody' (1956). During the 80s Mayerl's work was re-discovered by several leading pianists on CD release - Eric Parkin (Chandos), Susan Tomes (Virgin) and Peter Jacobs (Aspen). Eric Parkin has also recorded Mayerl's transcriptions of 20s and 30s popular songs for Priory Records (UK).

Selected albums: by Eric Parkin *Original Piano Compositions - Volumes 1, 2, 3* (Chandos 1988, 1990, 1993), *British Light Music Series - Billy Mayerl* (Marco Polo 1994).

Mayes, Pete

b. 1938, Houston, Texas, USA. Mayes was being given his first guitar by an uncle after experimenting with string and wire. According to his own story, by the age of 14 he had already worked with **Lester Williams**, although he did not meet **T-Bone Walker,** the doyen of all Texas guitarists, until 1954. During the next 20 years, he often worked with Walker and made the acquaintance of many other bluesmen who would later come to fame, most prominently, **Joe Hughes**. Mayes' first recordings were made in support of **Junior Parker** and, in 1978, he entered a studio again while in Paris on tour with **Bill Doggett**. In the meantime, he had three singles issued under his own name on the Ovide label. In 1984, he appeared in the film *Battle Of The Guitars*, the soundtrack of which was issued on album. His own debut album was recorded in Houston during 1984-85 for the Dutch company, Double Trouble.
Album: *I'm Ready* (1986).

Mayfield, Curtis

b. 3 June 1942, Chicago, Illinois, USA. As songwriter and vocalist with the **Impressions**, Mayfield established an early reputation as one of soul music's most intuitive talents. In the decade between 1961 and 1971, he penned a succession of exemplary singles for his group, including 'Gypsy Woman' (1961), 'It's All Right' (1963), 'People Get Ready' (1965), 'We're A Winner' (1968) and 'Choice Of Colours' (1969), the subjects of which ranged from simple, tender love songs to broadsides demanding social and political equality. Years later **Bob Marley** would lift lines from the anthemic 'People Get Ready' to populate his own opus, 'One Love'. Two independent record companies, Windy C and Curtom, emphasized Mayfield's statesman-like role within black music, while his continued support for other artists - as composer, producer or session guitarist - enhanced a virtually peerless reputation. **Jerry Butler**, **Major Lance**, **Gene Chandler** and **Walter Jackson** are among the many Chicago-based singers benefiting from Mayfield's involvement. Having parted company with the Impressions in 1970, the singer began his solo career with '(Don't Worry) If There's A Hell Below We're All Going To Go', a suitably astringent protest song. The following year Mayfield enjoyed his biggest UK success when 'Move On Up' reached number 12, a compulsive dance song which surprisingly did not chart in the US. There, the artist's commercial ascendancy was maintained with 'Freddie's Dead' (US R&B number 2/number 4 pop hit) and the theme from

'Superfly' (1972), a 'blaxploitation' film which he also scored. Both singles and the attendant album achieved gold status, inspiring further excursions into motion picture soundtracks, including *Claudine*, *A Piece Of The Action*, *Sparkle* and *Short Eyes*, the last of which featured Mayfield in an acting role. However, although the singer continued to prove popular, he failed to sustain this high profile, and subsequent work, including his production of **Aretha Franklin**'s 1978 album, *Almighty Fire*, gained respect rather than commercial approbation. In 1981, he joined the Boardwalk label for which he recorded *Honesty*, his strongest album since the halcyon days of the early 70s. Sadly, the death of label managing director **Neil Bogert** left an insurmountable gap, and Mayfield's career was then blighted by music industry indifference. The singer nonetheless remained a highly popular live attraction, particularly in Britain where '(Celebrate) The Day After You', a collaboration with the **Blow Monkeys**, became a minor hit. In 1990, a freak accident, in which part of a public address rig collapsed on top of him during a concert, left Mayfield permanently paralysed from the neck down. The effects, both personal and professional, may yet prove costly to an individual whose contribution to soul music has been immense. The material for *BBC Radio 1 Live In Concert* was gathered from the gig at London's Town And Country club during Mayfield's 1990 European tour. In 1993 Shanachie released, *A Tribute To Curtis Mayfield; People Get Ready*, with various artists; including **Lenny Kravitz**, **Whitney Houston**, Aretha Franklin, **Bruce Springsteen**, **Rod Stewart** and **Elton John**, as a tribute to the Mayfield songbook. A year later **Charly Records** reissued the majority of Mayfield's 70s albums on CD as well as several compilations.
Albums: *Curtis* (1970), *Curtis Live* (1971), *Roots* (1971), *Superfly* (1972, film soundtrack), *Back To The World* (1973), *Curtis In Chicago* (1973), *Sweet Exorcist* (1974), *Got To Find A Way* (1974), *Claudine* (1975), *Let's Do It Again* (1975), *There's No Place Like America Today* (1975), *Sparkle* (1976), *Give, Get, Take And Have* (1976), *Short Eyes* (1977), *Never Say You Can't Survive* (1977), *A Piece Of The Action* (1978), *Do It All Night* (1978), *Heartbeat* (1979), with Linda Clifford *The Right Combination* (1980), *Something To Believe In* (1980), *Love Is The Place* (1981), *Honesty* (1983), *We Come In Peace With A Message Of Love* (1985), *Live In Europe* (1988), *People Get Ready* (1990), *Take It To The Streets* (1990), *BBC Radio 1 Live In Concert* (Windsong 1994). Compilations: *Of All Time* (1990), *Get Down To The Funky Groove* (1994), *Groove On Up* (1994), *Tripping Out* (1994), *A Man Like Curtis - The Best Of* (1994)
Film: *The Groove Tube* (1974).

Mayfield, Percy

b. 12 August 1920, Minden, Louisiana, USA, d. 11 August 1984. A gifted performer, Percy Mayfield's first success came in 1950 with 'Please Send Me Someone To Love' on the **Specialty** label. A massive US R&B hit, it reportedly sold well in excess of one million copies and became an enduring composition through its many cover versions. Further chart entries, 'Lost Love' (1951) and 'Big Question' (1952), confirmed Mayfield's status, but it was nine years before he secured another best seller with 'River's Invitation'. 'Hit The Road Jack' enhanced Mayfield's standing as a gifted composer when it became an international hit for **Ray Charles**. This influential musician recorded several of Percy's songs; Mayfield, in turn, pursued his career on Charles' Tangerine outlet. The talented artist remained an active performer throughout the 70s and early 80s, and his later work appeared on several different labels. His death from a heart attack in 1984 robbed R&B of one of its most individual voices. **Johnny Adams** released an excellent tribute album in 1989 titled *Walking On A Tightrope*.
Albums: *My Jug And I* (1962), *Percy Mayfield* (1969), *Bought Blues* (1969), *Tightrope* (1969), *Percy Mayfield Sings* (1970), *Weakness Is A Thing Called Man* (1970), *Blues - And Then Some* (1971). Compilations: *The Incredible Percy Mayfield* (1972), *My Heart Is Always Singing Sad Songs* (1985), *The Voice Within* (1988), *Percy Mayfield: Poet Of The Blues* (1990), *Percy Mayfield Vol. 2: Memory Pain* (1992).

Mayhem

Formed in Norway by Euronymous (real name Oystien Aarseth) who was a young fan of the Satanic black metal played by bands like **Bathory** and **Venom**, Mayhem made their first impact with the 1984 demo, *Pure Fucking Armageddon*, which is regarded as something of a classic of extreme metal in underground circles. The black metal genre was losing popularity however, along with the leather and chains imagery and Satanic lyrics that were its trademark. Rather than follow heavy metal fashion and adopt the hardcore punk or death metal genres that were becoming popular, Euronymous opted to preserve purist black metal. In order to do this he opened a record shop in Oslo named Helvete (Norwegian for Hell) and founded the Deathlike Silence label, both dedicated solely to black metal. In 1987 he released *Deathcrush*, Mayhem's official debut which featured six songs in seventeen and a half minutes of frenzied angst. Then, in 1991, the band's vocalist shot himself (by way of black irony, he went under the stagename 'Dead'). Rather than halting Euronymous' black metal crusade, the tragedy only appeared to have redoubled his faith. Mayhem inspired a number of Scandinavian bands to readopt the musical style and imagery of black metal during the early 90s, while Euronymous became an increasingly melodramatic and popular spokesman on the extreme metal underground with his philosophies of cold hate and spite. A series of Norwegian church burnings in early 1993 were linked to the Black Metal Circle, a cult-like group centred around Euronymous' black metal crusade and dominated by members of bands like **Emperor**, Dark Throne and **Burzum**, all signed to Deathlike Silence. Euronymous revelled in the international publicity. Then, on August 10th 1993 he was found, stabbed 25 times, outside his Oslo apartment. Two weeks later Varg Vikernes (better known by his stagename of Count Grishnakh) of the band Burzum was arrested for the murder, and convicted the following year. Vikernes had been Euronymous' right-hand man, and it is not apparent whether the murder was committed because of a financial dispute over record royalties, over a woman, or because of darker doctrinal differences between the two. What does seem clear is that Euronymous was swallowed by the vivid world of pain and hate he had himself created, while the black metal revival he had inspired continues unabated. In 1994 *De Mysteriis Dom Sathanas*, Mayhem's last recording, was released posthumously. Sinisterly enough, it featured Grishnakh on bass guitar.

Albums: *Deathcrush* (Deathlike Silence 1987), *De Mysteriis Dom Sathanas* (Deathlike Silence 1994).

Maynard, Ken

b. 21 July 1895, Vevay, Indiana, USA, d. 23 March 1973, California, USA. Maynard, who could play guitar, banjo and fiddle, worked in rodeos until he broke into films as a stunt man. He became the first motion picture singing cowboy, when he sang in *The Wagon Master* in 1929. In this part-talkie (it was 40% silent), he sang 'The Lone Star Trail' and 'The Cowboy's Lament'. He recorded eight cowboy songs for Columbia in 1930. A cowboy song was used for a film title for the first time in Maynard's 1930 film *The Strawberry Roan.* His career as a singing cowboy basically ended with the film debut of **Gene Autry** in Maynard's 1934 film, *In Old Sante Fe.* His singing, which has been described as rustic, was not comparable to that of Autry, **Roy Rogers** or later singing cowboys but he continued for some years as a noted cowboy actor. (His brother Kermit Maynard [1898-1971] was also a cowboy actor.)

Mayor, Simon

b. 5 October 1953, Sheffield, England. Mayor taught himself guitar at the age of 10, and in his teens he added the whistle, mandolin and fiddle. He met Hilary James (b. 4 August 1952, Stoke On Trent, England; vocals/guitar/double bass), at the Reading University folk club, and began to work with her in various line-ups. After university, they formed Spredthick, a folk/blues/ragtime band. The group underwent many personnel changes at different times and featured musicians such as Andrew Mathewson (b. 1952; guitar) who was with them from 1973-76, Peter Jagger (b. 1954; guitar) from 1976-77, Andy McGhee (banjo) during 1978, and Phil Fentimen (b. 10 August 1954; guitar/double bass), from 1977-80. Spredthick released one album then disbanded.

Aside from working as a duo, Simon and Hilary make occasional outings fronting Slim Panatella And The Mellow Virginians, a bluegrass/western swing trio. For this they recruit the services of Andy Baum (b. 1953; vocals/guitar/mandolin). With Hilary, Simon has written topical songs for television programmes such as *Newsnight*, *Kilroy*, and children's songs for *Play School*, *Listening Corner*, and *Green Claws*. As a duo, they have played throughout Europe, and Singapore. Simon has also presented *The Song Tree* on BBC Radio 5 for six years. He has done much to revive interest in the much under-rated mandolin, via his mandolin album project, encompassing classical, bnaroque, and folk themes. The project featured Simon's own compositions alongside non-folk elements by composers including Vivaldi, Berlioz, and Handel. This series of albums received excellent reviews and a great deal of airplay.

Albums: *Spredthick* (1979), *Craving The Dew* (1981), *Musical Mystery Tour* (1985), *Slim Panatella And The Mellow Virginians* (1988), *Musical Mystery Tour 2 - Up In A Big Balloon* (1988), *Musical Mystery Tour 3 - A Big Surprise* (1989), *Musical Mystery Tour 4 - Snowmen And Kings* (1990), *The Mandolin Album* (1990), *The Second Mandolin Album* (1991), *Winter With Mandolins* (1992), with Hilary James *Burning Sun* (1993). Compilation: *Children's Favourites From The Musical Mystery Tour* (1990).

Mays, Curley

b. 26 November 1938, Maxie, Louisiana, USA. A nephew of **Gatemouth Brown** and a cousin of **Phillip Walker,** Mays was raised in Beaumont, Texas, where he taught himself to play guitar when he was in his early teens. He worked on the streets and in the clubs around Beaumont until his break came in 1959 when he began a three-year stint with the **Etta James** Revue. Over the years, he also worked with the Five Royales, **James Brown** and **Tina Turner**. After a period spent working in hotel bands in Las Vegas, Mays formed his own band in the mid-60s and returned to Texas, where he appeared regularly in clubs from San Antonio to Houston. Veteran Texas bluesman Zuzu Bollin remembered him as a consummate showman blessed with the ability to play the guitar with his bare feet!

Mays, Lyle

b. 27 November 1953, Wausaukie, Wisconsin, USA. The varied keyboard talents of Mays are regularly heard together with **Pat Metheny**. They met in 1975, and have since forged a musical partnership built upon respect and admiration for each other's work. While it is Metheny who rightly takes the limelight, the integral backbone of the music has much to do with May's fluid keyboard playing, thoughtful arrangements and superb composing ability. In addition to sharing the credits on

As Falls Wichita, So Falls Wichita Falls, he has played on virtually all of Metheny's impressive catalogue. He contributed to **Eberhard Weber**'s *Later That Evening,* and has so far released two critically acclaimed solo albums. The 'Alaskan Suite' in particular, shows the vast range of capabilities from this dedicated and unassuming musician.
Albums: with Pat Metheny *As Falls Wichita, So Falls Wichita Falls* (ECM 1981), *Lyle Mays* (Geffen 1986), *Street Dreams* (Geffen 1988), with John DeJohnette, Marc Johnson *Fictionary* (Geffen 1993).

Maytals

Arguably the Maytals were only ever kept from becoming 'international' artists by the runaway success of **Bob Marley And The Wailers** in the 70s. Rumour has it that **Island Records**' **Chris Blackwell** only originally signed the Wailers because he was unable to obtain the Maytals' signatures at the time! Frederick 'Toots' Hibbert, Nathaniel 'Jerry' Matthias/McCarthy and Henry 'Raleigh' Gordon came together in 1962 at the start of Jamaica's **ska** craze and began recording for **Coxsone Dodd**'s **Studio One** organisation. Ska vocalists needed to work very hard indeed to make themselves stand out against the heavy, frantic and often overpowering rhythms, and Toots sang himself hoarse in true Baptist preacher style, while Jerry and Raleigh filled in whatever gaps were left to make a solid, impenetrable wall of sound. Subtlety was not their strong point, but the sheer, vibrant joy of all that they were doing is evident in every note. It was not too long before the Maytals were the number one vocal group in Jamaica - a position they would maintain throughout the 60s and on into the 70s.
They left Coxsone after some massive hits and moved on to his ex-employee and arch-rival **Prince Buster**, celebrating with the vengeful 'Broadway Jungle'/'Dog War': 'We were caught in the jungle . . . In the hands of a man . . .' However, their stay with Buster was also short-lived and the Maytals moved on again to **Byron Lee**'s BMN stable. In 1965 they made Jamaican musical history when both sides of 'Daddy'/'It's You' topped both Jamaican charts, and in 1966 they won the prestigious Jamaican Festival Song Competition with 'Bam Bam'. Many of their releases in these early days were credited to 'The Vikings' or 'The Flames', for as Toots says: 'Promoters in Jamaica called us all kinds of different names because they didn't want us to get our royalties'. The future was looking bright for the group, but Toots was imprisoned in late 1966 for possession of ganja (marijuana) and he was not released until 1968. The Maytals began work for **Leslie Kong**'s Beverleys label, and their first release was a huge hit in Jamaica and the UK - '54-46 That's My Number' featured one of reggae's most enduring bass lines as Toots details his prison experiences in song (54-46 was his prison number). This was the beginning of a hugely successful period - both artistically and financially - for the group, and they recorded many classic records for Beverley's including 'Do The Reggay' one of the first songs ever to use 'reggae' in the title, 'Monkey Man', which actually made the UK charts, and 'Sweet and Dandy', which won the Festival Song Competition again for them in 1969. They also appeared in a cameo role in the hugely popular film *The Harder They Come,* singing one of their all- time favourites, 'Pressure Drop'.
Kong's untimely death in 1971 from a heart attack robbed them of their mentor. Many believed that their best work was recorded while at Beverley's; evidence of its popularity was found in the **2-Tone** craze in the late 70s when the new bands formed a large part of their repertoire from Toots Hibbert's Beverleys song book. They returned to Byron Lee - now the very successful owner of Dynamic Sounds, a state-of-the-art recording, mastering and record pressing complex. In 1972 the Maytals won the Festival Song Competition yet again with 'Pomps and Pride'. Through their work with Dynamic they attracted the attention of Chris Blackwell and became Toots And The Maytals. For the first time in 14 years they became widely known outside of reggae circles. Their UK and USA tours were sell outs, and Island Records released what was to be their biggest selling album ever, *Reggae Got Soul,* which took them into the UK album charts. They made history again in 1980 when, on 29 September, they recorded a live show at London's Hammersmith Palais which was mastered, processed, pressed and in the shops 24 hours later. Few live excursions have been able to capture the feel and spontaneity of this album, which showcases the Maytals at their best : live without any embellishments. By now they had left their Jamaican audiences far behind but their nebulous 'pop' audience soon moved on to the next big sensation. While the Maytals continued to tour and make records on into the 90s, real lasting international success always seemed to elude them. Toots dispensed with the services of Jerry & Raleigh for his 1982 tour and has even experimented with non reggae line-ups. It will be interesting to see what direction he will now take to match the myriad achievements of his illustrious past.
Selected albums: *The Sensational* (Wirl c.1965), *Never Grow Old* (Studio One c.1966), *Original Golden Oldies (Volume Three)* (Fab Prince Buster c. 1967), *Sweet & Dandy* (Beverley's 1969), *From The Roots* (Trojan 1970), *Monkey Man* (Trojan 1970), *Funky Kingston* (Dragon 1973), *In The Dark* (Dragon/Dynamic 1974), *Slatyam Stoot* (Dynamic), *Reggae Got Soul* (Mango/Island 1976), *Toots Live* (Mango/Island), *Life Could Be A Dream* (Studio One 1992). Compilations: *Reggae Greats* (Mango/Island 1988), *Do The Reggae 1966-70,* (Trojan 1988).

Maytime (Film Musical)

Although this 1937 screen version retained hardly

anything from the 1917 stage operetta other than the title and one of the songs, it remains one of the most accomplished and enjoyable films of its kind. Noel Langley's story, which is told in flashback, concerns the famous opera star Marcia Mornay (**Jeanette MacDonald**), who puts her career before her true love, Paul Allison (**Nelson Eddy**), and marries Nicolai Nazaroff (John Barrymore), the dominant figure in her life. The somewhat melodramatic climax comes when Allison, having been killed by Nazaroff while in a jealous rage, materialises in spiritual form and is serenaded by a remorseful Marcia. Among a strong supporting cast were Herman Bing, Lynne Carver, Tom Brown, Sig Ruman, Billy Gilbert, Harry Davenport, Walter Kingsford, Ivan Lebedeff, and Leonid Kinskey. The lovely 'Will You Remember (Sweetheart)?' (Rida Johnson Young-**Sigmund Romberg**), the song that survived from the original stage show, was sung with a glorious passion by Eddy and MacDonald, a feeling they also brought to bear on 'Czaritza', which consisted of excerpts from Tchaikovsky's Fifth Symphony, arranged by **Robert Wright** and **George Forrest**. The latter duo also wrote new lyrics to the folk song, 'Vive L'Opera', and the rest of the score - a mixture of songs and operatic excerpts, included 'Carry Me Back to Old Virginny' (James Bland), 'Love's Old Sweet Song' (James L. Molloy-G. Clifton Bingham), 'Le Regiment De Sambre Et Meuse' (Robert Planquette), and 'Ham And Eggs' (Herbert Stothart-Wright-Forrest). This lavish production, which is considered to be one of the best of Jeanette MacDonald and Nelson Eddy's eight films together, was produced by Hunt Stromberg for MGM and directed by Robert Z. Leonard. *Variety* reported that it grossed three and a half million dollars in US domestic theatre rentals, putting it among the most successful films of the decade.

Maytime (Stage Musical)

With his score for this highly popular operetta, which was based on a German production, *Wie Einst In Mai*, **Sigmund Romberg** finally stepped out of **Victor Herbert**'s shadow, and established himself as the leading composer of these gloriously musical, sentimental sagas. Rida Johnson Young wrote the book and lyrics, and the show's role-reversal story was set in New York, where well-off Ottilie Van Zandt (Peggy Wood) is prevented by her father, Matthew Van Zandt (William Norris), from marrying her true love, Richard Wayne (Charles Purcell), because, quite frankly, he comes from 'the other side of the tracks'. They go on to each marry their respective partners, although they meet socially and affirm their love for each other. When Ottilie's husband dies, she is left destitute, and her house and all her belongings are auctioned. Richard buys the house, and many years pass before their grandchildren encounter each other, and presumably find happiness together. The grandchildren were also played by Peggy Wood and Charles Purcell. The sweeping, romantic score included 'The Road To Paradise', 'Jump Jim Crow', 'In Our Little Home Sweet Home', 'Only One Girl For Me', and 'Will You Remember?', a lovely song which achieved wider recognition. One of the other numbers, 'Dancing Will Keep You Young', had music by Romberg and a lyric by Cyrus Wood. An enormously popular show - America's biggest hit of World War I - which all the soldiers aimed to see before they departed for the conflict. Its run of 492 performances in 1917 was, for the time, astounding. The 1937 film of *Maytime*, which starred **Jeanette MacDonald** and **Nelson Eddy**, changed the story and discarded all the songs except for 'Will You Remember?'. The song was sung superbly by **Jane Powell** and **Vic Damone** in the 1954 Sigmund Romberg bio-pic, *Deep In My Heart.*

Maytones

The Maytones comprised of Vernon Buckley and Gladstone Grant and began recording in the late 60s with Alvin 'GG' Ranglin. In 1970 they released, 'Black And White' which was considered to be the alternative reggae cut to **Greyhound**'s successful pop hit. They also enjoyed hits in the early 70s with, 'Preaching Love', 'If Loving You Was Wrong', 'Brown Girl' and 'Funny Man'. These successes were generally love songs but with the following releases they recorded in a more serious vein concentrating on a Rastafarian theme. 'Judas', 'Babylon A Fall' and 'Run Babylon' signalled the direction in which reggae was heading. Conscientious lyrics and a clarion call for black pride resulted in the duo achieving cult status. They continued releasing hits through to the mid-70s when returning to Ranglin producing at Channel One Recording Studio they scored with *Madness*, which surfaced in the UK through Burning Sounds. The group were inauspiciously overlooked by **Virgin Records** who were signing all the major acts in Jamaica. Fellow vocal group and Virgin signing the **Mighty Diamonds** had previously recorded as the Diamonds. This inspired Ranglin and Clement Bushay to promote the duo as the Mighty Maytones. The release of *Boat To Zion*, including the title track, was a hit within the West Indian community but failed to emulate the success of other Rastafarian-influenced vocal groups. The duo recorded in heavy patois and this possibly was the reason they were overlooked. Their image did not portray the typical Rastafarian, with no locks or red, gold and green outfits, and they therefore were ignored by the media. In 1980 Ranglin compiled a collection of the duo's work including recordings from 1976 sessions. Bushay also compiled a *Best Of* which featured tracks lifted from the two earlier releases.

Albums: *Madness* (Burning Sounds 1976), *Boat To Zion*

(Burning Sounds 1978). Compilations: *One Way* (GG 1980), *Best Of The Mighty Maytones* (Burning Sounds 1983), *Funny Man* (GG 1990).

Mayweather, Earring George

b. 27 September 1928, Montgomery, Alabama, USA, d. 12 February 1995, Boston Massachusetts, USA. Like **Little Sonny Willis**, young George received his first harmonica as a Christmas present when he was six, along with an apple and an orange. Although he heard John Lee **'Sonny Boy' Williamson**'s records, he was largely a self-taught musician until he arrived in Chicago in September 1949. There he befriended **Little Walter**, who helped him with harp selection and how to find keys in different positions. In 1951 he linked up with his next-door neighbour, **J.B. Hutto**, and with Eddie 'Porkchop' Hines on percussion, the group played at weekends on Maxwell Street market. But work was scarce, so Mayweather joined **Bo Diddley** and for a time alternated between both groups. He then formed a group with **Eddie Taylor**, refusing Walter's offer to replace him in **Muddy Waters**' band. He recorded with J.B. Hutto on the Chance session that produced 'Combination Boogie' and 'Pet Cream Man', and with Eddie Taylor on 'You'll Always Have A Home' and 'Don't Knock At My Door'. In the late 80s Mayweather moved to Boston where he established himself at the 1369 Jazz Club. *Whup It!*, recorded with the nucleus of **Luther Johnson**'s Magic Rockers, consists almost entirely of Chicago blues standards by **Howlin' Wolf**, Muddy, **Jimmy Rogers** and Little Walter, and just one original, 'Cheatin' On Me'. It represents an accurate and fitting memorial.
Album: *Whup It! Whup It!* (tone-Cool 1992).

Maze (featuring Frankie Beverly)

Frankie Beverly (b. 6 December 1946, Philadelphia, Pennsylvania, USA) had an apprenticeship in several Philadelphia groups. One such unit, Frankie Beverly And The Butlers, recorded several well-received singles in the 60s, but never managed to get more than local play. By the early 70s, however, impressed by **Santana** and **Sly And The Family Stone**, he formed a self-contained band, Raw Soul, and they moved to San Francisco where they became the houseband at a local club, the Scene. Discovered by a girlfriend of **Marvin Gaye**, the group subsequently supported the singer in concert, and it was he who suggested they change their name in deference to their now cooler sound. The septet, which featured Wayne aka Wuane Thomas, Sam Porter, Robin Duke, Roame Lowery, McKinley Williams, Joe Provost plus Beverly, thus became Maze. Their debut album was issued in January 1977, since which time Maze have remained one of soul's most consistent live attractions. Indeed, the group sold out six consecutive nights at London's Hammersmith Odeon during their 1985 tour. However, Beverly's brand of funk/R&B has failed to achieve the wider recognition it deserves and he remains something of a cult figure.
Albums: *Maze featuring Frankie Beverly* (1977), *Golden Time Of Day* (1978), *Inspiration* (1979), *Joy And Pain* (1980), *Live In New Orleans* (1981), *We Are One* (1983), *Can't Stop The Love* (1985), *Live In Los Angeles* (1986), *Silky Soul* (1989), *Back To Basics* (1993).

Mazzy Star

Highly regarded USA duo featuring the soothing timbre of singer Hope Sandoval's textured voice and guitarist David Roback. The partners had begun working together on a projected album as Opal (under which name Roback had formerly operated). Previous to which he had been a member of Paisley Underground legends the **Rain Parade**, and recorded the *Rainy Day* album with vocalists Susanna Hoffs (**Bangles**) and Kendra Smith. He met Sandoval while she was part of female duo Going Home. Enjoying a profitable working relationship, Roback and Sandoval adopted the name Mazzy Star for their sessions together, which eventually resulted in a critically lauded debut album. They released a comeback album on **Capitol Records** in 1993 after an absence that was mourned by many rock critics. Various musicians were employed, but the core of the project remained Roback and Sandoval (who would also contribute to the **Jesus And Mary Chain**'s 'Sometimes Always' single). Contrary to expectations established by its forerunner, the resultant album included a cover of the **Stooges**' 'We Will Fall'. Elsewhere, however, Roback's stinging lyrical poignancy and effortless song construction continued to hold sway.
Albums: *She Hangs Brightly* (Rough Trade 1990), *So Tonight That I Might See* (Capitol 1993).

Mbarga, Nico, Prince

b. 23 August 1950, Abakaliki, Nigeria. Vocalist and guitarist Mbarga, founder and leader of Rocafil Jazz, is one of Nigeria's few convincing highlife artists (generally speaking, the music is best performed by Ghanaians, its originators). Born of mixed Nigerian and Cameroonian parentage, he left Nigeria during the 60s civil war, basing himself in Cameroon, where he formed the Melody Orchestra. He returned home in 1971 and, two years later, fronting Rocafil, had his first hit, 'I No Go Marry My Papa', a song composed in 'panko' style (a mixture of highlife and Cameroonian makossa). In 1977, he enjoyed his - and, indeed, one of Africa's - biggest successes with 'Sweet Mother', sung in 'broken English' and so readily understandable throughout Anglophone West Africa. Hit albums followed: *Simplicity*, *Happy Birthday* and *Family Movement.* In 1981, Mbarga left his label, Rogers All Stars, during a dispute over foreign royalties for 'Sweet Mother' and, forming his own label, recorded the albums *Tribalism* and *Man Pass Man*. He returned to Rogers in 1985. Despite the international success of 'Sweet Mother', and a triumphant appearance at the WOMAD World Of Music Arts & Dance Festival in Britain in 1982, Mbarga has kept a realistic balance between the Nigerian and Western markets. He has been happy to tour Europe and the USA, but has not been prepared to de-Africanize his recorded output in order to appeal to Western audiences. In 1983, he built Sweet Mother hotels in two eastern Nigerian cities, and began to devote increasing amounts of his time to their management.

Albums: *Sweet Mother* (1976), *Simplicity* (1977), *Happy Birthday* (1979), *Family Movement* (1981), *Tribalism and Polygamy* (both 1982), *Man Pass Man* (1983), *The Best Of Prince Nico And Rocafil Jazz* (1984).

Mbulu, Letta

b. 23 August 1942, Johannesburg, South Africa. Resident in the USA since 1964, vocalist Mbulu - along with fellow expatriates and musical associates **Hugh Masekela**, **Miriam Makeba** and **Caiphus Semenya** - first came to prominence in South Africa in 1960, as a member of the cast of the musical *King Kong*. On arrival in the USA, she was still under a exclusive world contract with leading South African label Gallo which, afraid of reprisals from the Pretoria authorities, declined to offer her any new recording opportunities. For three years she continued her fruitless negotiations with Gallo's New York representatives, before unilaterally severing the agreement and signing to **Capitol**. For her new label she released two albums - *Letta Mbulu Sings* and *Letta Free Soul* - before Gallo re-emerged waving (but sadly, not waiving) her contract and threatening legal action. The continuing ramifications of this situation meant that Mbulu was unable to record for a further two years, instead spending much of her time on tour with, first, Masekela and, later, **Cannonball Adderley**. In 1970, she returned to the studios to record *Letta*, followed by *Naturally Letta Mbulu* and, in 1974, a live album with **Harry Belafonte**. In 1978, newly-signed to **A&M** through Masekela's connections with label boss **Herb Alpert**, she released *There's Music In the Air* and, in 1980, the Semenya-produced *Sound Of A Rainbow*, two masterpieces of black American and South African jazz/pop fusion. In 1981, she enjoyed considerable USA and UK dance-floor success with the single 'Kilimanjaro', co-written with Semenya. She continued to be active throughout the 80s, based in the USA but frequently touring Africa, the Far East and Europe.

Albums: *Letta Mbulu Sings* (1967), *Letta Free Soul* (1968), *Letta* (1970), *Naturally Letta Mbulu* (1973), with Harry Belafonte *Live* (1974), *There's Music In The Air* (1978), *Sound Of A Rainbow* (1980), *In The Music* (1982), *Streams Today Rivers Tomorrow* (1984), *Not Yet Uhuru* (1993).

MC 900ft Jesus

aka Dallas, Texas-based Mark Griffin, one of the more credible examples of white hip hop. Alongside his musical cohort DJ Zero, Griffin explores a wide variety of styles including jazz and industrial dance. The lyrics, especially on his second album, track a more personal, introspective path than many of his peers. He made his debut in 1989 with the self-titled *MC 900ft Jesus With DJ Zero* EP, which highlighted his distinctive vocal style, which could hardly be described as rap in conventional terms, and reflected more the spoken word narratives of the beat poets. However, he had certainly been listening to the rise of hip hop on the East Coast, as his liberal steals from **Public Enemy** testify. His debut album centred around club rather than studio directed material. Later, he scored a degree of infamy when his single, 'The City Sleeps Tonight', caused an outcry in Baltimore, where its inflammatory lyrics coincided with an outbreak of arson. Griffin moved to Rick Rubin's Def American label in time for a projected third album.

Albums: *Hell With The Lid Off* (Nettwerk/CIR 1990), *Welcome To My Dream* (CIR 1991), *One Step Ahead Of The Spider* (American 1995).

MC Breed

MC Eric Breed (b. c.1972, Flint, Michigan, USA) was originally supported by his cousin Al Breed (of **DFC** fame) in the early 90s, before that artist would go solo with the aid of T-Trouble E. Both Breeds would, however, remain firm friends, Eric going on to a support/advisory capacity on the latter's debut album. Under the title MC Breed And DFC, he had scored a crossover hit single (US number 66) with the debut album's 'Ain't No Future In Yo' Frontin'', a typical slice of hardnosed gangsta vanity (a theme revisited on the second set's 'Ain't To Be Fucked With', retitled 'Ain't To Be Flexed With' for single consumption). 'Ain't No Future In Yo' Frontin'' continues to enjoy a healthy half-life and has been much sampled by other rap artists. The album which bore it was produced with the aid of Bernard Terry, of **Ready For The World** fame. The follow-up set again saw him working with Terry and his DJ/Producer Flash Technology, its chart profile buoyed by a further three successful singles. After sessions for a third set were completed, he was invited to join **George Clinton** for his 'Paint The White House Black' ensemble single. When *The New Breed* emerged it brought a harder-edged sound, as might have been anticipated by its title. It featured guest apearances from **2Pac** ('Gotta Get Mine'), Clinton (on the video to 'Tight') and D.O.C. Production was assisted by **Warren G** and Colin Wolfe. D.O.C. also contributed a song, 'B.R. Double E. D', to Breed's fourth set. Other guests included DFC and Jamal of **Illegal** fame on an album whose high watermark was set by the 'Teach My Kids' cut.

Albums: *MC Breed & DFC* (S.D.E.G. 1991), *20 Below* (Wrap/Ichiban 1992), *The New Breed* (Wrap/Ichiban 1993), *Funkafied* (Wrap/Ichiban).

MC Buzz B

b. Shorn Braithwaite. Eco-conscious UK rapper who allies his intelligent, highly wordy raps to a jazz/soul-funk melange which is characterised beyond anything else by its cool, restrained vibe. He debuted for Manchester independent Play Hard with the 12-inch only 'Slaphead' in May 1988, following it with 'How Sleep The Brave' and 'The Sequel' the following year. It was enough to procure a contract from **Polydor** Records, who released his ironically-titled debut album in 1991. However, a series of singles, 'The Last Tree', 'Never Change' (delayed due to problems in obtaining clearance on a sample from **Bruce Hornsby**'s 'That's Just The Way It Is') and 'Don't Have The Time' during that period failed to break him, as he became yet another UK hip hop under-achiever. He made a comback in 1993 by providing the vocal to **Lionrock**'s 'Pocket Of Peace'.
Album: *Words Escape Me* (Polydor 1991).

MC Duke

Together with his DJ Leader One, this British MC released 'The Final Conflict' in 1990, which left substantial imprints in the relatively virgin soil of UK hip hop. Raised in east London, MC Duke made his recorded debut on Music Of Life's compilation, *Hard As Hell*. Later he would make his home there, releasing two relatively succesful solo albums. He picked up *Hip Hop Connection* magazine's 1990 award for Best British Recording Artist, and even broke the Top 75 of the UK charts with 'I'm Riffin''/'English Rasta', before the recession cut in. Despite two solid singles for the **Shut Up And Dance** label, his fortunes declined. Duke has gone on to produce the 90s compilation series *The Royal Family*, to showcase new British rap talent. In turn he set up his own label, Bluntly Speaking Vinyl, formed in conjunction with Dan Donnely (**Suburban Base** Records). The initial releases included a 12-inch by Phat Skillz (essentially MC Duke) and material from a new group, IQ Procedure.
Album: *Organised Rhyme* (Music Of Life 1989), *Return Of The Dread-I* (Music Of Life 1991).

MC Eric

b. Eric Martin, 19 August 1970, Cardiff, Wales. MC Eric, aka Me One, is of Jamaican descent, though he grew up in Wales as the youngest of twelve brothers and sisters. It was via his stint in **Technotronic** (notably the 'This Is Technotronic' refrain, appearing in said video with his notorious 'skyscraper' hairstyle) that he first graced television screens and stereos. He had been introduced to the band via his girlfriend, **Ya Kid K**. 'I was 18 and Ya Kid K was 17 when we came into Technotronic and we knew that the money wasn't good'. He has also contributed to material from artists as diverse as **Madonna** and **Jazzy Jeff**. His debut solo album, promoted by a single, 'Jealous', was an artistic success, with deceptively subtle shades to its musical spine, bouyed by piano motifs and lolloping bass. Following its release, however, he seems to have became another of rap's many yesterday men. In the meantime he had a child with Ya Kid K, one Eric Jnr.
Album: *I Beg Uno Ceasefire* (Polydor 1991).

MC Kinky

b. Caron Geary. This UK female rap artist grew up in north London, England, on a diet of reggae, **David Essex**, **Marc Bolan** and **Kate Bush**. After being expelled from sixth- form college, she worked in children's playcentres by day and in nightclubs after dark. MC Kinky met **Boy George** while working as a DJ at Fred's in Soho, London, and was signed to his More Protein label in 1989. Her first release was in conjunction with the E-Zee Posse - 'Everything Starts With An E' - which became an instant UK club hit and eventually, after several attempts, went high in the charts. Once mistakenly arrested by police for soliciting (she was actually window shopping) her first solo single, 'Get Over It', was released in 1991. After which the trail runs cold.

MC Lyte

b. Lana Moorer, 11 October 1970, Queens, New York, USA, but raised in Brooklyn. The daughter of First Priority boss Nat Robinson, and sister to the **Audio Two** brothers, Lyte began her career in fine style with the 45 'I Cram To Understand U (Sam)', released when she was still a teenager. The story told of personal deceit in a relationship, the narrator unable to compete for her boyfriend's attentions with his new mistress - crack. It was delivered with such force that it still has few peers in terms of adult, hardcore female rap. Lyte has gone on to underscore her patent scouring wit, often referring to the out of control egos of her male counterparts, with synthesizer and funk beats coalescing beneath. Her debut album additionally sampled **Ray Charles**, **Helen Reddy** and the **Four Seasons**. Her songs are populated by fully realised characters, though its an unfortunate truism that they often wind up dead (via AIDS, lung cancer, violence or drugs). Despite the contributions of **Grand Puba** on her second album, which was musically solid, there was a lack of lyrical progression which limited its appeal. At which time she has also found time to appear in the video to **Sinead O'Connor**'s 'I Want Your Hands (Show Me)'. *Ain't No Other* included attacks on fellow rappers **Roxanne Shanté** ('Steady F. King') and an answer record to **Apache**'s 'Gangsta Bitch' ('Ruffneck', which would go gold when released on single). Rap forerunner **KRS-1** introduced the tracks in a pseudo

ragga style. Like **Queen Latifah** and others before her, she has founded her own management company, Dupe The Moon Productions, which also handles **Isis** and Brooklyn rappers Born In Hell. She was also, again like Latifah, bitten by the acting bug.
Albums: *Lyte As A Rock* (First Priority 1988), *Eyes On This* (First Priority 1989), *Act Like You Know* (First Prioirty 1991), *Ain't No Other* (First Priority 1993).

MC Mell 'O'

b. Battersea, London, England. One of the earliest members of the UK's indigenous rap clan, Mell 'O' began his career in the best traditions of hip hop by breakdancing and body-popping in the streets of Covent Garden during the early 80s. He modelled himself on **Grandmaster Melle Mel**, calling himself Grandmaster Mellow in tribute, eventually abbreviating it to MC Mell 'O'. These activities would be followed by improvised jam sets at the Charing Cross Centre youth project. He also cruised with **sound systems** like First Class and Young Lion, and reggae remains a strong component in his Cockney-delivered rhymes (he was among the first British rappers to reject the process of imitating East or West Coast American accents). Together with fellow pupils **Monie Love**, **DJ Pogo** and **Sparkie D**, he formed the DETT (Determination, Endeavour and Total Triumph) collective, based on the New York **Native Tongues** principle. Together they released a solitary record, 'Freestyle', in 1987. This underground jamming scene lasted for several years, and it was not until 1989 that he released his first records. After a well-received debut album for Republic, he swiched to Jazzie B (**Soul II Soul**)'s Funki Dred label. However, he fell victim to record company politicking (when **Motown** pulled their finanical backing for Funki Dred). A completed album, due for release in 1992, was scrapped. Worse, Jazzie B held on to his contract meaning he wasn't released until December 1993. In the meantime his only sighting was as part of **Island Records**' *The Rebirth of Cool* set, with 'Open Up Your Mind'. Freed from Funki Dred at last, he signed to the **Stereo MC's**' Natural Response label in 1994. He had at least spent some of the intervening period working - notably on projects with **Izit** and the **Young Disciples**. His debut release for his new home was *The First Chronicles Of DETT*, in the summer of 1994. The first track on the record was 'I Hear Voices', which tackled the problem of mental illness in immigrant black generations, and was another intelligent, illuminating epistle from one of the genuine talents of the British hip hop scene.
Album: *Thoughts Released* (Republic 1989).

MC Pooh

b. Lawrence Thomas, USA. Rapper who emerged in the 90s with lyrical preoccupations including sex, money and murder (his debut album even housed one cut of that title). Other songs included the socio-political 'The Projects', but elsewhere the tasteless sexual jibes continued on 'I Eat Pussy' and 'Your Dick'.
Album: *Funky As I Wanna Be* (Jive 1992).

MC Ren

b. Lorenzo Patterson, Compton, Los Angeles, USA. Another of **NWA**'s personnel to launch a solo career, Ren has thus far failed to share the high profile of many of his former colleagues. He opened his slate with the *Kizz My Black Azz* EP, the title of which was a thinly veiled reference to the actions of **Vanilla Ice**. For his debut album Ren hooked up with a slew of producers, including Rhythm D, the Whole Click (which featured Ren's brother Juvenile) and Denmark-based crew Solid Productions. A deal with the latter was first mooted when Ren met them while they were working on the soundtrack to the *CB4* film, on which they encouraged Ren to participate. However, Ren has proved unable to replicate the lyrical incisiveness of **Ice Cube** nor the satisfying musical stance of **Dr Dre**. Allusions to the wisdom of the Nation Of Islam have revealed little in the way of insight or character.
Albums: *Kizz My Black Azz* (Ruthless 1992, mini-album), *Shock Of The Hour* (Ruthless 1993).

MC Serch

b. Michael Berrin, Queens, New York, USA. After splitting from white rap trio **3rd Bass**, Serch remained with **Def Jam** for the launch of his solo career in 1992. Shortly afterwards he would take up a position as A&R Vice President for **Wild Pitch** Records. His sole solo hit thus far proved to be 'Love Will Show Us'.
Album: *Return Of The Product* (Def Jam 1992).

MC Shan

b. Shawn Moltke, 8 September 1965, Queens, New York, USA. Moltke enjoyed an unusual start to his hip hop career. Rather than the drudgery of demo cassettes and auditions, he was first spotted by his future **Cold Chillin'** boss as he attempted to steal his car. Nevertheless, with the early guiding hand of cousin **Marley Marl**, Shan has gone on to provide an inconsistent but occasionally interesting legacy. His debut album was the archetypal B-boy artefact, replete with Marl's stripped down production and conscious and party rhymes (the best example of the former being the anti-drugs track 'Jane, Stop This Crazy Thing!', the worst instance of the latter 'Project 'Ho'). The follow-up was more musically varied, but Shan's voice lacked the agility to compete with some exquisite samples. He dispensed with Marl in time for *Play It Again, Shan*, which, as the title might suggest, saw a bid for more mainstream territory. Apart from 'It Ain't A Hip Hop Record', there was little to distinguish this collection and its lacklustre **Heavy D**-styled performance.

Albums: *Down By Law* (Cold Chillin' 1987), *Born To Be Wild* (Cold Chillin' 1988), *Play It Again, Shan* (Cold Chillin' 1990).

MC Shy D

b. Peter Jones, Bronx, New York, USA. Shy D is the cousin of **Afrika Bambaataa**, and grew up with the sounds and philosophy of the Zulu Nation. Moving to Atlanta in 1978, he made his name via his debut single 'Rapp Will Never Die' in 1985, before joining Luke Skywalker (now Luke) Records for 'I've Gotta Be Tough' and 'Shake It'. These releases, some of the first on the label, featured the prominent 'Miami bass' sound. After two well-received albums he set up his own Benz Records imprint in 1990, but his fortunes declined thereafter, 1991 being spent in the Georgia State Penal System. More fruitful was his liaison with Wrap/**Ichiban** Records, which saw the release of a quality single ('True To The Game') and album which re-acquainted him with the hip hop public.
Albums: *Gotta Be Tough* (Luke Skywalker 1987), *Comin' Correct* (Luke 1988), *Don't Sweat Me* (Benz Records 1990), *The Comeback* (Wrap/Ichiban 1993).

MC Solaar

b. Dakar, Senegal, but raised in Cairo and Paris, MC Solaar is the most prominent of the new breed of French rappers. His debut album (translating as Who Sows The Wind Will Reap The Beat) gave him four Top 10 French singles, the album itself moving over 200,000 copies. It brought him to the attention of the UK's **Talkin' Loud** imprint. They, like many others, were impressed by his free-flowing, relaxed style, and its easy musical backdrop, formulated by his DJ/producer Jimmy Jay. **Gang Starr** were so taken with the album that after a single hearing they asked if they could remix the title-track. Solaar also took part in many collaborative projects for the Talkin' Loud stable (**United Future Organization**, **Urban Species**) and the Guru of Gang Starr-orchestrated **Jazzamatazz** project. His own material most often concerns sad stories about malcontents in the stream of French life. The wordplay and nuances do not translate easily, but the musicality of the French language does. As well as rappers like **Big Daddy Kane**, Solaar draws his inspiration from the French literary tradition of Baudelaire and Jaques Prevert.
Albums: *Qui Seme Le Vent Recolte Le Tempo* (Talkin' Loud 1993), *Prose Combat* (Talkin' Loud 1994).

MC Trouble

b. Latasha Rogers, c.1972. MC Trouble became **Motown**'s first female rapper when she appeared in 1990 with a debut album and attendant singles ('High Roller' etc) at the tender age of 18. Backed by the soul undertow more familiar with the label, her rhymes were contrastingly harsh and cutting. Trouble's talents were obvious to many. Above and beyond being a talented contemporary rapper, she was also responsible for writing, arranging and producing her debut set. Her conscious raps included the likes of 'Black Line', which parodied black talk shows, while in a romantic mode cuts like 'Make You Mine' were offered a smooth, soulful sheen. A guest appearance by **Full Force** was pleasing but incidental. She passed away in the early 90s.
Album: *Gotta Get A Grip* (Motown 1990).

MC5

Formed in 1964 in Detroit, Michigan, USA, and originally known as the Motor City Five, the group was sundered the following year when its rhythm section left in protest over a new original song, 'Back To Comm'. Michael Davis (bass) and Dennis Thompson (drums) joined founder members Rob Tyner (b. Robert Derminer, 12 December 1944, Detroit, Michigan, USA, d. 18 September 1991; vocals), **Wayne Kramer** (guitar) and Fred 'Sonic' Smith (b. 1949, d. 4 November 1994; guitar) to pursue the radical direction this experimental composition offered. By 1967 their repertoire contained material drawn from R&B, soul and *avant garde* jazz, as well as a series of powerful original songs. Two singles, 'One Of The Guys'/'I Can Only Give You Everything' (1967) and 'Borderline'/'Looking At You' (1968), captured their nascent, high-energy sound as the group embraced the 'street' politics proselytized by mentor/manager John Sinclair. Now linked to this former DJ's Trans Love Commune and White Panther party, the MC5 became Detroit's leading underground act, and a recording deal with the **Elektra** label resulted in the seminal *Kick Out The Jams*. Recorded live at the city's Grande Ballroom, this turbulent set captured the quintet's extraordinary sound which, although loud, was never reckless. However, the Five were then dropped from their label's roster following several disagreements, but later emerged anew on **Atlantic**. Rock journalist Jon Landau, later manager of **Bruce Springsteen**, was invited to produce *Back In The USA* which, if lacking the dissolute thrill of its predecessor, showed a group able to adapt to studio discipline. 'Tonight', 'Shakin' Street' and a remade 'Lookin' At You' are among the highlights of this excellent set. A third collection, *High Time*, reasserted a desire to experiment, and several local jazz musicians added punch to what nonetheless remains a curiously ill-focused album on which each member, bar Davis, contributed material. A move to Europe, where the group performed and recorded under the aegis of **Rohan O'Rahilly**, failed to halt dwindling commercial prospects, while the departure of Davis, then Tyner, in 1972, brought the MC5 to an end. Their reputation flourished during the punk phenomenon, during which time each former member enjoyed brief notoriety. Davis later surfaced in

Destroy All Monsters, and Sonic Smith married **Patti Smith** (and was heavily featured on the singer/poet's 'comeback' album, *Dream Of Life*, in 1988). Both Kramer and Tyner attempted to use the MC5 name for several unrelated projects. They wisely abandoned such practices, leaving intact the legend of one of rock's most uncompromising and exciting acts. In September 1991 Rob Tyner died of a heart attack at the seat of his parked car in his home town of Ferndale, Michigan. Smith also passed away three years later. Kramer, however, relaunched a solo career in the same year, enlisting several prominent members of the US underground/alternative scene so inspired by the original MC5 as his new cohorts.

Albums: *Kick Out The Jams* (Elektra 1969), *Back In The USA* (Elektra 1970), *High Time* (Elektra 1971). Compilation: *Babes In Arms* (ROIR 1983), *Looking At You* (Receiver 1994).

Mchunu, Moses

b. 1953, Transvaal, South Africa. During the mid-70s and early 80s, Mchunu was one of the leading vocalists in the raucous Zulu 'jive' style which gave way to mbaqanga.

Albums: *Inkunzi Emnyama* (1976), *Baningi Abangithandayo* (1979), *Qhwayilhale* (1981), *Awukho Umuzi Wempholo* (1982).

Me And Juliet

Perhaps because it emerged into the bright lights of Broadway in the same season as hits such as ***Wish You Were Here***, ***Wonderful Town***, and ***Can-Can***, **Richard Rodgers** and **Oscar Hammerstein**'s *Me And Juliet* was regarded by critics and public alike to be well below their par. Certainly, after blockbusters such as ***Oklahoma!***, ***Carousel***, and ***The King And I***, a run of 358 performances was not remarkable by their standards. Unlike those three shows, *Me And Juliet* was not adapted from an existing work, but had an original book by Hammerstein. It opened at the Majestic Theatre in New York on 28 May 1953. The setting is a theatre, onstage and off, where a musical entitled *Me And Juliet* is playing. Jeannie (Isabel Bigley), a singer in the chorus, is being pleasantly pursued by Larry (Bill Hayes), the assistant stage manager, until electrician Bob (Mark Dawson), a nasty hard-drinking character, tries to muscle in on the romance to such an extent that he tries to murder her. The traditional 'fun-romance' situation that usually crops up in these kind of shows, in this case involves a dancer, Betty (Joan McCracken) and the stage manager, Mac (Ray Walston). The latter artist proved to be a memorable Luther Billis in the film of Rodgers and Hammerstein's ***South Pacific***, and he also gave a 'devil' of a good performance in ***Damn Yankees*** on both stage and screen. The score for *Me And Juliet* was light, and contained none of the composers' 'deeply meaningful songs' (such as 'You'll Never Walk Alone', 'Carefully Taught', etc.), but there were some pleasant songs, including 'Keep It Gay', 'It's Me', 'The Big Black Giant', 'A Very Special Day', 'I'm Your Girl', and 'Do I Love You Because You're Beautiful' and 'Marriage-Type Love', both of which achieved some modest popularity. Rodgers had used the melody of one of the other numbers, 'No Other Love', before, as part of the background score for the television documentary series, *Victory At Sea* (1952). The song became a big hit for **Perry Como** in America, and a UK number 1 for **Ronnie Hilton**. Rodgers remembered the song again, in 1957, and interpolated it into a US television version of *Cinderella*, which starred **Julie Andrews**. It was also present when *Cinderella* was adapted for the stage, and played the London Coliseum as a Christmas-time entertainment in 1958, with a cast that included **Tommy Steele**, Bruce Trent, **Yana**, Jimmy Edwards, Betty Marsden, and Kenneth Williams. Exactly 35 years after that, *Cinderella* was staged in America by the New York City Opera.

Me And My Girl

With music by **Noel Gay**, and a book and lyrics by Douglas Furber and L Arthur Rose, *Me And My Girl* opened in at the Victoria Palace in London on 16 December 1937. The immensely popular **Lupino Lane** starred as Bill Snibson, a Cockney barrow-boy who becomes involved with the 'toffs', but stays true to Sally (Teddy St. Dennis), a girl from his own background. *Me And My Girl* was the first West End production to be televised live from a theatre, and after excerpts were transmitted by the BBC, audiences flocked to see the show with its cheerful music and happy-go-lucky air. The show ran at the Victoria Palace until June 1940, a total of 1,646 performances, and, after a break, and a spell at the London Coliseum, it returned to the Palace for a further nine months in 1945/6. By that time everybody, it seemed, was doing 'The Lambeth Walk' and singing along with Bill and Sally to 'Me And My Girl'. There was yet another short-lived production at the Winter Garden in 1949/50. At this stage, Lupino Lane had played the lead in all of them. In February 1985, a revised version of the show, written by the humorist Stephen Fry, opened at the Adelphi Theatre in London. It was produced by Richard Armitage, Noel Gay's son, and starred the popular straight actor Robert Lindsay, and future Oscar-winner Emma Thompson. Also in the cast were veteran performers Frank Thornton and Ursula Smith, representing the 'toffs', who duetted the amusingly nostalgic 'If Only You Had Cared For Me'. Two other Noel Gay hits, ' Leaning On a Lamp Post' and 'The Sun Has Got His Hat On', were interpolated into the score, and coach parties galore continued to pour into the Adelphi for an incredible eight years. Along the way the show won **Laurence Olivier**

Awards for best musical and actor, Robert Lindsay, who reprised his role for the 1986 Broadway production. New York audiences loved it too, and the show earned **Tony Awards** for Lindsay, best actress (Maryann Plunkett), and choreographer Gillian Gregory. Many years before all that, in 1939, a film version was released, starring Lupino Lane, of course.

Mean Machine

Though somewhat unfairly consigned to the wastebasket of musical history, Mean Machine deserve their place in the hip hop hall of fame by dint of being the first crew to rap in Spanish, in 1979. As such they would serve as a signpost to subsequent generations of Latino rappers, from **Kid Frost** to **Mellow Man Ace**, to **Cypress Hill** and **K7**.

Meanstreak

Formed in New York, Meanstreak were formed in 1985 by guitarists Marlene Apuzzo and Rena Sands. Recruiting vocalist Bettina France, bassist Martens Pace and drummer Diane Keyser, they were the first all-female thrash metal band to record an album. Signing to the independent **Music For Nations** label, they released *Roadkill*, produced by **Alex Perialas** and ex-**Raven** drummer Rob Hunter. Recorded within a week, the pressure resulted in a set which betrayed its origins by being both shambolic and ill-focused. The songs, meanwhile, were rigidly formularized and were further scuppered by weak vocals. The album remains of interest to thrash aficionados, but even then on a historical rather than musical level.
Album: *Roadkill* (Music For Nations 1988).

Meat Loaf

b. Marvin Lee Aday, 27 September 1947, Dallas, Texas, USA. The name Meat Loaf originated at school, when aged 13, he was christened 'Meat Loaf' by his football coach, owing to his enormous size and ungainly manner. Two years later his mother died of cancer, and fights with his alcoholic father grew worse. He moved to Los Angeles in 1967 and formed Popcorn Blizzard, a psychedelic rock outfit which toured the club circuit, opening for acts including the **Who**, **Ted Nugent** and the **Stooges**. In 1969 Meat Loaf successfully auditioned for a role in ***Hair***, where he met soul vocalist Stoney. Stoney and Meat Loaf recorded a self-titled album in 1971, which spawned the minor ***Billboard*** chart hit, 'What You See Is What You Get'. *Hair* closed in New York in 1974, and Meat Loaf found new work in *More Than You Deserve*, a musical written by Jim Steinman, then took the part of Eddie in the film version of *The Rocky Horror Picture Show*. In 1976, he was recruited by **Ted Nugent** to sing lead vocals on his *Free For All*, after which he joined up with Jim Steinman again in the famous US satirical comedy outfit, the National Lampoon Roadshow. Meat Loaf and Steinman struck up a working musical relationship and started composing a grandiose rock opera. After a long search, they found **Epic** Records and producer **Todd Rundgren** sympathetic to their ideas and demo tapes. Enlisting the services of **Bruce Springsteen**'s E Street Band, they recorded *Bat Out Of Hell* in 1978. This was pieced together around the high camp of the title-track, an operatic horror melodrama which saw Meat Loaf raging against nature, and 'Paradise By The Dashboard Lights', with **Ellen Foley** providing female accompaniment. The album was ignored for the first six months after release, although Meat Loaf toured extensively, supporting **Cheap Trick**, among others. Eventually the breakthrough came, and *Bat Out Of Hell* rocketed towards the top of the charts in country after country. It stayed in the UK and US album charts for 395 and 88 weeks respectively, and sold in excess of thirty million copies worldwide, the third biggest-selling album release of all time. However, with success came misfortune. Meat Loaf split with his manager, David Sonenberg, causing all manner of litigation. He was drinking heavily to cope with his new found but barely anticipated stardom, and lost his voice. He also lost his songwriter too, as Steinman split to release solo what had been mooted as a thematic follow-up to *Bat Out Of Hell - Bad For Good*: 'I spent seven months trying to make a follow-up with him, and it was an infernal nightmare. He had lost his voice, he had lost his house, and he was pretty much losing his mind'. After a three-year gap, during which Meat Loaf declared himself voluntarily bankrupt, the eagerly anticipated follow-up, *Dead Ringer,* was released. Again it used Steinman's compositions, this time in his absence, and continued where *Bat Out Of Hell* left off, comprising grandiose arrangements, anthemic choruses and spirited rock 'n' roll. The title-song made the Top 5 in the UK and the album hit number 1, but it only dented the lower end of the Top 50 *Billboard* album chart. This was, seemingly, the last time Meat Loaf would be able to use Steinman's sympathetic songwriting skills, and the consequent weakening of standards undoubtedly handicapped the second phase of his career. Concentrating on Europe, relentless touring helped both *Midnight At The Lost And Found* and *Bad Attitude* to creep into the Top 10 UK album charts. Nevertheless, this represented a significant decline in popularity compared with his Steinman-penned albums. *Blind Before I Stop* saw Meat Loaf teaming up with **John Parr** for the single 'Rock'n'Roll Mercenaries', which, surprisingly, was not a hit. The album was, however, his strongest post-Steinman release and featured a fine selection of accessible, blues-based, hard rock numbers. With live performances, things had never been better; Meat Loaf's band included Bob Kulick (brother of **Kiss** guitarist Bruce Kulick, and now of **Skull**), and ex-**Rainbow** drummer Chuck Burgi. They delivered an electrifying show which ran for nearly three hours. Recorded at London's Wembley Stadium, *Meat Loaf Live* emerged in 1987, and featured raw and exciting versions of his finest songs. By now Meat Loaf was also a veteran of several films, including *Roadie*, *Americathon* and, in the 90s, *Wayne's World* and *Leap Of Faith*. Apart from re-releases and compilations, he maintained vinyl silence well into the 90s. However, he signed a new deal with **Virgin Records** in 1990, and as rumours grew that he was once again working with Steinman, the media bandwagon began to roll. *Bat Out Of Hell II - Back Into Hell*, from its title onwards, displayed a calculated, stylistic cloning of its precursor. The public greeted the familiarity with open arms, pushing lead-off single 'I'll Do Anything For Love (But I Won't Do That)' to number 1 in both the US and UK, its parent album performing the same feat. Though critics could point at the formulaic nature of their approach, Meat Loaf had no doubts that by working with Steinman again, he had recaptured the magic: 'Nobody writes like Jim Steinman. All these things - bombastic, over the top, self-indulgent. All these things are positives.'

Albums: *Bat Out Of Hell* (Epic 1978), *Dead Ringer* (Epic 1981), *Midnight At The Lost And Found* (Epic 1983), *Bad Attitude* (Arista 1985), *Blind Before I Stop* (Arista 1986), *Meat Loaf Live* (Arista 1987), *Bat Out Of Hell II: Back Into Hell* (Virgin 1993), *Alive In Hell* (Pure Music 1994). Compilation: *Hits Out Of Hell* (Epic 1984). With Bonnie Tyler: *Heaven & Hell* (1993).

Videos: *Live At Wembley* (1984), *Bad Attitude Live* (1986), *Hits Out Of Hell* (1986), *Meat Loaf Live* (1991), *Bat Out Of Hell II - Picture Show* (1994).

Further reading: *Meatloaf: Jim Steinman And The Phenomenology Of Excess*, Sandy Robertson.

Meat Puppets

Formed in Tempe, Arizona, USA, Curt Kirkwood (guitar/vocals), Cris Kirkwood (bass/vocals) and Derrick Bostrom (drums) made their debut in 1981 with a five-track EP, *In A Car*. *Meat Puppets*, released the following year on the influential hardcore label, **SST Records**, offered a mix of thrash punk with hints of country, captured to perfection on the alternative cowboy classic, 'Tumblin' Tumbleweeds'. Their affection for roots music was fully realised on *Meat Puppets II*, a captivating set marked by dramatic shifts in mood and Curt Kirkwood's uncertain, but expressive, vocals. *Meat Puppets II* hauled country back to the campfire. *Up On The Sun* showed the trio moving further from their punk roots, embracing instead neo-psychedelic melodies. This evolution was enhanced further on *Mirage*, yet another critically-acclaimed set. Having proclaimed an affection for **ZZ Top**, Curt Kirkwood introduced a more direct, fuzz-toned sound on *Huevos*, which was recorded in one marathon 72-hour session. Viewed by many longtime fans as a sell-out, the set's commercial appeal continued on *Monster*, the trio's heaviest, most 'traditional' set to date. Memorable hooklines were combined with hard-rock riffs and despite the qualms of those preferring the group's early work, the set was lauded as one of 1989's leading independent releases. Surprisingly the Meat Puppets then disbanded, reforming in 1991, buoyed by continued interest in their work and a proposed deal with **London Records**. Subsequent releases have kept interest in the group alive and in 1993 the Kirkwood brothers joined **Nirvana** on their now-legendary *Unplugged* appearance. Three songs from *Meat Puppets II*; 'Lake Of Fire', 'Plateau' and 'Oh Me', were immortalised during this affectionate collaboration.

Albums: *Meat Puppets* (SST 1982), *Meat Puppets II* (SST 1983), *Up On The Sun* (SST 1985). *Mirage* (SST 1987), *Huevos* (SST 1987), *Monsters* (SST 1989), *Forbidden Places* (London 1991), *Too High To Die* (London 1994). Compilation: *No Strings Attached* (SST 1990).

Meaux, Huey P.

b. 10 March 1929, Kaplan, Louisiana, USA. Meaux is an influential figure in Texas music circles, and often acted as go-between, arranging for labels to license masters brought to him. A shrewd judge of hit potential, he also prospered as a producer with a series of excellent, contrasting acts. **Barbara Lynn**'s 1962 hit, 'You'll Lose A Good Thing', helped finance Meaux's studios in Houston and Jackson, which in turn generated further success with **B.J. Thomas** ('I'm So Lonesome I Could Cry'), **Roy Head** ('Treat Her Right') and the **Sir Douglas Quintet** ('She's About A Mover'), the latter of which was released on Meaux's own Tribe label, one of several he would inaugurate. A conviction in 1967 for violation of the Mann Act (escorting a female across state lines for immoral purposes), resulted in his imprisonment. It was the mid-70s before Meaux recovered momentum with Tex-Mex star **Freddie Fender**, who rose from regional to national acclaim with Huey's excellent southern-style recordings. Among the many acts to use this intuitive individual's production skills are **Johnny Copeland**, **T-Bone Walker** and **Johnny Winter**. 'Before The Next Tear Falls' was a US number 1 single in 1975, and the producer continued this roots-based direction with several other acts, scoring a 1985 hit with Rockin' Sydney's version of the cajun 'standard', 'My Toot Toot'. He made an appearance as a disc jockey in **David Byrne**'s film, *True Stories*, in 1986.

Meco

Meco Monardo (b. 29 November 1939, Johnsonburg, Pennsylvania, USA) was a talented arranger who successfully moved into the pop field in the early 70s. He co-produced **Gloria Gaynor**'s 'Never Can Say Goodbye' and **Carl Douglas**'s 'Doctor's Orders' before finding fame in his own right in 1977. Totally entranced by the Steven Spielberg film *Star Wars*, which he saw 11 times, Meco was convinced that he could take the theme into the charts. After hiring musicians and employing his own talents as trombonist and pianist, Meco watched with equal fascination as 'Star Wars Theme'/'Cantina Band' effortlessly moved to number 1, outselling the official theme by the London Symphony Orchestra in the process. Thereafter, Meco became something of a specialist in movie themes, finding success with adaptations from *Close Encounters Of The Third Kind*, *The Wizard Of Oz*, *The Empire Strikes Back* and *Return Of The Jedi.*

Media Records

(see **Bortolotti, Gianfranco**)

Medicine

USA indie rock band featuring Beth Thompson (b. 12 June 1967, St Louis, Missouri, USA; vocals), Brad Laner (b. 6 November 1966, Los Angeles, California, USA; vocals, guitar), Jim Putnam (b. 30 September 1967, Hollywood, California, USA; guitar), Jim Goodall (b. 9 May 1952, Burbank, California, USA; drums) and Ed Ruscha (b. Edward Joseph Ruscha, 14 December 1968, Inglewood, California, USA; bass). Each of this membership had performed as part of other bands. Thompson had worked with Four Way Cross, Laner with **Savage Republic** and Steaming Coils, Putnam with SDF, Magic Beard and Bus Engines, Ruscha with SDF, Maids Of Gravity, Pita Hawks, Magic Beard and Dumb Speedway Children. The eldest member of the sect, Goodall has seen service with such established bands as the **Flying Burrito Brothers** and **Canadian Sweetheart**. Taking their name from an old **Throbbing Gristle** song, the group made their bow in Long Beach, California, in September 1991 (they had already been picked up for radio broadcast by west coast alternative radio guru Rodney Bingenheimer). Signed to English label **Creation Records**, they made their recorded debut in August 1992 with 'Aruca', which prefaced a well-received debut album. However, they left the UK independent's roster shortly afterwards, and sightings were fewer thenceforth until the release of *Sounds Of Medicine*, a mini-album with remixes by Billy Corgan (**Smashing Pumpkins**) and Robin Guthrie (**Cocteau Twins**). Again, this could hardly be described as light-hearted fare, but as Thompson declared to the press: 'I'm happy to make dark music. Fortunately you can't really make out our words so nobody's going to come to us and say we caused so and so's suicide.'

Albums: *Short Forth Self Living* (Creation 1992), *Sounds Of Medicine* (1994, mini-album).

Medicine Ball Caravan

This 1971 film followed several rock groups as they travelled across America. The guiding force behind the project was San Franciscan disc-jockey **Tom Donahue**, former proprietor of Autumn Records. Alternately known as *We Have Come For Your Daughters* after the motto pinned to the touring bus - which drew the ire of feminists - *Medicine Ball Caravan* was a thinly-veiled way of promoting Donahue's management clients, **Stoneground**. This expansive, revue-styled act was led by **Sal Valentino**, formerly of the **Beau Brummels**, and it also included several well-respected Bay Area musicians. **B.B. King**, **Alice Cooper**, **Delaney And Bonnie** and **Doug Kershaw** are among the other featured acts, but Stoneground remain at its core. Interesting rather than essential, *Medicine Ball Caravan* suggests a last-gasp attempt at exposing a 'gypsy-esque' notion of rock. It was not a great success and an attendant soundtrack album was also poorly received. Paradoxically, several portions featuring Stoneground were exhumed by **Warner Brothers Records** in a bid to help launch the group in Britain.

Medicine Head

John Fiddler (b. 25 September 1947, Darlaston, Staffordshire, England; guitar/vocals) and Peter Hope-Evans (b. 28 September 1947, Brecon, Powys, Wales; harmonica/jew's harp) were constrained to the small clubs of England's midlands, until a demo tape brought the duo to pioneering BBC disc jockey **John Peel**'s Dandelion label. Their debut album, *New Bottles Old Medicine,* offered delicate, sparse, atmospheric songs, and crude, rumbustious R&B, a contrast maintained on a second set, *Heavy On The Drum.* The duo enjoyed a surprise hit single when '(And The) Pictures In The Sky' reached number 22 in 1971, but their progress faltered when Hope-Evans left the group. Ex-**Yardbird** Keith Relf, at this point Medicine Head's producer, joined Fiddler and drummer John Davies for the group's third album, *Dark Side Of The Moon.* Hope-Evans and Fiddler resumed their partnership in 1972, although session musicians were employed on their subsequent album, *One And One Is One.* The title track became a number 3 UK hit in 1973, while a second single, 'Rising Sun', reached number 11; as a result, the line-up was expanded to include Roger Saunders (b. 9 March 1947, Barking, Essex, England; guitar), Ian Sainty (bass) and ex-**Family** member Rob Townsend (b. 7 July 1947, Leicester, Leicestershire, England; drums). Further ructions followed the release of *Thru' A Five* and by 1976, Medicine Head was again reduced to the original duo. *Two Man Band* marked the end of their collaboration. Fiddler then joined **British Lions**, which otherwise comprised former members of **Mott The Hoople**, and recorded several solo singles before fronting 'reformed' Yardbirds, Box Of Frogs, in 1983. He currently works as a solo act. Hope-Evans assisted **Pete Townshend** on his *White City* soundtrack (1985), and later played in several part-time groups.

Albums: *Old Bottles New Medicine* (1970), *Heavy On The Drum* (1971), *Dark Side Of The Moon* (1972), *One And One Is One* (1973), *Thru' A Five* (1974), *Two Man Band* (1976). Compilations: *Pop History Volume XXV* (1973), *Medicine Head* (1976).

Meditations

Jamaican vocal group comprising Ansel Cridland, Danny Clarke and Winston Watson. Clarke had previously been a member of The Righteous Flames, the group fronted by **Winston Jarrett** (who in turn had been formed from the ashes of **Alton Ellis**' Flames). He would go on to step out on his own in 1975, forming the Meditations alongside Cridland and Watson. The trio, a roots group closer to the **Mighty Diamonds** in style than anyone else, recorded a series of strong singles for producers **Dobbie Dobson** and **Lee Perry**: 'Running From Jamaica', 'No Peace', 'House Of Parliament' and 'Much Smarter', songs which cast them as righteous Rastafarians who had no truck with the system. Further hits for a variety of producers revealed their pedigree: 'Wake Up', 'Fly Your Natty Dread' and the massive 'Woman Is Like A Shadow' (1978). Their first LP, *Message From The Meditations*, was a minor classic. Resourceful beyond the limits of most bands, the Meditations rode out the **dancehall** era, cutting a series of strong, if hardly spectacularly successful albums for a variety of labels, including *Guidance* and *Wake Up*. Their 1986 set, *No More Friend*, was favourably received, and they remain revered ambassadors of rasta reggae, and retain much goodwill in America to this day.
Selected albums: *Message From the Meditations* (1977), *Wake Up* (Third World 1978), *No More Friend* (Greensleeves 1983), *For The Good Of Man* (Greensleeves 1988), *Return Of* (1993). Compilations: *Greatest Hits* (Greensleeves 1984).

Medley, Bill

b. 19 September 1940, Santa Ana, California, USA. After several successful years with the **Righteous Brothers**, Medley embarked on a solo career in late 1967. Several relatively barren years followed, until Medley received a major push from **A&M** in 1971. Again, no hits were forthcoming and, in 1974, the Righteous Brothers reunited. Medley's second attempt at a solo career took place in 1981, five years after the mysterious murder of his wife Karen. This time he enjoyed some minor hits, which reached fruition during the second half of the 80s with his contribution to the movie *Dirty Dancing*. Collaborating with **Jennifer Warnes**, Medley found the perfect song in '(I've Had) The Time Of My Life', which reached number 1 in the US charts. Further film-related material saw Medley enjoy minor successes, most notably with a cover of the **Hollies**' 'He Ain't Heavy, He's My Brother' from the soundtrack of *Rambo III*.

Albums: Bill Medley *100%* (MGM 1968), *Soft And Soulful* (MGM 1969), *A Song For You* (1971), *Sweet Thunder* (1981), *Right Here And Now* (1982). Compilation: *The All-Time Greatest Hits Of Bill Medley* (1988).

Meehan, Tony

Drummer Meehan (b. Daniel Joseph Anthony Meehan, 22 March 1943, Hampstead, London, England) worked with several late 50s' acts, including **Vince Eager**, **Vince Taylor** and the **Vipers**, before joining the Drifters, later the **Shadows**, in 1959. He left the group in 1961, in order to take up an A&R post with **Decca**, but later forged a successful partnership with another ex-Shadow. **Jet Harris And Tony Meehan** enjoyed three UK Top 5 singles, including the number 1 'Diamonds', before the former was involved in a serious car smash. Their partnership sundered, the drummer formed the Tony Meehan Combo for 'Song Of Mexico' (1964), but he failed to emulate earlier success. The short-lived group included bassist **John Paul Jones**, later of **Led Zeppelin**, but was disbanded when its leader reverted to backroom work. Meehan produced material for **Trash** and **Tim Hardin**, but his only reappearance as a performer was confined to 'Hooker Street' (1969), the b-side to his brother Keith's lone single.

Meek, Joe

b. Robert George Meek, 5 April 1929, Newent, Gloucestershire, England, d. 3 February 1967, London, England. Britain's premier independent record producer of the early 60s, Meek was equally renowned for his pioneering recording techniques and eccentric personality. His career began in 1954, when he joined IBC, the leading independent recording studio of the era. Originally an engineer, he worked on a number of hits, including **Lonnie Donegan**'s 'Cumberland Gap', **Frankie Vaughan**'s 'Green Door', **Johnny Duncan**'s 'Last Train To San Fernando' and **Humphrey Lyttelton**'s 'Bad Penny Blues'. He also turned his hand to songwriting, penning **Tommy Steele**'s 'Put A Ring On Her Finger' in 1958.
By 1960, he had set up Lansdowne Studios in west London, where he worked with producer Denis Preston on recordings by various popular jazz artists. An ill-advised expansion policy encouraged Meek to launch Triumph Records, which enjoyed a hit with **Michael Cox**'s 'Angela Jones' before rapidly winding down its activities. Thereafter, Meek concentrated on leasing tapes to major labels using the title, RGM Sound. He worked from a converted studio situated above a shop in Holloway Road, north London and it was here that he created the unusual sounds which were to become his hallmark. His first major hit as a producer was **John Leyton**'s 'Johnny Remember Me', an atmospheric, eerily echo-laden affair which topped the UK charts in 1961. Leyton followed-up with other

Meek-produced successes, including 'Wild Wind', 'Son, This Is She' and 'Lonely City'. With Geoff Goddard composing suitably ethereal material, Meek enjoyed further vicarious chart action with **Mike Berry** ('Tribute To Buddy Holly') and backing group the **Outlaws** ('Swingin' Low' and 'Ambush'). By 1962, the increasingly inventive producer had reached his apogee on the spacy instrumental 'Telstar', which took the **Tornadoes** to the top of the charts on both sides of the Atlantic. He was now hailed as a genuine original, with an innovative flair unmatched by any of his rivals. The accolades were to prove short-lived.
The mid-60s beat boom spearheaded by the **Beatles** seriously dented Meek's credibility and commercial standing. His work was increasingly regarded as novel, rather than important, and his love for gimmicks took precedence on recordings by **Screaming Lord Sutch** and others. Meek responded with the much publicized **Heinz,** who reached the Top 10 with the **Eddie Cochran** tribute, 'Just Like Eddie'. The swirling 'Have I The Right' provided a 1964 UK number 1 for the **Honeycombs**, but this was to be Meek's last major success. By 1965, he seemed something of an anachronism, and his production techniques seemed leaden and predictable rather than startling. The departure of songwriter Geoff Goddard weakened the supply of good material, and a motley series of flop records left record companies disenchanted. Meek's tempestuous personality and often violent behaviour alienated many old friends, while his homosexuality produced feelings of self-loathing and engendered a fear of imminent scandal. His mental instability worsened with successive personal and business problems, and on 3 February 1967, he was involved in a bizarre shooting incident in which he fatally shot his landlady before turning the gun on himself. It was the end of a sometimes brilliant but frustratingly erratic career.
Album: with the Blue Men *I Hear A New World* (1992).
Compilations: *The Joe Meek Story Volume 1* (1992), *Work In Progress* (1993).
Further reading: *The Legendary Joe Meek*, John Repsch.

Meet Me In St. Louis

Released by MGM in 1944, this enchanting film traces the adventures of the Smith family - all eight of them - as the seasons change from summer through to spring in the US city of St. Louis during 1903/4. Based on *The Kensington Stories* by Sally Benson, Irving Brecher and Fred Finklehoffe's screenplay focuses mainly on one of the Smiths' teenage daughter, Esther (**Judy Garland**), and her romance with the boy who lives next door to her in Kensington Avenue, John Truitt (Tom Drake). The rest of the cast was particularly fine: Esther's three sisters, Rose, Tootie and Agnes, were played by Lucille Bremer, Margaret O'Brien, and Joan Carroll; and the family group was completed by brother Lon Jnr. (Henry H. Daniels Jnr.), father and mother (Leon Ames and Mary Astor), grandpa (Harry Davenport) - and their long-time maid Katie, (Marjorie Main). Also featured were June Lockhart, Hugh Marlowe, Robert Sully, and Chill Wills. The seemingly ordinary day-to-day happenings involving collusion between Rose, her mother and Katie to advance the time of the evening meal by an hour so that it will not coincide with a long-distance telephone call from Rose's boyfriend, Tootie's Halloween night escapades, Esther and Tom's mutual joy at the Christmas dance, and the possibility of the whole family moving to New York, resulted in a most extraordinary film. To the relief of the majority, the move away from their beloved home does not materialize, and the whole family celebrate at the opening of 1904 St. Louis World Fair, singing 'Meet Me In St. Louis, Louis' (Andrew Sterling-Kerry Mills). **Hugh Martin** and **Ralph Blane** contributed three memorable songs for Judy Garland to sing: 'The Boy Next Door', 'Have Yourself A Merry Little Christmas', and the immortal 'The Trolley Song' which accompanied one of the most endearing sequences in any film musical. Garland also joined O'Brien for the charming 'Under The Bamboo Tree' (Bob Cole-J. Rosamond Johnson), and she and the rest of the young people (and audiences all over the world) brushed a tear from their eyes as Leon Ames (dubbed by **Arthur Freed**) and Mary Astor rendered the poignant 'You And I' (Freed-**Nacio Herb Brown**). The dances were staged by **Charles Walters**, and the film, which was directed with his usual style and flair by **Vincente Minnelli**, was photographed in Technicolor by George Folsey. *Meet Me In St. Louis* was an enormous commercial success, grossing over $5 million in US domestic theatre rentals alone - a fitting return for what is generally considered to be a masterpiece. Unfortunately, the magic did not extend to the 1989 Broadway stage adaptation which one critic called 'a lumbering and graceless project'. It ran for only 253 performances at the time, but revivals, complete with additional songs, were mounted in St. Louis in 1960 and 1991.

Mega Banton

Among the biggest reggae discoveries of the early 90s, Mega Banton's early career has been distinguished by the quality of his appearances for Maurice Johnson's Black Scorpio label, including an album shared with Ricky General. Often compared to the similarly-titled **Buju Banton** due to his gruff, haranguing delivery, Mega has enjoyed sizeable hits with 'Decision' and 'Dis The System'. However, with **ragga** and **dancehall** going overground, it may well be that he will enjoy his share of the crossover spotlight in the 90s.
Selected albums: with Ricky General *Showcase* (Black Scorpio 1993), *First Position* (VP 1994).

Mega City Four

Thrash pop outfit influenced by early punks such as **Stiff Little Fingers** and the **Buzzcocks**, stabilizing their output with a sustained melodicism and growing lyrical awareness. They started out in 1982 as Capricorn, who played a few gigs and recorded demos (including one 15 track affair entitled *The Good News Tape*). However, in 1986 original drummer Martin left, leaving the remaining members to undergo a re-think. A replacement, Chris Jones, was recruited from local bands Exit East and Moose Kaboose, joining Wiz (b. Darren Brown; vocals/guitar), Danny (b. Daniel Brown; rhythm guitar/backing vocals, brother of Wiz), and Gerry (b. Gerald Bryant; bass). Wiz had previously played one gig fronting a progressive rock band, Quilp, before joining Bryant in Capricorn, formed at Guildford technical college. On 1 January 1987, Mega City Four had their first practice. They took their name from the home base of *Judge Dredd*, the popular comic book enforcer. A demo appeared in March, and after nation-wide gigs a self-financed single, 'Miles Apart', was recorded in the autumn. Although it took six months to surface, reviews were impressive and DJ **John Peel** added his patronage. In the wake of its success it was reissued by **Vinyl Solution** subsidiary, Decoy Records, who became the band's permanent home. 'Distant Relatives' followed in November 1988, announcing Wiz's lyrical preoccupation with relationships, and was awarded Single Of The Week status by Steve Lamacq in ***New Musical Express***. Another single, 'Less Than Senseless', arrived during a relentless 300-gig touring schedule throughout 1989. These experiences would result in the title of their debut album, *Tranzophobia* - a term invoked to convey the horror of touring for extended periods out of the back of a transit van. Though at the time it perfectly described the earnest, hard-working nature of the band, later it became an albatross around their necks when they found themselves unable to escape the lack of sophistication it implied. Despite this, Mega City Four, alongside peers and friends the **Senseless Things**, helped revitalize a flagging UK live scene with wholly committed performances. Sadly *Who Cares Wins* saw many of the band's newly acquired critical following renounce their previous advocacy, on a set neutered by flat production. Frustrated by budget restrictions, the band elected to move to **Big Life Records** for future recordings. 'Words That Say' and 'Stop', the latter a Top 40 success in January 1992, prefaced the band's long playing debut for their new home. *Sebastapol Road* was titled after the group's Farnborough rehearsal studio and comprised a succinct, energized collection of three minute pop songs with more highly-evolved lyrical themes than had previously been the case. A live album, less perfunctory than efforts by bands without Mega City Four's on-stage fluency, preceded 1993's *Magic Bullets*. With increasingly introverted song writing from Wiz - though his words were as direct and anti-glamour as ever - this was another fine, considered set, its quality emphasized by the promotional single, 'Iron Sky'. However, the group's fans had also moved on, to new favourites like **Carter USM** (one of many bands who started out as support act to MC4), and sales proved disappointing.

Albums: *Tranzophobia* (Decoy 1989), *Who Cares Wins* (Decoy 1990), *Sebastapol Road* (Big Life 1991), *Inspiringly Titled (The Live Album)* (Big Life 1992), *Magic Bullets* (Big Life 1993). Compilation: *Terribly Sorry Bob* (Decoy 1991).

Megadeth

This uncompromising and intense thrash metal quartet was founded in San Francisco, California, USA, by guitarist Dave Mustaine (b. 13 September) after leaving **Metallica** in 1983 (he co-wrote four songs on the latter's debut album, though he did not actually appear on this). Recruiting bassist Dave Ellefson, guitarist Chris Poland and drummer Gars Samuelson, Mustaine negotiated a deal with the independent Combat label. Working on a tight budget, Megadeth produced *Killing Is My Business...And Business Is Good* in 1985. This was a ferocious blast of high-energy thrash metal, weakened by a thin production. Nevertheless, **Capitol Records**, realizing the band's potential, immediately signed them up, even though Mustaine was beginning to acquire a reputation for his outspoken and provocative manner. *Peace Sells...But Who's Buying?* was a marked improvement over their debut, both technically and musically. It was characterized by incessant, heavy duty riffing, bursts of screaming guitar and lyrics which reflected Mustaine's outspoken perception of contemporary social and political issues. In 1988 Mustaine fired Poland and Samuelson, bringing in Jeff Young and Chuck Behler as replacements before the recording of *So Far, So Good...So What!* This built on their aggressive and vitriolic style, and included a cover of 'Anarchy In The UK', with **Sex Pistols**' guitarist **Steve Jones** making a guest appearance. Following two years of heroin-related problems, and the enforced departure of Poland and Behler, Mustaine re-appeared in 1990 with guitar virtuoso **Marty Friedman** and drummer Nick Menza. *Rust In Peace* was released to widespread critical acclaim, combining an anti-nuclear message with the explosive guitar pyrotechnics of Friedman. *Countdown To Extinction*, meanwhile, was a bruising encounter which entertained more melody in the execution of its theme - that of impending ecological disaster. Reports of Mustaine's drug problems again overshadowed sessions for their sixth album, *Youthanasia*, recorded in Phoenix, Arizona, where three quarters of the band now live. It was produced by Max Norman (who co-produced *Countdown To Extinction* and mixed *Rust In Peace*). Along

with **Slayer**, **Metallica** and **Anthrax**, Megadeth remain at the forefront of the thrash metal genre, despite the vulnerability of their central creative force.
Albums: *Killing Is My Business...And Business Is Good* (Megaforce 1985), *Peace Sells...But Who's Buying?* (Capitol 1986), *So Far, So Good...So What!* (Capitol 1988), *Rust In Peace* (Capitol 1990), *Countdown To Extinction* (Capitol 1992), *Youthansia* (Capitol 1994).
Video: *Rusted Pieces* (1991).

Meisner, Randy

b. 8 March 1946, Scottsbluff, Nebraska, USA. Meisner's musical career began in the early 60s as a member of local act, the Dynamics. He subsequently moved to Colorado, where he joined the Soul Survivors, later known as the Poor; but although this folk/country-rock act was active between 1964 and 1968, its recorded legacy was constrained to two singles. Meisner then became a founder member of **Poco**, but having played on *Pickin' Up The Pieces*, left following a disagreement to join ex-Poor alumni Allen Kemp and Pat Shanahan in **Rick Nelson**'s Stone Canyon Band. In 1971, the bassist toured with **Linda Ronstadt** before joining fellow members **Bernie Leadon**, **Glenn Frey** and **Don Henley** in the **Eagles**. Meisner remained with this seminal act until 1977, when he left to pursue solo ambitions. The low-key *I Really Want You Here Tonight* was followed by the more successful *One More Song*, which spawned two US Top 30 hits in 'Deep Inside My Heart' and 'Hearts On Fire'. 'Never Been In Love' from *Randy Meisner* reached the same chart in 1982, but the artist then suspended his career. He re-emerged in 1989 when the original Poco line-up was reunited for *Legacy*, but former animosities quickly resurfaced. The following year, Meisner was involved in a new group, Black Tie, which enjoyed a hit on the country chart with a version of **Buddy Holly**'s 'Learning The Game'.
Albums: *I Really Want You Tonight* (1978), *One More Song* (1980), *Randy Meisner* (1982).

Mekons

Although initially based in Leeds, England, the Mekons made their recording debut for the Edinburgh-based Fast Product label in 1978. 'Never Been In A Riot', the outlet's first release, was the subject of effusive music press praise, and its joyous amateurism set the standard for much of the group's subsequent work. Having completed a second single, 'Where Were You', the Mekons were signed to **Virgin Records** where a line-up of Andy Carrigan (vocals), Mark White (vocals), Kevin Lycett (guitar), Tom Greenhalgh (guitar), Ross Allen (bass) and Jon Langford (drums, later guitar/vocals) completed *The Quality Of Mercy Is Not Strnen*. This unusual title was drawn from the axiom that, if you give a monkey a typewriter and an infinite amount of time, it would eventually produce the complete works of Shakespeare, a wry comment on the group's own musical ability. Nonetheless, the Mekons' enthusiasm, particularly in a live setting, was undoubtedly infectious and has contributed greatly to their long career. Despite numerous personnel changes (over 30 different members to 1995), they have retained a sense of naive adventurism, embracing world music, folk and roots material in their customarily ebullient manner. In the 90s three of the core members of the band (Greenhaigh, Langford and Sara Corina, Greenhaigh's violinist partner who joined in 1991) had relocated to Chicago, Illinois, USA, where the group enjoyed a loose recording contract with Quarterstick Records. This followed an unfortunate major label coalition with **A&M Records**. Other important contributors to the Mekons legacy include Sally Timms, vocalist and full-time member since the late 80s, who has released a brace of solo albums and is based in New York, and drummer Steve Goulding (ex-**Graham Parker And The Rumour**), a part-time journalist who has worked with Pig Dog Pondering. Langford would also work with Goulding on his part-time country band, Jon Langford & The Pine Valley Cosmonauts, who issued an album in Germany in 1994. He has also had numerous exhibitions of his paintings.
Albums: *The Quality Of Mercy Is Not Strnen* (Virgin 1979), *Mekons* (Red Rhino 1980), *Fear And Whiskey* (Sin 1985), *The Edge Of The World* (Sin 1986), *Honky Tonkin'* (Sin 1987), *New York Mekons* (ROIR 1987, cassette only), *So Good It Hurts* (Twin/Tone 1988), *Mekons Rock 'N' Roll* (A&M 1989), *The Curse Of The Mekons* (Blast First 1991), *I Love Mekons* (Quarterstick 1993), *Retreat From Memphis* (Quarterstick 1994). Compilations: *Mekons Story* (CNT 1982), *Original Sin* (RTD 1989).

Mel And Kim

One of **Stock, Aitken And Waterman**'s acts, Mel (b. Melanie Susan Appelby, 11 July 1966, London, England, d. 19 January 1990) and sister Kim (b. Kim Appelby, 28 August 1961, London, England) were two East End, London girls with a neat line in pop dance routines. They both started their careers as models - a fact which would come back to haunt them when topless pictures of Mel turned up in *Playboy* and *Penthouse* magazines. Picked up by the Stock, Aitken And Waterman team, they saw 'Showing Out (Get Fresh At The Weekend)' reach number 3 in the UK during 1986, and the following year they gave their mentors their first chart-topper as producers with 'Respectable'. The girls even stayed on top of the charts when the charity single 'Let It Be', by Ferry Aid, to which they contributed, supplanted 'Respectable'. The group was now such hot property that their name was hijacked at Christmas 1987 by Mel Smith and **Kim Wilde** for their version of 'Rockin' Around The Christmas Tree'. The title track of their debut album

(the initials *F.L.M.* stood for Fun, Love And Money) and 'That's The Way It Is' continued their string of UK Top 10 singles, but the hit records stopped when Mel was taken away from the 1988 Montreux Festival in a wheelchair. The official report was that she had a slipped disc, while press speculation intimated that it was something more serious. In late 1988, Kim smiled bravely in interviews and said that her sister was well on the way to recovery. However, the news soon broke that Mel was undergoing treatment for spinal cancer and she, too, showed her courage by allowing the press to publish pictures of her even though she was suffering the side effects of chemotherapy. Mel died in January 1990 from pneumonia. The following October, Kim carried on with her first solo single 'Don't Worry'.
Album: *F.L.M.* (1987). Kim Appleby solo *Breakaway* (1993).

Mel And Tim

Cousins Mel Hardin and Tim McPherson were born and raised in Holly Springs, Mississippi, USA, and later moved to St. Louis, Missouri. They were signed to **Gene Chandler**'s Bamboo label and reached the US Top 10 with 'Backfield In Motion' (1969). A vibrant single, it was followed by 'Good Guys Only Win In The Movies', after which Mel And Tim switched to **Stax**. The sumptuous 'Starting All Over Again', later covered by **Johnnie Taylor**, was another major R&B hit, but further singles, including 'I May Not Be What You Want' (from the film *Wattstax*), had less success.
Albums: *Good Guys Only Win In The Movies* (1969), *Starting All Over Again* (1972), *Mel And Tim* (1973).

Melachrino, George

b. George Militiades, 1 May 1909, London, England, d. 18 June 1965, London, England. An orchestra leader, composer, arranger, multi-instrumentalist and singer, Melachrino was the son of Greek parents. He learned to play a miniature violin, and wrote his first composition when he was five years old. He was already an accomplished musician at the age of 14 when he enrolled at the Trinity College Of Music, where he specialized in chamber music and the use of strings. At the age of 16, he wrote a string sextette which was performed in London. He resolved to learn every instrument in the orchestra, and succeeded, with the exception of the harp and piano. In 1927, he began his broadcasting career, playing and singing from the BBC studio at Savoy Hill. He strayed further and further away from his initial ambition to be a classical musician, playing jazz instead, and working in dance bands for leaders such as Bert Firman, Harry Hudson, **Ambrose** and **Carroll Gibbons**' Savoy Hotel Orchestra. In 1939, Melachrino formed his own dance band to play at the prestigious London venue, the Café de Paris, until 1940. During the period of the 'Battle of Britain', he joined the British Army as a military policeman, eventually becoming a Regimental Sergeant-Major. He later toured in the *Stars Of Battledress* and was musical director of the Army Radio Unit, as well as the leader of British Band of the Allied Expeditionary Forces. He also led the 50-piece 'Orchestra in Khaki', recruited from professional musicians serving in the ranks, who were much amused when he was introduced on broadcasts as 'the Sentimental Sergeant-Major'. The unit held its own against the American band led by **Glenn Miller** and the Canadian combination led by **Robert Farnon**, with both of whom Melachrino guested as vocalist on occasions during the war years.
While in the Forces, he experimented with large string sounds, and after the war he ran two outfits, the Melachrino Strings and the George Melachrino Orchestra, both purveying the sentimental mood music so popular in the 50s, especially in the USA. The full orchestra consisted of 30 strings, 10 reeds, seven brass, two percussion, a harp and a piano. He formed the Melachrino Music Organization, creating work in concerts, broadcasting, recordings and film music. His film scores included *Woman To Woman* (1946), *Code Of Scotland Yard* (1948), *No Orchids For Miss Blandish* (1948), *Story Of Shirley Yorke* (1948), *Dark Secret* (1949), *The Gamma People* (1956) and *Odongo* (1956). In 1947, he contributed the music, with book and lyrics by **Eric Maschwitz** and Matt Brooks, to the revue, *Starlight Roof*, which starred Fred Emney, **Pat Kirkwood** and Vic Oliver, and introduced **Julie Andrews** to London audiences. He also wrote the music for the ill-fated *Lucky Boy*, with lyrics by Ian Douglas. His other compositions included 'First Rhapsody' (his theme tune), 'Winter Sunshine', 'Vision D'Amour', 'Woodland Revel' and 'Portrait Of A Lady'. He had a UK chart entry in 1956 with the Italian melody, 'Autumn Concerto' but, like **Mantovani**, who also specialized in lush string arrangements, his albums sold more in the USA than in the UK. His US hits included *Christmas In High Fidelity*, *Under Western Skies* and *Immortal Ladies*, a set of standards with girls' names as their titles such as 'Laura', 'Dolores', 'Chloe' and 'Dinah'. Also popular was his series of mood records designed for various times of the day, such as *Music For Daydreaming*, *Music For Relaxation*, *Music For Two People Alone*, *Music For Dining*, *Music for Reading*, *Music To Help You Sleep*, and others. He died in 1965 following an accident at his home in Kensington, London. The Melachrino Strings and Orchestra continued to record into the 80s, conducted by Robert Mandell.
Selected albums: *Soft Lights And Sweet Music* (1954), *Christmas In High Fidelity* (1954), *Music For The Nostalgic Traveller* (1956), *Famous Themes For Piano And Orchestra* (1957), *Moonlight Concerto* (1958), *Great Show Tunes - Medleys* (1958), *Under Western Skies* (1959), *The World's Greatest Melodies* (1962), *The World Of George Melachrino* (1969), *The World Of George Melachrino, Volume Two*

(1972), *Strauss Waltzes* (1973), *The Immortal Melodies Of Victor Herbert And Sigmund Romberg* (1974), *Great British Light Orchestras-George-Melachrino* (EMI 1993).

Melanie

b. Melanie Safka, 3 February 1947, New York, USA. One of the surprise discoveries of the 1969 **Woodstock Festival** with her moving rendition of 'Beautiful People', Melanie briefly emerged as a force during the singer/songwriter boom of the early 70s. Although often stereotyped as a winsome 'earth-mother', much of her work had a sharp edge with a raging vocal style very different from her peers. Her first US hit, the powerful 'Lay Down' (1970), benefitted from the glorious backing of the **Edwin Hawkins Singers**. In Britain, she broke through that same year with a passionate and strikingly original version of the **Rolling Stones**' 'Ruby Tuesday'. *Candles In The Rain*, was a best seller on both sides of the Atlantic, with an effective mixture of originals and inspired cover versions. 'What Have They Done To My Song, Ma?' gave her another minor hit, narrowly outselling a rival version from the singalong **New Seekers**. Her last major success came in 1971 with 'Brand New Key', which reached number 1 in the USA and also proved her biggest hit in Britain. In 1972, Melanie founded Neighbourhood Records, and its parochial title seemed to define her career thereafter. Marginalized as a stylized singer/songwriter, she found it difficult to retrieve past glories. Sporadic releases continued, however, and she has often been seen playing charity shows and benefit concerts all over the world.
Selected albums: *Born To Me* (1969), *Affectionately Melanie* (1969), *Candles In The Rain* (1970), *Leftover Wine* (1970), *The Good Book* (1971), *Gather Me* (1971), *Garden In The City* (1972), *Stoneground Words* (1972), *Melanie At Carnegie Hall* (1973), *Madrugada* (1974), *As I See It Now* (1975), *From The Beginning* (1975), *Sunset And Other Beginnings* (1975), *Photogenic - Not Just Another Pretty Face* (1978), *Ballroom Streets* (1979), *Arabesque* (1982), *Seventh Wave* (1983), *Cowabonga - Never Turn Your Back On A Wave* (1989).

Melcher, Terry

b. 8 February 1942, New York City, New York, USA, d. 1991. The son of actress/singer **Doris Day** the artist's early recordings, credited to Terry Day, presaged his period as the youngest ever staff producer with the **Columbia/CBS** label. He brought singer **Bruce Johnston** to the company for *Surfin' 'Round The World* (1963), and together the pair oversaw the career of the Rip Chords, before recording a series of excellent singles as **Bruce And Terry**. Melcher's concurrent productions for **Paul Revere And The Raiders** proved particularly fruitful, engendering US Top 10 singles 'Kicks', 'Hungry' and 'Good Thing' (all 1966) and a run of eight consecutive albums. However, it is for work with the **Byrds** that this period is best recalled, and his empathetic skills enhanced the groups' early folk-rock sets, *Mr. Tambourine Man* and *Turn! Turn! Turn!*, as well as later selections, *Ballad Of Easy Rider*, *Untitled* and *Byrdmaniax*. In 1973, group members **Roger McGuinn**, **Chris Hillman** and **Clarence White** joined Johnston and **Ry Cooder** on *Terry Melcher*, but this introspective set failed to rise above cult status. The artist subsequently established his own label, Equinox, a name derived from an earlier production company. He enjoyed a measure of success with **David Cassidy**, but Terry's attempt to rekindle his solo career with *Royal Flush* proved less rewarding. In 1978, Melcher, who many believe was the intended victim of the infamous Sharon Tate murders, left the US for Britain, reportedly in fear of his life from the remnants of the Charles Manson tribe. He has subsequently remained out of the limelight.
Albums: *Terry Melcher* (1973), *Royal Flush* (1976).

Meldrum, Molly

b Ian Meldrum, 29 January 1946, in 'International Waters'. A likeable personality who has a high profile in the Australian rock industry. As compere of the long-running Australian television programme *Countdown* from 1974-87, Meldrum was in a position to influence and gain exposure for many up-and-coming bands, both local and international. With previous experience in television music and mime programmes, music journalism, management and production, he befriended many high-level music industry persons, and is credited as breaking **Abba** and **Madonna** in Australia. Since the show's demise, he has acted as consultant and has done media work, as well as supervising an offshoot of *Countdown*, called *Countdown Revolution*. His production of the **Johnny Young** song 'The Real Thing', sung by **Russell Morris**, ensures his place in Australian rock history.

Melle Mel And The Furious 5

Melle Mel (b. Melvin Glover, New York City, New York, USA) was a typical black 'ghetto child' whose interest in music originally stemmed from the **Beatles**. He soon embraced the earliest sounds of hip hop in the mid 70s, becoming a breakdancer with the D-Squad. As a DJ with his brother Kid Creole he was influenced by others in the profession like Klark Kent and Timmy Tim who used to talk rhymes whilst playing music. The pair started their own brand of rapping and around 1977 set up with another DJ, **Grandmaster Flash** - who gave Melle Mel his new name. Flash already had one MC - Cowboy - with him, and so the new team became Grandmaster Flash and the 3MCs. Over the next couple of years they were joined by Scorpio and then Rahiem. Spurred by the success Of 'Rapper's Delight' by the **Sugarhill Gang**, Flash's team recorded 'We Rap More Mellow' under the name The

Young Generation. Both it and a second single ('Sugar Rappin') flopped but then they signed to **Sugarhill Records** as Grandmaster Flash and the Furious Five. Together they recorded one of rap's greatest standards, 'The Message'. A hugely significant record which took hip hop away from braggadocio into social commentary, the featured vocalist was Melle Mel. Subsequent releases over the next few years came out under a wide variety of names and the battle for best billing plus squabbles with management and record company eventually led to the group splitting in two in 1984. A deep rift between Flash and Mel came about because, according to the latter: 'We'd known that Sugarhill was crooks when we first signed with 'em, so the plan had always been to build it up to a certain point where... they couldn't keep on taking the money that they was taking! That's what I'd been banking on, but those that left didn't seem to see it the same way'. Mel retained Cowboy and Scorpio and recruited another of his brothers King Louie III plus Tommy Gunn, Kami Kaze, and Clayton Savage. Flash had inaugurated a $5 million court action against Sylvia Robinson's Sugarhill label to attain full rights to the Grandmaster Flash name, which he lost. The group's new operating title was thus Grandmaster Melle Mel & The Furious Five. The name was forced on the band by Sugarhill, though it infuriated Flash and Mel himself was unhappy with it. Singles like 'Beat Street Breakdown Part 1', and 'We Don't Work For Free' would fail to break the upper echelons of the charts, though Mel did appear on the intro to **Chaka Khan**'s worldwide smash 'I Feel For You'. There was also a UK Top 10 hit with 'Step Off', after which his popularity cooled. By 1987 the mutual lack of success encouraged the separated parties to reunite as Grandmaster Flash, Melle Mel & The Furious Five for a **Paul Simon** hosted charity concert in New York. The intervening years between then and Mel's appearance on **Quincy Jones**' 'Back On The Block' were lost to drug addiction. Painfully ironic, considering that Mel's best known record remains 'White Lines (Don't Do It)', an anti-drug blockbuster which was credited to Grandmaster Flash and Melle Mel. It first hit the charts in 1983 and re-entered on several occasions. Originally targeted specifically at cocaine, it was revamped in 1989 by Sylvia Johnson because of the crack boom. Its pro-abstinence stance was not physically shared by the protagonists. When Mel was in the studio in 1982, laying down the vocal track, he admits that the 'only thing I was thinking about in that studio was listening to the record, joking and getting high'. In 1994 news broke that Mel was back and fighting fit (taking the trouble to perform press-ups for interviewers to prove the point), and working on a new album with former **Ice-T** collaborator Afrika Islam. He also linked with Flash for his 'Mic Checka' radio show.

Albums: *Work Party* (Sugarhill 1984), *Stepping Off* (Sugarhill 1985).

Mellencamp, John

b. 7 October 1951, Seymour, Indiana, USA. Mellencamp survived an early phase as a glam-rocker to become one of America's most successful mainstream rock singers of the past two decades. He played in local band Trash with guitarist Larry Crane (b. 1953), who remained with Mellencamp throughout the 80s. In 1976, **David Bowie**'s manager Tony de Fries signed him to a recording deal. His name was changed to Johnny Cougar, he was given a James Dean-style image and a debut album rush-released. *Chestnut Street Incident*, released as a demo and consisting of mainly cover versions, was credited to Johnny Cougar and did not chart. He left MainMan and moved back to Indiana, formed the Zone and recorded the self-penned *The Kid Inside*. Shortly afterwards he signed to Riva Records, owned by **Rod Stewart**'s manager **Billy Gaff** who presented him as 'the next **Bruce Springsteen**'. His first chart action came courtesy of *John Cougar*, which included the US Top 30 single 'I Need A Lover' in December 1979. Cougar and his band toured constantly, a strategy which paid off in 1982 when *American Fool* headed the US album chart while both 'Hurts So Good' and 'Jack And Diane' were million-sellers.

The following year he became John Cougar Mellencamp, eventually dropping 'Cougar' in 1989. With many of his songs dealing with social problems, Mellencamp was one of the organisers of the Farm Aid series of benefit concerts. His straight-ahead rock numbers also brought a string of big hits in the second half of the 80s. Among the most notable were 'Small Town', 'R.O.C.K. In The USA', 'Paper In Fire' (1987) and 'Cherry Bomb' (1988). *Lonesome Jubilee* used fiddles and accordions to illustrate bleak portraits of America in recession, while 'Pop Singer' from *Big Daddy* expressed Mellencamp's disillusionment with the current state of the music business. He took time off to concentrate on painting but returned with *Whenever We Wanted*, which recaptured the muscular rock sound of his earlier albums. In 1991, Mellencamp directed and starred in the film *Falling From Grace*. He has continued to hit the US charts with amazing rapidity and, up until early 1991, he had charted 21 singles in the US Hot 100 of which nine were Top 10, with one number 1, 'Jack And Diane' in 1982.

Albums: *Chestnut Street Incident* (1976), *A Biography* (1978), *John Cougar* (1979), *Nothing Matters And What If It Did* (1980), *American Fool* (1982), *Uh-Huh* (1983), *Scarecrow* (1985), *The Lonesome Jubilee* (1987), *Big Daddy* (1989), *Whenever We Wanted* (1991), *Human Wheels* (1993), *Dance Naked* (Mercury 1994).

Further reading: *American Fool: The Roots And Improbable Rise Of John Cougar Mellencamp*, Torgoff.

Mello K

Rapper Mello K boasts an intriguing marketing strategy: 'My rhymes are basically about females because they take to the music and they encourage guys to buy it'. Of West Indian descent, Mello K was brought up a native of New York, and first emerged as a serious artist in 1990. It was then that he was given the opportunity to work with Keith Sweat and Charlie Wilson from the **Gap Band**, subsequently forming his own posse, 40 Deep, hooking up with producer Monti Blues and reggae DJ Shawnie Ranks. Through Ranks Mello K debuted on his L.A. Boy Records. He also guested on the single 'Do Me', a slow-burning narrative reminiscent of lovers rock. It is this sort of material which gives Mello K his name, but he is equally capable of gruff, hard-nosed raps.

Album: *Hard & Mello* (L.A. Boy 1993).

Mello-Kings

The Mello-Kings were responsible for one of the most durable doo-wop hits of the 50s. Despite the fact that their only hit, 'Tonite Tonite', never got higher than number 77 in the US charts, that single was still considered one of the most popular group, harmony recordings of the era, more than three decades after its initial release. The group consisted of brothers Jerry and Bob Scholl, Eddie Quinn, Neil Arena and Larry Esposito. The quintet was formed in 1956 at a high school in Mount Vernon, New York, USA, under the guidance of manager Dick Levister. Originally named the Mellotones, the group was signed to the Herald label. 'Tonite Tonite' was written by Billy Myles, a staff composer for the label. The group was forced to change its name after the single's release, as another group had already claimed Mellotones. The record lasted only 10 weeks in the US charts, and the group was never able to repeat this success, although 'Tonite Tonite' returned in 1961, reaching number 95, due to a resurgence of interest in the doo-wop sound, and has been consistently voted among the top five doo-wop records of all time in radio polls, particularly in the New York area. A new Mello-Kings led by Jerry Scholl, whose brother died in 1975, was still touring the rock 'n' roll revival circuit in the early 90s.

Compilations: *Tonite, Tonite* (Relic 1991), *Tonight, Tonight* (Collectables 1992).

Mellotron

An early keyboard synthesizer, the mellotron was developed by Streetley Electronics of Sutton Coldfield in the West Midlands of England in the early 60s. It used pre-recorded tapes rather than electronic pulses to simulate various instruments, with each key triggering a different sound, from violin, guitar and brass to church organ and accordion. Early models offered a range of rhythms, including bossa nova, foxtrot, Dixieland and Viennese waltz. In the popular music field, jazz/R&B artist **Graham Bond** was a pioneer in using the Mellotron, and was the first person to extol its virtues by demonstrating the instrument to an amazed audience on UK television's *Ready Steady Go* in 1964 It soon became highly popular among progressive rock bands. It dominated the sound of the **Moody Blues**' concept album *Days Of Future Passed* and was also used on the **Beatles**' 'Strawberry Fields Forever' and in the work of **Barclay James Harvest**, **King Crimson** and **Procol Harum**. During the 70s, the Mellotron was overtaken by more sophisticated synthesizers produced by **Moog** and others, although both **Pink Floyd** and **Tangerine Dream** transferred Moog sounds onto mellotron tapes in order to play them in chords.

Mellow Man Ace

b. Ulpiano Sergio Reyes, 12 April 1967, Havana, Cuba, though he moved to the US at the age of four. Ace was brought up in Los Angeles, where he made his entrance in 1990 with a debut rap LP on **Capitol** that swtiched between his native Spanish and English. With production offered by the **Dust Brothers** and **Def Jef** (among others), the most successful exposition was a bilingual rap over **Santana**'s 'Evil Ways', entitled 'Mentirosa'. This was released as a single (US number 14), and he was among the key participants in the **Latin Alliance** project, but younger, more capable brothers have largely taken up the mantle of hispanic rap these days. These include his own blood brother, 'Sen Dog', of **Cypress Hill**.

Album: *Escape From Havana* (Capitol 1990), *Brother With 2 Tongues* (Capitol 1992).

Mellowmoods

An R&B vocal group from Harlem, New York City, New York, USA. The Mellowmoods began at the dawn of the doo-wop era, and made a brief impression on the recording scene with their deep street-corner sound. Members were Ray 'Buddy' Wooten, Bobby Williams, Monteith 'Monte' Owens, Alvin 'Bobby' Baylor, and Jimmy Bethea. Their one hit was 'Where Are You? (Now That I Need You)' (number 7 R&B) for **Bobby Robinson**'s Robin label in 1951. They failed on subsequent releases, 'I Couldn't Sleep A Wink Last Night', for Red Robin in 1952, and two more releases on Prestige. The group broke up after their last record in 1953, and Owens and Williams became members of the newly formed **Solitaires**.

Melly, George

b. 17 August 1926, Liverpool, Lancashire, England. Deeply involved in the UK trad scene of the late 40s and 50s, Melly sang with **Mick Mulligan**'s band. In the 60s he switched careers, exploiting his interest in and knowledge of both music and art to become one of

the UK's most ubiquitous critics and writers. He also became a popular television personality, and published the first volume in a series of three autobiographical works. In the early 70s Melly returned to music, performing regularly with **John Chilton**'s band. He has continued to sing with Chilton, touring extensively and entertaining audiences with his broadly-based repertoire which encompasses early blues, popular songs of 20s and 30s vaudeville, and a smattering of later material, some of it written especially by Chilton, which suits his highly personal, orotund singing style.
Selected albums: *George Melly With Mick Mulligan's Band* (1957), *George Melly* (1961), *Nuts* (WEA 1971), *Son Of Nuts* (WEA 1972), *At It Again* (1976), *Melly Sings Hoagy* (1978), *Ain't Misbehavin'* (1979), *It's George* (c.1980), *Let's Do It* (PRT 1981), *Like Sherry Wine* (1981), *Makin' Whoopee* (1982), *The Many Moods Of Melly* (1984), *16 Golden Classics* (Unforgettable 1986), *Running Wild/Hometown* (1986), *Anything Goes* (PRT 1988), *George Melly And Mates* (One-Up 1991), *Best Of George Melly* (Kaz 1992), *Frankie And Johnny* (D-Sharp 1992).
Further reading: *Owning Up*, George Melly. *Rum, Bum And Concertina*, George Melly. *Scouse Mouse*, George Melly. *Mellymobile, 1970-1981*, George Melly. *Scouse Mouse*, George Melly. *Revolt Into Style*, George Melly.

Melodians

Vocal trio comprising Brent Dowe, Tony Brevett and Trevor McNaughton. Robert Cogle was also a member of the group throughout their career. He made a major contribution as songwriter on many of the trio's biggest hits, but apparently not as a vocalist. They started singing in Kingston's amateur talent contests from 1960, but did not record until April 1966, when they made four titles for **Coxsone Dodd**, only two of which were released. During 1967-68 the Melodians recorded a series of big local hits for the Treasure Isle label owned by producer **Duke Reid** that endure to this day as classics of the **rocksteady** school. The trio's cool, precise harmonies are showcased to near-perfection on 'You Don't Need Me', 'I Will Get Along', 'I Caught You', all released in 1967, and 'Come On Little Girl' in 1968. Later in 1968, the group made two more massive local hits for **Sonia Pottinger**; 'Little Nut Tree', freely adapted from the nursery rhyme, and the celebratory 'Swing And Dine'. The following year, while still continuing to record occasional titles for Pottinger's Tip-Top label ('No Nola'), they began an association with the producer **Leslie Kong** which was to bring them international success, firstly with 'Sweet Sensation' and then with the Rasta-influenced, anthemic 'Rivers Of Babylon', the latter reputedly selling 75,000 copies in the UK alone.
They continued recording for Kong until his death in 1971, not only as a trio but as solo vocalists. Following this they recorded for **Lee Perry**, **Harry J**, Dynamics and Sonia Pottinger and Duke Reid again in 1972. Two years later the group split up. Brent Dowe recorded for Lee Perry in 1975 ('Down Here In Babylon'), and produced himself at **Channel One** the same year on the sublime 'Deh Pon The Wicked'. Tony Brevett enjoyed success again with 'Don't Get Weary', a self-production. In 1976, they re-formed, recording many of their old hits for producer **Harry J**, with backing by the **Soul Syndicate** band, but failed to maintain momentum. In the mid-80s the trio attempted a reunion, with little success; nonetheless, much of the music they made in the 60s remains emblematic of the best in rocksteady and reggae, and their recent stage shows at revival concerts have proved to be hugely popular.
Selected albums: *Rivers Of Babylon* (1970), *Sweet Sensation* (1976), *Sweet Sensation: The Original Reggae Hit Sound* (Island 1980), *Premeditation* (Skynote 1986), *Swing And Dine* (Heartbeat 1993).

Melodie MC

b. Kent Lövgren, Sweden. Dance/rap artist who began his career as a breakdancer at the age of 12 - proving good enough to be entered in major championship events throughout his native Sweden. He maintained his allegiance to the hip hop cause, releasing two moderately successful singles, 'Feel Your Body Movin' and 'Take Me Away', in 1992. His breakthrough came the following year with 'Dum Da Dum', whose dance stylings proved popular throughout Europe, especially in Germany where it sold some 200,000 copies. The follow-up, 'I Wanna Dance', was less strong, but repeated the chart success, and acted as a prelude to a debut album for the Sidelake Virgin label.
Album: *Northern Wonderland* (Sidelake Virgin 1993).

Melody Maker

The oldest-established pop music newspaper in the world was founded as the house journal of London music publisher Lawrence Wright in 1926, but soon became an independent monthly aimed primarily at dance band musicians. After founding editor Edgar Wright (1895-1967) left in 1929 to manage **Jack Hylton**'s band, *Melody Maker* increased its jazz coverage. Composer Spike Hughes took over as record reviewer, and the paper sponsored a 1933 concert tour by **Duke Ellington**. In that year, *Melody Maker* became a weekly with a newspaper format. Ray Sonin took over from P. Mathison Brooks as editor in 1940 and was succeeded in 1949 by Pat Brand. With Max Jones (b. 1917) as its top jazz writer, by 1955, *Melody Maker* was selling 97,000 copies. However, the hostility to rock 'n' roll of some columnists saw the paper lose ground to ***New Musical Express*** (founded 1952) and to the newly-launched *Record Mirror*. In 1956, *Melody Maker* published its first Top 20 singles chart but it did not wholeheartedly embrace the new pop music until 1963. When Jack Hutton replaced Brand, the paper was redesigned and Chris Welch was hired as its first pop journalist. One of the most important sections of *Melody Maker* was its classified advertisements, notably the 'musicians wanted' section. **Wishbone Ash** and **Camel** were among the numerous British rock bands that found drummers or guitarists through the *Melody Maker* small advertisements.

With the addition of other, younger writers, *Melody Maker* provided full coverage of the progressive rock and folk scenes of the 60s, until it was hit in 1970 by the defection of Hutton and most of the staff to set up a rival weekly, *Sounds*. Under Hutton's deputy, Ray Coleman, however, *Melody Maker* had its most successful period in the early 70s, with sales reaching a peak of 200,000. Although most of the staff were hostile to punk, Caroline Coon was brought in to sing its praises. The 80s were a period of falling sales for the paper and all its weekly rivals, as new teenybopper papers led by *Smash Hits* and monthlies for the older rock fan (*Q*, *Vox*) siphoned off sections of its audience. Despite an injection of new writing talent, notably from *Monitor*, a new wave fanzine based at Oxford University, *Melody Maker* turned inwards, writing about the latest indie rock bands in a style peppered with in-jokes. By 1991, *Sounds* and *Record Mirror* had disappeared, while the *New Musical Express* led the market, reviewing mainstream rock as well as independent label favourites. *Melody Maker* followed and seem likely to remain second fiddle in a market that has become less relevant with the appearance of magazines such as *Q*, *Mojo* and *Select*

Further reading: *Meoldy Maker Classic Rock Interviews*, ed. Allan Jones.

Meltdown

Meltdown are a five-piece band formed by ex-**Yardbirds**' drummer Jim McCarty. Previously responsible for writing epochal songs for the latter band including 'Shapes Of Things', 'Still I'm Sad' and 'Over Under Sideways Down', McCarty started Meltdown in the 90s as an avenue for full-blooded R&B, mixing original material with blues classics written by **Freddie King**, **Johnny Winter**, **Peter Green** and others. The cast list behind Meltdown was certainly impressive. Ray Majors (guitar/vocals) was formerly with **Mott The Hoople** and the **British Lions**, and had previously worked with McCarty as part of Box Of Frogs in 1984. He then joined the drummer's pre-Meltdown combo, the McCarty Band, for live work, replacing Top Topham. Sam Johnson provides Meltdown with expressive slide guitar, though he was still a teenager at the band's inception. Despite his tender years he had already worked with Pete Hogman of the **Five Dimensions** and Dick Taylor of the **Pretty Things**. The other youngster in the band is keyboard player Steve Corley, a jazz prodigy from the Royal Academy Of Music. Female bass player/vocalist Nikki Racklin had already recorded solo and opened shows for **Naked Truth** and **James**. The group then set about a series of live UK dates, before mini-tours of Sweden and France.

Melton, Barry

b. 1947, Brooklyn, New York, USA. This superb, fluid electric guitarist began his career in the Instant Action Jug Band, a politically-inspired unit from Berkeley, California, USA. The group subsequently evolved into **Country Joe And The Fish** with whom Melton remained until their demise in 1970. His first solo album, *Bright Sun Is Shining*, was recorded soon afterwards, but this soul-based selection was viewed as disappointing in the light of the artist's acid-rock credentials. In 1972, the guitarist joined forces with Jay Levy (keyboards), Rick Dey (bass; the composer of 'Just Like Me' for **Paul Revere And The Raiders**) and Tony Dey (drums) in Melton Levy And The Day Brothers. The group completed a low-key album before Barry left to form a new unit with **Grateful Dead** lyricist **Robert Hunter**. This pattern of short-lived associations continued over the years, during which time Melton would record a further five albums, each of intermittent interest, yet without fully harnessing his obvious talent. He rejoined **Country Joe McDonald** on several occasions and, despite embarking on a new career as a lawyer, maintains a voracious appetite for live appearances. Since 1982, Melton has also been a cornerstone in the **Dinosaurs**, the definitive, if irregular, Bay Area 'supergroup'.

Albums: *Bright Sun Is Shining* (1970), *The Fish* (1975), *Barry Melton* (1977), *We Are Like The Ocean* (1978), *Level With Me* (1980), *Next Great Depression* (1982).

Melvin, Harold, And The Blue Notes

Formed in Philadelphia in 1954, the Blue Notes - Harold Melvin (b. 25 June 1939, Philadelphia, Pennsylvania, USA), Bernard Wilson, Jesse Gillis Jnr., Franklin Peaker and Roosevelt Brodie - began life as a doo-wop group. In 1960, they scored a minor hit with a ballad, 'My Hero', but failed to make a significant breakthrough despite several excellent singles. By the end of the decade only Melvin and Wilson remained from that early group, with John Atkins and Lawrence Brown completing the line-up. Two crucial events then changed their fortunes. Theodore **'Teddy' Pendergrass**, drummer in the Blue Notes backing band, was brought into the frontline as the featured vocalist in place of the departing Atkins. A fifth singer, Lloyd Parkes, also joined the group which was then signed by producers **Gamble And Huff**, whose sculpted arrangements and insistent rhythm tracks provided the perfect foil for the Pendergrass voice. His imploring delivery was best heard on 'If You Don't Know Me By Now' (1972), an aching ballad which encapsulated the intimacy of a relationship. Further

singles, including 'The Love I Lost (1973) and 'Where Are All My Friends' (1974), enhanced Teddy's reputation and led to his demand for equal billing in the group. Melvin's refusal resulted in the singer's departure. However, while Pendergrass remained contracted to Philadelphia International and enjoyed considerable solo success, Melvin And The Blue Notes, with new singer David Ebo, moved to **ABC Records**. Despite securing a UK Top 5 hit with 'Don't Leave Me This Way' and a US R&B Top 10 hit with 'Reaching For The World' in 1977, the group was unable to recapture its erstwhile success. By the early 80s, they were without a recording contract, but continued to enjoy an in-concert popularity.
Albums: *Harold Melvin And The Blue Notes* (1972), *Black And Blue* (1973), *To Be True* (1975), *Wake Up Everybody* (1975), *Reaching For The World* (1977), *Now Is The Time* (1977), *Blue Album* (1980), *All Things Happen In Time* (1981). Compilations: *All Their Greatest Hits!* (1976), *Greatest Hits - Collector's Item* (1985), *Golden Highlights Of Harold Melvin* (1986), *Satisfaction Guaranteed - The Best Of* (1992), *Collection Gold* (1993).

Melvins

The late Kurt Cobain of **Nirvana** rated the Melvins as his favourite group. Unsurprising, perhaps, as they are the only other band of note to originate from his hometown Aberdeen (though they have since relocated to San Francisco), and he did once roadie for them. Drummer Dale Crover also played with Nirvana for a spell, while Cobain would guest and co-produce *Houdini* for the band. The other members of the Melvins, formed in 1984, numbered Buzz Osbourne (vocals/guitar) and Lori Beck (bass). Matt Lukin (**Mudhoney**) was also a floating member. Reputed to be more influenced by the heavy rock angle than many who have fallen under the generic title 'grunge', the Melvins are big fans of **Black Sabbath** and even released three solo albums in a tribute to the **Kiss** strategy of similar pretensions. A cover of **Flipper**'s 'Way Of The World' and 'Sacrifice' sat alongside **Alice Cooper**'s 'Ballad Of Dwight Fry' on cover album, *Lysol*. *Stoner Witch*, their second album for **Atlantic/East West**, saw Crover and Osbourne joined by bass player Mark Deutrom, who had previously produced the band's first two albums. This time they were working with Garth Richardson of **Red Hot Chili Peppers** and **L7** fame.
Albums: *Gluey Porch Treatments* (Alchemy 1986), *Ozma* (Boner 1987), *Bullhead* (Boner 1991), *Lysol* (Boner/Tupelo 1992), *Houdini* (Atlantic 1993), *Prick* (Amphetamine Reptile 1994), *Stoner Witch* (Atlantic 1994).

Members

One of the many UK bands inspired by punk, the Members came together in the summer of 1977, when former university student Nicky Tesco and French expatriate Jean-Marie Carroll, now a bank clerk in the UK, started working together. With Tesco on vocals and Carroll as guitarist and chief songwriter, they recruited Gary Baker on guitar, Adrian Lillywhite (brother of producer **Steve Lillywhite**) on drums, and a bass player. The bassist left after only a couple of months and was replaced by British Airways technician Chris Payne. They were based in Camberley, Surrey, England, where all the members (except Carroll) originated. The band's first recording - 'Fear On The Streets' - was for the **Beggars Banquet** punk compilation *Streets*. Despite this, it was **Stiff Records** that took the plunge and signed them. Their debut single, 'Solitary Confinement', was produced by **Larry Wallis** and earned them a contract with **Virgin Records** in November 1978, though by now Baker had departed and been replaced by Nigel Bennett. Their Virgin debut, 'Sound Of The Suburbs', was a hit in 1979, and was followed by the bloated but humorous reggae of 'Offshore Banking Business'. The b-side revisited 'Solitary Confinement', a song which the **Newtown Neurotics** would later update in the form of 'Living With Unemployment'. Their second album featured a guest appearance from **Joe Jackson** but it would be their last for Virgin, which they left in 1980. They were signed to **Island Records** briefly, but their third album came out on Albion Records, after which they disappeared. One other release of note is the Children Of 7's 'Solidarity' on Stiff, which featured both Carroll and Payne among the writing credits. More recently, 'Sound Of The Suburbs' featured as the title track to a nostalgic punk compilation which was advertised widely on UK television.
Albums: *At The Chelsea Nightclub* (Virgin 1979), *1980 The Choice Is Yours* (Virgin 1980), *Going West* (Albion 1983).

Membranes

Formed in Preston, Lancashire in 1977, this UK punk group was based in the seaside town of Blackpool, later immortalized as 'Tatty Seaside Town'. Founder member John Robb (b. 4 May, 1961; bass) was initially joined by Mark Tilton (guitar), Martin Kelly (drums) and Martin Critchley (vocals), the latter soon departing as Critchley sidestepped from drums to keyboards, with 'Goofy Sid' Coulthart taking over behind the drumstool. Robb was to prove himself nothing if not a trier, organizing compilation appearances and inaugurating the near legendary, near indecipherable *Blackpool Rox* fanzine. Their first vinyl single was the 3-track 'Muscles' in 1981, gaining single of the week awards for its defiant, brash optimism and gaining ascendancy on the turntable of Radio 1's **John Peel**. It remains one of the most memorable DIY efforts of the early 80s. Steve Farmery joined on guitar after its release, with Martin Kelly leaving the keyboard position vacant. They joined Rondolet Records for 'Pin

Stripe Hype', watching the label close down shortly after. This also saw off Farmery, leaving the band as a trio for much of the rest of their productive career. Missing out on the opportunity to be **Creation Records** first featured artists because of finance sent them down-market to Criminal Damage. It, too, proved a less than satisfactory home, and ultimately saw the group relocate to Manchester in 1983 in typically eternal optimism. The single which should have broken them was the acclaimed 'Spike Milligan's Tape Recorder', which somewhat pre-dated the guitar barrage of **Big Black** and **Sonic Youth**. However, distribution problems killed off the enthusiasm reciprocated by the media. The same problems applied to the 'Death To Trad Rock', 12-inch, after which Tilton left to be replaced by bass player, Stan. Although they finally made their postponed mark on Creation with the disappointing *Gift Of Life*, the band's fortunes were now in decline. Stan was replaced by Wallas as the band concentrated on the European circuit. Nick Brown was added on second guitar in 1987, followed in short order by Keith Curtis. Meanwhile, Robb was becoming more active as a freelance journalist for *Sounds*, and eventually ***Melody Maker*** and a host of other magazines. Despite the production services of Steve Albini (Big Black) on 1988's *Kiss Ass Godhead*, Wallas was the next departure, to be replaced by Paul Morley (ex-Slum Turkeys). However, total disintegration was imminent as Robb concentrated on his writing career, and launched his new dance project Sensurround.

Albums: *Gift Of Life* (Creation 1985), *Songs Of Love And Fury* (In Tape 1986), *Kiss Ass Godhead* (Homestead 1988), *To Slay The Rock Pig* (Vinyl Drip 1989). Compilations: *The Virgin Mary Versus Peter Sellers* (Vinyl Drip 1988), *Wrong Place At The Wrong Time* (Vinyl Drip 1993).

Video: *The Death To Trad Rock Special* (1988).

Memphis Horns

The Memphis Horns, an off-shoot of the **Mar-Keys**, boasted a fluid line-up throughout its history. The mainstays, trumpeter Wayne Jackson and tenor saxophonist Andrew Love, guided the group through its period at the **Stax** and Hi studios. Augmented by James Mitchell (baritone saxophone), Jack Hale (trombone) and either Ed Logan or Lewis Collins (tenor saxophone), the Horns appeared on releases by **Al Green**, **Ann Peebles**, **Syl Johnson** and many others. The group's eponymous debut album featured several members of the **Dixie Flyers** and, during the mid-70s, the Horns secured four R&B hits including 'Get Up And Dance' and 'Just For Your Love'. The 1978 album *Memphis Horns II*, featured as guest vocalists, **Michael McDonald**, Anita Pointer and James Gilstrap. The Memphis Horns are, however, better recalled for their contributions to many of southern soul's finest moments. Andrew Love and Wayne Jackson maintained the Memphis Horns' name throughout the 80s and made appearances on **U2**'s *Rattle And Hum* and **Keith Richards**' *Talk Is Cheap* (both in 1988). In 1990 the duo supported **Robert Cray**, and in 1991, 1992, and 1994 they played at the annual Porretta Terme Soul Festival in Italy which regularly attracts top soul acts from the Memphis area.

Albums: *Memphis Horns* (Cotillion 1970), *Horns For Everything* (Million 1972), *High On Music* (RCA 1976), *Get Up And Dance* (RCA 1977), *Memphis Horns Band II* (RCA 1978), *Welcome To Memphis* (RCA 1979), *Flame Out* (Lucky 7 1992).

Memphis Jug Band

Perhaps the most important and certainly the most popular of the jug bands, the Memphis Jug Band flourished on record, between 1927 and 1934, during which time they recorded some 80 tracks - first for Victor then later for **Columbia/OKeh Records**. Once they moonlighted for Champion using the name, the Picaninny Jug Band. Their repertoire covered just about any kind of music that anybody wanted to hear, and their personal appearances ran from fish-frys to bar mitzvahs. Recording for their own people, they restricted themselves to ballads, dance tunes (including waltzes), novelty numbers and blues. Normally a knockabout conglomeration, they could produce blues of feeling and beauty when required. The group had an ever-changing personnel that revolved around the nucleus of **Charlie Burse** and **Will Shade**. Other members included some of the stars of the Memphis blues scene such as **Memphis Minnie, Casey Bill Weldon,** Jab Jones, Milton Robey, Vol Stevens, Ben Ramey, Charlie Polk and **Hattie Hart**. Basically a string band augmented by such 'semi-legitimate' instruments as harmonicas, kazoos, washboards and jugs blown to supply a bass, the MJB had a constantly shifting line-up featuring violins, pianos, mandolins, banjos and guitars in different combinations. This, coupled with ever-changing vocalists, lent their music a freshness, vitality and variety that enables it to charm, entertain or move the listener as much today as it did during the great days of Beale Street. Although they ceased to record in 1934, this loose aggregation of musicians continued to work around Memphis until well into the 40s; some of its members being recorded again by researchers in the 60s.

Albums: *The Memphis Jug Band Vol 1* (1927-28), *Vol 2* (1928-29), *Vol 3* (1930), *Vol 5* (1932-34), *The Memphis Jug Band - Alternate Takes And Associates* (1991).

Memphis Minnie

b. Lizzie Douglas, 3 June 1897, Algiers, Louisiana, USA, d. 6 August 1973, Memphis, Tennessee, USA. Raised in Walls, Mississippi, Memphis Minnie learned banjo and guitar as a child, and ran away from home at the age of 13 to play music in Memphis; she worked for a time with Ringling Brothers Circus. When in Mississippi, she played guitar with **Willie Brown**, and in the 20s made a common-law marriage with **Casey Bill Weldon**. However, she was with **Kansas Joe McCoy** by the time of their joint recording debut in 1929. Her guitar playing had a strong rhythm, coupled with the ragtime influence common among the Memphis musicians, and her singing was tough and swaggering. 'Bumble Bee' was a hit, and Joe and Minnie recorded extensively, together and separately; their guitar duets were among the finest in blues. Apart from songs about sex and relationships, Minnie sang about her meningitis (calling it, with gallows humour, 'Memphis Minnie-jitis'), about her father's mule, 'Frankie Jean', and about the guitarist 'Mister Tango'. The McCoys moved to Chicago in the early 30s, but split up in 1935, apparently as a result of Joe's jealousy of his wife's success. By this time, Minnie's music was reflecting changing tastes, usually featuring a piano and string bass, and sometimes trumpet or clarinet and a drummer. She was a star of the Chicago club scene, as she continued to present herself on disc as the tough, independent woman she was in reality. In 1939, she began recording with her third husband, **Little Son Joe** (**Ernest Lawlars**) on second guitar. They were early users of amplification, and made swinging music, although it lacked the rich complexity of her early recordings. Her lyrics were of considerable originality, as on a graceful tribute to **Ma Rainey**, recorded in 1940, six months after Rainey's death. 'Me And My Chauffeur Blues', with its boogieing guitar, also became widely known. In the late 40s, Memphis Minnie ran a touring vaudeville company, and she continued to record after the war, playing tough electric guitar. Her efforts to keep up with trends were proving less successful, however, and in the mid-50s, she and Joe retired to Memphis. Joe was already unwell, and died in 1961, while Minnie was incapacitated from the late 50s, and lived out her life in nursing homes.

Selected albums: *Memphis Minnie & Kansas Joe Vols. 1-4* (1991), *Memphis Minnie 1935-41 Vols. 1-5* (1992), *The Postwar Recordings Vols. 1-3* (1992), *Blues Classics* (1993).

Further reading: *Woman With Guitar: Memphis Minnie's Blues*, Paul And Beth Garon.

Memphis Slim

b. Peter Chatman, 3 September 1915, Memphis, Tennessee, USA, d. 24 February 1988. One of the most popular performers of the blues idiom, Memphis Slim combined the barrelhouse/boogie-woogie piano style of the pre-war era with a sophisticated vocal intonation. A prolific songwriter, his best-known composition, 'Every Day I Have The Blues', has been the subject of numerous interpretations, and versions by **Count Basie** and **B.B. King** helped establish the song as a standard of its genre. Although Slim began his career in 1934, deputizing for pianist **Roosevelt Sykes**, his reputation did not prosper until moving to Chicago at the end of the decade. He supported many of the city's best-known acts, including **John Lee 'Sonny Boy' Williamson**, and, in 1940, became the regular accompanist to **Big Bill Broonzy**. The artist made his recording debut for the Bluebird label that year but remained with Broonzy until 1944,, when he formed his own group, the House Rockers. In 1949 Slim enjoyed an R&B number 1 with 'Messin' Around', the first in a series of successful singles, including 'Blue And Lonesome' (1949), 'Mother Earth' (1951) and 'The Come Back' (1953). He remained a popular attraction in Chicago throughout the ensuing decade, but following prestigious appearances at New York's Carnegie Hall and the Newport Jazz Festival, the artist moved to Paris, where he was domiciled from 1961 onwards. Slim toured and recorded extensively throughout Europe, an availability which, perversely, has irritated blues purists who view his work as overtly commercial. His later work certainly lacked the purpose of the young musician, but by the time of his death from kidney failure in 1988, Memphis Slim's role in the development of blues was assured.

Selected albums: *Memphis Slim At The Gate Of The Horn* (1959), *'Frisco Bay Blues* (1960), *Memphis Slim* (1961), *Broken Soul Blues* (1961), *Just Blues* (1961), *Tribute To Big Bill Broonzy* (1961), *Memphis Slim USA* (1962), *No Strain* (1962), *All Kinds Of Blues* (1963), *Alone With My Friends* (1963), *Steady Rolling Blues* (1964), *Memphis Slim* (1964), *The Real Folk Blues* (1966), *Legend Of The Blues* (1967), *Mother Earth* (1969), *Messin' Around With The Blues* (1970), *Born With The Blues* (1971), *Bad Luck And Trouble* (1971), *Blue Memphis* (1971), *South Side Reunion* (1972), *Old Times New Times* (1972), *Soul Blues* (1973), *Classical American Music* (1973), *Legacy Of The Blues, Volume 7* (1973), *Memphis Slim At Lausanne* (1974), *Memphis Slim Live* (1974), *Memphis Slim* (1974), *With Matthew Murphy* (1974), *Blues Man* (1975), *Going Back To Tennessee* (1975), *Rock Me Baby* (1975), *All Them Blues* (1976), *Chicago Boogie* (1976), *Fattening Frogs For Snakes* (1976), *Boogie Woogie* (1978), *Chicago Blues* (1978), *Blues Every Which Way* (1981), *Blues And Women* (1981).

Men At Work

Formed in Melbourne, Australia, in 1979, by singer Colin Hay (b. 29 June 1953, Scotland - emigrated to Australia aged 14) and guitarist Ron Strykert (b. 18 August 1957, Australia), initially as an acoustic duo. With the later addition of Greg Ham (b. 27 September 1953, Australia), John Rees (bass) and Jerry Speiser (drums), Men At Work performed for two years in small, inner-suburban pubs before being discovered and signed by **CBS** executive Peter Karpin. In 1981, the first single, 'Who Can It Be Now?', was an enormous Australian hit, soon followed by 'Down Under' and the album *Business As Usual.* The band's success surprised and infuriated home critics, who had written them off as derivative and insipid. However, blessed with three songwriters and supported by videos which showcased the band's sense of humour (and as a support act to **Fleetwood Mac**), Men At Work were able to achieve two US number 1 hits in 1982 with 'Who Can It Be Now?' and 'Down Under' and a US number 1 album that same year. Success followed again in the UK where 'Down Under' reached number 1 in early 1983, accompanied by *Business As Usual* topping the charts. By now, Men At Work could comfortably claim to be the world's most successful Australian pop group. The follow-up album, *Cargo,* sold well in the USA, reaching number 3, and provided two Top 10 singles in 'Overkill' and 'It's A Mistake'. Despite the album reaching the Top 10 in the UK, single success there was harder to sustain, with three singles reaching Top 40 status only. The third album, *Two Hearts,* sold less well, although it did achieve gold status in the USA, peaking at number 50. The original personnel had by now disintegrated, leaving Hay as the sole surviving member. The break-up in 1985 followed arguments over management and writing, and each member followed his own path. Hay, after recording a solo album, *Looking For Jack* (1987), recorded another, *Wayfaring Sons,* on MCA in 1990, as the Colin Hay Band, using Celtic music as its base.

Albums: *Business As Usual* (1981), *Cargo* (1983), *Two Hearts* (1985).

Men They Couldn't Hang

In their seven-year span, The Men They Couldn't Hang combined folk, punk and roots music to create an essential live act alongside a wealth of recorded talent. The band emerged as the **Pogues**' sparring partners but, despite a blaze of early publicity and praise, they failed to follow them upwards, dogged as they were by numerous label changes. Busking in Shepherds Bush, Welsh singer Cush met up with bassist Shanne (who had been in the Nips with the Pogues' Shane MacGowan), songwriter/guitarist Paul Simmonds, Scottish guitarist/singer Phil ('Swill') and his brother John on drums, in time for a ramshackle folk performance at London's alternative country music festival in Easter 1984. Labelled as part of some 'cowpunk' scene, the band were quickly signed by **Elvis Costello** to his Demon label, Imp. A cover of **Eric Bogle**'s 'Green Fields Of France' in October 1984 became a runaway indie success, and a favourite on BBC disc jockey **John Peel**'s show. While playing live, the Men matched their own incisive compositions with entertaining covers. June 1985's 'Iron Masters' was just as strong, if more manic, and was accompanied by an impressive and assured debut, *The Night Of A Thousand Candles.*

Produced by **Nick Lowe**, 'Greenback' was less immediate, but its success swayed **MCA** to sign the group, resulting in 'Gold Rush' in June 1986. The group's second album, *How Green Is The Valley* continued their marriage of musical styles and a political sensibility drawn from an historical perspective. 'The Ghosts Of Cable Street' exemplified these ingredients. A move to Magnet Records catalyzed perhaps their finest work, with the commercial 'Island In The Rain' and the listenable *Waiting For Bonaparte.* 'The Colours' received airplay, but only skirted the charts. Fledgling label Silvertone's Andrew Lauder (who had worked with the group at Demon) signed the group in time for 'Rain, Steam And Speed' in February 1989. Hot on its heels came *Silvertown.* Two further singles followed: 'A Place In The Sun' and 'A Map Of Morocco'.

In 1990 they recorded their final studio album, for which the personnel was increased to six, with the addition of Nick Muir. On the strength of it, they supported **David Bowie** at Milton Keynes. Shortly afterwards they disbanded, following a long farewell tour, and a live album, *Alive, Alive - O.*

Albums: *Night Of A Thousand Candles* (1985), *How Green Is The Valley* (1986), *Waiting For Bonaparte* (1987, reissued 1988), *Silvertown* (1989), *The Domino Club* (1990), *Well Hung* (1991), *Alive, Alive - O* (1991).

Men Without Hats

Formed in Montreal, Canada, in 1980, this act was the brainchild of siblings Ivan (vocals) and Jeremy (drums) Arrobas, who manufactured remaining accompaniment on their records with synthesizers. An independent EP, *Folk Of The 80s,* created overseas cult interest to the extent that it was re-issued on Britain's **Stiff** label, along with an edit of its 'Antarctica' track as a single. However, just after the release of 1981's 'Nationale Seven', Jeremy left to allow composer Ivan to front a Men Without Hats with the brothers Stefan (guitar/violin) and Colin Doroschuk (keyboards) plus Allan McCarthy (drums). Produced by manager Marc Durand, *Rhythm Of Youth* reached number 14 in the USA in the wake of 'Safety Dance', a global smash born of a truce between electro-pop and medieval jollity that carried an anti-nuclear message over into an arresting video. A sure sign of its impact was a parody by **Weird Al Yanovic**. No more hits came the group's way, but their recordings still received a fair critical consideration.

Albums: *Rhythm Of Youth* (1982), *Folk Of the 80s Part III* (1984), *Pop Goes The Word* (1987).

Menace To Society

Not related to the film of the same name, Menace To Society offer reality or slice of life raps about their immediate surroundings in Inkster, a suburb of Detroit, Michigan. The group's lead rapper is AGQ (b. Kevin Riley; AGQ being an acronym for American Genuine Quality) alongside Rhythm Layer Riccola (b. Andre Brintley) and Frank Nitty (b. Franchot Hayes). Their

debut single, 'Streets Of Hell', set out their agenda: 'Although some of our lyrics appear to be harsh, they come to you with the reality of today's street life.'
Album: *Life Of A Real One* (Cush/Ichiban 1993).

Mendes, Sergio

b. 11 February 1941, Niteroi, Brazil. A pianist, composer, arranger and bandleader, who is indelibly identified with the bossa nova boom of 60s. After touring North America with his own quintet, he settled there late in 1964, and worked on recordings with **Antonio Jobim** and **Art Farmer**. He founded Brasil '65, which later evolved into Brasil '66, a two women-four man, vocal-instrumental group which marketed 'a delicately-mixed blend of pianistic jazz, subtle Latin nuances, **John Lennon/Paul McCartney** style, some **Henry Mancini**, here and there a touch of **Burt Bacharach**, cool minor chords, danceable up-beat, gentle laughter and a little sex'. The initial ensemble consisted of Mendes (piano/vocals), Joses Soares (latin percussion/vocals), Bob Matthews (bass/vocals), Jao Palma (drums) and vocalists Janis Hansen and Lani Hall. Hall's husband, **Herb Alpert**, the owner, with Jerry Moss, of **A&M Records**, became Mendes' patron, and together in the late 60s, they produced a series of US chart albums. 'The Look Of Love', 'The Fool On The Hill', and 'Scarborough Fair' also made the US singles Top 20. During the 70s and 80s, Mendes recorded for several different labels, under a variety of names. His US and UK singles chart hit in 1983, 'Never Gonna Let You Go', was just credited to Sergio Mendes, and had vocals by Joe Pizzulo and Leza Miller. In 1984, he had minor success in the US with 'Alibis'. In 1990, when Sergio Mendes and Brasil 99 opened the new 600-seater Rio Showroom in Las Vegas, they gained 'resounding applause' and excellent reviews for the 'ascending American/Brazilian moods' of old favourites such as 'Manha De Carnaval' and 'Mas Que Nada'.
Selected albums: *Sergio Mendes & Brasil '66* (1966), *Equinox* (1967), *Look Around* (1968), *Sergio Mendes Favorite Things* (1968), *Fool On The Hill* (1968), *Crystal Illusions* (1969), *Ye-Me-Le* (1969), *Stillness* (1971), *Pais Tropical* (1971), *Primal Roots* (1972), *Love Music* (1973), *Vintage 74* (1974), *Sergio Mendes I* (1975), *Homecooking* (1976), *Sergio Mendes And The New Brasil '77* (1977), *Confetti* (1984), *Brasiliero* (Elektra 1992).

Mengelberg, Misha

b. 5 April, 1935, Kiev, Ukraine. Mengelberg was raised in Holland where, for 30 years, he has personified the Dutch *avant garde.* He characterizes himself as 'a rotten piano player' - if that is the case, wittier use has rarely been made of limitations. Mengelberg has consistently aligned himself with iconoclastic and provocative musicians, from straight music's Zen terrorists David Tudor and **John Cage** in the early 60s, to **Eric Dolphy** in 1963, to the members of the Dutch Instant Composers Pool, with whom he still works. Together with his long-standing ICP collaborator **Han Bennink**, he has been one of the main instigators behind three albums which have paid tribute to pianist **Herbie Nichols** - two with a small group that also featured **Steve Lacy**, and one with the ICP Orchestra. As an improviser, Mengelberg holds out for the 'responsibility to be different every day' and is against the jazzman's obsession with personal style and touch. All the same, his compositions reveal an identifiable preoccupation with irony, some pieces, in fact, dripping with sarcasm. The ICP Orchestra is currently the main outlet for his writing, but he also composes for the Berlin Contemporary Jazz Orchestra.
Albums: *Misha Mengelberg Trio* (1960), *Kwartet* (1966), *Driekusman Total Loss* (1966), with John Tchicai, Han Bennink *Instant Composers Pool* (1968), *Groupcomposing* (1970), with Tchicai, Bennink, Derek Bailey *Instant Composers Pool 1970* (1971), *Misha Mengelberg/Han Bennink* (1971), with Bennink *Het Scharrebroekse* (1972), with Bennink *Einepartietischtennis* (1974), with Bennink *Coincidents* (1975), with Bennink *Untitled Album* (1975), *Tenterett* (1977), with Bennink *Midwoud* (1977), *Pech Onderweg* (1978), with Dudu Pukwana, Bennink *Yi Yole* (1978), *ICP Tentet In Berlin* (1978), *Mengelberg-Bennink* (1979), with Paul Rutherford, Mario Schiano, Bennink *A European Proposal* (1979), with Peter Brötzmann, Bennink *Three Points And A Mountain* (1980), *ICP Orchestra Live In Soncino* (1980), *Japan Japon* (1982), *Change Of Season* (Soul Note 1984), *Impromptus* (FMP 1986), *Two Programs: ICP Performs Nichols/Monk* (1986), with Pino Minafra *Tropic Of The Mounted Sea Chicken* (1990), with others *Dutch Masters* (Soul Note 1992).

Menken, Alan

(see **Ashman, Howard**)

Mensah, E.T.

b. 1919, Accra, Ghana. Known throughout West Africa as 'The King Of Highlife', Mensah has been the single greatest influence on the development of the style, in a career which stretches back to the mid-30s. His father was a keen guitarist and encouraged his son to seek out formal musical training. At primary school, he studied fife and flute, and was a key player in the school's marching band, going on to serve his apprenticeship with the Accra Rhythmic Orchestra between 1936 and 1944, employed first as a roadie, then as a saxophonist. In 1945, he joined the legendary Black And White Spots, before switching to the Tempos Band in 1947, succeeding **Guy Warren** as its leader a year later. The Tempos inaugurated a new era in Ghanaian highlife, downplaying the role of jazz-based reed and brass soloing, and expanding the traditional drum and percussion section to give more prominence to folk-based rhythm patterns. At the same time, the band incorporated Afro-Cuban rumbas and cha chas into its repertoire. The resultant style became known as big band highlife. In 1952, the Tempos were signed to West African **Decca** and quickly established themselves as Ghana's top highlife band with a string of hit singles, including 'Sunday Mirror', 'School Girl', 'Cherry Red' and 'You Call Me Roko'. Mensah's reputation spread throughout West Africa. From the late 40s onwards, he regularly toured throughout the region, inspiring local bands who until then had played largely imported jazz or Latin music, and encouraging them to include a far greater proportion of roots rhythms and song structures in their output. Alongside his stylistic innovations, Mensah did much to the improve the lot of Ghanaian musicians in the 50s and early 60s - raising the wages of his sidemen to a level which permitted them to buy their own instruments (as opposed to the prevailing system of hiring them from the bandleader, to whom they were then effectively in a feudal relationship), and helping found the Ghana Musicians Union (at a time when royalty payments were practically unheard of). Under his leadership, the Tempos also served as finishing school to a large number of talented musicians, who went on to form important highlife bands under their own names - notable examples include the **Red Spots** and the **Rhythm Aces**.

In the late 60s, big band highlife began to be perceived as outmoded, and - despite the 1969 release of one of his greatest ever albums, *The King Of African Highlife Rhythm* - Mensah went on to spend much of the 70s and early 80s employed as a pharmacist. Happily, the inevitable revival occurred in the mid-80s, along with renewed interest in Mensah himself. In 1982, he travelled to Nigeria to record the album *Highlife Giants Of Africa* with **Victor Olaiya**. In 1986, some of his early material was re-released on the album *All For You*, and he undertook a critically-acclaimed tour of the UK, France and Holland.

Albums: *Tempos On The Beat* (1953), *King Of The Highlifes* (1963), *The King Of African Highlife Rhythm* (1969), *The King of Highiife* (1977), *E.T. Mensah Is Back Again* (1978), with Victor Olaiya *Highlife Giants Of Africa* (1982), *All For You* (1986).

Mental As Anything

Utilizing elements of rockabilly, rock and R&B combined with an energetic live act, Mental As Anything has proved a lasting, popular live and recording outfit. The group's debut album introduced Reg Mombasa (b. Chris O'Doherty, New Zealand; guitar/vocals), Wayne Delisle (b. Australia; drums) and the three songwriters: Martin Plaza (b. Martin Murphy, Australia; vocals/guitar), Greedy Smith (b. Andrew Smith, Australia; keyboards/harmonica/vocals) and Peter O'Doherty (b. New Zealand; bass). Despite their different writing styles, *Get Wet* achieved success, particularly with the enigmatically titled single 'The Nips Are Getting Better'. Their most fortuitous album, *Cats And Dogs*, saw the production smooth out the rough edges, and subsequent albums have maintained a high standard, with single releases constantly charting in Australia (two dozen to the end of 1990). Their single, 'Live It Up' gained considerable chart success in the UK in 1987, when it spent 13 weeks at number 3. Plaza has also released solo recordings which have enjoyed high sales in Australia.

Albums: *Get Wet* (1979), *Expresso Bongo* (1980), *Cats And Dogs* (1981), *Creatures Of Leisure* (1983), *Fundamental* (1985), *Mouth To Mouth* (1987), *Cyclone Raymond* (1989).

Menza, Don

b. 22 April 1936, Buffalo, New York, USA. In 1960, after military service, during which he had become adept as both an instrumentalist and an arranger, tenor saxophonist Menza joined the **Maynard Ferguson** band. He was then briefly with **Stan Kenton** but opted to return to his home town, showing a preference for small-group work. In the mid-60s, he lived and worked in Germany. In 1968, he returned to the USA, playing in the **Buddy Rich** big band. Resident in Los Angeles throughout the next decade, Menza developed his writing, both as arranger and composer. In particular, he wrote for **Louie Bellson**, with whom he also played and recorded. In the 80s, he played with several Los Angeles-based big bands, including that led by **Bill Berry**, and also led his own big bands and small groups. He toured extensively, at home and overseas, usually appearing as a single. His thorough musical background and eclectic tastes - he admires and has studied the work of many classical composers - has also allowed him to work in non-jazz contexts. A fiery, aggressive performer, Menza's writing shows his bebop leanings, which he brings even into his big band work.

Albums: with Stan Kenton *Adventures In Time* (1962), *Menza In Munich* (1965), with Buddy Rich *Mercy, Mercy* (1968), with Rich *Channel One Suite* (1968), with Louie Bellson *150 MPH* (1974), *Horn Of Plenty* (1979), *Burnin'* (1980), *Hip Pocket* (Palo Alto 1981), with Bellson *East Side Suite* (1987), *Ballads* (Fresh Souns 1988), with Bellson *Jazz Giants* (1989).

Mercedes Ladies

A very early hip hop group, the first all-female such aggregation, which featured Zena Z, Debbie D, Eva Deff, Sherry Sheryl, alongside DJs RC and Baby D. Their origins in the Bronx, they were often to be found supporting the Funky Four at house parties and jams. Baby D, whose sassy 'frontin'' earned her lessons at the hands of **Grandmaster Flash** himself, would go on to a contract for **East West**, then **Polydor**, recording the LPs *Dream About You* and *ESP*.

Mercer, Johnny

b. John Herndon Mercer, 18 November 1909, Savannah, Georgia, USA, d. 25 June 1976, Los Angeles, California, USA. A distinguished lyricist, composer and singer, Mercer was an important link with the first generation of composers of indigenous American popular music such as **Jerome Kern** and **Harry Warren**, through to post-World War II writers like **Henry Mancini**. Along the way, he collaborated with several others, including **Harold Arlen**, **Hoagy Carmichael**, **Gene DePaul**, **Rube Bloom**, **Richard Whiting**, **Victor Schertzinger**, **Gordon Jenkins**, **Jimmy Van Heusen**, **Duke Ellington**, **Billy Strayhorn**, Matty Malneck, **Arthur Schwartz** and more. Most of the time, Mercer wrote the most literate and witty lyrics, but occasionally the melody as well.

He moved to New York in the late 20s and worked in a variety of jobs before placing one of his first songs, 'Out Of Breath And Scared To Death Of You', (written with Everett Miller), in the ***The Garrick Gaieties*** *Of 1930*. During the 30s, Mercer contributed the lyrics to several movie songs, including 'If You Were Mine' from *To Beat The Band*, a record hit for **Billie Holiday** with **Teddy Wilson**, 'I'm An Old Cowhand' (words and music) (*Rhythm On The Range*), 'Too Marvellous For Words' (co-written with Richard Whiting for *Ready, Willing And Able*), 'Have You Got Any Castles, Baby?' (*Varsity Show*), 'Hooray For Hollywood' (*Hollywood Hotel*), 'Jeepers Creepers' (*Going Places*) and 'Love Is Where You Find It' (*Garden Of The Moon*).

Mercer's other songs during the decade included 'Fare-Thee-Well To Harlem', 'Moon Country', 'When A Woman Loves A Man' (with Gordon Jenkins and Bernard Hanighan), 'P.S. I Love You', 'Goody Goody', 'You Must Have Been A Beautiful Baby', 'And The Angels Sing', 'Cuckoo In The Clock', 'Day In - Day Out' and 'I Thought About You'. In the 30s he appeared frequently on radio, as MC and singer with **Paul Whiteman**, **Benny Goodman** and **Bob Crosby**. With his southern drawl and warm, good-natured style, he was a natural for the medium, and, in the early 40s, had his own show, *Johnny Mercer's Music Shop*. During this period, Mercer became a director of the songwriter's copyright organization, **ASCAP**. Also, in 1942, he combined with songwriter-turned-film-producer, **Buddy De Sylva**, and businessman, Glen Wallich, to form **Capitol Records**, which was, in its original form, dedicated to musical excellence, a policy which reflected Mercer's approach to all his work.

He had previously had record hits with other writers' songs, such as 'Mr Gallagher And Mr Sheen' and 'Small Fry', along with his own 'Mr. Meadowlark' (a duet with **Bing Crosby**), and 'Strip Polka'. For Capitol, he continued to register in the US Hit Parade with popular favourites such as 'Personality', 'Candy'; and some of his own numbers such as 'G.I. Jive', 'Ac-Cent-Tchu-Ate The Positive', 'Glow Worm'; and 'On The Atchison, Topeka, And The Santa Fe', which was also sung by **Judy Garland** in the film ***The Harvey Girls*** (1946), and gained Mercer his first Academy Award.

His other 40s song successes, many of them from movies, included 'The Waiter And The Porter And The Upstairs Maid' (from *Birth Of The Blues*); 'Blues In The Night' and 'This Time's The Dream's On Me' (*Blues In The Night*); 'Tangerine', 'I Remember You' and 'Arthur Murray Taught Me Dancing In A Hurry' (***The Fleet's In***), 'Dearly Beloved' and 'I'm Old Fashioned' (***You Were Never Lovelier***) (Kern); 'Hit The Road To Dreamland' and 'That Old Black Magic', **Billy Daniels**' identity song, (***Star Spangled Rhyth***m), 'My Shining Hour' (*The Sky's The Limit*) and 'Come Rain Or Come Shine', 'Legalize My Name' and 'Any Place I Hang My Hat Is Home', from the stage show *St. Louis Woman* (Arlen).

Two particularly attractive compositions were 'Fools Rush In' (with Rube Bloom), which was a big hit for **Glenn Miller** and the movie title song 'Laura', with Mercer's lyric complementing a haunting tune by David Raksin. Mercer's collaboration with Hoagy Carmichael produced some of his most memorable songs, such as 'Lazybones', 'The Old Music Master', 'Skylark', 'How Little We Know' and the Oscar-winning 'In The Cool, Cool, Cool Of The Evening', sung by Bing Crosby and Jane Wyman in the film *Here Comes The Groom* (1951). In the same year, Mercer provided both the music and lyrics for the Broadway show, *Top Banana*, a 'burlesque musical' starring Phil Silvers and a host of mature funnymen. The entertaining score included the witty 'A Word A Day'.

The 50s were extremely productive years for Mercer, with songs such as 'Here's To My Lady', 'I Wanna Be Around' (later successful for **Tony Bennett**), and yet more movie songs, including 'I Want To Be A Dancing Man', 'The Bachelor Dinner Song' and 'Seeing's Believing', sung by **Fred Astaire** in *The Belle Of New York*; 'I Like Men' (covered by **Peggy Lee**), 'I Got Out Of Bed On The Right Side' and 'Ain't Nature Grand' from ***Dangerous When Wet***; and 'Something's Gotta Give' and 'Sluefoot' (words and music by Mercer) from another Fred Astaire film, ***Daddy Long Legs***. Mercer also provided additional lyrics to 'When The World Was Young' ('Ah, The Apple Trees'), 'Midnight Sun', 'Early Autumn' and 'Autumn Leaves'. The highlight of the decade was, perhaps, ***Seven Brides For Seven Brothers*** (1954). Starring **Howard Keel** and **Jane Powell**, Mercer and Gene DePaul's 'pip of a score' included 'Spring, Spring, Spring', 'Bless Your Beautiful Hide', 'Sobbin' Women', 'When You're In Love', and 'Goin' Courtin', amongst others. Two years later Mercer and DePaul got together again for the stage show ***Li'l Abner***, starring **Stubby Kaye**, and including such songs as 'Namely You', 'Jubilation T. Cornpone' and 'The Country's In The Very Best Of Hands'. It ran on Broadway for nearly 700 performances and was filmed in 1959.

The early 60s brought Mercer two further Academy Awards; one for 'Moon River' from *Breakfast At Tiffany's* (1961), and the other, the title song to *The Days Of Wine And Roses* (1962). 'Moon River' was the song in which Mercer first coined the now- famous phrase, 'my huckleberry friend'. **Danny Williams** took the former song to the UK number slot in 1961, while namesake **Andy Williams** and Mercer's co-composer Henry Mancini both scored US Top 40 hits with the latter in 1963. Mancini also wrote other movie songs with Mercer, such as 'Charade', 'The Sweetheart Tree' (from *The Great Race*) and 'Whistling Away The Dark' (*Darling Lili*). In the early 70s, Mercer spent a good deal of time in Britain, and, in 1974, wrote the score, with **André Previn**, for the West End musical *The Good Companions*. He died, two years later, in 1976.

Several of his 1,000-plus songs became an integral part of many a singer's repertoire. In 1992, **Frank Sinatra** was still using 'One For My Baby' (music by Harold Arlen), 'the greatest saloon song ever written', as a moving set-piece in his concert performances. 'Dream' (words and music by Mercer), closed Sinatra's radio and television shows for many years, and the singer also made impressive recordings of lesser-known Mercer items, such as 'Talk To Me, Baby' and 'The Summer Wind'. Memories of his rapport with Bing Crosby in their early days were revived in 1961, when Mercer recorded *Two Of A Kind* with **Bobby Darin**, full of spontaneous asides, and featuring Mercer numbers such as 'Bob White' and 'If I Had My Druthers', plus other humorous oldies, like 'Who Takes Care Of The Caretaker's Daughter' and 'My Cutie's Due At Two-To-Two Today'. Several artists, such as **Marlene VerPlanck**, **Susannah McCorkle**, and Nancy LaMott, have devoted complete albums to his work, and in 1992 Capitol Records celebrated its 50th anniversary by issuing *Two Marvellous For Words: Capitol Sings Johnny Mercer*, which consistedof some of the label's most eminent artists singing their co-founder's popular song lyrics.

Selected albums: with Bobby Darin *Two Of A Kind* (1961). A*udio Scrap Book* (1964-74), *Johnny Mercer Sings Johnny Mercer* (Capitol c.70s), *Ac-Cent-Tchu-Ate The Positive*, *Johnny Mercer's Music Shop*, *My Huckleberry Friend* (Pye 1974), *An Evening With Johnny Mercer* (Laureate 1977).

Further reading: *Our Huckleberry Friend: The Life, Times And Song Lyrics Of Johnny Mercer*, B. Back and G. Mercer.

Mercer, Mabel

b. 3 February 1900, Birmingham, Staffordshire, England, d. 20 April 1984, Pittsfield, Massachusetts, USA. A celebrated and influential cabaret singer, as a young girl Mercer was educated at convent school, and underwent classical voice training. Her mother was a white variety singer and actress, her father a black American jazz singer who died before she was born. Her mother remarried and became popular in music hall in the UK, sometimes touring overseas. In her teens, Mercer became a professional dancer, and made one of her first appearances in a London production of Lew Leslie's ***Blackbirds***, which starred Florence Mills. By the early 20s, she had become a singer, performing in various parts of Europe and the Middle East. Before the end of the decade she had settled in Paris, and was soon a featured attraction at the renowned Bricktop's nightclub, mixing with and entertaining the 'lost generation' of American expatriates which included songwriters **Cole Porter** and **Vincent Youmans**, as well as leading literary figures such as Gertrude Stein and Ernest Hemingway. In 1938 Mercer visited New York, and by 1941 had begun the first of two long residencies in the city, at Tony's, and later at the Byline Room, which continued until 1957. In later years she also became associated with the Café Carlyle where **Bobby Short** regularly holds court, and recorded two live albums with him. In the 70s she worked at the St. Regis Room, appeared at Carnegie Hall and on UK television in *Miss Mercer In Mayfair*. In 1974 she received *Stereo Review Magazine*'s Award of Merit, which was renamed the Mabel Mercer Award in 1984. On being chosen as its first recipient, **Frank Sinatra** said: 'Mabel Mercer taught me everything I know, she is the finest music teacher in the world'. She retired in 1979, but was back on stage at the 1982 Kool Jazz Festival, singing a programme of songs by **Alec Wilder**. The composer is said to have written one of his most appealing songs, 'While We're Young', especially for her. Her final performance was at a charity benefit in November 1983, and in the same year she was awarded the Presidential Medal of Freedom, the nation's highest civilian award, by President Reagan. One of the most respected singers, greatly admired by fellow artists and also by the composers whose work she performs, Mercer's voice had a good range and a deep, melodious sound. Although she would sometimes use jazz phrasing, she was never a jazz singer, but remained one of the finest cabaret or supper-club singers of her generation. Her greatest talent lay in her masterly delivery of lyrics to which she brought intimacy and affection.

Albums: *Mabel Mercer Sings Cole Porter* (1955), *Midnight At Mabel Mercer's* (c.50s), with Bobby Short *At Town Hall* (Atlantic 1968), with Bobby Short *Second Town Hall Concert* (Atlantic 1969), *The Art Of Mabel Mercer* (c.60s), *Echoes Of My Life* (c.70s).

Further reading: *Mabel Mercer: A Life*, James Haskins.

Mercury Records

Mercury was founded in 1947 by booking agent Irving

Green, Jerry Fischer, Art Talmadge and Berle Adams. One of its first executives was **John Hammond** (Snr.) who hired **Mitch Miller** as musical director. With Nat Tarnapol (later to found **Brunswick**) and Clyde Otis (the first black A&R chief of a major company) were instrumental in the company's development. Mercury had R&B success with **Dinah Washington**, **Brook Benton** and **Eddie 'Cleanhead' Vinson**. In the rock 'n' roll era, Mercury had hits with both black vocal groups (the **Platters** and the **Penguins**) and white cover-version artists (**Georgia Gibbs**, and the **Crewcuts**). Through its southern A&R scout **Shelby Singleton**, Mercury also picked up artists like the **Big Bopper** and **Bruce Channel**.

In 1961, Mercury was purchased by the Dutch-owned Philips label, (soon to become PolyGram) but the management remained unchanged. There was a move into country with the Nashville-based Smash Records, run by producer Jerry Kennedy, who worked with **Jerry Lee Lewis**, **Charlie Rich** and **Tom T. Hall**. From 1964-67, the label ran Limelight, a jazz subsidiary (including **Oscar Peterson**), and the King/Starday catalogue of R&B and country recordings. In 1965, Philips/Mercury bought the famous King/Starday catalogue of R&B and country recordings.

During the 70s, the Mercury group was the main source of US talent for the giant Polygram corporation, providing hits from the **Ohio Players**, the **Gap Band**, **Rod Stewart**, **Graham Parker**, **10cc**, **Rush** and **Bachman-Turner Overdrive**. The company subsequently specialized in heavy metal talent, signing **Bon Jovi**, Cinderella, **L.A. Guns**, **Kiss** and, from its European sister companies, **Def Leppard** and the **Scorpions**. Its major rock acts were **John Mellencamp** and **INXS**. In the 80s, Mercury maintained its black music activities through a resuscitated Smash (for rap artists) and a new soul music label, Wing, whose early 90s roster included Vanessa Williams, Michael Morales and **Tony! Toni! Tone!**

Mercury Rev

A six piece band from Buffalo, New York State, Mercury Rev burst onto the music scene in 1991 to unanimous critical acclaim for their enterprising mix of **Pink Floyd** and **Dinosaur Jr** dynamics. However, the sounds produced by Jonathan Donahue (vocals/guitar; ex-**Flaming Lips**), David Fridmann (bass), Jimmy Chambers (drums), Sean 'Grasshopper' Mackowiak (guitar), Suzanne Thorpe (flute) and David Baker (vocals/guitar) remain difficult to classify. Their album, *Yerself Is Steam*, although practically ignored in their native country, created the sort of snowballing press acclaim in the UK which has rarely been accorded a debut. The ***Melody Maker***'s comment 'Universally acclaimed by UK critics as the draughtsmen behind the first, and so far only, great rock long player of 1991' was among the more conservative of the plaudits, and with only a handful of gigs under their belt they were to be seen filling support slots for the likes of **My Bloody Valentine** and, incredibly, **Bob Dylan**. DJ **John Peel** summed up their appeal by stating that: 'Unlike many bands, you can't tell what's in their record collection'. The press undoubtedly saw them as the next step forward from the previous wave of influential US guitar bands like the **Pixies**, **Sonic Youth** and Dinosaur Jr. However, the ability to capitalize on this flying start rested, rather precariously, on their ability to remain together as a collective unit. A variety of stories filtered through concerning their self-destructive, almost psychotic behaviour. Already banned from one airline due to Donahue trying to remove Mackowiak's eye with a spoon, another minor crisis concerned Fridmann's disposal of the band's entire advance for their 'Carwash Hair' single on a holiday for his mother in Bermuda, without telling anyone. The band's writing and recording takes place in a similar, reckless manner: 'Basically, its whoever shouts loudest, or who has the biggest punch'. However, even by Mercury Rev's standards David Baker offered an unsettled musical visage, often simply stepping off the stage during performances to fetch a drink, and enriching the surreal nature of their songs with lines like 'Tonight I'll dig tunnels to your nightmare room' in 'Downs Are Feminine Balloons'. This was drawn from *Boces*, another complex journey through multitudinous musical motifs and styles, producing a sonic anomaly drawing on the traditions of left field art rockers like **Wire**, **Pere Ubu** and **Suicide**. Baker was eventually deselected when his behaviour became intolerable in February 1994, with the miscreant electing to set out on a solo career instead. Reduced to a quintet, *See You On The Other Side* provided no other evidence of a reduction in the band's talents, revealing instead a more focused though no less exciting or adventurous sound.

Albums: *Yerself Is Steam* (Mint/Jungle 1991), *Boces* (Beggars Banquet 1993), *See You On The Other Side* (Beggars Banquet 1995). Compilation: *Yerself Is Steam/Lego My Ego* (Beggars Banquet 1992).

Mercury, Freddie

b. Frederick Bulsara, 5 September 1946, Zanzibar, Africa, d. 24 November 1991, London, England. Best known as the flamboyant lead singer of the multi-million selling UK group **Queen**, Mercury also branched out into extra-curricular musical activities. In 1973, while Queen were about to release their debut album, Mercury recorded a revival of the **Beach Boys**' 'I Can Hear Music' under the glam rock name Larry Lurex. It was not until late 1984 that he again attempted a solo work, this time with the UK Top 20 hit 'Love Kills', from the **Giorgio Moroder** soundtrack to the film *Metropolis*. A second solo single, 'I Was Born To Love You', reached the UK Top 20 early the next year. A solo album and some lowly-placed solo singles followed. In 1986, Mercury contributed some tracks to the cast recording of **Dave Clark**'s musical *Time*. His greatest solo success, however, came in 1987, with a kitsch revival of the **Platters**' 'The Great Pretender', which reached the UK Top 5. Later that year, Mercury emphasized his immemorial love of opera by teaming up with Monserrat Caballe for the grandiloquent 'Barcelona', another Top 10 success. An album of the same title was also successful and, in late 1988, the operatic duo played a major show at the Avinguda De Maria Cristina Stadium in Barcelona. Mercury retained a low profile thereafter, and, following much speculation over his health in November 1991, he finally admitted that he was suffering from AIDS. Within forty-eight hours, on 24 November, he died from bronchial pneumonia at his Knightsbridge home. A major concert was arranged in April 1992 at London's Wembley stadium. Known as the Freddy Mercury Aids Benefit, it attracted the largest world-wide viewing audience when televised live.

Albums: *Mr Bad Guy* (1985), with Monserrat Caballe *Barcelona* (1988).

Further reading: *The Show Must Go On: The Life Of Freddie Mercury*, Rick Sky. *A Kind Of Magic: A Tribute To Freddie Mercury*, Ross Clarke. *Mercury And Me*, Jim Hutton with Tim Wapshott.

Mercy

Formed by Jack Sigler Jnr. (b. 1950, Tampa, Florida, USA) in the late 60s, Mercy enjoyed one best-selling single in 1969, the ballad 'Love (Can Make You Happy)'. Following several membership changes (Sigler the only remaining original), the band were heard by movie producer George Roberts. He used the group's future hit, penned by Sigler, in a film called *Fireball Jungle,* but the film was never released. The group managed to place the single with the small Sundi label and, with distribution via **Warner Brothers**, made it to number 2 on the national US charts. The group managed one further minor chart single and an album before they disbanded owing to lack of commercial success.

Album: *The Mercy & Love (Can Make You Happy)* (1969).

Mercy Dee

b. Mercy Dee Walton, 30 August 1915, Waco, Texas, USA, d. 2 December 1962, Murphy's, California, USA. From an early interest in the piano, stimulated by the many local players of the instrument, Mercy Dee developed an instantly recognizable blues style, with much use of trills and crashing treble chords, complemented by lyrics packed with powerful, memorable imagery. After moving to California in his 20s, he recorded in a variety of settings between 1949 and 1955, even including rock 'n' roll and pop, but it was in slow blues, such as the much-covered 'One Room Country Shack' and humorous numbers like 'GI Fever', that he could be heard at his best. An album for **Arhoolie** recorded in the early 60s is particularly worthwhile, as it concentrated on those aspects of his music.

Albums: *Mercy Dee* (1961), *GI Fever* (1985), *Troublesome Mind* (1992).

Mercyful Fate

This seminal black metal act was formed in Copenhagen, Denmark, in 1980 by vocalist **King Diamond** (b. Kim Bendix Petersen, 14 June 1956, Copenhagen, Denmark) and guitarist Hank Shermann with Michael Denner (guitar), Timi Grabber Hansen (bass) and Kim Ruzz (drums). The band's first vinyl appearance was with 'Black Funeral' on the *Metallic Storm* compilation, before *A Corpse Without Soul* (aka *Nuns Have No Fun*) saw the full debut of their heavy yet intricate guitar-based approach, and of King Diamond's unique vocal style, which ranged from deep bass growls to falsetto shrieks. *Melissa*, with a name taken from the human skull then owned by Diamond and used as a stage prop, fulfilled Mercyful Fate's promise, and the band became one of the mainstays of the black metal underground with their occult lyricism and theatrical approach (though Diamond's facial make-up later drew legal action from **Kiss**' Gene Simmons over alleged similarities to his 'God Of Thunder' persona). *Don't Break The Oath* was a more mature work as the band reaped the benefits of extensive touring with a tighter sound. However, when they regrouped after further successful live work to record a third album, Shermann's determination to pursue a surprising AOR direction saw the band split, with Diamond going on to a solo career with Hansen and Denner in tow while Shermann formed Fate. The posthumous release of *In The Beginning*, containing the debut mini-album plus BBC session tracks, seemed to be an epitaph for Mercyful Fate. However, the heavier approach of Shermann and Denner's Zoser Mez led to the reformation of the old band, with Ruzz replaced by Morten Nielsen on *In The Shadows*, and by Snowy Shaw on tour (the latter taking up the position permanently). The record harked back to *Don't Break The Oath*'s style, and also featured a guest appearance by **Metallica**'s Lars Ulrich on 'Return Of The Vampire', a song resurrected form the band's second demo in 1982. Before 1994's *Time* Hansen would be replaced on bass by Sharlee D'Angelo, as the group toured the US with **Flotsam & Jetsam** and **Cathedral** (live recordings from which were released as *The Bell Witch* EP). When *Time* did emerge it provided unexpected diversions, with the Middle-Eastern flavour of 'The Mad Arab'

and the serenity of 'Witch's Dance' rubbing shoulders with more traditional Mercyful Fate concerns ('Nightmare Be Thy Name', etc.).
Albums: *A Corpse Without Soul* (Rave-On 1982, mini-album), *Melissa* (Roadrunner 1983), *Don't Break The Oath* (Roadrunner 1984), *In The Shadows* (Metal Blade 1993), *Time* (Metal Blade 1994). Compilations: *In The Beginning* (Roadrunner 1988, rec. 1982/1983), *Return Of The Vampire* (Roadrunner 1992).

Merlin

b. London, England. Hardly the 'new rap messiah' that his second album proclaimed him to be, Merlin nevertheless cut an intriguing figure in the British rap scene of the 90s. He was still a teenager when the record was released, but he had already chalked up a fair reputation for his late 80s releases on **Rhythm King** (including being arrested for stealing cheques from **Mute** Records just before he made an appearance on *Top Of The Pops*. One of the most notable examples of his craft was the single, 'Born Free', with its prototype UK hip hop lyrics.
Albums: *Merlin* (Rhythm King 1989), *The New Rap Messiah* (MCA 1991).

Merman, Ethel

b. Ethel Agnes Zimmermann, 16 January 1909, Astoria, New York, USA, d. 15 February 1984, New York, USA. One of the most celebrated ladies of the Broadway musical stage, a dynamic entertainer, with a loud, brash, theatrical singing style, flawless diction, and extravagant manner, who usually played a gutsy lady with a heart of gold. She worked first as a secretary, then sang in nightclubs, eventually graduating to the best spots. Noticed by producer Vinton Freedley while singing at the Brooklyn Paramount, she was signed for **George** and **Ira Gershwin**'s Broadway show ***Girl Crazy*** (1930), and was a great success, stopping the show with her version of 'I Got Rhythm', a song which became one of her life-long themes. She was equally successful in ***George White's*** *Scandals* (1931), in which she co-starred with **Rudy Vallee**, and sang 'My Song' and 'Life Is Just A Bowl Of Cherries'; and ***Take A Chance*** (1932), when her two big numbers were 'Eadie Was A Lady' and 'Rise 'N' Shine'. In 1934, Merman starred in ***Anything Goes***, the first of five **Cole Porter** musical shows in which she was to appear. The score was top drawer Porter, full of song hits such as 'I Get A Kick Out Of You', 'All Through The Night', 'You're The Top' (one of the composer's renowned 'list' songs'), 'Anything Goes' and 'Blow, Gabriel, Blow'. Merman also appeared in the 1936 film version of the show with **Bing Crosby**. The other Porter productions in which she appeared were ***Red, Hot And Blue!*** (1936), co-starring **Jimmy Durante** and **Bob Hope**, with the songs, 'Down In The Depths (On The Ninetieth Floor)', 'It's De-Lovely' and 'Ridin' High'; ***DuBarry Was A Lady*** (1939), with 'But In The Morning, No!', 'Do I Love You?', 'Give Him The Oo-La-La', 'Katie Went To Haiti' and 'Friendship'; ***Panama Hattie*** (1940), featuring 'I've Still Got My Health', 'Let's Be Buddies', 'Make It Another Old-Fashioned, Please' and 'I'm Throwing A Ball Tonight'; and *Something For The Boys* (1943) with 'Hey, Good Lookin'', 'He's A Right Guy', 'Could It Be You' and 'The Leader Of A Big Time Band'. Merman's longest-running musical was **Irving Berlin**'s ***Annie Get Your Gun*** (1946), which lasted for 1,147 performances. As the sharp-shooting Annie Oakley, she introduced such Berlin classics as 'They Say It's Wonderful', 'Doin' What Comes Naturally', 'I Got The Sun In The Morning', 'You Can't Get A Man With A Gun', and the song which was to become another of her anthems, 'There's No Business Like Show Business'. Merman's next Broadway show, ***Call Me Madam***, again had an Irving Berlin score. This time, as Sally Adams, ambassador to the mythical country of Lichtenburg, she triumphed again with numbers such as 'Marrying For Love', 'You're Just In Love', 'The Best Thing For You', 'Can You Use Any Money Today?', and 'The Hostess With The Mostes' On The Ball'.
She also starred in the 1953 film version of the show, with George Sanders, **Donald O'Connor**, and **Vera-Ellen**. Often cited as the peak of Merman's career, ***Gypsy*** (1959), with a score by **Jule Styne** and **Stephen Sondheim**, saw her cast as the domineering mother of stripper Gypsy Rose Lee, and Merman gave the kind of performance for which she had never before been asked. Her songs included 'Some People', 'Small World', 'You'll Never Get Away From Me', 'Together', 'Rose's Turn', and her triumphant hymn, 'Everthing's Coming Up Roses'. Apart from a brief revival of ***Annie Get Your Gun*** (1966), and a spell as a replacement in ***Hello, Dolly!***, (she had turned down the role when the show was originally cast), *Gypsy* was Merman's last Broadway musical appearance. Although the stage was her *metier*, she made several successful Hollywood films such as ***We're Not Dressing*** (1934), ***Kid Millions*** and *Strike Me Pink* (both 1935 with **Eddie Cantor**) ***Alexander's Ragtime Band*** (1938), with Tyrone Power, **Alice Faye**, and **Don Ameche**; and ***There's No Business Like Show Business*** (1954), in which she sco-tarred with **Dan Dailey**, **Donald O'Connor** and **Marilyn Monroe**.
There were also non-singing roles in comedy films such as *It's A Mad, Mad, Mad, Mad World* (1963), *The Art Of Love* (1965) and *Airplane!* (1980). Merman appeared regularly on television from the 50s through to the 70s in specials and guest spots, and also starred in cabaret. In 1953 she teamed up with another Broadway legend, **Mary Martin**, for the historic Ford 50th Anniversary Show, highlights of which were issued on a **Decca**

album. On the same label was her *Musical Autobiography* (2-album set). Besides the many hits from her shows, her record successes included 'How Deep Is The Ocean', 'Move It Over', and four duets with **Ray Bolger**, 'Dearie', 'I Said My Pajamas (And Put On My Prayers)', 'If I Knew You Were Comin' I'd've Baked A Cake', and 'Once Upon A Nickel'. After a distinguished career lasting over 50 years, Merman's final major appearance was at a Carnegie Hall benefit concert in 1982. A year after her death in 1984, a biographical tribute show entitled *Call Me Miss Birdseye: Ethel Merman - The Lady And Her Music*, was presented at the Donmar Warehouse Theatre in London. In 1994 the US Post Service somewhat optimistically mounted a search for an 'Ethel Merman Soundalike' ('no lipsynching!') in conjunction with the release of the Legends of American Music stamps. The first prize was, appropriately enough, an appearance in the Broadway hit musical ***Crazy For You***.
Selected albums: with Dick Haymes, Eileen Wilson *Call Me Madam* (Decca c.50s), *Memories* (Decca c.50s), *A Musical Autobiography* (Decca c.50s, double album), *Merry-Go-Round* (A&M 1967), *Merman Sings Merman* (Decca 1973), *Ethel's Ridin' High* (Decca 1975). Compilations: *Ethel Was A Lady* (MCA 1984), *The World Is Your Balloon* (MCA 1987), *Ethel Merman* (Nostalgia 1988), *Red. Hot And Blue!/Stars In Your Eyes* (AEI 1991), *Ethel Sings Merman-And More* (Decca/Eclipse 1992), *An Earful Of Merman* (Conifer 1994).
Further reading: *Who Could Ask For Anything More?* Ethel Merman and P. Martin. *Don't Call Me Madam*, Ethel Merman. *Merman*, Ethel Merman. *I Got Rhythm: The Ethel Merman Story*, B. Thomas.

Merrill, Bob

b. H. Robert Merrill Levan, 17 May 1921, Atlantic City, New Jersey, USA. A popular songwriter, for Tin Pan Alley and the musical theatre, Merril worked at a number of jobs in various parts of the USA, before he began singing in clubs and on the stage, where he was also an effective mimic. After military service during World War II, he spent some time in Hollywood as a dialogue director and also made a handful of acting appearances. It was while working on a film that he was asked by comedienne Dorothy Shay to write some songs for her forthcoming album. Merrill did as she suggested, and the financial rewards this brought encouraged him to pursue songwriting as a career. Among the early songs he wrote were 'Lover's Gold' (music by Morty Nevins), 'Fool's Paradise' and 'The Chicken Song' (with Terry Shand). In 1950 Merrill had his first hit with 'If I Knew You Were Coming I'd've Baked A Cake' (Al Hoffman and Clem Watts), which was followed by numerous others, such as 'Sparrow In The Treetop', 'My Truly, Truly Fair', 'She Wears Red Feathers' 'Pittsburgh, Pennsylvania', 'Chicka Boom' 'Feet Up', Belle Belle My Liberty Belle', 'Look At That Girl', 'Cuff Of My Shirt', (all successful for **Guy Mitchell**), '(How Much Is That) Doggie In The Window?', (a US number 1 for **Patti Page**), 'Let Me In', ''Walkin' To Missouri', 'Mambo Italiano', 'Where Will The Dimple Be?' and 'A Sweet Old-Fashioned Girl'. Despite the success of these songs, Merrill wanted to write for the musical theatre, and in 1956 he composed the score for ***New Girl In Town***, a musical adaptation of Eugene O'Neill's novel *Anna Christie*, which opened on Broadway in May 1957. Two years later Merrill wrote the music and lyrics for ***Take Me Along***, which was based on another O'Neill piece, *Ah, Wilderness!* Both productions enjoyed runs in excess of 400 performances, but Merrill's next show, ***Carnival*** (1961), did ever better, staying at the Imperial Theatre in New York for 719 performances. The score included several appealing songs such as 'Love Makes The World Go Round', 'Yes, My Heart' and 'Her Face'. In 1964 Merrill wrote two songs, 'Elegance' and 'Motherhood March' with **Jerry Herman** for his ***Hello, Dolly!***, before collaborating with composer **Jule Styne** on the smash hit ***Funny Girl*** which elevated **Barbra Streisand** to stardom, and was later filmed. Since then, Merrill has been unable to come up with another hit. *Breakfast At Tiffany's* (1966) closed during previews, and *Henry, Sweet Henry* folded after only 80 performances. He has subsequently worked with Styne again on *Prettybelle* (1971), which failed to reach Broadway, and ***Sugar***, based on the highly successful Billy Wilder film *Some Like It Hot*. Despite mixed reviews, it ran for 505 performances, and, retitled ***Some Like it Hot***, became a short-lived vehicle for the popular UK entertainer **Tommy Steele** in 1992. Merrill teamed with Styne once more in 1993 (under the pseudonym of Paul Stryker) to provide extra lyrics for ***The Red Shoes*** which lasted for just three days. In contrast, however, a new career as a screenwriter beckoned and, he also teaches at the University of California in Los Angeles.

Merrill, Helen

b. 21 July 1930, New York City, New York, USA. Merrill's early career found her singing in exalted bebop company. Among the major artists with whom she sang in the late 40s were **Charlie Parker**, **Miles Davis** and **Bud Powell**. She spent part of the 50s outside music, but continued to make a few records with notable figures such as **Clifford Brown**; by the end of the decade, was resident in Italy and a familiar figure at European festivals. In the early 60s, she returned to the USA but had difficulty in attracting the attention of either radio and television networks or the major record companies. She did make a handful of records backed by leading musicians such as **Thad Jones**, **Ron Carter**, **Richard Davis**, **Elvin Jones** and **Jim Hall**. By the late 60s, Merrill was again resident outside the USA, this time in Japan, where her

talents were much appreciated. Back in the USA in the mid-70s, she was still largely overlooked but was periodically recorded, again with excellent jazz backing from the likes of **Teddy Wilson**, **John Lewis** and **Pepper Adams**. In November 1994, Merrill reappeared on the scene, promoting a new album and planning a UK and European tour for 1995. One of the most musical of singers, Merrill customarily explores the emotional depths of the lyrics of the songs she sings, imbuing them with great passion.
Selected albums: *Helen Merrill Featuring Clifford Brown* (Emarcy 1954), *Helen Merrill With Hal Mooney And His Orchestra* i (1955), *Helen Merrill With Gil Evans And His Orchestra* (1956), *Helen Merrill With Hal Mooney And His Orchestra* ii (1957), *Helen Merrill* i (Philips 1957), *Helen Merrill* ii (1959), *Helen Merrill With Quincy Jones And His Orchestra* (1959), *Helen Merrill In Italy* (Liuto 1959-1962 recording), *Helen Merrill* iii (1964), *Autumn Love* (1967), *A Shade Of Difference* (Spotlite 1968), *Helen Merrill In Tokyo* (1969), with Teddy Wilson *Helen Sings, Teddy Swings* (c.1970), *Sposin'* (1971), *Helen Merrill/John Lewis* (1977), *Chasin' The Bird* (1979), *Case Forte* (1980), *The Rodgers & Hammerstein Album* (DRG 1982), *No Tears...No Goodbyes* (Owl 1984), *Music Makers* (Owl 1986), *Collaboration* (Emarcy 1988), *Just Friends* (Emarcy 1989), *Dream Of You* (Emarcy 1993, 1956 recording), *Clear Out Of This World* (Emarcy 1992), Brownie: *Tribute To Clifford Brown* (Verve 1994). Compilation: *Blossom Of Stars* (1954-1992 recordings).

Merrily We Roll Along

Two of the musical theatre's current heavyweights went into the Broadway ring during the the 1981/2 season, and the result of the contest gave theatre-goers on both sides of the Atlantic a foretaste of the significant shift in the balance of power that was about to take place during the next 10 years. The English champion, **Andrew Lloyd Webber** with his ***Joseph And The Amazing Technicolor Dreamcoat*** scored 747 performances, and the native New Yorker, **Stephen Sondheim**, with *Merrily We Roll Along*, only 16 performances. Prior to the latter show's debut at the Alvin Theatre on 16 November 1981, the smart money was on a Sondheim show that eschewed his usual brittle exposition of contemporary life, in favour of a more traditional style of entertainment - musical comedy - and that is what Sondheim claimed it was originally intended to be. George Furth's book was based on the 1934 play by **George S. Kaufman** and **Moss Hart**. The story, which is told in flashback, tells of a successful composer, Franklin Shepard (as a young man - Jim Walton; aged 43 - Geoffrey Horne), a lyricist, Charles Kringas (Lonny Price), and a mutual friend of the pair, Mary Flynn (Ann Morrison). Shepard is the central character, and the details of his wasted life - the betrayal of his wife and friends in the pursuit of money and glory over a period of some 20 years - are revealed before the final scene, in which - because in this piece the end is the beginning - the friends are meeting in 1957 for the first time. Sondheim constructed the score in what he called 'modular blocks' - the release of one song would be the verse of another, and the chorus of that one could serve as the release of the next, and so on. Some of the songs, such as 'Opening Doors', 'The Hills Of Tomorrow', and 'Good Thing Going'. were based on the same tune - it was Sondheim at his most inventive, and, at least, the composer was nominated for a Tony Award. The rest of the numbers included 'Not A Day Goes By', 'Franklin Shepard Inc.', 'Bobby And Jackie And Jack', 'Like It Was', 'It's A Hit', 'Now You Know', 'Meet The Blob', and 'Merrily We Roll Along'. Most aspects of the production came in for severe criticism: Eugene Lees's sparse sets, Larry Fuller's choreography, and a cast that was considered by many to be far too young and inexperienced. The celebrated partnership between Sondheim and director and producer **Hal Prince** came - perhaps temporarily to an end - with this production. As with most, if not all, Sondheim shows, this one continued to live on far beyond its two-weeks run in New York, via the excellent Original Cast album, and various provincial productions. One such, was mounted by the Leicester Haymarket Theatre in England, in 1992, the starting-off point for many fine original musicals and revivals. It starred Michael Cantwell, Maria Friedman, Evan Pappas, Gareth Snook, and Jacqueline Dankworth, the daughter of jazz musicians **John Dankworth** and **Cleo Laine**. The 1994 Off Broadway revival reminded *Variety*'s theatre critic that this is 'one of the best scores of any contemporary musical'.

Merritt, Max, And The Meteors

Formed in New Zealand in 1956. Max Merritt was influenced by black R&B and soul records imported by American Naval personnel stationed in New Zealand, which subsequently meant the Meteors were foremost in presenting this new music to New Zealand audiences on album and via several hit singles. Outgrowing their local market, the band visited Australia in late 1964, but soon relocated permanently. They released five singles, none of which sold well, but the high standard of musicianship within the group made it a popular live act, often winning praise from fellow musicians. A road accident left Merritt with one eye and the drummer, Stewie Spears, was permanently injured, which proved a difficult setback for the band to overcome. The band had an Australian hit single with 'Western Union Man' in late 1969. The accompanying album also sold well and the band departed for the UK in October 1970. After management problems which produced a state of limbo, they managed to ensconce themselves in the pub rock scene. By 1975, the group had signed with **Arista** and gained success with the single 'Slipping Away', and

two albums, *A Little Easier* and *Out Of The Blue*. Merritt spent much of 1978 in the USA, but despite a couple of more album releases, his career faded. Spears died in 1986, while Merritt retired to Los Angeles, where he is employed as a film set carpenter and otherwise tours occasionally in Australia.
Albums: *Max Merritt's Meteors* (1965), *Max Merritt & The Meteors* (1969), *Stray Cats* (1971), *A Little Easier* (1975), *Out Of The Blue* (1976), *Back Home Live* (1977), *Keeping In Touch* (1978), *Black Plastic Max* (1980).

Merry Widow, The

A perfect example of the kind of Viennese operetta that was so popular in the early part of the 20th century before it was overtaken by the more contemporary shows of **Jerome Kern** and the other pioneers of musical comedy. With its superb score by Franz Lehár, *The Merry Widow* was first offered to the public at the Theatre an der Wien in Vienna, on 30 December 1905, under the title of *Die Lustige Witwe*. The book, by Victor Leon and Leo Stein, was based on Henri Meilhac's play *L'Attaché d'Ambassade*. Eighteen months later, on 8 June 1907, when it was presented by George Edwardes at Daly's Theatre in London, the show had a new book by Basil Hood (who declined to be credited), and English lyrics by Adrian Ross. The classic story concerns the arrival in France of Sonia Sadoya (Lily Elsie), a wealthy widow from Marsovia, who is hunting for a husband. If she marries a Frenchman, her millions will be lost for ever to the impoverished principality, and Ambassador Baron Popoff (George Graves) will be out of a job. Prince Danilo (Joseph Coyne), a secretary to the legation, is instructed to make sure that a Franco-Marsovian union does not take place, preferably by marrying the lady himself. The joyous and memorable score contained several enduring favourites such as 'Maxim's', 'I Love You So' (also know as the 'Merry Widow Waltz'), 'Love In My Heart Awakening', 'Vilia', 'Women', 'Home', 'A Dutiful Wife', 'The Girls At Maxim's, and 'Silly, Silly Cavalier'. Enthusiastic audiences, with the ladies dressed in their 'Merry Widow' attire, flocked to the theatre for 778 performances - it was a tremendous success. The 1907 New York production, with Ethel Jackson, ran for a year, and was followed by several Broadway revivals through to the 40s. West End audiences, too, saw the show on many occasions, including 1958 (with June Bronhill), 1969 (with Lizbeth Webb), and 1985 (Helen Kuchareck). All the revivals to date have had revised books and scores. Many other professional and amateur productions are taking place constantly throughout the world, one of the most recent being that mounted by the Paper Mill Playhouse, New Jersey, USA, in 1991. Three film versions have been released: in 1925 (silent), in 1934 with **Jeanette Macdonald** and **Maurice Chevalier**, and a 1952 remake with Fernando Lamas and Lana Turner.

Merry-Go-Round

Formed in Hawthorne, California, USA, in 1966, the Merry-Go-Round were bit players in the Los Angeles pop scene at the same time groups such as the **Doors** and **Buffalo Springfield** were gaining national success. Original members **Emitt Rhodes** (keyboards/bass) and Gary Kato (lead guitar) were influenced by the harmonies and melodies of the **Beatles**. Completing the group with Bill Rinehart (guitar/bass) and Joel Larson (drums), they signed with **A&M Records** and recorded a single, 'Live', which was successful locally in southern California but barely gained notice in the rest of the US. A follow-up single, 'You're A Very Lovely Woman', and the group's only album, a self-titled effort also released in 1967, were ignored outside of LA. The group disbanded in 1969, and Rhodes embarked on a solo career, releasing four albums, before disappearing from the pop scene. **Rhino Records** issued a compilation of the group's issued and unissued recordings in 1985, and the **Bangles** recorded their 'Live' for their debut album.
Album: *The Merry-Go-Round* (1967). Compilation: *Best Of The Merry-Go-Round* (1985).

Merryweather, Neil

Having made his recording debut with John Richardson and Robin Boers, bassist Merryweather achieved minor fame in 1969 with the release of *Word Of Mouth*. Although ostensibly a vehicle for his group, the set is better recalled for stellar contributions made by **Steve Miller**, **Barry Goldberg** and **Charlie Musselwhite**, each of whom shared the artist's apprenticeship in Chicago's thriving R&B and blues circuit. The latter two musicians also contributed to *Ivar Avenue Reunion*, before Merryweather formed a more permanent group around Lynn Carey (vocals), J.J. Velker (keyboards), Ed Roth (keyboards) and Coffi Hall (drums). Having completed *Vacuum Cleaner*, credited to 'Merryweather And Carey', the bassist and vocalist formed Mama Lion in 1972. The itinerant Merryweather also established two subsequent units, the Spacerangers and Eyes, but despite such meritorious perseverance, has been unable to secure commercial success.
Albums: *Neil Merryweather, John Richardson and Robin Boers* (late 60s), *Word Of Mouth* (1969), *Ivar Avenue Reunion* (1970), *Vacuum Cleaner* (1971), *Space Ranger* (1974), *Kryptonite* (1975), *Differences* (1978).

Merseybeats

Originally called the Mavericks, this Liverpudlian quartet comprised Tony Crane (vocals/lead guitar), Billy Kinsley (vocals/bass), David Ellis (rhythm guitar) and Frank Sloan (drums). In 1962, long before the **Beatles** put Liverpool on the musical map, they rechristened themselves the Merseybeats. Early line-up changes saw Ellis and Sloan replaced by Aaron Williams and John Banks. By mid-1963, Beatlemania had engulfed the UK, and A&R representatives descended upon Liverpool in search of talent. The Merseybeats were scooped up by Fontana and initially signed by **Brian Epstein**, but left their new mentor within weeks, following an argument over image. **Burt Bacharach** and **Hal David**'s 'It's Love That Really Counts' gave them a minor hit, but it was the relatively unknown songwriter Peter Lee Stirling (see **Daniel Boone**) who penned their biggest hit, 'I Think Of You'. Although essentially balladeers on single, the group's EPs had a grittier edge. The *On Stage* EP, with its use of monochrome photography, was extremely progressive in design terms as it did not feature the band on the cover, while their debut album included a variety of old musical standards. Pop star pressures prompted founding member Billy Kinsley to leave the group briefly, but he returned in time for their third major hit, 'Wishin' And Hopin''. Other members included Bob Garner, who was himself replaced by Johnny Gustafson from the **Big Three**.

The eclipse of the Mersey Sound eventually took its toll on the group, though a change of management to **Kit Lambert** brought two more minor hits, 'I Love You, Yes I Do' and 'I Stand Accused'. In January 1966, the group split, paving the way for hit duo, the **Merseys**. In later years, Tony Crane reactivated the group, which still performs regularly on the cabaret circuit.

Album: *The Merseybeats* (1964). Compilation: *The Merseybeats: Beat And Ballads* (1982).

Merseys

From the defunct **Merseybeats,** Tony Crane (vocals/lead guitar) and Billy Kinsley (vocals/bass) emerged as the Merseys. For their backing group, they employed Liverpool hopefuls, the Fruit Eating Bears. With manager **Kit Lambert** encouraging a fresh direction, the duo covered an old **McCoys** b-side, 'Sorrow', which climbed to number 4 in the UK charts. Lambert next invited **Pete Townshend** to compose a follow-up, 'So Sad About Us', but despite some good reviews, it failed to chart. Further attempts with 'Rhythm Of Love' and 'The Cat' brought no success and the duo reluctantly moved into cabaret, employing various additional musicians under their old name, the Merseybeats. Kinsley later re-emerged as a hit artist in the 70s, leading **Liverpool Express**. A small footnote was added to the Merseys' career when their first two singles were belatedly covered by **David Bowie** and the **Jam,** respectively.

Merton Parkas

One of several late 70s mod revivalists to make the UK charts, the Merton Parkas began life as the Sneakers around 1975, playing old **Motown** classics. The line-up comprised brothers Mick (b. 11 September 1958; keyboards) and Danny Talbot (vocals), Neil Wurrell (bass) and Simon Smith (drums), and they chose their new name from Merton (the area of south London, they hailed from) and Parka (the ubiquitous item of mod attire). The Merton Parkas were great live favourites at the Bridgehouse in Canning Town, London but were unable to appear on the *Mods Mayday '79* live compilation because they were negotiating contracts with **Beggars Banquet**, after the label's first signing, the **Lurkers**, had recommended them. They were one of the first neo-mod bands to record, and their debut single, 'You Need Wheels' was a hit in August 1979. Unfortunately, the rather trite lyrics had the Mertons branded as a novelty act, and they were often unfairly dismissed as bandwagon jumpers. Subsequent singles such as 'Plastic Smile', 'Give It To Me Now' (produced by Dennis Bovell of Matumbi), and 'Put Me In The Picture' failed to match the success of their debut. Mick Talbot was meanwhile making his name as an in-demand keyboard player on the **Jam**'s *Setting Sons* and an album by the **Chords**. The Mertons soon disbanded and Talbot went on to join **Dexy's Midnight Runners** and the **Bureau** and appeared in the **Style Council**. Smith, meanwhile, joined the psychedelic revivalists **Mood Six**, and spent a while with the **Times**, before returning to the reformed Mood Six.

Album: *Face In The Crowd* (1979).

Mesner Brothers

Leo and Edward Mesner formed Philo Records in 1945 at Santa Monica Boulevard, Hollywood, California, USA, changing the label name to Aladdin the following year. The company had early sales with **Helen Humes**, **Wynonie Harris** and **Lester Young,** but enjoyed its biggest successes after signing Texan musicians **Charles Brown** and **Johnny Moore** ('Driftin' Blues'), Amos Milburn ('Chicken Shack Boogie') and **Lightnin' Hopkins** in 1945 and 1946. Aladdin continued to be one of the major west coast independents throughout the 40s and early 50s with recordings by **Floyd Dixon, Gatemouth Brown**, **Pee Wee Crayton**, Lloyd Glenn and **Peppermint Harris** (five more Texans), **Louis Jordan, Lowell Fulson**, **Big Jay McNeely**, **Lynn Hope**, and the **Five Keys**.These artists invariably benefitted from the instrumental and arrangemental expertise of Maxwell Davis. In the mid-50s, Aladdin's biggest sales came with the boy/girl duets of **Shirley And Lee** ('Let The Good Times Roll') and Gene And Eunice ('Ko Ko Mo'), but sales gradually decreased into the late 50s, despite the brief success of **Thurston Harris** in 1957, and the following year, the Mesners sold their label to Lew Chudd of Imperial Records.

Messiah

Ali Ghani and Mark Davies, from Hounslow,

Middlesex, England and Barnet, Hertfordshire, England respectively, met while students at the University Of East Anglia. They represent the talent behind the Messiah name, which moved from the independent **Kickin'** Records to WEA in 1993. The major doubtless saw Messiah as accessible rave which they could market. Their debut album was completed with the aid of Def American's Rick Rubin, who saw the group as the perfect embodiment of dance with which to convert an American audience. Old habits died hard however, and he hooked them up with Ian Astbury of the **Cult** to produce one of their debut album's tracks. He had picked the band up from their previous American base, **Moby**'s Instinct label. Their debut for WEA arrived with the aid of Precious Wilson's vocals, and included re-runs of their previous club favourites '20,000 Hardcore Members', 'Temple Of Dreams' (based on **This Mortal Coil**'s 'Song To The Siren'), 'I Feel Love' and 'There Is No Law'. The middle two of that quartet had given the band Top 20 crossover hits too. In addition they unveiled the impressive 'Thunderdome', with remixes from Spicelab, **Secret Knowledge** and Gods Underwater.
Albums: *Beyond Good And Evil* (Kickin' 1991), *21st Century Jesus* (WEA 1993).

Messiah Force

Formed in Jonquire, Canada, in 1984, the band consisted of Lynn Renaud (vocals), Bastien Deschênes (guitar), Jean Tremblay (guitar), Eric Parisé (bass) and Jean-Francois Boucher (drums). The band was essentially formed from the ashes of two local power metal bands, Exode and Frozen. Utilizing a sound that was reminiscent of early **Warlock**, the band released their debut, *The Last Day,* on the small, independent Haissem Records label in 1987. Though a strong power metal release, the album passed largely unnoticed resulting in the band's demise soon after its release.
Album: *The Last Day* (Haissem 1987).

Messina, Jim

(see **Loggins And Messina**)

Metal Church

Formed in Seattle, USA, in 1982, Metal Church initially comprised David Wayne (vocals), Kurt Vanderhoof (guitar), Craig Wells (guitar), Duke Erickson (bass) and Kirk Arrington (drums). Their first album was a phenomenal debut, brimming with energy and promise. The style was the then-evolving thrash metal sound, and Metal Church executed their own brand with precision. *The Dark* was a strong follow-up, but failed to top the debut, and Wayne left at this point to be replaced by Mike Howe for the recording of *Blessing In Disguise*, another commendable effort. Kurt Vanderhoof then retired from the band's ranks through his dislike of touring, and was replaced by John Marshall, previously guitar technician for **Metallica**. Metal Church have proved to be a consistently excellent band, but have failed to rise to the level of success suggested by their first album. Personnel changes and short tenures with their record companies have undoubtedly contributed to their under-achievement.
Albums: *Metal Church* (Ground Zero 1985), *The Dark* (Elektra 1987), *Blessing In Disguise* (Elektra 1989), *The Human Factor* (Epic 1991), *Hanging In The Balance* (Blackheart 1994).

Metalheads

UK Purveyors of 90s hardcore techno whose *Angel* EP invoked the rather over-employed 'intelligent hardcore' term. Whether or not it was correct for sections of the cognoscenti to herald it as a great leap forward for the genre remains to be seen. The main person behind the record was Goldie, an ex-Grafitti artist of some note, who has spent time in New York, Miami and Birmingham. Possibly his most famous illustration was his 'Change The World' mural at London's Queens Park Rangers football ground, Loftus Road. Before Metalheads he had recorded a solo white label EP under the name Ajaz Project, then 'Killer Muffin' on **Reinforced**, with whom he is now employed. His compatriots in the project are experienced DJs Fabio and Grooverider, both of whom have strong cult followings on their own terms. Further releases for Reinforced included the *Terminator* and *Enforcers* EPs, before in November 1994 he unveiled the much-heralded 'Inner City Life'. 22 minutes long in its full form, its urban narrative sought expression through three thematic 'movements'. It prefaced him signing an album deal with **London/ffrr**, for which he initially worked with **Simple Minds**' drummer Mel Gaynor.

Metallica

The most consistently innovative metal band of the late 80s and early 90s were formed during 1981 in California, USA, by Lars Ulrich (b. 26 December 1963, Copenhagen, Denmark; drums) and James Alan Hetfield (b. 3 August 1963, USA; guitar/vocals) after each separately advertised for fellow musicians in the classified section of American publication, *The Recycler.* They recorded their first demo, *No Life Til' Leather*, with Lloyd Grand (guitar), who was replaced in January 1982 by David Mustaine, whose relationship with Ulrich and Hetfield proved unsatisfactory. Jef Warner (guitar) and Ron McGovney (bass) each had a brief tenure with the group, and at the end of 1982 Clifford Lee Burton (b. 10 February 1962, USA; bass), formerly of Trauma, joined the band, playing his first live performance on 5 March 1983. Mustaine departed to form **Megadeth** and was replaced by Kirk Hammett (b. 18 November 1962; guitar). Hammett, who came to the attention of Ulrich and Hetfield while playing with rock band **Exodus**, played his first concert with Metallica on 16 April 1983. The Ulrich, Hetfield, Burton and Hammett combination endured until disaster struck the band in the small hours of 27 September 1987, when Metallica's tour bus overturned in Sweden, killing Cliff Burton. During those four years the group put thrash metal on the map with the aggression and exuberance of their debut, *Kill 'Em All*, the album sleeve of which bore the legend 'Bang that head that doesn't bang'. This served as a template for a whole new breed of metal, though the originators themselves were quick to dispense with their own rulebook. Touring with **N.W.O.B.H.M.** bands **Raven** and **Venom** followed, while **Music For Nations** signed them for European distribution. Although *Ride The Lightning* was not without distinction, notably on 'For Whom The Bell Tolls', it would be *Master Of Puppets* which offered further evidence of Metallica's appetite for the epic. Their first album for **Elektra** in the US (who had also re-released its forerunner), this was a taut, multi-faceted collection which both raged and lamented with equal conviction. After the death of Burton the band elected to continue, the remaining three members choosing to recruit Jason Newsted (b. 4 March 1963; bass) of **Flotsam And Jetsam**. Newsted played his first concert with the band on 8 November 1986. The original partnership of Ulrich and Hetfield, however, remained responsible for Metallica's lyrics and musical direction. The new line-up's first recording together would be *The $5.98 EP - Garage Days Revisited* - a collection of covers including material from **Budgie**, **Diamond Head**, **Killing Joke** and the **Misfits**, which also served as a neat summation of the group's influences to date. Sessions for *...And Justice For All* initially began with **Guns N'Roses** producer Mike Clink at the helm, before the group opted to return to Flemming Rasmussen, a realtionship they had begun with *Ride The Lightning*. A long and densely constructed effort, this 1988 opus included an appropriately singular spectuacular moment in 'One', also released as a single, while elsewhere the barrage of riffs somewhat obscured the usual Metallica artistry. Songs continued to deal with large themes - justice and retribution, insanity, war, religion and relationships, on 1991's *Metallica*. Compared to *Kill 'Em All* of nearly a decade previously, however, the group had grown from iconoclastic chaos to thoughtful harmony, hallmarked by sudden and unexpected changes of mood and tempo. The MTV-friendly 'Enter Sandman' broke the band on a stadium level. Constant touring in the wake of the album ensued, along with a regular itinerary of awards ceremonies for their last album and single at Grammy, *Rolling Stone* and MTV ceremonies. There could surely be no more deserving recipients, Metallica having dragged mainstream metal, not so much kicking and screaming as whining and complaining, into a bright new dawn when artistic redundancy seemed inevitable.

Albums: *Kill 'Em All* (Megaforce 1983), *Ride The Lightning* (Megaforce 1984), *Master Of Puppets* (Elektra 1986), *...And Justice For All* (Elektra 1988), *Metallica* (Elektra 1991), *Live Shit: Binge & Purge* (Elektra 1993, 3 CD).

Videos: *Cliff 'Em All* (1987), *One The Video* (1988), *Lick 'Em Up* (1988), *2 Of One* (1989), *A Year And A Half In The Life Of Metallica* (1992), *A Year In The Life Of Vols. 1 & 2* (1992), *Live Shit: Binge & Purge* (1993).

Further reading: *A Visual Documentary*, Mark Putterford. *In Their Own Words*, Mark Putteford. *Metallica Unbound*, K.J. Doughton. *Metallica's Lars Ulrich: An Up-Close Look At The Playing Style Of . . .*, Dino Fauci. *Metallica: The Frayed Ends Of Metal*, Chris Crocker.

Metcalf, Louis

b. 28 February 1905, Webster Groves, Missouri, USA, d. 27 October 1981. Metcalf was playing trumpet professionally by his early teenage years and spent some five years with Charlie Creath. The 20s were Metcalf's finest decade. Based in New York, he worked and sometimes recorded with blues singers and a galaxy of important jazz artists, including **Sidney Bechet**, **Duke Ellington**, **J.C. Higginbotham**, **James P. Johnson**, **Albert Nicholas**, **Luis Russell**, **Jelly Roll Morton** and **King Oliver**. In the 30s and 40s, Metcalf sometimes moved away from New York, frequently visiting Canada as a bandleader. Although his career profile was now much lower he still played with leading figures, including **Lester Young** and **Billie Holiday**. He played on through the 50s and 60s, often working at clubs in New York; but Metcalf's later years were overshadowed by his earlier successes. A gifted, blues-orientated trumpeter, with a precisely-articulated style, Metcalf's was an original talent whose recorded work offers only tantalizing glimpses of a major jazz artist.

Album: *Louis Metcalf At The Ali Baba* (1966). Compilations: *The Indispensable Duke Ellington Vols 1/2* (1927-29).

Meteors

The Meteors were the first UK group to combine punk's energy with raw 50s rockabilly and invent a new musical form - psychobilly. In the USA, the **Cramps** had discovered a similar formula, but theirs was less violent and more dramatic. Together, they influenced a whole movement and an accompanying youth culture during the 80s, which enabled the Meteors to record some 15 albums over 10 years. In the late 70s, P. Paul Fenech (singer/guitarist) and Nigel Lewis (double bass/vocals) were churning out rockabilly and rock 'n' roll standards in acts such as the Southern Boys and, as a duo, Rock Therapy. Around 1980, drummer Mark Robertson was recruited, coinciding with a name change to Raw Deal, and they appeared on Alligator Records' *Home Grown Rockabilly* compilation. After a name change to the Meteors, the band issued a debut EP, *Meteor Madness*, jammed with compulsive, raw rockabilly, with lyrics drawing inspiration from graveyards and vampiric legend, all performed in a crazed, headlong amphetamine rush to the end of the song. 'Radioactive Kid' followed suit, and *In Heaven* was issued on their own Lost Souls label. Around the same time, the Meteors recorded an EP featuring a cover of the **Electric Prunes**' 'Get Me To The World On Time' under the guise of the Clapham South Escalators. Robertson left soon afterwards and was replaced by Woody, but after releasing demos, Lewis also departed to form the Tall Boys. Fenech was left to soldier on, bringing in electric bassist Mick White and Russell Jones for August 1982's 'Mutant Rock'. Another personnel change (Steve 'Ginger' Meadham joining on drums) preceded the Meteors second album, *Wreckin' Crew*, early in 1983, featuring the previous single, a wild cover of **John Leyton**'s 'Johnny Remember Me'. That same year saw another departure, with White forming his own psychobilly act, the **Guana Batz**. His position was filled by Rick Ross for a national tour, captured on *Live*. Unfortunately, Ross left for the USA and in his place came Ian 'Spider' Cubitt, to record *Stampede*, 'I'm Just A Dog' and 'Fire, Fire'. *Monkey's Breath*, featuring new bassist Neville Hunt, surfaced in September 1985, alongside a cover of **Creedence Clearwater Revival**'s 'Bad Moon Rising'. After two more unofficial offerings (*Live II* and the *Live And Loud*), the Meteors covered **Jan And Dean**'s 'Surf City' and completed *Sewertime Blues*. *Don't Touch The Bang Bang Fruit* featured a version of the **Stranglers**' 'Go Buddy Go'. By this time, Spider's place had been filled by Toby 'Jug' Griffin and Austin H. Stones briefly deputized on bass. Lee Brown (ex-Pharaohs) took on a more permanent role on bass, in time for another punk cover in the **Ramones**' 'Somebody Put Something In My Drink'. Hot on its heels came *Only The Meteors Are Pure Psychobilly*, featuring new recordings of old 'classics'. Newer material was included on *Mutant Monkey And The Surfers From Zorch* later that year, although 'Rawhide' proved to be another popular cover. Even more powerful was *Undead, Unfriendly And Unstoppable*, which benefitted from new drummer Mark Howe. The release of 'Please Don't Touch' proved that, despite waves of imitators, the Meteors were still the most vibrant psychobilly band around. However, by the 90s the trail had finally run cold on the seemingly ever resilient Meteors.

Albums: *In Heaven* (Lost Soul 1981), *Wreckin' Crew* (ID 1983), *Live* (Wreckin' 1983), *Stampede* (Mad Pig 1984), *The Curse Of The Mutants* (Dojo 1984), *Monkey's Breath* (Mad Pig 1985), *Live II* (Dojo 1986), *Live And Loud* (Link 1986), *Sewertime Blues* (Anagram 1987), *Night Of The Werewolf* (Dojo 1987), *Don't Touch The Bang Bang Fruit* (Anagram 1987), *Only The Meteors Are Pure Psychobilly* (Anagram 1988), *Mutant Monkey And The Surfers From Zorch* (Anagram 1988), *Undead, Unfriendly And Unstoppable* (Anagram 1989). Compilation: *Teenagers From Outer Space* (Big Beat 1986).

Meters

This fundamental quartet, Art Neville (b. Arthur Lanon Neville; keyboards), Leo Mocentelli (guitar), George Porter (bass) and Joseph 'Zigaboo/Ziggy' Modeliste (drums) came together during informal sessions held in various New Orleans nightclubs. Initially known as Art Neville and the Neville Sounds, they were spotted by producers **Allen Toussaint** and Marshall Sehorn, who signed the unit to their Sansu label to work on sessions for the duo's other artists, including **Lee Dorsey** and **Betty Harris**. Redubbed the Meters, the group's first singles, 'Sophisticated Cissy' and 'Cissy Strut', reached the US R&B Top 10 in 1969. These tough instrumentals mixed the bare-boned approach of **Booker T. And The MGs** with the emergent funk of **Sly Stone**, a style consolidated on several further releases and the unit's three albums for the Josie label. This canvas was broadened on a move to **Warner Brothers/Reprise** in 1972, where a series of critically-acclaimed albums, including *Cabbage Alley* and *Rejuvenation*, reinforced their distinctive, sinewy rhythms. Such expertise also was heard on many sessions, including those for **Robert Palmer**, **Dr. John** and **Paul McCartney**, while in 1975, the group supported the **Rolling Stones** on their North American tour. Cyril Neville (vocals/percussion) was added to the line-up at this time, but the Meters found it difficult to make further commercial progress. In 1976, Art and Cyril joined Charles and **Aaron Neville** on a project entitled the Wild Tchoupitoulas. Led by an uncle, George Landry (Big Chief Jolly), this was the first time the brothers had played together. When the Meters split the following year, the quartet embarked on a new career, firstly as the Neville Family Band, then as the **Neville Brothers**.

Albums: *The Meters* (1969), *Look-Ka Py Py* (1970), *Struttin'* (1970), *Cabbage Alley* (1972), *Rejuvenation* (1974), *Fire On The Bayou* (1975), *Trick Bag* (1976), *New Directions* (1977), *Good Old Funky Music* (1979), *Uptown Rulers! Live On The Queen Mary* (1992, rec 1975). Compilations: *Cissy Strut* (1974), *Second Line Strut* (1980), *Here Come The Meter Men* (1986), *Original Funkmasters* (1992).

Metheny, Pat

b. 12 August 1954, Kansas City, Missouri, USA. Although classed as a jazz guitarist, Metheny has bridged the gap between jazz and rock music in the same way that **Miles Davis** did in the late 60s and early 70s. Additionally, he has played a major part in the growth of jazz with the younger generation of the 80s. His first musical instrument was a French horn, and surprisingly he did not begin with the guitar until he was a teenager. His outstanding virtuosity soon had him teaching the instrument at the University Of Miami and the **Berklee College Of Music** in Boston. He joined **Gary Burton** in 1974, and throughout his three-album stay, he contributed some fluid **Wes Montgomery**-influenced guitar patterns. Manfred Eicher of **ECM Records** saw the potential and initiated a partnership which lasted for 10 superlative albums. He became, along with **Keith Jarrett**, ECM's biggest selling artist, and his albums regularly topped the jazz record charts. Metheny is one of the few artists to make regular appearances in the pop album charts; such is the accessibility of his music. Both *Bright Size Life*, featuring the late **Jaco Pastorious** and *Watercolours*, though excellent albums, still showed a man who was feeling his way. His own individualistic style matured with *Pat Metheny Group* in 1978.

Together with his musical partner (and arguably, his right arm), the brilliant keyboardist **Lyle Mays**, he initiated a rock group format that produced album after album of melodious jazz/rock. Following a major tour with **Joni Mitchell** and Pastorious (*Shadows And Light*), Metheny released *New Chautauqua* and demonstrated an amazing dexterity on 12-string guitar and, against the fashion of the times, made the US Top 50. He returned to the electric band format for *American Garage,* which contained his country-influenced '(Cross The) Heartland'. The double set *80/81* featured **Michael Brecker**, **Jack DeJohnette**, **Charlie Haden** and **Dewey Redman**, and was more of a typical jazz album, featuring in particular the moderately *avant garde* 'Two Folk Songs' The record still climbed the popular charts. During this time, Metheny constantly won jazz and guitarist polls. Mays' keyboards featured prominently in the group structure, and he received co-authorship credit for the suite *As Falls Wichita, So Falls Wichita Falls.* Metheny had by now become fascinated by the musical possibilities of the guitar synthesizer or synclavier. He used this to startling effect on *Offramp*, notably on the wonderfully contagious and arresting 'Are You Going With Me?'. The double set *Travels* showed a band at the peak of its powers, playing some familiar titles with a new freshness. The short piece 'Travels', stands as one of his finest compositions, the low-level recording offers such subtle emotion that it becomes joyously funereal. *Rejoicing* was a modern jazz album demonstrating his sensitive interpretations of music by **Horace Silver** and **Ornette Coleman.** *First Circle* maintained the standard and showed a greater leaning towards Latin-based music, still with Metheny's brilliant ear for melody; additionally the track 'If I Could' displayed the same sparse subtlety of *Travels.* In 1985, he composed the film score for *The Falcon And The Snowman* which led to him recording 'This Is Not America' with **David Bowie**. The resulting Top 40 US hit (number 12 in the UK), brought Metheny many new young admirers. The concert halls found audiences bedecked in striped rugby shirts, in the style of their new hero.

Ironically, at the same time, following a break with ECM, Metheny turned his back on possible rock stardom and produced his most perplexing work, *Song X*, with free-jazz exponent Ornette Coleman. Reactions were mixed in reviewing this difficult album - ultimately the general consensus was that it was brilliantly unlistenable. He returned to more familiar ground with *Still Life (Talking)* and *Letter From Home*, although both showed a greater move towards Latin melody and rhythm. In 1990, *Reunion* was released, a superb meeting with his former boss Gary Burton and a few months later together with **Dave Holland** and **Roy Haynes** he made *Question And Answer*. Additionally he was heavily featured, along with **Herbie Hancock**, on the excellent Jack DeJohnette album, *Parallel Realities*. He continued into the 90s with *Secret Story*, an album of breathtaking beauty. Although the album may have made jazz purists cringe it was a realisation of all Metheny's musical influences. His second live album *The Road To You* did not have the emotion of *Travels* it was something to keep the fans quiet before he unleashed an exciting recording with John Scofield, both guitarists having been sharing the honours at the top of jazz polls for the past few years. *Zero Tolerence For Silence* can only be described as astonishing - for many this wall of sound guitar was a self-indulgent mess. After repeated play the music does not get any easier, but at least we can understand his motives more and appreciate what a bold move this thrash metal outing was. Metheny found himself reviewed in the Heavy Metal press for the first (and last) time. *We Live Here* was a return to familiar ground, and a familiar position at the top of the jazz charts. He has an extraordinary sense of melody and his work neither rambles nor becomes self-indulgent; much credit must also be given to the like-minded Lyle Mays, whose quiet presence at the side of the stage is the backbone for much of Metheny's music.

Albums: *Bright Size Life* (ECM 1976), *Watercolours* (ECM 1977), *Pat Metheny Group* (ECM 1978), *New Chautauqua* (ECM 1979), *American Garage* (ECM 1979), *80/81* (ECM 1980), *As Falls Wichita, So Falls Wichita Falls* (ECM 1981), *Offramp* (ECM 1982), *Travels* (ECM 1983), *Rejoicing* (ECM 1983), *First Circle* (ECM 1984), *The Falcon And The Snowman* (1985, film soundtrack), *Song X* (Geffen 1986), *Still Life (Talking)* (Geffen 1987), *Letter From Home* (Geffen 1989), with Gary Burton *Reunion* (Geffen 1990), *Question And Answer* (Geffen 1990), with Jack DeJohnette *Parallel Realities* (Geffen 1990), *Secret Story* (Geffen 1992), *The Road To You - Recorded Live In Europe* (Geffen 1993), with John Scofield *I Can See Your House From Here* (Blue Note 1994), *Zero Tolerance For Silence* (Geffen 1994), *We Live Here* (Geffen 1995).

Compilations: *Works* (ECM 1983), *Works 2* (ECM 1988).
Video: *More Travels* (1993).

Method Of Destruction

Following his work in legendary New York hardcore act **Stormtroopers Of Death**, vocalist Billy Milano formed M.O.D. (as they are commonly referred to) with Tim McMurtrie (guitar), Ken Ballone (bass) and Keith Davis (drums). The quality of the groove-based hardcore on *USA For MOD* was overshadowed by controversy over seemingly racist and near-fascist lyrics, although Milano later explained in an open letter to the press that his aim was to illustrate prejudice by writing from the bigot's perspective in the first person, thus stirring up truly negative reactions to these attitudes in the process; Milano subsequently noted that many of the most contentious lyrics were written by **Anthrax's** Scott Ian and had been part of the SOD set. The subsequent tour, while successful, proved unhealthy for MOD, with McMurtrie breaking his leg and continuing in a wheelchair, while Ballone broke his arm, and the line-up split after the tour. Milano was then joined by guitarist Louie Svitek, bassist John Monte (who had toured in place of the injured Ballone) and drummer Tim Mallare for the lyrically lighter *Surfin' MOD*, where Milano's sense of humour shone through, and the new band moved towards a metal/hardcore crossover style. *Gross Misconduct* maintained the quality, although Milano peppered the lyric sheet with explanations as he tackled serious subject matter once more. However, personal problems enforced Milano's departure from the music scene, with Svitek and Monte going on to form **Mindfunk**. MOD were revived as a trio in 1992 after the SOD reunion, with Milano (adopting the bassist role as he had in his days with the Psychos), drummer Dave Chavarri and the returning McMurtrie on guitar for *Rhythm Of Fear*, sounding as if the band had never been away. Despite a rather fluid line-up thereafter, *Devolution* showed that Milano - now rhythm guitarist with Rob Moscheti on bass - was still producing strong and relevant hardcore to match the likes of **Biohazard** and **Sick Of It All.**

Albums: *USA For MOD* (Megaforce 1987), *Surfin' MOD* (Megaforce 1988, mini-album), *Gross Misconduct* (Megaforce 1989), *Rhythm Of Fear* (Megaforce 1992), *Devolution* (Music For Nations 1994).

Metro, Peter

b. Donovan Harris, c.1960, Western Kingston, Jamaica, West Indies. After leaving school he worked as a welder following in the footsteps of many legendary reggae performers. In his leisure time he would go to the local dance and when given the opportunity to chat on the sound, the enthusiastic audience response inspired him to consider a career as a DJ seriously. He initially decided to call himself Peter Ranking but discovered another DJ went by that name and had enjoyed a minor hit with 'Sukiyaki'. Harris was a resident DJ on the sound Metromedia and adopted the pseudonym Peter Metro. He recorded his debut outing with, 'Jamaica Salute' and was soon found voicing a number of recordings for a variety of producers. An unusual characteristic in his recordings was to converse in Spanish which won him many fans in South America. Notably on 'Water Jelly' where in his inimitable singjay style the opening verse is Hispanic followed by an English chorus and a return to Spanish for the final verse. The intro to 'Fisherman Connection' is also in Spanish before switching to English when he advises, 'Don't catch the fish if you no eat it'. Another connection tune, 'Metric Connection' bemoans the advent of the metric system. As demonstrated in the lyrics, 'When you drive car - you drive it in metre, When you drink beer - you drink it in a litre, When you buy yam - you buy in kilogram, When you look pon woman - you look pon a good one'. Working with **Yellowman** and Fathead his popularity increased following the release of 'Water Pumpee'. He also recorded a version of **Michael Jackson**'s, 'The Girl Is Mine' in combination with Yellowman which became a massive seller in both the pre and released chart. Metro's success inspired his brother Squiddly Ranking to become resident DJ on the Gemini Sound System, where he frequently clashed with Yellowman. Being an innovative performer he recorded 'Yardie And Cockney' in combination with a white English DJ, Dominic, and is acknowledged as the first multi lingual toaster. The duo gave a conspicuously respectable performance at the 10th Reggae Sunsplash festival but the novelty was short lived.

Albums: with Yellowman, Fathead *Yellowman, Fathead And The One Peter Metro* (Abissa 1982), with Little John, Captain Sinbad *Sinbad And The Metric System* (CSA 1983), with various artists *Dedicated To You* (CSA 1984), *Live With Yellowman And Sassafrass* (White Label 1984), *No Problem* (VP 1989).
Video: *Reggae Sunsplash Dancehall X '87* (1987).

Metroplex

Juan Atkins' Detroit record label, which housed several of his greatest moments as Model 500 ('No UFO's', 'The Chase', 'Off To Battle', 'Interference'). In the 90s it has gone on to be operated under the aegis of Mike Banks' Submerge organisation.

Metsers, Paul

b. 27 November 1945, Noordwijk, Holland. In 1952, Metsers emigrated to New Zealand and was influenced by the American folk music that was available on record during the 60s. He bought his first guitar in 1963, and soon started writing songs. Paul arrived in the UK in 1980, and spent almost two years touring

round in a Volkswagen camper playing 'floor spots' in folk clubs to get himself noticed. He was rewarded with club and festival bookings the length and breadth of the country. The environment and 'green issues' have always figured largely in his songwriting, even before it became fashionable, and his first anti-pollution song, 'Now Is The Time', was written in 1969. By the time that *Caution To The Wind* was available, Metsers, was already established as an artist and performer of note. *In The Hurricane's Eye* contained the excellent 'Peace Must Come', and 'River Song'. The *Paul Metsers Songbook*, published in 1986, contained many of the songs from Paul's first four albums, but only one that would appear on *Fifth Quarter*. He was able to combine a busy touring schedule with campaigning for environmental pressure groups, but in November 1989, he decided to devote more time to his family. Now living in Cumbria, and working as a joiner as well as keeping bees, Metsers still performs occasionally.
Albums: *Caution To The Wind* (Highway 1981), *Momentum* (Highway 1982), *In The Hurricane's Eye* (Sagem 1984), *Pacific Pilgrim* (Sagem 1986), *Fifth Quarter* (Sagem 1987).

Mexican Hayride

Master showman Mike Todd was renowned for his spectacular productions, and this show, one of the most lavish and successful of the World War II period, was certainly no exception. It opened at the Winter Garden Theatre in New York on 28 January 1944, and was still around well over a year later. The book, by Herbert and **Dorothy Fields**, follows Joe Bascom (Bobby Clark), an ex-numbers racketeer from the USA who is on the run in Mexico from the police - and various ladies - through a series of hilarious adventures and disguises. **Cole Porter**'s Latin-styled score was full of good things such as 'I Love You', which was sung in the show by Wilbur Evans, and later became a US number 1 record for **Bing Crosby**. The other lively and attractive numbers included 'Sing To Me, Guitar', 'Abracadabra', 'Carlotta', 'There Must Be Someone For Me', 'Girls', and 'Count Your Blessings'. Bobby Clark was the man they all came to see, and he was at the top of his form. The veteran comedian had spent around 17 years in vaudeville in partnership with Paul McCullough before he broke through on Broadway in 1922. June Havoc, sister of the legendary Gypsy Rose Lee, was also in the cast of *Mexican Hayride*, along with George Givot, Luba Malina, Corinna Mura, Edith Meiser, Bill Callahan, Paul Haakon, and Candy Jones. The 1948 film version starred Abbott And Costello, but Porter's songs were dropped so the film was not classed as a musical.

Meyer, George W.

b. 1 January 1884, Boston, Massachusetts, USA, d. 28 August 1959, New York, USA. A prolific composer of popular songs from 1909 to the late 40s, Meyer was a self-taught pianist who worked in department stores in Boston and New York before getting a job as a song plugger with a firm of music publishers. He began to have his songs published in 1909, and these included 'I'm Awfully Glad I Met You' and 'You Taught Me How To Love You (Now Teach Me To Forget)' (with Jack Drislane and Alfred Bryan). Meyer composed several other songs with Bryan, including 'I've Got Your Number', 'Bring Back My Golden Dreams', 'Beautiful Anna Bell Lee' and 'Her Beaus Are Only Rainbows'. Several of his numbers were also used in early talkies such as *Broadway Babes* and *Footlights And Fools*, starring Colleen Moore. He also contributed songs to the 1916 Broadway musical *Robinson Crusoe Jnr.* ('Where Did Robinson Crusoe Go With Friday On Saturday Night?') and the 1924 all-black revue *Dixie To Broadway* (1924) ('Mandy, Make Up Your Mind' and 'I'm A Little Blackbird Looking For A Bluebird'). His 'In The Land Of Beginning Again' (lyric by Grant Clarke), written in 1919, was used in the popular **Bing Crosby** movie *The Bells Of St Mary's* (1945). Meyer's other songs included 'For Me And My Gal' (with **Edgar Leslie** and Ray Goetz), 'Everything Is Peaches Down In Georgia' (with Grant Clarke and **Milton Ager**), 'My Song Of The Nile', 'Tuck Me To Sleep In My Old 'Tucky Home', 'I Believe In Miracles', 'There Are Such Things', 'If He Can Fight Like He Can Love, Good Night Germany', 'I'm Sure Of Everything But You', 'I'm Growing Fonder Of You', 'If I Only Had A Match' and 'In A Little Book Shop'. In 1952 his 'Dixie Dreams', written with Arthur Johnston, Grant Clarke and Roy Turk, was included in *Somebody Loves Me*, the bio-pic of vaudeville headliners Blossom Seeley and Benny Fields, which starred **Betty Hutton**. Meyer's other collaborators included **Sam M. Lewis** and **Joe Young**. Together with two more contemporaries, **Edgar Leslie** and **Billy Rose**, Meyer formed the Songwriters' Protective Association in 1931.

Meyer, Joseph

b. 12 March 1894, Modesto, California, USA, d. 22 June 1987, New York, USA. A composer of popular songs, mainly for films and the stage, from the early 20s through the 40s, Meyer studied the violin in Paris and worked as a cafe violinist when he returned to the USA in 1908. After military service in World War I, he spent some time in the shipping business before taking up songwriting. In 1922, with **Harry Ruby**, he wrote 'My Honey's Lovin' Arms', which became a hit for **Benny Goodman**, **Isham Jones** and the California Ramblers, and was successfully revived on **Barbra Streisand**'s debut album in 1963. During the 20s and 30s, Meyer composed the songs for several stage shows, including *Battling Buttler* ('You're So Sweet' and 'As We Leave The Years Behind') and *Big Boy* (starring **Al Jolson** singing 'California, Here I Come'). Another song from *Big Boy*, 'If You Knew Susie', was later associated with **Eddie Cantor**. Meyer also contributed to *Gay Paree* ('Bamboo Babies'), *Andre Charlote's Revue Of 1925* ('A Cup Of Coffee, A Sandwich, And You'), *Sweetheart Time* ('Who Loves You As I Do?'), *Just Fancy* ('You Came Along'), *Here's Howe* ('Crazy Rhythm' and 'Imagination'), *Lady Fingers* ('There's Something In That', 'An Open Book' and 'I Love You More Then Yesterday'), *Wake Up And Dream, Jonica, Shoot The Works* ('Chirp, Chirp'), the ***Ziegfeld Follies*** *Of 1934* and *New Faces Of 1936* ('It's High Time I Got The Low-Down On You'). His film songs included 'I Love You, I Hate You' (*Dancing Sweeties*), 'Can It Be Possible?' (*The Life Of The Party*), 'Oh, I Didn't Know', 'It's An Old Southern Custom', 'It's Time To Say Goodnight', 'I Got Shoes, You Got Shoesies' and 'According To The Moonlight' (**George White**'s 1935 *Scandals*). His other popular numbers included 'Clap Hands, Here Comes Charley' (the signature tune of pianist, **Charlie Kunz**), 'Sweet So And So', 'Just A Little Closer', 'How Long Will It Last?' (used in the 1931 Joan Crawford-Clark Gable drama *Possessed*), 'Isn't It Heavenly?', 'I Wish I Were Twins', 'And Then They Called It Love', 'Hurry Home', 'Love Lies', 'Let's Give Love A Chance', 'Passe', 'But I Did', 'Fancy Our Meeting', 'I've Got A Heart Filled With Love', 'There's No Fool Like An Old Fool', 'Idle Gossip' and 'Watching The Clock'. His collaborators included Billy Moll, **Billy Rose**, **Al Dubin**, **Jack Yellen**, Cliff Friend, **Buddy De Sylva**, **Herb Magidson**, **Al Jolson**, Phil Charig, **Irving Caesar**, Carl Sigman, **Frank Loesser**, **Eddie De Lange**, and Douglas Furber. Meyer died after a long illness at the age of 93.

Meyers, Augie

b. 1941, San Antonio, Texas, USA. Meyers is best known as the organist in the **Sir Douglas Quintet** on their 60s hits, including 'She's About A Mover' and 'Mendocino'. He has recorded on his own, and more importantly, perhaps, has influenced the keyboard players in groups such as **Elvis Costello**'s **Attractions** and Joe 'King' Carrasco's Crowns. Meyers, who also plays accordion, first appeared on record in 1958, with a group called Danny Ezba And The Goldens. In 1964, producer **Huey P. Meaux** was assembling a Texan rock group to combat the British Invasion and teamed Meyers with San Antonio singer/songwriter/guitarist **Doug Sahm**. The Sir Douglas Quintet disbanded in 1967, when Sahm moved to San Francisco and Meyers formed Lord August and the Visions Of Lite. He then joined Sahm in San Francisco and the Quintet was reborn, only to break up again in 1971. Meyers began releasing a string of solo albums that year. In 1990, he teamed up with Sahm and fellow Texans **Flaco Jimenez** and **Freddy Fender** for an album called *Texas Tornados.*

Albums: *Augie's Western Head Music Co.* (1971), *You Ain't Rollin' Your Roll Rite* (1973), *Live At The Longneck* (1975), *Finally In Lights* (1977), *Still Growing* (1982), *August In New York* (1984), *Augie's Back* (1986), *My Main Squeeze* (1987), with Doug Sahm, Flaco Jimenez, Freddy Fender *Texas Tornados* (1990).

Mezzoforte

Until the arrival of the **Sugarcubes**, jazz-fusion band Mezzoforte were Iceland's best-known musical export. The group was formed in 1977 at a Rekjavik high school by Fridrik Karlsson (guitar), Eythor Gunnarsson (keyboards), Johann Asmundsson (bass), Gunnlaugur Briem (drums) and Kristin Svararsson (saxophone). They signed a recording contract with local label Steinar and the second album contained the exuberant 'Garden Party' which was a Top 20 hit in the UK in 1983. The tune was covered in the USA by **Herb Alpert** who performed it at half-speed, reportedly because he had learned the piece from a 45 rpm single accidentally played at 33. The follow-up 'Rockall' was only a minor hit but it was adopted as a signature tune by radio chart shows in Holland and Britain. For a brief period, the group was based in London and in the mid-80s Mezzoforte played the European jazz festival circuit with vocalists Chris Cameron and Noel McCalla, formerly with Moon and **Mike Rutherford**'s group. In 1990, Karlsson formed a jazz/funk band Point Blank featuring singer Ellen Kristjansdottor and members of Mezzoforte.

Albums: *Mezzoforte* (1981), *I Hakanum* (1982), *Thvilkt Og Annadeins* (1983), *Catching Up With Mezzoforte* (1983), *Surprise Surprise* (1983), *Observations* (1984), *Rising* (1984), *No Limit* (1987), *Playing For Time* (1989).

Mezzrow, Mezz

b. Milton Mesirow, 9 November 1899, Chicago, Illinois, USA, d. 5 August 1972. After playing club dates in and around his home town during the 20s, clarinettist Mezzrow moved to New York where he became a popular figure, partly owing to his other career as a supplier of marijuana. In the 30s he recorded with **Sidney Bechet** and **Tommy Ladnier** on the famous sessions organized by French critic Hugues Panassie, and in the 40s formed his own King Jazz record label to record Bechet and other important jazz artists. In the 50s, he moved to France, touring from a Paris base with visiting musicians (who included **Lionel Hampton**, **Lee Collins** and **Zutty Singleton**), recording and enjoying a level of adulation he had never achieved in his own country. A vehement anti-segregationist, Mezzrow wholly identified with black music and musicians, even to the extent of occasionally 'passing' for black in order to play with his idols. Much written about, critically by **Eddie Condon** and hyperbolically by himself, Mezzrow's image suffered and he was often dismissed by jazz commentators. In fact, despite the often outrageous claims he made in his racily extravagant autobiography, Mezzrow did much to foster jazz. In his early years in Chicago he encouraged many young musicians, even if later he claimed to have taught them how to play. He was tireless in setting up record dates and he boldly formed multi-racial bands during a period when such groups were rarely seen or heard. Mezzrow's clarinet style was earthy and at times elementary, but among the many records he made are flashes of a genuine feeling for the blues. His autobiography is witty, anecdotal and a classic of its kind.

Selected albums: with Lionel Hampton *The Hamp In Paris* (1953), with Lee Collins *Clarinet Marmalade* (1955). Selected compilations: with Sidney Bechet *The Panassie Sessions* (1938-39), with Bechet *Out Of The Galleon* (1945), with Bechet *Really The Blues* (1945), with Bechet *King Of Jazz Vols 1-5* (Storyville 1986), *The Chronological Mezz Mezzrow 1928-1936* (Original Jazz Classics).

Further reading: *Really The Blues*, Mezz Mezzrow.

MFSB

'Mother, Father, Sister, Brother' or MFSB (and there was a less flattering alternative), was the houseband employed by producers **Gamble And Huff**. Jesse James, Bobby Martin, Norman Harris, Ronnie Baker, Earl Young, Roland Chambers and Karl Chambers came to prominence as the uncredited performers on 'The Horse', a hit for **Cliff Nobles And Co.** in 1968. As the James Boys, the septet replicated with a cash-in release, 'The Mule', and the unit also recorded under other names, including the Music Makers and Family. It was as the instrumental muscle behind the **Philadelphia International** stable and artists such as the **O'Jays** and **Harold Melvin And The Blue Notes** that the group garnered its reputation. 'TSOP (The Sound Of Philadelphia)', the theme from television's *Soul Train* show, was a million-selling single in 1974, but later releases failed to match its exuberance and purpose. Undeniably rhythmic and undoubtedly competent, MFSB nonetheless lacked the focal point that the **Three Degrees**' voices provided on those early successes.

Albums: *MFSB* (1973), *Love Is The Message* (1974), *Universal Love* (1975), *Philadelphia Freedom!* (1975), *Summertime* (1976), *The End Of Phase 1* (1977), *The Gamble-Huff Orchestra* (1979), *Mysteries Of The World* (1981).

MGM Records

Founded in Hollywood, California in 1946, the label was initially viewed as an outlet for soundtracks derived from the parent Metro-Goldwyn-Mayer film company. Its roster was later expanded to include black ballad singers **Billy Eckstine** and **Ivory Joe Hunter**, as well as country star **Hank Williams**. The label was noticeably reticent about embracing rock 'n' roll, but in 1958, scored a major success with **Conway Twitty**'s 'It's Only Make Believe'. **Marvin Rainwater** and **Jimmy Jones** were briefly in the spotlight, but MGM enjoyed consistent chart placings with releases by **Connie Francis**. Between 1958 and 1963, this highly-popular singer scored 11 million-selling singles, including 'Lipstick On Your Collar' and 'Mama'. MGM secured brief success with **Sam The Sham And The Pharaohs**, whose 'Wooly Bully' became a staple part of mid-60s' groups' repertoires, and the label also enjoyed a fruitful relationship with English producer **Mickie Most** during the 'British Invasion', when proteges **Herman's Hermits** and the **Animals** secured several hit singles. The latter group's lead singer, **Eric Burdon**, remained with the label during his transformation from pop singer to counter-culture proselytizer, while a **Verve** subsidiary was responsible for 'progressive' signings, such as the **Velvet Underground** and **Mothers Of Invention**. A further diminution, Verve/Folkways, drew its initial releases from the **Folkways** roster, including such respected acts as **Dave Van Ronk** and the **New Lost City Ramblers**. Later renamed Verve/Forecast, this particular endeavour launched the **Blues Project**, **Tim Hardin**, **Richie Havens** and **Laura Nyro**. MGM itself attempted to gain a foothold in the underground movement with the notorious 'Boss Town' hype when, in 1968, they signed several undistinguished groups from the Boston area, including the **Ultimate Spinach**, the **Beacon Street Union** and **Orpheus**, in an attempt to create a 'second San Francisco'. The result was a commercial and financial disaster, and, having lost $4 million on the project, MGM invited entrepreneur **Mike Curb** to take control of the record company. Most of the staff were fired, 'drug-oriented' acts were dropped, but such draconian measures failed to reverse now-ailing fortunes. MGM later ceased recording new acts and while its back catalogue was absorbed by **Polydor**, the rights to its extensive film soundtrack library were later secured by **EMI**.

Miami Showband

Formed in Eire during 1961, the Miami comprised Jimmy Harte (vocals), Murty Quinn (trombone), Clem Quinn (lead guitar), Martin Phelan (saxophone), Tommy O' Rourke (trumpet), Denis Murray (bass guitar) and Tony Bogan (drums). After a year on the road, Harte emigrated to America and was replaced by **Dickie Rock**. It was at that point that the Miami scaled the Irish pop charts, with a string of number 1 hits courtesy of Dickie Rock's velvet tenor. Songs such as 'There's Always Me', 'From The Candy Store On The Corner' and 'Every Step Of The Way' were Rock classics in Eire. In addition to Rock's vocal contributions, however, other members of the Miami were featured vocalists. Clem Quinn followed the **Royal Showband**'s 'hucklebuck' craze by issuing 'Buck's Polka', which reached Eire's Top 10. Murty Quinn achieved a similar chart placing with 'One Kiss For Old Time's Sake' early the following year. A disagreement with Rock over money prompted Phelan, O'Rourke and the Quinns to form the offshoot **Sands** in 1967. A reformed Miami stayed with Rock until 1972, when he elected to continue as a soloist. Thereafter, vocalist Fran O'Toole assumed centre stage, and the band continued to enjoy occasional hits during the 70s, such as 'Clap Hands Stamp Your Feet'. In the early hours of 31 July 1975, the Miami were returning from a gig in Banbridge, when they were flagged down by several members of the Ulster Volunteer Force. A bomb was then planted in their van which unexpectedly exploded. The hostage musicians attempted to flee and were callously shot in the back by their captives. Fran O'Toole, Des Lee (Desmond McAlea) and Tony Geraghty were killed, while Stephen Travers was seriously injured. The appalling murders did irreparable damage to the showband scene in the north of Ireland, tolling the death knell for an era of musical innocence and non-sectarianism.

Miaow

(see **Carroll, Cath**)

Michael, George

b. Georgios (Yorgos) Kyriacos Panayiotou, 25 June 1963, Finchley, London, England. Michael first served his pop apprenticeship in the million-selling duo **Wham!**, the most commercially successful, teen-orientated group of the 80s. His solo career was foreshadowed in 1984's 'Careless Whisper', a song about a promiscuous two-timer with the oddly attractive line: 'Guilty feet have got no rhythm'. By the time Wham! split in 1986, Michael was left with the unenviable task of reinventing himself as a solo artist. The balladeering 'Careless Whisper' had indicated a possible direction, but the initial problem was one of image. As a pin-up pop idol, Michael had allowed himself to become a paste-board figure, best remembered for glorifying a hedonistic lifestyle and shoving shuttlecocks down his shorts in concert. The rapid transition from dole queue reject to Club Tropicana playboy had left a nasty taste in the mouths of many music critics. Breaking the Wham! icon was the great challenge of Michael's solo career, and his finest and most decisive move was to take a sabbatical before recording an album, to allow time to put his old image to rest. In the meantime, he cut the chart-topping 'A Different Corner', a song stylistically similar to 'Careless Whisper' and clearly designed to show off his talent as a serious singer-songwriter. Enlivening his alternate image as a blue-eyed soul singer, he teamed up with **Aretha Franklin** for the uplifting 'I Knew You Were Waiting', a transatlantic chart topper. Michael's re-emergence came in 1988, resplendent in leather and shades and his customary designer stubble. A pilot single, 'I Want Your Sex' was banned by daytime radio stations and broke his string of number 1s in the UK. *Faith* followed, and was not only well-received but sold in excess of 10 million copies. The album spawned a plethora of hit singles in the USA, including the title track, 'Father Figure', 'One More Try' and 'Monkey'. Equally adept at soul workouts and ballads, and regarded by some as one of the best new pop songwriters of his era, Michael seemed set for a long career. In 1990, he released his second album, *Listen Without Prejudice, Vol.1*, a varied work which predictably sold millions. The first single from the album, 'Praying For Time' reached number 1 in the USA. In the UK, however, the comeback single was merely a Top 10 hit, suggesting that his status as a singles exponent in his homeland had markedly declined. Still dissatisfied with his media image, Michael announced that he would cease conducting interviews in future and concentrate on pursuing his career as a serious songwriter and musician. In 1992 the *Sunday Times* announced his arrival as one of the richest men in the UK. However, a court clash with his record label Sony dominated his activities in 1993 and 1994 (and was estimated to have cost him $7 million), with Michael arguing that his contract rendered him a 'pop slave' and demanding to be released from it. Mr Justice Jonathan Parker ruled in Sony's favour and Michael stated he would appeal, and also insisted that he would never again record for the label. In July 1995 it looked likely that Michael had managed to free himself from Sony - but only at the cost of $40 million. The buy-out was financed by **David Geffen**'s new media empire, Dreamworks, and **Virgin**, who were also reputed to have paid him an advance of £30 million for two albums.

Albums: *Faith* (Epic 1987), *Listen Without Prejudice, Vol. 1* (Epic 1990).

Videos: *Faith* (1988), *George Michael* (1990).

Further reading: *Wham! (Confidential) The Death Of A Supergroup*, Johnny Rogan. *Bare*, George Michael with Tony Parsons. *George Michael: The Making Of A Super Star*, Bruce Dessau.

Michaels, Lee

b. 24 November 1945, Los Angeles, California, USA. This multi-instrumentalist, aka Mike Olsen, began his career with the Sentinels, a San Luis Obispo-based surf group which included **Merrell Fankhauser** and drummer John Barbata (later to join **Jefferson Airplane/Starship**). Michaels later joined Barbata in the Strangers, a group led by Joel Scott Hill, before moving to San Francisco in 1965. He enjoyed a spell in the **Family Tree**, a **Beatles**-influenced attraction, before embarking on a solo career in 1968. A popular fixture of the city's ballrooms, his dexterity was confirmed with *Recital*, on which he played all the instruments, as well as serving as producer and arranger. *Lee Michaels*, culled from a lengthy studio jam with drummer Frosty, reaped due commercial rewards, but the artist was unable to maintain a consistency. *5th* contained the US Top 10 hit, 'Do You Know What I Mean', but subsequent releases lacked a coherent purpose. Despite undoubted studio techniques and his gifted guitar and keyboard skills, Michaels later withdrew from active performing.

Albums: *Carnival Of Life* (1968), *Recital* (1969), *Lee Michaels* (1969), *Barrel* (1970), *5th* (1970), *Live* (1972), *Space And First Takes* (1972), *Lee Michaels* (1973), *Nice Day For Something* (1973), *Tailface* (1974), *Lee Michaels* (1975), *Saturn Rings* (mid-70s), *Absolutely Lee* (mid-70s).

Michel'le

b. Michele'le (pronounced Me-Shell-Lay) Toussaint, c.1972, Los Angeles, California, USA. One time girlfriend and protoge of **Dr Dre**, Michel'le's career exploded and then disappeared with equal velocity, after she retired to have a baby. She first came to prominence as a backing vocalist for Dre's **World Class Wreckin' Cru**, before guesting on the **D.O.C.**'s remarkable debut album. Her own 1990 set brought immediate platinum status, preceded as it was by the US Top 10 single, 'No More Lies'. She also appeared on the pro-awareness single 'We're All In The Same Gang' alonside other members of the **NWA** posse with **Hammer**, **Tone Loc**, **Digital Underground** and **Young MC**.

Album: *Michel'le* (Ruthless 1990).

Michelot, Pierre

b. 3 March 1928, Saint Denis, France. Michelot studied classical bass from the age of 16, but it was the playing of **Jimmy Blanton** and **Oscar Pettiford** which attracted him to jazz. He played with **Rex Stewart** in 1948, toured Europe with **Kenny Clarke** and recorded with **Coleman Hawkins**. Although such experience must have sharpened his playing, he only got the chance because he was already an accurate, melodic player who could provide a band with a springy rhythm. Throughout the 50s he worked in Paris clubs with **Django Reinhardt**, tenor players **Lester Young**, **Don Byas**, **Dexter Gordon**, **Zoot Sims** and **Stan Getz**. Among his recordings were sessions with **Miles Davis** in 1956/7, and pianist **Bud Powell** in the early 60s. Meanwhile he was writing arrangements for trumpeter **Chet Baker**, Kenny Clarke and for session work. For 15 years, from 1959, he worked with Jacques Loussier's Play Bach Trio and continued to work in the studios. He took part in the filming of Tavernier's film *Round Midnight* in 1986.

Albums: with Django Reinhardt *Blues For Ike* (1953), with Bud Powell *A Portrait Of Thelonius* (1961), with Dexter Gordon *Our Man In Paris* (1963), *Round About A Bass* (1963).

Mickey And Sylvia

McHouston 'Mickey' Baker (b. 15 October 1925, Louisville, Kentucky, USA) and Sylvia Vanderpool (b. 6 March 1936, New York City, New York, USA). This popular duo began recording together in 1956 and enjoyed an US R&B chart-topper that year with 'Love Is Strange', which peaked at number 11 in the US pop chart the following year. This enduring call and response song is rightly regarded as a classic of its genre, and later became a minor UK hit when recorded by the **Everly Brothers**. Mickey and Sylvia scored further success with 'There Oughta Be A Law' (1957) and, after a brief hiatus as a duo, 'Baby You're So Fine' (1961), but their career together was undermined by commitments elsewhere. Prolific session work for **Atlantic**, Savoy, King and Aladdin earned the former the epithet **Mickey 'Guitar' Baker**, while the latter had made her recording debut with jazz trumpeter **Oran 'Hot Lips' Page** as early as 1950. In 1973, she began recording as **Sylvia**,and later achieved notable success as an entrepreneur through her ownership of Sugar Hill Records.

Albums: *New Sounds* (1958), *Love Is Strange* (1965).

Microdisney

This incendiary pop/folk group were formed in Cork, Eire, in 1980. There was little cohesion in their early formations; 'We used to be much more frenzied in those days, a **Fall**-type mess, and our line-up was always changing. Originally Sean (O'Hagan) was going to play guitar and I (Cathal Coughlan) was going to recite poetry, then one week it was guitar, bass, drums, then guitar keyboard and violin, then we had a drum machine. . .' After settling on the more traditional formation of drums, guitars, bass and keyboards, the band began releasing singles which eventually were collected together on *We Hate You White South African Bastards*. The title was typically inflammatory, and in direct opposition to that of their long-playing debut, *Everybody Is Fantastic*. An early clue to their subversive nature, on the surface Microdisney were purveyors of accessible and restrained pop music. This attracted **Virgin Records**, but the band had a dark edge in Coughlan's bitter lyricism. Their Virgin debut, 'Town To Town', dented the lower regions of the charts and was quickly followed by *Crooked Mile*. However, Microdisney elected to bite the hand that fed them with the near hit 'Singer's Hampstead Home', which thinly masked an attack on Virgin's fallen idol, **Boy George**. They bowed out with *39 Minutes*, by which time the vitriol was really flowing, counter-balanced as ever by O'Hagan's delicate country guitar. Despite critical acclaim, Microdisney's sales had remained disappointingly in the cult bracket. O'Hagan went on

to release a solo album in 1990 (*High Llamas*), while Coughlan's **Fatima Mansions** has done much to spice up the late 80s and early 90s.
Albums: *Everybody Is Fantastic* (1984), *We Hate You White South African Bastards* (1984), *The Clock Comes Down The Stairs* (1985), *Crooked Mile* (1987), *39 Minutes* (1988), *Gale Force Wind* (1988).

Micus, Stephan

b. 19 January 1953, Stuttgart, Germany. Micus made his first overseas trip to Morocco at the age of 16. Since then he has travelled all over the world, studying traditional wind and string instruments, including the Japanese shakuhachi and sho, the Indian sitar and dilruba, as well as a range of percussion instruments from China, Korea, Bali, Java, Tibet and Ireland. For *East Of The Night* he designed a new type of 10- and 14-string guitar with resonant strings like that of the sitar. He has given concerts in Europe (including one in Düsseldorf with **Oregon**), the USA, Japan, Taiwan, Israel and Afghanistan. In 1977, his ballet, *Koan*, received its premiere in Cologne. Further performances included London, Paris and New York. *The Music Of Stones*, his compositions for the resonating stone sculptures of Elmar Daucher, were recorded in the atmospheric ambience of Ulm Cathedral and proved to be among his most inspired work. In the recording studio he has preferred to work as a soloist, making sensitive use of multi-track playback techniques. His compositions, often based on improvisation and always difficult to classify, have been widely acclaimed for their meditative and spiritual qualities. His expressed intention is not to play traditional music, but to search for fresh possibilities by using traditional instruments in unconventional combinations. Of this, the jazz writer Joachim E. Berendt, has said: 'He plays them with a profound internationalization of their tradition and spirituality, uniting their sounds in a musical river which makes the stream of inner consciousness audible'.
Selected albums: *Implosions* (ECM 1977), *Koan* (ECM 1981), *East Of The Night* (ECM 1985), *Ocean* (ECM 1986), *Twilight Fields* (ECM 1987), *Wings Over Water* (ECM 1988), *The Music Of Stones* (ECM 1989), *Darkness And Light* (ECM 1990), *Behind Eleven Deserts* (Verabra 1990), *To The Evening Child* (ECM 1992), *Till The End Of Time* (ECM 1993), *Listen To The Rain* (ECM 1993).

Middle Of The Road

Originally known as Los Caracas when they performed throughout Europe, this Scottish quartet featured singer Sally Carr, backed by Ian Lewis, Eric Lewis and Ken Andrew. An astute cover of a novelty Continental song 'Chirpy Chirpy Cheep Cheep' saw them outsell a rival version by **Mac And Katie Kissoon** and hog the UK number 1 spot for five weeks during the summer of 1971. The follow-up, 'Tweedle Dee, Tweedle Dum' (a song about two feuding Scottish clans) had already reached the top in Sweden, Denmark and Norway prior to its UK release, where it climbed to number 2. Further lightweight hits in the early 70s included 'Soley Soley', 'Sacramento' and 'Samson And Delilah', paving the way for many successful seasons in cabaret.
Albums: *Chirpy Chirpy Cheep Cheep* (c.70s), *Drive On* (c.70s).

Middleton, Velma

b. 1 September 1917, St. Louis, Missouri, USA, d. 10 February 1961, Sierra Leone. During the 30s, Middleton sang and danced in various clubs, sometimes as a solo, often in the chorus line. In 1942, she was hired to sing with the **Louis Armstrong** big band and remained when the All Stars were formed, touring the world and, as a result, becoming far more famous than many other, better singers. She was still touring with Armstrong when she collapsed and died in Sierra Leone in February 1961. Although her singing style was uninspired, Middleton had an earthily infectious sense of humour which blended with Armstrong's, and their performances together were always hugely entertaining.
Albums: with Louis Armstrong *Satchmo At Symphony Hall* (1947), *Louis Armstrong Plays W. C. Handy* (1954).

Midler, Bette

b. 1 December 1945, Paterson, New Jersey, USA. As a singer, comedienne and actress, Midler rose to fame with an outrageous, raunchy stage act, and became known as 'The Divine Miss M', 'Trash With Flash' and 'Sleaze With Ease'. Her mother, a fan of the movies, named her after Bette Davis. Raised in Hawaii, as one of the few white students in her school, and the only Jew, she 'toughened up fast, and won an award in the first grade for singing 'Silent Night'. Encouraged by her mother, she studied theatre at the University of Hawaii, and worked in a pineapple factory and as a secretary in a radio station before gaining her first professional acting job in 1965 in the movie *Hawaii*, playing the bit part of a missionary wife who is constantly sick. Moving to New York, she held jobs as a glove saleswoman in Stern's Department Store, a hat-check girl, and a go-go dancer, before joining the chorus of the hit Broadway musical ***Fiddler On The Roof*** in 1966. In February 1967, Midler took over one of the leading roles, as Tzeitel, the eldest daughter, and played the part for the next three years. While singing late-night after the show at the Improvisation Club, a showcase for young performers, she was noticed by an executive from the David Frost television show, and subsequently appeared several times with Frost, and on the *Merv Griffin Show*. After leaving *Fiddler On The Roof*, she performed briefly in the Off-Broadway musical *Salvation*, and worked again as a go-go dancer in a

Broadway bar, before taking a $50-a-night job at the Continental Baths, New York, singing to male homosexuals dressed in bath towels. Clad in toreador pants, or sequin gowns, strapless tops and platform shoes - uniforms of a bygone age - she strutted her extravagant stuff, singing songs from the 40s, 50s, and 60s - rock, blues, novelties - even reaching back to 1929 for the Harry Akst/Grant Clarke ballad 'Am I Blue?', which had been hit then for **Ethel Waters**. News of these somewhat bizarre happenings soon got round, and outside audiences of both sexes, including show people, were allowed to view the show. Offers of other work flooded in, including the opportunity to appear regularly on Johnny Carson's *Tonight* show.

In May 1971, she played the dual roles of the Acid Queen and Mrs Walker in the Seattle Opera Company's production of the rock opera ***Tommy*** and, later in the year, made her official New York nightclub debut at the Downstairs At The Upstairs, the original two-week engagement being extended to 10, to accommodate the crowds. During the following year, she appeared with Carson at the Sahara in Las Vegas, and in June played to standing room only at Carnegie Hall in New York. In November, her first album, *The Divine Miss M*, was released by **Atlantic Records**, and is said to have sold 100,000 copies in the first month. It contained several of the cover versions which she featured in her stage act such as the **Andrews Sisters**' 'Boogie Woogie Bugle Boy', the **Dixie Cups**' 'The Chapel Of Love', the **Shangri-Las**' 'The Leader Of The Pack' and **Bobby Freeman**'s 'Do You Want To Dance?'. The pianist on most of the tracks was **Barry Manilow**, who was Midler's accompanist and musical director for three years in the early 70s. The album bears the dedication: 'This is for Judith'. Judith was Midler's sister who was killed in a road accident on her way to meet Bette when she was appearing in *Fiddler On The Roof.* Midler's second album, *Bette Midler*, also made the US Top 10. In 1973, Midler received the *After Dark* Award for Performer Of The Year, and soon became a superstar, able to fill concert halls throughout the USA. In 1979, she had her first starring role in the movie ***The Rose***, which was loosely based on the life of rock singer **Janis Joplin**. Midler was nominated for an Academy Award as 'Best Actress', and won two Golden Globe Awards for her performance. Two songs from the film, the title track (a million-seller), and 'When A Man Loves A Woman', and the soundtrack album, entered the US charts, as did the album from Midler's next film, *Divine Madness*, a celluloid version of her concert performance in Pasadena, California. After all the success of the past decade, things started to go wrong in the early 80s. In 1982, the aptly-named black comedy, *Jinxed!*, was a disaster at the box office, amid rumours of violent disagreements between Midler and her co-star Ken Wahl and director Don Siegel. Midler became persona non-grata in Hollywood, and suffered a nervous breakdown. She married Martin Von Haselberg, a former commodities broker, in 1984, and signed to a long-term contract to the **Walt Disney** Studios, making her come-back in the comedy *Down And Out In Beverly Hills* (1985), with Nick Nolte and Richard Dreyfuss.

During the rest of the decade she eschewed touring, and concentrated on her acting career in a series of raucous comedy movies such as *Ruthless People* (1986) co-starring Danny De Vito, *Outrageous Fortune* (1987) and *Big Business* (1988). In 1988, *Beaches*, the first film to be made by her own company, All Girls Productions (their motto is, 'We hold a grudge'), gave her one of her best roles, and the opportunity to sing songs within the context of the story. These included standards such as 'Ballin' The Jack', **Cole Porter**'s 'I've Still Got My Health', 'The Glory Of Love', 'Under The Boardwalk', and 'Otto Titsling'. Also included was 'Wind Beneath My Wings', by Larry Henley and Jeff Silbar, which reached number 1 in the US charts. Midler's recording won Grammys in 1990 for 'Record Of The Year' and 'Song Of The Year'. In 1990, Midler appeared in *Stella*, a remake of the classic weepie, *Stella Dallas*, in which she performed an hilarious mock striptease among the bottles and glasses on top of a bar, and *Scenes From A Mall*, a comedy co-staring Woody Allen. Her appearance as a USO entertainer in World War II, alongside actor James Caan, in *For The Boys* (1991), which she also co-produced, earned her a Golden Globe award for Best Actress. The movie showed her at her best, and featured her very individual readings of 'Stuff Like That There' and 'P. S. I Love You'. In the same year, she released *Some People's Lives*, her first non-soundtrack album since the 1983 flop, *No Frills*. It entered the US Top 10, and one of the tracks, 'From A Distance', had an extended chart life in the USA and UK. By the early 90s she was planning to revive her musical career, and in 1993 brought a spectacular new stage show to Radio City Music Hall. The lavish three hour concert, her first for 10 years, was called *Experience The Divine*, and seemed as 'gaudy and outrageously tasteless as ever'. In 1994 Midler won an Emmy Nomination, along with Golden Globe and National Board of Review Awards for her outstanding performance as Rose in a CBS television musical production of ***Gypsy***. In 1995, she recorded her first studio a;bum for five years, *Bette Of Roses.*

Albums: *The Divine Miss M* (1972), *Bette Midler* (1973), *Songs For The New Depression* (1976), *Live At Last* (1977), *Broken Blossom* (1977), *Thighs And Whispers* (1979), *The Rose* (1979, film soundtrack), *Divine Madness* (1980, film soundtrack), *No Frills* (1983), *Beaches* (1989, film soundtrack), *Some People's Lives* (1990), *Best Of* (1993), *Bette Of Roses* (Atlantic 1995).

Further reading: *Bette Midler*, Rob Baker. *A View From A Broad*, Bette Midler. *The Saga Of Baby Divine*, Bette Midler.

Midnight Oil

Formed in Sydney, New South Wales, Australia, in 1975, and known as Farm, this strident band has pioneered its own course in Australian rock without relying on the established network of agencies and record companies. The original nucleus of the band comprised Martin Rotsey (guitar), Rob Hirst (drums) and Jim Moginie (guitar). They were later joined by law student Peter Garrett (lead vocals). The outfit became notorious for always insisting on total control over its recorded product and media releases, including photos, and when booking agencies denied the band gigs, the members organized their own venues and tours, taking advantage of the group's large following on the alternative rock scene. Joined by Dwayne 'Bones' Hillman (bass) in 1977 and changing their name to Midnight Oil, the group took a couple of album releases to refine its songwriting style, principally by Moginie and Hirst. As *Head Injuries* went gold in Australia, the imposing shaven-headed Garrett, who had by now received his law degree, began to make known his firm views on politics. Having signed a world-wide deal with **CBS/Columbia**, it was *10,9,8,7,6,5,4,3,2,1*, which saw the band gain mainstream radio airplay. Featuring songs about the environment, anti-nuclear sentiments, anti-war songs and powerful anthems of anti-establishment; it also propelled the band into the international market place. The band performed at many charity concerts, promoting Koori (Australian aborigines) causes in Australia and the loquacious Garrett almost gained a seat in the Australian Parliament in 1984 while standing for the Nuclear Disarmament Party. The following album saw the band tour the USA and Europe, and ***Rolling Stone*** writers voted the album one of the best of 1989, despite a low profile there. While many regard *Red Sails In The Sunset* as their best work, the subsequent albums have been equally highly regarded. The group's peak album chart positions in the UK and USA were achieved with *Diesel And Dust* reaching the UK Top 20 and US number 21, while in the US the follow-up, *Blue Sky Mining* emulated that position. The group continued its antagonistic attitude towards major industrial companies in 1990, by organizing a protest concert outside the Manhattan offices of the Exxon oil company which was responsible for the Valdez oil slick in Alaska.

Albums: *Midnight Oil* (1978), *Head Injuries* (1979), *Place Without A Postcard* (1981), *10,9,8,7,6,5,4,3,2,1* (1982), *Red Sails In The Sunset* (1985), *Diesel And Dust* (1987), *Blue Sky Mining* (1990), *Scream In Blue-Live* (1992), *Earth And Sun And Moon* (1993).

Further reading: *Strict Rules*, Andrew McMillan.

Midnite Follies Orchestra

The Orchestra was formed in the UK during 1978 by pianist **Keith Nichols** and arranger Alan Cohen to specialize in the repertoire of the 20s and 30s, and to play originals written in a similar style. After a memorable first night at London's 100 Club, the band were signed to **EMI** for which they have recorded since using the cream of British mainstream musicians - **Alan Elsdon**, **Digby Fairweather**, Pete Strange (trombone), John Barnes, Olaf Vas and Randolphe Colville (saxophones). The orchestra regularly play on radio and television, and in tribute concerts for artists, including **Louis Armstrong**, **Fats Waller** and **Duke Ellington**.

Albums: *Hotter Than Hades* (1978), *Jungle Nights In Harlem* (1981).

Midway Still

UK indie rock band whose profile initially rose through supports to the likes of **Cud** and the more musically similar **Mega City Four**. Boasting a sound which also earned comparisons to **Teenage Fanclub** or **Dinosaur Jr**, the band comprised Paul Thomson (guitar/vocals), Declan Kelly (drums) and Jan aka John Kanopka (bass). Both of the latter were formerly members of USMF. Their first single, 'I Won't Try', emerged on Roughneck records (a subsidiary of **Fire Records**) in July 1991. Thematically it was dedicated to their pet python and attempts to feed it with mice who bred exponentially. Thomson was an interesting character, having met Keith Moon (**Who**) on holiday as a child, and sharing baths with a young Michela Strachan. Also in chlildhood, alas. The band were easily distinguished by their taste in Hawaiian shirts, though their efforts at running a competition in the *New Musical Express* to get a reader to design a logo for them ended in disaster. So too did their short but entertaining career with diminishing press returns for their second long player in 1993. As its title suggested, life may indeed by too long, but musical careers can also be disastrously short.

Albums: *Dial Square* (Roughneck 1992), *Life's Too Long* (Roughneck 1993).

Mighty Avengers

This short-lived UK quartet - Tony Campbell (lead guitar/vocals), Teddy Mahon (rhythm guitar), Mike Linnell (bass/vocals) and 'Biffo' Beech (drums/vocals) - enjoyed the patronage of **Rolling Stones**' manager **Andrew Loog Oldham**. He produced the group's three singles, 'So Much In Love', 'Blue Turns To Grey' and '(Walking Through The) Sleepy City', each of which were exclusive Jagger/Richard songs. This altruism was fuelled by Oldham's desire to test the market for the songwriters' early efforts. 'So Much In Love' peaked at number 46 in November 1964, but Oldham's interest in the group waned when subsequent offerings failed to chart. The tracks remain interesting examples of Oldham's debt to producer **Phil Spector**.

'Blue Turns To Grey' later became a hit in the hands of **Cliff Richard** in 1966.

Mighty Avons

(see **Larry Cunningham**)

Mighty Baby

This UK rock group was formed in 1968 around Alan 'Bam' King (guitar), Mike Evans (bass) and Roger Powell (drums), all founder members of the **Action**, one of London's most exciting Mod groups. Late-period arrivals Martin Stone (guitar, ex-**Savoy Brown**) and Ian Whiteman (piano, saxophone) completed Mighty Baby, a name suggested by their manager, John Curd. The quintet's self-titled debut album, released on Curd's self-explanatory Head Records, was a skilful blend of strong melody and instrumental dexterity, exemplified on the opening composition, 'Egyptian Tomb'. Their improvisatory prowess was even greater on live performances, where Stone's imaginative soloing combined with Whiteman's woodwind and keyboard passages, creating a mesmerising sound. The group's second album, *A Jug Of Love*, issued on **Mike Vernon**'s **Blue Horizon** label, captured this spirit of adventure, but Mighty Baby's potential was suddenly shorn when Whiteman, Evans and Powell, who had each accepted the Sufi faith, left to form a new group, the Habibiyya. As such they recorded one album, **If Man But Knew**, in 1972, before pursuing careers as session musicians, notably for **Richard Thompson** and **Sandy Denny**. Stone latterly form **Chilli Willi And The Red Hot Peppers** with fellow guitarist Phil Lithman, before abandoning music in favour of antiquarian books. King meanwhile joined pub-rock favourites **Ace**.

Albums: *Mighty Baby* (1969), *A Jug Of Love* (1971)

Mighty Diamonds

One of the most famous Jamaican vocal groups of the 70s and 80s, the Diamonds consisted of Donald 'Tabby' Shaw (lead vocals), with Fitzroy 'Bunny' Simpson and Lloyd 'Judge' Ferguson providing the harmonies and occasional lead. They recorded unsuccessfully for **Stranger Cole** and **Rupie Edwards**, among others, before their breakthrough in 1975 with **Joe Joe Hookim**'s Channel One studio. 'Hey Girl' and 'Country Living' were big reggae hits, but their next release, 'Right Time' on Hookim's Well Charge label, brought everything together. The Diamonds initial success was due to a number of reasons: the influence of **Burning Spear**'s championing of Jamaican national hero, Marcus Garvey; the definitive three-part **rocksteady** harmonies of the **Heptones**, together with **Sly Dunbar**'s militant **rockers** style of drumming on 'do-overs' of timeless **Studio One** rhythms; and, of course, their own superb songwriting, vocal abilities and the odd knack of somehow managing to sound urgent and relaxed at the same time.

Jamaica erupted into Diamonds-mania while the Channel One 'rockers' sound they had brought to prominence was to dominate reggae music for the next few years, with every drummer in the business developing his very own **Sly Dunbar** impersonation. **Virgin Records** was busy acquiring reggae artists in 1976, and the Diamonds and Hookim signed with them for the release of their debut, *Right Time*. It was a classic collection, showcasing perfectly the Diamonds uncanny ability to write catchy, meaningful songs - whether about 'love' or 'reality' - and set them to updated versions of some of the greatest Studio One rhythms. They sold throughout the reggae world and picked up many crossover sales. Virgin sent the Diamonds to New Orleans to work with veteran producer **Allen Toussaint**, which resulted in *Ice On Fire*. It was not well-received, and sold poorly - mainly because its misguided approach baffled reggae fans, while the Diamonds name still meant very little to a wider audience.

They continued to work at Channel One, and many more hit singles came through during the 70s. In 1981, the **dub plates** of tunes they had recorded for **Gussie Clarke** were the most played on the Kingston and London **sound system** circuits. The most popular of these tunes was released on a 10-inch, dub plate style record in New York, a 7-inch in Jamaica and a 12-inch in England; 'Pass The Kouchie', an updating of a 60s Studio One instrumental 'Full Up', was a massive hit. This eventually became 'Pass The Dutchie' for the English group, **Musical Youth**, which was a worldwide pop hit. (A 'kouchie' is a pipe for smoking ganja, while a 'dutchie' is a type of cooking pot.) The rest of their work with Gussie was released on *Changes*, which consisted of the same combination of new songs and old rhythms, with some classic reggae songs, including 'Party Time' and 'Hurting Inside', performed in the inimitable Diamonds style.

For the rest of the decade and on into the 90s, the Diamonds have continued to consolidate their reputation as one of the best vocal harmony trios in the business with regular releases for a variety of different producers and some lovely self-produced records. Their harmonies are always tight, and their songs usually manage to avoid obvious and naive statements. In the constantly changing world of reggae, they are always a reliable and dependable source of top-quality music, and if their performances have not been quite up to the exalted standards of *Right Time* and *Changes*, it is perhaps too much to expect of them to change direction in a radical fashion at this stage in their careers.

Selected albums: *Right Time* (Well Charge/Virgin 1976, Shanachie 1984), *Ice On Fire* (Front Line 1977), *Stand Up To Your Judgement* (Channel One 1978), *Tell Me What's Wrong* (JJ 1979), *Planet Earth* (Virgin 1978), *Deeper Roots* -

Back To The Channel (Front Line 1979), *Changes* (Music Works 1981), *Vital Selection* (Virgin 1981), *Leader Of Black Countrys* (Mobiliser 1983), *Kouchie Vibes* (Burning Sounds 1984), *Struggling* (Live & Love 1985), *If You're Looking For Trouble* (Live & Love 1986), *The Roots Is There* (Shanachie 1987), *Real Enemy* (Greensleeves 1987), *Reggae Street* (Shanachie 1987), *Dubwise* (Music Works 1988), *Get Ready* (Greensleeves 1988), *Never Get Weary* (Live & Love 1988), *Live In Europe* (Greensleeves 1989), *Go Seek Your Rights* (Frontline 1990), *The Moment Of Truth* (Mango/Island 1992), *Bust Out* (Greensleeves 1993).

Mighty Lemon Drops

This UK independent label pop band broke through in 1985 with the highly-touted 'Like An Angel'. The band featured Paul Marsh (vocals/guitar), David Newton (guitar), Tony Linehan (bass) and Keith Rowley (drums), who had all enjoyed chequered careers in numerous Wolverhampton outfits. Newton had previously played with Active Restraint in 1982, which also included Marsh and Linehan. They in turn played regularly alongside Another Dream, and both bands featured on single releases by local label Watchdog Video And Records. Newton and Neal Cook of Another Dream put together the Wild Flowers, alongside Dave Atherton (also ex-Another Dream; guitar/keyboards), Pete Waldron (bass) and Dave Fisher (drums). After a further single and a support to **Simple Minds**, Newton moved on once more, forming the Mighty Lemon Drops with Marsh and Linehan. The temporary drummer was Martin Gilks (later with the **Wonder Stuff**), before Keith Rowley stepped in full-time. As part of the ***New Musical Express***' 'C-86' generation, they were snapped up by **Chrysalis Records**. Despite the charm of several singles in an **Echo And The Bunnymen** vein, they failed to translate independent chart success into hits. Although they were dropped by Chrysalis after three albums, they remained favourites on the US college circuit. Sadly this was not enough to sustain them, and they broke up in the early 90s leaving a compilation of live tracks and demos for release on Overground Records.

Albums: *Happy Head* (Chrysalis 1986), *World Without End* (Chrysalis 1988), *Sound* (Chyrsalis 1991), *All The Way - Live In Cincinnati* (Overground 1993).

Mighty Mighty

Like many of the UK indie guitar pop favourites of the mid-80s, Birmingham, UK's Mighty Mighty owed more than a passing debt to **Orange Juice** and the **Postcard Records** label. Hugh Harkin (vocals/occasional harp), Mick Geoghegan (guitar/lyric writer), brother Peter (organ/guitar), David Hennessy (drums) and Russell Burton (bass/vocals) first appeared as part of the ***New Musical Express***/ICA Rock Week gigs and accompanying *C86* cassette compilation. This coincided nicely with Mighty Mighty's debut single, the catchy 'Everybody Knows The Monkey', in May 1986; like July's 'Is There Anyone Out There?' 12-inch, it was issued on the band's own Girlie label. However, aspiring local label Chapter 22 soon snapped them up, for a string of classy pop tunes that fared well on the independent sector. After December's 'Throwaway' (originally half of a fanzine flexidisc) came the raunchy 'Built Like A Car' in May 1987, 'One Way' in October and the attractive 'Born In A Maisonette' in the New Year. Unfortunately, Mighty Mighty failed to develop, and by the time *Sharks* was released in February 1988, their formula had worn thin. Apart from the excellent 'Blue And Green', *Sharks* had little to offer in the way of new ideas at a time when the independent scene was rapidly hardening. The ensuing collapse of the band was inevitable.

Album: *Sharks* (Chapter 22 1988).

Mighty Sam

b. Sam McClain, 15 April 1943, Monroe, Louisiana, USA. Introduced to gospel as a child, McClain served his apprenticeship in a school-friend's R&B group. In 1963, he joined the Dothan Sextet and remained their lead singer for the next three years. Disc jockey 'Papa' Don Schroeder 'discovered' Sam and signed him to the Bell subsidiary Amy, where the artist recorded eight singles. The Fame studio houseband provided the perfect accompaniment to McClain's rasping interpretations, which evoked those of **Bobby 'Blue' Bland** and **Little Milton**. Ballads, including 'In The Same Old Way' (1967) and 'When She Touches Me' (1967), and the deep country-soul of 'Sweet Dreams' (1968) stand among his finest offerings. In 1970, following Schroeder's retirement, Mighty Sam joined **Atlantic Records** for two excellent singles before switching to **Malaco Records** for a solitary release. After years of neglect, during which the singer was almost penniless, he re-emerged on the Orleans label. A *Live In Japan* set followed. Sam's distinctive growl can also be heard on *Hubert Sumlin's Blues Party*, one of the finest blues collections of the late 80s.

Albums: *Mighty Soul* (1969), *Your Perfect Companion* (1986), *Live In Japan* (1987). Compilation: *Nothing But The Truth* (1988).

Migil Five

Red Lambert (guitar/vocals), Alan Watson (saxophone), Gil Lucas (piano), Lenny Blanche (bass) and Mike Felix (drums/lead vocals) achieved momentary fame when their 'Mockingbird Hill' single reached the UK Top 10 in 1964, on the strength of a fleeting bluebeat craze. Felix, Blanche and Lucas had previously worked as a jazz trio prior to embracing pop with the addition of Lambert. They recorded as the Migil Four before adding Watson at the suggestion of trumpeter **Kenny Ball**. Despite inordinate press

coverage, the group was unable to repeat this success. They later became stalwarts of the cabaret circuit before disintegrating when Felix began a solo career.
Album: *Mockingbird Hill* (1964).

Mihashi, Michiya

b. Michiya Kitazawa, 10 November 1930, Hakodate, Hokkaidô, Japan. After many years of training as a professional singer of Japanese folk-songs, Mihashi was signed by King Records as a singer of kayôkyoku (formerly the most common and typically Japanese form of popular song) with a debut single, 'Sake No Nigasa Yo' ('A Bitter Taste Of Sake') in 1954. Beginning with 'On 'Na Sendô Uta' ('A Song Of A Female Boatman') in 1955, he succeeded with many 'home-pining' songs in the late 50s, including 'Ringo-Mura Kara' ('From The Apple Village'), 'Osaraba Tokyo' ('Goodbye Tokyo') and 'Akai Yûi No Kokyô ('My Hometown With The Red Sunset'). These songs were particularly popular among the young workers who had streamed into large cities from rural areas. His nasal tenor, reminiscent of his background in folk-singing, and the nostalgic nature of his songs were familiar to Japanese households at least until the late 70s.
Compilations: *Zenkyokushû 1* (*Complete Works 1*) (1990), *Zenkyokushû 2* (*Complete Works 2*) (1990).

Mike And The Mechanics

Mike Rutherford (b. 2 October 1950, Guildford, Surrey, England; bass) formed the Mechanics in 1985, during a pause in the career of his band, **Genesis**, and while **Phil Collins** was engrossed in his solo career. The line-up comprised (ex-**Ace**, **Squeeze**, **Nick Lowe** member **Paul Carrack** (b. 22 April 1951, Sheffield, Yorkshire, England; vocals/keyboards), Paul Young (ex-**Sad Cafe**; vocals), Peter Van Hooke and Adrian Lee. Van Hooke was already an accomplished session musician, having played or toured with many singers, from **Van Morrison** to **Rod Argent**. The group's first hit came with 'Silent Running (On Dangerous Ground)' in 1986, which was used as the theme to the film *On Dangerous Ground*. However, it was late in 1988 before they scored their first big hit with the Rutherford/**B.A. Robertson** penned 'The Living Years', an emotive song expressing Rutherford's regret at the lack of communication he had with his father while he was alive. It also topped the US charts. Further chart success continued although the band were seen more as an album band. Quality singles such as 'Everybody Gets A Second Chance' and the highly emotive 'A Time And A Place' failed to make the UK Top 50, a sobering thought for future songwriters with high hopes of chart success. *Beggar On A Beach Of Gold* was preceeded by a lively single 'Over My Shoulder', unfortunately this proved to be the album's only ingot. The title track was written by B.A. Robertson and was a top 40 hit in the UK in 1995. Pedestrian covers of the **Miracles**' 'You Really Got A Hold On Me' and **Stevie Wonder**'s 'I Believe (When I Fall In Love Again It Will be Forever)' added nothing and the album, although competent, did not break any new ground. The band continue to be as fluid as its members' careers allow.
Albums: *Mike And The Mechanics* (WEA 1985), *The Living Years* (WEA 1988), *Word Of Mouth* (Virgin 1991), *Beggar On A Beach Of Gold* (Virgin 1995).

Miki And Griff

Miki (b. Barbara MacDonald Salisbury, 20 June 1920, Ayrshire, Scotland, d. 20 April 1989) was raised on Rothesay on the Isle of Bute. When she joined the **George Mitchell** Choir, she met Griff (b. Emyr Morus Griffith, 9 May 1923, Holywell, Wales). They learned vocal discipline and stagecraft there. They married in 1950, and leaving Mitchell, developed a comedy act with props and novelty numbers such as 'Spooks' and 'Ol' McDonald's Farm'. Griff's moustache became a recognizable trademark. In 1958, they fell in love with the **Everly Brothers**' album of traditional country ballads, *Songs Our Daddy Taught Us*, as well as country albums by the **Louvin Brothers**, and they would sing their songs for the own amusement in dressing-rooms. **Lonnie Donegan** heard them and invited them to perform those songs on his television series. He arranged a contract with Pye Records and produced their first records. In 1959, 'Hold Back Tomorrow' made the UK Top 30, and they made very successful EPs, *Rockin' Alone (In An Old Rockin' Chair)* and *This Is Miki - This Is Griff*, which topped the EP charts. They appeared on several of Donegan's own records, including 'Virgin Mary' and 'Michael Row The Boat'. Miki recorded a tender version of 'I Never Will Marry' with only Donegan's whistling and acoustic guitar for accompaniment, and they were to work with him until 1964. In 1962, Miki And Griff's only UK Top 20 hit came when they covered **Burl Ives**'s 'A Little Bitty Tear', and the following year they made the Top 30 with a cover of **Steve Lawrence** and **Eydie Gorme**'s US hit, 'I Want To Stay Here'. Lesser-known records such as 'This Time I Would Know', 'Oh, So Many Years' and **Harlan Howard**'s humorous 'Automation' were just as good. Although they often covered songs by other performers, their records were always instantly recognizable. Record producer **Tony Hatch** used to say, 'Miki can create a better harmony than I can ever write for her.' Visiting the USA, they received a standing ovation on **Roy Acuff**'s portion of the *Grand Ole Opry* in 1964. Miki And Griff are easily the most-recorded UK country act, with most of their recordings being for Pye. They did, however, record two albums for Major-Minor and included the weepie 'Two Little Orphans'. In later years, they performed as a duo to the accompaniment

of Miki's piano. Griff's humour was always evident, and his emotion-charged version of 'These Hands' was always a showstopper. Miki developed into a fine songwriter - in particular, 'God Was Here (But I Think He Left Early)'. They always had time for their fans, but Miki, who disguised her illness on stage for some months, died of cancer in April 1989. Understandably, Griff has not returned to performing since and, instead, cheers up the patients in the hospital where he visited Miki. The duo are fondly remembered by many listeners for introducing them to country music, and they were a fine, middle-of-the-road act in their own right.
Selected albums: *Miki And Griff* (1961), *The Country Style Of Miki And Griff* (1962), *I Want To Stay Here* (1963), *Those Rocking Chair People* (1969), *Two Little Orphans* (1970), *Tennessee Waltz* (1970), *Lonesome* (1970), *The Country Side Of Miki And Griff* (1972), *Let The Rest Of The World Go By* (1973), *Country Is* (1974), *Two's Company* (1975), *This Is Miki - This Is Griff* (1976), *Etchings* (1977), *Country* (1978), *The Best Of Miki And Griff* (1983), *At Home With Miki And Griff* (1987), *Little Bitty Tear* (1993).

Mikkelborg, Palle

b. 6 March 1941, Copenhagen, Denmark. Mikkelborg is a self-taught trumpeter who studied conducting at the Royal Music Conservatory, Copenhagen. After turning professional in 1960, he joined Danish Radiojazzgruppen (1963), of which he was the leader from 1967-72. He was also a member of Radioens Big Band from 1964-71. For both of these, he would write, arrange and conduct as well as play trumpet. In 1966, he formed a quintet with drummer Alex Riel which won first prize at the **Montreux Jazz Festival** and played at the **Newport Jazz Festival** (1968). Then he led an octet called V8 (1970-75) and an outfit called Entrance (1975-85). Mikkelborg has also worked with bandleaders **George Russell**, **Gil Evans**, **George Gruntz**, **Mike Gibbs** and **Maynard Ferguson** and a wide variety of musicians, including **Jan Garbarek**, **Terje Rypdal**, **Don Cherry**, **Abdullah Ibrahim** and **Charlie Mariano**. His trumpet playing is characterized by a clear, firm sound, a huge range and the successful incorporation of a variety of electronic effects. He has written many pieces for his various bands as well as a series of extended pieces for larger ensembles. In 1984, he wrote and later recorded *Aura*, a tribute to **Miles Davis**, for big band and soloists, featuring Davis himself.
Albums: *Ashoka Suite* (1970), with Entrance *Entrance* (1977), with Terje Rypdal *Waves* (1977), *Descendre* (1978), *Live As Well* (1978), with Shankar, Jan Garbarek *Visions* (1983), with George Gruntz *Theatre* (1984), *Journey To...* (1985), *Aura* (1985), *Heart To Heart* (Storyville 1986), with Niels-Henning Ørsted Pederson *Once Upon A Time* (1992).

Milburn, Amos

b. 1 April 1927, Houston, Texas, USA, d. 3 January 1980, Houston, Texas, USA. After service in the US Navy in World War II, Milburn formed his own blues and R&B band in Houston in which he played piano and sang, and in 1946 he was offered a contract by the **Aladdin** label. Between November 1948 and February 1954 he and his band, the Aladdin Chicken Shackers, had an extraordinary run of 19 consecutive Top 10 hits on the ***Billboard*** R&B chart, including four number 1's ('Chicken Shack Boogie', 'A&M Blues', 'Roomin' House Boogie' and 'Bad, Bad Whiskey'). His romping boogies about drinking and partying were hugely popular and for two years (1949 and 1950) he was voted Top R&B Artist by *Billboard*. Following the break up of his band in 1954 he never achieved the same level of success, and he left Aladdin in 1956. He then recorded as a duo with **Charles Brown** for the Ace label, and in 1963 recorded an album for **Motown**. In the 60s he played clubs around Cincinnati and Cleveland, Ohio, drawing heavily on his catalogue of old hits, but did not have any more hit records. In 1970 he suffered the first of a series of strokes. In 1972 he retired and returned to his home town of Houston where he died eight years later.
Albums: with Wynonie Harris *Party After Hours* (Aladdin 1955), *Rockin' The Boogie* (Aladdin 1955), *Let's Have A Party* (Score 1957), *Amos Milburn Sings The Blues* (Score 1958), *The Blues Boss* (Motown 1963), *13 Unreleased Masters* (Pathé-Marconi 1984). Compilations: *Million Sellers* (Imperial 1962), *Greatest Hits* (Official Records 1988, covers the Aladdin years).

Miles, Buddy

b. 5 September 1945, Omaha, Nebraska, USA. A teenage prodigy, this powerful, if inflexible drummer was a veteran of several touring revues prior to his spell with soul singer **Wilson Pickett**. In 1967, Miles joined the **Electric Flag** at the behest of guitarist **Mike Bloomfield**, whose subsequent departure left the drummer in control. Although the group collapsed in the wake of a disappointing second album, Miles retained its horn section for his next venture, the Buddy Miles Express. This exciting unit also included former **Mitch Ryder** guitarist Jim McCarthy. Their first album, *Expressway To Your Skull*, was full of driving, electric soul rhythms which had the blessing of **Jimi Hendrix**, who produced the album and wrote the sleeve notes. In 1969, Miles joined Jimi Hendrix in the ill-fated Band Of Gypsies. The drummer then continued his own career with the Buddy Miles Band and the rumbustious *Them Changes* album, the title track of which was a minor US hit. As an integral part of the artist's career, the song was not only featured on the *Band Of Gypsies* album, but provided one of the highlights of Miles' 1972 collaboration with **Carlos**

Santana, which was recorded live in an extinct Hawaiian volcano. Having participated in an ill-fated Electric Flag reunion, the drummer continued his prolific rock/soul output with a variety of releases. Despite enjoying a seemingly lower profile during the 80s, Miles has been the guiding musical force behind the phenomenally successful California Raisins, a cartoon group inspired by television advertising. In the mid-90s Miles reappeared with an accomplished album on Ryko which included his interpretations of 'All Along The Watchtower' and 'Born Under A Bad Sign'.
Albums: as the Buddy Miles Express *Expressway To Your Skull* (1968), *Electric Church* (1969); as the Buddy Miles Band *Them Changes* (1970), *We Got To Live Together* (1970), *Message To The People* (1971), *Live* (1971); with Carlos Santana *Carlos Santana and Buddy Miles! Live!* (1972); solo *Chapter VII* (1973), *Booger Bear* (1973), *All The Faces Of Buddy Miles* (1974), *More Miles Per Gallon* (1975), *Bicentennial Gathering* (1976), *Sneak Attack* (1981), *Hell And Back* (Ryko 1994).

Miles, Butch

b. Charles Thornton, 4 July 1944, Ironton, Ohio, USA. After playing the drums as a small child, Miles later studied music in college. As a teenager, he played with a rock band, but his admiration for **Gene Krupa** inclined him towards jazz drumming. Resident in Charleston, West Virginia, he began playing with small jazz groups and in 1972 became **Mel Tormé**'s regular drummer. In 1975, he quit Tormé and offered his services to **Count Basie**. When Basie's drummer, Ray Porello, was injured in a road accident, Miles deputized for a week and stayed for four and a half years. In 1979, he joined **Dave Brubeck**, and the following year was backing **Tony Bennett**. In the 80s Miles worked extensively with small groups, sometimes as leader, accompanying such artists as **Gerry Mulligan**, **Al Cohn**, **Buddy Tate**, **Bucky Pizzarelli**, **Glenn Zottola**, **Scott Hamilton** and **Bob Wilber**. Miles also sings occasionally, proving an engaging if uninspired vocalist with a limited range. As a drummer, he is a gifted performer with an eclectic style that revealed his admiration for such big band drummers as Krupa, **Chick Webb** and **Buddy Rich**. In a small group setting he is a self-effacing and supportive player but, stylistically, he seems better suited for big band work, where he ably continues the great tradition set by his idols.
Albums: with Mel Tormé *Live At The Maisonette* (1974), with Count Basie *Montreux '77* (1977), *Basie In Europe* (1977), *Miles And Miles Of Swing* (1977), *Butch's Encore* (1977-78), *Lady Be Good* (1978), with Dave Brubeck *Back Home* (1979), *Butch Miles Salutes Chick Webb* (1979), *Butch Miles Salutes Gene Krupa* (1982), *Hail To The Chief! Butch Miles Salutes Basie* (1982), *More Miles . . . More Standards* (1985), *Jazz Express* (1986).

Miles, Dick

b. 31 January 1951, Blackheath, London, England. From early days on the folk circuit, singer and concertina player, Miles turned professional in 1976. From 1977-85 he also played with the Suffolk Bell and Horseshoe Band, and was a founder member of the New Mexborough English Concertina Quartet from 1984-88. From 1988 until 1992, he toured occasionally, both at home and abroad, with songwriter Richard Grainger, in addition to pursuing his solo career. *The Dunmow Flitch*, recorded with his then wife Sue Miles, was an album of traditional English music, released on the now defunct Sweet Folk All label, and featured **Jez Lowe**. *Home Routes* includes 'The Alimony Run', a bitter song by **Pete Coe** about marital seperation and some of it's consequences. *Playing For Time* included a variety of songs such as Lennon and McCartney's 'Yesterday'/'All My Loving', and 'From Four Until Late' by blues guitarist **Robert Johnson**, as well as more traditional material, showing the range of the English concertina. Dick has established respect for himself on the folk circuit, where he is still much in demand as a soloist. In 1990, he recorded *On Muintavara* with the Irish group Suifinn, and then performed with them from 1991-92.
During his career Miles has appeared on *Folk On Two* on BBC radio, on numerous occasions, and has performed at both the Festival Hall, and Purcell Rooms on London's South Bank. Miles now lives in Ireland and tours regularly in Ireland, England and Holland. Apart from still working occasionally with Richard Grainger, he also plays with Ril-Gan-Anim, in addition to his solo work.
Albums: with Sue Miles *The Dunmow Flitch* (1981), *Cheating The Tide* (1984), *Playing For Time* (Greenwich Village 1987), *The New Mexborough English Concertina Quartet* (1987), *On My Little Concertina* (1989), with Richard Grainger *Home Routes* (1990), with Suifinn *On Muintavara* (1990).

Miles, Garry

b. James E. Cason, 27 November 1939, Nashville, Tennessee, USA. Miles had a busy career as solo singer, group member and songwriter in the 60s. His best-known song as Garry Miles was 'Look For A Star', a Top 20 hit in 1960 on **Liberty Records**. Before that, Cason had played guitar with **Brenda Lee** and performed as part of a trio called the Statues, who scored with a Top 100 cover version of the ballad 'Blue Velvet'. 'Look For A Star' had been featured in the UK film *Circus Of Horrors* in 1960. Released under the Miles pseudonym, it reached number 16. (NB; **Garry Mills**, who had a hit with the same song, was another artist.) A few other singles were issued under the Miles name, and as the Statues, but none were hits. Cason then recorded under his other nickname, Buzz Cason, for several labels but did not have any hits under that name. He did, however, co-write the hit 'Sandy' for **Ronny And The Daytonas**, and sang background for artists including **Elvis Presley, Kenny Rogers** and **Jimmy Buffett** .

Miles, John

b. 23 April 1949, Jarrow, Tyne And Wear, England. Miles achieved international fame in 1976 with the classic rock ballad 'Music' ('music was my first love and it will be my last/the music of tomorrow, the music of the past'). His beginnings in the music business found him manufacturing toilet signs by day, but by night performing in a semi-pro band called the Influences which also included Paul Thompson (later in **Roxy Music**) and Vic Malcolm (later in **Geordie**). After this band split, Miles formed his own John Miles Band, who were successful in their native north east and also recorded for the groups own Orange label. In 1975, Miles and bassist Bob Marshall moved to London and were signed to **Decca**. Recruiting Barry Black (and later adding pianist Gary Moberly) they reached the UK Top 20 with the **Alan Parson** produced 'Highfly'. The 1976 epic length follow-up 'Music' reached number 3 and earned the band an American tour with **Elton John**. The accompanying album portrayed Miles as a moody, James Dean figure and the artist came across as such when defending his composition from quarters of the music press who unfairly ridiculed the artist as pretentious. He had two further UK hits in 'Remember Yesterday' (Top 40, 1976) and 'Slow Down' (Top 10, 1977), but Miles was forever linked with his self-confessional epic. This ultimately proved to be a burden on Miles' development and although he continued to record into the 80s, he was never able to brush off the memory of that song. On 1983's *Play On*, Miles was using a 40-piece orchestra and Elton John's old producer **Gus Dudgeon**. In the early 90s Miles took to the road with artists including **Joe Cocker** and **Tina Turner**.

Albums: *Rebel* (1976), *Stranger In The City* (1977), *Zaragon* (1978), *More Miles Per Hour* (1979), *Miles High* (1981), *Play On* (1983), *Transition* (1985), *BBC Radio 1 Live In Concert* (1993), *Upfront* (1993).

Miles, Lizzie

b. Elizabeth Mary Pajaud, nee Landreaux, 31 March 1895, New Orleans, Louisiana, USA, d. 17 March 1963. As a teenager, Miles sang with outstanding early jazzmen from the age of 16, including **Joe 'King' Oliver**, **Freddie Keppard**, **Kid Ory** and **Bunk Johnson**. By the early 20s, she had established a reputation in Chicago and New York and she toured Europe in the middle of the decade. The late 20s found her resident in New York, singing in clubs and recording with Oliver and **Jelly Roll Morton**. Illness kept her out of the business for a few years, but she returned to work in New York and Chicago in the late 30s and early 40s. Miles then abandoned her career, but she returned to nightclub work in the 50s, made records and re-established her reputation in the wake of the dixieland revival, singing with **Bob Scobey**, **Sharkey Bonano** and **George Lewis**. She retired in 1959, turning her back on music to embrace religion. Often singing in Louisiana Creole patois, Miles had a robust and earthy style which made her a distinctive performer, despite a rather narrow vocal range. Miles was an all-round entertainer, applying her powerful delivery impartially to blues, pop songs, ballads, Creole songs, and improbable Creolized (French language) versions of 'Bill Bailey' and 'A Good Man Is Hard To Find'.

Albums: *George Lewis Live At The Hangover Club* (1953-54), *Moans And Blues* (1954), with Red Camp *Torch Lullabies My Mother Sang Me* (1955).

Miley, Bubber

b. James Wesley Miley, 3 April 1903, Aiken, South Carolina, USA, d. 20 May 1932. By his late teens, trumpeter Miley was working extensively in clubs in Chicago and New York and was on the road with **Mamie Smith**. In 1923, he became a member of **Elmer Snowden**'s band, staying on when **Duke Ellington** took over as leader. His heavy drinking made him unreliable and erratic, and he left the band in 1929, touring Europe that year with **Noble Sissle**. He briefly led his own band but was stricken with tuberculosis and died in May 1932. As a formative member of Ellington's orchestra, Miley's influence remained long after his departure. His dramatic use of the plunger mute, together with growls and other unusual sounds, helped to create many of the so-called 'jungle' effects which became an integral part of Ellington's music.

Compilation: *The Indispensable Duke Ellington Vols 1/2* (1927-29 recordings).

Milk And Honey

Jerry Herman's first Broadway score, and reputedly the first Broadway musical ever to have an Israeli setting - the block buster ***Fiddler On The Roof*** came along three years after *Milk And Honey* opened on Broadway at the Martin Beck Theatre on 10 October 1961. Don Appel's book deals mainly with the romantic relationship between Phil (Robert Weede) and Ruth (Mimi Benzell), two middle-aged American tourists in Israel. At the end of the piece, their on-off affair is still unresolved, mainly due to Ruth's not unreasonable misgivings concerning Phil's wife. Molly Picon played another American tourist - but one with a mission - a widow in determined pursuit of a new husband in the shape of Mr. Horowitz (Juki Arkin). Picon, a veteran of the Yiddish theatre, also starred in the film of ***Fiddler On The Roof***. Other members of the cast included Tommy Rall and Lanna Saunders. Herman's score was acclaimed as 'melodically inventive', and particular praise was reserved for Phil and Ruth's touching 'Shalom'. However, the rest of the songs, such as 'There's No Reason In The World', 'That Was Yesterday', 'Let's Not Waste A Moment', 'Like A Young Man', 'As Simple As That', 'Chin Up, Ladies', and 'Independence Day Hora', were extremely impressive, and lingered in the memory. *Milk And Honey* ran for 543 performances - without making a profit. Still, the money would soon be rolling in for Herman: his first smash-hit, ***Hello Dolly***, was set to make its elegant entrance on Broadway in 1964.

Milkshakes

This UK, Chatham, Kent-based group were originally conceived in the late 70s by Pop Rivit roadies Mickey Hampshire and Banana Bertie as Mickey And The Milkshakes. Often appearing on the same circuit as fellow Medway town bands, the **Dentists** and the **Prisoners**, the group performed as a 'psychobilly' outfit, supporting the Pop Rivits from time to time with **Wreckless Eric** covers. Pop Rivit leader Billy Childish then began writing with Hampshire and in 1980 formed a new version of Mickey And The Milkshakes. Eventually settling on a line-up of Childish and Hampshire (guitars/vocals), Russ Wilkins (bass) and Bruce Brand (drums), they started recording a string of albums featuring various R&B classics plus original material. After the first album they truncated their name. Later on, when John Agnew replaced Wilkins, they began to refer to themselves as Thee Milkshakes. In addition to their normal activities of gigging and recording, they also acted as the backing band to an all-girl vocal trio called the Del Monas. As prolific releasers of album material, The(e) Milkshakes were only modestly successful with singles, achieving two UK independent Top 20 hits with 'Brand New Cadillac' (1984) and 'Ambassadors Of Love' (1985). The group split in 1984 (although Milkshake material continued to be released long after), with Childish going on to form the equally productive Thee Mighty Caesars.

Albums: *Talkin' 'Bout Milkshakes* (1981), *Fourteen Rhythm And Blues Greats* (1982), *After School Session* (1983), *Milkshakes IV (The Men With The Golden Guitars)* (1983), *20 Rock And Roll Hits Of The 50s & 60s* (1984), *Nothing Can Stop These Men* (1984), *The Milkshakes In Germany* (1984), *Thee Knights Of Trash* (1984), *They Came, They Saw, They Conquered* (1985), *The Last Night Down At The Mic Club* (1986), *The 107 Tapes* (1986), *The Milkshakes Vs The Prisoners Live* (1987), *The Milkshakes Revenge* (1987), *Live From Chatham* (1987), *Still Talking 'Bout* (1992).

Millenium

This Los Angeles-based act emerged in 1967, when two former members of Ballroom, producer/songwriter **Curt Boettcher** and guitarist Lee Mallory, joined forces with singer/guitarist **Michael Fennelly**. Doug Rhodes (organ/bass), Sandy Salisbury (guitar) and Ron Edgar (drums) - all ex-**Music Machine** - and Joey Stec (guitar) completed the line-up of an act enhanced considerably by the production skills of **Gary Usher**. *Begin* offered the sweet, close harmonies of west coast contemporaries the **Association** and **Harper's Bizarre** but, despite considerable acclaim, it was not a commercial success, and the unit was officially disbanded soon afterwards. The musicians also contributed to the concurrent Boettcher/Usher project, **Sagittarius**, while Fennelly, Rhodes and Edgar subsequently formed Bigshot.

Album: *Begin* (1968).

Miller, Ann

b. Lucille Ann Collier, 12 April 1919 or 1923, Chireno, Texas, USA. A vivacious, long-legged tap dancer (500 taps per minute) who achieved stardom rather late in her career via several classic film musicals of the late 40s and early 50s. After her parents were divorced when she was about 10 years old, Miller, who is of Irish, French and Cherokee descent, moved with her mother to California and supplemented the family's finances by dancing in clubs. An RKO talent scout spotted her there, and in the late 30s she made a few films for the studio, including *New Faces Of 1937*, The *Life Of The Party*, *Stage Door*, *Having A Wonderful Time*, *Tarnished Angel*, *Room Service*, and *Radio City Revels*. In 1938 she was loaned out to Columbia for the Frank Capra comedy *You Can't Take It With You* which won the Oscar for best picture. A year later she thrilled Broadway audiences by dancing 'The Mexiconga', accompanied by the Loo Sisters and Ella Logan in ***George White's Scandals***. During the early 40s she was often one of the few artists worth watching in a series of mostly low-budget features which included *Melody Ranch*, *Time Out For Rhythm*, *Go West Young Lady*, ***Reveille With Beverley***, *What's Buzzin' Cousin?*, *Jam Session*, *Carolina Blues*, and *Eadie Was A Lady* (1945). In 1948 she had good role in ***Easter Parade*** with **Fred Astaire**, **Judy Garland**, and Peter Lawford, and provided one of the film's highspots with her scintillating solo dance number 'Shaking The Blues Away'. Her performance in that film merited a seven year MGM contract, and after performing a frenetic 'Dance Of Fury' with Ricardo Montalban and **Cyd Charisse** in ***The Kissing Bandit***, joined **Frank Sinatra**, **Gene Kelly**, **Vera-Ellen**, **Betty Garrett** and Jules Munshin in one of the all-time great movie musicals, ***On The Town*** (1949). She led them all a fine dance around the anthropology museum with the clever and amusing 'Prehistoric Man'. Although she was by now around 30 years of age, Miller continued to shine during the early 50s in movies such as *Texas Carnival*, *Two Tickets To Broadway*, ***Lovely To Look At***

(which included her highly individual interpretation of 'I'll Be Hard To Handle'), and *Small Town Girl* in which she excelled again, this time with 'I Gotta Hear That Beat'. In ***Kiss Me Kate*** (1953) she played what is said to be her favourite role of Bianca, and this film was arguably the highlight of her whole career. Her memorable performances of **Cole Porter**'s marvellous 'Too Darn Hot', 'From This Moment On', 'Tom, Dick And Harry', 'Why Can't You Behave?', 'Always True To You Darling In My Fashion', and 'We Open In Venice' were a joy to behold. By now, the golden era of MGM musicals was almost over, and after guesting in the **Sigmund Romberg** biopic ***Deep In My Heart***, and emphasising just how good she still was with a top-class routine to 'The Lady From The Bayou' in ***Hit The Deck***, Miller signed off in 1956 with the ordinary *The Opposite Sex* and the non-musical *The Great American Pastime* (about baseball, of course). Like so many others, in the 60s she turned to television and nightclubs and toured in stage revivals of shows such as ***Hello, Dolly!***, ***Panama Hattie***, and ***Can-Can***. She also made a television commercial for soup in which she danced on the top of an enormous can, surrounded by water fountains, a large orchestra, and a bevy of chorus girls. In 1969 she returned to Broadway after an absence of 30 years and took over the leading role in the hit musical ***Mame*** to wide critical acclaim. In the early 70s her extensive tours in ***Anything Goes*** were interrupted for more than a year while Miller recovered from an accident in which she was struck by a sliding steel curtain. In 1979 she joined **Mickey Rooney** in ***Sugar Babies***, a celebration of the golden era of American vaudeville which ran on Broadway for 1,208 performances before touring the US for several years, and spending a brief time in London's West End in 1988. Her honours include the **George M. Cohan** Award for Best Female Entertainer, the Sarah Siddons Award for Best Actress, and an award for Best Dance Number given to her by the Dance Awards of America. The University of California presented her with its Lifetime Award and endowed a yearly drama award and scholarship in her honour. Miller's colourful private life, which has involved admirers such as Conrad Hilton and Louis B. Mayer, and failed marriages to three American oil millionaires, is documented in her autobiography. She is also interested in the paranormal and is said to believe implicitly that she is a reincarnation of the first female Pharoah of Egypt.
Further reading: *Miller's High Life*, Ann Miller.

Miller, Bob

The instrumental group Bob Miller And The Millermen appeared regularly on UK television and radio programmes in the 50s and early 60s. After being noticed at several London gigs, including one at the Locarno Ballroom, Streatham, in London, on Coronation Day, 2 June 1953, Miller appeared on BBC television's *Dig This*. He subsequently toured with current pop stars, including **Cliff Richard**, **Bobby Darin**, the **Four Freshmen** and **Shirley Bassey**. Later, on shows such as *Drumbeat* (for eight years), and the radio series, *Parade Of The Pops* ('a review of the week's popular music, and prediction of hits to come'), they backed many of the UK's top vocalists, and had their own featured spots. Their records included 'Muchacha', 'Square Bash', 'Dig This', 'The Poacher', 'Little Dipper', 'In The Mood', 'My Guy's Come Back', 'The Busker's Tune', 'Manhunt', '77 Sunset Strip', and 'Joey's Song'. for much of his life, Miller's abiding interest has been yacht racing, and in June 1972 he participated in the Transatlantic Race, providing a day-by-day radio commentary.
Selected album: *The Exciting Sounds Of Bob Miller.* (c.50s), *Bob Miller & M* (1978).

Miller, Chuck

b. California, USA. Miller was a boogie-woogie piano player who had a 1955 Top 10 single with 'The House Of Blue Lights', a rocking version of an **Andrews Sisters**' song that had previously been a hit in 1946 for its co-author, **Frank Slack**. Recorded for **Mercury Records**, the cover was Miller's only major hit. Prior to his biggest recording, Miller had recorded some tracks for **Capitol Records** and, following the number US 9 hit, he continued to try for others, with no luck. His only other chart record was 'The Auctioneer', a country song that reached number 59 later in 1956.
Album: *After Hours.*

Miller, Clarence 'Big'

b. 18 December 1922, Sioux City, Iowa, USA. Miller moved to Kansas City as a child and his style is in that city's tradition of big-voiced, sophisticated blues singing. In the late 40s and early 50s, he worked with the big bands of **Jay Mcshann**, **Lionel Hampton**, **Duke Ellington** and others. Miller began recording in 1957 for the Savoy label, and continues to record and tour internationally, primarily in a jazz context, up to the present day.

Miller, Donnie

This American guitarist and singer/songwriter was most widely renowned for his leather-clad biker image. Influenced by **Steve Earle**, **Bruce Springsteen** and the old blues masters, he specialised in a laid-back, understated approach, with fluid but economical lead guitar breaks. Signed to **Epic** Records he released *One Of The Boys*, ably assisted by Vince Kirk (second guitar), Norman Dahlor (bass), Kurt Carow (keyboards) and Tim 'Kix' Kelly (drums). The album also featured guest appearances from **Cyndi Lauper** and **Tommy Shaw** (of **Damn Yankees**). 'The Devil Wears

Lingerie' attracted some attention as a single, with its provocative and sordid promotional video, but that was effectively the last sighting of the artist.
Album: *One Of The Boys* (Epic 1989).

Miller, Duncan

The studio boffin behind such 90s UK dance chart regulars as Esoterix (whose product includes 'Void', the first release on **Positiva**, and 'Come Satisfy My Love' for Union) and Monica De Luxe ('The Temperature's Rising' and 'Don't Let This Feeling Stop'). This is only the tip of the Miller iceberg, however. He garnered an *Echoes* Single Of The Week award for 'South By South West', from his jazz-based project, As One, on Wow Records, and another creation, Feelgood Factor's 'Jump Up In The Air' also showed strongly in several club listings. Miller operates out of his own West London studio, working alongside various DJs and musicians. In this role he produced 'U Don't Have To Say You Love Me' for **React Records**, and 'Bonour M. Basie' for Wow. He has also produced a track for **Robert Owens** and provided keyboard services for remixer Frankie Foncett. His own remixing projects included working with Paul Gotel on the **Well Hung Parliament** takes of **Nu Colours**' 'The Power', McKoy's 'Fight' and **Monie Love**'s 'Never Give Up'.

Miller, Eddie

b. Edward Raymond Müller, 23 June 1911, New Orleans, Louisiana, USA, d. 6 April 1991, Los Angeles, California, USA. Miller began playing clarinet as a child and in his early teens played in street bands. Before he was 17 years old he was on his way to New York where he played with several bands, including that led by Julie Wintz which had the unenviable task of playing opposite **Fletcher Henderson** at the Roseland Ballroom. While on this engagement, Miller met Henderson's star tenor saxophonist, **Coleman Hawkins**, with whom he formed a lifelong friendship. By this time Miller had also taken up the tenor and in 1930, at the age of 19 joined **Ben Pollack**'s band where he remained until its break-up in 1934. A founder-member of the co-operative group which became known as the **Bob Crosby** Orchestra, Miller was one of the leading soloists of the band and played an important part in its huge success. He was composer of 'Slow Mood', a hit for the band. In 1943, he briefly led his own unit before entering the US army. On his discharge, following illness, he reformed a band, but by the mid-40s he had become a studio musician in Hollywood where he remained for the next 10 years. Miller appeared in the film ***Pete Kelly's Blues*** (1955) and its television spin-off series, but by the late 50s was back on the jazz circuit. In the 60s, he played dates across the USA as a single and was also a member of the band led by **Pete Fountain** as well as that run by his former Crosby soulmates **Yank Lawson** and **Bob Haggart**, the **World's Greatest Jazz Band**. During the 70s and 80s Miller continued his career, touring as a single and working with the WGJB and its later version, the Lawson-Haggart Jazz Band. Amongst his associates in the band was pianist Lou Stein, with whom he recorded a duo album, *Lazy Mood For Two*. He also appeared at several Crosby reunions. He was still active when, while with the Lawson-Haggart band in 1988, he suffered a disabling stroke which ended his playing career. A later stroke was even more damaging and he eventually died in April 1991. A fluid player with a relaxed and smoothly elegant style, Miller was at his best on ballads, although his uptempo excursions with Crosby, especially on the numbers performed by the Bobcats, the band-within-the-band, lent weight to his status as one of the best white tenor players of his generation.
Albums: *Tenor Of Jazz* (1967), *A Portrait Of Eddie* (1971), *Live At Capolinea* (c.1976), with Lou Stein *Lazy Mood For Two* (1978), *It's Miller Time* (1979), *Street Of Dreams* (1983). Compilations: with Bob Crosby *South Rampart Street Parade* (1935-42), with Crosby *Big Noise From Winnetka* (1937-42), *Soft Jive* (1943-44), *Live At Michele's Silver Stope* (Audiophile 1988), *Piano Blues 1929-34* (Blues Document 1989).
Further reading: *Stomp Off, Let's Go!: The Story Of Bob Crosby's Bob Cats & Big Band*, John Chilton.

Miller, Ernest 'Punch'

b. Ernest Burden, 10 June 1894, Raceland, Louisiana, USA. d. 2 December 1971. Miller began playing cornet as a child, playing with local dance and early jazz bands. Shortly after World War I he settled in New Orleans for a while before joining the northward migration. Resident in Chicago from the mid-20s, he played with many bands including those led by **Freddie Keppard** and **Jelly Roll Morton**. From the mid-40s he was often in New York where he recorded with **Jimmy Archey**, **Ed Hall**, **Ralph Sutton** and others and also appeared on Rudi Blesh's *This Is Jazz* radio show. By the middle of the following decade, however, he had returned to New Orleans. In the early 60s he toured with **George Lewis**. A technically proficient trumpeter, Miller's playing mingled the New Orleans tradition with a deep feeling for the blues. His solos were often pungent and moving. He sang in a casual yet engaging manner, in this department, at least, displaying the influence of **Louis Armstrong**. In 1971 he was the subject of an exceptionally fine film documentary, ***'Til The Butcher Cuts Him Down***.
Albums: *Punch Miller And His Jazz Band* (1960), *Punch Miller's Hongo Fongo Players* (1961), *Punch Miller's Bunch And George Lewis* (1962), *Punch's Delegates Of Pleasure* (1962), *Preservation Hall* (1962), *The River's In Mourning* (1962), *George Lewis And His New Orleans All Stars In Tokyo* (1963), *Oh! Lady Be Good* (1967). Compilations: *Kid Punch*

Miller: Jazz Rarities (1929-30), *The Wild Horns* (1941), *Punch Miller And His All Star Band, New York 1947* (1947), *Delegates Of Pleasure* (Jazzology 1990).

Miller, Frankie

b. 1950, Glasgow, Scotland. Miller commenced his singing career in the late 60s group, the Stoics. Along with **Robin Trower**, Jim Dewar and Clive Bunker, he formed the short-lived Jude, whose potential was never captured on vinyl. With **Brinsley Schwarz** as his backing unit, Miller recorded his first solo album, *Once In A Blue Moon*, in 1972. The following year he moved to New Orleans to work with **Allen Toussaint** on the highly regarded *High Life*, which displayed Miller's throaty, blues-styled vocals to considerable effect. Although the album did not sell well, it provided hit singles for both **Three Dog Night** and **Bette Wright**. By 1975, Miller had formed a full-time band featuring **Henry McCullough**, **Mick Weaver**, Chrissie Stewart and Stu Perry. Their album, *The Rock*, was a solid effort, but met with middling sales. With a completely new band comprising Ray Minhinnit (guitar), Charlie Harrison (bass), James Hall (keyboards) and Graham Deacon (drums), Miller next recorded *Full House*. The band of the same name lasted a year before Miller reverted to a solo excursion for *Perfect Fit*. The latter provided a surprise Top 10 UK hit with 'Darlin'', but Miller could not build on that success. His frequent change of musicians and producers has resulted in an erratic career which has always remained tantalisingly short of a major leap into the top league of white blues performers. Nevertheless, his live performances are as popular as ever, while his back catalogue has grown substantially over the years.

Albums: *Once In A Blue Moon* (1972), *High Life* (1973), *The Rock* (1975), *Full House* (1977), *Double Trouble* (1978), *Falling In Love* (1979), *Perfect Fit* (1979), *Easy Money* (1980), *Standing On The Edge* (1982), *Rockin' Rollin' Frankie Miller* (1983), *Hey, Where Ya Goin'* (1984), *Dancing In The Rain* (1986). Compilation: *Best Of* (1992).

Miller, Gary

b. Neville Williams, 1924, Blackpool, Lancashire, England, d. 15 June 1968, London, England. Miller was a popular singer in the UK during the 50s and early 60s, with a smooth and polished style. As a young man, Miller was a talented soccer player and played for Blackpool Football Club as an amateur. During World War II, he served as a lieutenant in the Royal Navy Volunteer Reserve and, on release, enrolled as a student at London University with the intention of becoming a teacher of languages. After performing in college concerts, and with the experience of singing at a Welsh Eisteddfod festival as a schoolboy, Miller embarked on the learning process of small-time cabaret and concert tours, and made his first radio broadcast on *Beginners, Please*. As well as singing, he also included dancing in his act, and was involved in negotiations for a small part in the Ray Bolger movie, *Where's Charley?*, when it was being made in England, but nothing materialized. His first real break came when he was discovered by record executive and songwriter **Norman Newell** during a Variety appearance at Northampton, which led to him making a few tracks for **Columbia**. He also made regular appearances, singing and dancing, on television in *Shop Window*, and appeared on the fortnightly *Kaleidoscope* series. By 1954, he was headlining in variety on the Moss Empires circuit. After a spell with Newell at the newly-formed Philips Records in 1953, during which he released mostly romantic ballads, Miller switched to another new label, Pye Nixa, and started recording more uptempo material. His first hit, 'Yellow Rose Of Texas', in 1955, was overtaken by the US **Mitch Miller** version, but 'Robin Hood' made the Top 10 despite opposition from **Dick James**, who benefitted by having his version played over the titles during the weekly television show. During that era it was commonplace for several versions of the same song to jostle each other in the singles chart. This was the case with Miller's 'Garden Of Eden', which lost out to **Frankie Vaughan**. There was also strong competition on 'Wonderful, Wonderful' from **Ronnie Hilton**, and on 'The Story Of My Life' from **Michael Holliday**. Miller's record of the latter song is said to have suffered in popularity because he was touring North Africa at the time of its release. Perhaps in an effort to avoid the competition, Miller reached back to 1945 for his final chart entry, 'I've Heard That Song Before' (1961); it proved to be one of his best vocal performances. His first album, *Meet Mister Miller*, contained standards such as 'Manhattan', 'April Showers' and 'Stella By Starlight'. This was followed by *Gary On The Ball*, with the **Kenny Ball** Jazz Band. In 1964, Miller appeared in the West End production of *She Loves Me*, Jerry Bock and Sheldon Harnick's musical based on the Hungarian play, *Perfumerie*. He returned to the London stage in 1966 to play the role of the crooning Agent VO3 in Bryan Blackburn's comedy musical, *Come Spy With Me*, starring female impersonator Danny La Rue, at London's 'home of farce', the Whitehall Theatre. Two years later he died of a heart attack at his south London home.

Miller, Glenn

b. 1 March 1904, Clarinda, Iowa, USA, d. 15 December 1944. Miller was the first artist to be credited with a million-selling disc (for 'Chattanooga Choo Choo'), and was the toast of North American popular music during World War II for his uniformed orchestra's fusion of sober virtuosity, infectious dance rhythms and varied intonation of brass and woodwind. In Miller's hands, close harmony vocals - often wordless - were almost incidental in a slick repertoire that embraced Tin Pan Alley standards ('April In Paris', **Hoagy Carmichael**'s 'The Nearness Of You'), jump blues ('St. Louis Blues', **Jelly Roll Morton**'s 'King Porter Stomp'), western swing ('Blueberry Hill', once sung by **Gene Autry**) and mainstream jazz ('Jersey Bounce', 'Tuxedo Junction'), also exemplified by the 'hotter' big bands of **Artie Shaw** and **Jimmy Dorsey**. After his family moved to North Platts, Nebraska, Miller's trombone skills earned him places in bands operational within his Fort Morgan high school, and afterwards at the University of Colorado. On becoming a professional musician, he found work on the west coast and in New York as both a player and arranger - notably for **Victor Young**, whose Los Angeles studio orchestra accompanied **Judy Garland** and **Bing Crosby**. Other prestigious feathers in Miller's cap were his supervision of Britain's **Ray Noble** And The New Mayfair Orchestra's first USA tour and a scoring commission for **Columbia Records**. His earnings were ploughed back into the organization and rehearsal of his own band which, despite setbacks such as his wife's long illness in 1938, built up a huge following in New York, through dogged rounds of one-night-stands and record-breaking residencies in venues such as Pompton Turnpike roadhouse and the celebrated Glen Island Casino.

Signed to **RCA** in 1939, Miller proved a sound investment with immediate consecutive best-sellers in evocative classics such as 'Little Brown Jug' (written in 1869), 'In The Mood' and 'Sunrise Serenade'. The latter was coupled with 'Moonlight Serenade' - a strikingly effective extrapolation of a trombone exercise that became Miller's signature tune. As synonymous with him, too, was 1940's 'Chattanooga Choo Choo' with a chorus (by **Tex Beneke**, **Marion Hutton** and the **Modernaires**) atypically to the fore. This novelty was also among highlights of ***Sun Valley Serenade*** (1941), the orchestra's first movie (co-starring Norwegian ice-skating champion, Sonja Henie). Other Miller classics included the irresistible 'Pennsylvania 6-5000' and the haunting 'Tuxedo Junction'. At Miller's commercial peak the next year, ***Orchestra Wives*** (1942, with Ann Rutherford and Cesar Romero), enveloped a similarly vacuous plot with musical interludes that included another smash in '(I've Got A Gal In) Kalamazoo'. The enduring lyric brilliantly used the alphabet; 'a b c d e f g h I got a gal in Kalamazoo'. That same year also brought both Miller's lively hit arrangement of 'American Patrol' and his enlistment into the US Army. Even though he was too old for combat he still volunteered out of patriotism, was elevated to the rank of Captain and sent out to entertain the Allied forces. He was promoted to major in August 1944. Following a visit to Britain, his aircraft disappeared over the English Channel on 15 December 1944.

His death was an assumption that some devotees found too grievous to bear, and rumours of his survival persisted. In any case, his orchestra lived on - even if the economics of staying on the road, combined with the rise of rock 'n' roll, finished off lesser rivals. Universal Pictures produced the immensely successful 1954 bio-pic, ***The Glenn Miller Story*** (with James Stewart in the title role). An Oscar-nominated soundtrack album (directed by **Henry Mancini**) was released, and a re-issued 'Moonlight Serenade' reached number 12 in the UK singles charts. Miller's habit of preserving many of his radio broadcasts on private discs enabled the issue of another album, *Marvellous Miller Moods*. Also reaching the US chart in the late 50s was a 1939 Carnegie Hall concert recording and *The New Glenn Miller Orchestra In Hi-Fi*.

Miller's original arrangements were regarded as definitive by those multitudes who continued to put repackagings such as *The Real Glenn Miller And His Orchestra* high into the international charts as late as 1977. The sound was recreated so precisely by the **Syd Lawrence** Orchestra that it was employed in a 1969 television documentary of the late bandleader whose UK fan club booked Lawrence regularly for its annual tribute shows. Among best tributes paid were those by **Manhattan Transfer** in a 1976 version of 'Tuxedo Junction', and Jive Bunny And The Mastermixers whose 1989 medley, 'Swing The Mood' - a UK number 1 - was sandwiched between excerpts of 'In The Mood', sampled from Miller's 1938 recording. The arranging style perfected by Miller's staff arrangers, notably **Jerry Gray**, continued to influence several middle of the road writers and bandleaders during the next two or three decades. Curiously enough, for a musician whose work is now preserved eternally in its 40s style, Miller was always eager to move on. Shortly before his death he remarked to McKinley that the style that had made him famous was no longer of interest to him, 'I've gone as far as I can go with the saxophone sound. I've got to have something new'. The enduring quality of Miller's work is most forcibly underlined by the realization that his tunes have become part of the instant musical vocabulary of listeners young and old. In 1995, just over 50 years after Miller's death, a set of recordings made by the American Band of the AEF at the Abbey Road studios in London late in 1944, was released as a 2-CD set.

Selected albums: *The Glenn Miller Story* (1954), *Marvellous Miller Moods* (1957), *The New Glenn Miller Orchestra In Hi Fi* (1957), *The Glenn Miller Carnegie Hall Concert* (1958), *Glenn Miller Plays Selections From 'The Glenn MIller Story' And Other Hits* (1961), *The Best Of Glenn Miller* (1969), *The Nearness Of You* (1969), *A Memorial 1944-1969* (1970), *The Real Glenn Miller And His Orchestra Play The Original Music From The Film 'The Glenn Miller Story' And Other Hits* (1971), *A Legendary Performer* (1975), *A Legendary Performer Vol.2* (1976), *The Unforgettable Glenn Miller* (1977), *Glenn Miller Army Air Force Band (1943-44)* (1981), *Chesterfield*

Shows 1941-42 (1984), *Chesterfield Shows - Chicago 1940* (1984), *Chesterfield Shows - New York City 1940* (1984), *Glenn Miller Airforce Orchestra, June 10, 1944* (1984), *April 3, 1940 Chesterfield Show* (1989), *The Glenn Miller Gold Collection* (1993), *Live At The Café Rouge* (1994), *The Lost Recordings* (Happy Days 1995, 2-CD set).
Further reading: *Next To A Letter From Home - Major Glenn Miller's Wartime Band*, Geoffrey Butcher. *Glen Miller & His Orchestra*, George Thomas Simon.

Miller, Harry

b. 21 April 1941, Johannesburg, South Africa, d. 16 December 1983. A highly impressive and emotional bass player, Miller played R&B (with **Manfred Mann**) in South Africa. He moved to the UK in 1961, and then worked in bands on transatlantic liners, so that he heard New York jazz at first hand. Settling back in London, he made a reputation playing with **John Surman**, **Keith Tippett** (Ovary Lodge and Centipede), **Dudu Pukwana** (Spear), **Elton Dean** (Ninesense and Just Us), **Stan Tracey** (Tentacles and the Octet), **Alan Skidmore** (part of the quintet that won the 1969 Press prize at Montreux), **Louis Moholo**, Kenneth Terroade, **Chris McGregor**, **Mike Westbrook** and **Mike Osborne**, forming, with Louis Moholo, the superb Mike Osborne Trio for several years. He also worked in a trio with Moholo and **Peter Brötzmann**. He also led bands of his own, notably the ferocious and all-star Isipingo, and the Quartette A Tête, which he co-founded with Tippet, Radu Malfatti and Paul Lytton. He co-founded the Lambeth New Music Society and Ogun records, both of which showcased many of the best UK-based musicians. He also ran regular gigs through his Grass Roots agency. He died as a result of a road-accident in 1983. His widow, Hazel, continues to make an important contribution to the scene through Ogun, and by the intermittent, tenacious organisation of benefits and other gigs.
Selected albums: *Children At Play* (1974), with Isipingo *Family Affair* (1977), *In Conference* (1978), with Radu Malfatti *Bracknell Breakdown* (1978), with Peter Brötzmann, Louis Moholo *The Nearer The Bone The Sweeter The Meat* (1980), with Brötzmann, Moholo *Opened, But Hardly Touched* (1981), with Malfatti *Zwecknagel* (1981).

Miller, J.D. 'Jay'

b. c.1922, El Campo, Texas, USA. One of the best-known and most successful record producers from Louisiana, Miller started out as a musician, playing with country and Cajun bands around Lake Charles from the late 30s. After a spell in the services, he started to make records, aimed at a small localised market for Cajun music in southwest Louisiana; these, by obscure artists such as Lee Sonnier and Amidie Breaux, were among the first records in the idiom to appear after the war, and established his position as a pioneer in the field. He continued to record Cajun music and C&W on his Feature and Fais Do-Do labels, including the earliest records by **Jimmie C. Newman** and **Doug Kershaw**, and later on Kajun and Cajun Classics, which featured important figures such as Nathan Abshire and Aldus Roger. However, it was when he turned his attention in the mid-50s to black music that Miller began to develop his best-known and most enduring legacy. Between 1954, when he first recorded **Lightnin' Slim** and the early 60s, he established an extraordinary list of artists, including Slim, **Lonesome Sundown**, **Slim Harpo**, **Lazy Lester**, **Silas Hogan** and many others, whose work he leased to the Nashville label, Excello. He also continued to release records on labels of his own, Zynn and Rocko, including rockabilly and local pop by artists such as Johnny Jano and Warren Storm, and in the 70s, on Blues Unlimited. His list of artists is enormous, but just as important was the characteristic sound he achieved in his studio in Crowley, which has become inextricably linked with the indigenous sounds of Louisiana.

Miller, Jacob

b. c.1955, Jamaica, West Indies, d. 23 March, 1980. Miller recorded his first record for **Coxsone Dodd**, entitled 'Love Is A Message' (aka 'Let Me Love You') in 1968, aged just 13. The song did little business though, and Miller had to wait a few years before he returned to the studio. In 1974 he recorded a number of singles for **Augustus Pablo**, including 'Each One Teach One', 'Keep On Knocking', 'False Rasta', 'Who Say Jah No Dread' and 'Baby I Love You So', most of which were popular on the pre-release circuit in the UK. Unfortunately when **Island** released 'Baby I Love You So' they failed to credit Miller, and even relegated his vocal to the b-side in favour of its thrashing **King Tubby**'s/Pablo dub, 'King Tubby's Meets Rockers Uptown'. Miller's biggest hits would come as a member of **Inner Circle**. In 1976 they scored a couple of roots hits with 'Tenement Yard' and 'Tired Fe Lick Weed In A Bush' (both credited to Miller). These and Miller's explosive stage act made them the top act in Jamaica in the latter part of the 70s. Miller, an exuberant, amply proportioned man, possessed of a fine tenor which often employed a trademark stutter, went on to make a number of excellent records with Inner Circle, including 'All Night Till Daylight' and 'Forward Jah Jah Children'. He took part in the notorious 1978 One Love Peace Concert in Kingston, where **Bob Marley** joined hands with Edward Seaga and Michael Manley, flanked by representatives of Kingston's warring factions, and starred via an amusing cameo in the 1979 film, *Rockers*. He died in a road crash on March 23rd 1980.
Albums: *Killer Miller* (Top Ranking 1978, RAS 1988), *Natty Christmas* (Top Ranking 1978, RAS 1988),

Unfinished Symphony (Circle 1984), *Who Say Jah No Dread* (Greensleeves 1992). Compilations: *Reggae Greats* (Island 1985), *Greatest Hits* (RAS 1988).

Miller, Jimmy

b. 1942, New York, USA, d. 22 October 1994, Denver, Colorado, USA. Record producer Miller arrived in Britain during the mid-60s. His 1965 composition, 'Incense', was recorded by the Anglos, a studio group which featured **Steve Winwood** (as Steve Anglo) on vocals. Miller later co-wrote and produced 'I'm A Man', Winwood's final single with the **Spencer Davis Group**. Their association continued on Winwood's next venture, **Traffic**. Miller's unfussy style allowed the group to blossom, a feature prevalent in his work with another contemporary unit, **Spooky Tooth**. However, he gained his outstanding reputation for work with the **Rolling Stones**. *Beggar's Banquet* marked the group's return to basics in the wake of psychedelic ephemera, and Miller's natural but dynamic technique resulted in several classic performances, including 'Street Fighting Man', 'Sympathy For The Devil' and 'Stray Cat Blues'. His contribution to what is arguably the Stones' finest period, which encompassed *Let It Bleed*, *Sticky Fingers* and *Exile On Main Street*, cannot be over-emphasized, but their mutually beneficial collaboration ended with the release of *It's Only Rock 'N' Roll*. Miller's own profile diminished with this severance, but he remained one of the most important producers to emerge during the late 60s.

Miller, Jody

b. 29 November 1941, Phoenix, Arizona, USA, but raised in Blanchard, Oklahoma. Miller's father loved country music and played fiddle, and all her four sisters were singers. She led a folk trio while still at school and, after graduation, moved to California to pursue a singing career, but a severe car accident forced her to return home. She established herself locally, after appearing on **Tom Paxton**'s television show, and she gained a reputation as a folk singer. Actor Dale Robertson introduced her to **Capitol Records**, and her first album, *Wednesday's Child*, was a blend of folk and pop music. Her first US chart success was with 'He Walks Like A Man' and then she went to number 12 with the answer to **Roger Miller**'s 'King Of The Road', 'Queen Of The House'. As a result, she won a Grammy for the best female country performance. She recorded a dramatic teen anthem about being misunderstood, 'Home Of The Brave', which was more significant than its chart placings imply (US 25/UK49). This, however, was a one-off as she then recorded more conventional country hits, having some success with 'Long Black Limousine'. In 1968, she left the business to raise a daughter, but returned to work with producer **Billy Sherrill** in Nashville in 1970. Her first success was with a **Tony Hatch** song, 'Look At Mine'. She then scored with country versions of pop hits, 'He's So Fine', 'Baby I'm Yours' and 'Be My Baby'. A duet with **Johnny Paycheck**, 'Let's All Go Down The River', also fared well. She made little attempt to change with the times and in the early 80s, she retired to breed quarter horses on a 1,000 acre ranch in Blanchard, Oklahoma.

Albums: *Wednesday's Child Is Full Of Woe* (1963), *Jody Miller* (1965), *Home Of The Brave* (1965), *Queen Of The House* (1965), *Jody Miller Sings The Great Hits Of Buck Owens* (1966), *The Nashville Sound Of Jody Miller* (1969), *Look At Mine* (1970), *There's A Party Goin' On* (1972), *He's So Fine* (1972), *Good News* (1973), *House Of The Rising Sun* (1974), *Country Girl* (1975), *Will You Love Me Tomorrow?* (1976), *Here's Jody Miller* (1977).

Miller, Marcus

b. 14 June 1959, New York City, New York, USA. Taking up the electric bass in his teens, Miller's early musical experience came from the New York soul scene. Flautist **Bobbi Humphrey** gave him his first serious work in the jazz idiom in 1977, which was quickly followed by a tour with **Lenny White**'s group. Becoming competent on an impressive number of instruments, Miller's reputation grew in the New York studio world. By 1980, he had recorded for **Bob James**, **Grover Washington Jnr.**, **Roberta Flack**, and **Aretha Franklin**. In 1980, he joined **Miles Davis**, but left after two years for the financial lure of session work, producing and playing on several albums for **David Sanborn**. The second and more important period of Miller's relationship with Miles Davis began in 1986, when he played almost every instrument, and wrote most of the music for *Tutu*, Davis' first album for **Warner Brothers**. Davis had never before given away so much artistic control, but must have been pleased with the result, for Miller worked just as closely with him on his *Siesta* and *Amandlia* albums. He continues to work as one of New York's top studio musicians.

Albums: with Miles Davis *The Man With The Horn* (1981), with Davis *We Want Miles* (1981), with Davis *Tutu* (1986), with Davis *Siesta* (1988), with Davis *Amandlia* (1989) *The Sun Don't Lie* (Dreyfus Jazz Line 1993).

Miller, Mitch

b. Mitchell William Miller, 4 July 1911, Rochester, New York, USA. An oboist, record producer, arranger and one of the most commercially successful recording artists of the 50s and early 60s. He learned to play the piano at the age of six, and began studying the oboe when he was 12, and later attended Rochester's Eastman School of Music. After graduating in 1932, Miller played oboe with symphony orchestras in the area, before joining CBS Radio in 1932. For the next 11 years he was a soloist with the CBS Symphony, and played with **André Kostelanetz**, **Percy Faith**, the Saidenburg Little Symphony, and the Budapest String Quartet. In the later 40s he became director of **Mercury Records**' 'pop' division, and then, in 1950, was appointed head of A&R at **Columbia**. While at Mercury, Miller was responsible for producing several big hits, including **Frankie Laine**'s 'That Lucky Old Sun', 'Mule Train' and 'The Cry Of The Wild Goose'. Miller also conducted the orchestra on Laine's 'Jezebel' and 'Rose, Rose, I Love You'. Shortly after he left the label, **Patti Page** released 'The Tennessee Waltz', which became one of the biggest-selling singles ever. The original was by R&B singer, **Erskine Hawkins**, and the Page disc is sometimes credited as being the first really successful example of 'crossover' from country to pop, although Miller had already fashioned **Hank Williams**' 'Hey, Good Lookin'' into a minor hit for Frankie Laine and **Jo Stafford**. Miller developed this policy when he moved to Columbia, and recorded **Guy Mitchell** ('Singing The Blues' and 'Knee Deep In The Blues'), **Tony Bennett** ('Cold, Cold Heart'), **Rosemary Clooney** ('Half As Much'), Jo Stafford ('Jambalaya') and the little known **Joan Weber** ('Let Me Go Lover'). Miller's roster at Columbia also included **Johnnie Ray** ('Cry', 'The Little White Cloud That Cried', 'Just Crying In The Rain') and **Frank Sinatra**.

There was little empathy between Miller and Sinatra, and the singer rejected several songs which eventually became successful for Guy Mitchell. After he left Columbia, Sinatra sent telegrams to judiciary and senate committees, accusing Miller of presenting him with inferior songs, and of accepting money from writers whose songs he (Miller) had used. Certainly, Sinatra recorded some unsuitable material under Miller's auspices during his final years with label; although 'American Beauty Rose' and 'Goodnight, Irene', both with Miller's accompaniment, and 'Bim Bam Baby', paled in comparison with perhaps the most bizarre item of all, 'Mama Will Bark', on which Sinatra made barking and growling noises, and duetted with Miller's latest signing, a female named Dagmar.

Miller's own hit recordings, mostly credited to 'Mitch Miller And His Gang', began in 1950 with his adaptation of the Israeli folk song 'Tzena, Tzena, Tzena', complete with a happy vocal chorus which would typify his later work. After 'Meet Mr. Callaghan', 'Without My Lover', 'Under Paris Skies' and 'Napoleon' in the early 50s, he spent six weeks at number 1 with the million-selling 'The Yellow Rose Of Texas', one of the great marching songs from the American Civil War. This was followed by three instrumentals: 'Lisbon Antigua', 'Song For A Summer Night (Parts 1 & 2)', and 'March From The River Kwai And Colonel Bogey'. There was also the novelty 'The Children's Marching Song' from the 1959 film *The Inn Of The Sixth Happiness*. The previous year, Miller had started his series of *Sing Along With Mitch* albums, which featured an all-male chorus singing old favourites, many from before the turn of the century. Nineteen variations on the theme made the US Top 40 between 1958 and 1962, of which seven titles achieved million-selling status. The phenomenally successful *Sing Along* formula was developed as a popular television series which ran from 1961-66, and featured several solo singers such as Victor Griffin, Leslie Uggams and Louise O'Brien. Despite the obvious financial gain to Columbia from his records sales, Miller was constantly criticized for his negative attitude towards rock 'n' roll. He turned down **Buddy Holly**, among others, and was blamed for his company's relatively small market share in the rapidly changing music scene during his tenure as an influential executive. On the other hand, his promotion of the artists already mentioned, plus **Doris Day** ('Que Sera, Sera'), **Johnny Mathis**, Percy Faith, and many more, substantially aided Columbia. Out of place in the 'swinging 60s', he nevertheless emerged occasionally to conduct the orchestra on various light and classical music recordings.

Selected albums: *Sing Along With Mitch* (1958), *Christmas Sing Along...* (1958), *More Sing Along...* (1958), *Still More! Sing Along...* (1959), *Folk Songs Sing Along...* (1959), *Party Sing Along...* (1959), *Fireside Sing Along...* (1959), *Saturday Night Sing Along...* (1960), *Sentimental Sing Along...* (1960), *March Along...* (1960), *Memories Sing Along...* (1960), *Happy Times! Sing Along...* (1961), *TV Sing Along...* (1961), *Your Request Sing Along...* (1961), *Holiday Sing Along...* (1961), *Rhythm Sing Along...* (1962), *Family Sing Along...* (1962). Compilation: *Mitch's Greatest Hits* (1961).

Miller, Mrs

Mrs Miller (b. Elva Miller, California, USA) derives her chief notoriety from her popularity among collectors of musical exotica. Her *modus operandi* involves a seasoned though tuneless melodramatic delivery, accompanying whistles and wholly indulgent, untutored phrasing. Her versions of 'Catch A Falling Star' and 'A Hard Day's Night' reveal her as a natural precursor to the worst elements of karaoke, though she did manage chart entries for the atonal splendour of 'Downtown' and 'Lover's Concerto'.

Selected album: *Greatest Hits* (Capitol 1966).

Miller, Mulgrew

b. 13 April 1955, Greenwood, Massachusetts, USA. Miller learnt the piano while a child and studied music at university, all the while playing in local gospel and R&B groups. After playing with **Mercer Ellington**'s Orchestra in the late 70s, he joined vocalist **Betty Carter** before moving on to the quintet of **Woody Shaw** and **Art Blakey**'s **Jazz Messengers** (1983-86). He has added all the innovations of recent piano playing to this solid background, and fused them with a brilliant technique. In the late 80s he continued with his prolific studio career and played with the quintet of **Tony Williams**.

Albums: with Art Blakey *Blue Night* (1985), *Keys To The City* (1985), *Live At Sweet Basil's* (1985), *Work!* (1986), with James Spalding *Gotshabe A Better Way* (1988), with Benny Golson *Benny Golson Quartet* (1990), with Kenny Garrett *African Exchange Student* (1990), *Time And Again* (1992), *Hand In Hand* (1993).

Miller, Ned

b. Henry Ned Miller, 12 April 1925, Raines, Utah, USA. When Miller was a small child, the family moved to Salt Lake City, Utah where, after completing his education, he worked as a pipe fitter. He became interested in songwriting and country music, learned to play the guitar, but had no real inclination to be a performer. In the mid-50s, he married and moved to California, where he hoped to sell some of his songs and joined the Fabor label as a writer and/or performer. Early in 1957, a deal between Fabor and **Dot Records**, which gave the latter label first choice of all Fabor masters, saw two of his songs, 'Dark Moon' and 'A Fallen Star', both become US country and pop hits for **Bonnie Guitar** and **Jimmy C. Newman** respectively. Miller himself played guitar on the former recording, which also was a number 4 US pop hit for **Gale Storm**. The song became a UK Top 20 pop hit for **Tony Brent** and was also recorded by the **Kaye Sisters** and **Joe Loss** And His Orchestra. In July 1957, Miller's most famous song appeared when, as a result of a game of patience, he wrote 'From A Jack To A King'. Both his own version and a pop one by Jim Lowe were released by Dot, but created no major impression. From the start, Miller had little interest in a career as a singer and detested touring, he suffered constantly with stage fright and shyness, and was always a most reluctant performer. Stories are told of him on occasions actually sending a friend to perform as Ned Miller in his place. Although he made some further recordings, including 'Lights In The Street' and 'Turn Back', he achieved no chart success and concentrated on his writing. Between 1959 and 1961, he recorded briefly for Jackpot and **Capitol**.

In 1962, he persuaded Fabor Robison to reissue his recording of 'From A Jack To A King' and this time, despite Miller's reluctance to tour and publicise the song, it became a number 2 country and number 6 pop hit. Released in the UK on the London label, it also soon reached number 2 in the UK pop charts. 'From A Jack To A King', an old-fashioned, traditional sounding country song, was hardly a record that was ahead of its time, but it became an extraordinary success in Britain, where, in April 1963, it held the number 2 position for four weeks - in spite of the fact that there was no promotion from either the artist or label, and it went against the grain of songs that were hits at the time. It obviously says much for the quality of the song. Further Fabor recordings followed and Miller had Top 20 US country and pop hits with 'Invisible Tears' (1964) and 'Do What You Do Do Well' (1965). (The latter number also made a brief appearance in the British pop charts.) He returned to Capitol in 1965, and had five minor hits before being dropped by the label, again due to his unwillingness to tour. He moved to Republic where, in 1970, he achieved his last chart entry with 'The Lover's Song'. He then gave up recording and after moving to Prescott, Arizona, finally wrote his last song in the mid-70s. After eight years at Prescott, he settled in Las Vegas where he completely withdrew from all public appearances and gave up songwriting. In 1991, the German Bear Family label released a 31 track CD of his work, which included some previously unissued material.

Albums: *From A Jack To A King* i (1963), *Ned Miller (Sings The Songs Of Ned Miller)* (1965), *Teardrop Lane* (1967), *In The Name Of Love* (1968), *Ned Miller's Back* (1970), *From A Jack To A King* ii (1981), *From A Jack To A King* iii (1991).

Miller, Roger

b. 2 January 1936, Fort Worth, Texas, USA, d. 25 October 1992, Los Angeles, California, USA. Miller was brought up in Erick, Oklahoma, and, during the late 50s, moved to Nashville, where he worked as a songwriter. His 'Invitation To The Blues' was a minor success for **Ray Price**, as was '(In The Summertime) You Don't Want Love' for **Andy Williams**. Miller himself enjoyed a hit on the country charts, with the portentously titled 'When Two Worlds Collide'. In 1962, he joined **Faron Young**'s band as a drummer and also wrote 'Swiss Maid', a major hit for **Del Shannon**. By 1964, Miller was signed to **Mercury**'s Smash label, and secured a US Top 10 hit with 'Dang Me'. The colloquial title was reinforced by some humorous, macabre lyrics ('They ought to take a rope and hang me'). The song brought Miller several Grammy awards, and the following year, he enjoyed an international Top 10 hit with 'King Of The Road'. This stoical celebration of the hobo life, with its jazz-influenced undertones, became his best-known song. The relaxed 'Engine Engine No. 9' was another US Top 10 hit during 1965, and at the end of the year, Miller once more turned his attention to the UK market with 'England Swings'. This affectionate, slightly bemused tribute to swinging London at its zenith neatly summed up the tourist brochure view of the city ('bobbies on bicycles two by two . . . the rosy red cheeks of the little children'). Another international hit, the song was forever associated with Miller. The singer's chart fortunes declined the following year, and a questionable cover of **Elvis Presley**'s 'Heartbreak Hotel' barely reached the US Top 100. In 1968, Miller secured his last major hit with a poignant reading of

Bobby Russell's 'Little Green Apples', which perfectly suited his understated vocal style. Thereafter, Miller moved increasingly towards the country market and continued performing regularly throughout America. In 1982, he appeared on the album *Old Friends* with Ray Price and **Willie Nelson**. Miller's vocals were featured in the Walt Disney cartoon *Robin Hood*, and in the mid-80s he wrote a Broadway musical, ***Big River***, based on Mark Twain's *The Adventures Of Huckleberry Finn*.

Roger Miller finally lost his battle with cancer when, with his wife Mary and son Roger Jnr. at his bedside, he died on 25 October 1992. A most popular man with his fellow artists, he was also a great humorist and his general outlook was adequetly summed up when he once told the backing band on the *Grand Ole Opry*, 'I do this in the key of B natural, which is my philosophy in life.'

Albums: *Roger And Out* (1964), *The Return Of Roger Miller* (1965), *The 3rd Time* (1965), *Words And Music* (1966), *Walkin' In The Sunshine* (1967), *A Tender Look At Love* (1968), *Roger Miller* (1969). *Roger Miller* (1970), *Off The Wall* (1978), *Making A Name For Myself* (1980), *Motive Series* (1981), *Old Friends* (1982), *Roger Miller* (1987), *The Big Industry* (1988), Compilation: *Little Green Apples* (1976), *Best Of Roger Miller* (1978), *Greatest Hits* (1985).

Miller, Steve

b. 5 October 1943, Milwaukee, Wisconsin, USA. The young Miller was set on his musical path by having **Les Paul** as a family friend, and a father who openly encouraged music in the home. His first band, the Marksmen, was with school friend **Boz Scaggs**; also with Scaggs, he formed the college band, the Ardells, and at university they became the Fabulous Night Trains. He moved to Chicago in 1964, and became involved in the local blues scene with **Barry Goldberg**, resulting in the Goldberg Miller Blues Band. Miller eventually moved to San Francisco in 1966, after hearing about the growing hippie music scene, and formed the Miller Blues Band. Within a year he had built a considerable reputation and as the Steve Miller Band, he signed with **Capitol Records** for a then unprecedented $50,000, following his appearance at the 1967 **Monterey Pop Festival**. The band at that time included **Boz Scaggs**, Lonnie Turner, Jim Peterman and Tim Davis, and it was this line-up that was flown to London to record the **Glyn Johns**-produced *Children Of The Future*. The album was a critical success although sales were moderate, but it was *Sailor* later that same year which became his *pièce de résistance*. The clear production and memorable songs have lasted well and it remains a critics' favourite. Miller's silky-smooth voice and masterful guitar gave the album a touch of class that many of the other San Francisco rock albums lacked. The atmospheric instrumental 'Song For Our Ancestors' and well-crafted love songs like 'Dear Mary' and 'Quicksilver Girl' were just three of the many outstanding tracks. Scaggs and Peterman departed after this album, and Miller added the talented **Nicky Hopkins** on keyboards for *Brave New World*, which completed a trio of albums recorded in London with Johns. The blistering 'My Dark Hour' featured **Paul McCartney** (as Paul Ramon) on bass, while the epic 'Cow Cow' showed off Hopkins' sensitive piano.

The excellent *Your Saving Grace* maintained the quality of previous albums and repeated the success. Lonnie Turner and Hopkins left at the end of 1969, and Miller replaced Turner with Bobby Winkleman from local band **Frumious Bandersnatch**. *Number 5* completed a cycle of excellent albums which hovered around similar chart positions, indicating that while Miller was highly popular, he was not expanding his audience. He decided to change the format for *Rock Love*, by having half of the album live. Unfortunately, he chose to record a live set with arguably his weakest band; both Ros Valory and Jack King left within a year and the album sold poorly. Following a European tour, and in an attempt to reverse the trend of his last album, he released *Recall The Beginning . . . A Journey From Eden*, a perplexing album which showed Miller in a melancholic and lethargic mood; once again, Miller's fortunes declined further with poor sales.

After a gap of 18 months, Miller returned with the US chart-topping single 'The Joker', an easily contrived song over a simple riff in which Miller mentioned all references to his various self-titled aliases used in songs over the past years: 'Some people call me the Space Cowboy (*Brave New World*), some call me the Gangster Of Love (*Sailor*), some call me Maurice (*Recall The Beginning*) . . .'. The accompanying album was a similar success, stalling at number 2. His future had never looked brighter, but Miller chose to buy a farm and build a recording studio and he effectively vanished.

When he re-appeared on record three years later, only his loyal fans rated his commercial chances; however, the stunning *Fly Like An Eagle* became his best-selling album of all time and was a major breakthrough in the UK. This record, with its then state-of-the-art recording, won him many new fans, and finally put him in the major league as one of America's biggest acts. Almost as successful was the sister album *Book Of Dreams* (1977); they both gave him a number of major singles including the simplistic 'Rock 'N' Me' and the uplifting 'Jet Airliner'. Miller had now mastered and targeted his audience, with exactly the kind of songs he knew they wanted. Once again, he disappeared from the scene and a new album was not released for almost four years. The return this time was less spectacular. Although *Circle Of Love* contained one side of typical Miller - short, sharp, punchy melodic rock songs - side two was an over-long and self-indulgent epic, 'Macho City'. He once again corrected the fault by responding only six months later, with another US number 1, the catchy 'Abracadabra'. This gave him his second major hit in the UK, almost reaching the coveted top spot in 1982. In the USA, the album climbed near to the top and Miller was left with another million-plus sale. The momentum was lost over the following years, as a live album and *Italian X-Rays* were comparative failures. *Living In The 20th Century* contained a segment consisting of a tribute to **Jimmy Reed**, with whom Steve had played as a teenager. He opted out of the commercial market with the excellent *Born 2B Blue* in 1989. Together with his old colleague **Ben Sidran**, Miller paid homage to jazz and blues standards with some exquisite arrangements from Sidran. Songs like **Billie Holiday**'s 'God Bless The Child' and 'Zip-A-Dee-Doo-Dah', were given lazy treatments with Miller's effortless voice. The record was only a moderate success.

In the autumn of 1990, while Miller bided his time with the luxury of deciding what to do next, over in Britain Levi's jeans had used 'The Joker' for one of their television advertisements. Capitol quickly released it, and astonishingly, Maurice, the space cowboy, the gangster of love, found himself with his first UK number 1. *Wide River* in 1993 was a teturn to his basic rock formula but it was not one of his better efforts.

Albums: *Children Of the Future* (1968), *Sailor* (1968), *Brave New World* (1969), *Your Saving Grace* (1969), *Revolution* (1969, film soundtrack featuring three Miller tracks), *Number 5* (1970), *Rock Love* (1971), *Recall The Beginning . . . A Journey From Eden* (1972), *The Joker* (1973), *Fly Like An Eagle* (1976), *Book Of Dreams* (1977), *Circle Of Love* (1981), *Abracadabra* (1982), *Steve Miller Band - Live!* (1983), *Italian X Rays* (1984), *Living In The 20th Century* (1987), *Born 2B Blue* (1988), *Wide River* (1993). Compilations: *Anthology* (1972), *Greatest Hits (1974-1978)* (1978), *A Decade Of American Music: Greatest Hits 1976-1986* (1987), *The Best Of 1968-1973* (1990), *Pegasus* (box set) (1992).

Milli Vanilli

This soul duo consisted of Rob Pilatus, who was brought up in an orphanage, and Fabrice Morvan, who was training to be a trampoline athlete until a fall damaged his neck. Based in Germany, they worked as backing singers for various German groups, before forming their own duo combining rap and soul, taking their name from a New York club. They enjoyed big hits with 'Girl, You Know It's True' and the similar 'Girl, I'm Gonna Miss You' before they suffered a major backlash when they were exposed as front-men for a 'group' fabricated by producer **Frank Farian**. The duo had apparently been chosen for their looks and were effectively locked out of the studio when recording took place. After handing back music industry awards, they promised to return with a new contract and their own voices.

Albums: *All Or Nothing* (1988), *Two X Two* (1989).

Millican And Nesbitt

Alan Millican and Tom Nesbitt worked as coal miners for 20 years in Northumberland, the northern-most county in England and, in their spare time, sang as a duo in the local workingmen's clubs. In 1973, they appeared on the UK's top television talent show, *Opportunity Knocks*, and captured the hearts of millions with their sentimental rendition of 'Vaya Con Dios', which was light years away from **Les Paul** And Mary Ford's 1953 UK Top 10 version. They won their heat, and returned to the programme nine times in all. With 'Vaya Con Dios', they rubbed shoulders with **Gary Glitter** and **Diana Ross** in the UK chart for a few weeks, and had a minor hit with the follow-up, 'For Old Times Sake'. Voted 1973's top new talent by the Variety Club of Great Britain, they had hit albums with *Millican And Nesbitt* (which featured golden oldies such as 'Paper Roses', 'Keep A Light At The Window' and 'The Old Lamplighter') and *Everybody Knows Millican And Nesbitt*. During the late 70s, they also released *Golden Hour Of Millican And Nesbitt*, *Canadian Sunset* and *Country Roads*, before returning to the clubs.

Millie

b. Millicent Small, 6 October 1942, Clarendon, Jamaica. After leaving home at the age of 13 to further her singing career in Kingston, Millie recorded several tracks with producer **Coxsone Dodd**, who teamed her up with Roy Panton. As Roy And Millie, they achieved local success with 'We'll Meet' and 'Oh, Shirley' and caught the attention of entrepreneur **Chris Blackwell**. On 22 June 1964, Millie accompanied Blackwell to the UK and recorded Harry Edwards' 'Don't You Know', before being presented with the catchy 'My Boy Lollipop', formerly a US R&B hit for Barbie Gaye, which became a transatlantic Top 5 hit, the first crossover **ska** record. Such chart fame proved evanescent. A carbon copy follow-up, 'Sweet William', was only a minor hit, and 'Bloodshot Eyes' failed to breach the Top 40. Thereafter she languished in relative obscurity. Even a brief tie-up with **Jackie Edwards** in Jackie And Millie, and a nude spread in a men's magazine failed to revitalise her career. Ultimately handicapped by her novelty hit, Millie's more serious work, such as the self-chosen *Millie Sings Fats Domino*, was sadly ignored.

Selected album: *The Best Of* (Trojan 1970).

Millinder, Lucky

b. Lucius Millinder, 8 August 1900, Anniston, Alabama, USA, d. 28 September 1966, New York, USA. Growing up in Chicago, Millinder worked in clubs and theatres in the late 20s as a dancer and master of ceremonies. His engaging personality resulted in his being appointed leader of several bands in Chicago, New York, and on tour. In 1933, he brought

a band to Europe, playing as part of an all-black revue. The following year he was appointed leader of the **Mills Blue Rhythm Band**, fronting it at the Cotton Club in Harlem. Beginning in 1938, he had a few bad years, part of the time leading the **Bill Doggett** band but mostly suffering acute financial embarrassment. In 1940, he formed a new band of his own, hiring some quality musicians - including, at one time or another in the first few years, trumpeters **Dizzy Gillespie**, **Joe Guy** and **Freddie Webster**, saxophonists **Tab Smith**, **Eddie 'Lockjaw' Davis** and **Sam 'The Man' Taylor**, and in the rhythm section Doggett, Trevor Bacon and **David 'Panama' Francis**. Millinder also had **Sister Rosetta Tharpe** in the band for a while. He enjoyed considerable success, playing dance dates, often at the Savoy Ballroom in Harlem, broadcasting and touring, with occasional recording dates for good measure. Despite the changing times, Millinder kept the band afloat throughout the 40s, eventually calling it a day in 1952. Thereafter, he earned his living outside music, but formed occasional bands for special concerts. Although he was not a musician and could not read music, Millinder was an exceptional front man, conducting his bands with flair and showmanship. Given the fact that many of the arrangements used by his bands over the years were complex, he clearly had a good ear and was able to create the effect of leading when in reality he was following the musicians under his baton. Although it might be said with some justification that the Mills Blue Rhythm Band and his own band of the early 40s owed little to him musically, there can be little doubt that they owed him much for the success they enjoyed.
Selected compilations: *Big Bands Uptown!* (1931-43), *Lucky Millinder And His Orchestra 1941-1943* (1941-43), *Apollo Jump* (Affinity 1983), *Let It Roll Again* (Jukebox Lil 1985), *Shorty's Got To Go* (Jukebox Lil 1985), *Lucky Millinder And His Orchestra* (Hindsight 1987), *Ram-Bunk-Shush* (Sing 1988), *Stompin' At The Savoy 1943-44* (Bandstand 1988), *Lucky Millinder 1941-42* (Original Jazz Classics 1993).

Millns, Paul

b. Norfolk, England. Millns's first forays into music were undertaken playing piano in blues and soul bands, two musical styles which have maintained a strong influence on his output. After moving to London he found himself working in groups with **Alexis Korner**, **Eric Burdon**, **Bert Jansch**, **Jo Ann Kelly** and Chicago bluesman **Louisiana Red**. By the mid-70s his first solo album was released on **Phillips**. The following years saw him alternate between his own songwriting and session/touring duties with other artists. In 1979 he was invited to Germany and recorded a soundtrack of originals for the feature film, *Gibbi West Germany*. He has retained a strong reputation in that country via television appearances on music shows like *Rock Palast*, as well as appearing at major continental events and their domestic equivalents (including the Edinburgh Arts and Cambridge Folk Festivals). Further commissions for soundtrack work have been undertaken for the BBC, Thames, Channel Four etc., while artists like **Elkie Brooks** ('Too Much Between Us' on her *Pearls 2* set) have covered his songs. His circle of musical friends is also impressive, Bert Jansch, **Ralph McTell**, **Christine Collister** and members of **Pentangle** and **Fairport Convention** all guesting on his 1994 set, *Against The Tide*.
Albums: *Paul Millns* (Phillips 1975), *Gibbi West Germany* (Telefunken 1980, film soundtrack), *Heartbreaking Highway* (Telefunken 1981), *Till The Morning Comes* (Mays 1982), *Finally Falls The Rain* (Jeton 1985), *Reaching Out* (Plane 1987), *Secret Operations* (Ariola/Sad Mountain 1991), *Against The Tide* (Hypertension 1994). Compilation: *Simply Blue* (Hypertension 1993).

Mills Blue Rhythm Band

Late in 1929, a group of New York musicians, under the nominal leadership of drummer Willie Lynch, formed a big band which they named the Blue Rhythm Band. A succession of front men, who included pianist **Edgar Hayes** and singer **Cab Calloway**, led the band, but despite high musical standards, it failed to gather a large following. In 1931, **Irving Mills** took over management of the band and appended his name. The Mills Blue Rhythm Band became third string in Mills's stable, behind the bands of **Duke Ellington** and Calloway. Later conducted by Jimmy Ferguson ('Baron Lee') and then **Lucky Millinder**, the band made many fine records. Subsequently billed as the Instrumental Gentlemen From Harlem, the band eventually folded in 1938. During its existence, several top-flight musicians played in its ranks, among them trumpeters **Henry 'Red' Allen**, Shelton Hemphill, **Charlie Shavers**, **Harry Edison** and Edward Anderson, trombonist **J.C. Higginbotham**, saxophonists Charlie Holmes, Caster and Ted McCord, and clarinettist **Buster Bailey**. Especially in its middle and later years, the band was musically outstanding, playing fine arrangements by **Tab Smith**, **Joe Garland** and others. Regrettably, the band's lack of a charismatic frontman seemed to carry more weight with the public than its musical excellence, and the Mills Blue Rhythm Band sank into undeserved latterday obscurity. In the late 40s, the band was briefly reformed for record dates.
Selected compilations: *Henry 'Red' Allen And The Mills Blue Rhythm Band* (1934-35), *Big Bands* (1947), *Blue Rhythm* (Hep Jazz 1986 1930-31 recordings), 1937 (CJM 1987), *Rhythms Splash* (Hep Jazz 1987), *Savage Rhythm* (Hep Jazz 1987, 1931-32 recordings),*Rhythm Spasm* (Hep Jazz 1993, 1932-33 recordings).

Mills Brothers

The three permanent members of the group comprised Herbert Mills (b. 2 April 1912, d. April 1989, Las Vegas, Nevada, USA), Harry Mills (b. 9 August 1913, d. 28 June 1982) and Donald Mills (b. 29 April 1915). John Mills Jnr. (b. 11 February 1911, d. 1935), added vocal notes in string bass form and played guitar. All the brothers were born in Piqua, Ohio, USA, sons of a barber who had been a successful concert singer. By the mid-20s, they were singing in sweet, close harmony in local vaudeville, providing their own backing by accurately imitating saxophones, trumpets, trombones and bass. With the main trio still teenagers, they had their own show on Cincinnati radio before moving to New York in 1930. The brothers signed to **Brunswick Records** and had a hit in 1931 with their first disc, 'Tiger Rag', which they also sang in the movie ***The Big Broadcast***, featuring **Bing Crosby** and many other stars of US radio. They appeared in several other musical montage movies such as *Twenty Million Sweethearts* (1934), *Broadway Gondolier* (1935) and ***Reveille With Beverly*** (1943), *Rhythm Parade* (1943), *Cowboy Canteen* (1944) and *When You're Smiling* (1950). In the early 30s, Crosby featured on several of the brothers' record hits, including 'Dinah'/'Can't We Talk It Over', 'Shine' and 'Gems From George White's Scandals', which also included the **Boswell Sisters**. On later tracks, the Mills Brothers were also joined by **Louis Armstrong**, **Ella Fitzgerald** and **Cab Calloway**. Their early records were labelled: 'No musical instruments or mechanical devices used on this recording other than one guitar'. Other 30s hits included 'You Rascal, You', 'I Heard', 'Good-Bye, Blues', 'Rockin' Chair', 'St. Louis Blues', 'Sweet Sue', 'Bugle Call Rag', 'It Don't Mean A Thing (If It Ain't Got That Swing)', 'Swing It Sister', 'Sleepy Head' and 'Sixty Seconds Together'.

In 1935, John Mills died suddenly and the brothers' father, John Snr., took over as bass singer, and ex-bandleader Bernard Addison joined the group on guitar. During the late 30s, the Mills Brothers toured the USA and abroad, appearing in two UK Royal Command Performances. Their popularity peaked in 1943 with the record 'Paper Doll', which sold over six million copies. They had consistent chart success throughout the 40s with titles on the **Decca** label such as 'You Always Hurt The One You Love', 'Til Then', 'I Wish', 'I Don't Know Enough About You', ' Across The Alley From The Alamo', 'I Love You So Much It Hurts', 'I've Got My Love To Keep Me Warm', 'Someday (You'll Want Me To Want You)' and 'Put Another Chair At The Table'.

By 1950, the instrumental impressions having generally been discarded, the brothers were accompanied by ex-**Tommy Dorsey** arranger **Sy Oliver**'s orchestra on their hit 'Nevertheless (I'm In Love With You)' and again in 1952 on 'Be My Life's Companion'. That same year, 'The Glow Worm', gave them another blockbuster. This was a 1908 song from the German operetta *Lysistrata*, with a new lyric by **Johnny Mercer**. Other 50s favourites from the brothers included Sy Oliver's own composition 'Opus Number One', 'Say 'Si-Si'', 'Lazy River' and 'Smack Dab In The Middle'. In 1956, John Snr. retired, and the brothers continued as a trio. Their last hit on Decca was 'Queen Of The Senior Prom' in 1957. The switch to the **Dot** label gave them two US Top 30 entries, 'Get A Job' and their final chart success, 'Cab Driver', in 1968. After Harry Mills death in 1982, Herbert and Donald continued to perform their brand of highly polished, humorous entertainment with a substitute singer. However, when Herbert died seven years later, Donald, now walking with a cane, gained excellent reviews and favourable audience reaction when he played nightclubs with his son John, using mainly the old Mills Brothers catalogue, but with additional new material.

Selected albums: *Souvenir Album* (mid-50s), *Singin' And Swingin'* (mid-50s), *Memory Lane* (mid-50s), *One Dozen Roses* (mid-50s), *The Mills Brothers In Hi-Fi* (mid-50s), *Glow With The Mills Brothers* (mid-50s), *Barbershop Harmony* (mid-50s), *Harmonizing With The Mills Brothers* (mid-50s), *Mmmm, The Mills Brothers* (1958), *Great Barbershop Hits* (1959), *Merry Christmas* (1959), *The Mills Brothers Sing* (1960), *Yellow Bird* (1961), *San Antonio Rose* (1961), *Great Hawaiian Hits* (1961), *The Beer Barrel Polka And Other Hits* (1962), *The End Of The World* (1963), *Gems By The Mills Brothers* (1964), *Hymns We Love* (1964), *Say Si Si, And Other Great Latin Hits* (1964), *The Mills Brothers Sing For You* (1964), *These Are The Mills Brothers* (1966), *That Country Feelin'* (1966), *The Mills Brothers Live* (1967), *Fortuosity* (1968), with Count Basie *The Board Of Directors* (1968), *My Shy Violet* (1968), *Dream* (1969). Compilations: *The Mills Brothers Greatest Hits* (1958), *Ten Years Of Hits 1954-1964* (1965), *Greatest Hits* (1987, MCA label), in addition, there are a great many compilations available.

Film: *The Big Beat* (1957).

Mills, Frank

b. 1943, Toronto, Ontario, Canada. Mills is best remembered for his 1979 best seller 'Music Box Dancer', a Top 5 hit in the USA. He studied music in Montreal, joining a group called the Bells who recorded some of his compositions. In 1972, he left for a solo career and his first single, 'Love Me, Love Me, Love', on Sunflower Records, made the US charts, reaching number 46. He also had hits in Canada, but by 1974, he was without a record contract. His easy-listening sound had lost favour with the majority of the record-buying public. He recorded an a self-financed album during the mid-70s, which included his composition 'Music Box Dancer'. It was noticed in

1979 by a **Polydor Records** executive, released as a single, and ascended to number 3; the album was also reissued and reached number 21. One further single and album charted for Mills in 1979 but, by the turn of the decade, he was back to performing locally in Canada. He released another album, *Transitions*, in 1987, on **Capitol Records**.
Albums: *Music Box Dancer* (1979), *Transitions* (1987).

Mills, Garry

b. 13 October 1941, West Wickham, Kent, England. Mills was the nephew of jazz band leader **Nat Gonella**. Like many other UK pop singers of the late 50s, he started at London's 2 Is coffee bar and this led to his signing with **Dick Rowe** at Top Rank. He covered major US hits like 'Running Bear', 'Teen Angel', 'Hey, Baby', 'Seven Little Girls' and 'Footsteps' before charting with the b-side of the last single. The song, 'Look For A Star', had been written for the **Norman Wisdom** film *Follow A Star* but was actually used in the Hammer movie *Circus Of Horrors*. In America, Gary's (he dropped one 'r' for the USA) original soundtrack version was joined on the charts by three local covers, and, although he made the Top 40 in 1960, the biggest hit was by his near name-sake **Garry Miles** (aka Buzz Cason). The record was not only Garry's biggest success, it was also the first hit for composer Mark Anthony, better known as **Tony Hatch**. Mills, who was backed on the road by the **Flee-Rekkers**, had two smaller UK hits with the follow-up 'Top Teen Baby' and 'I'll Step Down' on **Decca** in 1961, and also appeared in the long forgotten films *London Nights* and *Treasure Island W.C.2*.

Mills, Gordon

b. 1935, Madras, India, d. 29 July 1986. The son of a Welsh army sergeant, Mills was brought up in Ton-y-Pandy, Wales. After leaving school, he entered national service, then worked as a bus conductor. His proficiency on the harmonica took him to London's Central Hall for the grandly-titled British Harmonica Championships. From there, he went on to Luxembourg to represent the UK at international level. Upon his return home, he joined the Morton Fraser Harmonica Gang and toured the world. In 1959, he broke away from the Gang with two junior members to form the **Viscounts**, one of the perennial support vocal groups of the early 60s. Mills was ambitious to succeed in different areas of the music business, and in 1963, made the brave decision to quit the group and pursue a career as a songwriter. He enjoyed several UK hits, including **Johnny Kidd And The Pirates**' 'I'll Never Get Over You' and 'Hungry For Love', plus **Cliff Richard**'s 'The Lonely One'. Mills' life changed again during a homecoming visit to Wales in 1964. One evening he was invited to see the group Tommy Scott And The Senators in concert, and was mightily impressed by the singer. As a result, Mills elected to become a manager and duly signed the vocalist whom he rechristened **Tom Jones**. Mills co-wrote his chart debut, 'It's Not Unusual', which reached number 1 in the UK in early 1965. Jones allowed his mentor to mastermind every aspect of his career. After several hits, both in the UK and USA, Mills decided to push Jones towards international stardom. Out went the sexy clothes and rabbit's foot that had launched his career, in favour of a more mature, tuxedoed image. Wisely, Mills retained the essential eroticism. During Christmas 1966, Jones topped the charts with 'Green, Green Grass Of Home', which sold in excess of one million copies in the UK alone, the first release on **Decca** ever to achieve this distinction. It would not be long before that feat was surpassed by another artist, also represented by Mills. Gerry Dorsey had been Mills' best man when he married fashion model Jo Waring, and he was chosen as the next star of the Welshman's hit stable. In one of his familiar rechristenings, Mills launched the singer as **Engelbert Humperdinck**. During 1967, the balladeer notched up two of the biggest- selling UK singles of the 60s, 'Release Me' and 'The Last Waltz'. By this time, millionaire status beckoned for Mills, and the operation was shifted to America. Both Jones and Humperdinck subsequently enjoyed massive success on the Las Vegas casino circuit, and indulged in a much-publicized hedonistic lifestyle. Back in the UK, Mills formed a record company/management empire MAM. Another major star, **Gilbert O'Sullivan**, emerged from this venture. He enjoyed many international hits, including one written in honour of Mills' daughter, Clair. During the 70s, Mills' operation ran smoothly, but slowly, complacency set in. Humperdinck left his manager, followed by O'Sullivan, who subsequently won substantial high court damages against his former employer. Following the case, Mills took stock of his empire and sold MAM to **Chrysalis**. His marriage was also over. Even the formidable zoo of animals he had accumulated over the years, including the largest collection of orangutans in the world, were donated to San Diego Zoo. The first gorilla born there in 20 years was named 'Gordon'. After all the recent changes, all that remained was the great partnership of Jones and Mills which had survived since the mid-60s. The pair entered a recording studio in the early summer of 1986, intent on re-establishing Jones as a chart act. During the session Gordon complained of a stomach upset. This was subsequently diagnosed as cancer. The manager was visited by his protege at the Cedars Sinai Hospital and demanded to know his chances of survival. '50-50', Jones said. Ever the gambler, Mills retorted: 'That's not bad odds'. The manager subsequently lapsed into unconsciousness and Jones broke down, crying : 'What am I going to do now?' On 29 July 1986, Mills the multi-faceted producer, writer,

singer, musician, manager and entrepreneur, passed away. His body was later flown to England and he was buried at St. Peter's Church, Hersham.
Album: *Do It Yourself* (1965).
Further reading: *Starmakers & Svengalis: The History Of British Pop Management*, Johnny Rogan.

Mills, Irving

b. 16 January 1884, New York City, New York, USA, d. 21 April 1985. After singing with dancebands in the early years of this century, Mills became very successful in the music publishing business in the 20s. Later in the decade, he entered the field of personal management, gathering under his wing some of the finest black musicians of the day, notably **Duke Ellington**, **Cab Calloway** and **Jimmie Lunceford**, all of whom were featured at the Cotton Club, an establishment with which Mills had strong links. Most of the artists Mills represented were tied to him by contracts with clauses so binding as to suggest a degree of unscrupulousness. His eye for business matters led to Mills forming record companies and organizing numerous record dates, many of which brought together some of the best jazz players of the day. This business sense also led Mills into the dubious practice of appending his name to various ventures, certain instances of which appear to be rather less than deserved. In some cases, his motive might have been little more than a desire to see his name in lights - for example, when he attached his name to another band he managed, the **Mills Blue Rhythm Band**, or to a pick-up group, **Irving Mills** And His Hotsy Totsy Gang (which was actually led by **Benny Goodman**). Much more questionable is the fact that his name appears as co-composer on most of **Duke Ellington**'s compositions of the late 20s and 30s, accreditations which can hardly be taken seriously. When Ellington finally split with Mills, the cause was a disagreement over financial matters. Although Mills continued his business activities into the 60s, his connections with the leading names of jazz were much reduced. For all the criticism which must be levelled at the manner in which Mills exploited the artists under contract to him, it should perhaps be acknowledged that he worked hard to ensure they achieved success - even if his motives in these endeavours were somewhat less than selfless.

Mills, Jeff

Hugely respected US techno DJ who relocated from his native Detroit (where he set up the **Underground Resistance** empire with 'Mad' Mike Banks) to the New York region. After the split he formed Axis, licensing the *Tranquilizer* EP to **Network**. Other releases on Axis include his 1994 single 'Cycle 30'. Robert Hood, who worked on several of Mills' productions, recorded his second EP, *Minimal Nation*, for Axis that year too.

Mills, Mrs.

Gladys Mills was a popular 50s performer when pianists of the calibre of **Winifred Atwell** were in vogue. Mills took all the popular tunes of old and ran them together in tinkly piano medleys. Never a massive success chart-wise, her albums sold reasonably well in the UK, and she made countless television appearances, including several on the *Wheeltappers And Shunters Social Club* and the *Billy Cotton Band Show*. She died on 25 February 1978.
Selected albums: *Come To My Party* (1966), *Mrs Mills' Party Pieces* (1968), *Let's Have Another Party* (1969), *I'm Mighty Glad* (1971), *All-Time Party Dances* (1978), *Piano Party Time* (1984), *An Hour Of Mrs Mills* (1987).

Mills, Stephanie

b. 1959, Brooklyn, New York, USA. Mills found fame when aged just nine, winning an influential talent show at Harlem's famous **Apollo Theater** six weeks running. Soon afterwards she appeared on Broadway in the play *Maggie Flynn*. She toured with the **Isley Brothers,** and in 1973, recorded her debut, *Movin' In The Right Direction*, for the Paramount label. Her debut single - 'I Knew It Was Love' - was issued in 1974. Already an established performer, Mills was still in her teens when, in 1975, she was offered the part of Dorothy in the stage show *The Wiz* - the all-black reworking of *The Wizard Of Oz*. It was a role she was to hold for several years, and she had hoped to continue it in the film version, until **Diana Ross** usurped her. During her run in the show, Mills was recommended to **Motown**'s **Berry Gordy** by **Jermaine Jackson** and recorded an album for the label. *For The First Time* was written and produced by **Burt Bacharach** and **Hal David**. Motown chose not to continue its association with Mills, and she signed to 20th Century for three albums, the second of which spawned the huge worldwide hit 'Never Knew Love Like This' in 1980. That same year, Mills married **Jeffrey Daniels** of **Shalamar**, though the marriage was short-lived. After working with **Teddy Pendergrass** in 1981, and charting with the duet 'Two Hearts', Mills signed a new deal with Casablanca and, in 1983, received a daytime television show on NBC. She reclaimed her role of Dorothy in a revival of *The Wiz* and had a further hit with 'The Medicine Song' from *I've Got The Cure*. This album was produced by David 'Hawk' Wolinski, formerly with the group **Rufus**.
Albums: *For The First Time* (1976), *Watcha Gonna Do With My Loving* (1979), *Sweet Sensation* (1980), *Stephanie* (1981), *Tantalizingly Hot* (1982), *Merciless* (1983), *I've Got The Cure* (1984), *Stephanie Mills* (1985), *If I Were Your Woman* (1987), *Something Real* (1993).

Milltown Brothers

60s revivalist pop band formed in Colne, Lancashire,

England, and featuring Matt Nelson (vocals), Simon Nelson (guitar), Barney James (keyboards), James Fraser (bass) and Nian Brindle (drums). Simon Nelson had the musical pedigree, performing in Blue Berlin whilst at university, then the Squire and The Word Association, who finally metamorphosed into the Milltown Brothers. They started out playing working men's clubs and then the college circuit, signing to **EMI Records** publishing long before they had a contract. Their debut release, 'Coming From The Mill', then 'Which Way Should I Jump', were housed on the indie label, Big Round. They would subsequently move on to **A&M Records** where 'Which Way Should I Jump' was re-released following the relative success of 'Apple Green'. It made the UK Top 40. 1993 saw them at work on a follow-up album, although by this time they had become part of a large clutch of **Byrds**-influenced indie pop bands (**Rain**, Resque, etc) trying to re-establish a profile which had been much higher in 1991. The trouble was exacerbated by difficulties with their label, stated manager Andrew Proudfoot: 'The band came up with new material, but it was darker than A&M wanted.' The result was a much delayed second offering which failed to sell, and the band broke up soon afterwards.
Albums: *Slinky* (A&M 1991), *Value* (A&M 1993).

Milsap, Ronnie

b. Ronnie Lee Millsaps, 16 January 1943, Robbinsville, North Carolina, USA. Milsap's mother had experienced a stillborn birth and the prospect of raising a blind child made her mentally unstable. Milsap's father took him to live with his grandparents and divorced his mother. What little vision young Ronnie had was lost after receiving a vicious punch from a schoolmaster; both eyes have now been removed. He studied piano, violin and guitar at the State School for the Blind in Raleigh, and although he had the ability to study law, he chose instead to be a professional musician. After some workouts with **J.J. Cale** and a 1963 single,'Total Disaster', for the small Princess label, he toured *Playboy* clubs with his own band from 1965. Among his recordings for Scepter were early compositions by **Ashford And Simpson,** including the memorable 'Let's Go Get Stoned', relegated to a b-side. A few months later it was a million-selling single for another blind pianist, **Ray Charles**. Following a residency at TJ's club in Memphis, Milsap performed at the 1969 New Year's Eve party for **Elvis Presley**. Presley invited him to sing harmony on his sessions for 'Don't Cry Daddy' and 'Kentucky Rain', ironically the only time he has been part of a UK chart hit. After several recordings with smaller labels, Milsap made *Ronnie Milsap*, for **Warner Brothers**, with top soul and country musicians. He worked throughout 1972 at **Roger Miller**'s King Of The Road club in Nashville, and then signed with **RCA**. *Where The Heart Is* was a tuneful, country collection including the US country hits, 'I Hate You' and 'The Girl Who Waits On Tables'. 'Pure Love' is among the most uplifting country singles of all time, while **Don Gibson**'s 'I'd Be A Legend In My Time' was even more successful. In 1975, Milsap came to the UK as **Glen Campbell**'s opening act, and the strength of his concert performances can be gauged from RCA's *In Concert* double-album, hosted by **Charley Pride**, in which he duets 'Rollin' In My Sweet Baby's Arms' with **Dolly Parton** and tackles a wild rock 'n' roll medley. His live album from the *Grand Old Opry*, shows a great sense of humour - 'You don't think I'm gonna fall off this stage, do you? I got 20 more feet before the edge. That's what the band told me.' He had a crossover hit - number 16 on the US pop charts - with **Hal David**'s, 'It Was Almost Like A Song'. Milsap bought a studio from **Roy Orbison**, GroundStar, and continued to record prolifically. In 1979, RCA sent an unmarked, pre-release single to disc jockeys, inviting them to guess the performer. The funky seven-minute disco workout of 'Hi-Heel Sneakers' was by Milsap, but, more often than not, he was moving towards the **Barry Manilow** market. Milsap also helped with the country music score for Clint Eastwood's film, *Bronco Billy,* and he recorded a flamboyant tribute album to **Jim Reeves**, *Out Where The Bright Lights Are Glowing.* A revival of **Chuck Jackson**'s 'Any Day Now (My Wild Beautiful Bird)' reached number 14 on the US pop charts and also became ***Billboard*'s** Adult Contemporary Song Of The Year. His *Lost In The Fifties Tonight* album had doo-wop touches, but the album should have remained completely in that mould. Milsap also recorded a duet with **Kenny Rogers**, 'Make No Mistake, She's Mine'. He moved away from synthesizers and sounded more country than ever on 'Stranger Things Have Happened'. Enjoying his 35th US country number 1 with a **Hank Cochran** song, 'Don't You Ever Get Tired (Of Hurtin' Me)', Milsap remains a formidable force in US country music, and only **Conway Twitty** and **Merle Haggard** have had more chart-toppers. It shows remarkable consistency by an artist with little traditional country to his name.
Albums: *Ronnie Milsap* (1971), *Where The Heart Is* (1973), *Pure Love* (1974), *A Legend In My Time* (1975), *Night Things* (1975), *A Rose By Any Other Name* (1975), *20-20 Vision* (1976), *Mr. Mailman* (1976), *Ronnie Milsap Live* (1976), *Kentucky Woman* (1976), *It Was Almost Like A Song* (1977), *Only One Love In My Life* (1978), *Images* (1979), *Milsap Magic* (1980), *Out Where The Bright Lights Are Glowing* (1981), *There's No Gettin' Over Me* (1980), *Inside* (1982), *Keyed Up* (1983), *One More Try For Love* (1984), *Lost In The Fifties Tonight* (1986), *Christmas With Ronnie Milsap* (1986), *Heart And Soul* (1987), *Stranger Things Have Happened* (1989), *Back To The Grindstone* (1991), *Greatest Hits Vol. 3* (1993), *True Believer* (1993), *The Essential Ronnie Milsap* (RCA 1995).

Further reading: *Almost Like A Song*, Ronnie Milsap with Tom Carter.

Milton, Roy

b. 31 July 1907, Wynnewood, Oklahoma, USA, d. 18 September 1983, Los Angeles, California, USA. Growing up on his Chickasaw grandmother's reservation, Milton encountered blues music when his family moved to Tulsa. In the late 20s, he was a vocalist with the **Ernie Fields** Orchestra; while on tour in Texas, he replaced the band's drummer after the latter was arrested. He left the Fields band in 1933 and moved to Los Angeles. After a couple of years he formed Roy Milton And The Solid Senders with pianist **Camille Howard**, Buddy Floyd and Hosea Sapp. In December 1945 they recorded 'R.M. Blues', which became an immediate hit, establishing both Roy Milton and **Specialty Records** and spearheading the wave of small R&B units that tolled the death knell of the big bands. Milton remained with Specialty for 10 years, recording ballads and pop tunes alongside more popular blues and boogie material like 'Milton's Boogie', 'Hop, Skip And Jump', 'T-Town Twist' and 'Best Wishes'. After Specialty, he recorded for Dootone, King and Warwick, but by the end of the 60s his style of music had become outdated. He appeared with **Johnny Otis** at the 1970 **Monterey Jazz Festival** and resumed a solo career that also brought him to Europe. He fell ill in 1982 and was confined to his home until his death a year later.

Albums: *Big Fat Mama* (Jukebox Lil 1986), *Roy Milton And His Solid Senders* (Specialty/Ace 1990), *Groovy Blues* (Specialty/Ace 1992), *Blowin' With Roy* (Specialty/Ace 1994).

Mimms, Garnet, And The Enchanters

b. Garrett Mimms, 26 November 1933, Ashland, West Virginia, USA. A former member of Philadelphia-based gospel groups the Evening Stars and the Norfolk Four, Mimms formed a secular quintet, the Gainors, in 1958. The line-up included future soul star **Howard Tate**, as well as Sam Bell, Willie Combo and John Jefferson. Over the next three years, the Gainors made several singles for **Cameo**, **Mercury Records** and Tally-Ho which, although unsuccessful, betrayed a contemporary soul feel. The group subsequently evolved into Garnet Mimms And The Enchanters, where the singer and Sam Bell were joined by Charles Boyer and Zola Pearnell. Signed to United Artists in 1963, they came under the tutelage of writer/producer **Jerry Ragovoy**. His inspired work helped create some of urban R&B's finest moments. The impassioned 'Cry Baby' was an immediate US hit, while 'Baby Don't You Weep' and 'For Your Precious Love' consolidated their arrival. The group split in 1964, when Garnet embarked on a solo career. Although the Enchanters found a new vocalist and continued to record, they were overshadowed by their former leader. Mimms' subsequent releases, 'Look Away', 'It Was Easier To Hurt Her' and 'I'll Take Good Care Of You', were artistic triumphs, pitting the singer's church roots against Ragovoy's sophisticated backdrop. Such excellent records were not always well-received, and in 1967, Garnet was demoted to United Artists' subsidiary, Veep. 'My Baby' and 'Roll With The Punches' followed, but the singer's now-tenuous position was confirmed when the latter was only released in Britain. Ragovoy then took Mimms to **Verve** (where he was also producing Howard Tate), but the four singles which appeared, although good, found little favour. It was not until 1977 that the singer returned to the chart. Credited to Garnet Mimms And The Truckin' Company, 'What It Is' was a minor R&B hit and even clipped the UK chart at number 44. Mimms is now a born-again Christian and has not recorded for many years.

Albums: with the Enchanters *Cry Baby (And 11 Other Hits)* (1963). Solo: *As Long As I Have You* (1964), *I'll Take Good Care Of You* (1966), *Garnet Mimms Live* (1967), *Garnet Mimms Has It All* (1978). Compilations: *Garnet Mimms And Maurice Monk* (1963), *Sensational New Star* (1963), *Warm And Soulful* (1965), *Warm & Soulful* (1984), *Roll With The Punches* (1986), *Cry Baby* (1991), *Garnet Mimms And The Enchanters* (1991), *The Best Of... Cry Baby* (1993).

Minami, Haruo

b. Bunji Kitazume, 1923, Tsukayama, Niigata, Japan. In 1939, in his mid-teens, Kitazume entered a school for rôkyoku, a popular art of narrative chant, and renamed himself Fumiwaka Nanjô before converting to the style of kayôkyoku (formerly the most common and typically Japanese form of popular song) and performing as Haruo Minami in 1957, when his three debut singles were released. The first couple, 'Chanchiki Okesa' (okesa is a kind of folk dance and chanchiki is an onomatopoeic word) and 'Funakatasan Yo' ('Halloa, Boatman') won Minami significant success and were followed by 'Yuki No Wataridori' ('A Wanderer In Snow') in the same year and 'Otone Mujô' ('Merciless Otone') in 1959, making him known as a singer of historical songs. Minami was hailed as a 'national singer' when his single, 'Tokyo Gorin Ondo' (Tokyo Olympic Dance), became a million-seller in 1964, the year of the Olympic Games in Tokyo for which the song was commissioned. His sinewy vocals and gaudy kimono-costumes, both of which are reminiscent of his rôkyoku background, have long been familiar to Japanese television audiences.

Compilations: *Daichûshingura* (1987), *Original Bests* (1988), *Best And Best* (1989), *Zenkyokushû* (*Complete Works*) (1989), *Meien: Chôhen Kayô-rôkyoku* (*Mastery Performance: Longer Pieces Of Kayô-rôkyoku*) (1990, three volumes).

Mince, Johnny

b. 8 July 1912, Chicago Heights, Illinois, USA. A highly accomplished clarinettist, Mince's early career saw him playing with several of the most sophisticated bands of the early swing era. At the age of 17, he was with **Joe Haymes**'s excellent danceband, and during the 30s, Mince moved on to **Ray Noble**, **Bob Crosby** and **Tommy Dorsey**. During the spell with Noble, Mince played an important part in helping to establish the 'sound' of **Glenn Miller**'s arrangements, a sound which Miller later developed with his own band. After military service, Mince was mostly active in studio work, but he returned occasionally to play jazz dates in clubs and on record. In later years, Mince became a familiar and popular figure at international jazz festivals, touring extensively with a variety of musicians, such as the Kings Of Jazz, and with the bands of Dixieland veterans led by **Yank Lawson** and **Bob Haggart** and by British trumpeter **Keith Smith**. On all such forays, Mince attracted the favourable attention of a new generation of fans through his superb technique and distinctive style.

Albums: *Summer Of '79* (1979), *The Master Comes Home* i (c.1980), *I Can't Give You Anything But Love* (1982), with others *Swingin' The Forties With The Great Eight* (1983), *The Master Comes Home* ii (1983). Compilations: with Tommy Dorsey *The Sentimental Gentleman* (1941-42).

Mindbenders

Originally a backing group for **Wayne Fontana**, the Mindbenders comprised Eric Stewart (b. 20 January 1945; guitar), Bob Lang (10 January 1946; bass) and Ric Rothwell (b. 11 March 1944; drums). In October 1965, they split with their leader and early the following year enjoyed a transatlantic number 2 hit with the **Carole Bayer Sager**/Toni Wine composition, 'Groovy Kind Of Love'. The excellent follow-up, 'Can't Live With You, Can't Live Without You', failed to chart, while its successor 'Ashes To Ashes' was only a minor hit. A cameo appearance in the film *To Sir With Love* maintained the group's profile and they continued to record material by name writers such as **Rod Argent** and **Robert Knight**, but to no avail. A brave stab with an average cover of the **Box Tops**' 'The Letter' scraped into the Top 50s but shortly after the release of 'Uncle Joe The Ice Cream Man' in March 1968, the group dissolved. Eric Stewart and latter-day Mindbender **Graham Gouldman** went on to form **Hotlegs** and **10cc**, while Bob Lang reappeared in **Racing Cars**.

Albums: *The Mindbenders* (1966), *With Woman In Mind* (1967).

Mindfunk

This intense American thrash-funk quintet were formed in 1989 by vocalist Patrick R. Dubar and rhythm guitarist Jason Coppola. Adding John Monte (ex-**MOD**; bass), Reed St. Mark (ex-**Celtic Frost**; drums) and Louis J. Svitek (ex-MOD; guitar), they signed to **Epic** and debuted with an aggressive and confident self-titled album the same year. **Slayer**, **Red Hot Chili Peppers** and **Anthrax** were obvious reference points, as were the hardcore origins of several of their membership. However, they were dropped by Epic shortly afterwards (a fact bitterly recalled in their second album's title) and in came Jason Everman (ex-**Nirvana**, **Soundgarden**) and Shawn Johnson for Coppola and St Mark respectively.

Albums: *Mindfunk* (Epic 1991), *Dropped* (Megaforce 1993).

Mindstorm

Mindstorm is the rock vision of vocalist Travis Mitchell. The group is in essence the Canadian equivalent of **Kingdom Come** or **Katmandu**. Employing Al Rodgers (guitar), Bruce Moffet (drums), Russ Boswell (bass) and Gary Moffet (keyboards), the songs are immaculately constructed and delivered with aplomb. However, their credibility and creativity is compromised through the overwhelming sense of *deja-vu* their recordings invoke. With monstrously aching riffs and thunderous drumming, Mindstorm careers along a well-worn rock 'n' roll path, with only the occasional musical detour. These include Eastern influences, simple acoustic bridges and brooding power ballads.

Albums: *Mindstorm* (Provogue 1987), *Back To Reality* (Provogue 1991).

Mineo, Sal

b. Salvatore Mineo, 10 January 1939, New York City, New York, USA, d. 12 February 1976. After a difficult childhood, Mineo studied dancing and made his Broadway debut in *The Rose Tattoo*. He followed this with an appearance in ***The King And I*** in 1952. In the mid-50s he went to Hollywood and began making films, usually appearing as a troubled teenager. Among his best-known films were *Rebel Without A Cause* (1955), for which he was nominated for an Oscar as Best Supporting Actor, *Somebody Up There Likes Me* and *Giant* (both 1956) and *Exodus* (1960), another unsuccessful Oscar nomination. He also played the title role in ***The Gene Krupa Story*** (1959). In the late 50s, Mineo made a number of records, including 'Love Affair', 'Start Moving (In My Direction)', 'Lasting Love' and 'You Shouldn't Do That'. He continued making films during the 60s and also returned to stage work. He directed and starred in *Fortune And Men's Eyes*, a play which reflected Mineo's own homosexuality. He was returning home from the theatre when he was stabbed to death in a Hollywood street.

Album: *Sal* (Epic 1958).

Mingus
Like its subject, this documentary made in 1968 is unflinching and at times uncomfortably honest. Mingus was being evicted from his home during the making of the film and these events are depicted as is the artist at work composing, rehearsing and performing. Amongst other musicians involved are **Charles McPherson** and **Dannie Richmond**.

Mingus, Charles
b. 22 April 1922, Nogales, Arizona, USA, d. 5 January 1979, Cuernavaca, Mexico. Mingus was never allowed the luxury of the feeling of belonging. Reactions to his mixed ancestry (he had British-born, Chinese, Swedish and African American grandparents) produced strong feelings of anger and confirmed his sense of persecution. However, this alienation, coupled with his own deep sensitivity and tendency to dramatize his experiences, provided substantial fuel for an artistic career of heroic turmoil and brilliance. Formative musical experiences included both the strictures of European classical music and the uninhibited outpourings of the congregation of the local Holiness Church, which he attended with his stepmother. The latter included all manner of bluesy vocal techniques, moaning, audience-preacher responses, wild vibrato and melismatic improvisation, along with the accompaniment of cymbals and trombones - all of it melding into an early gospel precursor of big band that heavily influenced Mingus's mature compositional and performance style. Other influences were hearing **Duke Ellington**'s band, and recordings of Richard Strauss's tone poems and works by Debussy, Ravel, Bach and Beethoven. Thwarted in his early attempts to learn trombone, Mingus switched from cello to double bass at high school.

He studied composition with Lloyd Reese and was encouraged by **Red Callender** to study bass with Herman Rheimschagen of the New York Philharmonic. He developed a virtuoso bass technique and began to think of the bass finger-board as similar to a piano keyboard. First professional dates as a bassist included gigs with New Orleans players **Kid Ory** and **Barney Bigard**, and then stints with the **Louis Armstrong Orchestra** (1943-1945) and **Lionel Hampton** (1947), but it was with the **Red Norvo** Trio (1950) that he first gained national recognition for his virtuosity. Work with other great pioneers of his generation such as **Charlie Parker**, **Miles Davis**, **Thelonious Monk**, **Bud Powell**, **Sonny Stitt**, **Stan Getz**, **Lee Konitz**, **Dizzy Gillespie**, **Quincy Jones** and **Teddy Charles** continued throughout the 50s. He joined Duke Ellington's band briefly in 1953, but a more artistically profitable association with his hero occurred with the trio album *Money Jungle*, which they made with **Max Roach** in 1962. Mingus was a pioneer of black management and artist-led record labels, forming Debut in 1953, and the Charles Mingus label in 1964. His early compositions were varying in success, often due to the difficulty of developing and maintaining an ensemble to realize his complex ideas.

He contributed works to the Jazz Composers' Workshop from 1953 until the foundation of his own workshop ensemble in 1955. Here, he was able to make sparing use of notation, transmitting his intentions from verbal and musical instructions sketched at the piano or on the bass. Mingus's originality as composer first began to flourish under these circumstances, and with players such as **Dannie Richmond**, **Rahsaan Roland Kirk**, **Jaki Byard**, **Jimmy Knepper** and **Booker Ervin** he developed a number of highly evolved works. Crucial amongst his many innovations in jazz was the use of non-standard chorus structures, contrasting sections of quasi-'classical' composed material with passages of freeform and group improvisations, often of varying tempos and modes, in complex pieces knitted together by subtly evolving musical motifs. He developed a 'conversational' mode of interactive improvisation, and pioneered melodic bass playing. Such pieces as *The Black Saint And The Sinner Lady* (1963) show enormous vitality and a great depth of immersion in all jazz styles, from New Orleans and gospel to bebop and free jazz. Another multi-sectional piece, 'Meditations For A Pair Of Wire Cutters', from the album *Portrait* (1964), is one of many that evolved gradually under various titles. Sections from it can be heard on *Mingus Plays Piano* (1963), there called 'Myself When I Am Real'. It was renamed 'Praying With Eric' after the tragic death of **Eric Dolphy**, who made magnificent contributions to many Mingus compositions, but especially to this intensely moving piece.

In the mid-60s, financial and psychological problems began to take their toll, as poignantly recorded in Thomas Reichman's 1968 film *Mingus*. He toured extensively during this period, presenting a group of ensemble works. In 1971, Mingus was much encouraged by the receipt of a Guggenheim fellowship in composition, and the publication of his astonishing autobiography, *Beneath The Underdog*. The book opens with a session conducted by a psychiatrist, and the work reveals Mingus's self-insight, intelligence, sensitivity and tendency for self-dramatization. Touring continued until the gradual paralysis brought by the incurable disease Amyotrophic Lateral Sclerosis prevented him doing anything more than presiding over recordings. His piece 'Revelations' was performed in 1978 by the New York Philharmonic under the direction of **Gunther Schuller**, who also resurrected *Epitaph* in 1989. Also in 1978, Mingus was honoured at the White House by Jimmy Carter and an all-star jazz concert. News of his death aged 56 in Mexico was marked by many tributes from artists of all fields.

Posthumously, the ensemble Mingus Dynasty continued to perform his works.

Mingus summed up the preoccupations of his time in a way which transcended racial and cultural divisions, whilst simultaneously highlighting racial and social injustices. Introducing the first 1964 performance of *Meditations*, Mingus tells the audience, 'This next composition was written when Eric Dolphy told me there was something similar to the concentration camps down South, [...] where they separated [...] the green from the red, or something like that; and the only difference between the electric barbed wire is that they don't have gas chambers and hot stoves to cook us in yet. So I wrote a piece called *Meditations* as to how to get some wire cutters before someone else gets some guns to us.' Off-mike, he can be heard saying to fellow musicians, 'They're gonna burn us; they'll try.' In the turmoil of his life and artistic achievements, and in his painful demise, Mingus became his own artistic creation. A desperate, passionate icon for the mid-20th century to which all can relate in some way, he articulated the emotional currents of his time in a way superior to that of almost any other contemporary jazz musician.

Selected albums: *Red Norvo Jazz Trio* (1951), with Spaulding Givens *Strings And Keys* (1951), *The Red Norvo - Charles Mingus - Tal Farlow Trio* (1951), *Autobiography In Jazz* (1953), *Strings And Keys* (Debut 1953), with others *Quintet Of The Year/Jazz At Massey Hall* (1953), *Jazz Composers Workshop* (Savoy 1954), *Jazz Experiments* (1954), *Charles Mingus And Thad Jones* (1955), Jazzical Moods, Vol 1 (Period 1955), Jazzical Moods Vol 2 (Period 1955), *Jazz Composers Workshop No 2* (Savoy 1956), *Mingus At The Bohemia* (Debut 1955), with Max Roach The Charles Mingus Quintet And Max Roach (Debut 1956), *Pithecanthropus Erectus* (Atlantic 1956), *The Clown* aka *Reincarnation Of A Lovebird* (Atlantic 1957), with Gunther Schuller, George Russell *Adventures In Sound* (1957), Jazz Experiment (Jazztone 1957), *Jazz Workshop Presents: Jimmy Knepper* (1957), *Duke's Choice* aka *A Modern Jazz Symposium Of Music And Poetry* (Bethlehem 1958), The Jazz Experiments Of Charles Mingus (Jazztone 1957), Mingus Three (Jubilee 1957), with Langston Hughes *Weary Blues* (1958), with Billie Holiday etc *Easy To Remember* (1958), East Coasting (Bethlehem 1958), *Wonderland* (United Artists 1959), *Jazz Portraits* (United Artists 1959), *Blues And Roots* (Atlantic 1959), *Mingus Ah-Um* (Columbia 1959), *Nostalgia In Times Square* (1959), *Mingus Dynasty* (Columbia 1960), *Pre-Bird* aka *Mingus Revisited* (Emarcy 1960), *Mingus At Antibes* (1960), *Charles Mingus Presents Charles Mingus!* (Candid 1960), *Mingus* (Candid 1960), *The Jazz Life* (1960), *Newport Rebels* (1960), with Tubby Hayes *All Night Long* (1960), *Oh Yeah!* (Atlantic 1961), *Pre Bird* (Mercury 1961), *Tonight At Noon* (Atlantic 1961), *Hooray For Charles Mingus* (1962), *J-For-Jazz Presents Charles Mingus* (1962), with Duke Ellington, Max Roach *Money Jungle* (1962), *Town Hall Concert* (United Artists 1962), *Chazz!* (Fantasy 1962), *The Black Saint And The Sinner Lady* (Impulse 1963), *Mingus Mingus Mingus Mingus Mingus* (Impulse 1963),*Tijuana Moods* (RCA 1964, rec 1957), *Town Hall Concert (Portrait)* (Original Jazz Classics 1964), *Live in Oslo* (rec 1964), *Charles Mingus Sextet Live In Europe Vols 1, 2* and *3* (1964), *The Great Concert Of Charles Mingus* (1964), *Mingus In Europe Vols 1 and 2* (1964), *Charles Mingus In Amsterdam* (1964), *Mingus In Stuttgart* (1964, 2 vols), *Right Now! Live At The Jazz Workshop* (Fantasy 1964), *Charles Mingus In Europe* (Enja 1964), *Mingus At Monterey* (Prestige 1964), *Music Written For Monterey 1965, But Not Heard* (1965), *My Favourite Quintet* (1965), *Statements* (1970), *Charles Mingus In Paris* (DIW 1970), *Pithy Canthropus Erectus* aka *Blue Bird* (1970), *Charles Mingus In Berlin* (1970), *Charles Mingus And The New Herd* (1971), *Let My Children Hear Music* (1971), *Charles Mingus And Friends In Concert* (1972), *Jazz Jamboree* (1972), *Charles Mingus Meets Cat Anderson* (1972), *Mingus Mingus* (1973), *Mingus At Carnegie Hall* (1974), *Cumbria And Jazz Fusion* (Atlantic 1977),*Three Or Four Shades Of Blue* (1977), *Lionel Hampton Presents: The Music Of Charles Mingus* aka *His Final Works* (1977), *Me Myself An Eye* (1978), *Something Like A Bird* (1978), *The Charles Mingus Memorial Album* (1978), with Joni Mitchell *Joni Mitchell - Mingus* (Geffen 1979). Selected compilations: *The Mingus Connection* (1957, rec 1951-53), *The Debut Recordings* (1951-57), *Vital Savage Horizons* (1952, 1961-62), *The Atlantic Years* (1956-1978), *Better Git It In Your Soul* (1959), *The Complete Candid Recordings Of Charles Mingus* (1960), *Charles Mingus/Cecil Taylor: Rare Broadcast Performances* (1962, 1966), *The Impulse Years* (1963), *Portrait* (1964, 1966), *Re-Evaluation: The Impulse Years* (1973, rec 1963-64), *The Art Of Charles Mingus* (1974), *Passions Of A Man* (1979, rec 1956-61, 1973, 1977), *Nostalgia In Times Square* (1979, rec 1959), *Great Moments With Charles Mingus* (1981, rec 1963-64), *Mingus, The Collection* (1985, rec c.50s), *Charles Mingus - New York Sketchbook* (1986, rec c.50s), *Charles Mingus - Shoes Of The Fisherman's Wife* (1988, rec 1959, 1971), *Abstractions* (1989, rec 1954, 1957), *Charles Mingus - Mysterious Blues* (1989, rec 1960), *Charles Mingus 1955-1957* (1990), *Charles Mingus* (1991), *Charles Mingus - The Complete Debut Recordings* (Debut 1991, 12-CD box set, rec c.50s), *Thirteen Pictures: The Charles Mingus Anthology* (Rhino, 1956-77 recordings), *Meditations On Integration* (1992, rec 1964).

Further reading: *Beneath The Underdog*, Charles Mingus. *Mingus: A Critical Biography*, Brian Priestley. *Revelations*, Charles Mingus. *Charles Mingus, Sein Leben, Seine Musik, Seine Schallplatten*, Horst Weber. *Mingus/Mingus*, Janet Coleman.

Video: *Charles Mingus Sextet* (KJazz 1994, rec 1964).

Ministry

'The difference between Ministry and other bands is that we sold out before we even started.' Alain Jourgensen (b. Havana, Cuba) began producing music under the Ministry name in the early 80s in Chicago, but was most unhappy with the Euro-pop direction in which his record company pushed him for *With Sympathy*. Ministry took on a more acceptable shape for Jourgensen after *Twitch*, with the addition of Paul Barker (b. Palo Alto, California, USA) on bass/keyboards and drummer Bill Rieflin to Jourgensen's guitar/vocals/keyboards. The band evolved their own brand of guitar-based industrial metal, considering *The Land Of Rape And Honey* to be their true debut, and employed a variety of guest musicians for both live and studio work, with regular contributions from ex-Rigor Mortis guitarist Mike Scaccia and ex-**Finitribe** vocalist Chris Connelly. Despite Jourgensen's dislike of touring, Ministry developed a stunning live show, with a backdrop of disturbing visual images to accompany the intense musical barrage, and the sinister figure of Jourgensen taking centre stage behind a bone-encrusted mike stand. *In Case You Didn't Feel Like Showing Up (Live)* displays the metamorphosis of the songs as the band extend themselves in concert. At this stage, Jourgensen and Barker were working on numerous other studio projects in a variety of styles, including Lard with **Jello Biafra**, but Ministry remained one of two main acts. The other, the outrageous **Revolting Cocks**, served as a more blatantly humorous outlet for the pair's creative talents, in contrast to the dark anger and socio-political themes of Ministry. As alternative culture became more acceptable to the mainstream, Ministry achieved major success with *Psalm 69* (subtitled *The Way To Succeed And The Way To Suck Eggs*), helped by the popularity on MTV of 'Jesus Built My Hotrod', featuring a guest vocal and lyric from **Butthole Surfer** Gibby Haynes. The band were a huge draw on the 1992 Lollapalooza tour, playing second on the bill, and their debut European tour later that year was also a resounding success. In 1994 Rieflin was replaced on drums by former **Didjits**' drummer Ray Washam.

Albums: *With Sympathy* (Arista 1983), *Twelve Inch Singles 1981-1984* (Wax Trax 1984), *Twitch* (Sire 1986), *The Land Of Rape And Honey* (Sire 1988), *The Mind Is A Terrible Thing To Taste* (Sire 1989), *In Case You Didn't Feel Like Showing Up (Live)* (Sire 1990), *Psalm 69* (Sire/Warners 1992).

Ministry Of Sound

London club whose unique atmosphere has led to a series of highly successful releases. The first of these was a compilation mixed by **Tony Humphries** in August 1993. Heralded by promotions man Jason Hill as 'a natural progression', it was among the fastest-selling items in dance shops throughout the UK in 1993, moving over 35,000 copies. This first set compiled a series of club classics, such as Mother's 'All Funked Up', **X-Press 2**'s 'London X-Press' and **Gabrielle**'s 'Dreams', the latter a staple at the club long before it scaled the national charts. A second, similarly successful set, followed in 1994. This time there were remixes from **Paul Oakenfold,** who helmed a live touring version of the club through 1994. The club also rose to prominence by projecting their logo onto the Houses Of Parliament as part of their second birthday celebrations, despite police objections.

Albums: Various: *The Ministry - Vol 1* (MOS 1993), *The Ministry - Vol 2* (MOS 1994).

Minit Records

Synonymous with both the New Orleans soul scene, and the tremendous impact producer, writer and musician **Allen Toussaint** had on the development of black American music, Minit Records took its name from the original intention to supply disc jockeys with short (i.e. Minit) records which maximised the possibility to play advertisements in-between. In fact, Toussaint was not present at the label's inception, in 1959, when Joe Banashak and Larry McKinley formed the company. The first release was 'Bad Luck And Trouble', by Boogie Jake. However, Boogie's moniker drew resistance from radio stations, ensuring that its local popularity did not translate to national acclaim, despite **Chess Records** licensing it for that purpose. Chess then reneged on its future options, though neither Boogie's follow-up (this time released under his real name, Matthew Jacobs) or a further single by Noland Pitts provided success. At this stage a twist in fortunes helped shaped Minit's future. Regular A&R representative Harold Batiste temporarily left, leaving Banashak and McKinley to recruit Toussaint, who had already successfully auditioned as a musician. When Batiste failed to return, the post became his on a permanent footing. Toussaint went on to define the Minit sound - writing much of the artistic repertoire, as well as arranging, producing and playing on the sessions. Minit's first hit, however, arrived with a rare artist's own composition - Jessie Hill's 'Ooh Poo Pah Doo'. Reaching number 28 in the ***Billboard*** charts and number 3 in its R&B division, it was followed by a second, lesser hit, 'Whip It On Me'. Meanwhile Toussaint had begun to shape the careers of Minit's roster. Ernie K-Doe (b. Ernest Kador) was a veteran of the Blue Diamonds, and later recorded for Specialty and Ember Records as a solo artist. K-Doe broke through with his third release for the label, a Toussaint composition entitled 'Mother-In-Law'. This rose to number 1 in the main *Billboard* charts and gave New Orleans its first ever such success. Follow-ups included 'Te-Ta-Te-Ta-Ta' and 'I Cried My Last Tear'. The latter was a double a-side featuring another Toussaint composition, 'A Certain Girl', which was later covered by the **Yardbirds**. Benny Speelman, who had provided additional vocals on K-Doe's 'Mother-In-Law' hit, was also a fellow Minit intern. He found fame under his own name with the 1962 double a-side,

'Lipstick Traces (On A Cigarette)'/'Fortune Teller'. The first-named title was later revived by both the **O'Jays** and **Ringo Starr**. More enduringly, **Aaron Neville** also began his career at Minit, beginning with 1960's 'Over You'. One of many songs Toussaint composed in tandem with Allen Orange (who also recorded solo for the label), it was a precursor to the artist's major breakthrough six years later with 'Tell It Like It Is'. Another staple of the early catalogue was the subsequently popular **Irma Thomas**, while the Showmen scored a 1961 hit for the label with 'It Will Stand'. Leader General Johnson would find subsequent success with **Chairman Of The Board**. However, by the time the Showmen's '30-21-46 (You)' had become another hit in 1963, Minit Records was in trouble. This coincided with Toussaint being drafted into the services, as well as the sale of Imperial Records (who distributed Minit) to **Liberty Records**. Minit was thus inactive until 1966, at which time Imperial revived the label, using it as a more generic soul outlet, meaning the subsidiary was now no longer dealing with exclusively New Orleans-based acts. The new roster included the Players, Jimmy Holiday, Jimmy McCracklin, Vernon Greene And The Medallions and the O'Jays, who moved over from Imperial. **Ike And Tina Turner** were also drafted from the parent label, and enjoyed their biggest success with Minit via the **Beatles**' cover, 'Come Together'. Another important name, that of **Bobby Womack**, also added to the discography, in his guise as lead singer of the Valentinos, before staying with the label when he became a solo artist. Minit's death knell arrived in 1971, when Liberty merged with United Artists and all subsidiary labels surrendered their artist rosters to the new conglomeration. A beautifully designed package was issued in 1994 with a full history.
Selected compilation: *The Mint Records Story* (EMI 1994).

Mink DeVille

The foundation of this unit was guitarist and songwriter **Willy DeVille** (b. 27 August 1953, New York City, New York, USA). He arrived in London in 1971 to form a band but, unable to find the right musicians, performed as a solo artist before heading to San Francisco and assembling the embryonic Mink DeVille. The basic trio became Willy (vocals, guitar, harmonica), Ruben Siguenza (bass) and Thomas R. Allen (drums). Allen had previously played with various blues musicians. They relocated to New York and recruited Louie X Erlanger on guitar. The band, by this time a wonderful live unit, recorded three tracks for the *Live At CBGB's* compilation and then in 1977 released their debut, which included the hit single 'Spanish Stroll'. The album, produced by **Jack Nitzsche**, also included a version of the **Patti And The Emblems**' classic, 'Mixed Up Shook Up'. The second album *Return To Magenta* was publicised by releasing 'Soul Twist' on purple vinyl, but overall the album was an unhappy compromise between the group's original new wave sound and Willy DeVille's more soulful ambitions. Like the debut, it included a Moon Martin cover, 'Rolene'. For the third album, *Le Chat Blue*, in 1980, the band comprised Willy and Erlanger, plus Kenny Margolis (keyboards), Jerry Scheff (bass), Ron Tutt (drums) and Steve Douglas (saxophone). Although it featured co-writing credits by songwriter **Doc Pomus** (**Joe Turner**, **Dion**, **Drifters**), the album failed to spark. *Savoir Faire* collected the best of the three Capitol albums, after which the band moved to **Atlantic Records**. Unfortunately, *Coup De Grâce* also failed to signal a revival. Despite Nitzsche returning to produce, only the occasional song had Mink DeVille's previous edge. Things improved, though, with the release of *Where Angels Fear To Tread* which removed some of the over-produced clutter from their sound. Willy DeVille's new songs paid tribute to his soul heroes without affecting the band's new-found strength. *Sportin' Life* continued the improvement, although afterwards De Ville left to renew his solo career.
Albums: *Mike DeVille* (Capitol 1977), *Return To Magenta* (Capitol 1978), *Le Chat Bleu* (Capitol 1980), *Coup De Grâce* (Atlantic 1981), *Where Angels Fear To Tread* (Atlantic 1983), *Sportin' Life* (Atlantic 1985), *Cabretta* (Razor 1987). Compilation: *Savoir Faire* (Capitol 1981).

Minnelli, Liza

b. Liza May Minnelli, 12 March 1946, Los Angeles, California, USA. An extremely vivacious and animated actress, singer and dancer, in films, concerts, musical shows and television. She was named Liza after the **George** and **Ira Gershwin-Gus Kahn** song- and May after the mother of her film-director father, **Vincente Minnelli**. Liza's mother was show-business legend **Judy Garland**. On the subject of her first name, Miss Minnelli is musically quite precise: 'It's Liza with 'zee', not Lisa with an 's'/'Cos Liza with a 'zee' goes 'zzz', not 'sss'. She spent a good deal of her childhood in Hollywood, where her playmates included Mia Farrow, although she also reputedly attended over 20 schools in the USA and Europe. At the age of two-and-a-half, she made her screen debut in the closing sequence of *In The Good Old Summer Time*, as the daughter of the musical film's stars, Garland and Van Johnson. When she was seven, she danced on the stage of the Palace Theatre, New York, while her mother sang 'Swanee'. In 1962, after initially showing no interest in a show-business career, Minnelli served as an apprentice in revivals of the musicals, ***Take Me Along*** and ***The Flower Drum Song***, and later played Anne Frank in a stock production. By the following year she was accomplished enough to win a Promising Personality Award for her third lead performance in an Off-Broadway revival of the 1941 **Ralph**

Blane/Hugh Martin Musical *Best Foot Forward*, and later toured in road productions of ***Carnival***, ***The Pajama Game***, and ***The Fantasticks***. She also made her first album, *Liza! Liza!* which sold over 500,000 copies shortly after it was released in 1964. In November of that year, Minnelli appeared with Judy Garland at the London Palladium. Comparatively unknown in the UK, she startled the audience with dynamic performances of songs such as 'The Travellin' Life' and 'The Gypsy In My Soul' - almost 'stealing' the show from the more experienced artist. Her Broadway debut in ***Flora, The Red Menace*** (1965), marked the beginning of a long association with songwriters **John Kander** and **Fred Ebb**, gained her a **Tony Award**, although the show closed after only 87 performances. In 1966 she made her New York cabaret debut at the Plaza Hotel to enthusiastic reviews, and in 1967 married Australian singer/songwriter, **Peter Allen**. Her film career started in 1968 with a supporting role in Albert Finney's first directorial effort, *Charlie Bubbles*, and in 1969, she was nominated for an Academy Award for her performance as Pookie Adams in the film of John Nichols' novel, *The Sterile Cuckoo*. She took time off from making her third film, *Tell Me That You Love Me, Junie Moon*, to attend the funeral of her mother, who died in 1969. In the following year she and Peter Allen announced their separation.

In 1972, Liza Minnelli became a superstar. The film of Kander and Ebb's Broadway hit, ***Cabaret***, won nine Oscars, including Best Film, and for her role as Sally Bowles, Minnelli was named Best Actress and appeared on the front covers of *Newsweek* and *Time* magazines in the same week. She also won an Emmy for her television special *Liza With A Z*, directed by **Bob Fosse**. Her concerts were sell-outs; when she played the Olympia, Paris, they dubbed her 'la petite Piaf Americano'. In 1973 she met producer/director Jack Haley Jnr. while contributing to his film project *That's Entertainment!* Haley's father had played the Tin Man in Judy Garland's most famous picture, ***The Wizard Of Oz***. Haley Jnr and Minnelli married in 1974, and in the same year she broke Broadway records and won a special Tony Award for a three-week series of one-woman shows at the Winter Garden. Her next two movies, *Lucky Lady* and *A Matter Of Time* received lukewarm reviews, but she made up for these in 1977,with her next film project, ***New York, New York***. Co-starring with Robert DeNiro, and directed by Martin Scorsese, Minnelli's dramatic performance as a young band singer in the period after World War II was a personal triumph. This was the last film she made until *Arthur* (1981), in which she played a supporting role to **Dudley Moore**. The musical theme for *Arthur*, 'Best You Can Do', was co-written by her ex-husband, Peter Allen. A renewed association with Kander and Ebb for the Broadway musical *The Act* (1977), was dismissed by some critics as being little more than a series of production numbers displaying the talents of Liza Minnelli. In brought her another Tony Award, but she collapsed from exhaustion during the show's run. In 1979, she was divorced from Jack Haley Jnr., and married Italian sculptor, Mark Gero. Rumours were appearing in the press speculating about her drug and alcohol problems, and for a couple of years she was virtually retired. In 1984 she was nominated for yet another Tony for her performance on Broadway in ***The Rink***, with **Chita Rivera**, but dropped out of the show to seek treatment for drug and alcohol abuse at the Betty Ford Clinic in California. She started her comeback in 1985, and in the following year, on her 40th birthday, opened to a sold-out London Palladium, the first time she had played the theatre since that memorable occasion in 1964; she received the same kind of reception that her mother did then. In the same year, back in the USA, Minnelli won the Golden Globe Award as Best Actress in *A Time To Live*, a television adaptation of the true story, *Intensive Care*, by Mary-Lou Weisman. During the late 80s she joined **Frank Sinatra** and **Sammy Davis Jnr.** for a world tour, dubbed *The Ultimate Event!*, and in 1989 collaborated with the UK pop group, the **Pet Shop Boys**, on the album *Results*. A single from the album, **Stephen Sondheim**'s 'Losing My Mind', gave Liza Minnelli her first UK chart entry, at number 6. She also appeared with Dudley Moore in the film *Arthur 2: On The Rocks*. In 1991, after co-starring with Julie Walters in the musical comedy *Stepping Out*, Minnelli used the film's title for a series of concerts she gave at Radio City Music Hall in New York which broke the venue's 59-year box office record. She later took the show to London's Royal Albert Hall, where she returned a year later for a one-off gala charity concert dedicated to the memory of her late friend Sammy Davis Jnr. Her other work in the early 90s included concerts with **Charles Aznavour** at the Palais des Congress and Carnegie Hall, and serving as host for the 1993 Tony Awards ceremony, during which she sang a medley of Broadway songs with her step-sister Lorna Luft. In June 1994 Minnelli was in Moscow, giving shows as part of the D-Day commemorations. Later in the year she underwent surgery to replace her right hip, after 'being in pain for 10 years'. Her career in film and music has enabled her to transcend the title, 'Judy Garland's daughter'.

Albums: *Best Foot Forward* (1963, Off-Broadway Cast), *Liza! Liza!* (1964), *It Amazes Me* (1965), *The Dangerous Christmas Of Red Riding Hood* (1965, film soundtrack), with Judy Garland *'Live' At The London Palladium* (1965), *Flora, The Red Menace* (1965, Broadway Cast), *There Is A Time* (1966), *New Feelin'* (1970), *Cabaret* (1972, film soundtrack), *Liza With A 'Z'* (1972, television soundtrack), *Liza Minnelli The Singer* (1973), *Live At The Winter Garden* (1974), *Lucky Lady* (1976), *Tropical Nights*

(1977), *Live! - At Carnegie Hall* (1988), *Results* (1989), *Live From Radio City Music Hall* (1992), *Aznavour/Minnelli Paris-Palais Des Congrès* (EMI 1995).
Further reading: *Liza*, James Robert Parish. *Judy And Liza*, James Spada. *Liza - Born A Star*, Wendy Leigh. *Liza: Her Cinderella Nightmare*, James Robert Parish.
Videos: *Visible Results* (1990), *Live At Radio City Music Hall* (1994).

Minnelli, Vincente

b. 28 February 1903, Chicago, Illinois, USA, d. 25 July 1986, Los Angeles, California, USA. A distinguished film director with a sophisticated style and flair, particularly in the use of colour and the innovative filming of the most exquisite dance sequences. Minnelli is credited, in collaboration with **Gene Kelly**, with being the main influence on the classic MGM musicals of the 50s. As a young child Minnelli appeared in plays produced by the family Minnelli Bros. Tent Theatre which toured the American Mid-West. After leaving school at 16 he studied at the Art Institute of Chicago and worked as a window and costume designer before moving to New York and designing the settings and costumes for two 1932 Broadway shows, the ***Earl Carroll Vanities*** and *The DuBarry*. From 1933-35 Minnelli was art director at the Radio City Music Hall where he staged a series of ballets and musicals. In 1935 he directed as well as designed the Beatrice Lillie musical ***At Home Abroad***, and throughout the 30s worked successfully on productions such as ***Ziegfeld Follies***, ***The Show Is On***, ***Hooray For What!***, and *Very Warm For May* (1939). From 1940-42, under the aegis of MGM producer **Arthur Freed**, Minnelli trained in different aspects of Hollywood film techniques and supervised speciality numbers in a number of films including ***Strike Up The Band***, ***Babes On Broadway***, and ***Panama Hattie***. He made his debut as a director in 1943 with the all-black musical ***Cabin In Sky***, which was followed by *I Dood It* a year later. Then came ***Meet Me In St. Louis*** (1944) a delightful piece of nostalgic Americana which became one of the most beloved musicals of all time. Minnelli married its star, **Judy Garland**, in 1945 (divorced 1951), and in the following year their daughter, **Liza Minnelli**, was born. Over the next 25 years Minnelli directed a number of musicals which met with varying degrees of success. *Yolande And The Thief* (1945), which starred **Fred Astaire**, was followed by the all-star spectacular ***Ziegfeld Follies*** (1946), and two films with Gene Kelly, the underrated ***The Pirate*** (1948), and ***An American In Paris*** (1951), which is often considered to be Minnelli's masterpiece. However, many would argue that another of the director's collaborations with Fred Astaire, ***The Band Wagon*** (1953), or the delightful ***Gigi*** (1958), were equally important events in the director's distinguished career. Certainly, whatever their merits - and they were not inconsiderable - few would submit ***Brigadoon*** (1954), ***Kismet*** (1955), ***Bells Are Ringing*** (1960), or *On A Clear Day You Can See Forever* (1970) as being prime examples of Vincente Minnelli's art. The latter film was made for Paramount after he had ended his association with MGM which had lasted for more than 25 years. Of course, the majority of Minnelli's films were not musicals. Over the years he made many other pictures in a wide variety of styles and moods, including *The Clock*, *Father Of The Bride*, *The Bad And The Beautiful*, *Lust For Life*, *Tea And Sympathy*, *The Cobweb*, *The Reluctant Debutante*, and *Some Came Running*. He finally achieved his ambition to work with his daughter, Liza Minnelli, on his last film *A Matter Of Time* in 1976. By then Minnelli's kind of films - particularly the musicals - were a thing of the past, and he lived quietly in retirement until his death at his home in Beverly Hills in 1986. The year of his birth has always been the subject of speculation. The one given above is that which was printed in the excellent obituary notice in *Variety*. In 1993 the young cabaret entertainer Jeff Harnar presented his solo revue *Dancing In The Dark - Vincente Minnelli's Hollywood* in New York.
Further reading: *I Remember It Well*, Vincente Minnelli.

Minogue, Dannii

b. 20 October 1970, Australia. One of two famous Minogue sisters, Dannii actually became a star in her native country before elder sister **Kylie Minogue**, though the latter hit the world arena first. Dannii made her television debut at the age of seven in *Skyways*, and followed it with a string of television shows, including *Young Talent Time*, a showcase for new young acts, on which she first appeared in 1979; three years later, she became its host for the next six years. It was not all smooth running, though; twice the two sisters went for the same role, with Kylie coming out on top to land parts in *The Sullivans* and *Neighbours*. Meanwhile, in 1985, Dannii launched her recording career with an Australian-only cover version of **Madonna**'s 'Material Girl'. She followed this with poppy stabs at **Europe**'s 'The Final Countdown', and the **Cars**' 'Let's Go'. *Now And Then* and *Phenomenon* were released in 1985 and 1987 respectively, but only in Australia. Her popularity in her homeland was such that she even designed and marketed her own fashion range. After leaving the talent show in 1988, Dannii took a role in *All The Way*. Shortly afterwards she was signed to Australia's Mushroom Records and was sent to New York with producers Vincent Bell and Alvin Moody to record a new single. However, before it could be finished, Dannii was offered the important role of Emma Jackson in *Home And Away* and decided to put her musical career on hold for about a year. After she left, the single 'Love And Kisses' was completed and released in Australia in March 1990. The following year, with *Home And Away* turning her into a star in the

UK, Dannii was signed to **MCA** and the single was remixed by Danny D of **D Mob**.
Albums: *Dannii* (1991), *Get Into You* (1993).

Minogue, Kylie

b. 28 May 1968, Melbourne, Australia. Heralding from a stage family, Minogue passed an audition for the Australian soap opera, *Neighbours*, which eventually led to her recording debut with **Little Eva**'s hit, 'The Locomotion'. When the television series was successfully screened in Britain, prolific hit producers **Stock, Aitken And Waterman** intervened to mould Kylie's attractive, wholesome, anodyne image to their distinctive brand of radio-centred pop. The first UK single, 'I Should Be So Lucky', soon reached number 1, presaging an impressive chart run of instantly hummable hits, including 'Got To Be Certain', 'Je`Ne Sais`Pas Pour Qui', 'Hand On Your Heart', 'Wouldn't Cange A Thing' and 'Never Too Late'. With solo success enhanced by duets with co-star **Jason Donovan,** Minogue has emerged as one of the most successfully marketed acts of the late 80s, with books and films, including *The Delinquents*. In 1991, the former soap star drastically changed her girl-next door image and adopted a sexier persona, which won her even more media coverage - particularly when she became romantically involved with **INXS** lead singer, Michael Hutchence. Surprisingly, she even won some acclaim in the music press and found her self championed as an unlikely 'pop goddess'.
Albums: *Kylie* (1988), *Enjoy Yourself* (1989), *Kylie* (1991), *Kylie Minogue* (Deconstruction 1994). Compilation: *Greatest Hits* (1992).
Further reading: *The Superstar Next Door*, Sasha Stone.

Minor Threat

One of the most influential US punk band of the 80s, Minor Threat's highly idealistic message, similar to that of **Crass** and the anarcho-punk bands of the UK, proved inspirational to a young audience disaffected with its political choices. Based in Washington D.C., the group was formed in 1980 from the ashes of local band, Teen Idles. The main spokesman Ian MacKaye (vocals) and drummer Jeff Nelson left that band to join Lyle Preslar (guitar) and Brian Baker (bass; ex-**Government Issue**) in Minor Threat. By this time Minor Threat had already recorded their anthem 'Minor Threat' and 'Straight Edge', the song that gave punk rock a new energy. Railing against the impotent whining of would-be rebels who spent all their energy on drink, drugs, abusive sex and shallow relationships, 'straight edge' stood for a code of abstinence which swept the US punk scene (no drugs, tobacco, alcohol or meat). By 1982 Steve Hansen had taken over on bass, and Baker switched to second guitar. The new line-up completed *Out Of Step*. This revealed a fastidiously executed, densely structured assault which sounded like nothing which had preceded it. Sadly, the enormous pressure the band was now under resulted in their demise. MacKaye, in particular, was struggling with the sort of deification that had been his last intention when he formed the band. MacKaye and Nelson continued to work together for **Dischord Records**, one of America's foremost underground labels. MacKaye went on to record with Egg Hunt (again with Nelson), Embrace (with members of his brother, Alec MacKaye's former band, Faith), Pailhead (with Al Jourgenson of **Ministry**) and finally **Fugazi** - the most permanent and important of those liaisons. Nelson worked with Three, Skewbald and **Senator Flux**, before concentrating full-time on Dischord's growth. Baker went on to stints in **Meatmen**, **Dag Nasty** and **Junkyard**. Preslar also worked with the Meatmen, while Hansen has recorded with Government Issue, Modest Proposal, Weatherhead and others.
Albums: *Out Of Step* (Dischord 1983, mini-album). Compilations: *First Two 7-inches* (Dischord 1984), *Complete Discography* (Dischord 1988).

Minott, Sugar

b. Lincoln Minott, 25 May 1956, Kingston, Jamaica, West Indies. Minott was, perhaps, reggae music's brightest hope throughout the early 80s, but his refusal to compromise and turn his back on either his roots or his ghetto companions has marginalized his influence, and he is now a peripheral figure, as opposed to the major force he arguably deserves to be. Minott first recorded in the mid-70s as one of the **African Brothers** with Tony Tuff and Derrick Howard for a variety of Kingston producers; a couple of all-time classics evolved from this period, including 'Torturing' and 'Party Night'. The African Brothers eventually arrived at **Studio One**, where Sugar's precocious talent was immediately recognised and he was taken on as a studio apprentice where he sang whatever was required, often providing percussion and guitar where necessary. His sweet vocals were only one facet of his talent, and his ability to write new songs to fit over existing rhythms was remarkable. The results, in many cases, eclipsed the originals. He had a few steady sellers for Studio One, but it was his debut long player, *Live Loving,* that made his name and extended his popularity. He became a bigger star in the UK than in his homeland, and his first release in Britain, the self-produced 'Hard Time Pressure', was a major underground hit in 1979. He travelled to England later that year, and stayed for a lengthy period, adding immeasurably to the indigenous reggae scene. He became a focus for UK reggae, while releasing many records in the accepted local **lovers rock** style, which demonstrated his ability to work successfully in any flavour of reggae music. A national chart hit, for Hawkeye Records, followed in 1980, and crossover success seemed to be the next obvious step for Minott.

He had previously parted company with Studio One because of his desire for independence, and set up his own Youth Promotion/Black Roots collective organisation to foster and develop the abundant talent in the Kingston ghettos. Consequently, when he was offered deals for recording and concert work with established companies, Minott refused to sign unless the rest of the Youth Promotion team were a part of the arrangement. This proved too altruistic for the large labels, and Minott continued to work in his own way, recording solo outings for many independent producers to finance his ideals. Sadly, his single-minded determination to help out the youths in the ghetto did not work in his favour, and many young singers and DJs who came to prominence on Sugar's Youth Promotion **sound system** (one of the top Kingston Sounds of the 80s) went on to greater success elsewhere, while his personal strength, too, seemed to be sapped by his constant caring for others less fortunate. His releases for the latter part of the decade were often lacklustre, relying too heavily on the stringing together of **dancehall** catchphrases and clichés. However, in the 90s he began to make some excellent records both for himself and other producers, including **King Jammy,** which at last recalled former glories.

Selected albums: *Live Loving* (Studio One 1978), *Showcase* (Studio One 1979), *Black Roots* (Island 1979), *Bittersweet* (Ballistic 1979), *Ghetto-Ology* (Trojan 1979), *Roots Lovers* (Black Roots 1980), *Give The People* (Ballistic 1980), *African Girl* (Black Roots 1981), *Good Thing Going* (RCA 1981), *Dancehall Showcase* (Black Roots 1983), *With Lots Of Extra* (Hitbound 1983), *Herbman Hustling* (Black Roots 1984), *Slice Of The Cake* (Heartbeat 1984), *Wicked A Go Feel It* (Wackies 1984), *Leader Of The Pack* (Striker Lee 1985), *Rydim* (Greensleeves 1985), *Time Longer Than Rope* (Greensleeves 1985), *Inna Reggae Dancehall* (Heartbeat 1986), *Sugar And Spice* (Taxi 1986), *Them Ah Wolf* (C&F 1987), *Jamming In The Streets* (Wackies 1987), *African Soldier* (Heartbeat 1988), *Buy Off The Bar* (Sonic Sounds 1988), *Sugar Minott And Youth Promotion* (NEC 1988), *Lovers Rock Inna Dancehall* (Youth Promotion 1988), *Ghetto Youth Dem Rising* (Heartbeat 1988), *Sufferer's Choice* (Heartbeat 1988), *The Boss Is Back* (RAS 1989), *Smile* (L&M 1990), *A Touch Of Class* (Jammys 1991), *Run Things* (Exterminator 1993). With the African Brothers: *Collectors Item* (Uptempo 1987). With Leroy Smart: *Rockers Award Winners* (Greensleeves 1985). Compilations: *Best Of Vol. 1* (Black Roots 1988), *The Artist* (L&M 1989, double album), *20 Super Hits* (Sonic Sounds 1990).

Video: *Official Sugar Minott Dance Hall Video* (1988).

Mint Juleps

This **a cappella** soul group from the East End of London, England, consisted of sisters Debbie, Lizzie, Sandra and Marcia Charles plus their friends Debbie and Julie. They all formerly worked together at the Half Moon Theatre in Putney, where they decided to form a group. They played at various benefits and toured with **Sister Sledge** and **Billy Bragg**, and worked as backing singers for **Bob Geldof**, the **Belle Stars** and **Dr. Feelgood**. They signed to **Stiff Records**, and were managed by former **Darts'** members Rita Ray and Rob Fish. The Mint Juleps recorded vocal versions of **Neil Young**'s 'Only Love Can Break Your Heart', **Robert Palmer**'s 'Every Kinda People', and the original 'Girl To The Power Of 6' (produced by **Trevor Horn**). They later moved away from a cappella into a kind of lightweight rap in the vein of **Salt 'N' Pepper**.

Album: *One Time* (1985).

Mint Tattoo

Guitarist Bruce Stephens founded this short-lived, late 60s San Franciscan trio with Burns Kellogg (bass) and Greg Thomas (drums). Their only, blues-based, album showed promise, but the group broke up prematurely when both Stephens and Kellogg joined heavy west-coast rockers **Blue Cheer**. The former was later a member of **Pilot** (USA), prior to embarking on a solo career.

Album: *Mint Tattoo* (1968).

Minter, Iverson

(see **Louisiana Red**)

Mintzer, Bob

b. 27 January 1953, New Rochelle, Westchester, New York, USA. Interested in music from childhood, he began serious studies shortly before he left high school. He went to Interlochen Arts Academy in Michigan by which time he was becoming adept on tenor saxophone and also was taking interest in arranging. Fellow students at Interlochen included **Peter Erskine** and two sons of **Dave Brubeck**. Mintzer then studied and played, mostly clarinet, at Hart College of Music in Hartford, Connecticut, then went to the Manhattan School of Music in New York. However, the active New York music scene proved to be a greater attraction and in 1974 he went on the road with Eumir **Deodato** and the following year began a two-year stint with **Buddy Rich** where his arranging talents blossomed. After leaving Rich he worked regularly with the **Thad Jones-Mel Lewis** Jazz Orchestra. He continued to develop as an arranger and preferred the context of a big band, playing with Stone Alliance, and the big bands of **Sam Jones** and **Jaco Pastorius**. In 1984 he formed his own big band before becoming a regular member of the popular **Yellowjackets**. In his playing, Mintzer acknowledges the influence of most of the leading tenor saxophone stylists of jazz from **Coleman Hawkins** through to **John Coltrane** but has developed his own powerful and distinctive style. As

an arranger he happily uses latterday musical movements, such as rock and post-rock, without ever losing the tradition of big band jazz. His arrangements, especially when playing by his own band are finely crafted and performed, tight and urgent.
Albums: with Stone Alliance *Heads Up* (PM 1980), *Papa Lips* (Sony 1984), *Incredible Journey* (DMP 1985), *Camouflage* (DMP 1986), *Spectrum* (DMP 1987), *Urban Contours* (DMP 1988), *Art Of The Big Band* (DMP 1989), with Peter Erskine *Sweet Soul* (BMG 1991), *One Music* (DMP 1991), *I Remember Jaco* (BMG 1991), with Yellowjackets *Greenhouse* (GRP c1990), with Yellowjackets *Run For Your Life* (GRP c.1990), *Departure* (DMP 1992), *Only In New York* (DMP 1994).

Minutemen

Formed in 1980 in San Pedro, California, USA, and originally known as the Reactionaries. This influential hardcore trio initially comprised D. Boon (guitar/vocals), Mike Watt (bass) and Frank Tonche (drums), but the last named was replaced by George Hurley prior to recording. Although the trio donated tracks to several independent compilations, notably for the pivotal Radio Tokyo Tapes and the Posh Boy and New Alliance labels, their association with SST Records resulted in some of the genre's most impressive recordings. The unfettered rage of their early work was less apparent on *Buzz Or Howl Under The Influence Of Heat* and *Project: Mersh*, ('Mersh' is San Pedro slang for 'commercial'), but *Double Nickels On The Dime* and *3-Way Tie (For Last)* showed an undeterred passion and commitment. The Minutemen came to a premature end in 1986 following the death of D. Boon. Watt and Hurley decided to drop the group's name, and in its place formed **Firehose** with guitarist Ed Crawford.
Albums: *The Punchline* (1980), *Bean Spill* (1982), *What Makes A Man Start Fires* (1983), *Buzz Or Howl Under The Influence Of Heat* (1983), *Politics Of Time* (1984), *Double Nickels On The Dime* (1984), *Project: Mersh* (1985), *3-Way Tie (For Last)* (1986), *Ballot Result* (1987). Compilations: *My First Bells* (1985), *Post-Mersh Volume 1* (1985), *Post-Mersh Volume 2* (1987), *Post-Mersh Volume 3* (1989), *What Makes A Man Start Fires* (1991).

Miracles

Of all the R&B vocal groups formed in Detroit, Michigan, USA, in the mid-50s, the Miracles proved to be the most successful. They were founded at the city's Northern High School in 1955 by **Smokey Robinson** (b. William Robinson, 19 February 1940, Detroit, Michigan, USA), Emerson Rogers, Bobby Rogers (b. 19 February 1940, Detroit, Michigan, USA), Ronnie White (b. 5 April 1939, Detroit, Michigan, USA) and Warren 'Pete' Moore (b. 19 November 1939, Detroit, Michigan, USA). Emerson Rogers left the following year, to be replaced by his sister Claudette, who in turn married Smokey Robinson in 1959. Known initially as the Matadors, the group became the Miracles in 1958, when they made their initial recordings with producer **Berry Gordy**.
He leased their debut, 'Got A Job' (an answer record to the **Silhouettes**' major hit 'Get A Job'), to End Records, produced a duet by Ron (White) And Bill (Robinson) for Argo, and licensed the classic doo-wop novelty, 'Bad Girl', to **Chess** in 1959. The following year, Gordy signed the Miracles directly to his fledgling **Motown** label. Recognizing the youthful composing talents of Smokey Robinson, he allowed the group virtual free rein in the studio, and was repaid when they issued 'Way Over There', a substantial local hit, and then 'Shop Around', which broke both the Miracles and Motown to a national audience. The song demonstrated the increasing sophistication of Robinson's writing, which provided an unbroken series of hits for the group over the next few years. Their raw, doo-wop sound was further refined on the Top 10 hit 'You Really Got A Hold On Me' in 1962, a soulful ballad which became a worldwide standard after the **Beatles** covered it in 1963. Robinson was now in demand by other Motown artists: Gordy used him as a one-man hit factory, to mastermind releases by the **Temptations** and **Mary Wells**, and the Miracles' own career suffered slightly as a result.
They continued to enjoy success in a variety of different styles, mixing dance-floor hits like 'Mickey's Monkey' and 'Going To A Go-Go' with some of Robinson's most durable ballads, like 'Oooh Baby Baby' and 'The Tracks Of My Tears'. Though Smokey sang lead on almost all the group's recordings, the rest of the group provided a unique harmony blend behind him, while guitarist Marv Tarplin - who co-wrote several of their hits - was incorporated as an unofficial Miracle from the mid-60s onwards. Claudette Robinson stopped touring with the group after 1965, although she was still featured on many of their subsequent releases. Exhausted by several years of constant work, Robinson scaled down his writing commitments for the group in the mid-60s, when they briefly worked with **Holland/Dozier/Holland** and other Motown producers. Robinson wrote their most ambitious and lasting songs, however, including 'The Tears Of A Clown' in 1966 (a belated hit in the UK and USA in 1970), and 'The Love I Saw In You Was Just A Mirage' and 'I Second That Emotion' in 1967. These tracks epitomized the strengths of Robinson's compositions, with witty, metaphor-filled lyrics tied to aching melody lines and catchy guitar figures, the latter often provided by Marv Tarplin. Like many of the veteran Motown acts, the Miracles went into a sales slump after 1967 - the year when Smokey Robinson was given individual credit on the group's records. Their slide was less noticeable in Britain, where Motown gained a Top 10 hit in 1969 with a reissue of 'The Tracks Of My Tears', which most listeners

imagined was a contemporary record. The success of 'The Tears Of A Clown' prompted a revival in fortune after 1970. 'I'm The One You Need' became another reissue hit in Britain the following year, while 'I Don't Blame You At All', one of their strongest releases to date, scored chart success on both sides of the Atlantic. In 1971, Robinson announced his intention of leaving the Miracles to concentrate on his position as vice-president of Motown Records. His decision belied the title of his final hit with the group, 'We've Come Too Far To End It Now' in 1972, and left the Miracles in the unenviable position of having to replace one of the most distinctive voices in popular music. Their choice was William 'Bill' Griffin (b. 15 August 1950, Detroit, Michigan, USA), who was introduced by Robinson to the group's audiences during a 1972 USA tour. The new line-up took time to settle, while Smokey Robinson launched a solo career to great acclaim in 1973. The group responded with *Renaissance*, which saw them working with Motown luminaries like **Marvin Gaye** and **Willie Hutch**. The following year, they re-established the Miracles as a hit-making force with 'Do It Baby' and 'Don'tcha Love It', dance-orientated singles which appealed strongly to the group's black audience. In 1975, 'Love Machine' became the Miracles' first US chart-topper, while the concept album *City Of Angels* was acclaimed as one of Motown's most progressive releases. This twin success proved to be the Miracles' last commercial gasp. Switching to **Columbia** in 1977, they lost Billy Griffin, who set out on a little-noticed solo career. Donald Griffin briefly joined the group in his place, but the Miracles ceased recording in 1978. Thereafter, Ronnie White and Bill Rogers steered the outfit into the new decade as a touring band, before the Miracles disbanded, without any fanfares only to be reformed by Bobby Rogers in 1982. He enlisted Dave Finlay and Carl Cotton as the new Miracles. Former members Billy Griffin and Claudette Robinson (ex-wife of Smokey) recorded solo tracks for **Ian Levine**'s Motor City label during 1988-91. Griffin issued *Technicolour* in 1992. Another reformed group comprising Griffin, Robinson, Rogers, Donald Griffin, Cotton and Finlay also recorded for Levine remaking 'Love Machine' in 1990.

Albums: as the Miracles *Hi, We're The Miracles* (1961), *Cookin' With The Miracles* (1962), *I'll Try Something New* (1962), *The Fabulous Miracles* (1963), *Recorded Live: On Stage* (1963), *Christmas With The Miracles* (1963), *The Miracles Doin' 'Mickey's Monkey'* (1963), *Greatest Hits From The Beginning* (1965), *Renaissance* (1973), *Do It Baby* (1974), *Don'tcha Love It* (1975), *City Of Angels* (1975), *The Power Of Music* (1976), *Love Crazy* (1977), *The Miracles* (1978), *Technicolour* (1992). As Smokey Robinson And The Miracles: *Going To A Go-Go* (1965), *Away We-A-Go-Go* (1966), *Make It Happen* (1967), *Greatest Hits Volume 2* (1968), *Special Occasion* (1968), *Live* (1968), *Time Out For Smokey Robinson And The Miracles* (1969), *Four In Blue* (1969), *What Love Has Joined Together* (1970), *A Pocketful Of Miracles* (1970), *The Season For Miracles* (1970), *One Dozen Roses* (1971), *Flying High Together* (1972), *1957-72* (1972), *Anthology* (1973).

Miranda Sex Garden

Widely tagged with the terms 'classical' and 'pretentious' by UK critics, Miranda Sex Garden have faced sterner tests than that, including facing 20,000 unimpressed **Depeche Mode** fans on tour. The group comprise singer/songwriter Katharine Blake, and her cohorts, Ben Golomstock (keyboards), Donna McKevitt (violin) and Trevor Sharpe (percussion), having dropped original member Kelly McClusker, who formed the band with Blake after graduating from music college (Purcell School Of Music). All are accomplished musicians, and the three women each have strong falsetto voices. They spent their early days busking sixteenth century madrigals on London's underground, with an impressed **Barry Adamson** catching one performance on Portobello Road. Later they would contribute to his *Delusion* soundtrack. Their debut release comprised two versions of the madrigal 'Gush Forth My Tears', an *a cappela* treatment on one side, and a dance version on the other. Their talents won them a reception which was roughly equal in incredulity and wonder, and their voices soon appeared on Derek Jarman's soundtrack to *Blue* (on an unlikely song entitled 'Muff Diving Size Queen'). *Fairytales*, meanwhile, concerned sado-masochism, and they have actually played gigs under the title of Waltzing Maggots at fetish clubs, which included Blake performing half naked in Nazi regalia (finally destroying utterly their early press reputation for Victorian-esque primness).

Albums: *Madra* (Mute 1991), *Iris* (Mute 1992, mini-album), *Suspiria* (Mute 1993), *Fairytales Of Slavery* (Mute 1994).

Miranda, Carmen

b. Maria do Carmo Miranda da Cunha, 9 February 1909, near Lisbon, Portugal, d. 5 August 1955, California, USA. A flamboyant singer, dancer and actress with an animated style and a penchant for exotic, colourful costumes, 10 inch-heeled shoes, and turbans decorated with significant amounts of artificial fruit. She was raised in Rio de Janeiro and began her career there on local radio. Later she made several films and appeared in nightclubs and theatres throughout South America. Lee Shubert, the oldest of the famous trio of producer brothers, took Miranda to the USA in 1939 where she introduced **Al Dubin** and **Jimmy McHugh**'s catchy 'South American Way' in the Broadway musical *The Streets Of Paris*. She sang it again (her peculiar accent turned it into 'Souse American Way') when she made her spectacular film debut with **Betty Grable** and **Don Ameche** in ***Down Argentine Way*** (1940). A year later she joined the comedy team of Olsen and Jolsen in another Broadway show, *Sons O' Fun*. However, her real impact was made in a series of film musicals in the 40s when she became known as the 'Brazilian Bombshell'. These included ***That Night In Rio***, *Weekend In Havana*, *Springtime In The Rockies*, ***The Gang's All Here***, *Four Jills In A Jeep*, *Greenwich Village*, *Doll Face*, *If I'm Lucky*, *Copacabana*, and *A Date With Judy*. By then her star had faded, and she made only two more pictures, *Nancy Goes To Rio* (1950) and *Scared Stiff* (1953), although in the late 40s and early 50s she continued to perform in theatres and nightclubs. She died suddenly of a heart attack in 1955 shortly after appearing with **Jimmy Durante** on his television show. A dynamic, much impersonated entertainer - **Mickey Rooney**'s wickedly accurate takeoff in ***Babes On Broadway*** immediately comes to mind - Carmen Miranda was indelibly associated with several lively and diverting songs, including 'The Lady With The Tutti Frutti Hat', 'I Yi Yi Yi Yi (I Like You Very Much)', 'Chica Boom Chic', 'When I Love, I Love', 'Cuanto La Gusta', 'Mama, Eu Quero (I Want My Mama)', and 'The Wedding Samba' (the last two with the **Andrews Sisters**).

Selected albums: *South American Way* (c.50s, re-released 1982), *By Popular Demand* (MCA 1995).

Further reading: *Brazilian Bombshell: The Biography Of Carmen Miranda*, M. Gil-Montero.

Miranda, Ismael

b. 20 February 1950, Aguada, Puerto Rico. Singer/songwriter Miranda was one of the most popular soneros (extemporizing salsa singers) of the 70s salsa boom. His parents and an uncle took him to live in Long Island, USA when he was four years old; later on he moved with his family to the Lower East Side in Manhattan, New York City. He started studying singing at about eight years old and by 11 years of age he had mastered the conga. He performed with the bands of Pipo, Benny Ortiz, Raúl González and Andy Harlow (**Larry Harlow**'s brother) before joining Joey Pastrana's orchestra at the age of 16. He made his recording debut with Pastrana on *Let's Ball* (1967), performing on the big hit track 'Rumbón Mélon'. Larry Harlow, who had seen Miranda sing with his brother Andy's band, recruited the young sonero to perform lead vocals for his Orchestra Harlow in July 1967. 'His voice was young, clear, strong and above all he had great presence . . . Ismael combines his Puerto Rican blood, Cuban flavour and American know-how into a dynamic style,' wrote Harlow in his liner notes to *Orchestra Harlow Presenta a Ismael Miranda*. Over the next five years Miranda and Harlow developed a highly creative and successful partnership. During this period, he made seven albums with Orchestra Harlow, contributing a number of co-written (with Harlow) and self-penned hits.

By 1973 it was clear Miranda had out-grown Orchestra Harlow, and he split, taking three Harlow sidemen (Frankie Rodríguez, conga; Joe Santiago, bass; and Nicky Marrero, timbales) with him to his own newly formed Orquesta Revelación. His debut with them, *Así Se Compone Un Son* (1973), was arguably his finest work. Revelación's personnel contained several future prominent salsa names, such as Marrero; Nelson González, tres guitar; and Oscar Hernández, piano. 'I was 18 years old and we recorded one album and worked our butts off for about one year,' recollected Hernández in *New York Latino* in 1991. 'We used to play five to eight gigs a week and it was a great group. And it consisted of the young bloods who were good musicians . . . We had a great rhythm section . . .' Problems arose in the band, so Miranda disbanded and relocated to Puerto Rico to work as a solo artist, though he continued to record in New York. During the following 12 years he released a dozen albums on Fania Records, notable were *En Fa Menor* (1974), which he co-produced; his 1976 reunion with Larry Harlow: *Con Mi Viejo Amigo*, and the collaborations with **Willie Colón** (*Doble Energía*, 1980) and Cuban musical institution **Sonora Matancera** (*Sonora Matancera - Ismael Miranda*, 1984). 1977's *No Voy Al Festival* was Miranda's first LP where he took sole charge of production.

Several of Miranda's hit compositions attained classic status, such as 'Arsenio' from Orchestra Harlow's 1971 *Tribute To Arsenio Rodríguez*, co-written with Harlow; 'Pa Bravo Yo' written for Justo Betancourt's 1972 album of the same title (the song became Betancourt's trademark); and 'Así Se Compone Un Son', the title track of Miranda and Orquesta Revelación's 1973 debut album.

He guested at the first New York Salsa Festival in 1975 (called Super Salsa 75) at Madison Square Garden; others on the bill included **Tito Puente**, **Ray Barretto**, Willie Colón with **Héctor Lavoe**, **Típica 73**, **Cheo Feliciano**, **El Gran Combo**, Johnny Ventura and **La Lupe**.

In 1984 Miranda produced and acted as musical director of Nelson González and his Orquesta Revelación on *Feliz y Contento* for the small Bernis Records label, with future salsa romántico star Alex D'Castro providing the lead vocals. Two years later he was backed by González and Revelación (with D'Castro in the chorus) on *Una Nueva Vision*, his last on Fania until the mid-90s.

After his departure from Fania, Miranda briefly released albums on his own IM Records label, including *Por El Buen Camino* (1987) and the Christmas album *La Mano Maestro* (1989). As his waistline thickened with advancing middle age (chronicled by his album photographs), it seemed that the harder edge of his younger, leaner years diminished in direct proportion. He signed a short term contract with RMM Records and released the weak salsa romántica sets *Hasta La Ultima Gota* (1991) and *Entre Sombras*

(1992). He returned to Fania for 1993's *Enamorado De Ti*.

Miranda was a founder member of the **Fania All Stars** and sang on 17 of their albums between 1968 and 1986, and appeared with them in the movies *Our Latin Thing (Nuestra Cosa)* (1972; which 'catapulted this young lion even higher in the eyes of the public,' wrote Izzy Sanabria in his liner note to *Así Se Compone Un Son*), *Live In Africa* (1974) and *Salsa* (1976). In 1994 he participated in the three city (San Juan, Miami and New York) reunion of the Fania All Stars to mark the 30th anniversary of the Fania label. His rendition of his self-penned 'Borinquen Tiene Montuno' (originally recorded for *En Fa Menor*, 1974) was reportedly one of the highlights of the tour.

He sang on **Tito Puente**'s second tribute album to **Beny Moré** (1979) and the same bandleader's Grammy Award nominated *The Mambo King: 100th LP* (1991). In 1993 young salsa romántica heart-throb Rey Ruiz (b. 21 June 1966, Havana, Cuba; he defected while with the Cuban Tropicana cabaret when they were visiting the Dominican Republic in 1991) interpreted Miranda's 'Así Se Compone Un Son' on *Los Soneros De Hoy Tributo A Los Soneros* (Today's Soneros Pay Tribute To The Soneros). Miranda's contribution to the hip Puerto Rican all-star Latin jam session double CD *Descarga Boricua* (1993) helped absolve him for his flabby, undistinguished albums of the early 90s.

Albums: with Orchestra Harlow *El Exigente* (1967), *Orchestra Harlow Presenta a Ismael Miranda* (1968), *Me And My Monkey - 'Mi Mono y Yo'* (1969), *Electric Harlow* (1970), *Abran Paso!* (1971), *Tribute To Arsenio Rodríguez* (1971), *La Oportunidad* (1972); with Orquesta Revelación *Así Se Compone Un Son* (1973), *En Fa Menor* (1974), *Este Es...Ismael Miranda* (1975); with Orchestra Harlow *Con Mi Viejo Amigo* (1976), *No Voy Al Festival* (1977), *Sabor, Sentimiento y Pueblo* (1978); with Willie Colón *Doble Energía* (1980), *La Clave del Sabor* (1981), *Exitos De Los 50* (1982), *The Master* (1983); with Sonora Matancera *Sonora Matancera - Ismael Miranda* (1984), *Exitos De Los 50, Vol. II* (1985); with Orquesta Revelación *Una Nueva Vision* (1986), *Por El Buen Camino* (1987); three Christmas albums *Motivos De Mi Tierra* (1987), *Felicitándote* (1988), *La Mano Maestro* (1989); *Hasta La Ultima Gota* (1991), *Entre Sombras* (1992), *Enamorado De Ti* (1993). Compilations: with Orchestra Harlow *Harlow's Harem* (1971), *The Best Of Orchestra Harlow & Ismael Miranda* (1976); solo *El Compositor Que Canta* (1978).

Miro

Leading lights of the late UK 80s acoustic music revival, Miro reflected pastoral traditions with a string section, guitars and **Nick Drake**-influenced songs, composed by the leader, Roddy Harris. The press were fond of using phrases such as 'Music for a Kensington bedsit' to describe their appeal.

Selected album: *Angel N.1.* (1990).

Misery Loves Co.

Formed in January 1993, Swedish duo Misery Loves Co. immediately picked up healthy press coverage with their blend of intelligent 90s metal and strong songwriting, *Kerrang!* stating 'the hottest new metal combo since the arrival of **Machine Head**'. Made up of Örjan Ôrnkloo (programming/guitar) and Patrik Wirén (vocals/guitar), the latter was formerly a member of thrash band Midas Touch (one album for Noise Records), while his partner played with female dance troupe the Bikinis. Putting their heads together, the group signed a Swedish deal with the MNW Zone label (also home to **Clawfinger**), and made their debut vinyl appearance on a compilation album, *Extreme Close Up*, before the release of a three track EP, *Private Hell*, in January 1994. Their debut album was licensed to **Earache Records** in the UK, while live appearances saw the duo augmented by the addition of Jim Edwards (guitar), Marre (bass) and Boss (drums).

Album: *Misery Love Co.* (MNW Zone 1994/Earache 1995).

Misex

Formed in New Zealand in 1977. The group comprised Steve Gilpin (lead vocals), Don Martin (bass), Murray Burns (keyboards), Kevin Stanton (guitar) and Richard Hodgkinson (drums). Misex originally played cover versions of UK new-wave material, and during the group's history have borrowed heavily from **Elvis Costello**, **Mink Deville** and **Graham Parker**, as well as cultivating an **Ultravox**-like electro-pop image. They relocated to Australia in 1978, toughened up their sound and began to perform originals. The band quickly grew in stature, touring incessantly, and by 1979, despite attracting derision from their contemporaries for their image, Misex were among the two or three top live acts in Australia, even surpassing their mentors, the Angels. Like **Mother Goose**, another New Zealand band, Misex had success with a novelty single 'Computer Games', which featured Gilpin's hiccuping styled vocals. Paul Dunningham replaced Hodgkinson in 1981. Their follow-up singles also charted well, as had their first album, but by the time the band had produced their most mature and strongest work, *Where Do They Go*, their following faded. They toured the USA twice, but without record company support, which set the band's back financially. By 1984, after several changes to personnel the band broke up. Steve Gilpin died in January 1991.

Albums: *Graffiti Crimes* (1979), *Shanghaied* (1981), *Space Race* (1980), *Where Do They Go* (1983). Compilation: *Misex Greatest Hits* (1984).

Misfits

Like the **13th Floor Elevators** in the 60s and the

New York Dolls in the early 70s, this US punk band was swiftly surrounded in a cloak of mythology and cult appeal. Long after their demise (they played their last live gig in 1983), their obscure US-only records were fetching large sums of money in collecting circles, by those fascinated by the band's spine-chilling mix of horror-movie imagery and hardcore. The Misfits were formed in New Jersey, New York, in 1977 by Gerry Only (bass) and Glenn Danzig (vocals) and, like many aspiring new wave acts, played in venues like **CBGBs**, adding guitarist Bobby Steele and drummer Joey Image. Later that year, 'Cough Cool' became their first single on their own Plan 9 label. A four-track EP, *Bullet* (in a sleeve showing J.F. Kennedy's assassination), was recorded before their debut album, and was followed by 'Horror Business'. A third single, 'Night Of The Living Dead', surfaced in 1979, the reference to the classic George A. Romero film revealing the Misfits' continued fascination with blood-and-guts horror. Then came an EP, *Three Hits From Hell*, recorded in 1980, but not issued until the following April, and a seasonal October single, 'Halloween'. Having now lost Steele to the **Undead**, replaced by Jerry's brother Doyle, Googy (aka Eerie Von) stepped in on drums during a European tour with the **Damned** as Joey's narcotic problems worsened. The Misfits rounded off 1981 by recording the seven-track mini-album *Evilive*, originally sold through the band's Fiend fan club, which also secured a German 12-inch release. The band's only original UK release was a 12-inch EP, *Beware*. Other Misfits releases included several patchy albums which failed to capture their live impact: 1982's *Walk Among Us*, *Earth A.D.* (aka *Wolfblood*) and the posthumous brace, *Legacy Of Brutality* and *Misfits*. Danzig issued his first solo single in 1981, 'Who Killed Marilyn?', later forming **Samhain** with Misfits' drummer Eerie Von. He was subsequently venerated in heavy metal magazines in the late 80s as his eponymous **Danzig** vehicle gained ground. The other Misfits mainstays, brothers Jerry and Doyle, formed the hapless Kryst The Conqueror, who releasd one five song EP with the help of **Skid Row** guitarist David Sabo.

Albums: *Beware* (Cherry Red 1979, mini-album), *Evilive* (Fiend 1981, mini-album), *Walk Among Us* (Ruby 1982), *Earth A.D.* (Plan 9 1983). Compilations: *Legacy Of Brutality* (Plan 9 1985), *The Misfits* (Plan 9 1986), *Evilive* (Plan 9 1987, expanded version of 1981 mini-album).

Misiani, Daniel

(see **Shirati Jazz**)

Misora, Hibari

b. Kazue Katô, 29 May 1937, Yokohama, Kanagawa, Japan. d. 1989. Katô began singing professionally at the age of nine at the Athens Theatre in Yokohama, and was given her stage name in 1948. 'Hibari' means a skylark and 'Misora', fair sky. After being refused by three record companies on the grounds that her performance sounded overtly pert and precocious, she was finally signed by **Columbia** in 1949, when her single 'Kanashiki Kuchibue' ('Plaintive Whistle'), a theme song for a film with the same title, was a Japanese hit. It was followed by more hits, including 'Tokyo Kid' and 'Watashiwa Machino Ko' ('I'm A City Girl') which gave encouragement to the defeated post-war Japanese, as did the film performances of this teen star singing grown-up songs. As well as her numerous chart successes, she also won many awards, and her stardom never waned until her death. She was undisputably the all-time queen of kayôkyoku (formerly the most common and typically Japanese form of popular song). Some critics regret, however, that her versatile talent was prevented from fully developing by commercial manipulation; she was, for example, flexible enough to deal adeptly with American musical styles, as shown in her earlier recordings.

Albums: *Kakureta Meikyokushû* (*Hidden Treasures*) (1987), *Jazzwo Utau* (*Sings Jazz*) (1988), *Eiga Shudaida-shû, 2 Volumes* (*Themes Songs Of Motion Pictures*) (1989), *Dôyôwu Utau* (*Sings Children's Songs*) (1989), *Min'yô Wo Utau* (*Sings Folksongs*) (1989), *Hauta Wo Utau* (*Sings Hauta*) (1989), *Jazz And Standards* (1990), *Hizô! Maboroshi No Mihatsubai Kyokushû* (*Treasury!: Previously Unreleased Songs*) (1990). Compilation: *Zenkyokushû* (*Complete Works*) (1986).

Further reading: *Misora Hibari*, Rô Takenaka. *Misora Hibari*, Eiji Ôshita.

Miss Hook Of Holland

One of the most popular London musicals in the early part of the century, this show was sub-titled a 'Dutch musical incident in two acts', when it opened at the Prince of Wales Theatre in London on 31 January 1907. The score was the work of Paul Rubens who had enjoyed great success five years earlier with ***A Country Girl***. Rubens collaborated with Austen Hurgon on the book which concerns Mr. Hook (G.P. Huntley), a liqueur distiller in Amsterdam. His daughter, Sally (Isabel Jay) boosts the company's sales by inventing a liqueur made of 61 different ingredients, which she calls 'Cream In The Sky'. However, the important recipe is stolen and passed from hand to hand during a romantic, but sometimes bewildering plot, before it is returned to Hook's safe. None of the songs endured, but there were several pleasant numbers including 'Little Miss Wooden Shoes', 'The Sleepy Canal', 'A Little Pink Petty From Peter', 'Tra-La-La', 'The House That Hook Built', and 'Cream Of The Sky'. An excellent London run of 462 performances was followed by a further 119 at the Criterion Theatre in New York in 1907. In the same year the show was presented in Vienna, and there were London revivals in 1914 and 1932.

Miss Liberty

Three years after his biggest success with ***Annie Get Your Gun*** in 1946, **Irving Berlin** came up with the score for this show, which, on the face of it, had all the right credentials: a book by Pulitzer Prize-winning playwright Robert E. Sherwood, choreography by **Jerome Robbins**, direction by **Moss Hart**, and, of course, music and lyrics by Berlin himself. It opened at the Imperial Theatre in New York on 15 July 1949, with Sherwood's cosy, patriotic story set in New York and Paris in 1885. The plot tells of how Horace Miller (Eddie Albert), an inept newpaper photographer, travels to France to find the model who posed for the Statue Of Liberty. He returns with the wrong one, and all sorts of complications have to be overcome before everyone gathers at the statue's dedication ceremony to sing 'Give Me Your Tired, Your Poor', Berlin's musical adaptation of the poem by Emma Lazarus. Monique Dupont, played by the accomplished ballerina, Allyn McLerie, was the lady that Horace fell for in Paris and took back with him to America, only to find that, waiting for him there was his girlfriend, Maisie Dell (Mary McCarty). Berlin's score contained two songs that became popular: 'Let's Take An Old Fashioned Walk' was a big hit for **Perry Como**, and for **Doris Day** with **Frank Sinatra**; and both Como and **Jo Stafford** took 'Just One Way To Say I Love You' into the US Hit Parade. The rest of the numbers included 'Little Fish In A Big Pond', 'I'd Like My Picture Took', 'Homework', 'Falling Out Of Love Can Be Fun', 'Paris Wakes Up And Smiles', 'Only For Americans', and 'You Can Have Him', an untypical ballad containing 'truth and sarcasm, and dedicated to the "other woman"' - ('You can have him/I don't want him/He's not worth fighting for/Besides, there's plenty more where he came from'), which received a sophisticated reading on the 1965 abum *The Nancy Wilson Show!* Despite its virtues, and its patriotic theme, *Miss Liberty* did not start any parades, and closed after 308 performances.

Miss London Ltd.

Released by Gainsborough Pictures in 1943, this comedy-musical is a typical example of the cheery, tuneful fare British cinema audiences flocked to see during the dark war years. It starred Arthur 'Hallo Playmates!' Askey, one of the country's most popular funny-men. He played Arthur Bowman, the manager of the Miss London Ltd. escort agency which is visited by its attractive American owner, Terry Arden (Evelyn Dall). The business needs a shake-up, and Arthur goes on a recruitment drive and comes up with railway station announcer Gail Martin (**Anne Shelton**). The ensuing complications involve some of Britain's top comedy talent, such as Jack Train as Arthur's right-hand man, Max Bacon as an hilariously coy head waiter, and Richard Hearne, who plays a jitterbugging commodore in the Navy, the service into which Arthur himself is being co-opted (by another fine comic actor, Ronald Shiner) when the closing titles roll. Other parts were taken by Peter Graves and Jean Kent. Manning Sherwin and Val Guest, wrote the songs, and Evelyn Dall had one of the film's best musical moments with the punchy 'Keep Cool, Calm - And Collect!'. She also joined Askey for the lively 'It's A Fine How-Do-You-Do'. Anne Shelton, who had the distinction of singing with the **Glenn Miller** Orchestra during the war, was splendid on 'If You Could Only Cook', 'You Too (Can Have a Lovely Romance)', and 'The Eight Fifty Choo Choo'. Val Guest and Marriott Edgar wrote the screenplay, and Guest also directed. The producer was Edward Black.

Miss Saigon

A re-working of Puccini's enduring *Madame Butterfly* as a Vietnam war tale, set in Saigon during the last days of the American presence there in 1975. The music was by **Claude-Michel Schönberg**, with lyrics by **Richard Maltby Jnr**. and **Alain Boublil** (adapted from the original French lyrics by Boublil) with additional material by Maltby. *Miss Saigon* opened at the Theatre Royal, Drury Lane in London on 20 September 1989. The dramatic story concerns a young marine, Chris (Simon Bowman), who falls in love with a would-be prostitute Kim (Lea Salonga). However, partly owing to the chaotic troop evacuation (aided by a stunning helicopter effect), he goes back to America without her. As with Puccini, the wartime liaison ends in tragedy, with the soldier returning to Saigon only to find the girl has commited suicide. The show was hailed as being 'savagely objective . . . a critical shot at the destabilizing and corrupting American role in Vietnam . . . more than a mature musical, a tough popular opera, clear-headed but romantic, warm as well as sordid and brutal'. Jonathan Pryce played the central role of the Engineer, the cynical and ruthless owner of the sleazy Dreamland Bar, and he had the show's big number, 'The American Dream', a savage attack on US commercialism. The remainder of a score containing some 24 songs, with lyrics that were 'sharp, hard-hitting, elegantly but bitterly sardonic', included 'The Heat Is On In Saigon', 'The Movie On My Mind', 'Why God, Why?', 'The Last Night Of The World', 'You Will Not Touch Him', 'I'd Give My Life For You', 'Sun And Moon', 'Now That I've Seen Her', and 'The Sacred Bird'. Jonathan Pryce and Lea Salonga both won **Laurence Olivier Awards** for their outstanding performances, and *Miss Saigon* was widely acclaimed, and settled in for a long stay. The Broadway transfer was in doubt for some time when American Equity banned Pryce from reprising his role because 'it would be an affront to the Asian community'. When producer **Cameron Mackintosh** reportedly threatened to cancel the production, they relented, and, after opening in April 1991, the show recouped its $10.9 million investment in 39 weeks. **Tony Awards** went to Pryce, Salonga, and featured actor (Hinton Battle). Since then, *Miss Saigon* has been successfully presented in many countries throughout the world, including Stuttgart and Toronto, where new theatres were designed specifically to house the German and Canadian productions. In December 1994, when *Miss Saigon* became the Theatre Royal's longest-running musical, eclipsing the 2,281-performance record set by *My Fair Lady*, it was estimated that the show had taken over £65 million at the London box office, and more than £400 million worldwide.

Further reading: *The Story Of Miss Saigon*, Edward Behr and Mark Steyn.

Missing Persons

Missing Persons consisted of Dale Bozzio (vocals), her husband Terry Bozzio (drums/keyboards; formerly of the **Frank Zappa** band and **U.K.**), Warren Cuccurullo (guitar) and Patrick O'Hearn (bass/keyboards), both also veterans of earlier Zappa formations. Outwardly bearing an image of space age sexuality they produced a radio-friendly power pop sound. They released a debut EP, having changed name from U.S. Drag, after which they signed to **Capitol Records** who re-released the EP with extra tracks as the *Missing Persons* mini-album. Their debut album, the anagramatical *Spring Session M*, brought Dale Bozzio's vocals to the fore, and managed to sound simultaneously playful and world-weary. The musical backing anticipated the synthesizer-led groups of the mid to late 80s, but the lyrics were largely in advance of anything those groups were using. *Rhyme & Reason* perfected the formula, igniting typical rock 'n' roll topics such as 'Surrender Your Heart' with an appealing subtext of intrigue and disaffection. For *Color In Your Life*, the band changed tack. Bernard Edwards (of **Chic**) took over the producer's role, and the addition of horns and funk rhythms did little to extend their appeal, and in many ways neutered it. An obvious attempt to make Missing Persons a credible dance pop band, the results were passable but disappointing given their previous work. The band broke up in consequence (the Bozzios having already done so on a personal level), leaving Cuccurullo to join **Duran Duran** and Dale to sign a solo contract with **Prince**'s Paisley Park imprint. O'Hearn went on to record several well-received instrumental albums for Private Music.

Albums: *Missing Persons* (Capitol 1982, mini-album), *Spring Session M* (Capitol 1982), *Rhyme & Reason* (Capitol 1984), *Color In Your Life* (Capitol 1986). Compilation: *The Best Of Missing Persons* (Capitol 1987). Dale Bozzio solo: As Dale: *Riot In English* (Paisley Park 1988).

Mission

UK rock band who evolved from the **Sisters Of Mercy**, when Wayne Hussey (b. 26 May 1959, Bristol, England; ex-Walkie Talkies, **Dead Or Alive**) and Craig Adams split from Andrew Eldritch. They quickly recruited drummer Mick Brown (ex-**Red Lorry, Yellow Lorry**) and guitarist Simon Hinkler (ex-**Artery**). The original choice of title was the Sisterhood, which led to an undignified series of exchanges in the press between the band and Eldritch. In order to negate their use of the name, Eldritch put out a single under the name Sisterhood on his own Merciful Release label. Thus the title the Mission was selected instead. After two successful independent singles on the Chapter 22 label, they signed to **Mercury** in the autumn of 1986. Their major label debut, 'Stay With Me', entered the UK singles charts while the band worked on their debut album. *God's Own Medicine* was the outcome, revealing a tendency towards straightforward rock, and attracting criticism for its bombast. A heavy touring schedule ensued, with the band's off-stage antics attracting at least as much attention as their performances. A particularly indulgent tour of America saw Adams shipped home suffering from exhaustion. His temporary replacement on bass was Pete Turner. After headlining the Reading Festival, they began work on a new album under the auspices of **Led Zeppelin** bass player John Paul Jones as producer. *Children* was even more successful than its predecessor, reaching number 2 in the UK album charts, despite the customary critical disdain. 1990 brought 'Butterfly On A Wheel' as a single, providing further ammunition for accusations that the band were simply dredging up rock history. In February, the long-delayed third album, *Carved In Sand*, was released, revealing a more sophisticated approach to songwriting. During the world tour to promote the album, both Hinkler and Hussey became ill because of the excessive regime. Hinkler departed suddenly when they reached Toronto, leaving Dave Wolfenden to provide guitar for the rest of the tour. On their return, Paul Etchells took over the position on a more permanent basis. Hussey had meanwhile joined with the **Wonder Stuff** in proposing a fund-raising concert in London under the banner The Day Of Conscience, but the event self-destructed with a barrage of allegations about commercial intrusion. In a similar vein over the Christmas period, members of the band joined with **Slade**'s Noddy Holder and Jim Lea to re-record 'Merry Xmas Everybody' for charity. However, 1992 would bring numerous further personnel difficulties. Craig Adams returned to Brighton, while Hussey brought in Andy Hobson (bass), Rik Carter (keyboards) and Mark Gemini Thwaite (guitar). A reflective Hussey, promoting the *Sum And Substance* compilation, would concede: 'We had an overblown

sense of melodrama. It was great - pompous songs, big grand statements. We've never attempted to do anything that's innovative'. A nation of rock critics found something to agree with Hussey on at last.
Albums: *God's Own Medicine* (Mercury 1986), *Children* (Mercury 1988), *Carved In Sand* (Mercury 1990), *Masque* (Mercury 1992). Compilations: *The First Chapter* (Mercury 1987), *Grains Of Sand* (Mercury 1990), *Sum And Substance* (Vertigo 1994), *Neverland* (Neverland 1995).
Videos: *South America* (1989), *Crusade* (1991), *Dusk To Dawn* (1991), *Waves Upon The Sand* (1991), *Sum And Substance* (1994).
Further reading: *The Mission - Names Are Tombstones Baby*, Martin Roach with Neil Perry.
Videos: *South America* (1989), *Waves Upon The Sand* (1991), *From Dawn To Dusk* (1991), *Crusade* (1991), *Sum And Substance* (1994).

Mission Of Burma

Once cited as 'the ultimate collision of punk and pop', Boston, Massachusetts band Mission Of Burma were compared by others to the UK's art terrorists **Wire**. Certainly, they invoked a similar level of rapture among US critics and, much like Wire, self-consciously avoided the glare of the mainstream. The original line-up of Clint Conley (bass), Peter Prescott (drums), and Roger Miller (guitar) were greatly influential to a number of more commercially viable outfits. They formed in 1979, when Miller and Conley moved to Boston from Ann Arbor and New York respectively. They briefly put together Moving Parts before joining with resident Bostonian Prescott. Burma kicked off with supports for the UK's **Gang Of Four**. These went well and the Leeds funksters continued to sponsor them early in their development. They would split in 1985 after a career which embraced well defined but chaotic live and recorded work. Through a series of reissues on the venerated underground label, Taang! Recordrs, critics have now reassessed their historical importance. Among their staunchest admirers are **R.E.M.**, who regularly covered 'Academy Flight Song' in their live sets. Prescott would go on to **SST** recording artists **Volcano Suns**.
Albums: *Vs* (Ace Of Hearts 1982), *The Horrible Truth About Burma Live* (Ace Of Hearts 1985), *Forget* (Taang! 1988), *Let There Be Burma* (Taang! 1990). Compilation: *Mission Of Burma* (Rykodisc 1988).

Mississippi Mass Choir

This gospel choir was formed in 1988 by Frank Williams who was a member of the Jackson Southernaires and an executive of the gospel division of **Malaco Records**. The choir signed immediately to Malaco under the musical directorship of David R Curry. Serving God Through Song is the motto of the choir. The group's first rehearsal was in 1988 followed by the release of their first CD and video, *The Mississippi Mass Choir Live*, recorded before an audience of 3,000 at the Jackson Municipal Auditorium. This release reached number 1 on the ***Billboard*** gospel chart and remained there for 45 consecutive weeks, setting a new record. In 1990 they released their second live project, *God Gets The Glory*, which again reached number 1 in the *Billboard* gospel chart and was named 1992 Gospel Record Of The Year by *Billboard*. Their third release in January 1993 was *It Remains To be Seen* and has been number 1 in the gospel charts for over one year and by the mid-90s spent 2 years in the charts. This release featured the last recorded performance of the choirs founder, Frank Williams who died in March 1993. In 1995 they released *Live At Jackson State University* with the Rev. James Moore .
Albums: *Live At Jackson, Mississippi* (Malaco), *God Gets The Glory* (Malaco), *It Remains To Be Seen* (Malaco), *Live With Rev. James Moore* (Malaco), *Rev. James Moore With Mississippi Mass Choir-Live At Jackson State University* (Malaco).

Mississippi Sheiks

This musical combination flourished between 1930 and 1935, during which time they recorded more than 80 tracks for various 'race' labels. The Sheiks was a string band made up of members and friends of the Chatman family, and included Lonnie Chatman (guitar/violin), Sam Chatman (guitar), Walter Vincson (guitar violin), Bo (Carter) Chatman, (guitar) and Charlie McCoy (banjo/mandolin). Vocal chores were handled by everybody. Most of these individuals pursued independent musical careers either at this time or later. The instrumental abilities of all members were extremely high and their repertoire covered all ground between popular waltzes to salacious party songs, with a fair quantity of high-quality blues thrown in. Their work also appeared under the names the Mississippi Mud Steppers, the Down South Boys and the Carter Brothers.
Albums: *Sitting On Top Of The World* (1972), *Stop And Listen Blues* (1973), *The Mississippi Sheiks* (1984).

Missourians

In the early 20s, St. Louis-based violinist Wilson Robinson formed a band which he named the Syncopaters. By 1924, the band was in New York and, now directed by another violinist, they were engaged as the house band at the Cotton Club. Incorporating the club's name in its title, the band was known as Andy Preer And His Cotton Club Orchestra. When the band was replaced at the club by **Duke Ellington**, Preer's group changed its name yet again, this time calling itself the Missourians. After Preer's death, the band secured another prestigious New York engagement, this time at the Savoy Ballroom under the leadership of George Scott. The band retained a good measure of

popularity with dancers at the Savoy, playing with a propulsive, free-flowing swing that reflected its now-distant Midwestern origins. Early in 1930, the band backed singer **Cab Calloway** on record dates, and soon thereafter became his permanent band, changing their name to the Cab Calloway Orchestra. In its early years at the Cotton Club, the band did much to foster the type of music which was associated with that venue and which Ellington later refined. The band had a number of fine soloists, among them trumpeter R. Q. Dickerson, whose use of the plunger mute helped to establish the so-called 'jungle' music with which the Cotton Club show bands were associated.
Compilation: *The Missourians* (1929-30 recordings).

Mister Rock And Roll

US DJ **Alan Freed** was a pivotal figure in the development of 50s' rock 'n' roll. His radio programmes helped expose the emergent music to a generation of teenagers and he later showcased many acts live in revue-styled concerts. A cavalcade of performers populated the films Freed was involved with, including ***Rock Around The Clock*** and ***Rock Rock Rock***, a premise equally prevalent on this 1957 feature. *Mister Rock And Roll* boasted a plot wherein Freed pondered why the record industry had hit a slump. Satori arrived in the shape of R&B, but Freed must first incur parental wrath, before trying to convert his denigrators. 'Young people. Show your parents how exciting your music is. Take them to see this picture,' ran the publicity blurb for a film showcasing **Little Richard**, **Chuck Berry**, **Frankie Lymon**, **LaVern Baker** and the **Moonglows**. Each performance was meritorious in itself, inspiring continued interest in the feature, but the notion of grafting memorable performances to witless plots was already undermining the true potential of celluloid pop.

Misty In Roots

One of Britain's foremost roots reggae groups, fronted by brothers Walford (lead vocals) and Delvin Tyson (rhythm guitar, vocals), with other regular members including Delbert McKay (guitar, vocals), Chesley Samson (lead guitar), Tony Henry (bass) and Dennis Augustine (rhythm guitar), who took over Delvin's role on the instrument when he elected to concentrate on vocal duties. Samson was replaced by Lorrance Crossfield in 1983, though this was just the most serious of numerous line-up revisions. Through eight **John Peel** Radio 1 sessions (he numbered them among his favourite groups for several years in the early 80s) they exhibited radically different line-ups for each, happily adding and subtracting musicians and vocalists as the occasion demanded.

The band's origins can be traced to Southall, Middlesex, where they first formed in 1974, backing Jamaican singer **Nicky Thomas** on his British tour a year later. From early on their commercial brand of reggae attracted supporters, but they relinquished the opportunity of singing to a major in order to set up their own People Unite label. On successive releases they honed a crafted, pleasing sound which would later see them become the first band in the reggae idiom invited to play Russia. They were also heavily involved in the Rock Against Racism movement playing alongside punk bands such as **999** and the **Ruts**. The fact that their staunch Rastafarian views were aired regularly on Radio 1 via Peel could only strengthen links between the two musical camps. Their Rasta beliefs were reinforced in the 80s by playing shows in their spiritual homeland of Africa, which helped them to define: 'A feeling which has always been there'. In 1987 the band toured West Africa, but the euphoria was marred when Delvyn Tyson drowned in a swinning accident. Alongside **Steel Pulse** and **Aswad**, Misty In Roots rank as the most important UK reggae band of their generation.
Albums: *Live At The Counter-Eurovision* (People Unite 1979), *Wise And Foolish* (People Unite 1981), *Earth* (People Unite 1983), *Musi O Tunya* (People Unite 1985), *Forward* (Kaz 1989).

Misunderstood

One of psychedelia's finest groups, the Misunderstood originated in Riverside, California, USA, and evolved from a local surfing group, the Blue Notes. Their first line-up - Greg Treadway (guitar), George Phelps (guitar) and Rick Moe (drums) - was augmented by Rick Brown (vocals) and Steve Whiting (bass), before adopting their new name in 1965. Phelps was then replaced by Glenn Ross 'Fernando' Campbell who played steel guitar. The quintet completed a single, 'You Don't Have To Go'/'Who's Been Talking?', before leaving for the UK on the suggestion of disc jockey **John** (**Peel**) Ravenscroft, then working in San Bernadino. Tredway was subsequently drafted, and his place was taken by Tony Hill (b. South Shields, Co. Durham, England). The group completed six masters during their London sojourn. 'I Can Take You To The Sun', a hypnotic, atmospheric and ambitious performance, was their only contemporary release although the rousing 'Children Of The Sun' was issued, after their break-up, in 1968. Campbell later re-established the name with several British musicians. Their two blues-cum-progressive singles shared little with the early, trail-blazing unit, and the latterday version then evolved into **Juicy Lucy**.
Compilations: *Before The Dream Faded* (1982, six UK-recorded masters and several early demos), *Golden Glass* (1984, material by the group's second incarnation).

Mitchell, Billy

b. 3 November 1926, Kansas City, Missouri, USA. Mitchell studied in Detroit and worked with Nat

Towles's band in the late 40s before moving to New York with **Lucky Millender**'s Orchestra. He spent a couple of months in **Woody Herman**'s Second Herd, and then lead his own bop quintet back in Detroit, which included **Thad Jones** on trumpet and **Elvin Jones** on drums (1950-53). In the mid-50s, after a couple of years with **Dizzy Gillespie**, he recorded with **Ray Charles** and joined **Count Basie**'s Orchestra. He co-led a sextet with ex-Basie trombonist **Al Grey**, and worked as musical director for **Stevie Wonder** in the mid-60s, before rejoining Basie (1966-67). He uses a tough, bluesy tone to construct fluent solo lines. In the 70s Mitchell settled in New York and undertook studio work, as well as teaching and performing with the Xanadu All Stars.
Albums: with Ray Charles *Soul Brothers* (1957), with Count Basie *One More Time* (1958), *Al Grey With Billy Mitchell* (1961), *Little Juicy* (1963), with Xanadu *Xanadu At Montreux* (1978), with Paul Lingle *Vintage Piano Vol 3* (Euphonic 1979), *De Lawd's Blues* (1980), *Faces* (Optimism 1987), *In Focus* (Optimism 1989).

Mitchell, Blue

b. Richard Allen Mitchell, 13 March 1930, Miami, Florida, USA, d. 21 May 1979. Mitchell's early professional career found him playing trumpet in a number of R&B bands, including that led in the mid-50s by **Earl Bostic**. Later in the decade he worked briefly with **Cannonball Adderley** in New York, and then joined **Horace Silver**'s band, an engagement which established Mitchell's reputation. When Silver disbanded in 1963, Mitchell formed his own group, employing most of his fellow musicians, with Silver's place being taken by **Chick Corea**. This band continued until the end of the decade, at which time Mitchell joined the band that was backing **Ray Charles**. During the early 70s, Mitchell played with a number of artists in fields outside jazz, notably bluesman **John Mayall** and popular singers such as **Tony Bennett** and **Lena Horne**. Resident in Los Angeles from the mid-70s, Mitchell played in both small and big bands, including those led by **Harold Land**, **Louie Bellson** and **Bill Berry**. A gifted, soulful player with a full, rich tone, Mitchell's frequent excursions into areas of music outside jazz never caused him to lower his standards. Indeed, he enhanced every record date, concert or club engagement on which he played with the sincerity of his playing and the beautiful sound he drew from his instrument.
Albums: *Big Six* (Original Jazz Classics 1958), with Horace Silver *Finger Poppin'* (1959), *Out Of The Blue* (Original Jazz Classics 1959), *Blue Soul* (Original Jazz Classics 1959), with Silver *Horace-Scope* (1960), *Blues On My Mind* (Original Jazz Classics 1960), *Blue Moods* (1960), *Smooth As The Wind* (1960), *A Sure Thing* (1962), *The Cup Bearers* (Original Jazz Classics 1963), *Step Lightly* (1963), *The Thing To Do* (Blue Note 1964), *Down With It* (1965), *Bring It Home To Me* (1966), *Boss Horn* (1966), *Heads Up!* (1967), *Collisons In Black* (1968), *Bantu Village* (1969), *Blue Mitchell* (1971), *Vital Blue* (1971), with John Mayall *Jazz Blues Fusion* (1971), *Blue's Blues* (1972-74), *Graffiti Blues* (Audio Fidelity 1973-74), *Many Shades Of Blue* (1974), with Bill Berry *Hot & Happy* (1974), *Stratosonic Nuances* (c.1975), *Funktion Junction* (1976), with Berry *Hello Rev* (1976), with Dexter Gordon, Al Cohn *True Blue* (1976), with Harold Land *Mapenzi* (1977), with Land *Best Of The West* (1977), *Last Dance* (1977), *African Violet* (1977), *Summer Soft* (1977).

Mitchell, Bobby

b. 16 August 1935, Algiers, Louisiana, USA, d. 17 March 1989, New Orleans, Louisiana, USA. After studying music in high school, Mitchell formed a vocal group, the Toppers, in June 1950. The group comprised various high school friends and they entered local talent shows. After being discovered by **Dave Bartholomew** in 1952, the group began recording for Imperial until they split up in 1955 upon graduation, leading Mitchell to a solo career and his biggest hit the following year, 'Try Rock And Roll'. This reached number 14 on ***Billboard***'s R&B chart - although he is probably better known as the originator of 'I'm Gonna Be A Wheel Someday' which was later covered by **Fats Domino**. Leaving Imperial in 1958, he recorded infrequently for small local labels like Ronn, Sho-Biz and Rip, and by the late 60s, he was working outside the music business.
Album: *I'm Gonna Be A Wheel Someday* (1979).

Mitchell, Chad, Trio

Chad Mitchell, Mike Kobluk and Mike Pugh were students at Gonzaga University in Spokane, Washington, USA, when they formed this influential folk group in 1958. They then crossed America, performing when able, before arriving in New York to secure a recording deal. The following year, Mike Pugh dropped out in favour of Joe Frazier, while the Trio's accompanist, Dennis Collins, was replaced by guitarist (Jim) **Roger McGuinn**, who later found fame with the **Byrds**. The group then embarked on their most successful era, when they became renowned for songs of a satiric or socially-conscious nature. Chad Mitchell left for a solo career in 1965. He was replaced by aspiring songwriter **John Denver**, but the restructured act, now known as the Mitchell Trio, found it difficult to sustain momentum. Frazier and Kobluk also left the group, which was then sued by its former leader for continuing to use the 'original' name. The trio then became known as Denver, Boise And Johnson, but split up in 1969 when first Johnson, then Denver, left to pursue independent projects.
Selected albums: *The Chad Mitchell Trio Arrives* (1960), *A Mighty Day On Campus* (Kapp 1961), *The Chad Mitchell Trio At The Bitter End* (Kapp 1962), *The Chad Mitchell Trio*

In Action aka *Blowin' In The Wind* (Kapp 1962), *Hootenanny Number 3* (Kapp 1963), *Singin' Our Minds* (1963), *The Chad Mitchell Trio In Concert* (Colpix 1964), *Reflecting* (1964), *The Slightly Irreverent Mitchell Trio* (1964), *Typical American Boys* (1965), *That's The Way It's Gotta Be* (1965), *Violets Of Dawn* (1966), *Alive* (1967). Compilations: *The Best Of The Chad Mitchell Trio* (Kapp 1963), *The Chad Mitchell Trio And The Gatemen In Concert* (1964), *Beginnings: The Chad Mitchell Trio Featuring John Denver* (1973).

Mitchell, George

b. 27 February 1917, Stirling, Scotland. Although he played the piano and sang as a youth, Mitchell intended to be an accountant, and followed his inclinations in the Royal Army Pay Corps during World War II. In his spare time he organized concerts with a mixed choir consisting of 16 ATS girls and Pay Corps personnel. In 1947, after his release, he formed the George Mitchell Choir for the BBC radio programme *Cabin In The Cotton*, and then, two years later, changed the name to the George Mitchell Glee Club, a group of 32 singers, that performed on popular radio shows such as *Stand Easy*, as well as having its own series. The Glee Club also toured the UK variety circuit and appeared in the Royal Variety Performance of 1950, the first of many in which Mitchell was involved. By 1957 the Mitchell singers were re-creating traditional minstrel shows for television, singing on fixed rostra, and wearing red facial make-up, which appeared to be black when the cameras were fitted with green filters. In 1958, masterminded by Mitchell and producer George Innes, the first *Black And White Minstrel Show* proper was transmitted, and continued, with occasional short breaks, in the Saturday night peak spot for 20 years. The original static format was transformed into 'the fastest moving show on television' when the male singers performed routines with the Television Toppers dance troupe. The company, and its three principal singers, Dai Francis, Tony Mercer and John Boulter, were joined at various times through the years by comedians such as Leslie Crowther, Stan Stennett and **George Chisholm**. Always at the heart of the show was a series of nostalgic medleys of (mostly) American popular music from the years 1920-50, cleverly arranged by Mitchell so that each number seemlessly segued into the next one. When the medleys were transferred to albums, beginning in 1960, the first three issued went to number 1 in the UK charts. In 1961 the *Black And White Minstrel Show* won the Golden Rose of Montreux for the best light entertainment programme. By then, a stage version, presented by Robert Luff, had toured the provinces, beginning in Bristol, and including a summer season at Scarborough, before moving into London's Victoria Palace in 1962. It stayed there, with a break of a few months, until 1972, by which time it was estimated that over seven million people had seen the show, which traditionally always closed with a half-tempo rendering of 'When The Saints Go Marching In'. During the 60s two more companies toured the UK, Australia and New Zealand. In 1978 the BBC axed the television show on the grounds that 'it might offend black people', and later refused to show clips in programmes celebrating BBC Television's history. Eventually, Mitchell and Luff issued a statement disassociating themselves from contemporary versions of the concept that had brought them so much success in the past, although the original format continued to tour Australia. A form of 'Minstrel' stage show remained a popular summer season attraction at UK seaside resorts, and, in 1985, undertook a 20-date Silver Anniversary Tour. In 1992, *That Old Minstrel Magic* played to capacity audiences in the provinces, but, following protests from the Commision for Racial Equality, no members of the cast appeared in black-face - an attempt by one of the lead singers to do so was rapidly quashed. By that time, Mitchell had retired and was spending most of each year in Florida, USA. His son, Rob, continued the family musical tradition, becoming a respected musical director on radio, and for various stage productions.

Selected albums: *The Black And White Minstrel Show* (1960), *Another Black And White Minstrel Show* (1961), *On Stage With The George Mitchell Minstrels* (1962), *On Tour With The George Mitchell Minstrels* (1962), *Spotlight On The George Mitchell Minstrels* (1963), *Magic Of The Minstrels* (1965), *Here Come The Minstrels* (1966), *Showtime* (1967), *Sing The Irving Berlin Songbook* (1968), *The Magic Of Christmas* (1970), *30 Golden Greats* (1977).

Mitchell, Guy

b. Albert Cernick, 22 February 1927, Detroit, Michigan, USA. An enormously popular singer in the USA and the UK, particularly during the 50s, with a straight-forward style and affable personality. Although his birthplace is often given as Yugoslavia, his parents' homeland, Mitchell confirmed in a 1988 UK interview that he was born in Detroit, and was brought up there until the family moved to Colorado, and then to Los Angeles, California, when he was 11 years old. In Los Angeles, he successfully auditioned for Warner Brothers and, for the next few years, was groomed for a possible movie career as a child star, besides singing on the Hollywood radio station KFWB. The possibility of the world having another **Mickey Rooney** was averted when the family moved again, this time to San Francisco. Mitchell became an apprentice saddle maker, and worked on ranches and in rodeos in the San Joaquin Valley, and sang on cowboy singer Dude Martin's radio show. His affection for country music stayed with him for the remainder of his career. After a spell in the US Navy, Mitchell joined pianist **Carmen Cavallero**, and made his first records with the band, including 'I Go In When The Moon Comes Out' and 'Ah, But It Happens'. He then spent some time in New York, making demonstration records, and also won first place on the *Arthur Godfrey Talent Show*. In 1949, he recorded a few tracks for King Records, which were subsequently reissued on *Sincerely Yours* when Mitchell became successful.

In 1950, he was signed to **Columbia Records** by **Mitch Miller**, who is said to have been responsible for changing Cernick to Mitchell, Miller's full Christian name. Their first success came in 1950, with 'My Heart Cries For You' and 'The Roving Kind', which were followed by a string of hits throughout the decade, mostly jaunty novelty numbers, usually with Miller arrangements which used French horns to considerable effect. Several of the songs were written by **Bob Merrill**, including 'Sparrow In The Tree Top', 'Pittsburgh, Pennsylvania', 'My Truly, Truly Fair', 'Feet Up (Pat Him On The Po-Po)', 'Belle, Belle, My Liberty Belle' and 'She Wears Red Feathers', which contained the immortal Merrill couplet: 'An elephant brought her in, placed her by my side/While six baboons got out bassoons, and played "Here Comes The Bride"!' Other US Top 30 entries during this period included 'You're Just In Love', a duet with another Miller protégé **Rosemary Clooney**, 'Christopher Columbus', 'Unless' (a 30s Tolchard Evans number), 'Sweetheart Of Yesterday', 'There's Always Room At Our House', 'I Can't Help It', 'Day Of Jubilo', "Cause I Love You, That's A-Why', 'Tell Us Where The Good Times Are' (the latter two duets with **Mindy Carson**), and 'Ninety-Nine Years (Dead Or Alive)'. 'Singing The Blues' (with **Ray Conniff** And His Orchestra), became his most successful record, which stayed at number 1 in the US charts for 10 weeks in 1956. In the UK, **Tommy Steele** had a hit with his cover, but Mitchell also succeeded by reaching number 1. Further infectious hits followed: 'Knee Deep In The Blues', the irritatingly catchy 'Rock-A-Billy' ('rock-a-billy, rock-a-billy, rock-a-billy rock, rock-a-billy rock-a-billy, ooh rock rock'), and his last US chart entry in 1959, 'Heartaches By The Number', (number 1).

Of these, five sold over a million copies. Most of Mitchell's US hits were also successful in the UK, where he was highly popular, touring regularly, appearing at the London Palladium for the first time in 1952, and in the 1954 Royal Variety Performance. Additional chart entries in the UK included 'Pretty Little Black-Eyed Susie', 'Look At That Girl' (number 1), 'Cloud Lucky Seven', 'Cuff Of My Shirt', 'Dime And A Dollar' and 'Chicka Boom'. The latter was featured in Mitchell's first movie, a 3-D musical entitled *Those Redheads From Seattle* (1953), with Rhonda Fleming, Gene Barry and **Teresa Brewer**. Brewer and Mitchell proved a pleasant combination on the **Johnny Mercer/Hoagy Carmichael** song 'I Guess It Was You All The Time'. In 1954, Mitchell appeared with Gene Barry again, in the spoof western movie *Red Garters*, which also starred Rosemary Clooney, and contained another Mitchell 'special', 'A Dime And A Dollar'. In contrast to the somewhat perky style, so effective on his singles, some of Mitchell's albums revealed him to be an excellent ballad singer, particularly *A Guy In Love*, with **Glenn Osser** and his Orchestra, which contained standards such as 'The Moon Got In My Eyes', 'Allegheny Moon', 'East Of The Sun' and 'East Side Of Heaven'. *Sunshine Guitar*, with its guitar choir, was 'carefree and breezy, full of infectious gaiety', with a country 'feel' on several of the numbers. With the 60s beat boom imminent, Mitchell's contract with Columbia ended in 1962, and he released some singles on the Joy and **Reprise** labels. In 1967, he signed for the Nashville-based Starday label, but shortly after his *Travelling Shoes* and *Singing Up A Storm* were released, the company went out of business. During some periods of the 60s and 70s, Mitchell ceased performing. He issued only a few tracks on his own GMI label - partly because of poor health and serious alcoholic problems.

In 1979, he toured Australia, and started to play nightclubs in the USA. In the 80s he made several appearances in the UK, and released the old **Elvis Presley** favourite, 'Always On My Mind', backed with 'Wind Beneath My Wings' from the **Bette Midler** hit movie *Beaches*. This was followed by *Garden In The Rain*, a set of British numbers which included 'My Kind Of Girl', 'Yesterday', 'I Hadn't Anyone Till You' and **Noël Coward**'s theme tune, 'I'll See You Again'. In the 90s, the old hits were still being repackaged and sold to a younger audience following Guy's appearance in John Byrne's UK television drama, *Your Cheatin' Heart*, in 1990. During the filming in the UK he took the opportunity to play a number of country festival gigs. In 1991 during a tour of Australia he had a horse riding accident which resulted in serious internal injuries. He spent some time in intensive care but made a complete recovery. Mitchell typified 50s pop more than any other performer, and his catalogue of hits remains formidable. His work is destined to endure.

Albums: *Songs Of The Open Spaces* (1952), UK title, *Guy Mitchell Sings* (1954), *Red Garters*, (Soundtrack) (1954), *The Voice Of Your Choice* (1955), *A Guy In Love* (1958), *Sincerely Yours* (as Al Grant) (1959), *Sunshine Guitar* (1960), *Traveling Shoes* (1967), *Singin' Up A Storm* (1968), *Heartaches By The Number* (1970), *The Roving Kind* (1981), *A Garden In The Rain* (1985), Compilations: *Guy's Greatest Hits* (1958), *Showcase Of Hits* (1958), *The Best Of Guy Mitchell* (1966), *American Legend - 16 Greatest Hits* (1977), *20 Golden Greats* (1979), *Hit Singles 1950-1960* (1981), *20 Golden Pieces Of Guy Mitchell* (1984), *Guy's Greatest Hits* (1984), *Singing The Blues* (1986), *Portrait Of A Song Stylist* (1989), *Sweep Your Blues Away* (1989), *Heartaches By The Number* (1990), *Your Cheatin' Heart* (Soundtrack)(1990), *16 Most Requested Songs* (1992), *The Essential Collection* (1993).

Further reading: *Mitchell Music* (privately published UK fanzine).

Mitchell, Joni

b. Roberta Joan Anderson, 7 November 1943, Fort McLeod, Alberta, Canada. After studying art in Calgary, this singer-songwriter moved to Toronto in 1964, where she married Chuck Mitchell in 1965. The two performed together at coffee houses and folk clubs, playing several Mitchell originals including 'The Circle Game'. The latter inspired was a response to Canadian **Neil Young** who had recently written 'Sugar Mountain', a paean to lost innocence that Mitchell herself included in her sets during this period. While in Detroit, the Mitchells met folk singer **Tom Rush**, who unsuccessfully attempted to persuade **Judy Collins** to cover Joni's 'Urge For Going'. He later recorded the song himself, along with the title track of his next album, *The Circle Game.* The previously reluctant Collins also brought Mitchell's name to prominence by covering 'Michael From Mountains' and 'Both Sides Now' on her 1967 album *Wildflowers.*

Following her divorce in 1967, Mitchell moved to New York and for a time planned a career in design and clothing, selling Art Nouveau work. Her success on the New York folk circuit paid her bills, however, and she became known as a strong songwriter and engaging live performer, backed only by her acoustic guitar and dulcimer. At this time the astute producer **Joe Boyd** took her to England, where she played some low-key venues and on her return she appearing at the Gaslight South folk club in Coconut Grove, Florida, Her trip produced several songs, including the comical tribute to 'London Bridge', based on the traditional nursery rhyme. The song included such lines as 'London Bridge is falling up/Save the tea leaves in my cup . . .' Other early material included the plaintive 'Eastern Rain', 'Just Like Me' and 'Brandy Eyes', which displayed Mitchell's love of sharp description and internal rhyme. Mitchell was initially discovered by budding manager Elliot Roberts at New York's Cafe Au Go-Go, and shortly afterwards in Coconut Grove by former **Byrds** member, **David Crosby**. She and Crosby became lovers, and he went on to produce her startling debut album *Joni Mitchell* aka *Songs To A Seagull.* Divided into two sections, 'I Came To The City' and 'Out Of The City And Down To The Seaside', the work showed her early folk influence which was equally strong on the 1969 follow-up *Clouds*, which featured several songs joyously proclaiming the possibilities offered by life, as well as its melancholic side. 'Chelsea Morning' presented a feeling of wonder in its almost childlike appreciation of everyday observations. The title of the album was borrowed from a line in 'Both Sides Now', which had since become a massive worldwide hit for Judy Collins. The chorus ('It's love's illusions I recall/I really don't know love at all') became something of a statement of policy from Mitchell, whose analyses of love - real or illusory - dominated her work. With *Clouds,* Mitchell paused for reflection, drawing material from her past ('Tin Angel', 'Both Sides Now', 'Chelsea Morning') and blending them with songs devoted to new-found perplexities. If 'I Don't Know Where I Stand' recreates the tentative expectancy of an embryonic relationship, 'The Gallery' chronicles its decline, with the artist as the injured party. The singer, however, was unsatisfied with the final collection, and later termed it her artistic nadir.

Apart from her skills as a writer, Mitchell was a fine singer and imaginative guitarist with a love of open tuning. Although some critics still chose to see her primarily as a songwriter rather than a vocalist, there were already signs of important development on her third album, *Ladies Of The Canyon.* Its title track, with visions of antique chintz and wampum beads, mirrored the era's innocent naivety, a feature also prevailing on 'Willy', the gauche portrait of her relationship with singer **Graham Nash**. Mitchell is nonetheless aware of the period's fragility, and her rendition of 'Woodstock' (which she never visited), a celebration of the hippie dream in the hands of **Crosby, Stills, Nash And Young**, becomes a eulogy herein. With piano now in evidence, the music sounded less sparse and the lyrics more ambitious. portraying the hippie audience as searchers for some lost Edenic bliss ('We are stardust, we are golden . . . and we've got to get ourselves back to the garden'). With 'For Free' (later covered by the Byrds), Mitchell presented another one of her hobbyhorses - the clash between commercial acceptance and artistic integrity. Within the song, Mitchell contrasts her professional success with the uncomplicated pleasure that a street performer enjoys. The extent of Mitchell's commercial acceptance was demonstrated on the humorous 'Big Yellow Taxi', a sardonic comment on the urban disregard for ecology. The single was a surprise UK number 11 hit and was even more surprisingly covered by **Bob Dylan**.

Following a sabbatical, Mitchell returned with her most introspective work to date, *Blue.* Less melodic than her previous albums, the arrangements were also more challenging and the material self-analytical to an almost alarming degree. Void of sentimentality, the work also saw her commenting on the American Dream in 'California' ('That was a dream some of us had'). Austere and at times anti-romantic, *Blue* was an essential product of the singer/songwriter era. On *Blue,* the artist moved from a purely folk-based perspective to that of rock, as the piano, rather than guitar, became the natural outlet for her compositions. **Stephen Stills** (guitar/bass), **James Taylor** (guitar), 'Sneaky' Pete Kleinow (pedal steel) and Russ Kunkel (drums) embellished material inspired by an extended sojourn travelling in Europe, and if its sense of loss and longing echoed previous works, a new maturity instilled a lasting resonance to the stellar inclusions, 'Carey', 'River' and the desolate title track. Any lingering sense of musical restraint was thrown off with *For The Roses*, in which elaborate horn and woodwind sections buoyed material on which personal themes mixed with third-person narratives. The dilemmas attached to fame and performing, first aired on 'For Free', reappeared on the title song and 'Blonde In The Bleachers' while 'Woman Of Heart And Mind' charted the reasons for dispute within a relationship in hitherto unexplored depths. 'You Turn Me On, I'm A Radio' gave Mitchell a US Top 30 entry, but a fifteen month gap ensued before *Court And Spark* appeared. Supported by the subtle, jazz-based LA Express, Mitchell offered a rich, luxuriant collection, marked by an increased sophistication and dazzling use of melody. The sweeping 'Help Me' climbed to number 7 in the US in 1974, bringing its creator a hitherto unparalleled commercial success. The emergence of Mitchell as a well-rounded rock artist was clearly underlined on *Court And Spark* with its familiar commentary on the trials and tribulations of stardom ('Free Man In Paris'). The strength of the album lay in the powerful arrangements courtesy of **Tom Scott**, and guitarist **Robben Ford**, plus Mitchell's own love of jazz rhythms, most notably on her amusing version of **Annie Ross**' 'Twisted'. The quality of Mitchell's live performances, which included stadia gigs during 1974, was captured on the live album *Miles Of Aisles*.

In 1975, Mitchell produced the startling *The Hissing Of Summer Lawns*, which not only displayed her increasing interest in jazz, but also world music. Her most sophisticated work to date, the album was less concerned with introspection than a more generalized commentary on American mores. In 'Harry's House', the obsessive envy of personal possessions is described against a swirling musical backdrop that captures an almost anomic feeling of derangement. The Burundi drummers feature on 'The Jungle Line' in which African primitivism is juxtaposed alongside the swimming pools of the Hollywood aristocracy. 'Edith And The Kingpin' offers a startling evocation of mutual dependency and the complex nature of such a relationship ('His right hand holds Edith, his left hand holds his right/what does that hand desire that he grips it so tight?'). Finally, there was the exuberance of the opening 'In France They Kiss On Main Street' and a return to the theme of 'For Free' on 'The Boho Dance'. The album deserved the highest acclaim, but was greeted with a mixed reception on its release, which emphasized how difficult it was for Mitchell to break free from her 'acoustic folk singer' persona. *The Hissing Of Summer Lawns* confirmed this newfound means of expression. Bereft of an accustomed introspective tenor, its comments on suburban values were surprising, yet were the natural accompaniment to an ever-growing desire to expand stylistic perimeters. However, although *Hejira* was equally adventurous, it was noticeably less ornate, echoing the stark simplicity of early releases. The fretless bass of **Jaco Pastorius** wrought an ever-present poignancy to a series of confessional compositions reflecting the aching restlessness encapsulated in 'Song For Sharon', an open letter to a childhood friend. The same sense of ambition marked with *Hejira*, Mitchell produced another in-depth work which, though less melodic and texturous than its predecessory, was still a major work. The dark humour of 'Coyote', the sharp observation of 'Amelia' and the lovingly cynical portrait of **Furry Lewis**, 'Furry Sings The Blues', were all memorable. The move into jazz territory continued throughout 1978-79, first with the double album, *Don Juan's Reckless Daughter*, and culminating in her collaboration with **Charlie Mingus**. The latter was probably Mitchell's bravest work to date, although its invention was not rewarded with sales and was greeted with suspicion by the jazz community. On *Mingus*, she adapted several of the master musician's best-known compositions. It was an admirable, but flawed, ambition, as her often-reverential lyrics failed to convey the music's erstwhile sense of spontaneity. 'God Must Be A Boogie Man' and 'The Wolf That Lives In Lindsay', for which Joni wrote words and music, succeeded simply because they were better matched.

A live double album, *Shadows And Light* featured **Pat Metheny** and Jaco Pastorius among the guest musicians. She signed a long-term contract with **Geffen Records** and the first fruits of this deal were revealed on *Wild Things Run Fast* in 1982, following this she married bassist Larry Klein, and Mitchell appeared to wind down her activities. . A more accessible work than her recent efforts, *Wild Things Run Fast* lacked the depth and exploratory commitment of its predecessors. The opening song, 'Chinese Cafe', remains one of her finest compositions, blending nostalgia to shattered hopes, but the remainder of the set was musically ill-focussed, relying on unadventurous, largely leaden arrangements. Its lighter moments were well-chosen, however, particularly on the humorous reading of **Leiber And Stoller**'s 'Baby, I Don't Care'. The **Thomas Dolby** produced *Dog Eat Dog* was critically underrated and represented the best of her 80s work. Despite such hi-tech trappings, the shape of the material remained constant with 'Impossible Dreamer' echoing the atmosphere of *Court And Spark*. Elsewhere, 'Good Friends', an uptempo duet with **Michael McDonald**, and 'Lucky Girl', confirmed Mitchell's newfound satisfaction and contentment. In interviews, Mitchell indicated her intention to pursue a career in painting, a comment which some took as evidence of the loss of her musical muse. *Chalk Mark In A Rain Storm* continued in a similar vein, while including two notable reworkings of popular tunes, 'Cool Water', which also featured **Willie**

Nelson, and 'Corrina Corrina', herein retitled 'A Bird That Whistles'. Their appearance inferred the change of perspective contained on *Night Flight Home*, issued in 1991 following a three-year gap. Largely stripped of contemporaneous clutter, this acoustic-based collection invoked the intimacy of *Hejira*, thus allowing full rein to Mitchell's vocal and lyrical flair. Its release coincided with the artist's avowed wish to pursue her painting talents - exhibitions of her 80s canvases were held in London and Edinburgh - and future musical directions remain, as always, open to question. Her remarkable body of work encompasses the changing emotions and concerns of a generation: from idealism to adulthood responsibilities, while baring her soul on the traumas of already public relationships. That she does so with insight and melodic flair accounts for a deserved longevity. With *Chalk Mark In A Rainstorm* and *Night Ride Home*, Mitchell reiterated the old themes in a more relaxed style without ever threatening a new direction. The creatively quiet decade that followed did little to detract from her status, though many were pleased to witness her renaissance in the 90s. Rumours abounded in the 90s that her addiction to cigarettes had caused a serious throat ailment (her voice had become progressively lower and huskier), although this was never confirmed she was told to quit smoking - which she promtly ignored. After contributing a track, 'If I Could', to **Seal**'s 1994 album, she embarked on her first live dates in 12 years on a tour of Canada, before settling in to the studio once more to record *Turbulent Indigo* with production support from Larry Klein in Los Angeles. She has since separated from Klein. Mitchell is one artist that deserves a detailed biography, while we wait, Bill Ruhlmann's revealing 25,000 word interview for *Goldmine* magazine will have to suffice. Still regarded as one of the finest singer/songwriters of her generation, Mitchell has displayed more artistic depth and consistency than most of her illustrious contemporaries from the 70s.

Albums: *Songs To A Seagull* (Reprise 1968), *Clouds* (Reprise 1969), *Ladies Of The Canyon* (Reprise 1970), *Blue* (Reprise 1971), *For The Roses* (Asylum 1972), *Court And Spark* (Asylum 1974), *Miles Of Aisles* (Asylum 1974), *The Hissing Of Summer Lawns* (Asylum 1975), *Hejira* (Asylum 1976), *Don Juan's Reckless Daughter* (Asylum 1977), *Mingus* (Asylum 1979), *Shadows And Light* (asylum 1980), *Wild Things Run Fast* (Geffen 1982), *Dog Eat Dog* (Geffen 1985), *Chalk Mark In A Rainstorm* (Geffen 1988), *Night Ride Home* (Geffen 1991), *Turbulent Indigo* (Warners 1994)

Further reading: *Joni Mitchell*, Leonore Fleischer.

Mitchell, Kim

Having dissolved **Max Webster** in 1982 Mitchell quickly found inspiration to pursue a solo career. After signing with Anthem Records he released a mini-album which followed closely in the Max Webster tradition. He then took a break from music until he signed with **Bronze Records**. His next release was the excellent and slightly offbeat *Akimbo Alogo* which also housed the single 'Go For Soda'. At times reminiscent of the excesses of **Frank Soda And The Imps** and **Neil Merryweather** (c.1974), Mitchell's approach was, at times, misunderstood by the press, but there was no mistaking his obvious talent as a guitarist. He finally achieved critical acclaim with *Rockland.*

Albums: *Kim Mitchell* (Anthem 1982, mini-album), *Akimbo Alogo* (Bronze 1985), *Shakin' Like A Human Being* (Anthem 1987), *Rockland* (Atlantic 1989).

Mitchell, McKinley

b. 25 December 1934, Jackson, Mississippi, USA, d. 1986, USA. A formative soul singer with George Leaner's early 60s Chicago-based One-derful label, Mitchell came from the Chicago blues-club scene to launch that label with his fine self-penned 'The Town I Live In', later re-cut during an even more productive soul period in the 70s with the **Malaco** subsidiary Chimneyville. After leading the Hearts Of Harmony gospel group at the age of 16, Mitchell tried secular music with a quintet in Springfield, Massachusetts, before moving to Philadelphia to front his own gospel group, the Mitchellairs. Subsequently, he travelled to Chicago, where he sang at several blues clubs, and worked with **Muddy Waters** at Pepper's Lounge. Ironically, his first recording, 'Rock Everybody Rock', was in a rock 'n' roll style, cut with members of **Howlin' Wolf**'s band for the Boxer label in 1959. In the local clubs, Mitchell had actually become known as McKinley 'Soul' Mitchell by the time he brought 'The Town I Live In' to Leaner in 1962. Despite this number 8 R&B hit, Mitchell's subsequent records for One-derful, although good examples of early 'tough' soul, sold poorly, and Mitchell embarked on a Chicago label-hopping exercise with the likes of St Lawrence, **Chess**, Spoonful, Sandman, Black Beauty and Big 3, often being produced by Chicago bluesman **Willie Dixon**. In 1976, Mitchell's Big 3 cut, 'Trouble Blues', received good southern coverage from Jackson's Malaco label, and it was followed by other superior soul sides for the same company's Chimneyville label, including the beautiful 'The End Of The Rainbow' and 'The Same Old Dream', as well as the fine re-make of 'The Town I Live In'. A good Chimneyville album, *Mckinley Mitchell*, was also released in 1978. In the 80s, Mitchell worked for James Bennett's Rettas label where he cut three singles and an album. Earlier material was reissued on both US and Japanese labels. Mitchell died prematurely from a heart attack in 1986, and was buried in his native Jackson.

Selected albums: *McKinley Mitchell* (1978), *I Won't Be Back For More* (1984), *The Last Of McKinley Mitchell* (c.1988). Compilations: *McKinley 'Soul' Mitchell* (1979), *The Complete Malaco Collection* (1992).

Mitchell, Red

b. Keith Moore Mitchell, 20 September 1927, New York City, New York, USA, d. 8 November 1992. After studying piano and alto saxophone, Mitchell took up the bass while serving in the armed forces. In the late 40s he played in bands led by **Jackie Paris**, **Mundell Lowe**, **Chubby Jackson** (with whom he played piano) and **Charlie Ventura**. He spent two years with **Woody Herman**, but was hospitalized with tuberculosis in 1951. In the early 50s he worked with **Red Norvo** and **Gerry Mulligan**, opting to stay in California when Mulligan headed back to New York. Resident in Los Angeles from 1954, Mitchell became an important figure on the west coast scene, accompanying and sometimes leading artists such as **Chet Baker**, **Bill Perkins**, **André Previn**, **Mel Lewis**, **Hampton Hawes**, **Don Cherry**, **Ornette Coleman** and **Harold Land**. In the late 60s, Mitchell moved to Sweden, remaining in Europe for 10 years, accompanying visiting American musicians and leading his own groups, which included Communication. During the 80s, Mitchell divided his time between Europe and the USA, playing and recording extensively with jazzmen including **Lee Konitz**, **Warne Marsh**, **Art Pepper** and **Jimmy Rowles**. Mitchell's playing in the 50s was advanced for its time, and in some of his technical developments he opened the way for artists such as **Scott La Faro**. His clean articulation made his solo work of particular interest and an unaccompanied album, *Home Suite*, clearly revealed his remarkable talent. (His brother Whitey Mitchell, also a bass player, was active in the 50s and 60s, but later left the jazz scene.)

Selected albums: *The Fabulous Gerry Mulligan Quartet* (1954), *The Red Mitchell Sextet* (1955), *Jam For Your Bread* (Affinity 1955), *Hampton Hawes Trio* (1955), *Sessions, Live* (1957), *Presenting Red Mitchell* (1957), with André Previn *Pal Joey* (1957), with Previn *West Side Story* (1959), *Red Mitchell At The Renaissance* (1960), with Harold Land *Hear Ye!* (1961), *The Red Mitchell Trio* (1969), *The Red Mitchell Quartet* (1972), with Konitz *I Concentrate On You* (1974), *Communication* (1974), *Red Mitchell Meets Guido Manusardi* (1974), *Blues For A Crushed Soul* (Sonet 1976), *Chocolate Cadillac* (1976), *Red Mitchell And Friends* (1978), *Jim Hall/Red Mitchell* (1978), *Red Mitchell Plays Piano And Sings* (1979), with Art Pepper *Straight Life* (1979), *Empathy* (1980), with Tommy Flanagan *You're Me* (1980), *Home Cookin'* (1980), *Soft And Warm And Swinging* (1982), *When I'm Singing* (1982), *Holiday For Monica* (1983), *The Jimmy Rowles/Red Mitchell Trio* (1985), *Home Suite* (1985), with Clark Terry *To Duke And Basie* (c.1986), with Terry *Jive At Five* (c.1986), with Kenny Barron *The Red Barron Duo* (1986), with Herb Ellis *Doggin' Around* (1988), with Putte Wickman *The Very Thought Of You* (1988), with Roger Kellaway *Alone Together* (Dragon 1988), *Talking* (1989), *Evolution* (1990).

Mitchell, Roscoe

b. 3 August 1940, Chicago, Illinois, USA. As a child Mitchell enjoyed listening to **Nat 'King' Cole**, **Lester Young** and **Charlie Parker**. He studied clarinet and baritone saxophone in high school, taking up alto saxophone in his senior year and continuing with it while in the army. He went to Europe with an army band, where he heard **Albert Ayler**, who was also playing in a military band. After demobilization, he played bop in an outfit with **Henry Threadgill**, but Ayler's music had been a revelation to him. Back in Chicago, he jammed with Threadgill, **Malachi Favors**, **Jack DeJohnette**, and **Muhal Richard Abrams**. Abrams was even more of an influence than Ayler. In 1965 Mitchell, was a charter member of the **AACM**, having played in the Experimental Band (organised by Abrams, the AACM President, inspirer and prime mover) since 1961. His debut *Sound* was the first and one of the most famous recordings to come out of the AACM, characterizing the Chicagoan's new emphasis on sound-as-texture and the importance of the relationship between sound and silence. On these tracks, wrote critic John Litweiller, 'Music is the tension of sounds in the free space of silence'. For a while Mitchell led his own groups, and it was from one of these (a quartet including **Lester Bowie**, Favors and **Phillip Wilson**) that the **Art Ensemble Of Chicago** grew. He once explained: 'It was my band, but I couldn't afford to pay those guys what they deserved, so everybody was shouldering an equal amount of responsibility. We became a co-operative unit in order to remain committed to one another and in order to survive.' Since co-founding the Art Ensemble in 1969, most of his work has been accomplished with them, but he has continued to lead bands of his own, including Space (a trio with saxophonist Gerald Oshita and vocalist Tom Buckner) and Sound (a quintet with trumpet, guitar, bass and percussion). He has also worked with Byron Austin, Scotty Holt and DeJohnette; and has assembled an impressive body of solo saxophone music. Like his partners in the Art Ensemble, Mitchell plays a dazzling number of instruments, the primary ones being soprano, alto, tenor and bass saxophones, oboe, flute, piccolo and clarinet as well as various percussion and 'little instruments'. He and Joseph Jarman represent the two poles of the Ensemble's art: Jarman brings the bulk of the theatrical impulse, while Mitchell - the one member of the group who does not habitually wear facepaint or costume - is the musical structuralist who, despite the apparent freedom of the Ensemble's music, worries about how true an improviser will be to the composer's intention. As a composer he has been an influence on **Anthony Braxton** and **Leo Smith**. There is an ascetic streak to his art, and it is not insignificant that as soon as he was able, he went to live on a 365-acre farm in Wisconsin, dissatisfied with the life-style necessitated by constant touring. Recent projects have included *Songs In The Wind*, which features Steve Sylvester on 'bull roarers and wind wands'; a meeting with the Stockholm-based Brus Trio (*After Fallen Leaves*); and *Four Compositions*, which shows Mitchell evolving into an impressive writer of classical chamber music.

Albums: *Sound* (Delmark 1966), *Solo Saxophone Concerts* (1974), *The Roscoe Mitchell Quartet* (1975), *Old/Quartet* (1975, rec 1967), *Nonaah* (1977), *L-R-G/The Maze/S II Examples* (1978), *Duets With Anthony Braxton* (1978), *Congliptious* (Nessa 1978), *Roscoe Mitchell* (Chief 1979), *Sketches From Bamboo* (1979), *Snurdy McGurdy And Her Dancin' Shoes* (1981), with Tom Buckner, Gerald Oshita *New Music For Woodwinds And Voice* (1981), *3x4 Eye* (1981), *More Cutouts* (Cecma 1981), *Concert Toronto 4/5 October 1975* (Sackville 1981), with Space *An Interesting Breakfast Conversation* (1984), *And The Sound And Space Ensembles* (1984), *Live At The Muhle Hunziken* (1986), *The Flow Of Things* (Black Saint 1987), *Four Compositions* (1987), *Live In Detroit* (1989), *Songs In The Wind* (Victo 1991), with Brus Trio *After Fallen Leaves* (Silkheart 1992, rec. 1989), *Live At The Knitting Factory* (Black Saint 1992, 1987 recording), with Muhal Richard Abrams *Solos And Duets At Merkin Hall* (Black Saint 1992), *This Dance Is For Steve McCall* (Black Saint 1993).

Mitchell, Walter

b. 19 March 1919, New Orleans, Louisiana, USA, d. 10 January 1990, Toledo, Ohio, USA. A harmonica player from the age of four, Mitchell travelled the south prior to military service, settling in Detroit in 1945. There he formed another version of his group, Little Walter Junior And The Boogie Blues Boys. The pseudonym presumably referred to his height of just over five feet. Mitchell's music owes most to **John Lee 'Sonny Boy' Williamson** and, unusually, much to **Sonny Terry**. Mitchell was closely associated with his Mississippian cousin **L.C. Greene**, on whose records he played; he also sang on a couple of titles issued as by Greene. His own records were in a strange format of piano, bass and two (often dissonant) harmonicas, the second being played by Robert Richard, whom Mitchell also backed as a singer in the same format.

Album: *Harp-Suckers!* (1983).

Mitchell, Willie

b. 3 January 1928, Ashland, Mississippi, USA. A veteran of several Memphis-based bands, Mitchell rose to prominence in the late 50s with an outfit which formed the basis for his production work and early solo recordings. The line-up included Lewis Steinberg and Al Jackson, both of whom would later appear in **Booker T. And The MGs**. By the 60s, Mitchell was leading the Hi Records houseband. The company was established on the success of **Bill Black**, the one-time **Elvis Presley** bassist whose economical instrumental singles suggested the style later forged across town at the **Stax** studio. Although Black died in 1965, releases bearing his name continued, with Mitchell's group supplying the music. Mitchell's own recording career prospered with such classic Memphis offerings as '20-75' and 'Percolatin'' (both 1964), as well as the **Junior Walker**-influenced groove of 'That Driving Beat' and 'Everything Is Gonna' Be Alright' (both 1966). 'Soul Serenade' was a Top 10 US R&B single in 1968, but his releases were latterly obscured by work with other artists. Mitchell became vice-president at Hi in 1970, and proceeded to mould its 70s sound with production work for **Al Green**, **Syl Johnson** and **Ann Peebles**. Other sessions at his Royal Studio included those of **Bobby Bland**, **Otis Clay** and **O.V. Wright**. During the early part of the decade, Mitchell's classic band - the Hodges brothers, Charles (organ), Teeny (guitar) and Leroy (bass), Howard Grimes or Al Jackson (drums) and the **Memphis Horns** - defined post-Stax southern soul, but the formula grew sterile as time progressed. Treasured moments still occurred, but the loss of Green, then Johnson, suggested an internal dissatisfaction. Mitchell resigned from Hi in 1979, three years after its acquisition by the Los Angeles-based Cream label, and joined the Bearsville label as a producer and artist. During the 80s he became a partner in a video production company and set up his Wayco outlet. In 1985, he was reunited with Al Green for the latter's *He Is The Light* and the following year's *Going Away*. In 1987, he produced *Popped In, Souled Out* for **Wet Wet Wet**.

Albums: *20-75* (1964), *It's Dance Time* (1965), *Driving Beat* (1966), *It's What's Happening* (1966), *Soul Serenade* (1968), *Willie Mitchell Live* (1968), *Solid Soul* (1969), *On Top* (1969), *Soul Bag* (1970), *Hold It* (1971), *Listen Dance* (1971), *Willie...Mitchell...Listen...Dance* (1981). Compilations: *The Best Of Willie Mitchell* (1977), *That Driving Beat* (1986).

Mitchell-Ruff Duo

Dwike Mitchell (b. 14 February 1930, Dunedin, Florida, USA; piano) and Willie Ruff (b. 1 September 1931, Sheffield, Alabama, USA; French horn/bass) first met while they were in the army, and afterwards played together in **Lionel Hampton**'s band. Mitchell has a formidable technique, and though Ruff sometimes solos on the horn, he usually plays bass. He is an academic musician who became a professor of music at Yale. They formed the duo in 1955, and were the first jazz musicians to appear in the USSR when they performed impromptu concerts during a tour with the Yale Russian Chorus in 1959. During the 60s they played regularly at their own club in New Haven, Connecticut, or at the Hickory House in New York - usually with the addition of a drummer, either Charlie Smith or Helicio Milito. In 1966, they were the first jazz musicians to be used by the State Department on a goodwill tour when they went to Mexico City with President Johnson. In 1967, they made a film in Brazil tracing the African roots of Brazilian music. They have continued performing together and toured China in 1981.

Albums: *Mitchell-Ruff Duo* (1955), *Appearing Nightly* (1957), *Ruff-Mitchell Duo Plus Strings And Brass* (1958), *Jazz Mission To Moscow* (1959), *Brazilian Trip* (1966), *Strayhorn* (1969), *Dizzy Gillespie And The Mitchell-Ruff Duo In Concert* (1970), *Dizzy Gillespie Live With The Mitchell Ruff Duo* (1971), *Virtuoso Elegance In Jazz* (1984).

Mittoo, Jackie

b. 1948, Kingston, Jamaica, West Indies, d. 1990. The self-effacing Jackie Mittoo was perhaps reggae's premier keyboard player, and had as much influence on the direction of reggae in the 60s and 70s as any single musician. Mittoo was taught to play the piano by his grandmother, first performing in public before he was 10 years old. After playing with local Kingston bands the Rivals and the Sheiks, Mittoo came to the attention of **Coxsone Dodd** at **Studio One**. At 15 Mittoo was playing piano and organ in the **Skatalites**, thereafter performing scouting and arranging duties for Dodd's labels. His own 'Got My Bugaloo' (1966) 45, a rare vocal outing, was one of the best records of the **ska** era and presaged the arrival of **rocksteady**, and his work with the Soul Brothers and, later, Soul Vendors bands, helped keep Studio One ahead of rival production houses. His playing behind the **Heptones, Cables, Wailers** and innumerable solo acts helped create the sound of reggae for years to come: later artists and studios, such as **Augustus Pablo, Channel One** and almost the entire **dancehall** movement of the early-80s based their rhythm arrangements on material that Mittoo had pioneered in the 60s. Dodd also issued solo albums by Mittoo from 1967 onwards, and they (*Now* and *Macka Fat* particularly) rank amongst the most artistically pleasing organ instrumental LPs outside of **Booker T** and jazz maestros like **Jimmy Smith**. For proof, try his radical arrangement of 'Eleanor Rigby' on *Now*, transforming a worn-out song with an astonishing roots sound.

In the mid-70s Mittoo left Dodd to work in Canada, where he set up the Stine-Jac label to moderate success, with music that was similar to that which he had left behind at Studio One, and cut several albums for producer **Bunny Lee** in both Jamaica and London. He also worked extensively on some fine sessions for **Sugar Minott**'s Youth Promotion outlet, still displaying the same taste and rhythmic acumen that had always been his trademark. He was deeply respected as an elder statesman amongst Sugar's young reggae guns. He died in 1990, an event that brought about a long-overdue reassessment of his work among reggae cognoscenti. Undoubtedly, if he had been an American musician, his name would be spoken in the same breath as the greats of black music.

Selected albums: With the Soul Vendors: *On Tour* (Studio One 60s). Solo: *Evening Time* (1967), *In London* (Coxsone 1967), *Keep On Dancing* (1969), *Now* (1969), *Macka Fat* (Studio One 1970), *Hot Blood* (1977), *Cold Blood* (1978), *Keyboard King* (1978), *Showcase* (Studio One 1983). Compilation: *The Original Jackie Mittoo* (Third World 1979).

Mix Tapes

An attempt in the UK during the early 90s to recreate the 'buzz' of live DJ performances, mix tapes are a musical format whose ancestry can be traced back to reggae's **yard tapes**. Often of similar dubious origins and quality, very few are clared through copyright, bearing in mind the number of samples and tracks involved in a single one or two hour set (However, the official lines, such as those promoted by *Mixmag*, have undergone this process.) It is a noble but inherently flawed medium, but also the closest recorded appromixation of a night clubbing or raving.

Mixmaster Morris

UK house guru, who arrived in the early 90s at the height of hardcore techno's domination (he titled his own music weirdcore), and whose name has subsequently graced dozens of releases, both as a producer and remixer. Morris' first live performances were at the ICA Rock Week in 1980, before he began to work with samplers in 1983. He has since claimed the honour of being 'the first to play a house set in the UK', at the Fridge in London in 1987 at his Madhouse nights. He also prepared pirate radio tapes for his 'Mongolian Hip Hop Show', and worked with experimental pirate TV. He met Colin Angus of the **Shamen** via mutual **Psychic TV** acquaintences, and began DJing on their Synergy tours. His musical style was certainly unique, often building a set to the centrepiece section, which would as likely be a **This Heat** track as anything more conventional. He also stressed the importance of providing DJ's with label information, not just bpm's but also the key a track was played in. In addition to his sampling and rhythmic wizardry, he has gone on to record in his own right. The first such release was 'Space Is The Place' on the **Rising High** label, a relationship with whom prospers to this day. Following late 80s singles 'Freestyle' and 'I Want You', his debut album arrived, also credited to The Irresistable Force, in 1992. It boasted a splendid holographic label, and was filled with samples taken from obscure and obtuse sources. A more detached, ambient based project, after a brief **Kraftwerk** parody on the intro it branched out into seamless 'chill-out' territory. This was the man, after all, who invented the phrase 'I think, therefore I ambient'. He has gone on to record with the new king of chill, **Peter Namlook**, as

part of the latter's Dreamfish project, and remixed for **Spiritualized** among others.
Albums: As the Irresistable Force *Flying High* (Rising High 1992, double album), with Peter Namlook *Dreamfish* (Rising High 1993).

Mize, Billy

b. 29 April 1929, Kansas City, Kansas, USA. Raised in the San Joaquin Valley of California, Mize first learned to play guitar as a child, but converted to steel guitar when he received one for his 18th birthday. Originally, he was influenced by the music of **Bob Wills** and when he moved to Bakersfield, he formed his own band and played residences and local venues. He also worked as a disc jockey on KPMC. In 1953, he appeared on *The Cousin Herb Trading Post Show* on KERO-TV Bakersfield, and became affectionately known as Billy The Kid. He was a regular with the show for 13 years, including hosting it at one stage. Mize still played his other appearances, and in 1955, began to appear on the ***Hank Penny*** *Show* on Los Angeles television. In 1957, his popularity grew to the extent that, for several years, he managed to appear on seven Los Angeles television stations weekly, including *Town Hall Party*, and still maintained his Bakersfield commitments. He naturally developed into a television personality and, in 1966 and 1967, he became host/singer of **Gene Autry**'s *Melody Ranch* network show on KTLA. He also commenced his own syndicated *Billy Mize Show* from Bakersfield. He first recorded for **Decca** in the 50s, and later for Challenge and **Liberty**, before making the US country charts in 1966 with his **Columbia** recording of 'You Can't Stop Me'. Between 1966 and 1977, he totalled 11 US chart entries, including his own composition 'Make It Rain'. Some of his songs were hits for other artists, such as 'Who Will Buy The Wine' (Charlie Walker), 'My Baby Walks All Over Me' (Johnny Sea) and 'Don't Let The Blues Make You Bad' (**Dean Martin**). He maintained rigorous schedules throughout the 60s and 70s, and appeared in the television series *RFD Hollywood*. He later became a television producer with his own production company. He has also worked as a musician on numerous recording sessions, including playing steel and rhythm guitar on many of **Merle Haggard** recordings. His brother Buddy (b. 5 August 1936, Wichita, Kansas, USA.) is a noted country songwriter, record producer and radio personality. He also relocated to Bakersfield, and his songs have been recorded by **Buck Owens, Johnny Cash, Marty Robbins, Hank Snow** and many others. In the early 80s, Buddy and Billy worked together on various television projects. Billy currently heads Billy Mize Productions, making television spectaculars with Merle Haggard.
Albums: *This Time And Place* (1969), *You're Alright With Me* (1971), *Love'N'Stuff* (1976).

Mizell, Hank

b. Bill Mizell, Asheville, North Carolina, USA. Mizell was a minor rockabilly artist best known for the 1957 recording 'Jungle Rock'. He served in the US Navy in 1947, and upon his discharge began both singing and preaching. In the early 50s he and his five-piece country band went to Montgomery, Alabama, to record. A disc jockey there nicknamed him Hank, after the recently deceased **Hank Williams,** and the name stuck. In 1957, working with guitarist Jim Bobo, drummer Bill Collins and pianist Eddie Boyd in Chicago, Mizell recorded 'Jungle Rock' for the local EKO label. **King Records** picked up distribution, but the record did not sell, and Mizell gave up performing professionally. He became a preacher and moved between Chicago, Mississippi and Nashville for the next few years. Although several country singles were recorded in the 60s and 70s, Mizell remained virtually unknown until 1976, when rockabilly collectors in Europe discovered the King single. 'Jungle Rock' transcended cult credibility to reach the UK Top 10, and prompted **Charly Records** to release other rediscovered Mizell recordings. Mizell made a few other rockabilly and country recordings in the 80s, but remained unknown outside of hardcore rockabilly circles.
Albums: *Jungle Rock* (1976), *Higher* (1977), *We're Gonna Bop Tonight* (1982).

Mlle. Modiste

Composer **Victor Herbert**'s first collaboration with librettist and lyricst Henry Blossom was a tremendous success. - in the long term. After its debut at the Knickerbocker Theatre in New York on 25 December 1905, it ran for 202 performances. That was a decent enough run in those days anyway, and it gained in popularity over the years mainly due to the its star, the lovely Fritzi Scheff, and her close identification with the operetta during its many tours and subsequent Broadway revivals. Scheff played the role of Fifi, who works in a hat shop owned by Mme. Cecil (Josephine Bartlett). She is in love with Captain Etienne de Bouvray (Walter Percival), but their romance is disapproved of by her employer, and the gentleman's uncle, Compte. de St. Mar (William Pruett). Josephine would also like to sing on the stage, and she confides her ambitions to a visiting American, the wealthy Hiram Bent (Claude Gillingwater). He is so taken by her charm and manner, that he offers to pay for an extensive course of singing lessons. Inevitably, when the dissenters hear her beautiful voice, they protest no more, and the marriage is allowed to take place. Fritzi Scheff, who had been with the Metropolitan Opera before she made her Broadway debut in the title role of Babette in 1903, introduced 'Kiss Me Again', one of the most cherished ballads in the history of operetta, and she also excelled on the delightful 'If I Were On The Stage' and 'The Mascot Of The Troops'. Pruett had the resolute 'I Want What I Want When I Want It', and Percival sang the engaging 'The Time, The Place And The Girl'. The rest of the score included 'Love Me, Love My Dog', 'When The Cat's Away', and 'The Nightingale And The Star'. Fritzi Scheff, who was born in Vienna in 1879, made her last Broadway appearance as Mlle. Modiste in 1929 when she was 50 years old. She died in New York on 8 April 1954.

MLO

A collaboration between UK-born Jon Tye and Pete Smith through the **Rising High** imprint, MLO's debut album was also the soundtrack to a film of the same name - shown as live accompaniment to **Pink Floyd** gigs in 1994. The project was put together in an intensive two week period inside one of the world's most advanced multi-media studios. The term ambient was almost inevitably invoked, though the duo opted to disassociate themselves from the bulk of the artists working within that genre. The album was titled after the seventh moon of Jupiter, the only entity in the solar system, aside from the earth, known to be volcanically active. As well as recording a film for use alongside their debut album, and producing videos for other artists, Tye has also recorded solo as Flutter ('Flutter').
Album: *Io* (Rising High 1994).

Mo Wax

An indepedent label run from Oxford, England, whose musical predilictions cover a territory which takes in **Acid Jazz** and the ambient strains of new dance gurus like the **Aphex Twin**. The label was formed by James Levelle (b. c.1973, Oxford, England), who started compiling his own electro tapes at the age of 10. Three years later he developed his interest in hip hop, going on to work experience at Bluebird Records in London, and DJing in his native Oxford. The eclecticism of his early musical tastes broadened through exposure to acid house then techno and jazz, as he worked in a record shop by day and wrote a column for *Straight No Chaser*. By the age of 20 he had established his record company, Mo Wax, bringing his diverse musical tastes to bear on its catalogue. The label's inventry kicked off with Repercussions' 'Promise' and Stylus' 'Many Ways'. Within a year of operation its discography boasted vital cuts like those by **RPM** ('2000'), DJ Krush ('Krush'), **DJ Shadow** (the superb 'In Flux'), and Lavelle's own Men From Uncle project. There was even a hip hop record remixed by techno ambassador **Carl Craig**, while the Federation (the Bristol based team of Alex Swift, St. John, Julie Lockhart and Stepchild) returned to a more conventional jazz groove. The boundaries were stretched further by invoking a second label, Smoke Filled Thoughts, through **London**.

Selected albums: Various: *Royalties Overdue* (Mo Wax 1994). The Federation: *Flower To The Sun* (Mo Wax 1994).

Mo-Dettes

Despite the name, the timing of their appearance on the music scene, and the fact that they covered the **Rolling Stones**' 'Paint It Black', the Mo-Dettes were not modettes and disliked anyone who said they were. They were originally formed for a one-off gig at the Acklam Hall, supporting the Vincent Units. Their line-up was built around Kate Korus (b. Katherine Corris, New York, USA; guitar), who played with the Castrators before lasting just three gigs with the earliest line-up of the **Slits**. She left (to be replaced by Viv Albertine) and attempted to form several bands. Korus took a long time finding musicians with whom she was happy, but gradually she came across (on the set of *The Great Rock 'N' Roll Swindle* where both had non-acting jobs) drummer June Miles-Kingston (the sister of Bob Kingston of **Tenpole Tudor**) and bassist Jane Crockford. Crockford had previously played in the Banks Of Dresden with Richard Dudanski. Through a mutual friend they met Ramona Carlier, a singer from Switzerland whose experience to date had been backing vocals at a few sessions plus a one-off party gig with a band called the Bomberettes, and had been in England about a year. The first product of their labours was 'White Mice' - on their own Mode label through **Rough Trade**. Ramona left late in 1981 to start a solo career, and was replaced by Sue Slack. Soon after, Korus split to be replaced by Melissa Ritter. The final split came shortly after in 1982, owing to further internal friction. Miles-Kingston moved on to **Fun Boy Three**'s backing band, before she produced a solo single for Go! Discs, joined the **Communards** and sang on various sessions. Kate Korus also released a single with Jenny of the **Belle Stars**.
Album: *The Story So Far* (1980).

Mobley, Hank

b. Henry Mobley, 7 July 1930, Eastman, Georgia, USA, d. 30 May 1986. Tenor saxophonist Mobley began his professional career with an R&B band in 1950. The following year, he was attracting the attention of such important beboppers as **Max Roach** and **Dizzy Gillespie**, and by 1954 his stature was such that he was invited to become a founder member of **Horace Silver**'s Jazz Messengers. When Silver reformed a band under his own name, bequeathing the Messengers to **Art Blakey**, Mobley went along, too. In the late 50s he was briefly with Blakey, then worked with **Dizzy Reece** and, in 1961, spent a short but memorable time with **Miles Davis**. Throughout the 60s, Mobley worked with many distinguished musicians, among them **Lee Morgan**, **Barry Harris** and **Billy Higgins**, often leading the bands, and recording several outstanding sessions for **Blue Note**. In the 70s, Mobley was dogged by poor health, but he worked sporadically, including a stint as co-leader of a group with **Cedar Walton**. Mobley played even less frequently in the 80s, but shortly before his death in 1986, he worked with **Duke Jordan**. The seemingly casual ease with which Mobley performed, comfortably encompassing complex rhythmical innovations, and the long period spent on the sidelines have tended to obscure the fact that his was a remarkable talent. Also militating against widespread appeal was his sometimes detached, dry and intimate sound, which contrasted sharply with the more aggressively robust style adopted by many of his contemporaries.

Selected albums: with Art Blakey *The Jazz Messengers At The Cafe Bohemia* (1955), *The Hank Mobley Quartet* (Blue Note 1955), *The Jazz Message Of Hank Mobley* (Savoy 1956), *Mobley's Message* (1956), *Mobley's Second Message* (Savoy 1956), *The Hank Mobley Sextet* (1956), *Hank Mobley-Lee Morgan: Hank's Shout* (1956), *Hank Mobley And His All Stars* (Blue Note 1957), *Hank Mobley With Donald Byrd And Lee Morgan* (Blue Note 1957), *The Hank Mobley Quintet* (1957), *Hank* (1957), *Hank Mobley* (Blue Note 1957), *Poppin'* (1957), *Peckin' Time* (Blue Note 1958), *Monday Night At Birdland* (1958), *Soul Station* (Blue Note 1960), *Roll Call* (Blue Note 1960), with Miles Davis *Carnegie Hall 1961* (1961), with Davis *At The Blackhawk* (1961), *Workout* (Blue Note 1961), *Another Workout* (1961), *Straight No Filter* (Blue Note 1963-65), *No Room For Squares* (Blue Note 1963), *The Turnaround* (1965), *Dippin'* (Blue Note 1965), *A Caddy For Daddy* (Blue Note 1965), *A Slice Of The Top* (1966), *Third Season* (1967), *Hi Voltage* (1967), *Far Away Lands* (Blue Note 1967), *Reach Out* (1968), *The Flip* (1969), *Thinking Of Home* (1970).

Moby

A New York DJ, recording artist, Christian, vegan and Philosophy graduate. Moby (b. Richard Melville Hall, c.1966, New York, USA) is so nicknamed because of the fact that he can trace his ancestry to the author of the famous Captain Ahab whaling tale. This is by no means the only interesting aspect of his idiosyncratic artistic life. He refuses to travel anywhere by car because of the environmental considerations, and generally displays little of the public anonymity that is the creed of the underground DJ. In 1991 he took the *Twin Peaks* theme, under the guise of 'Go', into the Top 10. Although that appealed to the more perverse natures of both mainstream and club audiences, the release of 'I Feel It'/'Thousand' in 1993 was yet more bizarre. The latter track was classified by the *Guinness Book Of Records* as the fastest single ever, climaxing at 1015 bpm. It was typical of Moby's playful, irreverent attitude to his work. In his youth he was a member of hardcore punk outfit the Vatican Commandos, and even substituted as singer for **Flipper** while their vocalist was in prison. He has brought these rock 'n' roll inclinations to bear on the world of dance: at the 1992 DMC/Mixmag Awards ceremony he trashed his keyboards at the end of his set. His introduction to dance music began in the mid-80s: 'I was drawn to it, I started reading about it, started hanging out in clubs. For me house music was the synthesis of the punk era.' He collected cheap, second hand recording equipment, basing himself in an old factory/converted prison in New York's Little Italy. He signed to leading independent **Mute** in 1993. *Ambient* was a collection of unissued cuts from 1988 to 1991, composed of barely audible atmospheric interludes. *Story So Far* gathered together a series of tracks he cut for Instinct Records. The following year Moby released 'Hymn', a transcendental religious techno odyssey, distinguished by a 35-minute ambient mix and a **Laurent Garner** remix. His own remix catalogue includes **Brian Eno**, **LFO** ('Tan Ta Ra'), **Pet Shop Boys**, **Erasure** ('Chorus'), **Orbital** ('Speed Freak'), **Depeche Mode** and even **Michael Jackson**.

Albums: *Ambient* (Mute 1993), *The Story So Far* (Mute 1993), *Everything Is Wrong* (Mute 1995).

Moby Dick

'A Whale Of A Tale' according to the publicity hand-outs - but 'a whale of a mistake', according to the critics. They harpooned the show right at the start, and even the financial clout of **Cameron Mackintosh** could not heal the wounds. *Moby Dick* was tried out at the tiny Old Fire Station in Oxford in the autumn of 1991, before opening at London's Piccadilly Theatre on 17 March 1992. In Robert Longden's book, sixth-form members of a girls' school bearing a remarkable resemblance to the infamous St. Trinian's, stage a production of Herman Melville's classic story in the school swimming pool. As one critic noted: 'The degree of camp, of music-hall smut and anachronism is extreme.' Cabaret singer Tony Monopoly played Miss Dorothy Hymen, the establishment's headmistress, who in turn played Captain Ahab (with a cricket pad where his peg leg should be) in the musical production of *Moby Dick*. When Ahab's ship sets sail, the schoolgirls, who are supposed to be sailors, appear scantily clad in gymslips and sexy stockings, and utter ancient jokes such as 'three years at sea and no sign of Dick'. Director and librettist Longden also wrote the lyrics, and the music was composed by Hereward Kaye. Their score, which contained more than 20 numbers - but no items that stood out - included 'Hymn', 'Forbidden Seas', 'Primitive', 'Love Will Always', 'Mr. Starbuck', 'Building America', 'Save The Whale', and 'Heave'. In the face of a vicious critical reaction and dwindling audiences, Mackintosh remained committed to the production until he was forced to close after a run of 15 weeks. He sanctioned the release of a double-CD which contained a recording of the show made over the sound system as a souvenir for the cast, and indicated that *Moby* was not sunk for ever. In 1993, a production was mounted by a theatre company in Boston, Massachusetts, and in the same year, a scaled-down, revised version, entitled *Moby!*, was presented in the English city of Exeter. The show surfaced again in 1995 at Hof, a small town in Northern Bavaria, with 'a new concept worked out by the authors and director Steven Dexter'.

Moby Grape

The legend that continues to grow around one of San Francisco's late 60s' groups is mainly based on their magnificent debut album, which fans vainly willed them to repeat. This iconoclastic band was formed in September 1966, with the seminal line-up of **Alexander 'Skip' Spence** (b. 18 April 1946, Windsor, Ontario, Canada; guitar/vocals), Jerry Miller (b. 10 July 1943, Tacoma, Washington, USA; guitar/vocals), Bob Mosley (b. 4 December 1942, Paradise Valley, California, USA; bass/vocals), Don Stevenson (b. 15 October 1942, Seattle, Washington, USA; drums) and Peter Lewis (b. 15 July 1945, Los Angeles, California, USA; guitar/vocals). With record companies queueing up to sign them, they decided to go with **CBS** and became marketing guinea pigs for an unprecedented campaign, whereupon 10 tracks (five singles plus b-sides) were released simultaneously. Not even the **Beatles** could have lived up to that kind of launch. Only one of the records dented the US chart: 'Omaha' reached a dismal number 88. Had the singles been released in normal sequence, they might have all been hits, as the quality of each song was outstanding. The band fell into immediate disarray, unable to cope with the pressure and hype. The resulting debut, *Moby Grape*, contained all these 10 tracks plus an additional three, and it deservedly reached the US Top 30 album charts. It is now recognized as a classic. The short, brilliantly structured, guitar-based rock songs with fine harmonies still sound fresh in the 90s.

Their follow-up was a similar success (yet a lesser work), and made the US Top 20 album chart. As with their debut, CBS continued with their ruthless marketing campaign, determined to see a return on their investment, as the Grape had originally held out for a considerable advance. *Wow* sported a beautiful surrealistic painting/collage by Bob Cato, depicting a huge bunch of grapes mixed with an 18th- century beach scene which came with a free album, *Grape Jam*. Additionally, one of the tracks was recorded at 78rpm, forcing the listener to get up and change the speed only to hear a spoof item played by Lou Waxman And His Orchestra. Amidst this spurious package were some of their finest songs, including Spence's 'Motorcycle Irene', Millers' 'Miller's Blues', Mosley's 'Murder In My Heart For The Judge' and arguably their best track, 'Can't Be So Bad'. Penned by Jerry Miller and featuring his stinging guitar solo, this furious-paced heavy rock item is suddenly slowed down and sweetened by an outstanding five-part **Mamas And The Papas**-style harmony. The song failed to chart anywhere.

Spence had departed with drug and mental problems by the release of *Moby Grape '69*, although his ethereal composition 'Seeing' is one of the highlights of this apologetic and occasionally brilliant album (the hype of the past is disclaimed by the 'sincere' sleeve notes). Other notable tracks included Lewis' hymn-like 'I Am Not Willing' and the straightforward rocker 'Truck Driving Man'. A disastrous European tour was arranged, during which the band was constantly overshadowed by the support act **Group Therapy**. Mosley left on their return to the USA, and allegedly joined the marines, leaving the rest to fulfil their contract by making a fourth album. He also made a solo album, as did Spence. The latter, who today lives in a men's hostal as a ward of the county, released an extraordinary album. *Oar* has become a cult classic since its release in 1968. It is painfully dark ('Diana') and hoplessly light ('Lawrence Of Euphoria'). It does at least reflect Spence's condition as a paranoid schizophrenic.

The poor-selling and lacklustre *Truly Fine Citizen* was badly received; the critics had already given up on them. The band then disintegrated, unable to use the name which was and still is owned by their manager, Matthew Katz. The remaining members have appeared as Maby Grope, Mosley Grape, Grape Escape, Fine Wine, the Melvills, the Grape, the Hermans and the Legendary Grape. During one of their many attempts at reformation, Mosley and Miller actually released a record as Fine Wine. The original five reunited for one more undistinguished album in 1971 *20 Granite Creek*. Out of the mire, only Mosley's 'Gypsy Wedding' showed some promise. Skip Spence delivered the quirky 'Chinese Song,' played on a koto, and the silk-voiced Lewis produced 'Horse Out In The Rain' with its unusual timing and extraordinary booming bass. A live album in 1978 delighted fans, and rumours constantly abound about various reformation plans. Some of the band still play together in small clubs and bars, but the magical reunion of the five (just like the five **Byrds**) can never be. Spence sadly is in no fit shape and unbelievably Mosely was also diagnosed as a schizophrenic and lives rough on the streets in San Diego. The myth around the band continues to grow as more (outrageous) stories come to light. The debut album is one of the true rock/pop classics of the past 30 years (along with **Loves**'s *Forever Changes*). Their influence is immense and they still have many followers (including long-standing fan **Robert Plant**). The 'grape sound' has shown up in many groups over the past 20 years including the **Doobie Brothers**, **R.E.M.**, the **Smithereens, Teenage Fanclub** and **Weezer**. They were, more than any other band from the Bay Area in 1967/68, the true embodiment of the music (but not the culture).

Albums: *Moby Grape* (CBS 1967), *Wow* (CBS 1967), *Grape Jam* (Columbia 1967), *Moby Grape '69* (CBS 1969), *Truly Fine Citizen* (CBS 1969), *20 Granite Creek* (Reprise 1971), *Live Grape* (1978). As Fine Wine *Fine Wine* (1976), Compilations: *Great Grape* (CBS 1973), *Vintage* 2CD box set with unreleased material and alternate takes (CBS/Legacy 1993). Skip Spence solo *Oar* (Columbia 1968). Bob Mosely solo *Bob Mosely* (Warner Bros 1972).

Mock Turtles

With their promising UK hit single, 'Can You Dig It?', the Mock Turtles followed a line of success stories that had emanated from Manchester, England, between 1989 and 1991. Like many of their contemporaries, the band had been playing the independent circuit for several years before realizing their potential. The band's lynch-pin was singer/guitarist/songwriter Martin Coogan, who had previously fronted Judge Happiness, won a Salford University talent contest and subsequently issued a single, 'Hey Judge', on the Mynah label in 1985. As the Mock Turtles, Coogan was joined by Steve Green (bass), Krzysztof Korab (keyboards) and Steve Cowen (drums), and their recordings surfaced on several of the Imaginary label's popular tribute compilations (covering **Syd Barrett**'s 'No Good Trying', **Captain Beefheart**'s 'Big-Eyed Beans From Venus', the **Kinks**' 'Big Sky', the **Byrds**' 'Why' and the **Velvet Underground**'s 'Pale Blue Eyes'), illustrating their eclectic tastez. Meanwhile, the band's first 12-inch EP, *Pomona*, was issued in 1987, and although it owed an obvious debt to early **David Bowie** and veered towards the overblown, the confidence of musicians, string arrangements and songwriting was obvious. Guitarist Martin Glyn Murray joined the band in time for 'The Wicker Man' (inspired by the film of the same name), followed by 'And Then She Smiles'. From pure folk to powerful songs verging on the pompous, the Mock Turtles conveyed a distinctive feel within their music. But it was their next single, 1990's 'Lay Me Down', which hinted at bigger things, sporting a sparse yet infectious shuffling backbeat. Hot on its heels came a well-received debut album, *Turtle Soup*, in June, which fared well on the independent chart, as did the band's collaboration with one of Coogan's long-time influences, **Bill Nelson**, 'Take Your Time' (the b-side of their next single, 'Magic Boomerang'). This was enough to lure Siren Records, and for their first major label single, the band chose to rework the b-side of 'Lay Me Down', 'Can You Dig It?'. The single was an instant hit with BBC television's ***Top Of The Pops*** appearances to match, and in its wake came another reissue of sorts, 'And Then She Smiles'. This failed to consolidate the success of 'Can You Dig It', and the Mock Turtles' highly commercial *Two Sides* suffered from a low profile, despite its abundance of musical muscle and carefully-crafted songs. In the meantime, Imaginary compiled most of their early single tracks on *1987-90*, for those newcomers who had missed them first time around. However, the Mock Turtle's rapid progress soon transmuted into an equally swift decline. The band dissolved when Coogan formed a new band with Korab and Green after Murray left to pursue an acting career.

Albums: *Turtle Soup* (Imaginary 1990) *Two Sides* (Two Sides 1991). Compilation: *1987-90* (Imaginary 1991).

Mockingbirds

Formed in Manchester, England, in 1964, when three former members of the Whirlwinds - **Graham Gouldman** (b. 10 May 1945, Manchester, England; guitar/vocals), Steve Jacobsen and Bernard Basso - were joined by ex-Sabres' drummer Kevin Godley (b. 7 October 1945, Manchester, England). However, although Graham's songwriting skills provided hits for the **Yardbirds**, **Hollies** and **Herman's Hermits**, his group was unable to gain a similar commercial ascendancy. Between 1965 and 1966, the Mockingbirds completed five singles, of which 'You Stole My Love' was the most ambitious. Although co-produced by **Giorgio Gomelsky** and **Paul Samwell-Smith**, and abetted by vocalist **Julie Driscoll**, the song was a commercial failure and the group's confidence was consequently undermined. Gouldman began a solo career upon the group's collapse, but later rejoined Godley for several studio projects, which in turn inspired the formation of **10cc**.

Models

The Models were Australia's premier 'new wave' band to emerge from the punk period in the second half of 1978. Original member Sean Kelly (guitar/vocals) and James Freud (bass; who joined in 1982), provided much of the Models' song material. Both had played together previously in Melbourne punk band, the Teenage Radio Stars. The fluctuating line-up of the Models has in the past included notables Andrew Duffield (keyboards; replaced in 1983 by Roger Mason), drummers Janis 'Johnny Crash' Friedenfields and Barton Price, Mark Ferrie (bass/vocals) and James Valentine (keyboards). The band recorded often, and despite having substantial success on the Australian alternative charts, toured frequently and extensively to repay debts that would eventually lead to acrimony between the principal songwriters. Commercial success finally came in 1985 with the 'Out Of Sight Out Of Mind' single and album, and the 'Barbados' single. The band's material was either dense rock music or melodic pop, which alienated its long-standing fans. Since the band broke up in 1987, Freud has recorded a solo album, but despite its high production costs, it did not perform very well. Kelly eased himself back into the

limelight by co-forming a band called the Absent Friends with various other well-known Australian musicians, including **INXS** bassist, Garry Beers. Initially conceived as a part-time affair, the band developed into a more fully-fledged outfit which earned high respect around Sydney.
Albums: *Alphabetacharliedeltaechofoxtrot* (1980), *Local And/Or General* (1981), *Pleasure Of Your Company* (1983), *Out Of Sight Out Of Mind* (1985), *Media* (1986). Absent Friends *Here's Looking Up Your Address* (1990).

Modern English

Formed in Colchester, Essex, England, in 1979, Modern English's debut, *Mesh And Lace* was released in suitably arty packaging by **4AD Records** two years later. It drew heavily on the gloom rock sound already patented by bands like **Joy Division**, and had little originality or focus. *After The Snow*, recorded by the same line-up of Robbie Gray (vocals), Gary McDowell (guitar/vocals), Richard Brown (drums), Mick Conroy (bass /vocals) and Stephen Walker (keyboards), was a minor revelation, as they introduced warmth and strong guitar harmonies, rejecting the tinny bleakness of the debut. It was well-received in the USA, and the band re-located to New York to consolidate a popularity encouraged by college radio. *Richochet Days* had a crisper production but less creative experimentation. By *Stop Start*, released by **Sire Records** in 1986, Stephen Walker and Richard Brown had left, and Aaron Davidson (keyboards/guitar) had joined. The band had tried too hard for commercial approval and was left with an unspecific rock/pop sound which caused them to split soon afterwards. Robbie Gray returned to England to form a new group. They reconvened in 1990 for *Pillow-Lips*, but to little interest
Albums: *Mesh And Lace* (4AD 1981), *After The Snow* (Sire 1982), *Richochet Days* (Sire 1984), *Stop Start* (Sire 1986), *Pillow Lips* (TVT 1990).

Modern Jazz Quartet

In 1951, four musicians who had previously played together in the **Dizzy Gillespie** big band formed a small recording group. Known as the **Milt Jackson** Quartet, the group consisted of Jackson (vibraphone), **John Lewis** (piano), **Ray Brown** (bass), and **Kenny Clarke** (drums). Brown's place was soon taken by **Percy Heath**, and by the following year, the group had adopted the name, Modern Jazz Quartet. Although initially only a recording group, they then began playing concert engagements. In 1955, Clarke dropped out to be replaced by **Connie Kay**. The new line-up of Jackson, Lewis, Heath and Kay continued performing as a full-time ensemble for the next few years, later reducing their collective commitments to several months each year. Seen as both a black response to the intellectualism of the **Dave Brubeck** quartet and New York's answer to west coast cool jazz, the MJQ were both very popular and very controversial, their detractors claiming that their music was too delicate and too cerebral. Whatever the case, there was certainly no denying that the group brought the dignity and professionalism of a classical quartet to their jazz performances. In 1974, the MJQ was disbanded, but reformed once more in 1981 for a concert tour of Japan. The success of this comeback convinced the members to reunite on a semi-permanent basis, which they did in the following year. Since 1982 they have continued to play concert and festival dates. Among the most sophisticated of all bop ensembles, the MJQ's directing influence has always been Lewis, whose sober performing and composing style was never more apparent than in this context. Lewis's interest in classical music has also been influential in MJQ performances, thus placing the group occasionally, and possibly misleadingly, on the fringes of third-stream jazz. The playing of Heath and Kay in this, as in most other settings in which they work, is distinguished by its subtle swing. Of the four, Jackson is the most musically volatile, and the restraints placed upon him in the MJQ create intriguing formal tensions which are, in jazz terms, one of the most exciting aspects of the group's immaculately played, quietly serious music.
Selected albums: *Django* (1953), *Concorde* (1955), The Artistry Of (Prestige 1956), *The MJQ At Music Inn* (1956), *Django* (Original Jazz Classics 1956), *Fontessa* (Atlantic 1956), *Live* (Jazz Anthology 1956), *One Never Knows* (1957), *Third Stream Music* (1957), *MJQ* (Original Jazz Classics 1957), *Concorde* (Original Jazz Classics 1957), *Live At The Lighthouse* (Atlantic 1957), *Plus* (1957-71), *At Music Inn: Vol 2* (Atlantic 1958), *Odds Against Tomorrow* (1959), *Longing For The Continent* (LRC 1959), *European Concert* (1960), *Pyramid* (Atlantic 1961), *Lonely Woman* (Atlantic 1962), *The Comedy* (Atlantic 1962), *The Sheriff* (Atlantic 1963), *A Quartet Is A Quartet Is A Quartet* (Atlantic 1963), *Blues At Carnegie Hall* (1966), *Under The Jasmine Tree* (Apple 1968), *Space* (1969), *Plastic Dreams* (Atlantic 1971), *The Legendary Profile* (Atlantic 1972), *Blues On Bach* (Atlantic 1974), *The Complete Last Concert* (Atlantic 1974), *In Memoriam* (1977), *Together Again!* (Pablo 1982), *Together Again!: Echoes* (Pablo 1984), *The Best Of The MJQ* (1984-85), *Three Windows* (Atlantic 1987), *For Ellington* (East West 1988), *MJQ & Friends* (Atlantic 1994), *A Celebration* (Atlantic 1994). Compilation: *MJQ 40* (Atlantic 4CD box set, 1952-88 recordings).

Modern Lovers

Formed in Boston, Massachusetts, USA, the Modern Lovers revolved around the talents of uncompromising singer/songwriter **Jonathan Richman** (b. May 1951, Boston, Massachusetts, USA). The group, which included **Jerry Harrison** (b. 21 February 1949,

Milwaukee, Wisconsin, USA; guitar - later of **Talking Heads**), Ernie Brooks (bass) and future **Cars** drummer David Robinson, offered an inspired amalgam of 50s pop, garage bands, girl groups and the **Velvet Underground**, a style which both engendered a cult following and attracted the interest of ex-Velvet member **John Cale**, then a staff producer at **Warner Brothers**. However, having completed a series of demos, a disillusioned Richman disbanded the line-up and retreated to Boston, although Cale marked their association by recording his protege's composition, 'Pablo Picasso' on *Helen Of Troy* (1975). In 1976, the unfinished tracks were purchased by the newly-founded Beserkley Records label, which remixed the masters, added two new performances and released the package as *The Modern Lovers*. The company also signed Richman, whose new album, *Jonathan Richman And The Modern Lovers*, was confusingly issued within months of the first selection. The second set revealed a less intensive talent, and his regression into almost child-like simplicity was confirmed on *Rock 'N' Roll With The Modern Lovers*. Richman's new group - Leroy Radcliffe (guitar), Greg 'Curly' Kerenen (bass) and D. Smart (drums) - was purely acoustic and featured a repertoire which, by including 'The Ice-Cream Man', 'Hey There Little Insect', 'The Wheels On The Bus' and 'I'm A Little Aeroplane', was deemed enchanting or irritating, according to taste. The Modern Lovers nonetheless enjoyed two surprise UK hits with 'Roadrunner' and 'Egyptian Reggae', which reached numbers 11 and 5, respectively, in 1977. However, as the unit was undeniably a vehicle for Richman's quirky vision, the Modern Lovers' name was dropped the following year when the singer embarked on a solo tour. He has nonetheless revived the title on occasions, notably on *It's Time For Jonathan Richman And The Modern Lovers* and *Modern Lovers 88*.

Albums: *The Modern Lovers* (Beserkley 1976), *Jonathan Richman And The Modern Lovers* (Beserkley 1976), *Rock 'N' Roll With The Modern Lovers* (Beserkley 1977), *The Modern Lovers Live* (Beserkley 1977), *It's Time For Jonathan Richman And The Modern Lovers* (Upside 1986), *Modern Lovers 88* (Rounder 1988). Compilations: *The Original Modern Lovers* (Bomp 1981, early recordings), *Jonathan Richman And The Modern Lovers - 23 Great Recordings* (Beserkley 1990).

Modern Mandolin Quartet

America's Modern Mandolin Quartet were co-founded by producer Mike Marshall, a native of Florida, whose early interests in bluegrass music were later qualified by his experiences as second mandolin player in the eclectic David Grisman Quartet, before he experienced full blooded modern jazz first hand with Montreaux. This circuitous passage was further complicated by a growing awareness of classical structures, which led in turn to him adapting string quartet literature to different musical forms. The MMQ was thus formed with Dana Rath in 1985. Rath's second mandolin was augmented by Paul Binkley on mandola and John Imholz on mandocello. The latter pair adopted responsibility for arranging the group's material. Binkley had previously performed on classical guitar with the San Francisco Symphony, Opera and Ballet. Marshall's intention was explicitly to 'take a folk instrument, and by tackling classical music bring the mandolin into the concert hall'. By 1988 they were sufficiently prepared to announce their self-titled debut. It was followed two years later by *Intermezzo*, featuring pieces drawn from the repertories of Shostakovisch, Ravel, Brahms and Bach. Continuing this thread, 1991's *Nutcracker Suite* became one of the top 35 Christmas releases in the US ***Billboard*** charts. The group's fourth album for Windham Hill Records was arguably their most audacious. *Pan-American Journeys: 20th Century Music Of The Americas, Vol. 1*, was exactly what its title suggested. Rather grandly, it invited the ensemble to adapt pieces drawing on the musical history of their continent, in an attempt to produce a patchwork map of classical music's evolution from ethnic forms. The featured writers included **George Gershwin**, Argentinean Astor Piazzolla, famous for his demonstrative tangos (his contribution, 'Four For Tango', was originally written for the **Kronos Quartet**), and Brazilian composer Heitor Villa-Lobos. Other contemporary writers consulted included Tully Cathey, whose 'Elements IV: Water', was inspired by the Colorado River that runs by his home. The set opened with 'Redonda', specially composed for the quartet by former Montreux drummer Tom Miller, and climaxed in an adaptation of a Cuban folk song, 'Ojos Brujos' ('Eye Of The Sorceror').

Albums: *Modern Mandolin Quartet* (Lost Lake Arts/Windham Hill 1988), *Intermezzo* (Windham Hill 1990), *The Nutcracker Suite* (Windham Hill 1991), *Pan-American Journeys: 20th Century Music Of The Americas, Vol. 1* (Windham Hill 1994).

Modern Romance

From the remnants of UK punk band, the (**Leyton**) **Buzzards,** crawled Geoff Deanne and David Jaymes. After becoming involved in the London club scene (alongside luminaries like Steve Strange), they formed a company called Business Art Productions with manager Brian O'Donoughue. Signed to WEA, they released 'Tonight'. This flopped, so in late 1980, Jaymes and Deanne formed a new line-up featuring Deanne (b. 10 December 1954; vocals), Jaymes (b. 28 November 1954; bass), brother Robbie Jaymes (b. 3 October 1962; keyboards), Paul Gendler (b. 11 August 1960; guitar) and Andy Kyriacou (b. 19 April 1958; drums, ex-**Linx** and Central Line). John Du Prez also featured on trumpet. Through their club connections they came across the Latin-American music salsa, which was set to be all the craze in the summer of 1981. They quickly recorded 'Everybody Salsa', which gave them their first hit. It was followed by other successful material in a similar vein; 'Ay Ay Ay Ay Moosey', 'Queen Of The Rapping Scene', and 'Cherry Pink And Apple Blossom White'. At this point Deanne left to release several solo singles and write for camp club act Divine. Former fireman Michael J. Mullins (b. 9 November 1956) was his replacement. Their hit run continued in 1983, with 'Best Years Of Our life', 'High Life' and 'Walking In The Rain'. A cover of Baltimora's 'Tarzan Boy' the following year fared less well. They disbanded shortly afterwards. David Jaymes released a solo single in 1988, while Deanne now writes comedy scripts. John Du Prez currently lives in Hollywood where he plays on film scores.

Albums: *Adventures In Clubland* (1981), *Trick Of The Light* (1983), *Party Tonight* (1983), *Move On* (1985).

Modugno, Domenico

b. 9 January 1928, Polignano a Mare, Italy, d. 6 August 1994, Lampeduso. Modugno disappointed his father, a civic dignitary, by rejecting higher education to seek a career as a film actor in Rome. However, though he passed an entrance examination to drama college, National Service postponed entry for two years. Among the parts he gained on graduation was that of a balladeer in 1955's *Il Mantello Rosso*. More conspicuous than expected in this role, he was contracted by both national radio and Fonit Records as a vocalist, with accompaniment that varied from his own lone guitar or accordion to full orchestra. In a developing repertoire were self-composed pieces such as 'Ninna Nanna' (a lullaby penned in 1943), 'Lu Piscispada' and - recorded by many other Latinate artists - 'La Donna Riccia'. While he was runner-up in 1957's Neopolitan Song Festival with 'Lazzarella', 'Nel Blu Dipinto Di Blu' (written with Franco Migliacci) was placed first at the more prestigious San Remo event the following year, and thus flung Modugno into a lucrative round of appearances in venues beyond Italy - including North America. With English lyrics by Mitchell Parish, the opus became better known as 'Volare', a Grammy-earning US chart-topper which also reached the UK Top 10 - despite covers by **Charlie Drake**, Marino Marini and **Dean Martin**. 1959's 'Piove' - another San Remo winner - was an international smash, too - if overtaken in Britain by a version from Marini - when translated by Parish (as 'Ciao Ciao Bambino'). This and lesser triumphs, like 'Addio Addio' and 1966's 'Dio Come Ti Amo', blessed Modugno with the dubious title of 'genius' - though many claim that his most enduring work was his earliest, as demonstrated by periodic revivals of 'Volare' from **Bobby Rydell** in 1960 to **David Bowie** in 1986's *Absolute Beginners* movie.

Moffatt, Hugh

b. 10 November 1948, Fort Worth, Texas, USA. Unlike most country performers, Moffatt played trumpet in his high school band and had a fondness for big band jazz. He obtained a degree in English from Rice University in Houston and learned to play the guitar. Moffatt played acoustic sets in Austin and Washington and then, in 1973, moved to Nashville. He says, 'I was interested in Nashville purely because of **Kris Kristofferson**. He proved that you can take the folk and the literary tradition, and you can be in Nashville, too.' In 1974, **Ronnie Milsap** recorded Moffatt's 'Just In Case'. Moffatt recorded two singles for **Mercury** - a cover of 'The Gambler' and his own 'Love And Only Love' - but the contract then terminated. In the early 80s he formed the band Ratz, which included Moffatt's wife, Pebe Sebert, and released a five-track EP, *Putting On The Ratz*. In 1987, his superb album *Loving You* was released, and included a song written with Sebert, 'Old Flames (Can't Hold A Candle To You)'. He admits, 'That title and the ideas were Pebe's. We wrote it three months after we were married. We spent three months writing it, as we wanted it to be right. Everybody knew it would be a hit.' The song has been successfully recorded by **Joe Sun**, **Dolly Parton** and **Foster And Allen**. The only other song they wrote together was 'Wild Turkey', which was recorded by **Lacy J. Dalton**. Other Moffatt songs include 'Love Games' (**Jerry Lee Lewis**), 'Praise The Lord And Pass Me The Money' (**Bobby Bare**), 'Why Should I Cry Over You?' (**George Hamilton IV**) and 'Words At Twenty Paces' (**Alabama**). His sister, Katy, is also a recording artist, at home on both acoustic and hard-rocking material. Her albums are *Walking On The Moon* (1988), *Child Bride* (1989) and *The Greatest Show On Earth* (1993). They have released a duet of 'Rose Of My Heart', which has also been recorded by **Johnny Rodriguez** and **Nicolette Larson**.

Albums: *Loving You* (1987), *Troubadour* (1989), *Live And Alone* (1991), with Katy Moffatt *Dance Me Outside* (1992).

Moffatt, Katy

b. 19 November 1950, Fort Worth, Texas, USA. Moffatt is a Texan singer-songwriter whose country-based folk has won a limited, yet loyal following. Originally from Fort Worth, her early influences included **Leonard Cohen** and **Tracy Nelson**. She spent the early 70s playing folk clubs and small rock venues, mainly in Colorado, before signing to **CBS**, and releasing two commercially slanted records in the mid to late 70s. Disillusioned with the music business, Moffatt kept a low profile during the early 80s, but during the mid-80s she received a nomination from the Academy Of Country Music as Best New Female Vocalist. Her appearance on the semi-legendary

compilation, *A Town South Of Bakersfield* (1985), was a key career move, and her performance at the Kerrville Folk Festival a year later was another important step; she met the respected songwriter, **Tom Russell**, and they began a fruitful collaboration. In 1989, Moffatt gained favourable reviews for *Walkin' On The Moon*, her first album for 11 years. Throughout her career she has supported many musicans including **Warren Zevon**, **Roy Orbison**, the **Everly Brothers**, and **Don Williams**, and has recorded regularly for a variety of independent labels.
Selected albums: *Katy* (CBS 1976), *Kissing In The California Sun* (CBS 1978), *Walkin' On the Moon* (1989), *Child Bride* (1989), *The Greatest Show On Earth* (Round Tower), with Hugh Moffatt *Dance Me Outside* (1992), *Indoor Fireworks* (1992), *The Greatest Show On Earth* (Round Tower Music 1993), *Hearts Gone Wild* (Round Tower 1994).

Moffett, Charles

b. 1 September 1929, Fort Worth, Texas, USA. Moffett began his career playing trumpet with local R&B groups, and in the same high school band as **Ornette Coleman**, but at the age of 16 he began to study percussion. In 1953 he gained a BA in music and went on to teach in Texas for eight years. Coleman had been best man at Moffett's wedding in 1952; in 1961 they met again, Moffett taking the drummer's stool in Coleman's band. During Coleman's lay off from performance in the early 60s, Moffett went back to teaching, but he was ready when the group reformed to tour Europe in 1965. In 1970, Moffett moved to California, where he resumed his teaching while playing with local players such as Steve Turre, Keshavan Maslak and Prince Lasha. He also formed groups with his students and with members of his family. During the 80s Moffett moved back to New York, where he teaches mentally retarded children and continues to play. Moffett's easy swing and perfect sense of time often seems to owe much to earlier styles while remaining a perfect foil for the *avant garde* musicians he most often accompanied. A recent, and rare, appearance on record was on **Frank Lowe**'s *Decision In Paradise* (c.80s).
Albums: with Ornette Coleman *At The Golden Circle Vols. 1&2* (1965), *The Gift* (1969), *Family* (1974).

Mogg, Ambrose

b. Andrew Morgan, 1 April 1941, Liverpool, England. Mogg, a catalyst amongst Merseybeat musicians, formed the Caterwaulers in the early 60s and enjoyed local success with 'The Cat Came Back' and other feline songs. He refused to sign with **HMV** because of the picture of the dog on the label. However, his short time with **Decca** in 1963 was fraught with problems. Forced to use pugnacious session musicians, Jackie Russell, Gordie Setter and 'Bulldog' Drummer, Mogg's desire to escape from the studio fast turned 'Mean Dog Blues' into a frantic rockabilly classic. Unfortunately for Mogg, the pressing plant was closing for its annual holiday and careless workers approved the record without a hole in its centre. Mogg raged at Decca, who cancelled his contract on grounds of insubordination, saying he should take lessons in manners from the **Rolling Stones**. A few weeks later, Mogg lost a leg at the Cavern when passionate fans pulled him first one way and then the other. He disappeared into the Catskill Mountains, while 'Mean Dog Blues' became a cult single although the drilling of the holes by collectors is rarely accurate. Mogg returned to Liverpool in 1989 with nothing in the kitty, but he is clawing his way back into the limelight with sterling work for the Merseycats charity.
Selected album: Purrfect Alibi (Whisker 1990).

Moholo, Louis

b. 10 March 1940, Cape Town, South Africa. Moholo is simply one of the great drummers, regardless of genre. In common with **Blackwell** and **Billy Higgins**, both alumni of **Ornette Coleman**'s Quartet, he has developed a sharp, clean, agile style, and shares with Higgins a remarkable ability to play with considerable dynamic restraint without losing strength and momentum. He is equally capable of thunderous, breakneck playing, which commands attention as much through its constant inventiveness as through its inexorable power. He grew up in a musical environment (his father a pianist, his mother and sister, singers). At the age of 16 he co-founded the Cordettes big band. In 1962, he won the Best Drummer award at the Johannesburg Jazz Festival and, together with four more of the best players at the Festival, he was invited by **Chris McGregor** to form a band. Thus the legendary Blue Notes were created. As a mixed-race band it was impossible for them to work under apartheid and so, in 1964, while touring Europe, they decided to stay in Switzerland. After a year there they settled in London, where, ultimately evolving into the Chris McGregor Group, they made a huge impact. As well as playing in the six-piece McGregor Group and the **Brotherhood Of Breath** big band, Moholo put his stamp on many fine bands, including **Elton Dean**'s Ninesense, the **Mike Osborne** Trio, and **Keith Tippett**'s extra-big band, Ark. In 1966, he toured South America with **Steve Lacy**, **Enrico Rava** and **Johnny Dyani**. In the 70s and 80s he often worked in Europe, particularly in trios with **Irène Schweizer** and Rudiger Carl, and **Peter Brötzmann** and **Harry Miller**, and recorded a duo concert with Schweizer in 1986. Moholo has also worked in duos with Tippett and **Andrew Cyrille**, and organized the African Drum Ensemble. He currently leads Viva La Black as well as a trio with Gary Curzon and **Paul Rogers** (recalling the classic Osborne trio) and plays in

a percussion duo with Thebe Lipere.
Albums: with Irène Schweizer, Rudiger Carl *Messer* (1975), *Blue Notes For Mongezi* (1976), with Schweizer, Carl *Tuned Boots* (1977), *Blue Notes In Concert Volume I* (1978), *Spirits Rejoice* (1978), with Peter Brötzmann, Harry Miller *The Nearer The Bone, The Sweeter The Meat* (1980), with Keith Tippett *No Gossip* (1980), with Brötzmann, Miller *Opened, But Hardly Touched* (1981), with Tippett, Larry Stabbins *Tern* (1982), *Irène Schweizer/Louis Moholo* (1987), *Blue Notes For Johnny* (1987), *Viva La Black* (1988), with Cecil Taylor *Remembrance* (1989), *Exile* (Ogun 1991), *Freedom Tour-Live In South Afrika 1993* 1995).

Moist

Vancouver, Canada-based band, featuring David Usher (vocals) and Mark Makowy (guitar), who met at a party hosted by mutual friend and keyboard player Kevin Young. Makowy brought in bass player Jeff Pearce, and eventually drummer Paul Wilcox completed the line-up. Following a demo cassette in early 1993, the band went on to release a debut album on their own label in February of the following year. Picked up by **EMI** Music Canada just one month later, the record would go platinum within their own country, mainly bolstered by a ferocious appetite for live appearances. Their most important early exposure in Europe came when they were invited on to the Annual *Smash Hits* Poll Winners' Party as a token rock presence (alongside that of **Terrorvision**).
Album: *Silver (*EMI 1994).

Mojo Men

This San Francisco-based group - Jimmy Alaimo (vocals/guitar), Paul Curcio (guitar), Don Metchick (organ) and Dennis DeCarr (drums) - was signed to Autumn, the city's leading independent label, in 1965. Here they enjoyed a fruitful artistic relationship with producer **Sly Stone**, which spawned a minor US hit in 'Dance With Me'. Jan Errico, from stablemates the **Vejtables**, replaced DeCarr in 1966 as the quartet switched outlets to **Reprise Records**. The following year they secured a US Top 40 hit with a charming version of **Buffalo Springfield**'s 'Sit Down I Think I Love You', which was engineered and arranged by **Van Dyke Parks**. The group truncated its name to Mojo in 1968 and, now trimmed to a trio on Metchick's departure, completed the Mojo Magic album before breaking-up. Paul Curcio meanwhile founded the Pacific Recording Studio in San Mateo, where **Santana** recorded their early releases.
Album: *Mojo Magic* (1968).

Mojos

Originally known as the Nomads, this Liverpool beat group was formed in 1962 by Stu James (vocals), Adrian Wilkinson (guitar), Keith Karlson (bass) and John Konrad (drums). They secured early minor fame by winning a songwriting contest which resulted in a recording deal. Pianist Terry O'Toole was added to the line-up prior to the release of the Mojos' debut single, and Nicky Crouch replaced Wilkinson before a follow-up, 'Everything's Alright', was recorded. This energetic 1964 single became a UK Top 10 hit, and the crafted excitement maintained throughout the performance assured its classic status. The group's later releases failed to match this quality, and although a revitalized line-up, consisting of James, Crouch, Lewis Collins (bass) and **Aynsley Dunbar** (drums) continued as Stu James and the Mojos, they broke up in December 1966. The singer then pursued a career in music publishing, while Dunbar joined **John Mayall**'s Bluesbreakers and Collins pursued a acting career, later starring in the popular UK television series, *The Professionals*.
Album: *Working* (1982).

Mole, Miff

b. Irving Milfred Mole, 11 March 1898, Roosevelt, Long Island, New York, USA, d. 29 April 1961. A youthful multi-instrumentalist, Mole had settled on the trombone by his mid-teenage years. Gigging extensively in and around New York, he worked with many small early jazz bands, including one led by pianist-turned-comedian **Jimmy Durante**, and was also a member of the **Original Memphis Five**, led by **Phil Napoleon**. In the mid-20s he became a close friend and musical associate of **Red Nichols**; they made many records together and generally encouraged one another's development. After a stint with **Roger Wolfe Kahn**'s popular society band, Mole began a long period of studio work, and in 1938 joined **Paul Whiteman**. In the early 40s Mole began teaching, worked briefly with **Benny Goodman**, and led his own small bands at nightspots in New York and Chicago. Ill-health restricted his career in the 50s. Although subsequently overshadowed by outstanding contemporaries such as **Jack Teagarden** and **Tommy Dorsey**, Mole played an important role in the development of jazz trombone. He was a major influence in elevating the instrument from its slightly jokey status as a purveyor of unusual sounds, ably demonstrating that it could be a tasteful, melodic vehicle on which to play effective jazz solos. His exceptional technique also provided a standard by which trombonists could be measured, at least until the arrival on the scene of latterday technical wizards. He died in April 1961.
Selected compilations: *Miff Mole's Molers '1927'* (Swaggie 1983, 1927 recording), *Miff Mole's Molers '1928/30'* (Swaggie 1983, 1928-30 recording), with Bobby Hackett *At Nick's* (1944).

Molly Half Head

This Manchester, England guitar band are led by Paul Bardsley's distinctive vocals, with the line-up completed by Phil Murphy (guitar), Aky (b. Graham Atkinson; bass) and Andy Pickering (drums), who came together after advertisements in *Loot* magazine. However, Molly Half Head have more unusual origins than the average indie band. An early incarnation of the group was reportedly an experimental coalition with a trombone player competing against a wall of noise and feedback. The band claim that said trombonist eventually went mad and has been ensconced in a mental asylum after murdering someone ever since. Veterans of that incarnation, Pickering and Murphy had recruited Atkinson and Bardsley by the time the group signed to Manchester independent Playtime Records in 1992. After an encouraging reception at the 1993 In The City festival/conference, the band released their debut single, 'Taste Of You'. Bearing in mind their own financial struggles, this was made available to the unemployed for 75 pence on the production of a valid UB40, and they also played a series of free-to-enter gigs. However, they were hardly the decade's most political band otherwise ('There's no great insights into life we're trying to convey'). A second single, 'Toe To Sand', preceded sessions for their debut album. The UK indie press quickly warmed to the band, whose offbeat attitude was confirmed by a series of semi-nude photos, and a resistance to any degree of preciousness. 'Barny', included on the debut, managed to gain daytime UK radio play on the *Steve Wright Show*, and featured an impressive collage of characters drawn from the band's home estate. *Dunce* saw the band move to **Columbia Records**, and though the press' interest had worn a little thin (particularly with the passing of the 'Madchester' phenomenon, where all bands from the Manchester area were briefly deemed newsworthy), it was another energetic collection of pop songs which rewarded repeated listening.
Albums: *Sulk* (Playtime 1993), *Dunce* (Columbia 1995).

Molly Hatchet

This **Lynyrd Skynyrd**-style, blues-rock boogie outfit emerged from the USA's deep south. The name is taken from a lady who beheaded her lovers with an axe after sleeping with them in 17th-century Salem. The initial line-up comprised guitarists Dave Hlubek, Steve Holland and Duane Roland plus bassist Bonner Thomas, vocalist Danny Joe Brown and drummer Bruce Crump. Their debut album, produced by **Tom Werman** (of **Cheap Trick** and **Ted Nugent** fame), was an instant success, with its three-pronged guitar onslaught and gut-wrenching vocals. Brown was replaced by Jimmy Farrar in 1980, before the recording of *Beatin' The Odds*. Farrar's vocals were less distinctive than Brown's, and an element of their identity was lost while the former fronted the band. Nevertheless, commercial success ensued, with both *Beatin' The Odds* and *Take No Prisoners* peaking on the ***Billboard*** album chart at number 25 and 36, respectively. In 1982 Danny Joe Brown rejoined the band, while Thomas was replaced by Riff West on bass. *No Guts...No Glory* emerged and marked a return to their roots: explosive guitar duels, heart-stopping vocals and steadfast rock 'n' roll. Surprisingly the album flopped and Hlubek insisted on a radical change in direction. Steve Holden quit and keyboardist John Galvin was recruited for the recording of *The Deed Is Done*. This was a lightweight pop-rock album, largely devoid of the band's former trademarks. Following its release the band retired temporarily to lick their wounds and reassess their future. In 1985 *Double Trouble Live* was unveiled, a triumphant return to former glories. It included stunning versions of their best-known songs plus a superb Skynyrd tribute in the form of 'Freebird'. Founder member Dave Hlubek departed, to be replaced by Bobby Ingram in 1989. They signed a new deal with **Capitol Records** and released *Lightning Strikes Twice*. This leaned away from their southern roots towards highly polished AOR. It featured covers of **Paul Stanley**'s 'Hide Your Heart' and Miller/Burnette's 'There Goes The Neighbourhood', but was poorly received by fans and critics alike. This despite the return of Danny Joe Brown, who had been plagued by illness due to diabetes.
Albums: *Molly Hatchet* (Epic 1978), *Flirtin' With Disaster* (Epic 1979), *Beatin' The Odds* (Epic 1980), *Take No Prisoners* (Epic 1981), *No Guts...No Glory* (Epic 1983), *The Deed Is Done* (Epic 1984), *Double Trouble Live* (Epic 1985), *Lightning Strikes Twice* (Capitol 1989).

Molton, Flora

b. 1908, Virginia, USA, d. 31 May 1990, Washington, DC, USA. Molton began preaching at the age of 17, not taking up guitar until 1943, when she moved to Washington, DC. Virtually blind, she supported herself by playing in the streets. From 1963, she made appearances on the folk circuit, and later signed-up by a European record company, when she visited Europe in 1987. Her slide guitar playing, in 'Vastopol' (open D) was basic, but intense, owing much to the blues whose verbal content she fiercely rejected. Her delivery, mainly, was reminiscent of an unsophisticated **Sister Rosetta Tharpe,** particularly when Molton was assisted by more skilful musicians.
Albums: *Flora Molton And The Truth Band* (1982), *Gospel Songs* (1988).

Moments

Formed in Hackensack, New Jersey, USA in the late 60s, this distinctive sweet soul trio comprised Al Goodman (b. 31 March 1947, Jackson, Mississippi, USA; ex-**Vipers** and **Corvettes**), Harry Ray (b. 15

December 1946, Longbranch, New Jersey, USA; ex-Sounds Of Soul and Establishment) and William Brown (b. 30 June 1946, Atlanta, Georgia, USA; ex-Broadways and Uniques). The falsetto-led, 50s-style harmony vocal group recorded for Sylvia Robinson's Stang label. According to Goodman, the original group led by Mark Greene was replaced by Ray, Goodman and Brown in 1969, after their first hit 'Not On The Outside'. It was this trio's fourth R&B Top 20 hit, 'Love On A Two-Way Street' in 1970, that gave them their biggest pop hit, reaching number 3 in the US charts. They had a further 21 R&B chart records, which included their self-penned Top 20 hit 'Sexy Mama' in 1973, and the R&B number 1 'Look At Me (I'm In Love)' in 1975. Their first UK success came in 1975 with 'Girls', made with fellow Stang group the **Whatnauts**. They had two further UK Top 10s: 'Dolly My Love' in 1975 and 'Jack In The Box' in 1977, neither of which charted in the USA. In 1979, they joined **Polydor** as **Ray**, **Goodman And Brown**.

Albums: *Not On The Outside* (1969), *A Moment With The Moments* (1970), *Moments Live At The New York State Women's Prison* (1971), *Love At The Miss Black America Pageant* (1971), *Those Sexy Moments* (1974), *Look At Me* (1975), *Moments With You* (1976), *Sharp* (1978). Compilations: *Moments Greatest Hits* (1970), *Best Of The Moments* (1974), *Greatest Hits* (1987), *Moments* (1988).

Momus

b. Nicholas Currie, 1960, Paisley, Scotland. After living in Canada for a spell as a teenager, Currie returned to the UK and, during the mid-80s, began recording on the independent circuit. His primary influence was **Jacques Brel**, whose earthy sexuality soon infiltrated Momus's work. An EP, *Beast With No Backs*, on El Records, garnered minor critical attention, as did the album *Circus Maximus*. Momus promised a follow-up, *The Poison Boyfriend*, but that title was abandoned after he signed with Alan McGee's **Creation Records**. Finally, in 1988, Momus returned with *Tender Pervert*, a lacerating document of sexual and emotional psychoanalysis. His strength was his strong narrative line, particularly on songs such as 'Love On Ice' and 'Bishonen'. The following year, he issued *Don't Stop The Night*, which featured a more electronic, dance-orientated approach in keeping with current fashion. One song, 'Righthand Heart', was a less effective reworking of an essentially acoustic song on the previous album. Momus's lack of live experience has so far prevented any major excursion into performing. His 1991 album, *Hippopotamomus*, was less well received and was greeted with a zero out of 10 rating in the ***New Musical Express*** as a result of its moral perversity. The artist no doubt appreciated the irony. The early 90s saw Currie build on his audience within the gay community (parts of which admired his openess), contributing one track, 'Cocksucking Lesbian Man', to Derek Jarman's *Blue* movie. *Philosophy Of Momus* continued Curry's forays into the netherworld of twisted sexuality, utilising a third person mechanism as a defence against accusations of amorality.

Albums: *Circus Maximus* (El 1986), *The Poison Boyfriend* (Creation 1987), *Tender Pervert* (Creation 1988), *Don't Stop The Night* (Creation 1989), *Hippopotamomus* (Creation 1991), *Voyager* (Creation 1992), *The Ultracomformist* (Creation 1992), *Timelord* (Creation 1993), *The Philosophy Of Momus* (Cherry Red 1995). Compilation: *Monsters Of Love - Singles 1985-90* (Creation 1990).

Further reading: *Lust Of A Moron: The Lyrics Of Momus*, Momus.

Monaco, James V.

b. 13 January 1885, Genoa, Italy, d. 16 October 1945, Beverly Hills, California, USA. A prolific composer, particularly for movies, whose career spanned more than 30 years. After moving to the USA with his family when he was six years old, Monaco taught himself to play piano, and began earning his living playing in Chicago clubs while still in his teens. By 1910 he was resident in New York, playing in saloons. The following year, he began writing songs, some of which were recorded and others used in Broadway shows. In 1912, he had his first hits with 'Row, Row, Row' (lyrics by William Jerome) and 'You Made Me Love You' (**Joseph McCarthy**). The latter was taken up by **Al Jolson**, a fact which ensured its enduring popularity. Monaco continued to compose, and his songs of the next few years included 'I Miss You Most Of All', (McCarthy) 'What Do You Want To Make Those Eyes At Me For?' (McCarthy), 'Caresses' and 'Dirty Hands, Dirty Face' (**Edgar Leslie** and Grant Clarke), which Jolson sang in the 1927 film ***The Jazz Singer***. Among Monaco's songs of the late 20s were 'Me And My Boyfriend' (Sidney Clare), 'Me And The Man In The Moon' (Leslie) and 'Through' (McCarthy). In the 30s, Monaco was active in Hollywood, where he began a fruitful collaboration with **Johnny Burke**. Among the results were a string of hits sung in films and recorded by **Bing Crosby,** including 'On The Sentimental Side', 'I've Got A Pocketful Of Dreams', 'An Apple For The Teacher', 'Too Romantic', 'That's For Me' and 'Only Forever'. He contributed to films such as *The Golden Calf, Doctor Rhythm*, ***Sing You Sinners***, *East Side Of Heaven, The Star Maker, If I Had My Way*, ***Road To Singapore***, *Rhythm On The River, Stage Door Canteen, Pin-Up Girl*, and ***The Dolly Sisters*** (1945). In the early 40s, Monaco had more popular successes with 'Six Lessons From Madame La Zonga' (Charles Newman), 'I Can't Begin To Tell You' (**Mack Gordon**), 'Ev'ry Night About This Time' (**Ted Koehler**), 'We Musn't Say Goodbye' (**Al Dubin**), and 'Time Will Tell' (Gordon). Monaco died from a heart attack in 1945.

Moncur, Grachan, III

b. 3 June 1937, New York City, New York, USA. An early starter (his father played bass with Al Cooper's **Savoy Sultans**), Moncur had already mastered several other instruments when, at the age of 11, he turned to the trombone. In his teens, Moncur worked with local bands and also studied music. In the early 60s he was with **Ray Charles**, and was a member of the **Art Farmer-Benny Golson** Jazztet. He also worked with **Jackie McLean** and **Sonny Rollins**, recorded for **Blue Note** and, by the late 60s, was a leading figure of the free jazz movement, playing with **Archie Shepp** in the USA and Europe. In the 70s, Moncur worked with the Jazz Composers' Orchestra, and in the 80s, with **Frank Lowe**, among others. In the last decade or so, his experience has also been applied to teaching and to several major compositions in musical areas ranging from jazz to ballet. An accomplished performer, Moncur's fluid style has helped to make his playing more readily accessible than that of many other free jazz trombonists. Through his teaching and recording he continues to exercise considerable influence upon the rising generation of musicians.

Albums: *Evolution* (Blue Note 1963), *Some Other Stuff* (1964), *New Africa* (Affinity 1969), with Jazz Composers Orchestra *Echoes Of Prayer* (1974).

Money, Eddie

Legend has it that Brooklyn native Eddie Mahoney was a New York police officer when first discovered by promoter **Bill Graham** (he was, in fact, a NYPD typist). Nevertheless, under Graham's managerial wing, Mahoney became Eddie Money and produced two hit singles in 'Baby Hold On' and 'Two Tickets To Paradise' from his self-titled debut, to begin a career which has seen him maintain arena headlining status in America with a series of consistently fine R&B-flavoured AOR records. *Life For The Taking* produced two more hits, 'Rock And Roll The Place' and 'Maybe I'm A Fool', as Money built a strong live following which set him free from the constraining need for radio or **MTV** airplay to sell albums or concert tickets, although the hits continued to come. *Where's The Party?* saw a slight dip in form, but Money stormed back with perhaps his best 80s album, *Can't Hold Back*, producing three huge hits in the title-track, 'I Wanna Go Back' and 'Take Me Home Tonight', where his warm, soulful vocals were augmented by **Ronnie Spector**'s production. 1991's *Right Here* saw Money move away from the keyboard-dominated sound of preceding albums towards the rootsier feel of his early work, producing another hit in a cover of **Romeo's Daughter**'s 'Heaven In The Backseat'. While European success continues to elude him, Money's future in his homeland seems secure.

Albums: *Eddie Money* (Columbia 1977), *Life For The Taking* (Columbia 1978), *Playing For Keeps* (Columbia 1980), *No Control* (Columbia 1982), *Where's The Party?* (Columbia 1984), *Can't Hold Back* (Columbia 1986), *Nothing To Lose* (Columbia 1988), *Right Here* (Columbia 1991). Compilation: *Greatest Hits: The Sound Of Money* (Columbia 1989).
Film: *Americation* (1979).

Money, Zoot

b. George Bruno Money, 17 July 1942, Bournemouth, Dorset, England. A veteran of his hometown's thriving music circuit, Money played in several local rock 'n' roll groups before forming the Big Roll Band in 1961. Its original line-up comprised Roger Collis (guitar), Kevin Drake (tenor saxophone), Johnny King (bass), Peter Brooks (drums) and Zoot on piano and vocals. By 1963, the singer was fronting an all-new unit of Andy Somers aka **Andy Summers** (guitar), Nick Newall (saxophone) and Colin Allen (drums), but he left the group for a temporary spot in **Alexis Korner**'s Blues Incorporated. Zoot remained in London when his tenure ended, and his band subsequently joined him there. The Big Roll Band secured a residency at London's prestigious Flamingo Club, and added two new members, Paul Williams (bass/vocals) and Clive Burrows (saxophone), before recording their debut single, 'The Uncle Willie'. In 1965, the group released its first album, *It Should've Been Me*, a compendium of soul and R&B material which enhanced the band's growing reputation. A second album, *Zoot!*, recorded live at Klook's Kleek, introduced newcomer **Johnny Almond**, who replaced Burrows. This exciting set included a superb **James Brown** medley and confirmed the unit's undoubted strength. However, a devil-may-care attitude undermined their potential, and only one of their excellent singles, 'Big Time Operator' (1966), broached the UK Top 30. Money became famed as much for dropping his trousers onstage as for his undoubted vocal talent, and several of the line-up were notorious imbibers. Yet this lifestyle was reversed in 1967, when Money, Somers and Alan embraced the emergent 'flower-power' movement with Dantallion's Chariot. However, by the following year Zoot had resumed his erstwhile direction with *Transition*, a disappointing release which was pieced together from several sessions.

In 1968, both Money and Somers joined **Eric Burdon** in his American-based New Animals. Zoot's vocals were heard on a number of tracks with Burdon, notably a lengthy re-working of his Dantallion's Chariot showpiece, 'Madman'. Additionally, his spoken dialogue was featured on some of Burdon's more self-indulgent efforts on *Everyone Of Us*. The singer completed *Welcome To My Head* on the group's demise before returning to London for *Zoot Money*. He continued an itinerant path with Centipede, Grimms

and Ellis, before joining Somers in the **Kevin Coyne** and **Kevin Ayers** bands. In 1980, Zoot released the low-key *Mr. Money*, since which he has played on numerous sessions and enjoyed a new career as a character actor in television drama and comedy. In the early 90s he could be found as music controller for Melody Radio but was back on the road by 1995.
Albums: *It Should've Been Me* (1965), *Zoot!* (1966), *Transition* (1968), *Welcome To My Head* (1969), *Zoot Money* (1970), *Mr. Money* (1980).

Monguito 'El Unico'

b. Ramón Quian, Manguito, Matanzas Province, Cuba. Titled 'El Unico' (The Unique), this Afro-Cuban vocalist, composer, bandleader, producer Monguito, sings in a typical Cuban style with an instantly recognizable, nasal voice. He performed with various bands in Cuba, and then Mexico, where he also worked in three films. In 1962, El Unico relocated to New York and initially joined **Orquesta Broadway**. The following year he made his album debut with **Arsenio Rodríguez**. In 1964, Monguito shared lead vocals with **Pete 'El Conde' Rodríguez** and sang coro (chorus) on *Pacheco At The N.Y. World's Fair* by, **Johnny Pacheco**. Pete departed and El Unico became co-lead singer with Chivirico Dávila on Pacheco's *Pacheco te Invita a Bailar* and *Viva Africa*. In 1966, Monguito appeared on the Tico All Stars' *Descargas At The Village Gate-Live* albums. He sessioned with Chivirico on **Herbie Mann**'s *Latin Mann*, and featured on **Larry Harlow**'s *Bajándote*, singing the hit title track, 'Cienfuegos'. Monguito went solo in 1967 with *Pacheco Presents Monguito*, and released a further three albums up to 1971. He sang lead on 'Me Gusto El Son' with the **Fania All Stars** on their debut *Live At The Red Garter, Vol.1* in 1968.
His 1979 release, *Yo No Soy Mentiroso*, produced by **Roberto Torres**, went gold. It was the third album issued on the new SAR label, founded by Sergio Bofill, Andriano García and Torres. Torres developed a highly successful house style tailored mainly for the West African and French-speaking Caribbean markets. This comprised stretching out Cuban son montunos and guajiras, often using old Cuban standards, with plenty of spaces for soloing. Monguito toured Africa in 1980, and recorded as a lead singer and musical director for the Ivory Coast-based Sacodis label. El Unico paralleled the SAR sound with Sacodis and used many leading New York-based musicians for the sessions, including pianist/arranger Alfredo Valdés Jnr., who was SAR's house arranger; violinists **Alfredo de la Fé** and **Pupi Legarreta**; vocalist **Adalberto Santiago**; saxophonist/flautist Mario Rivera. Torres produced his 1982 and 1984 albums on the Toboga label, which was a stablemate of SAR. In 1985, El Unico issued *Yo Soy La Meta* on Caiman Records, which was a successor of SAR.

Selected albums: with Johnny Pacheco *Pacheco At The N.Y. World's Fair* (1964), *Pacheco te Invita a Bailar*, with Herbie Mann *Latin Mann* aka *Big Boss Mann* (1965); with Pacheco *Viva Africa* (1966); with Larry Harlow *Bajándote* (1967); *Pacheco Presents Monguito* (1967); with the Fania All Stars *Live At The Red Garter, Vol.I* (1968); *El Unico y su Conjunto* (c.1969), *De Todo Un Poco* (c.1970), *Escuchame/Listen To Me* (1971), *Yo No Soy Mentiroso* (1979); as musical director *Charanga Para Todos, Doh Alberto A Manhattan USA: Salsa Africana Vol.3*; *Monguito El Unico And His All Star Band: Algo Diferente* (1980), *Monguito El Unico International* (1981), *Monguito El Unico* (1982), *Monguito El Unico And His All Star Band: Alto Songo* (c.1984), *El Unico!* (1984), *Yo Soy La Meta* (1985). Selected compilations with Pacheco: *La Crema* (1980), *Sabrosura* (1980). The CD *Monguito El Unico International* (late 80s) collected 11 tracks together from his Sacodis period.

Monitors

Sandra Fagin, John 'Maurice' Fagin, Warren Harris and Richard Street formed the Monitors in the early 60s, having each performed with Detroit-based vocal groups since the late 50s. In 1965, they were signed to **Motown**'s VIP subsidiary, for whom they issued six singles and an album over the next four years. Their doo-wop-influenced style was epitomized by the 1966 R&B hit 'Say You', and their cover of the Valadiers' 'Greetings (This Is Uncle Sam)' later that year - the most successful recording of a sly piece of social comment that was taped by several artists on the Motown roster. The Monitors were unable to establish themselves among the label's frontline artists, however, and they dissolved in 1969. Richard Street replaced **Eddie Kendricks** in the **Temptations** in 1971. In 1990 the band reformed with original members Harris and Fagin, Hershell Hunter (who joined the group in 1968), Darrell Littlejohn (who recorded for Motown as half of Keith & Darrell) and Harris's daughter Leah. They recorded with Ian Levine's Motor City label releasing *Grazing In The Grass*.
Albums: *Greetings . . . We're The Monitors* (1968), *Grazing In The Grass* (1990).

Monk, Meredith

b. 20 November 1943, Lima, Peru. In 1964, Monk graduated in performing arts from Sarah Lawrence College where she had been encouraged to mix the arts in a variety of projects. She saw herself as an 'orchestrator of music and image and movement', someone making 'live movies'. She first appeared in New York at Washington Square Gallery and was one of a group of artists, including painter Robert Rauschenberg, creating mixed-media pieces like Duet For Cat's Scream And Locomotive at Judson Church. She presented her theatre piece, *Juice*, at New York's Guggenheim Museum in 1969, and brought her group the House to Liverpool in 1972 to perform *The Vessel*. In the same year, she received a *Village Voice* Award for outstanding achievement in the Off-Broadway Theatre. She also performed solo vocal pieces like 'Raw Recital', from which 'a definite American Indian quality emerged'. She sees herself as performing ethnic music from a culture she has herself created. In 1978, she formed the Vocal Ensemble to perform compositions which consist of simple, often modal melodies or melodic cells which are repeated with small variations and contrasted with different material. These performances are sometimes accompanied by repetitive keyboard parts reminiscent of the minimalist movement, and usually depend on extended vocal techniques. The success of *Dolmen Music* and *Turtle Dreams* has brought the Ensemble to an international audience.

Albums: *Our Lady Of Late* (1973), *Key: An Album Of Invisible Theatre* (Lovely 1977), *Songs From The Hill* (1979), *Dolmen Music* (1980), *Dolmen Music* (ECM 1981), *Turtle Dreams* (ECM 1983), *Do You Be* (ECM 1987), *Book Of Days* (ECM 1990), with Robert Een *Facing North* (1992), *Atlas* (ECM 1993).

Monk, Thelonious

b. 11 October 1917, Rocky Mount, North Carolina, USA, d. 17 February 1982. Monk's family moved to New York when he was five years old. He started playing piano a year later, receiving formal tuition from the age of 11 onwards. At Stuyvesant High School he excelled at physics and maths, and also found time to play organ in church. In the late 30s he toured with a gospel group, then began playing in the clubs and became pianist in **Kenny Clarke**'s house band at Minton's Playhouse between 1941 and 1942. He played with **Lucky Millinder**'s orchestra in 1942, the **Coleman Hawkins** Sextet between 1943 and 1945, the **Dizzy Gillespie** Big Band in 1946 and started leading his own outfits from 1947. It was Hawkins who provided him with his recording debut, and enthusiasts noted a fine solo on 'Flyin' Hawk' (October 1944). However, it was the **Blue Note** sessions of 1947 (subsequently issued on album and CD as *Genius Of Modern Music*) that established him as a major figure. With **Art Blakey** on drums, these recordings have operated as capsule lessons in music for subsequent generations of musicians. An infectious groove makes complex harmonic puzzles sound attractive, with Monk's unique dissonances and rhythmic sense adding to their charm. They were actually a distillation of a decade's work. ''Round Midnight' immediately became a popular tune and others - 'Ruby My Dear', 'Well You Needn't', 'In Walked Bud' - have become jazz standards since. In his book, *Bebop*, **Leonard Feather** recognized Monk's genius at composition, but claimed his playing lacked technique (a slight he later apologised for). Monk certainly played with flat fingers (anathema to academy pianists), but actually his bare-bones style was the result of a modern sensibility rather than an inability to achieve the torrents of **Art Tatum** or **Oscar Peterson**. For Monk, the blues had enough romance without an influx of European romanticism, and enough emotion without the sometimes over-heated blowing of bebop. His own improvisations are at once witty, terse and thought-provoking.

A trumped-up charge for possession of drugs deprived Monk of his New York performer's licence in 1951, and a subsequent six-year ban from playing live in the city damaged his career. He played in Paris in June 1954 (recorded by Vogue Records). Riverside Records was supportive, and he found sympathetic musicians with whom to record - both under his own name and guesting with players such as **Miles Davis**, **Sonny Rollins** and **Clark Terry**. *Plays Duke Ellington* (1955) was a fascinating look at **Duke Ellington**'s compositions, with a non-pareil rhythm section in bassist **Oscar Pettiford** and drummer Clarke. *Brilliant Corners* in 1956 showcased some dazzling new compositions and featured Sonny Rollins on tenor saxophone. Regaining his work permit in 1957, Monk assembled a mighty quintet for a residency at the Five Spot club: **Shadow Wilson** (drums), **Wilbur Ware** (bass) and **John Coltrane** (tenor). Coltrane always spoke of what an education he received during his brief stay with the band - though the group was never recorded live, the studio albums that resulted (*Thelonious Monk With John Coltrane*, *Monk's Music*) were classics. Monk repaid **Coleman Hawkins**' earlier compliment, and featured the tenorman on these records: history and the future shook hands over Monk's keyboard. Previously considered too 'way out' for mass consumption, Monk's career finally began to blossom. In 1957, he recorded with **Gerry Mulligan**, which helped to expose him to a wider audience, and worked with classical composer Hall Overton to present his music orchestrally (*At Town Hall*, 1959). He toured Europe for the first time (1961) and also Japan (1964). He formed a stable quartet in the early 60s with **Charlie Rouse** on tenor, **John Ore** (later Butch Warren or Larry Gales) on bass and **Frankie Dunlop** (later **Ben Riley**) on drums. Critics tend to prefer his work with other saxophonists, such as **Harold Land** (1960) or **Johnny Griffin** (the late 50s), but the point was that Rouse really understood Monk's tunes. He may not have been the greatest soloist, but his raw, angular tone fitted the compositions like a glove.

In the early 70s, Monk played with **Pat Patrick** (**Sun Ra**'s alto player), using son T.S. Monk on drums. Illness increasingly restricted his activity, but he toured with the Giants Of Jazz (1971-72) and presented a big band at the Newport Festival in 1974. Two albums recorded for the English Black Lion label in 1971 - *Something In Blue* and *The Man I Love* - presented him in a trio context with **Al McKibbon** on bass and Blakey on drums: these were stunning examples of the empathy between drummer and pianist - two of Monk's best records. When he died from a stroke in 1982, at Englewood, New Jersey, leaving his wife (for whom he had written 'Crepuscule With Nellie') and son, he had not performed in public for six years. Monk's influence, if anything, increased during the 80s. **Buell Neidlinger** formed a band, String Jazz, to play only Monk and Ellington tunes; **Steve Lacy**, who in the early 60s had spent a period playing exclusively Monk tunes, recorded two solo discs of his music; and tribute albums by **Arthur Blythe** (*Light Blue*, 1983), **Anthony Braxton** (*Six Monk's Compositions*, 1987), **Paul Motian** (*Monk In Motian*, 1988) and Hal Wilner (*That's The Way I Feel Now*, 1984, in which artists as diverse as the **Fowler Brothers**, **John Zorn**, **Dr. John**, **Eugene Chadbourne**, and **Peter Frampton** celebrated his tunes) prove that Monk's compositions are still teaching everyone new tricks. His son, T.S. Monk, is a gifted drummer who continues a tradition by encouraging young musicians through membership of his band. One of the most brilliant and original performers in jazz, Thelonious Monk was also one of the century's outstanding composers. ''Round Midnight' is probably the most recorded jazz song of all time. His unique ability to weld intricate, surprising harmonic shifts and rhythmic quirks into appealing, funky riffs means that something special happens when they are played: his compositions exact more incisive improvising than anybody else's. In terms of jazz, that is the highest praise of all.

Selected albums: *Genius Of Modern Music, Vols One And Two* (Blue Note, rec. 1947-52), *Thelonious Monk Trio* (1953), *And Sonny Rollins* (1954), *Pure Monk* (1954), *Solo 1954* (Vogue 1955), *Plays Duke Ellington* (Original Jazz Classics 1956), *The Unique* (Original Jazz Classics 1956), *Brilliant Corners* (Original Jazz Classics 1957), *Thelonious Himself* (Original Jazz Classics 1957), *With John Coltrane* (Original Jazz Classics 1957), with Gerry Mulligan *Mulligan Meets Monk* (Original Jazz Classics 1957), *Art Blakey/Thelonious Monk* (1958), *Monk's Music* (Original Jazz Classics 1958), *Thelonious In Action* (Original Jazz Classics 1958), *Misterioso* (Original Jazz Classics 1958), *The Thelonious Monk Orchestra At Town Hall* (Original Jazz Classics 1959), *Five By Monk By Five* (Original Jazz Classics 1959), *Thelonious Alone In San Francisco* (Original Jazz Classics 1960), *At The Blackhawk* (Original Jazz Classics 1960), *Two Hours With Thelonious* (1961), *Criss Cross* (Columbia 1963), *Monk's Dream* (Columbia 1963), *Big Band And Quartet In Concert* (1964), with Miles Davis *Miles & Monk At Newport* (1964, rec 1963, 1958), *It's Monk's Time* (Columbia 1964), *Monk* (1964), *Solo Monk* (Columbia 1965), *Straight No Chaser* (Columbia 1966), *Monk's Blues* (Columbia 1968), *Underground* (Columbia 1968), *Epistrophy* (1971), *Something In Blue* (1972), *The Man I Love* (1972), *Sphere* (1979, rec. 1967), *April In Paris/Live* (1981, rec. 1971), *Live At The It Club* (Columbia 1982, rec. 1964), *Live At The Jazz Workshop* (Columbia 1982, rec. 1964), *Tokyo Concerts* (1983, rec. 1963), *The Great Canadian Concert Of Thelonious Monk* (mid-80s, rec. 1965), *1963 - In Japan* (1984, rec. 1963), *Live In Stockholm 1961* (1987, rec. 1961), *Solo 1954* (1993), *The Nonet Live* (Charly 1993, 1967 recording), Selected compilations: *Always Know* (1979, rec. 1962-68), *Memorial Album* (1982, rec. 1954-60), *The Complete Blue Note Recordings Of Thelonious Monk* (1983, rec. 1947-52, four-album box-set), *The Complete Black Lion And Vogue Recordings Of Thelonious Monk* (1986, rec. 1971, 1954, four-album box-set), *The Composer* (Giants Of Jazz 1987).

Videos: *American Composer* (1993), *Thelonious Monk: Live In Oslo* (1993).

Further reading: *Monk On Records: A Discography Of Thelonious Monk*, L. Bijl and F. Canté.

Monkees

Inspired by the burgeoning pop phenomena and armed with an advance from Columbia's Screen Gems subsidiary, US television producers Bob Rafelson and Bert Schneider began auditions for a show about a struggling pop group in 1965. When extant acts, including the **Lovin' Spoonful**, proved inappropriate, an advertisement in the *Daily Variety* solicited 437 applicants, including **Stephen Stills**, Danny Hutton (later **Three Dog Night**) and **Paul Williams**. Following suitably off-beat auditions, the final choice paired two musicians - **Michael Nesmith** (b. Robert Michael Nesmith, 30 December 1942, Houston, Texas, USA; guitar/vocals) and folksinger Peter Tork (b. Peter Halsten Thorkelson, 13 February 1944, Washington, D.C., USA; bass/vocals) - with two budding actors and former child stars - Davy Jones (b. 30 December 1945, Manchester, England; vocals) and ex-*Circus Boy* star Mickey Dolenz (b. George Michael Dolenz, 8 March 1945, Los Angeles, California, USA; drums/vocals). On 12 September 1966, the first episode of *The Monkees* was aired by NBC-TV and, despite low initial ratings, the show quickly became hugely popular, a feat mirrored when it was launched in the UK. Attendant singles 'Last Train To Clarksville' (US number 1) and 'I'm A Believer' (US and UK number 1), and a million-selling debut album confirmed the group as the latest teenage phenomenon, drawing inevitable comparisons with the **Beatles**. However, news that the quartet did not play on their records fuelled an already simmering internal controversy. Early sessions had been completed by Tommy **Boyce And** Bobby **Hart**, authors of 'Last Train To Clarksville', and their backing group, the Candy Store Prophets, with the Monkees simply overdubbing vocals. Musical supervision was later handed to Screen Gems executive **Don Kirshner**, who in turn called in staff songwriters **Gerry Goffin** and **Carole King**, **Neil Diamond** and **Jeff Barry** to contribute material for the show.

This infuriated the Monkees' two musicians, in particular Nesmith, who described the piecemeal *More Of The Monkees* as 'the worst album in the history of the world'.

Sales in excess of five million copies exacerbated tension, but the group won tacit approval from Schneider to complete several tracks under their own devices. An undeterred Kirshner coaxed Jones to sing on the already-completed backing track to 'A Little Bit Me, A Little Bit You' which was issued, without group approval, as their third single. The ensuing altercation saw Kirshner ousted, with the quartet gaining complete artistic freedom. Although not issued as a single in the USA, 'Alternate Title' (aka 'Randy Scouse Git'), Dolenz's ambitious paean to London, reached number 2 in Britain, while two further 1967 singles, 'Pleasant Valley Sunday' and 'Daydream Believer' (composed by **John Stewart**), achieved gold record status. *Headquarters*, the first Monkees album on which the group played, was a commercial and artistic success, consisting largely of self-penned material ranging from country-rock to vaudevillian pop. *Pisces, Aquarius, Capricorn And Jones Ltd* featured material drawn from associates **Michael Murphy**, Harry **Nilsson** and Chip Martin as the unyielding call on the group's talents continued. This creative drain was reflected in the disappointing *The Birds, The Bees And The Monkees* and its accompanying single, 'Valleri'. The track itself had been recorded in 1966, and was only issued when 'pirate' recordings, dubbed off-air from the television series, attracted considerable airplay. 'The Monkees are dead!', declared an enraged Nesmith, yet the song sold over a million copies, the group's last such success. The appeal of their series had waned as plots grew increasingly loose, and the final episode was screened in the USA on 25 March 1968. The quartet had meanwhile embarked on a feature film, *Head*, which contained many in-jokes about their artistic predicaments. Although baffling their one-time teenage audience, it failed to find favour with the underground circuit who still viewed the Monkees as bubblegum. However, *Head* has since been rightly lauded for its imagination and innovation. A dispirited Peter Tork left following its release, but although the remaining trio continued without him, their commercial decline was as spectacular as its ascendancy. Nesmith left for a solo career in 1969. and the following year the Monkees' name was dissolved in the wake of Dolenz/Jones recording *Changes*. However, in 1975, the latter-day duo joined their erstwhile songwriting team in *Dolenz, Jones, Boyce And Hart* which toured under the banner 'The Great Golden Hits Of The Monkees Show'. The project drew cursory interest, but the group's reputation was bolstered considerably during the 80s, when the independent **Rhino Records** label reissued the entire Monkees' back catalogue and the entire series was rescreened on **MTV**. Although Nesmith demured, Dolenz, Jones and Tork embarked on a highly successful, 20th-anniversary world tour which engendered a live album and a new studio set, *Pool It*. The group has since disbanded as members pursued contrasting interests, while attempts to create the New Monkees around Marty Roos, Larry Saltis, Jared Chandler and Dino Kovas in 1987 was aborted. Although reviled by many contemporary critics, the original group's work is now regarded as among the best American pop of its era.

Albums: *The Monkees* (1966), *More Of The Monkees* (1967), *Headquarters* (1967), *Pisces, Aquarius, Capricorn And Jones Ltd* (1967), *The Birds, The Bees And The Monkees* (1968), *Head* (1968, film soundtrack), *Instant Replay* (1969), *The Monkees Present...* (1969), *Changes* (1970), *Pool It* (1986), *20th Anniversary Concert Tour 1986* (1986). Compilations: *The Monkees Greatest Hits* (1969), *The Monkees Golden Hits* (1972), *Monkeemania* (1979), *The Monkees* (1981), *Monkee Business* (1982), *Monkee Flips* (1984), *The And Now...The Best Of The Monkees* (1986), *Missing Links* (1987), *The Monkees Live - 1967* (1987), *Hey! Hey! It's The Monkees Greatest Hits* (1989), *Missing Links Volume 2* (1990).

Film: *Head* (1968).

Further reading: *Love Letters To The Monkees*, Bill Adler. *The Monkees Tale*, Eric Lefcowitz. *The Monkees Scrapbook*, Ed Finn and T. Bone. *Monkeemania*, Glenn A. Baker. *The Monkees: A Manufactured Image*, Ed Reilly, Maggie McMannus and Bill Chadwick. *I'm A Believer-My Life Of Monkees, Music And Madness*, Mickey Dolenz with Mark Bego.

Monks

This uncompromising US group originated in 1962. Disenchanted US servicemen Gary Burger (guitar/vocals), Dave Day (guitar/vocals) and Larry Clark (organ) formed the Torquays in Gelnhausen, near Frankfurt, Germany with a local civilian recalled solely as 'Hans' (drums). Eddie Shaw (bass) joined the line-up soon afterwards, while a fifth inductee, Roger Johnson, became their permanent drummer in 1964. A highly popular live attraction, the Torquays completed a single, 'Boys Are Boys'/'There She Walks' for the tiny SCH label the following year before mutating into the Monks. Armed with a set comprising largely of original material and now free of army commitments, the quintet opted for a radical image. To complete the transition, the tops of their heads were shaved and each member wore a black shirt with a white noose around the neck in place of a tie. Musically the Monks were unlike any contemporaries and with Day switching to electric banjo, they unleashed a startlingly different sound. Barked vocals, chopped rhythms, thudding bass and screaming feedback coalesce on *Black Monk Time*, which owes something to R&B but is quite unlike any release from this period. A new version of 'Boys Are Boys' sat beside as 'Blast Off', 'Shut Up!' and 'I Hate You', uncompromising titles which merely hint at the stark power on offer. A gruelling series of one-night stands ensued before 'Love Can Tame The Wild'/'He Went Down To The Sea', released in 1967, showed the group embracing emergent psychedelic textures. However, conflict between Day and Clark undermined the unit, before Johnson left for Texas, tiring of strife and life in exile, Johnson left for Texas. The remaining Monks opted to disband. Burger and Shaw did reconvene in 1969 as Gary Alan And The Professionals. A three-track single, 'Jaded Figurine'/'Where There's A Will There's A Way'/'Pretty Suzanne' - the last of which was from their erstwhile group's repertoire - appeared on a local Minneapolis label, but the unit split up soon afterwards, closing the career of one of rock's most enigmatic bands.

Album: *Black Monk Time* (Polydor 1966).

Monochrome Set

Any all-encompassing classification of the Monochrome Set's music would be difficult. During a sporadic career that has spanned as many musical styles as it has record labels, they have been on the verge of breaking to a wider audience on a number of occasions. Formed in the UK during late 1976, Andy Warren (bass), Lester Square (guitar) and Bid (guitar/vocals) were playing in the B-Sides with **Adam Ant**. When the B-Sides became **Adam And The Ants**, Bid and Lester Square left. They formed the Monochrome Set in January 1978, later joined by Warren in 1979 after his role on the debut Ants album. With Jeremy Harrington (bass; ex-Gloria Mundi and Mean Street) and J.D. Haney (drums; ex-Art Attacks), the band issued singles during 1979-80 for **Rough Trade Records** including 'He's Frank', 'Eine Symphonie Des Graeuns', 'The Monochrome Set' and 'He's Frank (Slight Return)', each completely different in style and content. Their debut, *The Strange Boutique*, skirted the UK charts. After the title track came further singles '405 Lines' and 'Apocalypso', and a second album, *Love Zombies*. Lex Crane briefly sat in on drums before ex-**Soft Boys** member Morris Windsor joined for the release of the brilliant sex satire, 'The Mating Game', in July 1982, followed by 'Cast A Long Shadow' and the memorable *Eligible Bachelors*. By this time Carrie Booth had joined on keyboards while Nick Wesolowski took up the drums and Foz the guitar soon after. *Volume, Brilliance, Contrast*, compiled their Rough Trade recordings and selected BBC Radio 1 sessions, and coincided with another indie hit, 'Jet Set Junta' (like many Monochrome Set compositions deflating class/monetary division). 'Jacob's Ladder' seemed a sure-fire hit for 1985, but like 'Wallflower' later that year and the charming *The Lost Weekend*, eluded the charts. Disheartened, the band split and it was left to Cherry Red's El subsidiary to issue a sympathetic retrospective, *Fin! Live*, a year later. Various collections filtered out over the next three years (*Colour Transmission* featured much of the DinDisc material, while *Westminster Affair* highlighted their earliest recordings). In December 1989 the band reformed, with Bid, Lester and Warren joined by Orson Presence on guitar and keyboards, marking their return with *Dante's Casino*. From there on they have concentrated primarily on their cult following in the Far East, with frequent tours there.

Albums: *The Strange Boutique* (DinDisc 1980), *Love Zombies* (DinDisc 1980), *Eligible Bachelors* (Cherry Red 1982), *The Lost Weekend* (Blanco y Negro 1985), *Dante's Casino* (Vinyl Japan 1990), *Charade* (Cherry Red 1993), *Misere* (Cherry Red 1994). Compilations: *Volume, Brilliance, Contrast* (Cherry Red 1983), *Fin! Live* (El 1985), *Colour Transmission* (Virgin 1987), *Westminster Affair* (Cherry Red 1988).

Video: *Destiny Calling (Visionary)* (1994).

Monotones

Formed in 1955 in Newark, New Jersey, USA, the Monotones recorded one of the most memorable doo-wop novelty songs of the 50s, 'Book Of Love'. The group was a sextet, Warren Davis, George Malone, Charles Patrick, Frank Smith, and John and Warren Ryanes. They had sung in the same church choir as **Dionne Warwick** and **Cissy Houston** before forming their own group. In 1956, they appeared on the *Ted Mack's Amateur Hour* television programme, singing the **Cadillacs**' 'Zoom'. They won first prize and began to think more seriously about a career in music. Inspired by a television commercial for toothpaste ('You'll wonder where the yellow went when you brush your teeth with Pepsodent'), Patrick, Malone and Davis wrote 'Book Of Love' to a similar melody. They recorded it at Bell Studio in New York and it was released on the small Mascot label, a subsidiary of Hull Records. It was then picked up by Argo Records for national distribution and ultimately reached number 5 in the USA. The group was touring when their record entered the charts, and months went by before they had a chance to record a follow-up. A single called 'Tom Foolery' was released but failed to chart; the third, 'The Legend Of Sleepy Hollow', was a fine record and is still played on doo-wop radio programmes today, but also failed to chart in its own time. After a few more singles, the Monotones gave up, although some of the original members performed under that name in the 90s. (The two Ryanes brothers have died).

Compilation: *Who Wrote The Book Of Love?* (Collectables 1992).

Monro, Matt

b. Terry Parsons, 1 December 1932, London, England, d. 7 February 1985, Ealing, London, England. This velvet-voiced balladeer first played in bands under the pseudonym Al Jordan before adopting the name Monro, allegedly borrowed from **Winifred Atwell**'s father. Between stints as a bus driver and singer on the UK Camay soap commercial, he recorded for a number of labels, but his choice of material was generally too predictable. His interpretation of 'Garden Of Eden', for example, had to compete with four other versions by hit artists **Frankie Vaughan**, **Gary Miller**, **Dick James** and **Joe Valino**. Monro's luck changed when producer **George Martin** asked him to contribute a pseudo-**Frank Sinatra** version of 'You Keep Me Swingin'' to a Peter Sellers comedy album. This led to a contract with Parlophone and a Top 3 hit with 'Portrait Of My Love' (1960). For the next five years, Matt was a regular chart entrant with his classic up-tempo version of 'My Kind Of Girl', along with ballads such 'Why Not Now/Can This Be Love', 'Gonna Build A Mountain', 'Softly As I Leave You', and 'When Love Comes Along'. A cover of the James Bond movie theme 'From Russia With Love' and the emotive 'Walk Away' proved particularly successful, and the speedy release of a slick adaptation of the **Beatles**' 'Yesterday' underlined the sagacity of covering a song before your competitors. His 1962 album of **Hoagy Carmichael** songs, with arrangements by his regular musical director Johnny Spence, was right out of the top drawer.

A move to the USA in 1965 brought a decline in Monro's chart fortunes, but he sustained his career as an in-demand nightclub performer. The enduring commercial quality of his voice was recognised by **Capitol Records** with the Christmas release and television promotion of the compilation album, *Heartbreakers*, in 1980. Ill-health dogged the singer in the early 80s, and he died from cancer in 1985. Ten years later, his son Matt Jnr, who had carved out a career for himself as a golf professional, 'duetted' with his father on an album of some of Matt Snr.'s favourite songs.

Selected albums: *Blue And Sentimental* (1957), *Portrait* (1961), *Love Is The Same Anywhere* (1961), *My Kind Of Girl* (1961, USA), *Matt Monro Sings Hoagy Carmichael* (1962), *I Have Dreamed* (1965), *Matt Monro And Don Rennie* (1965), *Walk Away* (1965, USA), *Hits Of Yesterday* (1965), *This Is The Life!* (1966), *Here's To My Lady* (1967), *Invitation To The Movies* (1967), *These Years* (1967), *The Late Late Show* (1968), *Invitation To Broadway* (1968), *Here And Now* (1969), *We're Gonna Change The World* (1970), *Let's Face The Music And Dance* (1972), *For The Present* (1973), *The Other Side Of The Stars* (1975), *The Long And Winding Road* (1975), *If I Never Hear Another Song* (1979), *Heartbreakers* (1980), with Matt Monro Jnr. *Matt Sings Monro* (EMI 1995).

Monroe, Bill

b. William Smith Monroe, 13 September 1911, on a farm near Rosine, Ohio County, Kentucky, USA. The Monroes were a musical family; his father, known affectionately as Buck, was a noted step-dancer, his mother played fiddle, accordion and harmonica, and was respected locally as a singer of old time songs. Among the siblings, elder brothers Harry and **Birch** both played fiddle, and brother **Charlie** and sister Bertha, guitar. They were all influenced by their uncle, Pendleton Vanderver, who was a fiddler of considerable talent, and noted for his playing at local events. (Monroe later immortalized him in one of his best-known numbers, 'Uncle Pen', with tribute lines such as 'Late in the evening about sundown; high on the hill above the town, Uncle Pen played the fiddle, oh, how it would ring. You can hear it talk, you can hear it sing'). At the age of nine, Monroe began to concentrate on the mandolin; his first choice had been the guitar or fiddle, but his brothers pointed out that no family member played mandolin, and as the baby, he was given little choice, although he still kept up his guitar playing. His mother died when he was 10, followed soon after by his father. He moved in to live with Uncle Pen and they were soon playing guitar together at local dances. Bill also played with a black blues musician, Arnold Schultz, who was to become a major influence on the future Monroe music. After the death of his father, most of the family moved away in their search for work. Birch and Charlie headed north, working for a time in the car industry in Detroit, before moving to Whiting and East Chicago, Indiana, where they were employed in the oil refineries. When he was 18, Bill joined them, and for four years, worked at the Sinclair refinery. At one time, in the Depression, Bill was the only one with work, and the three began to play for local dances to raise money to live on.

In 1932, the three Monroe brothers and their girlfriends became part of a team of dancers and toured with a show organised by WLS Chicago, the radio station responsible for the *National Barn Dance* programme. They also played on local radio stations, including WAE Hammond and WJKS Gary, Indiana. In 1934, Bill, finding the touring conflicted with his work, decided to become a full time musician. Soon after, they received an offer to tour for Texas Crystals (the makers of a patent purgative medicine), which sponsored radio programmes in several states. Birch, back in employment at Sinclair and also looking after a sister, decided against a musical career. Bill married in 1935, and between then and 1936, he and Charlie (appearing as the Monroe Brothers) had stays at various stations, including Shenandoah, Columbia, Greenville and Charlotte. In 1936, they moved to the rival and much larger Crazy Water Crystals and, until 1938, they worked on the noted *Crazy Barn Dance* at WBT Charlotte for that company. They became a very popular act and sang mainly traditional material, often with a blues influence. Charlie always provided the lead vocal, and Bill added tenor harmonies.

In February 1936, they made their first recordings on

the Bluebird label of **RCA**-Victor, which proved popular. Further sessions followed, and in total they cut some 60 tracks for the label. Early in 1938, the brothers decided that they should follow their own careers. Charlie kept the RCA recording contract and formed his own band, the Kentucky Pardners. Since he had always handled all lead vocals, he found things easier and soon established himself in his own right. Prior to the split, Bill had never recorded an instrumental or a vocal solo, but he had ideas that he wished to put into practice. He moved to KARK Little Rock, where he formed his first band, the Kentuckians. This failed to satisfy him, and he soon moved to Atlanta, where he worked on the noted *Crossroad Follies,* at this time, he formed the first of the bands he would call the BlueGrass Boys. In 1939, he made his first appearance on the *Grand Ole Opry,* singing his version of 'New Muleskinner Blues', after which **George D. Hay** (the Solemn Old Judge) told him, 'Bill, if you ever leave the Opry, it'll be because you fire yourself'. (Over 50 years later, he was still there.)

During the early 40s, Monroe's band was similar to other string bands such as Mainer's Mountaineers, but by the mid-40s, the leading influence of Monroe's driving mandolin and his high (some would say shrill) tenor singing became the dominant factor, which set the Blue Grass Boys of Bill Monroe apart from the other bands. This period gave birth to a new genre of music, and led to Bill Monroe becoming known affectionately as the Father of Bluegrass Music. He began to tour with the *Opry* road shows, and his weekly network WSM radio work soon made him a national name. In 1940 and 1941, he recorded a variety of material for RCA-Victor, including gospel songs, old-time numbers and instrumentals such as the 'Orange Blossom Special' (the second known recording of the number). War-time restrictions prevented him from recording between 1941 and early 1945, but later that year, he recorded for **Columbia**. In 1946, he gained his first country chart hits when his own song, 'Kentucky Waltz', reached number 3, and his now-immortal recording of 'Footprints In The Snow' reached number 5 in the US country charts. By 1945, several fiddle players had made their impact on the band's overall sound, including Chubby Wise, Art Wooten, Tommy Magness, Howdy Forrester and in 1945, guitarist/vocalist **Lester Flatt** and banjo player **Earl Scruggs** joined. David '**Stringbean**' Akeman had provided the comedy and the banjo playing since 1942, although it was generally reckoned later that his playing contributed little to the overall sound that Monroe sought. Scruggs' style of playing was very different, and it quickly became responsible for not only establishing his own name as one of the greatest exponents of the instrument, but also for making bluegrass music an internationally identifiable sound. It was while Flatt and Scruggs were with the band that Monroe first recorded his now-immortal song 'Blue Moon Of Kentucky'.

By 1948, other bands such as the **Stanley Brothers** were beginning to show the influence of Monroe, and bluegrass music was firmly established. During the 40s, Monroe toured with his tent show, which included his famous baseball team (the reason for Stringbean's first connections with Monroe), which played against local teams as an attraction before the musical show began. In 1951, he bought some land at Bean Blossom, Brown County, Indiana, and established a country park, which became the home for bluegrass music shows. He was involved in a very serious car accident in January 1953, and was unable to perform for several months. In 1954, **Elvis Presley** recorded Monroe's 'Blue Moon Of Kentucky' in a 4/4 rock tempo and sang it at his solitary appearance on the *Opry*. A dejected Presley found the performance made no impact with the *Opry* audience, but the song became a hit. It also led to Monroe re-recording it in a style that, like the original, started as a waltz but after a verse and chorus featuring three fiddles, it changed to 4/4 tempo: Monroe repeated the vocal in the new style. (**Paul McCartney**'s 1991 album, *Unplugged,* contains a version in both styles). Monroe toured extensively throughout the 50s, and had chart success in 1958 with his own instrumental number, 'Scotland'. He used the twin fiddles of Kenny Baker and Bobby Hicks to produce the sound of bagpipes behind his own mandolin - no doubt his tribute to his family's Scottish ancestry. By the end of the decade, the impact of rock 'n' roll was affecting his record sales and music generally. By this time, (the long departed) Flatt and Scruggs were firmly established with their own band and finding success on television and at folk festivals. Monroe was a strong-willed person and it was not always easy for those who worked with him, or for him, to achieve the perfect arrangement. He had stubborn ideas and, in 1959, he refused to play a major concert in Carnegie Hall, because he believed that Alan Lomax, the organiser, was a communist. He was also suspicious of the Press and rarely, if ever, gave interviews. In 1962, however, he became friendly with Ralph Rinzler, a writer and member of the **Greenbriar Boys**, who became his manager.

In 1963, Monroe played his first folk festival at the University of Chicago. He soon created a great interest among students generally and, with Rinzler's planning, he was soon busily connected with festivals solely devoted to bluegrass music. In 1965, he was involved with the major Roanoke, Virginia, festival and in 1967, he started his own at Bean Blossom. During the 60s, many young musicians benefitted from their time as a member of Monroe's band, including **Bill Keith**, **Peter Rowan**, Byron Berline, Roland White and Del McCoury. In 1969, he was made an honorary Kentucky Colonel, and in 1970, was elected to the

Country Music Hall Of Fame in Nashville. The plaque stated 'The Father of Bluegrass Music. Bill Monroe developed and perfected this music form and taught it to a great many names in the industry'. Monroe has written many songs, including 'Memories Of Mother And Dad', 'When The Golden Leaves Begin To Fall', 'My Little Georgia Rose' and 'Blue Moon Of Kentucky' (the latter a much-recorded country standard) and countless others. Many have been written using pseudonyms such as Albert Price, James B. Smith and James W. Smith. In 1971, his talent as a songwriter saw him elected to the Nashville Songwriters Association International Hall Of Fame. He kept up a hectic touring schedule throughout the 70s, but in 1981, he suffered with cancer. He survived after treatment and, during the 80s, maintained a schedule that would have daunted much younger men. In 1984, he recorded the album *Bill Monroe And Friends,* which contains some of his songs sung as duets with other artists, including the **Oak Ridge Boys** ('Blue Moon Of Kentucky'), **Emmylou Harris** ('Kentucky Waltz'), **Barbara Mandrell** ('My Rose Of Old Kentucky'), **Ricky Skaggs** ('My Sweet Darling') and **Willie Nelson** ('The Sunset Trail'). **Johnny Cash,** who also appears on the album, presumably did not know any Monroe songs because they sang Cash's own 'I Still Miss Someone'.

Over the years since Monroe first formed his bluegrass band, some of the biggest names in country music have played as members before progressing to their own careers. These include **Clyde Moody**, Flatt And Scruggs, **Jim Eanes**, Carter Stanley, Mac Wiseman, Jimmy Martin, Sonny Osborne, **Vassar Clements**, Kenny Baker and son **James Monroe**. Amazingly, bearing in mind his popularity, Monroe's last chart entry was 'Gotta Travel On', a Top 20 country hit in March 1959. However, his records are still collected and the German Bear Family label has released boxed sets on compact disc of his **Decca** recordings. (Between 1950, when he first recorded for Decca and 1969, he made almost 250 recordings for the label) He continued to play the *Opry* and, in 1989, he celebrated his 50th year as a member, the occasion being marked by **MCA** (by then the owners of Decca) recording a live concert from the *Opry* stage, which became his first-ever release on CD format. He first visited the UK in 1966, did an extended tour in 1975, and has always been a very popular personality on the several occasions he has played the UK's Wembley Festival. He underwent surgery for a double coronary bypass on 9 August 1991, but by October, he was back performing and once again hosting his normal *Opry* show.

Albums: *Knee Deep In Bluegrass* (1958), *I Saw The Light* (1959), *Mr. Bluegrass* (1960), *The Great Bill Monroe & The BlueGrass Boys* (1961), *Bluegrass Ramble* (1962), with Rose Maddox *Rose Maddox Sings Bluegrass* (1962), *The Father Of Bluegrass Music* (1962), *My All-Time Country Favorites* (1962), *Early Bluegrass Music* (1963), *Bluegrass Special* (1963), *Sings Country Songs* (1964), *I'll Meet You In Church Sunday Morning* (1964), *Original Bluegrass Sound* (1965), *Bluegrass Instrumentals* (1965), *The High Lonesome Sound* (1966), *Bluegrass Time* (1967), *Bill Monroe And Lester Flatt* (1967), *A Voice From On High* (1969), *Bill Monroe & His Blue GrassBoys (16 Hits)* (1970), *Bluegrass Style* (1970), *Kentucky Bluegrass* (1970), *Country Music Hall Of Fame* (1971), *Uncle Pen* (1972), *Bean Blossom* (1973, double album), with James Monroe *Father And Son* (1973), *The Road Of Life* (1974), with Birch Monroe *Brother Birch Monroe Plays Old-Time Fiddle Favorites* (1975), with Doc Watson *Bill & Doc Sing Country Songs* (1975), *Weary Traveller* (1976), *Bill Monroe & His Bluegrass Boys 1950-1972* (c.1976), with Kenny Baker *Kenny Baker Plays Bill Monroe* (1976), *Sings Bluegrass, Body And Soul* (1977), *Bluegrass Memories* (1977), with James Monroe *Together Again* (1978), *Bill Monroe With Lester Flatt & Earl Scruggs:The Original Bluegrass Band* (1978), *Bean Blossom 1979* (1980), *Bluegrass Classic (Radio Shows 1946-1948)* (1980), *The Classic Bluegrass Recordings Volume 1* (1980), *The Classic Bluegrass Recordings Volume 2* (1980), *Orange Blossom Special (Recorded Live At Melody Ranch)* (1981), *Master Of Bluegrass* (1981), *Live Radio* (1982), *MCA Singles Collection Volumes 1, 2 & 3* (1983), *Bill Monroe & Friends* (1984), *Bluegrass '87* (1987), *Southern Flavor* (1988), *Muleskinner Blues* (1991), with the Bluegrass Boys *Live Recordings 1956-69* (Smithsonian Folkways 1994), with Doc Watson *Live Duet Recordings 1963-80* (Smithsonian Folkways 1994). As The Monroe Brothers *Early Bluegrass Music* (1963), *The Monroe Brothers, Bill & Charlie* (1969), *Feast Here Tonight* (1975). Compilations: *Bill Monroe BlueGrass 1950-1958* (Bear Family 1989, CD box set), *Bill Monroe BlueGrass 1959-1969* (Bear Family 1991, CD box set).

Further reading: *Bossmen: Bill Monroe And Muddy Waters,* J. Rooney. *Bill Monroe And His Blue Grass Boys,* Neil V. Rosenberg.

Monroe, Birch

b. 1901, on a farm near Rosine, Ohio County, Kentucky, USA, d. 15 May 1982. Birch was the fiddle-playing elder brother of **Bill Monroe** who, after the death of his parents, moved to Detroit with brother **Charlie Monroe**. Here, they worked for a time in the motor industry, before moving to work in the oil refineries at Whiting and East Chicago, Indiana. In 1929, they were joined by brother Bill, and during the Depression, the three began to play at local venues; eventually Bill and Charlie worked professionally together as the Monroe Brothers. From the mid-to late 40s, he worked with brother Bill's band, playing bass and taking bass vocals, as well as acting as their manager and booking agent. He remained connected with his brother's business enterprises, and from 1951 to the end of the 70s, he managed the country park at Bean Blossom, Indiana, which featured the weekly

Brown County Jamboree. His recording career was limited to those made with his brother's band, except in the mid-70s, when accompanied by the BlueGrass Boys and under the production of Bill, he recorded an album of fiddle music. Birch Monroe died in 1982, and is buried in the Monroe family plot on Jerusalem Ridge, Rosine, Kentucky.
Album: *Brother Birch Monroe Plays Old-Time Fiddle Favorites* (1975).

Monroe, Charlie

b. 4 July 1903, on a farm near Rosine, Ohio County, Kentucky, USA, d. 27 September 1975. Charlie was the elder brother of **Bill Monroe** who, after the death of his parents, moved to Detroit with fiddle-playing brother **Birch Monroe**. Here they worked for a time in the motor industry, before moving to work in the oil refineries at Whiting and East Chicago, Indiana. In 1929, they were joined by brother Bill and during the Depression, the three began to play at local venues; eventually Bill and Charlie worked professionally together as the Monroe Brothers. In 1938, they decided to pursue their own careers. At the time of the split, they had a contract with **RCA**-Victor, for whom they had recorded 60 songs; Charlie, who had always taken the lead vocals (though Bill had written many of their songs), kept this contract. Throughout the 40s, he toured and recorded for RCA-Victor, and at times his band, the Kentucky Pardners, which became one of North Carolina's most popular hillbilly bands, included notable musicians such as guitarist **Lester Flatt** and mandolin players Red Rector, Ira Louvin and Curly Sechler. He differed from his brother in that his band played a mixture of country and bluegrass, and Charlie, a highly respected guitarist, frequently used an electric guitar. He made many fine recordings, and though he never achieved a chart hit, Monroe is remembered for his versions of numbers such as 'Down In The Willow Garden' (an old folk song) and his own compositions 'Rubber Neck Blues', 'It's Only A Phonograph Record' and 'Who's Calling You Sweetheart Tonight?'. He joined **Decca** around 1950, although they made some concert appearances together, further recordings with brother Bill never materialized. In the early 50s, tired of the touring, he broke up his band and semi-retired to his Kentucky farm. In 1957, he supposedly retired to manage a coal mine and yard near Rosine, but made some special appearances and, during the early 60s, recorded two albums on the Rem label. His wife became ill with cancer, and to meet the medical expenses, Monroe left Kentucky and worked in Indiana for a lift company until his wife died. He remarried in 1969, when he moved to Tennessee, and in 1972, he was persuaded to appear with Jimmy Martin at a Gettysburg bluegrass festival, which led him to make some further appearances at similar events. He relocated to Reidsville, North Carolina, and in late 1974, he, too, was diagnosed as suffering from cancer. He made his last public performance in his old home area of Rosine, Kentucky, around early August, and died at his home in Reidsville in September 1975, but is buried in the Monroe family plot on Jerusalem Ridge, Rosine, Kentucky. Although his work was not as important as that of brother Bill, he nevertheless made a significant contribution to the formation of what is now known as bluegrass music.
Albums: *Bluegrass Sound* (1963), *Lord Build Me A Cabin* (1965), *Charlie Monroe Sings Again* (1966), *Who's Calling You Sweetheart Tonight?* (1969), *Noon-Day Jamboree (Radio Shows 1944)* (1970), *Songs Of Charlie Monroe & the Kentucky Pardners (Vintage Radio Recordings)* (1970), *Live At Lake Norman Music Hall* (1975), *Tally Ho* (1975), *Charlie Monroe & His Kentucky Pardners* (c.70s), one side of second album by Phipps Family *Memories Of Charlie Monroe* (1975, double album), *Charlie Monroe's Boys:The Early Years* (1982), *Vintage Radio 1944* (1990). As The Monroe Brothers: *Early Bluegrass Music* (1963), *The Monroe Brothers, Bill & Charlie* (1969), *Feast Here Tonight* (1975).

Monroe, Gerry

b. unknown, d. November 1989. After signing with the independent Chapter One label, this mild-mannered, bespectacled counter tenor made a startling television debut in May 1970 on BBC's *Top Of The Pops,* with a version of 'Sally', the signature tune of **Gracie Fields**, an entertainer he greatly admired. This reached number 4 in the UK, and although later singles, until 1972, were less successful, they all made the charts. Most of his a-sides were upper-octave revivals of sentimental ballads such as **Johnnie Ray**'s 'Cry' (1970, Top 40), the **Platters**' 'My Prayer' (1970, Top 10) and the evergreen 'It's A Sin To Tell A Lie' (1971, Top 20). However, the last two chart entries, 'Little Drops Of Silver' (1971, Top 40) and 'Girl Of My Dreams' (1972, Top 50), were composed especially for him. Monroes's cache of hits formed the backbone of his act when he returned to the working men's club netherworld from which he had emerged. While his voice remained a thing of wonder, failing health obliged him to cut back on engagements by the mid-80s.
Album: *World Of Gerry Monroe* (early 70s).

Monroe, James

b. James William Monroe, 1941. Son of **Bill Monroe**. James began his musical career in 1964, playing upright bass with his father's BlueGrass Boys. In 1969, he became the band's guitarist and also began to take lead vocals. He left the Bluegrass Boys in 1972, and formed his own bluegrass band, the Midnight Ramblers, but later recorded two albums with his father. In the mid-70s, he recorded several albums for Atteiram, including a tribute to his uncle, **Charlie**

Monroe, on which his father also appeared. Soon afterwards he drastically reduced his performing to help with the running of his father's business affairs.
Albums: with Bill Monroe *Father And Son* (1973), *Sings Songs of 'Memory Lane' Of His Uncle Charlie Monroe* (1976), *Together Again* (1978). With the Midnight Ramblers *Something New! Something Different! Something Good!* (1974), *Midnight Blues* (1976), *Satisfied Mind* (1984).

Monroe, Marilyn

b. Norma Jean Mortenson, 1 June 1926, Los Angeles, California, USA, d. 5 August 1962, Brentwood, California, USA. As well as being a talented comedienne and the number 1 sex symbol in movies during the 50s, Monroe proved to be an appealing interpreter of flirtacious ballads in several of her most popular films. As one of the *Ladies Of The Chorus* (1949), she made a promising start with Lester Lee and Allan Roberts's 'Every Baby Needs A Da-Da-Daddy', which, with its reference to 'Tiffany's', was a precursor to one of her most celebrated performances a few years later, when the same New York store cropped up 'Diamonds Are A Girl's Best Friend', from **Jule Styne** and **Leo Robin**'s score for ***Gentlemen Prefer Blondes*** (1953). In that film Monroe duetted with another of Hollywood's top glamour girls, Jane Russell, on 'Two Little Girls From Little Rock', 'Bye Bye Baby' and a **Hoagy Carmichael/Harold Adamson** number, 'When Loves Goes Wrong'. Co-starred with Robert Mitchum in *River Of No Return* (1954), Monroe's role as a saloon singer conveniently gave her the opportunity to put over the title song and 'I'm Gonna File My Claim', amongst others, and, in the same year, she registered strongly with a bundle of **Irving Berlin** numbers in ***There's No Business Like Show Business***. These included 'A Man Chases A Girl' (with **Donald O'Connor**), 'After You Get What You Want You Don't Want It', 'Heatwave', 'Lazy' and 'You'd Be Surprised'. In 1959 she made what was to become her most commercially successful film - arguably the highlight of her career. The classic *Some Like It Hot*, with Tony Curtis, Jack Lemmon and Joe E. (nobody's perfect) Brown, contained some of Monroe's most efective vocal peformances, such as 'I'm Through With Love', 'I Wanna Be Loved By You' and 'Running Wild'. She sang for the last time on screen in ***Let's Make Love*** (1960). Apart from contributing the film's highspot, a compelling version of 'My Heart Belongs To Daddy', Monroe duetted with a couple of European heart-throbs, Yves Montand and **Frankie Vaughan**, on **Sammy Cahn** and **Jimmy Van Heusen**'s 'Specialization', 'Incurably Romantic' and the title song. Her final performance, a sultry rendering of 'Happy Birthday Mr. President' and 'Thanks For The Memory', was given in May 1962 for President Kennedy's birthday celebrations in Madison Square Garden. Just over two months later she died, in mysterious circumstances, at the age of 36. One of the musical selections chosen for her funeral service was a recording of 'Over The Rainbow', sung by **Judy Garland**, another show business legend who met a tragic end. Since her death, it has been estimated that over 100 Monroe biographies have been published. She was also the subject of several songs, the most famous being **Elton John**'s 'Crying In the Wind'. Others included James Cunningham's 'Norma Jean Wants To Be A Movie Star' and 'Elvis And Marilyn' by **Leon Russell**.
Selected album: *Marilyn Monroe -The Complete Recordings* (1988, 2-CD set).
Further reading: *Marilyn*, Norman Mailer. *Marilyn Monroe: The Biography*, Donald Spoto. *Goddess: Secret Lives Of Marilyn Monroe*, Anthony Summers. *The Complete Films Of Marilyn Monroe*, Mark Ricci and Michael Conway.

Monroe, Melissa

b. Melissa Katherine Monroe, 1936, d. December 1990. Daughter of **Bill Monroe**. A singer and instrumentalist, Monroe toured with her father's road show during the 40s and 50s. She made some solo recordings for **Columbia** in the early 50s, but did not achieve any chart success.

Monroe, Michael

When **Hanoi Rocks** folded following the death of drummer Razzle in 1984, Monroe took several years off before deciding to start again and build a solo career. In 1988 *Nights Are So Long* emerged on the independent Yahoo label, featuring a mixture of originals and covers of songs by the **Heavy Metal Kids**, **Johnny Thunders**, **MC5** and the **Flamin' Groovies**. This low-key comeback was a soul-cleansing process for Monroe, before he signed to **Mercury Records**, and threw himself back into the spotlight with all guns blazing. Recruiting Phil Grande (guitar), Tommy Price (drums), Kenny Aaronson (bass) and Ed Roynesdal (keyboards), he recorded *Not Fakin' It*, a streetwise selection of sleazy rock 'n' roll numbers, delivered in Monroe's inimitable, alley cat style. The album was well received and the tour to support it was a further triumph, proving easily the most successful of the Hanoi Rock spin-off projects.
Albums: *Nights Are So Long* (Yahoo 1988), *Not Fakin' It* (Polygram 1989).

Monroe, Vaughn

b. 7 October 1911, Akron, Ohio, USA, d. 21 May 1973, Stuart, Florida, USA. Monroe was a Wisconsin State Trumpet Champion in 1926 with an ambition to become an opera singer. This eventually led him to join Austin Wylie And His Golden Pheasant Orchestra and Larry Funk And His Band Of A Thousand Melodies. He studied voice at the New England Conservatory Of

Music, and in 1939 sang and played for the Jack Marshard Orchestra. Monroe then formed his own band in Boston in 1940, and immediately had a big hit with 'There I Go', quickly followed by 'My Devotion', 'When The Lights Go On Again', 'Let's Get Lost' and his theme tune 'Racing With The Moon'. His robust baritone, sometimes called The Voice With Hairs On Its Chest, sold the band to the public, although Monroe also had some leading sidemen such as future **Glenn Miller** trumpeter Bobby Nichols, guitarist Carmen Mastren, drummer Alvin Stoller and vocalist Marilyn Duke. Throughout the 40s Monroe had great success in clubs, radio and especially on records. 'There I've Said It Again', 'Ballerina' and 'Riders In The Sky' each sold over a million, while 'Someday', 'Let It Snow! Let It Snow! Let It Snow!', 'Red Roses For A Blue Lady', 'The Trolley Song', 'Seems Like Old Times', 'How Soon' and 'Sound Off' all made the US Top 10. Monroe also made two films in the 40s: *Meet The People* (1944) with Lucille Ball and **Dick Powell**, and *Carnegie Hall* (1947), which featured Monroe with the New York Symphony Orchestra. He disbanded the orchestra in the early 50s and worked in television. Monroe was also involved in films such as *Singing Guns* (1950) and many other b-movie westerns, sometimes as a singing cowboy. In 1955 he also flirted with the 'rock' age by getting his recording of **Leiber And Stoller**'s 'Black Denim And Motor Cycle Boots' into the US Top 40. He was still active, touring, playing clubs and running his own Massachusetts restaurant until his death in 1973.

Albums: *There I Sing/Swing It Again* (1958), *Vaughn Monroe* (1958), *Surfer's Stomp* (1962), *Greatest Hits* (1962), *Themes Of Bands And Singers* (1963), *Great Gospels* (1964), *Racing With The Moon* (1965), *Dance With Me!* (1969). Compilation: *The Best Of Vaughn Monroe* (1987).

Monsieur Beaucaire

A romantic operetta with music and lyrics by André Messager and Adrian Ross, and a book by Fredererick Lonsdale, which was based on the novel by Brook Tarkington. Set in the stylish city of Bath, England, in the early 18th century, when it was ruled by the so-called King of Bath, Richard 'Beau' Nash, the familiar plot concerned yet another nobleman disguised as a commoner. In this instance, the Duc d'Orléans (Marion Green), son of the King of France, is masquerading as the barber Monsieur Beaucaire. In spite of stern opposition from the Duke of Winterset (Robert Parker) (a bounder who cheats at cards), the ducal barber wins the heart of Lady Mary Carlisle (Maggie Teyte), and eventually accedes to the throne of France. After opening at the Prince's Theatre in London on 19 April 1919, the show transferred to the Palace Theatre in July, and ran for 221 performances. The gay and lively score included songs such as 'Honour And Love', That's A Woman's Way', 'Lightly, Lightly', 'Say No More', 'Gold And Blue And White', 'Red Rose', 'The Honours Of War', 'Going To The Ball', and 'I Love You A Little'. Maggie Teyte, who had sung in leading operatic roles before turning to the musical stage, was outstanding. *Monsieur Beaucaire* was presented on Broadway in December 1919, and was produced in Paris in 1925, 1929, 1935, and 1954. A London revival played Daly's Theatre in 1931. The 1946 film version starred **Bob Hope** and Joan Caulfield.

Monsoon

The nucleus of UK-based Monsoon were producer/writer/musician Steve Coe and his collaborator Martin Smith. Together they produced a hybrid of raga-pop, fusing Indian and Western influences. They were fronted by the schoolgirl vocalist Sheila Chandra (b. 14 March 1965, Waterloo, London, England), and augmented by session musicians, particularly on percussion instruments. Chandra had previously acted in the UK children's television programme *Grange Hill*. Monsoon's brief UK success arrived in 1982 with 'Ever So Lonely' and the follow up 'Shakti (The Meaning Of Within)'. However, when 'The Wings Of Dawn' failed Chandra elected to take a solo career, recording four albums with the assistance of Coe. After a five-year break she returned with *Roots And Wings* (1990) and *Weaving My Ancestor's Voices* in 1992.

Album: *Third Eye* (1983).

Monster Magnet

This space-rock revivalist band was formed in New Jersey in 1989 by vocalist/guitarist David Wyndorf, with guitarist John McBain, bassist Joe Calendra and drummer Jon Kleinman. After a promising debut and the rather self-indulgent *Tab*, Monster Magnet suddenly found broad press and public support with *Spine Of God*, despite the back cover disclaimer that 'It's a satanic drug thing... you wouldn't understand'. The sound and songs drew on Wyndorf's obsession with late 60s psychedelia, music and culture, producing a hypnotic set which blended *Space Ritual*-era **Hawkwind** style with an **MC5/Black Sabbath** guitar barrage and a liberal sprinkling of drug references, all played with a 90s venom. The band were quick to capitalize, touring almost non-stop around Europe and the USA, and, following a US tour with **Soundgarden**, they lost McBain but gained a deal with **A&M**, who were happy to give the group creative freedom. The resultant *Superjudge*, with new guitarist Ed Mundell, was, if anything, more intense, and saw Monster Magnet pay tribute to Hawkwind with an affectionate blast through 'Brainstorm'. Their live shows remained an experience in themselves, with lighting engineer Tim Cronin's astral projection backdrop proving to be an essential component as the band whipped up a frenzy on stage, touring Europe with **Paw** and the US with **Raging Slab**.

Albums: *Monster Magnet* (Primo Scree 1991), *Tab* (Primo Scree 1991), *Spine Of God* (Primo Scree 1991), *Superjudge* (A&M 1993), *Dopes To Infiinity* (A&M 1995).

Montana Slim

(see **Carter, Wilf**)

Montana, Patsy

b. Rubye Blevins, 30 October 1912, Hot Springs, Arkansas, USA. Montana was the 11th child, and first daughter, of a farmer and in her childhood she learned organ, guitar, violin and yodelling. In 1928 she worked on radio in California as Rubye Blevins, the Yodelling Cowgirl from San Antone. In 1931 she joined **Stuart Hamblen**'s show, appearing on radio and at rodeos as part of the Montana Cowgirls. Hamblen renamed her Patsy as it was 'a good Irish name'. In 1933 she joined the Kentucky Ramblers who, because of their western image, became the **Prairie Ramblers**. In 1935 Montana recorded her self-penned 'I Want To Be A Cowboy's Sweetheart', the first million-seller by a female country singer. She recorded many other western songs including 'Old Nevada Moon' and 'Back On The Montana Plains' - several of her songs had Montana in the title. She appeared in several films including *Colorado Sunset* with **Gene Autry**. During the war, she recorded with the **Sons Of The Pioneers** and the Lightcrust Doughboys; her 'Goodnight Soldier' was very popular. She continued with her cowgirl image after the war but retired in 1952 and moved to California. She returned to touring in the 60s, often with her daughter Judy Rose, and recorded for Starday with **Waylon Jennings** on lead guitar. She won popularity in the UK with her appearances in country clubs. Montana, who presented a picture of independence through her cowgirl image, has inspired many yodelling singers including **Rosalie Allen**, Texas Ruby and Bonnie Lou.

Albums: *New Sounds Of Patsy Montana At The Matador Room* (1964), *Precious Memories* (1977), *Patsy Montana And Judy Rose - Mum And Me* (1977), *I Want To Be A Cowboy's Sweetheart* (1977), *Patsy Montana Sings Her Original Hits* (1980), *Early Country Favourites* (1983), *Patsy Montana And The Prairie Ramblers* (1984), *The Cowboy's Sweetheart* (1988).

Montañez, Andy

b. 7 May, Puerto Rico. For 15 years Montañez's rich and powerful voice was an essential part of **El Gran Combo**'s trademark sound. In 1977 **Dimensión Latina**, based in then oil wealthy Venezuela, made him a lucrative offer he could not refuse, and he joined them as a co-lead singer until 1980, when he left to go solo. He released a string of albums during the 80s and in 1990. His 1983 *Hoy . . . y Ayer* (Today and Yesterday), contained a medley of El Gran Combo hits to mark their 20th anniversary. Mirroring El Gran Combo, Montañez uses a line-up that contains two trumpets, two saxophones and a trombone, plus a rhythm section (conga, bongo, timbales, cowbell, maracas, bass, piano) and coro (chorus). The 1985 chart-topper, *Andy Montañez*, was one of his best. It contained the superb C. Curet Alonso composition 'Genio y Figura'. Ernesto Rivera wrote all the arrangements and Montañez's sons, Andy Jnr. and Harold, sang coro. The sons became members of Andy's gigging band, led by flamboyant timbales player Don Perignon, whom backed him on the hit *Mejor Acompañado Que Nunca* (*Better Accompanied Than Ever*), 1986. This was another fine album and contained the outstanding 'Me Lo Estas Poniendo Dificil' (You Are Making It Difficult For Me), arranged by Rivera. Andy and the band won awards in Colombia and Puerto Rico and made one more album together in 1988.

Andy Jnr. and Harold began recording as a duo in 1987 with *El Comienzo Del Camino . . .*, followed by *Siguiendo El Camino* in 1989. Both albums were produced by bandleader, trombonist, arranger, composer Julio 'Gunda' Merced. Don Perignon went solo as a bandleader and debuted on *La Buena Vida!* in 1989. His trio of lead vocalists included Luisito Carrión, who previously worked with 'Gunda' Merced's Salsa Fever, La Terrifica, and **Bobby Valentín**. In 1990, Carrión became a member of Sonora Ponceña (see **Papo Lucca**). Andy became the centre of controversy in early 1989 when the Kiwanis Club, which organize Miami's Calle Ocho Festival, vetoed his appearance because he had visited Cuba in 1979 while still a member of Dimensión Latina. Paradoxically, he had been allowed to perform at the festival during the previous four years. Andy retorted that his political views were private, and added that he was not a communist. The same year, Montañez and El Gran Combo appeared on the same bill at the New Orleans Jazz and Heritage Festival. Montañez returned in 1990 with *Todo Nuevo . . !*, recorded with some of Puerto Rico's finest session musicians. 'Fantasma', arranged by trumpeter Tommy Villariny, was the first hit from the album. In the tradition of the 70s Puerto Rico All Stars albums, which Andy participated in, Don Perignon assembled a mini-galaxy of Puerto Rico's current stars under the banner of La Puertorriqueña for *Festival De Soneros* in 1990. Besides Montañez, other artists involved were: **Gilberto Santa Rosa**, Pedro Brull (from **Mulenze**), Luisito Carrión, Primi Cruz (from **Willie Rosario**'s band), lead vocals were by **Tony Vega**, Alex D'Castro, coro; **Mario Ortiz**, trumpet; Humberto Ramírez, arranger, co-musical director and trumpet; Andy Guzmán, piano and arranger. Leading Puerto Rican composers C. Curet Alonso and Johnny Ortiz, were amongst those contributing songs.

Selected albums: with El Gran Combo *El Gran Combo . . . de Siempre* (1962), *Acángana* (1963), *Ojos Chinos - Jala Jala* (1964), *El Caballo Pelotero* (1965), *El Swing del Gran Combo* (1966), *El Gran Combo en Navidad, Maldito Callo, Esos Ojitos Negros, Fiesta con El Gran Combo, Boleros Románticos con El Gran Combo, Boogaloos con El Gran Combo, Tu Querias Boogaloo?, Pata Pata Jala Jala Boogaloo, Tangos Por El Gran Combo* (1967), *Los Nenes Sicodelicos, Latin Power, Smile It's El Gran Combo* (1968), *Este Si Que Es El Gran Combo* (1969), *Estamos Primeros* (1970), *De Punta A Punta* (1971), *Por El Libro* (1972), *En Acción* (1973), *El Gran Combo 5* (1973), *Disfrútelo Hasta El Cabo!* (1974), *El Gran Combo 7* (1975), *El Gran Combo* (1975); with the Puerto Rico All Stars *Puerto Rico All Stars* (1976); with El Gran Combo *Mejor Que Nunca* (*Better Than Ever*) (1976); with Dimensión Latina *Los Generales de la Salsa* aka *Presentanda: Andy Montañez* (1977); with the Puerto Rico All Stars *Los Profesionales* (1977); with Dimensión Latina *Dimensión Latina 78/780 Kilos de Salsa* (1977), *Inconquistable* (1978), *Dimension Latina '79* (1978); solo *Una Dimensión Desconocida* (1978); with Dimensión Latina *. . . Tremenda Dimensión!* (1978), *Combinación Latina No.4* (1979), *Dimensión Latina* (1980), *Dimensión Latina en el Madison Square Garden* (1980); solo *Salsa Con 'Cache'* (1980); with Dimensión Latina *Para Siémpre* (1981); solo *Andy Montañez* (1981), *Trovador del Amor, Para Ustedes . . . con Sabor!* (1981), *Solo Boleros* (1982), *Hoy . . . y Ayer* (1983), *Tania & Andy Montañez* (1983), *Versátil* (1984), *Andy Montañez* (1985); duo on one track with Milagros Hernández *La Milagros* (1986); *Mejor Acompañado Que Nunca* (1986), *El Eterno Enamorado* (1988), *Todo Nuevo . . !* (1990); with La Puertorriqueña *Festival De Soneros* (1990), *El Catedrático de la Salsa* (1991). Compilations: *14 Grandes Exitos* (1984), *Canta Sus Exitos* (1989).

Montclairs

An R&B vocal group from East St. Louis, Illinois, USA. Members were lead Phil Perry, David Frye, George McLellan, Kevin Sanlin, and Clifford 'Scotty' Williams. The Montclairs are well representative of the vocal group renaissance of the early 70s when falsetto lead and sweet-sound vocals were all the rage. The group recorded their first single in 1969, which was only distributed in the St. Louis area, and the following year began recording for bandleader/producer **Oliver Sain** at his Archway Studio. Sain arranged for the group to be signed with Paula Records based in Shreveport, Louisiana. Their outstanding hits for the label were 'Dreaming Out Of Season' (number 34 R&B) from 1972, and 'Make Up For Lost Time' (number 46 R&B) from 1974. Their last chart record was 'Baby You Know (I'm Gonna Miss You)' from 1974. After the Montclairs left Paula in 1975 they disbanded.

Selected album: *Dreaming's Out Of Season* (Paula 1972).

Monte Carlo

Slightly less risqué than ***The Love Parade*** (1929), *Monte Carlo*, which was released by Paramount a year later, was nevertheless a hot-bed of romance and intrigue in the hands of director-producer **Ernst Lubitsch**. **Jeanette Macdonald**, who had raised temperatures and blood pressures with her sizzling scenes in *The Love Parade*, exchanged her European co-star in that film for another - Britain's premiere suave and sophisticated song-and-dance man **Jack Buchanan**. In Ernest Vajda and Vincent Lawrence's screenplay, which was adapted from the play *The Blue Coast* by Ernest Mueller, MacDonald plays a countess who leaves her intended (titled) husband waiting at the church while she boards the Blue Express which takes her to Monte Carlo. After falling for a barber (Buchanan), her penchant for gambling pays off when he turns out to be a wealthy count. By this stage in his career, director Lubitsch was well into his stride as the leader in intelligent and integrated musicals. Acclaimed highlights of this particularly example of his outstanding work include his setting of the song 'Beyond The Blue Horizon', which MacDonald sings aboard the famous train accompanied by familiar sounds and movements of the train itself; and a novel operatic sequence which was based on Booth Tarkington's story *Monsieur Beaucaire*. The film's engaging score was written by **Richard Whiting** and W. Franke Harling (music) and **Leo Robin** (lyrics), and included a variety of numbers such as 'Trimmin' With Women', 'Give Me A Moment Please', 'Whatever It Is, It's Grand', 'Always In All Ways', and 'She'll Love Me And Like It'. Also in the cast were Claud Allister, ZaSu Pitts, Tyler Brooke, and Lionel Belmore.

Montenegro, Hugo

b. 1925, New York City, New York, USA, d. 6 February 1981. An accomplished and prolific composer, arranger and orchestral conductor for film music. After two years in the US Navy where he arranged for Service bands, Montenegro graduated from Manhattan College and entered the record industry in 1955. He served as staff manager to **André Kostelanetz**, and was conductor-arranger for several artists, including **Harry Belafonte**. Montenegro also made his own orchestral albums such as *Arriba!*, *Bongos And Brass*, *Boogie Woogie And Bongos*, *Montenegro And Mayhem*, *Pizzicato Strings*, *Black Velvet* and *American Musical Theatre 1-4*. After moving to California he wrote the score for Otto Preminger's 1967 film *Hurry Sundown*, a racial melodrama starring Jane Fonda and Michael Caine. In 1968, with his orchestra and chorus, he recorded **Ennio Morricone**'s theme from the Italian film *The Good, The Bad And The Ugly*. The record went to number 2 in the US, topped the chart in the

UK, and sold well over a million copies. The instrumental contrasted with Montenegro's big, romantic string sound, and the effects were startling. From the haunting introduction featuring **Arthur Smith** on the ocarina, the unusual instruments used included an electric violin, electric harmonica, and a piccolo trumpet, aided by a vocal group which featured the whistling of Muzzy Marcellino reinforced by grunting vocals. In 1969 Montenegro had a minor UK hit with the theme from *Hang 'Em High*, the film with which Hollywood attempted to match the brutal style of the 'spaghetti' originals, partly by using the same star, Clint Eastwood. The soundtrack album, *Music From 'A Fistful Of Dollars' & 'For A Few Dollars More' & 'The Good, The Bad And The Ugly'* made the US Top 10. There was a refreshing change from the usual film themes on *Broadway Melodies*, where the material included standards such as 'Varsity Drag', 'Thou Swell', 'Tea For Two' and 'I Got Rhythm'. Throughout the late 60s and 70s he continued to provide music for movies such as *The Ambushers* (1968) and *The Wrecking Crew* (1969), both Matt Helm adventures starring **Dean Martin**; *Lady In Cement*, featuring **Frank Sinatra** as private eye Tony Rome; *Charro!* (1969), an **Elvis Presley** western; *The Undefeated* (1969), starring John Wayne; *Viva Max!* (1969); *Tomorrow* (1972); and *The Farmer* (1977).
Albums: *Original Music From 'The Man From UNCLE'* (1966), *More Music From 'The Man From UNCLE'* (1966), *Hurry Sundown* (1967, film soundtrack), *Music From 'A Fistful Of Dollars' & 'For A Few Dollars More' & 'The Good, The Bad And The Ugly'* (1968), *Hang 'Em High* (1968), *Moog Power* (1969), *Arriba!* (70s/80s), *Bongos And Brass* (70s/80s), *Boogie Woogie And Bongos* (70s/80s), *Montenegro And Mayhem* (80s), *Pizzicato Strings* (80s), *Black Velvet* (80s), *American Musical Theatre 1-4* (80s), *Plays For Lovers* (1981). Compilations: *The Best Of Broadway* (1977), *The Best Of Hugh Montenegro* (1980).

Monterey Jazz Festival

Founded in 1958 by Jimmy Lyons and Ralph J. Gleason, the festival has been held every year since its inception and has become one of the most prestigious and popular of all jazz events in the USA. Lyons, a missionary's son born in Peking, China, was a DJ in Southern California in the early 40s and introduced many of the early broadcasts by the **Stan Kenton** band. During his army service in and after World War II he produced many 'Jubilee' shows for the Armed Forces Radio Service, including sessions with **Dizzy Gillespie, Charlie Parker** and **Milt Jackson**. He was also involved in recording the first **Jazz At The Philharmonic** concert staged by **Norman Granz**. After his military service was over Lyons became a DJ in San Diego, then was a publicist for the **Woody Herman** Four Brothers band. He settled in San Francisco in 1948, working again as a radio DJ, presenting a late night show with a strong orientation towards modern jazz. Lyons developed an ambition to establish a west coast jazz festival along the lines of those being staged in the east by **George Wein**. He had discussed this with jazz writer Gleason and, in 1953, when Lyons moved south of San Francisco to Big Sur, he decided that Monterey was the place in which to realize his ambition. With Gleason as advisor and Lyons as the enthusiastic generator of support from local businessmen, the festival was eventually under way. After the success of the first festival, which included **Louis Armstrong**, Gillespie, **John Lewis, Max Roach, Gerry Mulligan, Dave Brubeck, Harry James, Benny Carter** and **Billie Holiday**, Gleason recommended that Lewis should be appointed permanent musical director. Lewis retained the post until 1983, missing only occasional years when major tours clashed with the festival's regular late September date. For a few years after Lewis the musical director was **Mundell Lowe**, who was later replaced by **Bill Berry**. Among other artists who have played the festival have been **Chris Barber**, **George Lewis**, **Earl Hines**, Herman, **Coleman Hawkins**, **Ornette Coleman**, **Count Basie**, **Duke Ellington**, **Modern Jazz Quartet**, **Charles Mingus**, **Anita O'Day**, **Don Ellis**, **Gil Evans**, **Johnny Otis**, **Cannonball Adderley**, **Hampton Hawes**, **Sonny Stitt**, **Sarah Vaughan**, **Big Joe Turner**, **Art Blakey, Betty Carter**, **Tito Puente, Horace Silver**, **Jay McShann**, **JoAnne Brackeen**, **Cal Tjader**, **Billy Eckstine**, **Herbie Mann**, **Freddie Hubbard**. Several major musical works have been premiered at Monterey and the festival has also become a major showcase for emerging talent with regular appearances of all-star Californian high school bands. Much of the material played over each of the three-day festivals has been recorded and issued. Lyons was due to retire in 1991 but the festival he created looks set to continue for many more years.
Further reading: *Dizzy, Duke, the Count and Me: The Story Of The Monterey Jazz Festival*, Jimmy Lyons with Ira Kamin.

Monterey Pop Festival

16-18 June 1967. The burgeoning west coast American music scene was effectively launched at Monterey, California, USA in 1967. In a transition from 'pop music', performers and bands suddenly found that they were preaching their new music to a like-minded mass audience. The sounds became more adventurous as they explored other musical routes. Blues, jazz and folk became tinged with Eastern and African influences. This galvanization in turn made people more aware and tolerant of these ambitious and different styles. Nevertheless, the music was still labelled 'progressive pop' rather than rock. The festival was the brainchild of **John Phillips**, Alan Pariser, **Paul Simon** and **Lou**

Adler, who assembled a board of artists to help stage the event. **Derek Taylor** the skilful former press officer of the **Beatles** and the **Byrds** was enrolled. **Brian Wilson** of the **Beach Boys** pulled out prior to the event. The Beatles were notably missing. The **Rolling Stones,** although absent, were there in spirit, with **Brian Jones** on the advisory board seen wandering in the crowd throughout the proceedings.

The three day festival was a forerunner to **Woodstock**, and history has subsequently shown that Monterey was more 'musically' important, although by today's standards it was a comparatively small affair with only 35,000 people present at any one time. The festival gave birth to a movement and introduced major new artists to the general public. It was at Monterey that **Jimi Hendrix** first attracted mass attention with the public burning of his guitar. Likewise it was **Janis Joplin** with her band, **Big Brother And The Holding Company** who grabbed the audience's imagination with her orgasmic and electrifying performance, as did a quasi-live album by the Mama And Papas. **Otis Redding**'s accomplishment was memorable in that he brought together black soul and white rock music and became accepted by a predominantly white pop audience. His thrilling and frantic performance broke down all barriers, even though he wore a conservative blue suit instead of the regulation kaftan, beads and flowers. The first major pop music revolution since the Beatles was born at Monterey.

Among other artists who paraded their music at the festival were the **Grateful Dead**, **Electric Flag** (featuring the brilliant young **Mike Bloomfield**), **Canned Heat**, **Buffalo Springfield**, the **Byrds**, the **Mamas And The Papas**, **Eric Burdon And The Animals**, **Hugh Masekela**, **Jefferson Airplane**, **Ravi Shankar**, **Booker T. And The MGs**, the **Who**, **Moby Grape**, the **Steve Miller Band**, **Country Joe And The Fish**, **Simon And Garfunkel**, **Beverly** (**Martyn**), the **Paupers**, **Lou Rawls**, the **Association**, **Johnny Rivers**, **Quicksilver Messenger Service**, **Laura Nyro**, and the **Blues Project**. D.A. Pennebaker's 80 minute film *Monterey Pop* captured the event. No official album was ever released although a Jimi Hendrix/Otis Redding album included highlights of their performance. However, the show was broadcast on radio almost in its entirety in 1989 and further extracts from the festival have since been issued on CD.

Monterose, J.R.

b. Frank Anthony Monterose, 19 January 1927, Detroit, Michigan, USA, d. 26 September 1993. After gaining experience playing tenor saxophone in a number of mid-western bands of the 40s, He joined **Buddy Rich** in the early 50s. He became known on the New York bebop scene, playing and recording with a wide range of musicians, including **Charles Mingus** and **Kenny Dorham**. Although he has worked elsewhere, including a spell of some three years in Belgium, Monterose has chosen to spend much of his career in and around New York and Albany, thus limiting his international reputation. A soft-spoken, introverted individual, Monterose plays with a rich and warm sound and in an intensely melodic style.

Albums: *J. R. Monterose* (1956), *Straight Ahead* (1960), *In Action* (Studio 4 1964), *Live In Albany* (Uptown 1979), *Luan* (1979), with Tommy Flanagan *...And A Little Pleasure* (Uptown 1981), *Bebop Loose And Live* (1981), *The Message* (Fresh Sounds 1993).

Montez, Chris

b. Christopher Montanez, 17 January 1943, Los Angeles, California, USA. Teenage vocalist Montez was discovered by impresario Jim Lee in 1961, and having joined the latter's Monogram label, enjoyed an international hit the following year with 'Let's Dance'. This exciting, Lee-penned single, redolent of the Hispanic 'latino-rock' style of **Ritchie Valens** sold over 1 million copies and climbed to number 2 in the UK. A follow-up, 'Some Kinda Fun', reached the UK Top 10 in 1963, but a three year hiatus ensued before the singer resurfaced on **A&M** in the US with a version of the much-covered 'Call Me'. The charmingly simple 'The More I See You', gave Montez a second UK Top 3 entry, while minor US successes followed with 'There Will Never Be Another You' and 'Time After Time'. Re-released in the UK in 1972, 'Let's Dance' confirmed its timeless appeal by reaching the UK Top 10.

Albums: *Let's Dance And Have Some Kinda Fun!!!* (1963), *The More I See You/Call Me* (1966), *Time After Time* (1966), *Foolin' Around* (1967), *Watch What Happens* (1968).

Montgomery, Bob

b. 1936, Lambasas, Texas, USA. While attending Lubbock's Hutchinson High School, this rhythm guitarist was partnered by **Buddy Holly** as a 'Singer of Western and Bop' when entertaining at parents' evenings, parties and, indeed, 'anywhere we could get to a microphone'. Sometimes augmented by the younger Larry Welborn on double bass, they were heard regularly on local radio with Montgomery as main vocalist in a repertoire that embraced his (and Holly's) own compositions. Among these were 'Flower Of My Heart' and other items taped as demos in the mid-50s. With superimposed backing, these would be released after Holly's death gave them historical importance, because it was Buddy who was singled out by **Decca Records** in 1956 as the most commercial talent. However, not begrudging him his luck, Bob continued to write songs with his friend, among them 'Wishing', 'Love's Made A Fool Of You' and other Holly hits. After serving as engineer in Norman Petty's

Clovis studio, Montgomery moved to Nashville in 1959 where, as a songwriter, he provided **Wilma Burgess** with 'Misty Blue' (revived in 1976 by Dorothy Moore), 'Two Of A Kind' (written with Earl Sinks) for Sue Thompson and **Roy Orbison**, and 1965's 'Wind Me Up' for **Cliff Richard**. Among other recipients of Montgomery pieces were **Bob Luman** and **Mel Tillis**. In 1966 he became a United Artists staff producer. His most enduring labours in this sphere were for **Bobby Goldsboro** (including 'Honey' and 'Summer The First Time') but other ventures into what was to be named 'country-pop' included records by Bill Dees, **Johnny Darrell**, **Buddy Knox**, Del Reeves and Earl Richards. In the early 70s Montgomery founded House Of Gold, one of Nashville's most respected music publishing concerns.
Albums with Buddy Holly: *Holly In The Hills* (1965, re-issued as *Wishing* in 1968), *Western And Bop* (1977).

Montgomery, John Michael

b. 20 January 1965, Danville, Kentucky, USA. Montgomery arrived on the country music scene in 1993 with a debut album, *Life's A Dance*, that became the only million-seller on the country charts by a new artist that year. Its title track was a number 1 single, too. *Kickin' It Up* was also number 1 on both the US Country and Adult Contemporary charts, and produced two more successful singles, 'I Swear' and 'Rope The Moon'. However, Montgomery was unchanged by his success, and refused to leave Lexington to go to Nashville. Instead he continued to enjoy traditional rock 'n' roll pursuits such as fishing and golfing. His musical talent was initially encouraged by his father, who performed in a local country band and taught his son his first chords. Montgomery joined the family band as guitarist, before taking the lead singing role when his parents divorced. After that he made a frugal living on the local honky tonk scene as a solo artist playing what he referred to as 'working man's country'. Eventually, **Atlantic Records** signed him, although it was Montgomery himself rather than the record company who rejected his own material for inclusion on his debut ('Mine just weren't good enough'). There were problems during the recording, typified in the anecdote about a late-night call to the head of Atlantic that resulted in a change of producer. Atlantic's faith in their artist was subsequently rewarded by Montgomery's swift rise.
Albums: *Life's A Dance* (Atlantic 1993), *Kickin' It Up* (Atlantic 1994), *John Michael Montgomery* (Atlantic 1995).
Videos: *I Swear* (1993), *Kickin' It Up* (1994).

Montgomery, Little Brother

b. Eurreal Wilford Montgomery, 18 April 1906, Kentwood, Louisiana, USA, d. 6 September 1985, Chicago, Illinois, USA. Impressed by the piano players who visited his parents' house, including **Jelly Roll Morton** and **Cooney Vaughan**, Little Brother began playing at the age of five. At the age of 11 he ran away, and worked as a musician for the rest of his life. He played the southern jukes and lumber camps as a solo blues pianist, singing in his unmistakable voice, nasal and with a strong vibrato, yet somehow pleading and wistful. With Friday Ford and Dehlco Robert he developed 'The Forty-Fours' into one of the most complex themes in the repertoire, calling his own version 'Vicksburg Blues'. In the 20s Montgomery played jazz in New Orleans with Clarence Desdune and toured Mississippi with **Danny Barker;** he also worked briefly with **Buddy Petit,** and on the blues side toured with **Big Joe Williams**. In 1928 Brother headed for Chicago, playing blues at rent parties with **Blind Blake** among others, and recording as an accompanist in 1930, under his own name in 1931. During the 30s he returned south to Jackson, Mississippi, from where he travelled as leader of the jazz-playing Southland Troubadours until 1939. He continued to play blues, and on a single day in 1935 recorded no fewer than 18 titles and five accompaniments to other singers for Bluebird, including his instrumental masterpieces 'Shreveport Farewell' and 'Farish Street Jive', the latter a technically daunting blend of boogie and stride. In 1941 Montgomery settled in Chicago. He worked with **Kid Ory** at Carnegie Hall in 1949, and was for a long while a member of the Franz Jackson Band; he also continued to work solo (including a residency at an Irish tavern in the 60s) and to record, and was on the first releases by **Otis Rush** and **Magic Sam**. In 1960 he visited Europe for the first time, and began recording for a white audience. As well as promoting young protegees like Elaine McFarland (later 'Spanky' of **Spanky And Our Gang**)and Jeanne Carroll, Montgomery recorded himself at home, issuing material on his FM label, named from the initials of himself and his devoted wife Janet Floberg, whom he married in 1967. With her encouragement and support, he had active until not long before his death. Montgomery was a consummate musician, with a huge repertoire and an excellent memory, but his recordings mostly reflect the preferences, first of record companies in the 30s, then of the white audience of the 60s and after; he was a giant of the blues, but it should not be forgotten that he was also a capable pop singer, and an excellent jazz pianist.
Selected albums: *Tasty Blues* (1960), *Blues* (1961), *Little Brother Montgomery* (1961), *Farro Street Jive* (1961), *Church Songs* (1962), *Chicago: The Living Legends* (1962), *After Hour Blues* (1969), 1930-1969 (1971), *Little Brother Montgomery* (1972), *Bajes Copper Station* (1973), *Crescent City Blues* (1977), *Tishomingo Blues* (1980), *Unissued Recordings Vol. 1* (1987), *Unissued Recordings Vol. 2* (1988), *Little Brother Montgomery At Home* (1990).

Montgomery, Marian

b. 1934, Natchez, Mississippi, USA. Montgomery quit school to sing on television in Atlanta, Georgia. After working in advertising and publishing, performing in plays and singing in strip joints and jazz clubs, she became an established cabaret performer. She moved to the UK in 1965 to sing at a new London club, the Cool Elephant, with the **John Dankworth** Band. That same year she married composer and musical director **Laurie Holloway**. Possessing a voice which has been likened to 'having a long, cool glass of mint julep on a Savannah balcony', she expanded her career with a starring role in the 1969 West End revival of *Anything Goes*, and frequent appearances on radio and television, as well as concerts and cabaret in the UK and abroad. Her one-woman show was televised by the BBC in 1975. Besides her musical association with Holloway, she successfully collaborated with classical composer/pianist Richard Rodney Bennett on several projects, including *Puttin' On The Ritz*, *Surprise Surprise* and *Town And Country*. With an instantly recognizable, relaxed and intimate style, she has become one of a handful of American artists to take up permanent residence in the UK.

Selected albums: *Swings For Winners And Losers* (1963), *Let There Be Marian Montgomery* (1963), *Lovin' Is Livin'* (1965), *Marian Montgomery On Stage* (1979), with Richard Rodney Bennett *Town And Country* (1978), with Bennett *Surprise Surprise* (1981), with Bennett *Puttin' On The Ritz* (1984), *I Gotta Right To Sing* (1988), *Sometimes In The Night* (1989), *Nice And Easy* (1989).

Montgomery, Melba

b. 14 October 1938, Iron City, Tennessee, USA. Born into a musical family, Montgomery's father ran a church choir and both her brothers, Carl and Earl, became country songwriters, often supplying her with material. In 1958 she and her brothers were finalists in a nationwide talent contest sponsored by Pet Milk - another finalist was **Johnny Tillotson**. Her success led to an appearance on the *Grand Ole Opry* where she impressed **Roy Acuff**. He added her to his roadshow and she spent four years covering the USA and its military bases abroad. In 1962 she recorded two singles, 'Happy You, Lonely Me' and 'Just Another Fool Along The Way', for Lonzo and Oscar's Nugget label. She recorded prolifically for United Artists and Musicor, although she made the US country charts with 'Hall Of Shame' and 'The Greatest One Of All', Melba is better known for her duets with **George Jones** ('We Must Have Been Out Of Her Minds', which she wrote) and **Gene Pitney** ('Baby, Ain't That Fine'). Substantial successes eluded her at **Capitol**, although she recorded duets with **Charlie Louvin**, notably 'Something To Brag About'. She gave **Elektra** a number 1 country single with 'No Charge', written by Harlan Howard, although it was covered for the UK market by **J.J. Barrie**. She has spent the past decade raising her family.

Albums: with George Jones *What's In Our Heart* (1963), *Melba Montgomery - America's Number One Country And Western Girl Singer* (1964), *Down Home* (1964), with Jones *Bluegrass Hootenanny* (1964), *I Can't Get Used To Being Lonely* (1965), with Jones *Blue Moon Of Kentucky* (1966), *Country Girl* (1966), *Hallelujah Road* (1966), with Gene Pitney *Being Together* (1966), with Jones *Close Together* (1966), *The Mood I'm In* (1967), *Melba Toast* (1967), *Don't Keep Me Lonely Too Long* (1967), *I'm Just Living* (1967), with Jones *Let's Get Together/Party Pickin'* (1967), with Jones *Great Country Duets Of All Time* (1969), *The Big Country World Of Melba Montgomery* (1969), with Charlie Louvin *Somethin' To Brag About* (1971), with Louvin *Baby, You've Got What It Takes* (1971), *Melba Montgomery - No Charge* (1973), *No Charge* (1974), *Aching Breaking Heart* (1975), *Don't Let The Good Times Fool You* (1975), *The Greatest Gift Of All* (1975), *Melba* (1976), *Melba Montgomery* (1978), *Melba Montgomery* (1982).

Montgomery, Monk

b. William Montgomery, 10 October 1921, Indianapolis, Indiana, USA, d. 20 May 1982. One of three musical brothers, Montgomery began playing relatively late in life. After first taking up the acoustic bass he switched to the electric bass guitar in 1951. He toured with **Lionel Hampton**, recording in Paris in 1953, then became a member of the Montgomery-Johnson Quintet, which included his brothers Buddy, a pianist and vibraphonist, and **Wes Montgomery**. In the mid-50s he settled in San Francisco, often working with Buddy and less frequently with Wes. Montgomery continued playing throughout the 60s and 70s with leaders such as **Cal Tjader, Hampton Hawes** and **Red Norvo**. In the late 70s and early 80s he worked in Las Vegas, Nevada, as a studio and show band musician, as a radio disc jockey and as the founder and organizer of the Las Vegas Jazz Society.

Albums: with Lionel Hampton *He Swings The Most* (1953), with Hampton *The Complete 1953 Paris Session* (1953), *Jazz Showcase* (1957), with Wes Montgomery *Montgomeryland* (1958-59), *Grooveyard* (1961), with Hampton Hawes *The Green Leaves Of Summer* (1964), *It's Never Too Late* (c.1969), *Reality* (1974).

Montgomery, Wes

b. John Leslie Montgomery, 6 March 1923, Indianapolis, Indiana, USA, d. 15 June 1968. Montgomery was inspired to take up the guitar after hearing records by **Charlie Christian**. Nearly 20 years old at the time, he taught himself to play by adapting what he heard on records to what he could accomplish himself. Guided in part by Christian's example, but also by the need to find a way of playing which did not alienate his neighbours, he evolved a uniquely quiet style. Using the soft part of his thumb instead of a plectrum or the fingers, and playing the melody line simultaneously in two registers, Montgomery was already a distinctive stylist by the time he began to work with local bands . In 1948 he joined **Lionel Hampton**, touring and recording. In the early 50s he returned to Indianapolis and began playing with his brothers Buddy and **Monk Montgomery** in the Montgomery-Johnson Quintet (the other members being Alonzo and Robert Johnson). During an after-hours session at a local club, the visiting **Cannonball Adderley** asked him if he would like a record date. On Adderley's recommendation, Montgomery was recorded by Riverside in a series of trio albums which featured artists such as **Hank Jones** and **Ron Carter**. These albums attracted considerable attention and Montgomery quickly became one of the most talked about and respected guitarists in jazz. In the early 60s he worked with his brothers in Northern California and also played with **John Coltrane**. Further recordings, this time with a large string orchestra, broadened Montgomery's horizons and appealed to the non-jazz public. However, despite such commercially successful albums as *Movin' Wes*, *Bumpin'*, *Goin' Out Of My Head* and *A Day In The Life*, he continued to play jazz in small groups with his brothers and with **Wynton Kelly**, **Herb Alpert**, Harold Mabern and others. In 1965 he visited Europe, playing club and festival dates in England, Spain and elsewhere. His career was at its height when he died suddenly in June 1968. An outstanding guitarist with an enormous influence upon his contemporaries and countless successors, Montgomery's highly personal style was developed deliberately from Christian, and unwittingly shadowed earlier conceptions by musicians such as **Django Reinhardt**. In Montgomery's case he stumbled upon these methods not with deliberate intent but through what jazz writer Alun Morgan has described as 'a combination of naivety and good neighbourliness'.

Selected albums: *Far Wes* (1958-59), *The Wes Montgomery Trio/A Dynamic New Sound* (Original Jazz Classics 1959), *Movin' Along* (Original Jazz Classics 1960), *The Incredible Jazz Guitar Of Wes Montgomery* (Original Jazz Classics 1960), *So Much Guitar* (Original Jazz Classics 1961), *Far Wes* (Pacific 1961), *Full House* (Original Jazz Classics 1962), *Fusion* (Original Jazz Classics 1963), *Portrait Of Wes* (Original Jazz Classics 1963), *The Alternative Wes Montgomery* (Milestone 1960-63 recordings), *Boss Guitar* (Original Jazz Classics 1964), *Wes Montgomery Plays The Blues* (1964-66), *Goin' Out Of My Head* (1965), *Bumpin'* (1965), *'Round Midnight* (1965), *Straight No Chaser* (1965), *Movin' Wes* (Verve 1965), *Live In Paris* (1965), *Smokin' At The Half Note* (1965), *Tequila* (Verve 1966), *A Day In The Life* (1967), *Road Song* (1968). Compilation: *Verve Jazz Masters Wes Montgomery* (Verve 2-CD set).

Further reading: *Wes Montgomery*, Adrian Ingram.

Montoliu, Tete

b. Vincente Montoliu, 28 March 1933, Barcelona, Spain. Blind from birth, pianist Montoliu studied classical music as a child, but at the start of his teens was already listening to jazz and later played with **Don Byas**. In the mid-50s he regularly sat in with visiting American artists, including **Lionel Hampton**. By the end of the decade he had ventured north to play at a number of important European jazz festivals and had also played in Scandinavia. In the late 60s he played in New York, thereafter establishing an international reputation as a gifted soloist with enormous technical gifts which never obstruct his ability to generate a powerful swing. Among the musicians with whom he has worked are **Ben Webster**, **Anthony Braxton**, **Roland Kirk** and **Dexter Gordon**.

Selected albums: *The Tete Montoliu Trio* (1965), *Blues For Nuria* (1968), *Ben Webster Meets Don Byas In The Black Forest* (1968), *Interpreta A Serrat* (1969), *Ricordando A Line* (c.1971), *Songs For Love* (Enja 1971), *That's All* (Steeplechase 1971), *Body And Soul* (1971), *Lush Life* (Steeplechase 1971), *Temi Latino Americani* (1973), *Temi Brasiliani* (1973), *Music For Perla* (Steeplechase 1974), *Catalonian Fire* (Steeplechase 1974), *Tete* (Steeplechase 1974), *Vampyria* (1974), *Tete A Tete* (Steeplechase 1976), *Tootie's Tempo* (Steeplechase 1976), *Words Of Love* (1976), *Blues For Myself* (1977), *Yellow Dolphin Street* (Timeless 1977), *Secret Love* (1977), *Boleros* (1977), *Catalonian Folksongs* (Timeless 1977), *Al Palau* (1979), *Live At The Keystone Corner* (Timeless 1979), *Lunch In LA* (1980), *Catalonian Nights Vols 1-2* (Steeplechase 1980), *Boston Concert* (Steeplechase 1980), *I Wanna Talk About You* (1980), *Face To Face* (1982), *Carmina* (1984), *The Music I Like To Play Vols 1-2* (Soul Note 1986), with Peter King *New Year's Morning '89* (1989), *Sweet N' Lovely Vols 1-2* (Fresh Sound 1990), *The Man From Barcelona* (Timeless 1991), *A Spanish Treasure* (Concord 1992).

Montrell, Roy

b. 27 February 1928, New Orleans, Louisiana, USA. Guitarist Montrell joined **Roy Milton**'s Solid Senders upon his discharge from the US Army in 1951, but soon returned to New Orleans where he formed a trio called the Little Hawkettes, which worked various clubs along Bourbon Street. After touring with **Lloyd Price,** he began to do session work in New Orleans for Ace and **Specialty,** recording with artist including Edgar Blanchard and **Little Richard**. He only had two releases under his own name: one on Specialty in 1956 - the black rock 'n' roll classic 'Ooh Wow That Mellow Saxophone' - and another on Minit in 1960. Virtually the New Orleans session guitarist by 1960, Montrell played with **Allen Toussaint**'s band and **Harold Battiste**'s AFO combo, and in 1962 he took over from **Walter Nelson** as **Fats Domino**'s guitarist, becoming Domino's bandleader in the late 60s.

Montreux International Jazz Festival

Held at the Montreux Casino over 17 days in July, since its opening in 1967 the Montreux Jazz Festival has become one of the leading European festivals. Attracting large audiences and a host of major artists, the festival has benefitted through close association with record companies, notably Pablo, and regular filming for transmission over television networks in many countries. Among the recorded results have been masterly sets by the likes of **Dizzy Gillespie, Monty Alexander** and **Benny Carter**. More fusion-orientated than most jazz festivals, at times Montreux has proved less than wholly attractive to hardcore jazz fans but high standards of performance and presentation have helped it maintain its rightful place as a major venue.

Montrose

After working with **Van Morrison**, **Boz Scaggs** and **Edgar Winter**, guitarist **Ronnie Montrose** (b. Colorado, USA) formed Montrose in San Francisco in the autumn of 1973. Comprising vocalist **Sammy Hagar**, bassist Bill Church and drummer Denny Carmassi, they signed to **Warner Brothers** and released their self-titled debut the following year. Produced by **Ted Templeman**, *Montrose* was an album that set new standards in heavy metal; the combination of Hagar's raucous vocals with the guitarist's abrasive guitar sound was to become a blueprint against which new bands judged themselves for years to come. Including the classic recordings 'Bad Motor Scooter', 'Space Station No. 5' and 'Rock The Nation', the album still ranks as one of the cornerstones of the hard rock genre. Alan Fitzgerald replaced Bill Church on bass before the recording of the follow-up, *Paper Money*. Hagar was fired shortly after the tour to support it was completed. Bob James and Jim Alcivar were drafted in on vocals and keyboards, but they never recaptured the magic of the debut release. Hagar and Ronnie Montrose, the principal protagonists, would go on to solo careers, the latter joined by several ex-members of Montrose the band in **Gamma**. Carmassie would, in addition, re-emerge in the 90s as drummer for the **Coverdale/Page** project.

Albums: *Montrose* (Warners 1974), *Paper Money* (Warners 1975), *Warner Brothers Presents Montrose* (Warners 1975), *Jump On It* (Warners 1976).

Montrose, Ronnie

After rock guitarist Ronnie Montrose (b. Colorado, USA) dissolved his own band **Montrose** in 1976, he decided to pursue a solo career. Switching styles from hard to jazz-rock, he released *Open Fire*, an instrumental album that was unpopular with fans and critics alike. Disillusioned by this, he formed **Gamma**, who recorded three albums between 1979 and 1982. When Gamma ground to a halt in 1983, Ronnie recorded *Territory*, another low-key solo set. In 1987 he teamed up with vocalist Johnny Edwards (later **Foreigner**) and drummer James Kottak (later of **Kingdom Come**), both ex-**Buster Brown** and ex-Gamma bassist Glen Letsch. *Mean* was the result, an uncompromising hard rock record that had the guts and musical firepower of Montrose's debut, released 13 years earlier. This line-up was short-lived, with Johnny Bee Bedanjek replacing Edwards and the addition of synthesizer player Pat Feehan, before *The Speed Of Sound* was recorded. Adopting a more sophisticated, melody conscious approach, it lost much of the ground that had been recaptured by the previous album. Ronnie decided to go solo again, producing *The Diva Station* in 1990. This was a semi-instrumental affair and incorporated rock, metal, jazz and soul influences, including an astonishing version of the old **Walker Brothers**' hit, 'Stay With Me Baby'. Ronnie Montrose remains an extremely gifted guitarist, but as yet he has found it difficult to channel his energies in a direction which also brings commercial rewards. A situation which has seen him spend progressively more time on production work.

Albums: *Open Fire* (Warners 1978), *Territory* (Passport 1986), *Mean* (Enigma 1987), *The Speed Of Sound* (Enigma 1988), *The Diva Station* (Roadrunner 1990).

Monyaka

This six-piece Jamaican-born, Brooklyn, New York, USA based reggae act was led by guitarist/vocalist Errol Moore. At the time of their hit in 1983 other group members included Beres Barnet (guitar/vocals), Paul Henton (bass/vocals), Richard Bertram (drums/percussion), William Brown and John Allen (keyboards). Formed in 1974 as the Soul Supersonics they backed visiting reggae stars and released their first single, 'Rocking Time', in 1977. They followed this with *Classical Roots*, both records being released in the USA on their Hevyaka label. Under the new name Monyaka (Swahili for 'good luck') they recorded 'Stand Up Strong' in 1982. A year later, with just three original members left, they had a UK Top 20 hit with 'Go Deh Yaka'(patois for 'go to the top'), which cleverly fused reggae and contemporary R&B. The follow-up 'Reggae-matic Funk' failed to continue the interest and this unique band joined the ranks of reggae one-hit wonders.

Album: *Classical Roots* (Monyaka 1977).

Mood Six

Mood Six were central to the short-lived UK psychedelic revival that swept London's West End in the early 80s, and had evolved from various units with mod leanings. Drummer Simon Smith (b. 3 December 1958, Merton Park, London, England; ex-**Merton Parkas**), songwriter Tony Conway (b. 28 February

1958, Newbury, Berkshire, England) and Andy Godfrey (b. 28 December 1957, Ilford, Essex, England) were both drawn from Security Risk, Paul Shurey and Guy Morley came from **VIP's** leaving only Phil Ward without high profile previous experience. The group debuted on WEA's 1982's new psychedelia compilation, *A Splash Of Colour.* The band contributed two tracks, the catchy 'Plastic Flowers' and the atmospheric 'Just Like A Dream', although both owed as much to late 60s pop as psychedelia. The resulting publicity surrounding that scene led to an interview on BBC television's *Nationwide* and a deal with **EMI**. 'Hanging Around' (later covered by **Toni Basil**) became the band's first single but was commercially disappointing and the follow-up, 'She's Too Far (Out)', was scrapped as the band were dropped from the label. Mood Six re-emerged early in 1985 on the psychedelic reissue label Psycho, with *The Difference Is...*, which saw the introduction of Chris O'Connor. This was followed in May by a re-recording of 'Plastic Flowers'. The band then moved to the **Cherry Red** label for 1986's classy, 'What Have You Ever Done?', drawn from *A Matter Of!*. Unfortunately, although Mood Six were writing endearing pop music, the final sound was occasionally bland, lacking that spark of originality. Keyboard player Simon Taylor (b. 28 December 1960, Redhill, Surrey, England) was inducted before the release of 'I Saw The Light' in May 1987, after which the band's relationship with Cherry Red fizzled out, and Phil Ward was ousted from the group. Simon Smith recently turned up in **Small Town Parade**, another band with strong mod connections, as did Taylor, though Mood Six continued in a low-key manner. Phil Ward's replacement on vocals would be Gerry O'Sullivan (b. 25 March 1963, Paddington, London, England). A new album was released in 1993 on the band's own label.

Albums: *The Difference Is...* (Psycho 1985), *A Matter Of!* (Cherry Red 1986), *And This Is It* (Lost Recording Company 1993).

Moodswings

Formed by indie stalwarts JFT 'Fred' Hood, a drummer and friend of Johnny Marr (**Smiths**), plus producer Grant Showbiz (the **Fall**, Smiths), this was still a decidedly house-aimed project. They first interceded in the dance scene with the release of 1990's 'Spiritual High', a cover of the **Diana Ross** song with additional lyrics interspersed from the **Beatles**' 'Tomorrow Never Knows', with vocals from **Chrissie Hynde**. After appearing on a blue label it was snapped up by **Zoom** before **Arista** gave it a big push and stock release in 1991. However, instead of building on the acclaim they slaved over their debut album for five years before release.

Album: *Moodfood* (Arista 1993).

Moody Blues

The lengthy career of the Moody Blues has come in two distinct phases. The first from 1963-67, when they were a tough R&B-influenced unit, and the second from 1967 to the present, where they are regarded as rock dinosaurs performing a blend of pop utilizing symphonic themes which has been given many labels, among them pomp-rock, classical-rock and art-rock. The original band was formed in 1964 by **Denny Laine** (b. Brian Hines, 29 October 1944, Jersey; vocals, harmonica, guitar), Mike Pinder (b. 12 December 1942, Birmingham, England; piano, keyboards), Ray Thomas (b. 29 December 1942, Stourport on Severn, England; flute, vocals, harmonica), Graeme Edge (b. 30 March 1941, Rochester, Staffordshire, England; drums) and Clint Warwick (b. 25 June 1940, Birmingham, England; bass). During their formative months they established a strong London club following, and soon received their big break, as so many others did, performing live on the influential television show *Ready Steady Go*. A few months later their Bessie Banks cover, 'Go Now' topped the UK charts, complete with its striking piano introduction and solo. Although the single made the US Top 10, their commercial fortunes were on an immediate decline, although their following releases were impeccable.

Their splendid debut *The Magnificent Moodies* failed to sell as anticipated. Warwick and Laine departed in 1966 to be replaced by Justin Hayward (b. 14 October 1946, Swindon, Wiltshire, England) and John Lodge (b. 20 July 1945, Birmingham, England). So began phase two, which debuted with Hayward's classic, 'Nights In White Satin'. The accompanying *Days Of Future Passed* was an ambitious orchestral project with Peter Knight conducting the London Festival Orchestra and Tony Clark producing. The album was a massive success and started a run that continued through a further five albums, all involving Knight and Clark. The increased use of the mellotron gave an orchestrated feel to much of their work, and while they became phenomenally popular, they also received a great deal of criticism. During this period they founded **Threshold Records,** their own record label, and in 1973 reached the UK Top 10 with a re-entry for 'Nights In White Satin'.

The band parted company in 1974 to allow each member to indulge in spin-off projects. Hayward and Lodge became the Blue Jays, with great success, Thomas released *From Mighty Oaks* and Edge teamed with **Adrian Gurvitz** for *Kick Off Your Muddy Boots*. The group reunited for *Octave*, which became another huge hit, although shortly after its release Pinder decided to quit the business; he had been the only band member not to release a solo project. Further discontent ensued when Clark resigned. Patrick Moraz

from **Yes** and **Refugee** joined the band as Hayward's 'Forever Autumn' hit the charts. This track was taken from the **Jeff Wayne** epic, *The War Of The Worlds*. Each subsequent release has met with predictable glory both in Europe and America. The Moodies march on with the comforting knowledge that they will fill concert halls and sell vast amounts of records until the days of future have passed.
Albums: *The Magnificent Moodies* (1965), *Days Of Future Past* (1967), *In Search Of The Lost Chord* (1968), *On The Threshold Of A Dream* (1969), *To Our Children's Children* (1969), *A Question Of Balance* (1970), *Every Good Boy Deserves Favour* (1971), *Seventh Sojourn* (1972), *Caught Live + 5* (1977), *Octave* (1978), *Long Distance Voyager* (1981), *The Present* (1983), *The Other Side Of Life* (1986), *Sur La Mer* (1988), *Keys Of The Kingdom* (1991), *A Night At Red Rocks With The Colorado Symphony Orchestra* (Polydor/Threshold 1993). Compilations: *This Is The Moody Blues* (1974), *Out Of This World* (1979), *Voices In The Sky - The Best Of The Moody Blues* (1985), *Greatest Hits* (1989). Solo albums: Justin Hayward and John Lodge *Blue Jays* (1975); Ray Thomas *From Mighty Oaks* (1975), *Hope Wishes And Dreams* (1976); Mike Pinder *The Promise* (1976); John Lodge *Natural Avenue* (1977); Graeme Edge Band *Kick Off Your Muddy Boots* (1975), *Paradise Ballroom* (1977); Justin Hayward *Songwriter* (1977), *Night Flight* (1980), *Moving Mountains* (1985), *Classic Blue* (1989); Denny Laine *Japanese Tears* (1980), *Hometown Girls* (1985), *Weep For Love* (1985), *Wings On My Feet* (1987), *Lonely Road* (1988), *Master Suite* (1988), *Holly Days* (c.80s).
Videos: *Cover Story* (1990), *Star Portrait* (1991), *Legend Of A Band* (1991), *Live At Red Rocks* (1993).

Moody Boyz

Tony Thorpe's incarnation of the dub-house ethic, his most high-profile banner since 80s experimentalists **400 Blows**. After the demise of that tempestuous outfit he formed Warrior Records. This was superceded by his BPM label, which won its spurs releasing compilations like *Acid Beats* (1988), the musical tastes determined by Thorpe's immersion in the club scene (the legendary Spectrum nights in particular). Later he became in-house remixer for the **KLF**, before the Moody Boyz' name was first employed on a series of acid-inspired 12-inch releases such as 'Boogie Woogie Music', 'King Of The Funky Zulus' and the *Journey Into Dubland* EP. His debut long playing set as the Moody Boyz combined his traditional love of reggae bass with a strong philosophy of black emancipation, particularly on 'Fight Back (27-4-94)', dedicated to the democracy movement's victory in South Africa. There were also intriguing collaborations with **Black Dog** on 'Elite Doodz Presents Snooze', and the Italian Vibraphone set-up. Thorpe has also recorded as Voyager, House Addicts and Urban Jungle, and remixed for **Joi**, **Bocca Juniors** and **Fun-Da-Mental**. He also provides Channel 4 with much of its incidental music.
Albums: *Product Of The Environment* (Guerilla 1994). As Voyager: *Transmission* (Underworld/Virgin 1993).

Moody, Clyde

b. 19 September 1915, Cherokee, North Carolina, USA, d. 7 April 1989, Nashville, Tennessee, USA. Raised in Marion, North Carolina, Moody had learned the guitar by the age of eight and soon after became a professional musician. He left home when he was 14. He first worked with Jay Hugh Hall, initially as Bill And Joe on WSPA Spartanburg, South Carolina in 1929 but later with Steve Ledford, they became the Happy-Go-Lucky Boys. (He also played some semi-professional baseball with Asheville, South Carolina). Between 1937 and 1940, while continuing to appear as a duo, they also played with Wade Mainer's Sons Of The Mountaineers and recorded for Bluebird, both as a duo and with the group. They performed on many Carolina radio stations until they left Wade Mainer and joined his brother, **J.E. Mainer**, in Alabama. In 1941 Moody had a disagreement with both Hall and Mainer, and left to join **Bill Monroe** back in North Carolina. During his time with Monroe, Moody appeared on various recordings including the classic version of his own song 'Six White Horses', which was coupled with 'Mule Skinner Blues' as Monroe's Blue Grass Boys' first Bluebird single release. Moody soon left, and hiring **Lester Flatt** as his partner, he worked WHBB Burlington as the Happy-Go-Lucky Boys; however, in 1942, he rejoined Monroe and stayed with him until 1945. When he finally left, his place was taken by Flatt. Moody worked with **Roy Acuff** for a short time but soon went solo and made his first solo recordings that year. He played the *Grand Ole Opry* during the late 40s but left to work on early television in Washington DC. His 1947 recording of 'Shenandoah Waltz' (co-written with Chubby Wise) is reputed to be the top selling record for the King label, having had sales in excess of three million. The song is now a bluegrass standard, although most experts would say the Moody's original version is more that of a country ballad singer, such as **Red Foley**, than that of a bluegrass artist. He began to specialize in waltz numbers, having such success that he acquired the nickname of The Hillbilly Waltz King. In 1948, he had Top 20 US country chart hits with 'Carolina Waltz' and 'Red Roses Tied In Blue' and in 1950, his recording of 'I Love You Because' reached number 8. He left King in 1951 and recorded for **Decca** but from 1957 to the early 60s, he was less active on the music scene. He returned to North Carolina, where he developed business interests in mobile homes and for a long time hosted his own daily television show *Carolina In The Morning* in Raleigh. During the 60s, he recorded for Starday, Wango and Little Darlin'. He returned to Nashville in 1971 and once more became involved with the music scene. He guested on the *Opry*, played various bluegrass festivals,

toured extensively with his friend Rambling Tommy Scott's Medicine Show and recorded for Old Homestead. During the mid-70s, his health began to suffer but he continued to perform whenever he was able, until he died in Nashville on 7 April 1989.
Albums: *The Best Of Clyde Moody* (1964), *All Time Country & Western Waltzes* (1969), *Moody's Blues* (1972), *A Country Tribute To Fred Rose* (1976), with Tommy Scott *We've Played Every Place More Than Once* (1978), with Scott *Early Country Favorites* (1980).

Moody, James

b. 26 February 1925, Savannah, Georgia, USA. Beginning to play saxophones in his mid-teens, Moody developed his abilities as an instrumentalist during a spell in the American armed forces. Discharged in 1946, he joined **Dizzy Gillespie**'s big band (on tenor saxophone), later touring Europe (mostly playing alto saxophone). His 1949 recording of 'I'm In The Mood For Love' became a hit and greatly enhanced his reputation at home and abroad. During the 50s he led a number of small groups, some of which were R&B oriented. In the 50s he also began to play the flute. By the 60s he had become a major figure on the USA club scene and the international festival circuit. An able and melodic soloist on all three of his instruments, Moody is especially effective on ballads.
Selected albums: *Sax Talk* (Vogue 1952), *Hi Fi Party* (Original Jazz Classics 1955), *Wail Moody Wail*(Original Jazz Classics 1955), *Flute'n The Blues* (1956), *Moody's Mood For Blues* (Original Jazz Classics 1956), *Moody's Mood For Love* (1956), *Easy Living* (1956-63), *Last Train From Overbrook* (1958), *James Moody* i (1959), *Hey! It's James Moody* (1959), *Moody With Strings* (1961), *Cookin' The Blues* (1961), *Another Bag* (1962), *Great Day* (1963), *Comin' On Strong* (1963), *Running The Gamut* (1964), *Group Therapy* (1964), *The Blues And Other Colours* (1967), *Don't Look Away Now* (1969), *Heritage Hum* (c.1971), *Lush Life* (1971), *Too Heavy For Words* (1971), *Never Again!* (1972), *Feelin' It Together* (1973), *James Moody* ii (1973), *James Moody* iii (c.1975), *Beyond This World* (1977), *Something Special* (Novus 1987), with Stan Getz *Tenor Contrasts* (Esquire 1988), *Moving Forward* (Novus 1988), *Sweet And Lovely* (Novus 1990), *Honey* (Novus 1991). Compilations: *James Moody And His Modernists* (1948), *Bebop Revisited Vol. 4* (1948-50), *Bebop Enters Sweden* (1949), *The James Moody Story* (1951-53).

Moog, Robert A.

b. 1934, USA. Moog was responsible for designing the first commercially viable keyboard synthesiser. He started designing electronic musical instruments as a teenager and later trained as an electrical engineer. He began synthesiser research at New York University in the early 60s and with Donald Buchla, developed a system of voltage control where each note on a synthesiser keyboard produced a different voltage. By 1967, the Moog synthesiser was fully developed. It came to public attention through the 1968 recording, *Switched On Bach* by **Walter Carlos**. Although other firms like ARP and Buchla brought out their own versions of the synthesiser, Moog stuck as the generic name for the instrument. Among its earliest exponents were **Keith Emerson** and **Jan Hammer**. Moog's most commercially successful product was the mini-Moog launched in 1971. This was suitably for use in live performance and was capable of 'bending' notes in the same way as a guitar. Later models included the Polymoog (1976), a polyphonic synthesiser (it could play more than one note at a time), the pedal-operated Taurus system - used by **Rush** in the 80s - and the Memory Moog. Although the company did not join the trend towards digital synthesizers, **Herbie Hancock**, Hammer and **Gary Wright** were among those involved with its Source model. In the early 70s the Moog company was acquired by Norlin, owners of the Gibson guitar operation.

Moon Martin

b. John Martin, 1950, Oklahoma, USA. Emerging in 1979 with a style somewhere between new wave and nouveau 50s rock 'n' roll, Martin was nicknamed 'Moon' because he frequently employed lunar imagery in his songs. He began playing lead guitar in a straight C&W band Cec Wilson And The Panhandlers, then joined a **Beatles**-imitation group followed by a rockabilly unit called the Disciples. After moving to Los Angeles in the late 60s, he undertook session work for **Del Shannon** and **Jackie DeShannon**. In the meantime, the Disciples changed their name to Southwind and recorded three albums, all in a country rock vein. Martin continued his extra-curricular work, contributing to **Linda Ronstadt**'s *Silk Purse*, **Jesse Ed Davis**'s *Ululu* and some unreleased tracks by **Gram Parsons**. In 1974 Martin teamed-up with producer/arranger **Jack Nitzsche**, who took one of his songs, 'Cadillac Walk' to **Mink DeVille**. The song was a minor hit and DeVille recorded Martin's 'Rolene' on their second album. Martin next made a surprise appearance on **Michelle Phillips**' *Victim Of Romance*, for which he wrote three songs including the title track. After contributing two songs to an album by Lisa Burns, Martin worked on his debut solo album. *Shots From A Cold Nightmare*, an unusual sythesis of 50s/80s musical styles, was widely praised. After reaching the US Top 30 with 'Rolene', Martin released his second album, *Escape From Domination*, which had a stronger band feel with the inclusion of backing ensemble, the Ravens. Martin's homogeneous style lost some of its charm and bite by the third album and his subsequent work proved anti-climactic. He ended his association with **Capitol Records** and returned to songwriting.
Albums: With Southwind: *Southwind* (1969), *Ready To*

Ride (1971), *What A Place To Land* (1972). Solo: *Shots From A Cold Nightmare* (1978), *Escape From Domination* (1979), *Street Fever* (1980), *Mystery Ticket* (1982).

Moon Over Miami

This typically lavish 1941 20th Century-Fox Technicolor extravaganza was a remake of the same studio's somewhat less opulent *Three Blind Mice* which was produced three years earlier in 1938. The slight story concerns sisters Kay and Barbara Latimer (**Betty Grable** and Carole Landis) and their Aunt Charlotte (**Charlotte Greenwood**), who anxiously anticipate a substantial legacy. When the original $55,000 is whittled down to $4,287 and 96 cents (to be split three ways), the trio give up their jobs at a roadside diner and set off for Miami with the intention of finding Kay a rich husband. After going through the usual charades and complications, Kay lands the young well-heeled smoothie (Robert Cummings) - and then turns him down for the equally smooth but less well-off **Don Ameche**. In the sparkling supporting cast were funny-man Jack Haley, Cobina Wright Jnr., Robert Conway, Lynne Roberts, George Lessey, and dancers Jack Cole, the Condos Brothers and **Hermes Pan** (who also staged the dances). **Leo Robin** and **Ralph Rainger** came up with a bright and lively score which included 'You Started Something', 'Kindergarten Conga', 'I've Got You All To Myself', 'What Can I Do For You?', 'Oh Me, Oh Mi-ami', 'Is That Good?', 'Loveliness And Love', and 'Hurrah For Today'. The screenplay was written by Vincent Lawrence and Brown Holmes, and adapted by George Seaton and Lynn Starling from a 1938 English play by Stephen Powys. The director for this entertaining and colourful film was Walter Lang. Another remake appeared in 1946 entitled *Three Little Girls In Blue* and starring June Haver, George Montgomery and Celeste Holm.

Moon, Keith

b. 23 August 1947, Wembley, London, England, d. 7 September 1978. As the unpredictable, madcap drummer in the **Who**, Keith Moon cultivated a reputation as one of rock's great characters. His devil-may-care propulsiveness was always apparent in a drumming technique which eschewed conventional rhythm and goaded fellow instrumentalists into equally powerhouse retorts. His talent enhances the cream of the Who's output, including 'The Ox' (1965), 'I Can See For Miles' (1967) and 'Won't Get Fooled Again' (1971) while his quirky compositions for the group have included 'I Need You', 'Waspman', 'Cobwebs And Strange' and 'Tommy's Holiday Camp'. A life-long fan of surf music, Moon also inspired the **Beach Boys/Jan And Dean** selections on the 1966 EP *Ready Steady Who*.

This particular fascination was also apparent on the drummer's lone solo album, *Two Sides Of The Moon*, which included a version of **Brian Wilson**'s 'Don't Worry Baby'. The set featured material by **John Lennon**, **Harry Nilsson** and the Who, but a supporting cast drawn from the Los Angeles music fraternity failed to conceal it's self-indulgence. Its release emphasized the euphemistic 'rock 'n' roll life-style' in which Moon was now trapped, and having established a reputation for unconventional behaviour, he now felt compelled to live up to it. Tales of destruction were legendary, but Moon was now increasingly debilitated by drug and alcohol abuse, and his professional life inevitably suffered. Indeed 'Music Must Change', a track on *Who Are You* (1978), was left without a drum track when he was unable to hold the required beat. 'I'm still the best Keith Moon-style drummer in the world' he defiantly proclaimed, but the failure doubtless hurt. Sadly, the album was to be the last to feature Moon, who died in September 1978 as a result of an overdose of prescription drugs. Admired among both the rock and jazz fields, his talent was bound to his extrovert personality and the sound of the Who has been appreciably different without him. Since his death his standing as a musician has increased and many feel that like **Jimi Hendrix**, Moon was unique in his chosen field.

Album: *Two Sides Of The Moon* (1975).

Further reading: *Full Moon:The Amazing Rock & Roll Life Of Keith Moon, Late Of The Who*, Dougal Butler.

Moondoc, Jemeel

b. 5 August 1951, Chicago, Illinois, USA. Despite being a creative musician from Chicago, saxophonist Moondoc never touched base with the **AACM** - by the time he was looking for people to play with in the late 60s, **Anthony Braxton**, **Leroy Jenkins** and the **Art Ensemble Of Chicago** had left for Paris and New York. Turning down a career as an architect in the early 70s he studied music with **Ran Blake** in Boston, where he also played in the James Tatum Blues Band, and then followed **Cecil Taylor** to Wisconsin University and Antioch College, playing alto and soprano saxophones in Taylor's student orchestras. He moved to New York in 1972, where he met and played with *avant garde* luminaries such as bassist **William Parker** and trumpeter Roy Campbell, and also formed his Ensemble Munta, which lasted for nearly 10 years. In 1981 he toured Poland and recorded *The Intrepid* for the Poljazz label. In 1984 he formed the Jus Grew Orchestra, a wild 15-piece which had a residency at the Neither/Nor club on the Lower East Side. He says 'I try to speak through the horn - it's something I learned from **Jimmy Lyons** and **Ornette Coleman**', and he often plays deliberately sharp, like a free version of **Jackie McLean**. Moondoc's approach, which combines the looseness of bar-room blues with post-Ornette multi-key valency, found a willing accomplice in guitarist Bern Nix from Ornette's

harmolodic outfit Prime Time. Their band - with Parker on bass and **Dennis Charles** on drums - provided a tipsy, dislocated jazz that was excellently captured on *Nostalgia In Times Square*. Moondoc remains a strikingly individual musical mind in a jazz scene too often willing to conform to the standards of the past.
Albums: *First Feeding* (1977), *The Evening Of The Blue Men* (1979), *New York Live* (1981), *Konstanze's Delight* (1981), *The Intrepid Live In Poland* (1981), *The Athens Concert* (1982), *Judy's Bounce* (1982), *Nostalgia In Times Square* (1985).

Moondog

b. Louis Hardin, 26 May 1916, Marysville, Kansas, USA. This idiosyncratic composer lost his sight at age 16 following an accident with a dynamite cap. He was introduced to classical music at the Iowa School for the Blind, studying violin, viola and piano, but having moved to New York, opted for a life as a 'street musician'. He took the name Moondog in 1947 and established a pitch on the city's fabled Times Square. Such was his notoriety, Hardin successfully retained this sobriquet after issuing legal proceedings against disc jockey **Alan Freed**, who had claimed the 'Moondog' name for his radio show.
In a manner similar to fellow maverick Harry Partch, Moondog constructed his own instruments, claiming conventional scales could not reproduce the sounds heard in his head. This was immediately apparent on his first release, *On The Streets Of New York* (1953), a 45 rpm EP issued by **Epic** and **London/American**. Percussive devices, named the 'oo' and 'trimba', were at the fore of albums recorded for the **Prestige** label, notably *More Moondog* and *The Story Of Moondog*, although a distinctive jazz influence can also be detected. Further releases ensued, including *Moondog And His Honking Geese*, which the composer financed and distributed. Hardin also arranged an album of Mother Goose songs for singer **Julie Andrews**. During the 1960s Moondog continued to perform and beg on the city's streets, but his unconventional lifestyle and appearance - he wrapped himself in army surplus blankets and wore a Viking-styled helmet - found succour in the emergent counter-culture. He performed with anti-establishment comedian Lenny Bruce and eccentric singer **Tiny Tim**, while several groups, including **Big Brother and the Holding Company** and the **Insect Trust** recorded his distinctive musical rounds. In 1969, James Guercio, producer of the highly successful **Chicago**, introduced Moondog to **CBS**. Buoyed by a full orchestra, *Moondog* encapsulates twenty years of compositions, showing musical references to such diverse figures as Stravinsky and **Charlie Parker**, the latter of whom would often converse with Moondog. One particular selection, 'The Witch Of Endor', stands as one of his finest pieces. *Moondog 2* was a collection of rounds, inspired by the recognition afforded the composer by the hip cognoscenti. In 1974 Moondog undertook a tour of Germany where he opted to settle. 'I am a European at heart,' he later stated. A further series of albums maintained his unique musical vision, but although he has ceased recording, interest in this remarkable character continues to flourish.
Albums: *Moondog* (1955), *More Moondog* (1956), *The Story Of Moondog* (1957), *Moondog And His Friends*, *Moondog And His Honking Geese*, *Moondog* (1969), *Moondog 2* (1970), *Moondog In Europe* (1978), *H'Art Songs* (1979), *A New Sound Of An Old Instrument* (1980), *Selected Works* (1980).

Mooney, Art

b. 1911, Lowell, Massachusetts, USA. A popular bandleader in the late 40s and 50s, Mooney started out by leading a band mostly in Detroit and the midwest area during the 30s. After military service in World War II, he formed a new outfit with a similar style and sound to **Glenn Miller**, especially in the reed section. The band's arrangers included **Neal Hefti** and **George Williams**, and it made its New York debut in 1945, playing clubs, and appearing on radio. The big breakthrough came three years later, when Mooney recorded an old-fashioned version of **Mort Dixon** and **Harry Woods**' 1927 song 'I'm Looking Over A Four Leaf Clover', featuring the banjo playing of Mike Pingatore, an ex-**Paul Whiteman** sideman. The record sold over a million copies and put Mooney in the big money bracket for the band's personal appearances. Once down that lucrative road, he frequently used arrangements which featured the banjo and unison singing. His other hits, through to 1955, included 'Baby Face', 'Bluebird Of Happiness', 'Again', 'Beautiful Eyes', 'I Never See Maggie Alone', 'Toot Toot Tootsie (Goodbye)', 'Twenty Four Hours Of Sunshine', 'Hop Scotch Polka', 'M-I-S-S-I-S-S-I-P-P-I', 'Lazy River', 'Heartbreaker', 'Honey-Babe' and the band's theme, 'Sunset To Sunrise'. In 1955 he provided the orchestral backing for seven year-old **Barry Gordon**'s US Top 10 novelty, 'Nuttin' For Christmas'. By the late 50s Mooney's popularity had declined, but he played on through the 60s into the 70s, and toured with the *Big Band Cavalcade* from 1973-74. In 1988 he was still attracting enthusiastic crowds at venues such as the Erie County Fair in Hamburg, New York.
Selected albums: *Dance and Dream* (Coronet), *Banjo Bonanza* (MGM), *Art Mooney And His Orchestra In Hi-Fi Play For Dancing* (MGM) (all c.50s), *Songs Everybody Knows* (Decca 1962), *Best Of* (RCA 1967).

Mooney, John

b. 3 April 1955, East Orange, New Jersey, USA. Combining Delta guitar patterns with New Orleans second-line rhythms gives Mooney an edge when slide guitarists are under consideration. He was 12, living in

Rochester and playing guitar to **Ernest Tubb** songs on the radio when he first heard **Son House**'s records; four years later he was playing alongside House. After spending time in Arizona and California, he moved to New Orleans in 1976 and learned the city's complex rhythmic style from **Professor Longhair** and the **Meters**. He formed his band, Bluesiana, in 1983, which has since featured bass guitarists George Porter Jnr. and Glenn Fukunaga, drummers John Vidacovich and Kerry Brown, among others. *Sideways In Paradise* consisted of a series of acoustic duets with Jimmy Thackery recorded in Jamaica in 1984. *Testimony* enlisted the help of **Dr. John**, Jon Cleary and Ivan Neville, while *Travelin' On* was recorded live in Germany at the 1991 Breminale Festival.
Albums: *Comin' Your Way* (Blind Pig 1977), with Jimmy Thackery *Sideways In Paradise* (Seymour/Blind Pig 1985/1994), *Late Last Night* (Bullseye Blues 1990), *Telephone King* (Powerhouse 1991), *Tesimony* (Domino 1992), *Travelin' On* (CrossCut 1993).

Moonglows

This R&B vocal group was formed in Cleveland, Ohio, USA, in 1952. If there were any group that best signalled the birth of rock 'n' roll - by which R&B emerged out of its black subculture into mainstream teen culture - it was the Moonglows. The group's career paralleled that of their mentor, legendary disc jockey **Alan Freed**, who in his rise in rock 'n' roll made the Moonglows the mainstays of his radio programmes, motion pictures, and stage shows. Their membership comprised lead singer Bobby Lester (b. 13 January 1930, Louisville, Kentucky, USA, d. 15 October 1980), **Harvey Fuqua** (b. 27 July 1929, Louisville, Kentucky, USA), Alexander 'Pete' Graves (b. 17 April 1930, Cleveland, Ohio, USA), and Prentiss Barnes (b. 12 April 1925, Magnolia, Mississippi, USA). After recording for Freed's Champagne label in 1953, the group signed with Chicago-based Chance, where the group managed to get a few regional hits, most notably a cover of **Doris Day**'s 'Secret Love' in 1954. Freed used his connections to sign the Moonglows to a stronger Chicago label, the fast-rising **Chess Records**, and the group enjoyed a major hit with 'Sincerely' (number 1 R&B/number 20 pop 1954). Joining the group at this time was guitarist Billy Johnson (b. 1924, Hartford, Connecticut, USA, d. 1987).

Using a novel technique they called 'blow harmony', other great hits followed: 'Most Of All' (number 5 R&B 1955), 'We Go Together' (number 9 R&B 1956), 'See Saw' (number 6 R&B/number 25 pop 1956), all which featured Lester on lead; a remake of **Percy Mayfield**'s 'Please Send Me Someone To Love' (number 5 R&B/number 73 pop 1957) and 'Ten Commandments Of Love' (number 9 R&B/number 22 pop 1958), which featured Fuqua on lead. The original Moonglows disbanded in 1958, and Fuqua put together a new group that included **Marvin Gaye**. In 1960 Fuqua disbanded this group and he and Gaye went to Detroit to work in the industry there. Fuqua worked with **Berry Gordy**'s sister, Gwen Gordy on the Anna label and Gaye joined Berry Gordy's **Motown** operation. Fuqua carved out a very successful career as a producer and record executive, working with Motown artists in the 60s and a stable of Louisville artists in the 70s on the **RCA** label.
Albums: *Look! It's The Moonglows* (Chess 1959), *The Return Of The Moonglows* (RCA-Victor 1972), *The Moonglows On Stage* (Relic 1992). Compilations: *The Best Of Bobby Lester And The Moonglows* (Chess 1962), *The Flamingos Meet The Moonglows* (VeeJay 1962), *The Moonglows* (Constellation 1964), *Moonglows* (Chess 1976), *Their Greatest Sides* (Chess 1984), *Blue Velvet: The Ultimate Collection* (MCA/Chess 1993), *The Flamingos Meet The Moonglows: The Complete 25 Chance Recordings* (VeeJay 1993).

Moontrekkers

As the Raiders, Gary Le Port (lead guitar), Jimmy Rayther (rhythm guitar), Pete Johnson (bass) and Tony White (drums) were fronted originally by singer Robert Farrent (stage name: Bobby Shafto) but in 1960 it was with **Rod Stewart** that they were auditioned in a north London church hall by **Joe Meek** who was seeking an instrumental act to record an opus entitled 'Night Of the Vampire'. Submitting to the console boffin's masterplan, the group cast Stewart aside and, as the Moontrekkers, were rewarded with one week at number 50 in the UK Top 50 and a BBC ban because of this Parlophone single's sound effects (creaking coffin lid, wailing wind *et al*). When a second single, 'There's Something At The Bottom Of The Well', did not emulate this achievement, Johnson and White joined the Aristocats and, minus Rayther too, Le Port with new Moontrekkers went out in a blaze of glory when a 1963 **Decca** single, 'Moondust', entered Sweden's Top 10. The original personnel regrouped in 1991 for some Joe Meek memorial concerts and later semi-professional bookings.

Moore, 'Whistlin'' Alex

b. 11 November 1899, Dallas, Texas, USA, d. 20 January 1989, Dallas, Texas, USA. A lifelong individualist and eccentric, Moore came in later life to be regarded as a patriarch of Texas piano blues, although his inspirational technique wilfully avoided categorisation. He grew up in Freedman's Town, a section of Dallas where the children of slaves congregated. He became interested in piano while working as a delivery boy for a grocery store, and developed his style in the dives and whorehouses of North Dallas. He recorded six titles for **Columbia** in December 1929, including the first version of 'Blue

Bloomer Blues', and recorded this blues again for Decca in February 1937. With typical initiative, he financed his own session, recording eight titles, of which only two were later issued on album. A session for RPM in 1951 yielded five titles, two issued on a single, a third on album. In July 1960, Chris Strachwitz and Paul Oliver recorded him extensively for Arhoolie and Oliver's 'Conversations With The Blues' project. He was a member of the 1969 American Folk Blues Festival tour of Europe and recorded another album in Stuttgart, Germany. Throughout the 70s he was a feature of the festival circuit. In 1987 he received a Lifetime Achievement Award from the National Endowment for the Arts. Two years later, he recorded his last album for Rounder. Idiosyncratic to the end, he was returning home from a domino game at the Martin Luther King Centre in South Dallas and died on the bus, riding at the front, no doubt.
Selected albums: *Alex Moore* (1960), *Wiggle Tail* (1989), *Complete Recorded Works 1929-37* (Document 1994).

Moore, Arnold Dwight 'Gatemouth'

b. 8 November 1913, Topeka, Kansas, USA. At the age of 16, Moore went to Kansas City, where he sang with the bands of **Bennie Moten**, **Tommy Douglas** and **Walter Barnes**. Moore was one of the few survivors of the infamous 'Natchez Rhythm Club Fire' tragedy that wiped out most of Barnes' orchestra. His first recordings were made for the small K.C. labels, Chez Paree and Damon, and they caused enough of a stir to interest National Records. They brought Moore to Chicago and New York for four sessions in 1945-46 and were successful with Moore's 'I Ain't Mad At You, Pretty Baby', 'Did You Ever Love A Woman?' and 'Christmas Blues'. In 1947, Moore joined King Records and re-recorded his national hits along with a lot of new material. By the end of that year he had introduced **Wynonie Harris** to King and had discarded blues for a new career as the Reverend Moore. He became a gospel disc jockey and recorded gospel music in the early 50s for **Chess**/Aristocrat, Artists and Coral and recorded gospel albums for Audio Fidelity (1960) and Bluesway (1973). However, **Johnny Otis** did manage to persuade Moore to recreate some of his blues for a Blues Spectrum album in 1977.
Selected albums: *Gatemouth Moore* (c.50s), *Rev. Dwight 'Gatemouth' Moore & his Gospel Singers* (1960), *After Twenty-One Years* (1973), *Great R&B Oldies* (1977).

Moore, Bob

b. 30 November 1932, Nashville, Tennessee, USA. A popular studio musician who progressed from bass player to Musical director for country star **Red Foley** and pop artists **Brenda Lee** and **Connie Francis**, Moore then toured with **Elvis Presley**. His accompaniments for **Roy Orbison** earned him a solo contract with Monument Records (**London** in the UK) for his own combo, which made an impression with singles like 'Hot Spot', 'My Three Sons' and 'Mexico'. The first and last were issued back to back in Britain, the second and third as Moore's contribution to the anthological *Demand Performance* album, with other tracks by Orbison, **Billy Grammer**, **Jerry Byrd**, **Jack Eubanks** and the **Velvets**. 'Mexico' reached number 7 in the US charts and earned Moore a Gold Disc in 1961, but this was the peak of his achievement. Two albums were issued on London in the late 60s but little else has been heard from him in recent years.
Albums: *Mexico And Other Great Hits!* (Monument 1961), *Viva!* (c.60s), *Good Time Party* (c.60s).

Moore, Brew

b. Milton Aubrey Moore, 26 March 1924, Indianola, Mississippi, USA, d. 19 August 1973. After learning to play a range of instruments, Moore concentrated on tenor saxophone and in his teens sought work in various parts of the USA. A melodic player with a liquid ballad style, Moore's roots were in the style of the early **Lester Young**, and the advent of bebop restricted his progress. Nevertheless, he made many records in the 50s, then in 1961 became resident in Europe where, apart from a three-year return to the USA (1967-70), he remained for the rest of his life. Although his decision to stay away from America for so many years, allied to his refusal to move with the times, kept him out of the spotlight, it is now generally acknowledged that the quality of Moore's ballad playing was of the very highest order. His early death from a fall, attributed to his dependence upon alcohol, silenced a player whose talent, if not his career, was comparable to that of near-contemporaries such as **Stan Getz** and **Zoot Sims**.
Selected albums: *Brewer's Brew* (c.1949-50), *Fru And Brew* (1953), *The Brew Moore Quintet* (1955-56), *Danish Brew* (1959), *The Brew Moore Quartet* i (1962), *Svinget 14* (Black Lion 1963), *If I Had You* (1965), *I Should Care* (Speeplechase 1965), *Brew's Stockholm Dew* (1971), *No More Brew* (Storyville 1971). Compilations: *The Brew Moore Quartet* ii (1948 recording), *The Brew Moore Septet* (1949 recording), *Danish Brew* (Jazz Mark 1988).

Moore, Butch

(see **Capitol** (Eire))

Moore, Christy

b. 7 May 1945, Dublin, Eire. Moore's beginnings were fairly typical for a solo folk performer in the 60s: playing the club circuit in Eire, subsequently doing likewise in England while in between working on building sites and road gangs. Influenced by the American styles of **Woody Guthrie**, **Bob Dylan** and the British folk giant, **Ewan MacColl**, Moore performed in the UK folk clubs alongside the rising stars of the period. It was in England, in 1969, that he recorded his first album, a collaboration with **Dominic Behan**, *Paddy On The Road.* His first solo album led to the forming of **Planxty**, where he stayed until 1975. Having once again embarked on a solo career, he became involved in the mid-70s with the Anti-Nuclear Roadshow which featured performers, environmental activists and politicians. The 'Roadshow' established Moore's reputation as a campaigning and political performer and the ensemble's success made a heavy contribution to undermining the plans for a Irish nuclear power programme.

After a brief reunion with Planxty in the late 70s, Moore and fellow Planxty member Donal Lunny split in 1981 to form **Moving Hearts**. This progression from the former group fused folk with rock. Despite the group taking a similar ideologically agit-prop stance, Moore eventually felt uncomfortable within a group set-up and once again returned to solo work in 1982. Since that time, Moore's mixture of traditional songs with contemporary observations of Irish life, social and political, has also tackled the political problems of Central America and South Africa as well as the problems in his homeland and Ulster. His songs are notable not only for their spiky commentary but also an engaging humour. Christy Moore's standing in Irish folk music is of a stature unparalleled and his influence spills over into the field of pop and rock, winning critical favour, respect and debt, from such contemporary pop performers as the **Pogues**, **Elvis Costello**, **Billy Bragg** and **U2**.

Albums: with Dominic Behan *Paddy On The Road* (1969), *Prosperous* (1971), *Whatever Tickles Your Fancy* (1975), *Christy Moore* (1976), *The Iron Behind The Velvet* (1978), *Live In Dublin* (1978), *The Spirit Of Freedom* (1983), *The Time Has Come* (1983), *Ride On* (1984), *Ordinary Man* (WEA 1985), *Nice 'N' Easy* (1986), *Unfinished Revolution* (1987), *Voyage* (1989), *Smoke And Strong Whiskey* (1991), *King Puck* (1993), *Live At The Point* (Grapevine 1994). Compilation: *The Christy Moore Collection '81-'91* (1991).

Moore, Dorothy

b. 13 October 1947, Jackson, Mississippi, USA. Moore was one of the last great southern soul singers finding success in the late 70s when disco and funk were making deep soul increasingly a marginalized form limited to the south. She began her career at Jackson State University where she formed an all-female group called the Poppies. The group recorded for **Columbia Records**' Date subsidiary but never reached the national charts. She established a solo career in 1976 with a series of remarkable ballads for **Malaco Records**, hitting with 'Misty Blue' (number 2 R&B, number 3 pop) and 'Funny How Time Slips Away' (number 7 R&B, number 58 pop) in 1976 (the latter the **Willie Nelson** song); and 'I Believe You' (number 5 R&B, number 27 pop) in 1977. Moore's recordings in the next few years were not nearly as successful as she succumbed increasingly to the disco trend. She left the business for several years, but in 1986 recorded a fine gospel album in Nashville, *Giving It Straight To You* for the Rejoice label. It yielded a masterful remake of Brother Joe May's 'What Is This' that became a Top 10 gospel hit. Moore returned to secular music in 1988 recording, in the deep soul-style, two albums for the Volt subsidiary of Fantasy. In 1990 she began recording for her original label, Malaco.

Albums: as the Poppies *Lullaby Of Love* (Epic 1966), *Misty Blue* (Malaco 1976), *Dorothy Moore* (Malaco 1977), *Once More With Feeling* (Malaco 1978), *Definitely Dorothy* (Malaco 1979), *Talk To Me* (Malaco 1980), *Giving It Straight To You* (Rejoice 1986), *Time Out For Me* (Volt 1988), *Winner* (Volt 1989), *Feel The Love* (Malaco 1990), *Stay Close To Home* (Malaco 1992).

Moore, Dudley

b. 19 April 1935, Dagenham, Essex, England. After playing piano in a local youth club, Moore played semi-professionally in various jazz clubs. He studied music at Oxford University, graduating in the late 50s and thereafter playing with **Vic Lewis**. Early in the following decade he worked with **John Dankworth** before forming his own trio. For a while he successfully performed jazz while concurrently appearing in *Beyond The Fringe* in London and New York. With the trio, he also made records and appeared on television with the seminal *Not Only But Also*. By the mid-60s Moore's acting career had begun to take precedence over his jazz work and he later moved to Hollywood. His musical interests continued with the writing of scores for feature films including *The Wrong Box* (1966), *30 Is A Dangerous Age Cynthia* (1967), *Inadmissible Evidence* (1968), *Bedazzled* (1968) and *Staircase* (1969) and also for stage shows, plays and the ballet. His own acting career took off to such an extent that 'Cuddly Dudley' became a Hollywood star in such films as; *10* (1979), *Wholly Moses* (1980), *Arthur* (1981), *Six Weeks* (1982), *Lovesick* (1983), *Best Defence* (1984), *Micki And Maude* (1984) and *Santa Claus* (1985). Moore has cited **Erroll Garner** and **Oscar Peterson** as two of his main influences. His jazz playing is notable for his lightness of touch and deft right-hand filigrees although his eclecticism, allied to his absorption with other interests, has inhibited the development of a truly identifiable personal style. In recent years, having seemingly achieved everything as a 'movie star' Moore has returned to recording and performing, and has resurrected the definitive Dudley Moore Trio.

Selected albums: *The Dudley Moore Trio* i (1962), *The Dudley Moore Trio* ii (1965), *The Dudley Moore Trio* iii (1966), *Bedazzled* (1968), *The Dudley Moore Trio* iv (1968), *The Dudley Moore Trio* v (1968), *The Dudley Moore Trio* vi (1969), *Dudley Moore At The Wavendon Festival* (1976),

Dudley Down Under (1978), *Songs Without Words* (1992). Further reading: *Dudley*, Paul Donovan. *Off Beat: Dudley Moore's Book Of Musical Anecdotes*, Dudley Moore.

Moore, Freddie

b. 20 August 1900, Washington, North Carolina, USA, d. 1992. He began playing drums as a child and was soon working in tent shows, travelling throughout southern states. After playing with Charlie Creath and leading his own band, he moved to New York, joining Wilbur Sweatman, then toured with **King Oliver** and once again led his own band. During the 40s and 50s he was constantly in demand, mostly in New York but also for tours as far afield as Europe,. and played in bands led by, amongst others, **John Kirby**, **Sidney Bechet**, **Wilbur De Paris**, **Bob Wilber**, **Mezz Mezzrow**, **Sammy Price** and **Emmett Berry**. In the 60s and 70s he was still playing, with musicians such as **Tony Parenti** and **Roy Eldridge** but by the mid-80s had slowed down a little and mostly played washboard. A robust drummer steeped in the solid timekeeping tradition of early jazz, he took naturally to the mainstream and provided steady, fluid support to the front line horns with which he played.
Album: *Emmett Berry And His Orchestra* (Columbia 1956).

Moore, Gary

b. 4 April 1952, Belfast, Northern Ireland. This talented, blues-influenced singer and guitarist formed his first major band, **Skid Row**, when he was 16 years old - initially with **Phil Lynott**, who left after a few months to form **Thin Lizzy**. Skid Row continued as a three-piece, with Brendan Shields (bass) and Noel Bridgeman (drums). They relocated from Belfast to London in 1970 and signed a deal with **CBS**. After just two albums they disbanded, leaving Moore to form the Gary Moore Band. Their debut, *Grinding Stone*, appeared in 1973, but progress was halted the following year while Moore assisted Thin Lizzy after guitarist Eric Bell had left the band. This liaison lasted just four months before Moore was replaced by Scott Gorham and Brian Robertson. Moore subsequently moved into session work before joining **Colosseum** II in 1976. He made three albums with them, and also rejoined Thin Lizzy for a 10-week American tour in 1977 after guitarist Brian Robertson suffered a severed artery in his hand. Moore finally became a full-time member of Thin Lizzy, but he subsequently left midway through a US tour and formed a new band called **G-Force**, though this outfit soon floundered. Moore then resumed his solo career, cutting a series of commercially ignored albums until he scored hit singles in 1985 with 'Empty Rooms' and another collaboration with Phil Lynott, 'Out In The Fields'. His 1989 album, *After The War*, revealed a strong celtic influence, and also featured guest artists such as **Ozzy Osbourne** and Andrew Eldritch (**Sisters Of Mercy**). But his breakthrough to mainstream commercial acceptance came in 1990 with the superb, confident guitarwork and vocals of *Still Got The Blues*. Mixing blues standards and originals, Moore was acclaimed as one of the UK's foremost artists, a stature which the subsequent release of *After Hours* - featuring cameo appearances from **B.B. King** and **Albert Collins** - only confirmed. In 1994 with Jack Bruce and Ginger Baker, in a band called BBM, he released an accomplished and satisfying album. In 1995 he released the excellent *Blues For Greeny*, an album of songs written by **Peter Green** and played on Green's **Gibson** Les Paul guitar which was a gift from Green to Moore many years ago.
Albums: *Back On The Streets* (MCA 1979), *Corridors Of Power* (Virgin 1982), *Rockin' Every Night - Live In Japan* (Virgin 1983), *Live* (Jet 1984), *Run For Cover* (10 1985), *Wild Frontier* (10 1988), *After The War* (Virgin 1989), *Still Got The Blues* (Virgin 1990), *After Hours* (Virgin 1992), *Blues Alive* (Virgin 1993) *Blues For Greeny* (Virgin 1995). With Skid Row: *Skid Row* (CBS 1970), *Thirty Four Hours* (CBS 1971). Compilations: *Anthology* (Raw Power 1986), *The Collection* (Castle 1990, double album), *CD Box Set* (Virgin 1991), *Ballads + Blues 1982 - 1994* (Virgin 1994). With Gary Moore Band: *Grinding Stone* (CBS 1973). With Colosseum II: *Strange New Flesh Bronze* (MCA 1976), *Electric Savage* (MCA 1977), *War Dance* (MCA 1977). With Thin Lizzy: *Remembering Part 1* (Decca 1976), *Black Rose* (Vertigo 1979), *Live Life* (Vertigo 1983). With G-Force: *G-Force* (Jet 1979). With Greg Lake Band: *Greg Lake* (Chrysalis 1981), *Manoeuvers* (Chrysalis 1983). With BBM *Around The Next Dream* (Virgin 1994).
Videos: *Emerald Aisles* (1986), *Live In Sweden* (1988), *Video Singles* (1988), *An Evening Of The Blues* (1991), *Live Blues* (1993), *Ballads + Blues 1982-1994* (1994).
Videos: *Video Singles: Gary Moore* (1988), *Gary Moore: Live In Sweden* (1988), *Emerald Aisles* (1988), *Evening Of The Blues* (1991).

Moore, Glen

b. 28 October 1941, Portland, Oregon, USA. It was on sets with **Tim Hardin** and **Cyrus** that Moore came to public notice. However, upon uniting with **Ralph Towner**, **Paul McCandless**, and **Collin Walcott** within the fluid context of **Oregon** Moore's bass style was best showcased. Like his co-members he revealed an easy command of classical, folk, Eastern, and jazz overtones. Since Oregon was formed in 1970, Moore's distinctive upright bass sound has distinguished each of their albums, wherein he has also been known to play viola and flute. The intermittent development of Oregon has allowed Moore the freedom to pursue a parallel career in sessions.
Albums: with Tim Hardin *Bird On A Wire* (1970), with Annette Peacock *Bley/Peacock Synthesizer Show* (1971), with Cyrus *Cyrus* (1971), with Peacock *I'm The One* (1972), with Oregon *Music Of Another Present Era* (1973),

with Oregon *Distant Hills* (1974), with Oregon *Winter Light* (1974), with Larry Coryell *Restful Mind* (1975), with Oregon *In Concert* (1975), with Ralph Towner *Trios/Solos* (1975), with Oregon *Friends* (1975), with Oregon *Together* (1977), with Oregon *Violin* (1978), with Oregon *Out Of The Woods* (1978), with Oregon *Roots In The Sky* (1979), with Zbigniew Seifert *We'll Remember Zbiggy* (1980), with Oregon *In Performance* (1980), *Oregon* (1983), with Oregon *Crossing* (1984), with Oregon *Ecotopia* (1987), with Oregon *45th Parallel* (1989), with Oregon *Always, Never And Forever* (1991).

Moore, Grace

b. 5 December 1901, Slabtown, Tennessee, USA, d. 26 January 1947. Gifted with a remarkable singing voice, Moore first made her name on Broadway in musical comedies. The quality of her singing brought her to the attention of New York's Metropolitan Opera Company and from there she went to Hollywood where her physical beauty enhanced a number of 30s musicals. Moore's lyrical soprano voice was far better than anything offered by most singing actresses in Hollywood, as he demonstrated in *A Lady's Morals* (1930), *New Moon* (1931), ***One Night Of Love*** (for which she was nominated as Best Actress, 1934), *Love Me Forever* (1935), *The King Steps Out* (1936), *When You're In Love* (1937), *I'll Take Romance* (1937), and *Louise* (1940). In the 20s and 30s she made several successful recordings, including 'Listening', 'Tell Her In The Springtime', 'One Night Of Love', and 'Ciribiribin'. While on a concert tour of Europe, Moore was killed when the aircraft in which she was travelling crashed near Copenhagen. The 1953 film *So This Is Love* (UK title: *The Grace Moore Story*), in which she was portrayed by **Kathryn Grayson**, gave a reasonable account of her career and times.
Selected album: *The Art Of Grace Moore* (RCA 1987).
Further reading: *You're Only Human Once*, Grace Moore.

Moore, GT, And The Reggae Guitars

A popular act in London's pub and club circuit during the early 70s, this quintet comprised of former **Heron** member Gerald 'GT' Moore (guitar/vocals), Martin Hayward (guitar), Tim Jones (keyboards), Tom Whyte (bass) and Malcolm Mortimer (drums). Their melodic blend of rock and reggae was partially captured on the unit's self-titled debut, released in 1974, but like many contemporaries, GT Moore were unable to commit a live excitement to record. Their musicanship, however, was never in question and Whyte, Hayward and Moore made telling contributions to contemporaneous releases by **Shusha**. Tony Redunzo replaced Mortimer for *Reggae Blue*, but by this point the group was losing impetus and it was dissolved soon afterwards.
Albums: *GT Moore And The Reggae Guitars* (Charisma 1974), *Reggae Blue* (Charisma 1975).

Moore, Jackie

b. 1946, Jacksonville, Florida, USA. This powerful soul singer moved to Philadelphia in the late 60s and, with help, from top local R&B disc jockey Jimmy Bishop, had two releases on Shout and one on Wand. When success was not forthcoming she returned to Jacksonville and, partly thanks to her cousin, noted producer Dave Crawford, joined **Atlantic** in 1970. Crawford produced and co-wrote 'Precious, Precious', which after laying dormant for some months on a b-side, sold a million and became her only US Top 40 pop hit in 1970. After six Top 40 R&B hits she joined Kayvette Records in 1975 when she achieved her biggest R&B success 'Make Me Feel Like A Woman', which was produced by Brad Shapiro. Moore moved to **Columbia** in 1978 and continued to sell records in the USA soul market. She also had her only UK hit with 'This Time Baby', which narrowly missed the Top 40 in 1979. A consistent R&B hitmaker for over a decade, she increased her tally of US R&B chart entries to 15 in 1983 when she recorded on Catawba.
Albums: *Sweet Charlie Babe* (1973), *Make Me Feel Like A Woman* (1975), *I'm On My Way* (1979), *With Your Love* (1980). Compilation: *Precious Precious: The Best Of ...* (1994).

Moore, James

(see **Harpo, Slim**)

Moore, Johnny

b. John Dudley Moore, 20 October 1906, Austin, Texas, USA, d. 6 January 1969, Los Angeles, California, USA. The elder brother of guitarist **Oscar Moore**, Johnny began playing guitar with his violinist father's string band in 1934 and moved to the west coast, where Oscar joined **Nat 'King' Cole**'s Trio and Moore joined a group called the Blazes. Fired by that group in 1942, Moore decided to form his own group which he christened the Three Blazers. This featured Eddie Williams on bass and, briefly, pianist Garland Finney. When Finney left the trio the following year, Moore hired **Charles Brown**, a singer and pianist he had seen at an amateur talent show, and the Blazers began recording in 1944 for the small Atlas label. This was followed in 1945-48 by extensive recording for Exclusive, Philo/Aladdin and Modern. During this period the Blazers became a household name with huge hits like 'Driftin' Blues', 'Merry Christmas Baby', 'Sunny Road' and 'More Than You Know'. When Oscar Moore joined the group in 1947, it was the start of several major problems which resulted in a split, and Moore tried to replace Charles Brown with a succession of soundalikes. The most successful of these was Billy Valentine, who took the Blazers back to the R&B charts with **RCA**-Victor's 'Walkin' Blues' in 1949. After his 1949-50 association

with Victor, Johnny Moore's Blazers recorded for the gamut of Los Angeles labels, but was successful only with 1953's novelty 'Dragnet Blues' on Modern and 1955's morbid '**Johnny Ace**'s Last Letter' on Hollywood. Johnny Moore and Charles Brown were reconciled in the mid-50s and the real Three Blazers reunited for records on Aladdin, Hollywood and Cenco, however, by that time Moore's cool, sophisticated, melodic blues guitar was out of favour with R&B fans. He was an inspiration to most of the electric blues guitarists of the late 40s and early 50s (he is numbered among **B.B. King's** Top 10 guitarists of all time), and his solos on recordings by **Ivory Joe Hunter**, **Floyd Dixon** and Charles Brown, as well as tracks under his own group, bear witness that he was one of the unsung greats of his instrument.
Albums: with Charles Brown *Sunny Road* (1978), with Brown *Race Track Blues* (1981), with Brown *Sail On Blues* (1989), *This Is One Time, Baby* (1989), *Why Johnny Why?* (1989).

Moore, Johnny B.

b. 24 January 1950, Clarksdale, Mississippi, USA. Moore was first taught to play the guitar at the age of seven by his Baptist minister father. Four years later he was already playing in early evening sessions at local juke joints. In 1964 he moved north to Chicago to join his father who had moved there six years before. He learned to read music at school and after leaving to work in a lamp factory, played evenings and weekends around the city. In 1975, **Koko Taylor** asked him to join her band, the Blues Machine. Two years later, he was took part in the New Generation of Chicago Blues, a Berlin concert hosted by **Willie Dixon**. He subsequently toured Europe three times with Taylor and twice with Dixon, working with the latter until his death in 1992. His records show him to be a worthy performer, adept with a bottleneck and an adequate soloist in the post-**B.B. King** manner, who nevertheless conducts himself with undue restraint.
Albums: *Hard Times* (B.L.U.E.S. R&B 1987), *Lonesome Blues* (Wolf 1992), *911 Blues* (Wolf, 1994). Compilation: *From West Helena To Chicago* (Wolf 1988).

Moore, Melba

Based in New York City, Melba Moore first garnered attention in the Broadway production of ***Hair***. Although she has continued her thespian inclinations, winning an award for her performance in the musical *Purlie*, Moore has also forged a successful singing career. 'This Is It', a minor US hit, reached the UK Top 10 in 1976, and although her pop chart placings have since been inconsistent, Melba remained a fixture on the R&B lists over the following decade.
Albums: *Look What You're Doing To The Man* (1971), *Peach Melba* (1975), *This Is It* (1976), *Melba* (1976), *A Portrait Of Melba* (1978), *Dancin' With Melba Moore* (1979), *Melba* (1978), *Burn* (1979), *What A Woman Needs* (1981), *The Other Side Of The Rainbow* (1982), *Never Say Never* (1983), *Read My Lips* (1985), *A Lot Of Love* (1987), *I'm In Love* (1988).

Moore, Monette

b. 19 May 1902, Gainesville, Texas, USA, d. 21 October 1962, Garden Grove, California, USA. Moore was also known as Ethel Mayes, Nettie Potter, Susie Smith and Grace White. Interested in music from an early age, Moore taught herself piano in her early teens and became a fan of **Mamie Smith**. Among the first wave of classic blues singers, from 1923 onwards she was recording in New York City for Paramount, Vocalion, **Columbia** and **RCA** Victor. She also worked with the orchestras of **Charlie 'Fess' Johnson**, **Walter Page** and **Lucky Millinder** in myriad shows and revues. She was briefly married to singer/pianist/songwriter John Erby in the late 20s and in 1933 she opened her own nightclub, Monette's Place, but continued performing and recording. In the early 40s, she moved out to the west coast to record for various specialist labels with **Teddy Bunn**, **Hilton 'Nappy' Lamare** and **George Lewis**, then started a new career in television and films. In 1960 she secured a singing job on the Mark Twain Riverboat at Disneyland theme park in Anaheim, California, where she suffered a critical emphysema attack and died before reaching hospital. Although she did not enjoy an extensive recording career, Moore was a very effective jazz and blues stylist who easily coped with the various styles she encountered during her 40 year career.

Moore, Oscar

b. 25 December 1912, Austin, Texas, USA, d. 8 October 1981. Moore formed his first band with his brother Johnny (who was also a guitarist), while still in his mid-teens. In 1937 he became a founder member of the **Nat 'King' Cole** Trio, and for the next several years was an important part of the group's success. In 1947 Moore joined the Three Blazers, a group led by his brother, and also led his own groups for recording sessions. In the mid-50s he dropped out of music, but returned occasionally to gig and make record dates as a sideman. An outstanding guitarist in the mould of **Charlie Christian**, Moore was an exceptionally gifted soloist and an accompanist of rare distinction. The quicksilver exchanges between him and Cole on their early records provide eloquent testimony to his talent and make his long and presumably self-determined absence from the scene a matter of considerable regret.
Albums: *The Oscar Moore Quartet* (1954), *Tribute To Nat King Cole* (1965). Compilation: *The Complete Capitol Recordings Of The Nat 'King' Cole Trio* (1942-61).

Moore, R. Stevie

b. 1959, Nashville, Tennessee, USA. The son of a leading session bass-player, young Moore was recording with **Jim Reeves** at the age of seven, but grew up to have very different ambitions to his father. Absorbed in home-taping techniques, Moore waited many years before unleashing his songwriting and multi-instrumental talents upon an unsuspecting world. The early limited edition *Phonography* was followed by a handful of albums and a deluge of cassettes flowing from his New Jersey home. The most consistent feature of his material is its very unpredictability: a quirky, melodic writer, Moore covers a variety of musical and instrumental styles. Distancing himself from the music business, he continues to provide music of rare quality for his listeners.

Albums: *Everything* (1984), *What's the Point* (1984), *Verve* (1985), *Warning* (1988), *Has Beens And Never Weres* (1990).

Moore, Ralph

b. 1956, London, England. So assured, so steeped in the post-bop language and sensibility is Ralph Moore that it can come as a surprise that he is actually a British-born saxophonist (he has an English mother and an American father). He began learning the trumpet when he was 14, but was gradually seduced by the tenor saxophone. He moved to the USA at 15, settling on the west coast and served his apprenticeship in America's jazz hothouse environment until he reached a standard that enabled him to study at the prestigious **Berklee College Of Music** in Boston. Leaving after a couple of years, his innate ability and solid, raspy tone led to a period with the great drummer **Roy Haynes**, and then three years with the legendary hard-bop pianist and leader **Horace Silver**. With enough of a reputation to make it on the world's most competitive jazz scene, he moved to New York, and continued working with the greats, including **John Hicks**, **Dizzy Gillespie**, **Gene Harris** and **Freddie Hubbard**, as well as leading his own groups with some of the new wave of gifted, young hard-bop players, including trumpeter Brian Lynch, guitarist **Kevin Eubanks** and pianists Dave Kikoski, **Benny Green** and **Mulgrew Miller**. Ralph Moore's tenor work is characterised by an attractive, throaty tone, a little reminiscent of **Charlie Rouse**, and solid, self-assured phrasing. Hardly unorthodox but always creative and confident, he is undoubtedly one of the most promising of the new generation of bop saxophonists.

Albums: *Round Trip* (Reservoir 1985), *623 C Street* (Criss Cross Criss 1987), with Marvin 'Smitty' Smith *Keeper Of The Drums* (Concord 1987), with Bobby Hutcherson *Cruisin' The 'Bird* (Landmark 1988), *Rejuvenate!* (Criss Cross Criss 1988), *Furthermore* (Landmark 1990), with Roy Haynes *True Or False* (Freelance), with Freddie Hubbard *Bolivia* (Musicmasters/Limelight 1990/91).

Moore, Ray

b. 1942, Liverpool, England, d. 1988. A broadcaster and unlikely 80s records hitmaker, Moore left school in the summer of 1960 and started a good job in the then-thriving docks. However, a desire to do something different led him to Oldham Repertory Theatre where he became assistant stage manager. He managed to do some acting and even appeared in a b-movie called *A Touch Of Brass* made for the Billy Graham organization. After spending some more time in repertory, Moore joined Granada television as an announcer in 1962, working alongside Bernard Youens, later to star in *Coronation Street*. After a move to ATV in 1964, Moore was employed by BBC Manchester in television and as a radio disc jockey, hosting *Pop North* among other programmes. In the summer of 1967 he went to the BBC in London as a holiday stand-in for the *Saturday Club* show and was later invited to join Radio 2 when it was launched in September 1967. In 1986 he teamed up with the eccentric west country musician Shag Connors to record the novelty single 'My Father Had A Rabbit' which was a surprise hit with proceeds going to charity. By the time Moore and Connors recorded the follow-up 'Bog Eyed Jog' in the following year, Moore had learnt that he was suffering from cancer of the mouth. He soldiered on bravely until he was unable to speak, but sadly died in 1988. His biography subsequently became a best seller.

Further reading: *Tomorrow Is Too Late*, Ray Moore. *Tomorrow, Who Knows?*, Alma and Ray Moore.

Moore, Russell 'Big Chief'

b. 13 August 1912, nr. Sacaton, Arizona, USA, d. 15 December 1983. A native American, of the Pima tribe, Moore began playing trombone in the Chicago area before settling in the mid-30s in Southern California, where he played in one of **Lionel Hampton**'s first bands. By the end of the decade he had moved to New Orleans, where he became a regular musical associate of many of the older generation of traditional jazzmen. In 1944 he joined **Louis Armstrong** for a three-year spell, then worked in and around New York with **Sidney Bechet**, **Eddie Condon**, **Buck Clayton**, **Red Allen**, **Oran 'Hot Lips' Page**, **Pee Wee Russell** and many others. Occasional trips to Europe brought him to the attention of a wider range of fans and a short period with Armstrong's All Stars, beginning in 1964, further enhanced his reputation. He spent part of the 60s in Canada and led his own bands, recording occasionally on into the 70s. In the early 80s he was again on tour in Europe but died in 1983. Moore's style was well-suited to the ensemble playing of the traditional New Orleans-style band, but his soloing, especially in the 50s and 60s, had much to commend it.

Albums: *Russell 'Big Chief' Moore* (1953-74), *Russell 'Big Chief' Moore's Pow Wow Jazz Band* (1973).

Moore, Scotty

b. Winfield Scott Moore, 27 December 1931, Gadsden, Tennessee, USA. Guitarist Moore started playing at the age of eight and formed his first band while in the US Navy in 1948. After he left the service he joined the Memphis group Doug Poindexter And His Starlite Wranglers who also included bass player **Bill Black**. The band recorded Moore's 'My Kind Of Carryin' On' for **Sam Phillips' Sun** label and both Moore and Black played on several other Sun artists' recordings. In June 1954 Phillips invited a young singer he was trying out to Moore's apartment to rehearse some songs. That man was **Elvis Presley**. A week later Moore, Presley and Black went into Sun studios to record together for the first time. As a trio (later a quartet with drummer D.J. Fontana) they recorded some of Elvis's finest recordings. When Presley was sold to **RCA** for a 'king's ransom', Moore and Black were taken on as his sidemen on a relatively meagre salary. Moore, had acted as a kind of unpaid manager before Bob Neal and then **Colonel Tom Parker** took over the role. While Elvis was tied up filming *Loving You* Moore and Black headed for the Dallas State Fair where they performed as Scotty And Bill, Elvis' Original Backing Group. Scotty also went to work for the small Memphis label Fernwood Records whose most successful record was **Thomas Wayne**'s 'Tragedy'. Moore himself released a solo single called 'Have Guitar Will Travel'. During the same period he also did some sessions for **Dale Hawkins** at **Chess**. Unlike Black, Moore returned to play with Presley when he came out of the army in 1960, but not for long. Over the next few years he recorded infrequently with Elvis and went back to Sun as production manager. Later in the 60s he went to Nashville to start his own studio. Presley invited him back for the 1968 television special, which was the last time Moore played with, or even saw Presley. In 1970 Moore recorded an album with D.J. Fontana but by now he had virtually retired from playing to concentrate on production (most notably engineering **Ringo Starr**'s *Beaucoups Of Blues*). He was enticed out of retirement by **Billy Swan** to play on his self-titled 1976 album and later played on **Ral Donner**'s Elvis tribute album. By the 80s Moore had established a successful tape copying service in Nashville and rarely picked up his guitar.
Albums: *The Guitar That Changed The World* (1964), *What's Left* (1970), with Carl Perkins *706 Reunion-A Sentimental Journey* (1993).

Moore, Vinnie

b. 1965, USA. This jazz-trained virtuoso guitarist was playing the guitar competently by the age of 12. Picked up by talent scout Mike Varney, he was introduced to the techno-thrash band **Vicious Rumours**, with whom he recorded *Soldiers Of The Night* in 1985. He left the band as soon as the album was released to concentrate on a solo career. *Mind's Eye* emerged in 1986, a self-written guitar instrumental collection. This combined a fusion of classical jazz, blues and hard rock that was heavily melodic and technically brilliant, earning comparisons to **Joe Satriani**'s finest work. Two subsequent albums followed a similar pattern but were mellower still, after which he was employed by **Alice Cooper** as lead guitarist on his 1991 *Hey Stoopid* tour.
Albums: *Mind's Eye* (Shrapnel 1986), *Time Odyssey* (Squawk 1988), *Meltdown* (Squawk 1991).

Moore, Willie C.

b. 22 April 1913, Kinston, North Carolina, USA, d. 2 May 1971, Albany, New York, USA. Moore began playing guitar about 1930, and in 1934 won a talent contest organised by **J.B. Long**. It has been speculated that Moore recorded as Boll Weenie Bill for ARC, but this now seems unlikely. When located in 1970, he still possessed a wide repertoire, but died after preliminary recordings had been made.
Album: *Another Man Done Gone* (1978).

Moose

This UK group comprised Russell Yates (vocals), Kevin McKillop (guitar), Damien Warburton (drums) and Lincoln Fong (bass). They inadvertently began the so-called 'shoegazing' movement, so dubbed because of the static nature of bands who focused on the floorboards instead of their audience, when Yates read lyrics taped to the floor. They rose to notoriety with supports to **Lush**, from whom they borrowed Chris Acland when Warburton failed to appear at gigs. Another temporary change arose when McKillop attended his child's birth, and Tim Gane from **Sterolab** stepped in. Conversely Yates moonlights as a Stereolab guitarist and McKillop has played with See See Rider. It is this sort of activity which fuelled 'The Scene That Celebrates Itself' tag, summoned by the ***Melody Maker***s' Steve Sutherland to describe the incestuous nature of a clutch of upcoming bands who were not indulging in traditional rivalries. Three EPs comprised the original batch of recordings, the last of which was the first to confirm that the band could offer more than the voguish **My Bloody Valentine** influences. The C&W-tinged 'This River Will Never Run Dry' was applauded from almost all corners. Yates also achieved prominence through the Lillies, the brainchild of Stuart Mutler, editor of Tottenham Hotspurs' soccer magazine, *The Spur*. This included Miki Berenyi and Chris Acland from Lush, Yates and Kevin McKillop from Moose, and was masterminded by Simon Raymonde of the **Cocteau Twins**. Together they recorded a flexi-disc entitled: 'And David Seaman Will Be Very Disappointed About That'. Despite strong critical reaction in their favour,

Moose were dropped by **Virgin Records** subsidiary Circa when they failed to garner significant commercial reward for *XYZ*. The band relocated to Play It Again Sam, for whom *Honey Bee* further moved them away from indie rock territory, dabbling in soul, folk and country nuances. The critical response was still strong, but again did not provide an upsurge in sales.
Album: *XYZ* (Circa 1992), *Honey Bee* (Play It Again Sam 1993).

Morales, David

b. c.1961, Brooklyn, New York, USA. Born and bred in the capital, and of Puerto Rican parents, David Morales is the leader of the pack in terms of his country's leading remixers. His style, melodic garage house with a strong disco influence, belies his personal physique and presence, that of a pencil-bearded, tattooed body-builder. Married with a son, he works out for two hours every day, though he also employs a bodyguard for his regular evening shows (he was shot in his youth). As a young man he attended both the Loft and Paradise Garage, before being invited to play at the latter through Judy Weinstein's For The Record organisation. His other stomping grounds included all the major New York clubs, including the Ozone Layer, Inferno and Better Days. The Morales style has graced literally hundreds of records, his first remix being Insync's 'Sometimes Love'. He possibly works best in tandem with a strong garage vocalist (**Alison Limerick**, **Ce Ce Penniston**, **Yazz**, **Jocelyn Brown**, **Chimes** etc.). A good selection of his greatest work might be permed from the following: **Robert Owens**' 'I'll Be Your Friend', **Clive Griffin**'s 'I'll Be Waiting', Black Sheep's 'Strobelite Honey', **Pet Shop Boys**' 'So Hard', **Thompson Twins**' 'The Saint' or Limerick's 'Where Love Lives'. Many other remixes have been completed with longstanding friend **Frankie Knuckles** (as Def-Mix), who he also met through For The Record (Weinstein going on to manage both artists). His productivity is made possible by the fact that he is happy to churn out up to two remixes a week under his own auspices. His live sets, however, are often less glossy than the productions he is best known for: 'When I DJ I'm not as pretty as a lot of the records I make'. He has had trouble in constructing solo hits on his own account, though his debut album included guest appearances from **Sly Dunbar** and **Ce Ce Rogers**.
Album: *The Programme* (1993).

Morales, Noro

b. Norberto Morales, 4 January 1911, Puerta de Tierra, Puerto Rico, d. 14 January 1964, San Juan, Puerto Rico. Imposing and charismatic Latin pianist, bandleader, composer and 'arranger' Morales enjoyed considerable popularity with both Latino and non-Latino audiences in the 40s and early 50s. Born to a large musical family, Noro was initially tutored by his father and a sister; he first studied trombone and bass, but made better progress on the piano. In 1924 the Morales family were invited by the Venezuelan dictator President Juan Gómez to become his official court orchestra. His father died the same year and Noro took over leadership. After returning to Puerto Rico in 1930, the family orchestra disbanded and Noro freelanced with various bands (including Ralph Sánchez, The Midnight Serenaders, Carmelo Díaz Soler and Rafael Muñoz) before moving to New York in 1935. Following stints with Alberto Socarrás, Augusto Coen, Leo Marini and Johnny Rodríguez (**Tito Rodríguez**'s older brother), he founded a rumba band called the Hermanos Morales Orchestra in 1937 (renamed Noro Morales And His Orchestra in 1938). They were an immediate success and became the resident band at the El Morocco club for five years. In the early 40s Morales founded a big band which, along with the orchestras of **Machito**, Marcelino Guerra and Miguelito Valdés, became one of the most popular during the mid-40s. Some fine examples of his big band work are contained on the Tumbao CD *Rumbas And Mambo*. An early crossover hit composition by Noro, 'Bim Bam Bum', was introduced in 1942 by **Xavier Cugat**, sung by Tito Rodríguez (the recording is included on the Tumbao CD *Xavier Cugat And His Orchestra 1940-42*, 1991). Noro's 1942 self-penned hit 'Serenata Ritmica', which he was to record several more times and became his signature tune, consolidated his popularity with non-Latinos. That year, and for many after, his orchestra was hired to perform at the prestigious annual New York *Daily News* Harvest Moon Ball. During the 40s, Noro pioneered a hip piano and Latin percussion style (bass, bongo, conga and timbales, plus maracas and claves on occasion) that was commercially watered-down and sweetened by various imitators (he too succumbed to downtown commercial demands), whose vapidity encouraged a prejudice amongst many that obscured the genius of the original. Some of Noro's most highly regarded recordings in this piano and rhythm style were made for the Coda Record Company, founded in January 1945 by Gabriel Oller. 'On January 16, 1945, Noro was the first to record for Coda,' Oller told Max Salazar. 'He recorded 'Rumba Rhapsody', 'Bangin' The Bongo', 'Linda Mujer' and 'Begin The Beguine'. Our friendship began in the 30s . . . He was always well dressed, shoes shined, nails polished and reeked of expensive cologne . . . He loved women. He had to work steadily to pay the alimony his three wives collected . . . Noro made 12 great recordings for me.' The named tracks and other Coda cuts are included on the indispensable Tumbao CD *Rumba Rhapsody*. Noro adapted readily to the late 40s advent of the mambo (which peaked during the first half of the 50s), and his band remained popular during the early 50s. *Rumbas And Mambo* contains a couple of notable self-penned big band mambos Noro recorded for MGM in 1949: the outstanding '110th Street And 5th Avenue', which immortalized the New York corner meeting place for Latin musicians (near Tatay's Spanish Music Centre record store, opened by Oller and his brother Vicente in the early 30s); and 'Ponce', a tribute to the southern coastal Puerto Rican town known as 'la cuna de los musicos' (the musicians cradle). Noro continued to maintain his appeal to both Latinos and non-Latinos during the remainder of the 50s: at one stage he was practically the house band at the famous China Doll night club on Broadway, from where his shows were broadcast live on a daily basis. Many future major Latin names passed through Noro's band, including singers Machito (late 30s), Tito Rodríguez (mid-40s), Pellín Rodríguez, Vicentico Valdés, Dioris Valladares and Vitín Avilés; percussionists **Tito Puente**, Ray Romero (1942), Sabú Martínez, Manny Oquendo and **Willie Rosario**; saxophonist/arranger Ray Santos; and bass player Julio Andino. Jazz trumpeter **Doc Severinson** was a sideman between 1950 and 1951. Noro used a number of arrangers to write for him, including René Hernández, Joe Loco, **Arturo 'Chico' O'Farrill**, Ray Santos, Ben Pickering, Charlie Diamond (aka Carlos Diamante) and others. He worked particularly closely with Pickering and Diamond, dictating his ideas for them to transcribe. One of Noro's last albums was 1960's *His Piano And Rhythm* on Ansonia, which contained his elegant and haunting 'Maria Cervantes'. Noro became virtually blind due to chronic diabetes. From 1961, the last three years of his life were spent in Puerto Rico, where his big band, featuring Vitín Avilés, was contracted to play at the prestigious Hotel la Concha, and became one of the island's biggest attractions. In 1984 **Charlie Palmieri** revived the piano and rhythm format for his classic *A Giant Step*, which included his interpretation of 'Rumba Rhapsody'. According to Charlie's brother, **Eddie Palmieri**: 'Definitely, the inspiration for Charlie was Noro, because he owned all of his records and classic recordings of piano solos which he loved' (*Latin Beat*, 1991). One of the last surviving Latin pianists who was directly exposed to Noro is Dr. Ken 'Leo' Rosa (b. New York; Chiropractic Orthopaedist/1965; a 'Mr Universe' runner-up and a broadcaster), who refreshingly recreates, as well as extemporizes in, Noro's inimitable style.

Selected albums: *His Piano And Rhythm* (rec. 1960, reissued 1991), *Recordando Los Exitos De Noro Morales, Vol. 1* (rec. 1953-56, reissued 1992), with Miguelito Valdés *Mr. Babalú* (rec. 1949-51, reissued 1993), *Rumbas And Mambo* (rec. 1945-50, reissued 1993), *Rumba Rhapsody* (rec. 1945-51, reissued 1994).

Morand, Herb

b. 1905, New Orleans, Louisiana, USA. d. 23 February 1952. Beginning to play trumpet as a youth, Morand became a professional musician at the age of 18. He worked in bands led by Nat Towles, **Chris Kelly** and others, often in and around his home town. In Chicago from the late 20s, he played and recorded with many musicians, including **Johnny Dodds**, Rosetta Howard, and the Harlem Hamfats. In the early 40s he returned to New Orleans where he led his own bands, later joining **George Lewis**. A competent player raised in the New Orleans tradition, during his career Morand's playing took on characteristics of other styles of jazz. He remained a good ensemble player, his solo work seldom having the dash and fire of many of his contemporaries.

Albums: *Herb Morand And His New Orleans Band* (1950).

Morbid Angel

Formed in Florida, USA, in 1984, the band's original line-up consisted of Stering Von Scarborough (bass/vocals), Trey Azagthoth (guitar), Richard Brunelle (guitar) and Pete Sandoval (drums). They quickly gained a following on the underground death metal scene because of their extreme, ultra-fast musical approach. The band recorded the self-financed *Abominations Of Desolation* in 1986. However, unhappy with the resulting recordings, they decided not to release them, as had originally been intended, on their own, now defunct Gorque Records label. They then underwent a personnel change replacing the departed Scarborough with David Vincent (ex-**Terrorizer**), who gave the band much more of an identity with his strong, charismatic presence (he had previously produced *Abominations Of Desolation*). Morbid Angel continued to gain momentum and eventually attracted the attention of **Earache Records**, resulting in the band's official debut, *Altars Of Madness,* released in 1989. Death metal fans loved it and the band were soon elevated into the hierachy of that genre. By the release of *Blessed Are The Sick,* they had toured Europe extensively, building a strong following in the process. The album, like its forerunner produced by Tom Morris, was once again a marked improvement on previous efforts, and strengthened their position within a growing fan base. Owing to furious bootlegging and the band's burgeoning popularity, Earache Records released the original recordings of *Abominations Of Desolation* in 1991. For 1993's *Covenant*, released through Giant/**Warner** in the US, Flemming Rassmussen (**Metallica** etc.) was drafted in to produce, and their rising profile was cemented by a tour of that teritory supporting **Black Sabbath** and **Motörhead**. 1994 saw the replacement of Richard Brunelle by Eric Rutan (ex-Ripping Corpse).

Albums: *Altars Of Madness* (Earache 1989), *Blessed Are The Sick* (Earache 1991), *Abominations Of Desolation* (Earache 1991), *Covenant* (Earache 1993).

Mordred

Formed in San Francisco, USA, in 1985, Mordred were one of the first of a new breed of thrash metal bands that incorporated elements of funk into their high-speed onslaught. Comprising Scott Holderby (vocals), Danny White (guitar), James Sanguinetti (guitar), Art Liboon (bass) and Gannon Hall (drums), they signed to Noise Records and released *Fool's Game* in 1989. On their next album they recruited Aaron (Pause) Vaughn, a scratching disc jockey to give their sound a new dimension. This approach was thought to offer enormous crossover potential, combining elements of **Faith No More**, **Megadeth** and **Parliament**, but thus far the band have failed to gain a footing outside a strictly cult following.

Albums: *Fool's Game* (Noise 1989), *In This Life* (Noise 1991), *Vision* (Noise 1992).

More

This **N.W.O.B.H.M.** band was led by guitarist Kenny Cox with Paul Mario Day (vocals), Laurie Mansworth (guitar), Brian Day (bass) and Frank Darch (drums). Wild live shows which ended with most of the audience on stage, coupled with a promising session for BBC Radio One's *Friday Rock Show*, led to a deal with **Atlantic** as major N.W.O.B.H.M. acts such as **Saxon** and **Iron Maiden** began to make a serious impact. *Warhead* was a solid debut, but failed to match the live shows, and sales were poor despite a series of UK support performances which generally upstaged headliners **Krokus**, followed by an appearance in the opening slot of the 1981 **Donington Festival**. This lack of immediate success plus record company problems led to internal fighting, and by the release of *Blood And Thunder*, Cox had assembled an entirely new line-up of Nick Stratton (vocals), Andy John Burton (drums) and Barry Nicholls (bass). The album stuck faithfully to the riff-heavy style of *Warhead*, but without a UK release from a disinterested label, the band quickly faded.

Albums: *Warhead* (Atlantic 1980), *Blood And Thunder* (Atlantic 1982).

More American Graffiti

American Graffiti was not only a milestone in pop-orientated cinema, it remains one of the finest films of its era. Sadly, this 1979 sequel lacks its charm, atmosphere and characterization. Ron Howard, Paul LeMat and Candy Clark reprise their earlier roles as the action shifts from 1962 to a late 60s dominated by the Vietnam War, protest and counter-culture idealism. Where the canvas of *American Graffiti* was tight - the action unfolded over a single night - the attempt to compress several years of changing attitudes into the follow-up robbed it of potential resonance. However, appearances by **Country Joe And The Fish**, with their anti-war anthem 'I Feel Like I'm Fixin' To Die', and **Doug Sahm**, enliven the proceedings, while legendary disc jockey **Wolfman Jack** makes another welcome cameo. *More American Graffiti* did boast another stellar soundtrack. A succession of Tamla **Motown** classics, including 'Heatwave' (**Martha And The Vandellas**), 'Stop! In The Name Of Love' (the **Supremes**) and 'My Guy' (**Mary Wells**) are set beside folk-rock from the **Byrds**, **Bob Dylan** and **Simon And Garfunkel**. Garage bands **Sam The Sham And The Pharoahs** and **? And The Mysterions** give way to 'west coast' acolytes the **Doors**, **Grateful Dead** and **Frank Zappa** in a collection which, in microcosm, charts the development of US music during a highly-prolific decade.

Moré, Beny

b. Bartolomé Maximiliano Moré Gutiérrez, 24 August 1919, Santa Isabel de las Lajas, La Villas Province, Cuba, d. 19 February 1963. An outstanding singer ('his voice was like a bambo in the wind', said Cuban writer Miguel Barnet in 1984), bandleader, composer and arranger, the inimitable Moré, nicknamed 'El Bárbaro del Ritmo' (The Barbarian of Rhythm), is still idolized and the subject of tributes nearly three decades after his death. Beny worked with various groups, duos and trios before arriving in Havana in the early 40s. There he performed in the cafes and bars of the capital's bohemian society; sang with Cuarteto Cordero and Sexteto Cauto and debuted on Radio Mil Diez. In the mid-40s he joined the group of Miguel Matamoros (1894-1971; leader/composer/guitarist/vocalist; writer of the immortal 'Son de la Loma' and other classics), with whom he made his recording debut and travelled to Mexico. Matamoros returned to Cuba, but Moré remained and recorded prolifically with the orchestras of Cubans, Mariano Mercerón, Arturo Nuñez (with whom he had his first major hit 'Mucho Corazón') and **Pérez Prado**, and Mexican composer Rafael de Paz, among others. With Prado, he toured Mexico and performed at Carnival in Panama.

After his 1950 return to Cuba, Beny worked with the orchestras of Mariano Mercerón (again), Pacho Alonso, Fernando Alvarez and Bebo Valdés. In 1953, Moré organized a 21-piece aggregation which he named his Banda Gigante (Giant Band). Personnel included the great pianist/arranger Peruchín (Pedro Jústiz, 1913-1977), trumpeter **Alfredo 'Chocolate' Armenteros**, trombonist/arranger Generoso Jiménez and Beny's brother Delfín Moré. Moré and Banda Gigante had hit after hit and made a tremendous impact throughout the Latin Caribbean, Latin America and the North American Latino community. Salsa singer/songwriter and film star **Rubén Blades**, who was born and raised in Panama, said in 1986: 'Beny Moré for many reasons was a god-like man . . . this black man had a band of black guys who played as good as any white band

anybody had ever seen in the movies, you know, the big bands from the North. We had never seen so many guys from Latin America playing with that authority. And Beny himself had a fantastic voice'. Beny was reputed to have led a bohemian and bawdy lifestyle, which included lengthy drinking-bouts. He died at the early age of 44, reportedly from cirrhosis of the liver.
Albums: Collections have been issued on RCA, Discuba and the Cuban State label Areito (11 volumes of *Sonero Mayor*). A couple of his RCA classics, *Magia Antillana* and *The Most From Beny Moré*, have been reissued on CD.

More, Julian

b. 1929, England. A librettist and lyricist for some of the most successful British hit musical shows of the late 50s, More became interested in the theatre while at Cambridge University. He was involved as a performer and writer in undergraduate revues, and contributed the occasional item to the Watergate Theatre. In 1953 he wrote some material for the West End revue *Airs On A Shoestring*, which starred Max Adrian, Moyra Fraser and Betty Marsden. Two years later, he collaborated with composer James Gilbert for the Windsor Theatre production of a 'revusical', *The World's The Limit*, and, in the following year, they had a smash hit with ***Grab Me A Gondola***. Set at the Venice Film Festival, with the character of the film star heroine 'moulded' on Britain's Diana Dors, the show starred Joan Heal, Denis Quilley and June Wenham. It featured numbers such as 'That's My Biography', 'Cravin' For The Avon', 'A Man, Not a Mouse' and 'New To Me'. Even more successful was ***Irma La Douce*** (1958) for which More, with Monty Norman and **David Heneker**, provided the English book and lyrics translation to Marguerite Monnot's music. The story included such songs as 'Our Language Of Love' and 'Dis-Donc', and ran for 1,512 performances in London, and over 500 in New York. The More-Heneker-Norman team combined with Wolfe Mankowitz later in 1958 for ***Expresso Bongo***. The 'most important British musical for years' starred Paul Schofield, Hy Hazell and James Kenny, and ran for nine months. The score, which included 'The Shrine On The Second Floor' and 'I've Never Had It So Good', virtually disappeared from the innovative 1960 film version starring **Cliff Richard** and Laurence Harvey. The lead in the road version was taken by Colin Hicks, the brother of **Tommy Steele**. London's theatrical scene was changing and More was unable to match previous achievements. Throughout the 60s and 70s his offerings included *The Golden Touch* (with Gilbert), *The Art Of Living* (his last collaboration with both Norman and Heneker), *The Perils Of Scobie Prilt* (with Norman), *The Man From The West* (with David Russell), *Quick, Quick, Slow* (Norman), *Good Time Johnny* (Gilbert), *R Loves J* (with Alexander Ferris), and *Bordello* (with Americans Al Frisch and Bernard Spiro). In 1979 he was back with Monty Norman for *Songbook*, 'a burlesque tale' of the work of the prolific songwriter, Mooney Shapiro. Subsequently, More settled in France, with homes in Paris and Provence, and became a successful writer of travel books. Since then he has emerged occasionally, and wrote the book and lyrics to **Gilbert Becaud**'s music for the Broadway show *Roza* (1987), 'a maudlin and awkwardly constructed story with inferior songs'. He also adapted Abe Burrows' original book for a London revival of **Cole Porter**'s ***Can-Can*** (1988).

Morehouse, Chauncey

b. 11 March 1902, Niagara Falls, New York, USA, d. 3 November 1980. Morehouse's early career found him playing drums in the pit at silent-movie theatres, from which he graduated to danceband work. In 1922 he joined the popular band led by Paul Specht, with whom he came to New York. His recordings with **Frank Guarente**'s Georgians (a band drawn from the Specht group) attracted much favourable attention in the jazz world. After leaving Specht, Morehouse remained in New York, playing in the bands of **Ted Weems** and Howard Lanin. In 1925 he joined one of contractor **Jean Goldkette**'s bands, this one at the Goldkette flagship ballroom, the Greystone in Detroit. In the Goldkette band, Morehouse accompanied major jazz artists such as **Bix Beiderbecke** and **Frank Trumbauer**, making records which became classics of their kind. After the Goldkette band folded, Morehouse returned to New York and in 1930 began a gradual drift into studio work, which is where he remained for the next three decades. He retired at the end of the 60s, but played occasionally thereafter with bands such as the New York Jazz Repertory Orchestra and a revived Goldkette band.
Compilation: with Bix Beiderbecke *The Studio Groups - 1927* (1927).

Moreira, Airto

b. 5 August 1941, Itaiopolis, Brazil. Moreira moved to Rio de Janeiro when he was 16 years old. In the 60s he played in a quartet with the pianist/flautist Hermeto Pascal, travelling the length and breadth of Brazil collecting and using over 120 percussion instruments. He moved to Los Angeles in 1968 and then to New York in 1970. He was a musician who managed to be in the right place at the right time; jazz was being opened up to the kind of extra rhythmic subtlety a second percussionist could offer. Moreira describes how 'you look and listen for your own place in the music - your own space - and then you start to make sounds . . . music is like a picture; it's not just sound'. He worked with **Miles Davis** in 1970 as he sought to establish the changes announced in *Bitches Brew*. He played percussion on the **Weather Report** debut album in 1971 and then worked with **Chick Corea**'s **Return**

To Forever. Since then he has worked with tenor saxophonists **Stan Getz** and **Gato Barbieri** to the **Grateful Dead**'s drummer Mickey Hart with whom he recorded the percussion soundtrack for Francis Ford Coppola's film *Apocalypse Now*. He worked most regularly with his wife **Flora Purim**. In the mid-80s he played with the **Al DiMeola** Project, with which he came to Europe.

Albums: with Miles Davis *At Fillmore* (1970), *Black Beauty* (1970), *Live - Evil* (1970); *Weather Report* (1971), with Chick Corea *Return To Forever* (1972), *Fingers* (1973), with Stan Getz *Captain Marvel* (1975), with Mickey Hart *Rhythm Devils Play River Music* (1980), with Flora Purim *Colours Of Life* (In & Out 1988), *Struck By Lightning* (Virgin 1989), *The Other Side Of This* (Rykodisk 1992), *Forth World* (Jazz House 1992), with the Gods Of Jazz *Killer Bees* (B&W 1993).

Morello, Joe

b. 17 July 1928, Springfield, Massachusetts, USA. After studying violin Morello turned to playing drums while still at school. He played locally, accompanying fellow high school student **Phil Woods** among others. In the early 50s he moved to New York, performing with many bands in a wide variety of musical settings, including the big band of **Stan Kenton**. He was, however, most often to be found playing in small groups, notably those led by guitarists Johnny Smith, **Tal Farlow**, **Sal Salvador** and **Jimmy Raney**, pianist **Marian McPartland** and singers **Jackie Cain** and **Roy Kral**. He first attracted wide attention when he joined the **Dave Brubeck** Quartet in 1956. He remained with Brubeck for 12 years and, **Paul Desmond** apart, was that band's most accomplished jazzman. Indeed, Morello's playing with Brubeck was exemplary in its unassertive precision which, allied to a remarkably delicate swing, provided object lessons during a period when jazz drumming was notable for its aggression. After leaving Brubeck in 1967 Morello, who was partially-sighted from childhood, was involved mostly in teaching. He occasionally led small groups in the 70s and also made a handful of records with Brubeck, McPartland and Salvador. An outstanding small group drummer, Morello's long stint with Brubeck, while giving him a highly visible presence, resulted in a considerable loss to the wider world of jazz.

Albums: with Marian McPartland *Jazz at The Hickory House* (1953), with Tal Farlow *The Tal Farlow Album* (1954), with Dave Brubeck *Jazz Impressions Of The USA* (1956), with Brubeck *Time Out* (1959), *It's About Time* (1961), *The Dave Brubeck Quartet At Carnegie Hall* (1963), *The Dave Brubeck Quartet's 25th Anniversary Reunion* (1976), with Sal Salvador *Juicy Lucy* (1978).

Further reading: *All In Good Time*, Marian McPartland.

Morells

Formed in Springfield, Missouri, USA in 1982, the Morells recorded only one album, *Shake And Push*, on Borrowed Records. Although it never charted, this roots-rock group built a devoted following on the USA alternative circuit. Consisting of bassist Lou Whitney (who had once performed with soul singer **Arthur Conley**), his wife, Maralie (keyboards), D. Clinton Thompson (guitar) and Ron Gremp (drums), the group started in the late 70s as the Skeletons and then the Original Symptoms before settling in as the Morells, combining within their sound rockabilly, soul, blues and jazz. The group disbanded in the mid-80s. Lou Whitney went on to produce the debut album by New York rockers the **Del-Lords** before re-forming the Skeletons in 1988, with Thompson.

Album: *Shake And Push* (1982).

Morgan, Derrick

b. March 1940, Stewarton, Jamaica, West Indies. Morgan's recording career stretches back to the birth of the Jamaican record industry, c.1959-60. An imposing figure invariably topped with an almost brimless pork-pie hat, his cool, hip and rhythmic voice, enlivened by the occasional excited yelp, applied itself successfully to a variety of styles in those formative years, such as the Latin beat of 'Fat Man' (1960), the gospel fervour of 'I Pray For You' (1961) and the shuffling R&B of his Jamaican Independence anthem, 'Forward March' (1962). He duetted with female singer Patsy on a series of **Shirley And Lee**-styled numbers, that duo being currently popular in Jamaica, before settling into a **ska** style with 'Shake A Leg' (1962) and other recordings for **Prince Buster**. His split from Buster to join the Chinese-owned Beverley's Records led to an entertaining, and successful, exchange of insults on singles like Morgan's 'Blazing Fire' and Buster's unequivocal 'Blackhead China Man' (Buster resented the idea of the Jamaican music industry being controlled by non-blacks). Morgan recorded prolifically throughout the 60s and into the 70s, recording **rocksteady** cuts such as 'Greedy Gal' (1967). He quickly became a very popular figure with reggae's UK skinhead followers.About this time his sight, always impaired, deteriorated to the extent where he could see only 'light and clouds', and he is now musically less active, though as recently as 1990 he travelled to London for a ska revival concert.

Albums: *Forward March* (Island 1963), *Seven Letters* (1969), *Forward March* (Beverley's 1964), *Moon Hop* (1970), *In The Mood* (Magnet 1974), *Development* (1975), *People Decision* (Third World 1977). Compilations: *Blazing Fire Vol. 1 & 2* (1988), *I Am The Ruler* (Trojan 1993).

Morgan, Elaine

b. 11 February 1960, Cardiff, Wales A singer who has started to secure a place for her talent. Morgan started out by working in a Cardiff recording studio, supplying voice overs and vocals for jingles. Additionally, she supplied backing vocals for many of the recording artists using the studio, with the result that **Robin Williamson** recruited her to sing on his *Ten Of Songs* album. Elaine's next break came, in 1985, when she was asked to play support, with her new band Rose Among Thorns, to **Fairport Convention**. Since then, she has worked with **Ashley Hutchings** and the **Albion Band**, and has toured the UK, as support to **Ralph McTell**, on a number of occasions. Morgan's first solo release, *First Blush*, was produced by Ashley Hutchings and Phil Beer. The recording also featured other members of the Albion Band. Elaine has also appeared, in an acting capacity, in numerous television series. Despite one or two changes of personnel, the current line-up of Rose Among Thorns is her husband Derek Morgan (b. 14 October 1953, Cardiff, Wales; bass), John Turner (b. 30 January 1949, Cardiff, Wales; drums), and Tim Gray (b. 2 August 1961, Abercynon, Mid-Glamorgan, Wales; lead guitar). Dave Dutfield (electric and acoustic guitar), who had earlier been with the group, left in January 1993, to return to teaching. With Elaine's strong vocals, the sound has taken the group outside of the confines of the purely folk spectrum, into the more mainstream, and commercial, market.

Albums: *Masquerade-On The Wings Of Change* (1988), *First Blush* (1989), *Changing Moods* (1989), *Rose Among Thorns* (HTD 1991), *This Time It's Real* (1992).

Morgan, Frank

b. 23 December 1933, Minneapolis, Minnesota, USA. The west coast bebop altoist Frank Morgan's career was obscured for over 30 years by prison sentences for narcotics offences and it is only in recent times that his talents and imagination have been more widely displayed or discussed. Morgan began playing guitar under the tuition of his guitarist father then, after moving to Los Angeles in 1947, learned alto saxophone at LA's Jefferson High from the same teacher who taught **Dexter Gordon**, **Wardell Gray** and **Don Cherry**. He began on saxophone as a **Charlie Parker** admirer, then grew closer to the interpretation of his west coast contemporary, **Art Pepper**, whom he resembles in his sharply accented sounds, fragmented figures and blurted, episodic delivery. Morgan once told the American critic Francis Davis 'for me, prowess isn't as important as rapport' and he has always spaced out his statements with patience, artifice, a wide tonal palette and an avoidance of fireworks. At the age of 15 he won a television talent contest, which eventually led to a place in **Lionel Hampton**'s band. He also recorded as a sideman with **Ray Charles**, **Teddy Charles**, **Kenny Clarke** and others before releasing his debut as leader, *Introducing Frank Morgan*, in 1955. Since 1953 Morgan's drug problems have resulted in several prison sentences.

Although largely absent from the jazz scene he did continue to play (mostly inside prison). Morgan returned to the outside jazz world in the mid-80s to startle audiences with his exhilarating Parker-inspired style. Morgan was over 50 before he made his second record, *Easy Living*, which introduced his sparkling bebop to a new generation of admirers. With further releases and tours to his credit, he is now recognized as one of the premier bebop altoists of the day. Interviewed in 1988 by Stan Woolley for *Jazz Journal International*, Morgan declared that he was 'one of the old purists and proud of it.' New albums and appearances on the international circuit have brought his strikingly inventive playing to the attention of a new and admiring audience. His recovery from the problems which beset him during more than half his lifetime is fortunate and he appears to be well aware of how much he has lost. In the same interview he spoke of the present and future, remarking, 'I just want to take time and absorb everything.'

Albums: *Introducing Frank Morgan* (1955), *Easy Living* (1985), *Lament* (Contemporary 1986), *Double Image* (Contemporary 1987), *Bebop Lives!* (JVC 1987), *Quiet Fire* (Contemporary 1987), *Major Changes* (Contemporary 1987), *Yardbird Suite* (Contemporary 1989), *Reflections* (Contemporary 1989), *Mood Indigo* (Antilles 1989), *A Lovesome Thing* (Antilles 1991), *You Must Believe In Spring* (Antilles 1992), *Listen To The Dawn* (Antilles 1994).

Morgan, George

b. 28 June 1924, Waverley, Tennessee, USA, d. 7 July 1975. Morgan was raised in Barberton, Ohio and by the time he was nine, he was performing his own songs on guitar. He enlisted in the US Army during the War but was discharged three months later on medical grounds. He formed a band and found work on a radio station in Wooster, Ohio, and wrote 'Candy Kisses' after a broken romance. **RCA** showed an interest in Morgan, who performed 'Candy Kisses' on the *Grand Ole Opry* to great acclaim, but their tardiness led to US Columbia signing him instead. 'Candy Kisses' was a US country Number 1 in 1949 despite competition from cover versions from Elton Britt, **Red Foley** and Eddie Kirk. However, there was friction between Morgan and **Hank Williams**, who regarded 'Candy Kisses' as 'stupid' and its singer 'a cross-eyed crooner'. Morgan, a crooner in the vein of **Eddy Arnold**, called his band the Candy Kids and he consolidated his reputation with 'Please Don't Let Me Love You', 'Room Full Of Roses', 'Almost', 'You're The Only Good Thing' and 'Mr. Ting-A-Ling (Steel Guitar Man)'. In 1953 Morgan became the first country

performer to record with a symphony orchestra. In 1964 Morgan's duet of 'Slippin' Around' with Marion Worth was very successful, but by then Morgan was finding hits hard to come by. In 1967 he moved to Starday and then Nashville, Stop, US **Decca** and 4 Star, all with only minor successes. Morgan, a CB buff, suffered a heart attack whilst helping a friend install an aerial on his roof. Later that year, he celebrated his birthday at the *Opry* with the debut of his daughter, Lorrie. Within a few days he was undergoing open heart surgery but died on 7 July 1975. In 1979, a duet with Lorrie, 'I'm Completely Satisfied With You', made the US country charts. Lorrie Morgan married Keith Whitley and has been following a highly successful solo career since his death in May 1989.
Albums: *Morgan, By George* (1957), *Golden Memories* (1961), *Tender Lovin' Care* (1964), with Marion Worth *Slippin' Around* (1964), *Red Roses For A Blue Lady* (1965), *A Room Full Of Roses* (1967), *Candy Kisses* (1967), *Country Hits By Candlelight* (1968), *Steal Away* (1968), *Barbara* (1968), *Sounds Of Goodbye* (1969), *Misty Blue* (1969), *George Morgan Sings Like A Bird* (1969), *The Real George* (1969), *A Room Full Of Roses* (1971), *Red Roses From The Blue Side Of Town* (1974), *A Candy Mountain Melody* (1974), *George Morgan - From This Moment On* (1975), *Red Rose From The Blue Side Of Town* (1977), *George Morgan - Country Souvenirs Of The 1950s* (1990).

Morgan, Helen

b. Helen Riggins, 2 August 1900, Danville, Ohio, USA, d. 8 October 1941, Chicago, Illinois, USA. One of the first, and certainly one of the most accomplished torch singers in the history of popular music. After working at a number of unskilled jobs, Morgan began singing in small Chicago clubs. She graduated to revue, appearing in New York in ***George White's Scandals*** (1925), and *Americana* (1926) in which she was noticed by **Florenz Ziegfeld**, who signed her to play the role of Julie La Verne in the original production of **Jerome Kern**'s ***Show Boat*** (1927). Her performance of 'Bill' (lyric by **P.G. Wodehouse** and **Oscar Hammerstein II**) was a show-stopper. In fact, the song had been cut from ***Oh Lady! Lady!!*** (1918) and *Zip, Goes A Million* (1919), before Morgan gave it immortality in *Show Boat.* In the same show she also sang 'Can't Help Lovin Dat Man', and, 10 years later, introduced 'Why Was I Born?' and 'Don't Ever Leave Me' in another Kern-Hammerstein show, *Sweet Adeline.* She later appeared on Broadway in ***Ziegfeld Follies*** (1931) and the 1932 revival of *Show Boat*, and was in the 1929 and 1936 screen versions of ***Show Boat***. Here other film appearances included *Applause*, *Roadhouse Nights*, *Glorifying The American Girl*, *Marie Galante*, *You Belong To Me*, *Sweet Music*, ***Go Into Your Dance***, and *Frankie And Johnny* (1936). As well as the above songs from the shows, she had several hit records in the late 20s and early 30s, such as 'A Tree In The Park', 'Mean To Me', 'Body And Soul'. She is also particularly remembered for her version of **George** and **Ira Gershwin**'s 'The Man I Love'. By the late 30s her career was in disarray and she was heavily dependent upon alcohol. As owner of a number of Prohibition-era speakeasies she had ready access to liquor and her health rapidly deteriorated until she died of cirrhosis of the liver. Her life story was the subject of a 1957 screen biography, *The Helen Morgan Story* (UK title: *Both Ends Of The Candle*), in which she was played by Ann Blyth.
Further reading: *Helen Morgan, Her Life And Legend*, Gilbert Maxwell.

Morgan, Jane

b. Jane Currier, Boston, Massachusetts, USA. A popular singer with a clear, strong voice and an ability to sing in several languages, Morgan was accepted in many parts of the world during the 50s and 60s. Raised in Florida, she trained as a lyric soprano at the Juilliard School of Music in New York, supplementing her income by singing in night-clubs. At one of them, she was spotted by the French impresario Bernard Hilda, who offered her a contract to sing in Paris. Within weeks of arriving in France she became a major attraction and, during the next few years became established throughout Europe. On her return to the USA, she was billed as 'The American Girl From Paris', and appeared successfully on television and in night-clubs. Signed for Kapp Records, she had a minor hit in 1956 with 'Two Different Worlds', one of the several tracks she recorded with pianist Roger Williams.
In the following year she had a million seller with 'Fascination', adapted from the old French number 'Valse Tzigane', with an English lyric by **Dick Manning**, which became the theme for the Cary Grant-Audrey Hepburn movie *Love In The Afternoon.* Despite the rock 'n' roll revolution, she continued to be successful, especially in Europe, and in 1958, she had a UK number 1 with **Gilbert Becaud** and Carl Sigman's 'The Day The Rains Came'. Her French version of the song was on the b-side. Among her other hits in the early 60s, were 'If Only I Could Live My Life Again', 'With Open Arms' and 'Romantica', and her 1957 album, *Fascination*, made the US Top 20. Morgan's husband, Jerry Weintraub, was instrumental in **Elvis Presley**'s re-emergence in the early 70s, and managed several top US singers such as **John Denver**.

Morgan, Jaye P.

b. Mary Margaret Morgan, 1932, Mancos, Colorado, USA. Morgan performed with the Morgan Family Variety Troupe until her father's death in 1945. At 18, her voice had matured to the husky contralto that would land her a job as featured singer with Frank de Vol's orchestra and then that of **Hank Penny**, an **RCA** recording artist. Through Penny, the company signed Morgan who would reach a wider audience during two years of weekly radio exposure on New York's *Robert Q. Lewis Show* and, less regularly, on the nationally-transmitted *Stop The Music*. After 'That's All I Want From You' came close to topping the US chart in 1954, 'Danger! Heartbreak Ahead', 'The Longest Walk' and 'Pepper-Hot Baby' were smashes the following year - as were 'Chee Chee Oo Chee' and 'Two Lost Souls' (from Broadway musical, ***Damn Yankees***) - duets with **Perry Como**. However, a link-up on record with **Eddy Arnold** proved a flop, and, that Christmas, 'If You Don't Want My Love' barely scraped into the Top 40. Subsequently, though still planting feet in both the C&W and pop camps, only 1959's 'Are You Lonesome Tonight' and a 1960 version of **Johnny Cash**'s 'I Walk The Line' could be even remotely classed as 'hits'. Nevertheless, established as an all-American showbusiness 'personality', she would appear on television variety spectaculars and talk programmes as late as the mid-80s.

Morgan, Lanny

b. Harold Lansford Morgan, 30 March 1934, Des Moines, Iowa, USA. As a child he played violin before taking up the alto saxophone. When he was 10 his family moved to Los Angeles and he continued his studies. As a young man he played in big bands including those led by **Charlie Barnet**, **Terry Gibbs** and **Bob Florence**, then settled for a while in New York where he worked with **Maynard Ferguson**. Back on the west coast he played and recorded with several bands including **Supersax** and that led by **Bill Berry**. In addition to performing, Morgan also developed a reputation as a teacher. Since the mid-80s he had played mostly in small groups and has toured Europe and the UK as a single. A hard blowing saxophonist, with a crisply incisive tone, Morgan is a commanding musician and is much respected by his peers.
Albums: *Maynard Ferguson Sextet* (1965), with Bill Berry *Hello Rev* (Concord 1976), with Supersax *Dynamite!* (1978), *It's About Time* (Pausa 1981), with Jeff Hamilton *Indiana* (1982).

Morgan, Lee

b. 10 July 1938, Philadelphia, Pennsylvania, USA, d. 19 February 1972. Prodigiously talented, Morgan played trumpet professionally at the age of 15 and three years later joined **Dizzy Gillespie**'s big band. During this same period he recorded with **John Coltrane**, **Hank Mobley** and others. In 1958 the Gillespie band folded and Morgan joined **Art Blakey**'s **Jazz Messengers** where he made a tremendous impact not only nationally but around the world, thanks to the group's recordings. In the early 60s Morgan returned to his home town, where he played in comparative obscurity, but by 1963 he was back in New York, leading his own groups and also working for a while with Blakey in 1964. Morgan's popularity was enhanced by the success of a recording of his own composition, the irresistibly catchy 'The Sidewinder' which helped to spark a jazz/funk mini-boom and has remained a dance floor favourite ever since. Morgan's trumpet style was marked by his full-blooded vitality aided by the richness of his tone. Playing with the strictly-controlled Blakey band impacted his natural enthusiasm and the resulting tensions created some of the best hard-bop trumpet playing of the period. Indeed, despite the passage of time and the many fine trumpeters to have entered jazz in his wake, only a handful have attained Morgan's remarkable standards of emotional virtuosity. In the late 60s, Morgan's career was damaged for a while by personal problems but a woman friend helped him recover. Unfortunately, this same woman became jealous of a new relationship he had formed and on 19 February 1972 she shot and killed him at the New York nightclub, where his quintet were performing.
Selected albums: *Introducing Lee Morgan* (Savoy 1956), *Lee Morgan Indeed* (Blue Note 1956), *Lee Morgan Vol 2* (Blue Note 1957), with Hank Mobley *Hank's Shout* (1956), *City Lights* (Blue Note 1957), *Lee Morgan Vol 3* (Blue Note 1957), with John Coltrane *Blue Train* (1957), *The Cooker* (Blue Note 1958), *Peckin' Time* (1958), *Candy* (Blue Note 1959), with Thad Jones *Minor Strain* (1960), *Lee-Way* (Blue Note 1960), *Indestructible Lee* (Affinity 1960), with Art Blakey *The Freedom Rider* (1961), *Take Twelve* (Original Jazz Classics 1962), *Delightfulee Morgan* (Blue Note 60s), *The Sidewinder* (Blue Note 1963), *Search For The New Land* (Blue Note 1964), *Tom Cat* (Blue Note 1964), *Cornbread* (Blue Note 60s), *The Rumproller* (Blue Note 1965), *Infinity* (1965), *The Cat* (1965), *Charisma* (1966), *The Rajah* (Blue Note 1966), *The Procrastinator* (1967), with Mobley *Dippin'* (1965), *Caramba* (1968), *Live At The Lighthouse* (Fresh Sound 1970), *Capra Beach* (1971), *We Remember You* (Fresh Sound 1972).

Morgan, Lorrie

b. Loretta Lynn Morgan, 27 June 1959, Nashville, Tennessee, USA. The youngest daughter of country crooner and ***Grand Ole Opry*** star, **George Morgan**, she followed in father's footsteps. She naturally began singing with Dad and made her own *Opry* debut at the age of 13 at the old Ryman Auditorium, where her rendition of 'Paper Roses' gained her a standing ovation. After her father's death in 1975, she worked as a backing singing with **George Jones**' road show and for a time was married to Ron Gaddis, who played steelguitar in Jones' band. In 1979, she scored her first minor chart successes with 'Two People In Love' and 'Tell Me I'm Only Dreaming', as well as with a duet recording made earlier with her late father, 'I'm Completely Satisfied With You'. The same year, she had a daughter but her marriage ended and tiring of life on the road, she basically retired. In 1984, the lure of the music enticed her back; she became a member of the *Opry* and relaunched her career. She met and married singer **Keith Whitley** in 1986 but the marriage ended when Whitley's heavy drinking finally took his life in May 1989. (She later recorded a tribute to Whitley, 'If You Came Back From Heaven', which appeared on her 1994 album *War Paint*). In 1988, she joined **RCA** and scored a Top 20 hit with 'Trainwreck Of Emotion' but it was a number 9 weepy, 'Dear Me', entering the charts just a few weeks before Whitley's death, that finally established her as a major star. In 1990, she scored her first number 1 with 'Five Minutes' and from that point she has registered a regular stream of hit recordings. They include 'Til A Tear Becomes A Rose' (a duet made with Whitley), 'Except For Monday' and 'A Picture Of Me Without You' (a brave and very successful cover of a 1972 George Jones hit) on RCA. A change of label to BNA, in 1992, immediately produced a number 2 with 'Watch Me' and a further number 1 with 'What Part Of Me'. She is equally at home with up-tempo numbers or with ballads that call for the big voice technique such as her brilliant recording of 'Something In Red', which peaked at number 14. She attempted something different in 1993, when she recorded a Christmas album that had The New World Philharmonic Orchestra providing the music and contained duets with **Tammy Wynette**, **Andy Williams** and **Johnny Mathis**. (The music was recorded in London and the vocals added in Nashville, Branson or Los Angeles.)

Albums: *Leave The Light On* (RCA 1989), *Something In Red* (RCA 1991), *Watch Me* (BNA 1992), *Merry Christmas From London* (BNA 1993), *War Paint* (1994).

Videos: *War Paint - Video Hits* (1994), *I Didn't Know My Own Strength* (1995).

Morgan, Mike

b. 30 November 1959, Dallas, Texas, USA. Morgan was a motorcycle racer before applying himself seriously to playing blues guitar. He wears an eyepatch over his right eye as the result of a racing crash, making his appearance rather piratical. His band, the Crawl, was formed in the mid-80s with harmonica-player Lee McBee. The band's repertoire placed them alongside **Anson Funderburgh** And The Rockets and **Ronnie Earl**'s Broadcasters and successive albums have not seen any concerted stylistic change. In line with the **James Harman** and **William Clarke** bands, they have experimented with an acoustic approach without much success. Morgan stopped touring with the band in the early 90s. His 1994 collaboration with Jim Suhler of Monkey Beat pitted his more traditional stance against Suhler's post-SRV thrash without complete success.

Albums: *Raw & Ready* (Black Top 1990), *Mighty Fine Dancin'* (Black Top 1991), *Full Moon Over Dallas* (Black Top 1992), *Ain't Worried No More* (Black Top 1994), with Jim Suhler *Let The Dogs Run* (Black Top 1994).

Morgan, Russ

b. 29 April 1904, Scranton, Pennsylvania, USA, d. 7 August 1969. A popular bandleader, particularly during the 30s and 40s, who also wrote several durable songs, Morgan worked as a coalminer to finance his music lessons, becoming proficient on trombone and piano, as well as developing into a good arranger. After playing piano in local theatres, he switched to trombone, and in 1921 joined Billy Lustig's Scranton Sirens. He moved to New York in the early 20s and arranged for **Victor Herbert** and **John Philip Sousa**, then toured Europe with the Paul Specht band. In 1926 he joined **Jean Goldkette** in Detroit as an arranger, and then served briefly as musical director for radio station WXYX in Detroit. He spent the late 20s and early 30s in New York, and arranged for top names, **Fletcher Henderson**, **Chick Webb**, **Louis Armstrong**, the **Dorsey Brothers** and the **Boswell Sisters**, and wrote for Harlem's Cotton Club revues.

In 1934 he joined **Freddy Martin** as trombonist-arranger, and developed his distinctive muted, wah-wah style. He formed his own hotel-style band in 1935 with the aid of **Rudy Vallee**, and played important engagements at the Biltmore Hotels in New York and Los Angeles, and the Edgewater Hotel in Chicago. Morgan developed a very relaxed, easy style as a leader, along with his distinctive smooth singing voice, which was particularly effective on radio. With his tag-line, 'Music In The Morgan Manner', and his theme, 'Does Your Heart Beat For Me?', he featured on network radio in *The Rinso Show*, *The Lifebuoy Show*, and *The Philip Morris Program*. During the early part of World War II he lived on the west coast, playing a long engagement at the Claremont Hotel, Berkeley, California, and in 1946 he went into the Biltmore Bowl for a two-year run, and made several tours of eastern USA.

He had been recording with his own band since 1935, and had a string of US Top 10 hits through to 1948, including, 'Tidal Wave', 'Love Me Forever', 'In A Little Gypsy Tea Room', 'I'm In A Dancing Mood', 'When The Poppies Bloom Again', 'The Merry-Go-Round Broke Down' (number 1), 'Stop! You're Breaking My Heart', 'So Many Memories', 'Farewell My Love', 'The Dipsy Doodle', 'I Double Dare You', 'Bei Mir Bist Du Shoën', 'Will You Remember Tonight Tomorrow ?', 'I've Got A Pocketful Of Dreams' (number 1), 'Lambeth Walk', 'Wishing (Will Make It So)', 'Goodnight Wherever You Are', 'Dance With A Dolly (With A Hole In Her Stocking)', 'There Goes That Song Again' and 'I'm Looking Over A Four Leaf Clover'. Morgan was steady, rather than sensational, so it is not clear why, in 1949, he should suddenly become the year's number 1 recording artist, with hits such as 'Forever And Ever' (number 1), 'So Tired', 'Sunflower', 'Johnson Rag' and 'Cruising Down The River' (number 1, and the winner of a UK amateur songwriting contest, and his only million-seller). Morgan's own catalogue of songs, co-written with various composer-lyricists included 'Somebody Else Is Taking My Place', 'Flower Of Dawn', 'Please Think Of Me', 'Sweet Eloise', 'You're Nobody 'Till Somebody Loves You', 'So Tired', 'Does Your Heart Beat For Me?', 'So Long' (his closing theme), 'Whisper', 'California Orange Blossom', 'Don't Cry Sweetheart', 'Goodnight Little Angel' and 'It's All Over But The Crying'.

During the 50s Morgan appeared extensively on television, and had his own show in 1956 which featured ex-**Jimmy Dorsey** vocalist **Helen O'Connell**. Despite the general demise of the big bands he maintained his 17-piece unit until 1960, when he reorganized, and with a 12-piece unit played dates around Los Angeles. In 1965 he made his home in Las Vegas, and played regularly at 'The Top Of The Strip' in the Dunes Hotel. His band was still playing there when he died in 1969, after a short illness following a stroke. His son Jack, who had been with the band for 10 years, replaced him as leader.

Compilations: *One Night Stand* (1982), *Music In The Morgan Manner* (1987), *Golden Favorites* (1988), *The Best Of Russ Morgan* (1988), *Russ Morgan And His Orchestra 1937-38* (1988), *The Memory Lingers On* (1989).

Morgan, Sam

b. c.1895, Bertrandville, Louisiana, USA, d. 25 February 1936. Immensely popular in and around New Orleans, trumpeter Morgan's career was dogged by ill-health. Nevertheless, he achieved lasting fame thanks to some classic recordings made in 1927 which showed his to be a band of great style and attack, playing in the New Orleans manner. The band survived changing fashions but, following Morgan's second stroke, broke up in 1933. Morgan had two musical brothers: Isiah, who also played trumpet, and Al, who played bass with numerous bands including those of **Cab Calloway**, **Fats Waller** and **Les Hite** and also worked with **Louis Armstrong**, **Louis Jordan** and **Sabby Lewis**.

Compilations: with others *The Sound Of New Orleans* (1925-45), *The Get Happy Band* (1927).

Morillo, Erick 'More'

b. c.1971, USA. Morillo started DJing at the age of 11, playing sets in his local New Jersey that matched ragga with techno (a precursor to the sound of **Reel 2 Real**). As a student at New York's Centre For The Media Arts, he started collecting studio equipment, and became a self-taught maestro. He graduated to recording his own material by sampling Jamaican toasters on to DAT. One night a gentleman came forward from the crowd to enquire as to the source of a particular sampled voice. It transpired that the questioner, known as General, was the owner of said layrnx. Together they went on to record 'The Funky Buddha' and *Move It* album for **RCA**. Influenced by old school Chicago house like **Lil' Louis**, **Todd Terry** and **Kenny 'Dope' Gonzalez**, Morillo has gone on to build his own studio, Double Platinum, where **Little Louie Vega**'s *Hardrive* EP and **Barbara Tucker**'s 'Deep Inside' were recorded. His own productions included Deep Soul's 'Rhythms' (which featured future Smooth Touch collaborator Althea McQueen). He tried to get work at **Nervous** but was continually turned down by A&R head Gladys Pizarro. On the day he tried **Strictly Rhythm** instead Pizarro had just been installed in their offices, and this time she relented. He has gone on to be one of the leading lights of the Strictly Rhythm empire, for whom he released over 25 records, under nearly as many pseudonyms, within 1993 alone (His first release on the label having been Reel 2 Real's debut). Among his productions were Deep Soul's 'Rhythm', RAW's 'Unbe', Smooth Touch's 'Come And Take A Trip' and Club Ultimate's 'Carnival 93'. He was also represented by albums in 1994 by Deep Soul and Reel 2 Real (whose 'I Like To Move It' and 'Go On Move' were both massive worldwide hits), and recorded his own *More* EP. Part of the secret of Morillo's success may lie in his refusal to simply sample current rhythms and beats, preferring instead to write his own drum patterns and arrangements. He is nicknamed 'More' due to everybody connected being astonished at the number of different mixes he would put on to each of his releases.

Morley, Angela

In the 50s, 60s and into the 70s, Wally Stott was a highly respected conductor, arranger and composer on the UK music scene. In the early 70s he underwent a sex-change operation, and was subsequently known professionally as Angela Morley. Stott was born in 1924 in Sheffield, England. He attended the same Mexboro school as Tony Mercer, who went on to become one of the principal singers with the *Black And White Minstrel Show*. Mercer sang and played the piano accordion, while Stott concentrated on the saxophone. On leaving school, they each spent some time with Archie's Juveniles and **Oscar Rabin**'s Band. Stott's route to Rabin was via the bands of Billy Merrin and Bram Martin. By 1944, after some years with the Rabin Band, Stott was leading the saxophone section on alto, and had become the band's sole arranger: a great future was already being forecast for him. Stott's next move was to **Geraldo**, with whom he stayed for about four years, leaving in late 1948 to 'pursue arranging and film music work, which he is to make his future career'. He still managed to find the time to play the saxophone for outfits such as Jack Nathan's Coconut Grove Orchestra. In the early 50s Stott joined Philips Records, and soon became one of their key arrangers, along with **Peter Knight** and Ivor Raymonde. During the next 20 years he arranged and conducted for some of the UK's most popular artists, such as **Frankie Vaughan** ('Green Door', 'The Garden Of Eden' and 'The Heart Of A Man'), **Anne Shelton** ('Lay Down Your Arms' and *My Heart Sings*), **Harry Secombe** ('This Is My Song'), the **Beverley Sisters** ('Somebody Bad Stole De Wedding Bell' and 'Happy Wanderer'), Roy Castle (*Newcomer*), **Ronnie Carroll** ('Say Wonderful Things' and *Carroll Calling*), the **Kaye Sisters** ('Paper Roses'), **Shirley Bassey** ('Banana Boat Song' and 'As I Love You'), Muriel Smith ('Hold Me, Thrill Me, Kiss Me'), the Polka Dots (*Nice Work & You Can Buy It*) and many more, plus a few 'foreigners', too, as on ***Mel Tormé*** *Meets The British* (1959). Stott also made several of his own instrumental albums, sometimes augmented by a vocal chorus. He began writing music early in his career, and his first significant piece came to light in November 1954, when *Hancock's Half Hour* began. It proved to be one of BBC Radio's most popular programmes, later moving to television, and it's opening theme, played on a tuba over Tony Hancock's stuttering introduction, was composed by Stott. He also wrote and arranged the show's instrumental links, and conducted the orchestra for many other radio programmes, including *The Last Goon Show Of All*. Stott composed numerous pieces of mood music for London publishers, especially Chappell's, which included 'A Canadian In Mayfair' (dedicated to **Robert Farnon**, who gave Stott valuable advice on arranging and composition), 'Mock Turtles', 'Quiz', 'Travelling Along', 'Miss Universe', 'Flight By Jet', 'Casbah', 'Commenwealth March', 'Practice Makes Perfect', 'China', 'Focus On Fashion', and 'Skylight'. In the late 60s and early 70s, Stott wrote the music for several films, including *The Looking Glass War*, *Captain Nemo And The Underwater City* and *When Eight Bells Toll*, and for television productions such as *Hugh And I*, and the *The Maladjusted Busker*. Around that time, credits began to be given in the name of Angela Morley, and these include two Academy Award nominations, for her arrangements of **Alan Jay Lerner** and **Frederick Loewe**'s score for *The Little Prince* (1974), and **Richard M.** and **Robert B. Sherman**s' score for ***The Slipper And The Rose*** (1977). Morley also composed for the animated feature, *Watership Down*, the Italian production, *La Colina Dei Comali*, and for televison films such as *Friendships*, *Secrets And Lies*, *Madame X*, *Summer Girl*, *Two Marriages* and *Threesome* (1984). Most of this work has been completed in the USA, where Morley is reported to have been living for most of last 20 years.

Selected albums: *Wally Stott Tribute To George Gershwin* (1955), *Tribute To Irving Berlin* (1956), *Tribute To Jerome Kern* (1957), *London Pride* (1959), *Chorale In Concert* (1967), *Christmas By The Fireside* (1969).

Moroccos

This R&B vocal ensemble came from Chicago, Illinois, USA. With the impassioned lead work of the great Sollie McElroy (d. 1995), the Moroccos proved to be one of the finest doo-wop groups to come out of Chicago. They formed in 1952, and by 1954 when they were signed to United Records, consisted of Ralph Vernon (lead), George Prayer (d. 1992; baritone), Melvin Morrow (d. 1982; tenor), and Fred Martin (d. 1986; bass). Only after they added the ex-lead of the **Flamingos**, Sollie McElroy, did United release their recordings. The Moroccos' remake of the **Harold Arlen/E.Y. 'Yip' Harburg** tune, 'Somewhere Over The Rainbow' (1955), gave the group their biggest sales, but only regionally. Other fine regional hits were 'Pardon My Tears' (1955), 'What Is A Teen-Ager's Prayer' (1956), and 'Sad Sad Hours' (1957). On the latter George Prayer had been replaced with Calvin Baron from the **Sun Ra** organization. The Moroccos broke up in 1957. In 1966 soul singer **Joe Simon** had a big hit with 'Teenager's Prayer', a remake of the Moroccos' song.

Moross, Jerome

b. 1 August 1913, Brooklyn, New York, USA, d. 25 July 1983, Miami, Florida, USA. A highly regarded composer who wrote symphonic works as well as scores for films and Broadway shows. After graduating from New York University at the age of 18, Moross contributed some incidental music to the theatre, and then composed most of the score for the short-lived Broadway revue *Parade* in 1935. Later in that same year he was engaged by **George Gershwin** as assistant conductor and pianist for the last few weeks of the New York run of ***Porgy And Bess***, and subsequently for the west coast production. Moross moved to Hollywood in 1940 and spent the next decade orchestrating scores for a great many films, including *Our Town*, *Action In The North Atlantic*, and *Conflict*. He also worked on **Hugo Friedhofer**'s Oscar-winning score for *The Best Years Of Our Lives* (1946). In 1948 he was given the opportunity to compose his own original score for *Close-Up*, which was followed during the 50s and 60s by others such as *When I Grow Up*, *Captive City*, *The Sharkfighters*, ***Hans Christian Andersen*** (ballet music only), *Seven Wonders Of The World* (with **David Raksin** and Sol Kaplan), *The Proud Rebel*, *The Jayhawkers*, *The Adventures Of Huckleberry Finn* (1960), *The Mountain Road*, *Five Finger Exercise*, *The Cardinal*, *The War Lord*, *Rachel Rachel*, *Valley Of The Gwang!*, and *Hail, Hero!* (1969). His most acclaimed work during that time was undoubtedly for William Wyler's dramatic western, *The Big Country* (1958), for which he was nominated for an

Academy Award. The music, and particularly its electrifying main theme, is considered to be among the most memorable in the history of the cinema. His work was also heard regularly on television in such popular programmes as *Lancer* and *Wagon Train.* On Broadway, Moross collaborated twice with the author and librettist John Latouche. Firstly in 1948 for *Ballet Ballads*, a musical adaptation of three one-act plays; and again in 1954 for the innovative ***The Golden Apple***, which, although it folded after only 127 performances, won the New York Drama Critics Circle Award for best musical, and has since become a cult piece. One of its songs, the ballad 'Lazy Afternoon', has been recorded by several artists, including **Tony Bennett**. During his long and distinguished career, Moross also won two Guggenheim fellowship awards, in 1947 and 1948. He brought his own individual brand of folksy homespun Americana to his music for ballets such as *American Patterns*, *The Last Judgement*, and *Frankie And Johnny*, along with numerous orchestral works which included 'Biguine', 'A Tall Story', 'Paeans', 'Those Everlasting Blues', and 'First Symphony'. His last completed work was a one-act opera, *Sorry, Wrong Number*!

Morphine

Purveyors of quite startling, low-end alternative rock/jazz, US trio Morphine are one of the few in the field who do not use guitars. Even vocalist Mark Sandman's bass is a rudimentary affair, composed of only two strings. Together with Dana Colley (saxaphone) and Jerome Deupree (drums), the group was inaugurated by Sandman and Colley after the break-up the former's previous outfit, Treat Her Right. After playing a few tentative gigs they released their debut album, which, probably because no one had heard anything quite like it before, won many admirers. Their local community honoured them when they picked up Indie Debut Album Of The Year at the Boston Music Awards. Following its release Deupree departed, to be replaced by former Treat Her Right drummer Billy Conway. On the back of the attention they were receiving they picked up a deal with Rykodisc, while the band's music continued to be more influenced by literature, notably Jim Thompson, than musical peers. They came of age with *Yes* in 1995, having never compromised their line-up they are poised as one of the more interesting bands of the 90s. Rarely has jazz mixed with rock with such satisfying results. From this album 'Honey White' is a blistering romp with the baritone sax sounding like a 50s R&B band. Morphine is addictive, unusual and totally original.

Albums: *Good* (Accurate/Distortion 1992), *Cure For Pain* (Rykodisc 1993), *Yes* (Rykodisc 1995).

Morricone, Ennio

b. 11 October 1928, Rome, Italy. A distinguished and prolific composer, whose revolutionary scores for 'spaghetti Westerns' have made him one of the most influential figures in the film music world. He studied trumpet and composition before becoming a professional writer of music for radio, television and the stage as well as the concert hall. During the 50s he wrote songs and arrangements for popular vocalist Gianni Morandi and he later arranged **Paul Anka**'s Italian hit 'Ogni Volta' (1964). Morricone's first film score was for the comedy *Il Federale* in 1961. Three years later he was hired by Sergio Leone to compose music for *A Fistful Of Dollars.* Using the pseudonym Dan Savio, Morricone created a score out of shouts, cries and a haunting whistled phrase, in direct contrast to the use of pseudo-folk melodies in Hollywood Westerns. His work on Leone's trilogy of Italian Westerns led to collaboration with such leading European directors as Pontecorvo (*Battle Of Algiers* 1966), Pasolini (*Big Birds, Little Birds*, 1966) and Bertolucci (*1900*, 1976). In the 70s he began to compose for US films, such as *Exorcist II* (1977), *Days Of Heaven* (1978), *The Untouchables* (1987) and *Frantic* (1988). Morricone won an Oscar for Roland Joffe's *The Mission* (1986), where he used motifs from sacred music and native Indian melodies to create what he called 'contemporary music written in an ancient language'. In 1992 Morricone's score for *Bugsy* received an Oscar nomination. The composer's other scores in the early 90s included *Husbands And Lovers*, *City Of Joy*, *Tie Me Up! Tie Me Down!*, *Everybody's Fine*, *Hamlet*, *State Of Grace*, *Octopus 6 - The Force Of The Mafia*, *Jonah Who Lived In A Whale*, *In The Line Of Fire*, and *Cinema Paradiso - The Special Edition*, *La Scorta*, *Wolf*, and *Disclosure* (1994). The Spaghetti western sound has been a source of inspiration and samples for a number of rock artists including **BAD**, **Cameo** and **John Zorn** (*Big Gundown*, 1987). Morricone has recorded several albums of his own music and in 1981 he had a hit with 'Chi Mai', a tune he composed for a BBC television series. A double album for **Virgin Records** in 1988 included Morricone's own selection from the over 100 films which he has scored, while in the same year Virgin Venture issued a recording of his classical compositions.

Selected albums: *Moses* (1977), *Film Hits* (1981), *Chi Mai* (1981), *The Mission* (1986), *Chamber Music* (1988), *Frantic* (1988, film soundtrack), *The Endless Game* (1989), *Live In Concert* (1989), *Casualties Of War* (1990), *Morricone '93 Movie Sounds* (1993), *Wolf* film soundtrack (Columbia 1994), *Disclosure* film soundtrack (Virgin 1995). Compilations: *Film Music 1966-87* (1988), *The Very Best Of* (1992).

Morris Brothers

Wiley (mandolin/guitar/vocals) and Claude 'Zeke' Morris (guitar/vocals) are one of the many brother acts remembered for their fine harmony singing. At

different times both worked with other bands including those of **J.E. Mainer**, **Wade Mainer** and **Charley Monroe**. They made their first recordings (accompanied by fiddler Homer Sherrill) for Bluebird in January 1938 and their next session (in September) yielded their noted version of 'Let Me Be Your Salty Dog'. They retired in the late 40s but did make some rare appearances later including at the 1964 Newport Folk Festival and on a special television programme with **Earl Scruggs**. They were actually the first musicians ever to employ noted banjoists Earl Scruggs and **Don Reno** in their band. A third brother George Morris also played with them on occasions.
Album: with Homer Sherrill *Wiley, Zeke & Homer* (c.1973).

Morris Minor And The Majors

A UK comedy group, they had a novelty hit in 1987 with 'Stutter Rap'. The group comprised Morris Minor (b. Tony Hawkes, 27 February 1960), Rusty Wing (b. Paul Boross, 18 September 1959, London, England) and Phil Erup (b. Phil Judge, 13 February 1960). In 1985 songwriter Hawkes (author of a musical about strip cartoon character Bristow) had joined forces with actors Boross and Judge to perform a comic song on a television talent show. Afterwards, they continued with Morris Minor And The Majors as a comedy act on London's alternative cabaret circuit. 'Stutter Rap (No Sleep 'Til Bedtime') was a song from the cabaret act adapted to be a parody of the **Beastie Boys**' 'No Sleep 'Til Brooklyn'. Produced by Jakko M. Jakszyk (under the name Grandmaster Jellytot) and released by the **Virgin** subsidiary 10 Records, it swiftly rose into the UK Top 10. However, the follow-up, 'This Is The Chorus' (whose target was **Stock, Aitken And Waterman**) flopped. Soon afterwards Boross and Judge left the group when Hawkes was given a television comedy series. Under the name Morris And The Minors, he issued 'Morris Minor' (1989). Judge returned to acting, Hawkes to acting and scriptwriting for comedian Harry Enfield while Boross concentrated on songwriting, releasing a single as the Calypso Twins in 1991.

Morris, Gary

b. 7 December 1948, Fort Worth, Texas, USA. Morris sang in a church choir and learned guitar, playing along to the **Beatles**' records. When he and two friends auditioned for a club owner in Denver, they were told they were 'on in 15 minutes . . . providing they played country music'. They stayed at the club for five years and then Morris returned to Texas. He started campaigning for Jimmy Carter and in 1978, after Carter's election, Morris performed on a country show at the White House. As a result, he was signed to MCA but when the singles did not sell, he moved to Colorado and formed a band, Breakaway. Producer Norro Wilson, who had been at the White House, signed him to **Warners**, but when Wilson moved to **RCA**, Morris found himself in limbo. Eventually, he had US country hits with 'Headed For A Heartache', 'Dreams Die Hard', 'Don't Look Back' and 'Velvet Chains'. In 1983, he became the first artist to put 'The Wind Beneath My Wings' on the US country charts and also scored hits with 'The Love She Found In Me', 'Why Lady Why?' and a duet with **Lynn Anderson**, 'You're Welcome To Tonight'. He first appeared on the *Grand Ole Opry* in 1984, the same year he appeared on Broadway in *La Bohème* (alongside **Linda Ronstadt**). Morris had his first US country number 1 in 1985 with 'Baby Bye Bye' and he has had further US number 1 records with 'I'll Never Stop Loving You', 'Making Up For Lost Time' (a duet with **Crystal Gayle**), '100% Chance Of Rain' and 'Leave Me Lonely'. He returned to Broadway in 1987 for the main role in *Les Misérables* and was also featured on the 1988 symphonic recording. He moved from opera to soap opera by playing the blind country singer, Wayne Masterson, in *The Colbys*. Morris has the vocal and the acting ability to take his career in any number of directions, although his commercial standing had dropped substantially by the early 90s.
Albums: *Gary Morris* (1982), *Why Lady Why* (1983), *Faded Blue* (1984), *Anything Goes...* (1985), *Second Hand Heart* (1986), *Plain Brown Wrapper* (1986), with Crystal Gayle *What If We Fall In Love* (1987), *Stones* (1989), *Full Moon, Empty Heart* (1991).

Morris, Jenny

b. New Zealand. Morris has surprised many with her solo albums, writing most of the material herself. Arriving in Australia in 1980 with the Crocodiles, a new wave pop band from New Zealand, Morris joined QED, who recorded a warm, but sadly-neglected album in 1984. After this she worked as a backing singer with bands such as **INXS**. Now touring with her own band, Morris has found mainstream airplay with her strong, modern pop songs. She toured Europe during 1990 as support act to **Prince**, and is now presenting a more raunchy image.
Albums: *Body & Soul* (1987), *Shiver* (1989).
Video: *The Story So Far* (1992).

Morris, Joe

b. 1922, Montgomery, Alabama, USA, d. November 1958, Phoenix, Arizona, USA. Morris studied music at Alabama State Teachers' College, and toured with the college band led by the Trenier Twins. Heard by **Lionel Hampton** in Florida in 1942, Morris joined Hampton's Orchestra, where he became a valued writer/arranger as well as a trumpeter. He remained with Hampton until 1946, when he briefly joined **Buddy Rich**'s band. After forming his own band towards the end of 1946, Morris went on to record for

Manor, **Atlantic**, **Decca** and Herald, introducing new jazz and R&B stars such as **Johnny Griffin**, **Elmo Hope**, **Matthew Gee**, **Percy Heath, Philly Joe Jones**, **Laurie Tate** and **Faye Adams**. On the strength of his 'Blues Cavalcade' one of the first self-contained, touring R&B package shows, Morris had several hits including 'Any Time, Any Place, Anywhere' and 'Don't Take Your Love From Me' on Atlantic and, most notably, 'Shake A Hand' and 'I'll Be True' on Herald.
Albums: *Lowdown Baby* (1985), with Johnny Griffin *Fly Mister Fly* (1985).

Morris, Butch

b. Lawrence Morris, 10 February 1947, Long Beach, California, USA. Playing cornet on the west coast, Morris worked with bop tenor saxophonist **J.R. Monterose**, bassist George Morrow and *avant garde* players **Frank Lowe** and **Don Moye** as well as studying with well-known west coast mentors, **Horace Tapscott** and **Bobby Bradford** (which is where he first met his longtime associate **David Murray**). In 1975 he relocated to New York, playing free jazz in the Loft scene. From 1976-77 he lived in Paris, working with Lowe and bassist **Alan Silva**. In 1977 he joined Murray's seminal Octet, recording on *Ming*, *Home* and *Murray's Steps*. Morris developed what he called 'conduction', a method of leading improvisers with visual instructions, conducting the **David Murray** Big Band at Sweet Basil in 1984 (recorded for Black Saint). Meanwhile, Morris had also been recording his own music: *In Touch...But Out Of Reach* was a 1978 live concert with a sextet that included trombonist **Grachan Moncur III** and drummer **Steve McCall**; *The New York City Artists' Collective Plays Butch Morris* had him conducting an eight-piece group, which featured vocalist Ellen Christi, through a set of his own pieces. In 1985 he recorded a free-improvisation record with guitarist Bill Horvitz (*Trios*) and 1988 saw the appearance of two albums featuring a trio of Morris, Wayne Horvitz, and Robert Previte, (*Nine Below*, *Todos Santos*), the latter album showcasing the compositions of pianist/singer Robin Halcomb. In 1986 he released *Current Trends In Racism In Modern America*, an innovative music in which he led 10 musicians (including Lowe, **John Zorn**, harpist Zeena Parkins and drummer **Thurman Barker**) through poignant, desolate and highly charged 'free-improvisations'. *Homeing* (1987) and *Dust To Dust* (1991) continued his search for a new method of assembling musicians drawn from both the black *avant garde* and white avant-rock circles. In a period where conservatism has become the normal approach, Morris has bravely taken steps to provide a part of the future.
Albums: *In Touch...But Out Of Reach* (1982, rec 1978), *The New York City Artists' Collective Plays Butch Morris* (1984, rec 1982), with Bill Horvitz, J.A. Deane *Trios* (1985), *Current Trends In Racism In Modern America* (Sound Aspects 1986), *Homeing* (Sound Aspect 1988), with Robert Previte, Wayne Horvitz *Nine Below* (1988, rec 1986), with Previte, Wayne Horvitz *Todos Santos* (1988), *Dust To Dust* (New World 1991).

Morris, Russell

As leader of the Melbourne pop group Somebody's Image (1966-68), Morris came to the notice of **Molly Meldrum**, who soon became the group's, and subsequently Morris's, manager. Meldrum produced Morris's huge 1969 hit 'The Real Thing' which is regarded as the best psychedelic song of that era in Australia. The song featured a myriad of overdubs including snatches of speeches and ending, like one of its influences, with an atomic bomb exploding. Morris further developed his own songwriting skills sufficiently to release a low-key album release, *Bloodstone* which was greeted with luke-warm praise from the critics ('The Cell' often garnered praise), although little acknowledgement from the public. Deserted by Meldrum, Morris formed his own band and recorded several more albums which did achieve minor success. He moved to the USA in 1978, where he eventually obtained a green card, but was unable to establish himself in any musical niche. On his return to Australia, he formed the Rubes who backed him live and on record until they parted company in 1983. Since then he has played with a 60s' revival band and has remained unrecorded, although there have been plans to record in the early 90s. Morris possesses an excellent tenor voice, which is distinctive on his pop material but not suited to rock which he attempted on some of his later albums.
Albums: *Bloodstone* (1971), *Wings Of An Eagle* (1973), *Russell Morris* (1975), *Turn It On* (1976), *Foot In The Door* (1979), *Almost Frantic* (1980).

Morris, Sarah Jane

This UK singer rose to fame as joint vocalist on the **Communards** number 1 hit 'Don't Leave Me This Way' in 1986. Sarah Jane's previous work as a vocalist had principally comprised Berlin theatre songs with groups like the Happy End. As well as duetting on the Commmunards' hit she appeared on the group's debut album track 'Lover Man'. Her presence and husky tones, alongside Jimmy Somerville in live appearances became an integral part of the Communards' show, so much so, that audiences constantly link her with the group. Whether this has ultimately helped or hindered her solo career is subjective, for while her solo album on the Jive label received warm reviews it met with little UK chart success. A constant guest artist, her early 90s contributions have included an appearance on **Peter Hammill**'s *The Fall Of The House Of Usher*.
Albums: *Sarah Jane Morris* (1989), *Blue Valentine* (Ronnie Scott's Jazz House 1995).

Morrison, Van

b. George Ivan Morrison, 31 August 1945, Belfast, Northern Ireland. The son of a noted collector of jazz and blues records, Morrison quickly developed an interest in music. At the age of 12 he joined Deannie Sands And The Javelins, an aspiring skiffle group, but within two years was an integral part of the Monarchs, a showband which, by 1963, was embracing R&B and soul. Tours of Scotland and England were undertaken before the group travelled to Germany where they completed a lone single for **CBS**, 'Bozoo Hully Gully'/'Twingy Baby', before disbanding. The experience Morrison garnered - he took up vocals, saxophone and harmonica - proved invaluable upon his return to Belfast and a subsequent merger with members of local attraction the Gamblers in a new act, **Them**. This exciting group scored two notable hit singles with 'Baby Please Don't Go' and 'Here Comes The Night' (both 1965), while the former's b-side 'Gloria', a snarling Morrison original, is revered as a classic of the garage-band genre. The group's progress was hampered by instability and Morrison's reluctance to court the pop marketplace - a feature continued throughout his career - but their albums showed the early blossoming of an original stylist. His reading of **Bob Dylan**'s 'It's All Over Now, Baby Blue' (*Them Again*) is rightly regarded as one of the finest interpretations in a much-covered catalogue. Them was dissolved in 1966 following an arduous USA tour, but within months the singer had returned to New York at the prompting of producer **Bert Berns**. Their partnership resulted in 'Brown-Eyed Girl', an ebullient celebration of love in a style redolent of classic black harmony groups. The single deservedly reached the US Top 10, in turn inspiring the hurriedly-issued *Blowin' Your Mind*. Morrison later claimed the set was culled from sessions for projected singles and, although inconsistent, contained the cathartic 'T.B. Sheets', on which Van first introduced the stream-of-consciousness imagery re-occurring in later work. Berns' premature death brought this period to a sudden end, and for the ensuing 12 months Morrison punctuated live performances by preparing his next release.

Astral Weeks showed the benefit of such seclusion, as here an ambition to create without pop's constraints was fully realized. Drawing support from a stellar backing group which included **Miles Davis**' bassist Richard Davis and **Modern Jazz Quartet** drummer Connie Kay, Morrison created an ever-shifting musical tapestry, inspired by blues, soul and gospel, yet without ever aping their sound. His vocal performance was both assured and highly emotional and the resultant collection is justifiably lauded as one of rock's landmark releases. On *Moondance* the artist returned to a more conventional sense of discipline, on which tighter, punchier, jazzier arrangements formed the platform for the singer's still-soaring inflections. 'Caravan', 'Into The Mystic' and the title track itself (reminiscent of **Kenny Burrell**'s 'Midnight Blue'), became a staple part of Van's subsequent career, offering an optimistic spirit prevalent in the artist's immediate recordings. Both *Van Morrison, His Band And The Street Choir* and *Tupelo Honey* suggested a newfound peace of mind, as a now-married Morrison celebrated the idyll of his sylvan surroundings. 'Domino' and 'Wild Night' were the album's respective US hit singles, both of which invoked the punch of classic **Stax**-era soul, and if the former set offered a greater debt to R&B, its counterpart showed an infatuation with country styles. Both preoccupations were maintained on *St. Dominic's Preview*, one of Morrison's most enigmatic releases. Having opened the set with 'Jackie Wilson Said', an effervescent tribute to the great soul singer later covered by **Dexy's Midnight Runners**, Van wove a path through rock and late-night jazz culminating in two lengthy compositions, both laced with chiming acoustic 12-string guitar, 'Listen To The Lion' and 'Almost Independence Day'. Here he resumed vocal improvisation and by alternately whispering, pleading, shouting and extolling, created two intoxicating and hypnotic performances.

Morrison's next release, *Hard Nose The Highway*, proved disappointing as the artist enhanced an ever-widening palette with contributions by the Oakland Symphony Chamber Chorus and such disparate inclusions as 'Green', culled from the educational children's show, *Sesame Street*, and the folk standard 'Wild Mountain Thyme', herein retitled 'Purple Heather'. Despite the presence of 'Wild Love' and 'The Great Deception', the album is generally regarded as inconsistent. However, Morrison reclaimed his iconoclast position with the enthralling *It's Too Late To Stop Now*, an in-concert selection on which he was backed by the Caledonia Soul Orchestra. Van not only restated his own impressive catalogue, but acknowledged his mentors with a series of tight and outstanding recreations, notably of **Sonny Boy 'Rice Miller' Williamson** ('Take Your Hand Out Of Your Pocket'), **Ray Charles** ('I Believe To My Soul') and **Bobby 'Blue' Bland** ('Ain't Nothing You Can Do'). The result was a seamless tribute to R&B and one of rock's definitive live albums. It was succeeded by the pastoral *Veedon Fleece* a set inspired by a sabbatical in Ireland during 1973. Its sense of spirituality - a keynote of Morrison's later work - is best captured on 'You Don't Pull No Punches But You Don't Push The River', but 'The Streets Of Arklow' and 'County Fair' are equally evocative. The judicious use of uillean pipes and woodwind enhanced the rural atmosphere of a collection which, although received with mixed reviews, is, in retrospect, a lynchpin in the artist's subsequent development. A three-year hiatus ended with the release of *A Period Of Transition*, a largely undistinguished set on which the singer collaborated actively with **Dr. John**. *Wavelength*, which featured former Them organist **Peter Bardens**, was welcomed as a marked improvement and if lacking the triumphs of earlier work, contained none of its pitfalls and instead offered a mature musical consistency. Similar qualities abounded on *Into The Music* which included the noticeably buoyant 'Bright Side Of The Road', Van's first solo, albeit minor, UK chart entry. It also featured 'And The Healing Has Begun', wherein Morrison celebrated his past in order to address his future, and the shamelessly nostalgic 'It's All In The Game', a cover version of **Tommy Sands**' 1957 hit single. Although a general penchant for punchy soul suggested part of a continuing affinity, it instead marked the end of a stylistic era. On *Common One* Morrison resumed his introspective path and, on the expansive 'Somewhere In England', referred to the works of Wordsworth, Coleridge and T.S. Eliot in a piece whose gruff, improvisatory nature polarized critics proclaiming it either mesmerising or self-indulgent. A greater sense of discipline on *Beautiful Vision* resulted in another much lauded classic. Although noted for 'Cleaning Windows', a joyous celebration of the singer's formative Belfast years, the album contained several rich, meditative compositions, notably 'Dweller On The Threshold' and 'Across The Bridge Where Angels Dwell'.

Inarticulate Speech Of The Heart and *A Sense Of Wonder* continued in a similar vein, the former boasting the compulsive 'Rave On John Donne', wherein Van again places his work on a strictly literary pantheon, while the latter opened with the equally evocative 'Tore Down A La Rimbaud'. The title track of the latter set the style for many beautifully wandering and spiritually uplifting songs of the next fertile period. *Live At The Grand Opera House, Belfast* was an insubstantial resume, failing to capture the sense of occasion demonstrably apparent in person, but Morrison confirmed his artistic rebirth with *No Guru, No Method, No Teacher*. Here he openly acknowledged his musical past - the set included the punningly titled 'Here Comes The Knight' - as well as offering a searing riposte to those perceived as imitators on 'A Town Called Paradise'. 'Tir Na Nog' and 'One Irish Rover' continued his long-running affair with Celtic themes, a feature equally relevant on *Poetic Champions Compose*. The wedding of love and religion, another integral part of the artist's 80s' work, was enhanced by the sumptuous 'Sometimes I Feel Like A Motherless Child', on which the singer's contemplative delivery was truly inspirational. Morrison, many years into his career, was now producing an astonishingly high standard of work. His albums during this period were events, not mere releases.

Irish Heartbeat, a festive collaboration with traditional act the **Chieftains**, offered a joyous but less intensive perspective. Although the title song and 'Celtic Ray' were exhumed from Van's own catalogue, its highlights included moving renditions of 'She Moved Through The Fair' and 'Carrickfergus'. By this time (1988) Morrison was resettled in London and had invited R&B vocalist/organist **Georgie Fame** to join his touring revue. *Avalon Sunset* enhanced the singer's commercial ascendancy when 'Whenever God Shines His Light On Me', a duet with **Cliff Richard**, became a UK Top 20 single, Morrison's first since Them's halcyon days. The album had once again a strong spiritual feel combined with childhood memories. Morrison, however, was also able to compose and deliver quite immaculate love songs, including a cover of 'Have I Told You Lately That I Love You'. *Enlightenment* thus engendered considerable interest although Morrison, as oblivious to pop's trappings as always, simply maintained his peerless progress. The mixture was as before, from the pulsating opening track, 'Real Real Gone', itself once considered for *Common One*, through gospel and the biographical, where 'Days Before Rock 'N' Roll' recalls the singer's discovery, by radio, of **Ray Charles** and **Little Richard**. 1991 witnessed another unlikely collaboration when Morrison recorded several songs with **Tom Jones**, one of which, 'Carrying A Torch', was remade for *Hymns To The Silence*. This expansive double set confirmed the artist's prolific nature, yet reviews lauding its sense of grandeur also queried its self-obsession. *Too Long In Exile*, visited his R&B roots and includes a reworked 'Gloria', featuring a duet with **John Lee Hooker**. In Febraury 1994 he was honoured at the Brit Awards for his outstanding contribution to music. *Days Like This* was highly accessible, easy on the ear and probably the most 'contented' album he has made since *Tupelo Honey* 24 years previously. Morrison, whose disdain for the press is legendary, will doubtlessly remain unmoved, yet the paradox of a man capable of sumptuous music and a barking temper is indeed intriguing. It is a tribute that such aberrations can be set aside in order to enjoy his enthralling catalogue. Taken as a whole, this body of work is arguably one the most necessary, complete and important collections in rock music, and it is still growing.

Albums: *Blowin' Your Mind* (1967), *Astral Weeks* (1968), *Moondance* (1970), *Van Morrison, His Band And The Street Choir* (1970), *Tupelo Honey* (1971), *St. Dominic's Preview* (1972), *Hard Nose The Highway* (1973), *It's Too Late To Stop Now* (1974), *Veedon Fleece* (1974), *A Period Of Transition* (1977), *Wavelength* (1978), *Into The Music* (1979), *Common One* (1980), *Beautiful Vision* (1982), *Inarticulate Speech Of The Heart* (1983), *Live At The Grand Opera House, Belfast* (1984), *A Sense Of Wonder* (1984), *No Guru, No Method, No Teacher* (1986), *Poetic Champions Compose* (1987), with the Chieftains *Irish Heartbeat* (1988), *Avalon Sunset* (1989), *Enlightenment* (1990), *Hymns To The Silence* (1991), *Too Long In Exile* (1993), *A Night In San*

Francisco (Polydor 1994), *Days Like This* (Polydor 1995). Compilations: *The Best Of Van Morrison* (1971), *T.B. Sheets* (1973), *This Is Where I Came In* (1977), *The Best Of Van Morrison* (1990), *Bang Masters* (1991), *The Best Of Vol. 2* (1992).
Further reading: *Van Morrison: Into The Music*, Ritchie Yorke. *Van Morrison: The Great Deception*, Johnny Rogan. *Van Morrison: The Mystic's Music*, Howard A. DeWitt. *Van Morrison: Too Late To Stop Now*, Steve Turner.

Morrissey

b. Steven Patrick Morrissey, 22 May 1959, Davyhulme, Manchester, England. Morrissey began his career with the vague intention of succeeding as a music journalist. Unemployed in Manchester during the late 70s, he frequently wrote letters to the music press and was eventually taken on by *Record Mirror* as a freelance local reviewer. During this period, he also ran a **New York Dolls**' fan club and even wrote a booklet about them. Another small illustrated volume, *James Dean Is Not Dead*, briefly catalogued the career of another Morrissey obsession. Two other projects, on girl groups and minor film stars, failed to reach the printed page. In the meantime, Morrissey was attempting unsuccessfully to progress as a performer. He had played a couple of gigs with local group the Nosebleeds and failed a record company audition with a relaunched version of **Slaughter And The Dogs**. By the early 80s his chance of fame had apparently expired. In 1982, however, he was approached by Wythenshawe guitarist Johnny Maher (later Marr) with the idea of forming a songwriting team. They soon developed into the **Smiths**, the most important and critically-acclaimed UK group of the 80s. Morrissey's arch lyrics, powerful persona and general newsworthiness made him a pop figure whose articulacy was unmatched by any of his contemporaries. By the late summer of 1987, the Smiths disbanded, leaving Morrissey to pursue a solo career. Early the following year he issued his first post-Smiths single, 'Suedehead', with Vini Reilly filling the guitarist's spot. The track was irresistibly commercial and reached the UK Top 5. The subsequent *Viva Hate* hit the top soon after, indicating that the singer could look forward to a long and successful future with **EMI Records**. A further UK Top 10 single with the John Betjemen-influenced 'Everyday Is Like Sunday' reiterated that point. In spite of his successes, Morrissey was initially keen on promoting a Smiths reunion but the closest this reached was the equivalent of a farewell concert in the unlikely setting of Wolverhampton Civic Hall. On 22 December 1988, Morrissey performed alongside former Smiths, Andy Rourke, Mike Joyce and Craig Gannon for a 1,700 capacity audience, many of whom had queued for days in order to gain admittance to the venue. The following year brought several problems for Morrissey. Although he continued to release strong singles such as 'The Last Of The Famous International Playboys' and 'Interesting Drug', both reviews and chart placings were slighter less successful than expected. By the time of 'Ouija Board, Ouija Board', Morrissey suffered the most disappointing reviews of his career and, despite its charm, the single only reached number 18. Financial wrangles and management changes, which had characterized the Smiths' career, were repeated by Morrissey the soloist. A projected album, *Bona Drag*, was delayed and eventually cancelled, although the title served for a formidable hits and b-side compilation. In the meantime, Morrissey concentrated on the singles market, issuing some fascinating product, most notably the macabre 'November Spawned A Monster' and controversial 'Piccadilly Palace'. In March 1991, Morrissey issued the long-awaited *Kill Uncle*, a light yet not unappealing work, produced by Clive Langer and Alan Winstanley. By this time, the artist had not toured since the heyday of the Smiths, and there were some critics who wondered whether he would ever perform again. That question was answered in the summer and winter of 1991 when the singer embarked on a world tour, backed by a rockabilly group, whose raw energy and enthusiasm brought a new dimension to his recently understated studio work. The fruits of this collaboration were revealed on *Your Arsenal*, a neat fusion of 50s rockabilly influences and 70s glam rock. The presence of former **David Bowie** acolyte **Mick Ronson** as producer added to the effect. During 1992 Morrissey also hit the headlines when he issued a bitter attack on author Johnny Rogan. Prior to the publication of a book on the Smiths, which he had yet to read, Morrissey decreed: 'Personally, I hope Johnny Rogan ends his days very soon in an M3 pile-up.' The much publicised and long-running dispute merely served to focus attention on the book and heighten appreciation of his Smiths' work. Indications that interest may have peaked came as a result of the dismal failure of *Beethoven Was Deaf*, a live album which disappeared after only 2 weeks in the charts. However, Morrissey was now beginning to cultivate a following in the US way above the cult devotees who had followed the Smiths there. This offered welcome succour at a time when UK critics were predicting his imminent downfall and his domestic audience was undergoing a period of reduction. Then came the Madstock disaster - a live appearance in support of a reformed **Madness** that saw Morrissey bedecked in a Union Jack - which, when combined with song titles such as 'Bengali In Platforms' and 'The National Front Disco', saw a huge debate rage in the media over the artist's interpretation of 'Englishness'. *Vauxhall And I* (the title possibly alluding to his continuing battle with Johnny Rogan) ended the downward spiral, receiving 'born again' reviews throughout the UK music media. With the more sedate production from **Steve Lillywhite**, this was the closest the artist had come to matching his

lyricism with the right material components since the Smiths. Indeed, as *Select* magazine decreed: 'If he keeps making albums like this, you won't want the Smiths back.' Morrissey's odyssey seems set to continue for some time yet.
Albums: *Viva Hate* (HMV 1988), *Kill Uncle* (HMV 1991), *Your Arsenal* (HMV 1992), *Beethoven Was Deaf* (HMV 1993), *Vauxhall And I* (HMV 1994). Compilation: *Bona Drag* (HMV 1990), *World Of Morrissey* (Parlophone 1995).
Further reading: *Morrissey & Marr: The Severed Alliance*, Johnny Rogan. *Peepholism: Into The Art Of Morrissey*, Jo Slee. *Landsacapes Of The Mind*, David Bret. *Morrissey In His Own Words*, John Robertson. *Morrissey Shot*, Linder Sterling. *The Smiths: The Visual Documentary*, Johnny Rogan.
Video: *Live In Dallas* (1993).

Morrissey, Dick

b. 9 May 1940, Horley, Surrey, England. A self-taught tenor saxophonist who is also adept on clarinet, flute and soprano saxophone, Morrissey became a professional musician at the end of his teens. In 1960 he played in a band led by Harry South and soon afterwards formed his own quartet with South, Phil Bates and **Phil Seamen**. He maintained a small band throughout the 60s, playing club engagements in the UK, backing visiting American jazzmen (including **Jimmy Witherspoon**) and making records. In the 70s Morrissey was deeply involved in jazz-rock, co-leading the band highly respected **If**, working with **Herbie Mann**, and recording with the **Average White Band**. The most important of the bands in this idiom with which he was associated was the Morrissey-Mullen band he co-led with **Jim Mullen**. The band became one of the UK's best-known jazz-rock bands and remained in existence into the mid-80s, after which Morrissey returned to leading a more mainstream jazz-orientated group.
Selected albums: *It's Morrissey, Man!* (1961), *Have You Heard?* (1963), *Jimmy Witherspoon At The Bull's Head* (1966), *Storm Warning* (1967), *After Dark* (Coda 1983), *Resurrection Ritual* (Miles 1988), *Souliloquy* (Coda 1988). As Morrissey-Mullen *Up* (1977), *Cape Wrath* (1979), *Badness* (1981), *Life On The Wire* (1982), *It's About Time* (1983), *This Must Be The Place* (1985), *Happy Hour* (1988).

Morrissey, Louise

b. 23 March 1961, Bansha, Co. Tipperary, Eire. She grew up with a love of music and after completing her schooling, she began to sing with her brothers, Billy and Norman, as the Morrisseys Folk And Ballad Group. She made her first recording, 'Farewell To Carlingford', in 1978. The group recorded several successful albums, including *Ireland's Morrisseys* and *On Stage (Live From Olympia)*. In 1988, encouraged by the popularity of Irish singers such as Ray Lynam and **Philomena Begley**, she gave up folk music in favour of the ever popular country and Irish. (Norman became the bass guitarist in her band and Billy the band's manager.) Her second country music recording 'The Night Daniel O'Donnell Came To Town' (based on **Johnny Cash**'s hit 'The Night Hank Williams Came To Town') was a big hit for her in Ireland and quickly established her as a major Irish country singer. In 1990, in Zurich, competing against 14 countries, she won the European Country Music Gold Star Award singing 'Tipperary On My Mind' and since then she has continued to build her reputation with fine record releases. Her video *Memories Of Home* (1990) has sold in large numbers and she proved very popular on an appearance at the Wembley International Festival Of Country Music. Her touring has seen her play venues in the USA, Denmark and the Lebanon. On 26 September 1993, she survived a head-on car crash, when travelling to a concert. She was scheduled to fly to Nashville the following day to record another album and make USA concert appearances but her injuries were so severe that it was six months before she was able to perform again. During her absence the talented Trudi Lalor, a promising young vocalist, fronted Louise's band and fulfilled all her Irish and UK commitments. In 1995, completely recovered, Morrissey toured the UK with **Charley Pride**, receiving glowing tributes for her singing. She is equally at home with Irish ballads such as 'The Rose Of Allendale', country standards like 'Blue Eyes Crying In The Rain' or modern including 'Achy Breaky Heart', one of the 14 tracks she recorded on an earlier visit to Nashville. She is the possessor of one of the finest female voices currently performing around the Irish and UK country music scene.
Albums: *Louise* (CMR 1988), *When I Was Yours* (CMR (in Ireland) & Ritz (in England) 1990), *Here I Am In Love Again* (CMR/RTE 1991), *Silver Threads Among The Gold - Reflections* (CMR 1993), *You'll Remember Me* (Ritz 1994).
Video: *Memories Of Home* (1990).

Morrissey-Mullen

(see **Morrissey, Dick**; **Mullen, Jim**)

Morrow, Buddy

b. Muni Zudecoff, 8 February 1919, New Haven, USA. Morrow, after graduating from Juilliard, began his prolific career as a sideman with the hotel bands of **Eddy Duchin** and **Vincent Lopez**. He developed into a jazzman in Vocalion sessions with **Sharkey Bonano**'s Sharks Of Rhythm, a 1936 **Eddie Condon** Dixieland group. He reached swing band status with **Artie Shaw** the same year, under his real name then later Muni Morrow (his adopted name). He joined **Tommy Dorsey**'s trombone section in 1938 for 'Boogie Woogie' and 'Hawaiian War Chant', the next year playing with **Paul Whiteman**'s Concert

Orchestra in their **Decca/Brunswick** recording of **Gershwin**'s 'Concerto In F'. He joined **Tony Pastor** in 1940 on his way to replacing **Ray Conniff** with the **Bob Crosby** band (1941). (The next year saw him in the US Navy, with a one-off **Red McKenzie** jazz session for Commodore producing *inter alia* 'Sweet Lorraine' and 'Talk Of The Town'). On demob Morrow played with **Jimmy Dorsey** for a while ('Jumping Jehosaphat') then moved into radio; conducting in the studios gave him a taste for leading, and **RCA** Victor decided to back him with his own band in 1951. His first minor hit was a cross-over into R&B with 'Night Train', taken from **Duke Ellington**'s 'Happy Go Lucky Local' by **Jimmy Forrest**, who had his own hit on United. There was little room for big bands in subsequent years, on singles at least, and after more minor hits with 'Man With The Golden Arm' and 'Dragnet', Morrow concentrated in the late 50s and early 60s on albums of standards for **Mercury**, Victor and Camden, not all of which were issued in the UK. He returned to studio work, emerging on occasion to front revivals of the Dorsey and Miller bands.

Morse, Ella Mae

b. 12 September, 1924, Mansfield, Texas, USA. A singer with an appealing jazz/blues style, Morse first sang with a band organized by her pianist mother and her father who was a drummer. At the age of 12 she was heard at a Houston Jam session by **Jimmy Dorsey**, who hired her as replacement for June Richmond. Her stay with Dorsey was a brief one, and she returned to Texas and sang with local bands. Subsequently she was heard singing in a San Diego club by **Freddie Slack**, who had been the pianist when she had been with the Dorsey band. He signed her as the vocalist on his first **Capitol** recording session in 1942, which resulted in 'Cow Cow Boogie'. The record became a million-seller, and Morse had further hits in the 40s with 'Mr. Five By Five', 'Shoo Shoo Baby', 'Tess's Torch Song (If I Had A Man)', 'Milkman, Keep Those Bottles Quiet', 'The Patty Cake Man', 'Captain Kidd', 'Buzz Me', and 'House Of Blue Lights' (1946). She also appeared in a few minor films such as ***Reveille With Beverly***, *Ghost Catchers*, *South Of Dixie*, and *How Do You Do It?* Morse retired for a time, but made a spectacular comeback in 1952 with another enormous hit, 'Blacksmith Blues', on which she was accompanied by **Nelson Riddle** and his orchestra. She continued to perform over the years, and was spotted in 1987 at Michael's Pub in New York, sharing the billing with another 40s survivor, **Nellie Lutcher**.
Selected albums: *The Morse Code* (1957), *The Hits Of Ella Mae Morse* (c.50), *Sensational* (1986, recorded 1951-57), *Barrel House, Boogie And The Blues* (1984), *Hits Of* (1984), *Capitol Collectors* (1992).

Morse, Steve, Band

Instrumental rock guitarist Steve Morse (b. Ohio, USA) took his primary influence, like so many others, from the **Beatles**: 'When I saw the Beatles on Ed Sullivan I had an instantaneous attraction to the most commercial, listenable, yet quality music ever heard. It began right there. It was just a matter of finding a guitar and somebody to show me some chords.' Expanding his listening to include prevalent rock bands including the **Yardbirds**, **Jimi Hendrix** and **Led Zeppelin**, as well as a nascent interest in country music, Morse moved with his family to Georgia at the age of 13. There he was captivated by a live concert by classical guitarist Juan Mercadal, persuading the artist to give him lessons. He went on to study with Mercadal at the University of Miami, while also putting together his first band, **Dixie Dregs** (aka the Dregs). Inspired by a campus performance from John McLaughlin's original Mahavishnu Quartet, he dedicated himself to exploring the conventions and frontiers of instrumental rock music. The Dregs, essentially a vehicle for these experiments, would go on to record eight albums of bright, impressive fusion. Morse qualified as a pilot during this time, and flying remains his greatest passion outside of music. He also began his solo career after briefly joining with **Kansas** for two albums. The Steve Morse Band's debut, *The Introduction*, continued to mine a particularly adept blend of instrumental rock fusion, with a guest role for guitarist **Albert Lee**. There was more of a vocal presence for *Stand Up*, which featured an appearance from another renowned guitarist, **Eric Johnson**. By the advent of *Southern Steel* the Steve Morse Band was a core team of Morse, Berklee graduate Dave LaRue (bass) and Van Romaine (drums; ex-**Blood Sweat & Tears**, Kansas and **Naughty By Nature**). The acclaim surrounding Morse has hardly died down throughout his career - *Guitar Player* magazine made him ineligible for their Best Overall Guitarist poll after he won it five times in succession. He has also collaborated with artists including **Eddie Van Halen**, **Steve Howe** and **Lynyrd Skynyrd**, and accepted an invitation to join **Deep Purple** for a spell in the 90s. The Steve Morse Band's sixth album, *Structural Damage*, revealed an undiminished talent, with a range of songs spanning the Celtic-influenced 'Sacred Ground' and the cinematic 'Dreamland'.
Albums: *The Introduction* (Elektra 1984), *Stand Up* (Elektra 1985), *High Tension Wires* (MCA 1989), *Southern Steel* (MCA 1991), *Coast To Coast* (MCA 1993), *Structural Damage* (High Street 1995).

Morta Skuld

Milwaukee-based four-piece Morta Skuld specialize in a provocative cocktail of death metal and noise, brewed by Dave Gregor (vocals/guitar), Jason Hellman (bass), Jason O'Connell (guitar) and Kent Truckebrod

(drums). Their debut for Deaf Records was somewhat lacklustre, and several personnel difficulties erupted following its release, resulting in the band splitting in two. However, by the advent of a second long playing set the group had moved up a gear both in tempo and cohesion. The improvement was partially justified by the fact that, though their debut was released early in 1993, it had actually been written and recorded over a year previously. The newer material, akin to a skinnier **Obituary** sound, brought good reviews in the metal press.
Albums: *Dying Remains* (Deaf 1993), *As Humanity Fades* (Deaf 1994).

Morton, 'Jelly Roll'

b. Ferdinand Joseph Lemott (or La Menthe), 20 October 1890, New Orleans, Louisiana, USA, d. 10 July 1941. A gifted musician, Morton played various instruments before deciding to concentrate on piano. In the early years of the 20th century he was a popular figure on the seamier side of New Orleans nightlife. He played in brothels, hustled pool and generally lived the high-life. His reputation spread extensively, owing to tours and theatrical work in various parts of the Deep South and visits to Kansas City, Chicago, Los Angeles and other important urban centres. He also worked in Canada, Alaska and Mexico. From 1923 he spent five years based in Chicago, touring and recording with various bands, including the **New Orleans Rhythm Kings** and his own band, the Red Hot Peppers. He later worked with **Fate Marable** and **W.C. Handy**, and by the end of the 20s had moved to New York for residencies and more recording sessions. He also formed a big band, with which he toured throughout the east coast states. Various business ventures played a part in his life, often with disastrous financial consequences, but he remained musically active throughout the 30s, even though he was on the margins of the commercial success which many jazzmen enjoyed in that decade. During the 30s Morton moved to Washington, DC, where he made many recordings, also playing and reminiscing for **Alan Lomax** Snr. of the US Library of Congress. By 1940 his health was failing and he moved to Los Angeles, where he died in July 1941.
One of the major figures in jazz history and a significant musical conceptualist, in particular the role of the arranger, Morton's penchant for self-promotion worked against him and for many years critical perceptions of his true worth were blighted. Many of the recordings which he made during his stay in Chicago have proved to be classics, not least for the construction of those songs he composed and the manner in which they were arranged. Although some thought that carefully arranged music went contrary to the spirit of improvisation that was inherent in jazz, Morton's arrangements, to which he insisted his musicians should strictly adhere, inhibited neither soloists nor the ability of the ensembles to swing mightily. In his arrangements of the mid-20s, Morton foreshadowed many of the musical trends which only emerged fully a decade later as big band jazz became popular. Curiously, Morton failed to grasp the possibilities then open to him and preferred to concentrate on small group work at a time when popular trends were moving in the opposite direction. His compositions include many jazz standards, among them 'The Pearls', 'Sidewalk Blues', 'King Porter Stomp', 'Dead Man Blues', 'Grandpa's Spells', 'Doctor Jazz', 'Wolverine Blues', 'Black Bottom Stomp' and 'Mister Jelly Lord'. As a pianist, Morton's early work was ragtime-oriented; but unlike many of his contemporaries, he was able to expand the rather rigid concept of ragtime to incorporate emerging jazz ideas and his later playing style shows a vital and often exhilarating grasp of many styles. It was, however, as an arranger that Morton made his greatest contribution and he can be regarded as the first significant arranger in jazz. Morton himself certainly never underestimated his own importance; quite the opposite, in fact, since he billed himself as the Originator of Jazz, Stomps and Blues. Shortly before his death he became involved in a mildly embarrassing public wrangle over the origins of the music, denying (rightly, of course) that W.C. Handy was the 'originator of jazz and the blues' and counter-claiming that he had created jazz in 1902. This outburst of self-aggrandizement was ridiculed and created an atmosphere in which few fans, critics or fellow musicians took his work seriously. By the early 50s, however, some more perceptive individuals began to reassess his contribution to jazz and this reappraisal gradually swelled into a tidal wave of critical acclaim. By the 70s musicians were eager to play Morton's music, and through into the 90s many concerts and recordings in the USA and UK have been dedicated to his achievements.
Selected albums: *The Gennet Piano Solos* (1923-24), *Jelly Roll Morton Vols 1-3* (1926-30), *The Centennial: His Complete Victor Recordings* (RCA 1926-39), *The Complete Jelly Roll Morton Vols 1/2, 3/4, 5/6, 7/8* (RCA, 1926-40 recordings), *Library Of Congress Recordings Vols 1-8* (Swaggie 1938 recordings), *Rarities And Alternatives 1923-1940* (Suisa 1991), *Mr Jelly Lord* (Pickwick 1992).
Further reading: *Mister Jelly Roll: The Fortunes Of Jelly Roll Morton, New Orleans Creole And 'Inventor Of Jazz'*, Alan Lomax. *Jelly Roll Morton*, M. Williams. *Jelly Roll, Jabbo, And Fats*, Whitney Balliett. *Jelly Roll Morton's Last Night At The Jungle Inn*, Samuel B. Charters.

Morton, Benny

b. 31 January 1907, New York City, New York, USA, d. 28 December 1985. Largely self-taught, Morton played trombone in bands in and around New York during his teenage years and by 1926 was sufficiently

advanced to be hired by **Fletcher Henderson**. He subsequently played in bands led by **Chick Webb**, **Don Redman** and **Count Basie**; in 1940 he became a member of **Teddy Wilson**'s superb sextet. He also made record dates with **Billie Holiday**. In 1943 he joined **Edmond Hall**'s small group, then led his own band for a few years before becoming active in theatre pit bands in New York. In the 50s and 60s he was also busy in radio and recording studio bands, but occasionally turned up on record dates with artists such as **Buck Clayton** and **Ruby Braff**, and by the end of the 60s was mostly back on the jazz scene. He toured widely, playing in various bands including the Saints And Sinners package and outfits led by **Wild Bill Davison**, **Bobby Hackett** and **Sy Oliver**. A smooth and polished player with a relaxed and elegant style, Morton was one of the unsung heroes of the swing era.
Album: with Buck Clayton, Ruby Braff *Buck Meets Ruby* (1954). Compilation: with Count Basie *Swinging The Blues* (1937-39 recordings).

Morton, George 'Shadow'

b. 1942, Richmond, Virginia, USA. Shadow Morton - so named because he was never found where he was expected - began his career as a member of the Marquis. This New York vocal group often accompanied Ellie Gaye who, as **Ellie Greenwich**, later enjoyed success as a songwriter with husband **Jeff Barry**. In 1964 Morton brought her a demo of his first composition, '(Remember) Walkin' In The Sand', performed by the then-unknown **Shangri-Las**. Captivated by the ethereal performance, the couple placed the song with the nascent **Red Bird** label where it became the first of several atmospheric collaborations between the artist and this popular act. A US Top 5 hit, the single was succeeded by 'Leader Of The Pack' (a 1964 chart-topper), 'Give Him A Great Big Kiss', 'Out In The Streets' and 'I Can Never Go Home Anymore', but Morton then tired of the girl-group genre. In 1967 he helped launch the career of **Janis Ian** with the controversial 'Society's Child', but found greater fame for his production work for **Vanilla Fudge**. The melodramatic air of the Shangri-Las was herein blended to psychedelic pop, most notably on 'You Keep Me Hanging On', a funereally-paced interpretation of a former hit for the **Supremes**. This inspired rendition sold over one million copies and established a pattern for several subsequent releases. However, Morton left the music business having produced *Too Much Too Soon* (1974) for the **New York Dolls** and undertook a five-year sabbatical. His return in 1979 garnered some publicity, but he failed to recapture the success of the previous decade.

Morton, Pete

b. 30 July 1964, Leicester, England. Morton is one of the newer group of folk singer/songwriters to emerge in recent years who have gained a growing acceptance and respectability. During school days, he played in a punk band redolent of the **Ramones**, and subsequently moved into the folk scene. Having already 'discovered' **Bob Dylan**, Morton found a good deal of interest in the talent available on the circuit. He moved to Manchester in 1987, and was signed by Harbourtown Records, which released the highly acclaimed *Frivolous Love*. This brought Morton to the attention of a wider audience, and he began touring the UK. With the follow-up *One Big Joke* appearing a year later to good reviews, Morton undertook his first tour of the USA in 1989. His style is generally rock-orientated, but still based on traditional styles. 1992 saw the release of his third album, *Mad World Blues* and tours of the USA and Canada.
Albums: *Frivolous Love* (Harbourtown 1987), *One Big Joke* (Harbourtown 1988), with Roger Wilson, Simon Edwards *Urban Folk Volume One* (Harbourtown 1990), *Mad World Blues* (Harbourtown 1992).

Morton, Tex

b. Robert William Lane, 8 August 1916, Nelson, New Zealand, d. 23 July 1983, Sydney, Australia. A Maori neighbour taught Morton his first guitar chords and he became so obsessed with music that, at the age of 15, he ran away from home and busked on the streets of Waihi. When asked one day by the town's policemen if his name was Bobby Lane, he noticed a nearby garage sign that gave the name of 'Morton' and quickly informed the officer that his name was Bob Morton and that he was a street singer and entertainer. He worked on various jobs, including one with a travelling troupe known as the Gaieties Of 1932. He made some aluminium disc recordings in Wellington (never commercially released), which proved very popular on local radio and may well be the first country music records made outside the USA. In 1932, he moved to Australia and worked with travelling shows, where apart from singing, he worked as a magician, a boxing booth fighter, with wild animals, as the stooge for others and even rode as a Wall Of Death rider. In 1934, with a repertoire of Australian bush ballads as well as the early country songs that he had heard on record, he moved to Sydney. He undertook whatever jobs he could find, including going to sea as a stoker and electrician, and once worked as a labourer for the firm responsible for installing the lighting on Sydney Harbour Bridge. After eventually winning a major talent show, he made his first recordings for Regal Zonophone in February 1936 when, among the four tracks recorded, two, 'Happy Yodeller' and 'Swiss Sweetheart', were his own compositions. The records sold well, further sessions soon followed and by 1937, Tex Morton the Yodelling Boundary Rider was a nationally known star. When he played his first concert in Brisbane, the crowd totalled 50,000. He continued to record throughout the late 30s, the material ranging from known country songs and his own numbers to recitations of the works of famous Australian poets Henry Lawson and Banjo Patterson. He published his Tex Morton songbook and a newspaper even ran a comic strip of his adventures. In 1939, a major star, he had established his own travelling circus/rodeo, where apart from singing, he entertained with trick shooting, fancy riding, a memory act and magic. World War II forced him to close his show and he invested heavily in a dude ranch, losing all his money when the project failed. After the war, he reformed his rodeo, linked it with another major touring zoo and circus and toured all over Australia. In 1949, he decided to move to the USA and, having by then learned an act using hypnotism as well as his other talents, he moved to Los Angeles. After spending two years working as a singer and acting on radio and in some films, he began to appear as The Great Doctor Robert Morton - the World's Greatest Hypnotist. In 1951, he toured the USA and Canada with his one-man show on which he sang, did recitations, trick shooting, mind reading and hypnotism. He proved so popular that he set attendance records in many cities, including St. Louis, Boston and Vancouver and in Toronto his show outran *South Pacific*. Ever the showman, he used many gimmicks to attract the crowd, including stunts such as walking blindfold on the parapet of the tallest building in the town. In the early 60s, with many similar acts now performing, he gave up the hypnotism and, for a time, he worked on the stage and in films as Robert Morton. He returned to Australia in 1965, where he briefly and unsuccessfully resurrected The Great Morton. He toured for a while with a small rodeo show but soon found that television had made such entertainment no longer viable. He continued to record and in 1973, he scored a major Australian hit with his song 'The Goodiwindi Grey' (a tribute to a famous racehorse), recorded at what turned out to be his last recording session. Throughout the 70s, he appeared on television and in Australian films and although he often tried to leave out the old hillbilly and yodelling songs, the public would not let him. It is estimated that during his long career he recorded over 1000 songs and had many major national hits with numbers such as 'Beautiful Queensland', 'The Black Sheep' (his best selling song) and 'Good Old Droving Days'. Tex Morton died from pneumonia in July 1983.

Selected albums: *The Tex Morton Story* (1959), *Tex Morton Looks Back* (1961), *Songs Of The Outback* (1961), *The Versatile Tex Morton* (1962), *Sing, Smile And Sigh* (c.1964), *Encores* (60s), *Hallelujah I'm A Bum* (60s, double album), *The Travelling Showman* (60s), *Tex Morton Today* (c.1970), *Tex Morton's Australia* (1973), early tracks some with sister Dorrie *Red River Valley* (1975).

Morwells

Formed in 1973, Kingston, Jamaica, this group featured Maurice 'Blacka' Wellington (vocals/percussion) and Eric 'Binghi Buny' Lamont (vocals/guitar). Prior to forming the group, Wellington had been a record salesman, and Lamont had recorded with Bongo Herman for **Derrick Harriott**. The group's name is a contraction of Maurice Wellington. In 1974 they released 'Mafia Boss' and 'You Got To Be Holy' on their own Morwell Esquire label, and followed these with their debut, *Presenting The Morwells* (1975). The album is a blend of strong original songs and covers of hits by the **Melodians** and **Delroy Wilson**. A dub version of the album, *Dub Me*, was also released, and proved even more popular than the vocal album. In 1976 Wellington became an engineer and producer for **Joe Gibbs**, and Lamont became the rhythm guitarist with the Revolutionaries, **Channel One**'s houseband. This gave them fairly free access to the island's top musicians and studios, and in this period they reached peak form. Singles on Morwell Esquire included 'Proverb' (1976) and 'Crab In A Bag' (1977), and eight tracks from their first album plus four singles were released in the UK as *Crab Race*. Bassist Errol 'Flabba' Holt now joined the group on a permanent basis, and further singles in 1977 included ''77 Festival' for Joe Gibbs, 'Mix-up' for **Winston 'Niney' Holness** and 'Africa We Want To Go' for Tony Robinson. Excellent albums followed with *Cool Runnings* (1978), *Kingston 12 Toughie* (1979) and *The Best Of The Morwells* (1981). The group then broke up, with Maurice Wellington continuing with the Morwell label, and Eric Lamont and Errol Holt forming the **Roots Radics**.

Albums: *Presenting* (Morwells 1975), *Dub Me* (1975), *Crab Race* (Burning Sounds 1978), *Cool Runnings* (Bushays 1979), *Kingston 12 Toughies* (Carib Gems 1980). Compilation: *The Best Of The Morwells* (Night Hawk 1981).

Mosby, Johnny And Jonie

b. 26 April c.30s, Ft. Smith, Arkansas, USA. Mosby moved to Los Angeles when a child and during the 50s built a reputation around the local country circuit, soon fronting his own band. He first met Jonie (b. Janice Irene Shields, 10 August 1940, Van Nuys, Los Angeles, California, USA) when she successfully auditioned for the post of female vocalist with his band early in 1958; and that same year they married. They made their first recordings for a minor label in 1959 and had local chart success with 'Just Before Dawn'. They were later signed to **Columbia Records** and achieved their first US country chart entry in 1963 with a Harlan Howard song called 'Don't Call Me From A Honky Tonk'. They left **Columbia** and joined **Capitol** in 1964 and by 1973 had 16 further hits to their credit. These

included 'Trouble In My Arms', 'Keep Those Cards And Letters Coming In' and 'Just Hold My Hand'. They also showed a penchant for recording, with minor success, country versions of songs that were pop hits, such as 'Hold Me, Thrill Me, Kiss Me' (Mel Carter), 'I'm Leaving It Up To You' (**Dale And Grace**) and 'My Happiness' (**Connie Francis**). Jonie and Johnny limited their touring in favour of raising their family but appeared on various television shows and for several years had their own *Country Music Time* on Los Angeles television. They moved to Nashville in the 70s but achieved no chart hits after 1973.
Albums: *The New Sweethearts Of Country Music* (1965), *Mr & Mrs Country Music* (1965), *Make A Left And Then A Right* (1968), *Hold Me* (1969), *I'll Never Be Free* (1969), *Just Hold My Hand* (1969), *My Happiness* (1970), *Oh, Love Of Mine* (1970).

Mosca, Sal

b. Salvatore Joseph Mosca, 27 April 1927, Mount Vernon, New York, USA. A student, disciple and close friend of **Lennie Tristano**, pianist Mosca has followed his mentor's example by recording and touring only rarely. In the 50s he did play on several **Lee Konitz** albums, and some sessions with **Peter Ind** later appeared on the bassist's Wave label. In the 70s Mosca again worked with Konitz and with **Warne Marsh**, toured Europe as a solo artist and played at the Lennie Tristano Memorial Concert in 1979. In the 80s he was seldom heard as a performer, but remained active as a teacher. A remarkably subtle player, with the sophisticated harmonic ear characteristic of Tristanoites, Mosca can disguise the chord changes of the best-known standard so cleverly that he makes it virtually unrecognizable, creating an entirely new tune in the process.
Albums: With Peter Ind *At The Den* (1969, rec. 1959), *On Piano* (1969, rec 1955, 1959), *Sal Mosca Music* (1977), *For You* (1979), with others *Lennie Tristano Memorial Concert* (1979), with Warne Marsh *How Deep, How High* (1980, rec. 1977, 1979), *A Concert* (Jazz Records 1990, rec 1979).

Moses, Bob

b. 28 January 1948, New York, USA. Moses grew up surrounded by musicians like **Charlie Mingus**, for whom his father was press agent. Largely self-taught, he started to play drums when he was 10 years old and also played vibes in local Latin bands in his teens. He appeared with **Rahsaan Roland Kirk** in the mid-60s and formed Free Spirits with **Larry Coryell**, one of the first jazz-rock bands. After a short stay with **Dave Liebman**'s Open Sky he joined **Gary Burton**. In the early 70s he formed Compost with Harold Vick (tenor) and **Jack DeJohnette** and toured the UK with the **Mike Gibbs** Orchestra before returning to the groups of **Gary Burton** and **Pat Metheny**. At this stage he was also writing for large ensembles and formed his own label - Mozown Records - to release the results. The music was recorded by all-star line-ups of New York musicians and was accorded great critical acclaim. Moses makes personal use of a wide range of influences to create colourful, complex yet swinging music. In the 80s he played with the **Steve Kuhn/Sheila Jordan** Band (1979-82), **George Gruntz** Big Band and his own quintet. He is the author of the drum method *Drum Wisdom.*
Albums: with Rahsaan Roland Kirk *I Talk With the Spirits* (1966), with Kirk *Rip, Rig And Panic* (1966), with Gary Burton *Lofty Fake Anagram* (1967), with Compost *Life Is Round* (1971), with Mike Gibbs *The Only Chrome Waterfall Orchestra* (1975), with Pat Metheny *Bright Size Life* (1975), with Steve Swallow *Bittersweet In The Ozone* (1975), with Swallow *Home* (1979), with Swallow *When Elephants Dream Of Music* (1982), with Swallow *Visits With The Great Spirit* (Gramavision 1983), *Wheels Of Coloured Light* (Open Minds 1983), with Gibbs *Big Music* (Virgin 1988), *Story Of Moses* (Gala 1989), with Billy Martin *East Side* (ITM 1989).

Moses, J.C.

b. John Curtis Moses, 18 October 1936, Pittsburgh, Pennsylvania, USA, d. 1977. Moses began as a percussionist, learning congas and bongos, with drummer Paula Roberts. Between 1958 and 1960 he played with Walt Harper, then relocated to New York. His accurate, expansive timekeeping was embraced by the progressive jazz community, most notably **Eric Dolphy**, who used him on the sessions which produced the little-known masterpieces *Conversations* and *Iron Man* (1964). Other musical associates included pianists **Cedar Walton** and **Herbie Hancock** and bebop trumpeter **Kenny Dorham**. In 1963 he left for Europe with the short-lived New York Contemporary Five and later appeared on fellow-Fiver **Archie Shepp**'s *Fire Music* (1965) and *On This Night* (1966). Between 1965 and 1967 he drummed with **Roland Rahsaan Kirk**. For the next two years he freelanced, playing with **John Coltrane**, **Sonny Stitt**, **Jackie McLean**, **Hal Singer** and singer **Nancy Wilson**. In 1969 he left for Denmark and became house drummer at the famous Cafe Montmartre in Copenhagen. As well as working with fellow expatriates **Dexter Gordon** and **Kenny Drew,** he accompanied **Coleman Hawkins**, **Ben Webster**, **Ted Curson** and **Tete Monteliou**, and also recorded with **John Tchicai**'s Cadentia Nova Danica orchestra (*Afrodisiaca*, 1969). After 1970, problems with his kidneys limited his activities and he returned to Pittsburgh, where he played with **Nathan Davis** and Eric Kloss. His death in 1977, aged 41, deprived the world of a drummer who could relate both to New Thing iconoclasts and swing veterans.
Albums: with Eric Dolphy *Conversations* (1964), with

Dolphy *Iron Man* (1964), *Archie Shepp & The New York Contemporary Five* (c.60s, rec 1963).

Moses, Pablo

b. Pablo Henry, c.1953, Jamaica, West Indies. In 1975 Pablo made his debut recording 'I Man A Grasshopper'. It was immediately evident that an extraordinary talent was at work, an impression that was sustained by the release of 'We Should Be In Angola' (1976), produced by Clive Hunt. His first album, *Revolutionary Dream*, was released in 1977, and it still stands as a genuine mid-70s reggae classic. Pablo's detached delivery of his parable-like songs coalesced with Geoffrey Chung's brilliant production and arrangements to form a truly remarkable whole. Two further excellent albums under Chung's supervision followed: *A Song* (1980) and *Pave The Way* (1981). Pablo then decided to produce himself, but could not sustain the quality of his previous releases. Since the early 80s he has toured extensively, and gained a strong reputation internationally as a live performer.
Albums: *Revolutionary Dream* (Tropical Sound Track 1976), *A Song* (Island 1980), *Pave The Way* (Mango/Island 1981), *In The Future* (Alligator/Mercury 1983), *Tension* (Alligator/Mercury 1985), *Live To Love* (Rohit 1985), *We Refuse* (Profile 1990), *Charlie* (Profile 1990), *The Confessions Of A Rastaman* (Musidisc 1993).

Mosley, Snub

b. Lawrence L. Mosley, 29 December 1905, Little Rock, Arkansas, USA, d. 21 July 1981. Starting out on trombone, in the 20s Mosley joined in the popular **territory band** led by **Alphonso Trent**. Noted for his aggressive, attacking style, Mosley was dissatisfied with what he saw as the limitations of the trombone and invented his own instrument. This was a slide saxophone, which he thereafter preferred to a more orthodox instrument, although he still continued to play trombone. Leaving Trent in 1933, Mosley worked with some of the best-known bands of the period, including those led by **Claude Hopkins**, **Fats Waller** and **Louis Armstrong**. He also tried his hand at bandleading, but while he worked steadily throughout the 40s and into the 50s, accommodating shifts in musical tastes by playing and singing R&B, he never made the breakthrough to nationwide success. In the late 70s he became a popular figure on the international club and festival scene.
Album: *Snub Mosley Live At The Pizza Express* (1978).

Moss, Danny

b. 16 August 1927, Redhill, Surrey, England. By the late 40s tenor saxophonist Moss had established a reputation as an outstanding musician and was hired by many of the leading UK jazz and dancebands of the day, including those of **Ted Heath**, Oscar Rabin, **Vic Lewis**, **John Dankworth** and **Humphrey Lyttelton**. From the early 60s Moss led his own small groups, touring the UK and sometimes working with fellow UK musicians such as **Sandy Brown** and **Dave Shepherd**. Additionally, he was in great demand as an accompanist and featured soloist with visiting American artists, most notably with a succession of leading singers that included **Ella Fitzgerald**, **Sarah Vaughan** and **Rosemary Clooney**. In 1990 Moss, whose wife is singer Jeannie Lambe, took up residence in Australia. In the summer of the same year he was awarded an MBE in the Queen's Birthday Honours List. A committed jazzman, Moss's distinctive playing style shows him to be at ease whether on uptempo swingers, where his full-bodied sound is a delight, or on soulful ballads to which he brings great emotional depth.
Albums: *Danny Moss Quintet With Strings* (c.1966), *The Good Life* (1968), *Straighten Up And Fly Right* (1979), *Danny Moss Quartet With Geoff Simkins* (1979), *Jeannie Lambe* (1980), with Lambe *Blues And All That Jazz* (c.1982), with Simpkins *Danny Moss And Geoff Simpkins Vol 2* (Flyright 1982), with Lambe *The Midnight Sun* (1984).

Moss, Eugene 'Buddy'

b. 26 January 1914, Hancock County, Georgia, USA, d. October 1984, Atlanta, Georgia, USA. It was as a harmonica player that Moss first appeared on record, in 1930, as one of the Georgia Cotton Pickers, with **Barbecue Bob** and **Curley Weaver**. Although he apparently learnt guitar from Bob, his playing was distinctly in the ragtime-inflected Eastern blues tradition of artists such as **Blind Blake**. Moss had his own style, however, a carefully crafted blues sound that was to make his name as one of the most popular Atlanta-based singers of the 30s. He recorded prolifically between 1933 and 1935, sometimes backed by Weaver and occasionally **Blind Willie McTell**. On later dates he teamed up with **Josh White** and the two musicians accompanied each other on their respective recordings. Altogether, Moss made over 60 tracks in these three years, but there followed a long hiatus when he was sentenced to a prison term soon after the 1935 session. He was released in 1941 and recorded again, this time with **Sonny Terry** and **Brownie McGhee**. The outbreak of war cut short his prospects and he earned his living working outside music until he was rediscovered in the 60s, although this led to only a few new recordings and live appearances.
Selected albums: *Georgia Blues* (1983), *Red River Blues* (1984).

Most Happy Fella, The

Any show that opened in the same season as ***My Fair Lady*** was bound to be somewhat overshadowed by **Alan Jay Lerner** and **Frederick Loewe**'s masterpiece, which was so obviously going to be a smash hit. However, *The Most Happy Fella* was, in some ways, a more ambitious work than its female counterpart, and enjoyed a satisfactory run of 676 performances on Broadway. The show opened on 3 May 1956 at the Imperial Theatre, and immediately confused many of the critics: was it an opera? A play with music, perhaps? **Frank Loesser**, who wrote the music, lyrics, and libretto, settled on 'an extended musical comedy'. His adaptation of Sidney Howard's 1924 Pulitzer Prize-winning play, *They Knew What They Wanted*, was set in Napa Valley, California, and tells of an Italian vintner, Tony (Robert Weede, a former opera singer making his Broadway debut), who is maturing rather more quickly that grapes in his vineyard. He longs for a wife, and proposes by post to Rosabella (Jo Sullivan, who later became Loesser's wife), a waitress he has noticed in a San Francisco restaurant. To increase his chances of success, he includes a photograph of his handsome young foreman, Joey (Art Lund), and she comes hurrying on down to meet him. Even though he has deceived her, she still marries Tony - but tarries with Joey. When she discovers that she is to have Joe's baby she is determined to leave, but Tony forgives her and adopts the child as his own. With spoken dialogue at a minimum, *The Most Happy Fella* is a virtually sung-through show, and Loesser's score has moments of high emotion in songs such as 'Somebody Somewhere', My Heart Is Full Of You', and 'Joey, Joey'. Rosabella's friend, Cleo (Susan Johnson), who follows her out from San Francisco gets pretty friendly herself with one of the ranch hands, Herman (Shorty Long), and leads the company in a hymn to Dallas, the rousing 'Big 'D'. The show's big hit song was 'Standing On The Corner', which became popular in the US for **Dean Martin**, and the **Four Lads** who repeated their success in the UK, in competition with the **King Brothers**. Another of the show's lighter numbers, 'Happy To Make Your Acquaintance', also entered the UK chart in a version by **Sammy Davis Jnr**. and **Carmen McRae**. The rest of Loesser's highly distinguished score, which contained well over 30 songs in a wide variety of musical styles such as arias and choral pieces, included 'Ooh! My Feet', 'Mama, Mama', 'Warm All Over', 'I Like Everybody', 'Song Of A Summer Night', 'Sposalizio', 'How Beautiful The Days', 'Rosabella', 'The Most Happy Fella', and 'Abbondanza'. *The Most Happy Fella* was not everybody's idea of what a Broadway musical should be, but, during a 20 month stay on Broadway, it won the New York Drama Critics Award for best musical, and subsequently ran for 288 performances at the London Coliseum. Lund reprised his role in the West End, during which time he became quite a favourite of audiences there, and returned with **Richard Rogers**' ***No Strings*** in 1963. *The Most Happy Fella* was revived on Broadway in 1979, and presented by the New York City Opera in 1991, with Giorgio Tozzi in the lead. In the following year the show was back on Broadway again, via the Goodspeed Opera House and Los Angeles, this time with just a two-piano orchestration which Loesser himself had commissioned some years previously. Although critically acclaimed, the production ran for only 229 performances and lost most of its $1.4 million investment. It was nominated for four **Tony Awards**, but won just one - Scott Waara for best featured actor - being pipped at the post for 'best revival' by ***Guys And Dolls***, which is, of course, another Frank Loesser show. Unusually, the Original Cast album was recorded in 'real time' - in two long takes - just as the show was performed in the theatre. Even with part-retakes, the recording took only one day to complete, in comparison with the 1956 three-album set which needed a week of session time. In 1993, a concert performance of *The Most Happy Fella* became 'the first of its kind to be broadcast on BBC radio in England'.

Most, Mickie

b. Michael Peter Hayes, June 1938, Aldershot, Hampshire, England. In the late 50s Most toured and recorded for **Decca** as the Most Brothers with Alex Wharton who later produced the **Moody Blues**' hit 'Go Now'. From 1959-63 he worked in South Africa, producing his own hit versions of songs such as **Chuck Berry**'s 'Johnny B. Goode' and **Ray Peterson**'s 'Corrina Corrina'. He returned to Britain aiming to develop a career in production and after scoring a minor hit with 'Mister Porter', he became producer of the Newcastle R&B group the **Animals**. Beginning with 'Baby Let Me Take You Home' in 1964, Most supervised seven hit singles by the group and was now in demand as a producer. Much of his skill at this time lay in his choice of songs for artists such as the **Nashville Teens** and **Herman's Hermits**, for whom he found 'Silhouettes', 'I'm Into Something Good' and 'Wonderful World'. After his earliest UK successes Most was given a five-year retainer production deal by **CBS** in America, under which he produced records by **Lulu**, **Terry Reid**, **Jeff Beck** and **Donovan**, for whom he created a new electric sound on 'Sunshine Superman' (1966). He had later successes with artists such as **Mary Hopkin** (the 1970 Eurovision Song Contest entry, 'Knock Knock Who's There') and **Julie Felix** ('El Condor Pasa') but after 1969 he concentrated on running the **RAK** label. For over a decade, RAK singles were regularly to be found the the UK Top 10. The roster included **Hot Chocolate**, **Alexis Korner**'s **CCS**, **Smokie**, **Chris Spedding**, **Kim Wilde**, New World, **Suzi Quatro** and **Mud**. The last three acts were produced by **Nicky Chinn** and **Mike Chapman** for RAK. During the 70s Most was a member of the panel on the UK television talent show *New Faces* and with the arrival of punk, he presented *Revolver*, a short-lived show devoted to the new music. However, he was out of sympathy with much of punk and the subsequent New Romantic trend and after the RAK back catalogue was sold to **EMI** in 1983, Most was less active. Among his few later productions was 'Me And My Foolish Heart' an early record by **Johnny Hates Jazz** which included his son Calvin. After taking a brief sabbatical, Most returned in 1988 with a revived RAK label, producing Perfect Stranger which featured ex-**Uriah Heep** singer Peter Goalby. In 1995 Most appeared once more in the *Sunday Times* 'Britain's Richest 500', this time announcing a car collection worth over £1m and a new house costing £4m with claims that it is the largest private house in Britain.

Motello, Elton

Alan Ward had originally been the singer with UK punk hopefuls **Bastard**, which also included in its ranks future **Damned** guitarist Brian James. After the band split Ward assumed the pseudonym of Elton Motello, alternating between England and Belgium, where he had built up associations touring with Bastard. He made his debut appearance at the end of 1977 with 'Jet Boy, Jet Girl', first in Belgium on Pinball, followed a month later by a UK release on Lightning. The track achieved international success with the re-titled French version, 'Ca Plane Pour Moi', by pop-punk exponents **Plastic Bertrand**. Success for Motello's original was much more limited, even though it was released in many different countries. A few months later, 'Jet Boy, Jet Girl' was re-recorded to greater notoriety by **Captain Sensible** And The Softies. Towards the end of 1978 Motello recorded his debut album, *Victim Of Time*, which was released in March 1979 by Attic Records, but only in Canada. He was backed by various players including Peter (guitar), Nobby (drums) and Willie Change (bass), with the help of Jet Staxx (guitar), Tony Boast (guitar) and former **Pink Fairies** and **Pretty Things** drummer John 'Twink' Alder. In addition to the single, the album included a remake of the **Small Faces**' 'Sha La La La Lee' and another 11 compositions that fluctuated between pop and punk. With the new decade came two further releases: '20th Century Fox' and a second album, *Pop Art*.
Albums: *Victim Of Time* (Attic 1979), *Pop Art* (Attic 1980).

Motels

Formed in Berkeley, California, in the early 70s, the Motels comprised Martha Davis (vocals), Jeff Jourard (guitar), his brother Martin (keyboards/saxophone), former jazzer Michael Goodroe (bass) and UK session drummer Brian Glascock (ex-**Toe Fat**). Transferring to Los Angeles, the group assembled for appearances at Hollywood's Whiskey club throughout July 1978, attracting a modicum of music industry interest in the process. In 1979 their stunning debut album was issued by **Capitol Records**. Like its remaining tracks, the hit ballad, 'Total Control', was produced by John Carter and composed by central figure Davis, whose eclectic tastes included blues, Broadway musicals and Stravinsky. Her onstage presence was 'exceptionally charismatic', wrote *The Los Angeles Times*, wrongly predicting that she 'could become one of the most influential female performers in rock'. Her boyfriend, Tim McGovern (ex-Captain Kopter And The Fabulous Twirlybirds), replaced Jeff Jourard during sessions for *Careful*, with a sleeve adorned with a print of a Dougie Fields' painting. Though its singles, 'Whose Problem' and 'Days Are OK', flitted into the US and UK charts, they fared well in regional charts in Australasia, a territory where the group made its strongest impact. Their albums and tie-in singles tended to hover around the lower half of the UK Top 40 after *All Four One*, at number 16, marked the Motels' commercial zenith. In their homeland they scored two US Top 10 hits with 'Only The Lonely' (1982) and 'Suddenly Last Summer' (1983), but folded in 1987.
Albums: *The Motels* (Capitol 1979), *Careful* (Capitol 1980), *All Four One* (Capitol 1982), *Little Robbers* (Capitol 1983), *Shock* (Capitol 1985).

Moten, Bennie

b. 13 November 1894, Kansas City, Missouri, USA, d. 2 April 1935. In his youth, Moten gained a substantial reputation in and around his home town as a pianist; by 1920 he had become an established and respected bandleader. His unit, originally a small outfit, gradually expanded until it was a big band ready to take advantage of the upsurge in interest in this kind of ensemble. As a pianist and an accomplished arranger, Moten deftly blended New Orleans concepts into the freewheeling style popular in the midwest. Beginning its recording career in 1923, the band built a reputation far afield, and residencies in New York followed. Moten attracted many excellent musicians until his was the outstanding band of the region. Some of the best men were poached from **Walter Page**'s Blue Devils, among them Bill (not yet **Count**) **Basie**, **Oran 'Hot Lips' Page**, **Eddie Durham** and **Jimmy Rushing**. Eventually, Walter Page went along, too. Later additions to the band included **Ben Webster**, **Herschel Evans**, **Eddie Barefield** and **Lester Young**. By the mid-30s the band was not merely the finest in the region, but was superior to many of the headline bands in the east and elsewhere. In 1935 the unit visited Chicago to audition for a residency at the Grand Terrace Ballroom. When they headed for home Moten remained behind for a tonsillectomy and died when the surgeon's knife slipped and severed his jugular vein. The band subsequently broke up, but later many of the musicians reformed under the leadership of **Buster Smith** and Basie, and later still the band

became Basie's. As the leader of an outstanding band, Moten occupies an important position in the history of Kansas City jazz, even if he was understandably overshadowed by his musical legatees.
Selected compilation: *The Complete Bennie Moten Vols 1/2, 3/4, 5/6* (RCA, 1923-32 recordings).

Mother Earth (60s)

Formed in Texas in 1966, Mother Earth was one of several American groups to move to the more liberal San Francisco during the west coast beat boom of the late 60s. The original line-up featured three former members of the Wigs, John 'Toad' Andrews (guitar), Bob Arthur (bass) and George Rains (drums), as well as songwriter R. Powell St. John, who composed several songs for the **13th Floor Elevators**. Blues singer **Tracy Nelson** (b. 27 December 1944, Madison, Wisconsin, USA), was Mother Earth's featured vocalist, while the group was latterly augmented by Mark Naftalin (keyboards) and Martin Fierro (horns). The ensemble made its tentative debut on the soundtrack of the film *Revolution*, before completing a promising debut album in 1968. Nelson's powerful voice enhanced its blues-based foundation, while admirable cameos from guitarist **Mike Bloomfield** and fiddler Spencer Perkin added to the informal atmosphere. The following year Mother Earth moved to a farm on the outskirts of Nashville. Their music became increasingly country-orientated and by the release of a fourth album, *Satisfied*, only Nelson and Andrews remained from the group's first release. In 1973 they took the name Tracy Nelson/Mother Earth, but the group was dissolved when the singer's self-titled solo album won critical and commercial plaudits.
Albums: *Living With The Animals* (1968), *Make A Joyful Noise* (1969), *Presents Tracy Nelson Country* (1969), *Satisfied* (1970), *Bring Me Home* (1971), *Mother Earth* (1972), *Poor Man's Paradise* (1973).

Mother Earth (90s)

Matt Deighton (vocals/guitar), Neil Corcoran (bass guitar), Chris White (drums), Bryn Barklam (Hammond organ). The UK's 'acid jazz' craze gained momentum in the mid-80s, when the original Acid Jazz label began to capitalise on the swelling interest in jazz, by encouraging a series of crossover bands who were mixing the music with funk and creating a danceable but harmonically rich, essentially live sound. As more and more London musicians began looking to the 70s, and projects led by **Herbie Hancock**, **Billy Cobham** or **Lonnie Liston Smith**, for inspiration, Mother Earth came together in 1990, originally as a six-piece, with additional vocalists Shauna Greene and Bunny. Their first recordings – '5th Quadrant' and 'Riot On 103rd Street' on the *Totally Wired 6* and *Totally Wired 7* Acid Jazz compilations – swiftly gained the group a cult popularity and a contract with the label. A funky, Hammond organ-led affair very much in the jazz funk mould, *Stoned Woman* was released in 1992, and the band quickly followed up with a hectic tour schedule, establishing a trendy, retro stage image heavy on flared trousers and sheepskin. If *Stoned Woman* suffered from an occasional blandness and lack of musical direction, Mother Earth tightened things up in 1994, with the release of *The People Tree*. Harder and funkier, with catchier tunes, *The People Tree* featured guest appearances by **Paul Weller** and popular Acid Jazz percussionist Snowboy, and represented a significant change in direction for the band, who were now looking towards 70s funk rock for a tougher, **Santana**-influenced sound.
Albums: *Stoned Woman* (Acid Jazz 1992), *The People Tree* (Acid Jazz 1994).

Mother Goose

Formed in Dunedin, New Zealand in 1975 and finding themselves rejected by their home country, Mother Goose emigrated to Australia in 1976. Their first single 'Baked Beans' was a novelty hit which caused the band many problems in relating to a wider rock audience. Like the **Village People**, each member dressed in a character's costume, and their stage choreography meant that the audience were entertained musically and visually. The line-up comprised Kevin Collings (guitar), Denis Gibbins (bass), Craig Johnston (vocal), Marcel Rodeka (drums), Steve Young (keyboards) and Pete Dickson (guitar, replaced by American Justin McCarthy in 1979). The band was never able to shake off the novelty image even though its recorded output was of a high standard, and the mime and satire in its stage show had a serious edge. Although Mother Goose released three albums they never achieved significant radio success, despite being one of Australia's most popular live acts, with a fiercely loyal following. The band spent 1978-79 in the USA, but record company troubles prevented them making any inroads into that market. On return to Australia the band based itself in Perth. When the third album enjoyed some success in Canada the band moved there, working under the name Landing Party, before returning to Australia to break up in 1984.
Albums: *Stuffed* (1977), *Don't Believe In Fairy Tales* (1979), *This Is The Life* (1982).

Mother Love Bone

This short-lived, Seattle-based quintet comprised Andrew Wood (vocals), Greg Gilmore (drums), Bruce Fairweather (guitar), Stone Gossard (guitar; ex-**Green River**) and Jeff Ament (bass; ex-Green River). Drawing influences from the **Stooges**, **MC5** and the **Velvet Underground** they specialized in heavy-duty garage rock laced with drug-fuelled psychotic overtones. Signing to **Polydor**, they debuted with *Apple* in 1990 to widespread critical acclaim. Their promising

career was curtailed abruptly by the untimely death of vocalist Andrew Wood in March, shortly after the album was released. Gossard and Ament would go on to enjoy further success with **Temple Of The Dog** and, to a much greater extent, **Pearl Jam**.
Album: *Apple* (Polydor 1990). Compilation: *Stardog Champion* (Polydor 1992).

Mother Wore Tights

20th Century-Fox teamed their top pin-up girl, **Betty Grable**, with one of their most popular and likeable song-and-dance-men, **Dan Dailey**, in this 1947 release which was produced by Lamar Trotti. He was also responsible for the screenplay which was based on a book by Miriam Young. Set in the early part of the century and told in flashback, it was a warm-hearted tale about a married vaudeville couple, Burt and McKinley (Grable and Dailey) whose hoity-toity elder daughter (Mona Freeman) derides her parents' performing lifestyle ('my friends go to the opera and things') until the entire class of her swanky music school go to see the 'old folks' show' - and actually enjoy it. The wayward miss then realises what a fool she has been, and at her graduation ceremony sings 'You Do', one of her father and mother's big hit songs. **Josef Myrow** and **Mack Gordon** wrote that one, and several of the others, including 'There's Nothing Like A Song', 'This Is My Favourite City', 'Kokomo, Indiana', 'Rolling Down To Bowling Green', and 'On A Little Two-Seat Tandem'. Gordon also collaborated with **Harry Warren** on 'Tra-la-la', and there were several more nostalgic numbers by various composers, such as 'Burlington Bertie From Bow' (William Hargreaves). Musical director **Alfred Newman** won an Oscar for his work on the score. Connie Marshall played the younger (but more mature) daughter, and there were excellent performances from Vanessa Brown, Robert Arthur, Sara Allgood, William Frawley, Ruth Nelson, Anabel Shaw, Michael Dunne, George Cleveland, Veda Ann Borg, Sig Ruman, Lee Patrick, and especially the highly amusing Señor Wences. Seymour Felix and Kenny Williams handled the olde worlde dance sequences and the director was Walter Lang. *Mother Wore Tights* was one of the Top 20 musicals of the 40s, and Betty Grable's most financially successful picture.

Mother's Finest

Despite the 90s fixation with funk rock, Mother's Finest have long been considered as the world's finest in this musical field. Led by vocalist Baby Jean (b. Joyce Kennedy) and hailing from Atlanta, Georgia, USA, the band boasts the talents of Moses Mo (b. Gary Moore; guitar), Glen Murdock (guitar/vocals), Mike (keyboards), Wizzard (b. Jerry Seay; bass) and B.B. Queen (b. B.B. Borden; drums). Formed in 1972, their music was basically funk with a metal edge and Kennedy's vocals ranged from the sensual to all-out attack. The band never quite made the big league in their homeland and only gained a cult following in Europe, although they were successful in Holland. In 1983, following the release of *Iron Age*, probably their hardest and most enduring record, the band dissipated. B.B. Queen played with southern boogie merchants **Molly Hatchet** and then teamed up with former colleagues Moses Mo and B.B. Queen in Illusion. He would subsequently release two soul albums for **A&M**. Wizzard would hook up with Rick Medlocke's **Blackfoot**. The original line-up reformed in 1989 but the accompanying album failed to capture the fire and soul of earlier releases. Undaunted, they soldiered on and released a live recording, *Subluxation*, to critical acclaim. In its wake, and with a line-up now boasting just three original members; Baby Jean, Murdock and Wizzard, they provided the agenda-setting *Black Raido Won't Play This Record*.
Albums: *Mother's Finest* (RCA 1972), *Mother's Finest* (Epic 1976), *Another Mother Further* (Epic 1977), *Mother Factor* (Epic 1978), *Live Mutha* (Epic 1979), *Iron Age* (Epic 1982), *One Mother To Another* (Epic 1983), *Looks Could Kill* (Capitol 1989), *Subluxation* (Capitol 1990), *Black Radio Won't Play This Record* (Scotti Bros 1992).

Motherlode

Formed in London, Ontario, Canada in the late 60s, Motherlode were best-known for their Top 20 entry, 'When I Die'. The group consisted of saxophonist Steve Kennedy, keyboardist William 'Smitty' Smith, guitarist Kenny Marco and drummer Wayne 'Stoney' Stone. The band was working at Top 40 clubs when it was signed to the Canadian label Revolution Records. Their local soul-orientated single 'When I Die', written by Smith and Kennedy, was picked up by **Buddah Records** and ultimately reached number 18 in the US. An album of the same title made the bottom of the charts but follow-up recordings failed to sell and the group disbanded in the early 70s. Smith formed a new Motherlode group and the remaining three members continued as Dr. Music. Smith and Marco later went on to become successful session musicians.
Albums: *When I Die* (1969), *Tuffed Out* (1973).

Mothers Of Invention

This celebrated group was formed in 1965 when guitarist **Frank Zappa** (b. 21 December 1940, Baltimore, Maryland, USA) replaced Ray Hunt in the Soul Giants, a struggling R&B-based bar band. Ray Collins (vocals), Dave Coronado (saxophone), Roy Estrada (bass) and Jimmy Carl Black (drums) completed their early line-up, but Coronado abandoned the group when the newcomer unveiled his musical strategy. Now renamed the Mothers, the quartet was relocated from Orange County to Los Angeles where they were briefly augmented by several individuals, including **Alice**

Stuart, **James Guercio** and Henry Vestine, later guitarist in **Canned Heat**. These temporary additions found Zappa's vision daunting as the Mothers embarked on a disarming melange of 50s pop, Chicago R&B and *avant garde* music. They were embraced by the city's nascent Underground before an appearance at the famed Whiskey A Go-Go resulted in a recording deal when producer **Tom Wilson** caught the end of one of their sets.

Now dubbed the Mothers Of Invention, owing to pressure from the record company, the group added guitarist Elliott Ingber (Winged Eel Fingerling) before commencing *Freak Out*, rock music's first double album. This revolutionary set featured several exceptional pieces including 'Trouble Every Day', 'Hungry Freaks, Daddy' and 'The Return Of The Son Of Monster Magnet', each of which showed different facets of Zappa's evolving tableau. The Mothers second album, *Absolutely Free*, featured a radically reshaped line-up. Ingber was fired at the end of 1966 while Zappa added a second drummer, Billy Mundi, plus Don Preston (b. 21 September 1932; keyboards), Bunk Gardner (horns) and Jim 'Motorhead' Sherwood (saxophone) to the original group nucleus. A six-month residency at New York's Garrick Theater combined spirited interplay with excellent material and the set showed growing confidence. Satire flourished on 'Plastic People', 'America Drinks & Goes Home' and 'Brown Shoes Don't Make It', much of which was inspired by the 'cocktail-bar' drudgery the group suffered in its earliest incarnation. However, Zappa's ire was more fully flexed on *We're Only In It For The Money*, which featured several barbed attacks on the trappings of 'flower-power'. Housed in a sleeve which cleverly mocked the **Beatles**' *Sgt. Pepper's Lonely Hearts Club Band*, the set included 'The Idiot Bastard Son' ('The father's a Nazi in Congress today, the mother's a hooker somewhere in LA') and 'Who Needs The Peace Corps' ('I'll stay a week and get the crabs and take a bus back home') and indicated Zappa's growing fascination with technology. The album also introduced new member Ian Underwood (saxophone/keyboards), who became an integral part of the group's future work. *Cruising With Ruben And The Jets* was, to quote the liner notes; 'an album of greasy love songs and cretin simplicity'. Despite such cynicism, the group displayed an obvious affection for the 50s doo-wop material on offer, all of which was self-penned and included re-recordings of three songs, 'How Could I Be Such A Fool', 'Any Way The Wind Blows' and 'You Didn't Try To Call Me', first aired on *Freak Out*. However, the album was the last wholly new set committed by the 'original' line-up. Later releases, *Uncle Meat* (a soundtrack to the then unmade film), *Burnt Weeny Sandwich* and *Weasels Ripped My Flesh*, were all compiled from existing live and studio tapes as tension within the group pulled it apart. The musicians enjoyed mixed fortunes; Estrada joined newcomer **Lowell George** in **Little Feat**, third drummer Arthur Dyre Tripp III switched allegiance to **Captain Beefheart**, while Jimmy Carl Black formed **Geronimo Black** with brothers Buzz and Bunk Gardner.

A new Mothers was formed in 1970 from the musicians contributing to Zappa's third solo album, *Chunga's Revenge*, and the scatalogical 'on the road' documentary, *200 Motels*. Three former **Turtles**, Mark Volman, Howard Kaylan (both vocals) and Jim Pons (bass) joined **Aynsley Dunbar** (drums) and longstanding affiliates Ian Underwood and Don Preston in the group responsible for *Fillmore East - June 1971*. Here, however, the early pot-pourri of Stravinsky, **John Coltrane**, doo-wop and 'Louie Louie' gave way to condescending innuendo as Zappa threatened to become the person once the subject of his ire. Paradoxically, it became the group's best-selling album to date, setting the tone for future releases and reinforcing the guitarist's jaundiced view of his audience. This period was brought to a sudden end at London's Rainbow Theatre. A 'jealous' member of the audience attacked the hapless Zappa onstage, pushing him into the orchestra pit where he sustained multiple back injuries and a compound leg fracture. His slow recuperation was undermined when the entire new Mothers, bar Underwood, quit *en masse* to form what became known as **Flo And Eddie**. Confined to the studio, Zappa compiled *Just Another Band From L.A.* and used the Mothers epithet for the jazz big band on *The Grand Wazoo*. Reverting to rock music, the Mothers' name was re-established with a new, tighter line-up in 1973. However subsequent albums, *Over-Nite Sensation*, *Roxy And Elsewhere* and *One Size Fits All*, are indistinguishable from projects bearing Zappa's name and this now superfluous title was abandoned in 1975, following the release *Bongo Fury*, a collaboration with Captain Beefheart. Zappa's career has progressed to such a high-level that his entire catalogue has been remastered and re-issued with the advent of the compact disc. The quality of those early Mothers Of Invention recordings are by today's standards quite outstanding.

Albums: *Freak Out* (1966), *Absolutely Free* (1967), *We're Only In It For The Money* (1968), *Cruising With Ruben And The Jets* (1968), *Uncle Meat* (1969), *Burnt Weeny Sandwich* (1969), *Weasels Ripped My Flesh* (1970), *Fillmore East - June 1971* (1971), *200 Motels* (1971, film soundtrack), *Just Another Band From L.A.* (1972), *The Grand Wazoo* (1972), *Over-Nite Sensation* (1973), *Roxy And Elsewhere* (1974), *One Size Fits All* (1975), with Captain Beefheart *Bongo Fury* (1975). Compilations: *Mothermania* (19 69), *The Worst Of The Mothers* (1971).

Further reading: *No Commercial Potential*, David Walley. *Zappalog*, Norbert Obermanns. *The Real Frank Zappa Book*, Frank Zappa and Peter Occhigrosso. *Mother! The Frank Zappa Story*, Michael Gray.

Motian, Paul

b. 25 March 1931, Providence, Rhode Island, USA. Motian played guitar in Providence in his teens, then served a term in the US army. On his discharge in 1954 he went to New York to study music at the Manhattan School. By 1956 he was playing drums for **George Wallington** and Russell Jacquet. Between 1956 and 1958 he worked with **Tony Scott**, with whom he met the pianist **Bill Evans**. His work in the Evans trio (1959-64) has since achieved legendary status for delicacy and balance. Motian also played with **Oscar Pettiford**, **Zoot Sims** and **Lennie Tristano** in the late 50s. In the mid-60s he worked with singers **Mose Allison** and **Arlo Guthrie** and was part of the **Paul Bley** trio in 1964. Motian had met **Ornette Coleman**'s bassist **Charlie Haden** in 1959 and got a chance to work with him in **Keith Jarrett**'s band with **Dewey Redman** (1967-76); he also joined Haden's Liberation Music Orchestra for its debut recording in 1969 and toured with the re-formed Orchestra in the 80s. In the 70s he was active in the Jazz Composers' Orchestra and played on **Carla Bley**'s *Escalator Over The Hill* in 1972. He emerged as a leader in 1974, since when he has released an impressive series of albums on the **ECM**, Soul Note and JMT labels that have confirmed his stature as a drummer and composer. *Tribute* (1974) featured **Carlos Ward** on alto, while *Dance* and *Le Voyage* from the late 70s boast rare appearances by saxophonist **Charles Brackeen**. In the 80s he began long-term associations with guitarist **Bill Frisell**, whose arching, tremulous interpretations of Motian's melodies are particularly sympathetic, and the inventive tenorist **Joe Lovano**. In the late 80s he renewed his acquaintance with Paul Bley on a marvellous album of improvised duets (*Notes*), and joined with Haden and pianist **Geri Allen** to form one of the most thoughtful of contemporary piano trios; a guest appearance with **Marilyn Crispell**'s trio (*Live In Zurich*, 1991) proved he was also at home in more exploratory modes. Motian's examination of **Thelonious Monk** (*Monk In Motian*), standards (*Motian On Broadway*) and his piano-less tribute to Bill Evans (1991) show a questing musical mind, still working as keenly as ever.

Albums: *Conception Vessel* (ECM 1974), *Tribute* (ECM 1974), *Dance* (1977), *Le Voyage* (ECM 1979), *Psalm* (ECM 1982), *The Story Of Maryam* (ECM 1984), *It Should've Happened A Long Time Ago* (ECM 1985), *Jack Of Clubs* (ECM 1985), *Misterioso* (Soul Note 1986), with Paul Bley *Notes* (1987), with Geri Allen, Charlie Haden *Etudes* (1988), *Monk In Motian* (JMT 1988), *Paul Motian On Broadway Vol 1* (JMT 1989), with Allen, Haden *In The Year Of The Dragon* (1989), with Allen, Haden *Segments* (1989), *One Time Out* (Soul Note 1990), *Paul Motian On Broadway Vol 2* (JMT 1990), *Motian In Motian* (JMT 1989), *Bill Evans* (JMT 1991), with Allen, Haden *Live At The Village Vanguard* (1991), *Motian In Tokyo* (JMT 1992), *On Broadway Vol. 3* (JMT 1992), *And The Electric Bebop Band* (JMT 1992), with Keith Jarrett, Gary Peacock *At The Deer Head Inn* (ECM 1994), *Trioism* (JMT 1994).

Mötley Crüe

This heavy rock band were formed in 1980 by Nikki Sixx (b. Frank Faranno, 11 December 1958, California, USA; bass) and consisted of former members of several other Los Angeles-based groups. Tommy Lee (b. 3 October 1962, Athens, Greece; drums) was recruited from Suite 19; Vince Neil (b. Vince Neil Wharton, 8 February 1961, Hollywood, California, USA; vocals) from Rocky Candy; while Nikki himself had recently left **London**. Mick Mars (b. Bob Deal, 3 April 1956, USA; guitar) was added to the line-up after Sixx and Lee answered an advertisement announcing 'Loud, rude, aggressive guitarist available'. Their first single, 'Stick To Your Guns'/'Toast Of The Town', was issued in 1981 on their own Leathür label, followed by their self-produced debut, *Too Fast For Love*. The band signed to **Elektra** in 1982, and the album was remixed and reissued that August. The following year they recorded a new set, *Shout At The Devil*, with producer Tom Werman. He stayed at the helm for the two albums which broke them to a much wider audience in the USA, *Theatre Of Pain* (which sold more than two million copies) and *Girls, Girls, Girls*, which achieved the highest entry for a heavy metal album on ***Billboard***'s album chart since *The Song Remains The Same* by **Led Zeppelin** in 1976. These albums refined the raw sound of earlier releases, without hiding the influence which **Kiss** and **Aerosmith** have exerted on their work. This change in style, which saw Mötley Crüe experimenting with organs, pianos and harmonicas in addition to their traditional instruments, has been described as a move from 'club-level metal glam' to 'stadium-size rock 'n' roll'. The band have not been without their setbacks: in 1984, Vince Neil was involved in a major car crash in which **Hanoi Rocks** drummer Razzle was killed. The subsequent *Theatre Of Pain* was dedicated to his memory, and this grim incident helped inform the mood of the recording. Three years later, Nikki Sixx came close to death after a heroin overdose following touring with **Guns N'Roses**. Feuding with that same band, particularly that between Neil and Axl Rose, later provided the group with many of their column inches in an increasingly disinterested press. The band survived to appear at the Moscow Peace Festival in 1989 before more than 200,000 people, and then in 1991 to issue *Dr. Feelgood*, which gave them their first US number 1 chart placing. Vince Neil would be ejected from the band's line-up, unexpectedly, in 1992, starting the **Vince Neil Band** shortly thereafter. His replacement for 1994's eponymous album would be John Corabi

(ex-**Scream**), though the band's problems would continue with a record label/management split and disastrous North American tour.
Albums: *Too Fast For Love* (Leathur 1981), *Shout At The Devil* (Elektra 1983), *Theatre Of Pain* (Elektra 1985), *Girls, Girls, Girls* (Elektra 1987), *Dr. Feelgood* (Elektra 1989), *Mötley Crüe* (Elektra 1994). Compilations: *Raw Tracks* (Elektra 1988), *Decade Of Decadence* (Elektra 1991).
Videos: *Uncensored* (1987), *Dr. Feelgood, The Videos* (1989), *Decade Of Decadence* (1991).
Further reading: *Lüde, Crüde And Rüde*, Sylvie Simmons and Malcolm Dome (1994).

Motley, Frank

b. 30 December 1923, Cheraw, South Carolina, USA. Motley learned the rudiments of trumpet playing from **Dizzy Gillespie** and soon developed a novelty technique of playing two trumpets simultaneously, thereafter being known by the nicknames of 'Dual Trumpet' and 'Two Horn' Motley. After navy service, Frank studied music at Chicago and Washington D.C. and formed his own band in 1949. The Motley Crewe, included drummer **T.N.T. Tribble** and recorded for Lilian Claiborne who placed masters with Gotham, **RCA** Victor, **Specialty**, Gem, DC, Big Town, Hollywood and many other small labels. In the mid-50s, with the advent of rock 'n' roll, Motley married and moved north to Toronto, Canada, where he continued to play and perform until 1984 when he retired to Durham, North Carolina.
Albums: *Frank Motley* (1986), with T.N.T. Tribble *The Best Of Washington D.C. R&B* (1991).

Motorcycle Boy

This UK 'indie' pop group were formed in 1987 by former **Shop Assistants** singer Alex Taylor (vocals) with ex-Meat Whiplash personnel Michael Kerr (guitar), Paul McDermott (drums), Eddie Connelly (bass) and outsider, 'Scottie' (b. David Scott; guitar). Their debut single for **Rough Trade Records**, 'Big Rock Candy Mountain' (formerly a title for **Burl Ives**), reached number 3 in the UK independent chart. Despite this promising start, and much music press attention, they failed, largely from disorganisation, to set the live circuit alight and subsequently broke up soon after the release of their lone album which was recorded for major label **Chrysalis Records**. Alex Taylor was reportedly last spotted working as a shop assistant for a record store chain.
Album: *Scarlet* (Chrysalis 1989).

Motörhead

In 1975 Lemmy (b. Ian Fraiser Kilmister, 24 December 1945, Stoke, England; vocals/bass) was sacked from **Hawkwind** after being detained for five days at Canadian customs on possession charges. The last song he wrote for them was entitled 'Motörhead', and, after ditching an earlier suggestion, Bastard, this became the name of the band he formed with Larry Wallis of the **Pink Fairies** on guitar and Lucas Fox on drums. Together they made their debut supporting **Greenslade** at the Roundhouse, London, in July. Fox then left to join Warsaw Pakt, and was replaced by 'Philthy' Phil Taylor (b. 21 September 1954, Chesterfield, England; drums), a casual friend of Lemmy's with no previous professional musical experience. Motörhead was a four-piece band for less than a month, with Taylor's friend **'Fast' Eddie Clarke** (b. 5 October 1950, Isleworth, Middlesex, England) of Continuous Performance as second guitarist, until Wallis returned to the Pink Fairies. The Lemmy/Taylor/Clarke combination would last six years until 1982, in which time they became the most famous trio in hard rock. With a following made up initially of hell's angels (Lemmy had formerly lived with their president, Tramp, for whom he would write the biker epic 'Iron Horse'), the band made their debut with the eponymous 'Motörhead'/'City Kids'. A similarly-titled debut album charted, before the group moved over to Bronze Records. *Overkill* and *Bomber* firmly established the group's *modus operandi*, a fearsome barrage of instruments topped off by Lemmy's hoarse invocations. They toured the world regularly and enjoyed hit singles with 'Ace Of Spades' (one of the most definitive heavy metal performances ever, it graced a 1980 album of the same name which saw the band at the peak of their popularity) and 'Please Don't Touch' (as **Headgirl**). Their reputation as the best live band of their generation was further enhanced by the release of *No Sleep 'Til Hammersmith*, which entered the UK charts at number 1. In May 1982 Clarke left, citing musical differences, and was replaced by Brian Robertson (b. 12 September 1956, Glasgow, Scotland), who had previously played with **Thin Lizzy** and **Wild Horses**. This combination released *Another Perfect Day*, but this proved to be easily the least popular of all Motörhead line-ups. Robertson was replaced in November 1983 by Wurzel (b. Michael Burston, 23 October 1949, Cheltenham, England; guitar) - so-called on account of his scarecrow-like hair - and Philip Campbell (b. 7 May 1961, Pontypridd, Wales; guitar; ex-**Persian Risk**), thereby swelling the Motörhead ranks to four. Two months later and, after a final appearance on television's *The Young Ones*, Taylor left to join Robertson in Operator, and was replaced by ex-**Saxon** drummer Pete Gill. Gill remained with the band until 1987 and played on several fine albums including *Orgasmatron*, the title-track of which saw Lemmy's lyric-writing surpass itself. By 1987 Phil Taylor had rejoined Motörhead, and the line-up remained unchanged for five years during which time Lemmy made his acting debut in the *Comic Strip* film, *Eat The Rich*, followed by other celluloid appearances including the role of taxi driver in *Hardware*. In 1992 the group released *March Or Die*, which featured the American Mikkey Dee (ex-**King Diamond**) on drums and guest appearances by **Ozzy Osbourne** and Slash (**Guns N'Roses**). The title-track followed on from '1916' and revealed a highly sensitive side to Lemmy's lyrical and vocal scope, both songs dealing with the horrors of war. The idiosyncratic Lemmy singing style, usually half-growl, half-shout, and with his neck craned up at 45 degrees to the microphone, remained as ever. On a more traditional footing they performed the theme song to the horror film *Hellraiser 3*, and convinced the film's creator, Clive Barker, to record his first promotional video with the band. Lemmy also hammed his way through insurance adverts, taking great delight in his press image of the unreconstructed rocker.

Albums: *Motörhead* (Chiswick 1977), *Overkill* (Bronze 1979), *Bomber* (Bronze 1979), *On Parole* (United Artists 1979), *Ace Of Spades* (Bronze 1980), *No Sleep Till Hammersmith* (Bronze 1981), *Iron Fist* (Bronze 1982), *Another Perfect Day* (Bronze 1983), *What's Wordsworth* (Big Beat 1983), *Orgasmatron* (GWR 1986), *Rock'N'Roll* (GWR 1987), *Eat The Rich* (GWR 1987), *No Sleep At All* (GWR 1988), *1916* (Epic 1991), *March Or Die* (Epic 1992), *Bastards* (ZYX 1993). Compilations: *No Remorse* (Bronze 1984), *Anthology* (Raw Power 1986), *Dirty Love* (Receiver 1989), *From The Vaults* (Sequel 1990), *Best Of* (Action Replay 1990), *Collection* (Castle 1990), *Meltdown* (Castle 1991, 3-CD box set), *All The Aces* (Castle 1993).

Videos: *Deaf Not Blind* (1984), *Birthday Party* (1986), *Eat The Rich* (1988, film), *Toronto Live* (1989), *Best Of* (1991), *Everything Louder Than Everything Else* (1991).

Further reading: *Motörhead*, Alan Burridge. *Born To Lose*, Alan Burridge. *Motorhead*, Giovanni Dadomo.

Motors

The Motors were based around the partnership of Nick Garvey (b. 26 April 1951, Stoke-on-Trent, Staffordshire, England) and Andy McMaster (b. 27 July 1947, Glasgow, Scotland) who first met in the pub rock band **Ducks Deluxe**. McMaster had a long career in pop music, having played in several bands in the 60s including the Sabres, which also featured **Frankie Miller**. McMaster released a solo single, 'Can't Get Drunk Without You', on President, and joined Ducks Deluxe in November 1974. Garvey was educated at Kings College in Cambridge and was an accomplished pianist, oboeist and trumpeter. Before he joined Ducks Deluxe in December 1972 he had acted as a road manager for the **Flamin' Groovies**. The pair left the Ducks early in 1975, just a few months before the unit disbanded. Garvey joined a group called the Snakes (along with future **Wire** vocalist Rob Gotobed) and they released one single. McMaster, meanwhile, went to work for a music publisher. Garvey's friend and manager Richard Ogden suggested that Garvey form his own band in order to record the songs he had written. This led to him contacting McMaster and in January 1977 they recorded demos together. The following month they recruited Ricky Wernham (aka Ricky Slaughter) from the Snakes on drums - he is the cousin of Knox from the **Vibrators**. Guitarist Rob Hendry was quickly replaced by **Bram Tchaikovsky** and the Motors were up and running. They made their live debut at the Marquee Club, London in March 1977 and signed to **Virgin** in May.

A tour with the **Kursaal Flyers** and the **Heavy Metal Kids** led to the release of their debut single, 'Dancing The Night Away', and first album, produced by Mutt Lange. However, it was their second single, 'Airport', which became a huge hit in the UK. It is widely used to this day as a stock soundtrack when television programmes show film clips of aeroplanes taking off or landing. Despite this success, the group were already burning out. After performing at Reading in August the Motors decided to concentrate on writing new material. Wernham took the opportunity to leave, while Tchaikovsky formed his own band with the intention of returning to the Motors, though he never did. Garvey and McMaster eventually re-emerged with some new material for *Tenement Steps*. It was recorded with the assistance of former **Man** bassist Martin Ace, and drummer Terry Williams (ex-**Man** and Rockpile, future **Dire Straits**). After *Tenement Steps* the Motors seized up, but both Garvey and McMaster have since released solo singles.

Albums: *The Motors I* (1977), *Approved By The Motors* (1978), *Tenement Steps* (1980). Compilation: *Greatest Hits* (1981).

Motown Records

The history of Motown Records remains a paradigm of success for independent record labels, and for black-owned industry in the USA. The corporation was formed in 1959 by **Berry Gordy**, a successful R&B songwriter who required an outlet for his initial forays into production. He used an $800 loan to finance the release of singles by **Marv Johnson** and **Eddie Holland** on his Tamla label, one of a series of individual trademarks which he eventually included beneath the Motown umbrella. Enjoying limited local success, Gordy widened his roster, signing acts like the **Temptations** and **Marvelettes** in 1960. That year, the **Miracles**' 'Shop Around' gave the company its first major US. hit, followed in 1961 by their first number 1, the Marvelettes' 'Please Mr Postman'. Gordy coined the phrase 'The Sound Of Young America' to describe Motown's output, and the apparent arrogance of his claim quickly proved well-founded. By 1964, Motown were scoring regular hits via the **Supremes** and the **Four Tops**, while **Mary Wells**' 'My Guy' helped the label become established outside the USA. The label's vibrant brand of soul music, marked by a pounding rhythm and a lightness of touch which appealed to both pop and R&B fans, provided America's strongest response to the massive impact of the British beat group invasion in 1964 and 1965. At the same time, Gordy realized the importance of widening his commercial bases; in 1965, he overtly wooed the middle-of-the-road audience by giving the Supremes a residency at the plush Copa nightclub in New York - the first of many such ventures into traditional showbiz territory. The distance between Motown's original fans and their new surroundings led to accusations that the company had betrayed its black heritage, though consistent chart success helped cushion the blow.

In 1966, Motown took three steps to widen its empire, snapping up groups like the **Isley Brothers** and **Gladys Knight And The Pips** from rival labels, opening a Hollywood office to double its promotional capabilities, and snuffing out its strongest opposition in Detroit by buying the Golden World and Ric-Tic group of R&B companies. Throughout these years, Gordy maintained a vice-like grip over Motown's affairs; even the most successful staff writers and producers had to submit their work to a weekly quality control meeting, and faced the threat of having their latest creations summarily rejected. Gradually dissent rose within the ranks, and in 1967 Gordy lost the services of his A&R controller, **Mickey Stevenson**, and his premier writing/production team, **Holland/Dozier/Holland**. Two years of comparative failure followed before Motown regained its supremacy in the pop market by launching the career of the phenomenally successful **Jackson Five** in 1969. Gordy made a bold but ultimately unsuccessful attempt to break into the rock market in 1970, with his Rare Earth label, one of a variety of spin-off companies launched in the early part of the decade. This was a period of some uncertainty for the company: several major acts either split up or chose to seek artistic freedom elsewhere, and the decision to concentrate the company's activities in its California office in 1973 represented a dramatic break from its roots. At the same time, Gordy masterminded the birth of Motown's film division, with the award-winning biopic about **Billie Holiday**, *Lady Sings The Blues*. The burgeoning artistic and commercial success of **Stevie Wonder** kept the record division on course, though outsiders noted a distinct lack of young talent to replace the company's original stalwarts.

The mid-70s proved to be Motown's least successful period for over a decade; only the emergence of the **Commodores** maintained the label as a contemporary musical force. Motown increasingly relied on the strength of its back catalogue, with only occasional releases, like the Commodores' 'Three Times A Lady' and Smokey Robinson's 'Being With You', rivalling the triumphs of old. The departure of **Marvin Gaye** and **Diana Ross** in the early 80s proved a massive psychological blow, as despite the prominence of Commodores leader **Lionel Richie**, the company failed to keep pace with the fast-moving developments in black music. From 1986, there were increasing rumours that Berry Gordy was ready to sell the label: these were confirmed in 1988, when Motown was bought by MCA, with Gordy retaining some measure of artistic control over subsequent releases. After more than a decade of disappointing financial returns, Motown remains a record industry legend on the strength of its remarkable hit-making capacities in the 60s.

Compilation: *Hitsville USA: The Motwon Singles Collection 1959 - 1971* (4CD set 1993).

Videos: *The Sounds Of Motown* (1985), *The Sixties* (1987), *Time Capsule Of The 70s* (1987), *Motown 25th: Yesterday, Today, Forever* (1988).

Mott

This short-lived group was founded in 1975. Morgan Fisher (keyboards), Overend Watts (bass, vocals) and Dale Griffin (drums), each formerly of **Mott The Hoople**, decided to drop the earlier suffix upon adding Nigel Benjamin (vocals) and Ray Major (guitar) to the line-up. Their albums proved sadly disappointing, invoking unfavourable comparison with their previous, highly-successful incarnation. The departure of Benjamin precipitated yet another change and, having invited ex-**Medicine Head** singer John Fiddler to join, the unit changed its name to **British Lions**.

Albums: *Drive On* (CBS 1975), *Shouting And Pointing* (CBS 1976).

Mott The Hoople

Having played in a number of different rock groups in Hereford, England, during the late 60s, the founding members of this ensemble comprised: Overend Watts (b. Peter Watts, 13 May 1947, Birmingham, England; vocals/bass), Mick Ralphs (b. 31 March 1944, Hereford, England; vocals/guitar), Verden Allen (b. 26 May 1944, Hereford, England; organ) and Dale Griffin (b. 24 October 1948, Ross-on-Wye, England; vocals/drums). After dispensing with their lead singer Stan Tippens, they were on the point of dissolving when Ralphs sent a demo tape to **Island Records** producer **Guy Stevens**. He responded enthusiastically, and after placing an advertisement in ***Melody Maker*** auditioned a promising singer named **Ian Hunter** (b. 3 June 1946, Shrewsbury, England; vocals/keyboards/guitar). In June 1969 Stevens christened the group Mott The Hoople, after the novel by Willard Manus. Their self-titled debut album revealed a very strong **Bob Dylan** influence, most notably in Hunter's nasal vocal inflexions and visual image. With his corkscrew hair and permanent shades Hunter bore a strong resemblance to vintage 1966 Dylan and retained that style for his entire career.

Their first album, with its M.C. Escher cover illustration, included pleasing interpretations of the **Kinks**' 'You Really Got Me' and **Sonny Bono**'s 'Laugh At Me', and convinced many that Mott would become a major band. Their next three albums trod water, however, and it was only their popularity and power as a live act which kept them together. Despite teaming up with backing vocalist **Steve Marriott** on the **George 'Shadow' Morton**- produced 'Midnight Lady', a breakthrough hit remained elusive. On 26 March 1972, following the departure of Allen, they quit in disillusionment. Fairy godfather **David Bowie** convinced them to carry on, offered his assistance as producer, placed them under the wing of his manager, Tony De Fries, and even presented them with a stylish UK hit, 'All The Young Dudes'. The catchy 'Honaloochie Boogie' maintained the momentum but there was still one minor setback when Ralphs quit to form **Bad Company**. With new members Morgan Fisher and Ariel Bender (Luther Grosvenor) Mott enjoyed a run of further UK hits including 'All The Way From Memphis' and 'Roll Away The Stone'. During their final phase, Bowie's sideman **Mick Ronson** joined the group in place of Grosvenor (who had departed to join **Widowmaker**). Preparations for a European tour in late 1974 were disrupted when Hunter was hospitalized suffering from physical exhaustion, culminating in the cancellation of the entire tour. When rumours circulated that Hunter had signed a deal instigating a solo career, with Ronson working alongside him, the upheaval led to an irrevocable rift within the group resulting in the stormy demise of Mott The Hoople. With the official departure of Hunter and Ronson, the remaining members, Watts, Griffin and Fisher, determined to carry on, working simply as **Mott**.

Albums: *Mott The Hoople* (Island 1969), *Mad Shadows* (Island 1970), *Wild Life* (Island 1971), *Brain Capers* (Island 1971), *All The Young Dudes* (CBS 1972), *Mott* (CBS 1973), *The Hoople* (CBS 1974), *Live* (CBS 1974). Compilations: *Rock And Roll Queen* (Island 1972), *Greatest Hits* (CBS 1975), *Shades Of Ian Hunter - The Ballad Of Ian Hunter And Mott The Hoople* (CBS 1979, double album), *Two Miles From Heaven* (Island 1981), *All The Way From Memphis* (Hallmark 1981), *Greatest Hits* (CBS 1981, different to 1975 issue).

Further reading: *The Diary Of A Rock 'N' Roll Star*, Ian Hunter.

Mould, Bob

The former guitarist, vocalist and co-composer of **Hüsker Dü**, Mould surprised many of that leading hardcore act's aficionados with his reflective solo debut, *Workbook.* Only one track, 'Whichever Way The Wind Blows', offered the maelstrom of guitars customary in the artist's work and instead the set was marked by a predominantly acoustic atmosphere. Cellist Jane Scarpantoni contributed to its air of melancholy, while two members of **Pere Ubu**, Tony Maimone (bass) and Anton Fier (drums; also **Golden Palominos**), added sympathetic support, helping to emphasize the gift for melody always apparent in Mould's work. Maimone and Fier also provided notable support on *Black Sheets Of Rain*, which marked a return to the uncompromising power of the guitarist's erstwhile unit. The set included the harrowing 'Hanging Tree' and apocalyptical 'Sacrifice Sacrifice/Let There Be Peace', but contrasted such doom-laden material with a brace of sprightly pop songs in 'It's Too Late' and 'Hear Me Calling', both of which echoed **R.E.M.**. He also formed his own record company, SOL (Singles Only Label), which has issued material by, among others, **William Burroughs**. The artist abandoned his solo career in 1993, reverting to the melodic hardcore trio format with **Sugar**.

Albums: *Workbook* (Virgin 1989), *Black Sheets Of Rain* (Virgin 1990).

Mound City Blue Blowers

Formed in 1924 by **Red McKenzie** as a novelty group, the Mound City Blue Blowers expanded to include **Eddie Lang**, with whom they visited London in the mid-20s. Later the band became a more orthodox, and often much larger, Dixieland outfit under McKenzie's leadership. In its bigger form the band was occasionally home in the late 20s to leading musicians such as **Eddie Condon**, **Gene Krupa**, **Glenn Miller** and **Jack Teagarden**. McKenzie continued to record under this collective title into the mid-30s, using artists including **Yank Lawson**, **Bob Haggart**, **Dave Tough** and **Bunny Berigan**. Although the band's first record, 'Arkansas Blues' in 1924, was its biggest seller, the finest jazz performance came at a 1929 session featuring **Coleman Hawkins**, which included 'Hello Lola' and the classic '(If I Could Be With You) One Hour (Tonight)'.

Mounka, Pamelo

b. 30 October 1945, Ouesso, Congo-Brazzaville. Vocalist Mounka is one of the most popular Congo-Brazzaville recording artists, performing in a style which to Western ears is indistinguishable from that of the country's larger neighbour, Zaire. In fact, Mounka's first break in the music business came via Zairean bandleader **Rochereau**, who recorded him in 1963. A member of the Bantous for some years, Mounka went solo in the mid-60s, releasing an unbroken string of over 70 hit singles between then and 1980, when he was taken to Paris by the Eddyson label to record, a venture that resulted in the major-selling album *L'Argent Appelle L'Argent.* In 1983 he was reunited with Rochereau on the album *20 Ans De Carriere*, celebrating his 20 years in the record business. In 1985 he recorded the superb *En Plein Maturite*, which remains his finest work to date.

Albums: *Les Grands Succes Africains Vol.12* (1977), *L'Argent Appelle L'Argent* (1981), *20 Ans De Carriere* (1983), *En Plein Maturite* (1985), *Cynthia* (1986), *Bonne Chance* (1989).

Mount Rushmore

This third generation, late 60s San Francisco rock group comprised Glen 'Smitty' Smith (vocals), Mike 'Bull' Bolan (guitar), Terry Kimball (bass) and Travis Fullerton (drums). Although they failed to garner the same commercial or artistic plaudits of many contemporaries, the group's two albums revealed a competent, if unadventurous, act. Mount Rushmore disbanded in 1969 following the release of their second album, although Fullerton later found success as a member of **Sylvester** And The Hot Band.
Albums: *High On Mount Rushmore* (1968), *Mount Rushmore 69* (1969).

Mountain

Mountain were one of the first generation heavy metal bands, formed by ex-Vagrants guitarist **Leslie West** (b. Leslie Weinstein, 22 October 1945, Queens, New York, USA) and bassist **Felix Pappalardi** (b. 1939, Bronx, New York, USA, d. 17 April 1983) in New York in 1968. Augmented by drummer Corky Laing and Steve Knight on keyboards they played the **Woodstock** festival in 1970, releasing *Mountain Climbing* shortly afterwards. Featuring dense guitar lines from West and the delicate melodies of Pappalardi, they quickly established their own sound, although **Cream** influences were detectable in places. The album was an unqualified success, peaking at number 17 in the ***Billboard*** album chart in November 1970. Their next two albums built on this foundation, as the band refined their style into an amalgam of heavy riffs, blues-based rock and extended guitar and keyboard solos. *Nantucket Sleighride* (the title-track of which was used as the theme tune to television programme *World In Action*) and *Flowers Of Evil* made the *Billboard* charts at numbers 16 and 35, respectively. A live album followed, which included interminably long solos and was poorly received. The group temporarily disbanded to follow separate projects. Pappalardi returned to producing, while West and Laing teamed up with **Cream**'s **Jack Bruce** to record as **West, Bruce And Laing**. In 1974, Mountain rose again with Alan Schwartzberg and Bob Mann replacing Laing and Knight to record *Twin Peaks*, live in Japan. This line-up was short-lived as Laing rejoined for the recording of the disappointing studio album, *Avalanche*. The band collapsed once more and West concentrated on his solo career again. Pappalardi was shot and killed by his wife in 1983. Two years later, West and Laing resurrected the band with Mark Clarke (former **Rainbow** and **Uriah Heep** bassist) and released *Go For Your Life*. They toured with **Deep Purple** throughout Europe in 1985, but split up again soon afterwards.

Albums: *Mountain Climbing* (Bell 1970), *Nantucket Sleighride* (Island 1971), *Flowers Of Evil* (Island 1971), *The Road Goes On Forever-Mountain Live* (Island 1972), *Avalanche* (Epic 1974), *Twin Peaks* (CBS 1974), *Go For Your Life* (Scotti Bros 1985). Compilations: *The Best Of* (Island 1973), *Over The Top* (Legacy 1995).

Mountain Ash Band

The Mountain Ash Band produced yet another of those 'old friends get it together' albums, forming a UK folk/rock band from Colin Cripps' musical about an old tramp, *Job Senior*. They made the album, did the show, and then vanished. The music was very gritty, and at times reminiscent of **Bob Pegg**.
Album: *The Hermit* (1975).

Mourneblade

London band whose main claim to fame was that one member was a British skateboard champion. Formed in late 1984 the group comprised Derek Jasnock (keyboards), Richard Jones (guitar), Dunken Mullet (vocals), Jeff Ward (drums) and Clive Baxter (bass). They blended the heavier qualities of **Hawkwind** with the bass driven power of **Motörhead**. In keeping with that tradition they took their name from a novel by Michael Moorcock, and signed to the Hawkwind-allied Flicknife Records. It was their tenuous links with the latter band which first got them noticed, and their debut album contained six excellent songs, though it failed to impress the Hawkwind fraternity or rock fans in general. They vanished off the music scene for a couple of years before regrouping in 1988, gaining a session on the *Friday Rock Show* in July of the following year. This saw them unveil a new sound, which had already been sketched more fully in January, when their second album had arrived. This contained further Hawkwind-inspired tracks like the 'Hall Of The Mountain King', but also, sadly, grim tales like 'Lolita' and 'Blonde Beautiful And Dead'. A few gigs and poor record sales later they returned to obscurity.
Albums: *Times Running Out* (Flicknife 1985), *Live Fast, Die Young* (Plastic Head 1989).

Mouse And The Traps

This US group was formed in Tyler, Texas, USA in 1965 by guitarist/vocalist Ronnie 'Mouse' Weiss. Jerry Howell (keyboards) and Dave Stanley (bass), ex-colleagues from Jerry Vee And The Catalinas, joined him in this new venture which was completed by Bugs Henderson (lead guitar) and Ken Murray (drums). The quintet made its debut in February 1966 with 'A Public Execution' on which Weiss's **Bob Dylan** inflections topped a punk-style backing. 'Maid Of Sugar, Maid Of Spice' followed in a similar manner, while other notable singles included 'Lie, Beg, Borrow And Steal' (1967) and 'I Satisfy' (1968). By this point Doug Rhone had replaced Henderson. The Traps also recorded as

Positively Thirteen O'Clock (with singer Jimmy Rabbit), and backed **Dale Hawkins** on *L.A., Memphis And Tyler*. The singer reciprocated by producing the group's final singles, 'Wicker Vine' and 'Knock On My Door' (both 1969). Barring a brief 1972 reunion, these releases brought Mouse And The Traps to a close, although Weiss, Stanley and Murray remained together in a country-rock act, Rio Grande.

Mouskouri, Nana

b. 13 October 1934, Athens, Greece. This bespectacled vocalist was steeped in the classics and jazz but was sufficiently broadminded to embrace a native style of pop after a stint on Radio Athens in 1958 and an artistic (and marital) liaison with orchestra leader Manos Hadjidakis facilitated a debut single, 'Les Enfants Du Piree', which was aimed at foreign consumers. Well-received performances at several international song festivals were added incentives for her team to relocate to Germany, where 'Weiss Rosen Aus Athen' (derived from a Greek folk tune), a number from Wadjidakis' soundtrack to the 1961 film *Traumland Der Sehnsucht*, sold a million copies. Now one of her country's foremost musical ambassadors, Mouskouri undertook a US college tour which was followed by further record success, particularly in France with such songs as 'L'Enfant Au Tambour', 'Parapluies De Cherbourg' (a duet with **Michel Legrand**) and a 1967 arrangement of the evergreen 'Guantanamera'. From the late 60s in Britain, she scored almost exclusively with albums with *Over And Over* lingering longest on the lists. Sales were boosted by regular BBC television series on which her backing combo, the Athenians, were granted instrumental spots. A collection of Mouskouri favourites from a BBC season in the early 70s spent many weeks in the Top 30 but, other than a postscript Top 10 single ('Only Love') in 1986, her UK chart career climaxed with 1976's *Passport*. By then, however, she had mounted a plateau of showbusiness high enough to survive comfortably without more hits.

Selected albums: *Over And Over* (1969), *The Exquisite Nana Mouskouri* (1970), *Recital '70* (1970), *Turn On The Sun* (1971), *British Concert* (1972), *Songs From Her TV Series* (1973), *Spotlight On Nana Mouskouri* (1974), *Songs Of The British Isles* (1976), *Passport* (1976), *Roses And Sunshine* (1979), *Come With Me* (1981), *Ballades* (1983), *Nana* i (1984), *Farben* (1984), *Athens* (1984), *Nana Mouskouri* (1984), *Why Worry?* (1986), *Alone* (1986), *Live At The Herodes Hatticus Theatre* (1986), *Nana* ii (1987), *Love Me Tender* (1987), *Je Chante Avec Toi Liberte* (1988), *The Magic Of Nana Mouskouri* (1988), *The Classical Nana* (1990), *Gospel* (1990), *Oh Happy Day* (1990).

Moustaki, Georges

b. 1934, Alexandria, Egypt. A singer, songwriter, actor and film music composer of Greek ancestry, early in his life Moustaki studied French which enabled him to work in Paris as a journalist. He began to write songs, and played the piano and guitar in the College Inn in Montparnasse. He also met the gypsy musician Henri Crolla, a cousin of **Django Reinhardt**. Crolla introduced him to the legendary performer, **Edith Piaf,** and in 1958, he became her guitarist and lover. With Marguerite Monnet, who was involved with many of Piaf's songs, he wrote 'Milord', which became Piaf's last big hit before she died three years later. Her record spent 15 weeks in the UK chart in 1960, easily beating a version by **Frankie Vaughan**, which had an English lyric by **Decca** recording manager Bunny Lewis. Moustaki was driving the car late in 1959 when Piaf had her third serious car accident. He escaped unscathed, and accompanied the singer on her ninth tour of the USA, where their relationship was terminated following her collapse onstage at the Waldorf Astoria, and subsequent four-hour operation. In the 60s, long haired, with a grey beard, Moustaki toured the music festivals, writing and performing his own songs. These included the dramatic 'Le Gitan Et La Fille', 'Un Etranger', 'Les Orgues De Barbarie', 'Les Gestes', which was memorably sung by Serge Reggiani and 'Le Meteque' (the outcast), perhaps the song most identified with Moustaki, which ran: 'Look at me, a bloody foreigner/A wandering Jew, a Greek peasant/Hair all over the place, eyes washed out . . .' In the 70s Moustaki worked with Jacques Potrenaud on the film of Albert Cosseri's book, *Mendiants Et Orgueilleux*, and played the central character, Hadjis. He also composed the music for movies such as *The Man With Connections*, *Solo*, *The Five Leaf Clover* and *At The Brink Of The Bench*. Although little known outside the French-speaking world, in the early 90s Moustaki still had several albums in the UK catalogue.

Selected albums: *Troubador* (Polydor 1978), *Le Meteque* (Polydor 1984), *Georges Moustaki* (Polydor 1985)

Mouth And McNeal

Although former construction worker Willem Duyn ('Mouth') was a rock 'n' roll exponent, he teamed up with classically-trained vocalist Sjoukje Van't Spiijker ('McNeal') in 1971 after she heard a tape he made at Amsterdam's Phonogram studio. Recording a debut single, 'Hey Love You', in English, the pair anticipated the US million-seller, 1972's 'How Do You Do' (composed by Hans Van Hemert and Hans Van Hoff), when it was issued in North America, following chart triumphs in Austria and the Netherlands. As this overseas breakthrough could not be sustained, the duo concentrated on the European market, touring constantly both before and after their second - and last - international smash with 'I See A Star', a UK Top 10 entry and Holland's entry in 1974's Eurovision Song Contest.

Mouth Music

Formed by Martin Swan, a Sheffield born Scot, and an American, Talitha MacKenzie, Mouth Music made an impressive debut in 1990 with a fusion of Gaelic vocals, African percussion and synthesisers. An EP, *Blue Door, Green Sea*, released in 1992, confirmed their direction, and a constant stream of influences made their live shows exciting as well as experimental. One of the EP's tracks, a dance mix of their earlier, 'Sienn O', revealed a further advance. On *Mo-di* (1993), there were more apparent moves into the dance area, and it seems that the band's apparent folk origin is now only one aspect of its work, which includes samba and hip-hop. When Talitha MacKenzie departed, she was replaced by vocalist, Jackie Joyce. The group's live performances are usually augmented by a seven piece band.
Albums: *Mouth Music* (1990), *Mo-Di* (1993), *Shorelife* (Triple Earth 1994).

Mouzon, Alphonze

b. 21 November 1948, Charleston, South Carolina, USA. Mouzon started playing when he was four years old and was taught drums at high school. He relocated to New York when he was 17 and in 1969 played in the Broadway musical ***Promises, Promises***. He released his first record in the same year, with **Gil Evans**. He freelanced for a time before playing with **Weather Report** in 1971, **McCoy Tyner** (1972-73), **Larry Coryell**'s Eleventh House (1973-75) and in a trio with **Albert Mangelsdorff** and **Jaco Pastorius**. After that Mouzon again freelanced until he joined **Herbie Hancock** in the late 70s. Mouzon tries to bring 'jazz polyrhythms to a rock pulse' and in this he succeeds, with his furiously propulsive drumming which is as welcome in a rock setting as in straight jazz.
Albums: *Gil Evans* (1969), *Weather Report* (1971), with McCoy Tyner *Sahara* (1972), with Larry Coryell *Introducing The Eleventh House* (1973), *Funky Snakefoot* (1973), *Mind Transplant* (RPM 1975), with Albert Mangelsdorff, Jaco Pastorius *Trilogue-Live* (1976), with Herbie Hancock *Mr. Hands* (1980), *In Search Of A Dream* (MPS 1981), *Back To Jazz* (L&R 1986). Compilation: *Best Of Alphonse Mouzon* (Black Sun 1989).

Move

Formed in late 1965 from the ashes of several Birmingham groups, the original Move comprised **Roy Wood** (vocals/guitar), Carl Wayne (vocals), Chris 'Ace' Kefford (bass), Trevor Burton (guitar) and Bev Bevan (drums). Under the guidance of **Tony Secunda**, they moved to London, signed to **Decca**'s hit subsidiary **Deram**, and rapidly established themselves as one of the most inventive and accomplished pop groups on the live circuit. Their first two hit singles, the classically-inspired 'Night Of Fear' and upbeat psychedelic 'I Can Hear The Grass Grow' sounded fresh and abrasive and benefitted from a series of publicity stunts masterminded by Secunda. Like the **Who,** the Move specialized in 'auto-destruction', smashing television sets and cars onstage and burning effigies of Adolf Hitler, Ian Smith and Dr Veerwoord. In 1967, they signed to the reactivated Regal Zonophone label which was launched with the fashionably titled 'Flowers In The Rain', the first record played on BBC Radio 1. The mischievous Secunda attempted to promote the disc with a saucy postcard depicting Harold Wilson. The Prime Minister promptly sued for libel, thereby diverting Roy Wood's royalties to charity.
In February 1968, the group returned as strong as ever with the high energy, 50's inspired, 'Fire Brigade'. Soon afterwards, Ace Kefford suffered a nervous breakdown and left the group which continued as a quartet, with Burton switching to bass. The catchy but chaotic 'Wild Tiger Woman' fared less well than expected, as did their bizarrely eclectic EP *Something Else*. Management switches from Tony Secunda to **Don Arden** and **Peter Walsh** brought further complications, but the maestro Wood responded well with the evocative 'Blackberry Way', a number 1 in some UK charts. A softening of their once violent image with 'Curly' coincided with Burton's departure and saw Carl Wayne recklessly steering them on to the cabaret circuit. Increasing friction within their ranks culminated in Wayne's departure for a solo career, leaving the Move to carry on as a trio. The heavy rock sound of 'Brontosaurus' and 'When Alice Comes Down To The Farm' supplemented their diverse hit repertoire, and further changes were ahead. The recruitment of Jeff Lynne from the **Idle Race** encouraged them to experiment with cellos and oboes while simultaneously pursuing their career as an increasingly straightforward pop act. The final flurry of Move hits ('Tonight', 'Chinatown' and 'California Man') were bereft of the old invention, which was henceforth to be discovered in their grand offshoots, the **Electric Light Orchestra** (ELO) and **Wizzard**.
Albums: *The Move* (1968), *Shazam* (1970), *Looking On* (1970), *Message From The Country* (1971). Compilation: *The Early Years* (1992).

Movement Ex

A Los Angeles, California-based duo combining Lord Mustafa Hasan Ma'd and DJ King Born Khaaliq, whose Afrocentric/Muslim opinions (they support the Five Percent Nation Islamic creed) are frankly and sharply put. The production of their debut, recorded when they were still teenagers, was dense and tightly-wrought, engaging the listener with its austere atmosphere. Subjects included drugs, gun-running, ecology, history and sexually transmitted diseases.
Album: *Movement Ex* (CBS 1990).

Movin' Melodies

Label founded in March 1993 by DJ's Rob Boskamp and Patrick Prins. Boskamp had started as a mobile DJ at the age of 14 in his native Amsterdam, joining DMC Holland in 1986. He worked with Go! Bang and **ESP** before releasing his own material on MTMT Records. Boskamp's other labels include Urban Sound Of Amsterdam, Gyrate, Weekend, Dutch Volume, Looneyville, Ces, Dutch Club Culture, Mulatto, Fast Food and Red Skins. Prins started DJing in Vegas, learning drums and keyboards before taking a course in production/engineering, building up his own studio. The two partners were introduced in January 1993 by a Dutch dance magazine. The Movin' Melodies name was first invoked for an EP on Urban Sound Of Amsterdam in March 1993. The label was inaugurated properly by July's *French Connection* EP, then 'Bailando Guitarra' a month later. 1994 brought Peppermint Lounge ('Lemon Project') and Artemsia ('Bits & Pieces').

Moving Hearts

This Irish group was formed in 1981, by former **Planxty** members **Christy Moore** and Donal Lunny and was notable for its innovative use in Irish folk of traditional music of an eclectic array of instruments, which at times included saxophones, pipes, bouzoukis and synthesizers. All the original members had a history in Irish folk scene. The original line-up with Moore and Lunny comprised: Eoghan O'Neill (bass/vocals), **Davy Spillane** (uileann pipes/whistles), Brian Calnan (percussion/drums) and Keith Donald (saxophone). This exciting blend of folk music, jazz and electric rock challenged the popular pre-conceptions of Irish - indeed, British - folk music, although the group never gained the recognition it fully deserved. The song subject matter ranged from the traditional to the more contemporary, chronicling the internment of terrorist suspects ('On The Blanket') and nuclear weapons ('Hiroshima'). Moore ultimately found the group format uncomfortable and returned to solo work in 1982. He was replaced by Mick Hanly, who in turn was supplanted by Florence McSweeney in 1984. The costs of running such a large line-up led to the eventually demise of the group in 1985, although they have since reformed for special concerts as in 1986's Self-Aid benefit.

Albums: *Moving Hearts* (1981), *Dark End Of The Street* (1982), *Live Hearts* (1983), *The Storm* (1985).

Moving Pictures

Formed in Sydney, Australia in 1980, Moving Pictures had a monster single, 'What About Me?', in early 1982 which went to number 1 in Australia and made the US Top 30. The band Comprised Alex Smith (vocals), Ian Lees (bass), Garry Frost (guitar/vocals), Charlie Cole (keyboards/trumpet/vocals), Andrew Thompson (saxophone) and Mark Meyer (drums), Moving Pictures' debut album featured strong ballads, but its rock-orientated live act was successfully captured on their second album which was a minor success. The band continued for several more years releasing a series of unsuccessful singles and another album before disbanding. The group would probably have achieved more success in the USA had its label **Elektra** not struck difficulties just as the band first charted. Guitarist Gary Frost later formed 1927 which also had an excellent response from Australian radio and the public.

Albums: *Days Of Innocence* (1981), *Matinee* (1983), *Last Picture Show* (1987).

Moving Shadow Records

Rob Playford's hardcore label, founded in 1990 ('Hardcore is totally different from the rest of the music industry, cos its not showbiz. There's no band loyalty and nothing to read about in teeny mags'). Playford comes from a hip hop DJ background, and records on the label with various guest personnel as 2 Bad Mice (including 'Waremouse' and 'Bombscare', both of which featured the label's distinctive, heavy snare sound which was widely imitated/sampled subsequently). The label found its stride in 1992 with major releases from 2 Bad Mice ('Hold It Down'), Cosmo & Dibs ('Sonic Rush' - Playford and 'Little' Stevie 'T' Thrower's follow-up to 'Oh So Nice' and 'Star Eyes') and Blame ('Music Takes You'), which went to the top of the dance lists. By 1993 the roster included 'intelligent techno/ambient tunes like Omni Trio's 'Mystic Stepper' and 'Renegade Snares', Four Play's 'Open Your Mind' and Hyper-On-Experience's 'Lords Of The Null Lines'. The label also started the *Two On One* series of EPs, where two artists were encouraged to experiment on either side of one record. The label's biggest record in the first half of 1994 would be Deep Blue's 'The Helicopter Tune'. Playford also promotes parties and raves (Voodoo Magic etc), runs a record shop (Section 5) and the compilation label Reanimate.

Selected album: Various *Renegade Selector Issue 1* (Reanimate/Moving Shadow 1994).

Moving Sidewalks

Formed in Houston, Texas, USA, the Moving Sidewalks comprised of Billy Gibbons (lead guitar/vocals), Tom Moore (keyboards), Don Summers (bass) and Dan Mitchell (bass). They made their debut in 1967 with the powerful '99th Floor', which adeptly crossed a garage-band sound with emergent acid-rock. Further singles included a radical reappraisal of the **Beatles**' 'I Want To Hold Your Hand', while the superior *Flash* blended neo-psychedelic styles ('Flashback') with experimental material ('Eclipse' and

'Reclipse'), in which Gibbons' **Jimi Hendrix**-influenced guitar work was particularly memorable. The Moving Sidewalks began to disintegrate in 1970 when first Tom Moore, then Don Summers, were drafted into the armed forces. Lanier Greig (keyboards) joined Gibbons and Mitchell for the unit's final gigs, before the revamped trio took a new name, **Z.Z. Top**.
Album: *Flash* (1968).

Mowatt, Judy

b. c.1952, Kingston, Jamaica, West Indies. In her teens Mowatt joined a dance troupe which toured the Caribbean. There she met up with Beryl Lawson and Merle Clemonson, with whom she formed the Gaylettes (aka the Gaytones). Together they backed many artists on releases for the Federal label in the mid-60s, until Mowatt's two accomplices left for America in 1970. Deciding to press ahead with a solo career, she recorded widely in both soul and reggae styles, under a variety of names due to contractual complications. The most notable of these releases was 'I Shall Sing', the first of a string of reggae chart successes. Subsequently Mowatt joined the Twelve Tribes Of Israel organisation, aligning herself with fellow Jamaican musicians such as **Dennis Brown** and **Freddie McGregor**. She formed her own label, Ashandan, and in the early 70s joined **Marcia Griffiths** on stage, alongside **Rita Marley**. Eventually the three way partnership was cemented as the **I-Threes**, **Bob Marley** having been suitably impressed by their performance as a trio. While working with Marley she continued her solo career, and also managed to find time to raise a family. She also had the honour of being the first to record at Bob Marley's Tuff Gong studio in Kingston, sessions which produced *Black Woman*. It was the first time that a female artist had produced her own album in Jamaica. Not only was it an outstanding work in its own right, but it offered an articulate voice for Jamaican women, who had previously been either under or mis-represented in the reggae idiom. Largely self-penned (with notable contributions from Bob Marley and Freddie McGregor) it proved a landmark work with her sweet and plaintive voice. She has continued to forge a solo career which rivals that of her old sparring partner Griffiths for the title of Jamaica's first woman of reggae. However, attempts to crossover have been less successful, notably *Love Is Overdue* which included takes on 'Try A Little Tenderness' and **UB40**'s 'Sing Our Own Song'. The album did bring her a Grammy nomination though, the first occasion on which a female reggae artist had been so honoured.
Albums: *Mellow Mood* (Ashandan 1975), *Black Woman* (Tuff Gong/Shanachie 1979), *Only A Woman* (Shanachie 1982), *Mr D.J.* (Ashandan 1982), *Working Wonders* (Shanachie 1985), *Love Is Overdue* (Greensleeves 1986).

Moxy Fruvous

A cappella Toronto, Canada band Moxy Fruvous initially made their name opening for the likes of **Bob Dylan** and **Bryan Adams**. The members had, allegedly, previously met on a school trip to a pig-calling contest. They did not win, but shared instead the prize for 'Most Promising Pig-Caller'. Hence Mike Ford (guitar/percussion), Murray Foster (bass/guitar), Jean Ghomeshi (drums) and David Matheson (guitar/bass/accordion) formed a band, taken after the pigs' names; Moxy and Fruvous. They subsequently began to write and rehearse together at high school. However, one pair broke off to write three full-length musicals, while the others started a pop/funk combo called Tall New Buildings. They quartet regrouped while attending university in 1990 and began busking on the streets of Toronto. Their eclectic tastes saw them draw on rap, soca, folk and theatrical traditions. The single unifying factor was the band's distinctive four-part vocal harmonies. The irreverent and occasionally incisive lyrics offered an additional attraction, as on the single 'Stuck In The '90s', a grim take on counter-culture and the politics of protest. The band's debut album, *Bargainville*, was released early in 1994, the songs conducted with the type of alternating restraint and fervour which recalled the passionate melodicism of the **Proclaimers**.
Album: *Bargainville* (East West 1994).

Moye, Famoudou Don

b. 23 May 1946, Rochester, New York, USA. Moye studied at Wayne State University, Detroit and with trumpeter Charles Moore participated in the Detroit Free Jazz Artists' Workshop, where he met **Joseph Jarman**. In 1968 Moye began touring Europe and Morocco with Detroit Free Jazz, playing also with **Steve Lacy** in Rome, North Africa and Paris, where he joined the **Art Ensemble Of Chicago** in 1969. Since then most of his work has been with the Ensemble, and with the group he co-leads with Jarman and with the Leaders, an all-star post-bop group. He has also worked with the Gospel Messenger Singers, Sonny Sharrock, **Dave Burrell**, **Gato Barbieri**, **Pharoah Sanders**, **Randy Weston** and Alan Shorter, and in 1989 replaced Phil Wilson in **Lester Bowie**'s Brass Fantasy.
Albums: with Joseph Jarman: *Egwu-Anwu* (1978), with Jarman, Don Pullen *The Magic Triangle* (1979), with Jarman *Black Paladins* (1980), *Earth Passage - Density* (1981), with the Leaders *Mudfoot* (1986), with the Leaders *Out Here Like This* (1988), with the Leaders *Unforseen Blessings* (1989).

Moyet, Alison

b. 18 June 1961, Basildon, Essex, England. The former singer of the synthesizer duo **Yazoo**, Moyet embarked on a solo career in 1983, after critics had consistently praised her outstanding natural blues voice. The debut *Alf* was a superb recording produced and co-written by **Tony Swain** and **Steve Jolley**. 'Invisible', 'Love Resurrection' and 'All Cried Out' were all UK hits, while the album made number 1 and took root in the charts for nearly two years. In 1985 she abandoned pop and toured with a jazz band led by John Altman, performing standards which included a version of **Billie Holiday's** 'That Ole Devil Called Love', which became her biggest hit to date. The tour was not well-received and following her performance with **Paul Young** at the **Live Aid** concert, little was seen or heard of her, apart from a major UK hit with 'Is this Love' in 1986. During this time she gave birth to a daughter and experienced the break-up of her marriage. *Raindancing* appeared in 1987 and narrowly missed the number 1 position in the UK chart. Two single successes were the driving 'Weak In The Presence Of Beauty' and a sensitive cover of **Ketty Lester**'s 'Love Letters'. Once again Alison disappeared and resurfaced in 1991. During this second hibernation she had another child and experienced a bout of lack of self-confidence. She embarked on a UK tour and released a new album. *Hoodoo* was a diverse record that broke Moyet away from the mould she was anxious to escape. It was artistically satisfying, although commercially pedestrian and effectively enabled this highly talented singer to start again. *Essex* failed to redress the balance with material that was nowhere near as strong as her outstanding voice deserves. We were reminded of the quality of her past songs on *Singles* a well-compiled retrospective that reached number 1 in the UK album chart.

Albums: *Alf* (1984), *Raindancing* (1987), *Hoodoo* (1991), *Essex* (Columbia 1994). Compilation: *Alison Moyet Singles* (Columbia 1995).

Mr Bo

b. Louis Collins, 7 April 1932, Indianola, Mississippi, USA. As a child, Collins heard no blues and was obsessed by country musicians such as **Eddy Arnold**. That interest was maintained when he moved to Chicago aged 14 and was given a guitar by his brother Mack, who also gave him his nickname. Five years later, he moved to Michigan and settled eventually in Detroit. His interest in blues began when he saw **T-Bone Walker** at the city's Graystone Ballroom. Walker remained an influence until he witnessed **B.B. King** perform in 1959. Thereafter, King became the model for both his singing and guitar playing. In the interim he had joined **Washboard Willie**'s band in 1956, where he met harmonica player **Aaron 'Little Sonny' Willis**, and two years later formed his own band with his brother on bass. His debut, 'I'm Leaving Your Town', was issued on Northern in 1959; the remaining pair of titles and alternate takes of the single were later issued on Lupine. Further singles followed during the 60s on the Big D and Diamond Jim labels; one, 'If Trouble Was Money', was later recorded by **Albert Collins**. In 1973, he released 'Plenty Fire Below' on Gold Top, a label he owned with soul singer Lee Rogers. The same year he appeared at the Ann Arbor Blues Festival and 'Don't Want No Woman' appears on the CD compilation from that event.

Albums: *Three Shades Of Blues* (Lupine 1984), *'Please Mr. Foreman': Motor City Blues* (Sequel 1995).

Mr Fingers

b. Larry Heard, USA. Mr Fingers aka Gherkin Jenks. Fingers was given his nickname by his younger brothers, alluding to his long fingers which he would employ when spinning records. Before his career in house music Heard had been a percussionist in more conventional bands (notably Infinity), until he became fascinated by electronica and its possibilities. He made his recording debut in 1985 with Fingers Inc's 'Mystery Of Love' (the original copies credited it solely to Mr Fingers) on Chicago's **DJ International**, following it a year later with 'You're Mind'/'A Path'. He also put together the It with Harry Dennis, releasing two further important singles, 'Donnie' and 'Gallimaufry Gallery', named after a Chicago club (a companion album saw further **Gil Scott-Heron** styled interludes from Dennis). It has been said by some commentators that Fingers 'invented' acid house in 1986 via 'Washing Machine', included on a three-track single headed by 'Can You Feel It?' (on **Trax**), though both **DJ Pierre** and **Marshall Jefferson** probably have prior claim on the accolade. However, there was no arguing with the strength of his mid-80s releases like 'Slam Dance', or his production of **Robert Owens**' 'Bring Down The Walls' and 'I'm Strong'. Owens, who had also sung on 'Washing Machine' and other Fingers Inc projects (together with third contributor Ron Wilson), went on to a solo career. After label problems in Chicago he set up his own Alleviated, though this too was ill-fated. 1988 brought the House Factors' 'Play It Loud', and a first album as Fingers Inc. The following year found him in the engine room of projects with **Kym Mazelle** ('Treat Me Right'), **Lil' Louis** ('Touch Me'), Blakk Society ('Just Another Lonely Day') and Trio Zero ('Twilight'). His own contribution as Mr Fingers arrived with 'What About This Love?', which placed him on the **ffrr** roster for the first time. Inbetween times he would remix/produce sundry other artists including **Adamski**, **Electribe 101** and **Massive Attack**. The second album in 1992 included singles like 'Closer' and 'On A Corner Called Jazz'.

Albums: *Amnesia* (Trax 1989, double album), *Introduction* (MCA 1992). As Fingers Inc: *Fingers Inc* (Jack Trax 1988). As The It: *On Top Of The World* (1990).

Mr Lee

b. Lee Haggard, c.1968, Chicago, Illinois, USA. Haggard's introduction to music came via his elder brother, who taught him bass, drums and keyboards in the tradition of **James Brown**, **Parliament** and **Funkadelic**. By the time he was 18 he was to be caught DJing at local clubs and recording demo tapes at home, perfecting his own sound. Confident of his newfound abilities, he approached a friend, who brought him to the attention of Mitchball Records. A few singles emerged from the deal, but failed to sell. More success was to be found with the **Trax** label, for whom he recorded the hip house cut 'Shoot Your Best Shot'. Popular in his native Chicago, it paved the way for the follow-up, 'I Can't Forget', on which he sang for the first time, to become an international hit. However, from then on he changed his vocal delivery to that of a rapper, releasing singles like 'Pump Up Chicago' and 'Pump Up England'. While promoting these in the latter territory he was the subject of intense bidding by the majors, finally signing with **Jive**. Following singles like 'Do It To Me' (which featured an all-star cast, being produced by **Mr Fingers**, part-penned by **Stevie Wonder** and featuring samples of **Quincy Jones**' 'Betcha'), his debut album would sell over one million copies worldwide, the title-track reaching number 1 on the Billboard dance chart when released as a single. By the time of his second collection he was experimenting with the New Jack Swing sound, a new way of maintaining the blend of R&B/house and rap which had served him so well perviously. His adoption of the style was made explicit on album cuts like 'New House Swing'. The first single taken from it, 'Hey Love', featured labelmate **R. Kelly**, though there was a return to hip hop roots with the samples of Chuck D (**Public Enemy**)'s 'Bring The Noise' chant on 'Time To Party'.

Albums: *Get Busy* (Jive 1990), *I Wanna Rock Right Now* (Jive 1992).

Mr. Big (70s)

With their name taken from an album track by the disbanded **Free**, Jeff Dicken (vocals), Pete Crowther (guitar), Robert Hirschman (bass) and John Burnip (drums) attempted to fill this market void by ploughing a hard rock furrow with a similar blues-derived stalk. On stage, hirsute Dicken's tight-trousered gyrations ensured a healthy cluster of fans round the central microphone as the group garnered a grassroots following on the British and European club circuit, and an **EMI** contract, in 1975. More touring ensured that their two albums sold well without actually making the charts, though the second spawned the singles 'Romeo' and 'Feel Like Calling Home' which reached the UK Top 40. By 1977, Burnip had been replaced by Vincent Chaulk and then John Marter, and Crowther was replaced by Edward Carter. Despite enriching their sound on record with keyboards, the group were categorized as another outmoded 'heavy' act as they drowned in the rip-tide of punk.

Albums: *Sweet Silence* (1975), *Mr. Big* (1977).

Mr. Big (80s)

Mr. Big (not to be confused with the 70s group of the same name) are a supergroup project, featuring bassist Billy Sheehan (ex-**David Lee Roth**), guitarist Paul Gilbert (ex-**Racer X**), drummer Pat Torpey (ex-**Impelliteri** and **Robert Plant**) and vocalist Eric Martin (ex-Eric Martin Band). Signing to **Atlantic Records**, their self-titled debut was a high-energy blast of sophisticated hard rock. *Lean Into It*, released two years later, marked a considerable progression; the band had evolved their own style and sounded more comfortable together. Drawing on influences from a wider musical spectrum, the album was well received by the critics and charted on both sides of the Atlantic. The exposition of AOR which has graced the charts remains, however, in sharp contrast to their reputation for strong live performances.

Albums: *Mr. Big* (Atlantic 1989), *Lean Into It* (Atlantic 1991), *Live* (Atlantic 1992), *Bump Ahead* (Atlantic 1993).

Mr. Bloe

'Groovin' With Mr. Bloe', an instrumental dominated by harmonica, was put together by pianist Zack Laurence and issued on **DJM Records**, a division of **Dick James** Music. It was prevented from topping the UK chart in the summer of 1970 by **Mungo Jerry**'s 'In The Summertime'. The Mr. Bloe project was abandoned after efforts including 'Anyway You Want It', 'One More Time' fell on deaf ears, despite contributions of compositions by **Elton John** and other James associates. The influence of the hit single was felt, nevertheless, in 1977 on the overall sound of 'A New Career In A New Town' on **David Bowie**'s *Low*.

Album: *Groovin' With Mr Bloe* (1973).

Mr. Bungle

Originating in Eureka, California, USA, in the mid-80s, this bizarre punk-metal-jazz-*avant garde* amalgam was Mike Patton's first band prior to joining **Faith No More**, and the success of *The Real Thing* helped Patton find a record contract for his previous project. Patton and colleagues Trey Spruance (guitar), Trevor Dunn (bass) and Danny Heifetz (drums) adopted an oddly-costumed image to match their eclectic musical style, with Patton and Spruance adopting the respective pseudonyms Vlad Dracula and Scummy, enlisting jazz-noise experimentalist **John Zorn** to produce *Mr Bungle.* The album received surprisingly positive reviews considering its extreme, genre-hopping, improvisational format and strange lyrical themes, although Zorn's

sympathetic production helped to focus the eccentricity. *Mr Bungle* sold respectably on the strength of Patton's name, but his Faith No More commitments kept live shows to a minimum. Spruance subsequently replaced Jim Martin in Faith No More for the recording of *King For A Day...Fool For a Lifetime*, although he departed shortly afterwards, while Patton hinted at the possibility of a further Mr Bungle album.
Album: *Mr Bungle* (Warners 1991).

Mr. Cinders

The distinguished English composer, **Vivian Ellis**, enjoyed his first hit with this show which opened on 11 February 1929 at the Adelphi Theatre in London. Ellis's co-composer was Richard Myers, and the book and lyrics were by Greatrex Newman and Clifford Grey, with additional lyrics by Vivian Ellis and **Leo Robin**. As the title suggests, the book is a gender-reversal of the well-worn *Cinderella* story with **Bobby Howes** as Jim Lancaster, a young man whose father has married again, thereby providing Jim with two ugly step-brothers. **Binnie Hale** is the rich girl masquerading as a parlour maid who becomes his 'fairy godmother', and sings the show's big hit song, 'Spread A Little Happiness', while 'dressed as a parlourmaid, high-kicking around the stage with a feather duster'. The rest of the songs in a delightful and engaging score included 'On the Amazon', 'I'm A One-Man Girl', 'Ev'ry Little Moment', 'I've Got You', 'I Could Be True To Two', and 'I Want The World To Know'. Basil Howes, Jack Melford, and Lorna Lubbard were also in the cast, and *Mr. Cinders* was a tremendous hit right away. After five months at the Adelphi, the show transferred to the London Pavilion in March 1929, and continued to run for a total of 529 performances. A film version with Kenneth and George Western (the Western Brothers), Clifford Mollison and Zelma O'Neal, was released in 1934. A major London revival of *Mr. Cinders* opened in the West End in 1983 and stayed for two performances short of the original. It's star, Denis Lawson, won a **Laurence Olivier Award** for best actor. Probably sparked by the 1992 Vivian Ellis biographical revue, *Spread A Little Happiness*, London audiences saw *Mr. Cinders* again during the following year, but only briefly. All the revivals 'borrowed' the occasional Vivian Ellis song from his various other shows. This was also the case when *Mr. Cinders* was produced in 1988 at the Goodspeed Opera House in Connecticut, USA. The piece was finally given its New York premiere at the Mazur Theatre in 1992. That most appealing song, 'Spread A Little Happiness', has endured, and surfaces frequently. **Sting**, the ex-lead singer with the **Police**, sang it in the 1982 film *Brimstone And Treacle*, and it became his first solo chart hit in the UK. It was also used during the 80s in a television commercial for margarine.

Mr. Fox

One of the genre's forgotten acts, Mr. Fox's pioneering influence in folk/rock was equal to that of **Steeleye Span** and **Fairport Convention**. Concerned at the lack of a band that could play atmospheric English music, Ashley Hutchings and traditionalist Bob Pegg, recruited Pegg's wife, Carole (fiddle), Alun Eden (drums), Barry Lyons (bass), Andrew Massey (cello) and John Myatt (woodwinds). They recorded a powerful, haunting album for Transatlantic, for which Pegg wrote mature, gothic songs, inspired by his Yorkshire homeland. Economically unfeasible, the band was reduced to a rock four piece unit, and released the excellent *The Gypsy*. In 1971 they toured the festival circuit, but various aspects of their perfomance at Loughborough were heavily criticized. In the following year Alan Edun and Barry Lyons left the group, to join Trees, and were replaced by Nick Strutt (guitar) and Ritchie Bull (bass). This drastic move changed the band's character, and Carol Pegg's departure reduced Mr. Fox to a trio, after which they disbanded. Carole Pegg later worked with **Graham Bond**, and issued a solo record influenced by 'magic'. Bob Pegg continued to perform with Nick Strutt, and, in the late 70s, released a series of characteristically black folk albums. He has since remarried, and moved into theatrical education, although he still has a number of unreleased concept albums.
Albums: *Mr. Fox* (1970), *The Gypsy* (1971). Compilation: *The Complete Mr. Fox* (1975). As Bob & Carole Pegg *He Came From The Mountains* (1971), as Carole Pegg *Carolanne* (1973), as Bob Pegg & Nick Strutt *Bob Pegg & Nick Strutt* (1973), *The Shipbuilder* (1974), *Ancient Maps* (1975).

Mr. Mister

Although formed in Phoenix, Arizona, soft metal artists Mr Mister were based in Los Angeles and were the brainchild of Richard Page (bass/vocals) and Steve George (b. 20 may 1955; keyboards) who had previously played together in the Pages. They were both also experienced session men, working alongside **REO Speedwagon** and **John Parr**. 'It became really frustrating. We were having the big US hits, but weren't getting any of the credit'. The band were completed when Steve Farris (guitar) and Pat Mastelotto (drums) joined in 1982. Their debut in 1984, *I Wear The Face*, provided the minor US hit 'Hunters Of The Night'. The album was released in the UK two years later. The next album broke the band by scaling the top of the charts and delivering 2 US number 1 singles in 'Broken Wings' and 'Kyrie'. Its release coincided with a marathon **Tina Turner** support tour. Both singles also made the UK Top 20. After one more album Farris left and was replaced by the well-known session guitarist Buzzy Feiten. Page has

since resisted offers to become vocalist for both **Toto** and **Chicago**.
Albums: *I Wear The Face* (1984), *Welcome To The Real World* (1985), *Go On* (1987).

Mraz, George

b. Jírí Mraz, 9 September 1944, Písek, Czechoslovakia. A gifted musician as a child, Mraz studied formally at the music conservatory in Prague. Although skilled on several instruments, he settled eventually on the bass. He worked in his homeland and in Germany, then in 1968 emigrated to the USA. He entered **Berklee College Of Music** for further studies, after which he played with **Dizzy Gillespie**, **Oscar Peterson** and other leading jazzmen. In New York in the mid-70s he became a member of the **Thad Jones-Mel Lewis** Jazz Orchestra and also recorded with **Stan Getz**, **Pepper Adams**, **Zoot Sims**, **Stéphane Grappelli** and in duos with Walter Norris and his fellow Jones-Lewis rhythm section-mate, **Roland Hanna**. Towards the end of the decade he worked with the New York Jazz Quartet and with **John Abercrombie**. By the 80s Mraz, who became an American citizen in 1973, was established as a major force among jazz bass players.
Albums: *Stéphane Grappelli Meets The Rhythm Section* (1973), with Roland Hanna *Sir Elf + 1* (1977), with Zoot Sims *Warm Tenor* (1978), with John Abercrombie *M* (1980), with Pepper Adams *Urban Dreams* (1981).

Mrs Brown You've Got A Lovely Daughter

As well as being popular in their native country, British beat group **Herman's Hermits** also enjoyed considerable success in the USA. Their impish pop singles seemed to suggest a vision of 'Swinging England', one exacerbated by smash-hit recordings of music-hall standards, ''I'm Henry XIII, I Am' and 'Leaning On The Lamp Post', neither of which were issued as singles in the UK. Another exclusive song, 'Mrs Brown You've Got A Lovely Daughter', topped the US charts in 1965, the theme of which inspired this 1968 film. The group had already completed a 'quickie' feature, ***Hold On*** in 1966, but its jejune plot and direction were at least related to the era inspiring it. *Mrs Brown You've Got A Lovely Daughter* surfaced amid rock films exposing drugs, protest, psychedelia and the counter-culture, none of which touched this misguided vehicle. Here the group acquire a greyhound and travel to London to race it in the Greyhound Derby. The presence of veterans **Stanley Holloway** and Mona Washbourne only served to enhance its anachronistic premise. If there was ever any possibility that Herman's Hermits would slip from pop to rock in the manner of the **Pretty Things** or **Spencer Davis Group**, it ended with this film.

Ms Melodie

b. Ramona Parker, Flatbush, Brooklyn, New York, USA. Gruff female rapper whose self-written rhymes and couplets were aided and abetted by the production skills of her (now ex-) husband **KRS-1**, on her debut album. The conscious lyrics were occasionally insightful, with 'Remember When' added a fitting testimony to the growth of the hip hop movement: 'The street is the root of the tree that branches out to R&B'. Melodie had formerly served time on **Boogie Down Productions**' roster of artists. She came from a musical family; her father played saxophone and clarinet, while her mother and sisters were regulars in the local church choirs. Though her first love was soul, Melodie was immediately drawn into the emerging hip hop world when it hit her native Brooklyn streets. In additon to her work with BDP, she had also made a film appearance in the blaxploitation movie parody, *I'm Gonna Git You, Sucka*, in 1987. Her abilities also extended to fashion design which incorporated her 'sophiticated B-girl' look.
Album: *Diva* (Jive 1989).

Mseleku, Bheki

b. 1955, Durban, South Africa. Proper recognition of this fine multi-instrumentalist's (pianist, composer, vocalist, saxophonist) jazz talents seemed long overdue, but since 1991 this modest and dignified performer has been very much in the limelight, touring internationally and releasing an album annually. One of a number of supremely talented improvising musicians who have left South Africa and its oppressive apartheid system to take up residence in London, Mseleku made the move relatively recently, touring out of South Africa in the late 70s, moving to Sweden in 1980 and finally settling in London in 1985. A **Ronnie Scott**'s club debut in 1987, with some of the more prominent figures from London's jazz revival, including **Courtney Pine** and **Cleveland Watkiss**, did much to bring his talents to the notice of the local scene, and helped pave the way for *Celebration* - a star-studded, major label debut featuring London-based musicians Pine, **Steve Williamson**, Eddie Parker and Jean Toussaint and a high-power American rhythm section comprising Michael Bowie and Marvin 'Smitty' Smith. A lively and enthusiastic record, it mixed gentle, township-inspired compositions with modal, post-**John Coltrane** burnouts, and was marked by a hectic touring campaign and a deserved nomination for British Mercury Music Prize for Album Of The Year. After the media furore had died down, Mseleku resumed the solo performances in which he excels, accompanying overtly spiritual and dedicatory vocal-lines with gently rocking, township-inspired piano voicings, and punctuating the whole with sparkling, **McCoy Tyner**-style runs and one handed riffs on the

tenor saxophone. *Meditations*, a live recording from the Bath International Music Festival, captured this absorbing style on two long tracks. Signing to the **Verve**/Polygram label at the end of 1993, Mseleku's *Timelessness* found him in the company of some top American heavy-weights, including **Joe Henderson**, **Pharoah Sanders**, **Abbey Lincoln** and **Elvin Jones**, and was accompanied by another media furore.
Albums: *Celebration* (World Circuit 1992), *Meditations* (1993), *Timelessness* (Verve 1994).

MSG

After stints with **UFO** and the **Scorpions**, guitarist **Michael Schenker** (b. 10 January 1955, Savstedt, Germany) decided to step out into the spotlight on his own in 1980. Enlisting the services of Gary Barden (vocals), Simon Phillips (drums), Mo Foster (bass) and **Don Airey** (keyboards), the Michael Schenker Group (later shortened to MSG) was born. Their approach, characterized by Schenker's screaming guitar work, had much in common with both his previous bands. Schenker, now in complete control, hired and fired musicians at will, so the line-up of MSG has rarely been stable. Only Barden survived to record their second album; **Cozy Powell** (drums), Chris Glen (bassist, ex-**Sensational Alex Harvey Band**) and Paul Raymond (keyboards; ex-**UFO**) were the replacements. They enjoyed great success in the Far East, where they recorded a double live set at the Budokan Hall, Tokyo. This album finally helped to establish the band in Europe. **Graham Bonnet** replaced Barden on *Assault Attack* and ex-**Rory Gallagher** drummer Ted McKenna was also recruited. Bonnet insisted on making a significant contribution to the compositions and his influence can clearly be heard on the album, which is far more blues-orientated than previous releases. Schenker fired Bonnet shortly after the album's launch and welcomed back former vocalist Gary Barden. The next two album releases were rigidly formularized. Old ideas were simply re-hashed as the band remained stuck in a creative rut. Even the contribution of Derek St. Holmes (ex-**Ted Nugent** vocalist) could not elevate the very ordinary material. Barden left to form **Statetrooper** and MSG disintegrated. Schenker moved back to Germany and teamed up with singer Robin McAuley (ex-**Grand Prix**) to form the McAuley Schenker Group, still retaining the acronym MSG. They completed the new-look band, with Steve Mann, Rocky Newton and Bobo Schopf on keyboards, bass and drums, respectively. They also concentrated on a more melodic direction, as McAuley's prolific writing skills were, for once, accepted by Schenker. With the release of *Perfect Timing* and *Save Yourself*, they began to re-establish a solid fan base once more, though 1992's confusingly titled *MSG* was universally despised.
Albums: *The Michael Schenker Group* (Chrysalis 1980), *MSG* (Chrysalis 1981), *One Night At Budokan* (Chrysalis 1982), *Assault Attack* (Chrysalis 1982), *Built To Destroy* (Chrysalis 1983), *Rock Will Never Die* (Chrysalis 1984), *Perfect Timing* (EMI 1987), *Save Yourself* (Capitol 1989), *MSG* (EMI 1992).

Mtukudzi, Oliver

b. 1952, Harare, Zimbabwe. Along with **Thomas Mapfumo**, Mtukudzi, and his band the Black Spirits, has played one of the most prominent roles in the modernization of traditional Zimbabwean music, mixing African-American soul with mbira and other traditional beats. He recorded his first single, 'Pezuna', in 1976, after which he joined the Wagon Wheels Band, and recorded his first major hit, 'Dzandimometera'. The band was steeped in Zairean rumba, then hugely popular in Zimbabwe, and in 1977 Mtukudzi, keen to reflect more of Zimbabwe's culture in his music, left to form the Black Spirits. The band released their first album, *Ndipeyiozano*, in 1978. In 1979, when the wartime curfew and travel restrictions were lifted, Mtukudzi took the Black Spirits on the road and built up substantial followings in Zambia, Botswana and Malawi. Recent albums have offered a mixture of reggae, soul and deeper Zimbabwean sounds like the mbakumba and katekwe, and have helped maintain Mtukudzi's position as one of Zimbabwe's great innovators.
Selected albums: *Hwena Handirase* (1986), *Mbakumba* (1988), *Shoko* (1992).

MTV

The first television channel entirely devoted to music was launched in the USA in 1981. MTV was also *the* major influence on the growth of music video during the 80s. Although there had been numerous US rock television shows since *American Bandstand* in the 50s, the immediate predecessor of MTV was *Popclips*, a 30-minute show combining comedy with music videos. It was produced by **Michael Nesmith**'s Pacific Arts company in 1981 for the Nickelodeon cable television channel. In that year, Nickelodeon's owners Warner-Amex Television launched MTV (Music Television) with **Buggles**' 'Video Killed The Radio Star' as its first offering. Headed by Robert Pittman, the 24-hour station hired five V-Js (video-jockeys) from radio and the theatre to announce the videos. Starting from a small audience base, the station used 'I Want My MTV' promotional spots by artists such as **Pete Townshend**, **David Bowie**, **Mick Jagger** and **Pat Benetar** to increase its reach. (In 1986, **Dire Straits** affectionately parodied the slogan in 'Money For Nothing', which duly won that year's MTV Award for best video.) Soon, MTV plays for their promotional videos were boosting record sales for bands like the **Human League** ('Don't You Want Me'), **Duran Duran** ('Hungry Like The Wolf', 'Rio') and the US success in 1983-84 of such UK artists as **Haircut 100** and **A Flock Of Seagulls** was widely attributed to MTV airplay. The impact of MTV led to the formation of specialist cable channels for black music (Black Entertainment TV) and country (the Nashville Network). But a direct competitor launched by Ted Turner failed to dislodge MTV from its pre-eminence. Meanwhile, the growth in television video programming and its influence on the charts forced record companies to produce accompanying videos for almost every new single they issued.

By 1984, MTV was making annual profits of six million dollars and it began a programme of international expansion with outlets in Japan (1984), Australia (1987) and Brazil (1990). Opened in 1987, MTV Europe had built up a reach of 30 million households in 28 countries by 1991, and operated its own programming policy, using videos by local artists as well as programmes imported from the USA. In 1991, MTV Asia was launched from Hong Kong as a satellite channel, also with a pledge to feature local acts. Expansion in the USA took the form of the creation of VH-1, devoted to album and adult-orientated rock in 1987, shortly after MTV Networks was purchased by Viacom Ltd. In 1991, plans were announced for a further splitting of MTV itself into three separate musical strands. By then, the global audience for MTV was said to be 52 million.

Video: *MTV's Greatest Hits* (1993).

Mu

A Californian band of legendary proportions, this cult quartet named themselves after the lost continent of Mu (of which the Hawaiian Islands are the remnants.) Founder member **Merrell Fankhauser** began his career in a surfing act, the Exiles, a group evolving into Merrell and the Exiles upon embracing nascent West Coast pop. By the release of 'Sorry For Crying' (1965) the line-up featured Fankhauser (vocals/guitar), Jeff Cotton (lead guitar), Larry Willey (bass) and Randy Wimer (drums). The group split the following year - Fankhauser then founded Fapardokly and **HMS Bounty** while Cotton joined **Captain Beefheart**, appearing on *Strictly Personal* and *Trout Mask Replica* under the name Antennae Jimmy Semens. The above Exiles reconvened during sessions for the latter album and, taking the name Mu, began playing live in Los Angeles. A single, 'Nobody Wants To Shine'/'Ballad Of Brother Lew' (1971), was issued on the group's own Mantra label, *Mu* (aka *Lemurian Music*) followed later the same year. A wondrous blend of oriental blues guitar, chopped rock rhythms and **Beach Boys**' harmonies, it established Mu's reputation for unique music. United Artists gave the set a belated British release in 1974, adding both sides of the preceding single in the process. In 1972 the group, bar Willey, decamped to the island of Maui. They purchased a banana and papaya plantation to finance their recordings, two singles, 'One More Day'/'You've Been Here Before' (1972) and 'On Our Way To Hana'/'Too Naked For Demetrius' (1973) were issued on the MU label. Jeff Parker (bass) and Mary Lee (violin) had joined the fold, but Mu disintegrated in 1974 when both Wimer and Cotton announced they were leaving to become Christian ministers. The latter reportedly now refuses to play guitar and has since established a dry cleaning business. Fankhauser embarked on a fascinating solo career but, mindful of Mu's heritage licensed the group's proposed second album to the Italian Appaloosa label in 1982. *The Last Album* confirmed the special nature of the band's music. A second collection, *Children Of The Rainbow* was complied from re-recovered taped thought lost upon Mu's disintegration. Quieter and more gentle in tone than its predecessors, it provided the missing link between this innovative group and Fankhauser's first solo releases.

Albums: *Mu* (1971), *The Last Album* (1982), *Children Of The Rainbow* (1985). Compilation: *End Of An Era* (1988).

Muana, Tshala

b. May 1955, Lubumbashi, Zaire. Vocalist and dancer Muana was born into a musical family and began performing in public at the age of six. Her adult career began with dancing, but she switched to singing in the early 70s. In 1980 she settled in Cote D'lvoire, and from 1981-84 toured widely throughout West and Central Africa. She recorded her first album, *Kami*, in Paris in 1984, followed a year later by *Mbanda Matiere*, recorded during a tour of the USA.

Albums: *Kami* (1984), *Mbanda Matiere* (1985), *La Grande Maitresse Du Voix* (1988).

Muckram Wakes

This largely traditional folk UK group specialized in songs, and later, dance music of the Midlands. Formed in 1970, the original line-up comprised Roger Watson (b. 7 February 1946, Mansfield, Nottinghamshire, England; concertina, tuba, melodeon), Helen Wainwright (b. 16 May 1951, Marchington, Staffordshire, England; harmonium, whistle, piano, bouzouki) - Helen and Roger married in 1972 - and John Tams (fiddle, banjo, concertina). This unit survived until October 1973, when Tams left to join the **Albion Band**. Shortly afterwards John Adams (fiddle, banjo, trombone), and Suzie Adams (drum, percussion), were added. In this format they continued until 1980, gaining much respect on the folk circuit. They also contributed to the short-lived 11-piece **New Victory Band**, and their highly-regarded 1978 release *One More Dance And Then*. In 1980 a complete change of line-up, brought about by personal and professional break-ups, meant that the group comprised of John Adams, Keith Kendrick (concertina), Barry Coope (vocals) and Ian Carter. This group only lasted for a short while before disbanding. Roger Watson also performed and recorded with American banjo player and singer Debbie McClatchy, and he was also a member of the Robb Johnson Band. Watson is now director of TAPS (Traditional Arts Projects), in Berkshire.

Albums: *A Map Of Derbyshire* (1973), *Muckram Wakes* (1976), *Warble, Jangles And Reeds* (1980). Roger Watson: *The Pick And The Malt Shovel* (1974), *Mixed Traffic* (1981), *Chequered Roots* (1988), with Debbie McClatchy *Radioland* (1988), Suzie Adams And Helen Watson *Songbird* (1983)

Mud

Originally formed in 1966, this lightweight UK pop outfit comprised Les Gray (b. 9 April 1946, Carshalton, Surrey, England; vocals), Dave Mount (b. 3 March 1947, Carshalton, Surrey, England; drums/vocals), Ray Stiles (b. 20 November 1946, Carshalton, Surrey, England; bass guitar/vocals) and Rob Davis (b. 1 October 1947, Carshalton, Surrey; lead guitar/vocals). Their debut single for **CBS**, 'Flower Power', was unsuccessful but they continued touring for several years. The group's easy-going pop style made them natural contenders for appearances on *The Basil Brush Show*, but still the hits were not forthcoming. Eventually, in early 1973, they broke through in the UK with 'Crazy' and 'Hypnosis'. Their uncomplicated blend of pop and rockabilly brought them an impressive run of 12 more Top 20 hits during the next three years, including three UK number 1 hits: 'Tiger Feet', 'Lonely This Christmas' and 'Oh Boy'. The group continued in cabaret, but their membership atropied after the hits had ceased. Gray attempted a solo career with little success, while Stiles turned up unexpectedly in 1988 as a latter-day member of the **Hollies** at the time of their belatedly chart-topping 'He Ain't Heavy He's My Brother'.

Albums: *Mud Rock* (1974), *Mud Rock Vol. 2* (1975), *Use Your Imagination* (1975), *It's Better Than Working* (1976), *Mudpack* (1978), *Rock On* (1978), *As You Like It* (1979), *Mud* (1983). Compilation: *Mud's Greatest Hits* (1975), *Let's Have A Party* (1990).

Muddy Waters

b. McKinley Morganfield, 4 April 1915, Rolling Fork, Mississippi, USA, d. 30 April 1983, Chicago, Illinois, USA. One of the dominant figures of post-war blues, Muddy Waters was raised in the rural Mississippi town of Clarksdale, in whose juke-joints he came into contact with the legendary **Son House**. Having already mastered the rudiments of the guitar, Waters began performing and this early, country blues period was later documented by **Alan Lomax**. Touring the South making field recordings for the Library Of Congress, this renowned archivist taped Muddy on three occasions between 1941-42. The following year Waters moved to Chicago where he befriended **Big Bill Broonzy** whose influence and help proved vital to the younger performer. Muddy soon began using amplified, electric instruments and by 1948 had signed a recording deal with the newly-founded Aristocrat label, the name of which was later changed to **Chess Records**. Waters' second release, 'I Feel Like Goin' Home'/'I Can't Be Satisfied', was a minor R&B hit and its understated accompaniment from bassist Big Crawford set a pattern for several further singles, including 'Rollin' And Tumblin'', 'Rollin' Stone' and 'Walking Blues'.

By 1951 the guitarist was using a full backing band and among the musicians who passed through its ranks were **Otis Spann** (piano), **Jimmy Rogers** (guitar), **Little Walter**, **Walter 'Shakey' Horton** and James Cotton (all harmonica). This pool of talent ensured that the Muddy Waters Band was Chicago's most influential unit and a score of seminal recordings, including 'Hoochie Coochie Man', 'I've Got My Mojo Working', 'Mannish Boy', 'You Need Love' and 'I'm Ready', established the leader's abrasive guitar style and impassioned singing. Waters' international stature was secured in 1958 when he toured Britain at the behest of jazz trombonist **Chris Barber**. Although criticized in some quarters for his use of amplification, Muddy's effect on a new generation of white enthusiasts was incalculable. **Cyril Davies** and **Alexis Korner** abandoned skiffle in his wake and their subsequent combo, Blues Incorporated, was the catalyst for the **Rolling Stones**, the **Graham Bond** Organisation, **Long John Baldry** and indeed British R&B itself. Paradoxically, while such groups enjoyed commercial success, Waters struggled against indifference. Deemed 'old-fashioned' in the wake of soul music, he was obliged to update his sound and repertoire, resulting in such misjudged releases as *Electric Mud*, which featured a reading of the Rolling Stones' 'Let's Spend The Night Together', the ultimate artistic *volte-face*. The artist did complete a more sympathetic project in *Fathers And Sons* on which he was joined by **Paul Butterfield** and **Mike Bloomfield**, but his work during the 60s was generally disappointing. *The London Sessions* kept Waters in the public eye, as did his appearance in the **Band**'s *The Last Waltz*, but it was an inspired series of collaborations with guitarist **Johnny Winter** that signalled a dramatic rebirth. This pupil produced and arranged four excellent albums which recaptured the fire and purpose of Muddy's early releases and bestowed a sense of dignity to this musical giant's legacy. Waters died of heart failure in 1983, his stature as one of world's most influential musicians secured.

Selected albums: *Muddy Waters At Newport* (1960), *Muddy Waters, Folk Singer* (1964), *Muddy Waters Sings Big Bill Broonzy* (1964), *Muddy Brass And The Blues* (1965), *Down On Stovall's Plantation* (1966), *Electric Mud* (1968), *After The Rain* (1969), *Fathers And Sons* (1969), *They Call Me Muddy Waters* (1970), *The London Sessions* (1971), *Live At Mister*

Kelly's (1971), *Experiment In Blues* (1972), *Sail On* (1972), *Can't Get No Grinding* (1973), *Mud In Your Ear* (1973), *London Revisited* (1974), *Woodstock Album* (1975), *Unk In Funk* (1977), *Hard Again* (1977), *Muddy Waters Live* (1977), *Live* (1977), *I'm Ready* (1978), *King Bee* (1981), *Muddy Waters In Concert 1958* (1982). Compilations: *The Best Of Muddy Waters* (1964), *Real Folk Blues* (1965), *More Real Folk Blues* (1967), *Vintage Mud* (1970), *McKinley Morganfield* aka *Muddy Waters* (1972), *Back In The Early Days* (1977), *Chess Masters* (1981), *Trouble No More* (1989), *The Chess Box* 1947-67 (Charly 1990, 9 CD set), *Funky Butt* (1993, rec early 70s), *Gold Collection* (1993).
Further reading: *The Complete Muddy Waters Discography*, Phil Wight and Fred Rothwell.

Mudhoney

Mudhoney, forged from a host of hobbyist bands, can lay claim to the accolade 'godfathers' of grunge' more legitimately than most - whether or not they desire that title. The band comprises brothers Mark Arm (vocals) and Steve Turner (guitar), plus Matt Lukin (bass) and Dan Peters (drums). Arm and Turner were both ex-**Green River**, the band which also gave birth to **Pearl Jam**, and the less serious Thrown Ups. Lukin was ex-**Melvins**, Peters ex-Bundles Of Piss. Mudhoney were the band that first imported the sound of **Sub Pop Records** to wider shores. In August 1988 they released the fabulous 'Touch Me I'm Sick' single, one of the defining moments in the evolution of 'grunge', followed shortly by their debut mini-album. Contrary to popular belief, Turner chose the name *Superfuzz Bigmuff* after his favourite effects pedals rather than any sexual connotation. Early support included the admiration of **Sonic Youth** who covered their first a-side while Mudhoney thrashed through Sonic Youth staple 'Halloween' on the flip side of a split single. The first album proper was greeted as a comparative disappointment by many, though there were obvious standout tracks ('When Tomorrow Hits'). The EP, *Boiled Beef And Rotting Teeth*, contained a cover of the **Dicks**' 'Hate The Police', demonstrating a good grasp of their 'hardcore' heritage. They had previously demonstrated an ability to nominate a sprightly cover tune when **Spacemen 3**'s 'Revolution' had appeared on the b-side to 'This Gift'. The band also hold the likes of **Celibate Rifles** and **Billy Childish** is high esteem. Members of the former have helped in production of the band, while on trips to England they have invited the latter to join as support. It was their patronage which led to Childish's **Thee Headcoats** releasing material through Sub Pop. Meanwhile, Mudhoney's shows were becoming less eye-catching, and progressively close to eye-gouging. Early gigs in London saw Arm invite the audience, every single one of them, on to the stage, with the resultant near destruction of several venues. *Every Good Boy Deserves Fudge* was a departure, with Hammond organ intruding into the band's accomplished rock formula. It demonstrated their increasing awareness of the possibilities of their own song writing. They are certainly not the wooden-headed noise dolts they are sometimes portrayed as: each comes from a comfortable middle class background, and while Arm is an English graduate, Turner has qualifications in anthropology. After much speculation Mudhoney became the final major players in the Sub Pop empire to go major when they moved to **Warner Brothers Records**, though many would argue that none of their efforts thus far have managed to reproduce the glory of 'Touch Me I'm Sick' or other highlights of their independent days. *My Brother The Cow*, however, revealed a band nearly back at its best. Released after extensive world-wide touring with Pearl Jam, songs such as 'Into Your Schtick' reflected on the passing of one-time friend Kurt Cobain. **Jack Endino**'s production, meanwhile, added lustre and managed to capture the band's always compelling live sound better than had previously been the case.
Albums: *Superfuzz Bigmuff* (Sub Pop 1988), *Mudhoney* (Sub Pop 1989), *Every Good Boy Deserves Fudge* (Sub Pop 1991), *Piece Of Cake* (WEA 1992), *Five Dollar Bob's Mock Cooter Stew* (WEA 1993), *My Brother The Cow* (WEA 1995). Compilation: *Superfuzz Bigmuff Plus Early Singles* (Sub Pop 1993).
Video: *Absolutely Live* (1994).

Mudie, Harry

b. c.1940, Spanish Town, Jamaica, West Indies. One of the unsung pioneers of Jamaican recording, Mudie first developed his interest in music while a pupil at St. Jago High School during the mid-50s. His debut with the legendary Rasta drummer **Count Ossie** and saxophonist Wilton Gaynair, entitled 'Babylon Gone', aka 'Going Home', backed with 'So Long' by Winston And Roy, was released in the UK on the Blue Beat label in 1962. The same year he opened the Scaramouch Garden Amusement Center in Spanish Town. Little seems to have emerged, though, between 1962 and 1970, when **Trojan Records** began releasing his productions on the specially formed Moodisc label. A year later Rita and Benny King's R&B Discs Ltd created their own Moodisc label. Using a studio band led by pianist Gladstone Anderson, Mudie deftly combined sweet, tuneful melodies with heavy rhythms. The records issued on these and his Jamaican labels, including organist **Winston Wright**'s 'Musically Red', Winston Shand's 'Time Is The Master', the Eternal's 'Push Me In The Corner', the Ebony Sisters' 'Let Me Tell You Boy', **John Holt**'s 'It May Sound Silly', Dennis Walks' 'The Drifter' and 'Heart Don't Leap', Count Ossie's 'Whispering Drums', Lloyd Jones' 'Rome' and trumpeter Jo Jo Bennett's instrumental version 'Leaving Rome', established Mudie's name among the very best of the reggae producers of the day. He launched DJ **I Roy** on record with 'Musical Pleasure' and a version of 'The Drifter'. He was probably the first to use strings in the music, notably on John Holt's classic love song album, *Time Is The Master* (1973), and it is arguably this fact that seems to have prejudiced his standing among some of the more reactionary elements of the reggae audience.

In 1973 he scored a big reggae hit with Dennis Walks' calypso-flavoured 'Margaret', released on the Cactus label in the UK, following it with vibist Lennie Hibbert's version 'Margaret's Dream'. He also produced the **Heptones** on the classic 'Love Without Feeling', DJ tunes by Count Sticky, Big Joe ('Set Your Face At Ease' on the 'Rome' rhythm), and Jah Lloyd, and a plethora of 'Drifter' cuts by Bongo Herman and others. During the mid-70s Mudie issued three classic dub albums mixed by **King Tubby**, instrumental sets by Gladstone Anderson and Ossie Scott, vocal albums by Dennis Walks and Bunny Maloney, for whom he produced the popular Jamaican lovers favourite 'Baby I've Been Missing You', and two excellent various artists collections. During the 80s and 90s he concentrated on his back catalogue with re-presses and some excellent new compilations such as *Reggae History Volume One* and *Reggae Bible*, the latter being a whole album based on the 'Drifter' rhythm. This prolific period produced over 100 singles and several 12-inch 'discomix' singles as the decade closed. Mudie recorded a variety of other artists, including **Gregory Isaacs**, **Freddy McKay**, Joe White, **Cornell Campbell**, Jah Walton (now known as Joseph Cotton), and Prince Heron. During the 80s he kept a low profile, moving to Miami, Florida, issuing his back catalogue and an album by Bunny Maloney.

Selected albums: Rhythm Rulers *Mudies Mood* (1970), Jo Jo Bennett *Groovy Joe* (1970), Gladstone Anderson *It May Sound Silly* (1972), *Gladdy Unlimited* (1977), John Holt *Time Is The Master* (1973), Bunny Maloney *Magic Woman* (1978), Ossie Scott *Reggae Exposure With Sax* (1983), with King Tubby *Harry Mudie Meets King Tubby In Dub Conference Vols. 1, 2 & 3* (Mudies 1975/6/7), Harry Mudie & Friends *Let Me Tell You Boy 1970-71* (Trojan 1988), various *Quad Star Revolution Vol. 1* (1974), *Quad Star Revolution Vol. 2* (1976), *Reggae History Vol.* 1 (Moods 1985).

Mudlarks

Soprano Mary Mudd, baritone Fred Mudd and tenor Jeff Mudd were the Mudlarks: a clean-cut family pop trio from Bedford, Bedfordshire, England. They started singing in public as the Mudd Trio in 1951 when they were just 12, 14 and 16 years old. Discovered by disc jockey David Jacobs and produced on Columbia Records by **Norrie Paramor**, they had a hit in 1958 with their second single, 'Lollipop', a cover of the **Chordettes**' US hit. Their follow-up 'Book Of Love', originally by the **Monotones**, also made the UK Top 10. They were often seen on the pioneering UK television series, *6.5 Special*, and won the ***New Musical Express*** poll award as Top British Vocal Group for both 1958 and 1959. Jeff was called up by the army in early 1959 and David Lane replaced him until his return two years later. One of the few UK pop groups in the 50s, they recorded several more covers of US hits without further chart success.

Mueller-Westernhagen, Marius

b. 6 December 1948, Duesseldorf, Germany. This popular singer and performer made his first move into the entertainment industry via theatre acting and singing courses in Hamburg (where he currently lives) and Duesseldorf. He made his television debut in 1964, and has gone on to appear in over 50 movies since. Possibly the most famous of these was his role in 1980's *Theo Gegen Den Rest Der Welt.* In the meantime he had also provided vocals for a beat band titled the Rabbits, and a rock ensemble christened Harakiri. These pursuits eventually culminated in the release of a debut solo album in 1975, pursuing a path somewhere between the exploits of his two previous groups. With a fluctuating line-up of sidemen and accomplices who have included Eddie Taylor (saxophone), Simon Crowe (drums), Klaus Voorman (bass), Ian Parker (keyboards) and Dolphin Taylor (drums), Mueller-Westernhagen went on to become arguably Germany's biggest live attraction of the 80s, and was certainly the nation's biggest-selling popular music artist of the period. Empirical evidence of the continued favour he carried with his public came in 1992 when *JaJa* produced quadruple platinum sales figures. By this time his name had been abbreviated to simply 'Westernhagen'.

Albums: *Das Erste Mal* (1975), *Bittersuess* (1976), *Ganz Allein Krieg Ich's Nicht Hin* (1977), *Mit Pfefferminz Bin Ich Dein Prinz* (1979), *Sekt Oder Selters* (1980), *Stinker* (1981), *Das Herz Eines Boxers* (1982), *Geiler Is Schon* (1983), *Die Sonne Ist Rot* (1984), *Lausige Zeiten* (1986), *Westernhagen* (1987), *Halleluja* (1989), *Live* (1990), *Jaja* (1992).

Muhammad, Idris

b. Leo Morris, 13 November 1939, New Orleans, Louisiana, USA. Immaculate, imaginative and equally at home on contemporary jazz and more popular funk and soul sessions, Idris Muhammad is one of America's most impressive and swinging drummers. Playing since the age of eight, he began working professionally in the soul scene in the early 60s, accompanying vocalists **Jerry Butler**, **Sam Cooke** and the **Impressions**. The gifted bebop alto saxophonist **Lou Donaldson** hired Muhammad for his soul-jazz group in 1965, and work with guitarist **George Benson** followed. In the early 70s, Muhammad became house drummer for the Prestige label, again playing mainly an unadventurous soul/jazz that offered him little room to stretch out and

take advantage of his talents. Spells with **Roberta Flack** followed, but by the end of the 70s, Muhammad was able to put together his own band and started concentrating on modern jazz. Toward the end of the decade he joined hard-bop tenor saxophonist **Johnny Griffin**, and then began a celebrated spell with fellow tenor saxophonist **Pharoah Sanders**. He continues to work intermittently with Sanders, and recently toured internationally and recorded with an all-star saxophone-orientated band, that included **Chico Freeman**, **Arthur Blythe**, **Sam Rivers** and pianist **Don Pullen**.
Albums: with Charles Earland *Black Talk!* (1969), with George Coleman *Big George* (1977), with Johnny Griffin *NYC Underground* (1979), with Pharoah Sanders *Journey To The One* (1980), *Kabsha* (1981), with Lou Donaldson *Sweet Poppa Lou* (1981), *Heart Is A Melody* (1982), *Live* (1982), *Manhattan Panorama* (1983), with James Moody *Something Special* (1986), *Africa* (1987), with Tony Coe *Canterbury Song* (1988).

Muldaur, Geoff

b. c.1940, Pelham, New York, USA. Muldaur began performing at the folk haunts of Cambridge, Massachusetts while a student at Boston University. He worked as a soloist at the *Club 47*, as well as becoming a featured member of the **Jim Kweskin Jug Band**. Muldaur's debut, *Sleepy Man Blues*, boasted support from **Dave Van Ronk** and **Eric Von Schmidt**, and offered sterling interpretations of material drawn from country-blues singers **Bukka White**, **Sleepy John Estes** and **Blind Willie Johnson**. Despite this recording, the artist remained with Kweskin until the Jug Band splintered at the end of the 60s. He then completed two albums, *Pottery Pie* (1970) and *Sweet Potatoes* (1972) with his wife, **Maria Muldaur**, before joining **Paul Butterfield**'s 70s venture, Better Days. The singer resumed his solo career upon the break-up of both the band and his marriage. The **Joe Boyd**-produced *Geoff Muldaur Is Having A Wonderful Time* showed the artist's unflinching eclecticism, a facet prevailing on all his releases. A longstanding professional relationship with guitarist and fellow Woodstock resident Amos Garrett resulted in *Geoff Muldaur And Amos Garrett*, on which the former's penchant for self-indulgence was pared to a minimum. Despite this trait, Muldaur's entire catalogue is worthy of investigation and deserves respect for its attention to music's ephemera.
Albums: *Sleepy Man Blues* (1963), *Geoff Muldaur Is Having A Wonderful Time* (1975), *Motion* (1976), *Geoff Muldaur And Amos Garrett* (1978), *Blues Boy* (1979).

Muldaur, Maria

b. Maria Grazia Rosa Domenica d'Amato, 12 September 1943, Greenwich Village, New York, USA. Her name was changed to Muldaur when she married **Geoff Muldaur**, with whom she performed in the **Jim Kweskin Jug Band**. Although her mother was fond of classical music, Muldaur grew up liking blues and big band sounds. The 60s scene in Greenwich Village thrived musically, and she first joined the **Even Dozen Jug Band**, playing alongside **John Sebastian**, **Stefan Grossman**, **Joshua Rifkin** and **Steve Katz**. After leaving them she teamed up with the Jim Kweskin Jug Band. After two albums together, they split up, and Geoff and Maria were divorced in 1972. *Maria Muldaur*, her first solo effort, went platinum in the USA. It contained the classic single 'Midnight At The Oasis', which featured an excellent guitar solo by Amos Garrett. The album reached number 3 in the US charts in 1974, with the single making the US Top 10. A follow-up, 'I'm A Woman', made the Top 20 in the US charts in 1975. Muldaur toured the USA in 1975, and shortly after played in Europe for the first time. The US Top 30 album, *Waitress In A Donut Shop*, featured the songs of contemporary writers such as **Kate And Anna McGarrigle**, and with the assistance of musicians including Amos Garrett and **J.J.Cale**, she created a stronger jazz influence on the album. With sales of her records in decline, she was dropped by **WEA**, and since then has concentrated on recording with smaller labels such as Takoma, Spindrift, Making Waves and the Christian label Myrhh with whom she released *There Is A Love*. Shortly after *Live In London* was released, the label, Making Waves, folded. *On The Sunny Side* appeared on the largely unknown Music For Little People label. She has never been able to completely match the success of 'Midnight At The Oasis', but her soulful style of blues, tinged with jazz is still in demand.
Albums: *Maria Muldaur* (1973), *Waitress In A Donut Shop* (Reprise 1974), *Sweet Harmony* (1976), *Southern Winds* (1978), *Open Your Eyes* (1979), *Gospel Nights* (1980), *There Is A Love* (1982), *Sweet And Slow* (1984), *Transblucency* (1985), *Live In London* (1987), *On The Sunny Side* (1991), *Louisiana Love Call* (1992).

Muldowney, Dominic

b. 19 July 1952, Southampton, Hampshire, England. This highly talented composer has amassed a formidable list of accomplishments over the past decade for films, television and theatre. He is now Director of Music at the Royal National Theatre, London. His television and film credits include, *Betrayal*, *The Ploughman's Lunch*, *Loose Connections*, *The Big H*, *Bedroom Farce*, *Only Yesterday*, *1984*, *Singleton's Pluck*, *The Beggar's Opera*, *Defence Of The Realm*, *The Act*, *The Burston Rebellion*, *The Blasphemer's Banquet*, *Baal*, *The Ginger Tree*, *Available Light*, *The Black Candle* and *Growing Rich*. His series of classical concerto's for violin, saxophone, percussion, oboe and piano have been performed by some of the UK's major orchestras, yet he is equally at home composing popular music for artists such as

Sting and **David Bowie**. Muldowney also performs as a pianist and conductor and has done much to bridge classical and popular music in contemporary film and drama.

Mulenze

Puerto Rico-based Mulenze are led by bassist/producer Edwin Moráles. They are a salsa orquesta with a line-up of two trumpets, two trombones, rhythm section (conga, bongo, timbales, bass, piano) and three vocalists (lead and chorus). 'Edwin Moráles is a victim of his own good taste. Mulenze unfailingly produce almost excessively sophisticated albums. Two elements stand out: the arrangements, always an astonishing demonstration of how jazz can be harnessed to clave (the rhythmic heartbeat of salsa) to produce superb swing. And then, the marvellous Pedro Brull: blessed with a gorgeous voice, he has that timing which places him among the great soneros (improvising salsa singers). How bitterly disappointing that Mulenze are not better appreciated' (quote from Tomek, UK salsa broadcaster).

The band's first four albums were issued on the PDC label. They signed to **Bobby Valentín**'s Bronco Records and debuted on the label with the excellent *Con Pocas Palabras Basta . . .* (Just A Few Words Are Enough) in 1984. Pedro Brull sang lead on the outstanding track 'No Te Vayas Todavia', which was written by Pedro Arroyo (b. 9 November 1957, Mayagüez, Puerto Rico; composer/vocalist/bandleader), who has composed 10 other songs for the band to date. Ex-**Willie Rosario** pianist/arranger Javier Fernández arranged the song. Co-lead singer Kenny Cruz departed after *Con Pocas Palabras Basta . . .* and later appeared on *De Cara Al Pueblo* (1988) by Concepto Latino. This band's style was in a similar mould to Mulenze and contained several sidemen who had recorded with them. Rafy Andino replaced Cruz on *Te Damos Las Gracias*. Brull supplied the lead vocals to the stand-out cut 'La Crianza', which was written by prominent Puerto Rican composer Johnny Ortiz. He also wrote the superb 'Buscando Aventuras' (sung by Brull) and two other songs on *Mulenze No.7*. Mulenze switched to the Hitt Makers label for 1988's *Toco Madera*. The title track was one of the year's biggest successes. Keyboardist/arranger Andy Guzmán left to work with bandleader/timbales player Don Perignon and the romantic salsa stars, Luis Enrique and Pupy Santiago. In 1982, Guzmán played and arranged on *Mamey* by bandleader, conguero, flautist, singer, composer, producer Julio Castro, another Puerto Rican exponent of sophisticated salsa. Keyboardist/arranger Ricky Rodríguez occupied the vacancy on *Extravagante* in 1990. Rodríguez was a member of Willie Rosario's band between 1984 and 1988. In addition to writing charts for Rosario, Ricky arranged for Pedro Arroyo, Conjunto Chaney (see **Eddie Santiago**), Tito Rojas, Viti Ruiz, and others. On *Extravagante*, he arranged the Arroyo composition 'Quedate', which again featured the glorious lead vocals of Pedro Brull. Two trombonists who recorded with Mulenze, Eliut Cintron and Daniel Fuentes, together with Brull and Guzmán participated in Don Perignon's all-star La Puertorriqueña line-up for *Festival De Soneros* in 1990.

Albums: *Desde El Principio*, *. . . Que Cambio*, *Creciendo* (early 80s), *Otra Vez . . .* (early 80s), *Con Pocas Palabras Basta . . .* (1984), *Te Damos Las Gracias* (1985), *Mulenze No.7* (1986), *Toco Madera* (1988), *Extravagante* (1990). Compilations from their PDC period: *Lo Mejor de La Mulenze: Veneno* (1985), *Lo Mejor de La Mulenze 2da Etapa : La Vida* (1986). Collection from the band's Bronco catalogue: *Grandes Exitos* (1990).

Mullen, Jim

b. 26 November 1945, Glasgow, Scotland. After starting out on guitar while he was still a small child, Mullen switched to bass in his early teens. He played in various dance bands in his home town before forming his own trio and reverting to guitar. At the end of the 60s he relocated to London and moved into R&B. In the early 70s he was frequently associated with jazz-rock and other fusion bands including **Paz**, the **Average White Band**, **Kokomo** (UK) and **Herbie Mann**'s group. He also formed a group with **Dick Morrissey**, **Morrissey-Mullen**, which became one of the best known jazz-rock bands in the UK. The band remained in existence until 1985, after which Mullen led his own small bands. Towards the end of the decade he occasionally appeared again with Morrissey, performing at jazz festivals throughout the UK. A dynamic and forceful player, Mullen's years in jazz-rock and his deep affinity with the blues give his music a quality of earthy excitement.

Selected albums: *Thumbs Up* (Coda 1984), *Into The 90s* (Castle 1990), *Soundbites* (EFZ 1993). As Morrissey-Mullen *Up* (1977), *Cape Wrath* (1979), *Badness* (1981), *Life On The Wire* (1982), *It's About Time* (1983), *This Must Be The Place* (1985), *Happy Hour* (1988).

Mullican, Moon

b. Aubrey Mullican, 29 March 1909, Corrigan, Polk County, Texas, USA, d. 1 January 1967. Mullican was raised on a farm which was manned by black workers. One sharecropper, Joe Jones, taught Mullican how to play blues guitar. His father bought an old pump organ so that the family could practice hymn-singing, but the Aubrey preferred to pound out boogie-woogie and the blues. When Mullican was 14 years old, he went into a cafe in nearby Lufkin and sat at the piano; he came out two hours later with $40 in tips. When aged 16, and after an argument with his father, he moved to Houston and started playing the piano in brothels and honky tonks. He would work all night and sleep all day, hence his nickname 'Moon'. In the late 30s Mullican made his first recordings for US **Decca** as part of Cliff Bruner's Texas Wanderers, taking the lead vocal for 'Truck Driver Blues', arguably the first trucking song. He also recorded as part of Leon Selph's Blue Ridge Playboys. He helped musician **Jimmie Davis** became the State Governor of Louisiana and later joined his staff. In 1944 he invested his savings in 10 large jukeboxes but they were confiscated by the authorities because he refused to pay the appropriate tax. In 1946 he was signed by **Sid Nathan** to the new King label and 'New Pretty Blonde', a parody in pigeon French of 'Jole Blon', became a million-seller. He won another gold disc with 'I'll Sail My Ship Alone', and also found success with a tribute to mothers, 'Sweeter Than The Flowers', the double-sided 'Mona Lisa'/'Goodnight Irene' and 'Cherokee Boogie', which was one of a succession of boogie records.

In 1949 he wrote 'Jambalaya' with **Hank Williams**, although he was not given a credit. This is probably unjust because the style of the song - and the subject matter of food! - were more in keeping with Mullican's other work than Williams'. In the mid-50s, Mullican delighted in the advent of rock 'n' roll as he said he had been doing that all along. Backed by the hit-making **Boyd Bennett And His Rockets**, he recorded 'Seven Nights To Rock'. However, he was too portly and bald for teenage record buyers. **Jerry Lee Lewis** acknowledges Mullican as a major influence - in particular, Mullican's playing of the melody with just two fingers on his right hand - and has recorded 'I'll Sail My Ship Alone'. He recorded for Coral and Starday but alcohol and too much jambalaya got the better of him. When asked why he chose the piano, Mullican replied, 'Because the beer kept sliding off my fiddle.' In 1962, the 19-stone Mullican collapsed on stage in Kansas City. He stopped drinking and returned to performing, making an album for Kapp, *The Moon Mullican Showcase*, produced by **Jack Clement**. He recorded the novelty, 'I Ain't No Beatle (But I Want To Hold Your Hand)' for Spar. On New Year's Eve, 1966, he resolved to cut down on pork chops but died the following day. Governor Jimmie Davis sang at his funeral.

Albums: *Moon Over Mullican* (1958), *Moon Mullican Sings His All-Time Greatest Hits* (1958), *The Old Texan Sings And Plays 16 Of His Favorite Tunes* (1959), *The Many Moods Of Moon Mullican* (1960), *Instrumentals* (1962), *Mr. Piano Man* (1964), *Moon Mullican Sings 24 Of His Favorite Tunes* (1965), *Moon Mullican's Unforgettable Great Hits* (1967), *The Moon Mullican Showcase* (1969), *Seven Nights To Rock* (1983), *Just To Be With You* (1984), *Sweet Rockin' Music* (1984).

Mulligan, Gerry

b. 6 April 1927, New York City, New York, USA. Raised in Philadelphia, Mulligan started out on piano before concentrating on arranging. He also took up the saxophone, first the alto and a few years later the baritone. Among the name bands which used his arrangements were those led by **Gene Krupa** and **Claude Thornhill** and he occasionally played in their reed sections. While writing for Thornhill he met and began a musical association with fellow-arranger **Gil Evans**. In New York in 1948 Mulligan joined Evans and **Miles Davis**, for whom he wrote and played, by now almost exclusively on baritone. In the early 50s Mulligan led his own groups but continued to arrange on a freelance basis. In this capacity his work was performed by **Stan Kenton** (these charts also being performed in the UK by **Vic Lewis**). In 1952 Mulligan began a musical association which not only attracted critical acclaim but also brought him widespread popularity with audiences. This came about through the formation with **Chet Baker** of a quartet which was unusual for the absence of a piano. When Baker quit in 1953, Mulligan subsequently led other quartets, notably with **Bob Brookmeyer** in the mid-50s. Although the quartet format dominated Mulligan's work during this part of his career he occasionally formed larger groups and early in the 60s formed his Concert Jazz Band. This band was periodically revived during the decade and beyond. He interspersed this with periods of leading groups of various sizes, working and recording with other leaders, including **Dave Brubeck**, in frequently rewarding partnership with musicians such as **Paul Desmond**, **Stan Getz**, **Johnny Hodges**, **Zoot Sims** and **Thelonious Monk** and writing arrangements on a freelance basis. In the early 70s Mulligan led big bands, some of which used the name Age Of Steam, and small groups for worldwide concert tours, recording sessions and radio and television appearances. The 80s and early 90s saw him following a similar pattern, sometimes expanding the size of the big band, sometimes content to work in the intimate setting of a quartet or quintet. As an arranger, Mulligan was among the first to attempt to adapt the language of bop for big band and achieved a measure of success with both Krupa (who recalled for George T. Simon that Mulligan was 'a kind of temperamental guy who wanted to expound a lot of his ideas'), and Thornhill. For all the variety of his later work, in many ways his music, as writer and performer, retains the colours and effects of his 50s quartets. In these groups Mulligan explored the possibilities of scoring and improvising jazz in a low-key, seemingly subdued manner. In fact, he thoroughly exploited the possibilities of creating interesting and complex lines which always retained a rich melodic approach. His compositions from the 50s, including 'Night At The Turntable', 'Walkin' Shoes', 'Soft Shoe' and 'Jeru', and his arrangements for 'Bernie's Tune', 'Godchild' and others helped establish the sound and style of the so-called 'cool school'. The intimate styling favoured in such settings was retained in his big band work and his concert band recordings from the 60s retain interest not only for their own sake but also for the manner in which they contrast with most other big band writing of the same and other periods. As a player, the lightness of touch Mulligan uses in his writing is uniquely brought to the baritone saxophone, an instrument which in other, not always lesser hands sometimes overpowers the fragility of some areas of jazz. It is hard to see in Mulligan's work, whether as writer or performer, a clearly discernible influence. Similarly, despite the enormous popularity he has enjoyed over more than four decades, few if any writers or players seem to have adopted him as role model. At the least, this must be something to regret.

Selected albums: with Miles Davis *Birth Of The Cool* (Capitol 1951), *Mulligan Plays Mulligan* (Original Jazz Classics 1951), *Jazz Superstars* (1952), *The Gerry Mulligan Quartet With Chet Baker* (Pacific 1952-53), with Lee Konitz *Konitz Meets Mulligan* (1953), *California Concerts Vols 1 & 2* (1954), *Presenting The Gerry Mulligan Sextet* (1955), *Gerry Mulligan Live In Stockholm* (1955), *Mainstream Of Jazz* (1955), *At Storyville* (1956), *Gerry Mulligan, The Arranger* (1957), *Quartet Live In Stockholm* (Moon 1957), *Gerry Mulligan Meets Stan Getz* (1957), *Desmond Meets Mulligan* (1957), *Blues In Time* (Verve 1957), *Gerry Mulligan Meets The Saxophonists* (1957), with Thelonious Monk *Mulligan Meets Monk* (1957), with Monk *Alternate Takes* (1957), *At Storyville* (Pacific 1957), with Baker *Reunion* (Pacific 1957), *Gerry Mulligan Quartet At Newport* (1958), *I Want To Live* (1958), *What Is There To Say?* (Columbia 1959), with Ben Webster *Gerry Mulligan Meets Ben Webster* (Verve 1959), *Gerry Mulligan And The Concert Band On Tour* (1960), *New York-December1960* (Jazz Anthology 1960), *Gerry Mulligan And The Concert Band* i (1960), *Gerry Mulligan Meets Johnny Hodges* (1960), with Judy Holliday *Holliday With Mulligan* (1961), *Gerry Mulligan Presents A Concert In Jazz* (1961), *The Gerry Mulligan Quartet* (1962), *Jeru* (1962), *Gerry Mulligan And The Concert Band* ii (1962), with Paul Desmond *Two Of A Mind* (1962), *Gerry Mulligan And The Concert Band* iii (1963), *The Shadow Of Your Smile* (1965), *The Gerry Mulligan Quintet* (1965), *Gerry Mulligan Meets Zoot Sims* (1966), *Live In New Orleans* (1968), *The Age Of Steam* (A&M 1971), *Summit* (1974), *Tango Nuevo* (1974), *Carnegie Hall Concert* (1974), *Gerry Mulligan Meets Enrico Intra* (1975), *Idle Gossip* (1976), *Lionel Hampton Presents Gerry Mulligan* (1977), *Mulligan* (LRC 1977), with Benny Carter *Benny Carter/Gerry Mulligan* (LRC 1977), *Walk On The Water* (1980), *LA Menace* (1982), *Little Big Horn* (GRP 1983), with Barry Manilow *2 am Paradise Cafe* (1984), with Scott Hamilton *Soft Lights & Sweet Music* (Concord 1986), *Symphonic Dream* (Sion 1988), *Lonesome Boulevard* (A&M 1990), *Re-Birth Of The Cool* (GRP 1992). Compilations: *Gerry Mulligan And Chet Baker* (1951-65 recordings), *The Best Of The Gerry Mulligan Quartet With Chet Baker* (1952-57 recordings).

Further reading: *Gerry Mulligan's Ark*, Raymond Horricks. *Listen: Gerry Mulligan: An Aural Narrative In Jazz*, Jerome Klinkowitz.

Mulligan, Mick

b. 24 January 1928, Harrow, Middlesex, England. Mulligan taught himself to play trumpet during early jazz revival of the 40s. Ignoring the fact that he was practically a raw beginner, he promptly formed his own group which he named the Magnolia Jazz Band. With the enthusiastic support of sidemen such as Bob Dawbarn, **Roy Crimmins**, **Archie Semple**, Ian Christie and singer **George Melly**, the band became very popular. With radio broadcasts, occasional appearances on television and endless one-night stands at clubs, pubs and theatres throughout the UK, the band established itself as a driving force of the British trad boom. Later renamed Mick Mulligan's Jazz Band, the group continued until the early 60s before folding in the face of a new kind of popular music. Mulligan stayed on in music for a short while before retiring. A forceful player, Mulligan has left behind only a few records but his band's often hilarious exploits have been extensively recounted in books by Melly and the band's manager, Jim Godbolt. Although in its early days the Mulligan band was noted more for enthusiasm than skill, towards the end it had become one of the finest examples of UK trad even if, probably deliberately, it always remained engagingly unpolished.

Album: *George Melly With Mick Mulligan's Band* (1957).

Further reading: *Owning Up*, George Melly. *All This And Many A Dog*, Jim Godbolt.

Mulry, Ted

b. 8 September 1949, England. Mulry was a successful solo act, recording soft, romantic ballads and love songs, several of which entered the Australian charts during 1970-72. These included the number 1 'Julia' and he also made a name for himself as a songwriter for other artists. During this period, Mulry returned to the UK briefly to perform under the name of Steve Ryder. Back in Australia in 1972, with Herm Kovak (drums), Les Hall (guitar, replaced by Gary Dixon in 1974), Mulry formed the trio, the Ted Mulry Gang (later shortened to TMG), changing musical direction to a rock/pop vein. He revived old standards, such as 'Darktown Strutters Ball', wrote a hit, 'Jump In My Car', toured widely and appealed to young teenage fans, who loyally followed his career through seven albums and 15 singles. The band continued to perform as a popular act on the live circuit, without releasing any more records until the mid-80s, when Mulry retired to run a garage. The band was reformed for a 70s' revival show in 1990.

Albums: *Falling In Love Again* (1971), *I Won't Look Back* (1973), with the Ted Mulry Gang *Here We Are* (1974), *Struttin'* (1976), *Steppin' Out* (1976), *TMG LP* (1977),

Disturbing The Peace (1978), *TMG Live* (1979), *Locked In* (1980), *Re-Union* (1990). Compilation: *Greatest Hits* (1977).

Mundell, Hugh

b. 14 June 1962, Kingston, Jamaica, West Indies. Hugh Mundell made his first recording for producer **Joe Gibbs**, the unreleased 'Where Is Natty Dread', while barely in his teens. After this false start his career really got under way when his precocious talent impressed session player/producer **Augustus Pablo**. Pablo enlisted his services as a DJ alongside Jah Bull on his Rockers **sound system**, and produced his first single release, 'Africa Must Be Free', in 1975. Several more singles were released over the next two years, including 'My Mind', 'Don't Stay Away Too Long', 'Let's All Unite' and 'Book Of Life', before the classic *Africa Must Be Free By 1983*, which was released in 1978, swiftly establishing Mundell's name as a bright new roots star in the ascendant.

Pablo further recorded Mundell on such sides as 'That Little Short Man', 'Feeling Alright', 'Jah Says The Time Has Come', 'One Jah One Aim And Destiny' and 'Great Tribulation'. Sundry other recordings were undertaken in his DJ mode as Jah Levi, surfacing mainly on 12". In 1979 Mundell tried his hand at self-production on 'Stop Them Jah' and 'Blackman's Foundation', as well as producing the teenage 'Little' **Junior Reid** on his debut, 'Speak The Truth', which emerged on Pablo's Rockers label in Jamaica. Another excellent song, 'Rastafari's Call' appeared on Mundell's own Muni Music label, while 'Can't Pop No Style' surfaced in 1981 on **Greensleeves**, coupled with Junior Reid's 'Know Myself'. The same year Mundell issued a co-produced album with Pablo entitled *Time And Place*, containing many of those tracks previously released as singles listed above, after which he broke with Pablo altogether, going on to record 'Jah Fire Will Be Burning' for **Prince Jammy** and *Mundell* for **Henry 'Junjo' Lawes**. Ironically it was in 1983, the year he prophesised for Africa's emancipation on his first record, that Hugh Mundell was tragically shot and killed whilst sitting in his car after an argument over a fridge.

Albums: *Africa Must Be Free By 1983* (Message 1978), *Time & Place* (Ja Mun Rock 1981), *Mundell* (Greensleeves 1982), *Black Man Foundation* (Shanachie 1985), *Arise* (Atra 1987).

Mundy, Jimmy

b. 28 June 1907, Cincinnati, Ohio, USA, d. 24 April 1983. Formally taught as a classical musician, Mundy began to concentrate on arranging for big bands in the late 20s and by the beginning of the next decade was well-placed to take advantage of their popularity. During the 30s he wrote for the bands of **Earl Hines** ('Cavernism'), **Benny Goodman** ('Madhouse', 'Sing, Sing, Sing', 'Solo Flight') and **Gene Krupa**. His inclination towards medium and uptempo swingers with impressively orchestrated riffs attracted the interest of **Count Basie** ('Feather Merchant'), for whom he arranged throughout the 40s. Late in the decade he also wrote for **Dizzy Gillespie**. Inevitably, Mundy's tenor saxophone-playing career suffered from his emphasis on his arranging, but he did make some records and briefly led his own band. In the 50s he drifted out of jazz, continuing to arrange for large studio orchestras. He died in 1983.

Albums: *Jimmy Mundy And His Orchestra* i (1958), *Jimmy Mundy And His Orchestra* ii (1959). Compilation: *Groovin' High* (1946).

Mungo Jerry

Mungo Jerry - Ray Dorset (vocals/guitar), Colin Earl (piano/vocals), Paul King (banjo/jug/guitar/vocals) and Mike Cole (bass) - was a little-known skiffle-cum-jug band which achieved instant fame following a sensational appearance at 1970's Hollywood Pop Festival, in Staffordshire, England, wherein they proved more popular than headliners the **Grateful Dead**, **Traffic** and **Free**. The group's performance coincided with the release of their debut single, 'In The Summertime', and the attendant publicity, combined with the song's nagging commerciality, resulted in a runaway smash. It topped the UK chart and, by the end of that year alone, global sales had totalled six million. Despite an eight-month gap between releases, Mungo Jerry's second single, 'Baby Jump', also reached number 1. By this time Mike Cole had been replaced by John Godfrey and the group's jug band sound had grown appreciably heavier. A third hit, in 1971, 'Lady Rose', showed a continued grasp of melody (the maxi-single also included the controversial 'Have A Whiff On Me' which was banned by the BBC). This successful year concluded with another Top 20 release, 'You Don't Have To Be In The Army To Fight In The War'. Paul King and Colin Earl left the group in 1972 and together with bassist Joe Rush, an early member of Mungo Jerry, formed the King Earl Boogie Band. Dorset released a solo album, *Cold Blue Excursions* prior to convening a new line-up with John Godfrey, Jon Pope (piano) and Tim Reeves (drums). The new line-up scored another Top 3 hit in 1973 with 'Alright Alright Alright', but the following year the overtly sexist 'Longlegged Woman Dressed In Black' became the group's final chart entry. Dorset continued to work with various versions of his creation into the 80s, but was never able to regain the group's early profile. A short-lived collaboration with **Peter Green** and Vincent Crane under the name Katmundu resulted in the disappointing *A Case For The Blues* (1986), but Ray did achieve further success when he produced 'Feels Like I'm In Love' for singer **Kelly Marie**. This former Mungo b-side became a UK number 1 in August 1980.

Albums: *Mungo Jerry* (1970), *Electronically Tested* (1971), *You Don't Have To Be In The Army To Fight In The War* (1971), *Boot Power* (1972), *Long Legged Woman* (1974), *Impala Saga* (1976), *Lovin' In The Alleys, Fightin' In The Streets* (1977), *Ray Dorset And Mungo Jerry* (1978), *Six Aside* (1979), *Together Again* (1981). Compilations: *Greatest Hits* (1973), *Golden Hour* (1974), *File* (1977), *The Early Years* (1992). Solo albums: Ray Dorset *Cold Blue Excursion* (1972), Paul King *Been In The Pen Too Long* (1972), the King Earl Boogie Band *Trouble At Mill* (1972).

Muranyi, Joe

b. 14 July 1928, Martin's Ferry, Ohio, USA. Muranyi is of Hungarian descent and first played in a balalaika ensemble. He studied for three years with **Lennie Tristano** and played in New York with a variety of dixieland groups as well as joining the Red Onion Jazz Band (1952-54). He worked as a producer and sleevenote writer for major record labels while playing with trumpeters **Max Kaminsky**, **Yank Lawson** and **Jimmy McPartland**. Between 1967 and 1971 he played with **Louis Armstrong**'s All Stars, providing just the kind of elegant support Armstrong then required. Since Armstrong's death he has played with **Roy Eldridge**, the **World's Greatest Jazz Band** (1975) and the Classic Jazz Quartet (1983) as well as continuing his career as a record producer.

Albums: *Louis Armstrong And The All Stars* (1968), *Clarinet Wobble* (1970), *Classic Jazz Quartet* (1984), with Keith Ingham *Unsaturated Fats* (1990).

Murata, Hideo

b. Isamu Kajiyama, 17 January 1929, Ochi, Saga, Japan. Making a public appearance at the age of five as the son of performers of rôkyoku (a popular art of narrative chant), Kajiyama was hailed a 'rôkyoku genius'. Singing in this style, he won an award in 1954 and subsequently took the stage name, Hideo Murata. After having enjoyed a reputation through the experiments with sound effects and orchestral accompaniment in his rôkyoku performances, he converted, in 1958, to kayôkyoku (formerly the most common and typically Japanese form of popular song) at the confident recommendation of Masao Koga, a renowned kayôkyoku composer. Murata's first single, 'Muhômatsu No Isshô' ('The Life Of Outrageous Matsu') was a national hit, which was followed by 'Jinsei Gekijô' ('Life's Theatre) in 1959 and by the million-selling 'Oshô' ('The Chess King') in 1961. Common to all these songs is the image of a manly, industrious protagonist who is going through hardships, and this suitably matched Murata's deep vocals trained in his rôkyoku days. Other notable hits in the following years included 'Jûdô Ichidai' ('A Life Of Jûdo'), 'Hana To Ryû ('A Flower And A Dragon') and 'Jinsei Tôge' ('A Life's Ridge'), which also celebrated a man who bears the sorrows of life.

Compilations: *Zenkyokushû* (*Complete Works*) (1986), *New Best Now* (1987), *Best Now* (1989).

Murder Inc.

This *avant garde*/industrial metal band were formed in London during 1992 by ex-**Killing Joke** members and ex-**Revolting Cocks**' vocalist **Chris Connelly**. Utilizing two drummers in Martin Atkins and Paul Ferguson, their style was naturally dominated by a strong rhythmic element. Geordie Walker (guitar), Paul Raven (bass) and John Bechdel (guitar/keyboards) completed the line-up. Contracted to **Music For Nations** Records, the band debuted with a self-titled album in June 1992. This built on the brutal rhythms of Killing Joke's material, but, as with each of the spin-off projects, failed to inspire similar devotion to that enjoyed by the parent group.

Album: *Murder Inc.* (Music For Nations 1992).

Murk

US record label, based in Miami, who are probably best known for club hits such as the Funky Green Dogs From Outer Space's 'Reach For Me' (voted third best dance song of 1992 by the *New Musical Express*) and Coral Way Chiefs' 'Release Myself'. Ralph Falcon and Oscar Gaetan also remixed **D.O.P.**'s 'Oh Yeah' for **Guerilla**, and Karen Pollack's 'You Can't Touch Me' for **Emotive**. The group behind the majority of the label's product is also known as the Deep South Recording team, who were also responsible for providing **Warp** with their *Miami* sampler EP. In 1992 they bowed to consumer demand and released a three-track DJ sampler which combined the hard-to-find trio of Funky Green Dogs From Outer Space ('Reach For Me'), Liberty City ('Some Lovin'') and Interceptor ('Together'). In the wake of their cult success the label's product was licensed to **Network** in the UK.

Murmaids

This rock 'n' roll female group came from Los Angeles, California, USA. The members were sisters Carol (b. 1948) and Terry Fischer (b. 1946), and Sally Gordon (b. 1946). Their 'Popsicles And Icicles' went to number 3 on the pop chart in 1963. The song, written by **David Gates** of **Bread** and produced by Kim Foley, was as substantial as cotton-candy, but girl groups were the rage in 1963 and the song had an appealing young teen sound. The Murmaids were devoid of show business aspirations, having been brought to their label, Chattahoochee Records, by their parents, and having left the music business to go to college shortly after 'Popsicles And Icicles' was a hit. Chattahoochee Records continued the Murmaids name through the 60s by recruiting other female members.

Murphey, Michael Martin

b. c.1946, Dallas, Texas, USA. Having been influenced

by gospel music at an early age, Murphey aspired to become a Baptist minister. From 1965-70, as a staff songwriter for Screen Gems, Murphey was writing theme tunes and soundtrack material for television. He grew disillusioned with the poor financial rewards, and left. For a short while he was a member of the **Lewis And Clark Expedition**, which he formed, before going solo. *Geronimo's Cadillac* was produced in Nashville by Bob Johnston, who had originally got Murphey signed to **A&M Records**. The title track was released as a single, and achieved a Top 40 place in the USA. As well as folk, country and blues, Murphey's early gospel leanings are evident in the overall sound of what is an excellent album. He signed to Epic in 1973, after releasing *Cosmic Cowboy Souvenir* which continued the urban cowboy theme of his earlier work. His albums followed a more middle-of-the-road format after this, with occasional glimpses of his better work, as in *Peaks, Valleys, Honky-Tonks And Alleys*. However, he did reach number 3 in the US singles charts, achieving a gold disc, in 1975, with 'Wildfire'. Apart from *Blue Sky, Night Thunder* also achieved gold status. Murphey has never had the degree of commercial success his writing would indicate that he is capable of. However, as a writer, Murphey has had songs covered by **John Denver**, **Cher**, **Claire Hamill**, **Hoyt Axton**, **Bobby Gentry** and the **Monkees**, for whom he wrote 'What Am I Doin' Hangin' 'Round'. He also wrote songs for **Michael Nesmith** including 'The Oklahoma Backroom Dance'. Murphey later played at **Ronnie Scott**'s club in London, for a press presentation, and was supported on the occasion by **J.D. Souther**, **Don Henley,** Dave Jackson and Gary Nurm. *Geronimo's Cadillac* is probably his best remembered work. *Michael Martin Murphey* included a number of songs Murphey had co-written with **Michael D'Abo**. Murphey was featured in the film *Urban Cowboy* which included his song 'Cherokee Fiddle'. Much of the film was shot at **Mickey Gilley**'s Bar. Murphey has continued recording easy listening country and, in 1987, had a number l country single with a wedding song, 'A Long Line Of Love'. He had US country hits with 'A Face In The Crowd', a duet with **Holly Dunn**, and 'Talkin' To The Wrong Man', which featured his son, Ryan. *Cowboy Songs* saw him return to his roots.

Albums: with the Lewis And Clark Expedition *I Feel Good, I Feel Bad*, *Geronimo's Cadillac* (A&M 1972), *Cosmic Cowboy Souvenir* (1973), *Michael Murphey* (1973), *Blue Sky Night Thunder* (1975), *Swans Against The Sun* (Epic 1976), *Flowing Free Forever* (Epic 1976), *Lone Wolf* (1977), *Peaks, Valleys, Honky-Tonks And Alleys* (1979), *Michael Martin Murphey* (Liberty 1982), *The Heart Never Lies* (1983), *Tonight We Ride* (1986), *Americana* (1987), *River Of Time* (Warner Brothers 1988), *Land Of Enchantment* (1989), *Cowboy Songs* (1990), *Cowboy Christmas - Cowboy Songs II* (1991), *Cowboy Songs III* (1993). Compilation: *The Best Of Michael Martin Murphey* (1982).

Murphy, Delia

b. 1903, Mount Jennings, Claremorris, County Mayo, Eire, d. 1971. The daughter of wealthy farming parents, Murphy was educated at University College, Galway, and supplemented her studies by assimilating a diverse repertoire of Irish ballads. Her knowledge of the genre, both in English and Gaelic, was impressive enough to encourage the famous Irish tenor **John McCormack** to seek her assistance in enunciating the ballad 'Una Bhan'. Her rendition so struck a visiting A&R representative from **HMV Records** that she was duly signed to the label. One of her first recordings was the extraordinary 'The Spinning Wheel'. Written in 1899 by John Francis Waller, the song hauntingly evoked the courtship of young lovers measured by the inexorable winding of the spinner's wheel. Murphy's ethereal West Ireland brogue and Gaelic pronunciation was reinforced by a harp arrangement which was quite remarkable for the period. With songs such as 'If I Were A Blackbird', 'Coortin' In The Kitchen', 'Goodbye Mike And Goodbye Pat' and 'Nora Creina', Murphy established herself as a traditionalist with a tremendous sense of humour and pathos. She borrowed freely, not merely from standard Irish ballads, but from obscure songs that had their origin in tinker folklore. Other material such as 'The Moonshiner' and 'Boston Burglar' were American adaptations, expertly gaelicized by Murphy's distinctive brogue and unique diction. Her marriage to the Ambassador Dr. Thomas Kiernan (author of *British War Finances And Their Consequences*) took her to the Vatican in 1941, where she spent the War years. While there she translated her version of 'Three Lovely Lassies' into Italian. After touring the world with her ambassador husband, she retired to Eire's Liffey Valley, where she died at the age of 68.

Compilation: *The Legendary Delia Murphy* (1977).

Murphy, Mark

b. 14 March 1932, Syracuse, New York, USA. Murphy began singing as a child and in his mid-teens was performing with a band led by his brother. He worked in many parts of the USA, and had built a small reputation for himself in New York when the appearance of several albums in the late 50s announced that the jazz world had a new and important singer in its midst. During the 60s he continued to tour, visiting Europe and making more fine records with **Al Cohn** (*That's How I Love The Blues*) and a group drawn from the **Clarke-Boland Big Band** (*Midnight Mood*). In the middle of the decade he decided to settle in Europe and worked extensively on the Continent, with occasional visits to the UK. In the early 70s he returned to the USA, where he recorded with **Michael** and **Randy Brecker** on *Bridging A Gap* and the later *Satisfaction Guaranteed*, and continued to attract new audiences.

Murphy's repertoire is extensive and draws upon sources as diverse as **Big Joe Turner** and **Jon Hendricks**. An accomplished stylist who sings with panache, good humour and great vocal dexterity, Murphy has remained dedicated to jazz. This commitment has been unswayed by the fact that his warm voice and highly personable stage presentation would almost certainly have guaranteed him a successful and much more lucrative career in other areas of popular music. In the early 90s Murphy was still on tour, still pleasing his old audience, and still, remarkably, pulling in newcomers.
Albums: *Meet Mark Murphy* (Decca 1957), *Let Yourself Go* (Decca 1958), *Sessions, Live* (c.1958), *This Could be The Start Of Something* (Capitol 1959), *Hit Parade* (Capitol 1960), *Playing The Field* (Capitol 1960), *Rah!* (Original Jazz Classics 1961), *That's How I Love The Blues!* (1962), *A Swingin' Singin' Affair* (Fontana 1965), *Midnight Mood* (1967), *Bridging A Gap* (1972), *Mark II* (1973), *Red Clay: Mark Murphy Sings* (1975), *Mark Murphy Sings Dorothy Fields And Cy Coleman* (1977), *Stolen Moments* (1978), *Satisfaction Guaranteed* (1979), *Bop For Kerouac* (1981), *Mark Murphy Sings The Nat 'King' Cole Songbook, Vols. 1 & 2* (1983), *Beauty And The Beast* (Muse 1986), *Night Mood* (Milestone 1986), *Kerouac Then And Now* (Muse 1987), *September Ballads* (Milestone 1987), *What A Way To Go* (Muse 1991), *Very Early* (1993), with Sheila Jordan *One For Junior* (Muse 1994).

Murphy, Matt

b. 27 December 1929, Sunflower, Mississippi, USA. He moved to Memphis as a child and learned guitar in the 40s. He joined Tuff Green's band before becoming lead guitarist with **Junior Parker**'s Blue Flames, playing on recording sessions with Parker and **Bobby 'Blue' Bland**. Murphy's brother Floyd replaced him with Parker when Matt moved to Chicago in 1952. There he spent seven years in **Memphis Slim**'s band, also recording as the Sparks with Sam Chatman (bass/vocals) and John Calvin (saxophone). He toured Europe in 1963 with the Folk Blues package, recording with **Sonny Boy 'Rice Miller' Williamson** in Denmark. Murphy found a wider audience through his role in the film *The Blues Brothers* as **Aretha Franklin**'s husband and his subsequent tours with the **Blues Brothers** package. Floyd Murphy joined him for his first solo album, recorded for Antone's in 1990.
Album: *Way Down South* (1990).
Film: *The Blues Brothers* (1980).

Murphy, Noel

b. 27 November 1943, Killerney, County Kerry, Eire. Singer, guitar player, and storyteller, Murphy first visited London in 1962 and decided to stay. He went to a wide number of folk clubs, then springing up under the banner of the folk revival. Shortly afterwards, Murphy started out doing the obligatory 'floor spots' in the clubs, and was rewarded with offers of bookings. The residency of the famous London club Les Cousins in Soho followed. He then began playing a large number of folk festivals, including Norwich, Cambridge and Trowbridge. In 1965, Murphy released an EP, *Noel Murphy*, for **EMI**. Subsequent releases turned up on a variety of labels, including **Fontana**, and **RCA**. Noel had by now been working abroad a great deal, in places as diverse as Saudi Arabia, Bermuda, Kenya, and Hungary. However, in 1983, his throat was damaged when he choked on a piece of glass which was found in his drink. His full-time singing career now over, he left the scene for four years. During this time he developed his abilities as an after dinner speaker. As a result, he is now much in demand in his capacity as a storyteller at golf and rugby functions. In 1987, he released the single 'Murphy And The Bricks' aka 'Why Paddy's Not At Work Today', recounting the amusing excuse given for someone not turning up for work on the building site. Murphy's career spans over 25 years, and includes numerous radio and television appearances, with many in Eric Sykes' television shows and films. Noel now does very few folk club bookings since he began touring with his one man show - An Evening With Noel Murphy.
Albums: *Nyaah!* (Fontana 1967), *A Touch Of The Blarney* (MFP 1968), *Another Round* (Fontana 1969), *Murf* (The Village Thing 1972), *Noel Murphy Performs* (Plant Life 1975), *Caught In The Act* (RCA 1978), *Homework* (Murphy 1988).

Murphy, Peter

The former **Bauhaus** vocalist set out on his solo career after a brief stint as half of **Dali's Car**, with former **Japan** member **Mick Karn** (one album: *The Waking Hour*). Murphy was already famous in his own right for appearing as the enigmatic figure in a Maxell Tapes television advertisement. His first solo output was a cover version of **Magazine**'s 'The Light Pours Out Of Me', for the **Beggars Banquet** sampler *The State Of Things*. This was included on his debut album, which boasted a massive credit list including **Daniel Ash**, his old songwriting partner in Bauhaus, John McGeogh (of Magazine and **Siouxsie And The Banshees**; who played on the original of 'The Light Pours Out Of Me') and Howard Hughes. The debut set a precedent for critical apathy (in the UK at least) which has accompanied all subsequent recordings. 1987's *Love Hysteria* included a cover of **Iggy Pop**'s 'Fun Time', amongst other typically dramatic gestures. By the third album a regular band had been formed, consisting of Peter Bonas (guitar), Terl Bryant (drums), Eddie Branch (bass) and Paul Statham (keyboards/guitar). All four had played on the previous album, Branch and Bonas on the first as well. One of the better songs from *Deep*, 'Cuts You Deep', won the Top Modern Rock Track in the 1990 ***Billboard*** Year In Music Awards.

Albums: *Should The World Fail To Fall Apart* (1986), *Love Hysteria* (1987), *Deep* (1989), *Holy Smoke* (1992), *Cascade* (Beggars Banquet 1995).

Murphy, Ralph

b. 1944, Wallaceburg, Ontario, Canada. He wanted to be a songwriter from an early age and, getting little encouragement in Canada, tried both Los Angeles and Liverpool, even landing a recording contract as part of the Guardsmen in the UK in 1964. His first hit song was 'Call My Name' for James Royal. Moving back to Canada, Murphy formed Double M Records and produced April Wine and Roadhouse. His first US country hit was with 'Good Enough To Be Your Wife' (**Jeannie C. Riley**). Going into partnership with **Roger Cook**, they wrote 'Talking In Your Sleep' and 'Half The Way' (both **Crystal Gayle**), 'He Got You' (**Ronnie Milsap**) and '18 Wheels And A Dozen Roses' (**Kathy Mattea**). He re-established himself in Canada with 'Bad Day For Trains' for Patricia Conroy. In the 90s **Little Texas** had success with 'Inside'. Murphy is currently Director of Artists Relations for **ASCAP** in Nashville and believes that much of his work is helping songwriters learn their craft. His advice is 'Listen to the best because that is your real competition. Don't try and be as good as the guy playing down the street in the bar.' Another piece of advice might be to take Ralph's place when he cannot make a gig: when he couldn't make the Bluebird one night, **Garth Brooks** stepped in and got his **Capitol** recording contract!

Murphy, Rose

b. 1913, Xenia, Ohio, USA, d. 16 November 1989, Queens, New York, USA. Murphy was a singer and pianist with a high-pitched squeaky voice, a bubbly, infectious personality and a keyboard style that fully complemented her singing. She also provided her own percussion by stamping her feet on the floor. When she moved upmarket to venues that were carpeted, she used a wooden board on which to pound out her foot stomps. Murphy established a considerable reputation on the New York club circuit in the mid/late 40s, entering the US Top 20 with a version of 'I Can't Give You Anything But Love' in 1947. Known as the 'Chee Chee' girl, due to her use of that particular expression, and several other chirrups and twitterings to punctuate her vocals, she became popular in the UK during 1948 after frequent playings of her single 'Busy Line' by then-disc jockey Richard Attenborough. This record introduced the telephone signal, 'Brruup, Brruup', as yet another of her sound effects. Other UK hits included 'Me And My Shadow' and 'Girls Were Made To Take Care Of Boys'. In 1950 she played the London Palladium and thereafter continued to tour Europe occasionally through to the 80s. During the 60s she performed regularly at the Cookery in New York. She died in 1989 but received further press attention the following year when UK mobile telephone company Cellnet used 'Busy Line' as a television commercial theme, prompting **RCA** to reissue Murphy's original recording.
Albums: *Not Cha-Cha, But Chi-Chi* (mid-50s), *Jazz, Joy and Happiness* (mid-50s).

Murphy, Turk

b. Melvin Murphy, 16 December 1915, Palermo, California, USA, d. 30 May 1987. Murphy's early career was as a trombonist in popular dancebands such as that led by Mal Hallett, but in the late 30s he joined the revivalist band led by **Lu Watters** and remained there for most of the next decade. After leaving Watters he formed his own band, gaining just as much fame and popularity as Watters had, and a similarly high level of critical disdain. Murphy opened his own club, Earthquake McGoon's, in San Francisco and continued to lead his band there and around the world until shortly before his death in 1987. An earthy, sometimes raucous but always entertaining player, Murphy was one of the key figures in retaining public interest in traditional jazz during a period, and in a place (the west coast) that saw most critical attention directed to other styles of music.
Albums: *Turk Murphy's Jazz Band Favourites* (Good Time Jazz, 1949-51 recordings), *The Music Of Jelly Roll Morton* (1953), *Music For Losers* (1957), *Turk Murphy At The Newport Jazz Festival 1957* (1957), *Turk Murphy In Concert Vols 1 & 2* (1972), *Southern Stomps* (1980-86), *San Francisco Memories* (c.1986), *Concert In The Park* (Merry Makers 1986), with Jim Cullum *Turk At Carnegie Hall* (1987). Compilations: *San Francisco Jazz, Vol. 1* (1949-50 recordings), *San Francisco Jazz, Vol. 2* (1950-52 recordings), *Live At Easy Street Vols 1-3* (Dawn Club 1979), *The Best Of Turk Murphy* (Merry Makers 1993).

Murphy, Walter

b. 1952, New York City, New York, USA. Murphy was responsible for one of the biggest and most bizarre early disco hits, 'A Fifth Of Beethoven'. As its title suggests, the number 1 single was based on Beethoven's Fifth Symphony. Murphy was schooled in music as a child and worked for the *Tonight* show in the USA as a musical arranger after graduating from the Manhattan School of Music. He then worked as a jingle writer, scoring for television films. His first foray into the new disco sound was in 1975 with dance-oriented Christmas singles, which were not successful. Murphy came up with the idea for 'A Fifth Of Beethoven' in early 1976 and recorded his arrangement, playing nearly all of the instruments himself (despite billing the record as being by Walter Murphy And The Big Apple Band). It was released on Private Stock Records and by the autumn had risen to number 1 in the US. An album of similar material reached number 15 during the same period. A

follow-up single, 'Flight '76', based on Rimsky-Korsakov's 'Flight Of The Bumble Bee', hit number 44 in late 1976, and an album, *Rhapsody In Blue*, including Murphy's reworking of the **George Gershwin** title song, made the lower rungs of that chart. Murphy was out of the charts for six years, resurfacing in 1982 with 'Theme From E.T. (The Extra-Terrestrial)', from the hit film.
Albums: *A Fifth Of Beethoven* (1976), *Rhapsody In Blue* (1977), *Themes From E.T.* (1982).

Murray, Anne

b. 20 June 1946, Springhill, Nova Scotia, Canada. Sometimes known as 'The Singing Sweetheart Of Canada', Murray graduated from the University of New Brunswick with a degree in physical education, and then spent a year as a teacher. After singing simply for pleasure for a time, in 1964 she was persuaded to audition for *Sing Along Jubilee*, a regional television show, but was selected instead for the same network's *Let's Go*, hosted by Bill Langstroth (her future husband). Income from a residency on the programme and solo concerts was sufficient for Murray to begin entertaining professionally in a vaguely folk/country rock style, though she could also acquit herself admirably with both R&B and mainstream pop material. Like **Linda Ronstadt** - seen by some as her US opposite number - she was mainly an interpreter of songs written by others. Issued by Arc Records, *What About Me* (1968) created sufficient impact to interest **Capitol Records**, who signed her to a long term contract.
Two years later, her version of Gene MacLellan's remarkable 'Snowbird', taken from the album *This Was My Way*, soared into *Billboard*'s Top 10. Despite regular appearances on **Glen Campbell**'s *Goodtime Hour* television series, subsequent releases - including the title track to *Talk It Over In The Morning* - sold only moderately until 1973 when she scored another smash hit with 'Danny's Song', composed by **Kenny Loggins** (with whom she duetted 11 years later on 'Nobody Loves Me Like You Do', a country chart-topper). She was rated ***Billboard***'s second most successful female artist in 1976, but family commitments necessitated a brief period of domesticity before 'You Needed Me' won her a Grammy award for best female pop vocal performance in 1978. While revivals of **Bobby Darin**'s 'Things' and the **Monkees**' 'Daydream Believer' were aimed directly at the pop market, it was with the country audience that she proved most popular. 'He Thinks I Still Care' (originally a b-side) became her first country number 1. However, along with 'Just Another Woman In Love', 'Could I Have This Dance' (from the film *Urban Cowboy*), the bold 'A Little Good News' (1983) and other country hits, she had also recorded a collection of children's ditties (*Hippo In My Tub*), commensurate with her executive involvement with Canada's Save The Children Fund. In 1989 Springhill's Anne Murray Center was opened in recognition of her tireless work for this charity. Three years later she played Las Vegas, with a show which amply demonstrated her excellent delivery and superior choice of songs.
Albums: *What About Me* (1968), *This Was My Way* (1970), *Snowbird* (1970), *Anne Murray* (1971), *Talk It Over In The Morning* (1971), *Annie* (1972), *Anne Murray And Glen Campbell* (1972), *Danny's Song* (1973), *Love Song* (1974), *Country* (1974), *Highly Prized Possession* (1974), *Together* (1975), *Love Song* (1975), *Keeping In Touch* (1976), *Let's Keep It That Way* (1977), *Hippo In My Tub* (1979), *New Kind Of Feeling* (1979), *I'll Always Love You* (1980), *Somebody's Waiting* (1980), *Where Do You Go To When You Dream* (1981), *Christmas Wishes* (1981), *The Hottest Night Of The Year* (1982), *A Little Good News* (1983), *Heart Over Mind* (1985), *Something To Talk About* (1986), *Talk It Over In The Morning* (1986), *Christmas Wishes* (1986), *Songs Of The Heart* (1987), *Harmony* (1989), *Croonin'* (1993). Compilations: *A Country Collection* (1980), *Greatest Hits* (1980), *The Very Best Of Anne Murray* (1981), *Special Collection* (1990), *Croonin'* (1994).

Murray, David

b. 19 February 1955, Oakland, California, USA. Murray is regarded by many critics as the most important tenor saxophonist of his generation. While he was still an infant his family moved from the Oakland ghetto to integrated Berkeley. He learnt music from his mother, a church pianist, and took up the tenor saxophone at the age of nine years old, learning the fingering from his clarinet-playing older brother. Three years later he was leading R&B bands. On the day that Martin Luther King was assassinated he was asked, as president of the student body at his junior high school, to address his fellow students. He led the soul revue, the Notations Of Soul, in a two-hour session which helped avert violence in response to Dr. King's murder. He continued formal study at Pomona College, Los Angeles, where he was taught by Stanley Crouch and Margaret Kohn. He and Crouch later worked together as part of Black Music Infinity and in Murray's 1975 Trio. It was with this unit that Murray re-located to New York, becoming involved with the loft circuit of experimental musicians. He linked up with three of these (**Hamiet Bluiett**, **Oliver Lake**, and **Julius Hemphill**) to form the **World Saxophone Quartet** in 1977. In the early 80s he joined the comparable Clarinet Summit, led by **John Carter**. He also worked with Curtis Clarke, **Billy Bang**, **Fred Hopkins**, Phil Wilson, **Sunny Murray**, **Jack DeJohnette** (in duo and in the drummer's group Special Edition) and **James 'Blood' Ulmer** (with whom he also played in Music Revelation Ensemble), and, while still in California, he had played with **Bobby Bradford**, **James Newton**, **Arthur Blythe** and **Butch Morris**, the latter still supplying him with many of the tunes he records. In 1978 he established a big band, out of which distilled the more economically and logistically viable Octet.

Throughout the 80s he led a quartet as well as the octet and, when feasible, the big band. Each of these units has been highly-praised throughout the world. Murray's bands offer well-crafted, distinctive writing and adventurous, though equally well-crafted, solos. His own playing on tenor, soprano, bass-clarinet and flute welds traces of his R&B and gospel background, the freedom of **Albert Ayler** (one of his early heroes) and the classic quality of players like **Paul Gonsalves** into an individualist whole. He told Francis Davis: 'When I first came to New York I was playing more melodically, almost the way I play now. If you listen to my records chronologically you'll hear me gradually laying off the overblown notes, but I still use energy techniques as a kind of capper to my solos.' He is both a polished and a passionate improviser, whose other influences include **Coleman Hawkins**, **Ben Webster** and **Duke Ellington**. To date, the best of his work can be found among the many albums he recorded for **Black Saint** during the 80s (notably *Ming*, *Morning Song*, *Children*, *The Hill* and *I Want To Talk About You*) together with *Ming's Samba* on the Portrait label, and the set of four 1988 quartet records released by DIW: *Deep River*, *Lovers*, *Spirituals* and *Ballads*. His 90s output is (so far) considerable and to a high standard. Highly recommended are *Death Of A Sideman*, *Fast Life*, *Real Deal* and *Tenors*. Quite how many more albums he will have put out by the end of the century is mind expanding.

Selected albums: with others *Wild Flowers 4* (1976), *Flowers For Albert* (West Wind 1976), *Low Class Conspiracy* (1976), with Synthesis *Sentiments* (1976), with James Newton *Solomon's Sons* (1977), *And Low Class Conspiracy Volume 1: Penthouse Jazz* (1977), *And Low Class Conspiracy Volume 2: Holy Siege On Intrigue* (1977), *Live At The Lower Manhattan Ocean Club Vols 1 & 2* (India Navigation 1978), *Last Of The Hipmen* (1978), *Let The Music Take You* (1978), *Sur-Real Saxophone* (1978), *Conceptual Saxophone* (1978), *Organic Saxophone* (1978), *Interboogieology* (Black Saint 1978), *The London Concert* (1979), *3D Family* (Hat Art 1979), *Sweet Lovely* (Black Saint 1980), *Solo Live Vols 1 & 2* (1980), with Music Revelation Ensemble *No Wave* (1980), *Ming* (Black Saint 1980), *Home* (Black Saint 1982), *Murray's Steps* (Black Saint 1983), with Wilber Morris *Wilber Force* (1983), *Morning Song* (Black Saint 1984), with Clarinet Summit *Concert At The Public Theater* (1984, rec. 1982), *Live At Sweet Basil Volume 1* (Black Saint 1985), *Children* (Black Saint 1985), with Clarinet Summit *Concert At The Public Theater Volume 2* (1985, rec 1982), *Live At Sweet Basil Volume 2* (Black Saint 1986), *David Murray* (1986), with Jack DeJohnette *In Our Style* (DIW 1986), *New Life* (1987), with Randy Weston *The Healers* (Black Saint 1987), *The Hill* (Black Saint 1988, rec. 1986), with McCoy Tyner and others *Blues For Coltrane* (1988), *Lovers* (1988), with Clarinet Summit *Southern Belles* (1988), *Music Revelation Ensemble* (1988), *The People's Choice* (1988), *I Want To Talk About You* (Black Saint 1989, rec 1986), *Deep River* (DIW 1989), *Ming's Samba* (1989), with Kahil El' Zabar *Golden Sea* (1989), with others *Lucky Four* (Tutu 1990), *Ballads* (DIW 1990, rec. 1988), *Spirituals* (DIW 1990, rec. 1988), with Music Revelation Ensemble *Elec. Jazz* (1990), *Hope Scope* (Black Saint 1991, rec. 1987), *Special Quartet* (1991), *Live At The Peace Church* (1991, rec. 1976), *Remembrances* (DIW 1992), *Shakill's Warrior* (DIW 1992), *Big Band* (DIW 1992), *A Sanctuary Within* (Black Saint 1992), with Music Revelation Ensemble *After Dark* (1992), with Dave Burrell *In Concert* (1992), *Fast Life* (DIW 1993), with Milford Graves *Real Deal* (DIW 1993, rec. 1991), *Death Of A Sideman* (DIW 1993, rec 1991), *The Jazzpar Prize* (Enja 1993), *Tea For Two* (Fresh Sound 1993, rec 1990), *Black And Red* (Red Baron 1993), *Ballads For Bass Clarinet* (DIW 1993) *Live '93 Acoustic Octfunk* (Sound Hills 1994), *Tenors* (DIW 1994), *Picasso* (DIW 1994), *Body And Soul* (Black Saint 1994), *Saxman* (Red Baron 1994), *Jazzosaurus Rex* (Red Baron 1994).

Murray, Pauline, And The Invisible Girls

Following the demise of **Penetration**, Murray (b. 8 March 1958, Durham, England) departed, with bass guitarist Robert Blamire, to form a new group. Producers **Martin Hannett** and Steve Hopkins were claimed to be the 'Invisible' members, while the actual line-up consisted of John Maher (ex-**Buzzcocks**), Dave Rowbotham and Dave Hassell. The Invisible Girls would also act as studio and road band for **John Cooper Clarke**, and include among its ranks **Pete Shelley**, Karl Burns (the **Fall**), **Bill Nelson**, Vini Reilly (**Durutti Column**) and numerous others. A self-titled album and single, 'Dream Sequence', announced the arrival of Pauline Murray And The Invisible Girls, gaining strong critical support. The album featured guest appearances from Wayne Hussey (ex-**Dead Or Alive**, **Sisters Of Mercy**, the **Mission**) in addition to the previously mentioned Invisible luminaries. Despite this fine collection, the band split after two subsequent single releases from it: 'Searching For Heaven' and 'Mr. X'. Blamire went into production work while Murray took two years away from the music industry. 'I just . . . retreated from music really, just backed right out and decided what I wanted to do. Which took about a year to two years . . . I think Penetration to the Invisible Girls was such a vast leap that it lost everyone. It lost us as well'. Blamire and Murray reunited in the similarly short-lived Pauline Murray And The Storm.

Album: *Pauline Murray And The Invisible Girls* (1981).

Murray, Ruby

b. 29 March 1935, Belfast, Northern Ireland. One of

the most popular singers in the UK during the 50s, Murray toured Ulster as a child singer in various variety shows, and, after being spotted by producer Richard Afton, made her television debut at the age of 12. Stringent Irish laws regarding child performers held her back for two years, and she returned to school in Belfast until she was 14. In 1954 she travelled to London in comedian Tommy Morgan's touring revue, *Mrs. Mulligan's Hotel*, and was again seen by Afton, at the famous Metropolitan Theatre, Edgware Road. He offered her the part of resident singer on BBC television's *Quite Contrary*, replacing **Joan Regan** who was about to leave. Signed to UK Columbia by recording manager and musical director **Ray Martin**, Murray's first release, 'Heartbeat', made the UK Top 5 in 1954, and was followed by 'Softly, Softly'. The latter reached number 1 in 1955, and became an ideal theme song, reflecting her shy, indigenous image. In the early part of 1955 Murray had five singles in the Top 20 at the same time, an extraordinary record that lasted until the emergence of **Madonna** in the 80s. Murray's hits included 'Happy Days And Lonely Nights', 'Let Me Go Lover', 'If Anyone Finds This, I Love You' (with Anne Warren), 'Evermore', 'I'll Come When You Call', 'Real Love', 'Goodbye Jimmy, Goodbye' and 'You Are My First Love'. She sang the last number over the opening titles of the film musical ***It's Great To Be Young***. Murray's own film appearances included the comedy, *A Touch Of The Sun*, with Frankie Howerd and Dennis Price. During a hectic period in the mid-50s, she had her own television show, starred at the London Palladium in *Painting The Town* with **Norman Wisdom**, appeared in a Royal Command Performance, and toured the USA, Malta and North Africa. In 1957, while appearing in a summer season at Blackpool, she met Bernie Burgess, a member of the vocal group, the Jones Boys. They married in secret 10 days later. Burgess became her personal manager and, during the early 60s, they toured as a double act. In 1970 Murray had some success with 'Change Your Mind', and released an album with the same title which included contemporary songs such as 'Raindrops Keep Falling On My Head', and re-vamped some of her hits. In 1989 *Ruby Murray's EMI Years* included other songs regularly featured in her act such as 'Mr. Wonderful', 'Scarlet Ribbons' and 'It's The Irish In Me'. In the 90s, based in Torquay, Devon, with her second husband, impresario Ray Lamar, she was still performing in cabaret and in nostalgia shows with other stars of the 50s.

Selected albums: *Endearing Young Charms* (1959), *Ruby* (1960), *Ruby Murray Successes* (1962), *Irish-And Proud Of It* (1962), with various artists *St. Patrick's Day* (1964), *Your Favourite Colleen* (c.60s), *The Spinning Wheel* (c.60s), *This Is Ireland* (c.60s), *Change Your Mind* (1970). Compilation: *Ruby Murray's EMI Years* (1989).

Murray, Sunny

b. James Marcellus Arthur Murray, 21 September 1937, Idabel, Oklahoma, USA. Murray is probably the most influential and certainly the most controversial drummer to emerge from the 60s new wave. He began to teach himself drums at the age of nine, subsequently flirting briefly with trumpet and trombone. In 1956 he moved to New York and worked with figures as diverse as **Henry 'Red' Allen**, **Willie 'The Lion' Smith**, **Jackie McLean**, Rocky Boyd, **Ted Curson** and **Cecil Taylor**. In 1963 he went with Taylor and **Jimmy Lyons** to Europe, where he joined **Albert Ayler** in the legendary trio that produced *Ghosts* and *Spiritual Unity*. He later played on several more Ayler albums, including *New York Eye And Ear Control*, *Bells* and *Spirits Rejoice*, while Ayler guested on Murray's debut, *Sunny's Time Now*. He lived in France from 1968-71, then moved to Philadelphia, Pennsylvania, USA, where he worked with an equally influential drummer from the hard bop era, **Philly Joe Jones**. In the 70s and 80s Murray remained extremely active, co-leading the Untouchable Factor, running a trio (that included tenor tyro **David Murray** - no relation) and recording with pianists **Don Pullen** (*Applecores*) and **Alex Von Schlippenbach** (on the duo *Smoke*) as well as renewing his old association with Cecil Taylor (*It Is In The Brewing Luminous*) and Jimmy Lyons. A player with an abstract and oblique approach to the beat, paying at least as much attention to the cymbals as the drums, Murray nevertheless creates a strong feeling of pulse for the music. He has played with most of the major figures of *avant garde* jazz, including **Archie Shepp**, **Ornette Coleman**, **Don Cherry**, **John Coltrane**, **John Tchicai**, **Roswell Rudd**, and **Grachan Moncur III**.

Albums: *Sunny's Time Now* (1966), *Sunny Murray Quintet* (1966), *Sunny Murray* (ESP 1969), *Big Chief* (1969), *Homage To Africa* (1969), *Sunshine* (1969), *An Even Break (Never Gives A Sucker)* (Affinity 1970), *New American Music Vol. 1* (1973), with others *Wildflowers Vols. 1 & 5* (1977), with Untouchable Factor *Charred Earth* (1977), *Applecores* (Philly Jazz 1978), *Live At Moers Festival* (Moers Music 1979), *African Magic* (1979), with Jimmy Lyons *Jump Up/What To Do About* (1981), *Indelicacy* (West Wind 1987), with Alex Von Schlippenbach *Smoke* (1990).

Murtceps

This Australian outfit (aka the Indelible Murtceps) were the alter-ego of the Melbourne group **Spectrum**, one of Australia's most innovative, experimental bands. Formed in 1971, it allowed the members of Spectrum to sufficiently finance the mother group by performing as a dance band. This 'prostitution of their art' spawned the singles 'We Are Indelible' and 'Indelible Shuffle', and an album on the **Harvest** label. These uptempo, lighter songs were all original **Mike Rudd**

material. The bands co-existed for 12 months before both were disbanded.
Album: *Warts Up Your Nose* (1973). Compilation: with Spectrum *Testimonial* (1973).

Murvin, Junior

b. c.1949, Port Antonio, Jamaica, West Indies. Murvin first recorded for producers **Sonia Pottinger** and **Derrick Harriott** in the early 70s as Junior Soul (not to be confused with the New York-based reggae singer of the same name). 'Solomon', a traditional Jamaican air, sold fairly well in 1972, but shortly after, Murvin vanished from the public eye. In 1976 he turned up, guitar in hand, at **Lee Perry**'s Black Ark studio in Kingston, with a song that he had been working on for some time. No-one was aware that this singer, now calling himself Junior Murvin, had ever recorded before, but Perry liked what he heard and within weeks 'Police And Thieves' was the biggest-selling Jamaican record of the year. Its popularity crossed the Atlantic to the UK and, released on **Island**, became the anthem for that year's violence-troubled Notting Hill Carnival. Perry recorded another couple of versions of the rhythm before issuing a strong album of the same title in 1977. The single was finally a UK chart hit in 1978. Junior's **Curtis Mayfield**-styled falsetto (he covered Mayfield's 'People Get Ready' and 'Closer Together') worked well with Perry's silky, complex arrangements, but the pair never put together another album; Perry was about to crack up and demolish his studio. Murvin moved on to work with **Joe Gibbs**, **Mikey Dread**, **Henry 'Junjo' Lawes** and **Prince Jammy**, but he has never quite captured the moment as 'Police And Thieves' did. Murvin's influence spilled over into rock, however, with 'Police And Thieves' right-on rude-boy image suiting the **Clash**'s first album.
Albums: *Police And Thieves* (Island 1977), *Bad Man Posse* (Dread At The Controls 1982), *Muggers In The Street* (Greensleeves 1984), *Apartheid* (1986), *Signs And Wonders* (Live & Love 1989).

Muscle Beach Party

This 1964 entry to the American International Pictures production line of 'beach' movies starred genre stalwarts **Frankie Avalon** and **Annette** Funicello. The path of true love is threatened when the former becomes attracted to a wealthy socialite - much to the chagrin of her body-building beau, Mr. Galaxy - but Avalon returns to Funicello in time for the closing reel. Rising Tamla/**Motown** star 'Little' **Stevie Wonder** provides a welcome cameo, performing 'Happy Street', while surf guitar maestro **Dick Dale** plays the title tune and 'My First Love'. **Brian Wilson** of the **Beach Boys** and then-partner **Gary Usher** composed much of the soundtrack material, including Donna Loren's superbly rumbustuous 'Muscle Bustle'. Annette subsequently re-recorded several songs from the film for a solo outing, *Muscle Beach Party*, issued on the Disney outlet, Buena Vista.

Muscle Shoals

Situated in Alabama between the focal centres of Nashville and Memphis, Muscle Shoals was the natural melting pot for southern country-soul. During the 50s the Fairlanes, which included Rick Hall (b. 31 January 1932, Franklin County, Mississippi, USA) and **Billy Sherrill** in their line-up, were one of many groups performing in the area. In 1958 the two musicians formed a partnership with Tom Stafford, who ran a basic recording studio in a room above his father's drugstore. Entitled 'Fame: Florence Alabama Music Enterprises', the rudimentary company fell apart two years later, but the terms of the split left Hall with the name while Sherrill travelled to Nashville where he became a successful producer. Hall then purchased a tobacco warehouse in Muscle Shoals and transformed it into a four-track studio. He assembled a houseband with David Briggs (piano), Terry Thompson (guitar), Norbert Putnam (bass), Jerry Carrigan (drums) - and scored a smash hit with **Arthur Alexander**'s 'You Better Move On'. Having sold the master to **Dot Records**, Rick moved to larger premises at 603 East Avalon Avenue, where the studio remains situated. Over the next few years Hall established Fame as both a record label and recording centre. Hits for the **Tams** and **Joe Tex** cemented its reputation, although the departure to Nashville of Briggs, Putnam and Carrigan was a serious blow. A second classic houseband was forged around Jimmy Johnson (guitar), Jimmy Lowe (bass), **Spooner Oldham** (piano) and Roger Hawkins (drums). **Jerry Wexler** took **Wilson Pickett** to Fame in 1966, inaugurating a fruitful period for his **Atlantic** label and the studio. Many superb sessions followed, including those for **Aretha Franklin**, **King Curtis** and **Arthur Conley**, while newer musicians - Roger Hood (bass) and **Duane Allman** (guitar) - were drawn into the circle. However Hall's autocratic methods resulted in a second defection, when Hawkins, Beckett, Johnson and Hood left *en masse* to found their own set-up, Muscle Shoals Sound, in 1969. Hall continued undeterred but by the 70s, the studio was being increasingly used for pop and country productions. He closed down the Fame label in 1974, and tired of losing rhythm sections, latterly worked as an executive producer for his song publishing empire. The rival Muscle Shoals Sound was sited at 3614 Jackson Highway in nearby Florence. The new studio initially acquired much of Atlantic's R&B contracts, but diversified into other areas when the label directed its work to Criteria in Miami. **Paul Simon**, **Rod Stewart**, the **Rolling Stones** and **Bob Seger** are among the many acts to record successfully at Muscle Shoals, enabling the studio to move to a larger site on the banks of the Tennessee River.

Mushroom

This group was an early, if somewhat **Horslips**-like attempt to marry drug laced hippie lyrics with Irish traditional dance tunes. Both the name of the band and the cover of the album reveal a good deal about the music they played.
Album: *Early One Morning* (1973).

Music Box Revue

Irving Berlin and producer Sam H. Harris built their brand new Music Box Theatre on New York's West 45th Street as a showcase for Berlin's prolific output of songs. The composer had contributed many of his early numbers, such as 'A Pretty Girl Is Like A Melody' and 'You'd Be Surprised', to **Florenz Ziegfeld**'s elegant productions, and this lavish revue, a stylish mixture of comedy and songs, was the first of four annual editions to play at his own cosy 1,010-seater Music Box. It opened on 22 September 1921, with a cast that included William Collier, Wilda Bennett, Paul Frawley, Ivy Sawyer, Joseph Santley, Sam Bernard, and the Brox Sisters. Berlin himself, made a brief appearance in a scene with Miriam Hopkins, an actress who went on to a successful Hollywood career in the 30s, in films such as *Dr Jekyll And Mr Hyde*, *Trouble In Paradise*, and *Becky Sharp*. 'Say It With Music' was the show's outstanding number, sung by Bennett and Frawley, and it became a recurring theme during the rest of the series. The other songs included 'Everybody Step', 'The Schoolhouse Blues', 'In A Cozy Kitchenette Apartment', 'My Little Book Of Poetry', 'They Call It Dancing', and 'The Legend Of The Pearls'. Hassard Short, who was just starting out on a career during which he would be acclaimed for his imaginative design and staging, was responsible for this show, and the next two, giving way to John Murray Anderson for the final edition. Short's innovative work was recognized as a major factor in the *Music Box Revue*'s impressive run of 440 performances. The 1922 production marked the Broadway debut of several future Broadway favourites, including the actor and singer William Gaxton, who later made a habit of appearing in musicals with one of America's most cherished clowns, Victor Moore, and the comedy team of ex-vaudevillians Bobby Clark and Paul McCullough. Comedienne **Charlotte Greenwood**, another artist who subsequently spent much of her time in Hollyood and will be remembered particularly for her portrayal of Aunt Eller in the film of ***Oklahoma!***, was also in the cast, along with Grace La Rue, Margaret and Dorothy McCarthy, and the Fairbanks Twins. The songs included 'I'm Looking For A Daddy Long Legs', 'Crinoline Days', 'Will She Come From The East?', 'Pack Up Your Sins And Go To The Devil', and 'Lady Of The Evening', and the show ran for 330 performances. *The Music Box Revue of 1923* - Mark III - had some sketches by **George S. Kaufman** and Robert Benchley, who also personally introduced his famous 'Treasurer's Report'. Among the rest of the cast were Frank Tinney, Joseph Santley, and Ivy Sawyer. **Grace Moore**, who sang with the Metropolitan Opera in the late 20s, had the charming 'Tell Me A Bedtime Story', and 'The Waltz Of Long Ago', and she duettted with John Steel on 'An Orange Grove In California' and the plaintive 'What'll I Do?'. The latter song, one of Berlin's all-time standards, was interpolated during the run of the show. Audiences for these revues were gradully declining - the 1923 version ran for 273 performances, and the final, 1924 edition, only lasted for 184. For that one, Moore was back again, as were Clarke and McCullough, along with Claire Luce, Carl Randall, and Ula Sharon. The star was funny girl **Fanny Brice**, who sang 'Don't Send Me Back To Petrograd' and 'I Want To Be A Ballet Dancer'. Moore had the lovely 'Tell Her In Springtime' and 'Rockabye Baby', and, with Oscar Shaw, she also introduced the wistful 'All Alone'. The 1923 edition also played at the Palace Theatre in London, where it starred **Jessie Matthews**, Fred Duprez, and Joseph Santley. This series of shows served as a launching pad for Irving Berlin's long and illustrious career which peaked with ***Annie Get Your Gun*** in 1946, but endured for much longer than that.

Music Explosion

Formed in Ohio, USA. Jamie Lyons (lead vocals), Don (Tudor) Atkins (lead guitar), Rick Nesta (rhythm guitar), Butch Stahl (bass guitar/organ) and Bob Avery (harmonia) sprang to fame in 1967 with 'Little Bit O' Soul' which reached number 2 in the US chart. This driving, irresistible song was written by UK songwriting duo John Carter and Ken Lewis and had originally been recorded, unsuccessfully, by the Little Darlings. The Music Explosion secured another minor hit with 'Sunshine Games', but were unable to sustain a permanent career and the group was subsequently absorbed into the **Kasenetz/Katz** 'bubblegum' circus. Singer Lyons later emerged in the Capitol City Rockets, an early 70s anglophile pop band whose lone album was critically acclaimed.
Album: *Little Bit O' Soul* (1967).

Music In The Air

This delightful musical comedy, with just a hint of operetta, and a score by **Jerome Kern** and **Oscar Hammerstein**, opened at the Alvin Theatre in New York on 8 November 1932. With America staggering to its feet following the terrible Depression, Hammerstein chose to set the story in modern-day Bavaria. Music teacher Dr. Walter Lessing (Al Shean) travels from his home in Edenhorf to the the big city of Munich, in an effort to impress an old colleague with his new composition, 'I've Told Ev'ry Little Star'. He is accompanied by his daughter, Sieglinde (Katherine

Carrington), who loves to perform her father's compositions, and her friend, Karl (Walter Slezak). They are all introduced to the fiery actress and singer, Frieda Hatzfeld (Natalie Hall), who is rehearsing a musical show which has been written by her long-time lover, Bruno Mahler (Tullio Carminati). When Frieda flounces out just before the opening night, Bruno, who is quite partial to the young Sieglinde, tells her to 'go out there and come back a star'. Unfortunately, the young girl is totally lacking in star quality, and she and her father realise this, and decide to return to their quiet life in the country. The score is regarded as one of Kern's finest, with the songs skifully and sympathetically integrated into the plot. They included 'The Song Is You', 'There's A Hill Beyond A Hill', 'One More Dance', 'In Egern On The Tegern Sea', 'And Love Was Born', 'I'm Alone', 'I Am So Eager', 'We Belong Together', 'When Spring Is In The Air', and, of course, 'I've Told Ev'ry Little Star', which was introduced by Walter Slezak. *Music In The Air*'s Broadway run of 342 performances was followed by a further 275 in London, where **Mary Ellis** took the role of Frieda. The show returned to New York, with a revised book, for a brief spell in 1951. The 1934 film version starred Gloria Swanson, John Boles and Al Shean.

Music Machine

Formed in 1965 as the Ragamuffins by Sean Bonniwell (b. 1940, San Jose, California, USA; vocals/guitar), Keith Olsen (bass) and Ron Edgar (drums), the group became the Music Machine on the addition of Mark Landon (guitar) and Doug Rhodes (organ). The quintet is best recalled for a magnificent 1966 release, 'Talk Talk', one of the most exciting singles to emerge from America's garage-band genre. Several further excellent releases followed, all of which were penned by Bonniwell. Mismanagement prevented the group from achieving the success of contemporaries the **Seeds**, the **Doors** or **Love**, and the original members began to drift away. Holly McKinley (organ), Joe Bludd (guitar), Fred Thomas (bass) and Jerry Thomas (drums), augmented Sean for the Music Machine's later releases and the group's second album, *Bonniwell Music Machine*, featured material from both line-ups. Bonniwell subsequently abandoned the name and released a solo album, *T.S. Bonniwell*, in 1970. Following years of inactivity, the singer became a born-again Christian, and relaunched his career at the end of the 80s. Of the original line-up, Keith Olsen later became a successful producer for **Fleetwood Mac** and the **Grateful Dead**, while Edgar and Rhodes worked with several Los Angeles-based studio groups, including Sagittarius and the **Millenium**.

Albums: *(Turn On) The Music Machine* (1966), *The Bonniwell Music Machine* (1968). Compilation: *The Best Of The Music Machine* (1985).

Music Man, The (Film Musical)

Despite studio chief Jack Warner's efforts to get a male superstar such as Cary Grant to play the lead, **Robert Preston** was eventually invited to recreate his magnificent Broadway performance for this enjoyable screen version which was released in 1962. So, film-goers the world over were able to enjoy the sight of Professor Harold Hill (Preston), a con-man of the highest order, who descends on the town Iowa with the intention of selling (non-existent) musical instruments to the parents of the parish in order that their children can form a brass band - which he will lead. Such is his charm, that, after overcoming the initial resistance of Marion Paroo (**Shirley Jones**), the Balzac-loving librarian, they not only fall in love, but he is absolved of all charges of deception after deciding not to make a run for it after all. There were some lovely performances in the supporting roles, such as the Professor's assistant and look-out man (Buddy Hackett), the always-blustering mayor (Paul Ford) and his lady wife (Hermione Gingold), and Marion's mother-with-the-blarney (Pert Kelton). Other parts were played by Ronnie Howard, Timmy Everett, Susan Luckey, Mary Wickes, and the harmonising Buffalo Bills. **Meredith Willson**'s songs were all gems in their way, and included 'Rock Island', 'Iowa Stubborn', 'Piano Lesson', 'If You Don't Mind Me Saying So', 'Goodnight My Someone', 'Sincere', 'The Sadder But Wiser Girl', 'Pick-A-Little, Talk-A-Little', 'Marion The Librarian', 'Being In Love', 'Gary, Indiana', 'The Wells Fargo Wagon', 'Lida Rose', 'Will I Ever Tell You?', 'Shipoopi', and 'Till There Was You'. Preston's musical highspot came with 'Ya Got Trouble', in which he warned the population about the perils of having a pool table in their midst, and, in the film's exuberant finalé, he was at the head of the procession during the rousing 'Seventy Six Trombones'. Onna White was the choreographer, and musical director Ray Heindorf won an Oscar for his scoring. Marion Hargrove's screenplay was adapted from Meredith Willson's stage libretto. The producer-director was Morton DaCosta, and the film was shot in Technicolor and Technirama. There was some dismay at the time that **Barbara Cook**, who created the role of Marion on stage, was not asked to repeat her role on the screen. As it transpired, Shirley Jones was fine - and Robert Preston sensational.

Music Man, The (Stage Musical)

This musical came to the Majestic Theatre in New York on 19 December 1957 after experiencing a good many difficulties out of town. With book, music and lyrics by **Meredith Willson**, the show had undergone several rewrites but the author's persistence paid off, and on opening night the audience was caught up in the revivalist enthusiasm of the show's characters. The story concerns Harold Hill, an itinerant con-man who persuades the citizens of River City, Iowa, that what they need is a boys' band. He will teach them to play - and even supply the instruments. Naturally, not even a penny whistle materialises. *The Music Man* was filled with engaging old-fashioned charm with songs ranging from the soulful 'Goodnight, My Someone' and 'Till There Was You' to the rousing 'Seventy-Six Trombones', by way of 'Marian The Librarian', 'Shipoopi', 'My White Knight', 'The Sadder-But-Wiser Girl', 'Pick-A-Little, Talk-A-Little', 'Gary, Indiana', 'Wells Fargo Wagon', 'Sincere' ('How can there be any sin in sincere?/Where is the good in goodbye'), 'Piano Lesson' and 'Lida Rose'/'Will I Ever Tell You'. In casting film actor **Robert Preston**, who had never before danced or sung, in the central role of Harold Hill, the producers took a big chance because many of Willson's songs were far more complex than they appeared on the surface. As it turned out, it was inspired casting, with Preston ably charming his way through a minefield of counter melodies, rhythmic dialogue and strutting dance routines to earn rapturous applause and critical praise. He had a *tour de force* with 'Trouble', a grim warning regarding the moral danger of introducing a pool table into the community ('That game with the fifteen numbered balls is the Devil's tool'). Co-starring with Preston was **Barbara Cook** as Marion Paroo; other cast members included David Burns, Iggie Wolfington, Helen Raymond, Pert Kelton, and The Buffalo Bills. The show enjoyed success, and won Tony Awards for best musical, actor (Preston), featured actress (Cook), featured actor (Burns), and musical director (Herbert Green). Several companies toured the US, and the show was also staged in Europe; the 1961 London production, which ran for 395 performances, starred Hollywood heartthrob Van Johnson. Revivals were presented on Broadway in 1965, 1980, and 1993. A film version was released in 1962 with Shirley Jones as Marian and, thankfully, Robert Preston, thus allowing millions to appreciate the exuberance of his magnificent, larger-than-life performance as Professor Harold Hill.

Musical Youth

Formed at Duddeston Manor School, Birmingham, England, this pop/reggae-influenced group featured two sets of brothers, Kelvin and Michael Grant and Junior and Patrick Waite (d. February 18 1993). The latter pair's father, Fred Waite, was a former member of Jamaican group the **Techniques**, and sang lead with Junior at the start of the group's career in the late 70s. Although schoolboys, the group managed to secure gigs at certain Birmingham pubs and released a single, 'Political'/'Generals' on local label 021 Records. An appearance on BBC DJ **John Peel**'s evening show brought further attention to the group and they were signed to MCA Records. By that time, founding father Fred Waite had backed down to be replaced by Dennis Seaton as lead singer. During the winter of 1982, the group issued one of the fastest selling singles of the year in 'Pass The Dutchie'. Based on the **Mighty Diamonds**' 'Pass The Kouchie' (a song about marijuana), the title had been subtly altered to feature the patois 'Dutchie' (literally a 'cooking pot'). The infectious enthusiasm of the group's performance captured the public's imagination and propelled the record to number 1 in the UK charts. A US Top 10 hit also followed. The catchy follow-up 'Youth Of Today' also reached the UK Top 20 and early in 1983 'Never Gonna Give You Up' climbed to number 6. Minor successes with 'Heartbreaker' and 'Tell Me Why' were succeeded by a surprise collaboration with **Donna Summer** on the UK Top 20 hit 'Unconditional Love'. A revival of **Desmond Dekker**'s '007' saw them back in the Top 30, but after one final hit with 'Sixteen', they fell from commercial grace and subsequently split up in 1985 when Seaton left the band. Plans to reform were scotched when Patrick Waite, who had gone on to a career of juvenile crime, died of natural causes while awaiting a court appearance on drug charges. The Grant brothers remain involved in music, while Seaton has released a solo set and formed his own band, XMY.
Albums: *The Youth Of Today* (MCA 1982), *Different Style* (MCA 1983), Dennis Seaton *Imagine That* (Bellaphon, Germany 1989).
Further reading: *Musical Youth: Their Own Story*, no editor listed.

Musicraft Records

The company began recording jazz in the mid-40s. Guided by Albert Marx, Musicraft reissued much of the Guild catalogue of early bop recordings. Musicraft's mainstream roster was impressive, including **Artie Shaw**, **Duke Ellington**, **Sarah Vaughan** and **Georgie Auld**, while bop was represented by **Dizzie Gillespie** and others. In the early 50s, Musicraft was sold to Pickwick and its fortunes declined. In the late 70s, Marx reissued some of Musicraft's most important material on his Trend and Discovery labels.

Musselwhite, Charlie

b. 31 January 1944, Mississippi, USA. Musselwhite grew up in Memphis where he was inspired to learn harmonica by hearing **Sonny Terry** on the radio. In 1962, Musselwhite moved to Chicago, performing with **Johnny Young**, **Big Joe Williams** and **J.B. Hutto**. He also linked up with another white blues musician, **Mike Bloomfield** before the latter went on to join **Paul Butterfield**'s group, Musselwhite emigrated to California, making his first solo recordings for **Vanguard**. From 1974-75 he made two albums for Chris Strachwitz's Arhoolie label and later cut an instructional record for **Stefan Grossman**'s Kickin' Mule. A growing reputation made Musselwhite a

favourite on the festival circuits in the USA and Europe. *Mellow Dee* was recorded during a German tour while *Cambridge Blues* was recorded live at Britain's leading folk festival for **Mike Vernon**'s **Blue Horizon** label. In 1990, Musselwhite joined Alligator, where **John Lee Hooker** guested on his 1991 album. Although heavily influenced by **Little Walter**, **Louis Myers** and **Junior Wells** Musselwhite has made his own niche and is probably today's most popular white blues harmonica player.
Albums: *Stand Back, Here Comes Charlie Musselwhite* (1967), *Charlie Musselwhite* (1968), *Stone Blues* (1968), *Tennessee Woman* (1969), *Memphis, Tennessee* (1969), *Taking My Time* (1974), *Going Back Down South* (1975), *The Harmonica According To Charlie Musselwhite* (1979), *Curtain Call* (1982), *Memphis, Tennessee* (1984), *Mellow Dee* (1986), *Cambridge Blues* (1988), *Tell Me Where Have All The Good Times Gone* (1988), *Ace Of Harps* (1990), *Signature* (1991), *Memphis Charlie* (1993), *In My Time...* (Alligator 1994).

Musso, Vido

b. 13 January 1913, Carrini, Sicily, d. 9 January 1982. Musso's family emigrated to the USA in 1920, settling in Detroit, where he began playing clarinet. Relocating to Los Angeles in 1930, he became friendly with **Stan Kenton** and the two men worked together in various bands, including one led by Musso and one they co-led. In the mid-30s Musso, by now playing tenor saxophone, joined **Benny Goodman** and thereafter played in the big bands of **Gene Krupa**, **Harry James**, **Tommy Dorsey** and others, rejoining Kenton in 1946. He stayed only a year and then formed another band of his own, continuing to lead jazz-orientated dancebands until the mid-50s. An entirely untutored musician, Musso's powerful, buzzing sound and aggressive solo style inclined him to the more extrovert areas of jazz and big band music. Untouched by the changes which took place in jazz in the 40s, Musso became something of an anachronism and for the rest of his career he played in relatively obscure settings, often in Las Vegas show bands.
Albums: *Vido Musso And His Orchestra* i (1954), *Vido Musso And His Orchestra* ii (c.1955), *One Night Stand With Vido Musso* (Savoy 1982, 1947 recording). Compilations: *The Indispensable Benny Goodman Vols 3/4* (1936-37 recordings), *Stan Kenton's Greatest Hits* (1943-51 recordings), *Vido Musso's All Stars* (1946 recordings), *Loaded* (Savoy 1993).

Musto And Bones

A highly successful, albeit brief, liaison between **Tommy Musto** and **Frankie Bones**, which resulted in success with singles such as 'Dangerous On The Dance Floor' and 'All I Want Is To Get Away'. In retrospect 'Dangerous' might well have achieved more signifcant crossover success had it been more fully backed by the duo's record company, with a long time delay between its UK and domestic release. The partnership eventually dissolved after a solitary album as Bones spent more of his time DJing, while Musto remained in New York to oversee their company and studio projects: 'Basically, we also grew apart musically' is how Musto remembers this period. He would go on to become a hugely successful remixer to the stars, while his former partner persevered on the live circuit. The duo were still contracted to **Beggars Banquet** for another album, however, and subtle, but amicable, litigation proceeded until Bones could be removed from the contract, Musto offering instead his collaboration with **Victor Simonelli**, Colourblind.
Album: *The Future Is Ours* (Citybeat 1990).

Musto, Tommy

b. c.1963, New York, USA. Formerly recognised for his hit singles as part of **Musto And Bones**, under his own steam Musto has grown to become one of dance music's prime remixing talents, with close to half a century of projects under his belt. These include many major artists attempting to dip a toe into the world of dance (**Michael Jackson**, **Gloria Estefan**, **Cyndi Lauper**, **Erasure**). Musto grew up on a diet of Philly soul, before going on to present his own mix show on WAKT alongside the then-underground talents of **Shep Pettibone** and **Tony Humphries** on Kiss FM. He began remixing for other artists, the first example of which was Junior Byron's 'Woman' for Vanguard Records, and also taught himself keyboard skills. His first major label commission was **S'Express**' 'Nothing To Lose' in the early 90s. His biggest commercial break, however, was the opportunity to remix **Michael Jackson**'s 'In The Closet', which went gold. In 1994 he formed Colourblind with **Victor Simonelli**, partially to satisfy a contract that was still extant between his former Musto And Bones partnership and **Beggars Banquet**. After removing Bones from the contract, he teamed with Simonelli and added first **Barbara Tucker** then Dina Roche. They initially provided a single, written and produced by Musto, 'He's So Fine', before an album scheduled for late 1994. He also runs the Northcott Productions empire, home to **Experimental Records**.

Mutabaruka

b. Allan Hope, Jamaica, West Indies. A **dub poet** who combines social commentary with scathing personal analysis and endearing humour. Having published several volumes of poetry (also writing for *Swing* magazine), Mutabaruka reserves his aural adventures for his most effective tirades against hypocrisy, injustice, or more particularly, stupidity. His favoured means of denouncing his enemies rests strongly with the latter, vilifying them and the contradictions of their positions by means of a languid, inviting slur. His debut album for Earl 'Chinna' Smith's High Times imprint was a

genre classic. Muta tore through a set which railed against oppression on all fronts, aided and abetted by Chinna's imaginative rhythms and arrangements. 'Everytime A Ear De Soun', from the album, was also a big hit on 45. In the interim he has ensured his position as Jamaica's most popular, radical poet, with a series of inspiring albums. Despite such militancy, his metaphorical feet are kept on the ground by his day job: operating a health food store in Jamaica and broadcasting on Jamaica's Irie FM radio station.
Selected albums: *Check It* (High Times 1982), *The Mystery Unfolds* (Shanachie 1986), *Out Cry* (Shanachie 1987), *Any Which Way* (Greensleeves 1989), *Blakk Wi Black...Kkk* (Shanachie 1991).

Mute Records

Daniel Miller's brainchild was originally set up for a single under the guise of the Normal. 'T.V.O.D.'/'Warm Leatherette' became the first Mute single in early 1978, a pioneering utilization of electronics that paved the way for Mute's alignment with synthesized and hi-tech sounds. Several hundred albums later, Mute's singular artistic identity and experimental approach still cuts a distinctive chord through an apathetic music industry. Along with **Factory** and **Rough Trade Records**, Mute has demonstrated an ability to combine aesthetic autonomy with survival. Among the label's early group roster were **Fad Gadget**, **D.A.F.** and **Depeche Mode**. It was the success of the latter that convinced many that a post-punk independent label could succeed in producing a consistent chart act. Despite the offers made to the group from major labels, Depeche Mode resisted any temptation to move - a tribute to Miller's business acumen and his faith in Depeche Mode's artistic growth. The label has also been greatly assisted by ex-Depeche Mode member Vince Clark's series of projects from **Yazoo** through to **Erasure**. Owing to Depeche Mode and Erasure's continuing international success, Mute has been able to finance less commercial acts such as **Laibach**, **Crime And The City Solution**, **Diamanda Galas** and **Nitzer Ebb**. The label's acquisition of the back catalogues of **Cabaret Voltaire**, **Can** and **Throbbing Gristle** also ensured the continued availability of these seminal artists' output. In the 90s a subsidiary operation dealing with dance and techno, **Novamute**, was established, dealing with forerunning experimental artists such as **Moby**. On a more conventional front the parent label also signed the **Inspiral Carpets**, but the long-standing artist to best combine critical and commercial approbation has undoubtedly been **Nick Cave**.
Compilation: *International* (Mute 1991).

Mutiny!

It started with a concept album, this musical adaptation of *Mutiny On The Bounty* - a marketing ploy which had been used successfully by several authors and composers in the 70s, notably **Andrew Lloyd Webber** and **Tim Rice**. This time it was the British actor and singer **David Essex** who was behind the release of the 1983 recording of *Mutiny!*, which spawned his Top 10 hit 'Tahiti'. Essex wrote the music and collaborated with librettist Richard Crane on the lyrics for the stage production which eventually sailed into the Piccadilly Theatre in London on 18 July 1985. The distinguished actor Frank Finlay played Captain Bligh, with Essex as Fletcher Christian, but the main character was a fully rigged HMS Bounty which was mounted on an hydraulic system and spectacularly recreated the high seas by rocking and rolling the entire stage to and fro. The score turned out to be 'a sequence of pastiche modal folk songs, shanties, ominous marches, and one effectively syncopated hornpipe', and included 'New World', 'Friends', 'Failed Cape Horn', 'Saucy Sal', 'Will You Come Back?', 'Falling Angels Riding', 'I'll Go No More A-Roving', and, of course, 'Tahiti'. First night reviews such as 'Bounty in blunderland . . . caught in the doldrums . . . a very leaky showboat' should really have heralded the end of the voyage, but *Mutiny!* rode the storm for a considerable time. Just as it was about to be recast with the American pop singer **David Cassidy** taking over from Essex, the show floundered and closed in September 1986 after a run of 526 performances without recovering its investment.

Mutuzudzi, Oliver

b. 1952, Harare, Zimbabwe. Along with **Thomas Mapfumo**, **Mutuzudzi** is one of Zimbabwe's most important roots-orientated vocalists and bandleaders. He formed his band the Black Spirits in the late 70s, performing a mbaqanga-influenced style with a consistent emphasis on militant protest lyrics.
Albums: *Ndipwiwo Zano* (1978), *Hwena Nadirase* (1986).

Muzsikás

This Hungarian group features Márta Sebestyén (vocals/recorder), Sándor Csoóri (bagpipes/hurdy-gurdy/viola/vocals), Mihaly Sipos (violin/zither/vocals), Péter Eri (bouzouki/turkish horn/cello/viola/vocals) and Dániel Hamar (bass/hurdy-gurdy/vocals). The ensemble specializes in traditional music from the Transylvania region of their country. Prior to 1987 Sebestyén had performed in the UK with a band called Mosaic. While still young, Sebestyén had heard her mother singing folk songs, so the interest in folk music passed on. Having won a competition at the age of 13, she was awarded a record player, which enabled her to listen to a wider sphere of music. The style of music Muzsikas play is often patronizingly called 'gypsy music', but it is far more than just a tourist attraction. Changing from a high-speed dance one minute, to a slow and melancholy air, the music covers a whole range of emotions and tempos. Péter Eri had previously played with a group called Sebo, where he learned much about the background to folk music. The original Muzsikas was a trio consisting of Sipos, Hamar and Csoóri. Eri joined them in 1978 after leaving Sebo. They recorded *Muzsikas Ketto* in Holland, but were not satisfied with the singer who had joined on lead vocals, so they asked Sebestyén to join them in 1979. A number of earlier recordings, from 1976-82, for the state-run label Hungaroton, are no longer available, but with the growing interest in Eastern European folk music, the possibility of re-releases seems likely.

Albums: *Living Hungarian Folk Music Vol.1* (1978), *The Prisoner's Song* (1986), *Nem Arról Hajnallik, Amerröl Hajnallot* (1986), *Márta Sebestyén With Muzsikas* (1987), *Blues For Transylvania* (1990), *Maramaros - The Lost Jewish Music Of Transylvania* (1993).

MX-80 Sound

Bruce Anderson (guitar), Rich Stim (guitar/keyboards/vocals/saxophone), Dave Sophiea (bass), Dave Mahoney (drums) and Jeff Armour, later replaced by Kevin Teare (drums). Formed in Bloomington, Indiana, USA, MX-80 began as a trio of Anderson, Sophiea and Armour. In late 1975 they were joined by Stim and Mahoney. A single and EP on a local label were followed by their debut *Hard Attack* for **Island Records**. By this time they were based in San Francisco. *Hard Attack* achieved considerable attention; the avowed experimentation of the group (**Captain Beefheart** and **Frank Zappa** were often cited by critics) matched by a lyrical subject matter that fitted into the 'new wave' ethos of the period. The sound quality was also suitably murky. Signed to *Ralph*, the label run by the **Residents,** they produced two more albums and appeared on several compilations but their career tailed off in the early 80s. Stim entered law school and nothing further was heard except for Anderson's appearance in the **Henry Kaiser** Band. However, a clutch of tapes under a variety of names (Gizzards, Half-Life, O-Type) have appeared since 1987, apparently the work of Sophiea and Anderson, on the former's Quadruped label. These two, plus Stim and drummer Marc Weinstein, appear to constitute an MX for the 90s.

Albums: *Hard Attack* (1977), *Out Of The Tunnel* (1980), *Crowd Control* (1981).

My Bloody Valentine

It took several years for My Bloody Valentine to capture their ground-breaking hybrid of ethereal melodies and studio-orientated, discordant sounds which proved so influential on the independent scene of the late 80s. Their roots lay in Dublin, where singer/guitarist Kevin Shields joined drummer Colm O'Ciosoig in the short-lived Complex. Forming My Bloody Valentine in 1984, the pair moved to Berlin, joined by vocalist Dave Conway (vocals) and Tina (keyboards). A mini-album, *This Is Your Bloody Valentine*, on the obscure German Tycoon label in 1984, made little impression (although it was later reissued in the UK), so the band returned to London and recruited bassist Debbie Googe. The 12-inch EP, *Geek!* (and the accompanying, 'No Place To Go') emerged on Fever in mid-1986 which, like their debut, was strongly influenced by the **Cramps** and the **Birthday Party**. Later that year, the band signed with Joe Foster's fledgling Kaleidoscope Sound label for *The New Record By My Bloody Valentine* EP, which revealed a new influence, the **Jesus And Mary Chain**. A switch to the **Primitives**' label Lazy, produced 'Sunny Sundae Smile' (1987), which meshed bubblegum pop with buzzsaw guitars, a formula that dominated both the mini-album, *Ecstasy*, and 'Strawberry Wine', released later that year. The departure of Conway signalled a change in musical direction, reinforced by the arrival of vocalist Belinda Butcher. A further move to **Creation Records** allowed for a drastic reappraisal in recording techniques, first apparent on the formidable *You Made Me Realise* EP in 1988. Enticing melodic structures contrasted with the snarling, almost unworldly collage of noise, developed more fully that year on My Bloody Valentine's pivotal *Isn't Anything*, from which was drawn the barrage of guitars, 'Feed Me With Your Kiss'. At last, the group had unearthed a completely new sound. Since then, their status has mushroomed. The release of an EP, *Glider* (1990), alongside a remix from the in-demand DJ **Andy Weatherall**, flirted with both dance music and the charts while 'Tremelo' (1991) must rank as arguably the most extreme piece of music to reach the Top 30. To quote the band, it 'sounded like it was being played through a transistor radio'. My Bloody Valentine's increasing maturity saw the meticulously-produced *Loveless* album reinforce their reputation as one of the prime influences on the late 80s' UK independent scene - one that groups such as **Slowdive**, **Lush** and **Chapterhouse** owe a great deal. However, the massive studio bills run up during that time saw My Bloody Valentine leave Creation, moving instead to **Island Records**. At which point another agonising gestation period was embarked upon, allegedly due to difficulty installing equipment in their own purpose built studio in south London.

Albums: *This Is Your Bloody Valentine* (Tycoon 1984), *Ecstasy* (Lazy 1987, mini-album), *Isn't Anything* (Creation 1988), *Loveless* (Creation 1991).

My Dying Bride

From Bradford, Yorkshire, England, My Dying Bride proffer an intriguing blend of full-blooded doom metal, with more poise than most and a rare experimental streak. Vocalist Aaron's lyrics also depart somewhat from the herd - though he often concerns himself with biblical and religious matters, his stance is neither that of Christian or Satanist: 'The bible is a fantastic story...There's no heaven or hell as far as I'm concerned, it's just a nice story and I like to write about it because it affects so many people's lives'. After formation in 1990 they secured a deal with French label Listenable, through whom they provided their first official release, the 'God Is Alone' single. This was enough to interest UK label Peaceville who released their debut EP, *Symphonaire Infernus Et Spera Empyrium*. Their 1992 album, *As The Flower Withers*, followed shortly afterwards, featuring artwork by popular cult artist Dave McKean. My Dying Bride were already making a name for themselves as innovators in the doom genre, with a sound that combined the morbid grind of death metal with orchestral flourishes and haunting refrains. The resultant effect was one of grandiose tragedy. After recording another EP, *The Thrash Of Naked Limbs*, they took their session violinist and pianist, Martin Powell, on as a full member of the band, confirming their dedication to a path which combined classical and contemporary influences. A second album, *Let Loose The Swans*, saw Aaron singing, rather than growling in the traditional death metal style, and is their most distinctive and accomplished work to date. The vitality and colour of the band was enshrined in their 1994 release, the *I Am The Bloody Earth* EP, with the a-side featuring guest vocals from Ghost (of **G.G.F.H.**), while the b-side, 'Transcending (Into The Exquisite)', featured a challenging remix from local dance gurus **Drug Free America**. November 1994 saw the release of a box set containing their previous EPs, which sold sold out almost immediately, reflecting My Dying Bride's growing popularity.

Albums: *As The Flower Withers* (Peaceville 1992), *Let Loose The Swans* (Peaceville 1993).

My Fair Lady (Film Musical)

Alan Jay Lerner and **Frederick Loewe**'s Broadway masterpiece came to the screen in 1964 complete with a controversial choice of leading lady. **Julie Andrews**, who created the part of Eliza Doolittle on stage, had only just made her film debut in ***Mary Poppins***, and Audrey Hepburn (whose singing was dubbed by Marni Nixon) won the coveted role. Thankfully, after some bizarre alternative casting suggestions, **Rex Harrison** was once again the irascible confirmed bachelor, Professor Henry Higgins, who bets his companion, Colonel Pickering (Wilfred Hyde-White), that he can take an ordinary cockney flower girl and pass her off in high society just by teaching her to 'speak like a lady'. This he does in triumphant fashion, but only after much hard work and frustration, and some delicate negotiations with the girl's philosophical dustman father, Alfred P. Doolittle, who is superbly played by **Stanley Holloway** reprising his stage performance. Gladys Cooper as Higgins's mother (who sides with Eliza in all disputes) and Jeremy Brett as the toff who worships the pavements that Eliza walks on, were among the supporting cast which also included Mona Washbourne, Theodore Bikel, Isobel Elsom, Charles Fredericks, and John Holland. Not surprising with Lerner writing the screenplay, all the songs from the stage production were retained. The by-now classic overture preceded this extraordinary score: 'Why Can't The English?', 'Wouldn't It Be Loverly?', 'With A Little Bit Of Luck', 'I'm An Ordinary Man', 'Just You Wait', 'The Rain In Spain', 'I Could Have Danced All Night', 'Ascot Gavotte', 'On the Street Where You Live', 'Embassy Waltz', 'You Did It', 'Show Me', 'Get Me To The Church On Time', 'A Hymn To Him', 'Without You', and the sublime 'I've Grown Accustomed To Her Face'. That last number was part of an ending to the story contrary to the one in Bernard Shaw's *Pygmalion* on which the stage and film musicals were based. Shaw refused to have a happy resolution to Higgins's relationship with Eliza, but in *My Fair Lady*, the famous curtain line, 'Where the devil are my slippers?,' does seem to indicate that the teacher and his prize pupil are destined to stay together. Jack L. Warner produced the film for Warner Brothers and the choreographer was **Hermes Pan**. It was photographed in Technicolor and Super Panavision 70 and won eight Academy Awards including best picture, actor (Harrison), director (George Cukor), scoring (**André Previn**), and costumes and sets (Cecil Beaton). The latter's work, especially in such scenes as the marvellous 'Ascot Gavotte', was a major factor in the film's success - even without Julie Andrews. Some 30 years after its release, *My Fair Lady*, which had deteriorated to a great extent in the vaults, was brilliantly restored - visually and aurally - by experts Robert A. Harris and James C. Katz, and reissued in a letterbox format. On the new print Marni Nixon's voice on 'Wouldn't It Be Loverly?' was replaced by Audrey Hepburn's. The actress had apparently recorded several tracks for the film which were never used.

My Fair Lady (Stage Musical)

One of the most successful shows in the history of the American musical theatre, *My Fair Lady* opened to rave reviews at the Mark Hellinger Theatre in New York on 15 March 1956. The book, by **Alan Jay Lerner**, was based on George Bernard Shaw's play *Pygmalion*, and told of the attempts by Professor Henry Higgins (**Rex Harrison**) to transform a Cockney flower girl, Eliza Doolittle (**Julie Andrews**), into a society lady simply by teaching her to speak correctly. In the course of the story Higgins and Eliza fall in love and all ends happily, if a little differently from the way Shaw ended his play. Alan J. Lerner and **Frederick Loewe**'s score was full of marvellous songs which included 'Wouldn't It Be

Loverly?', 'I Could Have Danced All Night', 'On The Street Where You Live', 'Get Me To The Church On Time', 'With A Little Bit Of Luck', 'Show Me', 'I'm An Ordinary Man', 'Without You', 'Just You Wait', 'A Hymn To Him', 'Why Can't The English?' 'Ascot Gavotte', and 'I've Grown Accustomed To Her Face'. Harrison and Andrews were both superb. Their delight and joy when they realise that Eliza has finally 'got it', celebrating their triumph with 'The Rain In Spain', remains a memorable and endearing moment. A strong supporting cast included **Stanley Holloway** (Alfred P. Doolittle, Eliza's father), Robert Coote (Colonel Pickering), Michael King (Freddy Eynsford-Hill), and Cathleen Nesbitt (Mrs. Higgins). *My Fair Lady* ran on Broadway for six-and-a-half years, a total of 2,717 performances, and won **Tony Awards** for best musical, actor (Harrison), director (**Moss Hart**), musical director (Franz Allers); and Oliver Smith (scenic design) and Cecil Beaton (costumes), both of whom made outstanding contributions to the lavish and spectacular production. Numerous road companies toured the show across the USA and it was subsequently presented in many other countries around the world. Four of the principals, Harrison, Andrews, Holloway and Coote, recreated their roles for the London production which stayed at the Drury Lane Theatre Royal for five and a half years. The Broadway cast album spent over 300 weeks in the US chart, many of them at number 1. The 1981 US revival with the 73-year-old Harrison and Catherine Nesbitt, who by then was 92, toured the US before spending some time in New York. By all accounts it attempted to stay true to the original version, which is more than can be said for some of the later efforts. A 1991 UK provincial production, with a cast headed by Edward Fox, was described by its director Simon Callow, as 'a politically correct' version, and the 1993 Broadway revival, directed by Howard Davies, with **Richard Chamberlain** as Higgins and Stanley Holloway's son, Julian, as Doolittle, was 'stripped almost entirely of its romanticism and honed to a provocative post-modern edge', according to the *Variety* theatre critic. He went on: 'The famous "Ascot Gavotte" scene is recreated as a living Magritte canvas, the actors in colourful finery descending from the flies to hover above the action against a field of brilliant blue'. The 1964 film version was reasonably faithful to the original stage show though, and starred Harrison, Holloway, and - somewhat controversially - Audrey Hepburn as Eliza. In recent times, the American musical historian David Ewen suggested that one way or another *My Fair Lady* has generated approximately $800 million.

My Gal Sal

Another screen biography that played fast and loose with the true facts about its subject - in this case the late 19th century songwriter Paul Dresser. The screenplay, by Seton I. Miller, Darrell Ware and Karl Tunberg, was loosely based on Theodore Dreiser's book *My Brother Paul*, and purported to trace the rise of Dresser (he changed his name from Dreiser early in his career) from his time as a performer in medicine shows and as a blackface comedian in vaudeville, to fame and fortune as a great songwriter. In fact, Dresser was never a commercial success and he wrote his best-known song 'My Gal Sal' in 1905 just a year before he died of heart failure. Victor Mature, an actor guaranteed to make the hearts of female members of the audiences go all-a-flutter, played the composer, and **Rita Hayworth** was the musical comedy star he fell for in a big way. No wonder, because Hayworth (whose vocals were dubbed by Nan Wynn), looked beautiful and gave one of the best and most joyful performances of her illustrious career. Other roles were played by Carole Landis, John Sutton, James Gleason, Phil Silvers, Walter Catlett, Andrew Tombes, Curt Bois, and Mona Maris. **Hermes Pan** also made an appearance, and he and Val Raset staged the delightful dance sequences. Several of Dresser's own numbers were featured, including 'On The Banks Of The Wabash', 'Come Tell Me What's Your Answer', 'Liza Jane', 'The Convict And The Bird', 'Mr. Volunteer', 'If You Want Me', and, of course, 'My Gal Sal'. These were supplemented by others, by **Ralph Rainger** and **Leo Robin**, such as 'Me And My Fella', 'On The Gay White Way', 'Oh! The Pity Of It All', and 'Midnight At The Masquerade'. It all added up to a colourful and entertaining period piece, which was photographed in Technicolor by Ernest Palmer and produced by Robert Bassler for 20th Century-Fox in 1942. The director was Irving Cummings.

My Heart Goes Crazy

(see ***London Town***)

My One And Only

This production was similar in many ways to ***Crazy For You***, which came along nine years later. Both productions were based on vintage shows with scores by **George** and **Ira Gershwin**: in *Crazy For You*, the producers went back to ***Girl Crazy*** (1930), and for *My One And Only*, which opened at the St. James Theatre in New York on 1 May 1983, librettists Peter Stone and Timothy S. Mayer reached back even further, and used the 1927 **Fred Astaire** hit, ***Funny Face***, as their role model. *My My One And Only* starred **Tommy Tune**, Broadway's contemporary equivalent of Astaire, and he also shared the choreography chores with Thommie Walsh, so the accent was very definitely on the dance. Tune's co-star was Twiggy, the English 60s fashion model, who had appeared in Ken Russell's film of *The Boy Friend* in 1971. Tune and Charles 'Honi' Coles stopped the show each night with their terpsichorean treatment of the title song, and some other numbers were retained from the original *Funny Face*, including 'He Loves And She Loves', ''S Wonderful', and 'Funny Face'. The rest of the score was culled from other Gershwin shows including 'I Can't Be Bothered Now', 'How Long Has This Been Going On?', and 'Nice Work If You Can Get It'. The story, such as it was, had Twiggy as a record-breaking swimmer and Tune as an intrepid pilot, getting mixed up with some Prohibition-busting bootleggers in the late 20s world of Charles Lindbergh and non-stop flights to various capital cities of the world. Tommy Tune won the 1983 **Tony Award** for best actor, and shared the prize for choreography with Thommie Walsh. The elegant tap dancer, Charles 'Honi' Coles, an ex-vaudevillian who dropped out of the performing business for a while in the 60s and 70s, made a triumphant Broadway comeback in this show at the age of 73, and won the Tony for best supporting actor in a musical. He died in 1992, shortly after receiving the National Medal of the Arts from President Bush. *My One And Only* continued to sing and dance to that gorgeous Gershwin music for a total of 767 performances.

Myers, Amina Claudine

b. 21 March 1942, Blackwell, Arkansas, USA. As a young woman, Myers played piano and sang in church. In the mid-60s she moved to Chicago, became a member of the **AACM** and over the next 10 years or so worked frequently with fellow-members such as **Kalaparush Maurice McIntyre** (*Humility In The Light Of The Creator*), **Muhal Richard Abrams**, **Henry Threadgill** and **Lester Bowie** (*African Children, The 5th Power*). In the early 70s she also played with **Gene Ammons**, **Sonny Stitt** and **Little Milton** as well as leading her own trio. She moved to New York in the mid-70s and spent some time in Europe in the early 80s, recording there with **Frank Lowe** (*Exotic Heartbreak*) and with Martha and **Fontella Bass** and David Peaston on the highly-praised gospel set, *From The Root To The Source*. Her first recording as leader, for **London**'s **Leo Records** featured her on piano, organ and vocals, and were powerful, even stark, evocations of her blues and gospel roots. Inexplicably, later recordings - particularly an ill-judged couple of fusion-based albums for Novus - largely failed to capture the outstanding talents that have won her a high standing among her peers. From the mid-80s she has been playing with **Charlie Haden**'s Liberation Music Orchestra, recording with them on *Dream Keeper*.

Albums: *Song For Mother E* (Leo 1980), *Salutes Bessie Smith* (Leo 1980), *Poems For Piano: The Music Of Marion Brown* (1980), with Muhal Richard Abrams *Duet* (1981), *The Circle Of Time* (1983), *Jumping In The Sugar Bowl* (Minor 1984), *Country Girl* (Minor 1986), *Amina* (Novus 1988), *In Touch* (Novus 1989).

Myers, Dave

b. 30 October 1926, Byhalia, Mississippi, USA. The older brother of **Louis Myers**, Dave bought a guitar after the family moved to Chicago in 1941. During 1951 he became a member of the **Aces**, leaving in 1955, a year after Louis. In the late 50s and early 60s he was part of a rock 'n' roll band with Louis, and when the Aces reformed at the end of the 60s, he had the opportunity to record with them and as accompanist to artists, including **Carey Bell**, **Howlin' Wolf**, **Robert Lockwood**, **Jimmy Rogers**, **Homesick**, **James Williamson** and **Hubert Sumlin**.

Myers, Louis

b. 18 September 1929, Byhalis, Mississippi, USA. Growing up in a musical family, Myers began playing harmonica at the age of eight, and guitar about two years later. He moved to Chicago in 1941 and played with Big Boy Spires for three years. With his brother **Dave Myers**, **Junior Wells** and later, drummer Fred Below, he formed the **Aces** and in the 50s became known for his light, jazzy and swinging guitar blues artists (including some years with the re-formed Aces) and his own material has appeared on the Abco, Advent, and JSP labels. Although he is primarily known for his fluent guitar work, he can also be an impressive harmonica player in the modern amplified style.

Albums: *I'm A Southern Man* (1978), *Wailin' The Blues* (1983).

Myers, Sammy

b. 19 February 1936, Laurel, Mississippi, USA. Originally one of **Elmore James**' Broomdusters working the Chicago circuit, Sammy Myers' early fame rests on a song he recorded for Johnny Vincent's Jackson, Mississippi based Ace label. 'Sleeping In The Ground', with its **Jimmy Reed**-like lope supplied by The King Mose Royal Rockers, is one of the classic post-war harmonica blues. It was recorded in Jackson in 1957 and the partially blind singer/harmonica player, who also plays drums, went on to produce further singles for the Fury and Soft labels (the latter credited to Little John Myers) before moving back to seek his livelihood in the clubs. He recorded for Vincent again, seeing the results issued as part of an album in 1981. Later he formed an unlikely partnership with the much younger, Texan guitarist **Anson Funderburgh** performing, with much success, as featured artist with Funderburgh's group the **Rockets**.

Albums: *Kings Of The Blues, Vol. 2* (anthology) (1979), *Genuine Mississippi Blues* (1981), *My Love Is Here To Stay* (1986), *Sins* (1988), *Talk To You By Hand* (1991).

Myers, Stanley

b. 6 October 1930, London, England, d. 9 November 1993, London, England. A composer, arranger and musical director for films and television from 1966. In the 50s Myers worked in the theatre, and contributed music to several London West End shows including *A Girl Called Jo* and served as musical director for the **Julian More**-James Gilbert hit musical ***Grab Me A Gondola*** (1956). In 1966 he scored his first film, a comedy entitled *Kaleidoscope*, which teamed Warren Beatty with English actress Susannah York. Two other early projects included *Ulysses* and *Tropic Of Cancer* for the US director, John Strick. Throughout a career spanning over 60 feature films, Myers worked in several countries besides the UK, including the USA, Canada, Australia, and in Europe, particularly France and Germany. In the 70s his credits included *The Walking Stick*, *Age Of Consent*, *A Severed Head*, *Long Ago Tomorrow (The Raging Moon)*, *Summer Lightning*, *X, Y And Z*, *Little Malcolm And His Struggle Against The Eunuchs*, *The Apprenticeship Of Dudley Kravitz*, *The Wilby Conspiracy*, *Absolution* and *Yesterday's Hero* (1979). In 1978 Myers won his first **Ivor Novello** Award for the theme from the five times Oscar-winner *The Deer Hunter*. It was a UK Top 20 entry for classical guitarist **John Williams**, and was also successful for the Welsh singer Iris Williams under the title of 'He Was Beautiful', with a lyric by **Cleo Laine**. In the 80s, Myers collaborated on the music for several films with **Hans Zimmer**. Together they scored Jerzy Skolimowski's highly-acclaimed *Moonlighting*, starring Jeremy Irons, *Success Is The Best Revenge*, *Eureka*, *Insignificance*, *Taffin*, *The Nature Of The Beast* and *Paperhouse*, amongst others. Myers' solo scores during the 80s included *The Watcher In The Woods*, *Blind Date* (**Bruce Willis**'s big screen success), *The Chain*, *The Lightship*, *Conduct Unbecoming*, *Dreamchild*, *Castaway*, *Sammy And Rosie Get Laid*, *Wish You Were Here*, *The Boost* and *Scenes From The Class Struggle In Beverly Hills* (1989). In 1987 Myers received an award for 'the best artistic contribution' at Cannes for his music to *Prick Up Your Ears*, Steven Frear's 'realistic and evocative look' at the life of playwright Joe Orton, which included the song 'Dancing Hearts' (written with Richard Myhill).

Two years later, Myers won his second Ivor Novello Award for his score for *The Witches*, director Nicholas Roeg's treatment of a story by Roald Dahl. In the early 90s Myers' credits included *Rosencrantz And Guildenstern Are Dead*, *Iron Maze*, *Claude*, *Sarafina!*, and the French-German production *Voyager*. Myers also worked extensively in television, on UK programmes such as *All Gas And Gaiters*, *Never A Cross Word*, *Robin Hood*, *Dirty Money*, *Widows I And II*, *Diana*, *Nancy Astor*, *Wreath Of Roses*, *Scoop*, *Here To Stay*, *The Russian Soldier*, *The Most Dangerous Man In The World*, *My Beautiful Laundrette*, *Christabel* and many more. For US network television he composed music for *Summer Of My German Soldier*, *The Gentleman Bandit*, *The Martian Chronicles*, *Florence Nightingale*, *Monte Carlo*, *Tidy Endings* among others.

In the early 90s Myers was working with the saxophonist **John Harle**. They had just finished recording Myers' specially written piece, 'Concerto For Soprano Saxophone', when he died of cancer in November 1993. In the same year Myers won another Ivor Novello Award for his Stalag Luft television theme, and in 1995 there was a posthumous BAFTA Award and yet another 'Ivor' for his original television music (written with Christopher Gunning) for the highly popular *Middlemarch* series.

Myles, Alannah

Toronto-based vocalist Myles spent much of her early career unsuccessfully shopping for a recording deal in her native Canada, but when she and writing partner Christopher Ward changed tack, targeting an American deal with a David Tyson-produced demo and a video for 'Just One Kiss', they met with almost instant success. Tyson produced *Alannah Myles*, an excellent commercial hard rock debut on which the vocalist turned her deep, soulful voice to a variety of material, from gentle acoustic guitar-based ballads to raunchy rock 'n' roll. After the years of struggle, the debut ironically took off rapidly in Canada, with 'Love Is' helping Myles achieve major status in just three months, but the slow, steamy raunch of 'Black Velvet' brought much wider success. She suddenly found herself topping the US singles chart and hitting the Top 3 in the UK as 'Black Velvet' became a worldwide hit. *Alannah Myles* subsequently became the most successful debut in Canadian music history, selling more than five million copies globally, and Myles proved that she was no mere studio songbird, taking her band out on the road, supporting **Robert Plant** in the UK.

Albums: *Alannah Myles* (Atlantic 1989), *Rockinghorse* (Atlantic 1992).

Myles, Heather

b. 31 July 1962, Riverside, California, USA. He was raised on a horse ranch in Texas and her brother was a rodeo rider. Heavily influenced by **Merle Haggard** and **Buck Owens**, she spent several years playing the honkytonk circuit. **Dwight Yoakam**'s fiddler, Brantley Kearns, also plays for Myles. She made her recording debut on HighTone's Western Beat sampler, *Points West*, with her songs, 'Lovin' The Bottle' and 'Rum And Rodeo', which was written about old-time rodeo rider, Casey Tibbs. An excellent country writer, her debut album caused a stir, not so much because of the songs, but because she looked like Princess Diana on the cover.

Albums: *Just Like Old Times* (HighTone 1992), *Rum And Rodeo* (HighTone 1994), *Untamed* (Demon Fiend 1995).

Myrow, Joseph

b. 28 February 1910, Russia, d. 24 December 1987, Los Angeles, California, USA. A popular composer from the 40s to the late 50s, mostly for movies, Myrow was educated at the University of Pennsylvania, Philadelphia Conservatory of Music and the Curtis Institute of Music. He graduated as an accomplished pianist, and served as a guest soloist with several symphony orchestras, including those of Cleveland and Philadelphia. After working as musical director for some Philadelphia radio stations, Myrow started composing for nightclub revues in cities on the east coast. His early songs in the late 30s included 'Haunting Me', 'Overheard In A Cocktail Lounge', 'The Fable Of The Rose' and 'I Love To Watch The Moonlight'. In the early 40s he wrote 'Autumn Nocturne' (a big hit for **Claude Thornhill**) and 'Velvet Moon'. In 1946, he and **Eddie De Lange** contributed several songs to the movie *If I'm Lucky*. In the same year, Myrow began what was to be a 10-year association with lyricist **Mack Gordon**. Together they wrote eight songs for *Three Little Girls In Blue*, including 'Somewhere In The Night', 'Always A Lady', 'On The Boardwalk In Atlantic City' and 'You Make Me Feel So Young'; the latter eventually became indelibly linked with **Frank Sinatra**. From 1947-50 the team provided the songs for four movies starring **Betty Grable**, including ***Mother Wore Tights*** ('Kokomo, Indiana', 'There's Nothing Like A Song' and 'You Do', which was nominated for an Academy Award, and became a hit for **Dinah Shore** and **Vaughn Monroe**), *When My Baby Smiles At Me* ('By The Way' and 'What Did I Do?'), *The Beautiful Blonde From Bashville Bend* ('Every Time I Meet You') and ***Wabash Avenue*** ('Baby Won't You Say You Love Me' and 'Wilhelmina', which was also nominated for an Oscar). Myrow and Gordon continued into the 50s with *The I-Don't-Care Girl* ('This Is My Favorite City'); *I Love Melvin* starring **Donald O'Connor** and **Debbie Reynolds** ('A Lady Loves', 'Where Did You Learn To Dance?' and 'There You Are'); and *Bundle Of Joy*, in which Reynolds appeared with husband **Eddie Fisher**. Myrow also contributed several numbers to *The French Line*, with **Ralph Blane** ('Comment Allez-Vous?', 'What Is This I Feel?', 'Well, I'll Be Switched' and 'Wait Till You See Paris'). His other compositions included 'Five O'Clock Whistle' (a hit for **Glenn Miller**, **Erskine Hawkins** and **Ella Fitzgerald**); 'It Happens Every Spring' (movie title song), 'Endless Love', 'Love Is Eternal', 'Five Four Blues', 'Soft And Warm', 'Three Quarter Blues' and 'Someday Soon'. His other collaborators included Kim Gannon, Jean Stone and Bickley Reichner. Josef Myrow died of Parkinson's disease in 1987.

Mystery Of Edwin Drood, The

In this innovative musical which was 'suggested by the unfinished novel of the same name by Charles Dickens', a newcomer to Broadway, the author and songwriter **Rupert Holmes**, invited the audience themselves to vote for what they thought should be the outcome at the end of the evening - and it proved to be a popular notion. The show opened at the Imperial Theatre in New York on 2 December 1985, and the story was told as if it was being performed as a play within a play at a London music hall in the late 19th century. The traditional figure of the emporium's Chairman was played by George Rose, and the rest of the cast was led by **Betty Buckley**, who played Drood, **Cleo Laine** as Princess Puffer the keeper of an infamous opium den, and Howard McGillin. Holmes's imaginative and relevant songs included 'Perfect Strangers', 'The Wages Of Sin', 'Moonfall', 'Don't Quit While You're Ahead', 'Both Sides Of The Coin', 'Ceylon', 'Off To The Races', and 'No Good Can Come From Bad'. The show had an excellent run of 608 performances, and, in a very poor season for new musicals, scooped the **Tony Awards**, winning for best musical, book, score, actor (Rose), and director (Wilford Leach). The short-lived London production starred Julia Hills, the pop singer **Lulu**, and Ernie Wise, the surviving partner of one of Britain's best-loved comedy double acts, Morecambe And Wise.

Mystery Trend

An early but minor group in the San Francisco scene of the 60s, the Mystery Trend took its name after misunderstanding a line in **Bob Dylan**'s 'Like A Rolling Stone' which referred to a 'mystery tramp'. The group consisted of Ron Nagle (vocals), Bob Cuff (guitar), Larry Bennett (bass), Larry West (lead guitar) and John Luby (drums). They performed many concerts in the San Francisco ballrooms of the era, but released only one single, 'Johnny Was A Good Boy'/'A House On The Hill' on **Verve**, in early 1967, at which time West departed. Cuff left the band in the summer of 1967 and was replaced by John Gregory, who went on to join **Seatrain**. The Mystery Trend split up in 1968. Nagle recorded a solo album, *Bad Rice*, in 1970 and produced albums by **Paul Kantner** (of **Jefferson Airplane**) and **John Hiatt**. Nagle also formed a unit called **Durocs** during the 70s.

Mystics

This rock 'n' roll vocal ensemble came from Brooklyn, New York, USA. The members were brothers Phil (lead) and Albee Cracolici (baritone), Bob Ferrante (first tenor), George Galfo (second tenor), and Allie Contrera (bass). The Mystics helped popularize the Italian-American doo-wop sound that came out of New York City in the early 60s, but like many such groups they did it with only one hit, 'Hushabye' (US pop Top 20, 1959). The song was written by the great songwriting team of **Doc Pomus** and **Mort Shuman** and has become a staple of US oldie stations. A follow-up, 'Don't Take The Stars', scraped the bottom of the charts later in 1959. Failing to get another hit record, the Mystics broke up in the early 60s. They reunited in the 80s to perform at oldies shows and that led to a critically well-received album for a revival label, Ambient Sound, in 1982. By this time, however, the audience for doo-wop was limited to a passionate few on the Eastern seaboard and the album remained obscure.

Albums: with the Passions *The Mystics And The Passions* (1979), *Crazy For You* (1982), *The Complete Mystics* (1985), *Golden Classics* (1987).

Mythra

Judas Priest-influenced band from the north east of England who came together in 1979 at the height of the **New Wave Of British Heavy Metal** and released one of the most outstanding records of the era. Yet the band - Vince High (vocals), Mick Rundel (guitar), Barry Hopper (drums), Maurice Bates (rhythm guitar) and Pete Melsom (bass) - never achieved the greatness a band which sells 15,000 singles in 20 days deserves. The EP, *Death And Destiny*, first released on Guardian Records, was quickly re-issued on Street Beat Records to coincide with their appearance at the Bingley Hall festival with **Motörhead**. It too sold well and their battle cry of 'Death And Destiny' was sung by a thousand voices at said gig. Yet by 1981 their name was absent from the live listings, leaving the EP to command a high collectors' value and cult reputation. **Metallica** fans would do well to track it down to see how much *Kill 'Em All* owes to this band.

N

N'Dour, Youssou

b. 1959, Dakar, Senegal. Born in the Medina, or 'old town', district of Dakar, N'Dour is the son of Ndeye Sokhna Mboup, herself a well-known traditional musician, who gave him his grounding in the traditional music of the Wolof people. His first public performances came with two local music and drama groups, including Sine Dramatic, which he joined in 1972. The following year he made his first public appearance with a modern band, singing with Orchestre Diamono. In 1975, he toured the Gambia with the band, returning after his parents complained he was too young to start a life on the road. In 1976 N'Dour took the first steps in a career which would establish him as one of Senegal's greatest musical pioneers, joining the Star Band, who were the houseband at Dakar's leading nightspot, the Miami Club. With them N'Dour began to forge the fusion of western electric instrumentation and traditional Wolof rhythms and lyrics that became known as mbalax - a route that was simultaneously being explored by fellow Dakar bands **Orchestre Baobab** and Orchestre Le Sahel.

In 1979 N'Dour left the Star Band, and set up Etoile De Dakar, which in 1982 he re-formed as **Super Etoile De Dakar**. The mature mbalax style emerged at this time, as N'Dour added a variety of western instrumentation to the tough, multi-rhythmic Wolof folk songs he was re-interpreting: a base of rolling, flamenco-like guitars, fuzz-box guitar solos and stabbing, **Stax**-like horns. Slowly the sound developed. Ten cassette releases, starting with *Tabaski* in 1981, displayed an increasing fullness and power of arrangement. The lyric subject matter ranged from folk tales to celebrations of life in Dakar, and the problems faced by migrants to the cities. In Senegal, N'Dour's reputation increased. His prowess as a praise singer attracted rich and famous patrons, all of them keen to be immortalised in his songs and willing to pay large sums of money for the privilege. Poorer people, particularly the urban youth, identified with his pride in his Wolof roots while also enjoying the rock and soul edges his instrumentation and arrangements brought to the music. Outside Senegal his music received wider attention with the western release of two classic albums, *Immigres* (1985) and *Nelson Mandela* (1986), which picked up sustained critical praise and significant sales in the USA, UK and France. In 1987 N'Dour was invited to support **Peter Gabriel** on a lengthy USA tour, returning to Dakar with an Akai sampler with which to record and further explore the traditional sounds of Senegal. The results were to be heard on *The Lion* and its 1990 follow-up *Set*. For purists in the west, the albums showed rather too much western influence. His Senegalese audience, however, received them with huge enthusiasm. '7 Seconds' a duet with **Nenah Cherry** reached number 3 in the UK chart in 1994.

Selected albums: *A Abijan* (1980), *Xalis* (1980), *Tabaski* (1981), *Thiapathioly* (1983), *Absa Gueye* (1983), *Immigres* (1984), *Nelson Mandela* (1985), *The Lion* (1989), *African Editions Volumes 5-14* (1990, reissues, rec. early 80s), *Africa Deebeub* (1990, reissues, rec. early 80s), *Jamm La Prix* (1990, reissues, rec. early 80s), *Kocc Barma* (1990, rec. early 80s), *Set* (1990), *Eyes Open* (1992), *Hey You! The Best Of* (Music Club 1993), *Live - Bir Sorano Juin '93, Vols. 1 & 2* (Studio 1993), *The Guide: Wommat* (Columbia 1994).

N-Joi

Two brothers from Essex, England, 'brothers of hardness', N-Joi comprise Mark Franklin and Nigel Champion, plus singer Saffron. Their five minutes of fame arrived with 'Malfunction' (**DeConstruction** 1991), a completely over-wrought affair much admired by their near-neighbour, Liam Howlett (**Prodigy**). They released a recording of their stage set, *Live In Manchester*, for the same label in February 1992, which lasted over 28 minutes and included over a dozen separate tunes in the mix. They followed up with a more conventional EP, which included a **Moby** remix of their 'Mindflux' single for **RCA** in the US. Saffron attempted to launch herself solo with garage singles like 'One Love' for **WEA** in 1992.

N.R.T.

Formerly No Right Turn, N.R.T. are a hard working folk band from Derby, England, band who have an excellent repertoire of acidic roots rock. The focal point, Jayne Marsden, has a distinctive voice, put to effective use on a series of pacy releases which leave their folk prologues far behind. One of the best unsigned bands on the UK club circuit in the early 90s

Selected album: *New Rising Tide* (1992).

N.W.O.B.H.M.

(see **New Wave Of British Heavy Metal**)

N2-Deep

A white rap trio based in Vallejo, Calfornia, USA. They were formed by their DJ and producer, Johnny 'Z' Zunino, who introduced MCs Jay 'Tee' Trujillo and TL Lyon. The title-track of their debut gave them a substantial crossover hit (reaching US number 14), though their legitimacy as an act within the hardcore Profile fraternity was confirmed with cuts like 'What The Fuck Is Going On?'.

Album: *Back To The Hotel* (Profile 1992).

Na Fili

A band from Cork, playing straight Irish traditional music with depth and dedication. The name translates from old Irish as 'poets'. Certainly it is music with a rhythm and a rhyme.

Selected album: *Na Fili 3* (1973)

Nail, Jimmy

b. 16 March 1954, Newcastle-upon-Tyne, Tyne & Wear, England. Never the most natural pop star, the actor Jimmy Nail's efforts in front of a microphone have nevertheless brought him huge UK success. As the son of the boxer and Huddersfield Town footballer, Jimmy Bradford, Nail worked hard on misspending his youth and was expelled from school and was later jailed for football violence. After prison, though, he mended his alcoholic ways and began singing in pubs and clubs. He fronted the band King Crabs, with whom he wore a dress on stage, before embarking on his own songwriting. After a few small acting parts, he received his break when he got the part of the loveable philistine 'Oz' in the widely acclaimed ITV television series, *Auf Wiedersehen, Pet!* Subsequent acting roles have played upon a gritty, rough-edged demeanour. His musical career took off when his version of **Rose Royce**'s 'Love Don't Live Here Anymore' reached number 3 in the UK chart. However the follow-up single 'That's The Way Love Is' and his debut album flopped, and so he concentrated on his acting career, especially the detective series *Spender*, which ran for the next seven years. This drama, which Nail co-wrote with Ian LaFrenais, had a musical background. When Nail returned to music it was with the UK number 1 single 'Ain't No Doubt'. However, its follow-up, 'Laura', failed to breach the Top 50. Nail pressed on with a new television series, *Crocodile Shoes*, which followed the career of a down-at-heel pub-rocker on his way to Nashville and stardom. The album which accompanied it became the biggest-selling UK release of 1994, and featured guest writers that included **Prefab Sprout**'s Paddy McAloon. The title-track and 'Cowboy Dreams' (whose ***Top Of The Pops*** transmission featured an appearance by fellow Newcastle native **Sting**) also made the UK Top 10.

Albums: *Take It Or Leave It* (Virgin 1992), *Growing Up In Public* (East West 1992), *Crocodile Shoes* (East West 1994). Video: *Cowboy Dreams* (1995).

Nailbomb

A side-project for **Sepultura** vocalist/guitarist Max Cavalera and **Fudge Tunnel** singer/guitarist Alex Newport, both now residents of Phoenix, Arizona. Nailbomb arrived with the public thus: 'It was right after the last show on the **Ministry** tour. It was in San Diego and we were having a party. Me and Alex were talking 'cause the tour was over, the rest of the guys in Sepultura were going to Brazil, and I wasn't going because it was close to the time my son (Zyon) would be born. But I didn't want to stay and just do nothing in Phoenix...So I told Alex, 'why don't we get together and do some songs, just for the hell of it'. We didn't even think of recording anything'. Originally titled Hate Project, then Sickman, they eventually settled on Nailbomb because both partners wanted something 'real shocking'. A tape of the duo's demos reached Monte Conner at **Roadrunner**, who got them a studio budget to put together something a little more firm. The result was *Point Blank*, which improved on the quality of those demos but maintained the punk sound (a cross between **Big Black** and **Discharge**) which they had developed together. Contributions from Sepultura's lead guitarist Andreas Kisser and drummer Igor Cavalera were received, together with an appearance by **Fear Factory**'s Dino Cazares on '24 Hour Bullshit'.

Album: *Point Blank* (Roadrunner 1994).

Nakajima, Miyuki

b. 23 February 1952, Hokkaidô, Japan. After winning various amateur minor talent contests, singer-songwriter Nakajima was signed to Canyon Records when she won the 1975 national Japanese Yamaha Popular Music Contest. Her debut release for the label was the competition winner, 'Azamijono Lullaby' ('Miss Azami's Lullaby'). Her second single, 'Jidai' ('The Time') won a Grand Prix at the World Popular Song Festival in November 1975, making her one of the twin stars of Japanese 'new music', along with **Yumi Mattôya**. Nakajima's introspective songs, including such hits as 'Wakare Uta' ('Farewell Song') (1977) and 'Akujo' ('A Bad Woman') (1981), have since been appreciated by variety of audiences, including readers of modern poetry, and some half-a-dozen books have been written about Nakajima and her songs.

Albums: *Watashino Koega Kikoemasuka (Do You Hear My Voice?)* (1976), *Min'na Satteshimatta (Everybody Has Gone)* (1976), *A-ri-ga-tô (Thank You)* (1977), *Aishiteiruto Ittekure (Please Say 'I Love You)* (1978), *Shin'ainaru Monoe (To My Dear)* (1979), *Okaerinasai (Welcome Home)* (1979), *Ikiteitemo Iidesuka (Is It Alright For Me To Be Alive?)* (1980), *Ringetsu (Near Her Time)* (1981), *Kansuigyo (Cold-Water Fish)*

(1982), *Yokan (Presentiment)* (1983), *Hajimemashite (How Do You Do?)* (1984), *Oironaoshi (The Bride's Change Of Dresses)* (1985), *Miss M.* (1985), *36.5 C* (1987), *Nakajima Miyuki* (1988), *Goodbye Girl* (1988), *Utadeshika Ienai (You Can Only Say In Songs)* (1991). Compilations: *The Best Of Miyuki Nakajima* (1986), *Singles* (1987), *CD Box 10* (1988), *Presents Best Selection 16* (1989).
Further reading: *Nakajima Miyukiwo Motomete (Looking For Miyuki Nakajima)*, Taijirô Amasawa. *Kataomi (One-side Love)*, Miyuki Nakajima.

Naked City

Formed in 1990, this radical act revolves around alto saxophonist/composer **John Zorn** (b. 2 September 1953, New York City, New York, USA.) A leading figurehead of the 'downtown' avant-garde enclave, centred on New York's Lower East Side, Zorn drew increasing parallels between free jazz and sonic extremists **Napalm Death**, whom he consistently championed. His radical versions of **Ornette Coleman** compositions unveiled on *Spy Vs Spy* (1989) bore the legend "Fucking hardcore rules" and set the tone for the founding of Naked City. **Fred Frith** (bass), formerly of **Henry Cow**, **Bill Frisell** (guitar), Wayne Horvitz (keyboards) and Joey Baron (drums) joined Zorn for the group's self-titled album debut. Jazz, surf and noise gelled perfectly on this impressive collection, which merged original compositions with 'The James Bond Theme' and sundry film music, each of which was viciously deconstructed. Guest vocalist Yamatsuka Eye, from Japanese hardcore act the Boredoms (*Soul Discharge*, 1991), was billed as special guest, although he later became a full-time member. The sense of adventure on *Naked City* maintained on the equally compulsive *Torture Garden*, after which Zorn undertook an offshoot project, Painkiller (*The Guts Of A Virgin*, 1991), with Frisell and Napalm Death drummer Mick Harris. A film soundtrack, *Heretic Jeux Des Dames Cruelles*, released on the Japanese Avant label, maintained Naked City's uncompromising stance; track titles including 'Copraphagist Rituals' merely heightened the controversy. A second Avant disc, *Grand Guignol*, proved even more challenging, combining Debussy's 'La Cathedrale Engloutie' and Charles Ives' 'The Cage' with 32 virulent blasts of freeform noise, only three of which lasted more than one minute. Zorn and Naked City remain at the cutting edge of adventurous music.
Albums: *Naked City* (1990), *Torture Garden* (1990), *Heretic - Jeux Des Dames Cruelles* (1992), *Grand Guignol* (1993).

Naked Prey

This US group was founded in 1981 in Tucson, Arizona by Van Christian (guitar/vocals), formerly of the Serfers. David Seger (guitar/vocals), Richard Badenious (bass) and Sam Blake (drums) completed the line-up featured on the unit's mini-album debut. The set was produced by ex-Serfer Dan Stuart, guitarist in **Green On Red**, but although comparisons were naturally drawn between the two, Naked Prey offered a louder, heavier sound. This was more clearly heard on *Under The Blue Marlin*, on which Blake had been replaced by Tom Larkins. *40 Miles From Nowhere*, which featured the **Rolling Stones** 'Silver Train' and **Glen Campbell**'s 'Wichita Lineman', was regarded as a disappointment, and the group's musical momentum noticeably faltered. Van Christian nonetheless continues to front his creation, although it now seems doomed to cult status.
Albums: *Naked Prey* (1984), *Under The Blue Marlin* (1986), *40 Miles From Nowhere* (1987), *Kill The Messenger* (1989).

Naked Truth

This Atlanta, Georgia-based quartet originated in the local hardcore scene in 1988, although the individual band members arrived from far afield: vocalist Doug Watts came from Detroit, bassist Jeff from Harlem, New York, and drummer Bernard Dawson from Los Angeles, while Jimmie Westley was the only Georgia native, from Savannah. Life was initially tough for a black metal band in Georgia, but the dreadlocked group caught the interest of former **Clash** manager Bernie Rhodes, and he helped the band sign to Sony and relocate to London. *Green With Rage* introduced Naked Truth's raw, aggressive sound, which was given an individual slant by jazz and funk influences, but the homesick Jeff departed, and was replaced by London-born Kwame Boaten for the *Read Between The Lines* EP. The band were fortunate to pick up a UK tour with **Little Angels** after a **Motörhead** support slot was lost due to a tour cancellation, and despite the obviously different styles, Naked Truth went down well. The band built up a varied following, helped by a series of London residencies, before *Fight* appeared, showing the band's ability to mix styles as diverse as jazz and death metal seamlessly and convincingly, while Watts supplied varied vocals, from rap to all-out hardcore rage, and intelligent lyrics. The band were impressive as they supported **Living Colour** around the UK, but decided on a name change to Watts before releasing their second full album.
Albums: *Green With Rage* (Sony 1991, mini-album), *Fight* (Sony 1993).

Namlook, Peter

German born Namlook is comfortably the most prolific and arguably the best of the new wave of ambient/house artists of the early 90s. Before his immersion in the world of dance, he had experimented with the sitar and new age jazz. His early solo EPs were shrouded in mystery, the labels distinguished solely by the contact number Fax +49-69/454064 - which later transpired to be the title of the label. Since then his output has been fantastic, in both the literal and

accepted senses of the word. From his base in Frankfurt, Germany, two or three collaborations emerge every week on 12-inch, via a stable of co-conspirators who include Dr Atmo, Craig Peck, DJ Hubee, DJ Brainwave, DJ Criss, Pascal FEOS and **Mixmaster Morris** (the latter also recording with Namlook as Dreamfish on the Faxworld subsidiary). Releases are colour-coded to differentiate between the types of music - yellow for trance, black for hardcore, green for house and blue for ambient - the most popular genre in terms of sales reaction. Each is also recorded in a cycle of eight - one each with each collaborator, always beginning with DJ Criss (as Deltraxx). Only five or six hundred of any given release ever emerges, quickly selling out, before the 'cycle' is reissued on a compilation CD. As if that were not enough, Namlook also records ambient 'solo' records as Air, Sin or Silence (with Dr Atmo). These recordings are symptomatic of the 'chill-out' factor which hit European clubs in the early 90s. On several of the tracks it can take up to ten mintues for a distinctive beat for rhythm to appear, spending time building its atmospheric, neo-filmic musical soundscapes. Namlook has also found time for the Sequential project. Released in the UK via **Rising High**, this allows him to work with any of his roster, ironically, out of sequence. Namlook is now perceived to be at the forefront of what has been termed the 'ethno-trance' movement. Rather than riding the ambient bandwagon, he has an overview of this new music's place and purpose: 'I think it's very important to enhance the notion of a global ambient movement, and to realise that a lot of music which we didn't expect to be ambient is in fact very, very ambient. When you examine other cultures you discover that what we recognise as a very new movement is in fact incredibly ancient'.
Selected albums: with Dr Atmo *Silence* (Rising High 1993), *Air 2* (Fax 1994), with Bill Laswell *Psychonavigation* (Fax 1994).

Namyslowski, Zbigniew

b. 9 September 1939, Warsaw, Poland. Namyslowski's *Lola*, recorded during his visit to the UK in 1964, caused quite a stir, since few people in the West were aware of the state of the jazz art in Soviet bloc countries (formerly). However, it was not simply the surprise of Eastern European musicians playing modern, post-bop jazz at all that impressed: Namyslowski was very good indeed, with a hard, emotional tone and considerable facility on the alto saxophone. He had begun his musical studies on piano at the age of six, switching to the cello at 12. He also plays soprano saxophone, flute and trombone. He studied music theory at the Warsaw High School of Music and began his career playing trombone with a trad band and 'cello with a modern group. Concentrating on alto, he set up his quartet in 1963 and toured Europe, Asia and Australasia as well as the USSR. He plays with the kind of intensely personal passion one associates with **Jackie McLean** and **Mike Osborne**, weaving in strong strands of Polish folk music in both his writing and improvising. In the late 70s and early 80s he moved away from the more *avant-garde* side of his style and, without losing his individuality, used rock-fusion elements. There was also an adventurous album, *Zbigniew Namyslowski*, for orchestra and large jazz group. By the late 80s, he was back in the hard-bop mainstream, sounding a little less dangerous than in his early days, but just as sincere and inventive. He has also worked with Krzysztof Komeda and Air Condition, the fine Polish fusion band which he led in the early 80s.
Albums: *Lola* (1965), *Zbigniew Namyslowski Quartet* (1966), with Krzysztof Komeda *Astigmation* (1967), *Winobranie* (1973), *All Stars After Hours* (1974), *Kujaviek Goes Funky* (1975), with Michael J. Smith *Geomusic III* (1975), *Namyslowski* (1977), *Zbigniew Namyslowski* (1980), with Air Condition *Follow Your Kite* (1980), *Air Condition* (Affinity 1982), *Polish Jazz Vol 4:* (Polskie Nagrania, 1966-87 recordings), *Open* (1988), *The Last Concert* (Polonia 1992).

Nance, Ray

b. Willis Nance, 10 December 1913, Chicago, Illinois, USA, d. 28 January 1976. A gifted multi-instrumentalist, Nance studied formally for several years and played in various small bands, mostly in the Chicago area. By the early 30s he was a popular local entertainer, leading his own bands and playing several instruments, including trumpet and violin, as well as singing, dancing and performing engaging comedy routines. The 30s also saw him playing in the Chicago big bands led by **Earl 'Fatha' Hines** and **Horace Henderson**. He joined **Duke Ellington** in 1940 and quickly became an integral, valued and much-loved part of the organization. He left Ellington for a short spell in the mid-40s to lead his own band, but returned at the end of 1945; this time he remained virtually without a break, until 1963. From 1964 until his death he led his own small bands but returned regularly to guest with the Ellington band. Whether playing trumpet - later cornet - or violin, Nance was a highly distinctive musician and his contributions to the Ellington band's recordings are many and marvellous. His violin playing on 'Moon Mist' and his trumpet solo on the 1941 version of 'Take the 'A' Train' are particularly fine examples of his work. Outside the Ellington band he made some excellent recordings with ex-Ellingtonians **Paul Gonsalves** and **Johnny Hodges**, while a 1971 **Jimmy Rushing** recording includes a moving violin solo on 'When I Grow Too Old To Dream'.
Albums: *Duke Ellington Presents* (1956), with Johnny Hodges *Duke's In Bed* (1956), with Duke Ellington *Black, Brown And Beige* (1958), *Body And Soul* (1969), with Paul

Gonsalves *Just A-Sittin' And A-Rockin'* (1970), with Jimmy Rushing *The You And Me That Used To Be* (1971), *Huffin' 'N' Puffin'* (1971), *Ray Nance Quartet And Sextet* (Unique 1986). Compilation: with Ellington *The Blanton-Webster Years (1940-42)* (1987).

Nanton, Joe 'Tricky Sam'

b. Joseph N. Irish, 1 February 1904, New York City, New York, USA, d. 20 July 1946. After playing trombone with a number of small bands in the early and mid-20s, including two stints with **Cliff Jackson**, Nanton joined **Elmer Snowden** and by 1926 was in the re-formed band led by **Duke Ellington**. Along with **Bubber Miley**, Nanton was a major force in creating the distinctive 'jungle' sound of Ellington's early work. Although occasionally beset by illness, Nanton remained with Ellington until he suffered a stroke in 1945. An inventive soloist capable of producing fascinating excursions within a narrow range, and with a marked penchant for creating sounds which closely resembled the human voice, Nanton helped to establish a role for the trombone in the Ellington band which, thereafter, had to be followed, more or less faithfully, by most of his successors.
Compilations: *The Indispensable Duke Ellington Vols. 1/2, 3/4, 5/6 (1927-40)* (1983), with Duke Ellington *The Blanton-Webster Years (1940-42)* (1986).

Napalm Death

This quintet from Birmingham, England, was formed in 1981. Dispensing with their original style by the mid-80s, they then absorbed punk and thrash metal influences to create the new sub-genre of grindcore, arguably the most extreme of all musical forms. Side one of their debut album featured Justin Broadrick (guitar), Mick Harris (drums) and Nick Bullen (bass/vocals), but by side two this had switched to Bill Steer (guitar), Jim Whitely (bass) and Lee Dorrian (vocals), with Harris the only survivor from that first inception (though that too had been subject to numerous changes). Broadrick would go on to **Head Of David** and **Godflesh**. *Scum* largely comprised sub-two minute blasts of metallic white noise, over-ridden by Dorrian's unintelligible vocal tirade. The lyrics dealt with social and political injustices, but actually sounded like somebody coughing up blood. Their main advocate was Radio 1 DJ **John Peel**, who had first picked up on *Scum*, playing the 0.75 second-long track 'You Suffer' three times before inviting them to record a session for the programme in September 1987. This would come to be acknowledged as one of the 'Classic Sessions' in Ken Garner's 1993 book on the subject, and introduced new bass player Shane Embury (also Unseen Terror, who split after one album in 1988). Elsewhere Napalm Death were the subject of derision and total miscomprehension. They were, however, the true pioneers of the 'blast-snare' technique - whereby the tempo of a given beat is sustained at the maximum physical human tolerance level. They went on to attract a small but loyal cult following on the underground heavy metal scene. From *Enslavement To Obliteration*, consisting of no less than 54 tracks on the CD, was a state of the artless offering which easily bypassed pervious extremes in music. However, following a Japanese tour in 1989 both Dorrian and Steer elected to leave the band, the former putting together **Cathedral**, the latter **Carcass**. Despite the gravity of the split replacements were found in vocalist Mark 'Barney' Greenway (ex-**Bendiction**) and US guitarist Jesse Pintado (ex-**Terrorizer**). To maintain their profile the band embarked on the European *Grindcrusher* tour (in their wake grindcore had developed considerably and found mass acceptance among the rank and file of the metal world) with **Bolt Thrower**, **Carcass** and **Morbid Angel**, before playing their first US dates in New York. A second guitarist, Mitch Harris (ex-**Righteous Pigs**) was added in time for *Harmony Corruption*, which, along with the 12 inch 'Suffer The Children', saw Napalm Death retreat to a purer death metal sound. During worldwide touring in 1992 sole surviving original member Mick Harris became disillusioned with the band and vacated the drum stool for Danny Herrara, a friend of Pintado's from Los Angeles. A fourth album, *Utopia Banished*, celebrated the band's remarkable survival instincts, while the heady touring schedule continued unabated. By 1993 the band had played in Russia, Israel, Canada and South Africa in addition to the more familiar European and US treks. A cover of the **Dead Kennedys**' 'Nazi Punks Fuck Off', issued as a single, reinstated their political motives. As *Fear, Emptiness, Despair* confirmed, however, they remain the antithesis of style, melody and taste - the punk concept taken to its ultimate extreme, and a great band for all the difficulty of listening to them.
Albums: *Scum* (Earache 1987), *From Enslavement To Obliteration* (Earache 1988), *The Peel Sessions* (Strange Fruit 1989), *Harmony Corruption* (Earache 1990), *Utopia Banished* (Earache 1992), *Fear, Emptiness, Despair* (Earache 1994). Compilation: *Death By Manipulation* (Earache 1992).
Video: *Live Corruption* (1990).

Napier-Bell, Simon

b. 1939. Napier-Bell emerged from the fringes of British pop when he co-wrote the English lyric to **Dusty Springfield**'s UK number 1, 'You Don't Have To Say You Love Me'. He tentatively entered pop management with the soul duo Diane Scott and Nicki Ferraz, before accepting an invitation to handle the **Yardbirds**. Napier-Bell produced the group's last major hit, 'Over Under Sideways Down', and secured their role in *Blow Up*, Michelangelo Antonioni's film of 'swinging London', but their association was not

particularly happy. He subsequently managed **John's Children** and **Marc Bolan**, talents he briefly combined in 1967, but this particular liaison ended when the latter left to form **Tyrannosaurus Rex**, later **T. Rex**. When his other charges split up at the end of that year, Napier-Bell formed a partnership with songwriter Ray Singer. Together they touted schemes to pliant record companies, and having secured an advance, employed aspiring musicians to record the now-requisite album for as little cost as possible. Many of these projects were intentionally unsuccessful, thus permitting the duo to retain the remaining cash balance, but Fresh's *Fresh - Out Of Borstal* and the self-titled *Forevermore*, both on **RCA**, featuring future members of **Glencoe** and the **Average White Band** (respectively), generated some interest. Napier-Bell retired from music during the early 70s, but resumed management in 1975 with **Japan**. During the punk boom he signed the short-lived **London**, but later achieved notoriety with **Wham!**. Having extricated the duo from a punitive recording contract, he carefully cultivated their 'buddy' image and as a result helped establish one of the leading pop sensations of the 80s. Their relationship ended acrimoniously over an impending business deal which caused **George Michael** to announce a solo career. Napier-Bell attempted to fill the gap with Blue Mercedes and his new label, Music UK.
Further reading: *You Don't Have To Say You Love Me*, Simon Napier-Bell. *Starmakers And Svengalis: The History Of British Pop Management*, Johnny Rogan.

Napoleon XIV

The pseudonym of songwriter/performer/recording engineer Jerry Samuels, Napoleon XIV burst into the US/UK Top 10 in the summer of 1966 with the bizarre 'They're Coming To Take Me Away, Ha-Haaa!' Although clearly a novelty song, its subject matter, mental illness (brought on by the loss of the singer's dog), prompted a ban on many American radio stations. An attempted follow-up, 'I'm In Love With My Little Red Tricycle' failed to capture the public's imagination and Napoleon's credibility was further dented when it was revealed that the performer undertaking personal appearances to promote the record was not Samuels but a certain Richard Stern. The presence of Napoleon imitator **Kim Fowley** hardly helped matters. An album based round the hit with lyrics by comedy writer Jim Lehrer was rushed out but in spite of such amusing titles as 'Photogenic, Schizophrenic You', 'The Nuts In My Family Tree' and 'Bats In My Belfry', it failed to sell in vast quantities. Its final track was not even by Napoleon but instead featured the strains of Josephine XV warbling the acerbic 'I'm Happy They Took You Away, Ha-Haaa!'. In 1990, Napoleon's finest moment was given a fresh airing courtesy of former **Dead Kennedys** vocalist Jello Biafra whose new group Lard cut a startling version of the hit.
Album: *They're Coming To Take Me Away, Ha-Haaa!* (1966).

Napoleon, Marty

b. 2 June 1921, New York City, New York, USA. A member of a musical family (his father was a professional musician, as were several uncles of whom the most famous is **Phil Napoleon**), Marty played piano in several second-string big bands of the 40s, including those led by **Lee Castle** and **Joe Venuti**. Later, he joined **Charlie Barnet** and also spent a brief spell with **Gene Krupa**. In the 50s, Napoleon began playing with his uncle Phil's revived **Original Memphis Five** and then showed his versatility by becoming a member of **Charlie Ventura**'s Big Four. He next spent periods with **Louis Armstrong**'s All Stars, as well as bands led by his brother Teddy (who was also a professional musician), **Coleman Hawkins**, **Ruby Braff** and others. Since the beginning of the 60s he has worked mostly as a solo artist, but has made occasional appearances with small groups, which have included **Red Allen**, and also played return stints with Armstrong and Krupa. Napoleon's wide stylistic range, which has taken him from dixieland to the edges of bop, has tended to limit appreciation of his talent among those members of the jazz public who like to label musicians.
Albums: *Trio* (1955), with Ruby Braff *Little Big Horn* (1955), with Red Allen *Ride, Red, Ride In Hi-Fi* (1957), with Louis Armstrong *Louis* (1966).

Napoleon, Phil

b. 2 September 1901, Boston, Massachusetts, d. 30 September 1990. A child prodigy, Napoleon came from a very musical family, two of his nephews being **Marty** and **Teddy Napoleon**. He played trumpet in public at the age of five and made his first records 10 years later. In 1922 he was a founder-member of the **Original Memphis Five**, an exceptionally good dixieland band which made numerous records, many of which sold very well. By the end of the 20s, however, Napoleon had folded the band and gone into studio work where he remained for a decade or more. At the end of the 30s, after an unsuccessful attempt to run a big band, he stopped playing for some years. In the early 50s he returned to the music scene, reviving the Memphis Five and thereafter leading a succession of dixieland bands. He continued to play well into the 80s, often at his own club, Napoleon's Retreat, in Miami, Florida. A fiery player with an attacking style, Napoleon was never on a par with such near-contemporaries as **Bix Beiderbecke**, although he claimed to have been influential on Beiderbecke and **Red Nichols**. Nevertheless, his many records show him to have been a distinctive and clear-toned

trumpeter. These records, together with his remarkably long playing career, made him an important figure in the spread of jazz throughout the world.
Album: *Phil Napoleon And His Memphis Five* (1959). Compilations: with Red Nichols *New York Horns* (1924-29), *Bailey's Lucky Seven* (Queendisc 1983), *Red Nichols And Phil Napoleon* (Zeta 1991).

Napoleon, Teddy

b. 23 June 1914, New York City, New York, USA, d. 5 July 1964. Older brother of **Marty Napoleon** and nephew of **Phil Napoleon**, Teddy played piano in a band led by **Lee Castle** in the early 30s. After touring extensively with minor bands he arrived in New York at the end of that decade. He played in yet more minor dancebands but then, in 1944, joined **Gene Krupa**. Featured not only in the big band but also in Krupa's band-within-a-band, a trio which was often rounded out by **Charlie Ventura**, Napoleon continued this association even after Krupa had folded the big band. He toured the world with Krupa's trio in the 50s, making concert, club and festival appearances and several records. He also played and sometimes recorded with **Flip Phillips**, **Bill Harris** and his brother Marty.
Albums: with Gene Krupa *The Rocking Mr Krupa* (1953), with Krupa *Krupa Rocks* (1957). Compilation: *Drummin' Man Vol. 2 (1945-49)* (1987).

Nas

b. Nasir Jones, c.1974, Long Island, New York, USA. From the tough Queensbridge housing projects which brought the world **Marley Marl**, **MC Shan** and **Intelligent Hoodlum**, Nas is a highly skilled hip hop artist whose music is crafted with a degree of subtlety and forethought often absent from the genre. He was heavily influenced by his jazz-playing father, and started rapping at the age of nine, graduating to a crew entitled the Devastatin' Seven in the mid-80s. He met **Main Source** producer **Large Professor** in 1989, in the course of recording his first demo tape. The producer introduced him to the group itself, and he would see his debut on Main Source's 1990 album *Breaking Atoms*, guesting on the cut 'Live At The BBQ', where he was part of a skilled chorus line, alongside Large Professor and **Akinyele**. However, though he was widely applauded for his contribution he failed to build on the impact, drifting through life and becoming disillusioned by the death of his best friend Will, and the shooting of his brother. He may well have stayed on the outside of the hip hop game had not **MC Serch** (Nas had guested on his 'Back To The Grill') searched him out, to provide a solo track for the *Zebra Head* film. 'Half Time', again recorded with the Large Professor, was the result. A debut album followed, with contributions from the cream of New York's producers: Premier (**Gang Starr**), **Pete Rock** and Q-Tip (**A Tribe Called Quest**). A hefty unit which **Columbia** were happy to pay the bill for, judging Nas to be their priority rap act for 1994. Nas, who had by now dropped his 'Nasty' prefix, honed a rapping style that was at once flamboyant, but with a lyrical armoury that far surpassed the expected humdrum 'bitches and ho's' routines. Serch, now A&R head of **Wild Pitch**, once declared Nas: 'Pound for pound, note for note, word for word, the best MC I ever heard in my life'. There was now evidence to suggest he may have been correct.
Album: *Illmatic* (Columbia 1994).

Nascimento, Milton

b. 26 October 1942, Rio de Janeiro, Brazil. Singer/songwriter Nascimento draws much of his inspiration from Brazil's Portuguese heritage, where even the jolliest tune can be counted on to contain more than a *frisson* of melancholy. His biggest successes, both at home and abroad, came in the 70s with *Milagre Dos Peixes* (1973, re-released in the UK in 1990), and *Milton* (1977), the latter featuring contributions from **Herbie Hancock**, **Wayne Shorter**, **Airto Moreira**, Roberto Silva and Laudir De Oliviera. First teaming with Shorter on his 1975 album *Native Dancer*, Nascimento was widely taken up by the Los Angeles music fraternity over the next few years, most notably guesting on albums by **Flora Purim**, **Deodato** and **Charlie Rouse**.
Selected albums: *Milagre Dos Peixes* (1973), with Flora Purim *500 Miles High* (1976), *Milton* (1977), *Travessia* (Sign 1986), *Meetings And Farewells* (Polydor 1986), *Ship Of Lovers* (Verve 1987), *Yauarete* (CBS 1988), *Txai* (Columbia 1991), *Planeta Blue Estrada Do Sol* (1992), *Noticias Do Brasil* (Tropical 1993), *Angelus* (Warner 1994).

Nash, Graham

b. 2 February 1942, Blackpool, Lancashire, England. Guitarist/vocalist Nash embraced music during the skiffle boom. He formed the Two Teens with classmate Allan Clarke in 1955, but by the following decade the duo, now known as Ricky And Dane, had joined local revue Kirk Stephens And The Deltas. In 1961 they broke away to found the **Hollies**, which evolved from provincial status into one of Britain's most popular 60s attractions with Nash's shrill voice cutting through their glorious harmony vocals. Although their early hits were drawn from outside sources, Nash, Clarke and guitarist Tony Hicks subsequently forged a prolific songwriting team. However, Graham's growing introspection, as demonstrated by 'King Midas In Reverse' (1967), was at odds with his partners' pop-based preferences and the following year he left to join 'supergroup' **Crosby, Stills And Nash**. Nash's distinctive nasal tenor instilled a sense of identity to the trio's harmonies, and although his compositional talent was viewed as lightweight by many commentators, 'Marrakesh Express' (originally written for the Hollies), 'Teach

Your Children' and 'Just A Song Before I Go', were all highly successful when issued as singles. *Songs For Beginners* confirmed the artist's unpretentious, if naive style with material weaving political statements, notably 'Chicago', to personal confessions. Stellar support from his girlfriend **Rita Coolidge**, plus **Jerry Garcia** and **Dave Mason** brought precision to a set which silenced many of Nash's critics. However, the stark and dour *Wild Tales*, recorded following the murder of Nash's girlfriend Amy Gosage, proved less successful and not unnaturally lacked the buoyancy of its predecessor; nevertheless it contained some strong material, including 'Prison Song' and 'Another Sleep Song'. Graham then spent the remainder of the decade as half of **Crosby And Nash**, or participating in the parent group's innumerable reunions. He devoted considerable time and effort to charitable and political projects, including *No Nukes* and *M.U.S.E.*, but a regenerated solo career was undermined by the poor reception afforded *Earth And Sky*. Having completed a brief spell in a rejuvenated Hollies (1983), Nash resumed his on-off commitments to **Crosby, Stills, Nash And Young** and to date has only released one further solo effort. The perplexing *Innocent Eyes* matched Nash with modern technology: a surfeit of programmed drum machines. The record sounded synthesized and over-produced and was rejected by the critics and public. Nash's first love has always been CS&N, and history has shown that his best post-Hollies work has been unselfishly saved for group rather than solo activities. Nash's own stability has enabled him to help his colleagues through numerous problems; he takes much of the credit for **David Crosby**'s recovery from drug addiction.

Albums: *Songs For Beginners* (1971), *Wild Tales* (1973), *Earth And Sky* (1980), *Innocent Eyes* (1986).

Further reading: *Crosby, Stills And Nash*, Dave Zimmer.

Nash, Johnny

b. 9 August 1940, Houston, Texas, USA. The story of Nash's association with **Bob Marley** has been well documented. His background is similar to that of many Jamaican performers in that he sang in the church choir although not the fiery gospel type. By his early teens he performed cover versions of popular R&B hits of the 50s in a television show called *Matinee*. He was to enjoy his first US chart entry in 1957 with a cover of **Doris Day**'s, 'A Very Special Love'. **ABC** decided to market the young singer as another **Johnny Mathis** which did nothing to enhance his career. Disillusioned with the label he concentrated on a career in the movies. In 1958 he starred in *Take A Giant Step*, and in 1960 he appeared alongside Dennis Hopper in *Key Witness* which was critically acclaimed in Europe. Returning to the recording studio he persevered with middle-of-the-road material but was unable to generate a hit. A number of label and style changes did not embellish his chart potential. By 1965 he finally scored a Top 5 hit in the R&B chart with the ballad, 'Lets Move And Groove Together'. He was unable to keep up the winning formula but in 1967 his R&B hit was enjoying chart success in Jamaica. The good fortunes in Jamaica led Nash to the island to promote his hit. It was here that he was exposed to **ska** and arranged a return visit to the island to record at Federal Studios. Accompanied by **Byron Lee and The Dragonaires** the sessions resulted in 'Cupid', 'Hold Me Tight' and 'You Got Soul'. When he released 'Hold Me Tight' the song became an international hit including a Top 5 success in the UK as well as a return to the Jamaican chart. He formed a partnership with Danny Simms and a label, JAD (Johnny and Danny) releasing recordings by Bob Marley, Byron Lee, **Lloyd Price** and **Kim Weston** as well as his own material until the label folded in the early 70s. He returned to recording in Jamaica at **Harry J**'s studio where he met Marley who wrote, 'Stir It Up' which revived Nash's career by peaking at number 13 on the UK chart in June 1972. He continued to enjoy popularity with, 'I Can See Clearly Now' a UK Top 5 hit which was successfully covered by **Jimmy Cliff** in 1994 for the film, *Cool Runnings*. Other hits followed 'Ooh What A Feeling' and 'There Are More Questions Than Answers' but the further he drifted from reggae the less successful the single. He covered other Bob Marley compositions including 'Nice Time' and 'Guava Jelly' but they were not picked up for single release although the latter was on the b-side to 'There Are More Questions'. His career subsequently took another downward turn and was again revived when he returned to Jamaica to record an **Ernie Smith** composition, 'Tears On My Pillow' which reached number 1 in the UK Top 10 in June 1975. He also reached the UK chart with 'Let's Be Friends' and '(What) A Wonderful World' before choosing to devote more energy to films and his West Indian recording complex.

Albums: *A Teenager Sings The Blues* (ABC 1957), *I Got Rhythm* (ABC 1959), *Hold Me Tight* (JAD 1968), *Let's Go Dancing* (1969), *I Can See Clearly Now* (CBS 1972), *My Merry Go Round* (CBS 1973), *Celebrate Life* (CBS 1974), *What A Wonderful World* (1977), *Tears On My Pillow* (CBS 1975), *Stir It Up* (1981), *Johnny Nash* (1985), *Here Again* (1986). Compilations: *Greatest Hits* (CBS 1975), *The Johnny Nash Collection* (1977).

Nashville Teens

Formed in Weybridge, Surrey in 1962, the Nashville Teens initially comprised vocalists Arthur 'Art' Sharp (b. 26 May 1941, Woking, Surrey, England) and Ray Phillips (b. Ramon John Phillips, 16 January 1944, Tiger Bay, Cardiff, Wales), Michael Dunford (guitar), John Hawken (b. 9 May 1940, Bournemouth, Dorset, England; piano), Pete Shannon (b. Peter Shannon Harris, 23 August 1941, Antrim, Northern Ireland;

bass) and Roger Groom (drums). Dunford and Groom left the line-up the following year and the group was completed by John Allen (b. John Samuel Allen, 23 April, 1945, St. Albans, Hertfordshire, England; guitar), Barrie Jenkins (b. 22 December 1944, Leicester, England; drums) and third vocalist Terry Crow for a protracted tenure in Hamburg, Germany. This period is chronicled on *Jerry Lee Lewis; Live At The Star Club* on which the septet backed the veteran rock 'n' roll star. In 1964, and with Crow now absent, the Teens were aligned with producer **Mickie Most** for a pounding version of 'Tobacco Road', which deservedly climbed to number 6 in the UK. The similarly-styled 'Google Eye' also proved popular, reaching the Top 10, but a split with Most ended this brief ascendancy. Collaborations with **Andrew Loog Oldham** ('This Little Bird') and **Shel Talmy** ('The Hard Way') were minor hits, but at the expense of the unit's undeniable grasp of R&B. Groom rejoined the line-up in 1966 when Jenkins left for the **Animals**, but despite excellent versions of **Randy Newman**'s 'The Biggest Night Of Her Life' and **Bob Dylan**'s 'All Along The Watchtower', the Nashville Teens were unable to rekindle former success. A spate of defections - John Hawken later found fame with **Renaissance** - left Phillips the sole remaining original member. He continues to front this act and concurrently performs with the British Invasion All-Stars, which features musicians drawn from the **Downliners Sect**, **Creation** and the **Pretty Things**.
Album: *Live At The Red House* (1984). Compilation: *The Best Of* (1993)
Film: *Be My Guest* (1965).

Nashville West

A short-lived but pivotal California-based country group, Nashville West included former member of the **Kentucky Colonels**, Clarence White (b. 7 June 1944, Lewiston, Maine, USA; guitar), and three ex-members of the **Castaways**: Wayne Moore (guitar/bass/vocals), **Gene Parsons** (b. 14 September 1944, Los Angeles, California, USA; drums/vocals) and Gib Guilbeau (fiddle/vocals). Popular in Bakersfield and El Monte's Nashville West club, the quartet's archive recordings reveal a mixture of contemporary hits ('By The Time I Get To Phoenix', 'Ode To Billy Joe') and country favourites ('Send Me Back Home', 'Sweet Mental Revenge'). The group split up in August 1968 when Parsons and White joined the **Byrds**. However, the duo paid homage to their former ensemble by including the instrumental 'Nashville West' on *Dr. Byrds And Mr. Hyde*.
Album: *Nashville West* (1978).

Nasty Idols

This Swedish glam-metal quintet were formed in 1988 by vocalist Andy Pierce and guitarist Jonnie Wee, with Dick Qwarfort (bass), George Swanson (drums) and Roger White (keyboards) completing the line-up. They pursued a commercial hard rock direction in the style of **Bon Jovi** and **Whitesnake**, debuting with *Gigolos On Parole* to widespread indifference. Wee was soon replaced by Peter Espinoza on guitar, and his arrival marked a move towards a more glam-metal image, with **Mötley Crüe** and **Hanoi Rocks** influences taking over. *Cruel Intention* was the result, released in 1991. A marked improvement, it nevertheless failed to help them emulate this new set of influences in terms of commercial reward.
Albums: *Gigolos On Parole* (Black Mark 1989), *Cruel Intention* (Black Mark 1991).

Nasty Savage

This heavy metal/thrash quintet was formed in Brandigan, Florida, USA, during 1983 by vocalist and professional wrestler Nasty Ronnie and guitarist Ben Meyer. Assisted by David Austin (guitar), Fred Dregischan (bass) and Curtis Beeson (drums), they made their debut via demo tracks which subsequently appeared on the *Metal Massacre IV* and *Iron Tyrants* compilations in 1984. This led to a contract with Metal Blade Records, producing four albums over the ensuing five years. From an initial hard rock base of **Iron Maiden** and **Judas Priest**-styles, they gradually incorporated thrash elements into their music, drawing inspiration and ideas from **Metallica**, **Anthrax** and **Slayer**. They have been through four bass players in as many years, with the current guitarist Richard Bateman having taken up four string duties in 1988. Rob Proctor replaced Beeson on drums the following year. When they eventually sundered at the close of the decade they were chiefly lamented for a spectacular live show which featured their wild vocalist smashing television sets on stage and performing crude gymnastics.
Albums: *Nasty Savage* (Metal Blade 1985), *Indulgence* (Metal Blade 1987), *Abstract Reality* (Metal Blade 1988), *Penetration Point* (Metal Blade 1989).

Nathan, Sydney

b. 1904, Cincinnati, Ohio, USA, d. 1968. Nathan learned to play drums and piano in his childhood with the help of local black musicians, but entered the record-selling business in the 30s, although he became a successful songwriter under the pseudonym of 'Lois Mann'. In November 1943 his King Records was launched with releases by local hillbilly acts. These initial releases failed to sell due to the poor pressings; Nathan then decided to learn how to press his own records. In August 1943 King Records was incorporated as an outlet for hillbilly music, and scored early on with hits by the **Delmore Brothers** and **Cowboy Copas**. One year later, Syd started his Queen Records subsidiary as a showcase for jazz and

R&B acts, making particular use of his friend, **Lucky Millinder**'s Orchestra, with releases by Bullmoose Jackson, **Annisteen Allen**, **David 'Panama' Francis** and Sam Taylor - all Millinder alumni. In 1946 Queen Records began recording, issuing some of the finest gospel music by such artists as Swan's Silvertone Singers and Wings Over Jordan Choir. Nathan's name became synonymous with peerless gospel and exciting R&B thereafter. By August 1947 the Queen label was discontinued and all output - new and old - was issued or reissued on King Records. This switch brought about a change of luck for Nathan; he scored almost immediately with three big hits in Bullmoose Jackson's 'I Love You, Yes I Do', **Lonnie Johnson**'s 'Tomorrow Night' and **Wynonie Harris**' version of 'Good Rockin' Tonight' and about the same time, Nathan began leasing or acquiring masters from smaller independents like DeLuxe, Miracle and Gotham.

During the 50s and early 60s, King Records went from strength to strength with top-selling R&B artists like **Tiny Bradshaw**, **Earl Bostic**, **Bill Doggett**, **Sonny Thompson**, **Little Willie John** and **James Brown**, and on the new subsidiary label Federal with the **Dominoes**, **Freddie King** and others, but by 1964 Nathan's search for innovative recording talent was virtually at an end. King settled down to focus on James Brown's career and to repackage much of its back-catalogue on album. In 1968 Nathan merged with Don Pierce's Starday record company. After Nathan's death, Starday/King and all its off-shoots was sold to Gusto Records of Nashville, Tennessee.

Nati

b. José Natividad Martínez, 25 December 1959, Caracas, Venezuela. Nati played various instruments, including mandolin, piano and saxophone, before settling for the flute and percussion. He started performing professionally at the age of 10 with Grupo Fiebre and Acosta y sus Tremendos. He joined Grupo Nueva Gente in 1975. This was followed by a stint as director of La Magnifica, a charanga (flute, strings, rhythm section and voices band) formed by conga player Elio Pacheco, an ex-founder member of **Dimensión Latina**. He assisted Tabaco (b. Carlos Quintana, 15 September 1943, Venezuela; singer/bandleader) in enlarging his sextet to a brass-led orquesta (band), giving it more power and swing. Nati became an accompanist with La Amistad (the Friendship), a band organized by another two ex-members of Dimensión Latina: singer Rodrigo Mendoza and pianist Jesús 'Chuíto' Narváez. La Amistad's co-lead vocalist was Puerto Rican Tito Gómez, who had worked with Sonora Ponceña (see **Papo Lucca**), La Terrifica, **Ray Barretto**, Tito Valentín, Grupo Niche and as a solo artist. Nati formed his own charanga and teamed up with Panamanian singer Carlos 'El Grande' to record *A Base De Salsa* in 1982 on the Velvet label. El Grande, who was formerly with La Salsa Mayor, went solo and recorded *Sonero Con Clase* (1982) with the band of percussionist/vocalist José Mangual Jnr.; he later worked with pianist/bandleader/arranger Alfredo Valdés Jnr. and **Louie Ramírez**. Meanwhile Nati signed to Ralph Cartagena's Combo Records label. His 1985 release, *Yo No Soy Guapo* combined charanga instrumentation (violins/flute) with a brass-led orquesta. Nati composed half the tracks and handled arranging and production. He dropped the flute and violins on *Para Usted* (1986) and wrote all the arrangements for a trombone/trumpet frontline. In addition to producing the album, he composed over half the songs, including the two outstanding tracks 'Que Hablen' and 'La Engañada'. Nati faded from the scene after his next release. However, he reappeared in 1989 with the aptly-titled *Regresó* (Return) on **CBS**.

Selected albums: with Tabaco *Tabaco y sus Metales* (1978), with La Amistad *Presente y Pasado* (1979), *El Poder De . . . La Amistad* (1980), with Carlos 'El Grande' *A Base De Salsa* (1982), solo *Nati y su Charanga* (c.1983), *Yo No Soy Guapo* (1985), *Para Usted* (1986), *Tiene Razón Señora* (1986), *Regresó* (1989).

National Barn Dance, The

Many radio stations broadcast 'barn dance' programmes, with WBAP Fort Worth probably the first in 1923. One of the longest running and the one to gain the most nationwide acceptance was the *National Barn Dance* broadcast by WLS Chicago. WLS (World's Largest Store), owned by Sears-Roebuck Company, first broadcast in April 1924. The first barn dance programme was broadcast from the Sherman Hotel and featured the local **Isham Jones** dance band and a group of country musicians, who probably included fiddler Tommy Dandurand and banjo player Jesse Doolittle. The listeners enjoyed the programme and the development of the *National Barn Dance* began. It featured a mixture of popular numbers and folk/country songs and the show gradually began to produce its first stars. One of the best loved was singer Grace Wilson (b. 10 April 1890, Owesso, Michigan, USA), who sang on the show from 1924 until she retired in 1960. After 1925, the show took on a more hillbilly format, with the arrival of performers such as **Bradley Kincaid** and Chubby Parker. In the early days, the show's development owed much to its announcer, **George D. Hay** (the Solemn Old Judge), a journalist from Memphis. With regular blasts of his steamboat whistle to emphasise his words, he popularized the show, before heading for WSM Nashville, where in November 1925, he launched a barn dance programme that soon became the ***Grand Ole Opry***. Sears-Roebuck sold WLS to the *Prairie Farmer* newspaper in 1928, by which time the programme was well established and continued to produce its stars like Luther Ossenbrink who, as Arkie The Woodchopper, arrived in 1929 and stayed until WLS ended the programme in 1960. During the 30s, the show's popularity increased, owing to performers such as **Lulu Belle And Scotty**, the **Cumberland Ridge Runners**, **Karl And Harty, Red Foley** and **Gene Autry**. In 1932, WLS moved the show to the Eighth Street Theatre, where it remained until the late 50s. In 1933, an hour long Saturday evening section of the programme was sponsored by Alka-Seltzer and networked by NBC. (It remained a networked NBC programme until 1946.) This publicity led to tours being made by the show's performers and other radio stations broadcasting their own barn dance programmes. In 1944, Paramount Pictures released *The National Barn Dance* film, which described the programme as 'America's Favorite Radio Show'. It featured Lulu Belle And Scotty, **Dinning Sisters**, **Hoosier Hotshots,** Arkie and many others. The Kentucky Ramblers, who joined in 1933, remained a popular act until 1948. **Bob Atcher** achieved major success during his days on the show and in later years, **Rex Allen**, **Johnny Bond** and even **Bill Haley** were members. The show finally lost out to the much larger *Opry*. WLS dropped the programme in 1960 but it was broadcast by WGN Chicago until 1968, when the *National Barn Dance*, country music's first jamboree, finally played the last waltz.

National Health

This group was formed in August 1975 by Phil Miller (guitar) and Dave Stewart (organ), former members of **Hatfield And The North**. Amanda Parsons (vocals), Alan Gowen (synthesizer), Mont Campbell (ex-Egg; bass) and **Bill Bruford** (ex-**Yes** and **King Crimson**; drums) completed the group's original line-up, but the following year Neil Murray joined in place of Campbell who had opted for session work. National Health continued the quintessential English progressive rock style forged by **Soft Machine**, **Caravan** and **Matching Mole**, but despite judicious live appearances, failed to reap the same commercial rewards. Pip Pyle replaced Bruford prior to the recording of *National Health*, but further changes in the unit's line-up preceded *Of Queues And Cures*. Such instability doomed the group's commercial progress, although they remained a popular live attraction until the end of the decade. Stewart subsequently enjoyed a successful solo career recreating classic 60s singles with singers **Colin Blunstone** and **Barbara Gaskin**, in turn confirming the demise of National Health as a serious proposition. Despite continued interest from the Continent, the group was then disbanded.

Albums: *National Health* (1978), *Of Queues And Cures* (1978), *D.S. Al Coda* (1982).

National Jazz Ensemble

(see **Israels, Chuck**)

National Youth Jazz Orchestra

In 1965 **Bill Ashton**, a teacher at a London school, formed the London Schools Jazz Orchestra. This was an organization in which youngsters could pursue musical ambitions in a setting that related to music which interested them, rather than forms imposed upon them by the educational hierarchy. Thanks to Ashton's persistence in the face of establishment hostility the orchestra survived, later becoming known as the London Youth Jazz Orchestra and, eventually, the National Youth Jazz Orchestra. In 1974 NYJO became a fully professional organization and remains the UK's only full-time professional big band playing jazz. Although Ashton's conception was to create an atmosphere in which young musicians could develop their craft, NYJO has long since passed the stage of being either a training ground or even a 'youth' orchestra. The extraordinarily high standard of musicianship demanded by the band means that newcomers to its ranks must have already achieved a very high standard of technical competence before auditioning. Ashton's leadership is a mixture of democracy and benign autocracy. The band's members choose the music, which varies from the brand new to charts originally played by editions of NYJO that were on the road when present members were barely walking, and Ashton organizes the musicians' choices into an entertaining programme. Although the nature of the orchestra means that it is in an almost constant state of flux, NYJO has developed an identifiable sound. Much of the music that is played by the band is original, often written by members, and everything is especially arranged. While many arrangements are 'in-house', others come from outside. Amongst the arrangers are Paul Higgs, David Lindup, **Brian Priestley**, Chris Smith, Terry Catharine, Bill Charleson, **Neil Ardley**, Alec Gould and Ashton. Many exceptional talents have passed through NYJO's ranks over the years, including **Steve** and **Julian Argüelles**, **Chris Hunter**, Lance Ellington, Paul Hart, David O'Higgins, **Phil Todd**, Mark and Andy Nightingale, Stan Sulzmann, **Chris Laurence**, Richard Symons, Gerard Presencer and **Guy Barker**. Ashton's interest in songwriting has ensured a succession of good singers with the band, including Carol Kenyon, Helen Sorrell and Litsa Davies. Over the years NYJO has travelled extensively, appearing in various European countries and also visiting the USA. The band's many albums have proved successful and help spread the sound of a remarkable orchestra which, although effectively the creation of one man, has come to represent the best in big band jazz and consistently denies its name by being both international and fully mature in all musical respects.

Selected albums: *Return Trip* (1975), *Eleven Plus: Live At LWT* (1976), *In Camra* (1977), *The Sherwood Forest Suite* (1977), *To Russia With Jazz* (1978), *Mary Rose* (1979), *Down Under* (1980), *Why Don't They Write Songs Like This Any More?* (1982), *Playing Turkey* (1983), *Born Again* (1983), *Full Score* (1985), *Concrete Cows* (1986), *With An Open Mind* (1986), *Shades Of Blue And Green* (1987), *Big Band Christmas* (1989), *Maltese Cross* (NYJO 1989), *Rememberance* (NYJO 1990), *Cookin' With Gas* (NYJO 1990), *Looking Forward Looking Back* (NYJO 1992), *These Are The Jokes* (1992), *Merry Christmas And A Happy New Year* (NYJO 1993).

Native Hipsters

This London-based duo comprised William Wilding (b. 18 May 1953, Romford, Essex, England) and Blatt (b. Nanette Greenblatt, 9 March 1952, Cape Town, South Africa). Prior to 1980 they had worked under names such as the Wildings, then later as the Patterns with Robert Cubitt and Tom Fawcett. In that guise, they released the challenging but largely incoherent 'The B'Shop Is In The Fridge'. They next emerged as (And The) Native Hipsters, again with Cubitt and Fawcett. It was as the latter that Wilding and Blatt achieved national recognition with their 1980 release 'There Goes Concorde Again'. Blatt's repetitive child-like enthusiasm at the sighting of the famed 'silverbird' captured the attention of UK Radio One disc jockey, **John Peel**, resulting in the single peaking at number 5 in the UK independent charts. Wilding turned down an offer from producer **Tony Visconti** to re-cut the single for national consumption, preferring total artistic control. Their next release in 1982, a four track EP, *Tenderly Hurt Me*, won them a respect from the music press who had previously condemned them as quirky odd-balls. The Hipsters' inventive and bizarre mixture of surreal poetry, diverse musical styles, original and sampled sounds, plus a vast array of musical instruments of whatever came to hand, managed to establish a cult following. Variously assisted by friends such as Lester Square (guitar, from the **Monochrome Set**), **Annie Whitehead** (trombone), Chris Cornetto (cornet), Liduina Van Der Sman (saxophone) and Simon Davison (piano), Wilding and Blatt have over the years recorded countless sessions, live and in the studio, which were later compiled to form *Blatt On The Landscape*. During the early 90s Wilding performed on the London cabaret circuit as the iconoclastic Woody Bop Muddy, an act consisting of his passing a savage judgement on whatever and whoever's records passed through his hands, by way of smashing them with a hammer.

Albums: as the Wildings *Why Did I Buy Those Blue Pyjamas* (1979), as the Native Hipsters *Blatt On The Landscape* (1988, cassette only).

Native Tongues Posse

An informal gathering in the late 80s of artists based in New York, USA, which set about to confirm and celebrate the history of black women and men. Intrinsic to the rise of 'Afrocentricity' in rap music, the coalition included the **Jungle Brothers**, **De La Soul**, **A Tribe Called Quest**, **Queen Latifah** and **Monie Love**. A critical backlash ensued in due course, with some of the proponents, or at least some of their adherents, criticised for their obsession with 'Afrocentric trinkets'. However, the movement as a whole was one imbued with positivity and intelligence, and the Native Tongues Posse played no small part in shifting rap's agenda from the self to the social.

Natural Acoustic Band

This trio was formed in 1969, in Milngavie, Glasgow, Scotland. There were a number of personnel changes but the essential line-up was Tom Hoy (b. 5 February 1950, Glasgow, Scotland; guitar/vocals), Robin Thyne (b. 1 November 1950, Newcastle Upon Tyne, England; guitar/vocals), and Krysia Kocjan pronounced Kotsyan (b. 10 August 1953, Craigendoran, Scotland; vocals). Krysia had a Polish father and a Flemish mother. The group played their first gig on 5 November 1969, at Alloa Working Men's Club. Eventually, the press picked up on Kocjan's vocal talent, and they were increasingly billed as the Natural Acoustic Band, featuring Krysia Kocjan. Occasionally, the group were augmented by a Chinese drummer and an Australian bass player, a truly international line-up. The two albums for **RCA**, were both released in 1972; *Learning To Live* in May, and *Branching In* in October. Krysia left in late 1972, and Robin and Tom continued to work with Joanna Carlin. She then left to pursue a solo career, and is now better known as Melanie Harrold. Robin and Tom continued as a duo, until Tom joined **Magna Carta** in 1975. Initially this was as a sound engineer, but eventually as a full-time member of the group. Robin also joined the Magna Carta, in 1977. In 1979, both Hoy and Thyne left and formed Nova Carta, recording the sole album, *Roadworks*, for **CBS**, in Holland. Kocjan released a solo album in 1974, and has since worked with **Al Stewart**, **Ray Davies**, **Robin Williamson**, **Mike Heron**, and **Glenn Yarborough**. Now living in the USA, Kocjan is still busy with session work, and voice teaching, and has plans to record again. Robin continues to work in a solo capacity, whilst Tom works as a duo with his wife Geraldine as Tom And Gerry.

Albums: *Learning To Live* (1972), *Branching In* (1972).

Natural Four

An R&B vocal group from Oakland, California, USA. The Natural Four who had a series of moderate-sized hits during the soul era recorded a soft style of soul in

two configurations, both led by Chris James. The original members were Chris James, Allen Richardson, John January, and Al Bowden. This group first recorded in 1968 on a small local label called Boola-Boola. From there they went to **ABC Records**, and reached the national charts in 1969 with 'Why Should We Stop Now' (number 31 R&B). The group was unable to repeat their success. Before breaking up in 1971, they recorded an unnoticed single for Bay Area producer Ron Carson that was released on **Chess Records**. James organized a new group - Darryl Canady, Steve Striplin, and Delmos Whitney - and signed with **Curtis Mayfield**'s **Curtom** label in 1972, and the following year had a sizable hit with 'Can This Be Real' (number 10 R&B, number 31 pop), written by **Leroy Hutson**. Subsequent records were not nearly as engaging and the group faded. Their last chart record was in 1976.
Albums: *Natural Four?* (ABC 1970), *Natural Four* (Curtom 1974), *Heaven Right Here On Earth* (Curtom 1975), *Nightchaser* (Curtom 1976).

Naturals

Formed in Harlow, Essex, the Naturals - Ricki Potter (vocals), Curt Cresswell (lead guitar), Bob O'Neale (harmonica), Mike Wakelin (bass) and Roy Heather (drums) - were originally known as the Blue Beats and had recorded several singles under this early appellation. The quintet made their debut as the Naturals in 1964, scoring their only hit in the UK singles chart that same year with a version of the **Beatles**' song, 'I Should Have Known Better'. Suspicions that the song had been the success, rather than the performers, was confirmed when subsequent, inferior singles failed to make an impression.

Naturists

Seven-piece UK techno group (yes, really), led by Wilmott Doonican, who claims to be a relative of **Val Doonican**, and Sid Raven Following the release of a mini-album (which despite the 'Gimmick' was well-received in the press), they released an appropriate cover version in **Blue Pearl**'s 'Naked In The Rain', in mid 1994. 'We were all into naturism before we started making records', they claim, 'in fact we all met at a small naturist reserve near Reading'. Their lack of clothing attire apparently acts as a key ingredient in the recording process too. 'When we went into the studio and recorded naked we found that the sound was much better because the top end frequencies weren't absorbed by out clothes'.
Album: *Friendly Islands* (1993, mini-album).

Naughton, David

b. 13 February 1951, Hartford, Connecticut, USA. Naughton is best known for his 1979 US Top 5 hit 'Makin' It'. After studying English literature and acting, Naughton appeared in a series of Dr. Pepper soda commercials, singing and dancing. He was then hired to act in the US television series *Makin' It,* based on the film *Saturday Night Fever*. Naughton recorded the title song from the film, and it scaled the charts. The television programme lasted only two months, however, and Naughton did not record again. His one hit was used that same year in a comedy film titled *Meatballs*.

Naughty By Nature

From New Jersey, New York, USA, the trio of Treach (b. Anthony Criss, 2 December 1970, East Orange, New Jersey, USA), Vinnie (b. Vincent Brown, 17 September 1970, East Orange, New Jersey, USA) and DJ Kay Gee (b. Keir Gist, 15 September 1969, East Orange, New Jersey, USA) are a rap troupe utilising the funkier rather than darker aspects of gangsta hip hop. Heavily influenced by the patronage of **Queen Latifah**, the language was blue but not always in the overtly sexual sense. 'Ghetto Bastard', for example, was a master stroke, pickled in the atmosphere of the street and exact in its execution of ghetto vernacular. Unlike many other hardcore outfits, Naughty By Nature were not afraid of injecting a touch of soul into the mix (once more, ala Queen Latifah), which makes the best of their work all the more endearing. They gave **Tommy Boy** their biggest ever hit with the 12-inch 'OPP', the largest-grossing authentic rap single in the US in 1990, selling over a million copies ('OPP' stands for 'Other People's Pussy', incidentally, though that did not prevent several generations enthusiastically singing along to 'I'm down with OPP', making the record an American equivalent to the **Shamen**'s 'Ebeneezer Goode'). A second album upped the sleaze factor with some lyrics, but still maintained the group's best traditions elswhere. The single lifted from *19 Naughty III*, 'Hip Hip Hooray', became another monster hit, helped in no small part by a Spike Lee-filmed video. Treach himself was to be found in Houston acting in the film *Jason's Lyric*, though he had appeared previously in the widely-ridiculed *Meteor Man*. He has written his own film treatments, inbetween bungie jumping sessions in Daytona with close friend Pepa (**Salt 'N' Pepa**). He also launched the Naughty Gear clothing line. Kay Gee, meanwhile, earned a production deal with **Motown**, intial fruit from which was characterised by **Zhane**'s debut album and hit single, 'Hey Mr. Deejay'.
Albums: *Naughty By Nature* (Tommy Boy 1991), *19 Naughty III* (Tommy Boy 1993).

Naughty Marietta (Film Musical)

Jeanette MacDonald, who had enjoyed much success with **Maurice Chevalier** in early musicals such as ***The Love Parade***, ***One Hour With You***, and ***Love Me Tonight***, co-starred in this film with a new partner with whom she would always be indelibly associated - **Nelson Eddy**. In the screenplay, by John Lee Mahin, Frances Goodrich, and Albert Hackett, which was based on the 1910 stage operetta of the same name, Jeanette Macdonald plays a French princess who avoids an arranged marriage by boarding a ship bound for the Colonies. The brave Capt. Warrington (Nelson Eddy) saves her from a fate worse than death, and the couple find sanctuary in New Orleans before eventually settling down together 'Neath The Southern Moon'. That was just one of the numbers in **Victor Herbert**'s sumptuous score which included such delights as 'Ah! Sweet Mystery Of Life', 'Italian Street Song', 'I'm Falling In Love With Someone', and 'Tramp! Tramp! Tramp!' (all with lyrics by Rida Johnson Young), and 'Chansonette' (lyric by **Gus Kahn**). Veteran character actor Frank Morgan lead the supporting cast, which also included Elsa Lanchester, Joseph Cawthorn, Akim Tamiroff, Douglas Dumbrille, Edward Brophy, and Walter Kingsford. This first episode in the Macdonald-Eddy series, during which they became the screen's favourite romantic singing duo, was produced by Hunt Stromberg for MGM and directed by W.S. Van Dyke. The MGM studios were awarded an Oscar for the sound recording.

Naughty Marietta (Stage Musical)

A comic operetta with music by **Victor Herbert** and a book and lyrics by Rida Johnson Young. It opened on 7 November 1910 at the New York theatre with a story set in New Orleans in 1870, where Naples-born Marietta d'Altena (Emma Trentini) has travelled in search of a husband. She finds the man of her dreams (in more ways than one) when the upstanding Captain Dick Warrington (Orville Harrold) finds that he too has been dreaming of the same song, 'Ah! Sweet Mystery Of Life'. It was only one of several numbers that endured from the attractive and tuneful score. The remainder included 'Tramp! Tramp! Tramp!', 'I'm Falling In Love With Someone', ''Neath The Southern Moon', 'Italian Street Song', 'Naughty Marietta', and 'Live For Today'. Even with the magnificent Trentini, *Naughty Marietta* folded after only 136 performances, but was revived on Broadway in 1912. Since then it has been frequently performed throughout the world, and is a part of the repertoire of the New York City Opera. The 1935 film version starred **Jeanette MacDonald** and **Nelson Eddy**.

Naura, Michael

b. 19 August 1934, Memel, Lithuania. Naura is a self-taught pianist and flautist who studied philosophy, sociology and graphic arts in Berlin. In the 50s he and Wolfgang Schluter (vibes) started a band which sought to mix blues, bebop and European *avant garde* and which became one of the leading German bands of the 60s. Since 1971, he has worked as the Head of the Norddeutscher Rundfunk Jazz Department. He continues occasional work with bands and regularly accompanies Peter Ruhmkorf in poetry-jazz recitals. He is also president of Performers and Artists for Nuclear Disarmament (PANDA) in Germany.
Albums: with Peter Ruhmkorf *Kein Apolloprogramm Fur Lyrik* (1976), *Country Children* (1977).

Navarre, Ludovic

b. c.1967, Saint-Germaine-En-Laye, France. French techno/ambient artist who records as Modus Vivendi, Deepside, Hexagone, Soofle, LN's, Deep Contest, DS and Saint-Germaine-En-Laye (titled after his hometown). A mainstay of **Laurent Garnier**'s FNAC and F imprints of the early 90s, Navarre has contributed to over 90% of both label's output as a musician/technician. Each of the names he has employed for his own recordings see him adapt a different house style, from techno to electronic jazz. Among his more impressive outings have been his work as Saint-Germaine-En-Laye ('Alabama Blues', 'My Momma Said', 'Walk So Lonely'), Modus VIvendi ('Modus Vivendi') and DS (Volume 1, Volume 2).

Navarro, Fats

b. Theodore Navarro, 24 September 1923, Key West, Florida, USA, d. 7 July 1950. After starting to learn the tenor saxophone and piano, Navarro opted for trumpet and by his mid-teens was playing professionally. In 1943 he joined the **Andy Kirk** band, working alongside **Howard McGhee**, and two years later was in the trumpet section of **Billy Eckstine**'s bebop-oriented big band. He later settled in New York, where he played with leading beboppers such as **Kenny Clarke**, **Ernie Henry**, Howard McGhee, **Tadd Dameron**, **Bud Powell**, **Charlie Parker**, **Leo Parker**, **Sonny Rollins** and **Dizzy Gillespie**, the last of whom he had replaced in the Eckstine band. Navarro also played with mainstreamers like **Coleman Hawkins** and **Eddie 'Lockjaw' Davis**. Most of these musical associations resulted in a legacy of fine recordings, with the Dameron sessions proving to be especially fruitful. During his short life Navarro displayed a precocious talent, his rich full tone contrasting with the thin sound adopted by many of the other young bebop trumpeters of the day. In this respect his sound resembled that of an earlier generation of trumpeters who were a little out of fashion by the late 40s. His last years were dogged by ill-health, exacerbated by an addiction to heroin, and he died in 1950. Despite his brief life, Navarro proved to be one of the most accessible of the early bop trumpeters and was an influence on another similarly short-lived talent, **Clifford Brown**.
Selected albums: with Billy Eckstine *Together!* (1947), with Charlie Parker *One Night In Birdland* (1950), *The Tadd Dameron Band 1948, Vols. 1 & 2 (1948)* (1976), *The*

Fabulous Fats Navarro Vols. 1 & 2 (1947-49) (Blue Note 1983), *Fat Girl - The Savoy Sessions (1947)* (1985), *Memorial* (Savoy 1992).

Naylor, Jerry

b. Jerry Naylor Jackson, 6 March 1939, Stephenville, Texas, USA. Naylor sang country music from an early age; when aged only 14, he appeared on *Louisiana Hayride*. Whilst in the US Army, he broke his back, an injury that has continued to plague him since then. He befriended **Glen Campbell** in Albuquerque, New Mexico and in 1961 moved with him to Hollywood. He found work as a disc jockey and a single, 'You're Thirteen', was released in the UK. He and Campbell joined the **Crickets** in 1962 and is featured on 'Don't Ever Change', 'My Little Girl' and 'Teardrops Fall Like Rain'. In 1964 he had a heart attack brought about, he says, 'by the stress of being **Buddy Holly**'s replacement'. He played the leading role in a concept album, a country opera entitled *The Legend Of Johnny Brown* in 1966. He returned to the Crickets for their 1971 album, *Rockin' 50s Rock And Roll*, but mostly he has followed a solo career, making numerous singles for US labels including **Motown**'s country division. His best-known record is 'Is That All There Is To A Honky Tonk?' in 1975. He now works as a disc jockey in Angoura, California and he is known to Buddy Holly fans for his outrageous claims such as being a Cricket throughout their hitmaking years.
Albums: *Happy Birthday USA* (1976), *Love Away Her Memory* (1977), *Once Again* (1978).

Nazareth

Formed in 1968 in Dunfermline, Fife, Scotland, Nazareth evolved out of local attractions, the Shadettes. **Dan McCafferty** (vocals), Manny Charlton (guitar), Pete Agnew (bass) and Darrell Sweet (drums) took their new name from the opening line in 'The Weight', a contemporary hit for the **Band**. After completing a gruelling Scottish tour, Nazareth opted to move to London. *Nazareth* and *Exercises* showed undoubted promise, while a third set, *Razamanaz*, spawned two UK Top 10 singles in 'Broken Down Angel' and 'Bad Bad Boy' (both 1973). New producer **Roger Glover** helped focus the quartet's brand of melodic hard rock, and such skills were equally prevalent on *Loud 'N' Proud*. An unlikely rendition of **Joni Mitchell**'s 'This Flight Tonight' gave the group another major chart entry, while the Charlton-produced *Hair Of The Dog* confirmed Nazareth as an international attraction. Another cover version, this time of **Tomorrow**'s 'My White Bicycle', was a Top 20 entry and although *Rampant* did not yield a single, the custom-recorded 'Love Hurts', originally a hit for the **Everly Brothers**, proved highly successful in the US and Canada. Nazareth's popularity remained undiminished throughout the 70s but, having tired of a four-piece line-up, they added guitarist Zal Cleminson, formerly of the **Sensational Alex Harvey Band**, for *No Mean City*. Still desirous for change, the group invited Jeff 'Skunk' Baxter, late of **Steely Dan** and the **Doobie Brothers**, to produce *Malice In Wonderland*. While stylistically different from previous albums, the result was artistically satisfying. Contrasting ambitions then led to Cleminson's amicable departure, but the line-up was subsequently augmented by former **Spirit** keyboard player, John Locke. Baxter also produced the experimental *The Fool Circle*, while the group's desire to capture their in-concert fire resulted in *'Snaz*. Glasgow guitarist Billy Rankin had now joined the group, but dissatisfaction with touring led to Locke's departure following *2XS*. Rankin then switched to keyboards, but although Nazareth continued to enjoy popularity in the US and Europe, their stature in the UK was receding. Bereft of a major recording deal, Nazareth suspended their career during the late 80s, leaving McCafferty free to pursue solo ambitions (he had already released a solo album in 1975). A comeback album in 1992 with the addition of Billy Rankin produced the impressive *No Jive*, yet Nazareth's recent low profile in the UK will demand further live work to capitalize on this success.
Albums: *Nazareth* (Mooncrest 1971), *Exercises* (Mooncrest 1972), *Razamanaz* (Mooncrest 1973), *Loud 'N' Proud* (Mooncrest 1974), *Rampant* (Mooncrest 1974), *Hair Of The Dog* (Mooncrest 1975), *Close Enough For Rock 'N' Roll* (Mountain 1976), *Play 'N' The Game* (Mountain 1976), *Expect No Mercy* (Mountain 1977), *No Mean City* (Mountain 1978), *Malice In Wonderland* (Mountain 1980), *The Fool Circle* (NEMS 1981), *'Snaz* (NEMS 1981), *2XS* (NEMS 1982), *Sound Elixir* (Vertigo 1983), *The Catch* (Vertigo 1984), *Cinema* (Vertigo 1986), *Snakes & Ladders* (Vertigo 1990), *No Jive* (Mainstream 1992). Dan McCafferty: *Dan McCafferty* (1975). Compilations: *Greatest Hits* (Mountain 1975), *20 Greatest Hits: Nazareth* (Sahara 1985), *Anthology: Nazareth* (Raw Power 1988).
Video: *Razamanaz* (1990).

Nazz

Formed in Philadelphia, USA in 1967, the Nazz comprised of **Todd Rundgren** (guitar/vocals), Carson Van Osten (bass/vocals), both ex-members of bar-band Woody's Truck Stop, Stewkey (lead vocals/keyboards) and Thom Mooney (drums). Although the quartet made its live debut supporting the **Doors**, manager John Kurland deliberately cultivated an air of exclusivity which ultimately hampered progress. A lucrative recording deal with publishers Screen Gems resulted in *Nazz*, a synthesis of British and US pop invoking the **Who**, **Jimi Hendrix**, **Buffalo Springfield** and **Small Faces**. However, the unit's anglophilia and mod affectations proved unfashionable in the face of acid-rock which, when coupled with growing internal disharmony, sowed the seeds of their demise. *Nazz Nazz* emphasized the positive elements of its predecessor and although the same influences were still apparent, a sense of individuality was also present. Rundgren's departure for a solo career in 1970 brought the Nazz to an end, and *Nazz III*, compiled from material from the *Nazz Nazz* sessions, was issued posthumously. Stewkey and Mooney were later joined by Rick Neilsen and Tom Petersson (later of **Cheap Trick**) in a group which took a variety of names, but only Rundgren achieved lasting success outside the Nazz. Despite negligible commercial gain, his former group's work was later lauded as the precursor to a generation of British-influenced US bands, notably the **Raspberries**, **Stories** and **Sparks**.

Albums: *Nazz* (1968), *Nazz Nazz* (1969), *Nazz III* (1970). Compilation: *Best Of The Nazz* (1983).

Ndegé Ocello, Me'Shell

b. Me'Shell Ndegé Ocello, Berlin, West Germany. Introduced by her PR machine as a female equivalent to **Prince**, Me'Shell has embarked on a solo career which embraces both the hip hop and R&B markets. Like Prince, she is a multi-instrumentalist, and writes, produces and plays on all her songs. Her given name was Swahili, indicating 'Free Like A Bird'. After a nomadic life as the child of a US forces man, her first love was art rather than the jazz skills of her father and brother. She was, however, inexorably drawn to music as she grew, and much of her youth was spent in Washington's 'go-go' scene, where at one point she was actually shot at whilst on stage with Little Bennie and the Masters, at the Cherry Atlantic Skating Rink. Her interest in music had blossomed when her brother played guitar in a local band, whose bass player left his instrument lying around after rehearsal. She was a quick convert. At the age of 19, she uprooted for New York 'with my baby and my bass'. There she joined **Living Colour**'s Black Rock Coalition, and recorded sessions for artists of the calibre of **Caron Wheeler** and **Steve Coleman**. She was the musical director for **Arrested Development**'s *Saturday Night Live* show, though her own demos were receiving little response. Until, that is, **Madonna** stepped in, inviting her to become one of the first artists signed to her Maverick empire. A palpable maturity was at work on her debut, with a combination of acid jazz and R&B rhythms backing her beat poetry. She scored a breakthrough hit with 'If That's Your Boyfriend (He Wasn't Last Night)', a provocative post-feminist statement. Despite the sexual overtones of her packaging, she was not averse to strong political statements; material like 'Step Into The Projects' retaining a cutting edge. Or the line 'The white man shall forever sleep with one eye open' (from 'Shoot'n Up And Gett'n High'), which had an almost **Public Enemy**-like ring to it. The album was produced by **A Tribe Called Quest**'s Bob Power, alongside guests including DJ Premier (**Gang Starr**) and Geri Allen (**Blue Note**). Though she attracted some criticism for espousing the corporate rebellion angle, her connections with Maverick hardly passing unobserved, there was substance and fire in the best of her work.

Album: *Plantation Lullabies* (Maverick/WEA 1993).

Neagle, Anna

b. Marjorie Robertson, 20 October 1904, Forest Gate, London, England, d. 3 June 1986, Surrey, England. One of the most beloved and durable artists in the history of British showbusiness: an actress, dancer and singer in West End musicals and British films with a career spanning more than 60 years. She took dancing lessons as a child, and appeared in the chorus of *Charlot's Revue* and a similar production, *Tricks*, in 1925. In the late 20s she undertook more chorus work in ***Rose Marie***, *The Charlot Show Of 1926*, ***The Desert Song***, and two London Pavilion revues as one of 'Mr Cochran's Young Ladies'. Up to then she had been primarily a dancer, but she developed further in 1931 when she took the ingenue lead opposite **Jack Buchanan** in the hit musical comedy ***Stand Up And Sing***, duetting with him on the lovely 'There's Always Tomorrow'. **Herbert Wilcox** produced and directed her first film musical, ***Goodnight Vienna***, in 1932, and most of her subsequent pictures, and were married in 1943. As well as making a number of acclaimed dramatic films during the 30s, Anna Neagle continued to appear in screen musicals such as *The Little Damozel*, *Bitter Sweet*, *The Queen's Affair*, *Limelight*, and *London Melody* (1939). From 1940-41 she and Wilcox were in America to make films such as *Irene* (in which she sang and danced to the delightful 'Alice Blue Gown'), *No, No, Nanette*, and *Sunny*. They returned to England to make a series of light and frothy romantic comedies, with the occasional musical number, which included *Spring In Park Lane*, *The Courtneys Of Curzon Street*, and *Maytime In Mayfair* (1949). Anna Neagle's leading man was Michael Wilding, and this magical partnership ensured that the films were among the British cinema's top box office attractions of the time. In the 50s Anna Neagle returned to the stage for *The Glorious Days* (1953), co-starred with Errol Flynn (of all people) in the film version of that show, *Lilacs In The Spring*; and also appeared in the screen adaptation of *King's Rhapsody*. She then kicked up her heels with popular singer **Frankie Vaughan** in ***The Lady Is A Square*** (1958). That was her last appearance on screen, although she did produce three more of Vaughan's films, *These Dangerous Years*, *Wonderful Things!*, and *Heart Of A Man*. In the early 60s Wilcox went bankrupt when his film company and one or two of the couple's other business ventures failed. Part of their salvation came in the form of **David Heneker**'s smash hit musical ***Charlie Girl*** (1965). Neagle stayed with the show - apart from the occasional holiday - for the duration of its run of over 2,000 performances and subsequent tours. On the day

it was announced that she was to be made a Dame of the British Empire, the cast of *Charlie Girl* surprised her by singing 'There Is Nothing Like A Dame' at the end of the evening's performance. In 1973 the new Broadway production of ***No, No, Nanette*** arrived in London, and Anna Neagle played the role which had been taken by **Ruby Keeler** in New York. Four years later Herbert Wilcox died, but Anna Neagle continued to work. In 1977 she was back in the West End, with the musical *Maggie*; in 1978 she toured as Henry Higgins's mother in a revival of ***My Fair Lady***, and in 1982 played in the pantomime *Cinderella* at the Richmond Theatre. It was as the Fairy Godmother in *Cinderella* that she made her final stage bow at the London Palladium at Christmas 1986. A few weeks after it closed she went into a Surrey nursing home to rest, and died there in June.
Further reading: *It's Been Fun*, Anna Neagle. *There's Always Tomorrow*, Anna Neagle.

Neal, Kenny

b. 14 October 1957, New Orleans, Louisiana, USA. The oldest son in Baton Rouge's most famous musical family, six of whom are professional musicians, Neal has been groomed throughout the 90s for blues stardom, but in a time of transition it remains an aim rather than an achievement. He accompanied his father to gigs from an early age, was given his first harmonica by **Slim Harpo** at the age of three, played piano onstage three years later, and at 13 stepped into the breach when **Raful Neal** needed a bass player. In 1976, he played bass in **Buddy Guy**'s band. Four years later, he moved to Toronto and brought his brothers north to work as the Neal Brothers Blues Band. Later, he joined the Downchild Blues Band, then Canada's top blues band. In 1984, he moved back to Baton Rouge to put another band together. When he accompanied his father on the *Louisiana Legend* album, King Snake owner Bob Greenlee signed him to a solo deal. *Bio On The Bayou* created a stir on its release in 1987; Alligator boss Bruce Iglauer leased the album, remixed it and changed its title, and acquired Neal's contract. In 1991, he took a role in the Broadway production of *Mule Bone*, a musical version of a play written by poet Langston Hughes and folklorist Zora Neale Hurston. He won that year's Theatre World Award for the most outstanding new talent appearing in a Broadway play. *Walking On Fire* features two songs, 'Morning After' and 'Bad Luck Card', on which he set Hughes' poems to music. *Bayou Blood* dispensed with the horn sections normally present on his records, updating the 60s Excello sound. *Hoodoo Moon* reflected the increasing maturity of his several talents and the promise of his eventual success.
Albums: *Bio On The Bayou* aka *Big News From Baton Rouge* (King Snake/Alligator 1987/8), *Devil Child* (Alligator 1989), *Walking On Fire* (Alligator 1991), *Bayou Blood* (Alligator 1993), *Hoodoo Moon* (Alligator 1994).

Neal, Raful

b. 6 June 1936, Baton Rouge, Louisiana, USA. That rare thing in the blues, a late developer, Neal was not interested in music until seeing **Little Walter** play at the Temple Room in Baton Rouge in 1958. Buying a harmonica the next day, he was helped by a friend, Ike Brown, to learn its rudiments. Sometime later, he was engaged to join the road band of guitarist Little Eddie Lang. His own first group was called the Clouds, and featured **Buddy Guy** and drummer Murdock Stillwood. When Guy left, **Lazy Lester** was one of his replacements. The band toured Louisiana and East Texas, its first residency, the Streamline Club in Port Allen, where Neal took up residence. He recorded 'Sunny Side Of Love' for Peacock in 1968 with little success, and was then refused by Crowley producer, **Jay Miller**. 'Change My Way Of Living', recorded for La Louisianna in 1969, fared better, and was followed by two records on Whit. During the 70s, he brought his teenage son, Kenny Neal, into his band and, as time went by, other sons, Noel, Raful Jnr., Larry and Darnell, were also recruited. With Kenny now a star in his own right, Raful continues to play in the Baton Rouge area, with forays further afield to play festivals, and record.
Album: *I Been Mistreated* (1991).

Near, Holly

b. 6 June 1949, Ukiah, California, USA. For Near's first 10 years, her family lived on a farm but her adolescence was spent in urban Ukiah where she matured from a child television actor to a performer with the confidence to accept a role in a Broadway run of ***Hair***. She also participated in Jane Fonda's controversial *Free The Army* revue that toured Vietnam with a message demanding US withdrawal. However, Near was to leave the 70s as an artist in direct descent from the early 60s protest singers. Indeed, it was Ronnie Gilbert of the **Weavers** who helped encourage interest in her on the US folk club and campus circuit. As a yardstick of the respect that became hers in this sphere, Gilbert, **Pete Seeger** and **Arlo Guthrie** were guests on *Lifelines* which, like all of her country-tinged body of mostly self-composed material, was issued on her and Jeff Langley's own Ukiah-based Redwood label. Largely by word of mouth, Near's first four albums sold a collective 155,000 by 1979 when *Imagine My Surprise* was voted Album Of The Year by the National Association of Independent Record Distributors. That spring found her in a Los Angeles theatre on the same bill as the premiere of the Labor movement film, *With Babies And Banners*. She also played a Women Against Violence Against Women benefit concert that shamed **Warner Brothers** into banning the use of brutal images on record sleeves.

Albums: *Hang In There* (1973), *Live* (1974), *You Can Know All I Am* (1976), *Imagine My Surprise* (1979), *Fire In The Rain* (80s), *Speed Of Light* (80s), *Journeys* (1984), *Watch Out* (80s), *Lifelines* (80s), *Don't Hold Back* (1987).

Nectarine No.9

Formed in Edinburgh, Scotland, in 1993, Nectarine No.9 revolves around guitarist/vocalist Davey Henderson, an ex-member of both the **Fire Engines** and **Win**. Alan Horne, founder of **Postcard Records** took great interest in both groups and Henderson's newest venture was one of his first signings on reactivating the label. *The Nectarine No.9* reinstated Henderson's love of abrasive pop and quirky rhythms, inhabiting a musical world part **T. Rex** and part **Fall**. However, it lacked the focus of Henderson's previous work and critical reaction was muted. *Guitar Thieves*, which collected various BBC Radio 1 sessions, included versions of **Captain Beefheart**'s 'Frownland' and the **Velvet Underground**'s 'Inside Of Your Heart', as well as an original song, 'Pull My Daisy', the title of which was drawn from a film featuring **Allen Ginsberg** and Jack Kerouac.

Albums: *The Nectarine No.9* (Postcard 1993), *Guitar Thieves* (Nightracks/Postcard 1994).

Ned's Atomic Dustbin

Formed in the West Midlands in 1988 by local characters Jonn Penney (b. 17 September 1968; lead vocals), Rat (b. 8 November 1970; guitar), Matt Cheslin (b. 28 November 1970; bass), Alex Griffin (b. 29 August 1971; bass) and Dan Warton (b. 28 July 1972; drums). After dubious Gothic beginnings, Ned's Atomic Dustbin began to find their feet in 1989 when a series of tour supports, notably with regional contemporaries the **Wonderstuff**, attracted a strong following. Notable for having two bassists, uniformly crimped hair and an unequivocally daft name (taken from the BBC radio's *The Goon Show*), the Ned's urgent, aggressive sub-hardcore sound still managed to offset any gimmicky connotations, turning a potential freak show into a challenging pop act. Armed with a plethora of original merchandising ideas - within three years the band produced 86 different t-shirt designs - their 'Kill Your Television' single entered the Top 50 of the UK chart and resulted in a major contract with Sony Music (formerly **CBS**). With the financial wherewithal to back their imagination, Ned's Atomic Dustbin soon translated their ideas into a phenomenal commercial success, peaking when *God Fodder* entered the UK charts at number four in 1991. The rest of the year was filled by hectic touring commitments, with America followed by Japan, a prestigious spot at the British Reading Festival, a UK number 21 hit with 'Trust', back to America (with **Jesus Jones**) and then a British tour which resulted in singer Jonn Penney collapsing from exhaustion on the last night.

Albums: *God Fodder* (1991), *Are You Normal?* (1992).
Videos: *Nothing Is Cool* (1991), *Lunatic Magnets* (1993).

Nefertiti

b. c.1973, Chicago, Illinois, USA, but raised in Los Angeles. Hardcore Islamic rapper, who as a baby was held in the arms of none other than Elijah Muhammed himself. Both her grandparents were employed by the founder of the Nation Of Islam, and their views have found a new conduit in Nefertiti. She began rapping at the age of 14, but this is just one of the means of expression and communication employed by her. She also works alongside Californian activist Jim Brown on the Amer-I-Can programme, to stabilise inter-gang violence and maintain truces in Los Angeles. She also lectures widely on self-awareness and improvement. Her first recorded messages came as guest appearances on records by **Professor Griff** and **King Tee**, and from an early age she was warming up crowds before **Public Enemy** and Louis Farrakhan shows. Although she signed to a major label, she insisted on a far-sighted contract stipulation: that **Mercury** pay to put her through college. The first results of this was the *LIFE* set, standing for Living In Fear Of Extinction. This included controversial calls for repatriation to Africa, never mind an Islamic State. She was joined on the record by **MC Lyte**, with whom comparisons have most frequently been made. She is also not to be confused with the UK rapper of similar name.

Album: *LIFE* (Mercury 1994).

Neidlinger, Buell

b. 2 March 1936, Westport, Connecticut, USA. After studying piano, trumpet and bass, Neidlinger concentrated on teaching himself the last instrument more extensively. He led bands in high school, then attended Yale for a year, winding up as a disc jockey. In 1955 he relocated to New York, where he gigged with **Coleman Hawkins**, **Tony Scott** and **Zoot Sims**. He made his name with **Cecil Taylor**, negotiating the pianist's difficult compositions with astonishing aptitude; he was part of Taylor's famous residency at the Five Spot in 1957 and played with him in a 1960 staging of *The Connection*. Always one for a surprising career move, Neidlinger then worked in singer **Tony Bennett**'s band for six months. Subsequent work included stints with **Gil Evans** and **Steve Lacy**. He studied music at Buffalo State University (1964-66), played with the Budapest Quartet at Tanglewood in 1965 and gave several recitals of works for solo bass by Sylvano Bussotti and Mauricio Kagel. In the late 60s he became a member of the Boston Symphony Orchestra. In 1970 Neidlinger played bass on **Frank Zappa**'s suite for violinist **Jean-Luc Ponty**, 'Music For Electric Violin And Low Budget Orchestra', brought in, according to Zappa, 'because he's the only man I could think of who could play the bass part'. In 1971 he became professor of music at the California Institute of the Arts and was also busy in the Hollywood recording studios. Neidlinger's ability to relate to different kinds of music is only equalled by his interest in them: at various times he has played with **Willie 'The Lion' Smith**, **Roy Orbison**, **Barbra Streisand** and **Archie Shepp**. He has several bands; Buellgrass provides a unique blend of country and jazz: an updated western swing; Thelonious plays **Thelonious Monk** tunes exclusively; String Jazz interprets **Duke Ellington** and Monk on saxophone, drums and various string instruments. Most of his releases are on the K2B2 label, which he co-runs with tenor saxophonist Marty Krystall, a playing associate of his for over 20 years. A caustic interviewee, Neidlinger has continually involved himself with the cutting edge of jazz and has an inimitable sound on his instrument.

Albums: with Cecil Taylor *New York City R&B* (1961, reissued as *Cell Walk For Celeste*), *Cecil Taylor All Stars Featuring Buell Neidlinger* (1961, reissued as *Jumpin' Punkins*), *Ready For The 90s* (1980), *Our Night Together* (1981), *Big Day At Ojai* (1982), with Thelonious Monk *Thelonious* (1987), with String Jazz *Locomotive* (Soul Note 1988), *Big Drum* (KB Records 1991). Compilations: *The Complete Candid Recordings Of Cecil Taylor And Buell Neidlinger* (1989, rec. 1960-61, 6-album box-set), *Rear View Mirror* (KB Records 1991, rec. 1979-86).

Neil, Fred

b. 1937, St. Petersburg, Florida, USA. An important figure in America's folk renaissance, Neil's talent first emerged in 1956 when he co-wrote an early **Buddy Holly** single, 'Modern Don Juan'. By the following decade he was a fixture of the Greenwich Village circuit, both as a solo act and in partnership with fellow singer **Vince Martin**. The duo embarked on separate careers following the release of *Tear Down The Walls*. Neil's subsequent solo *Bleecker And MacDougal* was an influential collection and contained the original version of 'The Other Side Of This Life', later covered by the **Youngbloods**, **Lovin' Spoonful** and the **Jefferson Airplane**. The singer's deep, resonant voice was equally effective, inspiring the languid tones of **Tim Buckley** and **Tim Hardin**. A reticent individual, Neil waited two years before completing *Fred Neil*, a compulsive selection which featured two of the artist's most famous compositions, 'The Dolphins' and 'Everybody's Talkin''. The latter was adopted as the theme song to *Midnight Cowboy*, a highly-successful film, although it was a version by **Harry Nilsson** which became the hit single. Such temporary trappings were of little note to Neil, who preferred the anonymity of his secluded Florida base, from where he rarely ventured. An appearance at the Los Angeles club, the Bitter End, provided the material for *The Other Side Of This Life*, Neil's last album to date and an effective resume of his career. This informal performance also contained other favoured material, including 'You Don't Miss Your Water', which featured assistance from country singer **Gram Parsons**. A major, if self-effacing talent, Fred Neil has virtually withdrawn from music altogether. He refuses to record or be interviewed and rare live appearances are constrained to benefit events for his charity, Dolphin Project, which he established with marine biologist Richard O'Berry in 1970.

Albums: *Hootenanny Live At The Bitter End* (1964), *World Of Folk Music* (1964), with Vince Martin *Tear Down The Walls* (1964), *Bleecker And MacDougal* aka *Little Bit Of Rain* (1964), *Fred Neil* aka *Everybody's Talkin'* (1966), *Sessions* (1968), *The Other Side Of This Life* (1971). Compilation: *The Very Best Of Fred Neil* (1986).

Neil, Vince, Band

Following his surprise sacking from **Mötley Crüe**, frontman Vince Neil (b. Vincent Neil Wharton, 8 February 1961, Hollywood, California, USA) wasted no time in setting up his solo career, contributing 'You're Invited But Your Friend Can't Come' (co-written with **Damn Yankees** duo Jack Blades and Tommy Shaw) to the *Encino Man* (*California Man* outside the USA) soundtrack. After which he assembled a band with ex-**Billy Idol** guitarist Steve Stevens, ex-**Fiona** guitarist Dave Marshall, ex-**Enuff Z'Nuff** drummer Vikki Foxx, and bassist Robbie Crane, who had switched from rhythm guitar after original bassist Phil Soussan's departure. The Ron Nevison-produced *X-Posed* brought Neil a good deal of respect, demonstrating his songwriting ability on good-time arena metal which followed the direction in which he felt that Mötley Crüe should have moved. The Vince Neil Band picked up a high-profile opening slot with **Van Halen**, but throat problems for Neil held up subsequent live work, and Stevens departed with Brent Woods replacing him. Rumours abounded of a Mötley Crüe reunion while Neil and his band worked towards a second album, but the acrimony surrounding the split makes this seem unlikely.

Album: *X-Posed* (Warners 1993).

Nelson

The twin sons of early rock 'n' roll star **Rick Nelson** and wife Kris, Matthew and Gunnar Nelson were born on 20 September 1967, Los Angeles, California, USA. Musically-inclined as children, the boys learned to play bass and drums as well as singng. Their father booked studio time for them for their 12th birthday, and they recorded a self-penned song with vocal backing by the **Pointer Sisters**. By the early 80s the twins had joined a heavy metal band called Strange Agents, which later changed its name to the Nelsons. In 1990, now simply called Nelson, the twins, both sporting waist-length blond hair (which saw them nicknamed the 'Timotei

Twins'), signed with **David Geffen**'s new DGC record label and recorded a self-titled pop-rock album. The first single release, '(Can't Live Without Your) Love And Affection', reached number 1 in the US charts, while the album made the US Top 20. Afterwards, however, press reaction remained hostile towards any return.
Album: *Nelson* (DGC 1990).

Nelson, 'Big Eye' Louis

b. 28 January c.1885, New Orleans, Louisiana, USA, d. 20 August 1949. Nelson settled on playing the clarinet after trying out a wide range of instruments. Throughout his career he rarely played outside his home town, choosing to work in the emerging jazz bands and the traditional New Orleans marching and brass bands. Nelson is reputed to have played in **Buddy Bolden**'s band, on bass, and he also worked with leading New Orleans jazzmen such as **John Robichaux**, **Joe 'King' Oliver** and **Jelly Roll Morton**. Nelson made few records - a handful of tracks with **Kid Rena** in 1940, and a few more in 1949 with **'Wooden' Joe Nicholas** and as leader, using the name Louis DeLisle, under which he sometimes worked. From these recordings it is possible to understand the high regard in which Nelson was held by musicians such as **Baby Dodds** and **Sidney Bechet**, whom Nelson tutored for a while. He played with a full sound and employed a facile technique. His records with Rena provide interesting testimony to the skill and stylistic devices of the earliest New Orleans jazz musicians.
Selected albums: with Wooden Joe Nicholas *Wooden Joe's New Orleans Band* (1945-49), *Louis Delisle's Band* (1949).

Nelson, Bill

b. William Nelson, 18 December 1948, Wakefield, West Yorkshire, England. Although noted chiefly for his innovative guitar work with **Be-Bop Deluxe**, his solo releases actually form more than four-fifths of his total output. *Smile* was a dreamy, acoustic debut after he had played throughout his home county with pre-progressive rock outfits like the Teenagers, Global Village and Gentle Revolution. He fronted Be-Bop Deluxe for most of the 70s before responding to punk and techno-rock forces by assembling Bill Nelson's Red Noise. *Sound-On-Sound*, released in 1979, was an agitated but confused debut from Red Noise and afterwards Nelson returned to solo work. The single 'Do You Dream In Colour?' provided his highest UK solo chart placing at number 52. It was released on his own label, Cocteau Records. Following a short-lived deal with **Mercury Records** he continued to release introspective, chiefly home-recorded albums. He was in demand as a producer and worked on sessions with many new-wave bands including the **Skids** and **A Flock Of Seagulls**. Surprisingly, after the demise of Be-Bop Deluxe he showed little inclination to use the guitar and preferred to experiment with keyboards and sampled sounds, composing thematic pieces which have been used in films and plays. He recorded backing music for the Yorkshire Actors Company's version of both *Das Kabinett* and *La Belle Et La Bette*, issued later as albums. Many of his releases throughout the 80s were of a whimsical, self-indulgent nature and missed the input of other musicians. Numerous albums were issued via his fan club and the quality was rarely matched by the prolificacy, which twice ran to four-album boxed sets, *Trial By Intimacy* and *Demonstrations Of Affection*. In 1991 he moved markedly towards a stronger and more defined melodic style with *Luminous* on Manchester's independent label, Imaginary, and also spoke of returning to his first love, the guitar.
Albums: *Smile* (1971), *Sound On Sound* (1979), *Quit Dreaming And Get On The Beam* (1981), *Sounding The Ritual Echo* (1981), *Das Kabinett* (1981), *La Belle Et La Bette* (1982), *The Love That Whirls* (1982), *Chimera* (1983), *The Two Fold Aspect Of Everything* (1984), *Trial By Intimacy* (1984), *Map Of Dreams* (1984), *Aconography* (1986), *Chamber Of Dreams* (1986), *Summer Of God's Piano* (1986), *Chance Encounters In The Garden Of Light* (1988), *Optimism* (1988), *Pavillions Of The Heart And Soul* (1989), *Demonstrations Of Affection* (1989), *Duplex* (1989), *Luminous* (1991), *Blue Moons And Laughing Guitars* (1992). Compilation: *Duplex: The Best Of Bill Nelson* (1990).

Nelson, Gene

b. Gene Berg, 24 March 1920, Seattle, Washington, USA. An actor, director, and athletic dancer in the **Gene Kelly**-style who was in several popular musicals of the 50s. Nelson grew up in Los Angeles and attended the renowned Fanchon and Marco dancing school there. After graduating from high school when he was 18, he took up ice skating and joined Sonja Henie's touring company and appeared in two of her films, *Second Fiddle* and *Everything Happens At Night*. After enlisting in the US Signals Corps early in World War II, he became a member of the cast of **Irving Berlin**'s celebrated wartime musical, ***This Is The Army***, which opened on Broadway in 1942 and was then filmed before touring the UK and US military bases throughout the world. Following his discharge, Nelson went to Hollywood in 1947 and made the musical, *I Wonder Who's Kissing Her Now*, with June Haver. Ironically, it was while he was starring in the hit Broadway revue ***Lend An Ear*** (1949), that Nelson was noticed by a representative of Warner Brothers Pictures. After playing a minor role in *The Daughter Of Rosie O'Grady*, he was signed to a long-term contract and given the third-lead to **Doris Day** and **Gordon MacRae** in *Tea For Two* (1950). From then on, he appeared in a string of musicals for the studio, including *The West Point Story*, *Lullaby Of Broadway* (his first starring role, opposite Doris Day), *Painting The Clouds With Sunshine*, *She's Working Her Way Through College*, *She's Back On Broadway*, *Three Sailors And A Girl*, *So This Is Paris*, and ***Oklahoma!*** (1955). In the latter film he had the best role of his career - and two great numbers, 'Kansas City' and 'All Er Nothin'' (with Gloria Grahame as Ado Annie). In the late 50s Nelson appeared on television until he suffered a horse riding action which put an end to his dancing - at least for a while. He turned to directing, and in the 60s worked on some melodramas, and two musical films starring **Elvis Presley**, *Kissin' Cousins* (which he also co-wrote) and *Harum Scarum*. He also directed ***Your Cheatin' Heart***, a film biography of country singer **Hank Williams**. In 1971 he was back on Broadway with other veteran entertainers such as Yvonne De Carlo and Alexis Smith in **Stephen Sondheim**'s ***Follies***. Nelson played Buddy Plummer and had one of the show's outstanding numbers, the rapid-fire 'Buddy's Blues'. He continued to direct in the 70s and 80s, mostly for television, and worked on the top-rated series *Washington Behind Closed Doors*. In 1993 his projects included staging a US provincial production of Richard Harris's popular comedy *Stepping Out*.

Nelson, Jimmy 'T-99'

b. 7 April 1928, Philadelphia, Pennsylvania, USA. Nelson joined his brother (who later became famous as a singer with the **Johnny Otis** Orchestra under the stage name Redd Lyte) on the west coast in the mid-40s, and began shouting the blues after seeing **Big Joe Turner**. While singing with the Peter Rabbit Trio in 1951, Jimmy was signed to Modern's RPM subsidiary, with whom he had big R&B hits with his 'T-99 Blues' and 'Meet Me With Your Black Dress On'. In 1955 Nelson moved to Houston, Texas, where he recorded records for **Chess** and a host of small Texas and California independent labels. From the mid-60s worked outside the music business until he was recorded by Roy Ames in 1971 for Home Cooking Records with **Arnett Cobb's** band. In recent years he has begun performing again and has toured Europe.
Albums: *Jimmy 'Mr T-99' Nelson* (1981), *Watch That Action!* (1987), with Arnett Cobb And His Mobb *Sweet Sugar Daddy* (1990).

Nelson, Louis

b. 17 September 1902, New Orleans, Louisiana, USA, d. 5 April 1990. Nelson grew up in a cultured family; his mother was a graduate of the Boston Conservatory of Music, his father was a physician. After starting out on alto horn, he switched to trombone in the 20s. Working mostly with bands in and around New Orleans, including those led by **Oscar 'Papa' Celestin** and **Kid Rena**, he built a sound reputation during the 30s. During this period he also worked often with the popular big band led by Sidney Desvigne. In the early 40s he joined **Kid Thomas** and in the 50s was a regular member of the band led by **George Lewis**, with whom he toured extensively. In the 60s Nelson also worked with the New Orleans Joymakers, the Legends Of Jazz, **Kid Thomas**, **Peter Bocage**, **Sammy Rimington** and other leading New Orleans-style musicians. For many years he was a frequent performer at Preservation Hall in his home town. Although best known for his New Orleans playing, Nelson's style incorporated many elements foreign to the form; an attribute that is due, most observers believe, to the time spent with Desvigne. This gave him a somewhat different approach to music than that followed by stalwarts of the tradition, such as **Jim Robinson**. Indeed, many keen followers of Nelson's work consider his sophisticated trombone playing to be more akin to that of **Tommy Dorsey** rather than that of the earthier New Orleanians. Nelson could still be heard at Preservation Hall in the late 80s and into early 1990, when, in April, he was the victim of a hit-and-run accident. He continued working for a few days, but one night on the bandstand he complained of feeling unwell and collapsed. He died the following day.
Albums: *Kid Thomas At Moulin Rouge* (c.1955), *George Lewis And His New Orleans All Stars* (1963), *Peter Bocage At San Jacinto Hall* (1964), *Louis Nelson's Big Four Vols 1 & 2* (1964), *Skater's Waltz* (1966), *Louis Nelson's New Orleans Band* (1970), *New Orleans Tradition* (1971), with Kid Thomas *Preservation Of Jazz Vol. 2* (1973), *Everybody's Talkin' Bout The* (GHB 1986), *Louis Nelson All Stars Live In Japan* (1987), *April In New Orleans* (GHB 1989), *New Orleans Portraits Vol 3* (Storyville 1990).

Nelson, Oliver

b. 4 June 1932, St. Louis, Missouri, USA, d. 28 October 1975. After studying piano and alto saxophone, he settled on playing the latter instrument, paying his dues in various **territory bands**. In the late 40s he was with the popular **Jeter-Pillars Orchestra** as well as that led by Nat Towles. Early in the 50s he was briefly with **Louis Jordan** but then resumed his studies at universities in Washington, DC, and Missouri, also taking lessons from the respected composer Elliott Carter. In New York in the late 50s, he worked in bands led by **Erskine Hawkins** and **Louie Bellson**, then moved on to the bands of **Duke Ellington** and **Quincy Jones**. He was writing extensively at this time, both as arranger and composer, and made several records under his own name, the best-known with a small group that often featured leading jazz soloists such as **Eric Dolphy** and **Freddie Hubbard**. He later turned more to big band work, recording with numerous soloists who included **Johnny Hodges** and **Pee Wee Russell**. By the mid-60s Nelson was in great demand as a teacher and arranger and he was also called upon to write scores for films and television. His arrangements with **Jimmy**

Smith during this period were particularly fertile, and included orchestrations of *Bashin'* and *The Dymanic Duo* (with **Wes Montgomery**). He played much less often in these years but did lead a small band from time to time and also formed all-star big bands for festival appearances. Nelson's work ranged widely, covering R&B and modal jazz, and he also composed pieces in the classical form. Much of his writing suggests considerable facility, though at times slipping a little into being merely facile. Nevertheless his recordings as a performer, especially *The Blues And The Abstract Truth*, on which he is joined by Dolphy and Hubbard, are extremely rewarding, while many of those he made as composer-leader such as the excellent *Sound Pieces* are interesting for their unstinting professionalism. He died from a heart attack in 1975.

Selected albums: *Meet Oliver Nelson* (New Jazz 1959), *Takin' Care Of Business* (New Jazz 1960), *Screamin' The Blues* (New Jazz 1960), *Soul Battle* (Original Jazz Classics 1960), *Nocturne* (Moodsville 1960), *Straight Ahead* (New Jazz 1961), *The Blues And The Abstract Truth* (Impulse 1961), *Main Stem* (Original Jazz Classics 1961), *Taking Care Of Business* (Original Jazz Classics 1961), *Afro-American Sketches* (Prestige 1962), *Main Stem* (Prestige 1962), *Impressions Of Phaedra* (United Artists 1962), with Jimmy Forrest *Soul Battle* (Prestige 1962), *Full Nelson* (Verve 1963), *Fantabulous* (Argo 1964), *More Blues And The Abstract Truth* (Impulse 1965), *Michelle* (Prestige 1966), *Sound Pieces* (Impulse 1966), *Live From Los Angeles* (Prestige 1967), *Happenings* (Impulse 1967), *The Kennedy Dream* (Impulse 1967), *The Spirit Of '67* (Impulse 1967), *Soulful Brass* (Impulse 1968), *Leonard Feather Presents The Sound Of Feeling And The Sound Of Oliver Nelson* (Verve 1968), *Black, Brown And Beautiful* (RCA 1970), *Berlin Dialogue For Orchestra* (1970), *Swiss Suite* (1971), *Oliver Nelson With Oily Rags* (1974), *Stolen Moments* (1975).

Nelson, Ozzie

b. 20 March 1906, Jersey City, New Jersey, USA, d. 3 June 1975. While studying for the legal profession, Nelson ran a danceband as a hobby, but it was so successful that he abandoned law for music. He played many of the east coast's more prestigious venues, including Glen Island Casino and the New Yorker Hotel. Nelson's extremely relaxed singing style proved remarkably popular, as did the work of the band's female singer, **Harriet Hilliard** (1909-1994). Ozzie and Harriet married in 1935 and their romantic duets, coupled with their real-life romance, gave fans something to coo over. In the early 40s Nelson and the band appeared in a number of films, and he made a great impact with a US radio series, *The Adventures Of Ozzie And Harriet*, which began in 1944. In 1952, the show transferred to television and ran until 1966. Nelson's interests expanded into other areas of show business; he worked on the stage and also produced and directed on television. Also in the cast of the television show, when they were old enough, were Ozzie and Harriet's sons, David and **Ricky Nelson**. After the show closed, Ozzie continued to work in many different facets of show business.

Compilations: *On The Air* (1940), *Young America's Favorite* (1986), *Ozzie Nelson (1940-42)* (1988), *Ozzie Nelson 1937* (1988), *Satan Takes A Holiday 1936-41* (1988).

Further reading: *Ozzie*, Ozzie Nelson.

Nelson, Ricky

b. Eric Hilliard Nelson, 8 May 1940, Teaneck, New Jersey, USA, d. 31 December 1985, De Kalb, Texas, USA. Nelson came from a showbusiness family and his parents had sung in bands during the 30s and 40s. They had their own US radio show, *The Adventures Of Ozzie And Harriet*, soon transferred to television, in which Ricky and his brother David appeared. By 1957 Nelson embarked on a recording career, with the million selling, double-sided 'I'm Walkin''/'A Teenager's Romance'. A third hit soon followed with 'You're My One And Only Love'. A switch from the label **Verve** to **Imperial** saw Nelson enjoy further success with the rockabilly 'Be-Bop Baby'. In 1958 Nelson formed a full-time group for live work and recordings, which included **James Burton** (guitar), James Kirkland (later replaced by Joe Osborn) (bass), Gene Garf (piano) and Richie Frost (drums). Early that year Nelson enjoyed his first transatlantic hit with 'Stood Up' and registered his first US chart topper with 'Poor Little Fool'. His early broadcasting experience was put to useful effect when he starred in the Howard Hawks movie western, *Rio Bravo* (1959), alongside John Wayne and **Dean Martin**. Nelson's singles continued to chart regularly and it says much for the quality of his work that the b-sides were often as well known as the a-sides. Songs such as 'Believe What You Say', 'Never Be Anyone Else But You', 'It's Late', 'Sweeter Than You', 'Just A Little Too Much' and 'I Wanna Be Loved' showed that Nelson was equally adept at singing ballads and uptempo material. One of his greatest moments as a pop singer occurred in the spring of 1961 when he issued the million-selling 'Travelin' Man' backed with the exuberant **Gene Pitney** composition 'Hello Mary Lou'. Shortly after the single topped the US charts, Nelson celebrated his 21st birthday and announced that he was changing his performing name from Ricky to Rick.

Several more pop hits followed, most notably 'Young World', 'Teenage Idol', 'It's Up To You', 'String Along' (his first for his new label, **Decca**), 'Fools Rush In' and 'For You'. With the emergence of the beat boom, Nelson's clean-cut pop was less in demand and in 1966 he switched to country music. His early albums in this vein featured compositions from such artists as **Willie Nelson**, **Glen Campbell**, **Tim Hardin**, **Harry Nilsson** and **Randy Newman**.

In 1969 Nelson formed a new outfit the Stone Canyon

Band featuring former **Poco** member Randy Meisner (bass), Allen Kemp (guitar), Tom Brumley (steel guitar) and Pat Shanahan (drums). A version of **Bob Dylan**'s 'She Belongs To Me' brought Nelson back into the US charts and a series of strong, often underrated albums followed. A performance at Madison Square Garden in late 1971 underlined Nelson's difficulties at the time. Although he had recently issued the accomplished *Rick Sings Nelson*, on which he wrote every track, the audience were clearly more interested in hearing his early 60s hits. Nelson responded by composing the sarcastic 'Garden Party', which reaffirmed his determination to go his own way. The single, ironically, went on to sell a million and was his last hit record. After parting with the Stone Canyon Band in 1974, Nelson's recorded output declined, but he continued to tour extensively. On 31 December 1985, a chartered plane carrying him to a concert date in Dallas caught fire and crashed near De Kalb, Texas. Nelson's work deserves a place in rock history as he was one of the few 'good looking kids' from the early 60s who had a strong voice which, coupled with exemplary material, remains durable.

Albums: *Teen Time* (1957), *Ricky* (1957), *Ricky Nelson* (1958), *Ricky Sings Again* (1959), *Songs By Ricky* (1959), *More Songs By Ricky* (1960), *Rick Is 21* (1961), *Album Seven By Rick* (1962), *Best Sellers By Rick Nelson* (1962), *It's Up To You* (1962), *A Long Vacation* (1963), *Million Sellers By Rick Nelson* (1963), *For Your Sweet Love* (1963), *Rick Nelson Sings For You* (1963), *Rick Nelson Sings 'For You'* (1963), *The Very Thought Of You* (1964), *Spotlight On Rick* (1964), *Best Always* (1965), *Love And Kisses* (1965), *Bright Lights And Country Music* (1966), *On The Flip-Side* (1966, film soundtrack), *Country Fever* (1967), *Another Side Of Rick* (1968), *Perspective* (1968), *In Concert* (1970), *Rick Sings Nelson* (1970), *Rudy The Fifth* (1971), *Garden Party* (1972), *Windfall* (1974), *Intakes* (1977), *Playing To Win* (1981), *Memphis Sessions* (1985), *Live 1983-1985* (1988). Compilations: *It's Up To You* (1963), *Million Sellers* (1964), *The Very Best Of Rick Nelson* (1970), *Legendary Masters* (1972), *The Singles Album 1963-1976* (1977), *The Singles Album 1957-63* (1979), *Rockin' With Ricky* (1984), *String Along With Rick* (1984), *The Best Of Ricky Nelson* (1985), *All My Best* (1985).

Further reading: *Ricky Nelson: Idol For A Generation*, Joel Selvin. *The Ricky Nelson Story*, John Stafford and Iain Young. *Ricky Nelson: Teenage Idol, Travelin' Man*, Philip Bashe.

Nelson, Romeo

b. Iromeio Nelson, 12 March 1902, Springfield, Tennessee, USA, d. 17 May 1974, Chicago, Illinois, USA. A Chicago resident from the age of six (apart from a 1915-19 interlude in East St. Louis, where he learned piano) Nelson played rent parties and clubs until the early 40s, otherwise supporting himself by gambling. In 1929 he recorded four titles for Vocalion, among them 'Head Rag Hop' and 'Gettin' Dirty Just Shakin' That Thing', which are two of the finest rent party showpieces on record. Both are complex, endlessly inventive and full of puckish humour, the former track (based on **Pinetop Perkins**' 'Pinetop's Boogie Woogie') being taken at breakneck speed. When interviewed in the 60s, Nelson had retired from music altogether.

Compilation: *The Piano Blues Vol. 3 Vocalion* (1977).

Nelson, Sandy

b. Sander L. Nelson, 1 December 1938, Santa Monica, California, USA. Drummer Nelson began his career as a member of the Kip Tyler Band. Appearances in live rock 'n' roll shows led to his becoming an in-demand session musician, where he joined an *ad hoc* group of young aspirants including **Bruce Johnston** and **Phil Spector**. Nelson played on 'To Know Him Is To Love Him', a million-selling single written and produced by the latter for his vocal group, the **Teddy Bears**. Johnston meanwhile assisted the drummer on an early demo of 'Teen Beat', a powerful instrumental which achieved gold status in 1959 on reaching the Top 10 in both the US and UK. Two years later, Nelson secured another gold disc for 'Let There Be Drums', co-composed with Richie Podolor, who became a successful producer with **Three Dog Night** and **Steppenwolf**. The pattern was now set for a plethora of releases on **Imperial**, each of which combined a simple guitar melody with Nelson's explosive percussion breaks, a style echoing that of the concurrent surf craze. Its appeal quickly waned and 'Teen Beat '65' (1964) - recorded in the artist's garage studio - was his last chart entry. Guitarists **Glen Campbell** and Jerry McGee, later of the **Ventures**, as well as bassist **Carol Kaye** were among the musicians contributing to his sessions, but these lessened dramatically towards the end of the decade. During the 70s Nelson was featured in one of impresario Richard Nader's *Rock 'N' Roll Revival* shows, but he retired following the disappointing disco-influenced *Bang Bang Rhythm*. Despite being tempted into occasional, informal recordings, Nelson has remained largely inactive in professional music since 1978, although instrumental aficionados still marvel at the drummer's extensive catalogue.

Albums: *Teen Beat* (1960), *He's A Drummer Boy* aka *Happy Drums* (1960), *Let There Be Drums* (1961), *Drums Are My Beat!* (1962), *Drummin' Up A Storm* (1962), *Golden Hits* (retitled *Sandy Nelson Plays Fats Domino*) (1962), *On The Wild Side* aka *Country Style* (1962), *Compelling Percussion* aka *And Then There Were Drums* (1962), *Teen Age House Party* (1963), *The Best Of The Beats* (1963), *Be True To Your School* (1963), *Live! In Las Vegas* (1964), *Teen Beat '65* (1965), *Drum Discotheque* (1965), *Drums A Go-Go* (1965), *Boss Beat* (1966), *'In' Beat* (1966), *Superdrums* (1966), *Beat That #!!&* Drum* (1966), *Cheetah Beat* (1967), *The Beat*

Goes On (1967), *Souldrums* (1968), *Boogaloo Beat* (1968), *Rock 'N' Roll Revival* (1968), *Golden Pops* (1968), *Rebirth Of The Beat* (1969), *Manhattan Spiritual* (1969), *Groovy!* (1969), *Rock Drum Golden Disc* (1972), *Keep On Rockin'* (1972), *Roll Over Beethoven* aka *Hocus Pocus* (1973), *Let The Good Times Rock* (1974), *Bang Bang Rhythm* (1975). Compilations: *Beat That Drum* (1963), *Sandy Nelson Plays* (1963), *The Very Best Of Sandy Nelson* (1978), *20 Rock 'N' Roll Hits: Sandy Nelson* (1983).

Nelson, Shara

Former **Massive Attack** singer who began her solo career with 'Down That Road' on **Cooltempo Records** in July 1993. Both **Paul Oakenfold** and Steve Osbourne were involved in remixing the single, which marketed her as the new **Aretha Franklin**. She had always admitted to her **Motown** influences, and the arrangements on her debut album were sumptuous affairs, with heaped strings and gushing choruses. Not that she had deserted her dance/hip hop roots entirely, with co-writing credits for Prince B of **PM Dawn** ('Down That Road'), **Adrian Sherwood** (title-track) and **Saint Etienne** ('One Goodbye In Ten') offering a nice balance. The latter was the second single to be lifted from the album, bringing her a first major hit.
Album: *What Silence Knows* (Cooltempo 1993).

Nelson, Skip

A popular and versatile band singer in the 40s, Nelson sang with **Teddy Powell** before taking over from **Ray Eberle** with the **Glenn Miller** civilian band in late 1942. Nelson sang on such Miller hits as 'Dearly Beloved', 'Moonlight Becomes You', 'Moonlight Mood' and 'That Old Black Magic'. In the mid-40s he joined **Guy Lombardo**'s Orchestra, and featured on their big 1944 hit, 'It's Love-Love-Love'.

Nelson, Tracy

b. 27 December 1944, Madison, Wisconsin, USA. Tutored on both piano and guitar as a child, Nelson began a singing career while studying at Wisconsin University. She was a member of two bands, including the Imitations, prior to recording her solo debut, *Deep Are The Roots*, in 1965. **Charlie Musselwhite** (harmonica) and Peter Wolfe (guitar) added support to a set drawing much of its inspiration from blues singers **Ma Rainey** and **Bessie Smith**. In 1966 Nelson became a founder member of **Mother Earth**, an excellent country/blues attraction which she later came to dominate as original members pursued other projects. By 1973, when they were recording regularly in Nashville, the group had become known as Tracy Nelson/Mother Earth, and that year's *Poor Man's Paradise* was, effectively, a solo album. The singer's independent career was officially launched the following year with *Tracy Nelson*, which included a powerful version of **Bob Dylan**'s 'It Takes A Lot To Laugh It Takes A Train To Cry'. Ensuing recordings revealed a mature, self-confident vocalist working in an eclectic style redolent of **Bonnie Raitt**. Recording opportunities decreased during the 80s, although Nelson continues to perform live; in 1990 she completed several live dates in the UK.
Albums: *Deep Are The Roots* (1965), *Tracy Nelson* (1974), *Sweet Soul Music* (1975), *Time Is On My Side* (1976), *Home Made Songs* (1978), *Doin' It My Way* (1980), *Come See About Me* (1980), *In The Here And Now* (1993).

Nelson, Willie

b. Willie Hugh Nelson, 30 April 1933, Abbott, Texas, USA. Following their mother's desertion and the death of their father, Nelson and his sister Bobbie were raised by their grandparents. Bobbie was encouraged to play the piano and Willie the guitar. By the age of 7 he was writing cheating-heart-style songs. 'Maybe I got 'em from soap operas on the radio,' he said, 'but I've always seemed to see the sad side of things.' Bobbie married the fiddle player Bud Fletcher, and they both played in his band. When Fletcher booked western swing star **Bob Wills**, the 13-year-old Willie Nelson joined him for a duet. After graduation he enlisted in the US Air Force, but was invalided out with a bad back, which has continued to plague his career to the present day. In 1953 Nelson began a traumatic marriage in Waco, Texas. 'Martha was a full-blooded Cherokee Indian,' says Nelson, 'and every night was like Custer's last stand.' When they moved to Fort Worth, Texas, Nelson was criticized for playing beer-joints and inappropriately evangelising - he fortunately gave up the latter. A Salvation Army drummer, Paul English, has been his drummer ever since, and is referred to in 'Me And Paul' and 'Devil In A Sleepin' Bag'. Nelson's first record, 'Lumberjack', was recorded in Vancouver, Washington in 1956 and written by **Leon Payne**. Payne, then a radio disc jockey, advertised the records for sale on the air. For $1, a listener received the record and an autographed 8 x 10 photo of Nelson. 3,000 copies were sold by this method. In Houston he sold 'Family Bible' to a guitar scholar for $50 and when it became a country hit for **Claude Gray** in 1960, Nelson's name was not on the label. He also sold 'Night Life' for $150 to the director of the same school: **Ray Price** made it a country hit and there have now been over 70 other recordings. Nelson moved to Nashville where his off-beat, nasal phrasing and dislike of rhinestone trimmings made him radically different from other country musicians. He recorded demos in 1961, which he later rescued from a fire. The demos were spread over three collections, *Face Of A Fighter*, *Diamonds In The Rough* and *Slow Down Old World*, but they are often repackaged in an attempt to pass off old material as new. These one-paced collections are not meant to encourage new fans as the songs are bleak, very bleak or unbearably bleak. From time to time,

Nelson has re-recorded one of these songs for another album.

In 1961 three of Nelson's country songs crossed over to the US pop charts: **Patsy Cline**'s 'Crazy', **Faron Young**'s 'Hello Walls' and **Jimmy Elledge**'s 'Funny How Time Slips Away'. Ray Price employed Nelson playing bass with his band, the Cherokee Cowboys, not knowing that he had never played the instrument. Nelson bought a bass, practised all night and showed up the next day as a bass player. Touring put further pressures on his marriage and he was divorced in 1962. The following year Nelson had his first country hits as a performer, first in a duet with Shirley Collie, 'Willingly' and then on his own with 'Touch Me'. His 40 tracks recorded for **Liberty Records** were top-heavy on strings, but they included the poignant 'Half A Man' and the whimsical 'River Boy'. He also wrote a witty single for Joe Carson, 'I Gotta Get Drunk (And I Sure Do Dread It)'. When Liberty dropped their country performers, Nelson moved to Monument. He gave **Roy Orbison** 'Pretty Paper', which made the UK Top 10 in 1964 and became Nelson's most successful composition in the UK. Some Monument tracks were revamped for *The Winning Hand*, which gave the misleading impression that Nelson had joined forces with **Kris Kristofferson**, **Brenda Lee** and **Dolly Parton** for a double-album. In 1965 Nelson married Shirley Collie and took up pig-farming in Ridgetop, Tennessee. During the same year Ray Price refused to record any more of Nelson's songs after an accident when Nelson shot his fighting rooster. They eventually joined forces for an album. Chet Atkins produced some fine albums for Nelson on **RCA,** including a tribute to his home state, *Texas In My Soul.*

However, he was only allowed to record with his own musicians on the live *Country Music Concert* album, which included an emotional 'Yesterday' and a jazzy 'I Never Cared For You'. He recorded around 200 tracks for the label, including well-known songs of the day like 'Both Sides Now', 'Help Me Make It Through The Night' and, bizarrely, the UK comedy team, Morecambe And Wise's theme song, 'Bring Me Sunshine'. *Yesterday's Wine* remains his finest RCA album, although it begins rather embarrassingly with Nelson talking to God. Nelson wrote seven of the songs in one night, but he was unstable as he drank heavily and used drugs. 'What Can You Do To Me Now?' indicated his anguish.

During 1970 his show-business lawyer, Neil Rushen, thought Nelson should record for **Atlantic Records** in New York. The singer used his own band, supplemented by **Doug Sahm** and **Larry Gatlin**. Atlantic did not feel that *The Troublemaker* was right for the label and it only surfaced after he had moved to **Columbia**. *Shotgun Willie* was closer to rock music and included **Leon Russell**'s 'A Song For You' and the reflective 'Sad Songs And Waltzes'. *Phases And Stages* (1974), made in **Muscle Shoals**, Alabama, looked at the break-up of a marriage from both sides - the woman's ('Washing The Dishes') and the man's ('It's Not Supposed To Be That Way'). Nelson also recorded a successful duet with **Tracy Nelson** (no relation) of 'After The Fire Is Gone'. He toured extensively and his bookings at a rock venue, the Armadillo World Headquarters in Austin, showed that he might attract a new audience. Furthermore, **Waylon Jennings**' hit with 'Ladies Love Outlaws' indicated a market for 'outlaw country' music. The term separated them from more conventional country artists, and, with a pigtail and a straggly beard, Nelson no longer looked like a country performer. Ironically, they were emphasizing the very thing from which country music was trying to escape - the cowboy image. In 1975 Nelson signed with Columbia and wanted to record a lengthy, old ballad, 'Red Headed Stranger'. His wife suggested that he split the song into sections and fit other songs around it. This led to an album about an old-time preacher and his love for an unfaithful woman. The album consisted of Willie's voice and guitar and Bobbie's piano. Columbia thought it was too low-key, too religious and needed strings. They were eventually persuaded to release it as it was and *Red Headed Stranger* (1975) has since become a country classic. Nelson's gentle performance of the country standard, 'Blue Eyes Crying In The Rain', was a number 1 country hit and also made number 21 on the US pop charts in 1975.

With brilliant marketing, RCA then compiled *Wanted: The Outlaws* with Jennings, Nelson, **Jessi Colter** and **Tompall Glaser**. It became the first country album to go platinum and it included a hit single, 'Good Hearted Woman', in which Jennings' thumping beat and Nelson's sensitivity were combined beautifully. The first *Waylon And Willie* (1978) album included Ed Bruce's witty look at outlaw country, 'Mammas, Don't Let Your Babies Grow Up To Be Cowboys' and two beautifully restrained Nelson performances, 'If You Can Touch Her At All' and 'A Couple More Years'. Their two subsequent albums contained unsuitable or weak material and perfunctory arrangements, although the humorous *Clean Shirt* (1991) was a welcome return to form. Since then, they have added **Johnny Cash** and Kris Kristofferson for tours and albums as the Highwaymen. Nelson has also recorded two albums with **Merle Haggard**, including the highly successful 'Poncho And Lefty', as well as several albums with country stars of the 50s and 60s. His numerous guest appearances include 'Seven Spanish Angels' (**Ray Charles**), 'The Last Cowboy Song' (Ed Bruce), 'Are There Any More Real Cowboys?' (**Neil Young**), 'One Paper Kid' (**Emmylou Harris**), 'I Gotta Get Drunk' (**George Jones**), 'Waltz Across Texas' (**Ernest Tubb**), 'They All Went To Mexico' (**Carlos Santana**) and 'Something To Brag About' (Mary Kay Place). Utilizing modern technology, he sang with **Hank Williams** on 'I Told A Lie To My Heart'. He

invited **Julio Iglesias** to join him at the Country Music Awards and their duet of **Albert Hammond**'s 'To All The Girls I've Known Before' was an international success.
Nelson has recorded numerous country songs, including a tribute album to **Lefty Frizzell**, but, more significant has been his love of standards. He had always recorded songs like 'Am I Blue?' and 'That Lucky Old Sun', but *Stardust* (1978), which was produced by **Booker T. Jones** of the MGs, took country fans by surprise. The weather-beaten, top-hatted character on the sleeve *was* Willie Nelson but the contents resembled a **Bing Crosby** album. Nelson sang ten standards, mostly slowly, to a small rhythm section and strings. The effect was devastating as he breathed new life into 'Georgia On My Mind' and 'Someone To Watch Over Me', and the album remained on the US country charts for nearly 10 years. Nelson recorded 103 songs in a week with **Leon Russell** but their performance of standards falls far short of *Stardust.* Nelson tried to recapture the magic of *Stardust* on the lethargic *Without A Song*, which contained the first Nelson/Julio Iglesias duet, 'As Time Goes By'. In both performance and arrangement, his Christmas album, *Pretty Paper* (1979), sounds like a mediocre act at a social club, but the jaunty *Somewhere Over The Rainbow* (the **Harold Arlen/E.Y. 'Yip' Harburg** classic) is much better. In 1982 Johnny Christopher showed Nelson a song he had written, 'Always On My Mind'. Nelson wanted to record the song with Merle Haggard, but Haggard did not care for it, so Nelson recorded an emotional and convincing version on his own, which went to Number 5 in the US charts. It was some time before Nelson learnt that **Elvis Presley** had previously recorded the song. The resulting album, which included 'Let It Be Me' and 'A Whiter Shade Of Pale', showed his mastery of the popular song. Other modern songs to which he has added his magic include 'City Of New Orleans', 'Wind Beneath My Wings' and 'Please Come To Boston'. He sang another Presley hit, 'Love Me Tender', on the soundtrack of *Porky's Revenge.* When Robert Redford met Nelson at a party, he invited him to join the cast of *The Electric Horseman.* Willie had an entertaining role as Redford's manager, and he made a major contribution to the soundtrack with 'My Heroes Have Always Been Cowboys'. Redford wanted to star in the film of *Red Headed Stranger* (1987) but it was cast eventually with Nelson in the title role. His other films include *Barbarosa* (in which he played an old gunfighter), a re-make of *Stagecoach* with his outlaw friends, and the cliche-ridden *Songwriter* with Kris Kristofferson. He is more suited to cameo roles and has the makings of a latter-day Gabby Hayes.
Nelson's record label, Lone Star, which he started in 1978 with **Steven Fromholz** and the Geezinslaw Brothers, was not a commercial success, but he later developed his own recording studio and golf course at Pedernales, Texas. He often adds the passing vocal and he produced
Timi Yuro - Today there in 1982. He took over the Dripping Springs Festival and turned it into a festival of contemporary country music: Willie Nelson's Fourth of July Picnic. He has organized several Farm Aid benefits, and he and **Kenny Rogers** represented country music on the number 1 **USA For Africa** single, 'We Are The World'. With all this activity, it is hardly surprising that his songwriting has suffered and he rarely records new compositions now. He wrote 'On The Road Again' for the country music film in which he starred, *Honeysuckle Rose*, and he also wrote a suite of songs about the old west and reincarnation, *Tougher Than Leather*, when he was in hospital with a collapsed lung.
Among the many songs which have been written *about* Willie Nelson are 'Willy The Wandering Gypsy And Me' (**Billy Joe Shaver**), 'Willie, Won't You Sing A Song With Me' (George Burns), 'Crazy Old Soldier' (**Lacy J. Dalton**), 'Willon And Waylee' (**Don Bowman**), 'The Willie And Waylon Machine' (**Marvin Rainwater**), 'Willie' (**Hank Cochran** and Merle Haggard) and 'It's Our Turn To Sing With Ol' Willie' (Carlton Moody And The Moody Brothers). Nelson's touring band, Family, is a very tight unit featuring musicians who have been with him for many years. Audiences love his image as an old salt, looking rough and playing a battered guitar, and his headbands have become souvenirs in the same way as Elvis' scarves. His greatest testimony comes from President Jimmy Carter, who joined him onstage and said, 'I, my wife, my daughter, my sons and my mother all think he's the greatest'. Unfortunately, the USA's Inland Revenue Service took a different view and, in an effort to obtain $16 million in back taxes, they had Nelson make an acoustic album, which was sold by mail order. His collaboration with artists like **Bob Dylan** and **Paul Simon** on *Across The Borderline* brought him back into the commercial mainstream for the first time in several years. In 1991 Nelson married Annie D'Angelo and they now have a young family. Nelson is a true outlaw and probably the greatest legend and performer in country music since **Hank Williams**.
Albums: *...And Then I Wrote* (1962), *Here's Willie Nelson* (1963), *Country Willie - His Own Songs* (1965), *Country Favorites - Willie Nelson Style* (1966), *Country Music Concert (Live At Panther Hall)* (1966), *Make Way For Willie Nelson* (1967), *The Party's Over* (1967), *Texas In My Soul* (1968), *Good Times* (1968), *My Own Peculiar Way* (1969), *Both Sides Now* (1970), *Laying My Burdens Down* (1970), *Willie Nelson And Family* (1971), *Yesterday's Wine* (1971), *The Words Don't Fit The Picture* (1972), *The Willie Way* (1972), *Shotgun Willie* (1973), *Phases And Stages* (1974), *Red Headed Stranger* (1975), with Waylon Jennings, Jessi Colter, Tompall Glaser *Wanted: The Outlaws* (1976), *The Sound In Your Mind* (1976), *Willie Nelson - Live* (1976), *The*

Troublemaker (1976), *To Lefty From Willie* (1977), *Stardust* (1978), *Face Of A Fighter* (1978), *Willie And Family Live* (1978), with Jennings *Waylon And Willie* (1978), *The Electric Horseman* (1979), *Willie Nelson Sings Kristofferson* (1979), *Pretty Paper* (1979), *Danny Davis And Willie Nelson With The Nashville Brass* (1980), with Leon Russell *One For The Road* (1980), with Ray Price *San Antonio Rose* (1980), *Honeysuckle Rose* (1980), *Family Bible* (1980), *Somewhere Over The Rainbow* (1981), with Roger Miller *Old Friends* (1982), *Diamonds In The Rough* (1982), with Merle Haggard *Poncho And Lefty* (1982), with Johnny Bush *Together Again* (1982), *Always On My Mind* (1982), with Jennings *WWII* (1982), with Webb Pierce *In The Jailhouse Now* (1982), with Kris Kristofferson, Brenda Lee, Dolly Parton *The Winning Hand* (1982), *Without A Song* (1983), *Tougher Than Leather* (1983), with Jennings *Take It To The Limit* (1983), with Jackie King *Angel Eyes* (1984), *Slow Down Old World* (1984), *City Of New Orleans* (1984), with Kristofferson *Songwriter* (1984), with Johnny Cash, Jennings, Kristofferson *Highwayman* (1985), with Faron Young *Funny How Time Slips Away* (1985), with Hank Snow *Brand On My Heart* (1985), *Me And Paul* (1985), *Half Nelson* (1985), *The Promiseland* (1986), *Partners* (1986), with Haggard *Seashores Of Old Mexico* (1987), *Island In The Sea* (1987), with J.R. Chatwell *Jammin' With J.R. And Friends* (1988), *What A Wonderful World* (1988), A *Horse Called Music* (1989), with Cash, Jennings, Kristofferson *Highwayman 2* (1990), *Born For Trouble* (1990), with Jennings *Clean Shirt* (1991), *Who'll Buy My Memories - The IRS Tapes* (1991), *Across The Borderline* (1993), *Healing Hands Of Time* (Liberty 1994), *Moonlight Becomes You* (Columbia 1994), with Curtis Porter *Six Hours At Pedernales* (Step One 1994), with Don Cherry *Augusta* (Coast To Coast 1995).
Compilations: *Willie Nelson's Greatest Hits (And Some That Will Be)* (1981), *Country Willie* (1987), *The Collection* (1988), *Across The Tracks - The Best Of Willie Nelson* (1988), *20 Of The Best* (1991), *King Of The Outlaws* (1993), *Heartaches* (1993), *The Complete Liberty Recordings 1962-64* (1993).
Video: *Willie Nelson And Family In Concert* (1988), *The Best Of* (1990), *The Original Outlaw/On The Road Again* (Hughes Leisure 1994).
Further reading: *Willie Nelson Family Album*, Lana Nelson Fowler (ed.). *Willie Nelson - Country Outlaw*, Lola Socbey. *Willie*, Michael Bane. *I Didn't Come Here And I Ain't Leavin'*, Willie Nelson with Bud Shrake. *Heartworn Memories - A Daughter's Personal Biography Of Willie Nelson*, Susie Nelson. *Willie: An Autobiography*, Willie Nelson and Bud Shrake.

Nemesis

This rap trio are from Dallas, Texas comprising The Snake, Big Al and MC Azim. Their first single, 'Oak Cliff', appeared in 1987, but it would be four years down the line before their debut long player, *To Hell And Back*. It was promoted by the single, 'I Want Your Sex'. As their spokesman Azim was happy to point out, 'To be young gifted and black is a blessing that has been treated as a sin'. Undoubtedly this has played a part in holding back their career, as too has prejudice against Texan rappers generally.
Albums: *To Hell And Back* (Profile 1990), *Munchies For Your Bass* (Profile 1991).

Neon Cross

This Californian 'white metal' quartet was formed in 1984 by David Raymond Reeves (lead vocals) and Don Webster (guitar). Enlisting the services of Ed Ott (bass) and Michael Betts (drums), it took a further four years before the band made their debut with a track on 1988's *California Metal* compilation. A deal with Regency Records ensued and their self-titled debut album emerged as a competent amalgam of **Stryper**, **Barren Cross** and **Bloodgood**. It was, however, discredited somewhat by Reeves' limited vocal ability.
Album: *Neon Cross* (Regency 1988).

Neon Philharmonic

Neon Philharmonic was essentially the work of two musicians, the Nashville, Tennessee-based singer-songwriter Don Gant (b. 1942) and arranger/conductor/composer Tuppy Saussy. Gant's career included writing songs with **Roy Orbison** and singing solo and background for country artists such as **Don Gibson** and **John D. Loudermilk**. He produced records for many artists, including **Bobby 'Blue' Bland**, **Jimmy Buffett** and **Lefty Frizzell**. Gant also ran **ABC**-Dunhill Records and was president of the Nashville branch of the National Academy of Recording Arts and Sciences (NARAS). Gant teamed with Saussy in 1969 and recorded the latter's 'Morning Girl' for **Warner Brothers Records** with a chamber group comprised of members of the Nashville Symphony Orchestra. The record made the US Top 20 and one follow-up single also reached the charts. The 'group' released two albums and five further singles but the novelty had diminished. Gant died on the 6th March, 1987.
Albums: *Moth Confesses* (1969), *Neon Philharmonic* (1969).

Neon Rose

This progressive rock group was formed in Sweden in 1973 by vocalist Roger Holegard and guitarist Gunnar Hallin. Augmented by Piero Mengarelli (guitar), Beno Mengarelli (bass/vocals) and Thomas Wilkund (drums), they signed to **Vertigo** the following year. Inspired by **Iron Butterfly**, **Emerson, Lake And Palmer** and **Deep Purple**, Neon Rose were an experimental quintet that indulged in long, esoteric and frequently blues-based workouts. They debuted with *A Dream Of Glory And Pride* in 1974, which showcased the band's instrumental capabilities, but also highlighted their vocal shortcomings. Two further albums were released,

but the quality of material declined significantly. They disappeared from the scene in 1976, having only made an impact in their native Sweden.
Albums: *A Dream Of Glory And Pride* (Vertigo 1974), *Neon Rose Two* (Vertigo 1974), *Reload* (Vertigo 1975).

Neptune's Daughter

Following their successful portrayal of a pair of twins in the bullfighting musical *Fiesta* (1947), MGM re-united **Esther Williams** and Ricardo Montalban two years later for this Jack Cummings Technicolor production which proved to be one of the top screen musicals of the decade, grossing $3.5 million in North America alone. Williams plays an up-market swim-suit designer who falls for millionaire Montalban, a member of a visiting South American polo team. The two stars nearly had the film stolen away from them via an hilarious sub-plot which involved **Betty Garrett** and comedian Red Skelton. He is a simple polo club masseur, but she is convinced that he is the wealthy Montalban, and wants to play her own kind of games with him. Joining in the fun were Keenan Wynn, Mel Blanc, Ted De Corsia, Mike Mazurki, and **Xavier Cugat** And His Orchestra. Jack Donahue staged the dance sequences and the obligatory underwater ballet. **Frank Loesser**'s songs included 'My Heart Beats Faster', 'I Love Those Men', and the enduring 'Baby, It's Cold Outside', which was introduced by Williams and Montalban, and went on to win an Oscar. Dorothy Kingsley, who wrote the witty screenplay, later worked on major musicals such as ***Kiss Me Kate***, ***Seven Brides For Seven Brothers***, and ***Pal Joey***. This bright and entertaining film was directed by Edward Buzzell.

Nero And The Gladiators

This short-lived UK instrumental pop group was formed by guitarist Mike O'Neill who, having been informed that he resembled a Roman emperor, dubbed himself Nero and took to wearing a toga. His group, which also included Colin Green (guitar) and Rod 'Boots' Slade (bass), completed three rousing singles, including 'Entry Of The Gladiators' and Prokofiev's 'In The Hall Of The Mountain King', the latter of which incurred a BBC radio ban when Boots' spoken introduction was deemed disrespectful to a classical piece of music. The unit was disbanded in 1962 when Slade and Green opted to join **Georgie Fame** And The Blue Flames. Slade later surfaced in the **Alan Price Set**.

Nervous Norvus

b. Jimmy Drake, 1912, d. 1968. The Californian based ex-truck driver's first record was the country ballad 'Gambling Fury', which he recorded as Singing Jimmy Drake on the Indiana label, Claudra. He joined **Dot Records** in 1956 and had two of the biggest novelty hits of that year. His first hit 'Transfusion', concerned the thoughts of a drunk driver who is in need of a blood transfusion after a car crash. Despite the sick subject it was hilarious, though the British public were spared it when **London Records** refused its release. The follow-up to this US Top 10 hit was 'Ape Call', a tale about cave men recorded in hip language, with jungle calls courtesy of Red Blanchard. After his few months in the spotlight he returned to obscurity, despite later unsuccessful recordings on Big Ben and Embee.
Compilation: *Transfusion* (1985).

Nervous Records

New York based record label almost as familiar to its adherents via a range of clothing merchandise emblazoned with its distinctive cartoon logo, as it is for its bouncing house tunes. Nervous came into being in the summer of 1990, through the efforts of Michael Weiss and Gladys Pizarro (who would subsequently split to form **Strictly Rhythm**). The label was launched on to New York's club underground via three specially selected releases - Niceguy Soulman's 'Feel It' (**Roger 'S' Sanchez**), Swing Kids' 'Good Feeling' (**Kenny 'Dope' Gonzalez**) and Latin Kings' 'I Want To Know (Quiero Saber)' (**Todd Terry**). Since then the label, and its merchandising arm, has been run on the basis of continuous throughput. New music is recorded and released week on week, and clothes lines are changed on a similar timescale. The philosophy is that this is the one way in which the label can maintain its link to the street, although it doubtless also increases profit margins too. Trinidad's 'Philly'/'The Blunt' was produced on either side by Frankie Feliciano and Todd Terry, while Just Us' 'You Got It' was created by Frankie Cutlass and Andy Marvel, typifying the depth in talent employed by the label. Garage mainstay Paul Scott also chipped in with Sandy B's 'Feel Like Singing'. Some of the label's better known later cuts include Nu Yorican Soul's output and Loni Clark's 'Rushin'' and 'You'. However, Nervous' ambitions do not end at merely providing quality dance material from established stars. There are already three subsidiary labels, Wreck, Sorted, Weeded and Strapped. Wreck covers hip hop, scoring immediately with the signing of **Black Moon** (whose 'Who Got The Props' single moved over 200,000 units). Sorted documents more trance and ambient focused material, while Weeded hosts underground reggae and dub artists. The newest offshoot is Strapped, which is more funk-orientated. Despite a number of instant successes, the Nervous empire continues to maintain its commitment to its original vision: 'When we put out a record, it's from the street level, if it crosses over, that's just a plus, we don't tailor a record to become a crossover hit. We want to keep our roots in the street'.

Nesbitt, John

b. c.1900, Norfolk, West Virginia, USA, d. 1935. In the early 20s Nesbitt played trumpet with various bands before joining the band led by Bill McKinney, which eventually evolved into **McKinney's Cotton Pickers**. He stayed with the band for several years, playing and writing arrangements. In the early 30s he was resident in New York, playing in the bands of **Fletcher Henderson** and **Luis Russell**, before returning to **territory bands**, including those of Zack Whyte and Speed Webb.

Compilation: *McKinney's Cotton Pickers (1928-29)* (1983).
Further reading: *McKinney's Music: A Bio-discography Of McKinney's Cotton Pickers*, John Chilton.

Nesmith, Michael

b. Robert Michael Nesmith, 30 December 1942, Houston, Texas, USA. Although best-known as a member of the **Monkees**, Nesmith enjoyed a prolific career in music prior to this group's inception. During the mid-60s folk boom he performed with bassist John London as Mike and John, but later pursed work as a solo act. Two singles, credited to Michael Blessing, were completed under the aegis of **New Christy Minstrels**' mastermind Randy Sparks, while Nesmith's compositions, 'Different Drum' and 'Mary Mary' were recorded, respectively, by the **Stone Poneys** and **Paul Butterfield**. Such experience gave the artist confidence to demand the right to determine the Monkees' musical policy and his sterling country-rock performances were the highlight of the group's varied catalogue. In 1968 he recorded *The Witchita Train Whistle Sings*, an instrumental set, but his independent aspirations did not fully flourish until 1970 when he formed the First National Band. Former colleague London joined Orville 'Red' Rhodes (pedal steel) and John Ware (drums) in a group completing three exceptional albums which initially combined Nashville-styled country with the leader's acerbic pop, (*Magnetic South*), but later grew to encompass a grander, even eccentric interpretation of the genre (*Nevada Fighter*). The band disintegrated during the latter's recording and a Second National Band, on which Nesmith and Rhodes were accompanied by Johnny Meeks (bass; ex-**Gene Vincent** and **Merle Haggard**) and Jack Panelli (drums), completed the less impressive *Tantamount To Treason*. The group was disbanded entirely for the sarcastically-entitled *And The Hits Just Keep On Comin'*, a haunting, largely acoustic, set regarded by many as the artist's finest work. In 1972 he founded the Countryside label under the aegis of **Elektra Records**, but despite critically-acclaimed sets by **Iain Matthews**, Garland Frady and the ever-present Rhodes, the project was axed in the wake of boardroom politics. The excellent *Pretty Much Your Standard Ranch Stash* ended the artist's tenure with **RCA**, following which he founded a second label, Pacific Arts. *The Prison*, an allegorical narrative which came replete with a book, was highly criticized upon release, although recent opinion has lauded its ambition. Nesmith reasserted his commercial status in 1977 when 'Rio', culled from *From A Radio Engine To The Photon Wing*, reached the UK Top 30. The attendant video signalled a growing interest in the visual arts which flourished following *Infinite Rider On The Big Dogma*, his biggest selling US release. In 1982 *Elephant Parts* won the first ever Grammy for a video, while considerable acclaim was engendered by a subsequent series, *Michael Nesmith In Television Parts*, and the film *Repo Man*, which the artist financed. Having refused entreaties to join the Monkees' 20th Anniversary Tour, this articulate entrepreneur continues to pursue his various diverse interests including a highly successful video production company (Pacific Arts).

Albums: *The Wichita Train Whistle Sings* (1968), *Magnetic South* (1970), *Loose Salute* (1971), *Nevada Fighter* (1971), *Tantamount To Treason* (1972), *And The Hits Just Keep On Comin'* (1972), *Pretty Much Your Standard Ranch Stash* (1973), *The Prison* (1975), *From A Radio Engine To The Photon Wing* (1977), *Live At The Palais* (1978), *Infinite Rider On The Big Dogma* (1979). Compilations: *The Best Of Mike Nesmith* (1977), *The Newer Stuff* (1989).
Film: *Head* (1968).

Nestico, Sam

b. 6 February 1924, Pittsburgh, Pennsylvania, USA. Nestico studied music after completing military service, although by this time he had already gained experience playing trombone in a radio orchestra. During the 50s and 60s he worked as staff arranger for various military bands. In the late 60s he began writing for **Count Basie** and subsequently wrote for films and television. He is also a teacher and many of his arrangements have been written with college and university bands in mind. He is a cousin of the arranger **Sal Nistico**.

Albums: *Swingphonic (With Time Out For Seven)* (70s), by Count Basie *Basie Big Band* (1975), by Basie *Warm Breeze* (1981), *Dark Orchid* (1982), *Night Flight* (1985).

Network

London-based duo of Tim Laws and Ryan Lee, who were friends from the age of 12, and formed their first band at the age of 13. Two years passed before they became Two Extremes, playing the London rock circuit. Afterwards Laws set up a fully equipped 16-track studio in his parent's garden shed. He is also an accomplished guitarist, having contributed to five of the songs on the debut **Undercover** album. Lee, meanwhile, concentrated on his vocals, seeking guidance from **Elton John/Annie Lennox** coach Glynn Jones. The duo formed Network while playing together in a covers band, the Max Wall Experience. Immediately they broke the charts with 'Broken

Wings', following up with the 1993 release, 'Get Real'.

Network Records

Brimingham dance label which originally grew out of the underground success of Kool Kat Records. Kool Kat was formed in 1988 by the partnership of Neil Rushton and Dave Barker. Rushton was a well known northern soul DJ in the 70s and a journalist for *Echoes* and other periodicals, and in the 80s managed the Inferno record label which re-released northern soul records and material by psychedelic soul group Dream Factory. He stumbled on Detroit techno through his northern soul connections in the US, and met leading lights **Derrick May** then **Kevin Saunderson**, in time becoming the latter's manager. He subsequently compiled an album of Detroit techno for **Virgin** (the first in the UK, later packaging similar collections like the *Retro Techno/Detroit Definitive* sets for Network). His partner Dave Barker's background was as a jazz-funk DJ in the Midlands. Kool Kat began with a number of underground records (experimental techno, psychedelic techno and Chicago house). The policy from the outset was to combine the cream of US releases with plenty of upfront British material. They consequently took on board several local groups, the best known early example of which were **Nexus 21/Altern 8**. Proclaimed as one of the hip record labels of the day, funds still remained in short supply and the label was on the verge of collapse. The team had a rethink and formed a new label, Network. From the start Network has employed its own, hard imagery and defined, generic sleeves. The musical range, however, was much broader than had been the case with Kool Kat. The first record to be released was Neal Howard's 'Indulge', while the honour of first chart appearance came with Altern 8's 'Infiltrate'. 'Activ8', by the same group, would do even better, reaching number 3. Network's money problems were easing, and with the advent of **KWS** and 'Please Don't Go' they disappeared altogether. Neil Rushton had heard the track in a Birmingham club and saw the potential in making a pop record out of it. He approached **ZYX** who held the rights to the Double You? version of the **KC & The Sunshine Band** song, only available in Europe, but was turned down unceremoniously. So Rushton arranged for KWS, then recording for Network as B-Line, to re-record it. It stayed at number 1 for five weeks. The follow-up, another KC cover, 'Rock Your Baby', was also hugely successful, and soon a lawsuit from ZYX, still unresolved years later, was underway. After KWS the label delivered Altern 8's debut, which effectively summarised the high watermark of the rave generation, with Network personnel taking a full hand in the various pranks and schemes which became synonymous with the group. However, they ran into trouble in June 1992 over Manchester rave band Rhythm Quest's *The Dreams* EP, which used expletives to criticise police procedures in closing down raves. The police expressed their fears to Network that the record, which featured ex-boxer Mark Hadfield, could incite violence, and it was subsequently reissued in a 'cleaned up version', just missing the Top 40. By the end of 1992 the label had grown unhappy with their distribution set-up with Pinnacle, and at great expense bought themselves out with two years of the contract to run. They initially contacted Sony with a view to distribution only, but in the end the notion of a bigger tie-in was mooted. After eight months of negotiations Sony bought 49% of the shares in the company in August 1993, and Network officially became (on the headed notepaper rather than record labels) Best Beat Dance Limited. It immediately allowed the company far greater freedom. Disenchanted with the reputation given to Network by KWS, they launched SiX6 (most commonly referred to as Six By Six) for street level house. Again a strong generic look was invoked with different colours to distinguish releases. The first product for the imprint was 'Hell's Party' by Glam, an immediate success, which secured the more underground vibe and credibility which Six By Six had been searching for. The Sony deal had also given the company the power to distribute records themselves, and thus help out younger labels by offering them distribution (as long as they pass the Network taste barometer). Some of these 'third party' distributed labels include **Bostin'** (which is owned by a band called Mother, whose main man is DJ Lee Fisher), Other Records, the 'Journeys By DJ' series, **Good Boy**, **DiY**/Strictly 4 Groovers, **Sure Is Pure**'s Gem, the Ritmo Rival's **Planet Four**, Hott Records from London and Manchester's UFG and Silver City. In addition there are several labels that Network actually owns. In 1990 the company opened an office in New York, and the **First Choice** garage/disco label (also a recording studio based in Greenwich Village) grew out of that set-up. Baseroom Productions is similar to First Choice in that it grew out of a recording studio, based in Stoke On Trent. Artists like Sure Is Pure, **BIzarre Inc**, Altern 8 and **MC Lethal** had been recording there, and with the name cropping up so frequently Network investigated. They eventually bought out the Baseroom as part of their deal with Sony, and launched a label around the studio, specialising in techno and experimental ambient/non-vocal material. The label's principal artists include Aquarel and the System, and **Laurent Garnier** has also collaborated on projects emanating from there. As if that were not enough, there are additionally three or four labels with whom deals have been done where Network handle all the rights for releases in the UK. **KMS** UK was inaugurated via Rushton's management of Saunderson, which made the move inevitable. The label specialises in strong vocal house while spin-off label Eclipse offers the non-vocal techno for which Saunderson is famous.

Another Detroit label is Serious Grooves, an underground techno/disco imprint pioneered by **Terrence Parker**. It is overseen by DJ Tone (b. Antonio Echols), a well-known underground DJ and the keyboard player in **Inner City**'s live band. Vicious Muzik in New York is a label owned and run by **Johnny Vicious**, one of the most exciting new arrivals on the dance scene of the 90s. Other labels under the Network umbrella include Vinyl Addiction (underground house, and the outlet for the highly-regarded Stereogen), Stafford South (called from the motorway junction, where Mark Archer, who A&Rs the label, lives - the label logo being a photograph of that sign), Stafford North (a more hardcore sister label), Eu4ea (for trance releases), Hidden Agenda and One After D. Not bad for a company with a staff team of seven. Intriguingly, bearing in mind the label's early sponsorship of modern techno, the team work in Birmingham's oldest building (a 'haunted Elizabethan house').

Selected albums: Various: *Retro Techno/Detroit Definitive* (Network 1991). Altern 8: *Full On...Mask Hysteria* (Network 1992).

Neu

This pioneering 'prog' group, based in Dusseldorf, Germany, originally comprised Klaus Dinger (guitar/deliguitar/bass/vocals) and **Michael Rother** (guitar/Japanese banjo/percussion/vocals). Formerly of **Kraftwerk**, they broke away from this seminal act to form Neu in August 1971. A third ex-member, Eberhard Krahemann, joined them for live appearances. *Neu* established the duo's compulsive style in which metronomic rhythms and spartan melodies created a hypnotic effect. Respected producer Conny Plank helped define the group's sound on a release which established Neu as one of Germany's most popular attractions, alongside **Can** and **Amon Duul II**. The promise of this impressive debut was undermined by *Neu 2*, one side of which was devoted to several versions two songs, already issued as a single, played at different speeds. This deflected attention from the remaining selections, which proved as captivating as the previous recording. *Neu 75* affirmed their imaginativeness and the duo's work inspired, among others, **David Bowie**, in particular *Station To Station* and *Low*. Both individuals also enjoyed acclaim outside the group; Rother completed several fascinating solo albums, while Dinger formed the innovative **La Dusseldorf**. Subsequent Neu releases, while worthwhile, lacked the incision of early work.

Albums: *Neu* (Brain 1972), *Neu 2* (Brain 1973), *Neu 75* (Brain 1975), *Hallogallo* (Brain 1980), *Black Forest Gateau* (Cherry Red 1982).

Neuro Project

UK born Simon Sprince, Dave Nicoll and Stewart Quinn originally introduced themselves on **R&S Records** with the sublime techno hit, 'Mama' in the early 90s. Their 90-minute long playing debut arrived shortly afterwards on 3 Beat Music, but retained the promise of their first release, offering a wide array of styles and structures.

Album: *The Electric Mothers Of Invention* (3 Beat Music 1994, double album).

Neuropolitique

Detroit-influenced mannah often credited as 'organic techno'. This, the work of Matt Cogger, was first premiered by two limited edition EPs for London label Irdial. By the time a full-length album emerged its creator was still engaged in the ceaseless exporation of percussion patterns, though never to the detriment of a strong tune. His work was thus compared to that of **Carl Craig**.

Album: *Menage A Trois* (Irdial 1994).

Neville Brothers

The Nevilles represented the essence of 40 years of New Orleans music distilled within one family unit. The Nevilles comprised Art (b. Arthur Lanon Neville, 17 December 1937, New Orleans, Louisiana, USA; keyboards/vocals), Charles (b. 28 December 1938, New Orleans, Louisiana, USA; saxophone/flute), Aaron (b. 24 January 1941, New Orleans, Louisiana, USA; vocals/keyboards) and Cyril (b. 10 January 1948, New Orleans, Louisiana, USA; vocals). Each member was also a capable percussionist. They have, individually and collectively, been making an impression on R&B, rock 'n' roll, soul, funk and jazz since the early 50s. Art was the leader of the Hawkettes, whose 1954 **Chess** hit 'Mardi Gras Mambo' has become a New Orleans standard, reissued every year at Mardi Gras time. From 1957 he released solo singles on **Speciality**, and in the early 60s, both he and Aaron worked (separately) for the legendary producer **Allen Toussaint**. Aaron had emerged from vocal group the Avalons, and although he scored a minor R&B hit in 1960 with Toussaint's 'Over You', it was not until 1967 that he achieved fame with the soul ballad 'Tell It Like It Is', a million-seller which reached number 2 in the charts. Charles Neville, meanwhile, had been working - on the road, or back home as part of the Dew Drop Inn's houseband - with many legendary names: **B.B. King**, **Bobby 'Blue' Bland** and **Ray Charles** among them. In 1968 Art formed the **Meters**, one of the Crescent City's most innovative and respected outfits. Featuring Leo Nocentelli (guitar), George Potter Jnr. (bass), Joseph Modeliste (drums) and, later, Cyril Neville (percussion), they were New Orleans' answer to **Booker T. And The MGs**, and besides their own albums, they could be heard on early 70s' releases by **Paul McCartney**, **Robert Palmer**, **LaBelle** and **Dr. John**. 1976's *The Wild Tchoupitoulas*

was a transitional album, featuring the Meters' rhythm section and all four Neville Brothers; by 1978 they were officially a group. Despite a considerable 'cult' following, particularly among fellow musicians, it took them until 1989, and the release of the **Daniel Lanois**-produced *Yellow Moon*, to find a wider audience. A single, 'With God On Our Side' was extracted and became a minor hit; Aaron, duetting with **Linda Ronstadt**, achieved his greatest chart success since 'Tell It Like It Is', when 'Don't Know Much' reached US and UK number 2 and won them the first of two Grammy awards. In 1990, as a band, they released *Brother's Keeper* and appeared on the soundtrack of the movie *Bird On A Wire*.
Albums: *The Wild Tchoupitoulas* (1976), *The Neville Brothers* (1978), *Fiyo On The Bayou* (1981), *Neville-ization* (1984), *Neville-ization II* (1987), *Yellow Moon* (1989), *Brother's Keeper* (1990), *Family Groove* (1992), *Live On Planet Earth* (A&M 1994). Compilation: *Treacherous: A History Of The Neville Brothers 1955-1985* (1986).

Neville, Aaron

b. 24 January 1941, New Orleans, Louisiana, USA. Neville began performing in the Hawkettes, a group which also featured his brother, Art. Aaron was signed to **Minit Records** as a solo artist, but despite a minor hit with 'Over You' (1960), remained largely unknown until the release of 'Tell It Like It Is' (1966). This simple, haunting ballad showcased the singer's delicate delivery while the song's slogan-like title echoed the sentiments of the rising Black Power movement. Sadly, the single's outlet, Parlo, went bankrupt, and despite subsequent strong releases, Neville was unable to repeat its commercial success. In 1978, following the break-up of the **Meters**, Aaron joined Art, Cyril and Charles in the Neville Family Band, later they renamed themselves the **Neville Brothers**. He continued a parallel solo career and in 1989 scored an international hit with 'Don't Know Much', a duet with **Linda Ronstadt**.
Albums: *Tell It Like It Is* (Par-Lo 1967), *Orchid In The Storm* (1986), *Warm Your Heart* (A&M 1991), *The Grand Tour* (1993), *Soulful Christmas* (1993). Compilations: *Like It 'Tis* (Minit 1967), *Humdinger* (1986), *Make Me Strong* (1986), *Show Me The Way* (1989), *My Greatest Gift* (1991, a collection of late 60s/early 70s recordings).

Neville, Art

b. New Orleans, Louisiana, USA. Neville first attracted attention as a member of the Hawketts, a Crescent City act which scored notable local success in 1954 with 'Mardi Gras Mambo'. Although ostensibly a keyboard player - he appeared as session pianist on **Jerry Byrne**'s 'Lights Out' - Neville also undertook a singing career and, having signed with the renowned **Specialty Records**, enjoyed a regional hit with his debut single, 'Cha Dooky-Doo'. This progress was interrupted by a spell in the US armed forces, but upon being discharged, he completed a series of low-key singles for the Minit/Instant label. Neville later achieved considerable acclaim as a member of the **Meters**, which in turn evolved into the equally compulsive **Neville Brothers**, where Art was joined by siblings Cyril, Charles and **Aaron Neville**.
Albums: *Mardi Gras Rock 'N' Roll* (1986), *Rock 'N' Roll Hootenanny* (1988).

Nevins, Jason

A top New York producer/remixer of the 90s, whose first involvement with music was at his college radio station at Arizona State University, where his sets were primarily composed of techno. He went on to release product as Plastick Project, Crazee Tunes, the Experience and Jason Nevins Movement. 'The Viper Rooms', licensed to **Loaded Records** a UK record label in Brighton, Sussex, England. This was typical of his output, being completely unabashed in its use of samples. He has gone on to record with **Nervous**, **Logic**, **Strictly Rhythm** and **Tribal**. He has also remixed Ann Consuelo for **Champion**. He is also signed to **MCA** as Analogue.

New Bomb Turks

Pleasantly appointed but noisy Ohio, USA-based band, the New Bomb Turks' manifesto was to rid their genre of its more dour concerns, re-establishing the sheer adrenaline rush and hedonism implicit in the musical format. Contrary to expectations, however, the band were no supporters of idiocy or ignorance, having met while studying at Ohio State University. Each member - Eric Davidson (vocals), Jim Weber (guitar), Matt Reber (bass) and Bill Brandt (drums) - obtained English degrees. They first worked together as DJ's on student radio station WSOR, gradually pulling together as a band via a series of small pressing 7-inch singles. It was with their debut album, however, that their arrival was signalled, *Maximum Rock 'n' Roll* magazine announcing it to be 'album of the year, maybe of the last five years'. In its wake New Bomb Turks gagged under the pressure somewhat, taking their time before a follow-up set, then blasting through the recording sessions to produce *Information Highway Revisited* in just sixty hours.
Albums: *!!Destroy-Oh-Boy!!* (Crypt 1992), *Information Highway Revisited* (Crypt 1994).

New Celeste

This lively folk rock outfit from Scotland was formed by Iain Fergus, who originally wanted the group to be a 'Caledonian big band'. They have worked extensively on the continent, and employed some significant Scots musicians, including future members of **Hue And Cry** and **Runrig**. The highly regarded *On The Line*, contained a good deal of Fergus's witty material, and a batch of atmospheric electric folk numbers. During the

80s New Celeste only worked occasionally, but, by 1990, Fergus had completely reorganized the personnel for *The Celtic Connection*, a collection of old and new songs. The band also made a highly impressive appearance at the Cambridge Festival in 1991.
Albums: *High Sands And The Liquid Lake* (1978), *On The Line* (1979), *Live* (1980), *The Celtic Connection* (1990).

New Christy Minstrels

Randy Sparks (b. 29 July 1933, Leavenworth, Kansas, USA), formed this commercialized folk group in 1961. Determined to create a unit that was 'a compromise between the Norman Luboff Choir and the **Kingston Trio**', he added a popular Oregon quartet, the Fairmount Singers, to his own Randy Sparks Three. A third unit, the Inn Group, which featured **Jerry Yester**, was absorbed into the line-up, while other Los Angeles-based performers embellished these core acts. Fourteen singers made up the original New Christy Minstrels but although the ensemble was viewed as supplementary to the participants' other careers, interest in the unit's debut *Presenting The New Christy Minstrels*, led to it becoming a full-time venture. Most of these early recruits, including the entire Inn Group, abandoned Sparks' creation at this point, creating the need for further, wholescale changes. New enlistments, including **Barry McGuire**, Barry Kane and Larry Ramos, joined the Minstrels whose next release, *In Person*, documented a successful appearance at the famed Troubador club. The following year (1963) the group secured its first hit single with 'Green Green' which established the ensemble as a leading popular attraction. The group, however, remained volatile as members continued to come and go. **Gene Clark** disbanded his Kansas-based trio, the Surf Riders, in order to join the Minstrels, but left after a matter of months, frustrated at the rather conservative material the ensemble recorded. He later formed the **Byrds** with (Jim) **Roger McGuinn** and **David Crosby**. Randy Sparks ended his relationship with the Minstrels in the summer of 1964. Maligned for creating their MOR image, his departure did not result in the more daring direction several members wished to pursue. McGuire, who was increasingly unhappy with such material as 'Three Wheels On My Wagon' and 'Chim Chim Cheree', left the group after seeing several British groups perform during the Minstrels European tour that year. His gravelly rasp was soon heard on his solo international protest hit, 'Eve Of Destruction'. In 1966 Larry Ramos accepted an invitation to join the **Association** and although several excellent new vocalists, including **Kim Carnes** and **Kenny Rogers**, had been absorbed into the Minstrels, their influential days were over. Longstanding members Mike Settle and Terry Williams left when their new ideas were constantly rejected. They formed the First Edition with the equally ambitious Rodgers, and subsequently enjoyed the kind of success the parent group previously experienced. Although the New Christy Minstrels continued to exist in some form into the 80s, singing early hits, show tunes and standards, their halcyon days ended during the mid-60s.
Albums: *Presenting The New Christy Minstrels* (1962), *The New Christy Minstrels In Person* (1962), *The New Christy Minstrels Tell Tall Tales, Legends And Nonsense* (1963), *Ramblin' (Featuring Green, Green)* (1963), *Merry Christmas!* (1963), *Today* (1964), *Land Of Giants* (1964), *The Quiet Side Of The New Christy Minstrels* (1964), *The New Christy Minstrels Sing And Play Cowboys And Indians* (1965), *The Academy Award Winner - Chim Chim Cheree* (1965), *The Wandering Minstrels* (1965), *In Italy...In Italian* (1966), *New Kick!* (1966), *Christmas With The Christies* (1966), *On Tour Through Motortown* (1968), *Big Hits From Chitty Chitty Bang Bang* (1968), *You Need Someone To Love* (1970), *The Great Soap Opera Themes* (1976). Compilation: *Greatest Hits* (1966).

New Colony Six

Formed in Chicago, Illinois, USA, the New Colony Six were one of the first of the city's teenage groups to secure a national hit when 'I Confess' reached the US Hot 100 in February 1966. The sextet then moved to Los Angeles where they shared a house with **Paul Revere And The Raiders**, adopting the same 'Revolutionary War'-styled garb favoured by the latter act. The New Colony Six - Patrick McBride (vocals/harmonica), Ray Graffia (tambourine/vocals), Jerry Kollenburgh (lead guitar), Carug Kemp (organ), Wally Kemp (bass) and Chic James (drums) - initially pursued a hard, British-influenced sound, but a subsequent switch to a soft-rock style was rewarded in 1968 with two US Top 30 entries, 'I Will Always Think About You' and 'Things I'd Like To Say'. Newcomer Ronnie Rice was largely responsible for this particular direction, writing the bulk of the group's material and taking lead vocals, but although the unit continued to enjoy minor hits into the 70s, it was unable to rekindle the urgency of early recordings.
Albums: *Breakthrough* (1966), *Colonization* (1967), *Revelations* (1968), *Attacking A Straw Man* (1969).

New Edition

Upbeat US teenage pop stars New Edition were formed by Maurice Starr who modelled them on the **Jackson 5**. He recruited five handsome young men, **Bobby Brown** (b. Robert Brown, 5 February 1969, Roxbury, Massachusetts, USA), **Ralph Tresvant** (b. 16 May 1968, Boston, Massachusetts, USA), Michael Bivins (b. 10 August 1968), Ricky Bell (b. 19 September 1967), and Ronnie DeVoe (b. Ronald DeVoe, 17 November 1967), who originally performed high quality mainstream pop, with soul overtones. As their careers progressed, however, they began to incorporate the sound and style of hip hop, inadvertently becoming

forerunners for the New Jack Swing (aka swingbeat) hybrid which **Teddy Riley** then developed. Following the success of *Candy Girl*, New Edition fired Starr, who then repeated the trick and earned a good deal of money by masterminding the career of **New Kids On The Block**. The first rap exchanges occurred on *New Edition*, their **MCA Records** debut, where the quintet proved particularly effective on cuts such as 'School'. Shortly afterwards Brown left for a hugely successful solo career, which still embraced hip hop as well as harmonic soul ballads. New Edition continued with an idiosyncratic album of doo-wop covers, before the arrival of Johnny Gill for *Heartbreak*, which was produced by Terry Lewis and Jimmy Jam (**Jam And Lewis**). With sales and interest slumping the remaining members set out on more successful solo projects. **Bell Biv Devoe** comprised the adventures of the three named founder members, while both Gill and Tresvant followed the solo trail.
Albums: *Candy Girl* (Streetwise 1983), *New Edition* (MCA 1984), *All For Love* (MCA 1985), *Christmas All Over The World* (MCA 1985), *Under The Blue Moon* (MCA 1986), *Heart Break* (MCA 1988). Compilation: *Greatest Hits* (MCA 1991).

New England (UK)

This British hard rock quartet were formed in Deptford, London, in 1990 by original **Atom Seed** member Chris Huxter (bass). Enlisting the services of Paul McKenna (lead vocals), Dave Cook and Ian Winters (drums), they secured a deal with the independent Street Link label. *You Can't Keep Living This Way* emerged in 1991 and confused the critics; the music was awkward to tie down and not easily pigeonholed, fusing influences as diverse as **Led Zeppelin**, **Faith No More**, the **Doors** and **Van Halen**, with the attitude of punk not lagging far behind. However, this was not enough to find them a place in metal's first division, and they collapsed soon afterwards.
Album: *You Can't Keep Living This Way* (Street Link 1991).

New England (USA)

This American quartet comprised John Fannon (guitar/vocals), Jimmy Waldo (keyboards), Gary Shea (bass) and Hirsh Gardener (drums). Taken under the wing of **Kiss**'s manager, Bill Aucoin, they purveyed sophisticated, melodic rock in a vein similar to **Styx** and **Journey**. In 1979 they were given the chance to impress on a major stage, landing the support slot on the American leg of the **Kiss** tour. Although competent, their music lacked individuality and the band themselves had a nondescript image. After a third album, produced by **Todd Rundgren**, the band disintegrated in 1981, with Waldo and Shea eventually going on to join **Alcatrazz**.
Albums: *New England* (Infinity 1979), *Explorer Suite* (Elektra 1980), *Walking Wild* (Elektra 1981).

New Fast Automatic Daffodils

Manchester, UK based indie band whose arrival in 1989 coincided with their city's descent in to 'rave' culture and an upswing in the fortunes of 'baggy' bands **Stone Roses** and **Happy Mondays**. From their debut at the Manchester Polytechnic Poetry Society in 1988, they were described in one quarter as resembling 'a team of sex psychologists at a mass orgy'. The band, Andy Spearpoint (vocals), Justin Crawford (bass), Dolan Hewison (guitar), Perry Saunders (drums) and Icarus Wilson-Wright (percussion) signed to Belgian label Play It Again Sam in 1989. Among their early singles, the caustic but wry 'Music Is Shit' gained most prominence. 'Get Better' was remixed by **Joy Division** producer, **Martin Hannett**, before second album, *Body Exit Mind*, was recorded with Craig Leon (**Blondie**, **Ramones**, **Fall**) at the helm. Their literate exposition of post-punk pop won them many friends in the media, though record sales failed to transpose to chart placings outside the 'independent' sector.
Albums: *Pigeon Hole* (Play It Again Sam 1990), *Body Exit Mind* (Play It Again Sam 1992).
Video: *Wake Up And Make Love Before 8:30 In The Morning* (1993).

New Frontier

This melodic US pop-rock group was formed in 1988 by ex-**Billy Satellite** vocalist Monty Byron and ex-**Gamma** bassist Glen Letsch. Adding David Neuhauser (keyboards) and Marc Nelson (drums), they successfully negotiated a deal with the newly-formed Mika label. Their debut album was produced by Ritchie Zito (of **Heart** and **Cheap Trick** fame) and featured a collection of hi-tech AOR numbers that were targeted at the ***Billboard*** charts. Failing to generate media interest, the band disintegrated shortly after the album's release. Letsch went on to play with **Robin Trower**.
Album: *New Frontier* (Mika 1988).

New Girl In Town

Bob Merrill, previously known for writing novelty songs such as 'Sparrow In The Treetop', 'Feet Up (Pat Him On the Po-Po)', 'If I Knew You Were Comin' I'd've Baked A Cake', and '(How Much Is That) Doggie In The Window?', some of which became hits for **Guy Mitchell**, made his Broadway debut with this show which opened at the 46th Street Theatre in New York on 14 May 1957. **George Abbott**'s book, which was based on Eugene O'Neill's 1921 play, *Anna Christie*, was set in New York at the turn of the century and told of a prostitute, Anna (**Gwen Verdon**), who returns to live with to her bargee father (Chris Christopherson) for a while. He is unaware of her occupation, but is soon put wise by his unsavoury lady friend, Marthy (Thelma Ritter). Matt Burke (George Wallace), a sailor with whom Anna falls in love, leaves her for a time when he, too, discovers her lifestyle, but he eventually returns in the hope that they can make a more conventional life together. The lively score included 'It's Good To Be Alive', 'Sunshine Girl', 'Did You Close Your Eyes?', 'If That Was Love', 'You're My Friend Ain'tcha?', 'Look At 'Er', 'At the Check Apron Ball', 'Roll Yer Socks Up', and 'There Ain't No Flies On Me'. The engaging and reflective 'Flings' ('Are meant to be flung' . . . 'As a girl, you start seethin'/Over guys just finished teethin'/Now if they're alive and breathin'/That's enough!') was given an amusing treatment on record from **Carol Burnett** and Martha Raye. When she starred in this piece, Gwen Verdon, one of the American musical theatre's favourite gypsies (dancers), was in the middle of a purple patch with shows such as ***Can-Can***, ***Damn Yankees***, and ***Redhead*** - with ***Sweet Charity*** and ***Chicago*** in the future. She shared the 1958 **Tony Award** for best actress with Thelma Ritter. *New Girl In Town* ran for 431 performances - an encouraging start for Merrill - who followed it in 1959 with ***Take Me Along***, another adaptation of an O'Neill play, *Ah, Wilderness.*

New Grass Revival

The New Grass Revival evolved around the fiddle talents of Sam Bush, who also plays guitar, mandolin and sings. Another longstanding member is bas player, John Cowan, who, somewhat surprisingly, contributed soaring R&B-styled vocals to an acoustic band. The four-piece group had some success with the **Leon Russell** song, 'Prince Of Peace'. They toured with Russell and cut a live album and video together at Perkins' Palace in Pasadena. In 1984 the band moved to Sugar Hill Records and their albums, whilst essentially bluegrass, also include jazz, reggae and soul. Amongst the later members of the Revival is the highly respected banjo player, **Bela Fleck**. In 1991 **Emmylou Harris** formed an acoustic band, the Nash Ramblers, to accompany her, the leader of the group being Sam Bush. The New Grass Revival are the most significant acoustic country band in the USA, but Bush's involvement with Harris may limit their future activities.

Albums: *Arrival Of The New Grass Revival* (1973), *Fly Through The Country* (1975), *Commonwealth* (1976), *When The Storm Is Over* (1977), *Too Late To Turn Back Now* (1978), *Barren Country* (1980), *Leon Russell And The New Grass Revival* (1981), *On The Boulevard* (1984), *New Grass Revival* (1986), *Hold On To A Dream* (1987), *Friday Night In America* (1989).

New Idol Son

Formed in the artistic hothouse of the Bay Area of San Francisco during 1991, New Idol Son immediately saw the press compare them to a '90s rebirth of **MC5** meets **Black Sabbath**'. Vocalist/guitarist Matt Hizendragzer first met drummer Brent Hagin at a Mookie Blaylock (who later transmuted into Pearl Jam) show. Eventually Rich Carr (bass) and Mike Davis (guitar) were recruited via adverts in BAM magazine, with the band titled Difference Engine. Playing shows throughout the west coast as support to Downset, Fear Factory and others, they built a strong reputation among local press outlets until Pavement Music moved in for their signatures in 1994. However, at this point it was discovered that another band already held the rights to the name Difference Engine, and New Idol Son was born when Hizendragzer saw the legend on the back of a book in a second-hand store. Their debut album, *Reach*, offered crafted musical composition with emotive lyrics, sometimes imbued with quasi-religious overtones.

Album: *Reach* (Bulletproof 1994).

New Jazz Orchestra

The New Jazz Orchestra was founded in 1963 by Clive Burrows and resurrected and directed by **Neil Ardley** between 1964 and 1968. It provided the up-and-coming generation of British jazz musicians with the experience of working with a large jazz orchestra, its personnel including **Harry Beckett**, **Henry Lowther** and **Ian Carr** (trumpets), **Paul Rutherford** and **Mike Gibbs** (trombones), **Don Rendell**, **Trevor Watts**, **Dick Heckstall-Smith** and **Barbara Thompson** (saxophones), **Michael Garrick** (piano), **Jack Bruce** (bass) and **Jon Hiseman** (drums). It is not surprising that with such quality musicians *The Times* critic, Miles Kington, would write that the NJO 'makes most big bands sound like trained elephants with two tricks'. It was not the only purpose of the NJO to provide such invaluable big band experience for these musicians; it also fostered a workshop atmosphere to provide its arrangers with a chance to try out scores. Among those who wrote for the orchestra were Ardley, **Alan Cohen**, Gibbs, Rutherford, Garrick and Mike Taylor. 'I learnt by my mistakes,' Ardley said later and by the time he had become the leader he was producing major scores like 'Shades Of Blue' from the first album and 'Dejeuner Sur L'Herbe' from the second. All the material in the latter is derived from two/four bar motifs in the main theme. There are no repeated chord sequences or scales; rather, the piece grows organically in the manner of classical music. This is not merely a third stream piece but an attempt to write jazz in new way. It was the kind of experiment the NJO was formed to encourage and a score Ardley would have been lucky to get performed anywhere else. The NJO gave some concerts in London and at festivals. They also had a fruitful pairing with **Colosseum**. Despite what a contemporary described as its 'fiercely swinging

rhythm, first class solos and brilliant ensemble' it gained no recognition abroad though in time many of its members have become very well known on the continent.
Albums: *Western Reunion* (1965), *Le Dejeuner Sur L'Herbe* (1969).

New Kids On The Block

Formed in 1985, this pop group from Boston, Massachusetts, USA featured Joe McIntyre (b. 31 December 1972, Needham, Massachusetts, USA), Jordan Knight (b. 15 May 1970, Worcester, Massachusetts, USA), Jonathan Knight (b. 29 November 1968, Worcester, Massachusetts, USA), Daniel Wood (b. 14 May 1969, Boston, Massachusetts, USA) and Donald Wahlberg (b. 17 August 1969, Boston, Massachusetts, USA). They were discovered by producer/writer Maurice Starr, who had previously moulded the career of New Edition. It was Starr who presented his proteges with a rap song titled 'New Kids On The Block' from which they took their name. Their self-titled album, released in 1986, fused rap and pop and brought them popularity among a predominately white teenage audience. However, it was not until 1988 that they broke through to the US charts with 'Please Don't Go Girl'. In 1989, they became the biggest-selling group in America, enjoying sizeable hits with 'You Got It (The Right Stuff)', 'I'll Be Loving You (Forever)', 'Cover Girl' and 'Didn't I'. A reissue of 'You Got It (The Right Stuff)' climbed to number 1 in the UK, thereby establishing the quintet as an act of international teen appeal.
Albums: *New Kids On The Block* (1986), *Hangin' Tough* (1988), *Merry Merry Christmas* (1989), *Step By Step* (1990), *No More Games/Remix Album* (1991).
Further reading: *New Kids On The Block: The Whole Story By Their Friends*, Robin McGibbon. *New Kids On The Block*, Lynn Goldsmith.

New Kingdom

Hardcore hip hop duo from Brooklyn, New York, comprising rapper Nosaj (his real name Jason, backwards) and DJ Sebastian. Their debut single was 'Good Times', a rock hip hop crossover effort on **Gee Street** which used a sample of **Joe Walsh** (of **James Gang**)'s guitar playing and looped it. Their major influence is **Curtis Mayfield**, and their output reflects a good deal of his social vision. 'Good Times', for example, was written about their desire not to lose their appetite for life as they grow older. They take a full band on tour with them and have live skateboarding at their events, much in the mode of hardcore punk bands. There is certainly a 'cartoon' element to the band, their lyrics generally being abstract, non-linear collages. Their beats, however, are more restrained, as pointed out in the self-explanatory lyric: 'Pouring no lies, no suits, no ties, No need to rush, we love to fuck time'. A genuine return to the old school aural values, their debut album was produced by the band in conjunction with Scott Harding of the Lumberjacks.
Album: *Heavy Load* (Gee Street 1993).

New Lost City Ramblers

Mike Seeger (b. 15 August 1933, New York City, New York, USA; brother of folksinger **Pete Seeger**), John Cohen (b. 1932, New York, USA) and Tom Paley (b. 19 March 1928, New York, USA) formed this influential old-time string band in 1958. Rather than ape their immediate predecessors who popularized the style, the trio preferred to invoke the music's original proponents, including Gid Tanner And His Skillet Lickers and the Carolina Tar Heels. Seeger undertook numerous field recordings to preserve authenticity and while their adherence to traditional values made commercial acceptance difficult, the group enjoyed the admiration of their peers and was crucial in the development of the urban folk revival. The original line-up remained together until 1962, when Paley left to resume his teaching career. Replacement Tracy Schwarz (b. 1938, New York, USA) primarily played fiddle, but his arrival coincided with a broadening of the Ramblers' repertoire. They began to incorporate unaccompanied ballads and modern bluegrass music but although the trio remained a popular attraction on the college and coffee-house circuit, they began to drift apart during the latter half of the 60s. *Remembrance Of Things To Come* included British traditional, riverboat songs and even some early bluegrass. *American Moonshine And Prohibition* was more lighthearted, but not lightweight in its criticism of the government legislation on prohibition. Cohen initially pursued his interest in photography before producing a series of excellent documentary films. Schwartz and Seeger meanwhile performed with different musicians and together formed the short-lived Strange Creek Singers.
Albums: *New Lost City Ramblers* (Folkways 1958), *New Lost City Ramblers Vol. 2* (Folkways 1959), *Songs From The Depression* (Folkways 1959), *Old Timey Songs For Children* (Folkways 1959), *New Lost City Ramblers Vol. 3* (Folkways 1961), *New Lost City Ramblers Vol. 4* (Folkways 1961), *American Moonshine And Prohibition* (Folkways 1962), *New Lost City Ramblers Vol. 5* (Folkways 1963), *Gone To The Country* (Folkways 1963), *String Band Instrumentals* (Folkways 1964), *Old Timey Music* (1964), *Rural Delivery No. 1* (Folkways 1965), *Remembrance Of Things To Come* (Folkways 1966), *Modern Times-Rural Songs From An Industrial Society* (Folkways 1968), *On The Great Divide* (Folkways 1973), *20 Years-Concert Performances 1958-1977* (Flying Fish 1978), *20th Anniversary Concert, Carnegie Hall* (Flying Fish 1978). Compilations: *Tom Paley, John Cohen And Mike Seeger Sing Songs Of The New Lost City Ramblers* (Folkways 1961), *Twenty Years* (1979), *The Early Years 1958-62* (1991).

New Model Army

With their roots embedded in the punk era, New Model Army were formed in Bradford, Yorkshire, in 1980, and immediately outlined their manifesto by naming themselves after the Sir Thomas Fairfax/Oliver Cromwell revolutionary army. The group was and is led by Justin 'Slade The Leveller' Sullivan (b. 1956, Buckinghamshire, England; guitar/vocals), a former platform sweeper and Mars Bar production line worker, with the help of Jason 'Moose' Harris (b. 1968; bass/guitar) and Robb Heaton (b. 1962, Cheshire, England; drums/guitar). Their brand of punk folk/rock attracted a loyal cult following, much of whom shared the band's grievances towards the Tory government policies of the 80s. This was best executed on their debut album, which combined militant themes such as 'Spirit Of The Falklands' and 'Vengeance' (a vitriolic anthem about getting even with one's trespassers) with the haunting lament for childhood, 'A Liberal Education'. The group's championing of traditional working class ethics saw an unexpected boost for a dying art and trade; that of the clog. New Model Army made their first public appearance at Scamps Disco in Bradford in October 1980. After releasing singles on Abstract Records, scoring a number 2 UK independent chart hit with 'The Price' in 1984, they formed an unlikely alliance with the multi-national **EMI Records**, which saw the band acquire a higher profile and a significantly increased recording budget. They eventually broke through to a wider audience with 'No Rest' which peaked at number 28 on the UK singles chart in 1985 - a position they were never to beat in an impressive run of 12 UK chart singles between 1985 and 1991. With often inflammatory lyrics, the band have never compromised their beliefs for commercial gain. They ran into trouble with the BBC's *Top Of The Pops* chart show for donning t-shirts with the (albeit laudable) slogan, 'Only Stupid Bastards Use Heroin'. This attracted some derision from the 'anarcho-punk' traditionalists **Conflict**, who replied with their own motif: 'Only Stupid Bastards Help EMI'. They subsequently continued to release quality albums, with considerable crossover potential, always maintaining credibility with their original fan base. In December 1991 the group left EMI, eventually finding a new home on **Epic Records**. Their first single for the label revealed few concessions to the mainstream: 'Here Comes The War' featured a picture of a charred body, and a pull-out psoter instructing the user in how to prepare a nuclear bomb.

Albums: *Vengeance* (Abstract 1984), *No Rest For The Wicked* (EMI 1985), *Ghost Of Cain* (EMI 1986), *Radio Sessions* (Abstract 1988), *Thunder And Consolation* (EMI 1989), *Impurity* (EMI 1990), *Raw Melody Men* (EMI 1990), *The Love Of Hopeless Causes* (Epic 1993). Compilations: *The Independent Story* (Abstract 1987), *History* (EMI 1992).

New Moon, The

After a poor out-of-town tryout, *The New Moon* underwent drastic revisions before opening at the Imperial Theatre in New York on 19 September 1928. The story traced the adventures of Robert Mission, a French aristocrat in New Orleans in the late 18th Century. With music by **Sigmund Romberg** lyrics by **Oscar Hammerstein II**, and a book by Hammerstein, Frank Mandel and Lawrence Schwab, the lavish and spectacular production was a great success and ran for 509 performances. Amongst the songs were 'Lover, Come Back To Me', 'One Kiss', 'Softly, As In A Morning Sunrise', 'Wanting You', 'Love Is Quite A Simple Thing', and 'Stouthearted Men'. The two lovers, Robert and Marianne, were played by Robert Halliday and Evelyn Herbert. The 1929 London production, starring **Evelyn Laye** and Howett Worster, ran for 148 performances. *The New Moon* was revived in New York in 1942, 1944 and 1986. A film version, which changed the plot but retained most of the music, was released in 1930 with **Grace Moore** and Lawrence Tibbett, and the popular singing duo of **Jeanette MacDonald** and **Nelson Eddy** were in the 1940 remake.

New Musical Express

Founded in March 1952 from the danceband newsheet *Musical Express*, this most influential of UK music papers had an inauspicious start with sales as low as 20,000 per week. Within months, the paper was bought out by leading agent Maurice Kinn for £1,000 and soon thrived. On 14 November 1952, the paper launched Britain's first singles chart in Britain, an innovation that was soon followed by the famous *NME* Poll Winners' concert, in which the leading stars of the day would participate. *NME* found its niche as a youth-orientated organ and by 1962 was boasting sales in excess of 200,000, 'the world's largest circulation of any music paper'. The Merseybeat explosion of the following year pushed sales up still further to a record 275,000. Such was the paper's prestige that it was able to stage one of the most remarkable concert line-ups of all time at the Wembley Empire Pool *NME* Poll Winners concert on Sunday, 11 April 1965. The remarkable cavalcade of stars that year comprised: the **Beatles**, **Rolling Stones**, **Cliff Richard**, **Shadows**, **Kinks**, **Animals**, **Moody Blues**, **Searchers**, **Them**, **Freddie And The Dreamers**, **Gerry And The Pacemakers**, **Rockin' Berries**, **Bachelors**, **Cilla Black**, **Dusty Springfield**, **Georgie Fame**, **Twinkle** and **Sounds Orchestral**. An additional selling appeal of the *NME* during the 60s was its innovative use of a chart points table to document and dramatize the fortunes of the major pop

artists of the day. With an authoritative breakdown by Derek Johnson, the tables provided an intriguing insight into chart consistency, while also displaying the remarkable divergence in musical taste throughout this period. The *NME* brilliantly reflected this most democratic era of pop, interviewing all the major artists of the day from the Beatles and the Rolling Stones to **Ken Dodd** and **Val Doonican**. Although this was not the era of the celebrity journalist, the *NME* had its own major infiltrator into the lives of the stars in Keith Altham, who managed to secure regular and exclusive interviews with such gods as the Stones and **Walker Brothers**. Significantly, when Altham finally left the paper, he formed his own PR company with a roster that included some of the biggest UK acts of the day. Derek Johnson was also a major figure in *NME* mythology, best known as their perennial singles reviewer from the early 60s until the end of the decade. It was only towards the late 60s that the *NME* began to lose ground on its nearest rivals. The divergence of 'pop' and 'rock', the emergence of an underground culture and the increasing interest in 'progressive' music saw readers moving away to rival titles. The *NME* incorporated progressive music, but only in that area which had managed to translate into the mainstream. The idea of a non-chart act or cult performer was still anathema, and even album reviews tended to be short and superficial. Nevertheless, as the 60s closed, the *NME* offered a precarious pot-pourri of pop and rock, still intent on the democratizing process that managed to embrace acts as stylistically diverse as the **Lulu** and **Jethro Tull**. What was actually a bold policy failed to work in the marketplace as other papers, most notably the ***Melody Maker***, were effectively abandoning pop in favour of serious reporting on progressive music. By the early 70s, the *NME* took on its rivals by changing its musical and editorial policy almost overnight. With a format and logo that echoed rivals *Melody Maker*, the *NME* 'went heavy' with an abruptness that was vaguely disconcerting. So stringent was its revisionism that some of its finest features were abandoned in the process, most notably the Alley Cat gossip column, the poll concerts, the sense of pop history provided by chart points' analysis and the severe loss of Derek Johnson's singles page. Thereafter, no reviewer would ever command such power or maintain such continuity, as the singles page was rotated among the staff.
By 1973 the *NME* had assimilated several leading writers from the underground press, including Nick Kent and Charles Shaar Murray. Under the talented editorship of Ian Macdonald, this trio was responsible for some of the most analytical writing of the era and *NME* quickly moved ahead in terms of style and content. Perhaps learning from its past circulation errors, it did not sit on the fence during the musical changes of 1976-77 but plunged headlong into punk, even advertising for 'two young gunslingers' who emerged in the form of iconoclastic writers Tony Parsons and Julie Burchill. Stylistically hip, they nevertheless lacked the musical knowledge or critical clout of Kent and Macdonald and later moved into other lucrative areas of the media. Post-punk *NME* lived off its tradition as the most stylish and irreverent rock weekly and continued the cult of the personality rock writer, most notably through the quirky prose of Paul Morley and obdurate incoherence of Ian Penman. The upsurge of glossy titles, such as *Smash Hits* saw the *NME* lose much of its influential power during the early 80s and the fostered myth of its independence was placed in a more realistic light by the intervention of owners IPC at various moments of circulation crisis. Still reflecting its time, the *NME* now partly serves as a training ground for its more established writers, many of whom have moved into the comparative anonymity of the quality popular press. Although there was much talk of the redundancy of the serious music press at the beginning of the 80s, the NME has enjoyed a resurgence of sales which by early the 90s stood at a solid 118,000. It remains the biggest selling rock weekly, although now overtaken by the monthly magazines such as *Q* and *Select*.

New Musik

This UK pop group comprised Tony Mansfield (guitar/keyboards/vocals), Tony Hibbert (bass), Phil Towner (drums) and Clive Gates (keyboards). They came to prominence after a minor hit in 1979 with 'Straight Lines', during 1980 with three pop/synthesizer hits on the GTO label, 'Living By Numbers', 'The World Of Water' and 'Sanctuary'. Mansfield regarded their debut *From A To B* as rudimentary, but the succeeding *Anywhere* fared less well, despite its evident maturity. The change in style also took its toll on the band with the departure of Hibbert and Towner soon after its release. They were replaced by electronic percussionist Cliff Venner for the band's final and rather uninspired *Warp*. Full of empty electronic dance tracks it was notable for an daring attempt at the **Beatles'** *All You Need Is Love*. However, sales were very poor and they soon disbanded. Mansfield went on to produce hits for **Captain Sensible**, **Mari Wilson**, Naked Eyes and worked on **A-Ha's** debut album *Hunting High And Low*.
Albums: *From A To B* (1980), *Anywhere* (1981), *Warp* (1982).

New Order

When **Joy Division**'s Ian Curtis committed suicide in May 1980 the three remaining members, Bernard Sumner (b. Bernard Dicken, 4 January 1956, Salford, Manchester, England; guitar/vocals), Peter Hook (b. 13 February 1956, Manchester, England; bass) and Stephen Morris (b. 28 October 1957, Macclesfield,

Cheshire, England; drums) continued under the name New Order. Sumner took over vocal duties and the trio embarked upon a low-key tour of the USA, intent on continuing as an entity independent of the massive reputation Joy Division had achieved shortly before their demise. Later that same year they recruited Morris's girlfriend, Gillian Gilbert (b. 27 January 1961, Manchester, England; keyboards/guitar) and wrote and rehearsed their debut, *Movement*, which was released the following year. Their first single, 'Ceremony', penned by Joy Division, was a UK Top 40 hit in the spring of 1981, and extended the legacy of their previous band. Hook's deep, resonant bass line and Morris's crisp, incessant drumming were both Joy Division trademarks. The vocals, however, were weak, Sumner clearly at this stage feeling uncomfortable as frontman. Much was made, in 1983, of the band 'rising from the ashes' of Joy Division in the music press, when *Power, Corruption And Lies* was released. Their experimentation with electronic gadgetry was fully realised and the album contained many surprises and memorable songs. The catchy bass riff and quirky lyrics of 'Age Of Consent' made it an instant classic, while the sign-off line, on the otherwise elegiac 'Your Silent Face', 'You've caught me at a bad time/So why don't you piss off', showed that Sumner no longer felt under any pressure to match the poetic, introspective lyricism of Ian Curtis. As well as redefining their sound they clearly now relished the role of 'most miserable sods in pop'. 'Blue Monday', released at this time in 12-inch format only, went on to become the biggest selling 12-inch single of all-time in the UK. In 1983 'disco' was a dirty word amongst the independent fraternity and 'Blue Monday', which combined an infectious dance beat with a calm, aloof vocal, was a brave step into uncharted territory. As well as influencing a legion of UK bands, it would be looked back upon as a crucial link between the disco of the 70s and the dance/house music wave at the end of the 80s. New Order had now clearly established themselves, and throughout the 80s and into the 90s they remained the top independent band in the UK, staying loyal to Manchester's **Factory Records**. Their subsequent collaboration with 'hot' New York hip-hop producer **Arthur Baker** spawned the anti-climactic 'Confusion' (1983) and 'Thieves Like Us' (1984). Both singles continued their preference for the 12-inch format, stretching in excess of six minutes, and stressing their lack of concern for the exposure gained by recording with mainstream radio in mind. *Low Life* appeared in 1985 and is perhaps their most consistently appealing album to date. While the 12-inch version of *Low Life*'s 'Perfect Kiss' was a magnificent single, showing the band at their most inspired and innovative, the collaboration with producer John Robie on the single version of 'Subculture' indicated that their tendency to experiment and 'play around' could also spell disaster. Their next album, 1986's *Brotherhood*, although containing strong tracks such as 'Bizarre Love Triangle', offered nothing unexpected. It wasn't until the UK Top 5 single 'True Faith' in 1987, produced and co-written by **Stephen Hague** hot on the heels of his success with the **Pet Shop Boys** and accompanied by an award-winning Phillipe Decouffle video, that New Order found themselves satisfying long term fans and general public alike. The following year **Quincy Jones**' remix of 'Blue Monday' provided the group with another Top 5 hit. If the recycling of old songs and proposed 'personal' projects fuelled rumours of a split then 1989's *Technique* promptly dispelled them. The album, recorded in Ibiza, contained upbeat bass-and-drums-dominated tracks that characterized the best of their early output. Its most striking feature, however, was their flirtation with the popular Balearic style, as in the hit single, 'Fine Time', which contained lines like 'I've met a lot of cool chicks, But I've never met a girl with all her own teeth', delivered in a voice that parodied **Barry White**'s notoriously sexist, gravelly vocals of the 70s. Meanwhile the band had changed significantly as a live act. Their reputation for inconsistency and apathy, as well as their staunch refusal to play encores, was by now replaced with confident, crowd-pleasing hour-long sets. In the summer of 1990 they reached the UK number 1 position with 'World In Motion', accompanied by the England World Cup Squad, with a song that earned the questionable accolade of best football record of all time, and caused a band member to observe that 'this is probably the last straw for Joy Division fans'. Rather than exploiting their recent successes with endless tours, the group unexpectedly branched out into various spin-off ventures. Hook formed the hard-rocking **Revenge**, Sumner joined former **Smiths**' guitarist Johnny Marr in **Electronic** and Morris/Gilbert recorded an album under the self-effacing title, **The Other Two**. The extra-curricular work prompted persistent rumours that New Order had irrevocably split, but no official announcement or press admission was forthcoming. In the summer of 1991 the group announced that they had reconvened for a new album which was eventually released in 1993. *Republic* consequently met with mixed reviews reflecting critical confusion about their status and direction. While retaining the mix of rock and dance music successfully honed on *Technique*, the tone was decidedly more downbeat, even sombre. Sadly it arrived too late to help the doomed Factory label, and afterwards the band's membership would return to varied solo projects.

Albums: *Movement* (Factory 1981), *Power, Corruption And Lies* (Factory 1983), *Low Life* (Factory 1985), *Brotherhood* (Factory 1986), *Technique* (Factory 1989), *Republic* (London 1993). Compilations: *Substance* (Factory 1987), *The Peel Sessions* (Strange Fruit 1990), *Live In Concert* (Windsong 1992).

Videos: *Taras Schevenko* (1984), *Pumped Full Of Drugs*

(1988), *Substance 1989* (1989), *Brixton Academy April 1987* (1989), *neworderstory* (1993), *(The Best Of) New Order* (1995).
Further reading: *New Order & Joy Division: Pleasures And Wayward Distractions*, Brian Edge. *New Order & Joy Division: Dreams Never End*, Claude Flowers.

New Orleans

Jazz fans watching this US feature film made in 1947 are torn between embarrassment (at the corny jazz vs. classics storyline) and frustration at the waste of the talent available to the film's makers. **Billie Holiday** and **Louis Armstrong** have acting roles (as servants - what else?) and also perform on screen. Alongside them are musicians such as **Barney Bigard**, **Meade 'Lux' Lewis**, **Kid Ory**, **Zutty Singleton**, **Lucky Thompson** and **Woody Herman** And His Orchestra. Holiday longed to act in films and when she was cast for this part asserted her disappointment: 'I fought my whole life to keep from being somebody's damn maid. It was a real drag . . . to end up as a make-believe maid.'

New Orleans Rhythm Kings

After the hugely popular **Original Dixieland Jazz Band** created a storm of interest in Chicago in the early 20s other musicians decided to try their luck at the new jazz music. Amongst them were **Georg Brunis**, Jack Pettis, Arnold Loyacano, Louis Black, **Elmer Schoebel** and Frank Snyder. They formed a band they named the New Orleans Rhythm Kings for an engagement at the Friars Inn. With the ODJB safely on their way to international fame in New York and London, the NORK became Chicago's top jazz band. They recorded in 1922 and looked set to become one of the mainstays of the suddenly vital white jazz scene. With a few personnel changes the band was strengthened, but by 1925 they had folded, leaving behind a handful of records and a lasting impression upon the next generation of musicians who would form the basis of Chicago-style jazz.
Compilations: *The New Orleans Rhythm Kings 1922-23* (Swaggie 1988), *The New Orleans Rhythm Kings* 1923 (Swaggie 1988), *The New Orleans Rhythm Kings Vol 1* (King Jazz 1992), *The New Orleans Rhythm Kings Vol 2* (Village Jazz 1992).

New Riders Of The Purple Sage

Formed in 1969 the New Riders was initially envisaged as a part-time spin-off from the **Grateful Dead**. Group members **Jerry Garcia** (pedal steel guitar), **Phil Lesh** (bass) and **Mickey Hart** (drums) joined John Dawson (b. 1945, San Francisco, California, USA; guitar/vocals) and David Nelson (b. San Francisco, California, USA; guitar), mutual associates from San Francisco's once-thriving traditional music circuit. Although early live appearances were viewed as an informal warm-up to the main attraction, the New Riders quickly established an independent identity through the strength of Dawson's original songs. They secured a recording deal in 1971, by which time Dave Torbert had replaced Lesh, and Spencer Dryden (b. 7 April 1938, New York City, New York, USA), formerly of **Jefferson Airplane**, was installed as the group's permanent drummer. *New Riders Of The Purple Sage* blended country-rock with hippie idealism, yet emerged as a worthy companion to the parent act's lauded *American Beauty*. Sporting one of the era's finest cover's (from the renowned Kelley/Mouse studio), the stand-out track was 'Dirty Business'. This lengthy 'acid country' opus that featured some memorable guitar feedback. The final link with the Dead was severed when an over-committed Garcia made way for newcomer Buddy Cage (b. Canada). *Powerglide* introduced the punchier, more assertive sound the group now pursued which brought commercial rewards with the highly popular *The Adventures Of Panama Red*. Torbert left the line-up following *Home, Home On The Road* and was replaced by Skip Battin, formerly of the **Byrds**. In 1978 Dryden relinquished his drumstool in order to manage the band; while sundry musicians then joined and left, Dawson and Nelson remained at the helm until 1981. The New Riders were dissolved following the disastrous *Feelin' Alright*, although the latter musician subsequently resurrected the name with Gary Vogenson (guitar) and Rusty Gautier (bass). Nelson meanwhile resumed his association with the Dead in the Jerry Garcia Acoustic Band, and supervised several archive New Riders sets for the specialist Relix label.
Albums: *New Riders Of The Purple Sage* (1971), *Powerglide* (1972), *Gypsy Cowboy* (1972), *The Adventures Of Panama Red* (1973), *Home, Home On The Road* (1974), *Brujo* (1974), *Oh, What A Mighty Time* (1975), *New Riders* (1976), *Who Are These Guys* (1977), *Marin County Line* (1978), *Feelin' Alright* (1981), *Friend Of The Devil* (1991). Compilations: *The Best Of The New Riders Of The Purple Sage* (1976), *Before Time Began* (1976), *Vintage NRPS* (1988).

New Seekers

The original New Seekers comprised ex-Nocturnes Eve Graham (b. 19 April 1943, Perth, Scotland; vocals), Sally Graham (vocals), Chris Barrington (bass/vocals), Laurie Heath (guitar/vocals), and Marty Kristian (b. 27 May 1947, Leipzig, Germany - a Latvian who had been raised in Australia; guitar/vocals). This line-up recorded only one album, *The New Seekers*, before Heath, Barrington and Sally Graham were replaced by Lyn Paul (b. 16 February 1949, Manchester, England; ex-Nocturnes), Peter Doyle (b. 28 July 1949, Melbourne, Australia), and Paul Layton (b. 4 August 1947, Beaconsfield, England). Ex-**Seeker** Keith Potger was originally a member of the group, but retreated to the less public role of manager. The male contingent

played guitars in concert, but the act's main strengths were its interweaving vocal harmonies and a clean, winsome image. Their entertainments also embraced dance and comedy routines. Initially they appealed to US consumers who thrust a cover of **Melanie**'s 'Look What They've Done To My Song, Ma' and 'Beautiful People' - all unsuccessful in Britain - high up the ***Billboard*** Hot 100. A UK breakthrough came with 'Never Ending Song Of Love' which reached number 2, and, even better, a re-write of a Coca-Cola commercial, 'I'd Like To Teach The World To Sing', topping foreign charts too, and overtaking the **Hillside Singers**' original version in the USA. Their Eurovision Song Contest entry, 'Beg Steal Or Borrow' and the title track of 1972's *Circles* were also hits, but revivals of the **Fleetwoods**' 'Come Softly To Me' and **Eclection**'s 'Nevertheless' were among 1973 singles whose modest Top 40 placings were hard-won, though the year ended well with another UK number 1 in 'You Won't Find Another Fool Like Me'.
By 1974, Doyle had left the group and had been replaced by Peter Oliver (b. 15 January 1952, Southampton, England; guitar/vocals). He appeared on *Together* and *Farewell Album*. The next single 'I Get A Little Sentimental Over You' hurtled up the charts in spring 1974, but the five disbanded with a farewell tour of Britain. Two years later, however, the lure of a **CBS** contract brought about a reformation - minus Lyn Paul who had had a minor solo hit in 1975 and Oliver had now been replaced by Danny Finn - but no subsequent single could reconjure a more glorious past and, not-so-New anymore, the group disbanded for the last time in 1978.
Albums: *The New Seekers* (Phillips 1969), *Keith Potger & The New Seekers* (Phillips 1970), *New Colours* (Polydor 1971), *Beautiful People* (Phillips 1971), *We'd Like To Teach The World To Sing* (Polydor 1972, UK issue), *Live At The Royal Albert Hall* (Polydor 1972), *Never Ending Song Of Love* (1972), *Circles* (Polydor 1972), *Now* (Polydor 1973), *Pinball Wizards* (1973), *Together* (Polydor 1974), *Farewell Album* (Polydor 1974), *Together Again* (CBS 1976). Compilations: *Look What They've Done To My Song, Ma* (Contour 1972), *15 Great Hits* (1983), *The Best Of The New Seekers* (1985), *Greatest Hits* (1987). By Marty Kristian, Paul Layton and Peter Oliver *Peter Paul & Marty* (1973).

New Vaudeville Band

This parodic ensemble initially comprised studio musicians gathered to record a Geoff Stephens composition, 'Winchester Cathedral', a tale of lost love in deepest Hampshire, England, sung in the style of a Bertie Wooster character complete with megaphone vocals. The need for a permanent unit arose when in 1966 this contagious single became an international success, to the bizarre extent of winning a Grammy for 'Best Rock And Roll Record'. Having failed to tempt the nascent **Bonzo Dog Doo-Dah Band** into accepting the role, a group was assembled late in 1966 around Alan Klein aka Tristram, Seventh Earl of Cricklewood (b. 29 June 1942; vocals), Henri Harrison (b. 6 June 1943, Watford, Hertfordshire, England; drums), Stan Haywood (b. 23 August 1947, Dagenham, Essex, England; keyboards), Neil Korner (b. 6 August 1942, Ashford, Kent, England; bass), Mick Wilsher (b. 21 December 1945, Sutton, Surrey, England; guitar), Hugh 'Shuggy' Watts (b. 25 July 1941, Watford, Hertfordshire, England; trombone), Chris Eddy (b. 4 March 1942; bass), and the line-up was completed by Bob Kerr (b. 14 February 1943, London, England; trombone/saxophone), a refugee from the aforementioned Bonzos. The septet continued the 20's style of that debut release and scored a second UK Top 10 hit with 'Peek-A-Boo' in 1967. That same year, 'Finchley Central' and 'Green Street Green' also charted in the Top 40, but very soon their novelty appeal waned and the group underwent a gradual process of disintegration while playing out their days on the Las Vegas and English cabaret circuit. Kerr pursued the madcap angle with his new unit, Bob Kerr's Whoopee Band.
Albums: *Winchester Cathedral* (1966), *New Vaudeville Band On Tour* (1967).

New Victory Band

A highly talented group of UK country dance musicians, New Victory Band comprises: Pete (melodeon) and Chris Coe (hammer dulcimer, duet concertina), Roger (tuba, banjo, mouth organ) and Helen Watson (keyboards, whistles), John (trombone, fiddle, melodeon, tenor banjo, snare drum, harmonica) and Suzie Adams (banjo), Ian (percussion) and Linda Wordsworth (tap dance). They are one of those legendary bands that did much to loosen the woolly pully and tweed skirts image of English dance.
Album: *One More Dance And Then* (1978).

New Wave Of British Heavy Metal

The names speak for themselves - **Iron Maiden**, **Def Leppard, Saxon**, **Samson**, **Venom**, **Diamond Head**, **Girlschool** and **Praying Mantis**. Just a handful of the bands who made it during the period 1979 to 1981. The phrase was first coined by Geoff Barton at *Sounds*, but much credit is also due to DJ Neal Kay, whose help in giving bands like Iron Maiden and Praying Mantis (as well as many others) their first break was crucial. **EMI Records** were quick off the mark and with Kay's help they produced the compilation album, *Metal For Muthas*, which put many bands on the road to fame and others, like **Toad The Wet Sprockett**, on the road to obscurity. Well over 200 bands emerged during this period and many released records on their own labels - even more never got past the rehearsal stage, while others remained strictly

'bedroom' bands. This enthusiasm also helped to revitalise older bands and some, like **Gillan** and **Motörhead**, became spearheads for the movement. Yet by 1981 the corporate machine began to eat up the talent and American influences crept in to destroy the movement's identity. If, as has often been stated, the movement started with Iron Maiden's *Soundhouse Tapes* EP in 1979, then it would be equally true to say that the final nail in its coffin came in September 1981 when **Paul Di'Anno** left them. Just like punk in 1977, the ideas and attitude fell victim to clean living and commercialism.
Compilations: *Metal For Muthas Volume 1* (EMI 1980), *Metal For Muthas Volume 2 Cut Loud* (EMI 1980), *Brute Force* (MCA 1980), *New Electric Warriors* (Logo 1980), *The N.W.O.B.H.M. '79 Revisisted* (Vertigo 1990).

New World

USA heavy metal band New World were formed in February 1992 by guitarist Mike Polak, who completed the line-up with the addition of seasoned musicians Martin Koprax (vocals), Bernd Fuxa (bass) and Thomas Fend (drums). Polak had been featured on Mike Varney's 'Guitar On The Edge' series and teaches at the American Institute Of Music, Europe's biggest rock school, from where Fend was also drawn into the ranks. An eight-track demo, *The World We Created*, sold out quickly on the underground rock network, and as a consequence New World landed a deal with Rock The Nation Records. Their influences, ranging from jazz and classical to more conventional rock sources, saw comparisons to **Dream Theater** when their debut album was released in 1994.
Album: *Changing Times* (RTN 1994).

New York City

An R&B vocal group from New York City, New York, USA. New York City were one of the finest representatives of the renaissance of vocal harmony groups and the explosion of the Philadelphia recording scene during the early 70s. Members were Tim McQueen, John Brown (earlier a member of the **Five Satins**), Ed Shell, and Claude Johnson. The group first recorded for Buddah as Triboro Exchange, but it was not until their name change in 1972 and their signing to Chelsea Records that the group became successful. Under the aegis of ace Philadelphia producer/arranger **Thom Bell** the group flourished on the charts with such hits as 'I'm Doin' Fine Now' (number 14 R&B, number 17 pop), 'Quick, Fast, In A Hurry' (number 19 R&B, number 79 pop), and 'Happiness Is' (number 20 R&B). Their last chart record was in 1975, a time when standup vocal groups were becoming less of a factor in R&B. Their legacy was recalled in 1992 when in the UK the **Pasadenas** had a number 1 hit with 'I'm Doing Fine Now'.
Albums: *I'm Doing Fine Now* (Chelsea 1973), *Soulful Road* (Chelsea 1974). Compilations: *Best of New York City* (Chelsea 1976), *I'm Doing Fine Now* (Collectables 1993).

New York Dolls

One of the most influential rock bands of the last 20 years, the New York Dolls pre-dated the punk and sleaze metal movements which followed and offered both a crash course in rebellion with style. Formed in 1972, the line-up stabilized with **David Johansen** (b. 9 January 1950, Staten Island, New York, USA; vocals), **Johnny Thunders** (b. John Anthony Genzale Jnr., 15 July 1952, New York City, New York, USA, d. 23 April 1991, New Orleans, Louisiana, USA; guitar), Arthur Harold Kane (bass), **Sylvain Sylvain** (guitar/piano) and Jerry Nolan (d. 14 January 1992; drums), the last two having replaced Rick Rivets and Billy Murcia (d. 6 November 1972). The band revelled in an outrageous glam-rock image: lipstick, high-heels and tacky leather outfits providing their visual currency. Underneath they were a first rate rock 'n' roll band, dragged up on the music of the **Stooges**, **Rolling Stones** and **MC5**. Their self-titled debut, released in 1973, was a major landmark in rock history, oozing attitude, vitality and controversy from every note. It met with widespread critical acclaim, but this never transferred to commercial success. The follow-up, *Too Much Too Soon*, was an appropriate title - and indicated that alcohol and drugs were beginning to take their toll. The album remains a charismatic collection of punk/glam-rock anthems, typically delivered with 'wasted' cool. Given a unanimous thumbs down from the music press the band began to implode shortly afterwards. Johansen embarked on a solo career and Thunders formed the **Heartbreakers**. The Dolls continued for a short time before eventually grinding to a halt in 1975, despite the auspices of new manager **Malcolm McLaren**. The link to the **Sex Pistols** and the UK punk movement is stronger than that fact alone, with the Dolls remaining a constant reference point for teen rebels the world over. Sadly for the band, their rewards were fleeting. Jerry Nolan died as a result of a stroke on 14 January 1992 whilst undergoing treatment for pneumonia and meningitis. Thunders had departed from an overdose, in mysterious circumstances, less than a year previously. *Red Patent Leather* is a poor quality and posthumously-released live recording from May 1975 - *Rock 'N' Roll* offers a much more representative collection.
Albums: *New York Dolls* (Mercury 1973), *Too Much Too Soon* (Mercury 1974), *Red Patent Leather* (New Rose 1984). Compilations: *Lipstick Killers* (ROIR 1983), *Rock 'N' Roll* (Mercury 1994).
Further reading: *New York Dolls*, Steven Morrisey.

New York Jazz Repertory Orchestra

(see **Hyman, Dick**)

New York Skyy

This eight-piece soul/funk band formed in New York and was led by Randy Muller. They gained an underground cult following and reached the lower regions of the UK chart in 1982 with the exuberant 'Let's Celebrate'. Always a favourite on the dance/soul charts they found crossing over to the mainstream singles and albums a hard task and only achieved limited success. Very similar to **Earth, Wind And Fire**, they were a visual act that released a number of albums containing some rather run-of-the-mill-tracks.

Albums: *Skyy* (1979), *Skyyport* (1980), *Skyway* (1980), *Skyline* (1981), *Skyyjammer* (1982), *Skyylight* (1983), *From The Left Side* (1986). Compilation: *Greatest Hits* (1987).

New York, New York

Although greeted with mixed reviews at the time of its release in 1977, Martin Scorcese's vibrantly-directed film has two major virtues: Robert De Niro is extremely convincing as a big band tenor saxophonist who wants to play bop, and the simulation of the musical ethos of the era (the late 40s) which is remarkably accurate. Otherwise, much of the criticism might be thought fair, the film is too long and the leading roles (the other is **Liza Minnelli** as a band singer-turned-superstar) are rather unsympathetic. **Georgie Auld** dubbed for De Niro and the film's musical director was **Ralph Burns**.

New Yorkers, The

This early **Cole Porter** show is probably best remembered for the inclusion of the notorious 'Love For Sale'. With a lyric containing such lines as 'Appetizing young love for sale.' . . . 'If you want to buy my wares/Follow me and climb the stairs.', this 'threnody in which a frightened vocalist, Miss Kathryn Crawford, impersonates a lily of the gutters, vending her charms in trembling accents, accompanied by a trio of melancholy female crooners', was banned for some years by radio stations on both sides of the Atlantic. Sub-titled 'A Sociological Musical Satire', *The New Yorkers* opened at the Broadway Theatre on 8 December 1930. Herbert Fields's book, based on an idea of cartoonist Peter Arno's, propelled characters, swanky and seedy, around various Manhattan locations, both up-town and down. High society lady, Alice (Hope Williams), loves bootlegger and hoodlum, Al (Charles King), and they have 'Where Have You Been' and one of the score's best numbers, the supremely optimistic 'Let's Fly Away' ('And find a land that's so provincial/We'll never hear what Walter Winchell/Might be forced to say.'). The cast also included Frances Williams, who sang 'The Great Indoors' and 'Take Me Back To Manhattan'; and Barrie Oliver and Ann Pennington, who joined Frances Williams and Charles King for the witty 'I'm Getting Myself Ready For You'. The much-loved clown, **Jimmy Durante**, together with his vaudeville partners, Eddie Jackson and Lou Clayton, played three hoods. Durante stopped the show most nights with one of his own songs, an item called 'Wood', during which he littered the stage with a wide range of wood products. The clean-cut vocal instrumental group, **Fred Waring** And His Pennsylvanians, who had been discovered by the show's producer, Ray Goetz, while playing in Los Angeles, also used some of their own material, but, musically, the show belonged to Porter. Shortly after it opened, he interpolated a hymn to the 'Big Apple', 'I Happen To Like New York' ('I like the sight and the sound and even the stink of it.'), which was sung by Oscar 'Rags' Ragland. *The New Yorkers* ran for 168 performances, and despite being banned from airplay, 'Love For Sale' was a hit for **Libby Holman**, Fred Waring, and later, **Hal Kemp**. It also became widely-heard in a version by **Ella Fitzgerald** on one of her *Cole Porter Songbooks*.

Newbeats

This distinctive pop trio featured falsetto Larry Henley (b. 30 June 1941, Arp, Texas, USA) with brothers Marcus 'Marc' Mathis (b. 9 February 1942; bass) and Lewis 'Dean' Mathis (b. 17 March 1939, Hahira, Georgia, USA). Dean had joined Paul Howard's Western Swing Band in 1956 as a pianist and later moved to Dale Hopkin's Band, with Marc joining shortly afterwards. The Mathis brothers then performed and recorded as Dean And Marc; their version of 'Tell Him No' narrowly missed the US Top 40 in 1959. Henley briefly joined the act before they went their separate ways. After recording as the Brothers on Checker and Argo they also had releases on Check Mate and May before joining Hickory Records, where Henley had been recording fruitlessly as a soloist. Since neither act was successful they decided to record together as the Newbeats. Their first single, 'Bread And Butter', became their biggest hit, shooting to number 2 in the US charts and into the UK Top 20 in 1964. In the USA the shrill-sounding trio kept the Top 40 hits rolling with 'Everything's Alright' in 1964, 'Break Away (From That Boy)' and 'Run Baby Run' (a belated U028
K Top 10 hit in 1971), the last two in 1965. After a decade on Hickory the trio went to Buddah Records in 1973 and then in 1974 to Playboy. The trio split up that year, with Henley then recording without chart success for Capricorn and later for **Atco** and Epic. He then turned his attention to songwriting, and has been very successful since. His best known song was **Bette Midler**'s version of a 1983 country hit 'Wind Beneath My Wings'.

Albums: *Bread & Butter* (1964), *Big Beat Sounds By The Newbeats* (1965), *Run Baby Run* (1966). Compilation: *The Best Of* (1992).

Newbern, 'Hambone' Willie

b. c.1899, USA, d. c.1947, USA. **Sleepy John Estes**, who was taught guitar by Newbern, met him while working on medicine shows in Mississippi. Songs like 'She Could Toodle-Oo' and 'Way Down In Arkansas', made at his sole recording session in 1929, come from his medicine-show repertoire, but Newbern was also a master of the personal blues, composing a remarkable account of his arrest at Marked Tree, Arkansas. His surest claim to fame, however, rests in being the first to record 'Roll And Tumble Blues'. Estes later reported the rumour that Newbern's death was the result of an assault in prison.
Compilation: *The Greatest Songsters* (1990).

Newberry, Booker, III

b. 19 January 1956, Youngstown, Ohio, USA. This rotund soul singer started performing in his local group, Mystic Nights, in 1971. He moved to nearby Philadelphia to find fame and in the mid-70s formed and fronted the quintet Sweet Thunder. They had a Top 40 R&B hit in 1978 with 'Baby, I Need Your Love Today' which they recorded for WMOT Records and which was picked up by **Fantasy Records**. The group recorded three albums for WMOT: *Above The Clouds* (1976), *Sweet Thunder* (1978), which made the US Top 200 and *Horizons* (1979). The group split in 1979 and for a while Newberry worked with the group Impact. In 1983 he signed with Boardwalk Records and his recording of 'Love Town', though only a minor US R&B hit, shot into the UK Top 20 in its first week of release, peaking at number 6. His follow-up 'Teddy Bear' narrowly missed the UK Top 40 and he then soon faded from the public eye. He recorded on Malaco in 1984 and returned to the spotlight, albeit briefly, in 1986 when 'Take A Piece Of Me' on Omni put his name back on the US R&B chart.
Album: *Love Town* (1984).

Newborn, Phineas, Jnr.

b. 14 December 1931, Whiteville, Tennessee, USA, d. 26 May 1989. In the late 40s and early 50s Newborn, a gifted multi-instrumentalist who had studied extensively, played piano in a number of R&B and blues bands in and around Memphis, Tennessee. He had two brief spells with **Lionel Hampton** before military service interrupted his career. Subsequently, he led his own small group in New York, played with **Charles Mingus**, **Oscar Pettiford** and **Kenny Clarke** among others, made several records and appeared in the John Cassavetes film *Shadows* (1960). Relocated in Los Angeles in the 60s, he continued to record with artists such as **Howard McGhee**, **Teddy Edwards**, **Ray Brown** and **Elvin Jones**. His career then faltered, largely through a nervous breakdown and an injury to his hands, but the mid-70s saw his return to public performances. Newborn's early records were marked by displays of his phenomenal technique, while those made later suggested a growing maturity. Unfortunately, the interruptions to his career did not allow his potential full rein, and further illness prevented him from working for most of the 80s. Doctors discovered lung tumour in 1988; he died in 1989. The last years of his life are movingly recounted in a chapter of Stanley Booth's book on Memphis musicians, *Rhythm Oil.*
Albums: *Here Is Phineas* (1956), *Phineas Rainbow* (1956), *Phineas Newborn With Dennis Farnon Orchestra* (1957), *Phineas Newborn And His Orchestra* (1957), *Fabulous Phineas* (1958), *We Three* (1958), *Stockholm Jam Session Vol 1* and *2* (Steeplechase 1958 recording), *Phineas Newborn Plays Again* (1959), *Piano Portraits* (1959), *Newborn Piano* (1959), *A World Of Piano* (Original Jazz Classics 1961), *The Great Jazz Piano Of Phineas Newborn* (Original Jazz Classics 1962), *The Newborn Touch* (Original Jazz Classics 1964), *Please Send Me Someone To Love* (JVC 1969), *Harlem Blues* (Original Jazz Classics 1969), *Solo Piano* (Atlantic 1974), *Solo* (1975), *Look Out...Phineas Is Back* (Pablo 1976), *Phineas Is Genius* (1977).

Newbury, Mickey

b. Milton J. Newbury Jnr., 19 May 1940, Houston, Texas, USA. Newbury began by singing tenor in a harmony group, the Embers, who recorded for **Mercury Records**. He worked as an air traffic controller in the US Air Force and was stationed in England. He later wrote 'Swiss Cottage Place', which was recorded by **Roger Miller**. In 1963 he worked on shrimp boats in Galveston, Texas and started songwriting in earnest. In 1964 he was signed to **Acuff-Rose** Music in Nashville. Among his early compositions are 'Here Comes The Rain, Baby' (**Eddy Arnold** and **Roy Orbison**), 'Funny Familiar Forgotten Feelings' (**Don Gibson** and **Tom Jones**), 'How I Love Them Old Songs' (**Carl Smith**) and 'Sweet Memories' (**Willie Nelson**). In 1968 **Kenny Rogers** And The First Edition had a US pop hit with the psychedelic 'Just Dropped In (To See What Condition My Condition Was In)'. Newbury recorded low-key albums of his own but his voice was so mournful that even his happier songs sounded sad. After two albums for **RCA**, he moved to **Mercury** and wrote and recorded such sombre songs as 'She Even Woke Me Up To Say Goodbye' (later recorded by **Jerry Lee Lewis**), 'San Francisco Mabel Joy' (recorded by **John Denver**, **Joan Baez**, **David Allan Coe** and Kenny Rogers) and 'I Don't Think About Her (Him) No More', which has been recorded by **Don Williams** and **Tammy Wynette**, and also by **Bobby Bare,** under the title of 'Poison Red Berries'. Newbury, who by now lived on a houseboat, was intrigued by the way his wind chimes mingled with the rain, thus leading to the sound effects he used to link tracks with. This gave his albums of similar material a concept. His gentle and evocative 'American Trilogy' - in actuality a medley of three Civil War songs ('Dixie', 'The Battle Hymn Of The Republic' and 'All My Trials') - was a hit in a full-blooded version by **Elvis Presley** in 1972. Says Newbury, 'It was more a detriment than a help because it was not indicative of what I could do.' Nevertheless, his *Rusty Tracks* also features reworkings of American folk songs. Amongst his successful compositions are 'Makes Me Wonder If I Ever Said Goodbye' (**Johnny Rodriguez**) and 'Blue Sky Shinin'' (**Marie Osmond**). He has scarcely made a mark as a performer in the US country charts (his highest position is number 53 for 'Sunshine') but he was elected to the Nashville Songwriters International Hall of Fame in 1980. Ironically, he has released few new songs since and his 'new age' album in 1988 featured re-recordings of old material. Although he performs USA dates with violinist Marie Rhines, he makes a habit of cancelling UK tours.

Albums: *Harlequin Melodies* (1968), *Mickey Newbury Sings His Own* (1968), *Looks Like Rain* (1969), *'Frisco Mabel Joy* (1971), *Heaven Help The Child* (1973), *Live At Montezuma* (1973, also issued as a double-album with *Looks Like Rain*), *I Came To Hear The Music* (1974), *Lovers* (1975), *Rusty Tracks* (1977), *His Eye Is On The Sparrow* (1978), *The Sailor* (1979), *After All These Years* (1981), *In A New Age* (1988), *Nights When I Am Sane* (Winter Harvest 1994). Compilation: *Sweet Memories* (1988).

Newley, Anthony

b. 24 September 1931, London, England. A highly successful songwriter, actor and singer, Newley attended the Italia Conti Stage School in London before working as a child actor in several films, including *The Little Ballerina*, *Vice Versa*, and David Lean's acclaimed version of *Oliver Twist* (1948) in which he played the Artful Dodger. He made his London theatrical debut in John Cranko's revue, *Cranks* in 1955, and had character parts in well over 20 films before he was cast as rock 'n' roll star Jeep Jackson in *Idle On Parade* in 1959. Newley's four-track vocal EP, and his version of the film's hit ballad, **Jerry Lordan**'s 'I've Waited So Long', started a three-year UK chart run which included 'Personality', 'If She Should Come To You', 'And The Heavens Cried', the novelty numbers 'Pop Goes The Weasel' and 'Strawberry Fair' and two UK number 1 hits, 'Why' and **Lionel Bart**'s 'Do You Mind'. Newley also made the album charts in 1960 with his set of standards, *Love Is A Now And Then Thing.* He made further appearances in the charts with *Tony* (1961), and the comedy album *Fool Britannia* (1963), on which he was joined by his wife, Joan Collins and Peter Sellers. In 1961 Newley collaborated with **Leslie Bricusse** on the book, music and lyrics for the off-beat stage musical, ***Stop The World - I Want To Get Off***. Newley also directed, and played the central role of Littlechap. The show, which stayed in the West End for 16 months, ran for over 500 performances on Broadway, and was filmed in 1966. It produced several hit songs, including 'What Kind Of Fool Am I?', 'Once In A Lifetime' and 'Gonna Build A Mountain'.

In 1964 Bricusse and Newley wrote the lyric to **John Barry**'s music for **Shirley Bassey** to sing over the titles of the James Bond movie, *Goldfinger.* The team's next musical show in 1965, ***The Roar Of The Greasepaint - The Smell Of The Crowd***, with comedian **Norman Wisdom** in the lead, toured the north of England but did not make the West End. When it went to Broadway Newley took over (co-starring with Cyril Ritchard), but was not able to match the success of *Stop The World*, despite an impressive score which contained such numbers as 'Who Can I Turn To?', 'A Wonderful Day Like Today', 'The Joker', 'Look At That Face' and 'This Dream'. In 1967 Newley appeared with **Rex Harrison** and Richard Attenborough in the film musical ***Doctor Doolittle***, with script and songs by Bricusse. Despite winning an Oscar for 'Talk To The Animals', the film was considered an expensive flop, as was Newley's own movie project in 1969, a pseudo-autobiographical sex-fantasy entitled *Can Heironymus Merkin Ever Forget Mercy Humppe And Find True Happiness?* Far more successful, in 1971, was *Willy Wonka And The Chocolate Factory*, a Roald Dahl story with music and lyrics by Bricusse and Newley. **Sammy Davis Jnr.** had a million-selling record with one of the songs, 'The Candy Man'. Bricusse and Newley also wrote several numbers for the 1971 NBC television musical adaptation of ***Peter Pan***, starring Mia Farrow and **Danny Kaye**. The team's last authentic stage musical to date, *The Good Old Bad Old Days*, opened in London in 1972 and had a decent run of 309 performances. Newley sang some of the songs, including 'The People Tree', on his 1972 album, *Ain't It Funny*. In 1989, a London revival of *Stop The World - I Want To Get Off*, directed by Newley, and in which he also appeared, closed after five weeks, and, in the same year, he was inducted into the Songwriters' Hall Of Fame, along with Leslie Bricusse. In 1991, Newley appeared on UK television with his ex-wife, Joan Collins, in **Noël Coward**'s ***Tonight At 8.30***, with its famous 'Red Peppers' segment. In the following year, having lived in California for some years, Newley announced that he was returning to Britain, and bought a house there to share with his 90-year-old mother. In the early 90s he presented *Once Upon A Song*, an anthology of his own material, at the King's Head Theatre in London, and occasionally played the title role in regional productions of the musical ***Scrooge***, which Leslie Bricusse had adapted for the stage from his 1970 film. In 1994, Newley presented his accomplished cabaret act (in which he continually, and amusingly, bemoans the fact that he has not had a hit with one of his own songs) at London's Café Royal. In

the same year, Tara Newley, the daughter of Newley and Joan Collins, released her first record entitled 'Save Me From Myself'.
Albums: *Love Is A Now And Then Thing* (1960), *Tony* (1961), *Stop The World - I Want To Get Off* (1962, London Cast), with Peter Sellers, Joan Collins *Fool Britannia* (1963), *The Roar Of The Greasepaint - The Smell Of The Crowd* (1965, Broadway Cast), *Who Can I Turn To* (1965), *Newley Recorded* (1966), *Ain't It Funny* (1972), *The Singer And His Songs* (1978). Compilations: *The Romantic World Of Anthony Newley* (1970), *The Lonely World Of Anthony Newley* (1972), *Anthony Newley: Mr. Personality* (1985), *Greatest Hits* (1991).
Film: *Idle On Parade* (1959).

Newman, Alfred

b. 17 March 1901, New Haven, Connecticut, USA, d. 17 February 1970, Hollywood, California, USA. An important figure in the history of film music, Newman was a composer, conductor, arranger and musical director. A child prodigy on the piano, he went to New York before he was 10 years old, to study piano and harmony. At the age of 13 he was playing in several vaudeville shows a day, whilst also fitting in appearances as a soloist with various classical orchestras. In the 20s he conducted for the Broadway Theatre, and contributed the occasional song to shows such as *Jack And Jill* ('Voodoo Man', 1923). In 1930 he moved to Hollywood shortly after the movies had started to talk, and worked as an arranger and then a composer for United Artists, on films such as *The Devil To Pay*, *Indiscreet*, *The Unholy Garden* and *Arrowsmith.* His 'immortal' melancholy title theme for *Street Scene* (1931), echoed through the years in many a later film depicting urban decay. His scores for other 30s films included *I Cover The Waterfront* (1933), *Nana* (1934), *The Count Of Monte Cristo* (1934), *Clive Of India* (1935), *Les Miserables* (1935), *Dodsworth* (1936), *The Prisoner Of Zenda* (1937), *The Goldwyn Follies* (1938), *The Cowbay And The Lady* (1938), *Trade Winds* (1938), *Gunga Din* (1939), *Wuthering Heights* (1939), *Young Mr. Lincoln* (1939) and *Beau Geste* (1939). He also served as musical director for Sam Goldwyn (1933-39), and won Academy Awards for his work on ***Alexander's Ragtime Band*** (1938), *Tin Pan Alley* (1940), ***Mother Wore Tights*** (1947), ***With A Song In My Heart*** (1952), ***Call Me Madam*** (1953), ***The King And I*** (1956, with co-writer Ken Darby), ***Camelot*** (1967, again with Darby) and ***Hello, Dolly!*** (1969, with **Lennie Hayton**).
He gained further Oscars for his complete background scores to *The Song Of Bernadette* (1943) and *Love Is A Many Splendored Thing* (1955). His film credits during the 40s included *The Grapes Of Wrath* (1940), *The Blue Bird* (1940), *Lillian Russell* (1940), *How Green Was My Valley* (1941), *Charley's Aunt* (1941), *Life Begins At Eight Thirty* (1942), *The Black Swan* (1942), *Heaven Can Wait* (1943), *Claudia* (1943), *The Keys Of The Kingdom* (1944), *Wilson* (1944), *Leave Her To Heaven* (1945), *A Tree Grows In Brooklyn* (1945), *The Razor's Edge* (1946), *Captain From Castille* (1947), *Centennial Summer* (1946), *Unfaithfully Yours* (1948), *The Snake Pit* (1948), *A Letter To Three Wives* (1949), *Yellow Sky* (1948), *Twelve O'Clock High* and *Pinky* (1949). During the 40s Newman spent several years as musical director for 20th Century Fox with his brothers, Lionel and Emil, working for him. In 1950 while still at Fox, Newman wrote the score for 'the wittiest, most devastating, adult and literate motion picture ever made', *All About Eve*, starring Bette Davis and George Sanders. The remainder of his 50s music was of a superb standard, too, for films such as *Panic In The Streets* (1950), *David And Bathsheba* (1951), *What Price Glory?* (1952), *The Snows Of Kilimanjaro* (1952), *The Robe* (1953), *The Seven Year Itch* (1955), *Anastasia* (1956), *Bus Stop* (1956, with Cyril Mockridge), *A Certain Smile* (1958), *The Diary Of Anne Frank* (1959) and *The Best Of Everything* (1959). The latter film's title song (lyric by **Sammy Cahn**) became popular for **Johnny Mathis**, and several other earlier pieces of Newman's film music had lives of their own apart from the soundtracks. These included 'Moon of Manakoora' (lyric by **Frank Loesser**), sung by **Dorothy Lamour** in *The Hurricane*, and popularized by her fellow 'Road' traveller, **Bing Crosby**; 'Through A Long And Sleepless Night' (lyric by **Mack Gordon**), from *Come To The Stable*; and the title songs from *How Green Was My Valley*, *Anastasia* and *The Best Of Everything.* In the 60s his rousing scores for *How The West Was Won* and *The Greatest Story Ever Told* spawned best-selling albums. His music for the melodramatic *Airport* (1970), which featured the popular theme, was the last of Newman's works for the big screen. His son, David Newman (b. 1954), composed a number of television and feature film scores in the 80s and 90s, including *The Kindred*, *The Brave Little Toaster*, *Throw Momma From The Train*, *My Demon Lover*, *The Big Picture*, *Prince Of Pennsylvania*, *Heathers*, *Bill And Ted's Excellent Adventure*, *The War Of The Roses*, *Madhouse*, *The Freshman*, *Meet The Applegates*, *The Marrying Man*, *Bill And Ted's Bogus Journey*, *Don't Tell Momma The Babysitter's Dead*, *Paradise*, *Honeymoon In Las Vegas*, *The Mighty Ducks*, *That Night*, *Hoffa*, *Champions*, *The Sandlot*, *Undercover Blues*, *My Father*, *The Hero*, *The Air Up There*, *The Flintstones*, *The Sandlot Kids*, *I Love Trouble*, and *Boys On the Side* (1995).
Selected album: *Captain From Castile-Classical Film Scores.*

Newman, Chris

b. 30 October 1952, Stevenage, Hertfordshire, England. This highly-accomplished guitarist gave his first public performance at the age of five, and spent time as a teenager playing with **Diz Disley**. In 1974 Chris joined the **Pigsty Hill Light Orchestra**, but left within a couple of years. Newman became a sought-after session player during the 70s, and was also a very capable producer and arranger. This was

demonstrated in 1981 when he co-wrote, produced and arranged 'The Oldest Swinger In Town' by **Fred Wedlock**. The single reached number 4 in the UK charts, and topped a number of overseas charts, including Ireland and Israel. Chris received a silver disc for the production. He was then commissioned to write music for a variety of television and radio shows. At the same time, he was pursuing a career as a performer, touring Europe, the USA, Australia and the Middle East, both in a solo capacity and with other artists. Newman later teamed up with virtuoso harpist **Máire Ní Chathasaigh**, and together they have played worldwide to great acclaim. They performed in Australia in 1988 as part of Ireland's contribution to the Bicentennial celebrations, and again the following year, to take part in the Guinness Celebration of Irish Music. *The Living Wood* was voted Folk Album of the Year by the *Daily Telegraph*, and among the newspaper's top four albums of the decade. The album was used as background music and became a signature tune for the regional UK television series *Off The Hook*. Their recordings all exude refinement and explain why they are extremely popular as a live act.
Albums: *Chris Newman* (1981), *Chris Newman Two* (1983); as Chris And Máire: *The Living Wood* (1988), *The Carolan Album* (1991), *Out Of Court* (Old Bridge Music 1991).

Newman, Colin

A founder member of **Wire**, guitarist/vocalist Newman began a solo career upon the group's demise in 1980. The engaging *A-Z* unsurprisingly furthered the tenor of his former act's work - much of it was intended for a provisional fourth Wire album - and ex-colleagues Mike Thorne (keyboards/production) and Robert Gotobed (drums) were on hand to further the sense of continuity. The set ably showcased Newman's grasp of dissonant pop and an ability to subvert the form while engaging with its rules. *Provisionally Entitled The Singing Fish* was a purely instrumental set which the artist produced and contributed an array of different instruments to. Newman's discipline and dark humour was nonetheless still evident. Within months he issued *Not To*, which echoed the style of his debut. Significantly Thorne had dropped from the picture, and the absence of his sometimes overstated keyboards allowed space for guitarist Desmond Simmons to develop. Simon Gillham (bass) and the ever-faithful Gotobed added punch to a collection blending new material with Wire and *A-Z* leftovers. Challenging, minimalist and sometimes splintered rhythmically, *Not To* captures Newman at his best. Paradoxically, he then withdrew from music for a period but, having obtained a grant, journeyed to India to undertake a series of recordings. His return in 1984 sparked the seeds of Wire's reunion two years later. Newman remained committed to the group, later dubbed Wir on Gotobed's departure, but continued his solo career with *Commercial Suicide*. Aided by Malka Spigel and Sean Bonnar/Samy Birnach of **Minimal Impact** - whose 1985 album, *Raging Souls*, Newman produced - the singer herein offered a quieter, more introspective style than on previous recordings. *It Seems* featured the same core trio, while the additional use of horn and reed players added depth, but in 1994 he formed Oracle with Birnbach and Speigel (now Newman's wife). The sumptious *Tree* followed, issued on the collective's Swim label. The album, recorded over a five-year period, contained a haunting version of the **Lovin'Spoonful**'s 'Coconut Grove' and confirmed Newman's valued position on the periphary of modern music.
Albums: *A-Z* (Beggars Banquet 1980), *Provisionally Entitled The Singing Fish* (4AD 1981), *Not To* (4AD 1982), *Commercial Suicide* (Crammed Discs 1986), *It Seems* (Crammed Discs 1988).

Newman, David

(see **Newman, Alfred**)

Newman, David 'Fathead'

b. 24 February 1933, Dallas, Texas, USA. Newman was a tenor/baritone/soprano saxophone player and flautist, whose work contains elements of both jazz and R&B. In the early 50s he toured with Texan blues guitarist **'T-Bone' Walker** and recorded the classic 'Reconsider Baby' with **Lowell Fulson** in 1954. For the next 10 years Newman was part of **Ray Charles**' orchestra, appearing on landmark recordings such as 'I Got A Woman', 'What'd I Say' and 'Lonely Avenue'. Other tenures have included the saxophone position in **Herbie Mann**'s Family Of Mann (1972-74). He has recorded some two dozen albums as a leader since 1958, most tending towards mainstream and post-bop jazz with a funk edge, and has worked extensively as an accompanist in the blues, rock and jazz fields. He worked on **Natalie Cole**'s best-selling *Unforgettable* (1990), and received much acclaim for his involvement in the *Bluesiana Triangle* benefit projects in aid of the homeless. *Blue Greens And Beans* was a collection of bop standards also featuring another Texan player, Marchel Ivery.
Albums: as leader *Lonely Avenue* (1971), *Mr. Fathead* (1976), *Fire! Live At the Village Vanguard* (Atlantic 1989), *Blue Greens And Beans* (Timeless 1991), *Blue Head* (Candid 1991), with Art Blakey, Dr. John *Bluesiana Triangle* (1990), *Return To The Wide Open Spaces* (Meteor 1993). Compilation: *Back To Basics* (1990).

Newman, Jimmy C.

b. Jimmy Yves Newman, 27 August 1927, Big Mamou, Louisiana, USA. Since he was of half French origin, spoke both English and French and grew up in the heart of the cajun area of the State, it is no surprise that he went on to become one of the main artists to bring that genre of music into the field of country music. He left school prematurely when his father died to help support his eight siblings. Newman first became interested in country music through hearing his brother Walter play guitar and sing **Jimmie Rodgers**' songs. In the mid-40s he played in a local cajun band and made his first recording in French in 1946. Later, he formed his own band, played local radio and small venues around the State, and eventually got his own programme on KPLC-TV in Lake Charles, where his mixture of cajun and country music soon proved popular. In 1949 he recorded the original version of the **Webb Pierce** hit 'Wondering'. The release failed to chart but, determined to find a hit song, he wrote and recorded 'Cry Cry Darling'. Listeners to his early recordings will note a prominent hiss on his pronunciation of the letter 'S', caused by a badly fitted gold tooth. **Fred Rose** tried to eliminate the problem by changing lyrics, such as in 'Cry Cry Darling', where 'sunshine' became 'moonlight'. (A little later a partial denture replaced the offending tooth and permanently cured the problem). Also through the auspices of Fred Rose, Newman joined **Dot Records**. In 1954 a new recording of 'Cry Cry Darling' reached number 4 on the US country charts and led him to join the *Louisiana Hayride*. Between 1955 and 1957 he had five more Top 10 country hits, the biggest being his recording of **Ned Miller**'s 'A Fallen Star', which became a number 2 country and number 23 pop hit. Newman acquired the 'C' to his name when the drummer on the recording of the song, T. Tommy Cutrer, labelled him Jimmy 'Cajun' Newman and the initial stuck. He did not like rockabilly or novelty songs, but did record 'Bop-A-Hula' and the **Jim Reeves** song 'Step Aside Shallow Waters'.

In 1958 he moved to **MGM**, where Top 10 country hits included 'You're Making A Fool Out Of Me' and 'A Lovely Work Of Art'. In 1961 he left MGM because he felt he was losing his cajun roots. He joined **Decca** and in the next nine years charted 16 country hits including such popular recordings as 'DJ For A Day' and 'Artificial Rose' and cajun numbers including 'Alligator Man', 'Bayou Talk' and 'Louisiana Saturday Night'. His last chart hit came in 1970 with a song called 'I'm Holding Your Memory'. He later recorded for several minor labels including Plantation. From the mid-50s through the 70s he toured extensively throughout the USA, played some overseas concerts and has also appeared on all major network radio and television shows. He became a member of the ***Grand Ole Opry*** in 1956 and still maintains his regular appearances, often hosting one of the show's segments. Newman's plaintive tenor vocals and traditional fiddle and steel guitar backing were ideally suited to the country music of the 50s and 60s and at times, except for his cajun numbers, he was comparable in vocal work to Webb Pierce. He has always proved a great favourite with UK audiences on the occasions when he has appeared at the Wembley Festival and continues to tour with veteran cajun musicians like fiddle player Rufus Thibodeaux.

Albums: *This Is Jimmy Newman* (1959), *Jimmy Newman* (1962), *Songs By Jimmy Newman* (1962), *Folk Songs Of The Bayou Country* (1963), *Artificial Rose* (1966), *Country Crossroads* (1966), *A Fallen Star* (1966), *Sings Country Songs* (1966), *The World Of Country Music* (1977), *Born To Love You* (1968), *The Jimmy Newman Way* (1968), *The Jimmy Newman Style* (1969), *Country Time* (1970), *Progressive C.C* (1977), with Hank Locklin, Rita Remington *Carol Channing & Her Country Friends* (1977), *The Cajun Cowboy* (1978), *The Happy Cajun* (1979, *Cajun Country* (1982), *Wild 'N' Cajun* (1984), *Cajun & Country Too* (1987), *Lache Pas La Patate* (1987), *Bop A Hula* (1990), *The Alligator Man* (1991). Compilations: *Greatest Hits Volume 1* (1981), *Jimmy Newman & Al Terry - Earliest Recordings 1949-1952* (1981), *Cajun Country Classics* (1993).

Newman, Joe

b. 7 September 1922, New Orleans, Louisiana, USA, d. 4 July 1992. After playing with and leading a college band, trumpeter Newman joined **Lionel Hampton** in 1941. Two years later he joined **Count Basie** at the start of a long association. In the late 40s and early 50s he spent some time in bands led by **Illinois Jacquet** and **J.C. Heard** and also led his own bands for club and record dates. By 1952 he was back in the Basie fold and he remained with the band, handling most of the trumpet solos, until 1961. Subsequently, he toured world-wide, usually as a solo act, but occasionally in specially formed bands such as those led by **Benny Goodman** and Hampton. He also became active in jazz education. This pattern of work continued throughout the 80s and into the early 90s. A powerful player with a wide repertoire, Newman's style acknowledged latterday developments in jazz trumpet while remaining rooted in the concepts of his great idol, **Louis Armstrong**.

Albums: *Joe Newman And His Band* (1954), *Joe Newman And The Boys In The Band* (1954), *The Joe Newman Sextet* (1954), *All I Wanna Do Is Swing* (1955), *The Count's Men* (Fresh Sound 1955 recording), *I'm Still Swinging* (1955), *I Feel Like A Newman* (Black Lion 1955-56), *Salute To Satch* (1956), *The Joe Newman-Frank Wess Septet* (1956), *Jazz For Playboys* (Savoy 1957), *The Happy Cats* (Jasmine 1957), *The Joe Newman-Zoot Sims Quartet* (1957), *Soft Swingin' Jazz* (1958), *Joe Newman And His Orchestra* (1958), *Joe Newman And Count Basie's All Stars* (1958), *Jive At Five* (Original Jazz Classics 1960), *Good 'N' Groovy* (1961), *Joe's Hap'nin's* (1961), *The Joe Newman-Oliver Nelson Quintet* (1961), *In A Mellow Mood* (1962), *Shiny Stockings* (c.1965), *Way Down Blues* (c.1965), with Lionel Hampton *Newport Uproar!* (1967), *I Love My Baby* (1978), *Joe Newman-Jimmy Rowles Duets* (1979), *Similar Souls* (Vogue 1983), with Joe Wilder *Hangin' Out* (1984).

Newman, Lionel

b. 4 January 1916, New Haven, Connecticut, USA, d. 3 February 1989. A distinguished composer, musical director, conductor and arranger for movies for more than 30 years, Newman was a talented pianist as a child, and while in his teens started out as a rehearsal pianist for ***Earl Carroll's Vanities***, graduating to the position of musical director. He toured with other shows, played piano for Mae West for a while, and performed the same function at 20th Century-Fox when he joined them in 1943. Earlier in 1938, he had composed the title song (lyric by Arthur Quenzer) for the movie *The Cowboy And The Lady*, which had a score by his elder brother, **Alfred Newman**. In the late 40s Newman's songs included 'As If I Didn't Have Enough On My Mind' (with **Harry James**), sung by **Dick Haymes** in *Do You Love Me?*, as well as 'The Morning Glory Road', 'Ramblin' Around' and 'Sentimental Souvenirs'. He had a smash hit in 1948 with the romantic ballad 'Again' (lyric by Dorcas Cochrane), from the film *Road House*. It was successful at the time for **Doris Day**, **Gordon Jenkins** and **Vic Damone,** among others. Another of his numbers, *Never* (lyric by Eliot Daniel), sung by **Dennis Day** in *Golden Girl* (1951), was nominated for an Oscar. In his career as a musical director, Newman worked on such films as *Cheaper By The Dozen* (1950), *The Jackpot* (1950), *Mother Didn't Tell Me* (1950), *I'll Get By* (1950), *Dangerous Crossing* (1953), *Love Me Tender* (1956, **Elvis Presley**'s first film), ***The Best Things In Life Are Free*** (1956), *Mardi Gras* (1958), ***Doctor Dolittle*** (1967), *The Great White Hope* (1970) and *The Saltzburg Connection* (1972). He supervised all **Marilyn Monroe**'s movies for 20th Century-Fox, such as ***Gentlemen Prefer Blondes*** (1953), *River Of No Return* (1954) and ***There's No Business Like Show Business*** (1954). As the Studio's general music director, and senior vice-president in 1982, he was a powerful influence on the Fox output. His original music scores included *Don't Bother To Knock* (1952), *The Proud Ones* (1956), *A Kiss Before Dying* (1956), *Compulsion* (1959), *North To Alaska* (1960), *Move Over Darling* (1963), *The Pleasure Seekers* (1964, with Alexander Courage) and *Do Not Disturb* (1965). He was nominated for 11 Academy Awards, and won the Oscar, with **Lennie Hayton**, in 1969 for his adaptation of **Jerry Herman**'s score for the film version of ***Hello, Dolly!***. During the early 80s he conducted the Boston Pops Orchestra in the USA, and performed at London's Royal Albert Hall. He retired in 1985, but was persuaded by MGM to return to the business in 1987. He died two years later in California.

Newman, Randy

b. 28 November 1943, Los Angeles, California, USA. One of the great middle America songwriters, Newman is William Faulkner, Garrison Keillor, Edward Hopper and Norman Rockwell, all set to music. Newman's songs are uncompromising and humorous but are often misconceived as being cruel and trite. His early compositions were recorded by other people, as Newman was paid $50 a month as a staff songwriter for **Liberty Records** housed in the famous **Brill Building**, New York. Early hit songs included 'Nobody Needs Your Love' and 'Just One Smile' by **Gene Pitney**, 'I Don't Want To Hear It Anymore' recorded by **Dusty Springfield** and **P.J. Proby**, 'I Think It's Going To Rain Today', by **Judy Collins**, **UB40** and again by Dusty, as was the superb 'I've Been Wrong Before' which was also a hit for **Cilla Black**. **Alan Price** found favour with 'Simon Smith And His Amazing Dancing Bear' and 'Tickle Me', **Peggy Lee** succeeded with 'Love Story', and **Three Dog Night** and **Eric Burdon** did well with 'Mama Told Me Not To Come'. In addition, Newman's songs have been recorded by **Manfred Mann**, **Harpers Bizarre**, **Frankie Laine**, the **Walker Brothers**, the **Nashville Teens**, **Jackie DeShannon**, **Nina Simone**, **Ringo Starr** and **Ray Charles**. Newman's debut album came as late as 1968 and was the subject of bizarre advertising from **Reprise Records**. In February 1969 they announced through a hefty campaign that the record was not selling; they changed the cover and added a lyric sheet. This bold but defeatist ploy failed to increase the meagre sales. In 1970 he contributed to the *Performance* soundtrack and that same year his work was celebrated by having **Harry Nilsson** record an album of his songs. His introspective lyrics are never self-indulgent; he writes in a morose way but it all merely reflects the human condition. Songs like 'Old Kentucky Home' and 'Baltimore' have hidden warmth. 'Rednecks' and 'Short People' are genuine observations, but on these songs Newman's humour was too subtle for the general public and he received indignant protests and threats. In 1979's 'Story Of A Rock 'N' Roll Band' he castigated both **Kiss** and **ELO**. One of the first examples of his film music came in 1971, with *Cold Turkey*, and he was nominated for an Oscar in 1982 for his score to *Ragtime*, and again, in 1984, for *The Natural*. In 1983, his 'I Love Love L.A.' was used to promote the Los Angeles Olympic Games of the following year. In 1986 he wrote 'Blue Shadows', the theme for *The Three Amigos!*, which was performed in the hit movie by Steve Martin and Chevy Chase. More film scores followed, such as *Awakenings*, *Parenthood* (including the song, 'I Love To See You Smile'), *Avalon* (the last two films were nominated for Academy Awards), *The Paper*, and *Maverick* (1994). Among his most recent studio work was *Land Of Dreams*, ironically co-produced by one of the victims of his acerbic wit, **Jeff Lynne**. Newman continues to observe, infuriate and mock as his croaky voice turns out more masterpieces commenting on American society.

Albums: *Randy Newman* (1968), *12 Songs* (1970), *Performance* (1970), *Randy Newman/Live* (1971), *Sail Away* (1972), *Good Old Boys* (1974), *Little Criminals* (1977), *Born Again* (1979), *Ragtime* (1982, film soundtrack), *Trouble In Paradise* (1983), *The Natural* (1984, film soundtrack), *Land Of Dreams* (1988), *Parenthood* (1990, film soundtrack), *Awakenings* (1991, film soundtrack), *The Paper* (Reprise 1994, soundtrack). Compilation: *Lonely At The Top - The Best Of Randy Newman* (1987).

Newport Jazz Festival

Newport, Rhode Island, USA is not the kind of venue normally associated with music which began as lowlife entertainment, but the jazz festival, begun in 1954, blended comfortably into Newport's somewhat refined surroundings with considerable ease. The nature of the event, which was founded by two of Newport's top set, Louis and Elaine Lorillard and directed by **George Wein**, was exposed to the world at large thanks to a marvellous, if occasionally visually overwrought, evocation of the 1958 festival filmed by Bert Stern and released in 1960 under the title, *Jazz On A Summer's Day*. The artists at Newport that year included **Louis Armstrong**, **Gerry Mulligan**, **Dinah Washington**, **Thelonious Monk**, gospel singer **Mahalia Jackson** and, perhaps the most visually arresting sight of the festival, **Anita O'Day** in hip-hugging dress, gloves and cartwheel hat. Following crowd trouble in 1960, the 1961 festival was cancelled, but it was back the following year. However, more unsavoury events in 1971 caused it be moved permanently to New York City. Still under Wein's benignly autocratic direction, the festival gained in strength and has never lost is early importance. New York is where it remains, with events taking place over 10 days in June in venues ranging from Carnegie Hall to small intimate clubs, and even onto the streets of the city. Over the years the festival's name has changed slightly to accommodate different sponsors but most recently, in deference to the Japanese Victor Corporation, it has been known as the JVC Jazz Festival New York. Since 1984 Newport has once again had its own festival, with George Wein presenting a two-day show in August at Fort Adams State Park, again under the patronage of JVC.

Newton, David

b. 2 February 1958, Glasgow, Scotland. As a child he took lessons on piano, clarinet and bassoon, but while studying at the Leeds College of Music he decided to concentrate on piano. After playing in various bands as a semi-pro, he secured his first professional engagement leading a trio at a restaurant in Bradford, Yorkshire, in 1978. Around this time he also played in numerous other bands, ranging musically from traditional jazz to funk, from strict-tempo dancebands to classical. In the early 80s he worked extensively in the theatre, especially with Scarborough-based playwright Alan Ayckbourn. Newton then returned to Scotland, and from a base in Edinburgh quickly established himself as a rising star of the jazz world. He played in backing groups for many visiting jazzmen, including **Art Farmer**, **Bud Shank**, **Shorty Rogers** and **Nat Adderley**. He also recorded with **Buddy De Franco**. By the late 80s he had settled in London, recording with **Alan Barnes**, the Jazz Renegades, **Martin Taylor**, with whom he toured India, and also playing club dates with **Andy Cleyndert**, **Don Weller**, **Spike Robinson** and others. At the end of the decade he became accompanist and musical director to **Carol Kidd**, recording with her and making numerous concert appearances. An outstanding talent, Newton's wide-ranging experience has ensured that he is at home in most musical settings. Despite his eclecticism he has developed a distinctive and distinguished personal style. As he matures he appears likely to become one of Europe's leading jazz musicians, well-equipped to take the music into the 21st century.

Albums: with Alan Barnes *Affiliation* (1987), *Given Time* (GFM 1988), *Victim Of Circumstance* (Linn 1991), *Eye Witness* (Linn 1991), *Return Journey* (Linn 1993).

Newton, Frankie

b. 4 January 1906, Emory, Virginia, USA, d. 11 March 1954. In the late 20s and early 30s Newton played trumpet in a number of leading New York bands, including those led by **Charlie 'Fess' Johnson**, **Sam Wooding** and **Chick Webb**. He later joined **Charlie Barnet** and was briefly with **Andy Kirk**. The 40s saw him playing in various bands on the verge of the bigtime, including those led by **Lucky Millinder** and **Pete Brown**. Apparently without direction, his career drifted and he worked mostly in clubs in New York and Boston, sometimes in company with **James P. Johnson**, **'Big' Sid Catlett** and **Edmond Hall**. By the 50s he was playing only rarely. A gifted player with a full, burnished sound, Newton was especially attuned to the needs of singers and played on a number of memorable vocal recordings, including **Bessie Smith**'s last date, plus **Maxine Sullivan**'s 'Loch Lomond', and **Billie Holiday**'s 'Strange Fruit' sessions. Newton's briefly shining talent promised much, but his lack of ambition steadfastly countered any chance of popular success. But then, the easy-going life he led was perhaps what he really wanted.

Selected compilations: *At The Onyx Club 1937-1939* (Tax 1987), *Frankie's Jump* (Affinity 1993).

Newton, James

b. 1 May 1953, Los Angeles, California, USA. Already playing a host of reed instruments, Newton took up the flute when he was 17 years old. After three years in Stanley Crouch's Black Music Infinity (1972-75), Newton move to New York in 1978. By now working

only on flute, he led groups with **Anthony Davis**, an important association which continues. As well as experimenting with unusual flute techniques found in modern classical music, Newton has developed the art of humming and playing simultaneously to the degree of producing contrapuntal lines. He has recorded consistently.
Albums: *Hidden Voices* (1979), *Binu* (1979), *Axum* (1981), *James Newton* (1983), *Luella* (1984), *African Flower* (1986), *Echo Canyon* (1987), *Romance And Revolution* (1987), *In Venice* (1988).

Newton, Juice

b. Judy Kaye Cohen, 18 February 1952, Lakehurst, New Jersey, USA. This singing daughter from a military family spent most of her childhood in Virginia. While completing a formal education in California, she fronted Dixie Peach, a country-rock combo that was re-named Silver Spur for three **RCA** albums in the mid-70s. Despite assistance from top Los Angeles session musicians, immediate solo success was dogged by **Bonnie Tyler**'s version of 'It's A Heartache' eclipsing Newton's own, though she gained a US country hit by proxy when the **Carpenters** covered her self-composed 'Sweet Sweet Smile' in 1978. Two years later, she arrived in ***Billboard***'s Top 5 with a revival of **Chip Taylor**'s 'Angel Of The Morning' (her only UK hit) and then 'Queen Of Hearts' (also a hit for **Dave Edmunds**), while the *Juice* album containing both peaked at number 22. She enjoyed more hits in the pop charts with 'Love's Been A Little Hard On Me', *Quiet Lies* and a 1983 overhaul of the **Zombies**' 'Tell Her No', but it was the country market that came to provide the bulk of her success. After encouraging response when she performed 'The Sweetest Thing I've Ever Known' at 1981's annual Country Radio Seminar, this old Silver Spur track was re-mixed for a single to become a country number 1 the following year. Other genre successes included a reworking of **Brenda Lee**'s 'Break It To Me Gently', Dave Loggins' 'You Make Me Want To Make You Mine', 'Hurt' and a duet with **Eddie Rabbitt**, 'Born To Each Other'. She later married polo star Tom Goodspeed.
Albums: *Juice Newton And Silver Spur* (1975), *After The Dust Settles* (1977), *Come To Me* (1977), *Well Kept Secret* (1978), *Take A Heart* (1979), *Juice* (1981), *Quiet Lies* (1982), *Dirty Looks* (1983), *Can't Wait All Night* (1984), *Old Flame* (1986), *Friends And Lovers* (1986). Compilations: *Collection* (1983), *Greatest Hits* (1984).

Newton, Wayne

b. 3 April 1942, Roanoke, Virginia, USA. Newton began his singing career as a child and later became the most popular and highest-paid star on the Las Vegas nightclub circuit. Inspired by a visit to the *Grand Ole Opry* in Nashville, Newton's first professional singing engagement came at the age of six, when he was paid $5 for a performance. His family relocated to Phoenix, Arizona a few years later, where he learnt to play several instruments, including guitar and piano. He and his brother, Jerry, became a duo and by his early teens Wayne had landed his own television programme on station KOOL in Phoenix. At the age of 16, when the brothers were offered a five-year booking in Las Vegas, the family moved there. The Newton Brothers recorded one single for **Capitol Records** in 1959, 'The Real Thing'/'I Spy', before recording several singles for the small George Records. In 1962 they were heard by television star **Jackie Gleason**, who booked them on his programme in September. Wayne was clearly emerging as the star of the act, and brother Jerry dropped out in 1963. By this time he had signed a music publishing contract with **Bobby Darin**'s TM Music and returned to Capitol Records; Darin also oversaw the production of most of Newton's early Capitol recordings. Singing in a Las Vegas-lounge-lizard style, with minor traces of 'safe' rock, Newton's first single to chart was 'Heart (I Hear You Beating)', in 1963. 'Danke Schoen', co-written by **Bert Kaempfert**, followed and became a Newton trademark which he performed throughout his entire career. Newton's first album, sharing the single's title, was released in the autumn of 1963 and reached number 55.
One notable early single was 1965's 'Comin' On Too Strong', co-written by **Gary Usher**, who had written some music for the **Beach Boys**. The song included **Bruce Johnston** on backing vocals (along with arranger **Terry Melcher**). Newton continued to record for Capitol until 1967, when he briefly switched to **MGM Records** before returning to Capitol one last time in 1970. He then proceeded to Chelsea Records, for which he recorded his biggest hit, the number 4 single 'Daddy Don't You Walk So Fast', in 1972. He also charted twice, in 1979 and 1980, on the Aries II label. His total number of chart singles was 17, and 10 albums charted as well, but it became apparent by the 70s that Newton's strength was in his concert performances in Las Vegas. He not only commanded higher fees for those concerts than any other performer - reportedly $1 million per month - but invested in hotels in that city, becoming wealthy in the process. Newton has also made some nominal film appearances, including the 1990 *The Adventures Of Ford Fairlane.*
Selected albums: *Danke Schoen* (1963), *Sings Hit Songs* (1964), *In Person* (1964), *Red Roses For A Blue Lady* (1965), *Summer Wind* (1965), *Wayne Newton - Now!* (1966), *Old Rugged Cross* (1966), *It's Only The Good Times* (1967), *Walking On New Grass* (1968), *One More Time* (1968), *Daddy Don't You Walk So Fast* (1972), *Can't You Hear The Song* (1972), *While We're Still Young* (1973), *The Best Of Wayne Newton - Live* (1989). Compilation: *The Best Of Wayne Newton* (1967).

Newton-John, Olivia

b. 26 September 1948, Cambridge, England. Her showbusiness career began when she won a local contest to find 'the girl who looked most like Hayley Mills' in 1960 after the Newton-Johns had emigrated to Australia. Later she formed the Sol Four with schoolfriends. Though this vocal group disbanded, the encouragement of customers who heard her sing solo in a cafe led her to enter - and win - a television talent show. The prize was a 1966 holiday in London during which she recorded her debut single, **Jackie DeShannon**'s 'Till You Say You'll Be Mine' after a stint in a duo with Pat Carroll. Staying on in England, Olivia became part of Toomorrow, a group created by bubblegum-pop potentate **Don Kirshner**, to fill the gap in the market left by the disbanded **Monkees** (not to be confused with **Tomorrow**). As well as a science-fiction movie and its soundtrack, Toomorrow was also responsible for 'I Could Never Live Without Your Love,' a 1970 single, produced by the **Shadows**' Bruce Welch - with whom Olivia was romantically linked. Although Toomorrow petered out, Newton-John's link with **Cliff Richard** and the Shadows was a source of enduring professional benefit. A role in a Richard movie, tours as special guest in *The Cliff Richard Show*, and a residency - as an comedienne as well as a singer - on BBC television's *It's Cliff!* guaranteed steady sales of her first album, and the start of a patchy British chart career with a Top 10 arrangement of **Bob Dylan**'s 'If Not For You' in 1971. More typical of her output were singles such as 'Take Me Home Country Roads', penned by **John Denver**, 'Banks Of The Ohio' and, from the late John Rostill of the Shadows, 1973's 'Let Me Be There'. This last release sparked off by an appearance on the USA's *The Dean Martin Show* and crossed from the US country charts to the Hot 100, winning her a controversial Grammy for Best Female Country Vocal. After an uneasy performance in 1974's Eurovision Song Contest, Newton-John became omnipresent in North America, first as its most popular country artist, though her standing in pop improved considerably after a chart-topper with 'I Honestly Love You,' produced by John Farrar, another latter-day Shadow (and husband of the earlier mentioned Pat Carroll), who had assumed the task after the estrangement of Olivia and Bruce.

Newton-John also became renowned for her duets with other artists, notably in the movie of the musical **Grease** in which she and co-star **John Travolta** featured 'You're The One That I Want'. This irresistibly effervescent song became one of the most successful UK hit singles in pop history, topping the charts for a stupendous nine weeks. The follow-up, 'Summer Nights' was also a UK number 1 in 1978. Her 'Xanadu', the film's title opus with the **Electric Light Orchestra**, was another global number 1. However, not such a money-spinner was a further cinema venture with Travolta (1983's 'Two Of A Kind'). Neither was 'After Dark,' a single with the late **Andy Gibb** in 1980 nor *Now Voyager*' a 1984 album with his brother Barry. With singles like 'Physical' (1981) and the 1986 album *Soul Kiss* on **Mercury Records** she adopted a more raunchy image in place of her original perky wholesomeness.

During the late 80s/early 90s much of her time was spent, along with Pat (Carroll) Farrar, running her Australian-styled clothing business, Blue Koala. Following *The Rumour*, Olivia signed to **Geffen** for the release of a collection of children's songs and rhymes, *Warm And Tender*. The award of an OBE preceded her marriage to actor and dancer Matt Lattanzi; she remains a showbusiness evergreen although her life was clouded in 1992 when her fashion empire crashed, and it was announced that she was undergoing treatment for cancer. She subsequently revealed that she had won her battle with the disease, and in 1994 released an album which she had written, produced and paid for herself. At the same time, it was estimated that in a career spanning nearly 30 years, she has sold more than 50 million records worldwide.

Albums: *If Not For You* (1971), *Let Me Be There* (1973), *Olivia Newton-John* (1973), *If You Love Me Let Me Know* (1974), *Music Makes My Day* (1974), *Long Live Love* (1974), *Have You Never Been Mellow?* (1975), *Clearly Love* (1975), *Come On Over* (1976), *Don't Stop Believin'* (1976), *Making A Good Thing Better* (1977), with various artists *Grease* (1978, film soundtrack), *Totally Hot* (1978), with the Electric Light Orchestra *Xanadu* (1980, film soundtrack), *Physical* (1981), with various artists *Two Of A Kind* (1983, film soundtrack), *Soul Kiss* (1986), *The Rumour* (1988), *Warm And Tender* (1990), *Gaia: One Woman's Journey* (1994). Compilations: *Olivia Newton-John's Greatest Hits* (1977, US MCA issue), *Greatest Hits* i (1978, UK EMI issue), *Olivia's Greatest Hits, Volume 2* (1982, US MCA issue), *Greatest Hits* ii (1982, UK EMI issue), *Back To Basics: The Essential Collection 1971-1992* (Phonogram 1992).

Film: *Grease* (1978).

Further reading: *Olivia Newton-John: Sunshine Supergirl*, Linda Jacobs. *Olivia Newton-John*, Peter Ruff.

Newtown Neurotics

Formed in the English post-war 'new town' of Harlow, Essex, the Newtown Neurotics produced a fine blend of pop and punk rock with a strong left-wing political slant. Coming together in the spring of 1978, the group comprised Steve Drewett (vocals/guitars), Colin Dredd (bass/vocals) and Tiggy Barber (drums). 'Hypocrite' (1979) and 'When The Oil Runs Out' (1980) appeared on their own No Wonder label, after which Barber was replaced by Simon Lomond. The Neurotics became increasingly involved in the agit-pop and ranting poetry scenes throughout the 80s, regularly playing at benefit concerts and festivals with the likes of **Attila The**

Stockbroker. The strong socialist rhetoric was apparent on their third single on the short-lived but impressive CNT label, 'Kick Out The Tories', in May 1982, followed in December by an attack on Britain's 'Licensing Hours'. When CNT folded, the Newtown Neurotics moved to Razor Records for their debut album. *Beggars Can Be Choosers* was an entertaining yet pertinent mix of scathing observation and new wave power and was promoted on single by a cover of the **Ramones**' 'Blitzkrieg Bop'. November 1984 saw the band move back to their No Wonder label for 'Suzie Is A Heartbreaker' (again hinting at a Ramones' connection), before the Neurotics dropped the 'Newtown' from their name, signing to Jungle Records in the process. The first fruits of this deal emerged as *Repercussions* in 1985, showcasing a group who'd lost none of their musical vigour or political evangelism. 'Living With Unemployment' followed in 1986 (with the help of ranting comedian Porky The Poet and the rumbustious Attila), preceding *Kickstarting A Backfiring Nation*. The Neurotics turned up occasionally during the late 80s (with *Is Your Washroom Breeding Bolshovics?*, for example) while the new decade was celebrated with *45 Revolutions Per Minute*, a singles compilation of the band's 'twelve blazing rock anthems' from 1979-84. The band had actually broken up in October 1988 when then bassist Colin Dredd contracted pleurisy, going on to play a series of astonishing farewell shows in Harlow with a stand-in bass player. Drewett and Mac would go on to form the Unstoppable Beat.
Albums: *Beggars Can Be Choosers* (Razor 1983), *Repercussions* (Jungle 1985), *Kickstarting A Backfiring Nation* (Jungle 1986), *Is Your Washroom Breeding Bolshovics?* (Jungle 1988). Compilation: *45 Revolutions Per Minute* (Jungle 1990).

Nexus 21

Namely Mark Archer and Chris Peat, more famous (in some quarters) for their work as **Altern 8**. They began their career as Nexus 21 - their 'core' project - with the 'Still Life' 12-inch for Blue Cat in September 1989, following it a few months later with 'Rhythm Of Life', this time for Blue Chip. After a 12-inch promo, 'Self-Hypnosis', they delivered *Logical Progression* in October 1990 on **R&S**, a second EP, *Progressive Logic*, following two months later. The duo have also released two singles ('Another Night' and 'Flutes') under the name C&M Connection. Archer has also recorded solo for the Stafford North Imprint as DJ Nex (The *DJ Nex* and *Poundstretcher* EPs) and Xen Mantra (The *Midas* EP). In 1994 he formed Slo-Moshun with Danny Taurus, scoring immediately with the Top 30 'Bells Of New York' cut.

Ní Chathasaigh, Máire

b. Eire. Ní Chathasaigh is one of the British Isles' leading harp players. She learned the instrument during the 70s and also learnt to play piano, tin-whistle and fiddle. She later graduated from University College, Cork with a BA Honours degree in Celtic studies. She followed this by winning the All-Ireland and Pan-Celtic Harp Competitions on a number of occasions. She then gave concert performances, as well as master-classes, in Europe, the USA and Australia, and turned professional in 1981. In 1985 Máire became the first harpist to produce an album comprised mainly of Irish traditional dance music, *The New Strung Harp*. Teaming up with guitarist **Chris Newman** has added a new dimension to the playing, and taken it out of the purely folk tag, by including elements of rock, jazz, and bluegrass. As its title implies, *The Carolan Album* is devoted to the work of the blind Irish harpist and composer, Turlough O'Carolan. Newman and Ní Chathasaigh are joined on the album by musicians of the calibre of **Danny Thompson**, and **Liam O'Flynn**. Having recorded three albums with Newman, and secured an international reputation for concert performances, Ní Chathasaigh produced *The Irish Harper*, a book of her own arrangements, in 1991. Two years later she represented Ireland at the World Harp Congress held in Copenhagen, Denmark.
Albums: *The New Strung Harp* (1985). Máire and Chris: *The Living Wood* (1988), *The Carolan Album* (1991), *Out Of Court* (1991), with Joe Burke *The Tailor's Choice* (1993).
Further reading: *The Irish Harper*, Máire Ní Chathasaigh.

Niagara

This melodic rock group was formed in Madrid, Spain, during 1987 by Angel Arias (bass) and V. M. Arias (guitar). The line-up was completed with the addition of Tony Cuevas (lead vocals), Joey Martos (drums) and Ricky Castaneda (keyboards). Using English lyrics and concentrating on a style that embodied elements of **Europe** and **Whitesnake**, they built up a sizeable following on the European heavy rock scene. Produced by **Baron Rojo** guitarist Carlos de Castro, *Now Or Never* was an impressive debut that featured abrasive guitar work, coupled with razor-sharp arrangements.
Album: *Now Or Never* (Avispa 1988).

Nice

Originally the back-up band to soul singer **P.P. Arnold**, the Nice became one of the true originators of what has variously been described as pomp-rock, art-rock and classical-rock. The band comprised **Keith Emerson** (b. 1 November 1944, Todmorden, Yorkshire, England; keyboards), Brian 'Blinky' Davison (b. 25 May 1942, Leicester, England; drums), Lee Jackson (b. 8 January 1943, Newcastle-Upon-Tyne, England; bass/vocals) and David O'List (b. 13 December 1948, Chiswick, London, England; guitar). After leaving Arnold in October 1967 the Nice quickly built a reputation as one of the most visually exciting bands. Emerson's stage act involved, in true circus style, throwing knives into his Hammond Organ, which would emit outrageous sounds, much to the delight of the audience. Their debut, *The Thoughts Of Emerlist Davjack*, while competent, came nowhere near reproducing their exciting live sound. By the time of the release of its follow-up, *Ars Longa Vita Brevis*, O'List had departed, being unable to compete with Emerson's showmanship and subsequently joined **Roxy Music**. The album contained their notorious single, 'America', from *West Side Story*. During one performance at London's Royal Albert Hall, they burnt the American flag on stage and were severely lambasted, not only by the Albert Hall authorities, but also by the song's composer, **Leonard Bernstein**. The band continued their remaining life as a trio, producing their most satisfying and successful work. Both *Nice* and *Five Bridges Suite* narrowly missed the top of the UK charts, although they were unable to break through in the USA. The former contained an excellent reading of **Tim Hardin**'s 'Hang On To A Dream', with exquisite piano from Emerson. The latter was a bold semi-orchestral suite about working-class life in Newcastle-upon-Tyne. One of their other showpieces was an elongated version of **Bob Dylan**'s 'She Belongs To Me'. *Five Bridges* also contained versions of 'Intermezzo From The Karelia Suite' by Sibelius and Tchaikovsky's 'Pathetique'. Their brave attempt at fusing classical music and rock together with the Sinfonia of London was admirable, and much of what Emerson later achieved with the huge success of **Emerson, Lake And Palmer** should be credited to the brief but valuable career of the Nice. With Emerson's departure, Jackson floundered with **Jackson Heights**, while Davison was unsuccessful with his own band, **Every Which Way**. Jackson and Davison teamed up again in 1974 to form the ill-fated **Refugee**.

Albums: *The Thoughts Of Emerlist Davjack* (1967), *Ars Longa Vita Brevis* (1968), *Nice* (1969), *Five Bridges* (1970), *Elegy* (1971). Compilations: *Autumn 76-Spring 68* (1972), *20th Anniversary Release* (1987).

Nice & Smooth

Based in New York City, Gregg Nice (b. Greg Mays) and Smooth Bee (b. Daryl Barnes) emerged in the late 80s with an album for independent concern Fresh Records, a matter of weeks before the label closed its doors. Their self-titled album did emerge, however, as did the two singles it yielded, 'More & More Hits' and 'Funky For You'. They switched to **Def Jam** for an album and hit single, 'Sometimes I Rhyme Slow', which made US number 44. Album tracks like 'Hip Hop Junkies' suggested they were authentic converts to the history of the movement, and indeed they spanned several of its styles and lyrical concerns. For their second collection they enlisted the help of some of rap and dance music's biggest heavyweights: **Bobby Brown** ('Return Of The Hip Hop Freaks'), **Slick Rick** ('Let's All Get Down'), **Everlast** ('Save The Children') and Jo Jo Hailey of **Jodeci** ('Cheri'). The duo had been trying to arrange a collaboration with Brown for some time, Barnes having previously written lyrics for his *King Of Stage* album, singing back-up vocals on tours by the latter and **New Edition**. Despite the supporting cast it was a set that maintained Nice And Smooth's traditions of deep funk and lyrical pyrotechnics.

Albums: *Nice & Smooth* (Fresh 1989), *Ain't A Damn Thing Changed* (Def Jam 1991), *The Jewel Of The Nile* (Def Jam 1994).

Nice Jazz Festival

The first jazz festival held in Nice, in the south of France, took place in 1948, when it was headlined by **Louis Armstrong**. Although it was in some ways the touch-paper that lit the fire of enthusiasm for jazz festivals, it was not until 1974 that the Nice Jazz Festival became a regular and important event on the international jazz calendar. Today the Grande Parade du Jazz, held in July at the Jardins des Arénes de Cimiez, and presented by **George Wein**, is a major event attracting audiences approaching 75,000. It also draws leading artists from the USA, UK and the rest of the world.

Niche, Grupo

Emanating from Cali, Colombia, Grupo Niche are led by Jairo Varela, whose many roles include: composer, arranger, musical director, vocalist and percussionist. They made their recording debut in 1981 with *Querer Es Poder*. Tomek (the UK salsa broadcaster) reviewed the impact of the band's first decade: 'Who would have said barely 10 years ago that there would be half a dozen salsa bands in Colombia challenging the very best from Puerto Rico and New York? If one man can be responsible, it is Jairo Varela, whose body of work with Niche is the single most impressive songwriting and arranging achievement in salsa during the 80s. A musical illiterate, he has developed his own, inimitable sound by sheer talent. Others have had to transcribe his brilliant ideas. Many of the original Niche were related to the musicians in and took inspiration from Combo Vacana, the seminal Colombian coastal band of the 60s. Fittingly Niche's own achievements have fuelled the current salsa boom in Colombia'. For their albums between 1981 and 1986, Niche's salsa orquesta instrumentation included a front-line of saxophone, flute, two or three trumpets and one or two trombones, a rhythm section (timbales, conga, bongo, güiro, maracas, bass, piano) and voices (lead and chorus). On the first two albums, Varela and trombonist Alexis Lozano shared musical direction and arranging chores. *Querer Es Poder* featured a trio of lead singers: Alvaro del

Castillo, Homer 'Tuto' Jiménez and La Coco Lozano (Alexis's sister). Tuto and La Coco departed. Oscar Alberto Abueta shared lead vocals with del Castillo on the 1982 follow-up *Preparate...Grupo Niche Vol.2*. Abueta left and relocated to Miami (see **Alberto 'El Conejo' Barros**). Tuto returned to replace him on 1983's *Niche* (aka *Directo Desde New York*). Tres, a Cuban six or nine-string guitar, was added to the band. Varela became the sole musical director on *Niche* and remained so on the following six albums released between 1984 and 1988. Lozano played trombone and co-arranged (with Varela) on the record; he departed to found and lead Orquesta Guayacán, whose releases include: *Llego La Hora De La Verdad* (1986), *Que La Sangre Alborota* (1987), *Guayacán Es La Orquesta* (1988), *La Mas Bella* (1990), *5 Años: Aferrados Al Sabor* (1991).

After *Niche*, del Castillo left to record as a solo artist, releasing *Al Puerto* (1985), *Llegamos!* (1986), *Bueno Y Más!* (1987), *Que Se Aguante El Mundo* (1991). Tuto also departed and appeared on the 1987 and 1988 albums by La Cali Charanga.

Moncho Santana sang lead vocals on *No Hay Quinto Malo* (1984) and *Se Pasó!* (1985, aka *Triunfo*); the former contained Niche's anthem 'Cali Pachanguero' (Partying Cali). Varela's arrangements were transcribed by pianist and founder member, Nicolás Cristancho 'Macabí', on both albums. Alberto Barros played trombone and shared the task of transcription with Macabí on *Se Pasó!* and *Me Huele A Matrimonio* (1986). Santana left after *Se Pasó!* and recorded with Grupo Star and Manuel Bravo y su Orquesta Palenque (*Salsa Felina*, 1988), before making his solo debut with *Aqui Estoy!* in 1990. Puerto Rican Tito Gómez (see **Papo Lucca**, **Ray Barretto** and **Nati**) joined Niche as co-lead singer on *Me Huele A Matrimonio*. Niche and Gómez's voice, with its melancholic catch, blended splendidly. Macabí left after 1986's *Grupo Niche Con Cuerdas* to become a regular accompanist with Alberto Barros's Los Titanes as well as a busy session musician. He was replaced by Alvaro Cabarcas 'Pelusa' on the double *Historia Musical* in 1987, which contained re-recordings and re-arrangements of songs from Niche's previous albums. Sadly, Varela dropped saxophone and flute from the line-up on this and further albums. Venezuelan César Monge, former musical director, arranger and trombonist with **Dimensión Latina**, was hired to play and transcribe for the rejigged Niche, which sported a front-line of two trombones and two trumpets only.

Most of the band split from Varela after *Historia Musical* and adopted the name Orquesta Internacional Los Niches, with trumpeter Fabio Espinoza Jnr. as their musical director. They made their UK debut in 1988 with Moncho Santana on lead vocals. Young pianist/arranger/composer Danilo 'Danny' Rosales handled *Tocando Madera*'s production, and contributed arrangements and songs; he worked on albums by other bands, including Grupo Contraste, Hermes Manyoma y su Orquesta La Ley, La Gran Banda Caleña, Formula 8 and La Octava Dimensión. Rosales leads Grupo Changó, for which he and his bassist/arranger/composer brother, Ricardo, share the role of musical director; the band's releases include: *Con Todo!* (1988) and *Sensaciones En Salsa* (1990). In 1990 Los Niches issued *Salsa Por Siempre*. Varela continued with the name Grupo Niche and substantially new personnel. Gómez, Monge and Cabarcas were the only pre-split members who remained with him on 1988's *Tapando El Hueco*, which was up to Varela's usual high creative and imaginative standard. The Miami recorded album featured veteran Cuban bassist **Israel 'Cachao' López** and Colombians Diego Galé, percussion, and trombonist Morist Jiménez, who played alongside Monge in the horn section of three trombones and one trumpet. Tres was dropped from the line-up. Multi-talented Galé sessions extensively; he acted as musical director on Grupo Caneo's debut *Ella* (1989), and now leads his own band, Grupo Galé, whose releases include: *Frivolo* (1989) and *Nuestra Salsa* (1990).

Jiménez shared direction with Varela and played all three parts in the trombone only front-line on the slightly disappointing *Sutil Y Contundente* in 1989. Javier Vásquez (not to be confused with the veteran Cuban bandleader/pianist/arranger Javier Vázquez) joined Gómez and Varela as a lead singer on the album. Varela and Grupo Niche, featuring Gómez and Jiménez, made their UK debut in October 1989. Jiménez departed; he sessions widely and released the solo *Espectacular* in 1989. Gómez left and Vásquez was joined by co-lead vocalists Charlie Cardona and Ricardo Valdez (who doubled on synthesizer) on 1990's *Cielo De Tambores*, recorded in Varela's own Niche Professional Studios in Cali.y confirmed Varela's status. Trombonist/bassist/arranger/vocalist Andrés Viáfara, who played on *Historia Musical* and was amongst those who defected to Los Niches, came back to co-arrange and co-direct with Varela. Viáfara, who also worked in Alvaro del Castillo's Orquesta La Calentura and with **José Harbey Caicedo**, played alongside Monge in the brass section of three trombones and two trumpets. Varela delegated the writing of two arrangements to New York arranger/producer/keyboardist Sergio George. Tito Gómez returned to Puerto Rico where he recorded the solo *Un Nuevo Horizonte* (1991). The album was a Top 10 hit in the ***Billboard*** tropical/salsa chart and contained the Puerto Rican number 1 hit single 'Dejala', on which Gómez sang a duet with salsa romántica star Tito Rojas. By way of belated recognition of Colombian salsa's growing popularity by the traditionally New York and Puerto Rico-dominated US salsa industry, Niche, along with their compatriot **Joe Arroyo**, were included on the bill of the 14th annual New York Salsa Festival in 1989, 1990 and

1991. Albums: *Querer Es Poder* (1981), *Preparate...Grupo Niche Vol.2* (1982), *Niche* (1983, aka *Directo Desde New York*), *No Hay Quinto Malo* (1984), *Se Pasó!* (1985, aka *Triunfo*), *Me Huele A Matrimonio* (1986), *Grupo Niche Con Cuerdas* (1986), *Historia Musical* (1987), *Tapando El Hueco* (1988), *Sutil Y Contundente* (1989), *Cielo De Tambores* (1990). Various compilations are available.

Nicholas Brothers

Fayard Nicholas (b. c.1918) and Harold Nicholas (b. c.1924), constituted what was, without a doubt, the most talented and spectacular power tap-dancing duo in the history of show business. They grew up in Philadelphia where their parents played in the orchestra at the Standard Theatre, a vaudeville house for blacks. The brothers were soon in vaudeville themselves, billed initially as the Nicholas Kids. By 1932 they had graduated to the renowned Cotton Club in Harlem, where, for the next two years they delighted the all-white audiences and rubbed shoulders with great black entertainers such as **Ethel Waters**, **Duke Ellington**, and **Cab Calloway**. In 1936 the Nicholas Brothers made their Broadway debut with **Bob Hope** and **Fanny Brice** in ***Ziegfeld Follies***, and also appeared in London in **Lew Leslie**'s revue *Blackbirds Of 1936*. A year later they were back on Broadway in the **Richard Rodgers** and **Lorenz Hart** hit musical ***Babes In Arms***. Their film career had begun in 1932 with two short films, *Black Network* and *Pie Pie Blackbird* (featuring **Eubie Blake** And His Band), and it continued via *Calling All Stars* (1936), and the **Don Ameche-Betty Grable** musical ***Down Argentine Way*** (1940), in which the brothers did a breathtaking dance to the lively number 'Down Argentina Way'. The sequence was choreographed by Nick Castle who worked with the duo on most of their subsequent pictures, and gained them a five year contract with 20th Century-Fox. During the rest of the 40s the Nicholas Brothers contributed some electrifying and superbly acrobatic dances to films such as ***Tin Pan Alley***, ***The Great American Broadcast***, ***Sun Valley Serenade***, ***Orchestra Wives***, ***Stormy Weather***, and ***The Pirate*** (1948). In 1946 they both starred in the Broadway musical ***St. Louis Woman*** in which Harold introduced **Harold Arlen** and **Johnny Mercer**'s appealing 'Ridin' On The Moon' and (with Ruby Hill) the all-time standard, 'Come Rain Or Come Shine'. Of course, as blacks, in films they were only allowed to be a speciality act and were never considered for leading roles. This is apparently one of the main reasons why, in the 50s, they worked in Europe for several years where audiences and managements were more racially tolerant. When Fayard decided to return to the USA, Harold stayed in France and carved out a solo career for himself there. After seven years they were reunited in America and played in nightclubs and on television until Fayard contracted arthritis and underwent two hip-replacement operations. Harold continued as a solo performer and was top-cast in the musical *Back In The Big Time* (1986). Fayard was still active in non-performing areas of the business and won a **Tony Award** when he co-choreographed the 1989 Broadway musical *Black And Blue*, with Cholly Atkins, Henry LeTang and Frank Manning. In 1991 the Nicholas Brothers received Kennedy Center Honours for their outstanding work over a period of more than 60 years. A year later, a documentary film *We Sing & We Dance*, celebrated their wonderful careers and included tributes from Mikhail Baryshnikov, Gregory Hines, **M.C. Hammer**, and Clarke Peters. In 1994, members of the cast of *Hot Shoe Shuffle*, London's 'New Tap Musical', also paid tribute to their 'inspiration' - the Nicholas Brothers.

Nicholas, 'Wooden' Joe

b. 23 September 1883, New Orleans, Louisiana, USA, d. 17 November 1957. A well-known figure in his native city, Nicholas started out on clarinet but took up the cornet under the influence of **Buddy Bolden** and **Joe 'King' Oliver**. He worked in marching bands, forming his own, the Camelia Band, in 1918. A powerful player with an earthy, basic style, Nicholas embodied the traditions of the music but never managed to achieve the panache of his idols and mentors. His nephew was the distinguished clarinettist **Albert Nicholas**.

Albums: with others *Echoes From New Orleans (1945)* (1988), *Echoes From New Orleans Vol. 2 (1949-51)* (1988).

Nicholas, Albert

b. 27 May 1900, New Orleans, Louisiana, USA, d. 3 September 1973. After taking lessons from **Lorenzo Tio**, the young Nicholas, a nephew of **'Wooden' Joe Nicholas**, played the clarinet in bands led by several of his home town's leading musicians, who included **Buddy Petit**, **Joe 'King' Oliver** and **Manuel Perez**. Service in the US Navy during World War I interrupted his career, but after the war he returned to working in various New Orleans-based bands, some of which he led. Late in 1924 he joined Oliver in Chicago, leaving again in the autumn of 1926 to work in Shanghai, China. On the way back home he played in Cairo, Egypt, and Paris, France. Back in the USA at the end of 1928 he joined **Luis Russell** for a five-year stint. He then played with **Chick Webb**, **Sam Wooding**, **John Kirby**, **Louis Armstrong**, **Zutty Singleton** and others, mostly in and around New York. In the early 40s he dropped out of music, but returned in mid-decade to work with **Bunk Johnson**, **Kid Ory** and others who were benefiting from the resurgence of interest in traditional jazz. In the early 50s he toured Europe, settling in France for the rest of

his life, making occasional trips to the USA. One of the best of the New Orleans clarinettists, Nicholas played with a rich, full sound, favouring the chalumeau end of the instrument's range and liberally imbuing his solos with a strong feeling for the blues.
Albums: *Albert Nicholas Quartet* (1959), *Tribute To Jelly Roll Morton* (60s), *Memorial* (60s), *Albert Nicholas And The John Defferary Jazztet* (60s). Compilations: with Joe 'King' Oliver *Snag It Vol. 1* (1926-27), *The Luis Russell Story* (1929-30), with Jelly Roll Morton *Last Band Dates* (1940), with Baby Dodds *Jazz A La Creole* (1946).

Nicholas, Paul

b. 3 December 1945, London, England. Actor/singer Nicholas served a musical apprenticeship as pianist with **Screaming Lord Sutch** And The Savages. Then known as Paul Dean, he embarked on a singing career in 1964, but later changed his name to Oscar when this venture proved unsuccessful. Despite access to exclusive songs by **Pete Townshend** ('Join My Gang') and **David Bowie** ('Over The Wall We Go' - a comment on a contemporary rash of prison outbreaks), this second appellation brought no commercial comfort. However, it was during this period that the artist began his long association with manager **Robert Stigwood,** and he developed a career in pop musicals, appearing in some of the best onstage productions of the era. His debut in the love/rock musical ***Hair*** was followed by ***Jesus Christ Superstar***. He has appeared in several films, including Ken Russell's *Lisztomania*, and had a major role in the film *Stardust* (1974), starring **David Essex**. During the 80s and early 90s his stage appearances have included ***Cats***, ***Blondel***, ***Charlie Girl*** (1986 revival), ***Barnum***, *The Pirates Of Penzance*, *Jesus Christ Superstar* (20th anniversary concert tour) and ***Singin' In The Rain*** (1995). Prior to all that Nicholas finally achieved pop single success with several disco-style numbers for Stigwood's RSO label. 'Dancing With The Captain' and 'Grandma's Party' reached the UK Top 10 in 1976, but his musical career increasingly took a subordinate role to thespian ambitions. Nicholas has since become a highly popular actor on television, performing light comedy and dramatic roles with confidence. One of his most fondly remembered performances was in the top-rated television series *Just Good Friends*, in which he co-starred with Jan Francis. In more recent years Nicholas has turned successfully to production, and he co-presented the smash hit West End revival of the musical ***Grease*** which opened in 1993.
Selected albums: *Paul Nicholas* (1977), *Just Good Friends* (1986), *That's Entertainment* (1993), *Colours Of My Life* (First Night 1994).

Nicholls, Horatio

(see **Wright, Lawrence**)

Nicholls, Sue

b. Susan Frances Harmar Nicholls, 23 November 1943, Walsall, West Midlands, England. The daughter of a former Conservative Member of Parliament, she is one of the rare people to star in two top-rated television soap operas. With much stage work under her belt, she joined the cast of UK television's *Crossroads* in 1965 playing waitress Marilyn Gates. She became so popular that a song she performed in the show, 'Where Will You Be', which was written and produced by **Tony Hatch**, climbed into the UK Top 20 in 1968. The success of the record inspired her to quit *Crossroads* and to go on the road as a singer. However, when the follow-up 'All The Way To Heaven' failed she returned to acting. She later appeared in many other television programmes including popular situation comedies *The Rise And Fall Of Reginald Perrin* (as Mr. Perrin's secretary, Miss Jones) and *Up The Elephant And Round The Castle.* She joined the cast of *Coronation Street* in 1979 and has been a regular member of the top-rated soap opera since 1985 playing the role of Audrey Roberts, the wife of the corner grocer.

Nichols, Herbie

b. 3 December 1919, New York City, New York, USA, d. 12 April 1963. In the late 30s and early 40s Nichols played piano with numerous bands in a wide variety of styles. The bands included those of **Herman Autrey**, **Illinois Jacquet**, **Lucky Thompson**, **Edgar Sampson** and **Arnett Cobb**, while the styles ranged across small-group swing, dixieland and R&B. A remarkably original and talented musician, Nichols developed a personal music that owed a debt to bebop, particularly to its more idiosyncratic practitioners such as **Thelonius Monk**, but for much of his life the only gigs he could get were playing Dixieland music, which he came to dislike intensely. In the early 60s, he was able to work occasionally with modern musicians closer to his advanced thinking, among them **Roswell Rudd** and **Archie Shepp**, but by then he was terminally ill with leukaemia (though Rudd also blamed 'a broken heart' brought on by 'years of frustration, neglect and disillusionment'). In recent years Nichols's reputation has grown rapidly and there have been several tribute albums that feature his compositions, notably two on the Soul Note label and one by Holland's Instant Composers Pool Orchestra. Nichols's own recorded legacy, though small, is of outstanding quality: two **Blue Note** trio sessions, reissued as the double album *The Third World*, feature sympathetic support from **Art Blakey** and **Max Roach**. A later trio set for Bethlehem has George Duvivier and **Dannie Richmond**. These records mostly feature his own distinctive and delightful compositions, some of which - '2300 Skiddoo', 'Shuffle Montgomery', 'House Party Starting', 'Hangover Triangle' - look like becoming

established standards in the 90s. 'There is charm and interest all around you', Rudd wrote of Nichols's music, 'from bright ripples on down to heavy undercurrents. What a beautiful sense of space! What incredible lyricism! What soulfullness! What grace! What an expansive palette of sonorities!. Wit, taste, discretion, subtleties, nuances . . . and all so personal and individual.'
Selected albums: *The Herbie Nichols Quartet* (1952), *M+N N* (1952), *The Prophetic Herbie Nichols Vol.s 1 & 2/The Third World* (1955), *The Herbie Nichols Trio* (Blue Note 1955), *The Third World* (1955), *Out Of The Shadows* (Affinity 1957), *The Bethlehem Sessions* (Affinity 1957), *Love, Gloom, Cash, Love* (1957).
Further reading: *Four Lives In The Bebop Business*, A.B. Spellman.

Nichols, Keith

b. 13 February 1945, Ilford, Essex, England. Although he was playing the trombone and leading the band at school Nichols also became All-Britain junior accordion champion. He can now play most of the instruments in the bands he leads but excels on piano and trombone. He played with **Dick Sudhalter**'s Anglo-American Alliance (1969) before leading bands of his own like the New Sedalia in the early 70s. He led the Ragtime Orchestra which played scholarly versions of the repertoire, before going to the USA to record with the New **Paul Whiteman** Orchestra. He wrote arrangements for the **New York Jazz Repertory Company**, for **Dick Hyman** and for the **Pasadena Roof Orchestra**. By 1978 he was well equipped to found the **Midnite Follies Orchestra** with **Alan Cohen**. Their aim was to play the music of the 20s and 30s and original pieces in a similar vein. Nichols is an authority on ragtime and earlier styles of jazz, and he works ceaselessly to keep them being performed. In the mid-80s he played with **Harry Gold** (bass saxophone) and led the Paramount Theatre Orchestra. He now leads his own Cotton Club Band.
Albums: *Ragtime Rules OK?* (1976), *Hotter Than Hades* (1978), *Jungle Nights In Harlem* (1981), *Shakin' The Blues Away* (Stomp Off 1988), *Doctors Jazz* (Stomp Off 1988), *Chitterlin' Strut* (Stomp Off 1989), *Syncopated Jamboree* (Stomp Off 1992), *Keith Nichols* (Stomp Off 1992), *I Like To Do Things For You* (Stomp Off 1993).

Nichols, Red

b. Ernest Loring Nichols, 8 May 1905, Ogden, Utah, USA, d. 28 June 1965. Taught by his father, cornetist Nichols quickly became a highly accomplished performer. Strongly influenced by early white jazz bands, and in particular by **Bix Beiderbecke**, he moved to New York in the early 20s and was soon one of the busiest musicians in town. He recorded hundreds of tracks, using a bewildering array of names for his bands, but favouring the Five Pennies, a group which was usually eight pieces or more in size. In these bands Nichols used the cream of the white jazzmen of the day, including one of his closest friends, **Miff Mole** plus **Jimmy Dorsey**, **Joe Venuti**, **Eddie Lang**, **Pee Wee Russell**, **Benny Goodman** and **Jack Teagarden**. Although his sharp business sense and desire for formality and respect alienated him from hard-living contemporaries such as **Eddie Condon**, Nichols remained enormously successful, continuing to lead bands and record until the outbreak of World War II. After a brief spell outside music Nichols returned to performing with a short stint with **Glen Gray**, and then resumed his bandleading career from his new base in California. A sentimental Hollywood bio-pic, ***The Five Pennies*** (1959), starring **Danny Kaye**, gave his career a boost and during the last few years of his life he was as busy as he had ever been in the 20s. A polished player with a silvery tone and a bold, attacking style which reflected his admiration for Beiderbecke, Nichols at his best came close to matching his idol. As a bandleader he left an important recorded legacy of the best of 20s' white jazz.
Selected albums: *Syncopated Chamber Music* (1953), *Hot Pennies* (1957), with the Charleston Chasers *Thesaurus Of Classic Jazz, Vol. 3* (1961). Selected compilations: *Class Of '39 - Radio Transcriptions* (1979), with Miff Mole *Red And Miff, 1925-31* (Village 1982), *Rhythm Of The Day* (ASV 1983), *Feelin' No Pain (1920s-30s)* (Affinity 1987), *Great Original Performances 1925-30* (1988), *Red Nichols And Other Radio Transcriptions* (Meritt 1988), *Red Nichols And The Five Pennies Vols 1-5* (Swaggie 1989).

Nicholson, J.D.

b. James David Nicholson, 12 April 1917, Monroe, Louisiana, USA, d. 27 July 1991, Los Angeles, California, USA. Nicholson learnt to play the piano from the age of five in church. He later emigrated to the west coast where, influenced by the popular black recording artists of the day, he built up a solo act and travelled and performed all over California. In the mid-40s he teamed up with **Jimmy McCracklin** and they made their first recordings together; Nicholson played, McCracklin sang and both their styles were very much in the mould of **Walter Davis**. Over the next decade, Nicholson accompanied a number of well-known artists, such as **Lowell Fulson** and Ray Agee, and also made some records under his own name. Later in the 50s, he joined **Jimmy Reed**'s band, and also played with **Little Walter**. He made a few more records in the 60s.
Compilation: *Mr. Fullbright's Blues Vol. 2* (1990).

Nick And Nora

This show was based on Dashiell Hammett's witty 30s comedy-drama movie, *The Thin Man*, which starred William Powell and Myrna Loy, and spawned several sequels. Its transfer from Hollywood to Broadway provided yet another insight into the agonizing trials and tribulations endured by the creators - and, some would say, the audiences - concerned with a contemporary musical production. After several postponements, the show actually started its previews at the Marquis Theatre in New York on 8 October 1991. These continued for 71 performances - an unprecedented nine weeks - while the highly experienced team of Arthur Laurents (director and librettist), **Charles Strouse** (music) and **Richard Maltby Jnr.**, strove to get the show ready. After numerous changes to the cast, score and book, *Nick And Nora* finally faced the critics on December 8. The story, still set in the film world of the 30s, has Nora Charles (Joanna Gleason) doing a favour for her old girlfriend, the actress Tracy Gardner (Christine Baranski), by trying to find the murderer of studio book keeper, Lorraine Bixby (Faith Prince). Eventually, she gives way to husband Nick (Barry Bostwick), who comes out of retirement to solve the case himself. Not a show to appeal to feminists. There were high hopes for the score. Richard Maltby Jnr. was co-lyricist on ***Miss Saigon***, and his collaborations with David Shire, such as *Baby* and *Starting Here, Starting Now*, had been duly noted. Charles Strouse had composed the music for several big Broadway hits, but his record revealed six flops in a row since ***Annie*** in 1977. Their songs met with a mixed reception. They included 'Is There Anything Better Than Dancing?', 'Everybody Wants To Do A Musical', 'Swell', 'Not Me', 'As Long As You're Happy', 'Look Whose Alone Now', and 'Let's Go Home', which some unkind critics took literally. The number that attracted the most attention was 'Men', which was sung by Faith Prince, and that too, with its lyric, 'I was nuts . . . dropped my pants like a putz', was regarded as 'astonishingly coarse' by one critic, and 'absolute dynamite' by another. There was an air of doom surrounding the production, anyway, and it folded after only nine performances (not forgetting the 71 previews) with estimated losses in excess of $2.5 million.

Nicks, Stevie

b. Stephanie Nicks, 26 May 1948, Phoenix, Arizona, USA. When Stevie Nicks joined **Fleetwood Mac** in January 1975, she not only introduced her talents as a singer and songwriter, but provided a defined focal point during the group's live appearances. A former vocalist with Fritz, a struggling San Francisco band, Nicks moved to Los Angeles with her boyfriend and fellow ex-member **Lindsey Buckingham**. Together they recorded *Buckingham-Nicks*, a promising but largely neglected album, at the Second City Studio in Van Nuys. The collection was subsequently used to demonstrate the facilities to Mick Fleetwood. By coincidence both Stevie and Lindsey were in a nearby room and were introduced to the Fleetwood Mac drummer when he showed interest in their work. Within weeks the duo were invited to join his group to replace the departing **Bob Welch**. Their arrival brought a change in Fleetwood Mac's commercial fortunes. Stevie provided many of the group's best-known and successful songs, including the atmospheric 'Rhiannon' and the haunting 'Dreams'. The latter was one of several excellent compositions which graced the multi-million-selling *Rumours*, although the album itself signalled the collapse of two in-house relationships, including that of Buckingham and Nicks. In 1980, following the release of Fleetwood Mac's much-maligned *Tusk*, the singer began recording a solo album. *Bella Donna*, released the following year, which achieved platinum sales and remained on the ***Billboard*** album chart for over two years. It also spawned two US Top 10 singles in 'Stop Dragging My Heart Around', a duet with **Tom Petty** and 'Leather And Lace', which featured former **Eagles** drummer, **Don Henley**. A second selection, *The Wild Heart*, followed in 1983 and this best-seller also produced two major hits in 'Stand Back' and 'Nightbird'. Her third album, *Rock A Little*, was less successful, artistically and commercially, and following its release Nicks entered the Betty Ford Clinic to be treated for drug dependency. She then rejoined Fleetwood Mac for the exceptional *Tango In The Night*, which marked the departure of Lindsey Buckingham. Although his absence has created more space within the band's framework, a revitalised Nicks continues her solo activities, as exemplified in 1989's *The Other Side Of The Mirror.*

Albums: with Lindsey Buckingham *Buckingham-Nicks* (1973), *Bella Donna* (1981), *The Wild Heart* (1983), *Rock A Little* (1985), *The Other Side Of The Mirror* (1989), *Street Angel* (EMI 1994). Compilation: *Time Space* (1991).

Nico

b. Christa Paffgen (Pavolsky), 16 October 1938, Cologne, Germany, d. 18 July 1988. Introduced to a European social set which included film director Federico Fellini, Nico began an acting career with a memorable appearance in *La Dolce Vita.* Briefly based in London, she became acquainted with **Rolling Stones**' guitarist Brian Jones, and made her recording debut with the folk-tinged 'I'm Not Saying'. Nico then moved to New York, where she was introduced to Andy Warhol. She starred in the director's controversial cinema-verité epic, *Chelsea Girls*, before joining his newfound proteges, the **Velvet Underground**. Nico made telling contributions to this seminal group's debut album, but her desire to sing lead on all of the songs brought a swift rebuttal. She resumed a solo career in 1967 with *Chelsea Girl* which included three compositions by a young **Jackson Browne**, who accompanied Nico on live performances, and 'I'll Keep It With Mine', which **Bob Dylan** reportedly wrote with her in mind. **Lou Reed** and **John Cale**, former colleagues in the Velvet Underground, also provided memorable contributions, while the latter retained his association with the singer by producing her subsequent three albums. Here Nico's baleful, gothic intonation was given free rein, and the haunting, often sparse use of harmonium accentuated her impressionistic songs. In 1974 she appeared in a brief tour of the UK in the company of **Kevin Ayers**, John Cale and **Brian Eno**, collectively known as ACNE. A live album of the concert at the Rainbow Theatre in London was subsequently released. That same year, following the release of *The End*, the singer ceased recording, but re-emerged in the immediate post-punk era. Her Teutonic emphasis inspired several figures, including Siouxsie Sioux of **Siouxsie And The Banshees**, but Nico's own 80s' releases were plagued by inconsistency. Signs of an artistic revival followed treatment for drug addiction, but this unique artist died in Ibiza on 18 July 1988, after suffering a cerebral haemorrhage while cycling in intense heat.

Albums: *Chelsea Girl* (1967), *The Marble Index* (1968), *Desertshore* (1971), with ACNE *June 1, 1974* (1974), *The End* (1974), *Drama Of Exile* (1981), *Do Or Die* (1983), *Camera Obscura* (1985), *The Blue Angel* (1986), *Behind The Iron Curtain* (1986), *Live In Tokyo* (1987), *Live In Denmark* (1987), *En Personne En Europe* (1988), *Live Heroes* (1989), *Hanging Gardens* (1990).

Video: *Nico - Heroine* (1994).

Further reading: *The Life And Lies Of An Icon*, Richard Witts. *Songs They Never Play On The Radio: Nico, The Last Bohemian*, James Young.

Nico, Dr.

b. 1939, Luluaborg, Zaire, d. 1985, Kinshasa, Zaire. A member of **Joseph Kalle**'s African Jazz in the early 60s, guitarist and composer Nico went on to be a founder member, with **Rochereau**, of African Fiesta, one of the most popular and influential Zairean bands of the mid and late 60s. He retired from the music scene in the early 70s, but returned as a solo artist in 1983.

Albums: *Eternal Dr Nico 1963 - 1965* (1985), *Kassanda Wa Mikalaya* (1984), *Dieu De La Guitare* (1985).

Nicol, Simon

b. 13 October 1950, Muswell Hill, London, England. Vocalist/guitarist Nicol was the sole surviving member of the original **Fairport Convention** line-up. He has toured and recorded with **Dave Swarbrick**, and been involved in session work on a number of albums. He has also recorded and toured with, among others, **Al Stewart**, **John Martyn**, **Julie Covington** and the **Albion Country Band**. Many felt that Simon was overshadowed as a guitarist by former Fairport Convention member **Richard Thompson**. It was not until 1986 that Nicol's long-overdue solo *Before Your Time* was released, although the well-received record did not achieve the commercial success that it deserved. In 1990 Simon provided the music for a video *Singing Games For Children* and, the same year, was recruited for the recording of the debut album by **Beverley Craven**. Despite these other commitments, his recording and touring work with Fairport Convention continues. Although his solo career looks sparse Nicol remains one of the most experienced performers in the UK, playing sessions and touring with countless artists. His heart and soul will always belong to the Fairports, a band that by longevity he has now made his own. His vocal performance on their 1995 *Jewell In The Crown* is exemplary.

Albums: with Dave Swarbrick *Live At The White Bear* (1982), with Swarbrick *In The Club* (1983), with Swarbrick *Close To The Wind* (1984), *Before Your Time* (1987), *Consonant Please Carol* (1992).

Nicolette

b. Nicolette Okoh, c.1964, Glasgow, Scotland. **Shut Up And Dance**'s first female signing, whose approach to her vocal craft was more blues-based and less shrill than many garage divas. She also wrote her own songs, demonstrating a keen talent on singles like 'Wicked Mathematics'. However, she was quick to affirm that 'I really do see myself as a dance act', despite her debut album featuring more political material like 'No Government'. She was born in Glasgow but brought up in Nigeria, Paris, Geneva and Cardiff.

Nicols, Maggie

b. 24 February 1948, Edinburgh, Scotland. Nicols is a renowned vocalist in UK jazz and has worked at the roots of experimental jazz since the mid-60s. She started her career in song and dance as a child by enrolling at the Italia Conti Stage School in London's Soho. By the age of 15 she was dancing and singing at the Windmill Theatre and at 16 was singing in cabaret in a Manchester, subsequently appearing at the Moulin Rouge in Paris after undergoing a dancing tour of Europe. By the mid-60s Maggie had turned her attention to jazz and had become a member of the **Spontaneous Music Ensemble;** she was also involved in inaugurating a free-jazz workshop in south London which included therapy work with mental patients, using jazz vocal expression as an emotional outlet. She was responsible for the instigation of several groups including the quartet, **Voice**, which featured **Julie Tippetts** and Phil Minton and which utilized Nicols' own experimental 'scat' language. Her involvement with the Feminist Improvising Group (and its European counterpart, the EWIG) found her working with the *avant garde* bassist **Joëlle Léandre** and the former **Henry Cow** multi-instrumentalist **Lindsay Cooper,** as well as the free-jazz pianist **Irène Schweizer**. In 1982 she collaborated with

Léandre and Cooper to record the completely improvised *Live At The Bastille*. That same year, Nicols collaborated with Tippetts again on *Sweet And S'ours*. On this set there featured an example of the duo's idiosyncratic technique, with the use of vacuum-cleaner tubes (on 'Whailing'). 1985's joint effort with Peter Nu was released on **Leo Records** and was funded by the London Arts Council. Nicols has since continued to work in fringe theatre and various groups on the UK jazz scene.
Selected albums: with Voice *Voice* (1977), with Julie Tippetts *Sweet And S'ours* (1982), with Joëlle Léandre, Lindsay Cooper *Live At The Bastille* (1984, rec. 1982), with Peter Nu *Nicols 'N' Nu* (1985), with Irène Schweizer, Paul Lovens, Léandre, Cooper *Live At Taklos* (1986), with Keith Tippett, Julie Tippetts *Mr. Invisible And The Drunken Sheilas* (1989, rec. 1987).

Niehaus, Lennie

b. 11 June 1929, St. Louis, Missouri, USA. After completing his studies at university in California, to where his family had moved when he was seven years old, alto saxophonist Niehaus joined Jerry Wald and then **Stan Kenton** in 1951. Apart from a spell away in the army, he remained with the Kenton band until 1960. During this period Niehaus also recorded under his own name and played and recorded with other small groups, including that led by **Shorty Rogers**. From the 60s onwards Niehaus was active in film and television studios, writing scores for a number of films including two, *City Heat* (1984) and *Pale Rider* (1985), which starred Clint Eastwood. When Eastwood came to make his film about **Charlie Parker**, ***Bird*** (1988), he invited Niehaus to handle the complex musical problems, which included writing the score and 'engineering' Parker's solos so that they could be re-recorded with new accompaniments. The skill and integrity with which Niehaus accomplished this difficult task represent one of the highlights of the film. A brilliant technician, playing with a hard-edged sound, Niehaus sometimes fails to engage the emotions of his listeners, but for the most part overcomes this failing through his extraordinary rush of exciting ideas.
Albums: *Lennie Niehaus Vol. 1: The Quintet* (1954-56), *Lennie Niehaus Vol. 2: The Octet/Zounds!* (1954-56), *Lennie Niehaus Vol. 3* (1955), *The Lennie Niehaus Quintet With Strings* (1955), *The Lennie Niehaus Sextet* (1956), *Lennie Niehaus* (1957). Compilation: *Patterns* (Fresh Sounds 1990).

Nielsen-Chapman, Beth

Nielsen-Chapman sang harmony on **Tanya Tucker**'s 1988 US number 1 country single, 'Strong Enough To Bend', which she wrote with Don Schlitz. She also sang harmony and wrote **Willie Nelson**'s 1989 US country number 1, 'Nothing I Can Do It About It Now'. Her debut album for Warners failed to secure her role as a singer, however.
Albums: *Beth Nielsen-Chapman* (1990), *You Hold The Key* (1993).

Nieves, Tito

b. Humberto Nieves, 4 June c.1958, Rio Piedras, Puerto Rico. One of salsa's hit-makers in the late 80s and early 90s, Nieves's family migrated to Brooklyn, New York when he was two years old. The fact that his father played guitar with various trios and that his uncle was a renowned composer, singer and guitarist, created a family climate conducive to music, within which the young Tito studied bass, guitar and drums. Nieves began his professional career in 1975 as a vocalist with Orquesta Cimarrón, which was co-led by the band's lead singer Rafael de Jesús. This was followed by a stint with **Héctor Lavoe**. Tito made his recording debut as a lead vocalist in 1978 when the prominent Puerto Rican composer Johnny Ortiz hired him for *Johnny Ortiz y Taibori*. In 1979 he was invited by composer/producer Ramón Rodríguez to perform lead vocals on the first album by Julio Castro and his Orquesta La Masacre. The same year he became a founder member of **Clásico, Conjunto** with Rodríguez and executive producer/chorus singer/percussionist Raymond Castro, and appeared on eight of the band's albums before departing in the mid-80s. Nieves signed with Ralph Mercado's RMM Records and made his solo debut on *The Classic* in 1988. The album went gold and contained the hit 'Sonanbulo'. The single 'I'll Always Love You', from his 1989 follow-up *Yo Quiero Cantar*, achieved the distinction of being the first English language salsa tune to reach number 1 in the Puerto Rican hit parade and, with help from WBLS disc jockey Frankie Crocker, was a crossover success on some New York R&B radio stations. Crocker introduced Nieves at the 1990 New York Salsa Festival in Madison Square Garden. with The album won him another gold disc. In February 1990, Tito's stepson died while being arrested. Nieves and Alexandra (a female vocalist with the meringue group the New York Band) duetted on the New York chart-topping English lyrics single 'How Do You Keep The Music Playing', which was included on his 1991 release *Déjame Vivir* and the compilation *Put Your Heart On Salsa In English*.
Albums: with Johnny Ortiz *Johnny Ortiz y Taibori* (1978), with Julio Castro *New Generation Presenta Julio Castro & Orquesta La Masacre* (1979), with Conjunto Clásico *Los Rodríguez* (1979), *Felicitaciones* (1980), *Si No Bailan Con Ellos, No Bailan Con Nadie* (1981), *Clásicas de Clásico* (1982), *Las Puertas Abiertas* (1983), *El Panadero* (1985), *Llego La Ley* (1985), *Asi Es Mi Pueblo* (1986), *The Classic* (1988), *Yo Quiero Cantar* (1989), *Déjame Vivir* (1991), *Rompecabeza (The Puzzle)* (1994). Compilation: *Ray Castro Presenta...Lo Mejor de Conjunto Clásico con Tito Nieves* (1990).

Night And Day

Benny Green, the British author and critic, has often commented that if only the screenwriters of these lavish Hollywood film biographies had told the subject's real life story instead of writing the usual insipid puff, some fascinating pictures would have resulted. This theory could have been especially true in the case of *Night And Day* which was released by Warner Brothers in 1946. It was supposed to be a celebration of the smart and sophisticated songwriter **Cole Porter**, but hardly any of the important incidents in his life - apart from his tragic accident - were touched upon. The inclusion of a good many of his magnificent songs more than made up for the omissions, though, and these included 'I've Got You Under My Skin', 'Night And Day', 'Miss Otis Regrets', 'In The Still Of The Night', 'Begin The Beguine', 'What Is This Thing Called Love?', 'Just One Of Those Things', 'I Get A Kick Out Of You', 'Easy To Love', 'You Do Something To Me', 'Let's Do It', 'Old Fashioned Garden', 'Love For Sale', 'You've Got That Thing', and 'Anything Goes'. **Mary Martin** reprised 'My Heart Belongs To Daddy' which she originally introduced to rapturous acclaim in ***Leave It To Me!*** back in 1938, and several of the other numbers were sung by Ginny Simms and Jane Wyman. Cary Grant played Porter, and it was interesting, if unsatisfying, to hear his version of 'You're The Top', one of the composer's all-time great 'list' songs. Alexis Smith was Mrs. Porter, and also cast were Monty Woolley (as himself), Eve Arden, Alan Hale, Victor Francen, Dorothy Malone, Selena Royle, Donald Woods, Henry Stephenson, Sig Rumann, and Carlos Ramirez. Charles Hoffman, Leo Townsend and William Bowers were responsible for the screenplay, and the dances were staged by Leroy Prinz. **Arthur Schwartz**, a legendary songwriter himself, was the producer and Michael Curtiz provided the lack-lustre direction. It was photographed in Technicolor by J. Peverell Marley and William Skall. In spite of their obvious drawbacks, these kind of films were always crowd-pullers, and *Night And Day* proved to be no exception, grossing $4 million in North America alone.

Night Ranger

This talented and sophisticated American pomp-rock group released a string of first class albums between 1982 and 1988. Featuring Jack Blades (vocals/bass), Brad Gillis (guitar; ex-**Ozzy Osbourne**), Alan Fitzgerald (keyboards; ex-**Montrose**), Kelly Keagy (drums) and Jeff Watson (guitar), they gigged in and around their Californian hometown, San Francisco, as an extension of Gillis' club band, Ranger. They soon attracted the attention of promoter **Bill Graham**, who secured them support slots to **Santana**, **Judas Priest** and the **Doobie Brothers**. They also signed with Neil Bogart's short-lived Boardwalk label, though this decision would have a major impact on their later career when Boardwalk was swallowed up by **MCA** who had little sympathy for the band's rock roots. However, Night Ranger's first four albums made the ***Billboard*** Top 40 charts, with *Seven Wishes* reaching the Top 10 in June 1985. They also scored two Top 10 single hits in the USA with 'Sister Christian' and 'Sentimental Street' peaking at number 5 and 8, respectively. *Man In Motion* saw the departure of Fitzgerald as the band adopted a rockier direction. Produced by **Keith Olsen**, the album was their first commercial failure. The band split up shortly afterwards, with *Live In Japan*, featuring one of their 1988 concerts, emerging two years later. Jack Blades joined **Damn Yankees** with **Ted Nugent**, **Tommy Shaw** and Michael Cartellone. The name was resurrected in 1992 by Gillis and drummer/vocalist Kelly Keagy with new members, much to the disgust of Blades and Watson. It seems unlikely that this new formation can add much to the existing Nightranger legacy of solid US AOR.

Albums: *Dawn Patrol* (Boardwalk 1982), *Midnight Madness* (MCA 1983), *Seven Wishes* (MCA 1985), *Big Life* (MCA 1987), *Man In Motion* (MCA 1988), *Live In Japan* (MCA 1990). Compilation: *Greatest Hits* (MCA 1989).

Nighthawk, Robert

b. Robert McCollum, 30 November 1909, Helena, Arkansas, USA, d. 5 November 1967. Having left home in his early teens, McCollum initially supported himself financially by playing harmonica, but by the 30s had switched to guitar under the tutelage of Houston Stackhouse. The two musicians, together with Robert's brother Percy, formed a string band which was a popular attraction at local parties and gatherings. Robert left the South during the middle of the decade, allegedly after a shooting incident, and settled in St. Louis. He took the name Robert McCoy, after his mother's maiden name, and made contact with several Mississippi-born bluesmen, including **Big Joe Williams** and **John Lee 'Sonny Boy' Williamson**. McCoy accompanied both on sessions for the Bluebird label, who then recorded the skilled guitarist in his own right. His releases included 'Tough Luck' and the evocative 'Prowlin' Nighthawk', which in turn engendered the artist's best-known professional surname. Nighthawk then discovered the electric guitar which, when combined with his already dexterous slide technique, created a sound that allegedly influenced **Earl Hooker**, **Elmore James** and **Muddy Waters**. The last musician was instrumental in introducing Nighthawk to the Aristocrat (later **Chess**) label. It was here the artist completed his most accomplished work, in particular two 1949 masters, 'Sweet Black Angel' and 'Anna Lee Blues'. Both songs were procured from **Tampa Red**, whose dazzling, clear tone bore an affinity to jazz and was an inspiration on Nighthawk's

approach. However, his disciple was unable or unwilling to consolidate the success these recordings secured, and although he continued to record in Chicago, Robert often returned to Helena where he performed with his son, Sam Carr. The guitarist's last substantial session was in 1964 when he completed two tracks, 'Sorry My Angel' and 'Someday', with a backing band that included **Buddy Guy** and **Walter 'Shakey' Horton**. Robert Nighthawk died in his hometown on 5 November 1967, leaving behind a small but pivotal body of work.
Albums: *Bricks In My Pillow* (1977), with Elmore James *Blues In D Natural* (1979), *Complete Recordings, Vol. 1 1937* (1985), *Complete Recordings, Vol. 2 1938-40* (1985), *Live On Maxwell Street* (1988), *Black Angel Blues* (1988).

Nightingale, Maxine

b. 2 November 1952, Wembley, London, England. Although Maxine made her recording debut in 1968, early acclaim was garnered from a series of roles in the stage productions of ***Hair***, ***Jesus Christ Superstar*** and ***Godspell***. She resumed a solo career during the 70s, scoring an international hit with the compulsive 'Right Back Where We Started From'. This infectious performance, featured heavily in Paul Newman's cult movie *Slapshot*, reached number 8 in the UK and number 2 in the US, but although 'Love Hit Me' also reached the UK Top 20, the singer was unable to sustain consistent success. 'Lead Me On', a flop at home, climbed to number 5 in the USA in 1979, but proved to be her last substantial release.
Albums: *Right Back Where We Started From* (1976), *Love Hit Me* (1977), *Night Life* (1977), *Love Lines* (1978), *Lead Me On* (1979), *Bittersweet* (1981), *It's A Beautiful Thing* (1982).

Nightingales

After a series of low-key UK school bands, **Robert Lloyd** (b. 1959, Cannock, Staffordshire, England) formed the Prefects - one of the earliest punk bands - who toured with the **Clash**. They split up in 1979 and Lloyd assembled the Nightingales using the best of the musicians who had passed through the ranks of the Prefects. The first of many subsequent Nightingales line-ups were Alan and Paul Apperley, Joe Crow, Eamonn Duffy and Lloyd himself. They were ably championed by BBC disc jockey **John Peel**, for whom Lloyd has recorded more sessions under various guises than any other artist. Peel himself said of them: '(their performances) will serve to confirm their excellence when we are far enough distanced from the 1980s to look at the period rationally, and other, infinitely better known bands stand revealed as charlatans'. The Nightingales' debut single, 'Idiot Strength', was released in 1981 on the band's own Vindaloo label in association with **Rough Trade Records**. Joe Crow then departed and his replacements, Nick Beales and Andy Lloyd, two of 15 personnel who would pass through the ranks, brought a totally different sound to the band. The Cherry Red label picked them up and the band's career began in earnest. Lloyd soon established himself as one of the more interesting lyricists of the independent chart. Most of his tirades were draped in humour: 'I'm too tired to do anything today, but tomorrow I'll start my diet, and answer some of my fan mail ('Elvis: The Last Ten Days'). Alternatively: 'I worked in a bakery ... the jokes were handed down like diseases, I only worked there for the bread.' The lack of success of subsequent releases led Lloyd and friends to the new Red Flame label started by Dave Kitson, the promoter of the Moonlight Club in London's Hampstead. Still unhappy with the way record companies were handling his band's career, Lloyd decided to reactivate the Vindaloo label. Ironically, this led to the demise of the Nightingales as Lloyd needed to spend more time as songwriter, producer and label boss for his relatively successful roster of artists such as **We've Got A Fuzzbox And We're Gonna Use It** and comedien Ted Chippington. When Fuzzbox toured America, taking the Nightingales' keyboard player with them, Lloyd dissolved the group and concentrated on a solo career. The Nightingales' legacy was wrapped up in 1991 with a compilation album for Mau Mau Records with sleevenotes written by a still devoted John Peel.
Albums: *Pigs On Purpose* (Cherry Red 1982), *Hysterics* (Red Flame 1983), *Just The Job* (Vindaloo 1983), *In The Good Old Country Ways* (Vindaloo 1986). Compilation: *What A Scream* (Mau Mau 1991).

Nightmares On Wax

Nightmares On Wax are a UK duo of George E.A.S.E. Evelyn and Kevin 'Boy Wonder' Harper. After the bombast of the *Dextrous* EP and 'Aftermath' the club hits continued with 'A Case Of Funk'. Sampling funk rhythms and soca drumming to work up a strong groove has long been a distinctive and endearing trait, as revealed on subsequent issues like 'Set Me Free' and 'Happiness'. 'Set Me Free' saw the band using the vocals of Desoto, who had formerly appeared on UK television's *Junior Showtime* with a spring-heeled Bonny Langford.
Album: *A Word Of Science* (Warp 1991).

Nightwing

After the demise of UK band **Strife** in 1978, bassist/vocalist Gordon Rowley formed Nightwing, with Alec Johnson (guitar), Eric Percival (guitar), Kenny Newton (keyboards) and Steve Bartley (drums). They debuted in 1980 with *Something In The Air*, a grandiose AOR album in the style of **Styx**, **Kansas** or **Journey**. Percival quit shortly after it's release and the band continued as a four-piece to record *Black Summer*. This moved towards a more metallic style, in keeping

with the **New Wave Of British Heavy Metal** which was in full swing at the time. The band expanded once more to a five-piece with the arrival of vocalist Max Bacon for the rawer *Stand Up And Be Counted*. Bacon's stay was short-lived as he moved on to **Bronz**, with Johnson also breaking ranks soon afterwards. Dave Evans and Glynn Porrino were swiftly recruited to fill in on vocals and guitar, but their compositional abilities failed to match those of Johnson. Consequently *My Kingdom Come* represented the nadir of the band's creative capabilities. Nightwing were in their death throes and finally resigned hope after the disappointing *Night Of Mystery, Alive!, Alive!*
Albums: *Something In The Air* (Ovation 1980), *Black Summer* (Gull 1982), *Stand Up And Be Counted* (Gull 1983), *My Kingdom Come* (Gull 1984), *Night Of Mystery, Alive!, Alive!* (Gull 1985).

Nilsson

b. Harry Edward Nelson, 15 June 1941, Brooklyn, New York, USA, d. 15 January 1994, Los Angeles, California, USA. Nelson moved to Los Angeles as an adolescent and later undertook a range of different jobs before accepting a supervisor's position at the Security First National Bank. He nonetheless pursued a concurrent interest in music, recording demos of his early compositions which were then touted around the city's publishing houses. Producer **Phil Spector** drew on this cache of material, recording 'Paradise' and 'Here I Sit' with the **Ronettes** and 'This Could Be The Night' with the **Modern Folk Quartet**. None of these songs was released contemporaneously, but such interest inspired the artist's own releases for the Tower label. These singles - credited to 'Nilsson' - included 'You Can't Take Your Love Away From Me' and 'Good Times' (both 1966). The following year the **Yardbirds** recorded his 'Ten Little Indians', and Nilsson finally gave up his bank job upon hearing the **Monkees**' version of another composition, 'Cuddly Toy', on the radio. He secured a contract with **RCA Records** and made his album debut with the impressive *Pandemonium Shadow Show*. The selection was not only notable for Nilsson's remarkable three-octave voice, it also featured 'You Can't Do That', an enthralling montage of **Beatles**' songs which drew considerable praise from **John Lennon** and inspired their subsequent friendship. The artist's own compositions continued to find favour with other acts; the **Turtles** recorded 'The Story Of Rock 'N' Roll', **Herb Alpert** and **Blood, Sweat And Tears** covered 'Without Her', while **Three Dog Night** enjoyed a US chart-topper and gold disc with 'One'. Nilsson's own version of the last-named song appeared on *Ariel Ballet* - a title derived from his grandparents' circus act - which also included the singer's rendition of **Fred Neil**'s 'Everybody's Talking'. This haunting recording was later adopted as the theme to the film *Midnight Cowboy* and gave Nilsson his first US Top 10 hit. *Harry* included 'The Puppy Song', later a smash for **David Cassidy**, while *Nilsson Sings Newman* comprised solely **Randy Newman** material and featured the songwriter on piano. This project was followed by *The Point*, the soundtrack to a full-length animated television feature, but Nilsson's greatest success came with *Nilsson Schmilsson* and its attendant single, 'Without You'. His emotional rendition of this **Badfinger**-composed song sold in excess of 1 million copies, topping both the US and UK charts and garnering a 1972 Grammy for Best Male Pop and Rock Vocal Performance. Having completed the similarly-styled *Son Of Schmilsson*, this idiosyncratic performer confounded expectations with *A Little Touch Of Schmilsson In The Night*, which comprised beautifully orchestrated standards including 'Makin' Whoopee' and 'As Time Goes By'. Nilsson's subsequent career was blighted by well-publicized drinking with acquaintances John Lennon, **Keith Moon** and **Ringo Starr**. Lennon produced Nilsson's *Pussy Cats* (1974), an anarchic set fuelled by self-indulgence, which comprised largely pop classics, including 'Subterranean Homesick Blues', 'Save The Last Dance For Me' and 'Rock Around The Clock'. Starr meanwhile assisted the artist on his film soundtrack, *Son Of Dracula*. Ensuing releases proved inconsistent, although a 1976 adaptation of *The Point*, staged at London's Mermaid Theatre, was highly successful, and marked the reunion of former Monkees Davy Jones and Mickey Dolenz. By the 80s Nilsson had largely retired from music altogether, preferring to pursue business interests, the most notable of which was a film distribution company based in California's Studio City. However, in 1988 RCA released *A Touch More Schmilsson In The Night* which, in common with its 1973 predecessor, offered the singer's affectionate renditions of popular favourites, including two of **E.Y. 'Yip' Harburg**'s classics, 'It's Only a Paper Moon' and 'Over The Rainbow'. The unyielding paradox of Nilsson's career is that despite achieving recognition as a superior songwriter, his best-known and most successful records were penned by other acts.
Albums: *Pandemonium Shadow Show* (1967), *Ariel Ballet* (1968), *Harry* (1969), *Skidoo* (1969, film soundtrack), *Nilsson Sings Newman* (1970), *The Point* (1971), *Nilsson Schmilsson* (1971), *Son Of Schmilsson* (1972), *A Little Touch Of Schmilsson In The Night* (1973), *Son Of Dracula* (1974), *Duit On Mon Dei* (1975), *The Sandman* (1975), *That's The Way It Is* (1976), *Knillssonn* (1977), *Night After Night* (1979), *Flash Harry* (1980), *A Touch More Schmilsson In The Night* (1988). Compilations: *Early Years* (c.1970), *Ariel Pandemonium Ballet* (1973), *Early Tymes* (1977), *Nilsson's Greatest Music* (1978), *Harry And...* (1979), *Diamond Series: Nilsson* (1988).

Nina And Frederick

This Danish singing duo was popular in the late 50s

and early 60s. Nina Möller had married the wealthy Danish aristocrat Baron Frederik Jan Gustav Floris van Pallandt (b. 14 May 1934, Copenhagen, Denmark, d. 15 May 1994, Puerto Talera, Philippines) in 1954, and teamed up with her husband to record a string of duo hits, including 'Mary's Boy Child' (1959), 'Little Donkey' (1960) and 'Sucu Sucu' (1961). After having three children, they separated in 1969 largely because he wanted to retire and she did not (the marriage was dissolved in 1976). The Baron, a descendent of a Dutch ambassador to Denmark, became a virtual recluse on a farm in Ibiza (briefly purchasing the publishing rights to Burke's Peerage), then Mindoro in the Phillipines. Nina, meanwhile, ventured into cabaret and acting, making her film debut in Robert Altman's *The Long Goodbye* in 1973, co-starring with Elliot Gould. She was later implicated in a minor scandal in the early 70s when she went on holiday with Clifford Irving, the fraudulent biographer of Howard Hughes, who was later jailed. In 1980 she appeared briefly in *American Gigolo*, later adding a second Altman movie, *Long Goodbye*, to her resume. Although they were divorced in 1976, Nina flew out to the Philippines to bring Frederick's body back to Europe after he became the victim of a 'mysterious professional killing', along with his girlfriend Susannah, in 1994.
Selected albums: *Nina And Frederick* i (1960), *Nina And Frederick* ii (1961), *An Evening With Nina And Frederick At The Royal Albert Hall* (1966), *Dawn* (1967). Solo compilation: Nina *Golden Hour Presents Nina* (1978).

Nine

This musical adaptation of Federico Fellini's 1963 movie *Eight And A Half*, had a book by Arthur Kopit, and music and lyrics by the Broadway newcomer Maurey Yeston. It opened on 9 May 1982 at the 46th Street Theatre in New York. The story follows film director Guido Contini (Raul Julia) to Europe in his quest to recharge his physical and emotional batteries, and revitalize his personal life and career. This applies particularly to his continually changing relationships with the women in his life, such as his wife (Karen Akers), his first love, Saraghina (Kathi Moss), his mother (Taina Elg), his close friend and professional colleague, Liliane LaFleur (Liliane Montevecchi), his latest discovery, (Shelley Burch), and his current mistress, Carla (Anita Morris). Yeston's innovative and tuneful score was greeted with enthusiasm, and contained songs such as 'Be Italian', 'My Husband Makes Movies', 'Only With You', 'Be On Your Own', 'Folies Bergéres', 'A Call From The Vatican', 'Nine', 'Unusual Way', 'Simple', 'Getting Tall', and 'The Grand Canal'. **Tommy Tune** and Thommie Walsh were responsible for the choreography and reprised their collaboration a year later for ***My One And Only***. Tune also directed the piece, and his extraordinary staging of a production which only included one adult male, four boys, and 21 women, was generally acclaimed. He won a **Tony Award** for his work, and *Nine* gained further Tonys for best musical, score, and featured actress (Liliane Montevecchi). The show surprised many critics, and ran for 732 performances. Productions were mounted in other countries, including Australia, where it starred John Diedrich. A concert version was presented at London's Festival Hall in 1992, with Liliane Montevecchi and Jonathan Price, the versatile actor who came to prominence as the Engineer in ***Miss Saigon***. The resulting two-CD set featured Ann Crumb, **Elaine Paige**, and a chorus of over 100, and is regarded as the most complete recorded version of Yeston's score.

Nine Below Zero

A British rhythm & blues band of the late 70s, the group took its name from a song by **Sonny Boy Williamson II** and was led by guitarist/singer Dennis Greaves and virtuoso harmonica player Mark Feltham. With Peter Clark (bass/vocals) and Kenny Bradley (drums), Feltham recorded the EP *Packed Fair And Square* (1979). This led to a recording deal with **A&M** and a live recording at London's Marquee Club where Nine Below Zero had a residency. The producer was **Glyn Johns**. With Stix Burkey replacing Bradley, the second album included some original songs while *Third Degree* was a minor UK hit. The band dissolved in the mid-80s as Feltham concentrated on session work and Greaves went on to a solo career and became a member of the **Truth**. However, Feltham revived Nine Below Zero at the end of the decade, signing a new recording contract with the China label.
Albums: *Live At The Marquee* (1980), *Don't Point Your Finger* (1981), *Third Degree* (1982), *Live At The Venue* (1990), *Off The Hook* (1992).

Nine Inch Nails

Trent Reznor, the multi-instrumentalist, vocalist, and creative force behind Nine Inch Nails, trained as a classical pianist during his small-town Pennsylvania childhood, but his discovery of rock and early industrial groups, despite his dislike of the 'industrial' tag, changed his musical direction completely. Following a period working in a Cleveland recording studio and playing in local bands, Reznor began recording as Nine Inch Nails in 1988. The dark, atmospheric *Pretty Hate Machine*, written, played and co-produced by Reznor, was largely synthesizer-based, but the material was transformed on stage by a ferocious wall of guitars, and show-stealing Lollapalooza performances in 1991. Coupled with a major US hit with 'Head Like A Hole', it brought platinum status. Inspired by the live band, Reznor added an abrasive guitar barrage to the Nine Inch Nails sound for *Broken* (a subsequent remix set was titled *Fixed*), which hit the US Top 10, winning a Grammy for 'Wish'. 'Happiness In Slavery', however,

courted controversy with an almost-universally banned video, where performance artist Bob Flanagan gave himself up to be torn apart as slave to a machine, acting out the theme of control common to Reznor's lyrics. Reznor also filmed an unreleased full-length *Broken* video which he felt 'makes 'Happiness In Slavery' look like a Disney movie'. By this time, Reznor had relocated to Los Angeles, building a studio in a rented house at 10050 Cielo Drive, which he later discovered was the scene of the Tate murders by the Manson Family (much to his disgust due to eternal interview questions thereafter about the contribution of the house's atmosphere to *The Downward Spiral*). Occupying the middle ground between the styles of previous releases, *The Downward Spiral*'s multilayered blend of synthesizer textures and guitar fury provides a fascinating soundscape for Reznor's exploration of human degradation through sex, drugs, violence, depression and suicide, closing with personal emotional pain on 'Hurt': 'I hurt myself today, To see if I still feel, I focus on the pain, The only thing that's real'. *The Downward Spiral* made its US debut at number 2, and a return to live work with Robin Finck (guitar), Danny Lohneer (bass/guitar), James Woolley (keyboards) and Reznor's long-time friend and drummer Chris Vrenna drew floods of praise, with Nine Inch Nails being one of the most talked-about acts at the **Woodstock** anniversary show. 1994 saw the first non-Nine Inch Nails releases on Reznor's Nothing label, and the band also found time to construct an acclaimed soundtrack for Oliver Stone's film, *Natural Born Killers*. In the following year Reznor announced plans to record an album with circus 'freak show' specialist, Jim Rose, stating with typical bombast: 'the record will confront just about ever issue that upsets people. It will be non-PC in every way imaginable'.
Albums: *Pretty Hate Machine* (TVT 1989), *Broken* (Nothing 1992, mini-album), *Fixed* (Nothing 1992, mini-album), *The Downward Spiral* (Nothing 1994), *Further Down The Spiral* (Island 1995).

999

This London-based, UK punk band was formed in May 1977. Dispensing with earlier names such as the Dials, 48 Hours and the Fanatics, Nick Cash (b. Keith Lucas, 6 May 1950, Gosport, Hampshire, England; guitar/vocals) was a former **Kilburn And The High Roads** guitarist and studied at Canterbury College Of Art under **Ian Dury**. Cash teamed up with Guy Days (guitar), Jon Watson (bass) and Pablo LaBrittain (drums) who set out to establish themselves on the thriving live scene in the capital. After releasing the fiery 'I'm Alive' on their own LaBrittain Records, United Artists signed them and quickly re-issued it. Two further singles, 'Nasty Nasty' and 'Emergency' were equally memorable for their energetic melodies, though 1978's debut album featured several weaker tracks. *Separates* was stronger, with compelling numbers like the single 'Homicide' resorting to muscular choruses instead of simple speed. However, LaBrittain was the subject of a motoring accident on the band's return from Scandinavia, and was replaced by friend Ed Case. With high sales of all their product in the USA, the band undertook a series of lucrative tours across the Atlantic, which earned them a degree of resentment from domestic supporters. Following the return of LaBrittain to the fold, the group signed a new contract with Radarscope Records, eventually transferring to **Polydor**. *The Biggest Prize In Sport* and *Concrete* represented their most accomplished work, although two follow-up cover version singles were evidence that inspiration was in short supply. This observation is certainly true of 1983's *13th Floor Madness*, though their last studio album *Face To Face* was more convincing. By the end of 1985 Watson had left and was replaced by Danny Palmer, with the band once more concentrating on touring in Europe and America. More recently, in the 90s, they have been the subject of a welter of compilations and live albums in the wake of renewed interest in punk nostalgia.
Albums: *999* (1978), *Separates* (1978), *The Biggest Prize In Sport* (1980), *Concrete* (1981), *13th Floor Madness* (1983), *Face To Face* (1985), *In Case Of Emergency* (1986), *You Us It* (1994). Compilations: *Greatest Hits* (1984), *Lust Power And Money* (1987), *The Early Stuff - The UA Years* (1992).
Video: *Feelin' Alright With The Crew* (1987).

1994

This US melodic-rock quartet was formed in 1977 by ex-**L.A. Jets** duo Karen Lawrence (vocals) and John Desautels (drums). With the addition of Steve Schiff (guitar) and Bill Rhodes (bass), they signed to **A&M Records** and released a self-titled debut the following year. This was characterized by Lawrence's powerful vocals and a style that incorporated elements of **Heart**, **Aerosmith** and **Foreigner**. Guitarist Steve Schiff was replaced by Rick Armand on *Please Stand By*, which lacked the rough edges of their debut, and saw them move towards mainstream AOR. Success eluded the band and Lawrence quit in 1980. After a decade of less than successful projects, which have included collaborations with **Cheap Trick**, **Jeff Beck** and **Rod Stewart**, it was rumoured that she may reform 1994. However, the only firm evidence of any such move was the guest appearance of Steve Schiff on her 1986 solo album.
Albums: *1994* (A&M 1978), *Please Stand By* (A&M 1979). Solo: Karen Lawrence *Rip & Tear* (FM Revolver 1986).

1910 Fruitgum Company

The aptly-named Fruitgum Company were at the forefront of a brief wave of bubblegum-pop in the late 60s. Bubblegum was a form that offered solid dance

beats, infantile lyrics and catchy choruses built around instantly-hummable melody lines. The Super K production team of **Jeff Katz** and Jerry Kasenetz were masters of the form and specialized in studio in-house creations such as the Fruitgum Company. Writer Joey Levine was the voice behind the hits which began with the nursery game anthem 'Simon Says' in 1968 and continued with '1, 2, 3, Red Light', 'Goody Goody Gumdrops', 'Indian Giver' and 'Special Delivery'. A touring troupe headed by Levine was hastily assembled and kept this manufactured group alive until they became expendable at the end of the decade.
Albums: *Simon Says* (1968), *1, 2, 3, Red Light* (1968), *Indian Giver* (1969), *1910 Fruitgum Company And Ohio Express* (1969).

95 South

From the Chill Deal Boys (who recorded albums for Quality Records) stable, and part of Toy Productions, 95 South were credited with starting a mini-revival in electro hip hop with their huge 1993 hit, 'Whoot! There It Is'. Sampling **Afrika Bambaataa**'s epic 'Planet Rock', the single returned to good-time, basic beat-box tunes, with lyrics concentrating on the party angle, underpinned by the mighty Florida/Miami Bass sound. It was released in ompetition with **Tag Team**'s similarly themed record. and was followed by an album which, good as it was in its own right, offered more of exactly the same. The group comprises Bootyman, Church's, Black and DJ Marcus. Together they created a monster in 'Whoot!' that refused to die; after high profile appearances on programmes like *The Arsenio Hall Show* it was adopted by both the New Orleans' Saints and Philadelphia Fillies as their theme tune. All of which was lapped up by the protagonists: 'We are a group with a simple message. We are positive, not political or controversial. We make fun music that anyone can get into'.
Album: *Quad City Knock* (Wrap 1993).

Ninjaman

b. Desmond Ballantine, Kingston, Jamaica, West Indies. Notorious from his long history of fearless controversy on record, stage show and **sound system**, Ninjaman's popularity in the Jamaican dancehalls has been unrivalled. He began DJing when he was 12, progressing to the Black Culture sound system and then Kilimanjaro, where from 1984 onwards he was apprentice to **Supercat** and Early B, known as Double Ugly. When another DJ appeared with the same name he became Uglyman, recording his debut for the Soul Carib label. That name too was short-lived; a second Uglyman arrived and, determined to forge an invincible identity of his own, 'Ugly' quickly became Ninja. His first hit, 'Protection', was self-produced, and voiced alongside Courtney Melody in 1987. The following year Lloyd Dennis teamed him with Tinga Stewart for a notable string of hits including 'Cover Me' and then 'Zig It Up', duetted with Flourgon. His early producers included **King Jammys**, Witty, **Redman** and **Ini Kamoze**, but it was with the advent of the Gulf War in 1990 that he became transformed into the archetypal outlaw; brandishing the title of 'Original Front Tooth, Gold Tooth, Gun Pon Tooth Don Gorgon', recording a bounty of apocalyptic 'burial' tunes interspersed with the most uncompromising 'reality' lyrics heard from any DJ of the **ragga** era. His sense of melodrama and stuttering verbal walkabouts are unique; he spread his fiery invective over many fine sides for **Bobby Digital** ('Permit To Bury', 'Fulfilment'), King Jammys ('Border Clash'/'Reality Yuh Want'), Mr. Doo ('Murder Weapon'), **Gussie Clarke** ('Above The Law'), **Steely & Clevie** ('Murder Dem') and **Exterminator** throughout 1991-1992. Among his many targets have been **Shabba Ranks**, who has had to endure an incessant stream of taunts over the years. By the end of 1992, after surviving a bout of Christianity, arrest on gun charges and a flood of imitators, his talents had become over-exposed, though he remained one of the few genuinely original DJs to remain without a major record deal. Instead he made unremarkable albums for **Henry 'Junjo' Lawes** and then **Junior Reid**, still waiting for a much-deserved wider audience.
Selected Albums: *Super Star* (Witty 1989), *Kill Them & Done* (Tassa 1990), *Out Pon Bail* (Exterminator 1990), *Move From Here* (1990), *Run Come Test* (RAS 1990), *Reggae Sunsplash* (Pickout 1991), *Warning You Now* (Jammys 1991), *Nobody's Business But My Own* (Shanachie 1991), *My Weapon* (Mr Doo 1991), *Bounty Hunter* (Blue Mountain 1991), *Target Practice* (Jammys 1992), *Original Front Tooth, Gold Tooth, Gun Pon Tooth Don Gorgon* (Greensleeves 1992), *Sing-A-Ling-A-Ling School Pickney Sing Ting* (Greensleeves 1992), *Hardcore Killing* (Greensleeves 1993), *Booyakka! Booyakka!* (Greensleves 1994). With Courtney Melody: *Protection* (1989). With Capleton & Tony Rebel: *Real Rough* (1990). With Johnny P and Japanese: *Rough, Mean & Deadly - Ninja Man With Johnny P* (Pickout 1990).

Nirvana (UK)

Songwriters Patrick Campbell-Lyons (b. Dublin, Eire) and George Alex Spyropoulus (b. Athens, Greece) met during their brief employment with the Kassner Publishing House in London's Denmark Street. Having established a rapport, the duo formed a group, adding Ray Singer (guitar), Brian Henderson (bass), Michael Coe (viola/french horn) and Sylvia Schuster (cello). The quintet, dubbed Nirvana, secured a recording deal with **Island Records** and made their official debut in 1967, supporting **Traffic** and **Spooky Tooth** at the Saville Theatre, London (owned by **Brian Epstein**). Their exotic debut, *The Story Of Simon Simopath*, was an episodic fairy tale. It emerged in a startlingly colourful cover, featuring a winged child and miniature goddess and centaur, surrounded by stars, planets and three-dimensional block typography. A kitsch concept album that billed itself as a 'science-fiction pantomime', the mock libretto told of the hero's journey from a six-dimensional city to a nirvana filled with sirens. Although the songs generally lacked the weight of their epochal singles, there were some charming moments. The **Alan Bown** Set covered the singalong 'We Can Help You', which received considerable airplay, but narrowly failed to chart. Nirvana themselves were plugged by several discriminating disc jockeys but in spite of the innovative qualities of their singles, the group fell tantalizingly short of a major breakthrough. It contained the haunting 'Pentecost Hotel', a fragile, orchestrated ballad which brought the group critical approval. Campbell-Lyons and Spyropoulus then disbanded the group format and completed a second set as a duo. This melodic collection featured several of Nirvana's finest songs, including 'Tiny Goddess' and 'Rainbow Chaser'. The latter was a powerhouse phased-production, typical of Nirvana's grandiose majesty, and became a minor UK hit in 1968. That same year a strong album followed with *All Of Us,* but soon after the group left Island and their following albums, *Black Flower* and *To Markos III* were considerably low-key. The group's career had already begun to falter when their label rejected *To Markos III* The selection was placed with an American company which then went into liquidation. Spyropoulus dropped out of the partnership and moved into film work, leaving his colleague with the rights to the Nirvana trademark. Having completed a fourth album, *Local Anaesthetic*, Campbell-Lyons became a producer with the **Vertigo** label, while recording *Songs Of Love And Praise*, a compendium of new songs and re-recorded Nirvana favourites. This release was the last to bear the group's name. Patrick subsequently issued two solo albums before reuniting with Spyropoulus for a projected musical, *Blood.*

Albums: *The Story Of Simon Simopath* (1967), *All Of Us* (1968), *To Markos 3* (1969), *Local Anaesthetic* (1971), *Songs Of Love And Praise* (1972). *Black Flower* (1987, combines previously-released and archive material). Solo: Patrick Campbell Lyons *Me And My Friend* (1973), *The Electric Plough* (1981), *The Hero I Might Have Been* (1982).

Nirvana (USA)

Formed in Aberdeen, Washington, USA, in 1988, the Nirvana which the MTV generation came to love comprised Kurt Cobain (b. Kurt Donald Cobain, 20 February 1967, Hoquiam, Seattle, USA, d. 5 April 1994, Seattle; guitar/vocals), Krist Novoselic (b. 16 May 1965, Croatia, Yugoslavia; bass) and Dave Grohl (b. 14 January 1969; drums). Grohl was 'something like our sixth drummer', explained Cobain, and had been recruited from east coast band Dave Brammage, having previously played with Scream, who recorded for **Minor Threat**'s influential Dischord Records label. Their original drummer was Chad Channing; at one point **Dinosaur Jr**'s J. Mascis had been touted as a permanent fixture, along with Dan Peters from **Mudhoney**. Having been signed by the Seattle-based **Sub Pop Records**, the trio completed their debut single, 'Love Buzz'/'Big Cheese', the former a song written and first recorded by 60s Dutch group, Shocking Blue. Second guitarist Jason Everman was then added prior to *Bleach,* which cost a meagre $600 to record. Though he was pictured on the cover, he played no part in the actual recording (going on to join **Mindfunk**, via **Soundgarden** and Skunk). The set confirmed Nirvana's ability to match heavy riffs with melody and it quickly attracted a cult following. However, Channing left the group following a European tour, and as a likely replacement proved hard to find, Dan Peters from labelmates Mudhoney stepped in on a temporary basis. He was featured on the single, 'Sliver', Nirvana's sole 1990 release. New drummer David Grohl reaffirmed a sense of stability. The revamped trio secured a prestigious deal with **Geffen Records** whose faith was rewarded with *Nevermind*, which broke the band worldwide. This was a startling collection of songs which transcended structural boundaries, notably the distinctive slow verse/fast chorus format, and almost single-handedly brought the 'grunge' subculture overground. It topped the US charts early in 1992, eclipsing much-vaunted competition from **Michael Jackson** and **Dire Straits** and topped many Album Of The Year polls. The opening track, 'Smells Like Teen Spirit', reached the UK Top 10; further confirmation that Nirvana now combined critical and popular acclaim. In early 1992 the romance of Cobain and Courtney Love of **Hole** was sealed when the couple married (Love giving birth to a daughter, Frances Bean). It was already obvious, however, that Cobain was struggling with his new role as 'spokesman for a generation'. The first big story to break concerned an article in *Vanity Fayre* which alleged Love had taken heroin while pregnant, which saw the state intercede on the child's behalf by not allowing the Cobains alone with the child during its first month. Press interviews ruminated on the difficulties experienced in recording a follow-up album, and also Cobain's use of a variety of drugs in order to stem the pain arising from a stomach complaint. The recording of *In Utero*, produced by **Big Black/Rapeman** alumni Steve Albini, was not without difficulties either. Rumours circulated concerning confrontations with both Albini and record company Geffen over the 'low-fi' production. When the record was finally released the effect was not as immediate as *Nevermind,* though Cobain's songwriting remained inspired on 'Penny Royal Tea', 'All Apologies' and the evocative 'Rape Me'. His descent into self-destruction accelerated in

1994, however, as he went into a coma during dates in Italy (it was later confirmed that this had all the markings of a failed suicide attempt), before returning to Seattle to shoot himself on 5 April 1994. The man who had long protested that Nirvana were 'merely' a punk band had finally been destroyed by the success that overtook him and them. The wake conducted in the press was matched by public demonstrations of affection and loss, which included suspected copycat suicides. The release of *Unplugged In New York* offered some small comfort for Cobain's fans, with the singer's understated, aching delivery on a variety of covers and Nirvana standards one of the most emotive sights and sounds of the 90s. Grohl and Novoselic would play together again in the Foo Fighters, alongside ex-**Germs** guitarist Pat Smear (who had added second guitar to previous touring engagements and the band's *MTV Unplugged* appearance) following press rumours that Grohl would be working with **Pearl Jam** (much to Courtney Love's chagrin) or **Tom Petty**. In reality both former members would continue to work together under the Foo Fighters' moniker, with small club engagements in the US and the recording of a demo album.

Albums: *Bleach* (Sub Pop 1989), *Nevermind* (Geffen 1991), *In Utero* (Geffen 1993), *Unplugged In New York* (Geffen 1994). Compilation: *Incesticide* (Geffen 1992).

Video: *Live! Tonight! Sold Out!* (1994).

Further reading: *Come As You Are*, Michael Azerrad. *Nirvana And The Sound Of Seattle*, Brad Morrell. *Route 66: On The Road To Nirvana*, Gina Arnold. *Never Fade Away*, Dave Thompson. *Cobain - By The Editors Of Rolling Stone. Nirvana*, Susan Black. *Nirvana: Tribute*, Suzi Black. *Never Fade Away*, Dave Thompson.

Nistico, Sal

b. Salvatore Nistico, 12 April 1940, Syracuse, New York, USA, d. 3 March 1991. Nistico started out on alto saxophone, later switching to tenor and joining an R&B band. In the late 50s he joined the Jazz Brothers, a band led by Gap and **Chuck Mangione**. In 1962 he became a member of the **Woody Herman** band, to which he returned frequently during the next two decades. Also in the 60s he spent some time in the band of **Count Basie** and early in the 70s he was with **Don Ellis**. In the next few years he worked with **Buddy Rich** and **Slide Hampton**, with whom he visited Europe. Eventually he settled in Europe, working there through the 80s. A bristling, aggressive player in the post-bop tradition, Nistico's live and recorded performances are filled with excitement and a vitality that made his sudden death in 1991 all the more tragic.

Albums: with Chuck Mangione *Hey Baby!* (1961), *Heavyweights* (1961), *Comin' On Up* (1962), *Woody Herman, 1963* (1963), *Encore* (1963), with Herman *Woody's Winners* (1965), *The Buddy Rich Septet* (1974), *Just For Fun* (1976), *East Of Isar* (1978), *Neo/Nistico* (1978).

Nitty Gritty

b. Glen Augustus Holness, 1957, August Town, Kingston, Jamaica, West Indies, d. 24 June 1991, Brooklyn, New York, USA. Nitty Gritty rose to prominence as computerised rhythms took hold in Jamaica, alongside **Tenor Saw**, **King Kong** and Anthony Red Rose, all of whom shared a similar vocal style. Gritty's was a deep-throated, gospel-tinged wail distinguished by improvised catchphrases. He was born the second eldest of 11 children in a church-going family, and he trained as an electrician before founding a local group called the Soulites. In 1973 he sang 'Let The Power Fall On I' with **Dennis Brown**, George Nooks and the **Mighty Diamonds** for **Joe Gibbs**, but his first solo release, 'Every Man Is A Seller', did not arrive for another decade, being voiced for **Sugar Minott**'s Youth Promotion label. After a spell on the Zodiac **sound system** with Danny Dread he cut several sides at **Channel One**, and two for Eric 'Bubbles' Howard of the African Brothers, before moving on to George Phang in 1984. By the following April he had joined forces with **King Jammys** and their first release together, 'Hog In A Minty', was an instant success with its haunting vocal refrain and shuffling 'tempo' rhythm track. It was promptly followed by 'Good Morning Teacher', 'Sweet Reggae Music', 'Run Down The World' and 'Gimme Some Of Your Something', all of them sizeable hits. His debut album, *Turbo Charged,* arrived in 1986 as did *Musical Confrontation,* on which credits were shared with **King Kong**.

Soon afterwards he moved to London and then to New York, his output becoming more varied but lacking the impact of his work with Jammys. Singles appeared for Uptempo, Black Solidarity and Skengdon. He returned to form with *General Penitentiary*, recorded with the **Studio One** Band in 1987. This was far more like the Nitty Gritty of old. By 1989 an album for Blacker Dread had arrived with material dating back to his first visit to England in 1986, after which he became relatively inactive. At the age of 34 he was shot dead outside Super Power record shop in Brooklyn, New York.

Selected albums: *Turbo Charged* (Greensleeves 1986), *General Penitentiary* (Black Victory 1987), *Nitty Gritty* (Witty 1988), *Jah In The Family* (Blacker Dread/SCOM 1989). With King Kong: *Musical Confrontation* (Jammys 1986). With Tenor Saw: *Powerhouse Presents* (Powerhouse 1989).

Nitty Gritty Dirt Band

Formed in Long Beach, California in 1965, this enduring attraction evolved from the region's traditional circuit. Founder members Jeff Hanna (b. 11 July 1947; guitar/vocals) and Bruce Kunkel (guitar/vocals) had worked together as the New Coast

Two, prior to joining the Illegitimate Jug Band. Glen Grosclose (drums), Dave Hanna (guitar/vocals), Ralph Barr (guitar) and Les Thompson (bass/vocals) completed the embryonic Dirt Band line-up, although Groslcose and Dave Hanna quickly made way for Jimmie Fadden (drums/guitar) and **Jackson Browne** (guitar/vocals). Although the last musician only remained for a matter of months - he was replaced by John McEuen - his songs remained in the group's repertoire throughout their early career. *Nitty Gritty Dirt Band* comprised of jugband, vaudeville and pop material, ranging from the quirky 'Candy Man' to the orchestrated folk/pop 'Buy For Me The Rain', a minor US hit. *Ricochet* maintained this balance, following which **Chris Darrow**, formerly of **Kaleidoscope** (US), replaced Kunkel. The Dirt Band completed two further albums, and enjoyed a brief role in the film ***Paint Your Wagon***, before disbanding in 1969. The group reconvened the following year around Jeff Hanna, John McEuen, Jimmie Fadden, Les Thompson and newcomer Jim Ibbotson. Having abandoned the jokey elements of their earlier incarnation, they pursued a career as purveyors of superior country-rock. The acclaimed *Uncle Charlie And His Dog Teddy* included excellent versions of **Mike Nesmith**'s 'Some Of Shelly's Blues', **Kenny Loggins'** 'House At Pooh Corner' and **Jerry Jeff Walker**'s 'Mr. Bojangles', a US Top 10 hit in 1970. *Will The Circle Be Unbroken*, recorded in Nashville, was an expansive collaboration between the group and traditional music mentors **Doc Watson**, **Roy Acuff**, **Merle Travis** and **Earl Scruggs**. Its charming informality inspired several stellar performances and the set played an important role in breaking down mistrust between country's establishment and the emergent 'long hair' practitioners. Les Thompson left the line-up following the album's completion, but the remaining quartet, buoyed by an enhanced reputation, continued their eclectic ambitions on *Stars And Stripes Forever* and *Dreams*. In 1976 the group dropped its 'Nitty Gritty' prefix and, as the Dirt Band, undertook a pioneering USSR tour the following year. Both Hanna and Ibbotson enjoyed brief sabbaticals, during which time supplementary musicians were introduced. By 1982 the prodigals had rejoined Fadden, McEuen and newcomer Bob Carpenter (keyboards) for *Let's Go*. The Dirt Band were, by then, an American institution with an enduring international popularity. 'Long Hard Road (Sharecropper Dreams)' and 'Modern Day Romance' topped the country charts in 1984 and 1985, respectively, but the following year a now-weary McEuen retired from the line-up. Former **Eagles** guitarist **Bernie Leadon** augmented the group for *Working Band*, but left again on its completion. He was, however, featured on *Will The Circle Be Unbroken Volume Two*, on which the Dirt Band rekindled the style of their greatest artistic triumph with the aid of several starring names, including **Emmylou Harris**, **Chet Atkins**, **Johnny Cash**, **Ricky Skaggs**, **Roger McGuinn** and **Chris Hillman**. The set deservedly drew plaudits for a group about to enter the 90s with its enthusiasm still intact. *Acoustic* in 1994 was a credible and well-produced set.

Albums: *The Nitty Gritty Dirt Band* (Liberty 1967), *Ricochet* (Liberty 1967), *Rare Junk* (Liberty 1968), *Alive* (Liberty 1968), *Uncle Charlie And His Dog Teddy* (Liberty 1970), *All The Good Times* (United Artists 1972), *Will The Circle Be Unbroken* (United Artists 1972, triple album), *Live* (United Artists 1973), *Stars And Stripes Forever* (United Artists 1974, double album), *Dreams* (United Artists 1975). As Dirt Band: *Dirt Band* (United Artists 1978), *An American Dream* (United Artists 1979), *Make A Little Magic* (United Artists 1980), *Jealousy* (United Artists 1981). As Nitty Gritty Dirt Band: *Let's Go* (United Artists 1983), *Plain Dirt Fashion* (Warner Bros. 1984), *Partners, Brothers And Friends* (Warners 1985), *Hold On* (Warners 1987), *Workin' Band* (Warner Bros. 1988), *Will The Circle Be Unbroken Volume II* (Warner Bros. 1989, double album), *Rest Of The Dream* (MCA 1990), *Not Fade Away* (Liberty 1992), *Acoustic* (Liberty 1994). Compilations: *Pure Dirt* (Liberty UK 1968), *Dead And Alive* (Liberty UK 1969), *Dirt, Silver And Gold* (United Artists 1976, triple album), *Gold From Dirt* (United Artists UK 1980), *Early Dirt 1967-1970* (Decal UK 1986), *Twenty Years Of Dirt* (Warners 1987), *Country Store: The Nitty Gritty Dirt Band* (Country Store UK 1987), *The Best Of The Nitty Gritty Dirt Band Vol 2* (Atlantic 1988), *More Great Dirt: The Best Of The Nitty Gritty Dirt Band, Volume 2* (Warners 1989).

Nitzer Ebb

The driving force behind this electronic based band are Douglas McCarthy (b. 1 September 1966, Chelmsford, England; vocals) and Bon Harris (b. 12 August 1965, Chelmsford, England; percussion/vocals). Frustrated by their environment at school in Chelmsford, and inspired by bands like **D.A.F.**, **Bauhaus** and the **Birthday Party**, they began their first experiments with synthesizers and drum machines in 1983. They were joined in their strictly amateur pursuits by school-mate David Gooday. They had summoned enough experience and confidence to release their first single the next year, 'Isn't It Funny How Your Body Works', on Power Of Voice Communications. They were nothing if not prolific, releasing a further five singles over the next twelve months, which led to a deal with the premier UK independent stable, **Mute Records**, and **Geffen Records** in the US. 1987 saw their first album on the shelves, *That Total Age*, home to surging minimalist aggression, and the beginning of a long-term relationship with producer Flood, who would remix the single 'Join In The Chant'. On Gooday's departure Julian Beeston was enrolled. After a lengthy European trek with **Depeche Mode**, the band recorded *Belief*, and in 1989 followed up their own world tour with

Showtime. Their third album revealed a swing in attitude, with music that was less confrontational and more consumer friendly. This was particularly true in the US, where the single 'Fun To Be Had' peaked at Number 2 in the US dance charts. Their most recent album has confirmed their popularity with fans and a previously reluctant press. As McCarthy puts it: 'With the advent of *Ebbhead,* I think we've managed to twist listenability around to our way of thinking'.
Albums: *That Total Age* (Mute 1987), *Belief* (Mute 1988), *Showtime* (Mute 1989), *Ebbhead* (Mute 1991), *Big Hit* (Mute 1995).

Nitzinger, John

b. Texas, USA. This energetic and highly talented guitarist/vocalist specializes in blues-based hard rock and boogie, and has worked with **Bloodrock**, **Alice Cooper** and **Carl Palmer**'s P.M., supplying ferocious **Ted Nugent**-inspired guitar chords to each. Members of Bloodrock, for whom he also wrote songs, would return the favour by appearing on his solo material. His three albums on his own account are highly varied and explore a wider range of styles than might at first be imagined. Psychedelia, jazz, rock, blues and metal nuances have been integrated within his own extrovert approach, though since the mid-70s his recording career has taken a back seat to session work.
Albums: *Nitzinger* (Capitol 1971), *One Foot In History* (Capitol 1972), *Live Better...Electrically* (20th Century 1976).

Nitzsche, Jack

b. 22 April 1937, Chicago, Illinois, USA. Nitzsche's long career began in the late 50s when he joined a cabal of young, Los Angeles-based, aspiring entrepreneurs including **Lee Hazelwood**, **Lou Adler** and **Nick Venet**. He became acquainted with **Sonny Bono**, then head of A&R at **Specialty Records**, with whom he wrote 'Needles And Pins', later an international hit for the **Searchers**. Nitzsche established his reputation as an arranger through an association with **Phil Spector**. His contribution to recordings by the **Crystals**, **Ronettes**, **Righteous Brothers** and **Ike And Tina Turner** should not be under- emphasized, while a similar relationship with the **Rolling Stones** resulted in several of the group's classic releases, notably 'The Last Time', 'Satisfaction' and 'Get Off Of My Cloud'. Nitzsche also enjoyed success in his own right as a performer with 'The Lonely Surfer' (1963), before garnering further acclaim for his arranging/production skills for **Jackie DeShannon**, **P.J. Proby** and **Bob Lind**. In 1966 he co-produced 'Expecting To Fly' for **Buffalo Springfield**, a track essentially viewed as a solo vehicle for group guitarist **Neil Young**. Their relationship continued when the latter opted for a solo career and Nitzsche not only assisted with the recording of *Neil Young* and *Harvest,* but joined the on-tour backing group, **Crazy Horse**, contributing extensively to their debut album. Having scored the film *Performance,* Nitzsche won considerable approbation for similar work for *The Exorcist* and *One Flew Over The Cuckoo's Nest.* The artist also rekindled solo aspirations with the neo-classical *St. Giles Cripplegate,* before enjoying further success with arrangements for **Mac Davis**, **Randy Newman** and the **Tubes**. He remains an integral part of the US west coast music industry.
Albums: *The Lonely Surfer* (1963), *Dance To The Hits Of The Beatles* (1964), *Chopin '66* (1966), *St. Giles Cripplegate* (1972).

Nix, Don

b. 27 September 1941, Memphis, Tennessee, USA. Saxophonist Nix was one of several aspiring high-school musicians forming the basis of the **Mar-Keys**. This renowned instrumental group enjoyed several R&B-styled best-sellers and became the houseband for the **Stax** record company during the mid-60s, performing on sessions for **Otis Redding**, **Rufus Thomas**, **Wilson Pickett** and **Sam And Dave**. Nix moved to California in 1965 where he became acquainted with several 'southern' expatriates, notably **Leon Russell** and **Delaney And Bonnie**. Nix produced the latter's *Home,* then subsequently worked with **Albert King** and **John Mayall**, and completed several uneven, yet endearing albums. In 1972 he toured with the ambitious Alabama State Troupers, an *ad hoc* musical carnival which also included **Lonnie Mack**, Jeannie Greene, Marlin Greene and **Furry Lewis**. Although never a well-known figure, Nix retained the respect of his contemporaries.
Albums: *In God We Trust* (1971), *Living By The Days* (1971), *Hobos, Heroes And Street Corner Clowns* (1974), *Gone Too Long* (1976), *Skyrider* (1979).

Nix, Willie

b. 6 August 1922, Memphis, Tennessee, USA, d. 8 July 1991, Leland, Mississippi, USA. Starting as a dancer and comedian, Nix switched to drums, and worked in Mississippi, Arkansas and Tennessee from his Memphis base in the 40s and 50s. Recorded in 1951 by **Sam Phillips** as a blues singing drummer, Nix appeared on albums for **Sun**, RPM and Checker. Nix moved to Chicago in 1953 where he played the clubs, and recorded four tracks for Chance/Sabre. His recordings were intense and exuberant, always powered by his propulsive, swinging drumming. Returning to Memphis he supported himself by migrant labour and a little guitar playing. He was largely retired by the end of the 60s, and spent the rest of his life notoriously telling tall tales and behaving eccentrically.
Albums: *Chicago Slickers Vol. 2* (1981), *Sun Records The Blues Years* (1985).

Nixon, Elmore

b. 17 November 1933, Crowley, Louisiana, USA, d. June 1975, Houston, Texas, USA. Little is known of Nixon, although his piano is to be heard on many more records than he made under his own name. His family moved to Houston in 1939, where he would remain until his death. At some stage he trained to join the church, which is presumed to be where he learned to play piano. By his early teens, he was already backing **Peppermint Harris** on his Gold Star debut. Thereafter he recorded with many Texas artists as a member of alto saxophonist Henry Hayes' Four Kings, including Carl Campbell, Milton Willis, **L.C. Williams**, Hubert Robinson, **Ivory Lee** and **Hop Wilson**. His debut record, 'Foolish Love', was made in 1949 for Sittin In With with the Hayes band. His own music reflected the jump music of the time, having affinities with **Little Willie Littlefield.** Other sessions followed for Peacock, **Mercury**, Savoy and **Imperial,** the latter in 1955. During the mid-60s, he worked with **Clifton Chenier,** recording on Chenier's sessions for **Arhoolie** and with **Lightnin' Hopkins** for Jewel. At other times he led his own band, working around Texas and Louisiana. He underwent serious surgery in 1970 and was largely inactive until his death.

Selected album: *Shout And Rock* (1986).

Nixon, Hammie

b. 22 January 1908, Brownsville, Tennessee, USA, d. 17 August 1984, Brownsville, Tennessee, USA. Nixon was the leading blues harmonica player in Brownsville, and a frequent visitor to Memphis, playing in street bands on jug, kazoo and harmonica. In Brownsville he was an associate of **Sleepy John Estes** and **James 'Yank' Rachell**, contributing beautiful, mournful playing to both men's 20s and 30s recordings. He was a major early influence on **John Lee 'Sonny Boy' Williamson**, and later on **Little Walter**. When Estes was located in 1962, Nixon was found also (proving to be a cheery extrovert, despite his sorrowful harmonica sound), and came out of musical retirement to tour and record with Estes until the latter's death. Thereafter, Nixon continued to play concerts and festivals, and made occasional recordings, though these were often disappointing, as they often overemphasized his kazoo and his rudimentary guitar.

Albums: *Hammie Nixon* (1976), *Tappin' That Thing* (1984).

Nixons

Formed in Norman, Oklahoma, in 1991, US rock band the Nixons built their reputation on the back of a relentless touring schedule, playing 324 gigs in 18 months and 55 cities. Comprising Ricky Brooks (bass), John Humphrey (drums), Jesse Davis (guitar) and Zac Maloy (vocals/guitar), they found immediate success on US alternative charts with their 1994 debut, *Halo*. In the wake of its strong performance the band were signed by **MCA Records**, who had the band re-record seven of that album's songs, including regional hit 'Sister', alongside new compositions to form 1995's *Foma*. It was produced by Mark Dodson, who had previously helmed projects by **Suicidal Tendencies** and **Prong**. The unusual title was taken from a book, *Cat's Cradle*, written by Maloy's favourite author, Kurt Vonnegut, and related to 'harmless untruths intended to comfort simple souls'. The album demonstrated the band's varying influences - Maloy had grown up listening to his grandfather's country band, Buddy White & The Westerners, who played at the **Grande Ole Opry**, while Humphrey had joined the **Kiss** Army as a child.

Albums: *Halo* (RainMaker 1994), *Foma* (MCA 1995).

NME

(see ***New Musical Express***)

No Exqze

This melodic rock quartet from Holland was formed by ex-**Vandenberg** bassist Dick Kemper in 1987. Recruiting Geert Scheigrond (guitar), Leen Barbier (vocals) and Nico Groen (drums), they signed to Phonogram Records and debuted with *Too Hard Too Handle* in 1988. No Exqze allowed Kemper to indulge his writing talents, which had previously been suppressed in Vandenberg. Not without good reason, it might be argued. Produced by Tony Platt, the album was dominated by Barbier's soulful vocals, which added depth and character to Kemper's rather average AOR-style compositions.

Album: *Too Hard Too Handle* (Phonogram 1988).

No Means No

An 'artcore' trio from Victoria, British Columbia, Canada, No Means No have done much to expand the boundaries of the 'hardcore' genre, fusing funk and fuzz-pop with questioning lyrics. The line-up featured Andrew Kerr (guitar) and the brothers Rob Wright (bass) and John Wright (drums). Kerr joined shortly after their 1984 debut, *Mama.* Having taken their name from the phrase commonly used in connection with the rights of rape victims, the band composed lyrics exploring the middle ground between the individual and society. The tone was often one of self-disgust, as in 'nobody knows you and nobody wants to' from 'Body Bag'. Their early efforts lose impact through their disjointed nature, although by the time *Small Parts Isolated And Destroyed* was released the band had refined their sound into a more structured whole - despite it veering from thrash-jazz to *avant garde* experimentalism. *0 + 2 = 1* crystallised their sound, with the title-song offering a good guide to their approach: 'Yes and no are like day and night / One breaks as the other is

falling / Question the answers, stir the solutions / In the end, for light, you must burn your conclusions'. This song was described by Rob Wright as 'essentially about how things don't add up, and people who think they have it all added up are either fooling themselves or lying'. Their avoidance of the media, particularly their dislike of having their photos taken, has limited their appeal, although they do enjoy considerable cult øpopularity in Europe. However, in late 1991 Andy Kerr left the band. Many of the songs on *Why Do They Call Me Mr. Happy?* were written by Rob for his solo act, Mr Happy. The lyrics, though, had the same remorselessness as before, such as these lines from 'The River': 'Mothers tell your children the truth / Don't hide the fate that's waiting / When you're born you start to drown / There is no help, no safety'.
Albums: *Mama* (No label 1984), *Sex Mad* (Psyche Industry/Alternative Tentacles 1986), *The Day Everything Became Nothing* (Alternative Tentacles 1988, mini-album), *Small Parts Isolated And Destroyed* (Alternative Tentacles 1989), *Wrong* (Alternative Tentacles 1989), with Jello Biafra *The Sky Is Falling And I Want My Mommy* (Alternative Tentacles 1991), *Live And Cuddly* (Alternative Tentacles 1991), *0 + 2 = 1* (Alternative Tentacles 1991), *Why Do They Call Me Mr. Happy?* (Alternative Tentacles 1993). Compilation: *The Day Everything Became Isolated And Destroyed* (Alternative Tentacles 1988).

No Nukes

This 1980 documentary revolved around a series of events staged in New York the previous year. Five nights of benefit concerts were held at Madison Square Gardens between 19 and 23 September 1979, which in turn were succeeded by an outdoor gathering in Battery Park, in order to raise funds for Musicians United for Safe Energy. MUSE was a charity headed by John Hall, formerly of the **Ozark Mountain Daredevils**, who was determined to lobby for the replacement of nuclear power by solar energy. Many well-known 70s US artists lent support to the cause, and *No Nukes* captured several strong performances. **Bruce Springsteen** contributed the title song to the as yet unreleased *The River*, as well as powerful readings of **Gary 'U.S.' Bonds**' 'A Quarter To Three' and his own 'Thunder Road'. **Crosby, Stills And Nash** offer 'Suite Judy Blue Eyes' while **Jackson Browne** completed resonant versions of 'Running On Empty' and 'Before The Deluge'. The **Doobie Brothers**, **Bonnie Raitt**, **Jesse Colin Young**, **James Taylor** and **Carly Simon** are among the others featured in an all-star cast brought together by a common ecological concern. Several guested on each other's sets, notably on the 60s protest anthem, 'Get Together', which featured Browne, Nash and Stills alongside Young, whose group the **Youngbloods** first popularised the song. *No Nukes* was also the subject of an expansive three-record set which, when combined with the scale of the event itself, showed commitment from all those involved in the project.

No Strings

When **Oscar Hammerstein** died in 1960, composer **Richard Rodgers** lost the second of only two lyricists with whom he had worked throughout his illustrious career - the first, of course, being **Lorenz Hart**. Shortly after Hammerstein's death, Rodgers wrote both words and music to five new songs for the second remake of the film ***State Fair***, and then in 1962 he undertook the complete score for *No Strings* which opened at the 54th Street Theatre in New York on 15 March. Rodgers also produced the piece, for which the book was written by the celebrated playwright Samuel Taylor, who had impressed the composer with his comedies such as *Sabrina Fair* and *The Pleasure Of His Company*. The black actress Diahann Carroll, who was spotted by Rodgers on US television in the *Jack Paar Show*, was cast as an American fashion model, Barbara Woodruff, who has moved to Paris. While there, she falls in love with the former Pulitzer Prize-winning novelist David Jordan (Richard Kiley), whose life has disintegrated to the point that he has given up writing and is just living on hand-outs. She helps in his process of rehabilitation, but they decide to go their separate ways. Rodgers himself hinted later that the reason that the characters split up is because they anticipate racial prejudice on their return to the USA, although the authors were careful not to mention it directly. The director and choreographer, Joe Layton, introduced several innovative features, such as placing the orchestra onstage instead of in the pit, and having members of the cast move the mobile sets in full view of the audiences. Another neat idea was for Kiley and Carroll to sing the show's lovely hit song, 'The Sweetest Sounds', each accompanied by their own individual instrumental soloist, and this technique was also used on some of the other numbers. Carroll excelled throughout on such as 'Loads Of Love', 'You Don't Tell Me', 'An Orthodox Fool', and joined with Kiley for 'Nobody Told Me', 'Maine', 'Look No Further', and the title song. While not in the same money-making class as ***The Sound Of Music*** and the other Rodgers and Hammerstein blockbusters, *No Strings* had a decent run of 580 performances. Rodgers won the **Tony Award** for outstanding music - but not, ironically for lyrics - and joint Tonys also went to Diahann Carroll, who shared hers with Anna Marie Alberghetti (***Carnival***); and Joe Layton, whose choreography was adjudged to be equally as excellent as that of **Agnes de Mille**'s for ***Kwamina***. In 1963, *No Strings* was presented at Her Majesty's Theatre in London, where it starred Hy Hazell and Art Lund, and ran for 135 performances.

No Sweat

This Dublin-based, six-piece melodic rock group comprised Paul Quinn (lead vocals), Dave Gooding (guitar), Jim Phillips (guitar), P.J. Smith (keyboards), Jon Angel (bass) and Ray Fearn (drums). Together they impressed **Def Leppard** vocalist Joe Elliot**,** who took over production on their debut album and helped them secure a deal with **London Records**. The record company's public relations team subsequently launched an impressive and expensive campaign on their behalf. They supported **Thunder** on their 'Backstreet Symphony' tour in 1990 and were generally well-received by the press. Paul Quinn's voice oozed emotion, but their material failed to stamp its own identity. Accusations of hype followed, and the band quietly dissolved a year later.

Album: *No Sweat* (London 1990).

No, No, Nanette

Unusually for a Broadway musical, *No, No Nanette* was far more popular when it was revived than when it was first staged. With music by **Vincent Youmans,** lyrics by **Irving Caesar** and **Otto Harbach**, and a book by Harbach and Frank Mandel, the show included several admirable songs, including 'You Can Dance With Any Girl At All', 'Too Many Rings Around Rosie', 'The Call Of The Sea', 'Peach On the Beach', 'Take A Little One-Step', and two that became classics, 'I Want To Be Happy' and 'Tea For Two'. *No, No, Nanette* opened at the Palace Theatre in London on 11 March 1925, with **Binnie Hale** and George Grossmith in the leading roles, and ran for 665 performances. The New York production, which made its debut at the Globe Theatre on 16 September of 1925, starred Ona Munson, Donald Brian, Cecil Lean, and Jack McCauley. Although the show epitomised the happy-go-lucky all-singing, all-dancing atmosphere of the 20s, it closed after a disappointing run of 321 performances. Nearly half a century later, a strong cast which included **Ruby Keeler**, Helen Gallagher and Bobby Van, appeared in the 1971 New York revival which stayed around for over two years, and won **Tony Awards** for best actress (Gallagher), supporting actress (Patsy Kelly), choreographer (Donald Saddler), and costumes (Raoul du Bois). Touring companies proliferated, and there was another major production at Drury Lane in London with **Anna Neagle**, Anne Rogers, Tony Britton, and Thora Hird. There have been two film versions: in 1930 with Alexander Gray and Bernice Claire, and in 1940 with Anna Neagle and Victor Mature.

Further reading: *The Making Of No, No, Nanette*, Don Dunn.

Noack, Eddie

b. De Armand A. Noack Jnr., 29 April 1930, Houston, Texas, USA, d. 5 February 1978. Noack who gained degrees in English and Journalism at University of Houston made his radio debut in 1947 and first recorded for Goldstar in 1949. In 1951, he cut several songs for Four Star including 'Too Hot To Handle'. Leased to the TNT label, it drew attention to his songwriting and was recorded by several artists. He joined Starday in 1953 (beginning a long association with 'Pappy' Daily), where his immediate success came as a writer when several of his songg were recorded by top artists including **Hank Snow** who scored a maior hit with 'These Hands' in 1956. Noack moved with Daily to his D label where in 1958, after recording rockabilly tracks as Tommy Wood, he had a country hit with 'Have Blues Will Travel'. During the 60s, Noack quit recording to concentrate on songwriting and publishing and had many of his songs including 'Flowers For Mama', 'Barbara Joy', 'The Poor Chinee', 'A Day In The Life Of A Fool' and 'No Blues Is Good News' successfully recorded by **George Jones**. Noack did make some further recordings in the 70s, including arguably some of his best for his fine tribute album to **Jimmie Rodgers**. He moved to Nashville and in 1976, recorded an album that found release in Britain (where he had toured that year) on the Look label. He worked in publishing for Daily and in an executive role for the Nashville Songwriters Association until his death from cirrhosis in 1978. A fine performer somewhat in the style of **Hank Williams**, he is perhaps more appreciated today as a singer than he was in his own time.

Albums: *Remembering Jimmie Rodgers* (1972), *Eddie Noack* i (1976), *Eddie Noack* ii (1980), *Gentlemen Prefer Blondes* (c.1981).

Noakes, Rab

A veteran of Scotland's folk circuit, Noakes' debut *Do You See The Lights*, although heavily produced, announced the arrival of a gifted songwriter. He then briefly joined **Gerry Rafferty** in the original **Stealer's Wheel**, appearing on the latter's solo debut, *Can I Have My Money Back*, but subsequently preferred to follow his own direction. Rafferty did, however, guest on Noakes' 1972 solo collection. Signed to **Warner Brothers** in 1974, the artist's two albums for the company showed an increasingly American slant. *Red Pump Special* featured the famed **Memphis Horns** brass section, but despite critical acclaim, Noakes was unable to secure a commercial breakthrough. Further albums also met public indifference, and although he still pursues a performing career, this underrated singer is now a producer with BBC Scotland.

Albums: *Do You See The Lights* (1970), *Rab Noakes* i (1972), *Red Pump Special* (1974), *Never Too Late* (1975), *Restless* (1978), *Rab Noakes* ii (1980), *Under The Rain* (1984), *Standing Up* (Mediat 1994).

Noble, Ray

b. Stanley Raymond Noble, 17 December 1903, Brighton, Sussex, England, d. 3 April 1978, London, England. The son of a part-time songwriter and musician, Noble attended choir school, Dulwich College and Cambridge University before studying at the Royal College of Music. In 1926 he won a ***Melody Maker*** arranging contest and worked for music publisher **Lawrence Wright** and **Jack Payne**'s BBC Dance Orchestra before becoming a staff arranger at **HMV Records**, eventually succeeding **Carroll Gibbons** as Head of Light Music. He conducted the company's New Mayfair Orchestra and New Mayfair Novelty Orchestra before forming his own sweet-swing studio band which included top musicians Freddy Gardner, Alfie Noakes, Bill Harty, Tiny Winters, Max Goldberg, **Nat Gonnella**, Lew Davis and the most popular vocalist of the 30s, **Al Bowlly**. Bowlly's vocals on songs such as 'Time On My Hands', 'Close Your Eyes', 'How Could We Be Wrong' and 'Lazy Day' are considered outstanding examples of the orchestra's substantial output, alongside the singer's interpretations of Noble's own compositions. Noble wrote his first hit song, 'Goodnight Sweetheart', in 1931, and during the early 30s, followed it with 'By The Fireside', 'I Found You', and 'What More Can I Ask'. One of his biggest successes, 'Love Is The Sweetest Thing' attracted much attention because of the similarity of its first five notes to the first five of the British national anthem, 'God Save The King'.

Ray Noble's ensemble was the first British band to become popular on records in the USA, and, having had hits there since 1931, including 'Lady Of Spain', 'Love Is The Sweetest Thing' and 'The Old Spinning Wheel', Noble went to the USA in 1934, taking with him drummer/manager Bill Harty and Al Bowlly. **Glenn Miller** assisted him in organizing an American orchestra which included, at various times, future leaders **Claude Thornhill**, **Charlie Spivak**, **Pee Wee Irwin**, **Will Bradley**, and soloists **Bud Freeman** and **George Van Eps**. They had hits with 'Isle Of Capri', 'Paris In The Spring', 'Let's Swing It', 'I've Got You Under My Skin' and 'Easy To Love' (with Bowlly on vocals), along with Noble's own songs, 'The Very Thought Of You', 'Love Locked Out' (lyric by Max Kester), and 'The Touch Of Your Lips'. In 1936, after the orchestra's very successful engagement at New York's Rainbow Room, Bowlly returned to England, and in the following year the band broke up, reforming later in the 30s.

Noble went to Hollywood. He had been there in 1935 to appear in ***The Big Broadcast*** *Of 1936* in which **Bing Crosby** and **Ethel Merman** sang his song, 'Why The Stars Come Out Tonight'. This time he appeared as a 'silly ass' Englishman in the **Fred Astaire** movie ***A Damsel In Distress***, and later duetted with Astaire on the record version of his eccentric dance, 'The Yam', and accompanied him on songs such as 'Change Partners', 'Nice Work If You Can Get It' and 'A Foggy Day'. He also backed singer **Buddy Clarke** on his US number 1, 'Linda', and 'I'll Dance At Your Wedding'. Noble continued to have successful records in the US until the end of the 40s with songs such as 'I've Got My Love To Keep Me Warm', 'Alexander's Ragtime Band' and 'By The Light Of The Silvery Moon'. Recordings of his compositions 'Cherokee' (by **Charlie Barnet**) and 'I Hadn't Anyone Till You' were highlights of the Swing Era. After returning briefly to England in 1938 to play in variety, Noble worked consistently in America, playing musical and comedy roles on George Burns and Gracie Allen's radio show, and later through to the 50s, with ventriloquist Edgar Bergen on radio and television, sometimes playing stooge to Bergen's famous partner, Charlie McCarthy. When the latter series ended in the mid-50s Noble retired to Santa Barbara, California, subsequently spending some years in Jersey in the Channel Islands.

Selected compilations: *Golden Age Of British Dance Bands* (1969), *...Featuring Al Bowlly, Vols. 1 & 2 (1935-36)* (1976), *Ray Noble Plays Ray Noble* (1976), *Ray Noble/Al Bowlly, Vols. 1-4* (1979), *Ray Noble's Encores, Vols. 1-6* (1979), *Ray Noble And Joe Haymes 1935* (1979), *Dinner Music* (1982), with Carroll Gibbons *The New Mayfair Dance Orchestra - Harmony Heaven 1928-1930* (1983), *The HMV Sessions* (1984), *We Danced All Night* (1984), *Notable Noble* (1985), *Goodnight Sweetheart* (1988).

Noble, Steve

b. 16 March 1960, Streatley, Berkshire, England. Noble studied with the Nigerian master drummer Elkan Ogunde. His first professional engagement was with the *avant garde* jazz-pop group, **Rip Rig And Panic**, touring England and Europe and playing on *I'm Cold* (1982) and *Attitude* (1983). His precision and invention as a percussionist made it natural for him to gravitate towards free improvisation. In 1985 he appeared at the Thessalonika Jazz Festival with **Derek Bailey** and later took part in the **Company** Weeks of 1987, 1989 and 1990. In 1987 he toured Holland with Tristan Honsinger. In the late 80s, he was part of the **Alan Wilkinson** Trio and a member of Kahondo Style. A longstanding partnership with pianist **Alex Maguire** produced countless gigs and *Live At Oscars*. Noble, along with **Louis Moholo**, provided percussion for Maguire's Cat O' Nine Tails in 1989. Other collaborations include Katie Duck, Group O and the Bow Gamelan Ensemble. In 1991 he provided drums both for the rock band CC Sagar and an improvising trio with tenor saxophonist Tony Bevan and bassist **Paul Rogers**; he also recorded an improvised duo with upcoming reedsman **Alex Ward**. Noble's lightning responses, wit and catholic taste

promise a lot for the future.
Albums: with Company *Once* (1987), with Alex Maguire *Live At Oscars* (1987), with Kahondo Style *Green Tea & Crocodiles* (1988), with Alex Ward *Ya Boo, Reel & Rumble* (1991), with Tony Bevan, Paul Rogers *Bigshots* (1992).

Nobles, Cliff (And Co.)

Cliff Nobles (b. 1944, Mobile, Alabama, USA) had a background as a gospel singer. In an effort to break into something more commercial, he moved to Philadelphia and won a contract with **Atlantic Records**. He was dropped from the label after three unsuccessful singles, 'My Love Is Getting Stronger', 'Let's Have A Good Time' and 'Your Love Is All I Need', whereupon independent producer Jesse James took him on and recorded 'The More I Do For You' on the Phil LA Of Soul label. 'The Horse' (1968), Nobles' US number 2 hit was originally the b-side to the undistinguished 'Love Is Alright'. Ironically the former track did not feature the artist's regular group - Bobby Tucker (guitar), Benny Williams (bass) and Tommy Soul (drums) - but, instead, the James Boys, a collection of emergent Philadelphia session musicians put together by producer **Leon Huff**. This unit then rushed out a complementary single, 'The Mule', which had the same version of 'The Horse' on the reverse. Despite minimal input, Nobles' name still graced such follow-up singles as 'Horse Fever', although he later secured a minor R&B success with 'Feeling Of Loneliness' (1973). The James Boys; Jesse James, Bobby Martin, Norman Harris, Roland Chambers, Nat Chambers, Ronnie Baker and Karl Young, became **MFSB**, the Sigma Sound studio houseband.
Album: *The Horse* (1968).

Nock, Mike

b. 27 September 1940, Christchurch, New Zealand. Nock is largely a self-taught pianist who was able to work professionally when he was only 15 years old. When he was 18 he went to Australia playing in a hard bop trio before moving on to England. He did not settle but went to the **Berklee College Of Music** in Boston, Massachusetts on a scholarship in 1961. In the early 60s he was the house pianist in a Boston Club before joining **Yusef Lateef** for three years. In 1968 he moved to San Francisco and formed the jazz-rock group, Fourth Way, which was extremely successful until disbanding in 1971. Nock became involved in electronic music and composed numerous film scores. In 1985 he returned to Australia where he spent most of his time composing, though he also taught improvisation at the New South Wales Conservatorium in Sydney.
Albums: with Yusef Lateef *Live At Peps* (1964), with John Handy *Projections* (1968), with Fourth Way *The Fourth Way* (1969), with Fourth Way *The Sun And The Moon Have Come Together* (1969), with Fourth Way *Werewolf* (1970), *Magic Mansions* (1977), *Piano Solos* (1978), *Talismen* (1978), *Ondas* (1982).

Nocturnus

This innovative American death metal band was formed by drummer and vocalist Mike Browning following his departure from an early incarnation of **Morbid Angel**. *The Key* showed an original approach, mixing the frenzied yet intricate riffing of guitarists Sean McNenney and Mike Davis with the atmospheric keyboard washes of Louis Panzer. Critical acclaim abounded, but the sound proved rather too radical for much of the death crowd, and Nocturnus struggled to rise above cult status. *Thresholds* was recorded with new vocalist Dan Izzo taking the pressure off Browning, with permanent bassist Emo Mowery being recruited after the sessions to replace touring bassist Jim O'Sullivan (Chris Anderson played on the album). However, with no upturn in the band's fortunes they parted company with **Earache**, re-emerging in 1994 with an EP for new label, Moribund.
Albums: *The Key* (Earache 1990), *Thresholds* (Earache 1992).

Noel And Gertie

(see **Lawrence, Gertrude**)

Noiseworks

Formed in Sydney, Australia in 1985, Noiseworks feature seasoned players culled from various groups of the New South Wales area. The line-up of Steve Balbi (bass), Stuart Fraser (guitar), Kevin Nicol (drums), Justin Stanley (vocals) and **Jon Stevens** (lead vocals) have attracted much attention with its clean, hard rock sound, distinctive vocals and competent playing. Jon Stevens had gained years of experience, being something of a teen idol in his homeland of New Zealand, hence he obtained the attention of a young audience on television as well as radio. Noiseworks had been compared in some quarters as the natural inheritors of **INXS**'s crown of top Australian group. Their final album was a self-financed and produced affair which was rejected by their record company. Several new tracks were added which affected the continuity and feel of the album that the band had originally created. This could have caused their break-up, as they announced a 'temporary split' in 1992. Jon Stevens joined the stage cast of a revival of the rock opera, ***Jesus Christ Superstar***.
Albums: *Noiseworks* (1987), *Touch* (1988), *Love Versus Money* (1991).

Nokemono

This Japanese hard rock quintet was formed in 1978. Inspired by fellow countrymen **Bow Wow**, Yukihiro 'Ace' Nakaya (vocals) and Shigeo 'Rolla' Nakano (guitar) decided to put a band together along similar

lines. Recruiting Bunzo 'Bunchan' Satoh (guitar), Masaaki 'Cherry' Chikura (bass) and Tadashi 'Popeye' Hirota (drums), they were picked up by the local SMS label. The resultant *From The Black World* combined **Van Halen**, **Deep Purple** and **UFO** influences. It was an impressive debut somewhat marred by an inferior production. However, the band remained virtually unknown outside their own country and the album was to be their solitary contribution to Japanese metal.
Album: *From The Black World* (SMS 1979).

Nolan, Bob

b. Robert Clarence Nobles, 1 April 1908, Point Hatfield, New Brunswick, Canada, d. 16 June 1980. Bob Nolan was an important member of the **Sons Of the Pioneers**. Although Canadian, his father joined the US Army in World War I and served in France. He suffered gas poisoning and on discharge, changed his name to Nolan and relocated to Arizona for health reasons. During his father's absence, the young Bob received some education whilst living with aunts in Boston but at 14, he moved to Tucson to join his father. Whilst attending the University of Arizona, he began writing poetry, some of which became the basis for the songs that he later wrote. In 1927, a desire to travel led him to hobo his way west. The sound of the trains were the reason for his first song 'Way Out There' and the later sequel 'One More Ride'. In 1929, he moved to California, where he worked on beaches as a life-guard and sang with a group, which led him to seek a musical career. In mid 1931, he answered an advertisement in an Los Angeles newspaper placed by Leonard Slye (later **Roy Rogers**) for a tenor singer/yodeller to join the Rocky Mountaineers. The pair and fiddler Bob Nichols, worked for a time with the Mountaineers until Nolan, disheartened by their lack of success, quit to become a caddy at Bel Air Country Club. Late in 1933, Slye and **Tim Spencer** persuaded Nolan to be the third member of the Pioneer Trio. The trio subsequently went on to become the Sons Of The Pioneers, with Nolan a most important part of the act, not only for his singing but also for his songwriting. Rated by many as the most poetic of all the western songwriters, Nolan was responsible for many of the group's biggest hits. These include 'At The Rainbow's End', 'The Touch Of God's Hand', 'Chant Of The Wanderer' and his two classics 'Cool Water' and 'Tumbling Tumbleweeds'. He retired from active performing in 1949 but recorded with the group until 1957. He finally tired of the music scene and adopted a solitary existence. He was persuaded to record a solo album in 1979 which contained some of old hits and **Marty Robbins**' 'Man Walks Among Us', which included an appearance from the writer. Nolan died, following a heart attack, on 16 June 1980. His last request was that his ashes should be spread on the sands of the Nevada desert in the US.
Album: *Sound Of A Pioneer* (Elektra 1979).

Nolans

This highly-popular Irish family group originally consisted of brothers and sisters Tommy, Anne (b. 12 November 1950), Denise (b. 1952), Maureen (b. 14 June 1954), Brian, Linda (b. 23 February 1959), Bernadette (b. 17 October 1961) and Coleen Nolan (b. 12 March 1965, Blackpool, England). The Nolans lived in Dublin until 1962 when they emigrated to Blackpool. Parents Tommy and Maureen Nolan were singers and gradually brought their offspring into the act. In 1963 the entire family debuted as the Singing Nolans. After moving to London, the group's personnel was Anne, Denise, Linda, Bernadette, and Maureen. Their act proved very popular on UK television and variety shows. After recording their second album in 1977, and touring America with **Engelbert Humperdinck**, Denise left a year later in order to pursue a solo career. The sisters signed to **CBS** and were widely tipped to represent the UK in the Eurovision Song Contest but lost out to **Black Lace**. After a minor hit single with 'Spirit Body And Soul', Anne married and left the group for two years. She was replaced by the youngest sister, Coleen, and the quartet changed their name from the Nolan Sisters to the Nolans. A massive hit with the catchy 'I'm In The Mood For Dancing' brought them worldwide renown and even topped the charts in Japan. The Nolans had further UK Top 10 hits with 'Gotta Pull Myself Together' and 'Attention To Me', and, with Anne's return, became a quintet for a while until Linda married former **Harmony Grass** drummer Brian Hudson and retired from the group. Linda is sometimes known as the 'Naughty Nolan' because she launched her solo career by posing near-naked for publicity shots. Phenomenal success for the Nolans in Japan and Eire coincided with further minor chart appearances in the UK, as well as best-selling albums. Coleen, Bernadette and Denise have each recorded solo singles, while Linda and Coleen enjoyed a minor hit as the Young And Moody Band with 'Don't Do That'. In 1994 Coleen left to have a baby, and a year later, Anne and Maureen became a Nolans duo when Bernadette, who had been the lead singer with the group since she was 13, decided to go solo. Coleen is married to Shane Ritchie, who took over the leading role from Craig McLachlan in the acclaimed 1993 London revival of the musical, ***Grease***.
Albums: *The Singing Nolans* (1972), *The Nolan Sisters* (1977), *20 Giant Hits* (1978), *Best Of The Nolan Sisters Vol. 1* (1979), *Best Of The Nolan Sisters Vol 2* (1979), *Nolan Sisters* (1979), *The Nolan Sisters Collection* (1980), *Making Waves* (1980), *Portrait* (1982), *Altogether* (1982), *Harmony* (1983), *I'm In The Mood For Dancing* (1983), *Girls Just Wanna Have Fun* (1984), *Love Songs* (1985), *Tenderly*

(1986). Further reading: *In The Mood For Stardom: The Nolans*, Kim Treasurer.

Nolen, Jimmy

b. 3 April 1934, Oklahoma City, Oklahoma, USA, d. 18 December 1983, Atlanta, Georgia, USA. The inventor of the 'Chicken Scratch' and thus the father of funk guitar, Nolen was the archetypal sideman who also had a fitful solo recording career. After learning the violin, he took up the guitar at 14, inspired by **T-Bone Walker**. Singer Jimmy Wilson saw him in a Tulsa club and brought him back to Los Angeles, where Nolen began his recording career backing trumpeter Monte Easter and **Chuck Higgins**, and under his own name for John Fullbright's Elko label. In the autumn of 1956, he recorded three sessions for Federal, from which six singles were released to little effect. During this time, he also worked with **Johnny Otis**, playing on many sessions for Otis' Dig label and recording some sides of his own. He remained with Otis for a couple of years and played on 'Ma, He's Making Eyes At Me' and 'Willie And The Hand Jive'. In 1959, Nolen signed with **Specialty** subsidiary, Fidelity, from which just one single emerged. Much of the early 60s he spent backing harmonica player **George Smith** before joining **James Brown**'s band, where in February 1965 his guitar licks became the defining element of 'Papa's Got A Brand New Bag'. Apart from a two-year break between 1970 and 1972, Nolen remained with Brown for the rest of his career, which ended suddenly with a fatal heart attack while the band was in Atlanta, Georgia.

Album: with Pete 'Guitar' Lewis, Cal Green *Scratchin'* (Charly 1991). Compilations: *Mr Fullbright's Blues* (P-Vine 1977), *Blues Guitar Blasters* (Ace 1988), *Dapper Cats, Groovy Tunes & Hot Guitars* (Ace 1992), *Elko Blues Vol. 1* (Wolf 1995).

Nomad

Band whose press largely revolved around two facts. First their vocalist, Sharon Dee Clarke (b. c.1965), was formerly the black nurse in Dennis Potter's *The Singing Detective* UK television programme. She was also filmed in the bed next to Michelle when the latter was giving birth in *Eastenders*. Secondly, their single, 'Devotion', comprised samples from the British Poll Tax Riots and even transferred one of Thatcher's more rabid outbursts onto tape. It was also a huge hit, reaching number 2 in the charts and becoming the biggest dance single of 1991 in the process. It was co-written and produced by future **Undercover** producer Steve Mac. The other personnel in the band were rapper MC Mikee Freedom (b. c.1969, Bristol, England) and Damon Rochefort (b. c.1965, Cardiff, Wales). Freedom was discovered by former law student Rochefort while rapping on a song entitled 'Love Don't Live Here Anymore' by Fresh Connection. Rochefort himself had worked with Clarke on the FPI Project's 1990 hit, 'Going Back To My Roots'. Unfortunately their debut album was thin on original songs, comprising three versions of 'Devotion', while elsewhere formulaic Euro dance pop held sway. Though the follow-up single, 'Just A Groove', made the Top 20, subsequent efforts ('Something Special' - originally recorded by Clarke solo for a compilation album, 'Your Love Is Lifting Me' and '24 Hours A Day') failed to replicate their original success. Rochefort also embarked on a side project, Serious Rope, again featuring Clarke, who scored a 1993 hit with 'Happiness', recorded as a tribute to the Flesh club in Manchester. Freedom would go on to a solo career with TEK, beginning with 'Set You Free' for Dave Pearce's Reachin' label.

Album: *Changing Cabins* (Rumour 1991).

Nomi, Klaus

b. 1945, Berlin, Germany, d. 6 August 1983, New York, USA. Famed for his Mephistophelean make up and piercing tenor voice, Nomi claimed erroneously to have worked in the 70s as both a professional opera singer and as **David Bowie**'s dresser. By 1979 he was touring in Europe and the USA as a highly idiosyncratic cabaret act, performing barely recognisable, electronic reworkings of everything from Saint Saens' 'Samson And Delilah' and **Donna Summer**'s 'I Feel Love' to **Chubby Checker**'s 'The Twist'. In 1980 he signed to **RCA** and released a version of **Elvis Presley**'s 'Can't Help Falling In Love' as a single. He worked with Man Parrish, the New York electro and hi-NRG producer, on his self-titled debut album. Nomi was well received in the US, which precipitated a move to New York. He became a regular guest on *Saturday Night Live* and starred in the film *Urgh! A Music War*. In England his openness about his own homosexuality and outrageous dress sense alligned him with the New Romantic movement. He seemed to be playing upon his goofball appeal with American audiences on his second album, *Simple Man*, which included a version of 'Ding Dong The Witch Is Dead' from the musical *The Wizard Of Oz*. The record closed with Purcell's 'Death' leading into an arrangement of John Dowland's 'If My Complaints' - an oblique and moving eulogy to the first victims of Aids. The disease took his own life the following year, Nomi was one of the first celebrity victims of the disease. Two posthumous compilation albums have been released, and a recording of one of his early concert performances appeared in the USA.

Albums: *Klaus Nomi* (1981), *Simple Man* (1982), *Encore* (1984), *In Concert* (1986), *Collection* (1990).

Nookie

In 1994 Nookie (b. Gavin Chung, c.1971) arrived from Hitchin in Hertfordshire at the forefront of the new

jungle movement sweeping through the UK's dance scene. Singles like 'Only You' (1994) and 'The Sound Of Music' (1995) attempted to add spiritual resonance to the drum and bass formula, and added keyboard, piano and vocals to crunching rhythms and breakbeats. Nookie had served a long apprenticeship in jungle and its two main antecedents, hardcore and reggae. Aged 17 he made his vinyl debut, remixing Flourgon and Ninjaman's ragga track 'Zig It Up', as a member of the hip hop crew Main Attraction. His first release under his own steam (as 2 Boasters) was 'Large Southend Donut', which revealed his stylistic hallmarks of piano melding into a rhythmic onslaught. As well as Nookie, Chung also records under the name Cloud Nine for the highly-regarded hardcore stable **Moving Shadow**. He runs his own record shop, Parliament, in Hitchin and runs his own label, Daddy Armshouse, with partner Pedro, as well doing a lot of remixing.
Album: *The Sound Of Music* (Reinforced 1995).

Noone, Jimmie

b. 23 April 1895, Cut Off, Louisiana, USA, d. 19 April 1944. One of numerous students of Lorenzo Tio, Noone turned to the clarinet after first playing guitar. In the years immediately prior to World War I he played in bands led by notable New Orleans musicians such as **Freddie Keppard** and **Buddy Petit**. In 1918 he worked with **Joe 'King' Oliver** in Chicago and two years later was with Doc Cooke, remaining there for five years. In 1926 Noone took his own band into Chicago's Apex Club, thus beginning a remarkable period of sustained creativity during which he became the idol of countless up-and-coming young musicians, black and white, clarinettists and all. During part of its existence, the Apex Club band included **Earl 'Fatha' Hines**. Noone had made records during his stints with Oliver and Cooke, but now embarked on another series of recordings, including his theme, 'Sweet Lorraine', which remain classics of their kind. In the early 40s he moved to Los Angeles where he worked with **Kid Ory**, led his own band and appeared as a member of the New Orleans All Stars on Orson Welles's weekly radio show, as well as playing with the Capitol Jazzmen. Noone appeared well poised to capitalize upon the upsurge of interest in traditional music heralded by the Revival movement, but he died suddenly in April 1944. One of the most important of the New Orleans clarinettists, he had a remarkable technique and exercised full control of his instrument. Playing with a deep appreciation of the blues, his records stand as significant milestones in the history of jazz. His son, Jimmie Noone Jnr. (1938-1991), also played clarinet and from the 80s enjoyed a successful international career.
Selected compilations: *Jimmie Noone And His Apex Club Orchestra Vol. 1* (1979), *Jimmie Noone (1931-40)* (Queendisc 1981), *King Of New Orleans* (Jazz Bird 1982), *With The Apex Club Orchestra 1928* (Swaggie 1992), *Collection Vol 1* (Collectors Classics 1992), *The Complete Recordings Vol 1* (Affinity 1992).

Noone, Peter

b. Peter Blair Dennis Bernard Noone, 5 November 1947, Manchester, England. After studying singing at the Manchester School of Music and Drama, the teenage Noone won a part in the television series *Coronation Street*. After taking up piano and guitar he talked his way into the Heartbeats, which later became **Herman's Hermits**. In the Herman guise, Noone scored a series of million-selling singles in the 60s before finally launching a solo career in 1970. A cover of **David Bowie's** 'Oh You Pretty Things' made the UK Top 10, but subsequent releases were largely ignored. By 1980 he was fronting a more contemporary-sounding group, the Tremblers, but in spite of his change of image, no hits were forthcoming. Two years later he reverted to his original career, taking an acting role in *The Pirates Of Penzance*. He subsequently moved to the USA where he hosts a music television show
Film: *Hold On* (1965).

Nordenstam, Stina

b. 1969, Stockholm, Sweden. Nordenstam came to music early through the jazz records and amateur playing of her father. She took to the fiddle and piano, and precociously began writing her own classically inspired compositions. At 15 she was singing modern classical music, but her next move, backed by the Flippermen learned towards jazz. Signed up by Swedish indie label Telegraph, she debuted with *Memories Of A Colour*, an ethereally evocative and occasionally disturbing journey through her psyche, setting her short story songs or vignettes to impeccably skewed jazzy arrangements. This soared to such Scandinavian success that the next opening of the Swedish parliament was accompanied by a rare Nordenstam gig. The oft-heard comparisons with **Kate Bush** and **Joni Mitchell**, whom she admires, are misleading. Nordenstam had taken her early passions (**Cannonball Adderley**, **Erik Satie**, **John Coltane** and **Bartok**), fused them with post-feminist angst and sang the results in a spooky *Village Of The Damned* little girl whisper. 1994's *And She Closed Her Eyes* was more of the same but better, tending towards ambient jazz with contributions from **Jon Hassell** and more guitar from Nordenstam.
Albums: *Memories Of A Colour* (Telegram 1992), *And She Closed Her Eyes* (Telegram 1994).

Norma Jean

b. Norma Jean Beasley, 31 January 1938, near Wellston, Oklahoma, USA. Norma Jean showed an early interest in singing and after the family relocated to Oklahoma City, when she was five years old, she was given guitar tuition by an aunt. At the age of 13 she had her own thrice-weekly show on KLPR and in 1958, after working with several other artists including **Leon McAuliffe**, she became a regular on **Red Foley**'s *Ozark Jubilee* television show, where she first dropped her surname and where her melodic singing soon attracted nationwide attention. In 1960 she moved to Nashville and became the featured vocalist with **Porter Wagoner** on both his network television show and also on the *Grand Ole Opry*. She recorded for **Columbia** in the early 60s but she did not gain her first US country chart success, 'Let's Go All The Way', until 1964, by which time she had joined **RCA**. (The Columbia material is contained on her only Columbia album, *Country's Favorite*; released in 1966 on their Harmony subsidiary, it is now highly sought after by collectors.) Further hits followed, including country Top 10's with 'Go Cat Go' and 'I Wouldn't Buy A Used Car From Him' and a Top 5 recording of 'The Game Of Triangles' with **Bobby Bare** and **Liz Anderson**. Equally at home with up-tempo songs such as 'Truck Driving Woman', country monologues like 'Old Doc Brown' or a country weepy on the lines of 'There Won't Be Any Patches In Heaven', she built up a considerable reputation. She married in 1967 and left Wagoner's show and though she continued to record regularly into the early 70s, she cut out most of her public appearances to concentrate on her home - a 1000 acre farm near Oklahoma City. (Wagoner filled the vacancy with a young girl called **Dolly Parton**). She recorded in the 80s and at the time of writing, her last chart entry was a very minor hit in 1982, with a duet recording with **Claude Gray** of her first hit 'Let's Go All The Way'.

Albums: *The Porter Wagoner Show (With Norma Jean)* (1963), *Porter Wagoner In Person (with Norma Jean)* (1964), *Let's Go All The Way* (1964), *Pretty Miss Norma Jean* (1965), *Country's Favorite* (1966), with Wagoner *Live On The Road* (1966), *A Tribute To Kitty Wells* (1966), *Please Don't Hurt Me* (1966), *Sings Porter Wagoner* (1967), *Jackson Ain't A Very Big Town* (1967), with Bobby Bare, Liz Anderson *The Game Of Triangles* (1967), *The Body And Mind* (1968), *Heaven Help The Working Girl* (1968), *Heaven's Just A Prayer Away* (1968), *Love's A Woman's Job* (1968), *Country Giants* (1969), *It's Time For Norma Jean* (1970), *Another Man Loved Me Last Night* (1970), *Norma Jean* (1971), *Sings Hank Cochran Songs* (1971), *It Wasn't God Who Made Honky Tonk Angels* (1971), *I Guess That Comes From Being Poor* (1972), *Thank You For Loving Me* (1972), *The Only Way To Hold Your Man* (1973), *Norma Jean* (1978).

Norman, Jimmy

b. 12 August 1937, Nashville, Tennessee, USA. Norman is one of those talented and ubiquitous R&B performers who has made a modest but memorable impact on the music scene. His first professional experience was as a member of the Los Angeles group, the Chargers, who recorded a couple of doo-wop records for **RCA** during 1958-59. The Chargers broke up in 1959 and Norman began recording as a solo act under producer H.B. Barnum. In 1960 he and Barnum in an *ad hoc* group called the Dyna-Sores recorded a successful cover of the **Hollywood Argyles**' song 'Alley Oop', and their version made it to number 59 on the pop charts. Norman solo career then took off when he scored regionally with the haunting 'Here Comes The Night' in 1961. The following year he reached the national charts with the memorable New Orleans-style 'I Don't Love You No More' (number 21 R&B, number 47 pop). Nothing else he did came close, but his delightful 'Love Is Wonderful' was an east coast hit in 1963. Norman had one other national chart record, 'Can You Blame Me' (number 35 R&B) in 1966. In the 70s and 80s Norman performed as a member of the Cornell Gunther-led **Coasters** group, one of several competing on the revival circuit during that time. In the early 70s Norman recorded several singles for this Coasters group on the Turntable label, and made some records as lead singer in **Eddie Palmieri**'s Latin-R&B fusion group, the Harlem River Drive. In 1975 Norman returned to solo recording, releasing some singles for **Buddah**. Norman recorded his first album in 1987 for the tiny Badcat label.

Album: *Home* (Badcat 1987).

North, Alex

b. 4 December 1910, Chester, Pennsylvania, USA, d. 8 September 1991, Pacific Palisades, California, USA. An important composer for films, theatre, television, ballet and classical music, whose career ranged from the late 30s through to the 80s. After studying at Juilliard with the distinguished composer Aaron Copland, as well as at the Moscow Conservatory (1933-35), North composed for the Federal Theatre Project in the late 30s. During those years, through to 1950, he wrote the scores for government documentary and information films, and served in the US Army in World War II. In 1948 he composed the incidental score for Arthur Miller's landmark play, *Death Of A Salesman* on Broadway, and repeated the role for the film version in 1951. For that, and for his innovative jazz-tinged score to *A Streetcar Named Desire* (1951), he gained the first two of his 15 Academy Award nominations. Other early 50s film music included *The 13th Letter*, *Viva Zapata!* (considered an early milestone in his career), *Les Miserables*, the ballet music for **Fred Astaire** and **Leslie Caron** in ***Daddy Long Legs***, and *Unchained* (1955). The last film contained 'Unchained Melody' (lyric by **Hy Zaret**), a ballad of yearning which was nominated for an Academy Award, and became popular at the time for **Les Baxter** (US number 1), **Al Hibbler**, and **Jimmy Young** (UK number 1), amongst others, and through the years was constantly remembered and revived. The **Righteous Brothers**' 1965 smash-hit version accompanied an erotic scene in the popular 1990 movie *Ghost*, and in 1995 the song topped the UK chart once again in a version by Robson Green and Jerome Flynn, two actors from the popular television series *Soldier, Soldier*. North's other 50s scores included *The Man With The Gun* (1955), *I'll Cry Tomorrow* (1955), *The Rose Tattoo* (1955), *The Bad Seed* (1956), *The Rainmaker* (1956), *Four Girls In Town* (1956), *The King And Four Queens* (1956), *The Bachelor Party* (1957), *The Long Hot Summer* (1958), *Stage Struck* (1958), *Hot Spell* (1958), *The Sound And The Fury* (1959) and *The Wonderful Country* (1959).

Early in the 60s North began an association with director John Huston which lasted until Huston's death in 1987. Together they worked on such films as *The Misfits* (1961), *Wise Blood* (1979), *Under The Volcano* (1984), *Prizzi's Honor* (1985) and *The Dead* (1987), Huston's Swan-song. North's 60s film work began with the epic *Spartacus* ('magnificent score, staggering battle scenes'), followed, in complete contrast, by *The Children's Hour*. His other scores of the decade included another epic, *Cleopatra*, John Ford's *Cheyenne Autumn*, *The Agony And The Ecstasy*, *Who's Afraid Of Virginia Woolf?*, *The Shoes Of The Fisherman*, *Hard Contract*, and *A Dream Of Kings*. In the 70s, as his kind of spectacular, dramatic scores went out of style, North worked less for the big screen. However, in the later years he composed the music for movies such as *Pocket Money*, *Once Upon A Scoundrel*, *Bite The Bullet*, and *Somebody Killed Her Husband*. In the 80s, besides his collaborations with Huston, North was still being critically acclaimed for scores such as *Carny*, *Dragonslayer*, *Under The Volcano*, *Good Morning Vietnam*, and his final film, *The Penitent* (1988). In 1986 he became the first composer to receive an honorary Academy Award 'in recognition of his brilliant artistry in the creation of memorable music for a host of distinguished motion pictures'. He died, five years later, in 1991. As well as films, his occasional television work included the feature documentary, *Africa* (1967), music for the mini-series *The Word* which was nominated for an Emmy, and *Rich Man, Poor Man*, which won two; the telefeature, *Death Of A Salesman* (again), and music for other programmes, such as *Your Show Of Shows*, *77 Sunset Strip*, *Playhouse 90* and *The F.D.R. Story*. Many of his scores were made available on albums, and several individual items such as the title themes from *I'll Cry Tomorrow* and *The Long Hot Summer*, and 'Unchained Melody', of course, endure.

North, Freddie

b. 28 May 1939, Nashville,Tennessee, USA. In the mid-50s the soulful singer formed the Rookies, who recorded 'Money, Money, Money' on Federal. North later became a demo singer (often singing country songs) for a Nashville publisher. In 1959, under later hit producer **Billy Sherrill**, he had a single on **Sam Phillips**' Phillips label. North's record 'Okay, So What' on University in 1960 led to his appearing on *Bandstand* but no hit resulted. In 1962 he moved to **Capitol** and two years later recorded on Ric Records. In the mid-60s he joined Nashboro working in their stockroom. This led to his recording on their A-Bet label in 1968 where he released his debut *The Magnetic North*. In 1970 he moved to the Nashboro-distributed Mankind label and, produced by owner producer/songwriter Jerry Williams Jnr. (aka **Swamp Dogg** and Raw Spitt), had his first and biggest hit 'She's All I Got', a R&B Top 10 hit that made the US Top 40 in 1971. A year later, while working as Nashboro's national director of promotion, he had his second and last charter with 'You And Me Together Forever'.

Albums: *The Magnetic North* (A-Bet 1968), *Friend* (Mankind 1972), *Cuss The Wind* (Nashboro 1974), *I'm Your Man* (Broadway Sounds 1977). Compilation: *I'm Your Man* (Charly R&B 1989).

Northcott, Tom

b. 1943, Vancouver, Canada. Northcott began his career as a folksinger but embraced pop on hearing the **Beatles**. By 1964 he was starring on television's *Let's Go*, the houseband of which, the Vancouver Playboys, supported the singer on his debut single, 'She Loves Me, She Loves Me Not'. The following year later he established his own record label, New Syndrome. This outlet not only featured his group the Tom Northcott Trio (Northcott (guitar/vocals), Rick Enns (bass) and Mike 'Kat' Hendrikse (drums), but also early releases by the CFUN Classics, later known as the **Collectors**. His trio completed three vibrant singles, including the dazzling 'Just Don't', before Northcott opted for a solo career, having aligned New Syndrome to **Warner Brothers Records**. His first release for the label, a haunting version of **Donovan**'s 'Sunny Goodge Street' was succeeded by **Nilsson**'s '1941'. **Leon Russell** arranged the latter single, and its follow-up, 'Girl From The North Country', before **Jack Nitszche** assumed control for 'The Rainmaker'. Its expansive production cost in excess of $60,000, yet the anticipated hit failed to materialise. *The Best Of Tom Northcott* ensued, which collected several of these tracks, fleshing them out with material Northcott recorded with Canadian group Spring. In 1970 the singer switched to the UNI label. Although his original composition, 'Crazy Jane', was issued as a single, Northcott continued to rely on other songwriters, including **Carole King**, **Leonard Cohen** and **Randy Newman**. He retired from music in 1973, phasing our New Syndrome and selling his home-based Studio 3. Occasional demos aside, Northcott has preferred to study marine law.

Albums: *The Best Of Tom Northcott* (Warners 1969), *Upside Down* (UNI 1971). Compilation: *The Best Of Tom*

Northcott 1964 - 1971 (Neptoon 1987).

Northside

This UK independent label dance music band was formed in mid-1989 in Manchester by Warren 'Dermo' Dermody (vocals), Cliff Ogier (bass), Timmy Walsh (guitar) and Paul Walsh (drums). After signing to the premier Manchester independent, **Factory Records**, they released two singles in 1990, 'Shall We Take A Trip' and 'Rising Star', which benefited from the 'Madchester' explosion brought about by the success of label mates **Happy Mondays**. Pilloried in the press as being an opportunistic 'baggy' band, these releases and an attendant album did little to persuade critics of any real significance to their shambolic dance shuffles.

Album: *Chicken Rhythms* (Factory 1991).

Norum, John

Norum was formerly guitarist for the Swedish band **Europe** but quit just as the band were on the verge of worldwide recognition with 'The Final Countdown'. After completing the recording of the *Countdown* album, he decided to break ranks because he was unhappy with the pop-metal direction that vocalist Joey Tempest was intent on pursuing. Turning to a solo career, he enlisted the help of Marcel Jacob (bass; ex-**Yngwie Malmsteen**), Peter Hermansson (drums; ex-220 Volts) and Goran Edman (vocals; ex-Madison) to record *Total Control* in 1987. Musically this followed a similar path to that of his former employers, but featured more prominent rock guitar work and less polished vocals. Following the release of a live album and a collaboration with Don **Dokken,** he moved to Los Angeles to work on sessions with Glenn Hughes (ex-**Trapeze**, **Deep Purple**) which became *Face The Truth.*

Albums: *Total Control* (CBS 1987), *Live In Stockholm* (CBS 1988), *Face The Truth* (Epic 1992).

Norum, Tone

Tone is the younger sister of former **Europe** guitarist, **John Norum**. She debuted in 1986 with *One Of A Kind*, an album written, arranged and played on by Joey Tempest (also of Europe) and her brother. Predictably, the musical direction was very close to that of her sibling's concern; melodic pop-metal, with the occasional power ballad. *This Time* followed a similar pattern, but used session musicians and the Billy Steinberg/Tom Kelly writing team who had previously penned hits for **Madonna** and **Whitney Houston**. The result was a highly polished melodic rock album in the style of **Heart** and **Starship**. *Red* saw Tone move away from AOR towards folk-rock.

Albums: *One Of A Kind* (Epic 1986), *This Time* (Epic 1988), *Red* (Epic 1989).

Norvo, Red

b. Kenneth Norville, 31 March 1908, Beardstown, Illinois, USA. After playing in a marimba band, Norvo was hired by **Paul Whiteman** in the late 20s. With this band he played xylophone and was called upon largely to deliver novelty effects. While with Whiteman he met and married one of the band's singers, **Mildred Bailey**; in 1933 they went to New York and embarked upon a career which culminated with them being billed as 'Mr and Mrs Swing'. During the 30s Norvo played and recorded with many leading jazz musicians of the day and remained in demand into the mid-40s, at which time he joined **Benny Goodman** and switched to vibraphone. During the 40s Norvo worked with leading bop musicians such as **Dizzy Gillespie** and **Charlie Parker**, and in 1945 became a member of **Woody Herman**'s First Herd. In the early 50s he was resident in California (his marriage to Bailey had ended in 1945), working in a trio he formed with **Tal Farlow** and **Charles Mingus**. He continued to play throughout the 60s and on into the mid-70s, when he decided to retire. This decision proved to be only temporary and the 80s saw him engaged in a series of worldwide tours as a solo artist, performing with **Benny Carter**, and in a reunion with Farlow. Norvo's vibraphone style retains the sound and feel of his earlier xylophone work, a fact which ensures a rhythmic urgency to much of his playing and which might well be the motive behind his long-standing preference for working in groups without a drummer. The assurance with which he incorporated bop phrasing into his work makes him unusual among musicians of his generation and brings an added quality to his work which ensures that it is always interesting and exploratory.

Selected albums: *Time In His Hands* (1945), *Red Norvo's Nine* (1945), *The Red Norvo Septet* i (1947), *The Red Norvo Trio* i (c.1949-50), *The Red Norvo Trio* ii (1950), *The Red Norvo Trio* iii (1953), *The Red Norvo Trio* iv (1953), *The Red Norvo Trio* v (1954), *The Red Norvo Trio* vi (1955), *The Red Norvo Trio* vii (1955), *The Red Norvo Septet* ii (1956), *The Red Norvo Quartet* (1956), *The Red Norvo Sextet* (1957), *Music To Listen To* (1957), *Norvo - Naturally!* (1957), *The Forward Look* (Reference Recordings 1957), *Red Norvo And His Orchestra* (1958), *Sessions, Live* (1958), *The Red Norvo Septet* iii (1958), *Command Performance* (c.1959), *The Red Norvo Quintet* (1969), *Swing That Music* (Affinity 1969), *Vibes A La Red* (1975), *The Second Time Around* (1975), *Red In New York* (1977), *Live At Rick's Cafe Americain* (1978), with Ross Tompkins *Red & Ross* (1979), with Bucky Pizzarelli *Just Friends* (1983), with others *Swing Reunion* (1985), *Benny Carter All Stars* (1985). Compilations: *Red Norvo And His All Stars* (1933-38), *The Band Goes To Town* (1935), *Small Band Jazz* (1936-44), *Small Band Jazz: Rare Broadcasts* (1943).

Notations

An R&B vocal group from Chicago, Illinois, USA. Original members were Clifford Curry, LaSalle Matthews, Bobby Thomas, and Jimmy Stroud (replaced by Walter Jones in 1973). The Notations featured a delightful upbeat sound and made a modest impact during the 70s. The Notations came together in the late 60s and recorded unsuccessfully for a few local labels before achieving a hit nationally on the Twinight label with 'I'm Still Here' (number 26 R&B). They were signed by **Curtom Records** in 1975 to the company's Gemigo subsidiary and scored with 'It Only Hurts For A Little While' (number 27 R&B) and 'It's Alright (This Feeling)' (number 42 R&B). The Notations left Curtom in 1977, and three of the members - Curry, Matthews, and Thomas - made one more single, 'Judy Blue Eyes' for Mercury, before breaking up in 1978.

Album: *Notations* (Gemigo 1976).

Notes From The Underground

Based in Berkeley, California, USA, the NFTU were one of the region's first electric-folk bands. Fred Sokolow (b. 1945, Los Angeles, California, USA), an accomplished bluegrass musician, formed the group in 1965 with Mark Mandell (guitar), Joe Luke (drums) and David Gale. Mike O'Connor (bass) and Peter Ostwald (drums) replaced Gale and Luke while a pianist, Jim Work, also joined the unit prior to their recording debut, a privately-pressed EP. Work then left the line-up and his place was ultimately filled by Skip Rose. The quintet released their only album in 1968. *Notes From The Underground* was a remarkably eclectic set, featuring good-time music, jazz and Bay Area-styled interplay, but its disparate nature robbed the NFTU of any cohesion. The subsequent loss of several key members undermined their progress. In 1970 Sokolow and Mandell disbanded the group and re-emerged the following year with a new ensemble, Prince Bakaradi.

Album: *Notes From The Underground* (1968).

Noto, Sam

b. 17 April 1930, Buffalo, New York, USA. After playing trumpet in a number of leading 50s big bands, including that led by **Stan Kenton**, Noto worked in small groups until joining **Count Basie** for two spells in the mid- and late 60s. He then returned to small group format, co-leading a band with **Joe Romano**. After spending part of the 70s in show bands in Las Vegas, Noto moved to Canada where he worked with **Rob McConnell**, playing and arranging for the latter's big band. During the late 70s and throughout the 80s Noto played on the international festival circuit and also worked in clubs in his home town and in Canada. A fluent improviser, Noto's composing and arranging reveal an exceptional talent although his chosen locations for much of his best work has unwarrentedly kept him hidden from the attention of audiences.

Albums: *Entrance!* (Xanadu 1975), *Act One* (Xanadu 1975), with Rob McConnell *The Jazz Album* (1976), *Notes To You* (Xanadu 1977), *Noto-riety* (Xanadu 1978), *2-4-5* (Unisson 1988).

Notorious

This ill-fated pop-rock act seemed set to revive the careers of ex-**Diamond Head** singer Sean Harris and guitarist **Robin George**, but was aborted before it had a chance to get off the ground. With an expensively recorded debut for the relaunched Bronze label, with George contributing all instrumentation, the future seemed bright, but the duo were reluctant to recruit a touring band when pressed by the record company, as they viewed Notorious as a 'studio project'. The disagreement resulted in *Notorious* being deleted after only three weeks on release. The album itself was an under-rated effort, with **Robert Plant**'s solo work an obvious influence, and produced an excellent single in 'The Swalk'. Denied any real chance of success, the duo parted company, with Harris returning to a revived Diamond Head.

Album: *Notorious* (Bronze 1990).

Notting Hillbillies

On 31 May 1986, **Mark Knopfler** played a low key gig at the Grove pub in Holbeck, Leeds, with old friends Steve Phillips and **Brendan Croker**. They were billed as the Notting Hillbillies and each received the princely sum of £22 for their performance. Phillips first met Knopfler in 1968 when both interviewed a local blues and country guitarist (also called Steve Phillips) for the *Yorkshire Post*. As both journalists played guitar they formed the Duolian String Pickers duo and played together during the late 60s. They split when Knopfler went to university in 1970. When he finished studying three years later he went to London and eventually formed **Dire Straits**. Meanwhile, Phillips formed the Steve Phillips Juke Band to play rockabilly. In 1976 Bradford-born Croker met Phillips and when the Juke Band split they toured as Nev And Norriss. In 1980, Phillips temporarily retired from music to concentrate on art. Croker eventually got the 5 O'Clock Shadows together. In 1986 Knopfler, flushed with success through Dire Straits, decided the time was right to do something a little different and all three musicians came together. Dire Straits manager Ed Bicknell was recruited as drummer (he had previously played in Mogul Thrash) and with backing musicians like Guy Fletcher (guitar), Paul Franklin (pedal steel) and Marcus Cliff (bass, of the 5 O'Clock Shadows), they set out on a tour. They made just one album before returning to concentrate on their main bands.

Album: *Missing...Presumed Having A Good Time* (1990).

Nottingham, Jimmy

b. 15 December 1925, New York City, New York, USA. After a brief apprenticeship with **Cecil Payne**, trumpeter Nottingham served in the US Navy, where he was a member of a band directed by **Willie Smith**. After World War II, he joined **Lionel Hampton** and during the late 40s also worked in the big bands led by **Lucky Millinder** and **Charlie Barnet**. Then he joined **Count Basie**'s Orchestra, where he remained until 1950. In the 50s he played mostly in small groups and was also with bands specializing in Latin-American dance music. From the mid-50s until the mid-70s he was a staff musician with **CBS Records**, but continued to play jazz with artists such as **Dizzy Gillespie**, **Edgar Sampson**, **Quincy Jones** and **Benny Goodman**. From 1966 until the end of the decade, his Monday evenings were spent at the Village Vanguard as a member of the **Thad Jones-Mel Lewis** band. A powerful lead trumpeter with a searing high register, Nottingham's skill and versatility make him a notable member of any band in which he plays.

Albums: with Edgar Sampson *Swing Softly Sweet Sampson* (1956), with Thad Jones *Mel Lewis Live At The Village Vanguard* (1957), with Lionel Hampton *Newport Uproar!* (1967), with Jones-Lewis *Central Park North* (1969).

Nova Mob

(see **Hart, Grant**)

Nova, Aldo

b. Aldo Caparucio. Nova is a virtuoso guitarist of Italian descent. He arrived on the rock scene in 1982 with a self-titled debut of melodic AOR/pomp-rock that incorporated elements of **Boston** and **Styx**, with production offered by **Blue Öyster Cult**'s Sandy Pearlman. Momentum was lost however, with *Subject*, a disjointed and ultimately disappointing concept album. *Twitch* made amends somewhat, with a return to smooth, sophisticated and melody-conscious symphonic rock. Disillusioned by the lack of media response and complex legal wrangles and contractual commitments, he left the music business in 1985. After a near six-year break, he was lured back into the studio by his good friend, **Jon Bon Jovi** (having guested on the latter's *Blaze Of Glory* solo project). Together they wrote the material for *Blood On The Bricks*, a stunning collection of hard rock songs, saturated with infectious hooks and inspired guitar breaks. The album was well-received in the music press and drew comparisons with **Bryan Adams**, **Europe** and, naturally enough, Bon Jovi. It may prove the launching pad for the second phase of Aldo Nova's career.

Albums: *Aldo Nova* (Portrait 1982), *Subject: Aldo Nova* (Portrait 1983), *Twitch* (Portrait 1985), *Blood On The Bricks* (Polygram 1991).

Nova, Heather

b. 1968, Bermuda. Nova's early interest in music intensified when, aged 19, she moved to art school in Providence, Rhode Island. She did not join in with the local rock scene but wrote film music for her own films. Inspired by **Patti Smith** and **Lou Reed**, she soon started writing songs. A tape of her demos was sent to the indie Big Cat Records in London for whom she recorded a single, before supporting the **Violent Femmes** and **Bob Mould**. Basing herself in south London, she set up her own home studio, made further demos, and started working with Youth who became her producer for the 5,000-limited-edition *Glowstars*, which attracted favourable reviews. A raw live album, *Blow*, was recorded at The Mean Fiddler in early 1993 and released in October 1993. A European tour followed, and October 1994 brought the first full studio album, *Oyster*.

Albums: *Glowstars* (Butterfly 1993), *Blow* (Big Life 1993), *Oyster* (Big Life 1994).

Novamute

The dance/techno arm of **Mute Records** independent empire, launched in January 1992 with Mick Paterson (promotions, subsequently departed), Pepe Jansz (A&R) and Seth Hodder (production). Unlike many other established record companies trawling the backwaters of club music angling for financial reward, Mute had established its own tradition in commercial dance with **Depeche Mode** and **Erasure**, or more particularly **Renegade Soundwave** and **Nitzer Ebb**. They had also supported the fledgeling **Rhythm King** for several years, before that label branched out on its own in the 90s. The step to the burgeoning house/techno scenes was a natural one, particularly as the parent label had already released Exit 100's 1991 12-inch 'Liquid', the Underground Resistance mini-album *X101*, and licensed a Black Market compilation set. The original plan for Novamute then, was to license 12-inch white labels and imports and give them a proper release. In the US this was achieved via a distribution deal with independent rap label, **Tommy Boy**. Three compilations were crucial in establishing Novamute: *Tresor 1 (The Techno Sound Of Berlin* and *Tresor II (Berlin-Detroit: A Techno Alliance)* - from the Berlin based Tresor label, and *Probe Mission USA* - drawn from Canada's **Plus 8 Records**. Their roster of artists has grown to include **Moby**, **Richie Hawtin**/Plastikman, **3Phase**, **Juno Reactor**, Spirit Feel ('Forbidden Chant'), 3MB ('Jazz Is The Teacher'), Compufonic (aka **Hyper Go-Go**: 'Make It Move') and Doof ('Disposable Hymns To The Infinite').

Selected album: Various: *Version 1.1* (Novamute 1993).

Novello, Ivor

b. David Ivor Davies, 15 January 1893, Cardiff, Wales, d. 6 March 1951, London, England. A much-loved composer, lyricist, librettist and actor, Novello was born into a musical family, and was encouraged by his mother, a singing teacher. He soon became musically proficient, and quickly established a local reputation. That reputation spread throughout the UK with the publication of a song which encapsulated the feelings of many families torn apart by World War I. Setting to music a poem by the American Lena Guilbert-Ford, Novello's 'Keep The Home Fires Burning' (1915) was a huge popular success. He continued to write songs while serving in the Naval Air Service, but in 1919 turned mainly to acting and appeared in a number of silent films. With a classic profile that gained him matinee idol status amongst the film-going public, his screen career continued into the 30s, although he persisted in his desire to write for the stage. He contributed material to *Theodore & Co.* (1916) and *Arlette* (1917), before writing the music for *Tabs* (1918) and *Who's Hooper?* (1919). These were followed during the 20s by *The Golden Moth*, *Puppets*, *Our Nell*, and *The House That Jack Built* (1929), but real success eluded him until 1935 when he teamed up with lyricist Christopher Hassall for the hugely popular ***Glamorous Night*** ('Shine Through My Dreams', 'Fold Your Wings'), which was followed by equally lush and romantic productions such as ***Careless Rapture*** ('Love Made The Song', 'Why Is There Ever Goodbye?', 1936), *Crest Of The Wave* ('Rose Of England', 'The Haven Of Your Heart', 1937), ***The Dancing Years*** ('I Can Give You The Starlight', 'Primrose', 'Waltz Of My Heart', 'My Dearest Dear', 'My Life Belongs To You', 1939), ***Arc de Triomphe***, ('Man Of My Heart', 'Waking Or Sleeping', 1943), ***Perchance To Dream*** ('We'll Gather Lilacs', 'Love Is My Reason', 1945), and ***King's Rhapsody*** ('Someday My Heart Will Awake', 'Take Your Girl', 1949). His last show, ***Gay's The Word*** (lyrics by Alan Melville) in which **Cicely Courtneidge** introduced 'It's Bound To Be Right On The Night' and 'Vitality', opened in London in 1951, three weeks before Novello died. In a way, it lampooned the kind of lavish, brilliantly staged productions with which Novello had captured the imagination of London theatre audiences, and successfully challenged the ever-present American invasion. By customarily taking the non-singing romantic lead in several of his own productions, Novello also built an immense following with the female audience, despite the fact that in his private life he was homosexual. Apart from Hassall, who was the lyricist for six of his shows, Novello's other collaborators included **P. G. Wodehouse**, Clifford Grey, Harry Graham, Ronald Jeans, Howard Talbot, Dion Titheradge (especially for the song 'And Her Mother Came Too'), Adrian Ross, and Douglas Furber. In 1993, the centenary of his birth was marked by several celebratory shows around the UK, including one at the Players Theatre in London, and the tribute album, *Marilyn Hill Smith Sings Ivor Novello*, which contained 20 of his loveliest melodies.

Further reading: *Perchance To Dream: The World Of Ivor Novello*, Richard Rose. *Ivor Novello*, Sandy Wilson. *Ivor Novello: Man Of The Theatre*, Peter Noble.

Now Generation

One of the great unsung bands (or session teams) in the history of Jamaican music. Led by Geoffrey Chung on keyboards, the band included Mikey Chung on lead guitar, Val Douglas on bass, Mikey 'Boo' Richards on drums, Robert Lynn on keyboards and Earl 'Wire' Lindo on organ. They worked on sessions for all the top producers in the early 70s, including **Derrick Harriott**, **Herman Chin-Loy**, Ken Khouri, **Sonia Pottinger**, **Joe Gibbs** and some of the late **Duke Reid**'s reggae recordings. Their music was 'uptown' and soul influenced (they covered many soul classics), but they proved that they could provide raw roots records too - **Glen Brown**'s better work, or Herman's 'Aquarius Dub' being notable examples. Their tightness and all round panache distinguished them from other session bands at the time, but they have never, sadly, been quite as celebrated as other less skilful outfits - perhaps due to a lack of show and stage work. They certainly deserve much wider recognition.

Selected album: *For The Good Times* (Trojan 1974).

Nowherefast

This Californian melodic rock quartet was formed in 1981 by Steve Bock (vocals/bass) and Jeff Naideau (guitar/keyboards). Enlisting the services of Bob Frederickson (guitar) and Jimmy Hansen (drums), they soon struck a contract with the **WEA**/Scotti Brothers label. Incorporating elements of blues and funk into **Kansas** and **Journey**-like AOR, they delivered a self-titled debut in 1982. The album was unsuccessful and the band's name unfortunately proved a fair summation of the impact they had made.

Album: *Nowherefast* (Scotti Bros 1982).

NRBQ

Formed in Miami, Florida, USA, 1968, the origins of NRBQ (New Rhythm & Blues Quintet) were actually in Louisville, Kentucky a few years earlier. There, Terry Adams (keyboards) and Steve Ferguson (guitar) were members of a group called Merseybeats USA. Moving to Miami, the pair joined with New York musicians Frank Gadler (vocals) and Jody St. Nicholas (b. Joseph (Joey) Spampinato; bass/vocals), then working with a group named the Seven Of Us. Tom Staley (drums) completed the line-up and the group relocated to New Jersey. They were signed by

Columbia Records in New York and released their self-titled debut album in 1969. From the start NRBQ's music was an eclectic mix incorporating rockabilly, *avant garde* jazz, pop-rock, country, blues and novelty songs - their first album included songs by both early rocker **Eddie Cochran** and spacy-jazz musician **Sun Ra**. From the beginning and into the 90s, the group's live show included a large range of covers in addition to their own material - they claim a repertoire of thousands of songs. Humour marked both their recordings and concerts, where they would often grant audience requests to perform unlikely cover songs. Their second album, *Boppin' The Blues*, was a collaboration with rockabilly legend **Carl Perkins**. Like their debut, it was praised by critics but the group was dropped from Columbia. In the 70s they recorded for numerous labels, including Kama Sutra and **Mercury Records** before launching their own Red Rooster label in the late 70s.

Personnel changes during the 70s resulted in the group being trimmed to a quartet: Adams and Spampinato (reverting to his true name) remained from the original band, while guitarist Al Anderson, formerly of Connecticut's **Wildweeds**, joined in 1971; Tom Ardolino (drums) joined in 1974, since when the group has retained that line-up into the 90s. A good-time spirit and down-to-earth attitude towards performing marked NRBQ's live show, which could be unpredictable. The band recorded an album backing country singer **Skeeter Davis** (who later married Spampinato) and also the ex-**Lovin' Spoonful** singer **John Sebastian** in concert a number of times. For a while they were managed by a wrestling star, Captain Lou Albano, with whom they recorded a single. Spampinato appeared as a member of the houseband in the **Chuck Berry** concert film *Hail! Hail! Rock 'N' Roll* and Adams recorded with jazz artist **Carla Bley**. Anderson has released two solo albums. In 1989 NRBQ signed to **Virgin Records** and released *Wild Weekend,* their first album to chart since the 1969 debut.

Albums: *NRBQ* (1969), with Carl Perkins *Boppin' The Blues* (1970), *Scraps* (1972), *Workshop* (1973), *All Hopped Up* (1977), *At Yankee Stadium* (1978), *Kick Me Hard* (1979), *Tiddlywinks* (1980), *Tapdancin' Bats* (1983), *Grooves In Orbit* (1983), with Skeeter Davis *She Sings, They Play* (1985), *God Bless Us All* (1987), *Diggin' Uncle Q* (1988), *Wild Weekend* (1989), *Message For The Mess Age Forward* (Rhino 1994).

Nu Groove Records

Revered New York-based record label owned by Frank and Judy Russell but established in the public's mind and ears by house producers and twins Rheji and Ronnie Burrell, who had formerly recorded for **Virgin** subsidiary Ten as Burrell. It was originally created for them as 'an alternative outlet... because we had a lot of material that we were doing and we couldn't put it all out on Virgin', but went on to become their priority operation. The first record on the label was Tech Trax Inc's 'Feel The Luv' in August 1988, created by Rhji. Further early material arrived from Ronnie's Bas Noir project and Rheji's 'You Can't Run From My Love'. The original plan was to release a record by each brother every two weeks, and they have not fallen far short of that blistering schedule. Among their more successful vinyl expeditions have been 1989's 'It's Power House Brooklyn Style' - created by Powerhouse, aka **Masters At Work**, 1990's 'The Poem' and 'Rydims' (**Bobby Konders**) and Transphonic's 'Tune In Light Up' and 'Bug Out'. Most featured the keyboard talents of Peter Daou (formerly, and incredibly, a member of the Beirut Jazz Trio, where he grew up). Together with wife Vanessa he released 'Law Of Chants' and 'Part Two' (as Vandal). Rheji was also behind the *New York House N Authority* album (SBK 1990), a softer, more reflective affair. Another significant record from this time was 'Major Problem', an anti-drugs parody from Lennie Dee and Ralphie, which utilised samples from **Yello** and others. 1991 brought the *Metro* EP, a weighty, bass-driven house cut from Rheji, and Lost Entity's 'Bring That Back On'/'The Verge', which boasted the label's familiar deep soul feel. Other examples were Howie How and Little Carlos' 'Cause I Need You' (as the Divine Masters), the Vision's 'Laidback And Groovy', created by Eddie 'Satin' Maduro, and Transphonic ('Club Tools (Professional Use Only)'). 1992 brought Ize 2's 'House Trix' (a Isaac Santiago production). This was also the label which housed **Joey Negro**'s Mr Maize scam, when his club hit 'Together' was licensed to the US. When the single topped the dance charts journalists tried to hunt down the entirely fictional Mr Maize. Other notable appearances included **Victor Simonelli** (under the guise of Groove Committee) with 'Dirty Games', and the Houz Negroz 'How Do You Love A Black Woman', produced once more by the Burrell brothers. Tracing the Nu Groove discography remains an arduous but rewarding task for fans of class house music.

Nuclear Assault

Formed in New York, USA, in 1985, this extreme and influential group consisted of John Conelly (guitar/vocals), Anthony Bramante (guitar), Dan Lilker (bass) and Glenn Evans (drums). Lilker formed Nuclear Assault while still a member of **Anthrax**, making them one of the earliest thrash metal outfits. The sound of Nuclear Assault proved much more aggressive, however, merging the styles of hardcore and thrash with socially aware lyrics. Becoming popular through constant touring and a refusal to compromise in their recorded work, their audience built steadily throughout the 80s. Lilker, however, would quit the band in 1993 to concentrate on a new project, **Brutal Truth**.

Bramante was expelled around the same time, with the pair being replaced by Scott Metaxas and Dave DiPietro respectively, both formerly of **Prophet**. The transitional *Something Wicked* failed to provide any conclusive proof of artistic rejuvenation.

Albums: *Game Over* (Music For Nations 1986), *The Plague* (Music For Nations 1987), *Survive* (Music For Nations 1988), *Handle With Care* (Music For Nations 1989), *Out Of Order* (Music For Nations 1991), *Live At Hammersmith* (Music For Nations 1993), *Something Wicked* (Music For Nations 1993).

Video: *Radiation Sickness* (1988).

Nuclear Valdez

This unconventional AOR act were based in Miami, Florida, but drew from their ethnic origins for both musical and lyrical inspiration. Vocalist/guitarist Froilan Sosa's family originated in the Dominican Republic, while Jorge Barcala (lead guitar), Juan Diaz (bass) and Robert Slade LeMont (drums) are all of Cuban descent, and the band incorporated the Latin influences in their backgrounds to give an unusual and unique flavour to their sound. Lyrically, the band were not content with the AOR conventions of love and heartache, but explored themes closer to their collective heart, such as the Castro regime and the feelings of the Cuban exiles who long to return home, while their choice of band name with its clever ecological overtones served to confirm their more cerebral approach. *I Am I* established their characteristic rhythmic sound with classy guitar work from Barcala and passionate, smoky vocals from Sosa, and also produced a US hit with 'Summer'. *Dream Another Dream* confirmed their abilities with further strong material, but Nuclear Valdez remain a cult act.

Albums: *I Am I* (Epic 1990), *Dream Another Dream* (Epic 1992).

Nucleus

The doyen of British jazz-rock groups, Nucleus was formed in 1969 by trumpeter **Ian Carr**. He was joined by **Chris Spedding** (guitar, ex-**Battered Ornaments**), **John Marshall** (drums) and Karl Jenkins (keyboards). The quartet was signed to the distinctive progressive outlet, Vertigo, and their debut, *Elastic Rock*, is arguably their exemplary work. The same line-up completed *We'll Talk About It Later*, but Spedding's subsequent departure heralded a bewildering succession of changes which undermined the group's potential. Carr nonetheless remained its driving force, a factor reinforced when *Solar Plexus*, a collection the trumpeter had intended as a solo release, became the unit's third album. In 1972 both Jenkins and Marshall left the group to join fellow fusion act, **Soft Machine**, and Nucleus became an inadvertent nursery for this 'rival' ensemble. Later members **Roy Babbington** and **Alan Holdsworth** also defected, although Carr was able to maintain an individuality despite such damaging interruptions. Subsequent albums, however, lacked the innovatory purpose of those first releases and Nucleus was dissolved during the early 80s. Nucleus took the jazz/rock genre further into jazz territory with skill, melody and a tremendous standard of musicianship. Their first three albums are vital in any comprehensive rock or jazz collection.

Albums: *Elastic Rock* (1970), *We'll Talk About It later* (1970), *Solar Plexus* (1971), *Belladonna* (1972), *Labyrinth* (1973), *Roots* (1973), *Under The Sun* (1974), *Snake Hips Etcetera* (1975), *Direct Hits* (1976), *In Flagrante Delicto* (1978), *Out Of The Long Dark* (1979), *Awakening* (1980), *Live At The Theaterhaus* (1985).

Nudeswirl

This New Jersey, New York, USA, band was formed by guitarist/vocalist Shane M Greene and guitarist Diz Cortright with drummer Woody Newland and bassist Christopher Worgo, specialising in an indie guitar-driven heavy rock style which brought comparisons to acts as diverse as **Soundgarden**, **Nirvana**, the **Pixies** and **Trouble**. This was rather different to Greene and Cortright's occasional **They Might Be Giants** tribute band, known as They Might Be Vaginas, which played locally with Greene on vocals and accordion and Cortright on bass. Nudeswirl signed to Megaforce on the strength of chaotic live shows around the underground club circuit. *Nudeswirl* was a varied debut, with the band driving their weighty sound in a multitude of directions with unusual rhythms, with their use of **Gretsch** guitars lending the delivery a warm, earthy feel. However, the nuances of the album were rather lost in the live arena as the band toured Europe with **Mindfunk** and in the USA with **Flotsam And Jetsam** in addition to their own dates, producing some visually lifeless performances, and the band's future seems in doubt with the departure of Greene in mid-1994.

Album: *Nudeswirl* (Megaforce 1993).

Nudie

b. Nudie Cohen, 1902, Kiev, Russia, d. May 1984. The surname has also been given as Cohn but he is usually referred to as just 'Nudie'. His father was a bootmaker in the Russian army and as a boy he began to learn the trade of a tailor. Around 1911, because of Anti-Jewish purges in Russia, he and an elder brother emigrated to the USA, where they initially settled in Brooklyn. Around 1920, he began travelling around the USA, struggling to make a living. He had a brief and financially unrewarding career as a flyweight boxer, he appeared as a Hollywood film extra and did tailoring work in the costume department of Warner Brothers. In New York, he even worked on costumes for striptease acts. In the early 40s, in Los Angeles, he became friendly with country singer **Tex Williams** and persuaded Williams that he could make stage costumes for him and his band that would attract attention. Williams was delighted with the result, ordered further costumes and widely advertised their designer. The popularity of his suits quickly spread and soon other West Coast artist, especially singing cowboys such as **Gene Autry, Roy Rogers** and **Rex Allen** were wearing brightly coloured, rhinestone studded, Nudie creations. Nudie designed a 'free' suit, whose pattern included wagon wheels and cacti, for **Porter Wagoner**, then a struggling young hopeful. It was a very shrewd investment on Nudie's part. Wagoner, who continued to wear Nudie suits on the ***Grand Ole Opry*** for a great many years, became Nudie's best and longest running advert. The attraction soon passed on to other country singers and during the 40s and 50s, most of Nashville's major stars were dressed by Nudie. His first cowboy designs were mainly elaborately decorated western wear but for the country stars, he designed the clothes to, in some way, fit in with the individual as he had with the wagon wheels for Wagoner. **Hawkshaw Hawkins**' jacket had a large hawk on the back, **Ferlin Husky** had husky dogs and **Jimmy C. Newman** had alligators (after his hit 'Alligator Man'). **Hank Williams** regularly wore Nudie designed drape suits and was actually buried in one. Nudie also designed the stage costumes of **Bill Anderson** and his band and **Hank Snow**, another long time flamboyant dresser, regularly wore his rhinestone studded creations. It was Nudie who created the $10,000 gold lamé tuxedo worn by **Elvis Presley** and later the flashy suits worn by the **Flying Burrito Brothers**, which had marijuana leaves embroidered on them and stage costumes for the **Rolling Stones**. However, not all of his creations were so brightly coloured, since it was Nudie who was responsible for **Johnny Cash**'s Man in Black image. Nudie obviously became a wealthy man and his own suits usually attracted considerable interest as did his penchant for jewellery, which often saw him wearing $25,000 worth of gold. (He was once described as 'a caricature of an American cowboy drawn by an enraged Russian cartoonist'.) He was also noted for his famous white Pontiac convertible. The hood had giant Texas longhorn horn ornaments, while the interior contained patterned hand tool leather, with a silver saddle between the rear seats. There were 14 guns mounted in varying positions, which included Colt revolvers that worked as arm rests and door handles, gear lever and direction indicators and three rifles on the rear boot lid. The interior was decorated with hundreds of silver dollars, the front bumper had chrome quarter horses and the tape player could blast out a recording of a cattle stampede, whilst the horn played **Dale Evans** singing 'Happy Trails'. It seems that when they were going out together, Nudie's wife not surprisingly used to suggest that they took her car. Naturally, the car was stolen but the police obviously had little trouble finding it again. Later there were several other Nudie designed cars, which over the years have had several owners, including **Webb Pierce** and **Hank Williams Jnr**. Nudie died from natural causes in May 1984 but his wife continued to operate their store. Nudie who was once quoted as saying, 'If Tom Mix got out of his grave and saw my clothes, he'd get back in again,' was always proud of his achievements but never once forgot the early days of struggle. A reminder was the photograph sent to him by famous American strip artist, Lili St. Cyr, which she had autographed 'If I ever wear clothes, they'll be yours', which he proudly displayed in his store. For many years, clothes bearing a label that said 'Nudie's Rodeo Tailors, North Hollywood, California', were very much a status symbol to country artist. Nudie also played mandolin and apparently recorded an album featuring himself on that instrument but recording data is seemingly not readily available. (In 1974, Manual Cuevas, who had started to work for Nudie in the late 50s, left to form his own Manual's Western Wear in North Hollywood, from which he carried on the traditions of dressing film stars and singers, including **Dolly Parton** and **Dwight Yoakam**, in the styles that he had learned during his years with Nudie.)

Nugent, Ted

b. 13 December 1949, Detroit, Michigan, USA. Excited by 50s rock 'n' roll, Nugent taught himself the rudiments of guitar playing at the age of eight. As a teenager he played in the Royal Highboys and Lourds, but this formative period ended in 1964 upon his family's move to Chicago. Here, Nugent assembled the **Amboy Dukes**, which evolved from garage band status into a popular, hard rock attraction. He led the group throughout its various permutations, assuming increasing control as original members dropped out of the line-up. In 1974 a revitalized unit - dubbed Ted Nugent And The Amboy Dukes - completed the first of two albums for **Frank Zappa**'s DiscReet label, but in 1976 the guitarist abandoned the now-anachronistic suffix and embarked on a fully-fledged solo career. Derek St. Holmes (guitar), Rob Grange (bass) and Cliff Davies (drums) joined him for *Ted Nugent* and *Free For All*, both of which maintained the high-energy rock of previous incarnations. However, it was as a live attraction that Nugent made his mark - he often claimed to have played more gigs per annum than any other artist or group. Ear-piecing guitar work and vocals - 'If it's too loud you're too old' ran one tour motto - were accompanied by a cultivated 'wild man' image, where the artist would appear in loin-cloth and headband, brandishing the bow and arrow with which he claimed to hunt food for his family. Trapeze stunts, genuine guitar wizardry and a scarcely self-deprecating image ('If there had been blind people at the {my} show they would have walked away seeing') all added to the formidable Nugent persona. The aggression of a Nugent concert was captured on the platinum selling *Double Live Gonzo*, which featured many of his best-loved stage numbers, including 'Cat Scratch Fever', 'Motor City Madness' and the enduring 'Baby Please Don't Go'. Charlie Huhn (guitar) and John Sauter (bass) replaced St. Holmes and Grange for *Weekend Warriors*, and the same line-up remained intact for *State Of Shock* and *Scream Dream*. In 1981 Nugent undertook a worldwide tour fronting a new backing group, previously known as the D.C. Hawks, comprising of Mike Gardner (bass), Mark Gerhardt (drums) and three guitarists; Kurt, Rick and Verne Wagoner. The following year the artist left Epic for **Atlantic Records**, and in the process established a new unit which included erstwhile sidemen Derek St. Holmes (vocals) and **Carmine Appice** (drums; ex-**Vanilla Fudge**). Despite such changes, Nugent was either unwilling, or unable, to alter the formula which had served him so well in the 70s. Successive solo releases offered little new and the artist drew greater publicity for appearances on talk shows and celebrity events. In 1989 Nugent teamed up with **Tommy Shaw** (vocals/guitar; ex-**Styx**), Jack Blades (bass; ex-**Night Ranger**) and Michael Cartellone (drums) to form the successful 'supergroup', **Damn Yankees**.

Albums: *Ted Nugent* (Epic 1975), *Free For All* (Epic 1976), *Cat Scratch Fever* (Epic 1977), *Double Live Gonzo* (Epic 1978), *Weekend Warriors* (Epic 1978), *State Of Shock* (Epic 1979), *Scream Dream* (Epic 1980), *Intensities In Ten Cities* (Epic 1981), *Nugent* (Atlantic 1982), *Penetrator* (Atlantic 1984), *Little Miss Dangerous* (Atlantic 1986), *If You Can't Lick 'Em...Lick 'Em* (Atlantic 1988). Compilations: *Great Gonzos: The Best Of Ted Nugent* (Epic 1981), *Anthology: Ted Nugent* (Raw Power 1986).

Video: *Whiplash Bash* (1990).

Further reading: *The Legendary Ted Nugent*, Robert Holland.

Numan, Gary

b. Gary Anthony James Webb, 8 March 1958, Hammersmith, London, England. Originally appearing under the group name Tubeway Army, Numan enjoyed enormous success in the UK at the close of the 70s. His **Kraftwerk/David Bowie**-influenced electronic music saw Tubeway Army top the UK charts in May 1979 with 'Are Friends Electric?' By September 1979 Numan abandoned the group pseudonym for the follow-up single 'Cars' which also topped the UK charts and reached the US Top 10. At his peak, Numan was one of the bestselling artists in Britain and his albums *The Pleasure Principle* and *Telekon* both entered the charts at number 1. His science-fiction orientated lyrics and synthesizer-based rhythms brought further Top 10 successes with 'We Are Glass', 'I Die: You Die', 'She's Got Claws' and 'We Take Mystery (To Bed)'. As the decade progressed his record sales steadily declined and his glum-robotic persona was replaced by that debonair man-about-town who also enjoyed aviation. In March 1982 he attempted to fly around the world in his light aircraft and was arrested in India on suspicion of spying. The charge was later dropped. While his reputation among music critics atrophied amid accusations of anachronism, his fan base remained solid and his recordings continue to reach the lower placings in the UK charts.

Albums: as Tubeway Army *Tubeway Army* (1979), *Replicas* (1979), solo *The Pleasure Principle* (1979), *Telekon* (1980), *Living Ormanments 1979-80* (1981), *Dance* (1981), *I Assassin* (1982), *Warriors* (1983), *The Plan* (1984), *Berserker* (1984), *White Noise - Live* (1985), *The Fury* (1985), *Strange Charm* (1986), *Exhibition* (1987), *Metal Rhythm* (1988), *The Skin Mechanic* (1989), *Outland* (1991) *Machine And Soul* (1992), *Dream Corrosion* (Numa 1994). Compilations: *New Man Numan - The Best Of Gary Numan* (1982), *Document Series Presents* (1992).

Further reading: *Gary Numan By Computer*, Fred and Judy Vermorel. *Gary Numan: The Authorized Biography*, Ray Coleman.

Nunez, Alcide 'Yellow'

b. 17 March 1884, New Orleans, Louisiana, USA, d. 2 September 1934. One of his home town's most noted musicians, Nunez's career was dogged by bad luck and poor timing. After playing clarinet with several famous marching and brass bands, including Papa Laine's, Nunez visited Chicago, where he teamed up with **Nick La Rocca** and others to form a band. He fell out with La Rocca, however, and quit to work in vaudeville with a music and comedy act. Meanwhile, La Rocca and the band, calling themselves the **Original Dixieland Jazz Band**, went on to international fame and fortune. After working with obscure bands in Chicago, Nunez returned to New Orleans in 1927 and remained there for the rest of his life. Although an enormously skilled musician, Nunez displayed a penchant for the shrill, jokey, barnyard effects popular with audiences in the early years of this century. As a result, his few records have received attention more for their curiosity value than for their musical content.

Nunn, Bobby

b. Buffalo, New York, USA. Nunn made his initial funk recordings at home in the mid-70s, forming his own label to handle their distribution. The results impressed new **Motown** signing **Rick James**, who invited Nunn to play on his debut *Come Get It*. Bobby subsequently moved to Los Angeles, where he formed the dance band Splendor, who recorded one album for **CBS Records**. When this venture failed, Rick James arranged for him to sign with Motown in 1981. The label encouraged comparisons between the two singers, which were fulfilled by the suggestive lyrics and

rhythmic funk of Nunn's debut singles, 'She's Just A Groupie' and 'Got To Get Up On It'. A collaboration with **Tata Vega** on 'Hangin' Out At The Mall' was a dance hit in 1983, but this success was shortlived; Motown refused to issue the projected *Fresh*, and he was later dropped from the label.
Albums: *Second To Nunn* (1982), *Private Party* (1983).

Nunn, Gary P.

b. Austin, Texas, USA. Nunn is a singer/songwriter/guitarist who was living and working around Austin. He and some other musicians started working with the 70s progressive musician, **Jerry Jeff Walker,** and they eventually coalesced in the progressive country bands, the Lost Gonzo Band. The highspot of *Viva Terlingua!* in 1973 was when Walker generously allowed Nunn to take the lead vocals on his song about life on the road, 'London Homesick Blues'. It was also recorded by **David Allan Coe** and became the theme song for the long-running television series, *Austin City Limits*. The Lost Gonzo Band worked on four more albums with Jerry Jeff Walker and also recorded under their own name. Nunn himself was married to singer-songwriter, **Karen Brooks**, and their songs, 'Couldn't Do Nothin' Right' (Karen) and 'Kara Lee' (Gary), comment on their relationship. **Willie Nelson** has recorded his song, 'The Last Thing I Needed The First Thing This Morning'. Gary works with the Sons Of The Bunkhouse Band and he was reunited with Walker as part of the Gonzo Compadres on *Viva Luckenbach!* which included his lead vocal on 'What I Like About Texas'.
Albums: *Nobody But Me* (Turnrow 1980), *Home With The Armadillo* (Guacamole 1985), *Border States* (Dixie Frog 1988), *For Old Times Sake* (AO 1989).

Nunn, Trevor

b. 14 January 1940, Ipswich, Suffolk, England. Nunn was educated at Downing College, Cambridge, and in 1962 won an ABC Director's Scholarship to the Belgrade Theatre in Coventry where he produced a musical version of *Around The World In 80 Days*. In 1964 he joined the Royal Shakespeare Company, was made an associate director in 1965, and became the company's youngest-ever artistic director in 1968. He was responsible for the running of the RSC until he retired from the post in 1986. As well as his numerous productions for the RSC, he co-directed *Nicholas Nickleby* (winner of five **Tony Awards**), ***Peter Pan***, and ***Les Misérables***, which became one of the most-performed musicals in the world. Outside of the RSC he has directed the Tony Award-winning ***Cats***, along with other musicals including ***Starlight Express***, ***Chess***, ***The Baker's Wife***, and ***Porgy And Bess***, and operas such as *Cosi Fan Tutte* and *Peter Grimes*. He has also worked in television and directed several films including *Hedda* and *Lady Jane*. Nunn is credited, along with **Andrew Lloyd Webber** and the late poet T. S. Eliot, with the writing of 'Memory', the hit song from *Cats* which has been recorded by hundreds of artists. In 1992 he directed the RSC's highly acclaimed production of Pam Gems' musical play *The Blue Angel*, and a year later became the ninth recipient of the 'Mr. Abbott Award' given by the US Stage Directors and Choreographers Foundation. In the early 90s he was back with Lloyd Webber again, staging the London, Los Angeles and Broadway productions of ***Sunset Boulevard***. It was also reported that Nunn had decided to take a break from the theatre, and had signed a two year deal to produce films for the New Line Cinema studio.

Nuns

Formed in San Francisco, California, USA, in 1977, the Nuns were one of the city's leading punk/new wave attractions, forerunning the rock and outrage antics of the **Dead Kennedys**. Their insubstantial progress was further limited by continual line-up problems, but such frustrations coalesced to astonishing effect in their 'Savage'/'Suicide Child' single. Their work appeared on several compilations, including *Rodney On The Roq* and *Experiments In Destiny*, but having split up in 1979, they reformed the following year to complete *The Nuns*, only to disband again. Ritchie Detrick (vocals), Jeff Olener (vocals), Alejandro Escovado (guitar), Jennifer Miro (keyboards), Mike Varney (bass) and Jeff Raphael (drums) were among those passing through the Nuns' ranks, of whom Escavado subsequently joined **Rank And File**. The Nuns reformed again in 1986 to record a completely different record, the icy, dance-fixated *Rumania*.
Albums: *The Nuns* (Posh Boy 1980), *Rumania* (PVC 1986).

Nunsense

Originally presented at the Duplex nightspot in Greenwich Village in 1984, this spoof on the Catholic sisterhood - 'The Habit Forming Musical Comedy' - transferred to the Off Broadway Cherry Lane Theatre on 12 December 1985. It was the brainchild of Dan Goggin, who wrote the book (from an original libretto by Steve Hayes), music, and lyrics, and also staged it. The story concerns the efforts of the convent's five surviving nuns to raise money so that they can bury the last few of their 52 companions who died of botulism after having eaten a meal of vichysoise prepared by the convent chef, Sister Julia. The quintet are still around because they went out to bingo that night. Sister Julia is preparing a cook book containing some of her best recipes, (including barbecued spare-ribs) while the rest of the nuns decide to put on a musical so as to raise enough money to get rid of the bodies, thereby leaving more space in the deep-freeze. The energetic Mother Superior was played by comedienne Marilyn Farina, and the rest of a highly talented cast included Suzi Winston, Christine Anderson, Semina De Laurentis, and Vicki Belmonte. Among the lively and extremely relevant songs were 'Nunsense Is Habit-Forming', 'So You Want To Be A Nun', 'Tackle That Temptation', 'Growing Up A Catholic', 'I Want To Be A Star', 'Just A Coupl'a Sisters', 'I Could've Gone To Nashville', and 'Holier Than Thou'. The show ran and ran, and, in 1992, when it entered its eighth 'everlasting' year, was advertising itself as 'The longest-running show in Off-Broadway history'. But what about ***The Fantasticks***, which opened in 1960? An explanatory rider was attached which stated: '*The Fantasticks* is more than a show, it is an institution!'. In the early 90s, *Nunsense II: The Second Coming* was out of town on its way to New York, with the Mother Superior demanding more audience participation on numbers such 'Oh Dear, What Can The Matter Be', in which Franciscan nuns get locked in the lavatory.

Nussbaum, Adam

b. 29 November 1955, New York, USA. Nussbaum had initially learnt to play the piano and alto saxophone, then switched to studying drums with **Charlie Persip** and majoring in music at the Davis Centre, City College of New York. After freelancing in New York he played through the late 70s and 80s with the bands of **John Scofield**, **Dave Liebman**, **Stan Getz**, **Gil Evans**, **Randy Brecker**, **George Gruntz** and **Gary Burton**. Nussbaum has attained a wide knowledge of the history of jazz drumming. He has a bright, swinging style which he has been able to adapt to all these differing contexts.

Albums: with Dave Liebman *If Only They Knew* (1980), with John Scofield *Shinola* (1981), *Out Like A Light* (1981), with Bill Evans *Living On The Crest Of A Wave* (1983), with Gil Evans *Live At Sweet Basil* (1984).

Nutmegs

An R&B vocal group from New Haven, Connecticut, USA. Members were lead Leroy Griffin, first tenor James 'Sonny' Griffin, second tenor James Tyson, baritone Billy Emery, and bass Leroy McNeil. The group was formed in 1954. The Nutmegs are famed for just two records, 'Story Untold' (number 2 R&B) and the follow-up 'Ship Of Love' (number 13 R&B) both from 1955. The songs with their exotic warbling are a working definition of 'rockaballad', a valuable term of the era that helped define what vocal groups were about - the rock 'n' roll revolution. Most notable among the lesser songs are 'Whispering Sorrows', 'My Story', and the west coast-sounding 'My Sweet Dream'. Surviving less well in the Nutmegs canon were the rock 'n' roll jumps, which were mostly routine. The group after several years of declining fortunes and many personnel changes broke up in 1962. The Nutmegs were one of the cult groups of the east coast collecting scene, and during the early 60s **a cappella** practice versions of their songs launched a craze for a cappella doo-wop recordings. The group without lead Leroy Griffin (who died years earlier) worked the doo-wop revival circuit on the east coast during the 70s.

Compilations: *The Nutmegs Featuring Leroy Griffin* (Relic 1971, a collection of a cappella tracks), *Story Untold* (Relic 1993, a collection of studio tracks).

Nutz

This UK hard rock quintet was formed in 1973 by Dave Lloyd (vocals) and Mick Devonport (guitar). With the addition of Keith Mulholland (bass), Kenny Newton (keyboards) and John Mylett (drums), they gained a reputation as the ubiquitous support act. Playing competent, blues-based rock and boogie, their exuberant and high-energy live shows always overshadowed the drab and lifeless studio recordings. Their sexist album covers were typical of the genre, though less likely was Lloyd's contribution of a vocal to a *Crunchie* chocolate bar advertisement. Newton left to join **Nightwing** in 1978 while the band changed their name to **Rage** in a deliberate attempt to jump the **N.W.O.B.H.M.** bandwagon.

Albums: *Nutz* (A&M 1974), *Nutz Two* (A&M 1975), *Hard Nutz* (A&M 1976), *Live Cutz* (A&M 1977).

NWA

The initials stand for 'Niggers With Attitude' which was the perfect embodiment of this Los Angleles group's outlook. They comprised **Dr Dre** (b. Andre Young), DJ Yella (b. Antoine Carraby), **MC Ren** (b. Lorenzo Patterson) and **Eazy-E** (b. Eric Wright, 7 September 1973, Compton, California, USA, d. 26 March 1995, Los Angeles, California, USA). Founder member **Ice Cube** (b. Oshea Jackson, c.1970, South Central, Los Angeles, California, USA), arguably the most inspiring of the rapping crew, departed for a solo career after financial differences with the band's manager (which would later be recorded in a highly provocative song which attacked him for, amongst other things, being Jewish). However, all the band's members had long CV's: Dr Dre had DJ'd for **World Class Wreckin' Crew**, and had produced Ice Cube's first band, CIA. Both Eazy E and DJ Yella had recorded and produced several rap discs under their own names, the former funding his **Ruthless** label, allegedly, through illegal activities. Other early members of the posse included **Arabian Prince** and **D.O.C.** NWA's first single was 'Boyz N' The Hood', marking out their lyrical territory as guns, violence and 'bitches'. Though *N.W.A. And The Posse* was their debut album, they only performed four of the raps on it, and to all intents and purposes *Straight Outta Compton* counts as their first major release. For those attracted to the gangsta rappers first time round, this was more of the same only sharper and more succinct. A landmark release, in its aftermath rap became polarised into two distinct factions; traditional liberal (reflecting the ideas of Martin Luther King) and a black militancy redolent of Malcolm X, albeit much less focussed and reasoned. In 1989 the FBI investigated *Straight Outta Compton*'s infamous 'Fuck Tha Police', after which Cube left the group. It set a precedent for numerous actions against NWA, including the first time anyone in the music industry had received a threatening letter from the FBI. *Efil4zaggin* (Niggaz4life spelt backwards) which made US number 1, also topped the outrage factor of its predecessor by addressing gang rape and paedophilia, in addition to the established agenda of oral sex, cop killing and prostitution. Musically it contained furious blasts of raggamuffin and 70s funk, but that was somehow secondary. It did reveal some humour in the band; ie on 'Don't Drink That Wine' (which jokingly encourages drug abuse instead), or lines like; 'Why do I call meself a nigger, you ask me? Because my mouth is so muthafuckin' nasty, Bitch this bitch that nigger this nigger that, In the meanwhile my pockets are getting fat.' However, such wit was stretched paper thin over a clutch of expletives and obscenities. The UK government used the Obscene Publications Act to seize copies but were forced to return them following legal action. Ultimately the BPI withdrew their support from **Island** Marketing's successful action. Counsel for the defence was Geoffrey Robertson QC, who had played a similar role in the infamous *Oz* trial of 1971. Expert testimony from Wendy K of **Talkin' Loud Records**, rap author David Toop and psychologist Guy Cumberbatch of Aston University swung the case. This prompted a variety of statements from British MPs outlining their intention to toughen up the law. However, even the anti-censorship lobby must concede that NWA's by turns ludicrous ('Find 'Em Fuck 'Em And Flee') and dangerous ('To Kill A Hooker') songs have blurred the generally positive influence of the rap movement. As the decade progressed it became obvious that the remaining members of NWA were spending more time on their solo projects, Dr Dre in particular enjoying huge success both as an artist and producer. His acrimonious parting from Eazy-E over monies owed through Ruthless Records was celebrated in records by both artists. Yella has been quiet, co-production credits on Ruthlesss aside, while Ren released a disappointing solo ablum and EP.

Albums: *NWA And The Posse* (Ruthless 1987), *Straight Outta Compton* (Ruthless 1989), *Efil4zaggin'* (Ruthless 1991).

Nyame, E.K.

b. December 1927, Kwahu, Ghana, d. 19 January, 1977, Accra, Ghana. Along with **E.T. Mensah**, Nyame was one of the godfathers of modern Ghanaian highlife music. His particular contribution was the bringing together of rural 'palm wine' music typically performed by a vocalist accompanying himself on acoustic guitar, and played on street corners and in bars, and 'concert parties' - a peculiarly Ghanaian mixture of drama and music performed by touring troupes in villages across the country. Nyame's fusion of the two arts would be updated by bands like the **African Brothers** in the 60s and 70s. The music of the early concert parties was basically western ballroom music: foxtrots, quicksteps and ragtimes learnt from British Army marching bands and records played by European settlers. Nyame africanized the concert party by using palm wine-based music and rejecting English language lyrics and speech in favour of indigenous Ghanaian languages. A self-taught guitarist, Nyame joined his first band, Appiah Adjekum's Band, in 1948. In 1951 he left to form his own group, the Akan Trio, where he first combined palm wine music and the concert party. The innovation was an almost immediate success, and was adopted by countless other highlife bands. During the 50s Nyame recorded over 400 78 rpm discs for West African **Decca**, Queenaphone and **HMV** and through them built up a reputation throughout west Africa. He became President Nkrumah's favourite musician and accompanied him on many state visits (many of Nyame's songs and plays had supported Nkrumah and the independence movement during the final years of British colonial rule). When he died in 1977 Nyame's body was laid out on a golden bed and he was given a state funeral attended by an estimated 10,000 people.

Selected albums: *E.K.'s Favourites* (1963), *Famous E.K.* (1970), *Sankofa* (1974), *In Memory Of E.K.* (1981).

Nyman, Michael

b. 23 March 1944, London, England. A composer, pianist, orchestra leader, and author, Nyman studied at the London Academy of Music (of which he is a Fellow) and at King's College, London. To the public at large, he is probably best known for his music to Jane Campion's 1993 award-winning film, *The Piano*, and for the 18 'propulsively pounding' film scores he composed for the idiosyncratic director and screenwriter, Peter Greenaway. Most notable amongst these are *The Draughtsman's Contract* (1982), *A Zed And Two Noughts* (1985), *Drowning By Numbers* (1988), *The Cook, The Thief, His Wife And Her Lover* (1989), and *Prospero's Books* (1991). The two men parted after Nyman discovered that his original score for *Prospero's Books* had been overlayed with what he called 'awful phoney electronic music'. Nyman's film music is just a part of a prolific and extremely varied output which has consisted of several operas, (including *The Man Who Mistook His Wife For A Hat*), string quartets, a saxophone concerto ('Where The Bee Dances'), the libretto for Harrison Birtwhistle's dramatic pastoral, *Down By The Greenwoodside*, other classical works, and numerous commissions. He also collaborated on the Channel 4

film, *The Final Score*, in which he paid tribute to the game of football, and in particular to his own favourite club, Queen's Park Rangers. Nyman's score for *The Piano* received the Australian Film Institute Award for Best Original Music, was nominated for a Golden Globe Award, and won the first-ever Chicago Film Critics Award for Best Musical Score. Although the film was nominated for eight Oscars, Nyman's brilliant score was ignored. In 1995, London's South Bank Centre presented a celebratory festival, *Nyman On The South Bank*, which opened with an all-night showing of a number of films associated with him. It continued with performances by his various ensembles, which 'showed off the grandeur of Nyman's orchestral writing, the amplified power of the Michael Nyman Big Band, and the intimate delights of his chamber music'. Among the works performed at the festival were premieres of 'The Upside-Down Violin', with the Orquesta Andalusi de Tetuan from Morocco, Nyman's score for the film *Carrington*, as well as his 'Harpsichord Concerto' with Elisabeth Chojnacka, and 'Six Celan Songs', sung by Hilary Summers. His music, which effortlessly spans the pop/classical divide, has attracted great attention from concert-goers and critics alike, making him a unique figure in British contemporary music.
Selected albums: *Decay Music* (Obscure 1978), *Michael Nyman* (Sheet 1982), *The Kiss And Other Movements* (Editions EG 1987), *Michael Nyman: Box Set* (Venture 1989, 2-CD set), *And They Do/Zoo Caprices* (TER 1988), *The Essential Michael Nyman* (Argo/Decca 1992), *Time Will Pronounce* (Argo/Decca 1993), *The Piano* (Virgin 1993), *Michael Nyman Live* (Virgin 1995), and film soundtrack recordings.
Further reading: *Experimental Music: Cage And Beyond*, Michael Nyman.

Nymph Errant

A vehicle for the talented an glamorous **Gertrude Lawrence**, this show was unusual in that it was written specifically for the London stage by the celebrated American composer **Cole Porter**. It opened at the Adelphi Theatre on 6 October 1933, with book by Romney Brent which was based on James Laver's somewhat risqué novel. The story told of Evangeline Edwards (Gertrude Lawrence), who, after graduating from a Lausanne finishing school, travels around Europe in a fruitless, but amusing search for a man who will love her. Unsuitable candidates include a Russian violinist, a Greek slave trader and a Count of the Holy Roman Empire. The Adelphi's revolving stage was used to excellent effect by costume and set designer Doris Zinkeisen to conjure up stylish locations such as the Carnival at Venice, Athens by moonlight, and the stage of the Folies de Paris. **Elisabeth Welch** as Haidee Robinson, Austin Trevor as the French impresario André de Croissant, and Morton Selton in the role of a devilish rake, were all outstanding, but the evening belonged to Gertrude Lawrence. As usual, Porter's songs were both tuneful and witty, especially 'The Physician', in which Lawrence complained: 'He said my maxillaries were marvels/And found my sternum stunning to see/He did a double hurdle/When I shook my pelvic girdle/But he never said he loved me.' The rest of the songs, including 'It's Bad For Me', 'How Could We Be Wrong?, 'Nymph Errant', 'Solomon', and 'If You Like Les Belles Poitrines' were all of similarly high-class. The show was presented by impresario **Charles B. Cochran**, so it was inevitable that his 'Young Ladies' should turn up from time to time. Considering the quality of performers and the production, he must have been disappointed with a run of only 154 performances.

Nymphs

This band originated in the Los Angeles club scene around volatile vocalist Inger Lorre (b. Laurie Wenning), a former model from New Jersey, with a line-up which eventually stabilized with drummer Alex Kirst, guitarists jet freedom (who prefers to have his initials expressed in lower case) and Sam Merrick, completed by bassist Cliff D. The Nymphs signed to **Geffen** in 1989 bolstered by a wave of hype which suggested that the band were a female-fronted **Guns N'Roses** (in truth their sound owed more to **Lou Reed**, the **Stooges** and **Patti Smith**). A period of limbo ensued as the band fought to record a debut on their own terms. Tales of drug abuse, rehabilitation and mental hospitals escalated as the tension of being contractually prohibited from playing live took its toll. These problems were exacerbated when producer Bill Price was commandeered by Guns N'Roses to mix their *Use Your Illusion* albums. Lorre expressed the feelings of the Nymphs by crushing five poppies (to represent the band members) and urinating on them, all on top of the desk of her label's A&R chief. *Nymphs* eventually emerged in February 1992 to a fanfare of critical praise, a darkly enthralling set which mixed punk and grunge with Lorre's lyrical images of death, drugs and sex (often drawn from personal experience). Subsequent live shows were of variable quality, with internal tensions abounding due to Lorre's eccentric behaviour, and following *A Practical Guide To Astral Projection*, it was no surprise when the Nymphs disintegrated spectacularly on stage in Miami in September that same year. Lorre is reportedly currently concerned with writing children's stories.
Albums: *Nymphs* (Geffen 1992), *A Practical Guide To Astral Projection* (Geffen 1992, mini-album).

Nyro, Laura

b. Laura Nigro, 18 October 1947, The Bronx, New York City, USA. The daughter of an accomplished jazz trumpeter, Nyro was introduced to music at an early age, reputedly completing her first composition when she was only eight years old. Her main influences ranged from **Bob Dylan** to **John Coltrane**, but the artist's debut *More Than A New Discovery* (aka *The First Songs*) revealed a talent akin to **Brill Building** songwriters **Carole King** and **Ellie Greenwich**. Nyro's empathy for soul and R&B enhanced her individuality, although she later disowned the set, claiming its stilted arrangements were completed against her wishes. The set nonetheless contained several songs adapted by other artists, notably 'Stoney End' (**Barbra Streisand**), 'And When I Die' (**Blood, Sweat And Tears**) and 'Wedding Bell Blues' (**Fifth Dimension**). *Eli And The Thirteenth Confession* complied more closely to Nyro's wishes; while containing the highly popular 'Stone Souled Picnic', it revealed the growing sense of introspection that flourished on the following year's *New York Tendaberry*. Here the singer's dramatic intonation, capable of sweeping from a whisper to anguished vibrato within a phrase, emphasized a bare emotional nerve exposed on 'You Don't Love Me When I Cry' and 'Sweet Lovin' Baby'. Her frequent jumps in tempo irked certain critics, but the majority applauded its audacious ambition and peerless fusion of gospel and white soul. The extraordinary *Christmas And The Beads Of Sweat*, which included the startling 'Christmas Is My Soul', offered a similar passion while *Gonna Take A Miracle*, a collaboration with producers **Kenny Gamble** and **Leon Huff**, acknowledged the music which provided much of the artist's inspiration. Backed by the Sigma Sound Studio houseband and singing trio **Labelle**, Nyro completed enthralling versions of uptown R&B and **Motown** favourites. She then retired from music altogether, but re-emerged in 1975 upon the disintegration of her marriage. *Smile* showed the singer's talent had remained intact and included the powerful 'I Am The Blues', while an attendant promotional tour spawned *Season Of Lights*. *Nested* was, however, less impressive and a further domestically-inspired hiatus followed. *Mother's Spiritual* reflected Nyro's reactions to both parenthood and ageing; her comeback was confirmed in 1988 when she embarked on her first concert tour in over a decade. Laura Nyro remains a singularly impressive performer while her intonation has proved influential on several other female singers, notably **Rickie Lee Jones**.

Albums: *More Than A New Discovery* aka *The First Songs* (1967), *Eli And The Thirteenth Confession* (1968), *New York Tendaberry* (1969), *Christmas And The Beads Of Sweat* (1970), *Gonna Take A Miracle* (1971), *Smile* (1976), *Season Of Lights* (1978), *Nested* (1979), *Mother's Spiritual* (1985), *Live At The Bottom Line* (1990), *Walk The Dog And Light The Light* (Columbia 1993). Compilation: *Impressions* (1980).

O

O Lucky Man

Noted British film director Lindsay Anderson (*This Sporting Life*, *If*) cast Malcolm McDowell in the leading role of this enthralling 1973 feature. Arthur Lowe, Ralph Richardson, Rachel Roberts and Helen Mirren were among the first-class supporting players. Screened at the Cannes Film Festival in its original three-hour form, *O Lucky Man* was later trimmed for US audiences. The plot revolved around the antics of a self-serving young man, initially intent on gratification, who later attempts to make amends for his perceived wrong-doings. Anderson's acerbic political eye and skilled direction brought resonance to the proceedings which were suitably enhanced by a taught score from former **Animals**' pianist/vocalist **Alan Price**. Aided by guitarist Colin Green, formerly of **Georgie Fame**'s Blue Flames, Dave Markee (bass) and ex-**Jethro Tull** drummer Clive Thacker, Price committed some of his finest songs and performances to the project, notably 'Poor People', 'My Home Town' and the ironic title song. One of the finest British films of the early 70s, *O Lucky Man* demonstrates Price's maturity as a songwriter as well as Anderson's considerable cinematic gifts.

O'Brien, Floyd

b. 7 May 1904, Chicago, Illinois, USA, d. 26 November 1968. Throughout the 20s and early 30s trombonist O'Brien worked regularly, playing in numerous bands mostly in Chicago. In the mid-30s he also played in New York, appearing on record with the **Chocolate Dandies**, **Fats Waller**, **Eddie Condon**, **George Wettling** and other leading jazz groups. He spent the second half of the 30s in the orchestra led by popular singer-comedian Phil Harris, then joined successively **Gene Krupa** and **Bob Crosby**. During the 40s he played mostly in dixieland and New Orleans-style bands, some of which he led. This pattern continued into the 50s, when he recorded with **Albert Nicholas** and also established a reputation as a brass teacher. Although not as well-known as some of his contemporaries, O'Brien was a gifted trombonist and an often vital and exciting exponent of Chicago-style.
Albums: with Albert Nicholas *All Star Stompers* (1959). Compilations: with George Wettling *Chicago Jazz* (1939-40), with Bob Crosby *South Rampart Street Parade* (1935-42).

O'Connell, Helen

(see **Dorsey, Jimmy**)

O'Connor, Des

b. January 1932. O'Connor served an apprenticeship on UK pop package tours - including that headlined by **Buddy Holly** - in the 50s before elevation to television as a smooth comedian-interlocutor. In the wake of **Ken Dodd**'s mid-60s record success as a balladeer, **EMI** decided to try O'Connor's light baritone on a few exploratory singles in the same vein. He struck gold in 1967 when 'Careless Hands' reached the Top 10. The next year had him at the top with 'I Pretend' composed by **Les Reed** and **Barry Mason**. Further success followed with the excellent '1-2-3 O'Leary'. An up-tempo approach with 'Dick-A-Dum-Dum' (a paeon to London's fashionable King's Road) precipitated a gradual slip from the hit parade - though he retained a strong following in the UK. He was also the good-natured victim of derogatory *bon mots* from showbusiness peers about his singing but he enjoyed a measure of revenge in 1980 when his hosting of an ITV chat-show hoisted *Just For You* to number 17 - his highest position in the album chart since *I Pretend*.
Selected albums: *I Pretend* (1968), *With Love* (1970), *Sing A Favourite Song* (1972), *Des O'Connor Selection* (1978), *With Feelings* (1979), *Christmas With...* (1979), *Careless Hands* (1980), *Des O'Connor Remembers* (1980), *This Is Des O'Connor* (1980), *Just For You* (1980), *Golden Hits Des O'Connor* (1983), *Des O'Connor Now* (1984), *The Great Songs* (1985), *Anytime* (1986), *True Love Ways* (1987), *Portrait* (1992).

O'Connor, Donald

b. Donald David Dixon Ronald O'Connor, 30 August 1925, Chicago, Illinois, USA. One of the most likeable and nimble of all Hollywood's song-and-dance-men, who seems to have retained his youthful looks and casual charm throughout a career spanning well over 50 years. O'Connor was the seventh child of parents who were circus and vaudeville performers. After his father died, Donald (aged three) joined his mother and two of his brothers in the family act until he made his film debut in the minor musical *Melody For Two* in 1937. A year later, at the age of only 13, he made a big impact in ***Sing You Sinners*** in which he completely captivated cinema audiences in his role as the younger brother of Fred MacMurray and **Bing Crosby**. The trio's version of 'Small Fry' was the highlight of the picture. After a few straight parts and one other musical, ***On Your Toes***, O'Connor went back to vaudeville until 1941 when he signed a contract with Universal which resulted in supporting roles in musicals such as *What's Cookin?*, *Private Buckaroo*, *Get Hep To Love*, and *Give Out Sisters*. These led to better parts in *It Comes Up Love*, *When Johnny Comes Marching Home*, *Strictly In The Groove*, and especially *Mister Big*. He was top-billed for the first time in *Top Man* (1943) with soprano Susanna Foster. Funny-girl Peggy Ryan was also in *Top Man*, and she joined O'Connor in several other films around this time, including *Chip Off The Old Block*, *This Is The Life*, *Follow The Boys*, *Bowery To Broadway*, *The Merry Monahans* (all 1944) and *Patrick The Great* (1945). After service in the US Army, O'Connor 'stole' *Something In The Wind* from Universal's premiere female star, **Deanna Durbin**, and further re-established himself in *Are You With It?*, *Feudin' Fussin' And A-Fightin'*, and *Yes Sir, That's My Baby* for which he was teamed with **Gloria DeHaven**. He was paired with a rather more unusual partner next - a 'talking mule' named Francis. The popular series, which began with *Francis* (1950), continued until O'Connor called a halt, saying: 'When you've made six pictures and the mule still gets more mail than you do . . .' In 1950 O'Connor starred at the London Palladium, and, on his return to the US, joined **Gene Kelly** and **Debbie Reynolds** for what is probably his best-remembered film - ***Singin' In The Rain***. All the routines are classics, but O'Connor's marvellous solo moment, 'Make 'Em Laugh', a series of pratfalls and back-flips performed in the company of a headless dummy, was improvised by O'Connor himself, and remains one of the all-time great sequences from any movie musical. Ironically, he revealed recently that the first take was ruined by 'foggy film' in the camera, and he had to do the whole thing over again three days later. The early 50s were good times for O'Connor. He featured on television's *The Colgate Comedy Hour* for three years, and continued to sing, dance and clown his way through ***Call Me Madam***, *I Love Melvin*, *Walking My Baby Back Home*, ***There's No Business Like Show Business***, and ***Anything Goes*** (1956). After that, with the glossy big screen musical in a state of terminal decline, he returned to television, and played the big cabaret rooms and clubs throughout the USA. He continued to appear in the occasional straight roles in films such as *The Buster Keaton Story* (1957), *Ragtime* (with **James Cagney** in 1981), and *Toys* (1992). In the 80s he toured in revivals of immortal stage musicals such as ***Show Boat***, and, later in the decade, was attracting enthusiastic reviews in Las Vegas for his shows with fellow movie legends Debbie Reynolds and **Mickey Rooney**. In June 1994 he brought his classy cabaret act to London for the opening of the capital's latest (ill-fated) cabaret space, the Connaught Room.

O'Connor, Hazel

b. 16 May 1955, Coventry, England. O'Connor's introduction to showbusiness involved working as an dancer and starred with a minor movie role in *Girls Come First*. At the close of the 70s, she signed to the Albion label and issued the single 'Ee-I-Adio', which failed to sell. Her profile increased when she appeared in the film *Breaking Glass*, a melodramatic portrayal of a fictional rock star. O'Connor's aggressive singing style and confrontational appearance was used to good effect on the **Tony Visconti** produced 'Eighth Day' (complete with 'robotic' intonation) which reached the UK Top 5. The following year, she registered two further Top 10 singles, 'D-Days' and the uncharacteristic ballad 'Will You'. Various disputes with her record company and management slowed down her career. In 1984, she recorded *Smile* for **RCA** but the record sold poorly and the label declined to renew her option. O'Connor subsequently appeared in the musical *Girlfriends* in 1987.

Albums: *Breaking Glass* (1980), *Sons And Lovers* (1980), *Glass Houses* (1980), *Cover Plus* (1981), *Smile* (1984).

Film: *Breaking Glass* (1980).

Further reading: *Hazel O'Connor: Uncovered Plus*, Hazel O'Connor.

O'Connor, Mark

b. 4 August 1962, Seattle, Washington, USA. A naturally gifted instrumentalist, who first began to play the guitar at the age of six and won a University of Washington classical/flamenco guitar contest when he was aged 10. A year later, tiring of just the guitar, he turned to the fiddle and within weeks was playing it at square dances. Influenced by noted Texas fiddler Benny Thomasson, he played at festivals and contests. By the age of 14, he had already won two National Fiddle Championships, a Grand Masters Fiddle Championship, the National Guitar Flatpicking Championship and had also produced two albums. After graduation in 1979, he toured extensively on the festival circuits, where he worked with several noted bluegrass musicians. After touring Japan with Dan Crary, he became the guitarist with **David Grisman**'s quintet, where he also worked on a tour with the jazz violinist **Stéphane Grappelli**. In 1981, while O'Connor was recovering from a broken arm sustained in a skiing accident, Grisman reduced to a quartet and O'Connor became the fiddle player with the **Dixie Dregs**. He left in 1983 and began to work with many artists including John McKuen, **Peter Rowan**, **Chris Hillman** and the legendary **Doc Watson**. His multi-instrumental ability has seen him much in demand and he has played on countless recordings as a session musician. By the late 80s, his music mixed various genres including bluegrass, rock, jazz and classical. In 1990, he began to follow a more independent career and writing much of his own material, he began to concentrate more on his own recordings. His collaboration with the cream of country sessionmen on *New Nashville Cats* won him much critical acclaim, and his revival of **Carl Perkins**' 'Restless', with vocals by **Ricky Skaggs**, **Steve Wariner** and **Vince Gill**, won several CMA Awards. O'Connor then began work on a record of duets with famous violinists from the classical as well as country fields. His flatpicking guitar work has been compared to Doc Watson and many now rate him Nashville's top fiddle player. He is also an accomplished banjoist and in 1983, he won a World Mandolin Championship.

Albums: *Mark O'Connor Four-Time National Junior Fiddle Champion* (1975), *Pickin' In The Wind* (1976) *Texas Jam Session* (1977), *In Concert* (1977), *Markology* (1980), *On The Rampage* (1980), with Fred Carpenter *Cuttin' Loose* (1980), with David Grisman Quintet *Quintet '80* (1980), *Soppin' The Gravy* (1981), *False Dawn* (c.80s), with Doc and Merle Watson *Guitar Album* (1983), *Meanings Of* (1986), *Stones From Which The Arch Was Made* (1987), *Elysian Forest* (1988), *The Championship Years* (1990), *New Nashville Cats* (1991), *Heroes* (Warner Brothers 1993), *The Fiddle Concerto* (Warner Bros 1995).

Video: *The Devil Came Back To Georgia* (1993).

O'Connor, Sinead

b. 12 December 1966, Glenageary, Eire. This Irish vocalist has combined her highly distinctive vocal range with striking post-feminist imagery to great commercial effect on both sides of the Atlantic. She endured a turbulent youth and diagnoses of 'behavioural problems', which included shoplifting. O'Connor signed her first record deal with Ensign Records in 1985. Her previous experience was limited to sessions with Dublin pop band Ton Ton Macoute. Nigel Grainge, the label's co-manager, allowed her a full year to develop her knowledge of music and the industry by helping around the office, before the sessions for her debut album began. Through connections on the Dublin music scene, O'Connor provided the vocals to the **U2** guitarist The Edge film soundtrack for *The Captive*. The track 'Heroine' is released by **Virgin Records** and the track stirs some interest when aired on BBC television's *Old Grey Whistle Test* in 1986.

O'Connor's debut solo singe, the disappointing 'Troy', emerged as a single in late 1987, failing to capitalize on column inches seemingly generated only by the singer's shaven head. Early 1988 saw 'Mandinka' reach the UK Top 20, and proved a more suitable showcase for O'Connor's banshee-like attack. Although two subsequent singles failed to chart, *The Lion And The Cobra* sold well on the strength of 'Mandinka', and her media profile was bolstered by a series of highly opinionated interviews. 1989 saw a lull in her solo output as she worked on a variety of collaborative projects. She also appeared in her first film role as a 15-year-old Catholic schoolgirl in *Hush-A-Bye Baby*, a project developed by the Derry Film Workshop. It explored the moral dilemmas forced upon unmarried pregnant women in the province, and motherhood as a theme would become central in her work thereafter. To promote her second solo album, O'Connor chose the **Prince** written 'Nothing Compares 2 U', originally recorded by Family for the Paisley Park label. A remarkable ballad which demonstrated the strength and vulnerability which are pivotal elements in the singer's delivery, it transfixed audiences worldwide. The second album, *I Do Not Want What I Haven't Got*, saw similar global success. Her 1990 tour of the USA prompted the first stirrings of a backlash. At the Garden State Arts Centre in New Jersey she refused to go on stage after 'The Star Spangled Banner' was played. It was her protest at the censorship which was sweeping the USA, but this fact was obscured under a wave of nationalistic vitriol from **Frank Sinatra** amongst others. It emerged in interviews that the artist was as troubled privately as her public persona may have suggested. Although the mother of a son, Jake, a series of miscarriages had been emotionally draining, catalogued in the tender singles 'Three Babies' and 'My Special Child'. O'Connor is now established as one of the most potent forces in the left field of popular music. Further contoversy ensued in late 1992 when O'Connor tore up a photograph of the Pope on US television. Her appearance at the **Bob Dylan** celebration concert shortly after was highly charged as she defied numerous hecklers by staring them out. She became too overcome however, and was led from the stage by a reassuring **Kris Kristofferson**. In 1993 she appeared as a guest on **Willie Nelson**'s *Across The Borderline*, dueting a a substitute **Kate Bush** on **Peter Gabriel**'s 'Don't Give Up'. *Universal Mother*, compared to her previous efforts found only marginal success, maybe her sermonizing had begun to cloud the music.

Albums: *The Lion And The Cobra* (1988), *I Do Not Want What I Haven't Got* (1990), *Am I Not Your Girl?* (1993), *Universal Mother* (Ensign 1994).

Further reading: *Sinead O'Connor: So Different*, Dermott Hayes. *Sinead: Her Life And Music*, Jimmy Guterman.

O'Daniel, Wilbert Lee

b. 1890, Malta, Ohio, USA, d. 1969. The family relocated to Kansas, where he grew up and worked for several milling companies. In 1925, he moved to Fort Worth, Texas to become the sales manager of the Burrus Mill And Elevator Company. A very competent salesman, he soon made the sales of the company's Light Crust Flour increase enormously, an achievement that saw him promoted to general manager of Burrus Mill. In 1930, he believed he could boost sales further by means of a radio programme although he initially professed that he did not like hillbilly music. Early in 1931, the Light Crust Doughboys, which included both

Milton Brown and **Bob Wills,** began broadcasting, first on KFJZ before moving to the more powerful WBAP. O'Daniel, determined to get the advertising exactly as he wanted it, began to carry out all announcing duties himself. He wrote promotional ditties and songs, arranged tours for the band and in 1932, the band recorded for **RCA-Victor**. Eventually differences of opinion with O'Daniel saw both Brown and Wills leave to pursue their own careers. In 1935, when O'Daniel was fired by Burrus Mill (probably for promoting himself more than his employers), he formed his own company and began to market Hillbilly Flour. He also had aspirations of political office and to assist in this and to advertise his product, he formed his band, the Hillbilly Boys, which included his sons Pat and Mike, singer/yodeller Leon Huff and Kitty Williamson (aka Texas Rose). The band proved very popular and made recordings, which included material that O'Daniel wrote. It also proved a useful and popular attraction during his successful 1938 campaign for the office of State governor. He was re-elected in 1940 and in 1941, on the death of the State senator, in a campaign that was far from pleasant, he was elected to the Senate. (The person that he beat for the office was Lyndon Baines Johnson who, as Vice-President at the time of President Kennedy's assassination in 1963, served as President until 1969.) At the end of his term, O'Daniel retired and an attempted comeback in 1956 failed miserably. During his career, he composed several songs that have remained popular in country music including 'Beautiful Texas' and 'Put Me In Your Pocket'.

O'Day, Alan

b. 3 October 1940, Hollywood, Los Angeles, California, USA. After leaving school, O'Day began writing music for Hollywood b-movies before being signed to **Warner Brothers** Music as a staff writer. O'Day composed a number of hits including **Bobby Sherman**'s 'The Drum' and the **Righteous Brothers**' 'Rock 'n' Roll Heaven' before finally hitting number 1 with 'Angie Baby', recorded by **Helen Reddy**. In an inspired move, Warners decided to launch a subsidiary, Pacific Records, whose purpose was to exploit the work of promising songwriters. O'Day was invited to record the first single for the new company and came up with 'Undercover Angel'. Surprisingly, the song was banned on some US radio stations due to its alleged sexual connotations, but O'Day surmounted the controversy and went all the way to number 1 in July 1977. Unwilling to pursue his singing career to excessive lengths, O'Day continued his main job as a writer and accepted the mantle of a chart-topping one-hit-wonder.

O'Day, Anita

b. Anita Colton, 18 October 1919, Kansas City, Missouri, USA. As Anita Colton, in her early teens she scraped a living as a professional Walkathon contestant (marathon dancer). During this period she changed her surname to O'Day. Along with other contestants she was encouraged to sing and during one Walkathon was accompanied by Erskine Tate's orchestra, an event which made her think that singing might be a better route to showbiz fame than dancing. By her late teens she had switched to singing and was told by **Gene Krupa**, who heard her at a Chicago club, that if he ever had a slot for her he would call. In the meantime she failed an audition with **Benny Goodman**, who complained that she did not stick to the melody, and upset **Raymond Scott**, who disliked her scatting (vocalese) - actually, she had momentarily forgotten the words of the song. Eventually Krupa called and O'Day joined the band early in 1941, just a few weeks before **Roy Eldridge** was also hired. The combination of Krupa, Eldridge and O'Day was potent and the band, already popular, quickly became one of the best of the later swing era. O'Day helped to give the band some of its hit records, notably 'Let Me Off Uptown', (also a feature for Eldridge), 'Alreet', 'Kick It' and 'Bolero At The Savoy'. After Krupa folded in 1943, O'Day went with **Stan Kenton**, recording hits with 'And Her Tears Flowed Like Wine' and 'The Lady In Red'. In 1945 she was back with the reformed Krupa band for more hit records including, 'Opus No. 1'. In 1946 she went solo and thereafter remained a headliner. She made a number of fine albums in the 50s, including a set with **Ralph Burns** in 1952, and made a memorable appearance at the 1958 **Newport Jazz Festival**. This performance, at which she sang 'Tea For Two' and 'Sweet Georgia Brown', resplendent in cartwheel hat, gloves, and stoned out of her mind, was captured on film in *Jazz On A Summer's Day* (1958). Drug addiction severely damaged O'Day's life for many years, although she continued to turn out excellent albums, including *Cool Heat* with **Jimmy Giuffre**, *Trav'lin' Light* with **Johnny Mandel** and **Barney Kessel** and *Time For Two* with **Cal Tjader**. Extensive touring, high living and a punishing life style (not to mention a dozen years of heroin addiction) eventually brought collapse, and she almost died in 1966. Eventually clear of drugs, O'Day continued to tour, playing clubs, concerts and festivals around the world. She recorded less frequently, but thanks to forming her own record company, Emily, in the early 70s many of the albums that she did make were entirely under her control. In 1985 she played Carnegie Hall in celebration of 50 years in the business, and towards the end of the decade appeared in the UK at **Ronnie Scott**'s club and at the Leeds Castle Jazz Festival in Kent. O'Day's singing voice is throaty and she sings with great rhythmic drive. Her scat singing and the liberties she takes on songs, especially when singing up-tempo, result in some remarkable vocal creations. In her hey-days her diction was exceptional and even at the fastest tempos she articulated clearly and precisely. On ballads she is assured and distinctive, and although very much her own woman, her phrasing suggests the influence of **Billie Holiday**. On stage she displays enormous rapport with musicians and audience, factors which make some of her studio recordings rather less rewarding than those made in concert. Late in her career some of her performances were marred by problems of pitch but, live at least, she compensated through sheer force of personality. Her autobiography makes compulsive reading.

Selected albums: *Specials* (1951), *Singing And Swinging* (1953), *Collate* (1953), *Anita O'Day* (1954), *Anita O'Day Sings Jazz* (1955), *An Evening With Anita O'Day* (1956), *Anita* (1956), *Pick Yourself Up* (1956), *The Lady Is A Tramp* (1956), *Anita Sings The Most* (1957), *Anita Sings The Winners* (1958), *Anita O'Day At Mr Kelly's* (1958), *Cool Heat* (1959), *Anita O'Day Swings Cole Porter With Billy May* (1959), *Waiter, Make Mine Blues* (1960), *Incomparable!* (1960), *Anita O'Day And Billy May Swing Rodgers And Hart* (1960), *Trav'lin' Light* (1961), *All The Sad Young Men* (1961), *Time For Two* (1962), *Anita O'Day And The Three Sounds* (1962), *Anita O'Day In Tokyo 1963* (1963), *Once Upon A Summertime* (c.1969), *Live At The Berlin Jazz Festival* (1970), *Anita '75* (1975), *My Ship* (1975), *Live In Tokyo* (1975), *Live At Mingo's* (1976), *Skylark* (1978), *Angel Eyes* (1978), *Mello' Day* (GNP 1979), *Live At The City, Vols 1 & 2* (1979), *Misty* (1981), *A Song For You* (c.1984), *Wave* (Essential 1986), *In A Mellow Tone* (1989), *At Vine St Live* (Disque Suisse 1992), *Rules Of The Road* (Pablo 1994). Compilations: *Anita O'Day Sings With Gene Krupa* (1941-42), *Singin' And Swingin' With Anita O'Day* (1947), *Hi Ho Trailus Boot Whip* (1947), *Anita O'Day 1949-1950* (1949-50), *Tea For Two* (1958-66), *The Big Band Sessions* (1959-61), *1956-62* (1993).

Further reading: *High Times, Hard Times*, Anita O'Day with George Eells.

O'Day, Molly

b. LaVerne Lois Williamson, 9 July 1923, McVeigh, Pike County, Kentucky, USA, d. 5 December 1987. O'Day learned several instruments and first sang with her brother Cecil 'Skeets' Williamson on WCHS Charleston in 1939; initially using the name Mountain Fern but soon changing to Dixie Lee. In 1940, she joined the Forty Niners, a group led by singer/guitarist Leonard (Lynn) Davis, (b. 15 December 1914, Paintsville, Kentucky, USA) who she married in April 1941. In 1942, she changed her stage name to Molly O'Day and together with Davis, worked on a variety of radio stations, including WHAS Louisville and WNOX Knoxville. Between 1946 and 1951, with their band the Cumberland Mountain Folks, they recorded almost 40 sides for **Columbia**. These included such heart rending numbers as 'The Drunken Driver' and 'Don't Sell Daddy Any More Whiskey'. She was the first artist to record **Hank Williams**' songs, ('When God Comes To Gather His Jewels' and 'Six More Miles') after hearing Hank in 1942 singing 'Tramp On The Street', which also became one her most requested numbers. In the early 50s, she and her husband turned to religious work (Davis later becoming an evangelist) but her singing was slowed by tuberculosis, which led to the removal of part of a lung, although they later recorded some religious material for Rem and GRS. Throughout the 60s and 70s, they did limited radio work centred around their home in Huntington, West Virginia. O'Day is rated by many to be the greatest woman country singer of all time; her individual emotional style causing some to call her 'the female Hank Williams or **Roy Acuff**'. She died of cancer in 1987.

Albums: *Hymns For The Country Folks* (1960), *Molly O'Day Sings Again* (1961), *The Unforgettable* (1963), *The Living Legend Of Country Music* (1966), *A Sacred Selection* (c.1975), *Skeets Williamson & Molly O'Day* (c.1975), *Molly O'Day Radio Favorites* (1981), *The Soul Of Molly O'Day Volume 1* (1983), *The Soul Of Molly O'Day Volume 2* (1984), *In Memory* (1990), *Molly O'Day And The Cumberland Mountain Folks* (1992, 2-CD).

O'Dell, Kenny

b. Kenneth Gist, Jnr., c.early 40s, Oklahoma, USA. O'Dell began writing songs in his early teens and after completing his education, he formed his own Mar-Kay record label in California. In the early 60s, he recorded his own 'Old Time Love' but it failed to chart. After working for a time with **Duane Eddy**, he formed a group, Guys And Dolls, with which he toured for some five years. In 1966, he wrote and recorded 'Beautiful People', which became a smash hit in Atlanta. **Liberty Records** told **Bobby Vee** he could record a better version and have a national hit. Vee later said he should never have listened to them but in spite of split sales both versions made the US Top 40. After further unsuccessful attempts for chart successes, he moved to Nashville in 1969, where he managed **Bobby Goldsboro**'s publishing company. He continued with his songwriting, sometimes with Larry Henley and in 1972, after producer **Billy Sherrill** had heard O'Dell's own recording, **Sandy Posey** charted with their song 'Why Don't We Go Somewhere And Love'. Sherrill became interested in O'Dell's songs and had **Charlie Rich** record 'I Take It On Home'. In 1973, Rich had a smash country and pop hit with 'Behind Closed Doors', which won O'Dell the CMA's *Song Of The Year* award. (He actually played guitar on Rich's recording). In the latter half of the 70s, he tried to relaunch his singing career with Capricorn. He had a Top 10 country hit with 'Let's Shake Hands And Come Out Lovin'' in 1978 but 'Medicine Woman' in 1979 has proved so far to be his last country hit. He was infinitely more successful and will always be

remembered for his writing rather than his singing. Many artists have benefited by recording his songs including Anthony Armstrong Jones ('I've Got Mine'), **Tanya Tucker** ('Lizzie And The Rainman'), both **Billie Jo Spears** (1977) and the **Bellamy Brothers** & Forrester Sisters (1986) ('Too Much Is Not Enough'), **Dottie West** ('When It's Just You And Me'), the **Judds** ('Mama He's Crazy') and many others.
Albums: *Beautiful People* (1968), *Kenny O'Dell* (1974), *Let's Shake Hands And Come Out Lovin'* (1978).

O'Donnell, Daniel

b. 12 December, 1961, Kincasslagh, Co. Donegal, Eire. O'Donnell is without doubt the biggest selling act ever in the musical genre known as 'Country 'n' Irish'. He is a clean-cut and gimmick-free vocalist with leanings towards sentimental MOR material. He first emerged in Britain in 1985, although he was already popular in Ireland. His first attempts at singing came when he worked as backing vocalist in the band which backed his sister, folk/country singer Margo O'Donnell, during the early 80s, and his popularity among the female audiences increased at high speed. After a handful of early recordings, (later released after he came to fame as 'The Boy From Donegal') he signed to Michael Clerkin's Ritz Records, an Irish label based in London, and *Two Sides Of Daniel O'Donnell* was released in 1985. It was promoted by the first in a continuing series of nationwide UK tours which attracted capacity audiences (largely composed of fans of artists like the late **Jim Reeves**. O'Donnell usually features in his stage show a medley of songs connected with Reeves). 1986 brought a second O'Donnell release, *I Need You*, which was his first to reach the UK country album charts (which it did in March 1987). That year's album *Don't Forget To Remember* (featuring a cover of the hit by the **Bee Gees** as its title track), was O'Donnell's first to enter the UK country chart at number 1, which has also occurred with his five subsequent original albums, although the next one to be released in chronological terms, *The Boy From Donegal*, consisted mainly of material recorded in 1984 before he signed to Ritz, and was released in the UK by Prism Leisure.
In 1988, Ritz licensed O'Donnell's next release, *From The Heart*, to Telstar Records, a television marketing company, and as well as entering the UK country chart at number 1, the album also reached the UK pop album chart in the autumn of that year, while a video, *Daniel O'Donnell Live In Concert*, was released. 1989 brought *Thoughts Of Home*, an album and video which were both advertised on television by Telstar - the album made the Top 40 of the pop chart and the video became O'Donnell's first to reach the UK Music Video chart; once again, all subsequent videos have featured in the latter chart, which the original *Live In Concert* also entered in the wake of *Thoughts From Home*. By 1990, O'Donnell was back with an album, *Favourites*, (and a companion video, *TV Show Favourites*), which was composed of material filmed for a hugely successful Irish television series. However, of far greater interest in 1990 was the news that he was making an album with noted producer Allen Reynolds (who had enjoyed major success with **Don Williams**, **Crystal Gayle**, **Kathy Mattea** and latterly, **Garth Brooks**) in Nashville - the first since O'Donnell's breakthrough that he had recorded with his original producer John Ryan. Released in late 1990, *The Last Waltz* was somewhat closer to genuine country music than its predecessors, and once again entered the UK country album charts at the top and charted strongly in the UK pop equivalent, while another video, *An Evening With Daniel O'Donnell*, had been in the Top 20 of the UK Music Video chart for 18 months at the time of writing. During 1991, it was decided that nearly all of O'Donnell's album catalogue was MOR rather than country, and at a stroke, a UK country album chart - in which O'Donnell occupied the majority of the Top 10 - hardly featured his albums at all. This produced an avalanche of complaints (including one from a nun) and public demonstrations urging that the decision be reversed and his albums reinstated in the country list, which eventually occurred in late 1991. Another release, *The Very Best Of Daniel O'Donnell*, a compilation composed partly of previously released items along with some newly recorded material, continued O'Donnell's remarkable success story. In musical terms, what O'Donnell records is unadventurous, yet his immense popularity in the UK and Eire makes it clear that his output has been brilliantly targeted. As yet, he has not released an album in the USA, although imported albums have been sold prodigiously in areas with population composed of large numbers of people of Irish extraction, and several concert appearance, including one at New York's Carnegie Hall in 1991, have been commercial triumphs.
Albums: *Two Sides Of Daniel O'Donnell* (1985), *I Need You* (1986), *Don't Forget To Remember* (1987), *The Boy From Donegal* (1987), *From The Heart* (1988), *Thoughts From Home* (1989), *Favourites* (1990), *The Last Waltz* (1990), *Follow Your Dream* (1992), *Especially For You* (Ritz 1994).
Compilation: *The Very Best Of Daniel O'Donnell* (1991).
Videos: *Live In Concert* (1988), *Thoughts Of Home* (1989), *TV Show Favourites* (1990), *An Evening With* (1990), *Follow Your Dream* (1992), *And Friends Live* (1993), *Just For You* (1994).

O'Farrill, Arturo 'Chico'

b. 28 October 1921, Havana, Cuba. After playing trumpet in several Cuban-based bands throughout the 40s, O'Farrill moved to the USA where he concentrated on arranging. During the 50s his work was played and recorded by **Benny Goodman**, **Stan Kenton**, **Dizzy Gillespie** among others and he also collaborated with **Machito** on albums featuring such

leading American jazzmen as **Charlie Parker** and **Joe 'Flip' Phillips**. O'Farrill also toured and recorded with his own band. He spent the early 60s in Mexico, then returned to the USA taking up a staff post with **CBS** but retained his jazz links by arranging for **Count Basie**. In the 70s and 80s O'Farrill continued to be active but his jazz work gradually diminished. An outstanding exponent of Latin-American music, O'Farrill's arrangements consistently demonstrate his comprehensive grasp of the music's potential and are often far more imaginative than others who work in this field.
Albums: by Machito *Afro-Cuban Jazz Suite* (1950), *Chico O'Farrill And His Orchestra* i (1951), *Chico O'Farrill And His Orchestra* ii (1952), *Chico O'Farrill And His Orchestra* iii (1952), *Mambo Latin Dances* (c.1953), *Tropical Fever* (mid-50s), *Torrid Zone* (mid-50s), *Chico O'Farrill And His Orchestra* iv (1966), *Chico O'Farrill And His Orchestra* v (1966), with Dizzy Gillespie, Machito *Afro-Cuban Jazz Moods* (1975), *Latin Roots* (1976).

O'Flynn, Liam

b. Kill, County Kildare, Eire. O'Flynn, an uillean piper, is acclaimed as being one of the most influential pipers on the scene today. His father, a schoolteacher, had been a fiddle player, and Liam was brought up into a world rich in folk tradition. He first came into contact with the uillean pipes through Sergeant Tom Armstrong of the Garda in Co. Kildare. During the 60s, O'Flynn won prizes at the Oireachtas festival and the Fleadh Ceoil, but it was not until joining the influential Irish group **Planxty**, in 1972, that his name came to prominence. O'Flynn has worked with other well-known names, such as **John Cage** and **Kate Bush**. The film *Cal*, featured his piping in the soundtrack written by **Mark Knopfler**. Both Liam and classical guitarist **John Williams** performed the 'Brendan Voyage Suite' at the London's Royal Festival Hall, in London, as part of the South Bank Festival.
Albums: *David Balfour* (1978, film soundtrack), with Sean Davey *The Brendan Voyage* (1980), *Liam O'Flynn* (80s), *The Fine Art Of Piping* (1992), with Sean Keane, Matt Molloy *The Fire Aflame* (1993), *Out To Another Side* (Tara 1993).

O'Jays

The core of this long-standing soul group, Eddie Levert (b. 16 June 1942) and Walter Williams (b. 25 August 1942), sang together as a gospel duo prior to forming the Triumphs in 1958. This doo-wop influenced quintet was completed by William Powell, Bill Isles and Bobby Massey and quickly grew popular around its hometown of Canton, Ohio. The same line-up then recorded as the Mascots before taking the name the O'Jays after Cleveland disc jockey Eddie O'Jay, who had given them considerable help and advice. Having signed to **Imperial** in 1963, the O'Jays secured their first hit with 'Lonely Drifter', which was followed by an imaginative reworking of **Benny Spellman**'s 'Lipstick Traces' (1965) and 'Stand In For Love' (1966). Despite gaining their first R&B Top 10 entry with 'I'll Be Sweeter Tomorrow (Than I Was Today)' (1967), the group found it difficult to maintain a constant profile, and were cut to a four-piece following Isles' departure. In 1968 the group met producers (Kenny) **Gamble And** (Leon) **Huff** with whom they recorded, unsuccessfully, on the duo's short-lived Neptune label. The line-up was reduced further in 1972 when Bobby Massey left. Paradoxically the O'Jays then began their most fertile period when Gamble and Huff signed them to **Philadelphia International**. The vibrant 'Back Stabbers', a US Top 3 hit, established the group's style, but the preachy 'Love Train', with its plea for world harmony, established the 'protest' lyrics of later releases 'Put Your Hands Together' (1973) and 'For The Love Of Money' (1974). *Back Stabbers* is a classic album and arguably the finest cohesive example of Gamble And Huff's outstanding work.
In 1975 Sammy Strain joined the line-up from **Little Anthony And The Imperials** when ill health forced William Powell to retire from live performances. This founder member continued to record with the group until his death on 25 April 1976. 'Message In Our Music' (1976) and 'Use Ta Be My Girl' (1977) confirmed the O'Jays continued popularity as they survived many of Philly soul's changing fortunes. But as the genre felt the ravages of fashion so the group also suffered. The early 80s were commercially fallow, until *Love Fever* (1985) restated their direction with its blend of funk and rap. Two years later the O'Jays were unexpectedly back at the top of the soul chart with 'Lovin' You', confirming their position as one of soul music's most durable groups.
Albums: *Comin' Through* (1965), *Soul Sounds* (1967), *O'Jays* (1967), *Full Of Soul* (1968), *Back On Top* (1968), *The O'Jays In Philadelphia* (1969), *Back Stabbers* (1972), *Ship Ahoy* (1973), *Live In London* (1974), *Survival* (1975), *Family Reunion* (1975), with the Moments *The O'Jays Meet The Moments* (1975), *Message In The Music* (1976), *Travelin' At The Speed Of Thought* (1977), *So Full Of Love* (1978), *Identify Yourself* (1979), *Year 2000* (1980), *My Favourite Person* (1982), *When When I See You Again* (1983), *Love And More* (1984), *Love Fever* (1985), *Close Company* (1985), *Let Me Touch You* (1987), *Serious* (1990), *Emotionally Yours* (1991), *Heartbreaker* (1993). Compilations: *Collectors' Items* (1977), *Greatest Hits* (1984). *Working On Your Case* (1985), *From The Beginning* (1984), *Reflections In Gold 1973-1982* (1988), *The Best Of* (1993).

O'Kanes

Jamie O'Hara (b. Toledo, Ohio, USA) planned to be a professional American footballer until knee injuries forced him to change his mind. He says, 'My father gave me a guitar as a gift. Two years later, I was in Nashville. That either shows a lot of confidence, a lot of arrogance or a lot of stupidity.' He wrote 'Grandpa (Tell Me 'Bout The Good Old Days)' for the **Judds** and befriended another songwriter, Keiran Kane. Kane (b. Queens, New York, USA) had worked amongst rock acts in Los Angeles in the early 70s and then moved to Nashville. He wrote 'Gonna Have A Party' for **Alabama**. O'Hara and Kane became friendly, sharing their frustration at not getting songs recorded, and they began collaborating on material. They recorded demos in Kane's attic studio. **Columbia** thought they were good enough to release on their own account. The acoustic recordings (two guitars, bass, fiddle, mandolin, accordion, drums) made a stunning album debut in 1987. Their harmonies were reminiscent of a mellow version of the **Louvin Brothers**. They made the US country Top 10 with their first single, 'Oh Darlin' (Why Don't You Care For Me No More)' and then topped the chart with 'Can't Stop My Heart From Loving You'. Although their album was quiet and low-key, their rousing shows won them further acclaim. They were among the 'new traditionalists' in country music, but they stopped performing when Columbia failed to renew their recording contract. Their final chart entry was 'Rocky Road'.

Albums: *O'Kanes* (1987), *Tired Of The Runnin'* (1988), *Imagine That* (1990), *Oh Darlin'* (1993).

O'Keefe, Danny

b. 1943, Wenatchee, Washington, USA. O'Keefe developed his blues-influenced songwriting in Minnesota and New York before recording 'That Old Sweet Song' for the Seattle-based Jerden label. He next performed with Calliope, making one album for Buddah before a tape of his best-known song 'Good Time Charlie's Got the Blues' (subsequently covered by **Elvis Presley** and many other artists) persuaded **Ahmet Ertegun** to sign him to **Atlantic**'s Cotillion subsidiary. His second album was produced by Arif Mardin and included the reflective 'The Road', which was later taken up by **Jackson Browne**, while 'Magdalena' and 'Angel Spread Your Wings' from *Breezy Stories* were covered by **Leo Sayer** and **Judy Collins** respectively. During the mid-70s, O'Keefe played benefit concerts for conservation causes and in 1977 changed labels to **Warner Brothers**. Although critically acclaimed, his two albums for the company failed to sell and he performed only occasionally in the early 80s. O'Keefe set up his own label, Coldwater, to issue *The Day To Day* in 1985.

Albums: *Danny O'Keefe* (1971), *O'Keefe* (1972), *Breezy Stories* (1973), *So Long Harry Truman* (1975), *American Roulette* (1977), *Global Blues* (1979), *The Day To Day* (1985).

O'Keefe, Johnny

b. 19 January 1935, Sydney, New South Wales, Australia, d. 6 October 1978. If one person were to claim the title 'Australian Legend' Johnny O'Keefe would be the one to assume the mantle; his personal success and contribution to the fledgeling Australian rock industry can never be overstated. Single-handedly he persuaded promoters into staging rock concerts, pioneered rock on television and toured the length and breadth of the country. Prior to his efforts, rock was virtually unknown in Australia. After the film *Rock Around The Clock* was shown in Australia, Johnny O'Keefe took up the cause and organized a rock band, the Dee Jays, in early 1957, recruiting jazz players. Once he had demonstrated that teenagers were prepared to attend his dances, other promoters followed suit. Johnny O'Keefe, with his precociousness, bluffed his way onto national television and once he had achieved notoriety, was asked to host his own show, *Six O'Clock Rock*, on national television in 1959. O'Keefe used this show to foster the talent and careers of many other Australian acts. His recording career is easily the most extensive of any Australian rock/pop performer with 63 singles, 53 EPs and 66 albums released, since the first single of mid-1957. His career was initially based on covers of international hits, but eventually he wrote and co-wrote his own songs or recorded other local writers' material, thus promoting fellow artists. His career established in Australia, O'Keefe went to the USA in 1959 where he was known as the 'Kangaroo Kid', but despite a contract with **Liberty Records** he was unable to make any impact. His career faltered in mid-1960 after a car accident. He now suffered bouts of ill health and several nervous breakdowns, but his records continued to chart, until the arrival of Beatlemania. O'Keefe publicly denounced the 'long-haired' acts and lost most of his teenage following to the new trend. He then concentrated on the club and dance circuit, but seemed to fade almost into obscurity. A re-release of an earlier song in 1969 saw him in the charts for the first time in three years but another three-year hiatus followed before another re-release of an earlier song entered the charts. O'Keefe now concentrated on occasional tours as part of a rock 'n' roll revival show and devoted time to his management company. Following his death in 1978, his record sales noticeably increased.

Selected albums: *Shout* (1959), *Lee Gordon Presents The Big Show* (1960), *I'm Still Alive* (1961), *Oldies, But Goodies* (1962), *Twist* (1963), *Come On* (1963), *About Love* (1963), *Shake Baby Shake* (1964), *J. O'K Sound* (1964), *The J. O'K Story* (1964), *The Sun's Gonna Shine Tomorrow* (1965), *J. O'K's Ballads* (1966), *Where The Action Is* (1966), *My Heart Belongs To You* (1967), *She's My Baby* (1969), *Johnny B Goode* (1973), *The Wild One Rocks Again* (1973), *J. O'Keefe Live* (1974), *King Of Rock* (1975), *The Last Concert* (1988).

Compilations: *The Wild One's King Size Hits* (1962), *The Best Of Johnny O'Keefe* (1964), *Collector's Items From The 50s* (1969), *The Great J. O'K* (1970), *The Legend Of J. O'K* (1978), *A Tribute To J. O'Keefe* (1978).
Further reading: *The A To Z Of J. O'K: A Pictorial Discography Of Johnny O'Keefe*, D. Hudson and B. Ross.

O'Neal, Alexander

b. 14 November 1954, Minneapolis, Minnesota, USA. O'Neal was one of the best-known soul crooners of the late 80s. In 1978, he joined Flyte Tyme with future producers Jimmy Jam and Terry Lewis. The group became the backing band for **Prince**, although O'Neal was soon dismissed for insubordination. During the early 80s he began a solo career as a vocalist, making his first recordings with Jam and Lewis producing in 1984. The resulting album was issued by the local Tabu label, and contained R&B hits with 'A Broken Heart Could Mend', 'Innocent' (a duet with Cherelle) and 'If You Were Here Tonight'. The latter reached the British Top 20 in 1986, after Cherelle's 'Saturday Love' (which featured O'Neal) had been an even bigger success there. His career was interrupted by treatment for drug and alcohol addiction, but O'Neal broke through to the mainstream US audience 1987-88 with his second album and the singles 'Fake' and 'Never Knew Love Like This', another collaboration with Cherelle. He remained very popular in the UK with live performances (including a Prince's Trust concert) and a BBC television special. When, in 1991, he released his first album of new material for three years, it went straight into the UK Top 10. Jam and Lewis were again the producers.
Albums: *Alexander O'Neal* (1985), *Hearsay* (1986), *Hearsay All Mixed Up* (1988), *My Gift To You* (1988), *All True Man* (1991), *Love Makes No Sense* (1993). Compilation: *This Thing Called Love, The Greatest Hits* (1992).

O'Neal, Shaquille

b. c.1971, Newark, New Jersey, USA. O'Neal is the star of the previously obscure Orlando Magic basketball team ('Rookie Of The Year' in 1992). After the media picked up on his demonstrative play, notably his cult slam-dunk action, he emerged as a major multi-media star of the early 90s. So much so that a record contract was around the corner, and the format was hip hop. His generally sport-related raps like '(I Know I Got) Skillz' and 'Shoot Pass Slam' kept the cash-tills rattling, the latter song being the soundtrack to the Reebok commercials he was the high profile star of. He did possess some history in the hip hop idiom, having previously been a breakdancer in Newark until his size made the activity impossible/ludicrous. Later he moved to Germany where his father, Sgt Phillip Harrison, took a post. He relocated to San Francisco to attend high school, playing for 68-1, who won the state championship. From there he was picked up by Louisiana State University coach Dale Brown, from where he joined Orlando. Basketball and music are by no means his only interests. In February 1994 he appeared in his first film, *Blue Chips*, with Nick Nolte. Incredibly, he had already penned his own autobiography, at the age of 21. His recording career was recovering from critical reaction to his long playing debut, which featured over-familiar **Gap Band** breakbeats funnelled through maestros like Erick Sermon (**EPMD**), **Def Jef,** Ali Shaheed (**A Tribe Called Quest**) and **Fu-Schnickens**. The final set was delivered for the approval of no lesser men than **Scarface**, **Big Daddy Kane** and **Ice Cube**. At least it gelled a great deal better than Paul Gascoigne or Waddle/Hoddle's ill-advised attempts to crossover from sporting to musical superstardom.
Albums: *Shaq Diesel* (Jive 1993).
Further reading: *Shaq Attack* (1993), *Shaq Fu: Da Return* (Jive 1995).

O'Neill, Sharon

b. 23 November 1952, New Zealand. O'Neill was an established singer/songwriter in New Zealand where she won several 'Queen of Pop' awards, before relocating to Australia in 1980. Unlike other singer/songwriters her material was piano-based rather than guitar, but her music always involved a band. Her early albums quickly became popular with the public, culminating in platinum awards for *Maybe* and *Foreign Affairs*, plus several hit singles. Subsequent albums were not so successful and a dispute with her record company, **CBS**, kept her unrecorded between 1984 and 1986. A new contract with Polygram saw the release of *Dance In The Fire* in 1987. This album garnered good reviews and radio support but generated poor sales.
Albums: *This Heart, This Song* (1977), *Smash Palace Soundtrack* (1980), *Words* (1980), *Maybe* (1981), *Foreign Affairs* (1983), *Danced In The Fire* (1987).

O'Rahilly, Ronan

The inspirational figure behind UK pirate radio's classic era, O'Rahilly initially worked as a song plugger for the renowned Rik Gunnell Agency. When the BBC refused to entertain a **Georgie Fame** release he was touting, Ronan looked to Radio Veronica, a **pirate radio** ship anchored off the Dutch coast, and hatched plans for his own similar operation. He secured the requisite backing to purchase and refit the *Frederica*, a Danish passenger ferry, which began broadcasting as Radio Caroline on 28 March 1964. The station's name was taken from the daughter of the late US President, John F. Kennedy. Within four months O'Rahilly had absorbed an early rival, Radio Atlanta, into his organization. The original ship was relocated off the Isle of Man while the new acquisition, the *Mi Amigo*, was anchored off the east coast of England as Caroline

South. Several more stations followed in the wake of Ronan's vision, including Radio London and Radio City. Much of station's freewheeling style was curbed when the idealistic O'Rahilly went into partnership with the businessman **Phil Solomon**. Although beloved by loyal audiences, the 1967 Marine Offenses Bill came into effect on 15 August 1967, effectively closing the pirates' heyday. O'Rahilly was the only proprietor to defy the law and the *Mi Amigo* continued broadcasting, albeit intermittently, until 1973, when the entrepreneur leased the ship to the Radio Veronica consortium. Ronan's pursuance of alternative careers also included a role as executive producer on the **Marianne Faithfull** film, *Girl On A Motor Cycle*, and an unfulfilled plan to operate a pirate television service.

O'Sullivan, Gilbert

b. Raymond O'Sullivan, 1 December 1946, Waterford, Eire. O'Sullivan's family moved to Swindon, England, during his childhood and after attending art college there, the singer was signed to **CBS Records**. Under the name Gilbert he issued the unsuccessful 'What Can I Do?' and soon moved on to **Phil Solomon**'s Major Minor label, where 'Mr Moody's Garden' also failed. Seeking a new manager, Gilbert wrote to the starmaking **Gordon Mills**, who had already launched **Tom Jones** and **Engelbert Humperdinck** to international success. Mills was impressed by the demo tape enclosed and relaunched the artist on his new MAM label under the name Gilbert O'Sullivan. The debut 'Nothing Rhymed' had some clever lyrics and a strong melody. It reached the UK Top 10 in late 1970 and television audiences were amused or puzzled by the sight of O'Sullivan with his pudding basin haircut, short trousers and flat cap. The 'Bisto Kid' image was retained for the first few releases and the singer initially acted the part of an anti-star. At one point, he was living in the grounds of Mills' Weybridge house on a meagre £10-a-week allowance. His hit-making potential was undeniable and his ability to pen a memorable melody recalled the urbane charm of **Paul McCartney**. Early UK successes included 'We Will', 'No Matter How I Try' and 'Alone Again (Naturally)'. Any suspicions that O'Sullivan's charm was largely parochial were dashed when the latter single broke through in America, peaking at number 1 and selling over a million copies. The debut album, *Himself*, was also highly accomplished and included the radio favourite 'Matrimony', which would have provided a sizeable hit if released as a single. O'Sullivan went on to become one of the biggest selling artists of 1972. That year he enjoyed two consecutive UK number 1s with 'Clair' (written in honour of Mills's daughter) and 'Get Down'. These singles also reached the US Top 10. By this time, O'Sullivan's image had radically changed and he began to appreciate the superstar trappings enjoyed by Mills' other acts. O'Sullivan's second album, *Back To Front*, reached number 1 in the UK and his appeal stretched across the board, embracing teen and adult audiences. For a time, he seemed likely to rival and even excel **Elton John** as Britain's most successful singer/songwriter export. Although further hits were forthcoming with 'Ooh Baby', 'Happiness Is Me And You' and 'Christmas Song', it was evident that his appeal had declined by the mid-70s. Following the UK Top 20 hit 'I Don't Love You But I Think I Like You' in the summer of 1975, his chart career ceased. After a spectacular falling out with Mills, he left MAM and returned to CBS, the label that had launched his career. Five years on, only one hit, 'What's In A Kiss?', emerged from the association. Minus Mills, it seemed that the superstar of the mid-70s was incapable of rekindling his once illustrious career. His disillusionment culminated in a High Court battle against his former manager and record company which came before Justice Mars Jones in the spring of 1982. The judge not only awarded O'Sullivan substantial damages and had all agreements with MAM set aside, but decreed that all the singer's master tapes and copyrights should be returned. The case made legal history and had enormous repercussions for the British music publishing world. Despite his court victory over the starmaking Mills, however, O'Sullivan has so far failed to re-establish his career as a major artist. A series of albums have appeared on the Park label and Sullivan now caters for a small but loyal following.

Albums: *Himself* (1971), *Back To Front* (1972), *I'm A Writer Not A Fighter* (1973), *Stranger In My Own Backyard* (1974), *Southpaw* (1977), *Off Centre* (1980), *Life And Rhymes* (1982), *Frobisher Drive* (1988), *In The Key Of G* (Park 1991), *Sounds Of The Loop* (Park 1992), *Live In Japan 1993* (Park 1993), *By Larry* (Park 1994), *Every Song Has It's Play* (Park 1995). Compilations: *Greatest Hits* (1976), *20 Golden Greats* (1981), *20 Of The Very Best* (1981), *20 Golden Pieces Of Gilbert O' Sullivan* (1985), *16 Golden Classics* (1986).

Oak Ridge Boys

Originally called the Country Cut-Ups, the Oak Ridge Boys were formed in 1942 in Knoxville, Tennessee. They often performed at the atomic energy plant in Oak Ridge where, in the midst of a war, their optimistic gospel songs were welcomed, and so they were renamed the Oak Ridge Quartet. They recorded their first records in 1947 and there were many changes in personnel, although Wally Fowler (b. c.1916, d. 3 June 1994, Tennessee, USA) remained its leader. The group disbanded in 1956, only to emerge as the New Oak Ridge Quartet with a new leader, Smitty Gatlin. Handled by Fowler, they recorded their first records in 1947, moving their base to Nashville, but disbanded in 1956. A year later, they reformed in a revised line-up by an original member, Smitty Gatlin. They became full-time professionals in 1961 and the album on which they changed from the Oak Ridge Quartet to the Oak Ridge Boys included strings and horns, an unusual move for a gospel group. William Lee Golden (b. 12 January 1939, near Brewton, Alabama, USA), who had admired the group since he saw them as an adolescent, became their baritone in 1964. When Gatlin decided to become a full-time minister, Golden recommended Duane David Allen (b. 29 April 1943, Taylortown, USA) who became the group's lead vocalist in 1966. They established themselves as the best-loved white gospel group in the USA and they won numerous awards and Grammys. Further changes came in 1972 with bass singer, Richard Anthony Sterban (b. 24 April 1943, Camden, New Jersey, USA) and in 1973 with tenor Joseph Sloan Bonsall (b. 18 May 1948, Philadelphia, Pennsylvania, USA) becoming part of the group. Although most gospel fans enjoyed their high-energy, criss-crossing performances, they were criticized for adding a rock 'n' roll drummer to their band. They recorded a single, 'Praise The Lord And Pass The Soup', with **Johnny Cash** and the **Carter Family** in 1973. In 1975, they switched to country music but their first secular single, 'Family Reunion', only reached number 83 in the US country charts. Their total income fell to $75,000 in 1975 and they made a loss in 1976. **Columbia Records** dropped them, ironically at the same time as they were accompanying their labelmate, **Paul Simon**, on 'Slip Slidin' Away', which had sentiments diametrically opposite to gospel music. They opened for Johnny Cash in Las Vagas, played the USSR with **Roy Clark**, and had a major country hit with 'Y'All Come Back Saloon'. They topped the US country charts with 'I'll Be True To You' (a death disc), the classic 'Leavin' Louisiana In The Broad Daylight' and 'Trying To Love Two Women'. In 1981 they made number 5 on the US pop charts with 'Elvira' and followed it with 'Bobbie Sue' (number 12). Ronald Reagan, in a presidential address, said: 'If the Oak Ridge Boys win any more gold, they'll have more gold in their records than we have in Fort Knox.' Further country hits followed with 'American Made', 'Love Song', 'I Guess It Never Hurts To Hurt Sometime' (written by **Randy Vanwarmer**), 'Make My Life With You' and 'Come On In (You Did The Best You Could)'. In award ceremonies, they ousted the **Statler Brothers** as the top country vocal group, and their band has won awards in its own right. Golden, who stopped cutting his hair in 1979, became a mountain man, going bear hunting and sleeping in a teepee. When he was dismissed in 1986 for 'continuing musical and personal differences', he filed a $40m. suit, which was settled out of court. He released a solo album, *American Vagabond*, also in 1986, and has since formed a family group called the Goldens. His replacement was their rhythm guitarist, Steve Sanders (b. 17 September 1941, Richmond, Georgia, USA), formerly a child gospel performer and Faye Dunaway's son in the film *Hurry Sundown*. The Oak Ridge Boys continue with their philosophy to 'Keep it happy, keep it exciting' and do nothing which will tarnish their image. They turn down beer commercials and only sing positive songs. To quote Joe Bonsall, 'We're just an old gospel group with a rock 'n' roll band playing country music.'

Albums: *The Oak Ridge Boys Quartet* (1959), *Wall Fowler's All Nite Singing Gospel Concert Featuring The Oak Ridge Quartet* (1960), *The Oak Ridge Boys With The Sounds Of Nashville* (1962), *Folk Minded Spirituals For Spiritual Minded Folk* (1962), *Sing For You* (1964), *I Wouldn't Take Nothing For My Journey Now* (1965), *The Sensational Oak Ridge Boys From Nashville, Tennessee* (1965), *Sing And Shout* (1966), *At Their Best* (1966), *Solid Gospel Sound Of The Oak Ridge Quartet* (1966), *Together* (1966), *Sings River Of Love* (1967), as Wally Fowler And The Oak Ridge Quartet *Gospel Song Festival* (1970), *International* (1971), *Light* (1972), *Hymns* (1973), *Street Gospel* (1973), *Gospel Gold Heartwarming* (1974), *Oak Ridge Boys* (1974), *Super Gospel - Four Sides Of Gospel Excitement Heartwarming* (1974), *Sky High* (1975), *Old Fashioned, Down Home, Handclappin' Footstompin', Southern Style, Gospel Quartet Music* (1976), *Y'All Come Back Saloon* (1977), *Live* 1977), *Room Service* (1978), *The Oak Ridge Boys Have Arrived* (1979), *Together* (1980), *Fancy Free* (1981), *Bobbie Sue* (1982), *Christmas* (1982), *American Made* (1983), *The Oak Ridge Boys Deliver* (1983), *Friendship* (1983), *Seasons* (1985), *Step On Out* (1985), *Where The Fast Lane Ends* (1986), *Christmas Again* (1986), *Monongahela* (1987), *New Horizons* (1988), *American Dreams* (1989), *Unstoppable* (1991), *The Long Haul* (1992).

Further reading: *The Oak Ridge Boys - Our Story*, with Ellis Winder and Walter Carter.

Oakenfold, Paul

Renowned UK DJ and remixer Oakenfold was first active in club promotions during dance music's underground days. Having formerly trained as a chef he was introduced to the decks by his friend Trevor Fung at a Covent Garden bar in 1981. He eventually moved to New York and worked for **Arista**, before returning to England as **Profile**'s UK agent. He spent 1987 DJing at Ibiza clubs like Amnesia, and when he returned to England in November of that year he staged a near-legendary, invite-only 'Ibiza Reunion Party' at his Project Club in Streatham. During his various residencies he was of pivotal importance in the emergence of the hip hop, balearic and house movements. Famed for his sets at the Future Club (which he launched), Spectrum, Theatre Of Madness, Land Of Oz, Shoom (alongside **Andy Weatherall**) and Hacienda, he would go on to become synonymous with the **Ministry Of Sound** venue, playing a major role in preparing tracks for 'in-house' compilations. However, he had long since established his name as a remixer. Together with Steve Osborne he gave the

Happy Mondays' 'Wrote For Luck' a new club edge in 1989. It won them the plaudit 'Dance Record Of The Year' from the *New Musical Express*. Other remix clients tumbled quickly after, including the **Shamen**, **Massive Attack**, **M People**, **New Order**, **Arrested Development** and **U2** (mostly under the Perfecto nom de plume, indicating Oakenfold/Osborne). Perfecto also operated as a label, through **RCA**. Oakenfold would later tour with U2, spinning diverse selections including sections of the *Blade Runner* soundtrack (the film soundtrack album being among his favourite musical mediums). However, Oakenfold also made the rarer transition to full-blown producer on projects by the aforementioned Happy Mondays, Solid Gold Easy Action ('Enjoy' in 1990) and **Deacon Blue**. In 1991 he was nominated, alongside Osbourne, for a BRIT award for best producer. He maintained his sense of propriety on singles like Movement 98 (Featuring Carroll Thompson)'s 'Joy And Heartbreak' - part of his intention to pull down the bpm of dance records to 98. It predicted the rise of ambient house by including a snatch of **Erik Satie**'s 'Trois Gymnopee'. Just like Weatherall, he was signed up by a major in 1994 (in this case as A&R consultant for **East West**), and launched his own career with the single, 'Rise'. His more interesting recent remixing projects have included the **Stone Roses** and **Snoopy Doggy Dogg**.

Albums: *Journeys By DJ* (Music Unites 1994), *JD15 - Paul Oakenfold In The Mix* (Music Unites 1994).

Oaktown's 3-5-7

Half-hearted female rap troupe from the USA whose strings were pulled by an indulgent **Hammer**. Following the latter's defection from **Capitol** the group appear to have been washed up in the blood-letting. The group comprised local Oakland, Calfornia-rappers Sweet LD (b. Djuana Johnican), Terrible T (b. Tabatha King), Vicious C and Sweat P. The latter was formerly a cheerleader with the Oakland Raiders. By 1991 only Johnican and King remained.

Albums: *Wild And Loose* (Capitol 1989), *Fully Loaded* (Capitol 1991).

Oasis

From Manchester, England, Oasis became overnight sensations in 1994 on the back of sublime singles and exponentially increasing press interest, culminating in the fastest selling debut album of the 90s. Widely regarded in the press as natural successors to the **Happy Mondays**, Oasis proffered a similar working class roughneck chic. The group's creative axis is the Gallagher brothers, Noel (guitar/song writing) and Liam (vocals). They were brought up by Irish Roman Catholic parents in south Manchester suburb Burnage. While his younger brother was still in school, Noel, whose country and western DJ father has purchased a guitar for him at age 11, discovered punk, and like most of his peers happily engaged in truancy, burglary and glue-sniffing. After six month's probation for robbing a corner shop he began to take the instrument seriously at age 13, later finding his role model in Johnny Marr of the **Smiths**. Liam was not weaned on music until 1989 when his elder brother took him to see the **Stone Roses**. Afterwards Noel befriended Clint Boon of the **Inspiral Carpets**, subsequently becoming a guitar technician and travelling the world with them. When he rang home in 1991 he was informed by his mother that Liam had joined a band. Paul 'Bonehead' Arthurs (guitar), Tony McCarroll (drums) and Paul 'Guigs' McGuigan had been playing together as Rain (not the Liverpool group of similar moniker) before meeting with Liam, who became their singer, as they changed name to Oasis. When Noel returned to watch them play at Manchester's Boardwalk in 1992 he saw their promise, but insisted that they install him as lead guitarist and only perform his songs if he were to help them. Noel continued as roadie to the Inspiral Carpets to help purchase equipment, as the band set about establishing a local reputation. The incident which led to them being signed to **Creation Records** quickly passed into rock mythology. In May 1993 they drove to Glasgow with fellow denizens of the Boardwalk rehearsal studios, Sister Lovers, to support **18 Wheeler** at King Tut's Wah Wah Club. Strong-arming their way on to the bill, they played five songs early in the evening, but these were enough to hypnotise Creation boss Alan McGee who offered them a contract there and then. However, they would not sign until several months later, during which time a copy of the band's demo had been passed to Johnny Marr, who became an early convert to the cause and put the band in touch with **Electronic**'s management company, Ignition. With news spreading of the group's rise it seemed likely that the band would join any number of labels apart from Creation, with **U2**'s Mother imprint rumoured to guarantee double any other offer. However, loyalty to the kindred spirits at Creation won through by October 1993, and two months later the label issued the group's 'debut', a one-sided 12-inch promo of 'Columbia' taken straight from the original demo. BBC Radio 1 immediately playlisted it (an almost unheralded event for such a 'non-release'). 1994 began with a torrent of press, much of it focusing on the group's errant behaviour. Punch-ups and the ingestion of large quantities of drink and drugs leading to gig cancellations, while frequent, often violent bickering between the Gallagher brothers lent the group a sense of danger and mischief. 'Supersonic' reached the UK Top 40 in May 1995. 'Shakermaker', owing an obvious debt to the **New Seekers**' 'I'd Like To Teach The World To Sing', duly made number 11 two months later. High profile dates at the Glastonbury Festival and New York's New Music Seminar ensued, along with more stories of on the road indulgence. The **Beatles**-redolent 'Live Forever', with a sleeve featuring a photo of the house where **John Lennon** grew up, made the Top 10 in October. All of which ensured that the expectation for a debut album was now phenomenal. After scrapping the original tapes recorded at Monmouth's Monnow Studios, the songs had been completed with Mark Coyle and Anjali Dutt, with subsequent mixing by Electronic producer Owen Morris, at a total cost of £75,000. In August 1994 *Definitely Maybe* entered the UK charts at number 1, and, backed by a live version of the Beatles' 'I Am The Walrus', 'Cigarettes And Alcohol', a stage favourite, became the group's biggest UK singles success to date, when it reached number 7 in October 1994. In December they released 'Whatever' (not quite the Christmas number 1), a lush pop song with full orchestration that sounded astonishingly accomplished for a band whose recording career stretched over only eight months. Their assault on America began January 1995, and with a few gigs and word of mouth reports they were soon hovering around the US top 50. In mid-1995 it was announced that drummer McCarroll had amicably left the band. Few pop bands in recent years have created such a body of quality work in such a short time, and all done without resorting to media hype. No band since the Beatles has received such universal acclaim. Sadly our expectation of them is already immense.

Album: *Definitely Maybe* (Creation 1994).

Further reading: *Oasis: The Illustrated Story*, Paul Lester.

Obey, Ebenezer

b. 27 August 1942, Abeokuta, Nigeria. Obey's earliest musical experiences were as a member of the local church choir while a child in Abeokuta - his parents, both devout Christians, were also members. In 1955, he joined the local band Ifelode Mambo, which despite its name was actually a juju outfit, playing guitar and thumb piano. He also played briefly with Fatayi Rolling Dollar and the Federal Rhythm Brothers Orchestra before moving to Lagos in 1963 and forming his own juju band, the International Brothers, in 1964. Under Obey's leadership, the International Brothers forged a highly individual style of juju. Abandoning the percussion and single-guitar style developed by **I.K. Dairo**, Obey added two more frontline guitars and electric bass, speeded up the tempo and simplified the beat. The formula struck an immediate chord with Nigerian juju fans, and Obey enjoyed his first hit, 'Omo Lami', in 1965, followed by an even bigger success the following year with 'Olo Mi Gbo Temi'. By the early 70s, Obey was rivalling **King Sunny Ade** in album output and sales, achieving big local hits with *In London, On The Town, Board Members* and *Aiye Wa A Toro*. In 1971, he renamed his band the Inter Reformers and retitled his style miliki system (essentially a shrewd marketing move, for the music continued in the same juju style he had introduced with the International Brothers, heavier and faster than that played by most of his peers). In 1972, he opened his Lagos nightclub, the Miliki Spot, and for the next two or three years reigned as the city's pre-eminent juju bandleader.

By the mid-70s, however, Obey was beginning to be threatened by the younger Ade. Juju fans split into two camps: those who followed the Master Guitarist Ade, and those who favoured the sweetness of Obey's vocals and the philosophical nature of his lyrics. It was with their lyrics, above all, that the two men identified themselves. Ade's reflected his belief in traditional Yoruba religion, while Obey, always the perfect Christian gentleman, preached the orthodox values of love, the family and peace in the household. He also took on the role of Government spokesman, explaining the switch to the right-hand side that took place on Nigeria's roads in 1972, and the need to follow more recent campaigns, such as Operation Feed Yourself in 1976 (with *Operation Feed The Nation),* or the austerity measures that followed the end of Nigeria's oil-based boom in the early 80s. While Obey never achieved the international profile of Ade, he actually preceded the latter in the attempt. In 1980, he licensed six albums to the London-based OTI label (including *Current Affairs* and *What God Has Joined Together).* Lacking the promotional and financial muscle of a larger label like **Island**, with whom Ade would sign in 1982, OTI were, however, unable to sell Obey outside the expatriate Nigerian market and a small number of white enthusiasts. In 1983 he tried again, signing to **Virgin Records**, and releasing the adventurously funk and highlife infused *Je Ka Jo*. Grossly underpromoted, the album failed to convince expatriate Nigerians or make any impact on the growing white audience for juju. A similar fate befell the Virgin follow-up *Greatest Hits*. A third attempt, with yet another label, the specialist independent Sterns, produced *Solubon* - which, sadly, failed to live up to its name, at least as far as sales outside the expatriate community were concerned. Ever resilient, Obey next set his sights on the US market, touring there to great acclaim - but with little effect on record sales - in 1985 and 1986. He continues, however, to be a major recording and performing artist at home in Nigeria.

Selected albums: *In London* (1969), *Board Members* (1970), *The Horse The Man And His Son* (1973), *Around The World* (1974), *Murtala Mohammed* (1976), *Operation Feed The Nation* (1976), *Adam And Eve* (1977), *No Place Uke My Country Nigeria* (1978), *Celebration* (1982), *Je Ka Jo* (1983), *The Only Condition To Save Nigeria* (1984), *Solution* (1984), *Juju Jubilee* (1985), *My Father* (1989), *What God Has Joined* (1989).

Obiedo, Ray

b. San Francisco, California, USA. Contemporary jazz

composer and guitarist Obiedo had an eclectic musical background during his youth, spent in the Bay Area of San Francisco. Here the sounds of **Miles Davis**, **Henry Mancini**, **Antonio Carlos Jobim** and the imported soul and pop of **Motown Records** defined his early musical persona. Probably the greatest influence on his embryonic career, however, was the **James Brown** revue, whose funky, percussive guitar platform founded the platform on which Obiedo built his technique. In the early 80s his reputation grew as one of California's finest exponents of jazz, pop and fusion. He joined organist **Johnny 'Hammond' Smith** on tour, then **ECM** trombonist Julian Priester. His own fusion band, Kick, included **Sheila E.** on drums and **Sonny Rollins** associate Mark Soskin on keyboards. His other outlet during this time was the pop-rock vehicle, Rhythmus 21, wherein he worked with other prominent session musicians from the Bay Area. His own such session/touring experience is considerable, having partnered artists including **Herbie Hancock**, **George Duke**, **Lou Rawls**, **Rodney Franklin** and **Marc Russo**. His solo compositions also attracted acclaim, and saw interpretations from Sheila E., saxophonist Alex Murzyn, guitarist Bruce Forman and percussionist **Pete Escovedo**. Parts of this work have appeared on film soundtracks, most notably Michael Caine's *A Shock To The System* and Richard Gere's *Internal Affairs*, and he also collaborated with Teresa Tull on *Claire Of The Moon*. Such notoriety co-existed with Obiedo's rising status as a solo artist, recording a clutch of 90s albums for Windham Hill Records while leading the Ray Obiedo group on club dates and concerts. *Sticks And Stones* peaked at number 7 on ***Billboard***'s Contemporary Jazz chart, while *Zulaya* continued his exploration of Latin and Brazilian influences. Sheila E. was on hand to provide percussion, while the backing vocals of Claytoven Richardson, Annie Stocking, Sandy Griffith and Jenny Meltzer lent the compositions a new emotive depth and identity. It was the first album to be solely produced by the artist, ensuring a clarity of vision to match the pristine musical performances.
Albums: *Perfect Crime* (Windham Hill 1989), *Iguana* (Windham Hill 1991), *Sticks & Stones* (Windham Hill 1993), *Zulaya* (Windham Hill 1995).

Obituary

This intense and disturbing death metal group hails from Brandon, Florida, USA, where they formed in 1985. After recording a single and contributing two tracks to *Metal Massacre* compilations as Xecutioner, they changed their name to Obituary. This was initiated by the appearance of another, inferior act, who also travelled under the Xecutioner banner. Signed to Roadrunner Records, the band comprised John Tardy (vocals), Allen West (guitar), Trevor Peres (guitar), David Tucker (bass) and Donald Tardy (drums). *Slowly We Rot*, unveiled in 1989, was characterized by their vocalist's gurgling, sewer-like vocals, primarily employed as a musical instrument rather than a means of imparting lyrics, over a maelstrom of crashing powerchords and demonic drumming. Indeed, the indecipherable nature of John Tardy's outbursts helped insure them against some of the hysterical criticisms levelled at other death metal pioneers. *Cause Of Death* saw the band refine their unique style with ex-**Death** guitarist James Murphy and bassist Frank Watkins in place of West and Tucker respectively. Obituary, however, continued to specialize in a hideous and brutal musical carnage, taking the death metal concept to its ultimate conclusion. The release of *World Demise*, again recorded with long-time producer Scott Burns, did reveal a more considered approach, with the occasional snatch of audible lyric from Tardy (a press statement from Peres noted 'We're serious people, and we wanna be taken seriously'). By this time Tucker had been replaced by Frank Watkins, while Allen West was also enjoying his own side-project, Six Feet Under, with **Cannibal Corpse**'s Chris Barnes.
Albums: *Slowly We Rot* (Roadracer 1989), *Cause Of Death* (Roadracer 1990), *The End Complete* (Roadracer 1992), *World Demise* (Roadrunner 1994).

Obsessed

Spawned by the Washington DC underground of the early 80s, the Obsessed were ranked alongside **Minor Threat** and **Bad Brains** in the vicinity, yet never made the immediate transition to nationwide renown which those two outfits achieved. Though more obviously metal-inclined than either, notwithstanding odes to mysticism and **Black Sabbath** riffs, the Obsessed (Scott 'Wino' Weinrich, vocals/guitar, Mark Laue, bass, Ed Gulli, drums) proved influential to two rival camps of supporters, who could be delineated by the length of their hair. They made their debut with a three-track EP (*Sodden Jackyl*) for their own Invictus label, but otherwise relied on live shows and the circulation of demo tapes to establish their reputation. After several years of attrition, Weinrich hooked up with **Saint Vitus**, replacing vocalist Scott Reagers (on the latter's request), and moving to Los Angeles. The group would go on to cut several albums of ultra-heavy hardcore together between 1986 and 1991. Towards the end of this stint Saint Vitus' German label, Hellbound, approached Weinrich about the now legendary Obsessed demos, and an eponymous album was released in 1990 (also referred to as *The Purple Album*). A fine collection which overcame the obvious budget limitations, it immediately drew the kind of attention deprived the band in its infancy, but put Weinrich's tenure with Saint Vitus into question. Forced to choose by guitarist Dave Chandler, he elected to reform the Obsessed with Scott Reeder (bass)

and Greg Rogers (drums; ex-**Poison 13**). The raging *Lunar Womb* revealed a rejuvenated and ferocious band back at the peak of its powers. However, problems with Hellbound delayed progress, until **Columbia** stepped in to offer the Obsessed a recording contract, while Reeder (going on to join **Kyuss**) was replaced by part-time **B.A.L.L./Scream** member, Guy Pinhas. Despite landing with a major, however, the Obsessed, and Weinrich in particular, maintained an enviable status amongst their peers, the more high profile of their supporters including **L7**'s Jennifer Finch, **Corrosion Of Conformity**'s Pepper Keenan, **Fugazi**'s Ian MacKaye, **Pantera**'s Phil Anselmo, and **Henry Rollins**.
Albums: *The Obsessed* (Hellbound 1990), *Lunar Womb* (Hellbound 1991), *The Church Within* (Columbia 1993).

Obsession

This Connecticut, USA-based outfit was formed in 1983 by vocalist Mike Vescara and guitarist Bruce Vitale. Adding Art Maco (guitar), Matt Karugas (bass) and Jay Mezias (drums), they made their debut with a track on the *Metal Massacre* compilation album in 1983. Combining **Judas Priest**, **Venom** and **Anvil** influences, they subsequently recorded the *Marshall Law* mini-album; a high-speed, dual guitar onslaught, accentuated by Vescara's piercing howl. A contract with Enigma ensued and the two albums that resulted showed the band diversifying into more melodic territory. In mid-1988 Maco and Mezias quit, but the band finally folded when Vescara accepted the position of frontman with Japanese rockers, **Loudness**.
Albums: *Marshall Law* (Metal Blade 1984), *Scarred For Life* (Enigma 1986), *Methods Of Madness* (Enigma 1987).

Obus

This Spanish melodic metal band was formed in 1980 by vocalist Fortu, guitarist Francisco Laguna, Fernando Sanches (drums) and Juan Luis Serrano. Though restricting their potential audience by insisting on singing in their native tongue, this undoubtedly helped the authenticity of their sound, which was otherwise unoriginal. Signing to the local Chapa Discos label, they recorded three amateurish albums lacking in fresh ideas before dissolving in the mid-80s.
Albums: *Preparato* (Chapa Discos 1981), *Podoroso Como El Trueno* (Chapa Discos 1982), *El Que Mas* (Mausoleum 1984).

Ocean

A song that owed much of its stylistic origin to pure hand-clapping gospel gave Ocean from Canada their one and only true hit in the spring of 1971. 'Put Your Hand In The Hand', originally recorded by Anne Murray, was written by Gene MacLellan, who also composed Murray's hit 'Snowbird'. Ocean, who were initially called Leather And Lace, rearranged the song themselves and sent copies to radio stations, resulting in the US number 2 hit. Ocean consisted of Janice Morgan (lead vocals), Jeff Jones (bass), Dave Tamblyn (lead guitar), Greg Brown (keyboard/vocals) and Chuck Slater (drums). After three other minor chart singles, the group disbanded in 1975, although they remained together domestically living on a Canadian farm. Sadly, during the 80s, Chuck Slater committed suicide.
Albums: *Put Your Hand In The Hand* (1971), *Give Tomorrow's Children One More Chance* (1972).

Ocean, Billy

b. Leslie Sebastian Charles, 21 January 1950, Trinidad, West Indies. Raised in England, Ocean worked as a session singer between employment at the Dagenham Ford Motor Company plant before being signed by the GTO label as a solo artist. His early hits included 'Love Really Hurts Without You' (1976) and 'Red Light Spells Danger' (1977), two purposeful, if derivative performances. The singer's subsequent releases fared less well and for four years, between 1980-84, Billy was absent from the British charts. Paradoxically, it was during this period that he began to win an audience in America. Ocean moved there at the turn of the decade and several R&B successes prepared the way for 'Caribbean Queen (No More Love On The Run)', his first national US pop number 1. Now signed to the Jive label, this million-selling single introduced an impressive run of hits, including two more US chart toppers, 'There'll Be Sad Songs (To Make You Cry)' (1986) and 'Get Outta My Dreams, Get Into My Car' (1988). Despite securing a UK number 1 with 'When The Going Gets Tough, The Tough Get Going', (which was featured in the film T*he Jewel Of The Nile*) Ocean's luck with chart success in Britain constantly fluctuated. However his popular appeal secured him three UK Top 5 albums during this period including the *Greatest Hits* collection in 1989.
Albums: *Billy Ocean* (1975), *City Limit* (1980), *Nights (Feel Like Getting Down)* (1981), *Inner Feelings* (1982), *Suddenly* (1984), *Love Zone* (1986), *Tear Down These Walls* (1988), *Time To Move On* (1993). Compilation: *Greatest Hits* (1989).

Ochs, Phil

b. 19 December 1940, El Paso, Texas, d. 7 April 1976. A superior singer/songwriter, particularly adept at the topical song, Phil Ochs began his career at Ohio State University. He initially performed in a folksinging duo, the Sundowners, before moving to New York, where he joined the radical Greenwich Village enclave. Ochs' early work was inspired by **Woody Guthrie**, **Bob Gibson** and **Tom Paxton**, and its political nature led to his involvement with the *Broadside* magazine movement. The singer was signed to the prestigious **Elektra Records** label, and through his initial work was hailed as a major new talent. He achieved popular acclaim when **Joan Baez** took one of his compositions, 'There But For Fortune', into the pop charts. Ochs' own version later appeared on his *In Concert*, the artist's best-selling set which also featured the evocative 'When I'm Gone' and the wry 'Love Me I'm A Liberal'. Ochs' move to **A&M Records** in 1967 signalled a new phase in his career. *Pleasures Of The Harbour*, which included the ambitious 'Crucifixion', emphasized a greater use of orchestration, as well as an increasingly rock-based perspective. He remained a lyrical songwriter; his sense of melody was undiminished, but as the decade's causes grew increasingly blurred, so the singer became disillusioned. Although *Rehearsals For Retirement* documented the political travails of a bitter 1968, the sardonically-titled *Phil Ochs Greatest Hits* showed an imaginative performer bereft of focus. He donned a gold-lamé suit in a misguided effort to 'wed **Elvis Presley** to the politics of Che Guevara', but his in-concert rock 'n' roll medleys were roundly booed by an audience expecting overt social comment. This period is documented on the controversial *Gunfight At Carnegie Hall*. Ochs' later years were marked by tragedy. He was attacked during a tour of Africa and an attempted strangulation permanently impaired his singing voice. Beset by a chronic songwriting block, Phil sought solace in alcohol and although a rally/concert in aid of Chile, *An Evening With Salvador Allende*, succeeded through his considerable entreaties, he later succumbed to schizophrenia. Phil Ochs' was found hanged at his sister's home on 7 April 1976. One of the finest performers of his generation, he was considered, at least for a short time, **Bob Dylan**'s greatest rival.

Albums: *All The News That's Fit To Sing* (1964), *I Ain't Marching Anymore* (1965), *Phil Ochs In Concert* (1966), *The Pleasures Of The Harbour* (1967), *Tape From California* (1968), *Rehearsals For Retirement* (1968), *Phil Ochs Greatest Hits* (1970), *Gunfight At Carnegie Hall* (1975). Compilations: *Phil Ochs - Chords Of Fame* (1976), *Phil Ochs - Songs For Broadside* (1976), *Broadside Tapes* (1976), *A Toast To Those Who Are Gone* (1987), *There But For Fortune* (1989).

Further reading: *Phil Ochs: Death Of A Rebel*, Marc Elliott.

Oden, James Burke

b. 26 June 1903, Nashville, Tennessee, USA, d. 30 December 1977, Chicago, Illinois, USA. He was also known as St. Louis Jimmy, Big Bloke, Poor Boy and Old Man Oden. Although he was quite a capable pianist St. Louis Jimmy Oden's fame rests mainly on his prowess as a blues singer and composer. His most famous song 'Going Down Slow' has been recorded by many famous blues artists, an outstanding version by **Howlin' Wolf** aided by **Willie Dixon**, and was something of an anthem with white groups during the 60s. He was born, according to some sources, in 1905, to Henry Oden, a dancer, and Leana West. Both parents died before he was eight years old and his early life remains a blank, largely because he wished it so, until he turned up in St. Louis, Missouri at the age of 14 working in a barber's shop. St. Louis had a thriving blues community during the 20s and Jimmy Oden found himself a niche in it. He taught himself piano during this period but never played much professionally, believing that there were many better players than himself around who would be able to accompany him. His main influence would seem to be **Walter Davis** although his most constant companions were **Big Joe Williams** and **Roosevelt Sykes**. It was in the company of Sykes and violinist Curtis Mosby that he made his first foray into a recording studio in 1932. He moved north to Chicago in 1933 and was active in the blues scene of that city from then until the 50s performing, writing, and sometimes managing a band for **Eddie Boyd,** as well as being involved in the founding of the JOB record label. On one of his later sessions he was backed by the then emerging **Muddy Waters** and, after his activities were restricted by a serious car accident, he took up lodgings in the basement of Waters' house, paying his rent by supplying the odd song. He benefited briefly from the resurgence of interest in the blues during the 60s, recording albums for such labels as Delmark, Bluesville and Spivey. His death was due to bronchopneumonia.

Selected album: *Doghouse*.

Odetta

b. Odetta Holmes Felious Gorden, 31 December 1930, Birmingham, Alabama, USA. A classically-trained vocalist, Odetta sang in the chorus of the 1947 Broadway production of ***Finian's Rainbow***, before opting for a career in folk music. Successful residencies in San Francisco clubs, the Hungry i and Tin Angel, inspired interest in New York circles although her early releases revealed a still maturing talent. Odetta had been brought up in the blues tradition, but moved increasingly towards folk during the late 50s. Odetta had sung jazz and blues for the **RCA** and Riverside labels, and, only occasionally, folk for the Tradition label. Her blues was sung in the **Bessie Smith** tradition, but without the same emotion. Nevertheless, she recorded standards including 'House Of The Rising Sun' and 'Make Me A Pallet On Your Floor'. In 1960 she took to the solo acoustic guitar and moved to **Vanguard**. Possessed of a powerful voice, her style embraced gospel, jazz and blues, but eventually Odetta fell foul of the changing trends and fashions in music, and much was forgotten of her earlier work from the 50s and 60s. The singer was championed by **Pete Seeger** and **Harry Belafonte**, the latter of whom Odetta accompanied on a 1961 UK hit, 'Hole In The Bucket', while her solo career flourished with a succession of albums for the Vanguard label. The artist's emotional mixture of spiritual, ethnic and jazz

styles is best captured in person and thus *Odetta At Town Hall* and *Odetta At Carnegie Hall* remain her most representative sets by revealing the full extent of her varied repertoire.
Albums: *Odetta Sings Ballads And Blues* (1956), *Odetta At The Gate Of Horn* (1957), *My Eyes Have Seen* (1959), *Christmas Spirituals* (Vanguard 1960), *Odetta And The Blues* (Riverside 1962), *Sometimes I Feel Like Crying* (RCA 1962), *Odetta At Town Hall* (1962), *Odetta* (1963), *Odetta Sings Folk Songs* (1963), *One Grain Of Sand* (Vanguard 1963), *It's A Mighty World* (1964), *Odetta Sings Of Many Things* (1964), *Odetta Sings Dylan* (1965), *Ballads For Americans* (1965), *Odetta In Japan* (1965), *Odetta* (1967), *Odetta At Carnegie Hall* (Vanguard 1967), *Odetta Sings The Blues* (1968), *Odetta Sings* (1971), *It's Impossible* (1978). Compilations: *Best Of Odetta* (1967), *The Essential Odetta* (1989).

Odom, Andrew

b. 15 December 1936, Denham Springs, Louisiana, USA. Odom occasionally worked under the name of 'BV' or 'Big Voice'. He sang in a church choir as a child; his family moved north in the mid-50s, settling in St. Louis, Missouri. While there Odom sometimes worked with **Albert King** and reputedly recorded in the late 50s. He moved to Chicago in 1960 where he had long associations with **Earl Hooker** and **Jimmy Dawkins**. Singles under Odom's same have appeared on several local labels, and he made his debut album for Bluesway in 1969. Since then he has also recorded for Wasp Music and French labels MCM and Isabel. Odom is an intense, powerful blues singer, influenced by **B.B. King** and **Bobby 'Blue' Bland**.
Albums: *Farther On Down The Road* (1969), *Feel So Good* (1982).

Odyssey

Formed in New York City, vocalists Lillian, Louise and Carmen Lopez were originally known as the Lopez Sisters. Their parents came from the Virgin Islands, but they were born and raised in Stamford, Connecticut, USA. Carmen left the group in 1968 and was replaced by Tony Reynolds (b. Manila), who after the group's first album was replaced by Bill McEachern. Odyssey's 1977 release, 'Native New Yorker', reached the US Top 20, but the song proved more popular in the UK where it peaked at number 5. It was not until 1980 that Odyssey appeared in the UK chart with the first of several UK hits. 'Use It Up And Wear It Out' topped the chart in June of that year, while the beautiful soulful ballad, 'If You're Looking For A Way Out' gave them their third Top 10 hit. Two more effortless pop/soul offerings, 'Going Back To My Roots' (1981) and 'Inside Out' (1982), reached the Top 5. However the lack of a sustained success at home hampered the group's wider progress and they latterly broke up.
Albums: *Odyssey* (1977), *Hollywood Party Tonight* (1978), *Hang Together* (1980), *I Got The Melody* (1981), *Happy Together* (1982), *A Piping Journey* (1987). Compilations: *Best Of Odyssey* (1981), *Magic Moments With Odyssey* (1984), *Greatest Hits* (1987).

Of Perception

Between 1979 and 1984 Deviant (b. Stuart Powell, Enfield, England; vocals/guitar/keyboards) and Jellyfish (b. Kevin Nicholson, Tottenham, London, England; bass/vocals/keyboards), were the mainstay of the **New Wave Of British Heavy Metal** band Tooth. After playing in various other groups the two reunited in 1989 for a jam session with various friends and session men. Within a year they had put together a stable line-up with ex-Swamp Angels guitarist Dave Williams and former lighting engineer Pete Smith. After a few gigs and two demos they found ex-**Neil Christian** bassist Arthur Anderson to record/produce and mix an entire album in 24 hours. The resulting *So Join Mr Dreams* offered a marriage of **Doors**, **Motörhead** and **Hawkwind** influences. It found little favour in the UK but an audience emerged in Europe. Dejected after a tour of Holland fell through at the last moment in 1992 they headed off to the studio to record a new album with producer Brian Martin. The resultant *Lords So Strange R* was a much more ambitious project, with the debut of female backing vocalist Jazz J. Soon after they split up, which turned out to be a blessing in disguise. Absent from the music scene, they picked up a cult following in Spain and Germany as well as 'underground' magazines from around the world. The group reformed late in 1994 minus Jazz J and Smith, and after initial studio work were joined by session drummer 'Chops'.
Albums: *So Join Mr Dreams* (Hawke Park 1991), *Lords So Strange R* (Hawke Park 1992).
Video: *Of Perception* (1991).

Of Thee I Sing

After **George S. Kaufman**'s uncompromising book for ***Strike Up The Band*** had been replaced by a less contentious one by Morrie Ryskind, the two writers collaborated on the libretto for this show which has been called 'the greatest of all American musicals'. It opened at the Music Box Theatre in New York on 26 December 1931, complete with a sharp and witty plot in which most American institutions, especially family life and politics, come in for their fair share of satirical attention. John P. Wintergreen (William Gaxton) and his prospective Vice-President, Alexander Throttlebottom (Victor Moore), have discarded issues such as home and foreign affairs, and are running for office on a ticket of LOVE. In fact, Wintergreen issues a statement that he will propose to his Mary (Lois Moran) in every one of the 48 States. They are elected to the White House with a landslide victory, but, like so many presidents that followed him, Wintergreen's future is threatened by an indiscreet dalliance with the fairer sex - in his case, Diana Devereaux (Grace Brinkley), the current Miss America. Impeachment looms, but Wintergreen keeps his job after Throttlebottom offers to marry the beauty queen because, under the Constitution: 'When the President of the United States is unable to fulfil his duties, his obligations are assumed by the Vice President.' Gaxton and Moore were marvellous, and went on to star in several other musicals together, including ***Anything Goes***, ***Leave It To Me!***, and ***Louisiana Purchase***. Once again, **George** and **Ira Gershwin** wrote a score that was both tuneful and entirely complementary to the action. Two of the songs matured into standards, 'Who Cares?' and 'Love Is Sweeping The Country', and the spirited 'Of Thee I Sing (Baby)' was also a hit at the time for **Ben Selvin**. The remainder of the score consisted of 'Wintergreen For President', 'Hello, Good Morning', 'The Illegitimate Daughter', and 'Because, Because'. As one of 29 new Broadway musicals that season, *Of Thee I Sing* enjoyed an excellent run of 441 performances, and returned two years later for a brief spell at the Imperial theatre. The show became the first musical to be awarded the prestigious Pulitzer Prize for Drama, although composer George Gershwin's music and name was omitted from the citation. Over the years, *Of Thee I Sing* was a leading candidate for revival in the US, especially at election time. When the Arena Stage in Washinton D.C. presented the show in November 1992, each patron received a voting slip in their programme. The running total was chalked on the back wall of the auditorium, and, even early on in the campaign, there was a hint of things to come with the Clinton-Gore ticket regularly beating Bush-Quayle by about four to one.

Ofarim, Esther And Abi

Esther Ofarim (b. Esther Zaled, 13 June 1943, Safed, Israel) and Abraham Reichstadt (b. 5 October 1939, Tel Aviv, Israel) were a husband and wife team who shot to fame in their homeland during the early 60s. With a keen eye for the international market, Esther had represented Switzerland in the 1963 Eurovision Song Contest while the duo extended their appeal on the Continent via concert performances and foreign language recordings. An appearance on the high-rating *Eamonn Andrews Show* on UK television, in which Esther and Abi sang a novelty love duet, proved so popular that the song became an overnight smash. 'Cinderella Rockefella' (composed by **Mason Williams**) topped the British charts for three weeks in early 1968 and although the duo seemed likely one-hit-wonders they managed a successful follow-up with 'One More Dance'. The partnership subsequently broke up when their marriage was dissolved.

Albums: *2 In 3* (1968), *Ofarim Concert - Live '69* (1969).

Offenbach

Progressive rock outfit originating from Quebec, Canada. The band were assembled in 1975 by Gerard Boulet (vocals/keyboards) and Breen Laboeuf (vocals/bass). Following the addition of Jean Gravel (guitar), John McGale (guitar) and Pierre Ringuet (drums), they signed to **A&M Records** in 1976. Debuting with *Never Too Tender*, they initially opted for English lyrics, which sounded rather wooden in their extended psychedelic, blues-based workouts. Realizing this, they switched to singing in French from *Offenbach* onwards. Changing labels to **RCA** in 1979 saw a swing towards an earthy R&B style, not that dissimilar to **Joe Cocker**. Failing to find an audience with this new direction, they started to incorporate wind instruments, extend the length of compositions and move into the domain of symphonic folk-rock.

Albums: *Never Too Tender* (A&M 1976), *Offenbach* (A&M 1977), *Victoire D'Armour* (A&M 1978), *Traversion* (RCA 1979), *Encore* (RCA 1980), *Coup De Foudu* (RCA 1981).

Offitt, Lillian

b. 4 November 1938, Nashville, Tennessee, USA. On the evidence of her half dozen releases, Lillian Offit was a plain but lusty blues shouter, of small stature and commensurate talent. She was still attending college when she visited the offices of Nashboro Records in the hope of making a gospel record. Owner Ernie Young suggested that she try secular music, and 'Miss You So' was issued on Excello sometime in 1957. It was successful enough for her to turn professional, and two further singles were issued, with diminishing success. In 1958 she moved to Chicago to become featured singer with the **Earl Hooker** band at Robert's Show Lounge. Through Hooker, she met Me London, owner of Chief Records, and cut her first record for the label in February 1960. 'Will My Man Be Home Tonight', heavily featuring Hooker's slide guitar, became a hit in the Chicago area. 'My Man I A Lover', recorded May 1960, and 'Troubles' from a year later, repeated the downward curve of Excello releases. She left music to start a family, preventing her from joining the 1964 American Folk Blues Festival tour, her place taken by **Sugar Pie DeSanto**. She was last sighted in 1974 as part of the Streakers Rated—X Revue in St. Joseph, Michigan.

Selected album: *Chicago Calling* (1986).

Oh! Calcutta!

A musical revue, devised in 1969 by Kenneth Tynan, the drama critic, and literary manager of Britain's National Theatre for 10 years, *Oh! Calcutta!* is rarely discussed in theatrical reference books. One of the excuses given for its omission is that it was not very good; but the main reason is surely that in most of the sketches the artists appear in the nude, and perform simulated sex acts. Tynan recruited **John Lennon**, Samuel Beckett, Jules Feiffer, Joe Orton, Sam Shepard, and others, to write material that reflected the sexual revolution that was taking place in the 'swinging sixties'; music and lyrics were credited to Open Window. The show opened in New York in June 1969 at the Off Broadway Eden Theatre, and was such a success that within a few months it was promoted to Broadway, where it stayed for 1,314 performances. The 1970 London production, taking advantage of the abolition of theatre censorship in 1968, ran for 3,918 performances. However, that impressive total paled in comparison with the 1976 Broadway revival which notched up an incredible total of 5,852. For some years now the show has been in second place in the Broadway long-running stakes, just behind ***A Chorus Line*** (6,137), with **Andrew Lloyd Webber**'s ***Cats***, coming up very fast on the rails. More than 20 years after its inception, *Oh! Calcutta!* continues to be controversial. In 1991, a judge in Chattanooga, Tennessee, overruled local officials and allowed the show to go on in a city-owned theatre. In both London and New York, its prolonged existence was often attributed to the patronage of visiting Japanese businessmen, so it was somewhat ironic that an American production opened in Tokyo in 1993 - albeit with some concessions involving partial body stockings and body paint.

Oh, Boy!

This was the second musical comedy to be written by the young Anglo/American team of **Jerome Kern** (music), **Guy Bolton** (book), and **P.G. Wodehouse** (book and lyrics), and their first to be presented at the the tiny **Princess Theatre** in New York. When *Oh, Boy!* opened there on 20 February 1917, it blew like a wind of change through the cobwebs of operetta which were hanging around most of the other Broadway shows. It was a jolly, contemporary production, unpretentious and thoroughly entertaining. There were elements of farce, too - people did seem to enter and leave through windows rather a lot - but the story was really about George Budd (Tom Powers). His main problem is to prevent his guardian, Aunt Penelope (Edna May Oliver), from discovering that he has just got married to Lou Ellen (Marie Carroll). If she does - there goes his allowance. When they learn of her imminent arrival, the newly-weds decided to part for a time - Lou Ellen's parents have not been informed of the situation either - and from that moment on, a series of complicted events ensue, during which Tom rescues the lovely actress, Jackie Sampson (Ann Wheaton), from the clutches of an amorous Judge Carter ('Tootles' to her), who eventually turns out to be his (Tom's) father-in-law, and Aunt Penelope gives the happy couple (George and Lou Ellen) her blessing while under the influence of a glass of spiked lemonade. The cast played it all with a lot of style, aided by a marvellous score which included the romantic couple's naive and wistful 'You Never Knew About Me' ('I'd have let you feed my rabbit/Till the thing became a habit, Dear!/But I never knew about you/Or what might have been/And you never knew about me.'). Jackie and Tom's best chum, Jim (Hal Forde), combined on another of the best numbers, 'Nesting Time In Flatbush', but there was not a dud among the rest of the bunch, which included 'Ain't It A Grand And Glorious Feeling', 'Be A Little Sunbeam', 'Every Day', 'The First Day Of May', 'FlubbyDub, The Cave Man', 'Land Where The Good Songs Go', 'A Pal Like You', 'Words Are Not Needed', 'An Old-Fashioned Wife', and 'A Package Of Seeds.' Another of the songs, 'Till the Clouds Roll By' became popular through recordings by Ann Wheaton with James Harrod, the Prince's Orchestra, and Vernon Dalhart. The tremendous success of *Oh, Boy!*, which ran for 475 performances, meant that the next Kern-Bolton-Wodehouse show, ***Leave It To Jane***, which was originally intended for the Princess, had to be diverted to the much larger Longacre Theatre. In 1919, when the show was presented in London, it was retitled *Oh, Joy!*, and starred Beatrice Lillie in her first book musical. The title *Oh, Boy!* did eventually go up in lights in London's West End 60 years later, when a show starring pop stars such as **Joe Brown**, **Shakin' Stevens**, and **Alvin Stardust**, which was based on a the television show, played the Astoria Theatre.

Oh, Joy!

(see ***Oh, Boy!***)

Oh, Kay!

This show provides the perfect argument for those who believe that 'they don't write them like that any more'. **George** and **Ira Gershwin** introduced four of the their all-time standards in *Oh, Kay!* which opened at the Imperial Theatre in New York on 8 November 1926, and the rest of the score was in the same class. **Guy Bolton** and **P.G. Wodehouse**, fresh from their successes with **Jerome Kern**, wrote the book in which the Kay of the title (**Gertrude Lawrence** in her first Broadway book musical) helps her hard-up ducal brother (Gerald Oliver Smith) - a bootlegger - to illegally import alcoholic beverages into the USA. They stash the booze on the Long Island estate of young and wealthy Jimmy Winter (Oscar Shaw), who is normally away and too busy enjoying himself at various shindigs to notice their comings and goings. However, when he returns, complications ensue, and Kay actually has to take a job in the household for a time, before Jimmy - cold sober - rejects his legion of admirers and decides to marry his 'Dear Little Girl'. Although not one of the one of the hits from the show, it was a charming number, which **Julie Andrews** reprised in the

Gertrude Lawrence biopic, ***Star!*** (1968). Kay and Jimmy's romance can only flourish, of course, after the two lovers have duetted on 'Maybe' and 'Do, Do, Do', and danced the night away with 'Clap Yo' Hands'. A more poignant moment occurs when, disguised as a housemaid, Kay 'meditates musically' - as Ira Gershwin put it - with the tender ballad, 'Someone To Watch Over Me'. 'Fidgety Feet' was another lively number by the two Gershwin brothers, but 'Oh, Kay!' and 'Heaven On Earth' both had lyrics by **Howard Deitz** who helped out when Ira Gershwin was ill. Victor Moore, one of America's favourite funny-men, returned to Broadway for the first time in 15 years in *Oh, Kay!*, and the cast also included Harland Dixon, Marion and Madeleine Fairbanks, Gerald Oliver, and Sascha Beaumont. The show ran for 256 performances, and Gertrude Lawrence recreated her role in the 1927 London production which lasted for six months. *Oh, Kay!* was revived Off Broadway in 1960, and was back in a main house, the **Richard Rodgers** Theatre, in 1990. The latter production, which started out at the Goodspeed Opera House in 1989, moved the show's location from Long Island to Harlem, and included an all-black cast. It closed after 77 performances, and producer David Merrick's attempt to restage it ended during previews. A reasonably successful West End revival was mounted in 1974, and 10 years later the show was a big hit when it played a season in England at the Chichester Festival Theatre, with the highly acclaimed Michael Siberry as Jimmy.

Oh, Lady! Lady!!

Another of the celebrated **Princess Theatre** shows with a score by **Jerome Kern** and **P.G. Wodehouse**, and a book by Wodehouse and **Guy Bolton** It opened at the tiny theatre in New York on 1 February 1918, and proved to be the last really successful show that the team wrote together. This time the plot centres on the well-to-do Long Island home belonging to the parents of Mollie Farrington (Vivienne Segal). She is about to marry Willoughby 'Bill' Finch (Carl Randall), that is until May Barber (Carroll McComas) turns up and announces that, in the past, she and Bill have been more than just good friends. Mollie is aghast: could Bill really have a female skeleton in his closet? Actually, it's not Bill that May is after at all, but Mollie's parents' jewels. All ends happily when May is apprehended by Bill's associate (and former crook), Spike Hudgins (Edward Ebeles). A thoroughly entertaining score contained no immediately identifiable hits, although Kern's music and Wodehouse's lyrics were far superior than those of their contemporaries - always relevant to the libretto - and continually pushing musical comedy forward. The songs included 'Before I Met You', 'Dear Old Prison Days', 'Do Look At Him', 'Do It Now', 'I'm To Be Married Today', 'It's A Hard, Hard World For A Man', 'Little Ships Come Sailing Home', 'Moon Song' 'Not Yet', 'Our Little Nest', 'A Picture I Want To See Of You', 'Some Little Girl', 'Waiting Round The Corner', 'You Found Me And I Found You', and 'Greenwich Village'. The latter number was featured in a spectacular rooftop sequence set in that New York location. One song was discarded during rehearsals because it was not considered suitable for Vivienne Segal's voice. It almost got to Broadway via *Zip Goes A Million* in 1919, but eventually had to wait until 1927 before it was introduced to the world by **Helen Morgan** in the magnificent ***Show Boat***. The song in question was 'Bill'. Even without it, *Oh, Lady! Lady!!* had an excellent run of 219 performances.

Oh, What A Lovely War!

This 'British musical entertainment' started out at the Theatre Royal, Stratford East in March 1963 before transferring to Wyndham's Theatre on 29 June that year. The cast consisted mainly of members of the Theatre Royal's 'repertory company', such as George Sewell, Avis Bunnage, Brian Murphy, Victor Spinetti, *et al.* Some of them collaborated with librettist Charles Chilton on the book which purported to reflect the misery and sheer waste of human life during World War I from the coersive recruitment methods ('We Don't Want To Lose You, But We Think You Ought To Go') to the grim reality of the trenches. This was achieved in an intelligent and humorous fashion by the use of more than 20 popular songs of the period, such as 'Your King And Country Need You', 'I'll Make A Man Of You', 'Goodbye ee', 'When This Lousy War Is Over', 'Hush, Here Comes A Whizzbang', 'Belgium Put The Kibosh On the Kaiser', 'Keep The Home Fires Burning', 'I Want To Go Home', and **Jerome Kern**'s lovely ballad 'They Didn't Believe Me'. Although some aspects of what started out at Stratford as a bitter anti-war tract were softened somewhat for West End audiences, the message remained loud and clear, and *Oh, What A Lovely War!* continued to spell it out for more than two years, during which time it won the *Evening Standard* Award for best musical. The appeal proved not to be so great in America, although Victor Spinetti won a **Tony Award** for best supporting actor, and the show folded after three and a half months. The 1969 film, directed by Richard Attenborough, adopted a different, star-studded approach. A rare revival of *Oh, What A Lovely War!* was presented by the UK National Youth Theatre in 1994 at the Bloomsbury Theatre in London.

Ohio Express

Key players in the bubblegum trend of the late 60s, the Ohio Express evolved from the Mansfield, Ohio, USA-based group Rare Breed in 1967. The group consisted of Joey Levine (lead vocals), Dale Powers (lead guitar), Doug Grassel (rhythm guitar), Jim Pflayer (keyboards),

Dean Krastan (bass) and Tim Corwin (drums). Their first single, 'Beg, Borrow And Steal', had originally been recorded by the group under its old monicker in 1966 before it was reissued the following year by **Cameo Records**. There the group teamed up with producers **Jerry Kasenetz** and **Jeff Katz**, and reached number 29 in the autumn of 1967. A second Cameo single to chart was 'Try It', a song penned by Levine which was later covered by the **Standells**. In 1968 the Ohio Express signed with Neil Bogart's Buddah Records and released the bubblegum 'Yummy Yummy Yummy', which became their biggest hit, reaching the Top 5 on both sides of the Atlantic. By the end of 1969 they would chart on six more occasions, the final time with 'Sausalito (Is The Place To Go)', sung by **Graham Gouldman**, later of **10cc** fame. The Ohio Express released six albums, of which only *Ohio Express* and *Chewy Chewy* made any real impact on the US charts. The group carried on until 1972; Levine formed **Reunion** in 1974.

Albums: *Beg, Borrow And Steal* (1968), *Ohio Express* (1968), *Salt Water Taffy* (1968), *Chewy Chewy* (1969), *Mercy* (1969). Compilation: *Very Best Of The Ohio Express* (1970).

Ohio Players

Formed in Dayton, Ohio, USA in 1959, this multi-talented unit originated from three members of the Ohio Untouchables, Leroy 'Sugarfoot' Bonner, Clarence 'Satch' Satchell and Marshall Jones. They forged a reputation as a powerful instrumental group by providing the backing to the **Falcons**, whose R&B classic, 'I Found A Love' (1962), featured singer **Wilson Pickett**. The Players began recording in their own right that same year, but did not achieve a notable success until the following decade when they embarked on a series of striking releases for the Westbound label after brief sessions for both Compass and **Capitol Records**. The group's experimental funk mirrored the work **George Clinton** had forged with **Funkadelic** for the same outlet and in 1973 the septet - Bonner, Satchell, Jones, Jimmy 'Diamond' Williams, Marvin 'Merv' Pierce, Billy Beck, Ralph 'Pee Wee' Middlebrook - scored a massive R&B smash with the irrepressible 'Funky Worm'. The Players later switched to **Mercury** where their US hits included 'Fire' (1974) and 'Love Rollercoaster' (1975), both of which topped the soul and pop charts. 'Who'd She Coo?' became the group's last substantial hit the following year and although success did continue throughout the rest of the 70s, their releases grew increasingly predictable. The group had become renowned for their sexually explicit album covers, suggesting the possibilities of a jar of honey, or depicting macho males dominating scantily clad subservient females - and vice versa. However, their musical credibility was such that the unit's version of 'Over The Rainbow' was played at **Judy Garland**'s funeral. Williams and Beck left the line-up in 1979 to form a new group, Shadow. A re-shaped Ohio Players recorded throughout the 80s, and scored a minor soul hit in 1988 with 'Sweat'.

Albums: *First Impressions* (1968), *Observations In Time* (1968), *Pain* (1972), *Pleasure* (1973), *Ecstasy* (1973), *Skin Tight* (1974), *Climax* (1974, a collection of out-takes), *Fire* (1974), *Honey* (1975), *Contradiction* (1976), *Angel* (1977), *Mr. Mean* (1977), *Jass-Ay-Lay-Dee* (1978), *Everybody Up* (1979), *Tenderness* (1981), *Ouch!* (1982), *Graduation* (1985), *Orgasm* (1993). Compilations: *Greatest Hits* (1975), *Rattlesnake* (1975), *Ohio Players Gold* (1976), *Ohio Players* (1977).

Ohrlin, Glenn

b. 26 October 1926, Minneapolis, Minnesota, USA. Ohrlin's father was a Swedish immigrant, and his mother's parents were from Norway. Apart from learning basic tunes and songs, and guitar technique, Glenn wanted to be a horse rider. At the age of 14, Ohrlin's family moved to California, and two years later he left home to go to Nevada to work in rodeo. He also worked on ranches throughout the West, and served in the US Army from 1945-46. After World War II, Ohrlin continued to absorb musical influences, including Flamenco guitar style, and traditional songs, learned from Mexican cowboys. He continued riding, both bareback and saddle, and, in September 1954, he and his wife moved to Mountain View, Arkansas to raise cattle. Later still, in 1960, having realized that some of the songs he was singing were important from a historical perspective, he began to collect songs from his friends and relations. Many of these were recorded in the field during the mid-60s. In April 1963, Glenn played at a Mountain View Festival, organized by the Rackensack Folklore Society. In September of the same year, Ohrlin travelled to Memphis, Tennessee, to play on the coffee house circuit. This, however, did not inspire any great reaction on the part of the music listening public at the time. He made his last rodeo ride in October 1963, at Andalusia, Alabama, and in less than three months made his debut recording, *Glenn Ohrlin*, in Illinois, in December 1963. It appeared on the University of Illinois Campus Folk Song Club Records label. The recording featured some of the songs performed at the University Folk Song Club on 14 December 1963, with other tracks taken from recordings made between 13 December and 16 March 1964. Glenn had already been recorded by Bruce Jackson during the summer of 1964. Between 1965-66, Ohrlin collected and recorded a number of performers throughout the states of Arkansas, Minnesota, and North Dakota. The material ranged from unaccompanied works (some with guitar and fiddle), to material sung in Swedish and Norwegian. *The Hell-Bound Train* contained tracks from the concert recorded in 1963-64, at the Campus Folksong Club.

Albums: *The Hell-Bound Train - Glenn Ohrlin At The Campus Folksong Club* (1964), with other artists *The Midwinter Festival Of Traditional Music* (1970), *The Wild Buckaroo* (1983), with other artists *Roots Of Country Music* (1988). Other recorded works held in sound archives at Indiana University: *Glenn Ohrlin At The Indiana University Folksong Club* (1964), *Glenn Ohrlin At The Illinois Folksong Club* (1964), *Glenn Ohrlin At The Indiana Folksong Club* (1964), *Glenn Ohrlin At The Campus Folksong Club* (1968), *The Hell-Bound Train: A Cowboy Songbook* (1973).
Further reading: *Hell-Bound Train: A Cowboy Song*, Glenn Ohrlin.

Oi Polloi

This Scottish punk band were formed in Edinburgh in the early 80s, immediately gaining a reputation within both the anarchist and skinhead movements (their name, more than their actual music or attitudes, allied them to the nascent Oi! scene gathering pace in England). Although similarly influenced by the football terrace chanting aesthetic displayed by bands such as **Sham 69** and the **Cockney Rejects**, Oi Polloi quickly proved themselves to be more deft both in terms of song construction and ideology than the Oi! bands. Acutely socially-aware, emphasising a strong anti-racist, anti-homophobia, pro-environmental stance, their only constant member through five albums of searing protest was Deek Allan (vocals). By 1990's grim manifesto, *In Defence Of Our Earth*, they had moved to the WOW Records label, also home to **Blaggers ITA**. This was arguably their most compelling release, earning deserved respect from the anarchist/hardcore fraternity and some grudging reviews from a mainstream media who had effectively ignored the band up to this point.
Albums: *Unlimited Genocide* (1986, split album with AOA), *Skins 'N' Punks II* (1987, split album with the Betrayed), *Mad As Fuck (Don't You Think?)* (Green Vomit 1987, split album with Toxic Ephex), *Unite And Win* (1988), *In Defence Of Our Earth* (1990). Compilations: *Outraged By The Atomic Menace* (1991), *Live* (Released Emotions 1993).

Oingo Boingo

An eight-piece band from Los Angeles, California, USA, Oingo Boingo's prolific if unspectacular career has always been centred on the compositional skills of leader Danny Elfman. Their early recordings for **A&M Records** were mainly synthesizer-led songs accompanied by a three piece horn section, and many compared them to a 'west coast **Devo**'. They developed their sound, though, and on *Nothing To Fear*, for example, they attempted to achieve commercial recognition with electronic funk. *Good For Your Soul*, produced by Robert Margouleff, was more effective and included the notable 'Wake Up (It's 1984)', although too many of the band's songs remained slight and insubstantial. Elfman's solo debut, *So-Lo*, on which other members of the band played, gave prominence to his sometimes grandiose vocals and lyrical themes, but made little impression on the charts or the critics. *Dead Man's Party* anticipated Elfman's future solo career with material suited to film soundtracks (most obviously on 'Weird Science', which accompanied the movie of the same name and was released as a single). With forceful songs such as 'Help Me' and 'Stay', many see *Dead Man's Party* as Oingo Boingo's finest hour. *Boi-ngo* retreated to a more experimental stance, offering an intricate but difficult listening climate in which instruments vied with each other and stereo effects in an aural collage, but not one destined for repeated listening. In the 90s Elfman concentrated increasingly on film and television soundtrack work, finding particular success with *Batman*, *Dick Tracy*, *Scrooged* and *The Simpsons*. Despite this, he has continued to return to the Oingo Boingo format, releasing a double live album before a new studio set, *Dark At The End Of The Tunnel*, under his own name, in 1990.
Albums: *Oingo Boingo* (IRS 1980, mini-album), *Only A Lad* (A&M 1981), *Nothing To Fear* (A&M 1982), *Good For Your Soul* (A&M 1983), *Dead Man's Party* (MCA 1985), *Boi-ngo* (MCA 1987), *Boingo Alive: Celebration Of A Decade 1979-1988* (MCA 1988), *Dark At The End Of The Tunnel* (MCA 1990). Compilation: *Skeletons In The Closet: The Best Of Oingo Boingo* (A&M 1989). Solo: Danny Elfman *So-lo* (MCA 1984), *Music For A Darkened Theatre* (MCA 1990).

Oisin

This Irish folk group featured Geraldine MacGowan (vocals/bodhran), and Anne Conroy (accordion). For *Winds Of Change*, on Tara Records, was largely credited to MacGowan and Conroy but were supplemented by **Davy Spillane** (uillean pipes/low whistle), Tom McDonagh (bouzouki), Brian O'Connor (flute/whistle), Maire Bhreathnach (fiddle), Gerry O'Connor (fiddle), Steve Cooney (bass/synthesiser), Noel Bridgeman (percussion), and Shay MacGowan (vocals/guitar).
Albums: *Oisin* (1976), *Bealoideas* (1979), *Over The Moor To Maggie* (1980), *The Jeannie C* (1983), *Winds Of Change* (1987).

OK Jazz

(see **Franco**)

Okeh Records

One of the earliest labels to record black music, Okeh was founded by Otto Heineman in 1916 as a producer of all kinds of music. Its ethnic European music catalogue was especially strong. In 1920 the label launched the race music recording industry, when its musical director Fred Hagar hired songwriter Perry Bradford to produce 'Crazy Blues' by **Mamie Smith**. It was a massive hit in the black community and other labels soon followed the lead of Okeh. To market records to the black audience, the company coined the name 'race music' in its publicity. There was another first in 1923 when Hager's assistant **Ralph Peer** recorded performances by country music performer **Fiddlin' John Carson** in Atlanta, Georgia. Although it was sold to **Columbia** in 1926, Okeh remained the leading blues and jazz label of the 20s, recording tracks by **Louis Armstrong**, **Lonnie Johnson**, and many others. However, in common with the rest of the record business, its activities were drastically curtailed during the Depression, although **Bessie Smith** recorded for the label in 1933. After a hiatus for several years, Okeh was revived in 1940 as a home for R&B music, and in 1951 had a big hit with **Johnnie Ray**'s 'Cry'. Later Okeh artists included **Chuck Willis**, **Big Maybelle**, and **Screaming Jay Hawkins**, but by the early 60s the label was virtually moribund. In 1962, producer **Carl Davis** was put in charge of A&R for Okeh and working out of Chicago revived the label's fortunes while producing a number of soul music hits by such artists as **Billy Butler**, **Walter Jackson**, **Major Lance**, and the **Vibrations**. Okeh lost its major asset with the departure of Davis in 1965, but the label managed to linger on until 1970, before it closed its doors. The label was ressurrected once more in the 90s, issued via **Epic Records**. One of the label's most interesting prospects are funk/rappers G. Love And Special Sauce.

Album: *The Okeh Rhythm & Blues Story 1949-1957* (Epic/Legacy 1994). Compilation: *The Okeh Rhythm & Blues Story 1949-57* (Epic 1994, 3 stars in Q).

Okey Dokey Stompers

British blues band the Okey Dokey Stompers were formed in Dagenham, Essex, England, in September 1992 from the ashes of the Corn Beef City Blues Band and the Impossibles. Comprising Stevie 'Young Blood' Cook (lead guitar), 'Automatic' Nick Nichols (vocals/harp), Gary 'Reverend Coco' Choules (bass), Johnny 'Boy' (keyboards) and 'Marky' Mark Ward (drums), members had also taken part in gigging bands such as Big Joe Louis, the Hoods and Night Prowler. Of these former incarnations, the Impossibles earned the greatest notoriety, as finalists in the Best Of British Blues competition sponsored by Banks Brewery in 1990/1991. As the Okey Dokey Stompers the band played a shattering 400 gigs in their first two years, with a sound located somewhere between Texas and West Coast rhythm and blues. A strong following for their energetic live shows led to the recording of a debut CD, *Dangerman Blues*, which was distributed by Hot Shot Records.

Album: *Dangerman Blues* (Dyna-might 1994).

Oklahoma! (Film Musical)

The show that opened on Broadway in 1943, and is credited with being a significant turning point in the history of the musical theatre, was transferred to the screen in the not-so-glorious Todd-AO wide-screen process in 1955. The skilful integration of **Richard Rodgers** and **Oscar Hammerstein II**'s wonderful songs into the sentimental but sincere story for which the stage production is so rightly admired, was equally impressive in this celluloid version. The action takes place just after the turn of the century on and around a ranch in the Oklahoma Territory, where Laurey (**Shirley Jones**) lives with her Aunt Eller (**Charlotte Greenwood**). The handsome and decent Curly (**Gordon MacRae**) and the evil-looking and devious Judd (Rod Steiger) both want to take Laurey to the 'box social'. Her decision to spite Curly (who she really wants to go with) by accepting Jud's invitation, sets off a train of events which culminate in Jud's death, for which Curly is immediately charged, but just as swiftly exonerated. Jones and MacRae were perfect together, and the supporting cast was exceptionally fine, with **Gene Nelson** as Will Parker and Gloria Grahame as his girlfriend Ado Annie, who 'just cain't say no'. Eddie Albert played a travelling pedlar-man, Ali Akim, whose indiscriminate use of a kissing technique known in his native country as 'A Persian Goodbye', results in a shotgun wedding. Other parts were taken by James Whitmore, Marc Platt, Barbara Lawrence, Roy Barcroft. Dancers James Mitchell and Bambi Lynn were stunning in the ballet sequence to the music of 'Out Of My Dreams'. Most of the rest of Rodgers and Hammerstein's rich and varied score was retained, and included all the favourites such as 'Oh, What A Beautiful Mornin'', 'The Surrey With The Fringe On Top', 'Kansas City', 'I Cain't Say No', 'Many A New Day', 'People Will Say We're In Love', 'Poor Jud Is Dead', 'The Farmer And The Cowman', 'All Er Nothin'', and the rousing 'Oklahoma'. Choreographer **Agnes de Mille** and musical arranger **Robert Russell Bennett** adapted their original stage work for the film, and Russell Bennett, together with Jay Blackton and **Adolph Deutsch**, won Oscars for 'scoring of a musical picture'. It was photographed in Technicolor and produced for Magna by Arthur Hornblow Jnr. The director was Fred Zinnemann. Sonya Levian and William Ludwig's screenplay was adapted from the original libretto by Oscar Hammerstein II which was based on Lynn Riggs's play *Green Grow The Lilacs*.

Oklahoma! (Stage Musical)

If one show can be said to mark the turning-point in the history of the American musical theatre then it must be *Oklahoma!* Although many of the trend-setting features of the show had been tried before, sometimes successfully, never before had such features as a ballet sequence and a serious plot been blended so well into a production which had great dramatic merit and was yet

filled with many wonderful songs. Set in the early years of the 20th century, as a section of Indian territory is about to become the state of Oklahoma, the story traces the love lives of two contrasting couples, Curly and Laurey, and Will Parker and Ado Annie. Conflict between farmers and cowmen, a staple of western films, provided drama as did the personal struggle for Laurey between Curly and Jud Fry, a disreputable farmhand who is finally killed in a knife fight with Curly. An on-stage death in a musical was another 'first' for *Oklahoma!*. Based upon Lynn Riggs's play, *Green Grow The Lilacs*, the book and lyrics for *Oklahoma!* were written by **Oscar Hammerstein II** with music by **Richard Rodgers**, the first time the two men had collaborated. Producers and outside commentators were agreed in their pre-production reservations about the show. Many felt it was doomed to failure, that the basis of an only moderately successful play, along with a collaboration between Hammerstein, who had been without a hit for some time, and Rodgers, now without his long-time collaborator **Lorenz Hart**, was a too-shaky foundation. On opening night, the 31 March 1943, despite playing to a less than full house at the St. James Theatre in New York, all doubts vanished. The vivid staging, sparkling choreography by **Agnes de Mille**, strong central performances, and above all a string of superb songs, made this the most momentous musical event of several decades. The songs included 'Oh, What A Beautiful Mornin'', which opened the show, 'The Surrey With The Fringe On Top', 'Kansas City', 'I Cain't Say No', 'Many A New Day', 'People Will Say We're In Love', 'The Farmer And The Cowman', 'Pore Jud', 'Out Of My Dreams', 'All er Nothin'' and the rousing 'Oklahoma' with which the show ended. The original cast included **Alfred Drake** as Curly, Joan Roberts as Laurey, Lee Dixon as Will, Celeste Holm as Ado Annie, Howard Da Silva as Jud and Betty Garde as Laurey's Aunt Eller. By the time the show closed, after 2,248 performances, other artists had replaced one or another of the leads, amongst them **Howard Keel**, Shelley Winters and **John Raitt**. The 1947 London production starred Keel and Betty Jane Watson and ran for 1,151 performances. London audiences, still war-shocked and starved of spectacle - amongst many other things - were overwhelmed. The show profoundly affected the producers of British shows which were still rooted in the 30s sophistication of **Noël Coward** and the flimsy Ruritania of **Ivor Novello**. *Oklahoma!* was the opening wave of a transatlantic musical tide that would take three decades to reverse. The show became a near-permanent feature of the theatrical scenes of both the USA and UK with touring companies seemingly forever on the road. There were major New York revivals in 1951 and 1965, and the 1980 London production gave impresario **Cameron Mackintosh** one of the first of his many West End successes. The 1955 film version starred **Gordon MacRae** and **Shirley Jones**. In 1993, the show's 50th anniversary was marked by a special **Tony Award** and several more revivals worldwide.
Further reading: *OK! The Story Of Oklahoma!*, Max Wilk.

Okoshi, Tiger

b. 21 March 1950, Ashita, Japan. Tiger Okoshi moved to the USA in 1972 and played with artists including **Gary Burton** and **Bob Moses**. He has also had his own groups playing what he calls 'Baku music' - a Baku is a mythical creature which eats bad dreams. This is a form of jazz-rock fusion derived from the music **Miles Davis** was creating in the late 60s. Okoshi is an interesting composer and accomplished trumpeter.
Albums: *Tiger's Baku* (1981), *Mudd Cake* (1982), with Gary Burton *Times Square* (1977), with Bob Moses *Visit With The Great Spirit* (1983).

Okosun, Sonny

b. 3 April 1947, Benin, Nigeria. On leaving school, Okosun's first ambition was to be an actor, and he spent a year training with Eastern Nigeria Theatre before joining his first group, the Postmen, in 1964. Nicknamed the Local Beatles by Benin music fans, the group concentrated on covers of western pop hits and were a big draw throughout Eastern Nigeria until the outbreak of civil war in 1967 led to their break-up. Western rock and pop, however, remained a big influence on Okosun, who later added reggae to the mix in an attempt to find an African-based style with wide international appeal. In 1969, Okosun joined **Victor Uwaifo** and his Melody Maestros, staying with the group for two years, touring Japan and throughout West Africa. In 1971, he decided he was ready to form his own band, and set up Paperback Unlimited, based in Lagos. Instrumentation and arrangements gave the group a sound similar to UK underground bands like **Cream** or **Traffic**, but most of their material was in fact composed of reworkings of traditional local music. Paperback Unlimited stayed together until 1975 while Okosun refined his vision of an African-Western musical fusion. That year he began calling the style Ozidizm, after a river god worshipped by the Ijaw people, and reformed Paperback Unlimited as Ozzidi. The band's approach, mixing highlife, progressive rock and touches of soul, rapidly became a major live draw throughout Nigeria and was followed by four major-selling album releases - *Ozzidi*, *Living Music*, *Papa's Land* and *Ozzidi For Sale*. In 1977, Okosun began adding reggae elements to Ozzidizm, and went on to release his most successful albums to date - *Fire In Soweto*, which dealt with the struggle in South Africa, and *Holy Wars,* which looked to the day when Africa would be ruled by Africans.
By the early 80s, Okosun's fascination with reggae had played itself out, and he abandoned Ozzidizm in favour

of a new, still internationally-based style which he called Afro-carnival, combining rock, funk and traditional African folk styles. The first album in the new mould was 1981's *3rd World,* which was followed a year later by *Mother And Child,* a concept album marking the International Year of the Child. Despite the consistently outward-looking nature of his music, and regular tours of Britain and mainland Europe, Okosun by the mid-80s had failed to match the international impact of **Fela Anikulapo Kuti**, **King Sunny Ade** or **Manu Dibango**. In 1985, however, he embarked upon a well-received tour of the USA, to promote the release of his album *Liberation.* That same year he launched a further attack on the world market with the British release, through Jive Afrika, of his 1983 album *Which Way Nigeria?*, supported by a major UK tour. Despite the enthusiastic receptions for both his USA and UK tours, Okosun's record sales in both territories continued to be limited to the specialist market, and by the late 80s he had decided to suspend his efforts for international recognition and concentrate on the West African market.

Albums: *Ozzidi* (1976), *Ozzidi For Sale* (1976), *Living Music* (1977), *Papa's Land* (1977), *Fire In Soweto* (1978), *Holy Wars* (1978), *3rd World* (1981), *Mother And Child* (1982), *Which Way Nigeria?* (1983), *Liberation* (1984), *Africa Now Or Never* (1986), *Ozzidi/Ozone* (1989).

Olaiya, Victor

b. 1926, Ijebu, Nigeria. Vocalist, composer and trumpeter Olaiya is one of the founding fathers of modern Nigerian highlife, a music he first became enthused by during Ghanaian bandleader **E.T. Mensah**'s legendary and seminal tour of the country in 1952. During the 50s he led the Cool Cats, and during the 60s the All Stars, both hugely popular throughout west Africa. During the 70s he ran - and performed nightly at - his own club, the Papingo, in Lagos and was also active in the Nigerian Musicians Union. Still active during the 80s, he frequently toured Nigeria with his International Stars, playing a form of highlife that had changed little since the 60s.

Albums: *Olaiya's Victories* (1964), *Highlife Reincarnation* (1973), *Country Hard O!* (1986).

Olatunji, Babtunji

b. 1939, Ijaw, Nigeria. Drummer and bandleader Olatunji moved to the USA in the early 60s, where he enjoyed lucrative mainstream success with epic, and highly sanitized, versions of traditional Nigerian drum and percussion music.

Albums: *Drums Drums Drums* (1964), *Drums Of Passion* (1965), *More Drums Of Passion* (1965), *Flaming Drums* (1967).

Old And New Dreams

This group formed in 1976 and featured **Ornette Coleman** alumni, **Dewey Redman**, **Don Cherry**, **Charlie Haden**, **Ed Blackwell**. They came together to play music, particularly that of the early, acoustic bands. By the mid-70s Coleman had become committed to expressing his musical theory of Harmolodics through the medium of his electric band, Prime Time. Old And New Dreams set out to play in the spirit of, rather than recreate, the earlier acoustic groups by reworking compositions of the period as well as composing new numbers within the parameters of the Coleman style. The group has experienced a great deal of success, particularly on the European festival circuit, indicating the enduring quality of Coleman's early musical output.

Albums: *Old And New Dreams* (1976), *Playing* (1980), *Tribute To Ed Blackwell* (1990).

Old Swan Band

Formed in 1974 by Rod And Danny Stradling, the band comprised Rod Stradling (b. London, England; melodeon), Danny Stradling (b. London, England; tambourine/drum), Martin Brinsford (b. 17 August 1944, Gloucester, England; mouth organ/skulls), Fi Fraser (b. Fiona Mildred Newmarch Fraser, 31 July 1959, Barnet, Hertfordshire, England; fiddle/clarinet/hammer dulcimer), Jo Fraser (b. Jo-Anne Rachel Newmarch Fraser, 4 December 1960, St. Albans, Hertfordshire, England; whistle) and Ron Field (autoharp/banjo). The group played what was described as Southern English Country Dance music. At a time when the vast majority of other dance groups were performing Irish and Scottish dance music, the Old Swan Band were researching and revitalizing many English dance tunes that had been almost forgotten. As with many groups of the time, they were relatively short-lived due to the commitments of the various group members, with Brinsford joining **Brass Monkey** in 1981. Their influence resulted in a growing interest in English dance music, and the formation of a number of other groups who followed their example.

Albums: *No Reels* (1976), *Old Swan Brand* (1978), *Gamesters, Pickpockets And Harlots* (1981), *The Old Swan Band* (1984).

Oldfield, Mike

b. 15 May 1953, Reading, Berkshire, England. Multi-instrumentalist Oldfield will forever be remembered for a piece of symphonic length music he wrote before his 20th birthday. *Tubular Bells* sold 12 million copies world-wide and topped the charts in the USA and UK, staying in both for more than five years. He began his career providing acoustic guitar accompaniment to folk songs sung by his older sister, **Sally Oldfield**, who would often appear in Reading's pubs and clubs with **Marianne Faithfull**. Mike and Sally recorded *Sallyangie* together before he left to join **Kevin Ayers**

And The Whole World, with whom he played bass and guitar for a short period. He continued working on his own material and produced a demo of instrumental music which later became *Tubular Bells*. Several record companies rejected the piece but entrepreneur **Richard Branson**, the head of **Virgin** stores, recognized its marketing potential. He asked Oldfield to re-record the demo in the recently-acquired Manor Studios and it became one of Virgin's first releases. The 49-minute long piece was a series of basic melodies from folk, rock and classical sources which featured an array of different instruments, all played by Oldfield, and was introduced by guest master of ceremonies, **Viv Stanshall**. Excerpts from it were used in the horror film, *The Exorcist*, and a shortened version was released as a single in 1974.

On *Hergest Ridge* he attempted to capture Berkshire's pastoral beauty and largely succeeded, although matching the impact of *Tubular Bells* was clearly impossible and many critics dubbed the album 'Son of Tubular Bells' because of the similarity. It reached the top of the UK charts but, like all his subsequent album releases, it did not chart in the USA. Along with arranger, **Dave Bedford**, a former collaborator of Kevin Ayers, he scored *Tubular Bells* and a version recorded by the Royal Philharmonic Orchestra was released in 1975. *Ommadawn* featured the uillean pipes playing of the **Chieftains**' Paddy Moloney and a team of African drummers. It sold well but the critical response was that his introspective music had become over-formularized over the three albums. Virgin also saw the records as complementary works and packaged them together in 1976 as *Boxed*. Oldfield had two consecutive Christmas hits in 1975 and 1976 with the traditional 'In Dulci Jubilo' and 'Portsmouth'.

Around 1977-78, the shy, withdrawn Oldfield underwent a programme of self-assertiveness with the Exegesis method. The result was a complete reversal of personality and Oldfield took the opportunity in music press interviews to retaliate, almost to the point of parody, to accusations of limp, neo-hippy blandness and strongly defended himself against pillorying by the nascent punk movement. *Incantations* drew strongly on disco influences and *Exposed* was recorded at various concerts where Oldfield played with up to 50 other musicians. In 1979 Oldfield also recorded a version of the theme tune to the popular BBC television show, *Blue Peter*. Entitled 'Barnacle Bill', it was released as a charity single and was subsequently adopted by the programme as a revamped signature tune. It was retained as such up to the late 80s *Platinum*, *QE2* and *Five Miles Out* caught Oldfield slightly out of step with his contemporaries as he tried to hone his songwriting and avoid repeating himself. **Hall And Oates** recorded a version of 'Family Man', which had missed out as a single for Oldfield, and it became a Top 20 hit in the UK in 1983. Oldfield began working with soprano Maggie Reilly and she sang on the hit 'Moonlight Shadow' from *Crises* (where other guests included Roger Chapman (**Family/Chapman Whitney**). After *Discovery* he wrote the music for the award-winning film *The Killing Fields*. On *Islands* he was joined by further guest vocalists **Bonnie Tyler** and **Kevin Ayers**. Even though he was now writing to a more standard pop structure, Oldfield found himself no longer in vogue and his music was largely portrayed in the music press as anachronistic. *Earth Moving*, with contributions from Maggie Reilly, Anita Hegerland and Chris Thompson (ex-**Manfred Mann**) failed to challenge the prevailing modern view. It appears that *Tubular Bells* will always ring rather too loudly and diminish most of Oldfield's other work, certainly in terms of commercial acceptance, but he continues releasing records welcomed by a large cult following which apparently cares little about his low profile and the scarcity of live appearances. 1992 has found him working with Trevor Horn on *Tubular Bells II* to mark the 20th anniversary of the original album. The album's success resulted in increased sales for the original *Tubular Bells* and led to a spectacular live concert of the new version.

Albums: with Sally Oldfield *Sallyangie* (1968), *Tubular Bells* (1973), *Hergest Ridge* (1974), with the Royal Philharmonic Orchestra *The Orchestral Tubular Bells* (1975), *Ommadawn* (1975), *Incantations* (1978), *Exposed* (1979), *Platinum* (1979), *QE2* (1980), *Five Miles Out* (1982), *Crises* (1983), *Discovery* (1984), *The Killing Fields* (1984, film soundtrack), *Islands* (1987), *Earth Moving* (1989), *Amarok* (1990), *Heaven's Open* (1991), *Tubular Bells II* (1992), *The Songs Of Distant Earth* (WEA 1994). Compilations: *Boxed* (1976), *The Complete Mike Oldfield* (1985).

Videos: *The Wind Chimes* (1988), *Essential Mike Oldfield* (1988), *Elements* (1993).

Further reading: *True Story Of The Making Of Tubular Bells*, Richard Newman. *Mike Oldfield: A Man And His Music*, Sean Moraghan.

Oldfield, Sally

This UK-born vocalist was the sister of **Mike Oldfield**. Together with her brother she formed **Sallyangie** and released an album and a couple of singles to little success. By the early 70s the duo had gone their separate ways professionally. While Mike was making a name for himself with albums like *Tubular Bells* and *Hergest Ridge*, Sally joined a number of small bands, and appeared as guest vocalist on her brother's first four albums. In 1978 she released a solo album which included her debut and only hit 'Mirrors'. Four other albums appeared on the Bronze label, all to mixed reactions and little success. She re-emerged in 1987 with the backing of a major label and considerable press backing, but still she could not add to her initial success. She remains highly popular in

Europe, notably Germany and Holland.
Albums: with Mike Oldfield *Sallyangie* (1968), *Water Bearer* (1978), *Easy* (1979), *Celebration* (1980), *Playing With The Flame* (1981), *Strange Day In Berlin* (1983), *Femme* (1987). Compilation: *The Collection* (1988).

Oldham, Andrew Loog

b. 1944, England. A one-time office junior with designer Mary Quant, Oldham made several attempts at launching a pop career under such aliases as 'Chancery Lane' and 'Sandy Beach'. When these failed he took employment as a publicist for such disparate characters as **Don Arden** and **Brian Epstein**. It was during this period that Andrew became acquainted with American producer **Phil Spector**, who left an indelible mark on his thinking. Having spied a glowing testimony in *Record Mirror*, Oldham watched the **Rolling Stones** perform at Richmond's Crawdaddy club. Impressed, he persuaded the group to break an unofficial deal with impresario **Giorgio Gomelsky** and emerged as their manager and producer. Although he initially tried to cultivate a clean-cut image, Oldham quickly abandoned this in favour of a rebellious, unkempt approach which directly pitted his charges against the more sedate **Beatles**. Copy and publicity was honed for outrage, establishing an impression which haunts the group to this date. Several other charges, including **Marianne Faithfull**, the **Poets** and the **Mighty Avengers**, joined his management stable, and Oldham also began recording in his own right. Clearly still indebted to Phil Spector, he fronted the Andrew Loog Oldham Orchestra over a series of singles and albums which retain a curiosity, rather than musical, value. In 1965, Oldham established the Immediate label with associate **Tony Calder**. Despite initial success and an impressive roster which included the **Small Faces**, the **Nice**, **Chris Farlowe** and **Amen Corner**, the company was bankrupt by the end of the decade. Andrew's tenure with the Stones ended in 1967 when he was dismissed following a period of estrangement between the two parties. He later moved to New York, and having established a small office in Broadway's **Brill Building**, resumed his production career. In 1977 he returned to pop management with the Texan group, the Werewolves, and the following year produced their debut album. Oldham latterly married a Colombian film star and now spends several months of the year in Bogota, which he once claimed invokes the atmosphere of 50s London. Still in business with Calder they have recently resurrected the Immediate label and in 1994 they put their efforts into writing a book on **Abba**.
Albums: *16 Hip Hits* (1964), *The Andrew Oldham Orchestra Plays Lionel Bart's Maggie May* (1964), *East Meets West - Famous Hits Of The Beach Boys And The Four Seasons* (1965), *The Rolling Stones Songbook* (1965). Compilation: *Rarities* (1984).
Further reading: *The Name Of The Game*, Calder and Irwin Oldham.

Oldham, Spooner

b. Lindon Dewey Oldham. Oldham first came to prominence as an in-house pianist at the Fame recording studio. Here he met **Dan Penn** and the resultant songwriting partnership was responsible for scores of southern soul compositions, including hits for **James And Bobby Purify** ('I'm Your Puppet'). **Clarence Carter** ('She Ain't Gonna Do Right') and **Percy Sledge** ('Out Of Left Field'). Oldham later moved out to the California where he became a fixture as a session musician, appearing on albums by **Jackson Browne**, **Maria Muldaur**, **Linda Ronstadt** and the **Flying Burrito Brothers**. He also maintained his relationship with Penn and the duo subsequently formed an independent production company. During the 70s/80s Oldham appeared with **Neil Young** as a member of the Gone With The Wind Orchestra and the International Harvesters.

Olivencia, Tommy

b. mid-30s, Villa Palmeras, Santurce, San Juan, Puerto Rico. During the three and a half decades of its existence, Olivencia's band has acted as an 'incubator' for various notable solo salsa singers, including Marvin Santiago (see **Bobby Valentín**), Paquito Guzmán, **Lalo Rodríguez**, **Gilberto Santa Rosa**, Frankie Ruiz and Héctor Tricoche. Olivencia began as a singer at the age of 16, but he preferred the role of trumpeter and musical director. He became a bandleader when he was 22-years-old. He favours a frontline of trumpets and trombones, and used a combination of four trumpets and two trombones on most of his albums since 1978. Tommy released his early recordings on his own Tioly label. He signed with Inca Records and remained with them until 1978. He switched to TH (Top Hits) Records (now TH-Rodven) and released eight albums on the label between 1978-88. In 1990, Olivencia's band was one of a number of popular Puerto Rican salsa acts lured to the major record company **Capitol/EMI** Latin. He debuted with them the following year. Early vocalists with Olivencia's band included Chamaco Ramírez and ex-**Joe Quijano** band member Paquito Guzmán. Ramírez's last recording with Tommy was 1975's *Planté Bandera*; heavy drug addiction destroyed his health and Chamaco died shortly after releasing the 1979 solo set *Alive And Kicking*, which contained material that its producer and arranger, Javier Vázquez, had originally prepared for **Ismael Rivera** to record. Apart from Olivencia's 1975 and 1976 releases, Guzmán was co-lead singer on six of the bandleader's albums between 1972-79. During the same period, Guzmán issued several solo albums on Inca Records, including *Paquito Guzmán* (1972), *Escucha Mi Canción* (1975), *Mintiendo Se*

Gana Mas (1977) and the compilation *Peligro* in 1980. He signed as a solo performer with TH Records and after releasing *El Caballero de la Salsa* (1983) and *Paquito Guzmán Con Trio* (1985), he became one of the earliest artists to record in the salsa romántica style on his major 1986 hit *Las Mejores Baladas En Salsa*. So-called sexy salsa boosted the ageing singer's career and he continued in the same vein with *Tu Amante Romántico* (1987) and *Aquí Conmigo* (1989). In 1990 Guzmán defected to Capitol/EMI Latin for more of the same on *El Mismo Romántico*. Additionally, Guzmán recorded with the Puerto Rico All Stars in the 70s and has sessioned extensively as a coro (chorus) singer.

Another Olivencia co-lead vocalist, Sammy González, left after 1972's *Secuestro* to join **Roberto Roena**'s band Apollo Sound. Reinaldo Jorge, Olivencia's first trombonist, left the band, after 1974's *Juntos De Nuevo*. He relocated to New York and worked there with Los Kimbos, Fania All Stars, **Conjunto Libre**, Frankie Morales and **Rubén Blades**' Son del Solar, amongst others. In 1981, Jorge made his debut as a bandleader on *No Sufro*. Young trumpeter/arranger **Luis 'Perico' Ortiz** produced, performed on and contributed some first-rate arrangements to Tommy's albums between 1975-79. In 1976, 18-year-old singer/composer Lalo Rodríguez, who worked previously with **Eddie Palmieri**, joined Simón Pérez as co-lead vocalist on *Introducing Lalo Rodríguez & Simón Pérez*. The same year, Tommy won awards for the best band in Puerto Rico and best foreign band in Panamá. Rodríguez departed, but Pérez stayed on for three more albums with the band. In 1978 Olivencia won a Puerto Rican music industry Diplo award. The awards were created by Cuban Bernardo Hevia, editor of the salsa magazine *Farándula*, which he founded in 1958. Pérez was replaced in 1979 by Gilberto Santa Rosa on *Tommy Olivencia & His Orchestra*; after which Santa Rosa left to join **Willie Rosario**'s band. Tommy hired two new young lead singers for 1981's *Un Triángulo De Triunfo!*: Frankie Ruiz and Carlos Alexis. Ruiz hails from Paterson, New Jersey, USA, and formerly sang lead vocals with the Puerto Rican band La Solución; he appeared on their commendable *La Solución* in 1980. Alexis was succeeded by Héctor Tricoche, who sang previously with Mikey Cora's Orquesta Cabala and La Terrifica, on *Celebrando Otro Aniversario* in 1984, which was Ruiz's last album with Olivencia. That year, Olivencia oversaw the production and his band provided the accompaniment for the veteran Colombian singer Nelson Pinedo on *. . . Desde Puerto Rico*.

Three of Olivencia's hits performed by Ruiz: 'Primero Fui Yo' (from *Un Triángulo De Triunfo!*), 'Como Lo Hacen' (from *Tommy Olivencia*) and 'Te Estoy Estudiando' (from *Celebrando Otro Aniversario*), were written by veteran former heart throb singer/composer Raúl Marrero and arranged by guitarist/arranger Máximo Torres. Marrero recorded his own interpretation of the first two compositions as part of a medley on his 1988 release *El Señor de la Salsa*. In the latter part of the 80s, Máximo Torres became the director and arranger of the Salsa Selection band, which accompanied his son, singer Max Torres, on the bestsellers *Sensualmente Tropical* (1988) and *Aprenderé!* (1989). These were followed by the less successful Max Torres releases *Peligroso Amor* (1990) and *From Puerto Rico* (1991). Frankie Ruiz remained with TH (and TH-Rodven) and his first two solo releases: *Solista . . . Pero No Solo* (1985) and *. . . Voy Pa' Encíma!* (1987), both topped the ***Billboard*** tropical/salsa chart. *Historia Musical de Frankie Ruiz* was a compilation of the young superstar's 14 best tracks with La Solución, Olivencia and his own band. It was released in time for Christmas 1987 and was another runaway success. Ruiz's emotive and captivating voice sounded strained - probably due to his gruelling gigging schedule - on his 1988 *En Vivo Y . . . A Todo Color . . .!*, which did less well in chart terms. His imprisonment for a drugs offense did not prevent 1989's *. . . Mas Grande Que Nunca* reaching number 1 in early 1990. Meanwhile, Ruiz was replaced by Paquito (Junior) Acosta on Olivencia's *Ayer, Hoy, Mañana Y Siempre . . .!* in 1985. In 1987 Tommy celebrated three decades as a bandleader with the chart-topping *30 Aniversario*. The album contained the smash hit 'Lobo Domesticado', performed by Héctor Tricoche and arranged by Máximo Torres, and an anniversary medley of past hits. Olivencia mixed salsa romántica flavoured songs with his usual searing salsa on *El Jeque*, which was his 1988 parting shot on TH-Rodven. Tricoche left and made his solo debut in 1990 with the TH-Rodven release *Clase Aparte*, which spawned the Máximo Torres arranged hit 'Hacer El Amor'. That year, Héctor appeared at the second part of the New York Salsa Festival at Madison Square Garden. His 1991 follow-up *Motorizame* contained the hit single 'Macho Pérez'. In 1990, singer Héctor 'Pichy' Pérez left Sonora Ponceña (see **Papo Lucca**) to join Olivencia as Tricoche's replacement. He made his recording debut with the band on 1991's *Enamorado . . . Y Que!* on Capitol/EMI Latin.

Selected albums: *La Nueva Sensación* (mid-60s), *Jala Jala y Guaguanco* (mid-60s), *Fuego Fuego* (mid-60s), *A Toda Maquina* (c.1968), *Cueros, Salsa y Sentimiento* (c.1969), with Paquito Guzmán and Sammy González *Secuestro* (1972), with Chamaco Ramírez and Guzmán *Juntos De Nuevo* (1974), with Ramírez *Planté Bandera* (1975), *Introducing Lalo Rodríguez & Simón Pérez* (1976), with Guzmán and Pérez *El Negro Chombo* (1977), with Guzmán and Perez *La Primerisima* (1978), with Guzmán and Pérez *Sweat Trumpet Hot 'Salsa'* (1978), with Gilberto Santa Rosa and Guzmán *Tommy Olivencia & His Orchestra* (1979), with Frankie Ruiz and Carlos Alexis *Un Triángulo De Triunfo!* (1981), with Ruiz and Alexis *Tommy Olivencia* (1983), with Ruiz and Héctor Tricoche *Celebrando Otro*

Aniversario (1984), with Nelson Pinedo... *Desde Puerto Rico* (1984), with Tricoche and Paquito Acosta *Ayer, Hoy, Mañana Y Siempre..!* (1985), with Tricoche and Acosta *30 Aniversario* (1987), with Tricoche and Acosta *El Jeque* (1988), with Pichy Pérez, Acosta *Enamorado... Y Que!* (1991). Compilations: *Lo Mejor de/The Best Of Tommy Olivencia* (1975), *Fiesta De Soneros* (1978), *Las 12 Grandes De Tommy Olivencia* (1991).

Oliver! (Film Musical)

'Please sir, can I have some more' was not just the tragic cry of the young orphan in Charles Dickens' famous story, but the plea of theatregoers both in Britain and on Broadway when they witnessed the tremendous success of **Lionel Bart**'s stage musical ***Oliver!*** in the early 60s. So it is not surprising that the film adaptation of the stage hit, released in December 1968, with just two songs missing from the original score, did so well and became such a favourite with adults and children alike. Adapted for the screen by Vernon Harris, this musical version of the Dickens story follows young Oliver (Mark Lester) as he runs away from his desperately unhappy existence in a poor house and his job as an undertaker's assistant, only to find himself lost in the big city. Here he meets the worldly-wise Artful Dodger (Jack Wild), and falls in with a group of young pickpockets. At the head of this gang is Fagin (Ron Moody in the part he orginally played on stage), a scoundrel who always keeps one eye on his 'bank' balance and the other on the boys in his charge. It is in Fagin's hideout that Oliver has his first stealing lessons, but the innocent boy gets caught on one of his first attempts. His subsequent arrest leads to the discovery of a loving and wealthy relative, and, eventually a happy ending to the story. Oliver Reed gives a truly villainous performance as Bill Sikes, and Shani Wallis is more than adequate in the role of Nancy, the girl who loves him no matter how evil he becomes. Directed by Carol Reed, and produced by John Woolf, *Oliver!* is an enchanting film full of great musical sequences and emotional drama. Mark Lester is perfectly innocent in the leading role. His rendition of the plaintive 'Where is Love?' tugs at the audience's heartstrings, and the scene in Fagin's den when he joins Nancy for 'I'd Do Anything' is gentle and touching. Other highspots include Nancy's powerful reaffirmation of her love for Bill in 'As Long As He Needs Me', and Fagin's 'You've Got To Pick A Pocket Or Two' which is a quirky and irresistible celebration of villainy, while his indecision and frustration are perfectly captured in the witty lyrics of 'Reviewing The Situation'. However, it is not just the individual performances which make the film so successful. The ensemble musical numbers are often breathtaking, ranging from the fantasising of 'Food Glorious Food' to the brotherhood of 'Consider Yourself.' The rest of the fine score includes 'Boy For Sale', 'Who Will Buy?', and the joyous 'Oom-Pah-Pah'. Among the excellent supporting cast were **Harry Secombe**, Leonard Rossiter, Hugh Griffith, Fred Emney and James Hayter. The film was beautifully photographed in Technicolor and Panavision by Oswald Morris. *Oliver!* won five Oscars, for best picture, director, choreographer (Onna White), and remains one of the all-time great British movies.

Oliver! (Stage Musical)

As soon as it opened at the New Theatre in London on 30 June 1960, *Oliver!* was an instant success, winning rave reviews and ecstatic audiences. With book, music and lyrics by **Lionel Bart**, the show's storyline was reasonably faithful to *Oliver Twist*, the Charles Dickens novel upon which it was based. Filled with memorable songs, from sweet ballads to comic masterpieces, the show had the benefit of a strong cast and one performance that ranks amongst the genre's finest. Ron Moody's Fagin alone was worth the price of admission. Well supported by **Georgia Brown**, as Nancy, and with a succession of good Olivers and Artful Dodgers, *Oliver!* was excellent entertainment. Bart's songs included 'As Long As He Needs Me', 'Where Is Love?', 'Food, Glorious Food', 'Consider Yourself', 'You've Got To Pick A Pocket Or Two', 'Come Back Soon', 'I Shall Scream', 'Who Will Buy?', 'Oom-Pah-Pah', 'I'd Do Anything' and 'Reviewing The Situation'. The show also had the benefit of extraordinary sets by Sean Kenny, much-admired to the point of outright copying in later years. *Oliver!* ran for 2,618 performances in London, and Georgia Brown reprised her role, with Clive Revill as Fagin, for the 1963 New York production which ran for nearly two years. The show won **Tony Awards** for composer and lyricist (Bart), scenic designer (Kenny), and musical director-conductor (Donald Pippin). The 1968 film version dropped a song or two, inexplicably replaced Brown with Shani Wallis, but fortunately preserved Moody's performance for all time. There were also good child actors in Mark Lester as Oliver and, particularly, Jack Wild as the Artful Dodger. Other young stars in the role have included **Phil Collins** and **Steve Marriott**. Not surprisingly, *Oliver!* has been revived many times over the years by amateur and professional companies alike, most recently in **Cameron Mackintosh**'s major new production at the London Palladium which opened in December 1994 with a £7 million box office advance. Directed by Sam Mendes, it starred Jonathan Pryce as Fagin, Sally Dexter as Nancy, and featured Adam Searles as the Artful Dodger who almost stole the show. The lavish £3.5 million presentation was generally enthusiastically received by the critics - and Lionel Bart - who, courtesy of Cameron Mackintosh, recouped a portion of the show's rights which he sold many years ago.

Oliver, Joe 'King'

b. 11 May 1885, Louisiana, USA, d. 10 April 1938. Raised in New Orleans, cornetist Oliver became well-known through appearances with local marching and cabaret bands during the early years of this century. After playing with such notable early jazzmen as **Kid Ory** and **Richard M. Jones** in 1918, he left for Chicago and two years later was leading his own band. After a brief trip to California, Oliver returned to Chicago and performed an engagement at the Lincoln Gardens. This was in 1922 and his band then included such outstanding musicians as **Johnny** and **Baby Dodds**, **Lil Hardin** and **Honore Dutrey**. Not content with being merely the best jazz band in town, Oliver sent word to New Orleans and brought in the fast-rising young cornetist **Louis Armstrong**. His motives in hiring Armstrong might have been questionable. Hardin, who later married Armstrong, reported that Oliver openly stated that his intention was to ensure that by having the newcomer playing second cornet in his band he need not fear him as a competitor. Whatever the reason, the Oliver band with Armstrong was a sensation. Musicians flocked to hear the band, marvelling at the seemingly telepathic communication between the two men. The band's glory days did not last long; by 1924 the Dodds brothers had gone, dissatisfied with their financial arrangements, and Armstrong had been taken by his new wife on the first stage of his transition to international star. Oliver continued leading a band but he quickly discovered that his example had been followed by many, and that even if his imitators were often musically inferior they had made it harder for him to obtain good jobs. His own judgement was also sometimes at fault; he turned down an offer to lead a band at New York's Cotton Club because the money was not good enough and lived to see **Duke Ellington** take the job and the radio exposure that went with it. In the early 30s Oliver led a succession of territory bands with a measure of local success but he rarely played. He was suffering from a disease of the gums and playing the cornet was, at best, a painful exercise. By 1936 he had quit the business of which he had once been king and took a job as a janitor in Savannah, Georgia, where he died in 1938. An outstanding exponent of New Orleans-style cornet playing, Oliver was one of the most important musicians in spreading jazz through his 1923-24 recordings, even if these did not gain their internationally-accepted status as classic milestones until after his death. His role in the advance of Armstrong's career is also of significance although, clearly, nothing would have stopped the younger man from achieving his later fame. Stylistically, Oliver's influence on Armstrong was important although here again the pupil quickly outstripped his tutor in technique, imagination and inventiveness. Setting aside the role he played in Armstrong's life, and the corresponding reflected glory Armstrong threw upon him, Oliver can be seen and heard to have been a striking soloist and a massively self-confident ensemble leader. He was also a sensitive accompanist, making several fine records with popular blues singers of the day.

Compilations: *King Oliver And His Creole Jazz Band: The OKeh Sessions* (1923), *King Oliver Vol. 1 1923-1929* (CDS 1923-29 recordings), *Farewell Blues* (1926-27), *King Oliver And His Dixie Syncopators* (1926-28), *King Oliver Vol. 2* (1927-30), *King Oliver And His Orchestra* (1929-30), *New York Sessions* (RCA 1990), *Sweet Like This* (1929-30), *Complete Vocalion/Brunswick Recordings 1926 - 1931* (1992).

Further reading: *King Joe Oliver*, Walter C. Allen and Brian A.L. Rust. *'King' Oliver*, Laurie Wright. *King Oliver And Kings Of Jazz*, M Williams.

Oliver, Sy

b. Melvin James Oliver, 17 December 1910, Battle Creek, Michigan, USA, d. 28 May 1988. Born into a family in which both parents were music teachers, Oliver played trumpet as a child and at the age of 17 was a member of the popular **territory band** led by Zack Whyte. During this stint he began arranging, primarily to prove to his older and supposedly wiser fellow sidemen that his theories about harmony were sound. After the Whyte band, Oliver played in another important territory band, led by **Alphonso Trent**. Then, after some of his arrangements had been accepted by **Jimmie Lunceford**, Oliver took a job with his band, playing in the trumpet section, singing and arranging. Lunceford had already enjoyed the benefits of good arrangers in **Eddie Durham** and, especially, **Ed Wilcox**; but, more than anyone, it was Oliver who shaped the sound of the Lunceford band from 1933 until 1939, the period of its greatest commercial and aesthetic success. Oliver's use of two-beat rhythm, stop-time breaks, intricate saxophone choruses and ear-splitting brass explosions, brilliantly executed by Lunceford's musicians, in particular drummer **Jimmy Crawford** and lead alto saxophonist **Willie Smith**, not only sealed Lunceford's success but created a style of big band music which proved widely influential. Oliver's arranging style was especially suitable to the more commercial aspects of the swing era and was taken up and adapted by many of his contemporaries and successors. Although employed by Lunceford, Oliver did arrange for other bands too, including **Benny Goodman**'s, and his reputation in the business was enviable. Tiring of his work with Lunceford, Oliver decided to quit music and study law, but **Tommy Dorsey** made him an offer he could not refuse: $5,000 a year more than he'd earned with Lunceford. Oliver's arrangements for Dorsey propelled the band into a new era of success, which transcended what had gone before for both arranger and leader. 'Swing High', 'Well, Git It!', 'Sunny Side Of the Street' and 'Opus No. 1' were all massively popular and the records became big sellers. After military service during World War II, Oliver briefly led his own musically excellent but commercially unsuccessful big band and worked as a freelance arranger, his charts being used by Dorsey and by studios for recording orchestras' dates with singers such as **Ella Fitzgerald** and **Frank Sinatra**. In the 60s he once again tried bandleading, but as before was not prepared to bow to commercial pressures. In the late 60s and 70s he toured extensively, resumed trumpet playing and undertook several club residencies in New York, a pattern which persisted into the 80s. A major figure in the development of jazz arranging, Oliver was almost single-handedly responsible for the creation of what later became definable as mainstream big band music. His use of attacking brass and clean ensemble passages was picked up and modified, sometimes simplified, but rarely if ever improved.

Selected albums: *Sy Oliver And His Orchestra* i (1954), *Sy Oliver And His Orchestra* ii (1957), *Sy Oliver And His Orchestra* iii (1958), *Sy Oliver And His Orchestra* iv (1958), *Back Stage* (1959), *77 Sunset Strip* (1959), *Just A Minute* (c.1960), *Annie Laurie* (1960), *Four Roses Dance Party* (1961), *Sy Oliver And His Orchestra* v (c.1962), *Sy Oliver And His Orchestra* vi (c.1962), *Easy Walker* (1962), *Take Me Back* (1972), *Yes, Indeed!* (1973), *Sy Oliver And His Orchestra Play The Famous Rainbow Room* (1976). Compilations: *The Indispensable Tommy Dorsey, Vols 7/8* (1939 recordings), *The Complete Jimmie Lunceford* (1939-40 recordings).

Olivier, Laurence, Awards

These awards are presented by the Society of West End Theatre in recognition of distinguished artistic achievement in West End Theatre. They were established in 1976 as the Society of West End Theatre Awards. Lord Olivier agreed to have his name associated with them in 1984 and they are now regarded as the highlight of the British theatrical year. The Awards are judged by three separate panels; for theatre, opera, and dance. The Theatre Panel comprises seven people chosen for their specialist knowledge and professional experience, plus six members of the theatre-going public. Anyone who applies to be included in the latter group should be prepared to see some 80 productions during the Awards year. The musical categories consist of: best director choreographer, actress, actor, supporting performance, revival, and the American Express Award for Best Musical. A musical production, or those associated with it, can also conceivably win in other sections such as best entertainment, costume design, lighting design, set design, outstanding achievement, and lifetime achievement. In 1993, the musicals prizes all went to the highly acclaimed British productions of the American shows ***Carousel***, ***Crazy For You***, and ***Assassins***. The bronze Laurence Olivier Award itself was specially commissioned by the Society from the sculptor Harry Franchetti and represents the young Laurence Olivier as Henry V at the Old Vic in 1937.

Ollie And Jerry

The R&B duo of Ollie Brown and Jerry Knight came from Los Angeles, California, USA. This dance-music producing and writing team briefly charted courtesy of two soundtrack items from the motion picture *Breakin'*. Their 'Breakin' . . . There's No Stopping Us' went to number 3 in the US R&B chart and number 9 national in 1984, and later in the year 'Electric Boogie' proved to be a mild R&B hit at number 45. In the UK, 'Breakin' . . . There's No Stopping Us' went to number 5 in 1984, and 'Electric Boogaloo' went to number 57 in 1985. The Ollie and Jerry team was somewhat of an outgrowth of their work together on several albums for **Ray Parker, Jnr.**, and his **Raydio** group. Brown continued his career in Detroit in 1975, playing drums with **Edwin Starr, Stevie Wonder**, and the **Rolling Stones,** and beginning in 1978 as guest drummer for Raydio. By the early 80s he was producing for such acts as **Patti Austin** and Klique. Knight began his musical career as bass player in **Bill Withers**'s band, and then moved to Raydio, where he sang the high parts as well as played bass. He charted with three albums, *Jerry Knight* (1980), *Perfect Fit* (1981) and *Love's On Our Side* (1983) and six singles, notably 'Overnight Sensation' (USR&B number 17, 1980) and 'Perfect Fit' (1981), before teaming up with Ollie Brown on the soundtrack titles for *Breakin'*.

Film: *Breakdance - The Movie* (1984).

Olympic Records

Record company formed in Liverpool by James Barton and Andy Carroll, named after their respected club night. Barton was a DJ who served his apprenticeship on the Northern club scene, going on to launch one of the best known venues, Cream. He was then instrumental in setting up Olympic Records in 1992 with Carroll, who was also a DJ. The label earned its biggest success with Seven Grand Housing Authority (Terrence Parker)'s 'The Question'. Barton also furnished **K-Klass**, who remixed the record, with management services, and introduced them to their, and his, future employers, **DeConstruction**. He joined the latter label in early 1994 to take a hand in their A&R operation, though he retained his interests in Olympic and Cream.

Olympics

Originally known as the Challengers, this adaptable vocal group, Walter Ward (b. 1940, Jackson, Mississippi, USA; lead), Eddie Lewis (b. 1937, Houston, Texas, USA; tenor), Charles Fizer (b. 1940,

Shreveport, Louisiana, USA; baritone) and Walter Hammond (baritone) was formed in Compton, California in 1954. The Olympics' finest moment came with 'Western Movies' (1958), a humorous, novelty disc in the vein of the **Coasters** and the **Clovers**, which reached the Top 10 in the US and Top 20 in the UK. The song was produced and co-written by Fred Smith, who later worked with **Bob And Earl**. The same was true of 'Private Eye', another laconic tribute to 50s pulp-fiction culture, but it was 1960 before the group claimed another US hit with 'Big Boy Pete', by which time Melvin King (b. 1940, Shreveport, Louisiana, USA), had replaced Walter Hammond. Meanwhile, the sacked lead vocalist Fizer, whose troubled life had already resulted in a prison sentence for drugs possession, was shot by the National Guard during the Watts riots in 1965. A reshaped Olympics later went on to score hits with such dancefloor favourites as 'The Bounce' (1963), 'Good Lovin'' (1965 - later successfully covered by the **Young Rascals**) and 'Baby Do The Philly Dog' (1966), before being drawn towards the 'oldies' circuit.

Albums: *Doin' The Hully Gully* (1960), *Dance By The Light Of The Moon* (1961), *Party Time* (1961), *Do The Bounce* (1963), *Something Old Something New* (1966), *Soul Music* (1968). Compilations: *Greatest Hits* (1971), *The Official Record Album Of The Olympics* (1984).

Om Records

'The idea of Om is to cover the spectrum of house music and to do absolutely the best stuff that house can offer', explained DJ Nick Hook, who founded the UK label Om together with *New Musical Express* dance correspondent Sherman and **Morgan King**. The label was thus inaugurated with three double-pack EP's which displayed just that: a *pot pourri* of modern house, labelled *Absolute Om, 1 - 3*. Other bands on the label included mainstays Soundsource (essentially Morgan King, whose recordings, such as 'Take Me Up' and 'One High', also appear on Sweden's B-Tech imprint), ex-**Geurilla** act Euphoria, **Bump** and Marine Boy (who are one-time **Ruts** member Segz and engineer Steve Dub's deep house/ambient project, disinguished by releases of the calibre of 'Fluid'). 1994 releases included 108 Grand featuring Roy Galloway's 'Love U All Over'.

Omar

b. Omar Lye Fook, c.1968. Omar was born the son of a Chinese Jamaican father and an Indian Jamaican mother. A former principle percussionist of the Kent Youth Orchestra, he would later graduate from the Guildhall School Of Music. His debut singles were 'Mr Postman' and 'You And Me' (featuring backing vocals from **Caron Wheeler**), before his debut album was released, via Harlesden's Black Music Association's Kong Dance imprint, on a slender budget. Nevertheless, it made the Top 60. In its wake Omar's name suddenly started cropping up everywhere, be it as a singer, writer or producer. Following a high profile Hammersmith Odeon concert in December 1990 Gilles Peterson of **Talkin' Loud** persuaded financial backers **Phonogram** to open their wallets. The debut album was slightly remixed and re-released, the title-track having already earned its stripes as a club favourite. Although by definition a soul artist, Omar's use of reggae, ragga and particularly hip hop has endeared him to a wide cross-section of the dance community. **RCA** won the scramble to sign Omar after departing from Talkin' Loud in January 1993. Since then Omar has continued to collaborate with a number of premier R&B artists: songwriter **Lamont Dozier**, keyboard player David Frank (famed for his contribution to **Chaka Khan**'s 'I Feel For You'), bass player Derek Bramble (ex-**Heatwave**), Leon Ware (arranger for **Marvin Gaye**) and no less than **Stevie Wonder** himself, who contacted Omar after hearing his 'Music' cut.

Albums: *There's Nothing Like This* (Kongo Dance 1990, remixed and re-released Talkin' Loud 1991), *For Pleasure* (RCA 1994).

OMD

This UK synthesizer pop duo comprised Paul Humphreys (b. 27 February 1960, Liverpool, England) and Andy McCluskey (b. 24 June 1959, Liverpool, England). Originally combining in school band Equinox they moved on through VCL XI and Hitlerz Underpantz, and finally The Id. When that band split in 1978 McCluskey spent a short time with **Dalek I Love You** before he and Humphreys, together with Paul Collister, performed live in October 1978 under their full title Orchestral Manoeuvres In The Dark. Tony Wilson of **Factory Records** became interested in the band, releasing their debut 'Electricity'. It was quickly re-released when **Virgin** subsidiary DinDisc signed them. Its success subsequently allowed the group the chance to build their own studio. They replaced their 4-track recorder ('Winston') with real personnel Malcom Holmes (ex-Equinox and the Id) and Dave Hughes (Dalek I Love You). 1980 saw 'Red Frame/White Light' released as a single to preface the band's first, self-titled album. Their breakthrough, however, came with the UK Top 10 'Enola Gay', and its laboured nuclear war sentiments. *Organisation* followed quickly, with Martin Cooper replacing Dave Hughes shortly afterwards. The more sophisticated *Architecture And Morality* showed a new romanticism particularly in the singles 'Joan Of Arc' and 'Maid Of Orleans'. 1983's *Dazzle Ships* was a flawed attempt at progression, highlighting dilemmas forced on them by popularity and DinDisc's collapse (the band transferred to Virgin). *Junk Culture* faced similar critical disdain, and did not boast the presence of a hit single, as

'Locomotion' had done for Dazzle Ships. *Crush* was a less orchestrated and more immediate affair, featuring the return of political commentary alongside the permanent insertion of Graham and Neil Weir into the line-up. *The Pacific Age* was premiered on another of the band's frequent worldwide touring endeavours, but it was obvious from its chart position that their domestic popularity was slipping. The six-piece line-up was proving too cumbersome and the Weir brothers departed shortly afterwards. The rift was compounded when Holmes and Cooper and, more importantly, Humphreys joined the list of departures. McCluskey retained the name and, after a long restorative period, resurfaced in 1991 with 'Sailing On The Seven Seas'. The resultant album harkened back to the era of *Architecture And Morality*, including the use of choral effects. Meanwhile, Humphreys formed a new band under the name the Listening Pool.

Albums: *Orchestral Manoeuvres In The Dark* (1980), *Organisation* (1980), *Architecture And Morality* (1981), *Dazzle Ships* (1983), *Junk Culture* (1984), *Crush* (1985), *The Pacific Age* (1986), *Sugar Tax* (1991), *Liberator* (1993).

Further reading: *Orchestral Manoeuvres In The Dark*, Mike West.

Omen

This Los Angeles, USA-based, melodic power-metal outfit formed in 1984. Comprising J.D. Kimball (vocals), Kenny Powell (guitar; ex-Sacred Blade), Jody Henry (bass) and Steve Wittig (drums), they debuted with a track on the *Metal Massacre V* compilation. This led to a contract with Metal Blade and the release of *Battle Cry* the same year. This was a competent, if uninspired, collection of **Iron Maiden**-style rockers, which lacked distinction due to Kimball's weak vocals. Three more albums followed a similar pattern, with 1987's mini-opus *Nightmares* being the most interesting (it featured a strong cover of **AC/DC**'s 'Whole Lotta Rosie'). Coburn Pharr replaced Kimball in 1988 and helped the band produced *Escape From Nowhere*, their finest recorded work. Adding **Rush**-styled dynamics to their basic metal framework, it was characterized by Pharr's powerful and high-pitched vocals. Surprisingly, it failed to sell and Pharr left to join **Annihilator** in 1990.

Albums: *Battle Cry* (Roadrunner 1984), *Warning Of Danger* (Roadrunner 1985), *The Curse* (Roadrunner 1986), *Nightmares* (Roadrunner 1987), *Escape From Nowhere* (Roadrunner 1988).

On A Clear Day You Can See Forever

Alan Jay Lerner's long-time partnership with **Frederick Loewe** had lapsed by the early 60s partly owing to the composer's ill health, when he decided to write a Broadway show based on his absorbing interest in the subject of extrasensory perception (ESP). Lerner's first choice for a project which was originally entitled *I Picked A Daisy*, was **Richard Rodgers**, who had been searching for a new partner since the death of **Oscar Hammerstein II** in 1960. According to reports, the collaboration resulted in the irrisistable force meeting the immovable object, so Lerner turned instead to **Burton Lane**. The new show, now called *On A Clear Day You Can See Forever*, made its debut at the Mark Hellinger theatre on 17 October 1965. In Lerner's book, Dr. Mark Bruckner (John Cullum) discovers that one of his patients, Daisy Gamble (Barbara Harris), can not only foresee the future and persuade her plants to grow by just talking to them, but is prepared to go into details about her life as Melinda, an early feminist, who lived in 18th century London. They fall in love, but when Daisy begins to believe (mistakenly) that Mark is more interested in Melinda than in her, she walks out. Although miles away, she hears and responds when he gives out with 'Come Back To Me' ('Leave behind all you own/Tell your flowers you'll telephone/Let your dog walk alone/Come back to me!'). McCallum also had two lovely ballads, the title song, 'On A Clear Day (You Can See Forever)', and 'Melinda'. The remainder of a fine score included the delightful 'Hurray! It's Lovely Up Here', 'She Wasn't You', 'Wait Till We're Sixty-Five', 'When I'm Being Born Again', 'What Did I Have That I Don't Have?', 'Don't Tamper With My Sister', and 'Tosy And Cosh'. The show ran for an unsatisfactory 280 performances, and, as usual, while Lerner's lyrics were admired, his book came in for a deal of criticism. Barbara Harris was particularly applauded for her work, but, in the 1970 film, her role was taken by **Barbra Streisand**, who co-starred with Yves Montand.

On The Avenue

After enjoying tremendous success in partnership with several American leading ladies in movie musicals such as ***42nd Street***, ***Dames*** and the ***Gold Diggers*** series, **Dick Powell** teamed with English actress Madeleine Carroll for this picture which was released by 20th Century-Fox in 1937. Carroll plays wealthy socialite Mimi Caraway who objects violently to being lampooned in a satirical revue by Gary Blake (Dick Powell). Naturally, they eventually resolve their differences and fall in love. This leaves Blake's previous girlfriend, Mona Merrick (**Alice Faye**), out in the cold, but she consoles herself by singing the lion's share of **Irving Berlin**'s wonderful score, including the enduring 'This Year's Kisses', 'He Ain't Got Rhythm' and 'Slumming On Park Avenue' (the last two with the Ritz Brothers); and 'I've Got My Love To Keep Me Warm' and 'The Girl On The Police Gazette' (both with Dick Powell). Powell himself had the superior 'You're Laughing At Me', which later became popular for **Fats Waller**. Also among the cast of *On The Avenue* were Alan Mowbray, George Barbier, Cora Witherspoon, Walter Catlett, Billy Gilbert, and Stepin

Fetchit. Gene Markey and William Conselman wrote the amusing screenplay, the stylish dances were staged by Seymour Felix, and the film was directed by Roy Del Routh. The basic plot of this film was used again in ***Let's Make Love*** (1960) starring **Marilyn Monroe**, Yves Montand and **Frankie Vaughan**.

On The Riviera

Post-war cinema audiences got a double ration of **Danny Kaye** in this Sol C. Siegel Technicolor production when it was released by 20th Century-Fox in 1951. Henry and Phoebe Ephron's screenplay concerned a well-known nightclub entertainer who is the spitting image of a philandering businessman. If that plot sounds familiar, it is because it cropped up on the screen in ***Folies Bergère De Paris*** (1934) and ***That Night In Rio*** (1941), and, with a slight twist and another change in location, formed the basis of *On The Double* (1961). Kaye played both roles, of course, and had a great time with all the complications that naturally spring from this kind of situation. Gene Tierney was the businessman's wife who could not tell the difference between her real husband and his stand-in, and also taking part in the hilarious shenanigans were Corinne Calvert, Marcel Dalio, Clinton Sundberg, Henri Letondal, Sig Ruman, and Joyce McKenzie. Future dancing star **Gwen Verdon** was in the chorus. Sylvia Fine, Kaye's wife, tailored four songs especially for him: 'Popo The Puppet', 'Rhythm Of Romance', 'Happy Ending', and 'On The Riviera', and he also sang one of his much-loved favourites, the 1913 number 'Ballin' The Jack' (James Henry Burris-Chris Smith). Jack Cole staged the imaginative dance sequences, and the film was directed by Walter Lang.

On The Road With Duke Ellington

A remarkable film record, made originally in 1967 and updated after **Duke Ellington**'s death in 1974. In addition to Ellington talking about his life there are sequences showing him receiving honorary doctorates, rehearsing and recording his orchestra, playing the piano and, most intriguing of all, composing and arranging. If anything, the casual manner in which he does this simply adds to the mystique. Sprawled out on a couch, feet up, he and **Billy Strayhorn** put together a piece of music with such deceptive ease as to make even a Hollywood songwriter biopic seem forced. Apart from the Maestro, musicians such as **Harry Carney**, **Jimmy Hamilton**, **Johnny Hodges**, **Paul Gonsalves** and **Louis Armstrong** also make appearances.

On The Town (Film Musical)

Remembered particularly for its innovative staging of some of the musical sequences on the streets of New York, *On The Town* was released by MGM in 1949. **Betty Comden** and **Adolph Green**'s screenplay (they also wrote all the lyrics) was based on their book for the 1944 stage musical, which itself was inspired by choreographer-director **Jerome Robbins'** ballet *Fancy Free*. From the moment that the three sailors, played by **Gene Kelly**, **Frank Sinatra**, and Jules Munshin come dashing from their ship to the strains of the rousing 'New York, New York' (music-**Leonard Bernstein**), eager to enjoy the delights of New York on their 24-hours leave, the film sings and dances along in an exhilarating fashion. Naturally, they each find their ideal partner: Kelly first sees the girl of his dreams, **Vera-Ellen**, on a poster in the subway, and their delightful *pas-de-deux* 'Main Street' (music-**Roger Edens**) is one of the film's many highspots; Munshin is pursued through the Museum of Natural History by the anthropological **Ann Miller** who considers him to be a perfect example of a 'Prehistoric Man' (music-Edens); while the ingenuous Sinatra is invited to 'Come Up to My Place' (music-Bernstein) by the amusingly man-hungry taxi driver **Betty Garrett**. Stage musical buffs were offended by the way Bernstein's original Broadway score was 'decimated', with only five numbers surviving - the two already mentioned, plus 'I Feel Like I'm Not Out Of Bed Yet' and two ballets, 'Miss Turnstiles' and 'A Day In New York'. The substitutes, with music by Roger Edens, included 'You're Awful' and 'On The Town'. Edens was also co-musical director with **Lennie Hayton**, and both men won Oscars for music scoring. Alice Pearce recreated her original stage role as Betty Garrett's flatmate, a girl with a permanent cold, and also in the cast were Florence Bates, Carol Haney, Hans Conried, and George Meader. Gene Kelly and **Stanley Donen**'s first film together was photographed in Technicolor and produced by **Arthur Freed**.

On The Town (Stage Musical)

Opening on 28 December 1944, *On The Town* was based on the 20-minute ballet, *Fancy Free*, by choreographer **Jerome Robbins** and composer **Leonard Bernstein**. Robbins had been on Broadway before, as a dancer, but for Bernstein, and librettists and lyricists **Betty Comden** and **Adolph Green**, *On The Town* was their first taste of the glamorous New York musical theatre. The 'almost non-existent book' concerns three sailors, Gaby (John Battles), Ozzie (Adolph Green), and Chip (Cris Alexander) who are on leave in New York for just 24 hours. They meet three girls, Ivy (Sono Osato), Hildy (Nancy Walker), and Claire (Betty Comden), and all enthusiastically take in tourist spots such as Coney Island, The Museum of Natural History, Central Park, Carnegie Hall, Times Square, and a dive called Diamond Eddie's. The thrilling score ranged from the rousing 'New York, New York', through the amusing 'Ya Got Me', 'Come Up To My Place', 'I Can Cook, Too', and 'I Get Carried Way', to the lovely ballads, 'Lonely Town',

'Lucky To Be Me', and 'Some Other Time'. At the end of the boys' day of freedom, the girls see them off at the quay - and another batch of sailors come careering down the gangplank singing 'New York, New York', and the whole process begins all over again. *On The Town* enjoyed a run of 463 performances and was revived twice in New York, Off-Broadway in 1959 (Harold Lang, Wisa D'Orso, and Pat Carroll), and in a main house in 1971, with Ron Husman, Donna McKechnie, **Bernadette Peters** and Phyllis Newman (Mrs. Adolph Green). A 1963 London production folded after 53 performances. There was renewed interest in the show almost 30 years later, when, in June 1992, a semi-staged version, narrated by Comden and Green, was presented at London's Barbican Hall, and then, in 1993, the Goodspeed Opera House in Connecticut, USA, mounted a well-received production. The 1949 film starred **Frank Sinatra**, **Gene Kelly**, Jules Munshin, **Vera-Ellen**, **Ann Miller**, and Betty Garrett.

On The Twentieth Century

In the long history of the musical theatre, this was probably not the first occasion on which the critics inferred that 'the audience left the theatre whistling the scenery'. However, that phrase did crop up a lot (along with 'it ran out of steam') in the reviews for this show which opened at the St. James Theatre in New York on 19 February 1978, and was set mostly aboard the fondly remembered train, the Twentieth Century Limited, which used to run from Chicago to New York. The set was certainly spectacular - a splendid art-deco affair - designed by Robin Wagner. The book, by **Betty Comden** and **Adolph Green**, which was based on Ben Hecht and Charles MacArthur's farce, *Twentieth Century*, concerns the legendary producer-director, Oscar Jaffee (John Cullum), a Broadway legend - but not recently. He is at the bottom of the barrel, but his former lover and protegée, the temperamental movie star Lily Garland (Madeline Kahn), is at the top of the tree. His efforts to sign her for a project that will ensure his rehabilitation bring him into contact with the current rivals for her attention, actor Bruce Granit (played by Kevin Kline, himself a film heart-throb of the 80s and 90s), and the film producer Max Jacobs (George Lee Andrews). The veteran Broadway comedienne Imogene Coca, making a welcome comeback to the New York musical stage after an absence of over 30 years, played a cooky religious character with a great deal of fervour. The score was written by Comden and Green together with composer **Cy Coleman**. His music, which is usually jazz-based, like the man himself, was regarded this time as being too flamboyant and out of character, 'alternating much of the time between early nineteenth century comic-opera mannerisms and early twentieth century operetta', in songs such as 'I Rise Again', 'Veronique', 'On The Twentieth Century', 'Our Private World', 'Repent', 'We've Got It', 'She's A Nut', 'Legacy', 'Never', 'Life Is Like A Train', 'Together', 'Stranded Again', and 'Mine'. In spite of the criticism, the show won **Tony Awards** for score, book, Cullum, and Kline, and stayed on the rails for 449 performances. Cullum is said to have based his portrayal of the mogul on John Barrymore, who appeared with Carole Lombard in the 1934 film *Twentieth Century*. The 1980 West End production of *On The Twentieth Century* starred **Julia McKenzie**, one of the outstanding leading ladies of the London musical theatre, but it still ground to a halt after only 165 performances.

On With The Dance

Noël Coward's first revue for impresario **C. B. Cochran** opened at the London Pavilion on 30 April 1925. Coward wrote the book and most of the songs, with Philip Braham providing a few extra numbers. The cast included Hermione Baddeley, Douglas Byng, Ernest Thesiger, Greta Fayne, and Lance Lister. The star was Alice Delysia, who introduced 'Poor Little Rich Girl', a song which Cochran thought 'dreary', although it went on to become one of Coward's most enduring copyrights. The lavish, superbly presented show also contained two ballets created and danced by Leonide Massine, and enjoyed a run of 229 performances.

On Your Toes

Ballet came to Broadway in a big way, courtesty of choreographer George Balanchine, in this show which opened at the Imperial Theatre in New York on 11 April 1936. **Richard Rodgers** and **Lorenz Hart** wrote the book, along with **George Abbott**, and their complex plot involved Junior Dolan (**Ray Bolger**), who has given up the grind of the vaudeville circuit in favour of teaching music at the Knickerbocker University. When the Russian Ballet just happen to stage a production of a jazzy, insinuating ballet, 'Slaughter On Tenth Avenue', in the locale, Junior becomes involved, both onstage and off, with its prima ballerina, Vera Barnova (Tamara Geva). This Pavlovian *pas de deux* offends both Junior's girlfriend, Frankie Frayne (Doris Carson), and, more importantly, Vera's regular dancing partner, who tries to have Junior bumped off. Bolger, in a part that was originally created for **Fred Astaire**, was sensational in his first Broadway role, and soon developed into one of America's most cherished clowns. Balanchine's choreography, which included a second ballet, 'Princess Zenobia', was highly praised. The show also marked the acting debut of the former Yale professor, Monty Woolley, as the director of the Russian Ballet company. Rodgers and Hart's lively and tuneful score was right up to their highest standard, and contained the delightful 'There's A Small Hotel' and It's Got to Be Love', sung by Carson and Bolger, a poignant ballad, 'Glad To Be Unhappy', the comical 'Too Good For The Average Man', and other equally pleasing numbers such as 'The Heart Is Quicker Than The Eye', 'The Three B's', 'On Your Toes', and 'Quiet Night'. *On Your Toes* danced along for 315 performances, and in 1937 was presented at the Palace Theatre in London with Vera Zorina in the leading role. She also starred in a 1954 Broadway revival with Bobby Van and Elaine Stritch. When *On Your Toes* returned to Broadway again in 1983, the role of Vera was played by the celebrated ballerina, Natalia Makarova, during the early part of a run of 505 performances. Both revivals were staged by George Abbott. Makarova also co-starred with Tim Flavin in a further successful West End presentation in 1984. 'Slaughter On Tenth Avenue' reached a wider audience when it was danced by **Gene Kelly** and **Vera-Ellen** in the Rodgers and Hart biopic, ***Words And Music*** (1948).

Once Upon A Mattress

This is an expanded musical adaptation of the comical fairy tale, *The Princess And The Pea*, with music by Mary Rodgers, daughter of the famous composer, **Richard Rodgers**, and lyrics by Marshall Barer. The show opened Off Broadway at the Phoenix Theatre in New York on 11 May 1959, transferring to the Alvin Theatre on Broadway in November. The book, by Jay Thompson, Dean Fuller, and Barer, told of Princess Winnifred (**Carol Burnett**), who is unable to marry Prince Dauntless the Drab (Joseph Bova), until she can prove to his mother, Queen Agravain (Jane White), that she is a genuine princess of royal blood. She triumphs during a series of tests, the last of which is to get no sleep at all during a night spent on a heap of mattresses with just one pea underneath the bottom one. Comedienne extraordinaire, Carol Burnett, who later went on to star in her own top-rated television series via the the Gary Moore Show, made an auspicious Broadway debut, and the cast also included that ever-reliable funny-man, Jack Gilford. No hits emerged from the score, but there were several pleasant songs, such as 'Shy', 'Sensitivity', 'Normandy', 'Man To Man Talk', 'Many Moons Ago', 'Very Soft Shoes', 'In A Little While', 'Happily Ever After', 'The Swamp Of Home', and 'Yesterday I Loved You'. An encouraging New York run of 460 performances was followed by a brief, one month stay in London.

One Dam Thing After Another

This **C. B. Cochran** revue, written by Ronald Jeans, opened at the London Pavilion on 20 May 1927. The impressive cast included **Sonnie Hale**, **Leslie 'Hutch' Hutchinson**, Melvin Cooper, the accomplished American pianist Edythe Baker, and the delightful, vivacious **Jessie Matthews** in her first leading role. One song, 'The Birth Of The Blues', was written by **De Sylva, Brown And Henderson**, but the remainder were provided by **Richard Rodgers** and **Lorenz Hart**, and included 'My Lucky Star', 'I Need Some Cooling Off', and the enduring standard, 'My Heart Stood Still', which was introduced by Jessie Matthews. The latter number, with Hart's emotional and affecting lyric, played a significant part in the show's success. After the Prince of Wales attended the opening night, he asked for the song to be played at a subsequent function. The orchestra did not know it, so the royal personage hummed it for them. Naturally, the press gave the incident extensive coverage, and also printed the words and music of the song's first 16 bars. The royal seal of approval helped *One Dam Thing After Another* to overcome initially lukewarm reviews, and it became a hit, running for 237 performances.

One Dove

Glasgow, Scotland trio, who caught the nation's imagination in 1993 with their mellow musical depths. The group comprise Ian Carmichael (b. 1 June 1960, Glasgow, Scotland), Jim McKinven (b. David James McKinven, c.1959, Glasgow, Scotland) and former chemical engineering student Dot Allison (b. Dorothy Elliot Allison, 17 August 1969, Edinburgh, Scotland). McKinven had been in an early incarnation of the **Bluebells** (rehearsal only), but was best known for his stint in **Altered Images**. Carmichael owns Toad Hall Studios, and has engineered or produced for many Glaswegian acts (**Orchids**, **Bachelor Pad** etc.). The group made their first public appearance at the Rock Garden, Queens Street, Glasgow, in August 1991. The fact that **Andy Weatherall** got involved attracted some initial attention, but there was more to the group than merely another of his side projects. They had already broken into the rave scene's elite with the single 'Fallen', prior to their collaboration. It was released on **Soma**, before the band had changed their name from their original selection, Dove. However, litigation followed from representatives of **Supertramp** (the band had, inadvertently, used a sample from an Italian house record which in turn had sampled the prog-rockers). They met Weatherall in Rimini in 1991. After he agreed to work with them there was some discussion in the press that One Dove's debut album would signal another landmark episode, ala **Primal Scream**'s *Screamadelica*, but this was perhaps over-optimistic. It was at least a solid, musically enthralling collection conveying One Dove's biggest influence: **King Tubby** and Jamaican dub music.

Album: *Morning Dove White* (1993).

One Hit Wonder

Hailing from Long Beach, Orange County, California, and led by singer and principal songwriter Dan Root,

One Hit Wonder additionally comprise Randy Bradbury (bass), Trey Pangborn (guitar) and Chris Webb (drums). Their self-titled debut EP in 1995, produced by alternative rock team the Robb brothers (**Lemonheads**, **Buffalo Tom**), consolidated the impression laid by an initial batch of underground 7-inch singles for Lethal Records. The material on offer ('Break Your Heart', 'After Her Disasters') provided down at heel takes on life backed by focused metal riffing with power pop flourishes.

One Hour With You

This highly acclaimed musical, a delightful and sophisticated picture which was released by Paramount in 1932, reunited **Maurice Chevalier** and **Jeanette MacDonald** following their joint triumph two years earlier in ***The Love Parade***. As with that film, *One Hour With You* bore the unmistakeable touch of director **Ernst Lubitsch**, and was, in fact, a remake of his 1924 silent, *The Marriage Circle*. Samson Raphaelson's screenplay told of a happily married couple, played by Chevalier and MacDonald, whose domestic bliss is shattered when he becomes far too friendly with her flirtatious best friend (Genevieve Tobin). Also in the cast were Roland Young, Charlie Ruggles, Josephine Dunn, Donald Novis, and George Barbier. The songs, with music by Oscar Straus and **Richard Whiting** and lyrics by **Leo Robin**, included 'Three Times A Day', 'One Hour With You', 'We Will Always Be Sweethearts', 'What Would You Do?', 'It Was Only a Dream Kiss', 'Oh, That Mitzi', and 'What A Little Thing Like A Wedding Ring Can Do'. For various complicated reasons, Lubitsch shared directorial credit with George Cukor on a film that is considered a classic of its kind.

110 In The Shade

If only this show had not opened in the same 1963-64 Broadway season as ***Hello, Dolly!*** and ***Funny Girl***, things might have been different; it would probably have won some awards for a start. Even so, when it made its debut at the Broadhurst Theatre on 24 October 1963, *110 In The Shade* met with almost universal acclaim. The odd man out was Walter Kerr, the critic of the New York Herald Tribune, who called the song 'Little Red Hat' 'dirty and salacious', but lines such as 'I find us a spot/Where no one is at/Then I reach across and grab her little red hat', would hardly raise any eyebrows today. That number, and the rest of the score was written by **Tom Jones** and **Harvey Schmidt**, whose first collaboration in 1960 had resulted in ***The Fantasticks***, the record-breaking Off Broadway production. N. Richard Nash's book was adapted from his own 1954 play, *The Rainmaker*, and it was only after seeing that on US television that Jones and Schmidt came up with the idea of this musical. A feature film version, with Burt Lancaster and Katharine Hepburn had been released in 1956. The story is set in a bleak town in the American Midwest, where a self-styled rainmaker, the handsome Bill Starbuck (Robert Horton), has arrived to cure the problem ('Rain Song'). Lizzie Curry (Inga Swenson) has a problem of her own - she cannot find a husband ('Love Don't Turn Away'). Her father and brothers try to fix her up with the town's sheriff, File (Stephen Douglass), a shy divorcee ('A Man And A Woman'), but she prefers the glamorous Starbuck. He indulges in all the rigmarole that is needed to bring the much-needed rain, but is eventually revealed to be a con-man on the run. Even so, Lizzie is about to run away with him ('Is It Really Me?') until File at last reveals his own love for her ('Wonderful Music'). She decides to accept him, and settle for the quiet life. At that moment, the heavens open . . . Jones and Schmidt's lovely, tuneful score, complemented perfectly the folksy, sentimental feeling of the piece. The rest of the songs included 'Gonna Be A Hot Day', 'Lizzie's Comin' Home', 'Poker Polka', 'Hungry Men', 'You're Not Foolin' Me', 'Raunchy', 'Old Maid', 'Everything Beautiful Happens At Night', 'Little Red Hat', 'Melisande', and 'Simple Little Things'. *110 In The Shade* had a decent run of 330 performances, and Inga Swenson's performance was oustanding. She was widely tipped to win a **Tony Award**, but *Hello, Dolly!* simply swept the board. In 1992 the show was revived by the New York City Opera, with Karen Ziémba as Lizzie. It was taped for transmission on the *Great Performances* television series.

One Hundred Men And A Girl

'Anything can be achieved if you just try hard enough', was the message that came through loud and clear in this charming and delightful **Deanna Durbin** film which was produced by Charles Rogers and Joe Pasternak for Universal in 1937. In the wonderfully optimistic screenplay, by Bruce Manning, Charles Kenyon, and Hans Kraly, the 16-year-old female star uses all her unbounded energy and enthusiasm to persuade the celebrated maestro Leopold Stokowski to conduct an orchestra consisting of her father (Adolph Menjou) and a number of other out-of-work musicians. Given that scenario, the songs such as 'It's Raining Sunbeams' (Sam Coslow-Frederick Hollander) and 'A Heart That's Free' (Alfred Robyn-Thomas T. Reilly), were joined by several classical pieces including '2nd Hungarian Rhapsody' (Liszt), '*Lohengrin* Prelude' (Wagner), 'Alleluja' (Mozart), and 'La Traviata' (Verdi). Charles Previn, head of Universal Studio's music department, won an Oscar for the film's score. In the strong supporting cast were Alice Brady, Eugene Pallette, Mischa Auer, and Billy Gilbert. Henry Koster directed the film which immediately proved to have enormous box-office appeal and touched the hearts of all who saw it.

One In A Million

Forty years before John Curry, and then others such as Robin Cousins and Torvill And Dean, caused television ratings to soar with their graceful and imaginative ice dancing, Norwegian champion Sonja Henie was delighting cinema audiences with her own individual brand of ice skating. She made he screen debut in this 1936 film, playing the daughter of a Swiss innkeeper who trains her for the Winter Olympic Games. Naturally, after some hitches along the way, she wins a medal - and the heart of press reporter **Don Ameche**. He headed an impressive cast along with Adolph Menjou as a band-leading impresario, the always hilarious Ritz Brothers, Jean Hersholt, Arline Judge, Dixie Dunbar, Ned Sparks, Montagu Love, Leah Ray, and Borrah Minevitch and his Harmonica Rascals. Sidney Mitchell and Lew Pollack's songs, which cropped up occasionally throughout an amusing and entertaining picture, included 'We're Back In Circulation Again', 'The Moonlight Waltz', 'Who's Afraid Of Love?', 'Lovely Lady In White', and 'One In A Million'. Producer Darryl F. Zanuck, who produced the film for 20th Century-Fox, is credited with the inspiration for bringing Sonja Henie to Hollywood - an idea that paid off handsomely at the box-office. Leonard Praskins and Mark Kelly wrote the screenplay, the choreographers were Jack Haskell and Nick Castle, and *One In A Million* was directed by Sidney Lanfield.

One Little Indian Records

The roots of the UK One Little Indian record label lie in the anarcho-punk scene of the early 80s particularly in one of its pioneering bands, **Flux Of Pink Indians**. The precursor to One Little Indian was Spiderleg, which released records by the **System**, **Subhumans**, and **Amebix** in addition to Flux's own material. Both labels were run by Derek Birkett (b. 18 February 1961, London, England), Flux's bass player, alongside friends and colleagues from the independent punk scene. Early releases included ones by **Annie Anxiety**, **D&V** and the **Very Things**. Reflecting on the mistakes made earlier, the label used expensive and tasteful cover art by Paul White's Me Company. When the **Sugarcubes**, a band Birkett previously knew when they were Kukl, broke through, financial security was assured. While One Little Indian retains its identity as the 'ethical indie', the operation is constructed on level-headed business practices: 'Our motives are artistic and business is reality'. Unlike many labels, the roster of bands does not have a uniform image or sounds. Music on the label includes the bright and breezy pop of the **Popinjays**, **Heart Throbs** and the Sugarcubes, the dance sound of the **Shamen** and **Finitribe**, the delicate, crafted pop of **Kitchens of Distinction** and the shattering volume of **What? Noise**. The label was also the temporary home for **They Might Be Giants**, who released *Lincoln* and two singles. The recent mainstream success of the Shamen has consolidated their position in the independent charts. The massive success of **Björk** was long overdue and was financially very welcome, although other outfits, like **Daisy Chainsaw**, failed to fulfil expectations. Recent signings include **Compulsion**, **Credit To The Nation** and the revitalized **Chumbawamba**. The label has released several 'Best Of' compilations which act as a good introductions.

Selected albums: Sugarcubes: *Life's Too Good* (One Little Indian 1988). Heart Throbs: *Cleopatra Grip* (One Little Indian 1990). Shamen: *Boss Drum* (One Little Indian 1992). Björk: *Debut* (One Little Indian 1993). Credit To The Nation: *Take Dis* (One Little Indian 1993). Chumbawamba: *Anarchy* (One Little Indian 1994).

One Night Of Love

Grace Moore brought her wonderful world of opera to the screen for the first time proper in this classic musical which was released by Columbia in 1934. In the uncomplicated story, by S.K. Lauren, James Gow, and Edmund North, she plays a young American soprano whose eventual worldwide fame is mainly due to the efforts of her music mentor and guru played impressively by Tullio Carminati. Also in the cast were Lyle Talbot, Mona Barrie, Jessie Ralph, and Jane Darwell. The score was a mixed bag of extracts from popular operettas and arias, along with some classical songs such as 'Ciribiribin' (Rudolph Thaler-Alberto Pestalozza) and 'None But The Lonely Heart' (Peter I. Tchaikovsky). The title number, by the film's director **Victor Schertzinger** (music) and **Gus Kahn** (lyric), won an Academy Award for Thematic Music although the award went to Louis Silvers, head of Columbia's music department - that was the custom in those days. *One Night Of Love* won another Oscar for sound recording, and was nominated best film, actress (Moore), and director.

101ers

Formed in London in May 1974, the 101ers made their performing debut four months later at the Telegraph pub in Brixton. Led by guitarist/vocalist **Joe Strummer**, the group established itself on a fading pub-rock circuit about to be undermined by the advent of punk. Support slots by the **Sex Pistols** confirmed Strummer's growing agitation and he left to join the **Clash** in June 1976. The 101ers then broke up with Clive Timperley (guitar) later joining the **Passions**. Dan Kelleher (bass) moved on to the Derelicts and Richard Dudanski (drums) went on to work with the **Raincoats** and **Public Image Limited**. The group was commemorated by 'Keys To Your Heart', issued on the independent Chiswick label the following month. In 1981 Strummer sanctioned the release of

Elgin Avenue Breakdown, a collection of live recordings, BBC sessions and studio out-takes. The material ranged from traditional R&B - 'Too Much Monkey Business', 'Route 66' - to ebullient originals which showed the singer's abrasive delivery already in place.
Album: *Elgin Avenue Breakdown* (1981).

One Records

Record label run by Eddie Colon (pronounced 'Cologne'), a former Kiss FM DJ, former proprieter of Renegade Records and a recording artist in his own right (scoring a US hit with 'Upfront') and the celebrated **Roger Sanchez**. They first met in 1991 when Colon was still a struggling DJ. The first One record was 'No Way' by Countdown, produced by **Toddy Terry/Kenny 'Dope' Gonzalez**. The release schedule continued apace with material by **Murk**'s Oscar G, more **Kenny 'Dope' Gonzalez** ('Axis Project' etc.) and **Victor Simonelli** ('I Know A Place') - almost a who's who of US house producers. The label was invoked: 'to bring quality records out of New York...a souful, house type of sound. We want to start developing artists. I'm an old song guy and I don't like this whole track thing'. One would sign **Farley and Heller** as their remix team, as well as UK singer J.B. Braithwaite ('Love Me Tonite'). In January 1994 the operation unveiled Sanchez's first ever long playing release.
Selected album: Roger Sanchez: *Secret Weapons Vol. 1* (One 1994). Various: *The Sound Of One* (One 1994).

1,000 Violins

This late 80s UK independent label group were formed in Sheffield, Yorkshire, and comprised Darren Swindells (bass), Colin Gregory (guitar), Vincent Keenan (vocals), David Warmsley (keyboards/guitar) and Ian Addie (drums). Their brand of 60s, US-influenced pop gave them three UK independent chart hits, the biggest being 'Locked Out Of The Love-In' (1987), which reached number 16. Their lone album was released on the US run Immaculate Records.
Album: *Hey Man, That's Beautiful* (1988).

One Touch Of Venus

After making her initial impact on Broadway in 1938 with **Cole Porter**'s 'My Heart Belongs To Daddy' in ***Leave It To Me!***, **Mary Martin** shot to stardom five years later in this show which opened at the Imperial Theatre in New York on 7 October 1943. The music was written by **Kurt Weill**, a familiar name in the American musical theatre following his flight from Germany in 1933, but for the two celebrated humorists, poet Ogden Nash (lyrics) and his fellow librettist, S.J. Perelman, *One Touch Of Venus* was their first, and only, book musical. The authors' story, which was based on F. Anstey's *The Tinted Venus*, was a contemporary 'sophisticated and witty variation on the Pygmalion-Galatea myth'. Whitelaw Savory (John Boles) has discovered a 3,000 year-old statue of Venus which he has put on display at his New York museum. While viewing the piece, Rodney Hatch (Kenny Baker), a barber from Ozone Heights, puts his fiancée's ring on Venus's finger, and the statue immediately springs to life in the classic shape of Mary Martin. Complex, and sometimes hilarious situations then develop, during which Whitelaw falls for Venus, but she prefers Rodney - that is until she finds out that he is just a simple barber. Eventually, disillusioned with her animated existence, Venus returns to her marble state, and Rodney falls in love with a girl who looks remarkably like . . . Mary Martin. Weill and Nash's score in which the words and music are always in perfect sympathy, is usually remembered for the haunting torch song, 'Speak Low', but there were several other attractive numbers including 'I'm A Stranger Here Myself', 'How Much I Love You', 'One Touch Of Venus', 'West Wind', 'That's Him', 'Foolish Heart', 'The Trouble With Women', 'Wooden Wedding', 'Very, Very, Very', and two beautiful and highly effective ballets sequences, 'Forty Minutes For Lunch' and 'Venus In Ozone Heights', both of which were choreographed by **Agnes de Mille**. Elia Kazan directed a brilliant all-round cast which included Paula Laurence, Teddy Hart, Ruth Bond, Sono Osato, and Harry Clark. The show ran for a respectable 322 performances, and is regarded as one of the classic musical comedies. Surprisingly, revivals have been few and far between, but the Goodspeed Opera House mounted an acclaimed production in 1987 which starred Richard Sabellico, Semina De Laurentis, Michael Piontek, and Lynnette Perry.

One Trick Pony

This underrated 1980 feature was written, scored and directed by its star **Paul Simon**. He played a musician reduced to the club circuit, questioning his existence after 14 years on the road had yielded a solitary hit. The cast included Blair Brown as Simon's wife, who wants a divorce, and Joan Hackett as his mistress, while his band included real-life musicians **Eric Gale**, Tony Levin and **Richard Tee**. The star's frustrations and dilemmas are skilfully drawn and Simon's untutored thespian gifts enhance the air of uncertainty. This was not the singer's first celluloid adventure - he enjoyed a cameo role in Woody Allen's *Annie Hall* - but *One Trick Pony* suggested a broadening artistic palate, particularly in the wake of the hiatus in Simon's recording career. The rebirth ushered in by *Gracelands* was still some years away and the attendant soundtrack album, which included 'How The Heart Approaches What It Yearns' and 'God Bless The Absentee', was not a major success despite being uniformly high-quality. The same was true of this low-key film, which also offered notable contributions from various denizens of the New York music scene from the 60s to the 80s. A reformed

Lovin' Spoonful, **Lou Reed**, **Tiny Tim** and the **B-52s** make fascinating appearances in a feature which deserves reappraisal.

One-derful Records

A Chicago record company founded by George Leaner in 1962 to record the hard soul sounds of the city. George Leaner with his brother Ernie Leaner had been operating a distribution firm, United Distributors since 1950. The One-derful/Midas/M-Pac/Mar-V-lus label complex got notable national hits with **McKinley Mitchell**'s 'The Town I Live In', the **Five Dutones**' 'Shake A Tail Feather', **Harold Burrage**'s 'Got To Find A Way' and **Otis Clay**'s 'That's How It Is', all of which epitomized Leaner's hard soul vision for the label. His most successful artist, however, was on a recording act that could not sing, **Alvin Cash And The Crawlers**. Rather leader Cash chanted his way through such giant hits as 'Twine Time', 'The Barracuda', and 'Philly Freeze'. Leaner recorded his acts in One-derful's house studio at 1825 S. Michigan, using such producer talents as **Monk Higgins** (Milton Bland) and **Andre Williams**, and such songwriting talent as Otis Hayes, Eddie Silvers, and Larry Nestor. The label folded in 1968, but brother Ernie Leaner and nephew Tony Leaner continued the family's involvement in the record business by founding the Toddlin' Town label, signing some of the artists who had previously been on **One-derful**. It lasted until 1971.

Ongala, Remmy

b. Zaire, 1947. At the age of 17 Remmy Ongala chose music as a means of supporting his family, the task he was left with after the death of his mother. As leader of Orchestre Super Matimila, which he joined in 1981, Remmy has become one of the best-known musicians in Tanzania. In his home-town of Dar Es Salaam he is well known by the community and even has a bus-stop named after him. Remmy's insightful, inspirational songwriting has led to his fans nicknaming him the Doctor. His lyrics are serious considerations of the problems that he and his fellow people face - poverty, poor living conditions, the struggle of women and so on. These lyrics, combined with the bright, danceable, soukous-based music of Orchestre Super Matimila produce a unique combination. This can be heard on *Songs For The Poor Man* which, recorded in England, is the Doctor's second album to be available outside Africa.

Selected albums: *Malilia Minana* (1988), *Songs For The Poor Man* (1989), *Mambo* (1992).

Only Child

This US heavy rock group was put together by the multi-talented songwriter, vocalist and guitarist **Paul Sabu** in 1988. Featuring Tommy Rude (keyboards), Murril Maglio (bass) and Charles Esposito (drums), their self-titled debut consisted of melodic rock which partially justified the critical acclaim it received. The praise heaped upon the album by *Kerrang* magazine, in particular, was rather premature, as the overtly commercial riffs and obvious hooks soon wore thin. This was borne out by the shortfall in anticipated sales. Esposito was replaced by Tommy Amato in 1989 and they were signed by **Geffen Records** to start work on new material, but thus far Only Child have remained quiet.

Album: *Only Child* (Rampage 1988).

Only Ones

The Only Ones were formed in 1976 with a line-up comprising: Peter Perrett (vocals/guitar), John Perry (guitar), Alan Mair (bass) and Mike Kellie (drums). Although touted as a new wave group, the unit included several old lags; Mair had previously worked with the **Beatstalkers**, while Kellie had drummed with **Spooky Tooth**, **Peter Frampton** and **Balls**. Perrett's former band, England's Glory, would have their demos released retrospectively after the Only Ones' demise. After a promising independent single, 'Lovers Of Today', the group were signed by **CBS Records** and made their debut with the searing opus, 'Another Girl, Another Planet' - on eof the new wave's most enduring songs. Front man Perrett, with his leopard-skin jacket and **Lou Reed** drawl, won considerable music press attention and the group's self-titled debut album was very well-received. A second self-produced collection, *Even Serpents Shine,* was also distinctive, but internal group friction and disagreements with their record company hampered their progress. Producer Colin Thurston took control of *Baby's Got A Gun,* which included a guest appearance by **Pauline Murray**, but lacked the punch of their earlier work. With sales dwindling, CBS dropped the group from their roster and the Only Ones finally broke up in 1981, with Perrett by now in the throes of desperate drug addiction. Since that time the group, and in particular, Perrett, have frequently been hailed as influential figures. After over-coming his chemical dependencies, Perrett made known his intentions for a come-back in 1991. This eventually materialised when his new band, The One, took the stage at London's Underworld in January 1994. This coincided with reports that Perrett had now written over 40 new songs.

Albums: *The Only Ones* (CBS 1978), *Even Serpents Shine* (CBS 1979), *Baby's Got A Gun* (CBS 1980). Compilations: *Special View* (CBS 1979), *Remains* (Closer 1984), *Alone In The Night* (Dojo 1986), *The Only Ones Live In London* (Skyclad 1989; also released as *Only Ones Live,* Demon 1989), *The Peel Sessions* (Strange Fruit 1989), *The Immortal Story* (Columbia 1992), *The Big Sleep* (Jungle 1993).

Only The Lonely

This 'throbbing tribute' to **Roy Orbison**, which was conceived and produced by the ubiquitous Bill Kenwright for the Liverpool Playhouse, opened at London's Piccadilly Theatre on 27 September 1994. In Shirlie Roden and Jon Miller's 'inept' book, Orbison's life is retold for the benefit of his son, Wesley (Stephen Tremblay), by the late singer's best friend, Bobbie Blackburn (James Carroll Jordan). The 'Big O' himself was played by an uncanny sound- and look-alike, Larry Branson, a Canadian who toured North America for several years in shows which gave him plenty of opportunities to sing 'Running Scared', 'It's Over', 'Crawlin' Back', 'Oh, Pretty Woman', 'In Dreams', 'Blue Bayou', 'Only The Lonely' and the rest of the nearly 30 songs featured during the evening. Not content with noting Branson's 'unnervingly similar Orbison characteristics - wide, plump cheeks, unsmiling mouth, and dark glasses' - some unkind critics also thought that they saw a likeness to the notorious terrorist Carlos the Jackal! Martin Glyn Murray gave a riveting performance as **Bruce Springsteen**, and the rest of the cast pretended to be **Dusty Springfield**, **Patsy Cline**, **Bob Dylan**, and the **Beatles**, amongst others. No pretence was needed in May 1995 when a real life survivor from the 60s - a genuine icon - **P.J. Proby** joined the cast, and delighted audiences with his own 15 minute spot during each performance.

Ono, Yoko

b. 18 February 1933, Tokyo, Japan. Yoko Ono moved to the USA at the age of 14 and was later immersed in the New York *avant garde* milieu. A reputation as a film-maker and conceptual artist preceded her collaborations with **John Lennon** which followed in the wake of their meeting in 1966. The couple's links were both professional and personal - they married in 1969 - and whereas Lennon introduced Yoko to rock, she in turn brought an appreciation of electronic music. Early collaborations, *Two Virgins*, *Life With The Lions* and *Wedding Album*, were self-indulgent and wilfully obscure, but with the formation of the **Plastic Ono Band** the Lennons began to forge an exciting musical direction. Unfairly vilified as the architect of the **Beatles**' demise, Yoko emerged as a creative force in her own right with a series of excellent compositions, including 'Don't Worry Kyoto' and 'Listen, The Snow Is Falling'. *Yoko Ono/The Plastic Ono Band*, her companion collection to John's cathartic solo debut, was equally compulsive listening and a talent to captivate or confront was also prevalent on *Fly*, *Approximately Infinite Universe* and *Feeling The Space*. Several tracks, including 'Men Men Men' and 'Woman Power', addressed feminist issues while her music's sparse honesty contrasted with the era's penchant for self-indulgence. The couple's relationship continued to undergo public scrutiny, particularly in the wake of a highly-publicized separation, but the birth of their son Sean, following their reconciliation, resulted in a prolonged retirement. The Lennons re-emerged in 1980 with *Double Fantasy*, for which they shared creative responsibility, and were returning home from completing a new Yoko single on the night John was shot dead. The resultant track, 'Walking On Thin Ice', was thus imbued with a certain poignancy, but while not without merit, the artist's ensuing albums have failed to match its intensity. Yoko has also supervised the release of unpublished material - videos, writings and recordings - drawn from Lennon's archive and continues to pursue their pacifist causes. Yoko has tolerated much indifference and abuse over the years, initially because she dared fall in love with a Beatle and latterly because it was felt that she manipulated John. Through all the flack she has maintained her integrity and dignity, resulting in *The Ono Box* being reappraised in 1992, albeit 20 years too late.

Albums: *Yoko Ono/The Plastic Ono Band* (1970), *Fly* (1971), *Approximately Infinite Universe* (1973), *Feeling The Space* (1973), *Season Of Glass* (1981), *It's Alright (I See Rainbows)* (1982), *Starpeace* (1985). Compilation: *The Ono Box* (1992).

Further reading: *Grapefruit: A Book Of Instructions*, Yoko Ono. *Yoko Ono: A Biography*, Jerry Hopkins. *Yoko Ono - Arias And Objects*, Barbara Haskell and John G. Hanhardt.

Onslaught

This UK thrash quintet, originally conceived as a punk/metal hybrid, was formed in Bristol in 1983 by guitarist Nige Rockett and drummer Steve Grice. With the addition of vocalist Paul Mahoney and bassist Jason Stallord, they recorded *Power From Hell* on the independent Cor label in 1985. This opened the doors to a contract with Under One Flag, the thrash subsidiary of **Music For Nations**. *The Force* saw the band expand to a quintet, with the arrival of new vocalist Sy Keeler; Mahoney was relegated to bass and Stallord switched to rhythm guitar. The album was heavily reliant on the styles of **Slayer**, **Metallica** and **Anthrax**, with little original input of their own. Mahoney was replaced by James Hinder on bass shortly after the album was released. Moving to **London Records**, *In Search Of Sanity* was their make or break album. Before it was completed Steve Grimmett (ex-**Grim Reaper**) and Rob Trottman replaced Keeler and Stallord respectively. After a series of delays, the album finally surfaced in early 1989. Producer Stephan Galfas had watered down their aggressive sound in an attempt to court commercial success. Even the cover of **AC/DC**'s 'Let There Be Rock' proved less strong than expected, and the material generally lacked distinction. They had moved away from hard-line thrash towards mainstream metal with negative results. The album was slated by the

metal media and Grimmett quit in 1990. A replacement was found in the form of Tony O'Hara, but the band were dropped by their label soon after. Disillusioned, they went their separate ways in 1991.
Albums: *Power From Hell* (Music For Nations 1985), *The Force* (Music For Nations 1986), *In Search Of Sanity* (London 1989).

Onuora, Oku

b. Orlando Wong, March 1952, Kingston Jamaica, West Indies. In 1971 at the start of a 15-year prison sentence for his part in an armed robbery, Onuora began writing poetry. In true Robin Hood-style, the funds from the misdemeanour were to finance projects to help the underprivileged. Not considering himself a criminal the poems reflected his assertion that he was a political prisoner. In the mid-70s much of his work had been smuggled out against the wishes of the authorities. It was probably owing to the praise bestowed upon his writing by the Jamaican Literary Festival Commission that the Jamaican Government was compelled to grant an early release in 1977. Soon after securing freedom his first collection of poems, *Echo* was published in Jamaica by Sangsters and later in Europe by the Cultural Media Collective. Onuora's debut in the recording studio was at Tuff Gong where backed by the **Wailers** drum and bass duo, Aston 'Familyman' Barrett and Carlton Barrett he read 'Reflection In Red' over a heavy dub sound. The poem was a sceptical chronicle of the peace truce between rival gangs led by Bucky Marshall and Claudie Massop. Read in patois he says, 'De man Peter Wailer (Tosh) wailin' in de wilderness - Dere can be no peace until dere's equal rights and justice'. The single won critical acclaim but was not to make an impression in the reggae charts. He began performing his poetry around the world and incongruously appeared at the One Love Peace Concert, a commemoration of the reprieve, alongside **Jacob Miller**, **Culture**, **Leroy Smart**, **Big Youth**, **Peter Tosh** and **Bob Marley**. His numerous awards and notoriety inevitably led to a working relationship with the first successful dub poet **Linton Kwesi Johnson**. In 1982 following a tour of Europe with **Rico Rodriguez** he released, 'I A Tell' on his own Kuya label with 'Reflection in Red' on the b-side. By the mid-80s he released his debut, *Pressure Drop* with backing supplied by AK7 (Armageddon Knights Column 7) demonstrating his uncompromising lyrics and inventive reggae style. In the early 90s Oku began experimenting with dub working alongside Courtney Panton who played and programmed all the instruments. Although Onuora's recorded work is sporadic he enjoys a cult following and occasional releases are snapped up by his dedicated followers.
Albums: *Pressure Drop* (Heartbeat 1986), *New Jerusalem Dub* (ROIR 1991), *I A Tell Dubwise And Otherwise* (ROIR 1994).

Onyeka

b. 17 May 1961, Onitsha, Nigeria. Steering a course between middle-of-the-road international pop and her own eastern Nigerian roots music, Onyeka has various professional interests outside music. She trained originally as a journalist, taking a master's degree in communications in the USA and working at the United Nations headquarters in New York before returning home to work in Nigerian television. In 1984, for BBC television, she presented a programme titled *The Squandering Of The Riches*, a critical look at the management of the Nigerian economy. Onyeka's recording career began in 1981 when, with the help of **Sonny Okosun**, she released *Onyeka*. This was followed in 1983 with *Endless Life*. In 1985, dissatisfied with the accounting procedures used by Nigerian **EMI**, who had released both her albums, she set up her own label, Ayolo, and released *In The Morning Light*. Later that year she released a bizarre single, 'Trina 4', on London-based specialist label Sterns, a strangely compelling mixture of reggae rhythms and bagpipe melodies.
Albums: *Onyeka* (1981), *Endless Life* (1983), *In The Morning Light* (1985).

Onyx

Hardcore gangsta rappers from Queens, New York, fronted by Sticky Fingaz (b. Kirk Jones), Pedro, Big DS and Suave, whose intense, gun-fixated, hard as nails image has become a popular recepticle for ill-conceived teenage fantasies in both the US and UK. They originally recorded a solitary single for **Profile**, 'Ahh, And We Do It Like This' before switching to Columbia. Boasting titles like 'Blac Vagina Finda', bald heads, and bad attitudes, their debut album was co-produced by Jam Master Jay (**Run DMC**). Nevertheless, it sold by the truckload, arguably because the music itself, on cuts like 'Throw Ya Gunz', was undeniably exciting. Almost as if to live up to his image, Fingaz found himself in trouble for allegedly asaulting a passenger on a United Airlines flight to New York from Chicago O'Hare airport. The fracas was caused by Jones' refusal to remove his Walkman in line with flight dictates. Fingaz faced a misdemeanour charge in Chicago as a result. Group member Fedro apeared in Forest Whitaker's film *Strapped* in 1993.
Album: *Bacdafucup* (Columbia 1993).

Open Road

This short-lived quartet took their name from a 1970 album by singer/songwriter **Donovan**. A self-styled 'celtic rock' release, *Open Road* featured guitarist Barry (Young) Husband, former vocalist with pop group the **Warm Sounds**, and percussionist John 'Candy' Carr who met as members of Hapshash And The Coloured Coat. Simon Lanzon (keyboards) and Mike Thompson

(bass) completed the line-up when the group left Donovan for an independent career. *Windy Daze* continued the direction already pursued with their erstwhile mentor, but the album was not a commercial success and Open Road folded soon afterwards.
Album: *Windy Daze* (1971).

Ophichus

A folk/rock group from Wiltshire, England, with varying line-ups, who played 'rural English rock'. Often whimsical and certainly literate, they created music from rustic isolation and could well have earned the tag 'crusty' before the **Levellers**.
Album: *Pronounced Offeickus* (1989).

Opus III

UK vocalist Kirsty Hawkshaw (b. c.1969), attired with boots and mohican haircut coupled with dayglo beads, led this pop house outfit on their breakthrough single, 'It's A Fine Day'. An update of **Jane & Barton**'s faint ballad, mixing poetry with sweet, harranguing vocals, it added a generic backbeat and little else. Hawkshaw had led a gypsy lifestyle since leaving school (her father composes theme music for television programmes, including *News At Ten*, *Grange Hill* and *Countdown*). As a child she recorded cover versions of the hits of the day for cheap compilation albums, before travelling around the free festival circuit selling home-made jewellery (and MCing for **Spiral Tribe**). She met the outfit's boiler room staff; Ian Dodds, Kevin Walters and Nigel Munro, at a rave. They form part of the Ashebrooke Allstars, and also recorded as A.S.K. ('Freedom We Cry' for **MCA**). The follow-up single would be a cover of **King Crimson**'s 'I Talk To The Wind'. Nurtured by her record company and band as chanteuse straddling the pop/rave market, Kirsty has yet to provide adequate substance to sustain her strong visual image. However, the band did eventually return in 1994 with 'When You Made The Mountain', and a new, 'spiritual' album.
Albums: *Mind Fruit* (PWL 1992), *Guru Mother* (PWL 1994).

Oral

A rather sad four-piece all female UK band comprising 'glamour' models and Stripagram girls, the line-up of Oral (a suitably childish reference point) was filled out by Bev (vocals), Monica (guitar), Dee (drums) and Candy (bass). Candy had quit by the time their only album was released and as they played no gigs it is questionable whether any of them could play at all. Evidently the whole thing was done to further their day jobs and they gained a little publicity thanks to song titles like 'I Need Discipline' and 'Gas Masks Vicars And Priests'. Their debut album was entitled *Sex*, written so that anyone glancing at the sleeve would read simply 'Oral Sex'. Even the group's version of the **Sex Pistols**' 'Black Leather' was ill-advised.
Album: *Sex* (Conquest 1987).

Orange

This Yugoslavian hard rock quintet was formed in 1981 by Zlato Magdalenic (vocals), Mijo Popovic (guitar), Tomaz Zontar (keyboards), Marko Herak (bass) and Franc Teropic (drums). Together they secured a contract with the local RTB label. Musically, they incorporated elements of **AC/DC**, **Deep Purple** and **Accept**, but added little creative input of their own. The band were known as Pomeranca in Yugoslavia and attracted a small but loyal cult following after the release of their debut album in 1982. This featured native lyrics and consequently closed down a large section of their potential audience. *Madbringer* saw the band using English lyrics for the first time, but their crude enunciation failed to enhance their appeal.
Albums: *Peklenska Pomaranca* (RTB 982), *Madbringer* (RTB 1983).

Orange Juice

Formed in Scotland at the end of the 70s, this engaging and, in some quarters, revered, pop group comprised **Edwyn Collins** (b. 23 August 1959, Edinburgh, Scotland; vocals/lead guitar), James Kirk (vocals/rhythm guitar), David McClymont (bass) and Steven Daly (drums). They began their career on the cult independent label **Postcard Records** where they issued some of the best pop records of the early 80s, including 'Blue Boy' and 'Falling And Laughing'. Collins' coy vocal and innocent romanticism gave them a charm which was matched by strong musicianship. After signing to **Polydor Records** they issued *You Can't Hide Your Love Forever*, a highly accomplished effort that augured well for the future. At that point, the group suffered an internal shake-up with Kirk and Daly replaced by Malcolm Ross and Zeke Manyika. *Rip It Up* was another strong work, and the insistent title-track reached the UK Top 10. Further musical differences saw the group reduced to Collins and Manyika as they completed an energetic mini-album, *Texas Fever*, and an eponymous third album, which included the wistful 'What Presence?' Collins subsequently recorded a couple of singles with Paul Quinn, after which he embarked on a solo career that has only begun to fulfil its early promise in the mid-90s. Ross joined the line-up of Roddy Frame's **Aztec Camera**. Manyika also spawned solo projects on Polydor and **Parlophone Records**.
Albums: *You Can't Hide Your Love Forever* (Polydor 1982), *Rip It Up* (Polydor 1982), *Texas Fever* (Polydor 1984, mini-album), *Ostrich Churchyard* (Postcard 1992, live album). Compilations: *In A Nutshell* (Polydor 1985), *The Very Best Of* (Polydor 1992), *The Heather's On Fire* (Postcard 1993).

Orb

Basically the Orb is one man, Dr Alex Paterson (b. Duncan Robert Alex Paterson, hence the appropriation of the Dr title), whose specialist field is the creation of ambient house music. A former **Killing Joke** roadie, member of Bloodsport, and A&R man at EG Records, he formed the original Orb in 1988 with Jimmy Cauty of **Brilliant** fame (for whom he had also roadied). The name was taken from a line in Woody Allen's *Sleeper.* The band first appeared on **WAU! Mr Modo**'s showcase set *Eternity Project One* (released via **Gee Street**), with the unrepresentative 'Tripping On Sunshine'. However, their first release proper came with 1989's *Kiss* EP, again on WAU! Mr Modo (which had been set up by Paterson with Orb manager Adam Morris). It was completely overshadowed by the success of the band's subsequent release, 'A Huge Ever-Growing Pulsating Brain Which Rules From The Centre Of The Ultraworld'. It was an extraordinary marriage of progressive rock trippiness and ambience, founded on a centrepoint sample of Minnie Riperton's 'Loving You' (at least on initial copies, being voiced by a soundalike due to cle`arance worries later). The group signed with **Big Life**, but Cauty departed in April 1990. He had wished to take Paterson and the Orb on board in his new **KLF** Communications set-up. There was no little acrimony at the time and Cauty re-recorded an album, which was to have been the Orb's debut, deleting Paterson's contributions, and naming it *Space* (also the artist title). In the event the ethereal 'Little Fluffy Clouds', with co-writer Youth, was the next Orb release, though that too ran into difficulties when the sample of **Rickie Lee Jones**' attracted the artist's displeasure. Paterson did at least meet future co-conspirator Thrash (b. Kristian Weston) during these sessions, who joined in late 1991 from a punk/metal background, hence his name (though he had also been a member of **Fortran 5**). Their debut album (and the remix set of similar title) was based on a journey to dimensions beyond known levels of consciousness, according to the participants. It soared, or perhaps sleepwalked, to the top of the UK album charts, and led to a plunge of remixes for other artists (including **Front 242** and **Primal Scream**). The album was fully in tune with, and in many ways anticipating of, the blissed out rave subculture of the early 90s, mingled with dashes of early 70s progressive rock (**Pink Floyd** were an obvious reference point). There was also an LP's worth of the band's recordings for **John Peel**'s Radio 1 show. This included a 20 minute version of 'Huge Ever-Growing...' which prompted fellow DJ Andy Kershaw to ring the BBC to complain, mockingly, about the return of hippy indulgence on a gross scale polluting the nation's airwaves. The Orb signed to **Island** in 1993 following a departure from Big Life that took seven months and eventually the high court to settle. The deal with Island allowed Paterson to continue to work on collaborative projects, through their own label Inter-Modo, outside of the Orb name. Other projects included a remix album for **Yellow Magic Orchestra**, though a previous request by **Jean Michel Jarre** for them to do the same for his *Oxygene* opus was declined. They also took the opportunity to play live at unlikely venues like the Danish Island of Trekroner, and generally appeared to be having a hugely enjoyable time of their unlikely celebrity, Paterson even being awarded honorary president of Strathclyde University's Student Union. However, their first studio set for Island, *Pomme Fritz*, saw them witness the first signs of a critical backlash.

Albums: *The Orbs Adventures Beyond The Ultraworld* (WAU! Mr Modo/Big Life 1991), *Peel Sessions* (Strange Fruit 1991), *Aubrey Mixes, The Ultraworld Excursion* (WAU! Mr Modo/Big Life 1992), UFOrb (WAU! Mr Modo/Big Life 1992, double album, available as a triple in limited edition), *Live 93* (Island 1993), *Pomme Fritz* (Island 1994, mini album), *Orbvs Terrarvm* (Island 1995).

Orbison, Roy

b. 23 April 1936, Vernon, Texas, USA, d. 6 December 1988. Critical acclaim came too late for one of the leading singers of the 60s. He became the master of the epic ballad of doom-laden despair. Orbison possessed a voice of remarkable range and power, often finding it more comfortable to stay in the high register. The former reluctant rockabilly singer, who worked with **Norman Petty** and **Sam Phillips** in the 50s, moved to Nashville and became a staff writer for **Acuff-Rose** Music. He used his royalties from the success of 'Claudette', recorded by the **Everly Brothers**, and written for his first wife, to buy himself out of his contract with **Sun Records**. He signed with the small Monument label. Although his main intention was to be a songwriter, Orbison found himself glancing the US chart with 'Up Town' in 1960. A few months later his song 'Only The Lonely' was rejected by **Elvis Presley** and the Everly Brothers. Orbison then decided to record it himself. The result was a sensation. The song topped the UK charts and narrowly missed the top spot in the USA. The trite opening of 'dum dum dum dummy doo wah, yea yea yea yea yeah', leads into one of the most distinctive pop songs ever recorded. It climaxes with a glass-shattering falsetto, and is destined to remain a modern classic.

The shy and quietly-spoken Roy donned a pair of dark-tinted glasses to cover up his chronic astigmatism, although early publicity photos had already sneaked out. Over the next five years he enjoyed unprecedented success in Britain and America, repeating his formula with further stylish but doom-laden ballads, including 'Blue Angel', 'Running Scared', 'Crying', 'Dream Baby', 'Blue Bayou' and 'In Dreams'. Even during the take-over of America by the **Beatles** (with whom he became good friends), Roy was one of the few American artists to retain his ground commercially. During the Beatles peak chart year he scored two UK number 1 singles, the powerful 'It's Over' and the hypnotic 'Oh Pretty Woman'. The latter has an incredibly simple instrumental introduction with acoustic guitar and snare drum, and it is recognized today by millions. It was subsequently used for the late 80s blockbuster film *Pretty Woman.* Such was the art of Orbison, having the advantage of crafting his own songs to suit his voice and temperament. Although he continued to have hits throughout the 60s, none except 'It's Too Soon To Know' reached former heights; he regularly toured Britain, which he regarded as his second home. He experienced appalling tragedy when in 1966 his wife, Claudette, was killed as she fell from the back of his motorcycle, and in 1968 a fire destroyed his home, also taking the lives of his two sons. In 1967 he starred as a singing cowboy in *The Fastest Guitar Alive,* but demonstrated that he was no actor. By the end of the decade Roy's musical direction had faltered and he resorted to writing average MOR songs like the unremarkable 'Penny Arcade'.

The 70s were barren times for his career, although a 1976 compilation topped the UK charts. By the end of the decade he underwent open heart surgery. He bounced back in 1980, winning a Grammy for his duet with **Emmylou Harris** on 'That Lovin' You Feelin' Again' from the film *Roadie.* David Lynch used 'In Dreams' to haunting effect in his chilling film *Blue Velvet* in 1986. The following year Orbison was inducted into the Rock 'n' Roll Hall of Fame; at the ceremony he sang 'Oh Pretty Woman' with **Bruce Springsteen**. With Orbison once again in favour, **Virgin Records** signed him, and he recorded an album of his old songs using today's hi-tech production techniques. The result was predictably disappointing; it was the sound and production of those classics that had made them great. The video *A Black And White Night,* showed Roy being courted by numerous stars, including **Tom Waits**, Springsteen and **Elvis Costello**. This high profile led him to join **George Harrison**, **Bob Dylan**, **Tom Petty** and **Jeff Lynne** as the **Traveling Wilburys**. Their splendid debut album owed much to Orbison's major input. Less than a month after its critically acclaimed release, Roy suffered a fatal heart attack in Nashville. The posthumously released *Mystery Girl* in 1989 was the most successful album of his entire career, and not merely because of morbid sympathy. The record contained a collection of songs that indicated a man feeling happy and relaxed; his voice had never sounded better. The uplifting 'You Got It' and the mellow 'She's A Mystery To Me' were impressive epitaphs to the legendary Big 'O'.

Albums: *Lonely And Blue* (Monument 1961), *Exciting Sounds Of Roy Orbison (Roy Orbison At The Rockhouse)* (Sun 1961), *Crying* (Monument 1962), *In Dreams* (Monument 1963), *Oh Pretty Woman* (1964), *Early Orbison* (Monument 1964), *There Is Only One Roy Orbison* (MGM 1965), *Orbisongs* (Monument 1965), *The Orbison Way* (MGM 1965), *The Classic Roy Orbison* (1966), *Roy Orbison Sings Don Gibson* (MGM 1966), *Cry Softly, Lonely One* (MGM 1967), *The Fastest Guitar Alive* (MGM 1968), *Roy Orbison's Many Moods* (1969), *The Big O* (1970), *Hank Williams: The Roy Orbison Way* (1971), *Roy Orbison Sings* (1972), *Memphis* (1973), *Milestones* (1974), *I'm Still In Love With You* (1976), *Regeneration* (1977), *Laminar Flow* (1979), *Big O Country* (1983), *Problem Child* (1984), *In Dreams* (1987), *For The Lonely* (1988), *Mystery Girl* (Virgin 1989), *Best Love Standards* (1989), *Our Love Song* (1989), *Rare Orbison* (1989), *A Black And White Night Live* (Virgin 1989), *Roy Orbison/Ray Peterson* (1993). Selected compilations: *Roy Orbison's Greatest Hits* (Monument 1962), *More Of Roy Orbisons Greatest Hits* (Monument 1964), *The Very Best Of Roy Orbison* (Monument 1966), *The Great Songs Of Roy Orbison* (1970), *The Monumental Roy Orbison* (1975), *Golden Days* (1981), *The Sun Years* (1980, early recordings), *My Spell On You* (Hits Unlimited 1982), *In Dreams: The Greatest Hits* (Virgin 1987), *The Legendary Roy Orbison* (1988), *For The Lonely: A Roy Orbison Anthology 1956-1965* (Rhino 1988), *The Greatest Hits* (1988), *Best Love Standards* (1989), *King Of Hearts* (Virgin 1992), *Best Loved Moments* (1993).

Further reading: *Dark Star*, Ellis Amburn. *Only The Lonely*, Alan Clayson.

Film: *The Fastest Guitar Alive* (1966).

Orbit, William

b. William Wainwright, England. In addition to heading the **Bass-O-Matic** group, Orbit has remixed for the likes of **Prince**, **Madonna** ('Justify Your Love'), **Belinda Carlisle**, **S'Express**, **Shamen**, **Seal**, **Les Negresses Vertes**, the **Cure** ('Inbetween Days') and **Shakespeare's Sister**, though he gave up remixing in 1993 so it would not overshadow his own work. As a teenager Wainwright would make his own music by splicing tapes together to produce sound collages. He started cutting songs as part of Torch Song, and released two albums, *Wild Thing* in 1984 and *Exhibit A* in 1987, with Laurie Mayer. He then took the name Orbit and brought in vocalist Peta Nikolich for his debut, having retained Mayer as his co-writer. This set included bizarre cover versions of the **Psychedelic Furs**' 'Love My Way' and **Jackie Mittoo**'s 'Feel Like Jumping'. The club favourite 'Fire And Mercy' brought him to the attention of dance pundits. This was housed on *Strange Cargo*, a collection of soundscapes recorded between 1984 and 1987. *Strange Cargo II* also steered away from the electronic house music that had marked Orbit's work with Bass-O-Matic, and resembled instead the experimental pieces of **Brian Eno** or **Holger Czukay**. Eventually the Madonna remix brought him to the attention of Rob Dickins, chairman of Warner

Music, and together they set up the N-Gram Recordings label in 1995. (Orbit had previously founded **Guerrilla Records** which released progressive house artists such as **Spooky** and **D.O.P.** and which folded in 1984) The first release on N-Gram was a single by cellist Caroline Lavelle, whom Orbit discovered when she played on **Massive Attack**'s 'Home And Away'. An album followed, as well as Orbit's first release for his new label, a continuation of the *Strange Cargo* series. N-Gram also gave him the opportunity to work with the Torch Song trio once more, while *Pieces In A Modern Style* was an interpretation of 20th Century classical music.
Albums: *Orbit* (MCA 1987), *Strange Cargo* (MCA 1988), *Strange Cargo II* (IRS 1990), *Strange Cargo III* (IRS 1993), *Strange Cargo IV* (N-Gram 1995), *Pieces In A Modern Style* (N-Gram 1995).

Orbital

Ambient UK techno band who have done much to bring about the possibilities of improvisation to live electronic music. Unlike many other groups, their stage performances do not depend on DAT or backing tapes. They also have a more varied scrapbook of samples, using the **Butthole Surfers** on 'Satan', then **Crass** on 'Choice'. Comprising brothers Paul (b. 19 May 1968, Dartford, Kent, England) and Phillip Hartnoll (b. 9 January 1964, Dartford, Kent, England), the Orbital moniker was first suggested by their friend Chris Daly of the Tufty Club. With all the M25 dance parties happening so close to their homes in Dunton Green they named themselves after the UK's least adored stretch of road. It also helped convey the idea of tape loops which are so central to their craft. Before the band began its active life in 1987, Paul had played with an outfit by the name of Noddy & The Satellites and done some labouring odd jobs, while his brother had been a bricklayer and barman. They made their live debut in the summer of 1989 at the Grasshopper, Westerham, Kent, hooking up with the **ffrr** imprint shortly afterwards. They opened their account for the label with 'Chime' in March 1990, setting a pattern for a sequence of dramatic, one-word titles ('Omen', 'Satan', 'Choice', 'Mutations'). They moved to **Internal** for 'Raddiccio' in October 1992, while work continued apace on their remixing chores. These included work on releases by artists as diverse as the **Shamen**, **Queen Latifah**, **Meat Beat Manifesto** and **EMF**. In 1994 they appeared at the Glastonbury Festival and contributed to the *Shopping* film soundtrack.
Albums: *Untitled 1* (ffrr 1991), *Untitled 2* (Internal 1993), *Snivilisation* (Internal 1994).

Orchestra Makassy

Makassy, along with a number of other bands such as Orchestra Virunga and **Orchestre Super Mazembe**, were one of a number of largely Zairean line-ups who left their overcrowded domestic music scene in the 70s, to make a living in the neighbouring Kenyan and Tanzanian markets. During the UK's mid-80s African music boom, Makassy made a brief impact with Western audiences via a licensing deal with the **Virgin** label. Makassy took their name from their leader, vocalist/guitarist Mzee Makassy. Born in Zaire, he learned his music at school and in his late teens began sitting in with bands in the capital, Kinshasa. In the early 70s, he found work with various groups in Kenya and Uganda and in 1974 formed the first Orchestra Makassy, a 10-piece, with whom he spent a year recording and touring in Europe. Returning to Africa in 1975, the band spent a few months in Uganda, before the then oppressive political climate (under Idi Amin) encouraged them to set up base in Tanzania. Ironically, it was in Tanzania rather than Uganda that tragedy hit Makassy, when, in 1976, lead vocalist Isiak Baharia was stabbed and killed in a street fight. For a time, the group was in turmoil, until Mzee was able to stabilize the line-up again, with the addition of musicians from the **OK Jazz** stable. The new personnel had a huge East African hit in 1979 with the single 'Mosese 2000' (written by ex-OK Jazz guitarist Fan Fan, who would go on to lead British-based outfit Somo Somo in the mid-80s before returning to Makassy). In 1982, Makassy's album *Agwaya* was released in the UK by Virgin, along with the single 'Mambo Mado'. Both releases made substantial impacts on the UK's dance and African music scenes, but in the absence of any UK follow-up releases, this promising start remained undeveloped.
Albums: *Mosese 2000* (1979), *Agwaya* (1982), *Chapter And Verse* (1985).

Orchestra Wives

The marvellous music more than made up for a dull plot in this, the second of only two films in which the enormously popular **Glenn Miller** Orchestra appeared. The story concerns the glitz and the grind of a band on the road in the heyday of the Swing Era. Glamour-boy trumpeter George Montgomery cannot bear to leave his young sweetheart Ann Rutherford behind so he marries her and brings her aboard the bus - much to the chagrin of the hard-bitten wives of the other orchestra members who give the poor girl a hard time. After providing the Miller band with several hits in their previous movie, ***Sun Valley Serenade***, **Harry Warren** and **Mack Gordon** came up trumps this time with 'At Last', 'Serenade In Blue', 'People Like You And Me', and 'I Got A Gal In Kalamazoo'. The latter number was a speciality for **Tex Beneke** And The Modernaires, and they were joined by most of Miller's regular sidemen, including **Hal McIntyre**, **Ray Anthony**, **Billy May**, and singers **Marion Hutton** and **Ray Eberle**. Also in the cast were Cesar Romero, Lynn Bari, Carole Landis, Mary Beth

Hughes, **Jackie Gleason**, Virginia Gilmore, Tamara Geva, Harry Morgan, and the marvellously athletic dancing team, the **Nicholas Brothers**. Karl Tunberg and Darrell Ware wrote the screenplay, and Nick Castle choreographed the dances. The director was Archie Mayo and the film was released in 1942. A film to watch again and again - just for those historic musical sequences.

Orchestral Manoeuvres In The Dark

(see **OMD**)

Orchestre Baobob

Formed in 1971 by saxophonist Issi Cissokho, a John Coltrane disciple who brought along a jazz influence, and Laye M'Boup, a traditional folk musician, Baobob were early Senegalese fusionists, who paved the way for artists like **Youssou N'Dour** and **Toure Kunda**.
Album: *Coumba* (1979).

Orchestre Jazira

Of the several dozen bands who emerged in the UK during that country's sizeable growth of interest in African music during the early and mid-80s, Jazira were the least roots orientated and, perhaps for that very reason, arguably the most interesting. Formed in 1980, they had an almost continuously shifting line-up (usually 10-piece, sometimes even larger) during the seven years of their existence, although some stylistic continuity was provided by a core of more-or-less permanent members including founder vocalists Isaac Tagoe and Martin Nii-Moi, founder guitarists Ben Mandelson and Folo Graff, and a three-piece horn section. In part, the band's stylistic eclecticism was a result of the large number of nationalities, African and European, represented amongst the personnel, with no single national grouping overwhelming the others; in part it was a conscious effort by the founding members to create a pan-African, even global, sound - incorporating highlife, soukous, rock, jazz and practically anything else that took their fancy. After making unsuccessful approaches to a number of major labels, Jazira signed a singles deal with the independent Earthworks in 1982, releasing the critically acclaimed but commercially unsuccessful 'Love' towards the end of the year. By 1983, the band had left Earthworks and had signed a three-year deal with the larger, but still independent, label **Beggars Banquet** - and were looking for a mainstream breakthrough. To achieve this they drafted in London-based Sierra Leonean producer Akie Deen, who had achieved widespread African and Caribbean success in the late 70s with his 'discolypso' sound. The first fruit of the new partnership, 'Sakabo', mixed by dub maestro Dennis Bovell, combined highlife, soca, soukous and reggae to glorious - but still commercially unrequited - effect.
True to form, Jazira shifted direction yet again with *Nomadic Activities* in 1984. The album was consciously and defiantly at odds with what both the UK record business and its public then expected of an 'African' band - that is a simple, happy, all-night party sound. The approach was just too moody, complex and cosmopolitan to fit the bill. In a desperate attempt to gain radio play, Beggars Banquet persuaded Jazira to release one of the album's least iconoclastic tracks, 'Happy Day', as a single - and when that failed to do the commercial trick, let the band's contract expire. Over the next three years, Jazira slowly unwound, as members left to pursue solo careers or join other bands. Graff was one of the first to leave, followed by Mandelson and Nii-Moi, then saxophonists Jane Shorter and Sophie Hellborg, who moved to Paris to join **Mory Kante**'s band. Tagoe continued to lead a much reduced Jazira around the UK club circuit until the end of 1987, when the group finally broke up.
Album: *Nomadic Activities* (1984).

Orchestre Super Mazembe

With a varying line-up of between nine and 14 musicians, Mazembe (Zairois for earth movers) were one of the most popular Kenyan bands of the 80s, and for a brief while in mid-decade enjoyed a cult following in Europe, following their signing by the Virgin label and the UK release of the album *Kaivaska*. Although based in Kenya since the early 70s, the band's personnel is wholly Zairean - it being one of several outfits who decided to leave the overcrowded Kinshasa scene in the late 70s to move to the greener East African markets of Kenya and Tanzania. Like fellow expatriates **Orchestra Makassy**, Mazembe have recorded their most popular material in Nairobi with British producer Norman Mighell. In 1984, they enjoyed a sizeable international hit with a cover version of Nguashi Timbo's East African evergreen 'Shauri Yako', which had been included on *Kaivaska*. A second UK album, *Maloba D'Amor*, repackaged some of the *Kaivaska* tracks - including 'Shauri Yako' - while new material included a curiously faithful reading of the old **Buddy Holly** hit 'Words Of Love' (the title track).
Albums: *Mazembe* (1980), *Tenth Anniversary* (1981), *Double Gold* (1982), *Kaivaska* (1983), *Maloba D'Amor* (1990).

Oregon

This inventive and influential progressive jazz chamber group were formed in 1970 from the nucleus of the **Paul Winter** Consort, an aggregation led by Paul Winter. Oregon comprised **Ralph Towner** (b. 1 March 1940, Chehalis, Washington, USA; guitar/keyboards), **Collin Walcott** (b. 24 April 1945, New York City, USA, d. 8 November 1984; percussion/sitar/tabla/clarinet), **Glen Moore** (bass/violin/piano/flute) and **Paul McCandless** (b. 24 March 1947, Indiana, Pennsylvania, USA; alto saxophone/oboe/bass clarinet). Walcott's death from a car accident in 1984 seemed a fatal blow to the band, but after a year in mourning they returned. The recruitment of Walcott's friend **Trilok Gurtu** (b. 30 October 1951, Bombay, India; tabla/drums/percussion) gave them a fresh incentive. Their debut on **ECM Records** in 1983 was an eclectic, part-electric album. Oregon explore the boundaries of jazz, using uniquely disparate influences of classical, folk, Indian and other ethnic music. Their chamber-like approach encourages hushed auditoriums and intense concentration, which is required to get maximum benefit from their weaving style. Occasionally they will burst into a song of regular form and pattern, as if to reward a child with a treat. One such number is the evocatively rolling 'Crossing' from the same album. Another outstanding piece from their immense catalogue is 'Leather Cats'. Their refusal to compromise leaves them a lone innovative force and one of the most important jazz-based conglomerations of the past three decades.

Selected albums: *Music Of Another Present Era* (Vanguard 1972), *Distant Hills* (Vanguard 1973), *Winter Light* (Vanguard 1974), *In Concert* (1975), *Oregon/Jones Together* (1976), *Friends* (1977), *Out Of The Woods* (1978), *Violin* (1978), *Roots In The Sky* (1979), *Moon And Mind* (1979), *In Performance* (1980), *Oregon* (ECM 1983), *Crossing* (ECM 1985), *Ectopia* (ECM 1987), *45th Parallel* (Verabra 1989), *Always, Never, And Forever* (Verabra 1991).

Organization

Formed from the remnants of **Death Angel**, the USA band Organization are Rob Cavestany (vocals/guitar), Andy Galeon (drums/vocals), D. Pepa (bass) and Gus Pepa (guitar). The former band, while on tour supporting *Act III*, endured a bus crash with seriously injured drummer and youngest member Andy Galeon. When singer Mark Osegueda decided he was unable to wait for him to make a full recovery, Cavestany took over as singer and front man and the Organization was born. Marking their arrival with an appearance at the Dynamo Festival in Europe in 1992, the members had learned enough about the music industry to act in a more independent fashion, setting up their own Unsafe Unsane Recordings for the release of *Free Burning* (licensed to Bulletproof/**Music For Nations** in the UK).

Album: *Free Burning* (Unsafe Unsane Recordings 1993).

Organized Konfusion

Duo comprising Pharoahe Monch and Prince Poetry, whose music is distinguished by both a rare knack for samples/rhythm tracks and a smooth lyrical flow. Coming from Jamaica and New York respectively, the band's members absorbed everything from jazz and reggae to gospel in their youth. They met at high school in 1986, signing to a small independent after honing their skills. No vinyl emerged from the deal, and they switched instead to Disney-funded Hollywood Basic, scoring immediate success with the number 1 rap hit, 'Walk Into The Sun', and a well-received debut long player (which also included a second hit single in 'Open Your Eyes'). The title-track, 'Stress', from their second album set out their stall with an attack on racist taxi drivers, and music industry incompetents. Joined by Q-Tip (**A Tribe Called Quest**) on 'Let's Funk', these were just two of the best tracks on another excellent album, with Prince Po indeed the '...exec with the intellectual concepts that elevate you like steps' ('Let's Organize').

Albums: *Organized Konfusion* (Hollywood Basic 1991), *Stress: The Extinction Agenda* (Hollywood Basic 1994).

Oriental Brothers Band

A highlife band from Eastern Nigeria, the original Orientals were formed by the Opara brothers Warrior, Dan Satch and Godwin Kabaka in 1972. By the end of the decade, the group had released some 20 albums. In 1977, Godwin Kabaka left to form the Kabaka International Guitar Band, and the Orientals continued under the leadership of Warrior and Dan Satch. In 1980, Warrior left, to form Dr Sir Warrior And The Original Oriental Brothers. In 1983, the original line-up got back together to record the album *Onye Nwe Ala*, before Warrior and Godwin Kabaka left once more to re-establish their own groups.

Albums: *Orientals Specials* (1974), *Murtala Mohammed* (1977), *Nwanne Awu Enyi* (1978), *Obi Nwanne* (1981), *Onye Nwe Ala* (1983). Compilation: *Best Of The Oriental Brothers* (1979).

Original Concept

Long Island, New York, four-piece who made an early impression on hip hop's underground scene with their 1986 single, 'Knowledge Me'/'Can You Feel It', following it with the mighty 'Pump That Bass'. The former was mainly notable for being the first of several rap tracks to sample the **Art Of Noise**'s 'Close To The Edit'. On album Original Concept concentrated squarely on entertainment, using comedic raps over dance-orientated grooves. Mainman Dr Dre (not the Dre of **NWA**/solo fame) went on to DJ for the **Beastie Boys** and co-host *Yo! MTV Raps* with Ed Lover.

Album: *Straight From The Basement Of Kooley High* (Def Jam 1988).

Original Dixieland Jazz Band

In May 1916 several young white New Orleans musicians were working in Chicago, some in the same band. After a few changes the group settled down with its personnel consisting of Nick La Rocca (b. 11 April 1889, d. 22 February 1961; cornet) Eddie Edwards (b. 22 May 1891, d. 9 April 1963; trombone), Larry Shields (b. 13 September 1893, d. 21 November 1953; clarinet), pianist Henry Ragas (b. 1891, d. 18 February

1919) - his successor at the piano, J. Russell Robinson (b. 8 July 1892, d. 30 September 1963) and Tony Sbarbaro (Spargo) (b. 27 June 1897, d. 30 October 1969; drums). Under its somewhat hyperbolic and misleading title, the Original Dixieland Jazz Band, aided by widespread publicity, became known as the creators of jazz. Despite this hopelessly inaccurate and unfair description, the ODJB's 1917 recordings of 'Livery Stable Blues' and 'Dixie Jass Band One-Step' succeeded in bringing the emergent music to the attention of millions. They were also able to make far more prestigious public appearances than would have been possible had they been black. First at Resenweber's restaurant in New York and later at London's Palladium theatre, the ODJB offered audiences a mixture of vaudeville eccentricity and good jazz (rather more of the former than the latter) and helped boost the music from its limited origins into world-wide popularity. Synonymous with the Jazz Age, and sometimes having just as little to do with real jazz as that loose term for a sociological and cultural phenomenon, the ODJB quickly became legendary and thereafter didn't need to live up to the usually unfulfilled promise their name evokes. In its original form the ODJB broke up in 1925, reforming in 1936 for a brief and not too successful tour. The founding five had variable success after their ODJB days with Sbarbaro being perhaps the most active.
Compilations: *The Original Dixieland Jazz Band* (1979, rec. 1917-36), *Sensation* (1983).

Original Memphis Five

Formed by a group of white musicians who were based in New York, the band became hugely popular during the 20s. Founder members were **Phil Napoleon, Frank Signorelli, Miff Mole**, Jimmy Lytell and Jack Roth. The band filled an engagement at the Balconnades Ballroom in New York, USA, and then stayed together for a number of years and made many popular records, sometimes using other names. Later, other musicians graced the band's ranks but, by the end of the 20s, the band, which had been the inspiration of many young white jazzmen, broke up. Towards the end of the 40s Napoleon reformed the band and a little while later Signorelli also formed a band which used the same name and which included Mole and Lytell. Reunions and reformations continued during the 50s. Specializing in snappily played dixieland jazz, the band did much to popularize jazz in the early years of its development. Napoleon and Mole made notable individual contributions to the music, gaining many emulators.
Albums: *Connee Boswell And The Original Memphis Five In Hi-Fi* (1957), *Phil Napoleon And His Memphis Five* (1959).

Original Rockers

Midlands, UK, based dance outfit, led by DJ Dick (b. Richard Whittingham) and musician Glynn Bush, who have been compared to the **On-U Sound** troupe via their ambient dub/deep trance techniques. They made their debut in February 1992 with a single, 'Breathless', dedicated to DJ Dick's club of the same name. Their 1993 single 'Rockers To Rockers' was originally issued a year before as the b-side to limited edition promos of 'Push Push', (previously titled 'Come Again'). As is usual, it was based on deep dub grooves, with adventurous drum and bass patterns. Other singles include the sdelf-descriptive 'Stoned', recorded in collaboration with fellow-Birmingham outfit **Groove Corporation**.
Album: *Rockers To Rockers* (Different Drummer 1993).

Originals

Freddie Gorman, Walter Gaines, C.P. Spencer (aka Crathman Spencer and Spencer Craftman), Henry 'Hank' Dixon and Joe Stubbs, first recorded as the Originals in 1966. Several members were already an integral part of Detroit's music history. Gorman, who released several solo singles, also co-wrote 'Please Mr. Postman' for the **Marvelettes**, while Stubbs was a former singer with both the Falcons and the **Contours**. Between 1965 and 1969 the quintet was used primarily as a backing group before their career blossomed with 'Baby I'm For Real', a number 1 R&B single co-written and produced by **Marvin Gaye**. The singer's involvement continued on two further releases, 'The Bells' and 'We Can Make It Pretty Baby', but despite several excellent records, including *California Sunset*, a collection of **Lamont Dozier** songs, the group was unable to sustain this momentum. Now reduced to a quartet following Stubbs' departure for **100 Proof Aged In Soul**, the Originals underwent a further changes prior to their departure from **Motown** in 1978. By this point Ty Hunter, former singer with the Voice Masters and **Glass House**, had joined the line-up, but his death three years later effectively marked the end of this group. The original line-up teamed with the Supremes for 'Back By Popular Demand' on Ian Levine's Motor City label in 1992. Former members C.P. Spencer, Freddie Gorman and Joe Stubbs were also signed to Levine's label.
Albums: *Green Grow The Lilacs* aka *Baby I'm For Real* (1969), *Portrait Of The Originals* (1970), *Naturally Together* (1970), *Def.I.Ni.Tions* (1972), *Game Called Love* (1974), *California Sunset* (1975), *Communique* (1976), *Down To Love Town* (1977), *Another Time Another Place* (1978), *Come Away With Me* (1979), *Yesterday And Today* (1981).

Oriole Records

A contemporary of other UK independent labels **Top Rank, Triumph** and Ember, Oriole was established in London during the 50s. It enjoyed fleeting chart success with **Maureen Evans**, who scored five hits between 1960 and 1964, notably with 'Like I Do', and

Swedish instrumental combo the **Spotniks**, who reached the Top 10 with a wild interpretation of 'Hava Nagila'. However, the outlet is best known for the brief period is distributed material licenced from Tamla/**Motown**. Having secured the rights from **Fontana** in September 1962, Oriole issued 19 singles including the **Contours**' 'Do You Love Me' and **Marvin Gaye**'s 'Stubborn Kind Of Fellow'. One EP and seven albums also appeared under its banner. However, the arrangement proved temporary and in October 1963 the catalogue was acquired by **EMI**'s Stateside division. Oriole also issued the Donays' revered 'Devil In His Heart' in the UK and this classic was later covered by the **Beatles** on *With The Beatles*. The label's links with the Liverpool scene was enhanced further when A&R director/producer John Schroeder recorded several of the city's lesser-known beat groups on a two-volume series *This Is Merseybeat*. Schroeder's departure in 1964 to inaugurate the **Pye** subsidiary, Piccadilly, coupled with the generally tenuous existence UK independents enjoyed, sealed Oriole's fate. Singles by the Rats, a Blackpool group featuring future **David Bowie** musicians, **Mick Ronson** and Woody Moodmansey, were among its last releases. In 1965 its catalogue was absorbed by **CBS**.

Orioles

This R&B vocal group was formed in 1947 in Baltimore, Maryland, USA. Along with the **Ravens**, the Orioles were considered the pioneers of rhythm and blues vocal harmony. All born in Baltimore, the group consisted of lead Sonny Til (b. Earlington Carl Tilghman, 18 August 1928; lead), Alexander Sharp (tenor), George Nelson (baritone), Johnny Reed (bass) and guitarist Tommy Gaither. Gaither died in a car accident in 1950 and was replaced by Ralph Williams, and Nelson left in 1953 and was succeeded by Gregory Carroll. The Orioles launched their career with the quiet languorous ballad, 'It's Too Soon To Know', which went to number 1 in the R&B charts (number 13 pop) in 1948. The song was written by Deborah Chessler, the group's manager, and she wrote many of their subsequent hits. Most Orioles hits followed the same formula of Til's impassioned tenor lead with sleepy vocal support and almost invisible instrumental accompaniment in which the music was felt rather than heard. These included the US R&B hits '(It's Gonna Be A) Lonely Christmas' (number 8, 1948), 'Tell Me So' (number 1, 1949), 'Forgive And Forget' (number 5, 1949), 'Crying In The Chapel' (number 1 - and a pop number 11, 1953), and their last R&B chart record, 'In The Mission Of St. Augustine' (number 7, 1953). In 1955 the Orioles broke up with Sharp and Reed joining various **Ink Spots** groups. Til formed a new Orioles group from members of another group, the Regals, but could not revive the fortunes of the Orioles. George Nelson died around 1959, Alexander Sharp some time in the 60s, and Sonny Til on 9 December 1981.

Albums: *The Cadillacs Meet The Orioles* (1961), *Modern Sounds Of The Orioles Greatest Hits* (1962), *Sonny Til Returns* (1970), *Old Gold/New Gold* (1971), *Visit Manhattan Circa 1950's* (1981). Compilations: *The Orioles Sing: Their Greatest Hits, 1948-1954* (1988), *Hold Me, Thrill Me, Kiss Me* (1991), *Greatest Hits* (1991), *The Jubilee Recordings* (1993, 7-CD box set).

Orion

b. Jimmy Ellis, 1945, Orrville, Alabama, USA. Orion was an **Elvis Presley** sound-alike and look-alike who gained recognition following the death of the rock 'n' roll 'king'. In fact, Orion's following was largely the result of many Presley fans believing that he actually *was* Elvis Presley hiding behind a Lone Ranger-type mask. Ellis began singing in 1963, influenced by country singers **Marty Robbins**, **Eddy Arnold**, **Ray Price** and Presley. After graduating from high school and winning a talent contest, he turned professional, performing at nightclubs in the south. His first recorded single was, 'Don't Count Your Chickens Before They Hatch', for the small Dradco label in 1964. He then gave up the music business until the mid-70s. In 1974 he recorded a single for MCA Records and then several for the Boblo label through 1977. Always compared to Presley, Orion started capitalizing on the comparisons in 1978 when he recorded an album for Boblo titled *By Request: Ellis Sings Elvis*. In 1979 he signed to the revived **Sun Records**, which had been Presley's first label and continued to further the connection. To drive the point home, Ellis's first single was the same Elvis had recorded, 'That's All Right' coupled with 'Blue Moon Of Kentucky'. The record label released the single with no artist's name on the label, and rumours spread that Presley had not died but returned to his roots instead. The name Orion was adopted after receiving a phone call from a woman who had written a book titled *Orion*, a fictionalized version of the Presley story. Although he did not perform Presley material in his show, he interpreted music in Presley's style. After a few years of building his reputation, Orion removed his mask and attempted to rid himself of the Presley connection. He continued to record and maintained a popular following, but press coverage lessened after the hype died and he never had a hit record.

Selected albums: *By Request: Ellis Sings Elvis* (1978), *Reborn* (1978), *Sunrise* (1979), *Rockabilly* (1980), *Country* (1980), *Feelings* (1981), *Glory* (1981), *Fresh* (1981). Compilation: *20 All-Time Favorites* (1981).

Orlando, Tony

b. 4 April 1944, New York, USA. An engaging, commercially-minded singer, Orlando's early success came in 1961 when he scored two US Top 40 entries with 'Halfway To Paradise' and 'Bless You'. The former, a superb **Gerry Goffin/Carole King** composition, was later successfully covered by **Billy Fury**, but Orlando enjoyed an emphatic UK hit when the latter reached number 5. Subsequent releases, including 'Happy Times' (1961) and 'Chills' (1962) were less impressive and Orlando began forging a backroom career in the music business, eventually rising to general manager of **Columbia Records**'s April/Blackwood publishing division. In 1970 he was tempted back into recording when he formed the highly popular **Dawn**. A later solo album was recorded on the **Elektra** label. In 1986, Orlando celebrated 25 years in show business at Harrah's in Atlantic City, and, three years later, joined Dawn at the Hilton, Las Vegas, for a run through of most of their old hits, including 'Tie A Yellow Ribbon,' 'Candida', and 'Knock Three Times'.

Selected albums: *Bless You (And 11 Other Great Hits)* (1961), *Tony Orlando* (1978). Compilation: *Before Dawn* (1976).

Further reading: *Tony Orlando*, Ann Morse.

Orleans

This mid-70s US group comprised John Hall (b. 1948, Baltimore, Maryland, USA guitar/vocal), Lance Hoppen (b. 1954, Bayshore, New York, USA bass), Wells Kelly (organ/vocal), Larry Hoppen (guitar/keyboards/vocal) and Jerry Marotta (drums). Drawing a variety of sources - country, rock, soul and calypso - Orleans acquired a cult following as one of the more intelligent mainstream bands of their era. They signed with **ABC** in 1973, but were dropped after one album and were picked up by **Elektra-Asylum**. Success for their new label came immediately with 'Dance With Me' an American top 10 hit. They continued from strength to strength, until Hall left to pursue a solo career in 1977. Morotta departed soon afterwards. They were replaced by Bob Leinback and R.A. Martin, and although the new look Orleans were less well regarded, they enjoyed another US Top 10 hit in 1979 with 'Love Takes Time'.

Albums: *Orleans* (1973, later reissued as *Before The Dance*), *Let There Be Music* (1975), *Walking And Dreaming* (1976), *Forever* (1979), *Orleans* (1980), *One Of A Kind* (1982).

Orlons

A mixture of school friends and neighbours, this Philadelphia-based group was formed by Shirley Brickley (b. 9 December 1944), Steve Caldwell (b. 22 November 1942), **Rosetta Hightower** (b. 23 June 1944) and Marlena Davis (b. 4 October 1944). Introduced to **Cameo Records** by the lead singer of the **Dovells**, **Len Barry**, the Orlons' first hits, 'The Wah Watusi', 'Don't Hang Up' and 'South Street', cleverly exploited the male/female aspect of the group. Each of these releases reached the US Top 5, but their potential was undermined when 'Cross Fire!' (1963) and 'Rules Of Love' (1964) were only minor hits. Any lingering impetus was lost when Davis and Caldwell left the line-up, but although Audrey Brickley took their place, the Orlons broke up in 1968 when Rosetta Hightower moved to the UK to become a session singer.

Albums: *The Wah-Watusi* (1962), *All The Hits* (1963), *South Street* (1963), *Not Me* (1964), *Down Memory Lane* (1964). Compilations: *Biggest Hits* (1963), *Golden Hits Of The Orlons And The Dovells* (1963).

Ornadel, Cyril

b. 2 December 1924, London, England. A composer, arranger and conductor for the theatre and films, Ornadel studied piano, double bass, and composition at the Royal College of Music. He was with ENSA for a while, and later toured Europe with the popular singer Dorothy Carless. He led his own all-girls' band at Murray's Club in London, and later worked as a concert party pianist. After providing some musical and vocal arangements for the Players' Theatre, he was appointed musical director of the touring show *Hello Beautiful*, which led to his first London assignment as the conductor of a pantomime at the People's Palace in the Mile End Road. In 1950, he became the West End's youngest pit conductor when he took over the baton for the musical revue *Take It From Us* at the Adelphi Theatre. During the remainder of the 50s he conducted for the London productions of several successful American musicals, such as ***Kiss Me, Kate***, ***Call Me Madam***, ***Paint Your Wagon***, ***Wish You Were Here***, ***Pal Joey***, ***Wonderful Town***, ***Kismet***, ***Plain And Fancy***, and ***My Fair Lady***. Ornadel also collaborated with David Croft on the scores for regional productions of *Star Maker*, *The Pied Piper*, and the London Palladium's 1956 pantomime, *The Wonderful Lamp* (with Phil Park). For much of the 50s he was the resident musical director for the top-rated television programme, *Sunday Night At The London Palladium*. In 1960, he and lyricist Norman Newell won **Ivor Novello** Awards for their delightful ballad, 'Portrait Of My Love', which gave **Matt Monro** his first UK chart hit. Ornadel's other 'Ivors' (to date) came in 1963 for 'If I Ruled The World' (lyric by **Leslie Bricusse**), the hit song from his score for the immensely successful musical, ***Pickwick***, starring **Harry Secombe**; and the scores for two 'Best British Musicals', *Treasure Island* (1973) and *Great Expectations* (1975), both with Hal Shaper. After playing its initial UK dates several Canadian cities, Ornadel and Shaper rewrote the score for *Great Expectations*, and the revised version was presented at the Liverpool Playhouse (1989) and in Sydney, Australia (1991). Ornadel's other stage musicals have included *Ann Veronica* (1969, with

Croft), *Once More, Darling* (1978, with Newell), *Winnie* (1988, additional songs with Arnold Sundgaard), *Cyrano: The Musical* (with Shaper), and *The Last Flower On Earth* (1991, with Kelvin Reynolds). Over the years, Ornadel has also conducted and/or composed and orchestrated the music for numerous radio, films, and television productions, including *Some May Live, Subterfuge, The Waitors, I Can't, I Can't, Wedding Night, Man Of Violence, Europa Express, Cool It Carol, Die Screaming Marianne, Yesterday, The Flesh And The Blood Show, The Strauss Family* (series), *Edward VII* (series), *Christina, Brief Encounter* (1974 remake), and many more. His albums, especially those on which his Starlight Symphony Orchestra celebrated the great popular composers, have been extremely successful, especially in America. He also composed a series of children's records for EMI, and was the musical supervisor for the *Living Bible* records with Sir Laurence Olivier, and created the 'Stereoaction Orchestra' for RCA Records. A genial, and much-liked man, in the early 90s Cyril Ornadel was living and working in Israel.
Selected albums: *Musical World Of Lerner And Loewe, Opening Night-Broadway Overtures, Bewitched, Camelot, Carnival, Dearly Beloved, Enchanted Evening, Gone With The Wind, Musical World Of Jerome Kern, Musical World Of Cole Porter, Musical World Of Rodgers And Hammerstein, So Nice To Come Home To, The Music Man* (all 60s).

Orphan

This Canadian melodic heavy rock quartet was formed in 1982 by ex-**Pimps** duo Chris Burke Gaffney (vocals/bass) and Brent Diamond (keyboards). Enlisting the services of guitarist Steve McGovern and drummer Ron Boivenue, they negotiated a contract with the Portrait label the following year. Drawing inspiration from commercial rockers like **Bryan Adams** and **Queen**, they debuted with *Lonely At Night*, a sophisticated collection of accessible AOR anthems. *Salute* saw Boivenue succeeded by Terry Norman Taylor and the guest appearance of guitarist **Aldo Nova**, but the songs lacked the impact of those on their debut release and the band's progress dissipated.
Albums: *Lonely At Night* (Portrait 1983), *Salute* (Portrait 1985).

Orpheus

Of the three Boston, Massachusetts, USA groups (the others were **Ultimate Spinach** and the **Beacon Street Union**) signed to **MGM Records** in 1968 in an attempt to create a '**Bosstown Sound**' to rival San Francisco's scene, Orpheus was the only one to create music still remembered years later. The group formed in the mid-60s and was originally known as the Mods. At that time the members included guitarists/vocalists Bruce Arnold (guitar/vocals) and Jack McKenes (guitar/vocals), Eric Gulliksen (bass) and Harry Sandler (drums). Preferring a soft-rock sound, the band changed its name to Orpheus and signed to MGM, recording a self-titled album in 1968. Both it and the debut single, 'Can't Find The Time', hit the lower end of the charts, but the single found a home on easy listening radio stations in later years and was still receiving airplay in the early 90s. Orpheus recorded four albums and disbanded in the early 70s.
Albums: *Orpheus* (1968), *Ascending* (1968), *Joyful* (1969), *Orpheus* (1971).

Orquesta Reve

b. Elio Reve, 1930, Cuba. Reve and his band are among the most popular musicians in Cuba and are becoming increasingly revered on the western-music scene. Reve his been performing since his mid-20s and was the driving force behind two other successful Cuban groups - Ritmo Oriental and Loss Van Van. In the mid-80s he formed Orquesta Reve, a band whose rhythm section is made up of a host of percussionists playing a varied of instruments including claves, congas and maracas, with Reve on timbale. The band have popularized changui, a little known style of dance music originating from eastern Cuba. They have fused it with son, the popular style from the salsa originates, and rumba to produce a dynamic sound. *Rhumberos Latino Americano, La Explosion del Memento* and *Que Cuento* Es Ese! kept Orquesta Reve at the top of the Cuban charts throughout the 80s and won them two gold discs. Although these albums were not officially promoted outside of Cuba, the western version of *La Explosion del Momento!* takes highlights from them all.
Selected album: *La Explosion del Momento!* (1989).

Ørsted Pedersen, Neils-Henning

b. 27 May 1946, Osted, Denmark. Ørsted Pedersen first learned to play piano but took up the bass as his friend Ole Kock Hansen was also a pianist and they wanted to play duets together. He achieved an amazing facility on his new instrument while still in his mid-teens, making his first record at the age of 14. Playing regularly at the noted Montmartre Club in Copenhagen from early in 1961, he accompanied and occasionally recorded with visiting and ex-patriot American jazz stars, including **Brew Moore**, **Yusef Lateef**, **Sonny Rollins**, **Bud Powell** and **Bill Evans** (with whom he toured in the early 60s having earlier refused an invitation to join **Count Basie**). He recorded frequently in the 60s, 70s and 80s, happily ranging from mainstream through bop to free jazz with artists such as **Don Byas**, **Ben Webster**, **Tete Montoliu**, **Kenny Dorham**, **Dexter Gordon**, **Anthony Braxton** and **Albert Ayler**. By the end of the 70s he had sealed his international reputation, thanks in part to a long stint with **Oscar Peterson** which continued well into the 80s. He has made a number of fine duo albums with **Kenny Drew** (*Duo*), **Joe Pass** (*Chops*) and **Archie Shepp** (*Looking At Bird*).

A superbly accomplished technician, his brilliant virtuosity is underpinned with a great sense of time and dynamics. His solos are always interesting and display his awareness of the roots of jazz bass whilst acknowledging the advances made in more recent years.
Selected albums: *Oscar Peterson Big Six At The Montreux Jazz Festival 1975* (1975), *Jay Walkin'* (Steeplechase 1975), *Double Bass* (Steeplechase 1976), with Oscar Peterson *The Paris Concert* (1978), with Joe Pass *Chops* (1978), *Dancing On The Tables* (Steeplechase 1979), *Just The Way You Are* (1980), with Archie Shepp *Looking At Bird* (1980), with Count Basie *Kansas City Six* (1981), *The Viking* (1983), with Palle Mikkelborg *Once Upon A Time* (1992).

Ortiz, Mario

Trumpeter Ortiz is a prominent bandleader and arranger working out of Puerto Rico. In the 60s, he led a 14 to 16-piece orchestra, called All Star Band, and recorded with them on the Ramso and Remo labels. At the time, the bandleader's 'extreme youth' attracted comment. Mario participated in **Kako**'s 1963 Latin jam session recording, *Puerto Rican All-Stars Featuring Kako*, and in the 70s Puerto Rico All Stars albums. Also in the 70s, he wrote arrangements for **Roberto Roena**'s band Apollo Sound and recorded for **El Gran Combo**'s EGC label. In the first half of the 80s Mario appeared on four albums by bandleader **Willie Rosario**. Ortiz signed to Ralph Cartagena's Rico Records. His 1984 hit on the label, *Vamos A Gozar*, was exceptional. The 13-piece band on the album comprised of three trumpets, two saxophones (alto and tenor), bass, piano, timbales, bongo, conga and three vocalists. Mario wrote all the arrangements and played trumpet, as did his son, Mario Ortiz Jnr., who sessions widely on the Puerto Rican recording scene. Anthony Cruz (b. 5 January 1965, New Jersey, USA) and Primi Cruz shared the lead vocals. **Gilberto Santa Rosa** acted as artistic assistant on the album, and on four of Ortiz's other releases between 1985-90; he also sang in the chorus on this album and all of Mario's records issued during the same period.
Baritone saxophone and a fourth trumpet were added to Mario's band on *Ritmo y Sabor* in 1985. Ernesto Sánchez began his tenure as Ortiz's regular baritone saxophonist on 1986's *Dejenme Soñar!*, and contributed a few arrangements to subsequent albums. Sánchez sessioned outside the band and worked extensively as an arranger, mainly in the salsa romántica vein. He arranged **Lalo Rodríguez**'s enormous 1988 Latin hit 'Ven Devorame Otra Vez', and wrote arrangements for **Eddie Santiago**, **Andy Montañez**, Paquito Guzmán, **Oscar D'León**, Amilcar Boscan, Pupy Santiago, David Pabón, Rubby Haddock, Frankie Ruiz, Grupo Clase, Héctor Tricoche, Vitín Ruiz, and others. In 1986, Ortiz and El Gran Combo leader, Rafael Ithier, co-produced Gilberto Santa Rosa's solo debut *Good Vibrations*. Mario contributed arrangements to this album and Santa Rosa's next two releases. 1987's *Algo Diferente* was Primi Cruz's last album with Ortiz before he left to join Willie Rosario's band. Nelson Rodríguez joined as a third vocalist (lead and chorus) on the same album. Cruz's vacancy was filled by Luigi Valentín on *Sexy Salsa* (1988). Rodríguez was replaced by Roberto Dávila, who sang the hit title track of the Puerto Rican Top 10 album, *Que Sera De Mi?*, in 1990. Anthony Cruz departed to go solo and had a big hit with *Algo Nuevo*, released on Tony Moreno's Musical Productions label. For 1991's *The Trumpet Man*, Ortiz radically rejigged his front-line to two trumpets, two trombones and baritone saxophone. Vocalist José David replaced Cruz and Dominican merengue star, Bonny Cepeda, sang and composed one track. Ortiz played trumpet with La Puertorriqueña, a Puerto Rican all-star gathering co-ordinated by bandleader/timbales player Don Perignon for *Festival De Soneros* (1990). During the 80s and at the beginning of the 90s, Mario wrote arrangements for artists and bands, such as: Julio Castro, **Conjunto Clásico**, Puerto Rican Power, Pedro Conga, **Tony Vega**, **José Alberto** and Ray de la Paz.
Selected albums: *Mario Ortiz y su All Star Band*, *Swinging With Mario Ortiz All Star Band* (1964), with the Puerto Rico All Stars *Puerto Rico All Stars* (1976), with the Puerto Rico All Stars *Los Profesionales* (1977), *Vamos A Gozar* (1984), *Ritmo y Sabor* (1985), *Dejenme Soñar!* (1986), *Algo Diferente* (1987), *Sexy Salsa* (1988), *Que Sera De Mi?* (1990), *The Trumpet Man* (1991). Compilation: *The Best Of Mario Ortiz* (1964).

Ory, Edward 'Kid'

b. 25 December 1886, La Place, Louisiana, USA, d. 23 January 1973. A gifted, hard-blowing trombonist and a competitive musician, Ory came to New Orleans when in his mid-twenties and he quickly established a fearsome reputation. An aggressive music maker and a tireless self-promoter, he was determined to be successful and very soon was. By 1919 he was one of the city's most popular musicians and bandleaders but he left town on medical advice. Taking up residence in California, he became just as popular in Los Angeles and San Francisco as he had been in New Orleans. In 1922 Ory became the first black New Orleans musician to make records and the success of these extended his fame still further. In 1925 he travelled to Chicago, playing and recording with **Joe 'King' Oliver**, **Jelly Roll Morton** and **Louis Armstrong**, with whom he made many classic Hot Five and Hot Seven sides. In 1930 he was back in Los Angeles, joining **Mutt Carey**, who had taken over leadership of the Ory band. By 1933, however, Ory had tired of the business and the lack of success he was enjoying compared to that of his earlier days and quit music. He returned in

the early 40s, sometimes playing alto saxophone or bass. Encouraged by some prestigious radio dates, he was soon bandleading again and playing trombone and was thus well-placed to take advantage of the boom in popularity of traditional jazz which swept the USA. Throughout the 50s and into the early 60s he played successfully in San Francisco and Los Angeles, where he had his own club, touring nationally and overseas. He retired in 1966. A strong soloist and powerful ensemble player, Ory's work, while redolent of New Orleans-style jazz, demonstrated that his was a much richer and more sophisticated ability than that of many early trombonists. His compositions included 'Ory's Creole Trombone' and 'Muskrat Ramble', which became a jazz standard.
Selected albums: *Kid Ory's 'This Is Jazz' Broadcast* (1947), *Live At The Club Hangover Vol. 1* (1953), *Live At The Club Hangover Vol. 2* (1953), *Live At The Club Hangover Vol. 3* (1954), *Live At The Club Hangover Vol. 4* (1954), *Kid Ory's Creole Jazz Band* (1954), *Live In England* (1959). Compilations: *Louis Armstrong Hot Five And Hot Seven* (1925-28), *Edward 'Kid' Ory And His Creole Band* (1948), *This Kid's The Greatest!* (Contemporary 1983, 1953-56 recordings), *The Legendary Kid* (Good Time Jazz 1993), *Creole Jazz Band* (Good Time Jazz 1993), *Kid Ory Favourites* (Fantasy 1993).

Osadebe, Osita

b. 1936, Atani, Nigeria. Vocalist and bandleader Chief Stephen Osita Osadebe, one of the founding fathers of eastern Nigerian highlife, started as a percussion player, specializing in konkoma and other forms of street music. His real interest, however, lay in big band highlife, typified by the sophisticated sounds of legendary Ghanaian bandleader **E.T. Mensah** and, nearer home, Stephen Amechi and other Lagos-based outfits. In 1956, when Amechi's band visited his home town, Osadebe contacted them, asking for an audition as a vocalist and percussionist. Although he impressed Amechi, and was invited to join the line-up, the band split and it was two years later, when Amechi re-formed the group, that Osadebe played his first gig with them. After a few months, he left to join the Central Dance Band, playing drums, congas, percussion and alto saxophone. He released his first record under his own name, 'Lagos Life Na So So Enjoyment', in 1959, with accompaniment from trumpeter Zeal Onyia's band. The single was a sizeable local hit, and encouraged Osadebe to form his own band, the Nigeria Soundmakers International. The group met with wide, but by no means universal, acclaim: when Osadebe's father first heard his son's voice on Nigerian radio he had a telegram sent telling him he had died of shame. Happily, Osadebe's uncle was later able to effect a reconciliation and a resurrection. Since that first single, Osadebe has released over 200 albums, earning four gold discs and a platinum award for *Osadebe 75*. He remains a pillar of Nigerian highlife, continuing to perform in a style barely changed from that of his original inspiration, E.T. Mensah.
Selected albums: *Osadebe '75* (1975), *FESTAC Explosion 77* (1977), *Osadebe '78* (1978), *Agbalu Aka No Ano* (1980), *Onu Kwulonjo Okwue Nma* (1981), *Peoples Club Special* (1982), *Onye Kwusia* (1983), *Makajo* (1985), *Osadebe '87* (1987), *Abu Aku* (1989).

Osborne Brothers

Bobby Van (b. 7 December 1931; mandolin/vocals) and Sonny (b. 29 October 1937; banjo/vocals) both at Hyden, Kentucky, USA. A talented bluegrass duo, Bobby played with the Lonesome Pine Fiddlers in 1949 and in 1951, they recorded with Jimmy Martin. During Bobby's military service in 1952, Sonny, though barely 15 years old, was playing and appearing on the *Grand Ole Opry* with **Bill Monroe**. They were reunited in 1953, appeared on WROL Knoxville and made further recordings with Martin. From 1956-59, they played the WWVA *Wheeling Jamboree* and recording with Red Allen, they had a 1958 hit on MGM with 'Once More'. In 1963. they joined the *Opry* and after changing to the **Decca** label had several country chart successes including 'Rocky Top'. Never afraid to modernise their bluegrass, (Sonny actually once stated that he did not care too much for the genre), they added other musicians and used electrified instruments including a steelguitar, piano and drums, which caused some traditionalists to criticise their work. In spite of the instrumental innovations, their unique harmonies saw them readily accepted and they survived the competition of rock and pop music much better than some of the other bluegrass groups. They toured with major stars including **Conway Twitty** and **Merle Haggard** and also played non-country venues such as night clubs and even a concert at the White House. In the mid-70s. they began recording for the new CMH label and later recorded ceveral albums including one with **Mac Wiseman** with whom they charted 'Shackles And Chains' in 1979.
Albums: with Red Allen *Country Pickin' & Hillside Singin'* (1959), *Bluegrass Music* (1961), *Bluegrass Instrumentals* (1962), *Cuttin' Grass* (1963), *Voices In Bluegrass* (1965), *Up This Hill And Down* (1966), *Modern Sounds Of Bluegrass* (1967), *Yesterday, Today & The Osborne Brothers* (1968), *Favorite Hymns* (1969), *Up To Date & Down To Earth* (1969), *The Osborne Brothers* (1970), *Ru-Beeee* (1970), *Country Roads* (1971), *The Osborne Brothers* (1971), *Georgia Pinewoods* (1971), *Bobby & Sonny* (1972), *Bluegrass Express* (1973), *Midnight Flyer* (1973), *Fastest Grass Alive* (1974), *Pickin' Grass And Singin' Country* (1975), *Number One* (1976), *The Osborne Brothers & Red Allen* (1977), *From Rocky Top To Muddy Bottom* (1977, double album), *Bluegrass Collection* (1978, double album), with Buddy Spicher *Bluegrass Concerto* (1979), with Mac Wiseman *The Essential Bluegrass Album* (1979), *I Can Hear Kentucky*

Calling Me (1980), *Bluegrass Spectacular* (1982), *Bluegrass Gold* (1982), *Some Things I Want To Sing About* (1984), *Once More* (1986), *Favorite Memories* (1987), *Singing, Shouting Praises* (1988). Solo: Bobby Osborne *Bobby Osborne & His Mandolin* (1981). Sonny Osborne *Early Recordings Volumes 1, 2,.3* (1979), *Sonny Osborne & His Sunny Mountain Boys* (70s), *Songs Of Bluegrass, Five String In Hi-Fi.*

Osborne, Jeffrey

b. 9 March 1948, Providence, Rhode Island, USA. Osborne sang with LTD (Love, Togetherness And Devotion) from 1970 until its disbandment 12 years later. However, he remained subject to the LTD contract with **A&M Records** for whom he recorded five albums as a solo soul executant. Under **George Duke**'s supervision, the first of these contained the singles 'I Really Don't Need No Light' and 'On The Wings Of Love' which both reached the US Top 40 - and the latter was a 'sleeper' hit in the UK, when 'Don't You Get So Mad' and the title track of *Stay With Me Tonight* had made slight headway there. In 1984 'Don't Stop' was, nevertheless, his last UK chart entry. The album of the same name featured a duet with Joyce Kennedy - duplicated on her *Lookin' For Trouble*, which was produced by Osborne. *Emotional* was a strong album and the subsequent singles among them 'You Should Be Mine (The Woo Woo Song)', reached number 13, becoming his biggest US hit. For two years, he chose - perhaps unwisely - to rest on his laurels. He returned with *One Love One Dream* (co-written with Bruce Roberts) and, just prior to a transfer to **Arista**, he teamed up with **Dionne Warwick** for 1990's 'Love Power'. Airplay for his increasingly more predictable output was no longer automatic - and consumers had not restored him, even temporarily, to his former moderate glory.
Albums: *Jeffrey Osborne* (1982), *Stay With Me Tonight* (1983), *Don't Stop* (1984), *Emotional* (1986), *One Love One Dream* (1988), *Only Human* (1991).

Osborne, Mike

b. 28 September 1941, Hereford, England. Osborne played violin in the school orchestra, but when he went to the Guildhall School it was to study clarinet. He could play piano too, but since turning professional his main instrument has always been alto saxophone. His favourite players are **Phil Woods**, **Joe Henderson** and **Jackie McLean**, with whom he shares a sharp-edged, slightly distressed-sounding tone, but he is often compared with **Ornette Coleman** for the urgency of his sound and his ability to create long, intense, graceful skeins of free melody. He first came to notice with the **Mike Westbrook** Concert Band when it reformed after Westbrook's move to London from Plymouth. 'Ossie' sat in for a couple of gigs and was asked to join permanently in early 1963, when he was one of only two professional musicians in the orchestra. Over the next few years he was an important constituent of several fine bands, including the **Michael Gibbs** Band, **Chris McGregor**'s Brotherhood Of Breath, **Harry Miller**'s Isipingo and the group, ranging from a quartet to an octet, which he co-led with **John Surman** during 1968 and 1969. He also worked with John Warren, **Alan Skidmore**, Kenneth Terroade, Rik Colbeck, and **Humphrey Lyttelton**. In 1969 he established his own exceptionally exciting trio with Harry Miller and **Louis Moholo**, which, apart from many fine public gigs, recorded several superb sessions for BBC Radio's Jazz Club. In the early 70s he began a fruitful association with **Stan Tracey** in wholly improvised duets, which brought Tracey back from the brink of retirement through disillusion with the music business. In 1973 he co-founded S.O.S., probably the first regular all-saxophone band, with Alan Skidmore and **John Surman**. He was voted best alto saxophonist in the ***Melody Maker*** poll every year from 1969-73. During the late 70s he became increasingly ill and has been unable to play since 1980. His relatively small recorded oeuvre does show the range of his playing, from deeply moving but unsentimental ballad interpretations with Westbrook to scorchingly intense free explorations with Isipingo or the trio.
Albums: *Outback* (Future Music 1970), with Stan Tracey *Original* (1972), *Border Crossing* (Ogun 1975), *All Night Long* (Ogun 1975), *SOS* (1975), with Tracey *Tandem* (1976), *Marcel's Muse* (Ogun 1977), *Gold Hearted Girl* (Crosscut 1988), *A Case For The Blues* (Crosscut 1993).

Osborne, Tony, Sound

UK-born Osborne was nominal leader of a traditional jazz outfit whose 'Saturday Jump' was the opening and closing theme to the highly influential BBC Light Programme's *Saturday Club* pop series on which they appeared regularly in the late 50s. By 1960, Osborne had enlisted additional musicians of such exacting calibre that the Tony Osborne Sound was hired frequently as all-purpose accompanists to visiting Americans such as **Connie Francis**, whose million-selling 'Mama' was recorded in Britain with them. Signed to **HMV**, the orchestra spent a week in the Top 50 in February 1961 under their own name with the film tune, 'Man From Madrid'. Twelve years later, they notched up a fractionally less minor UK hit - on the Philips label - with 'The Shepherd's Song' featuring vocalist Joanne Brown. His son Gary has composed numerous songs, most notably with **Elton John**.

Osbourne, Johnny

b. c.1948, Jamaica, West Indies. During 1967 Osbourne became lead vocalist of the Wildcats, and recorded for producer **Winston Riley**, although nothing was issued. The Wildcats' manager then financed a session at **Cosxone Dodd**'s **Studio One**, from which his debut single, 'All I Have Is Love', was released. In 1969 he recorded an album, *Come Back Darling*, for Riley. It was a strong collection on which Johnny was supported by the **Sensations** on harmony vocals. On the day that he completed the album, he emigrated to Toronto, Canada, to join his family. After singing with various soul and reggae groups, he became lead vocalist for Ishan People, and recorded two albums with them. The group broke up in 1979, and Johnny decided to return to Jamaica. Shortly after returning, he recorded 'Forgive Them' and 'Jealousy, Heartache And Pain' for the Studio One label. Through late 1979 and early 1980 he recorded extensively for Dodd, with these sessions culminating in a stunning album, *Truths And Rights*. This beautifully understated set of classic songs is Osbourne's major work. In 1979 he also had a hit for **Prince Jammy** with 'Folly Ranking', and an excellent album of the same name followed in 1980. The success of these recordings made him one of the most in-demand vocalists on the island, and a glut of material was released, including *Fally Lover*, *Warrior*, *Innah Disco Style* and *Never Stop Fighting*, between 1980-82. In 1983, he began the year with two big hits, 'Yo Yo' and 'Lend Me A Chopper', and later in the year enjoyed massive success with 'Water Pumping', an adaptation of Hopeton Lewis' 'Take It Easy', which had also served as the basis for **Johnny Clarke**'s 1976 hit 'Rockers Time Now'. The hits continued with 'Get Cracking', 'Check For You', 'Rewind' (1984), 'Buddy Bye', 'No Sound Like We' and 'In The Area' (1985). In the late 80s he was particularly successful when recording for **Bobby Digita**l, and had hits with 'Good Time Rock' (1988) and 'Rude Boy Skank' (1988), both of which are included on the album *Rougher Than Them* (1989). Throughout the 80s he continued to record for Coxsone Dodd, and excellent singles included 'Keep That Light', 'Unity' and 'A We Run Things', but a long-promised second album from Dodd has not materialised. Johnny's versatility and talent have enabled him to remain at the forefront of reggae, and no matter how thin the lyrics he has sung have been, often no more than encouragements to dance or endorsements of a particular **sound system**, he always manages to inject artistry and vitality into the proceedings. He is doubtless capable of another *Truths And Rights*.

Albums: *Come Back Darling* (Trojan 1969), *Truths And Rights* (Studio One 1980), *Folly Ranking* (Jammys 1980), *Fally Lover* (Greensleeves 1980), *Never Stop Fighting* (Greensleeves 1982), *Water Pumping* (Greensleeves 1984), *Reggae On Broadway* (Vista Sounds 1984), *Dancing Time* (Londisc 1984), *Johnny Osbourne* (Lix 1984), *In The Area* (Greensleeves 1984), *Michael Palmer Meets Johnny Osbourne* (Vibes & Vibes 1984), *Rub A Dub Soldier* (Jammys 1985), *Bring The Sensi Come* (Midnight Rock 1985), *Reality* (Selection 1985), *Rock Me Rock Me* (Top Rank 1986), *Cool Down* (1989), *Johnny Osbourne* (Jetstar 1989), *Rougher Than Them* (1989), *Smiling Faces* (Blue Mountain 1989), *Nuh Dis (Come Ya Fe Drink Milk)* (Star 1990).

Osbourne, Ozzy

b. John Osbourne, 3 December 1948, Birmingham, England. In 1979 this highly individual and by now infamous vocalist and songwriter left **Black Sabbath**, a band whose image and original musical direction he had helped shape. His own band was set up with Lee Kerslake, formerly of **Uriah Heep**, on drums, **Rainbow**'s Bob Daisley (bass) and **Randy Rhoads**, fresh from **Quiet Riot**, on guitar. Rhoads' innovative playing ability was much in evidence on the debut, *Blizzard Of Oz*. By the time of a second album, Daisley and Kerslake had left to be replaced by **Pat Travers** drummer Tommy Aldridge, and Rudy Sarzo (bass). Throughout his post-Black Sabbath career, Osbourne has courted publicity, most famously in 1982 when he had to undergo treatment for rabies following an on-stage incident when he bit the head off a bat. In the same year his immensely talented young guitarist, Rhoads, was killed in an air crash. In came Brad Gillis, former guitarist in **Night Ranger**, but, so close was Rhoads' personal as well as musical relationship to Osbourne, many feared he would never be adequately replaced. *Speak Of The Devil* was released later in 1982, a live album which included Sabbath material. Following a tour which saw Sarzo and Gillis walk out, Osbourne was forced to re-think the line-up of his band in 1983 as Daisley rejoined, along with guitarist Jake E. Lee. Aldridge left following the release of *Bark At The Moon*, and was replaced by renowned virtuoso drummer **Carmine Appice**. This combination was to be short-lived, however, Randy Castillo replacing Appice, and Phil Soussan taking on the bass guitar. Daisley appears on *No Rest For The Wicked*, although Sabbath bassist Geezer Butler played on the subsequent live dates. The late 80s were a trying time for Osbourne. He went on trial in America for allegedly using his lyrics to incite youngsters to commit suicide; he was eventually cleared of these charges. His wife, Sharon (daughter of **Don Arden**), also became his manager, and has helped Osbourne to overcome the alcoholism which was the subject of much of his work. His lyrics, though, continue to deal with the grimmest of subjects like the agony of insanity, and *The Ultimate Sin* is concerned almost exclusively with the issue of nuclear destruction. In later years Osbourne has kept to more contemporary issues, rejecting to a certain extent the satanic, werewolf image he constructed around himself in the early 80s. He embarked on a farewell tour in 1992, but broke four bones in his foot which inhibited his performances greatly. He also donated $20,000 to the Daughters Of The Republic Of Texas appeal to help restore the Alamo, and performed his first concert

in the city of San Antonio since being banned for urinating on a wall of the monument in 1982. Predictably neither retirement nor atonement sat too comfortably with the man, and by late 1994 he was announcing the imminent release of a new solo album, recorded in conjunction with **Steve Vai**. He also teamed up with **Therapy?** to sing lead vocals on the track 'Iron Man' for the Black Sabbath tribute album, *Black Nativity*. Far less likely was his pairing with Miss Piggy of *The Muppet Show* on 'Born To Be Wild', for a bizarre Muppets compilation album. He also confesssed that his original partner on his 1992 **Don Was**-produced duet with actress Kim Basinger, 'Shake Your Head', was **Madonna**, although he had not actually recognised her. Other strange couplings had included one with the Scottish comedian Billy Connolly and the the popular UK boxer Frank Bruno on the 'Urpney Song', written by Mike Batt for the cartoon series, *Dreamstone*.
Albums: With Black Sabbath: *Black Sabbath* (Vertigo 1970), *Paranoid* (Vertigo 1970), *Master Of Reality* (Vertigo 1971), *Black Sabbath Vol. IV* (Vertigo 1972), *Sabbath Bloody Sabbath* (World Wide Artists 1974), *Sabotage* (NEMS 1975), *Technical Ecstasy* (Vertigo 1976), *Never Say Die* (Vertigo 1978). Solo: *Blizzard Of Oz* (Jet 1980), *Diary Of A Madman* (Jet 1981), *Talk Of The Devil* (Jet 1982), *Bark At The Moon* (Jet 1983), *The Ultimate Sin* (Epic 1986), *Tribute* (Epic 1987), *No Rest For The Wicked* (Epic 1988), *Just Say Ozzy* (Epic 1990), *No More Tears* (Epic 1991), *Live & Loud* (Epic 1993, double album).
Further reading: *Diary Of A Madman*, Mick Wall. *Ozzy Osbourne*, Garry Johnson.
Videos: *The Ultimate Ozzy* (1987), *Wicked Videos* (1988), *Bark At The Moon* (1990), *Don't Blame Me* (1992), *Live & Loud* (1993).

Osby, Greg

b. 1961, St Louis, Missouri, USA. New York-based saxophonist who has attached jazz's cool to a militant hip hop beat. Following his work with the M-Base project (including **Steve Coleman** and **Cassandra Wilson**), Osby decided he wanted to record a more free-ranging, one-off hip hop record: 'The purpose for this record was to function as an 'either/or', meaning that it could rest solely as a hardcore hip hop record without any jazz or musicians at all, and that it also would be a strong musical statement without breakbeats or anything. I wanted it to bridge the gap'. Alongside jazz musicians including **Geri Allen** and **Darrell Grant**, he enlisted the aid of hip hop producers Ali Shaheed Muhammed (**A Tribe Called Quest**) and Street Element, and a variety of rappers. Osby had actually begun life as an R&B musician, only discovering jazz when he attended college in 1978. Though setting up M-Base as a street-sussed jazz/hip hop enclave, he had little time for the work of **Gang Starr** or **Digable Planets**, who sample from jazz but do not, generally, work with live musicians. That did not stop him from being bracketed alongside those artists however.
Albums: *Greg Osby And Sound Theatre* (Watt 1987), *Mind Games* (JMT 1989), *Season Of Renewal* (JMT 1990), *Man Talk For Moderns Vol X* (Blue Note 1991), *3-D Lifestyles* (Blue Note 1993).

Oscar The Frog

A highly regarded UK folk band, surprisingly neglected. Oscar The Frog had far more energy than most of the competition of the time. Despite definite power pop overtones, they deserve consideration for adapting the **Ian Dury** hit to 'Hit Me With Your Morris Stick'.
Album: *Oscar The Frog* (1980).

Osibisa

Formed in London in 1969 by three Ghanaian and three Caribbean musicians, Osibisa played a central role in developing an awareness of African music - in their case, specifically, West African highlife tinged with rock - among European and North American audiences in the 70s. Since then, Osibisa have suffered the fate of many once-celebrated 70s African-oriented performers. Their pioneering blend of rock and African rhythms has either been overlooked or downgraded for its lack of roots appeal. There is, in truth, some justification for this: Osibisa's style was too closely hitched to western rock to survive the passing of that lumbering wagon, and too much of a fusion to survive the scrutiny of western audiences who, from the early 80s onwards, were looking for 'authentic' African music. But the group's towering achievements in the 70s should not be denigrated. The Ghanaian founder members of Osibisa - Teddy Osei (saxophone), Sol Amarfio (drums) and Mac Tontoh (trumpet, Osei's brother) - were seasoned members of the Accra highlife scene before they moved to London to launch their attack on the world stage. Osei and Amaflio had played in the Star Gazers, a top Ghanaian highlife band, before setting up the Comets, who scored a large West African hit with their 1958 single 'Pete Pete'. Tontoh was also a member of the Comets, before joining the Uhuru Dance Band, one of the first outfits to bring elements of jazz into Ghanaian highlife.
The other founder members of Osibisa were Spartacus R, a Grenadian bass player, Robert Bailey (b. Trinidad; keyboards) and Wendel Richardson (b. Antigua; lead guitar). They were joined soon after their formation by the Ghanaian percussionist Darko Adams 'Potato' (b. 1932, d. 1 January 1995, Accra, Ghana). In 1962, Osei moved to London, where he was eventually given a scholarship by the Ghanaian government to study music. In 1964, he formed Cat's Paw, an early blueprint for Osibisa which blended highlife, rock and soul. In 1969, feeling the need for more accomplished

African musicians within the line-up, he persuaded Tontoh and Amarfio to join him in London, where towards the end of the year Osibisa was born. The venture proved to be an immediate success, with the single 'Music For Gong Gong' a substantial hit in 1970 (three other singles would later make the British Top 10: 'Sunshine Day', 'Dance The Body Music' and 'Coffee Song').

Osibisa's self-titled debut album in 1971 also scored heavily. The timing of its release was fortuitous: rock music, after having been revitalized in the 60s, was in a creative slump, demanding passive, sometimes catatonic audiences for whom dancing was not only uncool but in many cases physically impossible, such was the extent of the fashionable ingestion of narcotic substances. Disco had yet to make its mark. Osibisa stepped into the breach with a music whose rock references, in the guitar solos and chord structures, combined with vibrant African cross rhythms to attract an immediate public response. Osibisa became almost an household name, with their albums to be found in student bed-sits across the country. But the band's true power only fully came across on stage, when African village scenarios and a mastery of rhythm and melody summoned up an energy and spirit lacking in other branches of Western pop. Their best work, *Woyaya*, like their debut stalled outside the UK Top 10 (at number 11). The title track was covered by **Art Garfunkel**, who produced a sensitive arrangement. The group followed up their onslaught on the UK by making inroads into many other countries' charts and touring circuits, and during the mid and late 70s they spent much of their time on extended world tours, capturing particularly large audiences in Japan, India, Australia and, of course, throughout Africa. In 1977 they were headliners at the Lagos-based Festac 77, the pan-African Olympics of music and culture, and in 1980 performed a special concert at the Zimbabwean independence celebrations. By this time, however, Osibisa's star was firmly in decline in Europe and the USA, as disco overwhelmed African music as the accepted invitation to dance. The band continued touring and releasing records, but to steadily diminishing audiences. Business problems followed. After an initial signing to MCA, Osibisa had changed labels several times, ending with Bronze. The moves reflected their growing frustration with British business, as each label in turn tried to persuade them to adapt their music to the disco style and thus maximize their appeal. Osibisa were prepared to make some concessions but, to their credit (and sadly, their financial debit) only up to a point. Beyond that they were not prepared to abandon their roots, culture or pride. In the mid-80s, the group directed their attention to the state of the music business in Ghana, planning a studio and theatre complex which came to nothing following the withdrawal of state funding, and helping in the promotion of younger highlife artists. In 1984, Tontoh formed a London band to back three visiting Ghanaian musicians - A.B. Crentsil, Eric Agyeman and Thomas Frempong. An album, *Highlife Stars*, followed on Osibisa's own Flying Elephant label. Now effectively disbanded, Osibisa occasionally stage reunion concerts.

Albums: *Osibisa* (1971), *Heads* (1972), *Woyaya* (both 1972), *Happy Children* (1973), *Superfly TNT* (1974), *Welcome Home* (1976), *Ojah Awake* (1976), *Black Magic Night* (1977), *Mystic Energy* (1980), *Celebration* (1983), *Live At The Marquee* (1984). Compilation: *The Best Of Osibisa* (1974).

Oslin, K.T.

b. Kay Toinette Oslin, 1943, Crossitt, Arkansas, USA. Oslin was raised in Mobile, Alabama and then in Houston. She loved **Hank Williams** and the **Carter Family**, but hated early 60s country music because 'it was middle-aged men singing about drinking whiskey and cheating on their wives'. She attended drama school and worked in Houston as a folk trio with **Guy Clark** and radio producer David Jones. A live album she made with Texas singer Frank Davis was never released. She was in the chorus for the Broadway production of ***Hello, Dolly!*** starring Betty Grable. For many years, she played bit parts, did session work and sang commercials. She sang harmony on the 1978 album, *Guy Clark*, but her 1981 **Elektra** singles of 'Clean Your Own Tables' and 'Younger Men (Are Startin' To Catch My Eye)', released as Kay T. Oslin, did not sell. In 1982 **Gail Davies** recorded her song, 'Round The Clock Lovin'', which prompted her to borrow $7,000 from an aunt to form a band for a Nashville showcase. The **Judds** recorded her song, 'Old Pictures', whilst her own piano-based ballad, '80's Ladies', was a Top 10 country single and an anthem for older, single women. (Oslin herself is unmarried.) An album of songs from the female perspective, also called *80's Ladies*, was a top-selling country album that crossed over to the pop market. **Tom T. Hall** described her as 'everybody's screwed-up sister'. Her number 1 country singles are 'Do Ya' (she stopped a faster take being released when she realized it worked much better at half-tempo), 'I'll Always Come Back' and the partly-narrated 'Hold Me'. Although it is unique for a woman of this age to first make her mark in country music, it is doubtful if she can maintain the momentum, particularly as she seems to have exhausted her original flow of songs. Certainly the long silence since she released the patchy, but still impressive, *Love In A Small Town*, and its number 1 single 'Come Next Monday', appears ominous.

Albums: *80's Ladies* (1987), *This Woman* (1988), *Love In A Small Town* (1990), *Songs From An Aging Sex Bomb* (1993).

Osmond, Donny

b. Donald Clark Osmond, 9 December 1957, Ogden,

Utah, USA. The most successful solo artist to emerge from family group, the **Osmonds**, Donny was particularly successful at covering old hits. His first solo success came in the summer of 1971 with a version of **Billy Sherrill**'s 'Sweet And Innocent', which reached the US Top 10. The follow-up, a revival of **Gerry Goffin/Carole King**'s 'Go Away Little Girl' (previously a hit for both **Steve Lawrence** and **Mark Wynter**) took Osmond to the top of the US charts. 'Hey Girl', once a success for **Freddie Scott**, continued his US chart domination, which was now even more successful than that of the family group. By the summer of 1972, Osmondmania reached Britain, and a revival of **Paul Anka**'s 'Puppy Love' gave Donny his first UK number 1. The singer's clean-cut good looks and perpetual smile brought him massive coverage in the pop press, while a back catalogue of hit songs from previous generations sustained his chart career. 'Too Young' and 'Why' both hit the UK Top 10, while 'The Twelfth Of Never' and 'Young Love' both reached number 1. His material appeared to concentrate on the pangs of adolescent love, which made him the perfect teenage idol for the period. In 1974, Donny began a series of duets with his sister **Marie Osmond**, which included more UK Top 10 hits with 'I'm Leaving It All Up To You' and 'Morning Side Of The Mountain'. It was clear that Donny's teen appeal was severely circumscribed by his youth and in 1977 he tried unsuccessfully to reach a more mature audience with *Donald Clark Osmond*. Although minor hits followed, the singer's appeal was waning alarmingly by the late 70s. After the break-up of the group in 1980, Donny went on to star in the 1982 revival of the musical ***Little Johnny Jones***, which closed after only one night on Broadway, and ceased recording after the mid-70s. A decade later, a rugged Osmond returned with 'I'm In It For Love' and the more successful 'Soldier Of Love' which reached the US Top 30. Most agreed that his attempts at mainstream rock were much more impressive than anyone might have imagined. In the early 90s, Osmond proved his versatility once more when he played the lead in Canadian and North American productions of **Andrew Lloyd Webber**'s musical ***Joseph And The Amazing Technicolor Dreamcoat***.

Albums: *The Donny Osmond Album* (1971), *To You With Love* (1971), *Portrait Of Donny* (1972), *Too Young* (1972), *My Best Of You* (1972), *Alone Together* (1973), *A Time For Us* (1973), *Donny* (1974), *Discotrain* (1976), *Donald Clark Osmond* (1977), *Soldier Of Love* (1988), *Eyes Don't Lie* (1991); with Marie Osmond: *I'm Leaving It All Up To You* (1974), *Make The World Go Away* (1975), *Donny And Marie - Featuring Songs From Their Television Show* (1976), *Deep Purple* (1976), *Donny And Marie - A New Season* (1977), *Winning Combination* (1978), *Goin' Coconuts* (1978).

Osmond, Little Jimmy

b. 16 April 1963, Canoga Park, California, USA. The youngest member of the **Osmonds** family, Jimmy unexpectedly emerged as a pre-teen idol in 1972. Overweight and cute, he was launched at the peak of Osmondmania and topped the Christmas charts in the UK with his singalong 'Long-Haired Lover From Liverpool'. In doing so, he became, at nine years of age, the youngest individual ever to reach number 1 in the UK up until that time. He returned to the charts during the next two years with **Lavern Baker**'s old hit 'Tweedle Dee' and **Eddie Hodges**' 'I'm Gonna Knock On Your Door'. His brief popularity in Britain was eclipsed by fan mania in Japan where he was known as 'Jimmy Boy'. When the hits ceased and he grew up, he became successful as an entrepreneur and rock impresario.

Album: *Killer Joe* (1972).

Osmond, Marie

b. 13 October 1959, Ogden, Utah, USA. Following the success of her elder siblings in the **Osmonds**, Marie launched her own singing career in late 1973. Her revival of **Anita Bryant**'s 'Paper Roses' reached the US Top 5 and did even better in the UK, peaking at number 2. Following two solo albums, she successfully collaborated with her brother **Donny Osmond** on a series of duets. They enjoyed a transatlantic Top 10 hit with a version of **Dale And Griffin**'s 'I'm Leaving It All Up To You' and repeated that achievement with a cover of **Tommy Edwards**' 'Morning Side Of The Mountain'. Marie simultaneously continued her solo career with a reworking of **Connie Francis**'s 'Who's Sorry Now?' The brother and sister duo next moved into the country market with a version of **Eddy Arnold**'s 'Make The World Go Away'. By early 1976, their popularity was still strong and they featured in a one-hour variety television show titled *Donny And Marie*. The programme spawned a hit album and another UK/US hit with a revival of **Nino Tempo And April Stevens**' 'Deep Purple'. By 1977, the Mormon duo were covering Tamla/**Motown** material, duetting on **Marvin Gaye** And **Tammi Terrell**'s 'Ain't Nothing Like The Real Thing'. The duets continued until 1978 and their last significant success was a cover of the **Righteous Brothers**' '(You're My) Soul And Inspiration'. That same year, Donny and Marie starred together in the movie *Goin' Coconuts*. Following the break-up of the Osmonds the sister continued with her own television series *Marie*. Thereafter, she moved successfully into country music and recorded several albums for the Curb label.

Albums: *Paper Roses* (1974), *In My Little Corner Of The World* (1974), *Who's Sorry Now?* (1975), *This Is The Way That I Feel* (1977), *There's No Stopping Your Heart* (1986), *I Only Wanted You* (1987), *All In Love* (1988); with Donny

Osmond *I'm Leaving It All Up To You* (1974), *Make The World Go Away* (1975), *Donny And Marie - Featuring Songs From Their Television Show* (1976), *Deep Purple* (1976), *Donny And Marie - A New Season* (1977), *Winning Combination* (1978), *Goin' Coconuts* (1978).

Osmonds

This famous family all-vocal group from Ogden, Utah, USA comprised Alan Osmond (b. 22 June 1949), Wayne Osmond (b. 28 August 1951), Merrill Osmond (b. 30 April 1953), Jay Osmond (b. 2 March 1955) and **Donny Osmond** (b. 9 December 1957). The group first came to public notice following regular television appearances on the top-rated ***Andy Williams*** *Show*. From 1967-69, they also appeared on television's *Jerry Lewis Show*. Initially known as the Osmond Brothers they recorded for Andy Williams' record label Barnaby. By 1971, their potential was recognized by Mike Curb, who saw them as likely rivals to the star-studded **Jackson 5**. Signed to **MGM Records**, they recorded the catchy 'One Bad Apple', which topped the US charts for five weeks. Before long, they became a national institution, and various members of the family including Donny Osmond, **Marie Osmond** and **Little Jimmy Osmond** enjoyed hits in their own right. As a group, the primary members enjoyed a string of hits, including 'Double Lovin'', 'Yo Yo' and 'Down By The Lazy River'. By the time Osmondmania hit the UK in 1972, the group peaked with their ecologically-conscious 'Crazy Horses', complete with intriguing electric organ effects. Their clean-cut image and well-scrubbed good looks brought them immense popularity among teenagers and they even starred in their own cartoon series. Probably their most ambitious moment came with the evangelical concept album, *The Plan*, in which they attempted to express their Mormon beliefs. Released at the height of their success, the album reached number 6 in the UK. During the early to mid-70s, they continued to release successive hits, including 'Going Home', 'Let Me In' and 'I Can't Stop'. Their sole UK number 1 as a group was 'Love Me For A Reason', composed by **Johnny Bristol**. Their last major hit in the UK was 'The Proud One' in 1975, after which their popularity waned. The individual members continued to prosper in varying degrees, but the family group disbanded in 1980. Two years later, the older members of the group re-formed without Donny, and moved into the country market. During the mid-80s, they appeared regularly at the Country Music Festival in London, but their recorded output lessened.

Selected albums: *Osmonds* (1971), *Homemade* (1971), *Phase-III* (1972), *The Osmonds 'Live'* (1972), *Crazy Horses* (1972), *The Plan* (1973), *Our Best To You* (1974), *I'm Still Gonna Need You* (1975), *The Proud One* (1975), *Around The World - Live In Concert* (1975), *Brainstorm* (1976), *The Osmonds Christmas Album* (1976), *Today* (1985). Compilation: *The Osmonds Greatest Hits* (1977).

Further reading: *At Last ... Donny!*, James Gregory. *The Osmond Brothers And The New Pop Scene*, Richard Robinson. *Donny And The Osmonds Backstage*, James Gregory. *The Osmond Story*, George Tremlett. *The Osmonds*, Monica Delaney. *On Tour With Donny & Marie And The Osmonds*, Lynn Roeder. *Donny And Marie Osmond: Breaking All The Rules*, Constance Van Brunt McMillan. *The Osmonds: The Official Story Of The Osmond Family*, Paul H. Dunn. *Donny And Marie*, Patricia Mulrooney Eldred.

Osser, Glenn

b. 28 August 1914, Munising, Michigan, USA. Son of Russian immigrants, Osser has had a successful career, arranging and conducting for many leading bands and singers. He has also achieved a distinctive string sound through his clever scoring, which he describes as 'voicing register, and composition of the counterpoint'. In his early career Osser concentrated on arranging, and his scores were accepted by **Bob Crosby**, **Charlie Barnet**, **Bunny Berigan**, **Paul Whiteman**, **Les Brown** and **Red Nichols**. During the 50s, while still regularly working with Whiteman (who was Musical Director of the ABC Network at that time), Osser was in demand to back many singers for albums: **Georgia Gibbs**, **Vic Damone**, **Jack Jones**, **Frankie Laine**, **John Raitt**, **Maurice Chevalier** and **Guy Mitchell**. Osser was also recording his own instrumental albums, notably some with **Bobby Hackett** and **Joe Bushkin**. Further albums found Osser backing **Johnny Mathis**, Jerry Vale, **Tony Bennett**, **Robert Goulet** and Leslie Uggams. Leaving US **Columbia** and moving to **RCA**, Osser worked with **Della Reese** and **Sam Cooke**. Until 1987 he was Music Director and arranger for the *Miss America Beauty Pageant* on television, with Osser and his wife contributing various original songs including 'Miss America, You're Beautiful' and 'Look At Her'. He has also written many works for Concert Bands which are still regularly performed by many High School and College bands in the USA.

Selected albums: Glenn Osser Orchestra *But Beautiful* (Kapp 1956), with Joe Bushkin *Midnight Rhapsody* (Capitol 1957), Marian McPartland *With You In Mind* (Capitol 1957), Georgia Gibbs *Swingin' With Her Nibs* (Mercury 1957), Vivian Blaine *Songs From Ziegfeld Follies* (Mercury 1957), Vic Damone *Angela Mia* (Columbia 1957), Jerry Vale *I Remember Buddy* (Columbia 1958), Red Buttons, Barbara Cook *Hansel And Gretel* (MGM 1958), *Maurice Chevalier Sings Songs Of Yesterday/Today* (MGM 1958), Guy Mitchell *A Guy In Love* (Columbia 1958), Johnny Mathis *Heavenly* (Columbia 1959), Leslie Uggams *The Eyes Of God* (Columbia 1959), *March Along Sing Along (Marching Band And Chorus)* (United Artists 1960), Della Reese *Della By Starlight* (RCA 1960), Sam Cooke *Cooke's Tour* (RCA 1960), Osser Orchestra *Be*

There At Five (Mercury 1960), *Tony Bennett Sings A String Of Harold Arlen* (Columbia 1960), *Diana Trask* (Columbia 1961), Dona Jacoby *Swinging Big Sound* (Decca 1962), Bobby Hackett *Most Beautiful Horn In The World* (Columbia 1962), Jack Jones *Gift Of Love* (Kapp 1962), George Maharis *Portrait In Music* (Epic 1962), Robert Goulet *Two Of Us* (Columbia 1962), Jerry Vale *Arrivederci Roma* (Columbia 1963), Barbara Carroll *Fresh From Broadway* (Warners 1964), Brook Benton *That Old Feeling* (RCA 1966), Jerry Vale *The Impossible Dream* (Columbia 1967), Johnny Mathis *Up Up And Away* (Columbia 1968), Bob Thiele *Those Were The Days* (Flying Dutchman 1972).

Ossian

This Scottish revival group, formed in 1976, performed traditional songs and tunes in an authentic setting combining contemporary instruments. The original line-up of Billy Jackson (b. Glasgow, Scotland; harp/uillean pipes/whistle/vocals), George Jackson (b. Glasgow, Scotland; cittern/guitar/whistle/flute), John Martin (b. Glasgow, Scotland; fiddle/viola), and Billy Ross (b. Glasgow, Scotland; guitar/vocals) changed in 1980 with the departure of Ross. He was replaced by Tony Cuffe (vocals/guitar/whistle/tiple). In 1981, Iain MacDonald (highland pipes/flute/whistle) joined the group. George and Billy Jackson and John Martin had played on the 1974 self-titled album by Contraband, fronted by singer **Mae McKenna**. The group provided music for a theatre group in Jura in 1976, which led to other theatrical music work, including providing music and songs for a play called 'Clanna Cheo'. This was a play based around the legend of Rob Roy, and it toured widely including London. *Ossian* was released on Springthyme Records. The various members have continued with other commitments outside of the group, including Billy Jackson teaming up with former member Billy Ross to record *Misty Mountain*, and George Jackson and Maggie MacInnes recording *Cairistiona*. More recent recordings have featured less Gaelic songs than before. Both Billy and George Jackson were touring with the Tag Theatre Company in 1991.
Albums: *Ossian* (1977), *St. Kilda Wedding* (1978), *Seal Song* (1981), *Dove Across The Water* (1982), *Borders* (1984), *Light On A Distant Shore* (1986). Compilation: *The Best Of...* (Iona 1994). Billy Ross and Billy Jackson *Misty Mountain* (1986). George Jackson and Maggie MacInnes *Cairistiona* (1986), with William Jackson *Heart Music* (1987), with William Jackson *St. Mungo: A Celtic Suite For Glasgow* (1991). Billy Ross And John Martin *Braes Of Lochiel* (1991).

Ostrogoth

This Belgian hard rock outfit was formed in Gent, Belguim, during 1983, by guitarist Rudy Vercruysse and drummer Mario Pauwels. After a series of false starts, the line-up stabilized with the addition of Marc Debrauwer (vocals), Marnix Vandekauter (bass) and Hans Vandekerckhove (guitar). They debuted with a mini-album, *Full Moon's Eyes*, a competent if predictable re-hash of **Iron Maiden** and **Judas Priest** riffs. This line-up recorded two further collections in the same vein, but received little recognition outside their native Belgium. The band splintered in 1985, with only the nucleus of Vercruysse and Pauwels remaining. They rebuilt Ostrogoth with Peter de Wint (vocals), Juno Martins (guitar), Sylvain Cherotti (bass) and Kris Taerwe (keyboards). In 1987 they produced *Feelings Of Fury*, which added a melodic slant to their previous enterprises. The group subsequently disbanded with Pauwels moving on to Shellshock and Hermetic Brotherhood.
Albums: *Full Moon's Eyes* (Mausoleum 1983, mini-album), *Ecstasy And Danger* (Mausoleum 1983), *Too Hot* (Mausoleum 1985), *Feelings Of Fury* (Ultraprime 1987).

Other Half

Although based in San Francisco, USA during the latter part of the 60s, this primitive group was rooted in a Los Angeles garage band, the **Sons Of Adam**. Randy Holden (guitar) and Mike Port (bass) joined the new venture, although Port's contribution was confined to that of auxiliary member. The Other Half made an immediate impression with the powerhouse 'Mr. Pharmacist', and this seminal 60s punk offering was later covered by the **Fall**. Jeff Nowlen and Geoff Westen were among those supporting Holden on his group's lone album, which included 'Feathered Fish', a rare **Arthur Lee** song which the Sons Of Adam had also recorded. The quartet broke up in 1968 when Holden replaced Leigh Stephens in **Blue Cheer**.
Album: *Other Half* (1968).

Other Two

The most pure dance-orientated of the three major **New Order** spin-offs, the Other Two features arguably the least attention-seeking of the Manchester quartet: Stephen Morris (b. 28 October 1957, Macclesfield, Cheshire, England) and Gillian Gilbert (b. 27 January 1961, Manchester, England). Recording at their own studio in rural Macclesfield, they debuted on the charts with the number 41-peaking 'Tasty Fish' in 1991. The follow-up, 'Selfish', came two years later, but featured fashionable remixes by both **Moby** and **Farley & Heller**. The Other Two would also tamper with the work of other artists, as well as earning several credits for television and soundtrack motifs.
Album: *The Other Two & You* (London 1993).

Otis, Johnny

b. 28 December 1921, Vallejo, California, USA. Born into a family of Greek immigrants, was raised in a largely black neighbourhood where he thoroughly absorbed the prevailing culture and lifestyle. He began playing drums in his mid-teens and worked for a while with some of the locally-based jazz bands, including, in 1941, Lloyd Hunter's orchestra. In 1943 he gained his first name-band experience when he joined **Harlan Leonard** for a short spell. Some sources suggest that, during the difficult days when the draft was pulling musicians out of bands all across the USA, Otis then replaced another ex-Leonard drummer **Jesse Price** in the **Stan Kenton** band. In the mid-40s Otis also recorded with several jazz groups including, **Illinois Jacquet**'s all-star band and a septet led by **Lester Young**, which also featured **Howard McGhee** and **Willie Smith**. In 1945 Otis formed his own big band in Los Angeles. In an early edition assembled for a recording session, he leaned strongly towards a blues-based jazz repertoire and hired such musicians as Eli Robinson, **Paul Quinichette**, **Teddy Buckner**, **Bill Doggett**, **Curtis Counce** and singer **Jimmy Rushing**. This particular date produced a major success in 'Harlem Nocturne'. He also led a small band, including McGhee and **Teddy Edwards**, on a record date backing **Wynonie Harris**. However, Otis was aware of audience interest in R&B and began to angle his repertoire accordingly. Alert to the possibilities of the music and with a keen ear for new talent, he quickly became one of the leading figures in the R&B boom of the late 40s and early 50s. Otis also enjoyed credit for writing several songs, although, in some cases, this was an area fraught with confusion and litigation. Amongst his songs was 'Every Beat Of My Heart', which was recorded by **Jackie Wilson** in 1951 and became a minor hit followed, a decade later, by a massive hit version from **Gladys Knight**. Otis was instrumental in the discovery of **Etta James** and **Willie Mae 'Big Mama' Thornton**. A highly complex case of song co-authorship came to light with 'Hound Dog', which was recorded by Thornton. Otis, who had set up the date, was listed first as composer, then as co-composer with its originators, **Leiber And Stoller**. After the song was turned into a multi-million dollar hit by **Elvis Presley** other names appeared on the credits and the lawyers stepped in. Otis had a hit record in the UK with an updated version of 'Ma, He's Making Eyes At Me' in 1957. During the 50s Otis broadcast daily in the USA as a radio disc jockey, and had a weekly television show with his band and also formed several recording companies; all of which helped to make him a widely recognized force in west coast R&B. During the 60s and 70s, Otis continued to appear on radio and television, touring with his well-packaged R&B-based show. His son, Johnny 'Shuggie' Otis Jnr., appeared with the show and at the age of 13 had a hit with 'Country Girl'. In addition to his busy musical career, Otis also found time to write a book, *Listen To The Lambs*, written in the aftermath of the Watts riots of the late 60s.

Albums: *Mel Williams And Johnny Otis* (1955), *Rock 'N' Roll Parade, Volume 1* (1957), *The Johnny Otis Show* (1958), *Cold Shot* (1968), *Cuttin' Up* (1970), *Live At Monterey* (1971), *The New Johnny Otis Show* (1982), *Spirit Of The Black Territory Bands* (1993).

Ottawan

This European disco duo consisted of Annette (b. 1960, Guadeloupe Islands, West Indies) and Patrick (b. 1956, Guadeloupe Islands, West Indies). Patrick moved to Paris in 1966 and Annette in 1976. He was already a star in France when they met and formed Ottawan. 'D.I.S.C.O.' was a hit on the continent in 1979 and was requested by returning holiday makers who helped make it a UK hit in 1980. Only the combined efforts of the **Police** ('Don't Stand So Close To Me') and **Barbra Streisand** ('Woman In Love') managed to hold Ottawan at number 2 for three weeks. The follow-ups, all in a very similar vein, were 'You're OK', 'Hands Up (Give Me Your Heart)' (which reached number 3), and 'Help, Get Me Some Help!'. By this time their audience was growing tired of their material, and Ottawan disbanded.

Album: *Ottawan* (1980). Compilations: *Ottawan's Greatest Hits* (1981), *The Very Best Of Ottawan* (1993).

Otway, John

b. 2 October, 1952, Aylesbury, Buckinghamshire, England. The enigmatic madcap John Otway first came to prominence in the early 70s with his guitar/fiddle-playing partner Wild Willie Barrett. Otway's animated performances and unusual vocal style caught the attention of **Pete Townshend**, who produced the duo's first two Track label singles, 'Murder Man' and 'Louisa On A Horse'. Extensive gigging, highlighted by crazed and highly entertaining stage antics, won Otway and Barrett a loyal collegiate following and finally a minor hit with 'Really Free' in 1977. Its b-side, 'Beware Of The Flowers ('Cause I'm Sure They're Going To Get You Yeh)' was equally appealing and eccentric and augured well for further hits. Although Otway (with and without Barrett) soldiered on with syllable-stretching versions of **Tom Jones**'s 'Green Green Grass Of Home' and quirky novelty workouts such as 'Headbutts', he remains a 70s curio, still locked into the UK college/club circuit.

Albums: *John Otway And Wild Willie Barrett* (1977), *Deep And Meaningless* (1978), *Where Did I Go Right* (1979), *Way And Bar* (1980), *All Balls And No Willy* (1982), *The Wimp And The Wild* (1989), *Under The Covers And Over The Top* (1992), *Live!* (Amazing Feet 1994). Compilations: *Gone With The Bin Or The Best Of Otway And Barre* (1981), *Greatest Hits* (1986).

Further reading: *Cor Baby That's Really Me*, John Otway.

Ougenweide

A punchy German electric folk band, who wrote in

their national folk style and adapted Bohemian drinking songs and ancient harmonies in a series of very successful, endemic records.
Selected album: *Eulenspigel* (1976).

Oui 3

Oui 3 are Blair Booth (b. California, USA, vocals, programming), Phillip Erb (b. Switzerland, keyboards) and Trevor Miles (lyrics, rapping). In addition their debut album featured the formidable rhythmic skills of Youth (**Killing Joke**, **Brilliant** etc), **Jah Wobble**, **Galliano** and the **Brand New Heavies**. It revealed an obvious debt to **PM Dawn**, with a flat, distinctively English rapping style. Booth was once a sidekick of Terry Hall of the **Specials/Fun Boy 3** (as part of Terry, Blair and Anouschka), while Erb worked alongside Billy MacKenzie (ex-**Associates**). Together they met unknown rapper Miles, who shared their interest in **George Clinton** and **Lee Scratch Perry**. Their speciality then, was a witty mix of vocals and raps, with clever observations on a series of tightly wound scenarios. 'Break From The Old Routine', for example, depicted a collapsing relationship: 'We ain't gelling these days - we're congealing'. They returned to their reggae roots with the 45 'Arms Of Solitude', which featured of all things, an **Augustus Pablo** mix.
Album: *Oui Love You* (MCA 1993).

Our Daughters Wedding

This New York, USA electronic trio comprised Keith Silva (vocal), Layne Rico (synthesizers/vocal) and Scott (keyboards). After extensive gigging, they relocated to the UK and signed to **EMI**. In the summer of 1981, they broached the UK Top 40 with the catchy 'Lawnchairs'. The follow-up EP *The Digital Cowboy* gained considerable press but proved less commercial. Despite a strong record company investment, the trio lost ground and their sole album was followed by their demise.
Album: *Moving Windows* (1982).

Our Kid

This school-aged Liverpool based quartet were Kevin Rown (b. 1964), Brian Farrell (b. 1963), Terry McCreight (b. 1961) and Terry Beccino (b. 1961). The well choreographed and groomed young vocal group were winners on UK television's top talent show *New Faces* and were quickly signed up by **Polydor Records**. Their first single 'You Just Might See Me Cry' in 1976, which was penned by the hit team of **Roger Greenaway** and Barry Mason, shot to the runner-up position on the UK chart. The future looked very bright for the polished and youthful foursome. However, the local educational authorities intervened and, because of their age, banned them from various television and live appearances. They had two more singles on Polydor but when neither charted they returned to their studies.
Album: *Our Kid* (1975).

Our Miss Gibbs

Another vehicle for the vivacious actress and singer, Gertie Millar, with music written for her by her husband, Lionel Monkton in collaboration with Ivan Caryll. *Our Miss Gibbs* opened at the Gaiety Theatre in London on 23 January 1909, and dwelt, like so many similar productions of the time, on the life and loves of the common shop girl. This time the shop is in the county of Yorkshire, England, and sells flowers. Mary Gibbs (Gertie Miller) loves bank clerk Harry Lancaster (J. Edward Fraser), and the romance is going swimmingly until she discovers he is really the well-heeled Lord Eynsford, who has made certain commitments, marriage-wise, to Lady Elizabeth Thanet (Julia James). Wanting to be alone, she dashes off to the 1908 Franco-British Exhibition at London's White City Stadium (capacity 70,000), and emerges to accept the good Lord's apology and nuptial proposal. Most of the songs were written by Monkton or Caryll with lyricists Adrian Ross and Percy Greenbank, but the popular 'Yip-I-Addy-I-Ay', which was sung in the show by George Grossmith Jnr. (as the Hon. Hughie Pierrepoint), was the work of Grossmith Jnr. himself, with Will Cobb and John Flynn. The bulk of the score consisted of 'My Yorkshire Lassie', 'Not That Sort Of Person', 'Yorkshire', 'Mary', 'Hats', 'Country Cousins', 'White City', and 'Our Farm'. The song that created quite a stir, and endured, was the charming 'Moonstruck', which was introduced by Gertie Millar, dressed as a Pierrot, in a party scene. *Our Miss Gibbs* had - for those days - a prodigious run of 636 performances, but, understandably, given its subject matter and setting, flopped in New York, even with Pauline Chase as Mary, and some interpolated songs from **Jerome Kern**.

Our Tribe

Our Tribe is essentially Rob Dougan and Rollo Armstrong. They first met when Armstrong travelled to Australia with his friend Will Mount (later to become **Gloworm**) after finishing university, where he studied gynaecology. He met Dougan, who was then training to be an actor in Australia, signing a deal together for the rooArt label (nothing was released). On his return to England Rollo became a successful producer in his own right, and when Dougan emigrated they teamed up again. Their debut release for **ffrr**, 'I Believe In You', became a number 1 in the dance lists in the early 90s. Mel Medalie of **Champion** soon came along with the offer of both recording opportunities and their own subsidiary label (Cheeky). It was this which housed the duo's 'Understand This Groove' (as Franke), Gloworm's 'I Lift My Cup' and the OT Quartet's 'Hold That Sucker Down', a Top 10 hit. Our Tribe went on to remix for **U2** ('Numb'), **Pet Shop Boys** ('Can You Forgive Her', 'Absolutely Fabulous'), **M People** ('How Can I Love U More?'), **Wonderstuff** ('Full Of Life'), Shola ('Love, Respect & Happiness'), 3rd Nation ('I Believe'), **Raze** ('Break 4 Love') and **Gabrielle** ('Dreams'). The duo were also behind the writing and production of Kristine W's 'Feel What You Want' and Our Tribe featuring Sabrina Johnston's 'What Hope Have I?'.

Out Cold Cops

This gang of law enforcement toughs caused the Detroit Police Department to launch an internal enquiry when it was discovered that the crew was made up of their officers. After peforming on television's the *Jerry Springer Show*, they released an album, *Diary Of A Killer*, which recounted the joys of brutalising prisoners and criminals, thereby presenting their employers with a PR nightmare.
Album: *Diary Of A Killer* (1994).

Out Of My Hair

Effectively a vehicle for UK lead singer and guitarist 'Comfort' (b. Simon Eugene, c.1970), so much so that he sacked the rest of the original line-up when they objected to his controlling influence, Out Of My Hair additionally comprise Sean Elliot (guitar), Kenny Rumbles (drums) and Jon George (bass). Formed in London, England, and signed to **RCA Records**, the sound was one of glamorous indie guitar pop, with Comfort offering a **Rolling Stones/Jimi Hendrix**-styled vocal performance at its heart. However, he and the band remained suspicious of the 'retro' tag that had dogged more mainstream artists like **Lenny Kravitz**: 'I'm not into all that hippie shit. I was watching **Woodstock** the other day and it just made me think, Fuck Off!'. Despite this, the group's debut single, 'In The Groove Again', had an obvious 60s, neo-acid rock feel. The follow-up, 'Heart's Desire', was less restrained and more sprawling, but still in the classic pop tradition. Or, as Comfort prefers to call it, 'psychedelic bubblegum folk'.

Outcasts

At one time the premier punk band stationed in Northern Ireland, the Outcasts line-up revolved around the three Cowan brothers; Greg (b. c.1961; bass/vocals), Martin (b. c.1955; guitar) and Colin (b. c.1957; drums). This was the nucleus, though Gordon Blair had temporarily replaced Greg when he was injured in a car crash. The line-up was completed by 'Getty' (b. Colin Getgood, c.1960; guitar) and Raymond Falls (b. c.1965; additional drums). An impressive early single, 'Magnum Force', earned them the support of BBC disc jockey **John Peel**. They went on to release a solid debut album, characterized by the heavy rhythms produced by the twin drummers. However, before the release of *Seven Deadly Sins*, Colin became the second of the brothers to be injured in a car crash, this time fatally.
Albums: *Blood And Thunder* (Abstract 1983), *Seven Deadly Sins* (New Rose 1984).

Outer Rhythm Records

A subsidiary of UK label **Rhythm King** Records, established in 1989 in order to license hot 'outside' product. Early releases on the label included **Leftfield**'s 1990 single, 'Not Forgotten', released before that band had become a duo. They also scored with Digital Excitation (**Frank De Wulf**)'s 1992 trance hit, 'Pure Pleasure', plus other material under license from **R&S**. They imported heavily from Detroit, notably Random Noise Generation's 'Falling In Dub' in early 1992, which had originally been housed on the 430 West imprint, and Germany's **Hithouse** stable. The label closed in June 1992 due to 'changing forces in the market place'.

Outkast

Atlanta, Georgia duo comprising Andre 'Dre' Benjamin and Antoine 'Big Boi' Patton, who broke big with 'Player's Ball' - produced by **TLC** backroom gang **Organized Noise**. It comprised tales of the streets of their local East Point and Decateur neighbourhoods. Sadly songs like 'Get Up And Get Out' introduced wholly regrettable lines like 'I learned the difference between a bitch and a lady, but I treated them all like ho's'. They are signed to **LA & Babyface**'s LaFace imprint.
Album: *Southerplayalisticadillacmuzik* (LaFace 1994).

Outlaw Posse

UK duo of the early 90s comprising DJ K Gee and rapper Bello, originally titled Brothers Like Outlaw, who saw the potential of their debut album neutered by a long-delayed release schedule. Disillusioned, it was some small time before the release of their next record, the 'Party Time' 45, which included a sample of the **Cookie Crew**'s 'Born This Way'. Here they worked with a singer (Alison Evelyn) and live percussion. Although some accused them of jumping the jazz-rap bandwagon, they had actually prefaced their interest in such things as long ago as their 1989 debut single, 'Original Dope', which sampled **Donald Byrd**. Bello rapped memorably on the **KLF**'s 'What Time Is Love', and also produced tracks for Upfront, while Karl has remixed for numerous artists inlcuding **Queen Latifah**, **Mica Paris**, **Young Disciples** and **Omar**. The group enlisted a live crew entitled Push, and gigged widely through Europe and Scandanavia during the 90s, eventually shortening their name to simply Outlaw. The group split shortly thereafter, Bello going on to record solo as Mister Bello. He also inaugurated his own label, Krazy Fly, to which he signed Upfront

Ruddies, a crew he also manages.
Album: *My Afro's On Fire* (Gee St 1990).

Outlaws

Formed in Tampa, Florida, USA in 1974, the Outlaws comprised Billy Jones (guitar), Henry Paul (guitar), Hugh Thomasson (guitar), Monty Yoho (drums) and Frank O'Keefe (bass) - who was superceded by Harvey Arnold in 1977. With Thomasson as main composer, they were respected by fans (if not critics) for a strong stage presentation and artistic consistency which hinged on an unreconstructed mixture of salient points from the **Eagles**, **Allman Brothers** and similarly guitar-dominated, denim-clad acts of the 70s. The first signing to **Arista**, their 1975 debut album - produced by **Paul A. Rothchild** - reached number 13 in ***Billboard***'s chart. The set included the riveting lengthy guitar battle 'Green Grass And High Tides', which was the highlight of the group's live act. Singles success with 'There Goes Another Love Song' and 'Lady In Waiting' (the title track of their second album) was followed by regular touring. A coast-to-coast tour in 1976 and further less publicized work on the road necessitated the hire of a second drummer, David Dix, who was heard on 1978's in-concert *Bring It Back Alive* - the first without Paul (replaced by Freddy Salem) whose resignation was followed in 1979 by those of Yoho and Arnold. In 1981 the band was on the edge of the US Top 20 with the title track of *Ghost Riders* - a revival of **Vaughn Monroe**'s much-covered ballad - but, when this proved their chart swansong, the outfit - with Thomasson the only remaining original member - disbanded shortly after *Les Hombres Malo*. Following modest success with two albums by the Henry Paul Band, its leader rejoined Thomasson in a reformed Outlaws who issued *Soldiers Of Fortune* in 1986.
Albums: *The Outlaws* (1975), *Lady In Waiting* (1976), *Hurry Sundown* (1977), *Bring It Back Alive* (1978), *Playin' To Win* (1978), *In The Eye Of The Storm* (1979), *Ghost Riders* (1980), *Les Hombres Malo* (1982), *Soldiers Of Fortune* (1986). Compilations: *Greatest Hits Of The Outlaws/High Tides Forever* (1982), *On The Run Again* (1986).

Outside

Namely one Matt Cooper (b. c.1973, England), who is widely recognised among club and genre cognoscenti as the most talented arrival on the jazz/funk scene in the last decade. Classically trained on the piano, he went on to a deal with **Dorado** Records that allowed him to install a new digital recording studio in his own North London abode. Their relationship began with the singles 'No Time For Change' and 'Big City', whose featured vocalists included Cleveland Watkiss, with a bass line from Gary Crosby, before collaborating with fellow Dorado interns **D*Note** and jazzmen like Steve Williamson and Ronnie Laws. A third single, "Movin' On', was completed as a typically strong and energetic debut album was assembled in late 1993. Outside also comprise Patrice Blanchard (bass) and Byron Wallen (trumpet), plus various session musicians as the occasion demands.
Album: *Almost In* (Dorado 1993).

Outside Edge

Formerly known as **Blackfoot Sue** and Liner, this UK band switched to the name Outside Edge in 1984 to pursue an AOR direction. Comprising Tom Farmer (vocals/bass), Eddie Golga (guitar), Pete Giles (keyboards) and Dave Farmer (drums), they signed to **Warner Brothers** and released a self-titled debut in 1985. This was Americanized melodic rock, but featured rough and ragged vocals from Farmer, in contrast to the musical stylisation. *Running Hot* followed in 1986 and was produced by Terry Manning (of **Z.Z. Top** fame), but Outside Edge were still unable to break through on a commercial level. The Farmer brothers left in 1989 and the remaining duo recruited new members to become Little Wing.
Albums: *Outside Edge* (Warners 1985), *Running Hot* (10 1986).

Outsiders

Based in Cleveland, Ohio, the Outsiders was the brainchild of Tom King, a guitarist, composer and arranger. He was born in the city in 1944, and the group evolved from a duo he had formed with vocalist Sonny Geraci (b. 1948, Cleveland, Ohio, USA). Initially known as Tom King And The Starfires, the line-up was completed by Bill Bruno (b. 1946, Pittsburgh, Pennsylvania, USA; guitar), Met Madsen (b. Denmark; bass) and Rick Biagiola/Baker (b. 1949, Cleveland, Ohio, USA; drums). The Outsiders scored a million-selling single in 1966 with their debut release, 'Time Won't Let Me'. An infectious slice of classic American pop, it introduced a series of similarly excellent songs, which included the original version of 'Help Me Girl', later a hit for **Eric Burdon** And The **Animals** in 1966. Madsen was replaced by Ritchie D'Amato (b. 1949, Cleveland, Ohio, USA). By the following year the Outsiders' brand of unassuming pop was deemed anachronistic and their brief spell in the spotlight ended. Geraci subsequently fronted a new group, **Climax**, who scored a gold disc in 1971 with 'Precious And Few'.
Albums: *Time Won't Let Me* (1966), *The Outsiders Album #2* (1966), *Happening Live!* (1967), *In* (1967).

Ovations

An R&B vocal group from Memphis, Tennessee, USA. Lead singer Louis Williams sounded very much like **Sam Cooke**, and the group built their career on the merger of the Sam Cooke sound with southern gospel harmonies. Recording for the Goldwax label, their first hit in 1965 was 'It's Wonderful To Be In Love' (number 22 R&B, number 61 pop). Although coming out with a score of southern hits, they had only one other national hit on Goldwax with 'Me And My Imagination' (number 40 R&B) in 1967. The original group soon broke up, and Williams formed a new Ovations group with three former members of Ollie And The Nightingales, Rochester Neal, Bill Davis and Quincy Billops Jnr. They got on the charts again with the **MGM**-subsidiary label, Sounds Of Memphis. Reverting to the parent label, the group had its biggest hit in 1973 by fully exploiting Williams ability to sound like Sam Cooke with a remake of the singer's 1962 hit, 'Having A Party' (number 7 R&B, number 56 pop). The group never was able to hit the charts again and soon disbanded.

Overbea, Danny

b. 3 January 1926, Philadelphia, Pennsylvania, USA, d. 11 May 1994, Chicago, Illinois, USA. Guitarist and singer Overbea, who came out of the Chicago R&B scene, was one of the earliest pioneers of rock 'n' roll. He began his music career in 1946 and first recorded in 1950 as a vocalist on an **Eddie Chamblee** track. Overbea joined **Chess Records** in 1952, producing his best known songs, 'Train Train Train' (number 7 R&B) and '40 Cups Of Coffee', the following year. Both were essentially rock 'n' roll songs before the concept of 'rock 'n' roll' had even emerged. In the pop market 'Train Train Train' was covered by **Buddy Morrow** and '40 Cups Of Coffee' by **Ella Mae Morse**. By 1955, when rock 'n' roll was making its breakthrough on the pop charts, **Bill Haley And His Comets** recorded '40 Cups Of Coffee', which even though it did not chart proved to be one of the group's better efforts. Famed disc jockey **Alan Freed** featured Overbea many times in his early rock 'n' roll revues in Ohio and New York; his acrobatic back-bend to the floor while playing the guitar behind his head was always a highlight of the shows. Overbea was also a talented ballad singer (in the mode of **Billy Eckstine**, having most success with 'You're Mine' (also recorded by the **Flamingos**) and 'A Toast To Lovers'. Overbea made his last records in 1959 and retired from the music business in 1976.

Overdose

First sighted contributing a track to the *Metal Massacre 9* compilation, Brazilian thrash band Overdose actually started their career alongside the better known **Sepultura**, each band supplying one side to the *Brutal Devastation/Seculo XX* album in 1985. Afterwards the fortunes of the two bands diverged, and Overdose looked like becoming merely a footnote in the Sepultura story (Overdose vocalist B.Z., a graphic artist, also designed their logo). Claudio David (guitar), Sergio Cichovicz (guitar), Eddie Weber (bass), Andre Marcio (drums) and B.Z. kicked their heels while contractual problems were sorted out. They sustained themselves with a rigorous South American touring schedule which helped define their bombastic and potent sound. They also recorded profusely. 1994's *Progress Of Decadence* would prove to be their sixth album, but the first to be released in Europe, the group having previously sustained themselves with a staunch following in their native territory.

Selected album: *Progress Of Decadence* (Under One Flag 1994).

Overkill

This New York thrash metal quartet was formed in 1984 by vocalist Bobby Ellsworth, guitarist Bobby Gustafson, bassist D.D. Vernie and drummer Sid Falck. Together they self-financed the recording of a mini-album. Desperately short of cash and exposure, they sold the rights to the small Azra label and made a net loss. They were soon picked up by Megaforce, however, and released their full debut album in 1985. *Feel The Fire* was a brutal speed-metal riff assault, but lacked the variation in light and shade to compete with groups such as **Metallica** and **Anthrax**. Three more albums followed a similar pattern, with *Under The Influence* elevating their profile and courting comparisons with **Testament**. Following *The Years Of Decay*, Gustafson quit and was replaced by Rob Cannavino and Merrit Gant (ex-**Faith Or Fear**). Expanded to a quintet, the band recorded *Horrorscope*, their finest work to date. Unlike their earlier releases, they varied their approach and only switched to hyperspeed at crucial moments, in order to maximize the impact of their delivery. The album also featured an incredible cover of **Edgar Winter**'s 'Frankenstein'. Their reputation has continued to increase, following successful support slots on **Helloween** and **Slayer** tours, and a second excellent album in *I Hear Black*.

Albums: *Overkill* (Azra 1984, mini-album), *Feel The Fire* (Megaforce 1985), *Taking Over* (Megaforce 1987), *Under The Influence* (Megaforce 1988), *The Years Of Decay* (Megaforce 1989), *Horrorscope* (Megaforce 1991), *I Hear Black* (Megaforce 1993).

Overlanders

This UK vocal trio - Paul Arnold (aka Paul Friswell), Laurie Mason and Peter Bartholemew - initially pursued a folk-based career, but scored a surprise, if minor, US hit in 1964 with their version of 'Yesterday's Gone'. Buoyed by the addition of Terry Widlake (bass) and David Walsh (drums), they enjoyed a UK number 1 the following year with an opportunistic version of the **Beatles**' 'Michelle', but the reshaped group was unable to shake off a somewhat anachronistic image. A strong follow-up to their chart-topper, 'My Life', unfortunately failed to chart. Arnold left for a solo

career in 1966, but despite the arrival of Ian Griffiths, the Overlanders failed to reap reward from their early success.
Album: *The Overlanders* (1966).

Overlord X

b. c.1968. Hackney, London, England. Overlord X is a Brit-rapper who first arrived on Music Of Life's *Hard As Hell* compilation. However, he made his name with the verve of two excellent albums for **Island** Records, which were particularly successful in Europe. Indeed *X Versus The World* went platinum in France, making it the most popular hardcore hip hop album in that territory. Although not immediately recognisable as hardcore in the musical sense, there remained a lyrical exactitude which defied compromise. The influence of **Public Enemy** and Chuck D in particular has always been self-evident, notably on cuts like 'Prologue 1990', which featured a sample of the former's 'Bring The Noise'. However, Overlord had little time for **NWA**'s ghetto-romanticism: 'Trying to say we're niggers, who the fuck are you? Coming from this brother with an attitude' ('You Can't Do It In London'). An alliance with ragga stars Midrange and Kandy on *X Versus The World* proved his diversity. He also produced their recordings as part of the **X-Posse**, and began work on his own film and a documentary about Hackney. Perhaps Overlord X's influence in the medium of television has had the greatest impact, however. Terry Jarvis, a well-known BBC producer, directed the promo clip, '14 Days In May', through which Janet Street-Porter commissioned him to provide continuity links between sections of *Def II*. He subsequently became producer for that show for 18 months, before providing the title-song and music for sit-com *The Real McKoy*. However, a 1992 record deal with Jarvis was less successful. His imprint, Down To Jam, was financed by **Motown**, but its life span was truncated by financial considerations. Overlord X, no longer employing that name, regrouped in 1994 as part of Benz.
Albums: *Weapon Is My Lyric* (Mango Street 1988), *X Versus The World* (Mango Street 1990).

Overstreet, Paul

b. 17 March 1955, Van Cleave, Missouri, USA. Overstreet moved to Nashville in 1973 and was married for a short time to **Dolly Parton**'s sister, Frieda. It was not until 1982 that he made an impression as a songwriter. **George Jones** had a US country hit with 'Same Old Me' and Overstreet was able to 'buy a lot of booze and drugs and a new car'. The country hits continued with 'Diggin' Up Bones', 'On The Other Hand' and 'Forever And Ever, Amen', all for **Randy Travis**, and 'You're Still New To Me', a duet for **Marie Osmond** and **Paul Davis**. In 1985 and with the help of his new wife, Julie, Paul Overstreet decided to giving up drinking and drugs and devote his time to God and his family. This new lifestyle is reflected in many of his songs. He was part of the band **SKO** in 1986/7 and then had another US country number 1 with 'I Won't Take Less Than Your Love', which he performed with **Tanya Tucker** and Paul Davis. He wrote 'When You Say Nothing At All' (**Keith Whitley**), 'A Long Line Of Love' (**Michael Martin Murphey**) and 'Love Can Build A Bridge' (**Judds**) as well as having his own country hits with 'Seein' My Father In Me', 'Richest Man On Earth' and 'Daddy's Come Around', which was a number 1.
Albums: *Paul Overstreet* (RCA 1982), *Sowin' Love* (RCA 1989), *Heroes* (RCA 1990), *Love Is Strong* (RCA 1992).

Overstreet, Tommy

b. Thomas Cary Overstreet, 10 September 1937, Oklahoma City, Oklahoma, USA. He grew up in Houston, the home town of his uncle, the 30s pop singer **Gene Austin**, and learned to play the guitar at the age of 14. Here he first appeared on KTHT radio and in a local production of *Hit The Road* but after completing high school, he moved to Abilene. During 1956-57, he studied radio and television production at the University of Texas and also featured on Slim Willett's local television show, at one time appearing as Terry Dean from Abilene. Between 1957 and 1964 (military service excepted), he toured with Gene Austin, after which he worked for a time as a songwriter with **Pat Boone**'s Cooga Music in Los Angeles. He recorded, without success, for Dunhill and eventually returned to Texas. In 1967, he moved to Nashville, where his University training saw him become manager of **Dot Records**' office. He also recorded for the label and after two minor hits, he scored a Top 5 US country and minor pop hit with 'Gwen (Congratulations)'. This launched his career and, during the 70s, he registered 27 ***Billboard*** country chart hits. Although he never achieved a number 1, he did have Top 3 hits with 'Ann (Don't Go Runnin')', 'Heaven Is My Woman's Love' and '(Jeannie Marie) You Were A Lady'. He was never solely a country performer and with his band Nashville Express, he toured extensively both in the USA and to Europe. (He played at the Wembley Festival in London in 1977). He was at one time especially popular in Germany, where a recording of 'Heaven Is My Woman's Love', sung in German, was a hit. He appeared on most of the top US television programmes and made guest appearances on the *Grand Ole Opry* and *Hee-Haw*. He left Dot in 1979 and had six minor hits on **Elektra**, including 'What More Could A Man Need', but by the early 80s he was recording for minor labels. By this time, he had become a polished cabaret style entertainer, far removed from any country roots. Many may perhaps doubt that any really ever existed. He had a minor chart hit with 'Next To You' in 1986.
Albums: *Gwen (Congratulations)* (1971), *This Is Tommy Overstreet* (1972), *Heaven Is My Woman's Love* (1972), *My Friends Call Me T.O.* (1973), *Woman Your Name Is My Song* (1974), *I'm A Believer* (1975), *Live From The Silver Slipper*

(1975), *Turn On To Tommy Overstreet* (1976), *Vintage '77* (1977), *Hangin' Around* (1977), *A Better Me (10th Anniversary Album)* (1978), *There'll Never Be Another First Time* (1978), *The Real Tommy Overstreet* (1979), *I'll Never Let You Down* (1979), *I Can Hear Kentucky Calling* (1980), *Tommy Overstreet* (1982), *Dream Maker* (1983).

Owen, Reg

b. February 1928, England. Owen was a British bandleader who reached the US and UK charts in 1959 with his version of the song 'Manhattan Spiritual', written by Billy Maxted. The song was issued on the small Palette label in the USA and began its climb in December 1958, ultimately reaching number 10 in February 1959. Meanwhile, the record was issued in England on Pye International, where it reached number 20. Owen placed one other single on the English chart, 'Obsession', in 1960, and although he continued to record, there were no further chart successes on either side of the Atlantic. None of his albums, including those recorded for **RCA Records** prior to the 'Manhattan Spiritual' success, charted in either country.

Albums: *I'll Sing You A Thousand Love Songs* (1958), *Girls Were Made To Take Care Of Boys* (1959), *Cuddle Up A Little Closer* (1959), *Manhattan Spiritual* (1959), *Fiorello* (1959).

Owens, Bonnie

b. Bonnie Campbell, 1 October 1932, Blanchard, Oklahoma, USA. Bonnie was a yodelling country singer, who married **Buck Owens** in 1947. Their son, Alvis Alan Owens (b. 22 May 1948), became the singer, Buddy Alan. Buck and Bonnie Owens toured together and had a radio series in Arizona. They divorced in 1953 but both moved to Bakersfield in the early 60s, where she made her first records, 'Dear John Letter', 'Why Daddy Don't Live Here Anymore' and 'Don't Take Advantage Of Me'. After a relationship with **Merle Haggard**'s manager, Fuzzy Owen, she married Haggard in 1965, becoming part of his stage-show and recording a successful duet album with him. Their marriage was unusual in that Owens tolerated Haggard's affairs - 'I don't care what you do so long as you don't flaunt it in my face', she is reputed to have said. In 1970 they co-wrote 'Today I Started Loving You Again'. She stopped performing in 1975 to look after their family and business interests. They divorced in 1978 but she is now an integral part of his road show.

Albums: *Don't Take Advantage Of Me* (1965), with Merle Haggard *Just Between The Two Of Us* (1966), *Your Tender Loving Care* (1967), *All Of Me Belongs To You* (1967), *Somewhere Between* (1968), *Hi-Fi To Cry By* (1969), *Lead Me On* (1969), *Mother's Favourite Hymns* (1971).

Owens, Buck

b. Alvis Edgar Owens Jnr., 12 August 1929, Sherman, Texas, USA. Buck Owens became one of the leading country music stars of the 60s and 70s, along with **Merle Haggard**, the leading exponent of the 'west coast sound'. Owens gave himself the nickname Buck at the age of three, after a favourite horse. When he was 10, his family moved to Mesa, Arizona, where Owens picked cotton and 13 years of age began playing the mandolin. He soon learned guitar, horns and drums as well. Owens performed music professionally at the age of 16, starring, along with partner Ray Britten, in his own radio programme. He also worked with the group Mac's Skillet Lickers, and at 17 married their singer, Bonnie Campbell, who later launched her own career as **Bonnie Owens**. The couple bore a son, who also had a country music career as Buddy Alan. In 1951 Owens and his family moved to Bakersfield, California, at the suggestion of an uncle who said work was plentiful for good musicians. Owens joined the Orange Blossom Playboys, with which he both sang and played guitar for the first time, and then formed his own band, the Schoolhouse Playboys. Owens made ends meet by taking on work as session guitarist in Los Angeles, appearing on recordings by **Sonny James**, **Wanda Jackson**, **Tommy Sands** and **Gene Vincent**. When the Playboys disbanded in the mid-50s Owens joined country artist **Tommy Collins** as singer and guitarist, recording a few tracks with him.

In 1955-56 Owens recorded his first singles under his own name, for Pep Records, using the name Corky Jones for rockabilly and his own name for country recordings. Owens signed to **Capitol Records** in March 1957. It was not until his fourth release, 'Second Fiddle', that he made any mark, reaching number 24 on ***Billboard***'s country chart. His next, 'Under Your Spell Again', made number 4, paving the way for over 75 country hits, more than 40 of which made that chart's Top 10. Among the biggest and best were 'Act Naturally' (1963), later covered by the **Beatles**, 'Love's Gonna Live Here' (1963), 'My Heart Skips A Beat' (1964), 'Together Again' (1964), 'I've Got A Tiger By The Tail' (1965), 'Before You Go' (1965), 'Waitin' In Your Welfare Line' (1966), 'Think Of Me' (1966), 'Open Up Your Heart' (1966) and a cover of **Chuck Berry**'s 'Johnny B. Goode' (1969), all of which were number 1 country singles. Owens recorded a number of duets, with singer Susan Raye, and also his son Buddy Alan. He also released more than 100 albums during his career. In addition, his compositions were hits by other artists, notably **Emmylou Harris** ('Together Again') and **Ray Charles** ('Crying Time'). Owens' band, the Buckaroos (guitarist Don Rich, bassist Doyle Holly, steel guitarist Tom Brumley and drummer Willie Cantu), was also highly regarded. Their down-to-basics, honky-tonk instrumental style helped define the Bakersfield sound - Owens' recordings never relied on strings or commercialized, sweetened pop arrangements. The Buckaroos also

released several albums on their own. In 1969, Owens joined as co-host the country music television variety programme *Hee Haw*, which combined comedy sketches and live performances by country stars. He stayed with the show until the mid-80s, long after his Capitol contract expired, and he had signed with **Warner Brothers Records** (1976). Although Owens continued to place singles in the country charts with Warners, his reign as a top country artist had faltered in the mid-70s and he retired from recording and performing to run a number of business interests, including a radio station and recording studio, in Bakersfield. In 1988, country newcomer **Dwight Yoakam** convinced Owens to join him in recording a remake of Owens' song 'Streets Of Bakersfield'. It reached number 1 in the country chart and shed new light on Owens. He signed with Capitol again late in 1988 and recorded a new album, *Hot Dog*, featuring re-recordings of old Owens songs and cover songs of material by Chuck Berry, **Eddie Cochran** and others. Although Owens had not recaptured his earlier status by the early 90s, he had become active again, recording and touring, including one tour as a guest of Yoakam.
Selected albums: *Buck Owens Sings Harlan Howard* (1961), *Under Your Spell Again* (1961), *Together Again/My Heart Skips A Beat* (1964), *The Instrumental Hits Of Buck Owens And The Buckaroos* (1965), *I've Got A Tiger By The Tail* (1965), *Carnegie Hall Concert* (1966), *Buck Owens In London* (1969), *Big In Vegas* (1970), with Susan Raye *We're Gonna Get Together* (1970), *I Wouldn't Live In New York City* (1971), *The Songs Of Merle Haggard* (1972), *Hot Dog* (1988), *Act Naturally* (1989), *Blue Love* (1993, CD reissue). Compilations: *The Best Of Buck Owens* (1964), *The Best Of Buck Owens, Volume 2* (1968), *The Buck Owens Story Vol. 1 (1956-64), Vol. 2 (1964-68), Vol. 3 (1969-89)* (Personality 1994).

Owens, Calvin

b. 1929, Houston, Texas, USA. His Creole mother told her son stories about **Louis Armstrong**, so when Calvin got to be 13 he wanted to play the trumpet. A year later, he joined up with the Leonard Dunkins Revue, a vaudeville band that played all kinds of music and at the time featured **Willie Mae Thornton** as one of its singers. After that, Owens led a series of bands of his own, as well as touring Texas, Oklahoma and Louisiana with various **territory bands**. During the 40s, his band backed men such as **Big Joe Turner** and **T-Bone Walker** when they were in town. Owens also worked with the young **Amos Milburn**, and also **Leroy Ervin** and **Lightnin' Hopkins**. In 1949, he toured briefly with the Brownskin Models before joining I.H. Smalley's band, who regularly backed guitarist **Lester Williams**. Owens also worked in the houseband at the Eldorado Ballroom until 1953, when **B.B. King** asked him to join his touring group. That gig lasted for four years and Owens ended up as King's music director. He returned to Houston in 1957 and became an A&R director for **Don Robey**, appearing on many Duke and Peacock recordings. In 1979, he returned to work for B.B. King for another five years, appearing on *Live At Ole Miss* and *Live In London*, for which he also wrote the arrangements. During this time he got married and settled in Belgium, his wife's home country. *True Blue* was recorded there, with guest appearances by King and **Johnny Copeland**, and it successfully recreated the heyday of big band blues, with lavish brass arrangements and driving rhythm.
Album: *True Blue* (Sequel 1993).

Owens, Jack

b. 1905, Bentonia, Mississippi, USA. Along with **Skip James** and the unrecorded Henry Stuckey, Owens was one of the originators of the distinctive blues style developed in Bentonia after World War I, featuring 'deep' lyrics much concerned with death and loneliness, given a high and melismatic delivery. The complex, three finger guitar accompaniment, often in an eerie E minor tuning, blends inextricably with the equally eerie vocal line. Owens was not recorded until 1966, but proved to be a major musician, playing very extended songs with long guitar breaks. He was proud of his guitar prowess and, though fondest of E minor, could play in seven tunings. He has lived in Bentonia all his life, farming and at one time operating a juke joint. His wife's death in 1985 allowed him to play a few concerts further afield; in 1989 he played in Chicago, still a master musician at 84.
Albums: *It Must Have Been The Devil* (1971), *Bentonia Country Blues* (1979), *50 Years - Mississippi Blues In Bentonia* (1991).

Owens, Jimmy

b. 9 December 1943, New York, USA. Owens went to the High School of Music and Art in New York when he was aged 14. He then studied composition with Henry Bryant and trumpet with **Donald Byrd**. In the 60s, after Marshall Brown's Newport Youth Band, he played with the bands of **Slide Hampton**, **Lionel Hampton**, **Maynard Ferguson**, **Gerry Mulligan**, **Charles Mingus** and **Herbie Mann**. Owens worked briefly with **Duke Ellington** and **Count Basie** and was a member of the **Thad Jones-Mel Lewis** band. During the early 70s he played with drummer **Billy Cobham** as well as in **Billy Taylor**'s band on the *Frost Show* and continued the work he had started with Collective Black Artists Inc. (1969) and Jazzmobile. He has been on the music panel of the New York State Council on the Arts and was musical director of the **New York Jazz Repertory Company** (1974). Owens has written many extended pieces for the Brooklyn Philharmonic Orchestra. The foundation of his music remains in the blues. He plays with a prodigious technique and clear, ringing tone. He

has had a special four valve fluegelhorn made for him. In 1979 he toured with the Mingus Dynasty band.
Albums: with Charles Mingus *The Black Saint And The Sinner Lady* (1963), with Mingus *Live At Monterey* (1965), with Gerald Wilson *The Golden Sword* (1966), *No Escaping It* (1970), *Young Man On The Move* (1976), *Heading Home* (1978), with Billy Cobham *Spectrum* (1973), with Mingus Dynasty *Chair In The Sky* (1979).

Owens, Robert

A long time collaborator with **Mr Fingers** in Fingers Inc, Owens provided the vocal for early house classics like 'Washing Machine' and 'Music Takes Me Up'. He also sang on classics like **Frankie Knuckles'** 'Tears' and (uncredited) on the **Bobby Konders**' production, Jus' Friends' 'As One'. Ownes grew up, inspired by **Stevie Wonder**, **Patti Labelle** and others, with a church choir background, going on to sing in several bands. As a youth he travelled between his Los Angeles-based mother and Chicago-stabled father, where he was first introduced to house music. Ironically his first experience of a warehouse party left him overpowered, and he left after fifteen minutes. He would later watch the assembled masses through a window, and decided to begin DJing himself, combining deck skills with his own vocals. It was at this point that he was introduced to Larry Heard, aka Mr Fingers. Owens would select from the tunes presented to him by Fingers and choose the ones he wished to write lyrics for. This paved the ground for Owens' breakthrough performance on Fingers Inc's 'Can You Feel It?'. When his songwriting partnership with Fingers broke up due to financial pressures, he recreated the method with **Frankie Knuckles** and **David Morales** (hardly a step down in quality) for his debut solo album. He was eventually dropped from his contract with **Island** in 1992 despite US success with 'I'll Be Your Friend' (which came out on **Paul Oakenfold**'s **Perfecto**, and was remixed by Morales and Satoshi Tomiie) and the self-produced 'You Gotta Work'. Owens remains one of house music's great showmen, offering uplifting live sets with his Freetown posse (which was also the name of the label he helped establish). Earlier he had been the star turn on the first house package tour to London which arrived on English shores in February 1987. 1994 saw him defect to the Musical Directions imprint.
Album: *Rhythms In Me* (4th & Broadway 1990).

Owens, Tex

b. Doie Hensley Owens, 15 June 1892, Killeen, Texas, USA, d. 9 September 1962, New Baden, Texas, USA. The eldest of the 13 children of a sharecropper family that included sister **Texas Ruby**, who married fiddler **Curly Fox**, and who was a very popular country singer at the time of her tragic death in 1963. The family relocated to Oklahoma where, at 15 as 'Tex', he worked on ranches and briefly with touring shows as a singer and guitarist. For some years, he drifted around and worked on oil fields and railroad bridge building. He married Maude Neal in 1916. From 1920-22, he was a town marshal in Kansas and in the mid-20s, was working as a mechanic for a Chevrolet dealer. In 1932, after beginning to write songs seriously, he had his own show on KMBC Kansas City, Missouri and also appeared on KMBC's *Brush Creek Follies*. In 1934, he made two recordings with a KMBC group, the Texas Rangers (who appeared on his show but were not his band) and four solo numbers including his now famous 'Cattle Call'. His show, which at times included his two daughters singing as Joy And Jane, proved so popular that it was networked by CBS and lasted on KMBC for over 11 years. It is possible that the show even appeared on early television broadcasts in 1932. Ten 1936 **RCA**-Victor recordings were unissued and seemingly are now lost. After KMBC, he starred on and co-hosted *Boone County Jamboree* in Cincinnati, before moving to KHJ Hollywood to do radio work and hopefully some film work. He broke his back when his horse fell on him during filming for the John Wayne film *Red River*. (Owens spent over a year in hospital and later found that his scenes had been cut from the movie). He made his final four recordings in Hollywood in 1953-54, with backing that included his guitarist brother Charles. In 1960, he retired to his native State where he died at New Baden, on 9 September 1962. He wrote over 100 songs and, in 1971, he was posthumously elected to the Nashville Songwriters Hall Of Fame. His song 'Cattle Call' has become a country standard, recorded by countless artists but none with more success than the million selling RCA-Victor version made by **Eddy Arnold** in 1955. Owens' eldest daughter (as **Laura Lee McBride**) later became known for her vocal work with **Bob Wills**.
Album: *Tex Owens - Cattle Call* (Bear Family 1994).

Owoh, Orlando

b. 1942, Owo, Nigeria. Guitarist, vocalist and composer Owoh is amongst the handful of Nigerian musicians who has remained within the highlife tradition throughout his career - even when the style was eclipsed by juju, apala and fuji and audiences and record sales dwindled. Playing in an acoustic style known as toye, he continues today to be popular with Yoruba audiences (although those audiences are of Owoh's own generation, with few younger people within them). He began playing professionally in the early 60s, as a percussionist, first with the Fakunle Major Band and then with Kehinde Adex. Moving to the capital, Lagos, in 1965, he learnt guitar from Fatai Rolling Dollar, and spent the years 1967-70 in the Nigerian army, then at war with the secessionist Biafran state. At the conclusion of the war, Owoh returned to music, forming his own Omimah Band and enjoying a sizeable local hit with the single 'Oriki Ilu Oke'. In 1976, now a major star throughout Western (Yoruba) Nigeria, he renamed the band the Young Kenneries. His last period of major success came in the early 80s, before the wholesale triumph of juju music, when he recorded a string of singles riddled with double entendres.

Albums: *In Great Britain* (1972), *Okiki Ojo* (1975), *Easter Special* (1977), *Money For Hand Back For Ground* (1979), *Ganja Part* 2 (1981), *In The Sixties* (1983), *Asotito Aiye* (1984), *Foufou* (1986).

Oxford, Vernon

b. 8 June 1941, Benton County, Arkansas, USA. Oxford comes from a musical, church-going family, and his father passed his fiddle-playing talent onto his son. He was given a guitar when he was 13-years-old and has been singing country and country/gospel ever since. In 1964 he moved to Nashville with his wife, Loretta, and, after being turned down by several companies, **RCA Records** signed him, releasing a single and an album, both called 'Woman, Let Me Sing You A Song'. Oxford's recordings are a throwback to the rural honky tonk sound of **Hank Williams** with a voice to match, but he claims, 'I am being me. I sing a lot of Hank's songs but I never set out intentionally to imitate him. I guess we're both country boys and we both sing from the heart.' RCA dropped Oxford when his records didn't sell, but a contingent of British fans lobbied RCA so hard that they reversed the decision. RCA released a UK double-album in its *Famous Country Music Makers* series, although Oxford was anything but famous at the time. Oxford won more British fans with UK appearances, particularly at Wembley Country Music Festivals. He made the US country charts with 'The Shadows Of My Mind' and then, in 1976, with his controversial 'Redneck! (The Redneck National Anthem)', written by Mitchell Torok, and, in the same vein, 'Redneck Roots' and 'A Good Old Fashioned Saturday Night Honky Tonk Barroom Brawl'. He also recorded a humorous duet with Jim Ed Brown called 'Mowing The Lawn'. He claims he just dreamed the words and music of his own songs, 'She's Always There' and 'Better Way Of Life'. Since 1977, Oxford has not had chart success in the USA, but that is not one of his objectives. He says, 'Going to church doesn't make you a Christian, and, in 1978, I was born again, even though I was a Baptist already'. However, Oxford, the subject of a BBC-television documentary, says, 'I do cheating songs but now I do them to represent what sin is: I use them to make a point about Jesus Christ. 'Redneck!' shows what I used to be before I was saved. I sing gospel songs at the end of every show and tell them about the Truth. Sometimes I combine singing with preaching. When I called a girl out of the audience once, the power of God knocked her down and she slithered like a snake across the floor. I have found peace and happiness and I would like to help others to find it too.'

Albums: *Woman, Let Me Sing You A Song* (1966), *Famous Country Music Makers* (1973), *By Public Demand* (1975), *America's Unknown Superstar* (1976), *I Just Want To Be A Country Singer* (1976), *Tribute To Hank Williams* (1978), *Nobody's Child* (1978), *If I Had My Wife To Love Over* (1979), *Keepin' It Country* (1979), *I Love To Sing* (1980), *His And Hers* (1980), *A Better Way Of Life* (1981), *Pure Country* (1982), *The Tradition Continues* (1983), *Power In The Blood* (1989), *100% Country* (1990).

Oxley, Tony

b. 15 June 1938, Sheffield, Yorkshire, England. Oxley began to teach himself piano at the age of eight, and did not pursue the drums seriously until he was 17. During his National Service (1957-60) he studied drums and theory and for the following four years he led his own group in Sheffield. From 1963-67 he worked with **Derek Bailey** and bassist/composer Gavin Bryars in developing an abstract, freely improvised genre. In 1966 he moved to London, and was for some years in the house band at **Ronnie Scott**'s club, backing many famous visiting musicians. He was also in Scott's octet, the Band, and worked with **Howard Riley**, **Gordon Beck**, **Alan Skidmore**, **Mike Pyne** and **Barry Guy**'s **London Jazz Composers Orchestra** (LJCO). In 1970 he co-founded Incus Records with **Evan Parker** and Bailey and was a founder member of the London Musicians' Co-operative, and from 1973 was an organizing tutor at the Barry Summer School in Wales. In the mid-70s he led his own band, Angular Apron, which included Riley, Guy and Dave Holdsworth. In 1978 he moved to East Germany, then (clandestinely) to West Germany in 1981, but has returned to the UK for concerts. He also plays in the trio SOH (with Skidmore and Ali Havrand), with **Didier Levallet** and in the Quartet. Since the late 80s he has been a regular associate of **Cecil Taylor**, playing in the pianist's Feel Trio and recording the *Leaf Palm Hand* duo with him at FMP's special Taylor festival in Berlin in 1988. His Celebration Orchestra comprised four brass players, six strings, piano and five drummers, but he enjoys small group improvising best: witness the excellence of the trio Coe, Oxley & Co. (with **Tony Coe** and **Chris Laurence**). Oxley is a highly-skilled and versatile drummer whose fierce dedication to his music has gained him a reputation for being a difficult person to deal with. His playing is, however, that of a responsive and supportive colleague.

Albums: *The Baptised Traveller* (1969), *Four Compositions For Sextet* (1970), *Ichnos* (1971), with Alan Davie *Duo* (1974), *Tony Oxley* (Incus 1975), *February Papers* (1977), *Nutty (On) Willisau* (1984), with Phil Wachsmann *The Glider And The Grinder* (1987), *Tomorrow Is Here* (1988), with Cecil Taylor *Leaf Palm Hand* (1989), *The Tony Oxley Quartet* (Incus 1993).

Oyster Band

The Oyster Band entry was withdrawn at the request of band member John James.

Albums: *Jack's Alive* (1980), *English Rock 'N' Roll - The Early Years 1800-1850* (1982), *Lie Back And Think Of England* (1983), *20 Golden Tie-Slackeners* (1984), *Liberty Hall* (1985), *Step Outside* (Cooking Vinyl 1986), *Wide Blue Yonder* (1987), *Freedom And Rain* (1990), *Deserters* (Cooking Vinyl 1992), *Holy Bandits* (1993).

Oz

This Finnish heavy metal outfit was formed by The Oz (vocals) and Eero Hamalainen (guitar) in 1977. Complemented by Kari Elo (bass) and Tauno Vajavaara (drums), they adopted an approach that fused elements of **Black Sabbath** and **Motörhead** into a violent power chord frenzy. It took five years before the band made their debut with *The Oz*, a heavy rock album, which suffered from a budget production and weak vocals. Elo and Hamalainen were fired shortly after the album's release, with bassist Jay C. Blade and guitarists Speedy Foxx and Spooky Wolff recruited as replacements. The band relocated to Sweden and produced *Fire In The Brain*, a collection of tough and uncompromising power-metal songs not dissimilar to the work of **Judas Priest**. It served to bring them to the attention of **RCA Records** who offered them a European deal. The two albums that followed, however, were disappointing. Oz had moved away from their metallic roots and experimented with a greater use of melody, and this approach did not suit. It came as no surprise when they lost their contract. Disillusioned, the band split up in 1987 before reforming two years later (with no original members). Comprising Ape De Martini (vocals), Mark Ruffneck (drums), T.B. Muen (bass), Michael Loreda (guitar) and Mike Paul (guitar), they entered the studio to start work on new material in vain pursuit of former glories.

Albums: *The Oz* (Kraf 1982), *Fire In The Brain* (Wave 1983), *III Warning* (RCA 1984), *Decibel Storm* (RCA 1986).

Ozark Mountain Daredevils

One of country-rock's more inventive exponents, the Ozark Mountain Daredevils featured the songwriting team of John Dillon (b. 6 February 1947, Stuttgart, Arkansas, USA; guitar/fiddle/vocals) and Steve Cash (b. 5 May 1946, Springfield, Missouri, USA; harmonica/vocals) with Randle Chowning (guitar/vocals), Buddy Brayfield (keyboards), Michael 'Supe' Granda (b. 24 December 1950, St. Louis, Missouri, USA; bass) and Larry Lee (b. 5 January 1947, Springfield, Missouri, USA; drums). The group were originally based in Springfield, Missouri. Their acclaimed debut album, recorded in London under the aegis of producer **Glyn Johns**, contained the US Top 30 single, 'If You Want To Get To Heaven', while a second success, 'Jackie Blue' which reached number 3, came from the group's follow-up collection, *It'll Shine When It Shines*. Recorded at Chowning's ranch, this excellent set showcased the Ozarks' strong harmonies and intuitive musicianship, factors maintained on subsequent releases, *The Car Over The Lake Album* and *Men From Earth*. A 1978 release, *It's Alive*, fulfilled the group's obligation to **A&M Records** and two years later they made their debut on **CBS**. Paradoxically the Ozarks' subsequent work lacked the purpose of those early releases although the unit continues to enjoy a cult popularity. The group was reactivated in the late-80s by Dillon and Cash with Granda, Steve Canaday (b. 12 September 1944, Springfield, Missouri, USA; drums) and D. Clinton Thompson (guitar) and the resulting album, *Modern History*, released on the UK independent Conifer label, found the Ozarks with a new lease of life.

Albums: *Ozark Mountain Daredevils* (1973), *It'll Shine When It Shines* (1974), *The Car Over The Lake Album* (1975), *Men From Earth* (1976), *Don't Look Down* (1978), *It's Alive* (1978), *Ozark Mountain Daredevils* (1980), *Modern History* (1989). Compilation: *The Best Of The Ozark Mountain Daredevils* (1983).

Ozone

Ozone were formed in Nashville, Tennessee, USA, in 1977 by three former members of the funk band the Endeavors, Benny Wallace, Jimmy Stewart and Charles Glenn. This trio recruited Thomas Bumpass, William White, Ray Woodard, Greg Hargrove and Paul Hines to lend them instrumental and vocal support. The group perfected a mix of up-tempo dance material and romantic ballads that was heavily influenced by the **Commodores**, and they were signed to the same record label as their mentors in 1979. **Motown** initially used Ozone as backing musicians for artists like **Billy Preston** and **Syreeta**, before allowing them to record the first in a series of low-key albums in 1980. The instrumental 'Walk On' brought them an initial taste of chart success, but like their subsequent black-music hits, it failed to cross over into the pop market.

Albums: *Walk On* (1980), *Jump On It* (1981), *Send It* (1981), *Li'l Suzy* (1982), *Glasses* (1983).

Ozone, Makoto

b. 1961, Kobe, Japan. Makoto is the son of one of Japan's best jazz pianists, Minoru Ozone. He started on the organ at the age of four and was later much impressed by the organ playing of **Jimmy Smith**. He took up the piano in his teens after hearing **Oscar Peterson**. Ozone has a prodigious technique and a wide knowledge of jazz piano styles. In 1980 he went to the USA to study composing and arranging at the **Berklee College Of Music**. He played a Carnegie Hall recital to open the Kool Jazz Festival of 1983. On Ozone's arrival at Berklee he immediately impressed **Gary Burton** and was playing regularly with his quartet in 1985 when he was also playing in a duo with **Michel Petrucciani**. Alongside his jazz activities he is studying classical piano playing.

Albums: *Makoto Ozone* (1984), with Chuck Loeb *My Shining Hour* (1988), with Gary Burton *Real Life Hits* (1985).

Ozric Tentacles

Predominantly an 80s UK festival band, Ozric Tentacles was originally a name conjured up by the band for a psychedelic breakfast cereal. Their original line-up featured Ed Wynne (guitar), his brother Roly (bass), Nick 'Tig' Van Gelder (drums), Gavin Griffiths (guitar) and Joie 'Ozrooniculator' Hinton (keyboards). They met at an open camp fire at Stonehenge in 1982. By the following year a second synthesizer player, Tom Brookes had joined. They started gigging in clubs such as the 'Crypt' in Deptford, south-east London. There they met their second percussionist, Paul Hankin. They soon became regulars at another psychedelic 'head' venue, the Club Dog, at the George Robey pub in Finsbury Park, north London. The band's long existence has seen a number of shifts in personnel. In 1984 Griffiths left to form the Ullulators, and Brookes left a year later. Hinton remained but also played for the aforementioned Ullulators and also the Oroonies. The next major change arrived in 1987 when Merv Peopler replaced Van Gelder. More recently Steve Everett has replaced Brookes on synthesizers, while Marcus Carcus and John Egan have added extra percussion and flute. Considering their lengthy career it might appear that the band have had a relatively sporadic, and recent, recording output. However, much of their work from the mid-80s onwards was made available on six cassette-only albums. Into the early 90s, with the British neo-hippy, new age travellers receiving a higher media profile and their role in organizing music festivals becoming increasingly important, bands such as the Ozric Tentacles and the **Levellers** benefited greatly and began to widen their audience.

Albums: *Pungent Effulgent* (Dovetail 1989), *Erp Land* (Dovetail 1990), *Strangeitude* (Dovetail 1991), *Jurassic Shift* (Dovetail 1993), *Aborescence* (Dovetail 1994).

Ozz

This American hard rock project was founded by vocalist Alexis T. Angel and guitarist Gregg Parker. Using session musicians to complete the band they debuted with *Prisoners* in 1980. Produced by Andy Johns, Parker's guitar work proved exemplary and provided the perfect foil for Angel's vocal acrobatics (comparisons to prime **Led Zeppelin** were frequently mooted). Parker then relocated to London in 1982 to form the short-lived Ninja, but interest remained high enough in his former project to generate the release of *Exploited*, a compilation of live material and studio out-takes.

Albums: *Prisoners* (Epic 1980), *Exploited* (Streamline 1983).

P.O.W.E.R.

Their initials standing for People Oppressed by the World's Empire Ruling elite, it would not take genre commentators long to predict a similarity in style and presentation to **Consolidated**. POWER too deal in doses of polemic rap spliced with heavy rhythmic surges and undulations. The group comprises Krys Kills and Che 'Minister Of Defence' - a rapper and DJ respectively who met while studying law at college in Portland, Oregon. Their debut single 'Racemixer' emerged on Nettwerk/Play It Again Sam Records, as did a follow-up album crammed with message-lyrics like 'Geurilla Warfare' and 'Modern Day Slavery'.
Album: *Dedicated To World Revolution* (Nettwerk 1994).

Pablo

b. Pablo Lubadika Porthos, 1952, Inongo, Zaire. Vocalist and guitarist Pablo first came to the attention of European African music enthusiasts in the early 80s, following the release of the **Island** label's soukous compilation album *Sound D'Afrique* and the tracks 'Mbanda' and 'Madeleina'. By this time he was already a major star in Zaire, having worked during the 70s with such bands as Orchestre Kara, Kim Bantous and Lovy Du Zaire. He was featured on **Sam Mangwana**'s first major hit 'Georgette Eckins'. Invited to join **Les Quatre Etoiles** in 1984, he declined, preferring to pursue a solo career as a vocalist, and a session career as a guitarist. His first UK release was *Pablo Pablo Pablo* in 1985.
Albums: *Idie* (1981), *Revient En Force* (1983), *En Action* (1984), *Pablo Pablo Pablo* (1985), with Tutu *Safula* (1987), *Concentration* (1988).

Pablo Cruise

Formed in 1973, this San Francisco-based group was founded when two ex-members of **Stoneground**, Cory Lerois (b. California, USA; keyboards) and Steve Price (b. California, USA; drums), were joined by Dave Jenkins (b. Florida, USA; guitar) and Bud Cockrell (b. Missouri, USA; bass) from **It's A Beautiful Day**. *Pablo Cruise* enjoyed critical acclaim for its astute blend of rich, jazz-influenced textures and accomplished instrumental work and while *Lifeline* enhanced this reputation, the quartet reaped commercial rewards when 'Whatcha Gonna Do?' from *A Place In The Sun* reached number 6 in the US singles chart. 'Love Will Find A Way' achieved the same position the following year, while promoting *Worlds Away* into the US Top 10, while 'Don't Want To Live Without It' also entered the Top 30 as the group adroitly added elements of disco to an already cosmopolitan approach. Former **Santana** bassist Bruce Day joined the group for *Part Of The Game*, replacing Cockrell, but he in turn was supplanted by John Pierce and second guitarist Angelo Rossi. Although *Reflector*, a collaboration with veteran R&B producer **Tom Dowd**, generated another hit in 'Cool Love', Pablo Cruise was increasingly viewed as moribund in the wake of the 'new wave'. Internal problems led to further wholesale changes and a period of inactivity followed the release of *Out Of Our Hands*, after which the line-up reverted to that of the original quartet.
Albums: *Pablo Cruise* (1975), *Lifeline* (1976), *A Place In The Sun* (1977), *Worlds Away* (1978), *Part Of The Game* (1979), *Reflector* (1981), *Out Of Our Hands* (1983).

Pablo, Augustus

b. Horace Swaby, c.1954, St. Andrew, Jamaica, West Indies. Pablo was responsible for putting the humble melodica on the musical map when one day in 1969 he walked into **Herman Chin-Loy**'s Aquarius Records shop clutching the instrument and was taken down to Randy's studio the following day to cut his first record, 'Iggy Iggy'. His next release for the same producer was the prototype 'Far East' sound of 'East Of The River Nile'. Moving from Chin-Loy to **Clive Chin** as his new producer at Randy's, the next single, 'Java', proved to be Pablo's biggest, and one of his most influential. Chin later worked on the classic instrumental set, *This Is Augustus Pablo,* on which Pablo played a number of lead keyboard instruments. He worked with other producers at this time, cutting 'Lovers Mood' for Leonard Chin, 'Hot And Cold' with **Lee Perry** and others for **Gussie Clarke**, **Keith Hudson** and **Bunny Lee**. Dissatisfied with the financial and artistic arrangements with the producers, Pablo set up his own label named Rockers, after the **sound system** he and his brother Garth operated. His first releases were a mixture of new versions of old **Studio One** rhythms; 'Skanking Easy' (from 'Swing Easy') and 'Frozen Dub' (from 'Frozen Soul'), plus original compositions 'Cassava Piece', '555 Crown Street' and 'Pablo's Theme Song'. *King Tubby Meets Rockers Uptown* is regarded by many as one of the finest dub albums of all time. It contains dubwise versions of most of Pablo's productions mixed by the legendary independent studio engineer **King Tubby**. Other artists have benefitted from Pablo's skills as a producer, notably **Jacob Miller**, **Hugh Mundell** and Tetrack. Pablo was also in demand as a session musician and played on countless recordings throughout the 70s. *East Of The River Nile* in 1978 remains his most compelling instrumental set after *This Is Augustus Pablo*. On this release, Pablo and his Rockers All Stars band, featuring guitarist Earl 'Chinna' Smith, created vast landscapes of rhythmic sound awash with Pablo's string synthesizer and melodica. The sound bore the unmistakable production stamp of Lee Perry's Black Ark studios.

The early 80s saw Pablo floundering somewhat in the early throes of the **dancehall** revolution, though he later rallied with his production of **Junior Delgado**'s 'Raggamuffin Year' single and album in 1986. Since then he has released a number of recordings with varying degrees of artistic success, both of his own music and that of artists such as **Yammie Bolo**, **Icho Candy**, Delroy Williams, Norris Reid and Blacka T. Ironically, he has managed to adapt to the new computerised technology that many of his fans blame for what they see as the decline in musicianship in reggae music in the 80s and 90s. A withdrawn slip of a man, often in ill-health, Pablo's music has, at its best, always reflected a humility and inner peace. Although most critics agree his influential and commercially successful period was over by the end of the 70s, his most recent instrumental set, *Blowing With The Wind*, was his best since *East Of The River Nile*, and belies criticisms of artistic demise.

Albums: *This Is Augustus Pablo* (Tropical 1974), *Thriller* (Tropical/Nationwide 1975), *Ital Dub* (Trojan 1975), *King Tubby Meets Rockers Uptown* (Clocktower 1977), *East Of The River Nile* (Message 1978), *Africa Must Be Free By 1983 Dub* (Greensleeves 1979), *Dubbing In A Africa* (Abraham 1979; same tracks as *Thriller*), *Earths Rightful Ruler* (Message 1982), *Rockers Meet King Tubby In A Fire House* (Shanachie 1982), *King David's Melody* (Alligator 1983), *Rising Sun* (Greensleeves 1986), *East Man Dub* (Greensleeves 1988), *Rockers Comes East* (Greensleeves 1988), *Blowing With The Wind* (Greensleeves 1990), *One Step Dub* (Greensleeves 1990), *Heartical Chant* (Rockers International 1992), *Pablo And Friends* (1992). With Junior Delgado: *Raggamuffin Dub* (Rockers International 1990). Compilations: *Original Rockers* (Greensleeves 1979), *Original Rockers 2* (Greensleeves 1989), *Authentic Golden Melodies* (Rockers International 1992).

Pacheco, Johnny

b. 25 March 1935, Santiago De Los Caballeros, Dominican Republic. The son of bandleader Rafael Azarias Pacheco, Johnny became a musician at an early age. He was 11 years old when his family emigrated to New York. While at school, he played tambora (a double-headed Dominican drum) at weekends with the meringue group of Dioris Valladares. He learnt to play the saxophone at school and formed a group called the Chuchulecos Boys with trombonist Barry Rogers, who later achieved fame with **Eddie Palmieri**'s band La Perfecta. Johnny later worked with artists such as **Pérez Prado**, **Xavier Cugat** and **Tito Puente**. In 1959 **Charlie Palmieri** encountered Pacheco playing flute at the Monte Carlo Ballroom in New York and recruited him to his band. Johnny initially played timbales, but when trumpeter Mario Cora departed to live in Puerto Rico, Pacheco took over on flute. He appeared on the 1960 debut album, *Let's Dance The Charanga!*, by Palmieri's flute, strings, rhythm section and voices band, Charanga 'La Duboney', on the United Artists label, which was reissued under the title *Echoes Of An Era*. The two musicians parted company in 1960. Most accounts have highlighted 'musical differences', but Latin music historian Max Salazar gives another perspective: '. . . this red-hot charanga (flute and violin) band was in great demand as its name began to appear on posters for two and three dances on the same evening. (Palmieri and Pacheco booked the gigs in different parts of town.) The dancers let Charlie know that they felt robbed and the high price of tickets entitled them to his band for an entire evening. When Palmieri decided that he alone would book the band, Pacheco left to form his own charanga band . . .' (quote from article 'Remembering Charlie Palmieri', 1989).

Pacheco debuted with his own band in 1960 on *Pacheco y su Charanga Vol. I*, which was the first album released on the Alegre label, founded by **Al Santiago**. The record was a best seller and contained the smash hit 'El Güiro De Macorina', which shot to the top of the *Farándula* New York chart in February 1961. Johnny and his charanga band issued a further four volumes on Alegre. His lead singers included Elliot Romero, Rudy Calzado and **Pete 'El Conde' Rodríguez**, who joined on volume four. Pacheco's was the most successful band during the charanga and pachanga craze from 1960-64. In 1961, Johnny played flute with the Alegre All-Stars on their first descarga (latin jam session) album. ' . . . I cut my own throat', said Al Santiago in a 1989 interview, 'when the album came out and I named Charlie (Palmieri) as leader of the Alegre All-Stars - Pacheco from that point down didn't want to have anything to do with the Alegre All-Stars. That's why he was never on any other album except the first.'

Pacheco befriended Jerry Masucci (b. 1935, Brooklyn, New York, USA), an Italian-American lawyer who had dealt with his divorce. When Masucci became aware that Johnny was discontented with his record company, he proposed that they form their own label. With an initial investment of five thousand dollars, they founded Fania Records in 1964. For the first release on the label, *Cañonazo*, Pacheco dropped flute and violins and adopted the Cuban conjunto format of trumpets, rhythm section and voices, calling the band his Nuevo Tumbao (New Rhythm). He switched to timbales. Despite some fellow musicians' viewpoint that the new group's sound was a copy of Sonora Matancera, Pacheco's 'new' sound was a huge success. The lead singer on *Cañonazo* was Pete Rodríguez, who also sang lead vocals on eight out of the 13 other titles Pacheco released between 1964 and 1973. Nuevo Tumbao's other vocalists and accompanists included **Monguito**, Chivirico Dávila, and pianist/arranger Héctor Rivera. For the 1965 descarga album, *Pacheco His Flute And Latin Jam*, Johnny assembled a group of veteran and young musicians, including Lino Frías (piano), Carlos 'Caito' Diaz (vocals), Barry Rogers (trombone), **Bobby Valentín** (trumpet), **Pupi Legarreta** (violin), Orestes Vilato (timbales, see **Típica 73**), Carlos 'Patato' Valdés (conga) and Osvaldo 'Chi Hua Hua' Martínez (güiro). Cuban saxophonist José 'Chombo' Silva, a participant on the first two Panart *Cuban Jam Session* volumes in 1956, was also involved. Chombo later said that the cut 'Sugar Frost (Azucare)' was one of his favourite recordings. Max Salazar cited this track and 'Echate Pa' Ila' from Chi Hua Hua's *Descarga Cubana Vol.1* (1966) on the Fonseca label, as two of the most notable descargas. Pacheco guested on the Tico All-Stars descarga albums recorded at New York's Village Gate in 1966. He became the musical director of the **Fania All Stars** in 1968 and made his only UK appearance (to date) with them in 1976.

In the early Fania days, Pacheco and Masucci made their own deliveries to the record stores. Johnny scouted for talent and acted as recording director. Jerry initially looked after administration in addition to running his law firm, but within three years, he had devoted himself full-time to the label. At the beginning of the 70s, the Fania subsidiary, Vaya Records, was launched, and by the middle of the decade, the rival labels of Inca, Cotique, Tico and Alegre had been swallowed up. Their roster included an impressive array of stars like **Willie Colón**, **Ray Barretto**, **Celia Cruz**, Tito Puente and **Rubén Blades**. In 1975, Fania accounted for more than 80 per cent of all salsa record sales in the USA and as well as owning a recording studio and a Seventh Avenue headquarters in Manhattan, having a pressing plant in Puerto Rico, sponsoring shows on seven radio stations nationally and making two movies on the Latin music scene (*Our Latin Thing (Nuestra Cosa)* in 1972, and *Salsa* in 1976), Fania's interests in magazines and nightclubs, along with production and distribution deals with **Columbia** and **Atlantic Records**, helped to make Fania the biggest salsa labels of all time.

Johnny began a successful collaboration with Celia Cruz in 1974 on *Celia & Johnny*. They released a further five albums together up to 1985. In 1975, smoky-voiced, Afro-Cuban singer Héctor Casanova replaced El Conde on Pacheco's *El Maestro*. He appeared on two other records with Johnny before issuing the solo albums *Casanova* (1980), *Montuno Y Las Muchachas* (1983) and *Solido* (1986). Previously, he recorded *En Una Nota!* in 1974 with Monguito Santamaría (son of **Mongo Santamaría** (b. 1946, Havana, Cuba; bandleader/pianist/composer/arranger). Pacheco released a series of albums on which he teamed up with veteran Latin stars like Pupi Legarreta (violin/flute), songwriters Angel Luis Silva 'Melón' (b. Mexico; vocals) and Daniel Santos (b. Puerto Rico; vocals), Celio González (b. Cuba; vocals), José Fajardo (flute) and Rolando La Serie (b. Cuba; vocals). La Serie had recorded previously with the bands of Ernesto Duarte, Bebo Valdés, Tito Puente, Porfi Jiménez and **Rafael Cortijo**. At the beginning of the 80s, Fania went into decline. Masucci sold the company to the Argentinian firm of Val Syn, but retained a consultancy role. During the remainder of the decade, a procession of artists departed to other labels and releases slowed to a trickle. Meanwhile, Pacheco engaged in 'extra-curricular' work for other labels, with artists such as Santiago Ceron, Israel 'Kantor' Sardiñas, Los Guaracheros de Oriente, Héctor Casanova, Lefty Pérez and Melcochita. Johnny and El Conde reunited to make four more albums between 1983 and 1989. Their 1987 release *Salsobita* was nominated for a Grammy Award. Pacheco appeared twice in the UK BBC 2 *Arena* television series in 1988: first in the film profile *My Name Is Celia Cruz* and then in a *Rhythms Of The World* programme devoted to concert footage of Celia teamed up with Tito Puente's big band (with Pacheco as a special guest) recorded at New York's **Apollo** Theater in 1987. Pacheco can be seen conducting and performing with the Fania All Stars in Zaire in 1974 on the UK video release *Salsa Madness* (1991).

Albums: *Pacheco y su Charanga Vol. I* (1960), *Pacheco y su Charanga Vol. II* (1961), with the charangas of Charlie Palmieri and José Fajardo *Las Charangas* (1961), *Pacheco y su Charanga Vol. III: Que Suene La Flauta* (1962), *Pacheco y su Charanga Vol. IV 'Suav'ito'* (c.1963), *Pacheco y su Charanga Vol. V: Spotlight On Pacheco* (1964), *Cañonazo* (1964), *Pacheco At The N. Y. World's Fair* (1964), *Pacheco te Invita a Bailar* (c.1965) *Pacheco His Flute And Latin Jam* (1965), *Viva Africa* (1966), *Pacheco y su Charanga - By Popular Demand* (1966), *Sabor Tipico* (1967) *Latin Piper* (c.1968), *Volando Bajito* (1968), *La Perfecta Combinación* (c.1970), *Los Compadres* (1971), with Justo Betancourt *Los Dinamicos* (1971), *Tres de Café y Dos de Azúcar* (1973), with Celia Cruz *Celia & Johnny* (1974), with Cruz *Tremendo Caché* (1975), *El Maestro* (1975), with Cruz, Justo Betancourt and Papo Lucca *Recordando El Ayer* (1976), *The Artist* (1977), with Pupi Legarreta *Los Dos Mosqueteros - The Two Musketeers* (1977), with Angel Luis 'Melón' Silva *Llegó Melón* (1977), with Cruz *Eternos* (1978), *Los Amigos* (1979), with Daniel Santos *Los Distinguidos* (1979), with Legarreta, José Fajardo and Javier Vázquez *Las*

Tres Flautas (1980), with Cruz and Pete 'El Conde' Rodríguez *Celia, Johnny and Pete* (1980), with Celio González *El Zorro De Plata Presenta Al Flaco De Oro* (1981), with Fajardo *Pacheco y Fajardo* (1982), with Rolando La Serie *De Pelicula* (1982), with Rodríguez *De Nuevo Los Compadres* (1983), with Silva *Flying High* (1984), with Cruz *De Nuevo* (1985), with Rodríguez *Jicamo* (1985), with Rodríguez *Salsobita* (1987), with Rodríguez *Celebración* (1989). Compilations: (by Pacheco and his charanga) *Habia Una Vez/Once Upon A Time* (1973), *Lo Mejor de/The Best of Pacheco* (1974); (with his conjunto) *10 Great Years* (1971), *The Champ* (1980). The UK compilation *Introducing...Johnny Pacheco* (1989) was an odd assortment of tracks from his 60s Alegre and 60s, 70s and 1980 Fania back catalogue.

Pacheco, Tom

b. 4 November 1948, Massachusetts, USA. Pacheco's father, Tony, had played guitar, in Europe, with **Django Reinhardt**. He later moved to a farm in Massachusetts, where he also owned a music store and taught guitar. Tom started playing guitar at the age of 10, studying both Flamenco and classical styles whilst in high school. Leaving home at the age of 16, and already writing his own songs, he moved into the Greenwich Village scene in New York during the 60s. Gradually he emerged into the non-traditional country field of music, his early albums for **RCA** and **CBS** not being too well received. During the late 70s, Pacheco turned towards rock 'n' roll, his song 'All Fly Away' being recorded by **Jefferson Starship** as the title track of their *Dragonfly* album. Spending 1982/3 playing, and living, in Austin, Texas, Pacheco continued to build a following for himself. He then spent two years in Woodstock, before moving to Nashville in 1986. The following year he moved to Oldcastle, County Meath, Eire, and then to Dublin. It was while there *Eagle In The Rain* was recorded, which contained the excellent 'You Will Not Be Forgotten', and 'Jesus In A Leather Jacket'. Apart from being produced by Arty McGlynn, of **Patrick Street** fame, the album brought Pacheco some overdue critical acclaim. Appearances at the Cambridge Folk Festival in 1990, and sharing the bill with **Townes Van Zandt** at the Berlin Independence Day celebrations in September 1990, and numerous UK appearances, have all helped to circulate his music to a wider audience. *Big Storm Coming* recorded with the Norwegian Steinar Albrigtsen, had, by June 1993, sold some 35,000 copies in Norway, and topped the Norwegian album charts, outselling acts such as **Guns N'Roses**.

Albums: *Pacheco And Alexander* (CBS 1969), *Swallowed Up In The Great American Heartland* (RCA 1973), *The Outsider* (RCA 1977), *Eagle In The Rain* (Round Tower Music 1989), *Sunflowers And Scarecrows* (Round Tower Music 1991), *Tales From The Red Lake* (Round Tower Music 1992), with Steinar Albrigtsen *Big Storm Coming* (Round Tower Music 1993).

Pacific Drift

This UK group, formed in the late 60s, comprised Barry Reynolds (guitar/vocals), Brian Shapman (keyboards/vocals), Graham Harrop (bass) and Lawrence Arendes aka Larry King (drums). King, formerly of Liverpool's Wimple Winch, founded this new quartet from the ashes of Sponge, a jazz-rock unit which imploded when saxophonist Jack Lancaster left in 1968 to join **Blodwyn Pig**. The quartet's debut single, a version of **Spirit**'s 'Water Woman', was followed by a self-titled album, on the **Decca**/Nova label, in 1970. However, although they appeared live at the requisite underground haunts and festivals, Pacific Drift were unable to sustain a career and split up by the end of the year.

Album: *Pacific Drift* (1970).

Pacific Gas And Electric

Formed in Los Angeles, California, USA in 1968, Pacific Gas And Electric was a quintet which merged blues, gospel, soul, jazz and rock. The members were Charlie Allen (vocals), Glenn Schwartz (lead guitar), Thomas Marshall (rhythm guitar), Brent Black (bass) and Frank Cook (drums), the latter an alumnus of **Canned Heat**. The group's first album, *Get It On*, was initially issued on the small Bright Orange label and then reissued on the band's own Power Records, scraping into the charts at number 159. An appearance at the Miami Pop Festival in December 1968 was considered a highlight of that event and the group came to the attention of **Columbia Records**, who subsequently signed them. A self-titled album was released on Columbia in August 1969 and fared somewhat better, reaching number 91. The group's third album, *Are You Ready*, did not fare as well, reaching only to number 101, but it did yield their only hit single in the title track, a gospel-influenced rocker which climbed to number 14 in mid-1970. One other album and a couple of further singles were issued but by 1971 the group was in disarray. Various personnel changes, including the addition of a horn section, left Allen the only original member by 1973, when the group's final album was issued on Dunhill Records.

Albums: *Get It On* (1968), *Pacific Gas And Electric* (1969), *Are You Ready* (1970), *PG&E* (1971), *Pacific Gas And Electric, Starring Charlie Allen* (1973). Compilation: *The Best Of* (1985).

Pacific Overtures

Sometimes known as **Stephen Sondheim**'s 'kabuki musical', this ambitious production opened at the Winter Garden, New York, on 11 January 1976. The book was by John Weidman, a student of law at Yale University. It traced the history of Japan from 1852, when naval officer Commander Matthew Perry, and four warships, attempted to establish 'friendly' relations with a 'isolated and peaceful country', through a period of some 120 years of continual change, culminating in the country's emergence as a dominant trading force in the western world. The story was told in an imaginative and original manner, with every aspect of the production heavily influenced by the traditional form of Japanese Kabuki theatre. Most of Sondheim's music was written in the Japanese pentatonic scale, and his lyrics used extremely simple language, with very few rhymes. The songs included 'Pretty Lady', 'Four Black Dragons', "There Is No Other Way', 'Chrysanthemum Tea', 'Please Hello', 'A Bowler Hat', 'Welcome To Kanagawa', 'Someone In A Tree', 'Next'. 'The Advantages Of Floating In The Middle Of The Sea', and 'Poems'. The actors, who included Mako, Soon-Teck Oh, Yukis Shimoda, and Sab Shimono, were all Asians, even those who played Americans. Director **Hal Prince** was prominent among the show's several **Tony Award** nominees for his staging of a project that was both daring and completely different from anything Broadway had seen in living memory, but the only winners were Florence Klotz (costumes) and Boris Aronson (scenic design). The show also won the New York Drama Critics' Circle Award for best musical. It ran for 193 performances, and was presented in a revised, small-scale version Off Broadway in 1984, and in a far more lavish Paul Kerryson production at England's Leicester Haymarket Theatre in 1993.

Paddy, Klaus And Gibson

Formed in 1965, this Liverpool-based 'supergroup' featured Paddy Chambers (lead guitar; ex-**Big Three** and **Escorts**), **Klaus Voorman** (bass) and Gibson Kemp (drums; ex-**Kingsize Taylor And The Dominoes**). Their three singles included a version of **Marvin Gaye**'s 'No Good Without You Baby' and the theme song to British television's *Quick Before They Catch Us*, but despite the patronage of **Beatles**' manager **Brian Epstein**, the trio failed to secure commercial success. Plans by **Pete Townshend** to amalgamate the group with part of the **Who** fell apart when tribulations within the latter act were settled. Paddy, Klaus And Gibson embarked on separate careers late in 1966 with Voorman securing subsequent fame as the illustrator of the **Beatles**' *Revolver* album cover and also as a member of **Manfred Mann** and the **Plastic Ono Band**.

Page, Cleo

Very much one of the mystery men of the blues, this singer/guitarist caused a minor stir in the 70s with his powerful, raw blue records which were issued on small Los Angeles labels including Goodie Train and Las Vegas. In 1979 JSP Records released enough material for an album which was described by Jim DeKoster in *Living Blues* as 'one of the most striking blues albums of the past year', but Page remains elusive. His music is largely tough, no-nonsense, mostly original blues with sometimes startling lyrics, though JSP also issued a more contemporary sounding risque single entitled 'Hamburger-I Love To Eat It', which was not on the album.

Album: *Leaving Mississippi* (1979).

Page, Jimmy

b. James Patrick Page, 9 January 1944, Heston, Middlesex, England. One of rock's most gifted and distinctive guitarists, Page began his professional career during the pre-beat era of the early 60s. He was a member of several groups, including **Neil Christian**'s Crusaders and Carter Lewis And The Southerners, the last of which was led by the popular songwriting team, **Carter And Lewis**. Page played rousing solos on several releases by Carter/Lewis proteges, notably the McKinleys' 'Sweet And Tender Romance', and the guitarist quickly became a respected session musician. He appeared on releases by **Lulu**, **Them**, **Tom Jones** and **Dave Berry**, as well as scores of less-renowned acts, but his best-known work was undertaken for producer **Shel Talmy**. Page appeared on sessions for the **Kinks** and the **Who**, joining an elite band of young studio musicians which included **Nicky Hopkins**, **John Paul Jones** and Bobby Graham. The guitarist completed a solo single, 'She Just Satisfies', in 1965, and although it suggested a frustration with his journeyman role, he later took up an A&R position with **Immediate** Records, where he produced singles for **Nico** and **John Mayall**. Having refused initial entreaties, Page finally agreed to join the **Yardbirds** in 1966 and he remained with this groundbreaking attraction until its demise two years later. The guitarist then formed **Led Zeppelin**, with which he forged his reputation. His propulsive riffs established the framework for a myriad of tracks - 'Whole Lotta Love', 'Rock 'N' Roll', 'Black Dog', 'When The Levee Breaks' and 'Achilles Last Stand' - now established as rock classics, while his solos have set benchmarks for a new generation of guitarists. His acoustic technique, featured on 'Black Mountain Side' and 'Tangerine', is also notable, while his work with **Roy Harper**, in particular on *Stormcock* (1971), was also among the finest of his career. Page's recordings since Led Zeppelin's dissolution have been ill-focused. He contributed the soundtrack to Michael Winner's film *Death Wish II*, while the **Firm**, a collaboration with **Paul Rodgers**, formerly of **Free** and **Bad Company**, was equally disappointing. However, a 1988 release, *Outrider*, did much to re-establish his reputation with contributions from **Robert Plant**, **Chris Farlowe** and Jason Bonham, the son of Zeppelin's late drummer, John. The guitarist then put considerable effort into remastering that group's revered back catalogue. *Coverdale/Page* was a successful but fleeting partnership with the former **Whitesnake** singer in 1993, but it was his reunion with Robert Plant for the ironically-titled *Unledded* project which really captured the public's imagination.

Albums: *Death Wish II* (Swan Song 1982, film soundtrack), with Roy Harper *Whatever Happened To Jugula* (Beggars Banquet 1985), *Outrider* (Geffen 1988), with David Coverdale *Coverdale/Page* (EMI 1993), with Robert Plant *Unledded/No Quarter* (Fontana 1994). Compilations: *Jam Session* (Charly 1982), *No Introduction Necessary* (Thunderbolt 1984), *Smoke And Fire* (Thunderbolt 1985).

Page, Larry

b. Leonard Davies, c.1938, Hayes, Middlesex, England. While working as a packer at the nearby **EMI Records** factory, Davies auditioned for his record company and was duly signed. After changing his name to Larry Page in honour of Larry Parks, the star of *The Jolson Story*, the teenager began a brief recording career. Dubbed 'the Teenage Rage' by showbusiness columnist Jack Bentley, Page lived up to his sobriquet with a series of exploits, including a whirlwind romance with a fan leading to a much publicized marriage. With his sharp suits, blue-tinted hair and monotone croon, Page was an unlikely pop star but became one of the first UK performers to cover a **Buddy Holly** song with 'That'll Be The Day'. After retiring from performance at the end of the 50s, Page joined Mecca Enterprises as a consultant manager and ran the Orchid ballroom in Coventry. This led to a meeting with music publisher Eddie Kassner and the formation of Denmark Productions. With a deal whereby he could select and manage acts, Page launched a selection of minor talent, including Johnny B. Great, the Orchids, Little Lenny Davis and Shel Naylor.

In 1964 Page was approached by two society gentlemen, Robert Wace and Grenville Collins, and offered the chance to co-manage a north London group known as the Ravens. Page rechristened them the **Kinks**, helped fashion their image and prevented their imminent dissolution following a celebrated quarrel between **Dave Davies** and Mick Avory, in which the former was hospitalized. An unsatisfactory US tour culminated in a dispute between Page and Ray Davies which festered into a High Court action. Recovering his poise, he promoted a couple of other groups, the Pickwicks and the **Riot Squad,** before finding another hit artist in the **Troggs**. On this occasion, Larry not only signed the group to a management deal but produced their records and made them the leading lights of Page One (the record company he had formed with publisher **Dick James**). Remarkably, his association with the Troggs ended in another High Court action yet, in spite of his litigious history, Page was never regarded as one of the unscrupulous managers of the 60s. His name was well-known during this period, not only because of frequent appearances in print but the instrumental albums his label released under the self-referential title the Larry Page Orchestra. When Page One ceased operating in the early 70s, Dick James went on to found **DJM Records** while Larry formed the inauspicious Penny Farthing label. Page rewrote history to some extent in the 70s/80s when he briefly regained managerial control of both the Troggs and the Kinks.

Selected album: *Rampage* (1978). Compilation: *This Is Larry Page* (1974).

Page, Oran 'Hot Lips'

b. 27 January 1908, Dallas, Texas, USA, d. 5 November 1954. In the 20s Page played trumpet mostly in his home state but also toured in bands accompanying some of the best of the day's blues singers, among them **Ma Rainey**, **Bessie Smith** and **Ida Cox**. Towards the end of the 20s Page joined **Walter Page**'s Blue Devils, a band formed in Oklahoma City out of the remnants of a touring band in which the trumpeter had worked. With the Blue Devils Page built a reputation as a powerful lead and solo trumpet, an emotional blues player and singer, and an inspirational sideman. In 1931 he was one of several Blue Devils enticed into **Bennie Moten**'s band, where he remained until Moten's death in 1935. The following year he joined **Count Basie** in Kansas City where he was heard by **Louis Armstrong**'s manager, Joe Glaser, who signed him up. Glaser's motives have been much-speculated upon. At the time Armstrong was suffering lip trouble and Glaser certainly needed a trumpeter/singer. However, the neglect displayed by the manager towards his new signing once Armstrong was back suggests that he might well have seen Page as a competitor to be neutralized. In the late 30s Page led bands large and small, mostly in and around New York and appeared at numerous after-hours sessions and on many record dates, including Ida Cox's comeback date after her retirement. At the start of the 40s he was briefly in **Artie Shaw**'s band, with which he made a superb recording of 'St James Infirmary'. The rest of this decade was spent much as he had spent the late 30s, playing and recording in a succession of bands mostly in the New York area. He also featured on several excellent record dates, including the excellent 1944 V-Disc sides. At the end of the 40s he made another hit record, this time 'Baby, It's Cold Outside' coupled with 'The Hucklebuck' with **Pearl Bailey**, a record which helped establish her stardom. In the early 50s Page often played in Europe until his death in 1954. Although he was strongly influenced by Armstrong during part of his career, Page was in fact an inventive and exceptionally interesting blues-orientated trumpet player in his own right as well as an excellent singer of the blues. Whatever the reason,

Page's career was partially overshadowed by Armstrong and during his lifetime he was rarely granted the critical appraisal his talents deserved. Almost four decades after his death, his re-evaluation remains incomplete.
Selected albums: *Hot Lips Page In Sweden* (1951), *Hot Lips Page* (1952-53), *Hot Lips Page 1951* (Jazz Society 1989). Compilations: *Hot Lips Page 1938-1940* (Official 1989, 1938-40 recordings), *Oran 'Hot Lips' Page Vols 1/2* (1942-53), with others *Midnight At V-Disc* (1944), *Play The Blues In B* (Jazz Archives 1993).

Page, Patti

b. Clara Ann Fowler, 8 November 1927, Tulsa, Oklahoma, USA. A popular singer who is said to have sold more records during the 50s than any other female artist; her total sales (singles and albums) are claimed to be in excess of 60 million. One of eight girls in a family of 11, Fowler started her career singing country songs on radio station KTUL in Tulsa, and played weekend gigs with Art Klauser and his Oklahomans. She successfully auditioned for KTUL's *Meet Patti Page* show, sponsored by the Page Milk Company, and took the name with her when she left. Jack Rael, who was road manager and played baritone saxophone for the Jimmy Joy band, heard her on the radio and engaged her to sing with them; he later became her manager for over 40 years. In 1948 Page appeared on the top rated *Breakfast Club* on Chicago radio, and sang with the **Benny Goodman** Septet. In the same year she had her first hit record, 'Confess', on which, in the cause of economy, she overdubbed her own voice to create the effect of a vocal group.
In 1949, she used that revolutionary technique again on her first million-seller, 'With My Eyes Wide Open I'm Dreaming'. The song was re-released 10 years later with a more modern orchestral backing. Throughout the 50s, the hits continued to flow: 'I Don't Care If The Sun Don't Shine', 'All My Love' (US number 1), 'The Tennessee Waltz' (said to be the first real 'cross-over' hit from country music to pop, and one of the biggest record hits of all time), 'Would I Love You (Love You, Love You)', 'Mockin' Bird Hill' (a cover version of the record made by **Les Paul** and **Mary Ford**, who took multi-tracking to the extreme in the 50s), 'Mister And Mississippi', 'Detour' (recorded for her first country music album), 'I Went To Your Wedding', 'Once In Awhile', 'You Belong To Me', 'Why Don't You Believe Me', '(How Much Is) That Doggie In The Window', written by novelty song specialist, **Bob Merrill**, and recorded by Page for a children's album; 'Changing Partners', 'Cross Over The Bridge', 'Steam Heat', 'Let Me Go, Lover', 'Go On With The Wedding', 'Allegheny Moon', 'Old Cape Cod', 'Mama From The Train' (sung in a Pennsylvanian Dutch dialect), 'Left Right Out Of Your Heart', and many more. Her records continued to sell well into the 60s, and she had her last US Top 10 entry in 1965 with the title song from the Bette Davis-Olivia De Havilland movie *Hush, Hush, Sweet Charlotte*. Page also appeared extensively on US television during the 50s, on shows such as the *Scott Music Hall*, the *Big Record* variety show, and her own shows for NBC and CBS. She also made several films, including *Elmer Gantry* (1960), *Dondi* (1961, a comedy-drama, in which she co-starred with David Janssen) and *Boys Night Out* (1962). In the 70s, she recorded mainly country material, and in the 80s, after many successful years with **Mercury** and **Columbia Records**, signed for the Nashville-based company Plantation Records, a move which reunited her with top record producer **Shelby Singleton**. In 1988, Page gained excellent reviews when she played the Ballroom in New York, her first appearance in that city for nearly 20 years.
Albums: *Let's Get Away From It All* (1955), *I've Heard That Song Before* (1955), *Patti Page On Camera* (1955), *Three Little Words* (1955), *The Waltz Queen* (1955), *Indiscretion* (1955), *Romance On The Range* (1955), *I'll Remember April* (1956), *Page I* (1956), *Page II* (1956), *Page III* (1956), *You Go To My Head* (1956), *In The Land Of Hi Fi* (1956), *Music For Two In Love* (1956), *The Voices Of Patti Page* (1956), *Page IV* (1956), *My Song* (1956), *The East Side* (1956), *Manhattan Tower* (1956), *Just A Closer Walk With Thee* (1957), *Sings And Stars In 'Elmer Gantry'* (1960), *Country And Western Golden Hits* (1961), *Go On Home* (1962), *Golden Hit Of The Boys* (1962), *Patti Page On Stage* (1963), *Say Wonderful Things* (1963), *Blue Dream Street* (1964), *The Nearness Of You* (1964), *Hush, Hush, Sweet Charlotte* (1965), *Gentle On My Mind* (1968), *Patti Page With Lou Stein's Music, 1949* (1988). Compilations: *Patti Page's Greatest Hits* (1961), *Patti Page's Golden Hits, Volume 2* (1963), *The Best Of Patti Page* (1984).

Page, Stu

b. 12 May 1954, Leeds, Yorkshire, England. Page, who has been playing the guitar since he was 10 years old, began his career by session work around Leeds. In 1973, after helping out an American bluegrass band, the Warren Wikeson Band, he was invited to join them in Boston for a year. When he returned to the UK, he took various day jobs, but played in several semi-pro bands. In 1984 he formed Stu Page And Remuda, and says, 'It's a word for a spare horse and that's what we were. We only got the gigs when someone had let the organizer down.' Besides being a talented guitarist, Page has a powerful voice which belies his small stature, and his band includes Terry Clayton (bass), Andy Whelan (guitar), Pat McPartling (drums) and Tim Howard (pedal steel). They have recorded several cassettes for sale at shows, together with the excellent album, *The Stu Page Band*, which was produced by Joe Butler of the **Hillsiders** for Barge Records. Page's major influence is **Merle Haggard** and the band's singles include 'He Made The Whole World Sing', 'Are

You Still In Love With Me?' and the double a-side, 'Florida Feelin''/'Honeysuckle Dreamin''.
Albums: *Radio Nights* (1984), *Front Page News* (1985), *The Stu Page Band* (1989), *Fresh Pages* (1990).

Page, Walter

b. 9 February 1900, Gallatin, Missouri, USA, d. 20 December 1957. Page was one of many pupils of Major N. Clark Smith who gained fame in jazz circles. In the early 20s, Page played bass with **Bennie Moten** in Kansas City. In 1925 Page was stranded in Oklahoma City when a band he was playing in folded. He decided to form his own group out of the wreckage and this band became the legendary Blue Devils. One of the outstanding **territory bands** of the southwest and instrumental in helping form the musical concept which eventually became known as Kansas City style, Page gathered many fine musicians into his band. Among them were **Oran 'Hot Lips' Page**, **Jimmy Rushing**, **Lester Young** and **Bill Basie** (in the days before he was ennobled). After Moten headhunted some of his best sidemen Page kept going for a while but eventually gave up the struggle and he too joined Moten. He later played in Basie's band where he became one fourth of the fabled All American Rhythm Section (with Basie, **Freddie Green** and **Jo Jones**). Leaving Basie in 1942 he played with several leading territory bands, including those led by Nat Towles and **Jesse Price**, and in the middle of the decade was back with Basie. Later, he played in various pick-up groups, often in New York but with occasional tours, a pattern of work which continued into the mid-50s. He died in 1957. A solid player with an impeccable sense of time, Page is generally credited as one of the originators of the 'walking bass', a style of playing in which the bassist plays passing notes, up or down the scale, in addition to the three or four root notes of the chord, thus creating a flowing line.
Compilations: *Kansas City Hot Jazz* (1926-30), incl. on *Sweet And Low Blues, Big Bands And Territory Bands Of The 20s* (1929), with Count Basie *Swinging the Blues* (1937-39).

Pagliaro

Michel Pagliaro was a photogenic Montreal-based French-Canadian pop/rock singer/songwriter. He recorded for Much records, a label owned by top Canadian radio station CHUM. His success in his homeland bought him to the attention of Peter Summerfield, an A&R representative for British record label Pye. The record company brought him over to England and put a big campaign behind his UK launch, which helped to put his debut single 'Loving You Ain't Easy' into the UK Top 40 in 1972. Encouraged by the initial success the label released a self-titled album and two more singles, 'Rainshowers' and 'Some Sing Some Dance' but none of the records made any impression on the the charts.
Album: *Pagliaro* (1972).

Paich, Marty

b. 23 January 1925, Oakland, California, USA. While still undergoing long and thorough academic training, Paich began writing arrangements. After military service, during which he was able to continue his musical career, he returned to his studies and by the end of the 40s had gained numerous qualifications. In the early 50s he worked with a number of dancebands and also with **Shelly Manne** and **Shorty Rogers**, with whom he appeared on the successful and influential album *Cool And Crazy*. Also in the early 50s he was for a while pianist and arranger for **Peggy Lee** and made arrangements for **Mel Tormé**. He also wrote charts for another highly successful west coast album, *Art Pepper Plus Eleven*. An inventive and inquiring mind is clearly at work in all Paich's writing, whether as arranger or composer, and he proved particularly adept at creating material for small to medium-sized groups that allows the bands to sound as though they involve many more musicians. His work with such singers as **Ella Fitzgerald**, **Ray Charles**, **Anita O'Day**, **Sammy Davis**, **Lena Horne** and **Sarah Vaughan**, whether as arranger or musical director and conductor, denotes an acute appreciation of the particular needs of interpreters of the Great American Songbook. In recent years Paich has been active writing for films and television but the late 80s saw him back on the road with Tormé and some of his former Dek-tette sidemen, reunions which updated past glories with no hint of repetition and resulted in some remarkable record albums.
Selected albums: *Tenors West* (GNP 1956 recording), *Mel Tormé With The Marty Paich Dek-tette* (1956), *What's New?* (1957), *I Get A Boot Out Of You* (1957), *The Picasso Of Big Band Jazz* (Candid 1958), with Mel Tormé *Reunion* (1988), *Hot Piano* (VSOP 1988), *In Concert Tokyo* (1988), *Moanin'* (1993).

Paige, Elaine

b. Elaine Bickerstaff, 5 March 1951, Barnet, Hertfordshire, England. An actress and singer, often called the first lady of contemporary British musical theatre, Elaine Paige was trained at the Aida Foster Stage School in Golders Green, North London. She had already appeared in several stage musicals in the 60s and 70s, including ***The Roar Of The Greasepaint-The Smell Of The Crowd***, ***Hair*** (her first West End show), *Maybe That's Your Problem*, *Rock Carmen*, ***Jesus Christ Superstar***, ***Grease***, ***Billy***, and before she was chosen to portray Eva Peron in **Tim Rice** and **Andrew Lloyd Webber**'s ***Evita*** in 1978. Although **Julie Covington** had sung the part on the original concept album and had a UK number 1 hit with 'Don't Cry For Me Argentina', Paige went on to make the role her own. In spite of the disappointment of being unable to play the part on Broadway (because of American union rules), *Evita* made Paige into a star almost overnight. She won a Society of West End Theatres Award for her outstanding performance, and was also voted Show Business Personality of the Year. In the 80s she starred in ***Cats*** (as Grizabella, singing 'Memory'), *Abbacadabra*, ***Chess***, and a West End revival of **Cole Porter**'s ***Anything Goes***. She topped the UK chart with a number from *Chess*, 'I Know Him So Well', in a duet with **Barbara Dickson**. Her first solo album, which came in 1981, featured a variety of songs, mostly with lyrics by Tim Rice. It was recorded with the assistance of Stuart Elliot (ex-**Cockney Rebel**), Ian Bairnson and David Paton from **Pilot**, and Mike Moran. As well as a version of **Paul Simon**'s 'How The Heart Approaches What It Yearns', there was a rare **Paul McCartney** instrumental ('Hot As Sun') with words by Rice. She was voted 'Recording Artist of the Year' by the Variety Club of Great Britain. Her most unusual album was released in 1988, and consisted of cover versions of **Queen** songs. In 1989 she turned her attention more to straight acting, and made two films for the BBC including the acclaimed *Unexplained Laughter*, with Diana Rigg. She had previously worked in television programmes such as *Crossroads*, *Lady Killers*, *Ladybirds*, *A View Of Harry Clark*, and *Tales Of The Unexpected*, as well as musical specials such as *Elaine Paige In Concert*. In 1990 her long-term relationship with Tim Rice dissolved and she threw herself into her work. During the 80s and 90s she embarked on concert tours of Europe, the Middle East, Scandanavia and the UK, most recently accompanied by a 26-piece symphony orchestra. In 1993 she was highly acclaimed for her powerful and dramatic performance as the legendary **Edith Piaf** in Pam Gems' play with music, ***Piaf***, at the Piccadilly Theatre in London. In May 1995, she took over from **Betty Buckley** in the leading role of Norma Desmond in the West End hit musical ***Sunset Boulevard***, and later in the year received an OBE in the Queen's Birthday Honours List.

Selected albums: with Peter Oliver *Barrier* (1978), *Elaine Paige* (WEA 1982), *Stages* (K-tel 1983), *Cinema* (K-tel 1984), *Sitting Pretty* (WEA 1985), *Love Hurts* (WEA 1985), *Christmas* (WEA 1986), *The Queen Album* (Virgin 1988), *The Collection* (Pickwick 1990), *Love Can Do That* (1991), with Barbara Dickson *Together* (1992), *Romance And The Stage* (1993), *Piaf* (WEA 1995), *Encore* (WEA 1995), and Original Cast recordings. Compilation: *Memories - The Best Of Elaine Paige* (Telstar 1987).

Pain Teens

The Pain Teens are an extraordinary US rock group, who were formed in the late 80s and consist of Scott Ayers (guitar/samples/drums), Bliss Blood (vocals/percussion), Kirk Carr (bass) and Frank Garymartin (drums). After two obscure albums for Anonmie Records at the turn of the decade the group moved to Trance Syndicate, the left-field label set up by King Coffey of the **Butthole Surfers**. The marriage was an obvious one, with the Pain Teens able to conduct their experimental approach to music without the hindrance of commercial expectation. Happily, this did not necessitate an unpleasant listening experience, though certainly the subject matter chosen by Pain Teens could be described as difficult. Samples drawn from television shows, especially the psycho-babble of confessional talk shows littered their albums of this period, the best of which was *Destroy Me, Lover*. A confrontational, multi-dimensional record, it was released in a classic 'pulp fiction' cover, the image of which (man assailing woman) took on a ghastly double meaning when Blood's vocals began to address the disturbing subject matter of 'Lisa Knew'. This exorcism of child abuse was accompanied by a complementary track, 'Body Memory', which explored the mind of an incest survivor. Some light relief was on offer with their string arrangement of **Leonard Cohen**'s 'Story Of Isaac', but the title of the sweet pop track, 'RU 486', was actually the serial number of an abortion pill. The Pain Teens are not a band to spare anyone the truth of just how brutal life can be.

Albums: *Pain Teens* (Anomie 1988), *Case Histories* (Anomie 1989), *Born In Blood* (Trance Syndicate 1990), *Stimulation Festival* (Trance Syndicate 1992), *Destroy Me, Lover* (Trance Syndicate 1993).

Paint Your Wagon (Film Musical)

Opinions vary widely as to the quality of this film, but, in general, the 'noes' seem to have it. *Paint Your Wagon* started its musical journey on Broadway in 1951, with music by **Frederick Loewe** and a book and lyrics by **Alan Jay Lerner**. Lerner's screenplay for this 1969 version was based on a fresh adaptation of the story by Paddy Chayevsky. The action still takes place during the California gold rush of the late 1800s, but the sometimes droll story now concerns the relationship between the lovely young Elizabeth (Jean Seberg) and the two men in her life, Ben Rumson (Lee Marvin) and 'Pardner' (Clint Eastwood). She wants to live in No Name City with both of them, which does not please Ben because he used part of his stake to buy her from a Mormon, and then made her his wife. Also up to their knees in the mud of the goldfields were Harve Presnell ('Rotten Luck Willie), Ray Walston ('Mad Jack' Duncan), Tom Ligon, Alan Dexter, William O'Connell, Ben Baker, Alan Baxter, Paul Truman, and a whole heap of others. Several of Lerner and Loewe's songs survived from the stage score, including the rousing 'Main Title (I'm On My Way)', and the contrasting 'They Call The Wind Maria' and 'There's A Coach Comin' In', both of which were sung admirably by Presnell. Eastwood surprised and delighted with his handling of 'I Still See Elisa' and 'I Talk To The Trees', and Marvin brought his very own individual treatment to 'Hand Me Down That Can O' Beans', and 'Wand'rin Star'. The latter number gave him a number 1 hit in the UK, but did not make the Top 40 in the USA. The rest of the numbers, with Lerner's lyrics and music by **André Previn**, consisted of 'The First Thing You Know', 'A Million Miles Away Behind The Door', 'The Gospel Of No Name City', 'Best Things', and 'Gold Fever'. **Nelson Riddle** and his impressive musical arrangements were nominated for an Oscar. Jack Baker staged the energetic dance sequences and the director was Joshua Logan. Alan Jay Lerner produced for Paramount, and the film was photographed in Technicolor and Panavision by William Fraker. In spite of the critics' reservations, *Paint Your Wagon* grossed well over $14 million in the USA, and was just outside the Top 10 musicals of the decade.

Paint Your Wagon (Stage Musical)

Despite having music by **Frederick Loewe** and a book and lyrics by **Alan Jay Lerner**, *Paint Your Wagon* had only modest success. It opened at the Shubert Theatre in New York on 12 November 1951, and ran for only 289 performances. Well-staged by Daniel Mann, and with some exhilarating choreography by **Agnes de Mille**, the show was set in California during the 1850s gold rush. James Barton, Tony Bavaar, Olga San Juan, Rufus Smith and James Mitchell, were among a cast of hard-bitten prospectors and their equally tough girlfriends. Lerner and Loewe's score, which complemented this rough and tumble situation perfectly, contained several appealing songs, including 'They Call The Wind Maria', 'I Still See Elisa', 'There's A Coach Comin' In', 'I Talk To The Trees', 'I'm On My Way', 'Another Autumn', 'Hand Me Down That Can O' Beans', and 'Wand'rin' Star'. In 1953, London audiences were delighted with the show and it ran at Her Majesty's Theatre for over a year with **Bobby Howes** and his real-life daughter Sally Ann Howes. In 1992, the Goodspeed Opera House in Connecticut gave theatregoers another chance to hear what is now - over 40 years on - regarded as an outstanding score.

Pajama Game, The (Film Musical)

Hardly any screen version of a hit Broadway musical is considered to better than the original, but this one in 1957 was. Perhaps it was because several members of the original stage team made the trip to Hollywood to recreate their original roles. Two of them, **George Abbott** and Richard Bissell, adapted their libretto (which had been based on Bissell's novel *Seven And A Half Cents*) for the screenplay. Based in and around the Sleep Tite Pajama Factory in Iowa, it concerns the efforts of union leader Babe Williams (**Doris Day**) and her Grievance Committee, to extract a rise in pay of seven and a half cents for their members from the new (and extremely dishy) new superintendent, Sid Sorokin (**John Raitt**). Naturally, Babe falls for Sid, in spite of her protests ('I'm Not At All In Love'), and the negotiations are satisfactorily concluded. This was one of only two scores that **Richard Adler** and **Jerry Ross** wrote together (the other was ***Damn Yankees***) before the latter's tragic death, and it was a complete joy. Not only did the principals, Day and Raitt, share 'Hey, There', 'Small Talk', and 'There Once Was A Man', but the gifted singer and dancer, Carol Haney, dazzled with 'Steam Heat' and 'Hernando's Hideaway', while Eddie Foy Jnr. was delightfully unconvincing as he assured Reta Shaw: 'I'll Never Be Jealous Again'. In addition there were pleasing ensemble pieces such as 'Once-A-Year-Day' and 'Racing With The Clock'. Also in the cast were Buzz Miller, Peter Gennaro, Barbara Nicholls, Thelma Pelish, and Kenneth LeRoy. **Bob Fosse**, a veteran of the stage show, was responsible for the lively and imaginative choreography (much of it alfresco), and the producer-directors were George Abbott and **Stanley Donen**. The film was shot in WarnerColor.

Pajama Game, The (Stage Musical)

This show opened at the St. James Theatre in New York on 13 May 1954 with only limited expectations. **Richard Adler** and **Jerry Ross**, who wrote the music and lyrics, were relatively unknown to Broadway audiences, as was choreographer **Bob Fosse**. However, the witty book was the work of veteran George Abbott and Richard Bissell, and the score was full of amusing and romantic numbers, such as 'I'll Never Be Jealous Again', 'There Once Was Man', 'Once A Year Day', 'Small Talk', 'I'm Not At All In Love' 'Hernando's Hideaway', 'Steam Heat', and 'Hey, There'. Set against the unlikely backdrop of a factory manufacturing pajamas, with an industrial dispute as its central dramatic device, there were strong performances from Janis Paige, **John Raitt** and Carol Haney. It won **Tony Awards** for best musical, featured actress (Haney), and Bob Fosse's choreography, which was an outstanding feature of the show. The 1955 London production, which ran for 501 performances and is remembered with great affection, starred Max Wall, Joy Nichols, **Edmund Hockridge**, and Elizabeth Seal. Hockridge was subsequently always associated with 'Hey, There', although in fact the song was a UK hit for **Rosemary Clooney**, **Johnnie Ray**, **Lita Roza**, and **Sammy Davis Jnr.** *The Pajama Game* was revived briefly on Broadway in 1973 with Barbara McNair, Hal Linden, and **Cab Calloway**. The 1957 film version achieved the impossible and actually improved upon the original with dazzling performances from **Doris Day**, Raitt, Haney, and Eddie Foy Jnr. In 1958, the musical *Say Darling*, which was based on Richard Bissell's experiences with *The*

Pajama Game, opened on Broadway and ran for 332 performances. The cast was headed by **Vivian Blaine**, David Wayne, and **Johnny Desmond**, and the score was by **Betty Comden** and **Adolph Green**.

Pal Joey

Pal Joey is merely the best known of New Yorker Joey Longo (b. c.1964)'s inumerable aliases. He earned his spurs with early house recordings on pivotal New York deep house imprint Apexton, also playing out regularly in Manhattan. Like so many others he began life working in a record shop, Vinyl Mania, before becoming an apprentice at a local studio. His more recent recordings, which have steadily built an audience in clubs, generally consist of loose, happy house textures, often released on his own label, Loop D' Loop. Examples include 'Flight 801' from 1991, or Espresso's 'Ping Pong' for Maxi Records from earlier the same year. Other names he hides behind include Earth People, Soho (not the UK outfit - scoring a big hit with 'Hot Music'), House Conductor, Espresso and Dream House. As Pal Joey his productions include 'Jump And Prance', arguably the first ska/house tune, for **Republic**. He has produced widely, notably for **Boogie Down Productions** (half of *Sex And Violence*, also appearing alongside **KRS-1** on **R.E.M.**'s 'Radio Song'). Other clients include **Deee-Lite** (remixing their 'What Is Love' and 'ESP'). More recently he is often to be found working under the CFM Band moniker (Crazy French Man).

Pal Joey (Film Musical)

This somewhat sanitized version of the 1940 Broadway show and John O'Hara's witty essays on which it was based, came to the screen in 1957. **Frank Sinatra** proved to be the ideal choice for the role of 'the heel of all-time', Joey Evans, the nightclub singer and compere, whose apparent mission in life is to seduce each 'mouse' in the chorus with the offer of 'shrimp cocktail, a steak, french fries, a little wine - the whole mish-mosh', so that he can 'help her with her arrangements'. The ingenuous Linda English (Kim Novak) accepts his offer, and, after the usual complications, and to the surprise of many who had read O'Hara's original short stories, goes off with him into the sunset. The musical highspot came when Joey sang an electrifying version of 'The Lady Is A Tramp' straight to the wealthy widow, Vera Simpson (**Rita Hayworth**), who had been known as 'Vanessa The Undresser' in her former life as a stripper. London film critics at the time thought it slightly ridiculous when some of their number applauded a piece of celluloid, but it was that kind of performance. Hank Henry, as the grumpy owner of the Barbary Coast nightspot where Joey 'operates', and Bobby Sherwood the leader of its orchestra, headed a supporting cast which also included Barbara Nicholls and Elizabeth Patterson. The majority of **Richard Rodgers** and **Lorenz Hart**'s fine stage score was retained, with four additional songs from their other shows. Sinatra was in great voice on 'I Could Write A Book', 'There's a Small Hotel' and 'What Do I Care For A Dame?', while Hayworth shimmied her way through 'Zip' and 'Bewitched' (vocals dubbed by Jo Ann Greer). Trudy Erwin's voice was behind Novak's sultry rendering of 'My Funny Valentine' and 'That Terrific Rainbow'. **Hermes Pan** was the choreographer, and Dorothy Kingsley's screenplay was adequate - O'Hara's version of events would never have been acceptable even in the late 50s - and this entertaining film grossed nearly $5 million in US rentals alone. It was produced in Technicolor for Columbia by Fred Kohlmar. The director was George Sidney.

Pal Joey (Stage Musical)

One of the first musical comedies to break with tradition, *Pal Joey* opened at the Ethel Barrymore Theatre in New York on Christmas Day 1940. With a libretto by John O'Hara, based on his own short stories, the plot had tough, realistic characters whose lives were concerned with sex and blackmail, and was far from the usual escapism. Also breaking new ground were the songs, which had music by **Richard Rodgers** and lyrics by **Lorenz Hart**. They were cleverly integrated into the plot, advancing both it and the development of characters. Joey was played by **Gene Kelly** and other cast members included Leila Ernst and Vivienne Segal (as just two of the women in his life), June Havoc and Van Johnson. The rich and amusing score included 'I Could Write A Book', 'Bewitched, Bothered, And Bewildered', 'That Terrific Rainbow', 'You Musn't Kick It Around', 'Do It The Hard Way', 'Take Him', 'The Flower Garden Of My Heart', 'What Is A Man?', 'Our Little Den Of Iniquity', and the intellectual striptease 'Zip'. *Pal Joey* ran for 374 performances but its 1952 revival did better, lasting for 542 performances, and winning **Tony Awards** for best featured actress (Helen Gallagher), choreographer (Robert Alton), and musical director (Max Meth). The remainder of the cast included Harold Lang, Vivienne Segal, and Elaine Stritch. The new production was widely applauded by critics and audiences who were by this time familiar with at least some of the shows songs and themes. The 1954 London production also starred Harold Lang with Carol Bruce. Over the years, revivals continue to be mounted, and in the early 90s the show was presented by the Goodspeed Opera House, Connecticut, the Long Beach Civic Light Opera, California, the Huntington Theatre Company in Boston, and the Old Vic in Bristol, UK.

Palais Schaumburg

News of German band Palais Schaumburg gradually

filtered through in 1981 via two singles on the Zick Zack label, 'Rote Lichter' and 'Telefon'. Frontman and bassist Holger Hiller (ex-Geister-Fahrer and Traneninvasion) was joined by drummer Ralf (ex-Abwarts, later replaced by Mufti), Thomas Fehlman (synthesizer) and Timo (bass/trumpet, ex-Immermanner), to create a dense, synthesized and at times experimental formula. A deal with the Kamera label in 1982 produced a one-off single, 'Wir Bauen Eine Neue Stadt', before Palais Schaumburg signed with **Mercury Records**. An album, *Lupa*, emerged later that year, but the band could only muster two further offerings. After 'Hockey' in 1983 and 'Beat Of Two' in the following year, Hiller left to pursue a solo career.

Album: *Lupa* (1982).

Pale

Three piece outfit from Dublin, Eire, featuring Matthew Deveraux (vocals), Shane Wearen (mandolin), and Sean Molloy (bass). **A&M** signed the band after their debut release, a limited edition cassette titled *Why Go Bold* (the band indeed, are well shorn), caused ripples throughout London's A&R departments. Their first single, 'Dogs With No Tails', was heavily promoted, but, despite its memorably bizarre display of Eastern European and pop traditions, it failed to achieve a strong chart placing. Their debut album was loaded with quirky but self-consciously 'weird' songs namechecking Airfix model kits and the like. There is enough evidence of the band's idiosyncratic talent but whether or not they will recieve the corporate backing they need to break them must now be a subject of conjecture.

Album: *Here's One We Made Earlier* (1992).

Pale Fountains

Formed in Liverpool in the early 80s by songwriter Michael Head (guitar/vocals) and Chris McCaffrey (bass) with Thomas Whelan (drums) and Andy Diagram, formerly of **Dislocation Dance** and the Diagram Brothers. Having been assimilated into the early 80s 'quiet pop'/'Bossa Nova' movement, Pale Fountains also drew upon such influences as the **Beatles**, the **Mamas And The Papas** and **Love**, but were probably better known for wearing short baggy trousers. Previously on the Operation Twilight label, the group attempted to break into the big-time when they signed to the **Virgin** label. Despite this lucrative move, this highly-touted group never broke out of their cult status. Their highest national chart position was the UK Top 50 'Thank You' in 1982.

Albums: *Pacific Street* (1984), *From Across The Kitchen Table* (1985).

Pale Saints

Indie band formed in Leeds, Yorkshire, England, in 1989 by Ian Masters (b. 4 January 1964, Potters Bar, Hertfordshire, England; bass), Chris Cooper (b. 17 November 1966, Portsmouth, England; drums) and Graeme Naysmith (b. 9 February 1967, Edinburgh, Scotland; guitar), following an advertisement in a music paper. Aided by occasional guitarist Ashley Horner, who eventually concentrated on his other band, Edsel Auctioneer, on a full time basis, the Pale Saints spent a year playing local venues and perfecting an idiosyncratic array of material which relied heavily on textures and effects rather than traditional arrangements or blatantly commercial choruses. That was not to say that they were unattractive: their first ever London gig in the spring of 1989 brought them a record deal with **4AD Records**, and their debut album of six months later, *The Comforts Of Madness*, earned the band much critical appreciation and the number 40 spot in the UK charts. Canadian emigrate Meriel Barham (b. 15 October 1964, Yorkshire, England) joined as a permanent guitarist/vocalist soon after, as Pale Saints continued their decidedly obtuse - if not downright perverse - path into the new decade with tours of Europe and Japan and an elegant cover version of **Nancy Sinatra**'s 'Kinky Love', which reached number 72 in the UK charts. The subsequent *In Ribbons* housed a non-charting single in 'Throwing Back The Apple', before the band re-emerged in 1994 with *Slow Buildings*. By this time Masters had departed, leaving Barham in charge of lyric writing, while Hugh Jones' crisp production gave new impetus to the band's familiar grandeur.

Albums: *The Comforts Of Madness* (4AD 1990), *In Ribbons* (4AD 1992), *Slow Buildings* (4AD 1994).

Pallas

This UK progressive rock outfit was formed in Aberdeen, Scotland, in 1975, by Euan Lowson (vocals), Niall Mathewson (guitar), Ronnie Brown (keyboards), Graeme Murray (bass) and Derek Forman (drums). They toured the British club circuit for many years, receiving constant rejections from A&R departments. Undeterred, they decided to self-finance the recording of a demo album. This materialized in 1983 as *Arrive Alive*, a quality collection of melodic songs. The set's modest success led to a deal with **EMI**, the services of **Yes** producer, Eddie Offord, and a large budget to record *The Sentinel* in Atlanta, Georgia, USA. This was an ambitious and intricate concept album which betrayed the group's **Marillion** and **Yes** influences. Lawson split at this juncture, to be replaced by Alan Reed. *The Wedge* followed and represented the pinnacle of the group's creativity. However, its commercial failure led to EMI severing links. Despite this the band remained together, but finally split when unable to find a new label sympathetic to their cause.

Albums: *Arrive Alive* (Kigg Cool 1983), *The Sentinel* (Harvest 1984), *The Wedge* (EMI 1986).

Palmer, Carl

(see **Atomic Rooster**; **Emerson, Lake And Palmer**; **Asia**)

Palmer, Clive

The 'forgotten one' from the **Incredible String Band**, Palmer founded the the group as a duo with **Robin Williamson**, and featured on the debut album. Subsequently, he moved to India, and, on his return, formed the Famous Jug band with Jill Johnson (vocals), Pete Berryman (guitar) and Henry Bartlett (jug), and himself on banjo. After recording *Sunshine Possibilities* (1969), he worked with C.O.B. (Clive's Original Band), along with John Bidwell (banjo) and Mick Bennett (percussion), on *Spirit Of Love* (1971) and *Moyshe Mcstiff And The Tartan Lancers Of The Sacred Heart* (1972). Since then, he has continued to work with a variety of units, and as a solo performer. A highly accomplished musician, the Original String Band would probably have sounded rather differently had he remained with them.

Selected album: *Just Me* (1978).

Palmer, Earl

b. 25 October 1924, New Orleans, Louisiana, USA. Palmer's mother was a vaudeville performer, and from an early age he began entertaining as a singer and dancer. Playing drums in his school band, he started listening to jazz drummers like **Big Sid Catlett** and **Panama Francis,** and joined **Dave Bartholomew**'s band in 1947. He recorded with the Bartholomew band and went on to play on many of his productions for Imperial Records, notably **Fats Domino**'s classic records. Palmer is probably featured on virtually every other Crescent City classic, including those Specialty rockers by **Little Richard**, and **Lloyd Price**, but in 1956 Aladdin Records hired him as a session arranger to handle their New Orleans sessions. In February 1957, he moved out to Los Angeles to work for Aladdin until the company was liquidated. He remained one of the busiest session drummers on the west coast throughout the 60s and 70s, recording with everyone from **Lightnin' Hopkins** to **Marvin Gaye** and subsequently wrote movie scores and advertising jingles.

Palmer, Michael

b. 1964, Maxfield Park, Kingston, Jamaica, West Indies. Inspired by his neighbour, **Leroy Smart**, Palmer began his career singing on the Echo Tone Hi Fi Sound. The **sound system** featured Big John, Flux and owner **General Echo** who were all killed in 1980 following a shooting incident in Kingston. Working with producer Oswald Thomas. Palmer's debut release 'Mr Landlord' faltered and with the demise of the sound system he maintained a low profile. By 1983 he was back in the studio with **Jah Thomas**, who had enjoyed success with Triston Palmer, resulting in the release of 'Ghetto Dance' with Jim Brown and 'Different Love'. A number of recordings followed with a variety of producers including **Prince Jammy**, **Sugar Minott** and **Joseph 'Joe Joe' Hookim**. Palmer's career began to prosper and whilst **Aswad** were recording in Jamaica they utilized Michael's voice for the release of 'Me Nah Run'. By the mid-80s his career was firmly established. He scored a number 1 in Jamaica with 'Lickshot' and his appearance at the Reggae Sunsplash festival was one of the high points of the event. A plethora of albums followed and those producers that did not have enough material to release a complete set compiled duo artist sets. As is often the case when a glut of material becomes available interest begins to dwindle and a lean period follows. He decided to test his production skills and enjoyed a smash hit with 'Haul And Pull Up' by Neville Brown. Palmer returned in fine style by the early 90s with a condemnation of licentiousness with the single 'Juggling' and alternatively 'Everyone Makes Love'.

Albums: *Star Performer* (Tonus 1983), *Lickshot* (Powerhouse 1984), *Pull It Up Now* (Greensleeves 1984), *Angelia* (Vista 1984), with Frankie Paul *Double Trouble* (Greensleeves 1984), with Frankie Jones *Showdown Volume 4* (Empire 1984), with Half Pint *Joint Favourites* (Greensleeves 1985), with Kelly Ranks *Chucky No Lucky* (Vista 1985).

Palmer, Robert

b. Alan Palmer, 19 January 1949, Batley, Yorkshire, England. Britain's leading 'blue-eyed soul' singer has served a musical apprenticeship over four decades in which time he has participated in many different styles of music. In the UK progressive music boom of the late 60s, Palmer joined the interestingly named Mandrake Paddle Steamer part-time, so as not to interfere with his day job as a graphic designer. Shortly afterwards he left for the lure of London to join the highly respected but commercially unsuccessful **Alan Bown** Set, replacing the departed **Jess Roden**. The following year he joined the ambitious conglomeration Dada, an experimental jazz/rock unit featuring **Elkie Brooks**. Out of Dada came the much loved **Vinegar Joe**, with which he made three albums. Already having sights on a solo career, Robert had worked on what was to become his debut *Sneakin' Sally Through The Alley* in 1974. Backed by the **Meters** and **Lowell George**, the album was an artistic triumph. A long-term relationship with **Chris Blackwell**'s **Island Records** began. Blackwell had faith in artists like Palmer and **John Martyn** and allowed their creativity to flow, over and above commercial considerations.

Little Feat appeared on his follow-up *Pressure Drop* after Palmer had relocated to New York. Still without significant sales, he moved to the luxury of the

Bahamas, where he lived for many years. In 1976 he released *Some People Can Do What They Like* to mixed reaction. Palmer persevered, although he was better known in America for many years. His first major US hit single came in 1979 with the R&B **Moon Martin** rocker, 'Bad Case Of Loving You'. He collaborated with **Gary Numan** on *Clues* which became a bigger hit in the UK than in America. The infectious 'Johnny And Mary' sneaked into the UK charts and two years later 'Some Guys Have All The Luck' made the Top 20. Seeming to give up on his solo career, he joined the **Duran Duran** based, **Power Station** in 1985. Continuing his own career, *Riptide*, released at the end of that year, gave him his biggest success. The album was a super-slick production of instantly appealing songs and it made the UK Top 5. In 1986, in addition to singing on John Martyn's *Sapphire*, he found himself at the top of the US charts with the beautifully produced 'Addicted To Love'. The record became a world-wide hit, making the UK Top 5. It was accompanied by a sexy (or sexist) video featuring a number of identical-looking girls playing instruments behind Palmer. He followed this with another catchy hit 'I Didn't Mean To Turn You On'. Following a move to Switzerland with his family he left Island after 14 years, and joined **EMI**. *Heavy Nova* was accompanied by the major hit 'She Makes My Day' in 1988. The next year a formidable compilation of his Island work was released, and found more success than *Heavy Nova.* He returned to the UK Top 10 with UB40 in 1990 with the **Bob Dylan** song 'I'll Be Your Baby Tonight' and in 1991, with a medley of **Marvin Gaye** songs, 'Mercy Mercy Me'/'I Want You'. *Honey* was another credible release with notable tracks such as 'Know By Now' and the title song. Palmer remains a respected artist, songwriter and the possessor of an excellent voice. He is also to be admired for his wardrobe of suits, having worn them when they were anathema to most rock stars. Nowadays, Palmer finds himself praised for being a well-dressed man.

Albums: *Sneakin' Sally Through The Alley* (1974), *Pressure Drop* (1975), *Some People Can Do What They Like* (1976), *Double Fun* (1978), *Secrets* (1979), *Clues* (1980), *Maybe It's Live* (1982), *Pride* (1983), *Riptide* (1985), *Heavy Nova* (1988), *Don't Explain* (1990), *Ridin' High* (1992), *Honey* (EMI 1994). Compilations: *The Early Years* (1987), *Addictions, Volume 1* (1989), *Addictions, Volume 2* (1992).

Palmer, Roy

b. c.1892, New Orleans, Louisiana, USA, d. 22 December 1963. Early in his career Palmer played guitar and trumpet but eventually settled on trombone. In the early years of the century he worked mostly in his home town. By 1920 he had moved to Chicago where he recorded with, amongst others, **Jelly Roll Morton, Johnny Dodds** and **Jimmy Blythe**. In the early 30s he quit full-time music but, according to jazz musician and writer **John Chilton**, he continued to teach into the 50s.

Palmer, Tony

b. 1941, this 'brilliant but difficult' ex-Lowestoft Grammar School pupil from Suffolk, England was an *Observer* reviewer for whom pop meant little, until a belated admiration for the latter-day **Beatles**' 'joyful music-making that only the ignorant will not hear'. He ventured into authorship with *Born Under A Bad Sign* (an encapsulation of his newspaper commentaries on pop) and television production with the popular culture magazine *How It Is* and the 17-part series, *All You Need Is Love.* Both as a BBC employee and freelance, Palmer was responsible for over 40 documentaries, including **Cream**'s farewell concert and portraits of diverse subjects such as **Jack Bruce**, **Liberace**, Benjamin Britten and Igor Stravinsky. Palmer wrote a superb account of the infamous Old Bailey 'Oz Trial', *The Trials Of Oz* (1971). With **Frank Zappa**, he co-directed 1973's *200 Motels*, a sluggish 'fantasy opera' of the **Mothers Of Invention**'s antics on tour - and the first cinema film to employ video equipment. However, after ructions with Zappa, Palmer washed his hands of the movie and tore it to pieces in his *Observer* column. In artistic debt to Ken Russell, the expensive *Wagner* (starring the late Richard Burton) was his first attempt at directing actors. Since then, his career has not been marked by success but more commercial ventures by Palmer in the future cannot be discounted.

Palmieri, Charlie

b. Carlos Manuel Palmieri Jnr., 21 November 1927, Bellevue Hospital, Manhattan, New York, USA; d. 12 September 1988, Jacobi Hospital, Bronx, New York, USA. Known in salsa as 'El Gigante de Las Blancas y Las Negras' (The Giant of the Keyboard), Palmieri's parents, Carlos Palmieri Manuel Villaneuva and Isabel Maldonado-Palmieri, migrated from Ponce, Puerto Rico to New York's El Barrio (Spanish Harlem), shortly before he was born. He was a child musical prodigy who could faultlessly copy a piece on the piano by ear. He began piano lessons at the age of seven and later studied at the Juilliard School of Music in New York. In 1941 Charlie and his five-year-old brother, **Eddie Palmieri**, won prizes in amateur talent contests and during this time, a guardian would take him to Latin big band dances. Charlie made his professional debut on 2 October 1943 with the band of Osario Selasie at the Park Palace Ballroom. A seven-month stint with Selasie was followed by one-and-a-half years with Orquestra Ritmo Tropical. After graduating from high school in 1946, he freelanced with various bands, including La Playa Sextet and Rafael Muñoz, with whom he made his recording debut on 'Se Va La Rumba'. In October 1947, he was hired to replace Joe Loco (b. José Estevez Jnr., 26 March 1921, New York,

USA; pianist/arranger/bandleader/composer) in Fernando Alvarez's band at the Copacabana club, by the band's then musical director **Tito Puente**. In 1948 he recorded on the Alba label with his first band, Conjunto Pin Pin. After leaving the Copacabana in 1951, Palmieri toured briefly with **Xavier Cugat**. The same year, he joined Puente's band and appeared on the 10-inch album *Tito Puente At The Vibes And His Rhythm Quartet, Vol. 6* on the Tico label (most of which was later incorporated on the late 50s album *Puente In Love*). He joined Pupi Campo's band and worked on Jack Paar's CBS daytime television show. In the early 50s, Charlie formed another band, which debuted at New York's famous Palladium Ballroom with lead vocalist Vitín Avilés (b. September 1925, Mayagüez, Puerto Rico). However, lack of gigs caused him to resume work as an accompanist. He performed with Johnny Seguí, **Tito Rodríguez**, Vicentico Valdés and Pete Terrace. A couple of tracks he recorded with Rodríguez in 1953 were included on the 1990 compilation *Ritmo y Melodia, 15 Joyas Tropicales*. He appeared on Terrace's mid-50s *A Night In Mambo-Jazzland*, and recorded as leader of a small latin jazz group on *El Fantastico Charlie Palmieri*. At the end of 1956, he organized a quintet for an extended residency in Chicago.

Shortly after Palmieri's return to New York, he discovered **Johnny Pacheco** playing flute with the band of Dominican singer/composer Dioris Valladares, who was on the same bill as Palmieri's group at the Monte Carlo Ballroom. He employed Pacheco, initially as a timbales player, and later as the flautist with his flute, strings, rhythm section and voices band, Charanga 'La Duboney'. The band signed with the major label United Artists, and their 1960 debut *Let's Dance The Charanga!*, featuring Vitín Avilés, generated several hits in New York's Latino market. Not only did La Duboney enjoy considerable success in their own right - playing two to three dances a night - but they also kicked off the early 60s charanga (flute and violin band) boom. After a short while, Pacheco split to found his own charanga. Palmieri was obliged to break his contract with United Artists when the company insisted that he record Hawaiian music! This was because the record contract of Tito Rodríguez, who signed with the label in 1960, stipulated that he would be the only artist to record latin music for them.

Charlie and Charanga 'La Duboney' switched to **Al Santiago's** Alegre label. They released three albums on the label between 1961 and 1963, and contributed two tracks to 1961's *Las Charangas*, which also featured the charangas of Pacheco and **José Fajardo**. The tracks 'Como Bailan La Pachanga' and 'La Pachanga Se Baila Asi' (co-written by **Joe Quijano** and Palmieri), from La Duboney's magnificent best-selling Alegre debut *Pachanga At The Caravana Club*, were both hits in *Farándula* magazine's New York Latin Top 15 during May 1961.

Palmieri directed (and performed on) and Santiago produced four superlative Alegre All-Stars latin jam session (descarga) volumes issued between 1961 and the mid-60s. These albums, which gave Charlie an opportunity to indulge his dual passion for jazz and Cuban music, involved artists such as **Kako**, Pacheco, **Willie Rosario**, **Cheo Feliciano**, Orlando Marín, Dioris Valladares, Barry Rogers, Joe Quijano, Bobby Rodríguez (the bassist), Osvaldo 'Chi Hua Hua' Martínez and Willie Torres. The Alegre All-Stars' recordings were a descendant of the *Cuban Jam Session* volumes recorded in Cuba on the Panart label in the second half of the 50s (see **Israel 'Cachao' López**). Cuban saxophonist José 'Chombo' Silva participated on both. In their turn, the Alegre All-Stars inspired a string of New York descarga recordings, which included releases by Kako, Johnny Pacheco, Osvaldo 'Chi Hua Hua' Martínez (*Descarga Cubana Vol. 1*, 1966, and *Latin Cuban Session Vol. 2*, c.1967), Tico All-Stars, Cesta All-Stars (see Joe Quijano), Salsa All-Stars, Fania All Stars and SAR All Stars (see **Roberto Torres**). Palmieri and Santiago made a significant input: Charlie guested on the Tico All-Stars' 1966 descarga volumes recorded at New York's Village Gate, and directed and played on the Cesta All-Stars' two albums, which Santiago co-produced; Santiago produced *Salsa All Stars* in 1968, which featured Palmieri on piano.

When the charanga sound declined in popularity, Palmieri replaced the flute and violins with three trumpets and two trombones to form the Duboney Orchestra for 1965's *Tengo Maquina Y Voy A 60* (Going Like Sixty). Puerto Rico-born Victor Velázquez, a Palmieri accompanist since 1961, sang lead vocals with the new Duboney, which also included young trumpeter **Bobby Valentín**. Palmieri left Alegre to record for the BG label, but returned in 1967 for *Hay Que Estar En Algo/Either You Have It Or You Don't!*, which contained some boogaloos, an R&B/latin fusion form that was the rage at the time. Charlie later admitted to Max Salazar: ' . . . I didn't care for the boogaloo, but I've learned that if you do not follow a popular trend, you're dead.' The following year he recorded *Latin Bugalu* for **Atlantic**, which was also released in the UK. The album was produced by **Herbie Mann** and contained his self-penned classic 'Mambo Show'. 1969 was an extremely lean year for Palmieri's band. He nearly suffered a nervous breakdown and contemplated relocating to Puerto Rico. However, he was dissuaded from doing so by Tito Puente, who hired him as musical conductor for his television show *El Mundo De Tito Puente*. When the series finished, Charlie started a parallel career as a lecturer in Latin music and culture, and taught in various educational institutions in New York.

Velázquez left for an eight month stint with Joe Quijano in Puerto Rico; he returned to Palmieri's band in 1972 to share lead vocals with Vitín Avilés, then departed to join **Louie Ramírez**'s band. Charlie began using organ, which imparted an element of kitsch to some of his recorded work. He rejigged his horn section to two trumpets and saxophone (played by Bobby Nelson, who doubled on flute). He issued three notable albums on Alegre between 1972 and 1975 with Avilés on lead vocals, and two on Harvey Averne's Coco label (in 1974 and 1975) with lead vocals by Velázquez. A number of Charlie's hit tunes from this period were written by veteran Puerto Rican composer/singer and former heart-throb, Raúl Marrero, including, 'La Hija De Lola' from *El Gigante Del Teclado* (1972) and 'La Vecina' from *Vuelve El Gigante* (1973). Palmieri only played organ with his band on the first Coco outing, *Electro Duro*, which was probably his most disappointing album. His second Coco release, *Impulsos*, was a more refined remake of the rawer (and better) *Charlie Palmieri* issued on Mary Lou Records in c.1969. Both versions featured Velázquez on lead vocals; he again departed and went on to co-lead Típica Ideal. In 1977, Charlie teamed up with veteran Panamanian singer/composer Meñique Barcasnegras for *Con Salsa Y Sabor* on the Cotique label. That year, he returned to Alegre to lead and perform on the Al Santiago produced 17th anniversary Alegre All-Stars reunion *Perdido (Vol. 5)*, which re-convened ten musicians from the 60s sessions, together with Louie Ramírez, **Bobby Rodríguez** and members of his band La Compañia. Palmieri remained with Alegre in 1978 for *The Heavyweight*, with singers Meñique and Julito Villot, and played and arranged on Vitín Avilés' solo *Con Mucha Salsa*. His brief return to Alegre was punctuated by the highly recommended compilation *Gigante Hits* in 1978, which selected tracks from his 1965-75 period with the label. In 1979, Charlie appeared in Jeremy Marre's UK television film *Salsa*.

In one or more of his capacities as A&R head, producer, keyboardist and arranger, Palmieri worked with a long list of artists, which included: Kako, brother Eddie, **Celia Cruz**, Tito Puente, **Ismael Rivera**, **Rafael Cortijo**, Herbie Mann, **Ismael Quintana**, Yayo El Indio, **Cal Tjader**, Raúl Marrero, Joe Quijano, Frankie Dante, Bobby Capó, Israel 'Cachao' López, Machito, **Mongo Santamaría** and **Ray Barretto**. In January 1980, Palmieri moved to Puerto Rico to escape New York's severe winters and frustrating, exploitative Latin club scene. He organized a successful band there, but sadly never recorded with them. Charlie returned to New York in February 1983 to discuss a proposed concert in Puerto Rico with his brother Eddie. However he suffered a massive heart attack and stroke and was hospitalized for six weeks. Upon his recovery, he continued to reside in New York and resolved to live at a slower pace. On 6 January 1984, New York's Latin music industry paid tribute to Palmieri at Club Broadway. The same year, he returned to a small group format (piano, bass, timbales, conga and bongo) for the latin jazz *A Giant Step* on the Tropical Budda label. He played on *El Sabor Del Conjunto Candela/86*, led by bongo/güiro player Ralphy Marzan, and on Joe Quijano's *The World's Most Exciting Latin Orchestra & Review* in 1988. Up to 1988, he gigged with Combo Gigante, which he co-led with Jimmy Sabater (see **Joe Cuba**). No recordings by the band have been released. He made his belated UK debut in June 1988 with a five-night residency at London's Bass Clef club accompanied by London-based Robin Jones' King Salsa. On 12 September 1988, Charlie arrived back in New York after a trip to Puerto Rico, where he had performed at the Governor's residence with veteran singer/composer Bobby Capó. Later in the day he suffered a further heart attack and died at the Jacobi Hospital in the Bronx. In 1990, the latin jazz CD *Mambo Show* was released on the resurrected Tropical Budda label, which congregated an all-star ensemble, including Palmieri (piano and co-producer), Mongo Santamaría (conga), Chombo (saxophone); Barry Rogers (trombone), Nicky Marrero (timbales), Johnny 'Dandy' Rodríguez (bongo), Ray Martínez (bass), David 'Piro' Rodríguez (trumpet).

Selected albums: *El Fantastico Charlie Palmieri* (1950s), *Easy Does It* (late 50s), *Let's Dance The Charanga!* (1960, reissued under the title of *Echoes Of An Era*), *Pachanga At The Caravana Club* (1961), with the charangas of Johnny Pacheco and José Fajardo *Las Charangas* (1961), *The Alegre All-Stars* (1961), *Viva Palmieri* (1962), *Salsa Na' Ma', Vol. 3* (1963), *The Alegre All-Stars Vol. 2 'El Manicero'* (1965), *Tengo Maquina Y Voy A 60* (1965), *The Alegre All-Stars Vol. 3 'Lost & Found'* (mid-60s), *The Alegre All-Stars Vol. 4 'Way Out'* (mid-60s), *Mas De Charlie Palmieri* (1966), *Hay Que Estar En Algo/Either You Have It Or You Don't* (1967), *Latin Bugalu* (1968), with the Cesta All-Stars *Live Jam Session* (1968), *Salsa All Stars* (1968), with Cesta All-Stars *Salsa Festival*, *El Gigante Del Teclado* (1972), *Vuelve El Gigante* (1973), with various artists *Tico-Alegre All Stars Recorded Live At Carnegie Hall, Volume 1* (1974), *Electro Duro* (1974), *Adelante, Gigante* (1975), *Impulsos* (1975), with Meñique *Con Salsa Y Sabor* (1977), with Alegre All-Stars *Perdido (Vol. 5)* (1977), *The Heavyweight* (1978), *A Giant Step* (1984), with an all-star ensemble *Mambo Show* (1990). Compilations: with the Alegre All-Stars *They Just Don't Mak'em Like Us Any More* (1976), *Gigante Hits* (1978).

Palmieri, Eddie

b. Eduardo Palmieri, 15 December 1936, South Bronx, New York, USA, of Puerto Rican parentage. The self-avowed pioneering 'oxygen cocktail' of contemporary salsa, pianist, bandleader, composer, arranger, producer Palmieri began playing the piano at the age of eight. Eddie also played timbales, and wanted to specialize in the instrument, but changed his mind after several gigs with his uncle's group. He developed into ' . . . a pianist with impeccable time, drive and endurance; a soloist of originality and daring and . . . has an unorthodox piano technique which has startled many conventionally trained pianists' (Louise Rogers, c.1964). Within the framework of typical Latin music, Palmieri progressed a unique approach to the genre characterized by free improvisation and experimentation. While attending Public School Number 52 in the Bronx, 14-year-old Palmieri formed a group with timbales player Orlando Marín, which included vocalist/percussionist **Joe Quijano**. Eddie left in 1955 to turn professional as a member of Johnny Seguí's orchestra, and the group became the Orlando Marín Conjunto. However, his over-zealousness resulted in his dismissal. 'The club said I broke the piano, hitting the keys too hard. Seguí told me, either you go or the band goes, so see you later'. He then replaced brother Charlie as pianist with the band of ex-**Tito Puente** lead singer, Vicentico Valdés, before joining **Tito Rodríguez**'s big band from 1958-60. Eddie had great respect for Rodríguez: 'He was just an incredible artist, a great vocalist . . . He was the most wonderful person you could imagine, except when he got on the bandstand. Then he became like a Jekyll and Hyde. That's the way he had to be - because of the excellence he demanded. He was sadistic - no emotion, no nothing' (quoted by John Ortiz).

In the liner notes to Eddie's first album, Charlie described his brother as a 'nut' for leaving the financial security of Rodríguez's successful band. Palmieri subsequently played weddings, funerals and local dances before forming La Perfecta in 1961. The line-up included John Pacheco and Barry Rogers (b. 1936, New York, USA; d. 19 April 1991, New York, USA; trombonist/arranger). Palmieri and Rogers developed a two trombone and flute frontline for Conjunto La Perfecta, which Charlie dubbed a 'trombanga'. They became one of Latin New York's busiest bands and signed with **Al Santiago**'s Alegre label, who produced their debut *Eddie Palmieri And His Conjunto La Perfecta* in 1962. In addition to Rogers, other key founder members of La Perfecta on the album were: **Ismael 'Pat' Quintana** (lead vocals), Manny Oquendo (timbales, see **Conjunto Libre**) and George Castro (flute). In 1963, Brazilian trombonist Jose Rodrigues joined La Perfecta; he became a regular Palmieri accompanist into the 80s and a busy session musician. Eddie and the band released a further two volumes on Alegre before switching to Tico Records in 1964 for *Echando Pa'lante (Straight Ahead)*. La Perfecta's seminal mid-60s trombanga line-up comprised of Rogers and Rodrigues (trombones), Castro (flute), Oquendo (timbales/bongo), Tommy López (conga), Dave Pérez (bass), Palmieri (piano), Quintana (vocals). Pérez was an ex-member of Johnny Pacheco's charanga and later worked with **Ray Barretto** and **Típica 73**. Eddie released a further five albums with La Perfecta, including two with latin jazz vibraphonist **Cal Tjader**, before the band fell apart in 1968. 'I just wasn't taking care of business - problems with money, cancelling gigs. Just getting there was all I could manage - just get there and bring some money home to eat. That's about what it came down to.' However, the band's legacy of recorded work provides ample testimony of what a brilliant, ferociously swinging outfit they were. In 1966, Eddie participated in the Tico All-Stars' descargas (latin jam sessions) recorded at New York's Village Gate and guested on the Fania All-Stars' debut album in 1968. After the break-up of La Perfecta, Palmieri used a variety of front-line instrumentation on his albums. The first, *Champagne* in 1968, featured the trumpet of **Alfredo 'Chocolate' Armenteros** and Rogers on trombone, together with bassist **Israel 'Cachao' López** and three lead vocalists: Quintana, **Cheo Feliciano** and Cynthia Ellis. It contained boogaloo material, the R&B/latin fusion style that was in vogue at the time. Palmieri later described boogaloo as embarrassing, and blamed its emergence on what he perceived as a decline in Latin music's creativity, caused by the isolation of Cuba from the USA.

Palmieri took up the issue of economic and social injustice in the USA on 1969's *Justicia*. He was joined on this album by young timbales player Nicky Marrero, who became a regular accompanist until the mid-70s. Marrero later joined the Fania All-Stars and Típica 73, and worked extensively as a session musician. Cuban **Justo Betancourt** sang in the chorus on *Justicia* and Eddie's next release *Superimposition* (1969), which contained a whole side of experimental instrumentals. Bassist Andy González, a member of Ray Barretto's band at the time, performed on this album; he eventually joined Palmieri's band in 1971, then split in 1974 to co-found Conjunto Libre with Manny Oquendo. Eddie added the saxophone of Ronnie Cuber to his horn section on *Vamonos Pa'l Monte* in c.1971. Cuber remained with Palmieri until the late 70s. Brother Charlie guested on organ on this album and Eddie's other 1971 recordings, which were issued between 1971 and 1974. These included Eddie's latin and R&B fusion experiments with the black group Harlem River Drive, and concerts at Sing Sing prison and the University of Puerto Rico. Palmieri signed with ex-bandleader Harvey Averne's Coco Records, and debuted on the label with 1973's *Sentido*. Quintana left to pursue a solo career and was replaced by 16-year-old **Lalo Rodriguez** on *Sun Of Latin Music* in 1974. In 1976, the album won the first ever Grammy Award in the newly created Latin record category. His next Coco release, 1976's *Unfinished Masterpiece*, which he did not want issued, took him back to Grammy land. Young Cuban violinist **Alfredo de la Fé** appeared on both albums. Eddie's subsequent five new releases between 1978-87 all received Grammy nominations.

After a break from recording due to contractual

wrangles, Eddie made *Lucumi Macumba Voodoo* for the major record company Epic in 1978, which took the African-derived religions of Cuba, Brazil and Haiti as its theme. The record flopped both in and outside the Latin market, and Palmieri later expressed disappointment about his experience with the label. He also regretted unwittingly joining the Fania Records empire. *La Verdad/The Truth* won him a fifth Grammy Award, and featured late 80s/early 90s hit-maker **Tony Vega** on lead vocals. 1981's *Eddie Palmieri* was Barry Rogers' last appearance on record with Eddie - he played all trombone parts and solos - and marked the one-off return of Ismael Quintana, who sang lead on two tracks. Eddie relocated to Puerto Rico in 1983, but lack of regular work due to rejection by many promoters and musicians, caused him to return to New York in frustration. He made his only UK appearance to date in 1986. Palmieri signed with another major company, **Capitol Records**, for the slightly disappointing *Sueño* in 1989. It contained four remakes of previous hits and featured jazz-fusion alto-saxophonist **David Sanborn**.

Albums: *Eddie Palmieri And His Conjunto La Perfecta* (1962), *El Molestoso Vol. II* (1963), *Lo Que Traigo Es Sabroso* (1964), *Echando Pa'lante (Straight Ahead)* (1964), *Azucar Pa' Ti (Sugar For You)* (1965), *Mozambique* (1965), *Molasses* (1966), with Cal Tjader *El Sonido Nuevo/The New Soul Sound* (1966), with Cal Tjader *Bamboleate* (1967, UK release 1989), *Champagne* (1968), *Justicia* (1969), *Superimposition* (1969), with various artists *Lluvia De Estrellas* (1970), *Vamonos Pa'l Monte* (1971), *Harlem River Drive* (1971), with Harlem River Drive *Live At Sing Sing* (1972), *Sentido* (1973), *Eddie Palmieri & Friends In Concert At The University Of Puerto Rico* (1973), *The Sun Of Latin Music* (1974), with Harlem River Drive *Live At Sing Sing, Vol.2* (1974), *Unfinished Masterpiece* (1976), *Lucumi Macumba Voodoo* (1978), *Eddie Palmieri* (1981), *Timeless* (1981, mid-60s live recording of La Perfecta), *Palo Pa' Rumba* (1984), *Solito* (1985), *La Verdad/The Truth* (1987), *Sueño* (1989).

Compilations: from Palmieri's Alegre and Tico catalogue - *Lo Mejor De Eddie Palmieri* (1974), *The History Of Eddie Palmieri* (1975), *Eddie's Concerto* (1976), *The Music Man* (1977); *Gold 1973-1976* (1978), *Exploration* (1978, Coco label), *EP* (1990, Fania label).

Pama Records

Once the chief rival to **Trojan**, Pama has since evolved into Jet Star, the main reggae distributors in the UK. Originally the brainchild of occasional Jamaican record producers, the Palmer Brothers, Pama was founded in London in 1967, releasing an almost endless supply of Jamaican productions on a series of labels that were less high-profile than Trojan's in the white market, but which were every bit as musically strong as its rival's. Among Pama's subsidiary labels were Pama Supreme, Supreme, Crab, Bullet, Gas, New/Nu Beat, Success, Camel, Escort, Unity and Punch, the latter perhaps epitomising reggae's attitude, depicting a fist punching through a top 10 pop chart. Through these labels the brothers worked with nearly all of the top reggae producers, including **Laurel Aitken** (chiefly Nu Beat), **Lee Perry** (chiefly Punch), **Rupie Edwards** (Success), **Bunny Lee** (Unity, which scored a massive hit with **Max Romeo**'s 'Wet Dream' in 1969) and virtually everyone who was anyone in reggae at the time. They also issued a series of *Straighten Up* albums in competition with Trojan's *Tighten Up* series, which remain highly collectable today, plus a scattering of non-reggae LPs, including *Butlins Red Coat Revue* and an album commemorating the investiture of the Prince Of Wales! By the mid-70s the business was chiefly in the hands of the youngest Palmer brother, Carl, who began to concentrate on setting-up a distribution network in the UK, which has gradually expanded to the point of ubiquity: if Jet Star don't distribute it, it's probably not reggae.

Selected albums: Various: *Crab's Biggest Hits* (Crab 1969), *Straighten Up Volume 1* (Pama 1970). The Upsetters: *Clint Eastwood* (Pama 1970). Max Romeo: *Let The Power Fall* (Pama 1972).

Pampini, Gabino

b. Gabino Espinosa, Panama. This renowned soneros (improvising salsa singer) artist originally worked with El Combo Impacto and Roberto y su Zafra. The tracks he recorded with these two bands were later compiled on *Otra Vez...Gabino Pampini*. Gabino relocated to Miami, USA, where he linked up with Colombian bandleader/pianist/arranger/composer/flautist Hernán Gutiérrez, who worked with Fruko in the 70s. Pampini shared lead vocals with Cuban Javier Oliva on Gutiérrez's *Y Ahora...La Tremenda Salsa De Hernán Gutiérrez y su Orquesta* in 1980, which was later issued in Colombia under Pampini's name with the title *La Hermandad Latina*. Three years later, Gabino, Colombian Oscar Alberto Abueta (see **Grupo Niche** and **Alberto Barros**) and ex-Los Van Van vocalist, Cuban Israel 'Kantor' Sardiñas, were lead singers on Gutiérrez's modern classic *Con Sacrificio*, which must rank as one of the top 10 best salsa albums of the 80s. Lamentably, Gutiérrez died shortly afterwards.

Pampini continued in a similar stylistic vein as a solo artist. He teamed up with bassist/arranger/composer Ricardo Lance (b. Barranquilla, Colombia) to co-lead the band Fuerza Noble, and released three albums with them between 1987 and 1988, all recorded in Miami. Fuerza Noble's line-up sported a frontline of two trumpets and two or three trombones plus rhythm section (bass, conga, bongo, timbales and piano) and voices. Ex-Sonora Ponceña (see **Papo Lucca**) lead singer, Yolanda Rivera, sang in the chorus on all three albums. Pampini later parted company with Lance. In 1989 he guested on *Frivolo*, recorded in Colombia by

Grupo Galé led by young Colombian percussionist/singer/producer Diego Galé. Gabino provided lead vocals to the album's smash hit track 'Mi Vecina'. Pampini signed with the major Latin record company, TH-Rodven, and debuted on the label in 1990 with the Miami-recorded *Las Aventuras Musicales de...Gabino Pampini*, which included four tracks arranged by Alberto Barros. Meanwhile, Lance made his solo debut as bandleader with *Ricardo Lance y su Grupo Sublime* in 1989. His Grupo Sublime, a three-trombone band, featured four ex-Fuerza Noble members. The following year, Lance was the musical director and wrote two arrangements on *Mas Alla Del Sabor!* by female singer/composer Arabella (b. María Margarita Pinillos, 15 June 1950s, Bogotá, Colombia).

Albums: with Hernán Gutiérrez *Y Ahora...La Tremenda Salsa De Hernán Gutiérrez y su Orquesta* (1980) with Gutiérrez *Con Sacrificio* (1984), *Fuerza Noble* (1987), *Fuerza Noble* (1987), *Fuerza Noble* (1988), with Grupo Galé *Frivolo* (1989), *Las Aventuras Musicales de...Gabino Pampini* (1990). Compilation: with El Combo Impacto and Roberto y su Zafra *Otra Vez...Gabino Pampini* (1988).

Pan, Hermes

b. Hermes Panagiotopulos, between 1905 and 1910, Memphis, Tennessee, USA, d. 19 September 1990, Beverly Hills, California, USA. A dancer and legendary choreographer who worked closely with **Fred Astaire** on most of his film musicals and television specials. Pan danced in clubs and in the singing chorus of the Broadway musical *Top Speed*, which featured **Ginger Rogers**, before moving to Hollywood in the early 30s. After serving as assistant to dance director Dave Gould on ***Flying Down To Rio***, Astaire and Rogers' first picture together, and the follow-up, ***The Gay Divorcee***, Pan choreographed all of Astaire's films at RKO, including ***Roberta***, ***Top Hat***, ***Follow The Fleet***, ***Swing Time***, ***Shall We Dance***, ***Carefree***, and ***The Story Of Vernon And Irene Castle***. He won an Oscar for his imaginative staging of the 'Fun House' sequence in another RKO feature, ***A Damsel In Distress*** (1937), in which Astaire appeared with George Burns and Gracie Allen. Pan also worked with Astaire on *Second Chorus*, ***Blue Skies***, ***The Barkleys Of Broadway*** (with Ginger Rogers again), *Three Little Words*, *Let's Dance*, ***Silk Stockings***, and *Finian's Rainbow* (1968) which was their last movie together. Pan also made one of his rare on-screen appearances in that one. Over the years, he had occasionally danced in films such as ***My Gal Sal***, *Sweet Rosie O'Grady*, ***Moon Over Miami***, ***Kiss Me Kate***, and *Pin-Up Girl*. However, for most of his career, he was content to make major stars - **Betty Grable**, **Rita Hayworth**, **Don Ameche**, **Howard Keel**, Juliet Prowse, **Alice Faye**, **Carmen Miranda**, **Ann Miller**, **Kathryn Grayson** and many others - look good in a variety of mostly entertaining musical pictures such as ***Billy Rose's Diamond Horseshoe***, *Song Of The Islands*, *That Night In Rio*, *Footlight Serenade*, *Springtime In The Rockies*, ***Coney Island***, *Lovely To Look At*, *That Lady In Ermine*, ***Hit The Deck***, ***The Student Prince***, *Meet Me In Las Vegas*, ***Pal Joey***, ***Can-Can***, ***Flower Drum Song***, ***My Fair Lady***, *Darling Lili*, and *Lost Horizon*. He also staged Cleopatra's spectacular entry into Rome for the Elizabeth Taylor-Richard Burton epic *Cleopatra* in 1963. Pan won Emmy Awards for his work on the highly acclaimed television specials *An Evening With Fred Astaire* (1959) and *Astaire Time* (1961). In 1981 he received the National Film Award for achievement in cinema, and six years later was presented with the prestigious Joffrey Ballet Award. A true innovator, many of the films in which he mixed ballet, jazz and tap, are now rightly regarded as classics.

Panama Hattie

Considered to be similar in some ways to ***Dubarry Was A Lady*** (1939), this show was nevertheless felt to be inferior to that one, although it employed the same creative team, and ran for some four months longer. *Panama Hattie* opened at the 46th Street Theatre on 30 October 1940, with a **Cole Porter** score, a book by Herbert Fields and **B.G. 'Buddy' DeSylva**, and with the dynamic **Ethel Merman** on hand to belt out the songs. She plays Hattie Maloney, the owner of a nightclub in Panama City. Outwardly cynical, but a real pussy-cat deep down inside (a perfect Merman character) her prospective marriage to well-heeled divorcé, Nick Bullitt (James Dunn), hangs on the approval of Geraldine - sometimes known as Jerry - (Joan Carroll), the precocious eight-year-old daughter from his first marriage. Hattie wins her over during the conciliatory 'Let's Be Buddies' (Hattie: 'Would you like a big box of chocolate creams?'/Jerry: 'No, for candy I never did care'/Hattie: 'Then will you let me get you a cute little dog?'/Jerry: 'Would you mind making it a bear?'). Merman had several other clever Porter numbers, including 'Make It Another Old Fashioned, Please', 'I'm Throwing A Ball Tonight', and 'I've Still Got My Health' ('I can't count my ribs, like His Nibs, **Fred Astaire**/But I've still got my health, so what do I care!'). The rest of the songs included 'All I've Got To Get Now Is My Man', 'Fresh As A Daisy', 'My Mother Would Love You', 'Who Would Have Dreamed?', and 'Visit Panama'. The cast included some familiar names of the future such as **Betty Hutton**, along with **June Allyson** and **Vera-Ellen** who were both in the chorus. *Panama Hattie*, which was the fourth in a series of five musicals that Porter and Merman did together, enjoyed a run of 501 performances. It marked the beginning of a decade during which they both produced some of their finest work: Porter with ***Kiss Me, Kate*** (1948), and Merman with ***Annie Get Your Gun*** (1946). *Panama Hattie* also had a decent run of 308 performances in London's West End, where it starred

Bebe Daniels, Max Wall, Ivan Brandt, Claude Hulbert, and Richard Hearne.

Pandemonium

This Alaskan heavy metal band was formed by the Resch brothers; Chris (vocals), Eric (bass) and David (guitar), in 1981. They relocated to Los Angeles, California, and teamed up with Chris Latham (guitar) and Dave Graybill (drums) the following year. Making their debut on the first *Metal Massacre* compilation with 'Fighting Backwards', it opened the door to a full contract with Metal Blade Records. Three albums followed over the next five years, with each successive release becoming less formularized (despite displaying the continually strong influence of **Van Halen**) but to little commercial advantage.
Albums: *Heavy Metal Soldiers* (Metal Blade 1984), *Hole In The Sky* (Metal Blade 1985), *The Kill* (Metal Blade 1988).

Pandora's Box

This one-off project was put together by US producer **Jim Steinman** to record his rock opera, *Original Sin*. The band featured Roy Bittan (piano), Jeff Bova (synthesizers), Jim Bralower (drums), Eddie Martinez (guitar) and Steve Buslowe (bass). Utilizing a series of guest vocalists, which included Elaine Caswell, **Ellen Foley**, Gina Taylor, Deliria Wild, Holly Sherwood and Laura Theodore, *Original Sin* was a grandiose concept album themed on sex. Featuring classical interludes, spoken introductions, atmospheric ballads and breathtaking rock 'n' roll, it was almost too ambitious. Despite state-of-the-art production (courtesy of Steinman) it never received the sort of recognition afforded his **Meat Loaf** projects.
Album: *Original Sin* (Virgin 1989).

Pantera

This Texan heavy metal quartet was formed in 1981. They initially comprised Terry Glaze (guitar/vocals), Darrell Abbott (guitar), Vince Abbott (drums) and Rex Rocker (bass). Drawing musical inspiration from **Kiss**, **Aerosmith** and **Deep Purple**, they debuted with *Metal Magic* in 1983. This well-received set led to prestigious support slots to **Dokken**, **Stryper**, and **Quiet Riot**. *Projects In The Jungle* indicated that the band were evolving quickly and starting to build a sound of their own. The **Kiss** nuances had disappeared and the band sounded, at times, similar to early **Def Leppard**, with anthemic cuts likes 'Heavy Metal Rules' and 'Out For Blood' leading the charge. The membership altered their names at this juncture with Glaze becoming Terence Lee, Darrell Abbott switching to Diamond Darrell and brother Vince emerging as Vinnie Paul. *Power Metal* saw Phil Anselmo take over on vocals, but the album lacked the depth and polish of previous efforts, and had yet to make the full conversion to extant thrash which would become their new trademark. Diamond Darrell turned down the offer to join **Megadeth** at this point in order to concentrate on new Pantera material. The decision proved crucial, as a return to form was made with 1990's *Cowboys From Hell*. This was an inspired collection of infectious hard rock, played with unabashed fervour, with Anselmo growing as a creative and visual force. *Vulgar Display Of Power*, meanwhile, belied half of its title by invoking a sense of genuine songwriting prowess to augment the bone-crushing arrangements. Building up a fierce reputation, it surprised few of the group's supporters when *Far Beyond Driven* entered both the UK and US album charts at number 1. Rock music had found powerful new ambassadors in the brutally honest and savagely executed thrash metal of Pantera.
Albums: *Metal Magic* (Metal Magic 1983), *Projects In The Jungle* (Metal Magic 1984), *I Am The Night* (Metal Magic 1985), *Power Metal* (Metal Magic 1988), *Cowboys From Hell* (Atco 1990), *Vulgar Display Of Power* (Atco 1992), *Far Beyond Driven* (East West 1994), *Driven Downunder Tour Tour '94 Souvenir Collection* (East West 1995).
Video: *Vulgar Video* (1994).

Papa Bue

(see **Jensen, Papa Bue**)

Papa Chuk

b. Charles Roberts, c.1969. Hardcore hip hop artist from Houston, Texas, where he moved in 1991 from his native Austin. As a child Papa Chuk, 'The Desolate One', practised rapping along to b-side instrumentals purchased for him by his mother, and was obviously strongly influenced by **Naughty By Nature**'s Treach in his delivery. His debut album saw him also introduce a Jamaican patois/dancehall style, notably on cuts like 'Make Way For The Rudeboy', though other tracks like 'Desert Dog' and 'Down And Dirty' needed more to distinguish them.
Album: *Badlands* (Pendulum 1994).

Papa Levi, Phillip

b. Phillip Williams. Papa Levi originally rose to fame on south London's Saxon **sound system** in the early 80s. His committed and uncompromising stance has, perhaps, denied him the kind of mainstream success that his talent deserves. As the premier **UK MC** of the period he was notable for a number of firsts: he was the first from the Saxon posse to make a record - 'Mi God Mi King' (for Paul Robinson aka **Barry Boom**), the first UK MC to have a number 1 record in Jamaica when the same record was released on the **Taxi** label - and the first to sign a major recording deal - with **Island Records**. But while others reaped the spin off benefits from these achievements Levi never moved from Saxon Sound System. Live on the mic. he dominated the proceedings and little was lost in the

transfer to vinyl, as demonstrated on 'Mi God Mi King' when he dropped into the 'fast style' at the end of the record. The effect really was shattering. The rest of the decade saw him notching up some notable away performances in both Kingston and New York with Saxon on tour. Sadly he has never actually recorded that often, although when he does the results are always of interest. The 90s have neither seen nor heard too much from Levi but judging by his past performances the fireworks will start again once he returns to the studio.
Albums: *Trouble In Africa* (1987), *Code Of Practice* (Ariwa 1990). Various: *Coughing Up Fire - Saxon Studio Live* (Greensleeves 1985), *Great British MCs* (Fashion 1985, includes 'Mi God Mi King').

Papa San

b. Tyrone Thompson, 1966, Spanish Town, Jamaica, West Indies. Probably the fastest DJ in the world and certainly one of the most inventive, Papa San began his career on the People's Choice, Small Axe and Creation **sound systems**, based around Spanish Town, where he spent most of his early years. In 1983 he joined Lee's Unlimited and by the following year could be heard on Metromedia. He first recorded in 1985. 'Animal Party' on Black Solidarity being one of his earliest releases, so too 'Talking Parrot' for Rosie's Uprising, and both were distinguished by an ingenious lyrical slant and a quick-fire delivery, inspired in part by the fast-talking style instigated by **UK MCs** on the Saxon sound system. Over the next two years he recorded for Isiah Laing's Supreme label, **Bunny Lee**, **Prince Jazzbo**, Harmodio, **King Jammys** and the late **King Tubby** among others, voicing mainly cultural material and intricate tales of ghetto living complete with vivid descriptions of local characters. In 1988, after a successful spell in New York with the African Love and Papa Mike sets, he recorded 'DJ Business' for **Fashion** Records in London, an eight minute *tour de force* that listed in detail the entire history of reggae DJs. By all accounts it was voiced in one take and remains an essential illustration of his unique abilities. **Fashion** later teamed him with **Tippa Irie** for their *JA To UK MC Clash (Vol. 2)* album.
The next two years were spent recording in Jamaica with varying degrees of success. **Gussie Clarke** reunited him with his former Creation partner Lady G for 'Round Table Talk', but it was not until 1990 that he found another winning streak, sharpening his skills with Black Scorpio on both sound and record, voicing for Mikey Bennett, **Captain Sinbad**, **Penthouse**, **Digital B** and **King Jammy**'s son, John John, before really getting into his stride around 1991-92. 'Strange' and the bizarre 'Maddy Maddy Cry' he produced himself. 'Hippity Hippity Hop' arrived on Robbie Shakespeare's Powermatic label, and fine tunes for **Exterminator**, Tan Yah, Shocking Vibes, Wild Apache and Lloyd Honeyghan tumbled after. He then began a rewarding stint with **Sly And Robbie**'s Taxi label in 1993, though in December of that year his elder brother **Dirtsman**, also a DJ, was shot and killed in Jamaica..
Selected albums: *Animal Party* (Sonic Sounds 1986), *Lyric Shop* (Black Solidarity 1988), *Style And Fashion* (Black Scorpio 1989), *Fire Inna Dancehall* (Pipper 1991). With Tippa Irie: *JA To UK MC Clash Vol. 2* (Fashion 1988).

Papadimitriou, Sakis

b. 1 May 1940, Kavala, Greece. Pianist, broadcaster, promoter, novelist and journalist Papadimitriou has been one of the moving forces behind the still-small Greek jazz scene. His radio programmes and articles in the magazine *TZAZ* helped build an informed audience for jazz at its most experimental. Papadimitriou's duo with Floros Floridis (saxophone/clarinet) was Greece's first free music group. Unfortunately, 'musical and personal differences' made it a short-lived one. Although Papadimitriou periodically works with other Greek musicians, his discography is composed almost entirely of solo piano recordings. Particularly striking is his use - alternately subtle and dramatic - of the piano's interior: plucking, strumming and striking the strings of the instrument.
Albums: with Floros Floridis *Improvisation At Barakos* (1979), *Piano Contacts* (1980), *Piano Plays* (1983), *First Move* (1985), *Piano Oracles* (1989), *Piano Cellules* (1991, rec.1986).

Papaíto

b. Mario Muñoz Salazar, 1920s, Buena Vista, Cuba. Papaíto is an elderly Afro-Cuban who possesses a captivating bitter-sweet voice which he effortlessly employs in his inspiraciones: the improvisational ingredient fundamental to traditional salsa singing. First and foremost he is a percussionist, and he worked with cha cha chá originator, Enrique Jorrín, in Orquesta América. He moved to Mexico, where he performed in various movies. While there, Papaíto joined the 'staff' of the legendary Cuban musical institution, Sonora Matancera, and remains a member up to the present day. He fled Fidel Castro's Cuba in 1960 and took up residence in the USA. His session work outside Matancera included appearances on two highly-regarded albums by compatriot Carlos 'Patato' Valdez: the 60s classic *Patato & Totico*, with Cuban vocalist/percussionist Eugenio 'Totico' Arango and tres guitar master **Arsenio Rodríguez**; and 1976's *Ready For Freddy*. On the latter, Papaíto sang the lead vocals of his self-penned 'La Ambulancia'. He performed on trombonist Mark Weinstein's late 60s *avant garde* 'underground culture hit' *Cuban Roots*, which was produced by **Al Santiago**. He participated on **Mongo Santamaría**'s *Up From The Roots* in 1972. The following year, Papaíto sessioned on the solo debut, *El*

Castigador, by former Orquesta Broadway and Sonora Matancera singer **Roberto Torres**. In 1977 he contributed percussion to **Israel 'Cachao' López**'s famed descarga (latin jam) outings on Salsoul Records. He signed with SAR Records, which was founded by Sergio Bofill, Andriano García and Roberto Torres, and released five highly successful solo albums as a lead singer on the label between 1979-84. Torres produced and performed on all five. On four of the albums, Papaíto was accompanied by a trumpet-led conjunto (group), augmented on some tracks by flute and violin. Three of these conjunto sets featured songs associated with Cheo Marquetti, a popular Cuban singer and composer of the 40s and 50s. Papaíto fronted a small charanga (flute, violins rhythm section and voices band), augmented by a tres, for his 1980 tribute to the great Cuban singer/composer Abelardo Barroso (1905-1972): *Papaíto Rinde Homenaje A Abelardo Barroso* - which was probably the best album to come out of the SAR stable. Papaíto became a member of the SAR house band, which recorded and performed under the name of the SAR All Stars. On 1981's *SAR All Stars Recorded Live In Club Ochentas, Album 2*, he sang lead vocals on a notable descarga interpretation of the classic 1931 hit 'El Manisero' (The Peanut Vendor). He appeared on SAR recordings by singer/composer Linda Leida (b. Villas, Cuba), **Henry Fiol** and Torres. Other artists Papaíto has sessioned with, include ex-Septeto Nacional vocalist Alfredo Valdés, his son, pianist/arranger Alfredo Valdés Jnr. and Peruvian singer/composer Melcochita. He made his UK debut in 1987 with a backing band that included Paris-based Cuban pianist **Alfredo Rodríguez**, who featured on *Ready For Freddy* and *Papaíto* (1982). In 1990, Papaíto was hired by composer/executive producer Victor Raúl Sánchez 'Patillas' to perform the lead vocals of two of his songs on *Valdesa Records Presenta Vol. 1: Salsa Sudada*.

Solo releases and albums on which Papaíto sang lead vocals: with Carlos 'Patato' Valdez *Ready For Freddy* (1976), *Roberto Torres Presenta A Su Amigo: Papaíto* (1979), *Papaíto* (1980), *Papaíto Rinde Homenaje A Abelardo Barroso* (1980), *SAR All Stars Recorded Live In Club Ochentas, Album 2* (1981), *SAR All Stars Interpretan A Rafael Hernández* (1981), *Papaíto* (1982), *Para Mis Amigos* (1984), with various SAR artists *Cañonazo De La SAR!* (1984), with Adalberto Santiago, Melcochita, Herman Olivera, Yayo El Indio *Valdesa Records Presenta Vol. 1: Salsa Sudada* (1990).

Papasov, Ivo

b. 1952, Kurdzhali, Thrace, Bulgaria. The most famous practitioner of Bulgaria's most favoured musical format; master clarinetist Ivo Papasov is the King Of Wedding Music. Though Western European eyebrows might be raised at such a title, it equates Papasov with the status of superstar in his native country. Papasov and his Orchestra tour the Balkans, playing several weddings a week (many couples will re-arrange the dates of their ceremonies to coincide with a blank entry in his diary). He descends from a long line of zurna (double-reed instrument) and clarinetists. After forming his first ensemble in 1974, he gradually evolved from a traditional Thracian repertoire into a jazz-inspired improvisational set. This new work nevertheless maintained the complex time-signatures required of traditional Bulgarian dance music. Papasov had stumbled over the incredibly popular formula which would see him become a national toast. Though he boasts many domestic releases, the two albums listed below were the first to be circulated internationally.

Selected albums: *Orpheus Ascending* (1989), *Balkanology* (1991).

Paper Lace

This UK pop group was formed in 1969, and comprised Michael Vaughan (b. 27 July 1950, Sheffield, England; guitar), Chris Morris (b. 1 November 1954, Nottingham, England), Carlo Santanna (b. 29 July 1947, nr. Rome, Italy; guitar), Philip Wright (b. 9 April 1950, Nottingham, England; drums/lead vocals) and Cliff Fish (b. 13 August 1949, Ripley, England; bass). All were residents of Nottingham, England, the lace manufacturing city that lent their mainstream pop group its name. A season at Tiffany's, a Rochdale club, led to television appearances, but a passport to the charts did not arrive until a 1974 victory in *Opportunity Knocks*, the ITV talent contest series, put their winning song, Mitch Murray and Peter Callender's 'Billy Don't Be A Hero', on the road to a UK number 1. Hopes of emulating this success in the USA were dashed by Bo Donaldson And The Heywoods' cover. The follow-up, 'The Night Chicago Died', set in the Prohibition era, was untroubled by any such competition and topped the US charts, narrowly missing out in the UK by peaking at number 3. 'The Black-Eyed Boys', a UK number 11 hit from Murray and Callender was the group's last taste of chart success - apart from a joint effort with local football heroes, Nottingham Forest FC, for the 1978 singalong, 'We've Got The Whole World In Our Hands'.

Albums: *Paper Lace And Other Bits Of Material* (1974), *First Edition* (1975). Compilation: *The Paper Lace Collection* (1976).

Pappalardi, Felix

b. 1939, New York City, New York, USA, d. April 17 1983. A highly respected bass player and arranger, Pappalardi was present at countless sessions, when folk musicians started to employ electric instruments on a regular basis. **Ian And Sylvia**, **Fred Neil**, **Tom Rush**, and **Richard** and **Mimi Farina** were among those benefiting from his measured contributions. He

later worked with the Mugwumps, a seminal New York folk-rock quartet which included **Cass Elliot** and Denny Doherty, later of the **Mamas And The Papas**, and future **Lovin' Spoonful** guitarist, **Zalman Yanovsky**. Pappalardi also oversaw sessions by the Vagrants and the **Youngbloods**, contributing several original songs, composed with his wife Gail Collins, to both groups' releases. An association with **Cream** established his international reputation. Felix produced the group's studio work from *Disraeli Gears* onwards, a position he maintained when bassist **Jack Bruce** embarked on a solo career in 1969. Cream's break-up left a vacuum which Pappalardi attempted to fill with **Mountain**, the brash rock group he formed with former Vagrant guitarist **Leslie West**. Partial deafness, attributed to exposure to the excessive volumes that Mountain performed at, ultimately forced the bassist to retire and subsequent work was confined to the recording studio. He recorded two albums in the late 70s, one of which, *Felix Pappalardi & Creation*, included the services of **Paul Butterfield** and Japanese musicians, Masayuki Higuchi (drums), Shigru Matsumoto (bass), Yoshiaki Iijima (guitar) and Kazuo Takeda (guitar). Pappalardi's life ended tragically in April 1983 when he was shot dead by his wife.
Albums: *Felix Pappalardi & Creation* (1976), *Don't Worry, Ma* (1979).

Parachute Men

Formed in Leeds, Yorkshire, England, in 1985 by Fiona Gregg (b. 26 July 1963, Norwich, Norfolk, England; vocals), Stephen H. Gregg (b. 29 November 1960, Bishop Auckland, Co. Durham, England; guitar), Andrew Howes (bass) and Mark Boyce (drums), the Parachute Men proved to have a bat's ear for a tune, yet were persistently undersold by circumstance. Signing to Fire Records in 1987 was a promising move, particularly when 'The Innocents' was released to warm approval, but soon after Andrew Howes and Mark Boyce departed acrimoniously, leaving Fiona and Stephen H. Gregg to tour as an acoustic set-up until Matthew Parkin (bass) and Paul Walker (b. 7 July 1966, West Yorkshire, England; drums) filled the vacancies. The second album was released well over a year after it was recorded, costing the band valuable momentum and causing Matthew Parker to be replaced by Colleen Browne (b. 25 August 1966, Kelowna, Canada), but the Parachute Men continued to create lovingly-textured guitar sounds. However, the lack of media focus, undoubtedly exacerbated by their northern location, ensured that their talents remained the knowledge of a privileged few, and they disbanded soon after the release of *Earth, Dogs And Eggshells*.
Albums: *The Innocents* (Fire 1988), *Earth, Dogs And Eggshells* (Fire 1990).

Parade

This excellent US pop/harmony act was ostensibly a studio group based around songwriter/producer Jerry Riopelle. Having established his reputation with Ramona King's original version of 'The Shoop Shoop Song (It's In His Kiss)', Riopelle enjoyed a brief association with **Phil Spector**, before pursuing his backroom career with **Nino Tempo And April Stevens** and Clydie King. The Parade, comprising Riopelle, Murray MacLeod and Smokey Roberds, made its debut in February 1967 with 'Sunshine Girl', a beautiful, summery group composition which reached number 20 in the US chart. Despite a craftedness redolent of the **Turtles** or **Association**, none of the Parade's subsequent five singles were hits and the group dissolved in 1968.

Paradis, Vanessa

b. c.1972, Paris, France. Model and singer Vanessa Paradis has widely been dubbed her home nation's 'Lolita' of the 90s. Her debut single, the insistent 'Joe Le Taxi', was released in 1987 while Paradis was still just 14 years old. It stayed at number 1 in the French charts for 11 weeks, and also found success in the UK and the rest of Europe. She had first entered the studio at the age of 12 under the wing of her uncle, actor Didier Pain. There she met Pain's friend Franck Langolff, who provided the music for her first two albums, which were only released domestically. Noted French writer **Serge Gainsbourg** wrote all the words for the second of these collections. Further notoriety arrived with an appearance in black feathers on a trapeze for the 1992 Coco Chanel perfume advert, directed by Jean Paul Goude, former husband of **Grace Jones**. She spent the first part of 1992 in New York, USA, recording her debut English-language album with the help of rumoured romantic paramour **Lenny Kravitz**. He wrote and produced the whole of the rather insubstantial *Vanessa Paradis*. Selections included a bizarre cover version of the **Velvet Underground**'s 'Waiting For The Man'. Another song, a hopelessly narcissistic effort entitled 'Lenny Kravitz', was written by Kravitz for Paradis to sing. The lines 'He is so funky and he's looking good, And he does it like a good man should' led to further debate in the press about the nature of their relationship. Her popularity in France remained huge despite the eventually lack of success which greeted the album internationally. 'Be My Baby' became another major seller, while on her promotional tour Paradis was able to sell out six nights at the Paris Olympia without any difficulty. Critics at home and abroad remained repelled not only by her songs, but also her 'little girl lost' sexuality and the largely middle-aged male company she kept. Paradis had a simple, appropriately Americanised answer, 'I don't give a shit.'

Album: *Vanessa Paradis* (1992), *Live* (Polydor 1994).
Video: *Vanessa Paradis: Tous Les Clips* (1994).

Paradise - Hawaiian Style

Elvis Presley's 60s film career was hampered by poor plots between which it is hard to distinguish. This 1966 feature compounds the problem by simply revisiting the location of one of the singer's most popular movies, ***Blue Hawaii***. It is there the comparisons end; *Paradise - Hawaiian Style* had little of the former's attractive points. Here Presley plays a helicopter pilot flitting from one mini-crisis to another on the way to true love. A soundtrack album, comprising a meagre 10 songs, was hastily recorded. Seen by Presley aficionados as one of his worst albums, it featured material of remarkably poor quality, notably 'Queen Wahine's Papaya', and also, interestingly, two 'out-takes' (of 'Datin'' and 'A Dog's Life') that featured studio chat that betrayed Presley's dissatisfaction with the material he was required to sing.

Paradise Lost

This Halifax, Yorkshire, England-based death metal quintet was formed in 1988, taking their name from Milton's famous composition (although vocalist Nick Holmes (b. 7 January 1970, Halifax, Yorkshire, England) would concede that the poem 'doesn't half go on'). Together with Gregor Mackintosh (b. 20 June 1970, Halifax, Yorkshire, England; guitar), Aaron Aedy (b. 19 December 1969, Bridlington, Yorkshire, England; guitar), Stephen Edmondson (b. 30 December 1969, Bridlington, Yorkshire, England; bass) and Matthew Archer (b. 14 July 1970, Leicester, Yorkshire, England; drums), they were signed to the independent Peaceville label on the strength of two impressive demos. They debuted in 1990 with *Lost Paradise*, which was heavily influenced by **Napalm Death**, **Obituary** and **Death**. It featured indecipherable grunting from Holmes, over a barrage of metallic white noise. *Gothic* saw a major innovation in the 'grindcore' genre; with female vocals, keyboards and guitar lines that for once, were not lost in the mix. Importantly, the tempo had also dropped: 'We started to play more slowly because all the others were playing as fast as possible'. Many, notably **Asphyx** and **Autopsy**, followed suit. With indications in the early 90s of the metal sub-genres becoming accepted within the mainstream, it came as no surprise when Paradise Lost found a wider audience with *Shades Of God*, their first effort for **Music For Nations**. Recorded with producer Simon Efemey (**Diamond Head**, **Wonder Stuff**), and with artwork from cult cartoonist Dave McKean, this release was heralded in the press as a 'coming of age'. Sold out shows in Europe followed, before the group returned to Longhome studios in the UK, with Effemy once again in attendance. The *As I Die* EP gained a strong foothold on MTV, with approving glances from peers including **Metallica**, before *Icon* was released in September 1993. If previous offerings had seen the band's fan base expand, *Icon* brought about an explosion of interest, and acclaim usually reserved for the US gods of death metal. Reactions to the band's live shows in the US with **Sepultura** were just as strong. However, before sessions for a fifth album could begin Archer amicably departed to be replaced by Lee Morris. The excellent *Draconian Times* was the culmination of what the band had been threatening for five years. It is a faultless work and one destined to become a classic heavy metal album to rival **Black Sabbath**, **Led Zeppelin** and **Metallica**.

Albums: *Lost Paradise* (Peaceville 1990), *Gothic* (Peaceville 1991), *Shades Of God* (Music For Nations 1992), *Icon* (Music For Nations 1993), *Draconian Times* (Music For Nations 1995).
Videos: *Live Death* (1990), *Harmony Breaks* (1994).

Paradons

Formed c.1959 in Bakersfield, California, USA. The Paradons were a vocal group which scored one US Top 20 hit in 1960 and was never heard from again. The group was comprised of lead singer West Tyler plus Billy Myers, William Powers and Chuck Weldon, all students at the same high school. They were discovered by Werly Fairburn and Madelon Baker, who were setting up a record label called Milestone, and were taken to Hollywood to record Tyler's 'Diamonds And Pearls'. It was the label's first release and reached number 18 nationally, but subsequent singles, 'Bells Ring' and 'I Had A Dream', failed to repeat its success. A switch to **Warner Brothers Records** yielded one more single which failed to chart and the group disbanded.

Paradox

This German thrash-metal outfit was formed in 1986 by ex-Warhead duo Charly Steinhauer (vocals/guitar) and Axel Blaha (drums). After a series of false starts and a track included on the *Teutonic Invasion Part 1* compilation, the line-up stabilized with the addition of Markus Spyth (guitar) and Roland Stahl (bass). Signing to UK label **Roadrunner**, they delivered *Product Of Imagination* in 1987, a collection of formulaic speed-metal material. *Heresy* saw a major personnel reshuffle and a marked improvement in their conversion of **Metallica** and **Anthrax** riffing. Stahl and Spyth had been replaced by Dieter Roth (guitar), Manfred Springer (guitar) and Armin Donderer (bass), with the expanded line-up allowing a greater degree of flexibility live and more depth to their studio sound.

Albums: *Product Of Imagination* (Roadrunner 1987), *Heresy* (Roadrunner 1989).

Paragons (R&B)

An R&B vocal group from Brooklyn, New York, New

York, USA. The Paragons with their high false falsetto and exotic warbling represent a rock 'n' roll doo-wop sound - sometimes called 'greasy' - that was extremely popular on the east coast in the late 50s. Members were lead Julius McMichael, Ben Frazier, Al Brown, Donald Travis, and Ricky Jackson. The group was signed by Paul Winley in 1957 and their first record on the Winley label, 'Florence'/'Hey Little School Girl' was a local New York hit in early 1957. Later that year they followed with another remarkable ballad, 'Let's Start Over Again'. The group had no more hits, but continued to record fine music into the 60s.
Selected compilations: *The Paragons Meet The Jesters* (Jubilee 1959), *The Paragons Vs. The Harptones* (Musicnote 1963), *Simply The Paragons* (Rare Bird 1974), *Paragons Meet The Jesters* (Collectables 1990), *The Best Of The Paragons* (Collectables 1990), *The Paragons Meet The Jesters* (Relic 1991), *'War': The Paragons Vs The Jesters* (Sting Music Ltd 1993).

Paragons (reggae)

One of the classic reggae vocal groups, the Paragons recorded extensively throughout the 60s, and, by the time of their disbandment in 1970, had left behind a string of classic sides that few of their rivals could compete with. Originally a quartet comprising Garth 'Tyrone' Evans, **Bob Andy**, Leroy Stamp and Junior Menz, the Paragons evolved from a group called the Binders. In 1964 Stamp left, and was replaced by **John Holt**, whose controlled lead vocals, supported by sumptuous, never-wavering harmonies, became the group's trademark. Junior Menz also left that year, to join the **Techniques**, his place taken by Howard Barrett. During 1964-65 the group cut a few singles for **Coxsone Dodd** at **Studio One**, including 'Good Luck And Goodbye'. In 1965 Bob Andy left to go solo, and in 1966 the trio began recording for **Duke Reid**, scoring a series of Jamaican number 1 hits in the new **rocksteady** style. Reid's productions were almost serene compared to those of his rivals, somehow utterly harmonious, and the Paragons came to epitomise the classy, warm sound of Reid's **Treasure Isle** Studio with a heap of wonderful releases: 'Happy Go Lucky Girl', 'On The Beach', 'Riding High On A Windy Day', 'Wear You To The Ball', 'The Tide Is High' and 'Only A Smile' among them. The trio also recorded a couple of marvellous singles that showed them to be just as adept at the more furious early reggae beat as they were at rocksteady: 'Left With A Broken Heart' and 'A Quiet Place'. In 1970 the trio split, with Holt rising to even dizzier heights as a solo act and Evans and Barrett relocating to New York, where Evans occasionally recorded for **Lloyd Barnes**' Bullwackies label. The pop world belatedly discovered the Paragons' genius in the following decade with the **Slits** murdering 'A Quiet Place' as 'The Man Next Door', and **Blondie** having a world-wide number 1 with an inferior remake of 'The Tide Is High'. Perhaps encouraged by this, the original trio reformed in 1983 to cut a few sides for **Island** Records under **Sly & Robbie**'s production aegis, but to little reward.
Albums: *On The Beach* (Treasure Isle 1968), *The Paragons With Roslyn Sweat* (1971), *The Paragons Return* (Island 1981), *Sly & Robbie Meet The Paragons* (Island 1981), *Now* (Starlite 1982). Compilations: *The Original Paragons* (Treasure Isle 1990), *My Best Girl Wears My Crown* (Trojan 1992), *Golden Hits* (1993).

Paramor, Norrie

b. 1913, London, England, d. 9 September 1979. The most prolific producer of UK pop chart-toppers was a mild, bespectacled gentleman who had studied piano, and worked as an accompanist, prior to playing and arranging with a number of London dance bands, among them Maurice Winnick's Orchestra. During his time in the RAF during World War II, Paramor entertained servicemen in the company of artists such as **Sidney Torch** and Max Wall, served as a musical director for Ralph Reader's Gang Shows, and scored music **Noël Coward**, **Mantovani** and **Jack Buchanan**. After the war he was the featured pianist with **Harry Gold** And His Pieces Of Eight, and toured with the lively dixieland unit for five years. In 1950 he cut some sides for the Oriole label with Australian singer, Marie Benson, and, two years later, joined **Columbia Records**, an **EMI** subsidiary, as arranger and A&R manager. In 1954, he produced the first of two UK number 1 hits for **Eddie Calvert**, and another for **Ruby Murray** the following year. Although quoted as believing that rock 'n' roll was 'an American phenomenon - and they do it best', he still provided Columbia with such an act in **Tony Crombie**'s Rockets but had better luck with the mainstream efforts of **Michael Holliday** and the **Mudlarks** - both backed by the Ken Jones Orchestra. Then, in 1958, a demo tape by **Cliff Richard** And The Drifters arrived on his desk. With no rock 'n' roller currently on his books, he contracted Cliff intending to play it safe with a US cover with the Jones band until persuaded to stick with the Drifters (soon renamed the **Shadows**) and push a group original ('Move It') as the a-side. Partly through newspaper publicity engineered by Paramor, 'Move It' was a smash, and a consequent policy was instigated of Richard recording singles of untried numbers - among them, at Paramor's insistence, **Lionel Bart**'s 'Living Doll'. Columbia was successful too with the Shadows - even if Paramor wished initially to issue 'Apache' - their first smash - as a b-side. Later, he offended Shadows purists by augmenting the quartet on disc with horn sections and his trademark lush string arrangements.
Other Paramor signings were not allowed to develop to the same idiosyncratic extent as Richard and his associates. **Ricky Valance** scored his sole chart-topper

with a cover of **Ray Peterson**'s US hit, 'Tell Laura I Love Her', while **Helen Shapiro** was visualized as a vague 'answer' to **Brenda Lee**; Paramor even booking and supervising some Shapiro sessions in Nashville in 1963. His greatest success during this period, however, was with **Frank Ifield**, who dominated the early 60s UK pop scene with three formidable number 1 hits. Even as late as 1968, Paramor racked up another number 1 with **Scaffold**'s 'Lily The Pink'. Throughout his career, Paramor wrote, and co-wrote, many hit songs, several of them for films, such as ***Expresso Bongo*** ('A Voice In The Wilderness', Cliff Richard), ***The Young Ones*** ('The Savage') and *The Frightened City* (title song), both performed by the Shadows; *Play It Cool* ('Once Upon A Dream', **Billy Fury**), ***It's Trad, Dad!*** ('Let's Talk About Love', Helen Shapiro) and *Band Of Thieves* ('Lonely', **Acker Bilk**). He also composed several complete movie scores, and some light orchestral works such as 'The Zodiac' and 'Emotions', which he recorded with his Concert Orchestra, and released several 'mood' albums in the USA, including *London After Dark*, *Amore, Amore!*, *Autumn*, and *In London, In Love*, which made the US Top 20. In complete contrast, the Big Ben Banjo, and Big Ben Hawaiian Bands, along with similar 'happy-go-lucky' 'trad jazz' line-up, were originally formed in 1955 purely as recording units, utilising the cream of UK session musicians. Paramor was in charge of them all, and their popularity was such, that 'live' performances had to be organized. The Big Ben Banjo Band appeared in the Royal Variety Performance in 1958, and was resident on BBC Radio's *Everybody Step* programme, as well as having its own **Radio Luxembourg** series. Two of the band's 'Let's Get Together' singles, and *More Minstrel Melodies*, reached the UK Top 20. One of the highlights of Paramor's career came in 1960 when he arranged and conducted for **Judy Garland**'s British recording sessions, and was her musical director at the London Palladium and subsequent dates in Europe. In the same year, with his Orchestra, he made the UK singles chart with 'Theme From A Summer Place' and in 1962, registered again with 'Theme From Z Cars'. From 1972-78 Paramor was the Director of the BBC Midland Radio Orchestra, but he continued to dabble in independent production for such as the Excaliburs, and his publishing company was still finding material for Cliff in the 70s. Paramor remains one of the most underrated figures in the history of UK pop and a posthumous reappraisal of his work is overdue.

Selected albums: *In London, In Love ...* (1956), *The Zodiac* (1957), *New York Impressions* (1957), *Emotions* (1958), *Dreams And Desires* (1958), *The Wonderful Waltz* (1958), *My Fair Lady* (1959), *Paramor In Paris* (1959), *Jet Flight* (1959), *Lovers In Latin* (1959), *Staged For Stereo* (1961), *Autumn* (1961), *The Golden Waltz* (1961), *Lovers In London* (1964), with Patricia Clark *Lovers In Tokio* (1964), *Warm And Willing* (1965), *Shadows In Latin* (1966), *Norrie Paramor Plays The Hits Of Cliff Richard* (1967), *Soul Coaxing* (1968), *BBC Top Tunes* (1974), *Radio 2 Top Tunes, Volume 1* (1974), *Radio 2 Top Tunes, Volume 2 and 3* (both 1975), *Love* (1975), *My Personal Choice* (1976), *Silver Serenade* (1977), *Norrie Paramor Remembers ... 40 Years Of TV Themes* (1976), *Temptation* (1978), *Rags And Tatters* aka *Ragtime* (1978), *Classical Rhythm* (1979). Compilations: *Paramagic Pianos* (1977), *The Best Of Norrie Paramor* (1984), *Ragtime* (1985).

Paramounts

Formed in Southend, Essex, England in 1961, the Paramounts evolved out of local beat attraction the Raiders. Comprising **Gary Brooker** (b. 29 May 1945, Southend, Essex, England; keyboards/vocals), **Robin Trower** (b. 9 March 1945, Southend, Essex, England; guitar), Chris Copping (b. 29 August 1945, Southend, Essex, England; bass) and Mick Brownlee (drums), the latter replaced by Barrie (B.J.) Wilson (b. 18 March 1947, Southend, Essex, England) in 1963. The group became one of the region's most popular R&B acts and by 1963 had secured a prestigious deal with **EMI Records**. Diz Derrick replaced the college-bound Copping prior to recording 'Poison Ivy', the quartet's debut single and sole UK Top 40 entry. Subsequent releases included material drawn from the **Coasters**, **Jackie DeShannon** and **P.F. Sloan**, but despite considerable acclaim, the Paramounts failed to achieve due commercial success. Later reduced to backing **Sandie Shaw** and **Chris Andrews**, they split up in October 1966. Brooker then formed a songwriting team with lyricist Keith Reid which in turn inspired the formation of **Procol Harum**. By 1969, and in the wake of numerous defections, this attraction contained the same line-up as that of the original Paramounts. Trower and Brooker pursued subsequent solo careers, while the latter also worked with **Joe Cocker** and **Eric Clapton**.

Compilation: *Whiter Shades Of R&B* (1983).

Paras, Fabio

London-based DJ renowned for his sets in the 90s at **Boy's Own** parties, and equally admired for his 'bongo mixes' and eclectic record collection (ie playing the **Clash** to bemused but still receptive punters). His remixes inlcude **React 2 Rhythm**'s 'I Know You Like It', **Aloof**'s 'On A Mission', **Deja Vu**'s 'Never Knew The Devil' and **Outrage**'s 'Drives Me Crazy' (which sampled the **Fine Young Cannibals** song of the same name) and 'Tall 'n' Handsome'. The last named cut was issued on his own label, Junk, which he set up to house percussion-based material. He has also released material for **Cowboy** as Charas. However, he is not one of the DJ fraternity to push his own name with any vigour: 'I'm happy doing my own stuff. I'm just a mellow geezer minding my own business'.

Parenti, Tony

b. 6 August 1900, New Orleans, Louisiana, USA, d. 17 April 1972. By his early teenage years, Parenti was playing clarinet in various local bands which performed an incipient style of jazz. While still in his teens he formed his own band and made some records. In the late 20s he tried his luck in New York, playing with several popular dance bands including those of Meyer Davis, **Ben Pollack** and **Freddie Rich**. He worked in the studios for many years in the 30s, but at the end of the decade joined **Ted Lewis** for a five-year stint. In the late 40s he played at several clubs in New York and Chicago. He spent the early 50s in Florida playing with local bands before returning to New York to lead bands for residencies that extended throughout the 60s at clubs such as **Eddie Condon**'s and Jimmy Ryan's. A fluent player in the dixieland tradition, Parenti deserves rather more attention than he has gained. His neglect results largely from his long periods in New York's clubland and a relatively small recorded output.
Albums: *Jazz, That's All* (1955), *Tony Parenti's Talking Records* (1958).

Parham, Tiny

b. Hartzell S. Parham, 25 February 1900, Winnipeg, Manitoba, Canada, d. 4 April 1943. Raised in Kansas City, pianist and organ player Parham played in a number of lesser-known **territory bands** in the early 20s. During the later years of the decade he recorded with blues singers and such jazzmen as **Johnny Dodds**. In the late 20s and early 30s he led his own small and big bands in and around Kansas City but by 1936 abandoned bandleading in favour of a career as a solo organist mostly in Chicago.
Selected compilations: *Tiny Parham And His Musicians* (1928-29), *Tiny Parham 1928-1929* (Swaggie 1988), *Tiny Parham 1929-1930,* (Neovox 1993), *Tiny Parham And His Musician's 1929-1940* (Classic Jazz Masters 1993).

Pariah (UK)

Formerly known as **Satan**, this Newcastle-Upon-Tyne, England group became Pariah in 1988, feeling that their original name may have led to misconceptions concerning their style. They were never a true black metal outfit as their original moniker suggested, but part of the **New Wave Of British Heavy Metal** scene instead. Pariah comprised Michael Jackson (vocals), Steve Ramsey (guitar), Russ Tippins (guitar), Graeme English (bass) and Sean Taylor (drums). They debuted with *The Kindred* in 1988, an album of hard, fast metal, characterized by the dual guitar onslaught of Ramsey and Tippins. Following *Blaze Of Obscurity*, Jackson quit and was replaced by Mark Allen, but there was to be no further significant progressin their career. Along with **Demon**, Pariah passed into history as one of the most talented metal acts of their generation to be lost to obscurity save for reference books.
Albums: *The Kindred* (Steamhammer 1988), *Blaze Of Obscurity* (Steamhammer 1989).

Pariah (USA)

This Florida, USA-based speed-metal quartet were formed in 1987 by the Egger brothers, with the full line-up comprising Garth Egger (vocals), Shaun Egger (guitar), Chris Egger (drums) and Wayne Derrick (guitar). Unable to secure a record deal in the US they were finally signed to the Dutch Moshroom label in 1988, for whom they debuted with *Take A Walk*, a mixture of styles that alternated between derivative **Anthrax/Metallica** thrash and the characterless pop-metal of **Europe** and **Bon Jovi**. The album failed commercially and nothing has been heard from the group since.
Album: *Take A Walk* (Moshroom 1988).

Paris

This UK power-trio was put together in 1975 by former **Fleetwood Mac** guitarist **Bob Welch** and ex-**Jethro Tull** bassist Glenn Cornick. Adding Thom Mooney on drums, they signed to **Capitol Records** in 1976 and released their self-titled debut album. Weaving mystical lyrical tapestries, within psychedelic, blues-based progressive rock, their strange and tormented style was ignored at the time of release, and remains an odd curio even today. Hunt Sales replaced Mooney on *Big Towne 2061* and the band adopted a more mainstream approach, with the lyrics taking on a religious emphasis. This also failed to find an audience and the band went their separate ways soon after its release. Welch embarked on what was to become a highly successful solo career. Sales joined **David Bowie** in **Tin Machine**.
Albums: *Paris* (Capitol 1975), *Big Towne 2061* (Capitol 1976).

Paris (rap)

b. c.1968, San Francisco, California, USA. Paris is a hardcore black Muslim rapper, widely shunned by the mainstream for his militant views. Based in San Francisco, Paris recorded his first single, 'Scarface Groove', in 1989. However, his breakthrough came with 'Break The Grip Of Shame', a typically informed and effective rant against the degradation of black communities and the need for change. It was a sublime piece of West Coast hardcore, the first fruits of his deal with **Tommy Boy**, which saw him hailed on MTV. The video was a provocative cocktail of footage containing uniformed revolutionaries in Africa, and images of Malcolm X and the Black Panthers. This was a fitting introduction to Paris' craft, a self-made man who remains responsible for his own production and management, backed only by DJ Mad Mike. He graduated from the University of California in 1990

with an economics degree, and is a supporter of Louis Farakhan and the Nation Of Islam. **Public Enemy** took him on tour and they could have found fewer more suitable warm-up acts. Despite being accused in some quarters of being dour and worthy, Paris nevertheless injected a focused, reasoning intelligence where discussions of evil reached beyond the lure of the bedroom or the villainy of the local law enforcement agency. However, tracks like 'Bush Killer' were openly inflammatory, even if they were also fun - a good example of his willingness to bookend cerebral discussion with revenge fantasies. He runs his own record label, Scarface, set up in 1987, which at one point looked likely to sign up **Ice-T** following his split with Warners. He did, however, produce several acts from the Bay Area, and also cut an album with the critically-acclaimed **Conscious Daughters**, though his excellent *Sleeping With The Enemy* set would not see a UK release. He was accused of assaulting Chris Joyce, an executive for the company which originally distributed Scarface Records, in 1994.
Albums: *The Devil Made Me Do It* (Scarface/Tommy Boy 1990), *Sleeping With The Enemy* (Scarface/Tommy Boy 1992).

Paris Angels

This UK pop band was formed in November 1989 and were subsequently signed to **Virgin Records**. The embryonic line-up of Scott Carey (bass/harmonica), Rikki Turner (vocals/wind instruments), Simon Worrall (drums) and Paul Wagstaff (guitar) were joined by Jayne Gill (vocals/percussion) and Mark Adge (rhythm guitar/percussion), formerly the group's sound engineer. They blossomed with the addition of the computer-literate Steven Tajti to help with programming and effects. After releasing a version of **David Bowie**'s 'Stay' they signed to Sheer Joy for 'Perfume' in June 1990. The group's blend of rock/dance pigeon-holed them as late arrivals to the Manchester scene and the award of a Single Of The Week in the ***New Musical Express*** and 10 weeks in the UK independent chart justified Virgin's decision to move in after two more singles on the independent label. The last of these, 'Oh Yes', in early 1991, became *Sounds* magazine's last ever single of the week, before the paper folded. However, their debut album and a re-recorded 'Perfume' failed to embrace the spirit of adventure that the single promised and the group floundered.
Album: *Sundew* (Virgin 1991).

Paris Blues

For a few moments at the beginning hopes are raised that this is a film to take seriously the problems of racial intolerance. Soon, however, jazz musicians Paul Newman and Sidney Poitier drift into stereotypes and there is little left for the audience to do except enjoy the scenes of Paris and the music. Fortunately, much of the latter, including the film's score, is in the hands of **Duke Ellington** which almost makes up for the disappointment in the dramatics. Apart from Ellington And His Orchestra, which includes **Cat Anderson**, **Willie Cook**, **Johnny Hodges**, **Ray Nance**, **Clark Terry** and **Sam Woodyard**, other musicians include **Max Roach**, **Philly Joe Jones** and local boys Joseph Reinhardt and **Guy Lafitte**. **Louis Armstrong** puts in an appearance and locks horns with Ellington ensemble in a rowdy nightclub sequence. The playing of Newman and Poitier was dubbed respectively by **Murray McEachern** and **Paul Gonsalves**. Directed by Martin Ritt, this 1961 film was based upon the novel by Harold Flender which did not dodge the issues and in which the black musician was the sole protagonist, his white sidekick being very much a minor character.

Paris Sisters

Priscilla, Albeth and Sherrill Paris began their long recording career in 1954, but did not achieve chart success until the following decade when they joined Gregmark, a short-lived label co-owned by **Lee Hazelwood**. The trio completed five singles for the outlet, each of which was produced by **Phil Spector**. Although 'I Love How You Love Me' reached number 5 in the US chart in 1961, other releases in the same feather-light style failed to emulate its success. The sisters nonetheless enjoyed a prolific career, latterly abandoning their conservative image with several excellent recordings under the aegis of Spector's arranger **Jack Nitzsche**, and a superb rendition of 'Greener Days', composed by **David Gates**. Priscilla, the undoubted focal point of the trio, embarked on a solo career in 1967, but although her excellent debut, 'He Noticed Me' augered well for the future, ensuing releases were less assured. She nonetheless completed three contrasting albums and in 1974 re-recorded 'I Love How You Love Me' with the British **Chinn And Chapman** production team.
Albums: *Golden Hits Of The Paris Sisters* (1966, re-recordings), *Sing From The Glass House* (1966), *The Paris Sisters Sing Everything Under The Sun* (1967). Solo: Priscilla Paris *Priscilla Sings Herself* (1974), *Priscilla Sings Billy* (mid-70s), *Love Is...* (1978).
Film: *It's Trad, Dad* ak. *Ring-A-Ding Rhythm* (1962).

Paris, Jackie

b 20 September 1926, Nutley, New Jersey, USA. From the early 40s Paris was active in New York as singer and guitarist. He worked mostly with bop groups and his singing soon became his primary activity. He achieved a considerable measure of critical acclaim but failed to attract a popular following amongst the jazz audience. During the 50s and 60s he worked steadily but mostly in clubs and resort hotels although he did

record with jazzmen such as **Donald Byrd**, **Gigi Gryce** and **Charles Mingus**. Paris sings with an urgent attack, his voice throaty and rhythmically infectious. At his best on up-tempo boppish numbers, he can also bring qualities of understanding and depth to ballads. His wife is singer Anne Marie Moss.
Albums: with Donald Byrd, Gigi Gryce *Modern Jazz Persepctives* (1957), *Jackie Paris* (Audiophile 1988), *Nobody Else But Me* (Audiophile 1988), with Marc Johnson, Carlos Franzetti *Jackie Paris/Marc Johnson/Carlos Franzetti* (Audiophile 1994).

Paris, Jeff

This American vocalist/guitarist started his career in the jazz-rock group Pieces. He subsequently played with a number of similar bands on a short-term basis, and built up a reputation as a quality backing vocalist and talented songwriter. He worked with **Cinderella**, **Y&T**, **Vixen** and **Lita Ford** in this capacity and was offered a solo recording deal by Polygram in 1986. He debuted with *Race To Paradise* the same year, a highly polished and melodic collection of AOR anthems, similar in style to **Michael Bolton** and **Eric Martin**. *Wired Up* saw Paris toughen up his approach. The album was typical North American rock and drew comparisons with **Bruce Springsteen** and **Bryan Adams**. However, both sets failed commercially and Polygram terminated his contract in 1988.
Albums: *Race To Paradise* (Polygram 1986), *Wired Up* (Polygram 1987).

Paris, Mica

b. Michelle Wallen, 27 April 1969, London, England. Having written, recorded and produced with the aid of heavyweights like Nile Rodgers (**Chic**), **Prince** and Rakim (**Eric B And Rakim**), Paris remains one of the UK's biggest talents to never make the great leap forward. It has not been for want of effort or ability, yet somehow no-one has yet found a way of getting the most out of one of the world's most delightful soul-dance performers. Stronger material would certainly help. There are examples from her debut album when she hits a perfect beat, as when she matches the tenor sax of **Courtney Pine** for its dexterity on 'Like Dreamers Do'. Her second album chose new, hot producers as a remedy (Charles Mantronik of **Mantronix**, and Dancin' Danny D of **D-Mob**). A sense of frustration still pervades her career, however.
Albums: *So Good* (4th & Broadway 1989), *Contribution* (4th & Broadway 1990).
Video: *Mica Paris* (1991).

Parish, Mitchell

b. 10 July 1900, Shreveport, Louisiana, USA, d. 31 March 1993, New York, USA. Growing up in New York City, Parish showed an early interest in literature, especially poetry. Despite working for a musical publishing firm, it was some years before his attempts at lyric-writing achieved success. He was in his late 20s when his first song was published and it was not until 1928 that he had his first huge hit with 'Sweet Lorraine'. He followed this auspicious, if late start, with another major contribution to the Great American Songbook when, in 1929, he wrote the lyric for **Hoagy Carmichael**'s song, 'Star Dust'. Throughout the 30s and with varying degrees of success, Parish wrote lyrics for songs written by numerous composers, among them 'Sophisticated Lady' (music by **Duke Ellington**), 'Stars Fell On Alabama' (Frank Perkins), 'Deep Purple' (Peter De Rose), 'Stairway To The Stars' (Matty Malneck and **Frank Signorelli**) and 'Moonlight Serenade' (**Glenn Miller**). In the 40s and 50s Parish's work continued with popular songs such as 'Orange Blossom Lane' (De Rose), 'Blue Tango' (**Leroy Anderson**), 'Tzena, Tzena' (Julius Grossman and Issacher Miron) and 'Volare' (Domenico Modugno). Changing patterns in popular music meant that from the 60s onwards, Parish's style declined in its appeal to the new audiences. Nevertheless, the quality of his earlier work, especially his lyrics for such classics as 'Deep Purple', 'Stars Fell On Alabama' and the ageless 'Star Dust', has made an indelible impression upon American popular music.

Park, Graeme

b. c.1963. Classically trained saxophonist and clarinetist turned DJ, famed for his sets at such venues as Manchester's Hacienda and London's **Ministry Of Sound**. He began his career in the music industry by working behind the counter (buying in second hand stock) at Nottingham's Select-A-Disc Records. His boss, Brian Selby, purchased a reggae club entitled Ad-Lib, but on opening night didn't have a DJ and hence asked his first lieutenant Park to take the job. Park carried on DJing there for several years, but as his listening tastes broadened (especially with the advent of hip hop and electro) he eventually began to incorporate more adenturous music into his sets. He went on to play at Sheffield's Leadmill, Nottingham's Kool Kat and the Hacidenda, alongside Mike Pickering (**M People**). His style could be categorised as deep house and garage, though as he prefers to state: 'If you look at my playlists over the past eight years, you'll find a common thread - songs'. His most famous remix was probably for **New Order** and the England World Cup Squad's 'World In Motion'. Other remix credits include **D-Influence**'s 'Good Lover' and work with **Temper Temper** and **Eddie 'Flashin'' Fowlkes**. He was voted *Mixmag* DJ of the year in 1992, but he remains a good-humoured and approachable representative of his craft: 'It's nice to be important, but it's more important to be nice'.

Park, Simon

b. March 1946, Market Harborough, Leicestershire,

England. An Oxford music graduate, Park began playing piano at the age of five. In 1972 he was commissioned to write the theme music to the new television detective thriller series *Van Der Valk*. The theme, called 'Eye Level', and credited to the **Simon Park Orchestra**, was initially released during the first series, but it only reached number 41 in the UK charts. Viewing figures for the second series increased and the theme was re-released by public demand. This time it climbed all the way to the top and became the final number 1 for **EMI**/Columbia label. Simon Park went on to produce a number of albums containing a mixture of originals and orchestrated classics. He continues to compose with great success.

Albums: *Eye Level* (1973), with the Ingman Orchestra *Something In Air* (1974), *Venus Fly Trap* (1975), *Danger UXB* (1979).

Parker, 'Little' Junior

b. Herman Parker Jnr., 3 March 1927, West Memphis, Arkansas, USA, d. 18 November 1971, Blue Island, Illinois, USA. Despite his later fame some confusion still exists regarding the parents and date and place of birth of Little Junior Parker. Clarksdale, Mississippi and 1932 are sometimes quoted and his parents names are given in combinations of Herman Snr., Willie, Jeanetta or Jeremeter. It is certain is that they were a farming family situated near enough to West Memphis for Little Junior, (who had started singing in church) to involve himself in the local music scene at an early age. His biggest influence in those early days was **Sonny Boy 'Rice Miller' Williamson** in whose band Junior worked for a while before moving on to work for **Howlin' Wolf**, before assuming the leadership of the latter's backing band. He was a member of the *ad hoc* group, the Beale Streeters, with **Bobby 'Blue' Bland** and **B.B. King**, prior to forming his own band, the Blue Flames in 1951, which included the well regarded guitarist **Auburn 'Pat' Hare**. His first, fairly primitive, recordings were made for Joe Bihari and **Ike Turner** in 1952 for the Modern label. This brought him to the attention of **Sam Phillips** and **Sun Records** where Junior enjoyed some success with his recordings of 'Feeling Good' although the period is better recalled for the doomy 'Mystery Train', which was later taken up by the young **Elvis Presley**. His greatest fame on record stemmed from his work on **Don Robey**'s Duke label operating out of Houston, Texas, and it was along with fellow Duke artist Bobby 'Blue' Bland that Little Junior headed the highly successful Blues Consolidated Revue which became a staple part of the southern blues circuit. His tenure with Robey lasted until the mid-60s with his work moving progressively away from his hard blues base. In his later, days Parker appeared on such labels as **Mercury**, United Artists and **Capitol**, enjoying intermittent chart success with 'Driving Wheel' (1961), 'Annie Get Your Yo-Yo' (1962) and 'Man Or Mouse' (1966). His premature death in 1971 occurred while he was undergoing surgery for a brain tumour and robbed R&B of one of its most influential figures.

Albums: with Bobby 'Blue' Bland *Blues Consolidated* (1958), with Bland *Barefoot Rock And You Got Me* (1960), *Driving Wheel* (1962), *Like It Is* (1967), *Honey-Drippin' Blues* (1969), *Blues Man* (1969), *The Outside Man* (1970), *Dudes Doing Business* (1971), *I Tell Stories, Sad And True...* (1973), *You Don't Have To Be Black To Love The Blues* (1974), *Love Ain't Nothin' But A Business Goin' On* (1974). Compilations: *The Best Of Junior Parker* (1966), *Sometime Tomorrow My Broken Heart Will Die* (1973), *Memorial* (1973), *The ABC Collection* (1976), *The Legendary Sun Performers - Junior Parker And Billy 'Red' Love* (1977), *I Wanna Ramble* (1982), *Junior's Blues: The Duke Recordings Vol. 1* (1993).

Parker, Andy, And The Plainsmen

b. 1913, Mangum, Oklahoma, USA. Little is known of Parker's childhood but he began a 12-year spell on local radio in the Midwest in 1926. Then, in 1938, after relocating to San Francisco, he began to appear as the Singing Cowboy in *Death Valley Days* on NBC radio. He also sang on KGO on *Dude Martin's Roundup*, before moving to Los Angeles. Here, in 1944, Parker, Charlie Morgan and Hank Caldwell became, the Plainsmen, a vocal trio and swing instrumentalists. They made their film debut in *Cowboy Blues* with Ken Curtis and by 1946, they had record releases on the Coast label. They appeared regularly on the *Hollywood Barn Dance* on CBS radio and *Sunrise Salute* on KNX Los Angeles. When Caldwell departed, he was replaced by Paul 'Clem' Smith and the act then became Andy Parker And The Plainsmen. They recorded for **Capitol**, including more than 200 radio transcription discs and appeared in eight **Eddie Dean** B-westerns and many television shows. Other artists who became band members over the years, include Deuce Spriggens (who later became a member of the **Sons Of The Pioneers**) and Noel Boggs. When Morgan decided to leave in 1956, Parker broke up the group. Parker wrote many songs, including the popular 'Trail Dust' and he and Morgan sang the theme song with **Marilyn Monroe** in the 1954 film, *River Of No Return*.

Parker, Bobby

b. 31 August 1937, Lafayette, Louisiana, USA. With a reputation based upon one record from 1961, guitarist Parker spent 30 years in obscurity before recording his first album. His family moved to East Los Angeles in 1943 and Parker got his first guitar three years later. While still in high school he formed a band with future rockers, **Don Harris** and Dewey Terry. After winning a talent contest at **Johnny Otis**'s Barrelhouse club, he was offered the guitar spot with Otis Williams & The Charms. From there, he worked in **Bo Diddley**'s touring band for three years and then joined **Paul 'Hucklebuck' Williams**' orchestra. While with them he made his first single, 'Blues Get Off My Shoulder', for Vee Jay in Chicago. The b-side, 'You Got What It Takes', turned up as a hit for **Marv Johnson** but with composer credits to **Berry Gordy** and Billy Davis. In 1961 Parker settled in Washington, DC and released his first and only hit, 'Watch Your Step' on V-Tone, basing the tune on **Dizzy Gillespie**'s 'Manteca'. The **Spencer Davis Group** covered it in England and **John Lennon** revealed that the **Beatles**' 'Day Tripper' was based on a variation of its main riff. In 1969 he toured England and recorded 'It's Hard But It's Fair' for Blue Horizon. Sessions for Lillian Clayborn's DC label and for producer Mitch Corday in the 60s are also rumoured to exist. Parker gave up music for five years during the 80s, but returned in 1989. *Bent Out Of Shape* showed that his talent was undiminished.

Album: *Bent Out Of Shape* (Black Top 1993).

Parker, Charlie 'Bird'

b. 29 August 1920, Kansas City, Kansas, USA, d. 12 March 1955. Although he was born on the Kansas side of the state line, Parker was actually raised across the Kaw River in Kansas City, Missouri. His nickname was originally 'Yardbird' due to his propensity for eating fried chicken - later this was shortened to the more poetic 'Bird'. Musicians talk of first hearing his alto saxophone as if it were a religious conversion. Charles Christopher Parker changed the face of jazz and shaped the course of 20th-century music. Kansas City saxophonists were a competitive bunch. **Ben Webster** and **Herschel Evans** both came from Kansas. Before they became national celebrities they would challenge visiting sax stars to 'blowing matches'. It is this artistically fruitful sense of competition that provided Charlie Parker with his aesthetic. Live music could be heard at all hours of the night, a situation resulting from lax application of prohibition laws by the Democrat Tom Pendergast (city boss from 1928-39). While in the Crispus Attucks high school Parker took up the baritone. His mother gave him an alto in 1931. He dropped out of school at the age of 14 and devoted himself to the instrument. A premature appearance at the High Hat Club - when he dried up mid-solo on 'Body & Soul' - led to him abandoning the instrument for three months; the humiliation was repeated in 1937 when veteran drummer **Jo Jones** threw a cymbal at his feet to indicate he was to leave the stage (this time Parker just went on practising harder). Playing in bands led by **Tommy Douglas** (1936-37) and **Buster Smith** (1937-38) gave him necessary experience. A tour with **George E. Lee** and instructions in harmony from the pianist Carrie Powell were helpful. His first real professional break was with the **Jay McShann** band in 1938, a sizzling swing unit (with whom Parker made his first recordings in 1941). Parker's solos on 'Sepian Bounce', 'Jumpin' Blues' and 'Lonely Boy Blues' made people sit up and take notice: he was taking hip liberties with the chords. Brief spells in the **Earl 'Fatha' Hines** (1942-43) and **Billy Eckstine** (1944) big bands introduced him to **Dizzy Gillespie**, another young black player with innovative musical ideas and a rebellious stance. Wartime austerities, though, meant that the days of the big bands were numbered.

Parker took his experience of big band saxophone sections with him to Harlem, New York. There he found the equivalent of the Kansas City 'cutting contests' in the clubs of 52nd Street, especially in the 'afterhours' sessions at Minton's Playhouse. Together with Dizzy and drummers **Kenny Clarke** and **Max Roach**, and with the essential harmonic contributions of **Charlie Christian** and **Thelonious Monk**, he pioneered a new music. Furious tempos and intricate heads played in unison inhibited lesser talents from joining in. Instead of keeping time with bass and snare drums, Clarke and Roach kept up a beat on the cymbal, using bass and snare for accents, whipping up soloists to greater heights. And Parker played *high*: that is, he created his solo lines from the top notes of the underlying chord sequences - ninths, 11ths, 13ths - so extending the previous harmonic language of jazz. Parker made his recording debut as a small combo player in **Tiny Grimes**'s band in September 1944.

In 1945 Savoy Records - and some more obscure labels like Guild, Manor and Comet - began releasing 78s of this music, which the press called 'bebop'. It became a national fad, Dizzy's trademark goatee and beret supplying the visual element. It was a proud declaration of bohemian recklessness from a black community that, due to wartime full employment, was feeling especially confident. Charlie Parker's astonishing alto - so fluent and abrupt, bluesy and joyous - was the definition of everything that was modern and hip. 'Koko', 'Shaw Nuff', 'Now's The Time': the very titles announced the dawning of a new era. A trip to the west coast and a residency at Billy Berg's helped spread the message.

There were problems. Parker's addiction to heroin was causing erratic behaviour and the proprietor was not impressed at the small audiences of hipsters the music attracted (apart from an historic opening night). In January 1946 **Norman Granz** promoted Charlie Parker at the LA Philharmonic and the same year saw him begin a series of famous recordings for Ross Russell's Dial label, with a variety of players that included **Howard McGhee**, **Lucky Thompson**, **Wardell Gray** and **Dodo Marmarosa**. However, Parker's heroin-related health problems came to a head following the notorious 'Loverman' session of July 1946 when, after setting his hotel-room on fire, the saxophonist was incarcerated in the psychiatric wing of the LA County Jail and then spent six months in a rehabilitation centre (commemorated in 'Relaxin' At Camarillo', 1947). When he emerged he recorded two superb sessions for Dial, one of them featuring **Erroll Garner**. On returning to New York he formed a band with **Miles Davis** and **Max Roach** and cut some classic sides in November 1947, including 'Scrapple From The Apple' and 'Klact-oveeseds-tene'. Parker toured abroad for the first time in 1949, when he played at a jazz festival in Paris. In November 1950 he visited Scandinavia. He felt that his music would be taken more seriously if he was associated with classical instrumentation. The 'With Strings' albums now sound hopelessly dated, but they were commercially successful at the time. Fans reported that Parker's playing, though consummate, needed the spark of improvisers of his stature to really lift off on the bandstand. A more fruitful direction was suggested by his interest in the music of Edgard Varese, whom he saw on the streets of Manhattan, but Parker's untimely death ruled out any collaborations with the *avant garde* composer.

His health had continued to give him problems: ulcers and cirrhosis of the liver. According to **Leonard Feather**, his playing at the Town Hall months before his death in March 1955 was 'as great as any period in his career'. His last public appearance was on 4 March 1955, at Birdland, the club named after him: it was a fiasco - Parker and pianist **Bud Powell** rowed onstage, the latter storming off followed shortly by bassist **Charles Mingus**. Disillusioned, obese and racked by illness, Parker died eight days later in the hotel suite of Baroness Pannonica de Koenigswarter, a wealthy aristocrat and stalwart bebop fan. His influence was immense. **Lennie Tristano** said, 'If Charlie wanted to invoke plagiarism laws, he could sue almost everybody who's made a record in the last ten years.' In pursuing his art with such disregard for reward and security, Charlie Parker was black music's first existential hero. After him, jazz could not avoid the trials and tribulations that beset the *avant garde*.

Selected albums: *The Charlie Parker Story* (Savoy 1945 recording), *Bird On 52nd Street* (1948), with Lester Young *Bird & Pres Carnegie Hall 1949* (1949), *Dance Of The Infidels* (1949), *Broadcasts* (1950), *Bird At St Nick's* (1950), *Just Friends* (1950), *Apartment Sessions* (1950), *One Night In Chicago* (1950), *At The Pershing Ballroom* (1950), *Bird In Sweden* (1950), *The Mingus Connection* (1951), *Norman Granz Jam Session* (1952), *Inglewood Jam* (1952), *Live At Rockland Palace* (1952), *New Bird Vols 1 & 2* (1952-53), *Yardbird* (1953), *Jazz At Massey Hall* (1953, reissued as part of *The Greatest Jazz Concert Ever*), *Birdland All Stars At Carnegie Hall* (1954), *One Night At Birdland* (1977, rec. 1950), *One Night In Washington* (1982, rec. 1953), *Charlie Parker At Storyville* (1985, rec. 1953). Compilations: *Charlie Parker On Dial, Vols. 1-6* (1974, rec. 1945-47), *Bird With Strings* (1977, rec. 1950-52), *Summit Meeting At Birdland* (1977, rec. 1951, 1953), *The Complete Savoy Studio Sessions* (1978, rec. 1944-48, five-album box-set), *The Complete Charlie Parker On Verve* (1989, rec. 1950-54, 10-CD box-set), *The Savoy Master Takes* (1989, rec. 1944-48), *The Legendary Dial Masters, Vols. 1 & 2* (1989, rec. 1946-47), *Bird At The Roost, Vols. 1-4* (1990, rec. 1948-49), *The Complete Dean Benedetti Recordings Of Charlie Parker* (Mosaic 1991, rec. late 40s, 7-CD box-set), *Gold Collection* (1993), *The Complete Dial Sessions* (Spotlight 1993).

Further reading: *Bird Lives!*, Ross Russell. *Bird: The Legend Of Charlie Parker*, Robert Reisner. *Cool Blues*, Mark Miller. *Discography Of Charlie Parker*, Jorgen Grunnet Jepsen. *Charlie Parker*, M. Harrison. *Bird Lives: The High Life And Hard Times Of Charlie (Yardbird) Parker*, Ross Russell. *To Bird With Love*, C. Parker and F. Paudras. *Charlie Parker*, Brian Priestley. *Charlie Parker*, Stuart Isacoff. *Celebrating Bird: The Triumph Of Charlie Parker*, Gary Giddins. *From One Charlie To Another*, Charlie Watts.

Parker, Evan

b. Evan Shaw Parker, 5 April 1944, Bristol, Avon, England. Soprano and tenor saxophonist Parker has one of the most awesome techniques in any field of music. When playing solo he combines circular breathing, multiphonics and tonguing tricks to build up complex, contrapuntal masses of sound which are credible only to those who have heard him live and can testify that there is no overdubbing involved. (However, with his 1991 album, *Process And Reality*, he has begun to experiment with multi-tracking techniques, but not simply to mimic his solo feats: the overdubbed tracks find him producing more lyrical, though equally complex interweaving lines.) He is also to be heard from time to time in conventional big band contexts (such as Orchestra UK led by **Kenny Wheeler** at the start of the 90s) and at all points between there and total abstract improvisation. (Not forgetting occasional work in the pop field, with **Scott Walker** and **Annette Peacock**, and with contemporary classical composers **Michael Nyman** and Gavin Bryars.) While he has created a unique style and sound-world, which would seem to exclude other players, he can glory in any type of jam, digging in for the gritty blues with the best of them, sparking off players like **Annie Whitehead**, **Dudu Pukwana**, **Mark Sanders**, **Paul Rogers** and **John Stevens** so that he and they play their best. His mother, an amateur pianist, introduced him to jazz in the shape of **Fats Waller**. He studied saxophone with James Knott from 1958 until 1962 when he went to Birmingham University to study botany. He left to concentrate on music, playing with **Howard Riley** from time to time and developing his taste for free improvisation. In 1966 he moved to London to play with Stevens's **Spontaneous Music Ensemble** and with **Derek Bailey**, with whom he co-founded the Music Improvisation Company in 1968 and the Incus Records label in 1970. As well as some remarkable solo concerts and albums, Parker has gigged or recorded with **Chris McGregor**, **Tony Oxley**, **Barry Guy**, Paul Lytton, **George Lewis**, the **Globe Unity Orchestra**, **Steve Lacy**, **Peter Brötzmann**, several **Company** line-ups, electronics expert Walter Prati and, with **Paul Lovens**, has long been a member of the regular trio led by **Alex Von Schlippenbach**. He currently leads his own trio too, with Paul Rogers on bass and **Mark Sanders** on drums, participates in **Jon Lloyd**'s Anacrusis and continues to develop his singular solo saxophone improvisations.

Albums: with Derek Bailey, Han Bennink *The Topography Of The Lungs* (1970), *Music Improvisation Company* (1971), *The Music Improvisation Company 1968-71* (1971), with Paul Lytton *Collective Calls (Urban) (Two Microphones)* (1972), with Lytton *At The Unity Theatre* (1975), with Bailey *The London Concert* (1975), *Saxophone Solos* (1975), with others *Company 1* (1976), with Bailey, Anthony Braxton *Company 2* (1976), with Lytton *RA 1+2* (1976), with John Stevens *The Longest Night Vols 1 & 2* (1977), with Alvin Curran, Andrea Centazzo *Real Time* (1977), *Monoceros* (1978), with Greg Goodman *Abracadabra* (1978), *At The Finger Palace* (1978), with others *Four Four Four* (1980), with Company *Fables* (1980), with George Lewis *From Saxophone & Trombone* (1980), *Six Of One* (1980), with Barry Guy *Incision* (1981), *Zanzou* (1982), with Guy, Lytton *Tracks* (1983), with Lewis, Guy, Lytton *Hook Drift & Shuffle* (1983), with Company *Trios* (1983), with Bailey *Compatibles* (1985), with Guy *Tai Kyoku* (1985), with Steve Lacy *Chirps* (1985), *The Snake Decides* (1986), with others *Supersession* (1988, rec. 1985), with others *The Ericle Of Dolphi* (1989, rec. 1985, 1977), with Cecil Taylor, Tristan Honsinger *The Hearth* (1989), with Guy *Duo Improvisations* (1990), with others *Dithyrambisch* (1990), *Atlanta* (Impulse 1990), with Walter Prati *Hall Of Mirrors* (1990), *Hall Of Mirrors* (MMT 1991), *Process And Reality* (FMP 1991), *Conic Sections* (Ah-Um 1993, rec. 1989), *Corner To Corner* (Ogun 1994). Compilation: *Collected Solos* (1989).

Parker, Fess

b. 16 August 1925, Fort Worth, Texas, USA. An actor and singer, Parker did some stage work before making his film debut in 1952 in *Untamed Frontier*, a western starring Joseph Cotton and Shelley Winters. Two years later he appeared as the famous Indian scout-legislator-Alamo defender Davy Crockett, in three episodes of the television series *Disneyland*. The shows were extremely popular, and the theme, 'The Ballad Of Davy Crockett', written by scriptwriter Tom Blackburn and George Bruns, became a US number 1 hit for **Bill Hayes**, well known on television himself for *Show Of Shows*. Subsequently, Parker's own version of the song made the US Top 10. When the big screen version, *Davy Crockett, King Of The Wild Frontier!*, was made in 1955, coonskin caps abounded, nationwide and beyond; the inevitable sequel, *Davy Crockett And The River Pirates*, was released in 1956. In the same year, Parker starred in **Walt Disney**'s *Westward Ho, The Wagons!*, which contained five new songs, including 'Wringle Wrangle', Parker's second, and last, chart success. His other movies, through to the 60s, included *The Great Locomotive Chase* (1956), *Old Yeller* (1957 (the first of the many Disney films about a boy and his dog), *The Hangman* (1959) and *Hell Is For Heroes* (1962) an exciting World War II drama, with Steve McQueen and **Bobby Darin**. Parker was also prominent on US television: in 1962 he co-starred with country singer **Red Foley** in a series based on Lewis R. Foster's classic, *Mr. Smith Goes To Washington.* Two years later he returned to the backwoods and portrayed yet another legendary American pioneer in *Daniel Boone*, which ran until 1968. In 1972 he played the tough sheriff in the US television movie *Climb An Angry Mountain.* After he retired from show business, Parker moved to Santa Barbara, California, and initially concentrated on a career in real estate. Since then, as the owner of Santa Barbara's Red Lion Resort and Parker Winery, he has become something of a tycoon, and by the early 90s his products were selling in over 30 states.

Selected albums: *The Adventures Of Davy Crockett* (1955), *Yarns And Songs* (50s/60s), *Cowboy And Indian Songs* (50s/60s), *Fess Parker Sings* (1964).

Parker, Graham

b. 18 November 1950, London, England. Having begun his career in aspiring soul groups the Black Rockers and Deep Cut Three, R&B vocalist Parker undertook menial employment while completing several demo tapes of his original songs. One such collection came to the attention of David Robinson, owner of a small recording studio within a building housing the north London, Hope & Anchor pub. Impressed, he pieced together a backing group - Brinsley Schwarz (guitar/vocals), Bob Andrews (keyboards/vocals), both ex-**Brinsley Schwarz,** Martin Belmont (guitar/vocals, ex-**Ducks Deluxe**), Andrew Bodnar (bass) and Steve Goulding (drums) - known collectively as the **Rumour**, and the new aggregation joined the dying embers of the 'pub rock' scene. The patronage of Radio London disc jockey **Charlie Gillett** helped engender a recording deal and both *Howlin' Wind* and *Heat Treatment* received almost universal acclaim. Parker's gritty delivery was both tough and passionate, placing the singer on a level with US contemporaries **Bruce Springsteen** and **Southside Johnny And The Asbury Jukes**. Although the artist also enjoyed two chart entries with *The Pink Parker* EP (1977) and 'Hold Back The Night' (1978). His momentum was effectively stalled by the divided critical opinion to the commercial *Stick To Me*, and a live-double set, *The Parkerilla.* While the public gave the them a UK Top 40 hit with 'Hey Lord, Don't

Ask Me Questions' and despite both albums attaining UK Top 20 status, many felt Parker and the Rumour were losing their original fire and bitter wrangles with his record company further undermined progress. *Squeezing Out Sparks*, his debut for **Arista Records** (in the USA), reclaimed former glories and was lauded in both ***Rolling Stone*** and *Village Voice*. Persistent contradictions between the critics and chart positions added fuel to the confusion in the group line-up. Their most successful UK chart album, 1980's *The Up Escalator* (released on **Stiff Records** in the UK), would mark the end of Parker's partnership with the Rumour. With the break-up, any magic that had remained from the early days had truly gone. The remainder of the 80s was spent rebuilding his career and personal life in the USA. In 1988 *Mona Lisa's Sister* proved a dramatic return-to-form rightly praised for its drive and sense of purpose. Ex-Rumour bassist Andrew Bodnar joined former **Attractions** Steve Nieve (keyboards) and Pete Thomas (drums) for *Human Soul*, an ambitious concept albums split between sides labelled 'real' and 'surreal'. This surprising departure indicates Parker's increasing desire to expand the perimeters of his exhilarating style. Into the 90s, Parker proved fully capable, and confident, of performing to large audiences solo, with acoustic guitar or with full backing. In early 1992 he changed record labels once more by signing to **Capitol Records** in the USA.

Albums: *Howlin' Wind* (1976), *Heat Treatment* (1976), *Stick To Me* (1977), *The Parkerilla* (1978), *Squeezing Out Sparks* (1979), *The Up Escalator* (1980), *Another Grey Area* (1982), *The Real McCaw* (1983), *Steady Nerves* (1985), *Mona Lisa's Sister* (1988), *Human Soul* (1989), *Live! Alone In America* (1989), *Struck By Lightning* (1991), *Burning Questions* (1992), *Live Alone! Discovering Japan* (1993). Compilation: *The Best Of Graham Parker And The Rumour* (1980).

Parker, John 'Knocky'

b. 8 August 1918, Palmer, Texas, USA, d. 3 September 1986. During the 30s Parker played piano in several Texas bands, some of which were only on the edges of jazz. In the mid-40s he was working on the west coast with leading traditional jazz musicians such as **Albert Nicholas**. Parker later went into education, teaching at colleges and universities, but still found time to play with **Omer Simeon**, **Tony Parenti** and others during the 50s and 60s. In the early 60s he undertook an extensive recording programme of ragtime music, notably including the works of **Scott Joplin** and James Scott. A few years later he turned his attention to early jazz piano with a set of music by **Jelly Roll Morton**. In the early 80s he recorded a fine album with **Big Joe Turner**.

Selected albums: *The Complete Piano Works Of Scott Joplin* (1960), *The Complete Piano Works Of James Scott* (1962), *Golden Treasury Of Ragtime* (1968), *The Complete Piano Works Of Jelly Roll Morton* (1970), *Big Joe Turner With Knocky Parker And His Houserockers* (1983), *From Cakewalk To Ragtime* (Jazzology 1986), *Texas Swing - And The Blues* (1987), *Texas Swing - Boogie Woogie* (1987), *Texas Swing - The Barrel-House* (1987), *Knocky Parker And Galvanised Washboard Band* (GHB 1994).

Parker, Johnny

b. 6 November 1929, Beckenham, Kent, England. Parker is a self-taught pianist with a great talent for solo ragtime and boogie woogie but who can fit easily into a band's rhythm section. In the early 50s he worked with **Mick Mulligan** and **Humphrey Lyttelton** playing the catchy boogie woogie on the latter's 'Bad Penny Blues' hit in 1956. He later played with **Monty Sunshine** and **Kenny Ball** but also with **Alexis Korner**'s Blues Incorporated to which he made an important contribution as the 60s blues boom got under way. His own bands at this time reflected his love of the music of **Sidney Bechet** and **Eddie Condon**. Latterly he has presented his own one-man show, worked regularly with vocalist Beryl Bryden and provided the backing for the vocal group, Sweet Substitute.

Albums: with Alexis Korner *R&B From The Marquee* (1962), with Korner *Alexis Korner's Blues Inc.* (1963), *Johnny Parker's Boogie Woogie* (1979).

Parker, Leo

b. 18 April 1925, Washington, DC, USA, d. 11 February 1962. Starting out on alto saxophone, an instrument on which he recorded with **Coleman Hawkins**, Parker switched to baritone in 1944 when he joined the bebop-orientated big band led by **Billy Eckstine**. For the next year or so was a member of the band's so-called 'unholy four'. Fellow saxophonists in the band included **Dexter Gordon**, **Sonny Stitt** and **Gene Ammons** but it was another Eckstine alumni, his namesake **Charlie Parker**, who appears to have exercised most musical influence upon him. After leaving Eckstine, Parker played in New York with **Dizzy Gillespie** and **Fats Navarro** before joining **Illinois Jacquet**'s popular band. A record date with **Sir Charles Thompson** featured Parker on a tune entitled 'Mad Lad' and this became his nickname. Despite several other fine record dates with Gordon, and club sessions with Stitt, Ammons, **Teddy Edwards**, **Wardell Gray** and others, at all of which he more than held his own, Parker's career proved short-lived. By 1947 drug addiction was severely affecting his health. He played on into the 50s, but only intermittently, making occasional record dates, on some of which he rallied sufficiently to play superbly. One of the major baritone saxophonists in jazz, Parker died in 1962.

Selected albums: *Leo Parker's All Stars* (1947), *Leo Parker's Sextette/Quintette* (1948), *Leo Parker And His Mad Lads* i (1950), *Leo Parker And His Mad Lads* ii (1950), *The Leo*

Parker Quintet (1951), *The Leo Parker Quartet* (1953), *Let Me Tell You 'Bout It* (Blue Note 1961), *Rollin' With Leo* (Blue Note 1961).

Parker, Maceo

(see **Maceo And The King's Men**)

Parker, Ray, Jnr.

b. 1 May 1954, Detroit, Michigan, USA. This accomplished musician gained his reputation during the late 60s as a member of the houseband at the 20 Grand Club. This Detroit nightspot often featured Tamla/**Motown** acts, one of which, the (**Detroit**) **Spinners**, was so impressed with the young guitarist's skills that they added him to their touring group. Parker was also employed as a studio musician for the emergent Invictus/Hot Wax stable and his choppy style was particularly prevalent on 'Want Ads', a number 1 single for **Honey Cone**. Ray also participated on two **Stevie Wonder** albums, *Talking Book* and *Innervisions*, an association which prompted a permanent move to Los Angeles. Here Parker continued his session work until 1977 when he formed Raydio with other Detroit musicians Arnell Carmichael, Jerry Knight, Larry Tolbert, Darren Carmichael and Charles Fearing. 'Jack And Jill', a pop/soul reading of the nursery rhyme, gave the group an international hit, while further releases consistently reached the R&B charts. 'A Woman Needs Love (Just Like You Do)', credited to Ray Parker Jnr. & Raydio, was a US Top 5 hit in 1981, while the following year the leader embarked on a solo path with 'The Other Woman'. In 1984 Parker secured a multi-million selling single with the theme song to the film *Ghostbusters*, although its lustre was somewhat tarnished by allegations that he had plagiarized a **Huey Lewis** composition, 'I Want A New Drug'. Nonetheless, Ray's success continued as the song secured him a 1984 Grammy Award for Best Pop Instrumental Performance.

Albums: as Raydio *Raydio* (1977), *Rock On* (1979); as Ray Parker Jnr. and Raydio *Two Places At The Same Time* (1980), *A Woman Needs Love* (1981); as Ray Parker *The Other Woman* (1982), *Woman Out Of Control* (1983), *Sex And The Single Man* (1985), *After Dark* (1987). Compilations: *Greatest Hits* (1982), *Chartbusters* (1984), *The Collection* (1993).

Parker, Robert

b. 14 October 1930, New Orleans, Louisiana, USA. An accomplished saxophonist, this versatile musician was first heard on numerous recordings by pianist **Professor Longhair**. Parker also appeared on sessions for **Irma Thomas**, **Ernie K-Doe** and **Joe Tex** while at the same time embarking on a singing career. His early releases were largely unsuccessful until 'Barefootin'', an irresistible dance record, became a hit in the US and the UK during 1966. The singer continued this instinctive blend of soul and New Orleans R&B on several further releases, but 'Tip Toe' (1967) was his only further chart entry.

Album: *Barefootin'* (1966). Compilation: *Get Ta Steppin'* (1987).

Parker, Sonny

b. 5 May 1925, Youngstown, Ohio, USA; d. 1957. Raised in Chicago by vaudeville act, **Butterbeans And Susie**, Parker developed into an all-round entertainer specializing in singing and dancing, and his powerful voice lent itself well to blues shouting. Recording with trumpeter King Kolax for **Columbia** in 1948, he came to the attention of bandleader **Lionel Hampton**, and recorded as Hamp's blues vocalist for **Decca** and **MGM** over the next three years, covering many of the top US R&B hits of the day ('Drinking Wine, 'Spo-Dee-O-Dee', 'For You My Love', 'Merry Christmas Baby', and 'I Almost Lost My Mind'). During the Hampton years, Sonny recorded sessions in his own name for Aladdin, Spire and Peacock, albeit usually featuring a contingent from the current Hampton orchestra. Later sessions were recorded in the mid-50s for **Brunswick**, Ultima and Hitts, but Parker continued to tour sporadically with Hampton. In 1957, Hampton brought Parker to Europe, and it was while touring France that Sonny became seriously ill and died.

Selected album: with Wynonie Harris, Jimmy Rushing, Big Joe Turner *The Best Of The Blues Shouters* (c.1970).

Parker, Terrence

USA born Parker burst into the UK public's imagination when 'The Question', by his nom de plume Seven Grand Housing Authority, was played by **Tony Humphries** at Cream in Liverpool. The track was taken from the *Soul Beats* EP, built over a sample of **Kenny Gonzales**' 'Axis Project'. Among those who were astonished by the track were **James Barton** of Olympic Records (who subsequently joined **deConstruction**), and he and others walked over to inspect the record's label. The track was soon licensed from Detroit's Simply Soul label to Olympic, arriving with a **K-Klass** remix. Parker had been making house music since 1988, at which point he joined **Mark Kinchen** to become Separate Minds for the techno soul track, 'We Need Somebody'. He also remixed and produced in Detroit under the aliases Express, Trancefusion, Transsonic and Simply Soul. His earlier releases included the 'Call My Name' recorded for Detroit label 430 West. He was additionally responsible for running Intangible Records - at all stages defying the musical bent of his geographical home by remaining faithful to his love of Chicago house rather than techno. In confirmation of this, 1994 saw the release of the *Disco Disciple* EP.

Parker, Tom, 'Colonel'

b. Andreas Cornelius van Kuijk, 26 June 1909, Breda, The Netherlands. There remains bitter division about Parker. Was he Sam Katzman's 'biggest con artist in the world' or merely an unsophisticated fairground barker sucked into a vortex of circumstances he was unwilling to resist? Arguments supporting either might be construed from the icy ruthlessness formidable to those accustomed to Tin Pan Alley's glib bonhomie, and his blunt stance in negotiation on behalf of **Elvis Presley**, his most famous managerial client. 'Don't criticize what you can't understand, son,' Elvis said in the Colonel's defence. 'You never walked in that man's shoes.' Parker was an illegal immigrant, without passport or papers, who settled into carnival life in the 20s. Over the next decade, he evolved into a cigar-chewing huckster of spectacular amorality - exemplified by his practice of snaring sparrows, painting them yellow and selling them as canaries. With duties that included palm reading, he served the Royal American, the Union's top travelling show, for a while before a seemingly steady job as promoter for a charity organization in Tampa, Florida. Extremely potent fund-raisers, he discovered, were shows headlined by a popular C&W artist - and so it was that Parker came to commit himself full-time to the genre by moving to Nashville where he became **Eddy Arnold**'s personal manager. Once, when this vocalist was indisposed, an unruffled Parker allegedly offered a substitute attraction in two unhappy 'dancing chickens' who high-stepped around a cage to ease feet scorched by an electric hot plate hidden under their straw.

After Arnold left him, the Colonel (an honorary title conferred by the Tennessee Militia in 1953) took on **Hank Snow** - and it was in a support spot on a Snow tour of the deep south that 19-year-old Presley was noticed by his future svengali. Via connections nurtured during proceedings concerning Arnold and Snow, Parker persuaded **RCA** to contract his new find. A few months later in March 1956, the boy committed himself formally to Parker for life - and beyond. From that month, 'Elvis has required ever minute of my time, and I think he would have suffered had I signed anyone else'. While facilitating Presley's captivation of a global 'youth market', the Colonel's instinct for the commercial and economic machinations of the record industry obliged RCA to accede to his every desire, such as the pressing of one million copies of every Elvis release, regardless of positioning research. Moreover, to the team fell an average of eight per cent of approved merchandise associated with Presley - and, when the time came for the King to act in films, producer Hal Wallis grew to 'rather try and close a deal with the Devil' than Parker. To publicize one Presley movie, Tom was not above hiring dwarfs to parade through Hollywood as 'The Elvis Presley Midget Fan Club'. He was also behind the taming of Elvis via the stressing of a cheerful diligence while on national service; the post-army chart potboilers; the overall projection of Presley as an 'all-round entertainer', and, arguably, the moulding of his reactionary leanings. Nor did Parker object to Katzman dashing off a Presley vehicle in less than a month, each one a quasi-musical of cheery unreality usually more vacuous and streamlined than the one before. This was almost all fans saw of the myth-shrouded Elvis until his impatient return to the stage in 1968, whether the Colonel liked it or not.

After Presley's death in 1977, there were rumours that Parker would be devoting himself professionally to **Rick Nelson** but only Elvis' posthumous career interrupted a virtual retirement in Palm Springs. Parker was a consummate showman and media manipulator, who clearly enjoyed turning down million of dollars whenever his charge was asked to headline some grand concert package. His handling of merchandising rights during the early part of Presley's career has been compared favourably to the business dealings of later starmakers such as **Brian Epstein**. The obsession with commerce and disavowal of artistry dominated the Colonel's thinking, however, which mainly explains the singer's appalling film-related output during the early/mid-60s. After Presley's death, Parker's business empire was threatened by the star's estate - in the form of Elvis's ex-wife Priscilla and daughter Lisa Marie. Parker fought tenaciously to protect his empire before settling in June 1983. Thereafter, he surrendered claims to all future Elvis income, but received two million dollars from RCA, and 50 per cent of all Presley's record royalties prior to September 1982. In January 1993, Parker made one of his rare public appearances, signing autographs to promote the newly issued Elvis Presley postage stamp.

Further reading: *Elvis*, Albert Grossman. *Elvis And The Colonel*, Dirk Vallenga and Mick Farren.

Parker, William

b. 10 January 1952, New York City, New York, USA. Parker played cello in junior school and acquired a bass in the last year of high school. He remembers being sent with 99 cents to the store to buy **Duke Ellington** records for his father. He found a cut-price record by **Ornette Coleman** and rapidly became interested in the New Thing: **John Coltrane**, **Albert Ayler** and **Archie Shepp**. He attended sessions at Studio We in the early 70s, playing with **Sam Rivers** and **Frank Lowe** amongst others, and was involved with a **Cecil Taylor** big band at Carnegie Hall in 1973. Parker married in 1974 and worked at his day-job for the housing authority for a short time, then quit to play the Five Spot with **Don Cherry**. He next played with drummer Rashid Baker in **Jemeel Moondoc**'s band and in 1980 also joined Taylor, with whom he has continued to work regularly throughout the 80s and

early 90s in a variety of settings, including the pianist's recent Feel Trio. Other long-term associates - in addition to Taylor and Moondoc - have included Peter Kuhn, **Billy Bang** and **Bill Dixon**, and Parker is also much in demand in New York's *avant garde* scene, appearing with experimenters such as **Wayne Horvitz**, **Butch Morris** and Ellen Christi. In 1989 Parker started a trio with **Peter Brötzmann** (saxophone) and **Milford Graves** (drums) and in 1990 recorded with drummer **Dennis Charles** in a trio led by upcoming saxophonist **Rob Brown** (*Breath Rhyme*). Parker has a warm sound, and whether he is setting up simple vamps or responding to the torrential Taylor, his playing is always strong and creative.
Albums: *Through Acceptance Of The Mystery Peace* (1979), with Jason Hwang *Commitment* (1980), with Wayne Horvitz and Butch Morris *Some Order Long Understood* (1982), with the Feel Trio *Looking (Berlin Version)* (1990).

Parkes, Lloyd

b. 1949, Walton Gardens, Jamaica, West Indies. After completing his studies in music Parkes toured the North Coast performing on stage with his uncle. He teamed up with Wentworth Vernon as the vocal duo the Termites. Recording at Studio One the duo enjoyed a number of hits produced by **Coxsone Dodd** including, 'Do It Right Now', 'Have Mercy Mr Percy', 'My Last Love' and the legendary, 'Rub Up Push Up'. After three years the duo split up and Parkes was drafted into the **Techniques** replacing **Pat Kelly**. His output with the group was limited as he was only part of the line-up for a brief period. He was reputed to have sung on the classic 'You Don't Care', which he later recorded as a soloist in a medley of his hits. His first solo recording, 'Stars' was a minor hit but it was his version of 'Slaving' that won him international acclaim. The song was used by **I. Roy** for his classic 'Black Man Time' and **Big Youth** for 'Honesty'. The hit was included on the compilation *Officially* and featured a remake of his Termite hit 'Corporal Jones' along with 'Don't Put All Your Eggs In One Basket' and 'I Specialise In Good Girls'. Although Parkes has recorded a number of songs he is regarded as one of Jamaica's top bassists and his work in the line-up of Skin Flesh And Bones alongside, **Sly Dunbar**, Errol Nelson, and Bertram 'Ranchie' Maclean is legendary. In 1974 **Al Brown** recorded a cover version of **Al Green**'s, 'Here I Am (Come And Take Me)' which was a smash hit resulting in a plethora of versions of the rhythm. The notable versions were 'Butter Fe Fish', 'Bammie Fe Fish' and 'Tit For Tat' the latter being a reference to the club where the group backed a number of the islands top performers. The group also released a cover of **Neil Diamond**'s, 'Solitary Man' which was a hit in the reggae chart. Whilst providing his skills as a sessionist Parkes also found time to continue releasing singles on his own Parkes label, entering the UK reggae charts with, 'Ghetto Guns', 'Mafia' and 'Time A Go Dread'. When Skin Flesh And Bones evolved into **Joe Gibbs**' house band, the Professionals, the group performed on classic mid-70s hits backing **Culture**, **Dennis Brown**, **Prince Far I**, **Trinity** and the UK number one hit for **Althea And Donna**, 'Up Town Top Ranking'. The sessions also resulted in a series of dub albums which still enjoy healthy sales nearly 20 years on. During his time with Gibbs Parkes also secured further chart placing for his own 'Baby Hang Up The Phone' and with Big Youth, 'No War Into This Dance'. Gibbs' golden touch began to wane and Parkes formed his own group the We The People Band touring primarily with Dennis Brown. In the 90s Parkes toured with fellow Studio One veterans **Freddie MacGregor** and **Marcia Griffiths**
Albums: with the Termites *Presenting The Termites* (Studio One 1968), *Officially* (Trojan 1974), *Girl In The Morning* (Trojan 1975), *Loving You* (Trojan 1976), with the Professionals *African Dub Chapters 1, 2, 3 & 4* (Joe Gibbs mid-70s), with the Professionals *Earthquake Dub* (Joe Gibbs 1978).

Parkinson, Doug

b. Newcastle, New South Wales, Australia. As the lead singer with the Questions, the band came second in the 1967 Australian Battle of the Bands contest. Parkinson gained more prominence with his next band, Doug Parkinson In Focus, formed in 1968. This group charted in Australia with 'Hair', 'Without You' and the **Beatles**' 'Dear Prudence'. Parkinson's deep, expressive voice was easily recognizable on these hits and he remains one of the best male voices in Australia alongside **Leo De Castro** and **Jeff Duff**. When In Focus broke up in 1970, he went to the UK and formed the ill-fated Fanny Adams, whose albums were not successful. He returned to Australia in 1971 and re-formed In Focus briefly, released the *No Regrets* solo album and fronted several big show-type bands. More ballad material was released until 1979's excellent interpretation of the (**Detroit**) **Spinners**' 'I'll Be Around' with his much rockier Southern Star Band. Much of Parkinson's career has been centred on stage and in rock musicals such as *Tommy*, *Ned Kelly* and *Jesus Christ Superstar*. Parkinson possesses a great voice, although many of his releases lean too much towards MOR to be of any great interest to the rock and pop audience.
Albums: *No Regrets* (1973), *Doug Parkinson And The Southern Star Band* (1979), *Rock Legend* (1980), *Heartbeat To Heartbeat* (1983), *Reflections* (1986).

Parks, Lloyd

b. 26 May 1948, Walton Gardens, Jamaica. A singer and bass player, Lloyd Parks began his career in the late 60s with the Invincibles band, whose personnel at that time also included **Ansell Collins** on organ, **Sly**

Dunbar on drums and Ranchie Mclean on guitar, and was half of the Termites who recorded one album for **Studio One**. He then replaced **Pat Kelly** as lead vocalist in the **Techniques** vocal trio, joining Dave Barker and producer **Winston Riley**. He cut his debut solo single for Riley - 'Say You Love Me' (1969) - and played bass on **Dave Barker** and Ansell Collins' international hits 'Double Barrel' (1970) and 'Monkey Spanner' (1970). By 1970 he was recording solo again, for producers **Sonia Pottinger** ('We Will Make Love') and **Harry 'J' Johnson** ('A Little Better'). He then joined the Thoroughbreds house band playing Kingston's 'Tit-for-Tat' club. He continued making records in an expressive falsetto/tenor voice for a variety of producers including **Glen Brown** ('Slaving') and Prince Tony Robinson. When Parks launched his own label in 1973 it was initially distributed from Prince Tony's shop. Among his Jamaican hits were the huge smashes 'Officially' (1974), 'Mafia' (1974), 'Girl In The Morning' and 'Baby Hang Up The Phone' (1975). Parks continued session work on bass with Skin Flesh and Bones, and by 1976 was playing bass in both the **Revolutionaries** and Professionals studio bands. In 1978 he formed We The People Band, recording and touring, principally with **Dennis Brown**. He continued to combine session work and touring with the same band into the early 90s.
Albums: *Officially* (Trojan 1974), *Girl In The Morning* (Trojan 1975), *Loving You* (Trojan 1976).

Parks, Van Dyke

b. c.1941, Mississippi, USA. A former child actor, Parks had appeared in several Hollywood films prior to embarking on a musical career. Having studied classical piano, he joined MGM, but rather than follow this direction, began writing and recording pop songs. One of his early compositions, 'High Coin', was later covered by several disparate acts, including **Jackie DeShannon**, **Bobby Vee**, the **West Coast Pop Art Experimental Band** and the **Charlatans**, while 'Come To The Sunshine', an early Parks single, was later recorded by **Harpers Bizarre**, a group he also produced. Although Van Dyke fulfilled a similar role with the **Mojo Men**, whose cover version of the **Buffalo Springfield**'s 'Sit Down I Think I Love You' was a US hit in 1966, this period is better recalled for his work with **Brian Wilson** who was infatuated with Parks' intellectual air. The pair collaborated on Wilson's most ambitious compositions - 'Heroes And Villains' and 'Surf's Up' - but the full fruit of their labours, the doomed *Smile* project, was eventually scrapped when the remainder of Wilson's group, the **Beach Boys**, objected to the dense, obscure (although quite brilliant) lyricism Parks had brought to their leader's new compositions.
Van Dyke's first solo, *Song Cycle*, continued the direction this relationship had suggested with a complex array of sounds and ideas abounding with musical puns, Tin Pan Alley themes and exhaustive, elaborate arrangements. Commercial indifference to this ambitious project was such that **Warner Brothers** took out a series of adverts under the banner, 'The once-in-a-lifetime Van Dyke Parks 1 cent sale' offering purchasers the chance to trade a second-hand copy for two new albums, one of which was to be passed on to a 'poor, but open friend'. Undeterred Parks still forged his idiosyncratic path, producing albums for **Ry Cooder**, **Randy Newman**, and **Arlo Guthrie**, as well as pursuing work as a session musician, first unveiled on the **Byrds** 'Fifth Dimension', with appearances on albums by **Tim Buckley**, **Judy Collins** and **Little Feat**. *Discover America*, Van Dyke's second album, showcased his love of Trinidadian music, and blended contemporary compositions with show tunes from an earlier era. *Clang Of The Yankee Reaper* continued this new-found, relaxed emphasis but Parks then withdrew from active recording and only re-emerged in 1984 with *Jump*, a musical interpretation of the *Brer Rabbit* stories. This challenging performer still refused to be easily categorized and a fifth collection, *Tokyo Rose*, showed Parks continuing to sail his own course. Parks has continued to write and arrange for other artists into the early 90s.
Albums: *Song Cycle* (1968), *Discover America* (1972), *Clang Of The Yankee Reaper* (1975), *Jump* (1984), *Tokyo Rose* (1989).

Parkway Records

(see **Cameo-Parkway Records**)

Parlan, Horace

b. 19 January 1931, Pittsburgh, Pennsylvania, USA. Parlan played piano from an early age, his first professional work being in R&B bands during the early and mid-50s. In 1957 he joined **Charles Mingus** in New York, later playing with **Lou Donaldson**, **Booker Ervin**, **Eddie 'Lockjaw' Davis**, **Johnny Griffin**, **Roland Kirk** and others. In the early 70s he settled in Denmark, playing with local and visiting musicians including **Dexter Gordon**, **Archie Shepp** and **Michal Urbaniak**. As a result of contracting polio as a child, Parlan suffered limitations in the use of his right hand; to compensate, he developed a powerful left hand and evolved a distinctive style in which echoes of bop and the blues blend comfortably and to great effect. Although he is always an interesting soloist, it is in the interplay with other musicians that he displays his talents to the full - a fine example is the set of two duo albums - one of blues, one of spirituals - which he recorded with Shepp.
Albums: *Movin' And Groovin'* (1960), *Headin' South* (1960), *Up And Down* (1961), *Happy Frame Of Mind* (Blue Note 1963), *Back From The Gig* (1963), *Arrival* (Steeplechase 1973), *No Blues* (Steeplechase 1975), *Blue Parlan*

(Steeplechase 1975), *Frank-ly Speaking* (1977), with Archie Shepp *Goin' Home* (1977), *Hi-Fly* (1978), *Musically Yours* (Steeplechase 1979), *The Maestro* (1979), with Shepp *Trouble In Mind* (1980), *Pannonica* (Enja 1981), *Glad I Found You* (Steeplechase 1984), with Shepp *Reunion* (1987), *Splashes* (1987), *Little Esther* (Soul Note 1987).

Parliament(s)

This exceptional US vocal quintet was formed in 1955 by **George Clinton** (b. 22 July 1941, Kannapolis, North Carolina, USA), Raymond Davis (b. 29 March 1940, Sumter, South Carolina, USA), Calvin Simon (b. 22 May 1942, Beckley, West Virginia, USA), Clarence 'Fuzzy' Haskins (b. 8 June 1941, Elkhorn, West Virginia, USA) and Grady Thomas (b. 5 January 1941, Newark, New Jersey, USA). George Clinton's interest in music did not fully emerge until his family moved to the urban setting of Plainfield, New Jersey. Here, he fashioned the Parliaments after the influential doo-wop group, **Frankie Lymon And The Teenagers**. Two singles, 'Poor Willie' and 'Lonely Island' mark this formative era, but it was not until 1967 that Clinton was able to secure a more defined direction with the release of '(I Wanna) Testify'. Recorded in Detroit, the single reached the US Top 20, but this promise was all but lost when Revilot, the label to which the band was signed, went out of business. All existing contracts were then sold to **Atlantic**, but George preferred to abandon the Parliaments' name altogether in order to be free to sign elsewhere. Clinton took the existing line-up and its backing group to Westbound Records, where the entire collective recorded as **Funkadelic**. However, the outstanding problem over their erstwhile title was resolved in 1970, and the same musicians were signed to the Invictus label as Parliament. This group unleashed the experimental and eclectic *Osmium* (1970) before securing an R&B hit with the irrepressible 'Breakdown'. For the next three years the 'Parliafunkadelicament Thang' would concentrate on Funkadelic releases, but disagreements with the Westbound hierarchy inspired Parliament's second revival. Signed to the Casablanca label in 1974, the group's first singles, 'Up For The Down Stroke', 'Chocolate City' and 'P. Funk (Wants To Get Funked Up)' were marginally more mainstream than the more radical material Clinton had already issued, but the distinctions became increasingly blurred. Some 40 musicians were now gathered together under the P. Funk banner, including several refugees from the **James Brown** camp including **Bootsy Collins**, **Fred Wesley** and **Maceo Parker**, while live shows offered elements of both camps. Parliament's success within the R&B chart continued with 'Give Up The Funk (Tear The Roof Off The Sucker)' (1976), and two 1978 best-sellers, 'Flashlight' and 'Aqua Boogie (A Psychoalphadiscobetabioaquadoloop)', where the group's hard-kicking funk was matched by the superlative horn charts and their leader's unorthodox vision. Their last chart entry was in 1980 with 'Agony Of Defeet', after which Clinton decided to shelve the Parliament name again when problems arose following Polygram's acquisition of the Casablanca catalogue.

Albums: as Parliament *Osmium* (1970), *Up For The Down Stroke* (1974), *Chocolate City* (1975), *Mothership Connection* (1976), *The Clones Of Doctor Funkenstein* (1976), *Parliament Live - P. Funk Earth Tour* (1977), *Funkentelechy Vs The Placebo Syndrome* (1977), *Motor-Booty Affair* (1978), *Gloryhallastoopid (Or Pin The Tale On The Funky)* (1979), *Trombipulation* (1980). Compilations: *Parliament's Greatest Hits* (1984), *The Best Of Parliament* (1986), *Tear The Roof Off 1974-80* (1993).

Parlophone Records

The label's roots go back to March 1911 when Carl Gesellschaft Lindstrom (b. 1867, d. 1932) launched the Parlophon (sic) label in Europe. In March 1920 it was taken over by the Transoceanic Trading Co of Holland who formed the Parlophone Co. Ltd in London on 8 August 1923. Taken under UK Columbia's wing in 1925, it subsequently became part of **EMI** when that organization was formed by the merger of Columbia and several other labels in April 1931. The label started to come into its own during the 50s when it was run by Oscar Preuss and his assistant **George Martin**, whom he had rescued from the BBC Gramphone Library. They released largely lightweight dance music and Scottish reels until 1955 when Preuss retired and Martin took over. Looking for a new angle he saw that comedy records were few and far between and began to make recordings of such people as **Flanders And Swan**, **Peter Sellers** and Mike and Bernie Winters. He moved into more contemporary music by releasing American rock 'n' roll records by Mac Curtis, **Boyd Bennett**, **Charlie Gracie** and others, as well as putting out home-grown talent like the **Vipers**, **Jim Dale**, Rory Blackwell and **Vince Eager**. As the 60s arrived, so did the bigger selling artists such as **Adam Faith**, **Mike Sarne**, **Shane Fenton** and the **Temperance Seven**, but it was in 1962 that George Martin ensured his place in pop history. Although not over impressed with the **Beatles** at first, he did think them a worthwhile signing! The Beatles, **Cilla Black**, **Billy J. Kramer**, **Cliff Bennett**, the **Hollies** and Adam Faith were all Parlophone recording acts that dominated the charts in the 60s. There were also less well-known names such as Byron Lee And The Dragonaires (Lee was a top Jamaican producer), **Kippington Lodge** (including **Nick Lowe**), Davy Jones (later known as **David Bowie**), the **Herd** (featuring **Peter Frampton**) and a very young **Marc Bolan**. Aside from the pop music Parlophone continued to release comedy material - most notably spin-offs from television satire programmes like *That*

Was The Week That Was. They even continued with the odd Scottish reel: **Jimmy Shand** would come down to London once a year, record several dozen tunes, return home and watch while they were slowly released as singles over a 12-month period. George Martin left in 1965 to form his own independent production company, AIR, and the Beatles set up their own Apple label - though their records were still released in Parlophone's sequence but with the Apple logo. By the early 70s only the solo Beatles releases were coming out in the Parlophone series. In 1979, however, the label underwent something of a revival and in 1982 on the anniversary of the release of 'Love Me Do' they issued '101 Damnations' by Beatles soundalikes **Scarlet Party**. Since then the label has been the home for releases by **Dexy's Midnight Runners**, the **Pet Shop Boys**, **Queen**, **EMF** and, boosting the label's credibility, signing UK 'indie' stars the **Sundays** in the early part of 1992.

Parnell, Jack

b. 6 August 1923, London, England. One of the best-known and most popular of post-World War II British jazzmen, Parnell was at his most prominent during a long stint with **Ted Heath**'s big band. Before then, however, he had already made a mark on the UK jazz scene. While still on military service he became a member of Buddy Featherstonehaugh's Radio Rhythm Club Sextet, playing alongside **Vic Lewis** and other jazz-minded servicemen. Between 1944 and 1946 Parnell also recorded with Lewis, and the Lewis-Parnell Jazzmen's version of 'Ugly Child' sold extremely well (50,000 78 rpm discs would probably have made it a hit had there been such a thing as a hit parade in those days). The Lewis-Parnell band played in clubs and also made a number of theatrical appearances. Following a minor disagreement over billing, Lewis took over sole leadership of the band while Parnell joined Heath, where he became one of the band's most popular figures. With the band he also sang, displaying an engaging voice and an attractive stage personality. Leaving Heath after seven years, Parnell became musical director of ATV, directing the pit band for the popular *Sunday Night At The London Palladium*, throughout the 60s. Among his later television credits, he was musical director for *The Muppet Show*. In the late 70s, after two decades in television, Parnell returned to the UK jazz scene. He has continued to play in clubs and at festivals, sometimes backing visiting American jazzmen, at other times working with leading British stars. During his early days with the Heath band Parnell had an image of gum-chewing showman drummer, an image which in fact concealed a skilful, swinging and often underrated artist. His later work, with the need for an image no longer necessary, reveals his subtle and propulsive playing. In 1994, Parnell took over as leader of the newly-formed London Big Band, 'the largest band in Britain', consisting of the 'cream' of the UK music business.

Selected albums: *Big Band Show* (1976), *Big Band Stereo Spectacular* (1981), *Plays Music Of The Giants* (1975), *The Portrait Of Charlie Gilbraith* (1977), *Braziliana* (1977), *50 Big Band Favourites* (1984).

Parnell, Lee Roy

b. 21 December 1956, Abilene, Texas, USA. **Bob Wills** was a close family friend and Parnell sang on stage with him when he was only six years old, an incident he mentions in his 1993 song, 'Country Down To My Soul'. Growing up in a household that loved western swing, Parnell found that his own tastes included blues and rock 'n' roll. He formed his own band when he was aged 19 and spent 10 years playing Texas honky tonks. In 1987 he moved with his family to Nashville and built up a reputation at the Bluebird Cafe. His first album was produced by R&B producer **Barry Beckett** and mixed soul with country. It did reasonably well but his career took off when he cut *Love Without Mercy* with a small rhythm group. It included his US country hits 'What Kind Of Fool Do You Think I Am' and 'The Rock' ('I am your rock, but I'm rolling away.') as well as a duet with **Delbert McClinton**, 'Road Scholar', a parody of **Kris Kristofferson** being a Rhodes scholar. Parnell's superb guitar-playing is highlighted on 'Workin' Man Blues' which he cut with **Steve Wariner** and **Diamond Rio**: he wanted to call their group, Merle Jam, but was persuaded to settle for the less witty Jed Zepplin. His video for 'On The Road' was very evocative, showing how some people are forced to seek a new life.

Albums: *Lee Roy Parnell* (1990), *Love Without Mercy* (Arista 1992), *On The Road* (Arista 1993).

Parnes, Larry

b. Laurence Maurice Parnes, 1930, Willesden, London, England, d. 4 August 1989, London, England. Parnes was the most famous British pop manager and impresario of the 50s, and one of the greatest of all time. After briefly working in the family clothing business, he took over a bar in London's West End called La Caverne. The establishment was frequented by many theatrical agents and producers and, before long, Parnes was inveigled into investing in a play titled *Women Of The Streets*. One night at a coffee bar he met publicist John Kennedy, who was then overseeing the affairs of singer Tommy Hicks. After seeing the boy perform at **Lionel Bart**'s suggestion Parnes was impressed and went into partnership with Kennedy. Hicks was rechristened **Tommy Steele** and became Britain's first rock 'n' roll celebrity. He later emerged as an all round entertainer and star of several musicals. Parnes specialized in discovering young boys, who would be systematically groomed, launched on the rock 'n' roll circuit, and finally assimilated into traditional showbusiness areas. The technique was habitual. Parnes played the part of the svengali, carefully renaming his acts with some exotically powerful surname that suggested power, virility or glamour. His second discovery proved another winner. Reg Smith was quickly snapped up by the starmaker, rechristened **Marty Wilde** and soon enjoyed a string of UK hits, before 'retiring' from rock 'n' roll at the close of the 50s.

By this time, Parnes had a network of contacts, including A&R managers like Hugh Mendl, **Dick Rowe** and **Jack Baverstock**, who would always take notice of a Parnes act. The bombastic television producer **Jack Good** also realized that supporting Parnes ensured a steady flow of teenage talent. Finally, there were the songwriters like Lionel Bart, who could provide original material, although cover versions of US hits were always popular. Parnes' third great discovery of the 50s was **Billy Fury**, one of the most important figures to emerge from British rock 'n' roll. Significantly, Parnes remained with the star for a considerable time and was still handling his business affairs during the late 60s. The irrepressible **Joe Brown** was another major find for Parnes, though their association was often stormy. Brown was an exceptional guitarist and was frequently used to back other Parnes acts. For every star he unearthed, however, there were a series of lesser talents or unlucky singers who failed to find chart success. Among the famous Parnes' 'stable of stars' were **Dickie Pride**, **Duffy Power**, **Johnny Gentle**, **Sally Kelly**, **Terry Dene**, **Nelson Keene** and Peter Wynne. Larry was also briefly associated with **Georgie Fame** and the **Tornados**. Beyond his management interests, Parnes was a great provider of package shows with grandiloquent titles such as 'The Big New Rock 'n' Roll Trad Show' and the 'Star Spangled Nights'. Parnes' influence effectively ended during the early to mid-60s when new managers and entrepreneurs such as **Brian Epstein** and **Andrew Oldham** took centre stage. Ironically, Parnes had two chances to sign the **Beatles** but passed up the opportunity. Like his stars, he seemed intent on abdicating his position in rock 'n' roll and increasingly moved into more conservative areas of British showbusiness and theatre. During the 60s, he was involved in such musicals as *Charlie Girl* and *Chicago*. During the 70s, he returned to management in a different sphere, administering the business affairs of ice-skater John Currie. He subsequently fell ill with meningitis and effectively retired. His public image remained contradictory and subject to caricature. As the prototype British pop svengali, he was used as the inspiration for the vapid, camp starmaker in the movie *Absolute Beginners*. Ever self-protective and litigious, his wrath descended upon the BBC, among others, when he won a substantial out-of-court settlement for an alleged libel by **Paul McCartney** on a most unlikely programme, *Desert Island Discs*.

Further reading: *Starmakers & Svengalis: The History Of British Pop Management*, Johnny Rogan.

Parr, John

b. 18 November 1954. This vocalist, guitarist, composer and producer specializes in highly melodic AOR. Though British, his success had been drawn largely from the US where his recordings for the **Atlantic** label have been compared to **Rick Springfield** and **Eddie Money**. Parr composed the themes for the movies *American Anthem* and *St. Elmo's Fire*, the second of which made the UK Top 10 singles chart in 1985. The follow-up, 'Naughty Naughty', achieved a paltry number 58. He also duetted with **Meat Loaf** on 'Rock 'N' Roll Mercenaries', but this failed to embellish either artist's profile, stopping just short of the Top 30. Producing two solo albums, his self-titled debut in 1985 and *Running The Endless Mile* in 1986, both fared poorly with the critics. His finest moment remains the energetic 'St. Elmo's Fire (Man In Motion)', to give it its full title.

Albums: *John Parr* (Atlantic 1985), *Running The Endless Mile* (Atlantic 1987).

Parsons, Alan

b. 20 December 1949. A staff engineer at **EMI**'s recording studios, Parsons first attracted attention for his work on the final **Beatles**' album, *Abbey Road*. Such skills were then employed on several of **Wings**' early releases, but the artist's reputation was established in the wake of his contributions to **Pink Floyd**'s multi-million seller, *Dark Side Of The Moon*, and his productions for **Pilot**, **Cockney Rebel** and **Al Stewart**. Inspired by the 'concept' approach beloved by the latter act, Parsons forged a partnership with songwriter Eric Woolfson and created the Alan Parsons Project. The duo's debut *Tales Of Mystery And Imagination*, in which they adapted the work of Edgar Allen Poe, set the pattern for future releases whereby successive creations examined specific themes, including science fiction (*I Robot*) and mysticism (*Pyramid*). By calling on a circle of talented sessionmen and guest performers, including **Arthur Brown**, **Gary Brooker,** Graham Dye (ex-**Scarlet Party**) and **Colin Blunstone**, Parsons and Woolfson created a crafted, if rather sterile, body of work. However, despite enjoying a US Top 3 single in 1982 with 'Eye In The Sky', the Project's subsequent recordings have failed to repeat the commercial success of those early releases.

Albums: *Tales Of Mystery And Imagination* (1975), *I Robot* (1977), *Pyramid* (1978), *Eve* (1979), *The Turn Of A Friendly Card* (1980), *Eye In The Sky* (1982), *Ammonia Avenue* (1984), *Vulture Culture* (1985), *Stereotomy* (1985), *Gaudi* (1987), *Try Anything Once* (1993). Compilations: *The Best Of The Alan Parsons Project* (1983), *Limelight - The Best Of*

The Alan Parsons Project Volume 2 (1988), *Instrumental Works* (1988).

Parsons, Bill

b. 8 September 1934, Crossville, Tennessee, USA). Parsons was a friend of country singer **Bobby Bare**. Prior to entering the US Army, Bare agreed to help Parsons, who was just leaving the service, make a record. Due to a mix-up at Fraternity Records, for which Bare recorded, the 1959 single, titled 'The All American Boy', co-written by Parsons and Bare (using the name Orville Lunsford), was credited to Parsons, although it was Bare singing on the record. It rose to number 2 in the US pop charts as the real Bill Parsons stood on the sidelines watching. As Bare had not yet gained any attention within country music, the deception was continued for one other single, which did not chart. Bare then reverted to his true name and, beginning in 1962, launched a very successful country career. As for the real Bill Parsons, he retired from the music business after recording two unsuccessful singles for Starday Records in 1960.

Parsons, Gene

b. Eugene Victor Parsons, 4 September 1944, Los Angeles, California, USA. Parsons began his musical career playing in the **Castaways** and subsequently formed a duo with Gib Guilbeau. This was followed by the formation of country group Nashville West, in which Parsons played alongside the celebrated guitarist **Clarence White**. When the latter was inducted into the **Byrds** in 1968, Parsons was soon enrolled as their drummer. He remained with them until 1972, appearing on the albums, *Dr Byrds & Mr Hyde*, *The Ballad Of Easy Rider*, *(Untitled)*, *Byrdmaniax* and *Farther Along*. Parsons' drumming skills were notable on the extended arrangement of 'Eight Miles High' that the Byrds included in their live sets and on an entire side of *(Untitled)*. Gene also was a guitarist, banjoist and talented songwriter. Arguably his finest moment as a composer occurred on the excellent 'Gunga Din' from *The Ballad Of Easy Rider*. His other compositions included 'Yesterday's Train' and, in conjunction with Clarence White, the instrumentals 'Green Apple Quick Step' and 'Bristol Steam Convention Blues'. Parsons and White were also responsible for inventing the 'String Bender', an instrument that duplicated the sound of a steel guitar. Following his dismissal from the Byrds, Parsons signed to **Warner Brothers** and released the impressive *Kindling*. Parsons subsequently joined a latter-day version of the **Flying Burrito Brothers** for two minor albums *Flying Again* and *Airborne*. His second solo album, *Melodies*, included a moving tribute to his former partner, the late Clarence White. He also appeared in various offshoot-Byrds reunion concerts, notably with Michael Clarke, before continuing his recording career with *Birds Of A Feather*, recorded with his wife Meridian Green.

Albums: *Kindling* (1973), *Melodies* (1979), as Parsons Green *Birds Of A Feather* (1987).

Further reading: *Timeless Flight: The Definitive Biography Of The Byrds*, Johnny Rogan.

Parsons, Gordon

b. 24 December 1926, Paddington suburb, Sydney, New South Wales, Australia, d. 17 August 1990. At the age of three the family relocated into the bush to Cooks Creek, where he grew up listening to the radio to break the monotony of the lonely area. He got his first guitar at 11 and initially influenced by recordings he heard of **Jimmie Rodgers**, he was soon known around the area, especially at local dances for his singing, yodelling and guitar playing. School held little attraction and he left home at 14, when he was offered a job cutting sleepers for the railroad. His father's words to the employer's invitation are reputed to be 'You might as well take the mongrel - he's no use here'. (He became a skilled axe-man, later winning several awards for his abilities). Gaining further influence from recordings of **Wilf Carter** and fellow Australians **Tex Morton** and **Buddy Williams**, he built a reputation as an entertainer. An appearance on a talent show led to him cutting six sides for Regal-Zonophone in May 1946. These included 'Where The Bellinger River Flows' and 'The Passing of Cobber Jack'. He toured with Goldwyn Bros Circus, where he met and married Zelda Ashton of the Ashton Circus family. (They eventually parted but their daughter, Gail, was born in 1949). He began to tour with various artists, including **Slim Dusty** and Tex Morton but he was unable to maintain regular work for long periods. He loved the quiet life and later saying 'I never could handle anything long and drawn out', he periodically just disappeared from the scene literally into the bush to write more songs - sometimes he worked on farms and on others he just 'went fishing'. During the 50s, he made further recordings but he was never a prolific recording artist, in fact, his total recorded output seemingly only amounted to 21 singles and seven albums. Undoubtedly, the best known song associated with him is 'The Pub With No Beer', which in 1957 became an international hit for his great friend Slim Dusty. There has been some controversy over the years regarding the actual authorship of the song. Parsons had once been given some lines of verse and from them, he had written the song. It was later found that a poem by Dan Sheahan called 'A Pub Without Beer', which contained many similarities in the wording, had been printed in a 1944 newspaper. Dusty, who later became Sheahan's friend and recorded several of his songs, has always maintained that Parsons had believed the lines that he had been given were from some anonymous work. Noted Australian writer Eric Watson summed up the controversy by saying that, in his opinion, Sheahan's was the better poem, whilst Parsons' was the better song. In any event, those who knew of Parsons' fondness for beer later jokingly said that he not only wrote the song, he actually caused it. The song is in fact credited with being Australia's only gold 78 although, surprisingly, it is not actually listed as a million seller in Murrells' *The Book Of Golden Discs*. During the 60s, he made further recordings, including his own version of 'The Pub' but his reluctance to maintain routine appearances disappointed his fans. He gradually withdrew from performing except for the odd show and at one time worked as a warden of a wild life sanctuary. He married for the third time in 1978 and relocated to Sydney, although he kept a caravan at a fishing place near Gosford, which offered him immediate escape from the humdrum of city life. In the 80s, he released three albums on the Selection label. Over the years, he has won several major awards for his contributions to Australian country music, including having his effigy in the wax museum at Tamworth. In 1982, he received the ultimate honour when he became only the seventh artist to be elected to the Country Music Roll Of Renown (Australia's equivalent to Nashville's Country Music Hall Of Fame). His songs have ranged from the comedy of 'The Pub', to the descriptive ballad 'Ellenborough Falls' and the sadness of 'The Passing Of Cobber Jack'. Known affectionately as the Old GP or just plain Ned, he earned a reputation as a pioneer of Australian country music. Many would say that as a fine singer/songwriter and yodeller, he could have become as well known as any of his contemporaries, had he so wished. When asked why he did not make records he would likely reply 'I dunno, Mate. I'd just as soon poke around the bush and split a few posts' or 'I'd rather be fishing than anything else'.

Albums: *Rhythm Of The Range* (EMI 70s), *Gordon Parsons* (Hadley 1976), *The Old G.P.* (Selection 1980), *Just Passin' Through* (Selection 80s), *Throw In A Line* (Selection 80s).

Parsons, Gram

b. Cecil Ingram Connor, 5 November 1946, Winter Haven, Florida, USA, d. 19 September 1973. Parsons' brief but influential career began in high-school as a member of the Pacers. This rock 'n' roll act later gave way to the Legends which, at various points, featured country singer **Jim Stafford** as well as Kent Lavoie, later known as **Lobo**. By 1963 Gram had joined the Shilos, a popular campus attraction modelled on clean-cut folk attraction the **Journeymen**. The quartet - Parsons, George Wrigley, Paul Surratt and Joe Kelly - later moved to New York's Greenwich Village, but Gram left the line-up in 1965 upon enrolling at Harvard College. His studies ended almost immediately and, inspired by the concurrent folk-rock boom, founded the International Submarine Band with John Nuese (guitar), Ian Dunlop (bass) and Mickey Gauvin (drums). Two excellent singles followed, but having relocated to Los Angeles, Parsons' vision of a contemporary country music found little favour amid the prevalent psychedelic trend. The group was nonetheless signed by producer **Lee Hazelwood**, but with Dunlop and Gauvin now absent from the line-up, Bob Buchanan (guitar) and Jon Corneal (drums) joined Gram and Nuese for *Safe At Home*. This excellent set is now rightly viewed as a landmark in the development of country-rock, blending standards with several excellent Parsons' originals, notably 'Luxury Liner'. However, by the time of its release (April 1968), the quartet had not only folded, but Gram had accepted an offer to join the **Byrds**.

His induction resulted in *Sweetheart Of The Rodeo* on which the newcomer determined the group's musical direction. This synthesis of country and traditional styles followed the mould of *Safe At Home*, but was buoyed by the act's excellent harmony work. Although Parsons' role as vocalist was later diminished by Hazelwood's court injunction - the producer claimed it breached their early contract - his influence was undeniable, as exemplified on the stellar 'Hickory Wind'. However, within months Gram had left the Byrds in protest over a South African tour and instead spent several months within the **Rolling Stones**' circle. The following year he formed the **Flying Burrito Brothers** with another ex-Byrd, **Chris Hillman**, 'Sneaky' Pete Kleinow (pedal steel guitar) and bassist Chris Ethridge (bass). *The Gilded Palace Of Sin* drew inspiration from southern soul and urban country music and included one of Parsons' most poignant compositions, 'Hot Burrito #1'. *Burrito Deluxe* failed to scale the same heights as internal problems undermined the unit's potential. Gram's growing drug dependency exacerbated this estrangement and he was fired from the group in April 1970. Initial solo recordings with producer **Terry Melcher** were inconclusive, but in 1972 Parsons was introduced to singer **Emmylou Harris** and together they completed *G.P.* with the assistance of **Elvis Presley**'s regular back-up band. An attendant tour leading the Fallen Angels - Jock Bartley (guitar), Neil Flanz (pedal steel), Kyle Tullis (bass) and N.D. Smart II (drums) - followed, but Parsons' appetite for self-destruction remained intact. Parsons lived the life of a true 'honky tonk hero' with all the excesses of **Hank Williams**, even down to his immaculate embroidered Nudie tailored suits. Sessions for a second album blended established favourites with original songs, many of which had been written years beforehand. Despite its piecemeal content, the resultant set, *Grievous Angel*, was a triumph, in which plaintive duets ('Love Hurts', 'Hearts On Fire') underscored the quality of the Parsons/Harris partnership, while 'Brass Buttons' and 'In My Hour Of Darkness' revealed a gift for touching lyricism. Gram's death in 1973 as a result of 'drug toxicity' emphasized its air of poignancy, and the mysterious theft of his body after the funeral, whereupon his road manager, Philip Kaufman cremated the body in the desert, carrying out Gram's wishes, added to the singer's legend. Although his records were not a commercial success during his lifetime, Parsons' influence on a generation of performers, from the **Eagles** to **Elvis Costello**, is a fitting testament to his talent. Emmylou Harris adopted his mantle with a series of superior of country-rock releases while an excellent concept album, *Ballad Of Sally Rose* (1985), undoubtedly drew on her brief relationship with this star-struck singer. Parson's catalogue is painfully small compared to his enormous importance in contemporary country/rock, and his work is destined to stand alongside that of his hero **Hank Williams**.

Albums: *G.P.* (Reprise 1972), *Grievous Angel* (Reprise 1973), *Sleepless Nights* (A&M 1976), *Gram Parsons And The Fallen Angels - Live 1973* (Sierra 1981). Compilations: *Gram Parsons* (Warner Brothers 1982), *The Early Years* (1984).

Further reading: *Gram Parsons: A Music Biography*, Sid Griffin (ed.). *Hickory Wind: The Life And Times Of Gram Parsons*, Ben Fong-Torres.

Partch, Harry

b. 24 June 1901, Oakland, California, USA, d. 3 September 1974, San Diego, California, USA. This composer's work was called 'the most original and powerful contribution to dramatic music on this continent'. He began composing when he was 14, and 15 years later burnt all that he had written, rejecting the conventional, 'restricting', 12-note scale, for his 43 tones to the octave scale. He was a hobo for several years during the Depression, and from 1930-47 played on just one instrument, his 'adapted viola', which he used to accompany himself singing Biblical passages, and the hitch-hikers inscriptions he included in his hobo epic *The Wayward* (1943). These consisted of *Barstow*, *The Letter*, *San Francisco* and *US Highball*, made up from names of railroad towns, newsboy cries and other effects, which he recited and sung, accompanied by guitar riffs. Later, he designed and built around 30 of his own instruments, such as the Zymo-Xyl, the Gourd Tree, the Spoils of War, the Mazda Marimba, Cloud-Chamber Bowls and the Cone Gong. These were made of materials such as hubcaps, kettle tops, liquor bottles, artillery shell casings, and two nose cone casings salvaged from a Douglas bomber aircraft. Although his admirers included jazz musicians **Gerry Mulligan**, **Chet Baker**, **Bob Brookmeyer** and **Gil Evans**, performances of Partch's works such as *The Bewitched* (1957), 'an enormous ritualistic music drama', were limited by the need to have specially trained musicians rehearsing for at least six months. Some of his compositions were distributed privately on his Gate 5 Records series, and Madeline Tourtelot made five films which featured his music. However, it was not until the last 10 years of his life that his work was made commercially available. In 1973 a filmed portrait entitled *The Dreamer That Remains* was released. A year later he died at his home in California.

Albums: *The Music Of Harry Partch*, *And On The Seventh Day Petals Fell In Petaluma*, *The World Of Harry Partch*, *Delusion Of The Fury*.

Further reading: *The Genesis Of A Music*, Harry Partch.

Partners In Crime

This short-lived UK 'supergroup' was put together by ex-**Status Quo** drummer John Coghlan. Enlisting the services of Noel McCalla (vocals; ex-**Moon**), Mark de Vanchque (keyboards; ex-**Wildfire**), Ray Major (guitar; ex-**Mott**) and Mac Mcaffrey (bass), they specialized in Americanized melodic rock. Debuting with *Organised Crime* in 1985, it was obvious that this set of seasoned musicians gelled together well. Produced by John Eden (Status Quo) and James Guthrie (**Pink Floyd**, **Queensrÿche**) it was a strong album in many respects, yet failed to stand out fom a plethora of other acts offering similar material. The band sundered soon after the album was released.

Album: *Organised Crime* (Epic 1985).

Parton, David

This singer/songwriter and producer was based in Stoke, England. Parton was the mainstay of the group Strange Fox, who were taken under the wing of **Tony Hatch** in the early 70s. Parton discovered the group Sweet Sensation and together with Hatch wrote and produced their hits, including the 1974 UK number 1 'Sad Sweet Dreamer'. Since he had a voice similar to **Stevie Wonder**, he was the ideal choice to cover Wonder's 'Isn't She Lovely', when Stevie decided he did not want to release his version on a single. Parton's version on Pye Records shot into the UK Top 10 in 1977 but it was to be his sole hit as an singer. He continues to work in production and songwriting in Stoke.

Parton, Dolly

b. 19 January 1946, Locust Ridge, Tennessee, USA, Dolly Rebecca Parton's poor farming parents paid the doctor in corn meal for attending the birth of the fourth of their 12 offspring. After her appearances as a singing guitarist on local radio as a child, including the *Grand Ole Opry* in Nashville, Parton left school in 1964. Her recorded output had included a raucous rockabilly song called 'Puppy Love' for a small label as early as 1958, but a signing to Monument in 1966 - the time of her marriage to the reclusive Carl Dean - yielded a C&W hit with 'Dumb Blonde' as well as enlistment in the prestigious *Porter Wagoner Show* as its stetsoned leader's voluptuous female foil in duets and comedy sketches. While this post adulterated her more serious artistic worth, she notched up further country smashes, among them 'Joshua', the autobiographical 'Coat Of Many Colours' and, with Wagoner, 'Last Thing On My Mind' (the **Tom Paxton** folk standard), 'Better Move It On Home' and 1974's 'Please Don't Stop Loving Me'.

On the crest of another solo hit with 'Jolene' on **RCA** that same year, she resigned from the show to strike out on her own - though she continued to record periodically with Wagoner. Encompassing a generous portion of her own compositions, her post-1974 repertoire was less overtly country, even later embracing a lucrative stab at disco in 1979's 'Baby I'm Burning' and non-originals ranging from 'House Of The Rising Sun' to **Jackie Wilson**'s 'Higher And Higher'. 'Jolene' became a 'sleeper' UK Top 10 entry in 1976 and she continued her run in the US country chart with such as 'Bargain Store' (banned from some radio stations for 'suggestive' lyrics), 'All I Can Do' and 'Light Of A Clear Blue Morning' (1977). That same year, 'Here You Come Again' crossed into the US pop Hot 100, and her siblings basked in reflected glory - mainly Randy who played bass in her backing band before landing an RCA contract himself, and **Stella Parton** who had already harried the country list with 1975's 'Ode To Olivia' and 'I Want To Hold You With My Dreams Tonight'.

Their famous sister next ventured into film acting, starring with Lily Tomlin and Jane Fonda in 1981's *9 To 5* (for which she provided the title theme), and with Burt Reynolds in the musical *Best Little Whorehouse In Texas*. Less impressive were *Rhinestone* and 1990's *Steel Magnolias*. She also hosted a 1987 television variety series which lost a ratings war. Nevertheless, her success as a recording artist, songwriter and big-breasted 'personality' remained unstoppable. As well as ploughing back royalties for 70s covers of Parton numbers by **Emmylou Harris, Linda Ronstadt** and **Maria Muldaur** into her Dollywood entertainment complex, she teamed up with **Kenny Rogers** in 1983 to reach the number 1 positon in the USA and the UK Top 10 with a **Bee Gees** composition, 'Islands In The Stream'. With Rogers too, she managed another US country number 1 two years later with 'Real Love'. Although other 80s singles such as 'I Will Always Love You' and 'Tennessee Homesick Blues' were not major chart hits, they became as well-known as many that did. *Trio* with Ronstadt and Harris won a Grammy for best country album in 1987. Her **CBS** debut, *Rainbow*, represented her deepest plunge into mainstream pop - though 1989's *White Limozeen* (produced by **Ricky Skaggs**) retained the loyalty of her multi-national grassroots following. Her celebration of international womanhood, 'Eagle When She Flies', confirmed her return to the country market in 1991. In 1992, **Whitney Houston** had the biggest selling single of the year in the UK with Parton's composition, 'I Will Always Love You', which she sang in the film, *The Bodyguard*.

Selected albums: *Hello, I'm Dolly* (1967), *Dolly Parton And George Jones* (1968), *Just Because I'm A Woman* (1968), with Porter Wagoner *Just The Two Of Us* (1969), with Wagoner *Always, Always* (1969), *My Blue Ridge Mountain Boy* (1969), with Wagoner *Porter Wayne And Dolly Rebecca* (1970), *A Real Live Dolly* (1970), with Wagoner *Once More* (1970), with Wagoner *Two Of A Kind* (1971), *Joshua* (1971), with Wagoner *We Found It* (1973), *Jolene* (1974), *Bargain Store* (1975), *Dolly* (1976), *All I Can Do* (1976), *New Harvest . . . First Gathering* (1977), *Here You Come Again* (1977), *Heartbreaker* (1978), *Dolly Parton And Friends At Goldband* (1979), *Great Balls Of Fire* (1979), *Dolly Dolly Dolly* (1980), *9 To 5 And Odd Jobs* (1980), *Heartbreak Express* (1982), *Burlap And Satin* (1983), *The Great Pretender* (1984), *Rhinestone* (1984, film soundtrack), *Once Upon A Christmas* (1984), with Linda Ronstadt, Emmylou Harris *Trio* (1987), *Rainbow* (1988), *White Limozeen* (1989), *Eagle When She Flies* (1991), *Straight Talk* (1992, film soundtrack), *Slow Dancing With The Moon* (1993), with Tammy Wynette, Loretta Lynn *Honky Tonk Angels* (1993), *Heartsongs - Live From Home* (Columbia 1994). Compilations: *The Best Of Porter Wagoner And Dolly Parton* (1974), *The Dolly Parton Collection* (1980), *Greatest Hits* (1982), *The Collection* (1993), *The Essential Dolly Parton - One* (RCA 1995).

Videos: *Dolly Parton In London* (1988), with Kenny Rogers *Real Love* (1988).

Further reading: *Dolly Parton: Country Goin' To Town*, Susan Saunders. *Dolly Parton*, Otis James. *The Official Dolly Parton Scrapbook*, Connie Berman. *Dolly*, Alanna Nash. *Dolly Parton*, Scott Keely. *Dolly Parton*, Robert K. Krishef. *Dolly, Here I Come Again*, Leonore Fleischer.

Parton, Stella

b. 4 May 1949, Locust Ridge, near Sevier County, Tennessee, USA. Parton, the sixth of 12 children, made her radio debut with her sister, **Dolly Parton**, in 1955. She sang in local clubs and arrived in Nashville in 1972. She recorded, without success, for the small Royal American and Music City labels and toured with a gospel group. She returned to country music in 1975 with a defence of **Olivia Newton-John**'s awards from the Country Music Association called 'Ode To Olivia'. She spent 18 weeks in the US country charts with 'I Want To Hold You In My Dreams Tonight' for the Country Soul label before switching to **Elektra**. She then made the US country Top 20 with 'Danger Of A Stranger', 'Standard Lie Number 1' and 'Four Little Letters'. Parton is a slim blonde but the cover of her 1978 album, *Stella Parton*, was airbrushed to give her the same assets as her famous sister! On that album, ten of the Parton family join her on 'Down To Earth', while she is also featured on the soundtrack of her sister's film, *Rhinestone*. She has also played in a stage version of the film *The Best Little Whorehouse In Texas*, taking the

role Dolly originally played in the film.
Albums: *I Want To Hold You In My Arms Tonight* (1975), *Country Sweet* (1977), *Stella Parton* (1978), *Love Ya* (1979), *So Far...So Good* (1982).

Partridge Family

David Cassidy (b. 12 April 1950, New York City, New York, USA), and his real life step-mother actress **Shirley Jones** (b. 31 March 1934, Smithton, Pennsylvania, USA), were the only members of the fictitious television family group to be heard on their records. Jones, who had starred in hit film musicals like *Oklahoma!, Carousel* and *The Music Man* married David's father actor Jack Cassidy in 1956. *The Partridge Family*, a humorous series about a family pop group (based loosely on the **Cowsills**) started on US television on 25 September 1970. It was an instant hit and sent their debut single 'I Think I Love You' to the top of the chart. In less than two years the fake family, whose records were produced by **Wes Farrell**, had put another six singles and albums into the US Top 40, including the Top 10 successes, 'Doesn't Somebody Want To Be Wanted' and 'I'll Meet You Halfway'. When their US popularity began to wane the series took off in the UK, giving them five UK Top 20 hits, most of which were less successful Stateside. The show made Cassidy a transatlantic teen idol and he also had a run of solo hits. By the time the television series ended in 1974 the hits for both acts had dried up.
Albums: *The Partridge Family Album* (1970), *Up To Date* (1971), *A Partridge Family Christmas Card* (1971), *The Partridge Family Sound Magazine* (1972), *The Partridge Family Shopping Bag* (1972), *The Partridge Family Notebook* (1972), *Crossword Puzzle* (1973). Compilations: *The Partridge Family At Home With Their Hits* (1972), *Only A Moment Ago* (1975).

Partridge, Andy

(see **XTC**; **Dukes Of Stratosphear**)

Partridge, Don

b. 1945, Bournemouth, Dorset, England. Self-styled 'King of the Street Singers', Partridge was discovered busking in London's Berwick Street market by former **Viscount** Don Paul, who in turn became his manager. 'Rosie', the singer's self-penned debut single, was reputedly recorded for the sum of £8, but became a surprise UK Top 5 hit in 1968. The artist's unconventional lifestyle and penchant for straight-talking resulted in good copy, and engendered greater publicity than his novelty status might otherwise suggest. 'Blue Eyes', Partridge's follow-up single, reached number 3, yet the song is less well recalled than its ebullient predecessor. The singer later supervised *The Buskers*, a various-artists compilation, and enjoyed one further chart entry with 'Breakfast On Pluto' in 1969. After this brief flirtation with fame, Partridge returned to busking roots and continued to perform into the 90s.
Album: *Don Partridge* (1968).

Party Posse

Afflicted with poverty at their inception, this band of Harlem, New York-rappers originally practiced in the most un-party-like space of their local graveyard. The trio of DJ Alphonse Constant and rappers Randall Barber and Tedd Lewis were undettered, believing that if they could 'party there, (they) could party anywhere'. In actual fact that piece of hallowed ground has achieved something approaching notoriety since, being used for a **Doug E. Fresh** video. They formed in Harlem in the late 80s, passing by unobserved until **Kool Moe Dee** visited their school. Inspired by him, they eventually won themselves a contract through his manager, who organised an audition for Moe Dee's home label, **Jive**. Moe Dee would also make an appearance on their debut album ('Just Look At Us'), which was characterised by old school positivity ('Strivin'') and locker room humour ('Steppin' In Doo Doo')
Album: *It's Party Time* (Jive 1989).

Pasadena Roof Orchestra

Britain's most commercially successful traditional jazz-based act of the 70s was formed in the mid-60s by baker John Arthey (bass) as a larger, slicker recreation of a 20s ragtime band than that of the **Temperance Seven**. Among its mainstays were John Parry (vocals), arranger **Keith Nichols** (piano), Mac White (clarinet) and trumpeters Clive Baker, Enrico Tomasino and Mike Henry. Transient members included **Viv Stanshall** (euphonium). Despite much interest from London's music press - especially the ***Melody Maker*** - the Orchestra had no major record hits, but their albums did brisk business in foyers on the European college circuit and at the more prestigious jazz festivals where they command high fees as a popular attraction of considerable longevity.
Albums: *The Show Must Go On* (1977), *A Talking Picture* (1978), *Night Out* (1979), *Puttin' On The Ritz* (1983), *Fifteen Years On* (1985), *Good News* (1987), *On Tour* (1987), *Happy Feet* (1988). Compilatons: *Anthology* (1978), *Everythin' Stops For Tea* (1984), *C'mon Along And Listen To* (1986), *Isn't It Romantic* (1987), *Collection* (1987), *Top Hat, White Tie And Tails* (1988), *Sentimental Journey* (1993).

Pasadenas

UK soul band formed in 1987 by the three Brown brothers - Rockin' Jeff (b. 12 December 1964), Michael (b. 15 February 1962), and David (b. 16 February 1962), plus Hamish (b. 11 August 1964) and Andre (b. 4 December 1964). They had previously been performing in an outfit titled Finesse since 1982. Finesse danced on videos by Animal Nightlife, **Freez**

and others, appearing in the film *Absolute Beginners*. The band's debut 45, 'Right On', was a paean to artists such as **Marvin Gaye**. Follow-ups, including 'Riding On A Train', 'Enchanted Lady' and 'I'm Doing Fine Now', established them as a chart act proper. As well as the traditions of doo-wop, the band are heavily influenced by the spirit and style of the decade, despite their own acknowledgement that 'being black in the 50s was not a nice thing'.
Albums: *To Whom It May Concern* (1988), *Elevate* (1991), *Yours Sincerely* (1992).

Pass, Joe

b. Joseph Anthony Passalaqua, 13 January 1929, New Brunswick, New Jersey, USA, d. 23 May 1994, Los Angeles, California, USA. In his mid and late teens guitarist Pass worked with a number of name bands, including those led by **Tony Pastor** and **Charlie Barnet**. From the early 50s until the beginning of the following decade, Pass dwelt in self-imposed obscurity playing when and where he could in order to sustain a drug habit for which he also served time. The 60s saw his rehabilitation and revealed an astonishing talent. Following his internment at the Synanon Foundation in Santa Monica, a self-help regime which allowed him to break his habit, Pass was returned to the outside world as a reformed character, and a media-worthy example of the powers of Synanon healing (since largely discredited). The new profile brought engagements with artists as diverse as **Julie London** and **Richard 'Groove' Holmes**. Through the patronage of **Norman Granz** of Pablo he moved on to work with jazz's biggest names, including duos with leading artists such as **Oscar Peterson** (winning a Grammy for his album with the latter and bassist **Niels-Henning Ørsted Pedersen**), **Jimmy Rowles** and **Zoot Sims**, or in small groups including **Count Basie**'s reformed Kansas City Six. He proved especially gifted as accompanist to singers, particularly **Ella Fitzgerald**. It was as a solo performer, however, that he most ably displayed his mastery of guitar, but despite the virtuoso standard of his playing his work never degenerated into a mere display of technical accomplishment. His phenomenal technique, coupled as it was with an intense jazz feel, made him welcome in almost any setting.
Selected albums: *The Complete 'Catch Me' Sessions* (1963), *Joe Pass-John Pisano Quartet* (1963), *Joy Spring* (1964), *For Django* (1964), *The Living Legends* (1969, one side only), *Intercontinental* (1970), *Virtuoso* (Pablo 1973), with Ella Fitzgerald *Take Love Easy* (1973), *Portraits Of Duke Ellington* (1974), *Joe Pass At The Montreux Jazz Festival* (1975), with Oscar Peterson *Porgy And Bess* (1976), *Virtuoso No 2* (Pablo 1976), *Guitar Player* (1976), *Quadrant* (1977), *Virtuoso No 3* (Original Jazz Classics 1977), *Live At Montreux '77* (Original Jazz Classics 1977), *Guitar Interludes* (c.1977), *Tudo Bem!* (Original Jazz Classics 1978), *Chops* (Original Jazz Classics 1978), *I Remember Charlie Parker* (Original Jazz Classics 1979), *Northsea Nights* (1979), *Digital III At Montreux* (1979), *Quadrant Toasts Duke Ellington - All Too Soon* (1980), with Jimmy Rowles *Checkmate* (1981), *Ira, George And Joe/Joe Pass Loves Gershwin* (1981), with Zoot Sims *Blues For Two* (1982), *Eximious* (1982), *Live At Long Beach City College* (1984), *We'll Be Together Again* (1985), *Whitestone* (Pablo 1985), *University Of Akron Concert* (Pablo 1985), *Blues For Fred* (Pablo 1988), *One For My Baby* (Pablo 1988), *Summer Nights* (Pablo 1990), *Appassionato* (Pablo 1990), *Vituoso Live!* (Pablo 1991), *My Song* (Telarc 1993).

Passion

Stephen Sondheim's third collaboration (following ***Sunday In The Park With George*** and ***Into The Woods***) with librettist and director James Lapine opened at the Plymouth Theatre in New York on 9 May 1994. Set in the late 19th century, and based on Ettore Scola's 1981 film *Passione d'Amore*, which was adapted from the 1869 novel *Fosca* by Igino Tarchetti, *Passion* opens with a 10-minute sequence in which Giorgio (Jere Shea), a handsome young army officer, and Clara (Marin Mazzie) are making rapturous love, naked on a bed. What follows is a complex and absorbing piece in which Giorgio, after being posted to a far outpost, finds himself the object of the obsessive desire of the unattractive Fosca (Donna Murphy), who is dying. Before the curtain falls, Fosca has changed Giorgio's whole conception as to what real love should be, even inveigling him into writing the kind of love letter she believes he should send to her. Sondheim's score, which critics noted contained some of his most 'direct' love songs, consisted of 'Happiness', 'First Letter', 'Second Letter', 'Third Letter', 'Fourth Letter', 'I Read', 'Transition', 'Garden Sequence', 'Trio', 'I Wish I Could Forget You', 'Soldiers' Gossip', 'Flashback', 'Sunrise Letter', 'Is This What You Call Love?', 'Forty Days', 'Loving You', 'Farewell Letter', 'No One Has Ever Loved You' and Finalé. As usual, Jonathan Tunick's arrangements were singled out for special praise, as were Jane Greenwood's sumptuous costume designs. *Passion* won Tony Awards for best musical, book, score, leading actress (Donna Murphy), and a Grammy for Best Musical Show album in 1995, but despite being hailed by *Variety* as 'the most emotionally engaging new musical Broadway has had in years', the show closed on January 1995 after 280 performances.

Passions (UK)

This English post-punk group, with definite pop leanings, was formed in June 1978 and comprised Barbara Gogan (b. Dublin, Eire; vocals/guitar), Mitch Barker (vocals), Clive Timperley (guitar/vocals), Claire Bidwell (bass/vocals) and Richard Williams (drums). All save Timperley had featured in Rivers Of Passion,

while all except Bidwell had spent time in the various incarnations of the Derelicts between 1974-76. During this time Timperley also played with Joe Strummer's **101er's**. Gogan left her Dublin home at the age of 18 and settled in France within a Marxist commune. She came to London in 1972 and moved into a 'squat' near Ladbroke Grove, where she became involved with the Derelicts, a loose collection of like-minded left wingers. Evolving into the Passions they released their first single, 'Needles And Pins', on the tiny Soho label, also home of the Nips and the **Inmates**. They lost Barker in 1979 when a broken leg put paid to his musical activities. Continuing as a four-piece they signed to Fiction Records for their debut album, and one single, 'Hunted'. Bidwell left in July 1980 to form Schwarze Kapelle and then joined the **Wall**. David Agar, once a member of the fledgling **Spandau Ballet**, replaced her. Three days later they were dropped by Fiction but fell immediately on their feet with a contract for **Polydor Records**. They finally found success in 1981 with their second single for the label, 'I'm In Love With A German Film Star'. It would be their only hit, despite the eloquence and strength of later material. Timperley left to run a health shop in December 1981, while the recruitment of Kevin Armstrong (ex-Local Heroes SW9) on guitar and Jeff Smith (ex-**Lene Lovich** band) on keyboards failed to put the brakes on their commercial slide. Armstrong himself left in August 1982 to be replaced by Steve Wright, but by this time the band was in its death throes.
Albums: *Michael And Miranda* (Fiction 1980), *Thirty Thousand Feet Over China* (Polydor 1981), *Sanctuary* (Polydor 1982).

Passions (USA)

A rock 'n' roll vocal group from Brooklyn, New York City, New York, USA. Members were lead Jimmy Gallagher, second tenor Albie Galione, first tenor Tony Armato, and baritone Vinny Acierno. The Passions were one of the first Italian-American vocal ensembles to make their presence felt on the rock 'n' roll scene, and typical of such groups their sound was smooth and sincere. The Passions were formed in 1958, and after signing with the local Audicon label in 1959 immediately found success with 'Just To Be With You' (USA number 69 pop) in 1959. It would be the group's only national hit, but in the New York metropolitan area the Passions' impact was far greater. They were local stars. Their double-sided follow-up in 1960, 'I Only Want You'/'This Is My Love', is still cherished by doo-wop fans. At this time Vinny Acierno was replaced by Lou Rotondo. The Passions' next single was a smooth version of the **Cadillacs**' classic ballad, 'Gloria' (1960), which although only achieved local success became an enduring legacy for the group and something of a doo-wop standard. The group was unable to sustain success with the singles it recorded in the next two years, and in 1964 disbanded.
Compilations: *Just To Be With You* (Clifton 1990), *Legendary Hits* (Crystal Ball, 1991), *Just To Be With You* (Relic 1992).

Pastels (UK)

Formed in Glasgow, Scotland, in 1982, the Pastels were one of the prime movers in the 80s 'shambling'/'anorak' independent scene that influenced later luminaries such as the **Flatmates** and **Talulah Gosh**. Group leader Stephen Pastel (b. Stephen McRobbie, Scotland; guitar/vocals) has since gone to great lengths to distance the Pastels from their past idolaters. Today they serve as a major influence on emerging Scottish bands like **Teenage Fanclub** (whose Norman Blake is a fan club member and would later play in the Pastels) and **Captain America/Eugenius**. However, their history has been characterized by the kind of lethargy which has doomed them to mere cultism: 'I just find careerism and naked ambition really ugly'. The Pastels themselves were motivated by a conglomeration of the **Monkees** and the **Ramones**. The early line-up also comprised Brian Superstar (b. Brian Taylor; guitar) and Chris Gordon (drums), but the latter's early departure signalled a recurring instability in the group's rhythm section. Their first release on the **Television Personalities**' Whaam! label, the *Songs For Children* EP, was the beginning of an unsettled relationship with a variety of labels including **Rough Trade**, **Creation** and Glass Records. Appearances on various compilations, not least a prestigious slot on the seminal *C86* collection ('Breaking Lines') from the ***New Musical Express*** increased their standing in the independent market, while their music combined ambitious vision with naive ability. A settled line-up; Pastel, Superstar, Aggi Wright (vocals), Martin Hayward (bass) and Bernice Swanson (drums) - completed two albums, *Up For A Bit With The Pastels* and *Sittin' Pretty*, wherein the group matured from the charming innocence of early releases to embrace a myriad of contrasting styles held together by McRobbie's commited vision. Material ranged from the bouyant 'Nothing To Be Done' to the lengthy 'Baby Honey' and 'Ditch The Fool', as the Pastels expanded their musical horizons with the temporary aid of Eugene Kelly (ex-**Vaselines**), Norman Blake and David Keegan, formerly of the **Shop Assistants** and Stephen's partner in the pivotal 53rd & 3rd Records label. By the early 90s Keegan had become a full-time member of the Pastels which, following a series of alterations, re-emerged centred around McRobbie, Wright (now on bass) and Katriona Mitchell (drums), the latter pursuing a concurrent path as a member of Melody Dog. Against the odds this trio was still in place for 1995's *Mobile Safari*, an enjoyable collection of raggamuffin odes to life in and outside of

an under-achieving indie band, punctuated by songs such as 'Yoga' and 'Classic Lineup'.
Albums: *Up For A Bit With The Pastels* (Glass 1987), *Sittin' Pretty* (Chapter 22 1989), *Mobile Safari* (Domino 1995). Compilation: *Suck On The Pastels* (Creation 1988).

Pastels (USA)

This R&B vocal group formed at a US Air Force base in Narsarssuak, Greenland in 1954. Members were **Big Dee Irwin** (b. DiFosco Ervin, 4 August 1939, New York City, New York, USA; lead), Richard Travis, Tony Thomas, and Jimmy Willingham. Members were later transferred to Washington, DC and the the Pastels were discovered by New York-based Hull Records in 1957. They were signed to the company's subsidiary label, Mascot, but after their first hit, 'Been So Long', all their records were leased to the **Chess** (**Records**) brothers' Argo label in Chicago. 'Been So Long', an R&B number 5 and pop Top 30 hit, was an utterly sublime doo-wop with haunting chorusing and for decades later was a staple on oldies radio shows. By 1958 all the Pastels had gotten out of the service, so the group was ready to exploit the success of their hit with follow-ups, but instead suffered a criminal failure in the lack of national chart success in 1958 for their equally sublime 'So Far Away' their third and final release. The following year the Pastels disbanded but Dee Irwin continued in the music business. In 1964 he enjoyed a Top 40 national pop hit with 'Swingin' On A Star', accompanied by the uncredited **Little Eva**. He continued behind the scenes as a songwriter, composing tunes for artists such as **Ray Charles**, **Arthur Prysock**, **Esther Phillips** and **Isaac Hayes**.

Pastor, Tony

b. 26 October 1907, Middletown, Connecticut, USA, d. 31 October 1969. As a teenager Pastor played tenor saxophone in a number of east coast-based bands, sometimes with **Artie Shaw** who was a neighbour. Pastor tried a hand at bandleading in the early 30s but with limited success. In the middle of the decade he joined Shaw's band, became one of its featured soloists and occasional singer. He appeared on a number of the band's most popular records, including 'Indian Love Call' and 'Rosalie'. After leaving Shaw he tried bandleading again, this time with considerably more success. Thanks to a series of radio broadcasts the band became well known and sufficiently popular to survive the winter of 1947 that saw so many big bands fold. Among the singers he hired were the sisters Betty and **Rosemary Clooney**. Pastor continued leading a big band until the end of the 50s. In the 60s he led a small group at casinos in Nevada, singing in a group which also featured his three sons. A tough-toned soloist, Pastor always tried to give his band a strong jazz flavour while still keeping a careful eye on commercial needs. He died in 1969.
Albums: *One Night Stand With Tony Pastor* (1949), *Tony Pastor And His Orchestra* i (1958), *Tony Pastor And His Orchestra* ii (1959), *Tony Pastor And His Orchestra* iii (1960). Compilations: *The Indispensable Artie Shaw Vols 1/2* (1938-39 recordings), *Just For Kicks* (1940-45 recordings), *Confessin'* (1940-49 recordings), *Tony Pastor And His Orchestra* (1940-57 recordings), *Tony Pastor With Rosemary And Betty Clooney* (1942-47 recordings), *The Film Tracks Of Tony Pastor* (1949 recordings).

Pastorius, Jaco

b. John Francis Pastorius, 1 December 1951, Norristown, Pennsylvania, USA, d. 21 September 1987, Fort Lauderdale, Florida, USA. Encouraged by his father, a drummer and vocalist, to pursue a career in music, Pastorius learned to play bass, drums, guitar, piano, and saxophone while in his teens. As a result of a football injury to his arm, his ambitions were mainly orientated towards the drums, but he soon found work playing bass for visiting pop and soul acts. After backing the **Temptations** and the **Supremes**, he developed a cult following, and his reputation spread. In 1975, Bobby Colomby, drummer with **Blood, Sweat And Tears**, was impressed enough to arrange the recording of Pastorius' first album, and a year later **Pat Metheny** asked him to play bass on his own first album for **ECM Records**, additionally he worked with **Joni Mitchell**. But the most important stage in Pastorius' career came in 1976: joining **Weather Report** to record the highly influential *Heavy Weather*, his astonishing technique on the fretless bass and his flamboyant behaviour on stage consolidated the band's popularity and boosted his own image to star status. He established his own band, Word Of Mouth, in 1980, and they enjoyed three years of successful tours, while Pastorius himself recorded intermittently with some of the top musicians in jazz. However, Pastorius suffered from alcoholism and manic depression. In 1987, after increasing bouts of inactivity, he suffered fatal injuries in a brawl outside the Midnight Club in his home town of Fort Lauderdale. Pastorius was one of the most influential bass players since **Charles Mingus**, and extended the possibilities of the electric bass as a melodic instrument in a way which has affected many bassists since.
Selected albums: *Jaco* (DIW 1974 recording), *Jaco Pastorius* (1975), with Weather Report *Heavy Weather* (1976), *Word Of Mouth* (WEA 1980), *Invitation* (1982), *PDB* (DIW 1987), *Honestly* (Jazzpoint 1986), *Heavy N' Jazz* (Jazzppoint 1987), *Jazz Street* (Timeless 1987), *Live In Italy* (Jazzpoint 1991, 1986 recording), *Holiday For Pans* (Sound Hills 1993, 1980-82 recording).

Pat Garrett And Billy The Kid

This 1973 feature starred James Cockburn and **Kris Kristofferson** in the respective title roles. Sam

Peckinpah directed the film in customary fashion; violent, blood-splattered images pepper many of the scenes. Critical reaction was divided; Stanley Kauffman declared it showed 'what Peckinpah can do when he doesn't put his mind to it.' The presence of Kristofferson and **Rita Coolidge** helped bring the rock and movie worlds together. However, interest in the film from music fans was owing to the presence of **Bob Dylan**. His role as the monosyllabic 'Alias' was initially much larger, but his scenes were among many cut from the final print. Dylan also contributed the low-key, but atmospheric soundtrack music. His album of the same name reached the UK Top 30 and although the main theme from the film, 'Knocking On Heaven's Door' was only a minor Top 20 hit when issued as a single, the song has since become one of the artist's most popular compositions, inspiring several cover versions. Its appeal has outlasted the film it is drawn from. If *Pat Garrett And Billy The Kid* retains any fascination, it is because of Dylan's role, rather than being the product of a director responsible for the superior *The Wild Bunch* and *Straw Dogs*.

Pate, Johnny

b. 1923, Chicago Heights, Illinois, USA. Pate was one of the most important producers and arrangers in the creation of the Chicago sound in soul music during the 60s. With his highly lyrical horn arrangements Pate was able to suggest a gospel-tinged feeling with the utmost in subtlety and nuance. This deft approach probably grew out of his 50s career as a bassist in his own cocktail lounge jazz combo that worked Chicago clubs for many years. He first began performing in these clubs with Coleridge Davis and Stuff Smith in the late 40s. By the early 50s Pate had formed his own unit. In 1958 performing as the Johnny Pate Quintet he achieved a national hit with 'Swingin' Sheppard Blues' (number 17 R&B, number 43 pop), a cover of the hit by the Moe Koffman Quartet. By the end of the 50s the nightclubs in the black community were closing down and the call for cocktail lounge jazz was highly diminished, so Pate began working freelance for various Chicago R&B labels as an arranger and producer. Beginning in 1962 he began writing most of the arrangements for the horn-driven **OKeh Records**' hits of **Major Lance** and **Billy Butler** produced by **Carl Davis**. A year later Pate started production and arrangement work with the **Impressions** on **ABC Records**. At ABC he served as A&R man and produced and arranged hits for another Chicago-based group, the **Marvelows**. When the Impressions moved to the **Curtom** label in 1970 so did Pate, but he only stayed until 1972, when he moved to the west coast.

Albums: *Johnny Pate At The Blue Note* (Stepheny 1957), *Jazz Goes Ivy League* (King 1958), *Swingin' Flute* (King 1958), *A Date With Johnny Pate* (King 1959).

Patinkin, Mandy

b. Mandel Patinkin, 30 November 1952, Chicago, Illinois, USA. An actor and singer with a 'wonderfully expressive voice', as a boy Patinkin sang in the choir at his Jewish temple, and performed in musicals such as ***Anything Goes***, ***Stop The World - I Want To Get Off*** and ***Carousel*** at the local youth centre. After attending the University of Kansas and studying drama at the Juilliard School of Music, he worked in regional theatre before spending most of the late 70s with the New York Festival Theatre. In 1980 he won a Tony Award for his portrayal of Che in the Broadway production of ***Evita***, and was nominated again, four years later, for his performance in the leading role of ***Sunday In The Park With George***. In 1985 Patinkin was one of the many stars of *Follies In Concert* which played for two nights only at the Avery Fisher Hall in New York. His version of 'Buddy's Blues', in particular, is one of the cast CD's many highlights. A year later, Patinkin featured on another fine album, a new CBS studio recording of **Richard Rodgers** and **Oscar Hammerstein II'**s classic ***South Pacific***, on which he was joined by opera singers Kiri Te Kanawa and Jose Carreras. The album went to number 5 in the UK chart, and Patinkin's sensitive version of 'Younger than Springtime' was released as a single. In 1989, his one-man show, *Mandy Patinkin In Concert: Dress Casual* played for a four week season at the Helen Hayes Theatre, in New York, and in 1990 Patinkin co-starred with Claire Moore in the world premiere of the Jason Carr/Julian Barry/Peter Hall musical *Born Again*, based on Eugene Ionesco's play *Rhinoceros*, at the Chichester Festival Theatre in England. Since making his film debut in *The Big Fix* in 1978, Patinkin has made highly effective appearances in several other movies, including *Ragtime*, ***Yentl***, *Dick Tracy* (in the role of 88 Keys, **Madonna**'s pianist), *True Colours*, *The Doctor*, and *The Music Of Chance* (1993). In 1991 he was back on Broadway, playing the hunchbacked uncle, Archibald Craven, in ***The Secret Garden***, and in January 1993 he succeeded Michael Rupert as Marvin in ***Falsettos***. In 1994 Patinkin played Sky Masterson in a BBC Radio 2 recording of ***Guys And Dolls***, and in 1995 was on international television screens, starring in the medical drama series *Chicago Hope*.

Selected albums: *Mandy Patinkin* (CBS 1989), *Dress Casual* (CBS 1991), *Experiment* (Elektra Nonesuch 1994), and Original Cast recordings.

Patitucci, John

b. 22 December 1959, Brooklyn, New York, USA. Patitucci is a technically gifted bassist best known for his work on both the electric and acoustic instruments for fusion keyboard legend **Chick Corea**. After playing some pop and rock in his brother's band in New York, he moved with his family to America's west

coast, the home of a fearsome tradition for jazz/rock fusion virtuosi, in 1972, and was introduced to the jazz tradition by bass teacher Chris Poehler. Studying the acoustic work of **Ron Carter**, **Dave Holland**, **Charlie Haden** and **Eddie Gomez**, and the electric bass techniques of **Larry Graham**, **Marcus Miller**, **Stanley Clarke** and, particularly, bass hero **Jaco Pastorius**, he developed quickly, working with pianist Gap Mangione (brother of **Chuck Mangione**), and veteran British-borne vibesman **Victor Feldman**. It was with Feldman that Chick Corea came across him, and asked him to join the newly formed Elektric Band. Patitucci stayed with the Elektric Band throughout its life, recording five albums, and played an important part in the Akoustic Band trio. Since the late 80s he has also been working as a leader on GRP and Stretch – Corea's own subsidiary of the **GRP** label. An incredible technician on both acoustic and six-string electric basses, Patitucci has unfortunately allowed his output to be dominated by material that works primarily as a means to demonstrate his technique. His best record so far is probably *Sketchbook*, featuring drummer **Peter Erskine**, tenor saxophonist **Michael Brecker** and guitarist **John Scofield**.
Albums: with Chick Corea *The Chick Corea Elektric Band* (1986), with Corea *Light Years* (1987), with Corea *Eye Of The Beholder* (1988), *John Patitucci* (1988), *Chick Corea Akoustic Band* (1989), *On The Corner* (1989), *Sketchbook* (1990), with Corea *Inside Out* (1990), *Beneath The Mask* (1992), *Alive* (1992), *Heart Of The Bass* (1992).

Paton, Tam

b. Prestonpans, Scotland. Paton's involvement in the music business began during the early 60s when he played piano in Scottish showband, the Crusaders. After they split he was persuaded to form a new 10-piece showband known as the Tam Paton Orchestra, which had a residency at Edinburgh's Palais de Dance. In 1967, he was approached by two young kids, Alan and Derek Longmuir, who had recently formed a group called the Saxons. By the time he auditioned them, however, they had changed their name to the **Bay City Rollers**. Paton managed the group who had an ever-shifting line-up over the next few years. It was not until 1971 that they received their big break when Paton persuaded a posse of record company talent spotters to witness their act in Edinburgh. Initially signed to **Tony Calder**'s production company, they released their work through **Dick Leahy**'s Bell Records. In the meantime, Paton retained another group, Kip, who served as a pool of replacements. Briefly, he had a managerial tie-up with **Peter Walsh** after which the Rollers swiftly became the biggest pop sensation of their day. The press predictably caricatured Paton as an aggressive hirer/firer and puppetmaster. Several people attempted to buy out Paton's interests in the Rollers but he always refused to surrender power. For Paton, the Rollers were not merely a business asset but the embodiment of all his frustrated dreams and ambitions. Sadly, the dream ended in the late 70s when the Rollers good boy image was exposed as a myth. Worse was to follow for Paton who was sentenced to three years' imprisonment at Edinburgh High Court for committing indecent acts with a number of youngsters aged between 15 and 20 years, supplying them with stupefying liquor and allowing blue movies to be shown at his home. His fall was undoubtedly the most spectacular of any manager in pop music history.

Patra

b. Dorothy Smith, c.1973, Kingston, Jamaica, West Indies. A DJ, singer and hopeful actor widely touted/hyped as the female equivalent of **Shabba Ranks**, Patra (formerly Lady Patra) signed to the same management, under the aegis of Clifton 'Specialist' Dillon, in 1989. She also shares the same record company, **Epic**. Accordingly, with the new, commercial expectations placed on her shoulders, her material has moved from strict **dancehall** to include smooth love songs. Patra was brought up singing in churches in Westmoreland, where she moved from Kingston at an early age. Her ambition as a child was always evident, and she soon entered neighbourhood singing/DJing competitions in high school. Early supporters, who included Major Mackerel, encouraged her to return to Kingston and try her luck in the studios. **Gussie Clarke** was the first to 'voice' her after she had been declined by several others. Such rejections were only a short-term problem, however. Following the sessions with Clarke she found herself in demand by Shocking Vibes, **Exterminator** and several others. Sides like 'Holler Fe The Wok', Visa Hole', 'Man Me Love' and 'Worky Worky' showcased her considerable talents. On the back of this moderate success she played her first major show at the Sting '88 celebrations. By the time the deal with Epic was struck, Patra's singing voice had taken precedence over her DJ skills, as highlighted by the single 'Sweet Memories', the first product of new sessions (though it was actually released by Tachyon's Sonny Ochai). Curiously, it rose to number 1 in the Japanese reggae charts, but Epic will surely demand more concrete domestic success in return for their investment.
Album: *Queen Of The Pack* (Epic 1993).

Patrick Street

After touring the USA in 1986, the musicians, Kevin Burke, Andy Irvine and Jackie Daly, returned to Ireland and formed a permanent group, adding guitarist Arty McGlynn. From 1987-1991, they issued three albums under the name of Patrick Street, and reunited for a further release and tour in 1993. Kevin Burke (fiddle) is of English/Irish parents, although his playing is influenced by the Sligo style. Before joining Patrick Street he played an important role in the **Bothy Band**'s success, and has recorded with **Arlo Guthrie** and **Christy Moore**. He released the solo albums, *If The Cap Fits* and *Up Close*. Andy Irvine (guitar, harmonica, mandolin, bouzuki), a founder member of both **Sweeny's Men** and **Planxty**, has worked with many other leading figures in Irish, Scottish and English folk. Jackie Daly (accordion) first came to international attention when he joined **De Dannan**. Like Daly, Arty McGlynn started out on the accordion, but switched to the guitar, inspired by the late 50s rock 'n' roll greats. At the age of 15, McGlynn joined an Irish showband and spent 18 years touring Irish dance halls. Feeling stifled, he switched to traditional music, and sang solo in folk clubs. His European tours with Andy Irvine led to his participation in Patrick Street. More recently, he was an important element in the high flying Four Men And A Dog. A true Irish supergroup, Patrick Street's main success has been in the USA, but their four albums have also registered strongly in their home country, and in the UK folk charts. The group has proved to be equal to the sum of its parts, and has effectively mixed dance tunes with stirring songs and ballads sung by Irvine.

Albums: *Patrick Street* (1987), *No. 2 Patrick Street* (1989), *Irish Times* (1991), *All In Good Time* (1993).

Patrick, Pat

b. November 1929, the mid-west, USA. Like most of **Sun Ra**'s long-term associates, Pat Patrick's origins are shrouded in mystery. He studied piano and drums as a child and received trumpet lessons from his father and from **Clark Terry**. At DuSable High School in Chicago he met tenor saxophonists **John Gilmore** and **Clifford Jordan** and bassist **Richard Davis**. Patrick began playing alto and baritone saxophones and clarinet. Having worked with some of the pre-eminent shakers of American music - **Muddy Waters**, **Lillian Armstrong**, **Nat 'King' Cole** and **Cab Calloway** - he joined Sun Ra in 1953. His strong technique and expansive imagination were perfect for Sun Ra's mind-bending compositions and he stayed with him until the mid-80s. In 1961 he contributed baritone to **John Coltrane**'s *Africa/Brass* album. In the early 70s he played in **Thelonious Monk**'s group, joined the Jazz Composers Orchestra, recording with them on projects led by **Grachan Moncur III** (*Echoes Of A Prayer*) and **Clifford Thornton** (*The Gardens Of Harlem*), and also worked for **Quincy Jones** and **Duke Ellington**. In 1978 he recorded on Jordon's *Inward Fire*, which also featured Davis and fellow Chicagoan **Muhal Richard Abrams**. In 1990 Patrick was reported to be living in Chicago and concentrating on playing tenor saxophone.

Patt, Frank 'Honeyboy'

b. 1 September 1928, Fostoria, Alabama, USA. After singing in church as a child, Patt taught himself guitar soon after emigrating to Los Angeles, California in 1952. There he formed a musical partnership with pianist **Gus Jenkins**, also from Alabama. Two years later Patt made his first record, with Jenkins, issued on the **Specialty** label, a powerful blues evoking the scene of a murder, 'Blood Stains On The Wall'. Although years later this came to be regarded as something of a classic, it made little impact at the time, and he had only one more record issued, in 1957, again with Jenkins. Over the next decade, he worked mostly outside the music business, but his career enjoyed a revival in the 70s, with further recording work and live appearances.

Album: *City Blues* (1973).

Patterson, Ottilie

b. 31 January 1932, Comber, Co. Down, Northern Ireland. Patterson came to England in 1955 to work with **Chris Barber**'s band and later married Barber. Her style was originally based firmly on the singing of the classic blues singers like **Bessie Smith** and she built her reputation on songs like 'Reckless Love' and 'St. Louis Blues'. Gradually her vocal performances loosened up considerably as she was influenced by the R&B and gospel music and performers regularly touring with the Barber Band, such as **Muddy Waters**, **Sister Rosetta Tharpe** and **Sonny Boy** (Rice Miller) **Williamson**. In the late 50s she had introduced Irish folk into her repertoire and later even sang settings of Shakespeare and Macleish. She fell ill in the 70s and forced to retire though in the 80s she was able, once again, to make occasional appearances with the Barber band.

Albums: *Ottilie Patterson With Chris Barber's Jazz Band* (1955), *That Patterson Girl, I* (1955), *That Patterson Girl, II* (1956), *Chris Barber At The London Palladium* (1961), *Madame Blues And Dr. Jazz* (1983).

Patto

Patto was formed in 1969 when four members of Timebox - Michael Patrick (Patto) McGrath (vocals), Peter 'Ollie' Halsall (guitar/vibes), Clive Griffiths (bass) and John Halsey (drums) - abandoned commercial constraints and embarked on a more progressive direction. Their debut, *Patto*, featured several of the group's most lasting performances. Although producer **Muff Winwood** opted for a rather rudimentary sound, the set contained a series of impressive songs, featuring complex signatures, excellent vocals and Halsall's superb guitar work. Sometimes frenzied, at other times restrained, his contributions enhanced an already outstanding collection. A second release, *Hold Your Fire*, exaggerated their jazz-rock persuasions, but

retained the urgency and fire of their debut. Judicious overdubs ensured a fuller sound, yet Patto's interplay and empathy remained intact. Faced by commercial indifference, the group embarked on a third collection vowing to capture the irreverent side of their music. *Roll 'Em, Smoke 'Em, Put Another Line Out* was only partially successful with 'Singing The Blues On Reds' and the compulsive 'Loud Green Song' being the stand-out tracks. The project fared no better than its predecessors and Patto broke up in 1973 when their label rejected a completed fourth album, *Monkey's Bum.* Mike Patto joined Spooky Tooth, appearing on their final album, *The Mirror,* in 1974. Halsall resurfaced in **Tempest** before forging a partnership with **Kevin Ayers**. He was reunited with Patto in 1975 as a member of **Boxer**, and subsequently worked alongside John Halsley in the **Beatles**' spoof, the **Rutles**. The latter joined Patto in the ad hoc 'supergroup' Hinkley's Heroes, but the career of this expressive vocalist was tragically cut short in March 1979 when he succumbed to throat cancer. Halsall remained an in-demand session guitarist until his untimely death in 1993.
Albums: *Patto* (1970), *Hold Your Fire* (1971), *Roll 'Em, Smoke 'Em, Put Another Line Out* (1972).

Patton, 'Big' John

b. 12 July 1935, Kansas City, Missouri, USA. Unusually for a Hammond organ supremo, Patton does not come from Philadelphia. His mother played piano in church, and Patton took it up in 1948. He played in the **Lloyd Price** band from 1954-59, quitting just as Price topped his 1952 hit 'Lawdy Miss Clawdy' with a string of three million-sellers. Patton moved to New York and switched to organ. He was signed to **Blue Note Records** on the recommendation of **Lou Donaldson**, debuting with *Along Came John* in 1963, which featured **Grant Green** on guitar. In the late 60s he worked with tenor saxophonist **Clifford Jordon** and guitarist **James 'Blood' Ulmer**, as well as sitting in with **Sun Ra**'s musicians. In the 70s he moved to East Orange, New Jersey. **John Zorn**'s use of him on a track of *The Big Gundown* in 1985 rekindled interest in his career and in 1989 he toured Britain with jazz musicians including tenor saxophonist Jean Toussaint (ex-**Jazz Messengers**).
Selected albums: *Along Came John* (1963), *The Way I Feel* (1964), *Oh Baby* (1964), *Blue John* (Blue Note 1964), *Got A Good Thing Goin'* (1965), *Let 'Em Roll* (Blue Note 1966), *Soul Connection* (Nilva 1984), *Blue Planet Man* (Paddlewheel 1993). Compilation: *The Organization!: The Best Of Big John Patton* (Blue Note 1994).

Patton, Charley

b. 1 May 1891, Bolton, Mississippi, USA, d. 28 April 1934, Indianola, Mississippi, USA. Charley Patton was small, but in all other ways larger than life; his death from a chronic heart condition at the age of 43 brought to an end a relentless pursuit of the good things then available to a black man in Mississippi - liquor, women, food (courtesy of women), music, and the avoidance of farmwork, which carried with it another *desideratum,* freedom of movement. By 1910, Patton had a repertoire of his own compositions, including 'Pony Blues', 'Banty Rooster Blues', 'Down The Dirt Road', and his version of 'Mississippi Bo Weavil Blues', all of which he was to record at his first session in 1929. He also acquired a number of spirituals, although the degree of his religious conviction is unclear. By the time he recorded, Charley Patton was the foremost blues singer in Mississippi, popular with whites and blacks, and able to live off his music. He was enormously influential on local musicians, including his regular partner Willie Brown, in addition to **Tommy Johnson** and **Son House**. **Bukka White**, **Big Joe Williams** and **Howlin' Wolf** were among others whose music was profoundly affected by Patton. His own sound is characteristic from the first: a hoarse, hollering vocal delivery, at times incomprehensible even to those who heard him in person, interrupted by spoken asides, and accompanied by driving guitar played with an unrivalled mastery of rhythm. Patton had a number of tunes and themes that he liked to rework, and he recorded some songs more than once, but never descended to stale repetition. His phrasing and accenting were uniquely inventive, voice and guitar complementing one another, rather than the guitar simply imitating the beat of the vocal line. He was able to hold a sung note to an impressive length, and part of the excitement of his music derives from the way a sung line can thus overlap the guitar phrase introducing the next verse. Patton was equally adept at regular and bottleneck fretting, and when playing with a slide could make the guitar into a supplementary voice with a proficiency that few could equal.
He was extensively recorded by Paramount in 1929-30, and by Vocalion in 1934, so that the breadth of his repertoire is evident. (It was probably Patton's good sales that persuaded the companies to record the singing of his accompanists, guitarist Willie Brown and fiddler Henry Sims, and Bertha Lee, his last wife.) Naturally, Patton sang personal blues, many of them about his relations with women. He also sang about being arrested for drunkenness, cocaine ('A Spoonful Blues'), good sex ('Shake It And Break It') and, in 'Down The Dirt Road Blues' he highlighted the plight of the black in Mississippi ('Every day, seems like murder here'). He composed an important body of topical songs, including 'Dry Well Blues' about a drought, and the two-part 'High Water Everywhere', an account of the 1927 flooding of the Mississippi that is almost cinematic in its vividness. Besides blues and spirituals, Patton recorded a number of 'songster' pieces, including 'Mississippi Boweavil Blues', 'Frankie

And Albert' and the anti-clerical 'Elder Greene Blues'. He also covered hits like 'Kansas City Blues', 'Running Wild', and even **Sophie Tucker**'s 'Some Of These Days'. It is a measure of Patton's accomplishment as a musician and of his personal magnetism that blues scholars debate furiously whether he was a clowning moral degenerate or 'the conscience of the Delta', and whether he was an unthinking entertainer or a serious artist. It is perhaps fair to say that he was a man of his times who yet transcended them, managing to a considerable degree to live the life he chose in a system that strove to deny that option to blacks. A similar verdict applies to his achievements as a musician and lyricist; Patton was not independent of and uninfluenced by his musical environment, but considering how young he was when the blues were becoming the dominant black folk music, around the turn of the century, his achievement consists to a remarkable degree, of taking the given forms and transmuting them by the application of his genius.
Albums: *Volume 1* (1990), *Volume 2* (1990), *Volume 3* (1990), *Founder Of The Delta Blues 1929-1934* (1991).
Further reading: *Charley Patton*, John Fahey.

Paul And Paula

Paul (b. Ray Hildebrand, 21 December 1940, Joshua, Texas, USA) and Paula (b. Jill Jackson, 20 May 1942, McCaney, Texas, USA) were college students prior to singing together on a local radio's cancer fund appeal. In November 1962 they auditioned a Hildebrand composition, 'Hey Paula', for Fort Worth producer Major Bill Smith, and within weeks the song topped the US chart. 'Hey Paula' captured a 'puppy-love' naivety beloved by middle-America in the immediate pre-**Beatles** era. 'Hey, hey, hey Paula, I wanna marry you', and the continuing simplistic call and answer lyric found a receptive audience. 'Young Lovers', which recounted the eve of the duo's wedding, provided another hit, but although subsequent releases, including 'Our First Quarrel', continued the storyline, Paul And Paula were unable to repeat the success of their million-selling debut and ended up sounding overly cloying.
Albums: *Paul And Paula Sing For Young Lovers* (1963), *We Go Together* (1963), *Holiday For Teens* (1963).

Paul, Billy

b. Paul Williams 1 December 1934, Philadelphia, Pennsylvania, USA. Although Paul had been an active singer in the Philadelphia area since the 50s, singing in jazz clubs and briefly with **Harold Melvin And The Blue Notes**, it was not until he met producer **Kenny Gamble** that his career prospered. After signing to the Neptune label, he enjoyed a successful spell on the **Philadelphia International** label. His instinctive jazz-based delivery provided an unlikely foil for the label's highly structured, sweet-soul sound but Paul's impressive debut hit, 'Me And Mrs Jones', nonetheless encapsulated the genre. A classic confessional tale of infidelity, Billy's unorthodox style enhanced the ballad's sense of guilt. His later releases included 'Thanks For Saving My Life' (1974), 'Let's Make A Baby' (1976) and 'Let 'Em In' (1977), the last of which adapted the **Paul McCartney** hit to emphasize lyrical references to Dr. Martin Luther King. Billy continued to make excellent records but his last chart entry, to date, came in 1980 with 'You're My Sweetness'.
Albums: *Ebony Woman* (1970), *Going East* (1971), *360 Degrees Of Billy Paul* (1972), *Feelin' Good At The Cadillac Club* (1973), *War Of The Gods* (1973), *Live In Europe* (1974), *Got My Head On Straight* (1975), *When Love Is New* (1975), *Let 'Em In* (1976), *Only The Strong Survive* (1977), *First Class* (1979) *Lately* (1985), *Wide Open* (1988).
Compilation: *Billy Paul's Greatest Hits* (1983).

Paul, Emmanuel

b. 2 February 1904, New Orleans, Louisiana, USA. Originally a banjo player, Paul switched to tenor saxophone during the 30s. He was with the Eureka Brass Band from 1940 and joined **Kid Thomas Valentine**'s Band in 1942, continuing his association with Valentine for many years, and playing with him at Preservation Hall in New Orleans into the 80s. From the start of the 60s he was a member of Harold Dejan's Olympia Brass Band, and his remarkable, broad vibrato imparted a special warmth and majesty to the time-honoured traditional New Orleans dirges and hymns. Echoes of players like Paul can be heard in the work of the 60s *avant garde* saxophonists, such as **Archie Shepp** and **Albert Ayler**, whose roots were always deep in the rich New Orleans sub-soil of the jazz tradition. The work of the originals, not least Dejan and Paul, has a depth and emotional effectiveness that prevent it from dating, despite reaching back nearly a century.
Albums: with Eureka Brass Band *New Orleans Parade* (1951), *Dejan's Olympia Brass Band In Europe* (1968), *The Olympia Brass Band Of New Orleans* (1970).

Paul, Frankie

b. Jamaica, West Indies. Blind from birth, Paul Blake had his sight partially restored as a child on a hospital ship. When **Stevie Wonder** visited Paul's special school he was encouraged by his school friends and teachers to sing for him. Legend has it that Stevie was so impressed by the youth's precocious talent that from then on Paul Blake decided to make singing his career. He first came to the record buying public's attention in a big way as Frankie Paul in the early 80s when he shared the honours with **Sugar Minott** (one side each) on a **Channel One** 'clash' album. Minott was the established superstar while Frankie was billed as the 'up and coming superstar' and it was not long before he became one of the most prolific singers in the history of reggae music. Every important (and not so important) producer in **dancehall** reggae from Jamaica, the USA and the UK queued up for Frankie Paul and his consistency was amazing. It seemed as if he only came alive in the studio and although, at first, the **Dennis Brown** and Stevie Wonder influences were apparent, it was not too long before Frankie became his own man. His voice had a power and dignity too often lacking in 80s reggae and his interpretations of other people's material were masterful.

Reggae singers and DJs are not usually contracted to any particular label or producer but they work for whoever is willing to record them if the price is right - usually little more than a session fee and the promise of royalties to come if the record sells. When this occurs, the market will be immediately flooded with every recording he has made up until that point on a variety of different formats and on a bewildering number of labels. Frankie was one of the very few with enough talent to overcome this overkill syndrome and the amount of records he released was staggering, especially when one takes into account just how good most of them are. He was one of the only 'real' singer of note to come through in reggae music for the whole of the decade, and a major label deal has to be on the cards for Paul, after a mooted arranagement with **Motown** fell through. No evidence has come to light of any new deal as yet, but if someone can harness some of Frankie's vibrant energy to specific projects and stop him recording for anyone and everyone, the results promise to be very exciting.

Albums: *Strange Feeling* (Techniques 1983), *Be My Lady* (Joe Gibbs 1984), *Strictly Reggae Music* (Londisc 1984), *Pass The Tu-Sheng-Peng* (Greensleeves 1984), *Tidal Wave* (Greensleeves 1985), *Rich And Poor* (Classic 1986), *Alesha* (Powerhouse 1987), *Sara* (Jammys 1987), *Warning* (RAS 1987), *Give Me That Feeling* (Moodies 1987), *Rub A Dub Market* (Mango/Island 1987), *Casanova* (Live & Love 1988), *The Classic* (Tappa Zukie 1988), *Easy Mover* (Vena 1988), *True* (Black Scorpio 1988), *Ripe Mango* (Scom 1988), *Reaching Out* (Blue Mountain 1988), *Shut Up B'way* (Ujama 1988), *Sizzling* (Skengdon 1988), *Slow Down* (Redman 1988), *Love Affair* (Techniques 1989), *Love Line* (Glory Gold 1989), *Frankie Paul* (Blacka Dread 1989), *Can't Get You Out Of My Mind* (Rohit 1990), *Heartical Don* (Superpower 1990), *Close To You* (Jammys 1991), *Star Of A Romance* (Black Scorpio 1991), *At His Best* (Techniques 1991), *At Studio One* (Studio One 1992), *Fire Deh A Mus Mus Tail* (1992), *Should I?* (Hearbeat 1992). With Little John: *Showdown Volume 6* (Empire 1984). With Michael Palmer: *Double Trouble* (Greensleeves 1985). With Leroy Sibbles: *The Champions Clash* (Kingdom 1988). With Pinchers: *Dancehall Duo* (RAS 1988), *Turbo Charge* (Super Supreme 1988). Compilations: *The Best Of* (Abraham 1988), *20 Massive Hits* (Sonic Sounds 1990), *FP The Greatest* (Fashion 1992).

Video: *Musical Explosion* (Jettisoundz).

Paul, Les

b. 9 June 1915, Wankesha, Wisconsin, USA. Paul began playing guitar and other instruments while still a child. In the early 30s he broadcast on the radio and in 1936 was leading his own trio. In the late 30s and early 40s he worked in New York, where he was featured on **Fred Waring**'s radio show. He made records accompanying singers such as **Bing Crosby** and the **Andrews Sisters**. Although his work was in the popular vein, with a strong country leaning, Paul was highly adapatable and frequently sat in with jazz musicians. One of his favourites was **Nat 'King' Cole**, whom he knew in Los Angeles, and the two men appeared together in a **Jazz At The Philharmonic** concert in 1944, on which Paul played some especially fine blues. Dissatisfied with the sound of the guitars he played, Paul developed his own design for a solid-bodied instrument, which he had made at his own expense. Indeed, the company, **Gibson**, were so cool towards the concept that they insisted that their name should not appear on the instruments they made for him. In later years, when it seemed that half the guitarists in the world were playing Les Paul-style Gibson guitars, the company's attitude was understandably a little different. Paul's dissatisfaction with existing techniques extended beyond the instrument and into the recording studios. Eager to experiment with a multi-tracking concept, he built a primitive studio in his own home. He produced a succession of superb recordings on which he played multi-track guitar, amongst them 'Lover', 'Nola', 'Brazil' and 'Whispering'. During the 50s Paul continued his experimentation with other, similar recordings, while his wife, Mary Ford (b. 7 July 1928, d. 30 September 1977), sang multiple vocal lines. Other major record successes were 'The World Is Waiting For The Sunrise', 'How High The Moon', which reached number 1, and 'Vaya Con Dios', another US number 1 hit. By the early 60s Paul had tired of the recording business and retired. He and Ford were divorced in 1963 and he spent his time inventing and helping to promote Gibson guitars. In the late 70s he returned to the studios for two successful albums of duets with **Chet Atkins**, but towards the end of the decade had retired again. A television documentary in 1980, *The Wizard Of Wankesha*, charted his life and revived interest in his career. In 1984 he made a comeback to performing and continued to make sporadic appearances throughout the rest of the decade. He was performing at the guitar festival in Seville, Spain in 1992. A remarkably gifted and far-sighted guitarist, Paul's contribution to popular music must inevitably centre upon his pioneering work on multi-tracking and his creation of the solid-bodied guitar. It would be sad, however, if his efforts in these directions wholly concealed his considerable abilities as a performer.

Selected albums: with Mary Ford *New Sound, Volume 1 & 2* (mid-50s), with Ford *Les And Mary* (1955), *Bye, Bye Blues* (mid-50s), with Ford *The Hitmakers* (mid-50s), with Ford *Les And Mary* (late 50s), with Ford *Time To Dream* (late 50s), with Ford *Lover's Luau* (1959), with Ford *Warm And Wonderful* (1962), with Ford *Bouquet Of Roses* (1962), with Ford *Swingin' South* (1963), *Les Paul Now* (1968), with Chet Atkins *Chester And Lester* (1977), with Atkins *Guitar Masters* (1978). Compilations: with Mary Ford *The Hits Of Les And Mary* (1960), *The Very Best Of Les Paul And Mary Ford* (1974), *The Capitol Years* (1989).
Video: *He Changed The Music* (1990).
Further reading: *Les Paul: An American Original*, Mary Alice Shaughnessy. *Gibson Les Paul Book: A Complete History Of Les Paul Guitars*, Tony Bacon and Paul Day.

Paupers

Formed in Toronto, Ontario, Canada in 1965, the Paupers have been described by former band leader Skip Prokop as 'heavy-duty folk-rock psychedelic'. Including Prokop (drums/vocals), Bill Marion (rhythm guitar/drums/lead vocals; replaced by Adam Mitchell in late 1966), Chuck Beal (lead guitar/mandolin) and Denny Gerard (bass/vocals; replaced by ex-Last Words' Brad Campbell prior to *Ellis Island*), the Paupers first released singles locally on Canadian labels Red Leaf and Roman before signing a management contract with **Albert Grossman**, the manager of **Bob Dylan** at the time. They were signed to the **Verve**/Forecast label in the USA, and released six singles and two albums between 1966 and 1968. The debut, *Magic People*, received much airplay on FM rock stations but only managed a number 178 placing on the US album charts. The group built a steady following on the road, and played the **Monterey Pop Festival** in June 1967. The Paupers disbanded in 1970. Prokop and Campbell guested on *Richard P. Havens 1983*. Following the Paupers' break-up, Campbell joined **Janis Joplin** in her Kozmic Blues Band and the Full-Tilt Boogie Band. Prokop played with **Al Kooper** and **Michael Bloomfield** on their 1968 *Super Session* album and went on to form **Lighthouse** in 1969. He recorded solo in the 70s, hosted a Christian radio programme and then retired from the music business.
Albums: *Magic People* (1967), *Ellis Island* (1968).

Pavageau, Alcide 'Slow Drag'

b. 7 March 1888, New Orleans, Louisiana, USA, d. 19 January 1969. During his early years Pavageau became known as a competent guitarist and an excellent dancer and he was almost 40 years old before he took up the bass. On this instrument he played with a number of leading New Orleans bands of the day, including **Buddy Petit**'s. His fame did not spread, however, until 1943, when he joined **George Lewis**. He toured and recorded with Lewis throughout the 40s and also worked with **Bunk Johnson**. His association with Lewis continued through the 50s and on into the early 60s. Despite his late start, Pavageau became one of the best known New Orleans-style bass players and if much of that fame rested on his long-term relationship with Lewis he was certainly an above-average player. Late in life he became a popular figure, leading street parades in his home town. For all that fame, it was on one of the city's streets that he was attacked and robbed, dying soon afterwards on 19 January 1969.
Album: with George Lewis *Jazz At Vespers* (1954). Compilation: *American Music By George Lewis* (1944-45 recordings).

Pavement

Darlings of the US independent scene, formed in Stockton, California, in 1989. college dropouts Pavement were originally a duo with Steve Malkmus (vocals/guitar) and Scott 'Spiral Stairs' Kannberg (guitar). Later they extended to a five-piece by adding Gary Young (b. c.1954; percussion), a venerable live attraction who was as likely to perform handstands on stage as any musical duties, plus John Nastanovich (drums) and Mark Ibald (bass). However, as three of the band were located on the east coast (New York), rehearsals were initially limited to perhaps once a year, and recording sessions and tours proved equally sporadic, resulting in songs that were 'meant to sound like **Chrome** or the **Clean**, but ended up sounding like the **Fall** and **Swell Maps**.' Their debut release was 1989's *Slay Tracks (1933-1969)*, the first in a series of EP's to charm the critics. The attraction, undoubtedly, was Malkmus' dry, free-ranging lyrics, with their acute observational scope. Young left the band in 1993 (replaced by Steve West) when his stage behaviour became unbearable, but neither this, nor the insistence of UK critics that the band were a pale imitation of the Fall, hindered their rise to the top of the US alternative scene. *Wowee Zowee!* offered a more angular, less instantly accessible formula, with many of the tracks opting for outright experimentalism. Malkmus defended it thus: 'Its still a warm and open record if people are willing to join us'.
Albums: *Perfect Sound Forever* (Drag City 191, mini-album), *Slanted And Enchanted* (Big Cat 1992), *Crooked Rain, Crooked Rain* (Big Cat 1994), *Wowee Zowee!* (Big Cat 1995). Compilation: *Westing (By Musket And Sextant)* (Big Cat 1993). Solo: Gary Young *Hospital* (Big Cat 1995).

Pavlov's Dog

Formed in St. Louis, Missouri, USA in 1973, the group initially comprised David Surkamp (vocals/guitar), Siegfried Carver (violin), Steve Scorfina (guitar, ex-**REO Speedwagon**), David Hamilton (keyboards), Doug Rayburn (mellotron/bass) and Mike Safron (drums). They were initially signed to the **ABC** label, for whom they recorded *Pampered Menial* under the

aegis of **Blue Öyster Cult** producer Sandy Pearlman. The sextet was then traded to **Columbia** in exchange for **Poco** and their impressive debut album reappeared on this new outlet. The set focused on Surkamp's remarkable high voice, pitched somewhere between those of **Jon Anderson** and **Tiny Tim**, which soared through the group's exceptional compositions in tandem with Carver's mesmerizing violin. Although not a commercial success, *Pampered Menial* enjoyed a considerable cult following, in particular for 'Julia', its memorable opening track. The following album, *At The Sound Of The Bell* introduced several changes within the group, the most crucial of which was the loss of Carver. Guitarist Tom Nickeson had been added to the line-up while Safron was replaced by **Bill Bruford**, formerly of **Yes** and **King Crimson**. Although of a high quality, this second set lacked the distinctive panache of its predecessor and failed to reverse waning fortunes. The group split up soon afterwards, but despite considerable interest, Surkamp's subsequent work has been confined to a collaboration with singer/songwriter **Iain Matthews**.
Albums: *Pampered Menial* (CBS 1974), *At The Sound Of The Bell* (CBS 1975).

Pavone, Rita

b. 23 August 1945, Turin, Italy. This freckled, diminutive daughter of a Fiat factory mechanic shone in an 'Unknowns Festival' organized in 1962 at Ariccia by freelance record producer Teddy Reno. Signed to **RCA** Italia, her first single, 'La Partita Di Pallone' ('The Football Song') sold a million. Her popularity was further strengthened with regular appearances on *Studio 1*, Italian television's top variety showcase. After 'Come To Non C'E' Nessumo' became the country's best-selling single of 1963, she branched out with foreign language recordings, earning chart placings in Spain, South America, Japan, Germany - and Britain where BBC and ITV slots in autumn 1966 reactivated the three-year-old 'Cuore', a **Barry Mann-Cynthia Weill** melody with Italian lyrics. Translated as 'Heart', this Luis Enriquez production (with an apt throbbing rhythm) jumped into the UK Top 30 over Christmas. It was also the apex of her career in terms of record sales but she continued to develop as an entertainer, even making slight headway in the USA with a spot on *The **Ed Sullivan** Show*, and making her silver screen debut in 1966's *Rita The Mosquito*.
Selected album: *Rita Pavone* (1964).

Paw

This Lawrence, Kansas, USA quartet formed in 1990 with brothers Grant (guitar) and Peter Fitch (drums) and bassist Charles Bryan, recruiting vocalist Mark Hennessy (b. Mark Thomas Joseph Brendan Hennessy, 6 May 1969, Kansas, USA) from local art-noise band King Rat, which Hennessy described as a period when 'I thought I was **Nick Cave**'. Paw were the leading local band, and picked up support gigs with **Nirvana** and the **Fluid** before recording their first seven-song demo at Butch Vig's Smart Studios in Wisconsin, which led to an enormous major label bidding war, won by **A&M Records**. *Newsweek* described Paw as 'the next Nirvana', but **Hüsker Dü**, **Dinosaur Jr** and the **Replacements** were perhaps better reference points for *Dragline*'s marriage of melody and raw guitar power, with a distinctive small-town storytelling aspect to the songs. 'Sleeping Bag' was perhaps the most poignant, telling the childhood story of a car crash which hospitalised the seriously injured Peter Fitch, and when older brother Grant feared the worst, he slept in Peter's sleeping bag, 'as corny as it sounds, just to be a little closer to him'. *Dragline* deservedly received universal acclaim, and the band toured exhaustively, earning an excellent live reputation, touring Europe with **Therapy?** and Hammerbox, the UK with **Tool**, and both the UK and USA with **Monster Magnet**, as singles 'Sleeping Bag, and 'Couldn't Know' brought them a wider audience. The band returned to the studio in late 1994, but without Bryan, who had tired of the endless touring.
Album: *Dragline* (A&M 1993).

Paxton, Gary S.

Paxton was one of several young songwriters and producers to emerge from the Los Angeles' pop scene of the late 50s. Half of the duo Skip And Flip, alongside future **Byrds** member Skip Battin, Paxton then joined **Kim Fowley** in the **Hollywood Argyles**, and scored a US number 1 with the novelty disc, 'Alley Oop' (1960). The two entrepreneurs then put a series of faceless groups together in an attempt to repeat the success, while Gary also founded several record labels, including Garpax, on which **Bobby 'Boris' Pickett**'s million-seller, 'Monster Mash', was first issued. Paxton later grew interested in country music and by the mid-60s was heavily involved in the Californian scene centred on Bakersfield. He then moved to Nashville where he forged a successful career as a songwriter.
Album: *Anchored In The Rock Of Ages* (1978).

Paxton, Tom

b. 31 October 1937, Chicago, Illinois, USA. Paxton's interest in folk music developed as a student at the University of Oklahoma. In 1960 he moved to New York and became one of several aspiring performers to frequent the city's Greenwich Village coffee-house circuit. Paxton made his professional debut at the Gaslight, the renowned folk haunt which also issued the singer's first album. Two topical song publications, *Sing Out!* and *Broadside*, began publishing his original compositions which bore a debt to the traditional approach of **Pete Seeger** and **Bob Gibson**. Tom also auditioned to join the **Chad Mitchell Trio**, but although he failed, the group enjoyed a 1963 hit with 'The Marvellous Toy', one of his early songs. The following year Paxton was signed to the **Elektra** label for whom he recorded his best known work. *Ramblin' Boy* indicated the diversity which marked his recorded career and contained several highly-popular performances including 'The Last Thing On My Mind', 'Goin' To The Zoo' and 'I Can't Help But Wonder Where I'm Bound'. Subsequent releases continued this mixture of romanticism, protest and children's songs, while 'Lyndon Johnson Told The Nation' (*Ain't That News*) and 'Talkin' Vietnam Pot Luck Blues' (*Morning Again*) revealed a talent for satire and social comment. *The Things I Notice Now* and *Tom Paxton 6* enhanced Paxton's reputation as a mature and complex songwriter, yet he remained better known for such simpler compositions as 'Jennifer's Rabbit' and 'Leaving London'. Paxton left Elektra during the early 70s and although subsequent recordings proved less popular, he commanded a loyal following, particularly in the UK, where he was briefly domiciled. *How Come The Sun* (1971) was the first of three albums recorded during this period and although his work became less prolific, Paxton was still capable of incisive, evocative songwriting, such as 'The Hostage', which chronicled the massacre at Attica State Prison. This powerful composition was also recorded by **Judy Collins**. Although Paxton was never fêted in the manner of his early contemporaries **Bob Dylan**, **Phil Ochs** and **Eric Andersen**, his work reveals a thoughtful, perceptive craftsmanship.

Albums: *Live At The Gaslight* (early 60s), *Ramblin' Boy* (1964), *Ain't That News* (1965), *Outward Bound* (1966), *Morning Again* (1968), *The Things I Notice Now* (1969), *Tom Paxton 6* (1970), *The Compleat Tom Paxton* (1971), *How Come The Sun* (1971), *Peace Will Come* (1972), *New Songs Old Friends* (1973), *Children's Song Book* (1974), *Something In My Life* (1975), *Saturday Night* (1976), *New Songs From The Briar Patch* (1977), *Heroes* (1978), *Up And Up* (1980), *The Paxton Report* (1981), *The Marvellous Toy And Other Gallimaufry* (1984), *In The Orchard* (1985), *One Million Lawyers And Other Disasters* (1985), *Even A Gray Day* (1986), *The Marvellous Toy* (1980), *And Loving You* (1988), *Politics-Live* (1989), *A Car Full Of Songs* (1990), *Suzy Is A Rocker* (1992). Compilations: *The Very Best Of Tom Paxton* (1988), *Storyteller* (1989).

Further reading: *Englebert The Elephant*, Tom Paxton and Steven Kellogg. *Belling The Cat And Other Aesop's Fables*, Tom Paxton and Robert Rayevsky.

Paycheck, Johnny

b. Donald Eugene Lytle, 31 May 1941, Greenfield, Ohio, USA. The title of Paycheck's 1977 country hit, 'I'm The Only Hell (Mama Ever Raised)', is apt as he has been in trouble throughout his life: the wild eyes on his album sleeves give the picture. Although only 5 feet 5 inches, he is tougher than most and he served two years for assaulting an officer whilst in the US Navy. He moved to Nashville and played bass and sometimes steel guitar for **Porter Wagoner**, **Faron Young**, **Ray Price** and chiefly, **George Jones**. He made several records with Jones, singing tenor on *I'm A People* and the hit singles, 'Love Bug' and 'The Race Is On'. At first, he recorded rockabilly as Donny Young in 1959 ('Shaking The Blues', written by Jones) and then sang country on **Mercury Records** ('On Second Thoughts'). Most people think the name Johnny Paycheck was a parody of **Johnny Cash**, but it came from a heavyweight boxer who was KO'd by Joe Louis in two rounds in 1940 and was close to Paycheck's own Polish family name. By now, he had developed Jones' mannerisms and he had country hits with 'A-11' and 'Heartbreak, Tennessee'. He wrote **Tammy Wynette**'s first hit, 'Apartment No. 9' and Ray Price's 'Touch My Heart'. He formed his own Little Darlin' Records in 1966 and had country hits with 'The Lovin' Machine', **Bobby Bare**'s composition 'Motel Time Again' and 'Don't Monkey With Another Monkey's Monkey'. His supposedly live album from Carnegie Hall was recorded in a studio on April Fool's Day, 1966. Paycheck became an alcoholic, the label went bankrupt and he was arrested for burglary. He moved to Los Angeles, living hand to mouth, spending what little money he had on drink and drugs. Record producer **Billy Sherrill** straightened him out and he had a massive country hit with 'Don't Take Her, She's All I Got' in 1971. This was followed by 'Someone To Give My Love To', 'Mr. Lovemaker' and 'Song And Dance Man'. Paycheck also had success on the US country charts with a gospel-flavoured duet with **Jody Miller**, 'Let's All Go Down To The River'. Further troubles led to bankruptcy and a paternity suit in 1976. In 1977, at the height of outlaw country, he had his biggest country hit with **David Allan Coe**'s anthem to working people, 'Take This Job And Shove It', and its b-side 'Colorado Cool-Aid' was successful in its own right. He is well known in country circles in the UK for his narration, 'The Outlaw's Prayer' from *Armed And Crazy*. His lifestyle is reflected in 'Me And The I.R.S.', 'D.O.A. (Drunk On Arrival)', and '11 Months And 29 Days', which was his sentence of passing a dud cheque at a Holiday Inn - a case of Johnny Badcheck. A law suit with his manager followed and his friends, George Jones and **Merle Haggard**, made albums with him. In 1981, after he went back to a woman's house after a concert, he was arrested for allegedly raping her 12-year-old daughter. The charges were reduced - he was fined and given probation - but he was dropped by Epic Records, although he maintained, 'I dropped them. I couldn't stand the back-stabbing stench there anymore'. Then, in 1985, he got into a bar-room argument with a stranger - and shot him. While awaiting trial, he recorded with the 'de-frocked' evangelist, John Wesley Fletcher. Paycheck served a

nine-year sentence and said, 'This will probably be my last time around. The fans have taken me back every time, but you only stay young for so long'. He was released in 1991 and resumed his career. Whatever happens, his extraordinary life story is a bankable tale. It may be the only way he can resolve his problems with the IRS.
Albums: *Johnny Paycheck At Carnegie Hall* (1966), *The Lovin' Machine* (1966), *Gospeltime In My Fashion* (1967), *Jukebox Charlie* (1967), *Country Soul* (1967), *Wherever You Are* (1969), *Johnny Paycheck Again* (1970), *She's All I Got* (1971), *Heartbreak, Tennessee* (1972), *Mr. Lovemaker* (1972), *Song And Dance Man* (1972), *Somebody Love Me* (1973), *Slide Off Your Satin Sheets* (1977), *Take This Job And Shove It* (1978), *Armed And Crazy* (1978), *11 Months And 29 Days* (1979), with George Jones *Double Trouble* (1980), *Everybody's Got A Family - Meet Mine* (1980), *New York Town* (1980), with Merle Haggard *Mr. Hag Told My Story* (1981), *Lovers And Losers* (1982), *Back On The Job* (1984), *I Don't Need To Know That Right Now* (1984), *Apartment No. 9* (1985), *Modern Times* (1987), *Honky Tonk And Slow Music* (1988), *Outlaw At The Cross* (1989), *Live In Branson, MO, USA* (1993), *The Difference In Me* (1993). Compilations: *Biggest Hits* (1983), *16 Greatest Hits* (1988).

Payne, Cecil

b. 14 December 1922, New York City, New York, USA. After first learning guitar, alto saxophone and clarinet, Payne took up the baritone saxophone. In 1946, a year in which he played and recorded with **J.J. Johnson** and **Roy Eldridge**, he joined **Dizzy Gillespie**'s big band for a three-year stint. Leaving Gillespie in 1949 he joined **Tadd Dameron**'s band, following this with appearances with **James Moody** and **Illinois Jacquet**. In the mid-50s he played with **Randy Weston**, **John Coltrane** and **Duke Jordan**. During the 60s he was with **Machito**, **Lionel Hampton**, **Woody Herman**, **Count Basie** and Gillespie again. In the 70s he worked again for Basie and also formed a double-act with his vocalist sister, Cavril. In the 80s he played in a trio with **Bill Hardman** and led by Richard Wyand. An accomplished player with a special affinity for bebop, Payne's technical command is on a par with that of many better-known players, whose greater charisma has kept them more in the public eye.
Selected albums: with Randy Weston *Jazz A La Bohemia* (1956), with Tadd Dameron *Fontainebleau* (1956), with John Coltrane *Dakar* (1957), *Bird's Night* (1957), *Patterns Of Jazz* (Savoy 1957), *Cool Blues* (1961), *The Connection* (Jazz Reactivation 1962), *Brookfield Andante* (Spotlite 1966), *The Cecil Payne Quintet* (c.1969-70), *Brooklyn Brothers* (1973), *Bird Gets The Worm* (Muse 1976), *Bright Moments* (Spotlite 1979), *Zodiac* (Strata East 1993).

Payne, Freda

b. Freda Charcilia Payne, 19 September 1945, Detroit, Michigan, USA. Schooled in jazz and classical music, this urbane singer attended the Institute Of Musical Arts and worked with **Pearl Bailey** prior to recording her debut album in 1963 for **MGM Records**. Payne signed to **Holland/Dozier/Holland**'s label Invictus and her first recording, 'The Unhooked Generation' introduced a new-found soul style, but it was the magnificent follow-up, 'Band Of Gold' (1970), which established Payne's reputation. This ambiguous wedding-night drama was a US number 3 and UK number 1 and prepared the way for several more excellent singles in 'Deeper And Deeper', 'You Brought The Joy' and 'Bring The Boys Home', an uncompromising anti-Vietnam anthem. Ensuing releases lacked that early purpose and were marred by Payne's increasingly unemotional delivery. The singer moved to **ABC**/Dunhill (1974), **Capitol** (1976) and Sutra (1982), but Payne was also drawn to television work and would later host a syndicated talk show, 'For You Black Woman'.
Albums: *After The Lights Go Down And Much More* (1963), *How Do You Say I Don't Love You Anymore* (1966), *Band Of Gold* (1970), *Contact* (1971), *Reaching Out* (1973), *Payne And Pleasure* (1974), *Out Of Payne Comes Love* (1975), *Stares And Whispers* (1977), *Supernatural High* (1978), *Hot* (1979). Compilations: *The Best Of Freda Payne* (1972), *Reaching Out* (1973), *Bands Of Gold* (1984), *Deeper And Deeper* (1989).

Payne, Jack

b. 22 August,1899, Leamington Spa, England, d. 4 December 1969, London, England. A leading bandleader in the UK during the 20s and 30s, Payne learnt to play the piano as a child, then joined the Royal Flying Corps. in 1917 and qualified as a pilot. He formed a small band for the officers' mess and decided on music as a career on demobilisation. After six years of insignificant dates in the Midlands he became leader of a band at London's Hotel Cecil where he stayed for four years, broadcasting regularly from the hotel, recording for Regal and Zonophone before they amalgamated, and playing his first stage show at the Holborn Empire. In 1928 he took over the BBC Dance Orchestra and his daily broadcasts at 5.15 pm were so popular that when he left the BBC four years later he was a great success on stage, being a natural showman second only to the great **Jack Hylton**. Two films were built around the band, *Say It With Music* (1932) scored by **Ray Noble**, and *Sunshine Ahead* (1933). Although a great show band, Payne's was never regarded as the musical equal of those led by Noble, **Hylton**, **Ambrose**, **Lew Stone** and **Carroll Gibbons**, for example, *vide* the paucity of reissues from the era. He went back to radio during the early war years, but by then his top-heavy orchestrations did not compare with the new modern styles of **Geraldo** and **Ted Heath**. During the 30s he had been recording

variously for **Columbia**, **Imperial**, Rex and **Decca**, and recorded a few wartime recordings for **HMV**. After the war, Payne disbanded to become a theatrical agent and impresario and then a BBC disc jockey. He left the music business and endured many financial setbacks and bouts of ill-health, before his death in 1969.
Compilations: *Radio Nights 1928-31* (1983), *The Golden Age Of Jack Payne* (1985), *Rhythmitis* (1986), *I'll String Along With You* (1988), *The Imperial Days* (1988).
Further reading: *Signature Tune*, Jack Payne. *This Is Jack Payne*, Jack Payne.

Payne, Jimmy

b. 12 April 1936, Leachville, Arkansas, USA. The family moved to Gideon, Missouri in 1944 and Jimmy enjoyed country music and singing in church. He had a gospel programme on the radio on Saturdays and was picking cotton during the week. In 1957, he moved to St. Louis to work as a professional country singer. He met Chuck Glaser whilst in the US Army and he played guitar with the Glaser Brothers band. Chuck Glaser took over his management when he formed his band, the Payne Gang. He made several singles including 'Ladder To The Sky', 'What Does It Take (To Keep A Woman Like You Satisfied)' and 'My Most Requested Song'. He first appeared on the *Grand Ole Opry* in 1966. He cut several singles including his own composition, 'Woman, Woman', which had national success in 1967 when it was recorded by **Gary Puckett And The Union Gap**. He continued to have only minor success as a solo artist - 'L.A. Angels', 'Rambling Man' and 'Turning My Love On' - but he wrote **Charley Pride**'s US number 1 country single, 'My Eyes Can Only See As Far As You'. He wrote the popular title track of his gospel album, *Walk With Me The Rest Of The Way*, with Jim Glaser. In 1986 he recorded a duet, 'Ugly Women And Pickup Trucks', with **Tompall Glaser**.
Albums: *Woman, Woman, What Does It Take* (1968), *Live At Broadmoor* (1976), *Walk With Me The Rest Of The Way* (1978), *The Best That Love Can Give* (1980), *The Album Version* (1986).

Payne, Leon

b. Leon Roger Payne, 15 June 1917, Alba, Texas, USA. Payne became blind as a young child following the application of the wrong medication for an eye complaint. Between 1924 and 1935, he attended the Texas School for the Blind in Austin, where he studied music and learnt to play guitar, banjo, organ, piano, trombone and drums. After graduating, he worked briefly as a one man band. In 1935, he appeared as a vocalist on KWET Palestine and during the 30s, he worked with several bands including, in 1938, that of **Bob Wills**. In spite of his blindness, he travelled extensively (often hitchhiking to venues) and appeared on many Texas stations as well as the *Louisiana Hayride*. In 1948, he played with Jack Rhodes Rhythm Boys but in 1949, he formed his own band, the Lone Star Buddies, and played the *Grand Ole Opry*. Although a fine vocalist, he is best remembered for his songwriting and from the late 40s, his songs were regularly hits for other artists. These included 'Cry Baby Heart' (**George Morgan**), 'Lost Highway' and 'They'll Never Take Her Love From Me' (**Hank Williams**), 'For Now And Always' and 'There Wasn't An Organ At Our Wedding' (**Hank Snow**), 'You Can't Pick A Rose In December' (**Ernest Ashworth**) and 'Blue Side Of Lonesome' (**Jim Reeves** and **George Jones**). There is little doubt that the song for which he will always be remembered is 'I Love You Because'. Written in 1949, for his wife Myrtie, it has been recorded by countless artists including **Ernest Tubb**, **Carl Smith**, **Johnny Cash** and **Elvis Presley**. In the UK, it is always associated with **Jim Reeves**, whose recording was a number 5 UK pop hit in 1964. The fact is often overlooked that, in 1949, Payne's own recording was a US country number 1; the only version to actually top the charts. In 1956, he recorded a cover version of Presley's 'My Baby Left Me', under the pseudonym of Rock Rogers. He refused to use his own name for rock 'n' roll, in case it upset country music fans. During his career, Payne recorded for various labels including **MGM**, Bluebird, Bullet, **Capitol**, **Decca** and Starday. One album made for the latter label featured songs appertaining to events of the Old West. In 1965, he suffered a heart attack and retired to San Antonio, where he died following a further heart attack on 11 September 1969. He was one of the first members elected to the Nashville Songwriters International Hall Of Fame, when it was founded in 1970. Two radically different performers have paid tribute to his work - **Elvis Costello** with a recording of Payne's most bizarre song, the mass-murder saga 'Psycho', and George Jones with an album devoted to Payne's compositions.
Albums: *Americana* (1963), *A Living Legend Of Country Music* (1963), *Gone But Not Forgotten* (1988).

Payne, Scherrie

b. 14 November 1944, Detroit, Michigan, USA. The sister of soul singer **Freda Payne**, Scherrie forsook her teaching position at Detroit's Grayling Observatory to join the **Glass House**. This short-lived group enjoyed a series of minor US hits, the most notable of which was 'Crumbs Off The Table', a US R&B Top 10 entry in 1969. Several unsuccessful solo singles followed upon the unit's demise, but Scherrie achieved a higher profile upon replacing Jean Terrell in the **Supremes**. She remained with the trio between 1974 and 1976, contributing to *High Energy* (1976) and *Mary, Scherrie And Susaye* (1976). After the break-up of the group, she made one unsuccessful album with fellow ex-Supreme,

Susaye Green, in 1979 before resuming her own career with 'Incredible'. A duet with Philip Ingram, and 'Testify' reached the lower reaches of the R&B chart during 1987, but the singer failed to consolidate her early promise.
Album: with Susaye Green *Partners* (1979).

Payne, Sonny

b. Percival Payne, 4 May 1926, New York City, New York, USA, d. 29 January 1979. Payne began studying drums at an early age, encouraged by the fact that his father, Chris Columbus, was a jazz drummer. Payne's first jobs included spells with **Oran 'Hot Lips' Page**, **Earl Bostic** and **Tiny Grimes**. In 1950 he joined the Erskine Hawkins band, where he spent three years, then led his own band for a couple of years before joining **Count Basie**. He was with Basie for over 10 years, leaving to form his own small group and working as staff drummer for **Frank Sinatra**. In 1966 he began another long engagement with a big band, this time led by **Harry James**. In 1973 he was back with Basie, then played with amongst others **Illinois Jacquet** during the mid-70s. An aggressive, showman-drummer, Payne was an indifferent timekeeper but brought a sense of sustained excitement to any band in which he played. Even the Basie band, accustomed to such immaculate timekeepers as **Jo Jones** and **Gus Johnson**, was given a lift by Payne when he was at his best and, even when he was at his worst, audiences loved him.
Albums: all with Count Basie *The Atomic Mr Basie* (1957), *Basie - Chairman Of The Board* (1959), *On My Way And Shoutin' Again* (1962).

Paz

This UK Latin-jazz band was formed in 1972 by vibraphone player Dick Crouch. They have been very popular on the club circuit and recorded a series of exciting albums the first of which was issued on an independent label and sold more than 2,000 copies in the first week. Musicians who have played with the band include **Lol Coxhill** and **Brian Smith** (saxophones), Ray Warleigh (saxophone/flute), **Geoff Castle** (piano/synthesizer), **Phil Lee** and **Jim Mullen** (guitar), Simon Morton and Chris Fletcher (percussion), Ron Matthewson (bass). The lively arrangements used by the band have been provided by Lee, Castle and Crouch who describes the music as 'today's form of bop'.
Albums: *Kandeen Love Song* (1977), *Paz Are Back* (1980), *Look Inside* (1983), *Always There* (1986), *The Message* (1989).

Peaches And Herb

Herb Fame (b. Herbert Feemster, 1 October 1942) and Francine Barker (b. Francine Hurd, 1947). These two Washington-based singers were signed separately to the same record label, Date, and met on a promotional tour. Producer Dave Kapralik put the couple together, and their easy, if unexceptional, voices took 'Close Your Eyes' into the US Top 10 in 1967. The duo continued to figure in the charts as 'United' (1968) and 'When He Touches Me (Nothing Else Matters)' (1969). However, although Barker was featured on these records, she had been replaced for live performances by former session singer Marlene Mack, (b. 1945, Virginia, USA). The 'sweethearts of soul' were ostensibly disbanded in July 1970 when a disillusioned Fame left music in favour of the Police Department, although a 'bogus' duo hurriedly stepped in to fill the gap. Herb resumed recording in 1976 with a new 'Peaches', Linda Greene (b. Washington, DC, USA). Following a brief spell at **MCA Records**, the reconstituted couple moved to Polydor where they scored a major hit with 'Shake Your Groove Thing' (1978). The following year 'Reunited' reached number 1 in the US and number 4 in the UK. They continued to enjoy success into the 80s, but such releases lacked the charm of their early work.
Albums: *Let's Fall In Love* (1967), *For Your Love* (1967), *Golden Duets* (1967), *Peaches And Herb* (1977), *2 Hot!* (1978), *Twice The Fire* (1979), *Worth The Wait* (1980), *Sayin' Something* (1981), *Remember* (1983). Compilation: *Peaches And Herb's Greatest Hits* (1968).

Peacock, Annette

b. New York, USA. A highly individual and challenging songwriter with a distinctive voice, Peacock was in the centre of the Milbrook, New York, psychedelic scene in the 60s, having been 'discovered' by Timothy Leary. Her mother was a classical musician, and she was brought up on chamber music. She discovered jazz for herself at an early age but came into contact with the *avant garde* after she eloped to New York City with **Gary Peacock**, who was then the bass-player with **Albert Ayler**. Gary then joined the trio of **Paul Bley**, who began to use her compositions as well as those of **Carla Bley**. Paul Bley's 1967 *Ballads* used Annette Peacock's tunes exclusively. Her compositions include such beautiful modern classics as 'Open, To Love' and 'Nothing Ever Was, Anyway'. Touring as the Annette And Paul Bley Synthesizer Show at the start of the 70s, they used what was then state-of-the-art hardware: machines the size of a Welsh Dresser, with wiring like a telephone exchange, which took 10 minutes to 'tune' and programme between numbers. Moogs were then intended only for studio use. Certainly on the road the results were primitive and rough by today's standards, but this was real pioneering stuff. Annette used the technology in her own solo, somewhat more rock-inclined, work to process her voice or, often, used her voice to generate electronic sounds through the synthesizer, as on *I'm The One*, an album which led **David Bowie** to ask her to record and tour with him. (She told him to learn the synthesizer himself.) So pioneering was her work in this field that recently an electronics expert tried to tell her that the processes she was using were impossible given the technology of the time. Her songs are raw and personal, with an unblinking frankness about emotions and human relationships, and as well as keyboards she plays vibes and electric bass. She set up her own label, Ironic, in 1978. She has worked with **Bill Bruford** over a number of years and has also played with controversial composer Karlheinz Stockhausen.

Albums: as the Annette And Paul Bley Synthesizer Show *Dual Unity* (1970), with the Synthesizer Show *Improvisie* (1970), *Improvisie* (1970), *Revenge* (1970), *I'm The One* (1972), *X-Dreams* (1978), with Bill Bruford *Feels Good To Me* (1978), *Perfect Release* (1979), *Sky Skating* (1982), *Been In The Streets Too Long* (1983, rec. 1975-83), *I Have No Feelings* (1986), *Abstract Contact* (1988).

Peacock, Gary

b. 12 May 1935, Barley, Idaho, USA. Peacock went to Germany in the late 50s playing the piano in a US Army band. During this period he took up the bass and when he left the army he stayed in Germany playing with local musicians including **Albert Mangelsdorff** and **Attila Zoller** and visiting Americans like saxophonists **Bud Shank** and **Bob Cooper**. In 1958 he moved to California where he played with a wide range of musicians including **Shorty Rogers**, **Paul Horn** and **Paul Bley**. He continued to work with Bley when he moved to New York in 1962 and got involved in the burgeoning *avant garde* scene. He played with **Bill Evans**, **Rahsaan Roland Kirk**, **George Russell**, **Roswell Rudd**, **Steve Lacy** and **Albert Ayler** with whom he worked in Europe (1964). He is technically an excellent musician with a very full tone able to create appropriate lines in many contexts. In the mid-60s he studied Eastern philosophy and medicine. He later had a brief stint with **Miles Davis** and played again with Paul Bley before he went to study in Japan, returning to Washington University in 1972 to study biology. In the mid-70s he once again worked with Bley and also in a trio with pianist **Keith Jarrett** and drummer **Jack DeJohnette**. In the 80s he taught at Cornish Institute of the Allied Arts in Seattle, Washington.

Selected albums: with Bill Evans *Trio '64* (1963), with Albert Ayler *New York Eye And Ear Control* (1964), with Paul Bley *Ballads* (1967), *Tales Of Another* (ECM 1977), *December Poems* (ECM 1979), *Shift In The Wind* (ECM 1980), *Voice From The Past* (ECM 1981), with Keith Jarrett *Standards* i (1983), with Jarrett *Changes* (1984), with Jarrett *Standards* ii (1985), *Guamba* (ECM 1987), *Partners* (Owl 1990), with Paul Bley, Franz Koglmann *Annette* (1993), with Jarrett, Paul Motian *At The Deer Head Inn* (ECM 1994).

Peanut Butter Conspiracy

Originally known as the **Ashes**, this Los Angeles quintet assumed the above name in 1966. The group, comprising Sandi Robinson (vocals), John Merrill (guitar), Lance Fent (guitar), Al Brackett (bass) and Jim Voigt (drums) made their debut with 'Time Is After You' for the locally-based Vault label, before securing a major deal with Columbia/**CBS** the following year. Here they were united with producer **Gary Usher**, who sculpted a harmonious sound redolent of the **Mamas And The Papas**, **Jefferson Airplane** and **Spanky And Our Gang**. *The Peanut Butter Conspiracy Is Spreading* included their anthem-like single, 'It's A Happening Thing' and the haunting 'Then Came Love', but the album failed to make a significant commercial breakthrough. Fent was replaced by Bill Wolff for *The Great Conspiracy* wherein the group showed a greater emphasis on instrumental prowess. 'Turn On A Friend' and 'Time Is After You' confirmed the unit's undoubted potential, but they were dropped from the label following the failure of 'I'm A Fool'/'It's So Hard', a non-album single. A reshaped line-up emerged to complete *For Children Of All Ages* on the Challenge label, but this lacklustre set was a great disappointment and the group then folded. Lance Fent subsequently worked with **Randy Meisner** while late-period member Ralph Shuckett (ex-**Clear Light**) reappeared in Jo Mama.

Albums: *The Peanut Butter Conspiracy Is Spreading* (1967), *The Great Conspiracy* (1968), *For Children Of All Ages* (1968). Compilation: *Turn On A Friend* (1989).

Pearce, Dick

b. 19 April 1951, London, England. A fine, clear-toned, lyrical trumpeter and flugelhorn-player, Pearce has shown his consistency and imagination over 10 years with **Ronnie Scott**'s band, playing regularly at Scott's club and on the road. He took trumpet lessons at the age of 13, but taught himself theory. From 1968-71 he was in the army, where he played in the band, and on discharge he joined **Graham Collier**, with whom he worked from 1971-72. As well as Scott's quintet he has played with **Mike Westbrook**, **Keith Tippett**, **Dudu Pukwana**, **Chris Biscoe**, Brian Abrahams, and **Gil Evans**'s UK Band. In September 1990 he was injured in a motorcycle accident, and was out of action for some months, but by the end of 1991 he was back leading his own quartet.

Albums: with Graham Collier *Portraits* (1972), with Mike Westbrook *The Cortege* (1982).

Pearl Harbor And The Explosions

Formed in San Francisco, California in 1979, this much-touted attraction was centred on vocalist Pearl Harbor (b. 1958, Germany, of a Filipino mother), who, as Pearl E. Gates, had previously been a dancer in the

Tubes live show. She subsequently joined Jane Dornacker in Leila And The Snakes, before taking the group's rhythm section - Hilary Stench (bass) and John Stench (drums) - in this new act. Their act continued the theatricality of the Tubes, but Gates was more interested in conventional rock 'n' roll. To this end she recruited Peter Bilt (guitar) and formed Pearl Harbor And The Explosions in October 1978. They specialized in old fashioned rock 'n' roll/rockabilly spiced with 'new wave' energy. Their debut single 'Drivin'' (which was later covered by **Jane Aire And The Belvederes**) came out on the independent 415 Records label and became an cult hit. Its success encouraged **Warner Brothers** to sign the group. Their self-titled debut was a strong, promising work, but the group failed to complete a follow-up. They split in June 1980 leaving Pearl to continue with a solo album *Don't Follow Me I'm Lost* under her new name Pearl Harbor. The album was produced by Nicky Gallagher (former member of **Ian Dury**'s Blockheads). The Stench brothers joined ex-**Jefferson Airplane** guitarist **Jorma Kaukonen** in Vital Parts, before embarking on an association with cult *avant garde* act Chrome.

Albums: *Pearl Harbor And The Explosions* (1979), as Pearl Harbor *Don't Follow Me, I'm Lost* (1981).

Pearl Jam

This revisionist (or, depending on your viewpoint, visionary) rock quintet were formed in Seattle, USA, in the early 90s, by Jeff Ament (bass) and Stone Gossard (rhythm guitar). Gossard had played with Steve Turner in the Ducky Boys, the latter moving on to perform with Ament in **Green River**. Gossard would also become a member of this band when Mark Arm (like Turner, later to join **Mudhoney**) switched from guitar to vocals. Gossard and Ament, however, elected to continue working together when Green River washed up, and moved on to **Mother Love Bone**, fronted by local 'celebrity' Andrew Wood. However, that ill-fated group collapsed when, four weeks after the release of its debut album, *Apple*, Wood was found dead from a heroin overdose. Both Gossard and Ament would subsequently participate in Seattle's tribute to Wood, **Temple Of The Dog,** alongside Chris Cornell of **Soundgarden** who instigated the project, Soundgarden drummer Matt Cameron, plus Gossard's schoolfriend Mike McCready (guitar) and vocalist Eddie Vedder (ex-Bad Radio), from San Diego. He had been passed a tape of demos recorded by Ament, Gossard and McCready by **Red Hot Chili Peppers**' drummer Jack Irons. Both Vedder and McCready would eventually hook up permanently with Ament and Gossard to become Pearl Jam, with the addition of drummer Dave Krusen (having originally dabbled with the name Mookie Blaylock). The band signed to **Epic Records** in 1991, debuting the following year with the powerful, yet melodic *Ten*. A bold diarama, it saw the band successfully incorporate elements of their native traditions (Soundgarden, Mother Love Bone, **Nirvana**) with older influences such as the **Doors**, **Velvet Underground**, the **Stooges** and the **MC5**. The self-produced recording (together with Rick Parashar) showed great maturity for a debut, particularly in the full-blooded songwriting, never better demonstrated than on hit single 'Alive'. Dynamic live performances and a subtle commercial edge to their material catapulted them from obscurity to virtual superstars overnight, as the Seattle scene debate raged and Kurt Cobain accused them of 'jumping the alternative bandwagon'. In the USA *Ten* was still in the Top 20 a year and a half after its release, having sold over 4 million copies in that country alone. The touring commitments which followed, however, brought Vedder to the verge of nervous collapse. He struggled back to health in time for the **Lollapalooza** II tour, an appearance on *MTV Unplugged*, and Pearl Jam's cameo as Matt Dillon's 'band', Citizen Dick, in the Cameron Crowe film, *Singles*. Vedder would also front a re-united Doors on their induction into the Rock 'n' Roll Hall Of Fame in Los Angeles at the Century Plaza hotel, performing versions of 'Roadhouse Blues', 'Break On Through' and 'Light My Fire'. The eagerly awaited 'difficult' follow-up was announced in October 1993, close on the heals of Nirvana's latest offering. Whilst reviews were mixed the advance orders placed the album on top of charts on both sides of the Atlantic. *Vitalogy* seemed overtly concerned with re-establishing the group's grass roots credibility, a strong clue to which arrived in the fact that the album was available for a week on vinyl before a CD or cassette release (a theme revisited on 'Spin The Black Circle'). There were also numerous references, some oblique, others not, to the death of Nirvana's Kurt Cobain. Ironically 1994 also saw drummer Dave Abbruzzese dispensed with, amid unfounded rumours that former **Nirvana** sticksman Dave Grohl would be invited in to the ranks.

Albums: *Ten* (Epic 1991), *Vs.* (Epic 1993), *Vitalogy* (Epic 1994).

Further reading: *Pearl Jam: The Illustrated Biography*, Brad Morrell. *Pearl Jam Live!*, Joey Lorenzo (compiler). *The Illustrated Story*, Allan Jones.

Pearl, Minnie

b. Sarah Ophelia Colley, 25 October 1912, Centerville, Tennessee, USA. The daughter of a prominent businessman, she, unlike many country artists, grew up in relative luxury though under the strict supervision of her mother, who played the local church organ. She developed an interest in the stage as a small child and later, when permitted, watched vaudeville shows at a Nashville theatre, being very impressed by the act of comedienne Elviry Weaver. After graduating from high school, she attended Nashville's Ward-Belmont

College, a fashionable finishing school for young ladies, where, in 1932, she acquired a degree in speech and drama. She worked as a teacher in her home town for two years, before finding work with a company that toured the south producing amateur plays in rural areas. In 1936, after meeting what was later described as 'an amusing old mountain woman' when touring in Alabama, she began to develop her *alter ego*. Colley worked hard over the next few years, gradually building her act and it was not until November 1940, that she first auditioned for the ***Grand Ole Opry***. Although the *Opry* management had some misgivings that she would be accepted as a country character, because of her known upper-class education, she was permitted to appear on the late evening show. **Roy Acuff** was impressed and a few weeks later signed her to his road show. The audience on the night were amused and Minnie Pearl was on the *Opry* to stay and destined to become one of its most popular stars. Minnie Pearl, dressed in her cheap frilly cotton dress and wearing a wide-brimmed hat with the price label still attached, became an *Opry* legend. After an opening catchphrase of 'How-dee, I'm just so proud to be here', she chattered incessantly about the community of Grinder's Switch (an actual small railway switching point near Centerville), told appallingly corny jokes, recited comic monologues, sang (badly), included a little dance and related how one day she would catch her boy friend, Hezzie.

Since 1940, Minnie Pearl has worked with most major country stars and once featured in popular routines with *Opry* comedian Rod Brasfield. In 1947, she appeared on the first country show to play Carnegie Hall, New York (she returned with a second show in 1961) and also married Henry Cannon, a commercial pilot, who became her manager. She later joked 'I married my transportation'. She has toured extensively with *Opry* and other shows in America and Canada and appeared in Europe, including a 1949-1950 tour with her friends **Hank Williams, Red Foley** and Rod Brasfield. Over the years she has appeared on all major network radio and television shows. She has recorded for several labels but not being a recognized vocalist failed to find chart success to match that of her stage act. Her only country chart entry came in 1966 with a Top 10 hit in 'Giddyup Go - Answer', the woman's reply to **Red Sovine**'s country number 1. During her long career she has received many awards, the most important being her election to the Country Music Hall of Fame in 1975. The plaque reads 'Humor is the least recorded but certainly one of the most important aspects of live country music'. Although somewhat of a legend in the USA, especially in Nashville, where there is now a Minnie Pearl Museum in the Opryland complex, her appallingly unfunny jokes and distinctly rural humour, coupled with a distinct lack of exposure outside of her homeland, have never quite established her to anywhere near the same status in Britain. She suffered a severe stroke in 1991, and was forced into semi-retirement: scores of country stars contributed to a television tribute to her while she was in hospital, testifying to the respect in which she is held within the industry.

Albums: *Howdee (Cousin Gal From Grinder's Switch At The Party)* (1963), *Laugh-A-Long* (1964), *America's Beloved Minnie Pearl* (1965), with various artists, narration by Minnie Pearl *The Country Music Story* (1966), *Howdy!* (1967), *Looking For A Feller* (1970), with Grandpa Jones *Grand Old Opry Stars* (1975).

Pearls Before Swine

Formed in Florida, USA in 1965, Pearls Before Swine comprised Tom Rapp (vocals/guitar), Wayne Harley (autoharp/banjo/mandolin/vibraphone), Lane Lederer (bass/guitar/horns) and Roger Crissinger (keyboards). The latter was replaced by Jim Bohannon in 1967. The group pursued a recording deal with the *avant garde* ESP label, opining that the home of the **Fugs** would welcome their surrealist folk-rock. The quartet's debut, *One Nation Underground*, was an enticing mixture of intimate ballads and **Bob Dylan**-influenced ire, while Rapp's lisping delivery gave the group its distinctiveness. *Balaclava* followed a similar path, but enhanced the air of mystery with a succession of sound effects, string arrangements and contributions from jazz musician **Joe Farrell**. Although the Pearls' original members were now dropping out of the group, Rapp continued to forge an idiosyncratic path. *The Use Of Ashes* included 'Rocket Man', the artist's interpretation of a Ray Bradbury short story, which inspired the **Elton John** song of the same title. Rapp's later work, although still inventive, embraced more conventional styles and showed a marked interest in country styles. Such releases bore either his own name, or that of his group, at the whim of the relevant record company. Having achieved all he felt possible, Rapp retired from music in 1975 and has since become a successful lawyer.

Albums: *One Nation Underground* (1967), *Balaclava* (1968), *These Things Too* (1969), *The Use Of Ashes* (1970), *City Of Gold* (1971), *Beautiful Lies You Could Live* (1971), *Familiar Songs* (1972), *Stardancer* (1973), *Sunforest* (1973).

Pearson, Duke

b. Columbus C. Pearson, 17 August 1932, Atlanta, Georgia, USA, d. 4 August 1980. After studying piano and trumpet, Pearson opted for the former and played professionally in various parts of the USA before settling in New York at the end of the 50s. Working as both performer and composer, he associated with several leading musicians, including **Donald Byrd**, **Art Farmer**, **Benny Golson** and **Pepper Adams**. In 1963 he succeeded **Ike Quebec** as A&R director of **Blue Note Records**, a post he held until 1971.

During the late 60s Pearson formed a strikingly good big band from New York-based session musicians and jazzmen. The band, designed to perform his own music, made some excellent albums, notably *Now Hear This*. In the 70s Pearson divided his time between performing, accompanying singers such as **Carmen McRae** and **Nancy Wilson**, directing his big band and fighting against the onset of multiple sclerosis.
Albums: *Profile* (1959), *Dedication* (1961), *Wahoo* (1964), *Sweet Honey Bee* (Blue Note 1966), *The Right Touch* (1967), *Introducing Duke Pearson's Big Band* (1967), *The Phantom* (1968), *Now Hear This* (1968), *How Insensitive* (Blue Note 1969), *Merry Ole Soul* (1969), *It Could Only Happen To You* (1970), *Wahoo* (Blue Note 1989), *Bags Groove* (Black Lion 1991).

Pecora, Santo 'Peck'

b. 31 March 1902, New Orleans, Louisiana, USA, d. 29 May 1984. Pecora's first important job was with the **New Orleans Rhythm Kings**, with whom he played trombone from 1924-25. In the late 20s and during the following decade Pecora's early formal studies helped him to obtain work with several theatre orchestras and in such pre-swing era big bands as that led by **Ben Pollack**. In the mid-to-late 30s he was often found in dixieland bands, playing with **Sharkey Bonano** and others. He went back to his home town in the early 40s and thereafter led bands in and around the city, with occasional trips to Chicago, and sometimes joining forces with Bonano. Pecora's musical training gave him a broader range than he customarily chose to use and he was happy to be heard playing in a rumbustious dixieland style.
Selected album: *Recorded Live In New Orleans* (1956).

Peddlers

Though short of 'teen appeal', this seated, short-haired jazz-styled combo was appreciated by other artists for their stylistic tenacity and exacting technical standards. For much of 1964, the polished jazz-pop concoctions of ex-**Tornado** Tab Martin (b. 24 December 1944, Liverpool, England; bass), ex-Faron's Flamingo Trevor Morais (b. 16 October 1943, Liverpool, England; drums) and the **Dowlands**' former backing guitarist Roy Phillips (b. 5 May 1943, Parkstone, Poole, Dorset, England; Hammond organ/vocals) were heard nightly at London's exclusive Scotch of St. James's club - and, the following January, their arrangement of Teddy Randazzo's 'Let The Sunshine In', delivered by Phillips in a blues-tinged snort, slipped fleetingly into the UK Top 50. It took over four years for the three to come up trumps again when an invigorating **CBS** contract launched *Freewheelers* into the album chart. This was the harbinger of a Top 10 strike with the self-penned 'Birth', a stunningly innovative composition. The follow-up, 'Girlie' was a minor success and the Peddlers fared well in the album lists with *Birthday*. The long-term benefits of this commercial Indian summer included the broadening of the group's work spectrum - notably in providing musical interludes for television chat-shows - and the command of larger fees for their stock-in-trade cabaret bookings. When the trio split in the mid-70s, Martin found employment as a session player, Phillips emigrated to Australasia and Morais joined Quantum Jump.
Selected albums: *The Fantastic Peddlers* (1966), *Freewheelers* (1968), *Birthday* (1970), *Georgia On My Mind* (1973). Compilation: *The Best Of The Peddlers* (1974).

Peebles, Ann

b. 27 April 1947, East St. Louis, Missouri, USA. An impromptu appearance at the Rosewood Club in Memphis led to Peebles' recording deal. Bandleader Gene Miller took the singer to producer **Willie Mitchell** whose skills fashioned an impressive debut single, 'Walk Away' (1969). Anne's style was more fully shaped with 'Part Time Love' (1970), an irresistibly punchy reworking of the **Clay Hammond**-penned standard, while powerful original songs, including 'Slipped Tripped And Fell In Love' (1972) and 'I'm Gonna Tear Your Playhouse Down' (1973), later recorded by **Paul Young** and **Graham Parker**, confirmed her promise. Her work matured with the magnificent 'I Can't Stand The Rain', which defined the **Hi Records** sound and deservedly ensured the singer's immortality. **Don Bryant**, Peebles' husband and a songwriter of ability, wrote that classic as well as '99 lbs' (1971). Later releases, '(You Keep Me) Hangin' On' and 'Do I Need You', were also strong, but Peebles was latterly hampered by a now-established formula and sales subsided. 'If You Got The Time (I've Got The Love)' (1979) was the singer's last R&B hit, but her work nonetheless remains among the finest in the 70s soul canon. After a return to the gospel fold in the mid-80s, Peebles bounced back in 1989 with *Call Me*. In 1992 the fine back-to-the-Memphis-sound, *Full Time Love*, was issued. She appeared that summer at the Porretta Terme Soul Festival in Italy and her rivetting preformance was captured on a CD of the festival, *Sweet Soul Music - Live!*, released by Italian label 103.
Albums: *This Is Ann Peebles* (1969), *Part Time Tove* (1971), *Straight From The Heart* (1972), *I Can't Stand The Rain* (1974), *Tellin' It* (1976), *If This Is Heaven* (1978), *Handwriting On The Wall* (1979), *Call Me* (Waylo 1989), *Full Time Love* (Rounder/Bullseye 1992). Compilations: *I'm Gonna Tear Your Playhouse Down* (1985), *99 lbs* (1987), *Greatest Hits* (1988), *Lookin' For A Lovin'* (1990), *Straight From The Heart/I Can't Stand The Rain* (1992), *Tellin' It/If This Is Heaven* (1992), *This Is Ann Peebles/The Handwriting On The Wall* (1993), *The Flipside Of ...* (1993), *U.S. R&B Hits* (1995) .

Peel, John

b. John Robert Parker Ravenscroft, 30 August 1939,

Heswall, Cheshire, England. Having moved to the USA during the early 60s to work in his father's cotton business, Peel's musical knowledge engendered several guest appearances on Dallas radio stations. By cultivating his near-Liverpool birthright, he became something of a local celebrity in the wake of Beatlemania which in turn led to a full-time job as a disc jockey on Oklahoma's KOMA station. By 1966 he was working at KMEN in San Bernadino, California, but the following year John returned to Britain where his knowledge of emergent US underground rock led to his joining the **pirate radio** ship Radio London. Now stripped of his 'Ravenscroft' surname in favour of a snappier appellation, Peel achieved almost instant fame for his late-night *Perfumed Garden* programme which introduced the then-mysterious delights of **Country Joe And The Fish**, the **Velvet Underground** and **Captain Beefheart And His Magic Band** to unsuspecting UK audiences. When the Marine Offences Bill effectively outlawed pirate radio, Peel moved to the BBC's new Radio 1 where he latterly took control of Sunday afternoon's *Top Gear*. Here, he continued to promote 'new' music, airing progressive acts from Britain and America and giving a plethora of groups, including **Pink Floyd**, **Soft Machine**, **Jethro Tull, Moby Grape, Grateful Dead, Jefferson Airplane, Buffalo Springfield** and **Fleetwood Mac**, their first substantive airings. Peel also established the ambitious Dandelion label, the roster of which included **Medicine Head** and **Kevin Coyne**, but his closest ties lay with **Marc Bolan** and **Tyrannosaurus Rex**, whose later success was due, in part, to Peel's unswerving support during their early career. **Rod Stewart** and the **Faces** were also strong favourites although the Peel's influence lessened during the early 70s as their music became increasingly predictable. Peel nonetheless promoted such experimental acts as Matching Mole and **Can**, as well as reggae and soul, before finding renewed enthusiasm with the advent of punk. Saturation airplay of the first **Ramones** album alienated many entrenched listeners, but it excited a new, and generally younger, audience. Once again Peel, with the guidance of ever-present producer **John Walters**, was in the vanguard of an exciting musical upheaval as he broadcast material by **Siouxsie And The Banshees**, **Joy Division**, the **Undertones** and the **Fall**, the latter two of which were particular favourites. John Peel remains an important and influential figure. The sole survivor of Radio 1's initial intake, his weekend shows still gnaw at the barriers of popular music, be it rap, hardcore, reggae or ethnic music. The highly-successful *Peel Sessions* EP series on the Strange Fruit label, drawn from the extensive library of live performances recorded for his programmes, are a tribute to his intuition.

Compilations: various artist sessions recorded especially for Peel's programmes *Before The Fall - The Peel Sessions* (1991), *Winters Of Discontent - The Peel Sessions* (1991), *The New Breed - The Peel Sessions* (1991), *Too Pure - The Peel Sessions* (1992).

Peeping Tom

A well-established rocking ceilidh band from Coventry, England, the line-up includes the talents of Ben Woodward (melodeon/guitar), Pete Smale (guitar/banjo/mandolin), John McIntosh (bass), Ian Wilson (keyboards/cittern/mandolin), and Colin Halliwell (drums/percussion). They have sworn never to play anything but dances, but did however become involved in a lively adaptation of *Lark Rise To Candleford* (1990) with the Criterion Theatre.

Album: *A Sight For Sore Eyes* (1993).

Peer, Ralph

b. Ralph Sylvester Peer, 22 May 1892, Kansas City, Missouri, USA, d. 19 January 1960, Hollywood, California, USA. A leading talent scout, recording engineer and record producer in the field of country music in the 20s and 30s, Peer went on to form the famous Southern Music Publishing Company. After working for his father, who sold sewing machines, phonographs and records, he spent several years with **Columbia Records**, in Kansas City, until around 1920, when he was hired as recording director of General Phonograph's **OKeh** label. In the same year he supervised what is said to be the first blues recording, **Mamie Smith**'s 'Crazy Blues', and followed that, in June 1923, with another 'first', when he set up mobile recording equipment in Atlanta, Georgia, to make what was reputedly the first genuine country record, **Fiddlin' John Carson**'s 'Little Old Log Cabin In The Lane'/'That Old Hen Cackled And The Rooster's Goin' To Crow'. Early in 1925 Peer recorded some sides with Ernest V. 'Pop' Stoneman, the pivotal figure of the **Stoneman Family**. Out of these sessions came 'The Sinking Of The Titanic', one of the biggest selling records of the 20s. In 1926 Peer moved to Victor Records, and began to tour the southern states in search of new talent. He struck gold in August of the following year, when he recorded **Jimmie Rodgers** and the **Carter Family** on the same session. Rodgers, who later became known as the 'Father Of Country Music', cut 'The Soldier's Sweetheart' and 'Sleep, Baby, Sleep', while the Carters' first sides included 'Single Girl, Married Girl'. Another historic session took place in 1931 when Peers recorded Rodgers and the Carters performing together. In 1928, together with Victor, Peer formed the Southern Music Company, to publish and promote the expanding catalogue of country music.

Within two years, he had extended his interests to jazz, having added the legendary names and songs of **Fats Waller**, **Jelly Roll Morton**, **Louis Armstrong** and

Count Basie to Southern's roster. Shortly afterwards Peer broadened his canvas even further by moving into popular music, with songs as diverse as **Hoagy Carmichael** and Stuart Gorrell's 'Georgia On My Mind' and the French waltz, 'Fascination', written by F.D. Marchetti, Maurice de Feraudy and **Dick Manning**. Ten years after 'Rockin' Chair', Southern published 'Lazy River', another Carmichael standard, which was successfully revived in 1961 by **Bobby Darin**. In 1932 Peer acquired sole ownership of Southern from Victor and, in the same year, opened a London office headed by Harry Steinberg. Steinberg was able to place Southern copyrights with top bandleaders such as **Henry Hall**, enabling them to be heard on the popular radio programmes of the day. The 30s were boom years for sheet music, and it was not uncommon to sell over a million copies of a particular tune. In 1934 Southern had a smash hit in the UK with Fred Hillebrand's 'Home James And Don't Spare The Horses', which was popularized by Elsie Carlisle and Sam Browne with the **Ambrose** Orchestra. Back in the USA, **Benny Goodman** opened and closed his programmes with 'Let's Dance' and 'Goodbye', both Southern copyrights. In the early 30s Peer had visited Mexico and picked up several songs such as 'Granada' and 'Maria Elena', but in 1938, Southern's situation completely changed, and the publishing company moved dramatically into the big league. After further journeys to Central America, Peer flooded the world market with that region's music, and transformed it into enormous hits. Songs such as 'Frenesi', 'Brazil', 'Tico Tico', 'Perfidia' (a hit in 1941 for **Glenn Miller** and revived 20 years later by the **Ventures**), 'Baia', 'Ba-Ba-Lu', 'Amor', 'Besame Mucho' and 'El Cumbanchero' endured as some of Southern's most lucrative copyrights. 'Time Was' ('Duerme'), successful for bandleader **Jimmy Dorsey** in 1941, was was still heard regularly in the UK in the 90s, in a version by **Nelson Riddle**'s Orchestra, as the signature tune of veteran broadcaster Hubert Gregg's long-running radio show, *Thanks For The Memory*. Southern had another big hit with the title song from the 1939 movie *Intermezzo*, which starred Ingrid Bergman and Leslie Howard. It was especially popular in the UK, where the film's title was *Escape To Happiness*. In 1940 there came another watershed when the dispute between the **ASCAP** and US radio stations, led to the inauguration of the rival Broadcast Music Incorporated (BMI). BMI supported music by blues, country and hillbilly artists, and Peer, through his Peer-International company, soon contributed a major part of BMI's catalogue.

During World War II, and just afterwards, Peer published many fondly remembered songs such as 'Deep In The Heart Of Texas' and 'You Are My Sunshine' (both hits for **Bing Crosby**), 'Humpty Dumpty Heart' (Glenn Miller), 'You're Nobody 'Till Somebody Loves You' (**Russ Morgan**), 'The Three Caballeros' (**Andrews Sisters**), 'Say A Prayer For The Boys Over There' (**Deanna Durbin**), 'I Should Care' and 'The Coffee Song' (both **Frank Sinatra**), 'That's What I Like About The South' (Phil Harris), 'You've Changed' (Connie Russell), 'I Get the Neck Of The Chicken' (**Freddie Martin**) and 'Can't Get Out Of This Mood' (Johnny Long). Hot on the trail of the liberating forces, Peer was back in Europe in 1945, and published Jean Villard and Bert Reisfeld's composition 'Les Trois Cloches' ('The Three Bells'), which was recorded by **Edith Piaf**, and subsequently became a hit for the Browns in 1952 when it was also known as 'The Jimmy Brown Song'. Around that time, Peer was still publishing such music as 'Mockingbird Hill', a million seller for **Patti Page**, and **Les Paul** And Mary Ford, 'Sway' (**Dean Martin** and **Bobby Rydell**), 'Busy Line' (**Rose Murphy**) and the novelty 'I Know An Old Lady' (**Burl Ives**). Then came the rock 'n' roll revolution, during which Southern published hits by **Buddy Holly**, **Little Richard**, the **Big Bopper** and the **Platters**. In 1956 Peer-Southern's Mexican office signed **Perez Prado**, who is credited with having created the Latin-American jazz music, the mambo. He added evergreens such as 'Patricia' and 'Mambo Jambo' to the catalogue. By then Peer had relinquished control of the Peer-Southern empire which was represented by over 20 offices throughout the world, and handed over to his son, Ralph Peer II. Peer Snr was devoting more time to copyright law, and to his absorbing interest in horticulture, especially camellias, on which he was a leading authority. In the 60s Southern had successful copyrights with songs such as 'Running Bear' (**Johnny Preston**), 'What In the World's Come Over You' (**Jack Scott**), 'Little Boy Sad' (**Johnny Burnette**), 'Clementine' (Bobby Darin), 'Love Me With All Your Heart' (**Karl Denver**), 'Catch The Wind' (**Donovan**), 'Detroit City' (**Bobby Bare**) and 'Winchester Cathedral' (**New Vaudeville Band**). The original country connection was retained with material such as **Mel Tillis**'s 'Ruby, Don't Take Your Love To Town', which was a big hit for **Kenny Rogers**. Sadly, Peer did not live to hear those songs.

Peers, Donald

b. Donald Rhys Hubert Peers, 9 August 1909, Ammanford, Dyfed, Wales, d. 9 August 1973, Brighton, England. An extremely popular singer during the late 40s and early 50s in the UK, especially with female audiences who swooned and screamed à la American bobbysoxers. His father, a Welsh colliery worker, was a prominent member of the Plymouth Brethren, and would never go inside a theatre to see and hear his son at work. Peers was to have been a schoolteacher, but ran away and became a house painter, a steward on a British tanker vessel, and a singer with a seaside concert party. He made his first

broadcast in 1927 with the popular comedy duo Clapham And Dwyer, and continued to have success in the medium. In 1940 he enlisted in the Armed Forces, and was invalided out on D-Day, 1944. In the same year he recorded 'In A Shady Nook (By A Babbling Brook)', written by E.G. Nelson and Harry Pease in 1927, and it became his life-long theme. Other 40s recordings included 'I Can't Begin To Tell You', 'Bow Bells', 'Far Away Places', 'On The 5.45' (a vocal version of 'Twelfth Street Rag', with a lyric by **Andy Razaf**), 'Powder Your Face With Sunshine' (one of his biggest successes), 'Lavender Blue', 'A Strawberry Moon (In A Blueberry Sky)', 'Everywhere You Go', 'Clancy Lowered The Boom', 'It Happened In Adano', 'A Rose In A Garden Of Weeds', 'I'll String Along With You' and 'Down In The Glen'. He toured the UK Variety circuit and spent lucrative summer seasons at top locations such as Blackpool, and in 1949 presented his one-man show at the Royal Albert Hall and the London Palladium. He also had his own radio show *Cavalier Of Song*, a television series *Donald Peers*, and he made several films including *Sing Along With Me*. His record success was sustained through the early 50s with songs such as 'The Last Mile Home', 'Dear Hearts And Gentle People', 'Out Of A Clear Blue Sky', 'Music! Music! Music!', 'If I Knew You Were Comin', I'd've Baked A Cake', 'Enjoy Yourself (It's Later Than You Think')', 'Dearie', 'I Remember The Cornfields', 'Beloved, Be Faithful', 'Me And My Imagination', 'Mistakes', 'In A Golden Coach' (a celebratory number for the Coronation of Queen Elizabeth II), 'Is It Any Wonder' and 'Changing Partners'. In the late 50s he worked often in South Africa, Australia and India, and on his return to the UK, had to rebuild his career via the northern club circuit which had taken over from the music halls. He had a Top 10 chart entry in 1968 with 'Please Don't Go', written by comedian Jackie Rae and **Les Reed**. In 1972 Peers returned to the stage after overcoming a severe back injury sustained in Australia, and had his last chart entry with the aptly titled 'Give Me One More Chance'.
Albums: *The Last Broadcast* (1974), *In A Shady Nook* (Empress 1995). Compilations: *The World Of Donald Peers* (1970), *The World Of Donald Peers, Volume Two* (1973), *The Donald Peers Collection* (1978), *The Golden Age Of Donald Peers* (1987), *The Very Best Of* (1993).

Pegg, Dave

b. Birmingham, England, 1947. After persuading his father to buy him a guitar, Pegg worked on the local rock scene with such as John Bonham (**Led Zeppelin**). He swapped bass guitar for a stand-up bass, and joined The Ian Campbell Folk Group, with whom he learnt to play the mandolin. More importantly, he was introduced to Dave Swarbrick, who, in 1969, enabled him to become the bass guitarist with **Fairport Convention**. It was the beginnning of a two-man partnership which steered Fairport through until 1979. Pegg then moved to **Jethro Tull**. In 1978, he bought an old Baptist chapel and converted it into Woodworm Studios, which became a recording Mecca for folk rock bands. Woodworm also acts as a label for various Fairport associates. In 1985, a reconvened Fairport Convention recorded for the first time for some years, and Pegg was firmly in control of both the band and the Cropredy reunion festivals - by then a regular August event. Three years previously he had released his only solo album, which, like Pegg himself, was jovial, none too serious, and filled with character. With his wife, Christine, Dave Pegg (Peggy) is now with **Simon Nicol** the acknowledged heart and soul of Fairport Convention.
Album: *The Cocktail Cowboy Goes It Alone* (1982).

Peggy-Ann

With a score by **Richard Rodgers** and **Lorenz Hart**, and a book by Herbert Fields, this show opened at the Vanderbilt Theatre in New York on 27 December 1926. It was sandwiched between *Lido Lady* and *Betsy*, two fairly unsatisfactory Rodgers and Hart shows that were produced in the same year. *Peggy-Ann* was sub-titled 'The Utterly Different Musical Comedy', and, in some respects, that proved to be true. To begin with, it was a hit, and although Fields's book was based on the Edgar Smith and A. Baldwin Sloane's 1910 musical *Tillie's Nightmare*, in which Marie Dressler had enjoyed great success, it had highly topical overtones. 1926 was the year of the Surrealists, a new movement in poetry and painting whose members believed in the 'omnipotence of the dream', and were heavily influenced by Sigmund Freud. The libretto for *Peggy-Ann* was liberally sprinkled with Freudian references, and follows Peggy-Ann Barnes (Helen Ford), a domestic servant in a boarding house in Glen Falls, New York, into her own private fantasy world. In a trice, she is travelling the globe, tasting the high-life at the race track, aboard a yacht, shopping on New York's Fifth Avenue - and getting married in her underwear. There were some other unusual touches, too: no songs were sung in the opening 15 minutes of the show, and there was no rousing finale. Also, the sets and props were moved around in full view of the audience, a device used by Rodgers again, 36 years later, in ***No Strings***. The songs, when they eventually came, were a pleasing bunch, and one of them, 'A Tree In The Park', achieved some popularity through recordings by **Helen Morgan** and Frank Black. 'Where's That Rainbow?' also endured, and is often performed by supper-club singers such as **Bobby Short**. The rest of the score included 'A Little Bird Told Me So' 'and 'Maybe It's Me'. A New York run of 333 performances was followed by a further 130 in London, where the role of Peggy-Ann was played by Dorothy Dickson.

Pell, Axel Rudi

This German heavy metal guitar virtuoso left **Steeler** in 1988 to concentrate on a solo career. Influenced by **Ritchie Blackmore**, **Yngwie Malmsteen** and **Tony Macalpine**, he offered explosive guitar pyrotechnics within a traditional metal framework. *Wild Obsession* featured vocalist Charlie Huhn (vocals), **Bonfire** member Jorg Deisinger (bass) and Jorg Michael (drums; ex-**Rage**). It was well-received by the music press, but this was not translated into sales, partly due to Pell's reluctance to take the band out on the road. *Nasty Reputation* represented a major leap forward in songwriting. The heart of the music was still in the early 70s, but the guitar work and the sheer energy of the delivery was quite remarkable. Bob Rock, now on vocals, gave the music great authority, with the expanded quintet also including two more new faces, Volker Krawczak (bass) and Kai Raglewski (keyboards).
Albums: *Wild Obsession* (Steamhammer 1989), *Nasty Reputation* (Steamhammer 1991), *The Ballads* (Steamhammer 1993).

Pendergrass, Teddy

b. Theodore Pendergrass, 26 March 1950, Philadelphia, Pennsylvania, USA. Pendergrass joined **Harold Melvin And The Blue Notes** in 1969, when they invited his group, the Cadillacs, to work as backing musicians. Initially their drummer, Teddy had become the featured vocalist within a year. His ragged, passionate interpretations brought distinction to such releases as 'I Miss You' and 'If You Don't Know Me By Now'. Clashes with Melvin led to an inevitable split and in 1976 Pendergrass embarked on a successful solo career, remaining with the **Philadelphia International** label. His skills were most apparent on slower material which proved ideal for the singer's uncompromisingly sensual approach, which earned him a huge following amongst women. 'The Whole Town's Laughing At Me' (1977), 'Close The Door' (1978) and 'Turn Off The Lights' (1979) stand among the best of his early work and if later releases were increasingly drawn towards a smoother, more polished direction, Pendergrass was still capable of creating excellent records, including a moving rendition of 'Love TKO', a haunting **Womack And Womack** composition. However, his life was inexorably changed in 1982, following a near-fatal car accident which left the singer confined to a wheelchair, although his voice was intact. Nonetheless, after months of physical and emotional therapy, he was able to begin recording again. 'Hold Me' (1984), Teddy's debut hit on his new outlet, **Asylum**, also featured **Whitney Houston**, while further success followed with 'Love 4/2' (1986) and 'Joy' (1988).
Albums: *Teddy Pendergrass* (1977), *Life Is A Song Worth Singing* (1978), *Teddy* (1979), *Teddy Live! (Coast To Coast)* (1979), *T.P.* (1980), *It's Time For Love* (1981), *This One's For You* (1982), *Heaven Only Knows* (1983), *Love Language* (1984), *Workin' It Back* (1985), *Joy* (1988). Compilations: *Greatest Hits* (1987), *Teddy Pendergrass* (1989), *Truly Blessed* (1991).

Penetration

Durham, England band Penetration may have had a suitably outrageous name for a punk band, but their music took them far from conventional 'no future' concerns. Vocalist **Pauline Murray** and bass player Robert Blamire wrote songs which did not need to be hidden behind three-chord bluster, and, along with the **Adverts**, theirs remains one of the great undiscovered legacies of the era. After only four gigs the band gained a lucky break by being invited to support **Generation X** at the Roxy Club, London, on 29 January 1977. Formed like so many others after witnessing the **Sex Pistols** play Manchester Free Trade Hall, the line-up was crystallised with the addition of Gary Chaplin (guitar) and Gary Smallman (drums). After cutting a demo in the summer, their name was passed to **Virgin Records** by the manager of the same company's shop in Newcastle, resulting in their November debut, 'Don't Dictate'. A sterling, defiant punk statement, it quickly became a genre classic. Neale Floyd replaced Chaplin in time for the following year's 'Firing Squad'. The first of two **John Peel** sessions was completed in July, with Fred Purser now adding a second guitar, before a third single, 'Life's A Gamble', and debut album in October. *Moving Targets*, produced by Mick Glossop and Mike Howlett, was a deeply challenging album, adding covers of the **Buzzcocks**' 'Nostalgia' and **Patti Smith**'s 'Free Money' to highly invigorating original songs like 'Future Daze' and 'Too Many Friends'. A second album, *Coming Up For Air*, followed in September 1979. Despite **Steve Lillywhite**'s production, this all-original collection was a rather uninspired affair, without the clarity or purpose of the consistently exciting debut. The band announced their intention to split on stage in Newcastle on 14 October, just a month after its release. As Murray confirmed to the ***New Musical Express***: 'I never wanted to be in Penetration and to be worrying all the time. I wanted it to be fun, not to be always thinking of hit singles and cracking America and writing for the next LP'. Posthumous releases included an official bootleg, while Murray went solo (originally with the Invisible Girls).
Albums: *Moving Targets* (Virgin 1978), *Coming Up For Air* (Virgin 1979), *Race Against Time* (Clifdayn 1979), split album with Ruts *BBC Radio 1 Live In Concert* (Windsong 1993).

Penguin Cafe Orchestra

This collection of accomplished musicians was inaugurated in the late-70s to cater for the musical eclecticism of leader Simon Jeffes (b. 1948). Ex-London

music student Jeffes nurtured a desire to create an ensemble capable of fusing musics from around the world, of different styles and cultures - literally an Utopian dream which came to him while suffering from food poisoning in the early 70s. After working on the fringes of the pop world, involving himself with production work with such groups as **Caravan** and **Camel**, Jeffes found a champion for his musical vision in **Brian Eno**. The Orchestra, which includes within its line-up Elizabeth Perry, Gavyn Wright, Bob Loveday (violins), Helen Liebmann (cello), Steve Nye (keyboards) and Neil Rennie (cuatro/ukulele), recorded their debut album on Eno's esoteric Obscure label. Jeffes continued his studio work, being hired at various points by the **Clash** and **Malcolm McLaren** with Sid Vicious. A follow-up would not appear until almost five years later, and using such esoteric song titles as 'The Ecstacy Of Dancing Fleas' and 'Cutting Branches For A Temporary Shelter' they betrayed a degree of pretentiousness. The music however, swayed between a studied seriousness and a sense of jolliness. The group have also drawn criticism over the years on account of being *too* clever and employing a dry approach to their music - an observation often levelled at classically-trained musicians seen to be straying outside their boundaries.
Albums: *Music From The Penguin Cafe* (1977), *Penguin Cafe Orchestra* (1981), *Broadcasting From Home* (1984), *Signs Of Life* (1987), *When In Rome - Live* (1988), *Union Cafe* (1993), *Concert Program* (Windham Hill 1995).

Penguins

Formed in 1954 in Fremont High School, Los Angeles, California, USA, the Penguins were one of the most important R&B vocal groups from the west coast in the early 50s. Their hit ballad 'Earth Angel' remains one of the most fondly recalled 'doo-wop' recordings to date. The group consisted of lead vocalist Cleveland 'Cleve' Duncan (b. 23 July 1935, Los Angeles, California, USA), Bruce Tate (baritone), Curtis Williams (first tenor) and Dexter Tisby (second tenor). Williams learned 'Earth Angel' from LA R&B singer **Jesse Belvin**, and passed it along to his group. Some sources give co-writing credit to Williams, Belvin and Gaynel Hodge, a member of vocal group the Turks. Hodge won a 1956 lawsuit recognizing his role in the writing of the song. However, most reissues of 'Earth Angel' still list only either Belvin, Williams or both. The Penguins, who took their name from a penguin on a cigarette pack, signed with the local DooTone Records, owned by Dootsie Williams. Their recording date was as a backing group for a blues singer, Willie Headon. They next recorded 'Hey Sinorita', an uptempo number. 'Earth Angel' was chosen as their first single's b-side but when both sides were played on LA radio station KGJF, listeners called in to request the 'Earth Angel' side be played again. It ultimately reached number 1 in the US ***Billboard*** R&B chart. It also reached the pop Top 10, but was eclipsed by a cover version by the white group the **Crew-Cuts**. The song has also charted by Gloria Mann (1955), **Johnny Tillotson** (1960), the **Vogues** (1969) and New Edition (1986). The Penguins continued to record other singles for DooTone (plus one album for the related Dooto label) and then **Mercury Records** before disbanding in 1959. Members Williams and Tate have since died, Tisby retired from music, and Duncan later formed new bands under the name Penguins and was still performing under that name in the early 90s.
Album: *The Cool, Cool Penguins* (1959).

Peniston, Ce Ce

b. Cecelia Peniston, c.1971, Phoenix, Arizona, USA. Ce Ce started acting at school when in her early teens. She went on to appear in numerous talent contests and also won the beauty pageants Miss Black Arizona and Miss Galaxy. She worked as a backing singer and whilst still at school wrote 'Finally', which would become her fist solo single. Fresh out of college, and with only the faintest hopes of a music career, she nevertheless sprang in to the Top 10 lists of both the UK and US on the back of a speculative demo. The music which backed 'Finally' had more than a passing resemblance to the **Ce Ce Rogers** (no relation) underground hit, 'Someday'. A singer and dancer slightly reminiscent of late 70s soul, most of her compositions are piano based with strong similarities to **Aretha Franklin** and **Whitney Houston**. While her modelling career has been put on the backburner, her attitude to singing remains refreshingly uncomplicated; 'What I know best is singing my lil' old heart out'. 'We Got A Love Thang' became a second hit early in 1992, as did the re-released 'Finally', before her debut album which was somewhat disjointed. She has also sung backing vocals on **Kym Sims**' 'Too Blind To See'. Her second album included contributions from house gurus **David Morales** and **Steve 'Silk' Hurley**, but was generally more R&B-focused.
Albums: *Finally* (A&M 1992), *Thought Ya Knew* (A&M 1994).

Penn, Dan

b. Wallace Daniel Pennington, 16 November 1941, Vernon, Alabama, USA. His reputation as a songwriter was secured when one of his early compositions, 'Is A Bluebird Blue?', was a hit for **Conway Twitty** in 1960. Penn also led a local group, the Mark V, which included David Briggs (piano), Norbert Putnam (bass) and Jerry Carrigan (drums). Also known as Dan Penn And The Pallbearers, these musicians later formed the core of the first Fame studio houseband. Their subsequent departure for a more lucrative career in Nashville left room for a second session group, among whose number was pianist **Spooner Oldham**. Over the next few years, Penn's partnership with this newcomer produced scores of excellent southern soul compositions, including 'Out Of Left Field', 'It Tears Me Up' (**Percy Sledge**), 'Slippin' Around' (**Clarence Carter**) and 'Let's Do It Over' (**Joe Simon**) and 'Dark End Of The Street', a classic guilt-laced 'cheating' ballad, first recorded by **James Carr**. Penn subsequently left Fame to work at the rival American Sound studio where he joined studio-owner **Chips Morman**, with whom he had also struck up a songwriting partnership (their 'Do Right Woman - Do Right Man' was the b-side of **Aretha Franklin**'s first hit-single for **Atlantic Records**). Later at American Studios Penn would also be responsible for producing the hit group, the **Box Tops**, but in 1969 he broke away to form his own studio, Beautiful Sounds. The 70s, however, were much less prolific. However, having flirted with a singing career with several one-off releases, he finally produced a fine solo album, *Nobody's Fool*, which included the first version of 'I Hate You', later covered by **Bobby 'Blue' Bland**. Dan also maintained his friendship with Oldham, but by the time the duo formed their own independent production company, the changing face of popular music rendered their talents anachronistic. However, in 1991 Oldham and Penn reunited to appear at the New York Bottom Line's In Their Own Words songwriter series. This live performance of self-penned songs was so successful that it inspired Dan to cut a new album of his own work, both old and new, the critically-acclaimed *Do Right Man*. To promote the album he played a further series of live dates including the 1994 Porretta Terme Soul Festival in Italy, and then at London' South Bank Centre to salute to southern songwriters under the banner The American South, which also included **Allen Toussaint** and **Joe South**.

Albums: *Nobody's Fool* (1973), *Do Right Man* (Sire/Warner Brothers 1994).

Penn, Dawn

A veteran of the Caribbean reggae scene with over 400 songs to her name (including material covered by **Bob Marley**, **Marcia Griffiths** and **Cat Stevens**), Penn shot to mainstream pop fame in 1994 when spending three consecutive weeks at number 3 in the UK charts with 'You Don't Love Me (No No No)'. Originally discovered by **Coxsone Dodd**, she has also provided backing vocals for others, notably **Johnny Nash** ('I Can See Clearly Now', 'There Are More Questions Than Answers', 'Hold Me Tight'). Her debut album was ably produced by **Steely And Clevie**.

Album: *No No No* (East West 1994).

Penny, Hank

b. Herbert Clayton Penny, 18 August 1918, Birmingham, Alabama, USA. His father, who became a hypnotist, learned to play the guitar and wrote poetry, after being disabled in a mine accident, gave him his first guitar tuition and the interest in entertaining. At the age of 15, he joined the act of Hal Burns on WAPI, playing banjo and learning comedy routines. In 1936, he moved to New Orleans where he worked with **Lew Childre** on WWL. He disliked the *Grand Ole Opry*'s hillbilly music and became somewhat obsessed by what he termed Texas fiddle music, being the Western-Swing music of **Bob Wills** and Milton Brown. He returned to Birmingham, formed his band the Radio Cowboys and began to present his swing music, first on WAPI and WKBC Birmingham and then at WDOD Chattanooga. Penny made his first recordings for ARC (with Art Satherley) in 1938, recording such uptempo swing-jazz-country tunes as 'Hesitation Blues'. In 1939, he moved to WSB Atlanta and joined the *Crossroads Follies*. Here, **Boudleaux Bryant** and steel guitarist Noel Boggs joined the band. In July 1939, he recorded 'Won't You Ride In My Little Red Wagon', which became his signature tune. The group disbanded in 1940 and for a time Penny worked solo on WSB but recorded with a 'pickup' band in 1941. In 1942, he moved to WLW Cincinnati, appeared regularly on the *Boone County Jamboree* and *Mid-Western Hayride* and worked with **Merle Travis** and **Grandpa Jones**. He toured with various shows and also fronted a group called the Plantation Boys, with whom he recorded for King Records in 1944.

He moved to Hollywood in 1945, re-formed his band and played the ballroom circuits of California. Later that year, he took over the band of Deuce Spriggins, played a residency at the famed *Riverside Rancho* and had his own show on KXLA and KGIL. He made further recordings for King and also appeared in four Charles Starrett b-movie westerns. He registered his first US country chart hits in 1946 with 'Steel Guitar Stomp' and 'Get Yourself A Redhead' (both reaching number 4). In 1947, apart from his band work, he played on ABC's network *'Roundup Time* as a comedian. He had a further number 4 country hit in 1950, with 'Bloodshot Eyes', which also was a hit for R&B artist **Wynonie Harris**. Penny also joined his friend Spade Cooley's network television show as a comedian but still maintained a rigorous schedule of playing dance halls with his band now known as the Penny Serenaders. He recorded for **RCA**-Victor in 1950, using an enlarged band that recorded as Hank Penny And His California Cowhands. In 1951, he left Spade Cooley and became the comedian with the Dude Martin stage and television show and he was also one of the founders of the Palomino Club in North Hollywood. He married country singer Sue Thompson in 1953, for a time hosted his own show on KHJ-TV and also moved from RCA to Decca. In the late 50s, the effects of rock music saw him move to Las Vegas and begin to include pop music in his repertoire. He divorced in 1963 but married his vocalist Shari Bayne in 1966. (During the

70s, Sue Thompson had chart successes with solo hits as well as duet hits with **Don Gibson** for Hickory Records.) Penny quit Las Vegas in 1968 and after a spell back in California, he moved to Nashville in 1970. Disliking the city and its music, he worked as a DJ on KFRM Wichita and with his wife, he played the local club circuit. In 1976, he returned to California, where he remained active, played in a few films and organized reunion concerts of some of the television and western-swing music celebrities of the 50s, including **Cliffie Stone**. He ranks as one of the most important exponents of western-swing music, although he rarely receives the publicity afforded to the likes of Wills, Brown and Cooley. There are several country musicians who benefited from their experience as a member of Hank Penny's band, including Herb Remington, Curly Chalker and **Roy Clark**.
Selected albums: *Tobacco State Swing* (1981), *Rompin', Stompin', Singin', Swingin'* (1983), *Country And Western Memories* (1986).

Pentagons

An R&B vocal group from San Bernadino, California, USA. Members were Joe Jones (lead), Carl McGinnis (bass), Otis Munson (tenor), and the brothers Ted (tenor) and Ken Goodloe (baritone/piano). The Pentagons helped make the early 60s the era of neo-doo-wop renaissance in which they sang classic 50s vocal harmonies that evoked the past but with full orchestrated support that reflected the coming soul era. The original Pentagons group, which came together in 1958, were the Goodloe brothers, McGinnis, plus Bill James as tenor and Johnny Torrence as lead. They recorded one unsuccessful single for **Specialty Records**, and then Torrence and James departed to be replaced by Jones and Munson respectively. Another single for Modern was released as by the Shields, and then in 1961 the group had a big hit with a Ken Goodloe song, 'To Be Loved (Forever)' (number 48 pop). It was released on Bob Keane's Donna label, but after one follow-up on Donna the group moved to the Jamie label. They got reached the charts again during 1961 with another Goodloe composition, 'I Wonder (If Your Love Will Ever Belong To Me)' (number 84 pop). **Ricky Nelson** was so impressed with the song he recorded it in 1964. Later Pentagons releases failed to make the charts, and the group broke up in 1962. The Goodloes put together another outfit in 1964, but this to disbanded in 1966 after a few failed singles. Ken Goodloe died 4 August 1991.
Compilations: *The Pentagons* (True Gems 1986), *Golden Classics* (Collectables 1990).

Pentagram

Amongst the best of the bands continuing the seminal heavy metal tradition of early **Black Sabbath**, the core of Pentagram was formed by Bobby Liebling (vocals) and Joe Hasselvander (drums) in the USA during 1978. Like Sabbath, their roots were in the lively white blues bands of the early 70s, which they translated into ominous, crunching riffs and dark, devilish lyrics. However, unlike Black Sabbath, who treat the infernal with ambivalence, Pentagram have always seemed much more comfortable with their Satanic themes. Their first album, *Pentagram*, was released in 1985, but by this time Hasselvander had left, dismayed at lack of label support, and joined **Raven**. Hasselvander (replaced by Stuart Rose) however had already laid down most of the tracks for their next album, *Day of Reckoning*. Strong local and cult support was not enough to sustain Pentagram's, increasingly unfashionable, approach and they split in 1990. But this same cult appeal saw the rights for their first two albums (with their debut retitled as *Relentless*) bought by UK label Peaceville and re-released in 1993. Inspired by this renewed interest Liebling reformed the band with the classic line up of Hasselvander (drums), Martin Swaney (bass), and Victor Griffin (guitar and keyboards) and released the new album *Be Forewarned*. While it would be difficult to call Pentagram original, their sinisterly infectious riffs and fidelity to metal's darker roots certainly justify the band's enduring appeal.
Albums: *Pentagram* (1985), *Day Of Reckoning* (Peaceville 1987), *Be Forewarned* (Peaceville 1994).

Pentangle

Formed in 1967, the Pentangle was inspired by *Bert And John*, a collaborative album by folk musicians **Bert Jansch** (b. 3 November 1943, Glasgow, Scotland) and **John Renbourn**. Vocalist Jacqui McShee, an established figure on the traditional circuit, joined **Danny Thompson** (b. April 1939; bass) and Terry Cox (drums), both of **Alexis Korner**'s Blues Incorporated, in a quintet which would also embrace blues and jazz forms. Their respective talents were expertly captured on *The Pentangle*, where the delicate acoustic interplay between Jansch and Renbourn was brilliantly underscored by Thompson's sympathetic support and McShee's soaring intonation. Stylish original material balanced songs pulled from folk's heritage ('Let No Man Steal Your Thyme', 'Brunton Town'), while the inclusion of the **Staple Singers** 'Hear My Call' confirmed the group's eclectism. This feature was expanded on the double-set *Sweet Child*, which included two compositions by jazz bassist **Charles Mingus**, 'Haitian Fight Song' and 'Goodbye Pork Pie Hat'. The unit enjoyed considerable commercial success with *Basket Of Light*, which included 'Light Flight', the theme song to the UK television series, *Take Three Girls*. However, despite an undoubted dexterity and the introduction of muted electric instruments, subsequent releases were marred by a sense of sterility, and lacked the passion of concurrent releases undertaken by the two guitarists. Pentangle was disbanded in 1972, following which Thompson began a partnership with **John Martyn**. Cox undertook a lucrative session career before backing French singer **Charles Aznavour**, and while Jansch continued his solo career, McShee fronted the John Renbourn Band between 1974-81. The original Pentangle reconvened the following year for a European tour and *Open The Door*, although defections owing to outside commitments led to considerable changes. McShee and Jansch were joined by Nigel Portman-Smith (bass) and Mike Piggott for *In The Round*, but by 1991 the latter had departed and Peter Kirtly (guitar) and Gerry Conway (drums) were now featured in the group. The future of this particular line-up was then jeopardized by plans to reunite the founding quintet, although by 1993 the band had continued to record.

Albums: *The Pentangle* (1968), *Sweet Child* (1968), *Basket Of Light* (1969), *Cruel Sister* (1970), *Solomon's Seal* (1972), *Open The Door* (1982), *In The Round* (1988), *So Early In The Spring* (1989), *One More Road* (1993). Compilations: *Reflections* (1971), *History Book* (1971), *Pentangling* (1973), *The Pentangle Collection* (1975), *Anthology* (1978), *The Essential Pentangle Volume 1* (1987), *The Essential Pentangle Volume 2* (1987), *People On The Highway 1968 - 1971* (1993), *One More Road* (1993).

Penthouse Records

(see **Germain, Donovan**)

People

Formed in San Jose, California, USA, in 1968, People consisted of Jeff Levin (guitar/vocals), Gene Mason, John Tristau and Larry Norman (vocalists), Albert Ribisi (keyboards), Rob Levin (bass) and Danny Friedkin (drums). They were signed to **Capitol Records** and released their first album, *I Love You*, that year. Both the album and the single 'I Love You', (originally by the **Zombies**), charted, the single making the US Top 20. The band underwent several personnel changes and recorded further singles for Capitol and Paramount, and two more albums. Without finding any further success, the group disbanded in 1971.

Albums: *I Love You* (1968), *Both Sides Of People* (1969), *There Are People And There Are People* (1970).

Peplowski, Ken

b. 23 May 1959, Cleveland, Ohio, USA. Peplowski took up the clarinet as a child and played his first professional engagement at the age of 10. He studied formally and played both classical music and jazz, appearing on radio and television in and around his home town. In 1978 his quartet played opposite the **Tommy Dorsey** Orchestra, at the time under the direction of **Buddy Morrow**, and he was promptly offered a job. Peplowski toured extensively with the band, including a visit to Europe. During this period he met and briefly studied with **Sonny Stitt**. After two and a half years with the orchestra he decided to settle in New York. He obtained work in many areas of music, playing with a touring company of the show *Annie*, in symphony orchestras, in studio bands for films and records, and with jazz groups which ranged from traditional to the *avant garde*. Among these engagements, the most prestigious was a television date and two albums with **Benny Goodman**. During the 80s his reputation spread and he appeared at several festivals, making a great impression at the 1990 Nice Jazz Festival. He has also made records with singers such as **Mel Tormé**, **Peggy Lee** and **Rosemary Clooney** and jazzmen **Hank Jones**, **George Shearing**, **Dan Barrett**, **Scott Hamilton** and **Howard Alden**. By the late 80s he was a frequent visitor to the UK and continued to appear at festivals, also making club dates and records. A highly gifted clarinettist who plays alto and tenor saxophones too, Peplowski is strongly rooted in the mainstream. The quality of his playing is such that he is one of a small number of musicians who are helping restore the fortunes of the clarinet in jazz.

Albums: *Double Exposure* (Concord 1987), *Sonny Side* (Concord 1989), *Mr Gentle And Mr Cool* (Concord 1990), *Illuminations* (Concord 1990), *The Natural Touch* (Concord 1992), with Howard Alden *Concord Duo Series Vol. 3* (1993), *Steppin' With Peps* (Concord 1993).

Pepper, Art

b. 1 September 1925, Gardena, Los Angeles, California, USA, d. 1 June 1982. Pepper started out on clarinet at the age of nine, switching to alto saxophone four years later. After appearing in school groups, he first played professionally with **Gus Arnheim**'s band. During his mid-teens he developed his jazz style sitting in with otherwise all-black bands along Los Angeles's Central Avenue. After leaving Arnheim he worked with **Dexter Gordon** in **Lee Young**'s band at the Club Alabam. He then joined **Benny Carter**, playing alongside artists such as **Gerald Wilson**, **Freddie Webster** and **J.J. Johnson**. In 1943 Pepper joined **Stan Kenton** but soon afterwards was drafted into the US Army, spending most of his war-time service in England. In 1946 he rejoined Kenton, staying with the band until 1951. That year he also recorded with **Shorty Rogers**, playing a marvellous version of 'Over The Rainbow', a tune he would play often over the years. Later, he appeared on Rogers's *Cool And Crazy* album. Pepper subsequently freelanced around Los Angeles, making many record dates, some under his own name, and usually playing extremely well. Nevertheless, his career in the 50s and 60s was marred by his drug addiction and interrupted by several prison sentences. At the end of the 60s Pepper began a slow, uphill fight against his addiction, a struggle which was eventually successful and heralded his re-emergence in the mid-70s as a major figure on the international jazz scene. In the last years of his life, he produced a rich crop of recordings, including *Winter Moon*, an album with strings (a long-held ambition of Pepper's), the three-album set *Live At The Village Vanguard* (a fourth volume appeared posthumously) and two records recorded live in London under the name of pianist **Milcho Leviev**, *Blues For The Fisherman* and *True Blues*. Early in his career Pepper played with a light airy tone, through which burned a rare intensity of emotion that reflected his admiration for **Charlie Parker** and the lessons he learned playing with Carter. After his rehabilitation and a period playing tenor saxophone, on which instrument he showed both the influence of **Lester Young** and an awareness of **John Coltrane**, Pepper developed a strong, bop-rooted alto style which retained much of the richly melodic elements of his earlier playing. Pepper's life story was memorably recounted in his candid autobiography and a subsequent film, *Art Pepper: Notes From A Jazz Survivor* (1982), which offered a potent and harshly unsentimental lesson for any young musician contemplating the use of addictive drugs.

Selected albums: *Two Altos* (Savoy 1952-54 recordings), *Art Pepper Quartet* (1954), *Surf Ride* (Savoy 1954), *The Way It Was* (1956), with Chet Baker *The Route* (1956), with Baker *Playboys* (1957), *The Art Pepper Quintet* (1957), *The Artistry Of Pepper* (Pacific 1957), *Modern Art* (Blue Note 1957), *The Art Of Pepper* (Blue Note 1957), *Art Pepper Meets The Rhythm Section* (1957), *Art Pepper + Eleven* (1959), *Gettin' Together* (Original Jazz Classics 1960), *Smack Up!* (1962, rec. 1960), *The Way It Was* (Original Jazz Classics 1961), *Modern Jazz Classics* (Original Jazz Classics (1960), *Intensity* (Original Jazz Classics 1963, rec. 1960), *Live At Donte's Vol. 1* (1968), *The Omega Man* (1974, rec. 1968), *I'll Remember April* (Syoryville 1975), *Living Legend* (Original Jazz Classics 1976), *The Trip* (Original Jazz Classics 1977), *A Night In Tinisia* (Storyville 1977), *No Limit* (Original Jazz Classics 1978), *Among Friends* (1978), *Live In Japan* (1978), *Art Pepper Today* (1978), *Straight Life* (1979), *Landscape* (1980), *Omega Alpha* (1980, rec. 1957), *So Much In Love* (1980), *Live At The Village Vanguard* (1981, rec. 1977), *Winter Moon* (1981), *Besame Mucho* (1981, rec. 1979), *One September Afternoon* (1981), *Darn That Dream* (1982), *Road Game* (1982), *Goin' Home* (Original Jazz Classics 1982), *Art Lives* (1983, rec. 1981), *Art Works* (1984, rec. 1979), *More For Les: Live At The Village Vanguard, Volume 4* (1985, rec. 1977). Selected compilations: with Wayne Marsh *The Way It Was* (1972, rec. 1956-60), *Early Art* (1976, rec. 1956-57), *Artistry In Jazz* (JVC 1987), *The Art Of Pepper, Volumes 1 & 2* (1988), *The Complete Galaxy Recordings* (Galaxy 1989, 16-CD box set), *Memorial Collection Vols 1-4* (Storyville 1990), *The Best Of Art Pepper* (Blue Note 1993).

Further reading: *Straight Life: The Story Of Art Pepper*, Art and Laurie Pepper.

Pepsi And Shirlie

Former backing singers to **Wham!**, Lawrie 'Pepsi' Damacque (b. 10 December 1958, Paddington, London, England) and Shirlie Holliman (b. 18 April 1962, Watford, Hertfordshire, England) embarked on a solo career after that group's break-up in 1986. This connection was put to great use in the UK teenage magazine market where their pop/dance style appealed to suburban audiences. Signing to **Polydor Records**, the duo achieved two UK top 10 singles in 1987 with 'Heartache' (a number 2 hit) and 'Goodbye Stranger'. Later singles fared less well and *Change* was released over three years after their debut. Though it included one song **George Michael** had written for them, 'Someday', it seemed that Pepsi And Shirlie's following had moved on. The album failed to chart and no single success resulted. Their attempts to rehabilitate their image to that of rave club divas in 1993 fooled no-one.

Albums: *All Right Now* (Polydor 1987), *Change* (Polydor 1991), *Heartache* (1993).

Perchance To Dream

When this show opened at the London Hippodrome on 21 April 1945, it was conceived as **Ivor Novello**'s 'victory presentation'. As an antidote to the grimness of post-war Britain in the streets outside, Novello set out to recreate the kind of musical nostalgia with which he had been linked so successfully in the 30s. His story, which traced the lives of members of a family over several generations from Regency times to the present, was sumptuous and romantic. In much the same manner as before the war, Novello unerringly found a buried desire in the hearts of London's theatre-goers for the kind of musical that had never really been truly British. Owing more to Viennese operetta of an earlier century than it did to the current innovative American imported productions such as ***Oklahoma!*** and ***Carousel***, *Perchance To Dream* proved to be one of the composer's greatest successes. With several of his regular favourites in the cast, amongst them Olive Gilbert, Roma Beaumont and Muriel Barron, and songs like 'A Woman's Heart', 'This Is My Wedding Day', and especially 'Love Is My Reason' and 'We'll Gather Lilacs', Novello had yet another major success on his hands. The show ran for 1,022 performances.

Percy

This 1971 British film, directed by Ralph Thomas, starred Hywel Bennett as the recipient of a penis transplant. Intrigued as to who the donor was, he embarks on a series of adventures to try to find out. Elke Sommer and Britt Ekland also feature in the cast of this sex comedy, packed with *double entendre* and innuendo, typical of the *Carry On* and *Confessions of a...* genres. The formula wore thin long before the film's conclusion, but a sequel, *Percy's Progress*, followed in

1974. However, *Percy* did boast a fine soundtrack, courtesy of Ray Davies and his group, the **Kinks**. 'Lola', the 1970 UK number 2 hit which effectively relaunched their career, was one notable inclusion. The score also featured some of Davies' best work from this period, such as 'Willsden Green', a satirical C&W number, and the poignant 'God's Children'. The set was far superior to the film from which it was derived.

Pere Ubu

Formed in Cleveland, Ohio, USA in 1975, and taking their name from Alfred Jarry's surrealist play, Pere Ubu evolved from several of the region's experimental groups, including Rocket From The Tombs and Foggy And The Shrimps. Their initial line-up, comprising **David Thomas** (vocals), Peter Laughner (guitar), Tom Herman (guitar/bass/organ), Tim Wright (guitar/bass), Allen Ravenstine (synthesizer/saxophone) and Scott Kraus (drums) completed the compulsive '30 Seconds Over Tokyo', while a second single, 'Final Solution', was recorded following Ravenstine's departure. Wright and Laughner then left the fold, but new bassist Tony Maimone augmented the nucleus of Thomas, Herman and Kraus before the prodigal Ravenstine returned to complete the most innovative version of the group. Two more singles, 'Street Waves' and 'The Modern Dance', were released before the quintet secured an international recording deal. Their debut, *The Modern Dance*, was an exceptional collection, blending new-wave art-rock with early **Roxy Music**. Rhythmically, the group evoked **Captain Beefheart**'s Magic Band while Thomas's vocal gymnastics were both distinctive and compelling. Two further releases, *Dub Housing* and *New Picnic Time*, maintained this sense of adventure although the demonstrable power of that debut set was gradually becoming diffuse. Nonetheless, the three albums displayed a purpose and invention which deservedly received considerable critical approval.

In 1979 Tom Herman was replaced by former **Red Crayola** guitarist Mayo Thompson, who introduced a sculpted, measured approach to what had once seemed a propulsive, intuitive sound. *The Art Of Walking*, was deemed obtuse, and the group became pigeon-holed as both difficult and inconsequential. A dissatisfied Kraus left the line-up, and Anton Fier (ex-**Feelies**) joined Pere Ubu for the disappointing *Song Of The Bailing Man*. This lightweight selection appeared following the release of *The Sound Of The Sand*, David Thomas's first solo album, and reflected a general disinterest in the parent group's progress. Maimone then joined Kraus in Home And Garden, Herman surfaced with a new group, Tripod Jimmie, while Ravenstine and Thompson collaborated within a restructured Red Crayola. Thomas meanwhile enjoyed the highest profile with a further five albums.

By 1985 both Maimone and Ravenstine were working with the singer's new group, the Wooden Birds. Scott Kraus set the seeds of a Pere Ubu reunion by appearing for an encore during a Cleveland concert. 'It walked like a duck, looked like a duck, quacked like a duck, so it was a duck,' Thomas later remarked and by the end of 1987, the Ubu name had been officially re-instated. Jim Jones (guitar) and Chris Cutler (drums) completed the new line-up for the exceptional *Tenement Year*, which coupled the charm of earlier work with a newfound accessibility. *Cloudland* emphasized this enchanting direction although the group's age-old instability still threatened their long-term ambitions. Both Cutler and Ravenstine left the line-up. The latter was replaced by Eric Drew Feldman, formerly of Captain Beefheart.

Albums: *The Modern Dance* (1977), *Dub Housing* (1978), *Datapanik In The Year Zero* (1979), *New Picnic Time* (1979), *The Art Of Walking* (1980), *390 Degrees Of Simulated Stereo - Ubu Live: Volume 1* (1981), *Song Of The Bailing Man* (1982), *The Tenement Year* (1988), *One Man Drives While The Other Man Screams - Live Volume 2: Pere Ubu On Tour* (1989), *Cloudland* (1989), *Worlds In Collision* (1991), *The Story Of My Life* (1993). Compilation: *Terminal Tower* (1985).

Perez, Manuel

b. 28 December 1871, New Orleans, Louisiana, USA, d. 1946. One of the Crescent City's legendary figures, Perez was a respected cornet player, bandleader and teacher. He rarely played anywhere else, working in dancehalls and leading the Onward Brass Band in street parades. He made few trips outside his home town, playing in Chicago in 1915 and again in 1928. Fellow musicians thought highly of him, suggesting that his technique and command were at least on a par with his better-known contemporaries. By the 40s he was inactive through ill-health and died in 1946.

Perfect Disaster

Having tested the water as Orange Disaster, then the Architects Of Disaster, these calamitously-inclined types finally settled on the Perfect Disaster in 1984 as the original rhythm section departed to form **Fields Of The Nephilim**. The initial UK-based line-up consisted of Phil Parfitt, Allison Pates, John Saltwell and Malcolm Catto, although personnel changes were to plague the band's career. Ignored by the British music scene, the Perfect Disaster took their twisted, broody guitar sound to France for their self-titled debut album in 1985. There followed a couple of years of blank struggle on both sides of the English Channel before the band signed to **Fire** Records at home and released the critically-acclaimed *Asylum Road*. Prior to this, Saltwell and Pates both left, disillusioned, to be replaced by bassist Josephine Wiggs (b. Josephine Miranda Cordelia Susan Wiggs, 26 February 1965, Letchworth, Hertfordshire, England) and long-term

guitarist Dan Cross. 1989 suggested that better prospects lurked over the horizon: the *Up* album, which stretched splendidly from fiery two-chord blasts to near-suicidal ramblings, coincided with prestigious live shows with the likes of the **Jesus And Mary Chain**. And the band's initial inspiration, based upon singer Parfitt's spell working at a Victorian mental institution, looked set to reap rewards. The public, alas, didn't share the critics' enthusiasm for the band. Wiggs left in 1990 to spend more time on the **Breeders**, a side project which also involved Tanya Donelly from **Throwing Muses** and Kim Deal of the **Pixies**, allowing John Saltwell to return on bass. The *Heaven Scent* album continued the Perfect Disaster's foray into the darker side of alternative music, but rumours of the band's demise, which persisted throughout 1991, were finally confirmed. Parfitt would go on to write alongside Jason Pierce (**Spiritualized**) before forming Oedipussy.
Albums: *The Perfect Disaster* (Kampa 1985), *Asylum Road* (Fire 1988), *Up* (Fire 1989), *Heaven Scent* (Fire 1990).

Perfect Jazz Repetory Quintet
(see **Hyman, Dick**)

Perfect, Christine
(see **McVie, Christine**)

Performance
One of the most beguiling rock-related films, *Performance* allowed **Mick Jagger** to exorcise the ghost of the hapless ***Ned Kelly*** and play a role suited to his complex persona. Directed by Nicolas Roeg and Donald Cammell - the latter of whom also wrote the screenplay - *Performance* features James Fox as a vicious gangster who takes refuge in Jagger's flat. The **Rolling Stones** vocalist plays the failing pop star to perfection and his decaying, bohemian lifestyle at first repulses, then absorbs, Fox. Their identities become intertwined and although Fox is latterly taken away by mobster enemies, it is Jagger's face which peers out from the rear window of the car. **Randy Newman** took charge of the soundtrack music, contributing his own memorable 'Gone Dead Train' and assembling work from such disparate acts as **Ry Cooder**, **Merry Clayton** and the **Last Poets**. Meanwhile, Jagger's own contribution, 'Memo From Turner', was an explosive song which accompanied one of the film's most powerful segments. In the first inkling of alter egos, Jagger repulsively imagines himself crime boss. Released in 1970, *Performance* is a dense, impressive film which bears - and is enhanced - by repeated viewings.

Pericoli, Emilio
b. 1928, Cesenatico, Italy. This sailor's son was a member of an amateur dramatic society while a trainee accountant in Milan. It was after he had taken the plunge as a professional thespian that he found himself, microphone in hand, one frolicsome 1960 evening in a local nightclub. From this casual beginning, he decided to concentrate on singing, and eventually won a contract with Ricordi Records. The vehicle that was to project Pericoli's vocal talent most commercially was 'Al Di La' which, performed by Betty Curtis, had won 1961's San Remo Song Festival for composers Guilio Rapetti and Carlo Donida. Though Pericoli's cover - one of many - garnered modest domestic sales, it was a more palpable hit in Latin America. Furthermore, after it was re-recorded with an English lyric (by Ervin Drake) for 1962's *Rome Adventure* film soundtrack, it was used again in *Lover's Must Learn* with Pericoli in handsome cameo. This exposure elicited airplay which pushed 'Al Di La' to number 6 in the USA and into Britain's Top 30. He had no further hits in English-speaking territories but Pericoli was still able to rely on 'Al Di La' as leverage to gain a New York cabaret season in 1965 as a brief tangent to a career as a television actor.

Perkins, Bill
b. 22 July 1924, San Francisco, California, USA. Having started out on a career as an electrical engineer, tenor saxophonist Perkins was in his mid-20s before he made an appearance in Jerry Wald's band in 1950. The following year he was with **Woody Herman**'s Third Herd and by 1953 was in **Stan Kenton**'s band. The rest of the 50s were spent alternating between Herman and Kenton during which time his reputation as a subtly inventive soloist grew steadily. His playing at this time was derived from **Lester Young** by way of **Stan Getz**, although he was also influenced by **Richie Kamuca**, who was with him in both the Herman and Kenton bands. His light, relaxed style made him a natural for the currently active west coast school of music. In 1956 he recorded with **John Lewis**, Richie Kamuca, **Art Pepper** and others and in 1959 was on Pepper's highly successful *Plus Eleven*. In the 60s he chose to turn his back on life on the road, taking a job with Pacific Jazz Records, but was active in the studios and playing occasional jazz gigs, a pattern which continued into the 70s. By the 80s he was touring widely, and appeared in the UK where he showed that he had lost none of his earlier inventiveness. A relaxed style and an elegant, dry-toned sound characterize his playing.
Selected albums: *The Woody Herman Band!* (1954), *Stan Kenton Plays The Music Of Bill Russo And Bill Holman* (1954), *Grand Encounter* (1956), *Bill Perkins At The Music Box Theatre* (1956), *Tenors Head-On* (1956), with John Lewis *2 Degrees East, 3 Degrees West* (1956), with Richie Kamuca, Art Pepper *Just Friends* (1956), *Bill Perkins With Strings* (1963), *Quietly There* (Original Jazz Classics 1967), *Bill Perkins Plays Lester Young* (1978), *Confluence* (1978), with Pepper Adams *Front Line* (Storyville 1979), *Many*

Ways To Go (1980), *Journey To The East* (1984), *Remembrance Of Dino's* (Interplay 1986), *The Right Chemistry* (Jazz Mark 1988), *Our Man Woody* (1991), *I Wished On The Moon* (Candid (1991), with Kamucha *Tenors Head On* (Pacific 1992), with Frank Strazzeri *Warm Moods* (Fresh Sounds 1993).

Perkins, Carl (jazz)

b. 16 August 1928, Indianapolis, Indiana, USA, d. 17 March 1958. Perkins was a self-taught pianist who, after playing in R&B bands, including those led by **Tiny Bradshaw** and **Big Jay McNeely**, settled in California in the late 40s. At this time he changed his musical direction, working in the 50s in jazz mainstream with **Illinois Jacquet** and **Oscar Moore** and in bebop with **Miles Davis**. In the mid-50s he became one of the most active figures on the west coast scene, playing and recording extensively with artists such as **Wardell Gray**, **Dexter Gordon**, **Jim Hall**, **Pepper Adams**, **Mel Lewis**, **Jack Sheldon** and **Art Pepper**. He was also a member, briefly, of the **Max Roach-Clifford Brown** group and of the **Curtis Counce** group. Although physically impaired through contracting polio as a child, Perkins developed a strong sound and his style showed him to be an endlessly inventive musician. As a rhythm section member he made a substantial contribution to jazz in the 50s, playing on many classic west coast albums. Unfortunately, his personal life was a mess and narcotics addiction brought about his early death in 1958.

Album: *Introducing Carl Perkins* (Boplicity 1955).

Perkins, Carl (rock 'n' roll)

b. Carl Lee Perkins, 9 April 1932, Ridgely, Tennessee, USA (his birth certificate misspelled the last name as Perkings). Carl Perkins was one of the most renowned rockabilly artists recording for **Sun Records** in the 50s and the author of the classic song 'Blue Suede Shoes'. As a guitarist, he influenced many of the next generation of rock 'n' rollers, most prominently **George Harrison** and **Dave Edmunds**. His parents, Fonie 'Buck' and Louise Brantley Perkins, were share-croppers during the 30s Depression and the family was thus very poor. As a child Perkins listened to the ***Grand Ole Opry*** on the radio, exposing him to C&W (or hillbilly) music, and he listened to the blues being sung by a black sharecropper named John Westbrook across the field from where he worked. After World War II the Perkins family relocated to Bemis, Tennessee, where he and his brothers picked cotton; by that time his father was unable to work due to a lung illness. Having taught himself rudimentary guitar from listening to such players as Butterball Page and **Arthur Smith**, Perkins bought an electric guitar and learned to play it more competently. In 1953 Carl, his brothers Jay (rhythm guitar) and Clayton (upright bass), and drummer W.S. 'Fluke' Holland formed a band that worked up a repertoire of hillbilly songs performing at local honky-tonks, primarily in the Jackson, Tennessee area, where Carl moved with his recent wife Valda Crider in 1954.

Borrowing some of his technique from the black musicians he had studied set Carl Perkins apart from the many other country guitarists in that region at that time; his style of playing lead guitar fills around his own vocals was similar to that used in the blues. Encouraged by his wife, and by hearing a record by **Elvis Presley** on the radio, Perkins decided in 1954 to pursue a musical career. That October the Perkins brothers travelled to Memphis to audition for **Sam Phillips** at **Sun Records**. Phillips was not overly impressed, but agreed the group had potential. In February 1955 he issued two songs from that first Perkins session, 'Movie Magg' and 'Turn Around', on his new Flip label. Pure country in nature, these did not make a dent in the market. Perkins' next single was issued in August, this time on Sun itself. One track, 'Let The Jukebox Keep On Playing', was again country, but the other song, 'Gone! Gone! Gone!' was pure rockabilly. Again, it was not a hit. That November, after Phillips sold Presley's Sun contract to **RCA Records**, Phillips decided to push the next Perkins single, an original called 'Blue Suede Shoes'. The song had its origins when **Johnny Cash**, another Sun artist, suggested to Perkins that he write a song based on the phrase 'Don't step on my blue suede shoes'. It was recorded at Sun on 19 December 1955, along with three other songs, among them the b-side 'Honey Don't', later to be covered by the **Beatles**. 'Blue Suede Shoes' entered the US ***Billboard*** chart on 3 March 1956 (the same day Presley's first single entered the chart), by which time several cover versions had been recorded, by a range of artists from Presley to **Lawrence Welk**. Perkins' version quickly became a huge hit and was also the first country record to appear on both the R&B chart and the pop chart, in addition to the country chart.

Just as Perkins was beginning to enjoy the fruits of his labour, the car in which he and his band were driving to New York was involved in a severe accident near Dover, Delaware, when their manager, Stuart Pinkham, fell asleep at the wheel. Perkins and his brother Clayton suffered broken bones; brother Jay suffered a fractured neck; and the driver of the truck they hit, Thomas Phillips, was killed. 'Blue Suede Shoes' ultimately reached number 2 on the pop chart, a number 1 country hit and an R&B number 2. Owing to the accident, Perkins was unable to promote the record, the momentum was lost, and none of his four future chart singles would climb nearly as high. In the UK, 'Blue Suede Shoes' became Perkins' only chart single, and was upstaged commercially by the Presley cover. Perkins continued to record for Sun until mid-1958, but the label's newcomers, Johnny Cash and

Jerry Lee Lewis, occupied most of Sam Phillips' attention. Perkins' follow-up to 'Blue Suede Shoes', 'Boppin' The Blues', only reached number 70, and 'Your True Love' number 67. While still at Sun, Perkins did record numerous tracks that would later be revered by rockabilly fans, among them 'Everybody's Trying To Be My Baby' and 'Matchbox', both of which were also covered by the Beatles. On 4 December 1956, Perkins was joined by Lewis and a visiting Presley at Sun in an impromptu jam session which was recorded and released two decades later under the title 'The Million Dollar Quartet'. (Johnny Cash, despite having his photograph taken with Presley, Lewis and Carl, did not take part in the 'million dollar session' - he went shopping instead.) One of Perkins' last acts while at Sun was to appear in the film *Jamboree*, singing a song called 'Glad All Over'. In January 1958, Perkins signed with **Columbia Records**, where Cash would soon follow. Although some of the songs he recorded for that label were very good, only two, 'Pink Pedal Pushers' and 'Pointed Toe Shoes', both obvious attempts to recapture the success of his first footwear-oriented hit, had a minor impression on the charts. Later that year Jay Perkins died of a brain tumour, causing Carl to turn alcoholic, an affliction from which he would not recover until the late 60s.

In 1963 Perkins signed with **Decca Records**, for which there would be no successful releases. He also toured outside of the USA in 1963-64; while in Britain he met the Beatles, and watched as they recorded his songs. Perkins, who, ironically, was becoming something of a legend in Europe (as were many early rockers), returned to England for a second tour in October 1964. By 1966 he had left Decca for the small Dollie Records, a country label. In 1967 he joined Johnny Cash's band as guitarist and was allotted a guest singing spot during each of Cash's concerts and television shows. In 1969, Cash recorded Perkins' song 'Daddy Sang Bass', a minor hit in the USA. By 1970, Perkins was back on Columbia, this time recording an album together with new rock revival group **NRBQ**. In 1974 he signed with **Mercury Records**. Late that year his brother Clayton committed suicide and their father died. Perkins left Cash in 1976 and went on the road with a band consisting of Perkins' two sons, with whom he was still performing in the 90s. A tribute single to the late Presley, 'The EP Express', came in 1977 and a new album, now for the Jet label, was released in 1978. By the 80s Perkins' reputation as one of rock's pioneers had grown. He recorded an album with Cash and Lewis, *The Survivors* (another similar project, with Cash, Lewis and **Roy Orbison**, *The Class Of '55*, followed in 1986). Perkins spent much of the 80s touring and working with younger musicians who were influenced by him, among them **Paul McCartney** and the **Stray Cats**. In 1985 he starred in a television special to mark the 30th anniversary of 'Blue Suede Shoes'. It co-starred Harrison, **Ringo Starr**, Dave Edmunds, two members of the Stray Cats, **Rosanne Cash** and **Eric Clapton**. In 1987 Perkins was elected to the Rock And Roll Hall of Fame. He signed to the Universal label in 1989 and released *Born To Rock*. His early work has been anthologized many times in several countries.

Selected albums: *The Dance Album Of Carl Perkins* (1957), *Whole Lotta Shakin'* (1958), *Teen Beat/The Best Of Carl Perkins* (1961), *Country Boy Dreams* (1968), *Greatest Hits* (1969), *Blue Suede Shoes* (1969), *On Top* (1969), with the NRBQ *Boppin' The Blues* (1970), *My Kind Of Country* (1974), *Carl Perkins Show* (1976), *From Jackson, Tennessee* (1977), *Ol' Blue Suede's Back* (1978), with Jerry Lee Lewis, Johnny Cash *The Survivors* (1982), *The Sun Years* (1982), *The Class Of '55* (1986), *Up Through The Years, 1954-1957* (1986), *Original Sun Greatest Hits* (1986), *The Heart And Soul Of Carl Perkins* (1987), *Honky Tonk Gal: Rare And Unissued Sun Masters* (1989), *The Classic Carl Perkins* (1990, box-set), *Born To Rock* (1990), *Friends, Family & Legends* (1992), *Restless* (1993), with Scotty Moore *706 Reunion-A Sentimental Journey* (1993).

Videos: *Rockabilly Session* (1986), *Carl Perkins & Jerry Lee Lewis Live* (1987), *This Country's Rockin'* (1993).

Further reading: *Discipline In Blue Suede Shoes*, Carl Perkins.

Film: *Jamboree* aka *Disc Jockey Jamboree* (1957).

Perkins, Pinetop

b. Joe Willie Perkins, 7 July 1913, Belzoni, Mississippi, USA. A barrelhouse blues pianist from before his teens, Perkins travelled through Mississippi and Arkansas, and north to St Louis and Chicago, playing piano, and sometimes guitar, behind **Big Joe Williams**, **Robert Nighthawk, John Lee 'Sonny Boy' Williamson** and others. He recorded for **Sun Records** in 1953, although only 'Pinetop's Boogie Woogie' was issued, many years later. He also accompanied **Earl Hooker** and **Boyd Gilmore** on Sun, and Nighthawk on Aristocrat. From the early 60s, he settled in Chicago. In 1969, Perkins replaced **Otis Spann** in the **Muddy Waters** Band, with which he toured up to and after the leader's death, also working as a solo act.

Selected albums: *Chicago Boogie Blues Piano Man* (c.1986), *Chicago Blues Session, Volume 12* (1989), *Boogie Woogie King* (1986), *The Ultimate Sun Blues Collection* (1991), *With Chicago Beau And The Blue Ice Band* (1992).

Perrson, Bent

b. 6 September 1947, Blekinge, Sweden. Perrson's powerful trumpet and cornet playing made him the star of Swedish bands like Maggie's Blue Five and Bent's Blue Rhythm Band throughout the 70s. During this time he was recording a four volume set of **Louis Armstrong**'s *Fifty Hot Choruses* which had been transcribed from cylinder recordings now lost, but

published by the Melrose Brothers in 1927. These accurate sounding recordings add significantly to what is available of Armstrong's early playing. In the 80s Perrson continued to perform in the re-creative style he favours. He has formed the Weatherbird Jazzband, worked with Tomas Ornberg (reeds) and recorded with vocalist **Maxine Sullivan**.
Album: *Louis Armstrong's Fifty Hot Choruses For Cornet As Re-created By Bent Perrson, Vols 1-4* (1974-79).

Perry, Joe, Project

b. 10 September 1950, Boston, Massachusetts, USA. Having severed an apprenticeship in the aspiring Jam Band, guitarist Perry then became a founder member of **Aerosmith**. This durable hard rock act became one of USA's leading attractions during the 70s, principally through the artist's exciting, riffing style and vocalist Steve Tyler's charismatic performances. Tension between the group's leading figures led to the former's departure in 1979. He subsequently formed the Joe Perry Project with Ralph Mormon (vocals), David Hull (bass) and Ronnie Stewart (drums) but neither *Let The Music Do The Talking* nor *I've Got The Rocks 'N' Rolls Again*, which featured new singer Charlie Farren, captured the fire of the guitarist's previous group. Perry then established a new line-up around Mach Bell (vocals), Danny Hargrove (bass) and Joe Pet (drums) for *Once A Rocker, Always A Rocker*, but once again the combination failed to generate commercial approbation. Former Aerosmith colleague Brad Whitford (guitar) was then added to the group, but it was disbanded in 1984 when a full-scale reunion of Aerosmith was undertaken. The ensuing *Done With Mirrors* featured the title-song of the Project's debut album, but Aerosmith's successful rebirth brought Perry's external aspirations to a premature close.
Albums: *Let The Music Do The Talking* (CBS 1980), *I've Got The Rocks 'N' Rolls Again* (CBS 1981), *Once A Rocker, Always A Rocker* (MCA 1984).

Perry, Lee

b. Rainford Hugh Perry, 28 March 1936, Hanover, Jamaica, West Indies, aka Scratch and the Upsetter. Small in stature, but larger than life, 'Little' Lee Perry began his musical career working for seminal producer **Coxsone Dodd** during the late 50s and early 60s acting as a record scout, organising recording sessions, and later supervising auditions at Dodd's record shop in Orange Street, Kingston. By 1963, as well as handling production and songwriting for **Delroy Wilson** ('Joe Liges', 'Spit In The Sky') and the **Maytals**, Perry had released the first of his own vocal records through Dodd. Featuring a bluesy, declamatory vocal style over superb backing from the legendary **Skatalites**, these tracks set a pattern from which Perry, throughout his career, would rarely deviate. Social and personal justice, bawdy, sometimes lewd sexual commentary, and, like the material he wrote for Delroy Wilson, stinging attacks on musical rivals - mainly former Coxsone employee **Prince Buster** - are all prefigured on these early tracks like 'Prince In The Pack', 'Trial And Crosses', 'Help The Weak', 'Give Me Justice', 'Chicken Scratch' (from which he acquired his nickname), 'Doctor Dick' with **Rita Marley** and the Soulettes on backing vocals, and 'Madhead', recorded between 1963 and 1966. Incidentally, there were obviously no hard feelings involved between Buster and Perry, as the latter often appeared on Buster's records, including 'Ghost Dance' and 'Judge Dread'. Also during his sojourn with Dodd he began an association with the **Wailers** that had further repercussions later in the decade.
In 1966 Perry fell out with Coxsone and began working with other producers including JJ Johnson, **Clancy Eccles** and, in 1968, **Joe Gibbs**, for whom he wrote songs and produced artists like **Errol Dunkley**, and the **Pioneers**. With Gibbs, he also voiced a bitter snipe directed at Dodd entitled 'The Upsetter' from which he gained his next apt epithet. On parting with Gibbs, Perry recorded several fine titles, including the big local hit, 'People Funny Boy' (1968), a vicious record, featuring a chugging rhythm in the new reggae style given to him by Clancy Eccles, wherein Perry took his former employer to task for allegedly ignoring his role in Gibbs' success, the slight made all the more pointed by employing the melody he had used for the **Pioneers**' hit 'Longshot'. 1968 also saw the setting up of his own Upsetter label in Jamaica, again with help from Clancy Eccles. Right away he began having hits with David Isaacs ('Place In The Sun') and the Untouchables ('Tighten Up', which lent its title to the classic series of early 70s reggae compilations on **Trojan Records**), and, in common with other early reggae producers, secured a deal with Trojan whereby his records were released under his imprint in the UK.
Perry experienced his first taste of UK chart success with tenor saxophonist Val Bennett's spaghetti western-inspired title, 'Return Of Django', which spent three weeks at number 5 in the UK charts during October 1969. At the same time he began producing the Wailers on a series of records including 'Small Axe', 'Duppy Conqueror', and 'Soul Rebel', mostly available on a number of recent compilations, which are now considered to be among that group's finest work. Just over 100 singles were released on Upsetter between 1969 and 1974 by artists such as Dave Barker (**Dave And Ansell Collins**) ('Shocks Of Mighty', 'Upsetting Station'), **Dennis Alcapone** ('Alpha & Omega'), the Stingers ('Give Me Power'), the Bleechers ('Come Into My Parlour', 'Check Him Out'), Neville Hinds ('Blackmans Time'), Leo Graham ('Newsflash'), **Big Youth** ('Mooving (sic) Version'), and the legendary **Junior Byles** ('Beat Down Babylon', 'Place Called Africa'). He also unleashed a welter of intense,

energetic, and just plain barmy instrumentals: 'Night Doctor', 'Live Injection', 'Cold Sweat', 'Django Shoots First', 'The Vampire' and 'Drugs & Poison'. Other productions such as 'Selassie' by the Reggae Boys, the instrumentals 'Dry Acid', 'Return Of The Ugly', 'Clint Eastwood', and many more, appeared on other B&C and **Pama** labels.

From 1972-74 Perry slowed the rhythm down and consolidated his position as one of the leading innovators in Jamaican music. He released instrumentals like 'French Connection', 'Black Ipa', and DJ tracks by artists such as **U-Roy** (who had cut two of his earliest records 'Earths Rightful Ruler' and the demented 'OK Corral' for Perry in the late 60s), **Dillinger**, **Dr. Alimantado**, **I Roy** and Charlie Ace (on the unique and bizarre cut-and-mix extravaganza, 'Cow Thief Skak'). Perry was also one of the first producers to utilise the talents of **King Tubby**, then just starting his own operations, and released important early dub albums like *Rhythm Shower* (1972) and the glorious *Blackboard Jungle Dub* (1973). Perry's productions from this period: the Gatherers' monolithic 'Words Of My Mouth', Milton Henry's 'This World' - whose rhythm also served Junior Byles' reading of **Little Willie John**'s 'Fever' and **Augustus Pablo**'s melodic workout 'Hot & Cold', Perry's own 'Jungle Lion', the Classics' 'Civilisation', and many others, are amongst the heaviest and most exciting reggae records of their day.

In 1974 Perry opened his own studio, dubbed the Black Ark, situated in his back yard at Washington Gardens, Kingston. Almost immediately he scored a big Jamaican hit with Junior Byles' hugely influential 'Curly Locks'. In 1975 his production of Susan Cadogan's seminal **lovers rock** tune 'Hurt So Good' reached number 4 in the UK charts. He also released the overlooked but innovative dub album *Revolution Dub* (1975), featuring some of his heaviest contemporary productions like Bunny And Rickey's 'Bushweed Corntrash', Junior Byles' 'The Long Way', and Jimmy Riley's 'Womans Gotta Have It', all garnished with Scratch's crazy sing-along rhymes and bursts of dialogue 'sampled' off the Perry TV. From 1975 he began to employ studio technology, notably phase shifters and rudimentary drum machines, to produce a dense, multi-layered mixing style that is instantly recognizable, and eminently inimitable. It is all the more remarkable for the fact that all this was achieved in a four-track studio. By 1976 **Island Records** had begun to release the fruits of this latest phase, including music by the **Heptones** (*Party Time*), **Max Romeo** (*War Inna Babylon*), **Bob Marley** And The Wailers ('Jah Live', 'Punky Reggae Party'), George Faith (*To Be A Lover*), **Junior Murvin** (*Police & Thieves*, the single of the same title being very popular in Jamaica at the time, and becoming a belated chart hit in the UK in May 1980), **Prince Jazzbo** (*Natty Passing Through*, released on Black Wax), and the **Upsetters** (the classic *Super Ape*). However, Island rejected his own vocal album *Roast Fish, Collie Weed & Corn Bread* (1978), and missed out on the **Congos** classic, *Heart Of The Congos*, which finally gained a UK release some years later on the **Beat**'s Go Feet label.

With commercial success now coming infrequently the frustrations and personal problems began to build. He was still making wonderful records; 'Mr Money Man' by Danny Hensworth, 'Open The Gate' by Watty Burnett, 'Garden Of Life' by Leroy Sibbles, and many others, but his style was now so far removed from the reggae mainstream that they met with little success in Jamaica or abroad. Perry's behaviour became increasingly strange and bewildering, and in 1980 he destroyed his studio and left for Britain, where he conducted a number of puzzling interviews that seemed to add credence to reports of his mental decline. Since then he has made a long series of eccentric, often self-indulgent solo albums with a variety of different collaborators including **Adrian Sherwood**, **Lloyd Barnes**, and Neil 'Mad Professor' Fraser (see **Ariwa Sounds**), totally outside the mainstream of Jamaican music. Simultaneously, his earlier work began to receive significant critical and cult attention as well as commanding high prices in the collectors market. After living in the Netherlands in the mid-80s he moved back to London, occasionally performing live. In 1990 he went to Switzerland, worked with a new management team, and reputedly married a Swiss millionairess. He also returned to Jamaica with the intention of rebuilding the trashed and burnt out Black Ark, though sadly this plan does not seem to have come to fruition so far. Whatever the future holds, Lee 'Scratch' Perry, the Upsetter, the man Bob Marley once described as a 'genius', has already made one of the most individual contributions to the development of Jamaican music, whether as producer/arranger/writer, or simply as a singularly powerful guiding force during several crucial phases.

Selected albums: As Lee Perry/Lee Perry And The Upsetters: *The Upsetter* (Trojan 1969), *Many Moods Of The Upsetter* (1970), *Scratch The Upsetter Again* (1970), *Africa's Blood* (1972), *Battle Axe* (1972), *Cloak & Dagger* (Rhino 1972), *Double Seven* (Trojan 1973), *Rhythm Shower* (Upsetter 1973), *Blackboard Jungle* (Upsetter 1974), *Kung Fu Meets The Dragon* (D.I.P. 1974), *D.I.P. Presents The Upsetter* (D.I.P. 1974), *Revolution Dub* (Cactus 1975), *The Super Ape* (Mango/Island 1976), *Return Of The Super Ape* (Lion Of Judah/Mango 1977), *Roast Fish, Collie Weed & Corn Bread* (Lion Of Judah 1978), *Scratch On The Wire* (Island 1979), *Scratch And Company: Chapter 1* (Clocktower 1980), *Return Of Pipecock Jackson* (Black Star 1981), *Mystic Miracle Star* (Heartbeat 1982), *History Mystery & Prophecy* (Mango/Island 1984), *Black Ark Vol. 1 & 2* (Black Ark 1984), *Black Ark In Dub* (Black Ark 1985), *Battle Of Armagideon: Millionaire Liquidator* (Trojan 1986), *Satan*

Kicked The Bucket (Wackies 1988), *Scratch Attack* (RAS 1988, CD only), *Chicken Scratch* (Heartbeat 1989), *Turn And Fire* (Anachron 1989), *Build The Ark* (Trojan 1990, triple album), *From The Secret Laboratory* (Mango/Island 1990), *Message From Yard* (Rohit 1990), *Blood Vapour* (La/Unicorn 1990), *Spiritual Healing* (Black Cat 1991), *God Muzick* (Network/Kook Kat 1991), *The Upsetter And The Beat* (Heartbeat 1992), *Soundz From The Hot Line* (Heartbeat 1993). With Dave Barker: *Prisoner Of Love: Dave Barker Meets The Upsetters* (Trojan 1970). With Dub Syndicate: *Time Boom X De Devil Dead* (On-U-Sound 1987), *Magnetic Mirror Master Mix* (Anachron 1990). With Prince Jazzbo: *Natty Passing Through* (Black Wax 1976) aka *Ital Corner* (Clocktower 1980). With Bullwackie: *Lee 'Scratch' Perry Meets Bullwackie - Satan's Dub* (ROIR 1990). With Mad Professor: *Lee Scratch Perry Meets The Mad Professor, Volumes 1 & 2* (Ariwa 1990), *Lee 'Scratch' Perry Meets The Mad Professor In Dub, Volumes 1 & 2* (Angella 1991). Compilations: *The Upsetter Collection* (Trojan 1981), *Reggae Greats* (Island 1984), *Best Of* (Pama 1984), *The Upsetter Box Set* (Trojan 1985), *Some Of The Best* (Heartbeat 1986), *The Upsetter Compact Set* (1988), *All The Hits* (Rohit 1989). With Jah Lion: *Colombia Colly* (Mango/Island 1976 - production only). As Lee Perry And Friends: Compilations: *Give Me Power* (Trojan 1988, early 70s recordings), *Open The Gate* (Trojan 1989, triple set, 70s recordings), *Shocks Of Mighty 1969-1974* (Attack 1989), *Public Jestering* (Attack 1990). As the Upsetters: *Version Like Rain* (Trojan 1990). Various: *Heart Of The Ark, Volume 1* (Seven Leaves 1982), *Heart Of The Ark, Volume 2* (Seven Leaves 1983), *Turn & Fire: Upsetter Disco Dub* (1989), *Megaton Dub* (Seven Leaves 1983), *Megaton Dub 2* (Seven Leaves 1983). Important productions: Bob Marley And The Wailers: *Soul Revolution 1 & 2* (Trojan 1988, double album).
Video: *The Ultimate Destruction* (1992).

Perry, Mark

One of the first to spot the oncoming onslaught of UK punk, Mark Perry (b. c.1957, London, England) was a bank clerk who, inspired by the **Ramones**, started the *Sniffin' Glue (And Other Rock 'N' Roll Habits)* fanzine in mid-1976. After leaving his job and shortening his name to Mark P., he and south London pals like Danny Baker became the unofficial media messiahs of punk rock. *Sniffin' Glue* only lasted until August 1977 but by that time Perry was working on several labels and his new band, with Alex Ferguson; **Alternative TV** (signifying Alternative *to* TV). He had previously played in a trio called the New Beatles with Steve Walsh and Tyrone Thomas. Perry soon adapted the new band's name to ATV as everyone was either mispronouncing or misspelling it anyway. Their first release was a flexi on the Sniffin' Glue label. This was later reissued on Deptford Fun City, a label set up by Perry (in conjunction with Miles Copeland). ATV released several albums on DFC before becoming the Good Missionaries in 1979. After one album, *Fire From Heaven*, Perry left and recorded as the Reflection, the Door And The Window, and as a solo artist. There were just two 1980 singles credited to him but he also cropped up on various compilations. ATV reformed in 1981 for *Strange Kicks* only to break up again. Perry's album, *Snappy Turns*, also appeared in that year. ATV reformed for a second time in 1984, initially for a gig at the Euston Tavern in Kings Cross and this reformation lasted about a year. They split up just long enough to give themselves time to reform again and stayed together until 1987. More recently Perry has been involved in a band called Baby Ice Dog.
Album: *Snappy Turns* (Deptford Fun City 1981).

Perry, Oliver 'King'

b. 1920, Gary, Indiana, USA. Starting with the violin, Perry learned a variety of instruments in his youth, including bass, trumpet, drums, piano, and clarinet, before the alto saxophone after seeing **Johnny Hodges** with **Duke Ellington**'s Orchestra. Perry ended up in Los Angeles, in 1945, after a tour with his small band and stayed, recording for Melodisc Records in July of that year. They went on to have records released on Excelsior/United Artists (not the well-known label from recent years) - finding success on the R&B charts with his 'Keep A Dollar In Your Pocket' which was covered by **Roy Milton**. He also recorded for DeLuxe, Specialty (with whom he had his only other substantial hit, 'Blue And Lonesome'), **Dot**, RPM, Lucky, Hollywood, Trilyte, Look and Unique through to the late 50s. He turned to selling real estate when work was scarce, but returned to music in 1967 and resumed his recording career on Accent in 1975. He continues to perform around the Bakersfield area and runs his own record company (Octive) and publishing company (Royal Attractions).
Selected album: *King Perry* (1986).

Perry, Ray

Born in Lancashire, England, this writer and solo folk performer began drawing on traditional and 60s/70s songwriting influences after being a member of several failed rock bands. Increasingly prolific, his main release, *Common Knowledge* (Crow), amply displays his impressive ability.
Album: *Common Knowledge.*

Perry, Richard

b 18 June 1942, Brooklyn, New York City, New York, USA. His work with artists ranging from **Barbra Streisand** and **Carly Simon** to **Tiny Tim** and **Captain Beefheart** made Perry the 'name' producer of the 70s. As a teenager he sang with New York group the Legends whose members included **Goldie** Zelkowicz (aka **Genya Ravan**). He began songwriting with Kenny Vance and produced singles for the Kama

Sutra and Red Bird labels. In 1967 Perry moved to Los Angeles, producing the debut album of **Captain Beefheart** And The Magic Band before joining **Warner Brothers** as a staff producer. In two years with the label, Perry displayed his versatility by supervising recordings by Tiny Tim, **Ella Fitzgerald**, actor **Theodore Bikel** and all-female rock group, **Fanny**. Next, he undertook the project which catapulted him into the forefront of US producers. **Columbia Records** wished to bring Broadway musical star Barbra Streisand to a mass audience and Perry chose a selection of contemporary material for the *Stoney End* album. The title track became a US Top 10 hit. Harry **Nilsson**, Carly Simon ('You're So Vain'), **Ringo Starr**, **Leo Sayer** and **Diana Ross** were among the other artists he worked with before setting up his own label, Planet, in 1978. Its most successful signing was the **Pointer Sisters**, who recorded six albums for the label before moving to **RCA** in 1986. Perry's later work included *Rock, Rhythm And Blues* (1989), a various artists album including contributions from **Chaka Khan**, the Pointer Sisters and **Rick James**.

Perry, Steve

Following the success of *Escape* and *Frontiers*, the members of US band **Journey** took an extended break in order to pursue solo projects. Vocalist Steve Perry (b. 22 January 1953, Hanford, California, USA) put together a team of respected session players to produce *Street Talk*, which displayed soul and R&B influences in both Perry's vocals and songwriting, and proved a superb showcase for his talents. *Street Talk* proved to be the most successful of the Journey solo efforts, producing an enormous US hit in 'Oh Sherrie', an emotive tribute to Perry's girlfriend, and its influence on the style of *Raised On Radio*, Journey's final album, was obvious. However, amid rumours of up to three follow-up records being scrapped, it was not until 1994 that *For The Love Of Strange Medicine* saw the resumption of Perry's career, with a more straightforward AOR style than on the previous album. Any doubts over the viability of the project after such a protracted absence were dispelled when the album made its US chart debut at number 15, and produced a US Top 10 hit with 'You Better Wait'.

Albums: *Street Talk* (Columbia 1984), *For The Love Of Strange Medicine* (Columbia 1994).

Perryman, Lloyd

b. Lloyd Wilson Perryman, 29 January 1917, Ruth, Arkansas, USA, d. 31 May 1977. An important member of the **Sons Of The Pioneers**. The family relocated to California in 1928, where Perryman learned to play guitar and showed his first interest in music during his high school years. He first appeared on radio on KERN Bakersfield but in 1932, he left home and moved to the Los Angeles area. During the next few years, he sang with various groups, including the 4-S Ranch Boys, the Beverly Hillbillies, Jack And His Texas Outlaws and Jimmy LeFevre And His Saddle Pals. In September 1936, **Bob Nolan** invited him to take over from **Tim Spencer** who was leaving the Sons Of The Pioneers. Spencer returned in 1938, by which time Perryman had become an important part of the Pioneers. Between April 1943 and January 1946, he was drafted for military service and his place in the group was taken by **Ken Carson**. In 1949, when Spencer and Nolan left, Perryman became the leader of the group. He acted as compere at their concerts and was also responsible for all vocal arrangements, although he actually wrote very few songs himself. Perryman, a natural baritone, originally sang tenor but it was a well known fact that he could sing any part in the trio harmonies of the group, for any of the hundreds of songs in their repertoire. He died after a short illness in May 1977.

Perryman, Rufus 'Speckled Red'

b. 23 October 1892, Monroe, Louisiana, USA, d. 2 January 1973. Although his singing and piano playing were barely adequate, Perryman's work has about it a rather endearing, basic earthiness. In this respect it is sometimes preferable to the blander styles which developed as the blues became an acceptable part of popular entertainment. He played mostly in the south, achieving wider popularity thanks to recordings, and in the late 50s and early 60s toured Europe. In 1970 he recorded music for the soundtrack of the film *Blues Like Showers Of Rain*. Perryman, who died in 1973, was an elder brother of William '**Piano Red**' Perryman.

Album: *The Dirty Dozen* (1961).

Perryman, William

(see **Piano Red**)

Persen, Mari Boine

b. Gamehisnjarqa, Norway. Mari is a Sami, one of a small population of Arctic Europe. Spread across the northern extremes of Finland, Norway, Sweden and the former Soviet Union, the Sami are divided by politics but unified by culture and tradition. Having left teaching for music, Mari has for over a decade been writing, recording and performing material often based on traditional poetry. She has released two albums in Scandinavia although only *Gula Gula - Hear The Voices Of The Fore-Mothers* - is available elsewhere. Mari works with a variety of musicians, many playing traditional instruments such as the dozo n'koni, ganga and darboka, and through them has created a cross-cultural style whose roots remain with the Sami.

Album: *Gula Gula - Hear The Voices Of The Fore-Mothers* (1990).

Persian Risk

The line-up of this heavy metal outfit, based in the north of England, was in a constant state of flux during their formative period in the early 80s. At one time Phil Campbell and Jon Deverill, later of **Motörhead** and the **Tygers Of Pan Tang** respectively, were involved. They debuted with a track on the *Heavy Metal Heroes Vol. 2* compilation, and later recorded a single for Neat Records. It took a further three years to record an album because of the regular line-up shuffles. *Rise Up* finally saw the light of day in 1986 with the team now comprising Carl Sentance (vocals), Phil Vokins (guitar), Graham Bath (guitar), Nick Hughes (bass) and Steve Hopgood (drums). Formularized and rather out-dated, the songs were rooted in the early phase of the **New Wave Of British Heavy Metal**, which, unlike Persian Risk, had matured and progressed considerably since its inception. The album was unsuccessful and the band disintegrated when Bath and Hopgood left to join **Paul Di'anno's Battlezone**.

Album: *Rise Up* (Razor 1986).

Persip, Charlie

b. 26 July 1929, Morristown, New Jersey, USA. After taking up drums as a child Persip began playing bop, moving to New York where he worked with **Tadd Dameron** in the early 50s. From 1953 he was associated with **Dizzy Gillespie**, playing in small groups and big bands. He also recorded with **Lee Morgan**, **Zoot Sims** and **Dinah Washington**. In 1960 he formed his own band with **Freddie Hubbard** but continued to record with such artists as **Gil Evans**, **Roland Kirk**, **Don Ellis** and **Gene Ammons**. In the late 60s he began a long association with **Billy Eckstine**, playing drums and conducting the touring orchestra. In the early 70s Persip teamed up with several other leading jazzmen to work with Jazzmobile in New York City, teaching and performing. In the mid- to late-70s he recorded with **Archie Shepp**, Kirk and others and also led his own big band. Hard driving and technically assured, Persip is an excellent bop drummer whose skills are best represented by his superb big band work.

Albums: with Dizzy Gillespie *World Statesman* (1956), with Gil Evans *Out Of The Cool* (1960), with Don Ellis *How Time Passes* (1960), *The Charlie Persip Sextet* (1960), with Ellis *New Ideas* (1961), with Rahsaan Roland Kirk *We Free Kings* (1961), *Charlie Persip and Gary La Furn's 17-Piece Superband* (1980), *In Case You Missed It* (Soul Note 1984), *No Dummies Allowed* (Soul Note 1988).

Person, Houston

b. 10 November 1934, Florence, South Carolina, USA. A late starter, Person took up the tenor saxophone in his late teenage and gained considerable experience in bands during his military service. In the 60s he was sometimes sideman, sometimes, leader of small groups cashing in on the organ-tenor fad. Late in the decade he began a long-lasting association with the singer, **Etta Jones**. Although his playing style is rooted in earthy R&B, he has also played with forward-thinking musicians such as **Ran Blake**.

Albums: *The Nearness Of You* (Muse 1977), *Wild Flower* (Muse 1977), with Etta Jones *Love Me With All Of Your Heart* (Muse 1983).

Persson, Aake

b. 25 February 1932, Stockholm, Sweden, d. 5 February 1975. From his teens Persson was active and respected in his own country, playing trombone with fellow Scandinavians such as Arne Domnerus, **Lars Guillin**, **Bengt Hallberg** and Harry Arnold. While a member of Arnold's popular big band Persson was heard by several Americans who played with the band during visits to Sweden. These included **Benny Bailey** and **Quincy Jones** and he made records with them and with **Roy Haynes**. He played briefly in one of the orchestras Jones led in Europe before becoming a member of a radio band in Germany, where he remained for 15 years. During this period he was also a founder member of the **Clarke-Boland Big Band**, occasionally joining touring big bands for brief spells. In this way he played with **Count Basie** and **Duke Ellington**. An outstanding soloist whose flow of ideas and inventiveness was enhanced by an exceptionally good technique, Persson was a major figure on the European jazz scene and might have been better remembered had he chosen to live and work in the USA.

Selected albums: with Harry Arnold *Big Band Classics* (1958), *Aake Persson-Benny Bailey-Joe Harris* (1959), with the Clarke-Boland Big Band *Jazz Is Universal* (1961).

Persuaders

An R&B vocal group from New York, New York, USA. The original members were lead Douglas 'Smokey' Scott, Willie Holland, James 'B.J' Barnes, and Charles Stodghill. The Persuaders were one of the myriad stand-up vocal groups that helped make the early '70s an era of vocal harmony renaissance, one that significantly shaped the popular music of the day. The arresting dry lead of Douglas set against the pristine sweet harmonizing of the rest of the group gave the Persuaders a distinctive sound. The group was organized in 1968 as the Internationals and soon met Richard and Robert Poindexter, who owned a small label and began recording the group. Nothing much happened until 1971, when the Internationals redubbed themselves the Persuaders and had a hit with 'Thin Line Between Love And Hate' (number 1 R&B, number 15 pop), a fabulous composition by the Poindexters. They followed with almost an equally attractive song, 'Love Gonna Pack Up (And Walk Out)'

(number 8 R&B, number 64 pop). The 1972 hit, 'Peace In The Valley Of Love' (number 21 R&B) featured a revised line-up, with Barnes and Stodghill being replaced by John Tobias and Thomas Lee Hill. The Persuaders got their second biggest hit in 1973 with 'Some Guys Have All The Luck' (number 7 R&B, number 39 R&B), and competed with **Gladys Knight And The Pips** on the charts in 1974 with a rival version of 'Best Thing That Ever Happened To Me' (number 29 R&B, number 85 pop). The Persuaders' last chart record was in 1977, and by that time only Smokey Scott remained from the original group.
Albums: *Thin Line Between Love And Hate* (Win Or Lose 1972), *The Persuaders* (Atco 1973), *Best Thing That Ever Happened To Me* (Atco 1974), *It's All About Love* (Calla 1976).

Persuasions

Formed in the Bedford-Stuyvesant area in New York City, this talented group has continued the **a cappella** tradition despite prevalent trends elsewhere. Jerry Lawson (b. 23 January 1944, Fort Lauderdale, Florida, USA; lead), Joseph 'Jesse' Russell (b. 25 September 1939, Henderson, North Carolina, USA; tenor), Little Jayotis Washington (b. 12 May 1941, Detroit, Michigan, USA; tenor), Herbert 'Tubo' Rhoad (b. 1 October 1944, Bamberg, South Carolina, USA; baritone) and Jimmy 'Bro' Hayes (b. 12 November 1943, Hopewell, Virginia, USA; bass) began working together in 1966. Having recorded for Minit, the Persuasions gained prominence four years later with *Accapella*, a part live/part studio album released on **Frank Zappa**'s Straight label. Their unadorned voices were later heard on several superb collections including, *Street Corner Symphony* and *Chirpin'*, while the group also supplied harmonies on **Joni Mitchell**'s *Shadows And Light* (1980). During 1973-74, Willie C. Daniel replaced Jayotis Washington in the group. On 8 December 1988 Rhoad died, leaving a four-man group. The Persuasions continue to pursue this peerless path, winding sinewy harmonies around such varied songs as 'Slip Sliding Away' and 'Under The Boardwalk'.
Albums: *Accapella* (1970), *We Came To Play* (1971), *Street Corner Symphony* (1972), *Spread The Word* (1972), *We Still Ain't Got No Band* (1973), *More Than Before* (1974), *I Just Wanna Sing With My Friends* (1974), *Chirpin'* (1977), *Comin' At Ya* (1979), *No Frills* (1984), *Stardust* (1987), *Good News* (1988), *Right Around The Corner* (Bullseye 1994).

Pestilence

This German speed/thrash metal quartet was put together by guitarists Randy Meinhard and Patrick Mameli in 1986. Enlisting the services of Marco Foddis (drums) and Martin van Drunen (vocals/bass), they debuted with a track on the *Teutonic Invasion II* compilation (1987) on the Rock Hard label. A deal with **Roadrunner** ensued and they cut *Mallevs Maleficarum*, a high speed metallic blur reminiscent of **Slayer** and **Testament**. Meinhard quit soon after the album was released to form Sacrosanct. Ex-Theriac guitarist Patrick Uterwijk stepped in as replacement and the band entered the studio to record *Consuming Impulse*. This marked a distinct technical and musical improvement over their enthusiastic, but slightly amateurish debut. Produced by Harris Johns, the album took off in the USA and Pestilence toured extensively with **Death** and **Autopsy** during 1990. However, van Drunen left shortly afterwards to front his own band, **Asphyx** (subsequently forming Submission and acting as guest vocalist on the second Comecon album), with Mameli taking over vocal duties. Pestilence finally split in 1994 with Mameli becoming increasingly hostile to the death metal fraternity which had devoured the band's work. Rumours abounded that Roadrunner were on the verge of dropping them anyway.
Albums: *Mallevs Maleficarum* (Roadrunner 1988), *Consuming Impulse* (Roadrunner 1989), *Testimony To The Ancients* (Roadrunner 1991), *Spheres* (Roadrunner 1993).

Pet Lamb

Formed in Dublin in 1991, the four members of Pet Lamb are Dylan Philips (guitar/vocals), Brian Mooney (guitar/vocals), Kevin Talbot (bass) and James Lillis (drums). Influenced by the hardcore assault of the **Butthole Surfers** and **Jesus Lizard**, with the songwriting shared between Phillips and Mooney, they admitted to their central inspiration being: 'a mixture of lust, beer, frustration and boredom'. The group were first adopted by small independent imprint Blunt, a liaison which produced two EPs, and brought about support slots to the musically sympathetic **Therapy?, No Means No, Babes In Toyland** and others. After a session for the **John Peel** programme **Roadrunner** snapped the band up, packing them off to Dublin's Sonic Studios to record their debut for the label, 'Black Mask' - 'a kind of teenage sex and death fantasy, featuring Satan'. In its wake came a debut album, *Sweaty Handshake*, propelled by songs like the defiant 'Insult To Injury' and self-loathing 'Fun With Maggots'.
Album: *Sweaty Handshake* (Roadrunner 1995).

Pet Shop Boys

Formed in 1981, this inventive UK pop duo featured Neil Tennant (b. 10 July 1954, North Shields, Northumberland, England; vocals) and Chris Lowe (b. 4 October 1959, Blackpool, Lancashire, England; keyboards). Lowe had previously played in a cabaret group, One Under The Eight, while Tennant was employed as a journalist on the UK pop magazine *Smash Hits*. After writing and recording demos, they came under the wing of New York dance music producer Bobby 'O' Orlando. In the summer of 1984, they issued the Orlando-produced 'West End Girls', which passed unnoticed. After being dropped from Epic Records, they were picked up by **EMI/Parlophone** the following year. A second single 'Opportunities (Let's Make Lots Of Money)' also failed but a re-recording of 'West End Girls', produced by Stephen Hague, began selling in late 1985. In January 1986, this hypnotic single topped the charts in the UK and repeated the feat later in the USA. The group's debut *Please*, 'Love Comes Quickly', a re-mixed version of 'Opportunities (Let's Make Lots Of Money)' and 'Suburbia' consolidated their position in the UK during 1986. The following year, the duo returned to number 1 with the **Cat Stevens**' influenced 'It's A Sin'. By this time, they were critically feted as one of the more interesting groups of their time, with an engaging love of pop irony, camp imagery and arch wordplay. The quality of their melodies was also evident in the successful collaboration with **Dusty Springfield**, 'What Have I Done To Deserve This?' which reached number 2. By the end of the year the duo were back at the top in their home country with a cover of the **Elvis Presley** hit, 'Always On My Mind'. After another well-received album, *Actually*, the group were featured in a film, *It Couldn't Happen Here*, which co-starred *Carry On* actress, Barbara Windsor. The film was given the cold shoulder by reviewers and was seen as mild hiccup in the duo's fortunes. A fourth UK number 1 with 'Heart' was followed by a production and songwriting credit on **Eighth Wonder**'s 'I'm Not Scared'. *Introspective* (1988) spawned further hits in 'Domino Dancing', 'It's Alright' and 'Left To My Own Devices'. Having previously eschewed live tours (they had hitherto performed one-off concerts only), the Pet Shop Boys undertook their debut in Japan and the Far East, before finally reaching the UK. In typical manner, the show's concept took them as far away from the traditional pop concert as possible and incorporated the use of actors, dancers and film. A surprise collaboration with **Liza Minnelli** gave her a hit with 'Results'. The duo's own inventive wit was again in evidence on the laconic 'Being Boring' and an odd fusion of **U2**'s 'Where The Streets Have No Name' and **Andy Williams**' 'Can't Take My Eyes Off You'. In 1991, the group issued one of the best compilation albums of the era with *Discography*. 'Can You Forgive Her' was a fine trailer to the new album released in 1993.

Albums: *Please* (1986), *Disco* (1986), *Actually* (1987), *Introspective* (1988), *Behaviour* (1990), *Very* (EMI 1993).
Compilation: *Discography* (1991).
Videos: *Projections* (1993), *Various* (PMI 1994).
Further reading: *Pet Shop Boys, Literally*, Chris Heath. *Pet Shop Boys: Introspective*, Michael Crowton. *Pet Shop Boys Versus America*, Chris Heath and Pennie Smith.

Pete Kelly's Blues

A marvellous opening sequence, depicting the funeral of a New Orleans jazz musician, is the best moment in what is otherwise a fairly predictable tale of jazzmen and gangsters in the 20s. Other bright spots are of singers **Peggy Lee** and **Ella Fitzgerald**. **Teddy Buckner** plays in the opening scene and elsewhere can be heard the likes of **Nick Fatool**, Matty Matlock, **Eddie Miller**, **George Van Eps** and **Joe Venuti**. The role of Pete Kelly is played by Jack Webb, who also directed, and his trumpet playing was dubbed by **Dick Cathcart**. Lee Marvin made the most unlikely-looking clarinettist in jazz history, with the possible exception of **Pee Wee Russell**. Four years later, in 1959, a television spin-off lasted 13 episodes.

Peter And Gordon

Both the sons of doctors and former pupils of the prestigious English public school Westminster Boys, this privileged pair were signed by producer Norman Newell, following a residency at London's Piccadilly Club. **Peter Asher** (b. 2 June 1944, London, England) and Gordon Waller (b. 4 June 1945, Braemar, Grampian, Scotland), had a crucial advantage over their contemporaries - the priceless patronage of **Paul McCartney**, who was then dating Peter's sister, Jane. The perfectly enunciated 'A World Without Love' quickly became a transatlantic chart topper and two more 1964 McCartney compositions, 'Nobody I Know' and 'I Don't Want To See You Again', brought further success. The Beatle connection was again evident on 'Woman', which McCartney composed under the pseudonym Bernard Webb. In the meantime, the duo had switched to successful revivals of 50s material, including **Buddy Holly's** 'True Love Ways' and the **Teddy Bears'** retitled 'To Know You Is To Love You'. Peter and Gordon's wholesome image was somewhat belied by Waller's appearances in the salacious British Sunday press, but this did little to affect their popularity in the USA. Although the partnership was strained by late 1966, the saucy 'Lady Godiva' provided a new direction and was followed by the similarly-quaint novelty numbers 'Knight In Rusty Armour' and 'Sunday For Tea'. One year later, they split. Waller subsequently pursued an unsuccessful solo career while Asher emerged as a formidable producer and manager.

Albums: *Peter And Gordon* (1964), *A World Without Love* (1964), *In Touch With Peter And Gordon* (1964), *I Don't Want To See You Again* (1965), *I Go To Pieces* (1965), *True Love Ways* (1965), *Hurtin' 'N' Lovin'* (1965), *The Hits Of Nashville* (1966), *Woman* (1966), *Somewhere* (1966), *Lady Godiva* (1967), *A Knight In Rusty Armour* (1967), *In London For Tea* (1967), *Hot, Cold And Custard* (1968).
Compilations: *Peter And Gordon's Greatest Hits* (1966), *The Best Of Peter And Gordon* (1983), *Hits And More* (1986).

Peter And The Test Tube Babies

Punk rock can hardly stand as Brighton's major claim to fame, but the southern coastal town in Sussex, England, had its moments. In between the **Piranhas**' flirtations with the UK charts, Peter And The Test Tube Babies gained notoriety during the early 80s, with their brand of good-time Oi!-inspired punk. The group comprised Chris Marchant (bass), Nicholas Loizides (drums), Peter Bywaters (vocals) and Derek Greening (guitar). Locals may have remembered them from their contribution to resident label Attrix's *Vaultage 1978* compilation, which featured the provocative 'Elvis Is Dead'. But it wasn't until 1982 that the Test Tube Babies' first single emerged on the No Future label. 'Banned From The Pubs' was followed by 'Run Like Hell' that same year, before the band set up their own label, Trapper. After the gruesome 'Zombie Creeping Flesh' and 'The Jinx' (both 1983), they at last emerged with an album's worth of indecent exposure, *The Mating Sounds Of South American Frogs*. The inelegantly titled *Pissed And Proud* followed one month later. The next two years saw the group release albums and singles with various labels, including their own, Hairy Pie. The idiosyncratically entitled cassette-only release, *Journey To The Centre Of Johnny Clarke's Head*, was followed by the *Rotting In The Fart Sack* EP (1985) and *Another Noisy, Loud, Blaring Punk Rock LP*. The album *Soberphobia* saw the Test Tube Babies through to the end of 1986, but since then, all has been quiet, leaving it safe to assume that the band have returned to the pub.

Albums: *The Mating Sounds Of South American Frogs* (Trapper 1983), *Pissed And Proud* (No Future 1983), *Journey To The Centre Of Johnny Clarke's Head* (Hairy Pie 1984, cassette only), *Another Noisy, Loud, Blaring Punk Rock LP* (Hairy Pie 1985), *3 X 45* (Trapper 1985), *Soberphobia* (Dojo 1986). Compilation: *The Best Of Peter And The Test Tube Babies* (Dojo 1988).

Peter Pan (Film Musical)

(see **Disney, Walt**)

Peter Pan (Stage Musical)

A musical adaptation of J. M. Barrie's classic story were presented in New York as early as 1905 when Maude Adams and Ernest Lawford starred in a Charles Frohman production. It was revived in 1924, with Marilyn Miller in the leading role, and included two **Jerome Kern** songs, 'The Sweetest Thing In Life' and 'Just Because You're You'. The 1950 version, which ran for 321 performances, starred Jean Arthur and Boris Karloff. **Leonard Bernstein** wrote the music and lyrics for several songs, such 'Who Am I?', 'Never-Land', 'Peter, Peter', and 'My House', and **Alec Wilder** also provided some incidental music. In the fourth interpretation, which opened at the Winter Garden in New York on 20 October 1954, **Mary Martin**, returning to Broadway for the first time since her triumph in ***South Pacific***, made a spirited, high-flying Peter, to Cyril Ritchard's amusingly degenerate Captain Hook. The initial score, which was written by Moose Charlap and **Carolyn Leigh**, contained songs such as 'Tender Shepherd', 'I've Got To Crow', 'I'm Flying', and 'I Won't Grow Up'. Before the show reached Broadway, director and choreographer **Jerome Robbins** asked **Jule Styne**, **Betty Comden** and **Adolph Green** to provide the music and lyrics for several additional numbers, including 'Captain Hook's Waltz', 'Wendy', 'Mysterious Lady', and the lovely 'Never Never Land', which is still sung occasionally, and received a sensitive reading from **Lena Horne** on her *Lena At The Sands*. Mary Martin received the **Tony Award** for best actress, and this version ran for 152 performances before it was taped, and shown on US television, giving non theatre-going audiences a rare opportunity to see a Broadway show. A 1979 New York revival, starring Sandy Duncan and George Rose, beat all the previous versions and lasted for 551 performances. Six years later the same basic production played the West End, with Joss Ackland, Judith Bruce, and Bonnie Langford. In 1990, Cathy Rigby and Stephan Hanon played Peter and Hook when *Peter Pan* looked in on Broadway again for a limited six-week engagement as part of its nationwide tour. Numerous, quite different adaptations of J. M. Barrie's *Peter Pan* have been presented in the UK, including two major London productions: one with music and lyrics by Stephen Oliver at the Barbican Theatre in 1982; and another, *Peter Pan: The British Musical*, with a score by Piers Chater-Robinson, which starred Ron Moody and played at the Cambridge Theatre in 1994.

Further reading: *The Peter Pan Chronicles*, Bruce K. Hanson.

Peter, Paul And Mary

Peter Yarrow (b. 31 May 1938, New York City, New York, USA), Noel Paul Stookey (b. Paul Stookey, 30 November 1937, Baltimore, Maryland, USA) and Mary Allin Travers (b. 7 November 1937, Louisville, Kentucky, USA) began performing together in the spring of 1961. They were brought together by **Albert Grossman**, one of folk music's successful entrepreneurs, in an attempt to create a contemporary **Kingston Trio**. The three singers were already acquainted through the close-knit coffee-house circuit, although **Dave Van Ronk** was briefly considered as a possible member. The group popularized several topical songs, including 'If I Had A Hammer' and were notable early interpreters of **Bob Dylan** compositions. In 1963 their version of 'Blowin' In The Wind' reached number 2 in the US chart while a follow-up reading of 'Don't Think Twice, It's Alright' also broached the Top 10. They were also renowned for singing children's songs, the most memorable of which was the timeless 'Puff The Magic Dragon'. The trio became synonymous with folk's liberal traditions, but were increasingly perceived as old-fashioned as the 60s progressed. Nonetheless a 1966 selection, *Album*, included material by **Laura Nyro** and featured assistance from **Paul Butterfield**, **Mike Bloomfield** and **Al Kooper**, while the following year's 'I Dig Rock 'N' Roll Music' became their fifth US Top 10 hit. Peter, Paul And Mary enjoyed their greatest success in 1969 with 'Leaving On A Jet Plane'. This melodramatic **John Denver** song reached number 1 in the US and number 2 in the UK, but by then the individual members were branching out in different directions. Yarrow had been the primary force behind *You Are What You Eat*, an eccentric hippie film which also featured **Tiny Tim** and **John Simon**, and in 1970 he, Travers and Stookey announced their formal dissolution. The three performers embarked on solo careers but were ultimately unable to escape the legacy of their former group. They reunited briefly in 1972 for a George McGovern Democratic Party rally, and again in 1978. They have since continued to perform material reminiscent of their golden era. Although criticized for a smooth and wholesome delivery, Peter, Paul and Mary was one of the era's most distinctive acts and played a crucial bridging role between two contrasting generations of folk music.

Albums: *Peter, Paul And Mary* (1962), *Peter, Paul And Mary - Moving* (1963), *In The Wind* (1963), *Peter, Paul And Mary In Concert* (1964), *A Song Will Rise* (1965), *See What Tomorrow Brings* (1965), *Peter, Paul And Mary Album* (1966), *Album 1700* (1967), *Late Again* (1968), *Peter, Paul And Mommy* (1969), *Reunion* (1978), *Such Is Love* (1982), *No Easy Walk To Freedom* (1988), *Peter, Paul And Mommy Too* (1993). Compilations: *10 Years Together/The Best Of Peter, Paul And Mary* (1970), *Most Beautiful Songs* (1973), *Collection* (1982). Solo: Peter Yarrow *Peter* (1972), *That's Enough For Me* (1973), *Hard Times* (1975). Paul Stookey *Paul And* (1971), *Band And Body Works* (1980). Mary Travers *Mary* (1971), *Morning Glory* (1972), *All My Choices* (1973), *Circles* (1974), *It's In Everyone Of Us* (1978).

Peterik, Jim

This US keyboardist/composer started his career as a session musician. His first taste of success came with 'Ides Of March' at the end of the 60s. It was 1977, however, before he actually got round to recording a solo album; *Don't Fight The Feeling* was a mature, melodic rock album, that drew comparisons with **Bob Seger**, **Bruce Springsteen** and **Michael Bolton**. However, it made little headway and Peterik returned to session work, guesting on **Sammy Hagar** and **.38 Special** albums. In 1978 he formed **Survivor** with guitarist Frankie Sullivan and went on to multi-platinum success.

Album: *Don't Fight The Feeling* (Scotti Bros. 1977).

Peters And Lee

After Lennie Peters (b. 1939, London, England, d. 10 October 1992, Enfield, North London, England) was blinded at the age of 16 in an accident which put paid to his ambitions to become a boxer, he began singing and playing piano in pubs around the Islington area of London. Dianne Lee (b. c.1950, Sheffield, Yorkshire, England) was a dancer with her cousin, working as the Hailey Twins, and after Lennie and Dianne met on a tour of clubs, they decided to form a duo. They achieved some popularity on the club and holiday camp circuit, and subsequently won Hughie Green's top-rated television talent show *Opportunity Knocks*. Their blend of **Tony Bennett** and **Ray Charles** numbers made them one of the most popular winners of the programme, and led to their releasing the country-flavoured 'Welcome Home' which topped the UK chart in 1973. The accompanying *We Can Make It* also reached number 1 - it was the first time since the **Beatles** that a single and album from the same act had simultaneously held the UK number 1 spots. As well as becoming regulars on various television variety shows, the duo had three Top 20 singles in the ensuing years, including the number 3 hit 'Don't Stay Away Too Long' (1974). After splitting up in 1980, they re-formed six years later and toured holiday camps until 1992 when it was announced that Peters was suffering from cancer. After his death, Dianne Lee turned to acting, and also performed in cabaret. In 1994 she played the title role in *Sinderella*, comedian Jim Davidson's bawdy pantomime. In the following year Pickwick Records resissued Peters and Lee's last album, *Through All The Years*, after their biggest hit, 'Welcome Home', was featured in a television commercial for Walker's Crisps.

Selected albums: *By Your Side* (1973), *We Can Make It* (1973), *Rainbow* (1974), *Favourites* (1975), *Invitation* (1976), *Serenade* (1976), *Smile* (1977), *Remember When* (1980), *The Farewell Album* (1980), *Through All The Years* (1992). Compilations: *Spotlight On Peters And Lee* (1979). Solo: Lennie Peters *Unforgettable* (1981).

Peters, Bernadette

b. Bernadette Lazzara, 28 February 1948, Ozone Park, Queens, New York City, New York, USA. Often called 'the finest singing actress since Streisand', Bernadette Peters is certainly one of the few leading ladies of the last decade whose name on a Broadway marquee can cause box-office queues to form before the show has gone into previews. She was tap-dancing and acting at an early age, and joined Actors' Equity when she was nine. Soon afterwards she changed her name to Peters, and played Tessie in the 1959 revival of ***The Most Happy Fella*** at the New York City Centre. After appearing in the role of Baby June in a road tour of ***Gypsy***, she gave up performing for a time, and studied acting and singing in her teens, before returning to the stage in a number of fairly mediocre productions. In 1968 she received favourable notices, and a Theatre World citation, for her portrayal of **George M. Cohan**'s sister in ***George M!***, and, in the same year, won a Drama Desk Award for her 'hilarious performance' as the zany Ruby in ***Dames At Sea***, a 30s movie-spoof which enjoyed a good run Off Broadway. In between several theatrical disappointments in the late 60s and early 70s, which included *La Strada* (one performance), a New York revival of ***On The Town***, *W.C.* (a musical about W.C. Fields), and ***Mack And Mabel*** (1974), she turned to films and television, often playing straight roles, but without any notable success. In 1977 Peters formed a private and professional partnership with the comedian Steve Martin, and they appeared together in two movies, *The Jerk* (1979), and the highly expensive box-office disaster *Pennies From Heaven* (1981), for which Peters won a Golden Globe Award. Her other films around this time included the musical ***Annie***, in which she played Lily, the fiendish social worker. In the 80s she starred in three Broadway musicals, two of which had scores by **Stephen Sondheim**, ***Sunday In The Park With George*** (1984) and ***Into The Woods*** (1987). She also won a **Tony Award** for her brilliant solo performance in **Andrew Lloyd Webber** and **Don Black**'s ***Song And Dance***. During the latter part of the decade, Peters developed her cabaret act which revolved around Broadway show tunes but also contained a lovely version of **Hank Williams**' 'I'm So Lonesome I Could Cry', and a highly effective **Harold Arlen** medley. In 1993 she was back on Broadway with Martin Short and Carol Woods in the eagerly awaited *The Goodbye Girl*. In spite of Neil Simon's witty book, and a score by **Marvin Hamlisch** and David Zippel, the show folded after only 188 performances.

Selected albums: *Bernadette Peters* (1980), *Now Playing* (1981), and Original Cast and film soundtrack recordings.

Peters, Brian

b. 15 December 1954, Stockport, Cheshire, England. Peters started playing guitar at the age of 15 and subsequently appeared in a college rock band. In 1978, he took up the concertina, to accompany his singing and started the round of folk club floor spots years later. His first professional booking was at the Unicorn Folk Club, Manchester, in September 1981. Combining a day job with club bookings, Brian started to learn to play the melodeon and was signed to Fellside Records in 1985. *Persistence Of Memory* was released to critical acclaim from the folk press. He appeared on BBC Radio's *Folk On 2* in 1988, and a year later signed to Harbourtown for his next release, *Fools Of Fortune*. This comprised largely of traditional tunes and songs arranged by Peters including 'Dallas Rag', a departure from the reels, jigs and hornpipes normally associated with concertina players. *Fools Of Fortune* was voted *Folk Roots* magazine's Album Of The Year, in the folk and country music category. In addition to touring clubs and festivals, Brian has also done session work for **Mike Harding**, and Hughie Jones, formerly of the **Spinners**. He has also performed with Sara Grey (b. Sara Lee Grey, 22 March 1940, Boston, Massachusetts, USA; banjo/vocals), and **Roger Wilson** (guitar/vocals), as the Lost Nation Band since 1990. *Seeds Of Time* was part funded by North West Arts. Peters continues to play folk clubs, both at home and abroad, and his following and popularity, continue to grow.

Albums: *Persistence Of Memory* (1986), *Fools Of Fortune* (Harbourtown 1989), *Seeds Of Time* (Harbourtown 1992), *Squeezing Out Sparks* (Harbourtown 1994).

Peterson, Lucky

b. Judge Kenneth Peterson, 13 December 1964, Buffalo, New York, USA. Peterson was an exceptionally gifted musician as a child, and this has left him with the problem of harnessing his natural gift to a definable personality. His father James owned a blues club, the Governor's Inn, and his son received frequent opportunities to play alongside visiting musicians, although a three-year-old playing organ and drums may have been as much a curiosity as a phenomenon. Two years later he recorded for **Willie Dixon**; the single, '1, 2, 3, 4', and a subsequent album brought him a degree of celebrity and he made appearances on *Tonight* and *The* ***Ed Sullivan*** *Show*. At 17, **Little Milton** asked him to join his band and after three years, he moved on to spend another three years backing **Bobby Bland**. While on a European tour with Bland, he cut his first album as an adult, *Ridin'*, in Paris. By this time, he had taken up the guitar and subsequent albums such as *Lucky Strikes!* emphasised his prowess on the instrument. Meanwhile, he became a frequent session musician for other King Snake and Alligator artists, usually as a keyboard player. His move to **Verve** and the release of *I'm Ready* and *Beyond Cool* perpetuated his image as a guitarist and allowed him to broaden the scope of his musicianship to interpretations of **Jimi Hendrix** and **Stevie Wonder** songs. His adoption of French horn and trumpet are yet to make their debut on record, but in trying to become the complete musician, Peterson risks subordinating the depth of his talent to a veneer of display.

Albums: *Ridin'* (Isabel 1984), *Rough And Ready* (King Snake 1988), *Lucky Strikes!* (Alligator 1989), *Triple Play* (Alligator 1990), *I'm Ready* (Verve/Gitanes, 1993), *Beyond Cool* (Verve/Gitanes 1994).

Peterson, Marvin 'Hannibal'

b. 11 November 1948, Smithville, Texas, USA. One of many fine musicians to graduate from North Texas State University, Peterson settled on trumpet having previously played cornet and drums. After graduation he moved to New York where he played with **Rahsaan Roland Kirk**, **Elvin Jones**, **Archie Shepp** and other leading jazzmen, notably **Gil Evans** with whom he formed a lasting musical relationship. Throughout the 60s he toured and recorded with these and other musicians, sometimes leading his own band. He continued performing in similar settings through the 70s, working again with Evans and Jones and also with **Pharoah Sanders** and **Roy Haynes**. In the 80s he was touring internationally. For a while in the mid-to-late 70s Peterson played free jazz with **Roswell Rudd**, but his best work comes in bop and post-bop settings. A sparkling virtuoso trumpeter, Peterson's brilliant technique allows him to do pretty much anything he sets his mind upon; as his playing and writing testify, this ranges over the entire spectrum of jazz.

Albums: with Pharoah Sanders *Black Unity* (1971), with Gil Evans *Svengali* (1973), *Children Of Fire* (1974), *Hannibal* (1975), *Hannibal In Berlin* (1976), *Gil Evans Live At New York Public Theater* (1980), *The Angels Of Atlanta* (1981), *Hannibal In Antibes* (Enja 1982), *Poem Song* (Mole 1983), *Kiss On The Bridge* (Ear Rational 1990).

Peterson, Oscar

b. Oscar Emmanuel Peterson, 15 August 1925, Montreal, Canada. Blessed with an attractive stage personality, this behemoth of mainstream jazz's fluid technique was influenced by **Art Tatum**, **Errol Garner** and, later, **George Shearing**. After studying trumpet, illness redirected him to the piano. His enthusiasm resulted in endless hours of practise which helped mould his remarkable technique. In his mid-teens, after winning a local talent contest in 1940, Peterson was heard regularly on radio in Canada and beyond. By 1944, he was the featured pianist with the nationally famous Johnny Holmes Orchestra before leading his own trio. Peterson was unusual in not serving an apprenticeship as an older player's sideman. Although early recordings were disappointing, he received lucrative offers to appear in the USA but these were resisted until a debut at New York's Carnegie Hall with **Norman Granz**'s **Jazz At The Philharmonic** in September 1949. **Louis Armstrong**, **Billie Holiday**, **Count Basie**, **Dizzy Gillespie**, **Zoot Sims**, **Ella Fitzgerald** and **Stan Getz** have been among Peterson's collaborators during a career that has encompassed hundreds of studio and concert recordings. With 1963's *Affinity* as his biggest seller, Peterson's output has ranged from albums drawn from the songbooks of **Cole Porter** and **Duke Ellington**; a **Verve** single of **Jimmy Forrest**'s perennial 'Night Train', and 1964's self-written *Canadiana Suite*. Although he introduced a modicum of **Nat 'King' Cole**-type vocals into his repertoire in the mid-50s, he has maintained a certain steady consistency of style that has withstood the buffeting of fashion.

Since 1970, he has worked with no fixed group, often performing alone, although at the end of the 70s Peterson had a long stint with bass player **Neils-Henning Ørsted Pedersen** which continued well into the 80s. The soundtrack to the movie *Play It Again Sam*; the hosting of a television chat show; a 1974 tour of Soviet Russia, and 1981's *A Royal Wedding Suite* (conducted by Russ Garcia) have been more recent commercial high points of a fulfilling and distinguished professional life. While musicians as diverse as **Steve Winwood**, **Dudley Moore** and **Weather Report**'s **Joe Zawinul** absorbed much from Peterson discs, younger admirers have been advantaged by his subsequent publication of primers such as *Jazz Exercises And Pieces* and *Peterson's New Piano Solos*. Peterson's dazzling technique and unflagging swing have helped make him one of the most highly regarded and instantly identifiable pianists in jazz. Although the technical qualities of his work have sometimes cooled the emotional heart of his material, Peterson's commitment to jazz is undeniable. The high standard of his work over the years is testimony to his dedication and to the care which he and his mentor, Granz, have exercised over the pianist's career. Throughout this time, Peterson has displayed through his eclecticism, an acute awareness of the history of jazz piano, ranging from stride to bop, from **James P. Johnson** to **Bill Evans**, but always with Art Tatum as an abiding influence. However this influence is one that Peterson has been careful to control. Tatum may colour Peterson's work but he has never shaped it. Thus, for all his influences, Peterson is very much his own man. Yet, for all the admiration he draws from other pianists, there is little evidence that he has many followers. He may well prove to be the end of the line of master musicians in the history of jazz piano.

Selected albums: *In Concert* (1952), *Jazz At The Philharmonic, Hartford 1953* (Pablo 1953 recording), *1953 Live* (Jazz Band Records 1953 recording), *Verve Jazz Masters* (Verve 1953-1962 recordings), *At Zardi's* (Pablo 1955 recording), *The Silver Collection* (Verve 1959-63 recordings), *A Jazz Portrait Of Frank Sinatra* (Verve 1960), *Plays The Cole Porter Songbook* (Verve 1960), *Plays Porgy And Bess* (Verve 1960), *The Trio Live From Chicago* (Verve 1962), *Very Tall* (Verve 1962), *West Side Story* (Verve 1962), *Night Train* (Verve 1963), *Bursting Out With The All Star Big Band!* (1963), *Affinity* (1963), *Exclusively For My Friends* (1964), *Oscar Peterson Trio + One* (1964), *Canadiana Suite* (1964), *We Get Requests* (Verve 1965), *My Favourite Instrument* (1968), *Exclusively For My Friends* (MPS 1963-68 recordings), *The Vienna Concert* (Philology 1969), *Motion's And Emotions* (MPS 1969), *Hello Herbie* (MPS 1969), *Tristeza On Piano* (MPS 1970), *Three Originals* (MPS 1970), *Tracks* (1970), *Reunion Blues* (MPS 1972), *Terry's Tune* (1974), *The Trio* (Pablo 1975), *The Good Life* (Original Jazz Classics 1975), with Sonny Stitt *Sittin' In*

(1975), with Dizzy Gillespie *Oscar Peterson And Dizzy Gillespie* (Pablo 1975), with Roy Eldridge *Oscar Peterson And Roy Eldridge* (Original Jazz Classics 1975), *At The Montreaux Jazz Festival* 1975 (Pablo 1976), *Again* (1977), *Oscar Peterson Jam* (1977), *The Vocal Styling Of Oscar Peterson* (1977), *Montreaux '77* i (Original Jazz Classics 1978), *Montreaux '77* ii (Original Jazz Classics 1978), *The Silent Partner* (1979), *The Paris Concert* (Pablo 1979), *Skol* (Original Jazz Classics 1980), *The Personal Touch* (Pablo 1981), *A Royal Wedding Suite* (Pablo 1981), *Live At The Northsea Jazz Festival* (Pablo 1981), *Nigerian Marketplace* (Pablo 1982), *Romance* (1982), with Stéphane Grappelli, Joe Pass, Mickey Roker, Neils-Henning Ørsted Pedersen *Skol* (1982), *In Russia* (Pablo 1982), *Oscar Peterson & Harry Edison* (Pablo 1982), *Carioca* (Happy Bird 1983), *A Tribute To My Friends* (Pablo 1984), *Time After Time* (Pablo 1984), *If You Could See Me Now* (Pablo 1984), *The George Gershwin Songbook* (1985), *Live!* (Pablo 1987), *Live At the Blue Note* (Telarc 1991), *Saturday Night At The Blue Note* (Telarc 1991), *Last Call At The Blue Note* (Telarc 1992). Selected compilations: *History Of An Artist* (Pablo 1982), *History Of An Artist, Volume 2* (Pablo 1987), *Compact Jazz: Oscar Peterson And Friends* (Verve 1988), *Compact Jazz: Plays Jazz Standards* (Verve 1988), *Exclusively For My Friends Vols. 1-4* (1992).
Further reading: *Oscar Peterson*, Richard Palmer. *Oscar Peterson: The Will To Swing*, Gene Lees. *Oscar Peterson Highlights Jazz Piano*, Oscar Peterson.

Peterson, Ray

b. 23 April 1939, Denton, Texas, USA. Peterson entertained other patients with his singing during lengthy treatment for polio in the Texas Warm Springs Foundation Hospital. On discharge, he performed in local clubs before moving to Los Angeles where he was spotted by manager Stan Shulman who procured an **RCA**-Victor recording contract. 'Let's Try Romance' (1958) paved the way for further failures in 'Tail Light', a cover of the **Little Willie John** hit 'Fever' and the uptempo 'Shirley Purley'. However, Peterson came up trumps with 'The Wonder Of You' (later a million-seller for **Elvis Presley**) in the US and UK Top 30 charts in 1959 and had a minor UK hit a year later with 'Answer Me'. In 1960, he swept into the US Top 10 with the original version of car crash epic 'Tell Laura I Love Her' - which financed the foundation of Dunes, Peterson's own record company. Its flagship acts were Curtis Lee - and Ray himself who was successful with the traditional 'Corrina Corrina', 'Missing You' (a **Gerry Goffin/Carole King** ballad), and 'I Could Have Loved You So Well' (1961). On transferring to **MGM**, he attempted to rise anew as a C&W star after a pop chart swan-song in 1963 with 'Give Us Your Blessing'.
Selected album: *Roy Orbison/Ray Peterson* (1993).

Petit, Buddy

b. Joseph Crawford, c.1897, White Castle, Louisiana, USA, d.4 July 1931. By his early teens Petit was well known in New Orleans and by 1916 was co-leading a band with **Jimmie Noone**. The following year he was in California with **Jelly Roll Morton**. By 1918, however, he was back in his home state and, apart from another brief trip to California, he lived and worked in New Orleans and its environs for the rest of his life. Petit's reputation rests upon the acclaim of fellow musicians - he never recorded - and if they are to be believed he was an outstanding trumpet player with a reputation second only to that of **Louis Armstrong**. He died after 'over-indulging' in food and drink at an Independence Day celebration in 1931.

Petra

One of the first US Christian hard rock bands, Petra (named after the ancient city in Jordan) are an excellent musical unit who have never been swayed by passing trends and have stuck fast to their own ideals and beliefs. The group was formed in 1972 by vocalist Greg Volz and guitarist Bob Hartman, recruiting Mark Kelly (bass), John Slick (keyboards) and Louie Weaver (drums) to their cause. Petra specialized in a varied musical approach that incorporated elements of the **Eagles**, **Joe Walsh**, **Kansas** and **Deep Purple**. They have released well over a dozen quality albums to date, with their popularity having gradually waned from its peak in 1984. At this time, they appeared in the US Top 12 best-attended bands list in *Performance* magazine, while *Not Of This World* sold in excess of a quarter of a million units. John Schlitt (ex-Head East) replaced Volz after 1986's *Back To The Street* and the band adopted a heavier direction thereafter. John Lawry and Ronnie Cates replaced Slick and Kelly on keyboards and bass respectively in 1988. Their two most recent releases owe much to **Kiss** and **Stryper** and are more aggressive than their earlier material.
Albums: *Petra* (Myrrh 1974), *Come And Join Us* (Myrrh 1977), *Washes Whiter Than* (Star Song 1979), *Never Say Die* (Star Song 1981), *More Power To Ya* (Star Song 1982), *Not Of This World* (Kingsway 1983), *Beat The System* (Kingsway 1985), *Captured In Time And Place* (Star Song 1986), *Back To The Street* (Star Song 1986), *This Means War* (Star Song 1987), *On Fire* (Star Song 1988), *Petra Means Rock* (Star Song 1989), *Petra Praise - The Rock Cries Out* (Dayspring 1989), *Beyond Belief* (Star Song 1990).
Video: *Captured In Time And Space* (1989).

Petrillo, James Caesar

b. c.1892, Chicago, Illinois, USA, d. 23 October 1984. Petrillo began his career playing trumpet and leading a danceband in Chicago when he was barely into his teens. At the age of 23 he was president of the

American Musicians Union but in 1918 he joined the rival American Federation of Musicians, eventually rising to become the union's head in June 1940. Autocratic and outspoken, Petrillo attracted most attention when, in 1941, he called a strike of musicians, effectively banning any new recordings. He feared that the increasing use of records on radio was threatening the jobs of musicians who might otherwise be employed in studio orchestras and in hotels and restaurants. Petrillo was also concerned that, while bandleaders usually had royalty deals with record companies, the sidemen in the bands received only union scale. (Sometimes, during the swing era which coincided with the Depression, they didn't get even that.) He demanded that record companies should refuse to permit their products to be played on the air and on juke boxes. To implement his demand he instructed his members - who included classical musicians, as well as danceband and jazz players - to refuse to play on record dates. The ban lasted from 1 August 1942 until September of the following year when cracks appeared in the record companies' opposition. Some of the major companies held out even longer and it was late in 1944 before everyone was toeing Petrillo's line. Petrillo's action had been taken against the advice of a report he had himself commissioned, which recognized the problem but suggested that a recording ban was not the solution. Bandleaders, who depended upon record sales for income and publicity, also opposed the ban. In the event, the ban was only partially successful.

Record companies got around it at first by stockpiling recordings and later by using unaccompanied singers, vocals groups and choirs (singers were not allowed to be members of the AFM) or by using orchestras made up of musicians employed on salary. The strike coincided with a massive surge in the popularity of singers and a corresponding decline in the fortunes of the big bands and many have blamed Petrillo directly for this. While his action was clearly reckless and doubtless a contributory factor, there were many other reasons for the decline, some of which were far more significant. After the ban an uncertain peace followed; but in so far as big bands were concerned, much of the damage was irreversible. In 1948, Petrillo, who remained convinced that his action was not only right and proper but had also been wholly successful, called for another recording ban - but this one lasted less than a year and its long-term effects were negligible. For all his dictatorial nature, Petrillo did have a sense of humour. On one occasion in New York he had to walk down 18 flights of stairs during an elevator operators' strike. Exhausted, he went into a bar for a beer where he wryly observed to columnist Earl Wilson, 'Goddamn unions will ruin the country'. Petrillo's brother, Caesar Petrillo (1898-1963), played trombone in the bands of **Paul Whiteman** and **Vincent Lopez** before becoming a theatre orchestra conductor. Petrillo was heartily disliked by many musicians, who believed that he had wrecked their careers through the strikes. Many also believed him to have opposed integration of AFM locals. Whether or not this was the case, once integration became a fact, pushed through by concerted action from the musicians themselves, Petrillo put his weight behind the move to such effect that President Lyndon B. Johnson invited him to participate in a conference on civil rights. On his retirement Petrillo waived his pension, asking that it be used instead to fund a musical education programme in schools. In 1975 an open-air music stage in Grant Park, Chicago, was named the James C. Petrillo Music Shell and in September 1984 the Chicago Local 10 renamed their headquarters the James C. Petrillo Building. Petrillo's brother, Caesar Petrillo (1989-1963), played trombone in the bands of **Paul Whiteman** and **Vincent Lopez** before becoming a theatre orchestra conductor.

Petrucciani, Michel

b. 28 December 1962, Montpelier, France. After playing with **Kenny Clarke** and **Clark Terry** at the age of 15, Petrucciani moved to Paris, recorded his first album, and formed a successful duo with **Lee Konitz** just two years later. Moving to California in 1982, he joined **Charles Lloyd**'s new quartet. However, it was a solo performance at Carnegie Hall as part of the Kool Jazz Festival that resulted in widespread critical acclaim. With hard-hit notes he echoes *Keith Jarrett*, but it is his delicate **Peterson**-like frills that make him a romantic giant. No pun is intended, because irrespective of his restricted growth, Petrucciani plays with astonishing confidence and beauty. In the mid-80s Petrucciani signed a contract with **Blue Note Records**, and this in turn gave him much greater exposure outside the jazz world. *Michel Plays Petrucciani* features all his own compositions and is an album that sets him free, way beyond the restriction of playing somebody else's material, even in a jazz context. This record brims with flowing music (and some sparkling guitar from **John Abercrombie**). Another necessary record in his catalogue is the solo piano excursion *Promenade With Duke*. From the dozens of Ellington tributes over the years this record oozes respect for the master, so much so that Petrucciani gained both respect and credibility that is already cast in stone. In addition to his solo career worked with **Wayne Shorter** in Manhattan Project. He is a melodic, thoughtful pianist and one of the brightest stars of jazz piano in recent years.

Albums: *Michel Petrucciani Trio* (Owl 1982), *Estate* (IRD 19 1983), *Oracles's Destiny* (Owl 1983), 100 Hearts (Concord 1983), *Note'n Notes* (Owl 1985), *Live At The Village Vanguard* (Concord 1985), *Pianism* (Blue Note 1986), *Power Of Three* (Blue Note 1986), *Cold Blues* (Concord 1986), *Michel Plays Petrucciani* (Blue Note

1988), *Music* (Blue Note 1989), *Playground* (Blue Note 1991), *Live* (1991), *Promenade With Duke* (1993), *Marvellous* (Dreyfus 1994), *Au Theatre Des Champs-Elysees* (Dreyfus 1995).

Pettibone, Shep

Famed for his late 80s/early 90s remix and production work for **Bros**, **Madonna** and other major league pop stars, Pettibone's early origins actually lie in hip hop. Together with **Arthur Baker** he was behind the Jazzy 5's groundbreaking 'Jazzy Sensation' release. He also pioneered the 'mastermixes' of Kiss FM Radio, introducing a new methodology by segueing records to build 'sequences', almost like movements in classical music. It was a parallel development to hip hop's scratching and DJ innovations, which were undoubtedly an ongoing influence. Afterwards he moved into a musical area which is probably best described as disco, reviving the sounds of **Loletta Holloway** to great success, ensuring his status as an in-demand mixer for large budget studio sessions.

Pettiford, Oscar

b. 30 September 1922, Okmulgee, Oklahoma, USA, d. 8 September 1960. Coming from a musical background, Pettiford was competent on several instruments, settling for bass in the early 40s. He played with **Charlie Barnet**, **Roy Eldridge**, **Coleman Hawkins**, **Ben Webster** and others; then in the middle of the decade, was active among the New York beboppers. He briefly co-led a band with **Dizzy Gillespie**, and later led his own groups. From 1945 he was with **Duke Ellington**, moving on in 1948 to the **Woody Herman** band. During the 50s he played in several bands, big and small, often leading his own groups, and was usually in the company of important musicians such as **Thelonious Monk**, **Lucky Thompson** and **Art Blakey**. In 1958 he toured Europe with a jazz concert package, remaining behind to take up residence in Denmark where he died in 1960. A major influence upon bop bass players, Pettiford played with a superb tone and clarity. Nevertheless, he was frequently dissatisfied with his own work and also played cello, an instrument which gave him an opportunity to develop ideas sometimes inhibited by the physical limitations of the bass.

Selected albums: *The Oscar Pettiford Memorial Album* (1954), *Oscar Pettiford Group* (1954), *Basically Duke* (1954), *Bohemia After Dark* (Affinity 1955), *Discoveries* (Savoy 1952-57 recordings), *The Oscar Pettiford Orchestra In Hi-Fi* (Jasmine 1957), *The Legendary Oscar Pettiford* (Black Lion 1959), *Radio Tapes* (Jazzline 1958-1960 recordings), *Blue Brothers* (Black Lion 1960), *Monmartre Blues* (Black Lion 1959-60), Compilation: *Oscar Rides Again* (Affinity 1986).

Pettis, 'Alabama' Junior

b. Coleman Pettis Jnr., c.1935, Alabama, USA, d. April 1988. Pettis worked under a variety of pseudonyms including Daddy Rabbit, Alabama Junior, and Junior Pettis. He learned to play guitar at the age of eight and moved to Chicago in 1952. He was strongly influenced by Lee Jackson, with whom he worked as rhythm guitarist, and is best known for his year spell working with **Magic Slim** from 1973-83. He can be heard on several of Slim's records, supplying excellent complementary work to the leader's tough playing, and he also provides occasional lead vocals and compositions. In 1987 he made his only album under his own name for the Wolf label, and he died of cancer at the beginning of April 1988.

Selected album: *Chicago Blues Sessions Volume Four* (1987).

Petty, Norman

b. 1927, Clovis, New Mexico, USA, d. 15 August 1984, Lubbock, Texas, USA. Petty studied piano during his youth but became a recording engineer on local radio in Texas until his Norman Petty Trio - with wife Violet (organ) and Jack Vaughn (guitar) - achieved moderate record success in 1954 with an arrangement of **Duke Ellington**'s 'Mood Indigo'. In similar cocktail lounge-style were smaller sellers, notably 'On The Alamo' and 1957's self-composed 'Almost Paradise' (revived in the 70s by **Roger Whittaker**). More immediate proceeds from these discs enabled him to build a private studio NorVaJak in Clovis for the sole use of the Trio until Petty realized that he was unwitting owner of the only such facility in New Mexico and West Texas. Confident in his own technical abilities as both engineer and producer, he went public in 1955 - with **Roy Orbison**'s Teen Kings among early customers. Petty was amenable to working at a paper loss in exchange for first refusal on publishing rights (for the Trio's own Nor Vi Jak Music) on items recorded. With a foot in various doors via 'Mood Indigo' *et al.*, he next tried to interest labels in those tracks he considered marketable. Through a lease deal with Roulette Records, the studio's first million-seller was **Buddy Knox**'s 'Party Doll' but the most famous of its clients was **Buddy Holly** who, with his **Crickets**, betrayed sufficient promise for Petty to want to manage them. Furthermore, he (and Violet) received writing and arranging credits for certain Holly smashes - including 'That'll Be The Day' - and, until their sale to **Paul McCartney** in 1973, retained rights to all items recorded by Holly. Indeed, in the years after Buddy's fatal aircraft accident in 1958, Petty felt entitled to overdub fuller backings to often sketchy material for commercial release. After Holly's death, Norman continued to record the Crickets but further hits were sporadic. 1961 brought him an international chartbuster in the **String-A-Longs**' 'Wheels' while **Jimmy Gilmer And The Fireballs** topped ***Billboard***'s Hot 100 in 1963 with 'Sugar Shack'. In the mid-60s, Petty assisted on two of **Brian Poole**

And The Tremeloes' UK chart entries. He maintained a practical interest in his increasingly more splendid studio until his death in August 1984 in Lubbock, Texas, home town of Buddy Holly - with whom Petty's name will always be synonymous.

Petty, Tom, And The Heartbreakers

The Heartbreakers were formed from the ashes of Petty's first professional band, Mudcrutch, in 1971. In addition to Tom Petty (b. 20 October 1953, Florida, USA; guitar) the band comprised; Mike Campbell (b. 1 February 1954, Florida, USA; guitar), Benmont Tench (b. 7 September 1954, Gainesville, Florida, USA; keyboards), Stan Lynch (b. 21 May 1955, Gainesville, Florida, USA; drums) and Ron Blair (b.16 September 1952, Macon, Georgia, USA; bass). Armed with a Rickenbacker guitar and a **Roger McGuinn** voice, Petty's debut was accepted more in England where anything **Byrds**-like would find an audience. McGuinn in fact later recorded 'American Girl' (and did a fine Petty impersonation). The tight-structured rock formula of the first album showed great promise and eventually it made a substantial impression on the US charts, over a year after release. Having received rave reviews following his visit to Europe he released a second collection *You're Gonna Get It* to excellent reviews. Petty was able to appeal both to the new wave and lovers of American west coast rock with his rock songs. *Damn The Torpedoes* followed after a lengthy legal battle during which time he filed for bankruptcy. His cash-flow soon improved as the album was only kept from the top of the US charts by the **Pink Floyd** as it went platinum. Petty's subsequent albums have been similarly satisfying although not as successful. In 1981 he duetted with **Stevie Nicks** on 'Stop Draggin My Heart Around', complete with an **MTV**-style video, and in 1983 he was one of the artists to encourage **Del Shannon** to record again, producing his album *Drop Down And Get Me*. In 1985 he had another major hit with 'Don't Come Around Here No More' aided by an imaginative and award -winning *Alice in Wonderland* video depicting him as the Mad Hatter. During the recording of *Southern Accents* Petty smashed his hand (in anger) on the recording console and had to have a metal splint permanaently fixed as the bones were too badly broken. Petty's outburst failed to stop the album becoming another million-seller. That same year he played **Live Aid** in Philadelphia. The following year he reunited with Nicks for a remake of the **Searchers**' 'Needles And Pins'. His association with **Bob Dylan** prospered and they toured together; additionally Petty performed on Dylan albums and co-wrote with him. The live album *Pack Up The Plantation* delighted old fans, but failed to break any new ground. Tradegy struck that year when Petty's home was burnt down. In 1988 **Jeff Lynne** and Petty struck up a friendship and together with **George Harrison**, **Roy Orbison** and Dylan, they formed the **Traveling Wilburys**. Lynne's high-tech and over crisp production was in evidence on *Full Moon Fever* (a solo project) and *Into The Great Wide Open*, and fortunately the strength of Pettys songs won through. Both albums combined much of Petty's great gift for melody and irresistible 'middle eights' while acknowledging his influences including the **Beatles**, **Byrds**, **R.E.M**. and the **Searchers**. A greatest hits album was released in 1993 and became a huge hit in his homeland (3 million sales to date. It served as an introduction to a younger audience who had seen Petty cited as a major influence to some of the 90s guitar based rock bands. This new wave of success seemed to have inspired Petty to deliver *Wildflowers*, probably most satisfying album. This overtly acoustic and mellow collection gave his lyrics a chance to be heard clearly and together with a lower and more mature vocal delivery it is a stunning work. Seasoned session drummer Steve Ferrone replaced the long serving Stan Lynch and together with Howie Epstein (bass) they have bolstered the permanent band members of Petty, Tench and Campbell into an unbeatable live band. Petty has succeeded in a fickle marketplace by playing honest, unpretentious catchy rock with irrisistible hook lines. He is one of the most durable American artists of the past two decades and one that is still being creative and not dwelling on his past glory.

Albums: *Tom Petty And The Heartbreakers* (Shelter 1976), *You're Gonna Get It* (Shelter 1978), *Damn The Torpedoes* (MCA 1979), *Hard Promises* (MCA 1981), *Long After Dark* (MCA 1982), *Southern Accents* (MCA 1985), *Pack Up The Plantation* (MCA 1985), *Let Me Up (I've Had Enough)* (MCA 1987), *Full Moon Fever* (MCA 1989), *Into The Great Wide Open* (MCA 1991), *Wildflowers* (Warner 1994). Compilation: *Greatest Hits* (MCA 1993).

Pez Band

This melodic US pop-rock outfit was formed in 1976 by vocalist Mimi Betinis and guitarist Tommy Gawenda. Enlisting the services of Mike Gorman (bass) and Mick Rain (drums), they made their debut with a self-titled album on the Passport label. The accent on the commercial dynamic was overt, with thin melodies and lightweight guitar work. The album flopped and the band changed direction to hard-driving, blues-based rock. *Laughing In The Dark* was a remarkable improvement and featured highly engaging lead guitar, reminiscent of **Gary Moore** and **Pat Travers**. This too failed to find favour (perhaps because the band were already labelled as an unsuccessful pop act). Disillusioned by the lack of media response, they bowed out with a live mini-album, *30 Seconds Over Schaumberg*. The group reformed temporarily in 1981, releasing *Cover To Cover*, but then disbanded for a final time.

Albums: *Pezband* (Passport 1977), *Laughing In The Dark* (Passport 1978), *30 Seconds Over Schaumberg* (Passport

1978), *Cover To Cover* (Passport 1981).

Phair, Liz

b. c.1967, USA. Phair was brought up in a wealthy suburb of Chicago, Illinois, by her adoptive father (a physician) and mother (an art-teacher). It was a perfectly happy childhood, during which she befriended the actor Julia Roberts (a friendship later recounted in the song 'Chopsticks'). Her first love was art, but at Oberlin College in Ohio she became involved in the local music scene, which included bands such as **Codeine**, **Bitch Magnet**, **Seam** and **Come**. Phair too began writing songs, and became friends with Chris Brokaw, the guitarist with Come, and after college they both moved to San Francisco, and began playing together. When Brokaw moved back east, Phair used to send him tapes of her music, which generally consisted of 14 new songs each. Brokaw recognized her talent and alerted others. Although Phair herself was not as confident in the quality of these still-evolving songs, she did agree to sign with Matador Records in the summer of 1992. Entering the studio with her drummer and co-producer Brad Wood, Phair announced her intention to make a 'female *Exile On Main Street*'. Ignoring traditional song structures, her approach allowed the low-key production to empower her confessional and occasionally abusive lyrics. With fellow musicians Casey Rice (guitar) and LeRoy Bach (bass) complementing her own playing (like her UK peer, **PJ Harvey**, reference is often made of her voice at the expense of her distinctive guitar playing), Phair produced an album which was widely acclaimed and which sold an impressive 200,000 copies. *Exile In Guyville* lifted the last word of its title from a lyric by Chicago friends **Urge Overkill** and was a sprawling and inspired double album. Her only flaw became apparent during the live shows, when her stage fright was increased by the presence of famous guests such as Wynona Ryder and Rosanna Arquette. This was, perhaps, not to be expected from a woman with the confidence to write the overtly sexual, 'Flower' ('Every time I see your face, I get all wet between my legs'). It was not simply the brash sexuality of her debut that was discarded for her second album, but also her desire to be part of the 'Guyville' set. As she explained in interviews, there was no reason to resent her exclusion now that she had proved herself and moved on. *Whip-Smart* was a more polished set, lacking some of her previous eccentricities. It was still, however, a genuinely exciting and turbulent album, welcomed once again by critics and fans alike.

Albums: *Exile In Guyville* (Matador 1993, double album), *Whip-Smart* (Matador 1994).

Phantom Blue

This guitar-orientated melodic rock outfit hailed from Los Angeles, California, USA. The all-female line-up, comprising vocalist Gigi Hangach (vocals), guitarists Nicole Couch (guitar), Michelle Meldrum (guitar), Kim Nielsen (bass) and Linda McDonald (drums), was impressive on a technical, visual and musical level. Under the guiding hand of Shrapnel Records' guitar supremo, Mike Varney, the girls were introduced to Steve Fontano and **Marty Friedman** (later of **Megadeth**), who became responsible for producing and arranging their debut album. Comprising nine originals, *Phantom Blue* was a credible and rewarding bout of mature, inividual rock which, with a sheen of production gloss to temper the screaming guitars, impressed widely. A second, long-delayed album, *Built To Perform*, saw Friedman guest once more, and included a cover of **Thin Lizzy**'s 'Bad Reputation', but much of the momentum had been lost. In 1994 Rana Ross replaced Nielson on bass as the band attempted to recapture lost ground.

Albums: *Phantom Blue* (Roadrunner 1989), *Built To Perform* (Roadrunner 1993).

Phantom Of The Opera, The

This is probably **Andrew Lloyd Webber**'s most highly regarded and critically acclaimed work to date. Of course, the vast majority of his other productions, including those he wrote with **Tim Rice** and the later ones where people pretend to be cats and trains, have been enormously successful all over the world for many years now, but *The Phantom Of The Opera* seems to be the show that gives audiences the deepest and most enduring satisfaction. It opened at Her Majesty's Theatre in London on 9 October 1986. The score was by Lloyd Webber (music) and Charles Hart (lyrics), with additional lyrics by **Richard Stilgoe**. Lloyd Webber and Stilgoe also wrote the book, which was based on Gaston Leroux's classic 1911 novel. The familiar story is set in the Paris Opera House during the 19th century, where the facially disfigured masked Phantom (**Michael Crawford**) haunts and terrorizes the occupants. He is obsessed with the young and beautiful soprano, Christine (**Sarah Brightman** or Claire Moore), and whisks her away below the theatre, steering her through the candlelit sewers to his richly furnished rooms deep under the streets of the city. He teaches her to sing 'like an angel' and she initially becomes entranced by him, but she still loves another. In his rage, the Phantom threatens to blow up the opera house if she refuses to stay with him. She agrees to his blackmail, but when she kisses him without any apparent sign of revulsion at his deformity, he is so moved that he releases her into the arms of Raoul (Steve Barton), her leading man. Lloyd Webber's 'ravishing' music was his most romantic and overtly operatic so far - and arguably his best. The score contained two outstanding love songs, 'All I Ask Of You', sung by Brightman and Barton, and 'The Music Of The Night', impressively rendered by Crawford, but there were others equally attractive, including 'Masquerade', 'Wandering Child', 'The Phantom Of The Opera', 'Angel Of Music', 'Think Of Me', 'Wishing You Were Somehow Here Again', and 'The Point Of No Return'. **Hal Prince**'s highly impressive staging featured the by-now famous scene in which the great chandelier crashes down from the ceiling on to the stage - one of the Phantom's pranks in reprisal for his protegée not being given the lead. Crawford, who maintains that he only got the job because Lloyd Webber heard him singing while waiting to collect his then wife, Sarah Brightman, from her own lesson, dominated in the leading role. After appearing on the London stage in the musicals ***Billy*** and ***Barnum***, and on film in ***Hello, Dolly!***, this show marked a new beginning in his career. He had a UK Top 10 hit with 'The Music Of The Night', and won the **Laurence Olivier Award** for best actor in a musical. The show itself won for best musical, while Sarah Brightman and **Cliff Richard** almost made the top of the UK chart (number 3) with their duet of 'All I Ask Of You'. While *The Phantom Of The Opera* settled in for a long London run, Crawford, Brightman, and Barton recreated their roles for the Broadway production which opened at the Majestic Theatre on 26 January 1988. 'A muted triumph' was the consensus of opinion, but there was nothing muted about the show's appeal when **Tony Awards** time came round. *The Phantom Of The Opera* won for best musical, actor (Crawford), featured actress (Judy Kaye), sets, costumes, lighting, and director (Prince). Since that time, both the UK and US productions have continued to be the hottest tickets in town, and touring versions have proliferated in many countries. In 1993, as the London production celebrated its seventh anniversary, a second company was dispatched to the provinces, and, in the same year, it was estimated that the show had grossed over $1 billion worldwide.

There have been several other musical adaptations of Gaston Leroux's famous story. The two best-known versions are *Phantom Of The Opera* by Ken Hill, and *Phantom* with a book by Arthur Kopit and music and lyrics by Maury Yeston. Ken Hill's show, which is billed as 'The Original Stage Musical', was first seen in 1984 at the Theatre Royal, Stratford East in London. After revisions, and the negative impact of the Lloyd Webber version, it ran for six months at the Shaftesbury Theatre in the West End from 1991-92, with Peter Straker as the Phantom, music by composers such as Offenbach, Gounod, Verdi, Weber, Bizet, and Mozart, and witty and original lyrics by Hill. The Yeston-Kopit version ('A New Musical Thriller') first emerged in 1990 as a four-hour mini-series on US television with Burt Lancaster and Charles Dance, and was later presented on stage at such venues as the Music Hall, Texas, and the Paper Mill Playhouse, New Jersey. The *Phantom* phenomenon continues in many forms, but as far as the public at large are concerned it probably all started with the 1925 film which starred Lon Chaney. Subsequent screen versions were released in 1943 (with Claude Rains, Susanna Foster and **Nelson Eddy**), 1962 (Herbert Lom, Heather Sears, and Thorley Walters), 1983 (Maxamilian Schell, Jane Seymour and Michael York), and 1989 (Robert Englund, Jill Schoelen and Alex Hyde-Whyte).

Further reading: *The Complete Phantom Of The Opera*, George Perry.

Pharcyde

Spaced-out rappers who first hit big with 'Ya Mama', a series of ridiculous and escalating insults (also referred to as 'Snaps' or 'Playing The Dozens') traded between the vocalists, on the **Delicious Vinyl** label. It was typical fare from this free-flowing West Coast crew, though somewhat derivative of **A Tribe Called Quest** and **Dream Warriors**. However, their observations remained genuinely funny, housed in swinging, almost harmonised rap couplets, jazz breaks and quirky narratives: 'We're all jigaboos - might as well take the money' was a half-stinging, half self-mocking assertion. The single, 'Passing Me By', even contained a definition of old school stylings. They contributed one of the most effective cuts on the **Brand New Heavies**' *Heavy Rhyme Experience* collection, and returned the favour by remixing the latter's 'Soul Flower'. Based in Los Angeles, their goofy, fast talking style defied the early 90s rash of gangsta vinyl from that area with a dogma-deflating blend of cool, loopy rhythms and cultural lyrics. The group comprise Romye, Tre, Imani, Fat Lip, DJ Mark Luv and J-Swift.

Album: *Bizarre Ride II The Pharcyde* (Delicious Vinyl 1992).

Phd

This UK pop duo comprised **Jim Diamond** (vocals), Tony Hymas (keyboards). Their debut album included the single 'I Won't Let You Down', which initially failed to chart. Convinced that the band had potential an extra push from the **WEA** label was put behind the record and finally it paid off when the single reached number 3 in the UK charts and repeated its success in Europe. However they found life hard afterwards with their second and final album, which did not sell as well. The duo went their separate ways and Diamond signed a solo deal with **A&M Records** and found further chart success.

Albums: *Phd* (1981), *Is It Safe ?* (1983).

Phenomena

This ambitious video and musical project was co-ordinated by Tom Galley (brother of former **Whitesnake** guitarist, Mel Galley) - the albums are concept affairs, centred on the theme of supernatural phenomena. However, utilizing an impressive list of guest musicians has not always guaranteed a good result, and Phenomena went some way towards proving this truism. With Neil Murray (bass), **Cozy Powell** (drums), Mel Galley (guitar) and Glenn Hughes (vocals) among the starting line-up, great things were evidently expected for *Phenomena*. However, the songs were often overtly complex and lacked a central melody line. *Dream Runner* released two years later suffered from similar problems, but the music was less of a disappointment. It featured an impeccable array of guests once more, with Ray Gillen, Max Bacon, Scott Gorham, Kyoji Yamamoto and **John Wetton** contributing in one form or another. The album received good reviews in the music media, but sold poorly. As a result, plans to make the Phenomena projects into films were aborted.

Albums: *Phenomena* (Bronze 1985), *Phenomena II - Dream Runner* (Arista 1987).

Phil The Fluter

This show began its life in Dublin as a radio play by Donal Giltinan, based on the life of the celebrated Irish entertainer Percy French, who composed such memorable songs as 'The Mountains Of Mourne' and 'Phil The Fluter's Ball'. The radio show evolved into the stage musical *The Golden Years* which was presented successfully at the Gaiety Theatre in Dublin where it caught the eye of one of London's leading theatrical producers, Harold Fielding. He determined to produce the show in London, and engaged Beverly Cross to collaborate with Giltinan on the book, and composer **David Heneker**, of ***Half A Sixpence*** fame, to supplement Percy French's original score. The result, *Phil The Fluter*, opened in the West End at the Palace Theatre on 13 November 1969. The popular singer **Mark Wynter**, in the role of Percy French, was retained from the cast of *The Golden Years*, and he was joined by comedian and impressionist Stanley Baxter and one of the most celebrated leading ladies of the London musical stage, **Evelyn Laye**. Her rendition of Heneker's poignant 'They Don't Make Them Like That Any More' ('In those days men gave orchids by the dozen/Today they think forget-me-nots will do') still burns brightly in the memory more than 20 years later. She also had a charming duet with Wynter, 'You Like It'. The remainder of the score, a mixture of French and Heneker, included 'If I Had A Chance', 'Mama', 'A Favour For A Friend', 'Good Money', 'How Would You Like Me?', 'Abdoul Abulbul Ameer', 'I Shouldn't Have To Be The One To Tell You', 'Follow Me', 'Are You Right There, Michael?', 'That's Why The Poor Man's Dead', and 'Wonderful Woman'. Following a set of mixed reviews, the show never really caught on with the public, and closed after 125 performances.

Philadelphia International Records

Founded in Philadelphia, Pennsylvania, USA in 1971, this much-respected record company defined the sweet, melodic style of early 70s urban soul. Initiators **Gamble And Huff** were already renowned songwriters and producers through collaborations with **Jerry Butler**, the **Soul Survivors** and the **Intruders**, although several early ventures into label ownership, notably with Gamble and Neptune, had folded prematurely. They nonetheless established a distinctive sound which eschewed Tamla/**Motown**'s cavernous bass lines in favour of a smooth, string-laden, silky approach, fashioned on **Burt Bacharach**'s early work with **Dionne Warwick**, but embellished with lush orchestration and arrangements often obscuring the punch of a crack rhythm section. Armed with a marketing and distribution deal with **Columbia Records**, Gamble and Huff founded Philadelphia International knowing the parent company would exploit the white market, leaving the duo free to concentrate their energies on black radio stations. The result was a series of marvellous cross-over hits, including 'Love Train' and 'Backstabbers' (the **O'Jays**), 'Me And Mrs Jones' (**Billy Paul**) and 'If You Don't Know Me By Now' (**Harold Melvin And The Blue Notes**), while the label's cool, sculpted formula was echoed by **Blue Magic**, the (**Detroit**) **Spinners** and the **Stylistics**. The duo's houseband - Roland Chambers and Norman Harris (guitars), Vince Montana (vibes), Ronnie Baker (bass) and Earl Young (drums) - also appeared on releases by the **Delfonics** and **First Choice**, while **David Bowie** used their Sigma Sound studio to record *Young Americans*. The rise of disco undermined the freshness of 'Philly Soul', but a recurrent controversy of payola allegations did more to undermine the company's collective confidence. Charges against Huff - that he offered inducements in exchange for airplay - were dropped in 1976, but Gamble was fined $2,500, although commentators have viewed the indictment as racially motivated. Philadelphia International continued to function in the 80s, but its pre-eminent position was usurped by a new generation of black acts. It nonetheless set benchmarks for quality and style in the same way as Motown had done during the previous decade.

Compilations: *Philadelphia Classics* (1978), *The Philadelphia Story* (1986, 14-album box-set), *TSOP: The Sound Of Philadelphia* (1988), *The Philadelphia Years, Volume One* (1989), *The Philadelphia Years Volume 2* (1989).

Philips Records

Founded as a division of the Dutch electronics firm, Philips was established as one of the UK's four major record companies by the mid-50s. However, early success was largely due to a licensing deal with US **Columbia** (**CBS**). **Doris Day**, **Frankie Laine**,

Rosemary Clooney and **Johnnie Ray** were among the acts enjoying UK chart-toppers through this association. Philips retained the rights to CBS until 1961, during which time they issued material ranging from sing-a-long (**Guy Mitchell**) to rural blues (**Robert Johnson**). **Mercury** and **Riverside** are another two labels for which Philips held the UK rights and between December 1961 and March 1962 the label licensed four singles from Tamla/**Motown**, before losing out to **Oriole**. During the 60s the superior folk-orientated outlet, **Vanguard** was marketed by Philips in the UK.

Winifred Atwell and **Anne Shelton** were among the homegrown acts who enjoyed success with the label in the 50s but the company did not fully enter the teenage market until the beat boom of the next decade. Howie Casey And The Seniors, whose 'Let's Twist' was issued in 1961 on the budget subsidiary Wing, enjoys the distinction of being the first 'Merseybeat' release. Either in its own imprint, or through its Fontana imprint, Philips signed several successful 60s acts, including the **Pretty Things**, **Merseybeats**, **Walker Brothers** and **Wayne Fontana And The Mindbenders**. A production deal with the fledgling **Island** label brought the **Spencer Davis Group** and **Millie** to the company's roster. In the meantime a US division was responsible for releases by, among others, the **Four Seasons**.

During the mid-60s Philips entered several marketing and distribution deals with independent producers who wanted a label of their own. **Andrew Loog Oldham** founded **Immediate**, **Shel Talmy** inaugurated Planet, while **Larry Page** set up Page One and had great success with the **Troggs**. In 1969 Philips established **Vertigo** as an outlet for progressive music, such as **Black Sabbath** and **Status Quo**. The Philips label still remained active into the 70s, but by this point the parent company had changed its name to **Phonogram**.

Phillips, Barre

b. 27 October 1934, San Francisco, California, USA. At the age of three Barre Phillips was giving solo song recitals. He studied romance languages at Berkeley and then moved to New York where he received double bass lessons from Frederick Zimmermann in the early 60s. In March and April 1963 he played with **Eric Dolphy** at Carnegie Hall, part of **Gunther Schuller**'s Twentieth-Century Innovations series, and from 1964 he was a member of **Jimmy Giuffre**'s revolutionary drumless trio. He worked with Hungarian guitarist **Attila Zoller** between 1965 and 1967 and also with **Archie Shepp**, playing on Shepp's side of the famous *New Thing At Newport* and on one track of his classic *On This Night.* In 1969 he played in an orchestral project led by **John Lennon** and **Yoko Ono**; with the improvising band **Gong** (*Magick Brother*) and with **Mike Westbrook**. Increasingly involved with the European scene, he played with Rolf and **Joachim Kuhn** (1969) and with English saxophonist **John Surman** and fellow-expatriate drummer Stu Martin as the Trio (1969-71). In 1971, in conjunction with **Dave Holland**, he led a whole band of bass players. In 1976 he began recording for **ECM Records** (*Mountainscape*), an arrangement that lasted until 1983. In the latter year he played and recorded with the classical ensemble Accroche Note and in 1988 with **Derek Bailey** and **Company**. 1989 saw him involved with several of British bassist **Barry John Guy**'s projects. Possessed of an acute rhythmic intelligence, Barre Philips is an important link between the free jazz of 60s America and the European free improvisation scene.

Albums: *Unaccompanied Barre* (1968), with John Surman, Stu Martin *The Trio* (1970), *Alors!!!* (1970), with Dave Holland *Music From Two Basses* (1971), *Mountainscape* (1976), *Three Day Moon* (1978), *Journal Violine II* (1980), *Music By* (1981), *Call Me When You Get There* (1983), with Accroche Note *En Concert* (1983), with the Trio *By Contact* (1987, rec. 1971), with Derek Bailey *Figuring* (1988), with Company *Once* (1988), *Camouflage* (1989), *Naxos* (1990), with Jon Rose *Violin Music For Restaurants* (1991).

Phillips, Bill

b. William Clarence Phillips, 28 January 1936, Canton, North Carolina, USA. Phillips grew up in an area steeped in country music and learned guitar and began singing before leaving high school to work as an upholsterer. In 1955, he joined the *Old Southern Jamboree*, on WMIL Miami and sang at local clubs, before moving to Nashville in 1957. He joined Cedarwood Publishing as a songwriter and soon gained attention when he penned **Webb Pierce**'s 1958 Top 10 country hit 'Falling Back To You'. This success saw Phillips signed to **Columbia** and in 1959 and 1960, he registered his first two Top 30 hits with 'Sawmill' and 'Georgia Town Blues', both with **Mel Tillis** and he appeared on the ***Grand Ole Opry***. He joined **Decca** in 1963 and by 1971, had registered 12 more hits, the biggest being 'Put It Off Until Tomorrow' (1966) which, with **Dolly Parton** (the song's co-writer) on harmony vocal, reached number 6. Other Top 10's included 'The Company You Keep' (1966), 'The Words I'm Gonna Have To Eat' and 'Little Boy Sad' (1969), the latter having previously been a 1961 pop hit for **Johnny Burnette**. During the 70s, he registered five more minor hits, when recording on the **United Artistes** or Soundwaves label. From the early 70s, he began to work as part of the **Kitty Wells-Johnny Wright** Show, although continuing to make a few recordings as a solo artist. In 1995, he suffered a stroke and Wells, Wright and other country music friends played a charity show to raise money for him.

Albums: *Bill Phillips Best* (Harmony 1964), *Put It Off Until Tomorrow* (Decca 1966), *Bill Phillips Style* (Decca 1967), *Country Action* (Decca 1968), *Little Boy Sad* (Decca 1970).

Phillips, Brewer

b. 16 November 1924, Coita, Mississippi, USA. Phillips was on the Chicago blues scene from the mid-50s, when he worked briefly with **Memphis Minnie,** and from 1957-75 he played rhythm guitar for Hound Dog Taylor, taking occasional solos, and contributing significantly to the Houserockers' brash, energetic sound. After Taylor's death he continued to work the Chicago clubs, making occasional wider forays, and recording tracks that had the unpretentious, funky drive of his former leader, and revealed him to be a capable blues singer.

Albums: *Whole Lotta Blues* (1982), *Ingleside Blues* (1982).

Phillips, Bruce 'Utah'

b. 1935, Cleveland, Ohio, USA. Phillips's family were labour organizers and in 1947 they moved to Utah. Bruce subsequently worked at Yellowstone National Park, and, while there, he was nicknamed 'Utah'. When he left the Army, after serving in Korea, he became politically active, campaigning for a number of causes committed to peace. He ran for the Senate in 1968, but did not pursue a political career. After travelling to New York, he attempted unsuccessfully to sell some of his songs for publication. He recorded his first album for Prestige in 1960. In 1969 Phillips started travelling and singing, doing his first show in Norfolk, Virginia. In 1974, he took up truck farming. While based on a farm near Spokane, Washington, he wrote essays and poetry. Phillips earlier 'hoboed' around the USA, playing at free concerts and for trade unionists and, not surprisingly given his background, he specialized in union and railroad travelling songs. With the demise of the railroads, one song he sang was particularly poignant, 'Daddy, What's A Train?'. His first release for Philo Records, *Good Though!* includes the story with the subtle title of 'Moose Turd Pie'. The whole album is given over to songs and stories about hoboing and trains. The later *All Used Up: A Scrapbook* includes the classic 'Hallelujah! I'm A Bum'. *El Capitan* featured songs taken from the point of view of the working man and included the song 'Enola Gay', about the dropping of the first atomic bomb. Phillips's songs have been recorded by other artists including **Joan Baez**.

Albums: *Bruce 'Utah' Phillips* (1960), *Welcome To Caffe Lena* (60s), *Good Though!* (Philo 1968), *El Capitan* (Philo 1969), *All Used Up: A Scrapbook* (1975), *We Have Fed You All For A Thousand Years* (1984).

Further reading: *Starlight On The Rails And Other Songs*, Utah Phillips.

Phillips, Don

b. 18 December 1913, d. 24 February 1994. A popular figure in both the world of theatre and music, Phillips made his reputation in the 50s and 60s as a musical arranger to **Shirley Bassey**, **Joan Regan**, **Donald Peers**, **Anne Shelton**, **Dickie Vlanetine**, **Alan Jones** and others. He would also play piano on stage for the Marx Brothers, and toured Cyprus with **Harry Secombe** to entertain troops. Phillips left school at the age of 14 with no musical training, but by the following year had began his career playing the piano in London pubs. Almost immediately he was spotted by music publisher **Lawrence Wright** who bought his songs. Among his many noteworthy compositions were 'Old Piano Rag', 'Skyscraper Fantasy', 'Concerto In Jazz' and 'A Live Show Is The Best Show', which became the theme tune to literally thousands of summer season seaside shows. 'Melody Of The Sea' brought him an **Ivor Novello** award in 1958, while many of his songs were entered in the **Eurovision Song Contest**: the best known pair being 'Love Is The Same Everywhere' (**Matt Monro**) and 'Girl With The Curl' (**Ronnie Carroll**). Earlier he had been granted a Royal Command Performance in 1954. He went on to become musical director of several travelling shows and pantomimes, maintaining an office in Denmark Street ('Tin Pan Alley') until the advent of Parkinson's Disease in the late 80s.

Phillips, Esther

b. Esther Mae Jones, 23 December 1935, Galveston, Texas, USA, d. 7 August 1984, Carson, California, USA. This distinctive vocalist was discovered by bandleader **Johnny Otis**. She joined his revue in 1949 where, as 'Little Esther', the teenage singer recorded two number 1 R&B singles, 'Double Crossing Blues' and 'Mistrustin' Blues'. She then worked solo following the band's collapse, but by the middle of the decade Phillips was chronically addicted to drugs. In 1954 she retired to Houston to recuperate and did not fully resume recording until 1962. Esther's version of 'Release Me', a country standard which was later a hit for **Engelbert Humperdinck**, mirrored the blend of black and white music found, contemporaneously, in **Ray Charles** and **Solomon Burke**. An album, *Release Me! - Reflections Of Country And Western Greats*, consolidated this style, but when Phillips moved to the **Atlantic** label, her recordings assumed a broader aspect. Polished interpretations of show tunes and standards contrasted a soul-based perspective shown in her retitled version of the **John Lennon/Paul McCartney** song, 'And I Love Him', a performance showcased on the syndicated television show, *Around The Beatles*. Her unique, nasal intonation was perfect for her 1966 hit, 'When A Woman Loves A Man', while her several collaborations with the **Dixie Flyers**, the

highly respected Criteria studio houseband, were artistically successful. The singer moved to Kudu Records in 1972 where she recorded the distinctly biographical 'Home Is Where The Hatred Is', an uncompromising **Gil Scott-Heron** composition. The same label provided 'What A Diff'rence A Day Makes' (1975), which reached the US Top 20 and the UK Top 10. She also completed two exceptional albums at this time, *From A Whisper To A Scream* and *Alone Again Naturally*, but was increasingly pushed towards a specialist rather than popular audience. Ill health sadly undermined this artist's undoubted potential, and in August 1984, Esther died of liver and kidney failure.
Albums: *Memory Lane* (1956), *Release Me! - Reflections Of Country And Western Greats* (1963), *And I Love Him* (1965), *Esther* (1966), *The Country Side Of Esther Phillips* (1966), *Burnin' - Live At Freddie Jett's Pied Piper LA* (1970), *From A Whisper To A Scream* (1972), *Alone Again Naturally* (1972), *Black-Eyed Blues* (1973), *Performance* (1974), *What A Difference A Day Makes* (1975), *Confessin' The Blues* (1975), with guitarist Joe Beck *Esther Phillips With Beck* (1975), *For All We Know* (1976), *Capricorn Princess* (1976), *You've Come A Long Way Baby* (1977), *All About Esther* (1978), *Here's Esther...Are You Ready* (1979), *A Good Black Is Hard To Crack* (1981). Compilation: *Little Esther Phillips - The Complete Savoy Recordings* (1984, her entire 1949-1959 sessions).

Phillips, Gene

b. Eugene Floyd Phillips, 25 July 1915, St. Louis, Missouri, USA. Phillips learned to play ukulele and switched to guitar at the age of 11, after which he began playing and singing for tips and graduated through several obscure local bands. Between 1941-43, he played guitar behind the **Mills Brothers**, relocating with them to Los Angeles, and later worked and recorded with Lorenzo Flennoy, **Wynonie Harris**, **Johnny Otis** and **Jack McVea**. Phillips' **Charlie Christian**-inspired guitar and jump-blues shouting began to be featured on his own recordings for Modern Records from 1945, supported by west coast stalwarts such as **Maxwell Davis** and Jack McVea. They produced such hits as 'Big Legs', 'Just A Dream' and 'Rock Bottom'. Phillips' later records for RPM, **Imperial**, Exclusive, Federal (with Preston Love) and Combo, were successful locally and he spent the 50s doing extensive session work with artists such as **Percy Mayfield**, who played on 'Please Send Me Someone To Love' and **Amos Milburn**, but retired from the music business with the advent of rock 'n' roll.
Albums: *Gene Phillips & His Rhythm Aces* (1986), *I Like 'Em Fat* (1988).

Phillips, Joe 'Flip'

b. 26 March 1915, New York City, New York, USA. After playing in small groups in the New York area, Phillips joined **Woody Herman**'s First Herd in 1944. By the time he left the band, Phillips's reputation as a tenor saxophonist was established nationally and on record. He then became a member of **Norman Granz**'s touring package, **Jazz At The Philharmonic**, a move which raised his international profile. He remained with JATP until the late 50s, toured Europe with **Benny Goodman** and then opted for working outside music by day and leading a small group by night in Florida. This lifestyle continued for 15 years, then, in 1975, Phillips moved to New York and became more active in jazz, touring Europe into the late 80s. A magnificent ballad player, early in his career Phillips was often obliged to play uptempo rabble-rousers which he did with enormous vitality. In later years, in control of his repertoire, he developed the ballad side of his playing and proved himself to be an outstanding interpreter of great songs.
Selected albums: *Flip* (1949), *Flip Phillips Quintet* i (1951), *Flip Phillips Trio* (1952), with JATP *Live At The Nichigeki Theatre Tokyo* (1953), *Flip Phillips Quintet* ii (1954), *Your Place Or Mine?* (1963), *Phillips' Head* (1975), *Together* (1978), *Flipenstein* (1981), *Flip Phillips And His Swedish Friends* (1982), *A Melody From The Sky* (Doctor Jazz 1986), *A Real Swinger* (1988), *A Sound Investement* (Concord 1988), *The Claw* (Chiaroscuro 1988), *Try A Little Tenderness* (Chiaroscuro1993).

Phillips, John

b. 30 August 1935, Parris Island, South Carolina, USA. Phillips began his recording career in 1960 as a member of pop singing group the Smoothies, but the following year formed the **Journeymen** with **Scott McKenzie** and Dick Weissman. This popular harmony folk act completed three albums marked by the artist's growing songwriting abilities. He relaunched his old group as the New Journeymen with his wife **Michelle Phillips** and Marshall Brickman. His compositions were by now being recorded by the **Kingston Trio**, but as traditional folk began embracing elements of rock, so Phillips forged a more contemporary perspective, notably with the **Mamas And The Papas**. Evocative songs, including 'California Dreamin'' (1965), 'Monday Monday' (1966) and 'Creeque Alley' (1967) helped established this act as one of the finest of its era, while Phillips also penned the anthemic 'San Francisco (Be Sure To Wear Flowers In Your Hair)' for former colleague McKenzie. The artist drew contemporaneous plaudits as chief organizer of the **Monterey Pop Festival**, but internal disaffection led to the demise of his group in 1968. In 1970 he completed *John Phillips: The Wolfking Of LA*, a superb set redolent of his erstwhile band but infused with C&W affectations, before completing an ill-fated Mamas And The Papas reunion album. John's recording career waned during the 70s. His third wife, Genevieve Waite, released one album, *Romance Is On The Rise*, which benefited considerably from Phillips'

involvement. A solo single, 'Revolution On Vacation', appeared in 1976, but although he produced several tracks for former wife Michelle Phillips' *Victim Of Romance*, he fell increasingly under the influence of hard drugs. A projected solo album, with **Keith Richard** and **Mick Jagger** assisting, fell apart in a narcotic haze. An equally disastrous attempt at a Broadway musical, *Man On The Moon*, further dented Phillip's standing. Convicted of trafficking in narcotics in 1981, Phillips entered a rehabilitation programme and, following his sentence, re-established the Mamas And The Papas as a touring attraction. In 1989, Phillips joined McKenzie in composing 'Kokomo' which, with additional contributions by Mike Love and **Terry Melcher**, became a US number 1 hit for the **Beach Boys**. By 1991 the Mamas And The Papas line-up included Phillips, Scott McKenzie, Elaine 'Spanky' McFarlane and Laura McKenzie Phillips, but whereas no further recordings have ensued, the artist's highly-successful autobiography provided a salutary overview of dashed 60s idealism and an extraordinary saga of Phillips' gigantic appetite for drugs. He is the father of Chynna Phillips from the multi-million selling group **Wilson Phillips**, and a track about John, written by his daughter is contained on *Shadows And Light*.
Album: *John Phillips: The Wolfking Of LA* (1970).
Further reading: *Papa John*, John Phillips with Jim Jerome.

Phillips, Michelle

b. Holly Michelle Gillian, 6 April 1944, Long Beach, California, USA. Originally a teenage model, Michelle was drafted into the folk group the New Journeymen by her future husband, **John Phillips**. By the mid-60s, she was enjoying chart success and international stardom as a member of the **Mamas And The Papas**. Michelle co-wrote the group's debut million seller 'California Dreamin'', plus several other compositions on their early albums. She also persuaded the group to record one of their biggest hits - a revival of the **Shirelles**' 'Dedicated To The One I Love'. Her relationship with her husband became strained following her affair with **Gene Clark** of the **Byrds** and she was briefly ousted from the Mamas And The Papas in 1966. She returned within a month and remained with them until their demise in 1968. Following the dissolution of her marriage to John, she pursued an acting career, gradually progressing from bit parts in *The Last Detail* and *Shampoo* to major parts in *Dillinger*, *Valentino*, *Broodline* and *The Man With Bogart's Face*. Apart from an ill-fated Mamas And Papas reunion album her recording career ceased until 1976 when she release the expressive 'No Love Today', backed by the extraordinary 'Aloha Louie'. The latter, which she co-wrote with her producer John Phillips, was a mischievous romantic letter to entrepreneur **Lou Adler**. In 1977, she finally released her long-awaited solo album, *Victim Of Romance*. Produced and arranged by **Jack Nitzsche**, the work was an unexpected triumph, with some excellent compositions, most notably from John **Moon Martin**. Thereafter, Michelle returned to acting and no further recordings have emerged. She is the mother of Chynna Phillips, a member of the successful **Wilson Phillips**.
Album: *Victim Of Romance* (1977).

Phillips, Phil

b. John Phillip Baptiste, 14 March 1931, Lake Charles, Louisiana, USA. Phillips wrote his one hit, 'Sea Of Love', to impress a would-be girlfriend in 1958. He was introduced to producer George Khoury, who recorded the song at the Goldband Recording Studio and released it on his own label, credited to Phil Phillips And The Twilights. Although the song never had the intended effect upon the girl, the single sold well locally, resulting in the larger **Mercury Records** picking up distribution and the ballad reached number 2 in the US national chart and number 1 in the R&B chart. The song was typical of the 'swamp-rock' sound that Cajun community of the bayou of southern Louisiana was producing by such artists as **Rod Bernard**, **Tommy McLain**, and Johnnie Allan. Phillips recorded several other songs during the next few years, but never again managed to chart. His song later resurfaced recorded by **Marty Wilde** (UK number 3, 1959), **Del Shannon** and the **Honeydrippers** (a rock supergroup with **Robert Plant**, **Jimmy Page**, **Jeff Beck**, and Nile Rodgers), the latter nearly matching the original's performance by reaching the US number 3 position in 1985. In 1989, Phillips' original recording made news again as the title song for Al Pacino's film of the same name. Phillips was working as a Louisiana disc jockey in the late 80s.

Phillips, Sam

b. 1923, Florence, Alabama, USA. Although harbouring ambitions as a criminal lawyer, Phillips was obliged to drop out of high school to support his family. In 1942 he took up a post as disc jockey at station WLAY in Muscle Shoals, before moving to WREC in Memphis as an announcer four years later. In 1950 he opened Sam's Memphis Recording Studio at 706 Union Avenue and although initial work largely consisted of chronicling weddings and social gatherings, Phillips' main ambition was to record local blues acts and license the resultant masters. **Howlin' Wolf**, **Bobby 'Blue' Bland**, **Ike Turner**, **B.B. King** and **Roscoe Gordon** were among the many acts Phillips produced for independent outlets **Chess**, Duke and RPM. Their success inspired the founding of **Sun Records** in February 1952, a venture which flourished the following year when **Rufus Thomas** scored a notable R&B hit with 'Bear Cat'. Success was maintained by **'Little' Junior Parker** and **Billy 'The Kid' Emerson**, while Phillips looked to expand the label's horizons by recording country acts. His wish to find a white singer comfortable with R&B was answered in 1954 with the arrival of **Elvis Presley**. The singer's five singles recorded with Phillips rank among pop's greatest achievements, and although criticized for allowing his protege to sign for **RCA Records**, the producer used the settlement fee to further the careers of **Carl Perkins**, **Johnny Cash** and, later, **Jerry Lee Lewis**. Phillips' simple recording technique - single track, rhythmic string bass and judicious echo - defined classic rockabilly and for a brief period the label was in the ascendant. The style, however, proved too inflexible and by the beginning of the 60s new Memphis-based studios, **Stax** and **Hi Records**, challenged Sun's pre-eminent position. Phillips also became increasingly distracted by other ventures, including mining concerns, radio stations and, more crucially, his share of the giant Holiday Inn hotel chain. In 1969 he sold the entire Sun empire to country entrepreneur **Shelby Singleton**, thus effectively ending an era. Sam Phillips is nonetheless still revered as one of the leading catalysts in post-war American music and, if nothing else, for launching the career of Elvis Presley.

Phillips, Sid

b. 14 June 1902, London, England, d. 23 May 1973. Deeply immersed in the music business from childhood, Phillips played clarinet in various bands, including one led by his brothers, and also worked in music publishing and for record companies. In the early 30s he was staff arranger for the popular band led by Bert **Ambrose** and later became a member of the band. He also began leading his own small group in the 30s, but it was the bands he led from 1949 onwards that built his reputation. Broadcasting regularly on the radio, Phillips also recorded and his band became one of the best-known dixieland groups in the UK. Among the many fine musicians he employed at one time or another were **George Shearing**, **Kenny Ball** and **Tommy Whittle**. A gutsy, full-toned clarinettist, Phillips was also a skilful arranger and composed jazz-oriented dance tunes and several classical works. Changes in popular taste meant that from the 60s onwards his music was not in great demand, but he continued working until his death in 1973.

Albums: *Sid Phillips And His Band* i (1960s), *Stardust* (60s), *Sid Phillips And His Band* (1962), *Sid Phillips And His Band* iii (1964), *Rhythm Is Our Business* (c.1970), *Sid Phillips And His Great Band Play Stomps, Rags And Blues* (1975), *Sid Phillips Plays Barrelhouse Piano* (1975). Compilations: *H'ors D'Ouvres* (1976), *Anthology, Volume 1 - Chicago* (1976), *Anthology, Volume 2 - Lonesome Road* (1977), *Anthology, Volume 3 - Way Down Yonder In New Orleans* (1978), *The Best Of Sid Phillips* (1977).

Phillips, Steve

b. Nicholas Stephen Phillips, 18 February 1948, London, England, son of sculptor Harry Phillips. Steve first started playing guitar in 1961, at the time emulating rockabilly artists from the **Sun** label. From the age of eight he had been hooked on **Elvis Presley**, when others of his age were discovering **Hank B. Marvin** and the **Shadows**. Phillips was influenced by such people as **Robert Johnson** and **Scotty Moore**, an influence that was to become more apparent later in Steve's country blues playing. Up until 1964, Phillips had played piano in a jug band, called Easy Mr. Steve's Bootleggers, but by 1965 he switched to blues. By the end of 1968, he was being booked regularly in the folk and blues clubs of his local area. During 1968, Steve met **Mark Knopfler**, at the time a junior reporter in Leeds, and together they formed a duo, the Duolian String Pickers. This lasted until Knopfler moved to London, later to form **Dire Straits**. From 1974-76 Phillips fronted the Steve Phillips Juke Band, which included his brother on bass. Steve met **Brendan Croker**, in 1976, and they played occasionally as a duo. During this time, Steve had been supporting his music working as a guitar repairer and a furniture and picture restorer. Following a brief period of unemployment, he took up landscape painting until 1986. Long-time friend Croker coaxed Phillips out of his 'retirement', by organizing bookings. BBC disc jockey Andy Kershaw, using the growing popularity of 'Roots Music', helped create a demand that enabled Phillips to turn professional in 1986. Phillips achieved a higher profile with his appearances as support to acts such as the **Blues Band** and **Nanci Griffith**. He was then approached by Knopfler, who offered to produce an album by Steve. The project grew into the **Notting Hillbillies**, which included Guy Fletcher from Dire Straits, and Brendan Croker. Steve Phillips' recorded output is limited and is no reflection on his obvious talent. In 1991, he recorded two tracks, 'Stones In My Passway' and 'When You Got A Good Friend', for a Robert Johnson compilation. *The Best Of Steve Phillips* consists of recordings made during the previous 10 years, but is not a compilation in the strict sense of the word.

Albums: *The Best Of Steve Phillips* (1987), *Steel Rail Blues* (1990), with the Notting Hillbillies *Missing Presumed Having A Good Time* (1990).

Phillips, Washington

b. c.1891, Freestone County, Texas, USA, d. 31 December 1938, Austin, Texas, USA. Phillips was unique on records in accompanying his plaintive gospel singing with the ethereal sounds of the dolceola, a zither equipped with a piano-like keyboard, of which only some 100 examples were made following its invention in 1902. Phillips recorded annually for

Columbia from 1927-29, and his simple moral homilies were the work of a man who proclaimed his lack of education, preferring to trust in faith. His most famous song is the two-part 'Denomination Blues', an attack on the squabbling of black Christian sects, so titled because it uses the tune of 'Hesitation Blues'.
Album: *Denomination Blues* (1980).

Phiri, Ray Chipika

b. 17 July 1950, Natal, South Africa. Guitarist, vocalist and producer Phiri developed a growing reputation in Europe and the USA in the late 80s, following his contributions to **Paul Simon**'s 1986 *Graceland* and his role on Simon's subsequent world tour. By this time he had already been a major star in South Africa since the early 70s. He joined his first band, Jabuva Queens, a mbaqanga outfit, in 1967. In 1968, the group had a substantial local hit with the single 'Spონono', which continued to sell for over 10 years, long after Jabuvu had broken up. In 1971, he joined the Cannibals, one of the bands which went on to dominate the Soweto soul boom of the mid and late 70s, playing a **Stax**-influenced style of township funk. Between then and 1978, the Cannibals released 29 gold singles and three gold albums. Following the death of lead vocalist Jacob Mparanyana Radebe in 1978, Jabuvu disbanded, and after a period working as a session musician in Johannesburg, Phiri formed Stimela, playing an exciting blend of mbaqanga and black American funk. Phiri's songwriting for Stimela found him convincingly assuming the role of social commentator and teacher, asking people to look inside, rather than outside, for the answer to life's problems; to fight back after failure, to avoid self-pity. But in a country where inflamed sensitivities and paranoid authoritarianism encourage all sorts of interpretations to be made of innocently straightforward material, his lyrics frequently brought him into conflict with the regime. His celebrated single 'Highland Drift', released at the height of Zimbabwe's struggle for independence, was banned by the South African Broadcasting Corporation, while 1986's 'Whisper In The Deep' faced the not unrelated phenomenon of a simultaneous radio ban and massive sales success. Since first working with Paul Simon in 1986, Phiri has continued to work with Stimela, but has made increasingly frequent guest appearances with other artists, African and American, while also attempting to launch a solo career in the West. In 1990, he signed to major French label Barclay and began work on his first solo album, recorded in South Africa and mixed in Paris.
Albums: all with Stimela *Fire Passion Ecstasy* (1984), *Shadows Fear And Pain* (1985), *Rewind* (1986), *Look Listen And Decide* (1986).

Phoenix

This UK group rose from the ashes of **Argent** in 1975. A trio, the band comprised John Verity (vocals/guitar), Robert Henrit (drums) and Jim Rodford (keyboards/bass). They continued in much the same vein as before; hard-rock infused with melody and a keen sense of dynamics, and debuted with a self-titled album in 1976, before landing the support slot to **Ted Nugent**'s UK tour. The band proved an excellent live proposition, but this was never translated into album sales, and they split up after just 12 months together. In 1979 Verity and Henrit reformed Phoenix with **Russ Ballard** (keyboards/vocals), Bruce Turgon (bass), Ray Minnhinnett (guitar) and **Michael Des Barres** (vocals). This short-lived collaboration produced *In Full View*, a non-descript melodic rock album that sold poorly. The band disintegrated shortly afterwards, with Verity and Henrit joining Charlie and then later forming Verity, under the vocalist's own surname.
Albums: *Phoenix* (CBS 1976), *In Full View* (Charisma 1980).

Photos

Three-quarters of the Photos had previously been three quarters of **DJM Records**' token punk band **Satans Rats**, who released three singles in the late 70s. Formed in Evesham, Worcestershire, this trio comprised Steve Eagles (b. 1958; guitar) and Ollie Harrison (drums), who were at college together, and Dave Sparrow (bass) who had been in the Ipswich-band Quorum. The boys were in a club when they came across the photogenic Wendy Wu (b. 29 November 1959, Winson Green, West Midlands, England) who had previously managed a small band and been a hotel receptionist. Recruiting Wendy as their vocalist they became the Photos and signed with **CBS** in 1979. Their debut single was the stunningly accurate, if perhaps a little conceited, 'I'm So Attractive'. The four track EP released in 1980 included their own tribute to the Birmingham night-club Barbarellas. None of their singles on CBS/Epic dented the charts despite **Tony Visconti** being called in as producer. Wendy left in 1981 and was briefly replaced by Che from the **Orchids**. By 1983 they had moved on to the Rialto label but soon split up. Wendy would later work with **Steve Strange** in the band Strange Cruise. Steve Eagles went on to join **Blurt** and more recently re-emerged in one the most promising new bands of 1992, **Bang Bang Machine**.
Album: *The Photos* (Epic 1980).

Phranc

b. 1958, Los Angeles, California, USA. Before her career as the self-styled 'Jewish-American lesbian folksinger' Phranc had served an apprenticeship, of sorts, by appearing in LA 'hardcore' groups (Gender, Catholic Discipline and Castration Squad). On her return to acoustic playing in 1980, Phranc's sets consisted of autobiographical, part-comic songs, at

times performed to similar hardcore audiences from her recent past. These appearances led to the gay coffee-house/folk circuit. Her warmly received *Folksinger* set a standard with titles such as 'Female Mudwrestling', 'Amazons' and 'One O'The Girls'. Her willingness to tackle such subjects as her sexuality, left-wing politics and her own family problems have so far prevented her from achieving anything beyond cult status. Phranc's third album was highlighted by her role as support act on **Morrissey**'s first full British tour of 1991.
Albums: *Folksinger* (1986), *I Enjoy Being A Girl* (1989), *Positively Phranc* (1991).

Piaf

Legend has it that when Pam Gems was writing this musical play about **Edith Piaf**, 'the mid-20th century chanteuse who took to young men, drugs and fame, and regretted nothing', she saw **Elaine Paige** in a West End show and decided that she would be the ideal choice for the lead. But in the early 70s Paige was too young, and had yet to make a name for herself, so the role went to Jane Lapotaire, whose nerve-shattering performance earned her a **Tony Award** when the show transferred to Broadway. Since then, Elaine Paige has established herself as one of the outstanding leading ladies on the London musical stage, and was therefore first in line to star in Peter Hall's revival which began its limited run on 13 December 1993. However, Miss Paige was not too happy with Hall's choice of theatre - the Piccadilly - because of its recent association with a series of flop musicals which included ***Mutiny!***, *Metropolis*, ***King***, ***Moby Dick***, and ***Which Witch***. She need not have worried: the critics were unanimous in their praise for her 'astonishingly poignant performance as the tiny, black-garbed creature - a powerhouse of emotion'. She matched Piaf vulgarity for vulgarity, but her finest moments came when she sang those resounding anthems, 'Mon Dieu', 'Je Ne Regrette Rein', and the impassioned aria of loss, 'Hymne A L'Amour'. Lapotaire still lingers in the memory, but, with her powerful vocal range and heart-rending, emotional vibrato, Elaine Paige was Edith Piaf to the life.

Piaf, Edith

b. Edith Giovanna Gassion, 19 December 1915, Paris, France, d. 11 October 1963. Born into desperate poverty, Piaf survived desertion by her mother and temporary childhood blindness, to eke a living singing on the streets of Paris. After a brief period living in the country she sang in the streets with her father, an impoverished entertainer. The owner of Cerny's cabaret, Louis Leplée, heard the little girl and not only encouraged her but, struck by her diminutive stature, nicknamed her 'piaf', Parisian argot for 'little sparrow'. Piaf's dramatic singing style and her anguished voice appealed to French audiences and by the outbreak of World War II she had become a star. She proved her capacity for survival when she maintained her popularity despite being held as a material witness to Leplée's murder and in the face of accusations of collaboration with the German occupying forces. After the war Piaf's reputation spread internationally and she appeared in New York, singing at Carnegie Hall. In her private life Piaf was as tormented as the heroines of her songs and she had many relationships, most causing her severe emotional damage. She collapsed in 1959 but came back to sung with renewed vigour even if her physical condition was visibly deteriorating. Among her many hits were several songs which she made her own, 'Les Tres Cloche's, 'Milord', 'La Vie En Rose' and, above all others if only because the sentiment expressed in title and lyric so eloquently expressed her attitude to life, 'Non, Je Ne Regrette Rien'.
Selected albums: *Sincerely* (1960), *Piaf At The Paris Olympia* (1961), *C'est La Piaf* (1962), *La Reine De La Chanson* (1963), *I Regret Nothing* (1971), *Her Legendary Live Recordings* (1979), *De L'Accordeoniste A Milord* (1983), *Edith Piaf, Volumes 1-4* (1986), *The Best Of Edith Piaf (1936-43), Volumes 1 & 2* (1986), *Heart And Soul* (1987), *25th Anniversary Album* (1988), *30eme Anniversaire* (1993, 2-CD set), *Edith Piaf 1946-1963* (1993, 10-CD set), *L'Immortelle* (1994), various artists *Edith Piaf Tribute* (D# Records 1994).
Further reading: *The Wheel Of Fortune: The Autobiography Of Edith Piaf*, Edith Piaf. *Piaf*, Monique Lange. *The Piaf Legend*, David Bret. *Piaf*, Margaret Crosland. *Piaf*, Simone Berteaut. *Edith Piaf: My Life*, Edith Piaf and Jean Noli.

Piano

The piano, or pianoforte, is a musical instrument with a keyboard which is struck by the fingers, each key being connected to a hammer which strikes a tuned string and then rebounds. The piano evolved to its present form towards the end of the 18th century, at which time it enjoyed widespread popularity both professionally and domestically. The piano has 88 keys (experimental and 'one-off' instruments vary) and a range of over seven octaves. The volume of sound varies according to the degree of force with which the player strikes the keys, while further changes to sound, and the attenuation or otherwise of notes, can be effected by foot-operated damper pedals. The construction of the instrument varies from the 'concert grand' to the domestic 'upright'. Manufacturers abound in Europe and the USA, with Japan becoming a late and prolific producer. Amongst the best-known of the long-established manufacturers are Bechstein, Bluthner and Steinway. By the beginning of the 20th century the piano was the most popular domestic instrument in the USA and UK. In many homes, even those of the less well-off, families gathered around the piano to sing popular songs of the day. Many establishments in which the public gathered, such as restaurants, cafes and saloons, had pianos. By the 20s, the place of the piano as a popular source of domestic entertainment had been affected by economic circumstances and was largely supplanted by the gramophone and the advent of radio. The instrument was quickly reduced to being used primarily for public performances.

In the USA in the closing years of the last century a form of popular music known as ragtime enjoyed a passing popularity. Essentially, ragtime was music for the piano and some of the form's exponents later moved into jazz, although the two forms were markedly different. Amongst ragtime entertainers, many of whom were also composers, were **Scott Joplin**, **Tony Jackson** and **Jelly Roll Morton**. Of these, only Morton moved successfully into jazz. During the 20s and 30s jazz was the form of popular music which made most use of the piano. Stylistically, the musical forms used by pianists developed through the blues into all areas of early jazz and by the advent of the swing era the instrument was to be found in most ensembles, regardless of size. Significant jazz pianists in these years include Morton, **Earl Hines**, **James P. Johnson**, **Fats Waller**, **Art Tatum** (a virtuoso performer), **Mary Lou Williams** and **Teddy Wilson**. Towards the end of the 30s, and in the midst of the swing era, developments in jazz piano playing began to anticipate future shifts into bebop. Pianists active in this period included **Nat 'King' Cole**, **Bud Powell** and **Thelonious Monk**. Other important figures in bebop were pianists **Horace Silver** and **Hampton Hawes**. To one side of the developing thrust of jazz piano are highly individualistic players, amongst whom are **Erroll Garner** and **Count Basie**. Also outside the mainstream was the briefly fashionable boogie woogie style, with practitioners such as **Clarence 'Pinetop' Smith**, **Jimmy Yancey**, **Albert Ammons** and **Pete Johnson**, also an outstanding blues player.

A number of bandleaders in jazz played piano, amongst them Hines, Basie, **Stan Kenton**, **Gil Evans** and the leading composer in jazz, **Duke Ellington**. During the 30s and 40s, piano players who also sang found a level of success, especially in urban centres such as New York. Singer-pianists of note include **Mabel Mercer**, **Charles Brown**, **Cleo Brown** and, later, **Rose Murphy** and **Blossom Dearie**. A corresponding trend occurred in the UK between the wars with a number of piano-playing entertainers and bandleaders, many of them non-British, enjoying considerable success: **Leslie 'Hutch' Hutchinson**, **Carroll Gibbons**, **Turner Layton** and **Charlie Kunz**. The tradition of the sophisticated singer-pianist has continued in jazz with artists such as **Dave Frishberg**, **Mose Allison** and **Dardanelle**. The rise in popularity of R&B found a number of pianists able to adapt to fashionable demands, amongst them **Bill Doggett**, **Little Willie Littlefield** and **Ray Charles**. Rock 'n' roll also had a number of performers who clung to the piano in the face of the growing popularity of the guitar, amongst them **Little Richard** and **Jerry Lee Lewis**. Both these performers thrashed their pianos with hard driving music. On the opposite side were artists like **Floyd Cramer**, whose legendary slip-note piano style arguably defined country piano music. **Ramsey Lewis** played soul/jazz utilizing the instrument.

In later years, a number of rock composers who were also performers played piano, notably **Elton John, Rick Wakeman, Steve Winwood, Keith Emerson** and **Randy Newman**. **Nicky Hopkins** was a highly regarded rock session pianist during the 70s and **Jools Holland** has been acclaimed in the 80s. The few headliners in early rock 'n' roll playing piano were matched by a similarly small number in soul, although **Aretha Franklin** was one exception, especially early in her career. In the UK during the 60s and early 70s, pianists enjoyed occasional popular and chart success, often composing their own material even if, at times, their style was limited and repetitious: examples are **Russ Conway, Winifred Atwell** and **Mrs. Mills**, an unpretentious pub pianist who mysteriously captured the British fancy with her knees-up style of music-making. More flamboyantly, in the USA, **Liberace** successfully took his mixture of popular classics and latterday tunes to the masses, usually in Las Vegas. Outside the trends and fashionable areas of popular music some important singing entertainers, such as **Nina Simone** (a classically-trained pianist), **Roberta Flack**, **Nellie Lutcher**, **Shirley Horn** and Barbara Carroll continued to use the piano as have others in the mainstream of popular music, such as **Barry Manilow** and **Harry Connick Jnr**. Meanwhile, jazz piano players had continued to abound with notable contributions from **Wynton Kelly**, **Bill Evans**, **Paul Bley** and **Cecil Taylor** (possibly the fastest and most physical of all jazz pianists), while the virtuoso playing of **Oscar Peterson** followed the tradition set by Tatum. Inevitably, electric pianos and other non-acoustic keyboard instruments found a place in jazz and rock music. Among the artists adapting to (and sometimes leading) such trends have been **Herbie Hancock**, **Joe Zawinul**, **Dave Grusin**, **Sun Ra**, **Chick Corea**, **Keith Jarrett**, **Alan Price** and **Georgie Fame**. In the 80s and early 90s some jazz pianists of earlier times enjoyed a resurgence of popularity and their use of acoustic piano was evidence of a return to popularity of the instrument: these artists included a revitalized **George Shearing** and **Marian McPartland**. Amongst newcomers making an impact were **David Benoit, Bennie Green, Dave Newton** and **Oliver Jones**, plus - at the more experimental end of jazz - **Marilyn Crispell**, **Geri Allen**, **Alex Maguire** and Georg Gräwe. In the UK in the 80s and 90s a number of resolutely ordinary pianists, such as **Richard Clayderman** and **Bobby Crush**, gained huge followings and sold many albums of their quasi-classical work.

Piano Red

b. William Lee Perryman, 19 October 1911, Hampton, Georgia, USA, d. 8 January 1985. The younger brother of blues artist **Rufus 'Speckled Red' Perryman**, this powerful keyboard player enjoyed several R&B best-sellers during 1950-51, including 'Rockin' With Red' and 'Red's Boogie'. He subsequently assumed another identity, Dr. Feelgood, and with his backing group, the Interns, secured further success with a series of pounding performances. His most influential releases included 'Right String Baby But The Wrong Yo Yo', the eponymous 'Doctor Feelgood', beloved by British beat groups, and 'Mister Moonlight', which was recorded by both the **Beatles** and the **Merseybeats**. Another of Perryman's whimsical offerings, 'Bald Headed Lena', was covered by the **Lovin' Spoonful**, but none of these versions matched the wry insistency of the originals. Perryman remained a popular live attraction, particularly in Europe, until his death in 1985.
Albums: *Piano Red In Concert* (1956), *Happiness Is Piano Red* (1970), *All Alone With His Piano* (1972), *Piano Red - Ain't Going To Be Your Low-Down Dog No More* (1974), as Dr. Feelgood *All Alone* (1975), *Percussive Piano* (1979), *Dr. Feelgood* (1979), with the Interns *What's Up Doc* (1984), *Music Is Medicine* (1988).

Piano Slim

b. Robert T. Smith, 1 August 1928, La Grange, Texas, USA. Slim began singing and playing saxophone in clubs in the late 40s, but after being shot in the chest he switched to drums, playing behind **Lightnin' Hopkins** for a spell. He became a pianist when working with a band in Odessa, Texas, and, on moving back to Houston, **Henry Hayes** taught him about music; he also claims to have recorded around this time. **Don Robey** recommended Slim to Bobbin Records in St. Louis, and they released a single by him in the late 50s. He remains based in St. Louis, and has played in innumerable bars and clubs. In 1981 he recorded his first album, mostly solo, although with guitarist Amos Sandford on some titles, then two years later he made an album with a band including two horns. Reviewing these two records, both issued by Swingmaster, *Living Blues* stated 'whether you prefer solo piano blues or rocking horn-backed material, Robert T. Smith can deliver the good'.
Selected albums: *Mean Woman Blues* (1981), *Gateway To The Blues* (1983).

Piazza, Rod

b. 18 December 1947, Riverside, California, USA. Piazza heard the R&B records his brothers bought in the 50s and formed a blues band when he was around 16 years old. He became friendly with **George Smith**, a hugh influence on his vocals and harmonica playing. Piazza made two albums with the Dirty Blues Band for **ABC**-Bluesway, and in the late 60s formed **Bacon Fat**, who made two albums for Blue Horizon. In the mid-70s he was singer/harmonica player for the Chicago Flying Saucer Band, which became the Mighty Flyers, a good-times blues group very influential in California. In the 80s Piazza also recorded two solo albums in order to showcase his harder blues approach. Additionally, he has recorded on numerous sessions, from **Jimmy Rogers** and **Big Joe Turner** to **Michelle Shocked**.
Albums: *Harpburn* (1986), *So Glad To Have The Blues* (1988), as Rod Piazza And The Mighty Flyers *Blues In The Dark* (1991), *Alphabet Blues* (Black Top 1992), *Live At BB King's* (Big Mo 1994).

Piazzolla, Astor

b. 30 January 1935, Buenos Aires, Argentina. An immensely innovative player of the Argentian bandonean (a close relation of the accordion), Piazolla has successfully taken the instrument - and tango music in general - onto the international concert stage, without diluting its roots in the working class dancehalls and dockland nightclubs of Buenos Aires. His international breakthrough came in the early 80s with his Quinteto Tango Nuevo (formed in 1976) featuring Fernando Suarez Paz (violin), Pablo Ziegler (piano), Horacio Malvicino (guitar) and Hector Console (bass) - and two albums recorded with the American producer Kip Hanrahan: *Tango Zero Hour* and *The Rough Dancer And The Cyclical Night*. Both are essential parts of any representative world music collection, as is the harder to find but outstanding live album *Concert A Vienne*.
Albums: *Essencia Musica* (1978), *Concert A Vienne* (1983), *Tango Zero Hour* (1986), *The Rough Dancer And The Cyclical Night* (1988), *Tanguedia De Amor* (1992), *The Lausanne Concert* (1993).

Piblokto!

Piblokto! (pronounced pye-block-toe) was the second backing group formed by poet/songwriter/singer **Pete Brown** (b. 25 December 1940, London, England). Drummer Rob Tait was retained from Brown's previous unit, the **Battered Ornaments**, and the line-up was completed by Jim Mullen (guitar), Dave Thompson (keyboard/saxophone) and Roger Bunn (bass). The quintet recorded their debut album, *Things May Come And Things May Go, But The Art School Dance Goes On Forever*, with the help of augmented musicians, and the collection remains one of the finest of the

progressive era. Brown's lyricism coupled with excellent musicianship from all of the various line-ups resulted in several classic moments including 'High Flying Electric Bird' and 'Flying Hero Sandwich'.
Bunn was replaced by Steve Glover prior to a second release, *Thousands On A Raft*, but this excellent album marked the end of Brown's association with Mullen, Thompson and Tait. The singer's sadness over their departure was captured on 'My Last Band', his first single with a new Piblokto! - Glover, Brian Breeze (guitar), Phil Ryan (keyboards) and John 'Pugwash' Weathers (drums). Sadly this line-up also proved unstable; Taff Williams and Ed Spevock replaced Breeze and Glover, but Piblokto! folded in 1971 when Brown began a brief association with **Graham Bond**.
Albums: *Things May Come And Things May Go But The Art School Dance Goes On Forever* (1970), *Thousands On A Raft* (1971). Compilation: with the Battered Ornaments *My Last Band* (1977).

Pic And Bill

Charles Edward Pickens and Bill(y) Mills (b. North Carolina, USA). Male soul duos were extremely popular in the 60s and 70s - **Sam And Dave** and **James And Bobby Purify** were perhaps the best-known, and most commercially successful examples. Pickens and Mills, along with several others like the Knight Brothers, Maurice And Mac, Eddie And Ernie, Sam And Bill, and Van And Titus, were less well-known but no less emotive, and were raised in the gospel-hotbed of North Carolina. From 1965 they were based for five years in Fort Worth, Texas, where they recorded extensively for **Major Bill Smith**, owner of the local Le Cam, Soft, Charay and Shalimar labels. Smith had sustained his small empire on the back of three massive 60s pop and country hits which he had successfully leased out to bigger labels: **Paul And Paula**'s teen-love anthem, 'Hey Paula', **Bruce Channel**'s 'Hey Baby', and **J. Frank Wilson**'s million-selling country hit 'The Last Kiss'. However, Pic And Bill were two big-voiced gospel and soul artists, and Charles Pickens had a hand in the production of their 11 singles and one album from this era, as well as writing many of the songs. They began in 1966 with the popish 'What Would I Do' for Charay, followed by the superb deep-soul 'All I Want Is You', coupled 'It's Not You' and 'Nobody But My Baby'. 'Just A Tear'/'Sad World Without You' was a big double-sided seller in the southern states, and 'A Man Without A Woman' was a cover of a side already recorded for Major Bill Smith by another of his male duos, Matt And Robert. In the late 60s, Charles Pickens went solo with his own soul-ballad, 'How Many Times', which was followed by the duo's cover of **Joe Hinton**'s 'Funny How Time Slips Away', the disappointing 'Together Till the End Of Time', and an impressive 1968 version of Sam And Dave's much-covered 'deep' classic, 'When Something Is Wrong With My Baby'. Then, Major Bill leased three Pic And Bill singles to the Mercury subsidiary Smash and one to Blue Rock. One of the Smash releases was a straight reissue of an earlier single, but the new recordings included a great, soulful version of **Paul McCartney**'s 'Yesterday', along with 'Don't Put Me Down', 'Moments Like These' and the 1955 ballad, 'Love Is A Many Splendoured Thing'. The Blue Rock single consisted of another deep ballad, 'Soul Of A Man' (not the **Fontella Bass** number) and the slightly funky 'Gonna Give It To You'. Major Bill also issued a Pic And Bill album, *Thirty Minutes Of Soul*, which was first released on Charay, and then, in the 70s, on both LeCam and Twelve O'Clock. Also in the 70s, their 'All I Want Is You' Charay side surfaced again on both LeCam and Zuma. Billy Mills cut some solo material for Major Bill that was not released at the time, and went on to record a session for the Nashville label Sound Stage 7, but no more was heard of Charles Pickens for a while. Then, in 1987, the duo got together again for the Bandit label out of Ashville, North Carolina, with Dave Smith producing's 'Hang On In There Baby' was a 12-inch single release and this, plus nine other sides cut for Bandit, appeared on the Japanese Vivid Sound CD, *Taking Up The Slack*. Much of the best of Pic And Bill's 'prime' output from their time with Major Bill Smith appeared on 1988 UK Charly, *Givin' It To You*.
Selected albums: *Thirty Minutes Of Soul* (c.1969), *Taking Up the Slack* (1987). Compilation: *Givin' It To You* (1988).

Picard, John

b. 17 May 1934, Wood Green, London, England. Picard is a self-taught trombonist whose shouting style was a part of **Humphrey Lyttelton**'s classic traditional band (1954-61). Picard's interests broadened in the 60s and he played with the bands of **Sandy Brown**, **Bruce Turner** and **Tony Coe**. Although Picard became semi-professional in later years his taste became ever more catholic. He recorded with pianist **Brian Lemon** and played in a septet as at home with **Charles Mingus**-style pieces as with **Duke Ellington** compositions. He was the lead trombone with the London Jazz Big Band (1975-83) for whom he wrote some very modern arrangements. He has played with **Rocket 88**, the band featuring **Alexis Korner** and boogie pianist Ian Stewart, as well as with Charlie Watts' Big Band.
Selected albums: with Humphrey Lyttelton *Swing Out* (1959), with Lyttelton *Triple Exposure* (1959), with Brian Lemon *Our Kind Of Music* (1970), with Charlie Watts' Big Band *The Live Album* (1986).

Pichon, Walter 'Fats'

b. 3 April 1906, New Orleans, Louisiana, USA, d. 25 February 1967, Chicago, Illinois, USA. Pichon spent his musical career in the area between jazz, blues and pop, leading his own bands occasionally, and working as a pianist for artist including **Luis Russell**, **Fess Williams**, **Ted Lewis**', **Mamie Smith**, **Elmer Snowden** and Armand Piron. He recorded a few hokum vocals for Russell under his own name; the accompanists on the latter included Hawaiian guitarist King Benny Nawahi, for whom Pichon returned the compliment. In the 40s he began a long residency at the Absinthe House, New Orleans, also working in New York and the Caribbean. He was still active in the 60s, although treatment for failing eyesight interrupted his playing for long periods.

Pickens, Buster

b. 3 June 1916, Hempstead, Texas, USA, d. 24 November 1964, Houston, Texas, USA. An early life as an itinerant musician, playing barrelhouses across the southern states, enabled Pickens to develop his downhome blues piano style, although it was firmly in the Texas idiom. Following military service in the World War II, he settled back in Houston, and made his first record, supporting the vocals of **Alger 'Texas' Alexander**, along with guitarist Leon Benton. He also played regularly with **Lightnin' Hopkins**, and appeared as accompanist on some of that artist's records for Prestige/Bluesville in the early 60s. He also made a solo album in 1960, which demonstrated his deep knowledge of the Texas blues style. The possibilities of a successful new career in the blues revival, however, were tragically curtailed when he was murdered a few years later.
Selected album: *Texas Barrelhouse Piano* (1960).

Pickett, Bobby 'Boris'

b. 11 February 1940, in Somerville, Massachusetts, USA. Bobby 'Boris' Pickett (And The Crypt-Kickers) recorded the US number 1 'Monster Mash' in 1962, a song which has remained alive for decades due to perennial radio airplay each Halloween. Pickett moved to Los Angeles in 1961, upon his release from military service, hoping to become an actor. Instead, he joined a singing group called the Cordials. Pickett, an avowed fan of actor Boris Karloff, worked an impression of the horror film star into some of the group's songs and he and the Cordials' Leonard Capizzi wrote 'Monster Mash' to cash in on the dance craze launched by **Dee Dee Sharp**'s 'Mashed Potato Time' hit of 1962. Pickett was signed to **Gary S. Paxton**'s Garpax label and 'Monster Mash' worked its way to the top of the charts in time for Halloween 1962. The record later returned to the US charts twice, this time on Parrot Records, reaching number 91 in 1970 and then hitting the Top 10 for a second time three years later. It was not until 1973 that the song made any significant impact upon the UK chart, when it reached number 3 in September. It was also successfully covered by the UK unit the **Bonzo Bog Doo-Dah Band**. Pickett had two other minor US chart singles in 1962-63, including the Top 30 'Monster's Holiday', but he is indelibly linked with the classic novelty number.
Albums: *The Original Monster Mash* (1962), *The Original Monster Mash* (1973, reissue of the previous title, minus four tracks).

Pickett, Dan

b. James Founty. Pickett was a singer and guitarist, whose August 1949 recordings prompted years of speculation. Many noted his stylistic links with the blues of the east coast, and it was through company files that critics discovered his real name. Pickett's repertoire was derived almost exclusively from 30s recordings, and his virtuosity went into the delivery, rather than the composition, of his songs, which sound as if they could have been recorded a decade or so earlier. However, the transformations to which he subjected many songs are the work of a true original. His guitar playing, influenced by **Tampa Red,** is complex but effortlessly fluent, and perfectly integrated with his intense but extrovert singing, which is often remarkable for the number of words crammed into a single line.
Album: *Dan Pickett & Tarheel Slim* (1991).

Pickett, Wilson

b. 18 March 1941, Prattville, Alabama, USA. Raised in Detroit, Pickett sang in several of the city's R&B groups. He later joined the Falcons, an act already established by the million-selling 'You're So Fine'. Pickett wrote and sang lead on their 1962 hit, 'I Found A Love', after which he launched his solo career. A false start at Correctone was overturned by two powerful singles, 'If You Need Me' and 'It's Too Late', recorded for **Lloyd Price**'s Double L outlet. The former track's potential was undermined by **Solomon Burke**'s opportunistic cover version on **Atlantic Records**, the irony of which was compounded when Pickett moved to that same label in 1964. An inspired partnership with guitarist **Steve Cropper** produced the classic standard, 'In The Midnight Hour', as well as, 'Don't Fight It' (both 1965), '634-5789 (Soulsville, USA)', 'Land Of A 1,000 Dances' (written by **Chris Kenner**), 'Mustang Sally' (all 1966) and 'Funky Broadway' (1967). The singer's other collaborators included erstwhile Falcon **Eddie Floyd** and former **Valentino**, **Bobby Womack**. The latter partnership proved increasingly important as the 60s progressed. A 1968 album, *The Midnight Mover*, contained six songs featuring Womack's involvement. Deprived of the **Stax** houseband due to their break with Atlantic, Pickett next recorded at Fame's **Muscle Shoals** studio. A remarkable version of 'Hey Jude', with **Duane Allman** on guitar, was the highlight of this period. A further experiment, this time with producers **Gamble And Huff**, resulted in two hits, 'Engine Number 9' (1970) and 'Don't Let The Green Grass Fool You'

(1971), while a trip to Miami provided 'Don't Knock My Love', his last Top 20 hit for Atlantic. Wilson switched to **RCA** in 1972, but the previous success was hard to regain. A mercurial talent, Pickett returned to Muscle Shoals for *Funky Situation* (1978), issued on his own Wicked label. More recently he worked alongside **Joe Tex**, **Don Covay**, **Ben E. King** and Solomon Burke in a revamped Soul Clan. Pickett was the invisible figure and role model in the award-winning soul music film *The Commitments* in 1991.

Albums: *It's Too Late* (1963), *In The Midnight Hour* (1965), *The Exciting Wilson Pickett* (1966), *The Wicked Pickett* (1966), *The Sound Of Wilson Pickett* (1967), *I'm In Love* (1968), *The Midnight Mover* (1968), *Hey Jude* (1969), *Right On* (1970), *Wilson Pickett In Philadelphia* (1970), *Don't Knock My Love* (1971), *Mr. Magic Man* (1973), *Miz Lena's Boy* (1973), *Tonight I'm My Biggest Audience* (1974), *Live In Japan* (1974), *Pickett In Pocket* (1974), *Join Me & Let's Be Free* (1975), *A Funky Situation* (1978), *I Want You* (1979), *The Right Track* (1981), *American Soul Man* (1987). Compilations: *The Best Of Wilson Pickett* (1967), *The Best Of Wilson Pickett Vol.2* (1971), *Greatest Hits* i (1987), *Greatest Hits* ii (1989), *A Man And A Half* (1992, double CD).

Pickettywitch

Naming their London-based outfit after a Cornish village, singers Polly Brown and Maggie Farran and their turnover of backing musicians came to public attention in 1969 via ITV's *Opportunity Knocks* television talent show with 'Solomon Grundy', composed and arranged by **Tony Macauley** and John McLeod. This filled the b-side of the outfit's debut single, 'You Got Me So I Don't Know' but it was their second Pye single, 'The Same Old Feeling' that took them into UK Top 5 during the spring of 1970. With choreographed head movements peculiar to themselves, Pickettywitch promoted '(It's Like A) Sad Old Kinda Movie' and 'Baby I Won't Let You Down' to lesser effect on *Top Of The Pops* and on the cabaret circuit. Polly Brown was also in the news for her publicized romance with disc jockey, Jimmy Saville. After further Macauley-McLeod creations like 'Bring A Little Light Into My World', 'Summertime Feeling' and 'Waldo P. Emerson Jones' plus an album, the group split up - though a new Pickettywitch containing neither Farran nor Brown tried again in the mid-70s. As a soloist, Brown re-entered the British charts in 1974 with 'Up In A Puff Of Smoke', and a later single, 'Honey Honey' was a US hit. Farran subsequently headed a successful London publicity agency.

Album: *Pickettywitch* (1970).

Pickwick

Devised as a vehicle for the popular British comedian and singer **Harry Secombe**, *Pickwick* had a book by Wolf Mankowitz which was based on Charles Dickens' novel, *The Pickwick Papers*. **Leslie Bricusse**, fresh from his triumph with ***Stop The World - I Want To Get Off***, wrote the lyrics, and the music was composed by **Cyril Ornadel**. *Pickwick* opened at the Saville Theatre in London on 4 July 1963, and was what one critic described as 'comic-strip Dickens'. Secombe made a jovial, likeable Pickwick, and his adventures with familiar characters such as Sam Weller (Teddy Green), Tony Weller (Robin Wentworth), Mrs. Bardell (Jessie Evans), Augustus Snodgrass (Julian Orchard), and Mr. Jingle (Anton Rodgers), made for an extremely enjoyable evening. The score, a mixture of lively and amusing numbers and one or two spirited ballads, included 'There's Something About You', 'That's What I Want For Christmas', 'The Trouble With Women', 'You Never Met A Feller Like Me', 'A Bit Of Character', 'Look Into Your Heart', 'Talk', 'Learn A Little Something', and 'Do As You Would Be Done By'. The show's big number, 'If I Ruled The World', is sung by Mr. Pickwick when he is mistaken for a parliamentary candidate. It gave Secombe a UK Top 20 hit, and is probably the song most associated with him. After a satisfying London run of some 20 months, *Pickwick* travelled to New York, via a successful stop-over in San Francisco, but Broadway audiences were unimpressed, and the show folded after only 56 performances. Roy Castle, the much-admired UK all-round entertainer, and a good friend of Secombe's, played the role of Sam Weller in the American production. Thirty years later, when *Pickwick* was revived at the Chichester Festival Theatre, prior to a season at London's Sadler's Wells, Castle joined Secombe again - this time as Sam's father, Tony.

Picou, Alphonse

b. 19 October 1878, New Orleans, Louisiana, USA, d. 4 February 1961. An enormously popular musician in his home town, clarinettist Picou worked in numerous bands, whether playing dance music, jazz or military marches. It was his adaptation of a piccolo descant in a military band piece for use in a performance of a jazz number, 'High Society', that ensured Picou's immortality. That descant became a part of 'High Society' and ever afterwards the skills of New Orleans and dixieland clarinettists were measured by the way they played his variation. Relatively inactive in the 30s, Picou returned to the jazz scene during the **Revival Movement**, recording with **Kid Rena** in 1940. He worked on through the 40s and the 50s, dying in 1961. A skilful player, Picou's work suggests that for all his fame he was much less committed to jazz than many of his fellow townsmen. Nevertheless, as long as dixieland jazz is played, clarinettists the world over will have to prove themselves by performing Picou's 'test piece'.

Selected albums: with Kid Rena *Down On The Delta* (1940), *Alphonse Picou And His Paddock Jazz Band* (1953).

Picture

This Dutch heavy metal quartet was formed in 1979 by Ronald van Prooyen (lead vocals) and Jan Bechtum (guitar). With the addition of bassist Rinus Vreugdenhil and drummer Laurens 'Bakkie' Bakker, they modelled themselves on British bands, most noticeably **Uriah Heep**, **Deep Purple** and **Motörhead**. They went through numerous line-up changes during their seven-year, seven-album career, but produced consistently high quality material throughout. Vocalists included Pete Lovell, Shmoulik Avigal and Bert Heerink (ex-**Vandenberg**) while Chris van Jaarsueld, Henry van Manen and Rob van Enhuizen were responsible for six-string duties at one time or another. The band folded in 1987, but played a one-off reunion concert the following year.

Albums: *Picture* (Backdoor 1980), *Heavy Metal Ears* (Backdoor 1981), *Diamond Dreamer* (Backdoor 1982), *Eternal Dark* (Backdoor 1984), *Traitor* (Backdoor 1985), *Every Story Needs Another Picture* (Backdoor 1986), *Marathon* (Touchdown 1987).

Pictures At An Exhibition

Progressive rock of the early 70s was epitomised by **Emerson, Lake And Palmer**, a supergroup formed by **Keith Emerson** (organ, ex-**Nice**), **Greg Lake** (bass/vocals, ex-**King Crimson**) and Carl Palmer (drums, ex-**Crazy World Of Arthur Brown**, **Atomic Rooster**). In 1972 the trio released a classics/rock fusion of Mussorsky's *Pictures At An Exhibition* which in turn inspired this film. Comprising in-concert footage interspersed with images from *Marvel* comics, this feature included some of the group's best-known compositions, including 'Take A Pebble', 'Knife Edge' and 'The Barbarian', drawn from their albums *Emerson, Lake And Palmer* and *Tarkus*, as well as the title piece. As if to prove they were not devoid of humour, the trio also offer a reading of 'Nut Rocker', a jokey adaptation of part of Tchaikovsky's 'Nutcracker Suite', originally recorded by **B. Bumble And The Stingers**. Ably directed, the strength of *Pictures At An Exhibition* depends on the viewer's enjoyment of the group's chosen *métier*.

Pied Piper, The

'Come, children of the Universe. Let **Donovan** take you away,' ran the faintly hysterical by-line of this 1971 feature, directed by French auteur, Jacques Demy. Donovan did indeed take centre stage, playing the title role, composing the soundtrack music and singing lead on each one. The meticulously hand-picked cast included Donald Pleasance, Michael Horden, Diana Dors and John Hurt, but despite some memorable cinematography, the final results veered awkwardly between *passé*, hippie-styled fantasy and self-conscious seriousness. Perhaps if the star had not passed his artistic peak the film may have proved more interesting. However an earlier feature, *Brother Sun, Sister Moon*, proved equally flawed.

Pied Pipers

Although the Pied Pipers are always remembered as a quartet, this smooth, musical vocal group started out in 1937 as an all male-septet formed by John Huddleston, Chuck Lowry, Hal Hopper, Woody Newbury, Whit Whittinghill, Bud Hervey and George Tait. They later became an octet with the addition of **Jo Stafford**, who had formerly sung with the Stafford Sisters Trio. The Pipers appeared with **Tommy Dorsey** on the *Raleigh-Kool* radio show in 1938, and he signed four of them as vocalists with his orchestra. Together with **Frank Sinatra**, they made their recording debut with Dorsey in February 1940, recording two tracks, 'What Can I Say After I Say I'm Sorry', and 'Sweet Potato Piper' from the **Bing Crosby** movie ***Road To Singapore***. By July of that year they were part of a number 1 hit single, also featuring Sinatra, 'I'll Never Smile Again'. The song was recorded earlier by **Glenn Miller**, but it was the Pipers' more intimate version that registered with the record buyers, providing Dorsey with one of his biggest ever record successes. The group - which in its most remembered form comprised Huddleston, Lowry, Stafford and Clark Yocum (the latter also being Dorsey's guitarist) - continued with Tommy until 1944, appearing in films with the band and featuring on such Top 10 hits as 'Stardust' (1940), 'Oh Look At Me Now', 'Do I Worry', 'Dolores', 'Let's Get Away From It All' (all 1941), 'Just As Though You Were Here', 'There Are Such Things' and 'It Started All Over Again' (all 1942). Jo Stafford featured as a soloist on some Dorsey items including a hit version of 'Yes Indeed' (1941). After leaving Dorsey, the Pipers worked on radio shows with **Bob Crosby**, Frank Sinatra, **Johnny Mercer** and others, signed for Mercer's **Capitol Records** and gave the young label a big hit with 'Mairzy Doats' (1944). This was followed by 'The Trolley Song' (1944), 'Dream' (a million seller in 1945), 'Mamselle' (1947) and 'My Happiness' (1948). When Jo Stafford left to go solo in 1944, she was replaced by June Hutton, who, several years later, was herself replaced by Virginia Marcy and Sue Allen. Though the popularity of the Pipers faded when big band sounds went out of style, the group kept on working, appearing on west coast television and forming part of the **Sam Donohue**-headed Tommy Dorsey band in the mid-60s.

Albums: *Dream* (1957), *Tribute To Tommy Dorsey* (50s), *The Smooth Styling Of The Pied Pipers* (50s), *Singin' & Swingin'* (1962). Compilation: *Good Deal MacNeal 1944-46* (1986).

Pierce, Billie

b. Wilhemina Goodson, 8 June 1907, Marianna,

Florida, USA., d. 29 September 1974. After working for many years as singer or pianist or both in obscure southern clubs (with a brief moment of reflected glory as accompanist to **Bessie Smith**), Pierce married **De De Pierce** in 1935 and thereafter played usually in his company. Once again this was out of the spotlight but in the mid-60s their joint careers were revived.
Selected albums: *Billie And De De* (1966), *New Orleans* (1992).

Pierce, De De

b. Joseph De Lacrois, 18 February 1904, New Orleans, Louisiana, USA, d. 23 November 1973. For many years, playing the cornet was only a secondary occupation to Pierce, who played the cornet and occasionally sang. This comment might well be applied to many of the older generation of New Orleans musicians, who traditionally and rightly regarded music as an unreliable business. In Pierce's case, however, he kept up a 'day job' rather longer than most and not until after his marriage in 1935 to singer-pianist Billie Goodson (see **Billie Pierce**) did he devote himself to a musical career. The husband and wife duo worked regularly, although still within a restricted area, until Pierce retired temporarily in the 50s through ill-health and failing eyesight. The duo made a comeback in the mid-60s achieving international fame with a succession of concert tours and records and, inevitably perhaps, regular appearances at Preservation Hall, where they entertained the tourists of New Orleans.
Selected albums: *New Orleans Jazz* (1959), *Blues In The Classic Tradition* (1961), *Jazz At Preservation Hall* (1962), *Billie And De De* (1966), *De De Pierce's New Orleans Stompers* (1966), *New Orleans* (1992).

Pierce, Nat

b. 16 July 1925, Somerville, Massachusetts, USA, d. 10 June 1992. After studying and playing in local bands in his home state, Pierce worked with a handful of name bands, including **Larry Clinton**'s, then briefly led his own band in 1949-51, instigating what is commonly regarded among fellow musicians as being the birth of the so-called 'rehearsal band' concept. In 1951 he joined **Woody Herman**, in whose band he played piano, arranged, and acted as straw boss until 1955. Thereafter he arranged for several bands and singers, including **Count Basie** and **Ella Fitzgerald**. In great demand as a session musician, he made countless record dates, on which he played with almost everyone who was anyone in the upper echelons of jazz. In 1957 he appeared in the television programme *The Sound Of Jazz*, on which he was responsible for several of the arrangements, including the classic performance of 'Dickie's Dream' which featured Basie, **Roy Eldridge**, **Coleman Hawkins**, **Ben Webster**, **Joe Newman**, **Vic Dickenson** and **Gerry Mulligan** among many others. In the late 50s he led a band which included **Buck Clayton** and which had the doubtful honour of being the last band to play at Harlem's 'Home of Happy Feet', the Savoy Ballroom, before it closed forever. Also in the late 50s he worked with **Pee Wee Russell**, **Quincy Jones**, Fitzgerald, Hawkins and others. In 1960 he returned to Herman for a brief spell as road manager and was back again the following year, this time in his former capacities, remaining until 1966. In the early 70s Pierce relocated to the west coast where he played in several bands, including those led by **Louie Bellson** and **Bill Berry**. In 1975 he joined **Frank Capp** as co-leader of a big band that mostly played his arrangements, many of which were in the Basie/Kansas City tradition. This band, which became known as **Juggernaut**, continued to play through the 80s and on into the 90s. Pierce also continued to write for other musicians and to appear on record dates. He toured extensively, appearing in the UK and Europe with several Basie-alumni bands and other concert packages. A superb pianist in his own right, Pierce's eclecticism was such that at various times he appeared at the piano as substitute for three of the best-known piano-playing bandleaders in big band history: Basie, **Duke Ellington** and **Stan Kenton**. In small groups he proved the lynch-pin of the rhythm section, swinging with unflagging enthusiasm. As an arranger, especially for big bands, Pierce made an invaluable contribution to jazz, effortlessly creating swinging charts which underscored the 60s success stories of both Herman and Basie. Apart from his performing and arranging, Pierce was also a major source of information on many aspects of jazz history; a history which, through his personal dedication and extensive contributions, he helped to create.
Selected albums: *The Nat Pierce-Dick Collins Nonet* (1954), *Nat Pierce And His Band* (1955), *The Nat Pierce Octet* (1955), *Kansas City Memories* (1956), *The Nat Pierce Big Band At The Savoy Ballroom* (1957), with various artists *The Real Sound Of Jazz* (1957, television soundtrack), *The Ballad Of Jazz Street* (1961), *Juggernaut* (1977), *Juggernaut Live At Century Plaza* (1978), *5400 North...In Concert With Mary Ann McCall* (1978), *Juggernaut Strikes Again* (1981), *Boston Bustout* (Hep Jazz 1981), *Juggernaut Live At The Alleycat* (1986).

Pierce, Webb

b. 8 August 1921, near West Monroe, Louisiana, USA, d. 24 February 1991, Nashville, Tennessee, USA. Pierce's father died when he was three months old, his mother remarried and he was raised on a farm seven miles from Monroe. Although no one in the family performed music, his mother had a collection of country records which, together with watching **Gene Autry** films, were his first country music influences. He learned to play guitar and when he was 15 was given his own weekly radio show on KMLB Monroe. During World War II he served in the Army, married Betty

Jane Lewis in 1942 and after his discharge they relocated from Monroe to Shreveport where, in 1945, he found employment in the men's department of the Sears Roebuck store. In 1947, he and his wife appeared on an early morning KTBS show as 'Webb Pierce with Betty Jane, the Singing Sweetheart'. He also sang at many local venues and developed the style that became so readily identifiable and was later described as 'a wailing whiskey-voiced tenor that rang out every drop of emotion'. He recorded for 4-Star in 1949 and soon afterwards moved to KWKH, where he became a member of the *Louisiana Hayride* on its inception that year.

In 1950, he and Betty Jane were divorced and Pierce began building his solo career. He founded Pacemaker Records and a publishing company with Horace Logan, the director of the *Hayride*. His recording of 'Drifting Texas Sands', labelled as 'Tillman Franks and the Rainbow Valley Boys', due to Pierce still being under contract to 4-Star, created attention. His growing popularity attracted US **Decca** and in March 1951 he made his first recordings for that label. His third Decca release, 'Wondering', a song from the 30s by Joe Werner and the Riverside Ramblers, began his phenomenal success as a recording artist when, in March 1952, it spent four weeks at number 1 in the US country charts and gave Pierce his nickname of 'The Wondering Boy'. Two more number 1s 'That Heart Belongs To Me' (a self-penned song) and 'Back Street Affair' followed - all three remaining charted in excess of 20 weeks. (The latter song also led to **Kitty Wells**' second chart hit with the 'answer' version 'Paying For That Back Street Affair' early in 1953). In November 1952 he married again, this time to Audrey Grisham and finally gave up his job at Sears Roebuck. He left the *Hayride* and replaced **Hank Williams** on the *Grand Ole Opry*. During his days at Shreveport his band included such future stars as Goldie Hill, **Floyd Cramer**, Jimmy Day, the **Wilburn Brothers** and **Faron Young**. He remained a member of the *Opry* roster until 1955, leaving because of his heavy touring commitments but rejoined briefly in 1956 before a disagreement with the management caused him to once again leave. The problem concerned the fact that Pierce was having to give up lucrative Saturday concerts elsewhere to return to Nashville to meet his Opry commitments for which he received only the standard Opry fee. Pierce's chart successes during the 50s and 60s totalled 88 country hits. Further number 1 singles included 'It's Been So Long', 'Even Tho'', 'More And More', 'I Don't Care', 'Love Love Love' and a duet with **Red Sovine** of **George Jones**' song 'Why Baby Why'.

Arguably his best remembered number 1 hits are his version of the old **Jimmie Rodgers**' song 'In The Jailhouse Now', which held the top spot for 21 weeks and his co-written, 'Slowly', which remained there for 17, both songs charting for more than 35 weeks. The recording of 'Slowly' is unique because of Bud Isaacs' electric pedal steel guitar, which created a style that was copied by most other country bands. He also had nine US pop chart hits, the biggest being 'More And More', which reached number 22 in 1954. Pierce recorded rockabilly and rock 'n' roll numbers having Top 10 country chart success with the first recorded version of 'Teenage Boogie' and with the **Everly Brothers** 'Bye Bye Love' but his vocal version of 'Raunchy' failed to chart. In the mid-50s Pierce and the Opry manager, Jim Denny, formed Cedarwood Music, which handled other artists songs as well as Pierce's own and also bought three radio stations. When Denny died in 1963, Pierce retained the radio stations and left the publishing company to his late partner's family. (He later acquired two more stations but eventually sold all five for a sum reputed to be almost $3 million.) He toured extensively and appeared in the films *Buffalo Guns* (his co-stars being **Marty Robbins** and **Carl Smith**), *Music City USA, Second Fiddle To A Steel Guitar* and *Road To Nashville* and during his career, dressed in rhinestone studded suits, he became known as one of the most flamboyant, even by country standard, of the singers of his era. During the 60s he had two Pontiac cars fancily studded with silver dollars, large cattle horns mounted as a decoration on the radiator, ornamental pistols and rifles and even leather seats that resembled saddles. Later his expensive Oak Hill, Nashville home with its guitar-shaped swimming pool brought so many tourist buses around the normally quiet area that he had problems with his neighbours, particularly **Ray Stevens**. Pierce totally ignored suggestions that he was bringing country music into disrepute, maintaining that the fans had paid for his pool and were therefore entitled to see it. After heated court proceedings he was forced to erect a sign warning fans to stay away. His comment on Stevens, who had been the organizer of the objectors, was 'That's what he gets for livin' across the street from a star'. **Johnny Cash** in his song 'Let There Be Country' mentions the event when he sings 'Pierce invites the tourists in and Ray keeps them away'.

After 'Honky Tonk Song' in 1957, he never gained another number 1 record but he did add eight further country hits during the 70s on either Decca or Plantation. When the **Columbia** duet version of 'In The Jailhouse Now', that he recorded with **Willie Nelson**, charted in 1982 to register his 97th and last country hit, it gave him the distinction of having charted records in four decades. In the early 1980s he sold his Oak Hill home and retired to the Brentwood area of Nashville. He retired from touring but made special appearances when it pleased him and reflecting on his career said 'I've been blessed with so much. I guess it turned out the way I wanted it'. In 1985 he made a good-time album concentrating on Pierce's songs, with his friends **Jerry Lee Lewis**, **Mel Tillis** and Faron Young, but contractual problems led to it being withdrawn shortly after issue. Asked about recording again in 1986 he commented 'Hell, I might get a hit and then everybody would be botherin' me again'. Late in the 80s his health began to fail, he survived open heart surgery but early in 1990 it was diagnosed that he was suffering with cancer. He underwent several operations but finally died in Nashville on 24 February 1991. He had been nominated for membership of the Country Music Hall of Fame in August 1990: most authorities expected that he would be elected but it was not to be. The honour may be bestowed before long but sadly it will come too late for him to know. Pierce was, without any doubt, one of country music's most successful and popular honky-tonk singers.

Albums: *Webb Pierce* (1955), *The Wondering Boy* (1956), *Just Imagination* (1957), *Bow Thy Head* (1958), *Webb* (1959), *Bound For The Kingdom* (1959), *The One & Only Webb Pierce* (1959), *Walking The Streets* (1960), *Webb With A Beat* (1960), *Fallen Angel* (1961), *Cross Country* (1962), *Hideaway Heart* (1962), *Bow Thy Head* (1963), *I've Got A New Heartache* (1963), *Sands Of Gold* (1964), *Country Music Time* (1965), *Just Webb Pierce* (1965), *Memory Number One* (1965), *Sweet Memories* (1966), *Webb Pierce* (1966), *Webb's Choice* (1966), *Where'd Ya Stay Last Night* (1967), *Fool, Fool, Fool* (1968), *Country Songs* (1969), *Saturday Night* (1969), *Webb Pierce Sings This Thing* (1969), *Love Ain't Never Gonna Be No Better* (1970), *Merry Go Round World* (1970), *Country Favorites* (1970), *Webb Pierce Road Show* (1971), *I'm Gonna Be A Swinger* (1972), *Without You* (1973), *Carol Channing & Webb Pierce-Country & Western* (1976), *Faith, Hope And Love* (1977), with Willie Nelson *In The Jailhouse Now* (1982), with Jerry Lee Lewis, Mel Tillis, Faron Young *Four Legends* (1985). Compilations: *Golden Favorites* (1961), *The Webb Pierce Story* (1964), *The Living Legend Of Webb Pierce* (1977), *Golden Hits Volume 1* (1977), *Golden Hits Volume 2* (1977), *Webb 'The Wondering Boy' Pierce 1951-1958* (1990), *The One And Only...* (1993), King Of The Honky Tonk (MCA 1994).

Pigbag

Pigbag will be for ever linked with their debut single, and only hit, 'Papa's Got A Brand New Pigbag' (a play on words on the mid-60s **James Brown** classic, 'Papa's Got A Brand New Bag'). A quirky but nevertheless catchy funk/soul instrumental, the single was first released in May 1981, but took almost a year to reach the charts, peaking at number 3. Word had it that their label, Y, had deleted the single and then reactivated it when the demand was sufficient. The band had formed around the Gloucestershire and Avon region from the ashes of hardline militant funk act the **Pop Group**; Simon Underwood (bass) joined up with James Johnstone (guitar/keyboards), Ollie Moore (saxophone), Chip Carpenter (drums) and Roger Freeman (percussion). By the time of their hit, Pigbag already issued two further singles, 'Sunny Day' and 'Getting Up'. The debut album, *Dr Heckle And Mr Jive*, subsequently reached the UK Top 20. Despite shrewd promotion, Pigbag's heyday was short-lived. 'Big Bean' (1982) peaked at number 40 and 'Hit The "O" Deck' (1983), failed to make any impact. After a live album, the band broke up, although 'Papa's Got A Brand New Pigbag' was later re-recorded in 1987, to coincide with *The Best Of Pigbag*.

Albums: *Dr Heckle And Mr Jive* (1982), *Pigbag - Live* (1983). Compilation: *The Best Of Pigbag* (1987).

Pigeon Pie Records

London record label headed by Joe Borgia which in its first few years of operation has earned itself a healthy reputation with its first dozen or so releases. The catalogue began with two La Comoora records, 'Oki-Dokey' and 'Te Quiero'/'What Is Love'. Subsequent releases included Rhythm Eclipse ('Feel It In The Air'/'Thru The Night'), Marco Polo ('Zuazuzua'), Cecer ('Skyline', 'I Need Your Love'), Delphine ('Baby Don't You Go'), Mind The Gap ('Mind The Gap'), FOD ('All It Takes), Jupiter ('Destiny') and **Love To Infinity** ('Somethin' Outta Nothin''). The latter, a garage cut from brothers Andrew and Peter Lee, was typically well-received by the dance music press.

Piglets

Another of **Jonathan King**'s (b. Kenneth King, 6 December 1944, England) pseudonyms, the Piglets followed in the wake of UK hits under his own name ('Everyone's Gone To The Moon', 'Let It All Hang Out', 'Lazy Bones', 'Hooked On A Feeling', and 'Flirt'), as Sakkarin ('Sugar Sugar'), and the Weathermen ('It's The Same Old Song'). Recorded in November 1971 by King and a variety of session men, the Piglets came up with 'Johnny Reggae', which encapsulated the current trend for reggae within a poppy novelty framework perfectly suited to the early 70s. 'Johnny Reggae' quickly became King's fastest selling record to date and reached number 3 on the Bell label in November 1971. The follow-up, 'This Is Reggae' appeared in 1972 on King's UK label which he started in July. It was not a hit and the only other related release was on Bell later in the year - 'Johnny Reggae's Don't Get Your Knickers In A Twist', at which juncture the Piglets were sent to market whilst King created: Shag, Bubblerock, 53rd and 3rd, One Hundred Ton And A Feather, Sound 9418, Father Apraphart and the Smurfs.

Pigsty Hill Light Orchestra

This group formed to play at **Fred Wedlock**'s New Years Party in 1968. All the members came from various UK folk groups: Dave Creech (b. 4 March 1938, Bristol, England; trumpet/vocals/jug/trumpet mouthpiece) from the Elastic Band, Barry Back (b. 10

April 1944, Bristol, England, d. 2 April 1992; guitar/vocals/kazoo) and Andy Leggett (31 March 1942, Much Wenlock, Shropshire, England; vocals/guitar/brass) from the Alligator Jug Thumpers, and John Turner (b. 2 January 1947, Bristol, Avon, England; vocals/bass) from the Downsiders folk group. The party, held at the Troubadour club in Clifton, Bristol, England, became the birthplace of the Pigsty Hill Light Orchestra. The style of music was loosely based on jazz and blues from the 20s and 30s, and a variety of unorthodox instruments were employed to produce what became a highly original sound. Whether it be a paraffin funnel, ballcock sections from toilets, jugs and so on, they played it. In 1970, they released *Phlop!*, and ***Melody Maker*** voted them one of the bands most likely to succeed. The following year, they made their first Cambridge Folk Festival appearance. Fred Wedlock's *The Folker* and *Frollicks*, released in 1971 and 1973 respectively, featured members from the PHLO. Sadly, after a busy time playing the club and college circuit both at home and abroad, the group disbanded in May 1979. During that time, there had been various personnel changes, Turner had left in 1970, and Back departed in 1972. That same year the group were augmented by Dave Paskett (b. Dave Paskett Smith, 3 June 1944, Potters Bar, Hertfordshire, England; vocals/guitar), who remained for only two years, and John Hays (percussion/vocals), who stayed until 1979. In 1974, with the departure of both Leggett and Paskett, **Chris Newman** (b. 30 October 1952, Stevenage, Hertfordshire, England; guitar/bass) joined, as did Henry Davies (bass/brass). More changes occurred in 1975 with the departure of Davies, when Ricky Gold (bass) joined them. A year later, in 1976, Robert Greenfield (b. 14 May 1949, Norfolk, England; guitar) joined as Newman had now left the group. Finally, after Greenfield left in 1978, they were joined by Patrick Small (guitar/kazoo/vocals). Bill Cole (bass), joined the group for a short while, and appeared on *Piggery Joker*. He had also played with the **Ken Colyer** band. Despite the fairly frequent changes in their line-up, the group were still able to secure a strong and loyal following, and continued recording. A chance telephone call came in 1988, asking Back to resurrect the line-up for a 'one-off' booking at the Village Pump Festival, Trowbridge, Wiltshire. The group, this time, included Hannah Wedlock, Fred's daughter, on vocals. In 1990, the band played the Sidmouth Folk Festival, and at the Tonder Festival, in Denmark, when they were on the bill with **Peggy Seeger** and **Arlo Guthrie**. The group are again playing clubs and festivals, and have reached a new audience, to add to those who knew them first time round. True to form, more changes occurred with the departure of both Small and Wedlock in December 1991. They were replaced by Jim Reynolds (b. 15 August 1950, Bristol, Avon, England; vocals/guitar) and Dave Griffiths (b. 23 August 1948, Leeds, West Yorkshire, England; mandolin/fiddle/bass/washboard), reverting the five-piece group to its early jug band sound.

Albums: *Phlop!* (The Village Thing 1970), *Piggery Joker* (The Village Thing 1972), *The Pigsty Hill Light Orchestra* (1976), *Back On The Road Again* (Big Dipper 1991).

Piirpauke

A jazz/rock band from Finland that take tunes from anywhere in the world and adapts them to their own style. Arguably, they predated the whole world music movement, and, because of their locality, benefitted little from it. Sakari Kukko (saxophone), still leads this excellent, but obscure group.

Selected album: *Algazara* (1987).

Pike, Dave

b. 23 March 1938, Detroit, Michigan, USA. Pike started playing drums when he was eight and is self-taught on vibes inspired by the playing of **Lionel Hampton** and **Milt Jackson**. He moved to Los Angeles in 1953 and played with musicians including **Elmo Hope** and the saxophonists **Harold Land** and **Dexter Gordon**. He played for two years with **Paul Bley**. In 1960 he moved to New York and started to experiment with ways of amplifying the vibraphone when he played with flautist **Herbie Mann** (1961-65). After playing at the 1968 Berlin Jazz Festival and recording with the **Clarke-Boland Big Band** he stayed on in Germany and formed the Dave Pike Set with local musicians. In the early 70s the Set twice toured South America for the Goethe Institute. Pike returned to California in 1973 and led a quartet at Hungry Joe's Club in Huntingdon Beach.

Albums: with Mann *Live At Newport* (1963), *Noisy Silence, Gentle Noise* (1969), *The Four Reasons* (1969), *Infra Red* (1969), *Live At The Philharmonic* (1970), *Album* (1971), *Salamao* (1973), *Times Out Of Mind* (1975), *Let The Minstrels Play On* (1979), *Moa Bird* (1981), *Pike's Groove* (1986).

Pil

(see **Public Image Limited**)

Pillow, Ray

b. 4 July 1937, Lynchburg, Virginia, USA. A singer, guitarist and songwriter, who had no initial thoughts of a singing career. He dropped out of high school in the eleventh grade and enlisted in the US Navy, where he actually completed his high school diploma. In 1958, he was discharged and entered college and one day for a dare, he deputized for the singer in the college rock band. He found he enjoyed singing and also learned to play the guitar but still had no immediate ideas of a singing career. In 1961, he travelled to Nashville and competed in the National Pet Milk Talent Contest. He did not win but the WSM radio judges placed him in

second place. He returned to Lynchburg and after completing his college degree, he found work with a trucking company. However, he found that now he wanted to be an entertainer and returned to Nashville. He played small clubs, honky tonks and local radio stations and gradually built enough of a reputation that in 1964, he was given a recording contract by **Capitol**. His first charted in 1965 with 'Take Your Hands Off My Heart' and followed it with a Top 20 hit in 1966 with 'Thank You Ma'am'. Capitol also paired him with **Jean Shepard** and the duo had major successes with 'I'll Take The Dog', 'Mr Do It Yourself' and 'Heart We Did All We Could'. Pillow joined the *Grand Ole Opry* in 1966 and for a time toured with the *Martha White Show*. Although he never achieved any further major hits, he continued to record for various labels including **ABC**, Mega and MCA having minor hits with such songs as 'Gone With The Wine', 'Wonderful Day', 'Countryfied' and 'Living In The Sunshine Of Your Love'. His last chart entry, 'One Too Many Memories', came in 1981 on First Generation. A fine singer with a pleasant style of delivery, Pillow continues to appear on the *Opry* and make personal appearances.
Albums: *Presenting Ray Pillow* (1965), with Jean Shepard *I'll Take The Dog* (1966), *Even When It's Bad It's Good* (1967), *Wonderful Day* (1968), *Ray Pillow Sings* (1969), *People Music* (1970), *Slippin' Around With Ray Pillow* (1972), *Countryfied* (1974), *Ray Pillow* (1982), *One Too Many Memories* (1984).

Pilot

Formed in Edinburgh, Scotland, in 1973, Pilot initially consisted of David Paton (b. 29 October 1951, Edinburgh; bass/vocals) and Billy Lyall (b. 26 March 1953, Edinburgh; synthesizer/piano/flute/vocals), two former members of the **Bay City Rollers** and Stuart Tosh (b. 26 September 1951, Aberdeen, Scotland; drums). The trio won a contract with **EMI Records** after recording a series of demos in London. Session guitarist Ian Bairnson (b. 3 August 1953, Shetland Isles, Scotland) was recruited in the autumn of 1974. Having secured a Top 20 hit with 'Magic', the group reached the number 1 spot in 1975 with 'January', a simple, but perfectly crafted pop song. The group enjoyed two minor chart entries with 'Call Me Round' and 'Just A Smile', but their increasingly lightweight style quickly palled. Tosh left to join **10cc**, while Bairnson and Paton pursued studio careers, which included sessions for **Kate Bush**'s debut *The Kick Inside* (1978) and several recordings for **Alan Parsons** and **Chris DeBurgh**. Billy Lyall recorded a solo album, which featured several former colleagues, and later joined **Dollar**. In December 1989, he died weighing less than five stone, a victim of an AIDS-related illness.
Albums: *From The Album Of The Same Name* (1974), *Second Flight* (1975), *Morin Heights* (1976), *Two's A Crowd* (1977). Compilation: *The Best Of Pilot* (1980).

Piltdown Men

It is not unusual for session musicians to jam together in the studio while waiting for a recording to start and that is exactly how the Piltdown Men were born. A team of seven regular Los Angeles-based **Capitol Records** musicians, including noted arranger Lincoln Mayorga and Ed Cobb from the **Four Preps**, were playing around with the children's nursery rhyme 'Old MacDonald' and the result was the saxophone-laden instrumental track known as 'MacDonald's Cave'. Mayorga quickly penned another track, 'Brontosaurus Stomp', and Capitol rushed a single out under a group name that suited the stone-age styled titles. To their surprise 'MacDonald's Cave' was a UK Top 20 hit in 1960 and the b-side made the lower reaches of the US Top 100. Interest in the anonymous group quickly faded in their homeland but they continued to make rockin' instrumental records for the UK market and had two more Top 20 hits with 'Piltdown Rides Again' and 'Goodnight Mrs. Flintstone', which were again based on well-known traditional songs. After a couple of non-chart singles the Piltdown Men vanished into pre-history.

Pinchers

When Pinchers first came to England from Jamaica in 1985, he had already recorded an album for Blue Trac, alongside Peter Chemist. It was the release of his 45, 'Abracadabra', that first won him significant attention. He followed-up with minor hits for a variety of producers, including **'Fatis' Burrell** and Redman. The single to make the breakthrough for him, however, was 'Agony', recorded for **King Jammy**. It quickly made him a minor celebrity in Jamaica, to the point where he was offered (and accepted) advertising endorsements from a local wine vineyard. His other notable hits include 'Bandolero', the wild west imagery of which neatly seduced the **dancehall** audience, whose preoccupation with guns and violence it echoed. However, Pinchers' main source of fame continues to centre on **sound system** 'specials', live appearances at which he excels, and on which he has built a considerable reputation as one of reggae's emerging stars.
Albums: *Agony* (Live & Love 1987), *Mass Out* (Exterminator/RAS 1987), *Lift It Up Again* (Exterminator/Vena 1987), *Got To Be Me* (Live & Love 1987), *Return Of The Don* (Supreme 1989), *Hotter* (Blue Mountain 1992), *Dirt Low* (Exterminator 1993). With Frankie Paul: *Dancehall Duo* (RAS 1988), *Turbo Charge* (Super Supreme 1988). With Pliers: *Pinchers With Pliers* (Black Scorpio 1988). With Sanchez: *Pinchers Meets Sanchez* (Exterminator 1989). With Tweetie Bird: *Two Originals* (King Dragon 1990).

Pine, Courtney

b. 18 March 1964, London, England. Like many of his generation of young, black, British jazz musicians, Pine came from a reggae and funk background. He had been a member of Dwarf Steps, a hard-bop band consisting of **Berklee College Of Music** graduates, before joining reggae stars Clint Eastwood and General Saint. His interest in jazz was fostered when he participated in workshops run by **John Stevens.** In 1986 he depped for **Sonny Fortune** in **Elvin Jones**'s band, and was involved in setting up the **Jazz Warriors**. He came to wider public notice as a result of playing with Charlie Watts' Orchestra, **George Russell**'s European touring band and with **Art Blakey** at the Camden Jazz Festival. Blakey invited him to join the Messengers, but he decided to stay in Britain. In 1987 he played at the Bath Festival with the Orchestre National de Jazz. By that time his reputation had spread far beyond jazz circles, and his first album was a massive seller by jazz standards. He appeared before a huge world-wide audience in the Nelson Mandela 70th Birthday Concert at Wembley, backing dancers IDJ, and was the main subject of a number of television arts programmes about jazz in the late 80s, his smart image and articulate seriousness about his music enabling him to communicate with many people who had never before given jazz a hearing. He became much in demand for film and television, and appeared, for example, on the soundtrack of Alan Parker's *Angel Heart* and over the titles of BBC television's *Juke Box Jury*. His current quartet comprises young American luminaries **Kenny Kirkland** (piano), Charnett Moffett (bass) and Marvin 'Smitty' Smith (drums). Many of his admirers feel that in some ways his high media profile has hindered his development, but his talent, dedication and level-headedness have ensured that he has never been diverted by the hype, and his most recent work illustrates an emotional depth matching his undoubted technical brilliance. He has also continued to play in reggae and other pop contexts (*Closer To Home*), and is a frequent collaborator with UK soul singer **Mica Paris**.

Albums: *Journey To The Urge Within* (Island 1986), *Destiny's Song And The Image Of Pursuance* (Island 1988), *The Vision's Tale* (Island 1989), *Within The Realms Of Our Dreams* (Island 1991), *Closer To Home* (Island 1992), *To The Eyes Of Creation* (Island 1992).

Pinera, Mike

b. 29 September 1948, Tampa, Florida, USA. Guitarist Pinera first achieved recognition as a member of the Los Angeles-based **Blues Image**. In 1970 he replaced Erik Brann in the then popular **Iron Butterfly**, contributing to *Metamorphosis* (1970) before leaving for the ill-fated Mother's Milk. In 1972 Pinera surfaced in Ramatam, which also featured former **Jimi Hendrix** drummer **Mitch Mitchell**, before switching to the New **Cactus** Band in 1973. This itinerant musician then formed Thee Image, a promising unit which completed two albums, before he embarked on a lucrative career as a session musician. Pinera was lead guitarist with Alice Cooper from 1979-82 his work appearing on *Special Forces* and *Zipper Catches Skin.* He also undertook two low-key albums in his own right. Amidst reforming the Iron Butterfly in 1992, Pinera was shopping for a label with a brand new solo album during 1993.

Albums: *Isla* (1978), *Forever* (1979).

Pink Fairies

The name 'Pink Fairies' was initially applied to a fluid group of musicians later known as Shagrat. The original Tolkein-inspired appellation was resurrected in 1970 when one of their number, Twink (b. John Alder), erstwhile drummer in **Tomorrow** and the **Pretty Things**, joined former **Deviants** Paul Rudolph (b. USA; guitar/vocals), Duncan Sanderson (bass/vocals) and Russell Hunter (drums). The Fairies' debut album, *Never Neverland*, was a curious amalgam of primeval rabble-rousing ('Say You Love Me') and English psychedelia ('Heavenly Man'). It also featured 'Do It' and 'Uncle Harry's Last Freak Out', two songs which became fixtures of the group's live set as they became stalwarts of the free festival and biker circuits. Twink left the band in 1971 and the remaining trio completed the disappointing *What A Bunch Of Sweeties* with the help of Trevor Burton from the **Move**. Rudolph, later to join **Hawkwind**, was briefly replaced by Mick Wayne before Larry Wallis joined for *Kings Of Oblivion*, the group's most exciting and unified release. The trio split up in 1974, but the following year joined Rudolph and Twink for a one-off appearance at London's Chalk Farm Roundhouse. A farewell tour, with Sanderson, Wallis and Hunter, extended into 1977, by which time Martin Stone (ex-**Chilli Willi And The Red Hot Peppers**) had been added to the line-up. The Pink Fairies were then officially dissolved, but the original line-up, without Rudolph, but including Wallis, were reunited in 1987 for *Kill 'Em 'N' Eat 'Em* before going their separate ways again.

Albums: *Never Neverland* (Polydor 1971), *What A Bunch Of Sweeties* (Polydor 1972), *Kings Of Oblivion* (Polydor 1973), *Live At The Roundhouse* (Big Beat 1982), *Previously Unreleased* (Big Beat 1984), *Kill 'Em 'N' Eat 'Em* (Demon 1987). Compilations: *Flashback* (Polydor 1975), *Pink Fairies* (1991).

Pink Floyd

One of the most predominant and celebrated rock bands of all time, the origins of Pink Floyd developed at Cambridge High School. Roger Keith **'Syd' Barrett** (b. 6 January 1946, Cambridge, England; guitar/vocals), **Roger Waters** (b. 9 September 1944,

Cambridge, England; bass/vocals) and **Dave Gilmour** (b. 6 March 1944, Cambridge, England; guitar/vocals) were pupils and friends there. Mutually drawn to music, Barrett and Gilmour undertook a busking tour of Europe prior to the former's enrolment at the Camberwell School Of Art in London. Waters was meanwhile studying architecture at the city's Regent Street Polytechnic. He formed an R&B-based group, Sigma 6, with fellow students Nick Mason (b. 27 January 1945, Birmingham, England; drums) and Rick Wright (b. 28 July 1945, London, England; keyboards). The early line-up included bassist Clive Metcalfe - Waters favoured guitar at this point - and (briefly) Juliette Gale (who later married Wright) but underwent the first crucial change when Bob Close (lead guitar) replaced Metcalfe. With Waters now on bass, the group took a variety of names, including the T-Set and the (Screaming) Abdabs. Sensing a malaise, Roger invited Barrett to join but the latter's blend of blues, pop and mysticism was at odds with Close's traditional outlook and the Abdabs fell apart at the end of 1965. Almost immediately Barrett, Waters, Mason and Wright reconvened as the Pink Floyd Sound, a name Syd had suggested, inspired by an album by Georgia blues' musicians Pink Anderson and Floyd Council.

Within weeks the quartet had repaired to the Thompson Private Recording Company, sited in the basement of a house. Here they recorded two songs, 'Lucy Leave', a Barrett original playfully blending pop and R&B, and a version of **Slim Harpo**'s 'I'm A King Bee'. Although rudimentary, both tracks indicate a defined sense of purpose. Ditching the now-superfluous 'Sound' suffix, Pink Floyd attracted notoriety as part of the nascent counter-culture milieu centred on the London Free School. A focus for the emergent underground, this self-help organisation inspired the founding of Britain's first alternative publication, *International Times*. The paper was launched at the Roundhouse on 15 October 1966; it was here Pink Floyd made its major debut. By December the group was appearing regularly at the UFO Club, spearheading Britain's psychedelic movement with extended, improvised sets and a highly-visual lightshow. Further demos ensued, produced by UFO-co-founder **Joe Boyd**, which in turn engendered a recording deal with EMI. Surprisingly, the band's hit singles were different to their live sound, featuring Barrett's quirky melodies and lyrics. 'Arnold Layne', a tale of a transvestite who steals ladies' clothes from washing lines, escaped a BBC ban to rise into the UK Top 20. 'See Emily Play', originally entitled 'Games For May' in honour of an event the group hosted at Queen Elizabeth Hall, reached number 6 in June 1967. It was succeeded by *The Piper At The Gates Of Dawn* which encapsulated Britain's 'Summer of Love'. Largely Barrett-penned, the set deftly combined childlike fantasy with experimentation, where whimsical pop songs nestled beside riff-laden sorties, notably the powerful 'Interstellar Overdrive'. Chart success begat package tours - including a memorable bill alongside the **Jimi Hendrix** Experience - which, when combined with a disastrous US tour, wrought unbearable pressure on Barrett's fragile psyche. His indulgence in hallucinogenic drugs exacerbated such problems and he often proved near-comatose on-stage and incoherent with interviewers. A third single, 'Apples And Oranges', enthralled but jarred in equal measures, while further recordings, 'Vegetable Man' and 'Scream Thy Last Scream', were deemed unsuitable for release. His colleagues, fearful for their friend and sensing a possible end to the band, brought Dave Gilmour into the line-up in February 1968. Plans for Syd to maintain a backroom role, writing for the group but not touring, came to naught and his departure was announced the following April. He subsequently followed a captivating, but short-lived, solo career.

Although bereft of their principle songwriter, the realigned Pink Floyd completed *A Saucerful Of Secrets*. It featured one Barrett original, the harrowing 'Jugband Blues', as well as two songs destined to become an integral part of their live concerts, the title track itself and 'Set The Controls For The Heart Of The Sun'. Excellent, but flop singles, 'It Would Be So Nice' (a rare Wright original) and 'Point Me At The Sky' were also issued; their failure prompted the group to disavow the format for 11 years. A film soundtrack, *More*, allowed Waters to flex compositional muscles, while the part-live, part-studio *Ummagumma*, although dated and self-indulgent by today's standards, was at the vanguard of progressive space-rock in 1969. By this point Pink Floyd were a major attraction, drawing 100,000 to their free concert in London the following year. Another pivotal live appearance, in the volcanic crater in Pompeii, became the subject of a much-loved, late-night film.

Atom Heart Mother was a brave, if flawed, experiment, partially written with avant-garde composer, **Ron Geesin**. It featured the first in a series of impressive album covers, designed by the **Hipgnosis** studio, none of which featured photographs of the band. The seemingly abstract image of *Meddle*, is in fact a macro lens shot of an ear. The music within contained some classic pieces, notably 'One Of These Days' and the epic 'Echoes', but was again marred by inconsistency. Pink Floyd's festering talent finally exploded in 1973 with *Dark Side Of The Moon*. It marked the arrival of Waters as an important lyricist and Gilmour as a guitar hero. Brilliantly produced - with a sharp awareness of stereo effects - the album became one of the biggest selling records of all time, currently in excess of 25 million copies. Its astonishing run on the *Billboard* chart spanned over a decade and at last the group had rid itself of the spectre of the Barrett era. Perhaps with this in mind, a moving eulogy to their former member, 'Shine On You Crazy Diamond', was one of the highpoints of *Wish You Were Here*. Syd apparently showed at **Abbey Road** studio during the sessions, prepared to contribute but incapable of doing so. 'Have A Cigar', however, did feature a cameo appearance; that of **Roy Harper**. Although dwarfed in sales terms by its predecessor, this 1975 release is now regarded by aficionados as the group's artistic zenith. *Animals* featured a scathing attack on the 'clean-up television' campaigner, Mary Whitehouse, while the cover photograph, an inflatable pig soaring over Battersea power station, has since passed into Pink Floyd folklore. However it was with this album that tension within the band leaked into the public arena. Two of its tracks, 'Sheep' and 'Dogs', were reworkings of older material and, as one of the world's most successful bands, Pink Floyd were criticised as an anathema to 1977's punk movement. At the end of the year, almost as a backlash, Nick Mason produced the **Damned**'s *Music For Pleasure*. Wright and Gilmour both released solo albums in 1978 as rumours of a break-up abounded. In 1979, however, the group unleashed *The Wall*, a Waters-dominated epic which has now become second only to *Dark Side Of The Moon* in terms of sales. A subtly-screened autobiographical journey, *The Wall* allowed the bassist to vent his spleen, pouring anger and scorn on a succession of establishment talismen. It contained the anti-educational system diatribe, 'Another Brick In The Wall', which not only restored the group to the British singles' chart, but provided them with their sole number 1 hit. *The Wall* was also the subject of an imaginative stage show, during which the group was bricked up behind a titular edifice. A film followed in 1982, starring **Bob Geldof** and featuring ground-breaking animation by Gerald Scarfe, who designed the album jacket.

Such success did nothing to ease Pink Floyd's internal hostility. Longstanding enmity between Waters and Wright - the latter almost left the group with Barrett - resulted in the bassist demanding Wright's departure. He left in 1979. By the early 80s relations within the band had not improved. Friction over financial matters and composing credits - Gilmour argued his contributions to *The Wall* had not been acknowledged - tore at the heart of the band. 'Because we haven't finished with each other yet,' was Mason's caustic reply to a question as to why Pink Floyd were still together and, to the surprise of many, another album did appear in 1983. *The Final Cut* was a stark, humourless set which Waters totally dominated. It comprised of songs written for *The Wall*, but rejected by the group. Mason's contributions were negligible, Gilmour showed little interest - eventually asking that his production credit be removed - and Pink Floyd's fragmentation was evident to all. One single, 'Not Now John', did reach the UK Top 30, but by the end of the year knives were drawn and an acrimonious parting ensued. The following year Waters began a high-profile but commercially moribund solo career. Mason and Gilmour also issued solo albums (Wright completed his in 1978), but none of these releases came close to the success of their former group. The guitarist retained a higher profile as a session musician, and appeared with **Brian Ferry** at the **Live Aid** concert in 1984.

In 1987 Mason and Gilmour decided to resume work together under the Pink Floyd banner; Rick Wright also returned, albeit as a salaried member. Waters instigated an injunction, which was over-ruled, allowing temporary use of the name. The cryptically titled *A Momentary Lapse Of Reason*, although tentative in places, sounded more like a Pink Floyd album than its sombre 'predecessor', despite the muted input of Wright and Mason. Instead Gilmour relied on session musicians, including Phil Manzanera of **Roxy Music**. A massive world tour began in September that year, culminating 12 months and 200 concerts later. A live set, *Delicate Sound Of Thunder* followed in its wake but, more importantly, the rigours of touring rekindled Wright and Mason's confidence. Galvanised, Waters led an all-star cast for an extravagant adaptation of *The Wall*, performed live on the remains of the Berlin Wall in 1990. Despite international television coverage, the show failed to reignite his fortunes. In 1994 his former colleagues released *The Division Bell*, an accomplished set which may yet enter the Pink Floyd lexicon as one of their finest achievements. 'It sounds more like a genuine Pink Floyd album than anything since *Wish You Were Here*', Gilmour later stated, much to the relief of fans, critics and the band themselves. With Wright a full-time member again and Mason on sparkling form, the group embarked on another lengthy tour ensued, judiciously balancing old and new material. The band also showcased their most spectacular lightshow to date during these performances. Critical praise was effusive, confirming the group had survived the loss of yet another nominally 'crucial' member. *Pulse* cashed in on the success of the tours and was a perfectly recorded live album. The packaging featured a flashing LED, which was supposed to last (in flashing mode) for 6 months. The legacy of those 'faceless' record sleeves is irrefutable; Pink Floyd's music is somehow greater than the individuals creating it.

Albums: *The Piper At The Gates Of Dawn* (1967), *Saucerful Of Secrets* (1968), *More* (1969, film soundtrack), *Ummagumma* (1969), *Atom Heart Mother* (1970), *Meddle* (1971), *Obscured By Clowns* (1972; film soundtrack), *Dark Side Of The Moon* (1973), *Wish You Were Here* (1975), *Animals* (1977), *The Wall* (1979), *The Final Cut* (1983), *A Momentary Lapse Of Reason* (1987), *Delicate Sound Of Thunder* (1988), *The Division Bell* (1994), *Pulse* (EMI 1995). Compilations: *Relics* (1971), *First Eleven* (1977, 11-album box-set), *A Collection Of Great Dance Songs* (1981), *Works* (1983), *Sine On* (8-CD box set) (1992).

Videos: *Pink Floyd: London '66-'67* (See For Miles 1994), *Delicate Sound Of Thunder* (Columbia 1994).
Further reading: *The Pink Floyd*, Rick Sanders. *Pink Floyd*, Jean Marie Leduc. *Pink Floyd: The Illustrated Discography*, Miles. *The Wall*, Roger Waters and David Appleby. *Syd Barrett: The Making Of The Madcap Laughs*, Malcolm Jones. *Pink Floyd: A Visual Documentary*, Miles and Andy Mabbett. *Pink Floyd: Bricks In The Wall*, Karl Dallas. *Sauceful Of Secrets: The Pink Floyd Odyssey*, Nicholas Schaffner *Pink Floyd Back-Stage*, Bob Hassall. *Pink Floyd*, W. Ruhlmann. *Complete Guide To The Music Of*, Andy Mabbett.

Pink Floyd At Pompeii

This 1971 film featured a performance by **Pink Floyd** in the deserted amphitheatre of the Roman city. The surrounding ruins added a chilling atmosphere to the quartet's performance, which included versions of their most popular live numbers, including 'A Saucerful Of Secrets', 'Set The Controls For The Heart Of The Sun', and 'Careful With That Axe, Eugene', as well as material which would later appear on *Meddle*: 'One Of These Days' and 'Echoes'. *Pink Floyd At Pompeii* captures the group at the peak of their improvisatory period. **Dave Gilmour**'s guitarwork and Rick Wright's organ playing are particularly well-served, helping to define this era's Pink Floyd sound. Spilt-screen shots and psychedelic imagery, although predictable, add to the atmosphere, although the interview material suggests the band speak best through their music. Ably directed by a joint French/Belgian/German company, *Pink Floyd At Pompeii* quickly became a firm favourite of late-night cinema audiences and while dated by today's standards, it remains a valuable aural and visual testament to the group's considerable power.

Pink Lady, The

After writing the music for several successful shows on the London stage between 1894 and 1909, Ivan Caryll moved to America and collaborated with C.M.S. McLellan on the celebrated operetta, *The Pink Lady*, which opened at the New Amsterdam theatre in New York on 13 March 1911. McLellan's book was based on a French play, *Le Satyre*, by Georges Berr and Marcel Guillemand, and concerns Lucien Garidel (William Elliot), who is soon to marry Angele (Alice Dovey). Before he 'puts the ball and chain on', he decides that he would like to 'bring champagne on', and invites an old flame, Claudine (Hazel Dawn), for one last farewell dinner. Unluckily for him, his future wife is dining at the same restaurant, and cannot help noticing Lucien's companion, who is known as 'The Pink Lady' because of her blushing wardrobe. The embarrassing situation leads to some bewildering twists and turns in the plot, culminating in the reunion of the happy couple as Lucien sings 'My Beautiful Lady' to his Angele. The lovely waltz became widely successful through versions by Lucy Isabelle Marsh, Grace Kerns, and Elizabeth Spencer, and another song from the show, 'By The Saskatchewan' ('Flow river, flow, down to the sea'), was made popular by Reinald Werrenrath and the Hayden Quartet, amongst others. The rest of a romantic and tuneful score included 'The Kiss Waltz', 'The Right To Love', 'Parisian Two-Step', 'Bring Along The Camera', 'The Hudson Belle', 'I Like It', and 'Donny Didn't, Donny Did'. Critics agreed that, unlike most operettas, the songs emerged quite naturally from the plot. It all added up to a tremendous success, and a run of 312 performances. Hazel North, who not only sang and danced in a charming manner, but also played the violin, delighted London audiences when *The Pink Lady* opened at the Globe theatre in 1912. Since those days it has been revived on many occasions.

Pink Military/Pink Industry

This late 70s UK act were a central part of Liverpool's thriving post-punk scene. Distinctive vocalist Jayne Casey had fronted a now impressive-looking line-up in **Big In Japan**. But after their demise in the summer of 1978, she teamed up with John Highway (guitar), Wayne Wadden (bass), Paul Hornby (drums) and a certain Nicky (keyboards), to form Pink Military. An experimental 12-inch EP, *Blood And Lipstick*, appeared on local label Eric's (also the name of Liverpool's premier venue of the era), in 1979, and caused quite a stir. A deal with **Virgin Records** ensued, resulting in the more overtly commercial single, 'Did You See Her', in 1980. However, this belied the wealth and diversity of sounds to be found on the accompanying album, *Do Animals Believe In God?* By this time, Chris Joyce had been recruited on drums, while Wadden had been replaced by Martin on bass. But the Virgin/Eric's collaboration soon fell apart, and their next EP, *Buddha Waking/Disney Sleeping*, came out on Last Trumpet Records. Pink Military soon split and gave way to Pink Industry, Casey collaborating with Ambrose Reynolds, later a member of an early **Frankie Goes To Hollywood** line-up. The first fruits were extremely promising and 'Is This The End?' (1982) stands as one of the year's most outstanding singles. *Low Technology* emerged just over a year later, exemplifying the band's off-beat, haunting qualities. *Who Told You You Were Naked* hinted at eastern influences, while further embracing new instrument and studio techniques. There was a two-year gap before *New Beginnings*, accompanied by a single, 'What I Wouldn't Give' (with a sleeve adorned by a photograph of **Morrissey**) in mid-1985. An increasingly reclusive existence since then has been broken only by a retrospective self-titled album on Cathexis, promoted by 'Don't Let Go' in 1987.
Albums: As Pink Military *Do Animals Believe In God?* (Eric's 1980). As Pink Industry *Low Technology* (Zulu

1983), *Who Told You You Were Naked* (Zulu 1983), *New Beginnings* (Zulu 1985). Compilation: *Pink Industry* (Cathexis 1988).

Pinkerton's Assorted Colours

Originally known as the Liberators, this Rugby, Warwickshire-based quintet comprised: Samuel 'Pinkerton' Kemp (vocals/autoharp), Tony Newman (guitar), Tom Long (guitar), Barrie Bernard (bass) and Dave Holland (drums). One of the lesser known UK pop groups of the period, they came under the wing of **Fortunes** manager **Reg Calvert**, who encouraged them to change their name and to each don a different pastel shade suit. This unusual stress on colour was reflected in various publicity stunts such as polluting the fountains of Trafalgar Square with red dye. The gimmicky use of a kazoo and autoharp, aided by extensive plugging on the **pirate radio** stations Radio City and Radio Caroline, proved sufficient to break their **Decca** debut single, 'Mirror Mirror'. A minor dispute between their manager and rival **Phil Solomon** over the ownership of various group names brought them even more publicity than their next single, 'Don't Stop Loving Me Baby', which barely scraped into the Top 50. **Stuart Colman** replaced Bernard in the line-up, but by that time the group were losing momentum and their prospects were further blighted by the tragic death of their manager. After a lean patch, the group abbreviated their name to Pinkerton's Colours, then Pinkerton and finally evolved into the **Flying Machine**. That last incarnation brought a happier ending for, in the summer of 1969, the spin-off group achieved a US Top 5 hit with 'Smile A Little Smile For Me'.

Pinocchio

(see **Disney, Walt**)

Pins And Needles

Originally presented by members of the USA International Ladies Garment Workers Union at the tiny Labor Stage (formerly the **Princess Theatre**) for the enjoyment of their fellow workers, this revue subsequently transferred to the Windsor Theatre (which had nearly three times as many seats), and ran for a (then) record 1,108 performances. Armed with a liberal, pro-union point of view, it opened on 27 November 1937, and proceeded to take a satirical swipe at the usual targets, Fascists, Nazis, and Britain's injustice to its long-established Empire. Anyone who could 'Sing Me A Song Of Social Significance', as its most popular number demanded, was OK, of course, and if you could take your partner for 'Doin' The Reactionary', well, that was even better. The sketches were by the show's director, Charles Freidman, amongst several others, and the music and lyrics wre provided by a newcomer to Broadway, **Harold Rome**. His other songs included 'Sunday In The Park', 'Nobody Makes A Pass At Me', 'One Big Union For Two', 'I've Got The Nerve To Be In Love', 'Chain Store Daisy (Vassar Girl Finds A Job)', 'It's Better With A Union Man', 'Not Cricket To Picket', and 'Four Little Angels Of Peace'. When it moved to the Windsor Theatre in 1939, the show was retitled *New Pins And Needles*, and continued on its honest, angry, but good-humoured way, constantly up-dating the material as it went.

Pinski Zoo

Like a more user-friendly **Last Exit**, the loud and joyful Pinski Zoo has combined the free jazz of the 60s, the funk-fusion beat of the 70s and the technology of the 80s to produce a powerful, accessible brand of harmolodics. Head-keeper Jan Kopinski claims **Yma Sumac**, **Jimi Hendrix** and **John Coltrane** as his seminal influences, though clearly **Albert Ayler** and **Ornette Coleman**'s Prime Time have also been inspirations. The band, one of the most lively and exhilarating working units around, was born in Nottingham, like Kopinski and fellow-founder member Steve Iliffe. Earlier editions included Tim Bullock (drums), Tim Nolan (bass) and Mick Nolan (percussion/vocals), but by the early 90s the personnel comprised Kopinski (soprano and tenor saxophones), Iliffe (keyboards), Karl Wesley Bingham (electric bass) and Steve Harris (drums). The unit won the best small group title in the 1990 *Wire/Guardian* readers' poll, and their albums *Rare Breeds* and *East Rail* were highly acclaimed by UK jazz critics. Kopinski and Bingham are two of the most exciting and individual talents in contemporary jazz.

Albums: *Introduce Me To The Doctor* (1981), *The Dizzy Dance Record* (1982), *The City Can't Have It Back* (1983), *Speak* (1984), *Live In Warsaw* (1985), *Rare Breeds* (JCR 1988), *East Rail East* (JCR 1990), *De-Icer* (Slam 1994).

Pioneers

The original Pioneers, formed in 1962, consisted of the brothers Sydney and Derrick Crooks, and **Glen Adams**. The latter later enjoyed a career as vocalist and studio musician, playing organ as a member of **Lee Perry**'s **Upsetters**. The Pioneers' debut, 'Sometime', was recorded for **Leslie Kong**'s Beverleys label during 1965. By late 1967 they were recording for the Caltone label, owned by Ken Lack, former road manager of the **Skatalites**. In 1968, Sidney teamed up with Jackie Robinson to record a series of local hits for producer **Joe Gibbs**, hitting number 1 in the Jamaican chart with their first attempt, 'Gimme Little Loving'. They followed up with another number 1, 'Long Shot', a song celebrating the victories of a famous Jamaican racehorse. Further successes for Gibbs included 'Dem A Laugh', 'No Dope Me Pony', 'Me Nah Go A Bellevue', 'Catch The Beat', and

'Mama Look Deh', which the **Maytals** used as the basis for their huge local hit of 1968, 'Monkey Man'. Sidney and Jackie then teamed up with **Desmond Dekker**'s brother George, and returned to record for Leslie Kong, initially releasing another local hit, 'Nana', under the group name the Slickers. Subsequent records for Kong were recorded under the name of the Pioneers, including their famous continuation of the racehorse saga, 'Long Shot Kick De Bucket', which tells how Long Shot and a horse named Combat died in a race at Caymanas Park track in Kingston. Other local hits for Kong included the Jamaican chart-topper, 'Easy Come Easy Go' (a return volley against rival group the **Royals**), the frenetic 'Samfie Man', about a confidence trickster, and 'Mother Rittie'. After their sojourn at Beverleys, they took up residence in England, where 'Long Shot Kick De Bucket' had reached the UK chart, peaking at number 21 in early 1970. They toured Egypt and the Lebanon later that year, returning in 1971 to record in a much more lightweight 'pop' reggae style. Their greatest success came with the **Jimmy Cliff**-penned 'Let Your Yeah Be Yeah' which reached number 5 in the autumn of 1971. Smaller success came with the cover versions '100 lbs Of Clay' and 'A Little Bit Of Soap'. Since 1973, George has pursued a singing and composing career, Jackie has been a solo vocalist, while Sidney Crooks has concentrated on production, since the late 80s operating his own studio in Luton, Bedfordshire, England. Their best records remain those they recorded for Joe Gibbs and Leslie Kong during 1968-70.

Albums: *Greetings From The Pioneers* (1968), *Long Shot* (Trojan 1969), *Battle Of The Giants* (Trojan 1970), *Let Your Yeah Be Yeah* (1972), *I Believe In Love* (1973), *Freedom Feeling* (1973), *Roll On Muddy River* (1974), *I'm Gonna Knock On Your Door* (1974), *Pusher Man* (1974). Compilation: *Greatest Hits* (1975).

Pipkins

This clownish duo of **Roger Cook** and **Tony Burrows** had first sung together professionally in the Kestrels. They were reunited in 1969 to record and promote 'Gimme Dat Ding!', an infuriatingly insidious ditty composed by Mike Hazelwood and **Albert Hammond** for the UK children's television series, *Oliver And The Overlord*. A polished production, it jostled to number 6 in the domestic hit parade in 1970 after several out-sized trouser-dropping plugs by Burrows and Cook on *Top Of The Pops*. The single also made the US Top 10 and an accompanying album reached the lower regions of the US Top 200 lists. This was the last the world saw of the Pipkins - but their triumph was but one in a golden year for Burrows who, in his capacity as a session vocalist, also ministered to 1970 hits by **Edison Lighthouse**, **White Plains** and **Brotherhood Of Man**.

Album: *Gimme Dat Ding* (1970).

Pippin

Although the book was written by Roger O. Hirson, much of the credit for the success of the stage musical *Pippin* is owed to **Bob Fosse**. As director and choreographer, and through his collaboration with Hirson in the writing of the show, Fosse gave *Pippin* the sparkle needed to attract critical plaudits. The show opened at the Imperial Theatre in New York on 23 October 1972 and starred Ben Vereen in the lead role. The revue format, with its fast paced great dancing, and the remarkable sets helped overcome any audience resistance to a story set in the Middle Ages. John Rubinstein played the title role, a character based upon Pepin, the son of Emperor Charlemagne. Eric Berry, Jill Clayburgh, Leland Palmer, and Irene Ryan (Grandma in television's *The Beverly Hillbillies*) were also in the original cast but Irene Ryan died during the show's run and was replaced by Dorothy Stickney. The score was by **Stephen Schwartz**, whose songs included 'Magic To Do', Morning Glow', 'On The Right Track', 'Corner Of The Sky', 'No Time At All', 'Simple Joy', and 'Extraordinary'. That last song title describes perfectly this show's success and its run of 1,944 performances. *Pippin* won **Tony Awards** for best actor (Vereen), director and choreographer (Fosse), scenic design (Tony Walton), and lighting design (Jules Fisher). The 1973 London production didn't appeal, in spite of the inclusion in the cast of John Turner, Patricia Hodge, Diane Langton, **Paul Jones**, and **Elisabeth Welch**, and folded after 85 performances.

Pirate Radio

Although UK pop was flourishing in the wake of the **Beatles** and the **Rolling Stones**, the means of greatest access - radio - was sorely constrained. The problem of limited air-time was made particularly apparent to record plugger **Ronan O'Rahilly** as he tried in vain to secure plays for a single by his client **Georgie Fame**. Inspired by Radio Veronica, anchored off the Dutch coast since 1960, O'Rahilly secured the financial backing to purchase and refit the *Frederica*, a 1930 Danish passenger ferry. Renamed the *Caroline* after the daughter of US President John F. Kennedy, the ship sailed from Greenore in the Irish Republic and was anchored off Felixstowe, Suffolk on 27 March 1964. Following a brief test transmission around midnight that evening, Radio Caroline began regular broadcasts at noon the next day, opening with the Beatles' 'Can't Buy Me Love'. The reaction was quick and positive. The BBC was taken completely by surprise and their bland formula of popular music was immediately ignored as millions turned over to 'Caroline on 199 your all-day music station'. Within months several other stations had appeared, broadcasting sometimes contrasting music in often

uncomfortable, even farcical, circumstances.
In July 1964 Radio Caroline acquired an early rival - Radio Atlanta. The original ship was relocated off the Isle Of Man while the Atlanta vessel, the *Mi Amigo*, now christened Caroline South, was sited off Frinton, Essex. Its main competitor was established the following December when a former minesweeper, the *Galaxy*, anchored off Walton-on-the-Naze, Essex, began broadcasts as Radio London. Recalled by many as the genre's exemplary station, its imaginative playlist, powerful transmitter and memorable jingles combined to create a unique character. Its staff included **John Peel**, Kenny Everett, Tommy Vance and **Tony Blackburn**, a contrast which ensured the station's balance. The Carolines also boasted their share of future celebrities. Blackburn and Vance spent time on the *Mi Amigo*, alongside Simon Dee, Emperor Roscoe, Mike Ahearn and Dave Lee Travis. Life on board any of the vessels was usually gruelling, yet despite cramped conditions, storms and seasickness, a spirit of adventure and camaraderie bonded the disc jockey and audience.
The pirates constructed their own charts, loosely based on those of the music press, but punctuated with singles peculiar to individual ships. It resulted in a curious double standard; record companies could not court them officially, yet the pirates were crucial in pushing material, particularly original American versions, which might not otherwise have been hits. 'You've Lost That Lovin' Feelin'' (the **Righteous Brothers**) and 'Elusive Butterfly' (**Bob Lind**) were two prime examples of the pirates' influence and the stations were also less apprehensive of controversial material, including death discs and protest songs. However, loyalty to a particular release was not simply borne out of altruism, and the Caroline organization later admitted that records could be bought into their chart. When **Phil Solomon** took over the programming of the station he mercilessly plugged the recordings of his own acts on the Major Minor label, such as the **Dubliners** and **David McWilliams**. Radio London's publishing house, Pall Mall Limited, owned the rights to a succession of b-sides, fuelling rumours that this would guarantee airtime to the partnership.
Despite the pervasive influence of the two major stations, many others were peppered around Britain's coastline. Radio Scotland, initially anchored off Dunbar in East Lothian, inspired a fierce loyalty, maintaining onshore links through its Clan Balls, which featured national and local groups. Its nominal counterpart, Radio England, provided the UK with its most overtly American system, based on a fast-moving, non-stop format. Johnny Walker, later of Caroline, began his career there.
Nearby was Radio 355, also known as Britain Radio while further north, off Scarborough, lay Britain 270. Ships, however, were not the only source and several stations were sited on the disused army and navy watch-towers embedded in the Thames Estuary. Radio Essex, later BBMS (Britain's Better Music Station) was based on Fort Knock John; Radio 390, recalled with affection for Mike Raven's R&B Show, broadcast from the sprawling Red Sands' edifice; while between the two, on Shivering Sands, lay Radio City. The station had begun life in May 1964 when the platform was seized by singer **Screaming Lord Sutch** who proclaimed it Radio Sutch. The novelty quickly palled; records and valves were in short supply and provisions appeared in exchange for free advertising, and by September control had passed to pop group manager **Reg Calvert**, who renamed it Radio City. Although the new owner initially announced that the venture was a success, he made an aborted attempt to sell the station to Caroline at the end of 1965. Six months later Calvert approached Radio London, but problems arose over ownership of City's transmitter. Major Oliver Smedley claimed it was his, then raided the complex, leaving behind him a posse of riggers who, it is said, were about to retrieve his property. On 21 June 1966, Calvert arrived at Smedley's home following a heated meeting earlier in the day. A scuffle broke out during which the Major fired a shotgun, killing Calvert instantly. Although his widow, Dorothy, tried to keep the station on air, it closed prematurely in February 1967 when the Rochford, Essex magistrate ruled that Shivering Sands lay within British territorial waters and was thus under the scope of the Wireless Telegraphy Act. The scandal, coupled with the tragic drowning of an engineer, a disc jockey and the co-proprietor of the short-lived Radio Invicta, fuelled the ire of an already seething establishment. Time was already running out; a 1965 Council of Europe declared all offshore broadcasting illegal and one by one the member states introduced laws forbidding their ports to be used as a base.
On 15 August 1967, the Marine Offences Act came into effect resulting, overnight, in the closure of every station, barring the irrepressible Radio Caroline. As midnight passed, renegade disc jockeys Johnnie Walker and Robbie Dale kept the flag flying. Excluded from British patronage, the owners looked to the Continent, but support from this source grew equally problematical. Caroline nonetheless remained a *cause célèbre* for many years, broadcasting for several months before disappearing again, only to resume transmission when all hope seemed lost. Its legacy was also maintained onshore with the proliferation of minority or community-based stations which sprang up during the 80s. These pirates viewed Radio 1 and its commercial counterparts as restrictive as O'Rahilly had viewed the old BBC Light Programme. Caroline's tempestuous story ended in 1989 in the wake of new British laws. In the most punitive action to date, the ship was holed below the waterline during a combined raid by British and Dutch authorities and all equipment

put 'out of action'. With this act the legacy of Britain's offshore pirate radio would appear to be over. Their influence on the UK popular music was colossal: they alone defined how pop radio should be delivered, and much of their legacy still exists in modern radio presentation
Further reading: *Pop Went The Pirates*, Keith Skues.

Pirate, The

Released by MGM in 1948, *The Pirate* is set on a Caribbean island in the early part of the 19th century, and tells the colourful story of Manuela (**Judy Garland**) who is betrothed to the fat and arrogant mayor, Don Pedro (Walter Slezak). Serafin (**Gene Kelly**), the leader of a group of wandering actors, discovers that Manuela dreams of being with the famous pirate Macoco - Mack the Black to his friends - and so he claims to be the renegade himself. At first Manuela is taken in by his ruse, but when Don Pedro is hypnotised by Serafin at one of the troupe's performances, he admits he is the real Mack the Black. Not surprisingly, Manuela then loses her overwhelming passion for pirates and realises that she really loves Serafin. Although not a commercial success by any means, the film is impressive, not only for its exuberant music and dance sequences, but for its attempt to do something different. Both Garland and Kelly gave appropriately stylised performances (Garland's furious antics when Serafin's disguise is revealed are hilarious - probably one of the best tantrums ever to be seen in a Hollywood musical). **Cole Porter**'s sophisticated score contained several good numbers including 'Nina', which accompanied a scintillating dance sequence during which Kelly makes his way through the town serenading every pretty young woman he meets; 'Mack The Black', a dream sequence in which Kelly imagines he is the awesome Macoco (somewhat reminiscent of Kelly's vision of serenading **Kathryn Grayson** in ***Anchors Aweigh***); 'You Can Do No Wrong' and 'Love Of My Life', two ballads which are handled beautifully by Garland; and 'Be A Clown', performed early in the film by Kelly and the amazing **Nicholas Brothers**, and later given the full circus treatment by Kelly and Garland. Also featured were Reginald Owen, Gladys Cooper, George Zucco, Lola Albright, Lester Allen, and Cully Richards. The spirited and innovative choreography was designed by Robert Alton and Gene Kelly, and Frances Goodrich and Albert Hackett's screenplay was adapted from a play by S.N. Behrman. **Vincente Minnelli** was the director, and the film, which was brilliantly photographed in Technicolor by Harry Stradling, was produced by the **Arthur Freed** MGM unit. All in all it proved to be an interesting and frenetic experience for all concerned - almost experimental in parts - and was certainly different from other musicals of that era.

Pirates

The original Pirates - Alan Caddy (lead guitar), Tony Docherty (rhythm guitar), Johnny Gordon (bass), Ken McKay (drums), Mike West and Tom Brown (backing vocals) - formed in 1959 to back singer **Johnny Kidd**. The line-up later underwent extensive changes, but by 1962 had settled around Mick Green (guitar), Johnny Spence (bass) and Frank Farley (drums), each of whom were former members of the Redcaps. Their recording commitments to Kidd aside, the trio also completed an excellent 'solo' single in 1964 which coupled rousing versions of 'My Babe' and 'Casting My Spell'. John Weider, later of the New **Animals** and **Family**, joined the Pirates when Green left to join the **Dakotas** later that year, but he in turn was replaced by Jon Morshead. The newcomer accompanied Spence and Farley on a second single, 'Shades Of Blue', recorded in 1966 upon splitting permanently from Kidd. However the trio was disbanded within weeks when the latter joined erstwhile colleague Green in the Dakotas, from where they subsequently moved into the **Cliff Bennett** Band. The pair then forged separate careers but revived the Pirates, with Spence, in 1976. Their inspired, uncluttered grasp of R&B proved highly popular and a series of powerful albums, although not major sellers, showed a group of undoubted purpose. They disbanded again in 1982, weary of incessant touring, but the Pirates remain one of British pop's most enduring acts. Green's distinctive, staccato, rhythm/lead style was later adopted by **Wilko Johnson** of **Dr. Feelgood**, and he remains one of the UK's most respected musicians.
Albums: *Out Of Their Skulls* (1977), *Skull Wars* (1978), *Happy Birthday Rock 'N' Roll* (1979), *A Fistful Of Dubloons* (1981).

Pisces

A contemporary UK trio of **Plainsong**-like guitar folk strummers, best known for delivering **Richard Digance** to the waiting world.
Album: *Pisces* (1971).

Pitch Shifter

Nottingham, England-based quartet comprising Jonathan Clayden (vocals), Jonathan Carter (guitar/programming), D (drums) and Mark Clayden (bass). In early 1991 they signed to Peaceville Records and lanched their career with the release of *Industrial*. Among those impressed with the group's visceral guitar assault (at that time also featuring second guitarist Stuart Toolin, and no drummer) was disc jockey **John Peel**, who invited them to perform three tracks on his show in May 1991. Moving over to **Earache Records**, they recorded their debut for the label in January of the following year, with the *Submit* mini-album. For its full length follow-up the group increased

the ratio of technology, though its application remained studiously intense. The lyrics built on the themes of oppression and social injustice, while the use of samplers and sequencers offered an extra aural dimension. Touring with **Treponem Pal**, **Consolidated**, **Neurosis** and **Biohazard** ensued - and this musical melting pot produced the germ of an idea within the band. The resultant *The Remix Wars* saw the band revisiting their back catalogue, allowing access also to other sympathetic hands, including **Therapy?**, Biohazard and rappers **Gunshot**.
Albums: *Industrial* (Peaceville 1991), *Submit* (Earache 1992, mini-album), *Desensitized* (Earache 1993), *The Remix Wars* (Earache 1994).
Video: *Deconstruction* (1992).

Pitchford, Lonnie

b. 8 October 1955, Lexington, Mississippi, USA. Through his adoption of the one-string 'diddley-bow' and tuition in the music of **Robert Johnson** from **Robert Lockwood**, Pitchford has put himself in danger of being regarded as a museum curator rather than an active bluesman. He began constructing one-string guitars while still a child and his musical education as a guitarist and pianist remained in isolation until he was discovered by enthomusicologist Worth Long. He was introduced to Robert Johnson when he met Lockwood at the World's Fair in Knoxville when Long arranged a concert featuring them along with **Sammy Myers** and Theodis Morgan. He and Lockwood played together for three years thereafter. Pitchford's re-creations of Johnson songs like 'Come On In My Kitchen' and 'Terraplane Blues' sound like self-conscious performance art alongside the band numbers on *All Around Man* and pose the question of which format most nearly represents the man's talent.
Album: *All Around Man* (Rooster 1994). Compilations: *Mississippi Moan* (L+R 1988), *Roots Of Rhythm & Blues: A Tribute to the Robert Johnson Era* (Columbia 1992), *Deep Blues* (Anxious 1992).

Pitney, Gene

b. 17 February 1941, Hartford, Connecticut, USA. Although Pitney began recording in 1959 ('Classical Rock 'N' Roll' was recorded with Ginny Mazarro as Jamie And Jane), his initial success came as a songwriter, providing the Kalin Twins with 'Loneliness', **Roy Orbison** with 'Today's Teardrops' and **Bobby Vee** with 'Rubber Ball'. His solo recording career took off in 1961 with the multi-tracked 'I Wanna Love My Life Away' and the dramatic film themes 'Town Without Pity' and 'The Man Who Shot Liberty Valance'. Throughout this period, he was still writing for other artists, creating big hits for **Ricky Nelson** ('Hello Mary Lou') and the **Crystals** ('He's A Rebel'). In 1963, Pitney toured Britain where his 'Twenty Four Hours From Tulsa' reached the Top 10. After meeting the **Rolling Stones**, he recorded **Mick Jagger** and **Keith Richards**' 'That Girl Belongs To Yesterday'. Despite the onslaught of the beat groups, Pitney's extraordinarily impassioned big ballads remained popular in the USA and especially in the UK. Among his hits from this era were **Barry Mann** and **Cynthia Weill**'s 'I'm Gonna Be Strong' (1964), 'I Must Be Seeing Things' (1965), 'Looking Through The Eyes Of Love' (1965), 'Princess In Rags' (1965), 'Backstage' (1966), **Randy Newman**'s 'Nobody Needs Your Love' (1966), 'Just One Smile' (1966) and 'Something's Gotten Hold Of My Heart' (1967). The controversial 'Somewhere In The Country' (about an unmarried mother) was less successful. In addition, Pitney recorded albums in Italian and Spanish, with one of his songs, 'Nessuno Mi Puo Guidicare' coming second in the 1966 San Remo Song Festival. There were also country music albums with **George Jones** and **Melba Montgomery**. By the late 60s, his popularity in America had waned but he continued to tour in Europe, having the occasional hit like 'Maria Elena' (1969), 'Shady Lady' (1970) and 'Blue Angel' (1974). In 1988 he had unexpected success when he sang on a revival of 'Something's Gotten Hold Of My Heart' with **Marc Almond**, which topped the UK charts. Pitney will be remembered for his impassioned vocals and his almost faultless choice of material to record.
Albums: *The Many Sides Of Gene Pitney* (Musicor 1962), *Only Love Can Break A Heart* (Musicor 1962), *Gene Pitney Sings Just For You* (Musicor 1963), *Gene Pitney Sings World-Wide Winners* (Musicor 1963), *Blue Gene* (Musicor 1963), *Gene Pitney Meets The Fair Young Ladies Of Folkland* (Musicor 1964), *Gene Italiano* (Musicor 1964), *It Hurts To Be In Love* (Musicor 1964), *For The First Time Ever! Two Great Singers* (with George Jones, Musicor 1965), *I Must Be Seeing Things* (Musicor 1965), *It's Country Time Again!* (Musicor 1965), *Looking Through The Eyes Of Love* (Musicor 1965), *Espanol* (Musicor 1965), *Being Together* (Musicor 1965), *Famous Country Duets* (Musicor 1965), *Backstage (I'm Lonely)* (Musicor 1966), *Messumo Mi Puo Guidicare* (Musicor 1966), *The Gene Pitney Show* (Musicor 1966), *The Country Side Of Gene Pitney* (Musicor 1966), *Young And Warm And Wonderful* (Musicor 1966), *Just One Smile* (Musicor 1967), *Sings Burt Bacharach* (Musicor 1968), *She's A Heartbreaker* (Musicor 1968), *This Is Gene Pitney* (Musicor 1970), *Ten Years After* (Musicor 1971), *Pitney Today* (1968), *Pitney '75* (1975), *Walkin' In The Sun* (1979). Selected compilations: *Big Sixteen* (Musicor 1964), *More Big Sixteen, Volume 2* (Musicor 1965), *Big Sixteen, Volume 3* (Musicor 1966), *Greatest Hits Of All Time* (Musicor 1966), *Golden Greats* (Musicor 1967), *Spotlight On Gene Pitney* (Design 1967), *The Gene Pitney Story* (Musicor 1968, double album), *The Greatest Hits Of Gene Pitney* (Musicor 1969), *The Man Who Shot Liberty Valance* (Music Disc 1969), *Town Without Pity* (Music Disc 1969), *Twenty Four Hours From Tulsa* (Music Disc 1969), *Baby I*

Need Your Lovin' (Music Disc 1969), *The Golden Hits Of Gene Pitney* (Musicor 1971), *The Fabulous Gene Pitney* (Columbia 1972, double album), *The Pick Of Gene Pitney* (West-52 1979), *Anthology 1961-68* (Rhino 1987), *Best Of* (K-Tel 1988), *All The Hits* (Jet 1990), *Greatest Hits* (Pickwick 1991), *The Original Hits 1961-70 (Jet 1991), The EP Collection* (See For Miles 1991).

Pitt, Kenneth

b. 10 November 1922, Southall, Middlesex, England. Pitt's career in music blossomed during the 50s as a publicist for bandleaders **Ted Heath**, **Jack Parnell** and **John Dankworth**. He acted as press agent for visiting US stars, including **Stan Kenton**, **Count Basie**, **Louis Armstrong** and **Mel Tormé**, the latter of whom Pitt subsequently managed. A more arduous task facing Pitt was conducting press relations for **Jerry Lee Lewis** during his notorious 'child bride' tour. Pitt's initial forays into management were equally taxing. His first discovery was Danny Purches, the 'Singing Gypsy' who, despite some vocal talent, proved too rebellious for the show-business establishment of the 50s. In 1963 Pitt encountered the Mann/Hugg Blues Brothers during their appearance at a Southall club. Impressed by Pitt's pedigree, the group asked him to manage them and, as **Manfred Mann**, they became one of the most popular acts of their era. **Crispian St. Peters**, the **Mark Leeman Five** and the Beatstalkers were later added to Pitt's roster, but he is best known for a four-year tenure managing **David Bowie**. Their association, the subject of *The Pitt Report* (1985), ended in 1970 and the entrepreneur subsequently pursued a career as a consultant. He acted on behalf of **Rod McKuen** until the latter retired in 1980 and, in contrast, assisted punk band **Slaughter And The Dogs** to extricate themselves from an existing record deal and secure a replacement. Pitt also retained the rights to Mark Leeman's recordings, which he licensed for re-release in 1991.

Further reading: *The Pitt Report*, Kenneth Pitt. *Starmakers And Svengalis: The History Of British Pop Management*, Johnny Rogan.

Pittman, Barbara

b. Memphis, Tennessee, USA. Pittman was one of the few women who recorded for the legendary **Sun Records**. She heard blues music on Beale Street in Memphis as a child and began performing in Memphis clubs such as the Eagle's Nest, where a young **Elvis Presley**, whom Pittman dated, also honed his act during the mid-50s. In 1955 she went on the road as a singer with cowboy movie star Lash LaRue's travelling show. In 1956 she signed with Sun; although she released a number of singles on the label, none were hits. During the 60s Pittman moved to California where she sang on soundtracks for such 'motorcycle movies' as *Wild Angels*, *Wild On Wheels* and *Hells Angels*, under the name Barbara And The Visitors. She also recorded for Del-Fi Records but nothing was ever released. Pittman never recorded an album under her own name.

Pixies

This US group was formed in Boston, Massachusetts, by room-mates Charles Michael Kittridge Thompson IV aka Black Francis (b. Long Beach, California, USA; vocals, guitar) and Joey Santiago (guitar). A newspaper advertisement, requiring applicants for a '**Hüsker Dü/Peter, Paul And Mary** band', solicited bassist Kim Deal who in turn introduced drummer David Lovering. Originally known as Pixies In Panoply, the quartet secured a recording deal on the UK independent label **4AD Records** on the strength of a series of superior demo tapes. Their debut release, *Come On Pilgrim*, introduced the band's abrasive, powerful sound and Francis' oblique lyrics. *Surfer Rosa*, produced by **Big Black**'s Steve Albini, exaggerated the savage fury of its predecessor and the set was acclaimed Album Of The Year in much of the UK rock press. The superlative *Doolittle* emphasized the quartet's grasp of melody, yet retained their drive, and this thrilling collection scaled the national Top 10, aided and abetted by the band's most enduring single, 'Monkey Gone To Heaven'. The Pixies were now a highly popular attraction and their exciting live performances enhanced a growing reputation, establishing clear stage favourites in 'Debaser', 'Cactus', 'Wave Of Mutilation' and 'Bone Machine'. 1990's *Bossanova* showed an undiminished fire with a blend of pure pop with 'Allison' and sheer ferocity in 'Rock Music'. The band found themselves the darlings of the rock press and were once again widely regarded for recording one of the top albums of the year. Kim Deal, meanwhile, attracted glowing reviews for her offshoot project, the **Breeders**. *Trompe Le Monde* was, if anything, an even harsher collections than those which had preceded it, prompting some critics to describe it as the 'Pixies' heavy metal album'. Following the rechristened **Frank Black**'s departure for a solo career in early 1993 the band effectively folded, but the group's reputation continues to outshine any of the membership's concurrent or subsequent projects.

Albums: *Come On Pilgrim* (4AD 1987), *Surfer Rosa* (4AD 1988), *Dolittle* (4AD 1989), *Bossanova* (4AD 1990), *Trampe Le Monde* (4AD 1991).

Pixies Three

The Pixies Three, an all-female trio from Hanover, Pennsylvania, USA, comprised lead Midge Bollinger, Debbie Swisher (b. 1948), and Kaye McCool (b. 1946). The group found brief success during the peak years of the 'girl group' phenomenon in which raucous and strident-sounding female voices had become one of the favourite sounds in rock 'n' roll. Swisher and McCool

founded the Pixies Three in 1957 while still in grade school, bringing Bollinger into the group after several months singing as a duo. They served a long five-year apprenticeship performing at weddings, civic clubs, and private parties before they gained their professional break in 1962 when they were signed by producers John Madara and David White (of **Danny And The Juniors**) to a recording contract for **Mercury Records**. The Pixies Three's 1963 debut, 'Birthday Party', was an exuberant workout that evoked Claudine Clark's 'Party Lights' from the previous year. It was a number 1 hit in many markets but a more modest one nationwide (number 40 pop). The follow-up in late 1963 was a double-sided chart record, and as usual in such cases the record's chart action suffered from split airplay. The a-side '442 Glenwood Avenue' (number 56 pop) was in the rock 'n' roll-mode of their first hit, and the b-side, 'Cold Cold Winter' (number 79 pop), was a subdued ballad. After this record Bollinger left the group. Swisher switched to lead and recruited Bonnie Long, an old friend from Hanover, to maintain the trio. The reformed Pixies in 1964 reached the charts with 'Gee' (number 89 pop), a remake of the 1954 hit by the **Crows**. Following a little regional action on 'Summertime U.S.A.' (1964), the Pixies Three broke up. Debbie Swisher was the only member of the group to continue in the music business, singing lead for the **Angels** from 1966-68 (she was lead on their **RCA** tracks). In the 90s the Pixies Three appeared in occasional reunion concerts.
Album: *Party With The Pixies Three* (Mercury 1964).

Pizzarelli, Bucky

b. 9 January 1926, Paterson, New Jersey, USA. Although a self-taught guitarist, Pizzarelli quickly showed a comprehensive grasp of the guitar's potential. He played in large dancebands and small combos, worked as a studio musician, and as accompanist to singers, and even ventured into the classical field. He became a regular sideman with the later bands formed by **Benny Goodman** and in the 70s also appeared with Soprano Summit, the fine small band co-led by **Bob Wilber** and **Kenny Davern**, sometimes playing banjo. The 70s also saw him working with fellow guitarist **George Barnes** and with **Zoot Sims**, **Bud Freeman** and **Stéphane Grappelli**. He has also toured as a solo and in the 80s formed a duo with his son, John Pizzarelli, also a gifted guitarist, with whom he recorded the album *Swinging Sevens*. One of the finest of the mainstream guitarists in jazz, Pizzarelli remains rather less well known than many of his fellows, a state of affairs which seems likely to change in the 90s thanks to the continued high standard of his performances.
Albums: *Midnite Mood* (1960), *Green Guitar Blues* (1972), *Bucky Plays Bix: Bix Beiderbecke Arrangements By Bill Challis* (c.1973), *Soprano Summit II* (1977), *Nightwings* (1975), *Bucky's Bunch* (c.1977), *2 x 7 = Pizzarelli* (1980), *New York, New York/Sounds Of The Apple* (1980), *Love Songs* (1981), *The Cafe Pierre Trio* (1982), with John Pizzarelli *I'm Hip* (1983), with John Pizzarelli *Swinging Sevens* (1984), with John Pizzarelli *Hit That Jive, Jack* (1985), *Solo Flight* (1986), with John Pizzarelli *My Blue Heaven* (1990).

Pizzicato Five

Pizzicato Five are a conglomeration of fashion models and satirists from Japan, started by band leader Konishi (b. 3 February 1959, Japan) in 1984, after being a college student obsessed with the **Monkees**. Konishi was born on the day **Buddy Holly**, **Richie Valens** and the **Big Bopper** died in an air crash, and this fact led to an enduring interest in all aspects of rock 'n' roll. He was joined in the misnomered Pizzicato Five by Maki Nomiya (b. 12 March) and 'Bravo'. Song titles like 'Audrey Hepburn Complex', 'Twiggy Vs James Bond' indicated a fascination with retro-chic, and led to their song, 'Twiggy Twiggy', being included on the soundtrack to the Robert Altman film, *Pret-A-Porter*. As had been the case with another Japanese band to earn notoriety in the West, **Shonen Knife**, Pizzicato Five had released a number of domestic albums (some 17 to 1995) and singles before making inroads in to the US and UK markets. They were helped in this pursuit by singles such as 'Magic Carpet Ride', unveiled on Matador Records in March 1995, released following the band's attendance at the 1993 New Music Seminar in New York. There the band's performance was viewed by future manager Trit Macmillan, who negotiated the group's deal with the **Atlantic Records**-affiliated label. A compilation album of the band's hits to date, titled *Made In USA*, followed at the end of March, shortly after an appearance on British television programme *The Word*.
Selected album: *Made In USA* (Matador 1995).

PJ Harvey

b. 9 October 1970, Corscombe, Dorset, England, Polly Jean Harvey, from whom her band's title is taken, was the daughter of hippie parents who exposed her to art rock bands like **Captain Beefheart** and folk singer-songwriters like **Bob Dylan** at an early age. After growing up on their farm and playing saxophone with eight-piece instrumental group Boulogne, she wrote her first songs as part of the Polekats, a folk trio who toured local pubs she was only just old enough to drink in. Afterwards she attended an art foundation course before joining Somerset based band Automatic Dlamini for two and a half years (from whence would come several future collaborators). Over this period she contributed saxophone, guitar and vocals, and toured Europe twice, also appearing on the chorus of local band Grape's 'Baby In A Plastic Bag' single, and singing backing vocals on Bristol-based **Family Cat**'s 'Colour Me Grey'. Bored with playing other people's material, she moved to London, ostensibly to attend a course in sculpture (her other love), and elected to work with bass player Ian Olliver and drummer and backing vocalist Rob Ellis, both fellow Automatic Dlamini travellers. Together they played live for the first time in April 1991, using the name PJ Harvey. Independent label **Too Pure Records**, home of **Th' Faith Healers** and **Stereolab**, were so convinced by these nebulous performances that they mortgaged their home to finance the debut single, 'Dress' (Olliver left to be replaced by Stephen Vaughan on 'five-string fretless bass' after its release). Together with the most impressive 'Sheila-Na-Gig' and debut album *Dry*, it was enough to bring her to the attention not only of **Island Records** but also the mainstream press. Subverting the traditions of the female singer-songwriter with outbreaks of fire and brimstone guitar, Harvey possessed the sort of voice which, whilst not cultured in the traditional sense, offered a highly emotive cudgel. Allied to lyrics which laid her own relationships and feelings naked, her revisionary attitude to feminism was demonstrated by the ***New Musical Express*** cover on which she appeared topless, with her back to the photographer. An evocative and disturbing songwriter, most considered that she would leave too bitter an aftertaste for a mass audience. A truism which was partially dispelled by support slots to **U2** but hardly the choice of producer for *Rid Of Me*, **Big Black/Rapeman** controversialist Steve Albini. A vicious stew of rural blues, with Harvey's voice and guitar sounding almost animalised by the production, its title-track centre piece offered one of the most fearsome declarations ('You're not rid of me') ever articulated by rock music. Obsessive, haranguing imagery accompanied by stunning, committed musical performances (especially the distinctive drumming of Ellis), this was an album of such vehemence that its follow-up, by necessity, was forced to lower the extremity threshold. In the interim PJ Harvey (now officially a solo artist) made a memorable appearance at the 1994 BRIT Awards, duetting with **Björk** on a version of the **Rolling Stones**' 'Satisfaction'. For *To Bring You My Love* Harvey abandoned some of the psychosis, replacing it with a haunting, sinister ambience. With U2 producer Flood working in tandem with namesake Mick Harvey (of **Nick Cave And The Bad Seeds**), Polly left behind some of the less pleasant subject matter of yore (bodily dysfunction, revenge). The new approach was typified by the video to promotional single 'Down By The Water', evocative of Ophelia-like madness and sacrifice. Her band now consisted of guitarist John Parrish (another former colleague from Automatic Dlamini), Jean-Marc Butty (b. France; drums), Nick Bagnall (keyboards/bass), Joe Gore (b. San Francisco; ex-**Tom Waits**' band; guitar) and Eric Feldman (b. San Francisco; keyboards) - all musicians Harvey had met on previous travels. It was obvious, however, that she was still having problems with her public perception: 'If I hadn't been tarred with the angst-ridden old bitch cow image, it'd be something else. Now it's, oh, she's gone back to the farm'.

Album: *Dry* (Too Pure 1992), *Demonstration* (Too Pure 1992, 'demo' album given away with initial copies of *Dry*), *Rid Of Me* (Island 1993), *4-Track Demos* (Island 1993), *To Bring You My Love* (Island 1995).
Video: *Reeling* (1994).

Plain And Fancy

Rock 'n' roll music had begun to take a hold in America by the mid-50s, but the 1954/5 Broadway season was full of more traditional fare, such as ***The Boy Friend***, ***Peter Pan***, ***Silk Stockings***, and ***Damn Yankees***, amongst others. One of the others was *Plain And Fancy*, which opened at the Mark Hellinger Theatre on 27 January 1955. Joseph Stein and Will Glickman's book was set in Bird-in-Hand, Pennsylvania, the home territory of the Amish people, members of a fundamentalist religious sect who have no time or use for even the most basic modern aids. Don King (Richard Derr) has inherited a farm in the area, and he travels there from New York with Ruth Winters (Shirl Conway) to try to sell it to an Amish farmer, Papa Yoder (Stefan Schnabel). Yoder's daughter, Katie (Gloria Marlowe), is about to go through with an arranged marriage to Ezra Reber (Douglas Fletcher Rodgers), but she is still in love with an old flame, Ezra's brother, Peter (David Daniels). Peter has left the Amish community, and, when he returns just before the wedding, he is shunned by the traditionalists. Matters resolve themselves when Peter's bravery in a crisis gains him the respect of Katie's father, and the young people are allowed to marry. Don and Ruth make it a double wedding. The score, by composer **Albert Hague** - whose first full Broadway score this was - and lyricist Arnold Horwitt, contained a ballad that many feel to be one of the loveliest of all popular songs, 'Young And Foolish'. It was introduced by Daniels and Marlowe, and they also had 'Follow Your Heart' with **Barbara Cook**, who made a favourable impression in the role of Hilda Miller. Cook sang 'This Is All Very New To Me', 'I'll Show Him', and 'Take Your Time And Take Your Pick' (with Richard Kerr and Shirl Conway). The remainder of the delightful and romantic score included 'You Can't Miss It', 'It Wonders Me', 'Plenty Of Pennsylvania', 'Why Not Katie?', 'It's A Helluva Way To Run A Love Affair', 'Plain We Live', 'How Do You Raise A Barn?' (a spectacular scene to open Act II), 'Follow Your Heart', and 'City Mouse, Country Mouse'. Sophisticated New York audiences obviously loved this folksy view of their country cousins, and *Plain And Fancy* had a decent run of 461 performances. Barbara Cook went on to become Broadway's favourite ingénue during the 50s in shows such as ***Candide***, ***The Music Man***, ***The Gay Life*** and ***She Loves Me***.

Planet 4

Stockport, Lancashire record label who moved to their own offices and studio in Manchester in 1993. Their noble roster of releases includes Coventry DJs Parkes and Wilson (formerly **Limbo** recording artists) with 'American Slide', under the name the Ritmo Rivals. Others include Ultracynic (formerly famous for 1992's 'Nothing Lasts Forever'), who recruited a new singer to record 'Got To Have It', plus one-time Evolution vocalist Yvonne Shelton ('I Chose') and Paramist ('Release Me'). The Ritmo Rivals followed up in 1994 with 'Believe In Me'. The label is distributed through **Network**.

Planet Dog Records

A band/label/multi-tentacled collective founded in Wood Green, London in 1985, who abhor their media definition of 'crusty techno'. They started running weekly nights at the Robey in Finsbury Park (Club Dog), as well as monthly all-night parties at the Rocket in Holloway (Megadog). Regular contributors to these performances included **Banco De Gaia**, **Suns Of Arqa** and the Ullulators. Other early associates were **Ozric Tentacles**, from whence came the more progressive (in the purest sense) **Eat Static**. Regular DJs included Quark and Phidget from underground **sound system** Zero Gravity, Michael Dog and *New Musical Express* journalist Sherman. They quickly acquired a reputation as an attractive alternative to conventional club culture: 'When we first started the Dog, we used to go to other people's clubs and feel terribly self-conscious'. Their Megadog bashes were distinguished by an open-door and open-minded policy. The central figures are the publicity shy Bob and Michael Dog. The enclave have additionally set up their own label, Planet Dog records, which focuses on ambient and psychedelic dance tracks. The label's first release came from **Eat Static** with 'Abduction'. They also run the Wolf Distribution network, catering for **Astralasia**, **Alpha And Omega**, the **Magic Mushroom Band**, **Zion Train**, Psychedelic Psauna and even **Hawkwind**. Planet Dog label signings, meanwhile, include techno act Timeshard, from Liverpool.

Plant, Robert

b. 20 August 1948, West Bromwich, West Midlands, England. Plant's early career was spent in several Midlands-based R&B bands, including the New Memphis Bluesbreakers and Crawling King Snakes, the last of which featured drummer and future colleague, John Bonham. In 1965 Plant joined Lee John Crutchley, Geoff Thompson and Roger Beamer in Listen, a **Motown**-influenced act, later signed to **CBS Records**. A cover version of 'You Better Run', originally recorded by the **(Young) Rascals** made little headway, and Plant was then groomed for a solo career with two 1967 singles, 'Laughing, Crying, Laughing' and 'Long Time Coming'. Having returned to Birmingham, the singer formed Band Of Joy in which his growing interest in US 'west coast' music flourished. This promising group broke up in 1968 and following a brief association with blues veteran **Alexis Korner**, Plant then joined another local act, Hobstweedle. It was during this tenure that guitarist **Jimmy Page** invited the singer to join **Led Zeppelin**. Plant's reputation as a dynamic vocalist and frontman was forged as a member of this highly-influential unit, but he began plans for a renewed solo career following the death of John Bonham in 1980. *Pictures At Eleven* unveiled a new partnership with Robbie Blunt (guitar), Paul Martinez (bass) and Jezz Woodruffe (keyboards) and while invoking the singer's past, also showed him open to new musical directions. *The Principle Of Moments* contained the restrained UK/US Top 20 hit, 'Big Log' (1983), and inspired an ambitious world tour. Plant then acknowledged vintage R&B in the **Honeydrippers**, an *ad hoc* group which featured Page, **Jeff Beck** and **Nile Rodgers**, whose mini-album spawned a US Top 3 hit in 'Sea Of Love'. Having expressed a desire to record less conventional music, Robert fashioned *Shaken 'N' Stirred*, which divided critics who either lauded its ambition or declared it too obtuse. The singer then disbanded his group, but resumed recording in 1987 on becoming acquainted with a younger pool of musicians, including Phil Johnstone, Dave Barrett, Chris Blackwell and Phil Scragg. *Now And Zen* was hailed as a dramatic return to form and a regenerated Plant now felt confident enough to include Zeppelin material in live shows. Indeed one of the album's standout tracks, 'Tall Cool One', featured a cameo from Jimmy Page and incorporated samples of 'Black Dog', 'Whole Lotta Love' and 'The Ocean', drawn from their former group's extensive catalogue. The singer's artistic rejuvenation continued on the acclaimed *Manic Nirvana* and the excellent *Fate Of Nations*, before joining up with Jimmy Page for the *Unledded/No Quarter* project, which at last satisfied those who would never have the vocalist forget his past.

Albums: *Pictures At Eleven* (Swan Song 1982), *The Principle Of Moments* (Swan Song 1983), *Skaken 'N' Stirred* (Esparanza 1985), *Now And Zen* (Esparanza 1989), *Manic Nirvana* (Atlantic 1990), *Fate Of Nations* (Fontana 1993), with Jimmy Page *No Quarter* (Fontana 1994).

Videos: *Knebworth 90* (1990), *Mumbo Jumbo* (1991).

Further reading: *Robert Plant*, Michael Gross. *Led Zeppelin's Robert Plant Through The Mirror*, Mike Randolph.

Planxty

This early 70s Irish group originally featured **Christy Moore** (b. 7 May 1945, Dublin, Eire; guitar/vocals),

Donal Lunny (guitar/bouzouki/synthesizer), **Liam O'Flynn** (uilleann pipes) and **Andy Irvine** (guitar/mandolin/bouzouki/vocals). After two albums, Lunny left, to be replaced by Johnny Moynihan (bouzouki). In 1974, Moore left and was replaced by **Paul Brady** (b. 19 May 1947, Co. Tyrone, Northern Ireland; vocals/guitar). The name Planxty is an Irish word for an air that is written to thank or honour a person. The group remained highly popular throughout its existence and their records sold well. Moynihan then left to join **De Dannan**. After splitting up, the original group re-formed, this time with Matt Molloy (flute), who later joined the **Chieftains** in September 1979. Moore and Lunny departed once more in 1981 to form **Moving Hearts**. *Words And Music* featured the **Bob Dylan** song 'I Pity The Poor Immigrant'. The group were only ever formed as an extension of the various group members' solo commitments, and though they were always in demand at festivals, personal career moves saw an end to the line-up. By the time *The Best Of Planxty Live* emerged, they were pursuing solo projects.

Albums: *Planxty* (1972), *The Well Below The Valley* (1973), *Cold Blow And The Rainy Night* (1974), *After The Break* (Tara 1979), *The Woman I Loved So Well* (Tara 1980), *Timedance* (1981), *Words And Music* (1983), *The Best Of Planxty Live* (1987). Compilations: *The Planxty Collection* (1976), *The High Kings Of Tara* (1980), *Ansi!* (1984).

Plasmatics

Formed in 1979 in New York City, USA, the Plasmatics were a theatrical hardcore band which incorporated such violent acts as blowing up Cadillacs and chainsawing guitars in half into its performances. Assembled by and masterminded by former pornography entrepreneur Rod Swenson, the original personnel of the group included vocalist Wendy O. Williams, a former star of sex shows, who wore see-through lingerie, but for the most part, appeared topless with strategically-placed masking tape. The remainder of the band comprised Richie Stotts (guitar), who wore a blue mohawk haircut and a pink tutu on stage, Wes Beech (guitar), Stu Deutsch (drums) and Chosei Funahara (bass, later replaced by Jean Beauvoir). After releasing two EPs on the independent Vice Squad label in 1979, the Plasmatics signed with **Stiff Records** in the USA and the UK, releasing *New Hope For The Wretched* in 1980. It was largely panned by the critics but sold as a cult item due to the group's extensive press coverage, as did such singles as 'Butcher Baby' and 'Monkey Suit'. A second album, *Beyond The Valley Of 1984*, was issued on Stiff in 1981, as was an EP, *Metal Princess*. In 1982 the Plasmatics signed to **Capitol Records** and released *Coup D'Etat*, but by then they had evolved into an outright heavy metal outfit and had lost most of their novelty appeal. Williams and Beauvoir recorded solo albums following the Plasmatics' mid-80s break-up.

Albums: *New Hope For The Wretched* (1980), *Beyond The Valley Of 1984* (1981), *Coup D'Etat* (1982). Solo: Wendy O. Williams *Deffest! And Baddest!* (1988). Jean Beauvoir *Drums Along The Mohawk* (1986), *Jacknifed* (1988).

Plastic Bertrand

Plastic Bertrand was the name adopted by Roger Jovet (b. 1958, Belgium), who was raised by his Russian father and made his first record as a child in 1966. After school he trained as a stage manager before becoming the drummer for Belgian punk trio Hubble Bubble, who made one album. During this spell he met producer Lou Deprijck who arranged for him to try his hand at a solo record. The result was the frenetic 'Ca Plan Pour Moi', (translated: 'This Life's For Me') which was a big hit in Europe. His UK follow-ups included the **Small Faces**'s 'Sha La La La Lee'. Further recordings failed in the UK but he continued to release records in his native Belgium and also in Canada. All his material was recorded using session musicians, including **Elton Motello** who recorded in his own right. Part of his second album was recorded in Los Angeles, but English and American audiences were not yet ready to accept foreign language new wave.

Albums: *Plastic Bertrand Anl* (1978), *J'Te Fais Un Plan* (1979).

Plastic Ono Band

Formed in 1969, the Plastic Ono band initially served as an alternative outlet for **John Lennon** and his wife **Yoko Ono** during the fractious final days of the **Beatles**. The group's debut single, 'Give Peace A Chance', was recorded live in a Montreal hotel room during the much-publicized 'Bed-In' and featured an assortment of underground luminaries attending this unconventional anti-war protest. A more structured group - Lennon, Ono, **Eric Clapton** (guitar), **Klaus Voorman** (bass) and Alan White (drums) - was assembled for a Canadian concert captured on *Live Peace In Toronto 1969*. This audio-verité release contrasted Yoko's free-form and lengthy 'Don't Worry Kyoto' with several rock 'n' roll standards and a preview airing of 'Cold Turkey', the nerve-twitching composition which became the second Plastic Ono single when the Beatles spurned John's initial offer. Bereft of the cosy sentiments of 'Give Peace A Chance', this tough rocker failed to emulate its predecessor's number 2 position, a fact noted by Lennon when he returned his MBE in protest at British passivity over conflicts in Biafra and Vietnam. An expanded version of the group performed at the Lyceum in London during a UNICEF benefit and the Plastic Ono name was also used in a supporting role on several ensuing John and Yoko releases, notably *John Lennon: The Plastic Ono Band*, the artist's first, and arguably finest, solo album. Inspired by Arthur Janov's Primal Scream

Therapy, the album was a veritable exorcism of all Lennon's past demons, and a harrowing yet therapeutic glimpse into the abyss of his soul from the bleak atheism of 'God' to the Oedipal 'Mother', the self-mocking 'Working Class Hero', the elegiac child-like wonderment of 'Remember', the confrontation with the self in 'Isolation' and the spine-chilling, macabre nursery rhyme ending, 'My Mummy's Dead'. Voorman was the sole survivor from the earlier version of the Plastic Ono Band, which had included **George Harrison** and **Ringo Starr**. Although the epithet also appeared on *Imagine*, *Sometime In New York City* and *Walls And Bridges* (where it was dubbed the Plastic Ono Nuclear Band), it simply applied to whichever musicians had made contributions and had ceased to have any real meaning.

Albums: *Live Peace In Toronto 1969* (1969), *John Lennon: The Plastic Ono Band* (1970), *Sometime In New York City* (1972, also contains the group's live Lyceum concert recording).

Plastic Penny

This immensely talented UK quartet came together in 1968 when three former members of the Universals, Brian Keith (vocals), Paul Raymond (keyboards) and Tony Murray (bass), joined Mick Grabham (lead guitar) and Nigel Olsson (drums) to record for **Larry Page**'s recently launched Page One record label. Their debut was the refreshing and melodic 'Everything I Am', originally recorded by the **Box Tops**. It became a UK Top 10 hit, but after the failure of the Bill Martin/**Phil Coulter** composition 'Nobody Knows If', the group drifted into other recording ventures. Singer Brian Keith was the first to quit, leaving before the completion of the group's sole album. One-hit-wonders on paper, Plastic Penny nevertheless established themselves as an excellent musicians' training ground. Grabham founded **Cochise** and later joined **Procol Harum**, Murray teamed up with the **Troggs**, Paul Raymond had spells with **Chicken Shack** and **Savoy Brown**, and Olsson collaborated with the **Spencer Davis Group** and **Elton John**.

Album: *Two Sides Of A Penny* (1968).

Platt, Eddie

Very little is known about this Cleveland-born bandleader and saxophonist who reached the US Top 20 in 1958 with his version of 'Tequila', the rock 'n' roll dance number made popular by the **Champs**. He released one further single, a cover later that same year of 'Cha-Hua-Hua' by the Pets, which scraped into the lower end of the charts. He apparently never recorded again.

Platters

One of the leading R&B vocal groups of the 50s, they were the first black group to be accepted as a major chart act and, for a short time, were the most successful vocal group in the world. The Platters were formed in Los Angeles in 1953 by entrepreneur/songwriter Buck Ram (b. 21 November 1907, Chicago, Illinois, USA, d. 1 January 1991). By means of owning the Platters' name, Ram was able to control the group throughout their career, but his talent for composing and arranging enabled the Platters to make a lasting impression upon popular music. Their original line-up, Tony Williams (b. 5 April 1928, Elizabeth, New Jersey, USA, d. 14 August 1992, New York, USA; lead tenor), David Lynch (b. 1929, St. Louis, Missouri, USA, d. 2 January 1981; tenor), Alex Hodge (baritone) and Herb Reed (b. 1931, Kansas City, Missouri, USA; bass), recorded unsuccessfully the following year, precipitating the arrival of two new members, Paul Robi (b. 1931, New Orleans, Louisiana, USA), who replaced Hodge, and Zola Taylor (b. 1934; contralto). Signed to the **Mercury** label, the Platters secured their first hit in 1955 with 'Only You' reaching the US Top 5, an effortlessly light performance which set the pattern for subsequent releases including 'The Great Pretender', 'My Prayer' and 'Twilight Time', each of which reached number 1 in the US charts. 'Smoke Gets In Your Eyes' (previously a hit for **Paul Whiteman** in 1934), was an international number 1 hit single in 1958-59, highlighted their smooth delivery and arguably remains the group's best-loved release. Lead singer Williams left for a solo career in 1961, taking with him much of the Platters' distinctive style. His departure led to further changes, with Sandra Dawn and Nate Nelson replacing Taylor and Robi. With Sonny Turner as the featured voice, the group began embracing a more contemporary direction, seen in such occasional pop hits as 'I Love You 1000 Times' (1966) and 'With This Ring' (1967). During the late 60s, and for a long time afterwards, personnel changes brought much confusion as to who were the legitimate Platters. Sonny Turner and Herb Reed formed their own version, while Tony Williams did like-wise. The Platters' legacy has since been undermined by the myriad of line-ups performing under their name, some of which bore no tangible link to the actual group. This should not detract from those seminal recordings which bridged the gap between the harmonies of the **Mills Brothers** and the **Ink Spots** and the sweet soul of the ensuing decade. In the late 80s, Buck Ram continued to keep an eagle eye on the Platters' sold out appearances at Las Vegas and other US cities.

Selected albums: *The Platters* (1955, released on Federal, King and Mercury labels), *The Platters, Volume 2* (1956), *The Flying Platters* (1957), *The Platters On Parade* (1959), *Flying Platters Around The World* (1959), *Remember When* (1959), *Reflections* (1960), *Encore Of Golden Hits* (1960), *More Encore Of Golden Hits* (1960), *The Platters* (1960), *Life Is Just A Bowl Of Cherries* (1961), *The Platters Sing For The Lonely* (1962), *Encore Of The Golden Hits Of The Groups*

(1962), *Moonlight Memories* (1963), *Platters Sing All The Movie Hits* (1963), *Platters Sing Latino* (1963), *Christmas With The Platters* (1963), *New Soul Campus Style Of The Platters* (1965), *I Love You 1000 Times* (1966), *Going Back To Detroit* (1967), *I Get The Sweetest Feeling* (1968), *Sweet Sweet Lovin'* (1968), *Encore Of Broadway Golden Hits* (1972), *Live* (1974), *The Original Platters - 20 Classic Hits* (1978), *Platterama* (1982), *Platters Collection* (1986), *Magic Touch: An Anthology* (1992), *Greatest Hits* (1993).
Films: *Carnival Rock* (1957), *Girl's Town* aka *The Innocent And The Damned* (1959).

Platz, David

b. 13 January 1929, Hanover, Germany, d. 20 May 1994, London, England. Born of Jewish stock in the volatile political climate of Germany, Platz was exiled, with his sister, Gina, to Neasden, in Middlesex, in the 30s. Placed in publishing by his guardian, Platz was initially disappointed to discover it was in music rather than literature. At age 14 he became an office boy for Southern Music in Denmark Street, London. Graduating from copyright to manager of an office specialising in Latin-American recordings, he eventually left to set up his own company, Essex Music. That company, with Platz at the helm, became arguably the leading publishing agency by the late 50s, with the **Rolling Stones** its first major coup. They were soon joined by major talents like the **Moody Blues**, **Who**, **Procol Harum**, **Ralph McTell**, **David Bowie** and **Marc Bolan**. The *modus operandi* with each such major songwriter was to form a separate division of the company, overlooked by Essex, so that artists maintained a financial and business incentive in their affairs. In addition he inaugurated two record labels, Fly and Cube. Platz also went on to help finance and publish songs from the world of stage musicals, including ***Stop The World - I Want To Get Off***, ***The Roar Of The Greasepaint - The Smell Of The Crowd*** and **Lionel Bart**'s ***Oliver***. Between 1973 and 1986 he was publishing director of the Performing Rights Society, but his entrepreneurial activities were finally curtailed by the onset of motor neurone disease in his mid-60s.

Play It Cool

Released in 1962, *Play It Cool* starred **Billy Fury** as rock 'n' roll singer Billy Universe. While not leading his group, the Satellites, he takes a feisty heiress around London haunts as she seeks to find her brother. Michael Winner, later famed for violent, vigilante-styled films starring Charles Bronson, directed this low-key feature which sadly failed to capture Fury's vulnerable image and talent. *Play It Cool* did allow the singer space to perform and its most notable inclusion, 'Once Upon A Dream', gave Fury a UK Top 10 hit when issued as a single. Among the other featured performers were **Helen Shapiro**, **Shane Fenton** And The Fentones, Danny Williams and US star **Bobby Vee**, included by the producers with a highly-optimistic eye on the American market. Each of these acts were about to be eclipsed by the emergent Mersey Beat, although Shapiro re-emerged some 20 years later as an accomplished jazz singer. Fenton meanwhile reinvented himself as **Alvin Stardust** during the glam-rock 70s, successfully capturing a further 15 minutes of fame.

Players

An R&B vocal group from Chicago, Illinois, USA. Original members of the group were lead Herbert Butler, Collis Gordon, and John Thomas. The Players were formed in 1966 when Gordon and Thomas recruited Butler to sing lead for them on a song they had written, 'He'll Be Back', a marvellous lament about the plight of a girl whose boyfriend was fighting in the jungles of Vietnam. The trio was recorded by Calvin Carter, the long-time producer at **VeeJay Records**, and signed with the west coast-based Minit subsidiary of **Imperial Records**. In the middle of the session Carter replaced Gordon and Thomas in the background with the veteran **Dells**. 'He'll Be Back' became a national hit (number 24 R&B), deservingly so, but the follow-up, 'I'm Glad I Waited' (number 32 R&B) lacking the back-up talent of the **Dells** and the songwriting talents of Gordon and Thomas was a pale reflection of the previous hit. The Players made an album and toured with a new line-up of Butler, Joe Brackenridge, Otha Lee Givens, and Tommie Johnson, but with no more forthcoming hits eventually faded.
Album: *He'll Be Back* (Minit 1966).

Playmates

This humorous US pop trio comprised Donny Conn (b. 29 March 1930), Morey Carr (b. 31 July 1932) and Chic Hetti (b. 26 February 1930), all from Waterbury, Connecticut, USA. They formed the comedy and music trio the Nitwits while studying at the University of Connecticut and started touring in 1952 with an act that relied more on humour than singing ability. Re-named the Playmates, they made their first record, 'I Only Have Myself To Blame', on Rainbow in 1956. They moved to Roulette Records in 1957 and their third single on that label, 'Jo-Ann', a cover of the Twin Tones record, hit the US Top 20 in 1958. Over the next four years the clean-cut vocal group chalked up another nine US chart entries including the Top 20 hits 'What Is Love?' and 'Beep Beep', which reached number 4 in the US. They later recorded on **ABC**-Paramount, Colpix, Congress and Bell but their sound proved too dated to sell in the 60s.

Pleasure Elite

Pleasure Elite were formed in winter 1990 in Seattle, USA, around pseudonymous musicians V. Blast

(vocals), Lord Hoop De' Luv (guitar/vocals/sequencer), the Deacon (keyboards), Razor Monkey (drums) and Father Shark (guitar). Boasting a frenetic live show which won them early supports with **KMFDM**, **Rage Against The Machine**, **Jesus Jones** and **Alien Sex Fiend**, the band's lyrical concerns included media manipulation, lust and corruption. They made their debut with *Bad Juju* in May 1994, an album which delighted in crossing sundry musical frontiers including industrial metal and more traditional rock structures. With production by **Pearl Jam** associate Don Gilmore, the collection was promoted by the release of a strong attendant single, 'Media Feed'.
Album: *Bad Juju* (Music For Nations 1994).

Pletcher, Stew

b. 1907, d. 29 November 1978, USA. While he studied at Yale University, Pletcher was a trumpeter and vocalist with the Yale Collegians. In the early 30s he led his own bands and recorded with **Ben Pollack** (1934), but his swinging, melodic trumpet playing came to prominence in the time he spent in vibes player **Red Norvo**'s band (1936-37). He continued to work professionally as a musician and later played with **Jack Teagarden** (in 1945 and 1955) and with **Hilton 'Nappy' Lamare** (in 1949).

Plethyn

Plethyn were formed during the 70s and comprised Linda Healy (b. 11 May 1958, Welshpool, Powys, Wales), Roy Griffiths (b. 15 December 1952, Welshpool, Powys, Wales) and John Gittins (b. 30 November 1951, Welshpool, Powys, Wales). The name Plethyn is meant to convey the notion of three harmonic voices blending together to form one sound, like the three strands in a plait. Having started with local performances, the group extended their territory to cover the whole of Wales. From initial appearances on Welsh television, and playing at a festival in Brittany, they released *Blas Y Pridd*, which combined traditional and contemporary folk songs. They performed at the National Eisteddfod during the same year. The trio performed 'Can I Cymru' ('Song For Wales'), at the Pan Celtic Festival, in Killarney, Eire, in 1980, and two years later toured Sardinia. *Caneuon Gwerin I Blant* was an album of traditional children's songs. In 1985, the group toured California, USA, and in 1990, Vancouver, Canada. With numerous television appearances and regular airplay on Radio Cymru, they achieved sufficient fame to be given their own television series, *Blas Y Pridd*, on Channel S4C in 1991.
Albums: *Blas Y Pridd* (Sain 1979), *Golau Tan Gwmwl* (Sain 1980), *Rhown Garreg Ar Garreg* (Sain 1981), *Teulu'r Tir* (Sain 1983), *Caneuon Gwerin I Blant* (Sain 1984), *Byw A Bod* (Sain 1987), *Drws Agored* (Sain 1991). Solo: Linda Healy *Amser* (1989).

Plimsouls

One of a group of bands from Los Angeles, California, USA, playing power-pop in the mid-80s, the Plimsouls consisted of **Peter Case** (vocals/guitar; ex-**Nerves**), plus Lou Ramirez (drums), Dave Pahoa (bass) and Eddie Munoz (lead guitar). Formed in 1979, they originally worked as Tone Dogs before changing names and earning a strong local live reputation. This culminated in the low-budget recording in 1980 of a debut EP *Zero Hour* on the band's own Beat Records which captured their live energy despite its lo-fi recording quality. Their love of 60s pop was more fully realised on *The Plimsouls* whose vibrant pop tunes were given a clearer production. However, disappointed by record sales the group's relationship with Planet deteriorated, and they signed to **Geffen Records**. Again the band stayed long enough to produce only a single recording, the widely acclaimed *Everywhere At Once*, which included 'A Million Miles Away', issued as a 12-inch single while the band were between labels. One of the album's most enduring tracks, 'How Long Will It Take?', seemed to amplify the Plimsouls' long-standing role as commercial underachievers, and it was to be their last studio release. Case went on to a solo career while the Plimsouls' legacy was wrapped up with the 1988 release of a 1981 live gig by French label Fan Club.
Albums: *The Plimsouls* (Planet 1981), *Everywhere At Once* (Geffen 1983), *One Night In America* (Fan Club 1988).

Plus 8

Record label based in Detroit, Michigan, run by **Richie Hawtin** (b. 1973, Canada) and John Acquaviva (b. c.1963, London, Canada). Plus 8 has become one of the most influential outlets for new techno and acid, and hybrids thereof. The idea started when Hawtin lived near a club in Detroit called the Shelter. This ensured that he was in the same vicinity as techno innovators **Derrick May**, **Juan Atkins** and **Kevin Saunderson**. It was in this club scene that he first met partner Acquaviva and fellow Canadian Dan Bell. The latter helped instruct them in translating theiir ambitions of making music from theory in to practice. Plus 8 was set up in May 1990, taking their name from the familiar Detroit practice of spinning discs at increased volume. Their breakthrough release was Cybersonic's 'Technarchy', which featured old pal Dan Bell alongside Hawtin and Acquaviva. Afterwards Bell would move on to his own label Accelerate. Plus 8 'signings' include **Speedy J** ('De-Orbit', and, as Public Energy, *Binaural Signal Generator* EP), Circuit Breaker (*Circuit Breaker* EP), Vapourspace (**Mark Gage**) and Sysex (*City Points* EP). In 1991 they launched the sister label Probe, which introduced itself with FUSE's 'F.U.'. Probe is intended to be the more steadfast hard techno label, allowing Plus 8 to dabble in ambience and other

realms. Recently the label has hooked up with **Mute Records** dance empire, **Novamute**, to license material in the UK. However, Hawtin and Acqaviva continue to oversee quality control, from inception to finished artwork. Other merchandise includes a comic book and Plus 8 condoms. The future seems to hold a shift towards ambient sounds, though Hawtin will continue to be revered as the man who brought the 303 back into vogue.
Selected album: Various: *From Our Minds To Yours* (Plus 8 1991).

PM Dawn

One of the few rap acts who also sing in a more conventional fashion, PM Dawn consist of brothers Prince Be (Attrell Cordes) and DJ Minute Mix (Jarrett Cordes). They are from New Jersey where their stepfather was a member of **Kool And The Gang**. Their backgrounds were shrouded in tragedy; their real father having died of pneumonia when they were children, and their brother Duncan drowning when he was two years old. They came from a highly musical family - 10 of their aunts and uncles were rappers and DJs in the genre's early days in the 70s, when Prince Be started rapping as a youngster at family parties. They were equally influenced by 60s pop and duly incorporated harmonies in their work - hence the later tag, Daisy Age Soul. They cut demos in 1989, including their first song, 'Check The Logic', at a Long Island studio. After signing to the **Gee St** label, they took the name PM Dawn, indicating 'the transition from dark to light'. A debut single, 'Ode To A Forgetful Mind', was released in January 1991. Its follow-up, 'A Watcher's Point Of View', broke the UK charts, introducing their melodic hip hop to a larger audience. Their debut album saw them turned away by representatives of the **Beatles** in their attempts to sample 'Let It Be'. They had been more successful in negotiations with **Spandau Ballet**, who allowed them to build the song 'Set Adrift On Memory's Bliss' out of 'True'. PM Dawn went as far as to promote the release with an old 'new romantic' picture of Hadley and co, confirming their mischievous humour. It hit number 3 in the UK charts. When the album emerged in September 1991, it saw them grow out of the **De La Soul** comparisons that had previously plagued them, as one of the most concise, creative forces in rap/dance. All seemed to be running smoothly for PM Dawn in 1991, until an unfortunate experience at the end of the year. While Prince Be took part in the live filming of a gig at New York's The Sound Factory, **Boogie Down Productions** main man **KRS-1** became anagered at what he considered disrespectful remarks made by Prince Be during a *Details* magazine interview, and forcefully evicted him from the stage, smashing a record on Minute Mix's turntable in the process. 1992 saw two minor UK hits, 'Reality Used To Be A Friend Of Mine' and 'I'd Die Without You', which featured on the soundtrack to Eddie Murphy's *Boomerang* film. With Prince Be also appearing in a Nike trainers' commercial, the latter 45 climbed to US number 3. Following the release of 'Looking Through Patient Eyes', which heavily sampled **George Michael**'s 'Father Figure', PM Dawn released a long-awaited second album in April 1993. While writing tracks for *The Bliss* album, Prince Be had **Boy George** in mind, and the former **Culture Club** singer duetted on 'More Than Likely', which also became a single. 'Fly Me To The Moon', meanwhile, sampled **U2**'s 'The Fly'. However, critics still considered it to be a lesser album than their stunning debut. Minute Mix, meanwhile, had changed his name to J.C. The Eternal, and Prince Be had become The Nocturnal. PM Dawn also contributed to the AIDS benefit *Red Hot And Dance*, as well as remixing for **Simply Red**, and several benefit shows (Earth Day, LIFEbeat's CounterAid, etc).
Albums: *Of The Heart, Of The Soul, Of The Cross, The Utopean Experience* (Gee St 1991), *The Bliss Album...? (Vibrations Of Love & Anger & The Ponderance Of Life & Existence)* (Island 1993).

Poacher

This UK group was formed in Warrington, Cheshire in 1977 by guitar and singer Tim Flaherty (b. 1950). 'I'd played in local bands but I'd always wanted to be in one that had a pedal steel and a banjo.' The original line-up featured Flaherty (vocals), Adrian Hart (lead guitar), Allan Crookes (bass), Pete Allen (steel guitar), Pete Longbottom (banjo) and Stan Bennett (drums). Within months of being formed, Poacher won a heat on UK television's *New Faces* and then the all-winners final with a new British country song, 'Silver Dollar Hero'. Their first single, 'Darling', made a minor impact on the UK charts and a few months later the song was a hit for **Frankie Miller**. Other versions come from **Tom Jones** and **Barbara Mandrell**, but Poacher's original made number 86 in the US country charts, no mean achievement for a British group. Despite several singles ('Star Love', 'You Are No Angel'), Poacher have not reached the UK charts, although they are a very popular cabaret and country club act. Flaherty's own song, the excellent 'I Want To Hear It From You', was scheduled for a 1990 release and then withdrawn. Flaherty and Crookes remain from the original line-up, and vocalist/guitarist Peter John Frampton is a talented addition. Frampton has written the first country song about Warrington, 'Buttermarket'. The contents of their albums are more adventurous than their titles.
Albums: *Poacher* (1978), *Alive And Gigging* (1981), *Along The Way* (1989).

Poco

This US group formed as Pogo in the summer of 1968

from the ashes of the seminal **Buffalo Springfield**, who along with the **Byrds** were pivotal in the creation of country-rock. The band comprised **Richie Furay** (b. 9 May 1944, Yellow Springs, Ohio, USA; vocals/guitar), **Randy Meisner** (b. 8 March, 1946, Scottsbluff, Nebraska, USA; vocal/bass), George Grantham (b. 20 November 1947, Cordell, Oklahoma, USA; drums/vocals), **Jim Messina** (b. 5 December 1947, Harlingen, Texas, USA; vocals/guitar) and Rusty Young (b. 23 February 1946, Long Beach, California, USA; vocals/pedal steel guitar). Following an objection from Walt Kelly, the copyright owner of the Pogo cartoon character, they adopted the infinitely superior name, Poco. Poco defined as a musical term means 'a little' or 'little by little'. Their debut *Pickin' Up The Pieces* was arguably more country than rock, but its critical success made Poco the leaders of the genre. Meisner departed (later to co-found the **Eagles**) following a disagreement and *Poco* was released by the remaining quartet, again to critical applause, and like its predecessor made a respectable showing mid-way in the US Top 100. The album's landmark was an entire side consisting of a latin-styled, mainly instrumental suite, 'El Tonto De Nadie Regresa'. On this Rusty Young pushed the capabilities of pedal steel to its limit with an outstanding performance, and justifiably became one of America's top players. The energetically live *Deliverin'* made the US Top 30, the band having added the vocal talent of Timothy B. Schmit (b. 30 October 1947, Sacramento, California, USA; bass/vocals) and from the **Illinois Speed Press**, Paul Cotton (b. 26 February 1943, Los Angeles, California, USA; vocal/guitar). The departing Jim Messina then formed a successful partnership, **Loggins And Messina**, with **Kenny Loggins**. The new line-up consolidated their position with *From The Inside*, but it was the superb *A Good Feelin' To Know* that became their most critically acclaimed work. Contained on this uplifting set are some of Furay's finest songs; there were no weak moments, although worthy of special mention are the title track and the sublime 'I Can See Everything'. Another strong collection, *Crazy Eyes*, included another Furay classic in the 10-minute title track. Richie was tempted away by a lucrative offer to join a planned supergroup with **Chris Hillman** and **J.D. Souther**. Poco meanwhile persevered, still producing fine albums, but with moderate sales. Looking over their shoulder, they could see their former support band the Eagles carrying away their mantle.

During the mid-70s the stable line-up of Cotton, Schmit, Grantham and Young released three excellent albums, *Head Over Heels*, *Rose Of Cimarron* and *Indian Summer*. Each well-produced record contained a palatable mix of styles with each member except Grantham, an accomplished writer, and as always their production standards were immaculate. Inexplicably the band were unable to broach the US Top 40, and like Furay, Schmit was tempted away to join the monstrously successful Eagles. Grantham left shortly after and the future looked decidedly bleak. The recruitment from England of two new members, Charlie Harrison (bass/vocals)and Steve Chapman (drums/vocals), seemed like artistic suicide, but following the further addition of American Kim Bullard on keyboards, they released *Legend* in 1978. Justice was seen to be done; the album made the US Top 20, became a million-seller and dealt them two major hit singles, 'Crazy Love' and 'Heart Of The Night'. This new stable line-up made a further four albums with gradually declining success. Poco sounded particularly jaded on *Ghost Town* in 1982; the magic had evaporated. A contract-fulfilling *Inamorata* was made in 1984. Fans rejoiced to see Richie Furay, Grantham and Schmit together again, and although it was a fine album it sold poorly. Poco then disappeared. Five years later rumours circulated of a new Poco, and lo, Furay, Messina, Meisner, Grantham and Young returned with the exhilarating *Legacy*. Ironically, after all the years of frustration, this was one of their biggest albums, spawning further hit singles. Poco remain, along with the Eagles, the undefeated champions of country-rock.

Albums: *Pickin' Up The Pieces* (Epic 1969), *Poco* (Epic 1970), *Deliverin'* (Epic 1971), *From The Inside* (Epic 1971), *A Good Feelin' To Know* (Epic 1972), *Crazy Eyes* (Epic 1973), *Seven* (Epic 1974), *Cantamos* (Epic 1974), *Head Over Heels* (ABC 1975), *Live* (Epic 1976), *Rose Of Cimarron* (ABC 1976), *Indian Summer* (ABC 1977), *Legend* (ABC 1978), *Under The Gun* (MCA 1980), *Blue And Gray* (MCA 1981), *Cowboys And Englishmen* (MCA 1982), *Ghost Town* (Atlantic 1982), *Inamorata* (Atlantic 1984), *Legacy* (RCA 1989). Compilations: *The Very Best Of Poco* (Epic 1975), *Songs Of Paul Cotton* (Epic 1980), *Songs Of Richie Furay* (Epic 1980), *Backtracks* (MCA 1983), *Crazy Loving: The Best Of Poco 1975-1982* (RCA 1989), *The Forgotten Trail* (Epic/Legacy 1990).

Poet And The One Man Band

Formed in 1969, Poet And The One-Man Band included the songwriting team Tony Colton (vocals/piano) and Ray Smith (guitar/vocals), whose compositions had been recorded by, among others, **Cream**, the **Merseybeats** and **Zoot Money**. William Davies (organ), Roger Coulson (organ), Pat Donaldson (bass), Barry Morgan (drums) and Neemoi 'Speedy' Aquaye (ex-**Georgie Fame**; congas) completed the line-up responsible for the group's lone album, which also featured assistance from **Nicky Hopkins** (piano) and **Jerry Donahue** (arrangements), the latter of whom then joined the unit as a guitarist. Although Davies and Morgan were later replaced by Mike O'Neill and Pete Gavin, Poet And The One Man Band broke up when their label, **MGM**, closed its operation in Britain. Donaldson and

Donahue resurfaced in **Fotheringay**, while the rest of the group formed the core of **Head, Hands And Feet**.
Album: *Poet And The One Man Band* (1969).

Poets

Formed in Glasgow, Scotland in 1961, the Poets were one of Britain's more adventurous acts. Although obliged to play contemporary hits, the group - George Gallagher (vocals), Hume Paton (guitar), Tony Myles (guitar), John Dawson (bass) and Alan Weir (drums) - brought original songs and R&B favourites into their early sets. By 1964 they had become a leading attraction, resplendent in frilled shirts and matching velvet suits. **Rolling Stones**' manager **Andrew Loog Oldham** signed the quintet to his management and production company, attracted by their image and self-composed material. The Poets' debut single 'Now We're Thru', reached number 31 in the UK charts. Its ethereal drone and echoed 12-string guitars enhanced Gallagher's nasal delivery and the performance was the template for subsequent releases. Although the group would not secure another hit, their versatile recordings included ballads and uptempo R&B, imbued with their unique approach. The Poets' line-up fragmented and by 1967 none of the original group remained. Andi Mulvey (vocals), Fraser Watson (guitar), Ian McMillan (guitar), Norrie Maclean (bass) and Raymond Duffy (drums - on loan from Dean Ford And The Gaylords) completed 'Wooden Spoon', the unit's last official single. Further fragmentation ensued, but the name was retained until the early 70s. The core of the group subsequently joined **Longdancer**, while McMillan formed **Blue** with late-period member Hughie Nicholson.

Pogues

The London punk scene of the late 70s inspired some unusual intermingling of styles and the Pogues (then known as Pogue Mahone) performed punky versions of traditional Irish folk songs in pubs throughout the capital. They were fronted by singer **Shane MacGowan** (b. 25 December 1957, Kent, England) and also included Peter 'Spider' Stacy (tin whistle), Jem Finer (banjo/mandolin), James Fearnley (guitar/piano accordion), Cait O'Riordan (bass) and Andrew Ranken (drums). MacGowan had spent his late teen years singing in a punk group called the Nipple Erectors (aka the Nips) which also contained Fearney. After several complaints the band changed their name (Pogue Mahone is 'kiss my arse' in Gaelic) and soon attracted the attention of the **Clash** who asked them to be their opening act. Record companies were perturbed by the band's occasionally chaotic live act where they would often fight onstage and Stacy kept time by banging his head with a beer tray. In 1984 **Stiff Records** signed them and recorded *Red Roses For Me,* containing several traditional tunes as well as excellent originals like 'Streams Of Whiskey' and 'Dark Streets Of London'. It announced a major songwriting talent in McGowan's evocative descriptions of times and places he had often visited first-hand. **Elvis Costello** produced *Rum, Sodomy And The Lash* on which Philip Chevron, formerly a guitarist with the Radiators From Space, replaced Finer who was on 'paternity leave'. The group soon established themselves as a formidable and unique live act and the record entered the UK Top 20. There were further changes when the multi-instrumentalist Terry Woods (a co-founder of **Steeleye Span**) joined and Cait O'Riordan was replaced by Darryl Hunt. She later married Elvis Costello. The group's intrinsicly political stance resulted in their video to accompany the single, 'A Pair Of Brown Eyes', having to be re-edited because the group were filmed spitting on a poster of Prime Minister, Margaret Thatcher. 'We represent the people who don't get the breaks. People can look at us and say, "My God, if that bunch of tumbledown wrecks can do it, so can I"', explained Chevron in a press interview. The band would later have their protest ballad, 'Birmingham Six', banned from airplay. The album this was to be found on, *If I Should Fall From Grace With God*, was produced by **Steve Lillywhite** and embraced Middle Eastern and Spanish sounds. It sold more than 200,000 copies in the USA and 'Fairytale Of New York', a rumbustuous but poignant duet by MacGowan and Lillywhite's wife, **Kirsty MacColl**, was a Christmas number 2 hit in the UK in 1987. In the autumn of 1989 there were fears for the future of the group when MacGowan's heavy drinking led to him pulling out of several shows. He was due to join the band in the USA for a prestigious tour with **Bob Dylan** when he collapsed at London's Heathrow Airport. He missed all the support spots with Dylan and the band played without him. 'Other groups in a situation like that would've either said, "Let's get rid of the guy" or "Let's split up", but we're not the sort to do that. We're all part of each other's problems whether we like it or not', said Chevron. *Peace And Love* featured songs written by nearly every member of the group and its eclectic nature saw them picking up the hurdy-gurdy, the cittern and the mandola. Its erratic nature drew criticism from some quarters, mainly from original fans who had preferred the early folk-punk rants. While the rest of the group were clearly strong players it was widely accepted that MacGowan was the most talented songwriter. His output had always been highly sporadic but there were now fears that the drinking that fuelled his earlier creativity may have slowed him to a standstill. In an interview in 1989 he said he had not been 'dead-straight sober' since he was 14 and that he drank in quantity because 'it opened his mind to paradise'. It was announced in September 1991 that MacGowan had left the band and had been replaced by the former **Clash** singer, Joe Strummer.

This relationship lasted until June the following year when Strummer stepped down and the lead vocalist job went to Spider Stacy. McGowan later re-emerged with his new band, the Popes, while his erstwhile colleagues continued to tour heavily, recording competent new material that lacked the flair of old.
Albums: *Red Roses For Me* (Stiff 1984), *Rum, Sodomy And The Lash* (Stiff 1985), *If I Should Fall From Grace With God* (Stiff 1988), *Peace And Love* (WEA 1989), *Hell's Ditch* (Pogue Mahone 1990), *Waiting For Herb* (PM 1993). Compilations: *The Best Of The Pogues* (PM 1991), *The Rest Of The Best* (PM 1992).
Further reading: *The Pogues: The Lost Decade*, Ann Scanlon. *Poguetry: The Illustrated Pogues Songbook*, Hewitt and Pike McGowan.

Point Blank

Essentially from the same mould as Texan blues boogie supremos, **Z.Z. Top**, Point Blank's first two releases were produced by Bill Ham who had also masterminded the latter's rise to fame. Point Blank's line-up has been somewhat fluid but in the main featured John O'Daniel (vocals), Rusty Burns (guitar), Kim Davis (guitar), Bill Randolph (bass), Mike Hamilton (keyboards) and Buzzy Gren (drums). Their third venture into the recording studio resulted in *Airplay* which saw a slightly less intensive boogie stance, but this was rectified on *The Hard Way*, a part-live release which saw the band in blistering form. Bobby Keith replaced John O'Daniel in 1981 and their last two albums reflected a more radio-friendly approach to their sound, but without commercial success.
Albums: *Point Blank* (Arista 1976), *Second Season* (Arista 1977), *Airplay* (MCA 1979), *The Hard Way* (MCA 1980), *American Excess* (MCA 1981), *On A Roll* (MCA 1982).

Point, The

Much-heralded singer/songwriter Harry **Nilsson** wrote the screenplay and score for this 1970 animated feature. First produced as a 90-minute film for television, *The Point* revolves around the tale of Oblio, a boy with a round head born into a world where a triangular shape is the norm. Dustin Hoffman narrated the original version, but Alan Barzman took his place for this new version of an engaging fable posing questions about racial prejudice. Nilsson's music was suitably captivating. It included the melodic 'Me And My Arrow', a US Top 40 entrant, 'Think About Your Troubles' and 'Are You Sleeping?', each of which exhibited the singer's craftsmanship. Such material was issued on an concurrent album, and the film's legacy continued to prosper into the next decade. A theatrical version was staged in London featuring Mickey Dolenz, formerly a member of the **Monkees**, for whom Nilsson had written several songs. *The Point* remains a captivating project, appealing to both children and adults alike.

Pointer Sisters

These four sisters, Anita (b. 23 January 1948), Bonnie (b. 11 July 1950), Ruth (b. 1946) and June (b. 1954), were all born and raised in Oakland, California, USA, and first sang together in the West Oakland Church of God where their parents were ministers. Despite their family's reservations, Bonnie, June and Anita embarked on a secular path which culminated in work as backing singers with several of the region's acts including **Cold Blood**, **Boz Scaggs**, **Elvin Bishop** and **Grace Slick**. Ruth joined the group in 1972, a year before their self-named debut album was released. During this early period the quartet cultivated a nostalgic 40s image, where feather boas and floral dresses matched their close, **Andrews Sisters**-styled harmonies. Their repertoire, however, was remarkably varied and included versions of **Allen Toussaint**'s 'Yes We Can Can' and **Willie Dixon**'s 'Wang Dang Doodle', as well as original compositions. One such song, 'Fairytale', won a 1974 Grammy for Best Country Vocal Performance. However, the sisters were uneasy with the typecast, nostalgia image restraining them as vocalists. They broke up briefly in 1977, but while **Bonnie Pointer** embarked on a solo career, the remaining trio regrouped and signed with producer **Richard Perry**'s new label, Planet. 'Fire', a crafted **Bruce Springsteen** composition, was a million-selling single in 1979, and the group's rebirth was complete. The Pointers' progress continued with two further gold discs, 'He's So Shy' and the sensual 'Slow Hand' while two 1984 releases, 'Jump (For My Love)' and 'Automatic', won further Grammy awards. June and Anita also recorded contemporaneous solo releases, but although 'Dare Me' gave the group another major hit in 1985, subsequent work lacked the sparkle of their earlier achievements.
Albums: *The Pointer Sisters* (1973), *That's A Plenty* (1974), *Live At The Opera House* (1974), *Steppin'* (1975), *Havin' A Party* (1977), *Energy* (1978), *Priority* (1979), *Special Things* (1980), *Black And White* (1981), *So Excited!* (1982), *Break Out* (1983), *Contact* (1985), *Hot Together* (1986), *Serious Slammin'* (1988), *Right Rhythm* (1990), *Only Sisters Can Do That* (1993). Compilations: *The Best Of The Pointer Sisters* (1976), *Pointer Sister's Greatest Hits* (1982), *Jump - The Best Of The Pointer Sisters* (1989), *The Collection* (1993). Solo: Anita Pointer *Love For What It Is* (1987). June Pointer *Baby Sitter* (1983).

Pointer, Bonnie

b. 11 July 1951, East Oakland, California, USA. One of the four siblings who made up the successful R&B vocal group the **Pointer Sisters**, Bonnie Pointer was featured on two of the group's major hit singles, 'Yes We Can Can' and 'How Long', and on five albums between 1973-78. She then signed a solo contract with **Motown**, where she substituted a modern disco style

for the 40s-influenced jazz she had recorded with her sisters. 'Free Me From My Freedom' was a major black music hit in 1978, followed a year later by a sterling rendition of the **Elgins**' 'Heaven Must Have Sent You'. The latter was the linchpin of Bonnie Pointer II, an ambitious set of revivals of classic Motown hits. Pointer's increasingly outspoken attitude towards the label's hierarchy led to her contract being cancelled in 1981. After two years of legal battles, she signed to Private I Records, where she scored a succession of minor hits in the mid-80s.
Albums: *Bonnie Pointer* (1978), *Bonnie Pointer II* (1980), *If The Price Is Right* (1984).

Poison

This heavy metal band was formed in Pennsylvania, USA, in the spring of 1983 by Bret Michaels (b. Bret Sychalk, 15 March 1962, Harrisburg, Pennsylvania, USA; vocals) and Rikki Rockett (b. Richard Ream, 8 August 1959, Pennsylvania, USA; drums). They were soon joined by Bobby Dall (b. Kuy Kendall, 2 November 1958, Miami, Florida, USA; bass) and Matt Smith (guitar). Legendarily, Slash from **Guns N'Roses** would also audition at one point. The quartet played local clubs as Paris, before moving to Los Angeles and changing their name. It was at this point that Smith left the band and was replaced by C.C. Deville (b. 14 May 1963, Brooklyn, New York, USA; guitar). They were signed by Enigma Records in 1985 and released their first album in 1986, which went double platinum in America and produced three hits. *Open Up And Say...Ahh!* gave them their first US number 1, 'Every Rose Has Its Thorn'. Four other singles were also released, including a cover of 'Your Mama Don't Dance' which was a major US hit for **Loggins And Messina** in 1972. Poison were originally considered a 'glam band' because of the make-up they wore, but by the release of *Flesh And Blood*, in 1990, this image had been toned down dramatically. That year they also played their first UK shows, and fans declared their love of songs like 'Unskinny Bop' and 'Talk Dirty To Me' when the band made their official UK debut in front of 72,500 people at the Donnington Monsters of Rock Festival on 18 August 1990. The following year saw Deville replaced on guitar by the much-travelled **Richie Kotzen**. *Native Tongue* also had the addition of brass with the Tower Of Power Horns and eastablished the band alongside **Bon Jovi** as purveyors of image-conscious hard melodic rock. As well as many supporters, this naturally also saw them pilloried by more purist elements in heavy metal fandom. 1994 saw Michaels' face on the newstands once more as he dated *Baywatch* star Pamela Anderson, before being unceremoniously 'dumped' when it was decided that Michaels' press image did not fit with hers.
Albums: *Look What The Cat Dragged In* (Enigma 1986), *Open Up And Say...Ahh!* (Capitol 1988), *Flesh And Blood* (Capitol 1990), *Native Tongue* (Capitol 1993).
Videos: *Sight For Sore Ears, A* (1990), *Flesh, Blood And Videotape* (1991), *7 Days Live* (1994).

Poison Girls

The UK-based Poison Girls' firebrand political pop was first heard on a shared 12-inch EP, *Fatal Microbes Meet The Poison Girls*, a co-release for **Small Wonder Records** and the band's own label, Xntrix, in 1979. Poison Girls shared much of **Crass**' ideology (anarchism and communal living), though often through a more accessible musical medium. Aided by the strangely named Bernhardt Rebours (bass), Lance D'Boyle (drums) and Richard Famous (guitar), middle-aged Vi Subversa (vocals) also injected a strong feminist stance into their music. For their second EP, *Hex* (1979), the band co-opted with Crass' label, but it was almost a year before they released 'Persons Unknown', another shared single, this time with Crass themselves. The Poison Girls' long-playing debut proper, *Chappaquidick Bridge*, originally contained a free flexi-disc, 'Statement'. After 'All Systems Go' (1981), the group parted with Crass and a live album, *Total Exposure*, appeared later that year. *Where's The Pleasure* followed in 1982, before the band moved to a new label, Illuminated Records. This relationship proved short-lived, and after 'One Good Reason' and 'Are You Happy Now?' (both 1983), the Poison Girls returned to Xntrix for *Seven Year Scratch* in 1984. That same year, '(I'm Not A) Real Woman' continued the band's lyrical tack, but their next album was to be their last. After *Songs Of Praise*, and a one-off 12-inch single for the Upright label (a memorable effort too in 'The Price Of Grain'), the Poison Girls broke up. In 1995 *Statement*, a 4-CD box set, was released to anthologise the group's output, and the group played a one-off reformation gig in London in June.
Albums: *Chappaquidick Bridge* (Crass 1980), *Total Exposure* (Xntrix 1982), *Where's The Pleasure* (Xntrix 1982), *Seven Year Scratch* (Xntrix 1984), *Songs Of Praise* (Antrix 1985). Compilation: *Statement - The Complete Recordings* (Cooking Vinyl 1995).

Poison Idea

These hardcore heavyweights' broad appearance (nearly all members of the band could look on the term obese as a description of kindness) gave little credence to the harsh, speedy rock path they pursued. Formed in Portland, Oregon, USA, in late 1980, their first incarnation featured Jerry A. (vocals), Pig Champion (guitar), Chris Tense (bass) and Dean Johnson (drums). They debuted with the unwieldy EP *Pick Your King* which contained no less than 13 tracks, packaged in a sleeve featuring **Elvis Presley** on one side and Jesus Christ on the other. By the time of *Kings Of Punk* they were slightly more tuneful, but no less belligerent. However, Johnson and Tense were both fired and

replaced by Steve 'Thee Slayer Hippy' Hanford (drums) and Tim Paul (ex-Final Warning, now **Gruntruck**; bass). The sound was also filled out with additional guitarist Vegetable (ex-**Mayhem**). However, Tim Paul only lasted one abortive gig (just one song, in fact) before being replaced by the returning Tense. His tenure, though slightly longer, lasted only until the release of *War All The Time*, after which Mondo (also ex-Mayhem) joined. The line-up wars continued after 'Getting The Fear' was released, with Vegetable sacked on New Year's Eve, replaced by Kid Cocksman (ex-Gargoyle; guitar), and Mondo quit after the appropriately titled 'Discontent'. Myrtle Tickner (ex-Oily Bloodmen) then became the band's fourth bass player. Aldine Striknine (guitar; ex-Maimed For Life) stepped in for the next casualty Kid Cocksman (apparently kicked out for being too thin) to record *Feel The Darkness*, after which Mondo returned once more, this time on second guitar. Despite the line-up confusions and obvious gimmickry, they produced a body of work of some substance, characterized by a lyrical preference for matters alcoholic and sexual, with some of the world's great song titles ('Record Collectors Are Pretentious Assholes', etc.). Live they were both enormously impressive, and impressively enormous. After *We Must Burn* Poison Idea disbanded with Tense and Johnson going on to form Apartment 3G.
Albums: *Kings Of Punk* (Pusmort 1986), *War All The Time* (Alchemy 1987), *Record Collectors Are Pretentious Assholes* (Bitzcore 1989), *Poison Idea* (In Your Face 1989), *Feel The Darkness* (Vinyl Solution 1990), *Pajama Party* (Vinyl Solution 1992), *Blank, Blackout, Vacant* (Vinyl Solution 1992), *We Must Burn* (Vinyl Solution 1993).

Pokrovsky, Dmitri

b. Dmitri Pokrovsky, Russia. Pokrovsky's research into the traditional folk songs of his native Russia won him the Gorbachev award, the former Soviet government's highest artistic accolade. After initially studying conducting at the Gnessin Institute in Moscow, he took inspiration from ancient songs he heard women singing in a small remote village. He travelled all over Russia studying the music of the peasants and formed his own 'living laboratory', a study of village life where artists work closely with psychologists and scientists. *The Wild Field* by the Dmitri Pokrovsky Ensemble is the result of their research - a catalogue of communal, wedding and dance songs and other aspects of musical life of a remote part of southern Russia.
Selected album: *The Wild Field* (1991).

Polcer, Ed

b. 10 February 1937, Paterson, New Jersey, USA. Polcer first displayed his musical talents at the age of six when he played the xylophone. He began playing cornet semi-professionally while studying engineering at university. The band there, Princeton's very own Stan Rubin's Tigertown Five, had the distinction of playing both at Carnegie Hall and at the 1956 wedding of Prince Rainier and Grace Kelly in Monaco. In the 50s Polcer played in New York's clubland, returning there permanently after military service in the early 60s. Although gigging regularly at Jimmy Ryan's, the Metropole and other clubs, he remained a semi-pro, continuing his simultaneous business career. Throughout the 70s and into the mid-80s he was steadily more active in jazz, becoming a full-time musician in 1975 and taking on co-ownership of **Eddie Condon**'s club. Apart from co-leading the house band (with Red Balaban, who was also co-owner of the club), he worked with a number of other bands, including recordings with **Dick Wellstood** and a spell in 1973 with **Benny Goodman**. In 1975 he toured the USA and Canada with Bob Greene's *World Of Jelly Roll Morton* show. In 1982 Polcer became president of the New York International Art of Jazz Organization, which promotes community and corporate involvement in jazz education and performance. Latterly, he has toured extensively, playing cornet and occasionally adding vibraphone too.
Albums: with Dick Wellstood, Jane Harvey *You Fats...Me Jane* (1975), with Red Balaban *A Night At The New Eddie Condon's* (1975), *Coast To Coast Swingin' Jazz* (Jazzology 1990).

Polecats

Equally bequiffed but more heavily made-up than their contemporaries, the Polecats were one of the more successful bands involved in the early 80s UK rockabilly revival. This UK band comprised, Bloomberg, M.J. Boorer, Norman and Rodney, their debut was the first release on the Nervous label which would later release more rockabilly both past and present. 'Chicken Shack' proved strong enough to attract the attention of **Mercury Records** who put them under the production auspices of **Dave Edmunds**. The first single for the label was a cover version of **David Bowie**'s 'John I'm Only Dancing' which made the UK Top 40 in early 1981 and was followed up with a re-recording of 'Rockabilly Guy' (the b-side to 'Chicken Shack') which was also a Top 40 hit. For their third Mercury single they covered **Marc Bolan**'s 'Jeepster', helped out by the song's original producer **Tony Visconti**. Boorer was a Bolan devotee, taking his hero's place in later reformations of **John's Children** which he helped instigate. The Polecats' debut album also charted briefly but the rockabilly surge was fading and neither the 1983 Edward's produced mini-album *Make A Circuit With Me*, nor its title track, lifted as a single, made the charts. The following year the band were back recording for Nervous where they released *Cult Heroes*. Boorer became **Morrissey**'s post-Johnny Marr musical collaborator.

Albums: *Polecats* (1981), *Make A Circuit With Me* (1983), *Cult Heroes* (1984), *Nine* (1992).

Police

The reggae-influenced minimalist pop sound of this highly talented UK trio was one of the musical high-points of the late 70s and early 80s. Their individual talent and egos ultimately got the better of them and they fragmented, although each of the strong-willed former members have never officially ruled out the possibility of a re-match. The group comprised Stewart Copeland (b. 16 July 1952, Alexandria, Egypt; drums/percussion/vocals), **Andy Summers** (b. Andrew Somers, 31 December 1942, Poulton Le Fylde, Lancashire, England; guitar) and **Sting** (b. Gordon Sumner, 2 October 1951, Wallsend, Tyne And Wear, England; bass/vocals). Masterminded by Miles Copeland, ex-**Curved Air** member Stewart and ex-Last Exit bassist Sting came together with the vastly experienced Summers, leaving the original member Henry Padovani no alternative but to leave. He had previously played on their independent chart hit 'Fall Out', released on Miles' Illegal label. Summers, a former session musician and ex-**Zoot Money**, Dantalians Chariot, **Eric Burdon** And The New **Animals**, **Soft Machine** and **Kevin Ayers**, blended instantly with Copeland's back-to-front reggae drum technique and Sting's unusual and remarkable voice. Summers added a sparse clean guitar utilizing a flanger with echo, a sound he arguably invented and most certainly popularized; he found many imitators during his career with the Police. The mixture of such unusual styles gave them a totally fresh sound which they honed and developed over five outstanding albums; each record was a step forward both in musical content and sales.

Astonishingly, their **A&M** debut 'Roxanne' failed to chart when first released, but this now-classic tale of a prostitute was a later success on the back of 'Can't Stand Losing You'. Their heavily reggae-influenced *Outlandos D'Amour* and *Regatta De Blanc* dominated the UK charts for most of 1979 and contained such chart-toppers as 'Message In A Bottle' and 'Walking On The Moon'. Sting's simple but intelligently written lyrics were complete tales. By the time *Zenyatta Mondatta* was released their punk-styled bleached hair had black roots; they were never to be touched up, as the Police were on their way to becoming one of the world's leading bands. This album was their big breakthrough in America, Europe, Japan and indeed the rest of the world. The group's third number 1 'Don't Stand So Close To Me', a tale of the temptations of being a schoolteacher (which Sting had been previously), was closely followed by the lyrically rich yet simply titled 'De Do Do Do De Da Da Da'. The following year, having now conquered the world, they released the outstanding *Ghost In The Machine*, which contained Sting's most profound lyrics to date and was enriched by Hugh Padgham's fuller production. The major hit singles from this album were the thought-provoking 'Spirits In The Material World', 'Invisible Sun', a brooding atmospheric comment on Northern Ireland and the joyous Caribbean carnival sound of 'Every Little Thing She Does Is Magic' which provided their fourth UK number 1.

Following yet another multi-million seller, the band relaxed in 1982 to concentrate on solo projects. Stewart resurrected his **Klark Kent** *alter ego*, releasing *Klark Kent*, and wrote the music for the film *Rumblefish*. Andy had a book of photographs published to coincide with an exhibition of his camera work and also made an album with **Robert Fripp**. Sting appeared in the film adaptation of Dennis Potter's *Brimstone And Treacle* and had the UK gutter press speculate on his sexual preferences. The Police re-convened in 1983 and released the carefully crafted *Synchronicity*; almost as if they knew this would be their last album. The package was stunning, a superb album containing numerous potential hit singles and a series of expertly made accompanying videos. The magnificent 'Every Breath You Take', arguably their greatest song, stayed at number 1 in the UK for four weeks, and for twice as many weeks in the USA, while the album stayed at the top for an astonishing 17 weeks. The collection varies from gentle songs like 'Tea In The Sahara' and 'Wrapped Around Your Finger' to the mercurial energy of 'Synchronicity II'. To finish on such a high and to depart as undefeated champions must have satisfied the band. In retrospect, it is better to have produced five classic albums than a massive catalogue of indifferent collections. Like the **Beatles,** they never out-stayed their welcome, and thus are fondly remembered.

Albums: *Outlandos D'Amour* (1978), *Regatta De Blanc* (1979), *Zenyatta Mondatta* (1980), *Ghost In The Machine* (1981), *Synchronicity* (1983). Compilations: *Every Breath You Take - The Singles* (1986), *Greatest Hits* (1992).

Video: *Outlandos To Synchronicities: A History Of The Police* (1995).

Further reading: *Message In A Bottle*, Rossetta Woolf. *The Police: L'Historia Bandido*, Phil Sutcliffe and Hugh Fielder. *The Police: A Visual Documentary*, Miles. *The Police*, Lynn Goldsmith.

Pollack, Ben

b. 22 June 1903, Chicago, Illinois, USA, d. 7 June 1971, Palm Springs, California, USA. After playing drums with the **New Orleans Rhythm Kings** in the early 20s, Pollack formed his own band, which he proceeded to stock with the best of the up-and-coming young white jazz and danceband musicians of the day. Among the future stars who played in Pollack's bands in the late 20s were **Benny Goodman**, **Glenn Miller** and **Jack Teagarden**. Despite this interest in

fostering emerging jazz talent, Pollack was primarily concerned with commercial success and this led to a number of disputes that often ended with one or another of the musicians quitting. By the mid-30s, Pollack had largely given up drumming to direct the band and concern himself with business affairs, the drum chair being taken over by **Ray Bauduc**. In his band at this time were **Yank Lawson**, **Gil Rodin** and **Eddie Miller**; when another argument broke out the bulk of the band left to form a co-operative unit, at the head of which they placed **Bob Crosby**. Pollack formed a new band, featuring another rising star, **Harry James**, who quit in 1936 to join another former Pollack sideman, Goodman, who was by now the country's most famous bandleader. The years of accumulated resentments propelled Pollack into suing everyone in sight: Goodman, Crosby, Victor Records, Goodman's sponsors, the Camel Cigarette Co., and a motion picture company. The exact reason for some of this litigation is obscure but was presumably directed at recovering some of the financial benefits that had accrued to his protégés. For a while Pollack stopped performing regularly, although he remained in the music business, spending the 40s running a record company and acting as an agent. He also ran a restaurant and occasionally returned to bandleading, achieving a modest success in all these activities. His depression over what he saw as his rightful heritage going to others never fully lifted however, and he took his own life, by hanging, on 7 June 1971.
Selected compilations: *Ben Pollack And His Orchestra (1933-34)* (1979), *Futuristic Rhythm (1928-29)* (Saville 1983).

Pollock, Marilyn Middleton

b. 25 October 1947, Chicago, Illinois, USA. While still at college and university in Chicago, Pollock began singing with folk groups. In the late 60s she continued to sing folk locally and also performed with rock bands. In the early 70s her career encompassed radio and television commercials, tours of the USA with the rock bands Hurricane, Thunder and others, and continued activity as a folk singer. In the early 80s Pollock visited Ireland where she sang with the Chicago-based folk band, the Irish Ramblers. She continued to mix folk and rock performances in her repertoire then, in 1985, she relocated to Glasgow, Scotland. Her folk album, *Nobody Knows You*, won the British Music Retailers Association Award for Excellence in 1989. That same year she began singing jazz, appearing on *Yonder Come The Blues*. In 1990, she consolidated her acceptance as a jazz singer with an appearance at the Bude Festival and the following year joined the **Max Collie** band. Since then, although still active as a folk singer, Pollock's career has moved more towards jazz. She has recorded several albums and has appeared at numerous festivals including the Edinburgh International Festival and the Burnley Blues Festival at both of which she performed her one-woman show, *Those Women of the Vaudeville Blues*. In 1992, in addition to recording and touring clubs and festivals, both as a single and with Collie, she produced a new one-woman vaudeville blues show, *Jazz Me Blues*. A powerful and dynamic singer with great style and stage presence, Pollock's deep interest in and knowledge of the folk, blues and vaudeville traditions lend her repertoire considerable depth. Her vibrant voice, ranging through sensitivity to raunchiness, is well suited to the breadth and content of her repertoire and since her move to the UK she has established herself as a major contributor to the international jazz scene. In addition to singing, Pollock has also taught herself to play several instruments including guitar and flute.
Albums: *Nobody Knows You* (Fellside 1988), *Yonder Come The Blues* (1989), *Those Women Of The Blues* (Lake 1990), *Max Collie's Mardi Gras Vol. 2* (1991), *A Doll's House* (Fellside 1992).

Polo, Danny

b. 22 December 1901, Toluca, Illinois, USA, d. 11 July 1949. After playing clarinet in bands in various parts of the mid-west, Polo joined **Elmer Schoebel** in Chicago in 1923. Throughout the 20s he was very active, playing in numerous bands in various parts of the USA and also visiting Europe, where he played in and sometimes led bands in Paris, Berlin and London. His European visit lasted from 1927 until 1935 and included a spell with Bert **Ambrose**. He then returned to the USA but made another visit to Paris and London before World War II. In the early 40s he worked with **Jack Teagarden** and **Claude Thornhill**, with whom he had first worked when both were still youngsters. Polo's recordings, whether with the likes of **Coleman Hawkins** and **Benny Carter** in New York or with Tommy McQuater in London, display a musicianly clarinettist with coolly understated gifts.
Compilation: *Danny Polo And His Swing Stars* (1937-39 recordings).

Polo, Jimmy

b. c.1966, Alabama, but raised in Chicago, Illinois. Polo sang in gospel choirs as a boy, before becoming a musician in his teens around the local circuit. His first recorded outing was 'Libra Libra' in 1985 on Chicago Collection. His breakthrough hit, 'Shake Your Body', also emerged on that label, but the artist later complained bitterly that no royalties were forthcoming. Consequently Polo moved to the UK to join **Champion**, but this led to the break up of Polo's original Libra Libra group. 1989 brought another genre classic in 'Free Yourself'/'Better Days', released on Urban Records in the UK, and played keyboards for **Soul II Soul**. He also immersed himself in the UK's nascent acid/rave scene, alongside flatmate **Adamski**, who dedicated his 1990 hit album to Polo

(they also recorded together on the 1992 single, 'Never Goin' Down'). The same year he signed to **Perfecto** for the soul-influenced 'Express Yourself' single, and released his first album.
Album: *Moods* (Perfecto 1992).

Poly Styrene

b. Marion Elliot. Hailing from Brixton, London, England, the singer and main writer of **X-Ray Spex**, Poly Styrene, was writing songs by the age of nine. In 1976, a release on GTO Records, 'Silly Billy' by Mari Elliot, is believed to be her debut. Her subsequent work experiences on the sweet stall of Woolworths, and as a trainee clothes buyer, provided her with just as much songwriting stimulus. When punk reared its head Marion saw it as 'anti-racism, anti-nazism, and anti-sexism', and she quickly affirmed her identity with it. She assembled X-Ray Spex, wrote most of their material, and picked her new name from an advert. She was recognized as one of the leading lights of the punk movement in January 1978 when the BBC arts programme, *Omnibus*, broadcast the documentary *Who Is Poly Styrene?*. X-Ray Spex burnt out quickly and in 1980 Poly released her first solo single, 'Talk In Toytown', and the disappointing *Translucence* - especially moderate compared with the outstanding *Germ Free Adolescence* two years before. She then announced she was giving up pop music to devote herself to the Spiritual Life and Krishna Consciousness Movement, using the spiritual name Maharani Devi. She did, however, continue to play devotional music and to record at the temple's own studio (donated by **George Harrison**). At the bequest of her spiritual master she returned to pop music in 1986 with the Eastern-flavoured EP, *Gods And Goddesses*. In 1991 she reformed X-Ray Spex and announced that she was working on a 'counter culture street musical explosion' to be staged in 1992. She also appeared on **Dream Academy**'s 1991 album, *A Different Kind Of Weather*, as vocalist on a version of **John Lennon**'s 'Love'.
Album: *Translucence* (United Artists 1980).

Polydor Records

The label was formed in Germany in 1946 as the pop division of Deutsche Grammophon Gesellschaft, which had been set up in 1898 by Emile Berliner, one of the pioneers of sound recording. A UK branch was opened in 1956 and among its first signings were **Pearl Carr And Teddy Johnson**, although for several years its main activity was to release continental recordings in Britain. The most successful of these was 'My Bonnie' by Tony Sheridan and the 'Beat Boys' (the **Beatles**), a minor hit in 1963. Soon afterwards, the company took the then unusual step of signing production deals with entrepreneurs like **Giorgio Gomelsky** (whose Marmalade company had **Brian Auger** and **Julie Driscoll**) and Chris Stamp and **Kit Lambert**, owners of the Track label which issued records by the **Who** and **Jimi Hendrix.** Polydor also had a long-running connection with **Robert Stigwood** who set up the Reaction and Creation labels and brought both the **Bee Gees** and **Cream** to Polydor. During the 70s, the company also distributed Stigwood's RSO label, with its massive global hits, *Saturday Night Fever* and *Grease*. Polydor's own A&R department adopted a broad-based policy, signing **Slade**, the **Rubettes**, **Rory Gallagher**, the **New Seekers** and, via its Irish office, **Planxty** and the **Bothy Band**. True to its German roots, the label also found great success with bandleader **James Last.** From America, Polydor had **James Brown** and the roster of its subsidiary label **MGM** included the **Osmonds**. During the late 60s, the company also held the UK licence for the **Stax** and **Atlantic**. labels. DGG/Polydor and Philips had combined their music interests as far back as 1962 but it was not until a decade later that the two were merged world-wide into the PolyGram group. Even then, Phonogram (as the Philips label was renamed) and Polydor remained under separate management in the UK until 1981 when they were centralised under the PolyGram umbrella. Despite these changes, Polydor continued to operate across the whole spectrum of popular music. The label had its punks (the **Jam**, **Sham 69**, **Siouxsie And The Banshees**), progressive rock acts (**Barclay James Harvest**, **Roxy Music**, **Jean-Michel Jarre**), pop (**Darts**, **Level 42**) and comedy from **Billy Connolly**. Entering the 90s, Polydor's eclecticism remained the label's main characteristic. Artists as diverse as chanteuse Cathy Dennis, stage star Michael Ball (who played the lead in **Andrew Lloyd Webber**'s *Aspects Of Love*), veteran groups the *Shadows* and *Moody Blues*, indie rockers the **Wonder Stuff** and Canadian country singer Rita McNeill shared the same logo.

Pomeroy, Herb

b. 15 April 1930, Gloucester, Massachusetts, USA. After extensive studies at what later became known as the **Berklee College Of Music** in Boston, Massachusetts, Pomeroy joined the faculty to become one of the most respected teachers of the trumpet in jazz. His experience as a performer included work with the big bands of **Lionel Hampton** and **Stan Kenton** and, although he also played in small groups with **Charlie Parker** and others, it is in a big band context that he has made his greatest mark. Numerous contemporary jazz stars have graduated from Berklee, many of them paying tribute to Pomeroy's contribution to their musical education. His big bands, usually formed from college students and graduates, maintain an enviably high standard of musicianship. Unlike many of the college and university bands, Pomeroy's are not merely showcases for exceptional musical ability but also display an awareness of the underlying emotional qualities of jazz. The fact that his students demonstrate a greater involvement in the music they play is a tribute to his dedication to pursuing aims that transcend the simple imparting of knowledge. Pomeroy has also taught at the Massachusetts Institute of Technology, the Lenox School of Jazz and was, in 1962, employed by the US State Department to direct the house orchestra at Radio Malaya.

Albums: *Jazz In A Stable* (1955), *Life Is A Many Splendoured Gig* (Fresh Sounds 1957), *Band In Boston* (1958), *Herb Pomeroy And His Orchestra* (1958), *Pramlatta's Hips: Live At The El Morocco* (1980).

Pomus, Doc

b. Jerome Felder, 27 June 1925, Brooklyn, New York, USA, d. 14 March 1991, New York, USA. Doc Pomus wrote the lyrics for several great rock 'n' roll songs of the 60s. With **Mort Shuman**, who composed the music, Pomus's credits included the **Drifters**' 'Save The Last Dance For Me', 'This Magic Moment', 'Sweets For My Sweet' and 'I Count The Tears'; **Elvis Presley**'s 'Little Sister', '(Marie's The Name) His Latest Flame', 'Viva Las Vegas', 'Surrender' and others; and **Dion**'s 'A Teenager In Love'. Pomus developed polio at the age of nine and used crutches to walk. (A fall in his adult life left him confined to a wheelchair.) At the age of 15, already playing saxophone and singing at jazz and blues clubs, he changed his name to avoid alerting his parents of his activities - they found out two years later. Pomus recorded a number of blues-influenced singles for independent companies beginning in his late teens, none of which were hits. At that time he also began writing. The first major placement for one of his compositions was 'Boogie Woogie Country Girl', the b-side of **Big Joe Turner**'s 'Corrina, Corrina', in 1956. That same year he wrote 'Lonely Avenue', recorded by **Ray Charles**. In 1957 Pomus teamed up with writers/producers **Leiber And Stoller** to pen 'Young Blood', a hit for the **Coasters**, as well as 'She's Not You', a hit for Presley. Pomus and Shuman (who had played piano on some of Pomus's recordings), officially teamed in 1958 and signed to the Hill & Range publishing company in New York. Although Pomus's first love was blues, he became an adept rock lyricist, and among his earliest hits were such pop songs as **Fabian**'s 'Turn Me Loose', 'I'm A Man' and 'Hound Dog Man'. Pomus-Shuman also wrote the **Mystics**' 'Hushabye', **Bobby Darin**'s 'Plain Jane', **Gary 'U.S.' Bonds**' 'Seven Day Weekend', **Gene McDaniels**' 'Spanish Lace', **Terry Stafford**'s 'Suspicion', **Andy Williams**' 'Wrong For Each Other', 'Can't Get Used To Losing You' (later covered by the **Beat**) and **Jimmy Clanton**'s 'Go, Jimmy, Go'. Presley recorded over 20 of their songs, 'Kiss Me Quick' and 'A Mess Of Blues' being among the other noteworthy titles. Pomus estimated he wrote over one thousand songs during his career. The Pomus-Shuman team separated in 1965 and Pomus kept a low profile throughout much of the late 60s and 70s. In the late 70s he was instrumental in helping assemble the **Blues Brothers** band and then began writing prolifically again. He co-wrote an album with **Mink DeVille**'s *Willy DeVille*, two with **Dr. John** and one with **B.B. King**, the Grammy-winning *There Must Be A Better World Somewhere*. Later Pomus co-compositions appeared in the films *Cry Baby* and *Dick Tracy*.

He remained a champion of the blues and blues musicians until his death and was an often-seen figure at New York clubs where both older and younger blues artists performed. In 1991 Pomus received the Rhythm and Blues Foundation's Pioneer Award, the first white to be so honoured. Pomus died of lung cancer at the age of 65 later that year. He was inducted into the Rock and Roll Hall of Fame in January 1992.

Ponce, Daniel

b. 21 July 1953, Havana, Cuba. Percussionist and bandleader Ponce - who first gained international recognition with his contributions to **Herbie Hancock**'s *Future Shock* - received his early musical education from his grandfather, a renowned player of the bata drum. At the age of 11, he was playing cowbell with a group called Los Brilliantes in the Callo Weso district of Havana. During his mid-teens he moved over to conga drums, with Comparso Federacion Estuniantil Universitario. Ponce arrived in the USA, at Key West, Florida in 1980 and within a few months had settled in New York. Invited to sit in at the Village Gate with brothers Andy and Jerry Gonzalez, he met the Cuban saxophonist Paquito D'Rivera, for whom he guested on two albums. He also did sessions for **Eddie Palmieri**. Ponce's career really took off, however, when he met bass guitarist and avant-funk and jazz producer **Bill Laswell** in 1983, who secured him the *Future Shock* sessions and went on to involve him in a multiplicity of productions for the Celluloid and OAO labels. In 1984, Ponce released the self-produced *New York Now* - a *tour de force* through the roots of traditional Cuban percussion-based music which also included contributions from D'Rivera and Laswell. He went on to lead two New York-based bands: New York Now and Jazzbata.

Album: *New York Now* (1984).

Pond

Based in Portland, Oregon, USA, Pond consist of Chris Brady (bass/vocals), Charlie Campbell (guitar/vocals) and Dave Griebwasser (drums). Campbell and Brady are from Alaska, and met Griebwasser (a fully qualified microbiologist) in the Seattle area. They made their debut with the single 'Young Splendor', followed by 'Wheel', both of which were released on T/K Records. They supported **Throwing Muses** on tour, but

reacted with indifference to press accusations that they peddled a mongrelised version of the grunge sound, 'We just wanted danceable, driving drums, and lotsa melodies and hooks, and it all seems to come out murky and thick.' A second album, *The Practice Of Joy Before Death*, used its title to debunk those press accusations, and offered varied, skewed rock, now more akin to **Pavement** than **Dinosaur Jr**.
Albums: *Pond* (Sub Pop 1993), *The Practice Of Joy Before Death* (Sub Pop 1995).

Poni-Tails

A US female trio known for the 1958 Top 10 hit 'Born Too Late', the Poni-Tails - who, naturally, sported that hairstyle - were lead vocalist Toni Cistone, Patti McCabe (d. 1989; low harmony - replacing original member Karen Topinka) and LaVerne Novak (high harmony). The group met at their high school in Lyndhurst, Ohio, USA, in 1957. They first recorded for Point Records, an RKO Pictures division, but their two singles for that label were not successful. The members were then signed to **ABC**-Paramount Records, and their first single for that company fared badly. The next one, 'Born Too Late', an innocent ballad about being passed over by an older boy, catapulted to number 7 in the US chart the following year. Two further singles for ABC reached the charts but came nowhere near hit status and the group disbanded, each member retiring from the music business.
Compilation: *Born Too Late* (South Bay 1994).

Ponty, Jean-Luc

b. 29 September 1940, Avranches, France. Ponty grew up in an intensely musical home environment. His father ran a local music school, teaching violin, and his mother taught piano. He was a proficient pianist and violinist while still very young and at the age of 11 he added clarinet to his instrumental arsenal. After studying classical violin at the Paris Conservatoire, he became a professional musician but also developed an interest in jazz. For a while he divided his musical loyalty between the classical violin and jazz clarinet and tenor saxophone. However, he began to play jazz on violin, making this his chief activity from the mid-60s. He played with numerous European musicians (recording with **Stuff Smith**), sometimes as leader (in HLP). He visited the USA and UK, recording with **Frank Zappa** on the jazz-rock album *Hot Rats* ('It Must Be A Camel') and thereafter joined **George Duke**. Zappa later produced Ponty's *King Kong* in 1970. In the early 70s he experimented with free jazz, played again with Zappa on *Overnite Sensation*, as a member of the Mothers, and with **John McLaughlin**'s **Mahavishnu Orchestra**, *Visions Of The Emerald Beyond* (1974). Subsequently, he led his own band playing jazz-rock and gaining a substantial international following. In the 80s he also recorded with other artists including **Cleo Laine** and **Stéphane Grappelli**. A master technician, Ponty was not the first violinist in jazz to use electronic enhancement but he was the first to integrate electronics fully into his playing style. Rather than settle merely for the greater volume, which had been enough for his predecessors, Ponty used electronics in a complex and advanced way. He uses a fully electric violin, not just an electronically-amplified instrument, and incorporates numerous devices to create effects. By switching from bop to rock to free jazz and back to bop again with bewildering ease, he continues to prove himself a musician of many styles and for all seasons of jazz fashion.
Selected albums: with Stuff Smith *Violin Summit* (1966), *Sunday Walk* (1967), *Electric Connection* (1968), with George Duke *The Jean-Luc Experience* (1969), *King Kong* aka *Cantaloupe Island* (Blue Note 1970), *Astrorama* (1970), *Open Strings* (1972), *Live In Montreux* (1972), *Portrait* (1972), *Upon The Wings Of Music* (1975), *Aurora* (Atlantic 1975), *Imaginary Voyage* (Atlantic 1976), *Enigmatic Ocean* (Atlantic 1977), *Cosmic Messenger* (Atlantic 1978), *A Taste For Passion* (1979), *Jean-Luc Ponty Live* (1979), *Sonata Erotica* (Atmosphere 1979), *Civilized Evil* (1980), *Mystical Adventures* (Atlantic 1981), *Individual Choice* (Atlantic 1983), with George Benson, Chick Corea *Open Mind* (Atlantic 1984), *Fables* (Atlantic 1985), *The Gift Of Time* (Columbia 1987), *No Absolute Time* (Fnac 1993).
Further reading: *The Musical Styles Of Jean-Luc Ponty*, Jean-Luc Ponty.

Pooh Sticks

Mix a slapstick parody of the archetypal UK independent guitar band, a wicked sense of humour and an uncanny knack of turning out catchy, astute pop tunes and that ably defines the Pooh Sticks. They were formed in October 1987 in Wales when Hue Williams (b. 4 March 1968; son of ex-**Man** and **Dire Straits** drummer, Terry Williams) and friend Paul teamed-up with three schoolgirls Trudi, Alison and Stephanie. The band released a single almost immediately on local label, Fierce Records. 'On Tape' (1988) was a send-up of the independent scene at its most clichéd and attracted a great deal of interest, particularly as the band flew to New York for their first live appearance. A five-disc one-track single boxed set which included the legendary 'I Know Someone Who Knows Someone Who Knows Alan McGee Quite Well' (referring to the **Creation Records** head) followed in the summer, although these were transferred onto a one-sided self-titled mini-album by the end of the year. 1989 saw two live albums, *Orgasm* on the Scottish 53rd & 3rd label and *Trademark Of Quality*, while the Poohs covered the Vaselines' 'Dying For It' in 1990. The lampoonery continued with *The Great White Wonder* in 1991 when they tackled weightier

icons from the 60s and 70s. In February of 1992 the Pooh Sticks signed a $1.2 million deal with the major BMG (formerly **RCA Records**) company in the USA.
Albums: *Pooh Sticks* (Fierce 1988, mini-album), *Orgasm* (53 & 3rd 1989), *Trademark Of Quality* (Fierce 1989), *Formula One Generation* (Sympathy For The Record Industry 1990), *Peel Sessions* (Overground 1991), *The Great White Wonder* (Sympathy For The Record Industry 1991), *Million Seller* (Zoo 1993), *Optimistic Fool* (Seed 1995).

Poole, Brian, And The Tremeloes

Formed in the late 50s and fronted by vocalist Brian Poole (b. 2 November 1941, Barking, Essex, England), this UK pop group were initially known as Brian Poole and the Tremilos when they made their debut at the Ilford Palais in 1960. Poole was originally known as a **Buddy Holly** imitator and even went as far as wearing spectacles filled with plain glass. After his backing musicians reverted to the title **Tremeloes**, the entire ensemble successfully auditioned for **Decca Records** on 1 January 1962 and were signed in favour of the **Beatles**. A cover of the **Isley Brothers**' 'Twist And Shout' brought them a UK Top 10 hit the following year. The follow-up, a reading of the **Contours**' 'Do You Love Me?' hit number 1 in the UK and 15 other countries. American success, however, remained frustratingly elusive. Appropriately, the group's manager **Peter Walsh** recruited Buddy Holly's former mentor **Norman Petty** to play piano on two further UK smashes, the wistful 'Someone Someone' and mawkish 'The Three Bells'. Thereafter, the group's popularity waned and they seemed increasingly dated in comparison to the more aggressive R&B-based UK pop outfits that emerged in 1964-65. Sensing a crisis, Poole elected to leave the group and branch out into the world of big ballads. He subsequently moved into cabaret, retired to the family butcher business, and later resurfaced with a record and publishing company. Against the odds, it was his backing group, the Tremeloes, that went on to achieve enormous chart success under their own name. In the 90s Poole and most of his original Tremeloes are back ploughing the rich vein of 60s nostalgia tours.
Albums: *Twist And Shout With Brian Poole And The Tremeloes* (1963), *It's About Time* (1965). Compilation: *Remembering Brian Poole And The Tremeloes* (1977).

Poole, Charlie

b. 22 March 1892, Alamance County, North Carolina, USA, d. 21 May 1931. A talented five-string banjo player who because of a childhood hand injury played in a thumb and three fingered picking style that was later further developed by **Earl Scruggs**. In 1917, Poole teamed up with fiddle player Posey Rorer (b. 22 September 1891, Franklin County, Virginia, USA, d. March 1935) and the two played throughout West Virginia and North Carolina. In 1922, they added a guitarist, initially Clarence Foust but when they made their first **Columbia** recordings on 27 July 1925, the regular guitarist was Norman Woodlieff. Perhaps due to their itinerant life style, they adopted the name of North Carolina Ramblers in 1923 and as such they became one of the most influential of the early string bands. They are still remembered for their recording of 'Don't Let Your Deal Go Down'. In 1926, Roy Harvey (b. 24 March 1892, Monroe County, West Virginia, USA) replaced Woodlieff and in 1928, following a disagreement, Poole replaced Rorer with Lonnie Austin. Working with other musicians, including his son Charlie Jnr. (b. James Clay Poole, 1913). Poole continued to play but made his last recordings on 9 September 1930. (Woodlieff and Rorer made further recordings with other musicians and Harvey also recorded with his own North Carolina Ramblers band.) Poole was in real life very much a rambler, a trait which saw an early end to his 1911 marriage. He was also a heavy drinker and met a premature death from a heart attack in 1931, while celebrating an offer to play music for a Hollywood Western. Posey Rorer died in 1935 and was buried near Poole.
Albums: *Charlie Poole & The North Carolina Ramblers 1925-1930, Volumes 1 - 4* (1965-71), *Charlie Poole & Ihe Highlanders*, *Charlie Poole 1926-1930* (1975).

Poor Cow

Poor Cow was based on the novel of the same name, written by Nell Dunn, author of ***Up The Junction***. Director Ken Loach brought a politically acerbic eye to this 1967 feature which starred Carol White (*Cathy Come Home*) and Terence Stamp. They play a married couple, but as the husband is in jail, the wife is required to survive in a harsh world portrayed as the antithesis of concurrent flower-power trivialities. Paradoxically, wan singer/songwriter **Donovan** provided the score, which included the haunting title track, issued on the b-side of his 1968 hit 'There Is A Mountain'. His music was incidental in the best sense of the word; *Poor Cow* is an excellent work, invoking the spirit of British 'kitchen sink' drama from earlier in the decade.

Poor Little Rich Girl

By the time she made this film in 1936, **Shirley Temple** was an eight-year-old superstar with nearly 20 pictures to her credit. Cinema audiences all over the world had taken her to their hearts, and she did not disappoint them in this latest outing which continued along the familiar well-trodden path. In the screenplay, by Sam Hellman, Gladys Lehman, and Harry Tugend, Shirley runs away from her wealthy workaholic father (Michael Whalen) and is co-opted into a vaudeville act (**Alice Faye** and Jack Haley). Family reconciliation is eventually accomplished, but only after the loveable youngster has wowed the crowds with numbers such as

'You Gotta Eat Your Spinach, Baby', 'Military Man', 'But Definitely', and 'When I'm With You'. **Harry Revel** and **Mack Gordon** wrote those, and some others including 'Oh, My Goodness' and 'Wash Your Necks With A Cake Of Beck's' (Shirley did a lot of work on sponsored radio shows). Gloria Stuart, Sara Haden, Claude Gillingwater, Jane Darwell, and Henry Armetta were in the cast, and future singing heart-throb **Tony Martin** also made a brief appearance. The dance directors were Jack Haskell and Ralph Cooper, and the film, which was directed by Irving Cummings, was produced for 20th Century-Fox by Darryl F. Zanuck and **Buddy De Sylva**.

Poor Righteous Teachers

Trenton, New Jersey-based trio comprising the gregariously named Wise Intelligent, Culture Freedom and Father Shaheed, all advocates of the Five Percent Islam creed. Their debut album inlcuded the hot 'Rock Dis Funky Joint' 45, and sold over 400,000 copies, crossing over into the pop market. Their second album included the groundbreaking pro-women single cut, 'Shakiyla (JHR)', but failed to match the sales of its predecessor. *Black Business* was a celebration of the progress made by their black brothers and sisters in commerce and business, and was produced by Shaheed with the aid of Tony D. It included the single 'Nobody Move', which was inspired by albino reggae toaster, **Yellowman**. Indeed, PRT's most distinctive attribute is Wise Intelligent's highly effective blending of the reggae DJ's intonation with his partners hip hop skills.
Albums: *Holy Intellect* (Profile 1990), *Pure Poverty* (Profile 1991), *Black Business* (Profile 1993).

Poormouth

A vehicle for the Irish-tinged folk rock songs of Jackie McAuley (ex-**Them** and **Trader Horne**). Their sound is a composite of heavy guitar and jigs and reels. The membership varies according to touring and recording demands.
Album: *Gaelforce* (1989).

Pop Art

Hip hop record label, based in Philadelphia, USA, controlled by Lawrence Goodman, the cousin of **Steady B**. The latter issued an impressive answer record to **LL Cool J**'s big hit, 'I Can't Live Without My Radio', which established the imprint. Its other high profile releases included another artist well versed in the tradition of answer records, **Roxanne Shanté**. Goodman is now the manager of **Da Youngsters**.

Pop Down

Released in 1968, this rarely-screened British film was an indulgent, flower-power-influenced yarn involving creatures from outer space. There was little new in what the hapless aliens encountered, bar the garb of the Earthlings on view, as this tired plot had already been well-mined by the US American International Pictures Company. Interest lies in the pop performers on view, many of which were rarely captured on film. One-man band/busker **Don Partridge**, famed for the memorable hit, 'Rosie', and soul singer **Brenton Wood** appear alongside raver-turned-psychedelic acolyte **Zoot Money**, who plays Sagittarius, and former **John's Children** vocalist Andy Ellison, who portrays Mr. Love. The former subsequently became a character actor on television, while the latter occasionally took work as a stunt man. However, it is two acts from the newly-founded Marmalade label which prove most captivating. **Julie Driscoll with Brian Auger And The Trinity** and **Blossom Toes** were two of the era's more engaging attractions and *Pop Down* enshrines their brief moment in the limelight. They inhabit an off-beat world inhabited by several unusual individuals, including Miss Offkey, Miss Withit, Perpetual Kisser and Nude On Camel. Cut from 96 minutes to 54 for release, *Pop Down* is an interesting period-piece, thanks to the music on offer, but a far cry from the 'film that turns on tomorrow', despite that contemporaneous publicity line.

Pop Gear

Mindful of the growing British Beat phenomenon, the Pathe film company filmed a succession of acts, spliced them with introductions from DJ Jimmy Saville, and added footage of the **Beatles** performing 'She Loves You' and 'Twist And Shout' live in Manchester. The cross-section of performers reflected the era's transitional nature and the inclusion of **Matt Monro** and **Susan Maughan** brought an MOR slant to the proceedings. Several of the acts were drawn from **Brian Epstein**'s NEMS stable, including **Billy J. Kramer And The Dakotas**, **Tommy Quickly**, **Sounds Incorporated** and the **Fourmost**, while **Herman's Hermits**, the **Four Pennies**, **Honeycombs** and **Rockin' Berries** encapsulated the period's unashamedly commercial air. Despite the sterile studio atmosphere, in which the groups and singers mimed, *Pop Gear* contained several memorable performances, including the **Animals**' 'House Of The Rising Sun', the **Nashville Teens**' 'Tobacco Road' and the **Spencer Davis Group** powerful rendition of 'Strong Love'. In an era of black-and-white television, the film allowed fans a rare glimpse of their idols in colour and *Pop Gear* was a popular adjunct to the main feature in British cinemas in 1965. It was released in the USA under a new title, *Go Go Mania*, and portions still surface to this day on archive resumes of a career or era.

Pop Group

This seminal UK punk group operated from Bristol, Avon, in the late 70s, combining abstracted funk with

chaos and expressionist vocals courtesy of **Mark Stewart**. The topics under consideration - starvation, war, exploitation - were similar to those expounded by anarcho-punks **Crass**, but the Pop Group's music was much more sophisticated. Their records are by turns inspirational and intolerable, some of the most extreme music to have been pressed onto vinyl. The masterpiece was *For How Much Longer Do We Tolerate Mass Murder*. No one is able to maintain such a pitch of intensity: bassist Simon Underwood left to form **Pigbag**, a welcome relief from the drabness punk conformity had created, a riot of bright shirts, ethnic rhythms and **James Brown** references. Guitarist and saxophonist Gareth Sagar formed the irrepressible **Rip Rig And Panic**. Only singer Mark Stewart kept to his bleak viewpoint, forming the Maffia with the rhythm team from **Sugarhill Records** and working with producer Adrian Sherwood.
Albums: *Y* (Radar 1979), *For How Much Longer Must We Tolerate Mass Murder* (Rough Trade 1980), *We Are Time* (Rough Trade 1980).

Pop Will Eat Itself

This UK group took its name from the headine of an article on Jamie Wednesday (later **Carter USM**) by David Quantick in the ***New Musical Express***. Having previously rehearsed and gigged under the names From Eden and Wild And Wondering, the group emerged as Pop Will Eat Itself in 1986 with a line-up comprising Clint Mansell (b. 7 November 1963, Coventry, England; vocals/guitar), Adam Mole (b. 1962, Stourbridge, England; keyboards), Graham Crabb (b. 10 October 1964, Streetly, West Midlands, England; drums, later vocals) and Richard Marsh (b. 4 March 1965, York, Yorkshire, England; bass). Making their live debut at the Mere, Stourbridge Art College, their first recording was the privately issued EP, *The Poppies Say Grr*, which was nominated as Single Of The Week in the *New Musical Express*. BBC Radio sessions followed and the group appeared in the independent charts with the follow-up EPs *Poppiecock* and *The Covers*. Already known for their hard pop and vulgarisms, they ran into trouble with the release of 'Beaver Patrol', which was criticized for its puerile sexism. Their debut album, *Box Frenzy*, followed in late 1987 and displayed their odd mix of guitar pop with sampling. The insistent 'There Is No Love Between Us Anymore' was their most impressive single to date and augured well for the future, as did 'Def Con One' in 1988. During that year they were invited to play in the USSR, and soon afterwards signed to the major, **RCA Records**. 'Can U Dig It' and 'Wise Up Sucker' were minor successes, as was their second album. A world tour sharpened their approach and during 1990 they achieved mainstream acclaim with 'Touched By The Hand Of Cicciolina', a paean addressed to the Italian porn star turned politician. Two further hit singles, 'X,Y & Zee' and '92 Degrees', followed in 1991. The group recruited a full-time (human) drummer in 1992 when Fuzz (b. Robert Townshend, 31 July 1964, Birmingham, England; ex-**Pig Bros**, **General Public**, **Ranking Roger**) joined, but following *Weird's Bar & Grill* a year later RCA dropped the band. Now effectively despised by the media, Pop Will Eat Itself continued despite expectations that this might signify the end of the band, forging a new contract with Infectious Records. The results of which have hardly endeared them to critics, though the title of the 1995 collection, *Two Fingers My Friends*, did at least underline their tenacity and self-sufficiency.
Albums: *Box Frenzy* (Chapter 22 1987), *Now For A Feast!* (Rough Trade 1989, early recordings), *This Is The Day, This Is The Hour, This Is This* (RCA 1989), *The Pop Will Eat Itself Cure For Sanity* (RCA 1990), *The Looks Or The Lifestyle* (RCA 1992), *Weird's Bar & Grill* (RCA 1993), *Dos Dedos Mes Amigos* (Infectious 1994), *Two Fingers My Friends!* (Infectious 1995).

Popguns

This Brighton, England-based group comprise Wendy Morgan (vocals), Simon Pickles (guitar), Greg Dixon (guitar), Pat Walkington (bass) and Shaun Charman (drums, ex-**Wedding Present**). The Popguns breezy power-pop and well-crafted songs, accompanied by Morgan's lyrics of boyfriend trouble 'n' bliss and post-teen alienation, found a ready audience. Despite a thin voice, she more than adequately made up for any shortcomings with an energetic, impassioned delivery. The two EPs released in 1989, *Landslide* and *Waiting For The Winter*, promised much, and were later compiled along with 1990's *Someone You Love* on *Eugenie* for the Midnight Music label. The Popguns' first full album release in 1991 boasted a production credit for fellow Brighton resident, **Psychic TV**'s Genesis P. Orridge. It achieved a healthy independent Top 10 chart position and promised further success, but gradually they were swept under by a music press ever watchful for the new, leaving them to stew in relative obscurity - though 1995's *Love Junky* still offered ambitious, bold songwriting.
Album: *Snog* (Midnight Music 1991), *Love Junky* (3rd Stone 1995). Compilation: *Eugenie* (Midnight Music 1990).

Popinjays

Formed in London in 1988 by songwriters Wendy Robinson (b. 6 April 1964, Huddersfield, Yorkshire, England; vocals), Polly Hancock (b. 16 July 1964, Berkshire, England; guitar/vocals) and a drum machine, the Popinjays evolved out of the influential Timebox Club at the Bull & Gate pub in Kentish Town, north London (the duo later ran their own Pop Club at the same venue), by striving to perfect the ultimate pop formula. Dana Baldinger (b. 26 December

1963, California, USA; bass) joined in 1989 as the offer of a combination of sweets, comics and biscuits won the band a record deal with **One Little Indian Records**. Dana departed after one single, to be replaced by fellow countrywoman Anne Rogers (b. 17 October 1962, New York, USA) a move which was followed by a plethora of critical recommendations for the debut album, *Bang Up To Date With The Popinjays.* Ever conscious of the importance of fun in music, their promo video for the 'Vote Elvis' single featured much **Monkees**-style running around with special guest Cathal Coughlan from **Fatima Mansions**. Drummer Seamus Feeney (b. 19 November 1964, Middlesex, England), caused the drum machine to be sacked at the close of 1990, just as the Popinjays were beginning to garner appreciative attention from America. 1992's *Flying Down To Mono Valley* did little to embellish their reputation, and it was left to their 1994 album to produce a significant stylistic departure. *Tales From The Urban Prairie* saw forays into country rock and singer/songwriter melancholia, an affecting performance but one which left their traditional fan base in some degree of confusion.

Albums: *Bang Up To Date With The Popinjays* (One Little Indian 1990), *Flying Down To Mono Valley* (One Little Indian 1992), *Tales From The Urban Prairie* (One Little Indian 1994).

Poppy

After a brief career in vaudeville, and appearances in several editions of the the ***Ziegfeld Follies***, W.C. Fields, the bulbous-nosed comic with the 'never-give-a-sucker-an-even-break' attitude, came to Broadway in this production which opened at the Apollo Theatre in New York on 3 September 1923. The star was supposed to be Madge Kennedy who plays Fields's foster child, Poppy, but, during the New York run and the subsequent tour, the comedian gradually emerged as the principal attraction. In Dorothy Donnelly's book, Professor Eustace McGargle (Fields) is a card-sharp, a juggler (Fields used to juggle in vaudeville), and an all-round trickster and con-man around the carnivals. Poppy is an orphan girl from the same background, who eventually discovers that she is an heiress. Donnelly also wrote the lyrics for several of the songs, with music by Stephen Jones and Arthur Samuels. These included 'Two Make A Home', 'Steppin' Around', 'Hang Your Sorrows In The Sun', 'When You Are In My Arms', and 'A Picnic Party With You'. However the most popular numbers were the interpolated 'What Do You Do Sunday, Mary?' (music: Jones, lyric: **Irving Caesar**), which was introduced by Luella Gear and Robert Woolsey, and became a hit for the American Quartet; and 'Alibi Baby' (music: Samuels, lyric: **Howard Dietz**). 'Alibi Baby' was Howard Dietz's first successful song. Years later, when he was doing some of his best work with **Arthur Schwartz**, it turned up in the US Hit Parade in a version by **Tommy Dorsey**. Fans of W.C. Fields continued to flock to see *Poppy* for 346 performances, and the London production, which starred W.H. Berry and Annie Croft, stayed at the Gaiety Theatre for five months. Fields dominated the two films that were based on the show: a 1925 silent, renamed *Sally Of The Sawdust*, and the 1936 *Poppy*, with Rochelle Hudson. Another, quite different show named *Poppy*, with music by Monty Norman and a book and lyrics by Peter Nichols, played in London's West End in 1982.

Poppy Family

This Canadian folk-rock quartet was fronted by **Terry Jacks** (b. Winnipeg, Manitoba, Canada) and Susan Jacks (b. Susan Peklevits, Vancouver, British Columbia, Canada). Vancouver-based Terry led local group the Chessmen before teaming with, and later marrying, singer Peklevits. They later added guitarist/organist Craig MacCaw and percussionist Satwan Singh (who had played tabla with **Ravi Shankar**). The group had a transatlantic Top 10 hit with Terry's song 'Which Way You Goin' Billy' in 1970, which they had recorded and originally released in the UK the previous year. They had four more US chart entries before Terry and Susan divorced and went separate ways professionally in 1973. Although Susan's voice was the main feature of the Poppy Family her later recordings on **Mercury** and Epic had little success. Terry however had further success with a plaintive version of a **Jacques Brel** and **Rod McKuen** song 'Seasons In The Sun'.

Albums: *Which Way You Goin' Billy* (1970), *Poppyseeds* (1971).

Popsicle

This Swedish indie pop outfit began to make an international breakthrough in 1993. The line-up initially comprised Andreas Mattson (vocals/guitar), Fredrik Norberg (vocals/guitar), Kenny Vikstrom (bass) and Per-Arne Wikander (drums), who met on a school trip to Stockholm. They formed in the mid-80s and experimented with a number of musical styles before shaping up as Popsicle in 1991. Their boisterous, Anglophile songs earned them a Scandinavian Grammy two years later, and they briefly enjoyed infamy upon its presentation. Freddy's inebriated acceptance speech included a death wish fatwa on Sweden's **Eurovision Song Contest** entrants. Vikstrom was replaced by Arvid Lind for *Abstinence.*

Albums: *Lacquer* (MNW 1993), *Abstinence* (Warners 1995).

Porcino, Al

b. 14 May 1925, New York City, New York, USA. While still in his teenage years, Porcino joined the **Louis Prima** band where his high-note trumpet playing attracted excited attention. In the 40s he played in many of the leading big bands of the day, including those led by **Tommy Dorsey**, **Gene Krupa**, **Stan Kenton** and **Woody Herman**. In the 50s he again worked with Kenton and Herman among others such as **Charlie Parker**, **Count Basie** and **Elliot Lawrence** before settling in Los Angeles, where he did studio work and also made regular appearances in jazz groups, usually big bands including **Terry Gibbs**'s 'dream bands'. He made many record dates with singers including **Frank Sinatra**, **Sarah Vaughan**, **Ella Fitzgerald**, **Judy Garland** and **Ray Charles**. He was co-leader with **Med Flory** of the Jazz Wave Orchestra. In the 60s he continued to play in big bands, adding **Buddy Rich** and the **Thad Jones-Mel Lewis** Jazz Orchestra to his list of credits. He rejoined Herman again and also formed his own band, with which he accompanied **Mel Tormé**. His career continued along similar lines in the 70s and then, in 1977, he settled in Munich, Germany, where he worked with radio bands and led his own big band. During the 80s he made many concert appearances with his big band, some of which were recorded, often in company with visiting American jazzmen such as **Al Cohn**. One of the outstanding lead trumpeters in big band history, Porcino set remarkably high standards of performance for himself and for his section mates and any band in which he played was assured of a first-rate trumpet section. His German band of the late 80s clearly benefits from his remarkable leadership.

Albums: with Stan Kenton *Contemporary Concepts* (1955), with Med Flory *The Jazz Wave Orchestra* (1957), with Terry Gibbs *Dream Band* (1959), with Gibbs *Live At The Summit* (1961), with Buddy Rich *Mercy, Mercy* (1968), with Jones-Lewis *Consummation* (1969), with Woody Herman *The Raven Speaks* (1972), with Mel Tormé *Live At The Maisonette* (1974), with Jones-Lewis *New Life* (1975), with Jones-Lewis *Live In Munich* (1976), with Al Cohn *In Oblivion* (Jazz Mark 1986), with Cohn *The Final Performance* (1987).

Porgy And Bess (Film Musical)

The last film of producer Sam Goldwyn's illustrious career, which was released by Columbia in 1959, proved to be an expensive and troubled affair. After various disputes with his first choice director, **Rouben Mamoulian** (who had staged the original 1935 Broadway production), Goldwyn replaced him with Otto Preminger whose work on this occasion was considered to be somewhat laboured and uninspired. For some reason the well-known story of the crippled beggar Porgy (Sidney Poitier), who lives in the Catfish Row slum area and loves the tempestuous Bess (Dorothy Dandridge) did not transfer at all well to the big screen. The supporting cast was excellent, with **Sammy Davis Jnr.** (Sportin' Life), **Pearl Bailey** (Maria), Brock Peters (Crown), Diahann Carroll (Clara), and Ruth Attaway (Serena), all turning in outstanding performances. Other roles were taken by Leslie Scott, Clarence Muse, and Joel Fluellen. Because of the extremely demanding operatic score by composer **George Gershwin** and lyricists DuBose Heyward and **Ira Gershwin**, several of the principals were dubbed, including Poitier (Robert McFerrin), Dandridge (Adele Addison), Carroll (Loulie Jean Norman), and Attaway (Inez Matthews). Even so, there were some reservations regarding the vocal quality of the production, but these were swept aside by the sheer magnificence of the songs, which included 'Summertime', 'Bess, You Is My Woman', 'There's A Boat Dat's Leavin' Soon For New York', 'I Loves You Porgy', 'A Woman Is A Sometimes Thing', 'I Got Plenty O' Nuttin'', 'It Ain't Necessarily So', 'My Man's Gone Now', and 'Oh Bess, Oh Where's My Bess'. **André Previn** and Ken Darby both won Oscars for 'scoring a dramatic picture', and Leo Shamroy was nominated for his superb photography in Technicolor and Panavision. **Hermes Pan**, who had been associated with many top musical films in his long career including the **Fred Astaire** and **Ginger Rogers** RKO series, staged the dances. The screenplay, by N. Richard Nash, was based on the original Broadway libretto and novel by Heyward, and his and Dorothy Heyward's play *Porgy*. In the early 90s, this film remained one of the few big musicals not to have been released on video. Cinema distribution has also been curtailed; the Gershwin estate has had this film firmly under lock and key for some years now.

Porgy And Bess (Stage Musical)

The most acclaimed and performed American opera, *Porgy And Bess* was premiered in Boston, Massachusetts, on 30 September 1935. Composed by **George Gershwin**, the opera was based upon the play *Porgy* by DuBose and Dorothy K. Heyward. DuBose Heyward was also librettist and co-author with **Ira Gershwin** of the lyrics. The cast included Todd Duncan as Porgy, Anne Brown as Bess, and John Bubbles as Sportin' Life. Among the songs were 'Summertime', 'Bess, You Is My Woman Now', 'Oh, I Got Plenty O' Nuttin''. 'It Ain't Necessarily So', 'A Woman Is A Sometime Thing' and 'There's A Boat Dat's Leavin' Soon For New York'. The story told of events in the lives of urban blacks, enduring conditions of acute deprivation and attempting to survive in the face of indifference and the temptation of drink and drugs. In choosing to set his major work in a context and with characters so far removed from anything to which white middle-class Americans were accustomed, Gershwin took a great risk. Despite a poor reception in New York where *Porgy And Bess* ran for just 24 performances, in the long term the composer's gamble paid off. Despite the lyricists' debasing of language in an attempt to recreate the speech patterns of black Americans, which today appears patronising but was commonplace for its time, *Porgy And Bess* must be regarded as a major accomplishment. Not only does it have merit as musical theatre but much of the music stands up out of context. 'Summertime' in particular has been recorded many times by a wide range of artists. Additionally, concert suites have been performed by symphony orchestras around the world. *Porgy And Bess* was produced in London in 1952 and was brought to the screen in 1959, heavily directed by Otto Preminger, and starring Sidney Poitier, Dorothy Dandridge, **Sammy Davis Jnr.**, Brock Peters and **Pearl Bailey**. In 1986 the opera was given a sumptuous production by **Trevor Nunn** at Glyndebourne with a cast including Willard White, Cynthia Haymon, Damon Evans and Harolyn Blackwell. The highly praised production repeated its triumph at the Royal Opera House, Covent Garden, in 1992, and was televised two years later.

Porky's Productions

'Hull's only record label' - which sprang to prominence when they unveiled **Opik** (Murray, Dean Dawson, Rob Everall and Chris Devril) and their 'Feel Yourself' monster, which **DeConstruction** went on to licence. By the time Opik became successful in the early 90s the Yorkshire, England-based label had already established itself with cuts such as Fila Brazilia's 'Mermaids' and Heights Of Abraham's *Tides* EP. Heights Of Abraham comprised ex-**Chakk** members Jake Harries and Sim Lister, the latter co-writer of **Cath Carroll**'s ***England Made Me*** album), plus **Ashley & Jackson** guitarist Steve Cobby.

Porno For Pyros

This theatrical rock act was formed by **Jane's Addiction** frontman Perry Farrell in 1992, following the demise of his previous act. Enlisting former bandmate Stephen Perkins (drums), bassist Martyn Lenoble and guitarist Peter DiStephano, Farrell began developing his new band's direction during their low-key live debut on the Lollapalooza II second stage. With Farrell's creative input and Perkins' rhythmic talents, similarities between Porno For Pyros and Jane's Addiction's recorded output were inevitable, but the subtle shift in musical direction became more obvious in the live setting. Porno For Pyros' shows were closer in character to a carnival, with Farrell as ringmaster, than a traditional rock show, with the band augmented not only by Matt Hyde's keyboards but also by a cast of dancers and performance artists, from the ballerina pirouetting to 'Orgasm', to the sharp contrast of the fire-breathing stripper who appeared during 'Porno For Pyros'. The band subsequently headlined at the 1993 UK Reading Festival in spectacular fashion, and appeared at the **Woodstock** Anniversary show in 1994.

Albums: *Porno For Pyros* (Warners 1993).

Portal, Michel

b. 27 November 1935, Bayonne, France. Portal was as comfortable playing a Mozart clarinet concerto as he was performing a Stockhausen intuitive piece, or scoring a film on bandoneon as playing free jazz on various reeds - Portal has always surprised. Francois Tusques, Sunny Murray, **Joachim Kuhn** and **John Surman** are just some of the artists who have made use of his talents in a jazz context. Although accused by some of being over-clinical as a soloist, he has produced a number of remarkable recordings with editions of his ever-changing unit. Many leading French and Swiss players have passed through the ranks, while his *Men's Land* from 1987 includes **Jack DeJohnette** and **Dave Liebman**.

Selected albums: *No, No, But It May Be* (1974), *Men's Land* (1987).

Porter, Cole

b. 9 June 1891, Peru, Indiana, USA, d. 15 October 1964, Santa Monica, California, USA. One of the outstanding composers and lyricists of the 20th century, Porter was born into a rich family, and studied music from an early age. In his teens he excelled in many academic subjects, and wrote songs and played the piano for his own amusement - activities he later pursued at Yale University. Later he attended Harvard Law School, but his interest in music overcame his legal studies, and while he was still at college, some of his songs were used in Broadway productions. In 1916, his first complete score, for *See America First* ('I've A Shooting Box In Scotland'), closed after just 15 performances. The Porter family's wealth allowed him to travel extensively and he visited Europe both before and after World War I, developing a life-long affection for Paris. He wrote several numbers for *Hitchy-Koo 1919*, including the moderately successful 'Old Fashioned Garden', and, during the 20s, contributed to several other musicals, including ***Greenwich Village Follies*** (1924, 'I'm In Love Again'), before having his first real hit with the slightly risqué 'Let's Do It, Let's Fall In Love', which was introduced by Irene Bordoni and Arthur Margetson in *Paris* (1928). That delightful 'Musicomedy' also contained another attractive number, 'Don't Look At Me That Way'. There followed a series of mainly successful shows, each containing at least one, and more often, several sophisticated and witty numbers. They included *Wake Up And Dream* (1919, London and New York, 'What Is This Thing Called Love?', 'Looking At You'), *Fifty Million Frenchmen* (1929, 'You Do Something To Me', 'You've Got That Thing', 'You Don't Know Paree'), ***The New Yorkers*** (1930, 'I Happen To Like New York', 'Let's Fly Away', 'Love For Sale'), ***Gay Divorce*** (1932, 'Night And Day', 'After You', 'How's Your Romance?', 'I've Got You On My Mind'), and

Nymph Errant (1933). The score for the latter show, which starred **Gertrude Lawrence**, **Elisabeth Welch**, and David Burns, and ran for 154 performances, contained several Porter gems, such as 'Experiment', 'It's Bad For Me', 'Solomon', and 'The Physician'. A year later, in the play, *Hi Diddle Diddle*, London audiences were introduced to 'Miss Otis Regrets', one of the songs Porter used to write simply for his friends' amusement. Later in 1934, back on Broadway Porter had his first smash hit with ***Anything Goes***. In that show, **Ethel Merman**, who had taken New York by storm four years previously in **George** and **Ira Gershwin**'s ***Girl Crazy***, triumphed all over again with Porter's terrific 'Anything Goes', 'Blow, Gabriel, Blow', 'I Get A Kick Out Of You' and 'You're The Top' (both with William Gaxton). Her dynamic presence and gutsy singing style gave a tremendous lift to four more Porter musicals. The first, ***Red, Hot And Blue!*** (1936, 'Down In The Depths (On The Ninetieth Floor'), 'It's De-Lovely', 'Ridin' High'), which also starred **Jimmy Durante** and **Bob Hope**, was not particularly successful, but the others such as ***Du Barry Was A Lady*** (1939, 'Friendship' [one of Porter's wittiest 'list' songs], 'Do I Love You?'), ***Panama Hattie*** (1940, 'Make It Another Old Fashioned, Please', 'I've Still Got My Health'), and ***Something For The Boys*** (1943, 'Hey, Good Lookin'', 'The Leader Of A Big-Time Band'), were all substantial hits. Although not all of Porter's shows in the 30s and 40s were long runners by any means (*Around The World*, which had book and direction by Orsen Welles, was a 75-performance flop in 1946), almost every one continued to have at least one memorable and enduring song, such as 'Begin The Beguine', 'Just One Of Those Things', and 'Why Shouldn't I?' (1935, ***Jubilee***), 'At Long Last Love', (1938, *You Never Know*), 'Get Out Of Town', 'My Heart Belongs To Daddy', and 'Most Gentlemen Don't Like Love' (1938, ***Leave It To Me!***), 'Ev'rything I Love', 'Ace In The Hole', and 'Let's Not Talk About Love' (1941, ***Let's Face It!***), 'I Love You' (1944, ***Mexican Hayride***), and 'Ev'ry Time We Say Goodbye' (1944, *Seven Lively Arts*). After a rather lean period in the mid-40s, in 1948 Cole Porter wrote the score for ***Kiss, Me Kate***, which is considered to be his masterpiece. It starred **Alfred Drake**, Patricia Morison, Harold Lang, and Lisa Kirk, and contained superb numbers such as 'Another Op'nin', Another Show', 'Brush Up Your Shakespeare', 'I Hate Men', 'Always True To You In My Fashion', 'So In Love', 'Too Darn Hot', 'Why Can't You Behave?', 'Were Thine That Special Face', and several more. *Kiss Me, Kate* ran for 1,077 performances on Broadway, and a further 501 in London. Another song, 'From This Moment On', which Porter wrote for the stage production of *Kiss Me, Kate*, was eventually used in the 1953 film version. Before that, it was tried out in *Out Of This World* (1950), a show which, in spite of the presence of the high-kicking **Charlotte Greenwood**, and a mixture of attractive ballads and novelties such as 'I Am Loved', 'Where, Oh Where?', 'Nobody's Chasing Me', and 'Cherry Pies Ought To Be You', ran for less than six months. Porter's last two shows for Broadway were ***Can-Can*** (1953, 'I Love Paris', 'It's All Right With Me', 'C'est Magnifique') and ***Silk Stockings*** (1955, 'All Of You', 'Josephine', 'Stereophonic Sound'). The first was a resounding hit, running for 892 performances, but although the latter was generally an unfortunate affair, it still stayed around for over a year.

As well as his work for Broadway, Cole Porter also enjoyed a prolific and equally satisfying career in Hollywood. He wrote his first film songs, 'They All Fall In Love' and 'Here Comes The Bandwagon', for the **Gertrude Lawence** movie, *The Battle Of Paris*, in 1929. Thereafter, some of his most outstanding work was featured in ***Born To Dance*** (1936, 'Easy To Love' [introduced by James Stewart], 'I've Got You Under My Skin', 'Swingin' the Jinx Away', 'Rap-Tap On Wood'), ***Rosalie*** ('In The Still Of The Night', 'Rosalie'), ***Broadway Melody Of 1940*** (1940, 'I've Got My Eyes On You', 'I Concentrate On You', 'Please Don't Monkey With Broadway'), ***You'll Never Get Rich*** (1941, 'So Near And Yet So Far', 'Dream Dancing', 'Since I Kissed My Baby Goodbye'), *Something To Shout About* (1943, 'You'd Be So Nice To Come Home To'), *Hollywood Canteen* (1944, 'Don't Fence Me In'), ***Night And Day*** (1946, a Porter biopic, in which he was played by Cary Grant), ***The Pirate*** (1948, 'Be A Clown', 'Love Of My Life', 'Nina'), *Stage Fright* (1950, 'The Laziest Gal In Town', sung by **Marlene Dietrich**), ***High Society*** (1956, 'True Love', 'You're Sensational', 'I Love You, Samantha', 'Well, Did You Evah?', 'Now You Has Jazz'), and ***Les Girls*** (1957, 'All Of You', 'Ladies In Waiting', 'Paris Loves Lovers'). In addition, several of Porter's original stage shows were adapted for the screen (twice in the case of *Anything Goes*), and several of his songs were revived in the 1975 Burt Reynolds/Cybill Shepherd movie, ***At Long Last Love***.

In 1937 Porter was seriously injured in a riding accident. Astonishingly, a series of more than two dozen operations, several years in a wheelchair, and almost constant pain seemed to have little effect on his creative ability. His right leg was amputated in 1958, and in the same year he wrote what is said to have been his last song, 'Wouldn't It Be Fun?' ('not to be famous'), for the television spectacular *Aladdin*. Marked by wit and sophistication often far ahead of the times in which he lived, Porter's music and lyrics set standards which were the envy of most of his contemporaries. When he died in 1964, his fellow songwriters in the American Society of Composers and Authors paid this tribute: 'Cole Porter's talent in the creation of beautiful and witty songs was recognized as unique throughout the world. His brilliant contributions in the field of musical theatre made him an international legend in his lifetime.' Although he ceased writing in the late 50s, his music continued to be used in films and on television, and he was the subject of television specials and numerous honours and awards. In 1991, the centenary of his birth, there were tributes galore. In a gala concert at Carnegie Hall, artists such as Julie Wilson, **Kathryn Grayson**, and Patricia Morison paid tribute to him, as did songwriters **Jule Styne**, **Sammy Cahn**, and **Burton Lane**. Among the other special events were an Off Broadway revue, *Anything Cole*, the West End production of *A Swell Party*, and a UK touring show entitled *Let's Do It*, starring **Elaine Delmar** and **Paul Jones**. The special occasion was also marked by the release of new recordings of his scores for *Nymph Errant* and *Kiss Me, Kate*, and the album *Red Hot And Blue*, which featured a number of well known rock stars, with the proceeds going to AIDS research.

Selected album: *Cole Porter Sings Cole Porter* (Koch International 1995).

Further reading: *The Cole Porter Story*, David Ewen. *Cole: A Biographical Essay*, Brendan Gill and Richard Kimball. *The Cole Porter Story*, Cole Porter and Richard Hubler. *Cole Porter: The Life That Late He Led*, George Eells. *Travels With Cole Porter*, Jean Howard. *Cole*, Brendan Gill. *Cole Porter*, Cole Schwarz.

Porter, David

b. 21 November 1941, Memphis, Tennessee, USA. Although better recalled for a partnership with **Isaac Hayes**, Porter had been an active, if unsuccessful, performer prior to their meeting, recording for several labels including Savoy and **Hi Records**. The singer was also present on several early **Stax** sessions. Porter first encountered his future colleague when he tried to sell Hayes life insurance, but the pair soon combined in one of the 60s soul era's most electric songwriting teams. Rightly applauded for their songs for **Sam And Dave**, including 'Hold On I'm Comin'', 'Soul Man' and 'When Something Is Wrong With My Baby', the duo also provided hits for **Carla Thomas** ('B-A-B-Y') and **Johnnie Taylor** ('I Had A Dream'). Their friendship was strained when Hayes secured an international best-seller with his *Hot Buttered Soul.* Porter then re-embarked on a solo career and in 1970 scored a Top 30 US R&B hit with 'Can't See You When I Want To'. His only other chart entry came in 1972 when 'Ain't That Loving You (For More Reasons Than One)' was a minor success. Credited to 'Isaac Hayes And David Porter', it ostensibly marked the end of their collaboration.

Albums: *Gritty, Groovy And Gettin' It* (1970), *David Porter: Into A Real Thing* (1971), *Victim Of The Joke* (1974).

Portishead

Portishead were named after the sleepy West Coast port where Geoff Barrow (b. c.1971) spent his teens. His intentions in forming the band were simple, 'I just wanted to make interesting music, proper songs with a proper life span and a decent place in people's record collections.' Barrow started out as a tape operator, working in a minor capacity with **Massive Attack** and **Neneh Cherry**, and also wrote songs for Cherry ('Somedays' was included on *Home Brew*). With the aid of an Enterprise Allowance grant he recruited jazz guitarist and musical director Adrian Utley (b. c.1957), drummer/programmer Dave and vocalist Beth Gibbons (b. c.1965), whom he encountered on a job creation scheme while she was singing **Janis Joplin** cover versions in a pub. Together they recorded a soundtrack and film, *To Kill A Dead Man*, with themselves as actors because 'we couldn't find anyone else to do the parts'. At this point they came to the attention of A&R man Ferdy Unger-Hamilton at the **Go! Discs** subsidiary, Go! Beat, who encouraged Barrow to remix **Gabrielle**'s 'Dreams'. He was sufficiently impressed with the results to sign the band immediately, despite several other interested parties. The singles 'Numb' and 'Sour Times' emerged to good press reaction, although the debut album slipped in and out of the charts with little fanfare. There was some problem with marketing the band - both Barrow and Gibbons were reluctant to do interviews, and had no initial interest in playing live. Instead the press campaign saw painted mannequin dummies distributed in strategic locations throughout London, ensuring press coverage outside of the expected media. Word of mouth continued to push the band's profile and, with virtually no radio support, the group's third single, 'Glory Box', entered the UK charts at number 13 in January 1995. Aided by a distinctive, gender-swapping video (visuals are central to the band's approach), its arrival came on the back of several 'album of the year' awards for *Dummy* from magazines as diverse as *Mixmag*, *ID*, *The Face* and ***Melody Maker***. Mixing torch songs with blues, jazz and hip hop, their sound became known as 'trip hop'. The interest also translated to America, where the album sold over 150,000 copies without the band even setting foot there. Following their success, the band were invited to contribute to several soundtracks, including two low-budget art films and *Tank Girl.*

Album: *Dummy* (Go! Beat 1994).

Portnoy, Jerry

b. 25 November 1943, Evanston, Illinois, USA. Portnoy's father owned a rug store on Chicago's Maxwell Street, and every Sunday his son could drink in the wealth of music to be heard in the bustling street market. Blues was an early influence but he took little interest in the piano lessons that began when he was 10, nor in the accordion or the guitar which he adopted during the folk boom. Portnoy did not take to the harmonica until he was 24 but within two years he had formed a duo with mandolinist **Johnny Young**. After a two-year stint, he joined **Johnny Littlejohn**'s band for a further two years before moving on to the **Sam Lay** Band. His career changed significantly in 1974 when **Muddy Waters** asked him to replace **'Mojo' George Buford**. For the next six years, he toured the world and appeared on Muddy's three Blue Sky albums, two of which received Grammy Awards. In 1980, he along with **Pinetop Perkins**, **Calvin Jones** and **Little Willie Smith** left Muddy, recruited **Louis Myers** and formed the Legendary Blues Band. The following year, they released *Life Of Ease*, followed in 1983 by *Red Hot 'n' Blue*. Portnoy left in 1986 and took a year off from music. He formed the Broadcasters with **Ronnie Earl** in 1987, but 18 months later split to form his own band, the Streamliners. That band made its recording debut, *Poison Kisses*, in 1991, the same year that **Eric Clapton** asked him to play the blues night at his annual Royal Albert Hall concert series. Portnoy returned in the same role in 1993 and took part in the sessions and subsequent tour for Clapton's 'return to the blues' album, *From The Cradle*.

Album: *Poison Kisses* (Modern Blues Recordings 1991).

Posey, Sandy

b. Martha Sharp, 1945, Jasper, Alabama, USA. As a teenager Posey moved to west Memphis where she embarked on a career as a studio session singer. Her contributions to innumerable records impressed producer Chips Moman, who encouraged the artist as both a songwriter and performer. Posey's debut single, 'Born A Woman', reached number 12 in the US charts in 1966, while its pithy lyric - 'If you're born a woman, you're born to be hurt' - brought a new maturity to the often-maudlin approach common to female country singers. 'Single Girl', its equally accomplished follow-up, scaled the UK and US Top 20s, before 'What A Woman In Love Won't Do', 'I Take It Back' and 'Are You Never Coming Home' (all 1967) continued her run of success. Posey was one of several singers backing **Elvis Presley** when he undertook sessions at Moman's American studios. She was featured on 'Mama Liked The Roses', and also appeared with the singer during his first Las Vegas engagement (1969). However, while retaining a popularity within the country market, Sandy's distinctive approach as a solo act latterly proved too specialized for pop.

Albums: *Born A Woman* (1966), *I Take It Back* (1967). Compilation: *Very Best Of Sandy Posey* (1974).

Posies

Formed in Seattle, Washington, USA, the Posies play powerfully melodic music which pays tribute to Merseybeat and the harmonies of the **Hollies**. Growing up in Bellingham, 90 miles north of Seattle, Jonathon Auer (vocals/guitar) and Ken Stringfellow (vocals/guitar) were both in bands in their early teens, and even joined their high school choir. Stringfellow is married to Kim Warnick of the **Fastbacks**, and has mixed and produced for various Seattle/**Sub Pop Records** bands. He has also guested for **Mudhoney**. However, the Posies are equally influenced by **Hüsker Dü** as by the songwriting prowess of **XTC**, **Elvis Costello** and **Squeeze**. The duo's debut was recorded (originally on their own label as a cassette, later on PopLlama Products) in 1988 and introduced their penchant for sanguine, everyday lyrical topics. Entitled *Failure*, its title marked them out as singularly lacking in ambition, a trait which later became enshrined in the 'slacker' ethos. However, they signed to **Geffen Records**, and enlisted a rhythm section (Dave Fox and Mike Musburger) and brought in **John Leckie** to produce their major label debut. A varied, multi-textured album, it was reminiscent of the **Stone Roses**, whom Leckie also produced. The Posies' third album, *Frosting On The Beater*, a reference to masturbation, was produced by **Don Fleming**, and attracted wide acclaim, finishing in the higher reaches of many end of year critical polls. The group supported **Teenage Fanclub** and their heroes **Big Star** on European tours, and Auer and Stringfellow both took part in the reformation of the latter band.

Albums: *Failure* (23 1988, cassette only), *Dear 23* (Geffen 1990), *Frosting On The Beater* (Geffen 1993).

Positiva

EMI's dance subsidiary headed by Nick Halkes (b. c.1967, Portishead, Bristol, England), who was headhunted after taking **XL** recordings to the forefront of the dance market with releases by the **Prodigy SL2**, **Liquid** and **House Of Pain**. He also crunched into the Top 10 alongside one-time partner Richard Russell with 'The Bouncer', recorded under the name Kicks Like A Mule. He had also worked as Life Like (on the **Depeche Mode**-sampling 'Like Life'), again with Russell. Halkes' attended Goldsmiths University in London before kidding his way into a DJ slot on WRLS, the New York black music station. While in the third year of his degree he had become the UK representative of Easy Street Records, before DJing in Ibiza in 1988. He also worked part-time for Secret Promotions (**Rebel MC**, **Massive Attack**), then Citybeat, eventually heading himself his own 'underground' dance label, **XL**. The success of which made his name a hot property in the UK dance market, with **EMI** eventually offering him adequate terms and conditions to set up Positiva at the beginning of 1993. His second-in-command was to be DJ and journalist Dave Lambert. Positiva's first release was Exoterix's 'Void'. However, it was the **Disco Evangelists**' 'De Niro' which was the first significant record, before the ongoing success of **Hyper Go-Go** ('Raise'), **Judy Cheeks** ('So In Love' etc.), **Barbara**

Tucker ('Beautiful People'), Critical ('Wall Of Sound') and **Reel 2 Real** (house-ragga crossover 'I Like To Move It') began to really pay back EMI's investment. All the hits were collected on the *Phase One* compilation, while the label was also responsible for July 1993's *Ambient Collection* - one of the best introductions to this music yet compiled (**Orb**, **Visions Of Shiva**, **Black Dog**, **Orbital**, **Aphex Twin**, **Irresistable Force**, **Moby**, **Beaumont Hannant** etc.). Halkes has indicated that the next objective of the label will be to take club acts and break them as album artists. Recent signings include rappers the **Whooliganz**.

Albums: Various: *The Positiva Ambient Collection* (Positiva 1993), *Phase One* (Positiva 1994).

Positive Force

This eight-piece jazz funk act were formed in Pennsylvania, USA by Brenda Reynolds and Albert Williams. Producer Nate Edmunds discovered them and brought them to Sylvia Robinson's Sugarhill label. Edmunds produced their first single 'We Got The Funk' which he had co-written with Reynolds and Williams. The record vanished without trace in their homeland although it became a big club hit in the UK and spent a week in the Top 20 in 1979. Despite appearances on shows like *Top Of The Pops* in the UK, it was the only taste of success for Reynolds and the groups other vocalist Vicki Drayton. They were however positive about the situation, saying they really enjoyed their five minutes of fame because to quote them, 'For once in our lives we had been treated like someone special'. Positive Force made a brief reappearance in the UK Top 75 the following year when 'We Got The Funk' was featured in the club/disco medley hit from **Calibre Cuts**.

Positive-K

From Queens, New York, Positive-K (b. c.1967, Bronx, New York, USA) is yet another of rap's mouthpieces to augment his B-boy/breakbeat hip hop with messages from the Nation Of Islam. After being inspired by his view of a **Grandmaster Flash** show in Echo Park from his grandmother's window, he immersed himself in hip hop culture as a child. He was 18 years old when he made his first appearance on vinyl with the *Fast Money* compilation, subsequently hooking up with First Priority. A second various artists' credit came with the label's 1988 compilation *Basement Flavor*. His releases for the label would include 'Quarter Gram Pam', 'Step Up Front' and 'I'm Not Havin' It', at the same time as he duetted with **Grand Puba** on **Brand Nubian**'s debut set. He moved over to his own Creative Control Records for the release of 'Night Shift', which was subsequently picked up by **Island**/4th & Broadway. It was produced by **Big Daddy Kane**, who also guest rapped. Positive had met him some years previously when enjoying a bus ride rap battle between New York and Philadelphia. More successful still, however, was 'I Got A Man', which established him both in his native country and the US. Somewhat less cerebral than previous efforts, it was still great fun, with lines boasting that 'I'm a big daddy longstroke, your man's Pee Wee Herman'. In the afterglow of its success his Creative Control empire flourished, signing artists like Raggedyman.

Album: *Da Skills Dat Pay Da Bills* (Island 1992).

Possessed

Formed in San Francisco, California, USA, in 1983, this heavy metal band consisted of Jeff Beccarra (bass/vocals), Mike Tarrao (guitar), Larry Lalonde (guitar) and Mike Sus (drums). Through early demos and their inclusion on the *Metal Massacre VI* compilation album, released on Metal Blade Records in 1984, the band attracted the attention of Combat Records who promptly signed the band. This resulted in their debut, *Seven Churches*, released in 1985. Growling vocals and ultra-fast **Slayer**-influenced riffs were the order of the day and the band quickly made their mark on the death metal underground. The next album, produced by ex-**Rods** drummer Carl Canedy. entitled *Beyond The Gates* released in 1986 the band had toured throughout Europe building a strong following. On their return to America the band recorded and released a mini-album entitled *The Eyes Of Terror*. Produced by guitar maestro **Joe Satriani**, the album was, as expected, heavily guitar-oriented but due to internal band wrangles the band folded soon after its release.

Albums: *Seven Churches* (Roadrunner 1985), *Beyond The Gates* (Under One Flag 1986), *The Eyes Of Terror* (Under One Flag 1987, mini-album).

Possum Dixon

Possum Dixon are from the 'coffee house scene' of Los Angeles, California, USA. Named after a fugitive spotted on the US television programme *America's Most Wanted*, the group have earned a good deal of international support based on their rangy, expressive musicianship and lyrics, and have been compared to the **Talking Heads**, **XTC** and the **Violent Femmes**. Robert Zabrecky (vocals/bass) helped set up the Jabber Jaw club in the late 80s, which showcased local bands, as well as an unannounced **Nirvana** gig. Recruiting band members from this scene, Zabrecky started to put the band together and they released three independent singles. They eventually signed a contract with Interscope Records. Zabrecky described their music thus, 'There's a side that's experimental music, a stream of consciousness, trying to mix poetry, bullshit, abusive relationships, drugs, sex and coffee, things like that.' Songs such as 'We're All Happy' tackled the problem of a woman who came to vibrators late in life and overdosed on the resultant happiness they brought her. Better still was the single, 'Watch That Girl

Destroy Me', produced by Earle Mankey, which followed acclaimed support slots to **Compulsion** in London.

Albums: *Possum Dixon* (Interscope/East West 1993).

Post, Mike

This US writer, arranger and producer is known mainly for his music for television. His career began in the early 60s as a guitarist and session musician. He moved to production work in 1967, making his debut with the first album by the First Edition, featuring **Kenny Rogers**. Post went on to produce **Mason Williams** and 'Classical Gas' which earned him his first Grammy Award for Best Instrumental Arrangement. In the 70s he became musical director of the ***Andy Williams** Show*, but he really began to make his name along with his partner Pete Carpenter, writing numerous complete telefilm scores, and some of the most memorable television theme songs of the last 20 years, for programmes such as *The Rockford Files*, *The A-Team*, *Magnum P.I.*, *Hill Street Blues* (featuring **Larry Carlton**, two Grammys), and *L.A. Law* (Grammy). In the 80s he began to compose the music for feature films, such as *Deep In The Heart*, *Running Brave*, *Hadley's Rebellion*, *Rhinestone*, *The River Rat*, *Renegade* (theme), and *Crime And Punishment.* He has also continued to produce major stars, working on **Dolly Parton**'s 1981 album *9 To 5 And Other Jobs* and the debut album from **Joey Scarbury**.

Albums: as the Mike Post Coalition *Fused* (1975), *Railhead Overture* (1975), *Television Theme Songs* (1982), *A-Team* (1984), *Mike Post* (1984), *Music From L.A. Law & Otherwise* (80s).

Postcard Records

After the impetus of punk's initial onslaught, like-minded individuals in every corner of Britain set about creating their own musical identity. If they could not play music, they went one better and founded their own label. Alan Horne set about realizing his ambition in late 70s Glasgow when he discovered local favourites **Orange Juice**. Here was a band that could be harnessed, and Horne set about creating Postcard Records with lead singer Edwyn Collins as the 'Sound Of Young Scotland'. Orange Juice's 'Falling And Laughing' was issued early in 1980, housed in distinctive foldaround, hand-coloured sleeves with a free flexi-disc. Much of the Postcard label's appeal would stem from the precious nature of its roster and the presentation of its releases as vital and desirable artefacts. To do this, Horne needed more than one band and after losing the **Fire Engines**, opted for manic Edinburgh act **Josef K**. Postcard's second release was also arguably their finest; Orange Juice's 'Blue Boy'. Their debut had caused a stir, certainly, but this formidable single, awash with frenetic guitar work and an unforgettably passionate melody, sent the critics reeling. Josef K's 'Radio Drill Time' was less accessible and more frenzied, but an aura had already surrounded the label.

Next came the **Go-Betweens**, an obscure Australian outfit whom Horne met while they were touring the UK. They promptly recorded 'I Need Two Heads', which became the fourth Postcard single, but this was to prove their only single for the label. Josef K's more relaxed 'It's Kinda Funny' and another Orange Juice classic, 'Simply Thrilled Honey' saw out 1980, and Horne took the end of year opportunity to redesign the label's image. The spartan brown labels (with a drum-beating pussycat) were replaced by a checked design to reflect the new sleeves, portraying a collage of Scottish national dress. In the meantime, Josef K hit a stumbling block. They were unhappy with the sound on their debut *Sorry For Laughing*, and eventually scrapped it before it reached the shops. Postcard instead relied on Orange Juice for 'Poor Old Soul', before introducing a new signing early in 1981, **Aztec Camera**. Fronted by the 16-year-old Roddy Frame, their debut, 'Just Like Gold', was more traditional than other Postcard material, but nonetheless endearing. Josef K teamed up with Belgian label Les Disques du Crépuscule for 'Sorry For Laughing' (the title track to the abandoned album), and followed this with 'Chance Meeting', a re-recording of their first single. By this time, mid-1981, Postcard was basking in the critical sunshine and Orange Juice succumbed to a seductive offer from **Polydor Records**. Their next single, 'Wan Light', was abandoned and from this point on, Postcard fell apart. Josef K finally took the plunge with a re-recorded album, *The Only Fun In Town*, and Aztec Camera continued to ply their acoustic sensibilities with 'Mattress Of Wire', but Horne soon moved on to pastures new, leaving numerous projects on the shelf. In addition to the first long player from Aztec Camera (*Green Jacket Grey*), Horne had allocated numbers to singles from the **Bluebells** (later to enjoy commercial success at **London**), the Jazzateers (who joined **Rough Trade**) and Secret Goldfish (reputedly an Orange Juice pseudonym). Aztec Camera and the Go-Betweens also moved to Rough Trade, and Josef K split up, while Horne eventually re-surfaced managing the labels Win and Swamplands.

Potter, Tommy

b. 21 September 1918, Philadelphia, Pennsylvania, USA, d. March 1988. After taking up the bass in his early 20s, having previously mastered piano and guitar, Potter was soon involved in early bebop. He played in the bebop-oriented big band led by **Billy Eckstine** in the mid-40s, then joined **Charlie Parker**. He recorded with Parker and many other leading bebop musicians, including **Fats Navarro**, **Max Roach** and **Bud Powell**. In the 50s and early 60s he worked with a broader range of musicians, such as **Stan Getz**,

Sonny Rollins, **Miles Davis**, **Artie Shaw** and **Harry Edison**, before retiring from full-time playing in the mid-60s. One of the leading bass players of bebop, Potter set a high standard of performance with clearly articulated lines and impeccable timekeeping.
Albums: *The Sonny Rollins Quartet* (1954), *The Tommy Potter Sextet In Sweden* (1956). Compilations: with Charlie Parker *The Legendary Dial Masters, Volume 4 (1946-47)* (1983), with Parker *The Complete Savoy Sessions, Volume 3 (1947)* (1985).

Pottinger, Sonia

b. c.1943, Jamaica, West Indies. In the mid-60s Pottinger opened her Tip Top Record Shop on Orange Street, Kingston, and in 1966, launched her career as a record producer with 'Every Night' by Joe White And Chuck with the Baba Brooks Band, recorded at Federal Recording Studios. This sentimental C&W ballad with an R&B beat became a massive hit which stayed high in the Jamaican charts for months. As the music changed to **rocksteady**, she recorded a string of sweet sounding hits such as 'The Whip' by the **Ethiopians** (1967), 'That's Life' by Delano Stewart (1968), and 'Swing And Dine' by the **Melodians** (1968), all released on her Gayfeet and High Note labels. In 1974, after **Duke Reid**'s death, she took over his business and reissued and repackaged the Treasure Isle catalogue. In the late 70s, she issued several best-selling albums by **Bob Andy**, **Marcia Griffiths** and **Culture**. She retired from the recording business in 1985.
Albums: Various: *Put On Your Best Dress* (Trojan 1990, rec. 1967-68), *Musical Feast* (Heartbeat 1990, rec. 1967-70).

Poulsen, Hans

b. 1945, Denmark. One of the overlooked artists in Australia, Poulsen was active in the late 60s. His music reflected the hippie lifestyle and 'alternative culture'. The whimsical Poulsen could produce contagious melodies with ease and was asked to write songs for other well-known mainstream performers, notably **John Farnham**. His second album lacked the commercial impact of its predecessor, which contained his hit single 'Boom Sha La La Lo'. Later in the 70s, he travelled the world whilst fighting cancer, which was threatening to destroy his career. Despite playing occasionally, he has not recorded any material in the 80s and 90s, except for several albums of children's songs.
Albums: *Natural High* (1970), *Lost And Found* (1973).

Pourcel, Franck

With the violin his chosen instrument, Pourcel found playing in downtime jazz combos a liberating change from his studies at the Paris Conservatoire. He became an admirer of **Stéphane Grappelli** whose mainstream style he emulated before assuming leadership of the French Fiddlers in the late 40s. Signed to Pathe-Marconi, the orchestra adjusted to the popular forum and was rewarded with encouraging sales for 1952's 'Blue Tango'. Seven years later, a novel instrumental version of the **Platters**' 'Only You' - attributed to Franck Pourcel And His Rockin' Strings - represented the commercial peak of Pourcel's career as it scaled the US Top 10. It also anticipated the early 60s 'Stringbeat' that proved beneficial to **John Barry** and **Adam Faith**. Collectively, the Fiddlers - under whatever name they called themselves - had sold 15 million records by the early 70s with comparatively few chart placings. In Britain, for example, only *This Is Pourcel* registered in the album list. Nevertheless, its perpetrator continued to cut a suave, dapper figure at international award ceremonies when nominated for this lush film score or that easy-listening arrangement.
Selected albums: *Latino Americano* (1966), *Magnifique* (1966), *The Sound Of Magic* (1967), *Pourcel Today* (1968), *The Franck Pourcel Sound* (1968), *The Importance Of Your Love* (1968), *Rhapsody In Blue* (1968), *The Versatile Franck Pourcel* (1969), *Franck Pourcel* (1970), *Impressions* (1970), with the Paris Concert Orchestra *The World's Favourite Classics* (1970), *This Is Pourcel* (1971), *Franck Pourcel Meets The Beatles* (1972), *Western* (1973), *And Now Pourcel* (1975), *Franck Pourcel Plays Abba* (1979), *Classical Favourites In Digital* (1980), with the London Symphony Orchestra *A Digital Experience* (1981), *New Sound Tangos* (1983), *Nostalgia Mood* (1984), *Les Hits Classiques* (1986). Compilation: *The Very Best Of Franck Pourcel* (1976).

POV

New Jersey four-piece comprising Marc Sherman (b. c.1974, aka The Rapper Extraordinaire), Ewarner 'E' Mills (b. c.1974), Hakim 'HB' Bell (b. c.1975) and Lincoln 'Link' DeVulgt (b. Virgin Islands) whose sound encompasses reggae and R&B, with the uniting structure of hip hop rhythms. Their initials stand for Point Of View. Within their line-up stands not only a conventional rapper, but also one (Link) who takes a reggae/dancehall DJ approach. They made their debut with 'Anutha Luv', under the tutelage of Hakim Abdulsamad (the **Boys** etc.). But it was Michael Bennet who decided to take the group to Jamaica, recording the sweet 'Summer Nights' single at his Kingston studio. They boast of distinguished parentage too; bandleader Hakim 'HB' Bell is the son of Robert 'Kool' Bell, of **Kool And The Gang** fame, who served as co-executive producer on their debut album. This comprised two quite distinct sides. The first, the 'Beat U Up' side, was formulated by uptempo dance and swing material, while the second, 'Beat U Down', offered Link's dancehall chants and Sherman's hip hop verses set to the impressive soulful harmonising of the whole group. It included their duet with **Jade**, 'All Thru The Nite'. Their backgrounds (Sherman's father

is an import/export director) have disabused them of any naivety about the music business, and each member owns their own separate publishing company. Hakim is also responsible for HB Productions, which handled (in tandem with Robert Bell) backroom duties on the band's debut album.
Album: *Handing' Out Beatdowns* (Giant/RCA 1993).

Powell, Bobby

b. c.1941. From Baton Rouge, Louisiana, Powell is a heavily gospel-influenced soul artist, who achieved modest success in the 60s and 70s recording for small southern labels. He began his career in the church and singing in gospel groups, and in 1965 began recording for Lionel Whitfield's Whit label in Shreveport, Louisiana. Powell secured his biggest success in 1965 with 'C.C. Rider' (number 1 on the *Cash Box* R&B chart), a remake of a 20s blues standard. He obtained another hit with the funky 'Do Something For Yourself' (number 21 R&B) from 1966, but his most impressive recording that year was 'I'm Gonna Leave You' (number 34 R&B), which with its stinging blues guitar and a shouting gospel chorus ranked as one of the funkiest, most downhome soul records in history. Powell achieved some regional success in 1969 with 'In Time', and reached the charts again in 1971 with a lowdown remake of **Baby Washington**'s 'The Bells' (number 14 R&B). Beginning in the late 70s Powell began recording for the Hep Me label, but despite some sizeable regional successes failed to hit the national charts. During the 80s Powell functioned as the ultimate opening act in Baton Rouge whoever came into town, he received the opening gig. By the early 90s Powell had abandoned R&B to sing gospel music exclusively.
Albums: *Thank You* (Excello 1973), *Bobby Powell Explains The Glory Of Love* (Hep Me early 80s), *Down By The Riverside* (Hep Me 80s). Compilations: *A Fool For You* (Charly 1988), *In Time* (P-Vine 1992), *Especially For You* (Ace 1993).

Powell, Bud

b. Earl Powell, 27 September 1924, New York City, New York, USA, d. 1 August 1966. After learning to play the piano in the classical tradition while still a child, Powell began working around New York's Coney Island, where he played in a band featuring **Valaida Snow** around 1940. During the next couple of years he became a regular visitor to Minton's Playhouse, where he heard the first stirrings of bebop. In particular he was influenced by **Thelonious Monk**'s harmonic innovations but quickly developed his own style. Despite his leanings towards the new music, he was hired by **Cootie Williams** for his big band. During his stay with Williams he was arrested in Philadelphia and reportedly badly beaten by police officers, an event usually cited as the beginning of the mental problems which were to dog him for the rest of his life. He retained his links with events on 52nd Street and was soon one of the most striking of the bebop pianists. By 1945, however, he was displaying the first overt signs of acute mental instability and was hospitalized - the first of many incarcerations in mental hospitals, during some of which he was given electro-convulsive therapy. Throughout the 50s he worked regularly, appearing with all the leading figures of bebop, including **Charlie Parker**, **Dizzy Gillespie** and **Max Roach**. During this same period his mental instability increased, the sudden death in 1956 of his brother **Richie Powell** adding to his problems. Additionally, his mental and physical health were being gravely damaged by his growing dependence on narcotics and alcohol. At the end of the decade he left New York for Paris, where he spent three years of popular success but was still plagued by his mental and addiction troubles. Back in New York in 1964, his performances became fewer and were frequently fraught with emotional and technical breakdowns. He died on 1 August 1966. At his performing peak, Powell's playing style displayed a startling brilliance, with remarkable ideas being executed with absolute technical mastery, often at extraordinary speeds. By the late 50s his personal problems were such that he rarely played at his best, although the flow of ideas continued, as can be deduced from some of his compositions from these years. He was a major figure in bebop and an influence, either directly or indirectly, upon most pianists in jazz since the 50s.
Selected albums: *Jazz Giant* (Verve 1950), with Charlie Parker *One Night In Birdland* (1950), with Parker *Jazz At Massey Hall: The Quintet Of The Year* (1953), *Broadcast Performances Vols 1 & 2* (1953), *Inner Fires* (1953), *Ornithology* (1953), *The Bud Powell Trio: The Verve Sessions* (1955), *Bouncing With Bud* (Storyville 1955), *The Lonely One* (1955), *Blues In The Closet* (1956), *Strictly Powell* (1956), *Swinging With Bud* (1957), *The Bud* (1957), *Bud Powell In Paris* i (1960), *Bud Powell In Concert* (1960), *Oscar Pettiford Memorial* (1960), *Bud Powell In Europe* (1961), *A Portrait Of Thelonious* (CBS 1961), *The Bud Powell Trio At The Golden Circle Vols 1 & 2* (1962), *The Bud Powell Trio In Copenhagen* (1962), *Bud Powell '62* (1962), *At The Golden Circle Vols 1-4* (Steeplechase 1962 recordings), *Budism* (Steeplechase 1962 recordings), *Bud Powell In Paris* ii (1963), *Blues For Bouffemont/The Invisible Cage* (1964), *The Bud Powell Quartet* (1964), *The Bud Powell Trio* (1964), *Salt Peanuts* (Black Lion 1964 recording), *Ups 'N' Downs* (1965), *The Return Of Bud Powell* (1965), *At The Blue Note Cafe, 1961* (1981), *The Complete Essen Jazz Festival Concert* (1988, rec. 1960). Compilations: The Genius Of Bud Powell (Verve 1978, 1950-51 recordings), *The Best Years* (1978), *The Amazing Bud Powell, Volumes 1 & 2 (1949-53)* (Blue Note 1982), *The Amazing Bud Powell, Volume 3 (1949-53)* (Blue Note 1984).
Further reading: *The Glass Enclosure: The Life Of Bud*

Powell, Alan Groves with Alyn Shipton. *Bud Powell*, Clifford Jay Safane (ed.).

Powell, Cozy

b. Colin Powell, 29 December 1947, England. Powell is a virtuoso drummer who has played with the likes of **Jeff Beck**, **Rainbow** and Emerson, Lake And Powell. His musical career began in 1965 when he was a member of the Sorcerers, before working with Casey Jones And The Engineers for a couple of months, then returning to his first band, who would change their name first to Youngblood, and then to Ace Kefford Stand. Powell then moved on to Big Bertha. In 1971 Jeff Beck founded a new group consisting of Robert Tench (vocals), Max Middleton (keyboards), Clive Chaman (bass), and Powell. The Jeff Beck group were among the premier exponents of R&B jazz-rock, and Powell appears on two of their albums. It was after his work with **Bedlam**, the band he formed in 1972 with Frank Aiello (vocals), Dennis Ball (bass) and Dave Ball (guitar), that Powell came to the attention of producer **Micky Most**. This gave Powell the opportunity to release hit singles such as 'Dance With The Devil' and 'The Man In Black'. This latter single was recorded whilst Powell was in Cozy Powell's Hammer, a group with Bedlam's Aiello as vocalist, along with newcomers **Don Airey** (keyboards), Clive Chaman (bass) and **Bernie Marsden** (guitar). This project came to an end in April 1975 when Powell decided to take a break and spend three months motor racing. Strange Brew was formed in July 1975, with Powell on drums, but this project lasted for little more than a month. He then joined **Ritchie Blackmore**'s **Rainbow**, with whom he played until 1980, his farewell concert with them being at the first Donington Rock festival. In 1981 Powell appeared on the **Michael Schenker** Group's *MSG*, and in the mid-80s replaced **Carl Palmer**, becoming the third member of Emerson, Lake And Powell. He also released three solo sets in the early 80s, working with **Gary Moore** among other name musicians. The album he recorded with Emerson, Lake And Powell had little chart success and his tenure with the group was short, as was now becoming customary for the artist (he also played for two years in **Whitesnake**). In 1990 Powell appeared on and produced **Black Sabbath**'s *Headless Cross*.

Albums: with Jeff Beck *Rough And Ready* (Epic 1971), with Beck *The Jeff Beck Group* (Epic 1972), with Bedlam *Bedlam* (Chrysalis 1973), with Rainbow *Rising* (Polydor 1976), with Rainbow *On Stage* (Polydor 1977), with Rainbow *Long Live Rock 'N' Roll* (Polydor 1978), *Over The Top* (Ariola 1979), with Rainbow *Down To Earth* (Polydor 1979), with the Michael Schenker Group *MSG* (Chrysalis 1981), *Tilt* (Polydor 1981), with Whitesnake *Saints 'N' Sinners* (Liberty 1982), *Octopus* (Polydor 1983), with Whitesnake *Slide It In* (Liberty 1983), with Emerson, Lake And Powell *Emerson, Lake And Powell* (Polydor 1985), with Forcefield *Forcefield* (President 1987), with Forcefield *Forcefield II* (President 1988), with Forcefield *Forcefield III* (President 1989), with Black Sabbath *Headless Cross* (IRS 1990), *The Drums Are Back* (1992).

Powell, Dick

b. Richard Ewing Powell, 14 November 1904, Mountain View, Arkansas, USA, d. 3 January 1963, Hollywood, California, USA. Powell was an extremely popular singing star of major 30s film musicals, with an appealing tenor voice, and 'matinee-idol' looks. He sang firstly as a boy soprano, and later, tenor, in school and church choirs, and learnt to play several musical instruments including the cornet, saxophone and banjo. In his late teens he was a member of the Royal Peacock Orchestra in Kentucky, and in the late 20s sang and played for Charlie Davis, with whom he made some early recordings, and other mid-west bands. In the early 30s he worked as a Master of Ceremonies and singer at the Circle Theatre, Indianapolis, and the Stanley Theatre in Pittsburg, where he was discovered by a Warner Brothers talent scout, and signed to a film contract. He made his film debut in *Blessed Event* (1932), followed by *Too Busy To Work* and *The King's Vacation* (1933), before making an enormous impact, along with another young newcomer, **Ruby Keeler**, in the spectacular **Busby Berkeley** back-stage musical ***42nd Street*** (1933). The film's score, by **Harry Warren** and **Al Dubin**, included the title song; 'Shuffle Off To Buffalo', 'You're Getting To Be A Habit With Me' and 'Young And Healthy'. Co-starring with Keeler, his wife Joan Blondell, and several more glamorous leading ladies, Powell embarked on a series of, mostly, lavish movie musicals for Warners, 20th Century-Fox, and other studios, through to the mid-40s.

Containing some of the classic popular songs of the time, the films included ***Gold Diggers** Of 1933* (1933), ('We're In The Money', 'Shadow Waltz', 'I've Got To Sing A Torch Song' and 'Pettin' In The Park'); ***Footlight Parade*** (1933), ('By A Waterfall'); *Twenty Million Sweethearts* (1934), ('I'll String Along With You'); ***Dames*** (1934), (the title song and 'I Only Have Eyes For You'); *Gold Diggers Of 1935* (1935), ('Lullaby Of Broadway' and 'The Words Are In My Heart'); *Broadway Gondolier* (1935), ('Lulu's Back In Town' and 'The Rose In Her Hair'); *Gold Diggers of 1937* (1936), ('With Plenty Of Money And You' and 'All's Fair In Love And War'); ***On The Avenue*** (1937), ('The Girl On The Police Gazette', This Year's Kisses', 'I've Got My Love To Keep Me Warm', Slumming On Park Avenue' and 'You're Laughing At Me'); *Varsity Show* (1937), ('Have You Got Any Castles Baby?') and *Going Places* (1938), ('Jeepers Creepers'). During this period, Powell was also very active on US radio, with programmes such as the *Old Gold* show with the **Ted Fio Rito** Band (1934), ***Hollywood Hotel*** (1934-37, with **Frances Langford**), *Your Hollywood Party* (1938, the show that gave **Bob Hope**'s career a big boost), *Tuesday Night Party* (1939), *American Cruise* (1941) and *Dick Powell Serenade* (1942-43). He also had several hit records, mostly with songs from his films. During the early 40s Powell concentrated more and more on comedy and dramatic film roles. In 1944, a year before he married actress **June Allyson**, he confirmed his change of direction when he appeared as private-eye Philip Marlowe in the highly-acclaimed movie *Farewell My Lovely* (aka *Murder My Sweet*). From then on, singing was abandoned, as he undertook a series of 'tough guy' roles in crime and detective movies, becoming just as popular as he had been in the musicals of the 30s. He was also a pioneer of early US television drama in the 50s, directing and producing, as well as performing. From 1959-61, he presented the popular television series *Dick Powell Theatre*. Despite some pressure, he never went back to singing, but was still working up to his death from cancer in 1963.

Compilations: *In Hollywood* (1974), *16 Classic Tracks* (1982), *Lullaby Of Broadway* (1986, London label double set), *Lullaby Of Broadway* (1986, Living Era label), *On The Avenue* (1988), *Rare Recordings 1934-1951* (1989).

Powell, Eleanor

b. 21 November 1912, Springfield, Massachusetts, USA, d. 11 February 1982, Beverly Hills, California, USA. Often billed as 'the world's greatest female tap dancer', Powell is regarded by many as the most accomplished of **Fred Astaire**'s screen partners, but without, of course, the indefinable magic of **Ginger Rogers**. She studied ballet at an early age and later took up tap dancing. After only a few lessons she is said to have achieved 'machine-gun rapidity' - up to five taps per second. Powell moved to New York in 1928 and appeared in *The Optimists* revue at the Casino de Paris Theatre, and a year later made her Broadway debut in the musical ***Follow Thru***. This was followed by more stage shows, suc as *Fine And Dandy*, *Hot-Cha*, and ***George White's Scandals*** (1932). A small, but highly impressive role in the film of ***George White's Scandals*** (1935), led to Powell being elevated to star status immediately after the release of ***Broadway Melody*** *Of 1936*. Signed to a seven year contract with MGM, her exhilarating tap dancing was on display in musicals such as ***Born To Dance***, *Broadway Melody Of 1938*, *Rosalie*, *Honolulu*, *Broadway Melody Of 1940*, *Lady Be Good*, *Ship Ahoy*, ***Thousands Cheer***, *I Dood It*, and *Sensations Of 1945*. By that stage, Powell, who married the actor Glenn Ford in 1943, had retired from show business to devote more time to her family. She made just one more film, *The Duchess Of Idaho*, in 1950. A devout Presbyterian, she became a Sunday school teacher in the 50s and starred in her own religious television programme, *Faith Of Our Children*, which won five Emmy Awards. After she and Ford were divorced in 1959, Powell made a brief comeback playing large clubs and showrooms in Las Vegas and New York with a classy cabaret act. Reminders of her remarkable terpsichorean skills flooded back in 1974, when the marvellous 'Begin The Beguine' routine she did with Fred Astaire in *Broadway Melody Of 1940* was included in MGM's *That's Entertainment!*. As **Frank Sinatra** said when he introduced the sequence in that film: 'You know, you can wait around and hope, but I'll tell you - you'll never see the likes of this again.'

Further reading: *Eleanor Powell: A Bio-Bibliography*, Margie Schultz.

Powell, Eugene

b. 23 December 1909, Utica, Mississippi, USA. Powell made his first blues records thanks to **Bo Carter**, who set up a 1936 session for Bluebird. Carter heavily influenced his guitar playing, in sometimes discordant duet with **Willie (Bill) Harris**. Powell's singing, though warmer than Carter's, had a similar clarity. Powell recorded as 'Sonny Boy Nelson', Nelson being his stepfather's name, and besides his own titles accompanied his then wife, Mississippi Matilda, and the harmonica player Robert Hill. Powell and Matilda separated in 1952, and he retired from music soon after. In the 70s, he was still a skilful guitarist, and was persuaded by Bo Carter's brother **Sam Chatmon** to perform for white audiences, although it was not long before he retired again because of his second wife's health problems, and subsequently his own.

Selected albums: *Police In Mississippi Blues* (1978), *Sonny Boy Nelson With Mississippi Matilda And Robert Hill* (1986).

Powell, Jane

b. Suzanne Burce, 1 April 1929, Portland, Oregon, USA. An petite, vivacious, actress and singer with a thrilling soprano voice who excelled in several popular MGM musicals of the 50s. After singing a mixture of classical and popular songs on local radio, she won a film contract with MGM when she was just 15 years old. Her debut in *Song Of The Open Road* was followed in the 40s and early 50s by *Delightfully Dangerous*, *Holiday In Mexico*, *Three Daring Daughters*, *A Date With Judy*, *Luxury Liner*, *Nancy Goes To Rio*, *Two Weeks With Love*, *Rich*, *Young And Pretty*, *Small Town Girl*, and *Three Sailors And A Girl* (1953). In 1951 she co-starred with **Fred Astaire** in ***Royal Wedding***, and they duetted on one of the longest song titles ever - 'How Could You Believe Me When I Said I Love You When You Know I've Been A Liar All My Life?'. Their recording became a million-seller. In 1956 Powell made the US Top 20 on her own with 'True Love' from ***High Society***. Her best film role came in 1954 when he joined **Howard Keel** in the marvellous ***Seven Brides For Seven Brothers***, and she continued to appear on the screen into the late 50s, in musicals such as *Athena*, ***Deep In My Heart***, ***Hit The Deck***, and *The Girl Most Likely* (1957). The

golden era of movie musicals was drawing to close by then, and Powell turned to provincial theatre and nightclubs. In the 70s she was active on US television in programmes such as *Murdoch*, *The Letters*, and *Mayday At 40,000 Feet*. She also succeeded **Debbie Reynolds** in the leading role of the 1973 Broadway revival of ***Irene***. In 1988 Powell married her fifth husband, Dick Moore, who was a child star himself, and is an authority on the genre having written a book entitled *Twinkle, Twinkle Little Star (But Don't Have Sex Or Take The Car)*. In the same year she appeared in concert at Carnegie Hall with **Skitch Henderson** and the New York Pops.
Selected albums: *Two Weeks With Love* (1950, film soundtrack), *Rich, Young And Pretty* (1951, film soundtrack), *Three Sailors And A Girl* (1953, film soundtrack), *Romance* (50s), *A Date With Jane Powell* (50s), *Athena* (1954, film soundtrack), *Alice In Wonderland* (50s), *Can't We Be Friends?* (50s). Compilation: *Songs From Her Films* (1989).

Powell, Jesse

b. 27 February 1924, Fort Worth, Texas, USA. Powell studied music at Hampton University, where he became inspired by **Count Basie**'s **Lester Young** and **Herschel Evans**, and played his tenor saxophone with the bands of **Oran 'Hot Lips' Page** (1942-43), **Louis Armstrong** (1943-44), and **Luis Russell** (1944-45). In 1946 he accepted an offer from Count Basie to replace **Illinois Jacquet** in the reed section. After briefly leading his own band in 1948 and being featured at that year's Paris Jazz Festival, he joined **Dizzy Gillespie**'s Orchestra (1949-50), but the R&B era found him with copious session work and, again, his own unit, which recorded for Federal (the infamous 'Walkin' Blues' sung by Fluffy Hunter) and Jubilee.

Powell, Jimmy

Originally from Birmingham, England, Powell predated many British Beat acts by recording his debut single, 'Sugar Baby Parts 1 & 2' as early as 1962. Despite the obvious enthusiasm therein, the singer is better remembered for two 1964 releases, 'That's Alright' and 'I've Been Watching You', the first of which was recorded while **Rod Stewart** was briefly a member of Jimmy's backing group, the Dimensions. Powell continued his pop soul/R&B approach on several later releases, but was unable to fulfil his early promise.
Album: *Hold On* (1973).

Powell, Mel

b. 12 February 1923, New York City, New York, USA. As a teenager Powell played piano at Nick's in New York City and soon thereafter joined **Muggsy Spanier**. His exceptional and at the time eclectic gifts attracted the attention of **Benny Goodman**, whom he joined in 1941. During his stint with Goodman he wrote several interesting charts, sometimes for his own compositions, which included 'The Earl', 'Clarinet A La King' and 'Mission To Moscow'. Powell was then briefly on the staff at **CBS** before military service threatened to disrupt his career. In fact, his army service had the opposite effect and he was soon a member of **Glenn Miller**'s Army Air Force band, playing in the dance band and in the small jazz group, the Uptown Hall Gang. After the war Powell made a few jazz records in Los Angeles, then in the early 50s recorded again with **Ruby Braff** and **Paul Quinichette**; he also appeared with Goodman around this same time, but that was the last the jazz world heard of him until the mid-80s. Powell had turned to classical music, playing largely for his own pleasure, teaching and composing classical music. During this same period Powell's health deteriorated and his movements were severely limited. However, his playing ability was unimpaired and his return to the jazz scene, with appearances on the Caribbean jazz cruise ship, the *SS Norway*, and new recordings showed that he had lost none of his capacity for performing inventive, dexterous solos.
Albums: *Classics In Swing: All Star Groups* (Commodire 1942 recording), *The Mel Powell Septet* (1953), *Mel Powell And His All Stars At Carnegie Hall* (1954), with Ruby Braff *Thingamagig* (Vanguard 1954), with Paul Quinichette *Trio* (1954), *Easy Swing* (Vanguard 1954), *Mel Powell And His Band* (1954), *Out On A Limb* (1955), *Bouquet* (Vogue 1980), *Piano Forte* (1986), *The Return Of Mel Powell* (1987). Compilation: with Joe Bushkin *The World Is Waiting, 1942-46* (1982).

Powell, Richie

b. 5 September 1931, New York City, New York, USA, d. 26 June 1956. After studying at college and with **Mary Lou Williams**, Powell emulated his older brother, **Bud Powell**, and embarked on a career in jazz. He played with **Jackie McLean**, a friend and neighbour, then joined **Johnny Hodges**. Attracted to bebop, Powell became a member of the **Max Roach-Clifford Brown** quintet in 1954. This engagement was one which allowed him to begin a potentially interesting development, but before he attained his full musical maturity he was killed in a road accident, with Brown, in 1956.
Albums: *Clifford Brown With Max Roach* (1955), with Clifford Brown, Max Roach *Study In Brown* (1955), *Sonny Rollins Plus Four* (1956). Compilation: *More Of Johnny Hodges* (1951-54).

Powell, Rudy

b. Everard Stephen Powell, 28 October 1907, New York City, New York, USA, d. 30 October 1976. Born and raised in a tough district of New York, Powell was one of a number of young men from the same neighbourhood who turned to music and enjoyed

distinguished careers (among others was **Benny Carter**). Taking up clarinet and alto saxophone, Powell worked extensively in the vibrant New York club scene of the late 20s and early 30s including stints with **Cliff Jackson**, **Rex Stewart**, **Red Allen** and, most notably, **Fats Waller**. In the late 30s and early 40s, Powell's skilful musicianship meant that he was in demand as a sideman in several big bands including those led by **Claude Hopkins**, **Fletcher Henderson** and **Don Redman**. In the late 40s he was with **Cab Calloway** and in the 50s and 60s he worked with several small groups and also with singers **Jimmy Rushing** and **Ray Charles**. In the mid-60s he played with the Saints And Sinners band and then played around his home town until the end of his life. An exciting, hot clarinet player, Powell's playing made a distinctive contribution to many Waller recordings.
Albums: with Fats Waller *My Very Good Friend The Milkman* (1935), *Saints And Sinners In Europe* (1968).

Powell, Seldon

b. 15 November 1928, Lawrenceville, Virginia, USA. Studying and working mostly in New York, tenor saxophonist Powell played and recorded extensively throughout the 50s. His musical associates were many and varied, including **Lucky Millinder**, **Sy Oliver**, **Neal Hefti**, **Johnny Richards**, Billy VerPlanck and **Benny Goodman**. Aided by his early training in classical music and his ability to play other instruments, especially the flute, Powell found work in the studios throughout the 60s and 70s. Nevertheless, he was active in jazz, recording with musicians such as **Buddy Rich**, **Louis Bellson**, **Richard 'Groove' Holmes**, **Gato Barbieri**, **Dizzy Gillespie** and **Anthony Braxton**. Powell's early training has allowed him to develop twin careers but within the framework of largely mainstream jazz he has established a sound reputation. As an improvisatory soloist, his work is perhaps less impressive than when he works within a tightly orchestrated framework where he excels.
Albums: *Seldon Powell Plays* (1955), *Seldon Powell Sextet* (1956), with Billy VerPlanck *Jazz For Play Girls* (1957), with others *We Paid Our Dues* (1961).

Powell, Teddy

b. 1 March 1906, Oakland, California, USA. As a boy Powell studied violin and music theory privately, then attended the San Francisco Conservatory of Music. In 1927 he was playing guitar and banjo with **Abe Lyman**'s band, staying with them until 1935 when he became a radio producer for an advertising agency. He also branched out as a songwriter, with hits such as 'Take Me Back To My Boots And Saddle', 'All I Need Is You', 'Snake Charmer' and 'March Winds And April Showers'. Royalties from these and other songs helped finance a big band in 1939, which included some key personnel from the **Tommy Dorsey** and **Benny Goodman** bands and had **Ray Conniff** contributing some arrangements. At first recording for **Decca**, some of the band's tracks appeared in the UK on **Brunswick** (Conniff's 'Feather Merchant's Ball'/'Teddy Bear Boogie' by Powell). After a year Powell moved to the Bluebird label, and Regal-Zonophone issued only four tracks in the UK: 'Straight Eight Boogi'/'Ode To Spring' and 'Sans Culottes'/'In Pinetops' Footsteps', all the work of new arranger Bob Mersey. The band opened at New York's Famous Door club to local acclaim but had less success further afield and, returning to Manhattan, Powell bought the club as a showcase for the group. It was a good, clean-sounding outfit with imaginative scores by Mersey and Conniff, and the leader maintained his policy of using jazzmen in key positions no matter how commercial the band's output. **Peggy Mann** and **Gene Barry** were the band's vocalists. After the swing era Powell adopted a more commercial policy for hotel work and eventually left the band business to return to songwriting and publishing.

Power

US quartet from New Jersey, New York, USA, built on the skills of Alan Tecchio (ex-Hades, Watchtower; vocals), Daniel Dalley (ex-solo; guitar), Mike Watt (drums) and Bill Krohn (bass). Watt had previously attended Boston's Berklee College Of Music, while acclaimed guitarist Dalley had released a solo instrumental album in 1989 as well as being a regular interviewee in musician's magazines.. However, frontman Tecchio was the best known member, in addition to his previous activities being concurrently part of Non-Fiction. Power signed to European label Rock The Nation Records for the release of *Justice Of Fire* in 1994, which typically addressed its thematic constructs against a background of riffing and power surges.
Album: *Justice Of Fire* (RTN 1994).

Power Station

This commercial rock band started out as a Tony Thompson (ex-**Patti LaBelle** and **Chic**; drums) solo project, but came to be viewed as a spin-off from **Duran Duran**. Andy Taylor (b. 16 February 1961, Cullercoats, Newcastle-upon-Tyne, England; guitar) saw it as a cross between Chic and the **Sex Pistols**, and was joined by fellow Duran Duran member John Taylor (b. 20 June 1960, Birmingham, England; bass) and vocalist **Robert Palmer** (b. 19 January 1949, Batley, Yorks, England). Thompson's Chic partner Bernie Edwards (b. 31 October 1952, Greenville, North Carolina, US) handled production duties. Palmer had previously met the Duran Duran members at a MENCAP charity concert. They hit almost immediately with 'Some Like It Hot' and a cover of **T. Rex**'s 'Get It On'. Both tracks reached the US Top 10.

Then, after a subsequent minor hit with 'Communication' marking their third success of 1985, they split. Their single album was recorded at the Power Station Studio in New York, from which they took their name. Palmer did not want to tour so he was replaced by former Silverhead and Detective vocalist **Michael Des Barres**. Following the band's quick exit John Taylor would return to Duran Duran while his namesake Andy went on to a solo career. He invited **Steve Jones** to guest on his debut solo album, fulfilling the prophecy of his stated ambition that Power Station should fuse the Sex Pistols and Chic by eventually working with members of both.
Album: *The Power Station* (1985).

Power, Duffy

Power was one of several British vocalists, including **Marty Wilde**, **Billy Fury** and **Dickie Pride**, signed to the **Larry Parnes** stable. Having completed a series of pop singles, including 'Dream Lover' and 'Ain't She Sweet', the singer embraced R&B in 1963 with a pulsating version of the **Beatles**' 'I Saw Her Standing There' on which he was backed by the **Graham Bond** Quartet. Power's later singles included 'Tired, Broke and Busted', which featured support from the **Paramounts**, but he later supplemented his solo career by joining **Alexis Korner**'s Blues Incorporated. The singer appeared on *Red Hot From Alex* (1964), *Sky High* (1966) and *Blues Incorporated* (1967), during which time group members **Jack Bruce** (bass), **Danny Thompson** (bass) and Terry Cox (drums) assisted on several informal sessions later compiled on Power's *Innovations* set. Guitarist **John McLaughlin** also contributed to the album, before joined the vocalist's next project, Duffy's Nucleus. Power resumed his solo career late in 1967 when this short-lived attraction disbanded, but an ensuing fitful recording schedule did little justice to this under-rated artist's potential.
Albums: *Innovations* aka *Mary Open The Door* (1970), *Little Boy Blue* (1971), *Duffy Power* (1973), *Powerhouse* (1976). Compilation: *Blues Power* (1992).

Powers, Joey

b. 1939, Canonsburg, Pennsylvania, USA. Powers reached the charts once with the singalong folkish tune 'Midnight Mary'. His family knew singing star **Perry Como**, who secured a job for Powers on a television keep-fit, exercise programme. Powers then taught wrestling at a university for a short time. By 1962, he was signed to **RCA Records**, the label for which Como recorded, but none of the songs he released became hits. The following year Powers met songwriters Artie Wayne and Ben Raleigh and they worked on their song 'Midnight Mary' together. Released on Amy Records in January 1964, the single peaked at number 10, just in time to see Powers' career cut short by the onslaught of 'Beatlemania'. All of his subsequent recordings failed to chart and he never made an album.

Pozo, Chano

b. Luciano Pozo y Gonzales, 7 June 1915, Havana, Cuba, d. 2 December 1948, New York, USA. Drummer and vocalist Pozo's first appearance in the USA was at a Carnegie Hall concert in September 1947, at which he played with **Dizzy Gillespie**. Thereafter he worked regularly with Gillespie, making a number of records which were enormously influential on many jazzmen who responded to the intriguing Latin-American rhythms he used. In December 1948, before the two men could fully exploit what was clearly a potentially exciting musical relationship, Pozo was murdered, shot in a Harlem bar.
Selected compilations: all with Dizzy Gillespie *Dizzy Gillespie Big Band* (1947-49 recordings), *Afro Cuban Suite* (1948 recordings), *Melodic Revolution* (1948 recordings), with Arsenio Rodriguez, Machito *Legendary Sessions* (Fresh Sounds 1993).

Prado, Perez

b. Damaso Perez Prado, 11 December 1916, Mantanzas, Cuba, d. 14 September 1989, Mexico City, Mexico. Prado played organ and piano in cinemas and clubs before becoming an arranger for the mambo-style local bands in 1942. He formed his own unit in 1948 in Mexico when the mambo beat was becoming very popular. Prado was 'King of the Mambo' in Latin America with his scorching brass and persuasive percussion, exemplified in his 1950 recording of 'Mambo Jambo'. He had some modest US success in 1953-54 with the title theme from the Italian movie *Anne*, and a South African song 'Skokiaan'. Strong indications that the mambo craze was beginning to catch on in the USA came in 1954, when **Perry Como** with 'Papa Loves Mambo', and 'Mambo Italiano' by **Rosemary Clooney**, reached the Top 10. Prado made his world-wide breakthrough in 1955 when **RCA Records** released 'Cherry Pink And Apple Blossom White', with an exciting trumpet solo by Billy Regis. It stayed at number 1 in the US charts for 10 weeks and was featured in the Jane Russell/Richard Egan film *Underwater!* (1955). In Britain, **Eddie Calvert** and the **Ted Heath** orchestra had their own best-selling versions. Prado's follow-up in 1958 was another instrumental, his own composition 'Patricia'. Another chart topper, it contained more than a hint of the current burgeoning pop sounds with its heavy bass and rocking organ rhythms, along with the cha-cha-cha beat, and was used by Federico Fellini as the theme song for the movie *La Dolce Vita* in 1960. By then Prado was out of the limelight, but in 1981 he featured in a musical revue entitled *Sun*, which enjoyed a long run in Mexico City. Persistent ill health led to the amputation

of one leg, and he eventually died from a stroke in 1989. Six years later, Prado just failed to reach the top of the UK chart with the exciting 'Guaglione', following it's use in a Guinness beer television commercial.
Selected albums: *'Prez'* (1959), *A Cat In Latin* (1964). Compilations: *Perez Prado* (1979), *Perez Prado And Orchestra* (1988), *Guantanamera* (1989), *Go Go Mambo* (1993).

Praga Khan

Comprising Jade 4U (b. Nikki Danlierop, Belgium) and Maurice Engelen (b. c.1974, Belguim), the latter an 80s DJ and 'New Beat' pioneer, by 1993 Praga Khan had sold over half a million records together under various guises, such as Lords Of Acid, Channel X, Digital Orgasm and Jade 4U solo. Danlierop was certainly a vivacious character, she had apparently been 'sacked' from the band at one stage for 'biting' her partner on stage, due to over-excitement. As Praga Khan they had enjoyed a 1991 rave hit with 'Injected With A Poison', which cased a furore when it entered the Top 20 due to perceived drug connotations. It went to number 1 in Japan. In the USA they were signed to Rick Rubin's **Def Jam** on a five album contract, where Rubin hoped to market them as his 'next big thing'. On the commercial breakthrough of their music they commented: 'We have to see techno/rave for what it is, as the rock 'n' roll of the 90s'.
Albums: as Digital Orgasm *Come Dancin'* (Dead Dead Good 1992), *Spoon Full Of Miracle* (Profile 1993).

Prairie Ramblers

The group was originally formed as the Kentucky Ramblers by Charles 'Chick' Hurt (b. 1901, d. 1967; mandolin) and 'Happy' Jack Taylor (b. c.1900, d. 1962; tenor banjo). Both men were born in the Summershade area, near Glasgow, Kentucky, USA. Hurt moved to Kewanne, Illinois, when a young man and there organized his first band, but a few years later was reunited with Taylor, his childhood friend. They joined forces with Shelby David 'Tex' Atchison (b. 1912; fiddle/lead vocals) and Floyd 'Salty' Holmes (guitar/harmonica/jug player), both being born near Rosine, Ohio County, Kentucky, USA. (Atchison was actually born on the farm adjoining that of **Bill Monroe**'s father). In 1932, they made their radio debut on WOC Davenport, Iowa and later the same year, they moved to WLS Chicago, first working on the *Merry-Go-Round* and then the *National Barn Dance*. In June 1933, they joined forces with **Patsy Montana**, who recorded with them when they made their first recordings for **RCA**-Victor's Bluebird label in December that year. By this time, with the growing interest in cowboy songs and music, the band had become the Prairie Ramblers. In 1934, they spent six months at WOR New York and returned to WLS specializing more in pop-styled cowboy songs and swing music. They emphasized the cowboy image, appeared at venues on horseback and western dress, even using the **Gene Autry** song, 'Ridin' Down The Canyon', as their signature tune.
They joined ARC records and by the end of 1936, they had recorded over 100 sides for that label. Their repertoire covered a wide variety of songs including gospel numbers like 'How Beautiful Heaven Must Be' but in 1935, they were persuaded to record some numbers that were somewhat *risqué*. Hurt was not keen and to change their overall sound, they added the clarinet and vocals of Bill Thawl and recorded them under the name of the Sweet Violet Boys, although it was an open secret whom the band really were. Some of the songs were written by Bob Miller (he also played piano on many of the Ramblers' recordings), who sought anonymity by copywriting them under the rather poorly camouflaged pseudonym of Trebor Rellim. Amongst the songs were numbers such as 'There's A Man Who Comes To Our House Every Single Day (Poppa Comes Home And The Man Goes Away)', 'Jim's Windy Mule' and 'I Love My Fruit' - a song that has been suggested as being the first gay hillbilly song. (It seems that they made the young Patsy Montana leave the studio when this material was being recorded.) Atchison and Holmes left in 1938 and were replaced by fiddler Alan Crockett and guitarist/vocalist Kenneth Houchens. In the early 1940s, they added the accordion of Augie Kline and electric guitarist George Barnes. Patsy Montana left around 1941 to pursue her solo career. The Ramblers appeared in various films, some with Gene Autry and also later recorded with **Rex Allen**. They made their final recordings for **Mercury Records** in December 1947, by which time their material was no longer of any specific type. At the time when they left WLS and disbanded in 1948, one of their songs was 'You Ain't Got No Hillbilly Anymore' - a fact many people agreed with. Hurt and Taylor continued to work around the Chicago area as a duo for a time until they eventually retired.
Compilations: *Tex's Dance* (1982), *Patsy Montana And The Prairie Ramblers* (1984), *Sing It Fast And Hot* (1989).

Praying Mantis

Formed in London, England, in 1977, Praying Mantis were at the forefront of the **New Wave Of British Heavy Metal**. The original line-up consisted of Tino 'Troy' Neophytou (guitar/vocals), Robert Angelo (guitar), Tino's brother Chris 'Troy' Neophytou (bass/vocals) and Mick Ransome (drums). Through early demo recordings the band attracted the attention of heavy metal club DJ Neal Kay, who helped them release an independent three-track EP, *The Soundhouse Tapes Vol. 2*, a title also used by **Iron Maiden** for their first release. The band's career can be closely linked with Iron Maiden during those early years as in

addition to both bands appearing on the *Metal For Muthas* compilation released by **EMI Records** in 1980, they also toured England together. Signing to **Arista Records** and replacing Robert Angelo (who joined **Weapon** in July 1981) and Mick Ransome with guitarist/vocalist Steve Carroll and ex-**Ten Years After** drummer Dave Potts, the band's debut, *Time Tells No Lies*, was released in 1981. It was not well received due to the lacklustre production and basic melodic rock sound. The band decided a line-up change was needed, replacing the departed Steve Carroll with ex-**Grand Prix** vocalist Bernie Shaw, and they also recruited keyboard player Jon Bavin. This line-up went on to record 'Turn The Tables' for a compilation album released on the Yet Records label in the mid-80s. Through a lack of media interest the band metamorphosised into **Stratus**, who specialized in standard melodic rock and also featured ex-Iron Maiden drummer Clive Burr. To celebrate the 10th anniversary of the N.W.O.B.H.M. the band reformed early in 1990 to tour Japan as part of the British All Stars. This new line-up consisted of founder members Tino and Chris Troy, ex-Iron Maiden vocalist **Paul Di'anno**, ex-Iron Maiden guitarist Dennis Stratton and ex-Weapon drummer Bruce Bisland.
Albums: *Time Tells No Lies* (Arista 1981), *Predator In Disguise* (1993).

Preager, Lou

b. 12 January 1906, London, England, d. 14 November 1978, Majorca, Spain. A pianist, accordionist, and the leader of a fine, swinging dance band for more than 30 years, Preager was playing piano in various outfits while still at school. After working at various jobs, he became a full time musician in his teens, and in the late 20s toured extensively abroad, and formed bands to play at smart London clubs and restaurants, including Ciro's, the Bon Viveur, Romano's and the Monseigneur. Several of these ensembles were led or co-led by others such as violinist Eugene Pina and accordionist and composer **Billy Reid**. Preager's signature tune around this time was 'Let's All Go Down The Strand', and his first recordings to be released were made early in 1935. During World War II, Preager served in the Intelligence Corps but was invalided out in January 1942 following an accident in which he seriously damaged his right arm. A few months later, he began his association with the Hammersmith Palais, one of the largest dancehalls in the UK, where he led the resident band for some 18 years. In the late 40s he featured the highly popular songwriting contest Write A Tune For £1000, which was broadcast by the BBC, and produced several agreeable songs, including the hit 'Cruising Down The River', written by two amateurs, Eily Beadell and Nell Tollerton. In the late 50s Preager ran the successful television competition *Find A Singer*, in which all the winners received a recording contract. After leaving the Palais in 1959, Preager suffered from persistent ill-health, and eventually retired in 1967. During his long and busy career, he won several honours, including three Carl Alan Awards for the best palais band. Over the years, many of Britain's up-and-coming musicians, such as **Don Lusher** and Johnny Gray, played with his bands, and his numerous vocalists included Paul Rich, Edna Kaye, Rita Williams, Steve Martin, **Elisabeth Welch**, Paula Green, Ann Lenner, Judy Shirley, Eileen Orchard, Ken Barry, Helen Clare and many more. Preager was also a shrewd businessman, with interests in book publishing, television, records and film production, and entertainment agencies.
Selected album: *On The Sunny Side Of The Street* (President).

Precious Metal

This US glam-metal rock group were formed in Los Angeles, California, in the mid-80s. They came to the public's attention via their 1985 debut, *Right Here, Right Now*, which was produced by AOR producer and guitar-hero, **Paul Sabu**. An all-female outfit, they featured Leslie Wasser (vocals), Janet Robin (guitar), Mara Fox (guitar), Alex Rylance (bass) and Carol Control (drums). Unfairly categorized alongside 70s female outfit the **Runaways**, Precious Metal set about forging an original style. They were hampered in this by the inability of the hard rock press to critically engage with female bands above and beyond obvious comparisons and cosmetic factors. Their second and third album releases demonstrated that, at the very least, there was more potential at work than they were being given credit for.
Albums: *Right Here, Right Now* (Polygram 1985), *That Kind Of Girl* (Chameleon 1988), *Precious Metal* (Chameleon 1990).

Prefab Sprout

The intricate tales and thoughts in the lyrics of songwriter Paddy McAloon indicate a major songwriter. His **Bob Dylan** imagery and **Elvis Costello** bluntness have made Prefab Sprout one of the most refreshing pop bands of the late 80s and beyond. The band was formed in 1982 and comprised: Paddy McAloon (b. 7 June 1957, Durham, England; guitar/vocals), Martin McAloon (b. 4 January 1962, Durham, England; bass), Wendy Smith (b. 31 May 1963, Durham, England; vocals/guitar) and Neil Conti (b. 12 February 1959, London, England). Following a self-pressed single 'Lions In My Own Garden', Paddy attracted the attention of the independent label Kitchenware. They had further hits in the UK independent charts and their debut *Swoon* made the national chart. *Swoon* was a wordy album featuring songs with many chord changes that ultimately concentrated on lyrics rather than melody. Later that year the excellent 'When Love Breaks Down' failed to excite the single-buying public. A remixed version by **Thomas Dolby** was released the following year, but once again it failed. When *Steve McQueen* was issued in 1985 the band became media darlings, with Paddy McAloon coming near to over-exposure. The album was a critics' favourite and displayed hummable songs with fascinating lyrics, and it made a respectable showing in the charts. At the end of the year 'When Love Breaks Down' was issued for a third time and finally became a hit.

In the USA, *Steve McQueen* was forcibly retitled *Two Wheels Good.* A striking work, the album included a tribute to **Faron Young** and the arresting 'Goodbye Lucille # 1' (aka 'Johnny Johnny'). *From Langley Park To Memphis* in 1988 was a major success world-wide; Paddy had now refined his art to produce totally accessible yet inventive pop music. The album represented a courageous change of direction with McAloon employing strings and composing melodies which recalled the great show musical writers of the pre-rock 'n' roll era. 'Nightingales' was very much in this vein, and the work ended with the strikingly melodramatic 'Nancy (Let Your Hair Down For Me)' and 'The Venus Of The Soup Kitchen'. Already the band had reached the stage of having superstar guests 'turning up on the album'. Both **Stevie Wonder** (harmonica solo on 'Nightingales') and **Pete Townshend** put in appearances. 'The King Of Rock 'N' Roll' became their biggest hit to date. *Protest Songs* was a collection scheduled to appear before their previous album and its success was muted by the continuing sales of both *Steve McQueen* and *From Langley Park To Memphis.* McAloon unleashed *Jordan: The Comeback* in 1990, and for many critics it was the album of the year. All McAloon's talents had combined to produce a concept album of magnificence. Over 64 minutes in length, the album boasted 19 tracks, full of striking melodies and fascinatingly oblique lyrics. The ghost of **Elvis Presley** haunted several of the songs, most notably the elegiac 'Moon Dog'. McAloon has so far failed to make any attempt in the 90s of his early potential. Their future seems uncertain.

Albums: *Swoon* (1984), *Steve McQueen* (1985), *From Langley Park To Memphis* (1988), *Protest Songs* (1989), *Jordan: The Comeback* (1990). Compilation: *A Life Of Surprises: The Best Of* (1992).

Further reading: *Myths, Melodies & Metaphysics, Paddy McAloon's Prefab Sprout,* John Birch.

Prelude

A light UK folk trio formed in 1970, when Irene Hume (b. Irene Marshall, 5 August 1948, Gateshead, Tyne And Wear, England; vocals/percussion) began singing with her husband Brian Hume (b. 21 June 1947, Gateshead, Tyne And Wear, England; guitar/vocals), and Ian Vardy (b. 21 March 1947, Gateshead, Tyne And Wear, England; guitar/vocals). They began to write their own material and built a following on the folk circuit. *How Long Is Forever?* was recorded at Rockfield studios in Wales, and it was from this release that the cover of **Neil Young**'s 'After The Goldrush' was taken. This single reached number 21 in the UK charts in January 1974 - and when re-issued eight years later got to number 28. Their first nationwide tour followed, with **Michael Chapman**. 'After The Goldrush' also charted in the US peaking at number 22, and the group subsequently toured the USA. They then toured the UK supporting artists such as **Ralph McTell** and **Joan Armatrading**. 'Platinum Blonde' reached number 45 in the UK charts in 1980, and in the same year the group made a comeback with *Prelude.* In 1981 they toured the UK with **Don McLean**. Apart from the release of 'Only The Lonely', which climbed to number 55 in the UK charts in 1982, the next few years were spent touring and recording, but nothing was released, and Vardy left the band in 1985. Irene and Brian continued as a duo until 1987, when they were joined by Jim Hornsby (guitar/dobro). By 1993, Hornsby had left and Prelude continued as a duo once more, still writing and performing on the folk circuit.

Albums: *How Long Is Forever?* (1973), *Dutch Courage* (1975), *Owl Creek Incident* (1976), *Back Into The Light* (1977), *Prelude* (1980).

Premiers

This Hispanic rock 'n' roll band originated from San Gabriel, California, USA. The members were George Delgado (guitar), Larry Perez (guitar), Phil Ruiz (saxophone), Joe Urzua (saxophone), Frank Zuniga (bass) and Johnny Perez (drums). They had only one hit, 'Farmer John', which went to number 19 in the US pop chart in 1964. The song, a remake of a **Don And Dewey** song, was recorded in a studio but crowd noises were added to give an impression that it was a live recording. On their only album the claim is made that the song and the album were recorded live at the Rhythm Room in Fullerton, California. 'Annie Oakley', the band's follow-up, failed to chart, and for the remainder of the decade the Premiers continued to record local records for the southern California Hispanic constituency.

Album: *Farmer John* (Warners 1964).

Presley, Elvis

b. Elvis Aaron Presley, 8 January 1935, Tupelo, Mississippi, USA, d. 16 August 1977, Memphis, Tennessee. The most celebrated popular music phenomenon of his era and, for many, the purest embodiment of rock 'n' roll, Elvis's life and career have become part of rock legend. The elder of twins, his younger brother, Jesse Garon, was stillborn, a tragedy which partly contributed to the maternal solicitude that affected his childhood and teenage years. Presley's first significant step towards a musical career took place at the age of eight when he won $5.00 in a local song contest performing the lachrymose **Red Foley** ballad, 'Old Shep'. His earliest musical influence came from attending the Pentecostal Church and listening to the psalms and gospel songs. He also had a strong grounding in country and blues and it was the combination of these different styles that was to provide his unique musical identity.

By the age of 13, Presley had moved with his family to Memphis and during his later school years began cultivating an outsider image with long hair, spidery sideburns and ostentatious clothes. After leaving school he took a job as a truck driver, a role in keeping with his unconventional appearance. In spite of his rebel posturing, Elvis remained studiously polite to his elders and was devoted to his mother. Indeed, it was his filial affection that first prompted him to visit **Sun Records**, whose studios offered the sophisticated equivalent of a fairground recording booth service. As a birthday present to his mother, Gladys, Elvis cut a version of the **Ink Spots**' 'My Happiness', backed with the Raskin/Brown/Fisher standard 'That's When Your Heartaches Begin'. The studio manager, Marion Keisker, noted Presley's unusual but distinctive vocal style and informed Sun's owner/producer **Sam Phillips** of his potential. Phillips nurtured the boy for almost a year before putting him together with country guitarist **Scotty Moore** and bassist **Bill Black**. Their early sessions showed considerable promise, especially when Presley began alternating his unorthodox low-key delivery with a high-pitched whine. The amplified guitars of Moore and Black contributed strongly to the effect and convinced Phillips that the singer was startlingly original. In Presley, Sam saw something that he had long dreamed of discovering: a white boy who sang like a negro.

Presley's debut disc on Sun was the extraordinary 'That's All Right (Mama)', a showcase for his rich, multi-textured vocal dexterity, with sharp, solid backing from his compatriots. The b-side, 'Blue Moon Of Kentucky', was a country song but the arrangement showed that Presley was threatening to slip into an entirely different genre, closer to R&B. Local response to these strange-sounding performances was encouraging and Phillips eventually shifted 20,000 copies of the disc. For his second single, Presley cut **Roy Brown**'s 'Good Rockin' Tonight' backed by the zingy 'I Don't Care If The Sun Don't Shine'. The more roots-influenced 'Milkcow Blues Boogie' followed, while the b-side 'You're A Heartbreaker' had some strong tempo changes which neatly complemented Presley's quirky vocal. 'Baby Let's Play House'/'I'm Left, You're Right, She's Gone' continued the momentum and led to Presley performing on the *Grand Old Opry* and *Louisiana Hayride* radio programmes. A series of live dates commenced in 1955 with drummer D.J. Fontana added to the ranks. Presley toured clubs in Arkansas, Louisiana and Texas billed as 'The King Of Western Bop' and 'The Hillbilly Cat'. Audience reaction verged on the fanatical, which was hardly surprising given Presley's semi-erotic performances. His hip-swivelling routine, in which he cascaded across the stage and plunged to his knees at dramatic moments in a song, was remarkable for the period and prompted near-riotous fan mania. The final Sun single, a cover of **Junior Parker**'s 'Mystery Train', was later acclaimed by many as the definitive rock 'n' roll single with its chugging rhythm, soaring vocal and enticing lead guitar breaks. It established Presley as an artist worthy of national attention and ushered in the next phase of his career, which was dominated by the imposing figure of **Colonel Tom Parker**.

The Colonel was a former fairground huckster who managed several country artists including **Hank Snow** and **Eddy Arnold**. After relieving disc jockey Bob Neal of Presley's managership, Parker persuaded Sam Phillips that his financial interests would be better served by releasing the boy to a major label. **RCA Records** had already noted the commercial potential of the phenomenon under offer and agreed to pay Sun Records a release fee of $35,000, an incredible sum for the period. The sheer diversity of Presley's musical heritage and his remarkable ability as a vocalist and interpreter of material enabled him to escape the cultural parochialism of his R&B-influenced predecessors. The attendant rock 'n' roll explosion, in which Presley was both a creator and participant, ensured that he could reach a mass audience, many of them newly-affluent teenagers.

It was on 10 January 1956, a mere two days after his 21st birthday, that Elvis entered RCA's studios in Nashville to record his first tracks for a major label. His debut session produced the epochal 'Heartbreak Hotel', one of the most striking pop records ever released. Co-composed by **Hoyt Axton**'s mother Mae, the song evoked nothing less than a vision of absolute funereal despair. There was nothing in the pop charts of the period that even hinted at the degree of desolation described in the song. Presley's reading was extraordinarily mature and moving, with a determined avoidance of any histrionics in favour of a pained and resigned acceptance of loneliness as death. The economical yet acutely emphatic piano work of **Floyd Cramer** enhanced the stark mood of the piece, which was frozen in a suitably minimalist production. The startling originality and intensity of 'Heartbreak Hotel' entranced the American public and pushed the single to number 1 for an astonishing eight weeks. Whatever else he achieved, Presley was already assured a place in pop history for one of the greatest major label debut records ever released. During the same month that 'Heartbreak Hotel' was recorded, Presley made his national television debut displaying his sexually-enticing gyrations before a bewildered adult audience whose alleged outrage subsequently persuaded producers to film the star exclusively from the waist upwards. Having outsold his former Sun colleague **Carl Perkins** with 'Blue Suede Shoes', Presley released a debut album which contained several of the songs he had previously cut with Sam Phillips, including **Little Richard**'s 'Tutti Fruitti', the R&B classic 'I Got A Woman' and an eerie, wailing version of **Richard Rodgers/Lorenz Hart**'s 'Blue Moon', which emphasized his remarkable vocal range.

Since hitting number 2 in the UK lists with 'Heartbreak Hotel', Presley had been virtually guaranteed European success and his profile was increased via a regular series of releases as RCA took full advantage of their bulging back catalogue. Although there was a danger of overkill, Presley's talent, reputation and immensely strong fan base vindicated the intense release schedule and the quality of the material ensured that the public was not disappointed. After hitting number 1 for the second time with the slight ballad 'I Want You, I Need You, I Love You', Presley released what was to become the most commercially successful double-sided single in pop history, 'Hound Dog'/'Don't Be Cruel'. The former was composed by the immortal rock 'n' roll songwriting team of **Leiber And Stoller**, and presented Presley at his upbeat best with a novel lyric, complete with a striking guitar solo and spirited handclapping from his backing group the **Jordanaires**. **Otis Blackwell**'s 'Don't Be Cruel' was equally effective with a striking melody line and some clever and amusing vocal gymnastics from the hiccupping King of Western Bop, who also received a co-writing credit. The single remained at number 1 in the USA for a staggering 11 weeks and both sides of the record were massive hits in the UK.

Celluloid fame for Presley next beckoned with *Love Me Tender*, produced by David Weisbert, who had previously worked on James Dean's *Rebel Without A Cause.* Elvis's movie debut received mixed reviews but was a box office smash, while the smouldering, perfectly-enunciated title track topped the US charts for five weeks. The spate of Presley singles continued in earnest through 1957 and one of the biggest was another Otis Blackwell composition, 'All Shook Up' which the singer used as a cheekily oblique comment on his by now legendary dance movements. By late 1956 it was rumoured that Presley would be drafted into the US Army and, as if to compensate for that irksome eventuality, RCA, Twentieth Century Fox and the Colonel stepped up the work-rate and release schedules. Incredibly, three major films were completed in the next two-and-a-half years. *Loving You* boasted a quasi-autobiographical script with Presley playing a truck driver who becomes a pop star. The title track became the b-side of '(Let Me Be Your) Teddy Bear' which reigned at number 1 for seven weeks. The third movie, ***Jailhouse Rock***, was Elvis's most successful to date with an excellent soundtrack and some inspired choreography. The Leiber and Stoller title track was an instant classic which again topped the US charts for seven weeks and made pop history by entering the UK listings at number 1. The fourth celluloid outing, ***King Creole*** (adapted from the Harold Robbins' novel, *A Stone For Danny Fisher*) is regarded by many as Presley's finest film of all and a firm indicator of his sadly unfulfilled potential as a serious actor. Once more the soundtrack album featured some surprisingly strong material such as the haunting 'Crawfish' and the vibrant 'Dixieland Rock'.

By the time *King Creole* was released in 1958, Elvis had already been inducted into the US Forces. A publicity photograph of the singer having his hair shorn symbolically commented on his approaching musical emasculation. Although rock 'n' roll purists mourned the passing of the old Elvis, it seemed inevitable in the context of the 50s that he would move towards a broader base appeal and tone down his rebellious image. From 1958-60, Presley served in the US Armed Forces, spending much of his time in Germany where he was regarded as a model soldier. It was during this period that he first met 14-year-old Priscilla Beaulieu, whom he would later marry in 1967. Back in America, the Colonel kept his absent star's reputation intact via a series of films, record releases and extensive merchandising. Hits such as 'Wear My Ring Around Your Neck', 'Hard Headed Woman', 'One Night', 'I Got Stung', 'A Fool Such As I' and 'A Big Hunk O' Love' filled the long two-year gap and by the time Elvis reappeared, he was ready to assume the mantle of an all-round entertainer. The change was immediately evident in the series of number 1 hits that he enjoyed in the early 60s. The enormously successful 'It's Now Or Never', based on the Italian melody 'O Sole Mio', revealed the King as an operatic crooner, far removed from his earlier raucous recordings. 'Are You Lonesome Tonight?', originally recorded by **Al Jolson** as early as 1927, allowed Presley to quote some Shakespeare in the spoken-word middle section as well as showing his ham-acting ability with an overwrought vocal. The new clean-cut Presley was presented on celluloid in *GI Blues.* The movie played upon his recent Army exploits and saw him serenading a puppet on the charming chart-topper 'Wooden Heart', which also allowed Elvis to show off his knowledge of German. The grandiose 'Surrender' completed this phase of big ballads in the old-fashioned style. For the next few years Presley concentrated on an undemanding spree of films including *Flaming Star*, *Wild In The Country*, *Blue Hawaii*, *Kid Galahad*, *Girls! Girls! Girls!*, *Follow That Dream*, *Fun In Acapulco*, *It Happened At The World's Fair*, *Kissin' Cousins*, *Viva Las Vegas*, *Roustabout*, *Girl Happy*, *Tickle Me*,

Harem Scarem, *Frankie And Johnny*, *Paradise Hawaiian Style* and *Spinout*. Not surprisingly, most of his album recordings were hastily completed soundtracks with unadventurous commissioned songs. For his singles he relied increasingly on the formidable **Doc Pomus/Mort Shuman** team who composed such hits as 'Mess Of Blues', 'Little Sister' and 'His Latest Flame'. More and more, however, the hits were adapted from films and their chart positions suffered accordingly. After the 1963 number 1 'Devil In Disguise', a bleak period followed in which such minor songs as 'Bossa Nova Baby', 'Kiss Me Quick', 'Ain't That Lovin' You Baby' and 'Blue Christmas' became the rule rather than the exception. Significantly, his biggest success of the mid-60s, 'Crying In The Chapel', had been recorded five years before, and part of its appeal came from the realization that it represented something ineffably lost.

In the wake of the **Beatles**' rise to fame and the beat boom explosion Presley seemed a figure out of time. Yet, in spite of the dated nature of many of his recordings, he could still invest power and emotion into classic songs. The sassy 'Frankie And Johnny' was expertly sung by Elvis as was his moving reading of **Ketty Lester**'s 'Love Letters'. His other significant 1966 release, 'If Everyday Was Like Christmas', was a beautiful festive song unlike anything else in the charts of the period. By 1967, however, it was clear to critics and even a large proportion of his devoted following that Presley had seriously lost his way. He continued to grind out pointless movies such as *Double Trouble*, *Speedway*, *Clambake* and *Live A Little, Love A Little*, even though the box office returns were increasingly poor. His capacity to register instant hits, irrespective of the material was also wearing thin as such lowly-placed singles as 'You Gotta Stop' and 'Long Legged Woman' demonstrated all too alarmingly. However, just as Elvis's career had reached its all-time nadir he seemed to wake up, take stock, and break free from the artistic malaise in which he found himself.

Two songs written by country guitarist **Jerry Reed**, 'Guitar Man' and 'US Male', proved a spectacular return to form for Elvis in 1968, such was Presley's conviction that the compositions almost seemed to be written specifically for him. During the same year Colonel Tom Parker had approached NBC-TV about the possibility of recording a Presley Christmas special in which the singer would perform a selection of religious songs similar in feel to his early 60s album *His Hand In Mine*. However, the executive producers of the show vetoed that concept in favour of a one-hour spectacular designed to capture Elvis at his rock 'n' rollin' best. It was a remarkable challenge for the singer, seemingly in the autumn of his career, and he responded to the idea with unexpected enthusiasm. The *Elvis TV Special* was broadcast in America on 3 December 1968 and has since gone down as one of the most celebrated moments in pop broadcasting history. The show was not merely good but an absolute revelation, with the King emerging as if he had been frozen in time for 10 years. His determination to recapture past glories oozed from every movement and was discernible in every aside. With his leather jacket and acoustic guitar strung casually round his neck, he resembled nothing less than the consummate pop idol of the 50s who had entranced a generation. To add authenticity to the proceedings he was accompanied by his old sidekicks Scotty Moore and D.J. Fontana. There was no sense of self-parody in the show as Presley joked about his famous surly curled-lip movement and even heaped passing ridicule on his endless stream of bad movies. The music concentrated heavily on his 50s classics but, significantly, there was a startling finale courtesy of the passionate 'If I Can Dream' in which he seemed to sum up the frustration of a decade in a few short lines.

The critical plaudits heaped upon Elvis in the wake of his television special prompted the singer to undertake his most significant recordings in years. With producer Chips Moman overseeing the sessions in January 1969, Presley recorded enough material to cover two highly-praised albums, *From Elvis In Memphis* and *From Memphis To Vegas/From Vegas To Memphis*. The former was particularly strong with such distinctive tracks as the eerie 'Long Black Limousine' and the engagingly melodic 'Any Day Now'. On the singles front, Presley was back in top form and finally coming to terms with contemporary issues, most notably on the socially aware 'In The Ghetto' which hit number 2 in the UK and number 3 in the USA. The glorious 'Suspicious Minds', a wonderful song of marital jealously with cascading tempo changes and an exceptional vocal arrangement, gave him his first US chart-topper since 'Good Luck Charm' back in 1962. Subsequent hits such as the maudlin 'Don't Cry Daddy', which dealt with the death of a marriage, ably demonstrated Elvis's ability to read a song. Even his final few films seemed less disastrous than expected. In 1969's *Charro*, he grew a beard for the first time in his portrayal of a moody cowboy, while *A Change Of Habit* dealt with more serious matter than usual. More importantly, Presley returned as a live performer at Las Vegas with a strong backing group including guitarist **James Burton** and pianist Glen D. Hardin. In common with **John Lennon**, who also returned to the stage that same year with the **Plastic Ono Band**, Presley opened his set with Carl Perkins' 'Blue Suede Shoes'. His comeback was well-received and one of the live songs, 'The Wonder Of You', stayed at number 1 in Britain for six weeks during the summer of 1970. There was also a revealing documentary film of the tour Elvis - *That's The Way It Is* and a companion album which included contemporary cover songs such as **Tony Joe White**'s 'Polk Salad Annie', **Creedence Clearwater Revival**'s 'Proud

Mary' and **Neil Diamond**'s 'Sweet Caroline'.

During the early 70s Presley continued his live performances, but soon fell victim to the same artistic atrophy that had bedevilled his celluloid career. Rather than re-entering the studio to record fresh material he relied on a slew of patchy live albums which saturated the marketplace. What had been innovative and exciting in 1969 swiftly became a tedious routine and an exercise in misdirected potential. The backdrop to Presley's final years was a sordid slump into drug dependency, reinforced by the pervasive unreality of a pampered lifestyle in his fantasy home, Graceland. The dissolution of his marriage in 1973 coincided with a further decline and an alarming tendency to put on weight. Remarkably, he continued to undertake live appearances, covering up his bloated frame with brightly coloured jump suits and an enormous, ostentatiously-jewelled belt. He collapsed onstage on a couple of occasions and finally on 16 August 1977 his tired, burnt-out body expired. The official cause of death was a heart attack, no doubt brought on by barbiturate usage over a long period. In the weeks following his demise, his record sales predictably rocketed and 'Way Down' proved a fittingly final UK number 1.

The importance of Presley in the history of rock 'n' roll and popular music remains incalculable. In spite of his iconographic status, the Elvis image was never captured in a single moment of time like that of **Bill Haley**, **Buddy Holly** or even **Chuck Berry**. Presley, in spite of his apparent creative inertia, was not a one-dimensional artist clinging to history but a multi-faceted performer whose career spanned several decades and phases. For purists and rockabilly enthusiasts it is the early Elvis who remains of greatest importance and there is no doubting that his personal fusion of black and white musical influences, incorporating R&B and country, produced some of the finest and most durable recordings of the century. Beyond Elvis 'The Hillbilly Cat', however, there was the face that launched a thousand imitators, that black-haired, smiling or smouldering presence who stared from the front covers of numerous EPs, albums and film posters of the late 50s and early 60s. It was that well-groomed, immaculate pop star who inspired a generation of performers and second-rate imitators in the 60s. There was also Elvis the Las Vegas performer, vibrant and vulgar, yet still distant and increasingly appealing to a later generation brought up on the excesses of 70s rock and glam ephemera. Finally, there was the bloated Presley who bestrode the stage in the last months of his career. For many, he has come to symbolize the decadence and loss of dignity that is all too often heir to pop idolatry. It is no wonder that Presley's remarkable career so sharply divides those who testify to his ultimate greatness and those who bemoan the gifts that he seemingly squandered along the way. In a sense, the contrasting images of Elvis have come to represent everything positive and everything destructive about the music industry.

Albums: *Rock 'N' Roll* (1956), *Rock 'N' Roll No. 2* (1957), *Loving You* (1957), *Elvis' Christmas Album* (1957), *King Creole* (1958), *Elvis' Golden Records, Volume 1* (1958), *Elvis* (1959), *A Date With Elvis* (1959), *Elvis' Golden Records, Volume 2* (1960), *Elvis Is Back!* (1960), *G.I. Blues* (1960), *His Hand In Mine* (1961), *Something For Everybody* (1961), *Blue Hawaii* (1961), *Pot Luck* (1962), *Girls! Girls! Girls!* (1963), *It Happened At The World's Fair* (1963), *Fun In Acapulco* (1963), *Elvis' Golden Records, Volume 3* (1964), *Kissin' Cousins* (1964), *Roustabout* (1964), *Girl Happy* (1965), *Flaming Star And Summer Kisses* (1965), *Elvis For Everyone* (1965), *Harem Holiday* (1965), *Frankie And Johnny* (1966), *Paradise, Hawaiian Style* (1966), *California Holiday* (1966), *How Great Thou Art* (1967), *Double Trouble* (1967), *Clambake* (1968), *Elvis' Golden Records, Volume 4* (1968), *Speedway* (1968), *Elvis - TV Special* (1968), *From Elvis In Memphis* (1970), *On Stage February 1970* (1970), *That's The Way It Is* (1971), *I'm 10,000 Years Old - Elvis Country* (1971), *Love Letters From Elvis* (1971), *Elvis Sings The Wonderful World Of Christmas* (1971), *Elvis Now* (1972), *He Touched Me* (1972), *Elvis As Recorded At Madison Square Garden* (1972), *Aloha From Hawaii Via Satellite* (1973), *Elvis* (1973), *Raised On Rock* (1973), *A Legendary Performer, Volume 1* (1974), *Good Times* (1974), *Elvis Recorded On Stage In Memphis* (1974), *Hits Of The 70s* (1974), *Promised Land* (1975), *Having Fun With Elvis On Stage* (1975), *Today* (1975), *The Elvis Presley Sun Collection* (1975), *From Elvis Presley Boulevard, Memphis, Tennessee* (1976), *Welcome To My World* (1977), *A Legendary Performer* (1977), *He Walks Beside Me* (1978), *The '56 Sessions, Vol. 1* (1978), *Elvis's 40 Greatest* (1978), *Elvis - A Legendary Performer, Volume 3* (1979), *Our Memories Of Elvis* (1979), *The '56 Sessions, Vol. 2* (1979), *Elvis Presley Sings Leiber And Stoller* (1980), *Elvis Aaron Presley* (1979), *Elvis Sings The Wonderful World Of Christmas* (1979), *The First Year* (1979), *The King...Elvis* (1980), *This Is Elvis* (1981), *Guitar Man* (1981), *Elvis Answers Back* (1981), *The Ultimate Performance* (1981), *Personally Elvis* (1982), *The Sound Of Your Cry* (1982), *Jailhouse Rock/Love In Las Vegas* (1983), *The First Live Recordings* (1984), *A Golden Celebration* (1984), *Rare Elvis* (1985), *Essential Elvis* (1986), *Elvis From Nashville To Memphis: The Essential '60s Masters I* (1993, 5-CD boxed-set).

Videos: *One Night With You* (1986), *Elvis Presley In Concert* (1986), *68 Comeback Special* (1986), *Memories* (1987), *This Is Elvis* (1988), *Graceland* (1988), *Great Performances Vol 2* (1990), *Great Vocal Performances Vol 1* (1990), *Young Elvis* (1991), *Sun Days With Elvis* (1991), *Elvis On Tour* (1991), *Elvis; A Portrait By His Friends* (1991), *56 In the Beginning* (1991), *Private Elvis* (1993), *Elvis In Hollywood* (1993).

Further reading: *I Called Him Babe: Elvis Presley's Nurse Remembers*, Cocke, Marian J. *The Three Loves Of Elvis Presley: The True Story Of The Presley Legend*, Holmes, Robert. *A Century Of Elvis*, Hand, Albert. *The Elvis They*

Dig, Hand, Albert. *Operation Elvis*, Levy, Alan. *The Elvis Presley Pocket Handbook*, Hand, Albert. *All Elvis: An Unofficial Biography Of The 'King Of Discs'*, Buckle, Philip. *The Elvis Presley Encyclopedia*, Barlow, Roy. *Elvis: A Biography*, Hopkins, Jerry. *Meet Elvis Presley*, Friedman, Favius. *Elvis Presley*, Taylor, Paula. *Elvis*, Hopkins, Jerry. *The Elvis Presley Scrapbook 1935-1977*, Paris, James Robert. *Elvis And The Colonel*, Mann, May. *Recording Sessions 1954-1974*, Holum, Torben; Jorgensen, Ernst and Rasmussen, Erik. *Elvis Presley: An Illustrated Biography*, Harbinson, W.A. *Elvis: The Films And Career Of Elvis Presley*, Zmijewsky, Steven & Zmijewsky, Boris. *Presley Nation*, Leigh, Spencer. *Elvis*, Jones, Peter. *Presley: Entertainer Of The Century*, James, Antony. *Elvis And His Secret*, Gripe, Maria. *On Stage, Elvis Presley*, Bowman, Kathleen. *The Elvis Presley American Discography*, Barry, Ron. *Elvis: What Happened*, West, Red; West, Sonny and Hebler, Dave. *Elvis: Tribute To The King Of Rock*, Tatham, Dick. *Elvis Presley*, Slaughter, Todd. *Elvis: Recording Sessions*, Jorgensen, Ernst: Rasmussen, Erick and Mikkelsen, Johnny. *The Life And Death Of Elvis Presley*, Harbinson, W. A. *Elvis: Lonely Star At The Top*, Hanna, David. *Elvis In His Own Words*, Farren, Mick & Marchbank, Pearce. *Twenty Years Of Elvis: The Session File*, Escott, Colin and Hawkins, Martin. *Starring Elvis*, Bowser, James W. *My Life With Elvis*, Yancey, Becky & Lindecker, Cliff. *The Real Elvis: A Good Old Boy*, Staten, Vince. *The Elvis Presley Trivia Quiz Book*, Rosenbaum, Helen. *A Presley Speaks*, Presley, Vester. *The Graceland Gates*, Lloyd, Harold. *The Boy Who Dared To Rock: The Definitive Elvis*, Lichter, Paul. *Eine Illustrierte Dokumentation*, King, Bernd and Plehn, Heinz. *Elvis Presley Speaks*, Holzer, Hans. *Elvis: The Legend Lives! One Year Later*, Grove, Martin A. *Private Elvis*, Cortez, Diego. *Bill Adler's Love Letters To Elvis*, Adler, Bill. *Elvis: His Life And Times In Poetry And Lines*, West, Joan Buchanan. *Elvis '56: In The Beginning*, Wertheimer, Alfred. *Elvis Presley: An Illustrated Biography*, Wallraf, Rainer and Plehn, Heinz. *Even Elvis*, Thornton, Mary Ann. *Elvis: Images & Fancies*, Tharpe, Jac L.. *Elvis In Concert*, Reggero, John. *Elvis Presley: A Study In Music*, Matthew-Walker, Robert. *Elvis; Portrait Of A Friend*, Lacker, Marty; Lacker, Patsy and Smith, Leslie E. *Elvis Is That You?*, Hatcher, Holly. *Elvis: Newly Discovered Drawings Of Elvis Presley*, Harper, Betty. *Trying To Get To You: The Story Of Elvis Presley*, Harms, Valerie. *Love Of Elvis*, Hamilton, Bruce and Liben, Michael L. *To Elvis With Love*, Canada, Lena. *The Truth About Elvis*, Stearn, Jess. *Elvis: We Love You Tender*, Presley, Dee; Stanley, Billy, Rick and David. *Presleyana*, Osborne, Jerry and Hamilton, Bruce. *Elvis: The Final Years*, Hopkins, Jerry. *When Elvis Died*, Gregory, Nancy and Joseph. *All About Elvis*, Worth, Fred L. and Tamerius, Steve D. *Elvis Presley: A Reference Guide And Discography*, Whisler, John A. *The Illustrated Discography*, Hawkins, Martin and Escott, Colin. *Elvis: Legend Of Love*, Greenfield, Marie. *Elvis Presley: King Of Rock 'N' Roll*, Wooton, Richard. *The Complete Elvis*, Torgoff, Martin. *Elvis Special 1982*, Slaughter, Todd. *Elvis*, Marsh, Dave. *Up And Down With Elvis Presley*, Crumbaker, Marge with Tucker, Gabe. *Elvis For The Record*, Covey, Maureen. *Elvis: The Complete Illustrated Record*, Carr, Roy and Farren, Mick. *Elvis Collectables*, Cranor, Rosalind. *Jailhouse Rock: The Bootleg Records Of Elvis Presley 1970*, Cotten, Lee and DeWitt, Howard A. *Elvis The Soldier*, Mansfield, Rex and Elisabeth. *All Shook Up: Elvis Day-By-Day, 1954-1977*, Cotten, Lee. *Elvis And Gladys*, Dundy, Elaine. *Elvis*, Townson, John; Minto, Gordon and Richardson, George. *Priscilla, Elvis & Me*, Edwards, Michael. *Elvis On The Road To Stardom: 1955-1956*, Black, Jim. *Return To Sender*, Banney, Howard F. *Elvis: His Life From A To Z*, Worth, Fred L. and Tamerius, Steve D. *Elvis And The Colonel*, Vallenga, Dirk with Farren, Mick. *Elvis: My Brother*, Stanley, Bill with Erikson, George. *Long Lonely Highway: 1950's Elvis Scrapbook*, Rijff, Ger J. *Elvis In Hollywood*, McLafferty, Gerry. *Reconsider Baby: Definitive Elvis Sessionography*, Jorgensen, E. *Elvis '69, The Return*, Tunzi, Joseph. *The Death Of Elvis: What Really Happened*, Thompson, Charles C. and Cole, James P. *Elvis For Beginners*, Pearlman, Jill. *Elvis, The Cool King*, Moreland, Bob and Van Gestel, Jan. *The Elvis Presley Scrapbooks 1955-1965*, Haining, Peter (ed.). *The Boy Who Would Be King. An Intimate Portrait Of Elvis Presley By His Cousin*, Greenwood, Earl and Tracy, Kathleen. *Elvis: The Last 24 Hours*, Goldman, Albert. *The Elvis Files*, Brewer-Giorgio, Gail. *Elvis, My Dad*, Adler, David and Andrews, Ernest. *Elvis Bootlegs Buyer's Guide, Pts 1& 2*, Robinson, Tommy. *Elvis: The Music Lives On - The Recording Sessions 1954-1976*, Peters, Richard. *.Dead Elvis: A Chronicle Of A Cultural Obession*, Marcus, Greil. *Elvis People: Cult Of The KIng*, Harrison, Ted. *In Search Of The King*, Gelfand, Craig, Blocker-Krantz, Lynn and Noguera, Rogerio. *Aren Med Elvis*, Ersson, Roger and Svedberg, Lennart. *King And I: Little Gallery Of Elvis Impersonators*, Barker, Kent and Pritikin, Karin. *Elvis Sessions: The Recorded Music Of Elvis Aron Presley 1953-1977*, Tunzi, Joseph. *Elvis: The Sun Years*, DeWitt, Howard A. *Elvis In Germany: The Missing Years*, Schroer, Andreas. *Graceland: The Living Legend Of Elvis Presley*, Flippo, Chet. *Elvis: The Secret Files*, Parker, John. *Last Train To Memphis: The Rise Of Elvis Presley*, Guralnick, Peter. *In His Own Words*, Farren, Mick. *Elvis: Murdered By The Mob*, Parker, John. *The Essential Guide To The Music Of...*, Robertson, John.

Films: *Jailhouse Rock* (1957), *G.I. Blues* (1960), *Flaming Star* (1960), *Blue Hawaii* (1961), *Girls Girls Girls* (1962), *Follow That Dream* (1962), *It Happened At The World's Fair* (1963), *Fun In Acapulco* (1963), *Harum Scarum* aka *Harem Holiday* (1965), *Girl Happy* (1965), *Frankie And Johnny* (1966), *Easy Come Easy Go* (1967), *Clambake* (1967), *Double Trouble* (1968), *Change Of Habit* (1969).

Presley, Elvis (country career)

One of Elvis' first nicknames was 'The Hillbilly Cat'

and there was a strong country music component in much of what he did. Although initially recording in a blues town, Memphis, he cut several country songs for Sun: his first single was an up-tempo revival of **Bill Monroe**'s 'Blue Moon Of Kentucky'. He appeared on the ***Grand Ole Opry*** (none too successfully) and ***Louisiana Hayride***, toured with country musicians, and his manager, **Tom Parker,** had previously worked with **Eddy Arnold** and **Hank Snow**. The relationship between established country performers and the new pretender was acted out, with some amusement, in the fictional film, *Loving You*. Over at **RCA**, Elvis worked with numerous country musicians including **Floyd Cramer** and **Chet Atkins,** and his singles regularly made the pop, country and R&B charts. His records include '(Now And Then There's) A Fool Such As I' (originally recorded by Hank Snow), 'Old Shep' (**Red Foley**) and 'Is It So Strange?' (**Faron Young**). His drab material of the 60s changed when he discovered **Jerry Reed** and cut 'Guitar Man' and 'U.S. Male'. From then on, his arrangements were overblown but there were many country songs, both in live performance and on record, including 'He'll Have To Go', 'She Thinks I Still Care' and 'I Really Don't Want To Know'. The maudlin nature of much country music appealed to him once his marriage was over. In all, Elvis recorded around 60 country songs including *Elvis Country* in 1970. Since his death, he has been a regular topic for country songwriters and many contemporary country performers paid tribute to him in Memphis in 1994 at the concert released as *It's Now Or Never*.

Pressgang

A noisy group of punk folksters from Reading, England, led by Damian Clarke, which change image with each successive release. A quote that sums up their musical ethos: 'We want to play it louder than **Deep Purple**'.

Selected album: *Rogues* (1989).

Pressure Drop

Originally Justin Langford (percussion), Mike Puxley (keyboards) and Gareth Tasker (guitar), Pressure Drop made their debut with 'Feeling Good - Touch 1 2 3' for Big World in March 1990. The group met at the Heavy Duty Club where Justin was DJing. It was he who obtained the bank loan in order to set up an eight-track studio in his front room. However, afterwards the group would re-emerge as a duo of Langlands and Dave Henley (a hairdresser at London's Kensington Market, and Langford's partner in Blood Brothers, who had remixed Pressure Drop's first record). whose four-track *Sampler* EP in 1991 made waves. This featured live Hammond organ, Joanna Law, **Galliano** and Mark Cornell and included Indian tabla and African drums. The most notable track was 'You're Mine', an adaptation of 'Transfusion', by the group's alter-ego, the Blood Brothers. However, despite selling over 30,000 copies on German independent label Boombastic, their debut album would not receive a UK release.

Album: *Upset* (Boombastic 1992).

Pressure Of Speech

Taking their name from a condition of manic depressives, a stage at which victims are unable to express the multitude of ideas and words engulfing their minds, it should come as no surprise that Mickie Mann was once a pyschiatric nurse in Aberdeen, Scotland. After a spell in the army he joined **Orbital**, the **Shamen**, **Meat Beat Manifesto** and **Ultramarine**, among others, as live sound engineer. Pressure Of Speech were formed with lighting expert Luke Losey and DJ Stika, formerly of **Fun-Da-Mental** and **Spiral Tribe**. They made their debut with the track 'Surveillance' on **Planet Dog**'s *Feed Your Head* compilation, before stepping out on their own with 'X-Beats' on the North South label. Their debut album proved to be one of the most specific and obvious assaults on the UK's Conservative government within the previously largely apolitical techno/dance movement. They also proved keen to take their music out to a live audience, touring as part of a Megadog-styled collective.

Album: *Art Of The State* (North South 1994).

Preston, Billy

b. 9 September 1946, Houston, Texas, USA. Preston's topsy-turvy musical career began in 1956 when he played organ with gospel singer, **Mahalia Jackson** and appeared in the film *St Louis Blues* as a young **W.C. Handy**. As a teenager he worked with **Sam Cooke** and **Little Richard** and it was during the latter's 1962 European tour that Billy first met the **Beatles** with whom he would later collaborate. Preston established himself as an adept instrumentalist recording in his own right, especially on the driving 'Billy's Bag'. He also appeared frequently as a backing musician on the US television show, *Shindig*. After relocating to Britain as part of the **Ray Charles**' revue he was signed to Apple in 1969. **George Harrison** produced his UK hit, 'That's The Way God Planned It', and Preston also contributed keyboards to the Beatles' 'Get Back' and *Let It Be*. The following year he made a guest appearance at the Concert For Bangla Desh. He subsequently moved to **A&M Records** where he had a successful run of hit singles, with 'Outa-Space' (1972), a US number 1 in 1973 with 'Will It Go Round In Circles', 'Space Race' (1973), and another US number 1 in 1974 with 'Nothing From Nothing'. His compositional talents were also in evidence on 'You Are So Beautiful', a US Top 10 hit for **Joe Cocker**. Preston meanwhile continued as a sideman, most notably with **Sly And The Family Stone** and on the 1975 **Rolling Stones**' US tour. A sentimental duet with **Syreeta**, 'With You I'm Born Again', was an international hit in 1980. In 1989 Preston toured with **Ringo Starr**'s All Star Band and recorded for Ian Levine's Motor City label in 1990-91, including further collaborations with Syreeta. He was arrested on a morals charge in the USA during 1991.

Albums: *Gospel In My Soul* (1962), *The Most Exciting Organ Ever* (1965), *Early Hits Of 1965* (1965), *The Apple Of Their Eye* (1965), *The Wildest Organ In Town!* (1966), *That's The Way God Planned It* (1969), *Greazee Soul* (1969), *Encouraging Words* (1970), *I Wrote A Simple Song* (1971), *Music Is My Life* (1972), *Everybody Likes Some Kind Of Music* (1973), *The Kids & Me* (1974), *Live European Tour* (1974), *It's My Pleasure* (1975), *Do What You Want* (1976), *Billy Preston* (1976), *A Whole New Thing* (1977), *Soul'd Out* (1977), *Gospel In My Soul* (1977), with Syreeta *Fast Break* (1979), *Late At Night* (1979), *Behold* (1980), *Universal Love* (1980), *The Way I Am* (1981), *Billy Preston & Syreeta* (1981), *Pressin' On* (1982). Compilations: *The Best Of Billy Preston* (1988), *Collection* (1989).

Preston, Johnny

b. John Preston Courville, 18 August 1939, Port Arthur, Texas, USA. This pop ballad and rock singer first performed in the Lamar University (Beaumont, Texas) group the Shades, in 1957, and was brought to the attention of **Mercury Records** by disc jockey and singer, the **Big Bopper** (Jape Richardson). Amongst the tracks Richardson wrote and produced for him was the novelty 'Running Bear', a sad tale of Red Indian love gone wrong. The record took four months to chart Stateside but it then went on to became a chart-topper in the US and UK during 1959/60 (after Richardson's tragic death in the plane crash with **Buddy Holly**). Despite a disastrous UK tour (cut three weeks short due to poor houses), he had transatlantic Top 20 successes with the follow-ups 'Cradle Of Love' and a revival of **Shirley And Lee**'s 'Feel So Fine'. He later recorded for **Imperial**, TCF Hall (including 'Running Bear '65'), **ABC** and Hallway, but never graced the charts again.

Album: *Johnny Preston Sings* (1960).

Preston, Mike

b. Jack Davis, 14 May 1934, Hackney, London, England. The ex-boxer and cartoon cameraman was discovered singing in a small club in London's West End by noted agent Dennis Preston. He was given his stage name in a competition by readers of Patrick Doncaster's pop music column in the *Daily Mirror* newspaper. This pop ballad singer's first single 'A House, A Car And A Wedding Ring', a **Jerry Lordan** composition with musical direction from Harry Robinson. The **Decca** release failed to create much interest in the UK but charted in the US in early 1958. This led to his visiting America for promotion and appearing on the shows of **Alan Freed** and **Dick Clark** amongst others. Preston, continued to work as a cameraman, until he had his biggest UK hit in 1959 with a cover of the **Fleetwoods**' 'Mr. Blue', which narrowly missed the Top 10. He later appeared in the film *Climb Up The Wall* with **Craig Douglas** and **Russ Conway**. In all, he had four UK Top 40 singles, the last, 'Marry Me' which peaked at number 14, was the winning song from the 1961 ITV television *Song Contest*. After leaving Decca he recorded without success on Emerald.

Preston, Robert

b. Robert Preston Meservey, 8 June 1918, Newton Highlands, Massachusetts, USA, d. 21 March 1987, Santa Barbara, California, USA. An actor and singer, Preston had already enjoyed a busy, but undistinguished career in Hollywood for nearly 20 years when he landed the role of a lifetime on Broadway in ***The Music Man*** (1957). He grew up in Hollywood, and spent several of his teenage years in the theatre before signing for Paramount and making his first movie, *King Of Alcatraz*, in 1938. From then, until 1942, he made some 15 films, including *Union Pacific*, *Beau Geste*, *Typhoon*, *Moon Over Burma*, *Northwest Mounted Police*, and *This Gun For Hire* (1942). After serving in the US Army Air Force during World War II, Preston resumed his film career in features such as *The Macomber Affair*, *Tulsa*, and *When I Grow Up*, until 1951 when he moved to New York. He appeared on Broadway in number of straight plays including *Twentieth Century*, *The Tender Trap*, and *Janus*, and was out of town in Philadelphia with *Boy Meets Girl* when he was asked to audition for *The Music Man*. His portrayal of the likeable con-man, Harold Hill, who travels to small US towns such as Iowa, selling band instruments (which never materialise) to parents for their children to play, made Preston a gilt-edged Broadway star. **Meredith Willson**'s fine score contained numbers such as 'Seventy-Six Trombones', ''Til There Was You', and Preston's *tour de force* 'Ya Got Trouble'. He won the **Tony Award** for best actor in a musical, and stayed with the show for over two years. After being virtually ignored during initial casting, he recreated the part in the 1962 film version. Cary Grant, was one of the actors to whom the role was offered, and he reportedly said: 'Not only won't I play it, but unless Robert Preston plays it, I won't even go see it.' After appearing in several more straight parts, Preston returned to the musical stage in 1964 with *Ben Franklin In Paris*, but, unlike the large on-stage floating balloon in which Preston rode, the show did not really take off. Much more satisfying was ***I Do! I Do!***, a two-hander with **Mary Martin** for which Preston won another Tony. His final Broadway musical appearance came in 1974 with ***Mack And Mabel***, which, despite a splendid **Jerry Herman** score, only lasted for six weeks. During the 50s and 60s he had continued to make films, and in the 70s and early 80s he appeared in several more, including the musical ***Mame*** (1973), with Lucille Ball, and *S.O.B.* and ***Victor/Victoria*** (1982), both with **Julie Andrews**. He also starred in several television movies, including the highly regarded *Finnegan Begin Again*, a poignant story of the love of an older man for a young woman played by Mary Tyler Moore. Preston died of lung cancer in 1987, and in the same year was awarded a special posthumous Tony, the Lawrence Langner Memorial Award for Distinguished Lifetime Achievement in the American Theatre.

Pretenders

Chrissie Hynde (b. 17 September 1951, Akron, Ohio, USA), came to England to seek her fortune during the early 70s. After meeting with ***New Musical Express*** writer and future boyfriend Nick Kent she joined the paper and gained entrance into the world of rock. During her pre-Pretenders days she worked at **Malcolm McLaren**'s shop, SEX, played with **Chris Spedding**, joined Jack Rabbit, formed the Berk Brothers and made a tasteless, unreleased single as the Moors Murderers. By the time she assembled the band in 1978, Hynde had gained a great deal of experience. The classic Pretenders' line-up comprised: Pete Farndon (b. 2 June 1952, Hereford, England, d. 14 April 1983; bass), **James Honeyman-Scott** (b. 4 November 1956, Hereford, England d. 16 June 1982; guitar) and Martin Chambers (b. 4 September 1951, Hereford, England; drums). Their debut was a **Nick Lowe** produced version of the **Kinks** 'Stop Your Sobbing' in 1978. It scraped into the UK Top 40 the following year, having received critical praise and much interest. 'Kid' and the superb 'Brass In Pocket' followed. The latter was accompanied by a superb black and white video with Hynde portrayed as a waitress, and reached the number 1 position in the UK. It was their debut album that eventually put them on the road to becoming one of the decade's most important groups. *Pretenders* was a *tour-de-force* and remains their finest work. In addition to their previous singles the album contained the reggae-styled 'Private Life' (later recorded by **Grace Jones**), the frenetic 'Precious', the **Byrds**-like 'Talk Of The Town' and the beautiful ballad 'Lovers Of Today'.

Throughout 1980 they became a major stadium attraction in the USA; it was in America that Chrissie met and fell in love with her musical idol, the **Kinks**' Ray Davies. Davies had already expressed an interest in Hynde during an interview in the rock magazine *Dark Star*. Their tempestuous relationship lasted four years, almost resulting in marriage. Davies stated that they had gone to a registry office by bus but spent so much time arguing that they changed their minds and came home. During their romance they brought each other onstage to play with their respective bands, much to the chagrin of the band members. *Pretenders II* came in 1982; it was another collection of melodious rock played with new-wave enthusiasm. Stand-out tracks were 'Message Of Love', the brilliantly confessional, 'The Adulteress' and another Davies' chestnut, 'I Go To Sleep', first recorded by the **Applejacks** in 1964. During the turbulent month of June, Pete Farndon, whose drug abuse had been a problem for some time, was fired. Two days later Honeyman-Scott was found dead from a deadly concoction of heroin and cocaine. Nine months later Hynde gave birth to a daughter; the father was Ray Davies. Two months after this happy event, tragedy struck again. Pete Farndon was found dead in his bath from a drug overdose.

The new full-time Pretenders were Robbie McIntosh (ex-**Average White Band**) on lead guitar, and bassist Malcolm Foster. They set about recording a third album and the band ended the year with another hit single, the Christmassy '2000 Miles'. *Learning To Crawl* was released at the beginning of another successful year. The album was erratic, but it did contain some gems, notably the epic 'Thin Line Between Love And Hate', the powerful 'Middle Of The Road' and the melodic, yet poignant tribute to Honeyman-Scott, 'Back On The Chain Gang'. The band embarked on another US tour, but Chrissie refused to be parted from her baby daughter who accompanied her, while Davies and his band were touring elsewhere. In May 1984, following a whirlwind affair, Hynde married Jim Kerr of **Simple Minds**. Back with the Pretenders she appeared at Live Aid at the JFK stadium in Philadelphia, and would enjoy success under her own name duetting with **UB40** on the chart-topping reggae re-make of **Sonny And Cher**'s 'I Got You Babe'. Following the birth of another daughter (Jim Kerr is the father), Chrissie effectively dismantled the band. *Get Close* was released at the end of 1987 and was well received. Both 'Don't Get Me Wrong' and 'Hymn To Her' were substantial hits. In 1988 a solo Hynde performed with UB40 at the Nelson Mandela Concert and the subsequent duet 'Breakfast In Bed' was a Top 10 UK hit. Hynde has since spent much of her time campaigning for Animal Rights. Her marriage to Kerr collapsed and in 1990 she returned with a new album *Packed*, still as the Pretenders. It was another critical and commercial success, demonstrating Hynde's natural gift for writing tight, melodic rock songs. Just at the time when it looked as though music was no longer important for Hynde she returned with one of hef finest collections. *Last Of The Independents*, reunited her with drummer Martin Chambers, alongside Adam Seymour (guitar) and Andy Hobson (bass). It was lyrical, fresh and above all played with the energy of old. The ballad 'I'll Stand By You' is a future classic and re-established Hynde as a major songwriter.

Albums: *Pretenders* (1980), *Pretenders II* (1981), *Learning To Crawl* (1984), *Get Close* (1986), *Packed* (1990), *Last Of The Independents* (Sire/Warner Brothers 1994). Compilation: *The Singles* (1987).
Further reading: *Pretenders*, Miles. *The Pretenders*, Chris Salewicz. *The Pretenders: With Hyndesight*, Mike Wrenn.

Pretty Maids

This Danish heavy metal quintet was formed in 1981 by vocalist Ronnie Atkins and guitarist Ken Hammer. Taking their musical brief from British acts **Deep Purple**, **Judas Priest** and **UFO**, their style was such that enthusiasm often outweighed originality. The band have been through numerous line-up changes, with the current outfit comprising Atkins and Hammer along with Ricky Marx (guitar), Allan Delong (bass) and Phil Moorhead (drums). Although competent musicians, at times their delivery, image, and song titles provoked **Spinal Tap** comparisons in the press. *Future World* from 1987 is the band's strongest release to date. The more recent **Roger Glover**-produced *Jump The Gun* failed to offer anything new, aside from affording the band the opportunity of working with one of their obvious heroes.
Albums: *Pretty Maids* (Bullet 1983), *Red, Hot And Heavy* (CBS 1984), *Future World* (CBS 1987), *Jump The Gun* (CBS 1990).

Pretty Things

One of England's seminal R&B bands, the Pretty Things were formed at Sidcup Art College, Kent, England, in September 1963. The original line-up featured a founder member of the **Rolling Stones**, Dick Taylor (b. 28 January 1943, Dartford, Kent, England; guitar), plus Phil May (b. 9 November 1944, Dartford, Kent, England; vocals), Brian Pendleton (b. 13 April 1944, Wolverhampton, West Midlands, England; rhythm guitar), John Stax (b. 6 April 1944, Crayford, Kent, England; bass) and Peter Kitley (drums), although the latter was quickly replaced by Viv Andrews. The group secured a recording deal within months of their inception. Their label then insisted that the luckless Andrews be removed in favour of Viv Prince, an experienced musician and ex-member of Carter-Lewis And The Southerners. The Pretty Things' debut single, 'Rosalyn', scraped into the UK Top 50, but its unfettered power, coupled with the group's controversial, unkempt appearance, ensured maximum publicity. Their brash, almost destructive, approach to R&B flourished with two exciting UK Top 20 singles, 'Don't Bring Me Down' and 'Honey I Need'. The unit's exuberant first album offered much of the same. Skip Alan (b. Alan Skipper, 11 June 1948, London, England) replaced the erratic Prince in November 1965. Although the Pretty Things' commercial standing had declined, subsequent singles, 'Midnight To Six Man' and 'Come See Me', were arguably their finest work, combining power with purpose. However, first Pendleton, then Stax, abandoned the group and sessions for a third album, *Emotions*, were completed with two former members of the Fenmen, Wally Allen (bass/vocals) and John Povey (b. 20 August 1944, London, England; keyboards/vocals). Initially hired on a temporary basis, the duo proved crucial to the Pretty Things' subsequent development.
By late 1967 the quintet was immersed in the emergent underground scene. Their music combined harmonies with experimentation, and two exceptional singles, 'Defecting Grey' and 'Talking About The Good Times', are definitive examples of English 'flower-power' pop. The group's newfound confidence flourished on *S.F. Sorrow*, an ambitious concept album which reportedly influenced the **Who**'s *Tommy*. The set was not a commercial success, and a recurring instability - Skip Alan was replaced by former **Tomorrow** drummer John 'Twink' Alder - only to rejoin again, also proved detrimental. Dick Taylor's departure in November 1969 was highly damaging, and although the group's subsequent album, *Parachute*, was lauded in *Rolling Stone* magazine, his distinctive guitar sound was notably absent. The Pretty Things collapsed in 1971, but reformed under a core of May, Povey and Skip Alan to complete *Freeway Madness*. This trio remained central through the group's subsequent changes until May embarked on a solo career in 1976. Two years later the *Emotions* line-up - May, Taylor, Povey, Allen and Alan - was reunited. The same quintet, plus guitarist Peter Tolson (b. 10 September 1951, Bishops Stortford, Hertfordshire, England), completed a studio album, *Cross Talk* in 1980, and since then the group has been revived on numerous occasions, notably with May and Taylor at the helm. In 1990 a revitalized unit released a rousing version of **Barry McGuire**'s 1965 US number 1 'Eve Of Destruction'.
Albums: *The Pretty Things* (1965), *Get The Picture* (1965), *Emotions* (1967), *S.F. Sorrow* (1968), *Parachute* (1970), *Freeway Madness* (1972), *Silk Torpedo* (1974), *Savage Eye* (1976), *Live '78* (1978), *Cross Talk* (1980), *Live At The Heartbreak Hotel* (1984), *Out Of The Island* (1988). The group also completed several albums of background music suitable for films: *Electric Banana* (1967), *More Electric Banana* (1968), *Even More Electric Banana* (1969), *Hot Licks* (1973), *Return Of The Electric Banana* (1978). Compilations: *We'll Be Together* (1966), *Greatest Hits 64-67* (1975), *The Vintage Years* (1976), *Attention* (1976), *Attention Volume 2* (1976), *Singles A's And B's* (1977), *Cried From The Midnight Circus* (1986), *Let Me Hear The Choir Sing* (1986), *Closed Restaurant Blues* (1987).
Further reading: *The Pretty Things: Their Own Story And The Downliners Sect Story*, Stax, Mike (1992).

Previn, André

b. 6 April 1929, Berlin, Germany. After studying music in Berlin and Paris, Previn moved to the USA in 1938 when his family emigrated. Resident in Los Angeles, he continued his studies and while still at school worked as a jazz pianist and as an arranger in the film studios. From the mid-40s he made records with some measure of success, but it was in the middle of the following decade that he achieved his greatest renown. The breakthrough came with a series of jazz albums with **Shelly Manne**, the first of which featured music from the popular show ***My Fair Lady***. Previn recorded with lyricist Dory Langdon, whom he later married. The marriage broke-up in 1965 and was controversially chronicled in **Dory Previn**'s later solo recordings. In the 60s Previn continued to divide his time between jazz and studio work but gradually his interest in classical music overtook these other fields. By the 70s he was established as one of the world's leading classical conductors. His term as conductor for the London Symphony Orchestra saw him emerge as a popular personality, which involved him television advertising and making celebrated cameo appearances for light-entertainers such as Morecambe And Wise. He became conductor of the Pittsburg Symphony Orchestra in 1976 and later the London Philharmonic, the Los Angeles Philharmonica. He continues to involve himself in many facets of music throughout the 80s and into the 90s - one of his most recent projects, in 1992, was a jazz album with opera singer Dame Kiri Te Kanawa and jazz bass player **Ray Brown**. In 1993, Previn took up his appointment as conductor-laureate of the London Symphony Orchestra, while the stage musical *Rough Crossing*, for which he has written the music, to playwright Tom Stoppard's book and lyrics, had its US regional premiere. In 1995, Previn toured the UK with his jazz trio.

Selected albums: *Previn At Sunset* (1945), *André Previn All-Stars* (1946), *André Previn Plays Fats Waller* (1953), *Let's Get Away From It All* (1955), *But Beautiful* (1956), with Shelly Manne *My Fair Lady* i (1956), *André Previn And His Friends: Li'l Abner* (1957), *André And Dory Previn* (1957), *Double Play* (1957), *Pal Joey* (1957), *Gigi* (1958), *Sessions, Live* (1958), *André Previn Plays Songs By Vernon Duke* (1958), *King Size* (1958), *André Previn Plays Songs By Jerome Kern* (1959), *West Side Story* (1959), with the David Rose Orchestra *Secret Songs For Young Lovers* (1959), *The Previn Scene* (c.1959), *Composer, Arranger, Conductor, Pianist* (60s), *The Magic Moods Of André Previn* (60s), *Like Love* (1960), *André Previn Plays Harold Arlen* (1961), *André Previn* (1960), *Give My Regards To Broadway* (1960), *Thinking Of You* (1960), *Music From Camelot* (1960), *A Touch Of Elegance* (1961), *André Previn And J.J. Johnson Play Mack The Knife And Bilbao Song* (1961), *André Previn And J.J. Johnson* (c.1962), *Two For The See-saw* (c.1962), *Sittin' On A Rainbow* (1962), *The Light Fantastic: A Tribute To Fred Astaire* (c.1963), *4 To Go!* (1963), *André Previn In Hollywood* (1963), *Soft And Swinging* (1964), *Sound Stage* (1964), *My Fair Lady* ii (1964), *Previn At Sunset* (1975), with Itzhak Perlman *A Different Kind Of Blues* (1981), with Perlman *It's A Breeze* (c.1981), *André Previn And Friends Play Show Boat* (Deutsche Grammophon 1995).

Further reading: *André Previn*, Michael Freedland. *Music Face To Face*, André Previn. *Orchestra*, André Previn. *André Previn's Guide To The Orchestra*, André Previn. *No Minor Chords: My Days In Hollywood*, André Previn.

Previn, Dory

b Dory Langdon, 27 October 1937, Woodbridge, New Jersey, USA, she was the daughter of a musician who became a child singer and dancer in New Jersey, graduating to musical theatre as a chorus line member. Her abilities as a songwriter next brought Langdon work composing music for television programmes. After moving to Hollywood, she met and married **André Previn** in 1959, the year in which he composed the tune 'No Words For Dory'. Now a lyricist for movie soundtracks, Dory Previn worked with Andre, **Elmer Bernstein** and others on songs for such films as *Pepe*, *Two For The Seesaw*, and *Valley Of The Dolls*, whose theme tune was a big hit for **Dionne Warwick** in 1967. By now the Previns had separated and in the late 60s Dory turned to more personal lyrics, publishing a book of poems before launching a recording career with United Artists. Produced by **Nik Venet**, her early albums were noted for angry, intimate and often despairing material like 'The Lady With The Braid' and 'Who Will Follow Norma Jean ?'. The title track of *Mary C. Brown & The Hollywood Sign* was based on a true story of a suicide attempt and was turned by Previn into a stage musical. In 1974, she left U.A. for **Warner Brothers** where Joel Dorn produced the 1976 album,. In that year she also published her memoirs, *Midnight Baby*.

Albums: *On My Way To Where* (1970), *Mythical Kings & Iguanas* (1971), *Reflections In A Mud Puddle* (1971), *Mary C. Brown & The Hollywood Sign* (1972), *Live At Carnegie Hall* (1973), *Dory Previn* (1975), *We Are Children Of Coincidence And Harpo Marx* (1976), *1 AM Phone Calls* (1977).

Further reading: *Midnight Baby: An Autobiography*, Dory Previn. *Bog-Trotter: An Autobiography With Lyrics*, Dory Previn.

Prevost, Eddie

b. 22 June 1942, Hitchin, Hertfordshire, England. As a teenager Prevost drummed for various trad and skiffle bands and later played jazz. In 1965 he, along with saxophonist **Leslie Gare** and guitarist Keith Rowe, formed AMM, an *avant garde*, improvising chamber group which remains as radical, uncompromising and *sui generis* in 1992 as it was at its inception. AMM has been one of Prevost's major projects for most of the last 30 years. Very active in all kinds of free improvisation,

Prevost frequently draws attention to the political resonances of playing free music - he also gives lectures and writes articles. His quartet, with Larry Stabbins (tenor saxophone), Veryan Weston (piano) and Marcio Mattos (bass), performed throughout the 70s and 80s and Prevost has also recorded with the collective groups Supersession, Resoundings and the Free Jazz Quartet, releasing their (and his) albums on his own label, Matchless Records. A 1987 album, *Flayed*, on the Californian Silent label, featured Prevost on one side only playing solo. In 1990, with AMM colleagues Gare and Rowe, Prevost formed The Masters Of Disorientation; in 1991 he undertook a brief UK tour in a duo with pianist **Marilyn Crispell**. An expert percussionist in every mode of improvisation, Prevost cites **Max Roach** and **Ed Blackwell** as the jazz drummers he most admires.

Albums: *Now-Here-This-Then* (Spotlite 1977), *Live, Volumes 1 & 2* (Matchless 1979), *Continuum* (Matchless 1985), with Resoundings *Resound* (1986), *Supersession* (Matchless 1988, rec. 1984), with Organum *Flayed* (1987), with the Free Jazz Quartet *Premonitions* (1989).

Price

This UK pop punk combo began in the mid-80s. Leigh was playing with the Others, whilst Mick partnered In The Dark. Both were locals from the Uxbridge area, and when the groups folded Mick volunteered his drumming skills for the proposed band Leigh was inaugurating. They found vocalist Malcolm through an advertisement in the weekly *Sounds* music paper and bass player Gary, a multi-instrumentalist, who was one of the Others' original drummers. However, when he emigrated they drafted in another Gary, but he was as short-lived as his namesake. Huggy then stepped in as the permanent bass player. The final shift came in 1991 when Pete (also ex-Others) replaced Mick. Their first release came with a single jointly sponsored by *So What!* fanzine, 'The Price You Pay'. 1989 saw them joining the Released Emotions roster where they found Paul Fox (ex-**Ruts**) to produce their best recording, 'Between The Lies'. Their first album followed several months later.

Album: *Table Of Uncles* (Released Emotions 1990).

Price, 'Big' Walter

b. 2 August 1917, Gonzales, Texas, USA. Like many other aspects of society today, the blues has personalities famous for being famous. Big Walter Price is one. Raised from the age of three by his uncle, C.W. Hull, and aunt, he moved with them to San Antonio in 1928. Throughout his schooling, he also worked in cottonfields, sold newspapers, shined shoes and washed dishes. Taking an interest in music, he played with the Northern Wonders gospel group. From school, he worked on the railroad until, in 1955, he made three records for TNT Records, the first 'Calling Margie' achieving local success. Thereafter, he cut 'Shirley Jean', on which his reputation rests, and four other singles for Peacock in Houston, several of them with **Little Richard's** old band, The Upsetters, masquerading as The Thunderbirds. In the next 10 years, he recorded for Goldband, Myrl, Jet Stream and Teardrop, while other tracks recorded for Roy Ames and featuring **Albert Collins** on guitar were issued later on Flyright and P.Vine. In July 1971, also for Ames, he recorded an album eventually issued in England 17 years later. His ebullient personality tended to minimise the effect of his rather wayward timing; though written of as an exponent of classic Texas piano blues, the influence is more geographical than musical.

Album: *Boogies From Coast To Coast* (1988).

Price, Alan

b. 19 April 1941, Fatfield, Co. Durham, England. From the age of eight Price taught himself the piano, guitar and bass and lost no time in playing with local bands, usually containing various members of the as yet unformed **Animals**. His first major band was variously known as the Kansas City Five, (or Seven or Nine), the Kontours, the Pagans and finally the Alan Price Rhythm And Blues Combo. The late **Graham Bond** recommended the combo to his manager **Ronan O'Rahilly** and the name was changed as the band prepared to infiltrate the London R&B scene. As the most musically talented member of the Animals, Price eventually found the constant high-profile and touring too much. Always an introvert and having a more sophisticated and broader musical palette than the rest of the band, it was only a matter of time before the mentally exhausted Price left the Animals. Fear of flying was given as the official reason in May 1965, although leaving the band at the peak of their success was seen as tantamount to professional suicide. That year he appeared in the classic D.A. Pennebaker movie *Don't Look Back* as one of **Bob Dylan**'s entourage. Within a very short time he had assembled the Alan Price Set, who debuted in August that year with 'Any Day Now'. Although not a hit, the record showed great promise. This was confirmed with their second release, a stirring version of **Screamin' Jay Hawkins**' 'I Put A Spell On You'. While the record featured Price's distinctive fast arpeggio organ sound, the public were happy to discover that he could also sing well.

He followed with further singles which showed an unashamedly pop bias. In 1967 he had two major hits written by **Randy Newman**; 'Simon Smith And His Amazing Dancing Bear' and 'The House That Jack Built'. In 1970 he teamed up with **Georgie Fame** as Fame And Price Together and had a hit with the MOR-sounding 'Rosetta'. That same year he wrote the score for two musicals, *Home*, written by Lindsay Anderson, and his own *The Brass Band Man*. Price was then commissioned to write the music for Anderson's film, *O Lucky Man!* in 1973, for which he won a BAFTA award. His apparent serious nature and 'straight' appearance kept him apart from the hipper music scene, of which his former colleague **Eric Burdon** was one of the leading lights. His vaudeville-tinged playing effectively allied him with an older audience. In 1974 Price once again went against the grain and hit the charts with 'Jarrow Song', having been bought up in the town famous for its workers' march of 1936. Price's social conscience was stirred, and he produced the excellent autobiographical album *Between Today And Yesterday*. The critical success of the album garnered him a BBC television documentary.

Price starred in *Alfie Darling* in 1975, winning the Most Promising New British Actor award. In 1978 and 1979 he dented the charts with 'Just For You', some copies of which were pressed in heart-shaped red vinyl. He enjoys a fruitful career, often appears on television and is always able to fill a concert hall, in addition to continuing to write stage musicals like *Andy Capp* and *Who's A Lucky Boy?* Price took part in two abortive Animals reunions in 1977 and 1983.

Albums: *The Price To Play* (1966), *The Price On His Head* (1967), *Fame And Price, Price And Fame Together* (1971), *O Lucky Man!* (1973, film soundtrack), *Between Today And Yesterday* (1974), *Metropolitan Man* (1974), *Performing Price* (1975), *Shouts Across The Street* (1976), *Rainbows End* (1977), *Alan Price* (1977), *England My England* (1978), *Rising Sun* (1980), *A Rock And Roll Night At The Royal Court* (1981), *Geordie Roots And Branches* (1983), *Travellin' Man* (1986), *Liberty* (1989), *Live In Concert* (1993).

Further reading: *Wild Animals*, Andy Blackford.

Price, Jesse

b. 1 May 1909, Memphis, Tennessee, USA, d. 19 April 1974. After playing drums locally, Price toured with blues singers (including **Ida Cox**) and tent shows until 1934, when he settled in Kansas City. There he worked in several **territory bands** and helped establish the free-flowing rhythmic pulse which is at the heart of the Kansas City style of jazz. He led his own band, was a familiar figure at after-hours jam sessions and then joined **Harlan Leonard**'s Rockets. In the early 40s he worked briefly with **Ella Fitzgerald** and with the big bands of **Louis Armstrong**, **Stan Kenton**, **Count Basie** and **Benny Carter**. Despite his importance in the early development of the style refined and polished by such peers as **Jo Jones**, Price worked in comparative obscurity during his later years and by the end of the 60s was in semi-retirement. In 1971 he appeared at the **Monterey Jazz Festival** as part of the 'Kansas City Revisited' set, leading a band which included **Harry Edison**, **Jimmy Forrest** and **Big Joe Turner**.

Compilations: *Harlan Leonard Vol. 2* (1940 recordings), *Stan Kenton's Greatest Hits* (1943-51 recordings).

Price, Kenny

b. 27 May 1931, Florence, Kentucky, USA, d. 4 August 1987, Florence, Kentucky, USA. Price was raised on a farm in Boone County, Kentucky and he was given a guitar when he was five years old. He played guitar as a teenager on a radio station in Cincinnati and then entertained troups when he was in the forces. His break came in 1957 when he was invited to appear on Arthur Godfrey's television show in what was the first colour transmission in the US - perhaps they were attracted to his highly-coloured Nudie suits! He moved to Nashville in the early 60s and, after signing with the new Boone label in 1965, he had several US country hits - 'Walkin' On New Grass', 'Happy Tracks', 'Pretty Girl, Pretty Clothes, Pretty Sad', 'Grass Won't Grow On A Busy Street' and 'My Goal For Today'. He was a comedian and because he was 20 stone, he was known as 'The Round Mound Of Sound'. He became a regular member of *Hee Haw* television show. He moved to **RCA** and had US Top 10 country singles with 'Northeast Arkansas Mississippi County Bootlegger', 'Biloxi' and 'The Sheriff Of Boone County'. In 1973 Craig Baguley, the editor of *Country Music People*, wrote a tribute to him, 'Kenny Price' which was recorded by the Johnny Young Four. His final chart entries included 'Afraid You'd Come Back', 'Well Rounded Travellin' Man' and, ironically, 'She's Leavin' (And I'm Almost Gone)'. Price later died of a heart attack in 1987.

Albums: *One Hit Follows Another* (1967), *Southern Bound* (1967), *Walkin' On New Grass* (1969), *Happy Tracks* (1969), *Heavyweight* (1970), *Northeast Arkansas Mississippi County Bootlegger* (1970), *The Sheriff Of Boone County* (1971), *The Red Foley Songbook* (1971), *Charlotte Fever* (1971), *Super Sideman* (1972), *You Almost Slipped My Mind* (1972), *Sea Of Heartbreak And Other Don Gibson Tunes* (1973), *30 California Women* (1973), *Turn On Your Lovelight And Let It Shine* (1974), *Best Of Both* (1980), with Roy Clark, Grandpa Jones, Buck Owens *Hee-Haw Gospel Quartet* (1981), *A Pocket Full Of Tunes* (1982).

Price, Lloyd

b. 9 March 1933, Kenner, Louisiana, USA. Price, who launched his career in the early 50s performing rocking R&B, New Orleans-style, was - like his Crescent City compatriot, **Fats Domino** - made for the rock 'n' roll era. He did not have to modify his approach one iota to become a rock 'n' roll hit-maker in the late 50s. Price formed his own band in New Orleans in 1949 and in 1952 was signed with the Los Angeles-based **Specialty Records**, which made a practice of recording New Orleans artists. His first hit, 'Lawdy Miss Clawdy' (US R&B number 1, 1952) established his career in the R&B field and he followed with four more Top 10 hits. Military service intervened and took Price out of action from 1954-56. On returning to civilian life he settled in

Washington, D.C. and set up a record company with Harold Logan. Price regained his place on the chart in 1957 with 'Just Because' (US R&B number 3 and pop Top 30). Signed to **ABC**-Paramount, the company transformed their R&B veteran into a rock 'n' roll hitmaker for the new teen market. He and Logan revamped an old blues, 'Stack-O-Lee', that had been a hit for **Ma Rainey** in the 20s and made it one of his biggest successes (US R&B and pop number 1, 1959). In the UK, it entered the Top 10. Price's chart career peaked in 1959, with such hits as 'Where Were You (On Our Wedding Day)' (US R&B number 4 and pop Top 30), 'Personality' (US R&B number 1 and pop number 2), 'I'm Gonna Get Married' (US R&B number 1 and pop number 3). In the UK, he found success in the pop charts with 'Where Were You' (number 15), 'Personality' (number 9), 'I'm Gonna Get Married' (number 23). The hits continued, to a lesser extent, the following year with 'Lady Luck' (US R&B number 3 and pop Top 20) and 'Question' (US R&B number 5 and number 19 pop). Three years later Price re-surfaced on the Double-L label (owned by Price and Logan), briefly making an impact on the emerging soul market with his reworking of jazz standards 'Misty' (US R&B number 11 and pop Top 30) and 'Bill Bailey' (US R&B Top 40 and pop Top 100 as 'Billy Baby'). Double-L also released **Wilson Pickett**'s first solo sides, and in the late 60s Price began another label called Turntable for which **Howard Tate**, amongst others, recorded. Price's last chart record was in 1976 on the LPG label, a label he formed in partnership with the notorious boxing promoter Don King.

Albums: *Lloyd Price* (1959), *The Exciting Lloyd Price* (1959), *Mr. Personality* (1959), *Mr. Personality Sings The Blues* (1960), *The Fantastic Lloyd Price* (1960), *Lloyd Price Sings The Million Sellers* (1961), *Cookin' With Lloyd Price* (1961), *The Lloyd Price Orchestra* (1963), *Misty* (1963), *Lloyd Swings For Sammy* (1965), *Lloyd Price Now* (1969), *To The Roots And Back* (1972), *The Nominee* (1978). Compilations: *Mr. Personality's Big 15* (1960), *The Best Of Lloyd Price* (1970), *Lloyd Price's 16 Greatest Hits* (1972), *Original Hits* (1972), *The ABC Collection* (1976), *Misty* (1977), *Mr. Personality Revisited* (1983), *Lawdy!* (1991), *Stagger Lee & All His Other Greatest Hits* (1993).

Price, Ray

b. Ray Noble Price, 12 January 1926, on a farm near Perryville, Cherokee County, Texas, USA. Price grew up on a farm and by the time he left high school, was already singing and playing guitar locally. In 1942, while studying veterinary medicine at Abilene's North Texas Agricultural College, he was drafted into the Marines. He returned to his studies in 1946, also began performing at local clubs and as the Cherokee Cowboy, he appeared on KRBC. He still had thoughts of a career as a rancher but in 1949, the opportunity to join the *Big D Jamboree,* in Dallas, finally convinced him that his future lay in country music. He first recorded for a minor label, Bullet, and had some success in Texas with 'Jealous Lies' but in 1952, he joined **Columbia** and had immediate US country Top 10 hits with 'Talk To Your Heart' and 'Don't Let The Stars Get In Your Eyes'. Price moved to Nashville, where he became a member of the *Grand Ole Opry*. He was also befriended by **Hank Williams**, with whom he lived for a time and on occasions worked with the **Drifting Cowboys** on shows that Hank missed. When he later formed his own band, the Cherokee Cowboys, quite apart from appearances by members of the old Hank Williams band, it was occasionally to include **Willie Nelson, Johnny Paycheck,** Johnny Bush**, Buddy Emmons** and **Roger Miller**. Price's vocals and the excellence of the Cherokee Cowboys represented some of the finest honky tonk country music of all time. The immense popularity Price gained may be judged by his chart successes. In the 20 years between 1954 and 1974 he amassed a total of 64 US country chart hits, only 11 of which failed to make the Top 20 and 13 also crossed over to the pop charts. He registered 7 country number 1 hits including 'Crazy Arms' (his first million-seller), 'My Shoes Keep Walking Back To You', 'City Lights' (his second million-seller, which also launched **Bill Anderson**'s songwriting career) and 'For The Good Times', a third million-seller which first introduced the songwriting talent of a young Nashville janitor called **Kris Kristofferson**. He also recorded what is probably the most popular country version of 'Release Me', a song that 13 years later became a UK pop chart number 1 for **Engelbert Humperdinck**. In 1967, Price varied from honky-tonk music to a more pop-orientated approach. His backings began to feature strong orchestral accompaniment, far removed from the traditional fiddle and steel guitar influence of his mentor, Hank Williams. Price maintained that most of his songs were ballads and that the strings provided the soul. In concert, he often used up to ten violins in his backing but for his records there were often many more, in fact, when he recorded his version of 'Danny Boy', the backing was by an orchestra that consisted of forty-seven musicians. He also dispensed with any western-style dress and took to appearing in smart evening suits; the Cherokee Cowboy was dead. He toured extensively and appeared on all major network radio and television shows.

By 1973, Price had grown rather tired of the touring and semi-retired to his ranch near Dallas to breed horses. Five years later, he found that he missed it all and once more was to be found back on the circuit. From the mid-70s, through to the late 80s, he recorded for Myrrh, **ABC**, Monument, Dimension, **Warner Brothers**, Viva and Step One and although there were few Top 20 hits after 1974, he continued regularly to register country charts entries. In 1980, in an effort to boost his somewhat flagging chart successes, he asked Willie Nelson to record an album with him. Willie obliged his old boss and their duet of 'Faded Love', from the album *San Antonio Rose*, charted at number 3. A feud had existed for many years between Price and Nelson dating back to when they were neighbours. Willie had shot and eaten one of Price's fighting roosters for killing some of his hens and Price swore he would never record another Nelson song. (The reason why Price kept fighting roosters is open to conjecture.) He eventually got over it, but Willie had no real reason to agree to the request to record the album since Price had not in fact recorded any of his songs for a long time. Price appeared in the Clint Eastwood film *Honkytonk Man*. From the mid-80s, some of his recordings were of dubious country content such as his versions of the **Frank Sinatra** pop hit 'All The Way' and the 1931 **Gene Austin** hit 'Please Don't Talk About Me When I'm Gone' but on others he tended to revert more to the simple country backings of his early days. When 'I'd Do It All Over Again' charted in December 1988, it took his tally of country hits to 108 and in the statistics produced by Joel Whitburn for his *Record Research*, based on country music chart success 1944-88, Price stands at number 6 in the Top 200 country artists of all time.

Albums: *Heart Songs* (1957), *Talk To Your Heart* (1958), with orchestra and chorus *Faith* (1960), *Sings San Antonio Rose (A Tribute To The Great Bob Wills)* (1962), *Night Life* (1963), *Love Life* (1964), *Burning Memories* (1965), *Western Strings* (1965), *The Other Woman* (1965), *Another Bridge To Burn* (1966), *Ray Price - Collector's Choice* (1966), *Touch My Heart* (1967), *Born To Lose* (1967), *Danny Boy* (1967), *She Wears My Ring* (1968), *Take Me As I Am* (1968), *I Fall To Pieces* (1969), *Christmas Album* (1969), *Sweetheart Of The Year* (1969), *For The Good Times* (1970), *The World Of Ray Price* (1970), *You Wouldn't Know Love* (1970), *Make The World Go Away* (1970), *I Won't Mention It Again* (1971), *Release Me* (1971), *The Lonesomest Lonesome* (1972), *She's Got To Be A Saint* (1973), *Like Old Times Again* (1974), *This Time Lord* (1974), *You're The Best Thing That Ever Happened To Me* (1974), *If You Ever Change Your Mind* (1975), *Say I Do* (1975), *Hank 'N' Me* (1976), *Rainbows And Tears* (1976), *Help Me* (1977), *How Great Thou Art* (1977), *Reunited - Ray Price And The Cherokee Cowboys* (1977), *Precious Memories* (1977), *There's Always Me* (1979), with Willie Nelson *San Antonio Rose* (1980), *Ray Price* (1981), *Town And Country* (1981), *Tribute To Willie & Kris* (1981), *Diamonds In The Stars* (1981), *Loving You* (1982), *Somewhere In Texas* (1982), *Master Of The Art* (1983), *Portrait Of A Singer* (1985), *Welcome To The Country* (1985), *A Revival Of Old Time Singing* (1987), *The Heart Of Country Music* (1987), *A Christmas Gift For You* (1987), *Just Enough Love* (1988), *By Request Greatest Hits Volume 4* (1988), *Hall Of Fame Series* (1992), *Sometimes A Rose* (1992), with Faron Young *Memories That Last* (1992).

Compilations: *Welcome To My World* (1971), *Ray Price's All-Time Greatest Hits* (1972), *Greatest Hits, Volume 1, 2 & 3* (1986), *By Request - Greatest Hits, Volume 4* (1988).

Price, Sammy

b. 6 October 1908, Honey Grove, Texas, USA, d. May 1992. After studying alto horn and piano at schools in Texas, Price won a dancing contest. Arising from this he was invited to tour with the **Alphonso Trent** band. Back in Texas he accompanied singers on record dates, playing occasional club gigs. He also formed a band of his own, then toured with a succession of popular entertainers. By 1930 he was becoming known in and around Kansas City, but by 1937 was resident in New York where he became house pianist for **Decca**, playing on countless record dates, mostly with singers. The 40s saw him working as a solo act, leading his own small band, the Bluesicians, and working with **Sidney Bechet**. Price also found time for a brief European tour in 1948. During the 50s he divided his time between Texas and New York, playing clubs and recording with artists such as **Henry 'Red' Allen**. In the 60s he was active in New York and once again toured Europe, a pattern of work which continued through the following decade and into the 80s, sometimes in company with other veterans like **Doc Cheatham**. Price was an effective singer and his blues piano playing was of a very high standard.

Selected albums: *Blues And Boogie* (1955), *Sammy Price: Concert In Fontainebleau/The Price Is Right* (1956), *Piano Solo* (1956), *Sidney Bechet With Sammy Price's Bluesicians Live In Paris* (1956), *Sammy Price And Doc Cheatham* (1958), *Rib Joint* (1959), *Sammy Price And His All Stars* (1959), *Sammy Price And His Bluesicians* (Circle 1961), *Midnight Boogie* (1969), *Barrelhouse And Blues* (1969), *Blues On My Mind* (1969), *Texas And Louisiana Piano* (1969, one side only), *Fire* (1975), *Rockin' Boogie* (1975), *Boogie And Jazz Classics* (1975), *The New Sammy Price* (1975), *Sammy Price With Fessor's Big City Band* (1975), with Torben Petersen *The Boogie Woogie Twins* (1975), *Just Right* (1977), *Blues And Boogie-Woogie* (1978), with Cheatham *Black Beauty: A Tribute To Black American Songwriters* (1979), *Sweet Substitute* (1979), *Play It Again, Sam* (Whiskey Women And Song 1983).

Further reading: *What Do They Want? A Jazz Autobiography*, Sammy Price and Caroline Richmond (ed.).

Pride, Charley

b. 18 March 1938, Sledge, Mississippi, USA. Charley Pride was born on a cotton farm, which, as a result of his success, he was later able to purchase. Pride says, 'My dad named me Charl Frank Pride, but I was born in the country and the midwife wrote it down as Charley'. Harold Dorman, who wrote and recorded 'Mountain of Love', also hails from Sledge and wrote 'Mississippi Cotton Pickin' Delta Town' about the area, for Pride. As an adolescent, Pride followed what he heard on the radio with a cheap guitar, breaking with

stereotypes by preferring country music to the blues. He played baseball professionally but he reverted to music when the Los Angeles Angels told him that he didn't have a 'major league arm'. In 1965 producer **Jack Clement** brought Pride to **Chet Atkins** at **RCA Records**. They considered not disclosing that he was black until the records were established, but Atkins decided that it was unfair to all concerned. 'The Snakes Crawl at Night' sold on its own merit and it was followed by 'Just Between You And Me' which won a Grammy for the best country record by a male performer. On 7 January 1967 **Ernest Tubb** introduced him at the *Grand Ole Opry*, 42 years after the first black performer to appear there, **DeFord Bailey** in 1925. Prejudice ran high but the quality of Pride's music, particularly the atmospheric live album from Panther Hall, meant that he was accepted by the red-neck community. At one momentous concert, **Willie Nelson** kissed him on stage. Pride has had 29 number 1 records on the US country charts including six consecutive chart-toppers between 1969 and 1971.
His most significant recordings include 'Is Anybody Goin' to San Antone?', which he learnt and recorded in 15 minutes, and 'Crystal Chandelier', which he took from a **Carl Belew** record and is still the most-requested song in UK country clubs. Strangely enough, 'Crystal Chandelier' was not a US hit, where his biggest single is 'Kiss An Angel Good Mornin''. Unfortunately, Pride fell into the same trap as **Elvis Presley** by recording songs that he published, so he did not always record the best material around. Nevertheless, over the years, Charley Pride has encouraged such new talents as **Kris Kristofferson**, **Ronnie Milsap**, **Dave And Sugar** (who were his back-up singers) and **Gary Stewart** (who was his opening act). In 1975 Pride hosted a live double-album from the *Opry*, *In Person*, which also featured Atkins, Milsap, **Dolly Parton**, **Jerry Reed** and Stewart. By the mid-80s, Pride was disappointed at the way RCA was promoting 'New Country' in preference to established performers so he left the label. He then recorded what is arguably his most interesting project, a tribute album to **Brook Benton**. Sadly, it was not released as he signed with 16th Avenue Records, who preferred new material. Records like 'I'm Gonna Love Her On The Radio' and 'Amy's Eyes' continue his brand of easy-listening country, but he has yet to recapture his sales of the late 60s. Pride has had a long and contented family life and his son, Dion, plays in his band. ('We took the name from **Dion And The Belmonts**. We just liked it.'). Seeing him perform in concert underlines what a magnificent voice he has. Sadly, he doesn't test it in other, more demanding musical forms, although he argues that 'the most powerful songs are the simple ones.'
Albums: *Country Charley Pride* (1966), *Pride Of Country Music* (1967), *The Country Way* (1967), *Make Mine Country* (1968), *Songs Of Pride...Charley, That Is* (1968), *Charley Pride - In Person* (1969), *The Sensational Charley Pride* (1969), *Just Plain Charley* (1970), *Charley Pride's Tenth Album* (1970), *Christmas In My Home Town* (1970), *From Me To You (To All My Wonderful Fans)* (1971), *Did You Think To Pray?* (1971), *I'm Just Me* (1971), *Charley Pride Sings Heart Songs* (1971), *A Sunshine Day With Charley Pride* (1972), *Songs Of Love By Charley Pride* (1973), *Sweet Country* (1973), *Amazing Love* (1973), *Country Feelin'* (1974), *Pride Of America* (1974), *Charley* (1975), *The Happiness Of Having You* (1975), *Sunday Morning With Charley Pride* (1976), *She's Just An Old Love Turned Memory* (1977), *Someone Loves You Honey* (1978), *Burgers And Fries* (1978), *You're My Jamaica* (1979), *There's A Little Bit Of Hank In Me* (1980), *Roll On Mississippi* (1981), *Charley Sings Everybody's Choice* (1982), *Live* (1982), *Night Games* (1983), *The Power Of Love* (1984), *After All This Time* (1987), *I'm Gonna Love Her On The Radio* (1988), *Moody Woman* (1989), *Amy's Eyes* (1990), *Classics With Pride* (1991), *My 6 Latest & 6 Greatest* (1993). Compilations: *The Best Of Charley Pride* (1969), *The Best Of Charley Pride, Volume 2* (1972), *The Imcomparable Charley Pride* (1973), *The Best Of Charley Pride, Volume 3* (1977), *Greatest Hits* (1981).
Further reading: *Charley Pride*, Pamela Barclay, *Pride; The Charley Pride Story*, Charley Pride with Jim Henderson.

Pride, Dickie

b. Richard Knellar, Thornton Heath, England. Pride, a former Royal College of Church Music chorister and trainee stonemason, was 'discovered' in 1958 singing rock 'n' roll in a London pub by **Russ Conway** who recommended him to both **EMI** producer **Norrie Paramor** and pop svengali **Larry Parnes**. Groomed and given a *nom de théâtre*, the diminutive youth's voice rather than his face was his fortune - though his onstage convulsions earned him the nickname 'The Sheik Of Shake'. The first that Britain at large saw of him was on ITV's *Oh Boy!*, plugging his 1959 cover of **Little Richard**'s 'Slippin' And Slidin'.' While his third single, 'Primrose Lane', touched the Top 30, the failure of later singles contradicted a notion some had that Pride was a potential rival to **Cliff Richard**. Nevertheless, he was still impressing audiences in 1960 when he recorded a creditable album of Tin Pan Alley chestnuts with **Ted Heath**'s orchestra. This ploy might have set him on the road of the 'all round entertainer' had not his dabbling with amphetamines alienated him from Parnes and precipitated a fall from grace that found him delivering coal and nursing debilities related to the drug abuse that brought him to an early grave.
Album: *Pride Without Prejudice* (1960).

Priest, Maxi

b. Max Elliot, 10 June 1962, Lewisham, London, England. Former carpenter Maxi Priest is now a hugely successful solo reggae artist. Named by his mother after

her fondness for **Max Bygraves**, Elliot took his new name upon his conversion to **Rastafarianism** (from Priest Levi, one of the figureheads of the 12 tribes of Israel). He made his initial music industry breakthrough by employing his artisan's skills in building **sound systems**. He went on to tour with Saxon International, the UK's premier reggae assembly, where he rubbed shoulders with Peter King, Phillip Levi, **Smiley Culture** and Asher Senator. He made his name and reputation as a 'singing' DJ, vocalising off the cuff observations over prime 70s roots music, but he soon progressed to a more soulful style which was captured by producer Paul Robinson (aka **Barry Boom**) on his debut, *You're Safe*. After recording this album, he started a run of hits in 1986 with 'Strollin' On', 'In The Springtime' and 'Crazy Love'. In 1987 he scored a minor hit single with a cover of **Robert Palmer**'s 'Some Guys Have All The Luck'. However, most successful was his 1988 cover of **Cat Stevens**' 'Wild World', though it owed more of a debt to the **Jimmy Cliff** reggae version. Further chart appearances followed with 'Close To You', 'Peace Throughout The World' and 'Human Work Of Art'. 1990's *Bona Fide* included contributions from, amongst others, **Soul II Soul**, a group undoubtedly influenced by Priest's mellow but evocative brand of **lovers rock**.
Albums: *You're Safe* (Virgin 1985), *Intentions* (Virgin 1986), *Maxi* (Ten 1987), *Bona Fide* (Ten 1990), *The Best Of Me* (Ten 1991), *Fe Real* (Ten 1992).

Priester, Julian

b. 29 June 1935, Chicago, Illinois, USA. Trombonist Priester began his professional career with **Muddy Waters** and **Bo Diddley**; he then changed direction to join **Sun Ra** And His Arkestra. In the late 50s Priester was with **Lionel Hampton**, **Dinah Washington** and **Max Roach**. Most of the 60s were spent in studio work in New York, with a brief spell with **Duke Ellington** at the end of the decade. In the early 70s he played with **Herbie Hancock**, then moved to San Francisco (along the way adopting the name Pepo Mtoto). In the late 70s he worked and recorded with Stanley Cowell and **Red Garland** and in the 80s was featured with the **George Gruntz** big band and in the **Dave Holland** quintet. A powerful player with an inquiring mind, Priester's 70s work, which included explorations of electronics and other artificially created musical sounds, took him from the centre of the jazz scene and into the world of contemporary composers such as John Cage.
Albums: *Spiritsville* (1958), *Love, Love* (1973), *Polarization* (1977).

Priestley, Brian

b. 10 July 1946, Manchester, England. Priestley studied piano as a child, later playing in bands whilst studying at university. In the early 70s he wrote arrangements for the **National Youth Jazz Orchestra** and played in various small groups. Later he was co-leader with Dave Gelly of Stylus. He worked with **Alan Cohen** on the music of **Duke Ellington**, recording 'Black, Brown, And Beige' in 1972 and making a public performance at the 1988 Ellington Convention. In the late 80s and early 90s, he led his own group, the Special Septet, recording both a tribute album to Ellington and a live concert with ex-Ellington musician, **Bill Berry**. In addition to his playing and arranging, Priestley was for many years a regular broadcaster on BBC Radio London. He has also written several books, including works on **Charles Mingus**, **Charlie Parker** and **John Coltrane**, and has contributed articles to several leading music magazines. With **Ian Carr** and **Digby Fairweather** he is co-author of *Jazz: The Essential Companion.*
Albums: with Alan Cohen *Black, Brown, And Beige* (1972), with Bill Berry *Live At The Pizza Express* (1987), *Love You Gladly* (Cadillac 1989), with Berry *Bilberry Jam* (1990).

Prima, Louis

b. 7 December 1911, New Orleans, Louisiana, USA, d. 24 August 1978. A self-taught trumpet player, Prima was working professionally in his home town from the mid-20s. He attracted a good local following and it was 1935 before he was lured away for more than a brief trip. In Chicago and Los Angeles he held long residencies, made films and records and for the rest of the 30s and throughout the 40s and 50s was rarely out of work, making a number of successful records with his then wife **Keely Smith** (whom he divorced in 1961). Although his later career was devised to suit nightclub and casino audiences from New York to Las Vegas, Prima could still turn in good jazz solos which recalled his 30s and 40s recordings. His hoarse singing voice was used to good effect on such records as 'That Old Black Magic' and 'Buena Sera' and on the soundtrack of the 1966 **Walt Disney** film ***Jungle Book*** (he was 'King Louis' the orang-utan). He died in August 1978, having long been in a coma following an operation for a brain tumour.
Selected albums: *A Nite On 52nd Street* (1939), *One Night Stand With Louis Prima* i (1944), *Louis Prima At Frank Dailey's Terrace Room* (1944), *One Night Stand With Louis Prima* ii (1947), *Louis Prima Swings* (1955), *The Wildest Show At Tahoe* (1955), *The Wildest* (1957), *Jump, Jive And Wail* (1958), with Keely Smith *Hey Boy! Hey Girl!* (1958), with Smith *Las Vegas Prima Style* (1958), *Call Of The Wildest* (1958), with Smith *Senior Prom* (1959), with Smith *Louis And Keely!* (1959), *Louis Prima* (1959), *Strictly Prima* (1959), with Smith *Together* (1960), *Wonderland By Night* (1960), *Doin' The Twist* (1961), *The Wildest Comes Home* (1962), *Plays Pretty For The People* (1964). Compilations: *The Hits Of Louis And Keely* (1961), *Jimmie Lunceford And Louis Prima, 1945* (1979), *Jump, Jive An'*

Wail (1986), *Live From Las Vegas* (1988), *Just A Gigolo 1945-50* (1988).

Primal Scream

The line-up which achieved so much success in 1991 consisted of Bobby Gillespie (b. 22 June 1964), Andrew Innes, Robert Young, Henry Olsen, Philip 'Toby' Tomanov, Martin Duffy and **Denise Johnson**, but Primal Scream had been going since the middle of the 80s. Bobby Gillespie was the central force throughout, forming the band after a stint as drummer in the **Jesus And Mary Chain**. Primal Scream achieved immediate popularity via the ***New Musical Express***'s *C86* cassette compilation with 'Velocity Girl', an 80-second piece of 60s guitar pop. After one album on Elevation of similarly melodic material, they veered towards rock territory in the late 80s. Gillespie, encouraged by guitarist Andrew Innes, developed an interest in the burgeoning dance and drug scene. Come the start of the 90s, Primal Scream had been reinvented, with the aid of name remixers such as **Andy Weatherall**, into a groove machine. The 'Loaded' single was the first proof of the band's transformation, stealing from rock's heritage and cult biker movies yet invading Britain's dancefloors to become a Top 10 hit in the UK charts. Their iconoclastic ideals persisted, no more so than on the road, where Primal Scream's hedonistic indulgences were well-publicized. 1991's *Screamadelica* emphasized the band's cultural diversities and reaped rich critical acclaim and massive sales, just before the band relocated to Tennessee to work on the follow up. This finally emerged in 1994, produced by veteran **Atlantic Records** soul man Tom Dowd, revealing a stylistic debt to the **Rolling Stones** rather than the dance scene. Dowd was assisted by contributions from **George Clinton** and **Black Crowes**' producer George Drakoulias. Though the critical reception was mainly frosty, Gillespie had once again brilliantly reinvented himself and his band.

Albums: *Sonic Flower Groove* (Creation 1987), *Primal Scream* (Creation 1989), *Screamadelica* (Creation 1991), *Give Out But Don't Give Up* (Creation 1994).

Prime Minister Pete Nice and Daddy Rich

After the break-up of US rappers **3rd Bass**, of the three former members MC Serch was the first to release a solo album, *Return of The Product*. The remaining two, DJ Daddy Rich and Pete Nice (b. Peter Nash) spent a year cutting their debut. The fact that Nice was still rapping about being white in a black market did not help, but there was much to like in the sustained intelligence of his rhymes, and Rich's convuluted rhythmic strutures. Nice also set up his own record label, Hoppoh, signing talented Latino newcomer **Kurious**.

Album: *Dust To Dust* (1993).

Prime Time

(see **Coleman**, **Ornette**)

Primer, John

b. 3 March c.1946, Camden, Mississippi, USA. Primer recalls hearing the music of **Muddy Waters** as a youngster, and he played a one-string instrument before moving to Chicago in 1963 and acquiring a guitar. He initially played in **Jimmy Reed**'s style. He began to take music more seriously around 1973 and played at the famed Chicago club Theresa's (1974-80), usually with Sammy Lawhorn, who gave Primer many tips on playing blues guitar. In the early 80s he was a member of the Muddy Waters band, and after Muddy's death he replaced **'Alabama' Junior Pettis** as second guitarist in **Magic Slim**'s band the Teardrops. Slim allows his accompanist some of the spotlight, and Primer has recorded for Austrian label Wolf; he is highly rated for his pure blues playing (particularly slide guitar) and singing. Primer is a worthy bearer of the old Chicago blues traditions.

Album: *Chicago Blues Session, Volume Six - Poor Man Blues* (1991).

Primes

Formed in Birmingham, Alabama in 1958, the Primes comprised **Eddie Kendricks** (b. 17 December 1939), Paul Williams and Kel Osborn. Unable to secure a recording contract for their R&B-styled vocal group material in Alabama, the group moved to Detroit in 1959, where they became established in the black neighbourhood housing projects. They encouraged a group of female friends to form a sister group called the **Primettes**; but the Primes disbanded in 1961 when Kendricks and Williams joined three members of another Detroit group, the Distants, to form the **Temptations**.

Primettes

This US vocal group comprised **Diana Ross** (b. 26 March 1944), **Mary Wilson** (b. 4 March 1944), **Florence Ballard** (b. 30 June 1943) and Betty Travis (b. c.1944), and was formed in Detroit in 1959 as a sister group to the **Primes** (who subsequently merged with the Distants to become the **Temptations**). In 1960 they auditioned for **Berry Gordy** at **Motown** who declined to sign them. Instead, they recorded for Lu-Pine in Detroit, most of which recordings were unissued until 1968. They also sang backing vocals on records by **Eddie Floyd**, Don Revel and Gene Martin. Betty Travis was replaced in 1960 by Barbara Martin, and this line-up requested a second chance from Gordy. They were finally signed to Motown in 1961, whereupon they were renamed the **Supremes**.

Albums: *Looking Back With The Primettes* (1968), *The Roots Of Diana Ross* (1973).